HAMMOND®
WORLD ATLAS

HAMMOND® AMBASSADOR

WORLD

ATLAS

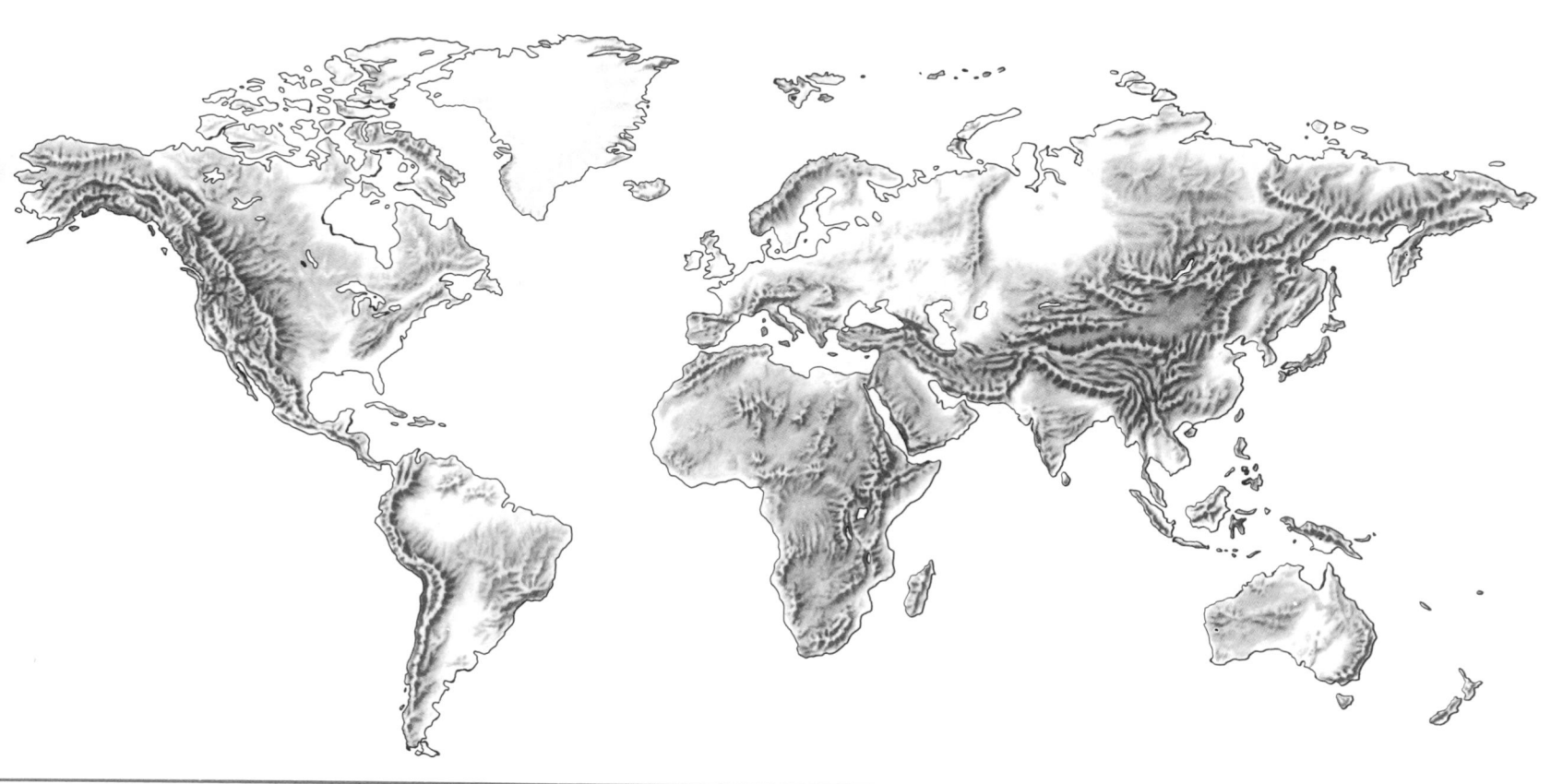

HAMMOND INCORPORATED   MAPLEWOOD, NEW JERSEY 07040

Library of Congress Cataloging in Publication Data
Hammond Incorporated.
    Hammond ambassador world atlas.
    Includes indexes.
    1. Atlases.   I. Title.   II. Title: Ambassador world
atlas.
G1021.H265   1985   912   85-675146
ISBN 0-8437-1242-2

Hammond Publications Advisory Board

Contents

Introduction to the World Atlas

As in previous editions, this Hammond World Atlas is organized to make the retrieval of information as simple and quick as possible. The guiding principle in organizing the atlas material has been to present separate subjects on *separate* maps. In this way, each individual map topic is shown with the greatest degree of clarity, unencumbered with extraneous information that is best revealed on separate maps. Of equal importance from the standpoint of good atlas design is the treatment of all current information on a given country or state as a single atlas unit. Thus, the basic reference map of an area is accompanied on adjacent pages by all supplementary information pertaining to that area. For example, the detailed index for a given map always appears on the same page as, or on the pages immediately following, the reference map. This same map index provides population data for the many cities, towns and villages shown on the map. Highlight information on the area, i.e., the total population and area, the capital, the highest point, is listed in the summary fact listings accompanying each unit. An adjacent locator map relates the subject area to the larger world beyond. A three-dimensional picture of the area is exhibited by means of the accompanying full-color topographic map. A separate economic map defines the vital agricultural, industrial and mineral resources of the area. In the case of the foreign maps, the flag of each independent nation appears on the appropriate page. Finally, certain country units contain special subject maps dealing with the history, climate, demography and vegetation of the area.

An outstanding feature of the atlas is the addition of ZIP codes to the index entries for each of the legion of communities shown on the state maps. With the exception of the U.S. Postal Service directories of limited availability, the ZIP code listings herein are the most extensive published. In addition to listing ZIP codes for the communities possessing post offices, ZIP codes of the nearest post offices are listed for communities without postal facilities. It may be said with a fair degree of certainty that this innovation in atlas content doubles the value of the work for home, office and school.

The back of the book contains a second type of index. This is a multi-paged "A-to-Z" index of all the world's places that appear on the maps. The use of this map index is essential when the name of a place is known but its country, state, or province is unknown. ZIP codes also are given here for each U.S. city, town, or community entry.

The numerous geographical changes of the decade are all recorded in the Hammond World Atlas. Over 8,000 changes, which occurred throughout the world since the last major revision, were entered on the maps. The state maps now reveal the many new towns and cities that have developed in the recent past. The majority of these are burgeoning suburbs on the fringes of our larger cities. On the other hand, large numbers of abandoned and defunct rural hamlets have been removed from the maps and map indexes. Hundreds of other changes are also recorded on the state maps: new national parks and monuments, new dams, new reservoirs, name changes, etc.

Of course, the maps of foreign areas have been thoroughly updated. These revisions echo the new nations, shifting boundaries and the fluid internal divisions of many countries. New communities generated by the opening up of resources in the developing nations are also noted.

In closing it may be said that the atlas has truly been designed for contemporary use. Just as the information presented on the following pages is as current and up to date as the editors and cartographers could issue it, so the design and organization has been as well planned as possible to create a work useful to present generations.

President
HAMMOND INCORPORATED

Gazetteer-Index of the World

This alphabetical list of continents, countries, states, colonial possessions and other major geographical areas provides a quick reference to their area in square miles and square kilometers, population, capital or chief town, map page number and index key thereon. The last name indicates the square on the respective page in which the name may be found. An indication of the population sources used is also included, and refers both to the total figures given in this Gazetteer-Index and to the populations appearing in greater detail with the maps throughout the atlas. The population figures used in each case are the latest reliable figures obtainable. A glance at the sources will show that the dates vary considerably throughout the world. In certain areas where no census has ever been taken, we must rely on official estimates. In other areas where censuses have been taken at infrequent intervals, we again rely on estimates. The key to the abbreviations used in the Gazetteer-Index follows:

aut = autonomous
boro = boroughs
cap = capital
CE = census (undetermined)
CIA = U.S. Central Intelligence Agency
cit = cities
co = counties
com = communes
dept = departments
dist = districts
div = divisions

est = estimates
excl = excluding
FC = final census
gov = governorates
incl = including
isl = islands
met = metropolitan
OE = official estimate
oth = other populations
par = parishes
PC = preliminary census
prov = provinces; provincial

reg = regions
rep = republics
S.S.R. = Soviet Socialist Republic
terr = territories; territory
TP = total population
U.K. = United Kingdom
UN = United Nations
U.S.A. = United States of America
U.S.S.R. = Union of Soviet Socialist Republics
ws = with suburbs

Country	Square Miles	Area Square Kilometers	Population	Capital or Chief Town	Page and Index Ref.	Sources of Population Data
*Afghanistan	250,775	649,507	15,540,000	Kabul	68/A 2	79 PC
Africa	11,707,000	30,321,130	469,000,000	....	102/......	80 UN est
Alabama, U.S.A.	51,705	133,916	3,893,888	Montgomery	195/......	80 FC & OE
Alaska, U.S.A.	591,004	1,530,700	401,851	Juneau	196/......	80 FC & OE
*Albania	11,100	28,749	2,590,600	Tiranë	45/E 5	TP—79 PC; cit over 6,000—70 OE; oth—63 OE
Alberta, Canada	255,285	661,185	2,237,724	Edmonton	182/......	81 FC
*Algeria	919,591	2,381,740	17,422,000	Algiers	106/D 3	77 PC
American Samoa	77	199	32,297	Pago Pago	87/J 7; 86/......	80 FC
Andorra	188	487	31,000	Andorra la Vella	33/G 1	TP—79 OE; cap—75 OE
*Angola	481,351	1,246,700	7,078,000	Luanda	114/C 6	TP—80 UN est; oth—70 FC
Anguilla	35	91	6,519	The Valley	156/F 3	74 FC
Antarctica	5,500,000	14,245,000	....	....	5/......	....
*Antigua and Barbuda	171	443	75,000	St. John's	161/E11; 156/G 3	TP—80 OE; oth—70 FC
*Argentina	1,072,070	2,776,661	28,438,000	Buenos Aires	143/......	TP—82 OE; oth—80 PC
Arizona, U.S.A.	114,000	295,260	2,718,425	Phoenix	198/......	80 FC & OE
Arkansas, U.S.A.	53,187	137,754	2,286,435	Little Rock	202/......	80 FC & OE
Armenian S.S.R., U.S.S.R.	11,506	29,800	3,031,000	Erivan	52/F 6	TP, cit over 50,000—79 PC; oth—70 FC
Aruba, Neth. Antilles	70	181	55,148	Oranjestad	161/E 9	TP—71 FC; cap—72 est
Ascension Island, St. Helena	34	88	719	Georgetown	102/A 5	76 FC
Ashmore & Cartier Islands, Australia	61	159	....	(Canberra, Austr.)	88/C 2	....
Asia	17,128,500	44,362,815	2,633,000,000	....	54/......	80 est
*Australia	2,966,136	7,682,300	14,576,330	Canberra	88/......	81 FC
Australian Capital Territory	927	2,400	221,609	Canberra	96/E 4	81 FC
*Austria	32,375	83,851	7,507,000	Vienna	40/B 3	TP—80 OE; cap, cit over 100,000—73 OE; oth—71 FC
Azerbaidzhan S.S.R., U.S.S.R.	33,436	86,600	6,028,000	Baku	52/G 6	TP, cit over 50,000—79 PC; oth—70 FC
Azores Islands, Portugal	902	2,335	264,400	Ponta Delgada; Angra do Heroísmo; Horta	32/......	TP—77 OE; oth—70 FC & PC
*Bahamas	5,382	13,939	209,505	Nassau	156/C 1	80 PC
*Bahrain	240	622	358,857	Manama	58/F 4	TP—81 PC; oth—71 FC
Baker Island, U.S.A.	1	2.6	....	....	87/J 5	....
Balearic Islands, Spain	1,936	5,014	558,287	Palma	33/H 3	70 FC
*Bangladesh	55,126	142,776	87,052,024	Dhaka	68/G 4	TP—81 PC; oth—74 FC
*Barbados	166	430	248,983	Bridgetown	161/B 8	80 PC
Belau (Palau)	188	487	12,116	Koror	86/D 5	80 FC
*Belgium	11,781	30,513	9,855,110	Brussels	27/E 7	TP—80 OE; oth—70 FC (com)
*Belize	8,867	22,966	144,857	Belmopan	154/C 2	TP, cap, cit over 1,000—80 PC; oth—70 PC
*Benin	43,483	112,620	3,338,240	Porto-Novo	106/E 6	TP—79 PC; cap, Cotonou—75 OE; oth—73 OE
Bermuda	21	54	67,761	Hamilton	156/H 3	80 PC
*Bhutan	18,147	47,000	1,298,000	Thimphu	68/G 3	TP—80 UN est; oth—70 OE
*Bolivia	424,163	1,098,582	5,600,000	La Paz; Sucre	136/......	TP—80 OE; cap, dept, dept cap—76 FC; oth—50 FC
Bonaire, Neth. Antilles	112	291	8,087	Kralendijk	161/E 9	TP—71 FC; cap—72 est
Bophuthatswana (rep.), South Africa	15,570	40,326	1,200,000	Mmabatho	119/D 5	TP—78 est; oth—70 FC
*Botswana	224,764	582,139	819,000	Gaborone	119/C 4	TP—80 OE; cap, Francistown—74 OE; Selebi-Pikwe—75 FC; oth—71 FC
Bouvet Island	22	57	....	....	5/D 1	....
*Brazil	3,284,426	8,506,663	119,098,992	Brasília	132/......	80 PC
British Columbia, Canada	366,253	948,596	2,744,467	Victoria	184/......	81 FC
British Indian Ocean Terr.	29	75	2,000	(London, U.K.)	54/L10	78 est
British Virgin Islands	59	153	11,006	Road Town	157/H 1	TP—80 FC; oth—70 FC
Brunei	2,226	5,765	192,832	Bandar Seri Begawan	85/E 4	81 PC
*Bulgaria	42,823	110,912	8,862,000	Sofia	45/F 4	TP—80 OE; oth—75 PC
*Burkina Faso	105,869	274,200	6,908,000	Ouagadougou	106/D 6	TP—80 UN est; oth—75 FC, 73 OE
*Burma	261,789	678,034	32,913,000	Rangoon	72/B 2	TP—79 OE; states, div. cit over 100,000—73 PC; oth—53 FC
*Burundi	10,747	27,835	4,021,910	Bujumbura	114/E 4	79 PC
*Byelorussian S.S.R. (White Russian S.S.R.), U.S.S.R.	80,154	207,600	9,560,000	Minsk	52/C 4	TP, cit over 50,000—79 PC; oth—70 FC
California, U.S.A.	158,706	411,049	23,667,565	Sacramento	204/......	80 FC & OE
*Cambodia (Kampuchea)	69,898	181,036	5,200,000	Phnom Penh	72/E 4	TP—79 CIA est; cap—80 est
*Cameroon	183,568	475,441	8,503,000	Yaoundé	114/B 2	TP—80 OE; cit over 21,000—76 FC; Ebolowa, oth—70 OE
*Canada	3,851,787	9,976,139	24,343,181	Ottawa	162/......	81 FC
Canary Islands, Spain	2,808	7,273	1,170,224	Las Palmas; Santa Cruz	32/B 4	70 FC
Cape Province, South Africa	261,705	677,816	5,543,506	Cape Town	118/C 6	TP—80 PC; oth—70 FC
*Cape Verde	1,557	4,033	324,000	Praia	106/B 8	TP—80 UN est; oth—70 PC
Cayman Islands	100	259	18,000	Georgetown	156/B 3	TP—81 OE; oth—79 FC

*Member of the United Nations.

Gazetteer-Index of the World

Country	Area Square Miles	Square Kilometers	Population	Capital or Chief Town	Page and Index Ref.	Sources of Population Data
Celebes, Indonesia	72,986	189,034	7,732,383	Ujung Pandang	85/G 6	71 PC
*Central African Republic	242,000	626,780	2,284,000	Bangui	114/C 2	TP—79 est; oth—75 FC
Central America	197,480	511,475	21,000,000	....	154/......	79 OE
Ceylon, see Sri Lanka						
*Chad	495,752	1,283,998	4,309,000	N'Djamena	111/C 4	TP—78 OE; oth—72 OE
Channel Islands	75	194	133,000	St. Helier; St. Peter Port	13/E 8	TP—81 OE; oth—71 FC
*Chile	292,257	756,946	11,275,440	Santiago	138/......	TP—82 PC; cit (part)—79 OE; oth—70 FC & PC
*China, People's Rep. of	3,691,000	9,559,690	958,090,000	Peking (Beijing)	77/......	TP, prov, Peking, Shanghai, Tianjin—78 OE; oth—70 est
China, Republic of (Taiwan)	13,971	36,185	16,609,961	Taipei	77/K 7	TP, cap, Penghu Isl., cit over 300,000—77 OE; oth—70 OE
Christmas Island, Australia	52	135	3,184	Flying Fish Cove	54/O11	80 OE
Ciskei (rep.), S. Africa	2,988	7,740	635,631	Bisho	119/D 6	80 PC
Clipperton Island	2	5.2	....		146/H 8	
Cocos (Keeling) Islands, Australia	5.4	14	555	West Island	54/N11	81 PC
*Colombia	439,513	1,138,339	27,520,000	Bogotá	126/......	TP—80 OE; oth—73 PC
Colorado, U.S.A.	104,091	269,596	2,889,735	Denver	208/......	80 FC & OE
*Comoros	719	1,862	290,000	Moroni	119/G 2	TP—78 est; cap—75 OE; oth—66 FC
*Congo, Republic of	132,046	342,000	1,537,000	Brazzaville	114/B 4	TP—80 UN est; cap—74 FC; oth—74 PC
Connecticut, U.S.A.	5,018	12,997	3,107,576	Hartford	210/......	80 FC & OE
Cook Islands	91	236	17,695	Avarua	87/K 7	81 PC
Coral Sea Islands, Australia	8.5	22	....		88/J 3	....
Corsica, France	3,352	8,682	289,842	Ajaccio; Bastia	28/B 6	75 FC
*Costa Rica	19,575	50,700	2,245,000	San José	154/E 5	TP—80 OE; oth—73 FC
*Cuba	44,206	114,494	9,706,369	Havana	158/......	TP—81 PC; prov, cap—81 PC; oth—81 & 70 PC
Curaçao, Neth. Antilles	178	462	145,430	Willemstad	161/G 7	TP—71 FC; cap—75 OE
*Cyprus	3,473	8,995	629,000	Nicosia	62/E 5	TP—80 OE; oth—73 FC, 72 OE
*Czechoslovakia	49,373	127,876	15,276,799	Prague	41/C 2	TP—80 PC; cap, cit over 100,000—75 OE; rep, reg—74 OE; oth—75 OE, 70 OE
Delaware, U.S.A.	2,044	5,294	594,317	Dover	245/R 3	80 FC & OE
*Denmark	16,629	43,069	5,124,000	Copenhagen	21/......	TP—80 OE; oth—75 OE, 71 OE, 70 FC
District of Columbia, U.S.A.	69	179	638,432	Washington	244/F 5	80 FC
*Djibouti	8,880	23,000	386,000	Djibouti	111/H 5	TP—79 est; cap—73 OE
*Dominica	290	751	74,089	Roseau	161/E 7	TP—80 PC; oth—70 FC
*Dominican Republic	18,704	48,443	5,647,977	Santo Domingo	158/D 6	81 PC
*East Germany (German Democratic Republic)	41,768	108,179	16,737,000	Berlin (East)	22/......	TP—80 OE; oth—75 OE
*Ecuador	109,483	283,561	8,644,000	Quito	128/C 3	TP—81 OE; oth—74 FC
*Egypt	386,659	1,001,447	41,572,000	Cairo	110/E 2	TP—79 OE; oth—76 FC
*El Salvador	8,260	21,393	4,813,000	San Salvador	154/C 4	TP—80 OE; oth—71 FC
England, U.K.	50,516	130,836	46,220,955	London	13/......	TP—81 PC; co, cap (boro & ws)—76 OE; cit—76 & 73 OE; oth—71 FC
*Equatorial Guinea	10,831	28,052	244,000	Malabo	114/A 3	TP—79 est; terr—68 OE; oth—60 FC
Estonian S.S.R., U.S.S.R.	17,413	45,100	1,466,000	Tallinn	52/C 3; 53/......	TP, cit over 50,000—79 PC; oth—70 FC
*Ethiopia	471,776	1,221,900	31,065,000	Addis Ababa	110/G 5	TP—80 OE; cap, Asmara—78 OE; prov—72 OE; oth—72 & 71 OE
Europe	4,057,000	10,507,630	676,000,000	....	7/......	80 est
Faeroe Islands, Denmark	540	1,399	41,969	Tórshavn	21/B 2	77 FC
Falkland Islands & Dependencies	6,198	16,053	1,813	Stanley	120/E 8; 143/D 7	80 FC
*Fiji	7,055	18,272	588,068	Suva	87/H 8; 86/......	80 FC
*Finland	130,128	337,032	4,788,000	Helsinki	18/O 6	TP—80 OE; prov—75 OE; oth—75 OE, 70 OE
Florida, U.S.A.	58,664	151,940	9,746,342	Tallahassee	212/......	80 FC & OE
*France	210,038	543,998	53,788,000	Paris	28/......	TP—80 OE; oth—75 FC
French Guiana	35,135	91,000	73,022	Cayenne	131/E 3	82 FC
French Polynesia	1,544	4,000	137,382	Papeete	87/L 8	77 FC
*Gabon	103,346	267,666	551,000	Libreville	114/B 4	TP—80 UN est; oth—70 FC
*Gambia	4,127	10,689	601,000	Banjul	106/A 6	TP—80 OE; oth—73 FC
Gaza Strip	139	360	400,000	Gaza	65/A 4	TP—76 OE; oth—67 CE
Georgia, U.S.A.	58,910	152,577	5,463,105	Atlanta	217/......	80 FC & OE
Georgian S.S.R., U.S.S.R.	26,911	69,700	5,015,000	Tbilisi	52/F 6	TP, cit over 50,000—79 PC; oth—70 FC
*Germany, East (German Democratic Republic)	41,768	108,179	16,737,000	Berlin (East)	22/......	TP—80 OE; oth—75 OE
*Germany, West (Federal Republic)	95,985	248,601	61,658,000	Bonn	22/......	TP—80 OE; states, cap—76 OE; oth—76 OE, 70 FC
*Ghana	92,099	238,536	11,450,000	Accra	106/D 7	TP—80 OE; oth—70 FC
Gibraltar	2.28	5.91	29,760	Gibraltar	33/D 4	79 OE
*Great Britain & Northern Ireland (United Kingdom)	94,399	244,493	55,672,000	London	10/......	TP—81 OE (see England, Wales, Scotland, Northern Ireland)
*Greece	50,944	131,945	9,599,000	Athens	45/F 6	TP—80 OE; oth—71 FC
Greenland	840,000	2,175,600	49,773	Nuuk (Godthåb)	4/B12	TP—80 OE
*Grenada	133	344	103,103	St. George's	161/D 9; 156/G 4	TP, cap—81 OE; oth—70 FC
Guadeloupe & Dependencies	687	1,779	328,400	Basse-Terre	161/A 5; 156/F 4	82 FC
Guam	209	541	105,979	Agaña	87/E 4; 86/......	80 FC
*Guatemala	42,042	108,889	7,262,419	Guatemala	154/B 3	TP—80 OE; oth—73 FC
*Guinea	94,925	245,856	5,143,284	Conakry	106/B 6	TP, cap (ws), Kankan, Kindia, Labé—72 FC; oth—67 OE
*Guinea-Bissau	13,948	36,125	777,214	Bissau	106/A 6	79 PC
*Guyana	83,000	214,970	793,000	Georgetown	131/B 3	TP—80 OE; cap, cit over 10,000—70 FC; oth—60 FC
*Haiti	10,694	27,697	5,053,792	Port-au-Prince	158/C 5	82 PC
Hawaii, U.S.A.	6,471	16,760	964,691	Honolulu	218/......	80 FC & OE
Heard & McDonald Islands, Australia	113	293	....	....	2/N 8	....
Holland, see Netherlands						
*Honduras	43,277	112,087	3,691,000	Tegucigalpa	154/D 3	TP—80 OE; oth—74 FC
Hong Kong	403	1,044	5,022,000	Victoria	77/H 7; 78/......	TP—81 PC; oth—76 FC
Howland Island, U.S.A.	1	2.6	....	....	87/J 5	....
*Hungary	35,919	93,030	10,709,536	Budapest	41/D 3	TP, cap, co—80 PC; oth—80 PC, 70 FC
*Iceland	39,768	103,000	228,785	Reykjavík	21/B 1	TP—80 PC; oth—70 FC
Idaho, U.S.A.	83,564	216,431	944,038	Boise	220/......	80 FC & OE

Country	Area Square Miles	Area Square Kilometers	Population	Capital or Chief Town	Page and Index Ref.	Sources of Population Data
Illinois, U.S.A.	56,345	145,934	11,426,596	Springfield	222/......	80 FC & OE
*India	1,269,339	3,287,588	683,810,051	New Delhi	68/D 4	TP & states—81 PC; oth—71 FC
Indiana, U.S.A.	36,185	93,719	5,490,260	Indianapolis	227/......	80 FC & OE
*Indonesia	788,430	2,042,034	147,490,298	Jakarta	85/D 7	TP—80 PC; cit—80 PC & 71 PC; isls.—71 PC
Iowa, U.S.A.	56,275	145,752	2,913,808	Des Moines	229/......	80 FC & OE
*Iran	636,293	1,648,000	37,447,000	Tehran	66/F 4	TP—80 OE; div, cit over 50,000—76 PC; oth—66 FC & PC, 56 FC
*Iraq	172,476	446,713	12,767,000	Baghdad	66/C 4	TP—79 OE; oth—65 & 57 FC
*Ireland	27,136	70,282	3,440,427	Dublin	17/......	TP—81 PC; oth—71 FC
Ireland, Northern, U.K.	5,452	14,121	1,543,000	Belfast	17/F 2	TP—81 OE; dist—76 OE; cap, Londonderry—73 OE; oth—71 FC
Isle of Man	227	588	64,000	Douglas	13/C 3	TP—80 OE; oth—71 FC
*Israel	7,847	20,324	3,878,000	Jerusalem	65/B 4	TP—80 OE; cap, cit over 100,000—77 OE; dist, cit over 5,000—72 PC; oth—61 FC
*Italy	116,303	301,225	57,140,000	Rome	34/......	TP—80 OE; oth—71 FC
*Ivory Coast	124,504	322,465	7,920,000	Abidjan	106/C 7	TP—79 OE; oth—75 PC
*Jamaica	4,411	11,424	2,184,000	Kingston	158/......	TP—80 OE; oth—70 & 60 FC
Jan Mayen	144	373	....	....	6/D 1	....
*Japan	145,730	377,441	117,057,485	Tokyo	81/......	TP—80 PC; oth—75 FC
Jarvis Island, U.S.A.	1	2.6	....	....	87/K 6	....
Java, Indonesia	48,842	126,500	73,712,411	Jakarta	85/J 2	71 PC
Johnston Atoll	.91	2.4	327	....	87/K 4	80 FC
*Jordan	35,000	90,650	2,152,273	Amman	65/D 3	TP—79 PC; cap, cit over 100,000—77 OE; gov, cit 9,000-100,000—73 OE; oth—61 FC
*Kampuchea (Cambodia)	69,898	181,036	5,200,000	Phnom Penh	72/E 4	TP—79 CIA est; cap—80 est
Kansas, U.S.A.	82,277	213,097	2,364,236	Topeka	232/......	80 FC & OE
Kazakh S.S.R., U.S.S.R.	1,048,300	2,715,100	14,684,000	Alma-Ata	48/G 5	TP, cit over 50,000—79 PC; oth—70 FC
Kentucky, U.S.A.	40,409	104,659	3,660,257	Frankfort	237/......	80 FC & OE
*Kenya	224,960	582,646	15,327,061	Nairobi	115/G 3	TP—79 PC; oth—69 FC
Kermadec Islands	13	33	5	....	87/J 9	81 FC
Kingman Reef	0.1	0.26	....	....	87/K 5	
Kirgiz S.S.R., U.S.S.R.	76,641	198,500	3,529,000	Frunze	48/H 5	TP, cit over 50,000—79 PC; oth—70 FC
Kiribati	291	754	56,213	Bairiki	87/J 6	TP—78 FC; oth—73 FC
Korea, North	46,540	120,539	17,914,000	P'yŏngyang	80/D 3	TP—80 UN est; cap—76 OE; Hamhŭng—72 OE; oth—70 OE
Korea, South	38,175	98,873	37,448,836	Seoul	80/D 5	TP—80 PC; oth—75 FC & PC
*Kuwait	6,532	16,918	1,355,827	Al Kuwait	58/E 4	80 PC
*Laos	91,428	236,800	3,721,000	Vientiane	72/D 3	TP—80 UN est; cap—66 FC; oth—58 OE
Latvian S.S.R., U.S.S.R.	24,595	63,700	2,521,000	Riga	52/B 3; 53/......	TP, cit over 50,000—79 PC; oth—70 FC
*Lebanon	4,015	10,399	3,161,000	Beirut	62/F 6	TP—80 UN est; cap—70 FC; Tarabulus—64 OE; oth—61 OE
*Lesotho	11,720	30,355	1,339,000	Maseru	119/D 5	TP—80 OE; oth—80 est
*Liberia	43,000	111,370	1,873,000	Monrovia	106/C 7	TP—80 OE; oth—74 FC
*Libya	679,358	1,759,537	2,856,000	Tripoli	110/B 2	TP—79 OE; oth—73 FC & PC
Liechtenstein	61	158	25,220	Vaduz	39/J 2	80 PC
Lithuanian S.S.R., U.S.S.R.	25,174	65,200	3,398,000	Vilna	52/B 3; 53/......	TP, cit over 50,000—79 PC; oth—70 FC
Louisiana, U.S.A.	47,752	123,678	4,206,312	Baton Rouge	238/......	80 FC & OE
*Luxembourg	999	2,587	364,000	Luxembourg	27/J 9	TP—79 OE; cap—74 OE; oth—70 FC
Macau	6	16	271,000	Macau	77/H 7	TP—78 OE; cap—70 FC
*Madagascar	226,657	587,041	8,742,000	Antananarivo	119/H 3	TP—80 UN est; prov, cap, cit over 40,000—75 PC; oth—71 OE
Madeira Islands, Portugal	307	796	262,800	Funchal	32/A 2	TP—77 OE; oth—70 FC & PC
Maine, U.S.A.	33,265	86,156	1,125,027	Augusta	243/......	80 FC & OE
*Malawi	45,747	118,485	5,968,000	Lilongwe	114/F 6	TP—80 OE; oth—77 PC
Malaya, Malaysia	50,806	131,588	11,138,227	Kuala Lumpur	72/D 6	TP, states, Kuala Lumpur—80 PC; cit over 100,000—70 FC; oth—70 PC
*Malaysia	128,308	332,318	13,435,588	Kuala Lumpur	72/D 6; 85/E 4	TP, states, Kuala Lumpur—80 PC; Kuching, Kota Kinabalu, cit over 100,000—70 FC; oth—70 PC
*Maldives	115	298	143,046	Male	54/L 9	78 FC
*Mali	464,873	1,204,021	6,906,000	Bamako	106/C 6	TP—80 OE; oth—76 PC
*Malta	122	316	343,970	Valletta	34/E 7	TP, cit—79 OE; oth—73 OE
Man, Isle of	227	588	64,000	Douglas	13/C 3	TP—80 OE; oth—71 FC
Manitoba, Canada	250,999	650,087	1,026,241	Winnipeg	179/......	81 FC
Marquesas Islands, French Polynesia	492	1,274	5,419	Atuona	87/N 6	77 FC
Marshall Islands	70	181	30,873	Majuro	87/G 4	80 FC
Martinique	425	1,101	328,566	Fort-de-France	161/D 5	82 FC
Maryland, U.S.A.	10,460	27,091	4,216,975	Annapolis	245/......	80 FC & OE
Massachusetts, U.S.A.	8,284	21,456	5,737,037	Boston	249/......	80 FC & OE
*Mauritania	419,229	1,085,803	1,634,000	Nouakchott	106/B 5	TP—80 UN est; oth—76 PC
*Mauritius	790	2,046	959,000	Port Louis	119/G 5	TP—80 OE; cap—77 OE; Curepipe, Quatre Bornes—74 OE; oth—72 PC
Mayotte	144	373	47,300	Dzaoudzi	119/G 2	TP—78 CE; cap—66 FC
*Mexico	761,601	1,972,546	67,395,826	Mexico City	150/......	TP, states, cap—80 PC; cap (ws), Guadalajara (ws), Monterrey (ws)—78 OE; oth—70 PC
Michigan, U.S.A.	58,527	151,585	9,262,078	Lansing	250/......	80 FC & OE
Micronesia, Federated States of	....	....	73,160	Kolonia	87/E 5	TP—80 FC
Midway Islands	1.9	4.9	453	....	87/J 3	80 FC
Minnesota, U.S.A.	84,402	218,601	4,075,970	St. Paul	255/......	80 FC & OE
Mississippi, U.S.A.	47,689	123,515	2,520,638	Jackson	256/......	80 FC & OE
Missouri, U.S.A.	69,697	180,515	4,916,759	Jefferson City	261/......	80 FC & OE
Moldavian S.S.R., U.S.S.R.	13,012	33,700	3,947,000	Kishinev	52/C 5	TP, cit over 50,000—79 PC; oth—70 FC
Monaco	368 acres	149 hectares	25,029	Monaco	28/G 6	75 FC
*Mongolia	606,163	1,569,962	1,594,800	Ulaanbaatar	77/E 2	TP—79 PC; prov, cap, Darhan—77 OE; oth—69 FC
Montana, U.S.A.	147,046	380,849	786,690	Helena	262/......	80 FC & OE
Montserrat	40	104	12,073	Plymouth	157/G 3	80 PC
*Morocco	172,414	446,550	20,242,000	Rabat	106/C 2	TP—80 OE; oth—71 FC
*Mozambique	303,769	786,762	12,130,000	Maputo	119/E 4	TP, prov, cap—80 PC; oth—70 FC
Namibia (South-West Africa)	317,827	823,172	1,200,000	Windhoek	118/B 3	TP—74 est; oth—70 PC
Natal, South Africa	33,578	86,967	5,722,215	Pietermaritzburg	119/E 5	TP—80 PC; oth—70 PC
Nauru	7.7	20	7,254	Yaren (district)	87/G 6	77 PC
Navassa Island	2	5	....	....	156/C 3	....
Nebraska, U.S.A.	77,355	200,349	1,569,825	Lincoln	264/......	80 FC & OE
*Nepal	54,663	141,577	14,179,301	Kathmandu	68/E 3	TP—81 PC; oth—71 FC
*Netherlands	15,892	41,160	14,227,000	The Hague; Amsterdam	27/F 5	TP—81 OE; oth—76 OE (com)

Gazetteer-Index of the World

Country	Area Square Miles	Square Kilometers	Population	Capital or Chief Town	Page and Index Ref.	Sources of Population Data
Netherlands Antilles	390	1,010	246,000	Willemstad	156/E 4	TP—78 OE; Willemsted—75 OE; oth—72 est.
Nevada, U.S.A.	110,561	286,353	800,493	Carson City	266/......	80 FC & OE
New Brunswick, Canada	28,354	73,437	696,403	Fredericton	170/......	81 FC
New Caledonia & Dependencies	7,335	18,998	133,233	Nouméa	87/G 8	76 FC
Newfoundland, Canada	156,184	404,517	567,681	St. John's	166/......	81 FC
New Hampshire, U.S.A.	9,279	24,033	920,610	Concord	268/......	80 FC & OE
New Hebrides, see Vanuatu						
New Jersey, U.S.A.	7,787	20,168	7,364,823	Trenton	273/......	80 FC & OE
New Mexico, U.S.A.	121,593	314,926	1,302,981	Santa Fe	274/......	80 FC & OE
New South Wales, Australia	309,498	801,600	5.126,217	Sydney	96/B 2	81 FC
New York, U.S.A.	49,108	127,190	17,558,072	Albany	276/......	80 FC & OE
*New Zealand	103,736	268,676	3,175,737	Wellington	100/......	TP, inc. places, isls.—81 FC; oth—76 FC
*Nicaragua	45,698	118,358	2,703,000	Managua	154/D 4	TP—80 OE; oth—71 PC
*Niger	489,189	1,267,000	5,098,427	Niamey	106/F 5	TP, cap, Maradi, Tahoua, Zinder—77 PC; oth—72 OE
*Nigeria	357,000	924,630	82,643,000	Lagos	106/F 6	TP—79 OE; prov—63 FC; oth—75 & 71 OE
Niue	100	259	3,578	Alofi	87/K 7	79 OE
Norfolk Island, Australia	13.4	34.6	2,175	Kingston	88/L 5	81 FC
North America	9,363,000	24,250,170	370,000,000	....	146/......	80 UN est
North Carolina, U.S.A.	52,669	136,413	5,881,813	Raleigh	281/......	80 FC & OE
North Dakota, U.S.A.	70,702	183,118	652,717	Bismarck	282/......	80 FC & OE
Northern Ireland, U.K.	5,452	14,121	1,543,000	Belfast	17/F 2	TP—81 OE; dist—76 OE; cap, Londonderry—73 OE; oth—71 FC
Northern Marianas	184	477	16,780	Capitol Hill	87/E 4	80 FC
Northern Territory, Australia	519,768	1,346,200	123,324	Darwin	93/......	81 FC
North Korea	46,540	120,539	17,914,000	P'yŏngyang	80/D 3	TP—80 UN est; cap—76 OE; Hamhŭng—72 OE; oth—70 OE
Northwest Territories, Canada	1,304,896	3,379,683	45,741	Yellowknife	187/G 3	81 FC
*Norway	125,053	323,887	4,092,000	Oslo	18/F 7	TP—80 OE; co, Svalbard—76 OE; oth—76 OE, 70 FC
Nova Scotia, Canada	21,425	55,491	847,442	Halifax	168/......	81 FC
Oceania	3,292,000	8,526,280	23,000,000	....	87/......	80 UN est
Ohio, U.S.A.	41,330	107,045	10,797,624	Columbus	284/......	80 FC & OE
Oklahoma, U.S.A.	69,956	181,186	3,025,290	Oklahoma City	288/......	80 FC & OE
*Oman	120,000	310,800	891,000	Muscat	58/G 6	TP—80 UN est; cap, Matrah—66 OE; Salala—68 OE
Ontario, Canada	412,580	1,068,582	8,625,107	Toronto	175, 177/......	81 FC
Orange Free State, South Africa	49,866	129,153	1,833,216	Bloemfontein	119/D 5	TP—80 PC; oth—70 FC
Oregon, U.S.A.	97,073	251,419	2,633,149	Salem	291/......	80 FC & OE
Orkney Islands, Scotland	376	974	17,675	Kirkwall	15/E 1	TP—76 OE; oth—71 FC
Pacific Islands, Territory of the	533	1,380	132,929	Saipan	87/F 5	80 FC
*Pakistan	310,403	803,944	83,782,000	Islamabad	68/B 3	TP—81 PC; Abbottabad, Bannu, cit over 50,000—72 PC; oth—61 FC
Palau (Belau)	188	487	12,116	Koror	86/D 5	80 FC
Palmyra Atoll	3.85	1	....	....	87/K 5	
*Panama	29,761	77,082	1,830,175	Panamá	154/G 6	TP, cit over 1,600—80 PC; oth—70 FC
*Papua New Guinea	183,540	475,369	3,010,727	Port Moresby	85/B 7; 87/E 6	80 PC
Paracel Islands	....	....	....	....	85/E 2	....
*Paraguay	157,047	406,752	2,973,000	Asunción	144/......	TP—79 OE; oth—72 PC
Pennsylvania, U.S.A.	45,308	117,348	11,863,895	Harrisburg	294/......	80 FC & OE
Persia, see Iran						
*Peru	496,222	1,285,215	17,031,221	Lima	128/......	81 PC
*Philippines	115,707	299,681	48,098,460	Manila	82/......	80 FC
Pitcairn Islands	18	47	54	Adamstown	87/O 8	81 FC
*Poland	120,725	312,678	35,815,000	Warsaw	47/......	TP—81 OE; prov, cap, Cracow, Łódź—75 OE; oth—70 FC
*Portugal	35,549	92,072	9,933,000	Lisbon	32/B 3	TP—80 OE; cap (ws)—76 OE; oth—70 FC & PC
Prince Edward Island, Canada	2,184	5,657	122,506	Charlottetown	168/E 2	81 FC
Puerto Rico	3,515	9,104	3,196,520	San Juan	161/......	80 FC
*Qatar	4,247	11,000	220,000	Doha	58/F 4	TP—80 UN est; cap—79 OE
Québec, Canada	594,857	1,540,680	6,438,403	Québec	172, 174/......	81 FC
Queensland, Australia	666,872	1,727,200	2,295,123	Brisbane	95/......	81 FC
Réunion	969	2,510	491,000	St-Denis	119/F 5	TP—80 OE; oth—74 FC
Rhode Island, U.S.A.	1,212	3,139	947,154	Providence	249/H 5	80 FC & OE
Rhodesia, see Zimbabwe						
*Romania	91,699	237,500	22,048,305	Bucharest	45/F 3	79 OE
Russian S.F.S.R., U.S.S.R.	6,592,812	17,075,400	137,551,000	Moscow	48/D 4	TP, cit over 50,000—79 PC; oth—70 FC
*Rwanda	10,169	26,337	4,819,317	Kigali	114/E 4	78 PC
Sabah, Malaysia	29,300	75,887	1,002,608	Kota Kinabalu	85/F 4	TP—80 PC; Kota Kinabalu—70 FC; oth—70 PC
*Saint Christopher and Nevis	104	269	44,404	Basseterre	156/F 3; 161/C11	TP, isl, cap—80 PC; oth—70 FC
Saint Helena & Dependencies	162	420	5,147	Jamestown	102/B 6	76 FC
*Saint Lucia	238	616	115,783	Castries	161/G 6	80 PC
Saint Pierre & Miquelon	93.5	242	6,034	Saint-Pierre	166/C 4	82 FC
*Saint Vincent & the Grenadines	150	388	124,000	Kingstown	161/A 8; 157/G 4	TP—80 OE; oth—70 FC
Sakhalin, U.S.S.R.	29,500	76,405	655,000	Yuzhno-Sakhalinsk	48/P 4	TP, cit over 50,000—79 PC; oth—70 FC
*Salvador, El	8,260	21,393	4,813,000	San Salvador	154/C 4	TP—80 OE; oth—71 FC
San Marino	23.4	60.6	19,149	San Marino	34/D 3	TP—76 FC; oth—77 OE
*São Tomé e Príncipe	372	963	85,000	São Tomé	106/F 8	TP—80 UN est; oth—70 PC
Sarawak, Malaysia	48,202	124,843	1,294,753	Kuching	85/E 5	TP—80 PC; Kuching—70 FC; oth—70 PC
Sardinia, Italy	9,301	24,090	1,450,483	Cagliari	34/B 4	71 FC
Saskatchewan, Canada	251,699	651,900	968,313	Regina	181/......	81 FC
*Saudi Arabia	829,995	2,149,687	8,367,000	Riyadh	58/D 4	TP—80 UN est; oth—74 PC
Scotland, U.K.	30,414	78,772	5,117,146	Edinburgh	15/......	TP—81 PC; reg—75 OE; cit—75 & 73 OE, 71 FC; oth—71 FC
*Senegal	75,954	196,720	5,508,000	Dakar	106/A 5	TP—79 OE; oth—76 PC
*Seychelles	145	375	63,000	Victoria	119/H 5	TP—79 OE; oth—77 FC
Shetland Islands, Scotland	552	1,430	18,494	Lerwick	15/G 2	TP—76 OE; oth—73 OE & 71 FC
Siam, see Thailand						
Sicily, Italy	9,926	25,708	4,628,918	Palermo	34/D 6	71 FC
*Sierra Leone	27,925	72,325	3,470,000	Freetown	106/B 7	TP—80 UN est; cap, Bo, Kenema, Makeni—74 PC; oth—63 FC
*Singapore	226	585	2,413,945	Singapore	72/F 6	80 FC
Society Islands, French Polynesia	677	1,753	117,703	Papeete	87/L 7	77 FC
*Solomon Islands	11,500	29,785	221,000	Honiara	87/G 6; 86/......	TP—79 OE; oth—76 OE
*Somalia	246,200	637,658	3,645,000	Mogadishu	115/H 3	TP—80 UN est; prov, cap—75 PC; oth—69, 68, 67, 63 & 62 OE

Gazetteer-Index of the World

Country	Area Square Miles	Square Kilometers	Population	Capital or Chief Town	Page and Index Ref.	Sources of Population Data
*South Africa	455,318	1,179,274	23,771,970	Cape Town; Pretoria	118/C 5	TP (excl Transkei, Bophuthatswana, Venda), prov—80 PC; Transkei, Bophuthatswana—78 est; Venda—79 est; oth—70 FC
South America	6,875,000	17,806,250	245,000,000	....	120/......	80 UN est
South Australia, Australia	379,922	984,000	1,285,033	Adelaide	94/......	81 FC
South Carolina, U.S.A.	31,113	80,583	3,121,833	Columbia	296/......	80 FC & OE
South Dakota, U.S.A.	77,116	199,730	690,768	Pierre	298/......	80 FC & OE
South Korea	38,175	98,873	37,448,836	Seoul	80/D 5	TP—80 PC; oth—75 FC & PC
South-West Africa (Namibia)	317,827	823,172	1,200,000	Windhoek	118/B 3	TP—74 est; oth—70 FC
*Spain	194,881	504,742	37,430,000	Madrid	33/......	TP—80 OE; met areas—75 OE; oth—70 FC
Spratly Island	....	....			85/E 4	....
*Sri Lanka	25,332	65,610	14,850,001	Colombo	68/E 7	TP—81 PC; cap, Jaffna—73 OE; oth—71 FC
*Sudan	967,494	2,505,809	18,691,000	Khartoum	110/E 4	TP—80 OE; cap, prov, prov cap—73 PC; oth—73 PC, 72 OE
Sumatra, Indonesia	164,000	424,760	19,360,400	Medan	84/B 5	71 PC
*Suriname	55,144	142,823	354,860	Paramaribo	131/C 3	TP, cap—80 PC; dist—71 PC; oth—64 FC
Svalbard, Norway	23,957	62,049	3,431	Longyearbyen	18/C 2	76 OE
*Swaziland	6,705	17,366	547,000	Mbabane	119/E 5	TP—80 OE; oth—76 FC
*Sweden	173,665	449,792	8,320,000	Stockholm	18/J 8	TP—81 OE; oth—75 FC
Switzerland	15,943	41,292	6,365,960	Bern	39/......	TP—80 FC; cantons—78 OE; cap, cit over 100,000 (& ws)—74 OE; cit (com) over 30,000 (& ws)—73 OE; oth—70 FC
*Syria	71,498	185,180	8,979,000	Damascus	62/G 5	TP—80 OE; oth—70 FC
Tadzhik S.S.R., U.S.S.R.	55,251	143,100	3,801,000	Dushanbe	48/G 6	TP, cit over 50,000—79 PC; oth—70 FC
Tahiti, French Polynesia	402	1,041	95,604	Papeete	87/L 7	77 FC
Taiwan	13,971	36,185	16,609,961	Taipei	77/K 7	TP, cap, Penghu Isl., cit over 300,000—77 OE; oth—70 OE
*Tanzania	363,708	942,003	17,527,560	Dar es Salaam	114/F 5	TP—78 PC; div, cap, cit over 17,000—78 PC; oth—67 FC
Tasmania, Australia	26,178	67,800	418,957	Hobart	99/......	81 FC
Tennessee, U.S.A.	42,144	109,153	4,591,120	Nashville	237/......	80 FC & OE
Texas, U.S.A.	266,807	691,030	14,229,288	Austin	303/......	80 FC & OE
*Thailand	198,455	513,998	46,455,000	Bangkok	72/D 3	TP—80 OE; oth—70 FC
Tibet, China	463,320	1,200,000	1,790,000	Lhasa	76/C 5	TP—78 OE; oth—70 est
*Togo	21,622	56,000	2,472,000	Lomé	106/E 7	TP—79 OE; oth—70 FC
Tokelau	3.9	10	1,575	Fakaofo	87/J 6	TP—76 FC; oth—72 FC
Tonga	270	699	90,128	Nuku'alofa	87/J 8	76 PC
Transkei (rep.), South Africa	16,910	43,797	2,000,000	Umtata	119/D 6	TP—80 est; oth—70 FC
Transvaal, South Africa	109,621	283,918	10,673,033	Pretoria	119/D 4	TP—80 PC; oth—70 FC
*Trinidad and Tobago	1,980	5,128	1,067,108	Port-of-Spain	157/G 5; 161/A10	80 PC
Tristan da Cunha, St. Helena	38	98	251	Edinburgh	2/J 7	79 OE
Tuamotu Archipelago, French Polynesia	341	883	9,052	Apataki	87/M 7	77 FC
*Tunisia	63,378	164,149	6,367,000	Tunis	106/F 1	TP—79 OE; oth—75 FC
*Turkey	300,946	779,450	45,217,556	Ankara	62/D 3	TP—80 PC; oth—75 FC
Turkmen S.S.R., U.S.S.R.	188,455	488,100	2,759,000	Ashkhabad	48/F 6	TP, cit over 50,000—79 PC; oth—70 FC
Turks and Caicos Islands	166	430	7,436	Cockburn Town, Grand Turk	156/D 2	80 PC
Tuvalu	9.78	25.33	7,349	Fongafale, Funafuti	87/H 6	79 FC
*Uganda	91,076	235,887	12,630,076	Kampala	114/F 3	TP, cap—80 PC; oth—69 FC
*Ukrainian S.S.R., U.S.S.R.	233,089	603,700	49,755,000	Kiev	52/D 5	TP, cit over 50,000—79 PC; oth—70 FC
*Union of Soviet Socialist Republics	8,649,490	22,402,179	262,436,227	Moscow	48/......	TP, S.S.R., cit over 50,000—79 PC; oth—70 FC
*United Arab Emirates	32,278	83,600	1,040,275	Abu Dhabi	58/F 5	TP—80 PC; oth—79 OE
*United Kingdom	94,399	244,493	55,672,000	London	10/......	TP—81 OE (see England, Wales, Scotland, Northern Ireland)
*United States of America	3,623,420	9,384,658	226,504,825	Washington	188/......	80 FC & OE
*Upper Volta (Burkina Faso)	105,869	274,200	6,908,000	Ouagadougou	106/D 6	TP—80 UN est; oth—75 FC, 73 OE
*Uruguay	72,172	186,925	2,899,000	Montevideo	145/......	TP—80 OE; oth—75 PC
Utah, U.S.A.	84,899	219,888	1,461,037	Salt Lake City	304/......	80 FC & OE
Uzbek S.S.R., U.S.S.R.	173,591	449,600	15,391,000	Tashkent	48/G 5	TP, cit over 50,000—79 PC; oth—70 FC
*Vanuatu	5,700	14,763	112,596	Vila	87/G 7	79 FC
Vatican City	108.7 acres	44 hectares	728	....	34/B 6	78 OE
Venda (rep.), South Africa	2,510	6,501	450,000	Thohoyandou	119/E 4	79 est
*Venezuela	352,143	912,050	14,313,000	Caracas	124/......	TP—81 OE; oth—71 FC
Vermont U.S.A.	9,614	24,900	511,456	Montpelier	268/......	80 FC & OE
Victoria, Australia	87,876	227,600	3,832,443	Melbourne	96/B 5	81 FC
*Vietnam	128,405	332,569	52,741,766	Hanoi	72/E 3	TP—79 FC; cap, Haiphong, Ho Chi Minh City—79 PC; oth cit over 100,000 (north)—70 est, (south)—73 & 71 OE; oth—69 OE, 60 FC
Virginia, U.S.A.	40,767	105,587	5,346,818	Richmond	307/......	80 FC & OE
Virgin Islands, British	59	153	11,006	Road Town	157/H 1	TP—80 FC; oth—70 FC
Virgin Islands, U.S.A.	132	342	96,569	Charlotte Amalie	161/A 4	80 FC
Wake Island	2.5	6.5	302	Wake Islet	87/G 4	80 FC
Wales, U.K.	8,017	20,764	2,790,462	Cardiff	13/D 5	TP—81 PC; co—76 OE; cit—76 & 73 OE; par—71 FC
Wallis and Futuna	106	275	9,192	Mata Utu	87/J 7	76 FC
Washington, U.S.A.	68,139	176,480	4,132,180	Olympia	310/......	80 FC & OE
West Bank	2,100	5,439	c. 800,000	....	65/C 3	TP—81 est; oth—67 CE & 61 FC
Western Australia, Australia	975,096	2,525,500	1,273,624	Perth	92/......	81 FC
Western Sahara	102,703	266,000	76,425		106/B 3	70 FC
*Western Samoa	1,133	2,934	158,130	Apia	87/J 7	81 PC
*West Germany (Federal Republic)	95,985	248,601	61,658,000	Bonn	22/......	TP—80 OE; states, cap—76 OE; oth—76 OE, 70 FC
West Virginia, U.S.A.	24,231	62,758	1,950,279	Charleston	312/......	80 FC & OE
*White Russian S.S.R. (Byelo-russian S.S.R.), U.S.S.R.	80,154	207,600	9,560,000	Minsk	52/C 4	TP, cit over 50,000—79 PC; oth—70 FC
Wisconsin, U.S.A.	56,153	145,436	4,705,521	Madison	317/......	80 FC & OE
World	(land) 57,970,000	150,142,300	4,415,000,000	....	1, 2/......	80 UN est
Wyoming, U.S.A.	97,809	253,325	469,557	Cheyenne	319/......	80 FC & OE
*Yemen, People's Democratic Republic of	111,101	287,752	1,969,000	Aden	58/E 7	TP—81 PC; oth—75 FC
*Yemen Arab Republic	77,220	200,000	6,456,189	San a	58/D 6	TP—80 OE; Mukalla, Seiyun—76 OE; cap—73 OE; Saihut—60 OE
*Yugoslavia	98,766	255,804	22,471,000	Belgrade	45/C 3	TP—81 OE; oth—71 FC
Yukon Territory, Canada	207,075	536,324	23,153	Whitehorse	186/E 3	81 FC
*Zaire	905,063	2,344,113	28,291,000	Kinshasa	114/D 4	TP—80 OE; prov, cap—70 FC; oth—70 FC & PC
*Zambia	290,586	752,618	5,679,808	Lusaka	114/E 7	80 PC
*Zimbabwe	150,803	390,580	7,360,000	Harare	119/D 3	TP—80 OE; cap, cit over 12,000—77 OE; oth—69 FC

Introduction to the Maps and Indexes

The following notes have been added to aid the reader in making the best use of this atlas. Though he may be familiar with maps and map indexes, the publisher believes that a quick review of the material below will add to his enjoyment of this reference work.

Arrangement — The Plan of the Atlas. The atlas has been designed with maximum convenience for the user as its objective. All geographically related information pertaining to a country or region appears on adjacent pages, eliminating the task of searching throughout the entire volume for data on a given area. Thus, the reader will find, conveniently assembled, political, topographic, economic and special maps of a political area or region, accompanied by detailed map indexes, statistical data, and illustrations of the national flags of the area.

The sequence of country units in this American-designed atlas is international in arrangement. Units on the world as a whole are followed by a section on the polar regions which, in turn, is followed by pages devoted to Europe and its countries. Every continent map is accompanied by special population distribution, climatic and vegetation maps of that continent. Following the maps of the European continent and its countries, the geographic sequence plan proceeds as follows: Asia, the Pacific and Australia, Africa, South America, North America, and ends with detailed coverage on the United States.

Political Maps — The Primary Reference Tool. The most detailed maps in each country unit are the *political maps.* It is our feeling that the reader is likely to refer to these maps more often than to any other in the book when confronted by such questions as — Where? How big? What is it near? Answering these common queries is the function of the political maps. Each political map stresses *political* phenomena — countries, internal political divisions, boundaries, cities and towns. The major political unit or units, shown on the map, are banded in distinctive colors for easy identification and delineation. First-order political subdivisions (states, provinces, counties on the state maps) are shown, scale permitting.

The reader is advised to make use of the *legend* appearing under the title on each political map. Map *symbols,* the special "language" of maps, are explained in the legend. Each variety of dot, circle, star or interrupted line has a special meaning which should be clearly understood by the user so that he may interpret the map data correctly.

Each country has been portrayed at a *scale* commensurate with its political, areal, economic or tourist importance. In certain cases, a whole map unit may be devoted to a single nation if that nation is considered to be of prime interest to most atlas users. In other cases, several nations will be shown on a single map if, as separate entities, they are of lesser relative importance. Areas of dense settlement and important significance within a country have been enlarged and portrayed in inset maps inserted on the margins of the main map. The scale of each map is indicated as a fractional representation (1:1,000,000). The reader is advised to refer to the linear or "bar" scale appearing on each map or map inset in order to determine the distance between points.

The *projection* system used for each map is noted near the title of the map. Map projections are the special graphic systems used by cartographers to render the curved three-dimensional surface of the globe on a flat surface. Optimum map projections determined by the attributes of the area have been used by the publishers for each map in the atlas.

A word here as to the choice of place names on the maps. Throughout the atlas names appear, with a few exceptions, in their local official spellings. However, conventional Anglicized spellings are used for major geographical divisions and for towns and topographic features for which English forms exist; i.e., "Spain" instead of "España" or "Munich" instead of "München." Names of this type are normally followed by the local official spelling in parentheses. As an aid to the user the indexes are cross-referenced for all current and most former spellings of such names.

Names of cities and towns in the United States follow the forms listed in the *Post Office Directory* of the United States Postal Service. Domestic physical names follow the decisions of the Board on Geographic Names, U.S. Department of the Interior, and of various state geographic name boards.

It is the belief of the publishers that the boundaries shown in a general reference atlas should reflect current geographic and political realities. This policy has been followed consistently in the atlas. The presentation of *de facto* boundaries in cases of territorial dispute between various nations does not imply the political endorsement of such boundaries by the publisher, but simply the honest representation of boundaries as they exist at the time of the printing of the atlas maps.

Indexes — Pinpointing a Location. Each political map is accompanied by a comprehensive index of the place names appearing on the map. If you are unfamiliar with the location of a particular geographical place and wish to find its position within the confines of the subject area of the map, consult the map index as your first step. The name of the feature sought will be found in its proper alphabetical sequence with a key reference letter-number combination corresponding to its location on the map. After noting the key reference letter-number combination for the place name, turn to the map. The place name will be found within the square formed by the two lines of latitude and the two lines of longitude which enclose the co-ordinates — i.e., the marginal letters and numbers. The diagram below illustrates the system of indexing.

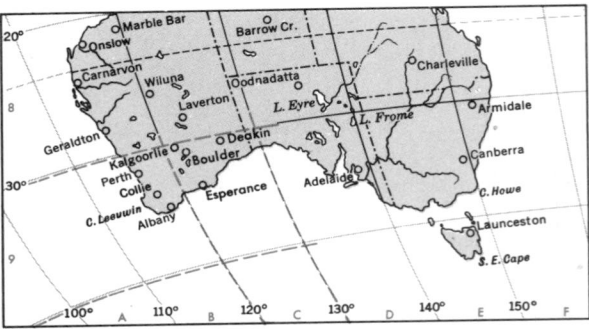

In the case of maps consisting entirely of insets, the place name is found near the intersection point of the imaginary lines connecting the co-ordinates at right angles. See below.

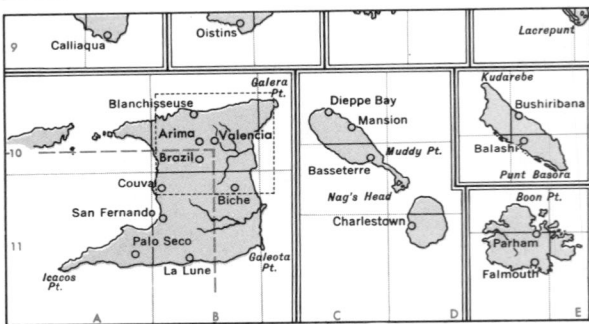

Where space on the map has not permitted giving the complete form of the place name, the complete form is shown in the index. Where a place is known by more than one name or by various spellings of the same name, the different forms have been included in the index. Physical features are listed under their proper names and not according to their generic terms; that is to say, Rio Negro will be found under Negro and not under Rio Negro. On the other hand, Rio Grande will be found under Rio Grande. Accompanying most index entries for cities and towns, and for other political units, are *population figures* for the particular entries. The large number of population figures in the atlas makes this work one of the most comprehensive statistical sources available to the public today. The population figures have been taken from the latest official censuses and estimates of the various nations. Dates and sources for the population figures are listed in the Gazetteer-Index of the World preceding this section.

Population and area figures for countries and major political units are listed in bold type *fact lists* on the margins of the indexes. In addition, the capital, largest city, highest point, monetary unit, principal languages and the prevailing religions of the country concerned are also listed. The Gazetteer-Index of the World on the preceding pages provides a quick reference index for countries and other important areas. Though population and area figures for each major unit area also found in the map section, the Gazetteer-Index provides a conveniently arranged statistical comparison contained in five pages. As mentioned, dates and sources of the population figures appearing in the country indexes are also listed in this section.

All index entries for cities and towns in the United States are preceded by a five-digit postal ZIP code number applying to the community. This useful feature permits the reader to address his mail so that it will be routed and delivered more efficiently and quickly by the U.S. Postal Service. A dagger (†) designates those places that do not possess a post office. The ZIP code number listed in such cases refers to that of the nearest post office. An asterisk (*) marks those larger cities which are divided into multiple ZIP code areas. Using the single ZIP code number listed in such cases will direct your letter to the proper city with dispatch. However, if the precise ZIP code number of the address within the city is needed, it is suggested that the reader refer to the latest National ZIP Code Directory at his local post office. This detailed guide lists every street in a multiple ZIP code city with the proper ZIP code for the street.

Relief Maps. Accompanying each political map is a relief map of the area. The purpose of the relief map is to illustrate the surface configuration (TOPOGRAPHY) of the region. A shading technique in color simulates the relative ruggedness of the terrain — plains, plateaus, valleys, hills and mountains. Graded colors, ranging from greens for lowlands, yellows for intermediate elevations to browns in the highlands, indicate the height above sea level of each part of the land. A vertical scale at the margin of the map shows the approximate height in meters and feet represented by each color.

Economic Maps — Agriculture, Industry and Resources. One of the most interesting features that will be found in each country unit is the economic map. From this map one can determine the basic activities of a nation as expressed through its economy. A perusal of the map yields a full understanding of the area's economic geography and natural resources.

The agricultural economy is manifested in two ways: color bands and commodity names. The color bands express broad categories of *dominant land use*, such as, cereal belts, forest lands, livestock range lands, nonagricultural wastes. The red commodity names, on the other hand, pinpoint the areas of production of *specific* crops; i.e., wheat, cotton, sugar beets, etc.

Major mineral occurrences are denoted by standard letter symbols appearing in blue. The relative size of the letter symbols signifies the relative importance of the deposit.

The manufacturing sector of the economy is presented by means of diagonal line patterns expressing the various *industrial areas* of consequence within a country.

The fishing industry is represented by names of commercial fish species appearing offshore in blue letters. Major waterpower sites are designated by blue symbols.

The publishers have tried to make this work the most comprehensive and useful atlas available, and it is hoped that it will prove a valuable reference work. Any constructive suggestions from the reader will be welcomed.

Sources and Acknowledgments

A multitude of sources goes into the making of a large-scale reference work such as this. To list them all would take many pages and would consume space better devoted to the maps and reference materials themselves. However, certain general sources were very useful in preparing this work and are listed below.

STATISTICAL OFFICE OF THE UNITED NATIONS.
Demographic Yearbook. New York. Issued annually.

STATISTICAL OFFICE OF THE UNITED NATIONS.
Statistical Yearbook. New York. Issued annually.

THE GEOGRAPHER, U.S. DEPARTMENT OF STATE.
International Boundary Study papers. Washington. Various dates.

THE GEOGRAPHER, U.S. DEPARTMENT OF STATE.
Geographic Notes. Washington. Various dates.

UNITED STATES BOARD ON GEOGRAPHIC NAMES.
Decisions on Geographic Names in the United States. Washington. Various dates.

UNITED STATES BOARD ON GEOGRAPHIC NAMES.
Official Standard Names Gazetteers. Washington. Various dates.

CANADIAN PERMANENT COMMITTEE ON GEOGRAPHICAL NAMES.
Gazetteer of Canada series. Ottawa. Various dates.

UNITED STATES POSTAL SERVICE.
National Five Digit ZIP Code and Post Office Directory. Washington. 1983.

UNITED STATES POSTAL SERVICE.
Postal Bulletin. Washington. Issued weekly.

UNITED STATES DEPARTMENT OF THE INTERIOR. BUREAU OF MINES.
Minerals Yearbook. 4 vols. Washington. Various dates.

UNITED STATES GEOLOGICAL SURVEY.
Elevations and distances in the United States. Reston, Va. 1980.

CARTACTUAL.
Cartactual — Topical Map Service. Budapest. Issued bi-monthly.

AMERICAN GEOGRAPHICAL SOCIETY.
Focus. New York. Issued ten times a year.

THE AMERICAN UNIVERSITY.
Foreign Area Studies. Washington. Various dates.

CENTRAL INTELLIGENCE AGENCY.
General reference maps. Washington. Various dates.

A sample list of sources used for **specific** countries follows:

Afghanistan
CENTRAL STATISTICS OFFICE.
Preliminary Results of the First Afghan Population Census 1979. Kabul.

Albania
DREJTORIA E STATISTIKES.
1979 Census. Tiranë.

Argentina
INSTITUTO NACIONAL DE ESTADISTICA Y CENSOS.
Censo Nacional de Población y Vivienda 1980. Buenos Aires.

Australia
AUSTRALIAN BUREAU OF STATISTICS.
Census of Population and Housing 1981. Canberra.

Brazil
FUNDAÇAO INSTITUTO BRASILEIRO DE GEOGRAFIA E ESTATISTICA.
IX Recenseamento Geral do Brasil 1980. Rio de Janeiro.

Canada
STATISTICS CANADA.
1981 Census of Canada. Ottawa.

Cuba
COMITE ESTATAL DE ESTADISTICAS.
Censo de Población y Viviendas 1981. Havana.

Hungary
HUNGARIAN CENTRAL STATISTICAL OFFICE.
1980 Census. Budapest.

Indonesia
BIRO PUSAT STATISTIK.
Sensus Penduduk 1980. Jakarta.

Kuwait
CENTRAL OFFICE OF STATISTICS.
1980 Census. Al Kuwait.

New Zealand
DEPARTMENT OF STATISTICS.
New Zealand Census of Population and Dwellings 1981. Wellington.

Panama
DIRECCIÓN DE ESTADISTICA Y CENSO.
Censos Nacionales de 1980. Panamá.

Papua New Guinea
BUREAU OF STATISTICS.
National Population Census 1980. Pòrt Moresby.

Philippines
NATIONAL CENSUS AND STATISTICS OFFICE.
1980 Census of Population. Manila.

Saint Lucia
CENSUS OFFICE.
1980 Population Census. Castries.

Singapore
DEPARTMENT OF STATISTICS.
Census of Population 1980. Singapore.

U.S.S.R.
CENTRAL STATISTICAL ADMINISTRATION.
1979 Census. Moscow.

United States
BUREAU OF THE CENSUS.
1980 Census of Population. Washington.

Vanuatu
CENSUS OFFICE.
1979 Population Census. Port Vila.

Zambia
CENTRAL STATISTICAL OFFICE.
1980 Census of Population and Housing. Lusaka.

Glossary of Abbreviations

A

A. A. F. — Army Air Field
Acad. — Academy
A. C. T. — Australian Capital Territory
adm. — administration; administrative
A. F. B. — Air Force Base
Afgh., Afghan. — Afghanistan
Afr. — Africa
Ala. — Alabama
Alb. — Albania
Alg. — Algeria
Alta. — Alberta
Amer. — American
Amer. Samoa — American Samoa
And. — Andorra
Ant., Antarc. — Antarctica
Ant. & Bar. — Antigua and Barbuda
Ar. — Arabia
arch. — archipelago
Arg. — Argentina
Ariz. — Arizona
Ark. — Arkansas
A. S. S. R. — Autonomous Soviet
    Socialist Republic
Aust. — Austria
Aust. Cap. Terr. — Australian Capital
    Territory
Austr., Austral. — Australian, Australia
aut. — autonomous
Aut. Obl. — Autonomous Oblast

B

B. — bay
Bah. — Bahamas
Barb. — Barbados
Battlef. — Battlefield
Bch. — Beach
Belg. — Belgium
Berm. — Bermuda
Bol. — Bolivia
Bots. — Botswana
Br. — Branch
Br. — British
Braz. — Brazil
Br. Col. — British Columbia
Br. Ind. Oc. Terr. — British Indian
    Ocean Territory
Bulg. — Bulgaria

C

C. — cape
Calif. — California
Can. — Canada
can. — canal
cap. — capital
Cent. Afr. Rep. — Central African
    Republic
Cent. Amer. — Central America
C. G. Sta. — Coast Guard Station
C. H. — Court House
chan. — channel
Chan. Is. — Channel Islands
Chem. Ctr. — Chemical Center
co. — county
C. of G. H. — Cape of Good Hope
Col. — Colombia
Colo. — Colorado
comm. — commissary
Conn. — Connecticut
cont. — continent
cord. — cordillera (mountain range)
C. Rica — Costa Rica
C. S. — County Seat
C. Verde — Cape Verde
Czech. — Czechoslovakia

D

D. C. — District of Columbia
Del. — Delaware
Dem. — Democratic
Den. — Denmark
depr. — depression
dept. — department
des. — desert
dist., dist's — district, districts
div. — division
Dom. Rep. — Dominican Republic

E

E. — East
Ec., Ecua. — Ecuador
E. Ger. — East Germany
elec. div. — electoral division
El Salv. — El Salvador
Eng. — England
Equat. Guinea, Eq. Guin — Equatorial
    Guinea

escarp. — escarpment
est. — estuary
Eth. — Ethiopia

F

Falk. Is. — Falkland Islands
Fin. — Finland
Fk., Fks. — Fork, Forks
Fla. — Florida
for. — forest
Fr. — France, French
Fr. Gui. — French Guiana
Fr. Poly. — French Polynesia
Ft. — Fort

G

G. — gulf
Ga. — Georgia
Game Res. — Game Reserve
Ger. — Germany
geys. — geyser
Gibr. — Gibraltar
glac. — glacier
gov. — governorate
Gr. — Group
Greenl. — Greenland
Gren. — Grenada
Gt. Brit. — Great Britain
Guad. — Guadeloupe
Guat. — Guatemala
Guinea-Biss. — Guinea-Bissau
Guy. — Guyana

H

har., harb., hbr. — harbor
hd. — head
highl. — highland, highlands
Hist. — Historic, Historical
Hond. — Honduras
Hts. — Heights
Hung. — Hungary

I

i., isl. — island, isle
I. C. — independent city
Ice., Icel. — Iceland
Ida. — Idaho
Ill. — Illinois
Ind. — Indiana
ind. city — independent city
Indon. — Indonesia
Ind. Res. — Indian Reservation
int. div. — internal division
inten. — intendency
Int'l — International
Ire. — Ireland
is., isls. — islands
Isr. — Israel
isth. — isthmus
Iv. Coast — Ivory Coast

J

Jam. — Jamaica
Jct. — Junction

K

Kans. — Kansas
Ky. — Kentucky

L

L. — Lake, Loch, Lough
La. — Louisiana
Lab. — Laboratory
lag. — lagoon
Ld. — Land
Leb. — Lebanon
Les. — Lesotho
Liecht. — Liechtenstein
Lux. — Luxembourg

M

Mad., Madag. — Madagascar
Man. — Manitoba
Mart. — Martinique
Mass. — Massachusetts
Maur. — Mauritania
Md. — Maryland
met. area — metropolitan area
Mex. — Mexico
Mich. — Michigan
Minn. — Minnesota
Miss. — Mississippi
Mo. — Missouri
Mon. — Monument
Mong. — Mongolia
Mont. — Montana
Mor. — Morocco

Moz., Mozamb. — Mozambique
mt. — mount
mtn. — mountain

N

N., No., North. — North, Northern
N. Amer. — North America
Nam., Namib. — Namibia
N. A. S. — Naval Air Station
Nat'l — National
Nat'l Cem. — National Cemetery
Nat'l Mem. Park — National Memorial
    Park
Nat'l Mil. Park — National Military
    Park
Nat'l Pkwy. — National Parkway
Nav. Base — Naval Base
Nav. Sta. — Naval Station
N. B., N. Br. — New Brunswick
N. C. — North Carolina
N. Dak. — North Dakota
Nebr. — Nebraska
Neth. — Netherlands
Neth. Ant. — Netherlands Antilles
Nev. — Nevada
New Bruns. — New Brunswick
New Cal., New Caled. — New Caledonia
Newf. — Newfoundland
New Hebr. — New Hebrides
N. H. — New Hampshire
Nic. — Nicaragua
N. Ire. — Northern Ireland
N. J. — New Jersey
N. Mex. — New Mexico
Nor. — Norway, Norwegian
North. — Northern
North. Terr., No. Terr. — Northern
    Territory
    (Australia)
N. S. — Nova Scotia
N. S. W., N.S. Wales — New South Wales
N. W. T., N. W. Terrs. — Northwest
    Territories
    (Canada)
N. Y. — New York
N. Z., N. Zealand — New Zealand

O

Obl. — Oblast
O. F. S. — Orange Free State
Okla. — Oklahoma
Okr. — Okrug
Ont. — Ontario
Ord. Depot — Ordnance Depot
Oreg. — Oregon

P

Pa. — Pennsylvania
Pac. Is. — Pacific Islands,
    Territory of the
Pak. — Pakistan
Pan. — Panama
Papua N. G. —Papua New Guinea
Par. — Paraguay
par. — parish
passg. — passage
P.D.R. Yemen — People's Democratic
    Republic of Yemen
P. E. I. — Prince Edward Island
pen. — peninsula
Phil., Phil. Is. — Philippines
Pk. — Park
pk. — peak
plat. — plateau
P. N. G. — Papua New Guinea
Pol. — Poland
Port. — Portugal, Portuguese
Pr. Edward I. — Prince Edward Island
pref. — prefecture
P. Rico — Puerto Rico
prom. — promontory
prov. — province, provincial
pt. — point

Q

Que. — Quebec
Queens. — Queensland

R

R. — River
ra. — range
Rec., Recr. — Recreation, Recreational
reg. — region
Rep. — Republic
res. — reservoir
Res. — Reservation, Reserve
R. i. — Rhode Island

riv. — river
Rom. — Romania

S

S. — South
Sa. — Sierra, Serra
S. Afr., S. Africa — South Africa
salt dep. — salt deposit
salt des. — salt desert
S. Amer. — South America
São T. & Pr. — São Tomé
    and Príncipe
Sask. — Saskatchewan
Saudi Ar. — Saudi Arabia
S. Aust., S. Austral. — South Australia
S. C. — South Carolina
Scot. — Scotland
Sd. — Sound
S. Dak. — South Dakota
Sen. — Senegal
sen. dist. — senatorial district
Seych. — Seychelles
S. F. S. R. — Soviet Federated Socialist
    Republic
Sing. — Singapore
S. Leone — Sierra Leone
S. Marino — San Marino
Sol. Is. — Solomon Islands
Sp. — Spanish
Spr., Sprs. — Spring, Springs
S. S. R. — Soviet Socialist Republic
St., Ste. — Saint, Sainte
Sta. — Station
St. Chris.-Nevis — Saint Christopher-
    Nevis
St. P. & M. — Saint Pierre and
    Miquelon
St. Vin. & Grens. — St. Vincent & The
    Grenadines
str., strs. — strait, straits
Sur. — Suriname
S. W. Afr. — South-West Africa
Swaz. — Swaziland
Switz. — Switzerland

T

Tanz. — Tanzania
Tas. — Tasmania
Tenn. — Tennessee
terr., terrs. — territory, territories
Tex. — Texas
Thai. — Thailand
trad. — traditional
Trin. & Tob. — Trinidad and Tobago
Tun. — Tunisia
twp. — township

U

U. A. E. — United
    Arab Emirates
U. K. — United Kingdom
Upp. Volta — Upper Volta
urb. area — urban area
Urug. — Uruguay
U. S. — United States
U. S. S. R. — Union of Soviet Socialist
    Republics

V

Va. — Virginia
Ven., Venez. — Venezuela
V. I. (Br.) — Virgin Islands (British)
V. I. (U. S.) — Virgin Islands (U. S.)
Vic. — Victoria
Viet. — Vietnam
Vill. — Village
vol. — volcano
Vt. — Vermont

W

W. — West, Western
Wash. — Washington
W. Aust., W. Austral. — Western
    Australia
W. Ger. — West Germany
W. Indies — West Indies
Wis. — Wisconsin
W. Samoa — Western Samoa
W. Va. — West Virginia
Wyo. — Wyoming

Y

Yugo. — Yugoslavia
Yukon — Yukon Territory

Z

Zim. — Zimbabwe

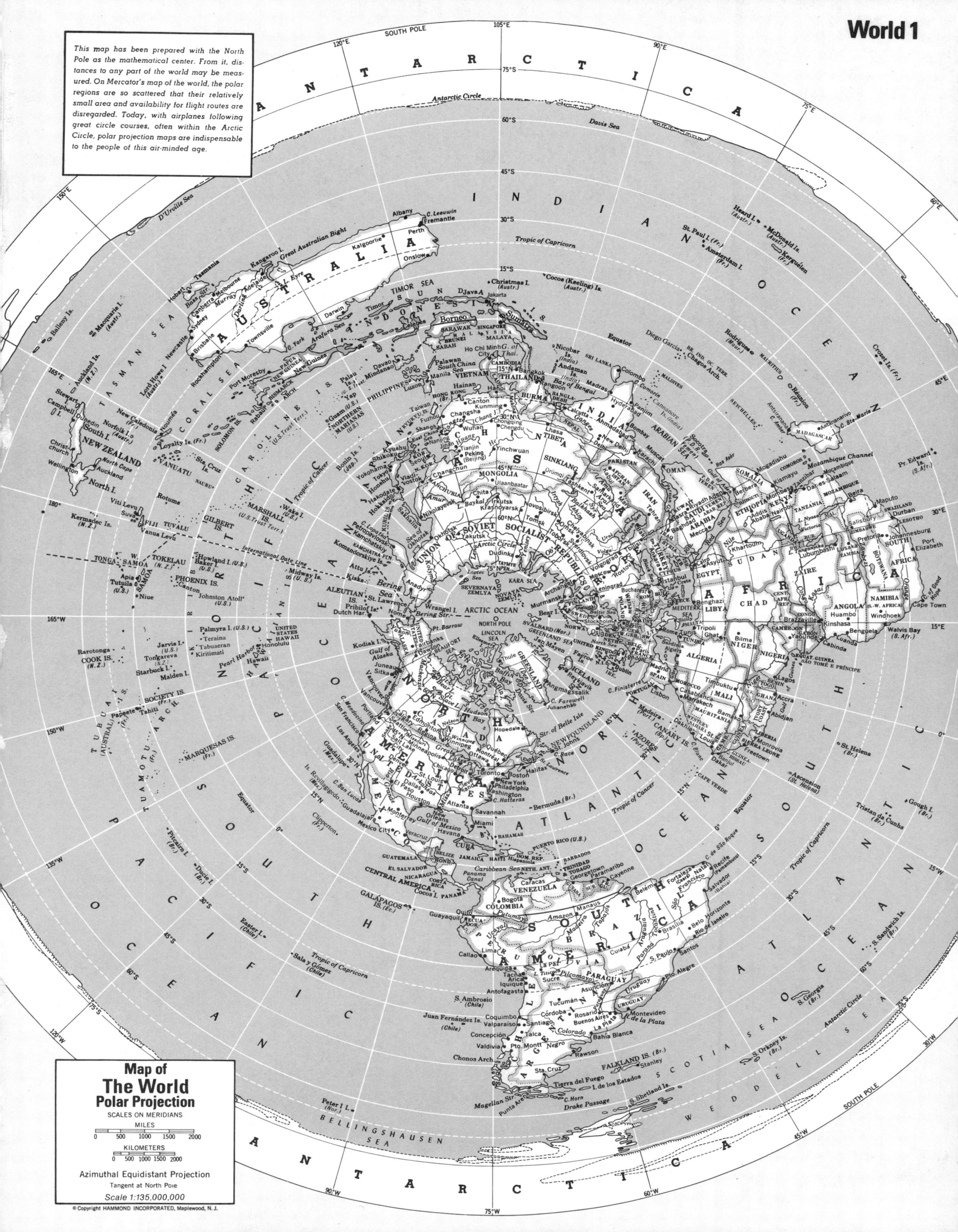

This map has been prepared with the North Pole as the mathematical center. From it, distances to any part of the world may be measured. On Mercator's map of the world, the polar regions are so scattered that their relatively small area and availability for flight routes are disregarded. Today, with airplanes following great circle courses, often within the Arctic Circle, polar projection maps are indispensable to the people of this air-minded age.

Map of The World Polar Projection

SCALES ON MERIDIANS

MILES

0   500   1000   1500   2000

KILOMETERS

0   500   1000   1500   2000

Azimuthal Equidistant Projection

Tangent at North Pole

Scale 1:135,000,000

© Copyright HAMMOND INCORPORATED, Maplewood, N. J.

The World

BRIESEMEISTER ELLIPTICAL
EQUAL-AREA PROJECTION

Capitals of Countries ....⊗
Other Capitals........................⊙
International Boundaries..... – – –

Scale 1:80,000,000

NORTH PACIFIC OCEAN

SOUTH PACIFIC OCEAN

NORTH AMERICA

SOUTH AMERICA

NORTH ATLANTIC OCEAN

SOUTH ATLANTIC OCEAN

CENTRAL AMERICA

CARIBBEAN SEA

GULF OF MEXICO

ANTARCTICA

MARIE BYRD LAND

GREENLAND (Den.)

UNITED STATES

CANADA

MEXICO

BRAZIL

ARGENTINA

CHILE

PERU

BOLIVIA

COLOMBIA

VENEZUELA

PARAGUAY

URUGUAY

ECUADOR

GUATEMALA

ALGERIA

SAHARA

MAURITANIA

MALI

NIGER

ALASKA

Honolulu — HAWAII — UNITED STATES

Time Zones

	Areas using half hour deviations.
STANDARD	
TIME	Areas not using zone system.
ZONES	

NOTE: Standard time zones in the U.S.S.R. are always advanced one hour.

INTERNATIONAL DATE LINE

MERIDIAN

GREENWICH

MONDAY / SUNDAY

LAND AREA 57,970,000 sq. mi.
(150,142,300 sq. km.)
WATER AREA 139,781,000 sq. mi.
(362,032,790 sq. km.)
TOTAL SURFACE AREA 197,751,000 sq.mi.
(512,175,090 sq. km.)
POPULATION 4,415,000,000

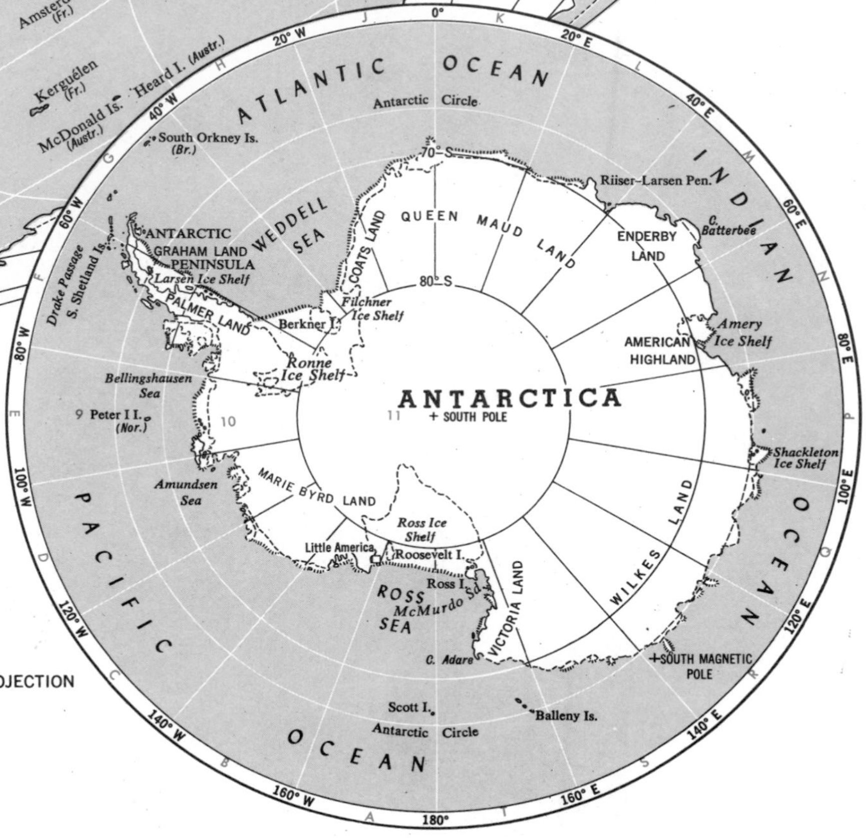

International Date Line

NORTH PACIFIC OCEAN

BERING SEA

Komandorskiye Is.
Anadyr
Kamchatka Pen.
Petropavlovsk–Kamchatskiy
New Siberian Is.
Verkhoyansk
Magadan
SEA OF OKHOTSK
Sakhalin
Nikolayevsk
Kuril Is.
Hokkaido
Sapporo
JAPAN
Tokyo
Honshu
Nagoya
Shikoku
Kyushu
Ryukyu
Yakutsk
Khabarovsk
Vladivostok
SEA OF JAPAN
Harbin
Changchun
Shenyang
N. KOR.
Seoul
S. KOR.
Kitakyushu
Osaka
Yokohama
Bonin Is.
Marshall Is.
TERR. OF THE PACIFIC ISLANDS (U.S. Trust Terr.)
NORTHERN MARIANAS (U.S.)
Guam (U.S.)
Gilbert Is.
KIRIBATI
NAURU
Caroline Is.
Bismarck Arch.
SOLOMON
VANUATU
New Caledonia (Fr.)
Nouméa
W. SAMOA
AM. SAMOA
FIJI
Suva
TONGA
Kermadec Is. (N.Z.)
Norfolk I. (Austr.)
Lord Howe I. (Austr.)

Severnaya Zemlya
Franz Josef Ld.
Barents Sea
Novaya Zemlya
Murmansk
SWEDEN
FINLAND
Baltic Sea
Riga
Minsk
Warsaw
Moscow
UNION OF SOVIET SOCIALIST REPUBLICS
SIBERIA
Arkhangelsk
Ob'
Yenisey
Noril'sk
Salekhard
Sverdlovsk
Omsk
Novosibirsk
Krasnoyarsk
L. Baykal
Irkutsk
Ulan Ude
Ulaanbaatar
MONGOLIA
Peking
Huang He
Lanzhou
CHINA
Tianjin
Nanjing
Shanghai
Yangtze
Wuhan
Fuzhou
Chengdu
Chongqing
Changsha
Canton
HONG KONG
MACAO
Taipei
Taiwan
Hainan
SOUTH CHINA SEA
Luzon
Manila
PHILIPPINES
Cebu
Mindanao
Davao
CORAL SEA
Townsville
Rockhampton
Brisbane
Gor'kiy
Kuybyshev
Volgograd
Kharkov
Kiev
Rostov
Astrakhan
Ufa
Chelyabinsk
Karaganda
L. Balkhash
Alma-Ata
Tashkent
Syrdar'ya
Aral Sea
Amudar'ya
Dushanbe
Samarkand
Kabul
Islamabad
SINKIANG
Urumqi
TIBET
Lhasa
NEPAL
Kathmandu
BHUTAN
Ganges
Delhi
New Delhi
Calcutta
BANGLADESH
BURMA
Rangoon
Huang
Kunming
Mekong
LAOS
THAILAND
Bangkok
CAMBODIA
VIETNAM
Hanoi
Ho Chi Minh City
MALAYSIA
Kuala Lumpur
SINGAPORE
Borneo
BRUNEI
SARAWAK
SABAH
CELEBES
Celebes Sea
Java Sea
Flores Sea
JAVA
INDONESIA
Jakarta
Sumatra
Christmas I. (Austr.)
Timor
Arafura Sea
Timor Sea
Darwin
NEW GUINEA
PAPUA NEW GUINEA
Port Moresby

Black Sea
Odessa
Bucharest
Istanbul
Ankara
TURKEY
CYP
LEB
SYRIA
Baghdad
IRAQ
IRAN
Tehran
Tbilisi
Baku
Caspian Sea
AFGHANISTAN
PAKISTAN
Indus
Karachi
Ahmadabad
Bombay
Hyderabad
INDIA
Madras
Bangalore
SRI LANKA
Colombo
C. Comorin
Tropic of Cancer
MALDIVES
Male
ARABIAN SEA
Muscat
U.A.E.
QATAR
KUWAIT
Basra
Riyadh
SAUDI ARABIA
Mecca
YEMEN ARAB REP.
P.D.R. YEMEN
Socotra (P.D.R. Yemen)
G. of Aden
Ras Asēr
DJIBOUTI
Addis Ababa
ETHIOPIA
SOMALIA
Mogadishu
Andaman Is.
Bay of Bengal
Cocos (Keeling) Is. (Austr.)
Equator

AUSTRALIA
Port Hedland
Kalgoorlie
Perth
Fremantle
C. Leeuwin
Adelaide
Melbourne
Sydney
Newcastle
Canberra
TASMAN SEA
Hobart
Tasmania
NEW ZEALAND
Auckland
Wellington
Christchurch
Dunedin
Auckland Is. (N.Z.)

LIBYA
EGYPT
Cairo
Suez
Alexandria
Benghazi
Tripoli
MEDITERRANEAN SEA
Athens
Red Sea
CHAD
N'Djamena
SUDAN
Khartoum
White Nile
CENT. AFR. REP.
Bangui
ZAIRE
Kinshasa
Brazzaville
Congo
UGANDA
Kampala
Nairobi
KENYA
Victoria
TANZANIA
Lake Tanganyika
Zanzibar
Dar es Salaam
COMOROS
MADAGASCAR
Antananarivo
C. Ste-Marie
ANGOLA
Luanda
Huambo
ZAMBIA
Lusaka
Lubumbashi
Lilongwe
L. Nyasa
Harare
ZIMBABWE
MOZAMBIQUE
Mozambique Chan.
MAURITIUS
Réunion (Fr.)
NAMIBIA
Windhoek
Walvis Bay (S.-W. Africa)
BOTSWANA
Gaborone
Pretoria
Johannesburg
SOUTH AFRICA
SWAZILAND
Maputo
LESOTHO
Durban
Cape Town
Cape of Good Hope
Orange
Pr. Edward Is. (S. Afr.)
Crozet Is. (Fr.)
SEYCHELLES
INDIAN OCEAN
Chagos Arch. (Br. Ind. Oc. Terr.)
Tropic of Capricorn
Amsterdam I. (Fr.)
St. Paul I. (Fr.)
Kerguélen (Fr.)
Heard I. (Austr.)
McDonald Is. (Austr.)

Antarctica
AZIMUTHAL EQUIDISTANT PROJECTION
Scale 1:62,000,000

ATLANTIC OCEAN
Antarctic Circle
South Orkney Is. (Br.)
ANTARCTIC
GRAHAM LAND
PENINSULA
Larsen Ice Shelf
PALMER LAND
Drake Passage
S. Shetland Is.
Bellingshausen Sea
Peter I I. (Nor.)
WEDDELL SEA
COATS LAND
Berkner I.
Filchner Ice Shelf
Ronne Ice Shelf
QUEEN MAUD LAND
ENDERBY LAND
Riiser-Larsen Pen.
Batterbee
AMERICAN HIGHLAND
Amery Ice Shelf
ANTARCTICA
+ SOUTH POLE
MARIE BYRD LAND
Amundsen Sea
Little America
Roosevelt I.
Ross Ice Shelf
Ross I.
McMurdo
ROSS SEA
VICTORIA LAND
WILKES LAND
Shackleton Ice Shelf
+ SOUTH MAGNETIC POLE
C. Adare
Scott I.
Balleny Is.
Antarctic Circle
PACIFIC OCEAN
INDIAN OCEAN
Cape Adare

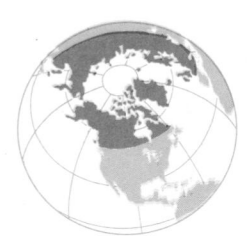

Arctic Ice

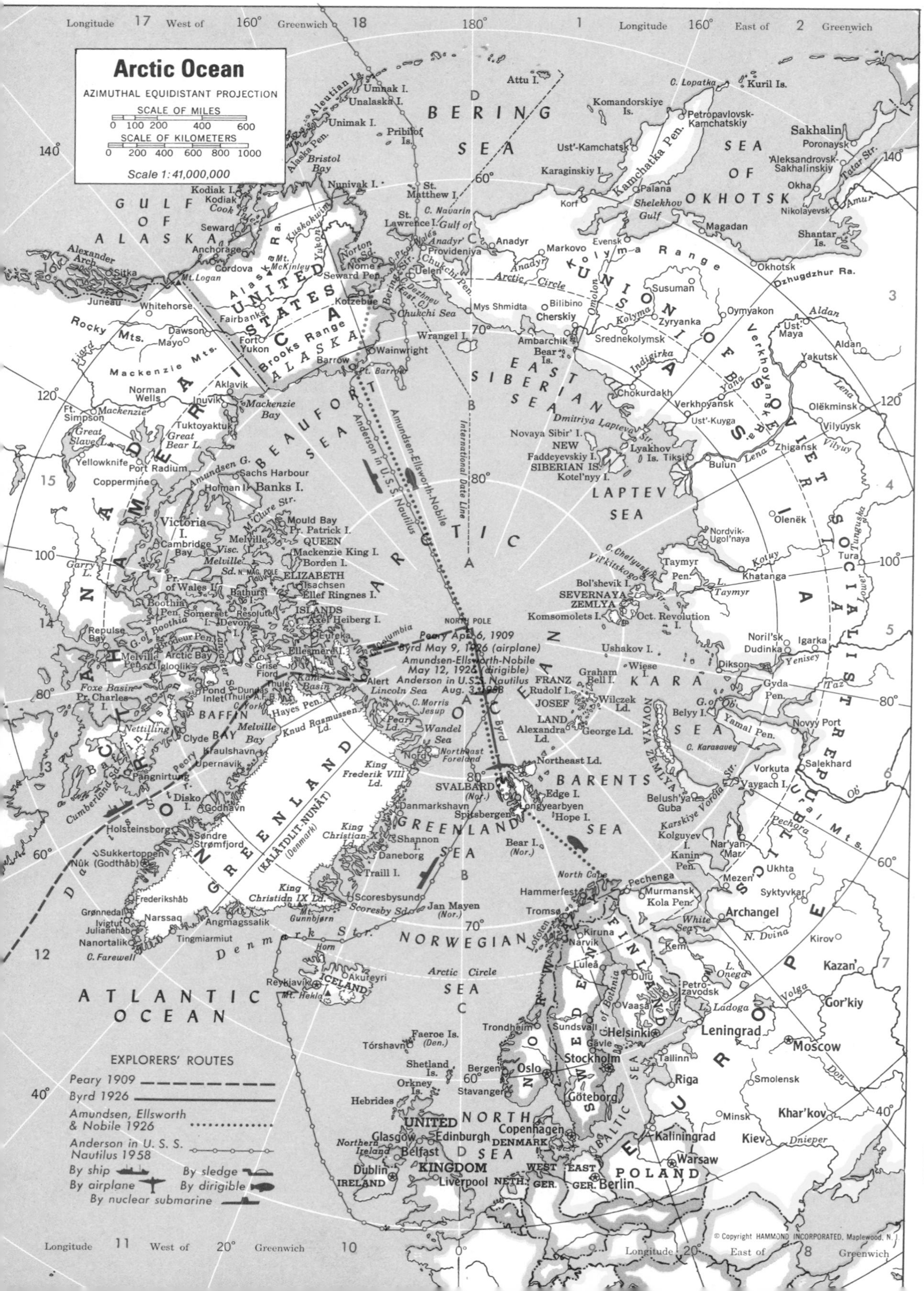

Arctic Ocean

AZIMUTHAL EQUIDISTANT PROJECTION

SCALE OF MILES
0 100 200 400 600

SCALE OF KILOMETERS
0 200 400 600 800 1000

Scale 1:41,000,000

EXPLORERS' ROUTES

Peary 1909
Byrd 1926
Amundsen, Ellsworth & Nobile 1926
Anderson in U.S.S. Nautilus 1958
By ship   By sledge
By airplane   By dirigible
By nuclear submarine

© Copyright HAMMOND INCORPORATED, Maplewood, N.J.

Antarctica
AZIMUTHAL EQUIDISTANT PROJECTION
SCALE OF MILES
0   200   400   600   800
KILOMETERS
0   200   400   600   800 1000
Scale 1:52,000,000
© Copyright HAMMOND INCORPORATED, Maplewood, N.J

A T L A N T I C   O C E A N

S C O T I A   S E A

W E D D E L L   S E A

Queen Maud Land

New Schwabenland

Enderby Land

I N D I A N   O C E A N

SOUTH AMERICA

Drake Passage

Bellingshausen Sea

Amundsen Sea

South Polar Plateau

AREA OF POLE OF INACCESSIBILITY

SOUTH POLE

Amundsen Dec. 14, 1911
Scott Jan. 18, 1912
Byrd Nov. 29, 1929 (airplane)
Fuchs Jan. 19, 1958

Marie Byrd Land

Ross Ice Shelf

Little America

Ross Sea

Wilkes Land

Davis Sea

QUEEN MARY COAST

P A C I F I C   O C E A N

T a s m a n   S e a

NEW ZEALAND

AUSTRALIA

Hobart
Tasmania
Melbourne

Dunedin

EXPLORERS' ROUTES

Palmer 1820
Amundsen 1910-12
Scott 1910-13
Byrd 1928-30
Fuchs 1957-58
By ship   By sledge   By airplane
By snow tractor

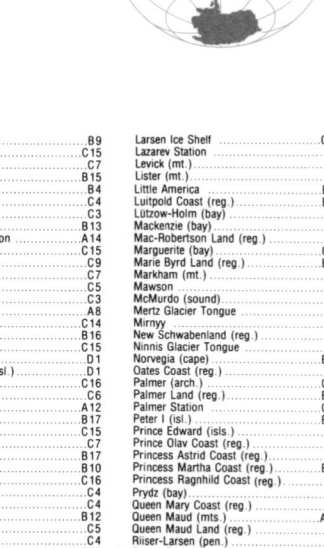

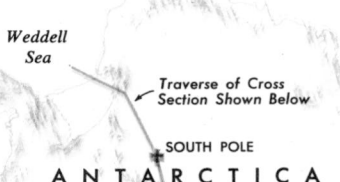

Weddell Sea

Traverse of Cross Section Shown Below

SOUTH POLE

A N T A R C T I C A

Ross Sea

Antarctic Cross Section: Weddell Sea to Ross Sea

Meters
3000
2000
1000
Sea Level
-1000
-2000

SOUTH POLE

Queen Alexandra Range

Ross Island

Whichaway Nunataks

Recovery Glacier

Beardmore Glacier

Weddell Sea

Filchner Ice Shelf

I C E

R O C K

R O C K

Ross Ice Shelf

Ross Sea

VERTICAL EXAGGERATION 95 TIMES

Information Based on American Geographical Society's "Antarctic Map Folio Series"

AREA 4,057,000 sq. mi.
(10,507,630 sq. km.)
POPULATION 676,000,000
LARGEST CITY Paris
HIGHEST POINT El'brus 18,510 ft.
(5,642 m.)
LOWEST POINT Caspian Sea -92 ft.
(-28 m.)

Population Distribution

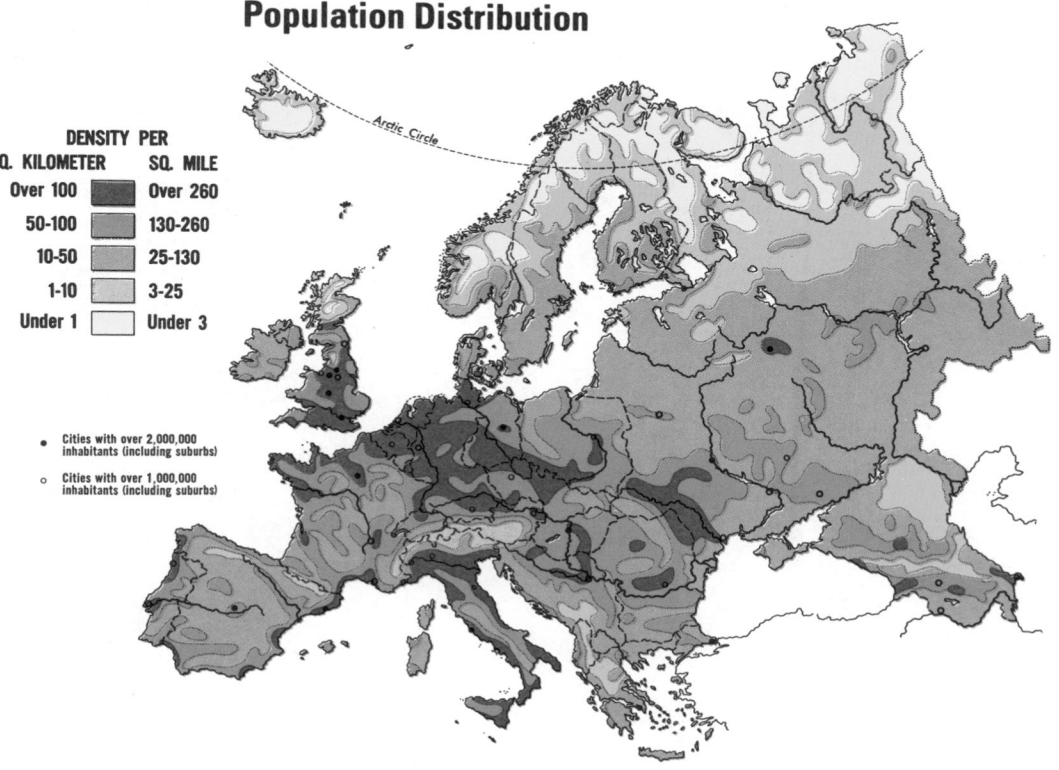

DENSITY PER

SQ. KILOMETER	SQ. MILE
Over 100	Over 260
50-100	130-260
10-50	25-130
1-10	3-25
Under 1	Under 3

● Cities with over 2,000,000
inhabitants (including suburbs)

○ Cities with over 1,000,000
inhabitants (including suburbs)

Vegetation

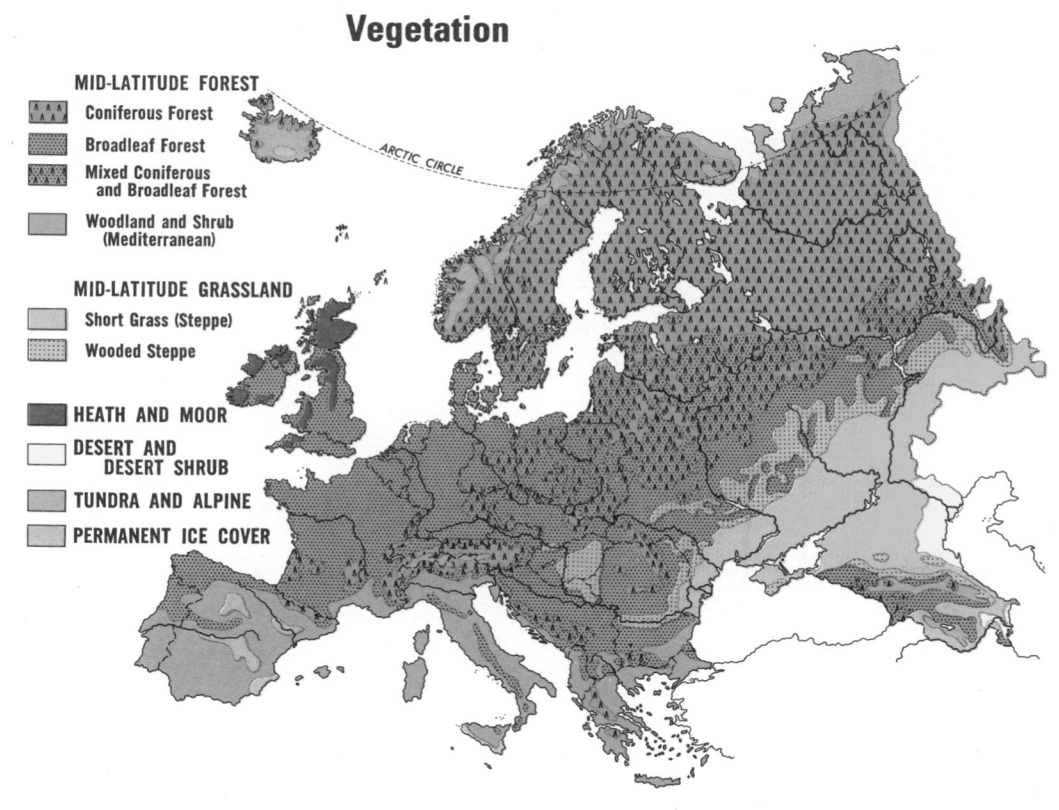

MID-LATITUDE FOREST
Coniferous Forest
Broadleaf Forest
Mixed Coniferous
and Broadleaf Forest
Woodland and Shrub
(Mediterranean)

MID-LATITUDE GRASSLAND
Short Grass (Steppe)
Wooded Steppe

HEATH AND MOOR

**DESERT AND
DESERT SHRUB**

TUNDRA AND ALPINE

PERMANENT ICE COVER

© Copyright HAMMOND INCORPORATED, Maplewood, N.J.

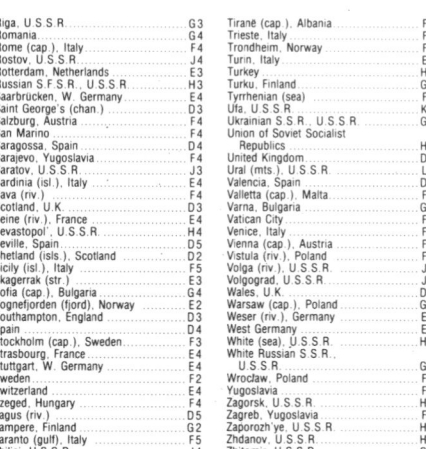

Vegetation/Relief

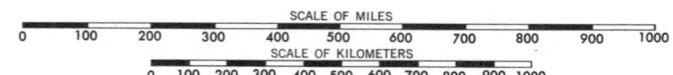

SCALE OF MILES
0 100 200 300 400 500 600 700 800 900 1000

SCALE OF KILOMETERS
0 100 200 300 400 500 600 700 800 900 1000

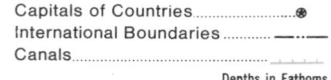

Capitals of Countries .... ⊛
International Boundaries .... — · —
Canals ....

Depths in Fathoms

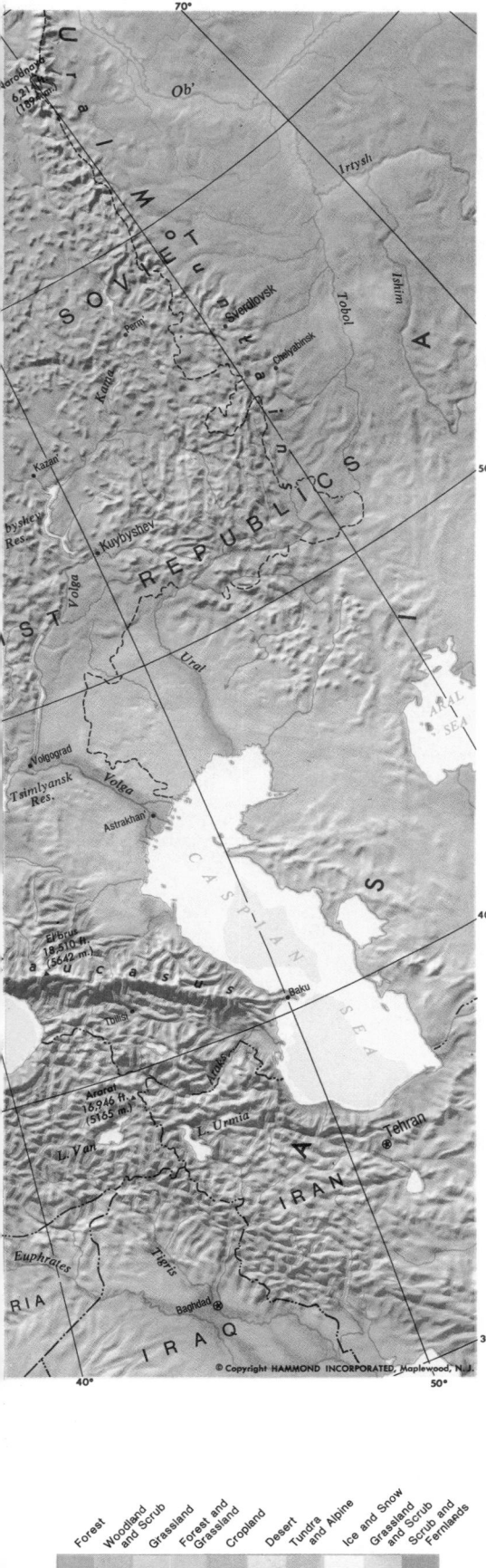

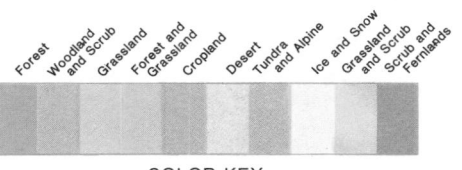

COLOR KEY

Forest | Woodland and Scrub | Grassland | Forest and Grassland | Cropland | Desert | Tundra and Alpine | Ice and Snow | Grassland and Scrub | Scrub and Farmlands

Rainfall

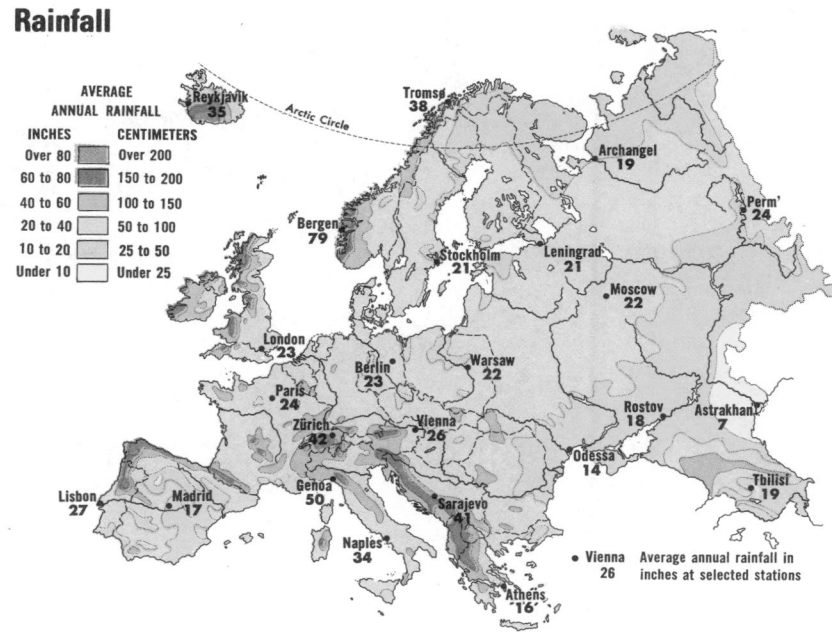

AVERAGE ANNUAL RAINFALL

INCHES	CENTIMETERS
Over 80	Over 200
60 to 80	150 to 200
40 to 60	100 to 150
20 to 40	50 to 100
10 to 20	25 to 50
Under 10	Under 25

Reykjavík 35
Tromsø 38
Archangel 19
Perm' 24
Bergen 79
Stockholm 21
Leningrad 21
Moscow 22
London 23
Berlin 23
Warsaw 22
Paris 24
Vienna 26
Rostov 18
Astrakhan' 7
Zürich 32
Odessa 14
Tbilisi 19
Lisbon 27
Madrid 17
Genoa 50
Sarajevo 41
Naples 34
Athens 16

• Vienna 26 Average annual rainfall in inches at selected stations

Average January Temperature

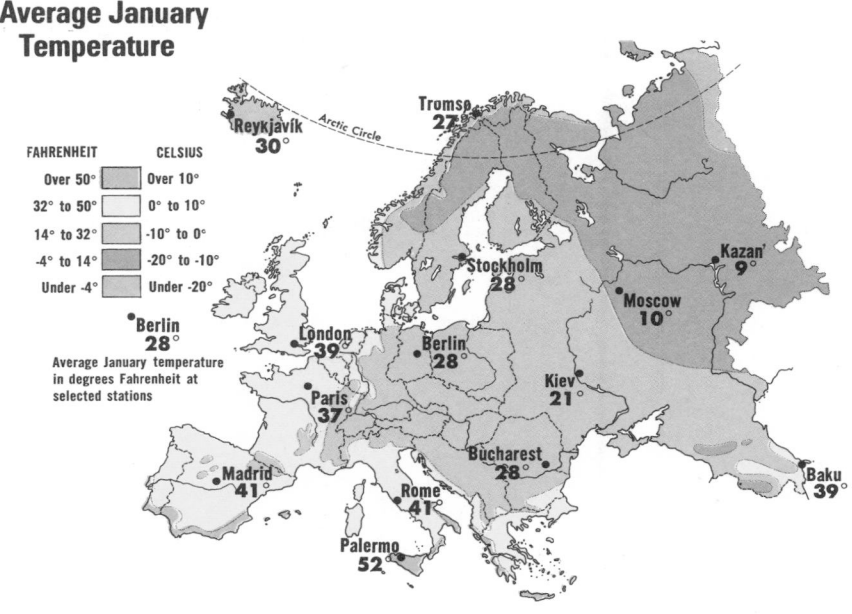

FAHRENHEIT	CELSIUS
Over 50°	Over 10°
32° to 50°	0° to 10°
14° to 32°	-10° to 0°
-4° to 14°	-20° to -10°
Under -4°	Under -20°

Reykjavík 30°
Tromsø 27°
Kazan' 9°
Stockholm 28°
Moscow 10°
• Berlin 28°
Average January temperature in degrees Fahrenheit at selected stations
London 39°
Berlin 28°
Kiev 21°
Paris 37°
Bucharest 28°
Baku 39°
Madrid 41°
Rome 41°
Palermo 52°

Average July Temperature

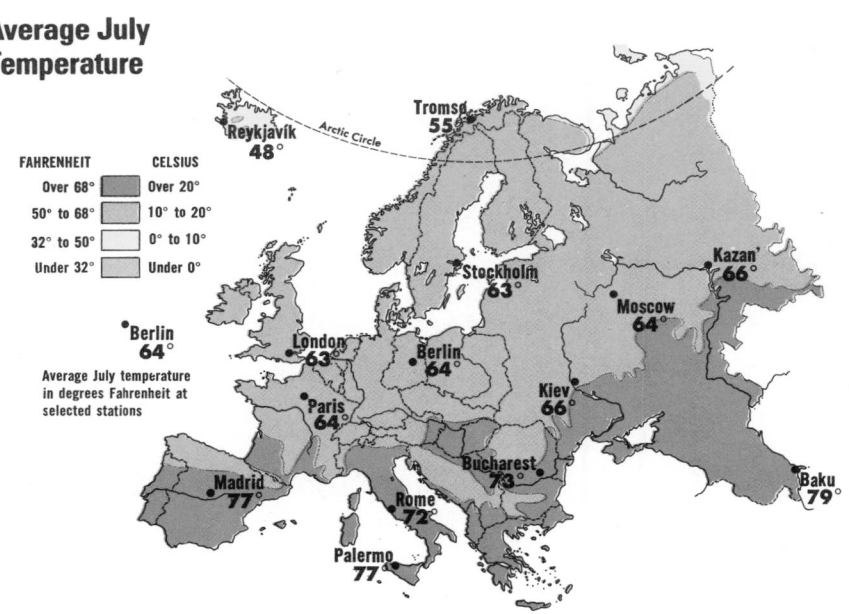

FAHRENHEIT	CELSIUS
Over 68°	Over 20°
50° to 68°	10° to 20°
32° to 50°	0° to 10°
Under 32°	Under 0°

Reykjavík 48°
Tromsø 55°
Kazan' 66°
Stockholm 63°
Moscow 64°
• Berlin 64°
Average July temperature in degrees Fahrenheit at selected stations
London 63°
Berlin 64°
Kiev 66°
Paris 64°
Bucharest 73°
Baku 79°
Madrid 77°
Rome 72°
Palermo 77°

© Copyright HAMMOND INCORPORATED, Maplewood, N.J.

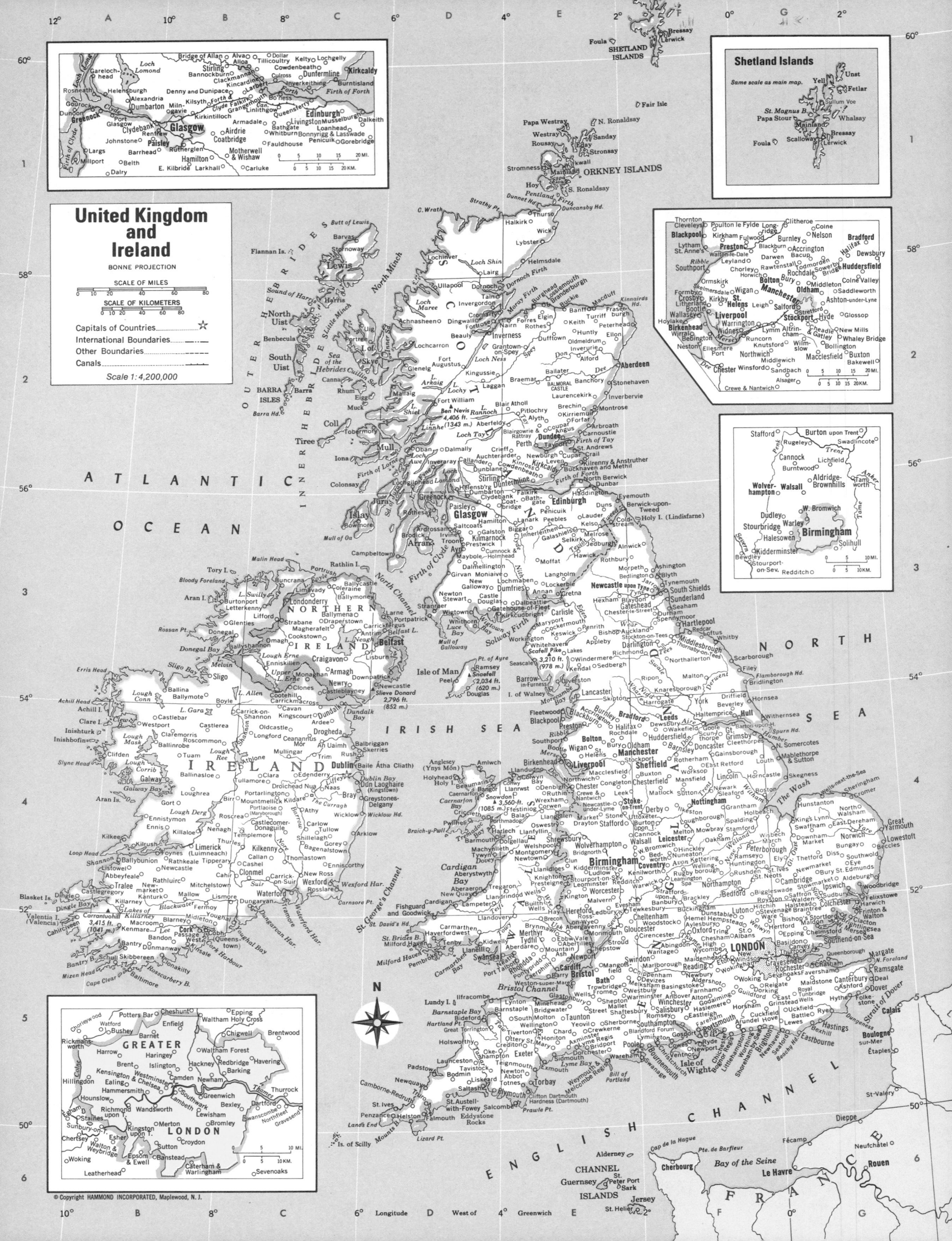

United Kingdom and Ireland

BONNE PROJECTION

SCALE OF MILES

SCALE OF KILOMETERS

Capitals of Countries..............★
International Boundaries..............
Other Boundaries..............
Canals..............

Scale 1:4,200,000

UNITED KINGDOM

AREA 94,399 sq. mi. (244,493 sq. km.)
POPULATION 55,672,000
CAPITAL London
LARGEST CITY London
HIGHEST POINT Ben Nevis 4,406 ft. (1,343 m.)
MONETARY UNIT pound sterling
MAJOR LANGUAGES English, Gaelic, Welsh
MAJOR RELIGIONS Protestantism, Roman Catholicism

IRELAND

AREA 27,136 sq. mi. (70,282 sq. km.)
POPULATION 3,440,427
CAPITAL Dublin
LARGEST CITY Dublin
HIGHEST POINT Carrantuohill 3,415 ft. (1,041 m.)
MONETARY UNIT Irish pound
MAJOR LANGUAGES English, Gaelic (Irish)
MAJOR RELIGION Roman Catholicism

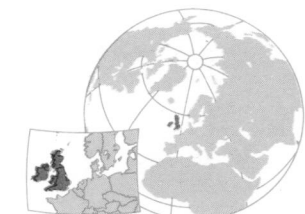

UNITED KINGDOM

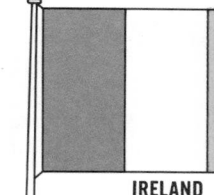

IRELAND

ENGLAND

COUNTIES

Avon, 920,200 . . . . E 6
Bedfordshire, 491,700 . . . . G 5
Berkshire, 659,000 . . . . F 6
Buckinghamshire, 512,000 . . . . . . G 6
Cambridgeshire, 563,000 . . . . G 5
Cheshire, 916,400 . . . . E 4
Cleveland, 567,900 . . . . F 3
Cornwall, 405,200 . . . . C 7
Cumbria, 473,600 . . . . D 3
Derbyshire, 887,600 . . . . F 5
Devon, 942,100 . . . . D 7
Dorset, 575,800 . . . . E 7
Durham, 610,400 . . . . F 3
East Sussex, 655,600 . . . . H 7
Essex, 1,426,200 . . . . H 6
Gloucestershire, 491,500 . . . . E 6
Greater London, 7,028,200 . . . . . . H 8
Greater Manchester, 2,684,100 . . . H 2
Hampshire, 1,456,100 . . . . F 6
Hereford and Worcester, 594,200 . . E 5
Hertfordshire, 937,300 . . . . G 6
Humberside, 848,600 . . . . G 4
Isle of Wight, 111,300 . . . . F 7
Isles of Scilly, 1,900 . . . . A 7
Kent, 1,448,100 . . . . H 6
Lancashire, 1,375,500 . . . . E 4
Leicestershire, 837,900 . . . . F 5
Lincolnshire, 524,500 . . . . G 4
London, Greater, 7,028,200 . . . . . H 8
Manchester, Greater, 2,684,100 . . H 2
Merseyside, 1,578,000 . . . . G 2
Norfolk, 662,500 . . . . H 5
Northamptonshire, 505,900 . . . . . G 5
Northumberland, 287,300 . . . . E 2
North Yorkshire, 653,000 . . . . F 3
Nottinghamshire, 977,500 . . . . . . F 4

Oxfordshire 541,800 . . . . F 6
Shropshire (Salop) 359,000 . . . . . E 5
Somerset 404,400 . . . . E 6
South Yorkshire 1,318,300 . . . . . . F 4
Staffordshire 997,600 . . . . E 5
Suffolk 577,600 . . . . H 5
Surrey 1,002,900 . . . . G 6
Sussex, East 655,600 . . . . H 7
Sussex, West 623,400 . . . . G 7
Tyne and Wear 1,182,900 . . . . . . H 3
Warwickshire 471,000 . . . . F 5
West Midlands 2,743,300 . . . . . . F 5
West Sussex 623,400 . . . . G 7
West Yorkshire 2,072,500 . . . . . . J 1
Wiltshire 512,800 . . . . E 6
Yorkshire, North 653,000 . . . . F 3
Yorkshire, South 1,318,300 . . . . . F 4
Yorkshire, West 2,072,500 . . . . . . J 1

CITIES and TOWNS

Abingdon, 20,130 . . . . F 6
Accrington, 36,470 . . . . H 1
Adwick le Street, 17,650 . . . . K 2
Aldeburgh, 2,750 . . . . J 5
Aldershot, 33,750 . . . . G 8
Aldridge-Brownhills, 89,370 . . . . . E 5
Alfreton, 21,560 . . . . F 4
Alnwick, 7,300 . . . . F 2
Altrincham, 40,800 . . . . H 2
Amersham, ⊙17,254 . . . . G 7
Andover, 27,620 . . . . F 6
Appleby, 2,240 . . . . E 3
Arnold, 35,090 . . . . F 4
Arundel, 2,390 . . . . G 7
Ashford, 36,380 . . . . H 6
Ashington, 24,720 . . . . F 2
Ashton-under-Lyne, 48,500 . . . . . H 2
Axminster, ⊙4,515 . . . . D 7
Aycliffe, ⊙20,203 . . . . F 3

Aylesbury, 41,420 . . . . G 7
Bacup, 14,990 . . . . H 1
Bakewell, 4,100 . . . . J 2
Banbury, 31,060 . . . . F 5
Banstead, 44,100 . . . . H 8
Barking, 153,800 . . . . H 8
Barnet, 305,200 . . . . H 7
Barnsley, 74,730 . . . . J 2
Barnstaple, 17,820 . . . . D 6
Barrow-in-Furness, 73,400 . . . . . D 3
Barton-upon-Humber, 7,750 . . . . . G 4
Basildon, 135,720 . . . . J 8
Basingstoke, 60,910 . . . . F 6
Bath, 83,100 . . . . E 6
Batley, 41,630 . . . . J 1
Battle, ⊙4,987 . . . . H 7
Bebington, 62,500 . . . . G 2
Bedford, 74,390 . . . . G 5
Bedlington, 27,200 . . . . F 2
Bedworth, 41,600 . . . . F 5
Beeston and Stapleford, 65,360 . . F 5
Benfleet, 49,780 . . . . J 8
Bentley with Arksey, 22,320 . . . . . F 4
Berkhamsted, 15,920 . . . . G 7
Beverley, 16,920 . . . . G 4
Bexhill, 34,680 . . . . H 7
Bexley, 213,500 . . . . H 8
Biddulph, 18,720 . . . . H 2
Birkenhead, 135,750 . . . . G 2
Birmingham, 1,058,800 . . . . F 5
Bishop Auckland, 32,940 . . . . F 3
Bishop's Stortford, 21,720 . . . . . . H 6
Blackburn, 101,670 . . . . H 1
Blackpool, 149,000 . . . . G 1
Blaydon, 31,940 . . . . H 3
Blyth, 35,390 . . . . F 2
Bodmin, 10,430 . . . . C 7
Bognor Regis, 34,620 . . . . G 7
Boldon, 24,430 . . . . J 3
Bolton, 154,480 . . . . H 2

Bootle 71,160 . . . . G 2
Boston 26,700 . . . . G 5
Bournemouth 144,100 . . . . F 7
Bracknell† 34,067 . . . . G 8
Bradford 458,900 . . . . J 1
Braintree and Bocking 26,300 . . . . H 6
Brent 256,500 . . . . H 8
Brentwood 58,690 . . . . J 8
Bridgwater 26,700 . . . . E 6
Bridlington 26,920 . . . . G 3
Bridport 6,660 . . . . E 7
Brigg 4,870 . . . . G 4
Brighouse 35,320 . . . . J 1
Brightlingsea 7,170 . . . . J 6
Brighton 156,500 . . . . G 7
Bristol 416,300 . . . . E 6
Broadstairs and Saint
   Peter's 21,670 . . . . J 6
Bromley 299,100 . . . . H 8
Bromsgrove 41,430 . . . . E 5
Buckfastleigh 2,870 . . . . C 7
Buckingham 5,290 . . . . G 6
Bude-Stratton 5,750 . . . . C 7
Bungay 4,120 . . . . J 5
Burgess Hill 20,030 . . . . G 7
Burnham-on-Crouch 4,920 . . . . . . H 6
Burnley 74,300 . . . . H 1
Burntwood† 23,088 . . . . F 5
Burton upon Trent 49,480 . . . . F 5
Bury 69,550 . . . . H 2
Bury Saint Edmunds 26,800 . . . . . H 5
Bushey 24,500 . . . . H 7
Buxton 20,050 . . . . J 2
Caister-on-Sea† 6,287 . . . . J 5
Camborne-Redruth 43,970 . . . . . . B 7
Cambridge 106,400 . . . . G 5
Camden 185,800 . . . . H 8
Cannock 56,440 . . . . E 5
Canterbury 115,600 . . . . H 6
Canvey Island 29,550 . . . . J 8

Carlisle, 99,600 . . . . D 3
Carlton, 46,690 . . . . F 5
Caterham and Warlingham, 35,840 . H 8
Chatham, 59,550 . . . . J 8
Cheadle and Gatley, 62,460 . . . . . H 2
Chelmsford, 58,320 . . . . J 7
Cheltenham, 75,910 . . . . E 6
Chertsey, 45,070 . . . . G 8
Chesham, 20,830 . . . . G 7
Cheshunt, 45,750 . . . . H 7
Chester, 117,200 . . . . G 2
Chesterfield, 69,480 . . . . J 2
Chester-le-Street, 20,720 . . . . . . J 3
Chichester, 20,940 . . . . G 7
Chigwell, 54,220 . . . . H 8
Chippenham, 18,550 . . . . E 6
Chorley, 31,800 . . . . G 2
Christchurch, 31,610 . . . . F 7
Cirencester, 14,500 . . . . E 6
Clacton, 39,380 . . . . J 6
Clay Cross, 9,630 . . . . J 2
Cleator Moor, ⊙7,686 . . . . D 3
Cleethorpes, 37,200 . . . . H 4
Clevedon, 15,140 . . . . D 6
Clun, ⊙1,261 . . . . D 6
Coalville, 28,740 . . . . F 5
Cockermouth, 6,480 . . . . D 3
Colchester, 79,600 . . . . H 6
Colne, 19,030 . . . . H 1
Colne Valley, 21,190 . . . . J 2
Congleton, 21,500 . . . . H 2
Consett, 35,080 . . . . H 3
Corby, 48,850 . . . . G 5
Coventry, 336,800 . . . . F 5
Cowes, 19,190 . . . . F 7
Crawley, 72,600 . . . . G 6
Crewe and Nantwich, 98,100 . . . . E 4
Cromer, 5,720 . . . . J 5
Crook and Willington, 21,120 . . . . E 3
Crosby, 56,750 . . . . G 2
Croydon, 330,600 . . . . H 8
Cuckfield, 26,500 . . . . G 6
Darlington, 85,120 . . . . F 3
Dartford, 44,130 . . . . J 8
Darton, 15,710 . . . . J 2
Darwen, 29,290 . . . . H 1
Deal, 26,840 . . . . J 6
Dearne, 24,780 . . . . K 2
Denton, 38,110 . . . . H 2
Derby, 213,700 . . . . F 5
Dewsbury, 50,560 . . . . J 1
Didcot, ⊙14,277 . . . . F 6
Doncaster, 81,530 . . . . F 4
Dorking, 22,410 . . . . G 8
Dover, 34,160 . . . . J 6
Downham Market, 4,120 . . . . H 5
Droitwich, 13,950 . . . . E 5
Dronfield, 20,000 . . . . J 2
Dudley, 187,110 . . . . E 5
Dunstable, 32,090 . . . . G 6
Durham, 88,800 . . . . J 3
Ealing, 293,800 . . . . H 8
Eastbourne, 73,200 . . . . H 7
East Grinstead, 19,420 . . . . G 6
Eastleigh, 46,340 . . . . F 7
East Retford, 18,260 . . . . G 4
Egham, 30,320 . . . . G 8
Eling, ⊙20,006 . . . . F 7
Ellesmere, ⊙2,630 . . . . E 5
Ellesmere Port, 63,870 . . . . G 2
Enfield, 260,900 . . . . H 7
Epsom and Ewell, 70,700 . . . . . . G 8
Esher, 63,970 . . . . H 8
Eston, ⊙46,219 . . . . F 3
Eton, 4,950 . . . . G 7
Evesham, 14,090 . . . . F 5
Exeter, 93,300 . . . . D 7
Exminster, ⊙3,181 . . . . D 7
Exmouth, 26,840 . . . . D 7
Falmouth, 17,530 . . . . B 7
Fareham, 86,300 . . . . F 7
Farnborough, 43,520 . . . . G 8
Farnham, 33,140 . . . . G 8
Farnworth, 26,110 . . . . H 2
Faversham, 15,010 . . . . H 6
Felixstowe, 19,460 . . . . J 6
Felling, 38,990 . . . . J 3
Filey, 5,660 . . . . G 3
Fleet, 22,930 . . . . G 8
Fleetwood, 30,070 . . . . D 4
Folkestone, 45,610 . . . . J 6
Formby, 24,850 . . . . G 2
Framlingham, ⊙2,258 . . . . J 5
Frimley and Camberley, 47,390 . . . G 8
Fulwood, 22,910 . . . . G 1
Gainsborough, 17,440 . . . . G 4
Gateshead, 91,230 . . . . J 3
Gillingham, Dorset, ⊙4,050 . . . . . E 6
Gillingham, Kent, 93,900 . . . . J 8
Glastonbury, 6,580 . . . . E 6
Glossop, 24,820 . . . . J 2
Gloucester, 91,600 . . . . E 6
Godalming, 18,840 . . . . G 8
Golborne, 28,720 . . . . G 2
Goole, 17,920 . . . . G 4
Gosport, 82,300 . . . . F 7
Grange, 3,520 . . . . E 3

Grantham 27,830 . . . . G 5
Gravesend 53,500 . . . . J 8
Great Grimsby 93,800 . . . . G 4
Great Torrington 3,430 . . . . C 7
Great Yarmouth 49,410 . . . . J 5
Greenwich 207,200 . . . . H 8
Guildford 58,470 . . . . G 8
Guisborough 14,860 . . . . F 3
Hackney 192,500 . . . . H 8
Hale 17,080 . . . . H 2
Halesowen 54,120 . . . . E 5
Halifax 88,580 . . . . J 1
Haltemprice 54,850 . . . . G 4
Haltwhistle† 3,511 . . . . E 2
Hammersmith 170,000 . . . . H 8
Haringey 228,200 . . . . H 8
Harlow 79,160 . . . . H 7
Harrogate 64,620 . . . . F 4
Harrow 200,200 . . . . B 5
Hartlepool 97,100 . . . . F 3
Harwich 15,280 . . . . J 6
Haslingden 15,140 . . . . H 1
Hastings 74,600 . . . . H 7
Hatfield† 25,359 . . . . H 7
Havant and Waterloo
   112,430 . . . . G 7
Haverhill 14,550 . . . . H 5
Havering 239,200 . . . . J 8
Hayle's 5,378 . . . . B 7
Hazel Grove and
   Bramhall 40,400 . . . . H 2
Heanor 24,590 . . . . F 4
Hebburn 23,150 . . . . J 3
Hedon 3,010 . . . . G 4
Hemel Hempstead 71,150 . . . . . . G 7
Hereford 47,800 . . . . E 5
Hertford 20,760 . . . . H 7
Hetton 16,810 . . . . J 3
Hexham 9,820 . . . . E 3
Heywood 31,720 . . . . H 2
High Wycombe 61,190 . . . . G 8
Hillingdon 230,800 . . . . G 8
Hinckley 49,310 . . . . F 5
Hindhead† 2,551 . . . . G 8
Hitchin 29,190 . . . . G 6
Hoddesdon 27,510 . . . . H 7
Holmfirth 19,790 . . . . J 2
Horley 18,593 . . . . H 8
Hornsea 7,030 . . . . G 4
Horsham 26,770 . . . . G 6
Horwich 16,670 . . . . G 2
Houghton-le-Spring 33,150 . . . . . J 3

Hounslow, 199,100 . . . . G 8
Hove, 72,000 . . . . G 7
Hoylake, 32,000 . . . . G 2
Hoyland Nether, 15,500 . . . . J 2
Hucknall, 27,110 . . . . F 4
Huddersfield, 130,060 . . . . J 2
Hugh Town, ⊙1,958 . . . . A 8
Hull, 276,600 . . . . G 4
Hunstanton, 4,140 . . . . H 5
Huntingdon and Godmanchester,
   17,200 . . . . G 5
Huyton-with-Roby, 65,950 . . . . . . G 2
Hyde, 37,040 . . . . H 2
Ilfracombe, 9,350 . . . . C 6
Ilkeston, 33,690 . . . . F 5
Immingham, ⊙10,259 . . . . G 4
Ipswich, 121,500 . . . . J 5
Islington, 171,600 . . . . H 8
Jarrow, 28,510 . . . . J 3
Kendal, 22,440 . . . . E 3
Kenilworth, 19,730 . . . . F 5
Kensington and Chelsea, 161,400 . G 8
Keswick, 4,790 . . . . D 3
Kettering, 44,480 . . . . G 5
Keynsham, 18,970 . . . . E 6
Kidderminster, 49,960 . . . . E 5
Kidsgrove, 22,690 . . . . E 4
King's Lynn, 29,990 . . . . H 5
Kingston upon Thames, 135,600 . . G 8
Kingswood, 30,450 . . . . E 6
Kirkburton, 20,320 . . . . J 2
Kirkby, 59,100 . . . . G 2
Kirkby Lonsdale, ⊙1,506 . . . . E 3
Kirkby Stephen, ⊙1,539 . . . . E 3
Knutsford, 14,840 . . . . H 2
Lambeth, 290,300 . . . . H 8
Lancaster, 126,300 . . . . E 3
Leatherhead, 40,830 . . . . G 8
Leeds, 744,500 . . . . J 1
Leek, 19,460 . . . . H 2
Leicester, 289,400 . . . . F 5
Leigh, 46,390 . . . . H 2
Leighton-Linslade, 22,590 . . . . . . F 7
Letchworth, 31,520 . . . . H 7
Lewes, 14,170 . . . . H 7
Lewisham, 237,300 . . . . H 8
Leyland, 23,690 . . . . G 1
Lichfield, 23,690 . . . . F 5
Lincoln, 73,700 . . . . G 4
Liskeard, 5,360 . . . . C 7
Litherland, 23,530 . . . . G 2
Littlehampton, 20,320 . . . . G 7

(continued on following page)

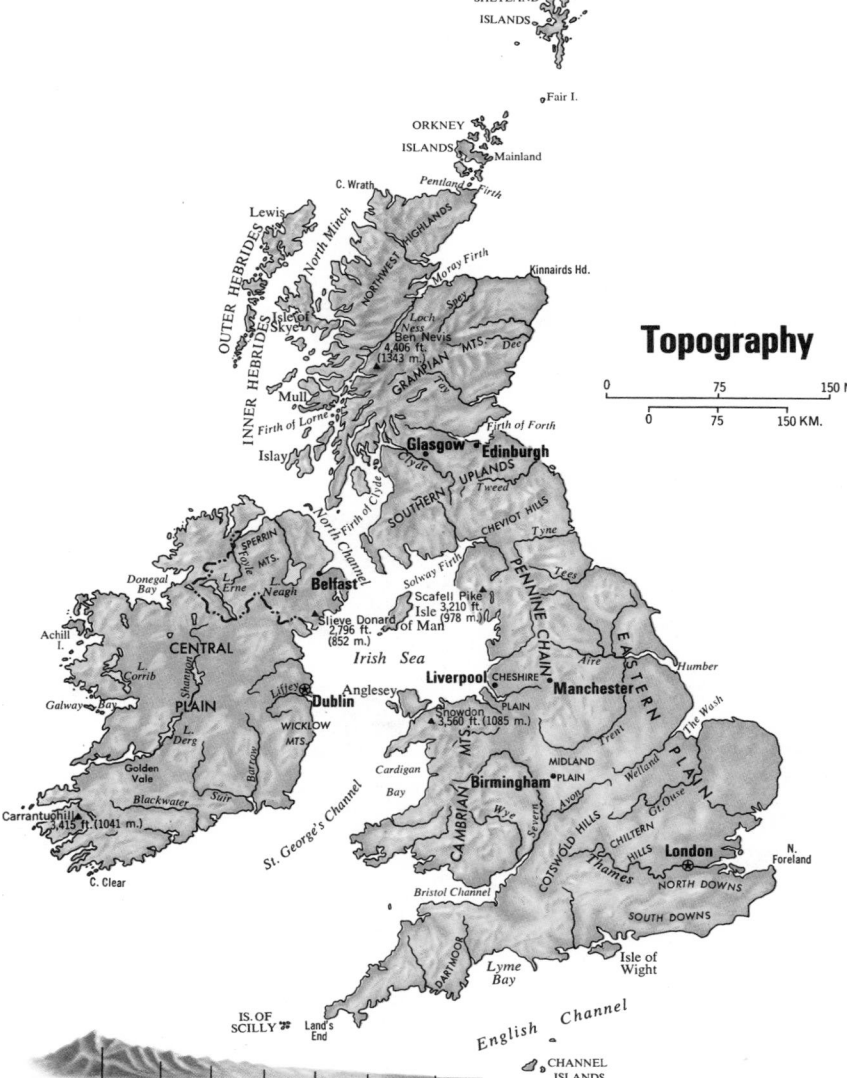

Topography

SHETLAND ISLANDS

Fair I.

ORKNEY ISLANDS

Mainland

C. Wrath
Pentland Firth
Lewis
OUTER HEBRIDES
NORTHWEST HIGHLANDS
Moray Firth
Kinnairds Hd.
Spey
Loch Ness
Ben Nevis 4,406 ft. 1343 m.
Dee
GRAMPIAN MTS.
INNER HEBRIDES
Skye
Firth of Lorne
Mull
Islay
Firth of Clyde
Glasgow
Edinburgh
Clyde
Firth of Forth
SOUTHERN UPLANDS
Tweed
CHEVIOT HILLS
Tyne
SPERRIN MTS.
North Channel
Solway Firth
Tees
Donegal Bay
L. Foyle
L. Erne
L. Neagh
Belfast
Slieve Donard 2,796 ft. (852 m.)
Scafell Pike 3,210 ft. (978 m.)
PENNINE CHAIN
Isle of Man
Irish Sea
Achill I.
CENTRAL PLAIN
L. Corrib
Galway Bay
Liverpool
CHESHIRE
Manchester
EASTERN PLAIN
Humber
Trent
The Wash
L. Derg
Golden Vale
WICKLOW MTS.
Dublin
Liffey
Anglesey
Snowdon 3,560 ft. (1085 m.)
Shannon
Blackwater
Suir
PLAIN
CAMBRIAN MTS.
Cardigan Bay
Wye
Severn
MIDLAND PLAIN
Avon
Welland
Gt. Ouse
Birmingham
Carrantuohill 3,415 ft. (1041 m.)
Galway Bay
St. George's Channel
C. Clear
COTSWOLD HILLS
CHILTERN HILLS
Thames
London
NORTH DOWNS
N. Foreland
Bristol Channel
SOUTH DOWNS
DARTMOOR
Lyme Bay
Isle of Wight
IS. OF SCILLY
Land's End
English Channel
CHANNEL ISLANDS

0   75   150 MI.
0   75   150 KM.

5,000 m. / 16,404 ft. · 2,000 m. / 6,562 ft. · 1,000 m. / 3,281 ft. · 500 m. / 1,640 ft. · 200 m. / 656 ft. · 100 m. / 328 ft. · Sea Level · Below

ENGLAND

AREA 50,516 sq. mi. (130,836 sq. km.)
POPULATION 46,220,955
CAPITAL London
LARGEST CITY London
HIGHEST POINT Scafell Pike 3,210 ft. (978 m.)

WALES

AREA 8,017 sq. mi. (20,764 sq. km.)
POPULATION 2,790,462
CAPITAL Cardiff
LARGEST CITY Cardiff
HIGHEST POINT Snowdon 3,560 ft. (1,085 m.)

SCOTLAND

AREA 30,414 sq. mi. (78,772 sq. km.)
POPULATION 5,117,146
CAPITAL Edinburgh
LARGEST CITY Glasgow
HIGHEST POINT Ben Nevis 4,406 ft. (1,343 m.)

NORTHERN IRELAND

AREA 5,452 sq. mi. (14,121 sq. km.)
POPULATION 1,543,000
CAPITAL Belfast
LARGEST CITY Belfast
HIGHEST POINT Slieve Donard 2,796 ft. (852 m.)

Liverpool, 539,700 G 2
Loftus, 7,850 G 3
London (cap.), 7,028,200 H 8
London, ★12,332,900 H 8
Long Eaton, 33,560 F 5
Longbenton, 50,120 J 3
Looe, 4,060 C 7
Loughborough, 49,010 F 5
Lowestoft, 53,260 J 5
Ludlow, ⊙7,466 E 5
Luton, 164,500 G 6
Lydd, 4,670 H 7
Lyme Regis, 3,460 E 7
Lymington, 36,780 F 7
Lynton, 1,770 D 6
Lytham Saint Anne's, 42,120 G 1
Mablethorpe and Sutton, 6,750 H 4
Macclesfield, 45,420 H 2
Maidenhead, 48,210 G 8
Maidstone, 72,110 J 8
Maldon, 14,350 H 6
Malmesbury, 2,550 E 6
Malton, 4,010 G 3
Malvern, 30,420 E 5
Manchester, 490,000 H 2
Mangotsfield, 23,000 E 6
Mansfield, 58,450 K 2
Mansfield Woodhouse, 25,400 F 4
March, 14,560 H 5
Margate, 50,290 J 6
Market Harborough, 15,230 G 5
Marlborough, 6,370 F 6
Matlock, 20,300 J 2
Melton Mowbray, 20,680 G 5
Merton, 169,400 H 8
Middlesbrough, 153,900 F 3
Middleton, 53,340 H 2
Middlewich, 7,600 H 2
Mildenhall, ⊙9,269 H 5
Millom, ⊙7,101 D 3
Milton Keynes, 89,900 F 5
Minehead, 8,230 D 6
Moretonhampstead, ⊙1,440 C 7
Morpeth, 14,450 F 2
Mundesley, ⊙1,536 J 5
Nelson, 31,220 H 1
Neston, 18,210 G 2
Newark, 24,760 G 4
Newbury, 24,850 F 6
Newcastle upon Tyne, 295,800 H 3
Newcastle-under-Lyme, 75,940 E 4
Newham, 228,900 H 8
Newhaven, 9,970 H 7
Newport, 22,430 F 7
New Romney, 3,830 J 7
Newton Abbot, 19,940 D 7
Newton-le-Willows, 21,780 H 2
New Windsor, 29,660 G 8
Northallerton F 3
Northam, 8,310 C 6
Northampton, 128,290 F 5
Northfleet, 27,150 J 8
North Sunderland, ⊙1,725 F 2
Northwich, 17,710 H 2
Norton, 5,580 G 3
Norton-Radstock, 15,900 E 6
Norwich, 119,200 J 5
Nottingham, 280,300 F 5
Nuneaton, 69,210 F 5
Oadby, 20,700 F 5
Oakham, 7,280 G 5
Okehampton, 4,000 D 7
Oldham, 103,690 H 2
Ormskirk, 28,860 G 2
Oswaldtwistle, 14,270 H 1
Oxford, 117,400 F 6
Padstow, ⊙2,802 B 7
Penryn, 5,660 B 7
Penzance, 19,360 B 7
Peterborough, 118,900 G 5
Peterlee, ⊙21,846 J 3
Plymouth, 259,100 C 7
Polperro, ⊙1,491 C 7
Poole, 110,600 E 7
Porlock, ⊙1,290 D 6
Portishead, 9,680 E 6
Portland, 14,860 E 7
Portslade-by-Sea, 18,040 G 7
Portsmouth, 198,500 F 7
Potters Bar, 24,670 H 7
Poulton-le-Fylde, 16,340 G 1
Preston, 94,760 G 1
Prestwich, 32,850 H 2
Queenborough, 31,550 H 6
Radcliffe, 29,630 H 2
Ramsbottom, 16,710 H 2
Ramsgate, 40,090 J 6
Rawtenstall, 20,950 H 1
Rayleigh, 26,740 J 8
Reading, 131,200 G 8
Redbridge, 231,600 H 8
Redcar, ⊙46,325 F 3
Redditch, 44,750 E 5
Reigate, 55,600 H 8
Richmond upon Thames, 166,800 H 8
Rickmansworth, 29,030 G 8
Ripley, 18,060 F 4
Rochdale, 93,780 H 2
Rochester, 56,030 J 8
Rothbury, ⊙1,818 E 2
Rotherham, 84,770 K 2
Royal Leamington Spa, 44,950 F 5
Royal Tunbridge Wells, 44,800 H 6
Rugby, 60,380 F 5
Rugeley, 24,440 E 5
Runcorn, 42,730 G 2
Rushden, 21,840 G 5
Ryde, 23,170 F 7
Rye, 4,530 H 7
Ryton, 15,170 H 3
Saddleworth, 21,340 J 2
Saint Agnes, ⊙4,747 B 7
Saint Albans, 123,800 H 7
Saint Austell-with-Fowey, 32,710 C 7
Saint Columb Major, ⊙3,953 B 7
Saint Helens, 104,890 G 2
Saint Ives, Cornwall, 9,760 B 7
Saint Neots, 17,940 G 5
Salcombe, 2,370 D 7
Sale, 59,060 H 2
Salford, 261,100 H 2
Salisbury, 35,460 F 6
Saltburn and Marske-by-the-Sea, 21,170 G 3
Sandbach, 14,280 H 2
Sandown-Shanklin, 14,800 F 7
Sandwich, 4,420 J 6
Saxmundham, 1,820 J 5
Scarborough, 43,300 G 3
Scunthorpe, 68,100 G 4
Seaford, 18,020 H 7
Seaham, 22,470 J 3
Seascale, ⊙2,106 D 3
Seaton, 4,500 D 7
Seaton Valley, 35,880 J 3
Sedbergh, ⊙2,741 E 3
Selsey, ⊙6,491 G 7
Sevenoaks, 18,160 J 8
Shaftesbury, 4,180 E 7
Sheffield, 558,000 J 2
Sherborne, 9,230 E 7
Sheringham, 4,940 J 5
Shildon, 15,360 F 3
Shoreham-by-Sea, 19,620 G 7
Shrewsbury, 56,120 E 5
Silloth, ⊙2,662 D 3
Sittingbourne and Milton, 32,830 H 6
Skelmersdale, 35,850 G 2
Skelton and Brotton, 15,930 G 3
Sleaford, 8,050 G 5
Slough, 89,060 G 8
Solihull, 108,230 F 5
Southampton, 213,700 F 7
Southend-on-Sea, 159,300 H 6
Southport, 86,030 G 1
South Shields, 96,900 J 3
Southwark, 224,900 H 8
Southwold, 1,960 J 5
Sowerby Bridge, 15,700 H 1
Spalding, 17,040 G 5
Spenborough, 41,460 J 1
Spennymoor, 19,050 F 3
Stafford, 54,860 E 5
Staines, 56,380 G 8
Stamford, 14,980 G 5
Stanley, 42,280 H 3
Staveley, 17,620 K 2
Stevenage, 72,600 G 6
Stockport, 138,350 H 2
Stockton-on-Tees, 165,400 F 3
Stoke-on-Trent, 256,200 E 4
Stourbridge, 56,530 E 5
Stourport-on-Severn, 19,430 E 5
Stowmarket, 9,020 J 5
Stratford-upon-Avon, 20,080 F 5
Stretford, 52,450 H 2
Stroud, 19,600 E 6
Sudbury, 8,860 H 5
Sunbury-on-Thames, 40,070 G 8
Sunderland, 214,820 J 3
Sutton, 166,700 H 8
Sutton Bridge, ⊙3,113 H 5
Sutton in Ashfield, 40,330 K 2
Swadlincote, 21,060 F 5
Swanage, 8,000 E 7
Swindon, 90,680 F 6
Tamworth, 46,960 F 5
Taunton, 37,570 D 6
Tavistock, ⊙7,620 C 7
Telford, ⊙79,451 E 5
Tenbury, ⊙2,151 E 5
Tewkesbury, 9,210 E 6
Thetford, 15,690 H 5
Thirsk, ⊙2,884 F 3
Thornaby-on-Tees, ⊙42,385 F 3
Thorne, ⊙16,694 F 4
Thornton Cleveleys, 27,090 G 1
Thurrock, 127,700 J 8
Tiverton, 16,190 D 7
Todmorden, 14,540 H 1
Tonbridge, 31,410 H 8
Torbay, 109,900 D 7
Torpoint, 6,840 C 7
Tower Hamlets, 146,100 H 8
Tow Law, 2,460 H 4
Trowbridge, 20,120 E 6
Truro, 15,690 B 7
Turton, 22,800 H 2
Tynemouth, 67,090 J 3
Upton upon Severn, ⊙2,048 E 5
Urmston, 44,130 H 2
Uttoxeter, 9,100 E 5
Ventnor, 6,980 F 7
Wainfleet All Saints, ⊙1,116 H 4
Wakefield, 306,500 J 2
Wallasey, 94,520 G 2
Wallsend, 45,490 J 3
Walsall, 182,430 E 5
Waltham Forest, 223,700 H 8
Waltham Holy Cross, 14,810 H 7
Walton and Weybridge, 51,270 G 8
Walton-le-Dale, 27,660 G 1
Wandsworth, 284,600 H 8
Wantage, 8,490 F 6
Ware, 14,900 H 7
Wareham, 4,630 E 7
Warley, 161,260 E 5
Warminster, 14,440 E 6
Warrington, 65,320 G 2
Warwick, 17,870 F 5
Washington, 27,720 J 3
Watchet, 2,980 D 6
Watford, 77,000 H 7
Wellingborough, 39,570 G 5
Wells, 8,960 E 6
Wells-next-the-Sea, 2,450 H 5
Welwyn, 39,900 H 7
Wem, ⊙3,411 E 5
West Bridgford, 28,340 F 5
West Bromwich, 162,740 F 5
West Mersea, 4,730 H 6
Westminster, 216,100 H 8
Weston-super-Mare, 51,960 D 6
Weymouth and Melcombe Regis, 41,080 E 7
Whickham, 29,710 J 3
Whitchurch, ⊙7,142 E 5
Whitehaven, 26,260 D 3
Whitley Bay, 37,010 J 3
Widnes, 58,330 G 2
Wigan, 80,920 G 2
Wigston, 31,650 F 5
Wilmslow, 31,250 H 2
Wilton, 4,090 F 6
Winchester, 88,900 F 6
Windermere, 7,860 E 3
Winsford, 26,920 G 2
Wirral, 27,510 G 2
Wisbech, 16,990 H 5
Witham, 19,730 H 6
Withernsea, 6,300 H 4
Wivenhoe, 5,630 J 6
Woking, 79,300 G 8
Wokingham, 22,390 G 8
Wolverhampton, 266,400 E 5
Wombwell, 17,850 K 2
Woodhall Spa, 2,420 G 4
Woodley and Sandford, ⊙24,581 G 8
Woodstock, 2,070 F 6
Wooler, ⊙1,833 F 2
Worcester, 73,900 E 5
Workington, 28,260 D 3
Worksop, 36,590 F 4
Worsbrough, 15,180 J 2
Worsley, 49,530 H 2
Worthing, 89,100 G 7
Wymondham, 9,390 J 5
Yateley, ⊙16,505 G 8
Yeovil, 26,180 E 7
York, 101,900 F 4

OTHER FEATURES

Aire (riv.) F 4
Atlantic Ocean A 7
Avon (riv.) F 5
Avon (riv.) F 7
Axe Edge (mt.) H 2
Barnstaple (bay) C 6
Beachy (head) H 7
Bigbury (bay) C 7
Blackwater (riv.) H 6
Bristol (chan.) C 6
Brown Willy (mt.) C 7
Cheviot (hills) E 2
Cheviot, The (mt.) E 2
Chiltern (hills) G 6
Cleveland (hills) F 3
Colne (riv.) G 8
Cornwall (cape) B 7
Cotswold (hills) E 6
Cross Fell (mt.) E 3
Cumbrian (mts.) D 3
Dart (riv.) D 7
Dartmoor National Park C 7
Dee (riv.) D 4
Derwent (riv.) G 3
Derwent (riv.) H 3
Don (riv.) F 4
Dorset Heights (hills) E 7
Dove (riv.) J 2
Dover (str.) J 7
Dungeness (prom.) J 7
Dunkery (hill) D 6
Eddystone (rocks) C 7
Eden (riv.) E 3
English (chan.) D 8
Esk (riv.) D 2
Exe (riv.) D 7
Exmoor National Park D 6
Fens, The (reg.) G 5
Flamborough (head) G 3
Formby (head) G 2
Foulness Island (pen.) J 5
Gibraltar (pt.) H 4
Great Ouse (riv.) H 5
Hartland (pt.) C 6
High Willhays (mt.) C 7
Hodder (riv.) H 1
Holderness (pen.), 43,900 G 4
Holy (isl.), 189 F 2
Humber (riv.) G 4
Irish (sea) B 4
Kennet (riv.) F 6
Lake District National Park D 3
Land's End (prom.) B 7
Lea (riv.) G 6
Lincoln Wolds (hills) G 4
Lindisfarne (Holy) (isl.), 189 F 2
Liverpool (bay) D 4
Lizard, The (pen.), 7,371 B 8
Lundy (isl.), 49 C 6
Lune (riv.) E 3
Lyme (bay) D 7
Manacle (pt.) B 7
Medway (riv.) H 6
Mendip (hills) E 6
Mersea (isl.), 4,423 J 6
Mersey (riv.) G 2
Morecambe (bay) D 3
Mounts (bay) B 7
Naze, The (prom.) J 6
Nene (riv.) H 5
New (for.) F 6
North (sea) J 4
North Downs (hills) G 6
North Foreland (prom.) J 6
Northumberland National Park E 2
North York Moors National Park G 3
Orford Ness (prom.) J 5
Ouse (riv.) G 4
Ouse (riv.) G 6
Parrett (riv.) E 6
Peak District National Park F 4
Peak, The (mt.) J 2
Peel Fell (mt.) E 2
Pennine Chain (range) E 3
Plymouth (sound) C 7
Portland, Bill of (pt.) E 7
Prawle (pt.) D 7
Purbeck, Isle of (pen.), 39,500 F 7
Ribble (riv.) E 4
Saint Alban's (head) F 7
Saint Bees (head) D 3
Saint Martin's (isl.), 106 A 8
Saint Mary's (isl.), 1,958 A 8
Scafell Pike (mt.) D 3
Scilly (isls.), 1,900 A 7
Selsey Bill (prom.) G 7
Severn (riv.) E 6
Sheppey (isl.), 31,550 J 6
Sherwood (for.) F 4
Skiddaw (mt.) D 3
Solent (chan.) F 7
Solway (firth) D 3
South Downs (hills) G 7
Spithead (chan.) F 7
Spurn (head) H 4
Stonehenge (ruins) F 6
Stour (riv.) E 7
Stour (riv.) H 6
Stour (riv.) J 6
Swale (riv.) F 3
Tamar (riv.) C 7
Taw (riv.) D 7
Tees (riv.) F 3
Test (riv.) F 6
Thames (riv.) H 6
Tintagel (head) C 7
Torridge (riv.) C 7
Trent (riv.) G 4
Tresco (isl.), 246 A 8
Tweed (riv.) E 2
Tyne (riv.) F 3
Ure (riv.) F 3
Ver (riv.) H 7
Walney, Isle of (isl.), 11,241 D 3
Wash, The (bay) H 5
Weald, The (reg.) H 6
Wear (riv.) F 3
Weaver (riv.) G 2
Welland (riv.) G 5
Wey (riv.) G 6
Wharfe (riv.) E 3
Wirral (pen.), 432,900 G 2
Witham (riv.) G 4
Wolds, The (hills) G 4
Wye (riv.) D 5
Wyre (riv.) G 1
Yare (riv.) J 5
Yorkshire Dales National Park E 3

CHANNEL ISLANDS

CITIES and TOWNS

Saint Anne E 8
Saint Helier (cap.), Jersey, ⊙28,135 E 8
Saint Peter Port (cap.), Guernsey, ⊙16,303 E 8
Saint Sampson's, ⊙6,534 E 8

OTHER FEATURES

Alderney (isl.), 1,686 E 8
Guernsey (isl.), 51,351 E 8
Herm (isl.), 96 E 8
Jersey (isl.), 72,629 E 8
Sark (isl.), 590 E 8

ISLE of MAN

CITIES and TOWNS

Castletown, 2,820 C 3
Douglas (cap.), 20,389 C 3
Laxey, 1,170 C 3
Michael, 408 C 3
Onchan, 4,807 C 3
Peel, 3,081 C 3
Port Erin, 1,714 C 3
Port Saint Mary, 1,508 C 3
Ramsey, 5,048 C 3

OTHER FEATURES

Ayre (pt.) C 3
Calf of Man (isl.) C 3
Langness (prom.) C 3
Snaefell (mt.) C 3
Spanish (head) C 3

WALES

COUNTIES

Clwyd, 376,000 D 4
Dyfed, 323,100 C 6
Gwent, 439,600 D 6
Gwynedd, 225,100 C 4
Mid Glamorgan, 540,400 D 6
Powys, 101,500 D 5
South Glamorgan, 389,200 A 7
West Glamorgan, 371,900 D 6

CITIES and TOWNS

Aberaeron, 1,340 C 5
Abercarn, 18,370 B 6
Aberdare, 38,030 A 6
Abertillery, 20,550 B 6
Amlwch, 3,630 C 4
Bala, 1,650 D 5
Bangor, 16,030 C 4
Barmouth, 2,070 C 5
Barry, 42,780 B 7
Beaumaris, 2,090 C 4
Bedwellty, 25,460 B 6
Bethesda, 4,180 D 4
Betws-y-Coed, 720 D 4
Brecknock (Brecon), 6,460 D 6
Brecon, 6,460 D 6
Bridgend, 14,690 B 7
Brynmawr, 5,970 B 6
Builth Wells, 1,480 D 5
Burry Port, 5,990 C 6
Caernarfon, 8,840 C 4
Caerphilly, 42,190 B 6
Cardiff, 281,500 B 7
Cardigan, 3,830 C 5
Chepstow, 8,260 E 6
Chirk, ⊙3,564 D 5
Colwyn Bay, 25,370 D 4
Criccieth, 1,590 C 5
Cwmamman, 3,950 D 6
Cwmbran, 32,980 B 6
Denbigh, 8,420 D 4
Dolgellau, 2,430 D 5
Ebbw Vale, 25,670 B 6
Ffestiniog, 5,510 D 5
Fishguard and Goodwick, 5,020 B 5
Flint, 15,070 G 2
Gelligaer, 33,820 A 6
Harlech, ⊙332 C 5
Haverfordwest, 8,930 B 6
Hawarden, ⊙20,389 G 2
Hay, 1,200 D 5
Holywell, 8,570 G 2
Kidwelly, 3,090 C 6
Knighton, 2,190 D 5
Llandeilo, 1,780 C 6
Llandovery, 2,040 D 5
Llandrindod Wells, 3,460 D 5
Llandudno, 17,700 D 4
Llanelli, 25,870 C 6
Llanfairfechan, 3,800 D 4
Llangefni, 4,070 C 4
Llangollen, 3,050 D 5
Llanguicke, ⊙15,029 D 6
Llanidloes, 2,390 D 5
Llantrisant, ⊙27,490 A 7
Llanwrtyd Wells, 460 D 5
Llwchwr, 27,530 D 6
Machynlleth, 1,830 D 5
Maesteg, 21,100 D 6
Menai Bridge, 2,730 C 4
Merthyr Tydfil, 61,500 A 6
Milford Haven, 13,960 B 6
Mold, 8,700 G 2
Montgomery, 1,000 D 5
Mountain Ash, 27,710 A 6
Mynyddislwyn, 15,590 B 6
Narberth, 970 C 6
Neath, 27,280 D 6
Nefyn, ⊙2,086 C 5
Newcastle Emlyn, 690 C 5
Newport, Dyfed, ⊙1,062 C 5
Newport, Gwent, 110,090 B 6
New Quay, 760 C 5
Newtown, 6,400 D 5
Neyland, 2,690 B 6
Ogmore and Garw, 19,680 A 6
Pembroke, 14,570 C 6
Penarth, 24,180 B 7
Penmaenmawr, 4,050 C 4
Pontypool, 36,710 B 6
Pontypridd, 34,180 A 6
Porthcawl, 14,980 D 6
Porthmadog, 3,900 C 5
Port Talbot, 58,200 D 6
Prestatyn, 15,480 D 4
Presteigne, 1,330 D 5
Pwllheli, 4,020 C 5
Rhondda, 85,400 A 6
Rhyl, 22,150 D 4
Risca, 15,780 B 6
Ruthin, 4,780 D 4
Saint David's, ⊙1,638 B 6
Swansea, 190,800 C 6
Tenby, 4,930 C 6
Tredegar, 17,450 B 6
Tywyn, 3,850 C 5
Welshpool, 7,370 D 5
Wrexham, 39,530 E 4

OTHER FEATURES

Anglesey (isl.), 64,500 C 4
Aran Fawddwy (mt.) C 5
Bardsey (isl.), 9 C 5
Berwyn (mts.) D 5
Black (mts.) D 6
Braich-y-Pwll (prom.) C 5
Brecon Beacons (mt.) D 6
Brecon Beacons National Park D 6
Caldy (isl.), 70 C 6
Cambrian (mts.) D 5
Cardigan (bay) C 5
Carmarthen (bay) C 6
Cemmaes (head) C 5
Dee (riv.) D 4
Dovey (riv.) D 5
Ely (riv.) B 7
Gower (pen.), 17,220 C 6
Great Ormes (head) C 4
Holy (isl.), 13,715 C 4
Lleyn (pen.), 25,800 C 5
Menai (str.) C 4
Milford Haven (inlet) B 6
Pembrokeshire Coast National Park C 6
Plynlimon (mt.) D 5
Preseli (mts.) C 6
Radnor (for.) D 5
Rhymney (riv.) B 6
Saint Brides (bay) B 6
Saint David's (head) B 6
Saint George's (chan.) B 5
Saint Gowans (head) C 6
Severn (riv.) E 5
Snowdon (mt.) D 4
Snowdonia National Park D 4
Taff (riv.) B 7
Teifi (riv.) C 5
Towy (riv.) D 6
Tremadoc (bay) C 5
Usk (riv.) B 6
Wye (riv.) D 5
Ynys Môn (Anglesey) (isl.), 64,500 C 4

★Population of met. area.
⊙Population of parish.

SCOTLAND

(map on page 15)

REGIONS

Borders, 99,409 E 5
Central, 269,281 D 4
Dumfries and Galloway, 143,667 E 5
Fife, 336,339 E 4
Grampian, 448,772 F 3
Highland, 182,044 D 3
Lothian, 754,008 E 5
Orkney (islands area), 17,675 E 1
Shetland (islands area), 18,494 F 2
Strathclyde, 2,504,909 C 4
Tayside, 401,987 E 4
Western Isles (islands area), 29,615 A 3

CITIES and TOWNS

Aberchirder, 877 F 3
Aberdeen, 210,362 F 3
Aberdour, 1,576 D 1
Aberfeldy, 1,552 E 4
Aberfoyle, 793 D 4
Aberlady, 737 F 4
Aberlour, 842 E 3
Abernethy, 776 E 4
Aboyne, 1,040 F 3
Acharacle, ⊙764 C 4
Achiltibuie, ⊙1,564 C 3
Achnasheen, ⊙1,078 C 3
Ae, 239 E 5
Airdrie, 38,491 C 2
Alexandria, 9,758 A 1
Alford, 764 F 3
Alloa, 13,558 C 1
Alness, 2,560 D 3
Altnaharra, ⊙1,227 D 2
Alva, 4,593 C 1
Alyth, 1,738 E 4
Ancrum, 266 F 5
Annan, 6,250 E 6
Annat, ⊙550 C 3
Annbank Station, 2,530 D 5
Applecross, ⊙550 C 3
Arbroath, 22,706 F 4
Ardavasar, ⊙449 B 3
Ardersier, 942 E 3
Ardgay, 193 D 3
Ardrishaig, 946 C 4
Ardrossan, 11,072 D 5
Armadale, 7,200 C 2
Arrochar, 543 D 4
Ascog, 230 A 2
Auchenblae, 339 F 4
Auchencairn, 215 E 6
Auchinleck, 4,883 D 5
Auchterarder, 1,738 E 4
Auchtermuchty, 1,426 E 4
Auldearn, 405 E 3
Aviemore, 1,224 E 3
Avoch, 776 D 3
Ayr, 47,990 D 5
Ayton, 410 F 5
Bailivanish, 347 A 3
Baillieston, 7,671 B 2
Balallan, 283 B 2
Balerno, 3,576 D 2
Balfron, 1,149 B 1
Ballantrae, 262 C 5
Ballater, 981 F 3
Ballingry, 4,332 D 1
Ballinluig, 188 E 4
Balloch, Highland, 572 D 3
Balloch, Strathclyde, 1,484 B 1
Baltasound, 246 G 2
Banchory, 2,435 F 3
Banff, 3,832 F 3
Bankfoot, 868 E 4
Bankhead, 1,492 F 3
Bannockburn, 5,889 C 1
Barrhead, 18,736 B 2
Barrhill, 236 D 5
Barvas, 279 B 2
Bathgate, 14,038 C 2
Bayble, 543 B 2
Bearsden, 25,128 B 2
Beattock, 309 E 5
Beauly, 1,141 D 3
Beith, 5,859 D 5
Bellsbank, 3,066 D 5
Bellshill, 18,166 C 2
Berriedale, ⊙1,927 E 2
Bieldside, 1,137 F 3
Biggar, 1,718 E 5
Birnam, 659 E 4
Bishopbriggs, 21,570 B 2
Bishopton, 2,931 B 2
Blackburn, 7,636 C 2
Blackford, 529 E 4
Blair Atholl, 437 E 4
Blairgowrie and Rattray, 5,681 E 4
Blanefield, 835 B 1
Blantyre, 13,992 B 2
Blyth Bridge, ⊙441 E 5
Bo'ness, 12,959 C 1
Boat of Garten, 406 E 3
Boddam, 1,429 G 3
Bonar Bridge, 519 D 3
Bonhill, 4,385 B 1
Bonnybridge, 5,701 C 1
Bonnyrigg and Lasswade, 7,429 D 2
Bowmore, 947 B 5
Braemar, 394 E 3
Breasclete, 234 B 2
Brechin, 6,759 F 4
Bridge of Allan, 4,638 C 1
Bridge of Don, 4,086 F 3
Bridge of Weir, 4,724 A 2
Brightons, 3,106 C 1
Broadford, 310 B 3
Brodick, 630 C 5
Brora, 1,436 E 2
Broxburn, 7,776 D 1
Buchlyvie, 412 B 1
Buckhaven and Methil, 17,930 F 4
Buckie, 8,145 E 3
Bucksburn, 6,567 F 3
Bunessan, ⊙585 B 4
Burghead, 1,321 E 3
Burnmouth, 300 F 5
Burntisland, 5,626 D 1
Cairndow, ⊙874 D 4
Cairnryan, 199 D 6
Callander, 1,805 D 4
Cambuslang, 14,607 B 2
Campbeltown, 6,428 C 5
Cannich, 203 D 3
Canonbie, 234 F 5
Caol, 3,719 C 4
Carbost, ⊙772 B 3
Cardenden, 6,802 D 1
Carloway, 178 B 2
Carluke, 8,864 E 5
Carnoustie, 6,838 F 4
Carnwath, 1,246 E 5
Carradale, 262 C 5
Carrbridge, 416 E 3
Carron, 2,626 C 1
Carsphairn, 186 D 5
Castlebay, 284 A 4
Castle Douglas, 3,384 E 6
Castle Kennedy, 307 D 6
Castletown, 902 E 2
Catrine, 2,681 D 5
Cawdor, 111 E 3
Chirnside, 888 F 5
Chryston, 8,322 C 2
Clackmannan, 3,248 C 1
Clarkston, 8,404 B 2
Closeburn, 225 E 5
Clovulin, ⊙315 C 4
Clydebank, 47,538 B 2
Coalburn, 1,460 E 5
Coatbridge, 50,806 C 2
Cockburnspath, 233 F 5
Cockenzie and Port Seton, 3,539 D 1
Coldingham, 423 F 5
Coldstream, 1,393 F 5
Coll, 305 B 2
Colmonell, 218 D 5
Comrie, 1,119 E 4
Connel, 300 C 4
Cononbridge, 914 D 3
Corpach, 1,296 C 4
Coupar Angus, 2,010 E 4
Cove and Kilcreggan, 1,402 A 1
Cove Bay, 765 F 3
Cowdenbeath, 10,215 D 1
Cowie, 2,751 C 1
Craigellachie, 382 E 3
Craignure, ⊙544 C 4
Crail, 1,033 F 4
Crawford, 384 E 5
Creetown, 769 D 6
Crieff, 5,718 E 4
Crimond, 313 G 3
Crinan, ⊙462 C 4
Cromarty, 492 E 3
Crosshill, 535 D 5
Crossmichael, 317 D 6
Cruden Bay, 528 G 3
Cullen, 1,199 F 3
Culross, 504 C 1
Cults, 3,336 F 3
Cumbernauld, 41,200 C 1
Cumnock and Holmhead, 6,298 D 5
Cupar, 6,607 E 4
Currie, 6,764 D 2
Dailly, 1,258 D 5
Dalbeattie, 3,659 E 6
Dalburgh, 261 A 3
Dalkeith, 9,713 D 2
Dalmally, 283 D 4
Dalmellington, 1,949 D 5
Dalry, 5,833 D 5
Dalrymple, 1,336 D 5
Darvel, 3,177 D 5
Daviot, ⊙513 D 3
Denholm, 581 F 5
Denny and Dunipace, 10,424 C 1
Dervaig, ⊙1,081 B 4
Dingwall, 4,275 D 3
Dollar, 2,573 E 4
Dornoch, 880 D 3
Douglas, 1,843 E 5
Doune, 859 D 4
Drongan, 3,609 D 5
Drumbeg, ⊙833 C 2
Drummore, 336 D 6
Drumnadrochit, 359 D 3
Drymen, 659 B 1
Dufftown, 1,481 E 3
Dumbarton, 25,469 B 1
Dumfries, 29,259 E 5
Dunbar, 4,609 F 4
Dunbeath, 161 E 2
Dunbeg, 939 C 4
Dunblane, 5,222 E 4
Dundee, 194,732 F 4
Dundonald, 2,256 D 5
Dunfermline, 52,098 D 1
Dunkeld, 273 E 4
Dunning, 564 E 4
Dunoon, 8,759 A 2
Dunragit, 323 D 6
Duns, 1,812 F 5
Duntocher, 3,532 B 2
Dunure E 5
Dunvegan, 301 B 3
Dyce, 2,733 F 3
Eaglesfield, 581 E 5
Eaglesham, 2,788 D 5
Earlston, 1,415 F 5
East Calder, 2,690 D 2
East Kilbride, 71,200 B 2
East Linton, 882 F 5
Eastriggs, 1,455 E 5
Ecclefechan, 844 E 5
Edinburgh (cap.), 470,085 D 1
Edzell, 658 F 4
Elderslie, 5,204 B 2
Elgin, 17,042 E 3
Elie and Earlsferry, 807 F 4
Ellon, 2,855 F 3
Embo, 260 E 3
Errol, 762 E 4
Evanton, 562 D 3
Eyemouth, 2,704 F 5
Fairlie, 1,029 D 5
Falkirk, 36,901 C 1
Falkland, 998 E 4
Fallin, 3,159 C 1
Fauldhouse, 5,247 C 2
Ferness, ⊙287 E 3
Ferryden, 740 F 4
Findhorn, 664 E 3
Findochty, 1,229 E 3
Fintry, 296 B 1
Fochabers, 1,238 E 3
Forfar, 11,179 F 4
Forres, 5,317 E 3
Fort Augustus, 670 D 3
Forth, 2,929 C 2
Fortrose, 1,150 D 3
Fort William, 4,370 C 4
Foyers, 276 D 3
Fraserburgh, 10,930 G 3
Friockheim, 807 F 4
Furnace, 220 C 4
Fyvie, 405 F 3
Gairloch, 125 C 3
Galashiels, 12,808 F 5
Galston, 4,256 D 5
Gardenstown, 892 F 3
Garelochhead, 1,552 A 1
Gargunnock, 457 B 1
Garlieston, 385 D 6
Garmouth, 352 E 3
Garrabost, 307 B 2
Gartmore, 253 B 1
Gatehouse-of-Fleet, 835 D 6
Giffnock, 10,987 B 2
Gifford, 575 F 5
Girvan, 7,597 D 5
Glamis, 190 F 4
Glasgow, 880,617 B 2
Glasgow, ★1,674,789 B 2
Glenbarr, ⊙691 C 5
Glencaple, 275 E 5
Glencoe, 195 C 4
Glenelg, ⊙1,468 C 3
Glenluce, 725 D 6
Glenrothes, 31,400 E 4
Golspie, 1,374 E 3
Gordon, 320 F 5
Gorebridge, 3,426 D 2
Gourock, 11,192 A 1
Grangemouth, 24,430 C 1
Grantown-on-Spey, 1,578 E 3
Greenlaw, 574 F 5
Greenock, 67,275 A 2
Gretna, 1,907 E 5
Gullane, 1,701 F 4
Haddington, 6,767 F 5
Halkirk, 679 E 2
Hamilton, 45,495 C 2
Hamnavoe, 307 G 2
Harthill, 4,712 C 2
Hatton, 315 G 3
Hawick, 16,484 F 5
Heathhall, 1,365 E 5
Helensburgh, 13,327 A 1
Helmsdale, 727 E 2
Hill of Fearn, 233 D 3
Hillside, 692 F 4
Hillswick, ⊙696 G 2
Hopeman, 1,248 E 3
Huntly, 4,078 F 3
Hurlford, 4,294 D 5
Inchnadamph, ⊙833 D 2
Innellan, 922 A 2
Innerleithen, 2,293 E 5
Insch, 881 F 3
Inveraray, 473 C 4
Inverbervie, 853 F 4
Invercassley, ⊙1,067 D 3
Invergordon, 2,385 D 3
Invergowrie, 1,389 E 4
Inverie, ⊙1,468 C 3
Inverkeithing, 6,102 D 1
Inverness, 35,801 D 3
Inverurie, 5,534 F 3
Irvine, 48,500 D 5
Isle of Whithorn, 222 D 6
Jedburgh, 3,953 F 5
John O'Groats, 195 E 2
Johnshaven, 544 F 4
Johnstone, 23,251 B 2
Kames, 230 C 5
Keiss, 344 E 2
Keith, 4,192 F 3
Kelso, 4,934 F 5
Kelty, 6,573 D 1
Kemnay, 1,042 F 3
Kenmore, 211 E 4
Kilbarchan, 2,669 A 2
Kilbirnie, 8,259 A 2
Kilchoan, ⊙764 B 4
Kildonan, ⊙1,105 E 2
Killearn, 1,086 B 1
Killin, 600 D 4
Kilmacolm, 3,348 A 2
Kilmarnock, 50,175 D 5
Kilmaurs, 2,518 D 5
Kilninver, ⊙247 C 4
Kilrenny and Anstruther, 2,951 F 4
Kilsyth, 10,210 B 1
Kilwinning, 8,460 D 5
Kinbrace, ⊙1,105 E 2
Kincardine, 3,278 C 1
Kinghorn, 2,163 D 1
Kingussie, 1,036 D 3
Kinlochewe, ⊙1,794 C 3
Kinlochleven, 1,243 D 4
Kinloch Rannoch, 241 D 4
Kinloss, 2,378 E 3
Kinross, 2,829 E 4
Kintore, 970 F 3
Kippen, 529 B 1
Kirkcaldy, 50,207 D 1
Kirkcolm, 346 C 6
Kirkconnel, 3,318 E 5
Kirkcowan, 354 D 6
Kirkcudbright, 2,690 E 6
Kirkhill, 210 D 3
Kirkintilloch, 26,664 B 2
Kirkmuirhill, 2,575 E 5
Kirkton of Glenisla, ⊙331 E 4
Kirkwall, 4,777 E 2
Kirriemuir, 4,295 E 4
Kyleakin, 268 C 3
Kyle of Lochalsh, 687 C 3
Kylestrome, ⊙745 D 2
Ladybank, 1,216 E 4
Laggan, 393 D 3
Lairg, 572 D 2
Lamlash, 613 C 5
Lanark, 8,842 E 5
Langholm, 2,509 E 5
Larbert, 4,922 C 1
Largs, 9,461 A 2
Larkhall, 15,926 E 5
Lauder, 639 F 5
Laurencekirk, 1,416 F 4

(continued)

England and Wales

CONIC PROJECTION

MILES

KILOMETERS

Capitals of Countries .... ⊛
Administrative Centers ....
Other Capitals .... ⊛
Canals ....

International Boundaries ....
County Boundaries ....
Other Boundaries ....

Scale 1:2,886,000

The administrative centers
for MID GLAMORGAN,
NORTHUMBERLAND and SURREY
are Cardiff, Newcastle upon
Tyne and Kingston upon Thames,
respectively.

© Copyright HAMMOND INCORPORATED, Maplewood, N.J.

Longitude West of Greenwich   Longitude East of Greenwich

Agriculture, Industry and Resources

DOMINANT LAND USE

Cereals (chiefly oats, barley)

Truck Farming, Horticulture

Dairy, Mixed Farming

Livestock, Mixed Farming

Pasture Livestock

MAJOR MINERAL OCCURRENCES

Ba	Barite	Na	Salt
C	Coal	O	Petroleum
F	Fluorspar	Pb	Lead
Fe	Iron Ore	Pe	Peat
G	Natural Gas	Sn	Tin
K	Potash	Zn	Zinc
Ka	Kaolin (china clay)		

⚡ Water Power

▨ Major Industrial Areas

Scotland

CONIC PROJECTION

MILES

KILOMETERS

Capital	⊛
Regional Centers	⊛
Canals	
International Boundaries	
Regional Boundaries	
Other Boundaries	

Scale 1:1,850,000
© Copyright HAMMOND INCORPORATED, Maplewood, N.J.

Former Counties

1 CLACKMANNAN
2 DUNBARTON
3 KINROSS
4 MIDLOTHIAN
5 PEEBLES
6 RENFREW
7 SELKIRK
8 STIRLING
9 W. LOTHIAN

Shetland Islands

IRELAND

Carlow 34,237 H6
Cavan 52,618 G4
Clare 75,008 D6
Cork 352,883 D7
Donegal 108,344 K2
Dublin 852,219 J5
Galway 149,223 D5
Kerry 112,772 H7
Kildare 71,977 H5
Kilkenny 61,473 G6
Laois 45,259 G6
Leitrim 28,360 E3
Leix (Laois) 45,259 G6
Limerick 140,459 D7
Longford 28,250 F4
Louth 74,951 J4
Mayo 109,525 C4
Meath 71,729 H4
Monaghan 46,242 H3
Offaly 51,829 F5
Roscommon 53,519 E4
Sligo 50,275 D3
Tipperary 123,565 F6
Waterford 77,315 F7
Westmeath 53,570 G5
Wexford 86,351 H7
Wicklow 66,295 J5

CITIES and TOWNS

Abbeydorney 188 B7
Abbeyfeale 1,337 C7
Abbeylara ‡290 F4
Abbeylex 1,033 G6
Achill Sound ‡1,163 D3
Aclare ‡336 D3
Adare 545 D6
Aghada-Farsid-Rostellan 461 E8
Aghadoe ‡497 B7
Aghagower ‡693 C4
Ahascragh 221 E5
Annagry 201 E1
Annascaul 236 B7
An Uaimh 4,605 H4
An Uaimh *6,665 H4
Ardagh Limerick 213 C7
Ardagh Longford ‡974 F4
Ardara 683 E2
Ardee *3,183 H4
Ardee 3,096 H4
Ardfert 286 B7
Ardfinnan 510 F7
Ardmore 233 F8
Ardrahan ‡239 D5
Arklow 6,948 J6
Arthurstown 1,188 H7
Arva 370 F4
Askeaton 341 J5
Askeaton 844 D6
Athboy 705 H4
Athea 308 C7
Athenry 1,240 D5
Athleague ‡955 E4
Athlone 9,825 F5
Athlone *11,611 F5
Athy 4,270 H6
Athy *4,654 H6
Aughrim 451 J6
Avoca ‡620 J6
Bagenalstown (Muinebeag) 2,321 H6
Baile Atha Cliath (Dublin) (cap.) 567,866 K5
Bailieborough 1,293
Balbriggan 3,741 J4
Balla 293 C4
Ballaghaderreen 1,121 E4
Ballina Mayo 6,063 C3
Ballina *6,369 C3
Ballina Tipperary 336 G4
Ballinagh 459 G4
Ballinakill 300 G6
Ballineen D8
Ballinamore 808 F3
Ballinasloe 5,969 E5
Ballincollig-Carrigrohane 2,110 D8
Ballindine 232
Ballingarry Limerick 422 D7
Ballingarry Tipperary ‡574 F6
Ballinlough 242 E4
Ballinrobe 1,272 C4
Ballintober ‡867 C4
Ballintra 197 E2
Ballisodare 486 E3
Ballivor 287 H4
Ballybay 754 G3
Ballybay *1,159 G3
Ballybofey-Stranorlar 2,214 F2
Ballybunion 1,287 B7
Ballycanew ‡460 J6
Ballycarney ‡294 C3
Ballycastle ‡724 C3
Ballyconnell 421 F3
Ballycotton 389 F8
Ballydehob 253 C8
Ballyduff 406 B7
Ballygar 359 E4
Ballygeary 725 J7
Ballyhaise 234 G3
Ballyhaunis 1,093 D4
Ballyheigue 450 B7
Ballyjamesduff 673 G4
Ballylanders 266 E7
Ballylongford 504 B6
Ballymahon 707 F4
Ballymakeery 272 C8
Ballymore 1,447 F5
Ballymore Eustace 433 J5
Ballymote 952 E3
Ballyporeen ‡810 E7
Ballyragget 519 G6
Ballyroan ‡478 G6
Ballyshannon 2,325 E3
Baltinore ‡580 H5
Baltimore 200 C9
Baltinglass 909 H6
Baltray 236 J4
Banagher 1,052 F5
Bandon 2,257 D8
Bandon *4,071 D8
Bannow ‡798 H7
Bansha 184 E7
Bantry 2,579 C8
Barna ‡1,734 C5
Belmullet 744 B3
Belturbet 1,092 G3
Bennettsbridge 367 G6
Birr 3,319 F5
Birr *3,881 F5
Blanchardstown 3,279 H5
Blarney 1,128 D8
Blessington 637 J5
Boherbue 372 C7
Borris 430 H6
Borris-in-Ossory 276 F6
Bornsokane 769 E6

Borrisoleigh 471 E6
Boyle 1,727 E4
Boyle *1,939 E4
Bray 14,467 K5
Bray *15,841 K5
Bri Chualann (Bray) 14,467 K5
Broadford 226 C7
Brosna 250 C7
Bruff 547 D7
Bruree 243 D7
Bunbeg-Derrybeg 878 E1
Bunclody-Carrickduff 929 H6
Buncrana 2,955 G1
Buncrana *3,334 G1
Bundoran 1,337 E3
Burtonport ‡1,288 E2
Buttevant 1,045 D7
Cahir 1,747 F7
Cahirciveen 1,547 A8
Callan 1,283 G6
Camolin 306 J6
Campile 231 H7
Cappamore 567 E6
Cappawhite 305 E6
Cappoquin 872 F7
Carbury ‡894 H5
Carlingford 559 J3
Carlow 9,588 H6
Carlow *10,399 H6
Carndonagh 1,146 G1
Carnew 570 H6
Carrickmacross 2,100 H4
Carrickmacross *2,475 H4
Carrick-on-Shannon 1,854 F4
Carrick-on-Suir 5,006 F7
Carriganolt ‡493 B6
Carrigaline 951 E8
Carrigallen 230 F4
Carrigart ‡753 F1
Carrigtwohill 622 E8
Carrowkeel ‡326 G1
Cashel 2,692 F7
Castlebar 5,979 C4
Castlebar *6,476 C4
Castlebellingham 407 J4
Castleblayney 2,118 H3
Castleblayney *2,395 H3
Castlecomer-Donaguile 1,244 G6
Castledermot 583 H6
Castlegregory 216 A7
Castleisland 1,929 B7
Castlemartyr 491 E8
Castlepollard 693 G4
Castlerea 1,752 D4
Castletown ‡504 F6
Castletownbere 812 B8
Castletownroche 399 D7
Castletownshend 170 C9
Causeway 215 B7
Cavan 3,273 G3
Cavan *4,312 G3
Ceanannus Mór 2,391 G4
Ceanannus Mór *2,653 G4
Celbridge 1,568 H5
Charlestown-Bellahy 677 D4
Charleville (Rathluirc) 2,232 D7
Ciara 2,156 F6
Claregalway ‡594 D5
Claremorris 1,718 D4
Clashmore ‡379 F8
Cliffen 790 B5
Cloghan 404 F5
Clogh-Chatsworth 324 G6
Cloghen 530 F7
Clogherhead 649 J4
Clonakilty 2,430 D8
Clonaslee 285 F5
Clondalkin 7,009 J5
Clonegal 202 H6
Clones 2,164 G3
Clonfert ‡430 E5
Clonmany ‡936 G1
Clonmel 11,622 F7
Clonmel *12,291 F7
Clonmellon 328 H4
Clonroche 222 H6
Clontuskert 351 E4
Cloone ‡460 F4
Cloughjordan 480 E6
Cloyne 654 E8
Coachford 290 D8
Cobh 6,076 E8
Coill Dubh 920 H5
Colon 262 J4
Collooney 546 E3
Cong 233 C4
Convoy 654 F2
Coolaney ‡352 E3
Coolgreany ‡603 J6
Cootehill 1,415 G3
Cootehill *1,542 G3
Cork 128,645 E8
Cork *134,430 E8
Corofin 342 C6
Courtmacsherry 210 D8
Courtown Harbour 291 J6
Creeslough 269 F1
Croagh ‡406 B9
Croom 756 D6
Crosshaven 1,222 E8
Crossmolina 1,077 C3
Crusheen ‡405 D6
Culdaff ‡621 G1
Daingean 492 G5
Delvin 223 G4
Dingle 1,401 A7
Doaghbeg ‡701 F1
Donabate 426 J5
Donegal 1,725 F2
Doneraile 799 D7
Dooagh-Keel 649 A4
Doon 387 E6
Douglas ‡4,448 E8
Drimoleague 415 C8
Drishane ‡1,548 C7
Drogheda 19,762 J4
Drogheda *20,095 J4
Droichead Nua 5,053 H5
Droichead Nua *6,444 H5
Dromahair 177 E3
Drumcar ‡1,215 J4
Drumconrath ‡1,044 H4
Drumkeerin ‡467 E3
Drumlish 205 F4
Drumshanbo 576 E3
Dublin (cap.) 567,866 K5
Dublin *679,748 K5
Duleek 658 J4
Duncannon 228 H7
Dundalk 21,672 H3
Dundalk *23,816 H3
Dunfanaghy 303 F1
Dungarvan 5,583 F7
Dunglое 940 E2
Dunkineely 288 E2
Dun Laoghaire 53,171 K5
Dun Laoghaire *98,379 K5
Dunlavin 423 H5

Dunleer 855 J4
Dunmanway 1,392 C8
Dunmore 522 D4
Dunmore East 656 G7
Dunshaughlin⊙ 283 H5
Durrow, Laois 596 G6
Durrow, Offaly⊙ 441 F5
Easky 184 D3
Edenderry 2,953 G5
Edenderry* 3,116 G5
Elphin 489 E4
Emyvale 281 G3
Ennis 5,972 D6
Ennis* 10,840 D6
Enniscorthy 5,704 J7
Enniscorthy* 6,642 J7
Enniskerry 772 J5
Ennistymon 1,013 C6
Eyrecourt 314 E5
Faha⊙ 1,423 G1
Falcarragh 506 E1
Feakle⊙ 398 D6
Fenit 360 B7
Ferbane 1,064 F5
Fermoy 3,237 E7
Fermoy* 4,033 E7
Ferns 712 J6
Fethard, Tipperary 1,064 F7
Fethard, Wexford⊙ 637 H7
Foxford 868 C4
Foynes 624 C6
Frankford (Kilcormac) 1,089 F5
Frenchpark⊙ 693 E4
Freshford 585 G6
Galbally 258 E7
Galway 27,726 C5
Galway* 29,375 C5
Geashill⊙ 751 G5
Glandore⊙ 695 C9
Glanmire-Riverstown 1,113 E8
Glanworth 335 E7
Glenbeigh 266 B7
Glencolumbkille⊙ 787 D2
Glengarriff 244 C8
Glenties 734 E2
Glenville⊙ 264 D7
Glin 623 C6
Golden⊙ 640 F7
Gorey 2,946 J6
Gorey* 3,024 J6
Gormanston⊙ 1,384 J4
Gort 975 D5
Gowran 402 G6
Graiguenamanagh-Tinnahinch 1,303 H6
Granard 1,054 F4
Greencastle 382 H1
Greenore 882 G3
Greystones-Delgany 4,517 K5
Gurteen 165 D3
Hacketstown 574 H6
Headford 673 C5
Holycross⊙ 802 F6
Hospital 525 E7
Inchigeelagh⊙ 516 C8
Inishannon 190 D8
Instioge 179 G6
Inniscrone 582 C3
Johnstown 303 G6
Kanturk 2,063 D7
Keel-Dooagh 649 A4
Kells⊙ 423 G6
Kells (Ceanannus Mór) 2,391 G4
Kenmare 903 B8
Kilbaha⊙ 491 B6
Kilbeggan 635 G5
Kilcar 273 D2
Kilcock 827 H5
Kilconnell⊙ 629 E5
Kilcoole 679 K5
Kilcormac 1,089 F5
Kilcullen 880 H5
Kildare 3,137 H5
Kildysart 209 C6
Kilfenora⊙ 441 C6
Kilfinane 561 D7
Kilgarvan 220 B8
Kilkee 1,287 B6
Kilkelly 225 D4
Kilkenny 9,838 G6
Kilkenny* 13,306 G6
Killala 368 C3
Killaloe 871 D6
Killarney 7,184 C7
Killarney* 7,541 C7
Killavullen 221 D7
Killenaule 592 F6
Killeshandra 432 F3
Killimor 221 E5
Killinaboy⊙ 297 C6
Killorglin 1,150 B7
Kilcuan-Rathwire 290 G4
Kilmacanogue⊙ 486 F1
Kilmacrennan 274 F1
Kilmacthomas 396 G7
Kilmallock 1,170 D7
Kilmeaden⊙ 262 G7
Kilmihill 284 C6
Kilmovee ‡
Kilmore Quay 273 H7
Kilmurry⊙ 387 C6
Kilnaleck 273 G4
Kilronan 243 B5
Kilrush 2,671 C6
Kilsheelan⊙ 665 F7
Kiltimagh 978 C4
Kilworth 360 E7
Kingscourt 1,016 H4
Kingstown (Dun Laoghaire) 53,171 K5
Kinlough 160 E3
Kinnegad 362 G5
Kinnitty⊙ 420 F5
Kinsale 1,622 D8
Kinsale* 1,989 D8
Kinvara 293 C5
Kircubbin
Knock⊙ 1,202 D4
Knocklong 248 D7
Knocknagashel 168 C7
Labasheeda⊙ 468 C6
Laghy⊙ 625 E2
Lahinch 455 C6
Lanesborough-Ballyleague 906 F4
Laracor⊙ 404 H4
Laytown-Bettystown-Mornington 1,882 J4
Leenaun⊙ 271 B4
Leighlinbridge 393 H6
Leitrim⊙ 544 F3
Leixlip 2,402 J5
Letterkenny 4,930 F1
Letterkenny* 5,207 F1
Lifford 1,121 F2
Limerick 57,161 D6
Limerick* 63,002 D6
Liscarroll 231 D7
Lisdoonvarna 459 C5
Lismore 884 F7

Lismore⊙ 1,041 F7
Listowel 3,021 C7
Littleton 322 F6
Longford 3,876 F4
Longford* 4,791 F4
Lorrha⊙ 685 E5
Loughrea 3,075 D5
Louisburgh 310 B4
Lucan-Doddsborough 4,245 J5
Luimneach (Limerick) 57,161 D6
Lusk 553 J4
Macroom 2,256 C8
Malahide 3,834 J5
Malin⊙ 552 G1
Mallow 5,901 D7
Mallow* 6,506 D7
Manorhamilton 858 E3
Manulla⊙ 660 C4
Maryborough (Portlaoise) 3,902 G5
Maynooth 1,296 H5
Meathas Truim 546 G4
Midleton 3,075 E8
Midleton* 4,666 E8
Milford 763 F1
Millstreet 1,319 D7
Milltown 260 A7
Milltown-Malbay 677 C6
Minard⊙ 397 A7
Mitchelstown 2,783 E7
Moate 1,378 F5
Mohill 868 F4
Monaghan 5,256 G3
Monasterevan 1,619 H5
Moneygall 282 F6
Monivea⊙ 405 D5
Mooncoin 413 G7
Mount Bellew 275 D5
Mountcharles 445 E2
Mountmellick 2,595 G5
Mountmellick* 2,864 G5
Mountrath 1,098 G5
Movie 1,089 G1
Moycullen⊙ 498 C5
Moynalty⊙ 583 H4
Muff 240 G1
Muinebeag 2,321 H6
Mullagh 293 H4
Mullaghmore⊙ 629 D3
Mullinahone 262 F7
Mullinavat 343 G7
Mullingar 6,790 G4
Mullingar* 9,245 G4
Naas 5,078 H5
Navan (An Uaimh) 4,605 H4
Nenagh 5,085 E6
Nenagh* 5,174 E6
Newbliss⊙ 547 G3
Newbridge (Droichead Nua) 5,053 H5
Newcastle 2,549 D7
Newcastle* 2,680 D7
Newmarket 886 C7
Newmarket-on-Fergus 1,052 D6
New Pallas⊙ 1,271 E6
Newport, Mayo 420 C4
Newport, Tipperary 582 E6
New Ross 4,775 H7
New Ross* 5,153 H7
Newtown Forbes⊙ 495 F4
Newtownmountkennedy 882 J5
Newtownsandes 268 C6
O'Briensbridge-Montpelier 237 D6
Oldcastle 759 G4
Old Leighlin⊙ 309 G6
Oola 348 E6
Oranmore 440 D5
Oughterard 628 C5
Passage East 408 G7
Passage West 2,709 E8
Patrickswell 415 D6
Pettigo 332 F2
Piltown 456 G7
Portarlington 3,117 G5
Portlaoise 3,902 G5
Portlaoise* 6,470 G5
Portlaw 1,166 G7
Portmarnock 1,726 J5
Portumna 913 E5
Queenstown (Cobh) 6,076 E8
Rahan⊙ 531 F5
Ramelton 807 F1
Raphoe 945 F2
Rathangan 868 H5
Rathcoole 1,740 J5
Rathcormac 191 E7
Rathdowney 892 F6
Rathdrum 1,141 J6
Rathgormuck⊙ 231 G7
Rathluirc 2,232 D7
Rathmore 437 C7
Rathnew 486 F1
Rathnew-Merrymeeting 954 J6
Rathowen⊙ 294 F4
Rathvilly 230 H6
Ratoath 300 J5
Riverstown 236 E3
Rockcorry 233 H3
Rosapenna⊙ 822 F1
Roscommon 1,556 E4
Roscommon* 2,821 E4
Roscrea 3,855 F6
Rosscarbery 259 C8
Rosses Point 464 D3
Rosslare Harbour (Ballygeary) 725 J7
Roundstone 204 A5
Roundwood 260 J5
Rush 2,633 J4
Saint Johnston 463 F2
Scarriff 619 E6
Schull 457 B8
Scotstown 264 H3
Shanagolden 231 C6
Shannon Airport 3,657 D6
Shannon Bridge 188 F5
Shercock 313 G4
Shillelagh 246 H6
Shinrone 365 F5
Shrule 204 C5
Sixmilebridge 567 D6
Skerries 3,044 J4
Skibbereen 2,104 C8
Slane 483 H4
Sligo 14,080 D3
Sligo* 14,456 D3
Spiddal⊙ 819 C5
Stepaside 760 J5
Stradbally, Laois 891 G6
Stradbally, Waterford 158 G7
Strokestown 543 E4
Swanlinbar 257 F3
Swinford 1,105 D4
Swords 4,133 J5
Taghmon 369 H7
Tallaght 6,174 J5

Tallow 883 F7
Tarbert 485 C6
Teltown ‡739 H4
Templemore 2,174 F6
Templetuohy 197 F6
Termonfeckin 328 J4
Thomastown 1,270 G7
Thurles 6,840 F6
Thurles *7,087 F6
Timoleague 257 D8
Tinahely 450 H6
Tipperary 4,631 E7
Tipperary *4,717 E7
Toomevara 272 E6
Tralee 12,287 B7
Tralee *13,263 B7
Tramore 3,792 G7
Trim 1,700 H4
Trim *2,255 H4
Tuam 3,808 D4
Tuam *4,952 D4
Tubbercurry 959 D3
Tulla 415 D6
Tullamore 6,809 G5
Tullamore *7,474 G5
Tullaroan ‡301 G6
Tullow 1,838 H6
Tullow *1,945 H6
Tynagh ‡452 E5
Tyrrellspass 289 G5
Urlingford 652 F6
Virginia 583 G4
Waterford 31,968 G7
Waterford *33,676 G7
Whitechurch 547 A8
Westport 3,023 C4
Wexford 11,849 H7
Wexford *13,293 H7
Whitegate 370 E8
Wicklow 3,786 K6
Wicklow *3,915 K6
Woodenbridge ‡620 J6
Woodford 198 E5
Youghal 5,445 F8
Youghal *5,626 F8

OTHER FEATURES

Achill (isl.) 3,129 A4
Allen (lake) E3
Allen, Bog of (marsh) H5
Aran (isl.) 773 B5
Aran (isls.) 1,499 B5
Arklow (bank) K6
Arrow (lake) E3
Awbeg (riv.) D7
Ballinskelligs (bay) A8
Ballycotton (bay) F8
Ballyheige (bay) B7
Ballyteige (bay) H7
Bandon (riv.) D8
Bann (riv.) J6
Bantry (bay) B8
Barrow (riv.) H7
Baurtregaum (mt.) B7
Bear (isl.) 288 B8
Blacksod (bay) A3
Blackstairs (mt.) H6
Blackwater (riv.) D7
Blackwater (riv.) H4
Blasket (isls.) A7
Bloody Foreland (prom.) E1
Blue Stack (mts.) E2
Boderg (lake) E4
Boggeragh (mts.) D7
Boyne (riv.) J4
Brandon (mt.) A7
Bride (riv.) E7
Broad Haven (harb.) B3
Bull, The (isl.) 5 A8
Caha (mts.) B8
Carlingford (inlet) J3
Carnsore (pt.) J7
Carrantuohill (mt.) B7
Clare (riv.) D5
Clare (isls.) 168 A4
Clear (cape) B9
Clear (isl.) 192 C9
Clew (bay) B4
Comeragh (mts.) F7
Conn (lake) C3
Connaught (prov.) 390,902 C4
Connemara (dist.) 7,599 B5
Cork (harb.) E8
Corrib (lake) C5
Courtmacsherry (bay) D8
Croagh, The H4
Dee (riv.) H4
Deel (riv.) D7
Deele (riv.) F2
Derg (lake) E6
Derravaragh (lake) G4
Derryveagh (mts.) E2
Dingle (bay) A7
Donegal (bay) D2
Drum (hills) F7
Dublin (bay) K5
Dundalk (bay) J4
Dunmanus (bay) B8
Dursey (isl.) 38 A8
Ennell (lake) G5
Erne (riv.) E3
Errigal (mt.) E1
Erris (head) A3
Fanad (head) F1
Fastnet Rock (isl.) 3 C9
Feale (riv.) C7
Fergus (riv.) D6
Finn (riv.) F2
Flesk (riv.) C7
Foyle (inlet) G1
Foyle (riv.) F2
Galley (head) D8
Galtee (mts.) E7
Galtymore (mt.) E7
Gara (lake) D4
Garadice (lake) F3
Gill (lake) E3
Glyde (riv.) H4
Golden Vale (plain) E7
Gorumna (isl.) 1,108 B5
Gowna (lake) G4
Grand (canal) H5
Grand (canal) H5
Gweebarra (bay) D2
Helvick (head) G7
Hook (head) H7
Horn (head) E1
Iar Connacht (dist.) 10,774 C5
Inishbofin (isl.) 236 A4
Inishbofin (isl.) 103 E1
Inisheer (isl.) 313 C6
Inishmaan (isl.) 319 C5
Inishmore (isl.) 864 B5
Inishowen (head) H1

Inishowen (pen.) 24,109 G1
Inishtrahull (isl.) 3 G1
Inishturk (isls.) 83 A4
Inny (riv.) A8
Inny (riv.) F4
Inver (bay) E2
Ireland's Eye (isl.) K5
Irish (sea) K4
Joyce's Country (dist.) 2,021 B4
Kenmare (riv.) A8
Kerry (head) A7
Key (lake) E4
Kilkieran (bay) B5
Killala (bay) C3
Killary (harb.) A4
Kinsale (harb.) E8
Knockboy (mt.) J5
Knockmealdown (mts.) F7
Lady's Island Lake (inlet) J7
Lambay (isl.) 24 K4
Laune (riv.) B7
Leane (lake) B7
Leane (lake) C7
Lee (riv.) D8
Leinster (mt.) H6
Leinster (prov.) 1,498,140 G5
Lettermullan (isl.) 221 B5
Liffey (riv.) H5
Liscannor (bay) B6
Long Island (bay) B9
Loop (head) A6
Lugnaquilla (mt.) H6
Macgillicuddy's Reeks (mts.) B7
Macnean (lake) F3
Maigue (riv.) D6
Maine (riv.) C7
Malin (head) G1
Mask (lake) C4
Maumturk (mts.) B5
Melvin (lake) E3
Mizen (head) B9
Moher (cliffs) B6
Monavullagh (mts.) F7
Moy (riv.) C3
Mulkear (riv.) E6
Mullaghareirk (mts.) C7
Mulroy (bay) F1
Munster (prov.) 882,002 D7
Mweelrea (mt.) B4
Mweenish (isl.) 198 B5
Nagles (mts.) E7
Nenagh (riv.) E6
Nephin (mt.) C3
Nore (riv.) G7
North (sound) B5
Omey (isl.) 34 A5
Oughter (lake) G3
Ovoca (riv.) J6
Owenmore (riv.) D3
Owey (isl.) 51 D1
Paps, The (mt.) C7
Partry (mts.) C4
Poliaphuca (res.) J5
Punchestown H5
Rathlin O'Birne (isl.) 3 C2
Rathlin (isl.) G7
Ree (lake) F5
Roaringwater (bay) B9
Rosses (bay) D1
Rosskeeragh (pt.) D3
Royal (canal) G4
Saint Finan's (bay) A8
Saint George's (chan.) K7
Saint John's (pt.) D2
Saint John's (isls.)
Seven (heads) D8
Seven Hogs, The (isls.) A7
Shannon (riv.) E6
Sheeffry (hills) B4
Sheelin (lake) G4
Sheep Haven (harb.) F1
Sheeps (head) B8
Sherkin (isl.) 82 C9
Silvermine (mts.) E6
Slieve Aughty (mts.) D5
Slieve Bloom (mts.) F5
Slieve Gamph (mts.) D3
Slievenaman (mt.) F7
Sligo (bay) D3
Slyne (head) A5
South (sound) B5
Stacks (mts.) B7
Suck (riv.) E4
Suir (riv.) G7
Swilly (inlet) F1
Tara (hill) H4
Tory (isl.) 273 E1
Tory (sound) E1
Tralee (bay) B7
Tramore (bay) G7
Ulster (part) (prov.) 207,204 G2
Valencia (Valentia) (isl.) 770 A8
Valentia (isl.) 770 A8
Waterford (harb.) G7
Wexford (bay) J7
Wicklow (head) K6
Wicklow (mts.) J5
Youghal (bay) F8

NORTHERN IRELAND

DISTRICTS

Antrim, 37,600 J2
Ards, 52,100 K2
Armagh, 47,500 H3
Ballymena, 52,200 J2
Ballymoney, 22,700 J1
Banbridge, 28,800 J3
Belfast, 368,200 K2
Carrickfergus, 27,500 K2
Castlereagh, 63,600 K2
Coleraine, 44,900 H1
Cookstown, 27,500 H2
Craigavon, 71,200 J3
Down, 48,800 K3
Dungannon, 43,000 H3
Fermanagh, 50,900 F3
Larne, 29,000 K2
Limavady, 25,000 H1
Lisburn, 80,800 J2
Londonderry, 86,600 G2
Magherafelt, 32,200 H2
Moyle, 13,400 J1
Newtownabbey, 71,500 J2
North Down, 59,600 K2
Omagh, 41,800 G2
Strabane, 35,500 G2

CITIES and TOWNS

Ahoghill, ‡1,929 J2
Annalong, 1,001 K3
Antrim, 8,351 J2
Ardglass, 1,052 K3
Armagh, 13,606 H3
Armoy, ‡1,051 J1

Augher, ‡1,986 G3
Aughnacloy, ‡1,885 H3
Ballycastle, 2,899 J1
Ballyclare, 5,155 J2
Ballykelly, 1,116 G1
Ballymena, 23,386 J2
Ballymoney, 5,697 J1
Ballynahinch, 3,485 J3
Banbridge, 7,968 J3
Bangor, 35,260 K2
Belfast (cap.), 353,700 K2
Belfast, *551,940 K2
Bellaghy, ‡2,265 H2
Belleek, ‡2,487 E3
Beragh, ‡2,137 G2
Bessbrook, 2,619 J3
Brookeborough, ‡2,534 G3
Broughshane, 1,288 J2
Bushmills, 1,288 J1
Caledon, ‡1,828 H3
Carnlough, 1,416 J2
Carrickfergus, 16,603 K2
Carrowdore, 2,548 K2
Castledawson, 1,162 H2
Castlederg, 1,766 F2
Castlewellan, 1,488 K3
Claudy, ‡2,507 G2
Clogher, ‡1,888 G3
Coalisland, 3,614 H2
Coleraine, 16,354 H1
Comber, 5,575 K2
Cookstown, 6,965 H2
Craigavon, 12,740 J3
Crossgar, 1,098 K3
Crossmaglen, 1,085 H3
Crumlin, 1,450 J2
Cullybackey, 1,649 J2
Derrygonnelly, ‡2,539 F3
Dervock, ‡1,191 J1
Donaghadee, 4,008 K2
Downpatrick, 7,918 K3
Draperstown, ‡2,247 H2
Dromore, Bainbridge, 2,848 J3
Dromore, Omagh, ‡2,224 G3
Drumquin, ‡1,982 F2
Dundrum, ‡2,245 K3
Dungannon, 8,190 H2
Dungiven, 1,586 H2
Dunnamanagh, ‡2,242 G2
Ederny and Kesh, ‡2,497 F2
Enniskillen, 9,679 F3
Feeny, ‡1,459 H2
Fintona, 1,190 G3
Fivemiletown, ‡1,649 G3
Garvagh, ‡2,363 H2
Gilford, 1,592 J3
Glenarm, ‡1,728 J2
Glenavy, ‡2,360 J2
Glynn, ‡1,872 K2
Gortin, ‡2,033 G2
Greyabbey, ‡2,646 K2
Hillsborough, 1,021 J3
Holywood, 9,892 K2
Irvinestown, 1,457 F3
Keady, 2,145 H3
Kells, ‡2,560 J2
Kesh, ‡2,497 F2
Kilkeel, 4,090 J3
Killough, ‡3,295 K3
Killyleagh, 2,359 K3
Kilrea, 1,196 H2
Kircubbin, 1,075 K3
Larne, 18,482 K2
Limavady, 6,004 H1
Lisburn, 31,836 J2
Lisnaskea, 1,443 G3
Londonderry, 51,200 G2
Loughbrickland, ‡2,056 J3
Maghera, 2,085 H2
Magherafelt, 4,704 H2
Markethill, ‡2,352 H3
Millisle, 1,172 K2
Moneymore, 1,178 H2
Moy, ‡2,349 H3
Moygashel, 1,086 H3
Newcastle, 4,647 K3
Newry, 20,279 J3
Newtownabbey, 58,114 K2
Newtownards, 15,484 K2
Newtownbutler, ‡2,663 G3
Newtownhamilton, ‡1,936 H3
Newtownstewart, 1,433 G2
Omagh, 14,594 G2
Pomeroy, ‡1,786 H2
Portaferry, 1,730 K3
Portavogie, 1,810 K2
Portglenone, ‡2,061 J2
Portrush, 5,376 H1
Portstewart, 5,085 H1
Randalstown, 2,799 J2
Rathfriland, 1,886 J3
Rostrevor, 1,617 J3
Saintfield, ‡2,198 K3
Sion Mills, 1,588 G2
Sixmilecross, ‡1,980 G2
Stewartstown, 1,759 H2
Strabane, 9,413 G2
Strangford, ‡1,987 K3
Tandragee, 1,725 J3
Tempo, ‡2,282 G3
Trillick, 12,167 G3
Warrenpoint, 4,291 J3
Whitehead, 2,642 K2

OTHER FEATURES

Bann (riv.) H2
Belfast (inlet) K2
Blackwater (riv.) H3
Bush (riv.) H1
Derg (riv.) F2
Down (bay) K3
Erne (lake) F3
Erne (riv.) F3
Foyle (inlet) G1
Foyle (riv.) G2
Giant's Causeway H1
Lagan (riv.) K2
Larne (inlet) K2
Magee, Island (pen.) 1,581 K2
Magilligan (pt.) H1
Main (riv.) J2
Mourne (mts.) J3
Mourne (riv.) G2
Neagh (lake) J2
North (chan.) J1
Oldstone (hills)
Red (bay) J1
Roe (riv.) H1
Saint John's (pt.) K3
Slieve Donard (mt.) K3
Sperrin (mts.) G2
Strangford (inlet) K3
Torr (head) J1
Ulster (part) (prov.) 1,537,200 F3
Upper Lough Erne (lake) F3

*City and suburbs
‡Population of district

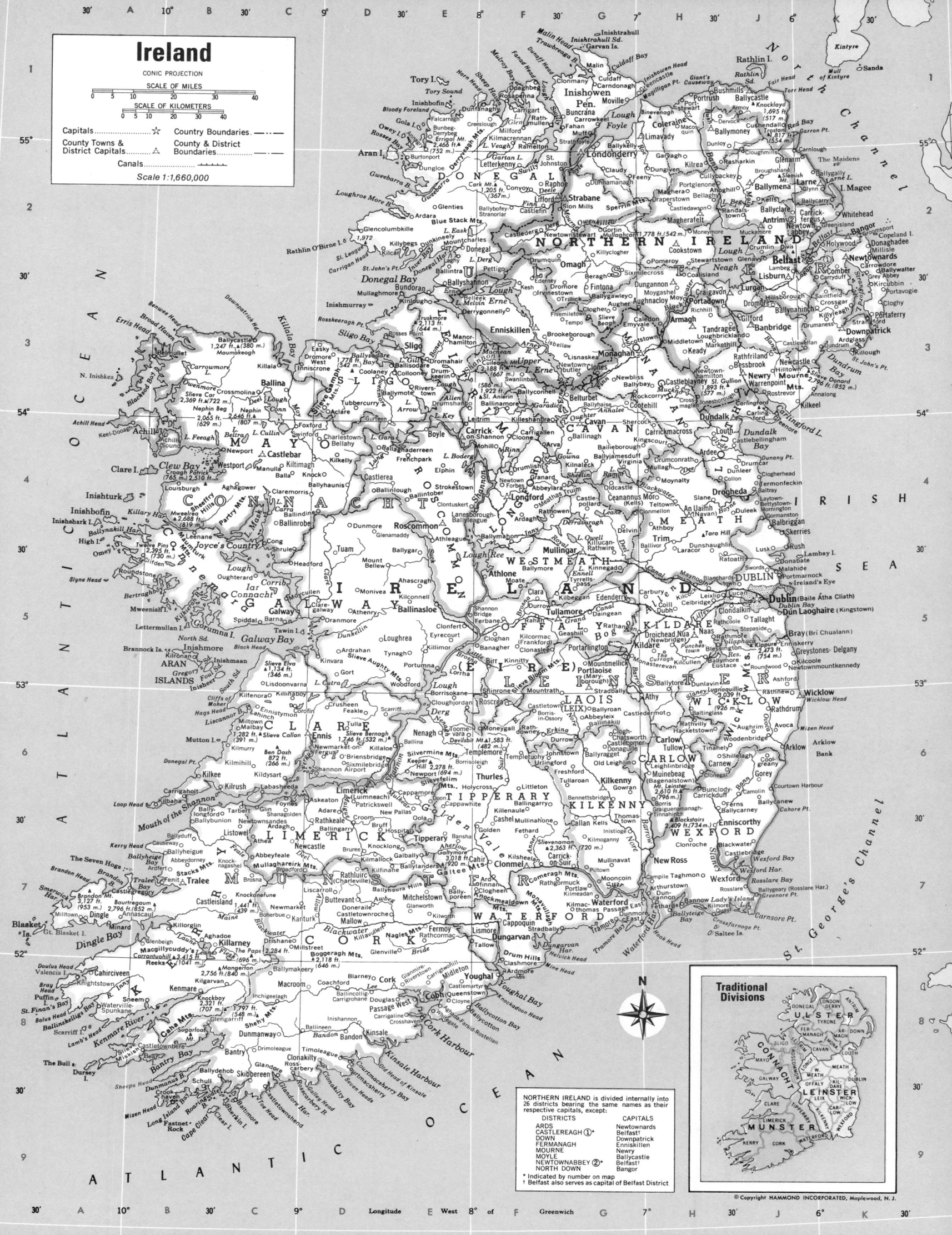

Ireland

CONIC PROJECTION

SCALE OF MILES

SCALE OF KILOMETERS

Capitals...........................★   Country Boundaries.._.._.._..

County Towns &   County & District
District Capitals.........△   Boundaries..............

Canals...........................

Scale 1:1,660,000

NORTHERN IRELAND is divided internally into
26 districts bearing the same names as their
respective capitals, except:

DISTRICTS	CAPITALS
ARDS	Newtownards
CASTLEREAGH ① *	Belfast
DOWN	Downpatrick
FERMANAGH	Enniskillen
MOURNE	Newry
MOYLE	Ballycastle
NEWTOWNABBEY ② *	Belfast
NORTH DOWN	Bangor

* Indicated by number on map
† Belfast also serves as capital of Belfast District

Traditional Divisions

ULSTER

CONNACHT

LEINSTER

MUNSTER

© Copyright HAMMOND INCORPORATED, Maplewood, N.J.

Norway, Sweden, Finland and Denmark

CONIC PROJECTION

Svalbard

SUBDIVISIONS
Indicated by Numbers
Counties in NORWAY

1 Akershus	G 6
2 Vestfold	G 7
3 Østfold	G 7
4 Oslo	G 7

Oslo is the administrative center for Akershus and Oslo County.

Counties in SWEDEN

5 Göteborg och Bohus	K 7
6 Västmanland	K 7
7 Södermanland	K 7
8 Östergötland	J 7
9 Malmöhus	H 9
10 Kristianstad	J 8

SCALE OF MILES
0 50 100 150

SCALE OF KILOMETERS
0 50 100 150 200

Capitals of Countries .... ☆
Administrative Centers .... △
International Boundaries .... — · · —
Internal Boundaries .... — · — ·
Canals .... ⌐⌐⌐⌐

© Copyright HAMMOND INCORPORATED, Maplewood, N.J.

AREA 125,053 sq. mi.
(323,887 sq. km.)
POPULATION 4,092,000
CAPITAL Oslo
LARGEST CITY Oslo
HIGHEST POINT Glittertinden
8,110 ft. (2,472 m.)
MONETARY UNIT krone
MAJOR LANGUAGE Norwegian
MAJOR RELIGION Protestantism

AREA 173,665 sq. mi.
(449,792 sq. km.)
POPULATION 8,320,000
CAPITAL Stockholm
LARGEST CITY Stockholm
HIGHEST POINT Kebnekaise 6,946 ft.
(2,117 m.)
MONETARY UNIT krona
MAJOR LANGUAGE Swedish
MAJOR RELIGION Protestantism

AREA 130,128 sq. mi.
(337,032 sq. km.)
POPULATION 4,788,000
CAPITAL Helsinki
LARGEST CITY Helsinki
HIGHEST POINT Haltiatunturi
4,343 ft. (1,324 m.)
MONETARY UNIT markka
MAJOR LANGUAGES Finnish, Swedish
MAJOR RELIGION Protestantism

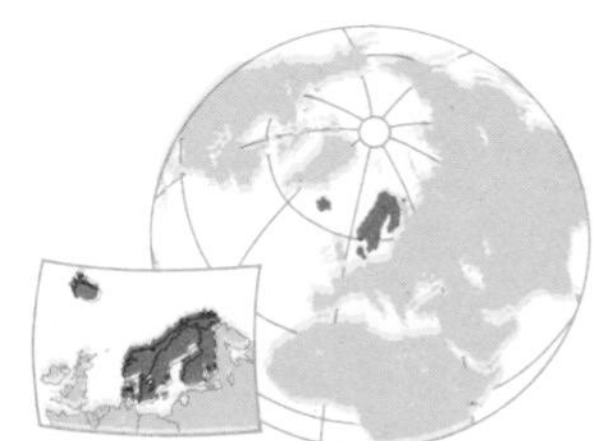

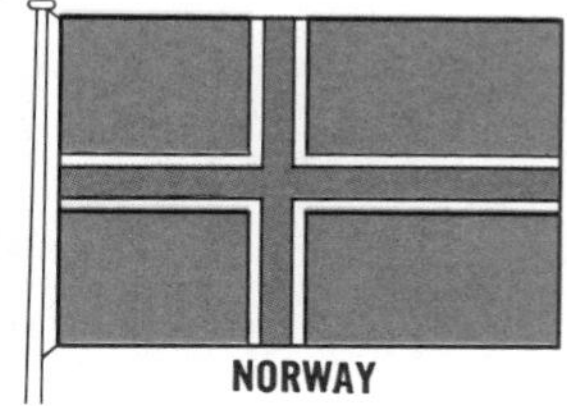

NORWAY

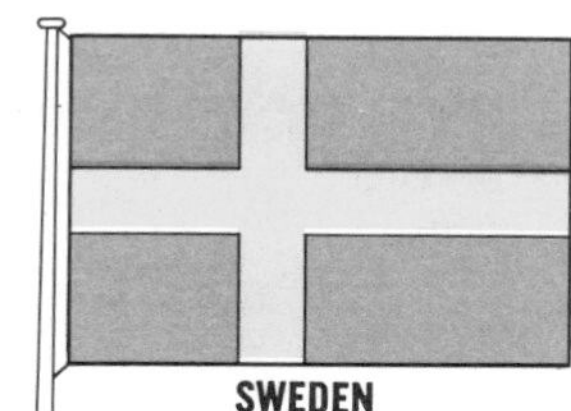

SWEDEN

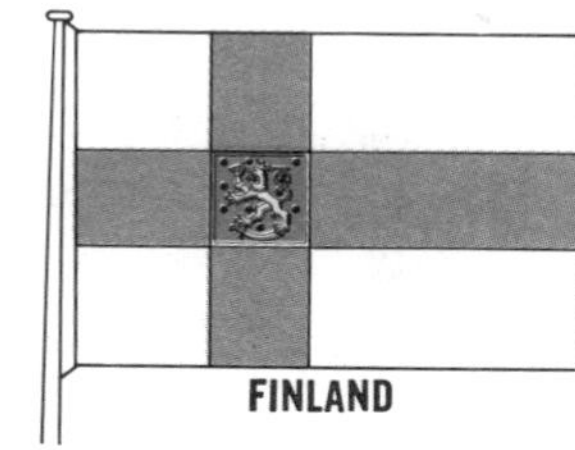

FINLAND

FINLAND

PROVINCES

Ahvenanmaa 22,380	L6
Åland (Ahvenanmaa) 22,380	L6
Häme 662,500	O6
Keski-Suomi 241,770	O5
Kuopio 252,023	P5
Kymi 346,478	Q6
Lappi 196,792	P3
Mikkeli 211,453	P6
Oulu 406,309	P4
Pohjois-Karjala 179,065	Q5
Turku ja Pori 697,988	N6
Uusimaa 1,085,625	O6
Vaasa 425,283	N5

CITIES and TOWNS

Äänekoski 10,725	O5
Åbo (Turku) 164,857	N6
Alavus 10,285	N5
Borgaå 18,740	O6
Ekenäs 7,391	N6
Espoo 117,090	O6
Forssa 18,442	N6
Haapajärvi 7,791	O5
Hämeenlinna 40,761	O6
Hamina 11,055	P6
Hangö 10,374	N7
Hanko (Hangö) 10,374	N7
Harjavalta 8,445	M6
Heinola 15,350	O6
Helsinki (cap.) 502,961	O6
Helsinki* 794,746	O6
Huutokoski† 6,458	P5
Hyvinkää 35,865	O6
Iisalmi 21,159	P5
Ikaalinen 8,364	N6
Imatra 35,590	Q6
Ivalo 2,661	P2
Jakobstad 20,397	N5
Jämsä 12,526	O6
Järvenpää 16,259	O6
Joensuu 41,429	Q5
Jyväskylä 61,209	O5
Jyväskylä* 84,185	O5
Kajaani 20,583	P4
Kalajoki 3,624	N4
Kankaanpää 12,564	M6
Karhula 21,834	P6
Karis 8,152	N6
Karjaa (Karis) 8,152	N6
Karkkila 8,678	N6
Kauniainen 6,219	O6
Kauttua 3,297	M6
Kellosekat† 8,200	Q3
Kemi 27,893	O4
Kemijärvi 12,951	P3
Kerava 19,966	O6
Kokemäki 10,188	N6
Kokkola 22,096	N5
Kotka 34,026	P6
Kotka* 60,235	P6
Kouvola 29,383	P6
Kouvola* 59,507	P6
Kristinankaupunki	
(Kristinestad) 9,331	N5
Kristinestad 9,331	N5
Kuhmo 4,150	Q4
Kuopio 71,684	Q5
Kurikka 11,177	M5
Kuusamo 4,449	Q4
Kuusankoski 22,342	P6
Lahti 94,864	O6
Lahti* 112,129	O6
Lappeenranta 52,682	P6
Lapua 15,189	N5
Lieksa 20,274	R5
Loimaa 6,575	N6
Lovisa 8,674	P6
Maarianhamina	
(Mariehamn) 9,574	M7
Mänttä 7,910	O6
Mariehamn 9,574	M7
Mikkeli 27,112	P6
Naantali 7,814	M6
Nokia 22,308	N6
Nurmes 11,721	Q5
Nykarleby 7,408	N5
Oulainen 7,322	O4
Oulu 93,707	O4
Oulu* 103,044	O4
Outokumpu 10,736	Q5
Parainen 10,170	M6
Parkano 8,518	N6
Pieksämäki 12,923	P5
Pietarsaari (Jakobstad) 20,397	N5
Pori 80,343	M6
Pori* 86,635	M6
Posiot 6,205	Q3
Pudasjärvi 12,594	P4
Raahe 15,379	O4
Raisio 14,271	M6
Rauma 29,081	M6
Riihimäki 24,106	O6
Rovaniemi 28,411	O3
Saarijärvi 2,714	O5
Salo 19,176	N6
Savonlinna 28,336	Q6
Seinäjoki 22,123	N5
Sodankyla 3,304	P3
Sotkamo 2,316	Q4
Suolahti 5,936	O5
Suonenjoki 9,286	P5
Tammisaari (Ekenäs) 7,391	N6
Tampere 168,118	N6
Tampere* 220,920	N6
Toijala 8,080	N6
Tornio 19,971	O4
Turku 164,857	N6
Turku* 217,423	N6
Turtola† 5,852	O3
Ulvilat 8,492	N6
Uusikaarlepyy	
(Nykarleby) 7,408	N5
Uusikaupunki 11,915	M6
Vaasa 54,402	M5
Vaasa* 58,224	M5
Valkeakoski 22,588	N6
Vammala 16,363	N6
Varkaus 24,450	Q5
Vasa (Vaasa) 54,402	M5
Vuotsot 10,186	P2
Ylivieska 10,827	O4

OTHER FEATURES

Åland (isls.)	L6
Baltic (sea)	K9
Bothnia (gulf)	M5
Finland (gulf)	P7
Hailuoto (isl.)	O4
Haltiatunturi (mt.)	M2
Hangöudd (prom.)	N7
Haukivesi (lake)	Q5
Iijoki (riv.)	O4
Inari (lake)	P2
Ivalojoki (riv.)	P2
Juojärvi (lake)	Q5
Kalajoki (riv.)	O4
Kallavesi (lake)	P5
Karlo (Hailuoto) (isl.)	O4
Keitele (lake)	O5
Kemijärvi (lake)	Q3
Kemijoki (riv.)	O3
Kiantajärvi (lake)	Q4
Kilpisjärvi (lake)	M2
Kitinen (riv.)	P3
Kivijärvi (lake)	O5
Koitere (lake)	R5
Kuusamojärvi (lake)	Q4
Längelmävesi (lake)	O6
Lapland (reg.)	O2
Lappajärvi (lake)	O5
Lapuanjoki (riv.)	N5
Lestijärvi (lake)	O5
Lokka (res.)	Q3
Muojärvi (lake)	R4
Muonio (riv.)	M2
Näsijärvi (lake)	N6
Onkivesi (lake)	P5
Orihvesi (lake)	Q5
Oulujärvi (lake)	P4
Oulujoki (riv.)	O4
Ounasjoki (riv.)	O3
Päijänne (lake)	O6
Pielinen (lake)	Q5
Puruvesi (lake)	Q6
Puulavesi (lake)	P5
Pyhäjärvi (lake)	O5
Pyhäjärvi (lake)	M6
Saimaa (lake)	Q6
Siikajoki (riv.)	O4
Simojärvi (lake)	P3
Simojoki (riv.)	O3
Tana (riv.)	P2
Tornio (riv.)	O3
Vallgrund (isl.)	M5
Ylikitka (lake)	Q3

NORWAY

COUNTIES

Akershus 355,196	G6
Aust-Agder 86,216	E7
Buskerud 209,684	F6
Finnmark 79,373	O2
Hedmark 183,465	G6
Hordaland 386,492	D6
Møre og Romsdal 231,944	E5
Nordland 243,233	J3
Nord-Trøndelag 122,886	H4
Oppland 178,259	F6
Oslo (city) 462,732	D3
Østfold 228,546	G7
Rogaland 287,653	E7
Sogn og Fjordane 103,135	E6
Sør-Trøndelag 241,361	G5
Telemark 158,853	F7
Troms 144,111	L2
Vest-Agder 131,659	E7
Vestfold 182,433	G7

CITIES and TOWNS

Ålesund 40,868	D5
Ålgård 2,322	D7
Alta 5,582	N2
Andalsnes 2,574	E5
Ardalstangen 2,360	F6
Arendal 11,701	F7
Arendal* 21,228	F7
Årnes 2,267	G6
Askim 8,413	E4
Bamble† 7,031	F7
Barentsburg	
Bergen 213,434	D6
Bodø 31,097	J3
Borget 3,294	H2
Brønnøysund 3,130	G4
Dombas 1,114	F5
Drammen 50,777	C4
Drammen* 56,521	C4
Drøbak 4,538	D4
Eidsvoll 2,906	G6
Eigersund 11,379	D7
Elverum 7,391	G6
Farsund 8,908	D7
Flekkefjord 8,750	E7
Flora 8,822	D6
Fredrikstad 29,024	D4
Fredrikstad* 51,141	D4
Gjøvik 25,963	G6
Grimstad 13,091	F7
Halden 27,087	F7
Hamar 16,418	G6
Hamar* 25,138	G6
Hammerfest 7,610	N1
Hammerfest* 8,005	N1
Harstad 21,125	K2
Haugesund 27,386	D7
Haugesund* 29,277	D7
Hermansverk 706	E6
Holmestrand 8,246	F7
Honningsvåg 3,780	O1
Horten 13,746	D4
Horten* 17,246	D4
Kirkenes 4,466	Q2
Kongsberg 19,854	F7
Kongsvinger 16,146	H6
Kopervik 4,221	D7
Kornsjø† 6,079	G7
Kragerø 5,249	F7
Kristiansand 59,488	F8
Kristiansund 18,847	D5
Kvinnheradt 2,898	D6
Larvik 9,097	C4
Larvik* 19,202	C4
Lenvikt 11,098	L2
Levanger 5,066	G5
Lillehammer 21,248	F6
Lillesand 3,028	F7
Lillestrøm† 11,550	E2
Longyearbyen	
Lysakert 81,612	D3
Mandal 11,579	E7
Meråkert 2,907	G5
Mo 21,033	J3
Molde 20,334	E5
Mosjøen 9,341	H4
Moss 25,786	D4
Moss* 27,430	D4
Mysen 3,760	G7
Namsos 11,452	G4
Narvik 19,582	K2
Nesttunt 11,519	D6
Nittedalt 8,889	D3
Notodden 12,970	F7
Odda 7,401	E6
Odda* 2,173	E6
Orkanger 3,685	F5
Oslo (cap.) 462,732	D3
Oslo* 645,413	D3
Porsgrunn 31,709	G7
Rakkestad 2,392	G7
Ringerike 3,156	C3
Risør 6,560	F8
Rjukan 5,334	F7
Røros 3,041	G5
Sandefjord 33,350	C4
Sandnes 33,934	D7
Sandvikat 34,337	C3
Sarpsborg 12,889	D4
Sarpsborg* 36,449	D4
Seljet 3,386	D5
Ski 9,081	D4
Skien 47,105	F7
Stavanger 86,639	D7
Stavern 2,604	D4
Steinkjer 20,553	G4
Stor-Elvdal† 2,993	G6
Sunndalsøra 5,114	F5
Svalgruva	D2
Sveagruva	
Svolvær 3,942	J2
Tønsberg 9,964	D4
Tønsberg* 36,374	D4
Tromsø 43,830	L2
Trondheim 134,910	F5
Ullensvang† 2,326	E6
Vadsø 6,019	Q1
Vardø 3,875	R1
Vik 1,019	E6
Volda 3,511	E5
Voss 5,944	E6

OTHER FEATURES

Alsten (isl.)	H4
Andøya (isl.)	J2
Bardelv (riv.)	L2
Bellsund	
Bjørnafjorden (fjord)	C2
Bjørnøya (isl.)	D6
Boknafjord (fjord)	D3
Bremanger (isl.)	D7
Dønna (isl.)	D6
Dovrefjell (hills)	H3
Edgeøya (isl.)	F5
Femundsjø (lake)	E2
Folda (fjord)	H3
Folda (fjord)	G4
Frohavet (bay)	J3
Frøya (isl.)	F5
Glittertinden (mt.)	F5
Hardangervidda (plat.)	E6
Hardangerfjord (fjord)	E6
Hinlopenstreten (str.)	D7
Hinnøya (isl.)	C1
Hitra (isl.)	K2
Hopen (isl.)	F5
Isfjorden (fjord)	E2
Jostedalsbreen (glac.)	E6
Kjølen (mts.)	E6
Kongsfjorden (fjord)	K3
Kvaløya (isl.)	B2
Lågen (riv.)	O1
Laksefjorden (fjord)	G6
Langøy (isl.)	P1
Lapland (reg.)	J2
Leka (isl.)	K2
Lindesnes (cape)	G4
Lista (pen.)	E8
Lofoten (isls.)	E7
Lopphavet (bay)	H2
Magerøya (isl.)	M1
Moskenesøya (isl.)	P1
Namsen (riv.)	H4
Nordaustlandet (isl.)	H4
Nordfjord (fjord)	D1
Nordkapp (pt.)	E6
Nordkinn (headland)	P1
Nordkinn (pen.)	Q1
North Cape (Nordkapp) (pt.)	P1
Norwegian (sea)	P1
Ofotfjorden (fjord)	F3
Oslofjord (fjord)	K2
Otra (riv.)	D4
Otterøya (isl.)	E7
Pasvikelv (riv.)	E5
Platen, Kapp (pt.)	Q2
Porsangen (fjord)	O1
Rana (riv.)	O1
Rauma (riv.)	H3
Ringvassøy (isl.)	F5
Romsdalsfjorden (fjord)	L2
Saltfjorden (fjord)	E5
Seiland (isl.)	J3
Senja (isl.)	N1
Skagerrak (str.)	K2
Smøla (isl.)	E7
Sognafjorden (fjord)	E5
Sørkapp (pt.)	D6
Sørøya (isl.)	C2
Spitsbergen (isl.)	N1
Storfjorden (fjord)	D2
Sulitjelma (mt.)	D2
Svalbard (isl.)	J3
Tana (riv.)	C3
Tanafjord (fjord)	P1
Tokke (riv.)	P1
Trondheimsfjorden (fjord)	F7
Tyrifjord (lake)	G5
Vaerøy (isl.)	C3
Vågavatn (lake)	H3
Vannøy (isl.)	F6
Varangerhalvøya (pen.)	L1
Varangerfjord (fjord)	Q1
Vega (isl.)	Q2
Vesterålen (isls.)	G4
Vestfjord (fjord)	J2
Vestvågøya (isl.)	H3
Vikna (isls.)	H3
	G4

SWEDEN

COUNTIES

Älvsborg 418,150	H7
Blekinge 155,391	J8
Gävleborg 294,595	K6
Göteborg och Bohus 714,660	G7
Gotland 54,447	L8
Halland 219,767	H8
Jämtland 133,559	J5
Jönköping 301,905	H8
Kalmar 240,768	J8
Kopparberg 281,082	J6
Kristianstad 272,090	J8

(continued on following page)

Topography

Horn • Fontur • Nordkapp (North Cape) • Varangerfjord • VATNA-JÖKULL • VESTER-ÅLEN • Inari • Faxaflói • Reykjavík • Hekla 4,891 ft. (1491 m.) • Hvannadals-shnúkur 6,946 ft. (2117 m.) • Iceland • LOFOTEN • Vestfjord • Haltiatunturi 4,343 ft. (1324 m.) • Muonio • Ivalo • Kebnekaise 6,946 ft. (2117 m.) • Torne • Kemi • Ylikitka • Uddjaur • Skellefte • Ume • Oulujärvi • Storsjön • Indals • Ångerman • Ljusna • Klar • Dal • Glåma • GULF OF BOTHNIA • Kumo • Saimaa • Helsinki • ÅLAND IS. • Nordfjord • Sognafjorden • Glittertinden 8,110 ft. (2472 m.) • Mjøsa • Oslo • Bergen • Hardanger fjord • Otra • Oslofjord • Stockholm • Vänern • Lindesnes • Skagerrak • Vättern • Göteborg • Göta Canal • Gotland • Öland • Kattegat • Yding Skovhoj 568 ft. (173 m.) • Copenhagen • Fyn • Sjaelland • Lolland • Bornholm

	0	100	200 MI.
	0	100	200 KM.

| Below Sea Level | 100 m. 328 ft. | 200 m. 656 ft. | 500 m. 1,640 ft. | 1,000 m. 3,281 ft. | 2,000 m. 6,562 ft. | 5,000 m. 16,404 ft. |

(continued)

Kronoberg 169,454 J8
Malmöhus 740,137 H9
Norrbotten 264,215 L3
Örebro 273,994 J7
Östergötland 387,104 J7
Skaraborg 263,382 H7
Södermanland 252,030 K7
Stockholm 1,493,052 L7
Uppsala 229,879 K7
Värmland 284,442 H7
Västerbotten 236,367 K4
Västernorrland 268,202 K5
Västmanland 259,872 K7

CITIES and TOWNS

Åhus 6,125 J9
Alingsås 18,892 H7
Älmhult 7,390 H8
Alvesta 7,261 J8
Älvsbyn 4,707 M4
Åmål 9,556 H7
Ånge 3,760 J5
Ängelholm 16,016 H8
Arboga 11,819 J7
Arbrå 2,734 K6
Årjäng† 2,596 H7
Arvidsjaur 4,194 L4
Arvika 13,934 H7
Åseda 2,465 J8
Askim 17,609 G8
Åtvidaberg 8,436 K7
Avesta 19,095 J6
Bålsta 8,243 G1
Båstad 2,452 H8
Bengtsfors 3,535 H7
Boden 19,590 M4
Bollnäs 13,305 K6
Bollstabruk 3,548 L5
Borås 67,537 H8
Borås* 187,710 H8
Borgholm 2,789 K8
Borlänge 40,158 J6
Brunflo 3,460 J5
Dalby† 4,013 H6
Danderyd† 36,596 H1
Dannemora 291 K6
Edsbyn 4,388 J6
Eksjö 9,686 J8
Emmaboda 5,652 J8
Enköping 18,541 G1
Eskilstuna 66,409 K7
Eslöv 13,629 H9
Fagersta† 14,778 J6
Falkenberg 14,148 H8
Falköping 15,126 H7
Falun 30,073 J6
Färjestaden 2,995 K8
Filipstad 7,835 H7
Finspång 16,346 J7
Flen 6,770 K7
Forshaga 6,000 H7
Frösö 10,274 J5
Frövi 2,583 J7
Gällivare 8,669 M3
Gamleby 3,666 J8
Gävle 67,454 K6
Gimo 3,154 K6
Gislaved 8,564 H8
Gnesta 3,835 G2
Göteborg 444,540 G8
Göteborg* 690,767 G8
Hagfors 8,060 H6
Hällefors 7,862 J7
Hallsberg 6,799 J7
Hallstahammar 13,583 K7
Hallstavik 5,162 L6
Halmstad 49,558 H8
Haparanda 5,031 N4
Härnösand 18,971 L5
Hässleholm 16,813 H8
Hedemora 7,039 K6
Helsingborg 80,986 H8
Helsingborg* 215,894 H8
Hjo 4,615 J7
Hofors 11,459 K6
Höganäs 10,866 H8
Holmsund 5,467 M5
Hörnefors 2,441 L5
Huddinge 48,339 H1
Hudiksvall 15,004 K6
Hultsfred 5,763 K8
Husum 2,517 L5
Hyltebruk 3,469 H8
Iggesund 4,448 K6
Järna 6,237 G2
Jokkmokk 3,186 L3
Jönköping 78,650 H8
Jönköping* 131,499 H8
Kalix 7,668 N4
Kalmar 32,049 K8
Karlshamn 17,447 J8
Karlskoga† 35,425 J7
Karlskrona 33,414 J8
Karlstad 51,243 H7
Katrineholm 22,884 K7
Kinna 13,676 H8
Kiruna 25,410 L3
Kisa 4,323 J7
Köping 20,059 J7
Kopparberg 3,942 J7
Kramfors 7,719 L5
Kristianstad 30,780 J9
Kristinehamn 21,146 H7
Kumla 11,451 J7
Kungälv† 12,764 G8
Kungsbacka† 11,986 G8
Kvissleby 3,413 K5
Laholm 3,898 H8
Landskrona 29,486 H9
Långshyttan 2,744 K6
Laxå 5,166 J7
Leksand 4,410 J6
Lessebo 2,991 J8
Lidingö 30,098 H1
Lidköping 21,001 H7
Lindesberg 8,247 J7
Linköping 80,274 K7
Linköping* 132,839 K7
Ljungby 12,969 J8
Ljusdal 7,075 J6
Ljusne 3,578 K6
Ludvika 18,217 J6
Luleå 42,139 N4
Lund 55,047 H9
Lycksele 8,586 L4
Lysekil 7,815 G7
Malmberget 10,239 M3
Malmö 241,191 H9
Malmö* 453,339 H9
Malung 6,211 H6
Mariefred 2,553 F1
Mariestad 16,454 H7
Markaryd 4,266 H8
Märsta 17,066 K7
Marstrand 1,168 G8
Mellerud 3,579 H7
Mjölby 12,488 J7
Mölndal† 47,248 H8
Mönsterås 5,005 K8
Mora 8,772 J6
Motala 29,454 J7
Nacka 19,708 H1
Nässjö 18,634 J8
Nora 5,515 J7
Norberg 5,438 K6
Norrköping 85,244 K7
Norrköping* 163,206 K7
Norrtälje 12,784 L7
Nybro 13,010 J8
Nyköping 30,352 K7
Nynäshamn 11,070 L7
Ockelbo 2,810 K6
Olofström 10,096 J8
Örebro 117,877 J7
Örebro* 171,440 J7
Örnsköldsvik 29,514 L5
Orrefors 919 J8
Orsa 5,099 J6
Oskarshamn 19,021 K8
Östersund 40,056 J5
Östhammar 1,783 L6
Oxelösund 13,862 K7
Piteå 16,169 M4
Rättvik 4,087 J6
Rimbo 3,404 L7
Ronneby 12,086 J8
Säffle 11,428 H7
Sala 11,216 K7
Saltsjöbaden 8,113 J1
Sandviken 27,994 K6
Säter 4,297 J6
Sävsjö 4,913 J8
Sigtuna 4,780 H1
Simrishamn 5,834 J9
Skanör med Falsterbo 4,909 H9
Skara 10,138 H7
Skellefteå 29,353 M4
Skövde 29,945 H7
Skutskär 7,174 K6
Smedjebacken 8,418 J6
Söderhamn 14,673 K6
Söderköping 5,310 K7
Södertälje 58,408 G1
Sollefteå 8,923 K5
Sollentuna† 40,905 H1
Solna† 53,992 H1
Sölvesborg 7,292 J9
Stenungsund 8,361 G7
Stockholm (cap.) 665,550 G1
Stockholm* 1,357,183 G1
Storuman 2,587 K4
Storvik 2,748 K6
Strängnäs 10,255 F1
Strömstad 4,735 G7
Strömsund 4,119 K5
Sundbyberg† 27,058 G1
Sundsvall 52,268 K5
Sunne 4,273 H7
Surahammar 6,509 J7
Sveg 2,608 J5
Svenljunga 3,189 H8
Täby† 41,285 H1
Tibro 8,476 J7
Tidaholm 8,039 J7
Tierp 5,005 K6
Timrå 11,416 K5
Tomelilla 5,371 J9
Torsby 3,632 H6
Torshälla 8,231 K7
Tranås 14,854 J7
Trelleborg 22,559 H9
Trollhättan 42,499 H7
Trosa 3,128 K7
Uddevalla 32,700 G7
Ulricehamn 7,827 H8
Umeå 49,715 M5
Uppsala 101,850 K7
Uppsala* 157,202 L7
Vadstena 5,294 J7
Vaggeryd 3,974 J8
Valdemarsvik 3,558 K7
Vallentuna 10,477 H1
Vänersborg 20,510 G7
Vännäs 3,876 L5
Vansbro 2,708 H6
Vara 3,049 H7
Varberg 19,467 G8
Värnamo 15,726 J8
Västerås 98,858 K7
Västerås* 147,508 K7
Västerhaninge 14,125 H1
Västervik 21,239 K8
Vaxholm† 3,744 J1
Växjö 40,328 J8
Vetlanda 12,358 J8
Vilhelmina 4,060 K4
Vimmerby 7,405 J8
Virserum 2,495 J8
Visby 19,886 L8
Ystad 14,286 H9

OTHER FEATURES

Ångermanälven (riv.) K5
Åsnen (lake) J8
Baltic (sea) K9
Bolmen (lake) H8
Bothnia (gulf) N4
Dalälven (riv.) K6
Fårö (isl.) L8
Göta (canal) J7
Göta (riv.) H7
Gotland (isl.) L8
Gräsö (isl.) L6
Hanöbukten (bay) J9
Hjälmaren (lake) J7
Hoburgen (cliff) L8
Hornslandet (pen.) K6
Indalsälven (riv.) H5
Kalixälv (riv.) N3
Kalmarsund (sound) K8
Kattegat (str.) G8
Kebnekaise (mt.) L3
Kölen (mts.) K3
Klarälv (riv.) H6
Lapland (reg.) M2
Ljusnan (riv.) H5
Luleälv (riv.) M4
Mälaren (lake) G1
Muonioälv (riv.) M2
Öland (isl.) K8
Öresund (sound) H9
Ornö (isl.) J2
Österdalälven (riv.) H6
Piteälv (riv.) M4
Siljan (lake) J6
Skagerrak (str.) F8
Sommen (lake) J8
Stora Lulevatten (lake) L3
Storsjön (lake) J5
Sulitelma (mt.) K3
Torneälv (riv.) M3
Uddjaur (lake) L4
Umeälv (riv.) L4
Vänern (lake) H7
Västerdalälven (riv.) H6
Vättern (lake) J7

*City and suburbs.
†Population of commune.
†Population of parish.

DENMARK

COUNTIES

Århus 534,333 D5
Bornholm 47,241 F9
Copenhagen (commune) 622,612 F6
Faerøe Islands 41,969 B2
Frederiksberg (commune) 101,874 F6
Frederiksborg 260,825 E5
Fyn 433,765 D7
København (Copenhagen) (commune) 622,612 F6
Københaven 616,571 F6
Nordjylland 457,165 D4
Ribe 198,153 B7
Ringkøbing 242,006 B5
Roskilde 154,314 E6
Sønderjylland 238,502 C7
Storstrøm 252,780 E7
Vejle 306,809 C6
Vestsjaelland 259,484 E6
Viborg 221,002 C4

CITIES and TOWNS

Åbenrå 15,196 C7
Åbybro 2,897 C3
Åkirkeby 2,001 F9
Ålborg 154,582 D4
Ålestrup 1,926 C4
Århus 245,941 D5
Års 4,266 C4
Årup 1,675 D7
AErøskøbing 1,223 D8
Agerbaek 935 B6
Allingaåbro 1,385 D5
Allinge-Sandvig 1,991 F8
Ansager 1,157 B6
Arden 1,303 C4
Asaå 1,344 D3
Askov 904 C7
Asnaes 1,413 E6
Assens, Århus 1,341 D4
Assens, Fyn 5,139 D7
Augustenborg 2,628 D8
Auning 1,516 D5
Avlum 1,729 B5
Baelum 1,169 D4
Bagenkop 776 D8
Ballerup 50,673 F6
Bandholm 693 E8
Bedsted 965 B4
Birkerød 13,663 F6
Bjerringbro 4,761 C5
Bogense 2,861 D6
Bolderslev 774 C8
Børkop 1,410 C6
Borup 1,591 E7
Braedstrup 2,163 C6
Bramming 3,678 B7
Brande 4,784 B6
Bredebro 1,173 B7
Broager 2,143 C8
Brønderslev 10,247 C3
Brørup 2,584 C7
Brovst 4,200 C3
Bryrup 579 C5
Christiansfeld 1,994 C7
Copenhagen (cap.) 603,368 F6
Copenhagen* 1,327,940 F6
Dronninglund 4,661 D3
Dybvad 805 D3
Ebeltoft 3,017 D5
Egernsund 1,323 C8
Egtved 1,311 C6
Ejby 1,372 C7
Esbjerg 68,097 B7
Faåborg 6,495 D7
Fakse 2,720 F7
Fakse Ladeplads 1,799 F7
Farsø 2,821 C4
Farum 9,936 F6
Fjerritslev 2,134 C3
Fredensborg 4,709 F6
Fredericia 36,157 C6
Frederiksberg 101,874 F6
Frederikshavn 24,846 D3
Frederikssund 11,272 E6
Frederiksvaerk 8,903 E6
Fuglebjerg 1,094 E7
Gedser 1,200 F8
Gedsted 1,006 C4
Gelsted 1,307 C7
Gentofte 77,744 F6
Gilleleje 2,943 F5
Give 2,366 C6
Glamsbjerg 2,226 D7
Glostrup 28,326 F6
Glumsø 1,027 E7
Glyngøre 1,071 C4
Gørding 1,261 B7
Gørlev 1,542 E7
Graested 1,654 F5
Gram 2,061 C7
Graåsten 2,947 C8
Grenaå 12,569 D5
Grindsted 7,558 B6
Haårby 1,506 D7
Haderslev 20,042 C7
Hadsten 3,914 C5
Hadsund 3,652 D4
Hals 1,654 D3
Hammel 3,247 C5
Hammerum 3,227 C5
Hanstholm 1,716 B3
Harboør 1,359 B4
Haårlev 1,228 F7
Hasle 18
Haslev 6,925 E7
Havdrup 1,833 F6
Hedensted 2,659 C6
Hellebaek 2,911 F5
Helsinge 3,613 F6
Helsingør 42,425 F6
Herning 32,973 B5
Hillerød 23,963 F6
Hinnerup 2,061 D5
Hirtshals 6,861 C2
Hjallerup 1,573 C3
Hjerm 647 B5
Hjørring 19,692 C3
Hobro 8,737 C4
Højer 1,416 B8
Højslev 1,641 C4
Holbaek 19,485 E6
Holeby 1,434 E8
Holstebro 25,006 B5
Holsted 1,390 B6
Høng 2,488 E7
Hornslet 2,561 D5
Horsens 44,120 C6
Hørsholm 19,346 F6
Hørve 1,139 E6
Hov 635 D6
Humlum 546 B4
Hundested 5,443 E6
Hurup 2,287 B4
Hvidbjerg 994 B4
Hvide Sande 2,129 A6
Ikast 9,222 C5
Jelling 1,540 C6
Jerslev 798 D3
Juelsminde 1,991 D6
Jyderup 2,901 E6
Kalundborg 12,248 D6
Karise 1,184 F7
Karup 1,694 C5
Kastrup† 17,391 F6
Kerteminde 5,007 D7
Kibaek 1,279 B5
Kjellerup 3,245 C5
Klitmøller 542 B3
København (Copenhagen) (cap.) 603,368 F6
Køge 18,608 F7
Kolding 41,602 C7
Kolind 1,036 D5
Korsør 15,502 E7
Kvaerndrup 891 D7
Langaå 2,320 C5
Lem 1,026 B5
Lemvig 6,448 B4
Løgstør 3,633 C4
Løgumkloster 2,091 B7
Lohals 580 D7
Løjt Kirkeby 1,203 C7
Løkken 1,345 C3
Løsning 1,967 C6
Lundby 747 E7
Lunderskov 1,494 C7
Lyngby 61,516 F6
Malling 1,584 D5
Mariager 1,692 D4
Maribo 5,287 E8
Marstal 4,124 D8
Middelfart 13,315 C7

Agriculture, Industry and Resources

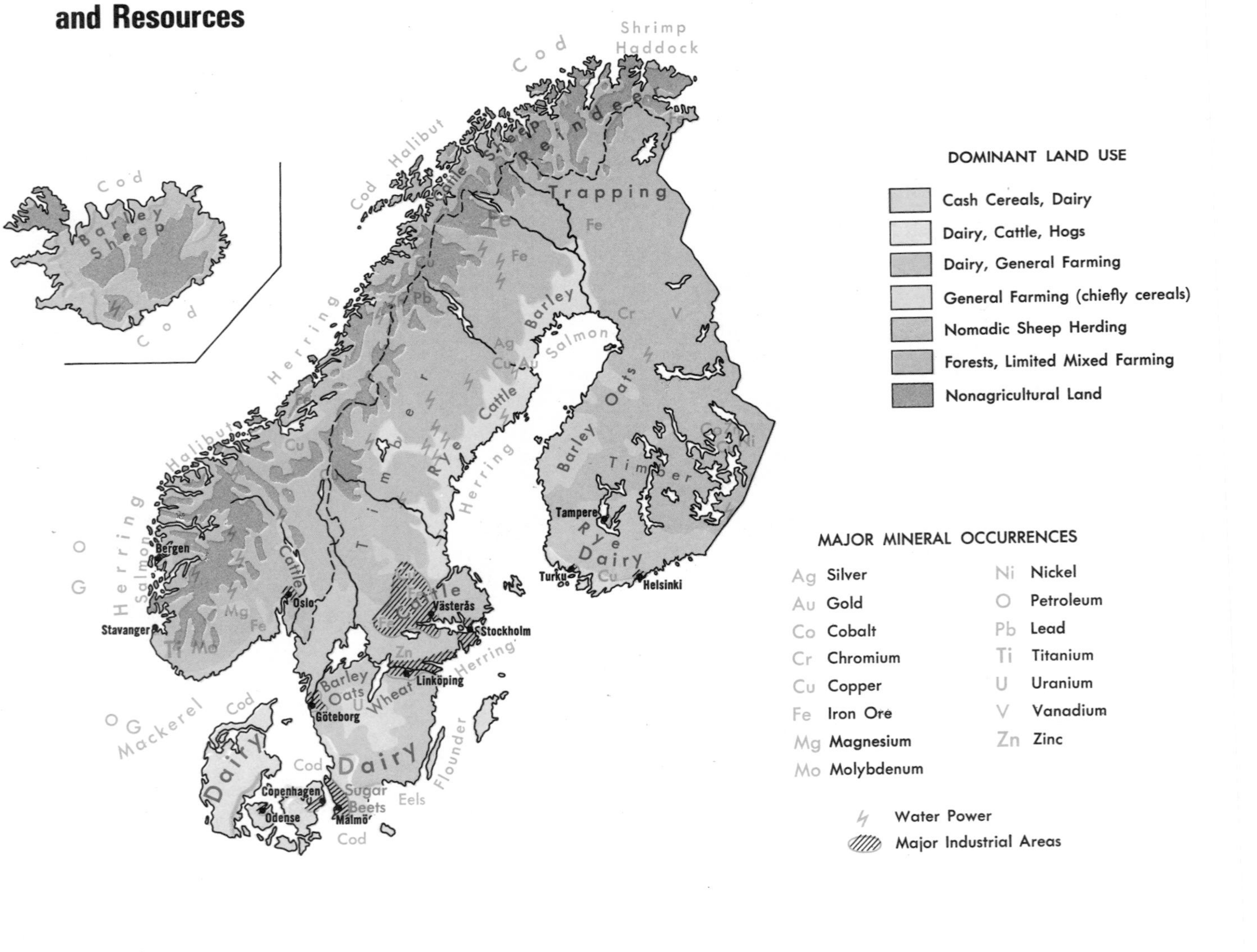

Shrimp
Haddock
Cod
Halibut
Reindeer
Trapping
Barley
Sheep
Herring
Salmon
Oats
Cattle
Timber
Rye
Dairy
Tampere
Turku
Helsinki
Bergen
Oslo
Stavanger
Västerås
Stockholm
Linköping
Göteborg
Wheat
Mackerel
Copenhagen
Odense
Malmö
Sugar Beets
Eels
Flounder
DOMINANT LAND USE
Cash Cereals, Dairy
Dairy, Cattle, Hogs
Dairy, General Farming
General Farming (chiefly cereals)
Nomadic Sheep Herding
Forests, Limited Mixed Farming
Nonagricultural Land
MAJOR MINERAL OCCURRENCES
Ag Silver
Au Gold
Co Cobalt
Cr Chromium
Cu Copper
Fe Iron Ore
Mg Magnesium
Mo Molybdenum
Ni Nickel
O Petroleum
Pb Lead
Ti Titanium
U Uranium
V Vanadium
Zn Zinc
Water Power
Major Industrial Areas

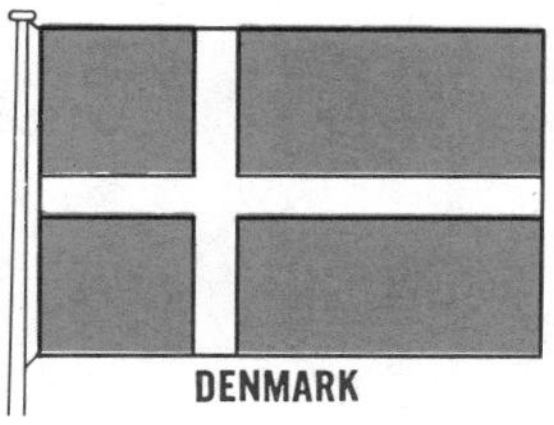

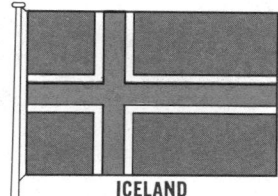

DENMARK

ICELAND

DENMARK

AREA 16,629 sq. mi. (43,069 sq. km.)
POPULATION 5,124,000
CAPITAL Copenhagen
LARGEST CITY Copenhagen
HIGHEST POINT Yding Skovhøj
568 ft. (173 m.)
MONETARY UNIT krone
MAJOR LANGUAGE Danish
MAJOR RELIGION Protestantism

ICELAND

AREA 39,768 sq. mi. (103,000 sq. km.)
POPULATION 228,785
CAPITAL Reykjavík
LARGEST CITY Reykjavík
HIGHEST POINT Hvannadalshnúkur
6,952 ft. (2,119 m.)
MONETARY UNIT króna
MAJOR LANGUAGE Icelandic
MAJOR RELIGION Protestantism

Denmark and Iceland

CONIC PROJECTION

SCALE OF MILES
0 10 20 30 40 50

SCALE OF KILOMETERS
0 10 20 30 40 50

Capitals of Countries _____ ★
Capitals of Counties (amter) ____ ⬡
International Boundaries _____
Internal Boundaries _____

Scale 1:2,300,000

Denmark is divided into fourteen Counties plus
Copenhagen and Frederiksberg communes.

© Copyright HAMMOND INCORPORATED, Maplewood, N.J.

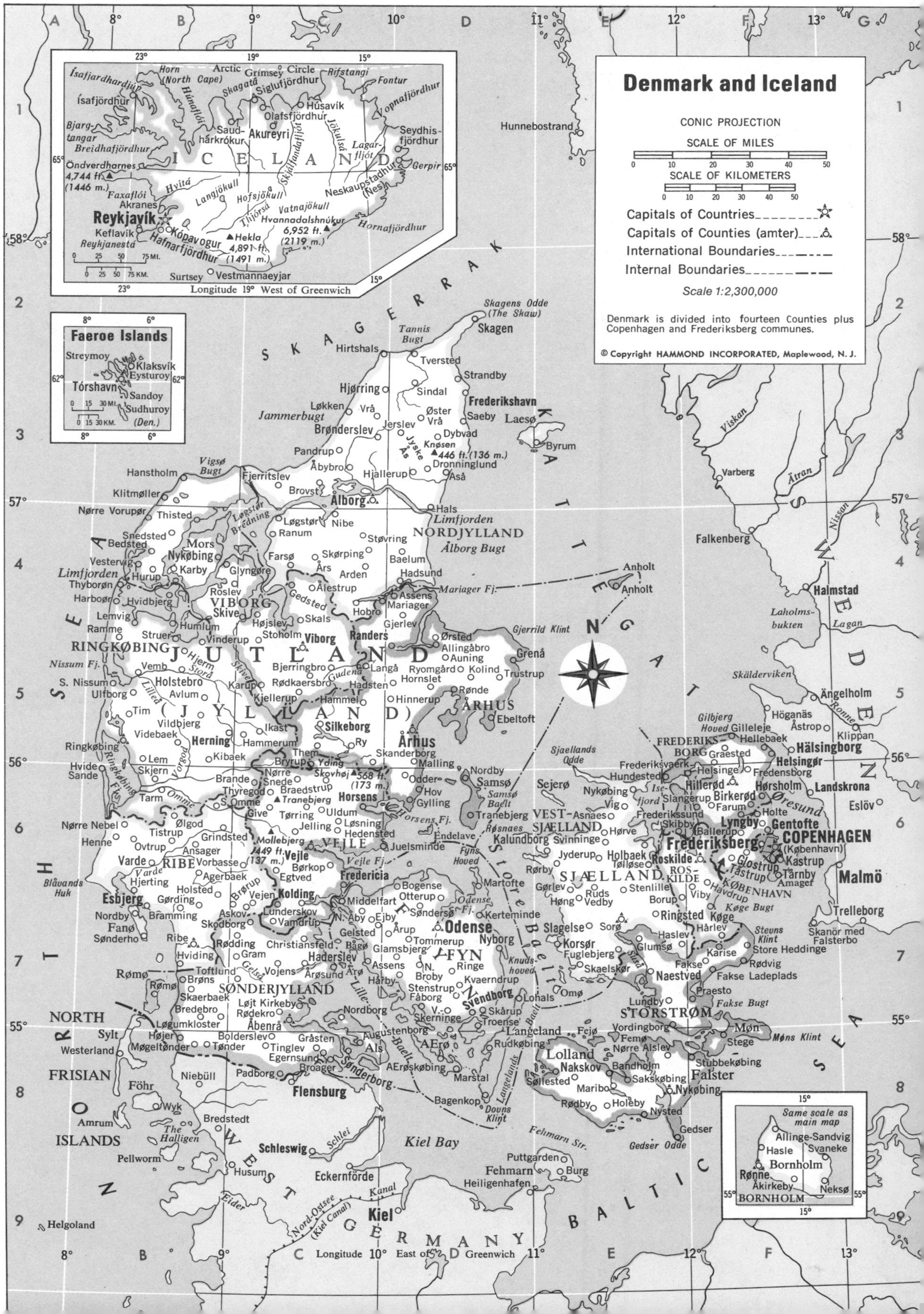

Germany

CONIC PROJECTION

SCALE OF MILES

SCALE OF KILOMETERS

Capitals of Countries .... ⭐
State and District Capitals .... ◉
International Boundaries ....
State and District Boundaries ....
Canals ....

Scale 1:3,040,000

East Germany is divided into districts bearing the same name as their respective capitals.

Berlin

© Copyright HAMMOND INCORPORATED, Maplewood, N.J.

AREA 95,985 sq. mi. (248,601 sq. km.)
POPULATION 61,658,000
CAPITAL Bonn
LARGEST CITY Berlin (West)
HIGHEST POINT Zugspitze 9,718 ft. (2,962 m.)
MONETARY UNIT Deutsche mark
MAJOR LANGUAGE German
MAJOR RELIGIONS Protestantism, Roman Catholicism

AREA 41,768 sq. mi. (108,179 sq. km.)
POPULATION 16,737,000
CAPITAL Berlin (East)
LARGEST CITY Berlin (East)
HIGHEST POINT Fichtelberg 3,983 ft. (1,214 m.)
MONETARY UNIT East German mark
MAJOR LANGUAGE German
MAJOR RELIGIONS Protestantism, Roman Catholicism

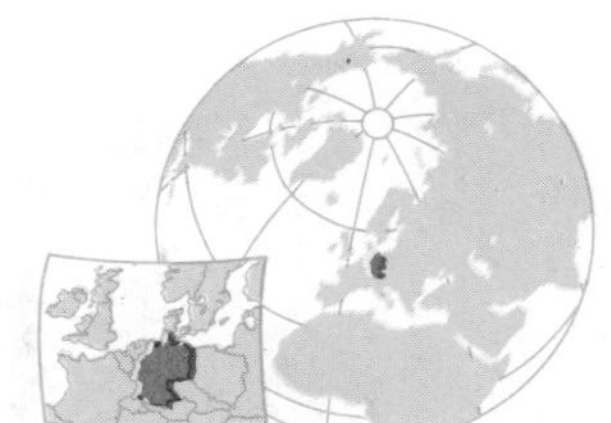

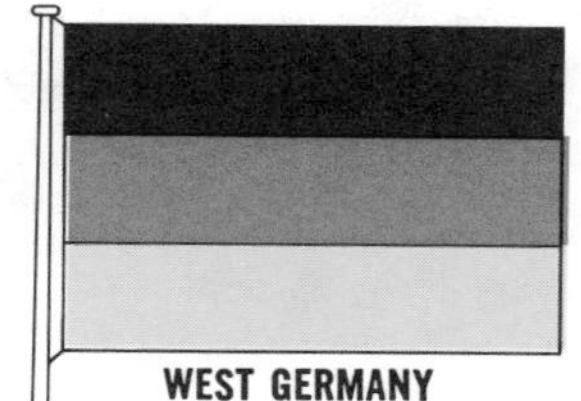

WEST GERMANY

EAST GERMANY

Topography

0 50 100 MI.
0 50 100 KM.

EAST GERMANY

DISTRICTS

Berlin 1,094,147 F4
Cottbus 872,242 F3
Dresden 1,845,459 E3
Erfurt 1,247,213 D3
Frankfurt 688,637 F2
Gera 738,847 D3
Halle 1,890,187 D3
Karl-Marx-Stadt 1,994,115 E3
Leipzig 1,457,817 E3
Magdeburg 1,297,881 D2
Neubrandenburg 628,686 E2
Potsdam 1,124,892 E2
Rostock 867,806 E1
Schwerin 592,334 D2
Suhl 550,497 D3

CITIES and TOWNS

Aken 11,742 D3
Altenburg 51,193 E3
Angermünde 11,786 E2
Anklam 19,099 E2
Annaberg-Buchholz 26,561 E3
Apolda 28,649 D3
Arnstadt 29,462 D3
Aschersleben 36,674 D3
Aue 32,622 E3
Auerbach 18,168 E3
Bad Doberan 12,541 D1
Bad Dürrenberg 15,192 D3
Bad Langensalza 166,282 D3
Bad Salzungen 17,277 C3
Barth 12,069 E1
Bautzen 45,851 F3
Bergen 13,244 E1
Berlin, East (cap.) 1,094,147 F4
Bernau bei Berlin 15,749 E2
Bernburg 44,428 D3
Bischofswerda 11,540 F3
Bitterfeld 27,062 E3
Blankenburg am Harz 18,784 D3
Boizenburg an der Elbe 12,428 D2
Borna 21,807 E3
Brandenburg 94,071 E2
Burg bei Magdeburg 29,027 D2
Calbe 15,976 D3
Chemnitz
(Karl-Marx-Stadt) 303,811 E3
Coswig, Dresden 22,149 E3
Coswig, Halle 12,473 E3
Cottbus 94,293 F3
Crimmitschau 28,845 E3
Delitzsch 24,076 E3
Demmin 17,270 E2
Dessau 100,820 E3
Döbeln 27,624 E3
Dresden 507,692 E3
Ebersbach 12,694 F3
Eberswalde-Finow 47,141 E2
Eilenburg 22,245 E3
Eisenach 49,954 D3
Eisenberg 13,450 D3
Eisenhüttenstadt 46,455 F2
Eisleben 29,297 D3
Erfurt 202,979 D3
Falkensee 25,295 E3
Falkenstein 14,367 E3
Finsterwalde 22,466 E3
Forst 28,084 F3
Frankfurt an der Oder 70,817 F2
Freiberg 50,815 E3
Freital 46,061 E3
Friedland E2
Fürstenwalde 31,065 F2
Gardelegen 12,987 D2
Genthin 15,916 E2
Gera 113,108 E3
Glauchau 30,927 E3
Görlitz 84,658 F3
Gotha 59,243 D3
Greifswald 53,940 E1
Greiz 37,612 E3
Grevesmühlen 12,005 D2
Grimma 17,100 E3
Grimmen 14,571 E1
Grossenhain 18,712 E3
Grossräschen 12,889 E3
Guben
(Wilhelm-Pieck-Stadt) 32,731 F3
Güstrow 36,824 E2
Halberstadt 46,669 D3
Haldensleben 19,194 D2
Halle 241,425 D3
Halle-Neustadt 67,956 D3
Havelberg D2
Heidenau 21,315 E3
Heiligenstadt 13,931 D3
Hennigsdorf bei Berlin 24,853 E3
Hettstedt 20,291 D3
Hildburghausen 11,372 D3
Hoyerswerda 64,904 F3
Ilmenau 22,021 D3
Jena 99,431 D3
Johanngeorgenstadt 10,328 E3
Jüterbog 13,477 E3
Kamenz 18,221 F3
Karl-Marx-Stadt 303,811 E3
Kleinmachnow 14,059 E4
Klingenthal 13,614 E3
Königs Wusterhausen 11,825 E2
Köpenick 130,987 F4
Köthen 35,451 E3
Kühlungsborn D1
Lauchhammer 26,939 E3
Leipzig 570,972 E3
Lichtenberg 192,063 F4
Limbach-Oberfrohna 25,706 E3
Löbau 18,077 F3
Lübben 14,224 E3
Lübbenau 22,350 F3
Luckenwalde 28,544 E2
Ludwigslust 13,280 D2
Magdeburg 276,089 D2
Markkleeberg 22,380 E3
Meerane 25,037 E3
Meiningen 26,134 D3
Meissen 43,561 E3
Merseburg 54,269 D3
Meuselwitz 13,585 E3
Mittweida 19,259 E3
Mühlhausen
(Thomas-Müntzer-Stadt) 44,106 D3
Nauen 11,940 E2
Naumburg 36,358 D3
Neubrandenburg 59,971 E2
Neuenhagen bei Berlin 12,603 F4
Neuruppin 24,888 E2
Neustrelitz 27,074 E2
Nordhausen 44,442 D3
Oelsnitz 15,084 E3
Oelsnitz im Erzgebirge 16,063 E3
Olbernhau 13,479 E3
Oranienburg 24,452 E2
Oschatz 18,974 E3
Oschersleben 17,377 D2
Pankow 136,527 F3
Parchim 22,927 D2
Pasewalk 15,099 F2
Peenemünde E1
Perleberg 15,029 D2
Pirna 49,771 E3
Plauen 80,353 E3
Pössneck 18,648 D3
Potsdam 117,236 E2
Prenzlau 22,738 E2
Pritzwalk 11,887 E2
Quedlinburg 29,796 D3
Radeberg 18,528 E3
Radebeul 38,383 E3
Rathenow 32,011 E2
Reichenbach 27,440 E3
Ribnitz-Damgarten 17,254 E1
Riesa 49,989 E3
Rosslau 16,520 E3
Rostock 210,167 E1
Rudolstadt 31,698 D3
Saalfeld 33,648 D3
Salzwedel 21,741 D2
Sangerhausen 32,721 D3
Sassnitz 13,857 E1
Schkeuditz 15,585 E3
Schmalkalden 15,017 D3
Schmölln 13,406 E3
Schneeberg 20,376 E3
Schönebeck 45,197 D2
Schwedt 45,729 F2
Schwerin 104,984 D2
Sebnitz 13,470 F3
Senftenberg 29,953 F3
Sömmerda 20,712 D3
Sondershausen 23,383 D3
Sonneberg 29,193 D3
Spremberg 22,862 F3
Stassfurt 26,225 D3
Stendal 39,647 D2
Stralsund 72,167 E1
Strausberg 21,334 F2
Suhl 36,642 D3
Tangermünde 12,898 D2
Teltow 16,171 E4
Templin 11,718 E2
Thale 17,248 D3
Thomas-Müntzer-Stadt 44,106 D3
Torgau 21,613 E3
Torgelow 14,320 F2
Treptow 127,448 F4
Ueckermünde 11,423 F2
Waldheim 11,925 E3
Waltershausen 13,893 D3
Waren 22,921 E2
Weida 11,816 D3
Weimar 63,144 D3
Weissenfels 43,191 D3
Weissensee 78,451 F3
Weisswasser 25,910 F3
Werdau 22,249 E3
Wernigerode 34,658 D3
Wilhelm-Pieck-Stadt 32,731 F3
Wismar 56,765 D2
Wittenberg 51,364 E3
Wittenberge 32,907 D2
Wolfen 27,570 E3
Wolgast 16,384 E1
Wurzen 20,501 E3
Zehdenick 12,651 E2
Zeitz 44,582 E3
Zella-Mehlis 16,301 D3
Zerbst 19,356 E3
Zeulenroda 13,452 D3
Zittau 42,298 F3
Zwickau 123,069 E3

OTHER FEATURES

Altmark (reg.) D2
Arkona (cape) E1
Baltic (sea) E1
Black Elster (riv.) E3
Brandenburg (reg.) E2
Elbe (riv.) D2
Elde (riv.) D2
Elster, Black (riv.) E3
Elster, White (riv.) E3
Erzgebirge (mts.) E3
Fichtelberg (mt.) E3
Harz (mts.) D3
Havel (riv.) E2
Lusatia (reg.) F3
Mecklenburg (bay) D1
Mecklenburg (reg.) E2
Mulde (riv.) E3
Neisse (riv.) F3
Oder (riv.) F2
Peene (riv.) E2
Pomerania (reg.) E2
Pomeranian (bay) F1
Rhön (mts.) D3
Rügen (isl.) E1
Saale (riv.) D3
Saxony (reg.) E3
Spree (riv.) F3
Spreewald (for.) F3
Thüringer Wald (for.) D3
Thuringia (reg.) D3
Ücker (riv.) E2
Unstrut (riv.) D3
Usedom (isl.) F1
Warnow (riv.) D2
Werra (riv.) D3
White Elster (riv.) E3

WEST GERMANY

STATES

Baden-Württemberg 9,152,700 C4
Bavaria 10,810,400 D4
Berlin (West) (free
city) 1,984,800 E4
Bremen 716,800 C2
Hamburg 1,717,400 D2
Hesse 5,549,800 C3
Lower Saxony 7,238,500 C2
North
Rhine-Westphalia 17,129,600 B3
Rhineland-Palatinate 3,665,800 B4
Saarland 1,096,300 B4
Schleswig-Holstein 2,582,400 C1

CITIES and TOWNS

Aachen 242,453 B3
Aalen 64,735 D4
Ahaus 27,126 B2
Ahlen 54,214 B3
Ahrensburg 24,964 D2
Alfeld 24,273 C2
Alsdorf 47,473 B3
Alsfeld 18,091 C3
Altena 26,753 B3
Altona C2
Alzey 15,190 C4
Amberg 46,934 D4
Andernach 27,132 B3
Ansbach 39,117 D4
Arnsberg 80,287 C3
Arolsen 15,619 C3
Aschaffenburg 55,398 C4
Augsburg 249,943 D4
Aurich 34,194 B2
Backnang 29,614 C4
Bad Berleburg 20,415 C3
Bad Driburg 17,478 C3
Bad Dürkheim 16,133 C4
Bad Ems 10,487 B3
Baden-Baden 49,718 C4
Bad Gandersheim 11,614 D3
Bad Harzburg 25,786 D3
Bad Hersfeld 29,248 C3
Bad Homburg vor der
Höhe 51,196 C3
Bad Honnef 20,903 B3
Bad Kissingen 22,279 D3
Bad Kreuznach 42,588 B4
Bad Lauterberg im Harz 14,715 D3
Bad Mergentheim 19,895 C4
Bad Münstereifel 14,340 B3
Bad Nauheim 25,916 C3
Bad Neuenahr-Ahrweiler 26,371 B3
Bad Oldesloe 19,640 D2
Bad Pyrmont 21,896 C3
Bad Reichenhall 13,048 E5
Bad Salzuflen 50,924 C2
Bad Schwartau 18,696 D2
Bad Segeberg 13,320 D2
Bad Tölz 12,458 D5
Bad Vilbel 25,012 C3
Bad Waldsee 14,296 C5
Bad Wildungen 15,418 C3
Bad Wimpfen 5,536 C4
Baiersbronn 14,845 C4
Balingen 29,310 C4
Bamberg 74,236 D4
Barsinghausen 32,873 C2
Bassum 14,113 C2
Bayreuth 67,035 D4
Bayrischzell 1,639 E5
Bebra 15,740 C3
Bendorf 15,943 B3
Bensheim 32,653 C4
Bentheim 13,681 B2
Berchtesgaden 8,558 E5
Bergisch Gladbach 99,517 B3
Berleburg (Bad
Berleburg) 20,415 C3
Berlin (West) 1,984,837 E4
Biberach an der Riss 28,891 C4
Bielefeld 316,058 C2
Bietigheim-Bissingen 34,042 C4
Bingen 24,541 B4
Birkenfeld 5,883 B4
Blaubeuren 11,652 C4
Böblingen 40,547 C4
Bocholt 65,460 B3
Bochum 414,842 B3
Bonn (cap.) 283,711 B3
Boppard 16,888 B3
Borghorst 17,238 B2
Borken 30,212 B3
Bornheim 32,847 B3
Bottrop 101,495 B3
Brake 18,089 C2
Bramsche 24,119 B2
Braunschweig
(Brunswick) 268,519 D2
Breisach am Rhein 9,230 B4
Bremen 572,969 C2
Bremerhaven 143,836 C2
Bremervörde 17,565 C2
Bretten 22,140 C4
Brilon 24,595 C3
Bruchsal 38,929 C4
Brühl 44,305 B3
Brunsbüttel 11,451 C2
Brunswick 268,519 D2
Buchholz in der
Nordheide 25,713 C2
Bückeburg 21,393 C2
Büdingen 16,845 C3
Bühl 21,596 C4
Bünde 40,021 C2
Büren 17,352 C3
Burg auf Fehmarn 5,874 D1
Burghausen 16,892 E4
Burgsteinfurt 31,367 B2
Butzbach 20,592 C3
Buxtehude 30,249 C2
Castrop-Rauxel 82,373 B3
Celle 74,347 D2
Cham 12,423 E4
Charlottenburg 201,732 E4
Clausthal-Zellerfeld 16,690 D3
Cloppenburg 19,757 B2
Coburg 46,244 D3
Coesfeld 30,617 B3
Cologne 1,013,771 B3
Crailsheim 24,506 D4
Cuxhaven 60,353 C2
Dachau 33,207 D4
Dahlem E4
Darmstadt 137,018 C4
Deggendorf 25,188 E4
Delmenhorst 71,488 C2
Detmold 65,629 C3
Diepholz 14,201 C2
Dillenburg 14,068 C3
Dillingen 21,369 B4
Dillingen an der Donau 11,601 D4
Dingolfing 13,325 E4
Dinkelsbühl 10,034 D4
Donaueschingen 17,578 C5
Donauwörth 17,077 D4
Dorsten 65,718 B3
Dortmund 630,609 B3
Duderstadt 23,255 D3
Dudweiler 27,877 B4
Duisburg 591,635 B3
Dülmen 37,013 B3
Düren 87,774 B3
Düsseldorf 664,336 B3
Eberbach 15,834 C4
Ebingen 22,594 C4
Eckernförde 22,938 D1
Ehingen 21,600 C4
Eichstätt 13,080 D4
Einbeck 29,821 C3
Eiserfeld 22,346 C3
Ellwangen 21,994 D4
Elmshorn 41,355 C2
Emden 53,509 B2
Emmendingen 24,722 B4
Emmerich 29,113 B3
Emsdetten 30,195 B2
Erlangen 100,671 D4
Eschwege 24,882 C3
Eschweiler 53,603 B3
Espelkamp 22,670 C2
Essen 677,568 B3
Esslingen am Neckar 95,298 C4
Ettlingen 35,159 C4
Euskirchen 43,558 B3
Eutin 17,701 D1
Fellbach 42,501 C4
Flensburg 93,213 C1
Forchheim 23,430 D4
Frankenberg-Eder 15,337 C3
Frankenthal 43,684 C4
Frankfurt am Main 636,157 C3
Frechen 41,453 B3
Freiburg im Breisgau 175,371 B5
Freising 31,524 D4
Freudenstadt 19,454 C4
Friedberg 24,762 C3
Friedrichshafen 51,544 C5
Fritzlar 15,079 C3
Fulda 58,976 C3
Fürstenfeldbruck 27,194 D4
Fürth 101,639 D4
Füssen 10,506 D5
Gaggenau 28,846 C4
Garbsen 56,337 C2
Garmisch-Partenkirchen 26,831 D5
Gatow E4
Geesthacht 24,745 D2
Geislingen an der
Steige 28,693 C4
Geldern 24,082 B3
Gelnhausen 17,889 C3
Gelsenkirchen 322,584 B3
Georgsmarienhütte 30,259 B2
Geretsried 17,330 D5
Germersheim 12,041 C4
Gerolstein 6,857 B3
Gifhorn 31,635 D2
Glückstadt 12,159 C2
Goch 28,213 B3
Göggingen 15,980 D4
Göppingen 54,365 C4
Goslar 53,957 D3
Göttingen 123,797 D3
Greven 27,479 B2
Grevenbroich 56,392 B3
Griesheim 18,548 C4
Gronau 40,527 B2
Gummersbach 49,316 B3
Günzburg 13,528 D4
Gunzenhausen 13,565 D4
Gütersloh 77,128 C3
Haar 18,824 D4
Hagen 229,224 B3
Haltern 29,750 B3
Hamburg 1,717,383 D2
Hameln 61,066 C2
Hamm 172,210 B3
Hammelburg 12,350 C3
Hanau 86,676 C3
Hannover 552,955 C2
Harburg-Wilhelmsburg C2
Hassloch 17,752 C4
Haunstetten 21,810 D4
Hechingen 15,926 C4
Heide 21,918 C1
Heidelberg 129,368 C4
Heidenheim an der Brenz 49,943 D4
Heilbronn 113,177 C4
Helmstedt 28,095 D2
Hennef 27,815 B3
Herford 64,385 C2
Herne 190,561 B3
Hildesheim 105,290 D2
Hockenheim 16,890 C4
Hof 54,357 D3
Hofgeismar 13,380 C3
Holzminden 23,650 C3
Homburg 41,861 B4
Horn-Bad Meinberg 16,927 C3
Höxter 32,759 C3
Hückelhoven 34,865 B3
Hünfeld 13,873 C3
Hürth 51,692 B3
Husum 24,984 C1
Hüttental 39,561 C3
Ibbenbüren 42,202 B2
Idar-Oberstein 37,179 B4
Immenstadt im Allgäu 13,720 C5
Ingolstadt 88,500 D4
Iserlohn 96,174 B3
Isny im Allgäu 12,367 D5
Itzehoe 35,077 C2
Jever 12,096 B2
Jülich 31,564 B3
Kaiserslautern 100,886 B4
Karlsruhe 280,448 C4
Kassel 205,534 C3
Kaufbeuren 42,224 D5
Kehl 29,861 B4
Kelheim 11,996 D4
Kempten 56,944 D5
Kevelaer 20,971 B3
Kiel 262,164 D1
Kirchheim unter Teck 31,666 C4
Kitzingen 19,116 C4
Kleve 44,043 B3
Koblenz 118,394 B3
Köln (Cologne) 1,013,771 B3
Königswinter 34,586 B3
Konstanz 70,152 C5
Korbach 22,998 C3
Kornwestheim 27,771 C4
Krefeld 228,463 B3
Kreuztal 30,473 C3
Kronach 11,538 D3
Kulmbach 25,711 D3
Lage 31,724 C3
Lahnstein 19,725 B3
Lahr 35,570 B4
Lampertheim 31,993 C4
Landau in der Pfalz 37,661 C4
Landsberg am Lech 15,862 D4
Landshut 55,858 E4
Langen 30,227 C4
Langenhagen 47,092 C2
Lauenburg an der Elbe 11,077 D2
Lauf an der Pegnitz 19,443 D4
Lauingen 8,778 D4
Lauterbach 15,007 C3
Leer 32,785 B2
Lehrte 38,272 D2
Lemgo 39,664 C2
Lengerich 20,836 B2
Leverkusen 165,947 B3
Lichtenfels 13,719 D3
Limburg an der Lahn 28,606 C3
Lindau 23,930 C5

(continued on following page)

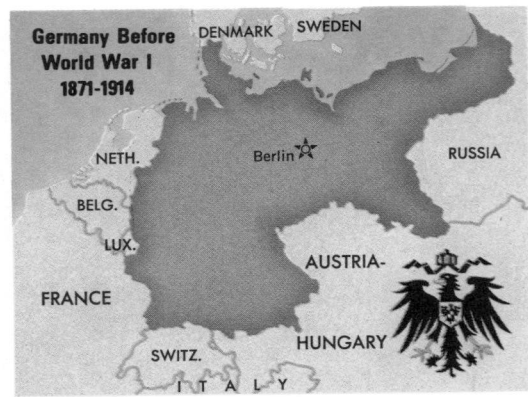

Germany Before World War I 1871-1914

Germany Between Wars 1919-1937

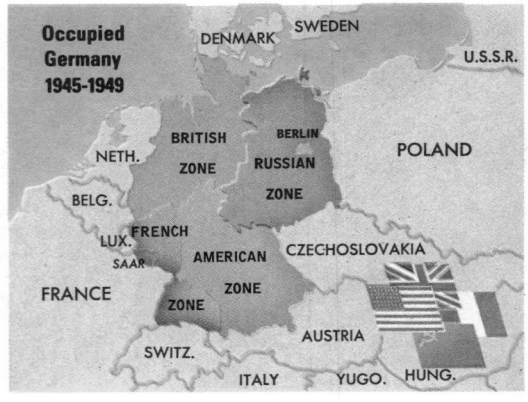

Occupied Germany 1945-1949

Agriculture, Industry and Resources

DOMINANT LAND USE

- Wheat, Sugar Beets
- Cereals (chiefly rye, oats, barley)
- Potatoes, Rye
- Dairy, Livestock
- Mixed Cereals, Dairy
- Truck Farming
- Grapes, Fruit
- Forests

MAJOR MINERAL OCCURRENCES

Ag	Silver	K	Potash
Ba	Barite	Lg	Lignite
C	Coal	Na	Salt
Cu	Copper	O	Petroleum
Fe	Iron Ore	Pb	Lead
G	Natural Gas	U	Uranium
Gr	Graphite	Zn	Zinc

⚡ Water Power

▨ Major Industrial Areas

AREA 15,892 sq. mi. (41,160 sq. km.)
POPULATION 14,227,000
CAPITALS The Hague, Amsterdam
LARGEST CITY Amsterdam
HIGHEST POINT Vaalserberg 1,056 ft. (322 m.)
MONETARY UNIT guilder (florin)
MAJOR LANGUAGE Dutch
MAJOR RELIGIONS Protestantism, Roman Catholicism

AREA 11,781 sq. mi. (30,513 sq. km.)
POPULATION 9,855,110
CAPITAL Brussels
LARGEST CITY Brussels (greater)
HIGHEST POINT Botrange 2,277 ft. (694 m.)
MONETARY UNIT Belgian franc
MAJOR LANGUAGES French (Walloon), Flemish
MAJOR RELIGION Roman Catholicism

AREA 999 sq. mi. (2,587 sq. km.)
POPULATION 364,000
CAPITAL Luxembourg
LARGEST CITY Luxembourg
HIGHEST POINT Ardennes Plateau 1,825 ft. (556 m.)
MONETARY UNIT Luxembourg franc
MAJOR LANGUAGES Luxembourgeois (Letzeburgisch), French, German
MAJOR RELIGION Roman Catholicism

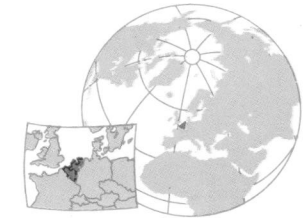

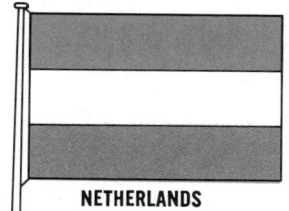

NETHERLANDS

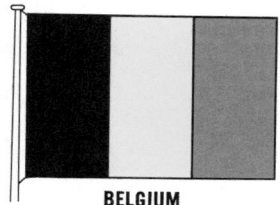

BELGIUM

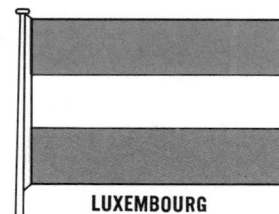

LUXEMBOURG

BELGIUM

PROVINCES

Antwerp 1,533,249	F6
Brabant 2,176,373	F7
East Flanders 1,310,117	D7
Hainaut 1,317,453	D7
Liège 1,008,905	H7
Limburg 652,547	G7
Luxembourg 217,310	H9
Namur 380,561	F8
West Flanders 1,054,429	B7

CITIES and TOWNS†

Aalst 46,659	D7
Aalter 9,173	C6
Aarlen (Arlon) 13,745	H9
Aarschot 12,474	F7
Aat (Ath) 11,842	D7
Aiken 8,677	G7
Alost (Aalst) 46,659	D7
Amay 7,617	G7
Andenne 8,091	G8
Anderlecht 103,796	B9
Anderlues 12,176	E8
Ans	H7
Antoing 3,426	C7
Antwerp 224,543	E6
Antwerp* 928,000	E6
Antwerpen (Antwerp) 224,543	E6
Ardooie 7,081	C7
Arendonk 9,919	G6
Arlon 13,745	H9
As 5,496	H6
Asse 6,583	E7
Ath 11,842	D7
Attert	H9
Aubange 3,761	H9
Audenarde (Oudenaarde) 26,615	D7
Auderghem 34,546	C9
Auvelais 8,287	F8
Aywaille 3,850	H8
Baerle-Hertog	F6
Balen 15,110	G6
Basse-Sambre	F8
Bastenaken (Bastogne) 6,816	H9
Bastogne 6,816	H9
Beernem	C6
Beloeil	D7
Berchem 50,241	F6
Berchem-Sainte-Agathe 19,087	B9
Bergen (Mons) 59,362	E8
Beringen	G6
Bertogne	H8
Bertrix 4,562	G9
Beveren 15,913	E6
Bilzen 7,178	G7
Binche 10,098	E8
Blankenberge 13,969	C6
Bocholt 6,497	H6
Boom 16,584	E6
Borgerhout 49,002	E6
Borgloon 3,412	G7
Borgworm (Waremme) 10,956	G7
Bourg-Léopold (Leopoldsburg) 9,593	G6
Boussu 11,474	D8
Braine-l'Alleud 18,531	E7
Braine-le-Comte 11,957	D7
Brecht	F6
Bredene 9,244	B6
Bree 10,389	H6
Bruges 117,220	C6
Brugge (Bruges) 117,220	C6
Brussels (cap.)* 1,054,970	C9
Bruxelles (Brussels)	
(cap.)* 1,054,970	C9
Cerfontaine	E8
Charleroi 23,689	E8
Charleroi* 458,000	E8
Chastre	F7
Châtelet 14,752	F8
Chièvres 3,283	D7
Chimay 3,288	E8
Chiny	G9
Ciney 7,536	G8
Comblain-au-Pont 3,582	G8
Comines 8,192	B7
Courcelles 17,015	E8
Courtrai (Kortrijk) 44,961	C7
Couvin 4,234	F8
Damme	C6
De Haan	C6
Deinze 16,711	C7
Denderleeuw 9,925	E7
Dendermonde 22,119	E6
De Panne 6,985	B6
Dessel 7,505	G6
Destelbergen	D6
Deurne 80,766	F6
Diest 10,799	F7
Diksmuide 6,669	B6
Dilbeek 15,108	B9
Dilsen	H6
Dinant 9,747	G8
Dison 8,466	H7
Dixmude (Diksmuide) 6,669	B6
Doische	F8
Doornik (Tournai) 32,794	C7
Dour 10,059	D8
Drogenbos 4,840	B10
Duffel 13,802	F6
Durbuy	H8
Ecaussinnes 6,630	E7
Edingen (Enghien) 4,115	D7
Eeklo 19,144	D6
Éghezée	F7
Eigenbrakel (Braine-l'Alleud) 18,531	E7
Ekeren 27,648	E6
Ellezelles 3,556	D7
Enghien 4,115	D7
Érezée	G8
Erquelinnes 4,471	E8
Esneux 6,183	H7
Essen 10,795	F6
Estampuis	C7
Etterbeek 51,030	B9
Eupen 14,879	J7
Evere 26,957	C9
Evergem 12,886	D6
Farciennes	G8
Fernelmont	F7
Ferrières	H8
Flémalle 8,135	G7
Fleurus 8,523	E8
Florennes 4,107	F8
Forest 55,135	B9
Fosses-la-Ville 3,972	F8
Frameries 11,224	D8
Froidchapelle	E8
Furnes (Veurne) 9,496	B6
Ganshoren 21,147	B9
Geel 29,346	F6
Geldenaken (Jodoigne) 4,132	F7
Gembloux-sur-Orneau 11,249	F7
Genk 57,913	H7
Gent (Ghent) 148,860	D6
Geraardsbergen 17,533	D7
Gerpinnes	F8
Ghent 148,860	D6
Ghent* 477,000	D6
Gistel	B6
Gooik	E7
Gouvy	H8
Grammont (Geraardsbergen) 17,533	D7
Grez-Doiceau	F7
Grimbergen	E7
Haacht 4,436	F7
Habay	H9
Hal (Halle) 20,017	E7
Halen 5,322	G7
Halle 20,017	E7
Hamme 17,559	E6
Hamois	G8
Hamont-Achel 6,893	H6
Hannuit (Hannut) 7,232	G7
Hannut 7,232	G7
Harelbeke 18,498	C7
Hasselt 39,663	G7
Hastière	F8
Heist-Knokke 27,582	C6
Heist-op-den-Berg 13,472	F6
Hensies	D8
Herentals 18,639	F6
Herne	E7
Herselt 7,412	F6
Herstal 29,600	H7
Herve 4,118	H7
Heuvelland	B7
Hoboken 33,693	E6
Hoei (Huy) 12,736	G8
Hoeselt 6,884	G7
Honnelles	D8
Hoogstraten 4,381	F6
Hotton	G8
Huy 12,736	G8
Ichtegem	B6
Ieper 20,825	B7
Ingelmunster 10,245	C7
Ittre	E7
Ixelles 86,450	C9
Izegem 22,928	C7
Jabbeke	C6
Jemappes 18,632	D8
Jette 40,013	B9
Jodoigne 4,132	F7
Kalmthout 12,724	F6
Kapellen 13,352	E6
Kasterlee	F6
Kinrooi	H6
Knokke-Heist 27,582	C6
Koekelare 7,807	B6
Koekelberg 17,570	B9
Koksijde	B6
Kontich 14,432	E6
Kortemark 5,904	C6
Kortrijk 44,961	C7
Kraainem 11,390	C9
La Louvière 23,310	E8
La Louvière* 113,259	E8
Lanaken 8,659	H7
Landen 5,740	G7
Langemark-Poelkapelle 5,457	B7
Lasne	F7
Lede 10,316	D7
Léglise	H9
Le Roeulx	E8
Lessen (Lessines) 8,906	D7
Lessines 8,906	D7
Leuven 30,623	F7
Leuze-en-Hainaut 7,185	D7
Libin	G9
Libramont-Chevigny 2,975	G9
Lichtervelde 7,459	C6
Liedekerke 10,482	D7
Liège 145,573	H7
Liège* 622,000	H7
Lier 28,416	F6
Lierre (Lier) 28,416	F6
Limbourg 3,762	J7
Limburg (Limbourg) 3,762	J7
Linkebeek 4,265	C10
Linter	G7
Lochristi	D6
Lokeren 26,740	D6
Lommel 21,984	G6
Lo-Reninge	H9
Lontzen	H9
Looz (Borgloon) 3,412	G7
Louvain (Leuven) 30,623	F7
Luik (Liège) 145,573	H7
Maaseik 8,622	H6
Maasmechelen	H6
Machelen 7,057	C9
Maldegem 14,474	C6
Malines (Mechelen) 65,466	F6
Malmedy 6,464	J8
Manage	E7
Manhay	H8
Marche-en-Famenne 4,567	G8
Marchin 4,206	G8
Mechelen 65,466	F6
Meerhout 8,567	G6
Meise	E7
Menen 22,037	C7
Menin (Menen) 22,037	C7
Merchtem 8,998	E7
Merelbeke 13,837	D7
Merksem 39,768	E6
Merksplas 5,065	F6
Messancy 3,150	H9
Mettet 3,372	F8
Meulebeke 10,458	C7
Middelkerke	B6
Moeskroen (Mouscron) 37,311	C7
Mol 28,623	G6
Molenbeek-Saint-Jean 68,411	B9
Momignies	E8
Mons 59,362	E8
Montigny-le-Tilleul	E8
Moorslede	B7
Mortsel 28,012	E6
Mouscron 37,311	C7
Namen (Namur) 32,269	F8
Namur 32,269	F8
Nassogne	G8
Nazareth	D7
Neerpelt 8,771	G6
Neufchâteau 2,670	G9
Nevele	D6
Nieuport (Nieuwpoort) 8,273	B6
Nieuwpoort 8,273	B6
Nijvel (Nivelles) 16,126	E7
Ninove 12,428	D7
Nivelles 16,126	E7
Ohey	G8
Onhaye	F8
Oostende (Ostend) 71,227	B6
Oostkamp 8,999	C6
Opwijk 9,699	E7
Ostend 71,227	B6
Oudenaarde 26,615	D7
Oudenburg	B6
Oud-Turnhout 9,245	F6
Oupeye	H7
Overijse 16,181	F7
Overpelt 10,470	G6
Paliseul	G9
Peer 7,201	G6
Péruwelz 7,878	D8
Philippeville 2,076	E8
Plombières	F7
Pont-à-Celles	E8
Poperinge 12,671	B7
Profondeville	F8
Putte 6,953	F6
Quaregnon 17,688	D8
Quévy	D8
Quiévrain 5,510	D8
Raeren 3,655	J7
Ravels	F6
Rebecq 3,744	E7
Renaix (Ronse) 25,056	D7
Rendeux	H8
Retie 6,619	G6
Rochefort 4,357	G8
Roeselare 40,428	C7
Ronse 25,056	D7
Roulers (Roeselare) 40,428	C7
Rouvroy	G9
Ruiselede	C6
Sainte-Ode	G9
Saint-Georges-sur-Meuse 6,003	G7
Saint-Gilles 55,055	B9
Saint-Hubert 3,091	G8
Saint-Josse-ten-Noode 23,633	C9
Saint-Nicolas	G7
Saint-Trond (Sint-Truiden) 21,473	G7
Saint-Vith (Sankt Vith) 3,001	J8
Sankt Vith 3,001	J8
Schaerbeek 118,950	C9
Schoten 29,914	F6
Seraing 40,545	G7
's-Gravenbrakel (Braine-le-Comte) 11,957	D7
Sint-Laureins	D6
Sint-Niklaas 49,214	E6

(continued on following page)

Agriculture, Industry and Resources

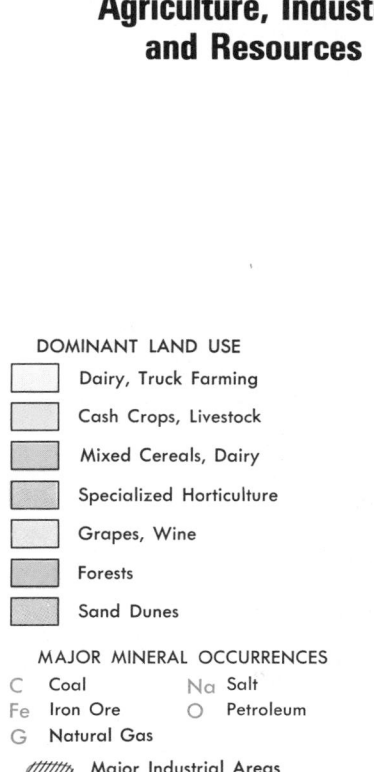

DOMINANT LAND USE

- Dairy, Truck Farming
- Cash Crops, Livestock
- Mixed Cereals, Dairy
- Specialized Horticulture
- Grapes, Wine
- Forests
- Sand Dunes

MAJOR MINERAL OCCURRENCES

- C Coal
- Fe Iron Ore
- G Natural Gas
- Na Salt
- O Petroleum

Major Industrial Areas

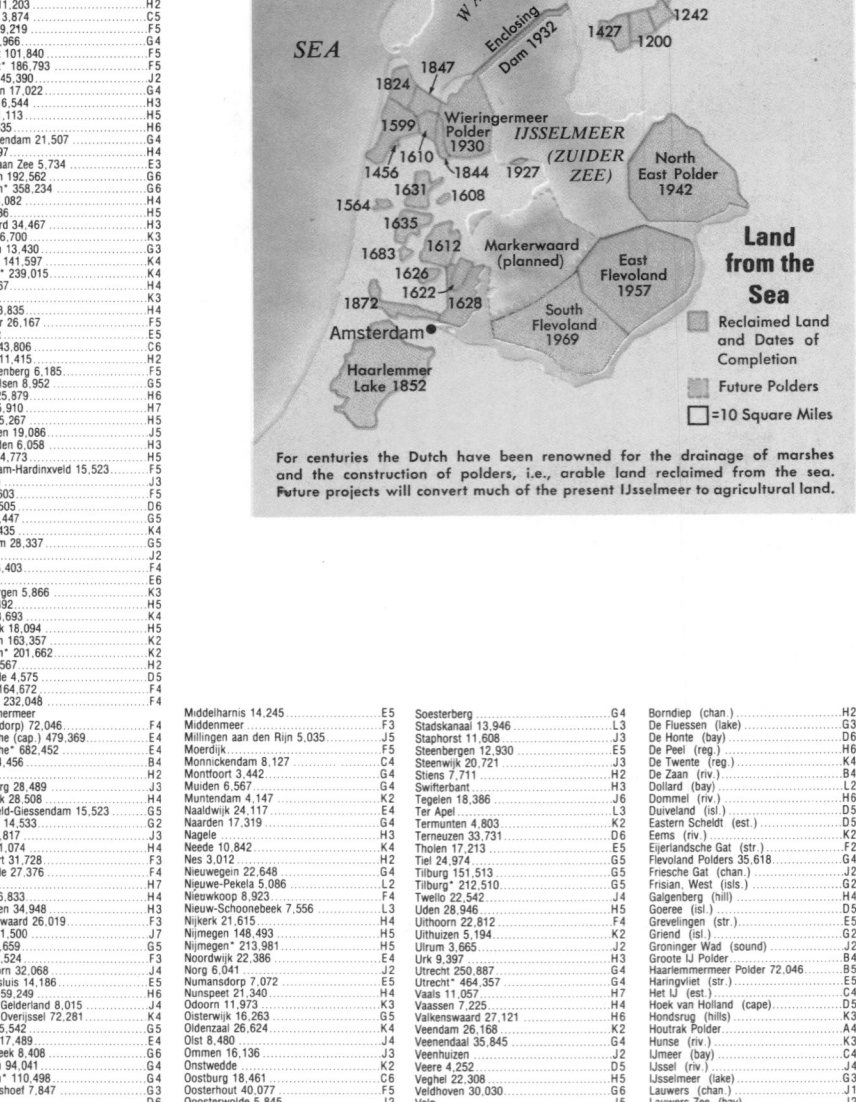

(continued)

Sint-Pieters-Leeuw 16,856 ....B9
Sint-Truiden 21,473 ....G7
Soignies 12,006 ....D7
Somme-Leuze G8
Spa 9,504 ....H8
Sprimont H8
Staden 5,499 ....B7
Stavelot 4,723 ....H8
Steenokkerzeel 4,037 ....C9
Stekene E6
Stoumont H8
Tamise (Temse) 14,950 ....E6
Tellin G8
Temse 14,950 ....E6
Tenneville H8
Termonde (Dendermonde) 22,119 ....E6
Tessenderlo 11,778 ....G6
Theux 5,316 ....H8
Thuin 5,777 ....E8
Tielt 14,077 ....C7
Tielt-Winge 3,743 ....F7
Tienen 24,134 ....F7
Tintigny G9
Tirlemont (Tienen) 24,134 ....F7
Tongeren 20,136 ....G7
Tongres (Tongeren) 20,136 ....G7
Torhout 15,156 ....C6
Tournai 32,794 ....C7
Trois-Ponts H8
Tubeke (Tubize) 11,507 ....E7
Tubize 11,507 ....E7
Turnhout 38,007 ....F6
Uccle 78,909 ....B9
Ukkel (Uccle) 78,909 ....B9
Vaux-sur-Sûre H9
Verviers 33,587 ....H7
Veurne 9,496 ....B6
Vielsalm 3,587 ....H8
Vilvoorde 34,633 ....F7
Vilvorde (Vilvoorde) 34,633 ....F7
Viroinval F8
Virton 3,558 ....H9
Visé 6,880 ....H7
Vleteren B7
Vorst (Forest) 55,135 ....B9
Vresse-sur-Semois F9
Waarschoot 7,905 ....D6
Wachtebeke D6
Waregem 17,725 ....C7
Waremme 10,956 ....G7
Waterloo 17,764 ....E7
Watermaal-Bosvoorde
(Watermael-Boitsfort C9
Watermael-Boitsfort 25,123 ....C9
Waver (Wavre) 11,767 ....F7
Wavre 11,767 ....F7
Wellin G8
Wemmel 12,631 ....B9
Wervik 12,672 ....B7
Westerlo 14,173 ....F6
Westmalle F6
Wetteren 20,816 ....D7
Wezembeek-Oppem 10,899 ....D9
Wezet (Visé) 6,880 ....H7
Willebroek 15,726 ....E6
Wilrijk 43,485 ....E6
Wingene 7,140 ....C6
Woluwe-Saint-Lambert 47,360 ....C9
Woluwe-Saint-Pierre 40,884 ....C9
Ypres (Ieper) 20,825 ....B7
Zaventem 10,625 ....C9
Zedelgem C6
Zeebrugge C6
Zele 18,585 ....E6
Zelzate 12,785 ....D6
Zemst E7
Zinnik (Soignies) 12,006 ....D7
Zonhoven 13,484 ....G6
Zottegem 21,461 ....D7
Zuienkerke C6

OTHER FEATURES

Albert, (canal) F6
Ardennes, (for.) F9
Botrange, (mt.) J8
Dender, (riv.) D7
Deûle, (riv.) B7
Dyle, (riv.) F7
Hohe Venn, (plat.) H8
Lesse, (riv.) F8
Lys, (riv.) B7
Mark, (riv.) F6
Meuse, (riv.) F8
Nethe, (riv.) F6
North, (sea) D4
Ourthe, (riv.) G8
Rupel, (riv.) F7
Sambre, (riv.) D8
Schelde (Scheldt), (riv.) C7
Scheldt, (riv.) C7
Schnee Eifel, (plat.) J8
Semois, (riv.) G9
Senne, (riv.) E7
Vaalserberg, (mt.) J7
Vesdre, (riv.) H7
Weisserstein, (mt.) J8
Yser, (riv.) B7
Zitterwald, (plat.) J8

LUXEMBOURG

CITIES and TOWNS

Clervaux 916 ....J8
Diekirch† 5,059 ....J9
Differdange 9,287 ....H9
Dudelange† 14,615 ....J10
Echternach† 3,792 ....J9
Esch-sur-Alzette† 27,574 ....J9
Ettelbruck† 5,990 ....J9
Grevenmacher† 2,918 ....J9
Luxembourg (cap.) 78,272 ....J9
Mamer 3,123 ....H9
Mersch 1,869 ....J9
Pétange 6,234 ....H9
Remich† 12,138 ....J9
Vianden† 1,520 ....J9
Wiltz 1,601 ....H9

OTHER FEATURES

Alzette, (riv.) J9
Clerf, (riv.) J8
Eisling, (mts.) H9
Mosel, (riv.) J9
Our, (riv.) J9
Sauer, (riv.) J9

NETHERLANDS

PROVINCES

Drenthe 405,924 ....K3
Dronten 15,343 ....H4
Friesland 560,614 ....H2
Gelderland 1,639,997 ....H4
Groningen 540,062 ....K2
Lelystad H4
Limburg 1,051,620 ....H6
North Brabant 1,967,261 ....F5
North Holland 2,295,875 ....F3
Overijssel 985,569 ....J4
South Holland 3,048,648 ....E5
Utrecht 867,909 ....G4
Zeeland 332,286 ....D6
Zuidelijke
IJsselmeerpolders 14,231 ....H4

CITIES and TOWNS†

Aalsmeer 20,779 ....F4
Aalten 17,486 ....K5
Aardenburg 3,869 ....C6
Akkrum 5,044 ....H2
Alkmaar 65,199 ....F3
Almelo 62,634 ....K4
Alphen aan de Rijn 46,065 ....F4
Amersfoort 87,784 ....G4
Amstelveen 71,803 ....B5
Amsterdam (cap.) 751,156 ....B4
Amsterdam* 987,205 ....B4
Andijk 5,301 ....G3
Apeldoorn 134,055 ....H4
Apeldoorn* 237,231 ....H4
Appingedam 13,295 ....K2
Arnhem 126,051 ....H4
Arnhem* 281,126 ....H4
Assen 43,783 ....K3
Asten 12,295 ....H6
Axel 12,072 ....D6
Baarle-Nassau 5,583 ....F6
Baarn 25,045 ....G4
Barneveld 34,189 ....H4
Bath E6
Beilen 12,948 ....K3
Bemmel 14,218 ....H5
Bergeijk 9,009 ....G6
Bergen 14,306 ....F3
Bergen op Zoom 40,770 ....E5
Bergum 28,047 ....H2
Berkel 9,367 ....F5
Berkhout 5,167 ....F3
Beverwijk 37,551 ....F4
Blerick J6
Bloemendaal 17,940 ....E4
Blokzijl H3
Bodegraven 15,848 ....F4
Bolsward 9,934 ....H2
Borculo 9,859 ....J4
Borger 12,017 ....K3
Borne 18,216 ....K4
Boskoop 12,985 ....F4
Boxmeer 12,662 ....H5
Boxtel 22,465 ....G5
Breda 118,086 ....F5
Breda* 151,182 ....F5
Breezand F3
Breskens C6
Brielle 10,620 ....E5
Brouwershaven 3,263 ....D5
Brummen 20,460 ....J4
Brunssum 26,116 ....J7
Buiksloot C4
Bussum 37,848 ....G4
Capelle 35,696 ....F5
Coevorden 13,089 ....K3
Colijnsplaat D5
Culemborg 17,682 ....G5
Cuyk 15,366 ....H5
Dalen 5,084 ....K3
De Bilt 32,588 ....G4
Dedemsvaart 12,975 ....J3
De Koog F2
Delft 86,103 ....E4
Delfzijl 23,316 ....K2
Den Burg 12,132 ....F2
Denekamp 11,533 ....L4
Den Helder 60,421 ....F3
Deurne 26,539 ....H6
Deventer 65,557 ....J4
Didam 14,263 ....J5
De Wijk 4,631 ....J3
Diemen 13,704 ....C5
Dieren J4
Diever 3,162 ....J3
Dinxperlo 7,296 ....K5
Dirksland 6,495 ....E5
Doesburg 9,759 ....J4
Doetinchem 34,915 ....J5
Dokkum 11,203 ....H2
Domburg 3,874 ....C5
Dongen 19,219 ....F5
Doorn 11,966 ....G4
Dordrecht 101,840 ....F5
Dordrecht* 186,793 ....F5
Drachten 45,390 ....J2
Driebergen 17,022 ....G4
Dronten 16,544 ....H3
Druten 11,113 ....H5
Echt 17,035 ....H6
Edam-Volendam 21,507 ....G4
Ede 79,897 ....H4
Egmond aan Zee 5,734 ....E3
Eindhoven 192,562 ....G6
Eindhoven* 358,234 ....G6
Elburg 18,082 ....H4
Elst 16,686 ....H5
Emmeloord 34,467 ....H3
Emmen 86,700 ....K3
Enkhuizen 13,430 ....G3
Enschede 141,597 ....K4
Enschede* 239,015 ....K4
Epe 32,267 ....H4
Erica K3
Ermelo 23,835 ....H4
Etten-Leur 26,167 ....F5
Europoort E5
Flushing 43,806 ....C6
Franeker 11,415 ....H2
Geertruidenberg 6,185 ....F5
Geldermalsen 8,952 ....G5
Geldrop 25,879 ....H6
Geleen 35,910 ....H7
Gemert 15,267 ....H5
Gendringen 19,086 ....J5
Genemuiden 6,058 ....H3
Gennep 14,773 ....H5
Giessendam-Hardinxveld 15,523 ....F5
Giethoorn J3
Gilze 19,603 ....F5
Goes 28,505 ....D6
Goirle 13,447 ....G5
Goor 11,435 ....K4
Gorinchem 28,337 ....G5
Gorredijk J2
Gouda 56,403 ....F4
Graauw E6
Gramsbergen 5,866 ....K3
Grave 9,492 ....H5
Groenlo 8,693 ....K4
Groesbeek 18,094 ....H5
Groningen 163,357 ....K2
Groningen* 201,662 ....K2
Grouw 8,567 ....H2
Haamstede 4,575 ....D5
Haarlem 164,672 ....F4
Haarlem* 232,048 ....F4
Haarlemmermeer
(Hoofddorp) 72,046 ....F4
Hague, The (cap.) 479,369 ....E4
Hague, The* 682,452 ....E4
Halfweg 4,456 ....B4
Hallum H2
Hardenberg 28,489 ....J3
Harderwijk 28,508 ....H4
Hardinxveld-Giessendam 15,523 ....G5
Harlingen 14,533 ....G2
Hasselt 5,817 ....J3
Hattem 11,074 ....H4
Heemskert 31,728 ....F3
Heemstede 27,376 ....F4
Heer H7
Heerde 16,833 ....H4
Heerenveen 34,948 ....H3
Heerhugowaard 26,019 ....F3
Heerlen 71,500 ....J7
Heesch 8,659 ....G5
Heiloo 20,524 ....F3
Hellendoorn 32,068 ....J4
Hellevoetsluis 14,186 ....E5
Helmond 59,249 ....H6
Hengelo, Gelderland 8,015 ....J4
Hengelo, Overijssel 72,281 ....K4
Heusden 5,542 ....G5
Hillegom 17,489 ....E4
Hilvarenbeek 8,408 ....G6
Hilversum 94,041 ....G4
Hilversum* 110,498 ....G4
Hippolytushoef 7,847 ....G3
Hoek D6
Hoek van Holland (Hook of
Holland) D4
Hoensbroek 22,441 ....H7
Holijsloot C4
Hollum H2
Holwerd H2
Hoofddorp
(Haarlemmermeer) 72,046 ....F4
Hoogeveen 42,673 ....J3
Hoogezand-Sappemeer 33,860 ....K2
Hoogkarspel 5,112 ....G3
Hook of Holland D4
Hoorn 24,609 ....G3
Horst 16,242 ....H6
Huissen 11,049 ....H5
Huizen 25,603 ....G4
Hulst 17,283 ....E6
IJmuiden 6,633 ....E4
IJsselstein 15,450 ....F4
Ilpendam 3,310 ....C4
Joure 14,329 ....H3
Kampen 29,488 ....H3
Katwijk aan Zee 37,437 ....E4
Kerkdriel 7,584 ....G5
Kerkrade 46,609 ....J7
Kesteren 8,257 ....G5
Klazienaveen 9,520 ....L3
Kollum 11,887 ....J2
Krimpen aan den IJssel 26,396 ....F5
Landsmeer 8,082 ....C4
Laren 13,615 ....G4
Leek 15,713 ....J2
Leerdam 15,030 ....F5
Leeuwarden 85,074 ....H2
Leiden 99,891 ....E4
Leiden* 167,554 ....E4
Lelystad H3
Lemmer 10,013 ....H3
Lisse 19,182 ....F4
Lith 5,088 ....G5
Lochem 17,274 ....J4
Lonneker K4
Loon op Zand 18,000 ....G5
Losser 20,688 ....L4
Maarssen 18,346 ....F4
Maasbree 9,462 ....H6
Maassluis 28,170 ....E5
Maastricht 111,044 ....H7
Maastricht* 145,862 ....H7
Margraten 3,318 ....H7
Medemblik 6,432 ....G3
Meerssen 8,414 ....H7
Meppel 21,057 ....J3
Middelburg 36,372 ....C6
Middelharnis 14,245 ....E5
Middenmeer F3
Millingen aan den Rijn 5,035 ....J5
Moerdijk F5
Monnickendam 8,127 ....C4
Montfoort 3,442 ....G4
Muiden 6,567 ....G4
Muntendam 4,147 ....K2
Naaldwijk 24,117 ....E4
Naarden 17,319 ....G4
Nagele H3
Neede 10,842 ....K4
Nes 3,012 ....H2
Nieuwegein 22,648 ....G4
Nieuwe-Pekela 5,086 ....L2
Nieuwkoop 8,923 ....F4
Nieuw-Schoonebeek 7,556 ....L3
Nijkerk 21,615 ....H4
Nijmegen 148,493 ....H5
Nijmegen* 213,981 ....H5
Noordwijk 22,386 ....E4
Norg 6,041 ....J2
Numansdorp 7,072 ....E5
Nunspeet 21,340 ....H4
Odoorn 11,973 ....K3
Oisterwijk 16,263 ....G5
Oldenzaal 26,624 ....K4
Olst 8,480 ....J4
Ommen 16,136 ....J3
Onstwedde K2
Oostburg 18,461 ....C6
Oosterhout 40,077 ....F5
Ooosterwolde 5,845 ....J2
Oostmahorn J2
Oostzaan 6,336 ....C4
Ootmarsum 3,901 ....K4
Oss 45,643 ....H5
Otterlo H4
Oud-Beijerland 14,251 ....E5
Ouddorp 9,091 ....D5
Oudenbosch 11,061 ....E5
Oude-Pekela 8,067 ....K2
Oudewater 6,870 ....F4
Purmerend 32,614 ....F4
Putten 18,243 ....H4
Raalte 23,598 ....J4
Renkum 34,547 ....H5
Reusel 6,901 ....G6
Rheden 49,755 ....J4
Rhenen 16,893 ....H5
Ridderkerk 45,069 ....F5
Rijnsburg 10,698 ....F4
Rijssen 20,008 ....J4
Rijswijk 54,123 ....E4
Roden 16,437 ....J2
Roermond 36,695 ....J6
Roosendaal 51,685 ....F5
Rotterdam 614,767 ....E5
Rotterdam* 1,016,505 ....E5
Rutten H3
Ruurlo 7,557 ....J4
Sappemeer-Hoogezand 33,860 ....K2
Schagen 13,929 ....F3
Scheveningen E4
Schiedam 78,068 ....E5
Schijndel 18,658 ....G5
Schiphol B5
Schoonhoven 10,753 ....F5
's Gravendeel 7,242 ....E5
's Gravenhage (The Hague)
(cap.) 479,369 ....E4
's Gravenhage* 682,452 ....E4
's Gravenzande 15,833 ....E4
's Heerenberg 18,326 ....J5
's Hertogenbosch 86,184 ....G5
Simpelveld 6,783 ....H7
Sint Annaland E5
Sint Jacobiparochie H2
Sittard 34,278 ....H6
Sliedrecht 21,839 ....F5
Slochteren 13,447 ....K2
Sloten, North Holland B5
Sloterdijk B4
Sluis 3,140 ....C6
Smilde 8,247 ....K3
Sneek 28,123 ....H2
Soest 40,165 ....G4
Soesterberg G4
Stadskanaal 13,946 ....L3
Staphorst 11,608 ....J3
Steenbergen 12,930 ....E5
Steenwijk 20,721 ....J3
Stiens 7,711 ....H2
Swifterbant H3
Tegelen 18,386 ....J6
Ter Apel L3
Termunten 4,803 ....K2
Terneuzen 33,731 ....D6
Tholen 17,213 ....E5
Tiel 24,974 ....G5
Tilburg 151,513 ....G5
Tilburg* 212,510 ....G5
Twello 22,542 ....J4
Uden 28,946 ....H5
Uithoorn 22,812 ....F4
Uithuizen 5,194 ....K2
Ulrum 3,665 ....J2
Urk 9,397 ....H3
Utrecht 250,887 ....G4
Utrecht* 464,357 ....G4
Vaals 11,057 ....H7
Vaassen 7,225 ....H4
Valkenswaard 27,121 ....H6
Veendam 26,168 ....K2
Veenendaal 35,845 ....G4
Veenhuizen J2
Veere 4,252 ....D5
Veghel 22,308 ....H5
Veldhoven 30,030 ....G6
Velp J5
Velsen 64,035 ....F4
Venlo 61,659 ....J6
Venraij 31,526 ....H6
Vianen 12,821 ....G5
Vlaardingen 78,311 ....E5
Vlagtwedde 16,719 ....L3
Vlijmen 13,515 ....G5
Vlissingen (Flushing) 43,806 ....C6
Volendam-Edam 21,507 ....G4
Voorburg 45,209 ....E4
Voorst 22,542 ....J4
Vorden 7,276 ....J4
Vriezenveen 16,025 ....K4
Vught 23,261 ....G5
Waalre 13,219 ....G6
Waalwijk 25,977 ....F5
Wageningen 28,659 ....H5
Wamel 8,979 ....H5
Warmenhuizen 3,818 ....F3
Weert 36,850 ....H6
Weesp 17,037 ....C5
West-Terschelling 4,542 ....G2
Wierden 20,618 ....K4
Wijhe 6,888 ....J4
Wijk bij Duurstede 7,927 ....G5
Wijk en Aalburg 9,266 ....F5
Winschoten 19,760 ....L2
Winsum 5,007 ....K2
Winterswijk 27,413 ....K5
Woensdrecht 9,101 ....E6
Woerden 22,064 ....F4
Wolvega 22,812 ....J3
Workum 4,135 ....G3
Zaandam (Zaanstad) 124,795 ....B4
Zaandam (Zaanstad)* 137,371 ....B4
Zaltbommel 8,010 ....G5
Zandvoort 16,289 ....E4
Zeist 58,630 ....G4
Zevenaar 26,560 ....J5
Zevenbergen 13,307 ....E5
Zierikzee 8,816 ....D5
Zundert 12,444 ....F6
Zutphen 29,188 ....J4
Zwartsluis 4,391 ....H3
Zwijndrecht 38,271 ....E5
Zwolle 77,826 ....J3

OTHER FEATURES

Alkmaardermeer (lake) F3
Ameland (isl.) H2
Bergumermeer (lake) J2
Beulaker Wijde (lake) H3
Borndiep (chan.) H2
De Fluessen (lake) G3
De Honte (bay) D6
De Peel (reg.) H6
De Twente (reg.) K4
De Zaan (riv.) B4
Dollard (bay) L2
Dommel (riv.) H6
Duiveland (isl.) D5
Eastern Scheldt (est.) D5
Eems (riv.) K2
Eijerlandsche Gat (str.) F2
Flevoland Polders 35,618 ....G4
Friesche Gat (chan.) J2
Frisian, West (isls.) G2
Galgenberg (hill) H4
Goeree (isl.) D5
Grevelingen (str.) E5
Griend (isl.) G2
Groninger Wad (sound) J2
Groote IJ Polder B4
Haarlemmermeer Polder 72,046 ....B5
Haringvliet (str.) E5
Het IJ (est.) C4
Hoek van Holland (cape) D5
Hondsrug (hills) K3
Houtrak Polder A4
Hunse (riv.) K3
IJmeer (bay) C4
IJssel (riv.) J4
IJsselmeer (lake) G3
Lauwers (chan.) J1
Lauwers Zee (bay) J2
Lek (riv.) F5
Lemelerberg (hill) J4
Lower Rhine (riv.) H5
Maas (riv.) G5
Mark (riv.) F6
Marken (isl.) G4
Markerwaard Polder G3
Marsdiep (chan.) F3
North (sea) E3
North Beveland (isl.) D5
North East Polder 34,467 ....H3
North Holland (canal) C4
North Sea (canal) F4
Old Rhine (riv.) E4
Oostzaan Polder 6,336 ....B4
Orange (canal) K3
Overflakkee (isl.) E5
Pinke Gat (chan.) H2
Regge (riv.) K4
Rhine (riv.) J5
Roer (riv.) J6
Rottumeplaat (isl.) J1
Rottumeroog (isl.) J1
Schiermonnikoog (isl.) J1
Schouwen (isl.) D5
Slotermeer (lake) H3
Sneekermeer (lake) H2
South Beveland (isl.) D6
Terschelling (isl.) G2
Texel (isl.) F2
Tjeukemeer (lake) H3
Tjonger (riv.) J3
Vaalserberg (mt.) J7
Vecht (riv.) F4
Vechte (riv.) J3
Veersche Meer (lake) D5
Veluwe (reg.) H4
Vlieland (isl.) F2
Vliestroom (str.) G2
Voorne (isl.) D5
Waal (riv.) G5
Waddenzee (sound) G2
Walcheren (isl.) C5
Wester Eems (chan.) K1
Western Scheldt (De Honte)
(bay) D6
West Frisian (isls.) F2
Westgat (chan.) F3
Wieringermeer Polder 11,870 ....G3
Wilhelmina (canal) G6
Willems (canal) G5

*City and suburbs.
†Population of cities in Belgium & Netherlands are communes

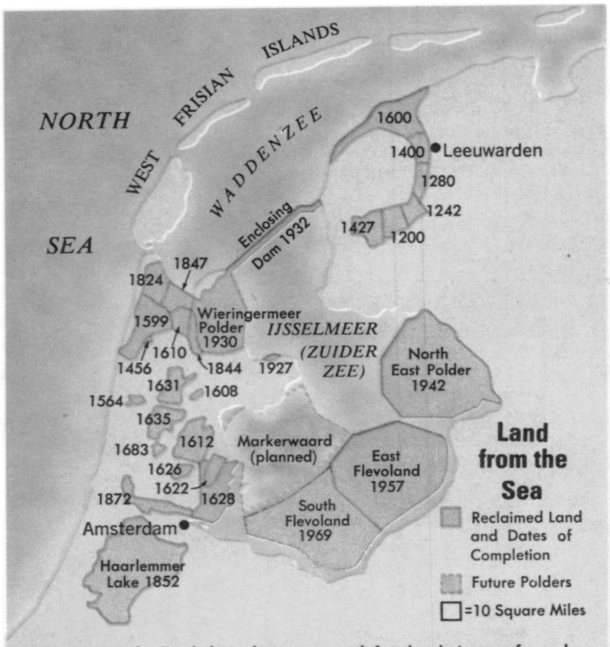

For centuries the Dutch have been renowned for the drainage of marshes and the construction of polders, i.e., arable land reclaimed from the sea. Future projects will convert much of the present IJsselmeer to agricultural land.

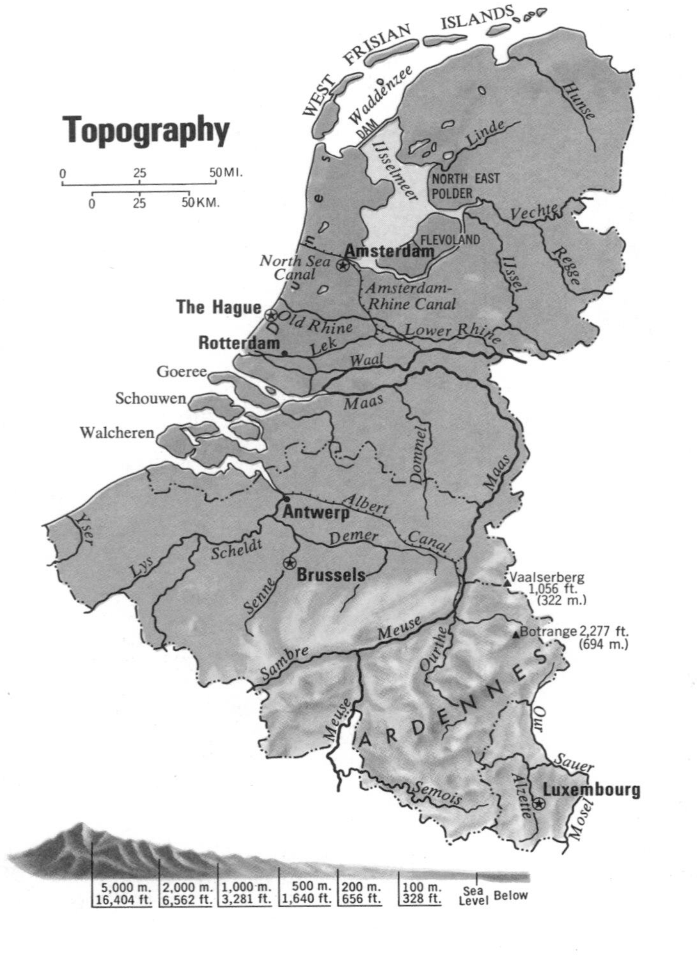

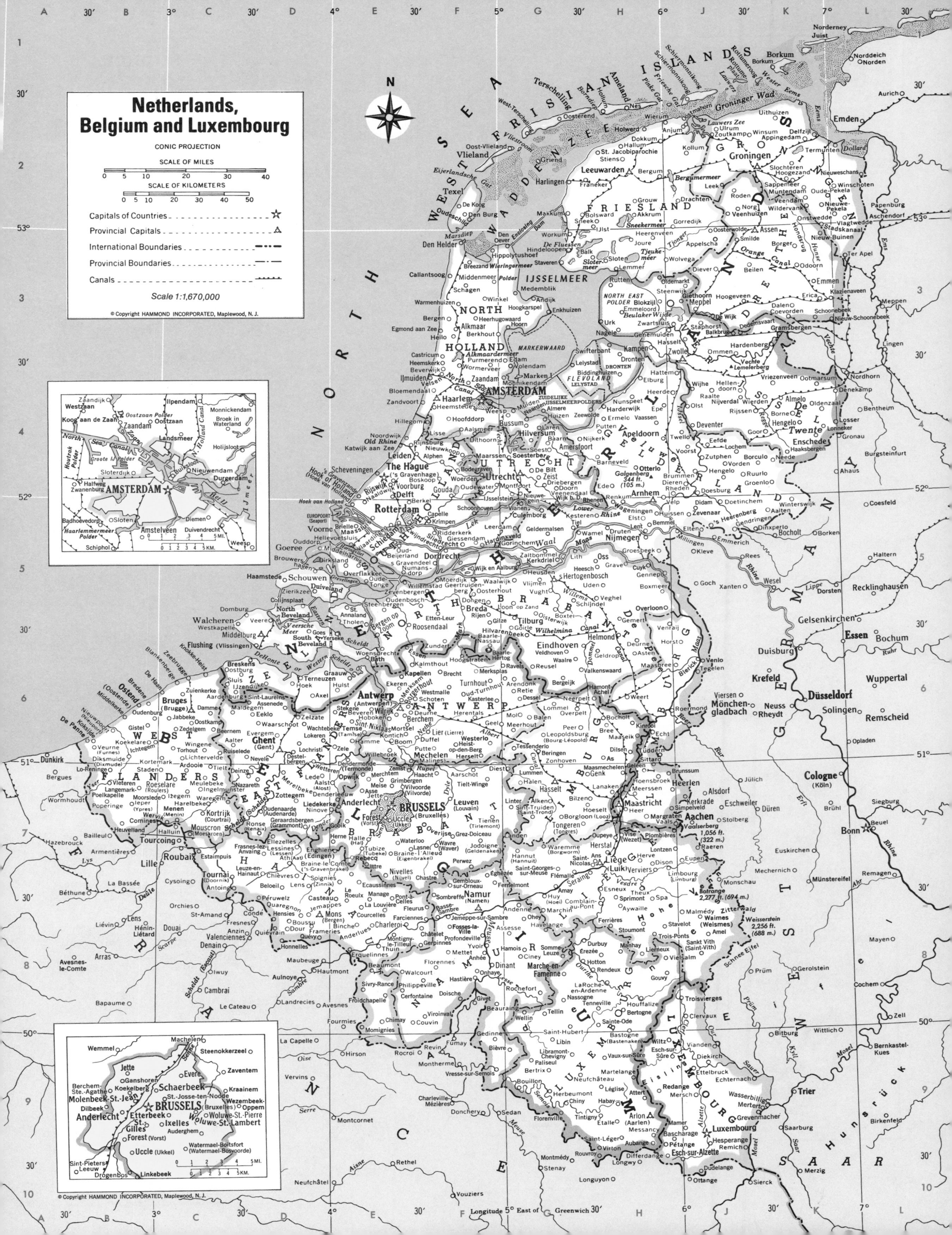

Netherlands, Belgium and Luxembourg
CONIC PROJECTION
SCALE OF MILES
0 5 10 20 30 40
SCALE OF KILOMETERS
0 5 10 20 30 40 50
Capitals of Countries
Provincial Capitals
International Boundaries
Provincial Boundaries
Canals
Scale 1:1,670,000
© Copyright HAMMOND INCORPORATED, Maplewood, N. J.
NORTH SEA
WEST FRISIAN ISLANDS
WADDEN ZEE
IJSSELMEER
GRONINGEN
FRIESLAND
DRENTHE
NORTH HOLLAND
OVERIJSSEL
GELDERLAND
UTRECHT
SOUTH HOLLAND
ZEELAND
NORTH BRABANT
LIMBURG
WEST FLANDERS
EAST FLANDERS
ANTWERP
BRABANT
HAINAUT
NAMUR
LIÈGE
LUXEMBOURG
GERMANY
FRANCE
SAAR
AMSTERDAM
The Hague
Rotterdam
Utrecht
Groningen
Leeuwarden
Haarlem
Arnhem
Nijmegen
Eindhoven
Maastricht
BRUSSELS
Antwerp
Ghent
Bruges
Liège (Luik)
Namur (Namen)
Mons
Luxembourg
Aachen
Cologne (Köln)
Düsseldorf
Essen
Bonn
Trier
Lille
Longitude 5° East of Greenwich
© Copyright HAMMOND INCORPORATED, Maplewood, N.J.

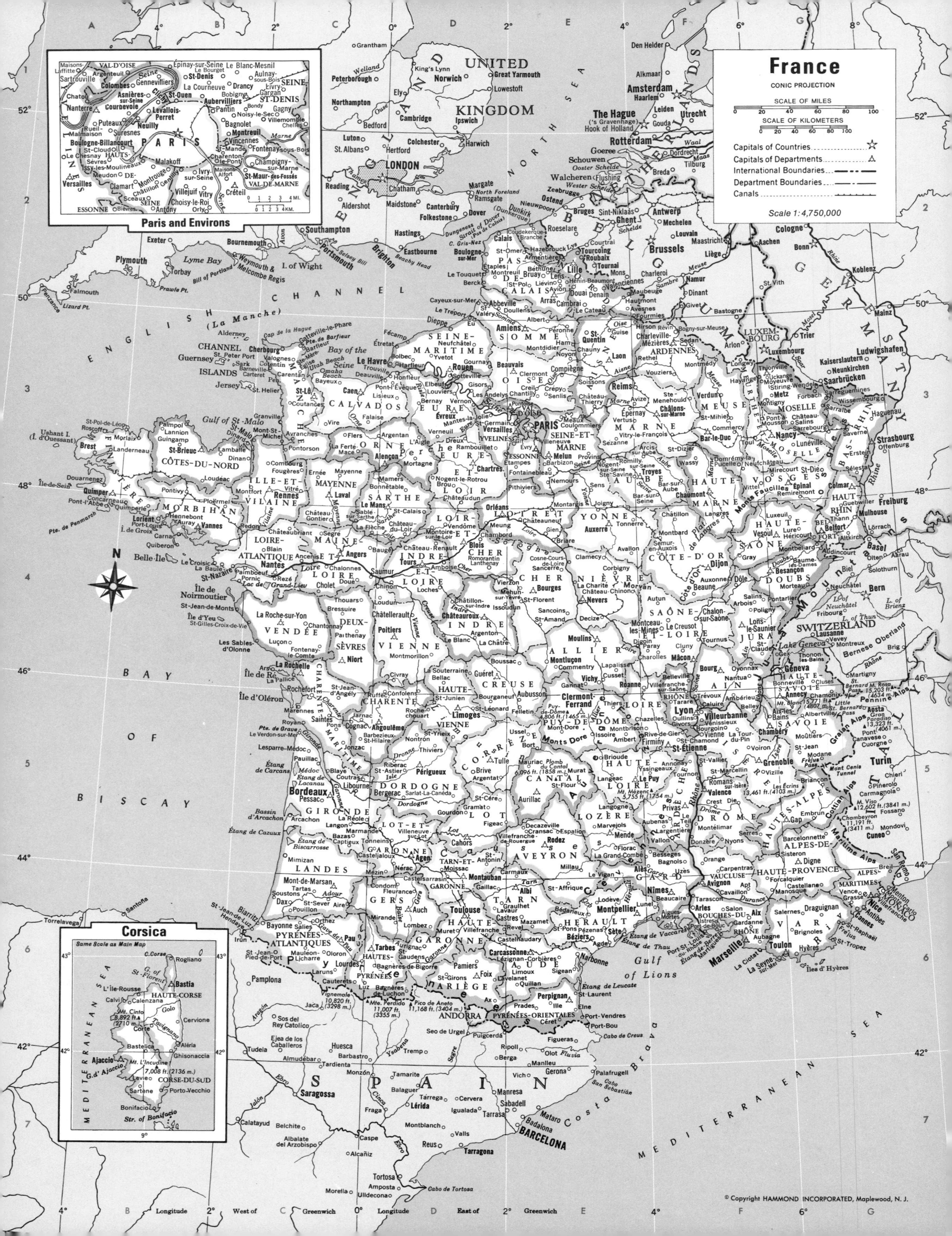
France
CONIC PROJECTION
SCALE OF MILES
0 20 40 60 80 100
SCALE OF KILOMETERS
0 20 40 60 80 100
Capitals of Countries
Capitals of Departments
International Boundaries
Department Boundaries
Canals
Scale 1: 4,750,000
Paris and Environs
Corsica
Same Scale as Main Map
UNITED KINGDOM
ENGLAND
LONDON
ENGLISH CHANNEL
(La Manche)
CHANNEL ISLANDS
NORTH SEA
NETHERLANDS
BELGIUM
LUXEMBOURG
GERMANY
SWITZERLAND
ITALY
MONACO
ANDORRA
SPAIN
BAY OF BISCAY
Gulf of Lions
MEDITERRANEAN SEA
PARIS
Brussels
Amsterdam
The Hague
BARCELONA
© Copyright HAMMOND INCORPORATED, Maplewood, N. J.
Longitude West of Greenwich
Longitude East of Greenwich

DEPARTMENTS

Ain 376,477 F4
Aisne 533,862 E3
Allier 378,406 E4
Alpes-de-Haute-Provence 112,178 G5
Alpes-Maritimes 816,681 G6
Ardèche 257,065 F5
Ardennes 309,306 F3
Ariège 137,857 D6
Aube 284,823 E3
Aude 272,366 E6
Aveyron 278,306 E5
Bas-Rhin 882,121 G3
Belfort (terr.) 128,125 G4
Bouches-du-Rhône 1,632,974 F6
Calvados 560,967 C3
Cantal 166,549 E5
Charente 337,064 D5
Charente-Maritime 497,859 C5
Cher 316,350 E4
Corrèze 240,363 D5
Corse du Sud 128,634 B6
Côte-d'Or 456,070 F4
Côtes-du-Nord 525,556 B3
Creuse 146,214 D4
Deux-Sèvres 335,829 C4
Dordogne 373,179 D5
Doubs 471,082 G4
Drôme 361,847 F5
Essonne 923,063 E3
Eure 422,952 D3
Eure-et-Loir 335,151 D3
Finistère 804,088 A3
Gard 494,575 F6
Gers 175,366 D6
Gironde 1,061,480 C5
Haute-Corse 161,208 B6
Haute-Garonne 777,431 D6
Haute-Loire 205,491 E5
Haute-Marne 212,304 F3
Hautes-Alpes 97,358 G5
Haute-Saône 222,254 G4
Haute-Savoie 447,795 G5
Hautes-Pyrénées 227,222 D6
Haute-Vienne 352,149 D5
Haut-Rhin 635,209 G4
Hauts-de-Seine 1,438,930 A2
Hérault 648,202 E6
Ille-et-Vilaine 702,199 C3
Indre 248,523 D4
Indre-et-Loire 478,601 D4
Isère 860,339 F5
Jura 238,856 F4
Landes 288,323 C5
Loire 742,396 F5
Loire-Atlantique 934,499 C4
Loiret 490,189 E4
Loir-et-Cher 283,686 D4
Lot 150,778 D5
Lot-et-Garonne 292,616 D5
Lozère 74,825 E5
Maine-et-Loire 629,849 C4
Manche 451,662 C3
Marne 530,399 F3
Mayenne 261,789 C3
Meurthe-et-Moselle 722,588 G3
Meuse 203,904 F3
Morbihan 563,588 B4
Moselle 1,006,373 G3
Nièvre 245,212 E4
Nord 2,510,738 E2
Oise 606,320 E3
Orne 293,523 C3
Paris (city) 2,299,830 B2
Pas-de-Calais 1,403,035 E2
Puy-de-Dôme 580,033 E5
Pyrénées-Atlantiques 534,748 C6
Pyrénées-Orientales 299,506 E6
Rhône 1,429,647 F5
Saône-et-Loire 569,810 F4
Sarthe 490,385 D3
Savoie 305,118 G5
Seine-et-Marne 755,762 E3
Seine-Saint-Denis 1,322,127 C1
Somme 538,462 E3
Tarn 338,024 E6
Tarn-et-Garonne 183,314 D5
Val-de-Marne 1,215,713 C1
Val-d'Oise 840,885 E3
Var 626,093 G6
Vaucluse 390,446 F6
Vendée 450,641 C4
Vienne 357,366 D4
Vosges 397,957 G3
Yonne 299,851 E4
Yvelines 1,082,255 D3

CITIES and TOWNS

Abbeville 25,252 D2
Agde 9,856 E6
Agen 33,763 D5
Aix-en-Provence 91,665 F6
Aix-les-Bains 21,884 G5
Ajaccio 47,065 B7
Albert 11,746 E2
Albertville 16,630 G5
Albi 43,942 E6
Alençon 32,917 D3
Alès 33,315 E5
Ambérieu-en-Bugey 9,294 F5
Amboise 10,498 D4
Amiens 129,453 D3
Ancenis 6,689 C4
Angers 136,603 C4
Angoulême 46,293 D5
Annecy 53,058 G5
Annonay 19,234 F5
Antibes 44,226 G6
Antony 57,450 B2
Apt 9,735 F6
Arcachon 13,856 C5
Argentan 16,063 D3
Argenteuil 101,542 A1
Arles 37,337 F6
Armentières 23,850 E2
Arras 45,804 E2
Asnières-sur-Seine 75,328 A1
Aubagne 26,145 F6
Aubenas 11,967 F5
Aubervilliers 72,859 B1
Auch 18,767 D6
Audincourt 18,570 G4
Aulnay-sous-Bois 77,982 B1
Auray 10,006 B4
Aurignac 744 D6
Aurillac 29,458 E5
Autun 19,441 F4
Auxerre 36,039 E4
Auxonne 6,414 F4
Avallon 8,518 E4
Avignon 73,482 F6
Avion 22,860 E2
Avranches 10,128 C3
Ax-les-Thermes 1,456 D6
Bagnères-de-Bigorre 9,080 D6
Bagnolet 35,858 B2
Bagnols-sur-Cèze 13,111 F5
Barbizon 1,189 E3
Barcelonnette 2,523 G5
Barfleur 701 C3
Bar-le-Duc 19,188 F3
Bar-sur-Aube 7,227 F3
Bastia 45,387 B6
Bayeux 13,381 C3
Bayonne 41,281 C6
Beaucaire 10,189 F6
Beaune 16,386 F4
Beauvais 53,493 E3
Belfort 54,469 G4
Belley 6,612 F5
Berck 14,104 D2
Bergerac 25,488 D5
Bernay 9,928 D3
Besançon 119,803 G4
Béthune 26,208 E2
Béziers 79,213 E6
Biarritz 27,453 C6
Blois 49,134 D4
Bobigny 43,041 B1
Bogny-sur-Meuse 6,845 F3
Bolbec 12,347 D3
Bondy 48,285 B1
Bonneville 6,717 G4
Bordeaux 220,830 C5
Boulogne-Billancourt 103,527 A2
Boulogne-sur-Mer 48,309 D2
Bourg-en-Bresse 40,052 F4
Bourges 75,200 E4
Bourgoin-Jallieu 18,504 F5
Bressuire 9,778 C4
Brest 163,940 A3
Briançon 8,523 G5

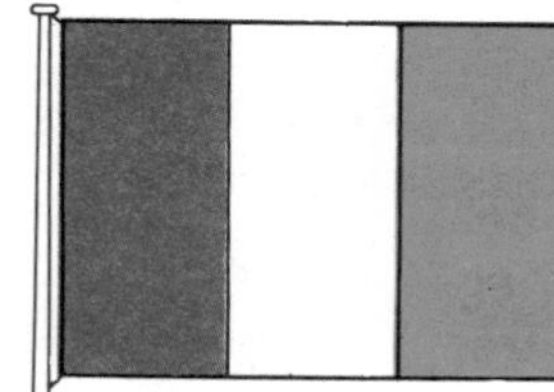

Brignoles 8,784 G6
Brioude 7,756 E5
Brive-la-Gaillarde 49,276 D5
Bruay-en-Artois 25,544 E2
Caen 116,987 C3
Cahors 19,288 D5
Calais 73,009 D2
Caluire-et-Cuire 43,024 F5
Cambrai 38,706 E2
Cannes 70,226 G6
Carcassonne 38,887 D6
Carmaux 11,970 E5
Carpentras 20,169 F5
Castelnaudary 8,947 E6
Castelsarrasin 6,562 D6
Castres 41,037 E6
Cavaillon 17,383 F6
Châlons-sur-Marne 50,870 F3
Chalon-sur-Saône 55,495 F4
Chambéry 52,286 F5
Chambord 166 D4
Chamonix-Mont-Blanc 6,246 G5
Champigny-sur-Marne 80,189 C2
Chantilly 10,517 E3
Charenton-le-Pont 20,383 B2
Charleville-Mézières 59,513 F3
Chartres 38,574 D3
Châteaubriant 12,417 C4
Château-du-Loir 5,598 D4
Châteaudun 14,634 D3
Château-Gontier 8,301 C4
Châteauroux 53,166 D4
Château-Thierry 13,379 E3
Châtellerault 33,811 D4
Châtillon 26,562 B2
Châtillon-sur-Seine 7,367 F4
Chatou 26,415 A1
Chaumont 26,568 F3
Chauny 14,324 E3
Chelles 24,192 C1
Cherbourg 31,333 C3
Chinon 5,378 D4
Choisy-le-Roi 38,629 B2
Cholet 49,887 C4
Clamart 52,881 A2
Clermont 7,834 E3
Clermont-Ferrand 153,379 E5
Clichy 47,731 B1
Cluny 4,335 F4
Cluses 12,713 G4
Cognac 21,567 C5
Colmar 58,585 G3
Colombes 83,241 A1
Commentry 8,074 E4
Commercy 6,918 F3
Compiègne 37,009 E3
Concarneau 15,096 A4
Cosne-Cours-sur-Loire 9,768 E4
Coudekerque-Branche 24,702 E2
Coulommiers 11,363 E3
Courbevoie 54,391 A1
Coutances 8,286 C3
Creil 31,893 E3
Crépy-en-Valois 10,661 E3
Créteil 58,665 B2
Cusset 13,672 E4
Dax 18,019 C6
Deauville 5,655 C3
Decazeville 9,318 E5
Decize 6,853 E4
Denain 26,096 E2
Dieppe 25,607 D3

AREA 210,038 sq. mi. (543,998 sq. km.)
POPULATION 53,788,000
CAPITAL Paris
LARGEST CITY Paris
HIGHEST POINT Mont Blanc 15,771 ft. (4,807 m.)
MONETARY UNIT franc
MAJOR LANGUAGE French
MAJOR RELIGION Roman Catholicism

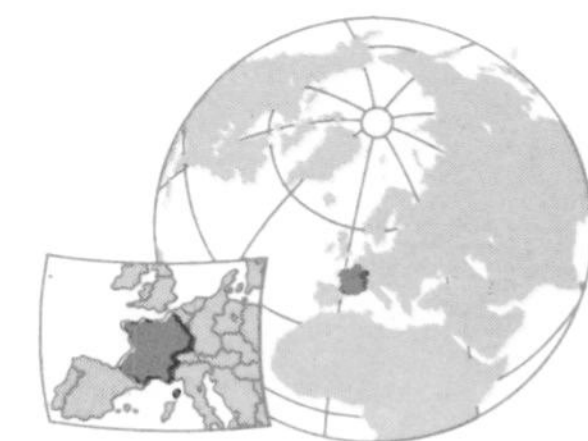

Topography

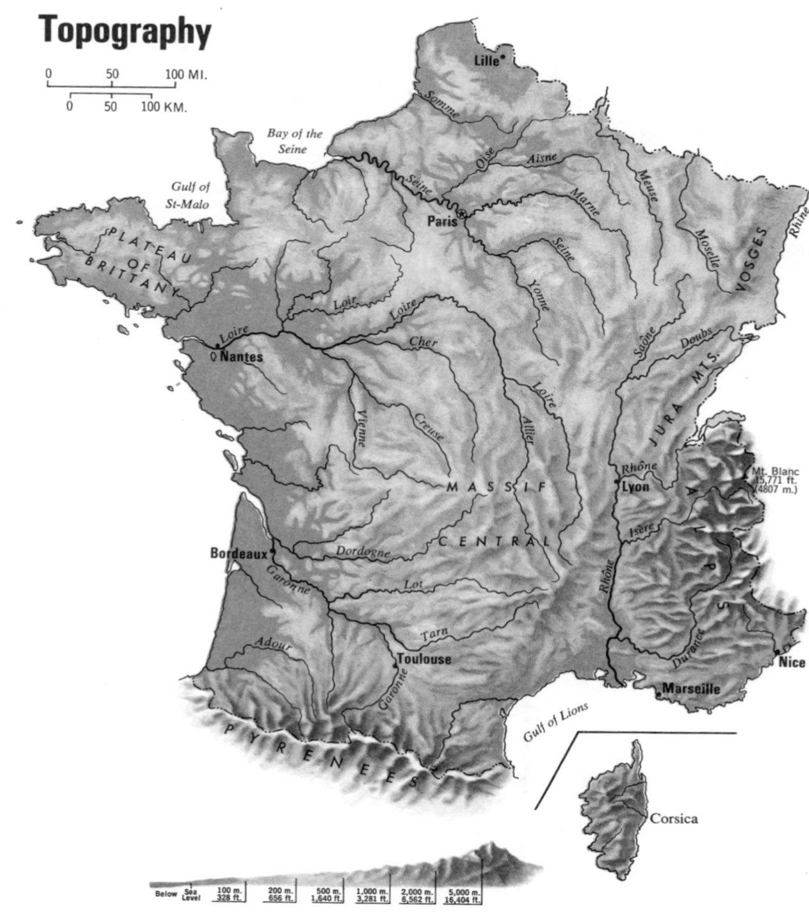

Historic Provinces

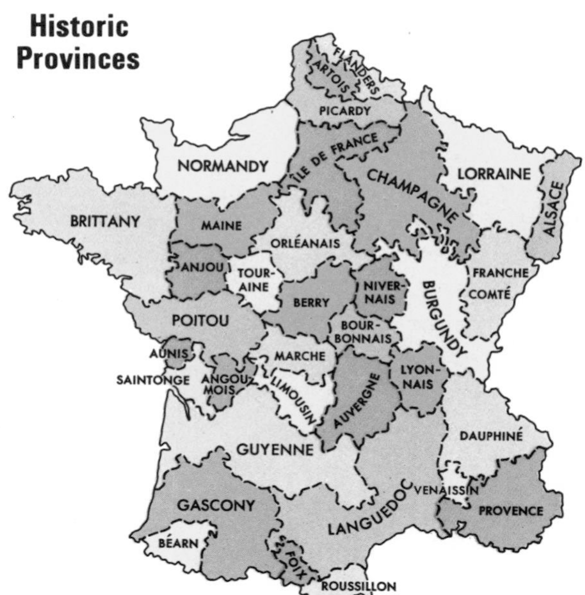

A resident of the city of Caen thinks of himself as a Norman rather than as a citizen of the modern department of Calvados. In spite of the passing of nearly two centuries, the historic provinces which existed before 1790 command the local patriotism of most Frenchmen.

Digne 13,140 G5
Digoin 10,449 F4
Dijon 149,899 F4
Dinan 13,303 B3
Dinard 9,211 B3
Dôle 28,109 F4
Domrémy-la-Pucelle 190 F3
Douai 43,954 E2
Douarnenez 17,851 A3
Doullens 6,806 E2
Draguignan 19,653 G6
Drancy 64,258 B1
Dreux 31,503 D3
Dunkirk (Dunkerque) 78,171 E2
Elbeuf 18,642 D3
Épernay 29,286 E3
Épinal 39,000 G3
Épinay-sur-Seine 46,458 B1
Erstein 6,494 G3
Étampes 18,810 E3
Étaples 10,423 D2
Eu 8,349 D3
Évreux 46,181 D3
Évry 15,300 E3
Falaise 8,133 C3
Fécamp 20,835 D3
Figeac 8,675 D5
Firminy 23,776 F5
Flers 18,590 C3
Foix 9,569 D6
Fontainebleau 16,436 E3
Fontenay-le-Comte 12,301 C4
Fontenay-sous-Bois 46,200 C2
Forbach 24,812 G3
Fougères 26,260 C3
Fourmies 15,318 F2
Fréjus 27,805 G6
Gagny 36,714 C1
Gaillac 7,653 D6
Gap 24,962 G5
Gardanne 8,175 F6
Gennevilliers 50,154 B1
Gentilly 16,843 B2
Gex 3,959 G4
Gien 13,817 E4
Gif 10,866 E3
Gisors 7,591 D3
Givet 7,787 F2
Givors 19,356 F5
Granville 12,869 C3
Grasse 24,260 G6
Graulhet 11,099 E6
Gray 8,718 F4
Grenoble 165,431 F5
Guebwiller 10,477 G4
Guéret 14,418 D4
Guingamp 9,269 B3

Guise 6,642 E3
Haguenau 23,023 G3
Harfleur 9,857 D3
Hautmont 19,130 F2
Hayange 8,479 F3
Hazebrouck 18,867 E2
Hendaye 9,404 C6
Hénin-Beaumont 26,296 E2
Hennebont 8,978 B4
Héricourt 8,481 G4
Hirson 11,909 F3
Honfleur 8,995 D3
Hyères 29,366 G6
Issoire 13,560 E5
Issoudun 15,065 D4
Issy-les-Moulineaux 47,355 A2
Istres 10,127 F6
Ivry-sur-Seine 62,804 B2
Joigny 10,825 E3
La Baule-Escoublac 13,854 B4
La Ciotat 29,290 F6
La Courneuve 37,917 B1
La Flèche 12,743 C4
La Grand-Combe 9,406 E5
L'Aigle 9,198 D3
Landerneau 13,983 B3
Langres 10,745 F4
Lannion 13,692 B3
Laon 27,420 E3
La Pallice C4
La Rochelle 72,936 C4
La Roche-sur-Yon 40,789 C4
La Seyne-sur-Mer 50,059 F6
Laval 50,734 C3
Lavelanet 9,278 E6
Le Blanc 7,431 D4
Le Blanc-Mesnil 49,062 B1
Le Bourget 10,520 B1
Le Cateau 8,680 E2
Le Chesnay 24,590 A2
Le Creusot 31,643 F4
Le Havre 216,917 C3
Le Mans 150,289 C3
Lens 39,973 E2
Le Puy 24,793 F5
Les Andelys 7,524 D3
Les Sables-d'Olonne 17,157 B4
Le Teil 7,993 F5
Le Tréport 6,463 D2
Levallois-Perret 52,460 A1
Lézignan-Corbières 6,929 E6
Libourne 21,265 C5
Liévin 33,040 E2
Lille 171,010 E2
Limoges 136,059 D5
Limoux 9,595 E6
Lisieux 24,972 D3

Livry-Gargan 32,879 C1
Lodève 7,131 E6
Longwy 20,107 F3
Lons-le-Saunier 20,897 F4
Lorient 68,655 B4
Loudéac 7,173 B3
Loudun 7,060 D4
Lourdes 17,685 C6
Louviers 17,919 D3
Luçon 8,834 C4
Lunel 12,392 E6
Lunéville 22,438 G3
Lure 8,538 G4
Luxeuil-les-Bains 10,061 G4
Lyon 454,265 F5
Mâcon 39,130 F4
Maisons-Alfort 53,963 B2
Maisons-Laffitte 23,465 A1
Malakoff 34,100 A2
Manosque 17,256 G6
Mantes-la-Jolie 42,408 D3
Marmande 13,223 C5
Marseille 901,421 F6
Martigues 26,850 F6
Maubeuge 34,152 F2
Mayenne 11,278 C3
Mazamet 13,148 E6
Meaux 41,831 E3
Mehun-sur-Yèvre 6,533 E4
Melun 36,913 E3
Mende 10,040 E5
Menton 24,736 G6
Metz 110,939 G3
Meudon 31,294 A2
Millau 20,401 E5
Mimizan 6,826 C5
Mirecourt 7,160 G3
Moissac 7,403 D5
Montargis 18,021 E3
Montauban 35,344 D5
Montbard 7,477 F4
Montbéliard 29,968 G4
Montbrison 9,945 E5
Montceau-les-Mines 28,093 F4
Mont-de-Marsan 24,812 C6
Mont-Dore 2,074 E5
Montélimar 25,422 F5
Montfort 2,701 C3
Montigny-les-Metz 24,208 G3
Montluçon 56,337 E4
Montmédy 1,859 F3
Montpellier 178,136 E6
Montreuil,
Seine-Saint-Denis 96,441 B2
Montrouge 40,189 B2
Mont-Saint-Michel 88 C3
Morlaix 15,919 B3

Morteau 6,515 G4
Moulins 25,856 E4
Moyeuvre-Grande 12,448 G3
Mulhouse 116,494 G4
Muret 13,041 D6
Nancy 106,906 G3
Nanterre 94,441 A1
Nantes 252,537 C4
Narbonne 36,525 E6
Nemours 11,159 E3
Neufchâteau 8,582 F3
Neuilly-sur-Seine 65,941 A1
Nevers 45,122 E4
Nice 331,002 G6
Nîmes 123,914 F6
Niort 59,297 C4
Nogent-le-Rotrou 12,284 D3
Noisy-le-Sec 37,674 B1
Noyon 13,784 E3
Oloron-Sainte-Marie 11,616 C6
Orange 19,847 F5
Orléans 88,503 D3
Orly 26,090 B2
Orthez 9,639 C6
Oullins 27,731 F5
Oyonnax 22,548 F4
Pamiers 12,906 D6
Pantin 42,651 B1
Paray-le-Monial 11,523 F4
Paris (cap.) 2,291,554 B2
Parthenay 12,549 C4
Pau 81,560 C6
Périgueux 34,779 D5
Péronne 8,358 E3
Perpignan 101,198 E6
Pessac 50,333 C5
Pézenas 6,768 E6
Pithiviers 9,976 E3
Poitiers 78,739 D4
Pont-à-Mousson 14,461 G3
Pontarlier 17,778 G4
Pontivy 9,478 B3
Pont-l'Abbe 6,618 A4
Pontoise 26,702 E3
Port-de-Bouc 20,448 F6
Port-Saint-Louis-du-Rhône 9,649 F6
Port-Vendres 5,448 E6
Privas 9,385 F5
Provins 12,281 E3
Puteau 35,366 A2
Quimper 50,856 A4
Quimperlé 9,783 B4
Rambouillet 18,446 D3
Redon 9,528 C4
Reims 177,320 E3
Remiremont 10,250 G3
Rennes 194,094 C3

(continued on following page)

Rethel 8,189 .... F3
Révin 11,459 .... F3
Reze 35,512 .... C4
Rive-de-Gier 17,369 .... F5
Roanne 54,999 .... E4
Rochechouart 2,953 .... D5
Rochefort 27,264 .... C5
Rodez 24,898 .... E5
Romans-sur-Isère 30,974 .... F5
Romilly-sur-Seine 17,276 .... E3
Romorantin-Lanthenay 15,727 .... D4
Roubaix 109,473 .... E2
Rouen 113,536 .... D3
Royan 17,978 .... C5
Rueil-Malmaison 62,504 .... A2
Sablé-sur-Sarthe 9,913 .... C4
Saint-Affrique 6,842 .... E6
Saint-Amand-Mont-Rond 11,896 .... E4
Saint-Brieuc 51,838 .... B3
Saint-Chamond 39,236 .... F5
Saint-Claude 12,651 .... F4
Saint-Cloud 28,052 .... A2
Saint-Denis 95,808 .... B1
Saint-Dié 22,834 .... G3
Saint-Dizier 36,377 .... F3
Sainte-Mère-Église 1,041 .... C3
Saintes 24,946 .... C5
Sainte-Savine 10,526 .... E3
Saint-Étienne 218,289 .... F5
Saint-Florent-sur-Cher 6,385 .... E4
Saint-Flour 6,900 .... E5
Saint-Gaudens 12,103 .... D6
Saint-Germain-en-Laye 35,351 .... D3
Saint-Gilles-Croix-de-Vie 6,569 .... B4
Saint-Girons 7,259 .... D6
Saint-Jean-d'Angély 8,801 .... C5
Saint-Jean-de-Luz 10,921 .... C6
Saint-Jean-de-Maurienne 9,525 .... G5
Saint-Jean-Pied-de-Port 1,725 .... C6
Saint-Junien 9,281 .... D5
Saint-Lô 21,670 .... C3
Saint-Malo 43,277 .... B3
Saint-Mandé 20,714 .... B2
Saint-Marcellin 6,768 .... F5
Saint-Maur-des-Fossés 80,797 .... B2
Saint-Mihiel 5,544 .... F3
Saint-Nazaire 65,228 .... B4
Saint-Omer 16,419 .... E2
Saint-Ouen 43,569 .... B1
Saint-Pol-de-Léon 6,571 .... A3
Saint-Quentin 69,956 .... E3
Saint-Raphaël 19,499 .... G6
Saint-Tropez 4,484 .... G6
Saint-Vallier 10,000 .... F5
Salon-de-Provence 31,783 .... F6
Sancerre 2,029 .... E4
Sarlat-La-Canéda 8,191 .... D5
Sarrebourg 12,442 .... G3
Sarreguemines 24,570 .... G3
Sartrouville 42,092 .... A1
Saumur 30,984 .... D4
Saverne 10,015 .... G3
Sceaux 19,651 .... A2
Sedan 23,867 .... F3
Sélestat 15,209 .... G3
Senlis 13,481 .... E3

Sens 25,621 .... E3
Sète 39,075 .... E6
Sèvres 21,100 .... A2
Sisteron 6,434 .... G5
Soissons 29,694 .... E3
Sotteville-les-Rouen 30,393 .... D3
Stiring-Wendel 12,665 .... G3
Strasbourg 251,520 .... H3
Suresnes 37,456 .... A2
Tarare 11,931 .... F5
Tarascon 8,522 .... F6
Tarbes 54,286 .... D6
Thann 8,508 .... G4
Thiers 14,534 .... E5
Thionville 37,943 .... G3
Thonon-les-Bains 24,673 .... G4
Thouars 11,835 .... C4
Tonneins 7,256 .... D5
Toul 16,141 .... F3
Toulon 180,508 .... F6
Toulouse 371,143 .... D6
Tourcoing 102,092 .... E2
Tournon 8,568 .... F5
Tournus 7,284 .... F4
Tours 139,560 .... D4
Troyes 71,600 .... F3
Tulle 18,375 .... D5
Uckange 11,552 .... G3
Ussel 9,816 .... E5
Uzès 6,470 .... F5
Valence 67,101 .... F5
Valenciennes 41,976 .... E2
Vannes 36,722 .... B4
Vence 7,332 .... G6
Vendôme 17,828 .... D4
Vénissieux 74,264 .... F5
Verdun-sur-Meuse 22,889 .... F3
Vernon 21,184 .... D3
Versailles 93,359 .... A2
Vesoul 17,883 .... F4
Vichy 32,107 .... E4
Vienne 25,981 .... F5
Vierzon 33,057 .... D4
Villefranche 6,600 .... G6
Villefranche-de-Rouergue 10,848 .... E5
Villefranche-sur-Saône 29,996 .... F4
Villejuif 28,684 .... B2
Villemomble 28,684 .... C1
Villeneuve-Saint-Georges 31,378 .... C2
Villeneuve-sur-Lot 17,818 .... D5
Villeurbanne 115,913 .... F5
Vincennes 44,256 .... B2
Vire 12,832 .... C3
Vitré 10,989 .... C3
Vitry-le-François 19,075 .... F3
Vitry-sur-Seine 87,119 .... B2
Vittel 6,791 .... F3
Vizille 6,810 .... F5
Voiron 17,879 .... F5
Wissembourg 6,679 .... G3
Yvetot 10,088 .... D3

OTHER FEATURES

Adour (riv.) C6

Ain (riv.) F4
Aisne (riv.) E3
Ajaccio (gulf) B7
Allier (riv.) E5
Auvergne (mts.) E5
Belle-Île (isl.) B4
Biscay (bay) B5
Blanc (mt.) G5
Bonifacio (str.) B7
Calais (Dover) (str.) D2
Causses (reg.) E5
Cévennes (mts.) E5
Charente (riv.) C5
Cher (riv.) D4
Corse (cape) B6
Corsica (isl.) B6
Côte-d'Or (mts.) F4
Cotentin (pen.) C3
Cottian Alps (range) G5
Creuse (riv.) D5
Dordogne (riv.) D5
Dore Alps (mts.) E5
Doubs (riv.) G4
Drôme (riv.) F5
Dronne (riv.) D5
Durance (riv.) F6
English (chan.) B3
Eure (riv.) D3
Faucilles (mts.) G3
Forez (mts.) E5
Gard (riv.) F5
Garonne (riv.) C5
Gave de Pau (riv.) C6
Geneva (lake) G4
Gers (riv.) D6
Gironde (riv.) C5
Graian Alps (range) G5
Groix (isl.) B4
Hague (cape) C3
Hérault (riv.) E6
Hyères (isls.) G6
Indre (riv.) D4
Isère (riv.) F5
Isle (riv.) D5
Langres (plat.) F4
Limousin (reg.) D5
Lions (gulf) F6
Little Saint Bernard (pass) G5
Loir (riv.) D4
Loire (riv.) C4
Lot (riv.) D5
Manche, La (English) (chan.) B3
Maritime Alps (range) G6
Marne (riv.) C2
Mayenne (riv.) C4
Mediterranean (sea) E7
Médoc (reg.) C5
Meuse (riv.) F3
Mont Cenis (tunnel) G5
Morvan (plat.) F4
Moselle (riv.) G3
Noirmoutier (isl.) B4
North (sea) E1
Oise (riv.) E3

Oléron (isl.) C5
Omaha (beach) C3
Orb (riv.) E6
Orne (riv.) C3
Ouessant (isl.) A3
Penmarch (pt.) A4
Perche (reg.) D3
Puy-de-Dôme (mt.) E5
Pyrenees (range) C6
Ré (isl.) C4
Rhine (riv.) G3
Rhône (riv.) F5
Risle (riv.) D3
Riviera (reg.) G6
Saint-Florent (gulf) B6
Saint-Malo (gulf) B3
Saône (riv.) F4
Sarthe (riv.) D4
Sein (isl.) A3
Seine (riv.) D3
Seine (bay) D3
Sologne (reg.) E4
Somme (riv.) D2
Tarn (riv.) E6
Ushant (Ouessant) (isl.) A3
Utah (beach) C3
Vaccarès (lag.) F6
Vilaine (riv.) D4
Vilaine (riv.) C4
Vosges (mts.) G3
Yonne (riv.) E3

MONACO

CITIES and TOWNS

Monte Carlo 11,599 .... G6

* City and suburbs

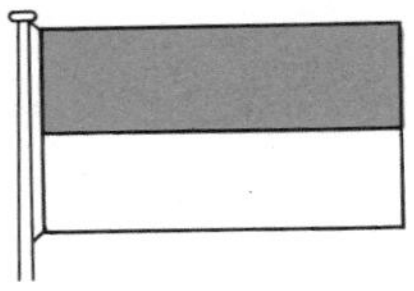

MONACO
AREA 368 acres
(149 hectares)
POPULATION 25,029

Wine Regions

Climate, soil and variety of grape planted determine the quality of wine. Long, hot and fairly dry summers with cool, humid nights constitute an ideal climate. The nature of the soil is such a determining influence that identical grapes planted in Bordeaux, Burgundy and Champagne, will yield wines of widely different types.

Agriculture, Industry and Resources

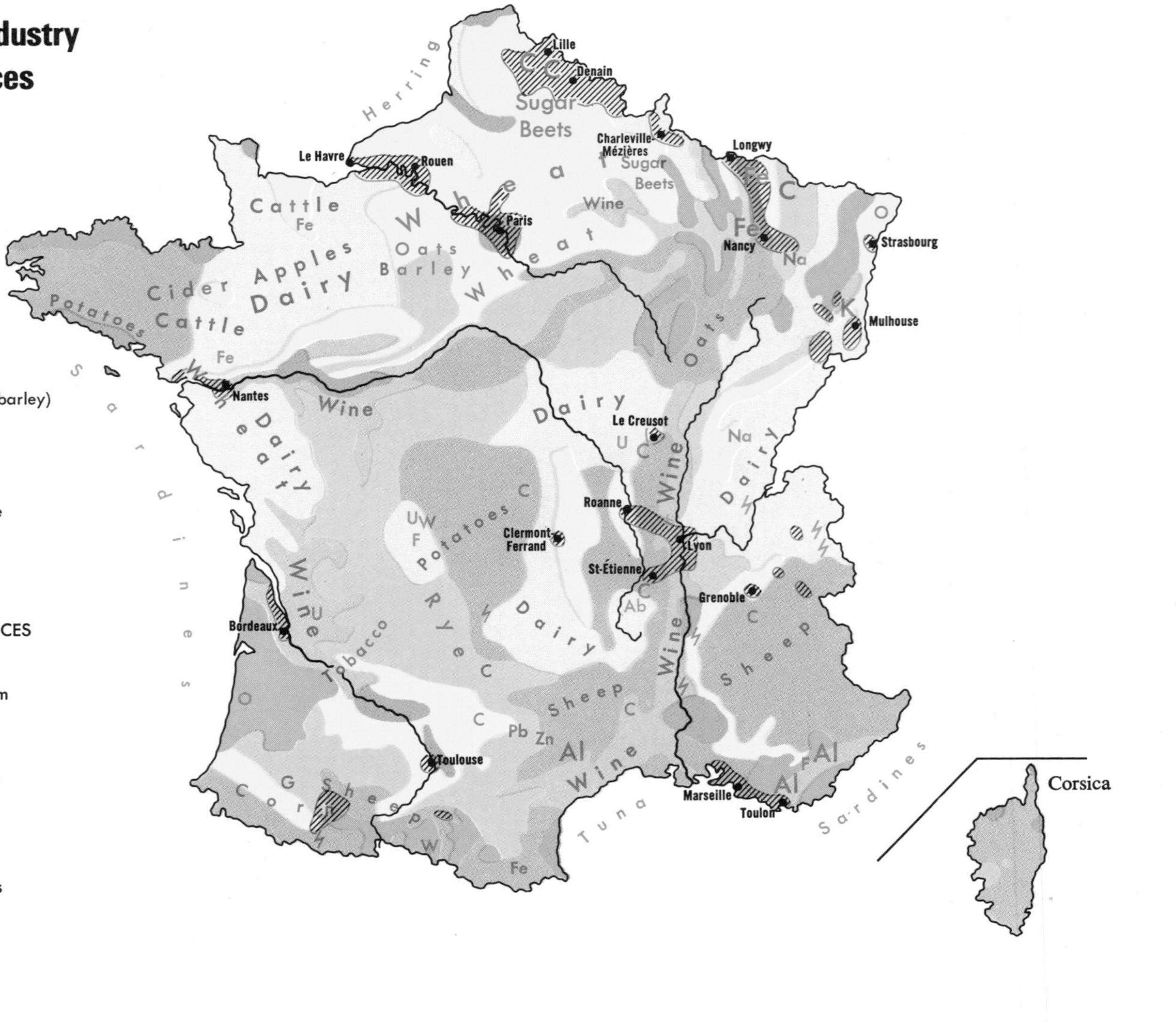

DOMINANT LAND USE

- Cereals (chiefly wheat)
- Cereals (chiefly rye, oats, barley)
- Dairy
- Pasture Livestock
- Truck Farming, Horticulture
- Grapes, Wine
- Forests

MAJOR MINERAL OCCURRENCES

Ab Asbestos
Al Bauxite
C Coal
F Fluorspar
Fe Iron Ore
G Natural Gas
K Potash

Na Salt
O Petroleum
Pb Lead
U Uranium
W Tungsten
Zn Zinc

⚡ Water Power
▨ Major Industrial Areas

Corsica

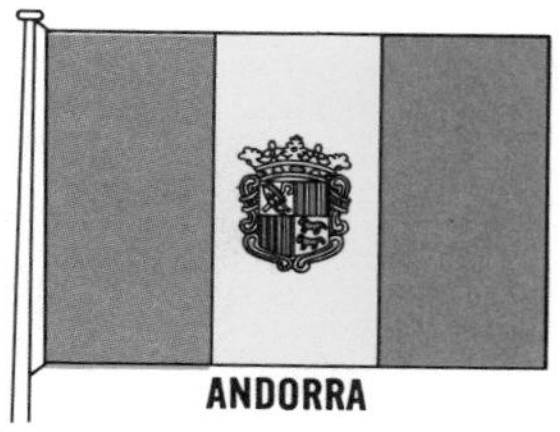

ANDORRA

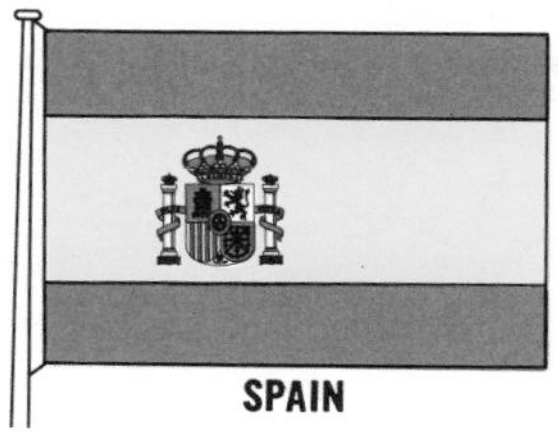

SPAIN

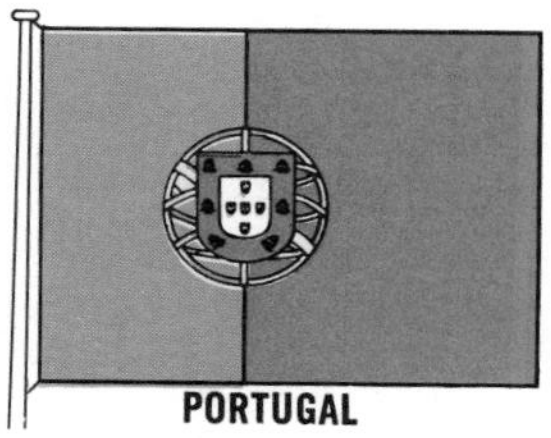

PORTUGAL

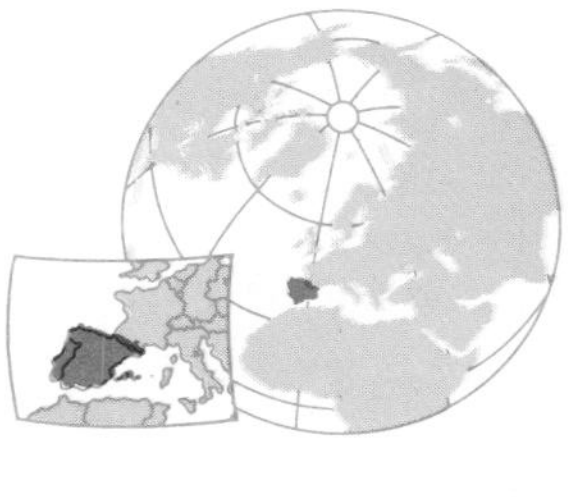

SPAIN

AREA 194,881 sq. mi. (504,742 sq. km.)
POPULATION 37,430,000
CAPITAL Madrid
LARGEST CITY Madrid
HIGHEST POINT Pico de Teide 12,172 ft. (3,710 m.) (Canary Is.); Mulhacén 11,411 ft. (3,478 m.) (mainland)
MONETARY UNIT peseta
MAJOR LANGUAGES Spanish, Catalan, Basque, Galician, Valencian
MAJOR RELIGION Roman Catholicism

ANDORRA

AREA 188 sq. mi. (487 sq. km.)
POPULATION 31,000
CAPITAL Andorra la Vella
MONETARY UNITS French franc, Spanish peseta
MAJOR LANGUAGE Catalan
MAJOR RELIGION Roman Catholicism

PORTUGAL

AREA 35,549 sq. mi. (92,072 sq. km.)
POPULATION 9,933,000
CAPITAL Lisbon
LARGEST CITY Lisbon
HIGHEST POINT Malhão da Estrela 6,532 ft. (1,991 m.)
MONETARY UNIT escudo
MAJOR LANGUAGE Portuguese
MAJOR RELIGION Roman Catholicism

GIBRALTAR

AREA 2.28 sq. mi. (5.91 sq. km.)
POPULATION 29,760
CAPITAL Gibraltar
MONETARY UNIT pound sterling
MAJOR LANGUAGES English, Spanish
MAJOR RELIGION Roman Catholicism

SPAIN

PROVINCES

Álava 204,323 E1
Albacete 335,026 E3
Alicante 920,105 F3
Almería 375,004 E4
Ávila 203,798 D2
Badajoz 687,599 C3
Baleares 558,287 H3
Barcelona 3,929,194 G2
Burgos 358,075 E1
Cáceres 457,777 C3
Cádiz 885,433 D4
Castellón 385,823 G2
Ciudad Real 507,650 D3
Córdoba 724,116* D3
Cuenca 247,158 E2
Gerona 414,397 H1
Granada 733,375 E4
Guadalajara 147,732 E2
Guipúzcoa 631,003 E1
Huelva 397,683 C4
Huesca 222,238 F1
Jaén 661,146 E4
La Coruña 1,004,188 B1
Las Palmas 579,710 C4
León 548,721 C1
Lérida 347,015 G2
Logroño 235,713 E1
Lugo 415,052 C1
Madrid 3,792,561 E2
Málaga 867,330 D4
Murcia 832,313 F4
Navarra 464,867 F1
Orense 413,733 C1
Oviedo 1,045,635 C1
Palencia 198,763 D1
Pontevedra 750,701 B1
Salamanca 371,607 C2
Santa Cruz de Tenerife 590,514 B5
Santander 467,138 D1
Segovia 162,770 D2
Sevilla 1,327,190 D4
Soria 114,956 E2
Tarragona 431,961 G2
Teruel 170,284 F2
Toledo 468,925 D3
Valencia 1,767,327 F3
Valladolid 412,572 D2
Vizcaya 1,043,310 E1
Zamora 251,934 D2
Zaragoza 760,186 F2

CITIES and TOWNS

Adra 10,851 E4
Aguilar 12,893 D4
Aguilas 15,525 F4
Alagón 5,114 F2
Alayor 5,124 J3
Albacete 82,607 F3
Albox 5,072 E4
Alburquerque 7,530 C3
Alcalá de Guadaira 28,781 D4
Alcalá de Henares 59,783 G4
Alcalá de los Gazules 5,262 D4
Alcalá la Real 9,849 E4
Alcanar 5,961 G2
Alcañiz 10,229 F2
Alcantarilla 19,895 F4
Alcaudete 8,557 E4
Alcázar de San Juan 24,620 E3
Alcira 30,493 F3
Alcora 6,711 F2
Alcoy 61,371 F3
Alfaro 8,766 F1
Algeciras 74,754 D4
Algemesí 21,158 F3
Alhama de Granada 6,148 E4
Alhama de Murcia 9,274 F4
Alicante 177,918 F3
Almadén 10,713 D3
Almagro 9,066 E3
Almansa 16,965 F3
Almendralejo 21,929 C3
Almería 104,008 E4
Almodóvar del Campo 7,310 D3
Almonte 9,960 C4
Almuñécar 7,812 E4
Álora 8,209 D4
Altea 7,262 G3
Amposta 11,767 G2
Andorra 6,485 F2
Andújar 25,962 D3
Antequera 28,039 D4
Aracena 5,390 C4
Aranda de Duero 18,183 E2
Aranjuez 28,559 E2
Archena 7,118 F3
Archidona 6,084 D4
Arcos de la Frontera 16,217 D4
Arenas de San Pedro 5,225 D2
Arenys de Mar 8,325 H2
Arévalo 5,807 D2
Argamasilla de Alba 6,192 E3
Arganda 11,876 G4
Arnedo 9,809 E1
Arrecife 21,310 C4
Arroyo de la Luz 8,130 C3
Artá 5,284 H3
Arucas 9,095 B5
Aspe 13,229 F3
Astorga 11,794 C1
Ávila de los Caballeros 30,958 D2
Avilés 67,186 C1
Ayamonte 9,897 C4
Ayora 5,249 F3
Azpeitia 7,835 E1
Azuaga 10,719 D3
Badajoz 80,793 C3
Badalona 162,888 H2
Baena 16,496 D4
Baeza 12,607 E4
Bailén 13,207 E3
Balaguer 11,676 G2
Bañolas 9,807 H1
Baracaldo 108,757 E1
Barbastro 13,243 F1
Barcarrota 5,012 C3
Barcelona 1,741,144 H2
Barcelona‡ 2,000,000 H2
Baza 14,290 E4
Beas de Segura 6,592 E3
Béjar 16,804 D2
Bélmez 5,161 D3
Benavente 11,779 D1
Benicarló 12,831 G2
Berga 11,163 G1
Berja 7,081 E4
Bermeo 16,714 E1
Betanzos 7,283 B1
Bilbao 393,179 E1
Bilbao‡ 450,000 E1
Binéfar 6,821 G2
Blanes 15,810 H2
Borjas Blancas 4,991 G2
Bujalance 8,236 D4
Bullas 8,131 F4
Burgos 118,366 E1
Burriana 21,298 G3
Cabeza del Buey 8,704 D3
Cabra 16,177 D4
Cáceres 53,108 C3
Cádiz 135,743 C4
Calahorra 16,315 E1
Calasparra 7,238 F3
Calatayud 16,524 F2
Calella 9,696 H2
Callosa de Ensarriá 5,701 G3
Calzada de Calatrava 5,751 E3
Campanario 7,722 D3
Campillos 7,014 D4
Campo de Criptana 12,604 E3
Candás 5,517 D1
Candeleda 5,153 D2
Cangas de Narcea 4,826 C1
Caniles 5,099 E4
Caravaca de le Cruz 10,411 E3
Carballo 5,542 B1
Carcagente 18,223 F3
Carmona 22,832 D4
Cartagena 52,312 F4
Caspe 8,766 G2
Cassá de la Selva 5,248 H2
Castellón de la Plana 79,773 G2
Castro del Río 10,087 D4
Castro-Urdiales 8,369 E1
Castuera 8,060 D3
Caudete 7,332 F3
Cazalla de la Sierra 5,382 D4
Cazorla 6,938 E4
Cehegín 9,661 F3
Cervera 5,693 G2
Ceuta 60,639 D5
Chiclana de la Frontera 22,986 C4
Chiva 5,394 F3
Ciempozuelos 9,185 F5
Cieza 22,929 F3
Ciudadela 13,701 H2
Ciudad Real 39,931 D3
Ciudad-Rodrigo 11,694 C2
Cocentaina 8,375 F3
Coín 14,190 D4
Colmenar de Oreja 4,930 G5
Colmenar Viejo 12,886 F4
Constantina 10,227 D4
Consuegra 10,026 E3
Córdoba 216,049 D4
Corella 5,850 F1
Coria 8,083 C3
Coria del Río 18,085 C4
Corral de Almaguer 8,006 E3
Crevillente 15,749 F3
Cuéllar 6,118 D2
Cuenca 33,980 E2
Cullera 15,128 F3
Daimiel 17,710 E3
Denia 14,514 G3
Dolores 5,420 F3
Don Benito 21,351 C3
Dos Hermanas 36,921 D4
Durango 20,403 E1
Écija 27,295 D4
Eibar 36,729 E1
Ejea de los Caballeros 9,766 F1
El Arahal 14,703 D4
Elche 101,271 F3
Elda 41,404 F3
Elizondo 2,516 F1
El Puerto de Santa María 36,451 C4
Espejo 5,925 D4
Estella 10,371 E1
Estepa 9,376 D4
Estepona 18,560 D4
Felanitx 9,100 H3
Ferrol del Caudillo 75,464 B1
Figueras 22,087 H1
Fraga 9,665 G2
Fregenal de la Sierra 6,826 C3
Fuengirola 20,597 D4
Fuente de Cantos 5,967 C3
Fuenterrabiá 2,350 E1
Fuentes de Andalucía 8,257 D4
Gandía 30,702 F3
Gerona 37,095 H2
Getafe 68,680 F4
Gijón 159,806 D1
Granada 185,799 E4
Granollers 30,066 H2
Guadalajara 30,924 E2
Guadix 15,311 E4
Guareña 7,706 C3
Guernica y Luno 12,046 E1
Haro 8,393 E1
Hellín 15,934 F3
Herencia 8,212 E3
Hinojosa del Duque 9,873 D3
Hortaleza G4
Hospitalet 241,978 H2
Huelma 5,260 E4
Huelva 96,689 C4
Huercal-Overa 5,158 F4
Huesca 33,076 F1
Huéscar 6,384 E4
Ibiza 16,943 G3
Igualada 27,941 G2
Inca 16,930 H3
Irún 38,014 F1
Iscar 5,192 D2
Isla Cristina 11,402 C4
Iznalloz 4,814 E4
Jaca 9,936 F1
Jaén 71,145 E4
Jaraíz de la Vera 6,379 D2
Játiva 20,934 F3
Jávea 6,228 G3
Jerez de la Frontera 112,411 C4
Jerez de los Caballeros 8,607 C3
Jijona 8,117 F3
Jódar 11,973 E4
Jumilla 16,407 F3
La Almunia de Doña Godina 4,835 F2
La Bañeza 8,480 C1
La Bisbal 6,374 H1
La Carolina 13,138 E3
La Coruña 184,372 B1
La Granja (San Ildefonso) 3,198 E2
La Guardia 4,967 B2
La Línea de la Concepción 51,021 D4
La Orotava 8,246 B4
La Palma del Condado 9,256 C4
La Puebla 9,923 H3
La Puebla de Montalbán 6,629 D3
La Rambla 6,525 D4
Laredo 9,114 E1
La Roda 11,460 E3
La Solana 13,894 E3
Las Palmas de Gran Canaria 260,368 B4
Las Pedroñeras 5,846 E3
La Unión 9,998 F4
Lebrija 15,081 D4
Leganés 57,537 F4
León 99,702 D1
Lérida 73,148 G2
Linares 45,330 E3
Liria 11,323 F3
Llerena 5,728 C3
Llivia 801 G1
Llodio 15,587 E1
Lluctmayor 9,630 H3
Logroño 83,117 E1
Loja 11,549 D4
Lora del Río 15,741 D4
Lorca 25,208 F4
Los Santos de Maimona 7,899 C3
Los Yébenes 5,477 E3
Lucena 21,527 D4
Lugo 53,504 C1
Madrid (cap.) 3,146,071 F4
Madrid‡ 3,500,000 F4
Madridejos 9,948 E3
Madroñera 5,397 D3
Mahón 17,802 J3
Málaga 334,988 D4
Málaga‡ 400,000 D4
Malagón 7,732 E3
Malpartida de Cáceres 5,054 C3
Manacor 20,266 H3
Mancha Real 7,547 E4
Manlleu 13,169 H1
Manresa 52,526 G2
Manzanares 15,024 E3
Marbella 19,648 D4
Marchena 16,227 D4
Marín 10,948 B1
Martos 16,395 E4
Mataró 73,129 H2
Medina del Campo 16,345 D2
Medina de Rioseco 4,874 D2
Medina-Sidonia 7,523 D4
Mérida 36,916 C3
Miajadas 8,042 D3
Mieres 22,790 D1
Minas de Ríotinto 3,939 C4
Miranda de Ebro 29,355 E1
Moguér 7,629 C4
Mollerusa 6,685 G2
Monesterio 5,923 C3
Monforte 14,002 C1
Monóvar 9,071 F3
Montehermoso 5,952 C2
Montellano 6,658 D4
Montijo 11,931 C3
Montilla 18,670 D4
Montoro 9,295 D3
Monzón 14,089 G2
Mora 10,523 E3
Moratalla 5,101 E3
Morón de la Frontera 25,662 D4
Mota del Cuervo 5,130 E3
Motril 25,121 E4
Mula 9,168 F3
Munera 5,003 E3
Murcia 102,242 F4
Navalcarnero 6,212 F4
Navalmoral de la Mata 9,650 D3
Nerja 7,413 E4
Nerva 10,830 C4
Novelda 16,867 F3
Nules 9,027 F3
Ocaña 5,603 E3
Oliva 16,717 F3
Oliva de la Frontera 8,560 C3
Olivenza 7,616 C3
Olot 18,062 H1
Olvera 9,825 D4
Onda 13,012 F3
Onteniente 23,685 F3
Orense 63,542 C1
Orihuela 17,610 F3
Osuna 17,384 D4
Oviedo 130,021 C1
Padul 6,377 E4
Palafrugell 10,421 H2
Palamós 7,679 H2
Palencia 58,327 D2
Palma 191,416 H3
Palma del Río 15,075 D4
Pamplona 142,686 F1
Pego 8,861 F3
Peñafiel 4,794 E2
Peñaranda de Bracamonte 6,094 D2
Peñarroya-Pueblonuevo 15,649 D3
Pinos-Puente 7,634 E4
Plasencia 26,897 C2
Pola de Lena 5,760 D1
Pollensa 7,625 H3
Ponferrada 22,838 C1
Pontevedra 27,118 B1
Porcuna 8,169 D4
Port-Bou 2,230 H1
Portugalete 45,589 E1
Posadas 7,245 D4
Pozoblanco 13,280 D3
Pozuelo de Alarcón 14,041 D2
Priego de Córdoba 12,676 D4
Puente-Genil 22,888 D4
Puertollano 50,609 D3
Puerto Real 13,993 D4
Puigcerdá 4,418 G1
Quesada 6,965 E4
Quintana de la Serena 5,171 D3
Quintanar de la Orden 7,764 E3
Reinosa 10,863 D1
Requena 9,836 F3
Reus 47,240 G2
Ripoll 9,283 H1
Ronda 22,094 D4
Roquetas 5,617 G2
Rosas 5,448 H1
Rota 20,021 C4
Rute 8,294 D4
Sabadell 148,223 H2
Sagunto 17,052 F3
Salamanca 125,132 D2
Sallent 7,118 H2
Salobreña 5,961 E4
Salt 5,572 H1
Sama 9,863 D1
San Carlos de la Rápita 8,946 G2
San Clemente 6,016 E3
San Felíu de Guíxols 12,006 H2
San Fernando 59,309 C4
San Ildefonso 3,198 E2

Agriculture, Industry and Resources

DOMINANT LAND USE

- Cereals (chiefly wheat)
- Livestock (chiefly sheep, goats)
- Mixed Cereals, Livestock
- Olives, Fruit
- Grapes, Fruit, Nuts, Mixed Cereals
- Forests
- Nonagricultural Land

MAJOR MINERAL OCCURRENCES

Ag	Silver	Na	Salt
C	Coal	O	Petroleum
Cu	Copper	Pb	Lead
Fe	Iron Ore	Py	Pyrites
G	Natural Gas	Sb	Antimony
Hg	Mercury	Sn	Tin
K	Potash	U	Uranium
Lg	Lignite	W	Tungsten
Mg	Magnesium	Zn	Zinc

Water Power
Major Industrial Areas

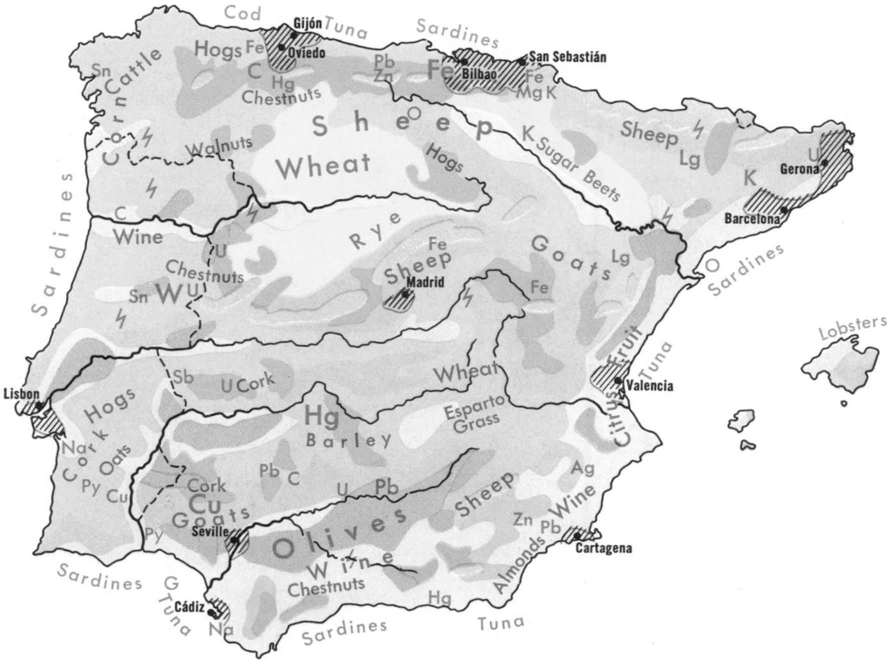

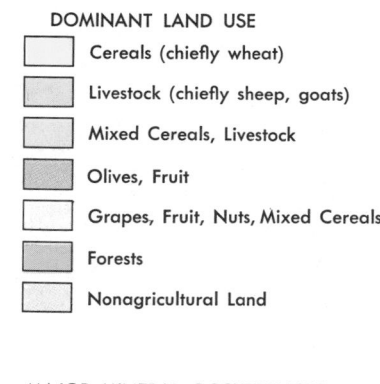

(continued on following page)

(continued)

San Lorenzo de El Escorial 8,098 E2
Sanlúcar de Barrameda 29,483 C4
Sanlúcar la Mayor 6,121 C4
San Roque 8,224 D4
San Sebastián 159,557 E1
Santa Cruz de la Palma 10,393 B4
Santa Cruz de Mudela 6,354 E3
Santa Cruz de Tenerife 74,910 B4
Santa Eugenia 5,946 B1
Santa Fé 8,990 E4
Santander 130,019 D1
Santiago 51,620 B1
Santo Domingo de la Calzada 5,638 E1
Santoña 9,546 E1
San Vicente de Alcántara 7,006 C3
Saragossa 449,319 F2
Saragossa‡ 500,000 F2
Segorbe 6,962 F3
Segovia 41,880 D2
Seo de Urgel 6,604 G1
Seville 511,447 D4
Seville‡ 560,000 D4
Sitges 8,906 G2
Socuéllamos 12,610 E3
Sóller 6,470 H3
Solsona 5,346 G2
Sonseca 6,594 D3
Soria 24,744 E2
Sotrondio 5,914 D1
Sueca 20,019 F3
Tabernes de Valldigna 13,962 G3
Tafalla 8,858 F1
Talavera de la Reina 39,889 D2
Tarancón 8,238 E3
Tarazona 11,067 E2
Tarazona de la Mancha 5,952 F3
Tarifa 9,201 D4
Tarragona 53,548 G2
Tarrasa 134,481 G2
Tárrega 9,036 G2
Tauste 6,832 F2
Telde 13,257 B5
Teruel 20,614 F2
Tobarra 5,887 F3
Toledo 43,905 D3
Tolosa 15,164 F1
Tomelloso 26,041 E3
Tordesillas 5,815 D2
Toro 8,455 D2
Torredonjimeno 12,507 D4
Torrejón de Ardoz 21,081 G4
Torrelavega 19,933 D1
Torremolinos 20,484 D4
Torrente 38,397 F3
Torrevieja 9,431 F4
Torrijos 6,362 D2
Torrox 5,583 E4
Tortosa 20,030 G2
Totana 12,714 F4
Trigueros 6,280 C4
Trujillo 9,024 D3
Tudela 20,942 F1
Úbeda 28,306 E3
Ubrique 13,166 D4
Utiel 9,168 F3
Utrera 28,287 D4
Valdemoro 6,263 F4
Valdepeñas 24,018 E3
Valencia 626,675 F3
Valencia‡ 700,000 F3
Valencia de Alcántara 5,963 C3
Valladolid 227,511 D2
Vall de Uxó 23,976 F3
Vallecas G4
Valls 14,189 G2
Valverde del Camino 10,566 C4
Vejer de la Frontera 6,184 C4
Vélez-Málaga 20,794 E4
Vendrell 7,951 G2
Vera 4,903 F4
Vergara 11,541 E1
Vicálvaro G4
Vich 23,449 H2
Vigo 114,526 B1
Vilafranca del Penedés 16,875 G2
Villacañas 9,883 E3
Villacarrillo 9,452 E3
Villafranca de los Barros 12,610 C3
Villagarcía 6,601 B1
Villajoyosa 12,573 F3
Villanueva de Córdoba 11,270 D3
Villanueva del Arzobispo 8,076 E3
Villanueva de la Serena 16,687 D3
Villanueva de los Infantes 8,154 E3
Villanueva y Geltrú 35,714 G2
Villarreal de los Infantes 29,482 G3
Villarrobledo 19,698 E3
Villarrubia de los Ojos 9,144 E3
Villaverde F4
Villena 23,483 F3
Vinaroz 13,727 G2
Vitoria 124,791 E1
Yecla 19,352 F3
Zafra 11,583 C3
Zalamea de la Serena 6,017 D3
Zamora 48,791 D2
Zaragoza (Saragossa) 449,319 F2

OTHER FEATURES

Alborán (isl.) E5
Alcaraz, Sierra de (range) E3
Alcudia (bay) H3
Almanzor (mt.) D2
Almanzora (riv.) F4
Andalusia (reg.) C4
Aneto (peak) G1
Aragón (reg.) F2
Arosa, Ria de (est.) B1
Asturias (reg.) C1
Balaitous (mt.) F1
Balearic (Baleares) (isls.) H3
Barbate (riv.) D4
Biscay (bay) E1
Cabrera (isl.) H3
Cádiz (gulf) C4
Cala Burras (pt.) D4
Canary (isls.) B4
Cantabrian (range) C1
Catalonia (reg.) G2
Cinca (riv.) G2
Columbretes (isls.) G3
Costa Brava (reg.) H2
Costa de Sola (Costa del Sol) (reg.) D4
Creus (cape) H1
Cuenca, Sierra de (range) F3
Demanda, Sierra de la (range) E1
Douro (riv.) C2
Duero (Douro) (riv.) C2
Ebro (riv.) G2
Eresma (riv.) D2
Esla (riv.) D2
Estats (peak) G1
Estremadura (reg.) C3
Finisterre (cape) B1
Formentera (isl.) G3
Formentor (cape) H2
Fuerteventura (isl.) C4
Galicia (reg.) B1
Gata (cape) F4
Gata (mts.) C2
Genil (riv.) D4
Gibraltar (str.) D5
Gomera (isl.) B5
Gran Canaria (isl.) B5
Gredos, Sierra de (range) D2
Guadalimar (riv.) E3
Guadalquivir (riv.) C4
Guadarrama, Sierra de (range) E2
Guadarrama (riv.) F4
Guadiana (riv.) D3
Gúdar, Sierra de (range) F2
Henares (riv.) G4
Hierro (isl.) A5
Ibiza (isl.) G3
Jalón (riv.) E2
Jarama (riv.) E2
Júcar (riv.) F3
Lanzarote (isl.) C4
La Palma (isl.) A4
León (reg.) C1
Llobregat (riv.) H2
Majorca (isl.) H3
Mallorca (Majorca) (isl.) H3
Mancha, La (reg.) E3
Manzanares (riv.) F4
Marismas, Las (marsh) C4
Mar Menor (lag.) F4
Mayor (cape) E1
Menorca (Minorca) (isl.) J2
Miño (riv.) B1
Minorca (isl.) J2
Moncayo, Sierra de (range) F2
Montserrat (mt.) G2
Morena, Sierra (range) E3
Mulhacén (mt.) E4
Murcia (reg.) F3
Nao (cape) G3
Navia (riv.) C1
Nevada, Sierra (mts.) E4
New Castile (reg.) E3
Odiel (riv.) C4
Old Castile (reg.) D2
Órbigo (riv.) D1
Palos (cape) F4
Peñalara (mt.) E2
Peñas (cape) D1
Peña Vieja (mt.) D1
Penibética, Sistema (range) E4
Perdido (mt.) G1
Pyrenees (range) F1
Rosas (gulf) H1
San Jorge (gulf) G2
Segre (riv.) G2
Segura (riv.) F3
Sil (riv.) C1
Tagus (riv.) D3
Tajo (Tagus) (riv.) D3
Teide, Pico de (peak) B5
Tenerife (isl.) B5
Ter (riv.) H1
Tinto (riv.) C4
Toledo (mts.) E3
Tortosa (cape) G2
Trafalgar (cape) C4
Turia (riv.) F3
Ulla (riv.) B1
Urgel, Llanos de (plain) G2
Valencia (gulf) G3
Valencia (reg.) F3
Valencia, Albufera de (lag.) G3
Vascongadas (reg.) E1

PORTUGAL

DISTRICTS

Aveiro 545,230 B2
Beja 204,440 C3
Braga 609,415 B2
Bragança 180,395 C2
Castelo Branco 254,355 C3
Çoimbra 399,380 B2
Évora 178,475 C3
Faro 268,040 B4
Guarda 210,720 C2
Leiria 376,940 B3
Lisbon 1,568,020 A1
Oporto (Porto) 1,309,560 B2
Portalegre 145,545 C3
Porto 1,309,560 B2
Santarém 427,995 B3
Sétubal 469,555 B3
Viano do Castelo 250,510 B2
Vila Real 265,605 C2
Viseu 410,795 C2

CITIES and TOWNS

Abrantes 11,775 B3
Águeda 9,343 B2
Albufeira 7,479 B4
Alcácer do Sal 13,187 B3
Alcântara 23,699 A1

Topography

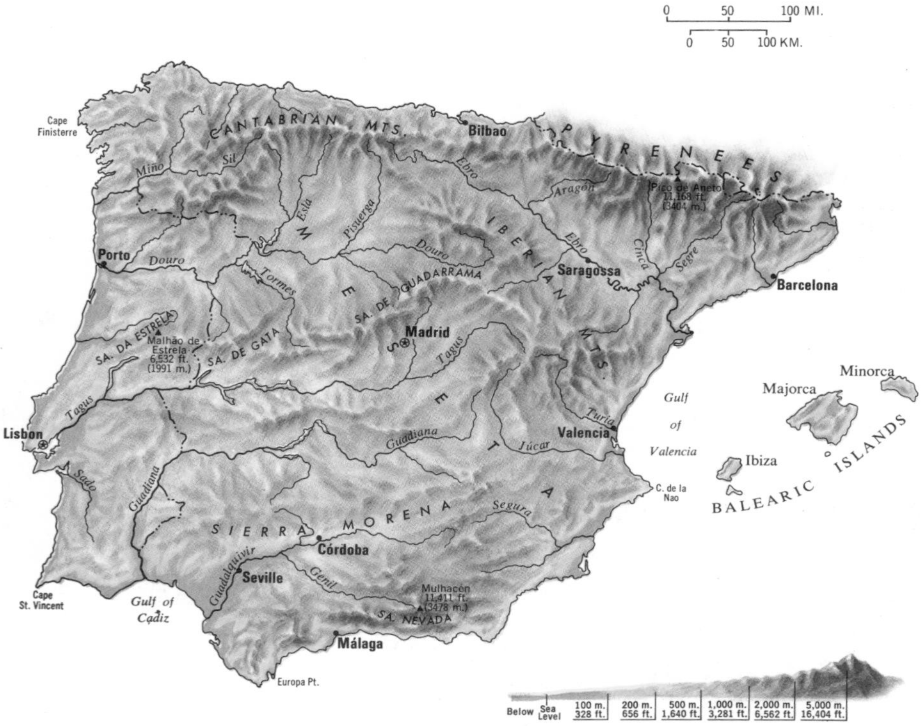

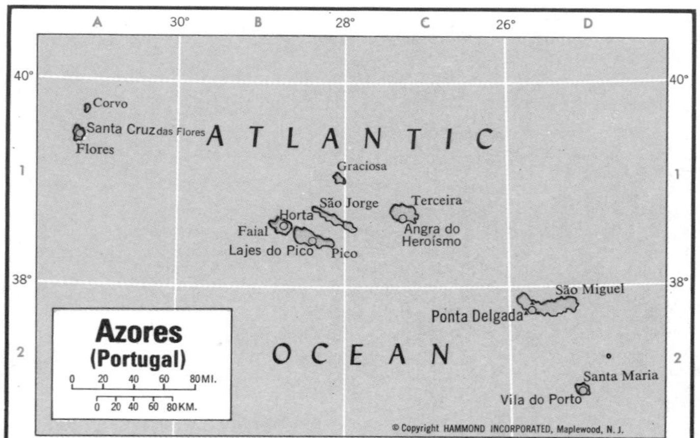

AZORES

INTERNAL DIVISIONS

Angra do Heroísmo (dist.) 83,500 C1
Horta (dist.) 38,700 A1
Ponta Delgada (dist.) 153,700 D2

CITIES and TOWNS

Angra do Heroísmo 13,795 C1
Horta 6,145 B1
Lajes do Pico 2,147 B1
Ponta Delgada 20,195 C2
Santa Cruz das Flores 1,880 A1
Vila do Porto 4,149 D2

OTHER FEATURES

Azores (isls.) A2
Corvo (isl.) A1
Faial (isl.) B1
Flores (isl.) A1
Graciosa (isl.) C1
Pico (isl.) C1
Santa Maria (isl.) D2
São Jorge (isl.) B1
São Miguel (isl.) D2
Terceira (isl.) C1

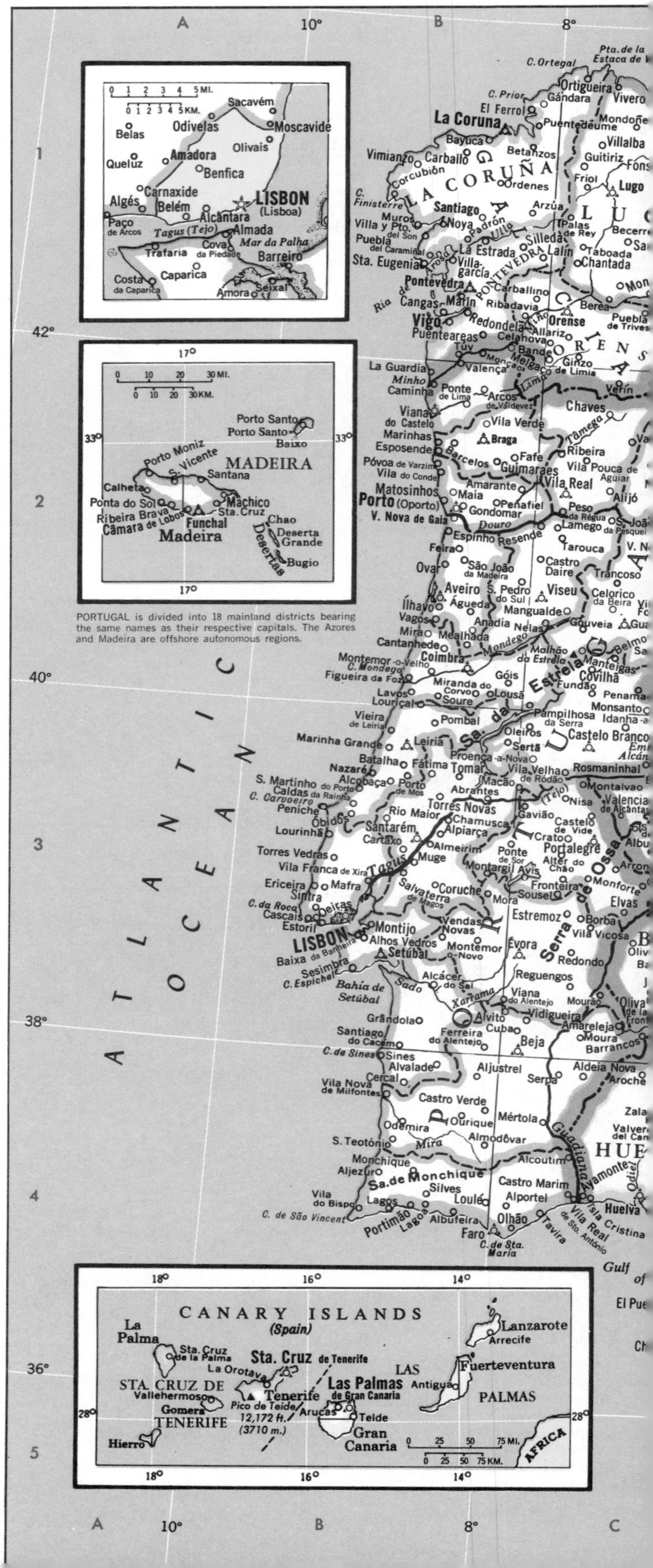

Alcobaça 4,799 ... B3
Aldeia Nova de São Bento 5,228 ... C4
Algés 18,010 ... A1
Alhos Vedros 7,915 ... B3
Aljustrel 7,473 ... B4
Almada 38,990 ... A1
Almeirim 8,780 ... B3
Alpiarça 7,623 ... B3
Alportel 7,632 ... C4
Amadora 65,870 ... A1
Amarante 6,067 ... B2
Amora 10,330 ... A1
Aveiro 19,905 ... B2
Avis 1,686 ... C3
Baixa da Banheira 18,550 ... B3
Barreiro 53,690 ... B1
Batalha 6,673 ... B3
Beja 14,760 ... C3
Belas 12,001 ... A1
Belém 19,043 ... A1
Benfica 39,459 ... A1
Borba 4,879 ... C3
Braga 48,735 ... B2
Bragança 9,310 ... C2
Caldas da Rainha 13,070 ... B3
Câmara de Lobos 14,068 ... A2
Campo Maior 7,405 ... C3
Cantanhede 6,734 ... B2
Caparica 13,315 ... A1
Carnaxide 38,309 ... A1
Cartaxo 6,628 ... B3
Cascais 14,925 ... B3
Castelo Branco 18,740 ... C3
Cercal 5,021 ... B4
Chaves 11,465 ... C2
Coimbra 55,985 ... B2
Coruche 17,461 ... B3
Cova da Piedade 21,000 ... A1
Covilhã 26,530 ... C2
Elvas 10,305 ... C3
Espinho 11,745 ... B2
Estoril 15,740 ... B3
Estremoz 9,565 ... C3
Évora 23,665 ... C3
Fafe 8,142 ... B2
Faro 20,470 ... B4
Fátima 6,433 ... B3
Feira 5,222 ... B2
Ferreira do Alentejo 6,153 ... B3
Figueira da Foz 10,485 ... B2
Funchal 38,340 ... A2
Fundão 5,081 ... C2
Gondomar 14,105 ... B2
Grândola 9,698 ... B3
Guarda 9,735 ... C2
Guimarães 24,280 ... B2
Ílhavo 11,083 ... B2
Lagoa 5,694 ... B4
Lagos 10,359 ... B4
Lamego 10,350 ... C2
Lavos 5,051 ... B2
Leiria 7,540 ... B3
Lisbon (Lisboa) (cap.) 769,410 ... A1
Lisbon‡ 1,100,000 ... A1
Loulé 12,777 ... B4
Louriçal 6,087 ... B3
Lourinhã 7,340 ... B3
Lousã 7,341 ... B2
Machico 10,905 ... A2
Mafra 7,149 ... B3
Mangualde 4,839 ... C2
Marinha Grande 18,548 ... B3
Matosinhos 22,505 ... B2
Mira 12,740 ... B2
Mirandela 5,203 ... C2
Monchique 8,155 ... B4
Montargil 5,070 ... B3
Montemor-o-Novo 9,284 ... B3
Montijo 26,730 ... B3
Moscavide 21,765 ... A1
Moura 9,351 ... C3
Nazaré 8,553 ... B3
Odemira 6,793 ... B4
Odivelas 26,020 ... A1
Oeiras 14,880 ... B3
Olhão 11,155 ... C4
Olivais 55,138 ... A1
Oporto (Porto) 300,925 ... B2
Ovar 16,004 ... B2
Paço de Arcos 11,791 ... A1
Penafiel 6,463 ... B2
Peniche 12,555 ... B3
Peso da Régua 5,376 ... C2
Pombal 12,508 ... B3
Ponta do Sol 5,599 ... A2
Ponte de Sor 9,951 ... C3
Portalegre 10,970 ... C3
Portimão 10,300 ... B4
Porto 300,925 ... B2
Póvoa de Varzim 17,415 ... B2
Proença-a-Nova 4,792 ... B3
Queluz 25,845 ... A1
Redondo 6,858 ... C3
Reguengos de Monsaraz 5,806 ... C3
Ribeira Brava 7,416 ... A2
Rio Maior 10,206 ... B3
Sacavém 12,625 ... A1
Salvaterra de Magos 6,265 ... B3
Santa Cruz 6,348 ... A2
Santarém 16,850 ... B3
Santiago do Cacem 5,887 ... B3
São Brás de Alportel (Alportel) 7,632 ... C4
São João da Madeira 14,225 ... B2
São Teotónio 6,146 ... B4
São Vicente 5,147 ... A2
Serpa 7,991 ... C4
Sertã 6,043 ... B3
Sesimbra 16,614 ... B3
Setúbal 49,670 ... B3
Silves 9,493 ... B4
Sines 6,996 ... B4
Sintra 15,994 ... B3
Soure 7,620 ... B2
Tavira 10,263 ... C4
Tomar 10,905 ... B3
Torres Novas 13,806 ... B3
Torres Vedras 14,833 ... B3
Trafaria 6,145 ... A1
Vagos 5,088 ... B2
Vendas Novas 8,979 ... B3
Viana do Castelo 12,510 ... B2
Vila do Conde 16,485 ... B2
Vila Franca de Xira 13,070 ... B3
Vila Nova de Gaia Gaia 50,805 ... B2
Vila Real Real 10,050 ... C2
Vila Real de Santo Antonio 10,320 ... C4
Viseu 16,140 ... C2

OTHER FEATURES

Atlantic Ocean ... A3
Carvoeiroeiro (cape) ... B3
Desertasrtas (isls.) ... A2
Douro (riv.) ... B2
Espichel (cape) ... B3
Estrela, Serra da (mts.) ... C2
Guadiana (riv.) ... C4
Lima (riv.) ... B2
Madeira (isl.) ...
Madeira (isls.) ... A2
Minho (riv.) ... B2
Mira (riv.) ... B4
Monchique, Serra de (mts.) ... B4
Mondego (riv.) ... B2
Monsanto (mt.) ... A1
Ossa, Serra da (mts.) ... C3
Palha, Mar da (bay) ... A1
Porto Santo (isl.) ... B2
Roca (cape) ... B3
Sado (riv.) ... B3
São Vincent (cape) ... B4
Santa María (cape) ... C4
Setúbal (bay) ... B3
Tagus (riv.) ... B3
Tâmega (riv.) ... C2
Tejo (Tagus) (riv.) ... B3
Xarrama (riv.) ... B3

ANDORRA

CITIES and TOWNS

Andorra la Vella (cap.) 12,000 ... G1

GIBRALTAR

Gibraltar 29,760 ... D4

PHYSICAL FEATURES

Europa (pt.) ... D4

‡Population of metropolitan area.

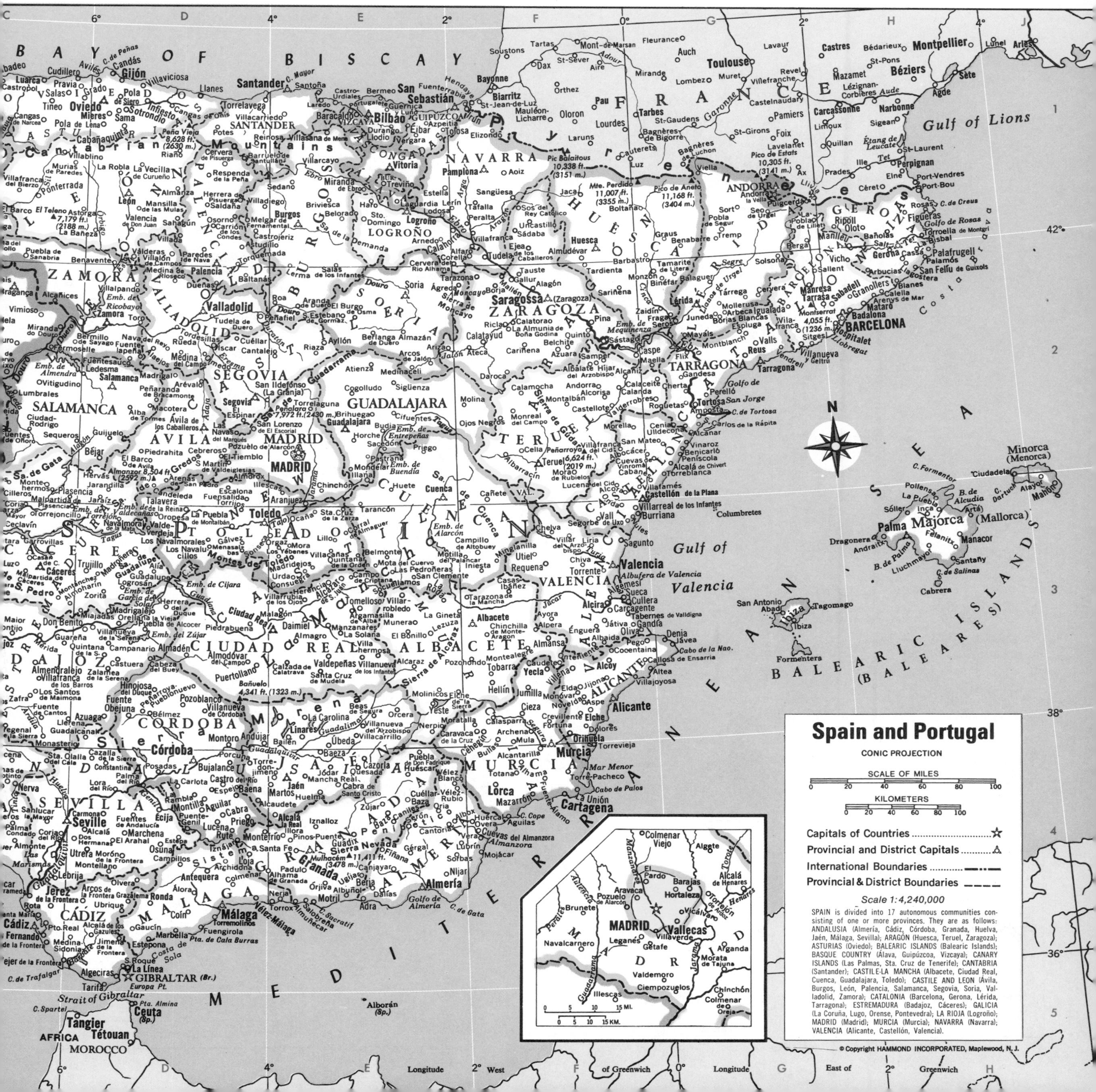

Spain and Portugal
CONIC PROJECTION
SCALE OF MILES
0 20 40 60 80 100
KILOMETERS
0 20 40 60 80 100
Capitals of Countries
Provincial and District Capitals
International Boundaries
Provincial & District Boundaries
Scale 1:4,240,000
SPAIN is divided into 17 autonomous communities consisting of one or more provinces. They are as follows: ANDALUSIA (Almería, Cádiz, Córdoba, Granada, Huelva, Jaén, Málaga, Sevilla); ARAGÓN (Huesca, Teruel, Zaragoza); ASTURIAS (Oviedo); BALEARIC ISLANDS (Balearic Islands); BASQUE COUNTRY (Álava, Guipúzcoa, Vizcaya); CANARY ISLANDS (Las Palmas, Sta. Cruz de Tenerife); CANTABRIA (Santander); CASTILE-LA MANCHA (Albacete, Ciudad Real, Cuenca, Guadalajara, Toledo); CASTILE AND LEON (Ávila, Burgos, León, Palencia, Salamanca, Segovia, Soria, Valladolid, Zamora); CATALONIA (Barcelona, Gerona, Lérida, Tarragona); ESTREMADURA (Badajoz, Cáceres); GALICIA (La Coruña, Lugo, Orense, Pontevedra); LA RIOJA (Logroño); MADRID (Madrid); MURCIA (Murcia); NAVARRA (Navarra); VALENCIA (Alicante, Castellón, Valencia).
© Copyright HAMMOND INCORPORATED, Maplewood, N.J.

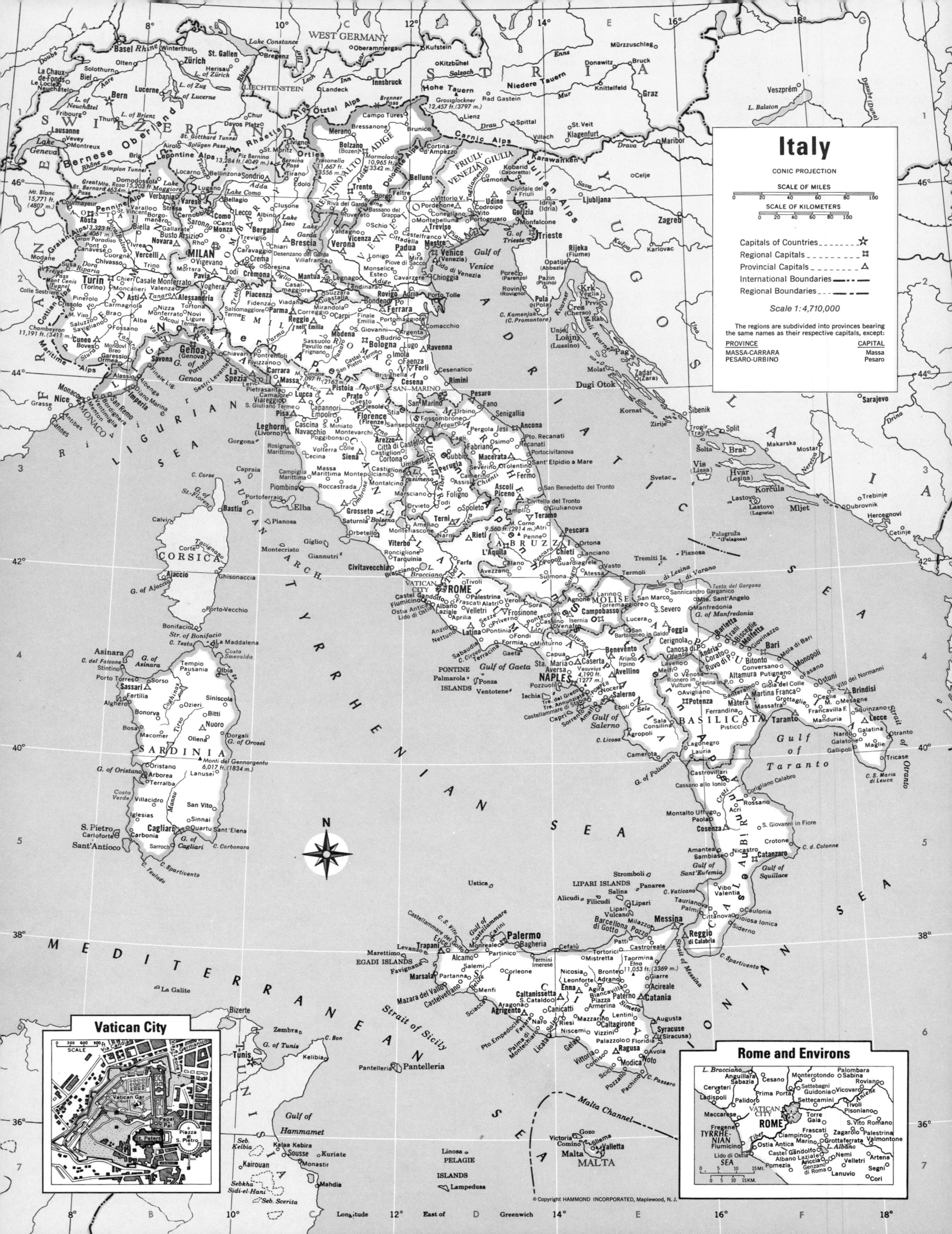

Italy
CONIC PROJECTION
SCALE OF MILES
0 20 40 60 80 100
SCALE OF KILOMETERS
0 20 40 60 80 100
Capitals of Countries
Regional Capitals
Provincial Capitals
International Boundaries
Regional Boundaries
Scale 1:4,710,000
The regions are subdivided into provinces bearing the same names as their respective capitals, except:
PROVINCE
CAPITAL
MASSA-CARRARA
Massa
PESARO-URBINO
Pesaro
Vatican City
Rome and Environs
SWITZERLAND
AUSTRIA
WEST GERMANY
LIECHTENSTEIN
YUGOSLAVIA
FRANCE
MONACO
SAN MARINO
VATICAN CITY
MALTA
TUNISIA
CORSICA
SARDINIA
SICILY
LIGURIAN SEA
TYRRHENIAN SEA
ADRIATIC SEA
IONIAN SEA
MEDITERRANEAN SEA
Gulf of Taranto
Strait of Sicily
Malta Channel
ROME
MILAN
NAPLES
Turin
Genoa
Venice
Florence
Bologna
Palermo
Bari
Longitude East of Greenwich
© Copyright HAMMOND INCORPORATED, Maplewood, N. J.

VATICAN CITY

AREA 108.7 acres (44 hectares)
POPULATION 728

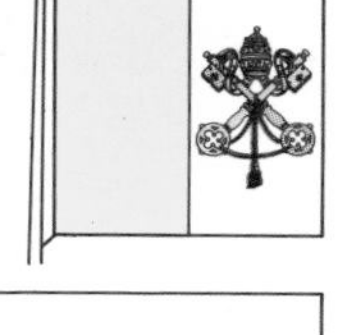

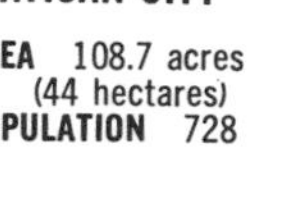

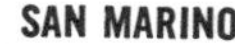

SAN MARINO

AREA 23.4 sq. mi. (60.6 sq. km.)
POPULATION 19,149

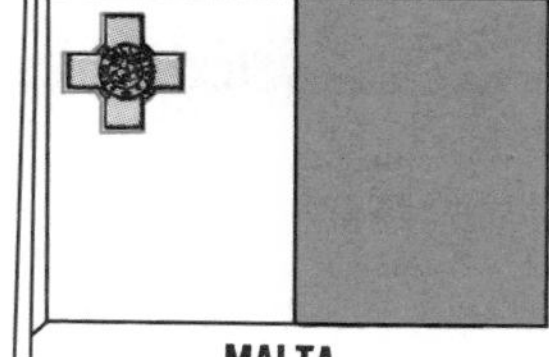

MALTA

AREA 122 sq. mi. (316 sq. km.)
POPULATION 343,970
CAPITAL Valletta
LARGEST CITY Sliema
HIGHEST POINT 787 ft. (240 m.)
MONETARY UNIT Maltese pound
MAJOR LANGUAGES Maltese, English
MAJOR RELIGION Roman Catholicism

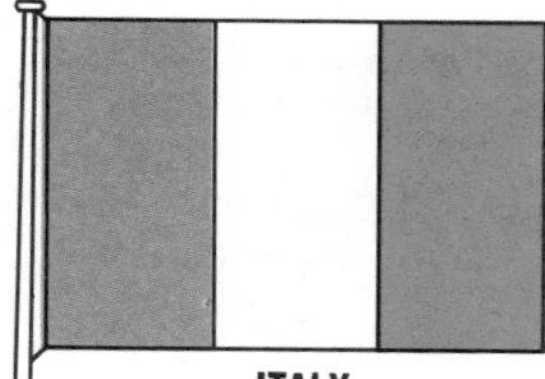

ITALY

AREA 116,303 sq. mi. (301,225 sq. km.)
POPULATION 57,140,000
CAPITAL Rome
LARGEST CITY Rome
HIGHEST POINT Dufourspitze (Mte. Rosa) 15,203 ft. (4,634 m.)
MONETARY UNIT lira
MAJOR LANGUAGE Italian
MAJOR RELIGION Roman Catholicism

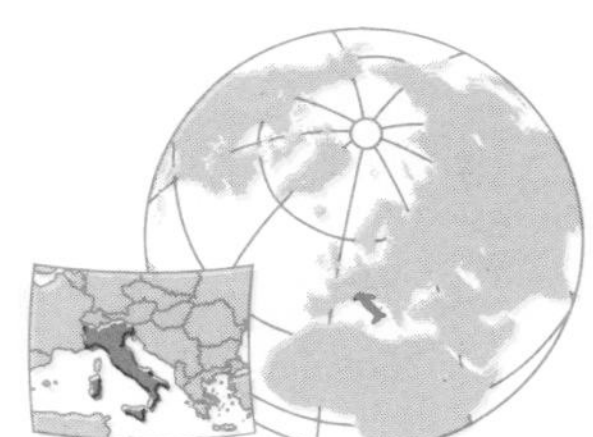

ITALY

REGIONS

Abruzzi 1,166,664 .... D3
Aosta 109,150 .... A2
Apulia (Puglia) 3,582,787 .... F4
Basilicata 603,064 .... F4
Calabria 1,988,051 .... F5
Campania 5,059,348 .... E4
Emilia-Romagna 3,846,755 .... C2
Friuli-Venezia Giulia 1,213,532 .... D1
Latium (Lazio) 4,689,482 .... D3
Liguria 1,853,578 .... B2
Lombardy 8,543,657 .... B2
Marche 1,359,907 .... D3
Molise 319,807 .... E4
Piedmont 4,432,313 .... A2
Sardinia 1,473,800 .... B4
Sicily 4,680,715 .... D6
Trentino-Alto Adige 841,886 .... C1
Tuscany 3,473,097 .... C3
Umbria 775,783 .... D3
Veneto 2,109,502 .... D3

PROVINCES

Agrigento 454,045 .... D6
Alessandria 483,183 .... B2
Ancona 416,611 .... D3
Aosta 109,150 .... A2
Arezzo 306,340 .... C3
Ascoli Piceno 340,758 .... D3
Asti 218,547 .... B2
Avellino 427,509 .... E4
Bari 1,351,288 .... F4
Belluno 221,155 .... D1
Benevento 286,499 .... E4
Bergamo 829,019 .... B2
Bologna 918,844 .... C2
Bolzano-Bozen 414,041 .... C1
Brescia 957,686 .... C2
Brindisi 366,027 .... G4
Cagliari 802,888 .... B5
Caltanissetta 282,069 .... D6
Campobasso 227,641 .... E4
Caserta 677,959 .... E4
Catania 938,273 .... E6
Catanzaro 718,069 .... F5
Chieti 351,567 .... E3
Como 720,463 .... B2
Cosenza 691,659 .... F5
Cremona 334,281 .... B2
Cuneo 540,504 .... A2
Enna 202,131 .... E6
Ferrara 383,639 .... C2
Florence 1,146,367 .... C3
Foggia 657,292 .... E4
Forlì 565,470 .... D2
Frosinone 422,630 .... D4
Genoa 1,087,973 .... B2
Gorizia 142,412 .... D2
Grosseto 216,315 .... C3
Imperia 225,127 .... B3
Isernia 92,166 .... E4
L'Aquila 293,066 .... D3
La Spezia 244,435 .... B2
Latina 376,238 .... D4
Lecce 696,503 .... G4
Leghorn 335,265 .... C3
Lucca 380,356 .... C3
Macerata 286,155 .... D3
Mantua 376,892 .... C2
Massa-Carrara 200,955 .... C2
Matera 194,629 .... F4
Messina 654,703 .... E5
Milan 3,903,685 .... B2
Modena 553,852 .... C2
Naples 2,709,929 .... E4
Novara 496,811 .... B2
Nuoro 273,021 .... B4
Padua 762,998 .... C2
Palermo 1,124,015 .... D5
Parma 395,497 .... C2
Pavia 526,389 .... B2
Perugia 552,936 .... D3
Pesaro e Urbino 316,383 .... D3
Pescara 264,981 .... E3
Piacenza 284,881 .... B2
Pisa 375,933 .... C3
Pistoia 254,335 .... C2
Pordenone 253,906 .... D2
Potenza 408,435 .... E4
Ragusa 255,047 .... E6
Ravenna 351,876 .... D2
Reggio di Calabria 578,323 .... E5
Reggio nell'Emilia 392,696 .... C2
Rieti 143,162 .... D3
Rome 3,490,377 .... F6
Rovigo 251,908 .... C2
Salerno 957,452 .... E4
Sassari 397,891 .... B4
Savona 296,043 .... B2
Siena 257,221 .... C3
Sondrio 169,149 .... B1
Syracuse 365,039 .... E6
Taranto 511,677 .... F4
Teramo 257,080 .... D3
Terni 222,847 .... D3
Trapani 405,393 .... D5
Trento 427,845 .... C1
Treviso 668,620 .... D2
Trieste 300,304 .... E2
Turin 2,287,016 .... A2
Udine 516,910 .... D1
Varese 725,823 .... B2
Venice 807,251 .... D2
Vercelli 406,252 .... B2
Verona 733,595 .... C2
Vicenza 677,884 .... C2
Viterbo 257,075 .... C3

CITIES and TOWNS

Acireale 34,081 .... E6
Acqui Terme 20,099 .... B2
Acri 8,150 .... F5
Adrano 31,988 .... E6
Adria 11,951 .... D2
Agira 11,262 .... E6
Agnone 3,965 .... E4
Agrigento 40,513 .... D6
Agropoli 9,413 .... E4
Alassio 13,512 .... A2
Alatri 5,710 .... D4
Alba 23,522 .... B2
Albano Laziale 15,561 .... F7
Albenga 13,397 .... B3
Albino 8,837 .... B2
Alcamo 41,448 .... D6
Alessandria 78,644 .... B2
Alghero 28,454 .... B4
Altamura 44,879 .... F4
Amalfi 4,205 .... E4
Amantea 6,132 .... E5
Amelia 4,331 .... D3
Ancona 88,427 .... D3
Andria 76,405 .... F4
Anguillara Sabazia 3,241 .... F6
Anzio 14,966 .... D4
Aosta 35,053 .... A2
Aprilia 18,412 .... D4
Aragona 11,213 .... D6
Arezzo 56,693 .... C3
Argenta 6,682 .... D2
Ariano Irpino 9,796 .... E4
Ariccia 7,287 .... F7
Artena 5,034 .... F7
Ascoli Piceno 43,041 .... D3
Assisi 4,630 .... D3
Asti 62,277 .... B2
Atessa 3,079 .... E3
Atri 4,686 .... D3
Augusta 32,501 .... E6
Avellino 44,750 .... E4
Aversa 46,536 .... E4
Avezzano 26,456 .... D3
Avigliano 5,400 .... E4
Avola 29,089 .... E6
Bagheria 32,465 .... D5
Barcellona Pozzo di Gotto 25,280 .... E5
Bari 339,110 .... F4
Barletta 75,116 .... F4
Bassano del Grappa 33,002 .... C2
Bellagio 3,258 .... B2
Belluno 22,180 .... D1
Benevento 48,523 .... E4
Bergamo 127,553 .... B2
Biancavilla 18,743 .... E6
Biella 46,453 .... B2
Bisceglie 45,014 .... F4
Bitonto 39,714 .... F4
Bitti 4,606 .... B4
Bologna 493,282 .... C2
Bolzano (Bolzen) 102,806 .... C1
Bondeno 7,451 .... C2
Bonorva 5,232 .... B4
Bordighera 8,994 .... A3
Borgo 4,013 .... C1
Borgomanero 16,655 .... B2
Borgo San Lorenzo 7,699 .... C2
Bosa 8,045 .... B4
Boves 3,896 .... A2
Bra 18,399 .... A2
Bracciano 7,681 .... C3
Brescia 189,092 .... C2
Bressanone 12,261 .... C1
Brindisi 76,612 .... G4
Bronte 17,823 .... E6
Brunico 5,175 .... D1
Budrio 5,635 .... C2
Busto Arsizio 72,400 .... B2
Cagli 4,356 .... D3
Cagliari 211,015 .... B5
Caltagirone 34,444 .... E6
Caltanissetta 52,838 .... D6
Camaiore 8,578 .... C3
Camerino 4,644 .... D3
Campobasso 35,551 .... E4
Campo Tures 1,325 .... C1
Canicattì 28,761 .... E6
Canosa di Puglia 30,263 .... E4
Cantù 28,617 .... B2
Capua 13,938 .... E4
Caravaggio 11,298 .... B2
Carbonia 23,031 .... B5
Carini 14,255 .... D5
Carloforte 6,671 .... B5
Carmagnola 16,469 .... A2
Carpi 41,789 .... C2
Carrara 56,236 .... C2
Casale Monferrato 35,156 .... B2
Casalmaggiore 6,374 .... C2
Cascina-Navacchio 28,263 .... C3
Caserta 51,621 .... E4
Cassano allo Ionio 9,661 .... F5
Cassino 14,747 .... D4
Castelfranco Veneto 16,042 .... D2
Castel Gandolfo 2,965 .... F7
Castellammare del Golfo 13,144 .... D5
Castellammare di Stabia 64,341 .... E4
Castel San Pietro Terme 6,985 .... C2
Castelvetrano 29,167 .... D6
Castiglion Fiorentino 3,797 .... C3
Castrovillari 15,207 .... F5
Catania 403,390 .... E6
Catanzaro 52,054 .... F5
Caulonia 3,402 .... F5
Cava de'Tirreni 33,868 .... E4
Cavarzere 7,917 .... D2
Cecina 19,415 .... C3
Cefalù 11,043 .... E5
Ceglie Messapico 17,512 .... F4
Celano 9,531 .... D3
Cerignola 44,648 .... E4
Cernobbio 8,026 .... B2
Cerveteri 5,239 .... E6
Cesano 2,883 .... F6
Cesena 49,915 .... D2
Cesenatico 12,805 .... D2
Chiari 12,017 .... C2
Chiavari 29,950 .... B2
Chieri 27,548 .... A2
Chieti 31,895 .... E3
Chioggia 24,044 .... D2
Chivasso 21,369 .... A2
Ciampino 36,728 .... F7
Cittadella 9,321 .... C2
Città di Castello 18,880 .... C3
Cittanova 11,045 .... F5
Cividale del Friuli 8,345 .... D1
Civitavecchia 41,305 .... C3
Clusone-Fiorine 6,428 .... C2
Codroipo 6,117 .... D2
Colle di Val d'Elsa 8,657 .... C3
Comacchio 10,437 .... D2
Comiso 24,508 .... E6
Como 73,257 .... B2
Conegliano 28,635 .... D2
Conversano 16,805 .... F4
Corato 38,163 .... F4
Cori 6,829 .... F7
Corigliano Calabro 14,518 .... F5
Corleone 11,057 .... D6
Correggio 11,415 .... C2
Cortina d'Ampezzo 7,285 .... D1
Cortona 3,482 .... C3
Cosenza 94,565 .... F5
Courmayeur 1,401 .... A2
Crema 26,061 .... B2
Cremona 75,988 .... B2
Crotone 44,081 .... F5
Cuneo 41,633 .... A2
Cuorgnè 6,752 .... A2
Desenzano del Garda 14,624 .... C2
Diano Marina 6,001 .... B3
Domodossola 18,562 .... A1
Dorgali 6,714 .... B4
Eboli 19,787 .... E4
Edolo 3,707 .... C1
Empoli 30,526 .... C3
Enna 27,351 .... E6
Este 12,992 .... C2
Fabriano 18,355 .... D3
Faenza 36,241 .... D2
Fano 31,238 .... D3
Fasano 21,247 .... F4
Favara 27,940 .... D6
Feltre 11,806 .... C1
Fermo 17,521 .... D3
Ferrandina 8,372 .... F4
Ferrara 97,507 .... C2
Fidenza 18,064 .... B2
Fiesole 3,772 .... C3
Finale Emilia 7,474 .... C2
Finale Ligure 11,461 .... B2
Firenze (Florence) 441,654 .... C3
Fiumicino 13,180 .... F7
Florence 441,654 .... C3
Floridia 16,562 .... E6
Foggia 136,436 .... E4
Foligno 26,887 .... D3
Fondi 16,472 .... D4
Forlì 83,303 .... D2
Formia 18,978 .... D4
Fossano 15,857 .... A2
Fossombrone 5,882 .... D3
Francavilla Fontana 30,347 .... F4
Frascati 14,217 .... F7
Frosinone 34,066 .... D4
Gaeta 21,973 .... D4
Galatina 22,137 .... G4
Galatone 13,880 .... F4
Gallarate 43,773 .... B2
Gallipoli 16,878 .... F4
Garessio 3,359 .... A2
Gela 66,845 .... E6
Gemona 6,863 .... D1
Genoa 787,011 .... B2
Genova (Genoa) 787,011 .... B2
Genzano di Roma 14,147 .... F7
Giarre 18,233 .... E6
Gioia del Colle 23,299 .... F4
Gioiosa Ionica 3,811 .... F5
Giovinazzo 17,768 .... F4
Giulianova 17,926 .... E3
Gorizia 35,912 .... D2
Gravina in Puglia 32,006 .... F4
Grosseto 48,309 .... C3
Grottaferrata 10,639 .... F7
Grottaglie 23,556 .... F4
Guardiagrele 4,122 .... E3
Guastalla 7,639 .... C2
Gubbio 12,371 .... D3
Guidonia 8,413 .... F6
Iglesias 24,472 .... B5
Imola 42,111 .... C2
Imperia 37,585 .... B3
Isernia 12,290 .... E4
Ivrea 26,530 .... B2
Jesi 33,011 .... D3
Ladispoli 6,625 .... E6
Lagonegro 5,613 .... E4
La Maddalena 10,405 .... B4
Lanciano 19,652 .... E3
Lanusei 5,508 .... B5
Lanuvio 2,970 .... F7
L'Aquila 36,233 .... D3
Larino 5,166 .... E4
La Spezia 121,254 .... B2
Latina 53,003 .... D4
Lauria 4,927 .... E4
Lavello 11,486 .... E4
Lecce 80,114 .... G4
Lecco 53,165 .... B2
Leghorn 170,369 .... C3
Legnago 15,534 .... C2
Lendinara 7,079 .... C2
Lentini 31,429 .... E6
Leonforte 16,317 .... E6
Lerici 5,407 .... B2
Licata 40,997 .... D6
Lido di Ostia 61,492 .... F7
Lido di Venezia 18,794 .... D2
Lipari 3,886 .... E5
Livigno 2,135 .... C1
Livorno (Leghorn) 170,369 .... C3
Lodi 42,489 .... B2
Lonigo 6,368 .... C2
Lucca 54,280 .... C3
Lucera 29,355 .... E4
Lugo 19,497 .... D2
Macerata 33,470 .... D3
Macomer 9,433 .... B4
Maglie 13,326 .... G4
Manduria 25,194 .... F4
Manfredonia 44,463 .... F4
Mantua 59,529 .... C2
Marino 12,135 .... F7
Marsala 34,150 .... D6
Marsciano 5,372 .... D3
Martina Franca 31,811 .... F4
Massa 56,591 .... C2
Massafra 22,610 .... F4
Massa Marittima 6,438 .... C3
Matera 43,026 .... F4
Mazara del Vallo 37,441 .... D6
Mazzarino 14,981 .... E6
Melfi 13,355 .... E4
Menfi 12,386 .... D6
Merano 30,951 .... C1
Mesagne 26,955 .... G4
Messina 203,937 .... E5
Mestre 184,818 .... D2
Milan 1,724,557 .... B2
Milazzo 18,576 .... E5
Minturno 2,428 .... D4
Mirandola 11,551 .... C2
Mira Taglio 10,194 .... D2
Mistretta 6,631 .... E6
Modena 149,029 .... C2
Modica 31,074 .... E6
Mola di Bari 23,778 .... F4
Molfetta 63,250 .... F4
Moncalieri 49,953 .... A2
Mondovì Breo 12,524 .... A2
Monfalcone 29,589 .... D2
Monopoli 29,776 .... F4
Monreale 19,348 .... D5
Monselice 9,047 .... C2
Montalto Uffugo 3,173 .... E5
Montebelluna 9,573 .... D2
Montefiascone 6,885 .... D3
Montepulciano 4,069 .... C3
Monterotondo 15,869 .... F6
Monte Sant'Angelo 17,756 .... F4
Montevarchi 16,849 .... C3
Monza 110,735 .... B2
Mortara 13,929 .... B2
Naples 1,214,775 .... E4
Nardò 24,142 .... F4
Narni 6,213 .... D3
Naro 13,171 .... D6
Nettuno 20,927 .... D4
Nicastro 27,206 .... F5
Nicosia 13,982 .... E6
Niscemi 23,925 .... E6
Nizza Monferrato 7,532 .... B2
Nocera Inferiore 44,415 .... E4
Noto 21,606 .... E6
Novara 92,634 .... B2
Novi Ligure 29,944 .... B2
Nuoro 30,551 .... B4
Olbia 20,998 .... B4
Oliena 7,030 .... B4
Orbetello 6,884 .... C3
Oristano 20,966 .... B5
Ortona 11,966 .... E3
Orvieto 8,813 .... D3
Osimo 12,034 .... D3
Ostia Antica 2,583 .... F7
Ostuni 27,241 .... F4
Otranto 3,707 .... G4
Ozieri 9,149 .... B4
Pachino 20,427 .... E6
Padua 210,950 .... C2
Palazzolo Acreide 8,981 .... E6
Palermo 556,374 .... D5
Palestrina 9,239 .... F7
Palma di Montechiaro 22,381 .... D6
Palmi 14,405 .... E5
Palombara Sabina 5,292 .... F6
Pantelleria 3,116 .... C6
Paola 11,330 .... E5
Parma 151,967 .... C2
Partanna 10,303 .... D6
Partinico 25,447 .... D6
Paterno 41,504 .... E6
Patti 7,500 .... E5
Pavia 80,639 .... B2
Pavullo nel Frignano 5,026 .... C2
Penne 5,889 .... D3
Pergine Valsugana 6,248 .... C1
Pergola 3,866 .... D3
Perugia 65,975 .... D3
Pesaro 72,104 .... D3
Pescara 125,391 .... E3
Pescia 9,918 .... C3
Piacenza 100,001 .... B2
Piazza Armerina 21,754 .... E6
Pietrasanta 6,620 .... B3
Pinerolo 33,935 .... A2
Piombino 35,641 .... C3
Piove di Sacco 7,035 .... C2
Pisa 91,156 .... C3
Pisticci 11,239 .... F4
Pistoia 55,403 .... C2
Poggibonsi 21,271 .... C3
Pomezia 11,915 .... F7
Pont Canavese 4,075 .... A2
Pontecorvo 5,986 .... D4
Pontinia 3,166 .... D4
Pontremoli 5,222 .... B2
Popoli 5,372 .... E3
Pordenone 43,230 .... D2
Portocivitanova 25,773 .... D3
Porto Empedocle 15,986 .... D6
Portoferraio 7,579 .... C3
Portofino 720 .... B2
Portogruaro 12,258 .... D2
Portomaggiore 6,343 .... C2
Porto Recanati 5,389 .... D3
Porto Torres 15,422 .... B4
Potenza 46,869 .... E4
Pozzallo 12,199 .... E6
Pozzuoli 53,546 .... D4
Prato 108,385 .... C3
Prima Porta 11,393 .... F6
Priverno 9,950 .... D4
Putignano 19,290 .... F4
Quartu Sant'Elena 29,715 .... B5
Ragusa 55,751 .... E6
Rapallo 22,272 .... B2
Ravenna 75,153 .... D2
Recanati 10,176 .... D3
Reggio di Calabria 110,291 .... E5
Reggio nell'Emilia 102,337 .... C2
Rho 39,206 .... B2
Riesi 15,855 .... E6
Rieti 26,775 .... D3
Rimini 101,579 .... D2
Rionero in Vulture 11,230 .... E4
Riva del Garda 8,513 .... C2
Roccastrada 2,629 .... C3
Rome (cap.) 2,535,018 .... F6
Ronciglione 5,900 .... C3
Rossano 12,119 .... F5
Rovereto 26,827 .... C2
Rovigo 31,124 .... C2
Ruvo di Puglia 23,133 .... F4

(continued on following page)

Topography

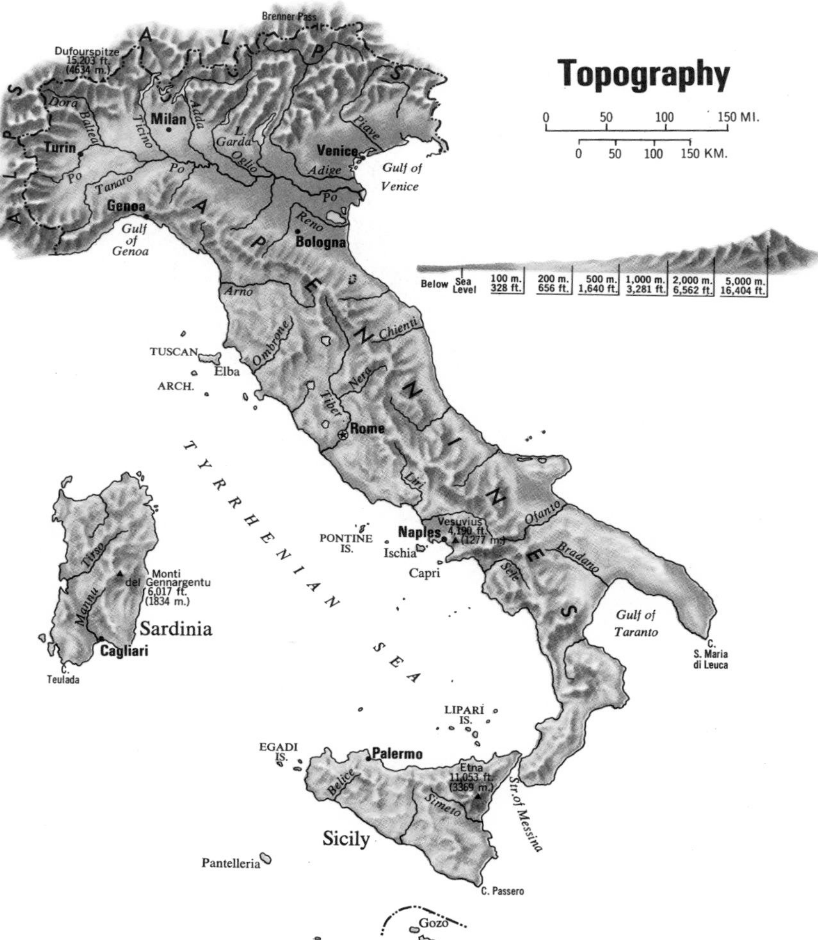
Brenner Pass
Dufourspitze 15,203 ft. (4634 m.)
ALPS
Milan
Turin
Venice
Gulf of Venice
Genoa
Gulf of Genoa
Bologna
APENNINES
Po
Adige
Reno
Arno
Tiber
Rome
TUSCAN ARCH.
Elba
TYRRHENIAN SEA
PONTINE IS.
Naples
Vesuvius 4,190 ft. (1277 m.)
Ischia
Capri
Gulf of Taranto
C. S. Maria di Leuca
Monti del Gennargentu 6,017 ft. (1834 m.)
Sardinia
Cagliari
C. Teulada
LIPARI IS.
EGADI IS.
Palermo
Etna 11,053 ft. (3369 m.)
Str. of Messina
Sicily
Pantelleria
C. Passero
Gozo
Malta
Lampedusa
0 50 100 150 MI.
0 50 100 150 KM.
Below Sea Level
100 m. 328 ft.
200 m. 656 ft.
500 m. 1,640 ft.
1,000 m. 3,281 ft.
2,000 m. 6,562 ft.
5,000 m. 16,404 ft.

Agriculture, Industry and Resources

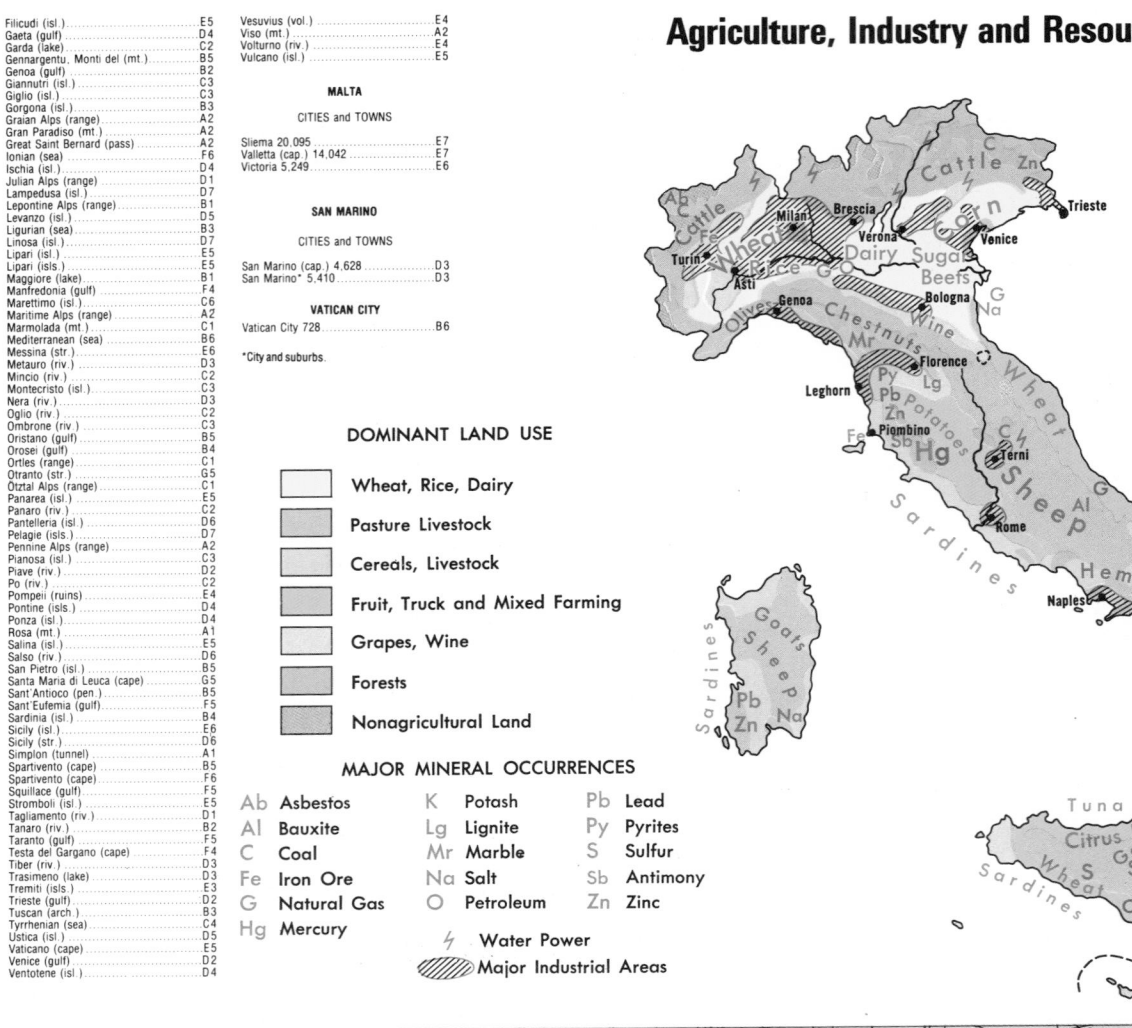

DOMINANT LAND USE

- Wheat, Rice, Dairy
- Pasture Livestock
- Cereals, Livestock
- Fruit, Truck and Mixed Farming
- Grapes, Wine
- Forests
- Nonagricultural Land

MAJOR MINERAL OCCURRENCES

Ab	Asbestos	K	Potash	Pb	Lead
Al	Bauxite	Lg	Lignite	Py	Pyrites
C	Coal	Mr	Marble	Na	Salt
Fe	Iron Ore	O	Petroleum	Sb	Antimony
G	Natural Gas	Zn	Zinc		
Hg	Mercury				

⚡ Water Power

▨ Major Industrial Areas

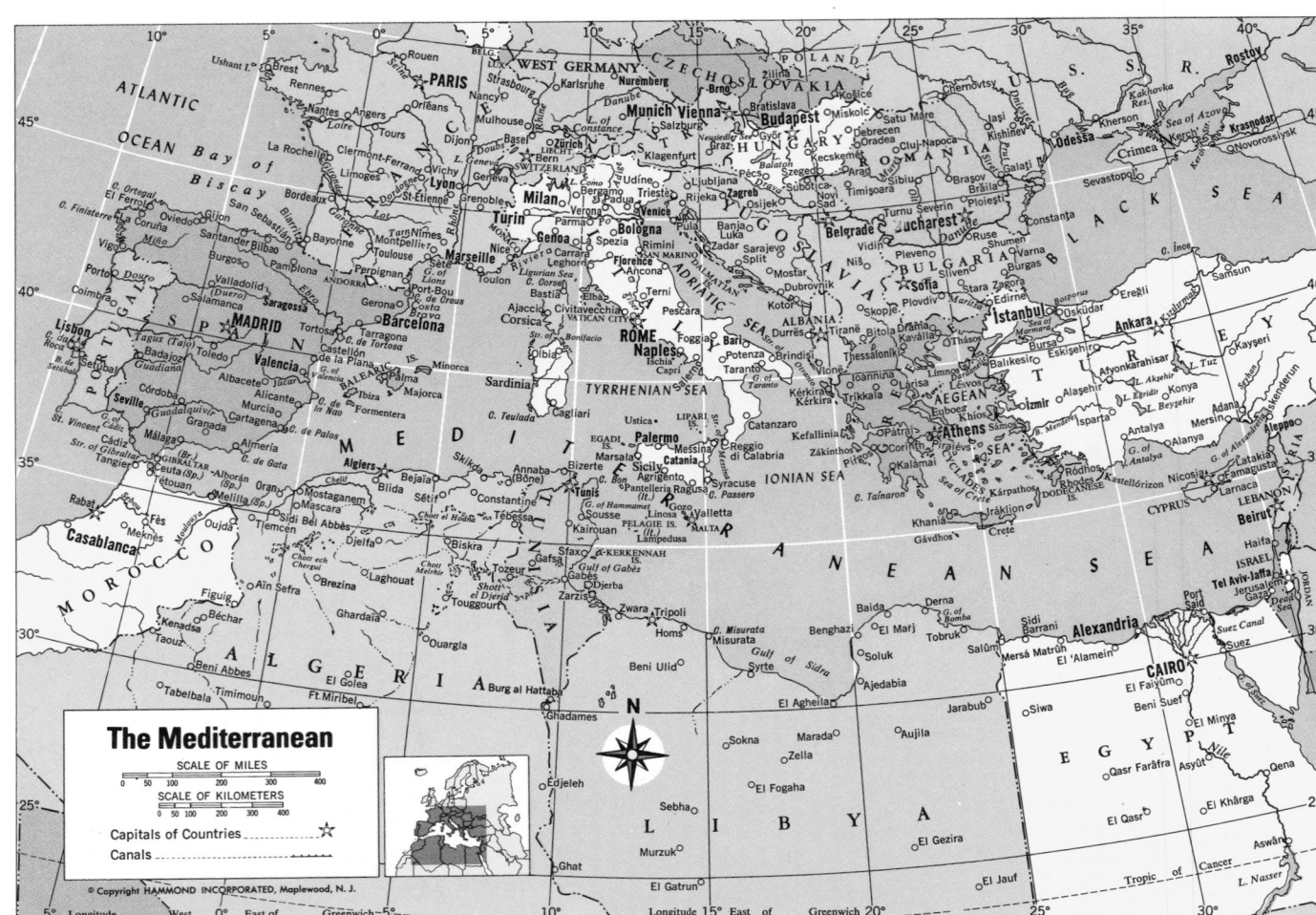

The Mediterranean

SCALE OF MILES

0 50 100   200   300   400

SCALE OF KILOMETERS

0 50 100 200   300   400

Capitals of Countries ....☆

Canals

© Copyright HAMMOND INCORPORATED, Maplewood, N. J.

SWITZERLAND
AREA 15,943 sq. mi. (41,292 sq. km.)
POPULATION 6,365,960
CAPITAL Bern
LARGEST CITY Zürich
HIGHEST POINT Dufourspitze
(Mte. Rosa) 15,203 ft. (4,634 m.)
MONETARY UNIT Swiss franc
MAJOR LANGUAGES German, French,
Italian, Romansch
MAJOR RELIGIONS Protestantism,
Roman Catholicism

LIECHTENSTEIN
AREA 61 sq. mi. (158 sq. km.)
POPULATION 25,220
CAPITAL Vaduz
LARGEST CITY Vaduz
HIGHEST POINT Grauspitze 8,527 ft.
(2,599 m.)
MONETARY UNIT Swiss franc
MAJOR LANGUAGE German
MAJOR RELIGION Roman Catholicism

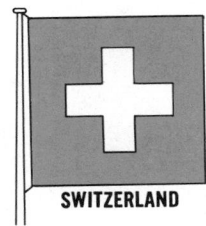

SWITZERLAND

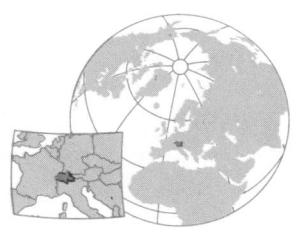

LIECHTENSTEIN

Languages

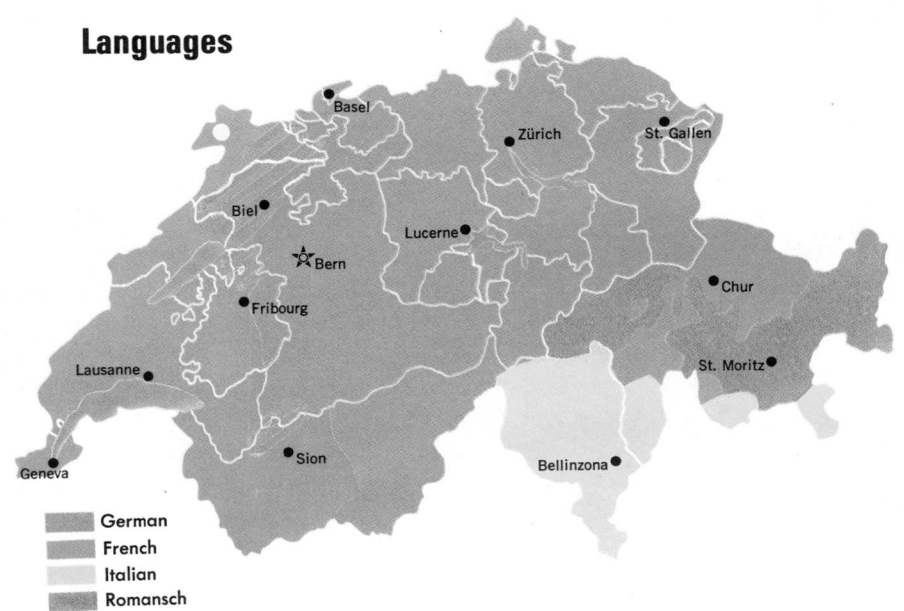

- German
- French
- Italian
- Romansch

Switzerland is a multilingual nation with four official languages. 70% of the people speak German, 19% French, 10% Italian and 1% Romansch.

SWITZERLAND

CANTONS

Aargau 442,400	F2
Appenzell, Ausser Rhoden 46,700	H2
Appenzell, Inner Rhoden 13,500	H2
Baselland 219,500	E2
Baselstadt 209,700	E1
Bern 920,900	D2
Fribourg 181,600	D3
Geneva (Genève) 338,600	B4
Glarus 35,700	H3
Graubünden (Grisons) 164,300	H3
Grisons (Graubünden) 164,300	H3
Jura 67,200	D2
Lucerne (Luzern) 292,900	F2
Luzern 292,900	F2
Neuchâtel 162,200	C3
Nidwalden 26,900	F3
Obwalden 25,400	F3
Sankt Gallen 385,000	H2
Schaffhausen 69,300	G1
Schwyz 93,100	G2
Soleure (Solothurn) 221,800	E2
Solothurn 221,800	E2
Thurgau 183,500	H1
Ticino 264,400	G4
Uri 34,000	G3
Valais 214,000	D4
Vaud 523,500	B3
Zug 73,600	G2
Zürich 1,117,300	G2

CITIES and TOWNS

Aadorf 3,022	G2
Aarau 16,881	F2
Aarau* 51,800	F2
Aarberg 3,122	D2
Aarburg 5,943	E2
Adelboden 3,326	E3
Adliswil 15,920	F2
Aeschi bei Spiez 1,402	E3
Affoltern am Albis 7,363	F2
Affoltern im Emmental 1,223	E2
Aigle 6,532	C4
Airolo 2,140	G3
Alle 1,615	D2
Allschwil 17,638	D1
Alpnach 3,277	F3
Altdorf 8,647	G3
Altstätten 9,084	J2
Amriswil 7,601	H1
Andelfingen 1,453	G1
Andermatt 1,589	G3
Appenzell 5,217	H2
Arbedo-Castione 2,456	G4
Arbon 12,227	H1
Arbon* 15,400	H1
Ardon 1,498	D4
Arosa 2,717	J3
Arth 7,580	F2
Ascona 4,086	G4
Attalens 1,116	C3
Au 4,944	J2
Aubonne 1,983	B4
Avenches 2,235	D3
Baar 14,074	G2
Baden 14,115	F2
Baden* 66,800	F2
Bad Ragaz 3,713	H2
Balerna 3,885	G5
Balsthal 5,607	E2
Bäretswil 2,733	G2
Basel 199,600	E1
Basel* 379,700	E1
Bassecourt 2,985	D2
Bätterkinden 1,757	E2
Bauma 3,159	G2
Beatenberg 1,263	E3
Beinwil am See 2,520	F2
Belfaux 1,075	D3
Bellinzona 16,979	H4
Bellinzona* 31,000	H4
Belp 6,981	D3
Berg 1,039	H1
Bern (cap.) 154,700	D3
Bern* 285,300	D3
Beromünster 1,552	F2
Bettlach 4,046	D2
Bex 5,069	D4
Biasca 4,696	H4
Biberist 7,769	D2
Biel 63,400	D2
Biel* 89,900	D2
Bière 1,252	B3
Binningen 15,344	D1
Bischofszell 4,233	H1
Blumenstein 1,049	E3
Bodio 1,425	G4
Boltigen 1,519	D3
Bonaduz 1,289	H3
Boncourt 1,528	C2
Bönigen 1,738	E3
Boswil 1,904	F2
Boudry 4,372	C3
Bourg Saint-Pierre 236	D5
Breil-Brigels 1,215	H3
Breitenbach 2,455	E2
Bremgarten 4,873	F2
Brienz 2,796	F3
Brig 5,191	F4
Brissago 2,120	G4
Brittnau 2,888	E2
Broc 1,842	D3
Brugg 8,635	F2
Brusio 1,344	K4
Bubendorf 2,070	E2
Bubikon 3,244	G2
Buchs 8,454	H2
Bülach 11,043	G1
Bulle 7,556	D3
Buochs 3,232	F3
Büren an der Aare 3,085	D2
Burgdorf 15,888	E2
Burgdorf* 18,400	E2
Bürglen, Thurgau 1,920	H1
Bürglen, Uri 3,401	G3
Bussigny-près-Lausanne 4,509	B3
Bütschwil 3,270	H2
Carouge 14,055	B4
Castagnola 4,430	G4
Cazis 1,687	H3
Cernier 1,717	C2
Chalais 1,651	E4
Cham 8,209	F2
Chamoson 2,049	D4
Charmey 1,155	D3
Château-d'Oex 3,203	D4
Châtel-Saint-Denis 2,842	C3
Chêne-Bougeries 8,670	B4
Chavornay 1,521	C3
Chexbres 1,607	C3
Chiasso 8,868	G5
Chippis 1,561	E4
Chur 32,400	H3
Churwalden 1,052	J3
Claro 1,143	G4
Collombey-Muraz 2,279	C4
Collonge-Bellerive 3,541	B4
Conthey 4,259	D4
Coppet 1,097	B4
Corcelles-près-Payerne 1,256	C3
Corgémont 1,645	D2
Cossonay 1,529	B3
Courgenay 1,954	D2
Courrendlin 2,656	D2
Courroux 1,788	D2
Courtelary 1,462	D2
Courtételle 1,864	D2
Couvet 3,481	C3
Cully 1,535	C4
Davos 10,238	J3
Degersheim 3,400	H2
Delémont 11,797	D2
Derendingen 4,917	E2
Dielsdorf 2,691	F1
Diemtigen 1,913	D3
Diepoldsau 3,311	J2
Diessenhofen 2,532	G1
Dietikon 22,705	F2
Disentis-Muster 2,319	G3
Domat-Ems 5,701	H3
Dombresson 1,109	C2
Dornach 5,258	E2
Döttingen 3,380	F1
Dübendorf 19,639	G2
Dürnten 4,820	G2
Dürrenroth 1,084	E2
Ebnat-Kappel 5,131	H2
Echallens 1,643	C3
Ecublens 6,379	B3
Egg 5,250	G2
Eggiwil 2,391	E3
Eglisau 2,160	G1
Egnach 3,466	H1

Agriculture, Industry and Resources

DOMINANT LAND USE

- Cereals, Dairy
- Pasture Livestock
- General Farming, Livestock
- Fruit, Truck, Mixed Farming
- Forests
- Nonagricultural Land

⚡ Water Power
▨ Major Industrial Areas

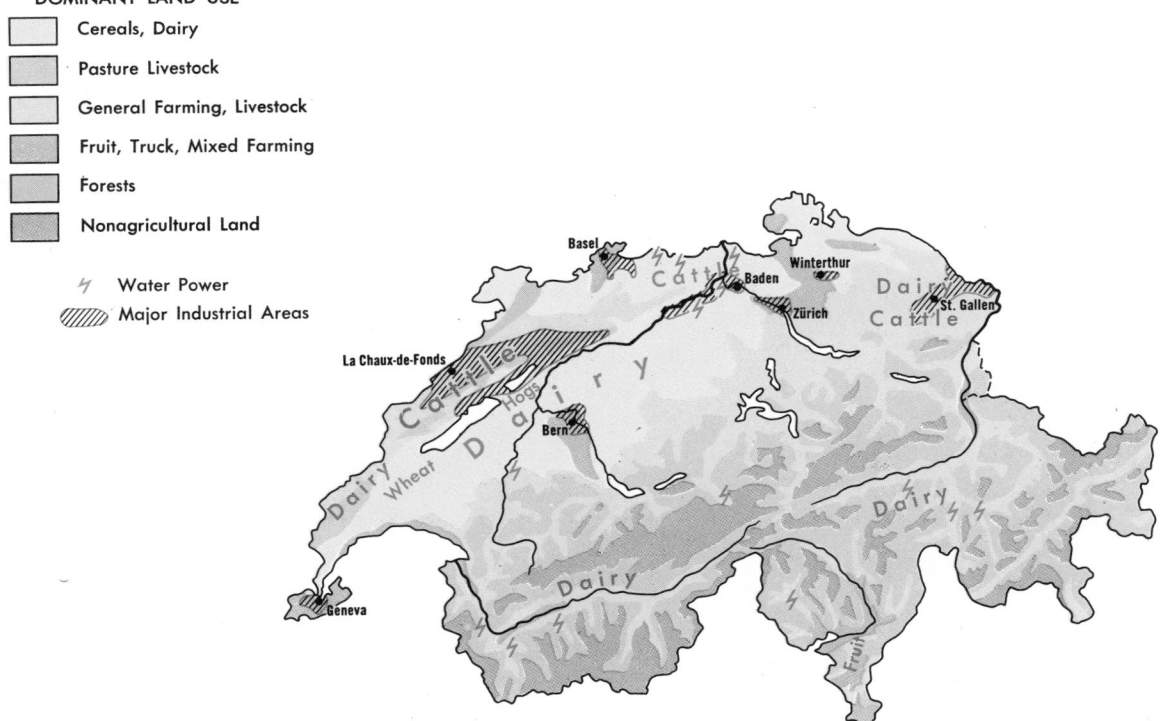

(continued on following page)

Topography

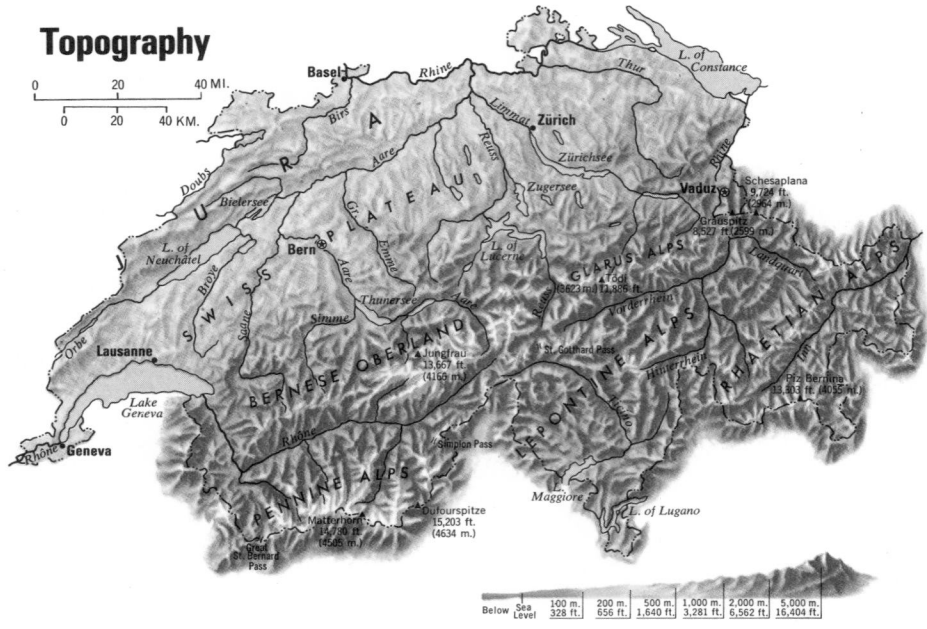

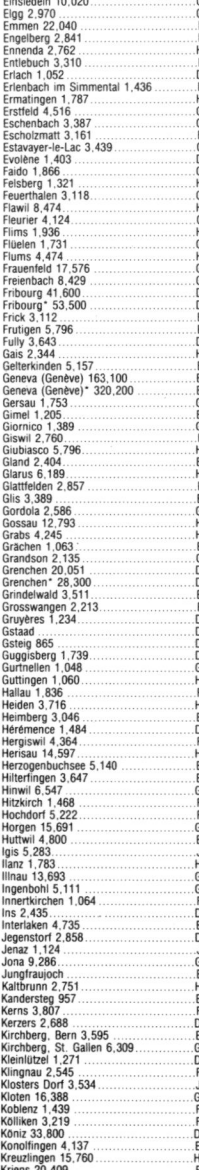

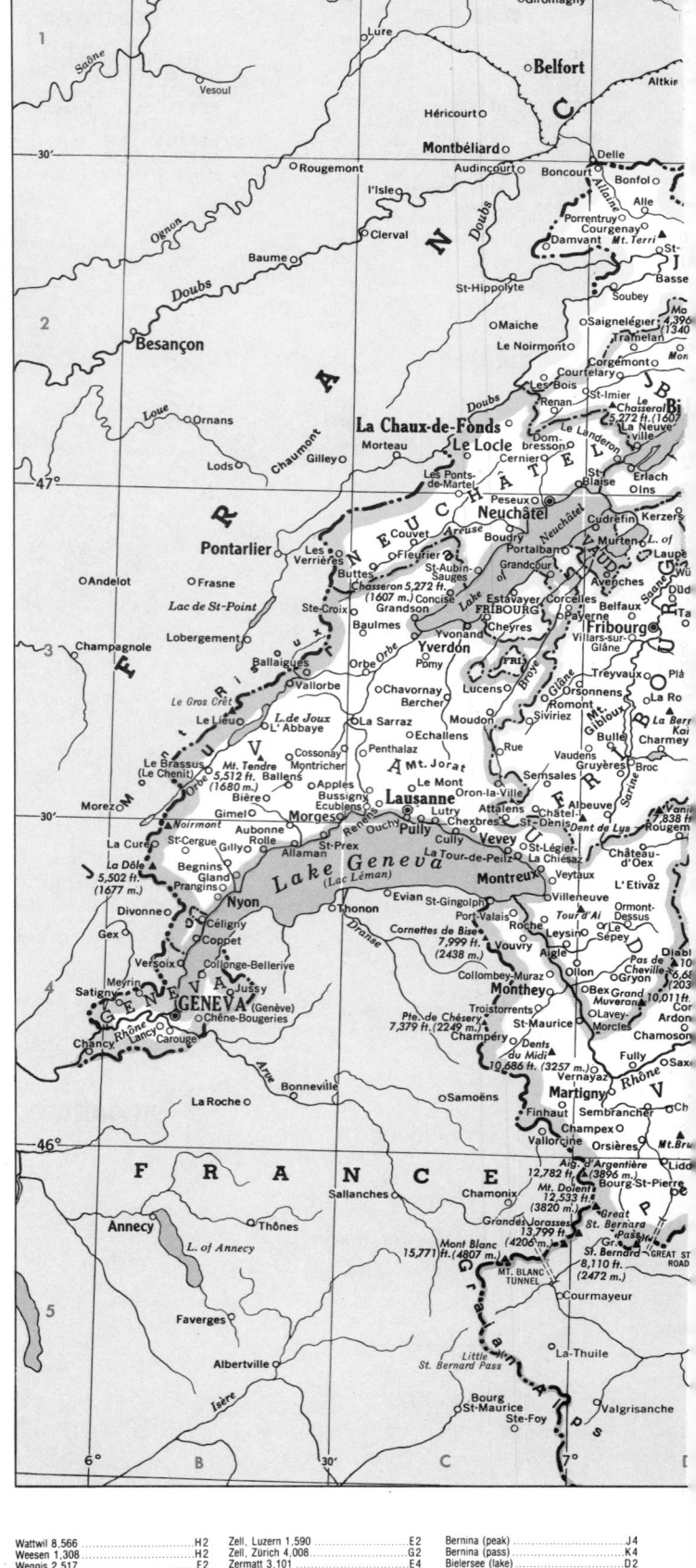

Below Sea Level	100 m. 328 ft.	200 m. 656 ft.	500 m. 1,640 ft.	1,000 m. 3,281 ft.	2,000 m. 6,562 ft.	5,000 m. 16,404 ft.

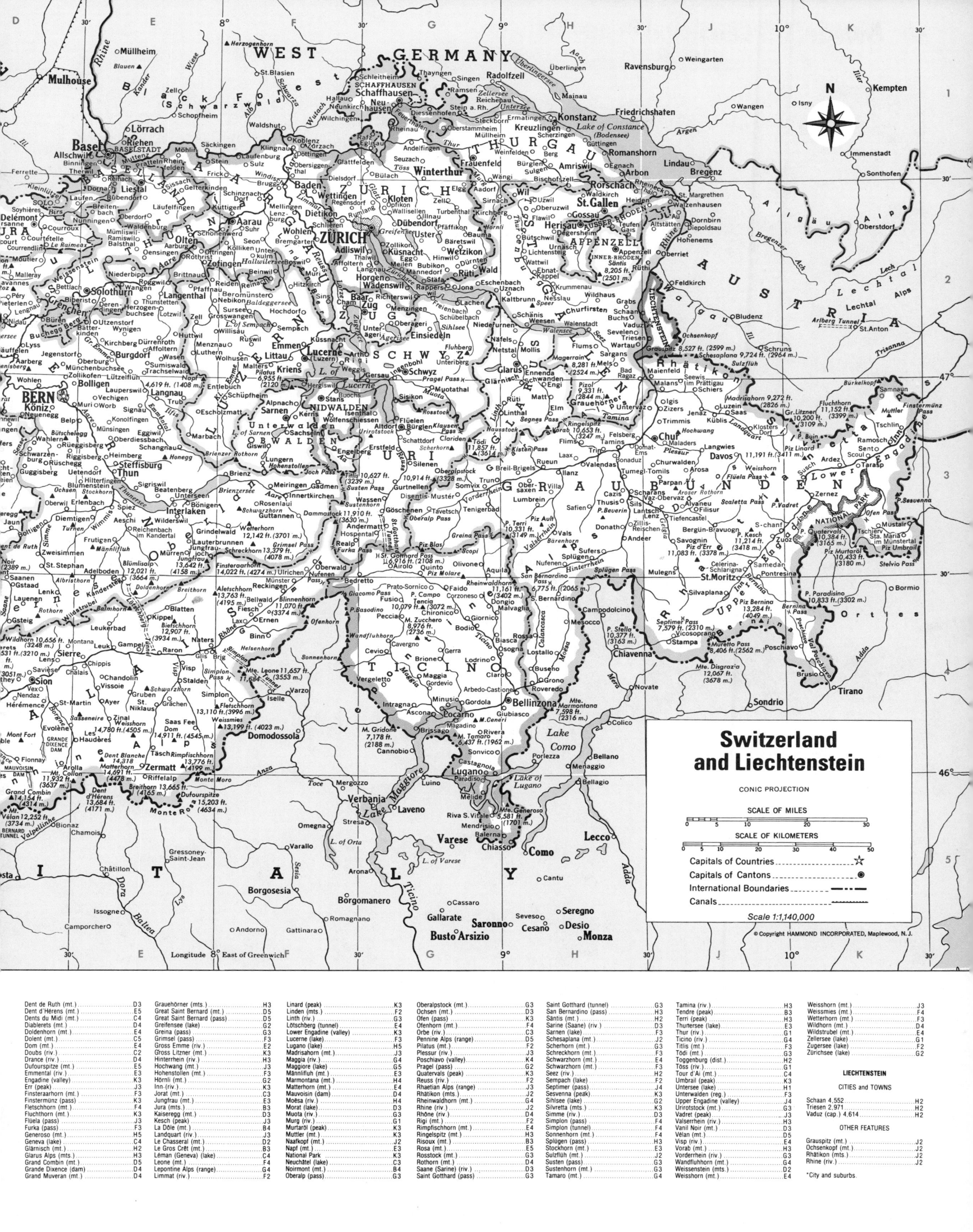

Switzerland and Liechtenstein

CONIC PROJECTION

SCALE OF MILES

SCALE OF KILOMETERS

Capitals of Countries .... ☆
Capitals of Cantons .... ◉
International Boundaries ....
Canals ....

Scale 1:1,140,000

© Copyright HAMMOND INCORPORATED, Maplewood, N.J.

AUSTRIA

PROVINCES

Burgenland 272,119 D3
Carinthia 525,728 B3
Lower Austria 1,414,161 C2
Salzburg 401,766 B3
Styria 1,192,442 C3
Tirol 540,771 A3
Upper Austria 1,223,444 B2
Vienna (city) 1,614,841 D2
Vorarlberg 271,473 A3

CITIES and TOWNS†

Admont 3,126 C3
Allentsteig 2,783 C2
Altheim 4,766 B2
Althofen 3,886 C3
Amstetten 13,330 C2
Andau 3,058 D3
Arnoldstein 6,740 B3
Aspang Markt 2,316 D3
Attnang-Puchheim 7,837 B2
Bad Aussee 5,039 B3
Baden 22,631 D2
Badgastein 5,228 B3
Bad Goisern 6,360 B3
Bad Hofgastein 5,525 B3
Bad Ischl 12,740 B3
Bad Leonfelden 2,712 C2
Bad Sankt-Leonhard im Lavanttal 4,882 C3
Berndorf 8,371 C3
Bischofshofen 9,417 B3
Bludenz 12,050 A3
Bramberg am Wildkogel 3,129 B3
Braunau am Inn 16,432 B2
Bregenz 22,839 A3
Bruck an der Leitha 7,506 D2
Bruck an der Mur 16,359 C3
Deutsch Feistritz 3,820 C3
Deutschkreutz 3,673 D3
Deutsch Landsberg 6,614 C3
Deutsch Wagram 4,481 D2
Dornbirn 33,810 A3
Ebenfurth 2,272 D3
Ebensee 9,413 B3
Eferding 3,014 B2
Eggenburg 3,730 C2
Ehrwald 2,198 A3
Horn 6,264 C2
Hüttenberg 3,251 C3
Imst 5,855 A3
Innsbruck 115,800 A3
Innsbruck* 167,200 A3
Jenbach 5,868 A3
Jennersdorf 4,210 C3
Judenburg 11,346 C3
Kapfenberg 26,001 C3
Kappl 2,156 A3
Kaprun 2,604 B3
Kindberg 6,128 C3
Kirchdorf an der Krems 3,471 C3
Kitzbühel 7,995 B3
Klagenfurt 74,326 C3
Klagenfurt* 112,600 C3
Klosterneuburg 21,912 D2
Knittelfeld 14,517 C3
Köflach 12,612 C3
Königswiesen 2,921 C2
Korneuburg 8,892 D2
Kössen 2,764 B3
Kötschach-Mauthen 3,740 B3
Krems an der Donau 21,733 C2
Kufstein 12,766 A3
Kundl 3,020 A3
Laa an der Thaya 5,455 D2
Laakirchen 7,664 B3
Lambach 3,301 C2
Landeck 7,388 A3
Längenfeld 2,838 A3
Langenlois 4,957 C2
Langenwang 4,071 C3
Lavamünd 4,120 C3
Leibnitz 6,646 C3
Lenzing 5,385 B3
Leoben 35,153 C3
Lienz 11,696 B3
Liezen 6,244 C3
Lilienfeld 3,126 C3
Linz 205,700 C2
Linz* 356,500 C2
Lustenau 15,239 A3
Mannersdorf am Leithagebirge 4,012 D3
Marchegg 2,678 D2
Mariazell 2,298 C3
Matrei in Osttirol 4,003 B3
Mattersburg 5,417 D3
Mattighofen 4,344 B2
Mauerkirchen 2,237 B2
Mautern in Steiermark 2,536 C3
Sankt Valentin 8,715 C2
Sankt Veit an der Glan 11,047 C3
Sankt Wolfgang im Salzkammergut 2,746 B3
Schärding 5,874 B2
Scheibbs 4,419 C2
Schladming 3,460 B3
Schrems 3,393 C2
Schruns 3,607 A3
Schwarzach im Pongau 3,616 B3
Schwaz 10,253 A3
Schwechat 14,997 D2
Schwertberg 3,881 C2
Sierning 8,162 C2
Sillian 1,988 B3
Solbad Hall in Tirol 12,335 A3
Spital am Pyhrn 2,315 C3
Spittal an der Drau 13,690 B3
Steinach 2,698 A3
Steyr 40,578 C2
Stockerau 12,634 D2
Strassburg 2,850 C3
Tamsweg 5,060 B3
Telfs 6,589 A3
Ternitz 10,287 D3
Traiskirchen 8,878 D2
Traun 20,843 C2
Trieben 4,639 C3
Trofaiach 8,731 C3
Tulln 7,705 D2
Velden am Wörthersee 7,306 C3
Vienna (cap.) 1,700,000 D2
Vienna* 1,858,700 D2
Villach 50,979 B3
Vöcklabruck 10,627 B2
Voitsberg 11,094 C3
Völkermarkt 10,772 C3
Vordernberg 2,508 C3
Waidhofen an der Thaya 4,200 C2
Waidhofen an der Ybbs 5,218 C3
Weitensfeld-Flattnitz 5,206 B3
Weitra 3,250 C2
Weiz 8,241 C3
Wels 47,279 C2
Weyer Markt 2,518 C3
Wien (Vienna) (cap.) 1,700,000 D2
Wiener Neustadt 34,774 D3
Wildon 2,002 C3
Wilhelmsburg 6,307 C2
Wolfsberg 31,176 C3
Wörgl 7,811 A3
Ybbs an der Donau 6,422 C2
Zams 3,120 A3
Zell am See 7,456 B3
Zell am Ziller 1,882 A3
Zeltweg 8,431 C3
Zirl 4,157 A3
Zistersdorf 3,412 D2
Zwettl-Niederösterreich 11,624 C2

OTHER FEATURES

AllgÄu Alps (mts.) A3
Bavarian Alps (mts.) A3
Bodensee (Constance) (lake) A3
Brenner (pass) A3
Carnic Alps (mts.) B3
Constance (lake) A3
Danube (riv.) C2
Donau (Danube) (riv.) D2
Drau (riv.) C3
Enns (riv.) C3
Grossglockner (mt.) B3
Hohe Tauern (range) B3
Inn (riv.) B2
Karawanken (range) C3
March (riv.) D2
Mühlviertel (reg.) C2
Mur (riv.) C3
Neusiedler See (lake) D3
Niedere Tauern (range) B3
Ötztal Alps (mts.) A3
Raab (riv.) C3
Rhine (riv.) A3
Salzach (riv.) B2
Salzkammergut (reg.) B3
Semmering (pass) C3
Thaya (riv.) C2
Traun (riv.) C2
Wildspitze (mt.) A3
Zugspitze (mt.) A3

CZECHOSLOVAKIA

REPUBLICS

Czech Socialist Rep. 9,964,338 B1
Slovak Socialist Rep. 4,670,409 E2

REGIONS

Bratislava (city) 333,000 D2
Jihočeský 662,002 C2
Jihomoravský 1,966,850 D2
Praha (city) 1,161,200 C1
Severočeský 1,122,035 C1
Severomoravský 1,849,286 D2
Středočeský 1,193,041 C2
Středoslovenský 1,436,351 E2
Východočeský 1,214,581 C1
Východoslovenský 1,298,481 F2
Západočeský 865,094 B2
Západoslovenský 1,610,542 D2

CITIES and TOWNS

Aš 120,000 B1
Austerlitz (Slavkov) D2
Bánovce nad Bebravou 11,400 E2
Banská Bystrica 53,000 E2
Banská štiavnica 7,486 E2
Bardejov 17,400 F2
Benešov 11,100 C2
Beroun 17,600 B2
Bílina 17,800 B1
Blansko 13,800 D2
Boskovice 8,531 D2
Brandýs nad Labem-Stará Boleslavv 333,000 C1
Bratislava 333,000 D2
Břeclav 21,100 D2
Brezno 14,800 E2
Brno 335,700 D2
Broumov 7,782 D1
Bruntál 12,300 D2
Bystřice nad Pernštejnem 6,471 D2
Bystřice pod Hostýnem 6,681 D2
Bytča 6,922 E2
Čadca 16,800 E2
Čalovo 6,591 D3
Čáslav 10,200 C2
Česká Lípa 18,600 C1
Česká Třebová 14,700 D2
České Budějovice 80,800 C2
Český Brod 6,640 C1
Český Krumlov 12,000 C2
Český Těšín 17,200 E2
Cheb 27,000 B1
Choceň 8,198 D1
Chodov 14,400 B1
Chomutov 44,200 B1
Chotěboř 6,692 C2
Chrudim 18,800 C2
Čierny Balog 6,435 E2
Děčín 46,500 C1
Detva 13,100 E2
Dobříš 6,378 C2
Dobruška 5,779 D1
Dolný Kubín 9,900 E2
Domažlice 9,100 B2
Dubnica nad Váhom 11,300 E2
Duchcov 9,712 B1
Dunajská Streda 13,000 D3
Dvory nad Žitavou 5,847 E3
Dvů Králové nad Labem 16,800 C1
Falknov (Sokolov) 23,900 B1
Fiľakovo 7,822 E2
Frenštát pod Radhoštěm 8,516 E2
Frýdek-Místek 43,800 E2
Frýdlant v. Čechách 5,948 C1
Frýdlant nad Ostravicí 6,250 E2
Galanta 12,300 D2
Gottwaldov 84,300 D2
Handlová 16,200 E2
Havířov 85,000 E2
Havlíčkův Brod 19,200 C2
Hlinsko 8,890 D2
Hlohovec 15,200 D2
Hlučín 15,300 E2
Hnúšťa-Likier E2
Hodonín 22,600 D2
Holešov 9,091 D2
Holíč 7,602 D2
Holice 6,151 C1
Horažďovice B2
Hořice v Podkrkonoší 7,715 C1
Horná Štubňa E2
Horní Benešov D2
Horní Libina D2
Hořovice 5,665 C2
Horšovský Týn B2
Hostinné C1
Hradec Králové 85,600 C1
Hranice 13,300 D2
Hrinova 7,800 E2
Hronov 9,767 D1
Hrušovany D2
Humenné 22,200 G2
Humpolec 7,810 C2
Hurbanovo E3
Hustopeče D2
Ilava E2
Ivančice 7,314 D2

Topography

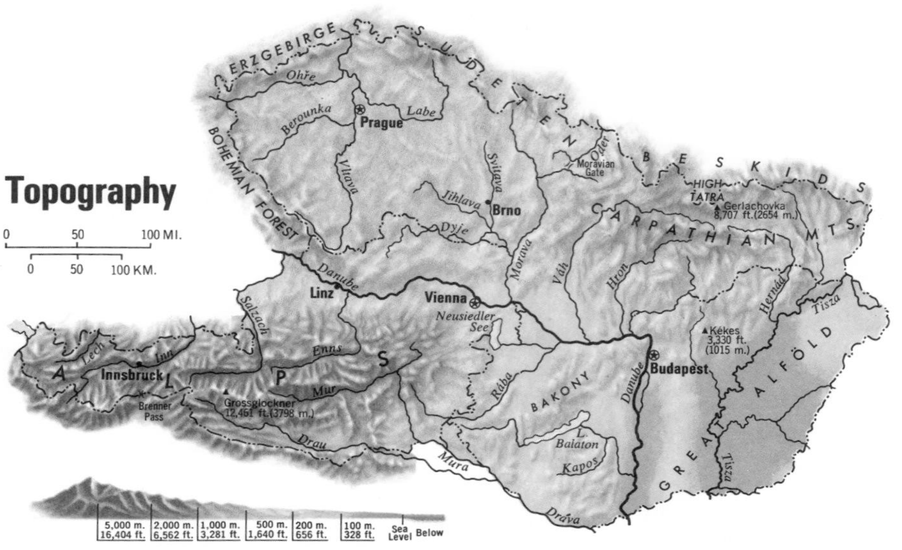

Eisenerz 11,563 C3
Eisenkappel-Vellach 3,761 C3
Eisenstadt 10,059 D3
Enns 9,622 C2
Feldbach 3,887 C3
Feldkirch 21,214 A3
Feldkirchen in Kärnten 11,188 B3
Ferlach 7,621 C3
Fieberbrunn 3,651 B3
Fohnsdorf 11,169 C3
Frankenmarkt 2,960 B3
Frauenkirchen 2,749 D3
Freistadt 5,956 C2
Freidberg 2,504 D3
Friesach 7,257 C3
Frohnleiten 5,081 C3
Fulpmes 2,553 A3
Fürstenfeld 6,054 C3
Gaming 4,181 C3
Gänserndorf 4,211 D2
Gleisdorf 4,921 C3
Gloggnitz 7,078 D3
Gmünd, Carinthia 2,267 B3
Gmünd, Lower Austria 6,323 C2
Gmunden 12,270 B3
Golling an der Salzach 3,089 B3
Götzis 7,931 A3
Gratwein 2,747 C3
Graz 251,900 C3
Graz* 314,200 C3
Grein 2,767 C2
f21Grieskirchen 4,519 B2
Grosssiegharts 3,288 C2
Grünburg 3,775 C3
Güssing 3,675 D3
Haag 5,060 C2
Hainburg an der Donau 6,009 D2
Hainfeld 3,897 C2
Hallein 14,371 B3
Hallstatt 1,303 B3
Hartberg 5,702 C3
Haslach an der Mühl 2,636 C2
Heidenreichstein 4,340 C2
Heiligenblut 1,324 B3
Hermagor-Preseggersee 7,531 B3
Herzogenburg 7,299 C2
Hohenau an der March 3,591 D2
Hohenberg 2,016 C3
Hohenems 11,487 A3
Hollabrunn 6,563 D2
Hopfgarten in Nordtirol 4,784 B3
Mauthausen 4,419 C2
Mauthen-Kötschach 3,750 B3
Mayrhofen 3,174 A3
Melk 5,108 C2
Mistelbach an der Zaya 6,306 D2
Mittersill 4,361 B3
Mödling 18,712 D2
Mondsee 2,141 B3
Murau 2,710 C3
Mürzzuschlag 11,564 C3
Neuberg an der Mürz 2,183 C3
Neumarkt am Wallersee 3,267 B3
Neunkirchen 10,922 C3
Neusiedl am See 3,999 D3
Neustift im Stubaital 2,789 A3
Ober Grafendorf 4,109 C2
Oberndorf bei Salzburg 3,293 B3
Obervellach 2,420 B3
Oberwart 5,661 D3
Paternion 5,805 B3
Perg 4,872 C2
Peuerbach 2,161 B2
Pfunds 2,043 A3
Pinkafeld 4,610 C3
Pöchlarn 3,199 C2
Pörtschach am Wörthersee 2,511 C3
Poysdorf 5,774 D2
Pregarten 3,249 C2
Raabs an der Thaya 4,194 C2
Radenthein 6,847 B3
Radkersburg 2,000 C3
Radstadt 3,585 B3
Rankweil 8,440 A3
Rechnitz 3,412 D3
Reichenau an der Rax 4,053 C3
Retz 4,780 D2
Ried im Innkreis 10,534 B2
Rottenmann 4,781 C3
Saalfelden am Steinernen Meer 10,172 B3
Salzburg 122,100 B3
Salzburg* 213,430 B3
Sankt Aegyd am Neuwalde 3,165 C3
Sankt Anton am Arlberg 2,086 A3
Sankt Johann in Tirol 5,942 B3
Sankt Michael im Lungau 2,839 B3
Sankt Michael in Obersteiermark 3,717 C3
Sankt Michael im Lungau 2,839 B3
Sankt Paul im Lavanttal 6,721 C3
Sankt Pölten 43,300 C2

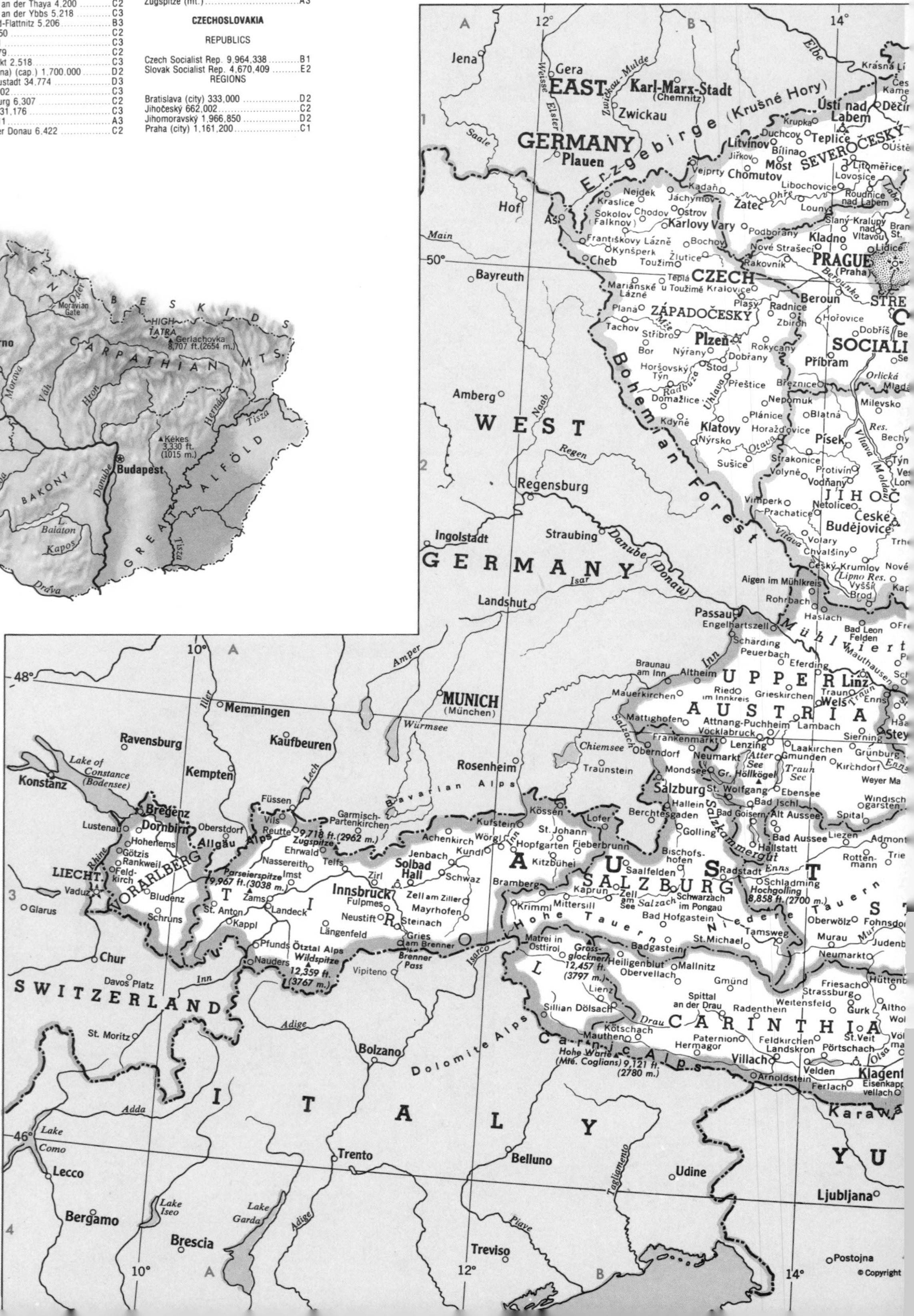

AREA 32,375 sq. mi. (83,851 sq. km.)
POPULATION 7,507,000
CAPITAL Vienna
LARGEST CITY Vienna
HIGHEST POINT Grossglockner
  12,457 ft. (3,797 m.)
MONETARY UNIT schilling
MAJOR LANGUAGE German
MAJOR RELIGION Roman Catholicism

AREA 49,373 sq. mi. (127,876 sq. km.)
POPULATION 15,276,799
CAPITAL Prague
LARGEST CITY Prague
HIGHEST POINT Gerlachovka 8,707 ft.
  (2,654 m.)
MONETARY UNIT koruna
MAJOR LANGUAGES Czech, Slovak
MAJOR RELIGIONS Roman Catholicism,
  Protestantism

AREA 35,919 sq. mi. (93,030 sq. km.)
POPULATION 10,709,536
CAPITAL Budapest
LARGEST CITY Budapest
HIGHEST POINT Kékes 3,330 ft.
  (1,015 m.)
MONETARY UNIT forint
MAJOR LANGUAGE Hungarian
MAJOR RELIGIONS Roman Catholicism,
  Protestantism

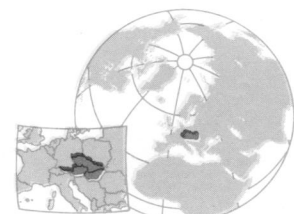

AUSTRIA

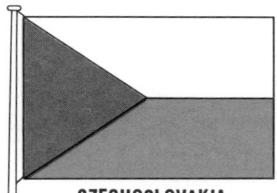

CZECHOSLOVAKIA

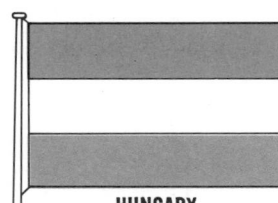

HUNGARY

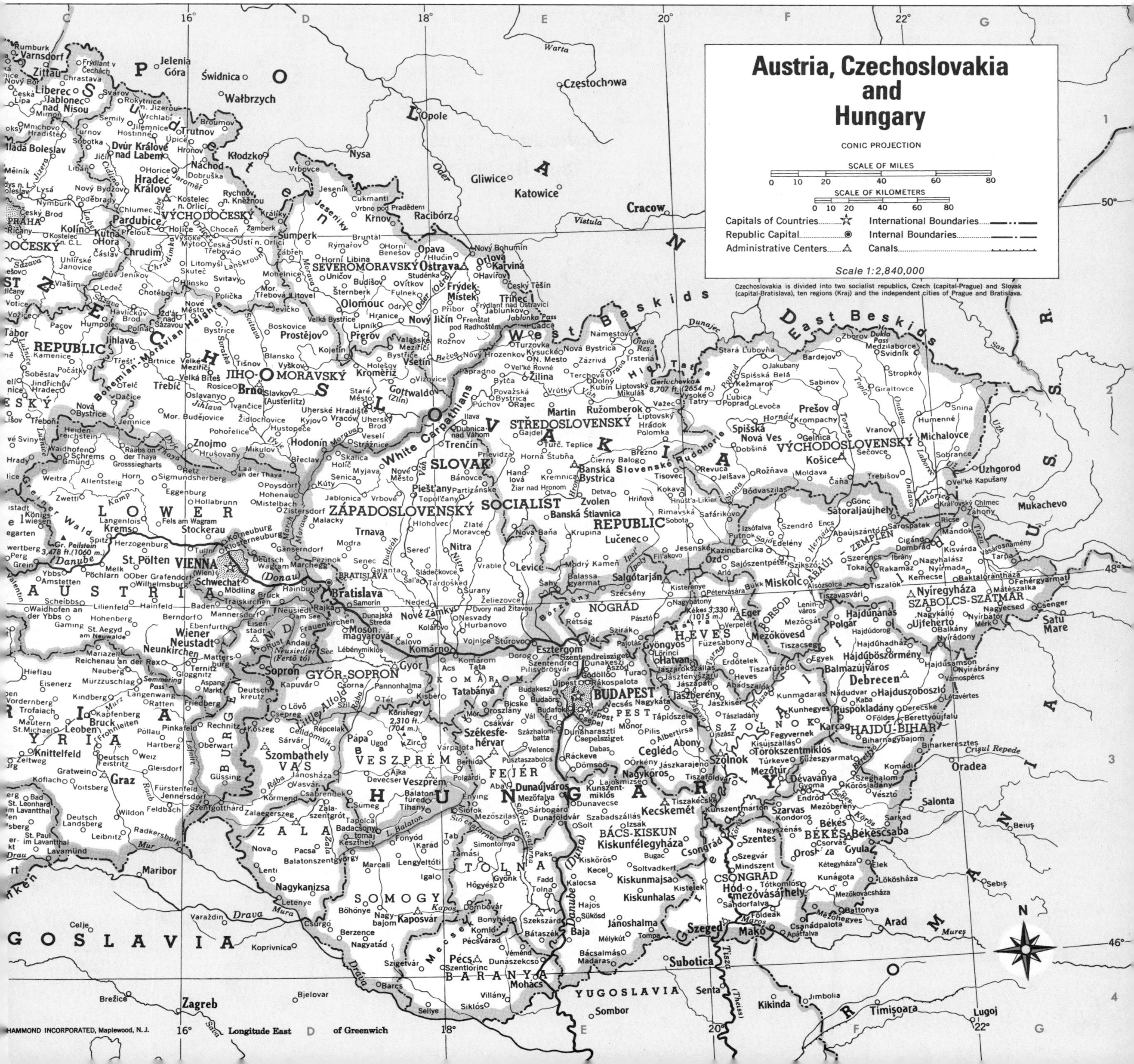

Austria, Czechoslovakia and Hungary

CONIC PROJECTION

SCALE OF MILES
0 10 20 40 60 80

SCALE OF KILOMETERS
0 10 20 40 60 80

Capitals of Countries .... ☆
Republic Capital .... ⊚
Administrative Centers .... △
International Boundaries ....
Internal Boundaries ....
Canals ....

Scale 1:2,840,000

Czechoslovakia is divided into two socialist republics, Czech (capital–Prague) and Slovak (capital–Bratislava), ten regions (Kraj) and the independent cities of Prague and Bratislava.

42 Austria, Czechoslovakia and Hungary

(continued)

Jablonec nad Nisou 36,300 C1
Jablonica D2
Jablunkov 9,405 E2
Jáchymov B1
Jakubany F2
Jaroměř 11,600 C1
Jelšava F2
Jemnice C2
Jeseník 10,900 D1
Jesenské F2
Jevíčko D2
Jičín 13,200 C1
Jihlava 44,500 C2
Jilemnice C1
Jindřichův Hradec 15,700 C2
Jiřkov 11,400 B1
Kadaň 18,100 B1
Kamenice C2
Kaplice C2
Karlovy Vary 43,300 B1
Karviná 79,100 E2
Kdyně B2
Kežmarok 11,000 F2
Kladno 61,200 B1
Klatovy 18,500 B2
Kojetín 5,852 D2
Kokava nad Rimavicou 5,391 E2
Kolárovo 10,500 D3
Kolín 29,100 C1
Komárno 28,200 D3
Košice 169,100 F2
Kostelec nad Orlicí 5,575 D1
Král'ovský Chlmec 5,329 G2
Kralupy nad Vltavou 16,900 C1
Kraslice 6,733 B1
Kremnica 5,941 E2
Krnov 25,000 D1
Kroměříž 23,200 D2
Krompachy 6,332 F2
Krupina 6,627 E2
Krupka 8,301 B1
Kutná Hora 19,200 C2
Kyjov 10,700 D2
Kynšperk 5,524 B1
Kysucké Nové Mesto 11,700 E2
Lanškroun 8,683 D2
Levice 19,000 E2
Levoča 10,100 F2
Libáň C1
Liberec 75,600 C1

Moravě 6,581 D2
Nové Město nad
Váhom 15,900 D2
Nové Strašecí B1
Nové Zámky 27,300 D3
Nový Bohumín 16,700 E2
Nový Bor 7,621 C1
Nový Bydžov 6,824 C1
Nový Hrozenkov E2
Nový Jičín 21,400 E2
Nymburk 13,600 C1
Nýřany 6,204 B2
Nýrsko B2
Odry D2
Olomouc 82,800 D2
Opava 53,800 E2
Orlová 25,500 E2
Ostrava 293,500 E2
Ostrov 18,200 B1
Pardubice 78,500 C1
Partizánske 15,100 E2
Pelhřimov 11,900 C2
Pezinok 13,100 D2
Piešt'any 25,400 D2
Písek 25,100 C2
Plzeň 155,000 B2
Počátky C2
Podbořany B1
Poděbrady 13,400 C1
Pohořelice D2
Polička 6,529 D2
Polná C2
Polomka E2
Poprad 25,800 F2
Považská Bystrica 19,300 E2
Prachatice 7,900 B2
Prague (Praha) (cap.) 1,161,200 C1
Přelouč 6,251 C1
Přerov 43,500 D2
Prešov 61,000 F2
Přeštice B2
Příbor 7,726 E2
Příbram 31,300 B2
Prievidza 30,900 E2
Prostějov 44,200 D2
Protivín C2
Púchov 9,306 E2
Radnice B2
Rajec E2
Rakovník 14,200 B1

Štúrovo 8,287 E3
Šumperk 25,900 D1
Šurany 6,693 E2
Sušice 10,300 B2
Svárov C1
Svidník 4,600 F2
Svitavy 15,000 D2
Tábor 28,100 C2
Tachov 11,400 B2
Telč 5,285 C2
Teplice 52,300 B1
Tišnov 8,263 D2
Topol'čany 17,500 D2
Třebíč 23,900 C2
Trebišov 13,700 F2
Třeboň 6,068 C2
Trenčín 38,800 E2
Třešt' 5,053 C2
Třinec 32,000 E2
Trnava 48,600 D2
Trutnov 24,500 D1
Turnov 13,600 C1
Turzovka 6,107 E2
Uherské Hradiště 32,100 D2
Uherský Brod 12,800 D2
Uničov 10,800 D2
Úpice 6,323 C1
Ústí nad Labem 74,900 C1
Ústí nad Orlicí 13,700 D2
Valašské
Meziříčí 19,400 D2
Varnsdorf 14,700 C1
Važec E2
Vejprty B1
Velká Bíteš D2
Velká Bystřice D2
Vel'ké Kapušany G2
Velké Meziříčí 7,590 D2
Vel'ké Rovné E2
Veselí nad Lužnicí C2
Veselí nad Moravou 11,500 D2
Vimperk 5,749 B2
Vítkov 5,138 D2
Vizovice D2
Vlašim 8,873 C2
Vodňany 5,620 C2
Vojnice E3
Volary B2
Volyně B2
Votice C2

Jablunka (pass) E2
Jeseniky (mts.) D1
Jihlava (riv.) D2
Krušné Hory (Erzgebirge)
(mts.) B1
Labe (riv.) C1
Lipno (res.) C2
Lužnice (riv.) C2
Moldau (Vltava) (riv.) C2
Morava (riv.) D2
Nitra (riv.) E2
Oder (Odra) (riv.) D2
Ohře (riv.) B1
Ondava (riv.) F2
Orava (riv.) E2
Orlická (res.) C2
Sázava (riv.) C2
Slovenské Rudohorie (mts.) E2
Sudeten (mts.) C1
Svitava (riv.) D2
Svratka (riv.) D2
Tatra, High (mts.) E2
Torysa (riv.) F2
Úhlava (riv.) B2
Váh (riv.) D2
Vltava (riv.) C2
White Carpathians (mts.) E2

HUNGARY

COUNTIES

Bács-Kiskun 568,532 E3
Baranya 434,030 E4
Békés 436,987 F3
Borsod-Abaúj-Zemplén 808,924 F2
Budapest (city) 2,060,170 E3
Csongrád 456,862 F3
Fejér 421,568 E3
Győr-Sopron 428,476 D3
Hajdú-Bihar 552,417 F3
Heves 350,874 F3
Komárom 321,579 E3
Nógrád 239,907 E3
Pest 973,486 E3
Somogy 360,308 D3
Szabolcs-Szatmár 593,746 G3
Szolnok 446,379 F3
Tolna 266,414 E3
Vas 285,527 D3

Csenger 4,792 G3
Csepel 71,693 E3
Csepreg 4,079 D3
Csongrád 22,202 E3
Csorna 12,131 D3
Csorvás 6,826 F3
Csurgó 5,463 D3
Dabas 13,075 E3
Debrecen 192,484 F3
Derecske 9,579 F3
Dévaványa 11,208 F3
Devecser 5,482 D3
Dombóvár 19,917 E3
Dombrád 6,328 F2
Dömsöd 6,545 E3
Dorog 10,754 E3
Dunaföldvár 10,318 E3
Dunaharaszti 15,788 E3
Dunakeszi 25,187 E3
Dunaszekcső 2,999 E3
Dunaújváros 60,694 E3
Dunavecse 4,521 E3
Edelény 9,559 F2
Eger 61,283 F3
Egyek 7,956 F3
Elek 6,032 F3
Enes 2,565 F2
Endrőd 8,136 F3
Enying 7,518 E3
Érd 41,210 E3
Erdőtelek 4,250 F3
Esztergom 30,476 E3
Fadd 4,805 E3
Fegyvernek 8,421 F3
Fehérgyarmat 6,729 G3
Földeák 3,855 F3
Földes 5,293 F2
Fonyód 3,957 D3
Füzesabony 6,965 F3
Füzesgyarmat 7,097 F3
Gödöllő 28,057 E3
Gönc 2,875 F2
Gyoma 10,392 F3
Gyöngyös 36,927 E3
Gyönk 2,507 E3
Győr 123,618 D3
Gyula 34,514 F3
Hajdúböszörmény 32,145 F3
Hajdúdorog 10,118 F3
Hajdúhadház 13,626 F3

Körmend 11,787 D3
Körösladány 6,565 F3
Kőszeg 12,705 D3
Kunágota 4,622 F3
Kunhegyes 10,116 F3
Kunmadaras 7,343 F3
Kunszentmárton 11,103 F3
Kunszentmiklós 7,952 E3
Lajosmizse 12,872 E3
Lébénymiklós 6,190 D3
Lengyeltóti 3,389 D3
Leninváros 18,667 F3
Lenti 8,106 D3
Létavértes 9,106 G3
Letenye 4,395 D3
Lőkösháza 2,514 F3
Lőrinci 10,679 E3
Madaras 4,519 E3
Makó 29,943 F3
Mándok 5,093 G2
Marcali 12,485 D3
Mátészalka 17,709 G3
Mélykút 7,640 E3
Mérk 3,211 G3
Mezőberény 12,702 F3
Mezőcsát 6,729 F3
Mezőfalva 5,008 E3
Mezőhegyes 8,631 F3
Mezőkovácsháza 7,473 F3
Mezőkövesd 18,435 F3
Mezőszilas 2,792 E3
Mezőtúr 22,018 F3
Mindszent 8,730 F3
Miskolc 206,727 F2
Mohács 21,385 E4
Monor 16,838 E3
Mór 12,066 E3
Mosonmagyaróvár 29,732 D3
Nádudvar 9,447 F3
Nagyatád 12,946 D3
Nagybajom 4,402 D3
Nagyecsed 8,225 G3
Nagyhalász 6,437 F2
Nagykálló 11,282 F3
Nagykanizsa 48,494 D3
Nagykáta 11,922 E3
Nagykőrös 27,900 E3
Nagyszénás 7,124 F3
Nyírábrány 4,509 G3
Nyíradony 7,146 G3

Szarvas 20,598 F3
Szécsény 5,690 E2
Százhalombatta 13,963 E3
Szeged 171,342 E3
Szeghalom 9,736 F3
Szegvár 6,395 F3
Székesfehérvár 103,197 E3
Szekszárd 34,592 E3
Szendrő 4,098 F2
Szentendre 16,844 E3
Szentes 35,326 F3
Szentgotthárd 5,837 D3
Szentlőrinc 3,926 E3
Szerencs 8,612 F2
Szigetvár 12,114 D3
Szikszó 6,419 F2
Szil 2,073 D3
Szolnok 75,203 F3
Szombathely 82,830 D3
Tab 3,922 E3
Tamási 7,602 E3
Tápiószele 5,575 E3
Tapolca 17,161 D3
Tarpa 3,436 G2
Tata 24,114 E3
Tatabánya 75,942 E3
Tét 4,441 D3
Tiszacsege 6,263 F3
Tiszaföldvár 12,560 F3
Tiszafüred 12,259 F3
Tiszakécske 12,378 E3
Tiszalök 6,230 F2
Tiszavasvári 13,292 F3
Tokaj 4,845 F2
Tolna 8,997 E3
Tompa 5,365 E3
Törökszentmiklós 25,551 F3
Tótkomlós 8,803 F3
Tura 8,235 E3
Túrkeve 11,393 F3
Újfehértó 14,412 F3
Újpest 80,384 E3
Újszász 7,098 F2
Vác 34,837 E3
Vál 2,488 E3
Vámospércs 5,213 F3
Várpalota 28,293 E3
Vásárosnamény 8,637 G2
Vasvár 4,275 D3
Vecsés 19,193 E3

Agriculture, Industry and Resources

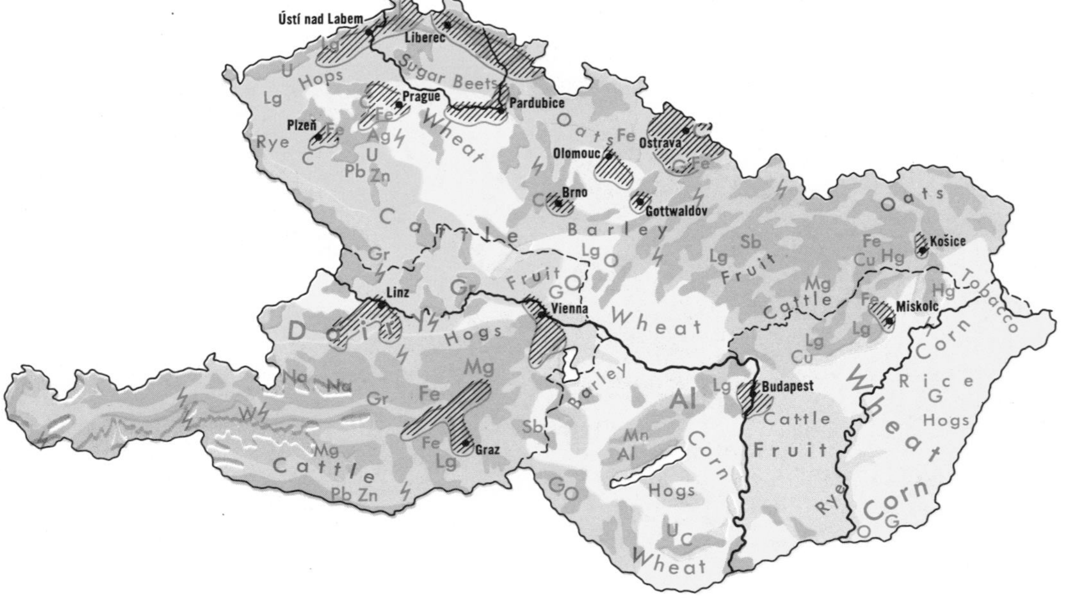

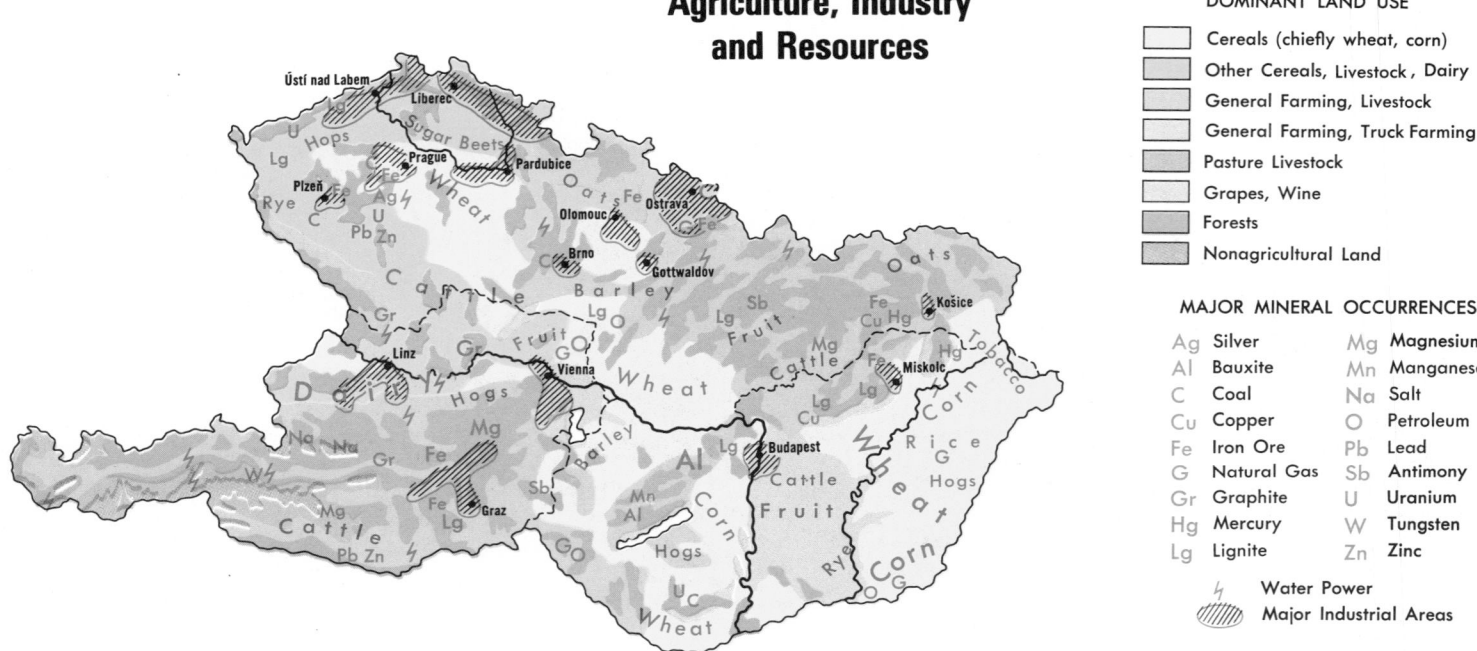

DOMINANT LAND USE

- Cereals (chiefly wheat, corn)
- Other Cereals, Livestock, Dairy
- General Farming, Livestock
- General Farming, Truck Farming
- Pasture Livestock
- Grapes, Wine
- Forests
- Nonagricultural Land

MAJOR MINERAL OCCURRENCES

Ag	Silver	Mg	Magnesium
Al	Bauxite	Mn	Manganese
C	Coal	Na	Salt
Cu	Copper	O	Petroleum
Fe	Iron Ore	Pb	Lead
G	Natural Gas	Sb	Antimony
Gr	Graphite	U	Uranium
Hg	Mercury	W	Tungsten
Lg	Lignite	Zn	Zinc

Water Power
Major Industrial Areas

Lidice C1
Lipník nad Bečvou 7,358 D2
Liptovský Mikuláš 19,400 E2
Litoměřice 19,700 C1
Litomyšl 8,112 D2
Litovel 5,805 D2
Litvínov 23,300 B1
Lomnice C2
Louny 15,200 B1
Lovosice 9,323 C1
L'ubica F2
Lučenec 23,300 E2
Lysá nad Labem 9,920 C1
Malacky 13,200 D2
Mariánské Lázně 14,600 B2
Martin 47,800 E2
Medzilaborce F2
Mělník 17,800 C1
Michalovce 23,600 G2
Mikulov 6,267 D2
Milevsko 7,091 C2
Mimoň 6,773 C1
Mladá Boleslav 36,900 C1
Mladá Vožice C2
Mnichovo Hradiště 5,239 C1
Modra 7,219 D2
Modrý Kameň 6,200 E2
Mohelnice 6,050 D2
Moldava nad Bodvou 5,397 F2
Moravská Třebová 9,052 D2
Moravské Budějovice 5,576 D2
Most 59,400 B1
Myjava 6,657 D2
Náchod 19,300 D1
Námestovo E2
Neded D2
Nejdek 8,187 B1
Nepomuk B2
Nesvady 5,453 E3
Netolice C2
Nitra 50,000 E2
Nová Baňa 6,218 E2
Nová Bystrica E2
Nová Bystřice C2
Nové Hrady C2
Nové Město na Moravě 6,581 D2

Revúca 5,901 F2
Říčany u Prahy 8,407 C2
Rimavská Sobota 5,800 E2
Rokycany 12,800 B2
Rokytnice nad Jizerou C1
Rosice D2
Roudnice nad Labem 11,800 C1
Rožňava 12,400 F2
Rožnov pod
Radhoštěm 11,600 E2
Rumburk C1
Ružomberok 22,600 E2
Rychnov nad Kněžnou 7,500 D1
Rýmařov 7,522 D2
Sabinov 5,473 F2
Šafárikovo F2
Šahy 5,049 E2
Šal'a 15,200 D2
Samorín 8,287 D2
Sečovce 5,744 F2
Sedlčany C2
Semily 8,200 C1
Senec 8,544 D2
Senica 12,300 D2
Sereď 12,500 D2
Skalica 11,100 D2
Skuteč D2
Sládečkovce 5,598 D2
Slaný 13,200 C1
Slavkov D2
Snina 10,900 G2
Soběslav 6,140 C2
Sobotka C1
Sobrance G2
Sokolov 23,900 B1
Spišská Belá F2
Spišská Nová Ves 26,100 F2
Stará L'ubovňa 5,800 F2
Staré Město 6,293 D2
Šternberk 13,700 D2
Stod B2
Strakonice 19,000 B2
Strážnice 5,482 D2
Stříbro B2
Stropkov 5,645 F2
Studénka 9,744 D2

Vráble E2
Vracov D2
Vranov nad Teplou 14,700 F2
Vrbno pod Pradědem 5,594 D1
Vrbovce D1
Vrbové D2
Vrchlabí 11,700 C1
Vrútky 5,756 E2
Vsetín 24,100 D2
Vyškov 15,100 D2
Vysoké Mýto 8,830 D2
Vysoké Tatry F2
Vyšší Brod C2
Zábřeh 11,300 D2
Žamberk 5,040 D1
Žatec 17,400 B1
Zázrivá E2
Zbiroh B2
Zborov F2
Žd'ár nad Sázavou 17,800 C2
Želiezovce 5,478 E2
Žiar nad Hronom 14,800 E2
Židlochovice D2
Žilina 56,000 E2
Zlaté Moravce 10,300 E2
Zlín (Gottwaldov) 84,300 D2
Žlutice B1
Znojmo 28,500 D2
Zvolen 29,000 E2

OTHER FEATURES

Berounka (riv.) C2
Beskids, East (mts.) F1
Beskids, West (mts.) E2
Bohemian (for.) B2
Bohemian-Moravian Heights
(hills) C2
Danube (riv.) C2
Dunajec (riv.) F2
Dyje (riv.) D2
Erzgebirge (mts.) B1
Gerlachovka (mt.) E2
Hornád (riv.) F2
Hron (riv.) E2
Ipel' (riv.) E2

Veszprém 386,740 D3
Zala 316,610 D3

CITIES and TOWNS

Aba 4,271 E3
Abádszalók 6,386 F3
Abaújszántó 4,209 F2
Abony 15,624 E3
Ács 8,423 E3
Ajka 29,601 D3
Albertirsa 11,252 E3
Alsózsolca 5,045 F2
Arló 4,203 F2
Aszód 6,218 E3
Bácsalmás 9,025 E3
Badacsonytomaj 2,933 D3
Baja 38,456 E3
Baktalórántháza 3,736 G2
Balassagyarmat 18,534 E2
Balatonfüred 12,599 D3
Balkány 7,667 G3
Balmazújváros 17,371 F3
Barcs 11,448 D4
Bátaszék 7,274 E3
Battonya 9,324 F3
Békés 22,287 F3
Békéscsaba 67,266 F3
Berettyóújfalu 16,406 F3
Berzence 3,406 D3
Bicske 10,720 E3
Biharkeresztes 4,788 F3
Biharnagybajom 4,093 F3
Böhönye 3,215 D3
Bonyhád 14,841 E3
Budafok 40,623 E3
Budaörs 13,958 E3
Budakeszi 10,429 E3
Budapest (cap.) 2,060,170 E3
Bugak 4,989 E3
Cegléd 40,567 E3
Celldömölk 12,533 D3
Cigánd 4,767 F2
Csabrendek 3,045 D3
Csákvár 5,238 E3
Csanádpalota 4,642 F3

Hajdúnánás 18,146 F3
Hajdúsámson 7,492 F3
Hajdúszoboszló 23,374 F3
Hajós 5,113 E3
Hatvan 24,790 E3
Heves 10,943 F3
Hódmezővásárhely 54,481 F3
Hőgyész 3,534 E3
Ibrány 7,037 F2
Izsák 7,686 E3
Izsófalva 6,816 F2
Jánoshalma 12,534 E3
Jánosháza 3,274 D3
Jászapáti 10,424 E3
Jászárokszállás 10,139 E3
Jászberény 31,347 E3
Jászfényszaru 6,869 E3
Jászkarajenő 4,101 E3
Jászkisér 6,816 F3
Jászladány 7,823 F3
Kaba 6,654 F2
Kalocsa 18,613 E3
Kaposvár 72,330 D3
Kapuvár 11,243 D3
Karád 2,754 D3
Karcag 25,264 F3
Kazincbarcika 37,481 F2
Kecel 10,493 E3
Kecskemét 91,929 E3
Kemecse 4,583 F2
Keszthely 21,671 D3
Kétegyháza 4,728 F3
Kisbér 4,562 D3
Kiskőrös 15,499 E3
Kiskunfélegyháza 35,339 E3
Kiskunhalas 30,552 E3
Kiskunmajsa 14,439 E3
Kispest 65,106 E3
Kistelek 8,544 E3
Kisterenye 6,844 E2
Kisújszállás 13,699 F3
Kisvárda 17,828 G2
Komádi 8,765 F3
Komárom 19,955 E3
Komló 30,301 E3
Kondoros 7,319 F3

Nyírbátor 13,388 G3
Nyíregyháza 108,156 F3
Nyírmada 4,744 F2
Örkény 5,013 E3
Orosháza 36,243 F3
Oroszlány 20,604 E3
Ózd 48,521 F2
Pacsa 1,984 D3
Paks 19,514 E3
Pannonhalma 3,731 D3
Pápa 32,202 D3
Pásztó 7,962 E3
Pécs 168,788 E3
Pécsvárad 3,672 E3
Pétervására 2,753 F3
Pilis 9,055 E3
Pilisvörösvár 10,217 E3
Polgár 9,429 F3
Polgárdi 5,767 E3
Püspökladány 15,730 F3
Pusztaszabolcs 5,794 E3
Putnok 7,103 F2
Ráckeve 7,534 E3
Rajka 2,448 D3
Rakamaz 5,407 F2
Rákospalota 60,983 E3
Répcelak 1,997 D3
Ricse 2,992 G2
Sajószentpéter 13,992 F2
Salgótarján 49,320 E2
Sándorfalva 5,949 F3
Sárbogárd 11,178 E3
Sarkad 11,937 F3
Sárospatak 15,316 F2
Sárvár 15,126 D3
Sátoraljaújhely 19,252 F2
Sellye 2,804 D4
Siklós 10,567 E4
Simontornya 4,892 E3
Siófok 20,084 E3
Solt 6,911 E3
Soltvadkert 7,934 E3
Sopron 53,930 D3
Sükösd 4,430 E3
Sümeg 6,229 D3
Szabadszállás 8,223 E3

Velence 3,463 E3
Vémend 2,293 E3
Verpelét 4,622 F2
Veszprém 54,898 D3
Vésztő 9,815 F3
Villány 2,764 E4
Záhony 3,049 G2
Zalaegerszeg 39,671 D3
Zalaszentgrót 5,346 D3
Zirc 5,980 D3

OTHER FEATURES

Bakony (mts.) D3
Balaton (lake) D3
Berettyó (riv.) F3
Bükk (mts.) F2
Csepelsziget (isl.) E3
Danube (riv.) E3
Dráva (riv.) D3
Duna (Danube) (riv.) E3
Fertő tó (Neusiedler See)
(lake) D3
Great Alföld (plain) F3
Hernád (riv.) F2
Kapos (riv.) D3
Kékes (mt.) E3
Körös (riv.) F3
Maros (riv.) F3
Mátra (mts.) E3
Mecsek (mts.) D3
Mura (riv.) D3
Rába (riv.) D3
Sajó (riv.) F2
Sárviz csatorna (canal) E3
Sió csatorna (canal) E3
Szentendreisziget (isl.) E3
Tisza (riv.) F3
Zala (riv.) D3

*City and suburbs.
†Population of Austrian cities
are communes.

YUGOSLAVIA

AREA 98,766 sq. mi. (255,804 sq. km.)
POPULATION 22,471,000
CAPITAL Belgrade
LARGEST CITY Belgrade
HIGHEST POINT Triglav 9,393 ft. (2,863 m.)
MONETARY UNIT Yugoslav dinar
MAJOR LANGUAGES Serbo-Croatian, Slovenian,
Macedonian, Montenegrin, Albanian
MAJOR RELIGIONS Eastern Orthodoxy,
Roman Catholicism, Islam

ALBANIA

AREA 11,100 sq. mi. (28,749 sq. km.)
POPULATION 2,590,600
CAPITAL Tiranë
LARGEST CITY Tiranë
HIGHEST POINT Korab 9,026 ft. (2,751 m.)
MONETARY UNIT lek
MAJOR LANGUAGE Albanian
MAJOR RELIGIONS Islam, Eastern Orthodoxy,
Roman Catholicism

ROMANIA

AREA 91,699 sq. mi. (237,500 sq. km.)
POPULATION 22,048,305
CAPITAL Bucharest
LARGEST CITY Bucharest
HIGHEST POINT Moldoveanul 8,343 ft.
(2,543 m.)
MONETARY UNIT leu
MAJOR LANGUAGES Romanian, Hungarian
MAJOR RELIGION Eastern Orthodoxy

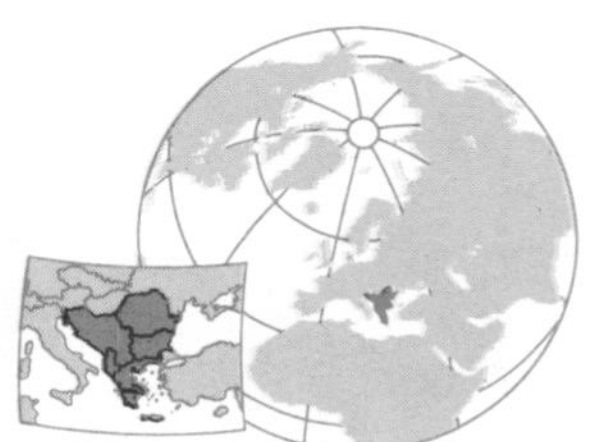

BULGARIA

AREA 42,823 sq. mi. (110,912 sq. km.)
POPULATION 8,862,000
CAPITAL Sofia
LARGEST CITY Sofia
HIGHEST POINT Musala 9,597 ft. (2,925 m.)
MONETARY UNIT lev
MAJOR LANGUAGE Bulgarian
MAJOR RELIGION Eastern Orthodoxy

GREECE

AREA 50,944 sq. mi. (131,945 sq. km.)
POPULATION 9,599,000
CAPITAL Athens
LARGEST CITY Athens
HIGHEST POINT Olympus 9,570 ft. (2,917 m.)
MONETARY UNIT drachma
MAJOR LANGUAGE Greek
MAJOR RELIGION Eastern (Greek) Orthodoxy

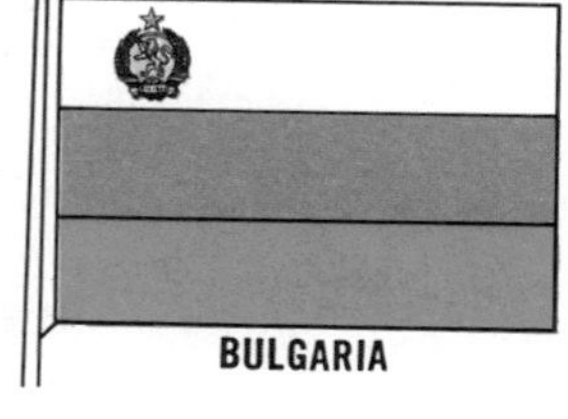
BULGARIA

GREECE

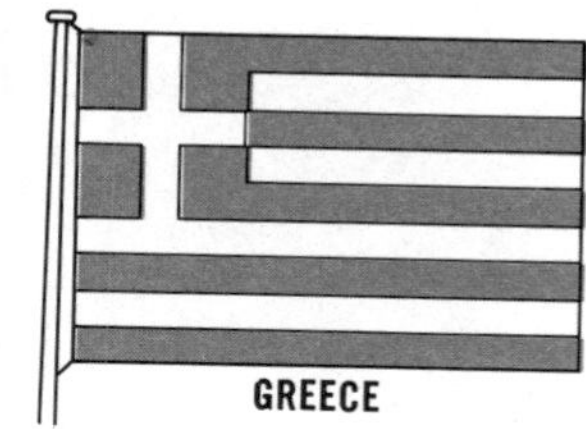
YUGOSLAVIA

ALBANIA

ROMANIA

Agriculture, Industry and Resources

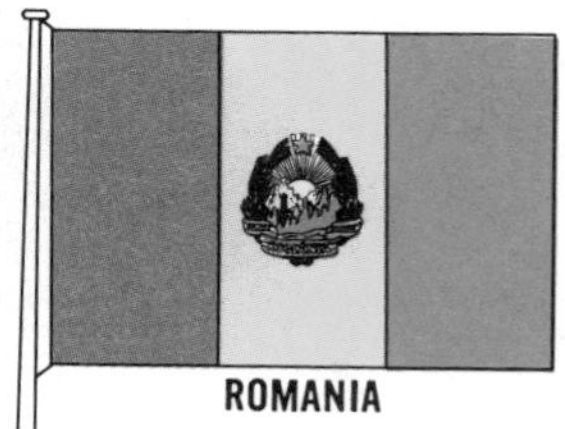

DOMINANT LAND USE

	Cereals (chiefly wheat, corn)
	Mixed Farming, Horticulture
	Pasture Livestock
	Tobacco, Cotton
	Grapes, Wine
	Forests
	Nonagricultural Land

MAJOR MINERAL OCCURRENCES

Ab	Asbestos	Mg	Magnesium
Ag	Silver	Mn	Manganese
Al	Bauxite	Mr	Marble
C	Coal	Na	Salt
Cr	Chromium	Ni	Nickel
Cu	Copper	O	Petroleum
Fe	Iron Ore	Pb	Lead
G	Natural Gas	Sb	Antimony
Hg	Mercury	U	Uranium
Lg	Lignite	Zn	Zinc

⚡ Water Power
▨ Major Industrial Areas

ALBANIA

CITIES and TOWNS

Berat 25.700	D5
Çorovodë	E5
Burrel	D5
Delvinë 6.000	D6
Durrës (Durazzo) 53.800	D5
Elbasan 41.700	E5
Ersekë	E5
Fier 23.000	D5
Gjirokastër 17.100	D5
Kavajë 18.700	D5
Korçë 47.300	E5
Krujë 7.900	D5
Kuçovë (Stalin) 14.000	D5
Kukës 6.100	E4
Leskovik	E5
Lezhë	D5
Lushnjë 18.900	D5
Memaliaj	E5
Pegin	D5
Përmet	E5
Peshkopi 6.600	E5
Pogradec 10.100	E5
Pukë	E4
Sarandë 8.700	D6
Shëngjin	D5
Shijak 6.000	D5
Shkodër 55.300	D5
Stalin	D5
Tepelenë	D5
Tiranë (Tirana) (cap.) 171.300	E5
Vlorë 50.000	D5

OTHER FEATURES

Adriatic (sea)	B4
Drin (riv.)	E4
Korab (mt.)	E5
Ohrid (lake)	E5
Otranto (str.)	D5
Prespa (lake)	E5
Sazan (isl.)	D5
Scutari (lake)	D4
Vijosë (riv.)	D5

BULGARIA

CITIES and TOWNS

Akhtopol 938	H4
Alfatar 3.249	H4
Ardino 5.080	G5
Asenovgrad 43.049	G5
Aytos 20.967	H4
Balchik 11.070	H4
Bansko 10.011	F5
Belogradchik 6.892	F4
Berkovitsa 16.253	F4
Blagoevgrad 50.043	F5
Botevgrad 17.789	F4
Bregovo 5.567	F3
Breznik 4.699	F4
Burgas 144.449	H4
Byala 10.564	G4
Byala Slatina 15.788	F4
Chirpan 20.595	G4
Devin 7.120	G5
Dimitrovgrad 45.596	G4
Dobrich (Tolbukhin) 86.184	H4
Dryanovo 9.804	G4
Elena 7.008	G4
Elin Pelin 5.499	F4
Elkhovo 12.397	H4
Gabrovo 75.034	G4
General-Toshevo 8.928	H4
Godech 5.225	F4
Gorna Oryakhovitsa 34.157	G4
Gotse Delchev 17.015	F5
Grudovo 9.871	H4
Ikhtiman 11.482	F4
Isperikh 10.500	H4
Ivaylovgrad 3.900	H5
Karapelit	H4
Karlovo 25.472	G4
Karnobat 21.480	H4
Kavarna 10.872	J4
Kazanlŭk 53.607	G4
Kharmanli 19.240	H5
Khaskovo 75.031	G5
Kotel 8.229	H4
Krumovgrad 5.211	H5
Kubrat 9.826	H4
Kula 5.667	F4
Kŭrdzhali 47.757	G5
Kyustendil 48.239	F4
Lom 30.538	F4
Lovech 43.858	G4

Lukovit 10.400	G4
Malko Tŭrnovo 4.233	H4
Maritsa 8.664	H4
Michurin 4.434	H4
Mikhaylovgrad 40.064	F4
Momchilgrad 8.185	G5
Nesebŭr 6.768	H4
Nikopol 5.563	G4
Nova Zagora 21.872	H4
Novi Pazar 15.751	H4
Omurtag 9.067	H4
Oryakhovo 14.012	F4
Panagyurishte 20.649	F4
Pazardzhik 65.577	G4
Pernik 87.432	F4
Peshtera 16.882	G4
Petrich 24.381	F5
Pirdop 8.248	G4
Pleven 107.567	G4
Plovdiv 300.242	G4
Pomorie 11.960	H4
Popina	H3
Popovo 19.428	H4
Provadiya 15.143	H4
Radomir 10.436	F4
Razgrad 42.486	H4
Razlog 13.690	F5
Rositsa	H4
Ruse 160.351	H4
Samokov 25.763	F4
Sandanski 19.003	F5
Sevlievo 24.421	G4
Shabla 4.471	J4
Shumen 83.525	H4
Silistra 58.270	H3
Simeonovgrad (Maritsa) 8.664	G4
Sliven 90.137	H4
Smolyan 29.032	G5
Smyadovo 5.020	H4
Sofia (cap.) 965.728	F4
Sozopol 3.877	H4
Stanke Dimitrov 42.034	F4
Stara Zagora 122.200	G4
Svilengrad 15.150	G5
Svishtov 29.412	G4
Teteven 12.555	G4
Tolbukhin 86.184	H4
Topolovgrad 7.230	H4
Troyan 23.692	G4
Tryavna 4.471	F4
Tŭrgovishte 38.796	H4
Tutrakan 11.447	H4
Varna 251.654	J4
Veliko Tŭrnovo 56.497	G4
Vidin 53.030	F4
Vratsa 61.265	F4
Yambol 75.861	H4
Zimnitsa	H4
Zlatograd 7.732	G5

OTHER FEATURES

Balkan (mts.)	G4
Black (sea)	J4
Danube (riv.)	H4
Dunav (Danube) (riv.)	H4
Emine (cape)	J4
Iskŭr (riv.)	G4
Kaliakra (cape)	J4
Maritsa (riv.)	G4
Mesta (riv.)	F5
Midzhur (mt.)	F4
Musala (mt.)	F4
Osŭm (riv.)	G4
Rhodope (mts.)	G5
Rujen (mt.)	F4
Struma (riv.)	F5
Timok (riv.)	F3
Tundzha (riv.)	G4
Vit (riv.)	G4

GREECE

REGIONS

Aegean Islands 417.813	G6
Athens, Greater 2.566.775	F7
Ayion Óros (aut. dist.) 1.732	G5
Central Greece and Euboea 966.543	F6
Crete 456.642	H4
Epirus 310.334	E6
Ionian Islands 184.443	D6
Macedonia 1.888.952	E5
Pelopónnisos 986.912	F7
Thessaly 659.913	F6
Thrace 329.582	G5

CITIES and TOWNS

Agrínion 30.973	E6
Aíyina 5.704	F7
Alyión 18.829	F6
Alexandroúpolis 22.995	H5
Alivérion 4.414	G6
Almirós 5.680	F6
Amaliás 14.177	E7
Amfílokhia 4.668	E6
Amfissa 6.605	F6
Andíssa 1.762	H6
Andravídha 3.046	E6
Ándros 1.827	G7
Ano Viánnos 1.431	G8
Andýa 2.750	G8
Ardhéa 3.555	F5
Árgos 18.890	F7
Argostólion 7.060	E6
Arkhángelos 3.016	J7
Arnaía 2.424	F5
Árta 19.498	E6
Astipálaia 787	H7
Atalándi 4.581	F6
Athens (cap.) 867.023	F7
Áyios 2.566.775	F7
Ayiá 3.241	F6
Áyios Kírikos 1.083	H7
Áyios Matthaíos 1.596	D6
Áyios Nikólaos 5.002	G8
Candia (Iráklion) 77.506	G8
Canea (Khaniá) 40.564	G8
Corinth 20.773	F7
Delfí 1.185	F6
Delvinákion 1.067	E6
Dhidhimótikhon 8.388	H5
Dhíkaia 1.222	H5
Dhimitsána 396	F7
Dhomokós 1.991	F6
Dráma 29.692	G5
Edhessa 13.967	F5
Elassón 7.200	F6
Elevtheroúpolis 4.888	G5
Ermoúpolis 13.502	G7
Fársala 6.967	F6
Filiátes 2.579	E6
Filiatrá 5.919	E7
Filippiás 3.248	E6
Flórina 11.164	E5
Gargaliánoi 5.888	E7
Grevená 8.106	E5
Ierápetra 7.055	G8
Igoumenítsa 4.109	E6
Ioánnina 40.130	E6
Íos 1.270	G7
Iráklion 77.506	G8
Istiaía 4.059	F6
Itháki 2.293	E6
Kalámai 39.133	F7
Kalampáka 5.453	E6
Kálavrita 1.948	F6
Kálimnos 6.492	H7
Kándanos 403	F8
Kardhítsa 25.685	E6
Kariá 1.350	E6
Karial 301	G5
Káristos 3.550	G6
Kárpathos 1.363	H8
Karpenísion 4.414	E6
Kastéllion (Kíssamos) 2.996	F8
Kastéllion 1.152	G8
Kastoría 15.407	E5
Katákolon 690	E7
Kateríni 28.808	F5
Kaválla 46.234	G5
Kéa 693	G7
Kérkira 28.630	D6
Khalkís 36.300	F6
Khaniá 40.564	G8
Khíos 24.084	G6
Khóra Sfakíon 246	G8
Kiáton 7.392	F6
Kilkís 10.538	F5
Kími 2.772	F6
Kiparissía 3.882	E7
Kíssamos 2.996	G8
Kíthira 349	F7
Komotiní 28.896	G5
Kónitsa 3.150	E5
Koropí 9.367	G7
Kos 7.828	H7
Kozáni 23.240	F5
Kranídhion 3.657	F7
Lagkadia 1.350	E7
Lamía 37.872	F6
Langadhás 6.707	F5
Langádhia	F7
Lárisa 72.336	F6
Lávrion 8.283	G7
Leonídhion 3.181	F7
Levádhia 15.445	F6
Levkás 6.818	E6
Limenária 1.507	G5

(continued on following page)

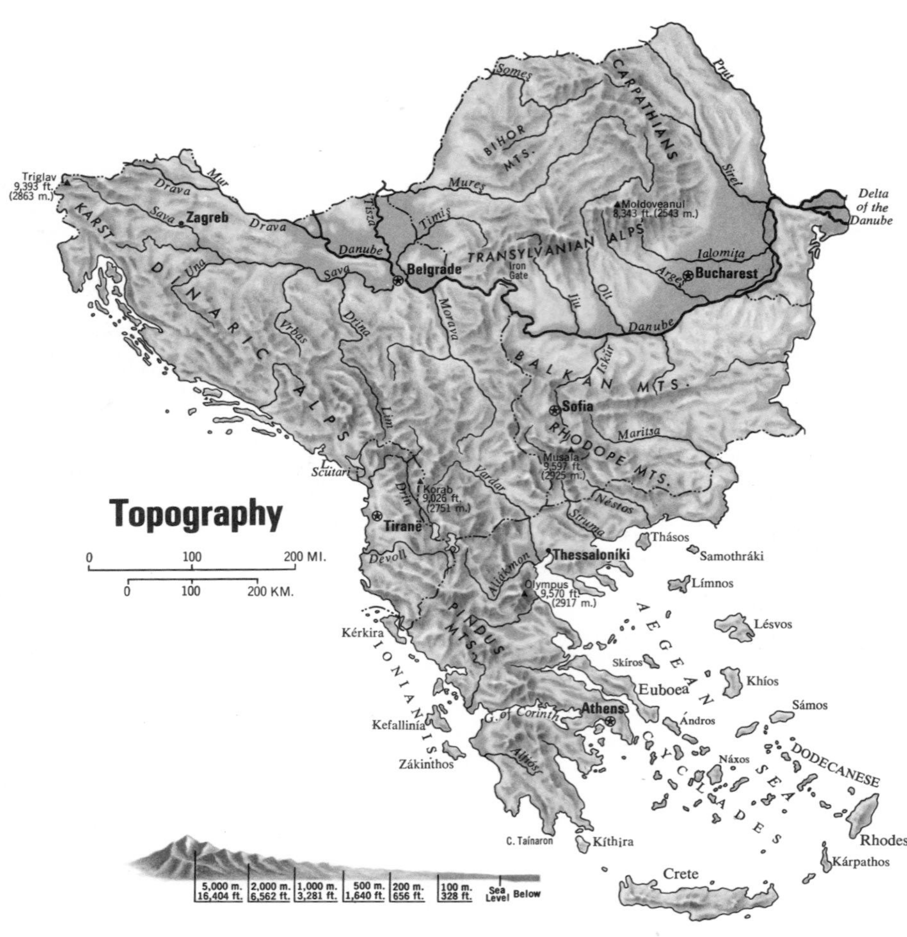
Topography
Triglav 9,393 ft. (2863 m.)
Mur
Drava
Sava
Zagreb
Drava
KARST
DINARIC ALPS
Una
Vrbas
Drina
Danube
Sava
Belgrade
Iron Gate
Morava
Tisza
Timiş
Mureş
Someş
BIHOR MTS.
CARPATHIANS
Prut
Siret
Moldoveanul 8,343 ft. (2543 m.)
TRANSYLVANIAN ALPS
Olt
Jiu
Argeş
Ialomiţa
Bucharest
Danube
Delta of the Danube
BALKAN MTS.
Iskur
Sofia
Maritsa
RHODOPE MTS.
Musala 9,597 ft. (2925 m.)
Nestos
Struma
Vardar
Lim
Scutari
Drin
Korab 9,026 ft. (2751 m.)
Tirane
Devoli
Thessaloníki
Aliákmon
Olympus 9,570 ft. (2917 m.)
PINDUS MTS.
Thásos
Samothráki
Límnos
Lésvos
AEGEAN SEA
Skíros
Euboea
Khíos
Sámos
Kérkira
IONIAN SEA
Kefallinía
Zákinthos
G. of Corinth
Athens
Ándros
Náxos
CYCLADES
DODECANESE
Rhodes
Kárpathos
C. Taínaron
Kíthira
Crete
0 100 200 MI.
0 100 200 KM.
5,000 m. 16,404 ft.
2,000 m. 6,562 ft.
1,000 m. 3,281 ft.
500 m. 1,640 ft.
200 m. 656 ft.
100 m. 328 ft.
Sea Level
Below

Límni 2,394 F6
Líndos 700 J7
Litókhoron 5,561 F5
Lixoúrion 3,364 E6
Loutrá Aidhipsoú 2,195 F6
Marathón 1,976 G6
Megalópolis 3,357 E7
Mégara 17,294 F6
Meligalá 1,724 E7
Mesolóngion 11,614 E6
Messíni 6,625 E7
Métsovon 2,823 E6
Mikínai 390 F7
Mílos 850 G7
Mírina 3,982 G6
Míthimna 1,414 G6
Mitilíni 23,426 H6
Moírai 2,948 G8
Moláoi 2,484 F7
Monólithos 247 H7
Moúdhros 1,024 G6
Náousa 17,375 F5
Návpaktos 8,170 F6
Návplion 9,281 F7
Náxos 2,892 G7
Neápolis 3,070 F7
Neméa 4,356 F7
Néon Karlóvasi 4,401 H7
Nestórion 1,143 E5
Nigríta 7,301 F5
Oinói 188 F6
Orestiás 10,727 H5
Paramithía 2,747 E6
Pátrai 111,607 E6
Pérdika 1,198 E6
Péta 2,116 E6
Pílos 2,258 E7
Piraiévs (Piraeus) 187,362 F7
Pírgos 20,599 E7
Píryí 1,455 G6
Píthion 1,047 H5
Plomárion 4,353 H6
Políkastron 5,279 F5
Políkhnitos 4,152 G6
Políyiros 3,707 F5
Póros 4,051 F7
Préveza 11,439 E6
Psakhná 4,650 F6
Psári 622 E7
Ptolemaís 16,588 E5
Réthimnon 14,969 G8
Rhodes (Ródhos) 32,092 J7
Salamís 18,256 F6
Salonika (Thessaloníki) 345,799 F5
Sámi 957 E6
Sámos 5,146 H7
Samothráki 508 G5
Sápai 2,456 G5
Sérrai 39,897 F5
Sérvia 3,834 F5
Siátista 4,852 E5
Sidhirókastron 6,363 F5
Símí 2,344 H7
Sitía 6,167 H8
Skíathos 3,707 F6
Skíros 1,925 G6
Skópelos 2,545 F6
Souflíon 5,637 H5
Sparta 10,549 F7
Spétsai 3,427 F7
Spíli 789 G8
Stavrós 1,700 F5
Stilís 4,427 F6
Thásos 2,052 G5
Thessaloníki 345,799 F5
Thessaloníki* 482,361 F5
Thíra 1,322 G7
Thívai 15,971 F6
Timbákion 3,229 G8
Tínos 3,423 G7
Tírnavos 10,451 F6
Tríkkala 34,794 E6
Trípolis 20,209 F7
Vámos 652 F8
Vartholomión 3,015 E7
Vathí 2,491 H7
Velvendós 4,063 F5
Véroia 29,528 F5
Vólos 51,290 F6
Vónitsa 3,324 E6
Vrondádhes 4,253 G6
Xánthi 24,867 G5
Yerolimín 73 F7
Yiannitsá 18,151 F5
Ýthion 4,915 F7
Zákinthos 9,339 E7
Zante (Zákinthos) 9,339 E7

OTHER FEATURES

Aegean (sea) G6
Akrítas (cape) E7
Aktí (pen.) G5
Amorgós (isl.) G7
Anáfi (isl.) G7
Andikíthira (isl.) F8
Ándros (isl.) G7
Árda (riv.) G5
Argolís (gulf) F7
Astipálaia (isl.) H7
Áthos (mt.) G5
Áyios Evstrátios (isl.) G6
Áyios Yeóryios (cape) G5
Cephalonia (Kefallinía) (isl.) E6
Corfu (Kérkira) (isl.) D6
Corinth (gulf) F6
Crete (isl.) G8
Crete (sea) G7
Cyclades (isls.) G7
Día (isl.) G8
Dodecanese (isls.) H8
Euboea (Évvoia) (isl.) G6
Évros (riv.) H5
Évvoia (isl.) G6
Gávdhos (isl.) F8
Ídhi (mt.) G8
Ikaría (isl.) G7
Ionian (sea) D7
Íos (isl.) G7
Itháki (Ithaca) (isl.) E6
Kafirévs (cape) G6
Kálimnos (isl.) H7
Kárpathos (isl.) H8
Kásos (isl.) H8
Kassándra (pen.) F6
Kéa (isl.) G7
Kefallinía (isl.) E6
Kérkira (isl.) D6
Khálki (isl.) H7
Khaniá (gulf) G8
Khíos (isl.) G6
Kímolos (isl.) G7
Kiparíssía (gulf) E7
Kíthira (isl.) F7
Kíthnos (isl.) G7
Kos (isl.) H7
Kriós (cape) F8
Kríti (Crete) (isl.) G8
Lakonía (gulf) F7
Léros (isl.) H7
Lésvos (isl.) G6
Levítha (isl.) H7
Levkás (isl.) E6
Límnos (isl.) G6
Maléa (cape) F7
Matapan (Taínaron) (cape) F7
Merabéllou (gulf) H8
Mesará (gulf) G8
Messíni (gulf) E7
Míkonos (isl.) G7
Mílos (isl.) G7
Mirtóön (sea) F7
Náxos (isl.) G7
Néstos (riv.) G5
Nísiros (isl.) H7
Northern Sporades (isls.) F6
Olympia (isls.) E7
Olympus (mt.) F5
Parnassus (mt.) F6
Páros (isl.) G7
Pátmos (isl.) H7
Paxoí (isl.) D6
Píndus (mts.) E6
Piniós (riv.) E6
Prespa (lake) E5
Psará (isl.) G6
Psevdhókavos (cape) G6
Rhodes (isl.) H7
Rhodope (mts.) G5
Salonika (Thermaic) (gulf) F6
Sámos (isl.) H7
Samothráki (isl.) G5
Saría (isl.) H8
Saronic (gulf) F7
Sérifos (isl.) G7
Sídheros (cape) H8
Sífnos (isl.) G7
Sími (isl.) H7
Síros (isl.) G7
Sithoniá (pen.) F5
Skíros (isl.) G6
Spátha (cape) F8
Strimón (gulf) G5
Strofádhes (isls.) E7
Taínaron (cape) F7
Thásos (isl.) G5
Thermaic (gulf) F6
Thíra (isl.) G7
Tílos (isl.) H7
Tínos (isl.) G7
Toronaic (gulf) F5
Vardar (riv.) E5
Voïvís (lake) F6
Vólvi (lake) F5
Voúxa (cape) F8
Zákinthos (Zante) (isl.) E7

ROMANIA

CITIES and TOWNS

Aiud 25,173 F2
Alba Iulia 44,552 F2
Alexandria 38,296 G3
Anina 11,594 E3
Arad 161,568 E2
Babadag 8,423 J3
Bacău 131,413 H2
Baia de Aramă 5,065 F3
Baia Mare 112,893 F2
Băile Herculane 4,606 F3
Băileşti 21,246 F3
Balş 16,091 G3
Beiuş 9,992 F2
Bereşti Tîrg H2
Bicaz 9,490 G2
Bîrlad 59,059 H2
Bistriţa 47,562 G2
Bivolari H2
Blaj 21,678 F2
Borşa 25,287 G2
Botoşani 69,881 H2
Brad 18,391 F2
Brăila 203,983 H3
Braşov 259,108 G3
Bucharest (Bucureşti) (cap.) 1,832,015 G3
Bucharest* 1,960,097 G3
Buhuşi 20,204 H2
Buzău 106,738 H3
Buziaş 8,310 E3
Calafat 16,421 F3
Călăraşi 58,960 H3
Caracal 31,159 G3
Caransebeş 27,429 F3
Carei 24,496 F2
Cernavodă 14,686 J3
Chişineu Criş 9,344 E2
Cîmpeni 7,722 F2
Cîmpia Turzii 23,745 F2
Cîmpina 33,259 H3
Cîmpulung 33,448 G3
Cîmpulung Moldovenesc 19,270 G2
Cisnădie 21,114 G3
Cluj-Napoca 274,095 F2
Cogealac J3
Comaneşti 18,177 H2
Constanţa 279,308 J3
Corabia 20,454 G4
Costeşti 10,446 G3
Craiova 220,893 F3
Cujmir F3
Curtea de Argeş 23,555 G3
Dăbuleni F4
Dăeni J3
Darabani 12,207 H1
Dej 35,396 F2
Deta 6,956 E3
Deva 68,290 F3
Dorohoi 23,121 H2
Drăgăneşti Olt 11,606 G3
Drăgăşani 16,290 F3
Drobeta-Turnu Severin 80,114 F3
Făgăraş 34,762 G3
Fălciu J2
Fălticeni 22,463 H2
Făurei 3,620 H3
Feteşti 28,730 H3
Focşani 62,275 H3
Folteşti H3
Găeşti 13,384 G3
Galaţi 252,884 H3
Gheorghe Gheorghiu-Dej 41,297 H2
Gheorghieni 20,592 G2
Gherla 19,303 G2
Giurgiu 53,241 G3
Haţeg 9,706 F3
Hîrlău 8,135 H2
Hîrşova 8,434 J3
Huedin 8,557 F2
Hunedoara 83,159 F3
Huşi 24,329 J2
Iaşi 262,493 H2
Ineu 10,414 E2
Isaccea 5,283 J3
Jibou F2
Jimbolia 15,325 E3
Lipova 12,427 E2
Luduş 15,771 G2
Lugoj 48,558 F3
Lupeni 28,251 F3
Mangalia 27,263 J4
Medgidia 43,691 J3
Mediaş 68,442 G2
Miercurea Ciuc 38,097 G2
Mizil 14,294 H3
Mociu G2
Moineşti 21,015 H2
Moldova Nouă 18,498 E3
Moreni 17,743 G3
Nădlac 8,407 E2
Năsăud 8,646 G2
Negreşti 7,435 H2
Ocna Mureş 16,381 G2
Odobeşti 8,440 H3
Odorheiu Secuiesc 33,392 G2
Olteniţa 25,536 H3
Oradea 175,400 E2
Orăştie 18,769 F3
Oraviţa 13,628 E3
Orşova 14,873 F3
Panciu 7,772 H3
Paşcani 26,937 H2
Pătulele F3
Pechea H3
Pecica E2
Periam E2
Petrila 25,087 F3
Petroşeni 42,316 F3
Piatra Neamţ 84,192 G2
Pîncota 7,494 E2
Piteşti 125,029 G3
Pleniţa F3
Ploieşti 207,009 H3
Poenari Burchi G3
Poiana Mare F4
Pucioasa 14,056 G3
Rădăuţi 24,222 G2
Reghin 31,948 G2
Reşiţa 90,698 E3
Rîmnicu Sărat 29,815 H3
Rîmnicu Vîlcea 75,070 G3
Roman 56,466 H2
Roşiori de Vede 28,832 G3
Săcele 29,391 G3
Salonta 19,698 E2
Satu Mare 108,152 F2
Săveni 7,913 H1
Sebeş 27,448 F3
Sebiş 6,401 F2
Segarcea 8,783 F3
Sfîntu Gheorghe 51,210 G3
Sfîntu Gheorghe J3
Sibiu 156,854 G3
Sighetu Marmaţiei 38,879 F2
Sighişoara 32,296 G2
Şimleul Silvaniei 14,780 F2
Sinaia 14,215 G3
Sînnicolaul Mare 13,565 E2
Siret 6,677 G1
Slănic 8,017 G3
Slatina 54,954 G3
Slobozia 35,207 H3
Solca 4,835 G2
Sovata 10,745 G2
Ştefăneşti H2
Strehaia 11,431 F3
Suceava 66,857 G2
Sulina 5,240 J3
Tăşnad 10,441 F2
Techirghiol 11,228 J3
Tecuci 37,928 H3
Timişoara 281,320 E3
Tinca E2
Tîrgovişte 71,533 G3
Tîrgu Cărbuneşti 7,536 F3
Tîrgu Frumos 6,428 H2
Tîrgu Jiu 70,629 F3
Tîrgu Mureş 129,284 G2
Tîrgu Neamţ 15,756 G2
Tîrgu Ocna 12,960 H2
Tîrgu Secuiesc 18,265 H2
Tîrnăveni 27,799 F2
Topliţa 14,347 G2
Tulcea 67,091 J3
Turda 57,972 F2
Turnu Măgurele 30,003 G4
Urlaţi 10,900 H3
Urziceni 13,500 H3
Vasile Roaită J3
Vaslui 44,134 H2
Vatra Dornei 16,748 G2
Videle 11,323 G3
Vişeul de Sus 20,697 F2
Viziru H3
Zalău 36,158 F2
Zărneşti 23,378 G3
Zimnicea 15,111 G4

OTHER FEATURES

Argeş (riv.) G3
Bîrlad (riv.) H2
Black (sea) J4
Brăila (marshes) H3
Buzău (riv.) H3
Carpathian (mts.) G2
Crişul Alb (riv.) F2
Crişul Repede (riv.) F2
Danube (delta) J3
Danube (riv.) H4
Ialomiţa (marshes) J3
Ialomiţa (riv.) H3
Jijia (riv.) H2
Jiu (riv.) F3
Moldoveanul (mt.) G3
Mureş (riv.) E2
Olt (riv.) G3
Peleaga (mt.) F3
Pietrosul (mt.) G2
Prut (riv.) J2
Siret (riv.) H2
Someş (riv.) F2
Timiş (riv.) E3
Tîrnava Mare (riv.) G2
Transylvanian Alps (mts.) G3

YUGOSLAVIA

INTERNAL DIVISIONS

Bosnia and Hercegovina (rep.) 3,710,965 C3
Croatia (rep.) 4,396,397 C3
Kosovo (aut. reg.) 1,240,919 E4
Macedonia (rep.) 1,623,598 E5
Montenegro (rep.) 527,207 D4
Serbia (rep.) 8,401,673 E3
Slovenia (rep.) 1,697,068 B2
Vojvodina (aut. prov.) 1,953,980 D3

CITIES and TOWNS

Aleksinac 11,943 E4
Apatin 17,501 D3
Arandjelovac 15,659 E3
Bačka Topola 16,028 D3
Bakar B3
Banja Luka 85,786 C3
Bar 3,594 D4
Bečej 26,616 E3
Bela Crkva 11,137 E3
Belgrade (cap.) 727,945 E3
Beli Manastir 7,325 D3
Beograd (Belgrade) (cap.) 727,945 E3
Berovo 5,053 F5
Bihać 24,155 B3
Bijeljina 24,888 D3
Bijelo Polje 9,298 D4
Bileća 4,083 D4
Biograd 3,595 B4
Bitola 64,467 E5
Bjelovar 21,019 C3
Blato 5,591 C4
Bled 4,710 A2
Bor 27,520 E3
Bosanska Dubica 9,191 C3
Bosanska Gradiška 9,742 C3
Bosanska Kostajnica 2,535 B3
Bosanska Krupa 8,947 C3
Bosanski Brod 10,113 D3
Bosanski Novi 9,861 C3
Bosanski Petrovac 4,113 C3
Bosanski Šamac 4,949 D3
Brčko 25,575 D3
Brežice 3,271 B3
Budva 2,483 D4
Bugojno 9,079 C3
Čačak 38,890 E4
Čakovec 11,766 C2
Čapljina 4,677 C4
Caribrod (Dimitrovgrad) 5,449 F4
Cazin 1,213 B3
Celje 30,827 B2
Cetinje 12,089 D4
Ćuprija 17,691 E4
Daruvar 8,478 C3
Debar 8,597 E5
Derventa 11,887 C3
Dimitrovgrad 5,449 F4
Djakovica 29,499 E4
Djakovo 15,833 D3
Doboj 18,073 D3
Donji Vakuf 4,928 C3
Drvar 6,237 C3
Dubrovnik 31,213 C4
Fiume (Rijeka) 128,883 B3
Foča 9,370 D4
Gacko 1,641 D4
Gevgelija 9,319 F5
Glamoč 2,627 C3
Gnjilane 21,359 E4
Gornji Milanovac 11,114 D3
Gornji Vakuf 2,429 C4
Gospić 8,238 B3
Gostivar 18,805 E5
Gračac 3,228 B3
Gračanica 9,302 D3
Gradačac 7,571 D3
Grubišno Polje 2,771 C3
Gusinje 2,616 D4
Herceg Novi 6,645 D4
Ivangrad 11,373 E4
Ivanjica 5,719 E4
Jajce 9,221 C3
Jesenice 16,163 A2
Kanjiža 11,348 D2
Karlovac 47,046 B3
Kavadarci 17,974 E5
Kičevo 14,189 E5
Kikinda 37,392 E3
Kladanj 3,255 D3
Ključ 3,466 C3
Knin 7,279 C3
Knjaževac 11,734 F4
Kočani 16,611 F5
Kočevje 7,277 B3
Kolašin 2,111 D4
Konjic 9,161 D4
Koper 16,683 A3
Koprivnica 16,398 C2
Kosovska Mitrovica 42,526 E4
Kostajnica 9,161 C3
Kotor 5,728 D4
Kragujevac 72,080 E3
Kraljevo 28,065 E4
Kranj 26,341 B2
Križevci 8,501 C2
Krk 1,500 B3
Krško 4,451 B3
Kruševac 29,902 E4
Kulen Vakuf 1,078 B3
Kumanovo 44,791 E4
Kutina 10,892 C3
Leskovac 46,050 E4
Livno 7,223 C4
Ljubinje 785 D4
Ljubljana 169,064 B3
Ljubuški 2,891 C4
Loznica 13,513 D3
Maglaj 5,869 D3
Makarska 6,589 C4
Maribor 94,976 B2
Modriča 7,406 D3
Mostar 47,821 D4
Murska Sobota 9,665 C2
Našice 5,836 C3
Negotin 11,325 F3
Nevesinje 3,077 D4
Nikšić 28,940 D4
Nin 1,782 B3
Niš 128,231 F4
Nova Gorizia A2
Nova Gradiška 11,765 C3
Novi 2,682 B3
Novi Pazar 28,696 E4
Novi Sad 143,591 D3
Novo Mesto 9,553 B3
Novska 5,168 C3
Ogulin 9,975 B3
Ohrid 26,352 E5
Omiš 3,515 C4
Opatija 9,238 A3
Osijek 94,989 D3
Pag 2,318 B3
Pančevo 53,979 E3
Paraćin 21,555 E4
Peć 41,783 E4
Petrinja 12,296 B3
Piran 5,485 A3
Pirot 29,658 F4
Plav 3,072 D4
Pljevlja 14,459 D4
Ploče 4,257 C4
Pola (Pula) 47,117 A3
Poreč 4,512 A3
Postojna 6,085 B3
Požarevac 33,336 E3
Preševo 7,634 E4
Priboj 12,556 D4
Prijedor 22,379 C3
Prijepolje 7,960 D4
Prilep 48,045 E5
Priština 71,264 E4
Prizren 41,875 E4
Prokuplje 20,617 E4
Prozor 1,420 C4
Ptuj 9,245 C2
Pula 47,117 A3
Rab 1,675 B3
Radoviš 9,373 F5
Ragusa (Dubrovnik) 31,213 C4
Raška 3,935 E4
Ravne na Koroškem 6,529 B2
Rijeka 128,883 B3
Rogatica 4,801 D4
Rovinj 8,998 A3
Rožaj E4
Ruma 24,180 D3
Šabac 43,539 D3
Samobor 7,821 B3
Sanski Most 8,718 C3
Sarajevo 245,058 D4
Senj 4,927 B3
Senta 24,694 D3
Šibenik 29,619 C4
Šid 11,867 D3
Sinj 4,705 C4
Sisak 37,215 C3
Sjenica 9,118 E4
Škofja Loka 4,971 A2
Skopje 308,117 E5
Skradin 893 B4
Slavonska Požega 18,160 C3
Slavonski Brod 38,829 D3
Smederevo 39,200 E3
Smederevska Palanka 18,837 E3
Sombor 44,210 D3
Split 150,739 C4
Srebrenica 3,101 D3
Sremska Mitrovica 32,569 D3
Štip 27,218 F5
Stolac 3,862 D4
Ston 407 C4
Struga 11,369 E5
Strumica 22,770 F5
Subotica 89,476 D2
Surdulica 7,048 F4
Svetozarevo 27,812 E4
Svilajnac 7,848 E3
Teslić 4,940 C3
Tetovo 35,293 E5
Titograd 54,639 D4
Titovo Užice 35,465 D4
Titov Veles 35,583 E5
Travnik 12,745 C3
Trbovlje 16,393 B2
Trebinje 3,553 D4
Trogir 6,162 C4
Trstenik 7,167 E4
Tržič 4,435 B2
Tuzla 53,836 D3
Ub 3,785 E3
Ulcinj 7,472 D5
Umag 3,228 A3
Uroševac E4
Valjevo 26,655 D3
Varaždin 34,662 B2
Vareš 7,632 D3
Velenje 11,225 B2
Velika Plana E3
Veliki Bečkerek (Zrenjanin) 60,201 E3
Vinkovci 29,257 D3
Virovitica 16,389 C3
Višegrad 4,753 D4
Visoko 9,365 D4
Vlasenica 4,033 D3
Vranje 25,909 F4
Vrbas 22,502 D3
Vršac 33,573 E3
Vučitrn 11,701 E4
Vukovar 29,500 D3
Žabljak 1,023 D4
Zadar 43,588 B3
Zagreb 561,773 C3
Zaječar 27,724 F4
Zara (Zadar) 43,588 B3
Zenica 49,522 C3
Žepče 3,177 D3
Zrenjanin 60,201 E3
Zvornik 8,498 D3

OTHER FEATURES

Adriatic (sea) B4
Bobotov Kuk (mt.) D4
Bosna (riv.) D3
Brač (isl.) C4
Cazma (riv.) C3
Cres (isl.) B3
Čvrsnica (mt.) C4
Dalmatia (reg.) C4
Danube (riv.) E3
Dinaric Alps (mts.) B3
Drava (riv.) C3
Drina (riv.) D3
Dugi Otok (isl.) B3
Hvar (isl.) C4
Ibar (riv.) E4
Istria (pen.) A3
Kamenjak (cape) A3
Kladovo F3
Korab (mt.) E5
Korčula (isl.) C4
Kornat (isl.) B4
Krk (isl.) B3
Kupa (riv.) B3
Kvarner (gulf) B3
Lastovo (Lagosta) (isl.) C4
Lim (riv.) D4
Lošinj (isl.) B3
Midzhur (mt.) F4
Mljet (isl.) C4
Morava (riv.) E3
Mur (riv.) B2
Neretva (riv.) C4
Ohrid (lake) E5
Pag (isl.) B3
Palagruža (Pelagosa) (isl.) C4
Prespa (lake) E5
Rab (isl.) B3
Rujen (mt.) F4
Sava (riv.) C3
Scutari (lake) D4
Slavonia (reg.) C3
Šolta (isl.) C4
Tara (riv.) D4
Timok (riv.) F3
Tisa (riv.) E3
Triglav (mt.) A2
Una (riv.) C3
Vardar (riv.) E5
Vis (isl.) C4
Vrbas (riv.) C3
Žirje (isl.) B4

*City and suburbs.

The Balkan States

CONIC PROJECTION

SCALE OF MILES

0 25 50 75 100 125 150 175

SCALE OF KILOMETERS

0 25 50 75 100 125 150 175

Capitals of Countries _____ ★
Administrative Centers _____ ⬡
International Boundaries _____
Major Internal Boundaries _____
Minor Internal Boundaries _____
Canals _____

Scale 1:6,150,000

BULGARIA and GREECE are divided into counties and departments, respectively. Because of the scale no attempt has been made to delimit and name these sub-divisions; their administrative centers have, however, been designated.

The larger divisions named in Greece are well-known geographical regions, without administrative function.

ROMANIA consists of thirty-nine counties and three cities of regional status, Bucharest, Constanţa and Petroşeni. Scale does not permit delimiting these counties.

ALBANIA is divided into twenty-seven districts. Scale does not permit the delimitation of these divisions.

YUGOSLAVIA is a federation of six republics. The Serbian republic includes an autonomous province (Vojvodina), and an autonomous region (Kosovo).

© Copyright HAMMOND INCORPORATED, Maplewood, N. J.

Topography

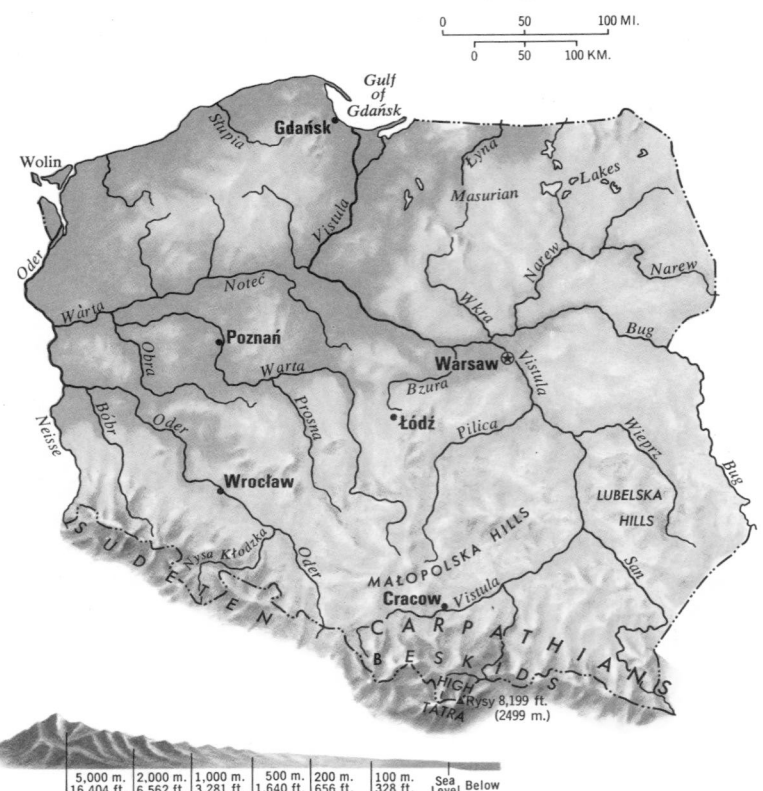

| 5,000 m. 16,404 ft. | 2,000 m. 6,562 ft. | 1,000 m. 3,281 ft. | 500 m. 1,640 ft. | 200 m. 656 ft. | 100 m. 328 ft. | Sea Level | Below |

Agriculture, Industry and Resources

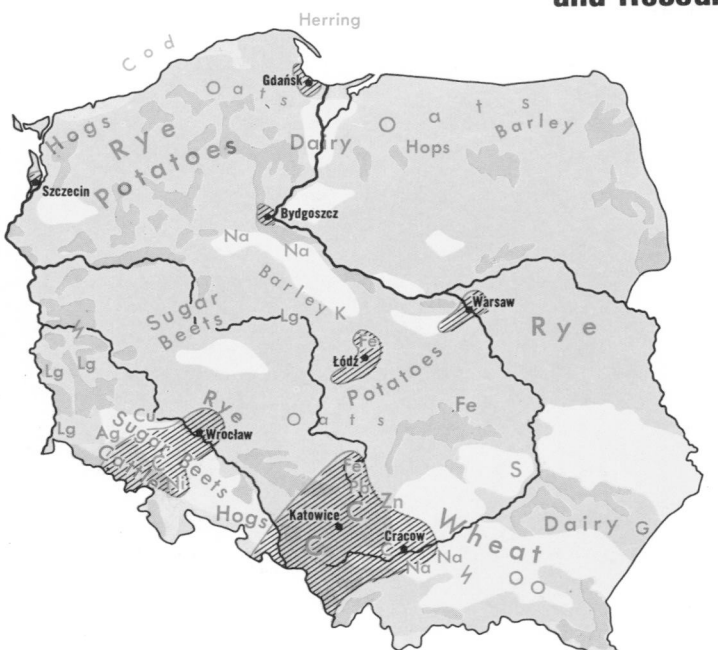

MAJOR MINERAL OCCURRENCES

Ag	Silver	Na	Salt
C	Coal	Ni	Nickel
Cu	Copper	O	Petroleum
Fe	Iron Ore	Pb	Lead
G	Natural Gas	S	Sulfur
K	Potash	Zn	Zinc
Lg	Lignite		

⚡ Water Power

▨ Major Industrial Areas

DOMINANT LAND USE

■ Cereals (chiefly wheat)

■ Rye, Oats, Barley, Potatoes

■ General Farming, Livestock

■ Forests

Poland 1938

0 50 100
MILES

Poland 1945

0 50 100
MILES

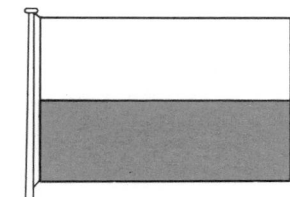

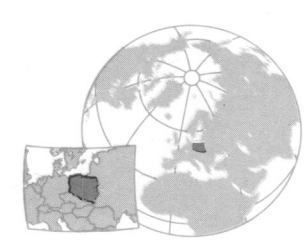

AREA 120,725 sq. mi. (312,678 sq. km.)
POPULATION 35,815,000
CAPITAL Warsaw
LARGEST CITY Warsaw
HIGHEST POINT Rysy 8,199 ft. (2,499 m.)
MONETARY UNIT zloty
MAJOR LANGUAGE Polish
MAJOR RELIGION Roman Catholicism

Braniewo 12,100 ..... D1
Breslau (Wrocław) 461,900 ..... C3
Brieg (Brzeg) 30,780 ..... C3
Brodnica 17,300 ..... D2
Brzeg 30,780 ..... C3
Brzeg Dolny 10,800 ..... C3
Brzesko 9,701 ..... E3
Busko Zdrój 11,100 ..... E3
Bydgoszcz 280,460 ..... C2
Bytom 186,993 ..... A3
Bytów 10,642 ..... C1
Chełm 38,789 ..... F3
Chełmno 17,906 ..... D2
Chełmza 14,200 ..... D2
Chodziez 14,100 ..... C2
Chojnice 23,500 ..... C2
Chojnów 11,000 ..... B3
Chorzów 151,338 ..... B4
Choszczno 9,800 ..... B2
Chrzanów 29,300 ..... B4
Ciechanów 28,500 ..... E2
Cieplice Śląskie-Zdrój 15,400 ..... B3
Cieszyn 25,234 ..... D4
Cracow 651,300 ..... E4
Czechowice-Dziedzice 25,400 ..... D4
Czeladź 31,843 ..... B4
Częstochowa 187,613 ..... D3
Dąbrowa Górnicza 61,660 ..... B3
Danzig (Gdańsk) 364,285 ..... D1
Darłowo 11,200 ..... C1
Dębica 22,900 ..... E3
Dęblin 14,600 ..... E3
Dębno 10,700 ..... B2
Działdowo 10,100 ..... E2
Dzierzoniów 32,800 ..... C3
Elbing (Elblag) 89,835 ..... D1
Ełk 27,188 ..... F2
Gdańsk 364,285 ..... D1
Gdynia 190,125 ..... D1
Gizycko 18,200 ..... E1
Gleiwitz (Gliwice) 170,912 ..... A4
Głogów (Glogau) 20,226 ..... C3
Głowno 12,800 ..... D2
Głubczyce 11,300 ..... C3
Głuchołazy 13,200 ..... C3
Gniezno 50,643 ..... C2
Goleniów 14,600 ..... B2
Gorlice 15,200 ..... E4
Gorzów Wielkopolski 74,267 ..... B2
Gostyń 13,000 ..... C3
Gostynin 12,000 ..... D2
Grajewo 11,200 ..... F2
Grodzisk Mazowiecki 20,400 ..... E2
Grójec 10,300 ..... E3
Grudziądz 75,511 ..... D2
Grünberg (Zielona Góra) 59,700 ..... B3
Gryfice 13,200 ..... B2
Guben (Gubin) 14,600 ..... B3
Hajnowka m4,345 ..... F2
Hindenburg (Zabrze) 199,400 ..... A4
Hirschberg (Jelenia Góra) 55,720 ..... B3
Hrubieszów 14,999 ..... F3
Iława 16,400 ..... D2
Inowrocław 54,817 ..... D2
Jarocin 18,100 ..... C3
Jarosław 29,000 ..... F4
Jasło 17,025 ..... E4
Jastrzębie Zdroj 34,400 ..... D3
Jaworzno 63,271 ..... B4
Jędrzejów 13,264 ..... E3
Jelenia Góra 55,720 ..... B3
Kalisz 81,227 ..... D3
Kamienna Góra 21,000 ..... B3
Kartuzy 10,558 ..... C1
Katowice 303,264 ..... B4
Kedzierzyn-Koźle 45,600 ..... C3
Kępno 10,151 ..... C3
Kętrzyn 19,300 ..... E1
Kielce 125,952 ..... E3
Kłobuck 12,600 ..... D3
Kłodzko 26,000 ..... C3
Kluczbork 18,000 ..... D3
Knurów 28,400 ..... A4
Kolberg (Kołobrzeg) 25,419 ..... B1
Koło 13,100 ..... D2
Kołobrzeg 25,419 ..... B1
Konin 40,600 ..... D2
Końskie 13,100 ..... E3
Konstantynów Łódzki 12,800 ..... D3
Kościan 18,700 ..... C2
Kościerzyna 18,914 ..... C1
Köslin (Koszalin) 64,414 ..... C1
Kostrzyń 11,200 ..... B2
Koszalin 64,414 ..... C1
Kraków (Cracow) 651,300 ..... E4
Krapkowice 13,800 ..... D3
Kraśnik Fabryczny 14,600 ..... F3
Krasnystaw 12,495 ..... F3
Krosno 26,500 ..... E4
Krotoszyn 21,900 ..... C3
Krynica 10,200 ..... E4
Küstrin 11,200 ..... B2
Kutno 30,000 ..... D2
Kwidzin 23,104 ..... D2
Łancut 12,049 ..... F3
Landsberg (Gorzów Wielkepolski) 74,267 ..... B2
Łaziska Górne 10,800 ..... A4
Lębork 25,000 ..... C1
Łęczyca 13,900 ..... D2
Legionowo 20,800 ..... E2
Legnica 75,843 ..... C3
Leszcyny 12,200 ..... A4
Leszno 33,890 ..... C3
Libiaz 10,600 ..... D3
Lidzbark Warmiński 12,900 ..... E1
Liegnitz (Legnica) 75,843 ..... C3
Lipno 10,900 ..... D2
Łódź 777,800 ..... D3
Łomza 25,500 ..... F2
Łowicz 20,400 ..... D2
Lubań 17,200 ..... B3
Lubartów 10,000 ..... F3
Lubin 28,400 ..... C3
Lublin 235,937 ..... F3
Lubliniec 19,800 ..... D3
Luboń 16,400 ..... C2
Lubsko 12,600 ..... B3
Łuków 15,500 ..... F3
Malbork (Marienburg) 30,900 ..... D1
Międzyrzec Podlaski 13,500 ..... F3
Międzyrzecz 14,900 ..... B2
Mielec 26,800 ..... E3
Mikłów 21,300 ..... B4
Mińsk Mazowiecki 24,200 ..... E2
Mława 20,007 ..... E2
Mońki 9,560 ..... F2
Morąg 9,681 ..... E2
Mrągowo 13,400 ..... E2
Myślenice 12,100 ..... E4
Mysłowice 44,737 ..... C4
Myszków 18,000 ..... D3
Nakło nad Notecia 16,800 ..... C2
Namysłów 11,076 ..... C3
Neisse (Nysa) 31,837 ..... C3
Nidzica 9,642 ..... E2
Nisko 10,000 ..... E3
Nowa Ruda 18,100 ..... C3
Nowa Sól 33,300 ..... B3
Nowy Dwór Mazowiecki 16,900 ..... E2
Nowy Sącz 41,103 ..... E4
Nowy Targ 21,900 ..... E4
Nysa 31,837 ..... C3
Oborniki 10,200 ..... C2
Oława 17,746 ..... C3
Oleśnica 27,500 ..... C3
Olkusz 15,800 ..... D3
Olsztyn 94,119 ..... E2
Opoczno 12,168 ..... E3
Opole 86,510 ..... C3
Oppeln 86,510 ..... C3
Orzesze 9,600 ..... A4
Ostróda 21,300 ..... D2
Ostrołęka 21,981 ..... E2
Ostrów Mazowiecka 15,000 ..... E2
Ostrów Wielkopolski 49,530 ..... C3
Ostrowiec Świętokrzyski 49,958 ..... E3
Oświęcim 39,600 ..... D3
Otwock 39,863 ..... E2
Ozorków 18,200 ..... D3
Pabianice 62,275 ..... D3
Piekary Śląskie 36,300 ..... B4
Piła 43,778 ..... C2
Pionki 13,600 ..... E3
Piotrków Trybunalski 59,683 ..... D3
Pisz 11,100 ..... E2
Pleszew 13,348 ..... C3
Płock 71,727 ..... D2
Płońsk 11,619 ..... E2
Police 12,700 ..... B2
Poznań 469,085 ..... C2
Prudnik 20,300 ..... C3
Pruszcz Gdanski 13,000 ..... D1
Pruszków 42,961 ..... E2
Przasnysz 11,100 ..... E2
Przemyśl 53,228 ..... F4
Puck 9,500 ..... D1
Puławy 34,800 ..... F3
Pułtusk 12,600 ..... E2
Rabka 10,700 ..... D4
Racibórz 40,418 ..... C3
Radom 158,640 ..... E3
Radomsko 31,179 ..... D3
Ratibor (Racibórz) 40,418 ..... C3
Rawa Mazowiecka 9,800 ..... E3
Rawicz 14,100 ..... C3
Ruda Śląska 142,407 ..... B4
Rumia 23,300 ..... D1
Rybnik 43,415 ..... D3
Rypin 10,029 ..... D2
Rzeszów 82,192 ..... F4
Sandomierz 16,800 ..... E3
Sanok 21,600 ..... F4
Schneidemühl (Piła) 36,600 ..... C2
Schweidnitz (Świdnica) 47,542 ..... C3
Siedlce 38,983 ..... F2
Siemianowice Śląskie 67,278 ..... B4
Sieradz 18,500 ..... D3
Sierpc 12,700 ..... D2
Skarzysko-Kamienna 39,194 ..... E3
Skawina 15,900 ..... D4
Skierniewice 25,590 ..... E2
Sławno 10,700 ..... C1
Słubice 12,000 ..... B2
Słupsk 68,311 ..... C1
Sochaczew 20,500 ..... E2
Sokółka 10,023 ..... F2
Sokołów Podlaski 9,569 ..... F2
Sopot 47,573 ..... D1
Sosnowiec 144,652 ..... B4
Śrem 15,600 ..... C2
Środa Śląska 10,259 ..... C3
Środa Wielkopolska 14,800 ..... C2
Stalowa Wola 29,768 ..... F3
Starachowice 42,807 ..... E3
Stargard Szeciński 44,400 ..... B2
Starogard Gdański 33,400 ..... D2
Stary Sacz 57,400 ..... E4
Stettin (Szczecin) 337,294 ..... B2
Stolp (Słupsk) 68,311 ..... C1
Strzegom 14,000 ..... C3
Strzelce Opolskie 14,700 ..... D3
Strzelin 9,800 ..... C3
Sulechów 10,200 ..... B2
Suwałki 25,360 ..... F1
Swarzędz 12,100 ..... C2
Świdnica 47,542 ..... C3
Świdnik 21,900 ..... F3
Świdwin 12,500 ..... B2
Świebodzice 18,500 ..... C3
Świebodzin 14,900 ..... B2
Świecie 17,900 ..... D2
Świętochłowice 57,633 ..... A4
Świnoujście (Swinemünde) 27,900 ..... B1
Szamotuły 14,600 ..... C2
Szczecin 337,204 ..... B2
Szczecinek 28,600 ..... C2
Szczytno 17,371 ..... E2
Szprotawa 11,200 ..... B3
Tarnobrzeg 18,800 ..... E3
Tarnów 85,514 ..... E4
Tarnowskie Góry 34,200 ..... A3
Tczew 40,794 ..... D1
Tomaszów Lubelski 12,329 ..... F3
Tomaszów Mazowiecki 54,911 ..... E3
Toruń 129,152 ..... D2
Trzcianka 10,900 ..... C2
Trzebinia-Siersza C4
Turek 18,500 ..... D2
Tychy 71,384 ..... B4
Ustka 9,900 ..... C1
Wąbrzeźno 11,800 ..... D2
Wadowice 11,700 ..... D4
Wągrowiec 15,600 ..... C2
Wałbrzych 125,048 ..... C3
Wałcz 18,900 ..... C2
Waldenburg (Wałbrzych) 125,048 ..... C3
Warsaw (Warszawa) (cap.) 1,377,100 ..... E2
Wejherowo 33,600 ..... D1
Wieliczka 13,600 ..... E3
Wieluń 14,300 ..... D3
Wisła 9,800 ..... D4
Włocławek 77,169 ..... D2
Wodzisław Śląski 25,600 ..... D4
Wolin 35,458 ..... B2
Wołomin 24,000 ..... E2
Wołów 10,500 ..... C3
Wrocław 523,318 ..... C3
Września 17,800 ..... C2
Wschowa 10,000 ..... C3
Wyszków E2
Ząbki 16,000 ..... E2
Ząbkowice Śląskie 13,800 ..... C3
Zabrze 197,214 ..... A4
Zagań 21,400 ..... B3
Zakopane 27,039 ..... D4
Zambrów 14,082 ..... E2
Zamość 34,734 ..... F3
Zary 28,300 ..... B3
Zawiercie 39,410 ..... D3
Zduńska Wola 29,066 ..... D3
Zgierz 42,838 ..... D3
Zgorzelec 28,400 ..... B3
Ziębice 9,700 ..... C3
Zielona Góra 73,156 ..... B3
Złocieniec 10,100 ..... C2
Złotoryja 12,200 ..... C3
Złotów 11,600 ..... C2
Znin 9,600 ..... C2
Zyrardów 33,196 ..... E2
Zywiec 22,400 ..... D4

OTHER FEATURES

Baltic (sea) B1
Beskids (range) D4
Brda (riv.) C2
Brynica (riv.) B4
Bug (riv.) F2
Danzig (Gdańsk) (gulf) D1
Dukla (pass) E4
Dunajec (riv.) E4
Gwda (riv.) C2
Hel (pen.) D1
High Tatra (range) D4
Kłodnica (riv.) A4
Łyna (riv.) E1
Mamry, Jezioro (lake) E1
Masurian (lkes) E2
Narew (riv.) E2
Neisse (riv.) B3
Noteć (riv.) B2
Nysa Kłodzka (riv.) C3
Nysa Łuzycka (Neisse) (riv.) B3
Oder (riv.) B2
Orava (res.) D4
Pilica (riv.) D3
Pomeranian (bay) B1
Prosna (riv.) C3
Przemsza (riv.) B4
Rysy (mt.) D4
San (riv.) F3
Słupia (riv.) C1
Śniardwy, Jezioro (lake) E2
Sudeten (range) B3
Uznam (Usedom) (isl.) B1
Vistula (riv.) D2
Warmia (reg.) D1
Warta (riv.) B2
Wieprz (riv.) F3
Wisła (Vistula) (riv.) D2
Wkra (riv.) E2
Wolin (Wollin) (isl.) B2

Poland
CONIC PROJECTION

SCALE OF MILES: 0 10 20 40 60 80
SCALE OF KILOMETERS: 0 10 20 40 60 80

Capitals of Countries
Other Capitals
International Boundaries
Internal Boundaries
Canals

Scale 1:4,500,000

Poland is divided into 49 provinces (bearing the same name as their capitals) and the autonomous cities of Warsaw, Łódź and Cracow.

Longitude 20° East of Greenwich

UNION REPUBLICS

Armenian S.S.R. 3,031,000	E6
Azerbaidzhan S.S.R. 6,028,000	E6
Estonian S.S.R. 1,466,000	C4
Georgian S.S.R. 5,015,000	E5
Kazakh S.S.R. 14,684,000	G5
Kirgiz S.S.R. 3,529,000	H5
Latvian S.S.R. 2,521,000	C4
Lithuanian S.S.R. 3,398,000	C4
Moldavian S.S.R. 3,947,000	D5
Russian S.F.S.R. 137,551,000	H6
Tadzhik S.S.R. 3,801,000	H6
Turkmen S.S.R. 2,759,000	F6
Ukrainian S.S.R. 49,755,000	D5
Uzbek S.S.R. 15,391,000	G5
White Russian S.S.R. 9,560,000	C4

INTERNAL DIVISIONS

Abkhaz A.S.S.R. 505,000	E5
Adygey Aut. Obl. 405,000	D5
Adzhar Aut. Obl. 354,000	E5
Aginsk Buryat Aut. Okr. 69,000	M4
Bashkir A.S.S.R. 3,849,000	F4
Buryat A.S.S.R. 900,000	L4
Chechen-Ingush A.S.S.R. 1,154,000	E5
Chukchi Aut. Okr. 133,000	R3
Chuvash A.S.S.R. 1,292,000	E4
Dagestan A.S.S.R. 1,628,000	E5
Evenki Aut. Okr. 16,000	K3
Gorno-Altay Aut. Obl. 172,000	J4
Gorno-Badakhshan Aut. Obl. 127,000	H6
Jewish Aut. Obl. 190,000	O5
Kabardin-Balkar	

A.S.S.R. 674,000	E5
Kalmuck A.S.S.R. 294,000	E5
Karachay-Cherkess Aut. Obl. 368,000	E5
Karakalpak A.S.S.R. 904,000	G5
Karelian A.S.S.R. 736,000	D3
Khakass Aut. Obl. 500,000	J4
Khanty-Mansi Aut. Okr. 569,000	H3
Komi A.S.S.R. 1,119,000	F3
Komi-Permyak Aut. Okr. 173,000	F4
Koryak Aut. Okr. 34,000	R3
Mari A.S.S.R. 703,000	E4
Mordvinian A.S.S.R. 991,000	E4
Nagorno-Karabakh Aut. Obl. 161,000	E5
Nakhichevan A.S.S.R. 239,000	E6
Nenets Aut. Okr. 47,000	F3
North Ossetian A.S.S.R. 597,000	E5
South Ossetian Aut. Obl. 98,000	E5
Tatar A.S.S.R. 3,436,000	F4
Taymyr Aut. Okr. 44,000	K2
Tuvinian A.S.S.R. 267,000	K4
Udmurt A.S.S.R. 1,494,000	F4
Ust'-Ordynskiy Buryat Aut. Okr. 133,000	L4
Yakut A.S.S.R. 839,000	N3
Yamal-Nenets Aut. Okr. 158,000	H3

CITIES and TOWNS

Abakan 128,000	K4
Abay 34,245	H4
Abaza 15,202	J4
Achinsk 117,000	K4

Agata	K3
Aginskoye 7,922	M4
Akmolinsk (Tselinograd) 234,000	H4
Aksay 10,010	F4
Aktas	G5
Aktash	J4
Aktyubinsk 191,000	F4
Aldan 17,689	N4
Aleksandrovsk-Sakhalinskiy 20,342	P5
Alekseyevka 18,041	J4
Aleysk 32,487	J4
Alga 12,000	F5
Aliskerovo	R3
Allakh-Yun'	N4
Alma-Ata 910,000	H5
Amderma	F3
Amursk 24,010	O4
Anadyr' 7,703	S3
Andizhan 230,000	H5
Androgov 239,000	D4
Angarsk 239,000	L4
Angren	H5
Anzhero-Sudzhensk 105,000	J4
Aral'sk 37,722	G5
Archangel (Arkhangel'sk) 385,000	E3
Arkalyk 15,108	G4
Armavir 162,000	D5
Arsen'yev 60,000	O5
Artem 69,000	O5
Artemovskiy	M4
Arys 26,414	G5
Arzamas 93,000	E4
Asbest 79,000	G4

Ashkhabad 312,000	F6
Asino 29,395	J4
Atbasar 37,228	G4
Ayaguz 35,827	J5
Ayan	O4
Aykhal	M3
Bagdarin	M4
Baku 1,022,000	F5
Baku* 1,550,000	F5
Balakovo 152,000	E4
Balashov 97,000	E4
Baley 27,215	M4
Balkash 78,000	H5
Balykshi 22,397	F5
Bam	N4
Barabinsk 37,274	H4
Baranovichi 131,000	C4
Barnaul 533,000	J4
Batagay 10,000	O3
Batumi 123,000	E5
Baykit	K3
Baykonur	G5
Bayram-Ali 31,987	G6
Belgorod 240,000	D4
Belogorsk 63,000	N4
Belomorsk 16,595	D3
Beloretsk 71,000	F4
Belovo 112,000	J4
Berdichev 80,000	C4
Berdsk 67,000	J4
Berezniki 185,000	F4
Berezovo 6,000	G3
Bikin 17,473	O5
Bira	O5

Birobidzhan 69,000	O5
Biruni	G5
Biysk 212,000	J4
Blagoveshchensk 172,000	N4
Bobruysk 192,000	C4
Bodaybo 19,000	M4
Borisoglebsk 68,000	E4
Borzya 27,815	M4
Bratsk 214,000	L4
Brest 177,000	C4
Brindakit	N4
Bryansk 394,000	D4
Bugul'ma 80,000	F4
Bukachacha 10,000	M4
Bukhara 185,000	G5
Bulun	N2
Buzuluk 76,000	F4
Chadan	K4
Chapayevsk 85,000	F4
Chara	M4
Chardzhou 140,000	G6
Chatkal 10,100	H5
Cheboksary 308,000	E4
Chegdomyn 16,499	O4
Chelkar 19,377	F5
Chelyabinsk 1,030,000	G4
Cheremkhovo 77,000	L4
Cherepovets 266,000	D4
Cherkessk 91,000	E5
Chernigov 238,000	D4
Chernogorsk 71,000	K4
Chernovtsy 219,000	C5
Chernyshevsk 10,000	M4
Chersky	O3
Chimbay 18,899	F5
Chimkent 322,000	H5
Chirchik 132,000	H5

Chita 303,000	M4
Chokurdakh	P2
Chumikan	O4
Dal'negorsk 33,506	O5
Dal'nerechensk 28,224	O5
Daugavpils 116,000	C4
Denau	G6
Dikson	J2
Dimitrovgrad 106,000	F4
Dnepropetrovsk 1,066,000	D5
Donetsk 1,021,000	D5
Drogobych 66,000	C5
Druzhba	J5
Druzhina	O3
Dudinka 19,701	J3
Dushanbe 494,000	G6
Dzerzhinsk 257,000	E4
Dzhalal-Abad 55,000	H5
Dzhalinda	M4
Dzhambul 264,000	H5
Dzhelinda	M2
Dzhezkazgan 89,000	G5
Dzhusaly 20,658	G5
Egvekinot	S3
Ekibastuz 66,000	H4
El'dikan	N3
Elista 70,000	E5
Emba 17,820	F5
Engel's 161,000	E4
Erivan 1,019,000	E6
Evensk	R3
Fergana 176,000	H5
Fort-Shevchenko 12,000	F5
Frolovo 33,398	E4
Frunze 533,000	H5

Gasan-Kuli	F6
Gol'chikha	J2
Gomel' 383,000	D4
Gor'kiy 1,344,000	E4
Gorno-Altaysk 34,413	J4
Gornyak 16,643	J4
Grodno 195,000	C4
Groznyy 375,000	E5
Gubakha 33,243	F4
Gulistan 30,879	G5
Gur'yev 131,000	F5
Gusinoozersk 10,000	L4
Gyda	H2
Igarka 15,624	J3
Igrim	G3
Ilanskiy 22,852	K4
Indiga	F3
Inta 51,000	G3
Iolotan' 10,000	G6
Irkutsk 550,000	L4
Ishim 63,000	H4
Isil'kul' 25,958	H4
Iul'tin	T3
Ivano-Frankovsk 150,000	C5
Ivanovo 465,000	E4
Ivdel 15,308	G3
Izhevsk (Ustinov) 549,000	F4
Izmail 83,000	C5
Kachug	L4
Kagan 34,117	G6
Kalachinsk 20,809	H4
Kalakan	M4
Kalinin 412,000	D4
Kaliningrad 355,000	B4
Kalmykovo	F5
Kaluga 265,000	D4
Kamen'-na-Obi 35,604	H4

Union of Soviet Socialist Republics

CONIC PROJECTION

SCALE OF MILES

0   100   200   300   400   500   600

SCALE OF KILOMETERS

0   100   200   300   400   500   600

Capitals — Boundaries
★ National
☆ Union Republic
◎ A.S.S.R.
◎ Autonomous Oblast
◎ Autonomous Okrug

Scale 1:30,400,000

AREA 8,649,490 sq. mi. (22,402,179 sq. km.)
POPULATION 262,436,227
CAPITAL Moscow
LARGEST CITY Moscow
HIGHEST POINT Communism Peak 24,599 ft. (7,498 m.)
MONETARY UNIT ruble
MAJOR LANGUAGES Russian, Ukrainian, White Russian, Uzbek,
Azerbaidzhani, Tatar, Georgian, Lithuanian, Armenian, Yiddish,
Latvian, Mordvinian, Kirgiz, Tadzhik, Estonian, Kazakh, Moldavian
(Romanian), German, Chuvash, Turkmenian, Bashkir
MAJOR RELIGIONS Eastern (Russian) Orthodoxy, Islam, Judaism,
Protestantism (Baltic States)

Kamenskoye	R3
Kamensk-Ural'skiy 187,000	G4
Kamyshin 112,000	E4
Kandalaksha 42,656	C3
Kansk 101,000	K4
Kapchagay	H5
Kara	G3
Karaganda 572,000	H5
Karasuk 22,637	H4
Karatau 26,962	H5
Karazhal 17,702	H5
Kargasok	J4
Karpinsk	F4
Karshi 108,000	G6
Kartaly 42,801	G4
Kattangli	P4
Kattakurgan 53,000	G5
Kaunas 370,000	C4

Kavalerovo 16,415	O5
Kazan' 993,000	F4
Kem' 21,025	D3
Kemerovo 471,000	J4
Kentau 52,000	G5
Kerki 10,000	G6
Khabarovsk 528,000	O5
Khandyga	O3
Khanty-Mansiysk 24,754	H3
Khar'kov 1,444,000	D4
Khatanga	L2
Kherson 319,000	D5
Khilok 17,000	M4
Khiva 24,139	F5
Khodzheyli 36,435	F5
Kholmsk 37,412	P5
Khorog 12,295	H6
Kiev 2,144,000	D4

UNION REPUBLICS

	AREA (sq. mi.)	AREA (sq. km.)	POPULATION	CAPITAL and LARGEST CITY
RUSSIAN S.F.S.R.	6,592,812	17,075,400	137,551,000	Moscow 7,831,000
KAZAKH S.S.R.	1,048,300	2,715,100	14,684,000	Alma-Ata 910,000
UKRAINIAN S.S.R.	233,089	603,700	49,755,000	Kiev 2,144,000
TURKMEN S.S.R.	188,455	488,100	2,759,000	Ashkhabad 312,000
UZBEK S.S.R.	173,591	449,600	15,391,000	Tashkent 1,780,000
WHITE RUSSIAN S.S.R.	80,154	207,600	9,560,000	Minsk 1,262,000
KIRGIZ S.S.R.	76,641	198,500	3,529,000	Frunze 533,000
TADZHIK S.S.R.	55,251	143,100	3,801,000	Dushanbe 494,000
AZERBAIDZHAN S.S.R.	33,436	86,600	6,028,000	Baku 1,022,000
GEORGIAN S.S.R.	26,911	69,700	5,015,000	Tbilisi 1,066,000
LITHUANIAN S.S.R.	25,174	65,200	3,398,000	Vilna 481,000
LATVIAN S.S.R.	24,595	63,700	2,521,000	Riga 835,000
ESTONIAN S.S.R.	17,413	45,100	1,466,000	Tallinn 430,000
MOLDAVIAN S.S.R.	13,012	33,700	3,947,000	Kishinev 503,000
ARMENIAN S.S.R.	11,506	29,800	3,031,000	Erivan 1,019,000

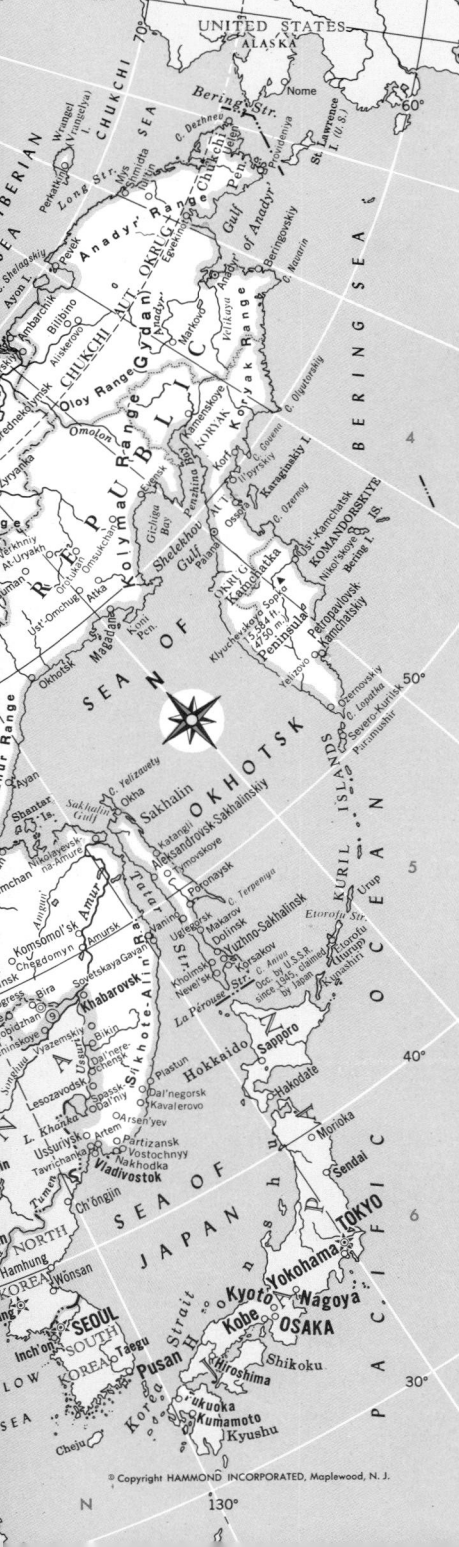

Kirensk 10,000	L4
Kirov 390,000	E4
Kirovabad 232,000	E5
Kirovograd 237,000	D5
Kirovskiy	H5
Kiselevsk 122,000	J4
Kishinev 503,000	C5
Kizel 46,264	F4
Kizyl-Arvat 21,671	F6
Klaipeda 176,000	B4
Kokand 153,000	H5
Kokchetav 103,000	H4
Kolomna 147,000	D4
Kolpashevo 24,911	J4
Komsomol'sk 15,385	G4
Komsomol'sk-na-Amure 264,000	O4
Kondopoga 27,908	D3
Kopeysk 146,000	G4
Korf	R3
Korsakov 38,210	P5
Koslan	E3
Kostroma 255,000	E4
Kotlas 61,000	E3
Kovel' 33,351	C4
Kovrov 143,000	E4
Kozhevnikovo	L2
Krasino	F2
Krasnodar 560,000	E5
Krasnokamensk 51,000	M4

Krasnokamsk 56,000	F4
Krasnotur'insk 61,000	G3
Krasnoural'sk 39,743	F4
Krasnovodsk 53,000	F5
Krasnoyarsk 796,000	K4
Kremenchug 210,000	D5
Krivoy Rog 650,000	D5
Kudymkar 26,350	F4
Kul'say 16,427	H5
Kulunda 15,264	H4
Kulyab 55,000	G6
Kum-Dag 10,000	F6
Kungur 80,000	F4
Kupino 20,799	H4
Kurgan 310,000	G4
Kurgan-Tyube 34,620	G6
Kursk 375,000	D4
Kushka	G6
Kustanay 165,000	G4
Kutaisi 194,000	E5
Kuybyshev 1,216,000	F4
Kuybyshev 40,166	H4
Kyakhta 15,316	L4
Kyusyur	N2
Kyzyl 66,000	K4
Kyzyl-Orda 156,000	G5
Labytnangi	N4
Lebedinyy	N4
Leninabad 130,000	G5

Leninakan 207,000	E5
Leningrad 4,073,000	D4
Leningrad* 4,588,000	D4
Leninogorsk 54,000	J5
Leninsk	K4
Leninsk-Kuznetskiy 132,000	J4
Leninskoye	O5
Lenkoran' 35,505	E6
Lensk 16,758	M3
Lesosibirsk	K4
Lesozavodsk 34,957	O5
Liepaja 108,000	B4
Lipetsk 396,000	D4
Luga 31,905	C4
Lutsk 137,000	C4
L'vov 667,000	C4
Lys'va 75,000	F4
Magadan 121,000	Q4
Magdagachi 15,059	N4
Magnitogorsk 406,000	F4
Makhachkala 251,000	E5
Makinsk 22,850	H4
Mama	N4
Markovo	S3
Mary (Merv) 74,000	G6
Maykop 128,000	D5
Mednogorsk 38,024	F4
Medvezh'yegorsk 17,465	D3
Mezen'	E3

Miass 150,000	G4
Michurinsk 101,000	E4
Millerovo 34,627	E5
Minsk 1,262,000	C4
Minsk* 1,276,000	C4
Minusinsk 56,000	K4
Mirnyy 23,826	M3
Mogilev 290,000	D4
Mogocha 17,884	N4
Molodechno 73,000	C4
Monchegorsk 51,000	C3
Moscow (cap.) 7,831,000	D4
Moscow* 8,011,000	D4
Motygino 10,000	K4
Mozyr' 73,000	C4
Murgab	H6
Murmansk 381,000	D3
Muynak 12,000	F5
Mys Shmidta	T3
Nadym	H3
Nagornyy	N4
Nakhichevan' 33,279	E6
Nakhodka 133,000	O5
Nal'chik 207,000	E5
Namangan 227,000	H5
Naminga	M4
Nar'yan-Mar 16,864	F3
Naryn 21,098	H5
Navoi 84,000	G6

Nazarovo 54,000	K4
Nazyvayevsk 15,792	H4
Nebit-Dag 71,000	F6
Nefteyugansk 52,000	H4
Nel'kan	O4
Nepa	L4
Neryungri	N4
Nevel'sk 20,726	P5
Nikolayev 440,000	D5
Nikolayevsk-na-Amure 30,082	P4
Nikol'skoye	R4
Nizhnevartovsk 39,743	K4
Nizhnevartovsk 109,000	H3
Nizhneyansk	O3
Nizhniy Tagil 398,000	G4
Nordvik-Ugol'naya	M2
Noril'sk 180,000	J3
Novaya Kazanka	F5
Novgorod 186,000	D4
Novokazalinsk 34,815	G5
Novokuznetsk 541,000	J4
Novomoskovsk 147,000	E4
Novorossiysk 159,000	D5
Novosibirsk 1,312,000	J4
Novozybkov 34,433	D4
Novyy Port	G3
Novyy Uzen' 18,073	F5
Novyy Urengoy	H3
Nukus 109,000	G5

Topography

Agriculture, Industry and Resources

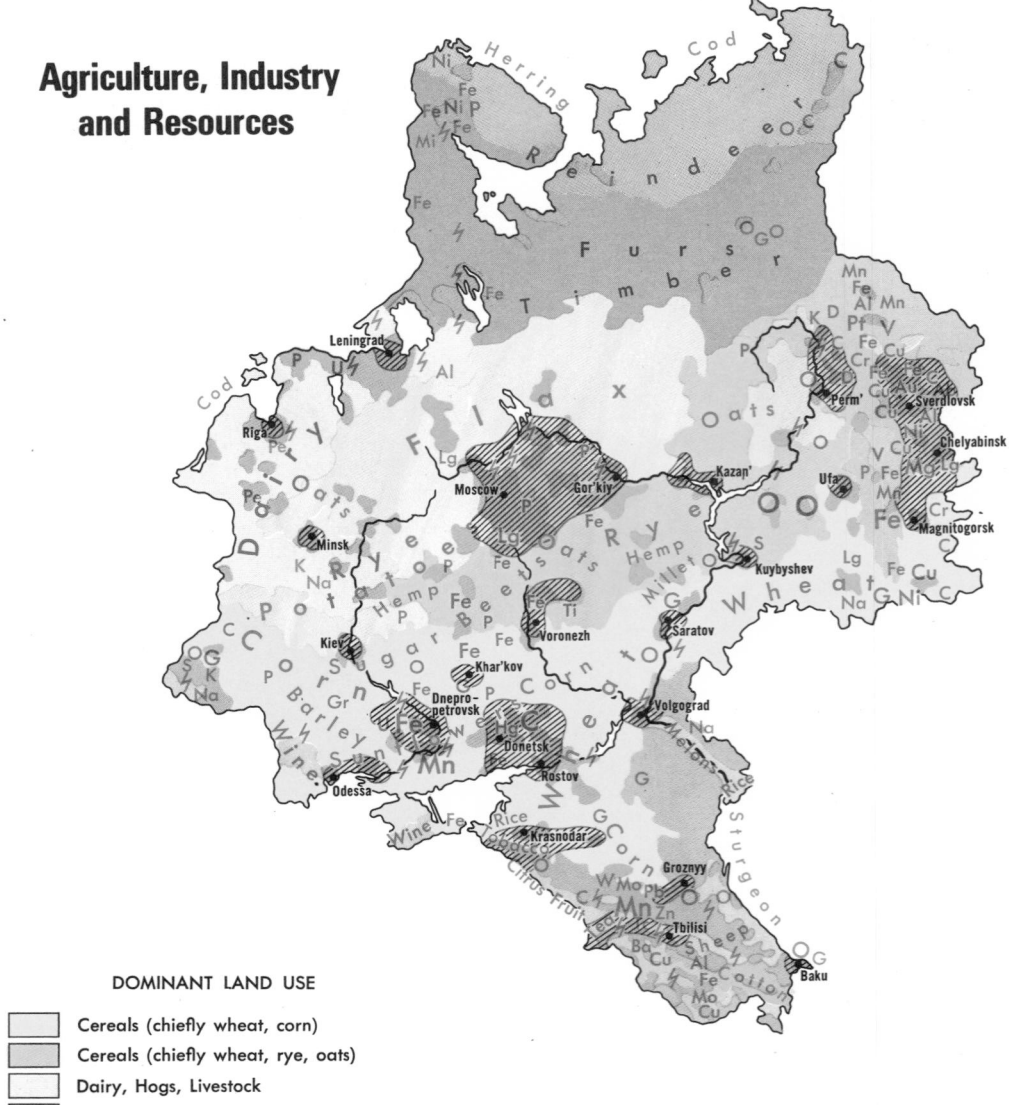

DOMINANT LAND USE

- Cereals (chiefly wheat, corn)
- Cereals (chiefly wheat, rye, oats)
- Dairy, Hogs, Livestock
- Livestock, Dairy
- Pasture Livestock
- Truck Farming, Potatoes, Vegetables, Dairy
- Flax, Dairy, Potatoes
- Cotton
- Vineyards, Orchards, Horticulture
- Sheep Herding, Limited Agriculture
- Forests
- Nonagricultural Land

MAJOR MINERAL OCCURRENCES

Ab	Asbestos	Hg	Mercury	Pb	Lead
Al	Bauxite	K	Potash	Pe	Peat
Au	Gold	Lg	Lignite	Pt	Platinum
Ba	Barite	Mg	Magnesium	S	Sulfur, Pyrites
C	Coal	Mi	Mica	Tc	Talc
Cr	Chromium	Mn	Manganese	Ti	Titanium
Cu	Copper	Mo	Molybdenum	U	Uranium
D.	Diamonds	Na	Salt	V	Vanadium
Fe	Iron Ore	Ni	Nickel	W	Tungsten
G	Natural Gas	O	Petroleum	Zn	Zinc
Gr	Graphite	P	Phosphates		

⚡ Water Power   ▨ Major Industrial Areas

Agriculture, Industry and Resources

DOMINANT LAND USE

- Cereals (chiefly wheat, corn)
- Livestock, Dairy
- Truck Farming, Potatoes, Vegetables, Dairy
- Cotton
- Sheep Herding, Limited Agriculture
- Forests
- Nonagricultural Land

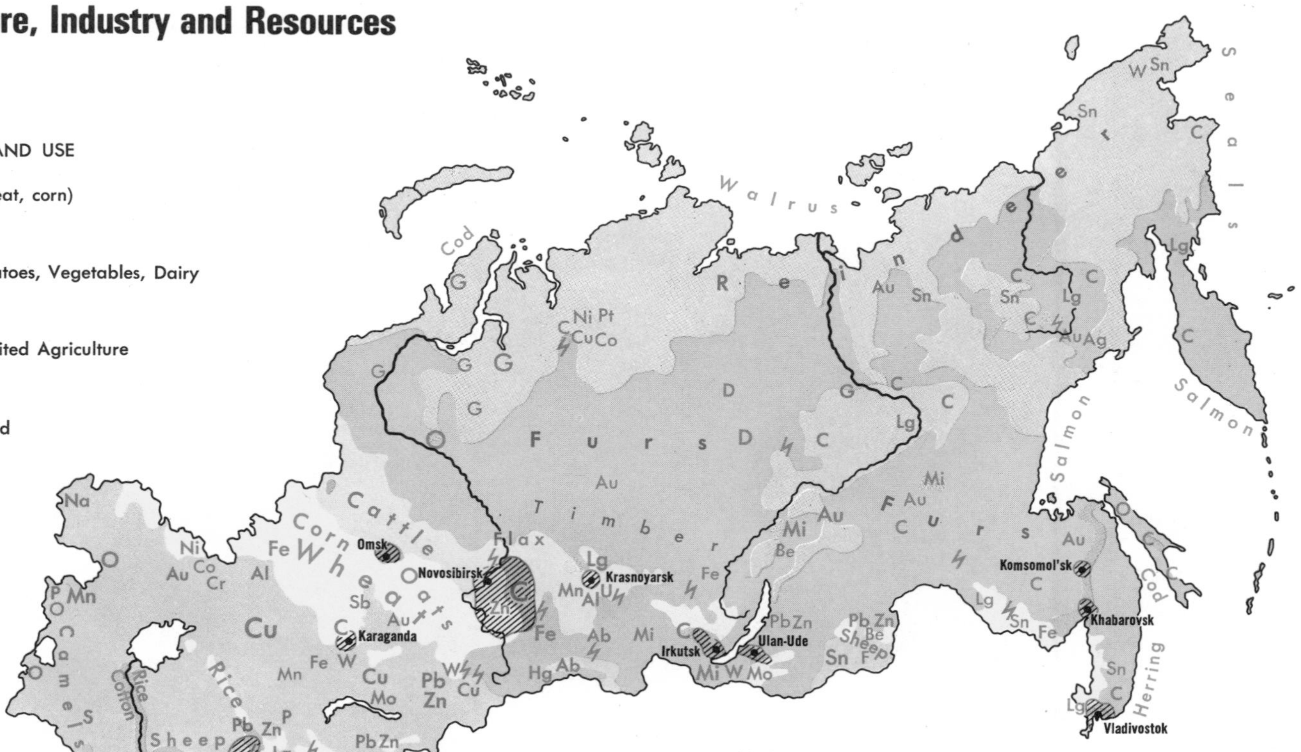

MAJOR MINERAL OCCURRENCES

Ab	Asbestos	Cu	Copper	Mi	Mica	Pt	Platinum
Ag	Silver	D	Diamonds	Mn	Manganese	S	Sulfur, Pyrites
Al	Bauxite	F	Fluorspar	Mo	Molybdenum	Sb	Antimony
Au	Gold	Fe	Iron Ore	Na	Salt	Sn	Tin
Be	Beryl	G	Natural Gas	Ni	Nickel	U	Uranium
C	Coal	Hg	Mercury	O	Petroleum	W	Tungsten
Co	Cobalt	Ka	Kaolin	P	Phosphates	Zn	Zinc
Cr	Chromium	Lg	Lignite	Pb	Lead		

⚡ Water Power ▨ Major Industrial Areas

U.S.S.R.—Railroads and Navigation

Principal Railroads
Navigable Rivers
Canals
Main Sea Routes
Major Russian Ports ⚓

SCALE OF MILES
0 500 1000
SCALE OF KILOMETERS
0 500 1000

© Copyright HAMMOND INCORPORATED, Maplewood, N.J.

(continued on following page)

Union of Soviet Socialist Republics
European Part

CONIC PROJECTION
SCALE OF MILES
0 50 100   300
SCALE OF KILOMETERS
0 50 100   200   300

National Capitals	⋆
Capitals of Union Republics	⬡
Administrative Centers	△
International boundaries	—·—
Union Republic boundaries	—··—
A.S.S.R., Oblast, Kray boundaries	⋯⋯
Autonomous Oblast boundaries	⋯⋯
Autonomous Okrug boundaries	⋯⋯

Scale 1:13,250,000

The government of the United States has not recognized the incorporation of Estonia, Latvia and Lithuania into the Soviet Union, nor does it recognize as final the de facto western limit of Polish administration in Germany (the Oder-Neisse line).

Administrative Divisions bear same names as their respective Capitals or Centers, except:

Abkhaz A.S.S.R.	Sukhumi	F6
Adygey Aut. Oblast	Maykop	F6
Adzhar A.S.S.R.	Batumi	F6
Bashkir A.S.S.R.	Ufa	J4
Chechen-Ingush A.S.S.R.	Groznyy	G6
Chuvash A.S.S.R.	Cheboksary	G3
Crimean Oblast	Simferopol'	D6
Dagestan A.S.S.R.	Makhachkala	G6
Kabardin-Balkar A.S.S.R.	Nal'chik	F6
Kalmuck A.S.S.R.	Elista	F5
Karachay-Cherkess Aut. Obl.	Cherkessk	F6
Karelian A.S.S.R.	Petrozavodsk	D2
Komi A.S.S.R.	Syktyvkar	H2
Komi-Permyak Aut. Okrug	Kudymkar	H3
Mari A.S.S.R.	Yoshkar-Ola	G3
Mordvinian A.S.S.R.	Saransk	G4
Nagorno-Karabakh Aut. Obl.	Stepanakert	G7
Nenets Aut. Okrug	Nar'yan-Mar	H1
North Ossetian A.S.S.R.	Ordzhonikidze	F6
South Ossetian Aut. Obl.	Tskhinvali	F6
Tatar A.S.S.R.	Kazan'	G3
Trans-Carpathian Oblast	Uzhgorod	B5
Udmurt A.S.S.R.	Ustinov	H3
Volyn Oblast	Lutsk	C4

© Copyright HAMMOND INCORPORATED, Maplewood, N.J.

(continued)

U.S.S.R. — EUROPEAN

UNION REPUBLICS

Armenian S.S.R. 3,031,000 F6
Azerbaidzhan S.S.R. 6,028,000 G6
Estonian S.S.R 1,466,000 C3
Georgian S.S.R. 5,015,000 F6
Latvian S.S.R 2,521,000 B3
Lithuanian S.S.R. 3,398,000 B3
Moldavian S.S.R. 3,947,000 C5
Russian S.F.S.R. 137,551,000 F3
Ukrainian S.S.R. 49,755,000 D5
White Russian S.S.R. 9,560,000 C4

INTERNAL DIVISIONS

Abkhaz A.S.S.R. 505,000 F6
Adygey Aut. Obl. 405,000 F6
Adzhar A.S.S.R. 354,000 F6
Bashkir A.S.S.R. 3,849,000 J4
Chechen-Ingush A.S.S.R. 1,154,000 G6
Chuvash A.S.S.R. 1,292,000 G3
Crimean Oblast 2,183,000 D6
Dagestan A.S.S.R. 1,628,000 G6
Kabardin-Balkar A.S.S.R. 674,000 F6
Kalmuck A.S.S.R. 294,000 F5
Karachay-Cherkess Aut. Obl. 368,000 F6
Karelian A.S.S.R. 736,000 D2
Komi A.S.S.R. 1,119,000 H2
Komi-Permyak Aut. Okr. 173,000 H3
Mari A.S.S.R. 703,000 G3
Mordvinian A.S.S.R. 991,000 G4
Nagorno-Karabakh Aut. Obl. 161,000 G7
Nakhichevan' A.S.S.R. 239,000 F7
Nenets Aut. Okr. 47,000 H1
North Ossetian A.S.S.R. 597,000 F6
South Ossetian Aut. Obl. 98,000 F6
Tatar A.S.S.R. 3,436,000 G3
Trans-Carpathian Oblast 1,155,000 B5
Udmurt A.S.S.R. 1,494,000 H3
Volyn Oblast 1,015,000 C4

CITIES and TOWNS

Abdulino 26,010 H4
Agdam 21,277 G6
Agryz 19,267 H3
Akhaltsikhe 18,972 F6
Akhtubinsk 43,466 G5
Akhty G6
Akhtyrka 41,354 E4
Akkerman (Belgorod-Dnestrovskiy) 32,928 D5
Alagir 18,161 F6
Alatyr' 43,499 G4
Alaverdi 21,311 F6
Aleksandriya 82,000 D5
Aleksandrovsk 18,286 J3
Alekseyevka 25,562 E4
Aleksin 67,000 E4
Ali-Bayramly 33,828 G7
Al'met'yevsk 110,000 H3
Alushta 22,016 D6
Amderma K1
Anapa 29,900 E6
Andropov 239,000 E3
Apatity 62,000 D1
Apsheronsk 32,867 F6
Archangel (Arkhangel'sk) 385,000 F2
Armavir 162,000 F5
Arzamas 93,000 F3
Astara G7
Astrakhan' 461,000 G5
Atkarsk 28,881 G4
Azov 75,000 E5
Bakhchisaray 15,912 D6
Baku 1,022,000 H6
Balakhna 36,542 F3
Balaklava D6
Balakovo 152,000 G4
Balashov 93,000 F4
Baltiysk 20,300 A4
Baranovichi 131,000 C4
Barysh 20,792 G4
Bataysk 90,000 E5
Batumi 123,000 F6
Belaya Tserkov' 151,000 C5
Belebey 32,460 H4
Belev 17,733 E4
Belgorod 240,000 E4
Belgorod-Dnestrovskiy 32,928 D5
Belomorsk 16,595 D2
Belorechensk 35,970 E6
Beloretsk 71,000 J4
Belozersk E3
Bel'tsy 125,000 C5
Belush'ya Guba H1
Bendery 101,000 C5
Berdichev 80,000 C5
Berdyansk 122,000 E5
Beregovo 27,308 B5
Berezniki 185,000 J3
Beslan 26,893 F6
Bezhetsk 30,030 E3
Birsk 29,607 J3
Bobrov 17,977 F4
Bobruysk 192,000 C4
Bologoye 33,949 D3
Bor 63,000 F3
Borislav 33,800 B5
Borisoglebsk 68,000 F4
Borisov 112,000 C4
Borovichi 60,000 D3
Brest 177,000 B4
Brezhnev 301,000 H3
Bryansk 394,000 D4
Bugul'ma 80,000 H4
Buguruslan 54,000 H4
Buturlinovka 21,643 F4
Buy 29,946 F3
Buynaksk 37,946 G6
Buzuluk 76,000 H4
Bykhov 17,371 C4
Cēsis 17,696 C3
Chadyr-Lunga 20,474 C5
Chapayevsk 85,000 G4
Chaykovskiy 48,034 H3
Cheboksary 308,000 G3
Cherepovets 266,000 E3
Cherkassy 228,000 D5
Cherkessk 91,000 F6
Chernigov 238,000 D4
Chernovtsy 219,000 C5
Chernushka 21,106 J3
Chervonograd 55,000 B4
Chiatura 25,474 F6
Chistopol' 64,000 H3
Chortkov 19,183 B5
Chudovo D3
Chusovoy 56,000 J3
Danilov 17,500 E3
Dankov 20,030 E4
Daugavpils 116,000 C3
Davlekanovo 20,123 H4
Derbent 70,000 G6
Dimitrovgrad 106,000 G4
Dneprodzerzhinsk 250,000 D5
Dnepropetrovsk 1,066,000 D5
Dobrush 16,809 D4
Dobryanka 18,349 J3
Donetsk 1,021,000 E5
Drogobych 66,000 B5
Dubna 55,000 E3
Dubna E4
Dubno 25,442 C4
Dvinsk (Daugavpils) 116,000 C3
Dyat'kovo 26,825 D4
Dzerzhinsk 257,000 F3
Dzhankoy 43,459 D5
Dzhul'fa G7
Echmiadzin 31,819 F6
Elektrostal' 139,000 E3
Elista 70,000 F5
El'ton G5
Engel's 161,000 G4
Erivan 1,019,000 F6
Fastov 51,000 C4
Feodosiya 76,000 D5
Frolovo 33,398 F5
Furmanov 40,155 F3
Gagra 23,025 E6
Galich 19,374 F3
Gandzha (Kirovabad) 232,000 G6
Gatchina 75,000 C3
Gay 28,250 J4
Gaysin 23,741 C5
Gdov C3
Gelendzhik 29,086 E6
Genichesk 20,031 E5
Georgiu-Dezh 52,000 E4
Glazov 81,000 H3
Glubokoye C3
Glukhov 27,096 D4
Gomel' 383,000 D4
Gori 56,000 F6
Gorki 22,117 D4
Gor'kiy 1,344,000 F3
Gorlovka 336,000 E5
Gorodets 34,229 F3
Gremikha E1
Gremyachinsk 29,975 J3
Grodno 195,000 B4
Groznyy 375,000 G6
Gryazi 41,292 F4
Gubakha 33,243 J3
Gubkin 65,000 E4
Gudauta F6
Gudermes 32,445 G6
Gukovo 68,000 F5
Gus'-Khrustal'nyy 72,000 F3
Imishli 17,839 G7
Inta 51,000 K1
Inza 19,060 G4
Ishimbay 57,000 J4
Ivano-Frankovsk 150,000 B5
Ivanovo 465,000 E3
Izberbash 17,299 G6
Izhevsk (Ustinov) 549,000 H3
Izmail 83,000 C5
Izyum 61,000 E5
Jēkabpils 22,440 C3
Jelgava 68,000 B3
Jurmala 61,000 B3
Kadiyevka (Stakhanov) 108,000 E5
Kafan 29,916 G7
Kagul 26,249 C5
Kakhovka 28,472 D5
Kalach 18,475 F4
Kalach-na-Donu 20,795 F5
Kalinin 412,000 E3
Kaliningrad, Kaliningrad 355,000 B4
Kaliningrad, Moscow Oblast 133,000 E3
Kalinkovichi 23,918 C4
Kaluga 265,000 E4
Kalush 60,000 B5
Kamenets-Podol'skiy 81,000 C5
Kamenka 30,067 F4
Kamensk-Shakhtinskiy 72,000 F5
Kamyshin 112,000 F4
Kanash 40,682 G3
Kandalaksha 42,656 D1
Kapsukas 28,763 B4
Karachayevsk F6
Karachev 15,972 E4
Kashin 17,678 E3
Kasimov 33,066 F4
Kaspiysk 38,990 G6
Kaunas 370,000 B4
Kazan' 993,000 G3
Kazatin 26,649 C5
Kem' 21,025 D2
Kerch' 157,000 E5
Keret' D1
Khachmas 22,313 G6
Khadyzhensk 17,856 E6
Khar'kov 1,444,000 E5
Khasavyurt 65,000 G6
Khashuri 24,469 F6
Kherson 319,000 D5
Khmel'nitskiy 172,000 C5
Khotin 10,319 C5
Khust 23,810 B5
Khvalynsk 16,249 G4
Kiev 2,144,000 D4
Kiliya 24,276 C5
Kimovsk 44,490 E4
Kimry 58,000 E3
Kinel' 39,373 H4
Kineshma 101,000 F3
Kirishi 27,252 D3
Kirov, Kaluga 29,355 D4
Kirov, Kirov 390,000 G3
Kirovabad 232,000 G6
Kirovakan 146,000 G6
Kirovo-Chepetsk 71,000 H3
Kirovograd 237,000 D5
Kirovsk 38,484 D1
Kirsanov 21,795 F4
Kishinev 503,000 C5
Kislovodsk 101,000 F6
Kizel 46,264 J3
Kizlyar 29,745 G6
Klaipeda 176,000 B3
Klintsy 67,000 D4
Kobrin 24,935 B4
Kobuleti 18,051 F6
Kohtla-Järve 73,000 C3
Kolomiya 52,000 B5
Kolomna 147,000 E4
Kolpino 114,000 D3
Kommunarsk 120,000 E5
Komrat 21,369 C5
Komsomol'skiy 17,078 K1
Kondopoga 27,908 D2
Königsberg (Kaliningrad) 355,000 B4
Konotop 82,000 D4
Konstantinovka 112,000 E5
Korenovsk 26,323 E5
Korosten' 65,000 C4
Korostyshev 21,153 C4
Koryazhma 33,230 G2
Kostopol' 17,548 C4
Kostroma 255,000 F3
Kotel'nich 29,196 G3
Kotel'nikovo 19,063 F5
Kotlas 61,000 G2
Kotovo 20,553 G4
Kotovsk, Odessa 36,463 C5
Kotovsk, Tambov 33,347 F4
Kovel' 33,351 C4
Kovrov 143,000 F3
Kovylkino 17,300 F4
Kramatorsk 178,000 E5
Krasnoarmeysk 60,000 G4
Krasnodar 560,000 E6
Krasnograd 18,386 E5
Krasnokamsk 56,000 H3
Krasnoslobodsk 17,749 G5
Krasnovishersk J2
Krasnyy Kut 17,087 G4
Krasnyy Luch 106,000 E5
Krasnyy Sulin 41,684 F5
Kremenchug 210,000 D5
Krichev 25,682 D4
Krivoy Rog 650,000 D5
Krolevets 18,307 D4
Kronshtadt 39,477 C3
Kropotkin 70,000 F5
Krymsk 41,430 E5
Kuba 18,871 G6
Kudymkar 26,350 H3
Kulebaki 46,252 F3
Kumertau 52,000 J4
Kunda C3
Kungur 80,000 J3
Kupyansk 30,055 E5
Kuressaare 12,140 B3
Kursk 375,000 E4
Kutaisi 194,000 F6
Kuvandyk 22,914 J4
Kuybyshev 1,216,000 H4
Kuznetsk 94,000 G4
Kuzomen' E1
Labinsk 54,000 F6
Lakhdenpokh'ya C2
Lebedin 29,240 D4
Leninakan 207,000 F6
Leningrad 4,073,000 C3
Leningrad* 4,588,000 C3
Leninogorsk 54,000 H4
Lenkoran' 35,505 G7
L'gov 25,110 E4
Lida 66,000 C4
Liepāja 108,000 B3
Likhoslavl' E3
Lipetsk 396,000 E4
Lisichansk 119,000 E5
Livny 37,290 E4
Lodeynoye Pole 19,632 D2
Lozovaya 53,000 E5
Lubny 54,000 D4
Luga 31,905 C3
Lutsk 137,000 B4
L'vov (Lwów) 667,000 B5
Lys'va 75,000 J3
Lyubertsy 160,000 E3
Lyubotin 33,324 E4
Lyudinovo 33,871 D4
Makeyevka 436,000 E5
Makhachkala 251,000 G6
Makharadze 21,679 F6
Malaya Vishera 15,381 D3
Malgobek 20,548 F6
Manturovo 21,510 F3
Marganets 50,000 E5
Mariupol' (Zhdanov) 503,000 E5
Marks 17,132 G4
Maykop 128,000 F6
Mednogorsk 38,024 J4
Medvezh'yegorsk 17,465 D2
Melenki 18,545 F3
Meleuz 24,851 J4
Melitopol' 161,000 D5
Memel (Klaipeda) 176,000 B3
Merefa 29,985 E5
Mezen' F1
Michurinsk 101,000 F4
Mikhaylovka 58,000 F4
Millerovo 34,627 F5
Mineral'nye Vody 67,000 F6
Mingechaur 60,000 G6
Minsk 1,262,000 C4
Minsk* 1,276,000 C4
Mirgorod 28,407 D5
Mogilev 290,000 C4
Mogilev-Podol'skiy 26,051 C5
Molodechno 73,000 C4
Molotov (Perm') 999,000 J3
Monchegorsk 51,000 D1
Morshansk 44,245 F4
Moscow (Moskva) (cap.) 7,831,000 E3
Moscow* 8,011,000 E3
Mozhaysk 20,321 E3
Mozhga 38,930 H3
Mozyr' 73,000 C4
Mtsensk 27,833 E4
Mukachevo 72,000 B5
Murmansk 381,000 D1
Murom 114,000 F3
Mytishchi 141,000 E3
Nakhichevan' 33,279 F7
Nal'chik 207,000 F6
Narva 73,000 C3
Nar'yan-Mar 16,864 H1
Neftekamsk 70,000 J3
Nelidovo 29,813 D3
Nerekhta 25,722 F3
Nevel' 17,804 D3
Nevinnomyssk 104,000 F6
Nezhin 70,000 D4
Nikel' 21,299 C1
Nikolayev 440,000 D5
Nikol'sk 20,740 G4
Nikopol' 146,000 D5
Nizhnekamsk 134,000 H3
Nizhniy Lomov 17,460 F4
Nizhniy Novgorod (Gor'kiy) 1,344,000 F3
Nosovka 19,430 D4
Novaya Kakhovka 52,000 D5
Novgorod 186,000 D3
Novgorod-Severskiy D4
Novoanninskiy 20,461 F4
Novocherkassk 183,000 F5
Novograd-Volynskiy 41,194 C4
Novogrudok 19,374 C4
Novokuybyshevsk 109,000 G4
Novomoskovsk 147,000 E4
Novopolotsk 67,000 C3
Novorossiysk 159,000 E6
Novoshakhtinsk 104,000 E5
Novotroitsk 95,000 J4
Novoukrainka 19,554 D5
Novouzensk G4
Novovolynsk 41,187 B4
Novovyatsk 26,408 G3
Novozybkov 34,433 D4
Nurlat 17,533 H4
Nyandoma 23,366 F2
Nytva 17,491 H3
Nyuvchim H2
Obninsk 73,000 E3
Ochamchira 18,718 F6
Odessa 1,046,000 D5
Oktyabr'sk 33,981 G4
Oktyabr'skiy 88,000 H4
Okulovka 19,194 D3
Olenegorsk 21,485 D1
Olonets D2
Omutninsk 28,777 H3
Onega 25,047 E2
Ordzhonikidze 279,000 F6
Orel 305,000 E4
Orenburg 459,000 J4
Orgeyev 25,798 C5
Orsha 112,000 C4
Orsk 247,000 J4
Osa 15,038 J3
Osipenko (Berdyansk) 122,000 E5
Osipovichi 19,705 C4
Ostashkov 23,419 D3
Ostrogozhsk 29,921 E4
Ostrov 22,369 C3
Otradnyy 44,426 H4
Panevežys 102,000 B3
Pärnu 51,000 C3
Pavlograd 107,000 E5
Pavlovo 68,000 F3
Pechenga D1
Pechora 56,000 J1
Penza 483,000 G4
Perm' 999,000 J3
Pervomaysk 72,000 D5
Petrokrepost' D3
Petrovsk 30,953 G4
Petrozavodsk 234,000 D2
Petsamo (Pechenga) D1
Pinsk 90,000 C4
Podol'sk 202,000 E3
Podporozh'ye 21,545 D2
Pokhvistnevo 26,125 H4
Polonnoye 22,484 C4
Polotsk 71,000 C3
Poltava 279,000 D5
Polyarnyy 15,321 D1
Ponoy F1
Poti 45,979 F6
Povenets E2
Povorino 20,591 F4
Prikumsk 35,768 F6
Priluki 65,000 D4
Primorsk C2
Primorsko-Akhtarsk 25,981 E5
Priozersk 16,652 D2
Privolzhskiy 23,041 G4
Priyutovo 21,051 H4
Prokhladnyy 40,074 F6
Pskov 176,000 C3
Pugachev 33,963 G4
Pushkin 90,000 C3
Pyatigorsk 110,000 F6
Rabocheostrovsk D1
Rakhov B5
Rakvere 17,891 C3
Rasskazovo 40,038 F4
Razdan 26,833 G6
Rechitsa 60,000 C4
Reni 19,625 C5
Revel (Tallinn) 430,000 B3
Rēzekne 30,803 C3
Riga 835,000 B3
Romny 53,000 D4
Roslavl' 56,000 D4
Rossosh' 36,438 E4
Rostov 30,815 E3
Rostov-na-Donu 934,000 F5
Rovno 179,000 C4
Rtishchevo 37,146 F4
Rubezhnoye 66,000 E5
Rustavi 129,000 G6
Ruzayevka 41,084 F4
Ryazan' 453,000 E4
Ryazhsk 25,425 F4
Rybinsk (Andropov) 239,000 E3
Rybnitsa 32,266 C5
Rzhev 69,000 D3
Safonovo 53,000 D3
Saki 24,208 D5
Salavat 137,000 H4
Sal'sk 57,000 F5
Sal'yany 24,228 G7
Samara (Kuybyshev) 1,216,000 H4
Sambor 29,253 B5
Saransk 263,000 G4
Sarapul 107,000 H3
Saratov 856,000 G4
Sasovo 27,228 F4
Segezha 28,810 D2
Semenov 23,633 F3
Semiluki 18,221 E4
Sengiley G4
Serdobol (Sortavala) 22,188 D2
Serdobsk 33,783 F4
Sergach 22,509 F3
Serpukhov 140,000 E4
Sevastopol' 301,000 D6
Severodonetsk 113,000 E5
Severodvinsk 197,000 E2
Severomorsk 50,000 D1
Shakhty 209,000 F5
Shakhun'ya 20,009 G3
Shar'ya 25,788 G3
Shchekino 70,000 E4
Shchigry 17,133 E4
Sheki 43,158 G6
Shemakha 17,986 G6
Shepetovka 38,707 C4
Shostka 82,000 D4
Shpola 19,806 D5
Shumerlya 33,816 G3
Shuya 72,000 F3
Šiauliai 118,000 B3
Sibay 37,656 J4
Simferopol' 302,000 D6
Skadovsk D5
Skopin 24,429 F4
Slantsy 41,146 C3
Slavuta 25,573 C4
Slavyansk 140,000 E5
Slavyansk-na-Kubani 54,000 E5
Slobodskoy 34,374 H3
Slonim 30,279 B4
Slutsk 35,609 C4
Smela 62,000 D5
Smolensk 276,000 D4
Sochi 287,000 E6
Sokol 48,243 F3
Soligorsk 65,000 C4
Solikamsk 101,000 J3
Sol'-Iletsk 22,227 J4
Sorochinsk 23,235 H4
Soroki 21,924 C5
Sortavala 22,188 D2
Sosnogorsk 24,688 H2
Sovetsk (Tilsit) 38,456 B4
Sovetsk 17,027 G3
Stakhanov 108,000 E5
Stalingrad (Volgograd) 929,000 F5
Staraya Russa 34,577 D3
Staryy Oskol 115,000 E4
Stavropol' 258,000 F5
Stepanakert 30,293 G7
Sterlitamak 220,000 J4
Stupino 70,000 E4
Sudak E6
Sukhumi 114,000 F6
Sumgait 190,000 G6
Sumy 228,000 E4
Svetlogorsk 55,000 C4
Svetlograd 40,265 F5
Syktyvkar 171,000 H2
Syzran' 178,000 G4
Taganrog 276,000 E5
Tallinn 430,000 B3
Tambov 270,000 F4
Tartu 105,000 C3
Taurage 19,461 B3
Tbilisi 1,066,000 F6
Telavi 21,179 G6
Telšiai 20,220 B3
Temryuk 23,172 E5
Ternopol' 144,000 C5
Teykovo 41,607 E3
Tiflis (Tbilisi) 1,066,000 F6
Tighina (Bendery) 101,000 C5
Tikhoretsk 64,000 F5
Tikhvin 59,000 D3
Tilsit (Sovetsk) 38,456 B4
Timashevsk 29,055 E5
Tiraspol' 139,000 D5
Togliatti (Tol'yatti) 502,000 G4
Tokmak 59,000 E5
Toropets 16,863 D3
Torzhok 45,443 D3
Troitsko-Pechorsk J2
Tskhinvali 30,311 F6
Tuapse 60,000 E6
Tula 514,000 E4
Tutayev 16,839 E3
Tuymazy 37,021 H4
Tver (Kalinin) 412,000 E3
Tyrnyauz 18,253 F6
Uchaly 21,808 J4
Ufa 969,000 J4
Uglich 35,463 E3
Ukmerge 21,663 C3
Ul'yanovsk 464,000 G4
Uman' 79,000 D5
Unecha 21,749 D4
Ungeny 17,228 C5
Uryupinsk 38,192 F4
Usinsk J1
Usman' 20,150 E4
Ustinov 549,000 H3
Uvarovo 24,946 F4
Uzhgorod 91,000 B5
Uzlovaya 65,000 E4
Valga 16,795 C3
Valmiera 20,331 C3
Valuyki 29,093 E4
Vasil'kov 26,741 D4
Velikiye Luki 102,000 D3
Velikiy Ustyug 36,737 F2
Vel'sk 21,899 F2
Ventspils 40,467 B3
Vereshchagino 23,585 H3
Vichuga 52,000 F3
Viipuri (Vyborg) 76,000 C2
Vileyka C4
Vilna (Vilnius) 481,000 C4
Vinnitsa 314,000 C5
Vinogradov 20,580 B5
Vitebsk 297,000 C3
Vladimir 296,000 F3
Vladimir-Volynskiy 28,412 B4
Volgodonsk 91,000 F5
Volgograd 929,000 F5
Volkhov 47,025 D3
Volkovysk 28,266 B4
Vologda 237,000 F3
Vol'sk 66,000 G4
Volzhsk 52,000 G3
Volzhskiy 209,000 G5
Vorkuta 100,000 K1
Voronezh 783,000 E4
Voroshilovgrad 463,000 E5
Voskresensk 76,000 E3
Votkinsk 90,000 H3
Voznesensk 36,457 D5
Vyatskiye Polyany 32,729 H3
Vyaz'ma 52,000 D3
Vyborg 76,000 C2
Vyksa 54,000 F3
Vyshniy Volochek 72,000 D3
Yalta 80,000 D6
Yanaul 20,115 J3
Yaroslavl' 597,000 E3
Yartsevo 36,662 D3
Yefremov 53,000 E4
Yelabuga 31,728 H3
Yelets 112,000 E4
Yenakiyevo 114,000 E5
Yershov 21,731 G4
Yessentuki 78,000 F6
Yevlakh 29,462 G6
Yevpatoria 93,000 D5
Yeysk 71,000 E5
Yoshkar-Ola 201,000 G3
Yur'yevets 20,144 F3
Zagorsk 107,000 E3
Zapolyarnyy 22,084 D1
Zaporozh'ye 781,000 E5
Zelenodol'sk 85,000 G3
Zelenokumsk 29,691 F6
Zernograd 20,324 F5
Zhdanov 503,000 E5
Zheleznodorozhnyy 76,000 H2
Zheleznogorsk 65,000 E4
Zhigulevsk 52,130 G4
Zhitomir 244,000 C4
Zhlobin 25,359 D4
Zhmerinka 36,195 C5
Zhodino 22,083 C4
Zhovtnevoye 31,102 D5
Znamenka 27,393 D5
Zolotonosha 27,639 D5
Zugdidi 39,896 F6
Zuyevka 17,001 H3

OTHER FEATURES

Apsheron (pen.) H6
Araks (riv.) G7
Azov (sea) E5
Baltic (sea) B3
Barents (sea) E1
Belaya (riv.) H3
Beloye (lake) E2
Black (sea) D6
Bug (riv.) B4
Bug (riv.) D5
Caspian (sea) G6
Caucasus (mts.) F6
Crimea (pen.) D5
Desna (riv.) D4
Dnieper (riv.) D5
Dniester (riv.) C5
Don (riv.) F5
Donets (riv.) E5
Dvina (bay) E2
Dvina, Northern (riv.) F2
Dvina, Western (riv.) C3
Dykh-Tau (mt.) F6
El'brus (mt.) F6
Finland (gulf) C3
Hiiumaa (isl.) B3
Il'men' (lake) D3
Imandra (lake) D1
Kakhovka (res.) D5
Kama (riv.) H2
Kandalaksha (gulf) D1
Kanin (pen.) G1
Kara (sea) K1
Karskiye Vorota (str.) J1
Kazbek (mt.) F6
Khoper (riv.) F4
Kola (pen.) E1
Kolguyev (isl.) G1
Kuban' (riv.) E5
Kura (riv.) G6
Kuybyshev (res.) G4
Ladoga (lake) D2
Lapland (reg.) D1
Mezen' (riv.) G1
Moksha (riv.) F4
Narodnaya (mt.) J1
Niemen (riv.) B4
Novaya Zemlya (isls.) H1
Oka (riv.) F4
Onega (bay) E2
Onega (lake) E2
Onega (riv.) E2
Pechora (riv.) H1
Peipus (lake) C3
Pripet (marshes) C4
Pripyat' (riv.) C4
Prut (riv.) C5
Riga (gulf) B3
Rybachiy (pen.) D1
Rybinsk (res.) E3
Saaremaa (isl.) B3
Samara (riv.) H4
Sevan (lake) G6
Seym (riv.) D4
Sura (riv.) G4
Svir' (riv.) D2
Timan (ridge) G1
Tsil'ma (riv.) H1
Tsimlyansk (res.) F5
Tuloma (riv.) D1
Ural (mts.) J2
Ural (riv.) J4
Usa (riv.) K1
Valday (hills) D3
Vaygach (isl.) K1
Velikaya (riv.) C3
Volga (riv.) G5
Volga-Don (canal) F5
Volgograd (res.) G5
Volkhov (riv.) D3
Vorskla (riv.) E4
Vyatka (riv.) H3
Vychegda (riv.) G2
Vyg (lake) E2
White (sea) E1
Yamantau (mt.) J4
Yugorskiy (pen.) K1

*City and suburbs.

The Baltic States

SCALE OF MILES 0 25 50 75 100
SCALE OF KILOMETERS 0 30 60 90 120 150 180

Capitals ☆
International Boundaries
Union Republic Boundaries
Prewar boundaries of the Baltic States where divergent from present boundaries

ESTONIA

LATVIA

LITHUANIA

The government of the United States has not recognized the incorporation of Estonia, Latvia and Lithuania into the Soviet Union, nor does it recognize other post-war territorial changes shown on this map. The flags shown here were the official flags of the independent Baltic States prior to 1939.

© Copyright HAMMOND INCORPORATED, Maplewood, N. J.

BALTIC STATES

Alytus 55,000 C3
Biržai 11,400 C2
Cēsis 17,696 C2
Daugava (Western Dvina) (riv.) D2
Daugavpils 116,000 D3
Dobele 10,100 B2
Druskininkai 11,200 C3
Dvina Western (riv.) C2
Finland (gulf) D1
Gauja (riv.) C2
Haapsalu 11,483 B1
Hiiumaa (isl.) B1
Jēkabpils 22,400 C2
Jelgava 68,000 B2
Jonava 14,400 C3
Jurmala 61,000 B2
Kapsukas 28,763 B3
Kaunas 370,000 C3
Kedainiai 19,677 C3
Kihnu (isl.) B1
Kingisepp (Kuressaare) 12,140 B1
Kiviõli 11,153 D1
Klaipeda 176,000 A3
Kohtla-Järve 73,000 D1
Kretinga 13,000 A3
Kuldīga 12,300 A2
Kuressaare 12,140 B1
Kuršenai 11,500 B2
Liepāja 108,000 A2
Lubāna (lake) D2
Mažeikiai 13,400 A2
Memel (Klaipeda) 176,000 A3
Muhu (isl.) B1
Narva 73,000 E1
Naujoji-Akmene 10,200 B2
Niemen (riv.) A3
Ogre 15,708 C2
Panevežys 102,000 C3
Pärnu 51,000 C1
Peipus (lake) D1
Plunge 13,600 B3
Radviliškis 16,841 B3
Rakvere 17,891 D1
Rēzekne 30,803 D2
Riga (cap.), Latvia 835,000 C2
Riga (gulf) B2
Saaremaa (isl.) B1
Saldus 10,000 B2
Šiauliai 118,000 B3
Sillamäe 13,505 D1
Šilute 12,400 A3
Tallinn (cap.), Estonia 430,000 C1
Tapa 10,037 C1
Tartu 105,000 D1
Taurage 19,461 B3
Telšiai 20,220 B2
Tukums 14,800 B2
Ukmerge 21,663 C3
Utena 13,300 C3
Valga 16,795 D2
Valmiera 20,331 C2
Venta (riv.) B2
Ventspils 40,467 A2
Viliya (riv.) C3
Viljandi 20,814 C1
Vilna (Vilnius) (cap.), Lithuania 481,000 C3
Vormsi (isl.) B1
Võrtsjärv (lake) D1
Võru 15,398 D2
Western Dvina (riv.) C2

Asia

LAMBERT AZIMUTHAL EQUAL-AREA PROJECTION

SCALE OF MILES
0 100 200 400 600 800 1000 1200

SCALE OF KILOMETERS
0 200 400 600 800 1000 1200

Capitals of Countries .... ⊛
Other Capitals .... ⊙
International Boundaries .... ▬▬▬▬
Other Boundaries .... ▬ ▪ ▬ ▪ ▬
Canals .... ▬▬▬

Scale 1:46,500,000

© Copyright Hammond Incorporated, Maplewood, N.J.

Population Distribution

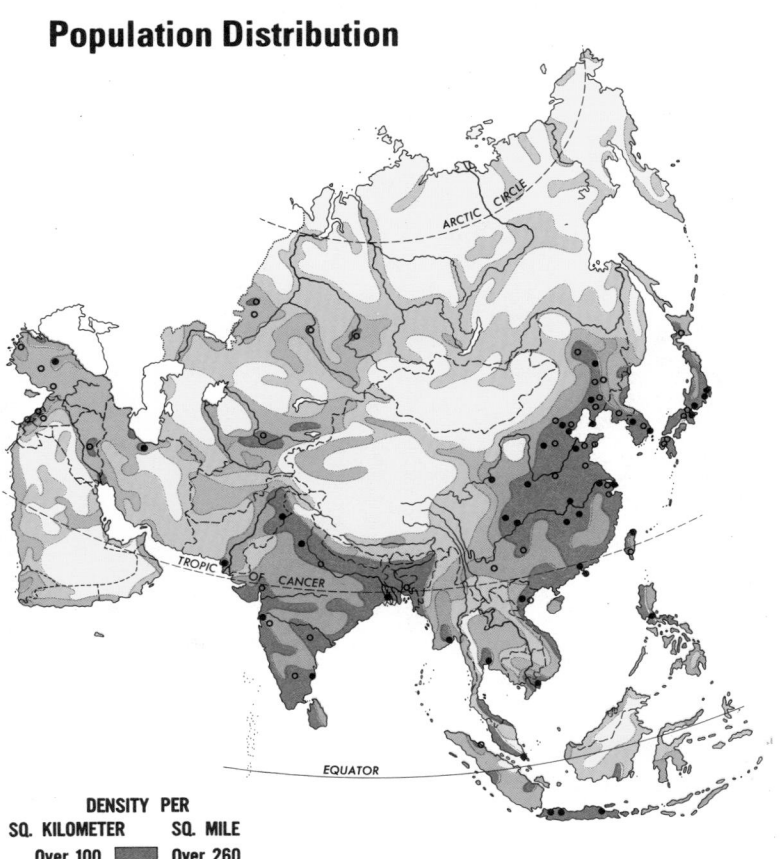

AREA 17,128,500 sq. mi.
(44,362,815 sq. km.)
POPULATION 2,633,000,000
LARGEST CITY Tokyo
HIGHEST POINT Mt. Everest 29,028 ft.
(8,848 m.)
LOWEST POINT Dead Sea -1,296 ft.
(-395 m.)

Vegetation

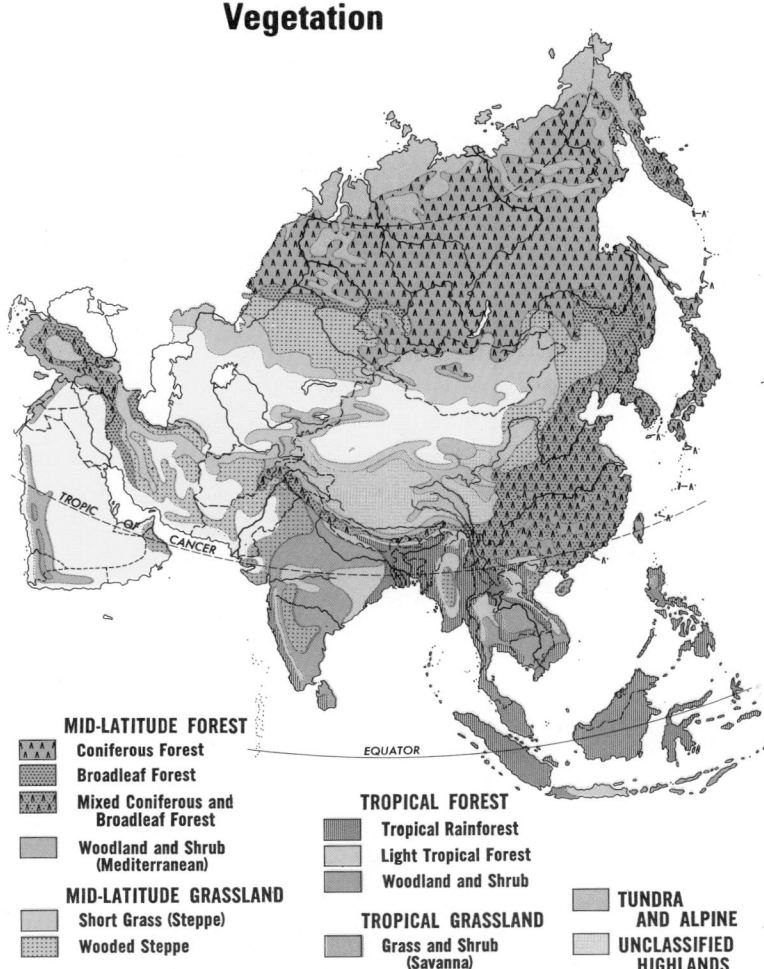

DENSITY PER

SQ. KILOMETER	SQ. MILE
Over 100	Over 260
50-100	130-260
10-50	25-130
1-10	3-25
Under 1	Under 3

● Cities with over 2,000,000 inhabitants (including suburbs)

○ Cities with over 1,000,000 inhabitants (including suburbs)

MID-LATITUDE FOREST
Coniferous Forest
Broadleaf Forest
Mixed Coniferous and Broadleaf Forest
Woodland and Shrub (Mediterranean)

MID-LATITUDE GRASSLAND
Short Grass (Steppe)
Wooded Steppe

DESERT AND DESERT SHRUB

TROPICAL FOREST
Tropical Rainforest
Light Tropical Forest
Woodland and Shrub

TROPICAL GRASSLAND
Grass and Shrub (Savanna)
Wooded Savanna

TUNDRA AND ALPINE

UNCLASSIFIED HIGHLANDS

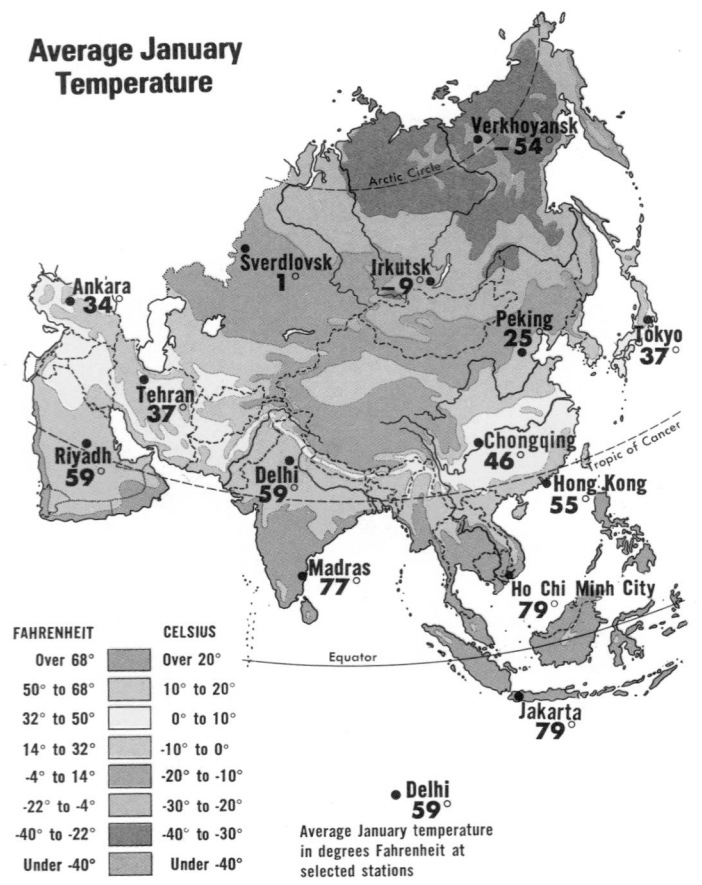

Average January Temperature

FAHRENHEIT	CELSIUS
Over 68°	Over 20°
50° to 68°	10° to 20°
32° to 50°	0° to 10°
14° to 32°	-10° to 0°
-4° to 14°	-20° to -10°
-22° to -4°	-30° to -20°
-40° to -22°	-40° to -30°
Under -40°	Under -40°

● Delhi
59°
Average January temperature in degrees Fahrenheit at selected stations

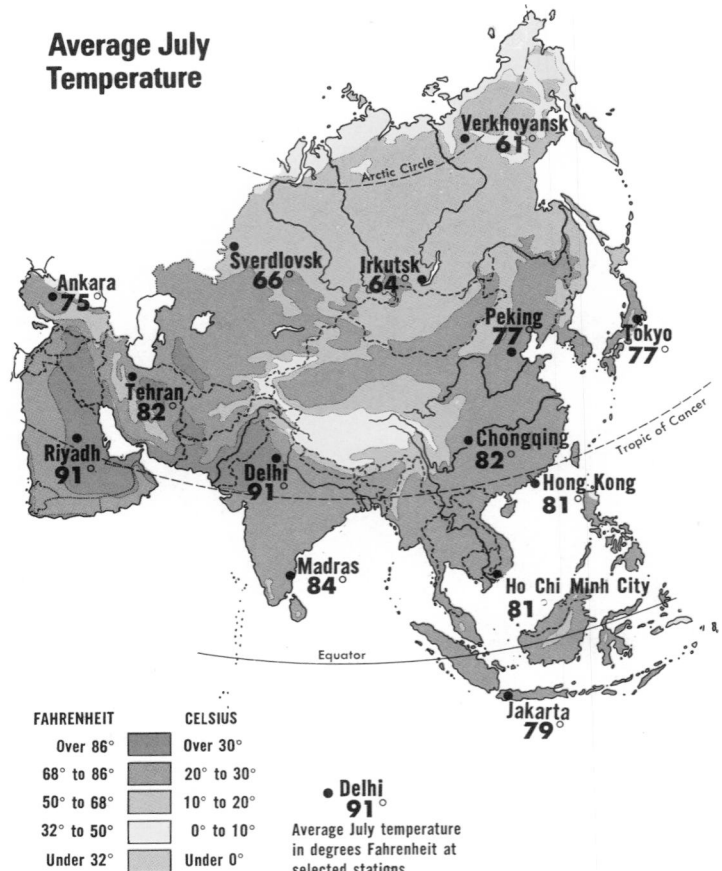

Average July Temperature

FAHRENHEIT	CELSIUS
Over 86°	Over 30°
68° to 86°	20° to 30°
50° to 68°	10° to 20°
32° to 50°	0° to 10°
Under 32°	Under 0°

● Delhi
91°
Average July temperature in degrees Fahrenheit at selected stations

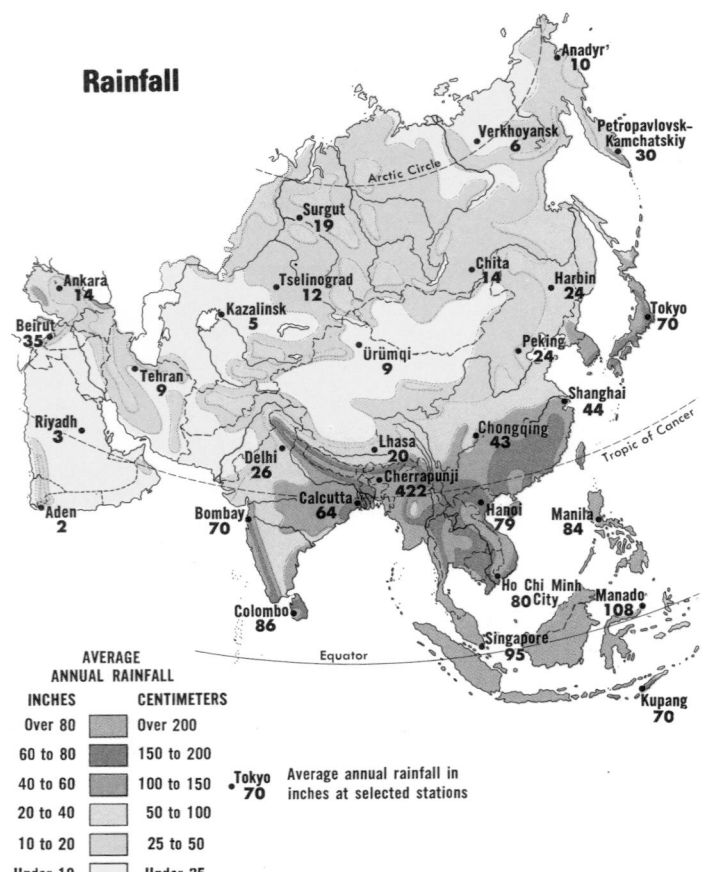

Rainfall

AVERAGE ANNUAL RAINFALL

INCHES	CENTIMETERS
Over 80	Over 200
60 to 80	150 to 200
40 to 60	100 to 150
20 to 40	50 to 100
10 to 20	25 to 50
Under 10	Under 25

● Tokyo
70
Average annual rainfall in inches at selected stations

Vegetation/Relief

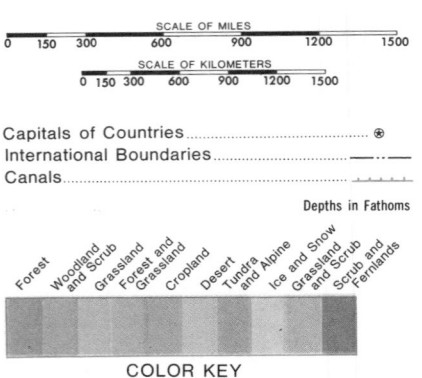

SCALE OF MILES
0   150   300   600   900   1200   1500

SCALE OF KILOMETERS
0   150   300   600   900   1200   1500

Capitals of Countries..............................⊛
International Boundaries...........................
Canals...

Depths in Fathoms

Forest · Woodland and Scrub · Grassland · Forest and Grassland · Cropland · Desert · Tundra and Alpine · Ice and Snow · Grassland and Scrub · Scrub and Fernlands

COLOR KEY

ATLANTIC OCEAN
ICELAND
GREENLAND
North Pole
Alaska
UNITED STATES
Bering Str.
C. Dezhnev
NORWEGIAN SEA
Arctic Circle
IRELAND
UNITED KINGDOM
London
NORTH SEA
PORTUGAL
SPAIN
Bay of Biscay
English Ch.
Paris
FRANCE
Rhine
Berlin
POLAND
BALTIC SEA
NORWAY
SWEDEN
FINLAND
Svalbard (Nor.)
Franz Josef Ld.
Nordkapp
BARENTS SEA
Novaya Zemlya
KARA SEA
ARCTIC OCEAN
Severnaya Zemlya
C. Chelyuskin
LAPTEV SEA
New Siberian Is.
EAST SIBERIAN SEA
BERING SEA
Aleutian Islands
Kolyma
Kamchatka Peninsula
C. Lopatka
SEA OF OKHOTSK
Sakhalin
Kuril Is.
PACIFIC OCEAN
EUROPE
Rome
Danube
ROMANIA
BLACK SEA
MEDITERRANEAN SEA
GREECE
Moscow
Volga
Ural
Ural Mountains
UNION OF SOVIET SOCIALIST REPUBLICS
Siberia
Ob'
Yenisey
Noril'sk
Lena
Vilyuy
Yakutsk
Aldan
Sverdlovsk
Chelyabinsk
Tobol
Omsk
Irtysh
Krasnoyarsk
Novosibirsk
Angara
Lake Baykal
Irkutsk
Yablonovyy Ra.
Amur
Khabarovsk
Hokkaido
Vladivostok
Harbin
SEA OF JAPAN
Honshu
Tokyo
JAPAN
CYPRUS
LEBANON
SYRIA
Damascus
ISRAEL
JORDAN
Cairo
EGYPT
Nile
Suez Canal
TURKEY
Caucasus
CASPIAN SEA
ARAL SEA
Karaganda
L. Balkhash
Altai Mts.
Ulaanbaatar
MONGOLIA
Gobi
Great Khingan Ra.
Shenyang
N. KOREA
Seoul
S. KOREA
Nagoya
Osaka
Shikoku
Kyushu
IRAQ
Baghdad
Euphrates
Tigris
Zagros Mts.
Tehran
IRAN
Syrdar'ya
Amudar'ya
Tashkent
Alma-Ata
Tien Shan
Ürümqi
Tarim
Takla Makan
Peking (Beijing)
Tianjin
Luda
YELLOW SEA
Hwang He
Huang He
Taiyuan
Lanzhou
Xi'an
Nanjing
Shanghai
EAST CHINA SEA
SAUDI ARABIA
KUWAIT
Persian Gulf
BAHRAIN
QATAR
U.A.E.
Riyadh
Mecca
RED SEA
SUDAN
AFRICA
Hindu Kush
Kabul
AFGHANISTAN
Helmand
K2 (Godwin Austen) 28,250 ft. (8611 m.)
Kunlun
Tibet
CHINA
Chengdu
Wuhan
Chang Jiang
Chongqing
Yangtze
Rub' al Khali
Gulf of Oman
Muscat
OMAN
Karachi
PAKISTAN
Indus
Lahore
Delhi
New Delhi
Himalaya
NEPAL
Mt. Everest 29,028 ft. (8848 m.)
BHUTAN
Brahmaputra
Jamuna
Kanpur
Ganges
Taipei
Tropic of Cancer
Taiwan
Ryukyu Is.
YEMEN ARAB REP.
PEOP. DEM. REP. YEMEN
Aden
Gulf of Aden
ETHIOPIA
SOMALIA
Socotra
Ras Asèr
INDIA
Ahmadabad
Narbada
BANGLADESH
Dhaka
Calcutta
Irrawaddy
Mekong
Red
Xi
Canton (Guangzhou)
HONG KONG (U.K.)
Hanoi
Hainan
C. Engaño
Luzon
ARABIAN SEA
Bombay
Godavari
Hyderabad
Kistna
Western Ghats
BURMA
BAY OF BENGAL
Salween
Rangoon
THAILAND
LAOS
VIETNAM
Bangkok
CAMBODIA
SOUTH CHINA SEA
Manila
PHILIPPINES
Mindanao
Palawan
SULU SEA
Madras
Bangalore
Andaman Is.
ANDAMAN SEA
Gulf of Siam
Ho Chi Minh City
C. Comorin
SRI LANKA (CEYLON)
Colombo
Dondra Head
MALDIVES
Nicobar Is.
MALAYSIA
BRUNEI
CELEBES SEA
New Guinea
Kuala Lumpur
SINGAPORE
Borneo
Celebes
SEYCHELLES
Equator
Sumatra
INDONESIA
BANDA SEA
COMOROS
INDIAN OCEAN
BRITISH INDIAN OCEAN TERR.
Sunda Islands
JAVA SEA
FLORES SEA
Jakarta
Java
Surabaya
Timor
TIMOR SEA
MADAGASCAR
Réunion (Fr.)
MAURITIUS
Tropic of Capricorn
AUSTRALIA

Longitude 70° East of Greenwich

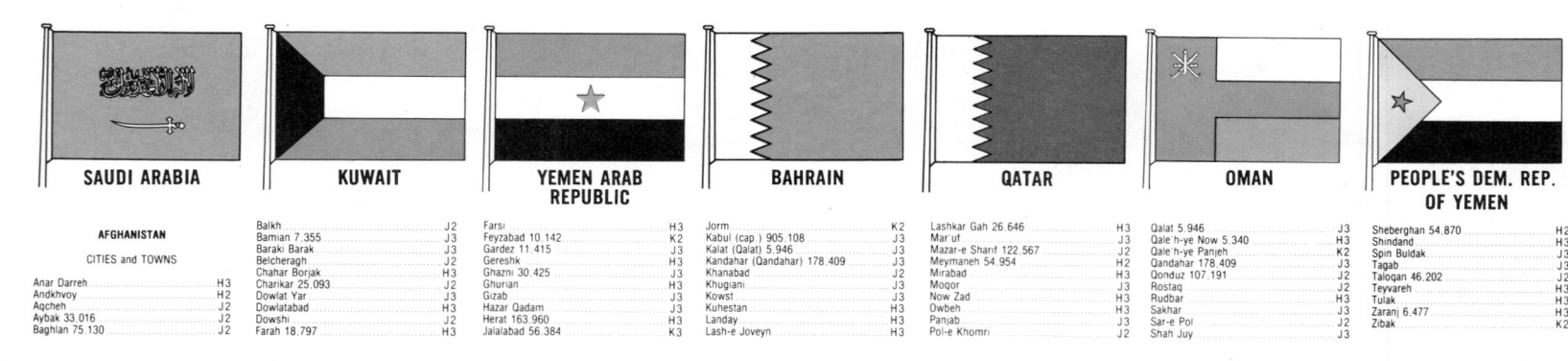

SAUDI ARABIA · KUWAIT · YEMEN ARAB REPUBLIC · BAHRAIN · QATAR · OMAN · PEOPLE'S DEM. REP. OF YEMEN

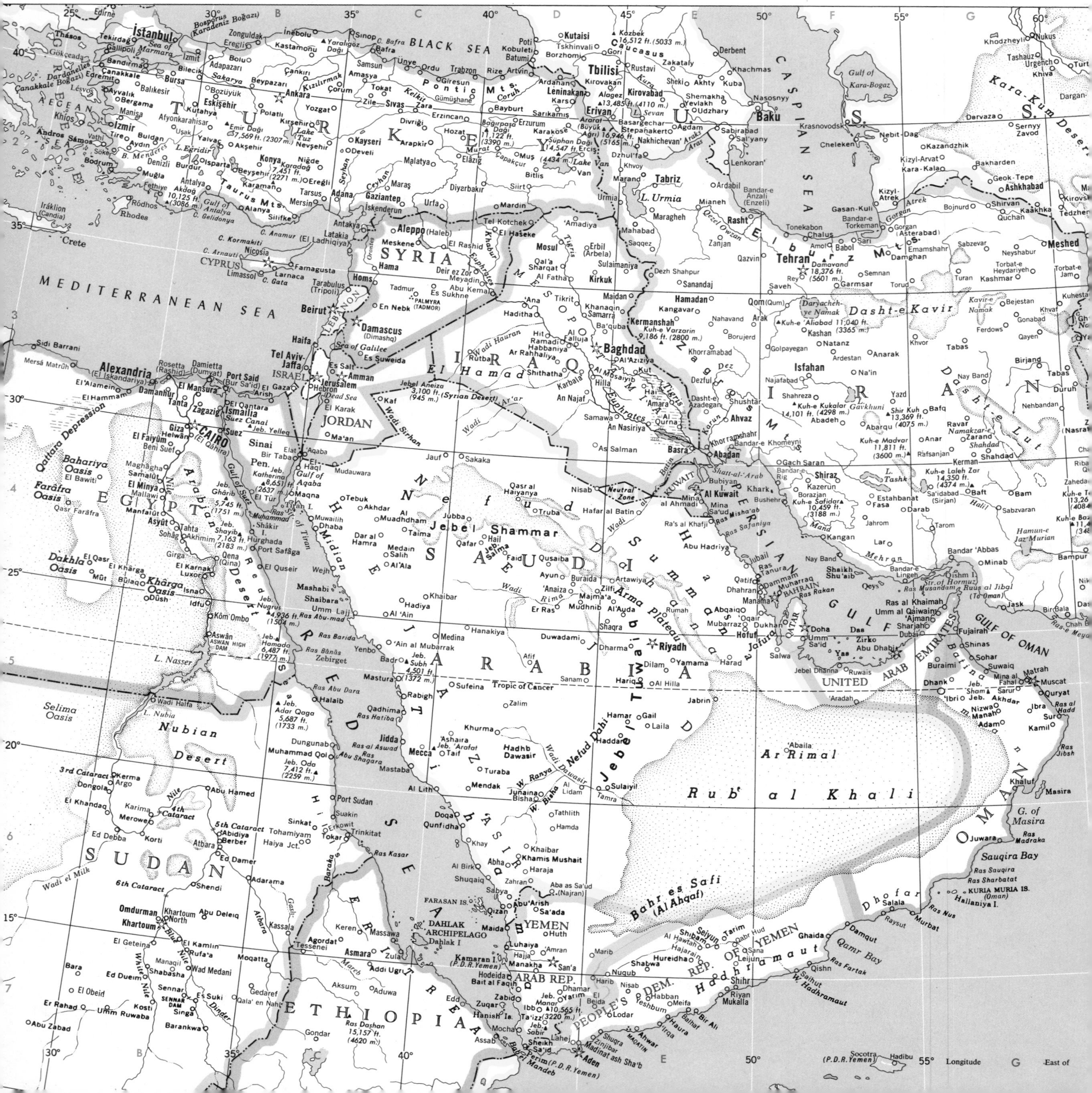

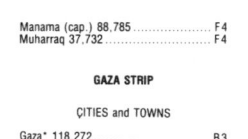

UNITED ARAB EMIRATES

OTHER FEATURES

Farah Rud (riv.)	H3
Gowd-e Zerreh (depr.)	H4
Harirud (riv.)	H3
Helmand (riv.)	J3
Hindu Kush (mts.)	J2
Kabul (riv.)	K3
Konar (riv.)	K2
Lurah (riv.)	J3

Margow, Dasht-e (des.)	H3
Murghab (riv.)	H2
Namaksar (salt lake)	H3
Paropamisus (mts.)	H3
Rigestan (reg.)	H3

BAHRAIN

CITIES and TOWNS

GAZA STRIP

CITIES and TOWNS

Gaza* 118,272	B3

Manama (cap.) 88,785	F4
Muharraq 37,732	F4

IRAN

CITIES and TOWNS

Abadan 296,081	E3
Abadeh 16,000	F3
Abarqu 8,000	F3
Ahvaz 329,006	E3

Amol 68,782	F2
Anar 463	G3
Anarak 2,038	F3
Arak 114,507	E3
Ardabil 147,404	E2
Ardestan 5,868	F3
Asterabad (Gorgan) 88,348	F2
Babol 67,790	F2
Bafq 5,000	G3
Baft 6,000	G4

(continued on following page)

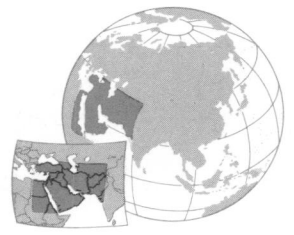

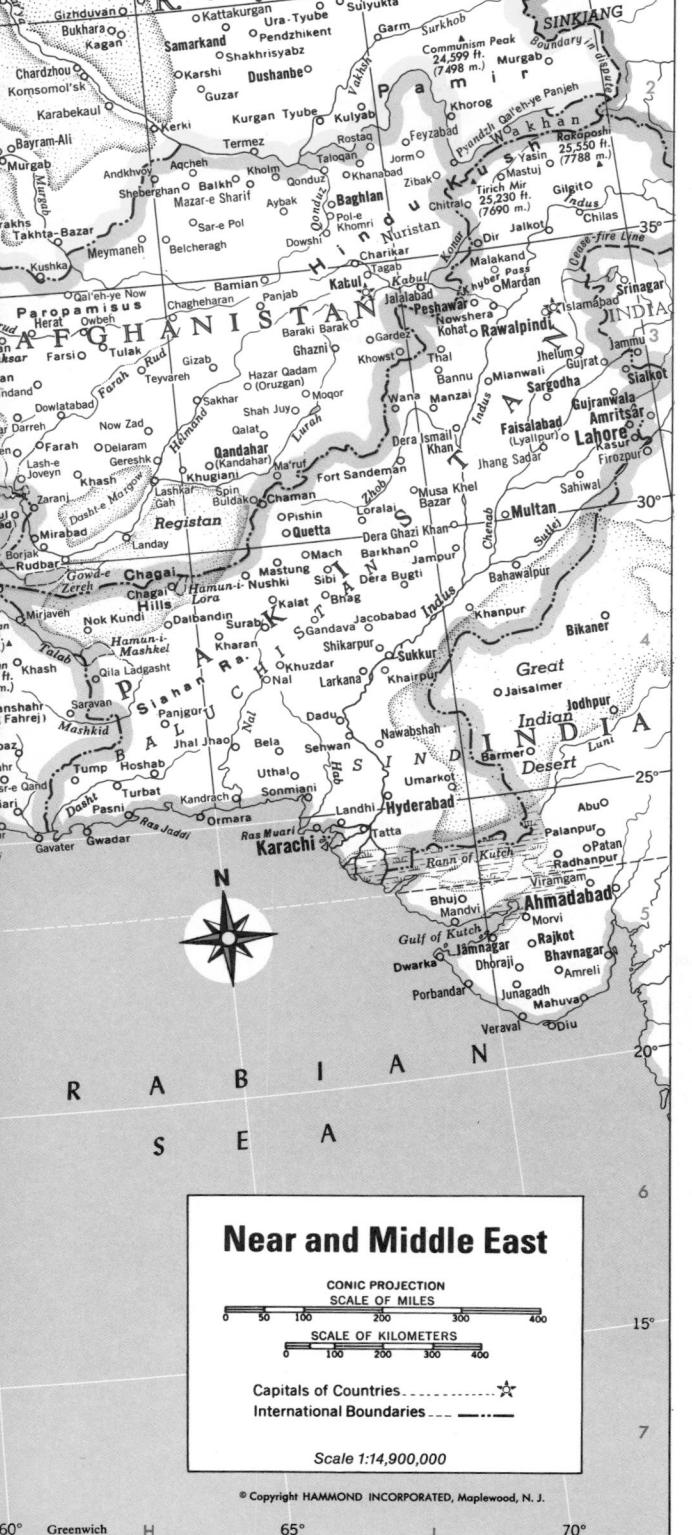

SAUDI ARABIA

AREA 829,995 sq. mi.
(2,149,687 sq. km.)
POPULATION 8,367,000
CAPITAL Riyadh
MONETARY UNIT Saudi riyal
MAJOR LANGUAGE Arabic
MAJOR RELIGION Islam

YEMEN ARAB REPUBLIC

AREA 77,220 sq. mi. (200,000 sq. km.)
POPULATION 6,456,189
CAPITAL San'a
MONETARY UNIT Yemeni rial
MAJOR LANGUAGE Arabic
MAJOR RELIGION Islam

QATAR

AREA 4,247 sq. mi. (11,000 sq. km.)
POPULATION 220,000
CAPITAL Doha
MONETARY UNIT Qatari riyal
MAJOR LANGUAGE Arabic
MAJOR RELIGION Islam

PEOPLE'S DEM. REP. OF YEMEN

AREA 111,101 sq. mi. (287,752 sq. km.)
POPULATION 1,969,000
CAPITAL Aden
MONETARY UNIT Yemeni dinar
MAJOR LANGUAGE Arabic
MAJOR RELIGION Islam

KUWAIT

AREA 6,532 sq mi. (16,918 sq. km.)
POPULATION 1,355,827
CAPITAL Al Kuwait
MONETARY UNIT Kuwaiti dinar
MAJOR LANGUAGE Arabic
MAJOR RELIGION Islam

BAHRAIN

AREA 240 sq. mi. (622 sq. km.)
POPULATION 358,857
CAPITAL Manama
MONETARY UNIT Bahraini dinar
MAJOR LANGUAGE Arabic
MAJOR RELIGION Islam

OMAN

AREA 120,000 sq. mi. (310,800 sq. km.)
POPULATION 891,000
CAPITAL Muscat
MONETARY UNIT Omani rial
MAJOR LANGUAGE Arabic
MAJOR RELIGION Islam

UNITED ARAB EMIRATES

AREA 32,278 sq. mi. (83,600 sq. km.)
POPULATION 1,040,275
CAPITAL Abu Dhabi
MONETARY UNIT dirham
MAJOR LANGUAGE Arabic
MAJOR RELIGION Islam

Near and Middle East

CONIC PROJECTION
SCALE OF MILES
0 50 100 200 300 400

SCALE OF KILOMETERS
0 100 200 300 400

Capitals of Countries .... ☆
International Boundaries ____ ___ ___

Scale 1:14,900,000

© Copyright HAMMOND INCORPORATED, Maplewood, N.J.

Topography

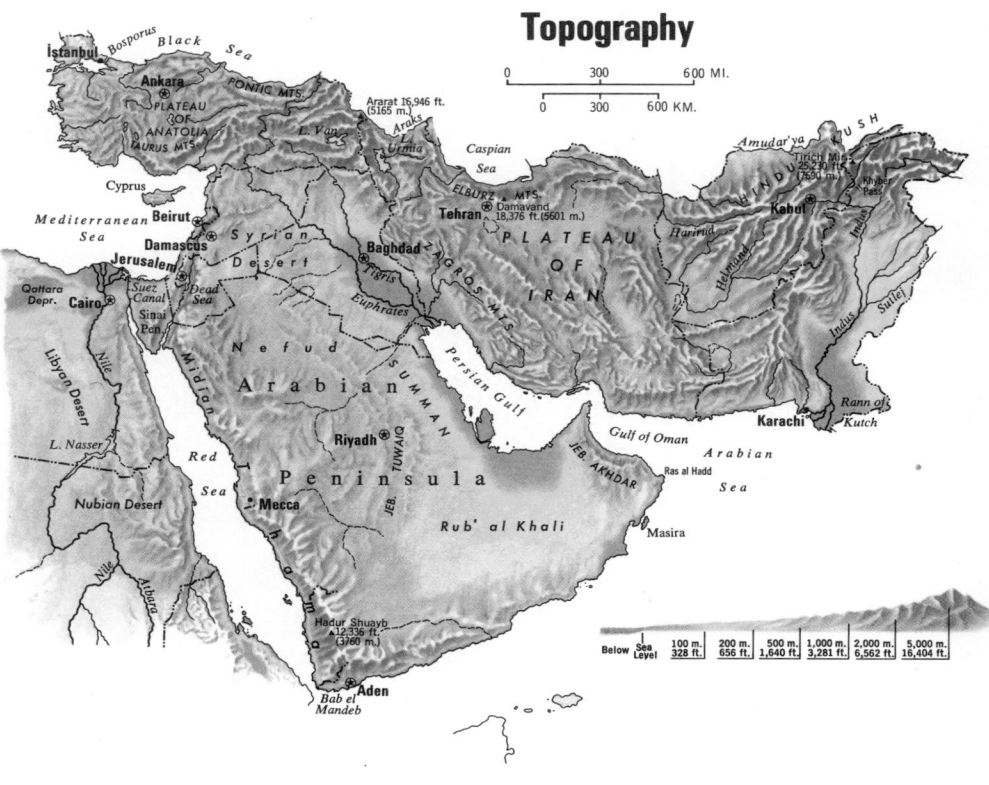

0 300 600 MI.
0 300 600 KM.

| Below Sea Level | 100 m. 328 ft. | 200 m. 656 ft. | 500 m. 1,640 ft. | 1,000 m. 3,281 ft. | 2,000 m. 6,562 ft. | 5,000 m. 16,404 ft. |

Agriculture, Industry and Resources

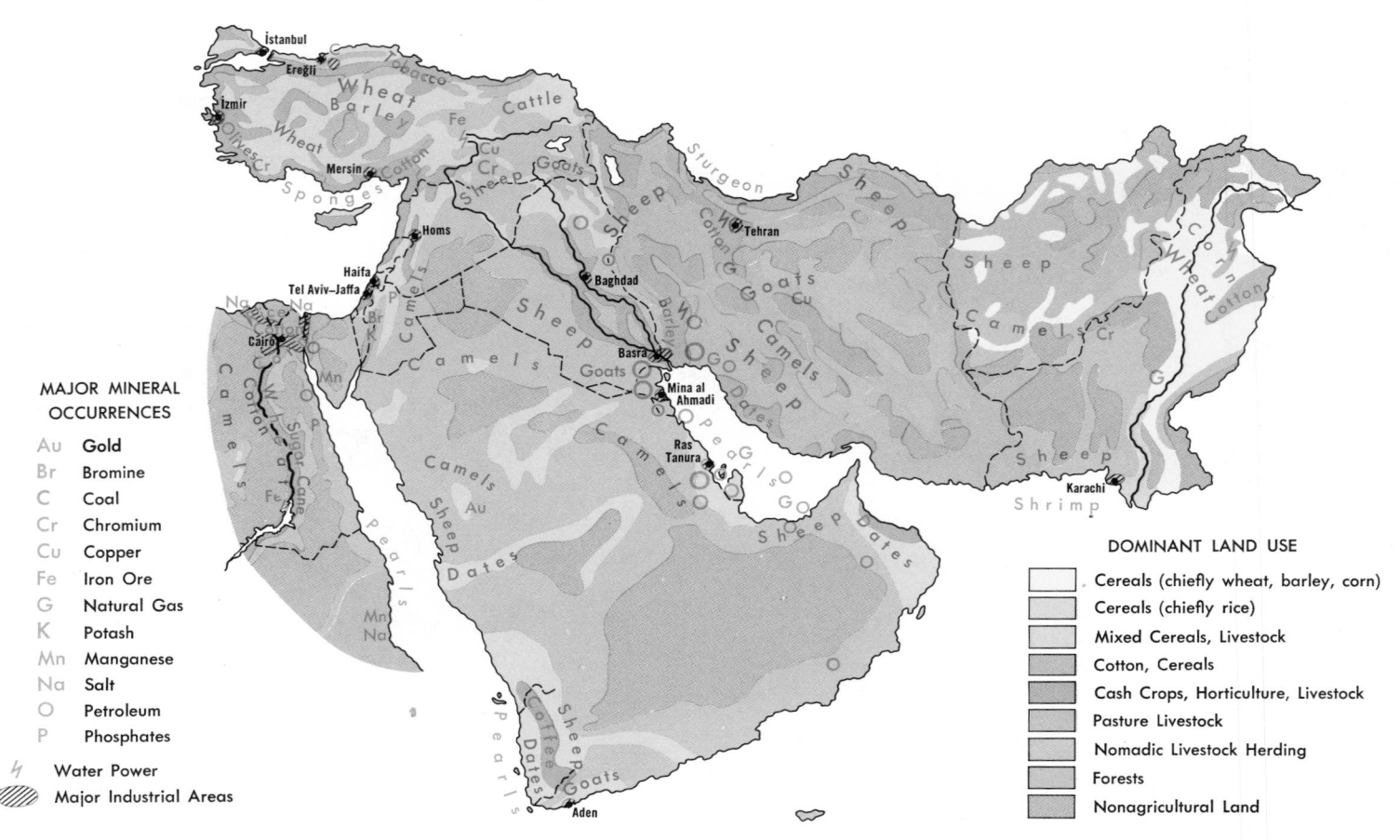

MAJOR MINERAL OCCURRENCES

Au Gold
Br Bromine
C Coal
Cr Chromium
Cu Copper
Fe Iron Ore
G Natural Gas
K Potash
Mn Manganese
Na Salt
O Petroleum
P Phosphates

⚡ Water Power
▨ Major Industrial Areas

DOMINANT LAND USE

Cereals (chiefly wheat, barley, corn)
Cereals (chiefly rice)
Mixed Cereals, Livestock
Cotton, Cereals
Cash Crops, Horticulture, Livestock
Pasture Livestock
Nomadic Livestock Herding
Forests
Nonagricultural Land

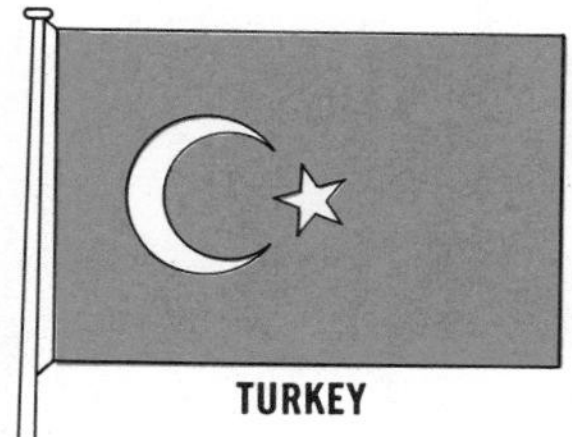

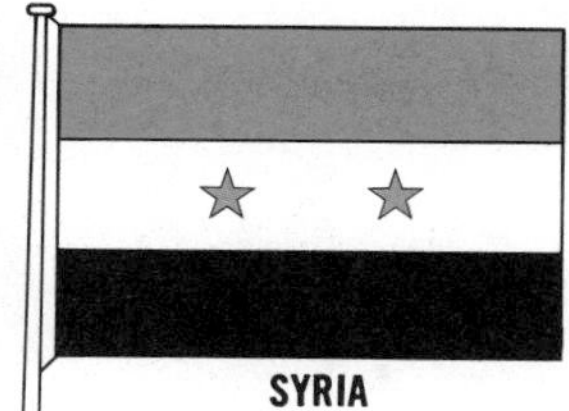

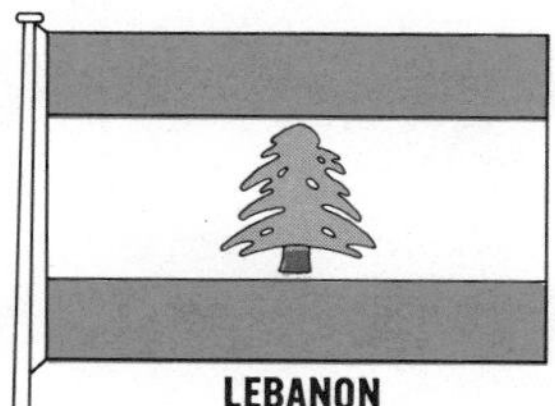

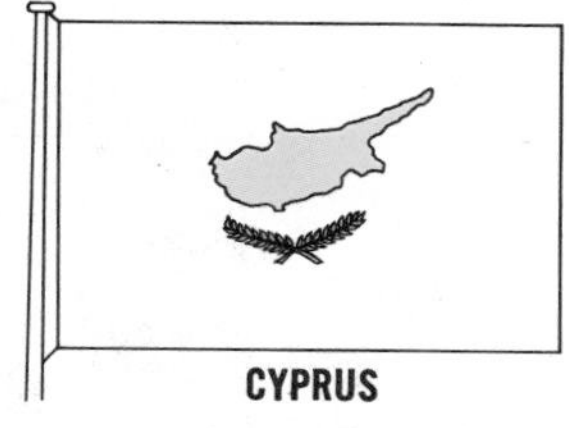

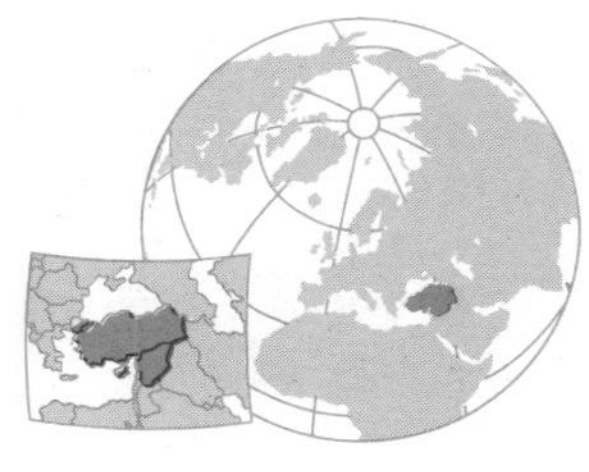

AREA 300,946 sq. mi. (779,450 sq. km.)
POPULATION 45,217,556
CAPITAL Ankara
LARGEST CITY Istanbul
HIGHEST POINT Ararat 16,946 ft. (5,165 m.)
MONETARY UNIT Turkish lira
MAJOR LANGUAGE Turkish
MAJOR RELIGION Islam

AREA 71,498 sq. mi. (185,180 sq. km.)
POPULATION 8,979,000
CAPITAL Damascus
LARGEST CITY Damascus
HIGHEST POINT Hermon 9,232 ft. (2,814 m.)
MONETARY UNIT Syrian pound
MAJOR LANGUAGES Arabic, French, Kurdish, Armenian
MAJOR RELIGIONS Islam, Christianity

AREA 4,015 sq. mi. (10,399 sq. km.)
POPULATION 3,161,000
CAPITAL Beirut
LARGEST CITY Beirut
HIGHEST POINT Qurnet es Sauda 10,131 ft. (3,088 m.)
MONETARY UNIT Lebanese pound
MAJOR LANGUAGES Arabic, French
MAJOR RELIGIONS Christianity, Islam

AREA 3,473 sq. mi. (8,995 sq. km.)
POPULATION 629,000
CAPITAL Nicosia
LARGEST CITY Nicosia
HIGHEST POINT Troödos 6,406 ft. (1,953 m.)
MONETARY UNIT Cypriot pound
MAJOR LANGUAGES Greek, Turkish, English
MAJOR RELIGIONS Eastern (Greek) Orthodoxy, Islam

CYPRUS

CITIES and TOWNS

Dhali 2,970 E5
Episkopi 2,150 E5
Famagusta 38,960 F5
Ktima E5
Kyrenia 3,892 E5
Kythrea 3,400 E5
Lapithos 3,600 E5
Larnaca 19,608 E5
Lefka 3,650 E5
Limassol 79,641 E5
Morphou 9,040 E5
Nicosia (cap.) 115,718 E5
Paphos 8,984 E5
Polis 2,200 E5
Rizokarpasso 3,600 F5
Yialousa 2,750 E5

OTHER FEATURES

Andreas (cape) F5
Arnauti (cape) E5
Gata (cape) E5
Greco (cape) F5
Kormakiti (cape) E5
Troodos (mt.) E5

LEBANON

CITIES and TOWNS

A'leih 18,630 F6
Amyun 7,926 F5
Baa'lbek 15,560 G5
Batrun 5,976 F5
Beirut (cap.) 474,870 F6
Beirut* 938,940 F6
Hermil 2,652 G5
Merj U'yun 9,318 F6
Rasheiya 6,731 F6
Rayak 1,480 G6
Saida 32,200 F6
Sidon (Saida) 32,200 F6
Sur 16,483 F6
Tripoli (Tarabulus) 127,611 F5
Tyre (Sur) 16,483 F6
Zahle 53,121 F6
Zegharta 18,210 G5

OTHER FEATURES

Lebanon (mts.) F6
Leontes (Litani) (riv.) F6
Litani (riv.) F6
Sauda, Qurnet es (mt.) G5

SYRIA

PROVINCES

Aleppo 1,316,872 G4
Damascus 1,457,934 G6
Deir ez Zor 292,780 H5
Dera' 230,481 G6
El Quneitra 16,490 F6
Es Suweida 139,650 G6
Hama 514,748 G5
Haseke 468,506 J4
Homs 546,176 G5
Idlib 383,695 G5
Latakia 389,552 G5
Rashid 243,736 H5
Tartus 302,065 G5

CITIES and TOWNS

Abu Kemal 6,907 J5
A'in el A'rab 4,529 H4
Aleppo 639,428 G4
Azaz 13,923 G4
Baniyas 8,537 F5
Busra G6
Damascus (cap.) 836,668 G6
Damascus* 923,253 G6
Deir ez Zor 66,164 H5
Dera' 27,651 G6
Dimashq (Damascus) (cap.) 836,668 G6
Duma 30,050 G6
El Bab 27,366 G4
El Haseke 32,746 J4
El Ladhiqiya (Latakia) 125,716 F5
El Quryatein G5
El Quneitra 17,752 F6
El Rashid 37,151 H5
En Nebk 16,334 G5
Es Suweide 29,524 G6
Et Tell el Abyad H4
Haffe 4,656 G5
Haleb (Aleppo) 639,428 G4
Hama 137,421 G5
Harim 6,837 G4
Homs 215,423 G5
Idlib 34,515 G5
Izra 3,226 G6
Jeble 15,715 F5
Jerablus 8,610 G4
Jisr esh Shughur 13,131 G5
Khan Sheikhun G5
Latakia 125,716 F5
Masyaf 7,058 G5
Membij 13,796 G4
Meskene H5
Meyadin 12,515 J5
Qala't es Salihiye J5
Qamishliye 31,448 J4
Quteife 4,993 G6
Raqqa (El Rashid) 37,151 H5
Sabkha 3,375 H5
Safita 9,650 G5
Selemiya 21,677 G5
Tadmur 10,670 H5
Tartus 29,842 F5
Telkalakh 6,242 F5
Zebdani 10,010 G6

OTHER FEATURES

A'mrit (ruins) F5
Arwad (Ruad) (isl.) F5
A'si (Orontes) (riv.) G5
Druz, Jebel ed (mts.) G6
El Furat (riv.) H4
Euphrates (El Furat) (riv.) H4
Hermon (mt.) F6
Khabur (riv.) J5
Orontes (riv.) G5
Palmyra (Tadmor) (ruins) H5
Ruwaq, Jebel er (mts.) G5

TURKEY

PROVINCES

Adana 1,240,475 F4
Adiyaman 346,892 H4
Afyonkarahisar 579,171 D3
Ağri 330,201 K3
Amasya 322,806 F2
Ankara 2,585,293 E3
Antalya 669,357 D4
Artvin 228,026 J2
Aydin 609,869 B4
Balikesir 789,255 B3
Bilecik 137,120 D2
Bingöl 210,804 J3
Bitlis 218,305 J3
Bolu 428,704 D2
Burdur 222,896 D4
Bursa 961,639 C2
Çanakkale 369,385 B2
Çankiri 265,468 E2
Çorum 547,580 F2
Denizli 560,916 C4
Diyarbakir 651,233 H4
Edirne 340,732 B2
Elâziğ 417,924 H3
Erzincan 283,683 H3
Erzurum 746,666 J3
Eskişehir 495,097 D3
Gaziantep 715,939 G4
Giresun 463,587 H2
Gümüşhane 293,673 H2
Hakkâri 126,036 K4
Hatay 744,113 G4
Içel 714,817 F4
Isparta 322,685 D4
Istanbul 3,904,588 C2
Izmir 1,673,966 B3
Kahramanmaraş 641,480 G4
Kars 707,398 K2
Kastamonu 438,243 E2
Kayseri 676,809 F3
Kirklareli 268,399 B2
Kirşehir 232,853 F3
Kocaeli 477,736 C2
Konya 1,422,461 E4
Kütahya 470,423 C3
Malatya 574,558 H3
Manisa 872,375 B3
Mardin 519,687 J4
Muğla 400,796 C4
Muş 267,203 J3
Nevşehir 249,308 F3
Niğde 463,121 F4
Ordu 664,290 G2
Rize 336,278 J2
Sakarya 495,649 D2
Samsun 906,381 F2
Siirt 381,503 J4
Sinop 267,605 F2
Sivas 741,713 G3
Tekirdağ 319,987 B2
Tokat 599,166 G2
Trabzon 719,008 H2
Tunceli 164,591 H3
Urfa 597,277 H4
Uşak 229,679 C3
Van 386,314 K3
Yozgat 500,371 F3
Zonguldak 836,156 D2

CITIES and TOWNS

Acigöl 3,934 F3
Acipayam 5,046 C4
Adalia (Antalya) 130,774 D4
Adana 475,384 F4
Adapazari 114,130 D2
Adilcevaz 9,022 K3
Adiyaman 43,782 H4
Afşin 18,231 G3
Afyonkarahisar 60,150 D3
Ağlasun 4,288 D4
Ağli 3,399 E2
Ağri (Karaköse) 35,284 K3
Ahlat 7,995 K3
Akçaabat 10,756 H2
Akçadağ 7,366 G3
Akçakoca 9,066 D2
Akdağmadeni 7,909 F3
Akhisar 53,357 B3
Aksaray 45,564 F3
Akşehir 35,544 D3
Akseki 5,141 D4
Akviran 3,799 E4
Akyazi 12,438 D2
Alaca 12,552 F2
Alacahan 2,321 G3
Alaçam 10,013 F2
Alanya 18,520 D4
Alaşehir 23,243 C3
Alexandretta (Iskenderun) 107,437 G4
Aliağa 5,727 B3
Alibeyköyü 33,387 D6
Almus 4,225 G2
Alpu 3,718 D3
Altindağ 512,392 E2
Altinova 6,980 B3
Altintaş 3,386 C3
Altinözü 5,158 G4
Alucra 7,070 H2
Amasra 4,369 E2
Amasya 41,496 G2
Anamur 21,475 E4
Andirin 5,018 G4
Ankara (cap.) 1,701,004 E3
Antakya 77,518 G4
Antalya 130,774 D4
Antioch (Antakya) 77,518 G4
Araç 3,594 E2
Aralik 4,155 L3
Arapkir 8,436 H3
Ardahan 16,285 K2
Ardeşen 7,980 J2
Ardanuç 2,942 K2
Arguvan 2,461 H3
Arhavi 6,311 J2
Arpaçay 2,651 K2
Arsin 6,557 H2
Artova 2,813 G2
Artvin 13,390 J2
Aşkale 10,817 J3
Avanos 8,635 F3
Ayancik 7,202 F1
Ayaş 4,575 E2
Aybasti 13,180 G2
Aydin 59,579 B4
Aydincik 6,739 E4
Ayranci 2,664 E4
Ayvacik 3,120 B3
Ayvalik 18,041 B3
Babadağ 5,890 C4
Babaeski 17,090 B2
Bafra 34,288 F2
Bahçe 10,212 G4
Bakirköy 200,942 D6
Baklan 3,327 C4
Balâ 4,107 E3
Balikesir 99,443 B3
Balya 2,362 B3
Banaz 6,264 C3
Bandirma 45,752 B2
Bartin 18,409 E2
Başkale 8,558 K3
Başmakçi 5,925 C4
Batman 64,384 J4
Bayat 4,671 F2
Bayburt 20,156 J2
Bayindir 14,078 B3
Baykan 2,690 J3
Bayramiç 6,385 B3
Bergama 29,749 B3
Beşiktaş 174,931 D6
Beşiri 4,165 J4
Besni 16,313 G4
Beykoz 76,804 D5
Beyoğlu 230,532 D6
Beypazari 14,963 D2
Beyşehir 15,060 D4
Beytüşşebap 2,766 K4
Biga 15,188 B2
Bigadiç 7,535 C3
Bilecik 11,269 D2
Bingöl (Çapakçur) 22,047 J3
Birecik 20,104 H4
Bismil 12,775 J4
Bitlis 25,054 J3
Bodrum 7,858 B4
Boğazliyan 10,329 F3
Bolu 32,812 D2
Bolvadin 29,218 D3
Bor 16,560 F4
Borçka 4,636 J2
Bornova 45,096 B3
Boyabat 13,139 F2
Bozdoğan 7,218 C4
Bozkir 5,294 E4
Bozkurt 2,948 F2
Bozova 5,462 H4
Bozüyük 15,197 C3
Bucak 15,090 D4
Bulancak 14,153 H2
Bulanik 8,296 K3
Buldan 11,115 C3
Bünyan 12,277 G3
Burdur 36,633 D4
Burhaniye 12,800 B3
Bursa 346,103 C2
Büyükada D6
Büyükdere D5
Çal 3,274 C3
Çala 2,450 K2
Caldiran 3,366 K3

(continued on following page)

Agriculture, Industry and Resources

DOMINANT LAND USE

- Cereals (chiefly wheat, barley), Livestock
- Cash Crops, Horticulture, Livestock
- Pasture Livestock
- Nomadic Livestock Herding
- Forests
- Nonagricultural Land

MAJOR MINERAL OCCURRENCES

- Ab Asbestos
- Al Bauxite
- C Coal
- Cr Chromium
- Cu Copper
- Fe Iron Ore
- Hg Mercury
- Mg Magnesium
- Na Salt
- O Petroleum
- P Phosphates
- Pb Lead
- Py Pyrites
- Sb Antimony
- Zn Zinc

Water Power
Major Industrial Areas

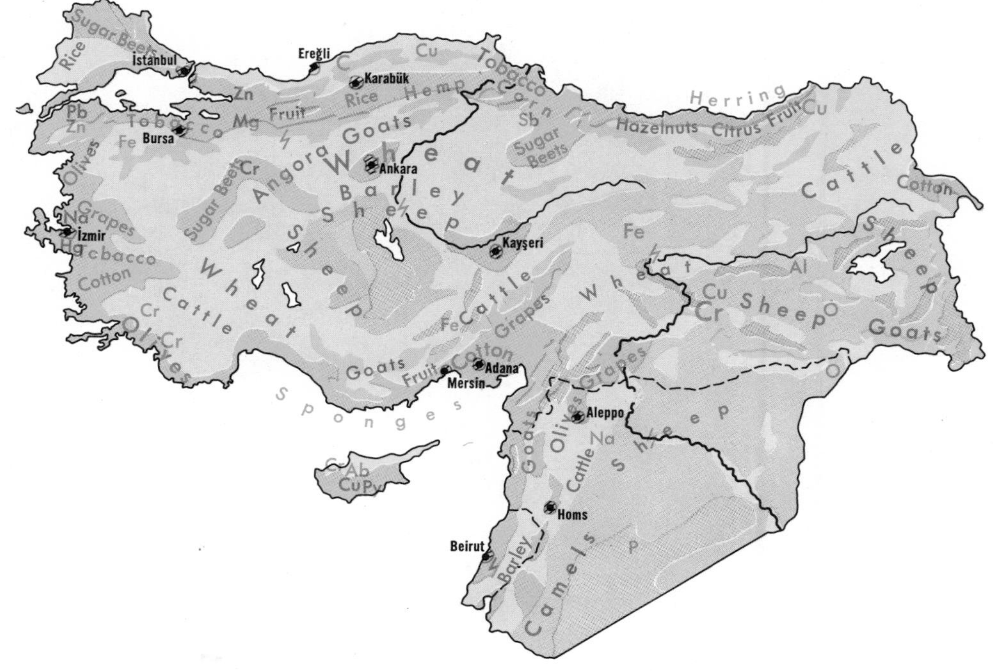

Name	Grid	Name	Grid	Name	Grid	Name	Grid	Name	Grid	Name	Grid	Name	Grid
Çalköy 3,002	C3	Çeşme 5,284	B3	Demirkent 4,204	E4	Eceabat 3,642	B6	Erzincan 60,351	H3	Gemerik 5,769	G3	Güdül 4,746	E2
Çamardı 2,419	F4	Çetinkaya 3,616	G3	Demirköy 4,257	B2	Edirne 63,001	B2	Erzurum 162,973	J3	Gemlik 20,704	C2	Günlar 6,344	E4
Çamlı 2,502	C4	Ceyhan 62,909	F4	Denizli 106,902	C4	Edremit 26,110	B3	Eskimalatya 10,182	H3	Genç 7,671	J3	Gülşehir 6,188	F3
Çamlıdere 4,386	E2	Çeylanpınar 20,171	H4	Dereli 4,188	H2	Eflâni 3,793	E2	Eskipazar 2,865	E2	Gercüş 4,393	J4	Gümüş 3,066	F2
Çan 11,797	B2	Çiçekdağı 3,203	F3	Derik 13,292	J4	Eğridir 9,799	D4	Eskişehir 259,952	D3	Gerede 8,259	E2	Gümüşhacıköy 12,789	F2
Çanakkale 30,788	B6	Cide 3,520	E1	Derinkuyu 5,618	F3	Elazığ 131,415	H3	Eşme 7,828	C3	Gerger 2,773	H3	Gümüşhane 11,166	H2
Çandır 6,986	F3	Çifteler 8,163	D3	Develi 17,323	F3	Elbistan 26,048	G3	Espiye 8,168	H2	Germencik 10,558	B4	Güney 7,154	C3
Çankaya 895,005	E2	Cihanbeyli 10,079	E3	Devrek 9,164	D2	Eldivan 3,392	E2	Eynesil 6,081	H2	Gerze 7,313	F2	Gürün 9,138	G3
Çankırı 28,512	E2	Çiftlik 2,260	K2	Devrekani 4,014	E2	Eleşkirt 8,202	K3	Eyüp 95,486	D6	Gevye 7,806	D2	Hacıbektaş 5,032	F3
Çapakçur 22,047	J3	Cimin 5,341	H3	Dicle 5,247	J3	Elmalı 10,184	C4	Ezbider 3,631	G3	Giresun 38,236	H2	Hacılar 15,622	F3
Çardak 4,232	C6	Çine 11,308	B4	Dikili 6,916	B3	Emet 6,239	C3	Ezine 9,359	B3	Gökçe 6,333	D2	Hadim 10,467	E4
Çarşamba 23,973	G2	Çivril 7,721	C3	Dinar 21,983	C3	Emirdağ 13,184	D3	Fakılı 4,173	F3	Gölbaşı 15,103	G3	Hafik 5,398	G3
Çatak 2,366	C2	Cizre 15,557	K4	Dirmil 3,476	C4	Emirgazi 5,244	E4	Fatih 504,127	D6	Gölbaşı 13,279	E2	Hakkâri (Çölemerik) 11,735	K4
Çatalca 7,693	C2	Çölemerik 11,735	K4	Divriği 12,302	H3	Enez 2,485	B2	Fatsa 19,758	G2	Gölköy 10,022	H2	Halfeti 3,689	G4
Çatalzeytin 2,271	F1	Çorlu 40,134	B2	Diyadin 5,094	K3	Erbaa 20,315	G2	Feke 5,375	F4	Gölmarmara 11,982	B3	Hamur 2,267	K3
Çay 12,200	D3	Çorum 64,852	F2	Diyarbakır 169,535	H4	Erciş 22,351	K3	Fethiye 12,700	C4	Gölpazarı 5,002	D2	Hanak 2,581	J2
Çaycuma 8,118	D2	Çubuk 13,793	E2	Doğanbey 3,077	D4	Erdemli 19,936	E4	Fevzipaşa 5,495	G4	Gönen 16,091	C3	Hani 7,559	J3
Çayeli 13,480	J2	Çukur 5,479	K4	Doğanhisar 9,487	D3	Ereğli 45,992	D2	Fındıklı 5,008	J2	Gördes 7,909	C3	Harput 3,231	H3
Çayıralan 8,071	F3	Çukurca 3,019	K4	Doğanşehir 10,280	G3	Ereğli 50,354	F4	Finike 4,200	C4	Görele 8,079	H2	Harunıye 12,837	G4
Çayırlı 4,580	J3	Çumra 19,225	E3	Döger 3,478	D3	Ergani 21,936	H3	Foça 4,829	B3	Göynücek 2,600	F2	Hassa 10,926	G4
Çekerek 3,796	F2	Çüngüş 2,616	H3	Doğubeyazıt 17,612	K3	Erkilet 3,924	F3	Gallipoli 13,466	C5	Göynük 2,519	D2	Hatay (Antakya) 77,518	G4
Çelikhan 3,066	H3	Daday 2,528	E2	Domaniç 2,729	C3	Ermenak 13,464	D4	Gaziantep 300,882	G4			Havran 7,552	B3
Çemişkezek 3,048	H3	Darende 8,055	G3	Dörtyol 19,390	F4	Eruh 5,340	K4	Gazipaşa 6,696	E4			Havsa 4,298	B2
Çerkes 3,780	E2	Dazkırı 3,912	D4	Dumlu 2,528	J2	Erzin 15,314	G4	Gediz 10,649	C3			Havza 15,341	F2
Çerkezköy 8,428	C2	Delice 3,462	F2	Durağan 3,259	F2			Gelibolu (Gallipoli) 13,466	C5			Haymana 6,123	E2
Çermik 9,749	H3	Demirci 15,016	C3	Dursunbey 8,615	C3								

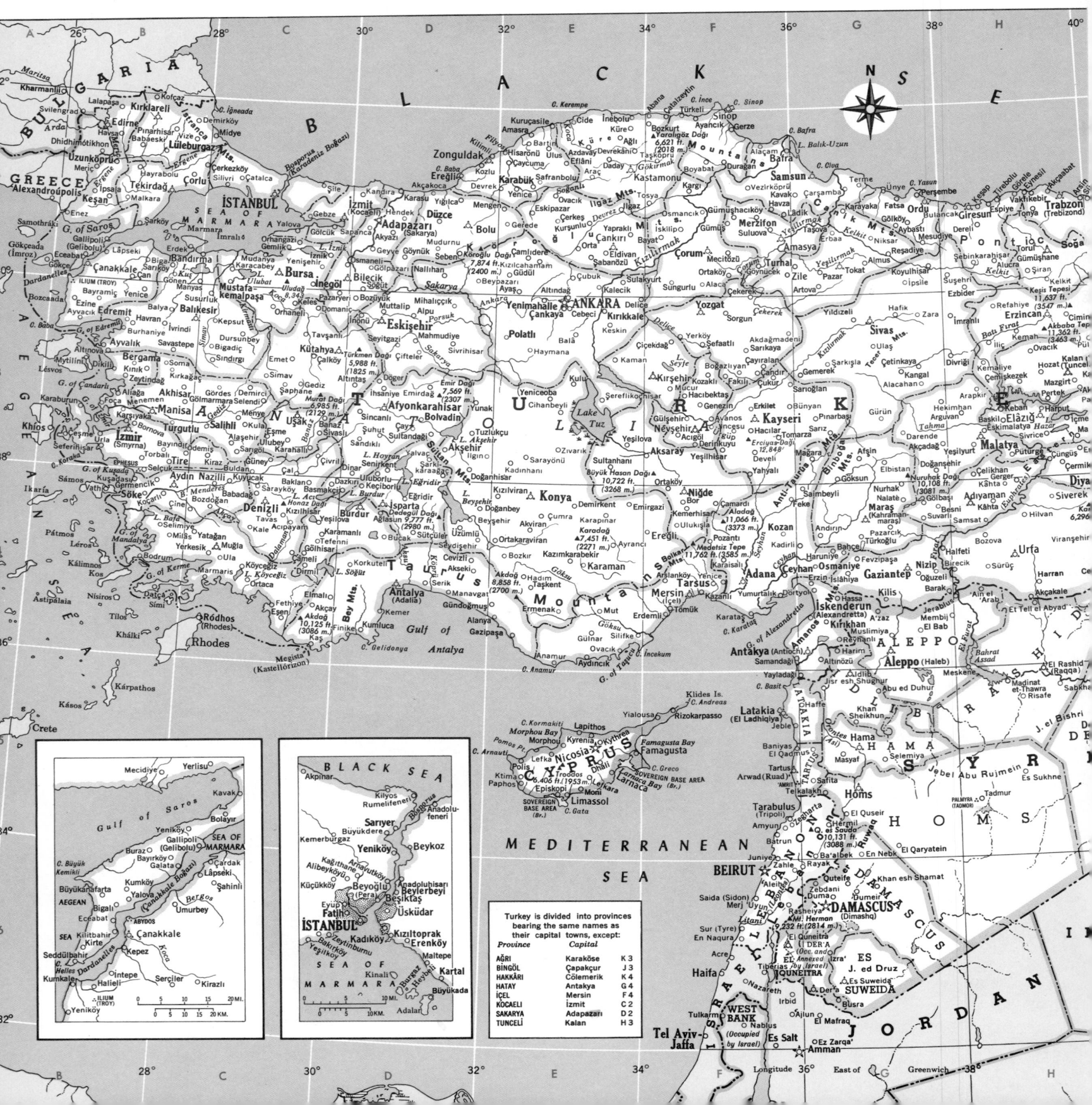

Turkey is divided into provinces bearing the same names as their capital towns, except:

Province	Capital	Grid
AĞRI	Karaköse	K3
BİNGÖL	Çapakçur	J3
HAKKÂRİ	Çölemerik	K4
HATAY	Antakya	G4
İÇEL	Mersin	F4
KOCAELİ	İzmit	C2
SAKARYA	Adapazarı	D2
TUNCELİ	Kalan	H3

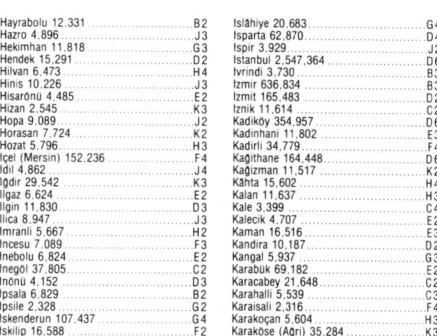

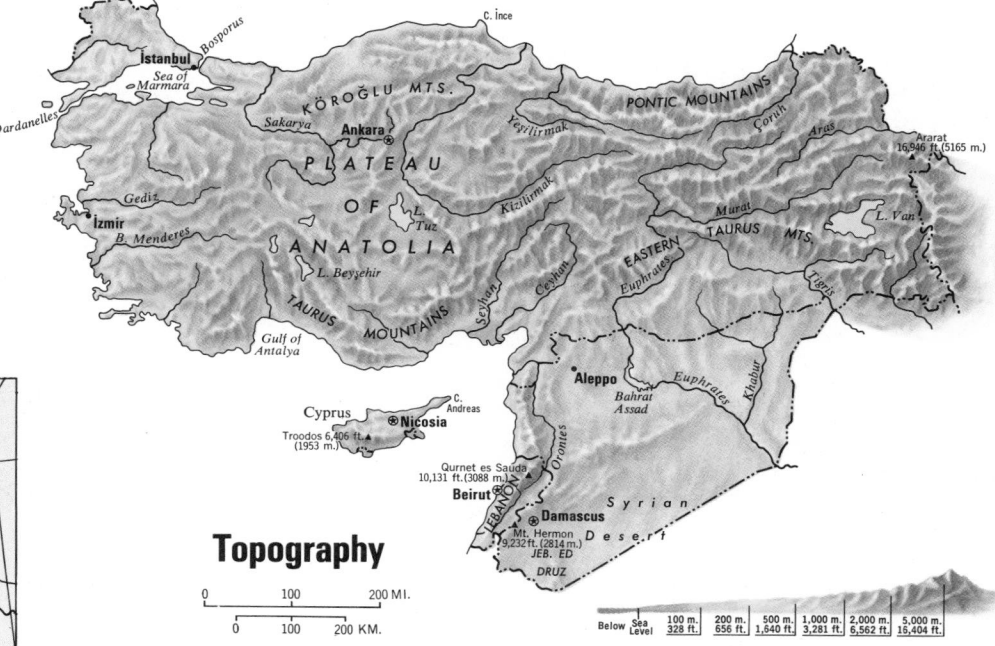

Topography

Scale: 0 — 100 — 200 MI. / 0 — 100 — 200 KM.

Below Sea Level	100 m. 328 ft.	200 m. 656 ft.	500 m. 1,640 ft.	1,000 m. 3,281 ft.	2,000 m. 6,562 ft.	5,000 m. 16,404 ft.

Turkey, Syria, Lebanon and Cyprus

© Copyright HAMMOND INCORPORATED, Maplewood, N.J.

SCALE OF MILES
0 — 25 — 50 — 75 — 100 — 125 — 150

SCALE OF KILOMETERS
0 — 25 — 50 — 75 — 100 — 125 — 150

Capitals of Countries ☆   Capitals of Provinces △

Provincial Boundaries ____

Scale 1:5,440,000

* City and suburbs

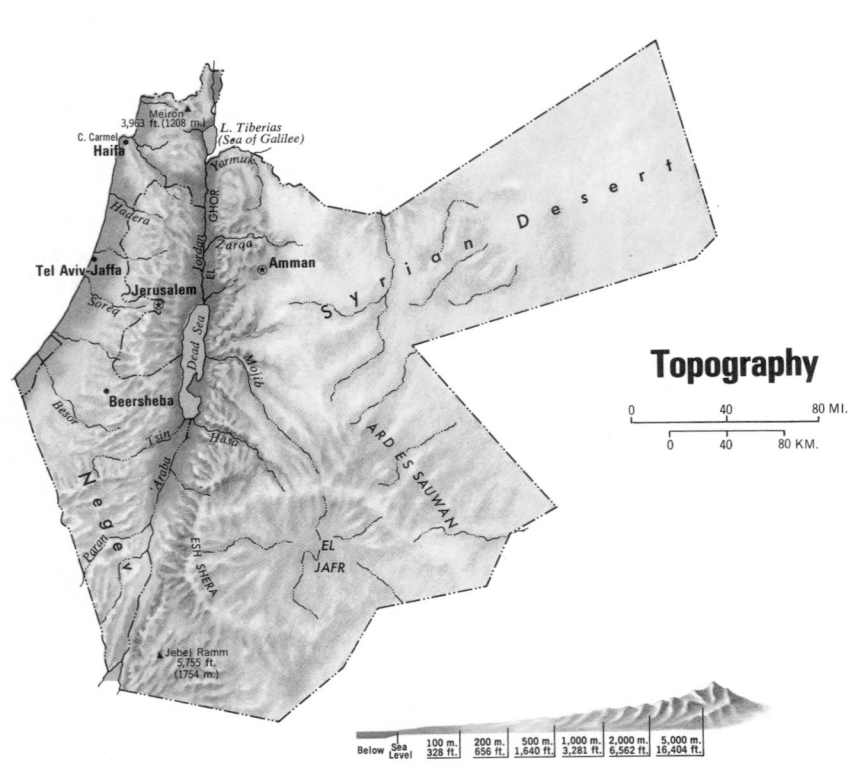

Topography

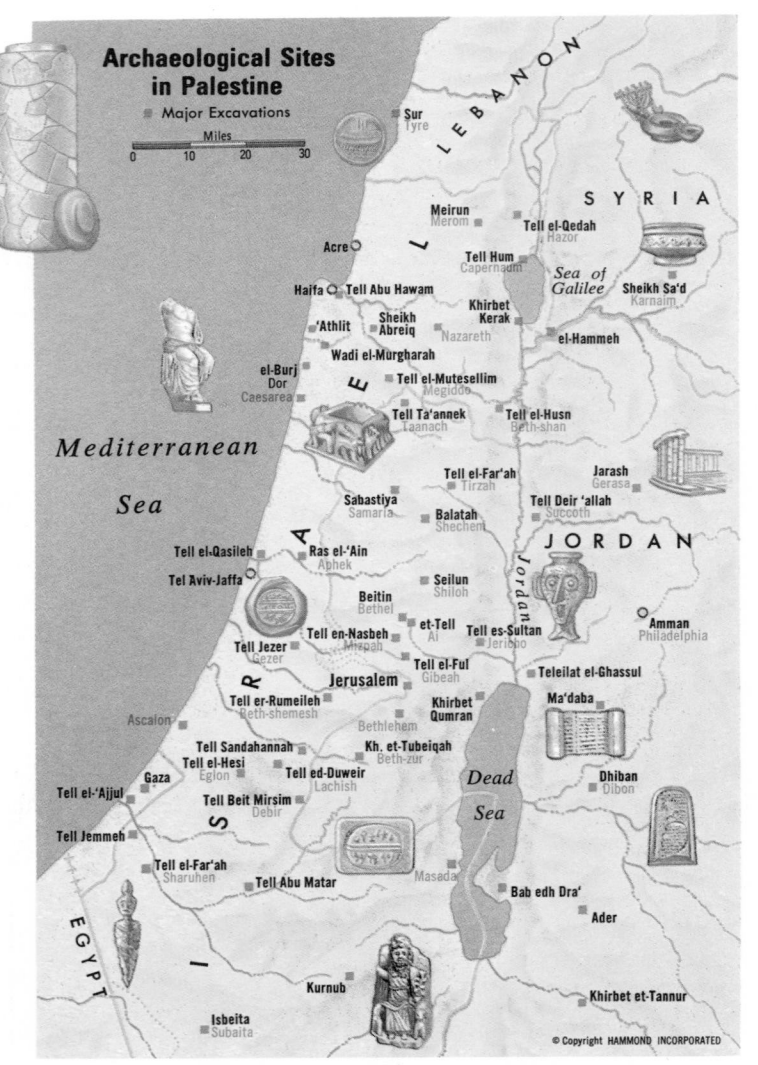

Archaeological Sites in Palestine

■ Major Excavations

Miles

Agriculture, Industry and Resources

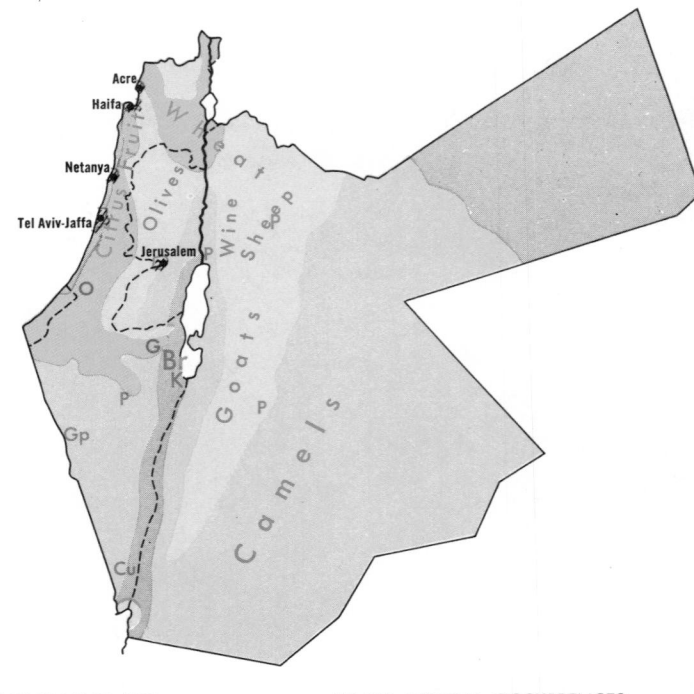

DOMINANT LAND USE

- Cereals, Livestock
- Cash Crops, Horticulture
- Nomadic Livestock Herding
- Nonagricultural Land

MAJOR MINERAL OCCURRENCES

- Br Bromine
- Cu Copper
- G Natural Gas
- Gp Gypsum
- K Potash
- O Petroleum
- P Phosphates
- Major Industrial Areas

© Copyright HAMMOND INCORPORATED

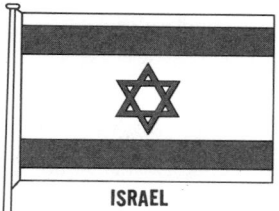

ISRAEL

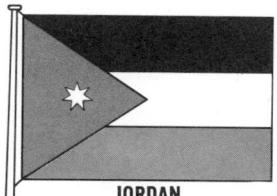

JORDAN

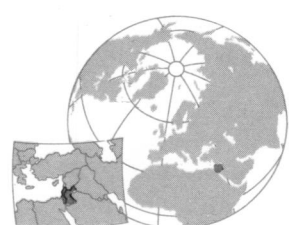

ISRAEL

AREA 7,847 sq. mi. (20,324 sq. km.)
POPULATION 3,878,000
CAPITAL Jerusalem
LARGEST CITY Tel Aviv-Jaffa
HIGHEST POINT Meiran 3,963 ft.
(1,208 m.)
MONETARY UNIT shekel
MAJOR LANGUAGES Hebrew, Arabic
MAJOR RELIGIONS Judaism, Islam, Christianity

JORDAN

AREA 35,000 sq. mi. (90,650 sq. km.)
POPULATION 2,152,273
CAPITAL Amman
LARGEST CITY Amman
HIGHEST POINT Jeb. Ramm 5,755 ft. (1,754 m.)
MONETARY UNIT Jordanian dinar
MAJOR LANGUAGE Arabic
MAJOR RELIGION Islam

Israel and Jordan

CYLINDRICAL PROJECTION

© Copyright HAMMOND INCORPORATED, Maplewood, N.J.

SCALE OF MILES
0   5   10   15   20   25   30
SCALE OF KILOMETERS
0 5 10 15 20 25 30

Capitals of Countries .... ☆
Internal Capitals .... ⊙
International Boundaries ....
Internal Boundaries ....

Scale 1:1,325,000

IRAN

INTERNAL DIVISIONS

Azerbaijan, East
(prov.) 3,194,543 ....E1
Azerbaijan, West
(prov.) 1,404,875 ....D1
Bakhtiari
(governorate) 394,300 ....F4
Boyer Ahmediyeh and Kohkiluyeh
(governor 244,750 ....G5
Bushehr (prov.) 345,427 ....G6
Central (Markazi)
(prov.) 6,921,283 ....G3
Esfahan (prov.) 1,974,938 ..H4
Fars (prov.) 2,020,947 .....H6
Gilan (prov.) 1,577,800 ....F2
Hamadan (governorate) 1,086,512 ..G3
Hormozgan (prov.) 463,419 ..J7
Ilam (governorate) 244,222 ..E4
Isfahan (prov.) 1,974,938 ..H4
Kerman (prov.) 1,088,045 ..K6
Kermanshahan (prov.) 1,016,199 ..E3
Khorasan (prov.) 3,266,650 ..K3
Khuzestan (prov.) 2,176,612 ..F5
Kordestan (Kurdistan)
(prov.) 781,889 ....E3
Lorestan (Luristan)
(governorate) 924,848 .....F4
Mazandaran (prov.) 2,384,226 ..H2
Semnan (governorate) 485,875 ..J3
Sistan and Baluchestan
(prov.) 659,297 ....M6
Yazd (governorate) 356,218 ..J5
Zanjan (governorate) 579,000 ..F2

CITIES and TOWNS

Abadan 296,081	F5
Abadeh 16,000	H5
Abarqu 8,000	H5
Abhar 24,000	G2
Agha Jari 24,195	F5
Ahar 24,000	E1
Ahwaz (Ahvaz) 329,006	F5
Amol 68,782	H2
Anarak 2,038	H4
Andimeshk 16,000	F4
Aradan 8,978	H3
Arak 114,507	F3
Ardabil 147,404	F1
Ardestan 5,868	H4
Asadabad 7,000	F3
Asterabad (Gorgan) 88,348	J2
Azaran 3,153	E2
Babol 67,790	H2
Babol Sar 7,237	H2
Bafq 5,000	J5
Baft 5,000	K6
Bajgiran 1,151	L2
Bam 22,000	L6
Bampur 1,585	M7
Bandar A'bbas 89,103	J7
Bandar-e Anzali (Enzeli) 55,978	F2
Bandar-e Deylam 3,691	G5
Bandar Khomeyni 6,000	F5
Bandar-e Lengeh 4,920	J7
Bandar-e Mas'hur 17,000	F5
Bandar-e Rig 1,889	G6
Bandar-e Torkeman 13,000	J2
Bandar Shahpur 6,000	F5
Bastak 2,473	J7
Bastam 3,296	J2
Behbehan 39,874	G5

Behshahr 26,032	H2
Bejestan 3,823	K3
Bijar 12,000	E3
Birjand 25,854	L4
Bojnurd 31,248	K2
Borazjan 20,000	G6
Borujerd 100,103	F4
Bostan 4,619	F5
Bowkan 9,000	E2
Bushehr (Bushire) 57,681	G6
Chah Bahar 1,800	M8
Chalus 15,000	H2
Damavand 5,319	H3
Damghan 13,000	J2
Darab 13,000	J6
Daran 4,609	G4
Darreh Gaz 11,000	L2
Dasht-e-Azadegan 21,000	F5
Dehkhvareqan 6,000	D2
Delijan 6,000	G3
Dezful 110,287	F4
Dizful (Dezful) 110,287	F4
Duzdab (Zahedan) 92,628	M6
Emamshahr 30,767	J2
Esfahan (Isfahan) 671,820	G4
Evaz 6,064	J7
Ezna 5,000	F4
Fahrej (Iranshahr) 5,000	M7
Fariman 8,000	L3
Farrashband 3,532	H6
Fasa 19,000	H6
Ferdows 11,000	K3
Firuzabad 8,718	H6
Firuzkuh 4,684	H3
Fowman 9,000	F2
Gach Saran	G5

Ganaveh 9,000	G6
Garmsar 4,723	H3
Gavater	M8
Ghaemshahr 63,289	H2
Golpayegan 20,515	G4
Golshan (Tabas) 10,000	K4
Gomishan 6,000	J2
Gonabad 8,000	L3
Gonbad-e Kavus 59,868	J2
Gonbadli 531	M2
Gorgan (Gurgan) 88,348	J2
Haft Gel 10,000	F5
Hamadan 155,846	F3
Hashtpar 5,000	F2
Hormoz 2,569	J7
Huzgan 4,722	H6
Ilam 15,000	E4
Iranshahr 5,000	M7
Isfahan 671,825	G4
Izeh 1,983	F5
Jahrom 38,236	H6
Jajarm 3,641	K2
Jask 1,078	K8
Kakhk 4,043	L3
Kangan 2,682	J4
Kangavar 9,414	F3
Karaj 138,774	G3
Kashan 84,545	G3
Kashmar 17,000	L3
Kazerun 51,309	H6
Kazvin (Qazvin) 138,527	F2
Khaf 5,000	L3
Khalkhal 5,000	M6
Khash 7,439	M6
Khiyav 9,000	E1
Khoman 3,054	F2
Khomeinishar 46,836	G4

Khorramabad 104,928	F4
Khorramshahr 146,709	F5
Khvaf 5,000	L3
Khvonsar 10,947	G4
Khvor 2,912	J4
Khvoy (Khoi) 70,040	D1
Kord Kuy 9,855	J2
Lahijan 25,725	F2
Lar 22,000	J7
Mahabad 28,610	D2
Mahallat 12,000	G4
Maku 7,000	D1
Malaher 8,000	F3
Malamir (Izeh) 1,983	F5
Malayer 28,434	F3
Maragheh 60,820	E2
Marand 24,000	D1
Marv Dasht 25,498	H6
Mashhad (Meshed) 670,180	L2
Masjed Soleyman 77,161	F5
Medishahr 9,000	H3
Mehran 664	E4
Meshed 670,180	L2
Meshed-i-Sar (Babol)	H2
Meybod 15,000	J4
Miandowab 19,000	D2
Mianeh 28,447	E2
Minab 4,228	K7
Mirjaveh 11,000	M6
Naft-e Shah 3,043	D4
Nahavand 24,000	F3
Na'in 5,926	H4
Najafabad 76,236	G4
Nasratabad (Zabol) 20,000	M5
Natanz 4,757	H4
Neyriz 16,114	J6
Neyshabur 59,101	L2

Nishapur (Neyshabur) 59,101	L2
Nosratabad 20,000	L6
Now Shahr 8,000	G2
Orumiyeh (Urmia) 163,991	D2
Oshnoviyeh 5,000	D2
Pahlevi (Enzeli) 55,978	F2
Pazanan 81	F5
Qasr-e Shirin 15,094	E3
Qayen 6,000	L4
Qazvin 138,527	F2
Qom 246,831	G3
Qorveh 2,929	E3
Qum (Qom) 246,831	G3
Rafsanjan 21,000	K6
Ramhormoz 9,000	F5
Rasht 187,203	F2
Ravar 5,074	K5
Resht (Rasht) 187,203	F2
Rey 102,825	G3
Reza'iyeh (Urmia) 163,991	D2
Rigan 8,255	L6
Rud Sar 7,000	G2
Sabzevar 69,174	K2
Sabzevaran 7,000	K6
Saeendey 4,195	E2
Sai'dabad 20,000	J6
Salmas 13,161	D1
Sanandaj 95,834	E3
Saqqez 17,000	E2
Sarab 16,000	E2
Sarakhs 3,461	M2
Saravan 4,012	N7
Sar Dasht 8,000	D2
Sari 70,936	H2
Savanat (Estahbanat) 18,187	J6
Saveh 17,565	G3
Semnan 31,058	H3

Shadegan 6,000	F5
Shahdad 2,777	K5
Shahistan (Saravan) 4,012	N7
Shahreza 34,220	H4
Shahr Kord 24,000	G4
Shahrud (Emamshahr) 30,767	J2
Sharafkhaneh 1,260	D1
Shiraz 416,408	H6
Shirvan 11,000	K2
Shush 1,433	F4
Shushtar 24,000	F5
Sinneh (Sanandaj) 95,834	E3
Sirjan (Sai'dabad) 20,000	J6
Sivand 1,811	H6
Songor 10,433	E3
Sultanabad (Kashmar) 17,000	L3
Tabas 10,000	K4
Tabriz 598,576	E1
Taft 7,000	J5
Takestan 13,485	F2
Tehran (cap.) 4,496,159	G3
Tonekabon 12,000	G2
Torbat-e Heydariyeh 30,106	L3
Torbat-e Jam 13,000	M3
Tun (Ferdows) 11,000	K3
Turbat-i-Shaikh Jam 13,000	M3
Tuysarkan 12,000	F3
Urmia 163,991	D2
Varamin 11,183	G3
Yazd (Yezd) 135,978	J5
Yazd-e Khvast 3,544	H5
Zabol 20,000	M5
Zahedan 92,628	M6
Zanjan 99,967	K5
Zarand 5,000	K6
Zarqam 7,000	H6
Zenjan (Zanjan) 99,967	F2

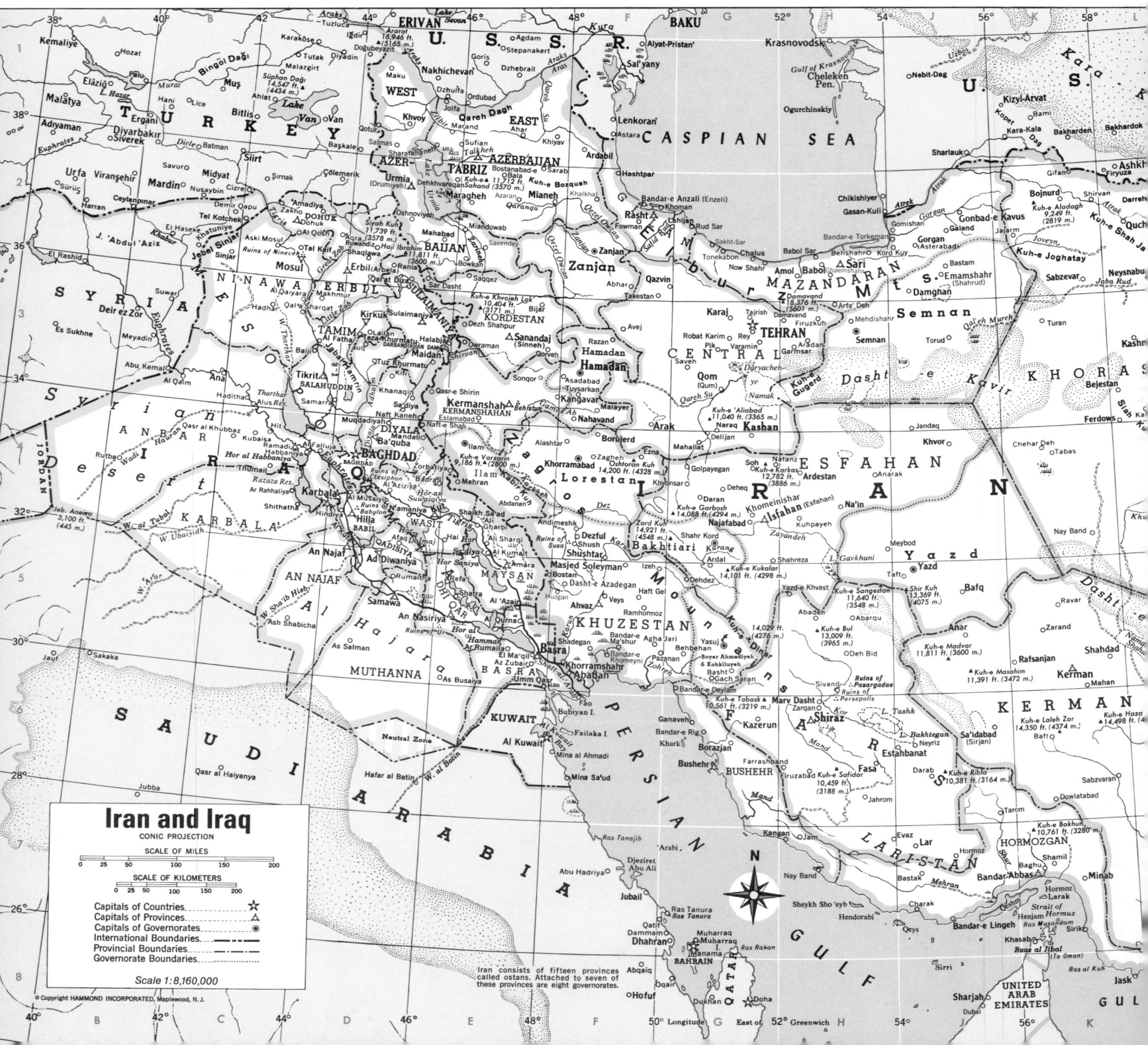

Iran and Iraq

CONIC PROJECTION

SCALE OF MILES

0   25   50   100   150   200

SCALE OF KILOMETERS

0 25 50 100   150   200

Capitals of Countries .... ★
Capitals of Provinces .... △
Capitals of Governorates .... ◉
International Boundaries ....
Provincial Boundaries ....
Governorate Boundaries ....

Scale 1:8,160,000

© Copyright HAMMOND INCORPORATED, Maplewood, N.J.

Iran consists of fifteen provinces
called ostans. Attached to seven of
these provinces are eight governorates.

OTHER FEATURES

Aji Chai (riv.) E1
A'rabi (isl.) G7
Araks (Aras) (riv.) E1
Atrak (Atrek) (riv.) J2
Bakhtegan (lake) J6
Baluchistan (reg.) M7
Bampur (riv.) M7
Behistun (ruins) E3
Caspian (sea) G1
Damavand (Demavend) (mt.) H3
Dez (riv.) F4
Elburz (mts.) G2
Farsi (isl.) G7
Gorgan (riv.) J2
Hari Rud (riv.) M3
Karkheh (riv.) E4
Karun (riv.) F5
Kashaf Rud (riv.) M2
Khark (Kharg) (isl.) G6
Kuh (cape) K8
Kurang (riv.) G4
Laristan (reg.) J7
Makran (reg.) M8
Mand Rud (riv.) G6
Mehran (riv.) J7
Namaksar (lake) M4
Nezwar (mt.) H3
Oman (gulf) M8
Pasargadae (ruins) H5
Persepolis (ruins) H6
Persian (gulf) F6
Qareh Su (riv.) E1
Qareh Su (riv.) G3
Qeshm (isl.) J7
Qezel Owzam (riv.) F2
Safid Rud (riv.) F2
Shaikh Shua'ib (isl.) H7
Shelagh (riv.) M5
Shirvan (riv.) E3
Shur (riv.) J7
Siah Kuh (mt.) L3
Silup (riv.) M8
Susa (ruins) F4
Talab (riv.) N6
Tashk (lake) J6
Urmia (lake) D2
Zagros (mts.) E4
Zarineh (riv.) E2
Zilbir (riv.) D1
Zohreh (riv.) F5

IRAQ

GOVERNORATES

Anbar B4
An Najaf C5
Babil D4
Baghdad D4
Basra E5
Dhi Qar E5
Diyala D4
Dohuk C2
Erbil C3
Karbala B4
Maysan E5
Muthanna D5
Ninawa B3
Qadisiya D4
Salahuddin C3
Sulaimaniya D3
Tamin D3
Wasit D4

CITIES and TOWNS

Ad Diwaniya 60,553 .... D5
A'faq 5,390 .... D4
Al A'ziziya 7,450 .... D4
Al Falluja 38,072 .... C4
Al Fatha† 15,329 .... C3
A'li Gharbi 15,456 .... E4
A'li Sharqi 8,398 .... E4
Al Kufa 30,862 .... D4
Al Musaiyib 15,955 .... D4
Al Q'aim 3,372 .... B3
Al Qaiyara 3,060 .... C3
Al Qosh 3,863 .... C2
Al Qurna 5,638 .... E5
A'madiya 2,578 .... C2
A'mara 64,847 .... E5
A'na 15,729 .... B3
An Najaf 128,096 .... D5
An Nasiriya 60,405 .... D5
A'qra 8,659 .... D2
Arbela (Erbil) 90,320 .... D2
Aski Mosul 643 .... C2
As Salman 1,789 .... D5
Az Zubair 41,408 .... E5
Badra 3,564 .... D4
Baghdad (cap.) 502,503 .... D4
Baghdad* 1,745,328 .... D4
Baiji 6,785 .... C3
Baq'uba 34,575 .... D4
Basra 313,327 .... E5
Dohuk 16,998 .... C2
Erbil 90,320 .... D2
Fao 15,399 .... F6
Habbaniya 14,405 .... C4
Haditha 6,870 .... C3
Hai 16,988 .... E4
Halabja 11,206 .... D3
Hilla 84,717 .... D4
Hindiya 16,436 .... C4
Hit 9,131 .... C4
Karbal'a 83,301 .... C4
Khanaqin 23,522 .... D3
Kifri 8,500 .... D3
Kirkuk 167,413 .... D3
Kirkuk* 176,794 .... D3
Kubaisa 4,023 .... C4
Kut 42,116 .... D4
Makhmur 2,556 .... C3
Mandali 11,262 .... D4
Mosul 315,157 .... C2
Muqdadiyah 12,181 .... D4
Naft Kaneh D3
Na'maniya 11,943 .... D4
Qal'at Diza 6,250 .... D2
Ramadi 28,723 .... C4
Rania 4,090 .... D2
Refai' 7,681 .... E5
Rumaitha 10,222 .... D5
Rutba 5,091 .... B4
Ruwandiz 5,801 .... D2
Sad'iya 5,285 .... D3
Samarra 24,746 .... C3
Samawa 33,473 .... D5
Shaikh Saa'd 2,958 .... E4
Shaqlawa 6,814 .... D2
Shatra 18,822 .... E5
Sinjar 7,942 .... B2
Sulaimaniya 86,822 .... D3
Tal Kaif 7,482 .... C2
Taza Khurmatu 2,681 .... D3
Tikrit 9,921 .... C3
Tuz Khurmatu 13,860 .... D3
Zakho 14,790 .... C2

OTHER FEATURES

Adhaim (riv.) D3
Aneiza, Jebel (mt.) A4
A'rab, Shatt-al- (riv.) F5
A'ra'r, Wadi (dry riv.) B5
Babylon (ruins) D4
Batin, Wadi al (dry riv.) E6
Ctesiphon (ruins) D4
Darbandikhan (dam) D3
Euphrates (riv.) D4
Great Zab (riv.) C2
Hauran, Wadi (dry riv.) B4
Little Zab (riv.) C3
Mesopotamia (reg.) B3
Nineveh (ruins) C2
Sad'iya, Hor (lake) E4
Saniya, Hor (lake) E5
Shai'b Hisb, Wadi (dry riv.) C5
Sinjar, Jebel (mts.) B2
Siyah Kuh (mt.) D2
Syrian (des.) B4
Tigris (riv.) E4
Ubaiyidh, Wadi (dry riv.) B5
Ur (ruins) E5

*City and suburbs.
†Population of commune.

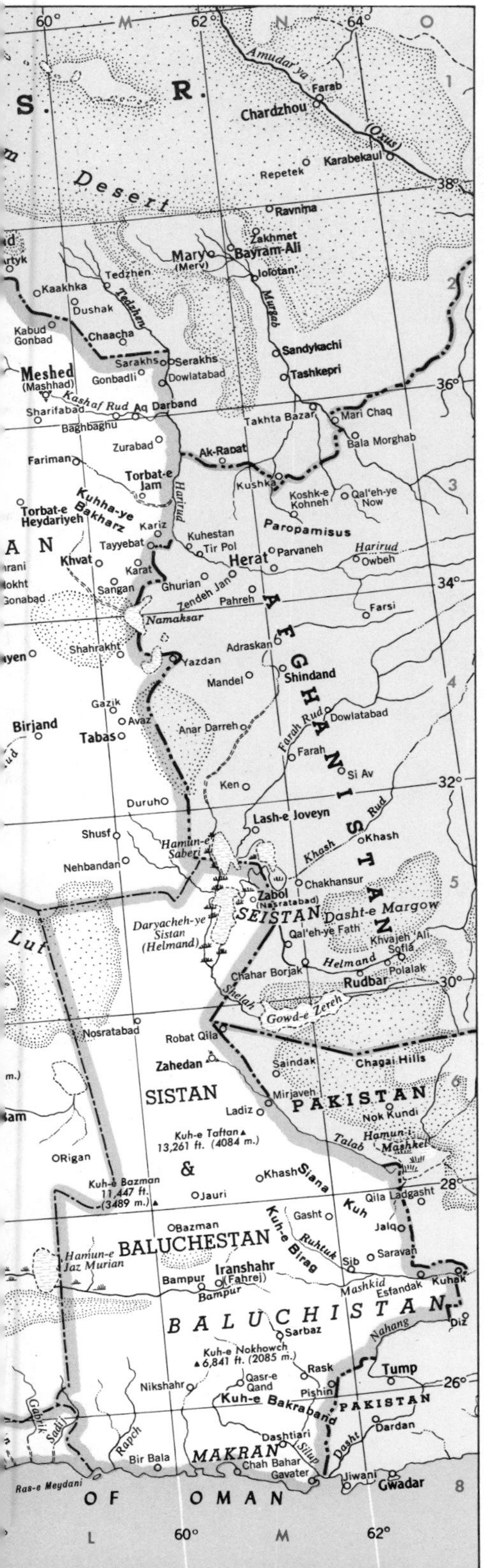

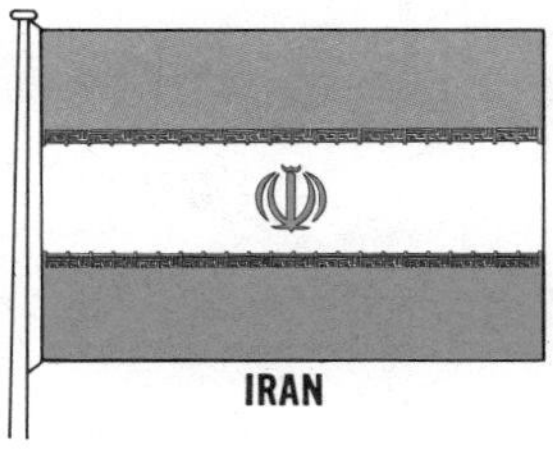

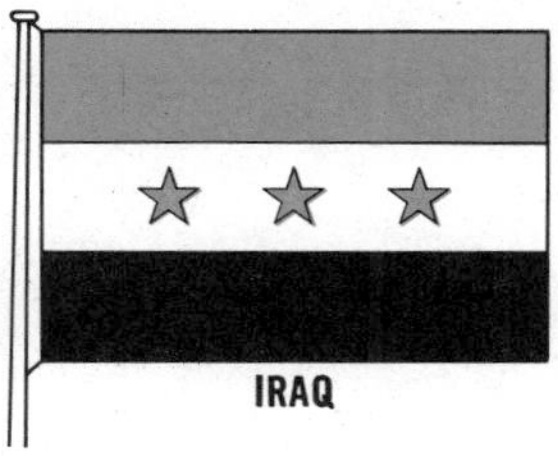

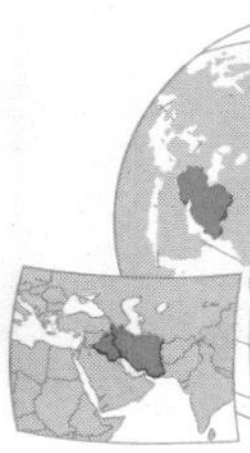

AREA 636,293 sq. mi. (1,648,000 sq. km.)
POPULATION 37,447,000
CAPITAL Tehran
LARGEST CITY Tehran
HIGHEST POINT Damavand 18,376 ft. (5,601 m.)
MONETARY UNIT Iranian rial
MAJOR LANGUAGES Persian, Azerbaijani, Kurdish
MAJOR RELIGION Islam

AREA 172,476 sq. mi. (446,713 sq. km.)
POPULATION 12,767,000
CAPITAL Baghdad
LARGEST CITY Baghdad
HIGHEST POINT Haji Ibrahim 11,811 ft. (3,600 m.)
MONETARY UNIT Iraqi dinar
MAJOR LANGUAGES Arabic, Kurdish
MAJOR RELIGION Islam

Topography

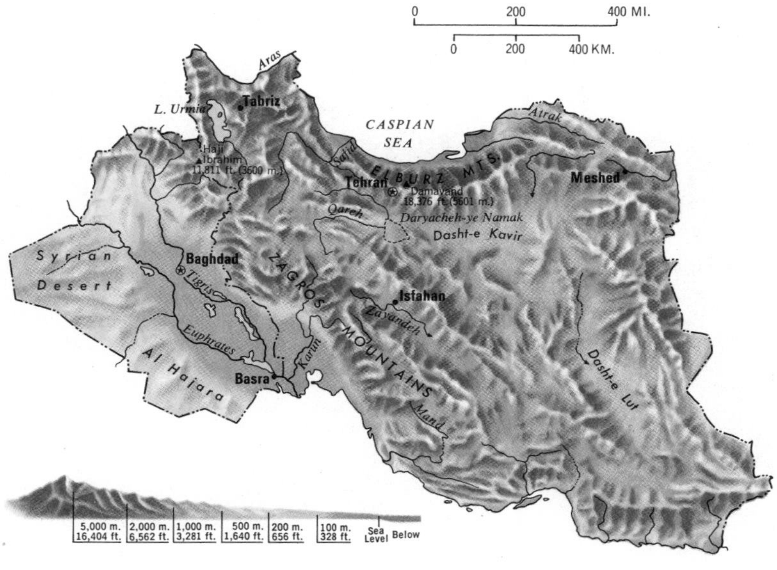

Agriculture, Industry and Resources

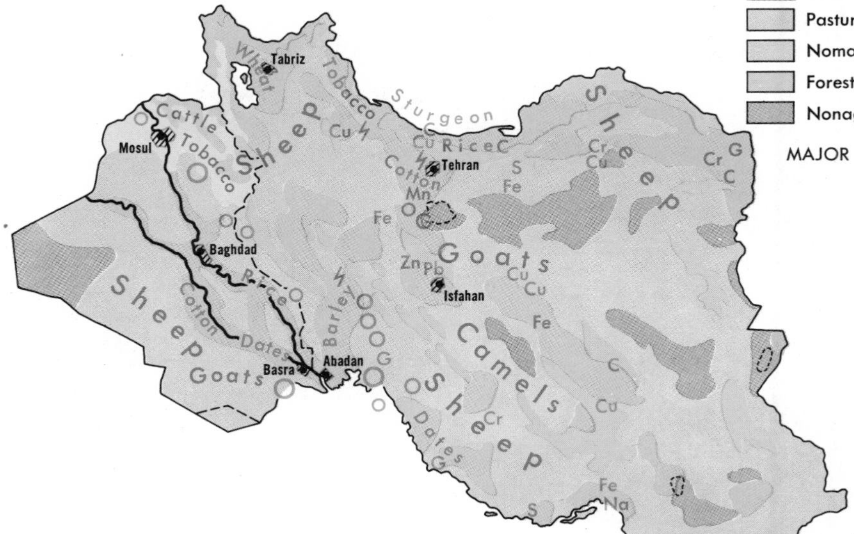

DOMINANT LAND USE

- Cereals, Livestock
- Cash Crops, Horticulture, Livestock
- Pasture Livestock
- Nomadic Livestock Herding
- Forests
- Nonagricultural Land

MAJOR MINERAL OCCURRENCES

- C Coal
- Cr Chromium
- Cu Copper
- Fe Iron Ore
- G Natural Gas
- Mn Manganese
- Na Salt
- O Petroleum
- Pb Lead
- S Sulfur, Pyrites
- Zn Zinc

- Water Power
- Major Industrial Areas

Indian Subcontinent and Afghanistan

CONIC PROJECTION

SCALE OF MILES

0   50   100   200   300

KILOMETERS

0   50   100   200   300

Capitals of Countries .... ☆
Provincial and State Capitals .... ◉
International Boundaries ....
Provincial and State Boundaries .....
Canals ....

Scale 1:14,500,000

© Copyright HAMMOND INCORPORATED, Maplewood, N.J.

Longitude East 85° of Greenwich

BOMBAY

CALCUTTA

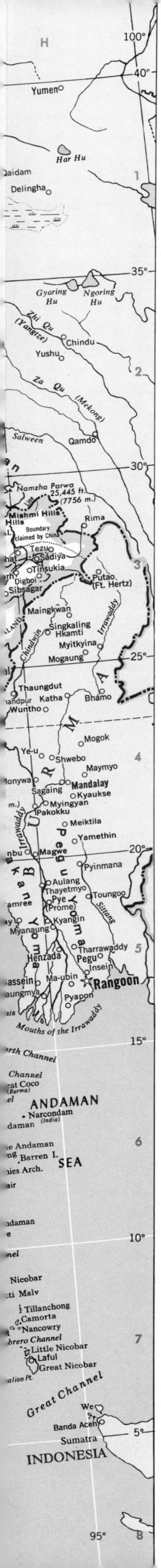

INDIA

AREA 1,269,339 sq. mi. (3,287,588 sq. km.)
POPULATION 683,810,051
CAPITAL New Delhi
LARGEST CITY Calcutta (greater)
HIGHEST POINT Nanda Devi 25,645 ft. (7,817 m.)
MONETARY UNIT Indian rupee
MAJOR LANGUAGES Hindi, English, Bihari, Telugu, Marathi, Bengali, Tamil, Gujarati, Rajasthani, Kanarese, Malayalam, Oriya, Punjabi, Assamese, Kashmiri, Urdu
MAJOR RELIGIONS Hinduism, Islam, Christianity, Sikhism, Buddhism, Jainism, Zoroastrianism, Animism

PAKISTAN

AREA 310,403 sq. mi. (803,944 sq. km.)
POPULATION 83,782,000
CAPITAL Islamabad
LARGEST CITY Karachi
HIGHEST POINT K2 (Godwin Austen) 28,250 ft. (8,611 m.)
MONETARY UNIT Pakistani rupee
MAJOR LANGUAGES Urdu, English, Punjabi, Pushtu, Sindhi, Baluchi, Brahui
MAJOR RELIGIONS Islam, Hinduism, Sikhism, Christianity, Buddhism

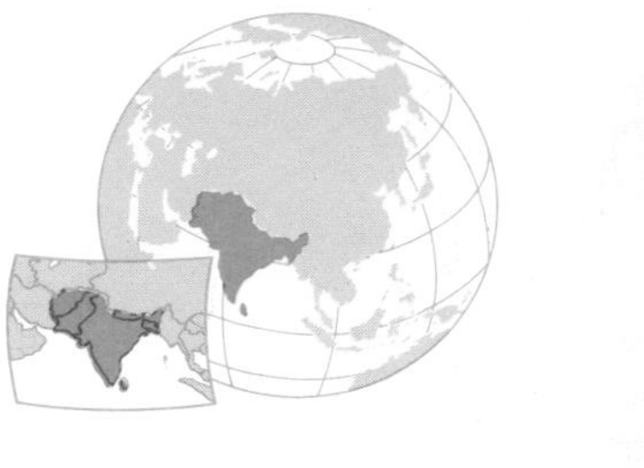

SRI LANKA (CEYLON)

AREA 25,332 sq. mi. (65,610 sq. km.)
POPULATION 14,850,001
CAPITAL Colombo
LARGEST CITY Colombo
HIGHEST POINT Pidurutalagala 8,281 ft. (2,524 m.)
MONETARY UNIT Sri Lanka rupee
MAJOR LANGUAGES Sinhala, Tamil, English
MAJOR RELIGIONS Buddhism, Hinduism, Christianity, Islam

AFGHANISTAN

AREA 250,775 sq. mi. (649,507 sq. km.)
POPULATION 15,540,000
CAPITAL Kabul
LARGEST CITY Kabul
HIGHEST POINT Nowshak 24,557 ft. (7,485 m.)
MONETARY UNIT afghani
MAJOR LANGUAGES Pushtu, Dari, Uzbek
MAJOR RELIGION Islam

NEPAL

AREA 54,663 sq. mi. (141,577 sq. km.)
POPULATION 14,179,301
CAPITAL Kathmandu
LARGEST CITY Kathmandu
HIGHEST POINT Mt. Everest 29,028 ft. (8,848 m.)
MONETARY UNIT Nepalese rupee
MAJOR LANGUAGES Nepali, Maithili, Tamang, Newari, Tharu
MAJOR RELIGIONS Hinduism, Buddhism

MALDIVES

AREA 115 sq. mi. (298 sq. km.)
POPULATION 143,046
CAPITAL Male
LARGEST CITY Male
HIGHEST POINT 20 ft. (6 m.)
MONETARY UNIT Maldivian rupee
MAJOR LANGUAGE Divehi
MAJOR RELIGION Islam

BHUTAN

AREA 18,147 sq. mi. (47,000 sq. km.)
POPULATION 1,298,000
CAPITAL Thimphu
LARGEST CITY Thimphu
HIGHEST POINT Kula Kangri 24,784 ft. (7,554 m.)
MONETARY UNIT ngultrum
MAJOR LANGUAGES Dzongka, Nepali
MAJOR RELIGIONS Buddhism, Hinduism

BANGLADESH

AREA 55,126 sq. mi. (142,776 sq. km.)
POPULATION 87,052,024
CAPITAL Dhaka
LARGEST CITY Dhaka
HIGHEST POINT Keokradong 4,034 ft. (1,230 m.)
MONETARY UNIT taka
MAJOR LANGUAGES Bengali, English
MAJOR RELIGIONS Islam, Hinduism Christianity

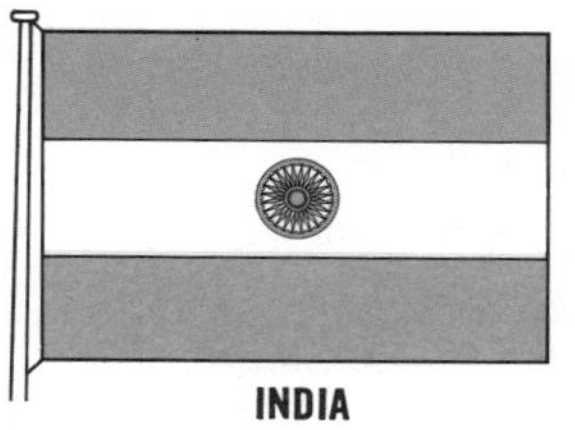
INDIA

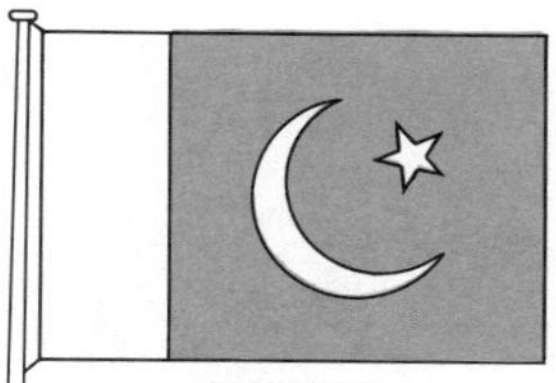
PAKISTAN

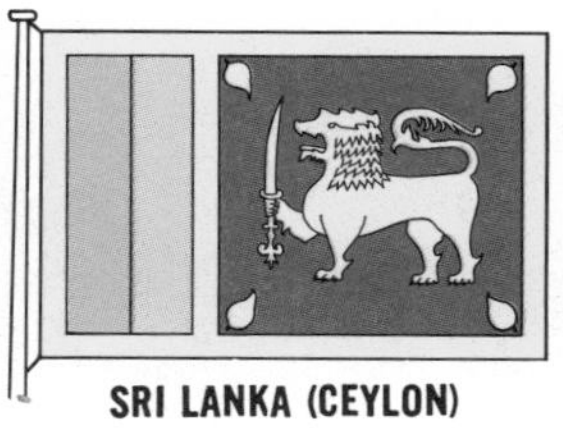
SRI LANKA (CEYLON)

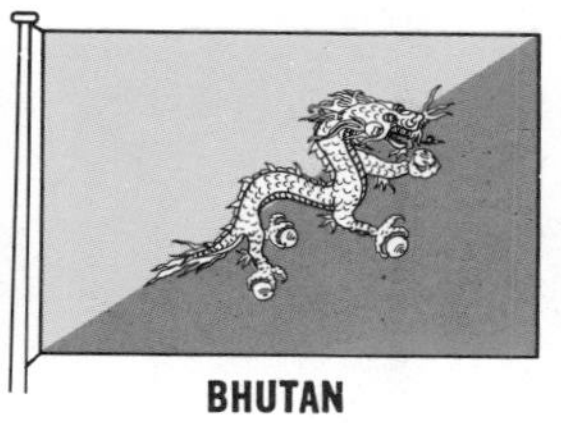
BHUTAN

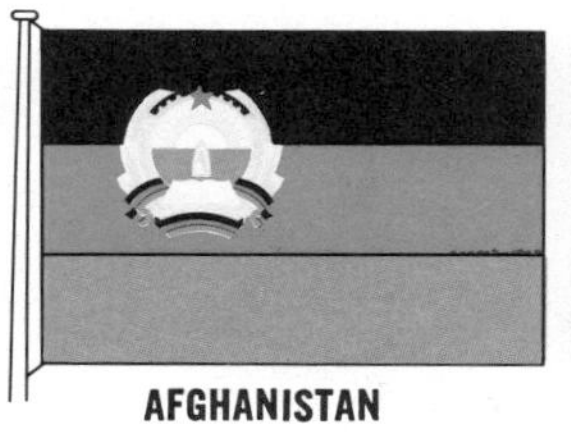
AFGHANISTAN

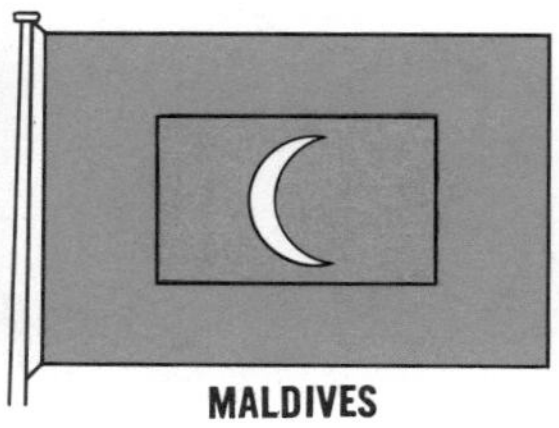
MALDIVES

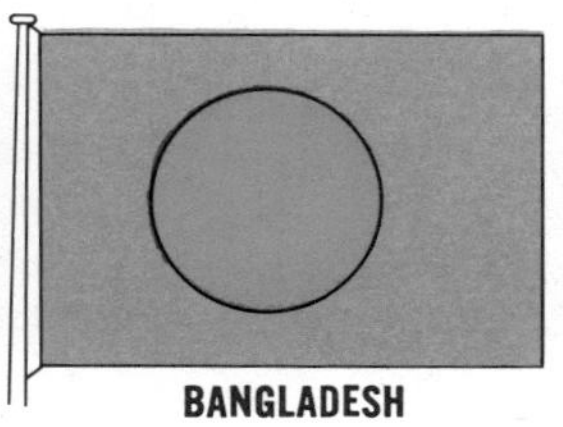
BANGLADESH

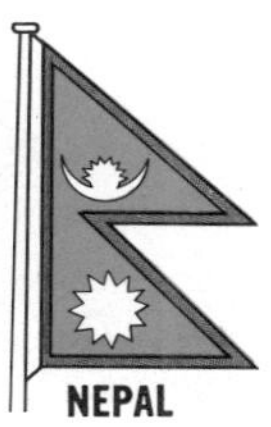
NEPAL

AFGHANISTAN

CITIES and TOWNS

Andkhvoy A1
Aqcheh B1
Aybak 33,016 .... B1
Baghlan 75,130 .... B1
Balkh B1
Bamian 7,355 .... B2
Belcheragh B1
Chaghcharan 2,974 .... B2
Chahar Borjak A2
Charikar 25,093 .... B1
Delaram A2
Dowlatabad A2
Dowlat Yar B2
Dowshi B1
Farah 18,797 .... A2
Farsi A2
Feyzabad 10,142 .... C1
Gardez 11,415 .... B2
Gereshk A2
Ghazni 30,425 .... B2
Ghurian A2
Gizab B2
Hazar Qadam B2
Herat 163,960 .... A2
Jalalabad 56,384 .... B2
Jorm C1
Kabul (cap.) 905,108 .... B2
Kalat (Qalat) 5,946 .... B2
Kandahar (Qandahar) 178,409 .... B2
Ken A2
Khanabad B1
Khash A2
Kholm B1
Khowst B2
Khugiani B2
Koshke-e Kohneh A2
Kowt-e 'Ashrow B2
Kuhestan A2
Landay A2
Lash-e Joveyn A2
Lashkar Gah 26,646 .... A2
Mar'uf B2
Mazar-e Sharif 122,567 .... B1
Meymaneh 54,954 .... A1
Mirabad A2
Moqor B2
Now Zad A2
Oruzgan (Hazar Qadam) B2
Owbeh A2
Panjab B2
Pol-e Khomri B1
Qalat 5,946 .... B2
Qale'h-ye Now 5,340 .... A1
Qale'h-ye Panjeh C1
Qandahar 178,409 .... B2
Qonduz 107,191 .... B1
Rostaq B1
Rudbar A2
Sakhar B2
Sar-e Pol B1
Shay Juy B2
Sheberghan 54,870 .... B1
Shindand A2
Spin Buldak B2
Tagab B2
Taloqan 46,202 .... B1
Teyvareh A2
Towraghondi A1
Tulak A2
Zaranj 6,477 .... A2
Zibak C1

OTHER FEATURES

Farah Rud (riv.) A2
Harirud (riv.) A1
Helmand (riv.) B2
Hindu Kush (mts.) B1
Kabul (riv.) C2
Konar (riv.) C1
Lurah (riv.) B2
Margow, Dasht-e (des.) A2
Namaksar (salt lake) A2
Paropamisus (range) A2
Tarnak (riv.) B2

BANGLADESH

CITIES and TOWNS

Barisal 98,127 .... G4
Bogra 47,154 .... F4
Chalna Port 14,590 .... F4
Chittagong 889,760 .... G4
Comilla 86,446 .... G4
Cox's Bazar (Maheshkhali) 15,720 .... G4
Dhaka (Dacca) (cap.) 1,679,572 .... G4
Dinajpur 61,866 .... F3
Faridpur 46,232 .... F4
Habiganj 16,281 .... G4
Jamalpur 60,261 .... F4
Jessore 76,168 .... F4
Khulna 437,304 .... F4
Kishorganj 35,605 .... G4
Madaripur 32,488 .... G4
Maheshkhali 15,720 .... G4
Mymensingh (Nasirabad) 182,153 .... G4
Narayanganj 270,680 .... G4
Nasirabad 182,153 .... G4
Nawabganj 46,059 .... F4
Noakhali 32,490 .... G4
Pabna 62,254 .... F4
Rajshahi 132,909 .... F4
Rangamati 20,473 .... G4
Rangpur 72,829 .... F3
Sirajganj 74,457 .... F4
Sylhet 59,546 .... G4
Teknaf G4

OTHER FEATURES

Bengal, Bay of (sea) F5
Brahmaputra (riv.) G3
Ganges (riv.) F3
Sundarbans (reg.) F4

BHUTAN

CITIES and TOWNS

Bumthang 10,000 .... G3
Paro 35,000 .... F3
Punakha 12,000 .... G3
Taga Dzong 18,000 .... G3
Thimphu (cap.) 50,000 .... G3
Tongsa Dzong 2,500 .... G3

OTHER FEATURES

Chomo Lhari (mt.) F3
Himalaya (mts.) E2
Kula Kangri (mt.) G3

INDIA

INTERNAL DIVISIONS

Andaman and Nicobar Isls. (terr.) 188,254 .... G6
Andhra Pradesh (state) 53,403,619 .... D5
Arunachal Pradesh (terr.) 628,050 .... G3

(continued on following page)

Topography

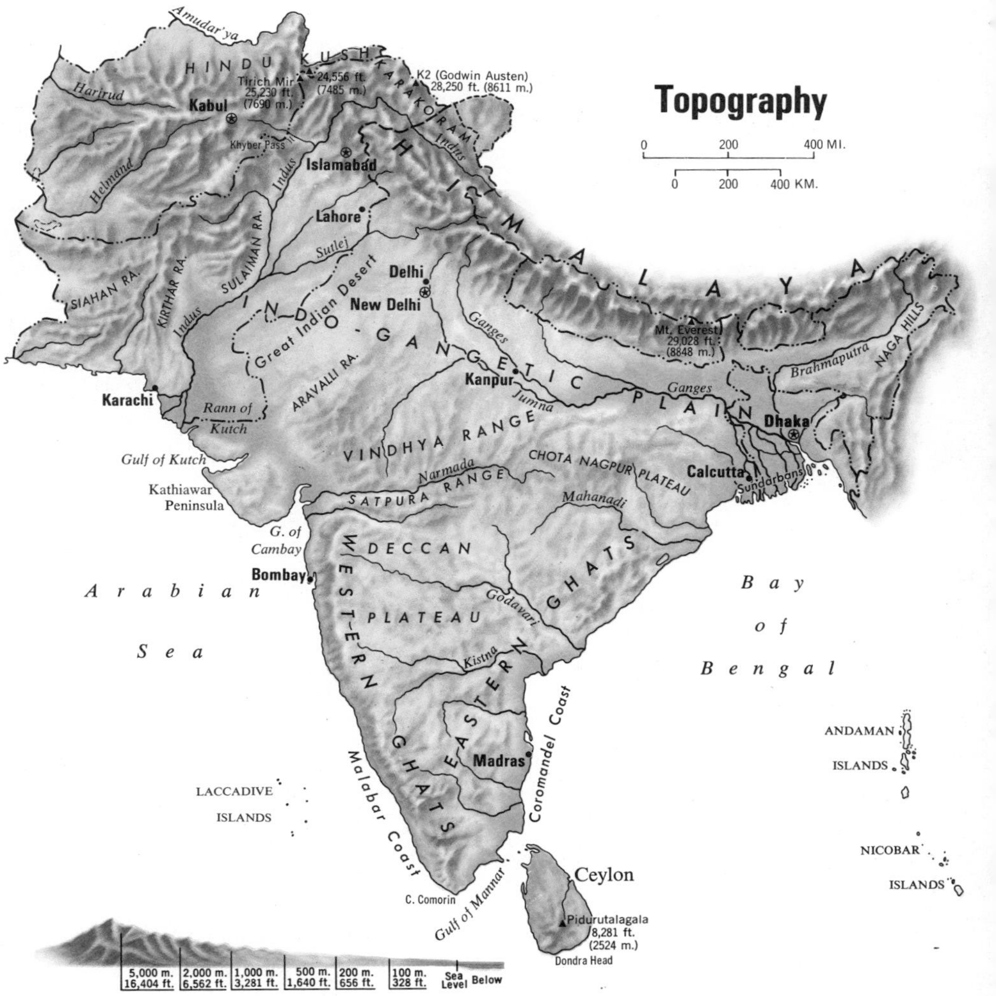

70 Indian Subcontinent and Afghanistan

(continued)

Assam (state) 19,902,826 ..... G3
Bihar (state) 69,823,154 ..... F4
Chandigarh (terr.) 450,061 ..... D2
Dadra and Nagar Haveli (terr.) 103,677 ..... C4
Delhi (terr.) 6,196,414 ..... D3
Goa, Daman and Diu (terr.) 1,082,117 ..... C4
Gujarat (state) 33,960,905 ..... C4
Haryana (state) 12,850,902 ..... D3
Himachal Pradesh (state) 4,237,569 ..... D2
Jammu and Kashmir (state) 5,981,600 ..... D2
Karnataka (state) 37,043,451 ..... D6
Kerala (state) 25,403,217 ..... D6
Lakshadweep (terr.) 40,237 ..... C6
Madhya Pradesh (state) 52,131,717 ..... D4
Maharashtra (state) 62,693,898 ..... C5
Manipur (state) 1,433,691 ..... G4
Meghalaya (state) 1,327,874 ..... G3
Mizoram (terr.) 487,774 ..... G4
Nagaland (state) 773,281 ..... G3
Orissa (state) 26,272,054 ..... E5
Pondicherry (terr.) 604,136 ..... E6
Punjab (state) 16,669,755 ..... D2
Rajasthan (state) 34,102,912 ..... C3
Sikkim (state) 315,682 ..... F3
Tamil Nadu (state) 48,297,456 ..... D6
Tripura (state) 2,060,189 ..... G4
Uttar Pradesh (state) 110,858,019 ..... D3
West Bengal (state) 54,485,560 ..... F4

CITIES and TOWNS

Abu 9,840 ..... C4
Abu Road 25,331 ..... C4
Achalpur 42,326 ..... D4
Addanki 10,223 ..... D5
Adilabad 30,368 ..... D5
Adoni 85,311 ..... D5
Agartala 59,625 ..... G4
Agartala□ 100,264 ..... G4
Agra 591,917 ..... D3
Agra□ 634,622 ..... D3
Ahmadabad 1,591,832 ..... C4
Ahmadabad□ 1,741,522 ..... C4
Ahmadnagar 118,236 ..... C5
Ahmadnagar□ 148,405 ..... C5
Aizwal 31,740 ..... G4
Ajanta D4
Ajmer 262,851 ..... C3
Akola 168,438 ..... D4
Alibag 11,913 ..... C5
Aligarh 252,314 ..... D3
Alipore F2
Allahabad 490,622 ..... E3
Allahabad□ 513,036 ..... E3
Alleppey-Cochin 160,166 ..... D7
Almora 19,671 ..... D3
Along 3,524 ..... G3
Alwar 100,378 ..... D3
Amalner 55,544 ..... C4
Ambala 83,633 ..... D2
Ambala□ 186,168 ..... D2
Ambikapur 23,087 ..... E4
Amravati 193,800 ..... D4
Amreli 39,520 ..... C4
Amritsar 407,628 ..... C2
Amritsar□ 458,029 ..... C2
Anakapalle 57,273 ..... E5
Anantapur 80,069 ..... D6
Anantnag 27,643 ..... D2
Andheri B7
Andul 3,602 ..... F2
Arcot 30,230 ..... D6
Arrah 92,919 ..... E3
Aruppukkottai 62,223 ..... D7
Arvi 26,494 ..... D4
Asansol 155,968 ..... F4
Asansol□ 241,792 ..... F4
Aurangabad, Bihar 18,714 ..... E4
Aurangabad, Maharashtra 150,483 ..... D5
Aurangabad□ 165,253 ..... D5
Azamgarh 40,963 ..... E3
Badagara 53,938 ..... D6
Bagalkot 51,746 ..... D5
Bahraich 73,931 ..... E3
Baidyabati 54,130 ..... F1
Balaghat 27,872 ..... E4
Balasore 46,239 ..... F4
Ballia 47,101 ..... E3
Bally 38,892 ..... F1
Balotra 17,595 ..... C3
Balrampur 36,191 ..... E3
Balurghat 67,088 ..... F3
Banda 50,575 ..... D3
Bandar (Machilipatnam) 112,612 ..... E5
Bandra B7
Bangalore 1,540,741 ..... D6
Bangalore□ 1,653,779 ..... D6
Bankura 79,129 ..... F4
Bansberia 61,748 ..... F1
Banswara 27,363 ..... C4
Baramati 27,912 ..... C5
Baramula 26,334 ..... C2
Baranagar 136,842 ..... F1
Barasat 42,642 ..... F1
Barbil 24,342 ..... F4
Bareilly 296,248 ..... D3
Bareilly□ 326,106 ..... D3
Baripada 28,725 ..... F4
Barmer 38,630 ..... C3
Baroda (Vadodara) 466,696 ..... C4
Barpeta 26,479 ..... G3
Barrackpore 96,889 ..... F1
Barrackpore□ 198,255 ..... F1
Barsi 62,374 ..... D5
Baruipur 20,501 ..... F2
Barwani 22,099 ..... D4
Basim 32,496 ..... D4
Basirhat 63,816 ..... F4
Bassein 30,594 ..... C5
Bastar E5
Batala 58,200 ..... D2
Baudh 8,891 ..... E4
Bauria 10,610 ..... E2
Beawar 66,114 ..... C3
Belgaum 192,427 ..... C5
Belgaum□ 213,872 ..... C5
Bellary 125,183 ..... D5
Benares (Varanasi) 583,856 ..... E3
Berhampore 72,605 ..... F4
Berhampur 117,662 ..... F5
Bettiah 51,018 ..... E3
Betul 30,862 ..... D4
Bhadrak 40,487 ..... F4
Bhadravati 40,203 ..... D6
Bhadravati□ 101,358 ..... D6
Bhadreswar 45,586 ..... F1
Bhagalpur 172,202 ..... F4
Bhandara 39,423 ..... E4
Bhandup B7
Bhanjanagar 12,353 ..... E4
Bharatpur 68,036 ..... D3
Bharuch 91,589 ..... C4
Bhatapara 20,980 ..... E4
Bhatinda 53,684 ..... C2
Bhatkal 18,732 ..... C6
Bhatpara 204,750 ..... F1
Bhavnagar 225,358 ..... C4
Bhavnagar□ 225,974 ..... C4
Bhawanipatna 22,808 ..... E5
Bhilai 157,173 ..... E4
Bhilwara 82,155 ..... C3
Bhimavaram 63,762 ..... E5
Bhimunipatnam 14,291 ..... E5
Bhind 42,371 ..... D3
Bhinmal 14,050 ..... C3
Bhir (Bir) 49,965 ..... D5
Bhiwandi 79,576 ..... C5
Bhiwani 73,086 ..... D3
Bhopal 298,022 ..... D4
Bhor 10,708 ..... C5
Bhubaneswar 105,491 ..... F4
Bhuj 52,177 ..... B4
Bhusawal 96,800 ..... D4
Bhusawal□ 104,708 ..... D4
Bidar 50,670 ..... D5
Bihar 100,046 ..... F3
Bijapur, Karnataka 103,931 ..... D5
Bijapur, Madhya Pradesh 5,289 ..... E5
Bijnor 43,290 ..... D3
Bikaner 188,518 ..... C3
Bikaner□ 208,894 ..... C3
Bilaspur 98,410 ..... E4
Bina-Itawa 33,106 ..... D4
Bir 49,965 ..... D5
Birmitrapur 28,063 ..... E4
Bobbili 30,649 ..... E5
Bodhan 37,589 ..... D5
Bodinayakkanur 54,176 ..... D6
Bolangir 35,748 ..... E4
Bombay (Greater)* 5,970,575 ..... B7
Bomdila 2,264 ..... G3
Broach (Bharuch) 91,589 ..... C4
Budaun 72,204 ..... D3
Budge-Budge 51,039 ..... F2
Bundi 34,279 ..... D3
Burdwan 143,318 ..... F4
Burhanpur 105,246 ..... D4
Calcutta 3,148,746 ..... F2
Calcutta□ 7,031,382 ..... F2
Calicut (Kozhikode) 333,979 ..... D6
Cambay 62,097 ..... C4
Cannanore 55,162 ..... C6
Cawnpore (Kanpur) 1,154,388 ..... E3
Chaibasa 35,386 ..... F4
Chamba 11,814 ..... D2
Champdani 58,596 ..... F1
Chanderi 10,294 ..... D4
Chandernagore 75,238 ..... F1
Chandigarh 218,743 ..... D2
Chandigarh□ 232,940 ..... D2
Chandrapur 75,134 ..... D5
Chapra 83,101 ..... F3
Chatrapur 10,835 ..... F5
Chembur B7
Cherrapunji⊙ 83,987 ..... G3
Chhatarpur 32,271 ..... D4
Chhindwara 53,492 ..... D4
Chidambaram 48,811 ..... E6
Chik Ballapur 29,227 ..... D6
Chikmagalur 41,639 ..... D6
Chingleput 38,419 ..... E6
Chiplun 20,942 ..... C5
Chirala 54,487 ..... E5
Chitorgarh 25,917 ..... C4
Chitradurga 50,254 ..... D6
Chittoor 63,035 ..... D6
Churachandpur 8,706 ..... G4
Churu 52,502 ..... D3
Chushul D2
Cocanada (Kakinada) 164,200 ..... E5
Cochin-Alleppey 439,066 ..... D6
Coimbatore 356,368 ..... D6
Coimbatore□ 736,203 ..... D6
Colachel 18,819 ..... D7
Cooch Behar 53,684 ..... F3
Coondapoor 23,831 ..... C6
Cuddalore 101,335 ..... E6
Cuddapah 66,195 ..... D6
Cumbum 9,745 ..... D5
Cuttack 194,068 ..... F4
Cuttack□ 205,759 ..... F4
Dabhoi 37,892 ..... C4
Daltonganj 32,367 ..... E4
Damoh 59,489 ..... D4
Dapoli 6,296 ..... C5
Darbhanga 132,059 ..... F3
Darjeeling 42,873 ..... F3
Datia 36,439 ..... D3
Davangere 121,110 ..... D6
Deesa 28,324 ..... C4
Dehra Dun 166,073 ..... D2
Dehra Dun□ 203,464 ..... D2
Delhi 3,287,883 ..... D3
Delhi□ 3,647,023 ..... D3
Demchok D2
Deogarh, Orissa 8,906 ..... E4
Deoghar, Bihar 40,356 ..... F4
Deolali 55,436 ..... C5
Deoria 38,161 ..... E3
Dewas 51,545 ..... D4
Dhamtari 34,546 ..... E4
Dhanbad 79,838 ..... F4
Dhanbad□ 434,031 ..... F4
Dhar 36,172 ..... C4
Dharmsala 10,939 ..... D2
Dharwar-Hubli 379,166 ..... C5
Dhenkanal 19,615 ..... E4
Dholpur 31,865 ..... D3
Dhond 16,583 ..... C5
Dhoraji 59,773 ..... C4
Dhubri 36,503 ..... G3
Dhulia 137,129 ..... C4
Dibrugarh 80,348 ..... G3
Digboi 16,538 ..... H3
Dindigul 128,429 ..... D6
Diphu 10,200 ..... G3
Dispur 1,725 ..... G3
Diu 6,214 ..... C4
Dohad 44,506 ..... C4
Domjor 10,896 ..... F1
Dudhi 5,084 ..... E4
Dum Dum 31,363 ..... F1
Dum Dum□ 273,812 ..... F1
Dungarpur 19,773 ..... C4
Durg 67,892 ..... E4
Durgapur 206,638 ..... F4
Dwarka 17,801 ..... B4
Eluru 127,023 ..... E5
English Bazar 61,335 ..... F3
Erode 105,111 ..... D6
Etawah 85,894 ..... D3
Faizabad-cum-Ayodhya 102,835 ..... E3
Faridabad 85,762 ..... D3
Farrukhabad-cum-Fatehgarh 102,768 ..... D3
Farrukhabad-cum-Fatehgarh□ 110,835 D3
Fatehpur, Rajasthan 34,929 ..... C3
Fatehpur, Uttar Pradesh 54,665 ..... E3
Firozabad 133,863 ..... D3
Firozpur 49,545 ..... C2
Gadag-Betgeri 95,426 ..... D5
Gadwal 21,828 ..... D5
Gandhinagar 24,055 ..... C4
Ganganagar 90,042 ..... C3
Gangapur 27,453 ..... D3
Gangtok 12,000 ..... F3
Garden Reach 154,913 ..... F2
Garulia 44,271 ..... F1
Gauhati 123,783 ..... G3
Gauhati□ 200,377 ..... G3
Gaya 179,884 ..... F4
Ghat Kopar 34,256 ..... B7
Ghaziabad 118,836 ..... D3
Ghaziabad□ 127,700 ..... D3
Ghazipur 45,635 ..... E3
Goalpara 16,703 ..... G3
Godhra 66,403 ..... C4
Gonda 52,662 ..... E3
Gondal 54,928 ..... C4
Gondia 77,992 ..... E4
Gorakhpur 230,911 ..... E3
Goregaon B7
Gudur 33,778 ..... D6
Gulbarga 145,588 ..... D5
Guna 40,006 ..... D4
Guntakal 66,320 ..... D5
Guntur 269,991 ..... D5
Gurais D2
Gwalior 384,772 ..... D3
Gwalior□ 406,140 ..... D3
Haflong 5,197 ..... G3
Hanle D2
Hanumangarh 30,017 ..... C3
Harda 28,504 ..... D4
Hardoi 46,639 ..... E3
Hardwar 77,864 ..... D2
Hassan 51,325 ..... D6
Hathras 74,349 ..... D3
Hazaribagh 54,818 ..... F4
Hindupur 42,959 ..... D6
Hinganghat 44,349 ..... D4
Hingoli 31,948 ..... D5
Hissar 89,437 ..... D3
Honavar 12,444 ..... C6
Hooghly-Chinsura 105,241 ..... F1
Hoshangabad 27,011 ..... D4
Hospet 65,196 ..... D5
Howrah 737,877 ..... F2
Hubli-Dharwar 379,166 ..... C5
Hyderabad 1,607,396 ..... D5
Hyderabad□ 1,796,339 ..... D5
Ichchapuram 15,850 ..... F5
Ichhapur 11,975 ..... F1
Imphal 100,366 ..... G4
Indore 543,381 ..... D4
Indore□ 560,936 ..... D4
Itanagar⊙ 18,787 ..... G3
Itarsi 44,191 ..... D4
Jabalpur 426,224 ..... D4
Jabalpur□ 534,845 ..... D4
Jagdalpur 31,344 ..... E5
Jagtial 30,900 ..... D5
Jaipur 615,258 ..... D3
Jaipur□ 636,768 ..... D3
Jaisalmer 16,578 ..... C3
Jajpur 16,707 ..... F4
Jalgaon 106,711 ..... D4
Jalna 91,099 ..... D4
Jalor 15,478 ..... C3
Jalpaiguri 55,159 ..... F3
Jamalpur 61,731 ..... F3
Jammu 155,338 ..... D2
Jammu□ 164,207 ..... D2
Jamnagar 214,816 ..... B4
Jamnagar□ 227,640 ..... B4
Jamshedpur 341,576 ..... F4
Jamshedpur□ 456,146 ..... F4
Jaora 37,235 ..... D4
Jaunpur 80,737 ..... E3
Jeypore 34,319 ..... E5
Jhalawar 20,035 ..... D4
Jhansi 173,292 ..... D3
Jhansi□ 198,135 ..... D3
Jharsuguda 24,727 ..... E4
Jhunjhunu 32,024 ..... D3
Jind 38,161 ..... D3
Jodhpur 317,612 ..... C3
Jorhat 30,247 ..... G3
Jubbulpore (Jabalpur) 426,224 ..... D4
Juhu B7
Jullundur 296,106 ..... D2
Jullundur□ 329,830 ..... D2
Junagadh 95,485 ..... B4
Kadayanallur 50,295 ..... D7
Kadiri 33,810 ..... D6
Kakinada 164,200 ..... E5
Kalyan 99,547 ..... C5
Kamarhati 169,404 ..... F1
Kamptee 53,412 ..... D4
Kanchipuram 110,657 ..... E6
Kanchrapara 78,768 ..... F1
Kandla 17,995 ..... C4
Kandukur 16,654 ..... E5
Kanker 9,278 ..... E4
Kannauj 28,187 ..... D3
Kanpur 1,154,388 ..... E3
Kanpur□ 1,275,242 ..... E3
Karad 42,329 ..... C5
Karaikudi 55,449 ..... D7
Karanja 31,150 ..... D4
Kargil 2,390 ..... D2
Karikal 26,080 ..... E6
Karkal 18,593 ..... C6
Karnal 92,784 ..... D3
Karwar 27,770 ..... C6
Kasaragod 34,984 ..... C6
Kasganj 46,467 ..... D3
Katarnian Ghat E3
Katihar 67,014 ..... F3
Katni (Murwara) 54,864 ..... E4
Kavali 29,616 ..... E6
Kavaratti 4,420 ..... C6
Kawardha 11,226 ..... E4
Kendrapara 20,079 ..... F4
Keonjhar 19,340 ..... F4
Khamgaon 53,692 ..... D4
Khamman 56,919 ..... D5
Khandwa 84,517 ..... D4
Kharagpur 61,783 ..... F4
Khardah 32,302 ..... F1
Khurda 15,879 ..... F4
Kirkee 65,497 ..... C5
Kishangarh 37,405 ..... D3
Kishtwar 5,276 ..... D2
Kohima 21,545 ..... G3
Kolar 43,418 ..... D6
Kolar Gold Fields 76,112 ..... D6
Kolhapur 259,050 ..... C5
Konnagar 34,424 ..... F1
Koppal 27,277 ..... D5
Koraput 21,505 ..... E5
Korba 30,963 ..... E4
Kota 212,991 ..... D3
Kottaguden 75,542 ..... E5
Kottayam 59,714 ..... D7
Kotturu 12,873 ..... D6
Kovur 16,846 ..... E6
Kozhikode 333,979 ..... D6
Krishnanagar 85,923 ..... F4
Kulu 8,958 ..... D2
Kumbakonam 113,130 ..... D6
Kumta 19,112 ..... C6
Kurla B7
Kurnool 136,710 ..... D5
Laful⊙ 8,161 ..... G7
Lansdowne 6,670 ..... D3
Latur 70,156 ..... D5
Leh 5,519 ..... D2
Lohardaga 17,087 ..... E4
Lucknow 749,239 ..... E3
Lucknow□ 813,982 ..... E3
Ludhiana 397,850 ..... D2
Ludhiana□ 401,176 ..... D2
Lumding 29,253 ..... G3
Lungleh 6,019 ..... G4
Machilipatnam 112,612 ..... E5
Madh B7
Madhubani 32,919 ..... F3
Madras 2,469,449 ..... E6
Madras□ 3,169,930 ..... E6
Madugula 8,376 ..... E5
Madurai 549,114 ..... D7
Madurai□ 711,501 ..... D7
Mahabaleshwar 7,318 ..... C5
Mahbubnagar 51,756 ..... D5
Mahe 8,972 ..... D6
Mahim 11,344 ..... C5
Mahoba 29,707 ..... D3
Mahuva 39,497 ..... C4
Malad B6
Malakanagiri 7,494 ..... E5
Malegaon 191,847 ..... C4
Maler Kotla 48,536 ..... D2
Malkapur 35,476 ..... D4
Malvan 17,579 ..... C5
Mandi 16,849 ..... D2
Mandla 24,406 ..... E4
Mandsaur 52,347 ..... C4
Mandvi 27,849 ..... B4
Manendragarh 11,936 ..... E4
Mangalore 165,174 ..... C6
Mangrol 27,183 ..... B4
Manmad 29,571 ..... C4
Mannargudi 42,783 ..... E6
Manori B6
Margao 41,655 ..... C5
Marmagao 44,065 ..... C5
Mathura 132,028 ..... D3
Mau 64,058 ..... E3
Mayuram 60,195 ..... D6
Meerut 270,993 ..... D3
Mehsana 51,598 ..... C4
Mercara 19,357 ..... D6
Mhow 59,037 ..... D4
Midnapore 71,326 ..... F4
Miraj 77,606 ..... D5
Mirzapur-cum-Vindhyachal 105,939 ..... E4
Modasa 22,483 ..... C4
Mokokchung 17,423 ..... G3
Monghyr 102,474 ..... F3
Mora B7
Moradabad 258,590 ..... D3
Morena 44,901 ..... D3
Morvi 60,976 ..... C4
Mulund B6
Murud 11,210 ..... C5
Murwara 54,864 ..... E4
Muzaffarnagar 114,783 ..... D3
Muzaffarpur 126,379 ..... E3
Mysore 355,685 ..... D6
Nadiad 108,269 ..... C4
Nagapattinam 68,026 ..... E6
Nagaur 36,448 ..... C3
Nagercoil 141,288 ..... D7
Nagina 37,066 ..... D3
Nagpur 866,076 ..... D4
Nagpur□ 930,459 ..... D4
Nahan 16,017 ..... D2
Naihati 82,080 ..... F1
Naini Tal 23,986 ..... D3
Nainpur 14,683 ..... E4
Nalgonda 33,126 ..... D5
Nander 126,538 ..... D5
Nandurbar 54,070 ..... C4
Nandyal 63,193 ..... D5
Narayanpet 21,744 ..... D5
Narnaul 31,875 ..... D3
Narsimhapur 25,552 ..... D4
Narsinghgarh 13,814 ..... D4
Nasik 176,091 ..... C5
Nasirabad 25,732 ..... C3
Navsari 72,979 ..... C4
Nellore 133,590 ..... E6
New Delhi (cap.) 301,801 ..... D3
Nhava-Sheva B7
Nimach 47,113 ..... D4
Nipani 35,116 ..... C5
Nirmal 28,529 ..... D5
Nizamabad 115,640 ..... D5
North Lakhimpur 20,094 ..... G3
Nova Goa (Panaji) 34,953 ..... C5
Nowgong, Assam 56,537 ..... G3
Nowgong, Madhya Pradesh 10,248 ..... D3
Okha Port 10,687 ..... B4
Ongole 53,330 ..... E5
Ootacamund 63,310 ..... D6
Orai 42,513 ..... D3
Osmanabad 27,279 ..... D5
Pachmarhi 1,212 ..... D4
Palanpur 42,114 ..... C4
Palayankottai 70,070 ..... D7
Palghat 95,788 ..... D6
Pali 49,834 ..... C3
Palni 49,575 ..... D6
Panaji 34,953 ..... C5
Panchur 59,021 ..... F2
Pandharpur 53,638 ..... D5
Panihati 148,046 ..... F1
Panipat 87,981 ..... D3
Panna 22,316 ..... E4
Panruti 34,065 ..... D6
Paradip F4
Parbhani 61,570 ..... D5
Parlakhemundi 26,917 ..... E5
Partapgarh 17,402 ..... C4
Parvatipuram 30,025 ..... E5
Pasighat 5,116 ..... G3
Patan 64,519 ..... C4
Pathankot 76,355 ..... D2
Patiala 148,686 ..... D2
Patiala□ D2
Patna 473,001 ..... F3
Patna□ F3
Pauni 17,781 ..... E4
Phalodi 17,379 ..... C3
Phulbani 10,677 ..... E4
Pilibhit 68,273 ..... D3
Pokaran 7,769 ..... C3
Pondicherry 90,537 ..... E6
Ponnani 35,723 ..... D6
Poona (Pune)□ C5
Porbandar 96,881 ..... B4
Porbandar□ B4
Port Blair 26,218 ..... G6
Porto Novo 17,412 ..... E6
Proddatur 70,822 ..... D6
Puduchcheri (Pondicherry) 90,537 ..... E6
Pudukkottai 66,384 ..... D6
Pune 856,105 ..... C5
Puri 72,674 ..... F5
Purli 31,078 ..... D5
Purnea 56,484 ..... F3
Purulia 57,708 ..... F4
Puttur 17,483 ..... D6
Quilon 124,208 ..... D7
Radhanpur 18,360 ..... C4
Raichur 79,831 ..... D5
Raigarh 46,745 ..... E4
Raipur 174,518 ..... E4
Raipur□ E4
Rajahmundry 165,912 ..... E5
Rajahmundry□ E5
Rajapalaiyam 86,952 ..... D7
Rajapur 9,017 ..... C5
Rajgarh 11,475 ..... D4
Rajkot 300,612 ..... C4
Rajnandgaon 41,183 ..... E4
Rajpipla 25,769 ..... C4
Rajpur 34,393 ..... F2
Rajpura 14,840 ..... D2
Rameswarem 16,755 ..... D7
Rampur, Him. Pradesh 2,623 ..... D2
Rampur, Uttar Pradesh 161,417 ..... D3
Ranchi 175,934 ..... F4
Ratangarh 31,506 ..... C3
Ratlam 106,666 ..... C4
Ratnagiri 37,551 ..... C5
Raurkela 47,076 ..... F4
Raxaul 12,064 ..... E3
Rayagada 25,064 ..... E5
Renigunta 8,567 ..... E6
Rewa 69,182 ..... E4
Rishra 63,486 ..... F1
Robertsganj 7,093 ..... E4
Roha 8,631 ..... C5
Rohtak 124,783 ..... C5
Sadiya⊙ 64,252 ..... H3

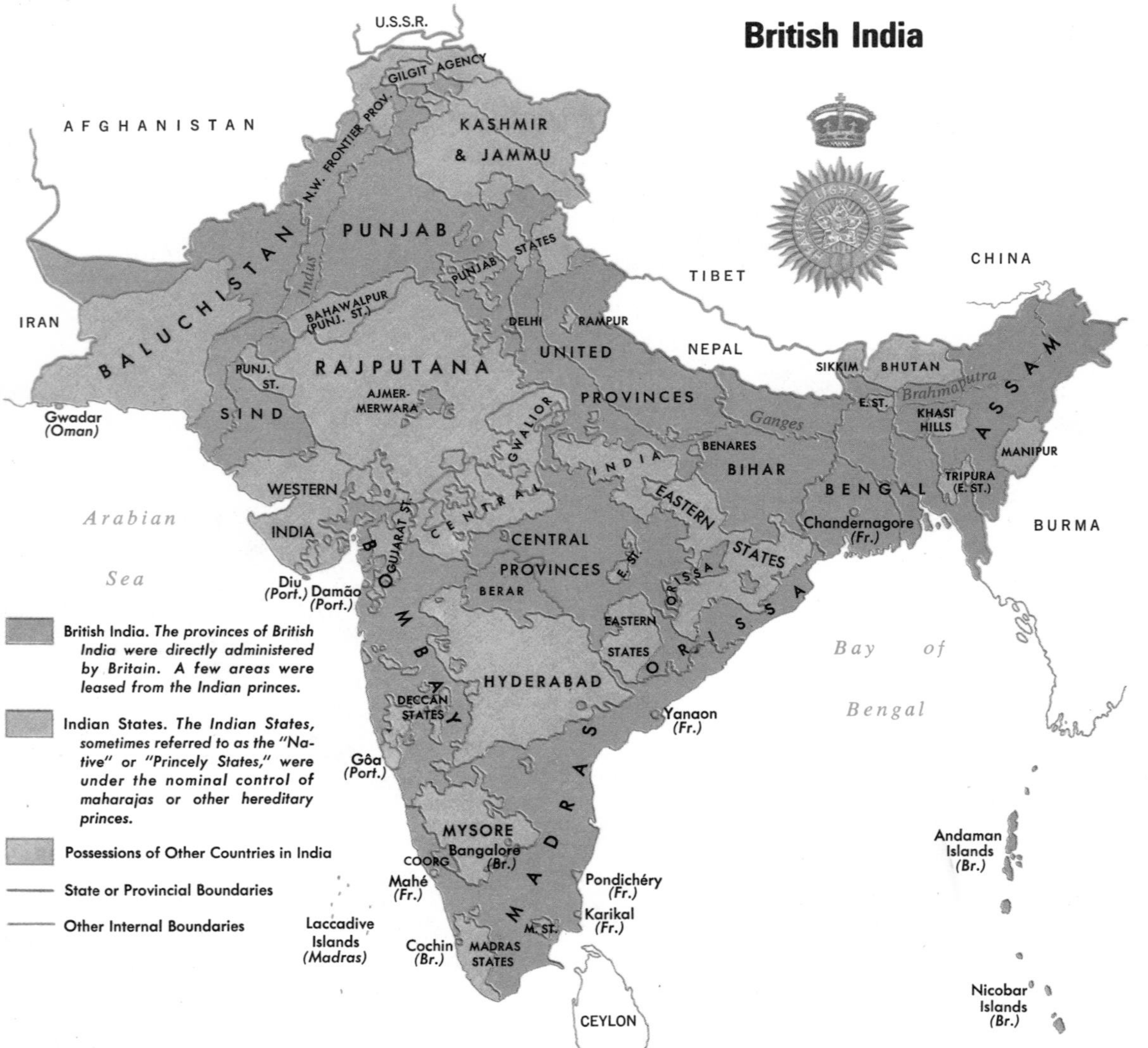

British India
U.S.S.R.
AFGHANISTAN
IRAN
TIBET
CHINA
NEPAL
BURMA
GILGIT AGENCY
KASHMIR & JAMMU
N.W. FRONTIER PROV.
PUNJAB
PUNJAB STATES
BALUCHISTAN
Indus
BAHAWALPUR (PUNJ. ST.)
DELHI
RAMPUR
UNITED PROVINCES
SIKKIM
BHUTAN
Brahmaputra
ASSAM
PUNJ. ST.
RAJPUTANA
AJMER-MERWARA
SIND
GWALIOR
Ganges
E. ST.
KHASI HILLS
MANIPUR
Gwadar (Oman)
BENARES
BIHAR
TRIPURA (E. ST.)
CENTRAL INDIA
WESTERN INDIA
BENGAL
EASTERN STATES
Chandernagore (Fr.)
Arabian Sea
GUJARAT ST.
CENTRAL PROVINCES
BERAR
E. ST.
ORISSA
Diu (Port.)
Damão (Port.)
BOMBAY
EASTERN STATES
HYDERABAD
DECCAN STATES
Bay of Bengal
Yanaon (Fr.)
Gôa (Port.)
MADRAS
MYSORE
Bangalore (Br.)
COORG
Mahé (Fr.)
Pondichéry (Fr.)
Karikal (Fr.)
M. ST.
Laccadive Islands (Madras)
Cochin (Br.)
MADRAS STATES
CEYLON
Andaman Islands (Br.)
Nicobar Islands (Br.)
British India. The provinces of British India were directly administered by Britain. A few areas were leased from the Indian princes.
Indian States. The Indian States, sometimes referred to as the "Native" or "Princely States," were under the nominal control of maharajas or other hereditary princes.
Possessions of Other Countries in India
State or Provincial Boundaries
Other Internal Boundaries

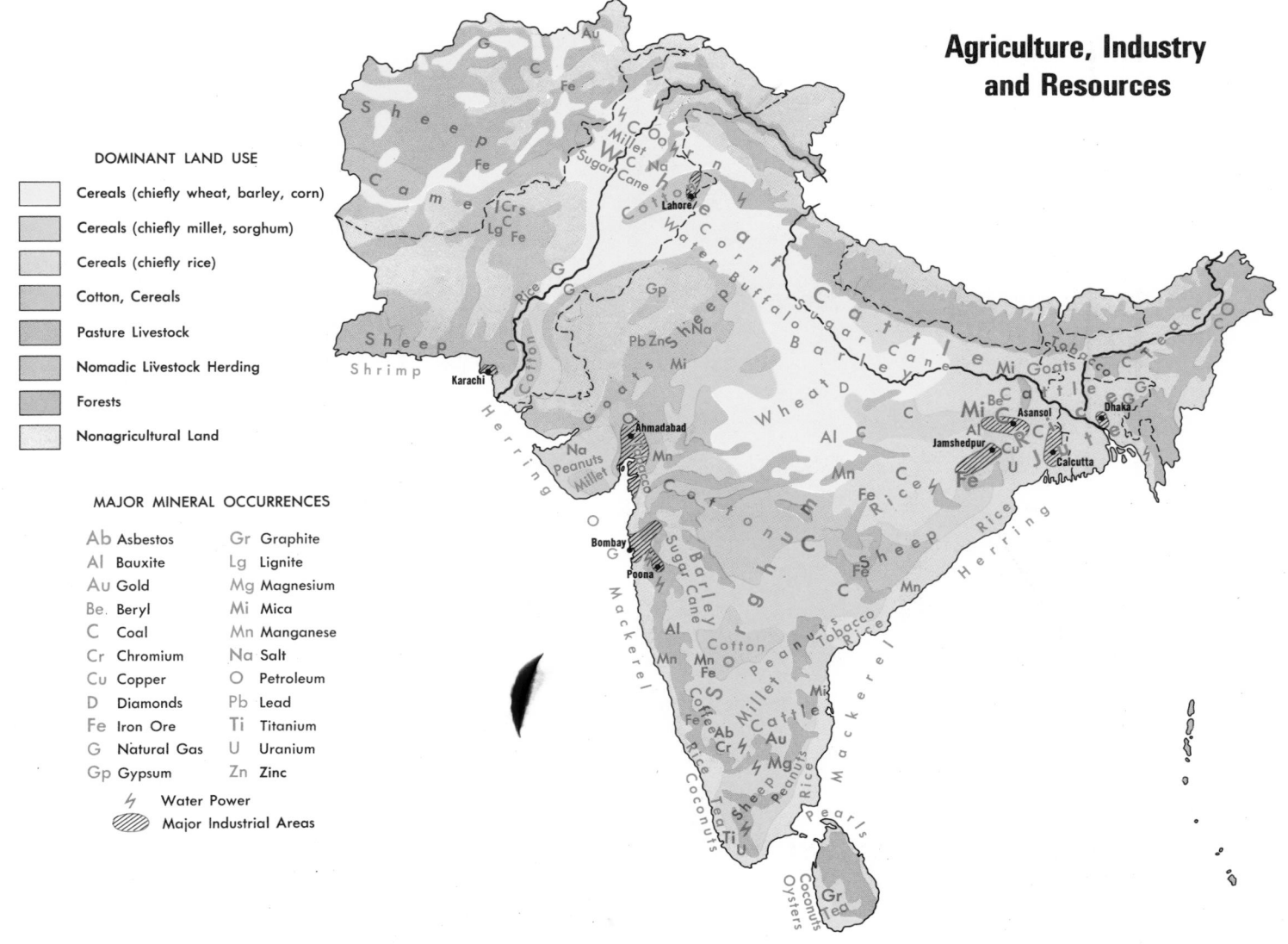

Agriculture, Industry and Resources

DOMINANT LAND USE

- Cereals (chiefly wheat, barley, corn)
- Cereals (chiefly millet, sorghum)
- Cereals (chiefly rice)
- Cotton, Cereals
- Pasture Livestock
- Nomadic Livestock Herding
- Forests
- Nonagricultural Land

MAJOR MINERAL OCCURRENCES

Ab	Asbestos	Gr	Graphite
Al	Bauxite	Lg	Lignite
Au	Gold	Mg	Magnesium
Be.	Beryl	Mi	Mica
C	Coal	Mn	Manganese
Cr	Chromium	Na	Salt
Cu	Copper	O	Petroleum
D	Diamonds	Pb	Lead
Fe	Iron Ore	Ti	Titanium
G	Natural Gas	U	Uranium
Gp	Gypsum	Zn	Zinc

⚡ Water Power

▨ Major Industrial Areas

Burma, Thailand, Indochina and Malaya

CONIC PROJECTION

SCALE OF MILES

SCALE OF KILOMETERS

International Boundaries _____
Division and State Boundaries _____
Capitals of Countries _____ ☆
Division and State Capitals _____ ◉

Scale 1:10,000,000

© Copyright HAMMOND INCORPORATED, Maplewood, N.J.

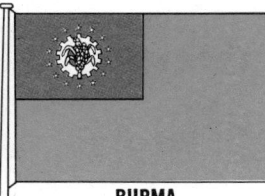

BURMA

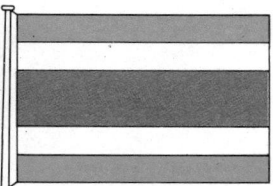

THAILAND

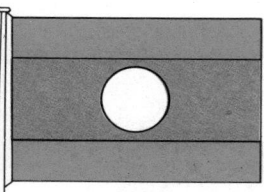

LAOS

CAMBODIA

VIETNAM

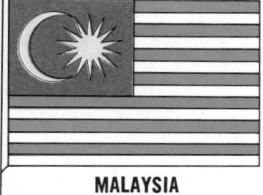

MALAYSIA

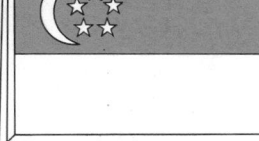

SINGAPORE

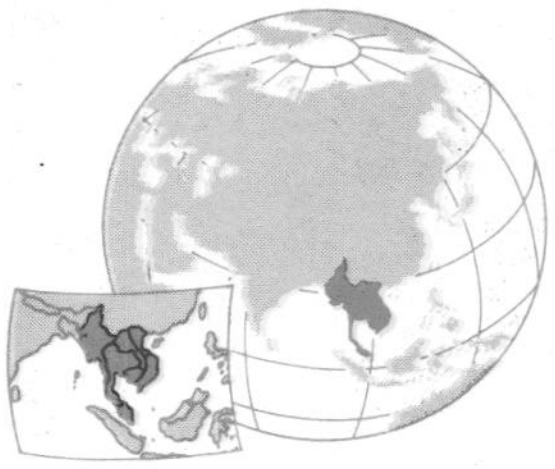

BURMA

AREA 261,789 sq. mi. (678,034 sq. km.)
POPULATION 32,913,000
CAPITAL Rangoon
LARGEST CITY Rangoon
HIGHEST POINT Hkakabo Razi 19,296 ft. (5,881 m.)
MONETARY UNIT kyat
MAJOR LANGUAGES Burmese, Karen, Shan, Kachin, Chin, Kayah, English
MAJOR RELIGIONS Buddhism, tribal religions

THAILAND

AREA 198,455 sq. mi. (513,998 sq. km.)
POPULATION 46,455,000
CAPITAL Bangkok
LARGEST CITY Bangkok
HIGHEST POINT Doi Inthanon 8,452 ft. (2,576 m.)
MONETARY UNIT baht
MAJOR LANGUAGES Thai, Lao, Chinese, Khmer, Malay
MAJOR RELIGIONS Buddhism, tribal religions

LAOS

AREA 91,428 sq. mi. (236,800 sq. km.)
POPULATION 3,721,000
CAPITAL Vientiane
LARGEST CITY Vientiane
HIGHEST POINT Phou Bia 9,252 ft. (2,820 m.)
MONETARY UNIT kip
MAJOR LANGUAGE Lao
MAJOR RELIGIONS Buddhism, tribal religions

CAMBODIA

AREA 69,898 sq. mi. (181,036 sq. km.)
POPULATION 5,200,000
CAPITAL Phnom Penh
LARGEST CITY Phnom Penh
HIGHEST POINT 5,948 ft. (1,813 m.)
MONETARY UNIT riel
MAJOR LANGUAGE Khmer (Cambodian)
MAJOR RELIGION Buddhism

VIETNAM

AREA 128,405 sq. mi. (332,569 sq. km.)
POPULATION 52,741,766
CAPITAL Hanoi
LARGEST CITY Ho Chi Minh City (Saigon)
HIGHEST POINT Fan Si Pan 10,308 ft. (3,142 m.)
MONETARY UNIT dong
MAJOR LANGUAGES Vietnamese, Thai, Muong, Meo, Yao, Khmer, French, Chinese, Cham
MAJOR RELIGIONS Buddhism, Taoism, Confucianism, Roman Catholicism, Cao-Dai

MALAYSIA

AREA 128,308 sq. mi. (332,318 sq. km.)
POPULATION 13,435,588
CAPITAL Kuala Lumpur
LARGEST CITY Kuala Lumpur
HIGHEST POINT Mt. Kinabalu 13,455 ft. (4,101 m.)
MONETARY UNIT ringgit
MAJOR LANGUAGES Malay, Chinese, English, Tamil, Dayak, Kadazan
MAJOR RELIGIONS Islam, Confucianism, Buddhism, tribal religions, Hinduism, Taoism, Christianity, Sikhism

SINGAPORE

AREA 226 sq. mi. (585 sq. km.)
POPULATION 2,413,945
CAPITAL Singapore
LARGEST CITY Singapore
HIGHEST POINT Bukit Timah 581 ft. (177 m.)
MONETARY UNIT Singapore dollar
MAJOR LANGUAGES Chinese, Malay, Tamil, English, Hindi
MAJOR RELIGIONS Confucianism, Buddhism, Taoism, Hinduism, Islam, Christianity

Topography

0   200   400 MI.
0   200   400 KM.

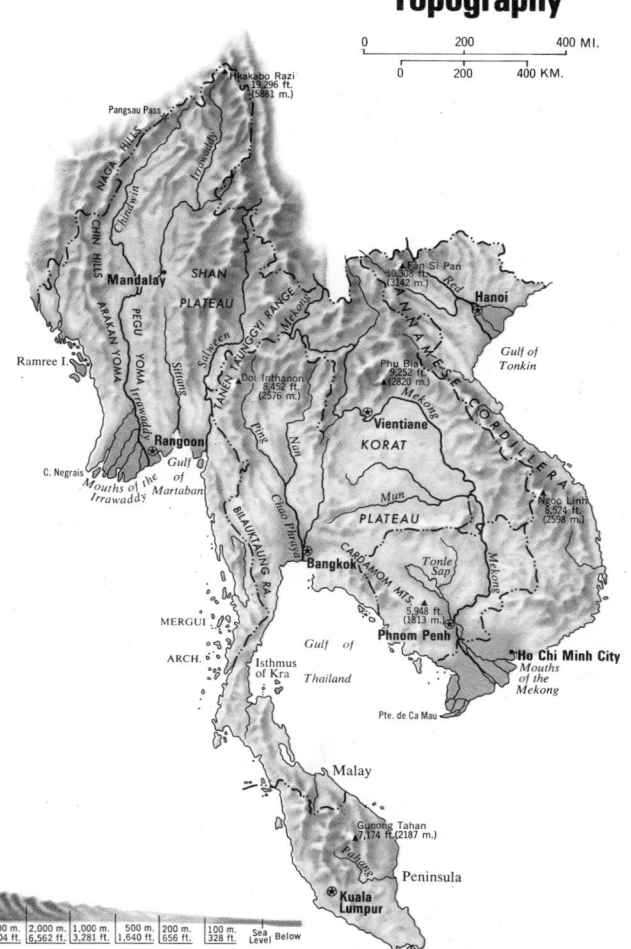

5,000 m. | 2,000 m. | 1,000 m. | 500 m. | 200 m. | 100 m. | Sea Level | Below
16,404 ft. | 6,562 ft. | 3,281 ft. | 1,640 ft. | 656 ft. | 328 ft. |

BURMA

INTERNAL DIVISIONS

Arakan (state) 1,710,913 ....B3
Chin (state) 323,094 ....B2
Irrawaddy (div.) 4,152,521 ......B3
Kachin (state) 735,144 ....C1
Karen (state) 865,218 ....C3
Kayah (state) 126,492 ....C3
Magwe (div.) 2,632,144 ....B2
Mandalay (div.) 3,662,312 ....B2
Mon (state) 1,313,111 ....C3
Pegu (div.) 3,174,109 ....C3
Rangoon (div.) 3,186,886 ....C3
Sagaing (div.) 3,115,502 ....B1
Shan (state) 3,178,214 ....C2
Tenasserim (div.) 717,607 ....C4

CITIES and TOWNS

Akyab (Sittwe) 42,329 ....B2
Allanmyo 15,580 ....B3
Amarapura 11,268 ....B2
Amherst 6,000 ....C3
An B3
Anin C4
Bassein 126,045 ....B3
Bhamo 9,821 ....C1
Chauk 24,466 ....B2
Danubyu B3
Falam B2
Fort Hertz (Putao) C1
Gawai C1
Gokteik C2
Gwa B3
Gyobingauk 9,922 ....B3
Haka B2
Henzada 61,972 ....B3
Hmawbi 23,032 ....B3
Homalin B1
Hsenwi C2
Hsipaw C2
Htawgaw C1
Insein 143,625 ....C3
Kamaing C1
Karathuri C5
Katha 7,648 ....C1
Kawludo C3
Kawthaung 1,520 ....C5
Keng Hkam C2
Keng Tung C2
Koma C4
Kunlong C2
Kyaikto 13,154 ....C3
Kya-in Seikkyi C3
Kyangin 6,073 ....B3
Kyaukme C2
Kyaukpadaung 5,480 ....B2
Kyaukpyu 7,335 ....B3
Kyaukse 8,659 ....C2
Labutta 12,982 ....B3
Lai-hka C2
Lamu B3
Lashio C2
Lenya C5
Letpadan 15,896 ....B3
Lewe C2
Loi-kaw C3
Lonton B1
Magwe 13,270 ....B2
Maingkwan C1
Maliwun C5
Mandalay 418,008 ....C2
Man Hpang C2
Martaban 5,661 ....C3
Ma-ubin 23,362 ....B3
Maungdaw 3,772 ....B2
Mawkmai C2
Mawlaik 2,993 ....B2
Mawlu C1
Maymyo 22,287 ....C2
Meiktila 19,474 ....B2
Mergui 33,697 ....C4
Minbu 9,096 ....B2
Minhla 6,470 ....B3
Mogaung 2,920 ....C1
Mogok 8,334 ....C2
Mohnyin C1
Möng Hsat C2
Möng Mau C3
Möng Mit C2
Möng Pan C2
Möng Si C2
Möng Tön C2
Möng Tung C2
Monywa 26,279 ....B2
Moulmein 171,977 ....C3
Mudon 20,136 ....C3
Myanaung 11,155 ....B3
Myaungmya 24,532 ....B3
Myingyan 36,439 ....B2
Myitkyina 12,382 ....C1
Myohaung 6,534 ....B2
Naba B1
Namhkam C2
Namlan C2
Namtu C2
Natmauk B2
Okkan 14,443 ....B3
Okpo 12,155 ....C3
Pakokku 30,943 ....B2
Palaw 5,596 ....C4
Paletwa B2
Pantha B2
Papun C3
Pasawng C3
Paungde 17,286 ....B3
Pegu 47,378 ....C3
Prome (Pye) 36,997 ....B3
Putao C1
Pyapon 19,174 ....B3
Pye 36,997 ....B3
Pyinmana 22,025 ....C3
Pyu 10,443 ....C3
Rangoon (cap.) 1,586,422 ....C3
Rangoon* 2,055,365 ....C3
Rathedaung 2,969 ....B2
Sadon C1
Sagaing 15,382 ....B2
Samka C2
Sandoway 5,172 ....B3
Shingbwiyang B1
Shwebo 17,827 ....B2
Shwenyaung C2
Singkaling Hkamti B1
Singu 4,027 ....C2
Sinlumkaba C1
Sittwe 42,329 ....B2
Sumprabum C1
Syriam 15,296 ....C3
Taunggdwingyi 16,233 ....C2
Taunggyi C2
Tavoy 40,312 ....C4
Tharrawaddy 8,977 ....C3
Thaton 38,047 ....C3
Thaungdut B1
Thayetmyo 11,649 ....B3
Thazi 7,531 ....C2
Thongwa 10,829 ....C3
Toungoo 31,589 ....C3
Wakema 20,716 ....B3
Yamethin 11,167 ....C2
Yandoon 15,245 ....B3
Ye 12,852 ....C4
Yenangyaung 24,416 ....B2
Yesagyo 7,880 ....B2
Ye-u 5,307 ....B2
Ywathit C3
Zadi C4
Zalun 899 ....B3

OTHER FEATURES

Amya (pass) C4
Andaman (sea) B4
Arakan Yoma (mts.) B3
Ataran (riv.) C4
Bengal, Bay of (sea) B3
Bentinck (isl.) C5

(continued on following page)

(continued)

Bilauktaung (range) C4
Chaukan (pass) C1
Cheduba (isl.) B3
Chin (hills) B2
Chindwin (riv.) B2
Coco (chan.) B4
Combermere (bay) B3
Daung Kyun (isl.) C4
Dawna (range) C3
Great Coco (isl.) B4
Great Tenasserim (riv.) C4
Heinze Chaung (bay) C4
Heywood (chan.) B3
Hka, Nam (riv.) C2
Hkakabo Razi (mt.) C1
Indawgyi (lake) C1
Inle (lake) C2
Irrawaddy (riv.) B3
Irrawaddy, Mouths of the (delta) B4
Kadan Kyun (isl.) C4
Kaladan (riv.) B2
Kalegauk (isl.) C4
Khao Luang (mt.) C5
Lanbi Kyun (isl.) C5
Launglon Bok (isls.) C4
Loi Leng (mt.) C2
Manipur (riv.) B2
Martaban (gulf) C4
Mekong (riv.) D2
Mergui (arch.) C5
Mon (riv.) B2
Mu (riv.) B2
Negrais (cape) B3
Pakchan (riv.) C5
Pangsau (pass) C1
Pawn, Nam (riv.) C2
Pegu Yoma (mts.) B3
Preparis (isl.) B4
Ramree (isl.) B3
Salween (riv.) C3
Shan (plat.) C2
Sittang (riv.) C3
Taungthonton (mt.) B1
Tavoy (pt.) C4
Tenasserim (isl.) C4
Teng, Nam (riv.) C2
Three Pagodas (pass) C4
Victoria (mt.) B2

CAMBODIA (KAMPUCHEA)

CITIES and TOWNS

Batdambang (Battambang) D4
Choam Khsant E4
Kampong Cham E4
Kampong Chhnang D4
Kampong Khleang E4
Kampong Saom D5
Kampong Spoe E5
Kampong Thum E4
Kampong Trabek E5
Kampot E5
Kaoh Nhek E4
Kracheh E4
Krong Kaoh Kong D4
Krong Keb E5
Kulen E4
Lumphat E4
Moung Roessei D4
Pailin D4
Paoy Pet D4
Phnom Penh (cap.) c. 300,000 ..... E5
Phnum Tbeng Meanchey E4
Phsar Ream D5
Phumi Banam E5
Phumi Phsar E4
Phumi Prek Kak E4
Phumi Samraong D4
Pouthisat D4
Prek Pouthi E5
Prey Veng E5
Pursat (Pouthisat) D4
Rovieng Tbong E4
Sambor E4
Senmonoron E4
Siempang E4
Siemreab D4
Sisophon D4
Sre Ambel D5
Sre Khtum E4
Stoeng Treng E4
Suong E5
Svay Rieng E5
Takev E5
Virochey E4

OTHER FEATURES

Angkor Wat (ruins) E4
Dangrek (mts.) D4
Drang, Ia (riv.) E4
Joncs (plain) E5
Khong, Se (riv.) E4
Kong, Kaoh (isl.) D5
Mekong (riv.) E4
Rung, Kaoh (isl.) D5
San, Se (riv.) E4
Sen, Stoeng (riv.) E4
Srepok (riv.) E4
Tang, Kaoh (isl.) D5
Thailand (gulf) D5
Tonle Sap (lake) D4
Wai, Poulo (isls.) D5

LAOS

CITIES and TOWNS

Attapu 2,750 ..... E4
Ban Khon E4
Ban Lahanam E3
Borikan D3
Champasak 3,500 ..... E4
Dônghén E3
Khamkeut⊙ 31,206 ..... E3
Louang Namtha 1,459 ..... D2
Louangphrabang 7,596 ..... D3
Muang Hinboun 1,750 ..... E3
Muang Kènthao D3
Muang Khammoun 5,500 ..... E3
Muang Không 1,750 ..... E4
Muang Khôngxédôn 2,000 ..... E4
Muang Khoua D2
Muang May E4
Muang Ou Tai D2
Muang Paktha D2
Muang Phin E3
Muang Tahoi E3
Muang Vapi E4
Muang Xaignabouri (Sayaboury) 2,500 ..... D3
Mounlapamôk E4
Napè E3
Nong Het E3
Pakxé 8,000 ..... E4
Phiafai⊙ 17,216 ..... E4
Phôngsali 2,500 ..... D2
San Nua (Sam Neua) 3,000 ..... E2
Saravan 2,350 ..... E4
Savannakhét 8,500 ..... E3
Sayaboury (Muang Xaignabouri) 2,500 ..... D3
Thakhek (Muang Khammouan) 5,500 ..... E3
Tourakom D3
Viangchan (Vientiane) 132,253 ..... D3
Vientiane (cap.) 132,253 ..... D3
Xiangkhoang 3,500 ..... D3

OTHER FEATURES

Bolovens (plat.) E4
Hou, Nam (riv.) D2
Jars (plain) D3
Mekong (riv.) D3
Ou, Nam (riv.) D2
Phou Bia (mt.) D3
Phou Cô Pi (mt.) E3
Phou Loi (mt.) D2
Rao Co (mt.) E3
Se Khong (riv.) E4
Tha, Nam (riv.) D2
Xianghoang (plat.) D3

MALAYA, MALAYSIA*

STATES

Federal Territory 937,875 ..... D7
Johor (Johore) 1,601,504 ..... D7
Kedah 1,102,200 ..... D6
Kelantan 877,575 ..... D6
Melaka 453,153 ..... D7
Negeri Sembilan 563,955 ..... D7
Pahang 770,644 ..... D7
Perak 1,762,288 ..... D6
Perlis 147,726 ..... D6
Pinang (Penang) 911,586 ..... D6
Selangor 1,467,441 ..... D7
Terengganu 542,280 ..... D6

CITIES and TOWNS

Alor Gajah 2,222 ..... D7
Alor Setar 66,260 ..... D6
Bandar Maharani (Muar) 61,218 ..... D7
Bandar Penggaram (Batu Pahat) 53,291 ..... D7
Batu Gajah 10,692 ..... D6
Batu Pahat 53,291 ..... D7
Bentong 22,683 ..... D7
Butterworth 61,187 ..... D6
Chukai 12,514 ..... D6
Gemas 5,214 ..... D7
George Town (Pinang) 269,603 ..... C6
Ipoh 247,953 ..... D6
Johor Baharu (Johore Bharu) 136,234 ..... F5
Kampar 26,591 ..... D6
Kangar 8,758 ..... D6
Kelang 113,611 ..... D7
Keluang 43,272 ..... D7
Kota Baharu 55,124 ..... D6
Kota Tinggi 8,725 ..... F5
Kuala Dungun 17,560 ..... D6
Kuala Lipis 9,270 ..... D6
Kuala Lumpur (cap.) 451,977 ..... D7
Kuala Lumpur* 937,875 ..... D7
Kuala Pilah 12,508 ..... D7
Kuala Rompin 1,384 ..... D7
Kuala Selangor 3,132 ..... D7
Kuala Terengganu 53,320 ..... D6
Kuantan 43,358 ..... D7
Kulai 11,841 ..... F5
Lumut 3,255 ..... D6
Malacca (Melaka) 87,160 ..... D7
Mawai F5
Melaka 87,160 ..... D7
Mersing 18,246 ..... E7
Muar 61,218 ..... D7
Pekan 4,682 ..... D7
Pekan Nanas 9,003 ..... E5
Pinang (George Town) 269,603 ..... C6
Pontian Kechil 8,349 ..... E5
Port Dickson 10,300 ..... D7
Port Kelang D7
Port Weld 3,233 ..... D6
Raub 18,433 ..... D7
Segamat 17,796 ..... D7
Seremban 80,921 ..... D7
Sungai Petani 35,959 ..... C6
Taiping 54,645 ..... D6
Tanah Merah 7,012 ..... D6
Telok Anson 44,524 ..... D6
Tumpat 10,673 ..... D6

OTHER FEATURES

Aur, Pulau (isl.) E7
Belumut, Gunong (mt.) D7
Gelang, Tanjong (pt.) D6
Johor, Sungai (riv.) E5
Johore (str.) E6
Kelantan, Sungai (riv.) D6
Langkawi, Pulau (isl.) C6
Ledang, Gunong (mt.) D7
Lima, Pulau (isl.) F6
Malacca (str.) C6
Malay (pen.) D6
Pahang, Sungai (riv.) D7
Pangkor, Pulau (isl.) D6
Perak, Gunong (mt.) D6
Perhentian, Kepulauan (isls.) D6
Pulai, Sungai (riv.) E5
Ramunia, Tanjong (pt.) F6
Redang, Pulau (isl.) D6
Sedili Kechil, Tanjong (pt.) F5
Tahan, Gunong (mt.) D6
Temiang, Bukit (mt.) D6
Tenggol, Pulau (isl.) D6
Tinggi, Pulau (isl.) E7

SINGAPORE

CITIES and TOWNS

Jurong 50,974 ..... E6
Nee Soon 37,641 ..... F6
Serangoon 89,558 ..... F6
Singapore (cap.) 2,413,945 ..... F6

OTHER FEATURES

Keppel (harb.) F6
Main (str.) F6
Singapore (str.) F6
Tekong Besar, Pulau (isl.) F6

THAILAND (SIAM)

CITIES and TOWNS

Ang Thong 7,267 ..... C4
Ayutthaya (Phra Nakhon Si Ayutthaya) 37,213 ..... D4
Ban Aranyaprathet 12,276 ..... D4
Bangkok (cap.) 1,867,297 ..... D4
Bangkok* 2,495,312 ..... D4
Bang Lamung D4
Bang Saphan C5
Ban Kantang 9,247 ..... C6
Ban Kapong C5
Ban Khlong Yai D5
Ban Kui Nua D4
Ban Ngon D3
Ban Pak Phanang 13,590 ..... D5
Banphot Phisai C3
Ban Pua D3
Ban Sattahip D4
Ban Tha Uthen D3
Bua Chum D4
Buriram 16,431 ..... D4
Chachoengsao 22,106 ..... D4
Chai Badan D4
Chai Buri D3
Chainat 9,944 ..... D4
Chaiya C5
Chaiyaphum 12,540 ..... D4
Chang Khoeng C3
Chanthaburi 15,479 ..... D4
Chiang Dao C3
Chiang Khan D3
Chiang Mai 83,729 ..... C3
Chiang Rai 13,927 ..... C3
Chiang Saen C2
Chon Buri 39,367 ..... D4
Chumphon 11,643 ..... C5
Den Chai C3
Hat Yai 47,953 ..... C6
Hot C3
Hua Hin 21,426 ..... D4
Kalasin 14,960 ..... D3
Kamphaeng Phet 12,378 ..... C3
Kanchanaburi 16,397 ..... C4
Khanu C3
Khemmarat E4
Khon Kaen 29,431 ..... D3
Khorat (Nakhon Ratchasima) 66,071 ..... D4
Krabi 8,764 ..... C5
Krung Thep (Bangkok) (cap.) 1,867,297 ..... D4
Kumphawapi D3
Lae D3
Lampang 40,100 ..... C3
Lamphun 11,309 ..... C3
Lang Suan 4,020 ..... C5
Loei 10,137 ..... D3
Lom Sak 10,597 ..... D3
Lop Buri 23,112 ..... D4
Mae Hong Son 3,981 ..... C3
Maha Sarakham 19,707 ..... D3
Mukdahan E3
Nakhon Nayok 8,185 ..... D4
Nakhon Pathom 34,300 ..... C4
Nakhon Phanom 20,385 ..... D3
Nakhon Ratchasima 66,071 ..... D4
Nakhon Sawan 46,853 ..... D4
Nakhon Si Thammarat 40,671 ..... D5
Nan 17,738 ..... D3
Nang Rong D4
Narathiwat 21,256 ..... D6
Ngao D3
Nong Khai 21,150 ..... D3
Pattani 21,938 ..... D6
Phanat Nikhom 10,514 ..... D4
Phangnga 5,738 ..... C5
Phatthalung 13,336 ..... D6
Phayao 20,346 ..... C3
Phet Buri 27,755 ..... C4
Phetchabun 6,240 ..... D3
Phichai D3
Phichit 10,814 ..... D3
Phitsanulok 33,883 ..... D3
Phon Phisai D3
Phrae 17,555 ..... D3
Phra Nakhon Si Ayutthaya 37,213 ..... D4
Phuket 34,362 ..... C6
Phutthaisong D4
Prachin Buri 14,167 ..... D4
Prachuap Khiri Khan 9,075 ..... D5
Pran Buri C4
Rahaeng (Tak) 16,317 ..... C3
Ranong 10,301 ..... C5
Rat Buri 32,271 ..... C4
Rayong 14,846 ..... D4
Roi Et 20,242 ..... D3
Rong Kwang D3
Sakon Nakhon 18,943 ..... E3
Samut Prakan 46,632 ..... D4
Samut Sakhon 33,619 ..... D4
Samut Songkhram 23,574 ..... C4
Sara Buri 25,025 ..... D4
Satun 7,315 ..... C6
Sawankhalok 8,387 ..... C3
Selaphum E3
Sing Buri 9,050 ..... D4
Singora (Songkhla) 41,193 ..... D6
Sisaket 13,662 ..... E4
Songkhla 41,193 ..... D6
Sukhothai 15,488 ..... D3
Suphan Buri 18,768 ..... C4
Surat Thani 24,923 ..... C5
Surin 16,342 ..... D4
Suwannaphum D4
Tak 16,317 ..... C3
Takua Pa 7,825 ..... C5
Thoen C3
Thon Buri 628,015 ..... D4
To Mo D6
Trang 32,985 ..... C6
Trat 7,917 ..... D4
Ubon 40,650 ..... E4
Udon Thani 56,218 ..... D3
Uthai Thani 10,525 ..... C4
Uttaradit 12,022 ..... D3
Warin Chamrap 21,520 ..... E4
Yala 30,051 ..... D6
Yasothon 12,079 ..... D4

OTHER FEATURES

Amya (pass) C4
Bilauktaung (range) C4
Chang, Ko (isl.) D4
Chao Phraya, Mae Nam (riv.) D4
Chi, Mae Nam (riv.) D3
Dangrek (Dong Rak) (mts.) D4
Doi Inthanon (mt.) C3
Doi Pha Hom Pok (mt.) C2
Doi Pia Fai (mt.) D4
Kao Prawa (mt.) C3
Khao Luang (mt.) C5
Khwae Noi, Mae Nam (riv.) C4
Kra (isth.) C5
Kut, Ko (isl.) D5
Laem Pho (cape) D6
Laem Talumphuk (cape) D5
Lanta, Ko (isl.) C6
Luang (mt.) C5
Mae Klong, Mae Nam (riv.) C4
Mekong (riv.) E3
Mun, Mae Nam (riv.) D4
Nan, Mae Nam (riv.) D3
Nong Lahan (lake) D3
Pakchan (riv.) C5
Pa Sak, Mae Nam (riv.) D4
Phangan, Ko (isl.) D5
Phuket, Ko (isl.) C5
Ping, Mae Nam (riv.) C3
Samui (str.) D5
Samui, Ko (isl.) D5
Siam (Thailand) (gulf) D5
Tao, Ko (isl.) C5
Tapi, Mae Nam (riv.) C5
Terutao, Ko (isl.) C6
Tha Chin, Mae Nam (riv.) C4
Thale Luang (lag.) D6
Thalu, Ko (isls.) C5
Three Pagodas (pass) C4
Wang, Mae Nam (riv.) C3

VIETNAM

CITIES and TOWNS

An Loc (Binh Long) 15,276 ..... E5
An Nhon F4
An Tuc (An Khe) F4
Ap Long Ha F5
Ap Vinh Hao F5
Bac Can E2
Bac Giang E2
Bac Lieu 53,841 ..... E5
Bac Ninh 22,560 ..... E2
Ba Don E3
Bai Thuong E3
Ban Me Thuot 68,771 ..... F4
Bao Ha D2
Bao Lac E2
Bien Hoa 87,135 ..... E5
Binh Long (An Loc) 15,276 ..... E5
Binh Son F4
Bo Duc E4
Bong Son (Hoai Nhon) F4
Cam Ranh 118,111 ..... F5
Can Tho 182,424 ..... E5
Cao Bang E2
Cao Lanh 16,482 ..... E5
Chau Phu 37,175 ..... E5
Chu Lai F4
Con Cuong E3
Cua Rao E3
Da Lat 105,072 ..... F5
Dam Doi E5
Da Nang 492,194 ..... E3
Dien Bien Phu D2
Dong Hoi E3
Duong Dong D5
Gia Dinh E5
Go Cong 33,191 ..... E5
Ha Giang E2
Haiphong* 1,279,067 ..... E2
Hanoi (cap.)* 2,570,905 ..... E2
Ha Tien E5
Ha Tinh E3
Hau Bon E4
Hoa Binh E2
Hoa Da F5
Hoai Nhon F4
Ho Chi Minh City (Saigon)* 3,419,678 ..... E5
Hoi An 45,059 ..... F4
Hoi Xuan E2
Hon Chong E5
Hon Gai 100,000 ..... E2
Hue 209,043 ..... E3
Huong Khe E3
Ke Bao E2
Khanh Hoa F4
Khanh Hung 59,015 ..... E5
Khe Sanh E3
Kien Hung E5
Kontum 33,554 ..... E4
Lac Giao (Ban Me Thuot) 68,771 ..... E4
Lai Chau D2
Lang Son 15,071 ..... E2
Lao Cai E2
Loc Ninh E5
Long Xuyen 72,658 ..... E5
Mo Duc F4
Mong Cai E2
Muong Khuong E2
My Tho 119,892 ..... E5
Nam Dinh E2
Nghia Lo D2
Nha Trang 216,227 ..... F4
Ninh Binh E3
Phan Rang 33,377 ..... F5
Phan Thiet 80,122 ..... F5
Phu Cuong 28,267 ..... E5
Phu Lang Thuong (Bac Giang) E2
Phuc Loi E3
Phu Dien E3
Phu Ly E2
Phu My F4
Phu Qui E3
Phu Rieng E5
Phu Tho 10,888 ..... E2
Phu Vinh 48,485 ..... E5
Pleiku 23,720 ..... E4
Quang Nam E4
Quang Ngai 14,119 ..... F4
Quang Tri 15,874 ..... E3
Quang Yen E2
Quan Long 59,331 ..... E5
Qui Nhon 213,757 ..... F4
Rach Gia 104,161 ..... E5
Ron E3
Sa Dec 51,867 ..... E5
Saigon (Ho Chi Minh City)* 3,419,678 ..... E5
Song Cau F4
Son Ha F4
Son La D2
Son Tay 19,213 ..... E2
Tam Ky 38,532 ..... F4
Tam Quan F4
Tan An 38,082 ..... E5
Tay Ninh 22,957 ..... E5
Thai Binh 14,739 ..... E2
Thai Nguyen E2
Thanh Hoa 31,211 ..... E3
Thanh Tri E5
That Khe E2
Tien Yen E2
Tra Vinh (Phu Vinh) 48,485 ..... E5
Truc Giang 68,629 ..... E5
Trung Khanh Phu E2
Tuyen Quang E2
Tuy Hoa 63,552 ..... F4
Van Hoa E2
Van Ninh F4
Van Yen E2
Vinh 43,954 ..... E3
Vinh Long 30,667 ..... E5
Vinh Yen E2
Vu Liet E3
Vung Tau 108,436 ..... E5
Xuan Loc E5
Yen Bai E2

OTHER FEATURES

Bach Long Vi, Dao (isl.) F2
Ba Den, Nui (mt.) E5
Bai Bung, Mui (Ca Mau) (pt.) E5
Black (riv.) D2
Ca Mau (Mui Bai Bung) (pt.) E5
Cam Ranh, Vinh (bay) F5
Cat Ba, Dao (isl.) E2
Chon May, Vung (bay) F3
Cu Lao, Hon (isls.) F5
Deux Frères, Les (isls.) E5
Dinh, Mui (cape) F5
Fan Si Pan (mt.) D2
Ia Drang (riv.) E4
Joncs (plain) E5
Kontum (plat.) E4
Khoai, Hon (isl.) E5
Lang Bian, Nui (mts.) E4
Lay, Mui (cape) E3
Mekong, Mouths of the (delta) E5
Nam Tram, Mui (cape) F4
Nightingale (Bach Long Vi) (isl.) F2
Panjang, Hon (Hon Tho Chau) (isl.) D5
Phu Quoc, Dao (isl.) D5
Rao Co (mt.) E3
Red (riv.) E2
Se San (riv.) E4
Sip Song Chau Thai (mts.) D2
Song Ba (riv.) F4
Song Ca (riv.) E3
Song Cai (riv.) E4
South China (sea) F4
Tonkin (gulf) E3
Varella, Mui (cape) F4
Wai, Poulo (isls.) E4
Yang Sin, Chu (mt.) F4

*See Southeast Asia, p. 85 for other part of Malaysia.

*City and suburbs.

⊙Population of district.

Agriculture, Industry and Resources

DOMINANT LAND USE

- Rice
- Diversified Tropical Crops
- Livestock Grazing, Limited Agriculture
- Tropical Forests

MAJOR MINERAL OCCURRENCES

Ag	Silver	Cu	Copper	O	Petroleum	Sn	Tin
Al	Bauxite	Fe	Iron Ore	P	Phosphates	Ti	Titanium
Au	Gold	G	Natural Gas	Pb	Lead	W	Tungsten
C	Coal	Mn	Manganese	Sb	Antimony	Zn	Zinc
Cr	Chromium						

Water Power

Major Industrial Areas

CHINA (MAINLAND)
AREA 3,691,000 sq. mi. (9,559,690 sq. km.)
POPULATION 958,090,000
CAPITAL Peking (Beijing)
LARGEST CITY Shanghai
HIGHEST POINT Mt. Everest 29,028 ft.
  (8,848 m.)
MONETARY UNIT yuan
MAJOR LANGUAGES Chinese, Chuang, Uigur,
  Yi, Tibetan, Miao, Mongol, Kazakh
MAJOR RELIGIONS Confucianism, Buddhism,
  Taoism, Islam

CHINA (TAIWAN)
AREA 13,971 sq. mi. (36,185 sq. km.)
POPULATION 16,609,961
CAPITAL Taipei
LARGEST CITY Taipei
HIGHEST POINT Yü Shan 13,113 ft. (3,997 m.)
MONETARY UNIT new Taiwan yüan (dollar)
MAJOR LANGUAGES Chinese, Formosan
MAJOR RELIGIONS Confucianism, Buddhism,
  Taoism, Christianity, tribal religions

MONGOLIA
AREA 606,163 sq. mi. (1,569,962 sq. km.)
POPULATION 1,594,800
CAPITAL Ulaanbaatar
LARGEST CITY Ulaanbaatar
HIGHEST POINT Tabun Bogdo 14,288 ft.
  (4,355 m.)
MONETARY UNIT tughrik
MAJOR LANGUAGES Khalkha Mongolian,
  Kazakh (Turkic)
MAJOR RELIGION Buddhism

HONG KONG
AREA 403 sq. mi. (1,044 sq. km.)
POPULATION 5,022,000
CAPITAL Victoria
MONETARY UNIT Hong Kong dollar
MAJOR LANGUAGES Chinese, English
MAJOR RELIGIONS Confucianism, Buddhism,
  Christianity

MACAU
AREA 6 sq. mi. (16 sq. km.)
POPULATION 271,000
CAPITAL Macau
MONETARY UNIT pataca
MAJOR LANGUAGES Chinese, Portuguese
MAJOR RELIGIONS Confucianism, Buddhism,
  Taoism, Christianity

CHINA (MAINLAND)

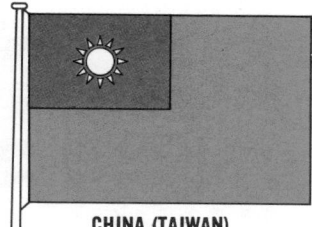

CHINA (TAIWAN)

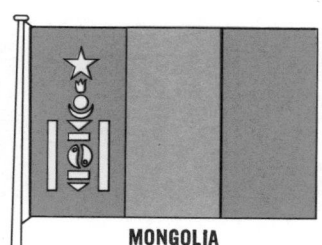

MONGOLIA

(continued on following page)

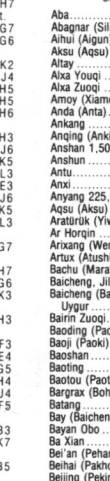
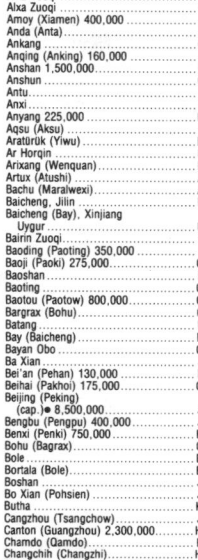

China and Mongolia Transportation

Railroads	
Under Construction	
Connecting Roads	
Navigable Rivers	
Canals	
Major Seaports	‡

© Copyright HAMMOND INCORPORATED, Maplewood, N.J.

Scale of Miles
0   500   1000

Scale of Kilometers
0   500   1000

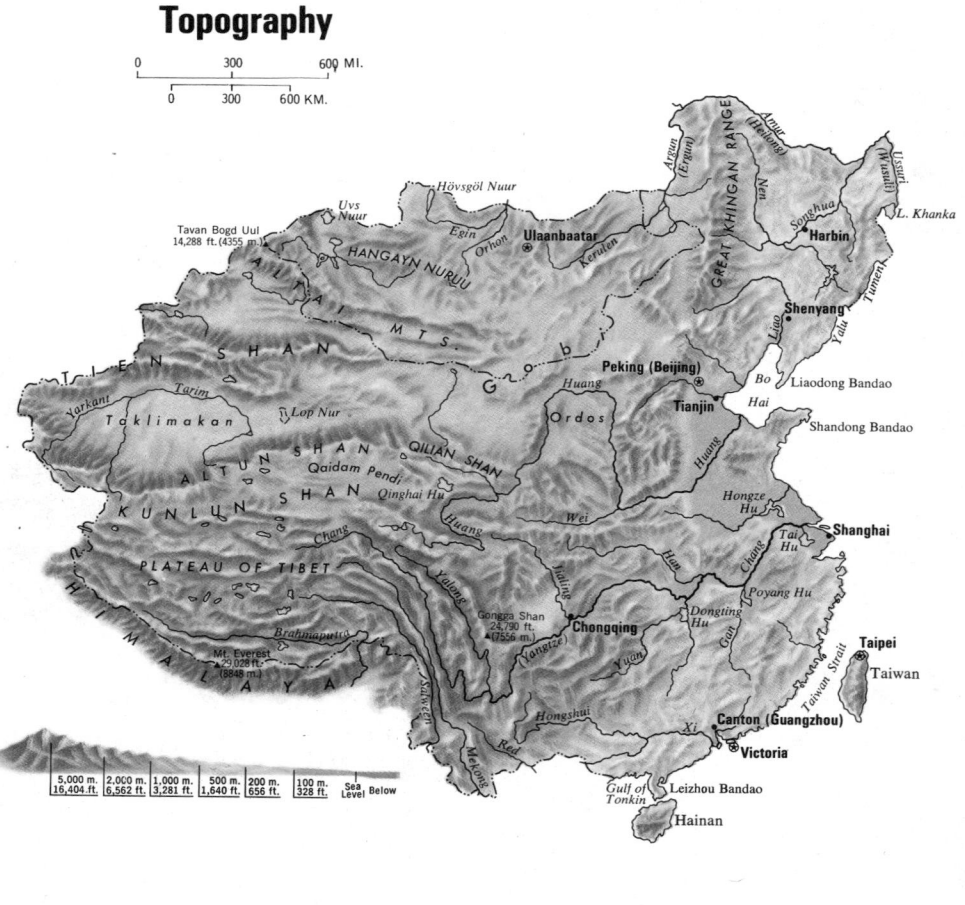

Topography

0 — 300 — 600 MI.
0 — 300 — 600 KM.

5,000 m. / 16,404 ft. | 2,000 m. / 6,562 ft. | 1,000 m. / 3,281 ft. | 500 m. / 1,640 ft. | 200 m. / 656 ft. | 100 m. / 328 ft. | Sea Level | Below

On this map Chinese place-names have been rendered according to the Pinyin spelling system within the area controlled by the People's Republic of China. Alphabetically listed below are selected Chinese place-names spelled in the traditional manner, followed by the equivalent Pinyin form.

(continued on following page)

China and Mongolia

SCALE OF MILES
0   100   200   300   400   500

SCALE OF KILOMETERS
0   100   200   300   400   500

Capitals of Countries .... ●   International Boundaries ....
Provincial Capitals .... ●   Provincial Boundaries ....
Canals ....   Walls ....

Scale 1:19,100,000

© Copyright HAMMOND INCORPORATED, Maplewood, N.J.

Mazu (Matsu) (isl.) K6
Mekong (Lancang Jiang) (riv.) .. F7
Min Jiang (riv.) J6
Mudan Jiang (riv.) L3
Muztag (mt.) B4
Muztagata (mt.) A4
Nam Co (lake) D5
Namzha Parwa (mt.) H6
Nan Ling (mts.) H6
Nen Jiang (riv.) K2
Ngangzê Co (lake) C5
Ngoring Hu (lake) E5
Nu Jiang (riv.) E6
Nyainêntanglha Shan
  (range) D5
Olwanpi (cape) K7
Ordos (reg.) G4
Penghu (Pescadores)
  (isls.) 113,397 .... J7
Pingtan (isl.) A3
Pobeda (peak) J6
Poyang Hu (lake) J6
Pratas (Dongsha) (isl.) J7
Qaidam Pendi (basin) (swamp) D4
Qarqan He (riv.) C4
Qilian Shan (range) E4
Qinghai Hu (lake) F4
Qiongzhou Haixia (str.) G7
Quemoy (Jinmen) (isl.) J7
Qumar He (riv.) D4
Salween (Nu Jiang) (riv.) E6
Siling Co (lake) C5
Songhua Hu (lake) L3
Songhua Jiang (Sungari)
  (riv.) M2
South China (sea) J7
Tachen (Taizhou) (isls.) K6
Tai Hu (lake) J5
Taiwan (Formosa)
  (isl.) 16,609,961 .... K7
Taiwan (Formosa) (str.) J7
Taizhou (Tachen) (isls.) K6
Takla Makan (Taklimakan Shamo)
  (des.) .... B
Tanggula Shan (range) D5
Tangra Yumco (lake) C5
Tarim He (riv.) B3
Tarim Pendi (basin) B4
Tian Shan (range) C3
Tibet (reg.) B5
Tongtian He (Zhi Qu) (riv.) E5
Tonkin (gulf) G7

Tumen (riv.) L3
Ulu Muztag (mt.) C4
Ulungur He (riv.) C2
Ulungur Hu (lake) C2
Ussuri (Wusuli Jiang) (riv.) M2
Wei He (riv.) G5
Wu Jiang (riv.) G6
Wusuli Jiang (Ussuri) (riv.) M2
Wuyi Shan (range) J6
Xiang Jiang (riv.) H6
Xi Jiang (riv.) H7
Yagradagzê Shan (mt.) D4
Yalong Jiang (riv.) F6
Yalu (riv.) L3
Yangtze (Chang Jiang) (riv.) K5
Yarkant He (riv.) A4
Yellow (Huang He) (riv.) J4
Yellow (sea) K4
Yin Shan (mts.) G3
Yuhuan (isl.) K6
Yu Shan (mt.) K7
Yushan (isls.) K5
Zhoushan (arch.) K5

HONG KONG
CITIES and TOWNS

Kowloon* 2,378,480 .... H7
Victoria (cap.)* 1,026,870 ...... H7

MACAU (MACAO)
CITIES and TOWNS

Macau (Macao) (cap.) 226,880 .... H7

MONGOLIA
PROVINCES

Arhangay 90,500 .... F2
Bayamhongor 64,900 .... E2
Bayan-Ölgiy 73,300 .... C2
Bulgan 45,700 .... E2
Dornod 51,100 .... H2
Dornogovi 36,400 .... G3
Dundgovi 37,800 .... G2
Dzavhan 87,600 .... E2
Govi-Altay 59,200 .... E3
Hentiy 49,900 .... H2

Hovd 68,300 .... D2
Hövsgöl 89,600 .... E1
Ömnögovi 32,200 .... F3
Övörhangay 84,100 .... F2
Selenge 53,700 .... G2
Sühbaatar 44,100 .... H2
Töv 74,900 .... G2
Uvs 76,300 .... D1

CITIES AND TOWNS

Altay 10,000 .... E2
Arvayheer 9,100 .... F2
Baatsagaan 800 .... E2
Baruun-Urt 8,200 .... H2
Bayanbaraat 400 .... G2
Bayandalay 500 .... F3
Bayanhongor 400 .... F3
Bayanhongor 11,300 .... E2
Bayan-Öndör 300 .... E3
Bayan-Uul 1,200 .... E2
Beger 800 .... E2
Bulgan, Bulgan 9,800 .... F2
Bulgan, Hovd 3,100 .... D2
Bulgan, Ömnögovi 700 .... F3
Bürentsogt 3,000 .... H2
Buyant 700 .... G2
Choybalsan 20,500 .... J2
Chandman 700 .... D2
Choybalsan 400 .... G3
Dalandzadgad 6,600 .... G3
Darhan (Darkhan) 32,900 .... G2
Dashbalbar 1,100 .... H2
Dashinchilen 600 .... F2
Delgertsogt 500 .... G2
Dzamiin Üüd 1,500 .... H3
Dzüünharaa 8,100 .... G2
Dzuunmod 7,200 .... G2
Erdenesagaan 1,500 .... J2
Ereen 700 .... H2
Hanbogd 300 .... G3
Hanh 500 .... F2
Hatgal 5,000 .... E1
Hongor H2

Mönhhaan 400 .... H2
Mörön (Muren) 10,700 .... F2
Nalayh (Nalaikha) 14,000 .... G2
Nomgon 500 .... G3
Noyon 300 .... F3
Onon 2,600 .... C2
Öndörhaan (Undur
  Khan) 7,900 .... G2
Onon 2,600 .... H2
Sayhan-Ovoo 400 .... F2
Saynshand 10,000 .... H3
Selenge 1,300 .... F2
Sühbaatar (Sukhe
  Bator) 10,000 .... G1
Sulanheer 300 .... G3
Tamsagbulag J2
Tsagaannuur 2,000 .... C2
Tsagaan-Ovoo 900 .... H2
Tsagaan-Uul 1,700 .... F2
Tsetseg 700 .... D2
Tsetserleg 12,400 .... F2
Ulaanbaatar (Ulan Bator)
  (cap.) 345,000 .... G2
Ulaangom (Ulangom) 14,000 .... D2
Ulegei (Ölgiy) 11,700 .... C2
Uliastay (Jibhalanta) 13,000 .... E2
Urga (Ulaanbaatar)
  (cap.) 345,000 .... G2
Yaruu 700 .... E2

OTHER FEATURES

Altai (mts.) C2
Dörgön Nuur (lake) D2
Dzavhan Gol (riv.) D2
Ghenghis Khan Wall (ruins) H2
Gobi (des.) G3
Hangayn Nuruu (mts.) E2
Har Us Nuur (lake) D2
Herlen Gol (Kerulen) (riv.) H2
Hovd Gol (riv.) D2
Hövsgöl Nuur (lake) F1
Hyargas Nuur (lake) D2
Ider Gol (riv.) F2
Karakorum (ruins) F2
Kerulen (riv.) H2
Munku-Sardyk (mt.) F1
Orhon Gol (riv.) F2
Selenge Mörön (riv.) G2
Tannu-Ola (range) D1
Tavan Bogd Uul (mt.) C2
Uvs Nuur (lake) D1

● Population of municipality
*City and suburbs

† Populations of mainland cities, excluding Peking (Beijing), Shanghai and Tianjin (Tientsin), courtesy of Kingsley Davis,
Office of Int'l Pop. and Research, Inst. of Int'l Studies Univ. of California.

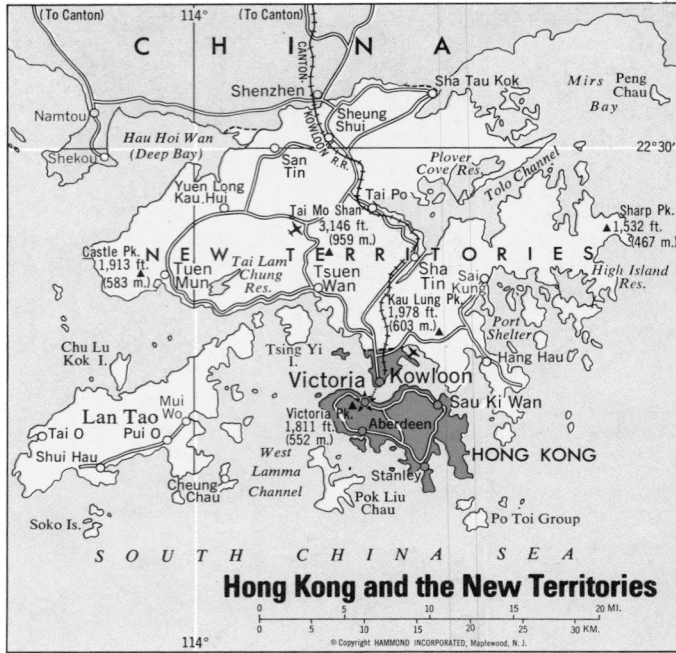

Hong Kong and the New Territories

Agriculture, Industry and Resources

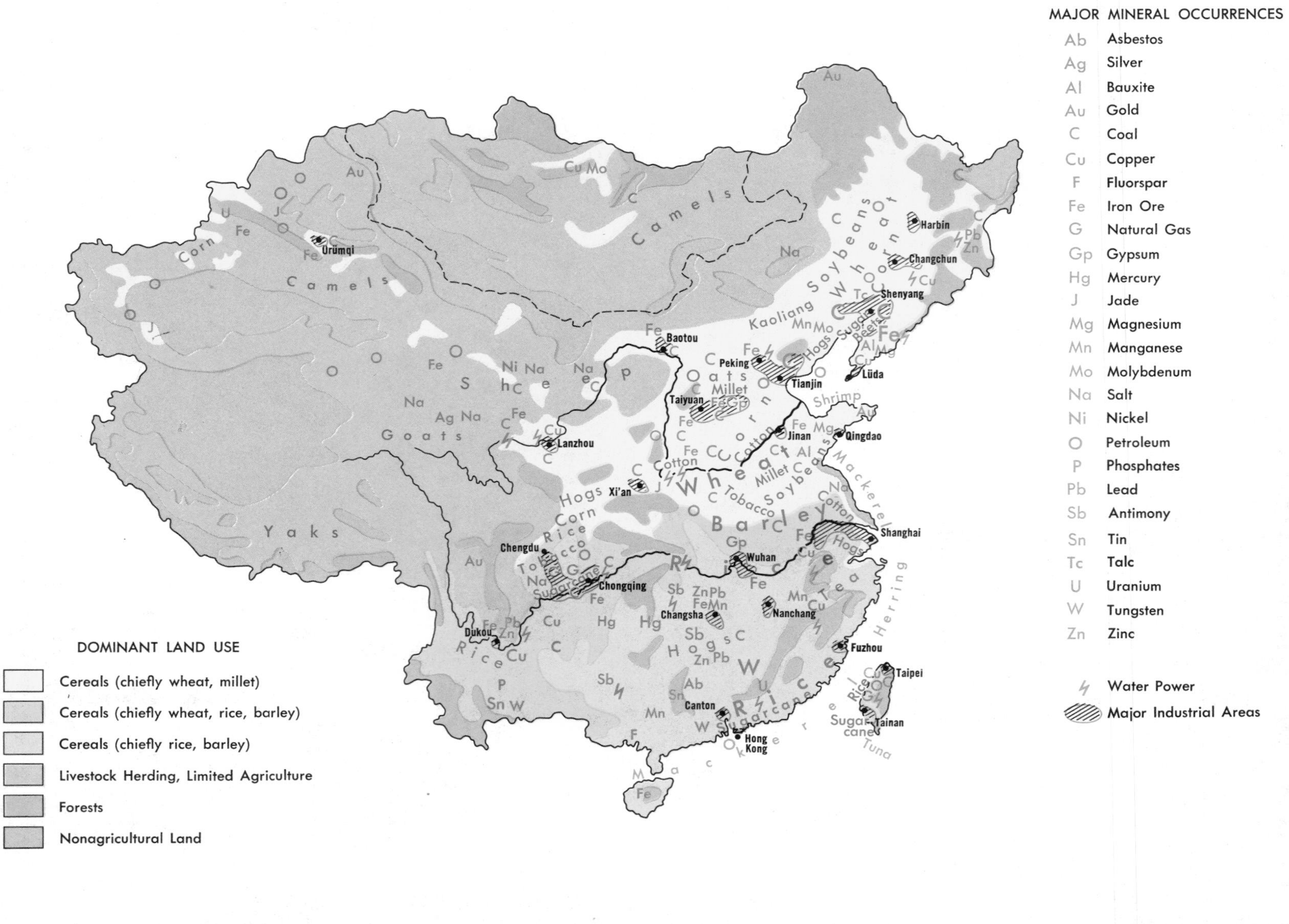

MAJOR MINERAL OCCURRENCES

Ab	Asbestos
Ag	Silver
Al	Bauxite
Au	Gold
C	Coal
Cu	Copper
F	Fluorspar
Fe	Iron Ore
G	Natural Gas
Gp	Gypsum
Hg	Mercury
J	Jade
Mg	Magnesium
Mn	Manganese
Mo	Molybdenum
Na	Salt
Ni	Nickel
O	Petroleum
P	Phosphates
Pb	Lead
Sb	Antimony
Sn	Tin
Tc	Talc
U	Uranium
W	Tungsten
Zn	Zinc

⚡ Water Power

▨ Major Industrial Areas

DOMINANT LAND USE

- ▢ Cereals (chiefly wheat, millet)
- ▢ Cereals (chiefly wheat, rice, barley)
- ▢ Cereals (chiefly rice, barley)
- ▢ Livestock Herding, Limited Agriculture
- ▢ Forests
- ▢ Nonagricultural Land

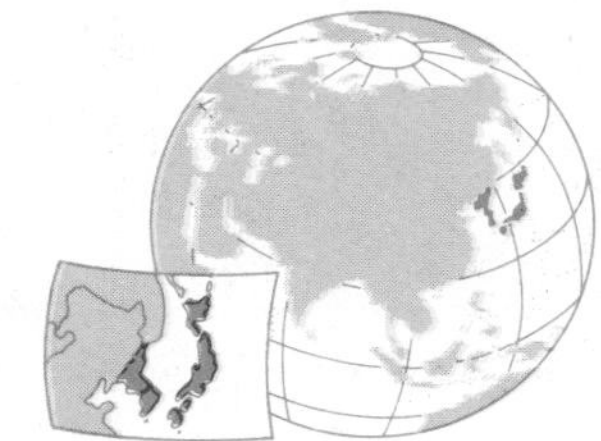

AREA 145,730 sq. mi. (377,441 sq. km.)
POPULATION 117,057,485
CAPITAL Tokyo
LARGEST CITY Tokyo
HIGHEST POINT Fuji 12,389 ft. (3,776 m.)
MONETARY UNIT yen
MAJOR LANGUAGE Japanese
MAJOR RELIGIONS Buddhism, Shintoism

AREA 46,540 sq. mi. (120,539 sq. km.)
POPULATION 17,914,000
CAPITAL P'yŏngyang
LARGEST CITY P'yŏngyang
HIGHEST POINT Paektu 9,003 ft. (2,744 m.)
MONETARY UNIT won
MAJOR LANGUAGE Korean
MAJOR RELIGIONS Confucianism, Buddhism, Ch'ondogyo

AREA 38,175 sq. mi. (98,873 sq. km.)
POPULATION 37,448,836
CAPITAL Seoul
LARGEST CITY Seoul
HIGHEST POINT Halla 6,398 ft. (1,950 m.)
MONETARY UNIT won
MAJOR LANGUAGE Korean
MAJOR RELIGIONS Confucianism, Buddhism, Ch'ondogyo, Christianity

JAPAN

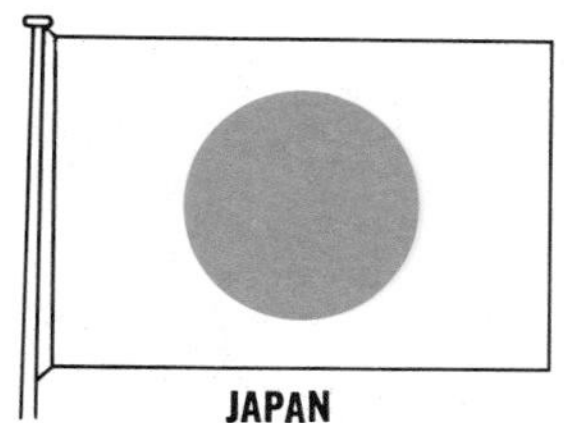

NORTH KOREA

SOUTH KOREA

JAPAN

PREFECTURES

Aichi 5,923,569	H6
Akita 1,232,481	J4
Aomori 1,468,646	K3
Chiba 4,149,147	P2
Ehime 1,465,215	F7
Fukui 773,599	G5
Fukuoka 4,292,963	D7
Fukushima 1,970,616	K5
Gifu 1,867,978	H6
Gumma 1,756,480	J5
Hiroshima 2,646,324	E6
Hokkaido 5,338,206	K2
Hyogo 4,992,140	H7
Ibaraki 2,342,198	K5
Ishikawa 1,069,872	H5
Iwate 1,385,563	K4
Kagawa 961,292	G6
Kagoshima 1,723,902	E8
Kanagawa 6,397,748	O2
Kochi 808,397	F7
Kumamoto 1,715,273	E7
Kyoto 2,424,856	J7
Mie 1,626,002	H6
Miyagi 1,955,267	K4
Miyazaki 1,085,055	E8
Nagano 2,017,564	J5
Nagasaki 1,571,912	D7
Nara 1,077,491	J8
Niigata 2,391,938	J5
Oita 1,190,314	E7
Okayama 1,814,305	F6
Okinawa 1,042,572	N6
Osaka 8,278,925	J8
Saga 837,674	E7

Saitama 4,821,340	O2
Shiga 985,621	J7
Shimane 768,886	F6
Shizuoka 3,308,799	H6
Tochigi 1,698,003	K5
Tokushima 805,166	G7
Tokyo 11,673,554	O2
Tottori 581,311	G6
Toyama 1,070,791	H5
Wakayama 1,072,118	H6
Yamagata 1,220,302	K4
Yamaguchi 1,555,218	E6
Yamanashi 783,050	J6

CITIES and TOWNS

Abashiri 43,825	M1
Ageo 146,358	O2
Aikawa 13,546	H4
Aizuwakamatsu 108,650	J5
Aigasawa 18,086	J3
Akashi 234,905	H8
Aki 24,480	F7
Akita 261,246	J4
Akeshi 16,778	M2
Akune 30,299	E7
Amagasaki 545,783	H8
Amagi 42,725	E7
Anan 60,439	G7
Aomori 264,222	K3
Asahi 34,028	K6
Asahikawa 320,526	L2
Ashibetsu 36,520	L2
Ashikaga 162,359	J5
Ashiya 76,211	H8
Atami 51,437	H6
Atsugi 108,955	O2
Awaji 9,623	H8

Ayabe 43,490	G6
Beppu 133,894	E7
Bibai 38,416	L2
Biratori 9,331	L2
Chiba 659,356	P2
Chichibu 61,798	J5
Chigasaki 152,023	O3
Chitose 61,031	K2
Chofu 175,924	O2
Choshi 90,374	K6
Daito 110,829	J8
Ebetsu 77,624	K2
Eniwa 39,884	K2
Esashi, Hokkaido 10,172	L1
Esashi, Hokkaido 14,409	J3
Esashi, Iwate 36,336	K4
Fuchu, Hiroshima 50,217	F6
Fuchu, Tokyo 182,474	O2
Fuji 199,195	J6
Fujieda 90,358	J6
Fujisawa 265,975	O3
Fukagawa 36,000	L2
Fukuchiyama 60,003	G6
Fukue 32,018	D7
Fukui 231,364	H5
Fukuoka 1,002,201	D7
Fukushima 246,531	K5
Fukuyama 329,714	F6
Funabashi 423,101	P2
Furukawa 54,356	K4
Gifu 408,707	H6
Gobo 30,272	G7
Gose 37,554	J8
Gosen 39,376	J5
Goshogawara 49,040	K3
Gotsu 27,992	F6
Habikino 94,160	J8
Haboro 13,624	K1

Hachinohe 224,366	K3
Hachioji 322,580	O2
Hadano 103,663	O3
Hagi 52,724	E6
Hakodate 307,453	K3
Hakui 28,726	H5
Hamada 50,316	E6
Hamamatsu 468,884	H6
Hanamaki 65,826	K4
Hanno 55,926	O2
Haramachi 43,483	K5
Hayama 24,026	O3
Higashiosaka 524,750	J8
Hikone 85,066	H6
Himeji 436,086	G6
Himi 61,789	H5
Hino 126,847	O2
Hirakata 297,618	J7
Hirara 29,301	L7
Hirata 30,942	F6
Hiratsuka 195,635	O3
Hiroo 11,399	L2
Hirosaki 164,911	K3
Hiroshima 852,611	E6
Hitachi 202,383	K5
Hitachiota 35,322	K5
Hitoyoshi 41,118	E7
Hofu 105,540	E6
Hondo 40,432	E7
Honjo 40,488	J4
Hyuga 53,448	E7
Ibusuki 32,339	E8
Ichihara 194,068	P3
Ichikawa 319,291	P2
Ichinohe 21,433	K3
Ichinomiya 238,463	H6
Ichinoseki 59,122	K4

Ide 9,112	J7
Iida 77,112	H6
Iizuka 75,417	E7
Ikeda, Hokkaido 12,306	L2
Ikeda, Osaka 100,268	H7
Ikoma 48,848	J8
Ikuno 6,658	G6
Imabari 119,726	F6
Imari 60,913	D7
Imazu 11,519	G6
Ina 54,468	H6
Isahaya 73,341	D7
Ise 104,957	H6
Ishigaki 34,657	L7
Ishige 19,220	P2
Ishinomaki 115,085	K4
Ishioka 43,679	K5
Itami 171,978	H7
Ito 68,072	J6
Itoigawa 36,646	H5
Itoman 39,363	N6
Iwaizumi 20,219	K4
Iwaki 330,213	K5
Iwakuni 111,069	E6
Iwami 16,063	G6
Iwamizawa 72,305	L2
Iwanai 25,823	K2
Iwasaki 4,437	J3
Iwata 67,665	H6
Iwatsuki 83,825	O2
Iyo 27,805	F7
Izuhara 18,460	D6
Izumi 118,237	J8
Izumiotsu 66,250	J8
Izumisano 86,139	G6
Izumo 71,568	F6
Joetsu 123,418	H5
Joyo 58,923	J7

Kadoma 143,238	J7
Kaga 61,599	H5
Kagoshima 456,827	E8
Kaizuka 79,506	H8
Kakogawa 169,293	G6
Kamaishi 68,981	L4
Kamakura 165,552	O3
Kameoka 58,184	J7
Kamiisco 27,229	K3
Kaminoyama 37,858	J4
Kamiyaka 8,668	E8
Kamo 8,953	J7
Kanazawa 395,263	H5
Kanonji 44,131	F6
Kanoya 67,951	E8
Kanuma 81,799	J5
Karatsu 75,224	D7
Kaseda 24,969	D8
Kashihara 95,701	J8
Kashiwa 203,065	P2
Kashiwa 63,586	H8
Kashiwazaki 80,351	J5
Kasugai 213,857	H6
Kasukabe 121,639	O2
Katsuta 79,996	K5
Katsuura 26,755	K6
Kawachinagano 66,936	J8
Kawagoe 225,465	O2
Kawaguchi 345,538	J6
Kawanishi 115,773	H7
Kawasaki 1,014,951	O2
Kesennuma 66,616	K4
Kikonai 10,034	K3
Kimitsu 76,016	O3
Kiryu 134,239	J5
Kisarazu 96,840	P3
Kishiwada 174,952	J8
Kitaibaraki 44,332	K5

Kitakami 48,759	K4
Kitakata 37,471	J5
Kitakyushu 1,058,058	E6
Kitami 91,519	L2
Kizu 11,890	J7
Kobayashi 38,325	E8
Kobe 1,360,605	H7
Kochi 280,962	F7
Kodaira 156,181	O2
Kofu 193,879	J6
Koga 55,973	J5
Koganei 102,714	O2
Kokubu 31,660	E8
Komagane 30,318	H6
Komatsu 100,273	H5
Koriyama 264,628	K5
Koshigaya 195,917	P2
Koyama 16,394	E8
Kubohama 17,817	F7
Kuji 38,122	K3
Kuki 45,797	O2
Kumagaya 131,485	J5
Kumamoto 488,166	E7
Kumano 27,026	G7
Kumashima 11,540	J7
Kurashiki 392,755	F6
Kurayoshi 50,785	F6
Kure 242,655	F6
Kuroiso 42,349	K5
Kurume 204,474	E7
Kushikino 30,456	E8
Kushima 30,038	E8
Kushiro 18,997	G7
Kushiro 206,840	M2
Kyonan 13,067	O3
Kyoto 1,461,059	J7
Machida 255,305	O2
Maebashi 250,241	J5
Maihara 12,845	G6
Maizuru 97,780	G6
Makubetsu 18,444	L2
Makurazaki 29,685	O3
Mashike 9,312	K2
Masuda 50,734	E6
Matsubara 132,662	H8
Matsue 127,440	F6
Matsumae 18,307	J3
Matsumoto 185,595	H5
Matsusaka 108,893	H6
Matsuto 36,170	H5
Matsuyama 367,323	F7
Mihara 83,679	F6
Miki 53,731	H7
Mikuni 21,602	G5
Minamata 36,782	E7
Minobu 10,345	J6
Minoo 19,621	J7
Misawa 37,437	K3
Mitaka 164,950	O2
Mito 197,953	K5
Mitsukaido 38,820	P2
Miura 47,888	O3
Miyako 61,912	L4
Miyakonojo 118,289	E8
Miyazaki 234,347	E8
Miyazu 30,194	G6
Miyoshi 37,193	F6
Mizusawa 52,266	K4
Mobara 64,942	K6
Mombetsu 32,825	L1
Monbetsu 15,029	L2
Mooka 47,345	K5
Mori 17,030	K2
Moriguchi 178,383	J7
Morioka 216,223	K4
Motobu 17,823	N6
Muko 45,886	J7
Murakami 32,939	J4
Muroran 158,715	K2
Muroto 26,660	G7
Musashino 139,508	O2
Mutsu 44,646	K3
Nachikatsuura 23,596	H7
Nagahama, Ehime 13,144	F7
Nagahama, Shiga 54,064	H6
Nagano 306,637	J5
Nagaoka, Kyoto 65,557	J7
Nagaoka, Niigata 171,742	J5
Nagaokakyo 65,557	J7
Nagasaki 450,194	D7
Nagato 27,327	E6
Nago 45,210	N6
Nagoya 2,079,740	H6
Naha 295,006	N6
Nakaminato 33,147	K5
Nakamura 34,437	F7
Nakasato 14,248	K3
Nakatsu 59,111	E7
Nanao 49,493	H5
Nankoku 42,832	F7
Nara 257,538	J8
Narashino 117,852	P2
Nayoro 35,145	L1
Naze 46,359	O5
Nemuro 45,817	M2
Neyagawa 254,311	J7
Nichinan 52,171	E8
Niigata 423,188	J5
Niihama 131,712	F6
Niimi 30,014	F6
Niitsu 58,970	J5
Nishinomiya 400,622	H8

(continued on following page)

Agriculture, Industry and Resources

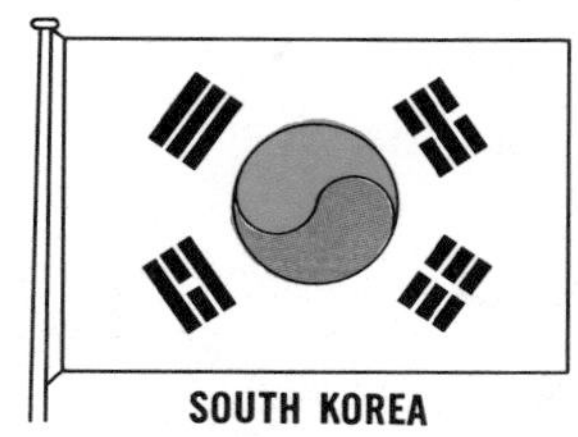

DOMINANT LAND USE

- Cereals, Cash Crops
- Truck Farming, Horticulture
- Mixed Farming, Dairy
- Rice
- Forests, Scrub

MAJOR MINERAL OCCURRENCES

Ag	Silver	Mn	Manganese
Au	Gold	Mo	Molybdenum
C	Coal	O	Petroleum
Cu	Copper	Pb	Lead
Fe	Iron Ore	Py	Pyrites
G	Natural Gas	U	Uranium
Gr	Graphite	W	Tungsten
Mg	Magnesium	Zn	Zinc

⚡ Water Power

▨ Major Industrial Areas

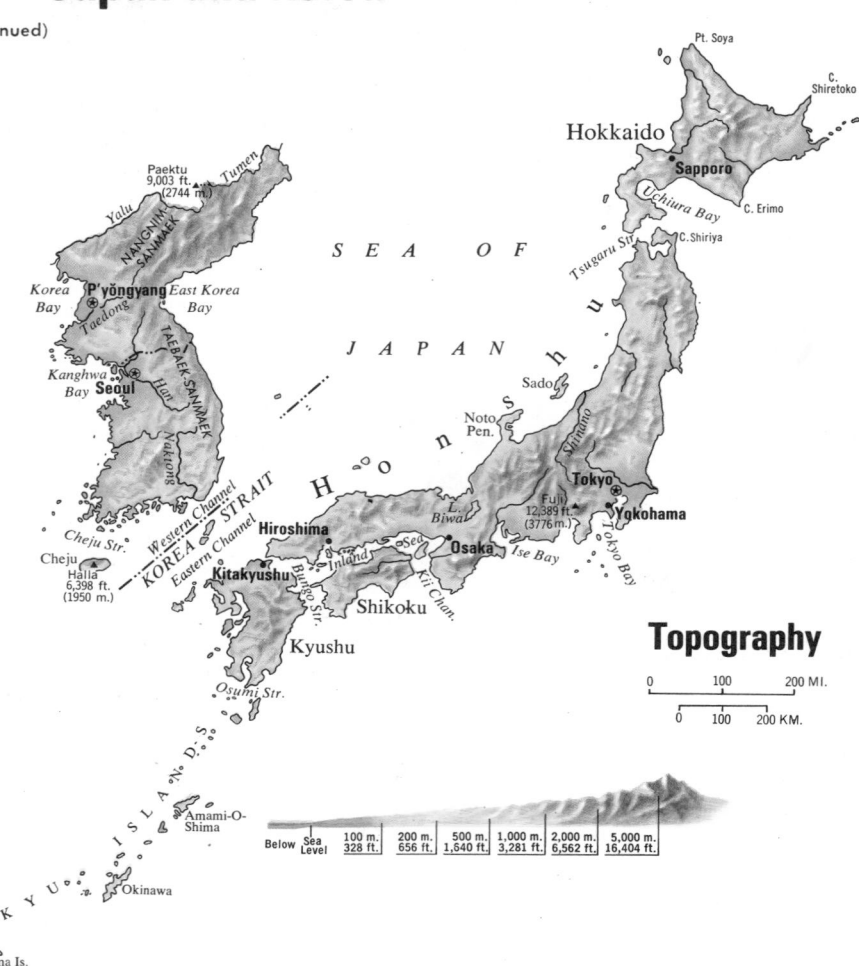

Hokkaido

Sapporo

SEA OF

JAPAN

P'yŏngyang

Seoul

Kitakyushu

Hiroshima

Osaka

Tokyo

Yokohama

Fuji 12,389 ft. (3776 m.)

Shikoku

Kyushu

RYUKYU ISLANDS

Amami-O-Shima

Okinawa

Sakishima Is.

Topography

Below Sea Level | 100 m. 328 ft. | 200 m. 656 ft. | 500 m. 1,640 ft. | 1,000 m. 3,281 ft. | 2,000 m. 6,562 ft. | 5,000 m. 16,404 ft.

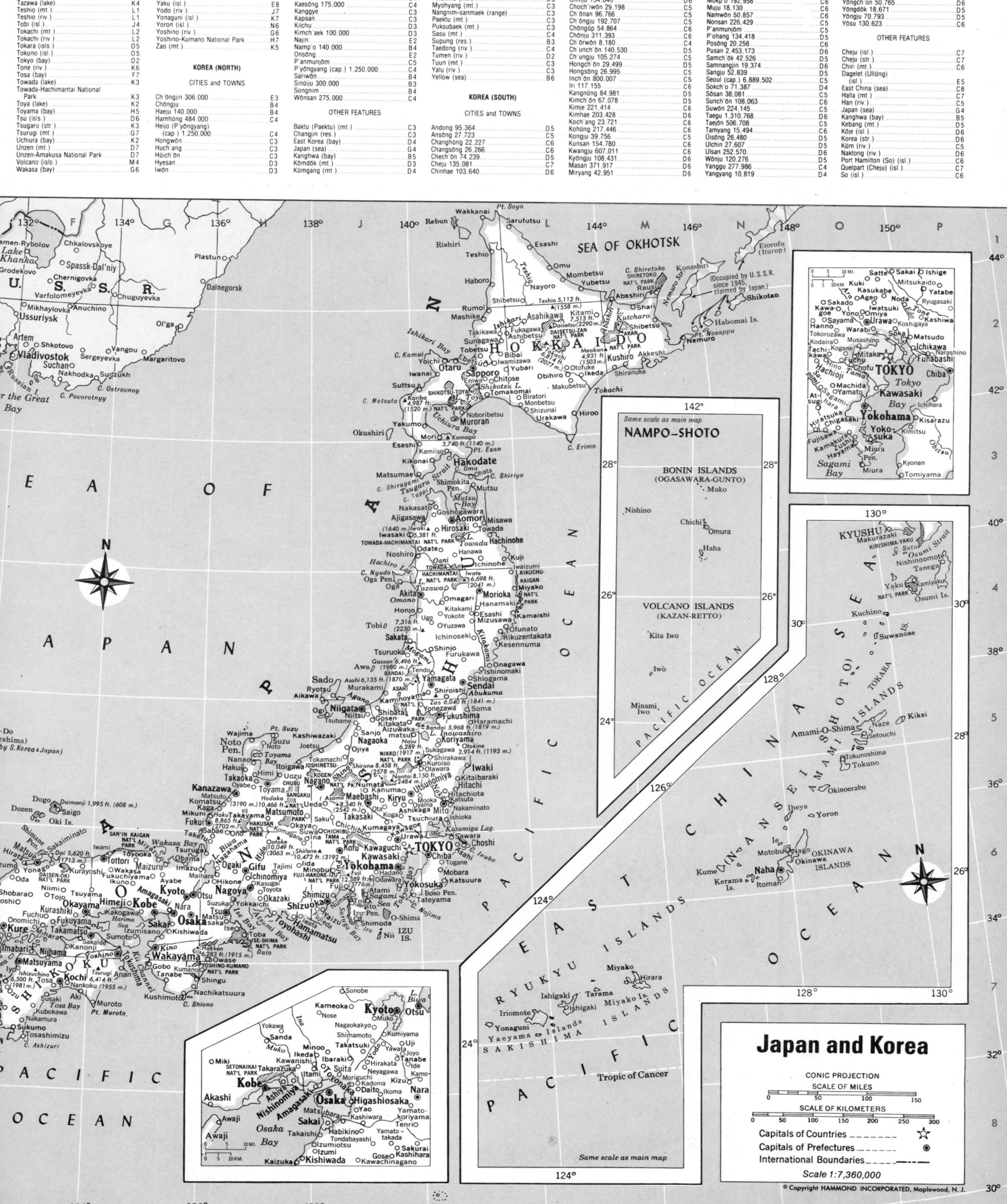

Japan and Korea

CONIC PROJECTION

SCALE OF MILES

SCALE OF KILOMETERS

Capitals of Countries ☆
Capitals of Prefectures ⊙
International Boundaries

Scale 1:7,360,000

© Copyright HAMMOND INCORPORATED, Maplewood, N.J.

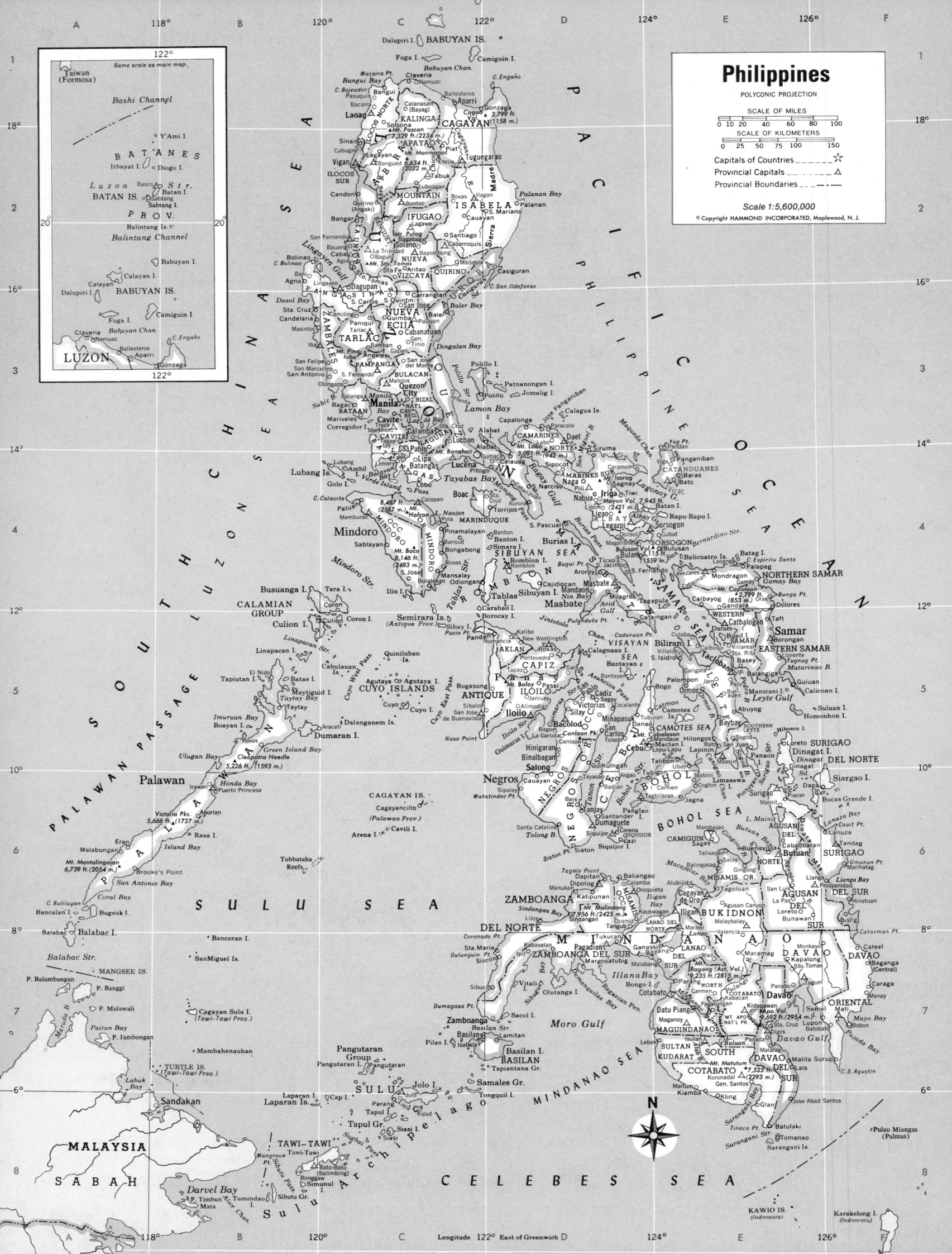

Philippines

POLYCONIC PROJECTION

SCALE OF MILES

0 10 20 40 60 80 100

SCALE OF KILOMETERS

0 25 50 75 100 150

Capitals of Countries _____ ☆
Provincial Capitals _____ △
Provincial Boundaries _____

Scale 1:5,600,000

© Copyright HAMMOND INCORPORATED, Maplewood, N.J.

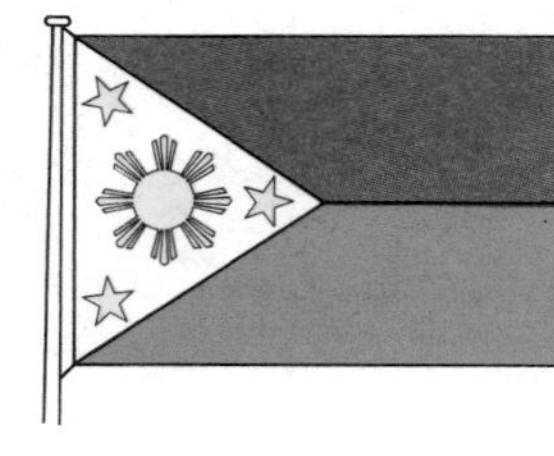

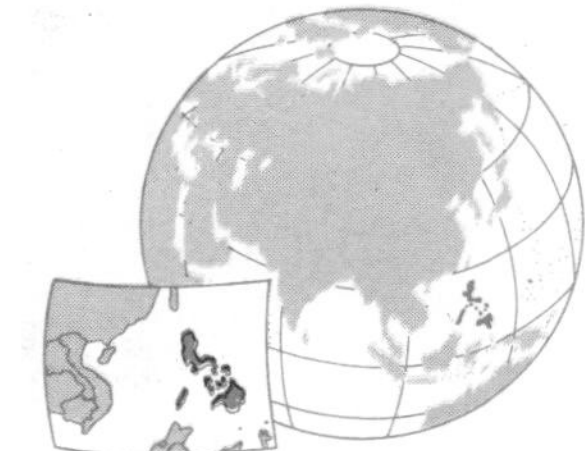

AREA 115,707 sq. mi. (299,681 sq. km.)
POPULATION 48,098,460
CAPITAL Manila
LARGEST CITY Manila
HIGHEST POINT Apo 9,692 ft. (2,954 m.)
MONETARY UNIT piso
MAJOR LANGUAGES Pilipino (Tagalog), English, Spanish, Bisayan, Ilocano, Bikol
MAJOR RELIGIONS Roman Catholicism, Islam, Protestantism, tribal religions

PROVINCES

Abra 160,198 ....C2
Agusan del Norte 365,421 ..E6
Agusan del Sur 631,634 ....E6
Aklan 324,563 ....D5
Albay 809,177 ....D4
Antique 344,879 ....D5
Aurora 107,145 ....C3
Basilan 201,407 ....D7
Bataan 323,254 ....C3
Batanes 12,091 ....A2
Batangas 1,174,201 ......C4
Benguet 354,751 ....C2
Bohol 806,031 ....E6
Bukidnon 631,634 ....E6
Bulacan 1,098,046 ....C3
Cagayan 711,476 ....C1
Camarines Norte 368,007 ..D3
Camarines Sur 1,099,346 ..D4
Camiguin 57,126 ....E6
Capiz 492,231 ....D5
Catanduanes 175,247 .....E4
Cavite 771,320 ....C3
Cebu 2,091,602 ....D5
Davao 725,153 ....E7
Davao del Sur 1,133,599 ..E7
Davao Oriental 339,931 ...F7
Eastern Samar 320,637 ....E5
Ifugao 111,368 ....C2
Ilocos Norte 390,666 ....C1
Ilocos Sur 443,591 ......C2
Iloilo 1,433,641 ....D5
Isabela 870,604 ....C2
Kalinga-Apayao 185,063 ...C1
Laguna 973,104 ....C3
Lanao del Norte 461,049 ..E6
Lanao del Sur 404,971 ....E7
La Union 452,578 ....C2
Leyte 1,302,648 ....E5
Maguindanao 536,546 .....E7
Manila 5,925,884 ....C3
Marinduque 173,715 ......C4
Masbate 584,526 ....D4
Misamis Occidental 386,328 D6
Misamis Oriental 690,032 .E6
Mountain 103,052 ....C2
National Capital Region
  (Manila) 5,925,884 .....C3
Negros Occidental
  1,930,301 ....D6
Negros Oriental 819,399 ..D6
North Cotabato 564,599 ...E7
Northern Samar 378,516 ...E4
Nueva Ecija 1,069,409 ....C3
Nueva Vizcaya 241,690 ....C2
Occidental Mindoro 222,431 C4
Oriental Mindoro 448,938 .C4
Palawan 371,782 ....B6
Pampanga 1,181,590 ......C3
Pangasinan 1,636,057 ....C3
Quezon 1,129,277 ....C3
Quirino 83,230 ....C2
Rizal 555,533 ....C3
Romblon 193,174 ....D4
Siquijor 70,300 ....D6
Sorsogon 500,685 ....E4
South Cotabato 770,473 ...E7
Southern Leyte 298,294 ...E5
Sultan Kudarat 303,784 ...E7
Sulu 360,588 ....C7

Surigao del Norte 363,414 ..F5
Surigao del Sur 377,647 ..F6
Tarlac 638,457 ....C3
Tawi-Tawi 194,651 ....B8
Western Samar 501,439 ....E5
Zambales 444,037 ....C3
Zamboanga del Norte
  588,015 ....D6
Zamboanga del Sur
  1,183,845 ....D7

CITIES and TOWNS

Angeles 188,834 ....C3
Aparri 45,070 ....C1
Bacolod 262,415 ....D5
Bagac 13,109 ....C3
Bago 99,631 ....D5
Baguio 119,009 ....C2
Balanga 39,132 ....C3
Baler 18,349 ....C3
Balimbing (Bato-Bato)
  22,189 ....C8
Bamban 26,072 ....C3
Basco 4,341 ....A2
Batangas 143,570 ....C4
Bato-Bato 22,189 ....C8
Baybay 74,640 ....E5
Bislig 81,615 ....F6
Boac 37,005 ....C4
Bontoc 17,091 ....C2
Burauen 48,058 ....E5
Butuan 172,489 ....E6
Cabanatuan 138,298 ......C3
Cabarroquis 17,450 ......C2
Cadiz 129,632 ....D5
Cagayan de Oro 227,312 ...E6
Calamba 121,175 ....C3
Calbayog 106,719 ....E4
Carigara 34,377 ....E5
Cauayan 70,017 ....D6
Cavite 87,666 ....C3
Cebu 490,281 ....D5
Cotabato 83,871 ....D7
Dagupan 98,344 ....C2
Davao 610,375 ....E7
Digos 70,065 ....E7
Escalante 71,293 ....D5
General Santos 149,396 ...E7
Gingoog 79,937 ....E6
Guihulngan 84,156 ....D5
Guimba 58,847 ....C3
Iba 22,791 ....B3
Ilagan 79,336 ....C2
Iligan 167,358 ....E6

Iloilo 244,827 ....D5
Infanta 27,914 ....C3
Jaro 29,739 ....E5
Jolo 52,429 ....C8
Koronadal 80,566 ....E7
Lagawe 15,075 ....C2
Lapu-Lapu 98,723 ....E5
Legazpi 99,766 ....D4
Ligao 69,860 ....D4
Lingayen 65,187 ....C2
Lipa 121,166 ....C4
Lucena 107,880 ....C4
Maganoy 45,845 ....E7
Mainit 18,078 ....E6
Malabang 18,955 ....D7
Malolos 95,699 ....C3
Mandaue 110,590 ....E5
Manila (cap.) 1,630,485 ..C3
Mariveles 48,594 ....C3
Mati 78,178 ....F7
Naga 90,712 ....D4
Olongapo 156,430 ....C3
Ormoc 104,978 ....E5
Ozamiz 77,832 ....D6
Pagadian 80,861 ....D7
Palo 31,124 ....E5
Palompon 40,242 ....E5
Panabo 71,098 ....E7
Prosperidad 33,824 ......F6
Puerto Princesa 60,234 ...B6
Quezon City 1,165,865 ....C3
Romblon 24,251 ....D4
Roxas 81,183 ....D5
Sagay 99,118 ....D5
San Antonio 42,969 ......B3
San Carlos, Negros Occ.
  91,627 ....D5
San Carlos, Pangasinan
  101,243 ....C3
San Fernando, La Union
  68,410 ....C2
San Fernando, Pampanga
  110,891 ....C3
San Jose 64,254 ....D7
San Jose del Monte 90,732 C3
San Pablo 131,655 ....C3
Santa Fe 6,338 ....C2
Santiago 69,877 ....C2
Silay 111,131 ....D5
Surigao 79,745 ....E6
Tacloban 102,523 ....E5
Tagaytay 16,322 ....C3
Tagum 86,201 ....E7
Tarlac 175,691 ....C3

Toledo 91,668 ....D5
Tuguegarao 73,507 ....C2
Zamboanga 343,722 ....C7

OTHER FEATURES

Agusan (riv.) E6
Alabat (isl.) D3
Apo (vol.) E7
Babuyan (isl.) B2
Balabac (isl.) A7
Balayan (bay) C4
Balintang (chan.) A2
Baloy (mt.) D5
Bantayan (isl.) D5
Banton (isl.) D4
Bashi (chan.) A1
Basilan (isl.) D7
Batan, Albay (isl.) E4
Batan, Batanes (isl.) ...B2
Batan (isls.) A2
Bay, Laguna de (lake) ...C3
Biliran (isl.) E5
Bohol (isl.) E6
Bojeador (cape) C1
Borocay (isl.) D5
Bucas Grande (isl.) F6
Bugsuk (isl.) A6
Buliluyan (cape) A6
Bunga (pt.) E4
Burias (isl.) D4
Busuanga (isl.) B4
Cabalcan (isl.) E5
Cabulauan (isls.) C5
Cagayan (isl.) C6
Cagayan (isls.) C7
Cagayan (riv.) C2
Cagayan Sulu (isl.) B7
Cagua (vol.) D1
Calagua (isls.) D3
Calamian Group (isls.) ..B4
Calayan (isl.) A2
Calicoan (isl.) E5
Camiguin, Cagayan (isl.) .B3
Camiguin, Camiguin (isl.) .E6
Camotes (isls.) E5
Camotes (sea) E5
Canigao (chan.) E5
Canlaon (peak) D5
Capotoan (mt.) E4
Carabao (isl.) D4
Catanduanes (isl.) E4
Cebu (isl.) D5
Celebes (sea) D8
Cleopatra Needle (mt.) ...B5
Coron (isl.) C5

Topography

0	100	200 MI.
0	100	200 KM.

BABUYAN IS.

C. Engaño

Luzon

Lingayen Gulf

C. Bolinao

CORDILLERA

SIERRA MADRE

PHILIPPINE SEA

Bataan Pen.

Manila

Manila Bay

Lamon Bay

Catanduanes

Marindu Mayon Vol.
7,943 ft. (2421 m.)

Mindoro

Aue Sibuyan Sea

Busuanga

CALAMIAN GROUP

Masbate

Samar Sea

Visayan Sea

Samar

Panay

Leyte

Leyte Gulf

Cebu

Palawan

Negros

Bohol

Bohol Sea

SULU SEA

Mindanao

Apo Vol.
9,692 ft. (2954 m.)

Moro Gulf

Pulangi

Agusan

Davao Gulf

Balabac

Basilan

Jolo

Mindanao Sea

SULU ARCH.

Tawi-Tawi

Tinaca Pt.

Below Sea Level	Sea Level	100 m. 328 ft.	200 m. 656 ft.	500 m. 1,640 ft.	1,000 m. 3,281 ft.	2,000 m. 6,562 ft.	5,000 m. 16,404 ft.

Agriculture, Industry and Resources

Cu

Tobacco

Au

Ag

Cu

Sugar Cane

Rice

Pb U

Manila

Coconuts

Fe

Abaca

Batangas

Cu

Rice

Bacolod

Mn

Sugar

Coconuts

Rice

Fe

Mn

Pearls

Coconut

Abaca

Iligan

Corn

Coconut

DOMINANT LAND USE

☐ Cereals (chiefly rice, corn)
▨ Cash Crops
▧ Tropical Forests

MAJOR MINERAL OCCURRENCES

Ag Silver
At Asphalt
Au Gold
C Coal
Cr Chromium
Cu Copper
Fe Iron
Hg Mercury
Mn Manganese
Ni Nickel
O Petroleum
Pb Lead
U Uranium

⚡ Water Power
▨ Major Industrial Areas

Corregidor (isl.) C3
Culion (isl.) B5
Cuyo (isl.) C5
Cuyo (isls.) C5
Daram (isl.) E5
Davao (gulf) E7
Dinagat (isl.) E5
Diuata (mts.) E6
Dumanquilas (bay) D7
Dumaran (isl.) C5
Engaño (cape) D1
Espíritu Santo (cape) ...E4
Fuga (isl.) A3
Guimaras (isl.) D5
Halcon (mt.) C4
Hibuson (isl.) E5
Homonhon (isl.) E5
Honda (bay) B6
Iligan (bay) E6
Ilin (isl.) C4
Illana (bay) D7
Imuruan (bay) B5
Island (bay) B6
Itbayat (isl.) A2
Jintotolo (chan.) D5
Jolo (isl.) C7
Jomalig (isl.) D3
Lagonoy (gulf) E4
Lamon (bay) C3
Lanao (lake) E7
Laparan (isls.) B8
Lapinin (isl.) E5
Leyte (gulf) E5
Leyte (isl.) E5
Limasawa (isl.) E6
Linapacan (isl.) B5
Lingayen (gulf) C2
Lubang (isls.) B4
Luzon (isl.) C3
Luzon (str.) A2
Macajalar (bay) E6
Malindang (mt.) D6

Mangsee (isls.) A7
Manila (bay) C3
Mantalingajan (mt.) A6
Maqueda (chan.) D3
Maraira (pt.) C1
Marinduque (isl.) C4
Masbate (isl.) D4
Mayon (vol.) D4
Maytiguid (isl.) B5
Mindanao (isl.) D7
Mindanao (riv.) E7
Mindoro (isl.) C4
Mindoro (str.) C4
Mompog (passg.) D4
Moro (gulf) D7
Mount Apo National Park ..E7
Naso (pt.) C5
Negros (isl.) D6
Olutanga (isl.) D7
Pacsan (mt.) C2
Palawan (isl.) B6
Palawan (passg.) A6
Panaon (isl.) E5
Panay (isl.) D5
Panglao (isl.) D6
Pangutaran (isl.) C7
Pangutaran Group (isls.) .C7
Patnanongan (isl.) D3
Philippine (sea) D3
Pilas (isl.) C7
Pinatubo (mt.) C3
Polillo (isl.) C3
Pujada (bay) F7
Pulangi (riv.) E7
Ragang (vol.) E7
Ragay (gulf) D4
Rapu-Rapu (isl.) D4
Romblon (isl.) D4
Sabtang (isl.) B2
Sacol (isl.) D7
Samal (isl.) E7
Samales Group (isls.) ...D7

Samar (isl.) E5
Samar (cape) E4
San Agustin (cape) F7
San Bernardino (str.) ...E4
San Miguel (bay) D3
San Pedro (bay) E5
Santo Tomas (mt.) C2
Semirara (isls.) C5
Siargao (isl.) F6
Sibay (isl.) C5
Sibuguey (bay) D7
Sibutu Group (isls.) B8
Sibuyan (isl.) D4
Sibuyan (sea) D4
Sierra Madre (mt.) D2
Simunul (isl.) B8
Siquijor (isl.) D6
South China (sea) B3
Subic (bay) C3
Sulu (arch.) B8
Sulu (sea) B6
Suluan (isl.) F5
Surigao (str.) E6
Taal (lake) C4
Tablas (isl.) D4
Tablas (str.) C4
Tagapula (isl.) E4
Tagolo (pt.) D6
Tanon (str.) D6
Tapul (isl.) C8
Tapul Group (isls.) C8
Tara (isl.) C4
Tawi-Tawi (isl.) B8
Tayabas (bay) C4
Ticao (isl.) D4
Tinaca (pt.) E8
Tongquil (isl.) D8
Tumindao (isl.) B8
Turtle (isls.) B7
Verde Island (passg.) ...C4
Victoria (peaks) B6
Visayan (sea) D5

BRUNEI

CITIES and TOWNS

Bandar Seri Begawan 63,868 E4
Seria 23,511 E5

INDONESIA

CITIES and TOWNS

Adaut J7
Agats K7
Ambon (Amboina) 208,898 H6
Amuntai F6
Amurang G5
Atambua G7
Aubá H7
Baa G8
Bagansiapiapi C5
Balikpapan 280,675 F6
Banda Aceh 72,090 A4
Bandanaira H6
Bandung 1,462,637 H2
Banggai G6
Banjarmasin 381,286 E6
Banyumas J2
Batang J2
Batavia (Jakarta) (cap.) 6,503,449 H1
Baukau H7
Bekasi H2
Belawan B5
Bengkulu 64,783 C6
Beo H5
Biak K6
Binjai 76,464 B5
Bintuhan C6
Blitar 78,503 K2
Bogor 247,409 H2
Bojonegoro J2
Bukittinggi 70,771 B6
Bula J6
Bulukumba G7
Buntok F6
Cianjur H2
Cimahi H2
Cirebon 223,776 H2
Demta L6
Denpasar E7
Dili H7
Djambi (Jambi) 230,373 C6
Djokjakarta (Yogyakarta) 398,727 J2
Dobo J7
Donggala F6
Enaratoli K6
Ende G7
Fakfak J6
Garut H2
Gorontalo 97,628 G5
Hollandia (Jayapura) K6
Indramayu H2
Jailolo H5
Jakarta (cap.) 6,503,449 H1
Jambi 230,373 C6
Jayapura (Hollandia) K6
Jogjakarta (Yogyakarta) 398,727 J2
Jombang K2
Kaimana J6
Kampung Baru (Tolitoli) G5
Kediri 221,820 K2
Kendari G6
Kepi K7
Ketapang E6
Kokonau K6
Kolonodale G6
Kotabaharu E6
Kotabaru F6
Kotawaringin E6
Kragen K2
Kupang G8
Kutaraja (Banda Aceh) 72,090 A4
Labuha H6
Labuhan G2
Laiwui H6
Larantuka G7
Lekitobi H6
Longiram F5
Madiun 150,562 K2
Magelang 123,484 J2
Majalengka H2
Makassar (Ujung Pandang) 709,038 F7
Malang 511,780 K2
Malili G6
Manado 217,159 G5
Manokwari J6
Maumere G7
Medan 1,378,955 B5
Menggala D6
Merauke K7
Mindiptana L7
Mojokerto 68,849 K2
Muarasiberut B6
Nangatayap E6
Pacitan J2
Padang 480,922 B6
Padangpanjang 34,517 B6
Padangsidempuan B5
Pakanbaru 186,262 C5
Palangkaraya 60,447 E6
Palembang 787,187 D6
Pangkalanbuun E6
Pangkalpinang 90,096 D6
Parepare 86,450 F6
Pasangkayu F6
Pasuruan 95,864 K2
Payakumbuh 78,836 C6
Pekalongan 132,558 J2
Pemalang J2
Pematangsiantar 150,376 B5
Pinrang F6
Plaju D6
Pontianak 304,778 D6
Probolinggo 100,296 K2
Purbolinggo J2
Raha G6
Rantauprapat C5
Rembang K2
Sabang, Celebes F5
Sabang, Weh 23,821 B4
Salatiga 85,849 J2
Samarinda 264,718 F6
Sampit E6
Sarmi K6
Sawahlunto 13,561 C6
Seba G8
Semarang 1,026,671 J2
Semitau E5
Serui K6
Sibolga 59,897 B5
Sigli B4
Sinabang B5
Singaraja F7
Solo (Surakarta) 469,888 J2
Solok 31,724 C6
Sorong J6
Sragen J2
Subang H2
Sukabumi 109,994 H2
Sumbawa Besar F7
Sumedang H2
Surabaya 2,027,913 K2
Surakarta 469,888 J2
Tanahmerah K7
Tanjungbalai 41,894 C5
Tanjungkarang 284,275 D7
Tanjungpinang C5
Tanjungselor F5
Tarakan F5
Tebingtinggi 92,087 B5
Tegal 131,728 J2
Telukbayur C6
Tepa H7
Terempa D5
Tjilatjap (Cilicap) H2
Tjirebon (Cirebon) 223,776 H2
Tolitoli G5
Tuban K2
Ujung Pandang 709,038 F7
Vikeke H7
Wahai H6
Waigama H6
Wajabula H5
Waren K6
Weda H5
Wonreli H7
Yogyakarta 398,727 J2

OTHER FEATURES

Anambas (isls.) 29,572 D5
Arafura (sea) J8
Aru (isls.) 34,195 K7
Babar (isl.) H7
Bali (isl.) 2,074,438 F7
Banda (sea) H7
Banggai (arch.) 169,025 G6
Bangka (isl.) 298,017 D6
Banyak (isls.) 1,980 B5
Barisan (mts.) C6
Barito (riv.) E6
Batu (isls.) 16,390 B6
Bawean (isl.) 64,551 K1
Belitung (Billiton) (isl.) 128,694 D6
Berau (bay) J6
Biak (isl.) K6
Billiton (isl.) 128,694 D6
Binongko (isl.) 11,549 G7
Bone (gulf) G7
Borneo (isl.) E5
Bosch, van den (cape) J6
Bunguran (Great Natuna) (isl.) D5
Buru (isl.) 23,034 H6
Butung (isl.) 188,173 G6
Celebes (Sulawesi) (isl.) 7,732,383 G5
Celebes (sea) G5
Cenderawasih (bay) K6
Dampier (str.) J6
Digul (riv.) K7
Doberai (pen.) J6
Enggano (isl.) 1,082 C7
Ewab (Kai) (isls.) 108,328 J7
Flores (isl.) 860,328 G7
Flores (sea) F7
Frederik Hendrik (Kolepom) (isl.) K7
Geelvink (Cenderawasih) (bay) K6
Great Kai (isl.) 38,748 J7
Halmahera (isl.) 122,521 H5
Irian Jaya (reg.) 923,440 J6
Jambuair (cape) B4
Jamursba (cape) J5
Java (head) C7
Java (isl.) 73,712,411 J2
Java (sea) D6
Jaya, Puncak (mt.) K6
Jayawijaya (range) K6
Jemaja (isl.) 5,628 D5
Kabaena (isl.) G7
Kai (isls.) 108,328 J7
Kalao (isl.) G7
Kalaotoa (isl.) G5
Kalimantan (reg.) 4,956,865 E5
Kangean (isl.) F7
Kapuas (riv.) D6
Karakelong (isl.) H5
Karimata (arch.) 9,398 D6
Karimunjawa (isls.) 5,025 J1
Kerinci (mt.) C6
Kisar (isl.) H7
Komodo (isl.) 30,407 F7
Krakatau (Rakata) (isl.) C7
Laut (isl.) 55,711 F6
Leuser (mt.) B5
Lingga (arch.) 46,658 D5
Lingga (isl.) 18,027 D6
Lombok (isl.) 1,581,193 F7
Madura (isl.) 1,509,774 K2
Mahakam (riv.) F6
Makassar (str.) F6
Malacca (str.) C5
Mamberamo (riv.) K6
Maoke (mts.) K6
Mapia (isls.) J5
Mentawai (isls.) 30,107 B6
Misool (isl.) J6
Molucca (sea) H6
Moluccas (isls.) 944,240 H6
Morotai (isl.) 27,333 H5
Muli (str.) K7
Müller (mts.) E5
Muna (isl.) 156,186 G7
Musi (riv.) C6
Natuna (isls.) 23,893 D5
Ngunju (cape) F8
Nias (isl.) 356,093 B5
Numfoor (isl.) J6
Obi (isls.) 12,437 H6
Ombai (str.) H7
Pantar (isl.) 28,259 G7
Perkam (cape) K6
Puting, Borneo (cape) E6
Puting, Sumatra (cape) C7
Raja Ampat Group (isls.) H6
Rakata (isl.) C7
Rantekombola (mt.) F6
Raya (mt.) E6
Riau (arch.) 483,230 C5
Rokan (riv.) C5
Roti (isl.) 76,270 G8
Salawati (isl.) J6
Sangihe (isl.) H5
Sangihe (isls.) 183,000 G5
Sawu (isls.) 51,002 G8
Sawu (sea) G7
Schouten (isls.) 110,148 K6
Schwaner (mts.) E6
Sebuku (bay) F5
Selatan (cape) E6
Selayar (isl.) 92,342 G7
Semeru (mt.) K2
Siau (isl.) 46,801 H5
Siberut (str.) B6
Simeulue (isl.) 29,147 A5
Singkep (isl.) 28,631 D6
Sipura (isl.) 6,051 B6
Slamet (mt.) J2
Sorikmerapi (mt.) B5
South Natuna (isls.) D5
Sudirman (range) K6
Sula (isls.) 36,922 H6
Sulawesi (isl.) 7,732,383 G6
Sumatra (isl.) 19,360,400 B5
Sumba (isl.) 291,190 F7
Sumba (str.) F7
Sumbawa (isl.) 621,140 F7
Sunda (str.) C7
Tahulandang (isl.) 21,493 H5
Talaud (isls.) 46,395 H5
Taliabu (isl.) 18,303 G6
Tambelan (isls.) 4,032 D5
Tanimbar (isls.) 55,405 J7
Tariku (riv.) K6
Tidore (isl.) 28,655 H5
Timor (reg.) 1,435,527 H7
Timor (sea) H7
Toba (lake) B5
Tolo (gulf) G6
Tomini (gulf) G6
Tukangbesi (isls.) 73,106 G7
Vals (cape) K7
Vogelkop (Doberai) (pen.) J6
Waigeo (isl.) J5
Wakde (isl.) K6
Wangiwangi (isl.) 28,469 G7
We (isl.) B4
Wetar (isl.) H7
Yapen (isl.) 50,888 K6

MALAYSIA

STATES

North Borneo (Sabah) 1,002,608 F3
Sarawak 1,294,753 E5

CITIES and TOWNS

Beaufort 2,709 F4
Bintulu 4,424 E5
Kabong E5
Kampong Sibuti E5
Kapit 1,929 E5
Keningau 2,037 F4
Kota Kinabalu 40,939 F4
Kuching 63,535 E5
Kudat 5,089 F4
Labuan 7,216 E4
Lahad Datu 5,169 F5
Lamag F4
Marudi 4,700 E5
Miri 35,702 E5
Mukah 1,717 E5

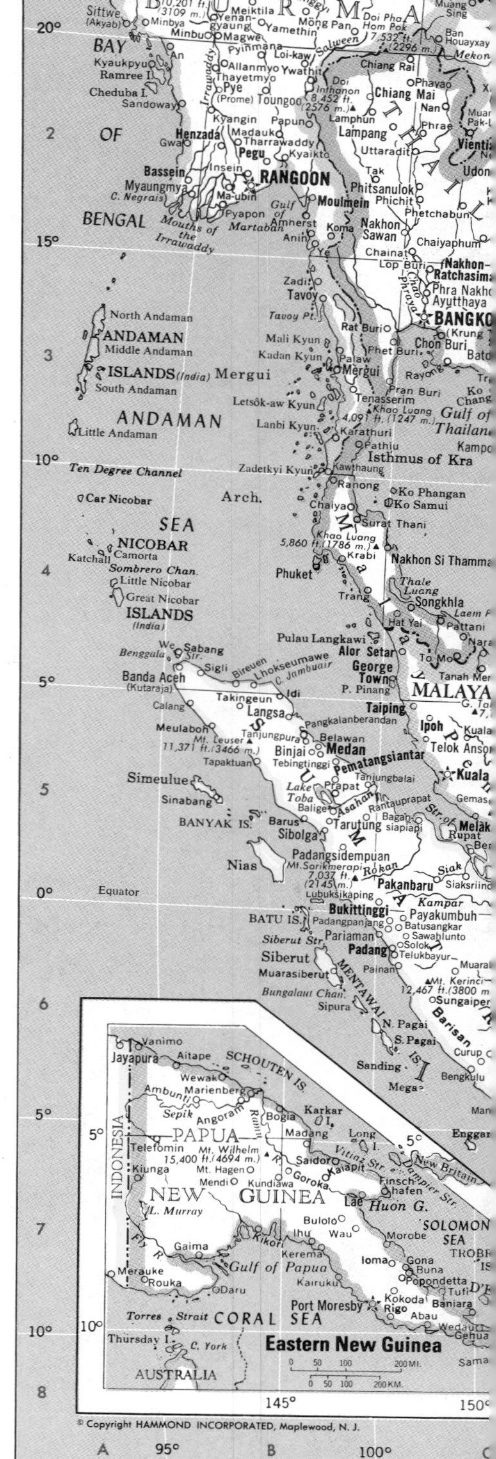
Mandalay
Rangoon
Moulmein
Bangkok
Andaman Sea
Nicobar Islands (India)
Isthmus of Kra
Gulf of Thailand
Malaya
Kuala Lumpur
Medan
Padang
Equator
Eastern New Guinea
Port Moresby
Papua New Guinea
Coral Sea
Australia
© Copyright HAMMOND INCORPORATED, Maplewood, N. J.

Topography

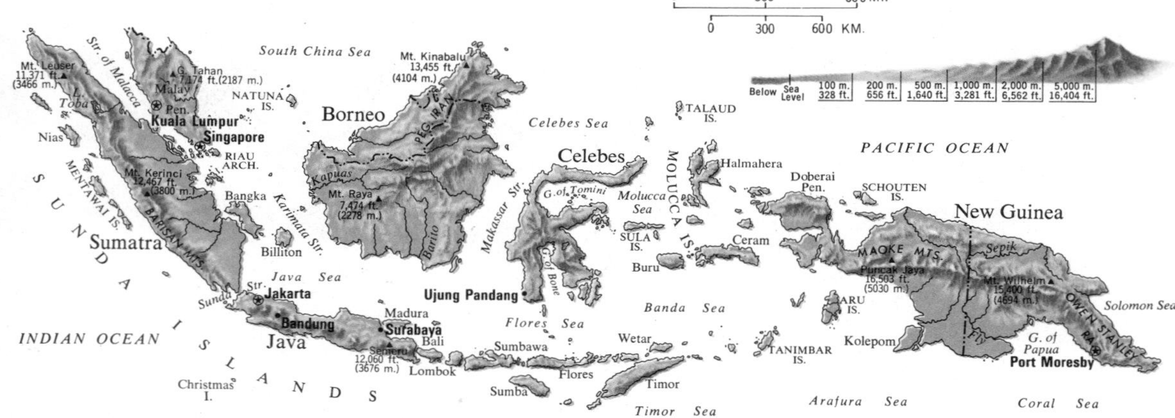
South China Sea
Mt. Kinabalu 13,455 ft. (4104 m.)
Borneo
Celebes Sea
Talaud Is.
Pacific Ocean
Celebes
Halmahera
Doberai Pen.
Schouten Is.
New Guinea
Molucca Sea
Sumatra
Kuala Lumpur
Singapore
Riau Arch.
Bangka
Billiton
Java Sea
Jakarta
Bandung
Java
Surabaya
Madura
Bali
Lombok
Ujung Pandang
Flores Sea
Banda Sea
Sumbawa
Flores
Sumba
Timor
Timor Sea
Arafura Sea
Coral Sea
Solomon Sea
Port Moresby
Kolepom
Tanimbar Is.
Ceram
Buru
Sula Is.
Nias
Mentawai Is.
Indian Ocean
Sunda Islands
Christmas I.
Below Sea Level
100 m. 328 ft.
200 m. 656 ft.
500 m. 1,640 ft.
1,000 m. 3,281 ft.
2,000 m. 6,562 ft.
5,000 m. 16,404 ft.
0 300 600 MI.
0 300 600 KM.

Agriculture, Industry and Resources

Pearls
Rubber
Rice
Millet
Spices
Coconuts
Coffee
Singapore
Jakarta
Corn
Sugar cane
Tobacco
Turtles
Tea

DOMINANT LAND USE

- Cereals (chiefly rice, corn)
- Diversified Tropical Crops
- Forests

MAJOR MINERAL OCCURRENCES

Al Bauxite
Au Gold
C Coal
Cu Copper
Fe Iron Ore
G Natural Gas
Mn Manganese
Ni Nickel
O Petroleum
Sn Tin

Major Industrial Areas

INDONESIA

AREA 788,430 sq. mi. (2,042,034 sq. km.)
POPULATION 147,490,298
CAPITAL Jakarta
LARGEST CITY Jakarta
HIGHEST POINT Puncak Jaya 16,503 ft. (5,030 m.)
MONETARY UNIT rupiah
MAJOR LANGUAGES Bahasa Indonesia, Indonesian and Papuan languages, English
MAJOR RELIGIONS Islam, tribal religions, Christianity, Hinduism

PAPUA NEW GUINEA

AREA 183,540 sq. mi. (475,369 sq. km.)
POPULATION 3,010,727
CAPITAL Port Moresby
LARGEST CITY Port Moresby
HIGHEST POINT Mt. Wilhelm 15,400 ft. (4,694 m.)
MONETARY UNIT kina
MAJOR LANGUAGES pidgin English, Hiri Motu, English
MAJOR RELIGIONS Tribal religions, Christianity

BRUNEI

AREA 2,226 sq. mi. (5,765 sq. km.)
POPULATION 192,832
CAPITAL Bandar Seri Begawan
LARGEST CITY Bandar Seri Begawan
HIGHEST POINT Pagon 6,070 ft. (1,850 m.)
MONETARY UNIT Brunei Dollar
MAJOR LANGUAGES Malay, English, Chinese
MAJOR RELIGIONS Islam, Buddhism, Christianity, tribal religions

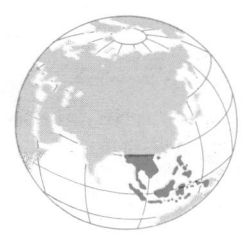

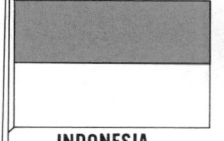

INDONESIA

PAPUA NEW GUINEA

BRUNEI

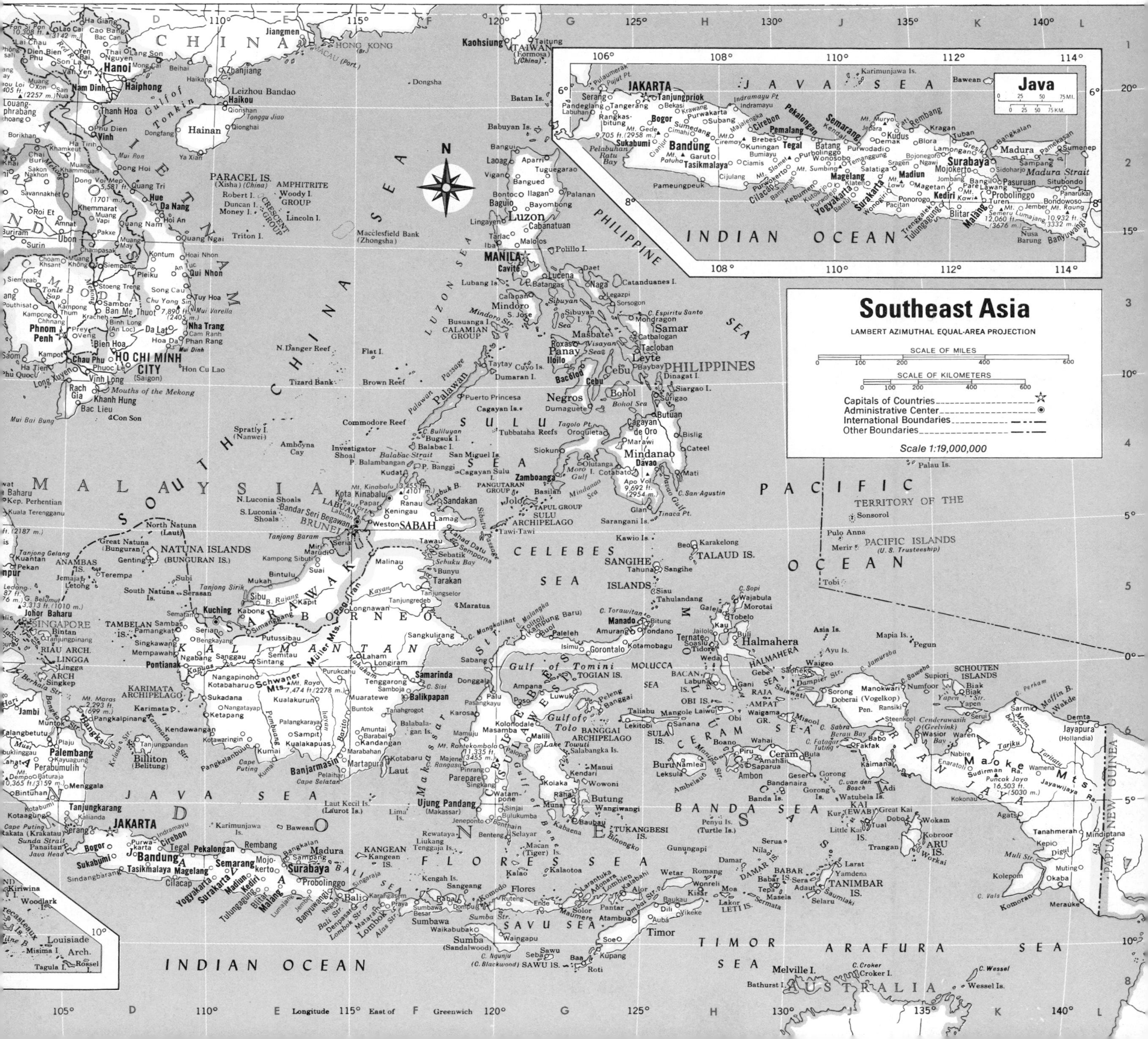

FIJI

AREA 7,055 sq. mi. (18,272 sq. km.)
POPULATION 588,068
CAPITAL Suva
LARGEST CITY Suva
HIGHEST POINT Tomaniivi 4,341 ft. (1,323 m.)
MONETARY UNIT Fijian dollar
MAJOR LANGUAGES Fijian, Hindi, English
MAJOR RELIGIONS Protestantism, Hinduism

KIRIBATI

AREA 291 sq. mi. (754 sq. km.)
POPULATION 56,213
CAPITAL Bairiki (Tarawa)
HIGHEST POINT (on Banaba I.) 285 ft. (87 m.)
MONETARY UNIT Australian dollar
MAJOR LANGUAGES I-Kiribati, English
MAJOR RELIGIONS Protestantism, Roman Catholicism

NAURU

AREA 7.7 sq. mi. (20 sq. km.)
POPULATION 7,254
CAPITAL Yaren (district)
MONETARY UNIT Australian dollar
MAJOR LANGUAGES Nauruan, English
MAJOR RELIGION Protestantism

SOLOMON ISLANDS

AREA 11,500 sq. mi. (29,785 sq. km.)
POPULATION 221,000
CAPITAL Honiara
HIGHEST POINT Mount Popomanatseu 7,647 ft. (2,331 m.)
MONETARY UNIT Solomon Islands dollar
MAJOR LANGUAGES English, pidgin English, Melanesian dialects
MAJOR RELIGIONS Tribal religions, Protestantism, Roman Catholicism

TONGA

AREA 270 sq. mi. (699 sq. km.)
POPULATION 90,128
CAPITAL Nuku'alofa
LARGEST CITY Nuku'alofa
HIGHEST POINT 3,389 ft. (1,033 m.)
MONETARY UNIT pa'anga
MAJOR LANGUAGES Tongan, English
MAJOR RELIGION Protestantism

TUVALU

AREA 9.78 sq. mi. (25.33 sq. km.)
POPULATION 7,349
CAPITAL Fongafale (Funafuti)
HIGHEST POINT 15 ft. (4.6 m.)
MONETARY UNIT Australian dollar
MAJOR LANGUAGES English, Tuvaluan
MAJOR RELIGION Protestantism

Abaiang (atoll) 3,296 . . . . . H 5
Abemama (atoll) 2,300 . . . . . H 5
Adamstown (cap.), Pitcairn Is. 54 . . . . . N 8
Admiralty (isls.) . . . . . E 6
Agaña (cap.), Guam 896 . . . . E 4
Agrihan (isl.) . . . . . E 4
Ailinglapalap (atoll) 1,385 . . G 5
Ailuk (atoll) 413 . . . . . H 4
Aitutaki (atoll) 2,348 . . . . . K 7
Alofi (cap.), Niue 960 . . . . . K 7
Alotau 4,310 . . . . . E 7
Ambrym (isl.) 6,324 . . . . . G 7
Anaa (atoll) 444 . . . . . M 7
Angaur (isl.) 243 . . . . . D 5
Apataki (atoll) 1,487 . . . . . M 7
Apia (cap.), W. Samoa 33,100 . J 7
Arno (atoll) 1,487 . . . . . H 5
Arorae (atoll) 1,626 . . . . . H 6
Atafu (atoll) 577 . . . . . J 6
Atiu (isl.) -1,225 . . . . . L 8
Austral (isls.) 5,208 . . . . . L 8
Avarua (cap.), Cook Is. . . . . . L 8
Babelthuap (isl.) 10,391 . . . D 5
Bairiki (cap.), Kiribati 1,777 . H 5
Baker (isl.) . . . . . J 5
Banaba (isl.) 2,314 . . . . . G 6
Banks (isls.) 3,158 . . . . . G 7
Belau (Palau) 12,116 . . . . . D 5
Belep (isls.) 624 . . . . . G 7
Bellona (reefs) . . . . . G 8
Beru (atoll) 2,318 . . . . . H 6
Bikini (atoll) . . . . . G 4
Bismarck (arch.) 218,339 . . . E 6
Bonin (isls.) 1,879 . . . . . E 3
Bora-Bora (isl.) 2,572 . . . . L 7
Bougainville (isl.) 71,761 . . . F 6
Bounty (isls.) . . . . . H 10
Bourail 3,149 . . . . . G 8
Butaritari (atoll) 2,971 . . . . H 5
Canton (isl.) . . . . . J 6
Capitol Hill (cap.), No. Marianas 592 . . . . . E 4
Caroline (isl.) . . . . . M 7
Caroline (isls.) . . . . . E 5
Chichi (isl.) . . . . . E 3
Choiseul (isl.) 10,349 . . . . F 6
Christmas (Kirimati) (isl.) 674 . L 5
Cook (isls.) 17,695 . . . . . K 7
Coral (sea) . . . . . F 7
Danger (Pukapuka) (atoll) 797 . . . . . K 7
Daru 7,127 . . . . . E 6
Disappointment (isls.) 373 . . . N 7
Ducie (isl.) . . . . . O 8
Easter (isl.) 1,598 . . . . . Q 8
Ebon (atoll) 887 . . . . . G 5
Efate (isl.) 18,038 . . . . . G 7
Enderbury (isl.) . . . . . J 6
Enewetak (Eniwetok) (atoll) 542 . . . . . G 4
Erromanga (isl.) 945 . . . . . H 7
Espiritu Santo (isl.) 16,220 . . G 7
Fais (isl.) 207 . . . . . E 5
Fakaofo (atoll) 654 . . . . . J 6
Fanning (Tabuaeron) (isl.) 340 L 5
Faraulep (atoll) 132 . . . . . E 5
Fatuhiva (isl.) 386 . . . . . N 7
Fiji 588,068 . . . . . H 8
Flint (isl.) . . . . . L 7
Fly (riv.) . . . . . E 6
Fongafale (cap.), Tuvalu . . . . H 6
French Polynesia 137,382 . . . L 8
Funafuti (atoll) 2,120 . . . . . H 6
Futuna (Hoorn) (isls.) 3,173 . . J 7
Gambier (isls.) 556 . . . . . N 8
Gardner (isl.) . . . . . J 6
Gilbert (isls.) 47,711 . . . . . H 6
Greenwich (Kapingamarangi) (atoll) 508 . . . . . F 5
Guadalcanal (isl.) 46,619 . . . F 7
Guam (isl.) 105,979 . . . . . E 4
Hall (isls.) 647 . . . . . F 5
Hawaiian (isls.) 964,691 . . . J 3
Henderson (isl.) . . . . . O 8
Hivaoa (isl.) 1,159 . . . . . N 6
Honiara (cap.), Solomon Is. 14,942 . . . . . F 6
Hoorn (isls.) 3,173 . . . . . J 7
Howland (isl.) . . . . . J 5
Huahine (isl.) 3,140 . . . . . L 7
Hull (isl.) . . . . . J 6
Huon (gulf) . . . . . E 6
Ifalik (atoll) 389 . . . . . E 5
Iwo (isl.) . . . . . E 3
Jaluit (atoll) 1,450 . . . . . G 5
Jarvis (isl.) . . . . . K 6
Johnston (atoll) 327 . . . . . K 4
Kadavu (Kandavu) (isl.) 8,699 H 7
Kapingamarangi (atoll) 508 . . F 5
Kavieng 4,633 . . . . . E 6
Kermadec (isls.) 5 . . . . . J 9
Kieta 3,491 . . . . . F 6
Kimbe 4,662 . . . . . F 6
Kingman (reef) . . . . . K 5
Kiribati 57,500 . . . . . J 6
Kirimati (isl.) 674 . . . . . L 5
Kolonia (cap.), Micronesia 5,549 . . . . . F 5
Koror (cap.), Belau 6,222 . . . D 5
Kosrae (isl.) 5,491 . . . . . G 5
Kwajalein (atoll) 6,624 . . . . G 5
Lae 61,617 . . . . . E 6
Lau Group (isls.) 14,452 . . . J 7
Lavongai (isl.) . . . . . F 6
Lifu (isl.) 7,585 . . . . . G 8
Line (isls.) . . . . . K 5
Little Makin (atoll) 1,445 . . . H 5
Lord Howe (Ontong Java) (isl.) 1,082 . . . . . G 6
Lord Howe (isl.) 287 . . . . . G 9
Lorengau 3,986 . . . . . E 6
Louisiade (arch.) . . . . . F 7
Loyalty (isls.) 14,518 . . . . G 8
Luganville 4,935 . . . . . G 7
Madang 21,335 . . . . . E 6

Majuro (atoll) (cap.), Marshall Is. 8,583 . . . . . H 5
Makin (Butaritari) (atoll) 2,971 H 5
Malaita (isl.) 50,912 . . . . . G 6
Malden (isl.) . . . . . L 6
Malakula (isl.) 15,931 . . . . G 7
Maloelap (atoll) 763 . . . . . H 5
Mangaia (isl.) 1,364 . . . . . L 8
Mangareva (isl.) 556 . . . . . N 8
Manihiki (atoll) 405 . . . . . K 7
Manua (isls.) 1,459 . . . . . K 7
Manus (isl.) 25,844 . . . . . E 6
Marcus (isl.) . . . . . F 3
Maré (isl.) 4,156 . . . . . G 8
Marianas, Northern 16,780 . . E 4
Mariana Trench . . . . . E 4
Marquesas (isls.) 5,419 . . . . N 6
Marshall Islands 30,873 . . . . G 4
Marutea (atoll) . . . . . N 8
Mata Utu (cap.), Wallis and Futuna 558 . . . . . J 7
Mauke (isl.) 684 . . . . . L 8
Melanesia (reg.) . . . . . E 5
Micronesia (reg.) . . . . . E 4
Micronesia, Federated States of 73,160 . . . . . F 5
Midway (isls.) 453 . . . . . J 3
Mili (atoll) 763 . . . . . H 5
Moen (isl.) 10,351 . . . . . F 5
Moorea (isl.) 5,788 . . . . . L 7

Mururoa (isl.) . . . . . M 8
Nadi 6,938 . . . . . H 7
Namonuito (atoll) 783 . . . . E 5
Namorik (atoll) 617 . . . . . G 5
Nanumea (atoll) 844 . . . . . H 6
Nauru 7,254 . . . . . G 6
Ndeni (isl.) 4,854 . . . . . G 7
New Britain (isl.) 148,773 . . . F 6
New Caledonia 133,233 . . . . G 8
New Caledonia (isl.) 118,715 . G 8
New Georgia (isls.) 16,472 . . F 6
New Guinea (isl.) . . . . . E 6
New Ireland (isl.) 65,657 . . . F 6
Ngatik (atoll) 560 . . . . . F 5
Ngulu (atoll) 21 . . . . . D 5
Niuatoputapu (isl.) 1,650 . . . J 7
Niue (isl.) 3,578 . . . . . K 7
Niutao (atoll) 866 . . . . . H 6
Nomoi (isls.) 1,879 . . . . . F 5
Nonouti (atoll) 2,223 . . . . . H 6
Norfolk Island (terr.) 2,175 . . G 8
Northern Marianas 16,780 . . E 4
Nouméa (cap.), New Caled. 56,078 . . . . . G 8
Nouméa *74,335 . . . . . G 8
Nui (atoll) 603 . . . . . H 6
Nuku'alofa (cap.), Tonga 18,356 . . . . . J 8
Nukuhiva (isl.) 1,484 . . . . M 6
Ocean (Banaba) (isl.) 2,314 . . G 6

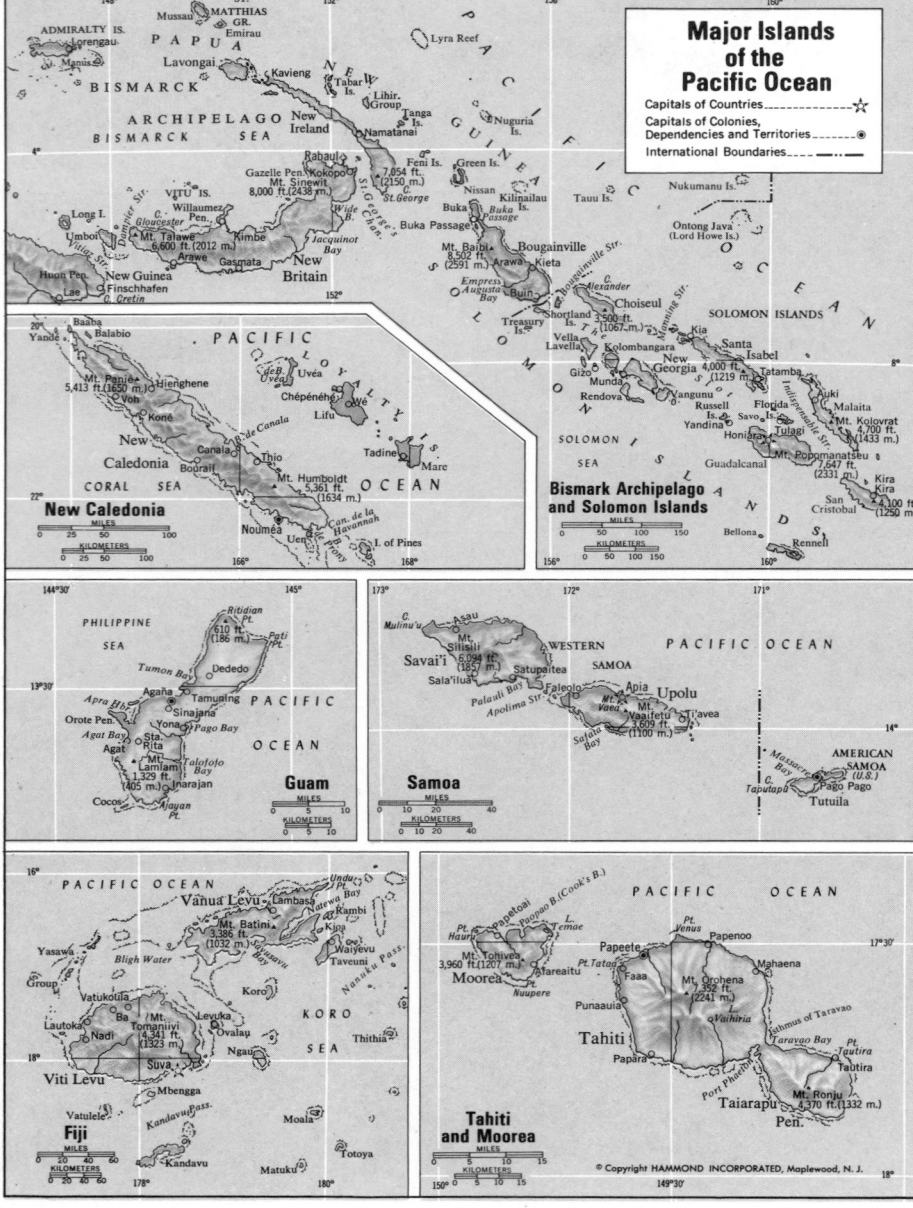

Major Islands of the Pacific Ocean

Capitals of Countries ....☆
Capitals of Colonies, Dependencies and Territories ......●
International Boundaries ....——·——

New Caledonia

Bismark Archipelago and Solomon Islands

Guam

Samoa

Fiji

Tahiti and Moorea

© Copyright HAMMOND INCORPORATED, Maplewood, N.J.

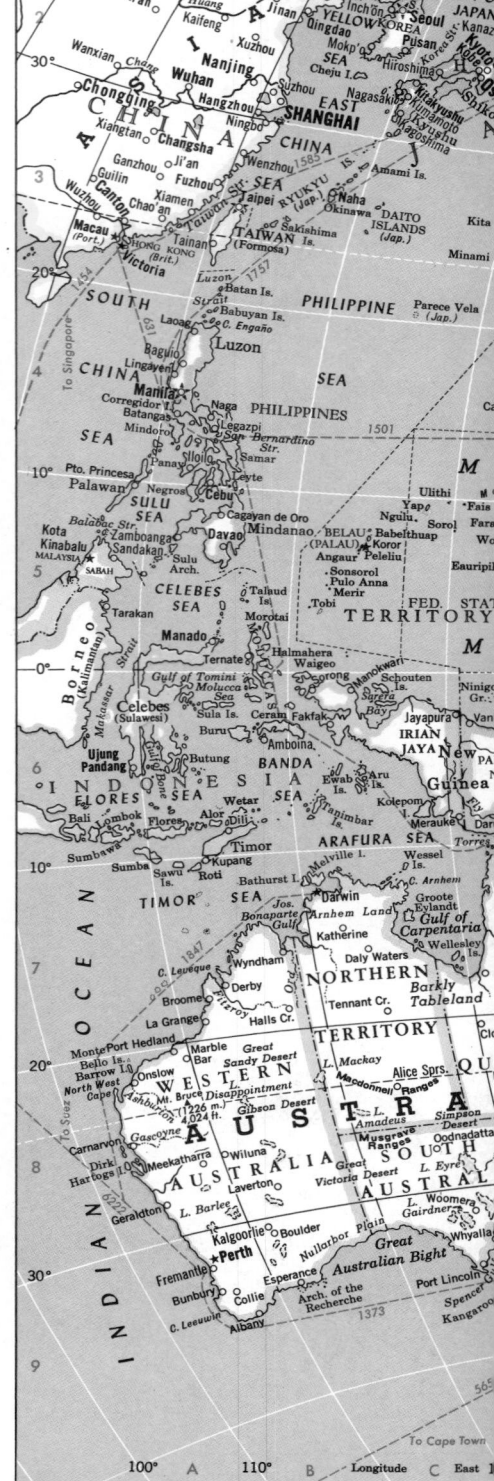

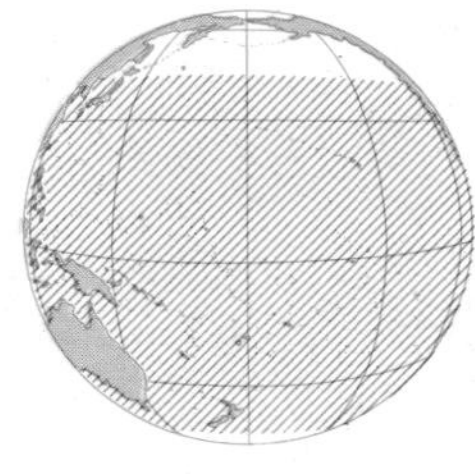

VANUATU

AREA 5,700 sq. mi. (14,763 sq. km.)
POPULATION 112,596
CAPITAL Vila
HIGHEST POINT Mt. Tabwemasana
  6,165 ft. (1,879 m.)
MONETARY UNIT vatu
MAJOR LANGUAGES Bislama, English,
  French
MAJOR RELIGIONS Christian, animist

WESTERN SAMOA

AREA 1,133 sq. mi. (2,934 sq. km.)
POPULATION 158,130
CAPITAL Apia
LARGEST CITY Apia
HIGHEST POINT Mt. Silisili 6,094 ft.
  (1,857 m.)
MONETARY UNIT tala
MAJOR LANGUAGES Samoan, English
MAJOR RELIGIONS Protestantism,
  Roman Catholicism

FIJI

TONGA

KIRIBATI

TUVALU

NAURU

VANUATU

SOLOMON ISLANDS

WESTERN SAMOA

Pacific Ocean

LAMBERT AZIMUTHAL EQUAL-AREA PROJECTION

©Copyright HAMMOND INCORPORATED, Maplewood, N.J.

NAUTICAL MILES
0 200 400 600 800 1000 1200
STATUTE MILES
0 200 400 600 800 1000 1200
KILOMETERS
0 200 400 600 800 1000 1200

Capitals of Countries .... ☆
Capitals of Colonies,
  Dependencies, States and Territories ... ★
Administrative Centers .... •
International Boundaries ....
Internal Boundaries ....
Railroads ....
Distances Between Points 5444
  (nautical miles)

Scale 1:50,000,000

Australia

CONIC PROJECTION

MILES

0 50 100 200 300 400 500

KILOMETERS

0 50 100 200 300 400 500

Capital of Country .... ⊛
State & Territorial Capitals .... ⊛
International Boundaries ....
State & Territorial Boundaries ....

Scale 1:19,000,000

© Copyright HAMMOND INCORPORATED, Maplewood, N.J.

AREA 2,966,136 sq. mi. (7,682,300 sq. km.)
POPULATION 14,576,330
CAPITAL Canberra
LARGEST CITY Sydney
HIGHEST POINT Mt. Kosciusko 7,310 ft.
(2,228 m.)
LOWEST POINT Lake Eyre -39 ft. (-12 m.)
MONETARY UNIT Australian dollar
MAJOR LANGUAGE English
MAJOR RELIGIONS Protestantism,
Roman Catholicism

Population Distribution

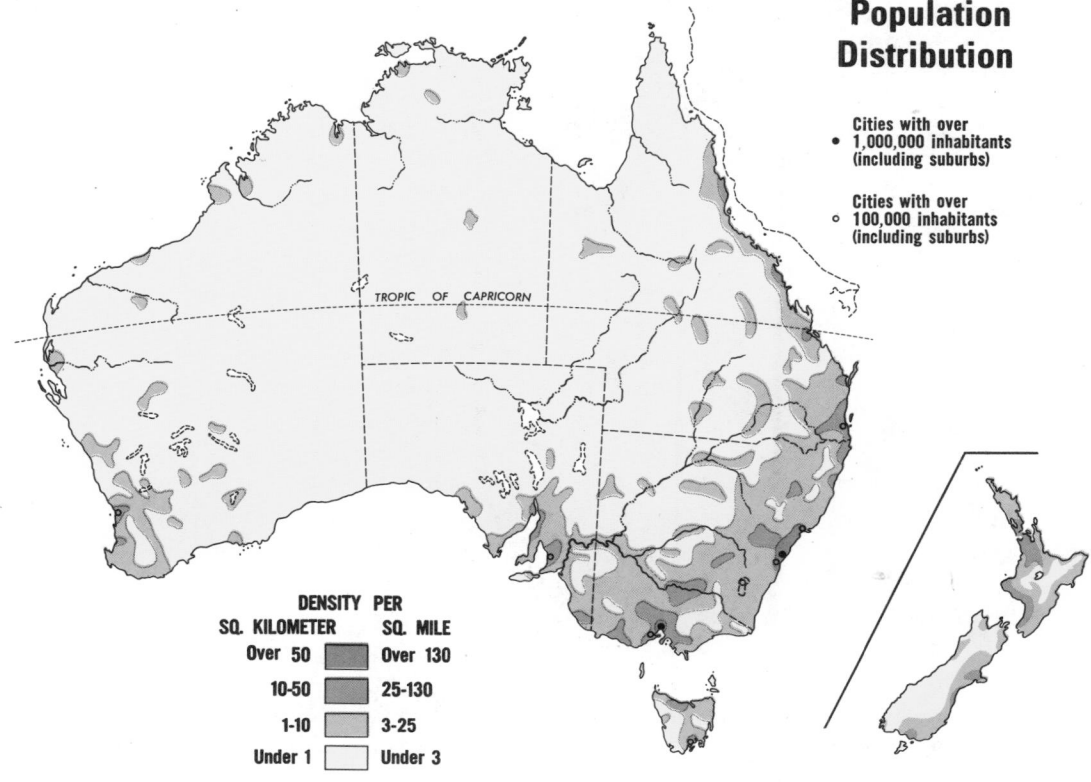

● Cities with over
1,000,000 inhabitants
(including suburbs)

○ Cities with over
100,000 inhabitants
(including suburbs)

DENSITY PER

SQ. KILOMETER		SQ. MILE
Over 50		Over 130
10-50		25-130
1-10		3-25
Under 1		Under 3

Vegetation

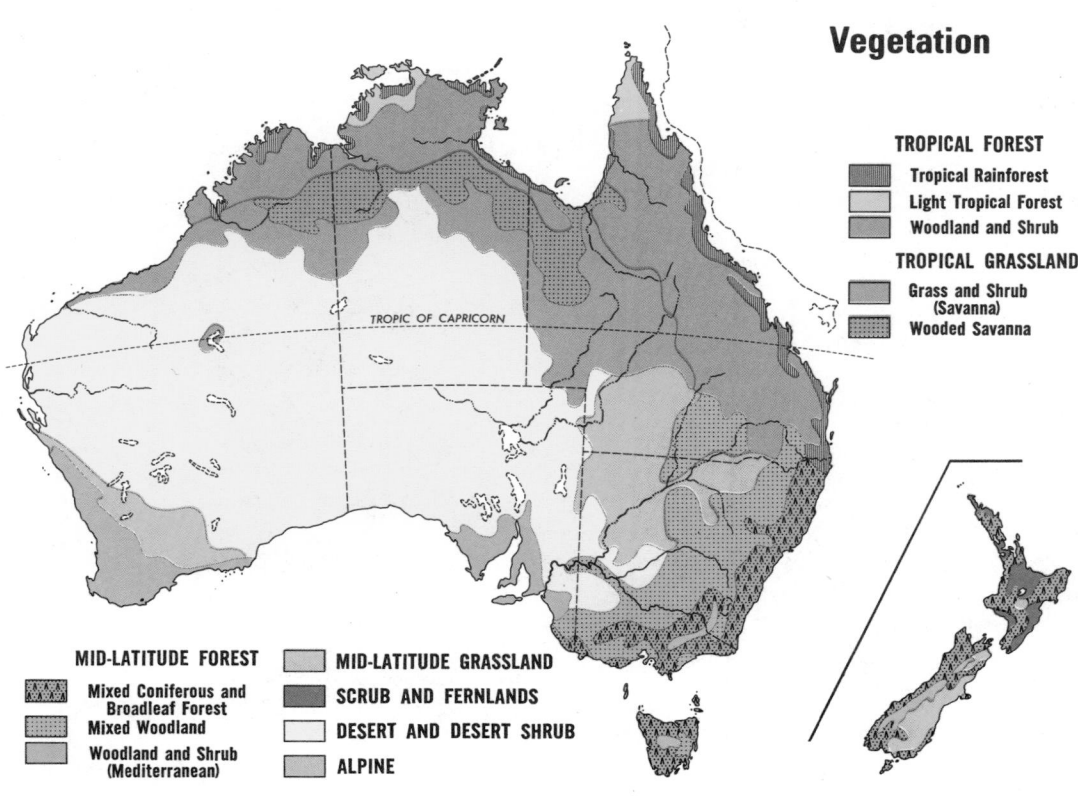

TROPICAL FOREST
Tropical Rainforest
Light Tropical Forest
Woodland and Shrub

TROPICAL GRASSLAND
Grass and Shrub
(Savanna)
Wooded Savanna

MID-LATITUDE FOREST
Mixed Coniferous and
Broadleaf Forest
Mixed Woodland
Woodland and Shrub
(Mediterranean)

MID-LATITUDE GRASSLAND
SCRUB AND FERNLANDS
DESERT AND DESERT SHRUB
ALPINE

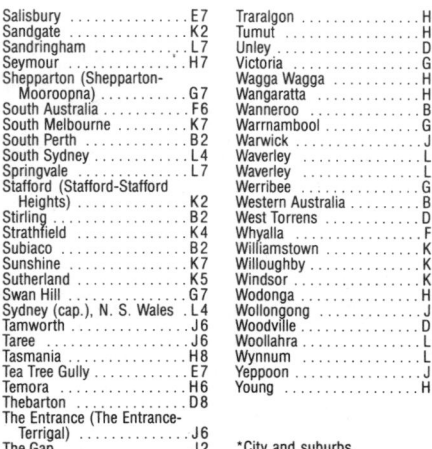

*City and suburbs.
†Population of met. area.
‡Population of urban area.

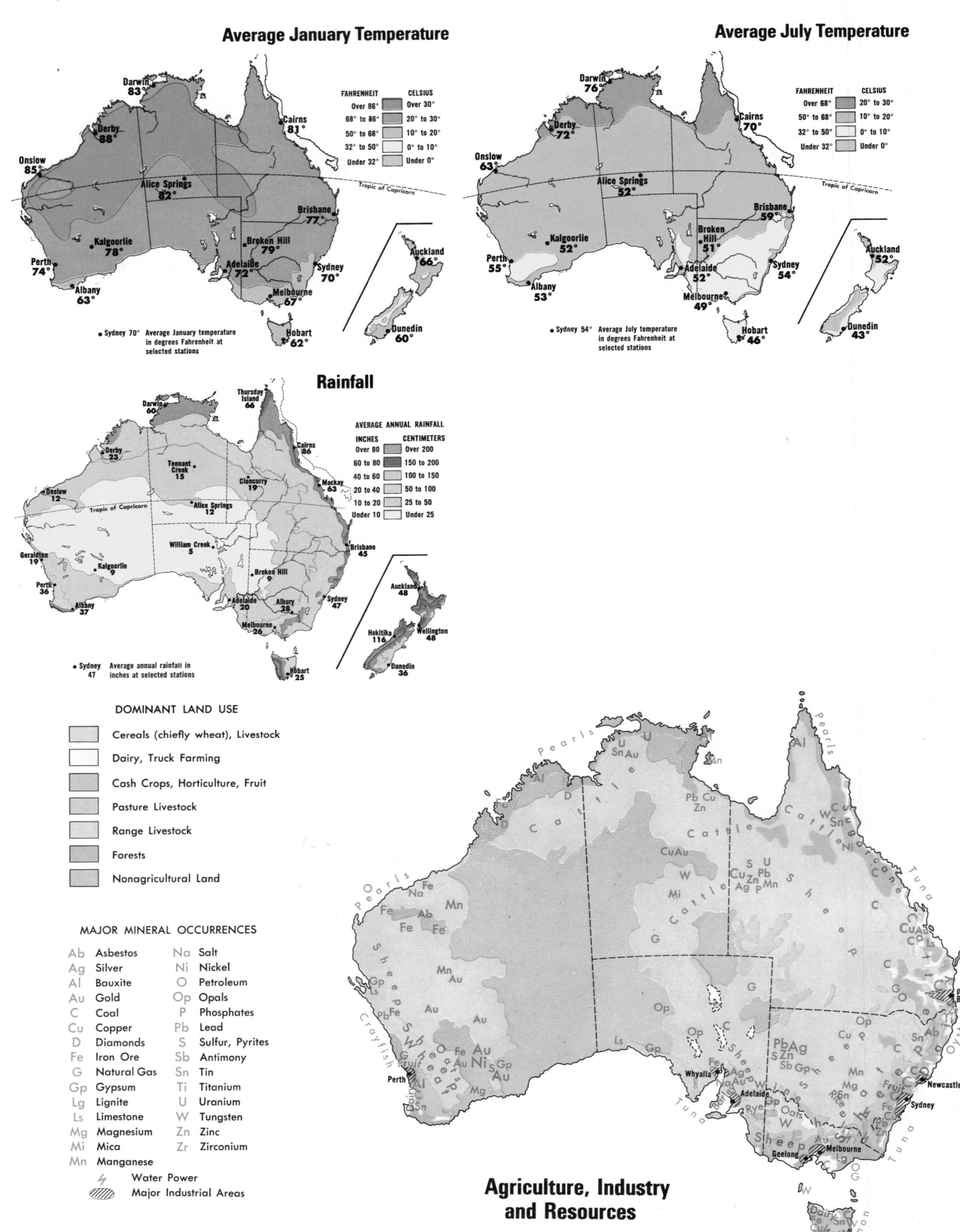

Average January Temperature

FAHRENHEIT	CELSIUS
Over 86°	Over 30°
68° to 86°	20° to 30°
50° to 68°	10° to 20°
32° to 50°	0° to 10°
Under 32°	Under 0°

Darwin 83°
Derby 88°
Onslow 85°
Alice Springs 82°
Cairns 81°
Brisbane 77°
Broken Hill 79°
Kalgoorlie 78°
Adelaide 72°
Perth 74°
Sydney 70°
Albany 63°
Melbourne 67°
Hobart 62°
Auckland 66°
Dunedin 60°
Tropic of Capricorn

• Sydney 70° Average January temperature in degrees Fahrenheit at selected stations

Average July Temperature

FAHRENHEIT	CELSIUS
Over 68°	20° to 30°
50° to 68°	10° to 20°
32° to 50°	0° to 10°
Under 32°	Under 0°

Darwin 76°
Derby 72°
Onslow 63°
Alice Springs 52°
Cairns 70°
Brisbane 59°
Broken Hill 51°
Kalgoorlie 52°
Adelaide 52°
Perth 55°
Sydney 54°
Albany 53°
Melbourne 49°
Hobart 46°
Auckland 52°
Dunedin 43°
Tropic of Capricorn

• Sydney 54° Average July temperature in degrees Fahrenheit at selected stations

Rainfall

AVERAGE ANNUAL RAINFALL	
INCHES	CENTIMETERS
Over 80	Over 200
60 to 80	150 to 200
40 to 60	100 to 150
20 to 40	50 to 100
10 to 20	25 to 50
Under 10	Under 25

Thursday Island 66
Darwin 60
Cairns 86
Derby 23
Tennant Creek 15
Cloncurry 19
Mackay 63
Onslow 12
Alice Springs 12
Brisbane 45
Geraldton 19
William Creek 5
Kalgoorlie 9
Broken Hill 9
Perth 36
Adelaide 20
Albury 28
Sydney 47
Albany 37
Melbourne 26
Auckland 48
Hokitika 116
Wellington 48
Hobart 25
Dunedin 36
Tropic of Capricorn

• Sydney 47 Average annual rainfall in inches at selected stations

DOMINANT LAND USE

- Cereals (chiefly wheat), Livestock
- Dairy, Truck Farming
- Cash Crops, Horticulture, Fruit
- Pasture Livestock
- Range Livestock
- Forests
- Nonagricultural Land

MAJOR MINERAL OCCURRENCES

Ab	Asbestos	Na	Salt
Ag	Silver	Ni	Nickel
Al	Bauxite	O	Petroleum
Au	Gold	Op	Opals
C	Coal	P	Phosphates
Cu	Copper	Pb	Lead
D	Diamonds	S	Sulfur, Pyrites
Fe	Iron Ore	Sb	Antimony
G	Natural Gas	Sn	Tin
Gp	Gypsum	Ti	Titanium
Lg	Lignite	U	Uranium
Ls	Limestone	W	Tungsten
Mg	Magnesium	Zn	Zinc
Mi	Mica	Zr	Zirconium
Mn	Manganese		

Water Power
Major Industrial Areas

Agriculture, Industry and Resources

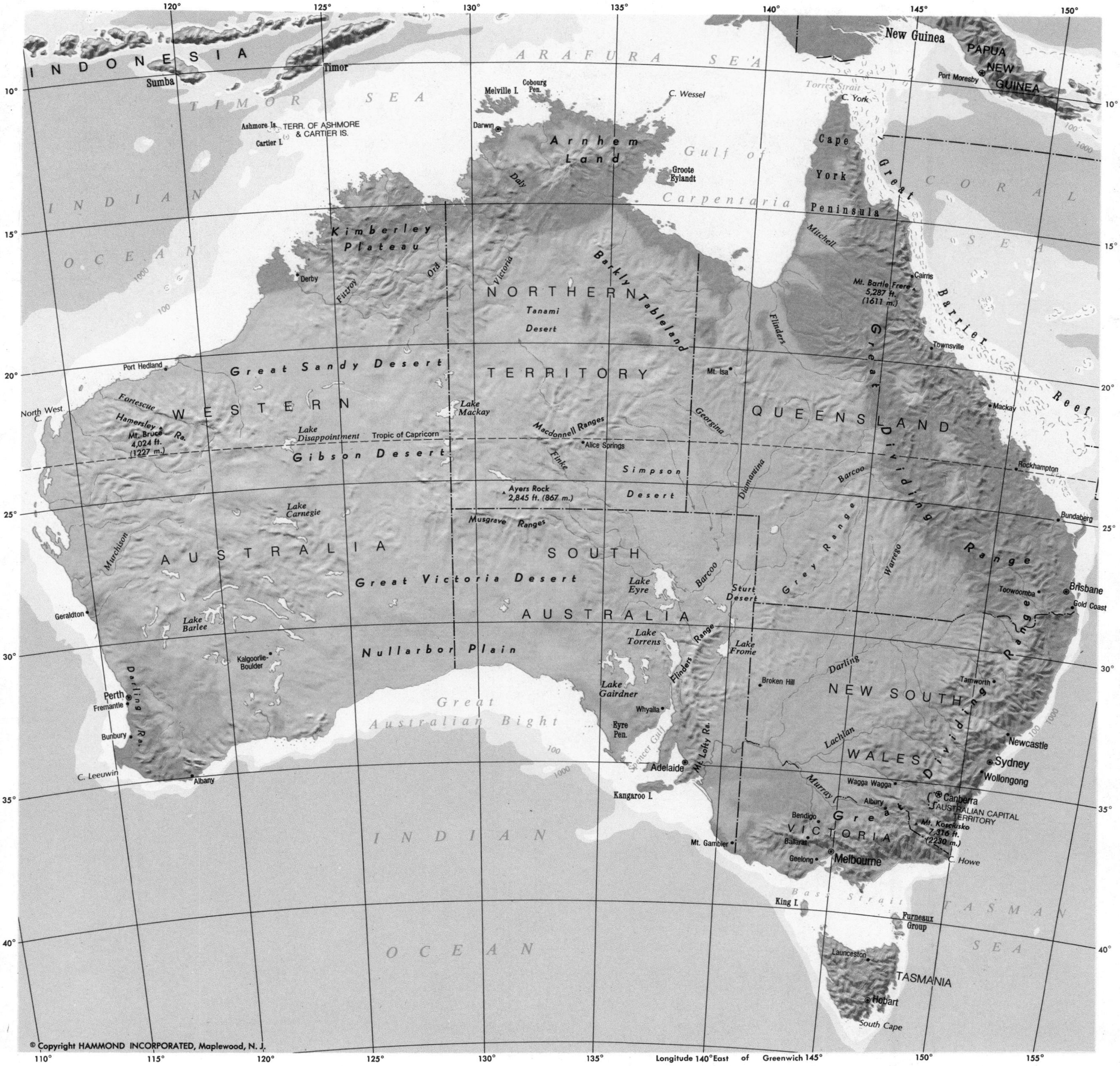

Vegetation/Relief

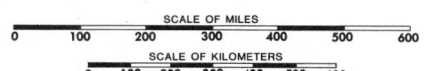

SCALE OF MILES
0 100 200 300 400 500 600

SCALE OF KILOMETERS
0 100 200 300 400 500 600

Capital of Country...................................⊛
State and Territorial Capitals........................⦿
International Boundaries.............................._____
State and Territorial Boundaries..............._ . _ . _

Depths in Fathoms

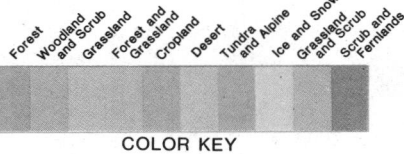

Forest Woodland and Scrub Grassland Forest and Grassland Cropland Desert Tundra and Alpine Ice and Snow Grassland and Scrub Scrub and Fernlands

COLOR KEY

© Copyright HAMMOND INCORPORATED, Maplewood, N.J.

Longitude 140° East of Greenwich

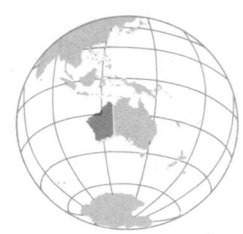

AREA 975,096 sq. mi.
(2,525,500 sq. km.)
POPULATION 1,273,624
CAPITAL Perth
LARGEST CITY Perth
HIGHEST POINT Mt. Bruce 4,024 ft.
(1,227 m.)

Topography

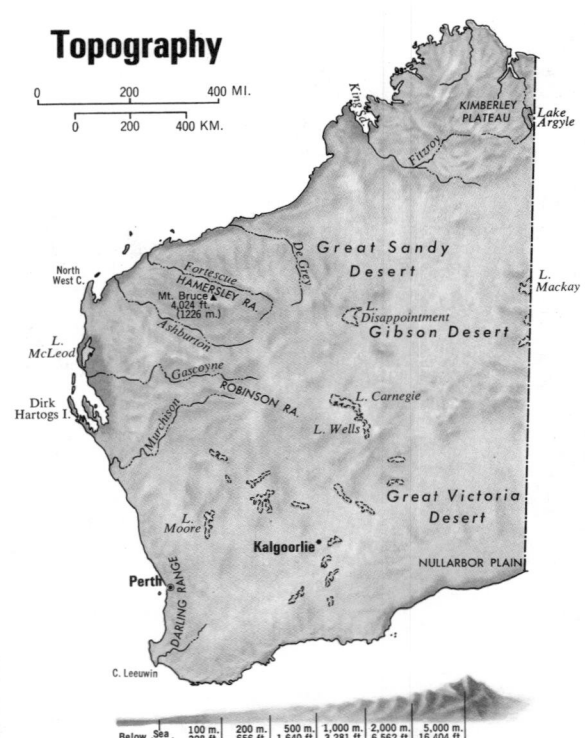

CITIES and TOWNS

Albany 15,222 .... B6
Augusta 588 .... A6
Australind 1,681 .... A2
Balladonia D6
Beverley 756 .... B1
Boddington 367 .... B2
Boulder-Kalgoorlie 19,848 .... C5
Boyanup 365 .... A2
Bridgetown 1,521 .... B6
Brookton 595 .... B2
Broome 3,666 .... C2
Bruce Rock 565 .... B5
Brunswick Junction 889 .... A2
Bunbury 21,749 .... A2
Busselton 6,463 .... A6
Canning 52,816 .... A1
Capel 680 .... A2
Carnamah 422 .... A5
Carnarvon 5,053 .... A4
Collie 7,667 .... B2
Coolgardie 891 .... C5
Coorow 226 .... B5
Corrigin 841 .... B6
Cranbrook 316 .... B6
Cuballing ○647 .... B2
Cue 320 .... B4
Cunderdin 731 .... B5
Dalwallinu 639 .... B5
Dampier 2,471 .... B3
Dandaragan ○1,748 .... A5
Darkan 242 .... B2
Denham 402 .... A4
Denmark 985 .... B6
Derby 2,933 .... C2
Dongara-Port Denison 1,155 A5
Donnybrook 1,197 .... A2
Dwellingup 453 .... B2
Esperance 6,375 .... C6
Eucla E5
Exmouth 2,583 .... A3
Fitzroy Crossing D2
Fremantle 22,484 .... A1
Geraldton 20,895 .... A5
Gingin 382 .... A1
Gnowangerup 872 .... B6
Goldsworthy 923 .... B3
Goomalling 600 .... B1
Halls Creek 966 .... D2
Harvey 2,479 .... A2
Hopetoun C6
Hyden B6
Jarrahdale 315 .... B2
Kalbarri 820 .... A4
Kalgoorlie 9,145 .... C5
Kalgoorlie-Boulder 19,848 .... C5
Kambalda 4,463 .... C5
Karratha 8,341 .... B3
Katanning 4,413 .... B6
Kellerberrin 1,091 .... B5
Kojonup 544 .... B6
Koolyanobbing 277 .... B5
Kununurra 2,081 .... E2
Kwinana New Town 12,355. A1
Lake Grace 575 .... B6
Laverton 872 .... C5
Learmonth A3
Leonora 524 .... C5
Madura D5
Mandurah 10,978 .... A2
Manjimup 4,150 .... B6
Marble Bar 357 .... C3
Margaret River 798 .... A6
Meekatharra 989 .... B4
Melville 61,211 .... A1
Menzies 232 .... C5
Merredin 3,520 .... B5
Mingenew 368 .... A5
Moora 1,677 .... B5
Morawa 694 .... A5
Mount Barker 1,519 .... B6
Mount Magnet 618 .... B4
Mukinbudin 370 .... B5
Mullewa 918 .... A5
Mundijong 356 .... A2
Nannup 552 .... B6
Narrogin 4,969 .... B2
Nedlands 20,257 .... A1
Newman 5,466 .... B3
New Norcia A5
Norseman 1,895 .... C6
Northam 6,791 .... B1
Northampton 750 .... A5
Northcliffe B6
Nungarin ○332 .... B5
Onslow 594 .... A3
Pannawonica 1,170 .... B3
Paraburdoo 2,357 .... B3
Pardoo B3
Pemberton 871 .... A6
Perenjori 257 .... B5
Perth (cap.) 809,035 .... A1
Perth *898,918 .... A1
Pingelly 937 .... B2
Pinjarra 1,336 .... A2
Port Denison-Dongara 1,155 A5
Port Hedland 12,948 .... B3
Quairading 741 .... B1
Ravensthorpe 327 .... B6
Rockingham 24,932 .... A2
Roebourne 1,688 .... B3

Sandstone ○133 .... B4
Shay Gap 853 .... C3
Southern Cross 798 .... B5
South Perth 31,524 .... A1
Stirling 161,858 .... A1
Three Springs 638 .... A5
Tom Price 3,540 .... B3
Toodyay 560 .... B1
Turkey Creek 212 .... E2
Wagin 1,488 .... B2
Walpole 291 .... B6
Wandering ○470 .... B2
Wanneroo 6,745 .... A1
Waroona 1,462 .... A2
Wickham 2,387 .... B3
Williams 453 .... B2
Wiluna 221 .... C4
Wittenoom 247 .... B3
Wongan Hills 947 .... B5
Wundowie 720 .... B1
Wyalkatchem 453 .... B5
Wyndham 1,509 .... E1
Yalgoo ○315 .... B5
Yampi Sound C2
York 1,136 .... B1

Exmouth (gulf) A3
Fitzroy (riv.) D2
Flinders (bay) A6
Forrest River Aboriginal Res. D1
Fortescue (riv.) B3
Garden (isl.) A1
Gascoyne (riv.) B4
Geelvink (chan.) A5
Geographe (bay) A6
Geographe (chan.) A4
Gibson (des.) D3
Great Australian (bight) E6
Great Sandy (des.) C3
Great Victoria (des.) D5
Hamersley (range) B3
Hann (mt.) D1
Hopkins (lake) E4
Houtman Abrolhos (isls.) A5
Indian Ocean A5
Johnston, The (lakes) C6
Joseph Bonaparte (gulf) E1
King (plat.) D2
King (sound) C2
King Leopold (range) D2
Koolan (isl.) C1
Leeuwin (cape) A6
Le Grand (cape) C6
Lévéque (cape) C2
Londonderry (cape) D1
Lyons (riv.) A4
Macdonald (lake) E3
Mackay (lake) E3
McLeod (lake) A4
Minigwal (lake) C5
Monte Bello (isls.) A3
Moore (lake) B5
Murchison (riv.) A4
Murray (riv.) A2
Naturaliste (cape) A6
Naturaliste (chan.) A4
North West (cape) A3
North-West Aboriginal Res. E4
Nullarbor (plain) D5
Oakover (riv.) C3
Ord (mt.) D2
Ord (riv.) D1
Percival (lakes) D3
Peron (pen.) A4
Petermann (ranges) E4
Rason (lake) D5
Rebecca (lake) C5
Recherche (arch.) C6
Robinson (ranges) B4
Roebuck (bay) C2
Rottnest (isl.) A1
Saint George (ranges) D2
Shark (bay) A4
Southesk Tablelands D3
Sturt (creek) D2
Swan (riv.) A1
Timor (sea) C1
Tomkinson (ranges) E4
Wanna (lakes) D4
Warburton Aboriginal Res. .. D4
Way (lake) C4
Weld (lake) C4
Weld (range) A4
Wells (lake) C4
Whalebake (mt.) B3
Wooramel (riv.) A4
York (mt.) D1

OTHER FEATURES

Adele (isl.) C1
Admiralty (gulf) D1
Aloysius (mt.) E4
Argyle (lake) E2
Arid (cape) C6
Ashburton (riv.) A3
Augustus (mt.) B4
Austin (lake) B4
Australia Aboriginal Res. E4
Bald (head) B6
Balwina Aboriginal Res. E3
Barlee (lake) B5
Barrow (isl.) A3
Beaglebay Aboriginal Res. .. C2
Bluff Knoll (mt.) B6
Bonaparte (arch.) D1
Bougainville (cape) D1
Brassey (range) C4
Bruce (mt.) B3
Brunswick (bay) D1
Buccaneer (arch.) C1
Carey (lake) C5
Carnegie (lake) C4
Central Aboriginal Res. E3
Churchman (mt.) B5
Collier (bay) C1
Cosmo Newbery Aboriginal Res. C5
Cowan (lake) C5
Cundeelee Aboriginal Res. .. C5
Dale (mt.) B1
Dampier (arch.) B3
Dampier Land (reg.) C2
Darling (range) B1
De Grey (riv.) B3
D'Entrecasteaux (pt.) A6
Dirk Hartogs (isl.) A4
Disappointment (lake) C3
Drysdale (riv.) D1
Dundas (lake) C6
Egerton (mt.) B4
Eighty Mile (beach) C2
Enid (mt.) B3
Esperance (bay) C6

○ Population of district.
*Population of met. area.

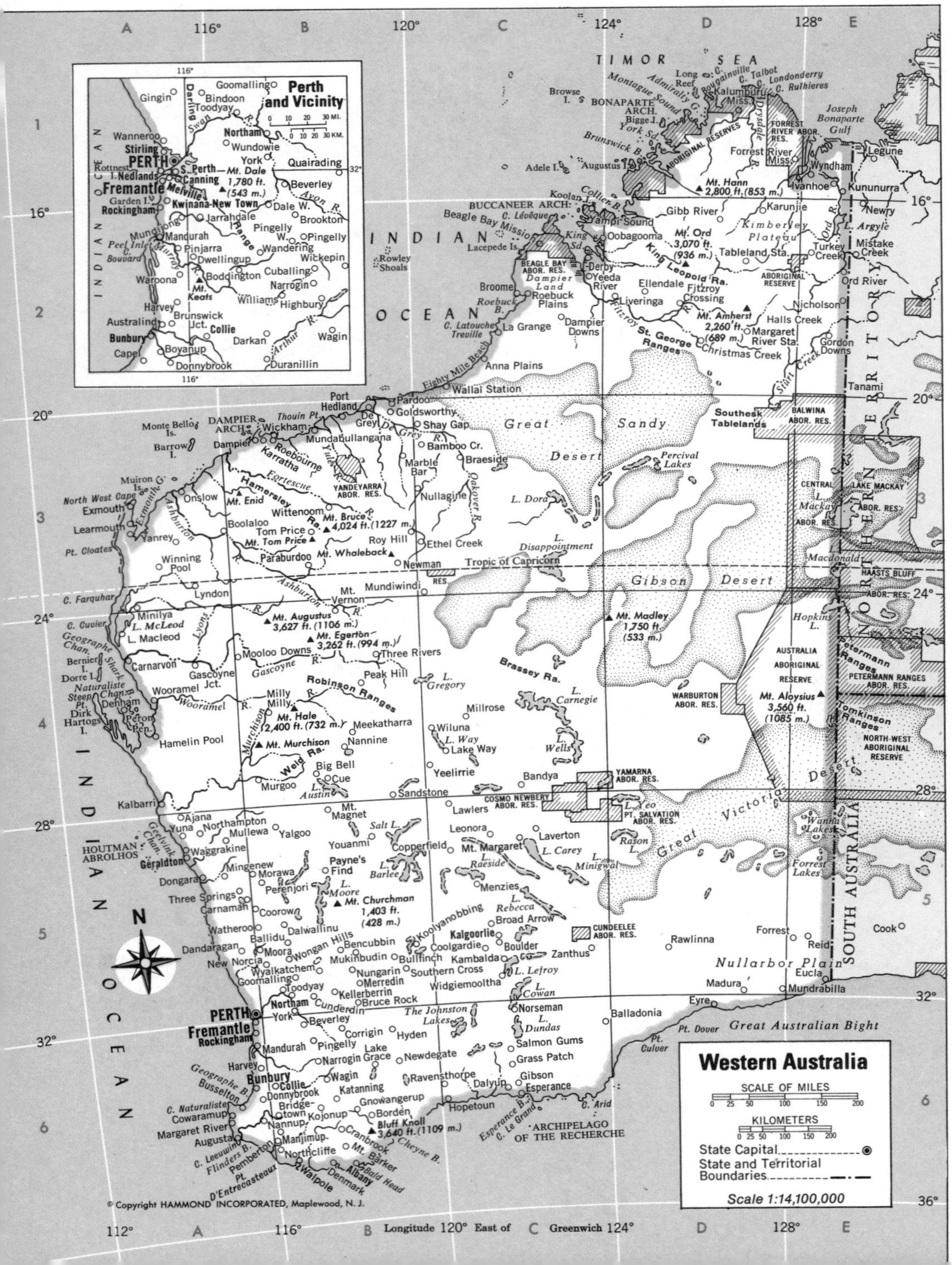

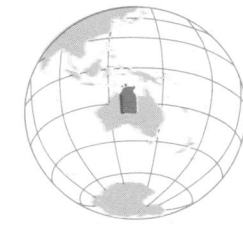

CITIES and TOWNS

Adelaide River	B2
Aileron	C7
Alice Springs 18,395	D7
Alyangula 1,181	E2
Angurugu 597	E3
Anthony Lagoon	D4
Areyonga	C8
Arltunga	D7
Avon Downs	E5
Bamyili-Beswick 685	C3
Banka Banka	C5
Barrow Creek	D6
Batchelor	B2
Bathurst Island 1,032	B1
Birdum	C3
Birrimbah	C3
Birrindudu	A5
Borroloola 420	E4
Bundooma	D8
Burramurra	E6
Charlotte Waters	D8
Claravale	B3
Coniston	C7
Coolibah	B3
Creswell Downs	E4
Croker Island Mission	C1
Daly River	B2
Daly Waters	C4
Darwin (cap.) 56,482	B2
Docker River 217	A8
Elliott	C4
Epenarra	D6
Erldunda	C8
Eva Downs	D5
Ewaninga	D7
Goulburn Island 277	C1
Gove (Nhulunbuy) 3,879	E2
Harts Range	D7
Hatches Creek	D6
Helen Springs	C5
Henbury	C8
Hermannsburg 541	C7
Hooker Creek 671	B5
Humpty Doo	B2
Katherine 3,737	B3
Kildurk	A4
Koolpinyah	B2
Kulgera	C8
Kurundi	D6
Lake Nash	E6
Larrimah	C3
Legune	A3
Limbunya	B4
Lucy Creek	E7
Mainoru	C3
Maningrida 702	C2
Mataranka	C3
Milingimbi 564	D2
Mistake Creek	A4
Montejinnie	C4
Mount Cavenagh	C8
Mount Doreen	B7
Murray Downs	D6
Napperby	C7
Newcastle Waters	C4
Nhulunbuy 3,879	E2
Numbulwar 422	D3
Oenpelli 452	C2
O. T. Downs	D4
Papunya 635	B7
Pine Creek 214	C2
Plenty River Mine	D7
Port Keats 819	A3
Powell Creek	C4
Rankine Store	E5
Robinson River	E4
Rockhampton Downs	D5
Rodinga	D8
Rum Jungle	B2
Santa Teresa 479	D7
Soudan	E6
Stirling Station	E6
Tanami	A5
Tarlton Downs	E7
Tea Tree Well	C7
Tempe Downs	C8
Tennant Creek 3,118	C5
The Granites	B6
Top Springs	C4
Ucharonidge	D4
Umbakumba 247	E2
Umbeara	C8
Urapunga	D3
Utopia	D7
Victoria River Downs	B4
Warrabri 459	D6
Warrego 991	C5
Wave Hill	B4
White Quartz Hill	D7
Willeroo	B3
Willowra	C6
Wollogorang	F4
Yambah	C7
Yirrkala 543	E2
Yuendumu 687	B7

OTHER FEATURES

Amadeus (lake)	B8
Arafura (sea)	D1
Arnhem (cape)	E2
Arnhem Land (reg.)	D2
Arnhem Land Aboriginal Res.	C2
Arnold (riv.)	D3
Ayers Rock Nat'l Park	B8
Barkly Tableland	D4
Bathurst (isl.)	A1
Beagle (gulf)	A2
Beatrice (cape)	E3
Bennett (lake)	B7
Beswick Aboriginal Res.	C3
Bickerton (isl.)	E2
Blaze (pt.)	B2
Carpentaria (gulf)	E3
Central Wedge (mt.)	B7
Clarence (str.)	B2
Cobourg (pen.)	C1
Conner (mt.)	B8
Croker (cape)	C1
Daly (riv.)	B2
Daly River Aboriginal Res.	A2
Davenport (mt.)	B7
Dundas (str.)	B1
East Alligator (riv.)	C2
Ehrenberg (range)	B7
Elcho (isl.)	D1
Finke (riv.)	C8
Fitzmaurice (riv.)	A3
Ford (cape)	A2
Georgina (riv.)	E6
Goulburn (isls.)	C1
Goyder (riv.)	D2
Groote Eylandt (isl.) 2,230	E3
Haasts Bluff Aboriginal Res.	B7
Hale (riv.)	D8
Hanson (riv.)	C6
Hay (dry riv.)	E7
Hogarth (mt.)	E6
Hopkins (lake)	A8
Joseph Bonaparte (gulf)	A3
Katherine (riv.)	C3
Lake MacKay Aboriginal Res.	A6
Lander (riv.)	C6
Leisler (mt.)	A7
Limmen (bight)	D3
Limmen Bight (riv.)	D4
Macdonald (lake)	A7
Macdonnell (ranges)	C7
MacKay (lake)	A7
Mann (riv.)	D2
Marshall (riv.)	D7
Melville (bay)	E2
Melville (isl.)	B1
Mount Olga Nat'l Park	B8
Murchison (range)	D6
Napier (mt.)	A4
Neale (lake)	A8
Newcastle (creek)	C4
Nicholson (riv.)	E5
Olga (mt.)	B8
Peron (isls.)	A2
Petermann (ranges)	A8
Petermann Ranges Aboriginal Res.	A8
Port Darwin (inlet)	B2
Ranken (riv.)	E6
Robinson (riv.)	E4
Roper (riv.)	C3
Sandover (riv.)	D6
Simpson (des.)	E8
Singleton (mt.)	B6
Sir Edward Pellew Group (isls.)	E3
South Alligator (riv.)	C2
Stanley (mt.)	B7
Stewart (cape)	D1
Stirling (creek)	A4
Sturt (plain)	C4
Tanami (des.)	C5
Timor (sea)	A2
Todd (riv.)	D8
Vanderlin (isl.)	E3
Van Diemen (cape)	A1
Van Diemen (gulf)	B1
Victoria (riv.)	B3
Wagait Aboriginal Res.	B2
Warwick (chan.)	E3
Wessel (cape)	E1
Wessel (isls.)	E1
West Baines (riv.)	A4
White (lake)	A6
Woods (lake)	C4
Young (mt.)	D3
Ziel (mt.)	C7

AREA 519,768 sq. mi.
(1,346,200 sq. km.)
POPULATION 123,324
CAPITAL Darwin
LARGEST CITY Darwin
HIGHEST POINT Mt. Ziel 4,955 ft.
(1,510 m.)

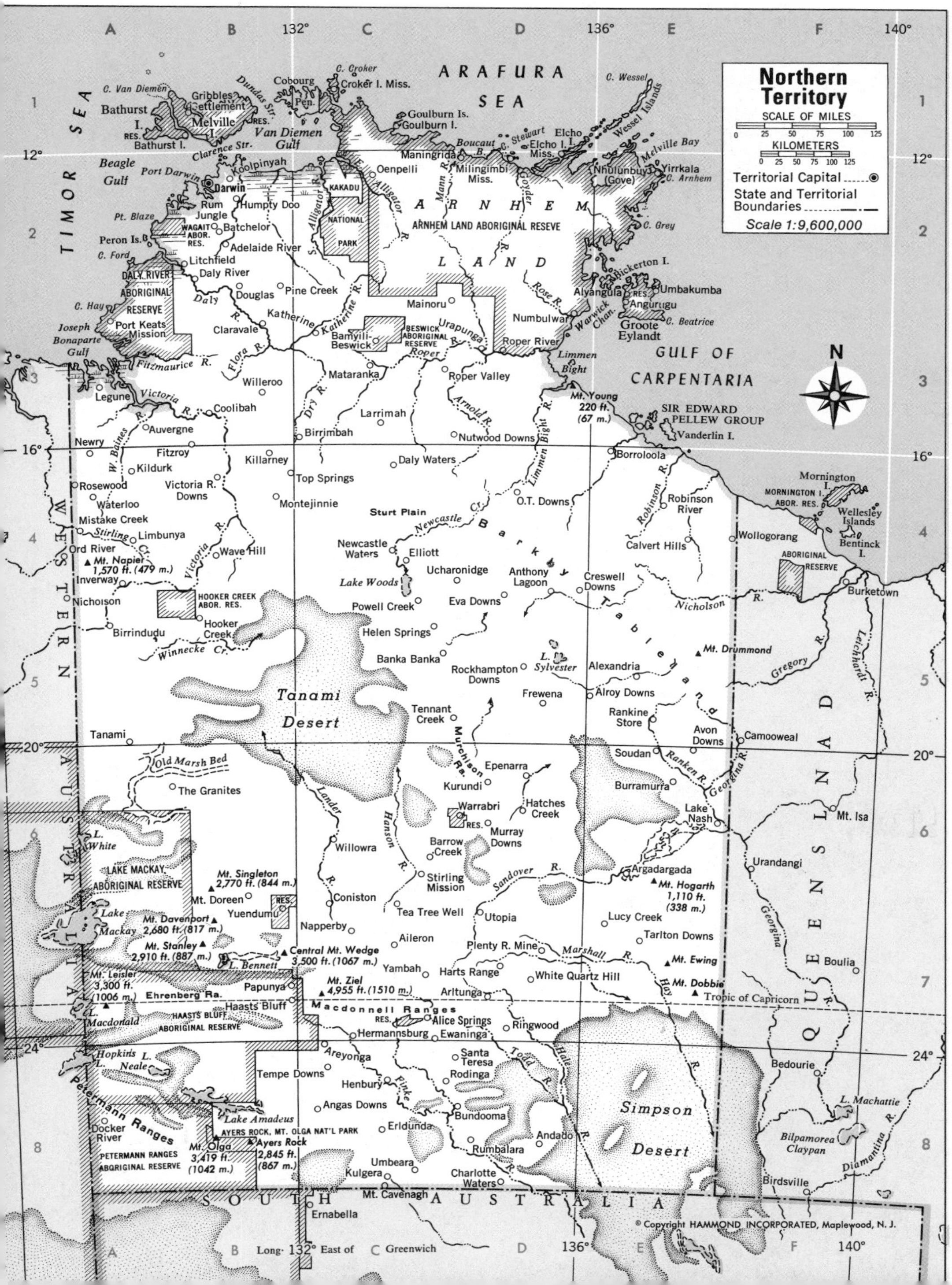

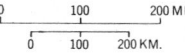

Topography

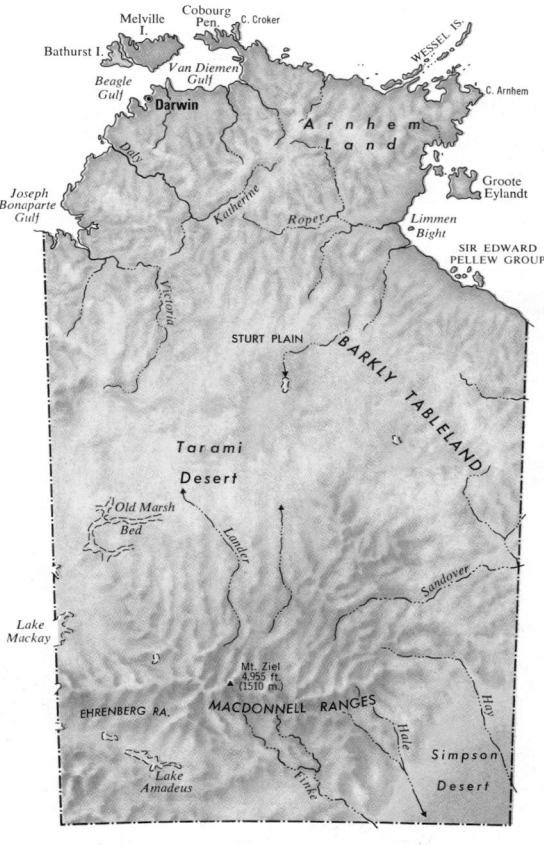

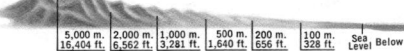

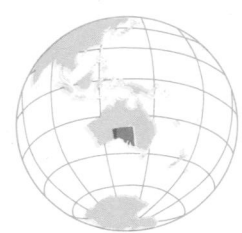

AREA 379,922 sq. mi. (984,000 sq. km.)
POPULATION 1,285,033
CAPITAL Adelaide
LARGEST CITY Adelaide
HIGHEST POINT Mt. Woodroffe 4,970 ft.
(1,515 m.)

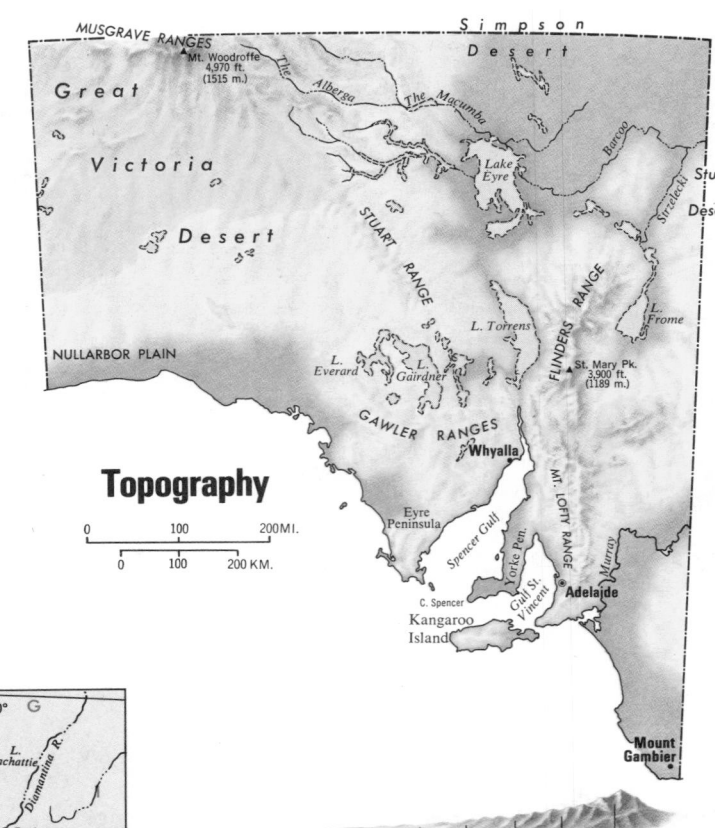

Topography

Adelaide and Vicinity

South Australia

SCALE OF MILES

KILOMETERS

State Capital . . . . ⊚
State and Territorial
Boundaries . . . . _____
Scale 1:9,790,000

® Copyright HAMMOND INCORPORATED, Maplewood, N.J.

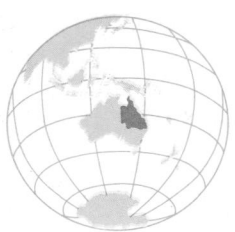

CITIES and TOWNS

AREA 666,872 sq. mi. (1,727,200 sq. km.)
POPULATION 2,295,123
CAPITAL Brisbane
LARGEST CITY Brisbane
HIGHEST POINT Mt. Bartle Frere 5,287 ft.
(1,611 m.)

Topography

NEW SOUTH WALES

AREA 309,498 sq. mi.
(801,600 sq. km.)
POPULATION 5,126,217
CAPITAL Sydney
LARGEST CITY Sydney
HIGHEST POINT Mt. Kosciusko
7,310 ft. (2,228 m.)

VICTORIA

AREA 87,876 sq. mi.
(227,600 sq. km.)
POPULATION 3,832,443
CAPITAL Melbourne
LARGEST CITY Melbourne
HIGHEST POINT Mt. Bogong
6,508 ft. (1,984 m.)

Topography

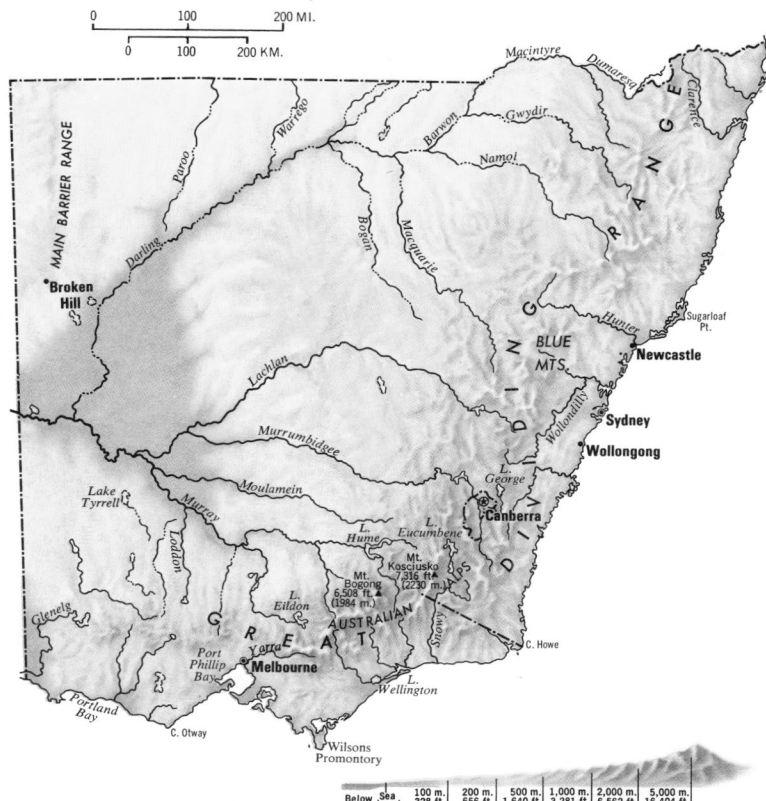

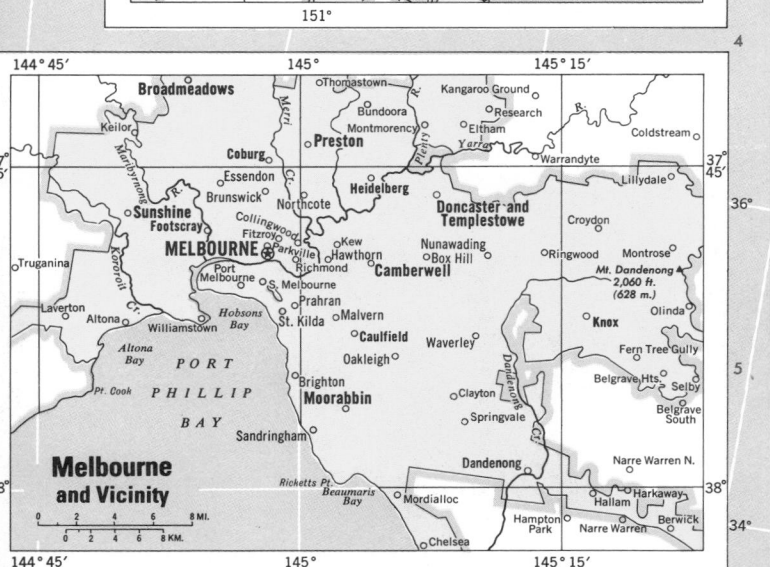

New South Wales and Victoria

SCALE OF MILES
0   25   50   100   150

SCALE OF KILOMETERS
0   25   50   100   150

Capital of Country .... ⊛
State Capitals .... ✪
State and Territorial Boundaries ....

Scale 1:5,280,000

Lord Howe I.

Sydney and Vicinity

Melbourne and Vicinity

(continued on following page)

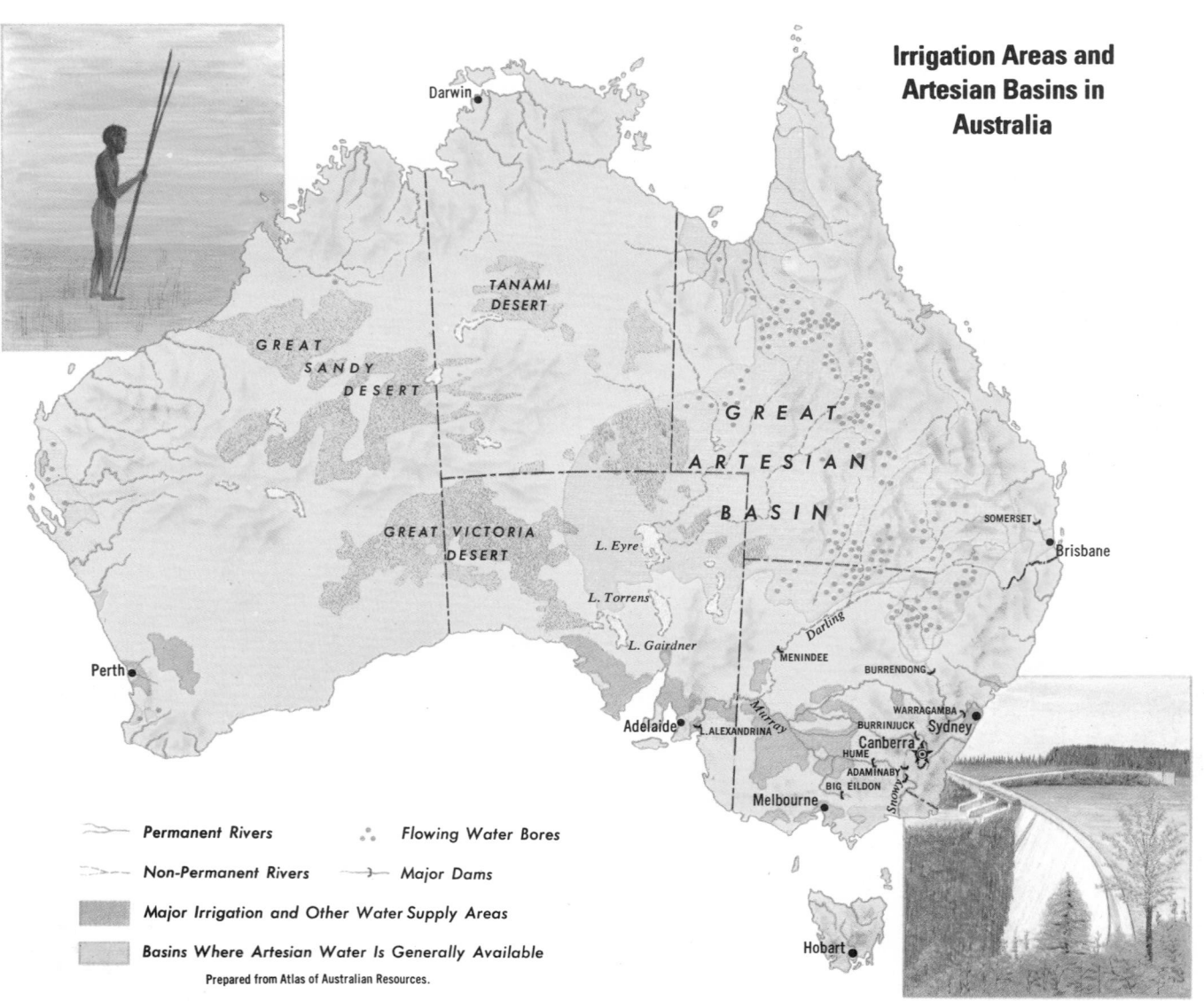

Irrigation Areas and Artesian Basins in Australia

Darwin

TANAMI DESERT

GREAT SANDY DESERT

GREAT VICTORIA DESERT

Perth

L. Eyre

L. Torrens

L. Gairdner

GREAT ARTESIAN BASIN

SOMERSET

Brisbane

Darling

MENINDEE

BURRENDONG

Adelaide

L. ALEXANDRINA

Murray

WARRAGAMBA

Sydney

BURRINJUCK

Canberra

HUME

ADAMINABY

BIG EILDON

Snowy

Melbourne

Hobart

Permanent Rivers
Non-Permanent Rivers
Flowing Water Bores
Major Dams

Major Irrigation and Other Water Supply Areas

Basins Where Artesian Water Is Generally Available

Prepared from Atlas of Australian Resources.

Topography

SCALE: 0 30 60 MI. / 0 30 60 KM.

Below Sea Level | 100 m. 328 ft. | 200 m. 656 ft. | 500 m. 1,640 ft. | 1,000 m. 3,281 ft. | 2,000 m. 6,562 ft. | 5,000 m. 16,404 ft.

TASMANIA

AREA 26,178 sq. mi. (67,800 sq. km.)
POPULATION 418,957
CAPITAL Hobart
LARGEST CITY Hobart
HIGHEST POINT Mt. Ossa 5,305 ft.
(1,617 m.)

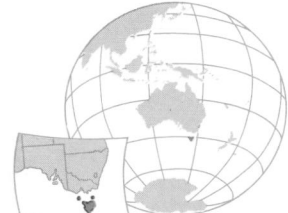

Forth (riv.)	C3	King (riv.)	B4	Ouse (riv.)	C4	South Bruny (isl.)	D5
Frankland (cape)	D1	King William (lake)	C4	Oyster (bay)	E4	South East (cape)	C5
Frankland (range)	B4	Lake (riv.)	D3	Pedder (riv.)	B4	South Esk (riv.)	D3
Franklin (riv.)	B4	Legges Tor (mt.)	D3	Phoques (bay)	A1	South West (cape)	B5
Frenchmans Cap (mt.)	B4	Leven (riv.)	B3	Picton (mt.)	C5	Stanley (mt.)	A1
Freycinet (pen.)	E4	Lofty (range)	B3	Pieman (riv.)	B3	Stokes (pt.)	A1
Furneaux Group (isls.) 1,039	E1	Low Rocky (pt.)	B4	Pillar (cape)	E5	Storm (bay)	D5
Gordon (lake)	C4	Lyell (mt.)	B4	Port Davey (inlet)	B5	Strzelecki (mt.)	D2
Gordon (riv.)	B4	Maatsuyker (isls.)	C5	Portland (cape)	D2	Tamar (riv.)	D3
Great (lake)	C3	Macquarie (harb.)	B4	Ramsey (mt.)	B3	Tasman (head)	D5
Great Western Tiers (mts.)	C3	Macquarie (riv.)	D3	Raoul (cape)	D5	Tasman (isl.)	E5
Grim (cape)	A2	Maria (isl.)	E4	Reid (rapid)	B1	Tasman (sea)	E4
Hartz (mt.)	C5	Marion (bay)	E4	Ringarooma (bay)	D2	Three Hummock (isl.)	B2
Hibbs (pt.)	B4	Mersey (riv.)	C3	Robbins (isl.)	B2	Vansittart (isl.)	E2
Hogan Group (isl.)	D1	Munro (mt.)	E2	Saint Clair (lake)	C4	West (cape)	A2
Hummock (isl.)	D2	Naturaliste (cape)	E2	Saint Helens (pt.)	E3	West Sister (isl.)	D1
Hunter (mt.)	A2	Nive (riv.)	C4	Saint Vincent (cape)	B5	Wickham (cape)	A1
Hunter (isls.)	B2	Norfolk (bay)	D4	Savage (riv.)	B3	
Huon (riv.)	C5	North (pt.)	E1	Schouten (isl.)	E4	
Indian Ocean	A4	North Bruny (isl.)	D5	Sorell (cape)	B4	
Kent Group (isls.)	D1	North Esk (riv.)	D3	Sorell (lake)	D4	
King (isl.) 2,592	A1	Ossa (mt.)	C3	South (cape)	C5	

○ Population of district.
*Population of met. area.

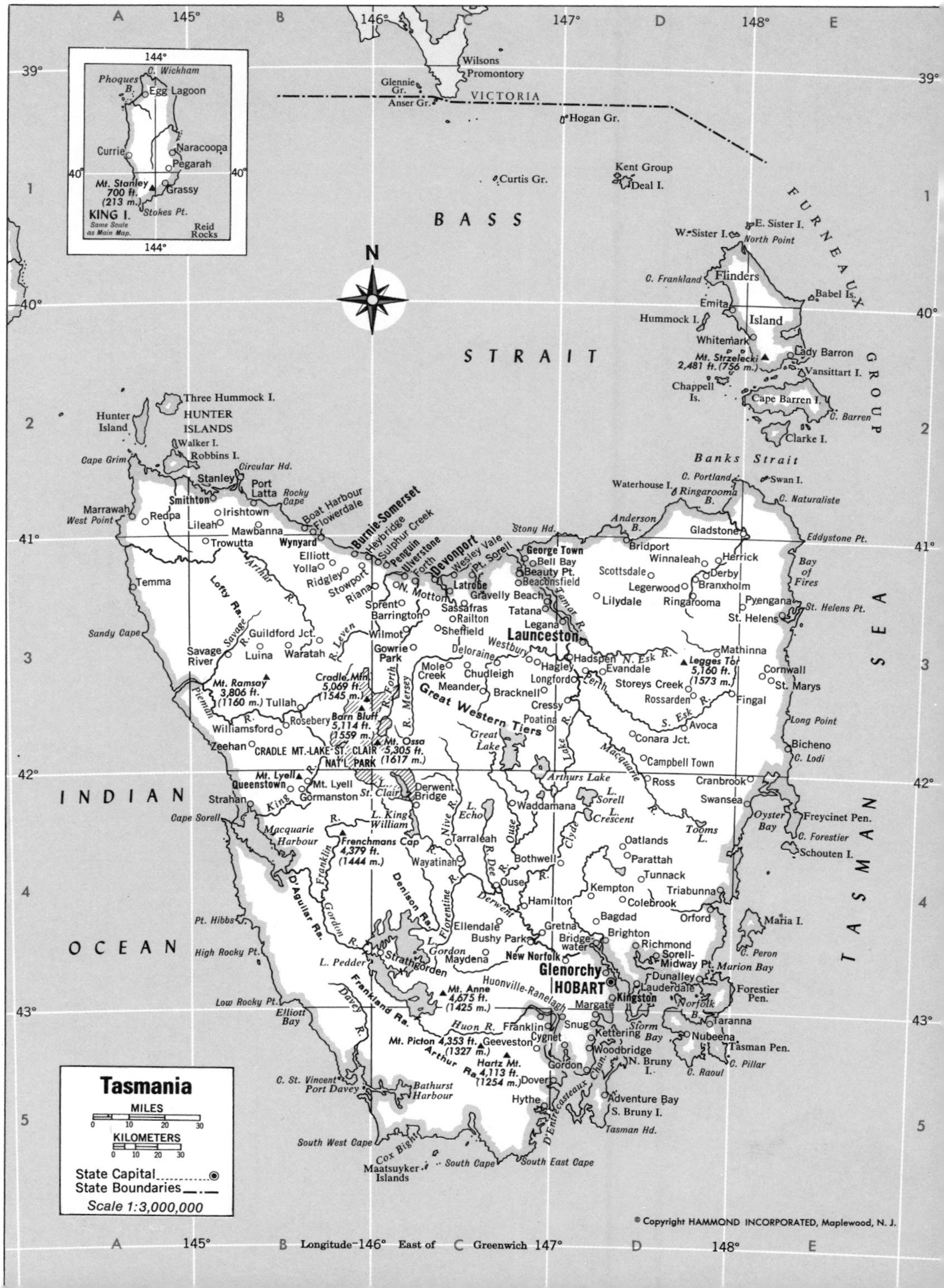

CITIES and TOWNS

Adventure Bay	D5	Ringarooma 223	D3
Avoca	D3	Roseberry 2,675	B3
Bagdad	D4	Ross 289	D4
Beaconsfield 898	C3	Rossarden 365	D3
Beauty Point 998	C3	Saint Helens 1,005	E3
Bell Bay	C3	Saint Marys 653	E3
Bicheno 674	E3	Sassafras	C3
Boat Harbour	B2	Savage River 1,141	B3
Bothwell 356	C4	Scottsdale 2,002	D3
Bracknell 347	C3	Sheffield 945	C3
Branxholm 273	D3	Smithton 3,378	A2
Bridgewater 6,880	D4	Snug 684	D5
Bridport 885	D3	Sorell-Midway Point 2,544	D4
Brighton 9,441	D4	Stanley 603	B2
Burnie 19,994	B3	Storeys Creek	D3
Campbell Town 879	D3	Strahan 402	B4
Chudleigh	C3	Strathgordon	C4
Colebrook	D4	Sulphur Creek 367	C3
Cressy 640	C3	Swansea 428	D4
Currie 859	A1	Tarraleah 498	C4
Cygnet 715	C5	Temma	A3
Deloraine 1,923	C3	Triabunna 924	D4
Derwent Bridge	C4	Tullah 1,894	B3
Devonport 21,424	C3	Ulverstone 9,413	C3
Dover 570	C5	Waratah 342	B3
Dunalley 203	D4	Wesley Vale	C3
Evandale 614	D3	Westbury 1,161	C3
Exeter 353	C3	Whitemark	D1
Fingal 424	E3	Woodbridge 259	D5
Forth 273	C3	Wynyard 4,582	B3
Franklin 479	C5	Zeehan 1,750	B3
Geeveston 860	C5		
George Town 5,592	C3	**OTHER FEATURES**	
Glenorchy 41,019	D4		
Gormanston 126	B4	Anderson (bay)	D2
Gowrie Park	C3	Anne (mt.)	C4
Grassy 780	B1	Anser Group (isls.)	C1
Gravelly Beach 535	C3	Arthur (lake)	D4
Hadspen 908	D3	Arthur (range)	C5
Hagley 232	C3	Arthur (riv.)	B3
Hamilton 2,488	C4	Babel (isl.)	E1
Heybridge 395	C3	Banks (str.)	D2
Hobart (cap.) 128,603	D4	Barn Bluff (mt.)	B3
Hobart *168,359	D4	Barren (cape)	E2
Huonville-Ranelagh 1,347	C5	Bass (str.)	C1
Kettering 288	D5	Bathurst (gulf)	C5
Kingston 8,556	C3	Cape Barren (isl.)	E2
Latrobe 2,401	C3	Chappell (isls.)	D2
Lauderdale 2,117	C3	Circular (gulf)	B2
Launceston 31,273	C3	Clarke (isl.)	E2
Launceston *64,555	C3	Clyde (riv.)	D4
Legana 964	C3	Cox (bight)	C5
Lilydale 308	D3	Cradle (mt.)	B3
Longford 2,027	C3	Cradle Mt. Lake St. Clair	
Luina 522	B3	Nat'l Park	B3
Margate 476	D4	Crescent (lake)	D4
Maydena 461	C4	Curtis Group (isls.)	C1
Meander	C3	D'Aguilar (range)	B4
Mole Creek 303	C3	Davey (riv.)	B4
New Norfolk 6,243	C4	Deal (isl.)	D1
Nubeena 225	D5	Dee (riv.)	C4
Oatlands 545	D4	Denison (range)	C4
Orford 378	D4	D'Entrecasteaux (chan.)	D5
Penguin 2,616	C3	Derwent (riv.)	C4
Perth 1,229	D3	East Sister (isl.)	E1
Poatina	C3	Echo (lake)	C4
Port Sorell 859	C3	Eddystone (pt.)	E2
Queenstown 3,714	B4	Elliott (bay)	B5
Railton 857	C3	Fires (bay)	E3
Richmond 587	D4	Flinders (isl.) 2,150	D1
Ridgley 452	B3	Florence (riv.)	C4
		Forestier (chan.)	E4
		Forestier (pen.)	E4

Tasmania

MILES 0 10 20 30
KILOMETERS 0 10 20 30

State Capital ⊙
State Boundaries —·—
Scale 1:3,000,000

® Copyright HAMMOND INCORPORATED, Maplewood, N.J.

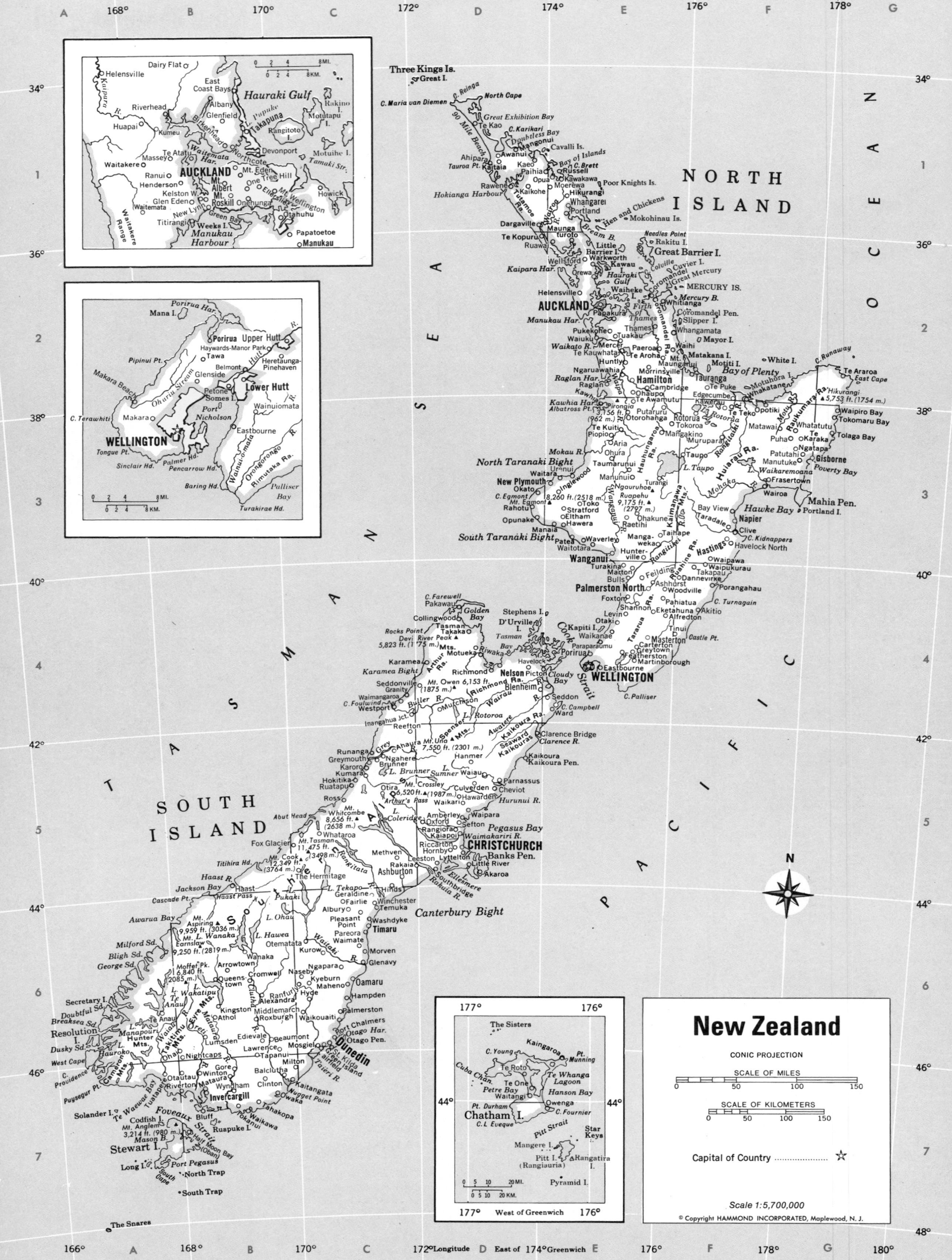

New Zealand

CONIC PROJECTION

SCALE OF MILES

0   50   100   150

SCALE OF KILOMETERS

0   50   100   150

Capital of Country .... ☆

Scale 1:5,700,000

© Copyright HAMMOND INCORPORATED, Maplewood, N. J.

Topography

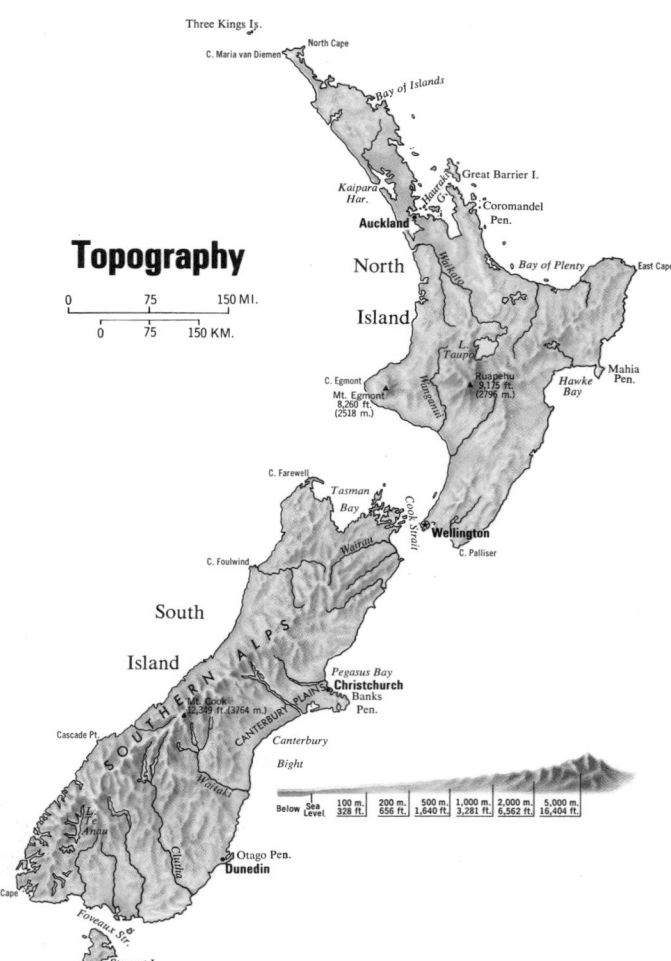

0   75   150 MI.
0   75   150 KM.

AREA 103,736 sq. mi. (268,676 sq. km.)
POPULATION 3,175,737
CAPITAL Wellington
LARGEST CITY Auckland
HIGHEST POINT Mt. Cook 12,349 ft.
(3,764 m.)
MONETARY UNIT New Zealand dollar
MAJOR LANGUAGES English, Maori
MAJOR RELIGIONS Protestantism,
Roman Catholicism

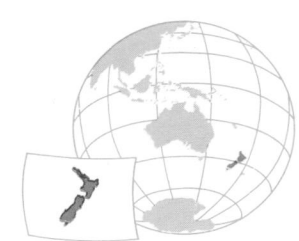

Wellington †321,004 . . . . . A3
Wellsford 1,621 . . . . E2
Westport 4,686 . . . . C4
Whakatane 12,286 . . . . F2
Whangamata 1,566 . . . . . . F2
Whangarei 36,550 . . . . E1
Whangarei †40,212 . . . . . . E1
Whitianga 1,960 . . . . E2
Winton 2,035 . . . . B7
Woodville 1,647 . . . . F4

OTHER FEATURES

Arthur's (pass) C5
Aspiring (mt.) B6
Banks (pen.) D5
Bream (bay) E1
Brett (cape) E1
Buller (riv.) D4
Campbell (cape) E4
Canterbury (bight) D6
Cascade (pt.) B6
Chatham (isls.) 751 . . . . . D7
Cloudy (bay) E4
Clutha (riv.) B6
Coleridge (lake) C5
Colville (cape) E2
Cook (mt.) C5
Cook (str.) E4
Coromandel (pen.) F2
Devil River (peak) D4
D'Urville (isl.) D4
Dusky (sound) A6
East (cape) G2
Egmont (cape) D3
Egmont (mt.) D3
Ellesmere (lake) D5
Farewell (cape) D4
Foulwind (cape) C4
Fournier (cape) E7
Foveaux (str.) A7
Golden (bay) D4
Great Barrier (isl.) 572 . . . E2
Haast (pass) B6
Hauraki (gulf) C1
Hawke (bay) F3
Hikurangi (mt.) G2
Hokianga (harb.) D1
Huiarau (range) F3
Hutt (riv.) C2
Islands (bay) E1
Jackson (bay) B5
Kaikoura (range) D5
Kaimanawa (range) F3
Kaipara (harb.) D2
Karamea (bight) C4
Kawhia (harb.) E3
Kidnappers (cape) F3
Mahia (pen.) G3
Manapouri (lake) A6
Manukau (harb.) B1
Maria van Diemen (cape) . D1
Mataura (riv.) B6
Mercury (isls.) F2
Milford (sound) A6
Needles (pt.) E2
Nicholson, Port (inlet) B3
Ninety Mile (beach) D1
North (cape) D1
North (isl.) 2,322,989 . . . . F1
North Taranaki (bight) D3
Otago (pen.) C6
Owen (mt.) D4
Palliser (cape) E4
Pegasus (bay) D5
Pitt (isl.) E7
Plenty (bay) F2
Port Nicholson (inlet) B3
Port Pegasus (inlet) B7
Pukaki (lake) B6
Puysegur (pt.) A7
Rakaia (riv.) C5
Rangitata (riv.) C5
Rangitikei (riv.) E3
Raukumara (range) F3
Reinga (cape) D1
Resolution (isl.) A6
Richmond (range) D4
Rocks (pt.) C4
Rotorua (lake) F3
Ruahine (range) F4
Ruapehu (mt.) E3
Ruapuke (isl.) B7
South (cape) A7
South (isl.) 852,748 . . . . . B5
Southern Alps (range) C5
South Taranaki (bight) D3
Spenser (mts.) D5
Stewart (isl.) 600 . . . . A7
Tararua (range) E4
Tasman (bay) D4
Tasman (mt.) C5
Tasman (mts.) D4
Tasman (sea) B4
Taupo (lake) F3
Tauroa (pt.) D1

Te Anau (lake) A6
Tekapo (lake) C5
Terawhiti (cape) A3
Thames (firth) E2
Three Kings (isls.) D1
Turakirae (head) B3
Una (mt.) D5
Waiheke (isl.) 3,223 . . . . . E2
Waikato (riv.) E2
Waimakariri (riv.) D5
Waipa (riv.) E2
Wairau (riv.) D4
Waitaki (riv.) C6
Waitemata (harb.) B1
Wakatipu (lake) B6
Wanaka (lake) B6
Wanganui (riv.) E3
West (cape) A6
Whitcombe (mt.) C5

†Population of urban area.

Agriculture, Industry and Resources

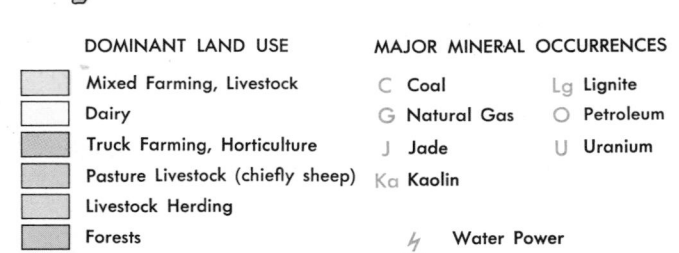

CITIES and TOWNS

Albany 2,001 . . . . B1
Alexandra 4,348 . . . . B6
Ashburton 14,151 . . . . C5
Ashhurst 1,906 . . . . E4
Auckland 144,963 . . . . B1
Auckland †769,558 . . . . . . B1
Balclutha 4,495 . . . . B7
Belmont 2,402 . . . . B2
Birkenhead 21,324 . . . . . . B1
Blenheim 17,849 . . . . D4
Bluff 2,720 . . . . B7
Bulls 1,839 . . . . E4
Cambridge 8,514 . . . . E2
Carterton 3,971 . . . . E4
Christchurch 164,680 . . . . D5
Christchurch †289,959 . . . D5
Cromwell 2,364 . . . . B6
Dannevirke 5,663 . . . . F4
Dargaville 4,747 . . . . D1
Devonport 10,410 . . . . C1
Dunedin 77,176 . . . . C6
Dunedin †107,445 . . . . . . C6
Eastbourne 4,561 . . . . B3
East Coast Bays 28,866 . . B1
Edgecumbe 1,929 . . . . F2
Eltham 2,411 . . . . E3
Ellerslie 5,404 . . . . C1
Eltham 2,411 . . . . E3
Fairfield 1,849 . . . . C6
Featherston 2,458 . . . . . . E4
Feilding 11,522 . . . . E4
Foxton 2,719 . . . . E4
Geraldine 2,128 . . . . C6
Gisborne 29,986 . . . . G3
Gisborne †32,062 . . . . G3
Glen Eden 9,406 . . . . B1
Glenfield 3,691 . . . . B1
Gore 9,185 . . . . B7
Green Bay 3,035 . . . . B1
Green Island 6,899 . . . . . . C7
Greymouth 8,103 . . . . C5
Greytown 1,797 . . . . E4
Half Moon Bay (Oban) 2,448 B7
Hamilton 91,109 . . . . E2
Hamilton †97,907 . . . . E2
Hastings 36,083 . . . . F3
Hastings †52,563 . . . . F3
Havelock North 8,507 . . . . F3
Hawera 8,400 . . . . E3
Helensville 1,360 . . . . B1
Henderson 6,645 . . . . B1
Heretaunga-Pinehaven 6,171 B2
Hokitika 3,414 . . . . C5
Hornby 8,215 . . . . D5
Howick 13,866 . . . . C1
Huntly 6,534 . . . . E2
Hutt (Upper and Lower)
†131,257 . . . . B2
Inglewood 2,839 . . . . E3

Invercargill 49,446 . . . . . . B7
Invercargill †53,868 . . . . . B7
Kaiapoi 4,894 . . . . D5
Kaikohe 3,663 . . . . D1
Kaikoura 2,180 . . . . D5
Kaitaia 4,737 . . . . D1
Kawerau 8,593 . . . . F3
Kumeu 3,414 . . . . B1
Levin 14,652 . . . . E4
Lower Hutt 63,245 . . . . . . B2
Lyttelton 3,184 . . . . D5
Manukau 159,362 . . . . C1
Marton 4,858 . . . . E4
Masterton 18,785 . . . . E4
Mataura 2,345 . . . . B7
Milton 2,193 . . . . B7
Morrinsville 5,080 . . . . E2
Mosgiel 9,264 . . . . C6
Motueka 4,693 . . . . D4
Mount Albert 26,462 . . . . . B1
Mount Eden 18,305 . . . . . . B1
Mount Maunganui 11,391 . . E2
Mount Roskill 33,577 . . . . . B1
Mount Wellington 19,528 . . C1
Murupara 2,964 . . . . F3
Napier 48,314 . . . . F3
Napier †51,330 . . . . F3
Nelson 33,304 . . . . D4
Nelson †43,121 . . . . D4
New Lynn 10,445 . . . . B1
New Plymouth 36,048 . . . . D3
New Plymouth †44,095 . . . D3
Ngaruawahia 4,435 . . . . . . E2
Northcote 10,061 . . . . B1
Oamaru 13,043 . . . . C6
Oban (Half Moon Bay) 2,448 B7
Onehunga 15,386 . . . . B1
One Tree Hill 11,078 . . . . . B1
Opotiki 3,388 . . . . F3
Orewa 5,552 . . . . E2
Otahuhu 10,298 . . . . C1
Otaki 4,301 . . . . E4
Otorohanga 2,574 . . . . E3
Paeroa 3,702 . . . . E2
Pahiatua 2,599 . . . . F4
Paihia 1,740 . . . . D1
Palmerston North 60,105 . . E4
Palmerston North †66,691 . E4
Papakura 22,473 . . . . E2
Papatoetoe 21,700 . . . . . . C1
Patea 1,938 . . . . E3
Petone 8,113 . . . . B2
Picton 3,220 . . . . D4
Pinehaven (Heretaunga-
Pinehaven) 6,171 . . . . . . C2
Porirua 41,104 . . . . B2
Port Chalmers 2,917 . . . . . C6
Pukekohe 9,070 . . . . E2
Putaruru 4,222 . . . . E3
Queenstown 3,367 . . . . . . B6

Raetihi 1,247 . . . . E3
Raglan 1,414 . . . . E2
Rangiora 6,385 . . . . D5
Reefton 1,200 . . . . C5
Riccarton 6,709 . . . . D5
Richmond 6,847 . . . . D4
Riverton 1,479 . . . . B7
Rotorua 38,157 . . . . F3
Rotorua †48,314 . . . . F3
Runanga 1,264 . . . . C5
Russell 932 . . . . E1
Saint Kilda 6,147 . . . . C7
Shannon 1,465 . . . . E4
Stratford 5,518 . . . . E3
Taihape 2,586 . . . . E3
Takapuna 64,844 . . . . B1
Tapanui 1,042 . . . . B6
Taradale 4,681 . . . . F3
Taumarunui 6,541 . . . . E3
Taupo 13,651 . . . . F3
Tauranga 37,099 . . . . F2
Tauranga †53,097 . . . . F2
Tawa 12,216 . . . . B2
Te Anau 2,610 . . . . A6
Te Aroha 3,331 . . . . E2
Te Atatu 14,713 . . . . B1
Te Awamutu 7,922 . . . . . . E3
Te Kauwhata 842 . . . . E2
Te Kuiti 4,795 . . . . E3
Temuka 3,771 . . . . C6
Te Puke 4,577 . . . . F2
Thames 6,456 . . . . E2
The Hermitage C5
Timaru 28,412 . . . . C6
Timaru †29,225 . . . . C6
Titirangi 8,426 . . . . B1
Tokoroa 18,713 . . . . F3
Tuakau 1,982 . . . . E2
Tuatapere 884 . . . . A7
Turangi 5,517 . . . . E3
Upper Hutt 31,405 . . . . . . B2
Waihi 3,538 . . . . E2
Waikanae 4,818 . . . . E4
Waikouaiti 858 . . . . C6
Waimate 3,393 . . . . C6
Wainuiomata 19,192 . . . . . B3
Waipawa 1,732 . . . . F4
Waipukurau 3,648 . . . . F4
Wairoa 5,439 . . . . F3
Waitangi D7
Waitara 6,012 . . . . E3
Waitemata 87,452 . . . . B1
Waiuku 3,654 . . . . E2
Waanaka 1,155 . . . . B6
Wanganui 37,012 . . . . E3
Wanganui †39,595 . . . . . . E3
Warkworth 1,734 . . . . E2
Washdyke 949 . . . . C6
Waverley 1,239 . . . . E3
Wellington (cap.) 135,688 . A3

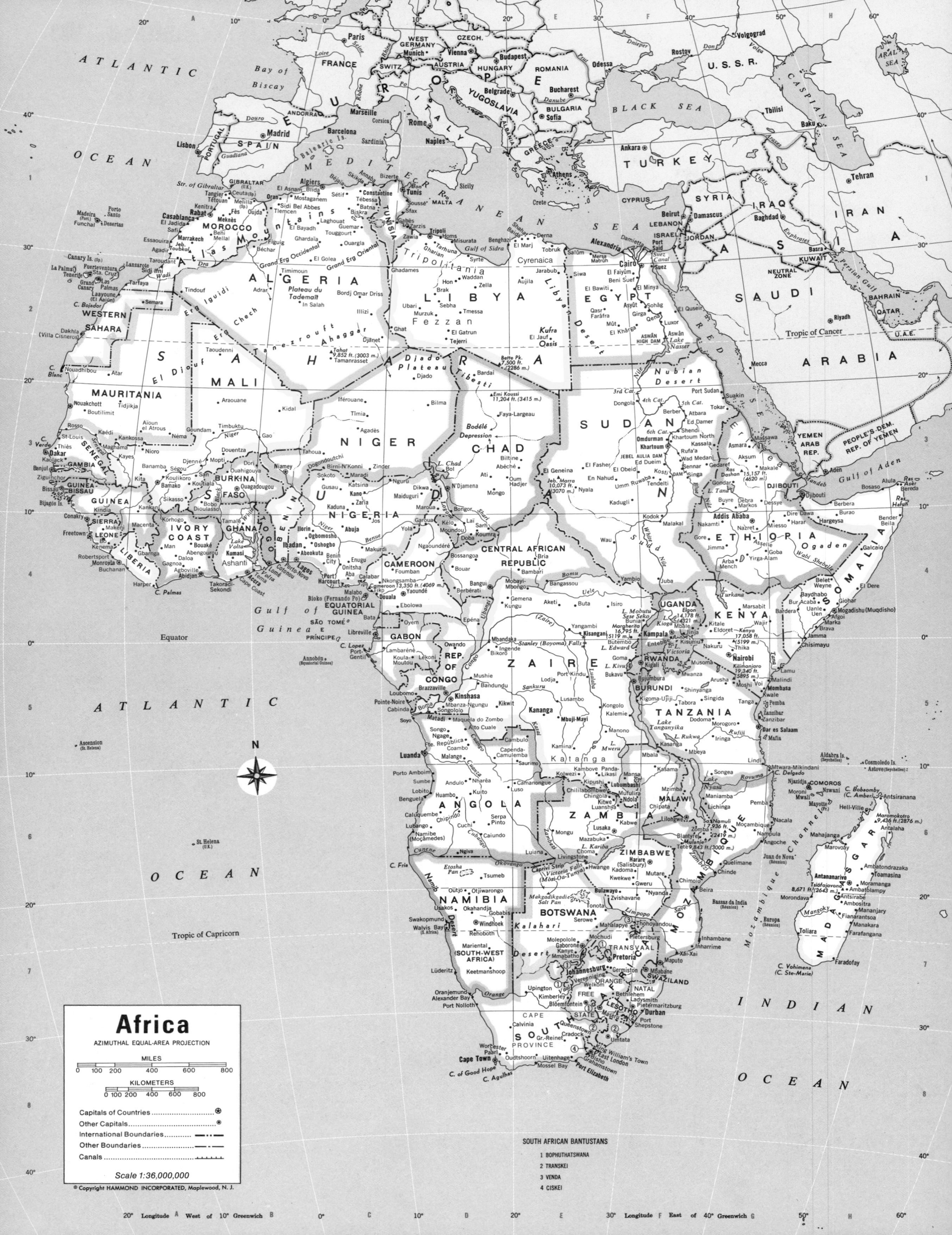

Africa

AZIMUTHAL EQUAL-AREA PROJECTION

MILES
0 100 200   400   600   800

KILOMETERS
0 100 200   400   600   800

Capitals of Countries .... ⊛
Other Capitals .... ⊙
International Boundaries .... ▬▬▬▬
Other Boundaries .... ▬ ▬ ▬
Canals .... ╾╼╾╼

Scale 1:36,000,000

® Copyright HAMMOND INCORPORATED, Maplewood, N.J.

SOUTH AFRICAN BANTUSTANS

1 BOPHUTHATSWANA
2 TRANSKEI
3 VENDA
4 CISKEI

Population Distribution

AREA 11,707,000 sq. mi. (30,321,130 sq. km.)
POPULATION 469,000,000
LARGEST CITY Cairo
HIGHEST POINT Kilimanjaro 19,340 ft. (5,895 m.)
LOWEST POINT Lake Assal, Djibouti -512 ft. (-156 m.)

Vegetation

DENSITY PER

SQ. KILOMETER	SQ. MILE
Over 100	Over 260
50-100	130-260
10-50	25-130
1-10	3-25
Under 1	Under 3

● Cities with over 1,000,000 inhabitants (including suburbs)

○ Cities with over 350,000 inhabitants (including suburbs)

TROPICAL FOREST
- Tropical Rainforest
- Light Tropical Forest
- Woodland and Shrub

TROPICAL GRASSLAND
- Grass and Shrub (Savanna)
- Wooded Savanna

MID-LATITUDE FOREST
- Mixed Coniferous and Broadleaf Forest
- Woodland and Shrub (Mediterranean)

MID-LATITUDE GRASSLAND
- Short Grass (Steppe)

RIVER VALLEY AND OASIS

DESERT AND DESERT SHRUB

UNCLASSIFIED HIGHLANDS

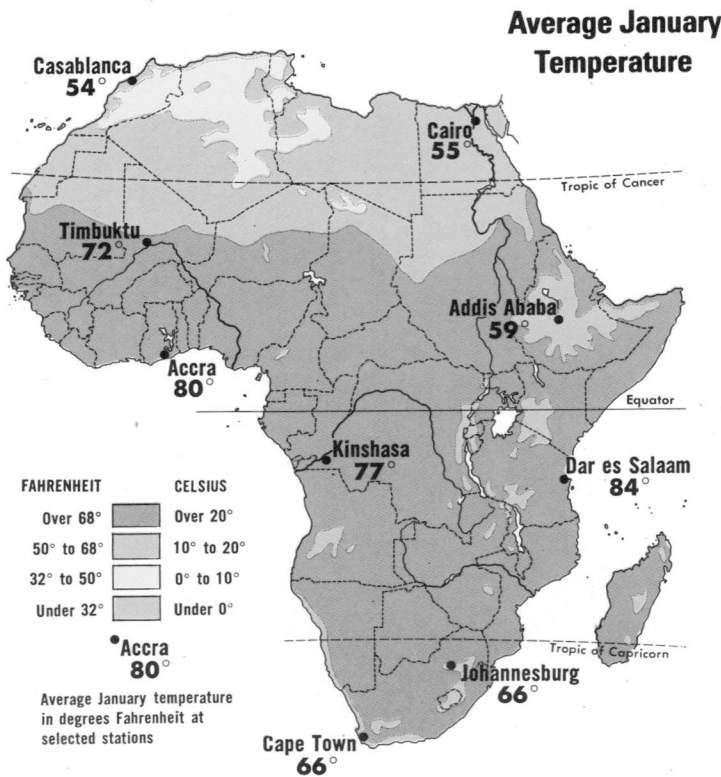

Average January Temperature

Casablanca 54°

Cairo 55°

Timbuktu 72°

Accra 80°

Addis Ababa 59°

Kinshasa 77°

Dar es Salaam 84°

Tropic of Cancer

Equator

FAHRENHEIT
- Over 68°
- 50° to 68°
- 32° to 50°
- Under 32°

CELSIUS
- Over 20°
- 10° to 20°
- 0° to 10°
- Under 0°

Johannesburg 66°

Cape Town 66°

Tropic of Capricorn

•Accra 80°
Average January temperature in degrees Fahrenheit at selected stations

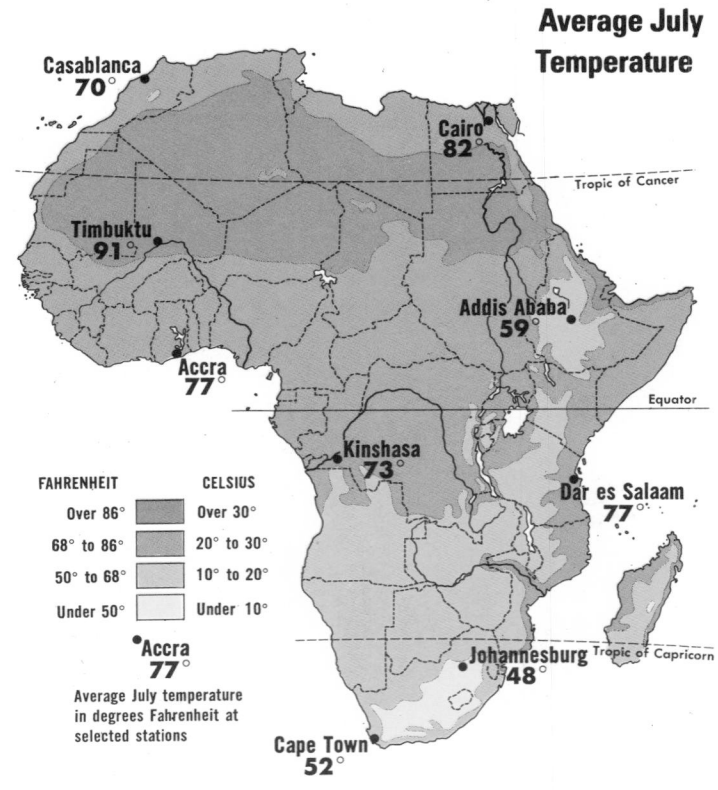

Average July Temperature

Casablanca 70°

Cairo 82°

Timbuktu 91°

Accra 77°

Addis Ababa 59°

Kinshasa 73°

Dar es Salaam 77°

Tropic of Cancer

Equator

FAHRENHEIT
- Over 86°
- 68° to 86°
- 50° to 68°
- Under 50°

CELSIUS
- Over 30°
- 20° to 30°
- 10° to 20°
- Under 10°

Johannesburg 48°

Cape Town 52°

Tropic of Capricorn

•Accra 77°
Average July temperature in degrees Fahrenheit at selected stations

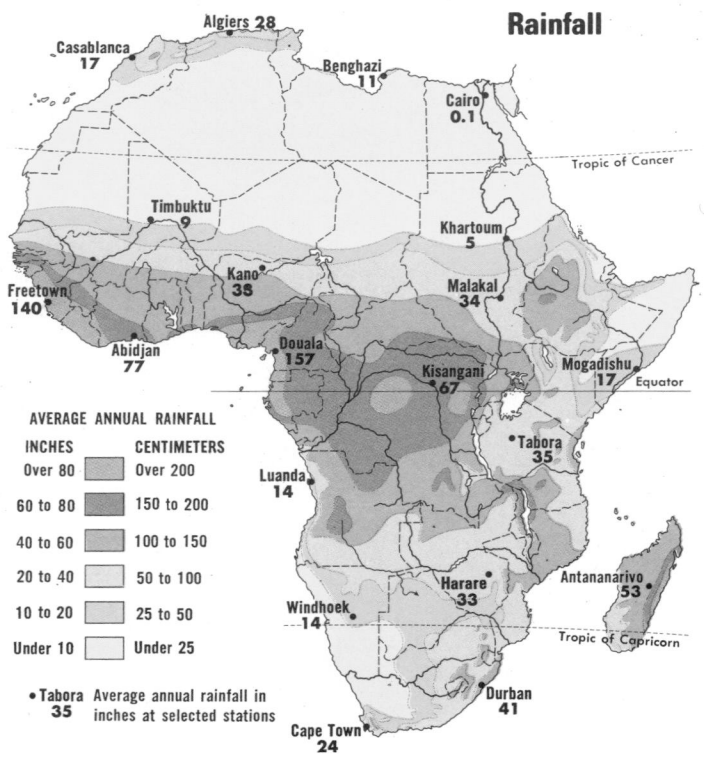

Rainfall

Algiers 28

Casablanca 17

Benghazi 11

Cairo 0.1

Tropic of Cancer

Timbuktu 9

Khartoum 5

Kano 35

Malakal 34

Freetown 140

Abidjan 77

Douala 157

Kisangani 67

Mogadishu 17

Equator

Tabora 35

Luanda 14

AVERAGE ANNUAL RAINFALL

INCHES
- Over 80
- 60 to 80
- 40 to 60
- 20 to 40
- 10 to 20
- Under 10

CENTIMETERS
- Over 200
- 150 to 200
- 100 to 150
- 50 to 100
- 25 to 50
- Under 25

Harare 33

Antananarivo 53

Windhoek 14

Tropic of Capricorn

Durban 41

Cape Town 24

•Tabora 35 Average annual rainfall in inches at selected stations

Vegetation/Relief

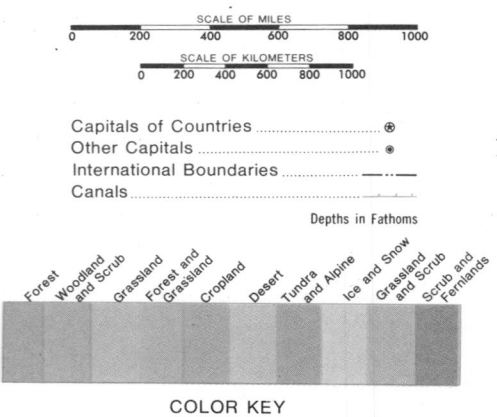

SCALE OF MILES
0 200 400 600 800 1000

SCALE OF KILOMETERS
0 200 400 600 800 1000

Capitals of Countries .... ⊗
Other Capitals .... ⊙
International Boundaries ....
Canals ....

Depths in Fathoms

Forest · Woodland and Scrub · Grassland · Forest and Grassland · Cropland · Desert · Tundra and Alpine · Ice and Snow · Grassland and Scrub · Scrub and Fernlands

COLOR KEY

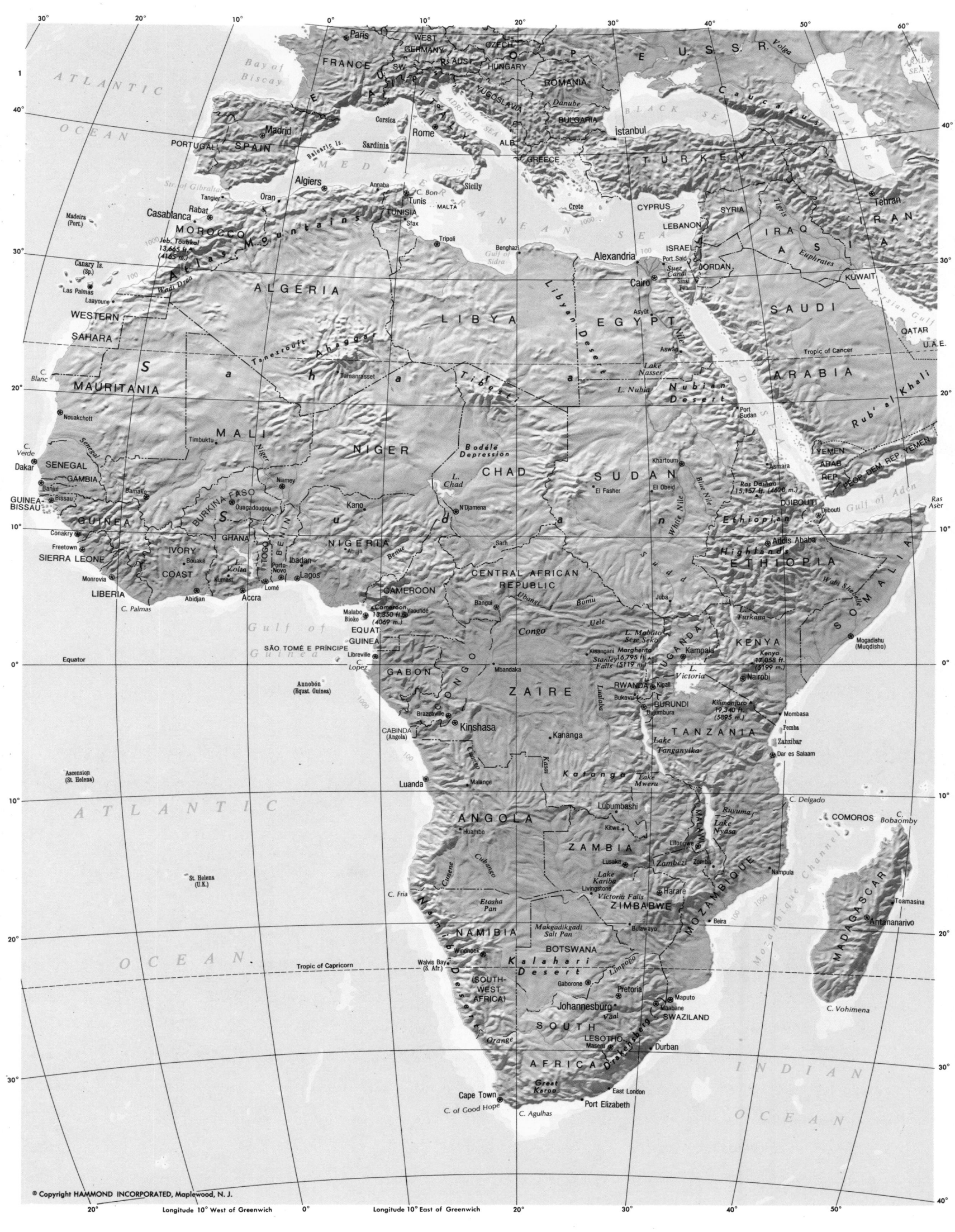
ATLANTIC OCEAN
Bay of Biscay
FRANCE
Paris
WEST GERMANY
CZECH.
AUST.
SW.
HUNGARY
ROMANIA
YUGOSLAVIA
BULGARIA
U. S. S. R.
Volga
Caucasus
BLACK SEA
CASPIAN SEA
ARAL SEA
Danube
ITALY
ADRIATIC SEA
Corsica
Sardinia
Rome
Madrid
SPAIN
PORTUGAL
Balearic Is.
ALB.
GREECE
Istanbul
TURKEY
MEDITERRANEAN SEA
Str. of Gibraltar
Tangier
Oran
Algiers
Annaba
C. Bon
Tunis
Sicily
MALTA
TUNISIA
Sfax
Crete
CYPRUS
SYRIA
LEBANON
ISRAEL
JORDAN
IRAQ
IRAN
Tehran
Tigris
Euphrates
KUWAIT
Persian Gulf
QATAR
U.A.E.
SAUDI ARABIA
ASIA
Rub' al Khali
Madeira (Port.)
Rabat
Casablanca
MOROCCO
Jeb. Toubkal 13,665 ft. (4165 m.)
Atlas Mountains
Canary Is. (Sp.)
Las Palmas
Laayoune
Wadi Draa
WESTERN SAHARA
ALGERIA
Tripoli
Benghazi
Gulf of Sidra
Alexandria
Port Said
Suez Canal
Sinai Pen.
Cairo
LIBYA
EGYPT
Libyan Desert
Asyût
Nile
Aswân
Lake Nasser
L. Nubia
Nubian Desert
RED SEA
Port Sudan
Tropic of Cancer
C. Blanc
MAURITANIA
Tanezrouft
Ahaggar
Tamanrasset
Tibesti
Sahara
Nouakchott
MALI
Timbuktu
Niger
NIGER
Bodélé Depression
CHAD
L. Chad
N'Djamena
SUDAN
Khartoum
El Fasher
El Obeid
Blue Nile
White Nile
Asmara
YEMEN ARAB REP.
PEOP. DEM. REP. YEMEN
Ras Dashan 15,157 ft. (4620 m.)
DJIBOUTI
Djibouti
Gulf of Aden
Ras Aser
C. Verde
Dakar
SENEGAL
Senegal
GAMBIA
Banjul
Bamako
Niamey
GUINEA-BISSAU
Bissau
GUINEA
Conakry
BURKINA FASO
Ouagadougou
Kano
Sudan
Ethiopian Highlands
Addis Ababa
ETHIOPIA
SOMALIA
Wabi Shebelle
Freetown
SIERRA LEONE
IVORY COAST
GHANA
TOGO
BENIN
NIGERIA
Abuja
Benue
Sarh
Sudd
Bouaké
L. Volta
Kumasi
Porto-Novo
Ibadan
Lagos
CENTRAL AFRICAN REPUBLIC
Monrovia
LIBERIA
Abidjan
Accra
Lomé
CAMEROON
Ubangi
Bomu
Juba
C. Palmas
Malabo
Bioko
Cameroon 13,350 ft. (4069 m.)
Yaoundé
Bangui
Uele
L. Turkana
Gulf of Guinea
EQUAT. GUINEA
Congo
L. Mobutu Sese Seko
Margherita 16,795 ft. (5119 m.)
UGANDA
Kampala
KENYA
Mogadishu (Muqdisho)
SÃO TOMÉ E PRÍNCIPE
Libreville
C. Lopez
Kisangani
Stanley Falls
Mbandaka
Kenya 17,058 ft. (5199 m.)
Equator
GABON
CONGO
L. Victoria
Nairobi
Annobón (Equat. Guinea)
ZAIRE
RWANDA
Kigali
Bukavu
BURUNDI
Bujumbura
Kilimanjaro 19,340 ft. (5895 m.)
Mombasa
Lualaba
Brazzaville
Kinshasa
CABINDA (Angola)
Kananga
TANZANIA
Pemba
Zanzibar
Dar es Salaam
Lake Tanganyika
Kasai
Cuanza
Luanda
Malange
Katanga
Lake Mweru
Ascension (St. Helena)
Lubumbashi
C. Delgado
COMOROS
C. Bobaomby
ANGOLA
Huambo
Kitwe
MALAWI
Ruvuma
Lake Nyasa
Lilongwe
ZAMBIA
Zomba
Lusaka
Zambezi
Cunene
Cubango
Lake Kariba
Livingstone
Victoria Falls
Harare
MOZAMBIQUE
Nampula
Mozambique Channel
St. Helena (U.K.)
C. Fria
Etosha Pan
ZIMBABWE
Toamasina
MADAGASCAR
Antananarivo
Beira
Makgadikgadi Salt Pan
NAMIBIA
Bulawayo
BOTSWANA
Windhoek
Walvis Bay (S. Afr.)
Kalahari Desert
Limpopo
Tropic of Capricorn
Namib Desert
(SOUTH-WEST AFRICA)
Gaborone
Pretoria
Maputo
Johannesburg
Vaal
Mbabane
SWAZILAND
C. Vohimena
SOUTH AFRICA
LESOTHO
Maseru
Drakensberg
Orange
Durban
INDIAN OCEAN
Great Karoo
East London
Cape Town
Port Elizabeth
C. of Good Hope
C. Agulhas
Longitude 10° West of Greenwich
Longitude 10° East of Greenwich

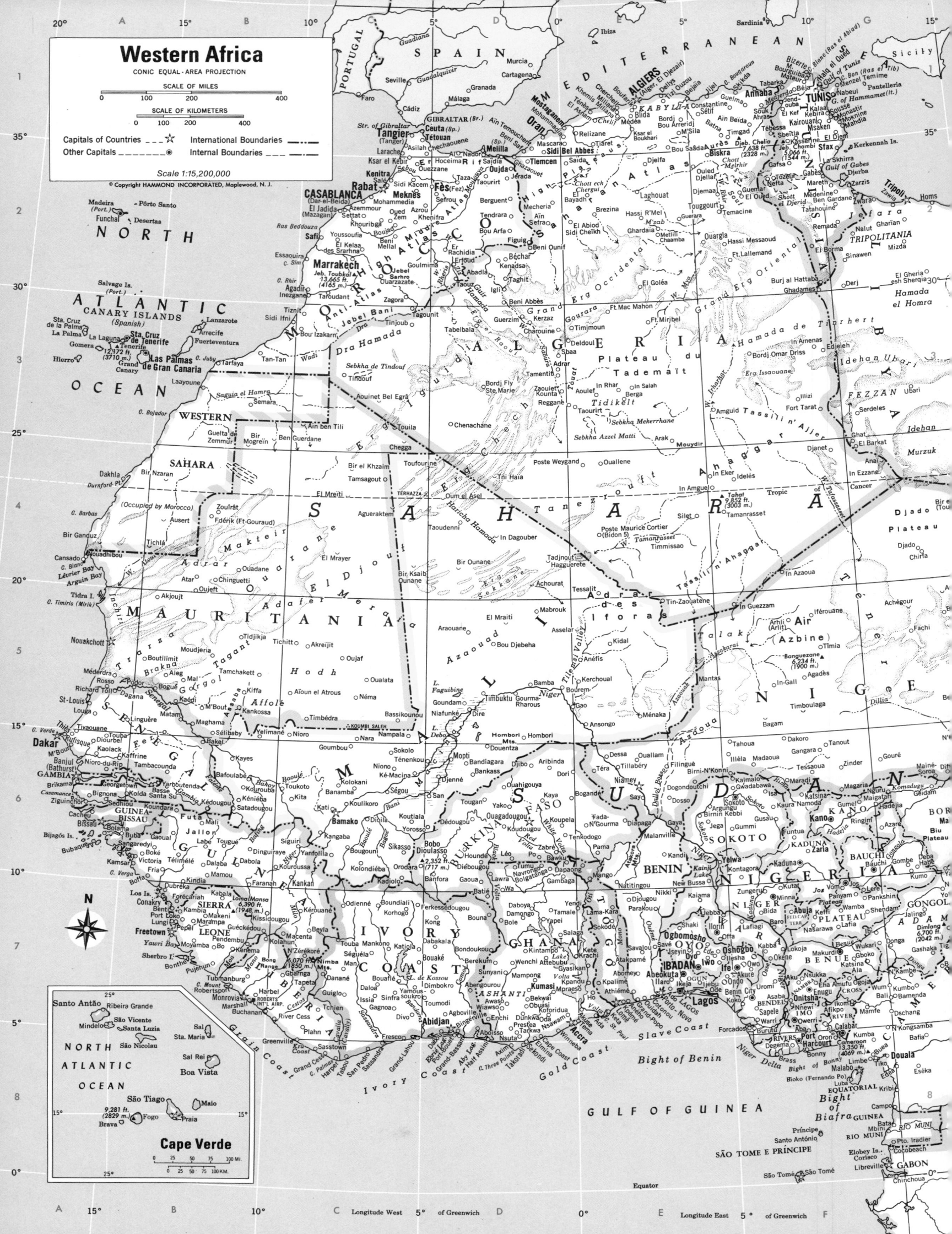

Western Africa

CONIC EQUAL·AREA PROJECTION

SCALE OF MILES

0   100   200   400

SCALE OF KILOMETERS

0 100 200   400

Capitals of Countries ___ ☆   International Boundaries ___·___

Other Capitals ___ ⊙   Internal Boundaries ___·___

Scale 1:15,200,000

© Copyright HAMMOND INCORPORATED, Maplewood, N.J.

Cape Verde

ALGERIA

AREA 919,591 sq. mi. (2,381,740 sq. km.)
POPULATION 17,422,000
CAPITAL Algiers
LARGEST CITY Algiers
HIGHEST POINT Tahat 9,852 ft. (3,003 m.)
MONETARY UNIT Algerian dinar
MAJOR LANGUAGES Arabic, Berber, French
MAJOR RELIGION Islam

BENIN

AREA 43,483 sq. mi. (112,620 sq. km.)
POPULATION 3,338,240
CAPITAL Porto-Novo
LARGEST CITY Cotonou
HIGHEST POINT Atakora Mts. 2,083 ft. (635 m.)
MONETARY UNIT CFA franc
MAJOR LANGUAGES Fon, Somba, Yoruba, Bariba, French, Mina, Dendi
MAJOR RELIGIONS Tribal religions, Islam, Roman Catholicism

CAPE VERDE

AREA 1,557 sq. mi. (4,033 sq. km.)
POPULATION 324,000
CAPITAL Praia
LARGEST CITY Praia
HIGHEST POINT 9,281 ft. (2,829 m.)
MONETARY UNIT Cape Verde escudo
MAJOR LANGUAGE Portuguese
MAJOR RELIGION Roman Catholicism

GAMBIA

AREA 4,127 sq. mi. (10,689 sq. km.)
POPULATION 601,000
CAPITAL Banjul
LARGEST CITY Banjul
HIGHEST POINT 100 ft. (30 m.)
MONETARY UNIT dalasi
MAJOR LANGUAGES Mandingo, Fulani, Wolof, English, Malinke
MAJOR RELIGIONS Islam, tribal religions, Christianity

GHANA

AREA 92,099 sq. mi. (238,536 sq. km.)
POPULATION 11,450,000
CAPITAL Accra
LARGEST CITY Accra
HIGHEST POINT Togo Hills 2,900 ft. (884 m.)
MONETARY UNIT cedi
MAJOR LANGUAGES Twi, Fante, Dagbani, Ewe, Ga, English, Hausa, Akan
MAJOR RELIGIONS Tribal religions, Christianity, Islam

GUINEA

AREA 94,925 sq. mi. (245,856 sq. km.)
POPULATION 5,143,284
CAPITAL Conakry
LARGEST CITY Conakry
HIGHEST POINT Nimba Mts. 6,070 ft. (1,850 m.)
MONETARY UNIT syli
MAJOR LANGUAGES Fulani, Mandingo, Susu, French
MAJOR RELIGIONS Islam, tribal religions

GUINEA-BISSAU

AREA 13,948 sq. mi. (36,125 sq. km.)
POPULATION 777,214
CAPITAL Bissau
LARGEST CITY Bissau
HIGHEST POINT 689 ft. (210 m.)
MONETARY UNIT Guinea-Bissau escudo
MAJOR LANGUAGES Balante, Fulani, Crioulo, Mandingo, Portuguese
MAJOR RELIGIONS Islam, tribal religions, Roman Catholicism

IVORY COAST

AREA 124,504 sq. mi. (322,465 sq. km.)
POPULATION 7,920,000
CAPITAL Abidjan
LARGEST CITY Abidjan
HIGHEST POINT 5,745 ft. (1,751 m.)
MONETARY UNIT CFA franc
MAJOR LANGUAGES Bale, Bete, Senufu, French, Dioula
MAJOR RELIGIONS Tribal religions, Islam

LIBERIA

AREA 43,000 sq. mi. (111,370 sq. km.)
POPULATION 1,873,000
CAPITAL Monrovia
LARGEST CITY Monrovia
HIGHEST POINT Wutivi 5,584 ft. (1,702 m.)
MONETARY UNIT Liberian dollar
MAJOR LANGUAGES Kru, Kpelle, Bassa, Vai, English
MAJOR RELIGIONS Christianity, tribal religions, Islam

MALI

AREA 464,873 sq. mi. (1,204,021 sq. km.)
POPULATION 6,906,000
CAPITAL Bamako
LARGEST CITY Bamako
HIGHEST POINT Hombori Mts. 3,789 ft. (1,155 m.)
MONETARY UNIT Mali franc
MAJOR LANGUAGES Bambara, Senufu, Fulani, Soninke, French
MAJOR RELIGIONS Islam, tribal religions

MAURITANIA

AREA 419,229 sq. mi. (1,085,803 sq. km.)
POPULATION 1,634,000
CAPITAL Nouakchott
LARGEST CITY Nouakchott
HIGHEST POINT 2,972 ft. (906 m.)
MONETARY UNIT ouguiya
MAJOR LANGUAGES Arabic, Wolof, Tukolor, French
MAJOR RELIGION Islam

MOROCCO

AREA 172,414 sq. mi. (446,550 sq. km.)
POPULATION 20,242,000
CAPITAL Rabat
LARGEST CITY Casablanca
HIGHEST POINT Jeb. Toubkal 13,665 ft. (4,165 m.)
MONETARY UNIT dirham
MAJOR LANGUAGES Arabic, Berber, French
MAJOR RELIGIONS Islam, Judaism, Christianity

NIGER

AREA 489,189 sq. mi. (1,267,000 sq. km.)
POPULATION 5,098,427
CAPITAL Niamey
LARGEST CITY Niamey
HIGHEST POINT Banguezane 6,234 ft. (1,900 m.)
MONETARY UNIT CFA franc
MAJOR LANGUAGES Hausa, Songhai, Fulani, French, Tamashek, Djerma
MAJOR RELIGIONS Islam, tribal religions

NIGERIA

AREA 357,000 sq. mi. (924,630 sq. km.)
POPULATION 82,643,000
CAPITAL Lagos
LARGEST CITY Lagos
HIGHEST POINT Dimlang 6,700 ft. (2,042 m.)
MONETARY UNIT naira
MAJOR LANGUAGES Hausa, Yoruba, Ibo, Ijaw, Fulani, Tiv, Kanuri, Ibibio, English, Edo
MAJOR RELIGIONS Islam, Christianity, tribal religions

SÃO TOMÉ E PRÍNCIPE

AREA 372 sq. mi. (963 sq. km.)
POPULATION 85,000
CAPITAL São Tomé
LARGEST CITY São Tomé
HIGHEST POINT Pico 6,640 ft. (2,024 m.)
MONETARY UNIT dobra
MAJOR LANGUAGES Bantu languages, Portuguese
MAJOR RELIGIONS Tribal religions, Roman Catholicism

SENEGAL

AREA 75,954 sq. mi. (196,720 sq. km.)
POPULATION 5,508,000
CAPITAL Dakar
LARGEST CITY Dakar
HIGHEST POINT Futa Jallon 1,640 ft. (500 m.)
MONETARY UNIT CFA franc
MAJOR LANGUAGES Wolof, Peul (Fulani), French, Mende, Mandingo, Dida
MAJOR RELIGIONS Islam, tribal religions, Roman Catholicism

SIERRA LEONE

AREA 27,925 sq. mi. (72,325 sq. km.)
POPULATION 3,470,000
CAPITAL Freetown
LARGEST CITY Freetown
HIGHEST POINT Loma Mts. 6,390 ft. (1,947 m.)
MONETARY UNIT leone
MAJOR LANGUAGES Mende, Temne, Vai, English, Krio (pidgin)
MAJOR RELIGIONS Tribal religions, Islam, Christianity

TOGO

AREA 21,622 sq. mi. (56,000 sq. km.)
POPULATION 2,472,000
CAPITAL Lomé
LARGEST CITY Lomé
HIGHEST POINT Agou 3,445 ft. (1,050 m.)
MONETARY UNIT CFA franc
MAJOR LANGUAGES Ewe, French, Twi, Hausa
MAJOR RELIGIONS Tribal religions, Roman Catholicism, Islam

TUNISIA

AREA 63,378 sq. mi. (164,149 sq. km.)
POPULATION 6,367,000
CAPITAL Tunis
LARGEST CITY Tunis
HIGHEST POINT Jeb. Chambi 5,066 ft. (1,544 m.)
MONETARY UNIT Tunisian dinar
MAJOR LANGUAGES Arabic, French
MAJOR RELIGION Islam

BURKINA FASO (UPPER VOLTA)

AREA 105,869 sq. mi. (274,200 sq. km.)
POPULATION 6,908,000
CAPITAL Ouagadougou
LARGEST CITY Ouagadougou
HIGHEST POINT 2,352 ft. (717 m.)
MONETARY UNIT CFA franc
MAJOR LANGUAGES Mossi, Lobi, French, Samo, Gourounsi
MAJOR RELIGIONS Islam, tribal religions, Roman Catholicism

WESTERN SAHARA

AREA 102,703 sq. mi. (266,000 sq. km.)
POPULATION 76,425
HIGHEST POINT 2,700 ft. (823 m.)
MAJOR LANGUAGE Arabic
MAJOR RELIGION Islam

Topography

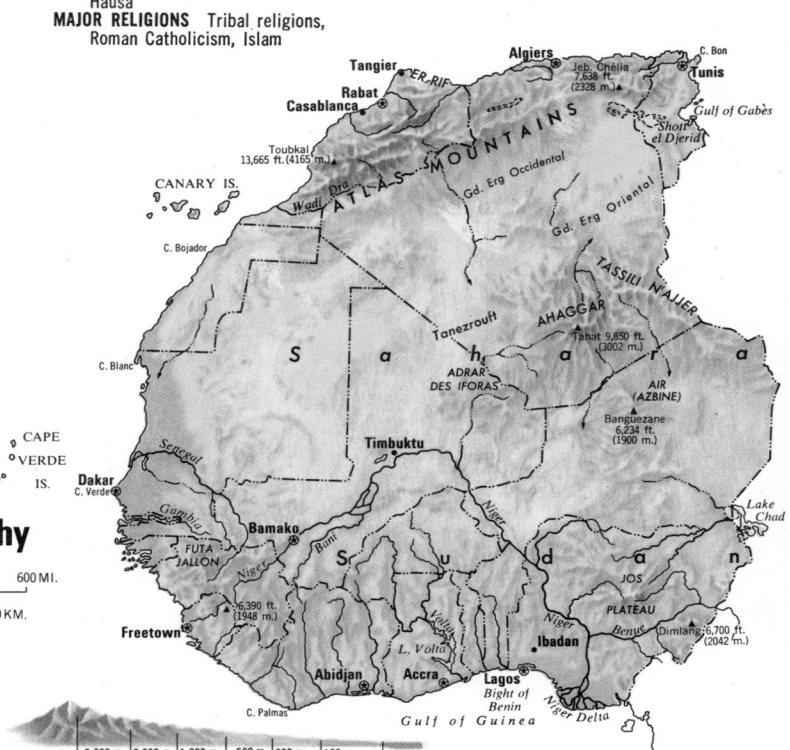

ALGERIA

CITIES and TOWNS

Abadla 12,200 D2
Adrar 22,800 D3
Aïn Beïda 26,976 F1
Aïn Sefra 22,400 D2
Aïn Temouchent 42,000 D1
Algiers (cap.) 1,365,400 E1
Amguid F3
Annaba 255,900 F1
Aoulef 17,200 E3
Arak E3
Batna 112,100 F1
Béchar 72,800 D2
Bejaïa 89,500 F1
Beni Abbès 5,000 D2
Beni Ounif 7,500 D2
Beni Saf 30,700 D1
Berga E3
Bidon 5 (Poste Maurice Cordier) E4
Biskra 90,500 F2
Blida 160,900 E1
Bône (Annaba) 255,900 F1
Bordj Bou Arreridj 65,000 E1
Bordj Fly Sainte Marie D3
Bordj Omar Driss 1,900 F3
Boufarik 50,000 E1
Bougie (Bejaïa) 89,500 F1
Bou Saâda 50,000 E1
Brezina 10,000 E2
Charouine D3
Chenachane D3
Cherchell 36,800 E1
Constantine 335,100 F1
Deldoul E3
Dellys 29,700 E1
Djanet 5,300 F4
Djelfa 51,000 E2
Djemaa 34,600 F2
Edjeleh F3
El Abiod Sidi Cheikh 15,300 E2
El Asnam 106,100 E1
El Bayadh 38,500 E2
El Djezair (Algiers) (cap.) 1,365,400 E1
El Goléa 24,400 E2
El Oued 72,100 F2
Fort Lallemand F2
Fort MacMahon E3
Fort Miribel E3
Fort Tarat F3
Ghardaïa 70,500 E2
Ghazaouet 25,900 D2
Guelma 60,100 F1
Guemar F2
Guerara 22,300 E2
Guerzim D3
Hassi Messaoud F2
Hassi R'Mel E2
Idelès F4
Igli 3,400 D2
Illizi 4,600 F3
In Amenas 4,200 F3
In Amguel E4
In Eker F4
In Guezzam F5
In Rhar E3
In Salah 18,800 E3
Jijel 49,800 F1
Kenadsa 7,600 D2
Kerzaz 2,900 D3
Khemis Miliana 57,800 E1
Ksar el Boukhari 41,200 E1
Laghouat 59,200 E2
Mascara 62,300 D1
Mecheria 22,600 D2
Médéa 72,300 E1
Metlili Chaamba 21,300 E2
Miliana 36,400 E1
Mohammadia 53,700 D1
Mostaganem 101,600 D1
M'Sila 49,100 E1
Oran 491,900 D1
Orléansville (El Asnam) 106,100 E1
Ouallene E4
Ouargla 77,400 F2
Ouled Djellal 22,700 F2
Philippeville (Skikda) 107,700 F1
Poste Maurice Cortier E4
Poste Weygand D4
Reggane 11,300 D3
Relizane 60,000 E1
Saïda 62,100 E2
Sbaa D3
Sétif 144,200 F1
Sidi Bel-Abbes 116,000 D1
Silet E4
Skikda 107,700 F1
Souk Ahras 60,200 F1
Tabelbala 3,100 D3
Taghit 3,500 D2
Tamanrasset 23,200 F4
Tamentit D3
Taourirt D3
Tébessa 67,200 F1
Temacine F2
Ténès 30,100 E1
Tiaret 62,900 E1
Tiguentourine F3
Timgad 9,800 F1
Timimoun 20,500 E3
Tindouf 6,500 C3
Tinjoub C3
Tin-Zaouatene E5
Tizi Ouzou 73,100 E1
Tlemcen 109,400 D2
Touggourt 75,600 F2
Zaouiet Kounta 13,800 D3

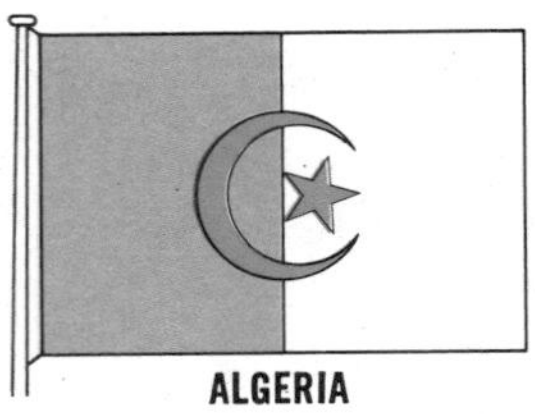

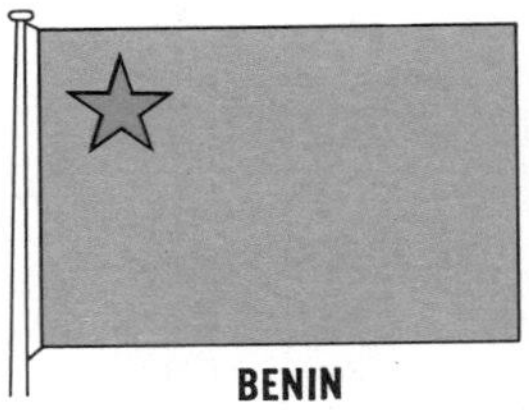

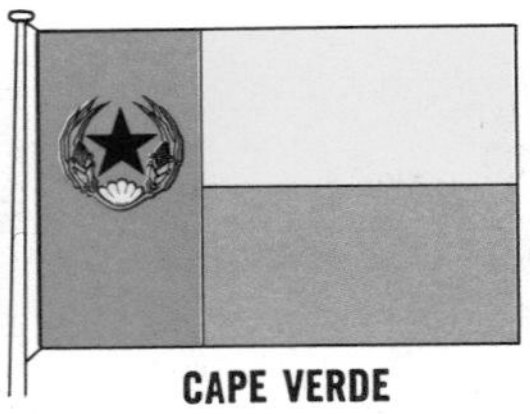

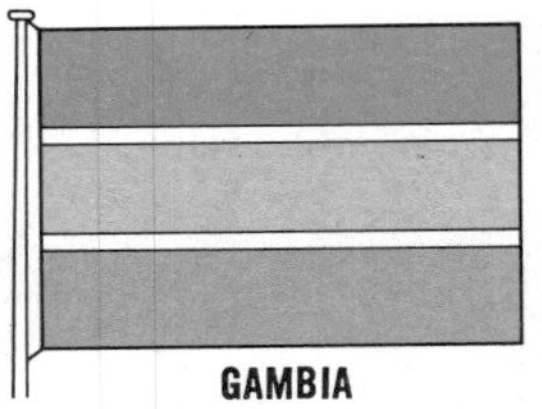

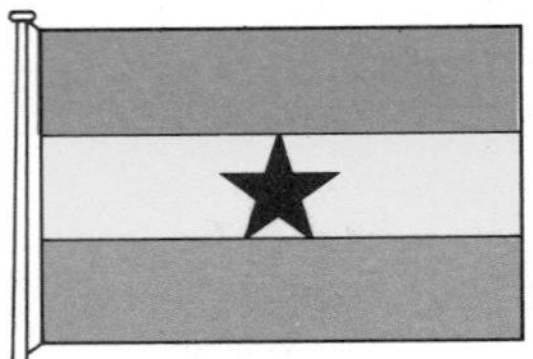

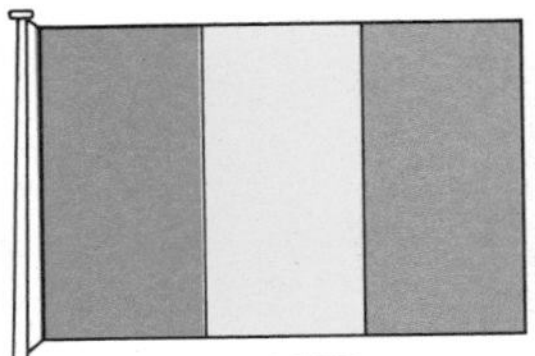

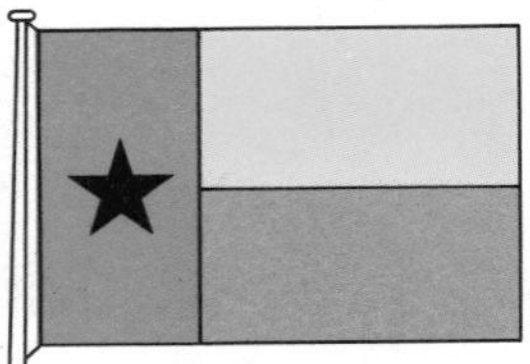

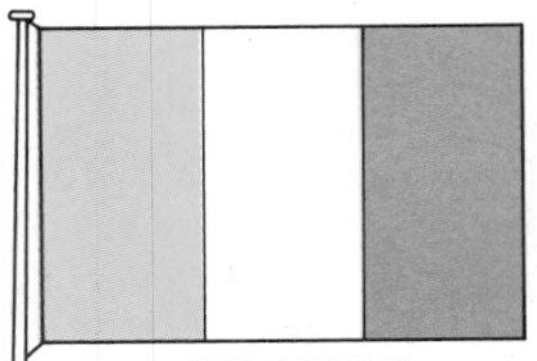

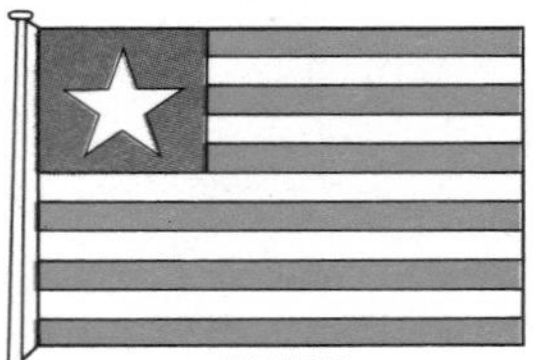

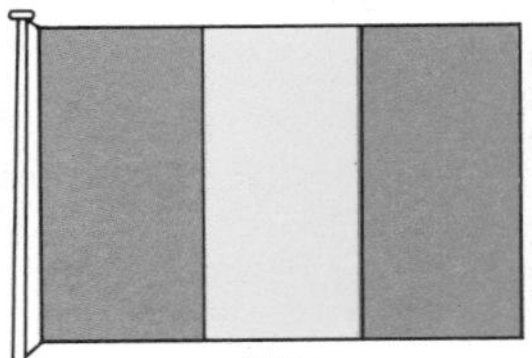

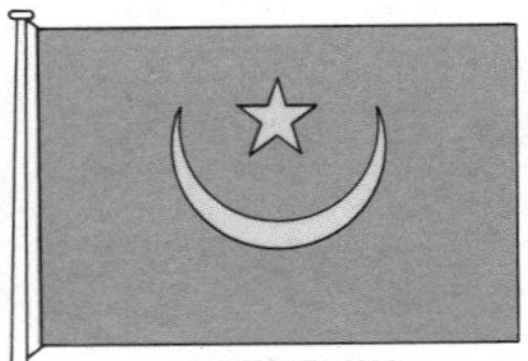

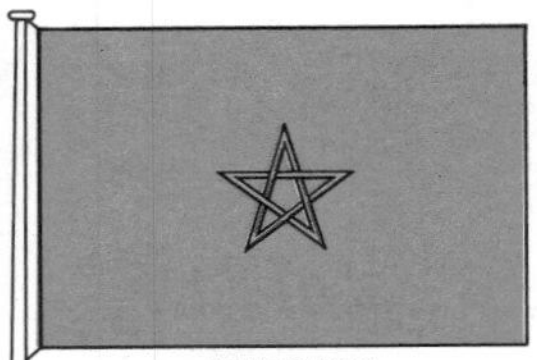

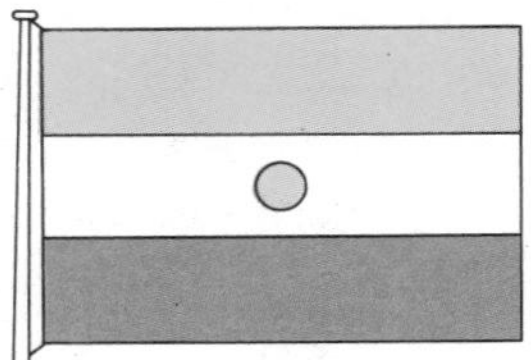

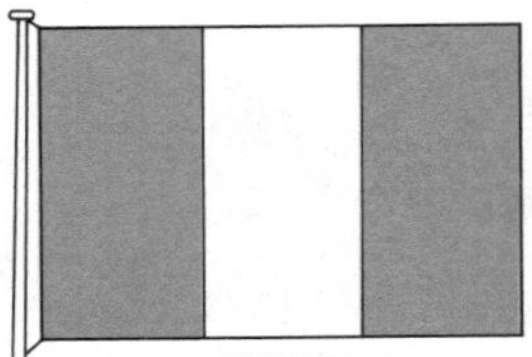

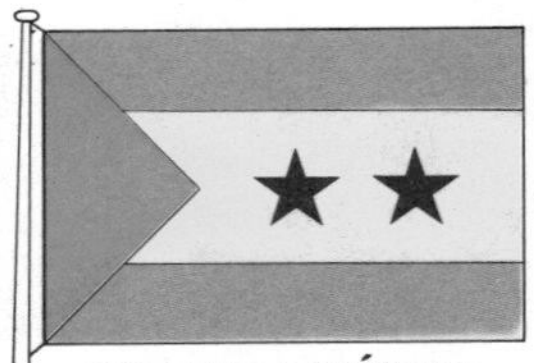

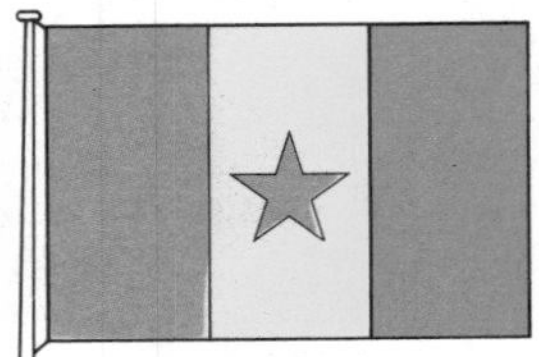

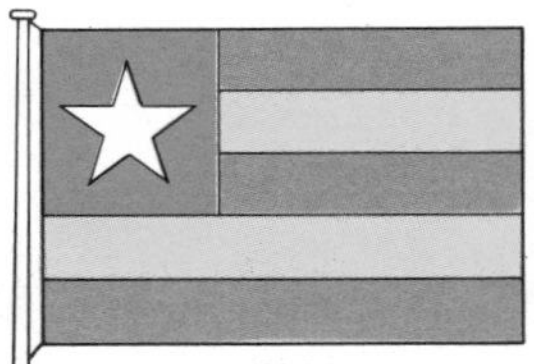

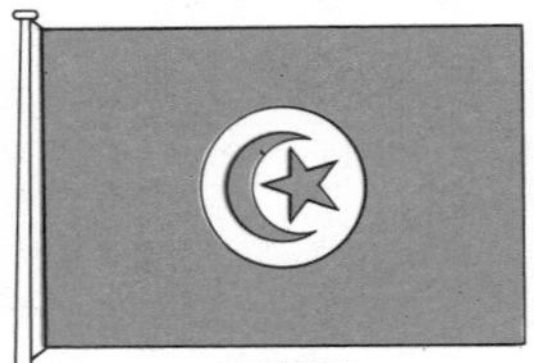

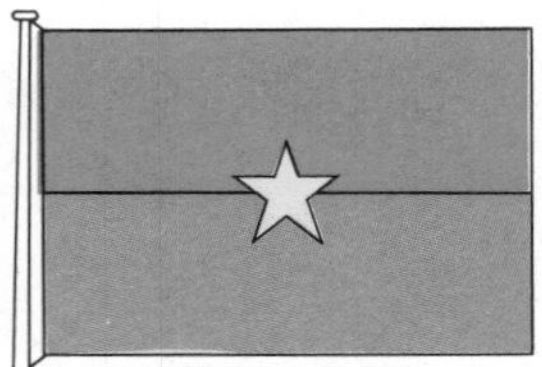

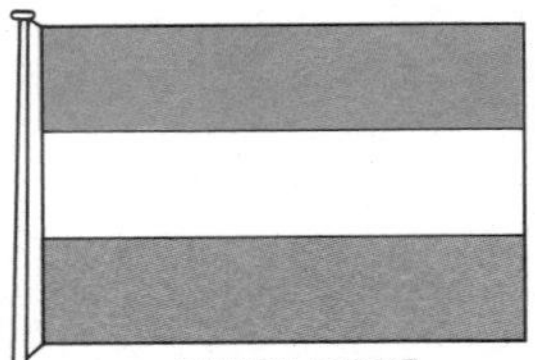

OTHER FEATURES

Adrar des Iforas (plat.) E5
Ahaggar (range) F4
Anaï (well) G4
Aouinet Bel Egrâ (well) C3
Atlas (mts.) E2
Aurès (lag.) F1
Azzel Mati, Sebkha (lake) E3
Bougaroun (cape) F1
Chech, Erg (des.) D3
Chelia (mt.) F1
Chelif (riv.) E1
Chergui, Chott Ech (salt lake) E2
Gourara (oasis) E3
Grand Erg Occidental (des.) E2
Grand Erg Oriental (des.) F2
Guir Hamada (des.) D2
High Plateaus (ranges) D2
Iguidi, Erg (des.) C3
In Ezzane (well) G4
Irharhar, Wadi (dry riv.) F3
Issaouane Erg (des.) F3
Kabylia (reg.) E1
Mediterranean (sea) E1
Medjerda (riv.) F1
Melrhir, Chott (salt lake) F2
Mouydir (mts.) E3
Mya, Wadi (dry riv.) E2
M'zab (oasis) E2
Raoui, Erg er (des.) D3
Rhir, Wadi (dry riv.) F2
Sahara (des.) E4
Saharan Atlas (ranges) E2
Saoura, Wadi (dry riv.) D3
Souf (oasis) F2
Tademaït, Plateau du (plat.) E3
Tafassasset, Wadi (dry riv.) F4
Tahat (mt.) F4
Tamanrasset, Wadi (dry riv.) E4
Tanezrouft (des.) E4
Tassili N'Ahagger (plat.) E4
Tassili N'Ajjer (plat.) F3
Tidikelt (oasis) E3
Timmissao (well) E4
Tindouf, Sebkha de (salt lake) C3
Tinrhert, Hamada de (des.) F3
Tni Haïa (well) D4
Touat (oasis) E3
Touila (well) C3

BENIN

CITIES and TOWNS

Abomey 38,000 E7
Cotonou 178,000 E7
Djougou E7
Grand-Popo E7
Kandi E6
Lokossa 6,000 E7
Malanville E6
Natitingou 49,000 E6
Nikki E7
Ouidah E7
Parakou 21,000 E7
Porto-Novo (cap.) 104,000 E7
Savalou E7
Savé E7

OTHER FEATURES

Atakora (mts.) E6
Benin (bight) E8
Guinea (gulf) E8
Mono (riv.) E7
Niger (riv.) E6
Ouémé (riv.) E7
Slave Coast (reg.) E7
Sudan (reg.) E6

CAPE VERDE

CITIES and TOWNS

Mindelo 28,797 A7
Praia (cap.) 21,494 B8
Ribeira Grande 1,892 B7
Sal Rei 1,296 B8
Santa Maria 956 B8

OTHER FEATURES

Boa Vista (isl.) B8
Brava (isl.) B8
Fogo (isl.) B8
Maio (isl.) B8
Sal (isl.) B7
Santa Luzia (isl.) B8
Santo Antão (isl.) A7
São Nicolau (isl.) B8
São Tiago (isl.) B8
São Vicente (isl.) B7

GAMBIA

CITIES and TOWNS

Banjul (cap.) 39,476 A6
Basse Santa Su 2,899 B6
Brikama 9,483 A6
Georgetown 2,510 A6

GHANA

CITIES and TOWNS

Accra (cap.) 564,194 D7
Accra* 738,498 D7
Ada 4,285 E7
Akuse 3,791 E7
Attebubu 6,630 D7
Awaso 5,449 D7
Axim 8,107 D8
Bawku 20,567 D6
Bekwai 11,287 D7
Berekum 14,296 D7
Bole 4,772 D7
Bolgatanga 18,896 D6
Cape Coast 51,653 D7
Daboya 1,872 D7
Damongo 7,760 D7
Dunkwa 15,437 D7
Elmina 11,401 D8
Enchi 4,382 D7
Gambaga 3,730 D6
Gyasikan 6,403 D7
Half Assini 5,429 D8
Ho 24,199 E7
Keta 14,446 E7
Kete Krachi 5,097 E7
Kintampo 7,149 D7
Koforidua 46,235 D7
Kpandu 12,842 E7
Kumasi 260,286 D7
Kumasi* 345,117 D7
Lawra 2,709 D6
Mampong 13,895 D7
Mpraeso 5,908 D7
Navrongo D6
Nsawam 25,518 D7
Nsuta 3,854 D7
Obuasi 31,005 D7
Oda 20,957 D7
Prestea 15,143 D7
Salaga 6,413 D7
Sekondi 33,713 D8
Sekondi-Takoradi* 160,868 D8
Sunyani 23,780 D7
Takoradi 58,161 D8
Tamale 83,653 D7
Tarkwa 14,702 D7
Tema 60,767 E7
Tumu 4,366 D6
Wa 21,374 D6
Wenchi 13,836 D7
Wiawso 5,558 D7
Winneba 30,778 D7
Yapei 1,203 D7
Yendi 22,072 D7

OTHER FEATURES

Ashanti (reg.) D7
Benin (bight) E8
Black Volta (riv.) D6
Gold Coast (reg.) D8
Guinea (gulf) E8
Oti (riv.) E7
Red Volta (riv.) D6
Saint Paul (cape) E7
Three Points (cape) D8
Volta (lake) D7
Volta (riv.) E7
White Volta (riv.) D6

ALGERIA

BENIN

CAPE VERDE

GAMBIA

GHANA

GUINEA

GUINEA-BISSAU

IVORY COAST

LIBERIA

MALI

MAURITANIA

MOROCCO

NIGER

NIGERIA

SÃO TOMÉ E PRÍNCIPE

SENEGAL

SIERRA LEONE

TOGO

TUNISIA

BURKINA FASO (UPPER VOLTA)

GUINEA

CITIES and TOWNS

Beyla C7
Boffa B6
Boké B6
Conakry (cap.)* 525,671 B7
Dabola B6
Dalaba B6
Dinguiraye B6
Dubréka B7
Faranah B6
Forécariah B7
Fria B6
Gaoual B6
Guéckédou B7
Kamsar B6
Kankan 85,310 C6
Kérouané C7
Kindia 79,861 B6
Kissidougou B7
Koundara 6,000 B6
Kouroussa C6
Labé 79,670 B6
Macenta C7
Mali B6
Mamou B6
N'Zérékoré 23,000 C7
Sangaredyi B6
Siguiri C6
Telimélé 12,000 B6
Tougué B6
Victoria B6

OTHER FEATURES

Bafing (riv.) B6
Bakoy (riv.) B6
Futa Jallon (lag.) B6
Los (isls.) B7
Milo (riv.) C7
Moa (riv.) B7
Niger (riv.) C6
Nimba (lag.) C7
Verga (cape) B6

GUINEA-BISSAU

CITIES and TOWNS

Bissau (cap.) 109,486 A6
Bolama 9,133 A6
Bubaque 6,706 B6
Bubaque 8,441 A6
Cacheu 15,194 A6

OTHER FEATURES

Bijagós (isls.) A6

IVORY COAST

CITIES and TOWNS

Abengourou 31,239 D7
Abidjan (cap.) 685,828 D7
Aboisso 14,272 D7
Agboville 27,192 D7
Bingerville 18,218 D7
Bondoukou 19,111 D7
Bouaflé 15,917 C7
Bouaké 173,248 D7
Bouna 5,787 D7
Boundiali 9,869 C7
Dabakala 3,272 D7
Dabou 23,870 D7
Daloa 60,958 C7
Danané 19,872 C7
Dimbokro 30,986 D7
Divo 37,896 C7
Ferkessédougou 25,307 D7
Fresco 1,865 C7
Gagnoa 42,362 C7
Grand-Bassam 25,808 D7
Grand-Lahou 4,070 C8
Guiglo 10,441 C7
Issia 11,143 C7
Katiola 21,559 C7
Kong 2,551 D7
Korhogo 47,657 C7
Man 50,315 C7
Mankono 6,570 C7
Odienné 13,864 C7
Port-Bouet 72,616 D7
San Pedro 27,616 C8
Sassandra 9,404 C8
Séguéla 12,587 C7
Sinfra 16,399 C7
Tabou 7,255 C8
Touba 5,256 C7
Toumodi 12,983 D7

OTHER FEATURES

Aby (lag.) D8
Bagoé (riv.) C6
Bandama (riv.) C7
Baoulé (riv.) C6
Black Volta (riv.) D6
Cavally (riv.) C7
Comoé (riv.) D7
Ebrié (lag.) D8
Guinea (gulf) E8
Ivory Coast (reg.) C8
Kossou, Lac de (lake) C7
Nimba (lag.) C7
Sassandra (riv.) C7

LIBERIA

CITIES and TOWNS

Buchanan 23,999 B7
Gbarnga 6,896 C7
Grand Cess C8
Greenville 8,462 C8
Harbel 11,445 B7
Harper 10,627 C8
Kolahun C7
Marshall B7
Monrovia (cap.) 166,507 B7
Plahn C7
River Cess 2,041 C7
Robertsport 2,562 B7
Sasstown C8
Tapeta 3,927 C7
Tchien 6,094 C7
Tubmanburg 14,089 B7

OTHER FEATURES

Bong (range) B7
Cavalla (riv.) C7
Cestos (riv.) C7
Grain Coast (reg.) B8
Kru Coast (reg.) C8
Mano (riv.) B7
Mount (cape) B7
Nimba (lag.) C7
Palmas (cape) C8
Roberts Field Int'l Airport C7

MALI

CITIES and TOWNS

Anéfis E5
Ansongo 3,485 E5
Araouane D5
Bafoulabé 2,163 B6
Bamako (cap.) 404,022 C6
Bamba D5
Banamba 6,776 C6
Bandiagara 8,920 D6
Bankass 3,229 D6
Bou Djebeha D5
Bougouni 17,246 C6
Bourem 4,538 E5
Dioïla 4,953 C6
Dire 8,941 D5
Djenné 10,251 D6
Douentza 6,746 D6
Gao 30,714 E5
Goundam 10,262 D5
Gourma-Rharous 4,671 D5
Hombori D5
Kadiolo 3,991 C6
Kangaba 3,184 C6
Kati 24,991 C6
Kayes 44,736 B6
Ké-Macina 5,426 C6
Kéniéba 4,510 B6
Kerchoual E5
Kidal 3,308 E5
Kita 17,538 C6
Kolokani 8,923 C6
Kolondiéba 5,882 C6
Koulikoro 16,376 C6
Kouroula B6
Koutiala 27,497 C6
Mabrouk D5
Ménaka 3,693 E5
Mopti 53,885 D6
Nampala C5
Nara 6,091 C5
Niafunké 6,399 C5
Niono 12,290 C6
Nioro 11,617 C5
San 22,962 D6
Satadougou B6
Ségou 64,890 C6
Sikasso 47,030 C6
Sokolo C6
Taoudenni D4
Ténenkou 4,708 C6
Tessalit E4
Timbuktu (Tombouctou) 20,483 D5
Toukoto C6
Yanfolila 3,809 C6
Yelimané 1,481 B5
Yorosso 2,390 C6

OTHER FEATURES

Achourat (well) D4
Adrar des Iforas (plat.) E5
Asselar (well) D5
Azaouad (reg.) D5
Azaouak (dry riv.) E5
Bafing (riv.) B6
Bagoé (riv.) C6
Bakoy (riv.) B6
Bani (riv.) C6
Baoulé (dry riv.) C6
Baoulé (riv.) C6
Bir Ounane (well) D4
Chech, Erg (des.) D4
Debo (lake) D5
El Mraïti (well) D5
Faguibine (lake) D5
Falémé (riv.) B6
Haricha Hamada (des.) D4
Hombori (mts.) D5
In Dagouber (well) D4
Macina (depr.) D6
Niger (riv.) D5
Oum el Asel (well) D4
Sahara (des.) D4
Sekkane, Erg (des.) D4
Senegal (riv.) B5
Sudan (reg.) D6
Tadjnout Hagguerete (well) D4
Terhazza (ruins) C4
Tilemsi (valley) E5
Toufourine (well) C4

MAURITANIA

CITIES and TOWNS

Aloun el Atrous C5
Akjoujt 8,044 B5
Akreïjit C5
Aleg 6,415 B5
Atar 16,326 B4
Bassikounou C5
Bir Mogreïn B3
Boutilimit 7,261 B5
Bogué 8,056 B5
Chinguetti B4
Fderik (Fort-Gouraud) 2,160 B4
Kaédi 20,848 B5
Kankossa B5
Kiffa 10,629 B5
Maghama B5
M'Bout B5
Méderdra A5
Néma 8,232 C5
Nouakchott (cap.) 134,986 A5
Nouadhibou 21,961 A4
Ouadane B4
Oualata C5
Oujaf C5
Ouijeft B4
Rosso 16,466 A5
Sélibaby 5,994 B5
Tamchakett B5
Tamsagout C4
Tazadit B4
Tichit C5
Tidjikja 7,870 B5
Timbédra 5,317 C5
Zouîrât 17,474 B4

OTHER FEATURES

Adafer (reg.) B5
Adrar (reg.) B4
Affolé (reg.) B5
Aguerakten (well) C4
Aïn ben Tili (well) C3
Arguin (bay) A4
Assaba (reg.) B5
Atoui, Wadi (dry riv.) B4
Ben Guerdane (well) B3
Bir el Khzaim (well) C4
Blanc (cape) A4
Brakna (reg.) B5
Chegga (well) C3
Djouf, El (des.) C4
El Mrayer (well) C4
El Mreïti (well) C4
Gorgol (reg.) B5
Hodh (reg.) C5
Iguidi, Erg (des.) C3
Inchiri (reg.) A5
Koumbi Saleh (ruins) C5
Lévrier (bay) A4
Maktelr (des.) B4
Meraïa (reg.) C5
Mirik (Timiris) (cape) A5
Ouarane (reg.) B4
Sahara (des.) C4
Senegal (riv.) B5
Tagant (reg.) B5
Tidra (isl.) A5
Timiris (cape) A5
Touila (well) C3
Trarza (reg.) A5

MOROCCO

CITIES and TOWNS

Agadir 61,192 C2
Al Hoceima 18,686 D1
Asilah 14,074 C1
Azemmour 17,182 C2
Azrou 20,756 C2
Beni Mellal 53,826 C2
Berguent 3,356 D2
Bou Arfa D2
Bou Izakarn 2,342 C3
Boujad 18,838 C2
Casablanca 1,506,373 C2
Chechaouene 15,362 D1
Dar-el-Beida (Casablanca) 1,506,373 C2
El Jadida 55,501 C2
El Kelaa des Srarhna 17,163 C2
Erfoud 5,400 D2
Er Rachidia 16,775 D2
Essaouira 30,061 B2
Fedala (Mohammedia) 70,392 C2
Fès (Fez) 325,327 D2
Figuig 13,660 D2
Goulmima 4,056 C2
Inezgane 11,495 C2

Jerada 30,633 D2
Kenitra 139,206 C2
Khenifra 25,526 C2
Khouribga 73,667 C2
Ksar el Kebir 48,262 C2
Larache 45,710 C1
Marrakech 332,741 C2
Mazagan (El Jadida) 55,501 C2
Meknès 248,369 C2
Mogador (Essaouira) 30,061 B2
Mohammedia 70,392 C2
Nador 32,490 D1
Ouarzazate 11,142 C2
Oued Zem 33,323 C2
Ouezzane 33,267 C2
Oujda 175,532 D2
Petitjean (Sidi Kacem) 26,831 C2
Port-Lyautey (Kénitra) 139,206 C2
Rabat (cap.) 367,620 C2
Safi 129,113 C2
Saïdia D2
Salé 155,557 C2
Sefrou 28,607 D2
Settat 42,325 C2
Sidi Ifni 13,650 B3
Sidi Kacem 26,831 C2
Tagounite C3
Tangier (Tanger) 187,894 C1
Tan-Tan 10,772 B3
Taourirt 15,580 D2
Taouz D2
Tarfaya 1,104 B3
Taroudant 22,272 C2
Taza 55,157 D2
Tendrara D2
Tétouan 139,105 C1
Tiznit 11,391 B3
Youssoufia 22,435 C2
Zagora 5,306 C2

OTHER FEATURES

Anti-Atlas (ranges) C3
Atlas (mts.) C2
Bani, Jebel (mts.) C3
Beddouza, Ras (cape) C2
Dra, Wadi (dry riv.) C3
Er Rif (range) D2
Gibraltar (str.) C1
High Atlas (ranges) C2
Juby (cape) B3
Mediterranean (sea) D1
Middle Atlas (ranges) C2
Moulouya (riv.) D2
Rhéris, Wadi (dry riv.) D2
Rhir (cape) B2
Rif, Er (range) D2
Sarhro, Jebel (mts.) C2
Sebou (riv.) C2
Sim (cape) B2
Toubkal, Jebel (mt.) C2
Ziz, Wadi (dry riv.) D2

NIGER

CITIES and TOWNS

Agadès 11,000 F5
Arhli (Arlit) F4
Bilma G5
Birni-N'Konni 10,000 E6
Bosso G6
Chirfa G4
Dakoro F6
Dessa E6
Diffa G6
Djado G4
Dogondoutchi 9,000 E6
Dosso E6
Fachi G5
Filingué 10,000 E6
Gangara F6
Gaya 5,000 E6
Gouré G6
Iférouane F5
Illéla 9,000 F6
In-Gall F5
Madama G4
Madaoua F6
Magaria F6
Mainé-Soroa G6
Maradi 45,852 F6
N'Guigmi G6
Niamey (cap.) 225,314 E6
Quallam E6
Say E6
Tahoua 31,265 F6
Tanout F6
Téra 8,000 E6
Tessaoua 5,000 F6
Tillabéry E6
Timia F4
Zinder 58,436 F6

OTHER FEATURES

Achégour (well) G5
Agadem (well) G5
Air (mts.) F5
Anaye (well) G5
Assakarai (dry riv.) F5
Azaoua (reg.) E5
Azbine (Air) (mts.) F5
Bagam (well) F5
Banguezane (mt.) F5
Bedouaram (well) G5
Chad (lake) G6
Dallol Bosso (dry riv.) E6
Dillia (dry riv.) G5
Djado (plat.) G4
El War (well) G4
In Azaoua (well) F4
Komadugu Yobe (riv.) G6
Mantas (well) E5
Niger (riv.) E6
Sahara (des.) F4
Sudan (reg.) F6
Tafassasset, Wadi (dry riv.) F4
Talak (reg.) E5
Ténéré (des.) G5
Timboulaga (well) F5
Tummo (El War) (well) G4
Zoo Baba (well) G5

NIGERIA

STATES

Anambra 2,300,000 F7
Bauchi 2,496,329 F6
Bendel 2,336,000 F7
Benue 2,641,496 F7
Borno 2,853,553 G6
Cross River 3,633,582 F7
Gongola 1,585,200 G7
Imo 5,000,000 F7
Kaduna 4,098,303 F6
Kano 5,775,000 F6
Kwara 1,600,600 E7
Lagos 1,100,000 E7
Niger 2,900,000 F7
Ogun 1,448,966 E7
Ondo 2,727,676 F7
Oyo 5,208,884 E7
Plateau 1,367,450 F7
Rivers 1,544,314 F8
Sokoto 1,367,450 F6

CITIES and TOWNS

Aba 177,000 F7
Abeokuta 253,000 E7
Abuja F7
Ado 213,000 E7
Afikpo F7
Aku F7
Akure F7
Argungu E6
Asaba F7
Azare G6
Baga G6
Bama G6
Baro F7
Bauchi F6
Benin City 136,000 F7
Bida F7
Birnin Kebbi E6
Biu G6
Bonny F8
Brass F8
Burutu F7
Calabar 103,000 F7
Deba Habe G6
Degema F8
Dikwa G6
Donga G7
Ede 182,000 E7
Eha Amufu F7
Enugu 187,000 F7
Forcados E7
Funtua F6
Gashaka G7
Gbogo F7
Geidam G6
Gombe G6
Gumel F6
Gummi F6
Gusau F6
Gwadabawa F6
Hadejia G6
Ibadan 847,000 E7
Ibi F7
Ife 176,000 E7
Ijebu-Ode E7
Ikeja E7
Ikom F7
Ilesha 224,000 F7
Ilorin 282,000 E7
Isa F6
Iseyin 115,083 E7
Iwo 214,000 E7
Jalingo G7
Jebba E7
Jega E6
Jos F7
Kabba F7
Kaduna 202,000 F6
Kaiama E7
Kalmalo F6
Kano 399,000 F6
Katsina 109,424 F6
Katsina Ala F7
Kaura Namoda F6
Keffi F7
Koko F7
Kontagora F6
Kukawa G6
Kumo G7
Kuta F7
Lafia F7
Lafiagi F7
Lagos (cap.) 1,060,848 E7
Laro E7
Lere F7
Lokoja F7
Maiduguri 189,000 G6
Maigatari F6
Makurdi F7
Minna F7
Mubi G6
Nasarawa F7
New Bussa E6
Nguru G6
Nnewi F7
Nsukka F7
Offa E7
Ogbomosho 432,000 E7
Ogoja F7
Okene F7
Ondo F7
Onitsha 220,000 F7
Oron F8
Oshogbo 282,000 F7
Owerri F7
Owo F7
Oyo 152,000 E7
Pankshin F7
Panyam F7
Port Harcourt 242,000 F8
Ringim F6
Sapele F7
Shaki E7
Shendam F7
Sokoto F6
Toungo G7
Uromi F7
Vom F7
Wamba F7
Warri F7
Wukari F7
Yan G7
Yelwa F6
Yola G7
Zaria 224,000 F6
Zungeru F7

OTHER FEATURES

Adamawa (reg.) G7
Benin (bight) E8
Benue (riv.) F7
Biafra (bight) F8
Biu (plat.) G6
Bonny (bight) F8
Chad (lake) G6
Cross (riv.) F7
Dimlang (mt.) G7
Donga (riv.) G7
Foge (isl.) E6
Gongola (riv.) G6
Guinea (gulf) E8
Hadejia (riv.) F6
Jos (plat.) F7
Kaduna (riv.) F7
Kainji (res.) E6
Kebbi (riv.) E6
Komadugu Yobe (riv.) G6
Niger (delta) F8
Niger (riv.) F7
Osse (riv.) F7
Slave Coast (reg.) E7
Sokoto (riv.) F6
Sudan (reg.) F6

PORTUGAL-Madeira

CITIES and TOWNS

Funchal (cap.) 38,340 A2

OTHER FEATURES

Desertas (isls.) A2
Madeira (isl.) A2
Pôrto Santo (isl.) A2
Salvage (isls.) A2

SÃO TOMÉ E PRINCIPE

CITIES and TOWNS

Santo António 1,618 F8
São Tomé (cap.) 7,681 F8

OTHER FEATURES

Guinea (gulf) E8
Príncipe (isl.) F8
São Tomé (isl.) F8

SENEGAL

CITIES and TOWNS

Bakel 6,339 B6
Bignona 14,537 A6
Dagana 10,506 A5
Dakar (cap.) 798,792 A6
Diourbel 50,618 A6
Kaolack 106,899 A6
Kédougou 7,575 B6
Kaffrine 11,211 A6
Kolda 19,302 B6
Linguère 7,890 B5
Louga 35,063 A5
Matam 10,002 B5
M'Bour 37,663 A6
Nioro-du-Rip 7,824 A6
Podor 6,914 B5
Richard Toll A5
Rufisque A6
Saint-Louis 88,404 A5
Sedhiou 9,421 A6
Tambacounda 25,147 B6
Thiès 117,333 A5
Tivaouane 17,351 A5
Touba A6
Yarboutenda B6
Ziguinchor 72,726 A6

OTHER FEATURES

Casamance (riv.) A6
Falémé (riv.) B6
Ferlo (reg.) B6
Gambia (riv.) B6
Senegal (riv.) B5
Verde (cape) A6

SIERRA LEONE

CITIES and TOWNS

Bo 42,216 B7
Bonthe 6,230 B7
Freetown (cap.) 274,000 B7
Kabala 4,610 B7
Kambia 3,700 B7
Kenema 33,880 B7
Lungi 2,170 B7
Marampa B7
Makeni 28,684 B7
Moyamba 4,564 B7
Pendembu 2,696 B7
Pepel 3,793 B7
Port Loko 5,809 B7
Pujehun 1 B7

OTHER FEATURES

Loma, Mansa (lag.) B7
Mano (riv.) B7
Moa (riv.) B7
Sherbro (isl.) B7
Yawri (bay) B7

SPAIN-Canary Islands, Ceuta and Melilla

CITIES and TOWNS

Arrecife 21,310 B3
Ceuta 60,639 C1
La Laguna A3
Las Palmas de Gran Canaria 260,368 B3
Melilla 64,942 D1
Santa Cruz de la Palma 10,393 A3
Santa Cruz de Tenerife 74,910 A3

OTHER FEATURES

Canary (isls.) A3
Fuerteventura (isl.) B3
Gomera (isl.) A3
Grand Canary (isl.) A3
Hierro (isl.) A3
Lanzarote (isl.) B3
La Palma (isl.) A3
Tenerife (isl.) A3

TOGO

CITIES and TOWNS

Aného (Anécho) 10,889 E7
Atakpamé 17,440 E7
Dapaong 10,100 E6
Kpalimé 19,801 E7
Kpémé 3,600 E7
Lama-Kara 9,400 E7
Lomé (cap.) 148,443 E7
Mango 9,600 E6
Sokodé 29,623 E7

OTHER FEATURES

Benin (bight) E8
Guinea (gulf) E8
Mono (riv.) E7
Oti (riv.) E7
Slave Coast (reg.) E7

TUNISIA

CITIES and TOWNS

Béja 39,226 F1
Ben Gardane 6,593 G2
Bizerte 62,856 F1
Burj al Hattaba F2
El Borma F2
El Djem 10,666 G1
El Kef 27,939 F1
Gabès 40,585 F2
Gafsa 42,225 F2
Halq el Oued 41,912 G1
Jendouba 18,127 F1
Kairouan 54,546 F1
Kalaa-Kebira 23,508 F1
Kasserine 22,594 F1
La Goulette (Halq el Oued) 41,912 G1
La Skhirra 4,565 G2
Le Kef (El Kef) 27,939 F1
Mahdia 25,711 G1
Mareth 2,185 F2
Mateur 19,645 F1
Médenine 15,826 F2
Menzel Bourguiba 42,111 F1
Menzel Temime 18,857 G1
Moknine 26,035 G1
Monastir 26,759 G1
Msaken 33,559 G1
Nabeul 30,476 G1
Nefta 12,476 F2
Remada 6,100 F2
Sbeitla 8,039 F1
Sfax 171,297 G2
Sousse 69,530 G1
Tabarka 3,140 F1
Tatahouine 10,399 G2
Tozeur 16,772 F2
Tunis (cap.) 550,404 G1
Tunis* 873,515 G1
Zarzis 14,420 G2

OTHER FEATURES

Abiad, Ras el (Blanc) (cape) G1
Blanc (cape) G1
Bon (cape) G1
Chambi, Jebel (mt.) F2
Djerba (isl.) G2
Djerid, Shott el (salt lake) F2
Gabès (gulf) G2
Grand Erg Oriental (des.) F2
Hammamet (gulf) G1
Jefara (reg.) G2
Kerkennah (isls.) G2
Mediterranean (sea) F1
Medjerda (riv.) F1
Tib, Ras el (Bon) (cape) G1
Tunis (gulf) G1

BURKINA FASO (UPPER VOLTA)

CITIES and TOWNS

Aribinda D6
Banfora 12,358 D6
Batié D7
Bobo Dioulasso 115,063 D6
Bogandé E6
Dédougou D6
Diapaga E6
Diébougou D6
Djibo D6
Dori D6
Fada-N'Gourma 12,000 E6
Gaoua D6
Houndé D6
Kaya 18,000 D6
Koudougou 36,838 D6
Koupela E6
Léo D6
Ouagadougou (cap.) 172,661 D6
Ouahigouya 25,690 D6
Pama E6
Po D6
Tenkodogo E6
Tougan D6
Yako D6
Zabré D6

OTHER FEATURES

Black Volta (riv.) D6
Comoé (riv.) D7
Oti (riv.) E7
Red Volta (riv.) D6
Sudan (reg.) D6
White Volta (riv.) D6

WESTERN SAHARA

CITIES and TOWNS

Dakhla 6,554 A4
El Aaiún (Laayoune) 24,519 B3
Semara 2,655 B3
Villa Cisneros (Dakhla) 6,554 A4

OTHER FEATURES

Atoui, Wadi (dry riv.) B4
Ausert (well) B4
Barbas (cape) A4
Bir Ganduz (well) A4
Bir Nzaran (well) B4
Blanc (cape) A4
Bojador (cape) B3
Durnford (pt.) A4
Guelta de Zemmur (well) B3
Saguia el Hamra (dry riv.) B3
Tichlá (well) B4

*City and suburbs.
○Population of sub-district or division.

Agriculture, Industry and Resources

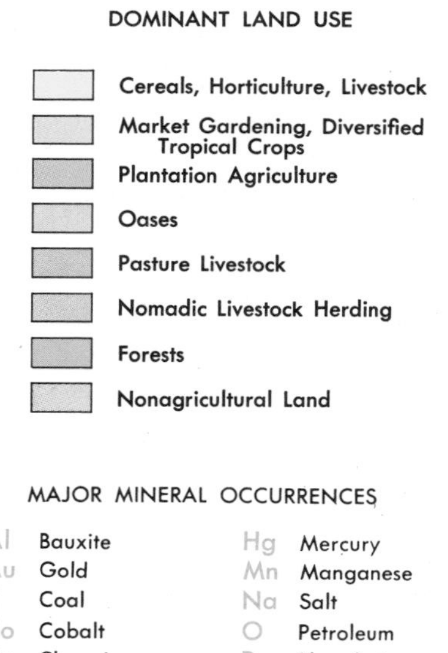

DOMINANT LAND USE
Cereals, Horticulture, Livestock
Market Gardening, Diversified Tropical Crops
Plantation Agriculture
Oases
Pasture Livestock
Nomadic Livestock Herding
Forests
Nonagricultural Land
MAJOR MINERAL OCCURRENCES
Al Bauxite
Au Gold
C Coal
Co Cobalt
Cr Chromium
Cu Copper
D Diamonds
Fe Iron Ore
G Natural Gas
Gn Granite
Gp Gypsum
Hg Mercury
Mn Manganese
Na Salt
O Petroleum
P Phosphates
Pb Lead
Sb Antimony
Sn Tin
Ti Titanium
U Uranium
Zn Zinc
Water Power
Major Industrial Areas

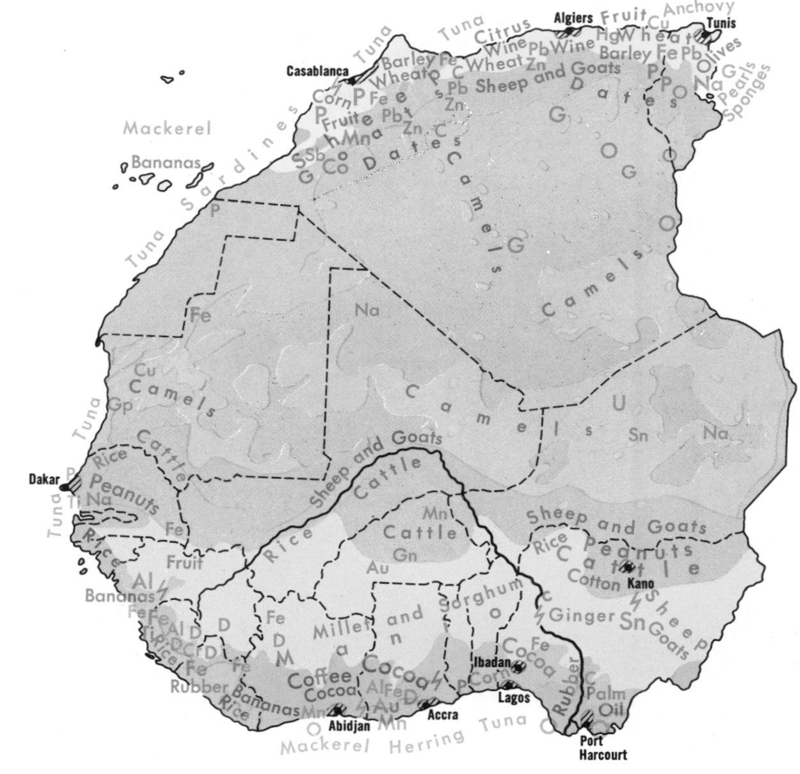

Algiers
Tunis
Casablanca
Dakar
Kano
Ibadan
Lagos
Abidjan
Accra
Port Harcourt
Tuna
Fruit
Anchovy
Citrus
Wine
Wheat
Barley
Olives
Sheep and Goats
Dates
Corn
Pearls
Sponges
Mackerel
Bananas
Sardines
Camels
Rice
Cattle
Peanuts
Millet and Sorghum
Ginger
Coffee
Cocoa
Rubber
Palm Oil
Mackerel
Herring

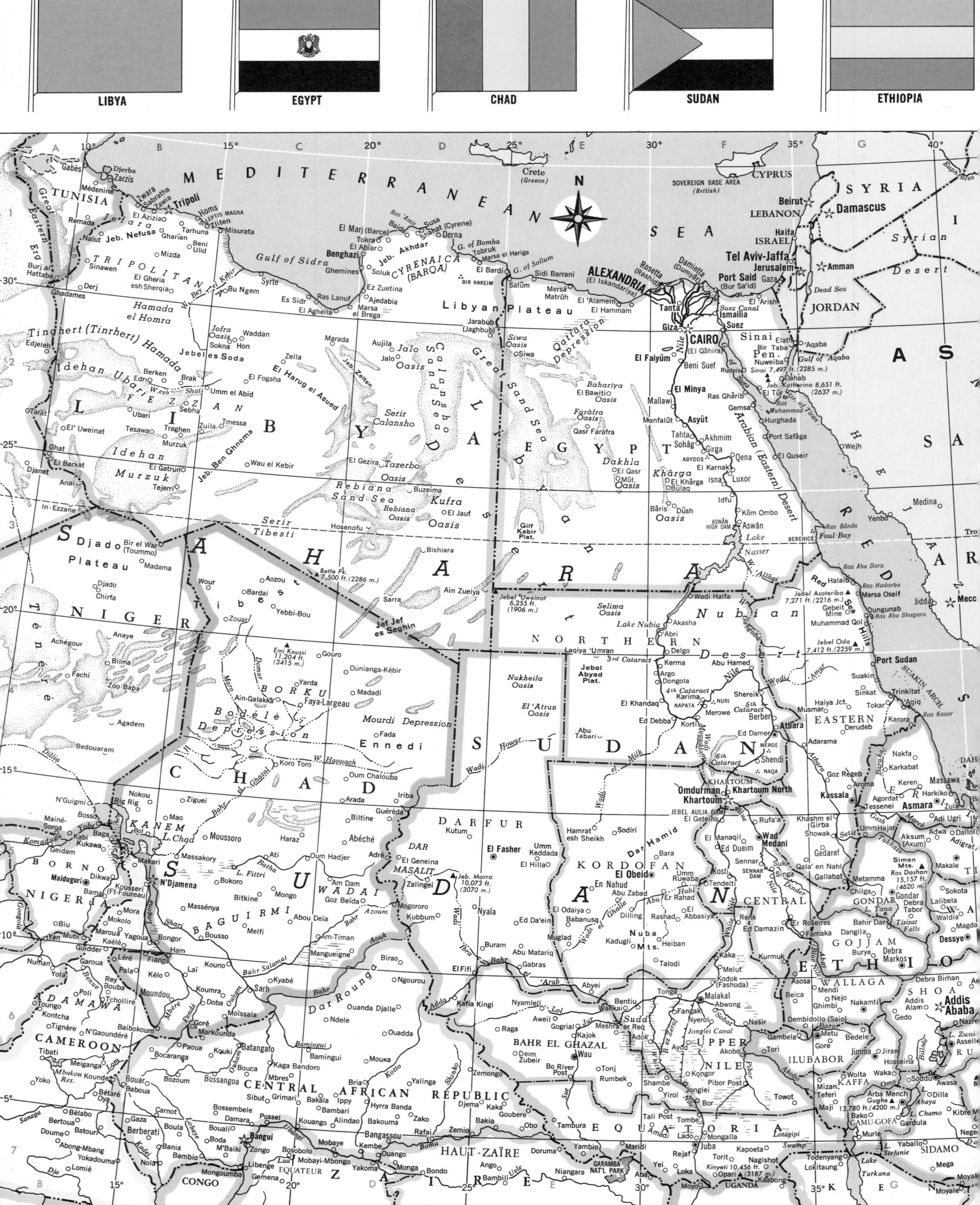

LIBYA
EGYPT
CHAD
SUDAN
ETHIOPIA
MEDITERRANEAN SEA
CYPRUS
SYRIA
Damascus
Beirut
LEBANON
ISRAEL
Tel Aviv-Jaffa
Jerusalem
Amman
JORDAN
Syrian Desert
Crete (Greece)
TUNISIA
Tripoli
Gulf of Sidra
Benghazi
CYRENAICA (BARQA)
TRIPOLITANIA
ALEXANDRIA (El Iskandariya)
Port Said
Suez
CAIRO (El Qâhira)
Giza
Sinai Pen.
Gulf of Aqaba
Libyan Plateau
Qattara Depression
Great Sand Sea
LIBYA
EGYPT
Arabian (Eastern) Desert
Aswân
Lake Nasser
Jebel 'Uweinat 6,255 ft. (1906 m.)
SAHARA
Tibesti
Emi Koussi 11,204 ft. (3415 m.)
BORKU
Bodélé Depression
Ennedi
NIGER
CHAD
N'Djamena
L. Chad
KANEM
BAGUIRMI
WADAI
DARFUR
El Fasher
Jeb. Marra 10,073 ft. (3070 m.)
SUDAN
NORTHERN
Nubian Desert
Port Sudan
Khartoum
Omdurman
Khartoum North
KORDOFAN
El Obeid
Nuba Mts.
EASTERN
CENTRAL
BAHR EL GHAZAL
UPPER NILE
EQUATORIA
Juba
Sudd
ETHIOPIA
Asmara
Addis Ababa
GOJJAM
GONDAR
SHOA
ILUBABOR
KAFFA
WALLAGA
SIDAMO
GAMU-GOFA
L. Tana
Simen Mts. Ras Dashan 15,157 ft. (4620 m.)
Red Sea
Jidda
Medina
CENTRAL AFRICAN REPUBLIC
Bangui
CAMEROON
NIGERIA
ADAMAWA
BORNO
CONGO
ZAIRE
HAUT-ZAÏRE
EQUATEUR
UGANDA
L. Turkana

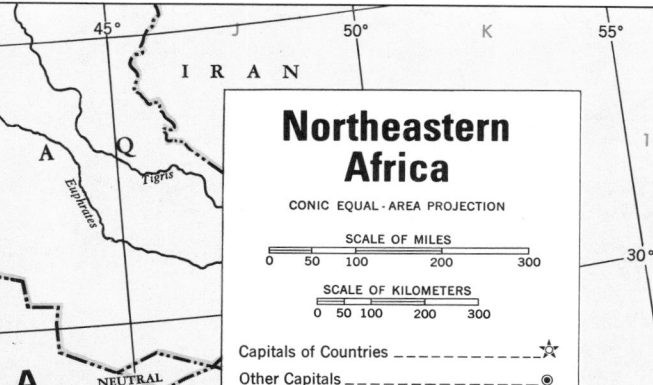

LIBYA

AREA 679,358 sq. mi. (1,759,537 sq. km.)
POPULATION 2,856,000
CAPITAL Tripoli
LARGEST CITY Tripoli
HIGHEST POINT Bette Pk. 7,500 ft. (2,286 m.)
MONETARY UNIT Libyan dinar
MAJOR LANGUAGES Arabic, Berber
MAJOR RELIGION Islam

EGYPT

AREA 386,659 sq. mi. (1,001,447 sq. km.)
POPULATION 41,572,000
CAPITAL Cairo
LARGEST CITY Cairo
HIGHEST POINT Jeb. Katherina 8,651 ft. (2,637 m.)
MONETARY UNIT Egyptian pound
MAJOR LANGUAGE Arabic
MAJOR RELIGIONS Islam, Coptic Christianity

CHAD

AREA 495,752 sq. mi. (1,283,998 sq. km.)
POPULATION 4,309,000
CAPITAL N'Djamena
LARGEST CITY N'Djamena
HIGHEST POINT Emi Koussi 11,204 ft. (3,415 m.)
MONETARY UNIT CFA franc
MAJOR LANGUAGES Arabic, Bagirmi, French, Sara, Massa, Moudang
MAJOR RELIGIONS Islam, tribal religions

SUDAN

AREA 967,494 sq. mi. (2,505,809 sq. km.)
POPULATION 18,691,000
CAPITAL Khartoum
LARGEST CITY Khartoum
HIGHEST POINT Jeb. Marra 10,073 ft. (3,070 m.)
MONETARY UNIT Sudanese pound
MAJOR LANGUAGES Arabic, Dinka, Nubian, Beja, Nuer
MAJOR RELIGIONS Islam, tribal religions

ETHIOPIA

AREA 471,776 sq. mi. (1,221,900 sq. km.)
POPULATION 31,065,000
CAPITAL Addis Ababa
LARGEST CITY Addis Ababa
HIGHEST POINT Ras Dashan 15,157 ft. (4,620 m.)
MONETARY UNIT birr
MAJOR LANGUAGES Amharic, Gallinya, Tigrinya, Somali, Sidamo, Arabic, Ge'ez
MAJOR RELIGIONS Coptic Christianity, Islam

DJIBOUTI

AREA 8,880 sq. mi. (23,000 sq. km.)
POPULATION 386,000
CAPITAL Djibouti
LARGEST CITY Djibouti
HIGHEST POINT Moussa Ali 6,768 ft. (2,063 m.)
MONETARY UNIT Djibouti franc
MAJOR LANGUAGES Arabic, Somali, Afar, French
MAJOR RELIGIONS Islam, Roman Catholicism

CHAD

CITIES and TOWNS

Abéché 28,100	D5
Abou Dela	C5
Adré	C5
Ain-Galakka	C4
Am-Dam	C5
Am-Timan 4,200	D5
Arada	D4
Ati 7,500	C5
Baibokoum 5,500	C6
Bardai	C3
Biltine 3,900	D5
Bitkine 5,000	C5
Bokoro 6,500	C5
Bol 2,500	B5
Bongor 14,300	C5
Bousso 4,500	C5
Doba 13,300	C6
Fada	D4
Faya-Largeau 6,800	C4
Fianga 10,000	C6
Goré	C6
Gouro	C3
Goz Belda	D5
Guéréda	D4
Ham	C5

Haraz	C5
Iriba	D4
Kélo 16,800	C5
Koro Toro	C4
Koumra 17,000	C6
Kouno	C5
Kyabé 5,000	C6
Lal 10,400	C6
Léré	B6
Madadi	D3
Mangueigne	D5
Mao 4,900	C5
Massakory	C5
Massenya	C5
Melfi	C5
Mogororo	D5
Molssala 5,100	C6
Mongo 8,300	C5
Moundou 39,600	C6
Moussoro 7,700	C5
N'Djamena (cap.) 179,000	C5
Nokou	B5
Oum Chalouba	D4
Oum Hadjer 5,600	D5
Ounianga-Kébir	D4
Pala 13,200	B6
Rig Rig	B5
Sarh 43,700	C6
Wour	C3
Yarda	C4

Yebbi-Bou	C3
Ziguei	C5
Zouar	C3

OTHER FEATURES

Azoum, Bahr	D5
Baguirmi (reg.)	C5
Bahr el Ghazal (dry riv.)	C5
Batha (riv.)	C5
Bodélé (depr.)	C4
Borku 72	C4
Chad (lake)	C5
Domar (dry riv.)	C4
Emi Koussi (mt.)	C4
Ennedi (plat.)	D4
Fittri (lake)	C5
Haouach, Wadi (dry riv.)	C4
Jef Jef es Seghin (plat.)	D3
Kanem (reg.)	C5
Logone (riv.)	C5
Maro (dry riv.)	C6
Mbéré (riv.)	C6
Mourdi (depr.)	D4
Ouham (riv.)	C6
Pendé (riv.)	C6
Sahara (des.)	C3
Salamat, Bahr (riv.)	C5
Sara (riv.)	C5
Shari (riv.)	C5

Sudan (reg.)	C5
Tibesti (mts.)	C3
Wadai (reg.)	D5

DJIBOUTI

CITIES and TOWNS

Ali Sabieh	H5
Dikhil	H5
Djibouti (cap.) 96,000	H5
Obock	H5
Tadjoura	H5

OTHER FEATURES

Abbe (lake)	H5
Aden (gulf)	J5
Bab el Mandeb (str.)	H5

EGYPT

CITIES and TOWNS

Abnûb 39,343	J4
Abu Qurqâs	J4
Akhmim 53,234	F2
Alexandria 2,318,655	J2

(continued on following page)

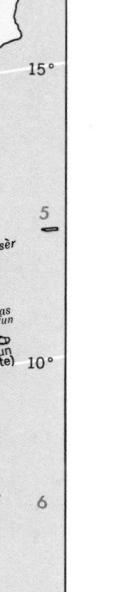

Topography

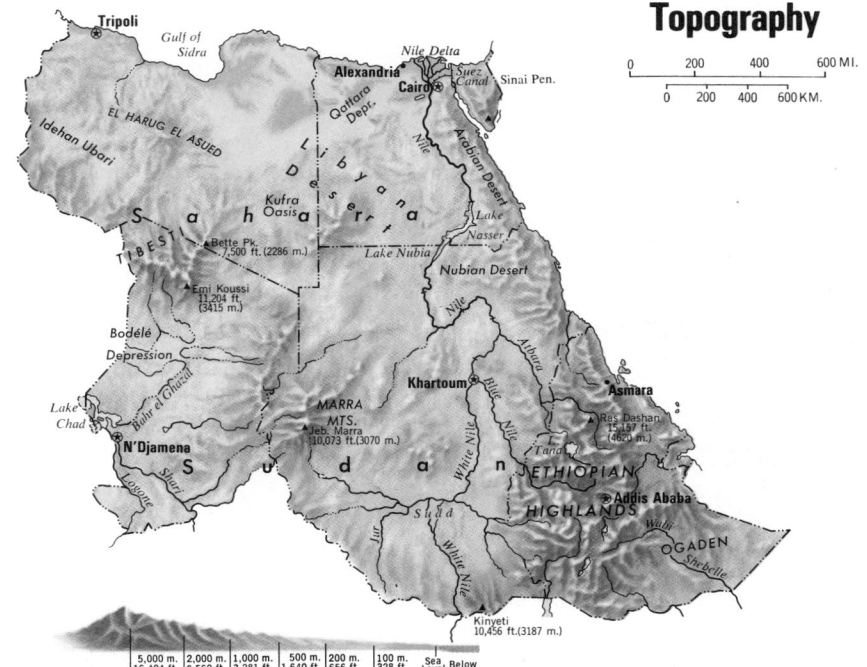

(continued on following page)

Northeastern Africa

(continued)

Aswan 144,377 F3
Asyût 213,983 J4
Bâris F3
Benha 88,992 J3
Beni Mazar 39,373 J4
Beni Suef 118,148 J3
Biba 33,074 J4
Bûlaq F2
Bur Sai'd (Port Said) 262,620 K2
Cairo (cap.) 5,084,463 J3
Dahab F2
Dairût 31,624 J4
Damanhur 188,927 J3
Damietta 93,546 J3
Disûq 58,650 J3
Dumyât (Damietta) 93,546 J3
Dûsh F3
El A'lamein E1
El A'rish F1
El Bawiti E2
El Faiyûm 167,081 J3
El Fashn 33,506 J4
El Hammam 6,588 E1
El Iskandariya (Alexandria) 2,318,655 J2
El Karnak F2
El Khârga 26,375 F2
El Mahalla el Kubra 292,853 J3
El Mansûra 257,866 K3
El Minya 146,423 J4
El Qâhira (Cairo) (cap.) 5,084,463 J3
El Qantara 919 K3
El Qasr E2
El Quseir 12,297 F2
El Tûr F2
El Wasta 17,659 J3
Gemsa F2
Girga 51,110 F2
Giza 1,246,713 J3
Heliopolis J3
Helwân J3
Hurghada F2
Idfu 34,858 F3
Imbâba J3
Ismailia 145,978 K3
Isna 34,186 F2
Karnak (El Karnak) F2
Kôm Ombo 44,531 F3
Luxor 92,748 F2
Maghâgha 40,802 J4
Mallawi 74,256 J4
Manfalût 41,126 J4
Mersâ Matrûh 27,857 E1
Minûf 55,131 J3
Mût 8,032 E2
Nuweiba F2
Port Fuad K3
Port Safâga F2
Port Said 262,620 K2
Port Taufiq K3
Qalyub 62,739 J3
Qasr Farâfra E2
Qena 94,013 F2
Ras Ghârib F2
Rashid (Rosetta) 42,962 J2
Rudeis F2
Salûm 4,161 E1
Samalût 48,146 J4
Shibin el Kom 102,844 J3
Sidi Barrani 1,574 E1
Sinnûris 42,022 J3
Siwa 4,999 E2
Sohâg 101,758 F2
Suez 194,001 K3
Tahta 45,242 F2
Tanta 284,636 J3
Zagazig 202,637 K3
Zifta 50,410 J3

OTHER FEATURES

Abu Qir (bay) J2
Abydos (ruins) F2
A'ilaqi, Wadi (dry riv.) F3
A'qaba (gulf) G2
Arabian (des.) F2
Aswân (dam) F3
Aswân High (dam) F3
Bahariya (oasis) E2
Bahr Yusef (stream) J4
Bânâs, Ras (cape) G3
Berenice (ruins) F3
Birket Qârûn (lake) J3
Bir Taba (well) F2
Bitter (lkes) K3
Dakhla (oasis) E2
Eastern (Arabian) (des.) F2
El Sollum (gulf) E1
Farâfra (oasis) E2
Foul (bay) G3
Ghard Abu Muharik (des.) J4
Gilf Kebir (plat.) E3
Great Sand Sea (des.) D2
Katherina, Jebel (mt.) F2
Khârga (oasis) F2
Libyan (des.) E2
Libyan (plat.) E1
Mediterranean (sea) E1
Memphis (ruins) J3
Muhammad, Ras (cape) F2
Nasser (lake) F3
Nile (riv.) F2
Pyramids (ruins) J3
Qattara (depr.) E2
Red (sea) G3
Sahara (des.) E3
Sinai (mt.) F2
Sinai (pen.) F2
Siwa (oasis) E2
Suez (canal) K3
Suez (gulf) J3
Tiran (str.) F2
U'weinat, Jebel (mt.) E3

ETHIOPIA

PROVINCES

Arusi 852,900 G6
Bale 707,800 H6
Eritrea 1,947,600 G4
Gamu-Gofa 698,800 G6
Gojjam 1,750,100 G5
Gondar 1,355,800 G5
Harar 3,359,200 H6
Ilubabor 688,800 F6
Kaffa 1,693,000 G6
Shoa 5,369,500 G6
Sidamo 2,479,800 G7
Tigre 1,828,900 H5
Wallaga 1,269,100 G6
Wallo 2,459,900 H5

CITIES and TOWNS

Addis Ababa (cap.) 1,196,300 G6
Addis Alam 5,500 G6
Adigrat 9,400 G5
Adi Ugri 12,800 G5
Adwa 16,400 G5
Afdem H6
Agordat G4
Aksum 12,800 G5
Ankober H6
Arba Mench 7,660 G6
Asmara 393,800 G4
Asosa F5
Assab 16,000 H5
Asselle 19,390 G6
Awareh H6
Awasa 16,790 G6
Awash H6
Axum (Aksum) 12,800 G5
Bahir Dar 25,100 G5
Burye G5
Callafo H6
Chilga G5
Dagabur H6
Dallol G5
Dangila G5
Debra Birhan 16,700 G6
Debra Markos 30,260 G5
Debra Tabor 8,700 G5
Dembidollo 7,600 F6
Dessye 49,750 G5
Dilla 13,800 G6
Dire Dawa 63,700 H6
Dolo H7
Domo J6
Edd H5
El Carre H6
El Der H6
Filtu H6
Gabredarre H6
Galadi J6
Gambela F6
Gardula 5,800 G6
Gedo G6
Gerlogubi H6
Ghimbi 8,300 G6
Ginir H6
Goba 13,500 H6
Gondar 38,600 G5
Gore 8,500 G6
Gorrahei H6
Harar 48,440 H6
Harkiko G4
Hosseina 8,500 G6
Imi H6
Jijiga 8,000 H6
Jimma 47,360 G6
Jiran G6
Karkabat G4
Keren G4
Kibre Mengist 8,300 G6
Lalibela G5
Magdala G5
Maji G6
Makale 30,780 G5
Massawa 19,800 G4
Mega G7
Mendi G6
Mersa Fatma H5
Metamma G5
Metu G6
Miesso H6
Mizan Teferi G6
Moyale G7
Murle G6
Mustahil H6
Nakamti 18,310 G6
Nakfa G4
Nazret 42,900 G6
Negelli 8,800 G6
Nejo G6
Saio (Dembidollo) 7,600 F6
Soddu 11,900 G6
Sokota G5
Tesseni G4
Thio H5
Tori F6
Umm Hajar G5
Waka G6
Waldia 9,600 G5
Wardere J6
Wolta G6
Yaballo G6
Zula G4

OTHER FEATURES

Abay (riv.) G5
Abaya (lake) G6
Akobo (riv.) F6
Assale (lake) H5
Atbara (riv.) G4
Awash (riv.) H5
Bale (mt.) G6
Baraka (riv.) G4
Baro (riv.) G6
Billate (riv.) G6
Blue Nile (Abay) (riv.) G5
Buri (pen.) H4
Chamo (lake) G6
Dahlak (arch.) H4
Dahlak (isl.) H4
Danakil (reg.) H5
Dawa (riv.) G7
Fafan (riv.) H6
Ganale Dorya (riv.) H6
Gash Mareb (riv.) G5
Gughe (mt.) G6
Haud (reg.) J6
Kasar, Ras (cape) G4
Ogaden (reg.) H6
Omo (riv.) G6
Ras Dashan (mt.) G5
Red (sea) H4
Rudolf (Turkana) (lake) G7
Simen (mts.) G5
Stefanie (lake) G7
Takkaze (riv.) G5
Tana (lake) G5
Tisisat (fall) G5
Turkana (lake) G7
Wabi (riv.) H6
Wabi Shebelle (riv.) H6
Zwai (lake) G6

LIBYA

CITIES and TOWNS

Ajedabia○ 53,170 D1
Aujila○ 6,695 D2
Baida○ 59,765 D1
Barce (El Marj)○ 55,444 D1
Benghazi (cap.)○ 286,943 C1
Beni Ulid○ 19,113 B1
Berken B2
Brak○ 12,507 B2
Bu Ngem C1
Cyrene (Shahat)○ 17,157 D1
Derj○ 2,152 B1
Derna○ 44,145 D1
Edri B2
El Abiar○ 17,685 D1
El Agheila C1
El Azizia○ 34,077 B1
El Bardi○ 4,330 D1
El Barkat○ 2,139 B3
El Fogaha C2
El Gatrun B3
El Gezira D2
El Jauf○ 6,481 D3
El Marj○ 55,444 D1
El' Uweinat B2
Es Sidr○ 706 C1
Ez Zuetina○ 7,256 D1
Ghadames○ 6,172 A2
Gharfan○ 65,224 B1
Ghat○ 6,924 B3
Ghemines○ 4,313 C1
Homs○ 66,890 B1
Hon○ 2,766 C2
Jaghbub (Jarabub)○ 1,436 D2
Jalo D2
Jarabub○ 1,436 D2
Marada○ 3,201 C2
Marsa el Brega○ 2,618 D1
Marsa el Hariga○ 5,043 D1
Mekili D1
Misurata○ 102,439 C1
Mizda○ 11,472 B1
Murzuk○ 22,185 B2
Nalut○ 23,535 B1
Ras Lanuf○ 1,990 C1
Sabrathaa○ 30,836 B1
Sebha○ 35,879 B2
Shahat○ 17,157 D1
Sinawen○ 1,549 B1
Sokna○ 3,757 C2
Soluk○ 6,501 D1
Susa D1
Syrte○ 22,797 C1
Tarhuna○ 52,657 B1
Tejerri B3
Tesawa B2
Tmessa C2
Tobruk○ 58,384 D1
Tokra○ 10,714 D1
Traghen B2
Tripoli (cap.)○ 550,438 B1
Ubari○ 19,132 B2
Umm el Abid C2
Waddan○ 5,347 C2
Wau el Kebir C2
Zawia○ 72,092 B1
Zella○ 4,835 C2
Zliten○ 58,981 C1
Zuila C2
Zwara○ 15,078 B1

OTHER FEATURES

Ain Zueiya (well) D3
Akhdar, Jebel (mts.) D1
A'mir, Ras (cape) D1
Barqa (Cyrenaica) (reg.) D1
Ben Ghnema, Jebel (mts.) C2
Bette (peak) C3
Bey el Kebir, Wadi (dry riv.) B1
Bir Hakeim (ruins) D1
Bishiara (well) D3
Bomba (gulf) D1
Buzeima (well) D3
Calansho Sand Sea (des.) D2
Calansho, Serir (des.) D2
Cyrenaica (reg.) D1
Fezzan (reg.) B2
Great Sand Sea (des.) D2
Harug el Asued, El (mts.) C2
Homra, Hamada el (des.) B2
Hosenofu (well) D3
Idehan Ubari (des.) B2
Idehan Murzuk (des.) B2
Jalo (oasis) D2
Jefara (reg.) B1
Jef Jef es Seghin (plat.) D3
Jofra (oasis) C2
Kufra (oasis) D3
Leptis Magna (ruins) B1
Libyan (des.) D2
Libyan (plat.) D1
Mediterranean (sea) C1
Nefusa, Jebel (mts.) B1
Rebiana○ (oasis) D3
Rebiana Sand Sea (des.) D3
Sahara (des.) C3
Sarra (well) D3
Shati, Wadi esh (dry riv.) B2
Sidra (gulf) C1
Soda, Jebel es (mts.) C2
Tazerbo○ (oasis) D2
Tibesti, Serir (des.) C3
Tinghert Hamada (Tinrhert) (des.) B2
Tripolitania (reg.) B1
U'weinat, Jebel (mt.) E3
Zelten, Jebel (mts.) D2

SUDAN

PROVINCES

Bahr el Ghazal E6
Central F5
Darfur D5
Eastern G4
Equatoria E6
Khartoum F4
Kordofan E5
Northern E3
Upper Nile F6

CITIES and TOWNS

A'bri F3
Abu Hamed F4
Abu Matariq E5
Abu Zabad E5
Abwong F6
Abyei E6
Adarama G4
Adok F6
Akasha F3
Akobo F6
Amadi F6
A'qiq G4
Argo F4
Aroma G4
Atbara 66,000 F4
Aweil E6
Ayod F6
Babanusa E5
Bara F5
Bentiu E6
Berber F4
Bor F6
Bo River Post E6
Buram E5
Damazin (Ed Damazin) 12,000 F5
Deim Zubeir E6
Delgo F3
Derudeb G4
Dilling E5
Dongola 6,000 F4
Dungunab G3
Ed Dae'in E5
Ed Damer 17,000 F4
Ed Damazin 12,000 F5
Ed Debba F4
Ed Dueim 27,000 F5
El Abbasiya F5
El Fasher 52,000 E5
El Fifi D5
El Geneina 33,000 D5
El Geteina F5
El Hilla E5
El Khandaq E4
El Managil F5
El Obeid 90,000 E5
El Odaiya E5
En Nahud 23,000 E5
Er Rahad F5
Er Roseires F5
Famaka F5
Fangak F6
Fashoda (Kodok) F6
Gabras E5
Gallabat G5
Gebeit Mine G3
Gedaref 92,000 G5
Gogrial E6
Goz Regeb G4
Haiya Junction G4
Halaib G3
Heiban F5
Jonglei F6
Juba 57,000 F7
Kadugli 18,000 E5
Kafia Kingi D6
Kajok E6
Kaka F5
Kapoeta F7
Karima F4
Karora G4
Kassala 99,000 G4
Kerma F4
Khartoum (cap.) 334,000 F4
Khartoum North 151,000 F4
Khashm el Girba G5
Kodok F6
Kongor F6
Korti F4
Kosti 57,000 F5
Kubbum D5
Kurmuk F5
Kutum D5
Lado F6
Loka F7
Malakal 35,000 F6
Maridi E7
Marsa Oseif G3
Melut F5
Merowe F4
Meshra er Req E6
Mongalla F6
Muglad E5
Muhammad Qol G3
Musmar G4
Nagishot F7
Nasir F6
Nimule F7
Nyala 60,000 E5
Nyamlell E6
Nyerol F6
Omdurman 299,000 F4
Opari F7
Pibor Post F6
Port Sudan 133,000 G4
Qalae'n Nahl F5
Raga E6
Rashad F5
Rejaf F7
Renk F5
Rufaa' F5
Rumbek 17,000 E6
Sennar F5
Shambe F6
Shendi F4
Shereik F4
Showak G5
Singa F5
Sinkat G4
Sodiri E5
Suakin G4
Suki F5
Tali Post F6
Talodi F5
Tambura E6
Tendelti F5
Tokar G4
Tombe F6
Tonga F6
Tonj E6
Torit F7
Towot F6
Trinkitat G4
Umm Keddada E5
Umm Ruwaba F5
Wadi Halfa F3
Wad Medani 107,000 F5
Wankai E6
Wau 53,000 E6
Yambio 7,000 E7
Yei F7
Yirol F6
Zalingei D5

OTHER FEATURES

Abu Dara, Ras (cape) G3
Abu Habl, Wadi (dry riv.) F5
Abu Shagara, Ras (cape) G3
Abu Tabari (well) E4
Adda (riv.) D6
Akobo (riv.) F6
A'mur, Wadi (dry riv.) G4
Asoteriba, Jebel (mt.) G3
Atbara (riv.) G4
Bahr Azoum (riv.) D5
Bahr el A'rab (riv.) E6
Bahr ez Zeraf (riv.) F6
Baraka (riv.) G4
Blue Nile (riv.) F5
Dar Hamid (reg.) F5
Dar Masalit (reg.) D5
Dinder (riv.) F5
El A'trun (oasis) E4
Fifth Cataract F4
Fourth Cataract F4
Gabgaba, Wadi (dry riv.) F3
Gezira, El (reg.) F5
Ghalla, Wadi el (dry riv.) E5
Hadarba, Ras (cape) G3
Howar, Wadi (dry riv.) E4
Ibra, Wadi (dry riv.) D5
Jebel Abyad (plat.) E4
Jebel Aulia (dam) F4
Jur (riv.) E6
Kasar, Ras (cape) G4
Kinyeti (mt.) F7
Laqiya U'mran (well) E3
Libyan (des.) E3
Lol (dry riv.) E6
Lotagipi Swamp (plain) F6
Marra, Jebel (mt.) D5
Meroe (ruins) F4
Milk, Wadi el (dry riv.) E4
Muqaddam, Wadi (dry riv.) F4
Napata (ruins) F4
Naqa (ruins) F4
Nile (riv.) F4
Nuba (mts.) E5
Nubia (lake) F3
Nubian (des.) F3
Nukheila (oasis) E4
Nuri (ruins) F4
Oda, Jebel (mt.) G3
Pibor (riv.) F6
Red (sea) G3
Sahara (des.) E3
Second Cataract F3
Selima (oasis) E3
Sennar (dam) F5
Setit (riv.) G5
Sixth Cataract F4
Sobat (riv.) F6
Suakin (arch.) G4
Sudan (reg.) E5
Sudd (swamp) F6
Sue (riv.) E6
Third Cataract E4
U'weinat, Jebel (mt.) E3
White Nile (riv.) F5

○Population of sub-district or division.

Agriculture, Industry and Resources

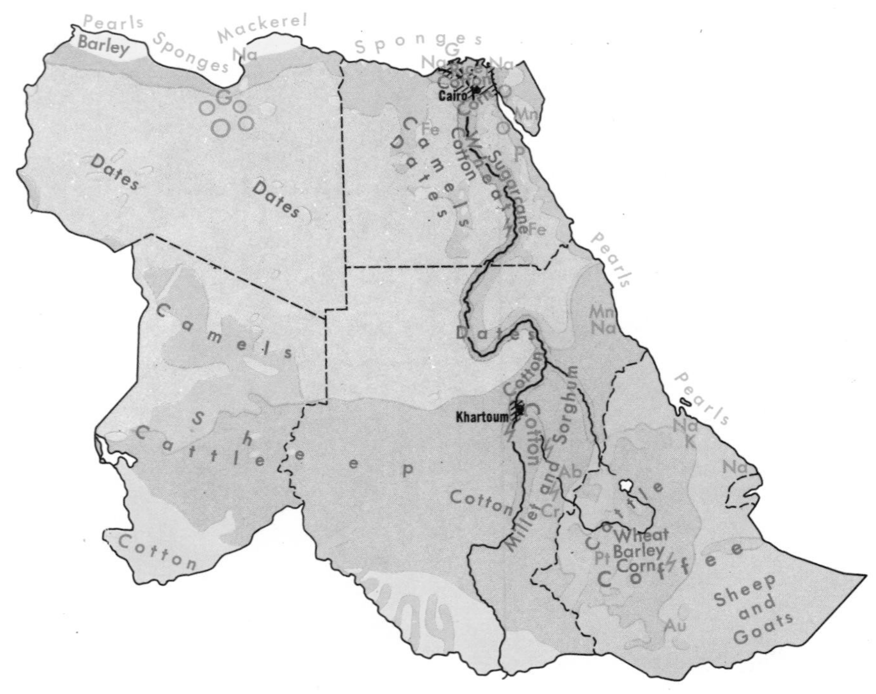

DOMINANT LAND USE

Cereals, Horticulture, Livestock
Cash Crops, Mixed Cereals
Cotton, Cereals
Market Gardening, Diversified Tropical Crops
Plantation Agriculture
Oases
Pasture Livestock
Nomadic Livestock Herding
Forests
Nonagricultural Land

MAJOR MINERAL OCCURRENCES

Ab Asbestos
Au Gold
Cr Chromium
Fe Iron Ore
G Natural Gas
K Potash
Mn Manganese
Na Salt
○ Petroleum
P Phosphates
Pt Platinum

Water Power
Major Industrial Areas

ANGOLA

AREA 481,351 sq. mi. (1,246,700 sq. km.)
POPULATION 7,078,000
CAPITAL Luanda
LARGEST CITY Luanda
HIGHEST POINT Mt. Moco 8,593 ft. (2,620 m.)
MONETARY UNIT kwanza
MAJOR LANGUAGES Mbundu, Kongo, Lunda, Portuguese
MAJOR RELIGIONS Tribal religions, Roman Catholicism

BURUNDI

AREA 10,747 sq. mi. (27,835 sq. km.)
POPULATION 4,021,910
CAPITAL Bujumbura
LARGEST CITY Bujumbura
HIGHEST POINT 8,858 ft. (2,700 m.)
MONETARY UNIT Burundi franc
MAJOR LANGUAGES Kirundi, French, Swahili
MAJOR RELIGIONS Tribal religions, Roman Catholicism, Islam

CAMEROON

AREA 183,568 sq. mi. (475,441 sq. km.)
POPULATION 8,503,000
CAPITAL Yaoundé
LARGEST CITY Douala
HIGHEST POINT Cameroon 13,350 ft. (4,069 m.)
MONETARY UNIT CFA tranc
MAJOR LANGUAGES Fang, Bamileke, Fulani, Duala, French, English
MAJOR RELIGIONS Tribal religions, Christianity, Islam

CENTRAL AFRICAN REP.

AREA 242,000 sq. mi. (626,780 sq. km.)
POPULATION 2,284,000
CAPITAL Bangui
LARGEST CITY Bangui
HIGHEST POINT Gao 4,659 ft. (1,420 m.)
MONETARY UNIT CFA franc
MAJOR LANGUAGES Banda, Gbaya, Sangho, French
MAJOR RELIGIONS Tribal religions, Christianity, Islam

CONGO

AREA 132,046 sq. mi. (342,000 sq. km.)
POPULATION 1,537,000
CAPITAL Brazzaville
LARGEST CITY Brazzaville
HIGHEST POINT Leketi Mts. 3,412 ft. (1,040 m.)
MONETARY UNIT CFA franc
MAJOR LANGUAGES Kikongo, Bateke, Lingala, French
MAJOR RELIGIONS Christianity, tribal religions, Islam

EQUATORIAL GUINEA

AREA 10,831 sq. mi. (28,052 sq. km.)
POPULATION 244,000
CAPITAL Malabo
LARGEST CITY Malabo
HIGHEST POINT 9,868 ft. (3,008 m.)
MONETARY UNIT ekuele
MAJOR LANGUAGES Fang, Bubi, Spanish
MAJOR RELIGIONS Tribal religions, Christianity

GABON

AREA 103,346 sq. mi. (267,666 sq. km.)
POPULATION 551,000
CAPITAL Libreville
LARGEST CITY Libreville
HIGHEST POINT Ibounzi 5,165 ft. (1,574 m.)
MONETARY UNIT CFA franc
MAJOR LANGUAGES Fang and other Bantu languages, French
MAJOR RELIGIONS Tribal religions, Christianity, Islam

KENYA

AREA 224,960 sq. mi. (582,646 sq. km.)
POPULATION 15,327,061
CAPITAL Nairobi
LARGEST CITY Nairobi
HIGHEST POINT Kenya 17,058 ft. (5,199 m.)
MONETARY UNIT Kenya shilling
MAJOR LANGUAGES Kikuyu, Luo, Kavirondo, Kamba, Swahili, English
MAJOR RELIGIONS Tribal religions, Christianity, Hinduism, Islam

MALAWI

AREA 45,747 sq. mi. (118,485 sq. km.)
POPULATION 5,968,000
CAPITAL Lilongwe
LARGEST CITY Blantyre
HIGHEST POINT Mulanje 9,843 ft. (3,000 m.)
MONETARY UNIT Malawi kwacha
MAJOR LANGUAGES Chichewa, Yao, English, Nyanja, Tumbuka, Tonga, Ngoni
MAJOR RELIGIONS Tribal religions, Islam, Christianity

RWANDA

AREA 10,169 sq. mi. (26,337 sq. km.)
POPULATION 4,819,317
CAPITAL Kigali
LARGEST CITY Kigali
HIGHEST POINT Karisimbi 14,780 ft. (4,505 m.)
MONETARY UNIT Rwanda franc
MAJOR LANGUAGES Kinyarwanda, French, Swahili
MAJOR RELIGIONS Tribal religions, Roman Catholicism, Islam

SOMALIA

AREA 246,200 sq. mi. (637,658 sq. km.)
POPULATION 3,645,000
CAPITAL Mogadishu
LARGEST CITY Mogadishu
HIGHEST POINT Surud Ad 7,900 ft. (2,408 m.)
MONETARY UNIT Somali shilling
MAJOR LANGUAGES Somali, Arabic, Italian, English
MAJOR RELIGION Islam

TANZANIA

AREA 363,708 sq. mi. (942,003 sq. km.)
POPULATION 17,527,560
CAPITAL Dar es Salaam
LARGEST CITY Dar es Salaam
HIGHEST POINT Kilimanjaro 19,340 ft. (5,895 m.)
MONETARY UNIT Tanzanian shilling
MAJOR LANGUAGES Nyamwezi-Sukuma, Swahili, English
MAJOR RELIGIONS Tribal religions, Christianity, Islam

UGANDA

AREA 91,076 sq. mi. (235,887 sq. km.)
POPULATION 12,630,076
CAPITAL Kampala
LARGEST CITY Kampala
HIGHEST POINT Margherita 16,795 ft. (5,119 m.)
MONETARY UNIT Ugandan shilling
MAJOR LANGUAGES Luganda, Acholi, Teso, Nyoro, Soga, Nkole, English, Swahili
MAJOR RELIGIONS Tribal religions, Christianity, Islam

ZAIRE

AREA 905,063 sq. mi. (2,344,113 sq. km.)
POPULATION 28,291,000
CAPITAL Kinshasa
LARGEST CITY Kinshasa
HIGHEST POINT Margherita 16,795 ft. (5,119 m.)
MONETARY UNIT zaire
MAJOR LANGUAGES Tshiluba, Mongo, Kikongo, Kingwana, Zande, Lingala, Swahili, French
MAJOR RELIGIONS Tribal religions, Christianity

ZAMBIA

AREA 290,586 sq. mi. (752,618 sq. km.)
POPULATION 5,679,808
CAPITAL Lusaka
LARGEST CITY Lusaka
HIGHEST POINT Sunzu 6,782 ft. (2,067 m.)
MONETARY UNIT Zambian kwacha
MAJOR LANGUAGES Bemba, Tonga, Lozi, Luvale, Nyanja, English
MAJOR RELIGIONS Tribal religions

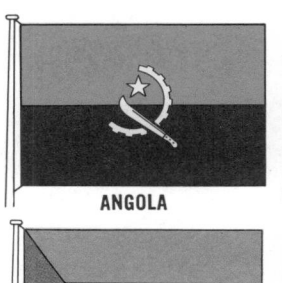

ANGOLA

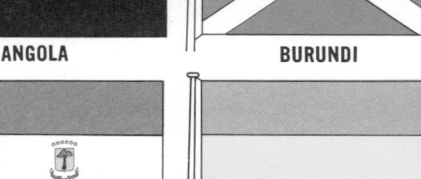

BURUNDI

CAMEROON

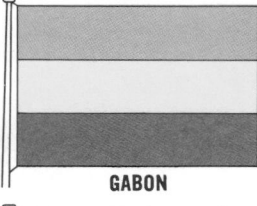

CENTRAL AFRICAN REP.

CONGO

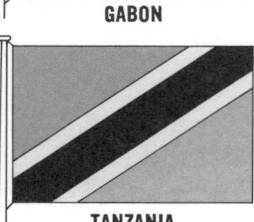

EQUATORIAL GUINEA

GABON

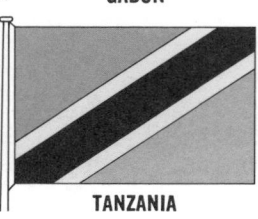

KENYA

MALAWI

RWANDA

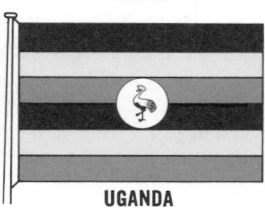

SOMALIA

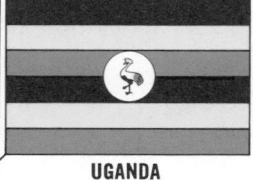

TANZANIA

UGANDA

ZAIRE

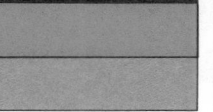

ZAMBIA

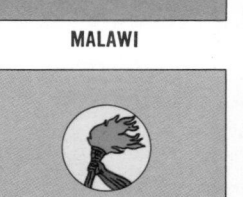
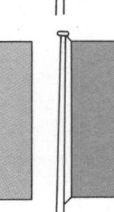
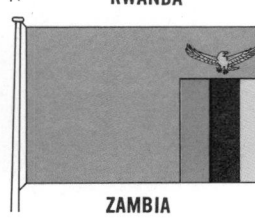

(continued on following page)

Kounde B2
Mbaïki 12,346 .... C3
Mbres 2,622 .... D2
Mobaye 4,220 .... D3
Ndele 5,858 .... D2
Ngourou D2
Nola 6,703 .... C3
Obo 2,570 .... E2
Ouadda 3,009 .... D2
Paoua 7,052 .... C2
Possel C2
Sibut 13,341 .... C2
Zako D2
Zemio 3,259 .... D2

Zemongo E2

OTHER FEATURES

Bamingui (riv.) C2
Bomu (riv.) D2
Dar Rounga (reg.) D2
Gao (mt.) D2
Kadeï (riv.) C3
Kotto (riv.) D2
Lobaye (riv.) C3
Mberé (riv.) B2
Ouham (riv.) C2
Pende (riv.) C2
Sanga (riv.) C3

Sara (riv.) C2
Shari (riv.) C2
Shinko (riv.) D2
Ubangi (riv.) C3

CONGO

CITIES and TOWNS

Abala C4
Boko B4
Brazzaville (cap.) 298,967 .. C4
Boundji C4
Djambala B4

Dongou C3
Enyellé C3
Epéna C3
Etoumbi B3
Ewo B4
Gamboma C4
Ikelemba C3
Impfondo C3
Kellé B4
Kibangou B4
Kindama C4
Kinkala C4
Komono B4
Loubomo 29,600 .... B4
Loudima B4

Madingo-Kayes B4
Madingou B4
Makoua C3
Mbinda B4
Mindouli B4
Mossaka C4
Mossendjo B4
M'Vouti B4
Nkayi 30,600 .... B4
Okoyo C4
Ouesso C3
Owando C4
Oyo C4
Pangala B4
Pointe-Noire 141,700 .... B4
Sembé B3
Sibiti B4
Souanké B3
Zanaga B4

OTHER FEATURES

Alima (riv.) B4
Congo (riv.) C4
Crystal (mts.) B4
Dja (riv.) B3
Ivindo (riv.) B3
Kadeï (riv.) C3
Kouilou (riv.) B4
Likouala (riv.) C3
N'Gounié (riv.) B4
Ogooué (riv.) A4
Sangha (riv.) C3
Ubangi (riv.) C3

EQUATORIAL GUINEA

TERRITORIES

Bioko 78,000 .... A3
Rio Muni 203,000 .... B3

CITIES and TOWNS

Bata 27,024 .... A3
Luba 19,933 .... A3
Malabo (cap.) 37,237 ...... A3
Mbini 14,503 .... A3

OTHER FEATURES

Biafra (bight) A3
Bioko (isl.) A3
Corisco (isl.) A3
Elobey (isls.) A3
Fernando Po (Bioko)
(isl.) A3

GABON

CITIES and TOWNS

Banda B4
Bitam 5,936 .... B3
Booué B3
Chinchoua A4
Cocobeach A3
Fougamou B4
Franceville 9,345 .... B4
Iguéla A4
Kango A3
Kemboma B3
Koula-Moutou 8,032 .... B4
Lalara B3
Lambaréné 17,770 .... B4
Lastoursville B4
Lekoni B4
Libreville (cap.) 105,080 ... A3
Makokou 5,005 .... B3
Mayumba A4
M'Bigou B4
Médouneu B3
Mekambo B3
Mimongo B4
Minvoul B3
Mitzic B3
Moanda 10,709 .... B4
Mouila 15,016 .... B4
Mounana 4,000 .... B4
N'Dendé B4
N'Djolé B4
Nyanga A4
Okondja A4
Owendo A4
Oyem 12,455 .... B3
Port-Gentil 48,190 .... A4
Setté-Cama A4

OTHER FEATURES

Daua (riv.) H3
Elgon (mt.) F3
Formosa (bay) H4
Galana (riv.) G4
Gedi (ruins) G4
Kavirondo (gulf) F4
Kenya (mt.) G4
Lak Dera (dry riv.) H3
Lorian (swamp) H3
Natron (lake) G4
Nyiru (mt.) G3
Patta (isl.) H4

Tchibanga 14,001 .... B4

OTHER FEATURES

Crystal (mts.) B4
Ibounzi (mts.) B4
Ivindo (riv.) B4
Lopez (cape) A4
N'Dogo (lag.) B4
N'Gounié (riv.) B4
N'Komi (lag.) A4
Ogooué (riv.) A4
Onangué (lake) A4
Pongara (pt.) A3

KENYA

PROVINCES

Central 1,675,647 .... G4
Coast 944,082 .... G4
Eastern 1,907,301 .... G4
Nairobi 509,286 .... G4
North-Eastern 245,757 ..... G3
Nyanza 2,122,045 .... F4
Rift Valley 2,210,289 ...... G3
Western 1,328,298 .... G3

CITIES and TOWNS

Buna G3
Bunyala H4
Bura H4
Eldoret 18,196 .... G3
El Wak H3
Embu 3,998 .... G4
Fort Hall 4,750 .... G4
Galole 3,908 .... G4
Garba Tula G3
Garissa G4
Garsen G4
Gilgil 4,178 .... G4
Isiolo 8,201 .... G3
Kakamega 6,244 .... F3
Kangundo G4
Kericho 10,144 .... F4
Kiambu 2,776 .... G4
Kilifi 5,080 .... H4
Kipini H4
Kisii 6,080 .... F3
Kisumu 32,431 .... G3
Kitale 11,573 .... G3
Kitui 3,071 .... G4
Kolbio G4
Konza G4
Laisamis H4
Lamu 7,403 .... H4
Lodwar G3
Lokitaung 4,090 .... G3
Lolgorien F4
Machakos 6,312 .... G4
Magadi G4
Malindi 10,757 .... H4
Mambrui H4
Maralal 3,878 .... G3
Marsabit 6,635 .... G3
Meru 4,475 .... G4
Moyale G3
Nairobi (cap.) 509,286 .... G4
Naivasha 6,920 .... G4
Nakuru 47,151 .... G4
Namanga G4
Nanyuki 11,624 .... G4
Narok 2,608 .... G4
North Horr G3
South Horr G3
Taveta G4
Thika 18,387 .... G4
Thomson's Falls 7,602 .... G3
Todenyang G3
Tsavo G4
Vanga G4
Voi 5,313 .... G4
Wajir H3
Wamba 2,650 .... G3

Rudolf (Turkana) (lake) G3
Tana (riv.) G4
Tsavo Nat'l Park G4
Turkana (lake) G3
Victoria (lake) F4
Winam (bay) F4

MALAWI

CITIES and TOWNS

Bandawe F6
Blantyre 222,153 .... F7
Chilumba F6
Chipoka F7
Chiromo F7
Chitipa 3,079 .... F5
Dedza 5,448 .... F7
Karonga 11,873 .... F5
Kasungu F6
Lilongwe (cap.) 102,924 ... F6
Livingstonia F6
Mangochi 3,341 .... G6
Mzimba 4,962 .... F6
Nkhata Bay 4,024 .... F6
Nkhotakota 10,312 .... F6
Nsanje 6,091 .... G7
Rumphi 3,998 .... F6
Salima 4,646 .... F6
Thyolo 4,186 .... F7
Zomba 21,000 .... G7

OTHER FEATURES

Chilwa (lake) G7
Malawi (Nyasa) (lake) F6
Mulanje (mts.) G7
Nyasa (lake) F6
Shire (riv.) G7

RWANDA

CITIES and TOWNS

Butare 21,691 .... E4
Cyangugu 7,042 .... E4
Gisenyi 12,436 .... E4
Kigali (cap.) 117,749 ...... E4
Nyabisindu 8,587 .... F4

OTHER FEATURES

Kagera Nat'l Park E4
Karisimbi (mt.) E4
Kivu (lake) E4
Ruzizi (riv.) E4
Virunga (range) E4

SOMALIA

PROVINCES

Bakool 100,000 .... H3
Bari 155,000 .... J1
Bay 302,000 .... H3
Galguduud 182,000 .... J2
Gedo 212,000 .... H3
Hiiraan 147,000 .... J2
Jubbada Hoose 246,000 .... H3
Mogadiscio 371,000 .... J2
Mudug 215,000 .... J2
Nugaal 85,000 .... J2
Sanaag 146,000 .... J1
Shabeellaha Dhexe 237,000 . J3
Shabeellaha Hoose 398,000 . H3
Togdheer 258,000 .... J2
Woqooyi Galbeed 440,000 .. H1

CITIES and TOWNS

Adadle H2
Afgoi J3
Afmadu 2,580 .... H3
Alula J1
Ankhor J1
Audegle J3
Baduen J2
Barawa (Brava) H3
Bardera H3
Bargal K1
Baydhabo 14,962 .... H3
Belet Weyne 11,426 .... J3
Bender Beila K2
Bender Cassim (Bosaso) ... J1
Berbera 12,219 .... J1
Bereda J1
Bircao H4
Bohodleh J2
Borama 3,244 .... H1

(continued on following page)

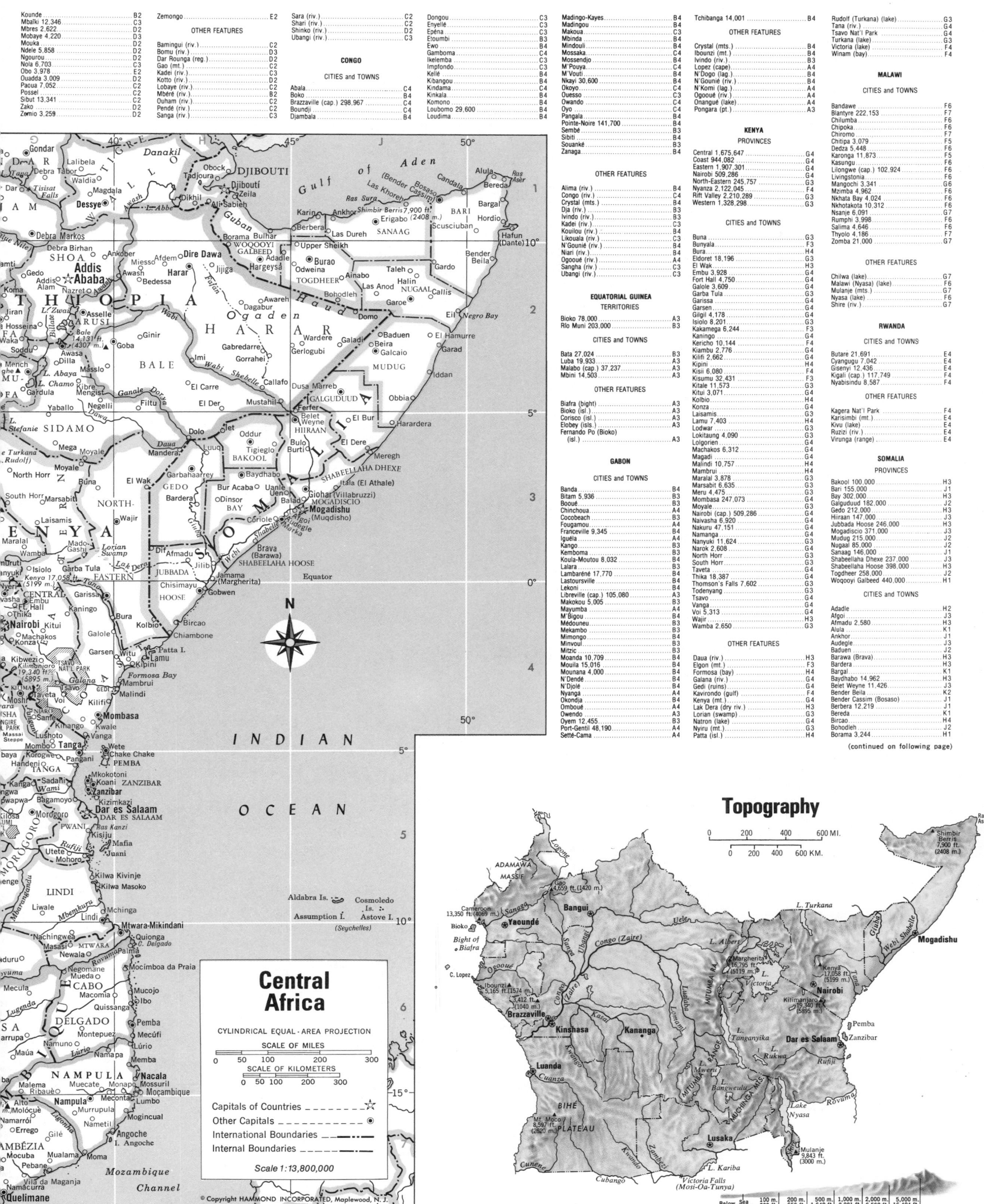

Central Africa

CYLINDRICAL EQUAL-AREA PROJECTION

SCALE OF MILES
0   50 100   200   300

SCALE OF KILOMETERS
0 50 100   200   300

Capitals of Countries .... ☆
Other Capitals .... ◉
International Boundaries ____
Internal Boundaries -------

Scale 1:13,800,000

© Copyright HAMMOND INCORPORATED, Maplewood, N.J.

Topography

0   200   400   600 MI.
0   200   400   600 KM.

Below Sea Level | 100 m. 328 ft. | 200 m. 656 ft. | 500 m. 1,640 ft. | 1,000 m. 3,281 ft. | 2,000 m. 6,562 ft. | 5,000 m. 16,404 ft.

(continued)

Bosaso J1
Brava 6,167 .... H3
Bulhar H1
Bulo Burti 5,247 .... J3
Bur Acaba H3
Burao 12,617 .... J2
Callis J2
Candala J1
Chisimayu 17,872 .... H4
Chiambone H4
Coriole 4,341 .... H3
Dante (Hafun) K1
Dif H3
Dinsor H3
Dusa Marreb J2
Eil J2
El Athale (Itala) J3
El Bur J3
El Dere J3
El Hamurre J2
Erigabo 4,279 .... J1
Ferfer J2
Galcaio J2
Garad J2
Garbahaarrey H3
Gardo J2
Garoe J2
Giohar 13,156 .... J3
Gobwen H4
Hafun K1
Halin J2
Harardera J3
Hargeysa 40,254 .... H2
Hordio K1
Iddan J2
Iet H3
Itala J3
Jamama 5,408 .... H3
Jilib 3,232 .... H3
Karin J1
Kismayu (Chisimayu) 17,872 .... H4
Las Dureh J1
Luuq H3
Margherita (Jamama) H3
Marka (Merka) 17,708 .... H3
Mogadishu (cap.) 371,000 .... J3
Muqdisho (Mogadishu)
(cap.) 371,000 .... J3
Obbia J2
Oddur H3
Taleh J2
Uanle Uen H3
Upper Sheikh J2
Villabruzzi (Johar) J3
Zeila 1,226 .... H1

OTHER FEATURES

Aden (gulf) J1
Asèr, Ras (cape) K1
Giuba (riv.) H3
Guban (reg.) H1
Hafun, Ras (cape) K1
Haud (plat.) J2
Lak Dera (dry riv.) H3
Negro (bay) J2
Nogal (reg.) J2
Shimbir Berris (mt.) J1
Sura, Ras (cape) J1
Surud Ad (mt.) J1
Webi Shabelle (riv.) H3

TANZANIA

REGIONS

Arusha 928,478 .... G4
Dar es Salaam 851,222 .... G5
Dodoma 971,921 .... G5
Iringa 922,801 .... G5
Kagera 1,009,379 .... F4
Kigoma 648,950 .... F4
Kilimanjaro 902,394 .... G4
Lindi 527,902 .... G5
Mara 723,295 .... F4
Mbeya 1,080,241 .... F5
Morogoro 939,190 .... G5
Mtwara 771,726 .... G5
Mwanza 1,443,418 .... F4
Pemba 205,870 .... H5
Pwani (Coast) 516,949 .... G5
Rukwa 451,897 .... F5
Ruvuma 564,113 .... G6
Shinyanga 1,323,482 .... F4
Singida 614,030 .... F5
Tabora 818,049 .... F5
Tanga 1,088,592 .... G5
Zanzibar Mjini 143,616 .... G5
Zanzibar Shambani North 77,424 .... G5
Zanzibar Shambani South 52,325 .... G5

CITIES and TOWNS

Arusha 55,281 .... G4
Babati G4
Bagamoyo 5,112 .... G5
Bukoba 20,430 .... F4
Chake Chake 4,862 .... H5
Dar es Salaam (cap.) 757,346 .... G5
Dodoma 45,703 .... G5
Geita 3,066 .... F4
Handeni G5
Ifakara G5
Iringa 57,182 .... G5
Itigi F5
Kahama 3,211 .... F4
Kaliua F5
Kanga G5
Karema F5
Kasanga F5
Kasulu F4
Kibara F4
Kibaya G5
Kibondo F4
Kigoma-Ujiji 50,044 .... E4
Kilosa 4,458 .... G5
Kilwa Kivinje 2,790 .... G5
Kilwa Masoko G5
Kinyangiri G4
Kipili F5
Kisiju G5
Kitunda F5
Kizimkazi G5
Kondoa 4,514 .... G4
Kongwa G5
Korogwe 6,675 .... G5
Lindi 27,308 .... G5
Liuli F6
Liwale G5
Longido G4
Mahenge G5
Makumbako G5
Manda F6
Manyoni G5
Masasi G6
Mbamba Bay G6
Mbeya 76,606 .... F5
Mbulu G4
Mchinga H5
Mohoro G5
Mombo G4
Morogoro 61,890 .... G5
Moshi 52,223 .... G4
Mpanda F5
Mtakuja F5
Mtwara-Mikindani 48,510 .... H6
Murongo F4
Musoma 32,658 .... F4
Muwale F5
Mwadui 7,383 .... F4
Mwanza 110,611 .... F4
Mwaya F5
Mwesi F5
Nachingwea 3,751 .... G6
Newala G6
Ngara F4
Njombe F5
Pangani 2,955 .... G5
Rungwa F5
Sadani G5
Same G4
Sekenke F4
Shinyanga 21,703 .... F4
Singida 29,252 .... F4
Songea 17,954 .... G6
Sumbawanga 28,586 .... F5
Tabora 67,392 .... F5
Tanga 103,409 .... G4
Tukuyu 4,089 .... F5
Tunduru G6
Urambo F4
Utete G5
Uvinza F5
Wete 8,469 .... G4
Zanzibar 110,669 .... G5

OTHER FEATURES

Eyasi (lake) F4
Great Ruaha (riv.) G5
Juani (isl.) G5
Kalambo (falls) F5
Kanzi (cape) G5
Kilimanjaro (mt.) G4
Kilombero (riv.) G5
Mafia (isl.) H5
Manyara (lake) G4
Masai (steppe) G4
Mbarangandu (riv.) G5
Mbemkuru (riv.) G5
Meru (mt.) G4
Mikumi Nat'l Park G5
Natron (lake) G4
Ngorongoro (crater) F4
Njombe (riv.) F5
Nyasa (lake) F6
Olduvai Gorge (canyon) G4
Pangani (riv.) G4
Pemba (isl.) H5
Rovuma (riv.) G6
Rufiji (riv.) G5
Ruaha Nat'l Park F5
Rukwa (lake) F5
Rungwa (riv.) F5
Rungwe (mt.) F5
Serengeti Nat'l Park F4
Tanganyika (lake) E5
Tarangire Nat'l Park G4
Victoria (lake) F4
Wami (riv.) G5
Wembere (riv.) F4
Zanzibar (isl.) G5

UGANDA

CITIES and TOWNS

Arua 10,837 .... F3
Atura F3
Butiaba 261 .... F3
Entebbe 21,096 .... F4
Fort Portal 7,947 .... F3
Gulu 18,170 .... F3
Hoima 2,339 .... F3
Jinja 52,509 .... F3
Kabale 8,234 .... E4
Kampala (cap.) 478,895 .... F3
Kasese 7,213 .... F3
Kilembe F3
Kitgum 3,242 .... F3
Lira 7,340 .... F3
Masaka 12,987 .... F4
Masindi 2,100 .... F3
Mbale 23,544 .... F3
Mbarara 16,078 .... F4
Moroto 5,488 .... F3
Moyo 2,656 .... F3
Mubende 6,004 .... F3
Rhino Camp 198 .... F3
Soroti 8,130 .... F3
Tororo 15,977 .... F3

OTHER FEATURES

Albert (Mobuto Sese Seko)
(lake) F3
Edward (lake) E4
Elgon (mt.) F3
George (lake) F4
Kabalega (falls) F3
Kagalega Nat'l Park F3
Kidepo Nat'l Park F3
Kioga (lake) F3
Margherita (mt.) E3
Mobuto Sese Seko (lake) F3
Owen Falls (dam) F3
Ruwenzori (range) E3
Sese (isls.) F4
Victoria (lake) F4
Virunga (range) E4
Virunga Nat'l Park F4

ZAIRE

PRUVINCES

Bandundu 2,600,556 .... C4
Bas-Zaïre 1,504,361 .... B4
Equateur 2,431,812 .... D3
Haut-Zaïre 3,356,419 .... E3
Kasai-Occidental 2,433,861 .... D4
Kasai-Oriental 1,872,231 .... D5
Kinshasa 1,323,039 .... C4
Kivu 3,361,883 .... E4
Shaba 2,753,714 .... E5

CITIES and TOWNS

Aba 7,600 .... F3
Abumombazi D3
Aketi 17,200 .... D3
Andoma E3
Ango E3
Ankoro E5
Bagata C4
Balangala D3
Bambesa E3
Bambili E3
Banalia E3
Banana B5
Bandundu 74,467 .... C4
Baraka E4
Basankusu C3
Basoko 9,100 .... D3
Basongo D4
Befale D3
Bena-Dibele D4
Beni 22,800 .... E3
Bikoro C4
Boende 12,800 .... D4
Bokote D4
Bokungu D4
Bolobo 10,300 .... C4
Bolomba 7,200 .... C3
Boma 61,100 .... B5
Bomboma C3
Bomongo C3
Bondo 10,000 .... D3
Bongandanga 12,900 .... D3
Bosobolo 11,100 .... D3
Budjala C3
Bukama E5
Bukavu 134,861 .... E4
Bulungu 16,300 .... C4
Bumba 34,700 .... D3
Bunia 28,800 .... E3
Bunkeya 5,100 .... E6
Businga 11,000 .... D3
Busu-Djanoa D3
Buta 19,800 .... D3
Butembo 27,800 .... E3
Dekese D4
Demba 22,000 .... D5
Dibaya 11,400 .... D5
Dibaya-Lubue 7,900 .... C4
Dilolo 14,000 .... D6
Dimbelenge D5
Djolu D3
Djugu F3
Dongo C3
Doruma E3
Dungu 9,100 .... E3
Etoile E6
Faradje 10,400 .... E3
Feshi C5
Fizi E4
Gandajika 60,100 .... D5
Gemena 37,300 .... D3
Goma 48,600 .... E4
Gungu C5
Idiofa C4
Ikela D4
Ilebo 32,200 .... D4
Imese C3
Ingende C4
Inongo 14,800 .... C4
Irumu 9,300 .... E3
Isangi D3
Isiro 49,300 .... E3
Kabalo 22,600 .... E5
Kabambare E4
Kabare 12,600 .... E4
Kabinda 60,500 .... D5
Kabongo 6,500 .... E5
Kahemba C5
Kalehe E4
Kalemie 62,300 .... E5
Kalima 27,500 .... E4
Kama 17,700 .... E4
Kambove 18,900 .... E6
Kamina 56,300 .... D5
Kampene 14,600 .... E4
Kananga 428,960 .... D5
Kanda-Kanda D5
Kaniama D5
Kapanga D5
Kasaji D6
Kasangulu 11,900 .... C4
Kasenga E6
Kasenyi E3
Kasese E4
Kasongo 37,800 .... E4
Kasongo-Lunda C5
Katako-Kombe D4
Katenga E5
Kazumba D5
Kenge 17,500 .... C4
Kiambi E5
Kibombo E4
Kikwit 111,960 .... C5
Kilembe C5
Kilwa E5
Kilo E3
Kinda D5
Kiniama E6
Kinshasa (cap.) 1,323,039 .... C4
Kipushi 32,900 .... E6
Kiri C4
Kirundu E4
Kisangani 229,596 .... E3
Kole, Kasai-Oriental D4
Kole, Haut-Zaïre E3
Kolwezi 81,600 .... E6
Komba D3
Kongolo 14,800 .... E5
Kungu C3
Kutu 10,000 .... C4
Kwamouth C4
Libenge 12,500 .... C3
Likasi, Panda- 146,394 .... E6
Likati D3
Lisala D3
Lodja 20,300 .... D4
Lokolama D4
Lomela D4
Loto D4
Luashi D6
Lubefu D4
Lubero E4
Lubudi 6,000 .... E5
Lubumbashi 318,000 .... E6
Lubutu E4
Luebo 21,800 .... D5
Luishia E6
Luiza D5
Lukolela, Equateur C4
Lukolela, Kasai-Oriental D5
Lukula 9,400 .... B5
Luozi 7,000 .... B5
Lusambo 13,100 .... D4
Makanza C3
Malemba-Nkulu E5
Mambasa 7,400 .... E3
Mangai 15,200 .... C4
Manono 44,500 .... E5
Masi-Manimba 6,300 .... C4
Masisi E4
Matadi 110,436 .... B5
Mbandaka 107,910 .... C3
Mbanza-Ngungu 55,800 .... C5
Mbuji-Mayi 256,154 .... D5
Mitwaba E5
Moanda 6,400 .... B5
Mobayi-Mbongo D3
Moliro E5
Monga D3
Monkoto D4
Mulongo E5
Mungbere E3
Mushie 13,700 .... C4
Mutshatsha D6
Muyumba E5
Mwadingusha E6
Mwanza E5
Mweka 24,900 .... D4
Mwene-Ditu 71,200 .... D5
Mwenga E4
Niangara 9,200 .... E3
Niemba E5
Nyunzu 11,300 .... E5
Opala D4
Oshwe C4
Panda-Likasi 146,394 .... E6
Pangi E4
Penge D5
Poko E3
Popokabaka C5
Port Kindu 42,800 .... E4
Punia E4
Pweto E5
Rutshuru E4
Sakania E6
Sampwe E5
Sandoa D5
Seke-Banza B5
Sentery 24,300 .... E5
Shabunda 6,900 .... E4
Songololo 4,600 .... B5
Tenke E6
Titule E3
Tshela 10,700 .... B4
Tshikapa 38,900 .... D5
Tshofa D5
Ubundu 6,300 .... E4
Uvira 15,900 .... E4
Virunga 21,900 .... E5
Waka D3
Walikale E4
Wamba 11,500 .... E3
Watsa 21,300 .... E3
Yahuma D3
Yakoma D3
Yangambi 22,600 .... D3
Zongo C3

OTHER FEATURES

Albert (Mobuto Sese Seko)
(lake) F3
Aruwimi (riv.) E3
Bomu (riv.) D3
Boyoma (Stanley) (falls) D3
Chicapa (riv.) D5
Congo (riv.) C4
Edward (lake) E4
Elila (riv.) E4
Fimi (riv.) C4
Garamba Nat'l Park E3
Giri (riv.) C3
Itimbiri (riv.) D3
Ituri (for.) E3
Karisimbi (mt.) E4
Kasai (riv.) C4
Kivu (lake) E4
Kwa (riv.) C4
Kwango (riv.) C5
Kwilu (riv.) C5
Lindi (riv.) E3
Livingstone (falls) B5
Loange (riv.) C5
Lokoro (riv.) C4
Lomami (riv.) D4
Lomela (riv.) D4
Lowa (riv.) E4
Lua (riv.) C3
Lualaba (riv.) E4
Luapula (riv.) E6
Lubilash (riv.) D5
Lufira (riv.) E5
Luilaka (riv.) C4
Lukenie (riv.) D4
Lukuga (riv.) E5
Lulua (riv.) D5
Luvua (riv.) E5
Mai-Ndombe (lake) C4
Malebo (Stanley Pool) (lake) C4
Margherita (mt.) E3
Marungu (mts.) E5
Mobuto Sese Seko (lake) F3
Mweru (lake) E5
Ruwenzori (range) E3
Ruzizi (riv.) E4
Salonga Nat'l Park D4
Sankuru (riv.) D4
Stanley (falls) D3
Stanley Pool (lake) C4
Tanganyika (lake) E5
Tshuapa (riv.) D4
Tumba (lake) C4
Ubangi (riv.) C3
Uele (riv.) E3
Ulindi (riv.) E4
Upemba (lake) E5
Upemba Nat'l Park E5
Virunga (range) E4
Virunga Nat'l Park E4
Zaire (Congo) (riv.) C4

ZAMBIA

CITIES and TOWNS

Abercorn (Mbala) 11,179 .... F5
Bancroft
(Chililabombwe) 61,928 .... E6
Broken Hill (Kabwe) 143,635 .... E6
Chibwe E6
Chilanga 12,503 .... E7
Chililabombwe 61,928 .... E6
Chingola 145,869 .... E6
Chinsali 4,211 .... F6
Chipata 32,291 .... F6
Choma 17,943 .... E7
Fort Rosebery (Mansa) 34,801 .... E6
Isoka 6,832 .... F6
Kabompo 5,357 .... D6
Kabwe 143,635 .... E6
Kafue 29,794 .... E7
Kalabo 7,398 .... D6
Kalomo 5,878 .... E7
Kaoma 6,731 .... D6
Kapiri Mposhi 13,677 .... E6
Kasama 38,093 .... F6
Kasempa 3,063 .... E6
Kataba D7
Kawambwa 7,235 .... E5
Kitwe 314,794 .... E6
Lealui D6
Livingstone 71,987 .... E7
Luanshya 132,164 .... E6
Lundazi 4,083 .... F6
Lusaka (cap.) 538,469 .... E7
Luwingu 3,763 .... E6
Mansa 34,801 .... E6
Mazabuka 29,602 .... E7
Mbala 11,179 .... F5
Mkushi 4,104 .... E6
Mongu 24,919 .... D7
Monze 13,141 .... E7
Mpika 25,880 .... F6
Mporokoso 6,008 .... F5
Mpulungu 6,354 .... F5
Mufulira 149,778 .... E6
Mulobezi 2,589 .... E7
Mumbwa 7,570 .... E6
Mwinilunga 3,169 .... D6
Nakonde 4,599 .... F5
Namwala 3,008 .... E7
Ndola 282,439 .... E6
Petauke 7,531 .... F6
Senanga 7,204 .... D7
Serenje 6,008 .... F6
Sesheke 3,500 .... D7
Solwezi 15,032 .... E6
Zambezi 8,166 .... D6

OTHER FEATURES

Bangweulu (lake) F6
Barotseland (reg.) D7
Chambeshi (riv.) F6
Cuando (riv.) D7
Dongwe (riv.) D6
Kabompo (riv.) D6
Kafue (riv.) E7
Kafue Nat'l Park E6
Kalambo (falls) F5
Kariba (dam) E7
Kariba (lake) E7
Luangwa (riv.) F6
Luapula (riv.) E6
Lungwebungu (riv.) D6
Mosi-Oa-Tunya (Victoria)
(falls) E7
Mulungushi (dam) E6
Mweru (lake) E5
Sunzu (mt.) F5
Tanganyika (lake) E5
Victoria (falls) E7
Zambezi (riv.) D7

Agriculture, Industry and Resources

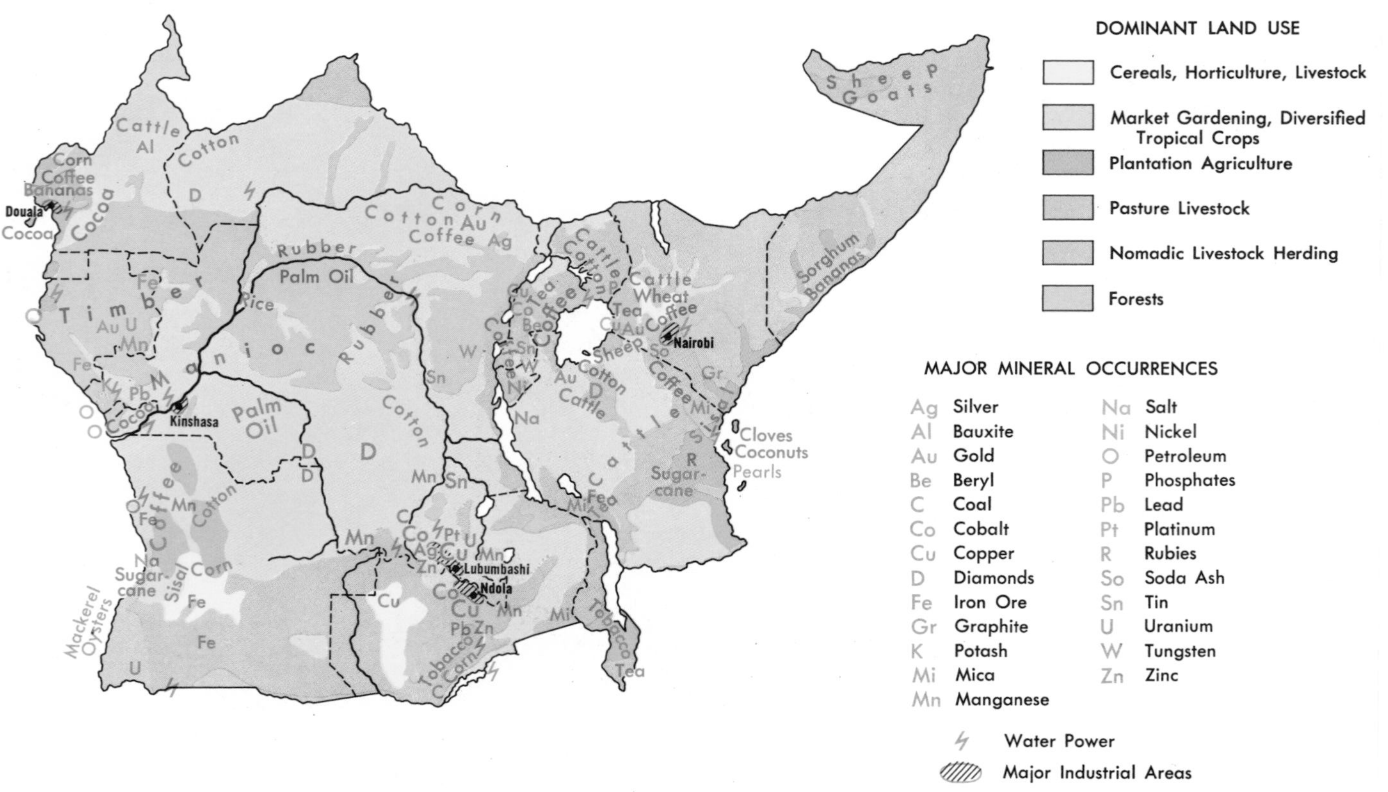
DOMINANT LAND USE
Cereals, Horticulture, Livestock
Market Gardening, Diversified Tropical Crops
Plantation Agriculture
Pasture Livestock
Nomadic Livestock Herding
Forests
MAJOR MINERAL OCCURRENCES
Ag Silver
Al Bauxite
Au Gold
Be Beryl
C Coal
Co Cobalt
Cu Copper
D Diamonds
Fe Iron Ore
Gr Graphite
K Potash
Mi Mica
Mn Manganese
Na Salt
Ni Nickel
O Petroleum
P Phosphates
Pb Lead
Pt Platinum
R Rubies
So Soda Ash
Sn Tin
U Uranium
W Tungsten
Zn Zinc
Water Power
Major Industrial Areas
Douala
Kinshasa
Nairobi
Lubumbashi
Ndola
Sheep
Goats
Cattle
Cotton
Coffee
Bananas
Cocoa
Timber
Rubber
Palm Oil
Manioc
Sorghum
Bananas
Cloves
Coconuts
Pearls
Sugar-cane
Sisal
Tobacco
Tea
Mackerel
Oysters

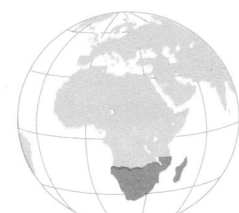

NAMIBIA (SOUTH-WEST AFRICA)

AREA 317,827 sq. mi. (823,172 sq. km.)
POPULATION 1,200,000
CAPITAL Windhoek
LARGEST CITY Windhoek
HIGHEST POINT Brandberg 8,550 ft.
(2,606 m.)
MONETARY UNIT rand
MAJOR LANGUAGES Ovambo, Hottentot,
Herero, Afrikaans, English
MAJOR RELIGIONS Tribal religions,
Protestantism

SOUTH AFRICA

AREA 455,318 sq. mi. (1,179,274 sq. km.)
POPULATION 23,771,970
CAPITALS Cape Town, Pretoria
LARGEST CITY Johannesburg
HIGHEST POINT Injasuti 11,182 ft. (3,408 m.)
MONETARY UNIT rand
MAJOR LANGUAGES Afrikaans, English,
Xhosa, Zulu, Sesotho
MAJOR RELIGIONS Protestantism,
Roman Catholicism, Islam, Hinduism,
tribal religions

LESOTHO

AREA 11,720 sq. mi. (30,355 sq. km.)
POPULATION 1,339,000
CAPITAL Maseru
LARGEST CITY Maseru
HIGHEST POINT 11,425 ft. (3,482 m.)
MONETARY UNIT loti
MAJOR LANGUAGES Sesotho, English
MAJOR RELIGIONS Tribal religions,
Christianity

BOTSWANA

AREA 224,764 sq. mi. (582,139 sq. km.)
POPULATION 819,000
CAPITAL Gaborone
LARGEST CITY Francistown
HIGHEST POINT Tsodilo Hill 5,922 ft.
(1,805 m.)
MONETARY UNIT pula
MAJOR LANGUAGES Setswana, Shona,
Bushman, English, Afrikaans
MAJOR RELIGIONS Tribal religions,
Protestantism

MOZAMBIQUE

AREA 303,769 sq. mi. (786,762 sq. km.)
POPULATION 12,130,000
CAPITAL Maputo
LARGEST CITY Maputo
HIGHEST POINT Mt. Binga 7,992 ft.
(2,436 m.)
MONETARY UNIT metical
MAJOR LANGUAGES Makua, Thonga,
Shona, Portuguese
MAJOR RELIGIONS Tribal religions,
Roman Catholicism, Islam

SWAZILAND

AREA 6,705 sq. mi. (17,366 sq. km.)
POPULATION 547,000
CAPITAL Mbabane
LARGEST CITY Manzini
HIGHEST POINT Emlembe 6,109 ft.
(1,862 m.)
MONETARY UNIT lilangeni
MAJOR LANGUAGES siSwati, English
MAJOR RELIGIONS Tribal religions,
Christianity

ZIMBABWE

AREA 150,803 sq. mi. (390,580 sq. km.)
POPULATION 7,360,000
CAPITAL Harare
LARGEST CITY Harare
HIGHEST POINT Mt. Inyangani 8,517 ft.
(2,596 m.)
MONETARY UNIT Zimbabwe dollar
MAJOR LANGUAGES English, Shona,
Ndebele
MAJOR RELIGIONS Tribal religions,
Protestantism

MADAGASCAR

AREA 226,657 sq. mi. (587,041 sq. km.)
POPULATION 8,742,000
CAPITAL Antananarivo
LARGEST CITY Antananarivo
HIGHEST POINT Maromokotro 9,436 ft.
(2,876 m.)
MONETARY UNIT Madagascar franc
MAJOR LANGUAGES Malagasy, French
MAJOR RELIGIONS Tribal religions,
Roman Catholicism, Protestantism

COMOROS

AREA 719 sq. mi. (1,862 sq. km.)
POPULATION 290,000
CAPITAL Moroni
LARGEST CITY Moroni
HIGHEST POINT Karthala 7,746 ft.
(2,361 m.)
MONETARY UNIT CFA franc
MAJOR LANGUAGES Arabic, French,
Swahili
MAJOR RELIGION Islam

MAURITIUS

AREA 790 sq. mi. (2,046 sq. km.)
POPULATION 959,000
CAPITAL Port Louis
LARGEST CITY Port Louis
HIGHEST POINT 2,711 ft. (826 m.)
MONETARY UNIT Mauritian rupee
MAJOR LANGUAGES English, French,
French Creole, Hindi, Urdu
MAJOR RELIGIONS Hinduism, Christianity,
Islam

SEYCHELLES

AREA 145 sq. mi. (375 sq. km.)
POPULATION 63,000
CAPITAL Victoria
LARGEST CITY Victoria
HIGHEST POINT Morne Seychellois
2,993 ft. (912 m.)
MONETARY UNIT Seychellois rupee
MAJOR LANGUAGES English, French,
Creole
MAJOR RELIGION Roman Catholicism

RÉUNION

AREA 969 sq. mi. (2,510 sq. km.)
POPULATION 491,000
CAPITAL St-Denis

MAYOTTE

AREA 144 sq. mi. (373 sq. km.)
POPULATION 47,300
CAPITAL Dzaoudzi

ZIMBABWE	BOTSWANA	SOUTH AFRICA	LESOTHO	SWAZILAND
MOZAMBIQUE	COMOROS	MADAGASCAR	MAURITIUS	SEYCHELLES

Agriculture, Industry and Resources

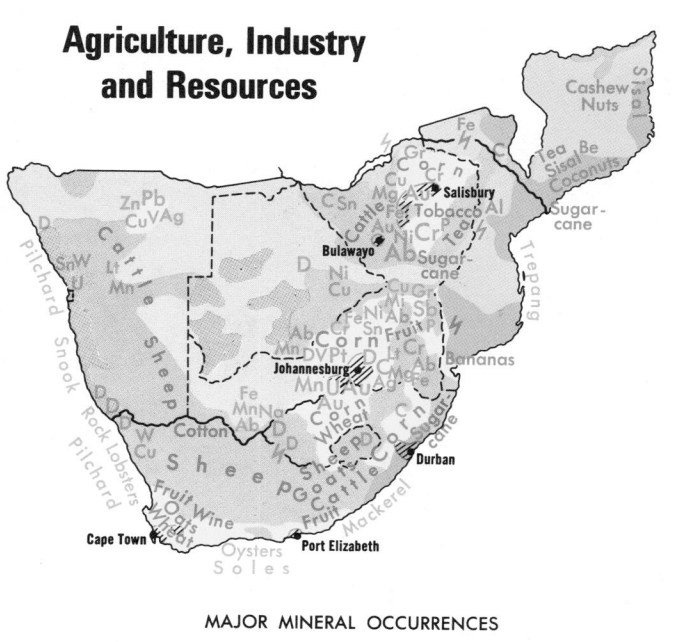
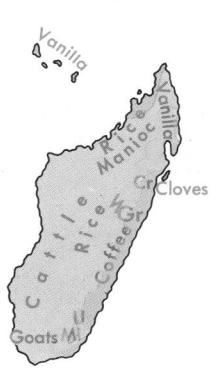

Salisbury
Bulawayo
Johannesburg
Cape Town
Durban
Port Elizabeth

DOMINANT LAND USE

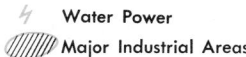

- Cereals, Horticulture, Livestock
- Market Gardening, Diversified Tropical Crops
- Plantation Agriculture
- Pasture Livestock
- Nomadic Livestock Herding
- Forests
- Nonagricultural Land

MAJOR MINERAL OCCURRENCES

Ab	Asbestos	Cu	Copper	Pb	Manganese	Sb	Antimony
Ag	Silver	D	Diamonds	Pt	Salt	Sn	Tin
Al	Bauxite	Fe	Iron Ore	Mn	Nickel	U	Uranium
Au	Gold	Gr	Graphite	Na	Phosphates	V	Vanadium
Be	Beryl	Lt	Lithium	Ni	Lead	W	Tungsten
C	Coal	Mg	Magnesium	P	Platinum	Zn	Zinc
Cr	Chromium	Mi	Mica				

⚡ Water Power
▨ Major Industrial Areas

(continued on following page)

Topography

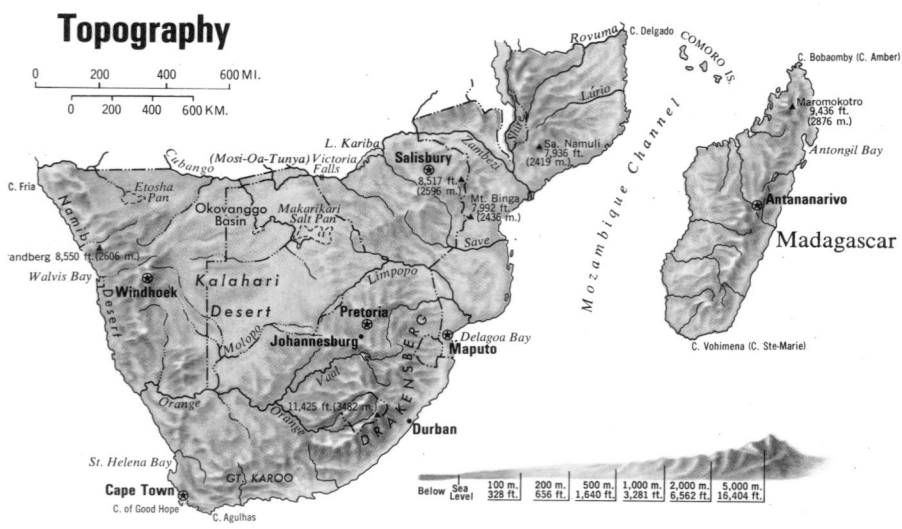

0 200 400 600 MI.		
0 200 400 600 KM.		

Below Sea Level | 100 m. 328 ft. | 200 m. 656 ft. | 500 m. 1,640 ft. | 1,000 m. 3,281 ft. | 2,000 m. 6,562 ft. | 5,000 m. 16,404 ft.

Topography map showing Southern Africa and Madagascar with labeled features: Rovuma, C. Delgado, COMORO IS., C. Bobaomby (C. Amber), L. Kariba, (Mosi-Oa-Tunya)Victoria Falls, Salisbury, Zambezi, Sa. Namuli, Maromokotro 9,436 ft. (2876 m.), Antongil Bay, Antananarivo, Madagascar, Mozambique Channel, Etosha Pan, Okovanggo Basin, Mukarikari Salt Pan, Mt. Binga, Save, Kalahari Desert, Windhoek, Pretoria, Johannesburg, Delagoa Bay, Maputo, C. Vohimena (C. Ste-Marie), Walvis Bay, Limpopo, Orange, DRAKENSBERG, Durban, St. Helena Bay, GT. KAROO, Cape Town, C. of Good Hope, C. Agulhas

Hawston 2,501	G7	Kuilsrivier 8,132	F6	Newcastle 14,407	E5
Heidelberg 12,521	J7	Kuruman 5,758	C5	Nigel 41,179	J7
Heilbron 8,258	J7	Ladybrand 8,757	D5	Noupoort 7,403	C6
Hermanus 4,956	G7	Ladysmith 28,920	D5	Nyanga 15,655	F6
Hopetown 3,273	C5	Lambert's Bay 3,247	B6	Nylstroom 6,906	D4
Houtbaai 5,691	E6	Lombardy 3,395	H6	Odendaalsrus 15,603	D5
Howick 12,429	E5	Louis Trichardt 8,906	E4	Okiep 4,983	B5
Humansdorp 4,215	C6	Lydenburg 7,427	E4	Oudtshoorn 26,907	C6
Ingwavuma 718	F5	Macassar 882	C5	Paarl 49,244	B6
Jagersfontein 4,142	D5	Maclear 3,279	D6	Parow 60,768	B6
Jameson Park 2,280	J7	Mafikeng (Mafeking) 6,515	C5	Pauls 17,447	B5
Johannesburg☐ 1,417,818	H6	Malmesbury 9,314	B6	Phalaborwa 7,543	E4
Johannesburg 654,232	H6	Margate 4,410	E6	Pietermaritzburg 114,822	E5
Keimoes 4,534	C5	Matatiele 3,853	D6	Pietermaritzburg☐ 174,179	E5
Kempton Park 37,205	J6	Melkbosstrand 453	D4	Pietersburg 27,174	D4
Kenhardt 3,230	C5	Messina 12,121	E4	Piet Retief 10,056	E5
Kimberley☐ 105,258	C5	Meyerton 8,654	H7	Piketberg 3,638	B6
Kimberley☐ 108,609	C5	Middelburg, C. of Good		Pinelands 11,769	F6
King William's Town 15,798	D6	Hope 11,121	D4	Pinetown 22,721	F6
Kirkwood 5,151	D6	Middelburg, Transvaal 26,942	D5	Pniel 1,596	F6
Kleinmond 1,175	F7	Milnerton 10,893	H6	Port Alfred 8,640	D6
Klerksdorp 53,558	D5	Modderfontein 8,538	H6	Port Elizabeth 392,231	D6
Knysna 13,479	C6	Molteno 5,825	D6	Port Elizabeth☐ 413,961	D6
Koffiefontein 3,672	D5	Montagu 5,504	C6	Port Nolloth 2,893	B5
Kokstad 10,227	D6	Moorreesburg 4,945	B6	Port Saint Johns	
Kraaifontein 10,286	F6	Mossel Bay 17,574	C6	(Umzimvubu) 1,817	D6
Kroonstad 51,988	D5	Nababeep 8,293	B5	Port Shepstone 5,581	E6
Krugersdorp 92,725	H6	Nelspruit 25,092	E5	Postmasburg 9,020	C5

Miandrivazo 2,371	G3	Chinde 742	F3
Midongy Atsimo 1,068	H4	Cóbuè 770	F2
Mitsinjo 3,118	H3	Cuamba 1,416	F2
Moramanga 10,806	H3	Dona Ana (Mutarara) 686	F3
Morombe 6,967	G4	Dondo 2,112	F3
Morondava 19,061	G3	Erego 418	F3
Nosy-Varika 1,252	H4	Espungabera 405	F4
Port-Bergé 4,734	H3	Fingoè 1,137	E2
Sambava 6,215	J2	Funhalouro☐ 42,366	E4
Soanierana-Ivongo 2,876	H3	Gorongoza 435	E3
Sosumav 10,946	H2	Guija 530	E4
Tamatave (Toamasina) 77,395	H3	Homolne 1,122	F4
Tambohorano 1,383	G3	Ibo 1,015	G2
Tananarive (Antananarivo)		Inhambane 4,975	F4
(cap.) 451,808	H3	Inhaminga 1,607	F3
Tanjanony 6,952	H4	Inharrime 856	F4
Toamasina 77,395	H3	Lichinga 3,011	F2
Toliara (Tuléar) 45,676	G4	Lumbo 11,080	G3
Tsihombe 1,008	H5	Lúrio 13,417	G2
Tsiroanomandidy 11,444	H3	Mabalane☐ 13,158	E4
Tsivory 1,036	H4	Maboto 28,970	E4
Vangaindrazo 2,593	H4	Machanga 15,754	F4
Vatomandry 4,202	H3	Machaze 42,255	E4
Vohibinany 1,741	H3	Macia 1,203	E4
Vohimarina (Vohémar) 4,289	J2	Macomia 730	G2
Vohipeno 2,736	H4	Magude 1,502	E4
		Malema 430	F2
OTHER FEATURES		Mandie☐ 24,382	E3
		Mandimbao 7,634	F2
Alaotra (lake)	H3	Manhica 1,680	E5
Amber (Bobaomby) (cape)	H2	Maniambao 2,045	F2
Antongil (bay)	J3	Manica 1,529	E4
Betsiboka (riv.)	H3	Manjacaze 641	E5
Bobaomby (Amber) (cape)	H2	Maputo (cap.) 755,300	E5
Mangoky (riv.)	G4	Marracuene 1,342	E5
Mangoro (riv.)	H3	Marromeu 1,330	F3
Maromokotro (mt.)	H2	Marrupa 824	F2
Masoala (pen.)	J3	Massangena☐ 3,301	E4
Mozambique (chan.)	G3	Massinga 517	F4
Nosy Be (isl.)	H2	Maxixe 902	F4
Nosy Boraha (isl.)	J3	Meconta 1,051	F3
Onilahy (riv.)	G4	Memba 379	G2
Saint-André (cape)	G3	Metangula 1,502	F2
Sainte-Marie (Vohimena)		Milanje 1,048	F3
(cape)	J3	Moamba 643	E5
Sainte-Marie (Nosy Boraha)		Mocímboa da Praia 935	G2
(isl.)	J3	Mocuba 2,293	F3
Tsiafajavona (mt.)	H3	Moma 433	F3
Tsiribihina (riv.)	G3	Monapo 902	G2
Vohimena (cape)	G5	Montepuez 2,837	F2
		Morrumbala 415	F3
MAURITIUS		Morrumbene 1,121	F4
		Mualama☐ 34,992	F3
CITIES and TOWNS		Mucojo 15,867	G2
		Mueda 1,583	G2
Curepipe 52,709	G5	Murrupula 444	F3
Mahébourg 15,463	G5	Mutarara (Dona Ana) 686	F3
Port Louis (cap.) 141,022	G5	Nacala 4,601	G2
Poudre d'Or 1,799	G5	Namacurra 399	F3
Quatre Bornes 51,638	G5	Namapa 440	F3
Souillac 3,361	G5	Nametil 453	F3
		Nampula 23,072	F3
OTHER FEATURES		Negomano☐ 656	F2
		Nova Lusitânia 1,363	E3
Mascarene (isls.)	F5	Nova Mambone 883	F4
		Nova Sofala 274	F4
MAYOTTE		Patúrio 2,599	E4
		Pemba 3,629	G2
CITIES and TOWNS		Quelimane 10,522	F3
		Quiongao 3,181	G2
Dzaoudzi (cap.) 196	H2	Quissico 2,615	F4
		Ribaué 437	F3
MOZAMBIQUE		Songo 1,350	E3
		Tete 4,549	E2
PROVINCES		Ulongue 451	E2
		Vila de Sena☐ 21,074	E3
Cabo Delgado 940,000	F2	Vilanculos 887	F4
Gaza 999,900	E4	Xai-Xai 5,234	E5
Inhambane 977,000	E4		
Manica 541,200	E4	OTHER FEATURES	
Maputo 491,800	E5		
Maputo (city) 755,300	E5	Angoche (isl.)	G3
Nampula 2,402,700	F3	Bazaruto, Ilha do (isl.)	F4
Niassa 514,100	F2	Binga (mt.)	E3
Sofala 1,055,200	F3	Changane (riv.)	E4
Tete 831,000	E2	Chilwa (lake)	F2
Zambézia 2,500,000	F3	Delagoa (bay)	E5
		Delgado (cape)	G2
CITIES and TOWNS		Ligonha (riv.)	F3
		Limpopo (riv.)	E4
Alto Molócuè 415	F3	Lugenda (riv.)	F2
Angoche 1,714	G3	Lúrio (riv.)	F2
Bartolomeu Dias☐ 6,102	F4	Mazoe (riv.)	E3
Beira 46,293	F3	Mozambique (chan.)	F3
Beira* 130,398	F3	Namuli, Serra (mt.)	F2
Bela Vista 851	E5	Nyasa (lake)	F2
Benga 1,398	E3	Olifants (riv.)	E4
Catandica 663	E3	Rovuma (riv.)	F2
Chemba 588	E3	São Sebastião (pt.)	F4
Chibuto 23,763	E4	Save (riv.)	E4
Chicualacuala 2,050	E4	Shire (riv.)	E3
Chimoio 4,507	E3	Zambezi (riv.)	E3

NAMIBIA (SOUTH-WEST AFRICA)	
CITIES and TOWNS	
Aroab 783	B5
Aus 767	B5
Berseba	B5
Bethanie 1,207	B5
Gibeon	B5
Gobabis 4,428	B4
Grootfontein 4,627	B3
Kalkfeld 587	B4
Kamanjab 713	A3
Karasburg 2,693	B5
Karibib 1,653	B4
Katima Mulilo	C3
Keetmanshoop 10,297	B5
Khorixas 1,299	A4
Koes 514	B5
Lüderitz 6,642	A5
Maltahöhe 1,313	B4
Mariental 4,629	B4
Ohopoho	A3
Okahandja 1,688	B4
Omaruru 2,783	B4
Ondangua	B3
Ongwediva	B3
Oranjemund 2,594	B5
Otavi 1,814	B3
Otjiwarongo 8,018	B4
Outjo 2,545	B4
Rehoboth 5,363	B4
Runtu 521	B3
Stampriet 271	B4
Swakopmund 5,681	A4
Tsumeb 12,338	B3
Usakos 2,334	B4
Warmbad 810	B5
Windhoek (cap.) 61,369	B4
Witvlei 303	B4
OTHER FEATURES	
Brandberg (mt.)	A4
Caprivi Strip (reg.)	C3
Chobe (riv.)	C3
Cubango (riv.)	B3
Damaraland (reg.)	B4
Diamond Coast (reg.)	A5
Elephant (riv.)	B5
Etosha Pan (salt pan)	B3
Fish (riv.)	B5
Great Namaland (reg.)	B5
Hottentot (bay)	A5
Kalahari (des.)	C4
Kaokoveld (reg.)	A3
Kaukauveld (mts.)	C3
Namib (des.)	A4
Nossob (riv.)	B4
Okavango (riv.)	C3
Ovamboland (reg.)	B3
Skeleton Coast (reg.)	A3
Swakop (riv.)	B4
Zambezi (riv.)	C3

La Digue (isl.)	J5
Mahé (isl.)	H5
North (isl.)	H5
Praslin (isl.)	H5
Silhouette (isl.)	H5
SOUTH AFRICA	
PROVINCES	
Cape Province 5,543,506	C6
Natal 5,722,215	E5
Orange Free State 1,833,216	D5
Transvaal 10,673,033	D4
AUTONOMOUS REPUBLICS	
Bophuthatswana 1,200,000	D5
Ciskei 345,191	D6
Transkei 2,000,000	D6
Venda 450,000	E4
CITIES and TOWNS	
Aberdeen 4,968	C6
Adelaide 7,227	D6
Alberton 23,988	H6
Alexandra 57,240	H6
Alexander Bay 2,675	B5
Aliwal North 12,311	D6
Barberton 12,382	E5
Barkly East 4,023	D6
Beaufort West 17,862	C6
Bellville 49,026	F6
Benoni 151,294	J6
Benoni☐ 164,543	J6
Bethlehem 29,918	D5
Bethulie 4,918	D6
Bloemfontein 149,836	C5
Bloemfontein☐ 182,329	C5
Bloubergstrand 378	D4
Boksburg 106,126	J6
Botrivier 743	F7
Brakpan 73,210	J6
Brandvlei 1,337	B6
Bredasdorp 3,264	B6
Brentwood Park 5,296	J6
Brits 12,182	D5
Brittstown 3,039	C6
Burgersdorp 8,340	D6
Butterworth (Gcuwa) 2,769	D6
Caledon 5,406	G7
Calvinia 6,386	B6
Cape Town (cap.) 697,514	B6
Cape Town☐ 833,731	E6
Carltonville 40,641	G7
Carnarvon 5,199	C6
Ceres 9,230	B6
Christiana 6,882	D5
Clanwilliam 2,724	B6
Clayville 3,994	H6
Colesberg 7,088	D6
Constantia 7,220	E6
Cradock 20,822	D6
De Aar 18,057	C6
Delmas 6,424	J6
Dibeng 945	C5
Douglas 4,335	C5
Dundee 17,162	E5
Dunnottar 3,089	J6
Durban 736,852	E5
Durban☐ 975,494	E5
Durbanville 7,438	F6
East London 119,727	D6
East London☐ 126,671	D6
Edenburg 3,710	D5
Edenvale 25,126	H6
Eersterivier 1,459	F6
Elliot 3,739	D6
Eloff 1,134	J6
Elsburg 3,501	H6
Eisiesrivier 63,706	F6
Empangeni 7,532	E5
Ermelo 19,036	E5
Eshowe 4,152	E5
Estcourt 10,922	D5
Firgrove 2,551	F6
Fort Beaufort 11,640	D6
Franschhoek 1,216	F6
Garies 1,339	B6
Gcuwa 2,769	D6
George 24,625	C6
Germiston 221,972	H6
Germiston☐ 293,257	H6
Glencoe 10,513	E5
Goodwood 31,592	E6
Gordon's Bay 1,112	F7
Graaff-Reinet 22,392	C6
Grabouw 4,286	F7
Grahamstown 41,302	D6
Grassy Park 32,709	F6
Greytown 9,028	E5
Griquatown 2,996	C5
Halfway House 3,639	H6
Harrismith 16,082	D5

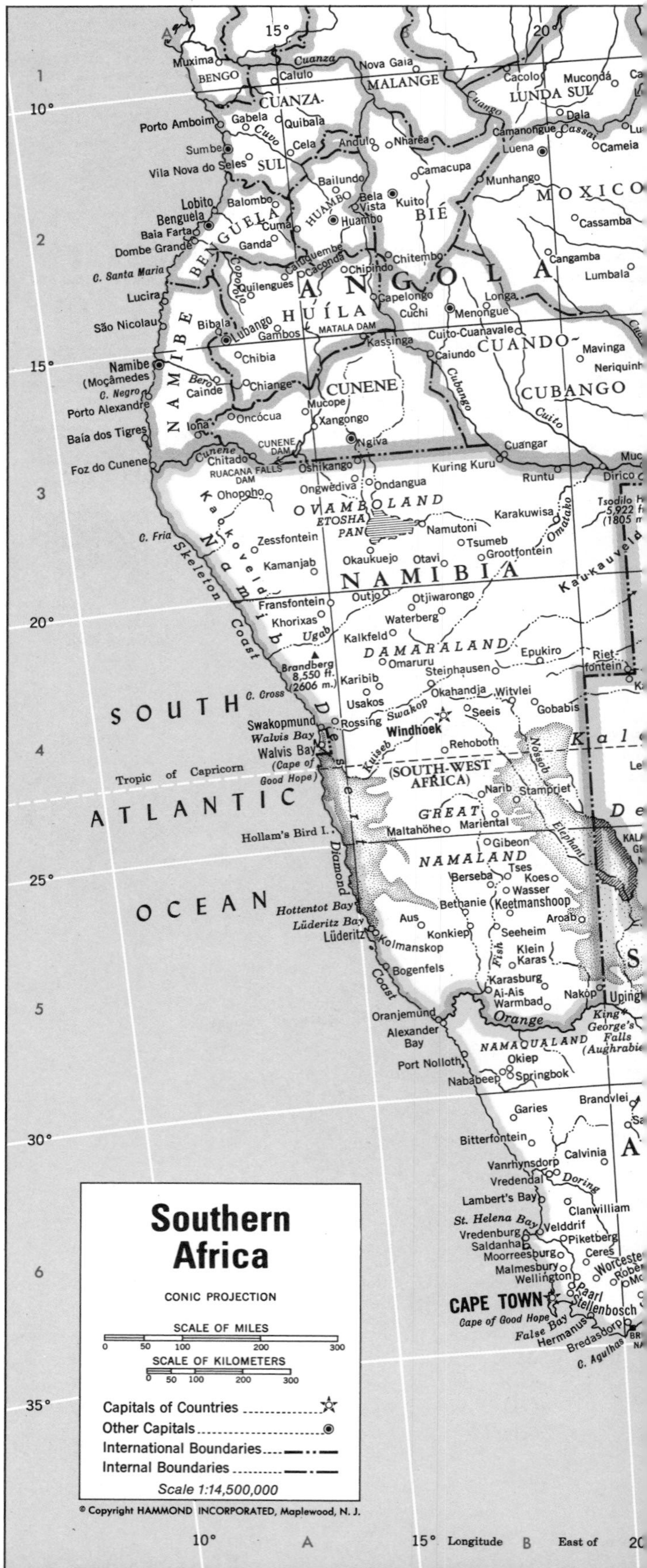

REUNION	
CITIES and TOWNS	
Le Port 21,564	F5
Saint-André 6,584	G5
Saint-Benoît 7,778	G5
Saint-Denis (cap.) 80,075	F5
Saint-Denis* 104,603	F5
Saint-Joseph 8,928	G6
Saint-Louis 10,252	F5
Saint-Pierre 21,817	F5
OTHER FEATURES	
Bassas da India (isl.)	F4
Europa (isl.)	G4
Glorioso (isls.)	H2
Juan de Nova (isl.)	G3
Piton des Neiges (mt.)	G5

SEYCHELLES	
CITIES and TOWNS	
Anse Boileau† 3,420	H5
Anse Royale† 3,182	H5
Cascadet 2,600	H5
Victoria (cap.) 15,559	H5
Victoria* 23,012	H5
OTHER FEATURES	
Aldabra (isls.)	H1
Assumption (isl.)	H1
Astove (isl.)	H2
Cosmoledo (isls.)	H1
Frigate (isl.)	J5

Map (right side):

Southern Africa

CONIC PROJECTION

SCALE OF MILES
0 50 100 200 300

SCALE OF KILOMETERS
0 50 100 200 300

Capitals of Countries ☆
Other Capitals ◉
International Boundaries
Internal Boundaries

Scale 1:14,500,000

© Copyright HAMMOND INCORPORATED, Maplewood, N.J.

Map labels include: Muxima, BENGO, CUANZA, MALANGE, LUNDA SUL, Nova Gaia, Calulo, Porto Amboim, Gabela, Quibala, Camanongue, Dala, Vila Nova de Seles, SUL, Bailundo, Munhango, Lobito, Benguela, HUAMBO, BIÉ, MOXICO, Baía Farta, Dombe Grande, C. Santa Maria, ANGOLA, Lumbala, Lucira, HUÍLA, Capelongo, Luena, São Nicolau, Caiundo, CUANDO-, Mavinga, Namibe (Moçâmedes), CUNENE, CUBANGO, C. Negro, Chibia, Porto Alexandre, Baía dos Tigres, Foz do Cunene, Oshikango, NAMIBIA, OVAMBOLAND, ETOSHA PAN, Namutoni, Grootfontein, Tsumeb, DAMARALAND, Otjiwarongo, Windhoek, Walvis Bay, SOUTH ATLANTIC OCEAN, Tropic of Capricorn, NAMALAND, Lüderitz, NAMAQUALAND, Port Nolloth, Springbok, CAPE TOWN, Cape of Good Hope, C. Agulhas

15° 20° 10° 15° Longitude B East of 20°

Potchefstroom 57,443	D5	Standerton 21,038	D5	Vishoek 6,721	E7	Bredasdorp Nat'l Park	C6	Sak (riv.)	C6	Bulawayo 359,000	D3

Potchefstroom 57,443 ....D5
Potgietersrus 6,667 ....D4
Pretoria (cap.) 545,450 ....D5
Pretoria 573,283 ....D5
Prieska 8,521 ....C5
Prince Albert 3,346 ....C6
Queenstown 39,304 ....C6
Randburg 43,257 ....H6
Randfontein 50,481 ....G6
Rensburg 2,042 ....J7
Richards Bay 598 ....E5
Richmond 3,185 ....D6
Riversdale 6,165 ....C6
Robertson 10,237 ....C6
Roodepoort 115,366 ....H6
Rustenburg 22,303 ....D5
Saldanha 4,994 ....B6
Senekal 9,124 ....D5
Sesfontein 2,731 ....J6
Simonstown 12,137 ....E7
Sishen 2,692 ....C5
Somerset East 10,383 ....D6
Somerset West 11,828 ....F6
Soweto 602,043 ....H6
Springbok 4,357 ....B5
Springs 142,812 ....J6
Springs 146,831 ....J6

Standerton 21,038 ....D5
Stanger 11,064 ....E5
Stellenbosch 29,955 ....F6
Strand 24,503 ....F7
Stutterheim 12,077 ....D6
Sundra 2,088 ....J6
Swellendam 6,423 ....C6
Taung 1,316 ....C5
Tembisa 81,821 ....H6
Thabazimbi 6,711 ....D4
Thohoyandou E4
Tzaneen 4,331 ....E4
Uitenhage 70,517 ....E5
Ulundi E5
Umtata 25,216 ....D6
Umzimkulu 1,817 ....D6
Upington 28,632 ....C5
Vaalplas 5,699 ....C6
Vanderbijl Park 78,754 ....D5
Vanrhynsdorp 2,279 ....B6
Veldrif 3,361 ....B6
Ventersburg G6
Vereeniging 172,549 ....D5
Vereeniging 200,078 ....D5
Victoria West 3,407 ....C6
Villiersdorp 2,349 ....G6

Vishoek 6,721 ....E7
Volksrust 10,238 ....D5
Vrede 6,309 ....D5
Vredenburg 6,094 ....B6
Vredendal 5,377 ....B6
Vryburg 16,916 ....C5
Vryheid 16,992 ....E5
Warmbad 8,343 ....H6
Warrenton 9,614 ....C5
Waterval-Bo 6,951 ....D5
Welkom 67,472 ....D5
Wellington 17,092 ....E4
Westonaria 36,253 ....H7
Willowmore 3,540 ....C6
Winburg 6,761 ....D5
Witbank 37,456 ....D5
Wolmaransstad 7,219 ....D5
Worcester 41,198 ....B6
Zastron 4,483 ....D6
Zeerust 6,972 ....D5
Zwelitsha 2,349 ....D6

OTHER FEATURES

Addo Nat'l Park D6
Agulhas (cape) B6
Bot (riv.) G7

Bredasdorp Nat'l Park C6
Cape (pen.) E7
Crocodile (riv.) H6
Drakensberg (range) D6
False (bay) F7
Good Hope (cape) E6
Great Fish (riv.) D6
Great Kei (riv.) D6
Great Karoo (reg.) C6
Groote (riv.) C5
Hartbees (riv.) C5
King George's (falls) B5
Klip (riv.) H6
Kruger Nat'l Park E4
Limpopo (riv.) D5
Molopo (riv.) C5
Mountain Zebra Nat'l Park D6
Olifants (riv.) B5
Orange (riv.) B5
Palmiet (riv.) F7
Plettenberg (bay) C6
Pondoland (reg.) D6
Robben (isl.) E7
Royal Natal Nat'l Park D5
Saint Helena (bay) B6
Saint Lucia (lake) E5

Sak (riv.) C6
Sand (riv.) D4
Slangkop (pt.) E7
Sneeuwkop (mt.) F6
Table (bay) E6
Table (mt.) E6
Vaal (riv.) D5
Walvis (bay) A4
Witwatersberg (range) G6
Witwatersrand (reg.) H7
Zonderend (riv.) G6
Zululand (reg.) E5

SWAZILAND

CITIES and TOWNS

Manzini 28,837 ....E5
Mbabane (cap.) 23,109 ....E5
Siteki 1,362 ....E5

ZIMBABWE

CITIES and TOWNS

Beitbridge 1,986 ....E4
Bindura 17,000 ....E3

Bulawayo 359,000 ....D3
Chegutu 12,000 ....D3
Chimanimani 667 ....E3
Chinhoyi 25,000 ....E3
Chipinge 2,350 ....E3
Chivhu 1,669 ....E3
Dete 2,473 ....D3
Gwanda 9,120 ....D3
Gwaaki 2,710 ....D3
Gwanda 2,049 ....D3
Gweru 68,000 ....D3
Harare (Salisbury) (cap.) 601,000 ....E3
Hwange 33,000 ....D3
Inyanga 733 ....E3
Kadoma 32,000 ....D3
Kariba 3,943 ....D3
Kwekwe 54,000 ....D3
Marondero 23,000 ....E3
Masvingo 22,000 ....D4
Matopos 11,330 ....D3
Mount Darwin 904 ....E3
Mutare 61,000 ....E3
Mvuma 1,525 ....D3
Mwenezi 7,830 ....D4
Plumtree 2,041 ....D3
Rusape 5,286 ....E3
Salisbury (Harare) (cap.) 601,000 ....E3
Shamva 785 ....E3
Shurugwi 8,387 ....E3

Tuli 340 ....D4
West Nicholson 1,929 ....D4
Zvishavane 20,000 ....E4

OTHER FEATURES

Inyanga Nat'l Park E3
Kariba (lake) D3
Lundi (riv.) D4
Mashonaland (reg.) 1,875,700 ....E3
Matabeleland (reg.) 969,220 ....D3
Mazoe (riv.) E3
Mushandike Nat'l Park D4
Sabi (riv.) E3
Sanyati (riv.) D3
Shangani (riv.) D3
Shashe (riv.) D4
Umvukwe (range) D3
Victoria (falls) D3
Zambezi (riv.) D3
Zimbabwe Nat'l Park E4

*City and suburbs.
†Population of parish.
○Population of subdivision.
□Population of urban area.

South America
AZIMUTHAL EQUAL-AREA PROJECTION
MILES
0 100 200 400 600
KILOMETERS
0 100 200 400 600
Capitals of Countries
Other Capitals
International Boundaries
Canals
Scale 1:27,000,000
© Copyright HAMMOND INCORPORATED, Maplewood, N. J.
Longitude West 50° of Greenwich
CARIBBEAN
SEA
ATLANTIC
OCEAN
PACIFIC
OCEAN
NETHERLANDS ANTILLES
ST. VINCENT AND THE GRENADINES
BARBADOS
WEST INDIES
GRENADA
TRINIDAD & TOBAGO
Port of Spain
PANAMA
Panamá
G. of Panamá
Panama Canal
COLOMBIA
Bogotá
Medellín
Cali
Barranquilla
Cartagena
VENEZUELA
Caracas
Maracaibo
Lake Maracaibo
Ciudad Bolívar
Guiana Highlands
Angel Fall
Mt. Roraima 9,094 ft. (2772 m.)
GUYANA
Georgetown
SURINAME
Paramaribo
FRENCH GUIANA
Cayenne
ECUADOR
Quito
Guayaquil
Gulf of Guayaquil
Chimborazo 20,561 ft. (6267 m.)
Equator
PERU
Lima
Callao
Cusco
Arequipa
Huascarán 22,205 ft. (6768 m.)
BOLIVIA
La Paz
Sucre
Lake Titicaca
Lake Poopó
Nev. Ancohuma 21,489 ft. (6550 m.)
BRAZIL
Brasília
Rio de Janeiro
São Paulo
Belo Horizonte
Salvador
Recife
Fortaleza
Belém
Manaus
Amazon
Ilha de Marajó
Selvas
Planalto de Mato Grosso
Brazilian Highlands
Caatingas
PARAGUAY
Asunción
Gran Chaco
Tropic of Capricorn
URUGUAY
Montevideo
Río de la Plata
ARGENTINA
Buenos Aires
Córdoba
Rosario
Mendoza
Cerro Aconcagua 22,831 ft. (6959 m.)
Pampa
Patagonia
Golfo San Matías
Golfo San Jorge
CHILE
Santiago
Valparaíso
Atacama Desert
ARCHIPIÉLAGO DE LOS CHONOS
Strait of Magellan
Tierra del Fuego
Cape Horn
FALKLAND ISLANDS (U.K.)
Stanley
I. de San Félix (Chile)
I. San Ambrosio (Chile)
JUAN FERNÁNDEZ IS. (Chile)
Malpelo I. (Col.)

Population Distribution

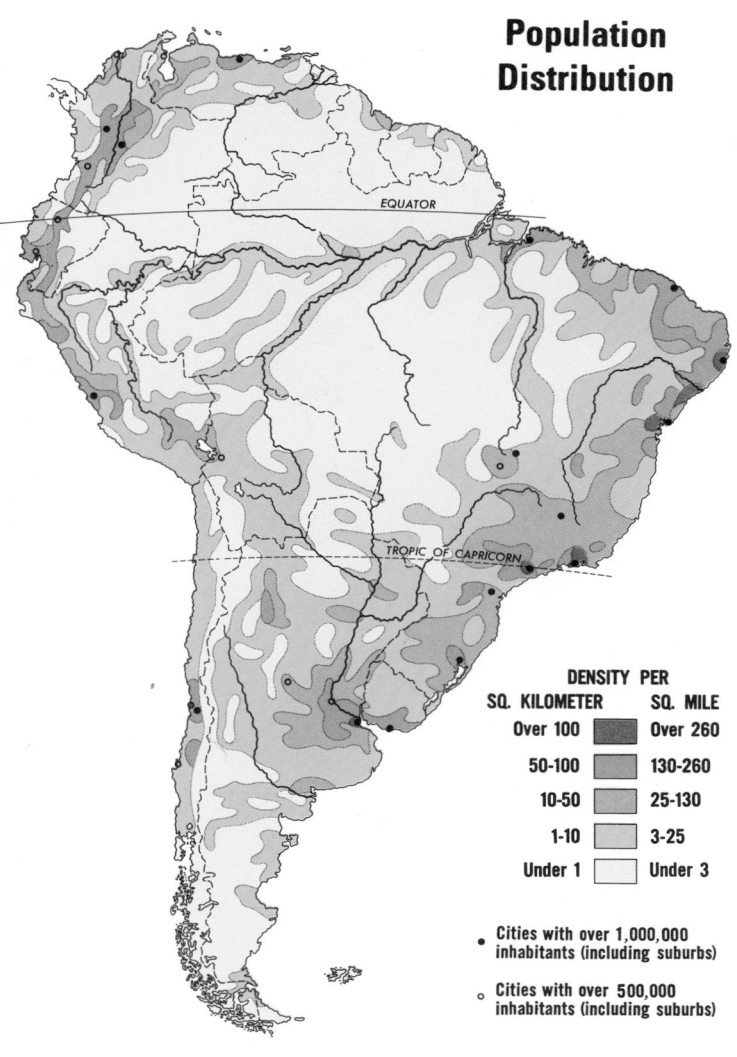

AREA 6,875,000 sq. mi. (17,806,250 sq. km.)
POPULATION 245,000,000
LARGEST CITY São Paulo
HIGHEST POINT Cerro Aconcagua 22,831 ft. (6,959 m.)
LOWEST POINT Salina Grande -131 ft. (-40 m.)

Vegetation

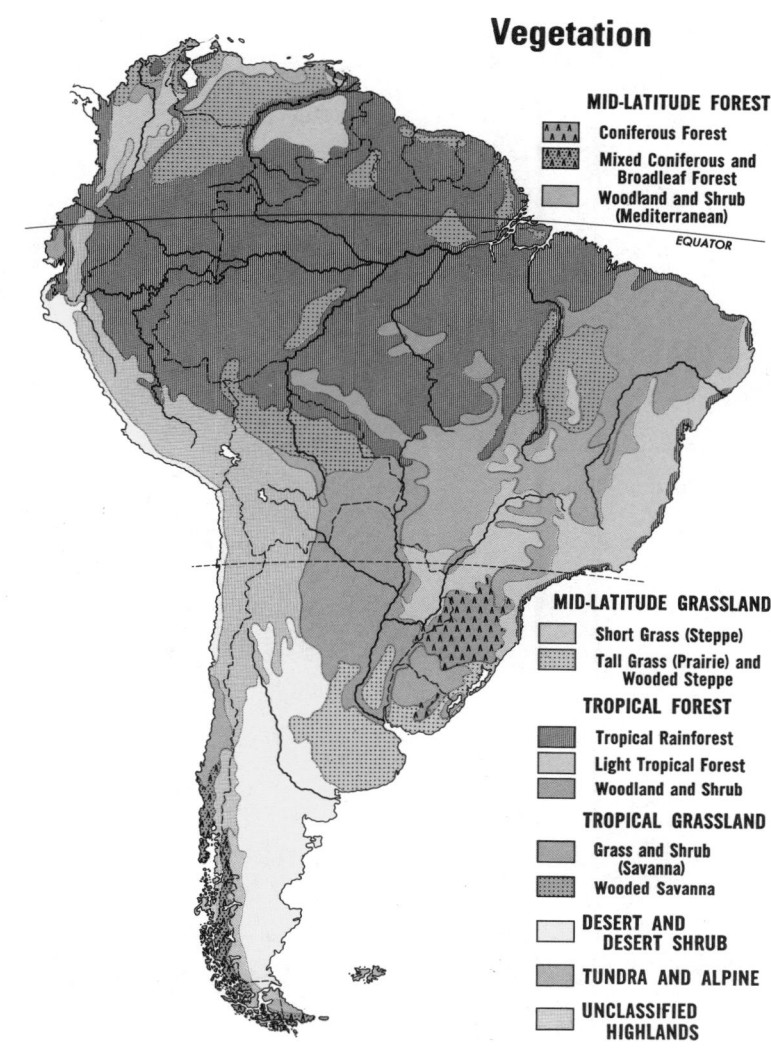

DENSITY PER

SQ. KILOMETER	SQ. MILE
Over 100	Over 260
50-100	130-260
10-50	25-130
1-10	3-25
Under 1	Under 3

• Cities with over 1,000,000 inhabitants (including suburbs)

○ Cities with over 500,000 inhabitants (including suburbs)

MID-LATITUDE FOREST
- Coniferous Forest
- Mixed Coniferous and Broadleaf Forest
- Woodland and Shrub (Mediterranean)

MID-LATITUDE GRASSLAND
- Short Grass (Steppe)
- Tall Grass (Prairie) and Wooded Steppe

TROPICAL FOREST
- Tropical Rainforest
- Light Tropical Forest
- Woodland and Shrub

TROPICAL GRASSLAND
- Grass and Shrub (Savanna)
- Wooded Savanna

DESERT AND DESERT SHRUB

TUNDRA AND ALPINE

UNCLASSIFIED HIGHLANDS

Average January Temperature

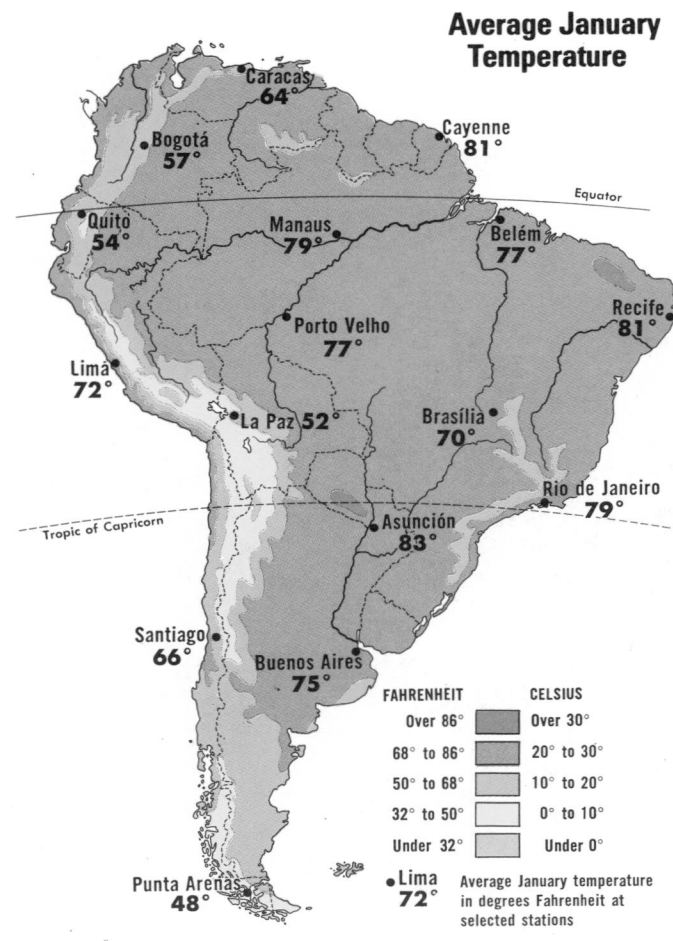

Caracas 64°
Bogotá 57°
Cayenne 81°
Equator
Quito 54°
Manaus 79°
Belém 77°
Porto Velho 77°
Recife 81°
Lima 72°
La Paz 52°
Brasília 70°
Rio de Janeiro 79°
Tropic of Capricorn
Asunción 83°
Santiago 66°
Buenos Aires 75°
Punta Arenas 48°

FAHRENHEIT		CELSIUS
Over 86°		Over 30°
68° to 86°		20° to 30°
50° to 68°		10° to 20°
32° to 50°		0° to 10°
Under 32°		Under 0°

• Lima 72°   Average January temperature in degrees Fahrenheit at selected stations

Average July Temperature

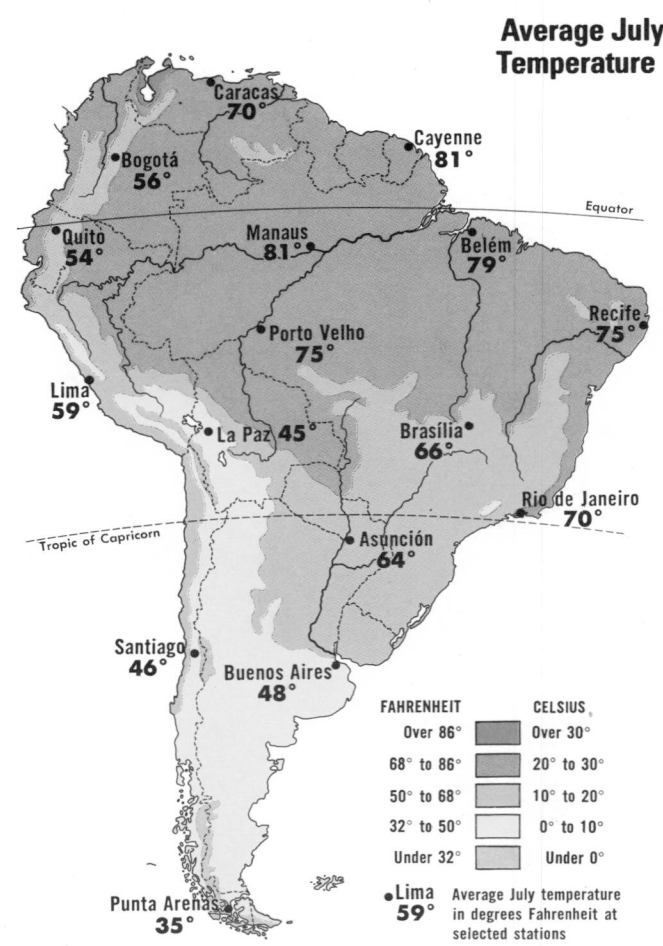

Caracas 70°
Bogotá 56°
Cayenne 81°
Equator
Quito 54°
Manaus 81°
Belém 79°
Porto Velho 75°
Recife 75°
Lima 59°
La Paz 45°
Brasília 66°
Rio de Janeiro 70°
Tropic of Capricorn
Asunción 64°
Santiago 46°
Buenos Aires 48°
Punta Arenas 35°

FAHRENHEIT		CELSIUS
Over 86°		Over 30°
68° to 86°		20° to 30°
50° to 68°		10° to 20°
32° to 50°		0° to 10°
Under 32°		Under 0°

• Lima 59°   Average July temperature in degrees Fahrenheit at selected stations

Rainfall

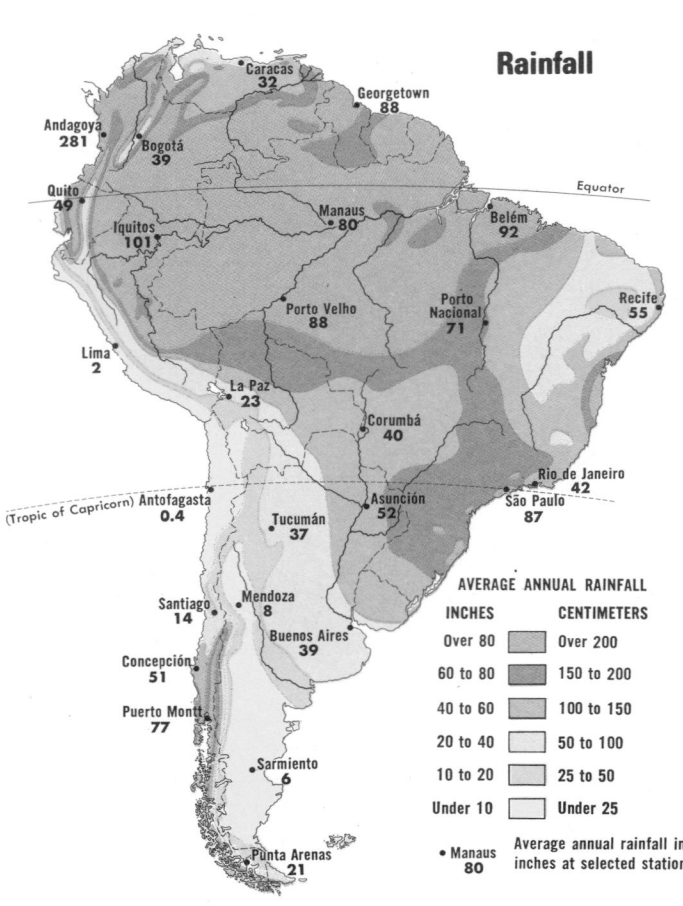

Caracas 32
Georgetown 88
Andagoya 281
Bogotá 39
Quito 49
Equator
Iquitos 101
Manaus 80
Belém 92
Porto Velho 88
Porto Nacional 71
Recife 55
Lima 2
La Paz 23
Corumbá 40
Rio de Janeiro 42
(Tropic of Capricorn) Antofagasta 0.4
Tucumán 37
Asunción 52
São Paulo 87
Santiago 14
Mendoza 8
Buenos Aires 39
Concepción 51
Puerto Montt 77
Sarmiento 6
Punta Arenas 21

AVERAGE ANNUAL RAINFALL

INCHES		CENTIMETERS
Over 80		Over 200
60 to 80		150 to 200
40 to 60		100 to 150
20 to 40		50 to 100
10 to 20		25 to 50
Under 10		Under 25

• Manaus 80   Average annual rainfall in inches at selected stations

Vegetation/Relief

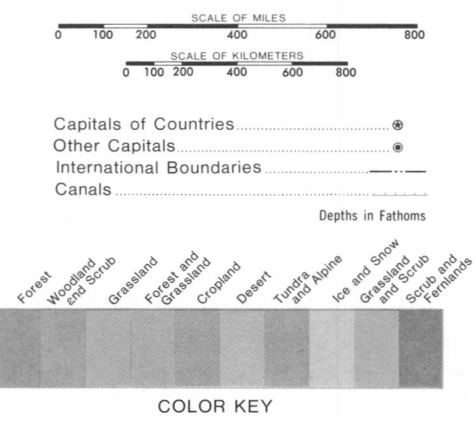

SCALE OF MILES
0 100 200 400 600 800

SCALE OF KILOMETERS
0 100 200 400 600 800

Capitals of Countries .... ⊛
Other Capitals .... ⊚
International Boundaries .... ____
Canals ....

Depths in Fathoms

Forest | Woodland and Scrub | Grassland | Forest and Grassland | Cropland | Desert | Tundra and Alpine | Ice and Snow | Grassland and Scrub | Scrub and Fernlands

COLOR KEY

CARIBBEAN SEA

NETH. ANTILLES

G. of Venezuela

Pta. Gallinas

Aruba
Curaçao
Bonaire
Willemstad

GRENADA

BARBADOS

West Indies

Tobago

TRINIDAD & TOBAGO

Port of Spain

Trinidad

Barranquilla

Maracaibo

Caracas

L. Maracaibo

Pico Bolívar
16,427 ft. (5007 m.)

Orinoco

Ciudad Guyana

VENEZUELA

Guri Res.

Georgetown

Paramaribo

Cayenne

Panama
G. of Panama

PANAMÁ

Medellín

Magdalena

Bucaramanga

Arauca

Meta

Angel Fall

GUYANA

Mt. Roraima
9,094 ft.
(2772 m.)

SURINAME

FRENCH
GUIANA

Bogotá

Cali

COLOMBIA

Orinoco

Caroní

Branco

Guiana Highlands

Cauca

Putumayo

Vaupés

Pico Phelps
(Pico da Neblina)
9,889 ft.
(3014 m.)

Japurá

Negro

Jari

Amazon

I. de Marajó

Bôca de Marajó

Equator

Quito
Chimborazo
20,561 ft.
(6267 m.)

ECUADOR

Içá

Iça

Amazon

Iquitos

Amazon

Manaus

Belém

São Luís

Guayaquil
Gulf of Guayaquil

Yavarí

Juruá

Tapajós

Xingu

Tocantins

Fortaleza

Pta. Aguja

S   e   l   v   a   s

Huascarán
22,205 ft.
(6768 m.)

Marañón

Ucayali

Purus

Madeira

Teles-Pires

Araguaia

Teresina

Cabo de
São Roque

Natal

Callao

Lima

Apurimac

Cuzco

Beni

Guaporé

Aripuanã

Juruena

B   R   A   Z   I   L

Caatingas

Recife

Maceió

Grande

Mamoré

Planalto de

Pôrnaíba

Paraguaçu

Salvador

Nev. Ancohuma
21,489 ft.
(6550 m.)

BOLIVIA

Mato Grosso

São Francisco

Brazilian

Lake
Titicaca

La Paz

Cochabamba

Grande

Goiânia

Brasília

Jequitinhonha

Arica

Lake
Poopó

Sucre

Planalto

Highlands

Pico da Bandeira
9,482 ft. (2890 m.)

Belo Horizonte

Tropic of Capricorn

Antofagasta

Volcán Llullaillaco
22,057 ft.
(6723 m.)

Pilcomayo

Bermejo

Chaco

Paraguay

Paraná

PARAGUAY

Campo Grande

Grande

Tietê

Paraíba

C. de São Tomé

São Paulo

C. Frio

Rio de Janeiro

Santos

I. de San Félix
(Chile)

I. San Ambrosio
(Chile)

CHILE

San Miguel de
Tucumán

Nev. Ojos del Salado
22,572 ft.
(6880 m.)

Salado del Norte

Asunción

ITAIPU
DAM

Iguazú
Falls

Iguaçu

Curitiba

Serra do

I. de Santa Catarina

Córdoba

Santa Fé

Rosario

Gran Chaco

Paraná

Uruguay

Pôrto Alegre

Lagoa dos Patos

I. Alejandro Selkirk

I. Robinson Crusoe

Juan Fernandez Is.
(Chile)

Valparaíso

Santiago

Cerro Aconcagua
22,831 ft. (6959 m.)

Mendoza

Salado

Negro

URUGUAY

Lagoa Mirim

Buenos Aires

La Plata

Montevideo

Río de la Plata

Concepción

Bahía Blanca

C.
San Antonio

Colorado

P   a   m   p   a   s

Puerto Montt

Negro

Golfo San Matías

Pen. Valdés

Isla de Chiloé

Chubut

Archipiélago
de los
Chonos

Golfo San Jorge

Pen. Taitao

Deseado

C. Tres Puntas

G. de Penas

Archipiélago
Reina Adelaida

Bahía
Grande

Falkland Islands
(U.K.)

Stanley

Str. of Magellan

Tierra del Fuego

Str. of Magellan

Punta
Arenas

Cape Horn

A   R   G   E   N   T   I   N   A

P   A   T   A   G   O   N   I   A

A   N   D   E   S

A   T   A   C   A   M   A

D   E   S   E   R   T

A   M   A   Z   O   N   I   A

CORDILLERA

PACIFIC OCEAN

ATLANTIC OCEAN

30° Longitude West of Greenwich 20°

STATES

Amazonas (terr.) 21,696 .... E5
Anzoátegui 506,297 .... F3
Apure 164,705 .... D4
Aragua 543,170 .... E3
Barinas 231,046 .... D3
Bolívar 391,665 .... E3
Carabobo 659,339 .... D2
Cojedes 94,351 .... D3
Delta Amacuro (terr.) 48,139 .... H3
Dependencias Federales (terr.) 463 .... E2
Distrito Federal 1,860,637 .... E2
Falcón 407,957 .... D2
Guárico 318,905 .... E3
Lara 671,410 .... C3
Mérida 347,095 .... C3
Miranda 856,272 .... E2
Monagas 298,239 .... G3
Nueva Esparta 118,830 .... G2
Portuguesa 297,047 .... D3
Sucre 469,004 .... G2
Táchira 511,346 .... C4
Trujillo 381,334 .... C3
Yaracuy 223,545 .... D2
Zulia 1,299,030 .... B2

CITIES and TOWNS

Acarigua 56,743 .... D3
Achaguas 4,633 .... D4
Adícora 707 .... D2
Aguada Grande 2,901 .... D2
Agua Fría E5
Agua Linda E5
Aguasay 1,752 .... G3
Altagracia 11,116 .... C2
Altagracia de Orituco 18,717 .... E3
Amuay C2
Anaco 29,487 .... F3
Aparurén G5
Apurito 740 .... D4
Arabopó H5
Aragua de Barcelona 9,107 .... F3
Aragua de Maturín 4,051 .... G3
Araure 22,466 .... D3
Aricagua 231 .... C3
Arichuna 1,204 .... E4
Aripao 296 .... F4
Aroa 5,418 .... D2
Atapirire 337 .... F3
Bachaquero C2
Bachaquero 2,513 .... B3
Baragua 659 .... D2
Barbacoas 2,513 .... E3
Barcelona 78,201 .... F2
Barinas 56,329 .... C3
Barinitas 9,644 .... C3
Barquisimeto 330,815 .... D2
Barrancas, Barinas 4,489 .... C3
Barrancas, Monagas 5,738 .... G3
Betijoque 5,851 .... C3
Biruaca 2,266 .... E4
Biscucuy 6,114 .... D3
Bobare 1,204 .... D2
Bobures 2,468 .... C3
Boca de Aroa 2,756 .... D2
Boca del Mangle F3
Boca del Pao 403 .... F3
Bocono 15,915 .... C3
Borbón F4
Borojó 423 .... D2
Bruzual 941 .... D3
Buena Vista, Anzoátegui F3
Buena Vista, Apure D4
Buena Vista, Falcón 944 .... C2
Cabimas 118,037 .... C2
Cabruta 1,927 .... E4
Cabudare 14,593 .... D3
Cabure 1,673 .... D2
Cachipo G3
Cacurí F5
Cagua 29,601 .... E3
Caicara 6,092 .... G3
Caicara de Orituco 6,867 .... E4
Calabozo 37,282 .... E3
Calderas 1,195 .... C3
Camaguán 4,143 .... E3
Camatagua 3,335 .... E3
Campo Claro 1,832 .... C3
Candelaria E4
Cantaura 15,839 .... F3
Capatárida 1,375 .... C2
Capibara E6
Carabobo, Bolívar H4
Carabobo, Carabobo D3
Caracas (cap.) 1,035,499 .... E2
Caracas* 2,183,935 .... E2
Carache 3,966 .... C3
Carapa 119 .... C2
Cariaco 6,549 .... G2
Caribén E4
Caripe 4,729 .... G2
Caripito 19,053 .... G2
Carirubana 15,701 .... C2
Carmelo 2,556 .... C2
Carora 36,115 .... C2
Carúpano 50,935 .... G2
Casanay 4,985 .... G2
Casigua, Falcón 460 .... C2
Casigua, Zulia 3,665 .... B3
Caucagua 6,218 .... E2
Cazorla 700 .... E3
Chaguaramas 2,748 .... E3
Chichiriviche 3,236 .... D2
Chivacoa 19,210 .... D2
Choroní 534 .... E2
Churuguara 6,636 .... D2
Ciudad Bolívar 103,728 .... G3
Ciudad Bolivia 4,864 .... C3
Ciudad de Nutrias 769 .... D3
Ciudad Guayana 143,540 .... G3
Ciudad Ojeda 83,083 .... C2
Ciudad Piar 3,965 .... G4
Clarines 2,099 .... F3
Cojoro C2
Colón E6
Comunidad E6
Coporito H3
Coro 68,701 .... D2
Corozo Pando E3
Cúa 9,953 .... E2
Cubiro 1,988 .... D3
Cuchivero F4
Cumaná 119,751 .... F2
Cumanacoa 9,179 .... G2
Cunaviche 795 .... E4
Curiapo H3
Dabajuro 4,516 .... C2
Delicias 1,616 .... B4
Democracia D3
Dolores 1,454 .... D3
Duaca 7,519 .... D2
Ejido 11,170 .... C3
El Almacén G4
El Amparo de Apure 2,015 .... D4
El Baúl 1,715 .... D3
El Callao 4,270 .... G4
El Calvario 384 .... E3
El Chaparro 768 .... F3
El Cristo G2
El Dorado 1,888 .... H4
El Empedrado 1,788 .... C3
El Guapo 1,231 .... F2
El Manteco 1,962 .... G4
El Miamo 335 .... H4
Elorza 3,184 .... D4
El Oso H5
El Palmar 2,758 .... G4
El Pao, Anzoátegui 761 .... F3
El Pao, Bolívar 1,259 .... G3
El Pao, Cojedes 1,715 .... D3
El Perú H4
El Pilar 3,278 .... G2
El Rastro 903 .... E3
El Samán de Apure 1,399 .... D4
El Socorro E3
El Sombrero 8,373 .... E3
El Tigre 49,801 .... F3
El Tocuyo 19,351 .... C3
El Toro H3
El Vigía 20,970 .... C3
El Vínculo D1
Encontrados 5,607 .... B3
Esperanza E6
Espino 559 .... C3
Garcitas C3
Guacara 35,111 .... D2
Guachara 577 .... D4
Guadarrama 334 .... G5
Guaina G5
Guana G5
Guanare 34,148 .... D3
Guanarito 3,150 .... D3
Guarenas G2
Guanta 9,017 .... F2
Guardatinajas 1,206 .... E3
Guarero B2
Guárico 3,259 .... D3
Guariquén 619 .... G2
Guasdualito 7,793 .... C4
Guasimal 582 .... H4
Guasipati 4,807 .... G4
Guayabal, Amazonas E5
Guayabal, Guárico 1,403 .... E3
Güiria 13,905 .... G2
Guri G4
Guzmán Blanco E6
Higuerote 5,008 .... E2
Icabarú H5
Independencia 4,897 .... B4
Irapa 4,470 .... G2
Juangriego 6,062 .... G2
Judibana D1
Juseplín G3
Kavanayen H5
La Aduana D3
La Asunción 6,381 .... G2
La Canoa G3
La Ceiba, Apure C4
La Ceiba, Trujillo 212 .... C2
La Concepción B2
La Concepción 13,885 .... C2
La Esmeralda F6
La Esperanza H3
La Fría 8,134 .... B3
La Grita 9,954 .... C3
La Guaira 20,344 .... E2
Lagunetas C3
Lagunillas C2

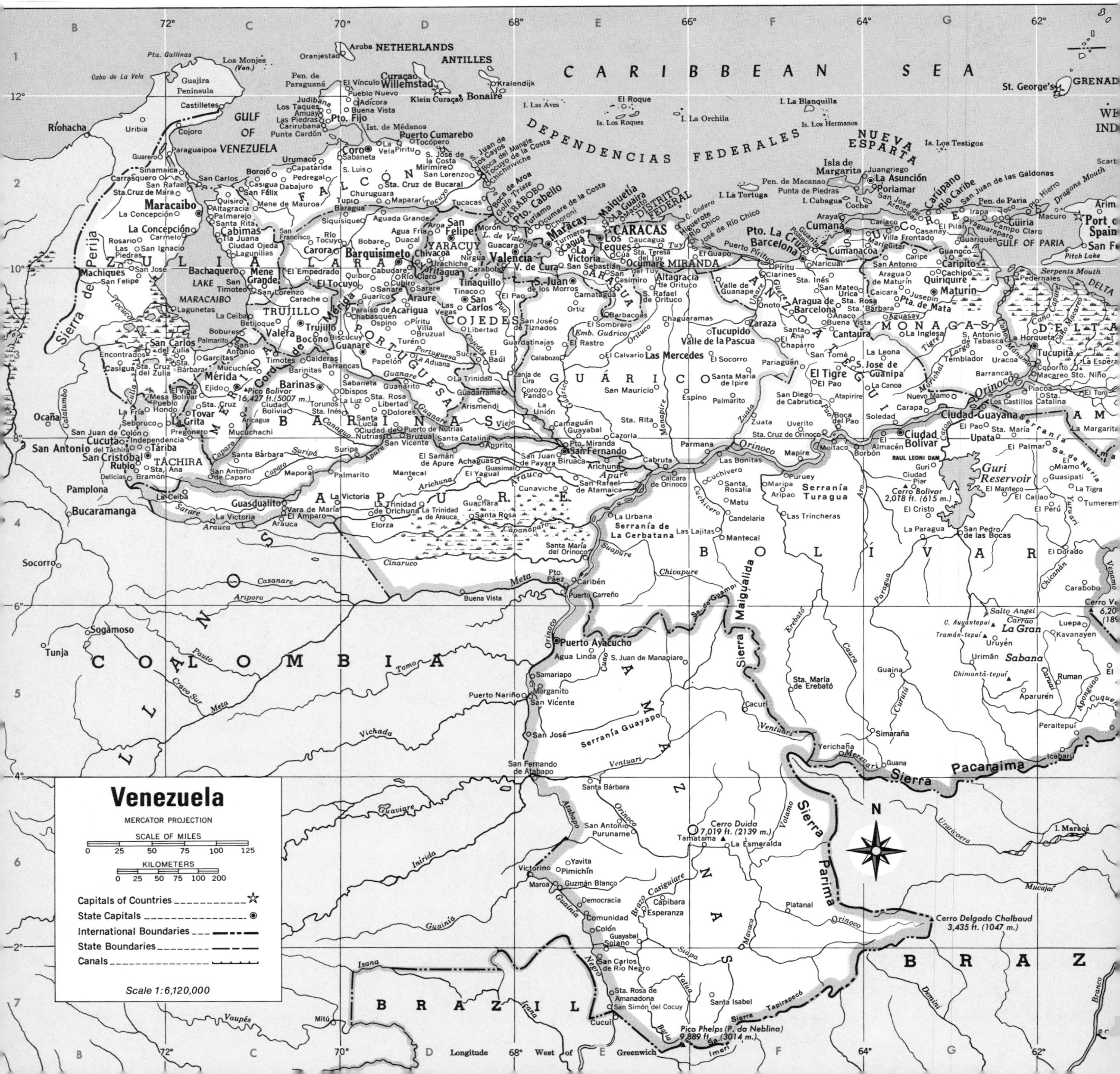

Venezuela

MERCATOR PROJECTION

SCALE OF MILES
0 25 50 75 100 125

KILOMETERS
0 25 50 75 100 200

Capitals of Countries _____ ☆
State Capitals _____ ◉
International Boundaries ___ ___ ___
State Boundaries _____
Canals _____

Scale 1:6,120,000

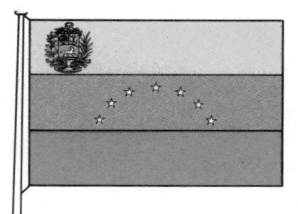

AREA 352,143 sq. mi. (912,050 sq. km.)
POPULATION 14,313,000
CAPITAL Caracas
LARGEST CITY Caracas
HIGHEST POINT Pico Bolívar 16,427 ft. (5,007 m.)
MONETARY UNIT Bolívar
MAJOR LANGUAGE Spanish
MAJOR RELIGION Roman Catholicism

La Horqueta....G3
La Inglesa....G3
La Leona....G3
La Luz 672....D3
La Margarita....H3
La Paragua 1,676....G4
Las Bonitas 343....F4
Las Lajitas....F4
Las Mercedes 6,739....E3
Las Piedras, Falcón....C2
Las Piedras, Zulia 4,583....B2
Las Trincheras....F4
Las Vegas 3,212....D3
La Tigra 129....H4
La Trinidad 129....H4
La Trinidad de Arauca....D4
La Trinidad de Orichuna 665....D4
La Unión 713....E3
La Urbana 661....E4
La Vela de Coro 7,172....D2
La Victoria, Apure 689....D4
La Victoria, Apure....C4
La Victoria, Aragua 40,731....E2
Libertad, Barinas 2,072....D3
Libertad, Cojedes 1,919....D3
Los Castillos....G3
Los Teques 63,106....E2
Macareo Santo Niño....H2
Machiques 18,898....B3
Macuro 1,122....H2
Macuto 11,704....E2

Maiquetía 59,238....E2
Mantecal, Apure 1,136....D4
Mantecal, Bolívar....F4
Maparari 1,376....D2
Mapire 1,195....F4
Maporal 249....C4
Maracaibo 651,574....B2
Maracay 255,134....E2
Marigüitar 5,645....G2
Maripa 913....F4
Maroa 408....E6
Matu....G3
Maturín 98,188....G3
Mene de Mauroa 4,336....C2
Mene Grande 11,498....C3
Mérida 74,214....C3
Mesa Bolívar 956....C3
Mirimire 3,424....D2
Moitaco 458....F4
Morganito....E5
Morón 19,451....D2
Mucuchachí 472....C3
Mucuchíes 1,625....C3
Naricual 1,047....G2
Nirgua 11,918....D2
Nuevo Mamo....G3
Obispos 1,140....C3
Ocumare de la Costa 2,840....E2
Ocumare del Tuy 24,229....E2
Onoto 1,991....F3
Ortiz 1,793....E3
Ospino 3,544....D3
Palmarejo....C2
Palmarito, Apure 926....D4
Palmarito, Guárico....F4
Palmarito, Mérida 988....C3
Papelón 774....D3
Paraguaipoa 3,850....C2
Paraíso de Chabasquén 2,094....D3
Pariaguán 8,173....F3
Parmana....F4
Pedernales....G3
Pedregal 1,317....C2
Peraitepul....H5
Piacoa....H3
Pimichín....E6
P'ritu, Anzoátegui 2,479....F2
P'ritu, Falcón 1,186....D2
P'ritu, Portuguesa 8,128....D3
Platanal....F6
Porlamar 31,985....G2
Pozuelos 45,391....F2
Pregonero 3,598....C3
Pueblo Hondo....C3
Pueblo Nuevo 3,426....D1
Puerto Ayacucho 10,417....E5
Puerto Cabello 72,103....E2
Puerto Cumarebo 10,064....D2
Puerto de Nutrias 675....D4
Puerto Hierro....H2
Puerto La Cruz 63,276....F2
Puerto Miranda....E4
Puerto Páez 954....E4
Puerto Píritu 3,495....F2
Punta Cardón 18,182....C2
Punta de Mata 7,777....F3
Punta de Piedras 2,826....F2
Punto Fijo 5,548....D2
Puruey....F4
Puruname....E6
Quíbor 12,216....D3
Quiriquire 7,304....G3
Quisiro 1,383....C2
Río Caribe 8,963....G2
Río Chico 4,491....F2
Río Claro 2,460....D3
Río Tocuyo 916....C2
Rosario....B2
Rubio 19,156....B4
Sabaneta, Barinas 4,680....D3
Sabaneta, Falcón 650....D2
Samariapo....E5
San Antonio, Amazonas....E6
San Antonio, Monagas 4,235....G2
San Antonio, Zulia....C3
San Antonio de Caparo 289....C4
San Antonio del Táchira 20,342....B4
San Antonio de Tabasca....G3
Sanare 6,717....D3
San Carlos, Cojedes 21,029....D3
San Carlos, Zulia 749....C2

San Carlos del Zulia 26,762....C3
San Carlos de Río Negro 515....E7
San Casimiro 4,843....E3
San Cristóbal 151,717....B4
San Diego de Cabrutica 432....F3
San Felipe, Yaracuy 43,801....D2
San Felipe, Zulia....B3
San Félix 379....G3
San Fernando de Apure 38,960....E4
San Fernando de Atabapo 1,537....E5
San Francisco, Lara 861....C2
San Ignacio....B2
San José, Amazonas....E5
San José, Zulia 4,498....B3
San José de Amacuro....H3
San José de Areocuar 985....G2
San José de Guanipa 22,530....G3
San José de la Costa....D2
San José de Río Chico 3,600....F2
San José de Tiznados 666....E3
San Juan de Colón....B3
San Juan de los Galdonas 1,196....G2
San Juan de los Cayos 1,692....C2
San Juan de los Morros 38,265....E3
San Juan de Manapiare....E5
San Juan de Payara 1,018....E4
San Lorenzo, Falcón 716....D2
San Lorenzo, Zulia....C3
San Luis 1,405....D2
San Mateo 2,424....F3
San Mauricio....E3
San Pedro de las Bocas....G4
San Rafael 10,910....C2
San Rafael de Atamaica 635....E4
San Rafael de Orituco 1,378....E3
San Sebastián 5,582....E2
San Simón del Cocuy....E7
Santa Ana, Anzoátegui 3,558....F3
Santa Ana, Táchira 5,116....B4
Santa Bárbara, Amazonas....E6
Santa Bárbara, Barinas 6,155....C4
Santa Bárbara, Monagas 2,034....G3
Santa Bárbara, Zulia....C3
Santa Catalina, Barinas 1,077....D4
Santa Catalina, Delta Amacuro....H3
Santa Cruz....C3
Santa Cruz de Bucaral 2,904....D2
Santa Cruz del Zulia 4,221....B3
Santa Cruz de Mara 5,773....C2
Santa Cruz de Orinoco 513....F3
Santa Elena 608....H5
Santa Inés, Anzoátegui 1,049....F3
Santa Inés, Barinas 391....C3
Santa Isabel....F7
Santa Lucía 619....D3
Santa María, Bolívar....G3
Santa María de Erebato....F5
Santa María de Ipire 3,307....F3
Santa María del Orinoco....E4
Santa Rita, Guárico....E3
Santa Rita, Zulia 15,668....C2
Santa Rosa, Anzoátegui 954....F3

Santa Rosa, Apure....D4
Santa Rosa, Barinas 1,514....D3
Santa Rosa de Amanadana....E7
Santa Rosalía 513....F4
Santa Teresa 10,220....E2
San Timoteo 3,635....C3
San Tomé....F3
San Vicente, Amazonas....E5
San Vicente, Apure 365....D3
Sarare 4,236....D3
Seboruco 2,616....B3
Simaraña....G5
Sinamaica....B2
Siquisique 3,821....D2
Solano....E6

Soledad 7,108....G3
Sucre 608....D3
Suripa....D4
Tamatama....F6
Táriba 15,683....B4
Temblador 5,380....G3
Tía Juana....C2
Timotes 3,229....C3
Tinaco 7,263....D3
Tinaquillo 12,015....D3
Tocópero 1,033....D2
Tocuyo de la Costa 4,023....C2
Torunos 739....C3
Tovar 12,814....C3
Trujillo 25,921....C3

Tucacas 4,780....D2
Tucupido 9,522....F3
Tucupita 21,417....H3
Tumeremo 5,036....H4
Tupi 88....D3
Turén....D3
Turiamo....E2
Turmero 43,832....E2
Upata 22,793....G3
Urachiche 4,759....D2
Uracoa 1,165....G3
Urica 1,881....F3
Urimán....G5
Urumaco 829....C2
Uruyén....G5
Uverito 468....F3
Valencia 367,171....E2
Valera 76,740....C3
Valle de Guanape 3,468....F3
Valle de la Pascua 36,809....F3
Vara de Marla....C4
Villa Bruzual 14,003....D3
Villa de Cura 27,832....E2
Villa Frontado 1,600....G2
Yaguaraparo 3,931....G2
Yaritagua 21,363....D2
Yavita....E6
Yerichaña....F5
Yoco 2,196....G2
Zanja de Lira....E3
Zaraza 15,480....F3
Zuata 914....F3

OTHER FEATURES

Amacuro (riv.)....H4
Angel (fall)....G5
Aponguao (riv.)....H5
Apure (riv.)....E4
Arauca (riv.)....D4
Arichuna (riv.)....D4
Aro (riv.)....F4
Atabapo (riv.)....E6
Auyantepui (mt.)....G5
Baria (riv.)....E7
Bolívar, Cerro (mt.)....G4
Bolívar, Pico (peak)....C3
Canagua (riv.)....C4
Caño Capure (riv.)....E4
Caño Macareo (riv.)....H3
Caño Mánamo (riv.)....G3
Capanaparo (riv.)....E4
Caparo (riv.)....C4
Caroní (riv.)....G4
Carrao (riv.)....G5
Caruai (riv.)....H5
Casiquiare, Brazo (riv.)....E6
Catatumbo (riv.)....B3
Caura (riv.)....F5
Chicanán (riv.)....H4
Chimantá-tepui (mt.)....G5
Chivapure (riv.)....D4
Cinaruco (riv.)....E5
Coche (isl.)....F2
Codera (cape)....F2
Cojedes (riv.)....D3
Cuao (riv.)....E5
Cubagua (isl.)....F2
Cuchivero (riv.)....F4
Cuquenán (riv.)....H5
Curutú (riv.)....E5
Cuyuni (riv.)....H4
Delgado Chalbaud, Cerro (mt.)....F7
Dragons Mouth (str.)....H2
Duida, Cerro (mt.)....F6
Erebato (riv.)....F5
Gran Sabana, La (plain)....G5
Guainía (riv.)....E6
Guampí, Sierra de (mts.)....F4

Guanare (riv.)....D3
Guanare Viejo (riv.)....D3
Guanipa (riv.)....G3
Guárico (res.)....E3
Guárico (riv.)....E3
Guayapo, Serranía (mts.)....E5
Güere (riv.)....F3
Guri (res.)....G4
Icabarú (riv.)....G5
Imataca, Serranía (mts.)....H4
Imeri, Sierra (mts.)....F7
La Blanquilla (isl.)....F1
La Orchila (isl.)....E1
La Gran Sabana (plain)....G5
La Tortuga (isl.)....F2
Las Aves (isls.)....E1
Los Hermanos (isls.)....F2
Los Monjes (isls.)....C1
Los Roques (isls.)....E1
Los Testigos (isls.)....G2
Macanao (pen.)....F2
Maiguálida, Sierra (range)....F4
Manapire (riv.)....F3
Maracaibo (lake)....C3
Margarita (isl.)....F2
Mavaca (riv.)....F6
Médanos (isth.)....D2
Merevari (riv.)....F5
Mérida, Cordillera de (range)....C3
Meta (riv.)....D4
Morichal Largo (riv.)....G3
Neblina (Phelps) (peak)....E7
Negro (riv.)....E7
Nuria, Sierra de (mts.)....H4
Ocamo (riv.)....F6
Orinoco (delta)....H3
Orinoco (riv.)....G3
Orituco (riv.)....E3
Pacaraima, Sierra (mts.)....G5
Pao (riv.)....F3
Pao (riv.)....D3
Paragua (riv.)....G4
Paraguaná (pen.)....C1
Paria (gulf)....H2
Paria (pen.)....G2
Parima, Sierra (mts.)....F6
Perijá, Sierra de (mts.)....B2
Phelps (peak)....E7
Portuguesa (riv.)....D3
Roraima (mt.)....H5
Salto Angel (fall)....G5
Sarare (riv.)....C4
Serpents Mouth (passage)....H3
Siapa (riv.)....F7
Sipapo (riv.)....E5
Suapure (riv.)....F4
Suripá (riv.)....C4
Tapirapecó, Sierra (mts.)....F7
Tigre (riv.)....G3
Tocuco (riv.)....B3
Tocuyo (riv.)....D2
Tramán-tepui (mt.)....G5
Triste (gulf)....D2
Turagua, Serranía (mts.)....F4
Tuy (riv.)....E2
Unare (riv.)....F2
Valencia (lake)....E2
Venamo, Cerro (mt.)....H4
Venamo (riv.)....H4
Venezuela (gulf)....C2
Venturi (riv.)....E5
Votomo (riv.)....F6
Yatua (riv.)....E7
Yuruní (riv.)....H4
Yuruari (riv.)....H4
Zuata (riv.)....F3
Zulia (riv.)....B3

*City and suburbs

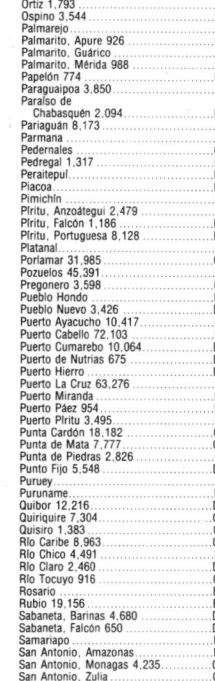

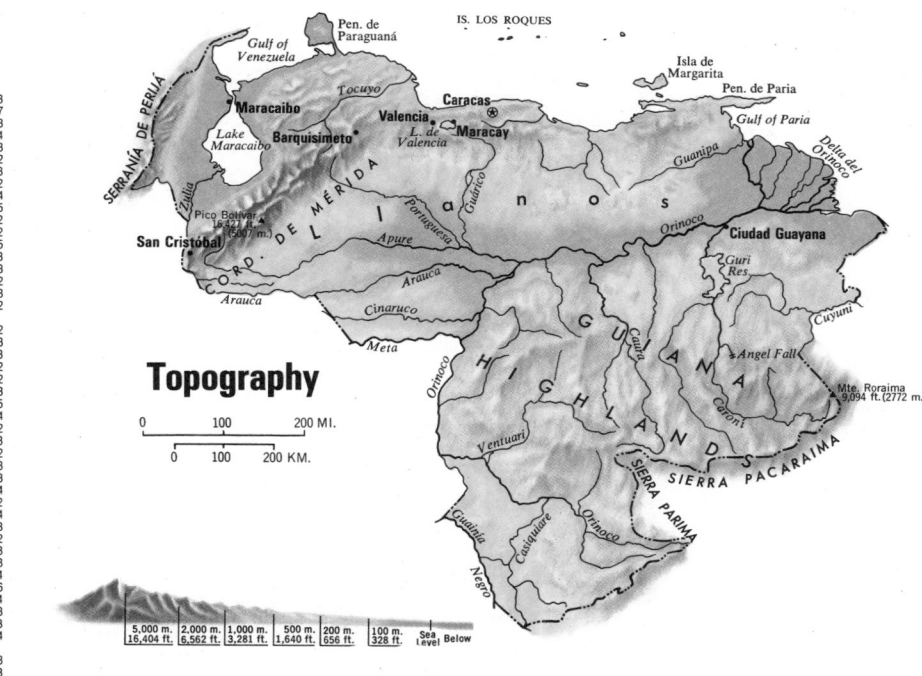

Topography

0   100   200 MI.
0   100   200 KM.

| 5,000 m. 16,404 ft. | 2,000 m. 6,562 ft. | 1,000 m. 3,281 ft. | 500 m. 1,640 ft. | 200 m. 656 ft. | 100 m. 328 ft. | Sea Level | Below |

Agriculture, Industry and Resources

MAJOR MINERAL OCCURRENCES

Al Bauxite
Au Gold
C   Coal
D   Diamonds
Fe Iron Ore
G   Natural Gas
Mn Manganese
Na Salt
O   Petroleum

⚡ Water Power
▨ Major Industrial Areas

DOMINANT LAND USE

Diversified Tropical Crops (chiefly plantation agriculture)
Upland Cultivated Areas
Upland Livestock Grazing, Limited Agriculture
Extensive Livestock Ranching
Forests

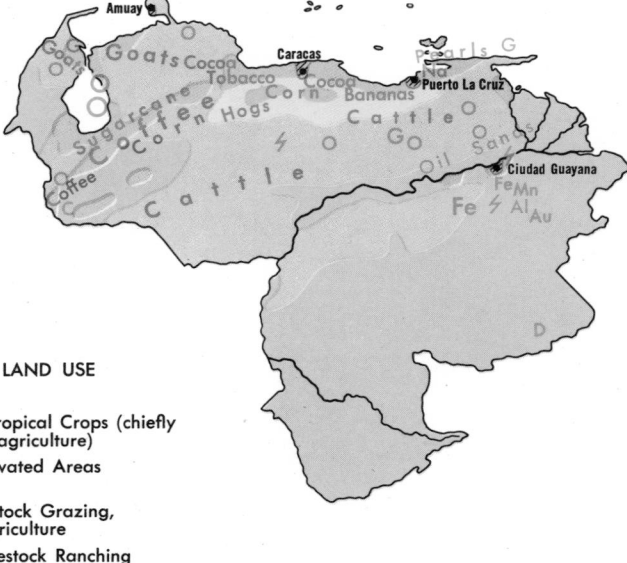

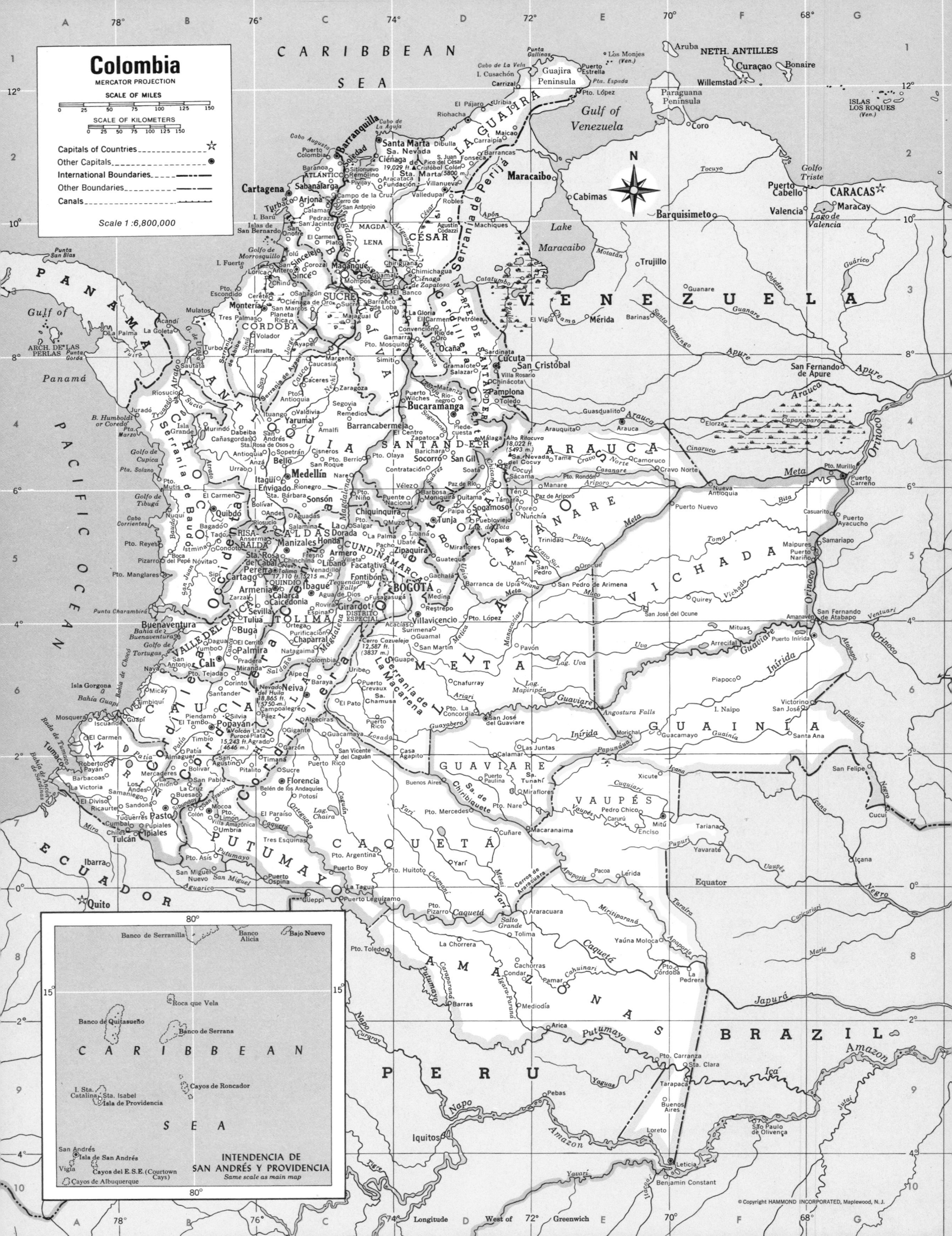
Colombia
MERCATOR PROJECTION
SCALE OF MILES
0 25 50 75 100 125 150
SCALE OF KILOMETERS
0 25 50 75 100 125 150
Capitals of Countries
Other Capitals
International Boundaries
Other Boundaries
Canals
Scale 1:6,800,000
CARIBBEAN SEA
PANAMA
PACIFIC OCEAN
ECUADOR
PERU
BRAZIL
VENEZUELA
NETH. ANTILLES
Aruba
Curaçao
Bonaire
Willemstad
CARACAS
Gulf of Venezuela
Lake Maracaibo
Maracaibo
Cabimas
Barquisimeto
Valencia
Maracay
Puerto Cabello
Coro
Paraguana Peninsula
Guajira Peninsula
Trujillo
Mérida
San Cristóbal
San Fernando de Apure
Gulf of Urabá
Gulf of Panamá
Panamá
ARCH. DE LAS PERLAS
Quito
Tulcán
Ibarra
Iquitos
Leticia
Benjamin Constant
LA GUAJIRA
MAGDALENA
ATLÁNTICO
CÉSAR
BOLÍVAR
SUCRE
CÓRDOBA
ANTIOQUIA
CHOCÓ
NORTE DE SANTANDER
SANTANDER
ARAUCA
BOYACÁ
CASANARE
VICHADA
CUNDINAMARCA
CALDAS
RISARALDA
QUINDÍO
TOLIMA
VALLE DEL CAUCA
CAUCA
NARIÑO
HUILA
PUTUMAYO
CAQUETÁ
META
GUAVIARE
GUAINÍA
VAUPÉS
AMAZONAS
DISTRITO ESPECIAL
BOGOTÁ
Barranquilla
Cartagena
Santa Marta
Riohacha
Valledupar
Sincelejo
Montería
Medellín
Quibdó
Bucaramanga
Cúcuta
Tunja
Manizales
Pereira
Armenia
Ibagué
Cali
Popayán
Neiva
Pasto
Florencia
Mocoa
Villavicencio
Yopal
Arauca
Mitú
Puerto Inírida
Puerto Carreño
San José del Guaviare
Buenaventura
Tumaco
Sa. Nevada de Sta. Marta
Serranía de Perijá
Cordillera Oriental
Cordillera Central
Cordillera Occidental
Serranía de Baudó
Serranía de la Macarena
Magdalena
Cauca
Meta
Orinoco
Guaviare
Vaupés
Caquetá
Putumayo
Amazon
Apaporis
Inírida
Japurá
Negro
Equator
INTENDENCIA DE SAN ANDRÉS Y PROVIDENCIA
Same scale as main map
Banco de Serranilla
Banco Alicia
Bajo Nuevo
Roca que Vela
Banco de Quitasueño
Banco de Serrana
Cayos de Roncador
I. Sta. Catalina
Sta. Isabel
Isla de Providencia
San Andrés
Isla de San Andrés
Vigía
Cayos del E.S.E. (Courtown Cays)
Cayos de Albuquerque
Longitude West of Greenwich
© Copyright HAMMOND INCORPORATED, Maplewood, N. J.

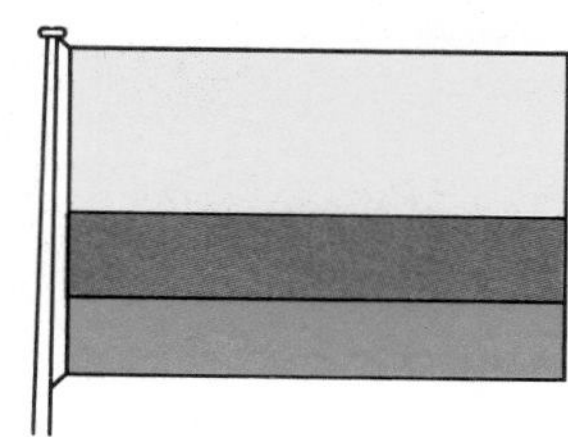

AREA 439,513 sq. mi. (1,138,339 sq. km.)
POPULATION 27,520,000
CAPITAL Bogotá
LARGEST CITY Bogotá
HIGHEST POINT Pico Cristóbal Colón 19,029 ft. (5,800 m.)
MONETARY UNIT Colombian peso
MAJOR LANGUAGE Spanish
MAJOR RELIGION Roman Catholicism

INTERNAL DIVISIONS

Amazonas (comm.) 6,825 D8
Antioquia (dept.) 2,976,153 B4
Arauca (inten.) 19,884 E4
Atlántico (dept.) 958,560 C2
Bolívar (dept.) 802,407 C3
Boyacá (dept.) 1,084,766 D5
Caldas (dept.) 700,954 C5
Caquetá (inten.) 57,103 C7
Casanare (inten.) B3
Cauca (dept.) 603,894 B6
César (dept.) 339,843 D3
Chocó (dept.) 201,915 B4
Córdoba (dept.) 645,478 C3
Cundinamarca (dept.) 1,106,626 C5
Distrito Especial 2,855,065 C5
Guainía (comm.) 1,792 F6
Guajira, La (dept.) 180,520 D2
Guaviare (comm.) D7
Huila (dept.) 469,834 C6
La Guajira (dept.) 180,520 D2
Magdalena (dept.) 536,122 C3
Meta (dept.) 245,176 D6
Nariño (dept.) 807,112 B7
Norte de Santander (dept.) 693,298 D3
Putumayo (inten.) 22,916 C7
Quindío (dept.) 321,677 C5
Risaralda (dept.) 452,626 B5
San Andrés y Providencia (inten.) 22,719 B10
Santander (dept.) 1,130,977 D4
Sucre (dept.) 354,412 C3
Tolima (dept.) 903,520 C5
Valle del Cauca (dept.) 2,204,722 B6
Vaupés (comm.) 6,923 E7
Vichada (comm.) 2,172 F5

CITIES and TOWNS

Acacías 9,238 D6
Acandí 2,358 B3
Agrado 2,771 C6
Aguachica 16,771 D3
Aguadas 9,995 C5
Agua de Dios 9,689 C5
Agustín Codazzi 21,932 D3
Aipe 3,794 C6
Algeciras 5,022 C6
Almaguer 1,518 B7
Amalfi 6,494 C4
Andes 14,957 C5
Anserma 15,559 B5
Antioquia 6,841 B4
Anzá 647 C4
Aracataca 7,511 D2
Arauca 7,613 E4
Arauquita 1,096 E4
Arjona 20,571 C2
Armenia 135,615 B5
Armero 19,567 C5
Ayapel 7,475 C3
Bagadó 1,575 B5
Baranoa 18,397 C2
Baraya 2,581 C6
Barbacoas 4,653 A7
Barbosa 7,960 D5
Barichara 2,548 D4
Barrancabermeja 87,191 C4
Barrancas 2,979 D2
Barranco de Loba 2,215 C3
Barranquilla 661,009 C2
Belén de los Andaquíes 2,190 C7
Bello 115,119 C4
Bogotá (cap.) 2,696,270 D5
Bogotá* 2,855,065 D5
Bolívar, Antioquia 13,259 C5
Bucaramanga 291,661 D4
Buenaventura 115,770 B6
Buesaco 2,763 B7
Buga 71,016 B6
Cáceres 7,154 C4
Caicedonia 23,567 C5
Calamar, Bolívar 5,867 C2
Calarcá 29,349 C5
Cali 898,253 B6
Campoalegre 11,799 C6
Campo de la Cruz 13,137 C2
Cañasgordas 3,900 B4
Cartagena 292,512 C2
Cartago 69,154 B5
Caucasia 19,348 C4
Cereté 18,788 C3
Cerro de San Antonio 3,394 C2
Chaparral 14,546 C6
Chimichaqua 6,382 D3
Chinácota 4,478 D4
Chinchiná 24,891 C5
Chinú 10,023 C3
Chiquinquirá 21,727 C5
Chiriguaná 6,611 D3
Ciénaga 42,546 C2
Ciénaga de Oro 10,607 C3
Cisneros 7,226 C4
Colombia 2,903 C6
Colón 1,306 B7
Condoto 4,798 B5
Contratación 3,057 D4
Convención 7,545 D3
Corinto 6,933 B6
Corozal 17,419 C3
Cravo Norte 771 F4
Cúcuta 219,772 D4
Cumbal 2,891 B7
Dabeiba 7,600 B4
Dagua 5,392 B6
Duitama 36,551 D5
El Banco 20,756 D3
El Carmen, Chocó 1,879 B5
El Carmen, Norte de Santander 2,362 D3
El Carmen de Bolívar 23,392 C3
El Cerrito 17,357 B6
El Cocuy 2,740 D4
El Tambo 2,179 B6
Envigado 63,584 C4
Espinal 32,475 C5
Facatativá 27,892 C5
Florencia 31,817 C7
Fonseca 9,988 D2
Fresno 8,141 C5
Fundación 17,497 C2
Fusagasugá 25,456 C5
Gachalá 1,364 D5
Gamarra 5,071 D3
Garzón 13,783 C6
Gigante 4,880 C6
Girardot 59,165 C5
Gramalote 2,880 D4
Guamal, Magdalena 4,986 C3
Guamal, Meta 2,854 D6
Guapí 5,005 B6
Guateque 6,032 D5
Honda 21,506 C5
Ibagué 176,223 C5
Inírida 1,792 F6
Ipiales 30,871 B7
Iscuandé 561 A6
Istmina 5,575 B5
Itagüí 96,972 C4
Ituango 5,561 C4
Juradó 935 B4
La Cruz 4,353 B7
La Dorada 30,962 C5
La Gloria 2,632 D3
La Palma 5,430 C5
La Plata 8,047 C6
La Unión 5,392 B7
Leticia 6,285 F10
Líbano 19,132 C5
Lorica 18,251 C3
Los Andes 1,414 B7
Magangué 34,396 C3
Maicao 21,645 D2
Majagual 2,329 C3
Málaga 10,645 D4

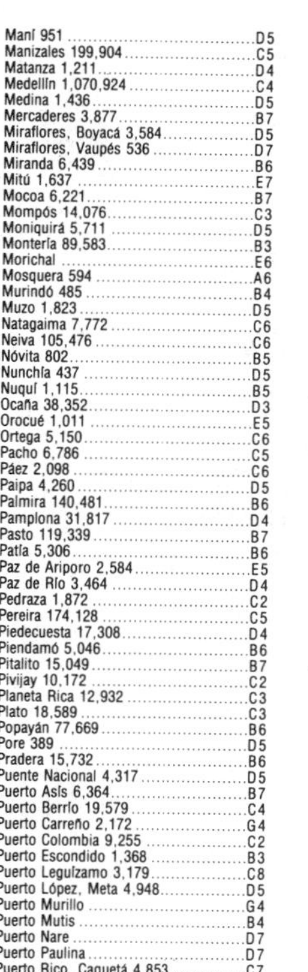

Maní 951 D5
Manizales 199,904 C5
Matanza 1,211 D4
Medellín 1,070,924 C4
Medina 1,436 D5
Mercaderes 3,877 B7
Miraflores, Boyacá 3,584 D5
Miraflores, Vaupés 536 D7
Miranda 6,439 B6
Mitú 1,637 E7
Mocoa 6,221 B7
Mompós 14,076 C3
Moniquirá 5,711 D5
Montería 89,583 B3
Morichal E6
Mosquera 594 A6
Murindó 485 B4
Muzo 1,823 D5
Natagaima 7,772 C6
Neiva 105,476 C6
Nóvita 802 B5
Nunchía 437 D5
Nuquí 1,115 B5
Ocaña 38,352 D3
Orocué 1,011 E5
Ortega 5,150 C6
Pacho 6,786 C5
Páez 2,098 C6
Paipa 4,260 D5
Palmira 140,481 B6
Pamplona 31,817 D4
Pasto 119,339 B7
Patía 5,306 B6
Paz de Ariporo 2,584 E5
Paz de Río 3,464 D4
Pedraza 1,872 C2
Pereira 174,128 C5
Piedecuesta 17,308 D4
Piendamó 5,046 B6
Pitalito 15,049 B7
Pivijay 10,172 C2
Planeta Rica 12,932 C3
Plato 18,589 C3
Popayán 77,669 B6
Pore 389 D5
Pradera 15,732 B6
Puente Nacional 4,317 D5
Puerto Asís 6,364 B7
Puerto Berrío 19,579 C4
Puerto Carreño 2,172 G4
Puerto Colombia 9,255 C2
Puerto Escondido 1,368 B3
Puerto Leguízamo 3,179 C8
Puerto López, Meta 4,948 D5
Puerto Murillo G4
Puerto Mutis B4
Puerto Nare D7
Puerto Paulina D7
Puerto Rico, Caquetá 4,853 C7
Puerto Rondón 1,010 E4
Puerto Salgar 6,396 C5
Puerto Tejada 18,315 B6

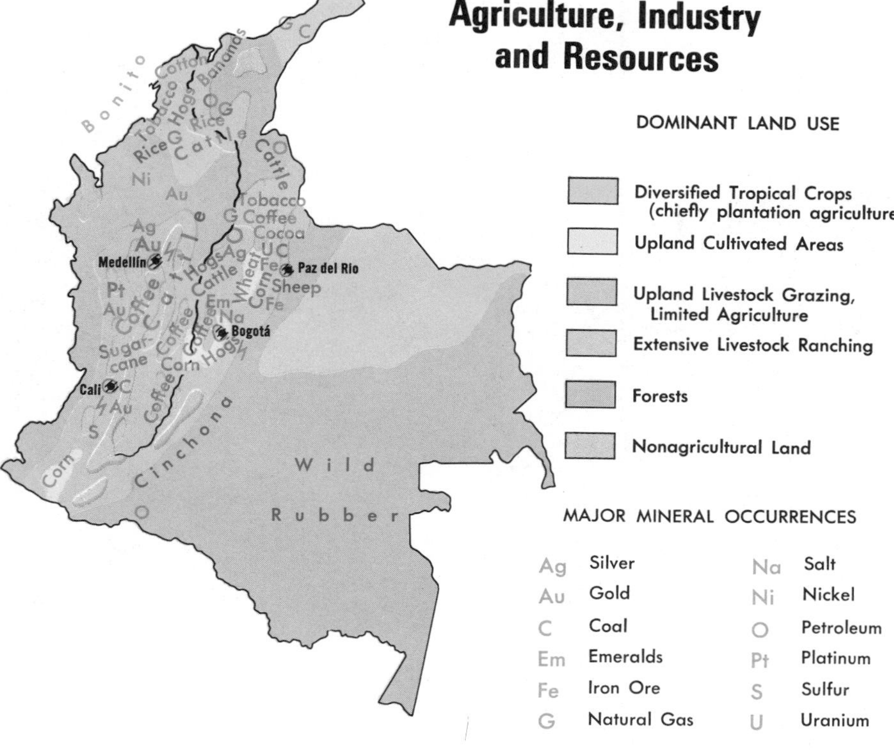

Agriculture, Industry and Resources
DOMINANT LAND USE
Diversified Tropical Crops (chiefly plantation agriculture)
Upland Cultivated Areas
Upland Livestock Grazing, Limited Agriculture
Extensive Livestock Ranching
Forests
Nonagricultural Land
MAJOR MINERAL OCCURRENCES
Ag Silver
Au Gold
C Coal
Em Emeralds
Fe Iron Ore
G Natural Gas
Na Salt
Ni Nickel
O Petroleum
Pt Platinum
S Sulfur
U Uranium
Water Power
Major Industrial Areas
Medellín
Paz del Río
Bogotá
Cali
Bonito
Tobacco
Coffee
Bananas
Cotton
Rice
Hogs
Cattle
Cocoa
Sheep
Wheat
Corn
Sugar-cane
Cinchona
Wild Rubber

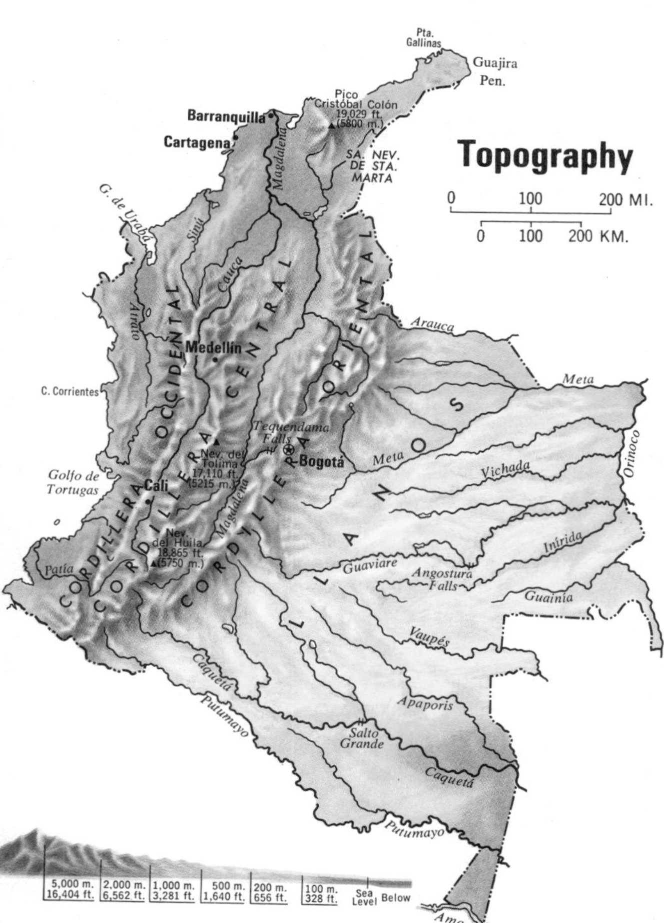

Topography
0 100 200 MI.
0 100 200 KM.
Pta. Gallinas
Guajira Pen.
Barranquilla
Cartagena
Pico Cristóbal Colón 19,029 ft. (5800 m.)
SA. NEV. DE STA. MARTA
G. de Urabá
Medellín
C. Corrientes
Arauca
Meta
Tequendama Falls
Nev. del Tolima 17,110 ft. (5215 m.)
Bogotá
Cali
Golfo de Tortugas
Nev. del Huila 18,865 ft. (5750 m.)
Patía
CORDILLERA OCCIDENTAL
CORDILLERA CENTRAL
CORDILLERA ORIENTAL
LLANOS
Vichada
Orinoco
Inírida
Guaviare
Angostura Falls
Guainía
Vaupés
Caquetá
Apaporis
Putumayo
Salto Grande
Amazon
Magdalena
Cauca
Atrato
Sinú
5,000 m. 16,404 ft.
2,000 m. 6,562 ft.
1,000 m. 3,281 ft.
500 m. 1,640 ft.
200 m. 656 ft.
100 m. 328 ft.
Sea Level
Below

Puerto Wilches 5,282 D4
Pupiales 2,723 B7
Purificación 8,164 C6
Quibdó 28,040 B5
Remedios 4,681 C4
Remolino 3,408 C2
Restrepo 2,704 D5
Ricaurte 1,205 A7
Río de Oro 2,985 D3
Riohacha 19,604 D2
Rionegro, Antioquia 22,654 C4
Rionegro, Santander 3,491 D4
Riosucio, Caldas 11,619 C5
Riosucio, Chocó 2,184 B4
Roberto Payán 445 A7
Robles 5,422 D2
Rovira 5,105 C5
Sabanalarga 26,542 C2
Sácama 69 D4
Sahagún 18,717 C3
Salamina 12,136 C5
Salazar 2,791 D4
Samaniego 4,790 B7
San Agustín 4,532 B7
San Andrés, Antioquia 2,003 C4
San Andrés, San Andrés y Providencia 14,428 A9
San Antero 7,129 C3
Sandoná 7,222 B7
San Francisco 1,654 B7
San Gil 21,679 D4
San Jacinto 13,459 C3
San José del Guaviare 4,138 D6
San Juan del César 9,468 D2
San Marcos 10,415 C3
San Martín 8,281 D6
San Onofre 7,899 C3
San Pablo 3,662 B7
San Roque 4,972 C4
Santa Bárbara 11,848 C5
Santa Marta 102,484 D2
Santander 13,625 B6
Santa Rosa de Cabal 28,368 C5
Santa Rosa de Osos 8,593 C4
San Vicente del Caguán 3,182 C6
Sardinata 3,726 D3
Segovia 10,000 C4
Sevilla 31,143 C5
Sibundoy 2,853 B7
Silvia 3,045 B6
Simití 3,062 C4
Sincé 11,909 C3
Sincelejo 68,797 C3
Sipí 153 B5
Sitionuevo 5,919 C2
Soatá 4,294 D4
Socorro 15,596 D4
Sogamoso 48,891 D5
Soledad 64,469 C2
Sonsón 15,990 C5
Sopetrán 5,223 C4
Tadó 3,102 B5
Támara 947 D5
Tame 4,811 E4
Tibaná 1,100 D5
Tierralta 7,950 C3
Timaná 4,262 C7
Timbío 4,755 B6
Timbiquí 1,048 B6
Toledo 2,942 D4
Tolú 9,118 C3
Trinidad 729 E5
Tuluá 86,736 B5
Tumaco 38,742 A7
Tunja 51,620 D5
Túquerres 12,058 B7
Turbaco 19,360 C2
Turbo 16,070 B3
Ubaté 7,716 D5
Uribia 2,193 D2
Urrao 8,577 B4
Valdivia 4,318 C4
Valledupar 87,425 D2
Vélez 8,241 D4
Venadillo 8,383 C5
Villanueva 9,836 D2
Villa Rosario 8,668 D4
Villavicencio 82,869 D5
Villeta 6,507 C5
Yarumal 21,333 C4
Yopal 5,851 D5
Yumbo 28,011 B6
Zapatoca 6,258 D4
Zaragoza 9,660 C4
Zarzal 21,370 B5
Zipaquirá 25,413 D5

OTHER FEATURES

Abibe, Serranía de, (mts.) B3
Aguarico, (riv.) B7
Aguja, La, (cape) C2
Albuquerque, (cays) A10
Alicia, (bank) B8
Alto Ritacuva, (mt.) D4
Amazon, (riv.) E9
Ancón de Sardinas, (bay) A7
Angostura, (falls) E6
Apaporis, (riv.) F8
Araracuara, Cerros de, (mts.) E7
Arauca, (riv.) E4
Ariari, (riv.) D6
Ariguaní, (riv.) D3
Ariporo, (riv.) E4
Atabapo, (riv.) G6
Atrato, (riv.) B4
Augusta, (cape) C2
Ayapel, Serranía de, (mts.) C4
Bajo Nuevo, (shoal) C8
Barú, (isl.) C2
Baudó, Serranía de, (mts.) B5
Baudó, (riv.) B5
Bita, (riv.) F5
Buenaventura, (bay) B6
Caguán, (riv.) C7
Cahuinari, (riv.) E8
Caquetá, (riv.) E8
Caraparaná, (riv.) D8
Casanare, (riv.) E4
Catatumbo, (riv.) D3
Cauca, (riv.) C4
Cazueleja, Cerro, (mt.) C6
Central, Cordillera, (range) C5
César, (riv.) D2
Chaira, Laguna, (lake) C7
Chamusa, Sierra, (mts.) C6
Charambirá, (pt.) B5
Chicamocha, (riv.) D4
Chiribiquete, Sierra de, (mts.) D7
Cinaruco, (riv.) F4
Chocó, (bay) B6
Cocuy, Sierra Nevada del, (mts.) D4
Coredó (Humboldt), (bay) B4
Corrientes, (cape) B5
Courtown (Este Sudeste), (cays) A10
Cravo Norte, (riv.) E4
Cravo Sur, (riv.) E5
Cristóbal Colón, Pico, (peak) D2
Cuemaní, (riv.) D7
Cupica, (gulf) B4
Cuquiari, (riv.) E7
Cusachón, (isl.) D1
Cusiana, (riv.) D5
Espada, (pt.) E1
Este Sudeste, (cays) A10
Fuerte, (isl.) B3
Gallinas, (pt.) E1
Gorgona, (isl.) A6
Grande, (isl.) B4
Grande, Salto, (falls) D8
Guainía, (riv.) F6
Guajira, (pen.) E1
Guapi, (bay) A6
Guaviare, (riv.) F6
Guayabero, (riv.) D6
Huila, Nevado del, (mt.) C6
Humboldt, (bay) B4
Igara-Paraná, (riv.) D8
Inírida, (riv.) F6
Isana, (riv.) F7
La Aguja, (cape) C2
La Macarena, Serranía de, (mts.) D6
La Vela, (cape) D1
Lebrija, (riv.) D4
Llanos, (plains) D5
Losada, (riv.) C6
Macarena, Serranía de La, (mts.) D6
Magdalena, (riv.) C3
Manacacías, (riv.) D6
Mapiripán, Laguna, (lake) E6
Marzo, (pt.) B4
Mesai, (riv.) D7
Meta, (riv.) E5
Metica, (riv.) D6
Mira, (riv.) A7
Miritiparaná, (riv.) E8
Morrosquillo, (gulf) C3
Muco, (riv.) E5
Naipo, (isl.) F6
Nechí, (riv.) C4
Negro, (riv.) G7
Occidental, Cordillera, (range) B5
Oriental, Cordillera, (range) D5
Orinoco, (riv.) G5
Orteguaza, (riv.) C7
Papunáua, (riv.) E6
Papurí, (riv.) F7
Patía, (riv.) B6
Pauto, (riv.) E5
Perijá, Serranía de, (mts.) D2
Providencia, (isl.) B9
Puracé, (vol.) B6
Putumayo, (riv.) E9
Quitasueño, (bank) A8
Roca que Vela, (cay) B8
Roncador, (cays) B9
Saldaña, (riv.) C6
Salto Grande, (falls) D8
San Andrés, (isl.) A10
San Bernardo, (isls.) C3
San Jorge, (riv.) C3
San Juan, (riv.) B5
San Miguel, (riv.) B7
Santa Catalina, (isl.) A9
Santa Marta, Sierra Nevada de, (range) D2
Serrana, (bank) B9
Serranilla, (bank) B8
Sinú, (riv.) B3
Sogamoso, (riv.) D4
Solano, (pt.) B4
Suárez, (riv.) D4
Sucio, (riv.) B4
Taraira, (riv.) F8
Tequendama, (falls) C5
Tibugá, (gulf) B5
Tolima, Nevada del, (mt.) C5
Tomo, (riv.) F5
Tortugas, (gulf) B6
Tota, Laguna de, (lake) D5
Truandó, (riv.) B4
Tumaco, Rada de, (bay) A6
Tunahí, Sierra, (mts.) E7
Upía, (riv.) D5
Urabá, (gulf) B3
Uva, Laguna, (lake) E6
Uva, (riv.) E6
Vaupés, (riv.) E7
Vela, La, (cape) D1
Vela, Roca que, (cay) B8
Vichada, (riv.) F5
Vigía, (cay) A10
Yarí, (riv.) D8
Zapatosa, Ciénaga de, (swamp) D3

*City and suburbs.

Peru and Ecuador
BIPOLAR OBLIQUE CONIC CONFORMAL PROJECTION
SCALE OF MILES
0 50 100 150 200
SCALE OF KILOMETERS
0 50 100 150 200
Capitals of Countries
Other Capitals
International Boundaries
Other Boundaries
Scale 1:8,000,000
PROVINCES OF ECUADOR INDICATED BY NUMBERS
1 Imbabura C-2
2 Cotopaxi C-3
3 Tungurahua C-3
4 Los Ríos C-3
5 Bolívar C-3
6 Chimborazo C-3
7 Cañar C-4
8 El Oro C-4
© Copyright HAMMOND INCORPORATED, Maplewood, N. J.
Galápagos Islands (Archipiélago de Colón)
(Ecuador)
Same scale as main map
PACIFIC OCEAN
I. Culpepper (Darwin)
I. Wenman (Wolf)
I. Pinta
I. Marchena
I. Genovesa
Equator
I. San Salvador (Santiago)
B. de Banks
I. Fernandina
I. Baltra
I. Sta. Cruz (Chaves)
Pinzón
Pto. Ayora
Isla Isabela
I. Sta. Fe
I. S. Cristobal
Baquerizo Moreno
El Progreso
Pto. Villamil
Floreana (Sta. María)
I. Sta. María (Floreana)
I. Española
COLOMBIA
ECUADOR
BRAZIL
BOLIVIA
CHILE
PACIFIC OCEAN
Equator
Gulf of Guayaquil
Quito
Guayaquil
Cuenca
Iquitos
LIMA
Callao
Arequipa
Cusco
Trujillo
Chiclayo
Piura
Huancayo
Puno
Lake Titicaca
La Paz
Amazon
Marañón
Ucayali
ESMERALDAS
PICHINCHA
NAPO
PASTAZA
MANABÍ
GUAYAS
AZUAY
LOJA
ZAMORA CHINCHIPE
MORONA SANTIAGO
CARCHI
TUMBES
PIURA
LAMBAYEQUE
CAJAMARCA
AMAZONAS
SAN MARTÍN
LORETO
LA LIBERTAD
ANCASH
HUANUCO
PASCO
JUNÍN
LIMA
HUANCAVELICA
ICA
AYACUCHO
APURÍMAC
CUSCO
MADRE DE DIOS
PUNO
AREQUIPA
MOQUEGUA
TACNA
Longitude 76° West of Greenwich

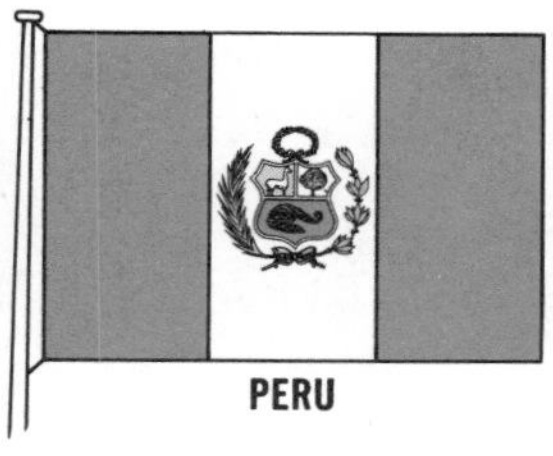

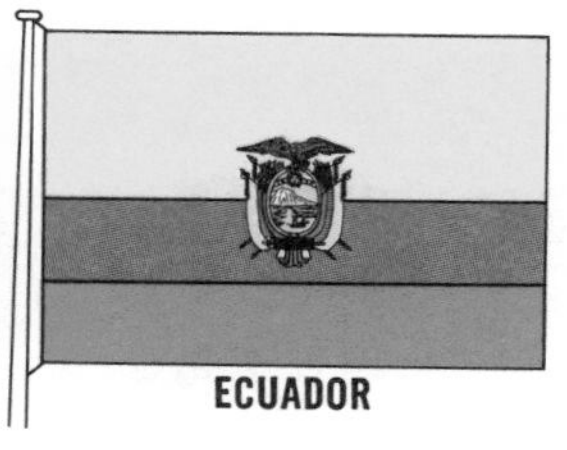

PERU

AREA 496,222 sq. mi. (1,285,215 sq. km.)
POPULATION 17,031,221
CAPITAL Lima
LARGEST CITY Lima
HIGHEST POINT Huascarán 22,205 ft. (6,768 m.)
MONETARY UNIT sol
MAJOR LANGUAGES Spanish, Quechua, Aymara
MAJOR RELIGION Roman Catholicism

ECUADOR

AREA 109,483 sq. mi. (283,561 sq. km.)
POPULATION 8,644,000
CAPITAL Quito
LARGEST CITY Guayaquil
HIGHEST POINT Chimborazo 20,561 ft. (6,267 m.)
MONETARY UNIT sucre
MAJOR LANGUAGES Spanish, Quechua
MAJOR RELIGION Roman Catholicism

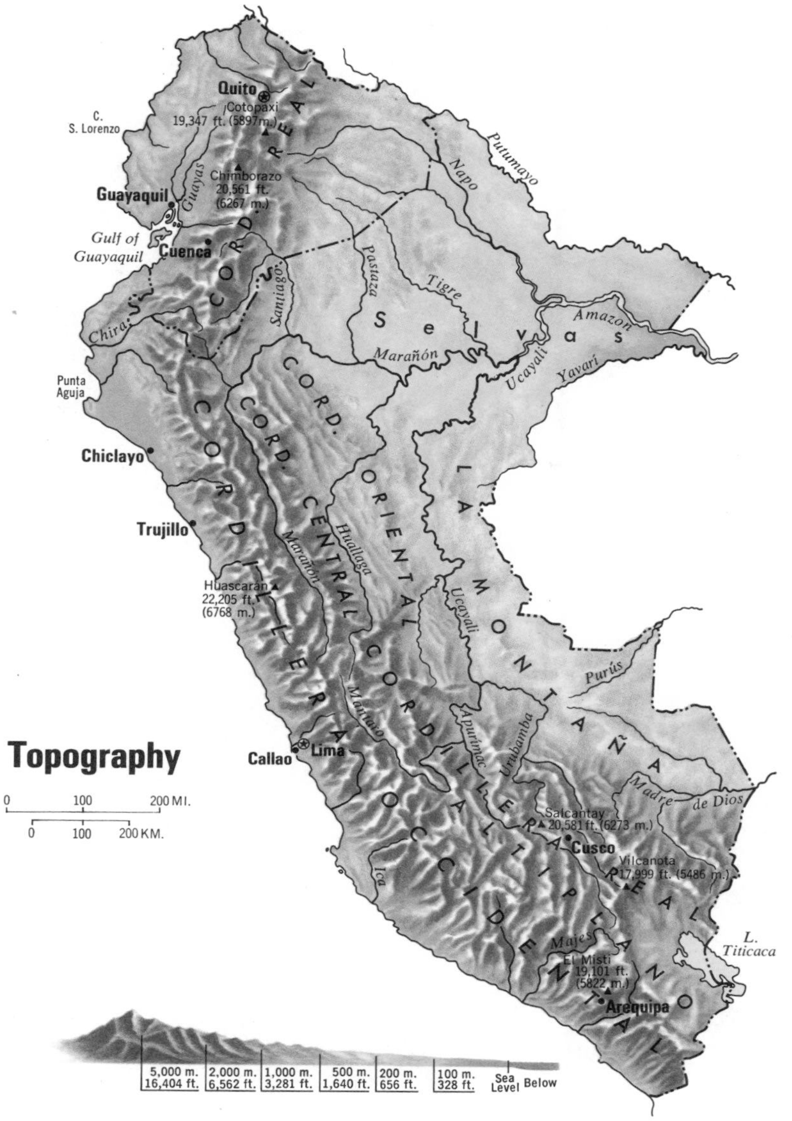

PERU

DEPARTMENTS

Amazonas 256,460 ... C5
Ancash 815,646 ... D7
Apurímac 321,936 ... F10
Arequipa 702,308 ... F10
Ayacucho 500,732 ... E9
Cajamarca 1,044,689 ... C6
Callao (prov.) 446,730 ... D9
Cusco 829,294 ... F9
Huancavelica 346,460 ... E9
Huánuco 481,924 ... D7
Ica 431,442 ... E10
Junín 848,993 ... E8
La Libertad 960,537 ... C6
Lambayeque 683,425 ... B6
Lima 4,738,266 ... D8
Loreto 446,316 ... E5
Madre de Dios 36,555 ... G8
Moquegua 99,287 ... G11
Pasco 221,219 ... E8
Piura 1,168,442 ... B5
Puno 893,586 ... G10
San Martín 319,670 ... D6
Tacna 133,240 ... G11
Tumbes 103,979 ... B4
Ucayali 200,085 ... E6

CITIES and TOWNS

Abancay 19,807 ... F9
Acarí 4,907 ... E10
Acobamba 2,156 ... E9
Acolla 5,717 ... E8
Acomayo, Cusco 1,419 ... G9
Acomayo, Huánuco 2,883 ... E7
Acora 1,910 ... H11
Acuracay 1,282 ... F5
Aija 1,843 ... D7
Alca 755 ... F10
Ambo 3,060 ... D8
Ananea 668 ... H10
Ancón 8,610 ... D8
Andahuaylas 7,654 ... F9
Andamarca 470 ... E8
Anta 3,703 ... F9
Antabamba 2,223 ... F10
Aplao 1,941 ... F11
Aquia 970 ... D8
Arequipa 107,858 ... G11
Arequipa* 447,431 ... G11
Ascope 12,070 ... C6
Astillero ... H9
Atalaya 2,229 ... E8
Atico 2,316 ... F11
Ayabaca 4,543 ... C5
Ayacucho 68,535 ... F9
Ayaviri 11,067 ... G10
Azángaro 7,658 ... H10
Bagua 9,735 ... C5
Balsapuerto 164 ... D5
Bambamarca 6,867 ... C6
Barranca, Lima 31,312 ... C8
Barranca, Loreto 1,351 ... D5
Bartra Antiguo ... E4
Bartra Nuevo ... E4
Bayóvar ... B5
Bellavista 4,906 ... C5
Bolívar 1,106 ... D6
Bolognesi ... F6
Bolognesi 661 ... F8
Borja 215 ... D5
Bretaña 1,035 ... E5
Buldibuyo 582 ... D7
Cabana 1,804 ... C7
Cabo Blanco ... B5
Cahuapanas 304 ... D5
Cailloma 1,187 ... G10
Cajabamba 7,282 ... C6
Cajacay 668 ... D8
Cajamarca 60,280 ... C6
Cajatambo 1,721 ... D8
Calca 6,112 ... G9
Callalli 819 ... G10
Callao 260,581 ... D9
Callao* 441,374 ... D9
Camaná 11,386 ... F11
Candarave 1,207 ... G11
Cangallo 1,584 ... E9
Canta 3,431 ... D8
Capachica 307 ... H10
Caraz 6,376 ... D7
Caravelí 1,827 ... F10
Carhuás 3,147 ... D7
Carumás 1,031 ... G11
Cascas 2,638 ... C6
Casma 12,725 ... C7
Castrovirreyna 1,749 ... E9
Catacaos 30,927 ... B5
Celendín 8,538 ... D6
Cerro Azul 2,314 ... D9
Cerro de Pasco 71,558 ... D8
Chachapoyas 11,919 ... D6
Chala 1,646 ... E10
Chalhuanca 3,071 ... F10
Chancay 18,993 ... D8
Chao ... C7
Chepén 29,919 ... C6
Chicama 11,160 ... C6
Chiclayo 280,244 ... C6
Chilca (Pucusana) 3,329 ... D9
Chilete 2,537 ... C6
Chimbote 216,406 ... C7
Chincha Alta 237,475 ... D9
Chiquián 3,521 ... D8
Chirinos 1,061 ... C5
Chivay 3,296 ... G10
Chosica ... D8
Chota 8,299 ... C6
Chulucanas 34,977 ... B5
Chupaca 5,422 ... E9
Chuquibamba 2,630 ... F10
Chuquibambilla 2,147 ... F9
Churín 1,801 ... D8
Cocachacra 5,985 ... G11
Cocama ... G8
Cojata 888 ... H10
Colasay 721 ... C5
Colcamar 1,216 ... D6
Conaica 1,154 ... E9
Concepción 7,129 ... E8
Concordia 1,372 ... E5
Contamana 5,718 ... E6
Contumazá 2,491 ... C6
Coracora 4,598 ... F10
Córdova 453 ... E10
Corongo 1,762 ... D7
Cotahuasi 1,301 ... F10
Culebras ... C7
Cumaría ... F7
Cusco (Cuzco) 85,044 ... F9
Cusco* 181,604 ... F9
Cutervo 6,890 ... C6
Cuyocuyo 1,101 ... H10
Desaguadero 2,682 ... H11
Deustua 544 ... G10
Dos de Mayo 574 ... E6
Echarate 1,071 ... F9
El Portugués ... C7
Esperanza 375 ... G7
Espinar 6,381 ... G10
Ferreñafe 22,200 ... C6
Francisco de Orellana 445 ... F4
Guadalupe 7,613 ... E9
Güeppi ... E3
Huacho 43,402 ... D8
Huacrachuco 1,210 ... D7
Hualgayoc 1,691 ... C6
Hualla 4,042 ... F9
Huallanca, Ancash 930 ... D7
Huallanca, Huánuco 4,806 ... D7
Huamachuco 8,273 ... D6
Huancabamba 4,393 ... C5
Huancané 5,227 ... H10
Huancapi 2,539 ... E9
Huancavelica 20,889 ... E9
Huancayo 165,132 ... E9
Huanchaco 6,005 ... C7
Huanta 11,213 ... E9
Huánuco 52,628 ... E7
Huaral 34,235 ... D8
Huaráz 45,116 ... D7
Huari 2,344 ... D7
Huariaca 2,671 ... E8
Huarmey 11,094 ... C8
Huarochirí 1,828 ... D9
Huarocondo 2,498 ... F9
Huaura 9,338 ... D8
Huaylas 1,344 ... C7
Iberia 2,307 ... F5
Ica 111,087 ... E10
Ichuña 277 ... G11
Ilave 9,891 ... H11
Ilo 31,549 ... G11
Imperial 20,894 ... D9
Iñapari 188 ... H8
Intutu 746 ... E4
Iparia 278 ... E7
Iquitos 173,629 ... F4
Jaén 24,356 ... C5
Jauja 14,630 ... E8
Jayanca 6,401 ... B6
Jeberos 1,493 ... D5
Juanjuí 9,324 ... D6
Juli 5,575 ... H11
Juliaca 77,976 ... G10
Jumbilla 1,035 ... C5
Junín 8,988 ... E8
Lagunas 4,601 ... E5
La Huaca 5,161 ... B5
La Jalca 1,769 ... D6
La Joya 5,000 ... G11
Lamas 8,937 ... D6
Lambayeque 23,746 ... B6
Lampa 4,319 ... G10
Lamud 2,405 ... C6
Lanlacuni Bajo 405 ... G9
La Oroya 33,305 ... D8
Las Piedras ... H9
Las Yaras 759 ... G11
La Unión 2,828 ... D7
Leimebamba 1,957 ... D6
Lima (cap.) 375,957 ... D8
Lima* 3,968,972 ... D8
Limbani 728 ... H10
Lircay 5,213 ... E9
Llata 2,922 ... D7
Lobitos 2,975 ... B5
Locumba 369 ... G11
Lomas 287 ... E10
Lucerna ... H9
Lurín 14,405 ... D9
Machupicchu 544 ... F9
Macusani 3,389 ... G10
Madre de Dios 660 ... G9
Máncora 5,358 ... B5
Manú 234 ... G9
Marcapata 369 ... G9
Marcona 25,962 ... E10
Margos 1,622 ... D8
Masisea 1,586 ... E7
Matarani ... F11
Matucana 4,196 ... D8
Mavila ... H8
Mazán 281 ... F4
Mazocruz 1,580 ... H11
Mendoza 1,902 ... D6
Mishagua ... F8
Moho 2,560 ... H10
Mollendo 21,206 ... F11
Monsefú 17,186 ... C6
Moquegua 21,488 ... G11
Morales 4,370 ... D6
Morococha 11,234 ... D8
Morropón 7,611 ... C5
Motupe 3,411 ... C6
Moyobamba 14,319 ... D6
Nauta 4,083 ... F5
Nazca 22,756 ... E10
Negritos 12,476 ... B5
Nuñoa 3,613 ... G10
Ocoña 1,062 ... F11
Ocros 1,037 ... D8
Ollachea 1,308 ... G9
Ollantaytambo 1,500 ... F9
Olmos 7,946 ... C5
Omaguas ... F5
Omas 249 ... D9
Omate 1,131 ... G11
Orcotuna 3,359 ... E8
Orellana 2,886 ... E6
Otuzco 5,765 ... C6
Oxapampa 5,233 ... E8
Oyón 6,279 ... D8
Pacasmayo 17,588 ... C6
Pachiza 889 ... D6
Paiján 12,699 ... C6
Paita 18,749 ... B5
Palpa 3,393 ... E10
Pampachiri 428 ... F10
Pampacolca 2,010 ... F10
Pampas 3,850 ... E9
Panao 1,363 ... E7
Pantoja 457 ... E3
Parinari 375 ... E5
Paruro 1,727 ... F9
Pataz 759 ... D6
Paucarbamba 534 ... E9
Paucartambo, Cusco 1,620 ... G9
Paucartambo, Pasco 3,497 ... E8
Pevas 1,325 ... G4
Picota 2,288 ... D6
Pimentel 9,129 ... B6
Pinquén ... G9
Pisac 1,566 ... G9
Pisco 53,414 ... D9
Piura 186,354 ... B5
Pizacoma 400 ... H11
Pomabamba 2,489 ... D7
Porvenir ... E5
Pozuzo 326 ... E8
Puca Barranca ... E4
Pucallpa 91,953 ... E7
Pucará 2,268 ... G10
Pucaurco 628 ... G4
Pucusana 3,329 ... D9
Puerto Alianza ... D5
Puerto América 240 ... D5
Puerto Arturo ... F3
Puerto Bermúdez 1,133 ... E8
Puerto Caballas ... E10
Puerto Chicama 3,136 ... C6
Puerto Eten 2,575 ... B6
Puerto Inca 1,286 ... E7
Puerto José Pardo ... D4
Puerto Leguía, Loreto ... D4
Puerto Leguía, Puno ... G9
Puerto Maldonado 12,609 ... H9
Puerto Morín ... C7
Puerto Ocopa 1,088 ... E8
Puerto Pardo ... F7
Puerto Pizarro ... B4
Puerto Portillo 86 ... F7
Puerto Prado 328 ... E8
Puerto Samanco 1,435 ... C7
Puerto Tahuantinsuyo ... G9
Puerto Victoria ... E7
Puno 66,477 ... G10
Punta de Bombón 4,647 ... F11
Punta Moreno ... C6
Puquina 1,026 ... G11
Puquio 8,099 ... F10
Putina 5,414 ... H10
Querecotillo 10,637 ... B5
Quicacha 255 ... F10
Quilca 235 ... F11
Quillabamba 16,837 ... F9
Quince Mil ... G9
Ramón Castilla 1,811 ... G5
Recuay 2,764 ... D7
Requena 8,270 ... F5
Reventazón ... B6
Rioja 9,876 ... D6
Salaverry 5,539 ... C7
Saña 40,144 ... C6
Sandia 1,682 ... H10
San José 4,070 ... B6
San José de Sisa 3,782 ... D6
San Juan ... E10
San Lorenzo 124 ... H8
San Martín ... E3
San Miguel, Ayacucho 1,440 ... F9
San Miguel, Cajamarca 1,798 ... C6
San Pedro de Lloc 11,463 ... C6
San Ramón 7,145 ... E8
Santa 20,490 ... C7
Santa Clotilde 1,068 ... E4
Santa Cruz, Cajamarca 2,739 ... C6
Santa Cruz, Loreto 449 ... E5
Santa Elena 368 ... F5
Santa María de Nanay 294 ... F4
Santiago 5,092 ... E10
Santiago de Cao 22,119 ... C6
Santiago de Chocorvos 525 ... E9
Santiago de Chuco 5,189 ... C7
Santo Tomás, Amazonas 1,093 ... C6
Santo Tomás, Cusco 2,755 ... G10
Santo Tomás de Andoas 272 ... D4
San Vicente de Cañete 15,277 ... D9
Saposoa 4,541 ... D6
Saquena 2,755 ... F5
Satipo 9,208 ... E8
Sauce 2,263 ... D6
Sayán 5,129 ... D8
Sechura 11,724 ... B5
Sicuani 21,176 ... G10
Sihuas 2,178 ... D7
Sullana 80,947 ... B5
Sumbay ... G10
Sumbilca 1,155 ... D8
Supe 10,061 ... D8
Tacna 92,640 ... G11
Tahuamanu 2,619 ... H8
Talara 55,122 ... B5
Tambo de Mora 2,790 ... D9
Tambo Grande 10,087 ... B5
Tamshiyacu 2,040 ... F5
Tarapoto 33,429 ... D6
Tarata 2,624 ... H11
Tarma 34,369 ... E8
Tarqui ... E3
Tayabamba 1,649 ... D7
Ticaco 781 ... H11
Tingo María 25,030 ... D7
Tiruntán 723 ... E6
Tocache 5,940 ... D7
Tonegrama ... D4
Topará ... D9
Toquepala ... G11
Torata 6,320 ... G11
Tournavista ... E7
Trujillo 354,557 ... C7
Tumbes 48,187 ... B4
Ubinas 422 ... G11
Uchiza 2,471 ... D7
Unini ... F8
Urcos 4,155 ... G9
Urubamba 4,686 ... F9
Vinchos 735 ... E9
Virú 6,587 ... C7
Vitor 416 ... G11
Yambrasbamba 277 ... D5
Yanahuanca 5,109 ... D8
Yanaoca 1,152 ... G10
Yauca 1,805 ... E10
Yauli 1,020 ... D8
Yauyos 1,296 ... E9
Yunguyo 7,253 ... H11
Yurimaguas 22,858 ... E5
Zarumilla 9,713 ... B4
Zorritos 4,497 ... B4

OTHER FEATURES

Acarí (riv.) ... E10
Aguaytía (riv.) ... E7
Aguja (pt.) ... B5
Amazon (riv.) ... F4
Andes, Cordillera de los (mts.) ... F10
Apurímac (riv.) ... F9
Azángaro (riv.) ... G10
Azul, Cordillera (mts.) ... E7
Blanca, Cordillera (mts.) ... D7
Blanco (cape) ... B5
Blanco (riv.) ... F6
Boquerón, El (pass) ... E7
Cañete (riv.) ... D9
Casma (riv.) ... C7
Chimbote (bay) ... C7
Chincha (isls.) ... D9
Coles (pt.) ... G11
Cóndor, Cordillera del (range) ... C5
Coropuna, Nudo (mt.) ... F10
Corrientes (riv.) ... E4
El Boquerón (pass) ... E7
El Misti (mt.) ... G11
Ene (riv.) ... E8
Ferrol (pen.) ... C7
Grande (riv.) ... E10
Guañape (isls.) ... C7
Heath (riv.) ... H9
Huallaga (riv.) ... D5
Huasaga (riv.) ... D4
Huascarán (mt.) ... D7
Huayabamba (riv.) ... D6
Ica (riv.) ... E10
Inambari (riv.) ... H9
Independencia (bay) ... D10
Independencia (isl.) ... D10
Junín (lake) ... E8
Juruá (riv.) ... F7
Lachay (pt.) ... D8
Lobos de Afuera (isls.) ... B6
Lobos de Tierra (isl.) ... B6
Locumba (riv.) ... G11
Madre de Dios (riv.) ... G9
Majes (riv.) ... F11
Mantaro (riv.) ... E8
Manú (riv.) ... G8
Marañón (riv.) ... E5
Mayo (riv.) ... D6
Misti, El (mt.) ... G11
Montaña, La (reg.) ... F8
Morona (riv.) ... D5
Nanay (riv.) ... E4
Napo (riv.) ... F4
Negra, Cordillera (mts.) ... D7
Negra (pt.) ... B6
Ñermete (pt.) ... B5
Occidental, Cordillera (range) ... F10
Ocoña (riv.) ... F11
Oriental, Cordillera (range) ... H10
Pachitea (riv.) ... E7
Paita (bay) ... B5
Pampas (riv.) ... E9
Paracas (pen.) ... D9
Parinacochas (lake) ... F10
Pariñas (pt.) ... B5
Pastaza (riv.) ... D5
Pativilca (riv.) ... D8
Perené (riv.) ... E8
Pichis (riv.) ... E8
Piedras, Las (riv.) ... G8
Pisco (bay) ... D9
Pisco (riv.) ... D9
Piura (riv.) ... B5
Puinagua, Canal de (riv.) ... E5
Purús (riv.) ... G8
Putumayo (riv.) ... G4
Rímac (riv.) ... D9
Salcantay (mt.) ... F9
Sama (riv.) ... G11
San Gallán (isl.) ... D9
San Lorenzo (isl.) ... D9
San Nicolás (bay) ... E10
Santa (riv.) ... C7
Santiago (riv.) ... D4
Sechura (bay) ... B5
Tahuamanu (riv.) ... H8
Tambo (riv.) ... G11
Tambopata (riv.) ... H9
Tapiche (riv.) ... E6
Tigre (riv.) ... E4
Titicaca (lake) ... H10
Tumbes (riv.) ... B4
Ucayali (riv.) ... F5

(continued on following page)

Agriculture, Industry and Resources

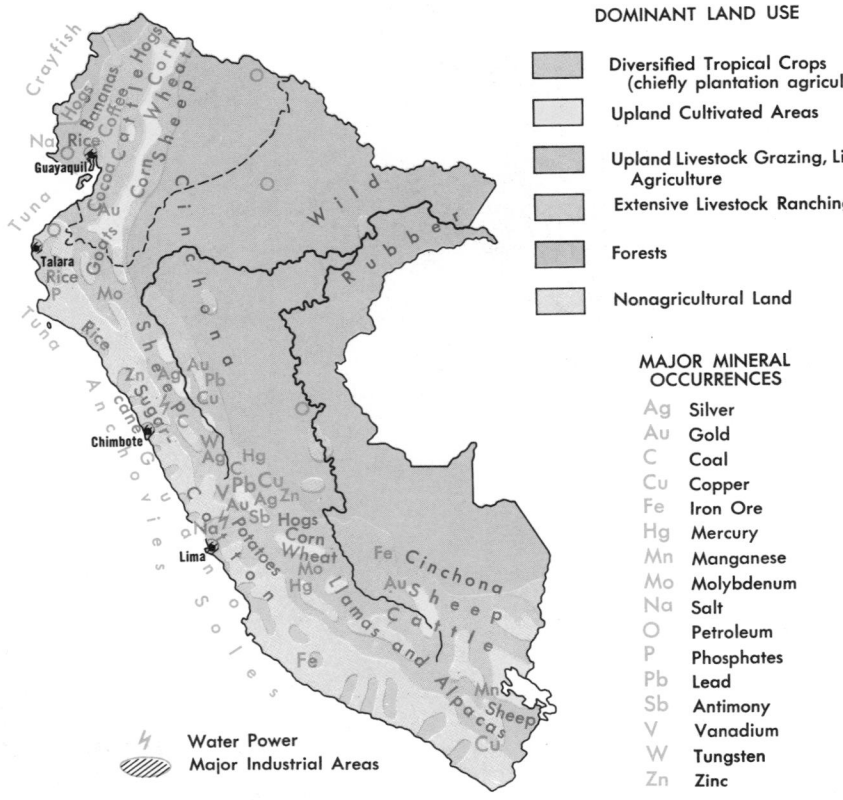

DOMINANT LAND USE

- Diversified Tropical Crops (chiefly plantation agriculture)
- Upland Cultivated Areas
- Upland Livestock Grazing, Limited Agriculture
- Extensive Livestock Ranching
- Forests
- Nonagricultural Land

MAJOR MINERAL OCCURRENCES

Ag	Silver
Au	Gold
C	Coal
Cu	Copper
Fe	Iron Ore
Hg	Mercury
Mn	Manganese
Mo	Molybdenum
Na	Salt
O	Petroleum
P	Phosphates
Pb	Lead
Sb	Antimony
V	Vanadium
W	Tungsten
Zn	Zinc

⚡ Water Power
▨ Major Industrial Areas

Agriculture, Industry and Resources

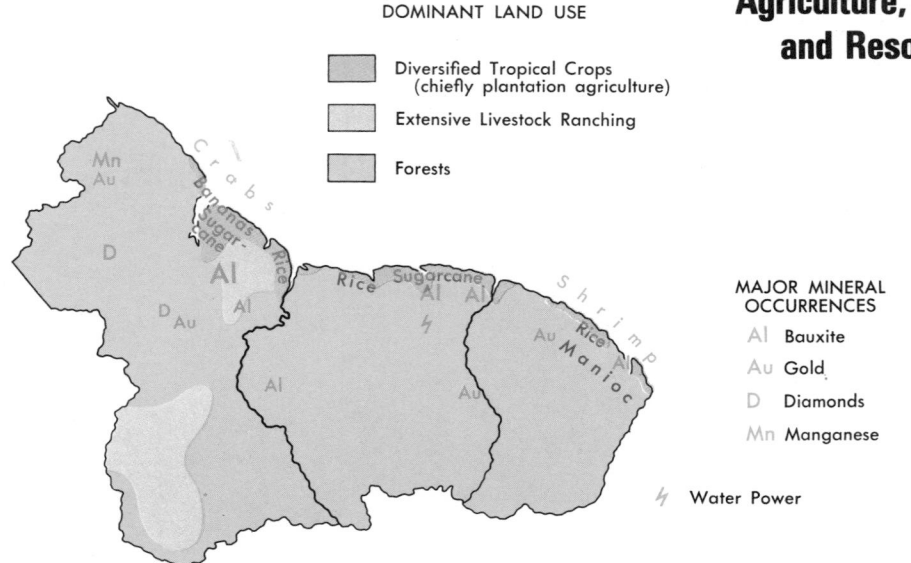

DOMINANT LAND USE

- Diversified Tropical Crops (chiefly plantation agriculture)
- Extensive Livestock Ranching
- Forests

MAJOR MINERAL OCCURRENCES

Al	Bauxite
Au	Gold
D	Diamonds
Mn	Manganese

⚡ Water Power

★ City and suburbs
○ Population of district.

GUYANA

AREA 83,000 sq. mi. (214,970 sq. km.)
POPULATION 793,000
CAPITAL Georgetown
LARGEST CITY Georgetown
HIGHEST POINT Mt. Roraima 9,094 ft. (2,772 m.)
MONETARY UNIT Guyana dollar
MAJOR LANGUAGES English, Hindi
MAJOR RELIGIONS Christianity, Hinduism, Islam

SURINAME

AREA 55,144 sq. mi. (142,823 sq. km.)
POPULATION 354,860
CAPITAL Paramaribo
LARGEST CITY Paramaribo
HIGHEST POINT Julianatop 4,200 ft. (1,280 m.)
MONETARY UNIT Suriname guilder
MAJOR LANGUAGES Dutch, Hindi, Indonesian
MAJOR RELIGIONS Christianity, Islam, Hinduism

FRENCH GUIANA

AREA 35,135 sq. mi. (91,000 sq. km.)
POPULATION 73,022
CAPITAL Cayenne
LARGEST CITY Cayenne
HIGHEST POINT 2,723 ft. (830 m.)
MONETARY UNIT French franc
MAJOR LANGUAGE French
MAJOR RELIGIONS Roman Catholicism, Protestantism

Courantyne (riv.)	C3
Cuyuni (riv.)	B2
Demerara (riv.)	B3
Enwarak (mt.)	B3
Essequibo (riv.)	B3
Great (fall)	B3
Ireng (riv.)	B3
Kaieteur (fall)	B3
Kamaria (falls)	B3
Kuyuwini (riv.)	B4
Kwitaro (riv.)	B4
Leguan (isl.)	B2
Marudi (mts.)	B5
Mazaruni (riv.)	A2
Moruka (riv.)	B2
New (riv.)	C4
Pakaraima (mts.)	A3
Playa (riv.)	B1
Pomeroon (riv.)	B2
Potaro (riv.)	B3
Puruni (riv.)	B2
Roraima (mt.)	B3
Rupununi (riv.)	B4
Sororieng (mt.)	B3
Surwakwima (fall)	A2
Takutu (riv.)	B4
Venamo (mt.)	A3
Waini (riv.)	B2
Wenamu (riv.)	A2

Albina 1,000	D3
Asidonhoppo	D4
Berg en Dal	D3
Bitagron	C3
Brokopondo	D3
Burnside	C2
Calcutta 1,100	C3
Cottica	D4
Domburg 1,200	D3
Groningen 600	D2
Huwelijkszorg	D2
Majoli	D4
Mariënburg 3,500	D2
Moengo 2,100	D3
Nieuw-Amsterdam 1,400	D2
Nieuw-Nickerie 7,400	C2
Paramaribo (cap.) ⊙ 167,905	D2
Paranam	D3
Totness 1,300	C3
Uitkijk	D3
Wageningen 800	C3
Zanderij	D3

OTHER FEATURES

SURINAME

DISTRICTS

Brokopondo 17,763	D4
Commewijne 18,740	D3
Coronie 3,251	C3
Marowijne 25,911	D4
Nickerie 35,178	C3
Para 16,635	D3
Paramaribo 102,297	D2
Saramacca 13,554	D3
Suriname 151,585	D3

CITIES and TOWNS

Ajoewa	C4
Alalapadu	C4

Bakhuys (mts.)	C3
Coeroeni (riv.)	C4
Commewijne (riv.)	D3
Coppename (riv.)	C3
Corantijn (riv.)	C3
Cottica (riv.)	D3
Eilerts de Haan (mts.)	C4
Frederik Willem IV (falls)	C4
Julianatop (mt.)	C4
Kayser (mts.)	C4
Lely (mts.)	D3
Litani (riv.)	D4
Marowijne (riv.)	D3
Nickerie (riv.)	C3
Orange (mts.) j.	D4
Saramacca (riv.)	D3
Sipaliwini (riv.)	C4
Suriname (riv.)	D3
Tapanahoni (riv.)	D4
Toekomstig (res.)	C3
Van Blommestein (lake)	D3
Wilhelmina (mts.)	C3

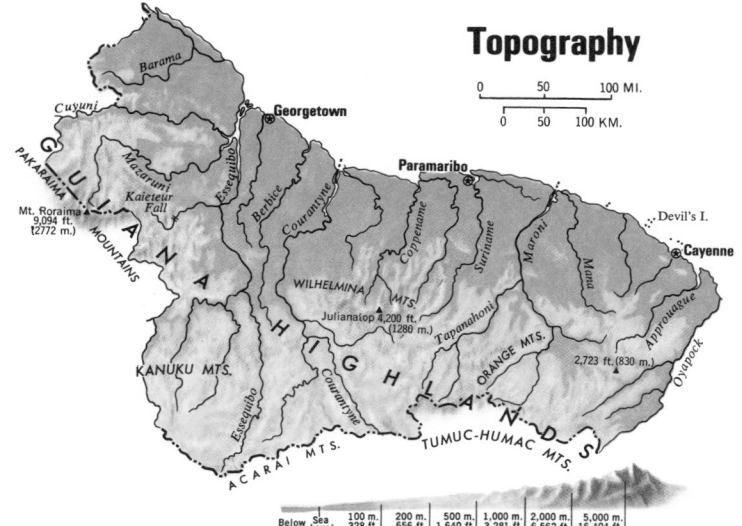

Topography

0   50   100 MI.
0   50   100 KM.

Below Sea Level	100 m. 328 ft.	200 m. 656 ft.	500 m. 1,640 ft.	1,000 m. 3,281 ft.	2,000 m. 6,562 ft.	5,000 m. 16,404 ft.

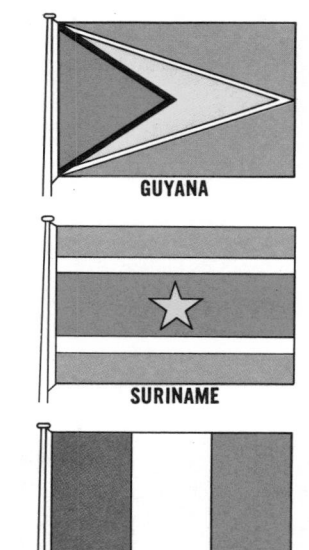

GUYANA

SURINAME

FRENCH GUIANA

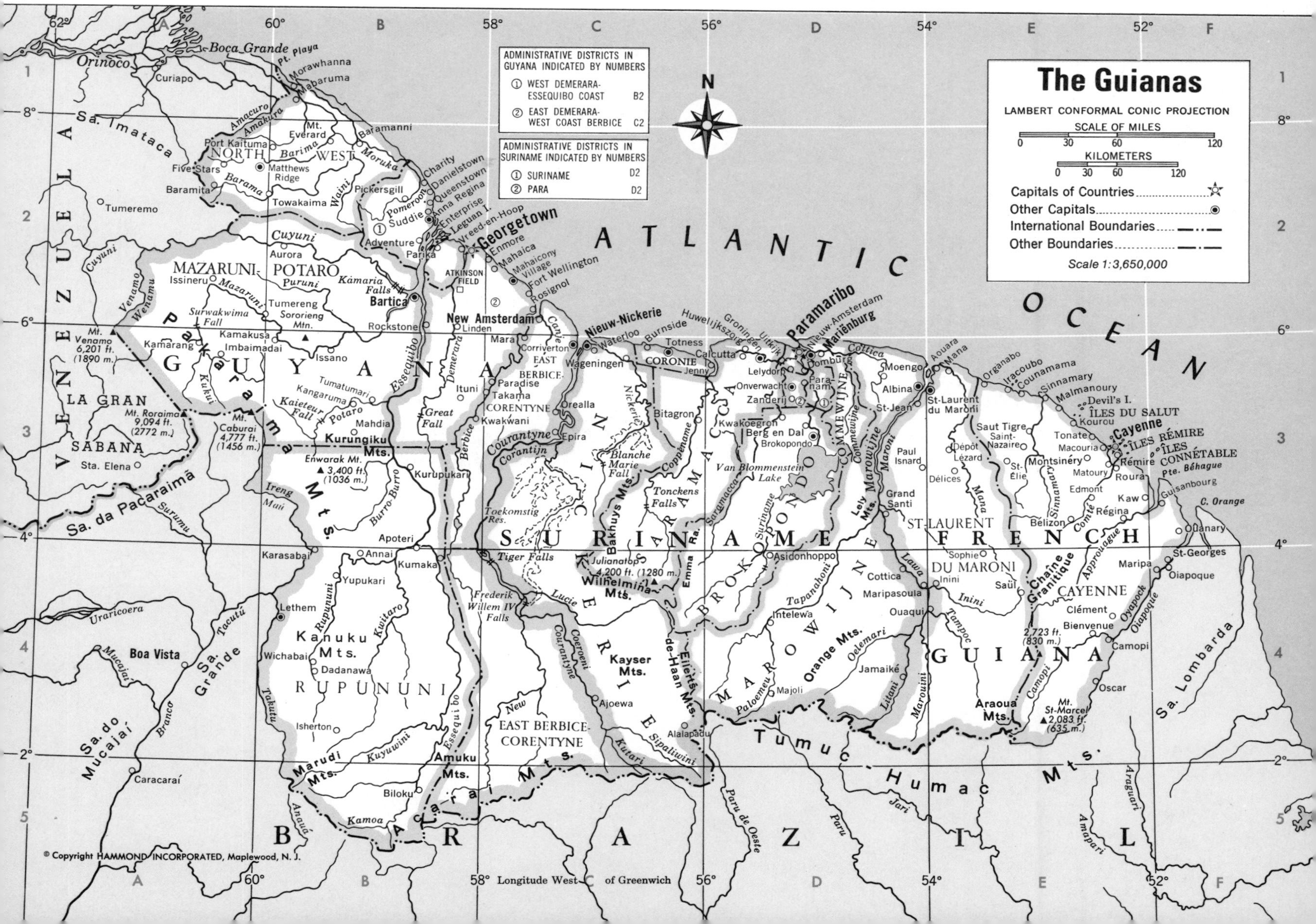

The Guianas

LAMBERT CONFORMAL CONIC PROJECTION

SCALE OF MILES
0   30   60   120

KILOMETERS
0   30   60   120

Capitals of Countries .... ☆
Other Capitals .... ⊙
International Boundaries .... — · —
Other Boundaries .... — ·· —

Scale 1:3,650,000

ADMINISTRATIVE DISTRICTS IN GUYANA INDICATED BY NUMBERS
① WEST DEMERARA-ESSEQUIBO COAST B2
② EAST DEMERARA-WEST COAST BERBICE C2

ADMINISTRATIVE DISTRICTS IN SURINAME INDICATED BY NUMBERS
① SURINAME D2
② PARA D2

© Copyright HAMMOND INCORPORATED, Maplewood, N. J.

Brazil
BIPOLAR OBLIQUE CONIC CONFORMAL PROJECTION
SCALE OF MILES
0 50 100 200 300
KILOMETERS
0 50 100 200 300
Capitals of Countries
State Capitals
International Boundaries
State Boundaries
Scale 1:14,700,000
© Copyright HAMMOND INCORPORATED, Maplewood, N. J.
GUYANA
SURINAME
FR. GUIANA
AMAPÁ
PARÁ
AMAZONAS
RORAIMA
RONDÔNIA
MATO GROSSO
MATO GROSSO DO SUL
MARANHÃO
PIAUÍ
CEARÁ
RIO GRANDE DO NORTE
PARAÍBA
PERNAMBUCO
ALAGOAS
SERGIPE
BAHIA
GOIÁS
FEDERAL DISTRICT
Brasília
MINAS GERAIS
ESPÍRITO SANTO
RIO DE JANEIRO
SÃO PAULO
PARANÁ
SANTA CATARINA
RIO GRANDE DO SUL
BOLIVIA
PARAGUAY
ARGENTINA
URUGUAY
ATLANTIC OCEAN
Tropic of Capricorn
BRAZIL WESTERN PART
COLOMBIA
VENEZUELA
PERU
ACRE
Longitude 48° West of Greenwich 44°

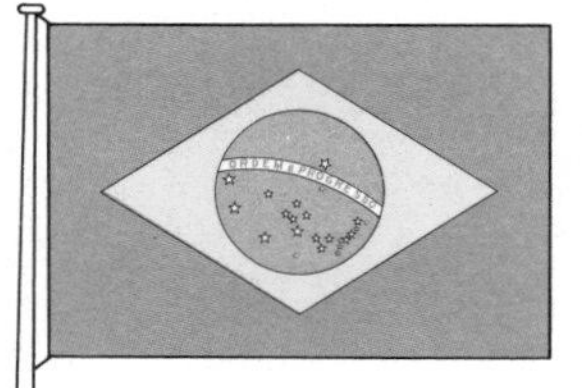

AREA 3,284,426 sq. mi. (8,506,663 sq. km.)
POPULATION 119,098,992
CAPITAL Brasília
LARGEST CITY São Paulo (greater)
HIGHEST POINT Pico da Neblina 9,889 ft. (3,014 m.)
MONETARY UNIT cruzeiro
MAJOR LANGUAGE Portuguese
MAJOR RELIGION Roman Catholicism

Topography

0 200 400 MI.
0 200 400 KM.

5,000 m. 16,404 ft. | 2,000 m. 6,562 ft. | 1,000 m. 3,281 ft. | 500 m. 1,640 ft. | 200 m. 656 ft. | 100 m. 328 ft. | Sea Level | Below

STATES and TERRITORIES

Acre 301,605 ... G10
Alagoas 1,987,581 ... G5
Amapá (terr.) 175,634 ... D2
Amazonas 1,432,066 ... G9
Bahia 9,474,263 ... F6
Ceará 5,294,876 ... G4
Espírito Santo 2,023,821 ... F7
Federal District 1,177,393 ... E6
Goiás 3,865,482 ... D6
Maranhão 4,002,599 ... E4
Mato Grosso 1,141,661 ... B6
Mato Grosso do Sul 1,370,333 ... C7
Minas Gerais 13,390,805 ... E7
Pará 3,411,868 ... C4
Paraíba 2,772,600 ... G4
Paraná 7,630,466 ... D9
Pernambuco 6,147,102 ... G5
Piauí 2,140,066 ... F4
Rio de Janeiro 11,297,327 ... F8
Rio Grande do Norte 1,899,720 ... G4
Rio Grande do Sul 7,777,212 ... C10
Rondônia (terr.) 492,810 ... H10
Roraima (terr.) 79,153 ... H8
Santa Catarina 3,628,751 ... D9
São Paulo 25,040,698 ... D8
Sergipe 1,141,834 ... G5

CITIES and TOWNS

Abaeté 12,861 ... E7
Abaetetuba 33,031 ... D3
Acaraú 7,144 ... F3
Acopiara 10,747 ... G4
Açu 20,544 ... G4
Agudos 18,790 ... *B3
Alagoa Grande 14,204 ... H4
Alagoinhas 76,377 ... G6
Alcobaça 3,430 ... G7
Alegre 9,441 ... *F2
Alegrete 54,786 ... B10
Além Paraíba 23,028 ... *E2
Alenquer 16,477 ... C3
Alfenas 31,815 ... *D2
Altamira 24,846 ... C3
Altos 13,621 ... F4
Amambaí 12,507 ... C8
Amapá 2,676 ... D2
Amarante 6,848 ... F4
Amargosa 11,118 ... F6
Americana 121,794 ... *C3
Amparo 26,970 ... *C3
Anápolis 160,520 ... D7
Anchieta 5,741 ... F8
Andaraí 2,476 ... F6
Andradina 42,036 ... D8
Andrelândia 8,737 ... *D2
Angra dos Reis 24,894 ... *D3
Antonina 11,950 ... *B4
Aparecida 27,265 ... *D3
Apiaí 7,809 ... *B4
Aquidauana 21,514 ... C8
Aracaju 288,106 ... G5
Aracati 20,282 ... G4
Araçatuba 113,486 ... *A2
Araçuaí 12,292 ... F7
Araguari 73,302 ... D7
Araranguá 22,468 ... D10
Araraquara 77,202 ... *B2
Araras 54,323 ... *C3
Araxá 51,339 ... E7
Arcoverde 40,646 ... G5
Areia Branca 12,979 ... G4
Assis 57,217 ... *A3
Avaré 40,716 ... *B3
Bacabal 43,229 ... E4
Bagé 66,743 ... C10
Bahia (Salvador) 1,496,276 ... G6
Baixo Guandu 13,714 ... F7
Balsas 13,566 ... E4
Bambuí 14,172 ... *C2
Barão de Cocais 11,950 ... *E1
Barbacena 69,675 ... *E2
Barcelos 1,846 ... H9
Bariri 15,372 ... *B3
Barra 10,809 ... F5
Barra do Corda 19,280 ... E4
Barra do Piraí 51,214 ... *E3
Barra Mansa 123,421 ... *D3
Barras 8,904 ... F4
Barreiras 30,355 ... E6
Barreiros 19,419 ... H5
Barretos 65,294 ... *B2
Batatais 30,478 ... *C2
Baturité 12,388 ... G4
Bauru 178,861 ... *B3
Bebedouro 39,070 ... *B2
Bela Vista 11,936 ... C8
Belém 758,117 ... E3
Belém †1,000,349 ... E3
Belo Horizonte 1,442,483 ... *D1
Belo Horizonte †2,541,788 ... *D1
Benjamin Constant 6,563 ... G9
Bento Gonçalves 40,323 ... C10
Betim 71,599 ... *D2
Bicas 8,611 ... *E2
Birigui 45,348 ... *A2
Blumenau 144,819 ... D9
Boa Esperança 17,394 ... *D2
Boa Vista 43,131 ... H8
Bocaiúva 16,616 ... E7
Bom Conselho 13,196 ... G5
Bom Despacho 22,941 ... *D1
Bom Jesus da Lapa 19,978 ... F6
Bom Sucesso 10,331 ... *D2
Borba 5,366 ... H9
Bragança Paulista 61,021 ... *C3
Brasiléia 4,835 ... G10
Brasília (cap.) 411,305 ... E6
Brasília de Minas 10,171 ... F7
Brejo 5,859 ... F3
Breves 31,452 ... D3
Brumado 24,663 ... F6
Brusque 37,898 ... D9
Cabedelo 18,581 ... H4
Cabo Frio 40,668 ... *F3
Caçador 25,287 ... D9
Caçapava 45,258 ... *D3
Caçapava do Sul 15,180 ... C10
Cáceres 33,472 ... B7
Cachoeira 11,520 ... G6
Cachoeira do Sul 59,967 ... C10
Cachoeiro de Itapemirim 84,994 ... G8
Caeté 23,331 ... *E1
Caetité 8,823 ... F6
Caiapônia 9,358 ... C7
Caicó 30,777 ... G4
Cajazeiras 30,834 ... G4
Cajuru 9,670 ... *C2
Camaquã 28,078 ... C10
Cambará 13,218 ... *A3
Cambuí 8,552 ... *C3
Cametá 15,539 ... D3
Camocim 19,921 ... F3
Campina Grande 222,229 ... G4
Campinas 566,517 ... *C3
Campo Belo 30,392 ... *D2
Campo Formoso 10,324 ... F5
Campo Grande 282,844 ... C8
Campo Largo 34,506 ... *B4
Campo Maior 24,009 ... F4
Campos 174,218 ... *F2
Cananéia 5,581 ... *C4
Canavieiras 14,076 ... G6
Canindé 18,573 ... G4
Canoas 214,115 ... D10
Canoinhas 25,880 ... D9
Capanema 28,272 ... E3
Capão Bonito 24,081 ... *B4
Caraguatatuba 22,932 ... *D3
Carangola 15,621 ... *E2
Caratinga 39,621 ... *E1
Caravelas 3,704 ... G7
Carazinho 41,913 ... C10
Carolina 10,136 ... E4
Caruaru 137,636 ... G5
Casa Branca 13,739 ... *C2
Cascavel 16,238 ... G4
Cássia 10,701 ... *C2
Castanhal 51,797 ... E3
Castelo 9,162 ... F8
Castro 21,079 ... *B4
Castro Alves 11,286 ... G6
Cataguases 40,659 ... *E2
Catalão 30,516 ... E7
Catanduva 64,813 ... *B2
Catolé do Rocha 12,165 ... G4
Caxambu 16,221 ... *D2
Caxias 56,755 ... F4
Caxias do Sul 198,824 ... D10
Ceará (Fortaleza) 648,815 ... G3
Ceará-Mirim 17,097 ... H4
Ceres 13,671 ... D6
Chapecó 53,198 ... C9
Coari 14,841 ... H9
Codajás 4,923 ... H9
Codó 11,593 ... E4
Colatina 61,057 ... F7
Conceição do Araguaia 18,143 ... D5
Concórdia 17,973 ... D9
Conselheiro Lafaiete 66,262 ... *E2
Corinto 17,056 ... E7
Cornélio Procópio 31,201 ... D8
Coroatá 16,070 ... F3
Coromandel 11,604 ... E7
Corumbá 66,014 ... B7
Coxim 14,876 ... C7
Crateús 29,905 ... F4
Crato 49,244 ... G4
Criciúma 74,003 ... D10
Cristalina 10,521 ... E7
Cruz Alta 53,315 ... C10
Cruzeiro 55,175 ... *D3
Cruzeiro do Sul 11,189 ... G10
Cubatão 78,327 ... *C3
Cuiabá 167,894 ... C6
Curitiba 843,733 ... *B4
Curitiba †1,441,743 ... *B4
Currais Novos 25,663 ... G4
Cururupu 10,358 ... E3
Curvelo 37,734 ... E7
Diamantina 20,197 ... F7
Divinópolis 108,344 ... *D2
Dois Córregos 11,811 ... *B3
Dom Pedrito 25,773 ... C10
Dores do Indaiá 13,058 ... E7
Dourados 76,838 ... C8
Duque de Caxias 306,057 ... *E3
Erexim 46,927 ... C9
Esperança 12,964 ... G4
Esplanada 9,822 ... G5
Estância 28,250 ... G5
Feira de Santana 225,003 ... G5
Fernandópolis 39,737 ... *A2
Floriano 35,761 ... F4
Florianópolis 153,547 ... E9
Fonte Boa 3,278 ... G9
Formiga 36,681 ... *D2
Formosa 29,304 ... E6
Fortaleza 648,815 ... G3
Fortaleza †1,581,588 ... G3
Foz do Iguaçu 93,619 ... C9
Franca 143,630 ... *C2
Frutal 22,955 ... *B2
Garanhuns 64,854 ... G5
Garça 26,527 ... *B3
Goiana 30,108 ... H4
Goiânia 703,263 ... D7
Goiás 15,768 ... D6
Governador Valadares 173,699 ... F7
Grajaú 11,147 ... E4
Guacuí 12,715 ... *F2
Guajará-Mirim 19,992 ... H10
Guarapuava 17,189 ... C9
Guaratinguetá 68,370 ... *D3
Guarujá 67,730 ... *C4
Guarulhos 395,117 ... *C3
Guaxupé 23,637 ... *C2
Guiratinga 8,981 ... C7
Gurupi 27,319 ... D5
Humaitá 10,004 ... H10
Ibaiti 11,352 ... *A3
Ibiá 11,161 ... E7
Ibicaraí 18,202 ... G6
Ibitinga 23,359 ... *B2
Icó 13,007 ... G4
Igarapava 15,342 ... *C2
Igarapé-Miri 12,172 ... D3
Iguape 16,827 ... *C4
Iguatu 39,611 ... G4
Ijuí 51,925 ... C10
Ilhéus 71,240 ... G6
Imbituba 9,998 ... D10
Imperatriz 111,818 ... E4
Inhumas 23,455 ... D7
Ipameri 14,163 ... E7
Ipu 12,787 ... F4
Irati 21,956 ... *A4
Itabaiana, Paraíba 17,843 ... H4
Itabaiana, Sergipe 26,055 ... G5
Itaberaba 27,590 ... F6
Itabira 57,691 ... F7
Itabirito 22,978 ... *E2
Itabuna 129,938 ... G6
Itacoatiara 26,737 ... B3
Itaituba 19,644 ... C4
Itajaí 78,867 ... D9
Itajubá 53,506 ... *D3
Itanhaem 26,181 ... *C4
Itapecerica 10,234 ... *D2
Itapecuru-Mirim 12,216 ... F3
Itapemirim 16,829 ... F8
Itaperuna 34,644 ... *F2
Itapetinga 36,897 ... G6
Itapetininga 61,344 ... *B3
Itapeva 36,551 ... *B3
Itapipoca 19,463 ... G3
Itapira 36,308 ... *C3
Itápolis 13,750 ... *B2
Itaporanga 8,988 ... G4
Itaqui 23,136 ... B10
Itararé 24,368 ... *B4
Itatiba 35,537 ... *C3
Itaúna 49,372 ... *D2
Itu 62,211 ... *C3
Ituaçu 1,749 ... F6
Ituiutaba 65,178 ... D7
Itumbiara 56,602 ... D7
Iturama 12,363 ... *A1
Ituverava 21,323 ... *C2
Jaboatão 67,120 ... H5
Jaboticabal 40,276 ... *B2
Jacareí 103,652 ... *D3
Jacarezinho 23,684 ... *A3
Jacobina 26,723 ... F5
Jacupiranga 7,044 ... *B4
Jaguaquara 11,336 ... F6
Jaguarão 18,165 ... C11
Jaguariaíva 8,566 ... *B4
Januária 20,484 ... E6
Jataí 40,957 ... D7
Jaú 59,522 ... *B3
Jequié 84,792 ... F6
Jequitinhonha 10,900 ... F7
Ji-Paraná 31,724 ... H10
Joaçaba 16,195 ... D9
João Pessoa 290,424 ... H4
João Pinheiro 17,013 ... E7
Joinvile 217,074 ... D9
Juazeiro 60,940 ... G5
Juazeiro do Norte 125,248 ... F4
Juiz de Fora 299,728 ... *E2
Jundiaí 210,015 ... *C3
Lages 108,768 ... D9
Laguna 27,743 ... D10
Lambari 9,722 ... *D2
Lapa 13,314 ... D9
Laranjeiras do Sul 19,329 ... C9
Lavras 35,345 ... *D2
Leme 40,155 ... *C3
Leopoldina 28,554 ... *E2
Limeira 137,812 ... *C3
Limoeiro 36,088 ... H4
Limoeiro do Norte 13,112 ... G4
Linhares 51,575 ... F7
Lins 44,633 ... *B2
Londrina 258,054 ... D8
Lorena 51,276 ... *D3
Luís Correia 3,576 ... F3
Luz 10,068 ... *D1
Luziânia 67,284 ... E7
Macaé 39,644 ... *F3
Macaíba 17,036 ... H4
Macapá 89,081 ... D2
Macau 17,543 ... G4
Maceió 376,479 ... H5
Machado 16,164 ... *C2
Mafra 26,226 ... D9
Magé 37,597 ... *E3
Mamanguape 16,321 ... H4
Manacapuru 17,016 ... H9
Manaus 613,068 ... H9
Manhuaçu 22,678 ... *E2
Manhumirim 11,085 ... *E2
Manicoré 9,532 ... H9
Marabá 41,564 ... D4
Maracaju 9,699 ... C8
Maragogipe 13,512 ... G6
Maranguape 20,098 ... G3
Marechal Deodoro 9,400 ... H5
Mariana 11,785 ... *E2
Marília 103,904 ... *A3
Maringá 158,047 ... D8
Mata de São João 23,741 ... G6
Mato Grosso (Vila Bela da Santíssima Trindade) 1,401 ... B6
Maués 10,846 ... B3
Mazagão 1,824 ... D3
Mineiros 16,844 ... C7
Miracema 15,545 ... *E2
Mirassol 25,173 ... *B2
Mococa 33,682 ... *C2
Mogi das Cruzes 122,265 ... *C3
Mogi-Mirim 41,827 ... *C3
Monte Alegre 10,646 ... C3
Monte Aprazível 9,767 ... *A2
Monteiro 11,051 ... G4
Montenegro 27,246 ... D10
Montes Claros 151,881 ... E7
Morrinhos 20,154 ... D7
Mossoró 118,007 ... G4
Muriaé 50,040 ... *E2
Muzambinho 8,803 ... *C2
Nanuque 34,445 ... F7
Natal 376,552 ... H4
Nazaré 18,068 ... G6
Niquelândia 8,828 ... D6
Niterói 386,185 ... *E3
Nova Cruz 12,824 ... H4
Nova Era 11,126 ... *E1
Nova Friburgo 88,943 ... *E3
Nova Iguaçu 491,802 ... *E3
Nova Lima 35,035 ... *E2
Nova Russas 10,021 ... F4
Novo Hamburgo 132,066 ... D10
Novo Horizonte 18,439 ... *B2
Óbidos 17,143 ... C3
Oeiras 12,406 ... F4
Olímpia 24,376 ... *B2
Olinda 266,392 ... H4
Oliveira 22,642 ... *D2
Oriximiná 12,078 ... C3
Orlândia 22,924 ... *C2
Osasco 376,689 ... *C3
Ourinhos 52,698 ... *B3
Ouro Preto 27,821 ... *E2
Palmares 40,624 ... H5
Palmas 15,823 ... C9
Palmeira 11,521 ... *B4
Palmeira das Missões 23,943 ... C9
Pará (Belém) 758,117 ... E3
Paracatu 29,911 ... E7
Pará de Minas 37,127 ... *D1
Paraguaçu Paulista 17,399 ... D8
Paraíba do Sul 13,510 ... *E3
Paranaíba 21,305 ... D7
Paranaguá 68,366 ... *B4
Parati 8,684 ... *D3
Parintins 29,369 ... B3
Parnaíba 78,718 ... F3
Passo Fundo 103,121 ... D10
Passos 56,998 ... *C2
Patos 58,735 ... G4
Patos de Minas 59,896 ... E7
Patrocínio 29,520 ... E7
Pau dos Ferros 12,985 ... G4
Paulo Afonso 62,066 ... G5
Pederneiras 18,864 ... *B3
Pedra Azul 13,615 ... F6
Pedreiras 30,843 ... E4
Pedro Segundo 9,693 ... F4
Pelotas 197,092 ... C10
Penápolis 32,168 ... *A2
Penedo 27,064 ... G5
Pernambuco (Recife) 1,184,215 ... H5
Petrolina 73,436 ... G5
Petrópolis 149,427 ... *E3
Picos 33,098 ... F4
Piedade 13,054 ... *C3
Pilar 14,778 ... H5
Pindamonhangaba 51,174 ... *D3

(continued on following page)

Pinhal (Espírito Santo do
  Pinhal) 23,235 . . . . *C3
Pinheiro 19,556 . . . . E3
Piquete 10,316 . . . . *D3
Piracanjuba 11,151 . . . . . . D7
Piracicaba 179,395 . . . . . . *C3
Piracuruca 9,419 . . . . F3
Piral do Sul 13,709 . . . . . . *B4
Piraju 16,288 . . . . *B3
Pirapora 31,533 . . . . E7
Pirassununga 32,510 . . . . . *C2
Pires do Rio 16,659 . . . . . . D7
Piripiri 29,497 . . . . F4
Pitangui 12,116 . . . . *D1
Piúi 17,327 . . . . *D2
Poções 16,036 . . . . F6
Poconé 12,960 . . . . B7
Poços de Caldas 81,448 . . . *C2
Pombal 14,831 . . . . A3
Pompéia 11,282 . . . . *B4
Ponta Grossa 171,111 . . . . . D9
Ponta Porã 25,807 . . . . C8
Ponte Nova 34,807 . . . . *E2
Porangatu 21,192 . . . . D6
Porto Alegre 1,108,883 . . . . D10
Porto Alegre †2,232,370 . . . D10
Porto Feliz 19,680 . . . . *C3
Porto Nacional 19,052 . . . . . E5
Porto Seguro 5,007 . . . . G7
Porto União 19,426 . . . . D9
Porto Velho 101,644 . . . . . . H10
Pouso Alegre 50,517 . . . . . . *D3
Presidente Dutra 14,506 . . . . E4
Presidente Prudente
  127,623 . . . . D8
Presidente Venceslau 26,720 D8
Propriá 19,034 . . . . G5
Promissão 15,333 . . . . *B2
Prudentópolis 8,645 . . . . . . D9
Quaral 15,091 . . . . C10
Quixadá 25,149 . . . . G4
Quixeramobim 14,387 . . . . . F4
Raposos 11,078 . . . . *E2
Raul Soares 10,055 . . . . *E2
Recife 1,184,215 . . . . H5
Recife †2,348,362 . . . . H5
Registro 28,702 . . . . *C4
Remanso 13,067 . . . . F5
Resende 36,633 . . . . *D3
Ribamar (São José de
  Ribamar) 17,560 . . . . F3
Ribeirão Preto 300,704 . . . . *C2
Rio Bonito 20,561 . . . . *E3
Rio Branco 87,462 . . . . G10
Rio Claro 103,174 . . . . *C3
Rio de Janeiro 5,093,237 . . . *E3
Rio de Janeiro †9,018,637 . . *E3
Rio do Sul 33,408 . . . . D9
Rio Grande 124,706 . . . . . . D11
Rio Negro 15,851 . . . . D9
Rio Pardo 18,370 . . . . C10
Rio Pomba 9,319 . . . . *E2
Rio Tinto 12,511 . . . . H4
Rio Verde 47,639 . . . . D7
Rio Verde de Mato Grosso
  10,001 . . . . C7
Rosário 11,669 . . . . F3
Rosário do Sul 30,753 . . . . . C10
Russas 16,259 . . . . G4
Sabará 22,883 . . . . *E1
Sacramento 10,524 . . . . *C1
Salgueiro 25,915 . . . . G5
Salinas 12,613 . . . . F7
Salinópolis 10,395 . . . . E3
Salto 42,351 . . . . *C3
Salvador 1,496,276 . . . . G6
Salvador †1,772,018 . . . . . . G6
Santa Cruz 13,172 . . . . G4
Santa Cruz do Rio Pardo
  20,507 . . . . *B3
Santa Cruz do Sul 52,050 . . . C10
Santa Helena de Goiás
  20,067 . . . . D7
Santa Leopoldina 1,217 . . . . G7
Santa Maria 151,202 . . . . . . C10
Santa Maria da Vitória
  16,294 . . . . F6
Santana do Ipanema 15,311 . G5
Santana do Livramento
  58,165 . . . . C10
Santarém 101,534 . . . . *C3
Santa Rita do Sapucaí
  15,005 . . . . *D3
Santa Vitória do Palmar
  14,758 . . . . C11
Santiago 30,406 . . . . C10
Santo Amaro 29,627 . . . . . . G6
Santo Ângelo 50,161 . . . . . . C10
Santo André 549,278 . . . . . . *C3
Santo Antônio da Platina
  21,284 . . . . *A3
Santos 411,023 . . . . *C3
Santos Dumont 31,053 . . . . *E2
São Bento 9,607 . . . . E3
São Bernardo do Campo
  381,261 . . . . *C3
São Borja 41,598 . . . . C10
São Carlos 109,231 . . . . *C3
São Cristóvão 11,720 . . . . . . G5
São Fidélis 11,713 . . . . *F2
São Francisco 12,011 . . . . . E6
São Francisco do Sul
  13,914 . . . . E9
São Gabriel 40,497 . . . . C10
São Gonçalo 221,278 . . . . . . F8
São João da Boa Vista
  45,712 . . . . *C2
São João del Rei 53,401 . . . . *D2
São João dos Patos 12,848 . . F4
São João Nepomuceno
  12,752 . . . . *E2
São Joaquim da Barra
  26,273 . . . . *C2

São José 37,562 . . . . D9
São José do Rio Pardo
  21,914 . . . . *C2
São José do Rio Prêto
  171,982 . . . . *B2
São José dos Campos
  268,073 . . . . *D3
São José dos Pinhais
  53,422 . . . . D9
São Leopoldo 94,864 . . . . . . D10
São Lourenço 23,047 . . . . . . *D3
São Lourenço do Sul
  13,251 . . . . C10
São Luís 182,466 . . . . F3
São Luís Gonzaga 29,188 . . . C10
São Manuel 17,028 . . . . *B3
São Mateus 22,522 . . . . G7
São Miguel do Guamá 9,929 . E3
São Miguel dos Campos
  18,495 . . . . G5
São Paulo 7,033,529 . . . . . . *C3
São Paulo †12,588,439 . . . . *C3
São Paulo de Olivença 3,102 . G9
São Raimundo Nonato 8,574 . F5
São Roque 26,118 . . . . *C3
São Sebastião 11,065 . . . . . *D3
São Sebastião do Paraíso
  28,482 . . . . *C2
São Vicente 192,770 . . . . . . *C4
Senador Pompeu 10,109 . . . G4
Sena Madureira 6,668 . . . . . G10
Senhor do Bonfim 33,811 . . . F5
Serra do Navio 415 . . . . C2
Serra Talhada 28,912 . . . . . G4
Serrinha 23,920 . . . . G5
Sertânia 11,410 . . . . G5
Sete Lagoas 94,502 . . . . E7
Sobral 69,072 . . . . G3
Socorro 12,111 . . . . *C3
Sorocaba 254,718 . . . . *C3
Soure 11,306 . . . . D3
Taguatinga 480,109 . . . . . . D6
Taquaritinga 28,018 . . . . . . *B2
Tarauacá 6,889 . . . . G10
Tatuí 44,816 . . . . *C3
Tatubaté 155,371 . . . . E8
Tefé 14,670 . . . . G9
Teófilo Otoni 83,108 . . . . . . F7
Teresina 339,264 . . . . F4
Teresópolis 78,782 . . . . *E3
Tijucas 8,979 . . . . D9
Timon 55,318 . . . . F4
Tocantinópolis 8,427 . . . . . . D4
Touros H4

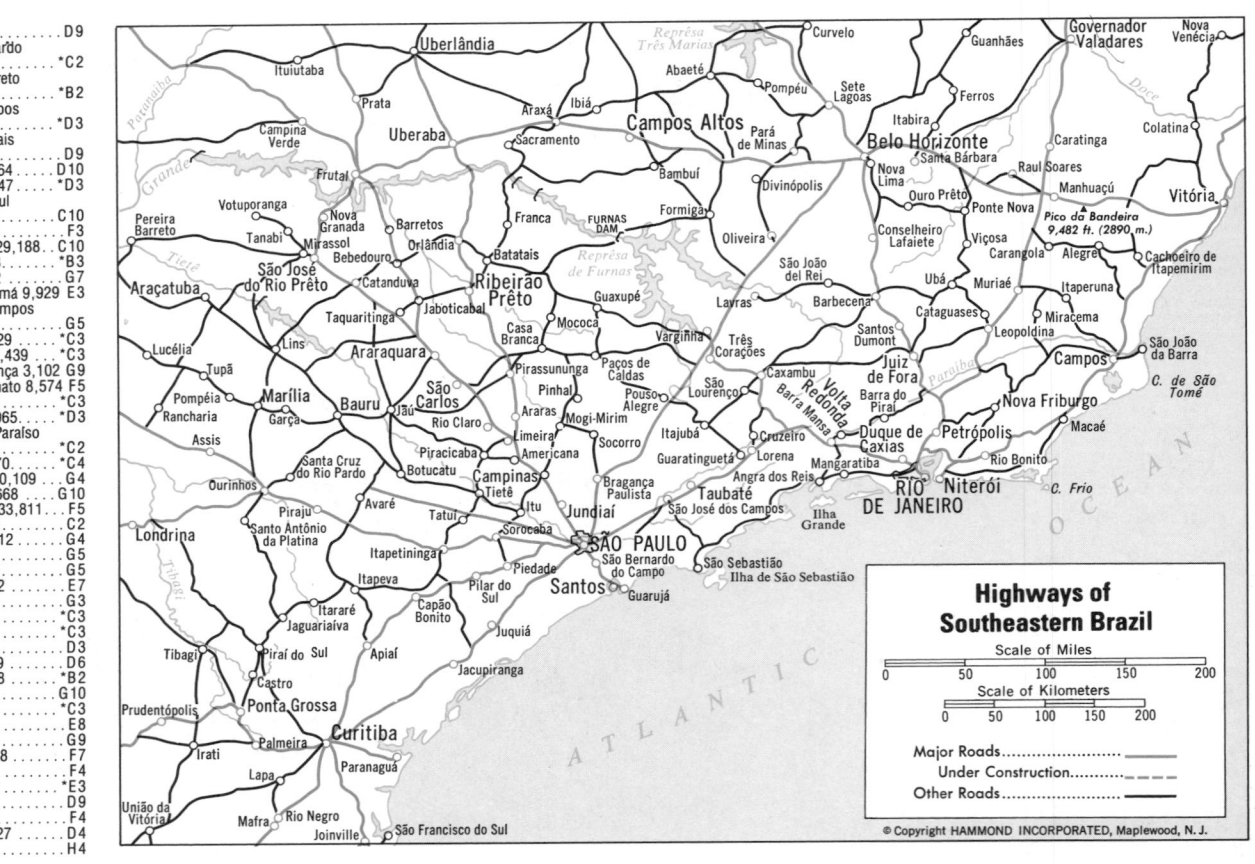

Highways of Southeastern Brazil

Scale of Miles

| 0 | 50 | 100 | 150 | 200 |

Scale of Kilometers

| 0 | 50 | 100 | 150 | 200 |

Major Roads . . . .
Under Construction . . . .
Other Roads . . . .

© Copyright HAMMOND INCORPORATED, Maplewood, N.J.

Agriculture, Industry and Resources

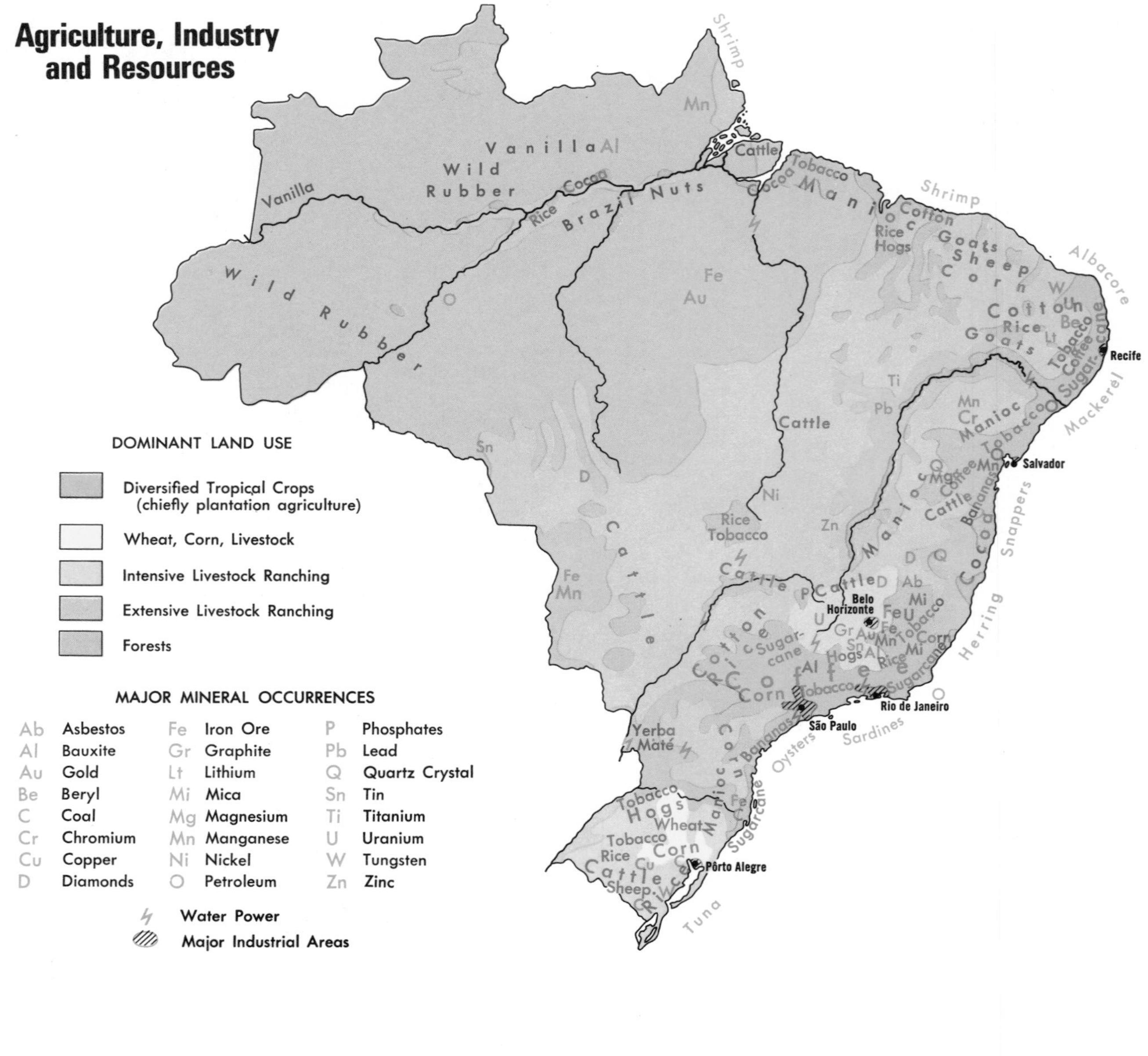

DOMINANT LAND USE

Diversified Tropical Crops
(chiefly plantation agriculture)

Wheat, Corn, Livestock

Intensive Livestock Ranching

Extensive Livestock Ranching

Forests

MAJOR MINERAL OCCURRENCES

Ab	Asbestos	Fe	Iron Ore	P	Phosphates
Al	Bauxite	Gr	Graphite	Pb	Lead
Au	Gold	Lt	Lithium	Q	Quartz Crystal
Be	Beryl	Mi	Mica	Sn	Tin
C	Coal	Mg	Magnesium	Ti	Titanium
Cr	Chromium	Mn	Manganese	U	Uranium
Cu	Copper	Ni	Nickel	W	Tungsten
D	Diamonds	O	Petroleum	Zn	Zinc

⚡ Water Power

▨ Major Industrial Areas

Brasilia

Southeastern Brazil

POLYCONIC PROJECTION

SCALE OF MILES

SCALE OF KILOMETERS

State Capitals.................................⊙

State Boundaries............................ ———

Scale 1:4,480,000

© Copyright HAMMOND INCORPORATED, Maplewood, N.J.

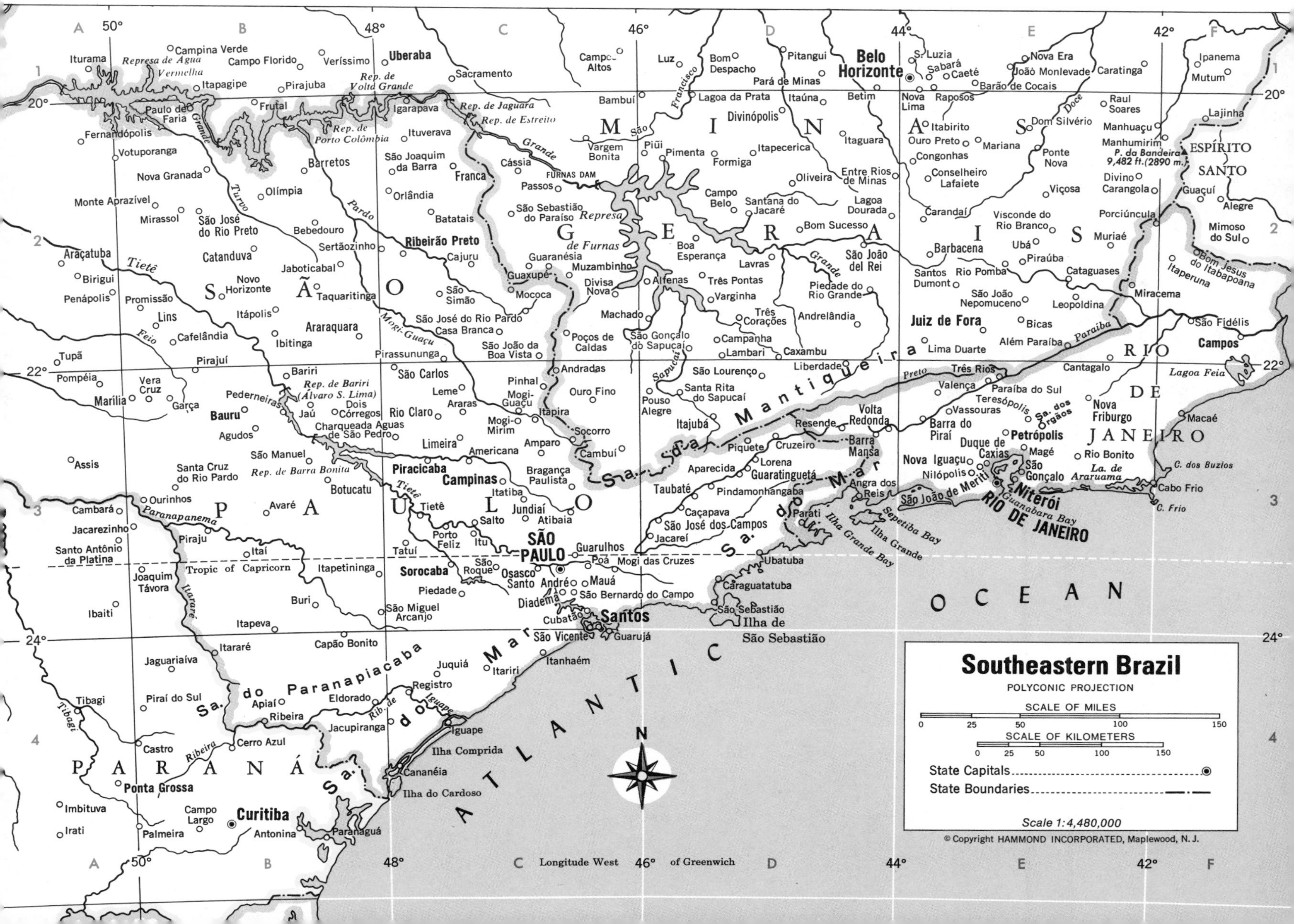

DEPARTMENTS

Beni, El 168,367 .... C3
Chuquisaca 358,516 .... C6
Cochabamba 720,952 .... C6
El Beni 168,367 .... C3
La Paz 1,465,078 .... A4
Oruro 310,409 .... A6
Pando 34,493 .... B2
Potosí 657,743 .... B7
Santa Cruz 710,724 .... E5
Tarija 187,204 .... D7

CITIES and TOWNS

Abapó 466 .... D6
Acchilla 208 .... C7
Achacachi 3,621 .... A5
Aiquile 3,465 .... C6
Alcala 236 .... C6
Alejandría‡ 198 .... C3
Alto Seco‡ 3,414 .... D6
Amarete 992 .... A4
Ananea 302 .... A4
Ancoraimes 769 .... A4
Andamarca‡ 5,187 .... B6
Añimbo 443 .... C7
Anzaldo 1,056 .... C5

Apolo 1,043 .... A4
Aracá‡ 3,537 .... B5
Arampampa 829 .... A5
Arani 2,200 .... C5
Arcopongo‡ 2,223 .... A5
Aromat 873 .... B6
Arque 1,254 .... C6
Arroyo Grande C3
Ascención (Añez) D4
Asunción B2
Asunta 45 .... B5
Atén 199 .... A4
Atocha‡ 3,964 .... B7
Ayacucho 729 .... A4
Ayata 479 .... A4

Azurduy 1,234 .... C6
Barrera B3
Baures 592 .... D3
Bella Flor A2
Bella Vista E3
Berenguela‡ 2,412 .... A5
Betanzos 1,097 .... C6
Bolívar B3
Bolpebra A2
Boyuibe 537 .... D7
Buena Vista, Santa Cruz D5
Cabezas 298 .... C6
Cachuela Esperanza 1,073 .... C2
Caiza 838 .... C7
Cajuata 447 .... B5

Calacoto 415 .... A5
Calamarca 802 .... A5
Callapa 636 .... A5
Camacho‡ 875 .... C7
Camargo 1,609 .... C7
Camatindi‡ 297 .... D7
Camiri 4,969 .... D7
Candelaria‡ 468 .... F5
Canquella 148 .... A7
Capinota 1,734 .... C5
Capirenda D7
Caquiavíri 760 .... A5
Carabuco 626 .... A4
Caracollo 909 .... A5
Caraparí 291 .... C6
Caranavi‡ 525 .... B4

Carandaiti 1,403 .... D7
Caraparí 351 .... D7
Carmen‡ 845 .... B2
Caticaicahua 3,240 .... B6
Cavari 249 .... B5
Cavinas‡ 1,011 .... A6
Chachacomani 159 .... A6
Chacomat 330 .... A6
Chaguaya 643 .... C7
Challacollo 284 .... B6
Challana‡ 1,206 .... B4
Challapata 2,529 .... B6
Chapacura‡ 152 .... A2
Chaqui 291 .... C6
Charagua 1,185 .... D6

Charaña 794 .... A5
Chayanta 1,272 .... B6
Chiguana 154 .... A7
Chiñijo 27 .... A4
Chivet 336 .... A3
Chocaya 444 .... B7
Choquecota‡ 1,976 .... A5
Choquecotat 330 .... A5
Chulumani 2,362 .... B5
Chuma 931 .... A4
Chuquichambi‡ 1,094 .... A5
Chuquichuqui‡ 1,892 .... C6
Cliza 3,121 .... C5
Cobija 3,650 .... B2
Cocani‡ 658 .... C6
Cocapata 2,855 .... B5

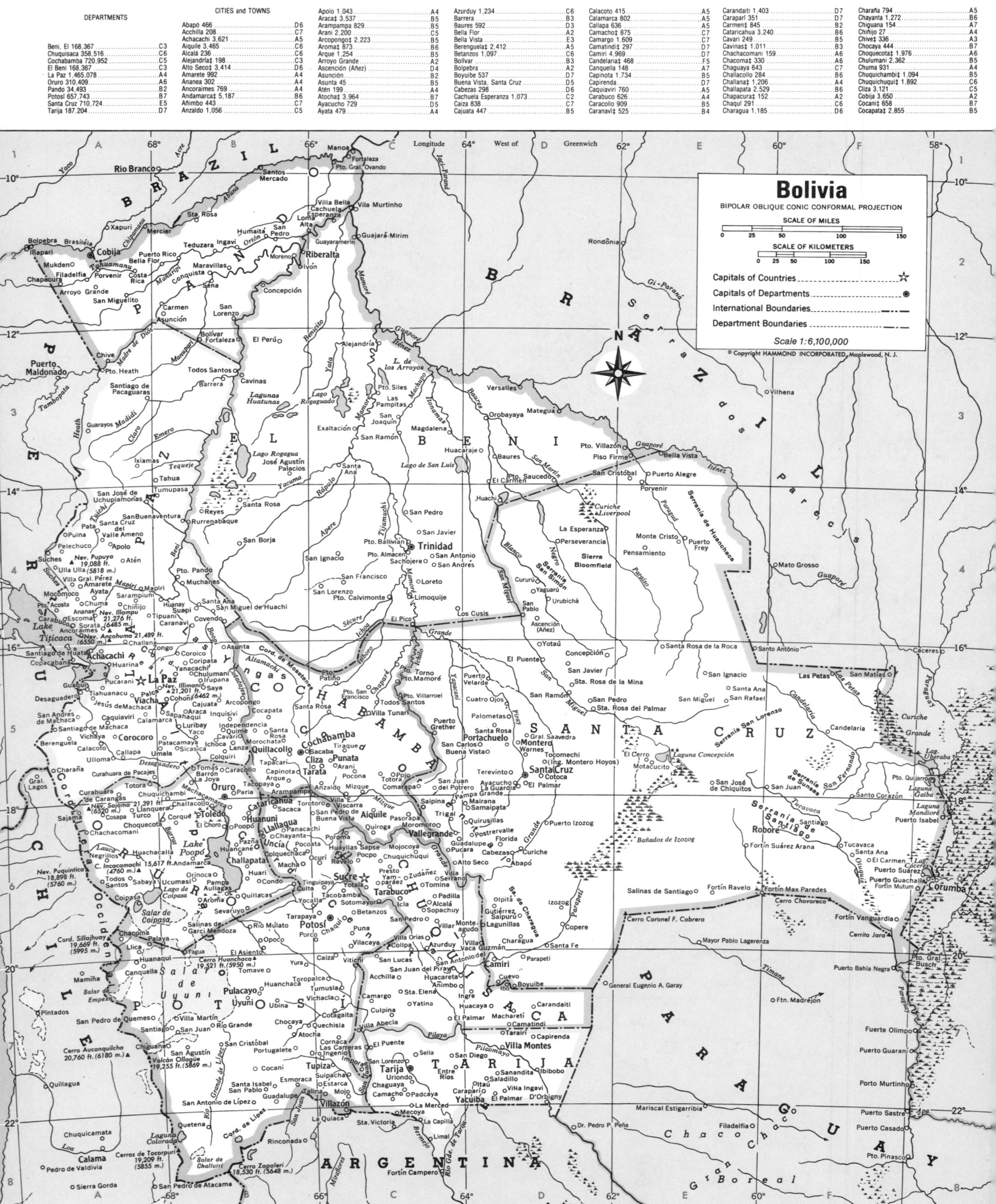

Bolivia

BIPOLAR OBLIQUE CONIC CONFORMAL PROJECTION

SCALE OF MILES
0 25 50 100 150

SCALE OF KILOMETERS
0 25 50 100 150

Capitals of Countries .... ☆
Capitals of Departments .... ◉
International Boundaries .... —·—·—
Department Boundaries .... —·· —··

Scale 1:6,100,000

© Copyright HAMMOND INCORPORATED, Maplewood, N.J.

Cochabamba 204,684 .... C5
Cohoni 890 .... B5
Coipasa‡ 202 .... A6
Collpa 481 .... C6
Colquechaca 1,070 .... B6
Colquiri 806 .... B5
Comarapa 1,096 .... C5
Concepción, El Beni‡ 61 .... B2
Concepción, Santa Cruz 1,056 .... D5
Condo‡ 5,525 .... B6
Conquista‡ 1,162 .... B2
Copacabana 1,981 .... A5
Copere D6
Coripata 1,647 .... B5
Cornaca 264 .... C7
Corocoro 4,431 .... A5
Coroico 2,235 .... B5
Corque 423 .... B6
Cosapa 297 .... A6
Costa Rica‡ 43 .... A2
Cotagaita 1,353 .... C7
Cotoca 915 .... D5
Covendo 71 .... B4
Cuatro Ojos‡ 465 .... D5
Cuevo 902 .... D7
Culpina 981 .... C7
Culta‡ 4,412 .... B6
Curahuara de Carangas 235 .... A5
Curahuara de Pacajes 510 .... A5
Curiche 257 .... D6
Cururú D4
Desaguadero 201 .... A5
D'Orbigny‡ 214 .... D7
El Asiento B6
El Carmen, El Beni 232 .... D3
El Carmen, Santa Cruz F6
El Cerro 117 .... E5
El Choro 224 .... B6
El Palmar, Chuquisaca‡ 772 .... D7
El Palmar, Santa Cruz 437 .... D5
El Palmar, Tarija 832 .... D7
El Perú B3
El Pico C4
El Puente, Santa Cruz‡ 1,185 .... D5
El Puente, Tarija‡ 1,310 .... C7
Entre Ríos 1,011 .... C7
Escoma 220 .... A4
Esmoraca‡ 1,137 .... B7
Estarca‡ 2,331 .... C7
Exaltación, El Beni 405 .... C3
Filadelfia‡ 942 .... A2
Florida, Santa Cruz 128 .... D6
Fortaleza‡ 765 .... B3
Fortaleza C1
Fortín Campero‡ 87 .... C8
Fortín Max Paredes F6
Fortín Mutum F6
Fortín Ravelo E6
Fortín Suárez Arana F6
Fortín Vanguardia F6
General Saavedra 1,006 .... D5
Guadalupe, Potosí 71 .... B7
Guadalupe, Santa Cruz 2,355 .... C6
Guaqui 2,266 .... A5
Guayaramerín 1,470 .... C2
Huacaraje 673 .... D3
Huacareta 239 .... C7
Huacaya 229 .... D7
Huachacalla 801 .... A6
Huachi D4
Huanaqui 359 .... A7
Huanay 574 .... B4
Huancané 148 .... B6
Huanchaca B7
Huanuni 5,696 .... B6
Huari 1,070 .... B6
Huarina 1,151 .... A5
Huayllas 206 .... C6
Humaitá‡ 429 .... B2
Ibibobo D7
Ibo D7
Ichoca 591 .... B5
Icla 196 .... C6
Impora 274 .... C7
Independencia 1,742 .... B5
Ingavi‡ 111 .... B2
Ingeniero Montero Hoyos
(Tocomechi) 575 .... D5
Ingre 162 .... D7
Inquisivi 530 .... B5
Irupana 1,937 .... B5
Itaú 102 .... D7
Ivón‡ 772 .... C2
Ixiamas 292 .... A3
Izozog‡ 2,759 .... D6
Jesús de Machaca 529 .... A5
José Agustín
Palacios‡ 2,273 .... B3
La Capilla‡ 1,870 .... C8
La Esmeralda D8
La Esperanza D4
La Guardia 470 .... D5
Lagunillas 840 .... D6
La Joya 401 .... B5

La Merced‡ 688 .... C8
Lanza 526 .... B5
La Paz (cap.) 635,283 .... B5
Las Carreras 155 .... C7
Las Pampitas‡ 71 .... C3
Las Petas‡ 383 .... F5
Limal‡ 524 .... C8
Limoquije C4
Llallagua 6,719 .... B6
Llanquera 613 .... A6
Llica 560 .... A6
Loma Alta B2
Loreto 589 .... C4
Los Cusis D4
Luribay 392 .... B5
Macha 1,050 .... B6
Machacamarca 1,746 .... B5
Machareti‡ 1,164 .... D7
Magdalena 1,724 .... C3
Mairana 508 .... D6
Manoa C1
Mapiri 289 .... B4
Maravillas B2
Mateguá 38 .... D3
Mecoya‡ 585 .... C8
Mercier‡ 272 .... B2
Mizque 870 .... C5
Mocomoco 977 .... A4
Mojo 469 .... C7
Mojocoya 498 .... C6
Monteagudo 971 .... D6
Monte Cristo E4
Montero 2,713 .... D5
Moreno B2
Morochata 461 .... B5
Moromoro 556 .... C6
Motacucito‡ 585 .... E5
Muchanes B4
Mukden‡ 84 .... A2
Negrillos 85 .... A6
Ocurí 1,531 .... C6
Opoco B6
Orinoca‡ 2,380 .... B6
Orobayaya‡ 1,132 .... D3
Oro Ingenio‡ 945 .... C7
Oruro 124,213 .... B5
Padcaya 324 .... C7
Padilla 2,462 .... C6
Palaya 300 .... A6
Palca 887 .... A5
Palometas‡ 3,453 .... D5
Pampa Aullagas‡ 1,834 .... B6
Pampa Grande 727 .... D5
Panacachi 952 .... B6
Paria 335 .... B5
Pasorapa 1,016 .... C6
Pata 122 .... A4
Patacamaya 1,278 .... B5
Pazña 671 .... B6
Pelechuco 873 .... A4
Pensamiento E4
Perseverancia D4
Piso Firme D3
Pocoata 859 .... B6
Pocona 518 .... C5
Pocpo‡ 2,791 .... C6
Pojo 1,047 .... C5
Poopó 736 .... B6
Porco 817 .... B6
Poroma 171 .... C6
Portachuelo 2,456 .... D5
Portugalete‡ 1,590 .... B7
Porvenir, Pando‡ 846 .... A2
Porvenir, Santa Cruz E4
Postrervalle 750 .... D6
Potosí 77,397 .... C6
Presto 725 .... C6
Pucara 762 .... C6
Pucarani 1,041 .... A5
Puerto Acosta 1,302 .... A4
Puerto Alegre E3
Puerto Almacen 358 .... C4
Puerto Ballivián C4
Puerto Calvimonte C4
Puerto Frey E4
Puerto General Ovando 50
Puerto Grether C5
Puerto Guachalla F6
Puerto Heath‡ 570 .... A3
Puerto Isabel F6
Puerto Izozog D6
Puerto Mamoré C5
Puerto Pando B4
Puerto Patiño C5
Puerto Quijarro G5
Puerto Rico‡ 539 .... B2
Puerto San Francisco C5
Puerto Saucedo D3
Puerto Siles 357 .... C3
Puerto Suárez 1,159 .... F6
Puerto Torno C5
Puerto Velarde D5
Puerto Villarroel C5
Puerto Villazón D3

AREA 424,163 sq. mi. (1,098,582 sq. km.)
POPULATION 5,600,000
CAPITALS La Paz, Sucre
LARGEST CITY La Paz
HIGHEST POINT Nevada Ancohuma 21,489 ft. (6,550 m.)
MONETARY UNIT Bolivian peso
MAJOR LANGUAGES Spanish, Quechua, Aymara
MAJOR RELIGION Roman Catholicism

Topography

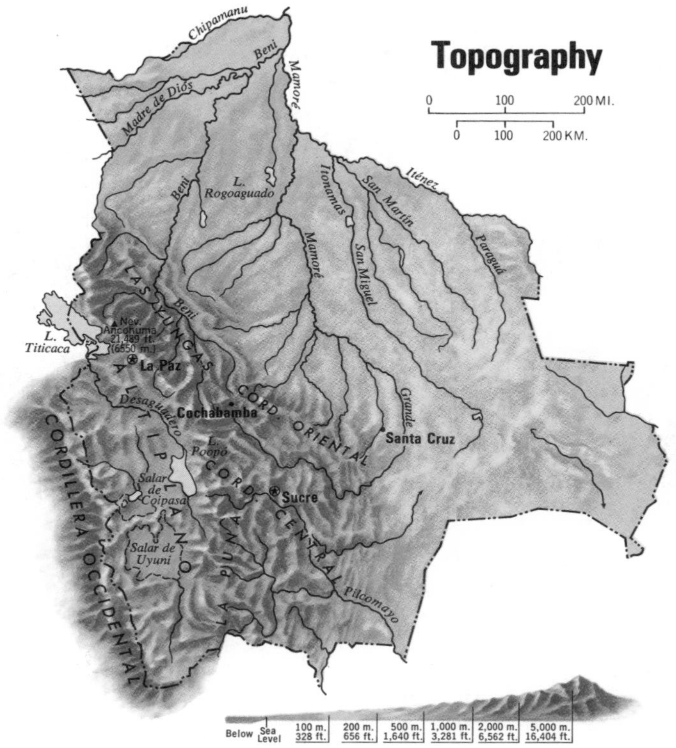

Puina A4
Pulacayo 7,984 .... B7
Puna 852 .... C6
Punata 5,014 .... C5
Quechisla 171 .... C7
Queteña 183 .... B8
Quillacas 1,170 .... B6
Quillacollo 9,123 .... B5
Quime 1,256 .... B5
Quiroga‡ 3,467 .... C6
Quirusillas 433 .... D6
Ravelo 907 .... C6
Reyes 1,404 .... B4
Riberalta 6,549 .... C2
Río Grande 281 .... B7
Río Mulato 381 .... B6
Roboré 3,715 .... F6
Rurrenabaque 1,225 .... B4
Sabaya 649 .... A6
Sacaba 2,752 .... C5
Sacaca 1,778 .... B6
Sachojere 401 .... C4
Saipina 573 .... C6
Sajama 231 .... A6
Saladillo‡ 1,315 .... D7
Salinas de Garci Mendoza 335 .... B6
Salinas de Santiago E6
Samaipata 1,656 .... D6
San Agustín‡ 810 .... B7
Sanandita 379 .... D7
San Andrés 399 .... C4
San Andrés de Machaca 101 .... A5
San Antonio, El Beni 436 .... C4
San Antonio de Lípez‡ 177 .... B7
San Antonio del
Parapetí 497 .... D7
San Borja 708 .... B4
San Buenaventura 307 .... A4
San Carlos 570 .... D5
San Cristóbal,
Potosí‡ 1,200 .... B7
San Cristóbal, Santa Cruz E3
San Diego‡ 773 .... D7
San Francisco, El Beni 185 .... C4
San Ignacio, El Beni 1,757 .... C4
San Ignacio, Santa Cruz 1,819 .... E5
San Javier, El Beni 233 .... C4
San Javier, Santa Cruz 564 .... D5
San Joaquín 1,959 .... C3
San José de Chiquitos 1,933 .... E5
San José de
Uchupiamonas 277 .... A4
San Juan, Potosí 131 .... B7
San Juan, Santa Cruz‡ 1,482 .... F5
San Juan del Piray 541 .... C7
San Juan del Potrero 263 .... C5
San Lorenzo, El Beni 496 .... C4
San Lorenzo, Pando‡ 317 .... B2
San Lorenzo, Tarija 785 .... C7
San Lucas 925 .... C7
San Matías 887 .... F5
San Miguel 502 .... E5
San Miguel de Huachi 25 .... B4
San Miguelito A2
San Pablo, Potosí 11 .... B7
San Pablo, Santa Cruz D4
San Pedro, Chuquisaca 182 .... C6
San Pedro, El Beni 262 .... C4
San Pedro, Pando‡ 312 .... B2
San Pedro, Santa Cruz 80 .... D5
San Pedro de Buena Vista 1,094 .... C6
San Pedro de Quemes‡ 290 .... A7
San Rafael‡ 1,282 .... E5
San Ramón, El Beni 1,161 .... C3
San Ramón, Santa Cruz 379 .... D5
Santa Ana, El Beni 2,225 .... C3
Santa Ana, La Paz 171 .... B4

Santa Ana, Santa Cruz 275 .... E5
Santa Ana, Santa Cruz 663 .... F6
Santa Cruz, Santa Cruz 254,682 .... D5
Santa Cruz del Valle
Ameno 442 .... A4
Santa Elena‡ 4,474 .... C7
Santa Fe D6
Santa Isabel‡ 323 .... B7
Santa Rosa, Cochabamba‡ 942 .... B5
Santa Rosa, Cochabamba‡ 276 .... C5
Santa Rosa, El Beni 765 .... B4
Santa Rosa, Pando‡ 105 .... B2
Santa Rosa, Santa Cruz 995 .... D5
Santa Rosa de la Mina 99 .... D5
Santa Rosa de la Roca 101 .... E5
Santa Rosa del Palmar 441 .... E5
Santiago, Potosí 172 .... A7
Santiago, Santa Cruz 765 .... F6
Santiago de Huata 948 .... A5
Santiago de Machaca 218 .... A5
Santiago de Pacaguaras A3
Santo Corazón‡ 963 .... F5
Santos Mercado B1
Sapahaqui 55 .... B5
Sapse‡ 89 .... C6
Sarampiuni 138 .... A4
Saya 339 .... B5
Sella C7
Sena‡ 660 .... B2
Sevaruyo 475 .... B6
Sicasica 1,486 .... B5
Sopachuy 713 .... C6
Sorata 2,087 .... A4
Sotomayor 510 .... C6
Suapi‡ 1,750 .... B4
Suches‡ 231 .... A4
Sucre (cap.) 63,625 .... C6
Suipacha‡ 2,701 .... C7
Tacobamba‡ 6,933 .... C6
Tacopaya 795 .... B5
Tagua B6
Tahua B3
Talina 122 .... B7
Tapacarí 980 .... B5
Tarabuco 2,833 .... C6
Tarairí‡ 394 .... D7
Tarapaya 357 .... B6
Tarata 3,016 .... C5
Tarija 38,916 .... C7
Teduzara‡ 271 .... B2
Terevinto‡ 3,790 .... D5
Tiahuanacu 1,227 .... A5
Tinguipaya 766 .... C6
Tipuani‡ 1,216 .... B4
Tiraque 1,390 .... C5
Tocomechi 575 .... D5
Todos Santos, Cochabamba 408 .... C5
Todos Santos, La Paz B3
Todos Santos, Oruro 68 .... A6
Toledo 3,273 .... B6
Tomás Barrón 1,852 .... B5
Tomave 201 .... B7
Tomina 708 .... C6
Toropalca‡ 199 .... B7
Torotoro 1,233 .... C6
Totora, Cochabamba C5
Totora, Oruro A5
Trigal 749 .... C6
Trinidad, El Beni 27,487 .... C4
Trinidad, Pando‡ 332 .... B2
Tucavaca F6
Tumupasa 349 .... B4
Tumusla‡ 526 .... C7
Tupiza 8,248 .... C7
Turco 131 .... A6
Ubina‡ 462 .... B7
Ucumasi‡ 1,040 .... B6

Ulla Ulla 52 .... A4
Ulloma 116 .... A5
Umala 481 .... B5
Uncía 4,507 .... B6
Uriondo 860 .... C7
Urubichá 1,369 .... D4
Uyuni 6,968 .... B7
Vallegrande 5,094 .... C6
Versalles 83 .... D3
Viacha 6,607 .... A5
Vichacla 317 .... C7
Vichaya 422 .... A5
Vilacaya 200 .... C6
Villa Abecia 539 .... C7
Villa Bella 88 .... C2
Villa E. Viscarra 658 .... C6
Villa General Pérez 802 .... A4
Villa Ingavi 122 .... D7
Villa Martín 543 .... B7
Villa Montes 3,105 .... D7

Villa Orías 404 .... C6
Villar 322 .... C6
Villa Serrano 1,570 .... C6
Villa Tunari 510 .... C5
Villa Vaca Guzmán 699 .... D6
Villazón 6,261 .... C7
Vitichi 1,515 .... C7
Warnes 1,571 .... D5
Yaco 835 .... B5
Yacuiba 5,027 .... D7
Yaguarú D4
Yamparaéz 725 .... C6
Yanacachi‡ 1,964 .... B5
Yatina‡ 1,850 .... C7
Yocalla‡ 1,814 .... B6
Yotala 1,554 .... C6
Yotaú D5
Yura 136 .... B7
Zongo 141 .... B5
Zudáñez 1,868 .... C6

OTHER FEATURES

Abuná (riv.) B2
Altamachi (riv.) B5
Ancohuma, Nevada (mt.) A4
Apere (riv.) C4
Arroyas, Los (lake) C3
Barras (riv.) B6
Baures (riv.) D3
Beni (riv.) B2
Benicito (riv.) C3
Bermejo (riv.) C8
Blanco (riv.) D4
Bloomfield, Sierra (mts.) D4
Boopi (riv.) B4
Cáceres (lag.) G6
Candelaria (riv.) F5
Capitán Ustarés, Cerro
(mt.) E6
Central, Cordillera (range) C6
Challviri (salt dep.) B8
Chaparé (riv.) C5
Charagua, Sierra de (mts.) D6
Chipamanu (riv.) A2
Chovoreca, Cerro (mt.) F6
Claro (riv.) A3
Coipasa (lake) B6
Coipasa (salt dep.) A6
Colorada (lag.) A8
Concepción (lag.) E5
Coronel F. Gabrera E6
Cotacajes (riv.) B5
Desaguadero (riv.) B5
Emero (riv.) B3
Empexa (salt dep.) A7
Gaiba (lag.) F5
Grande (marsh) F5
Grande (riv.) C4
Grande (riv.) C6
Grande de Lípez (riv.) B7
Guaporé (riv.) C3
Heath (riv.) A3
Huanchaca, Cerro (mt.) B7
Huanchaca, Serranía de
(mts.) E4
Huatunas (lag.) B3
Ichilo (riv.) C5
Ichoa (riv.) C4
Illampu, Nevada (mt.) A4
Illimani, Nevada (mt.) B5
Incacamachi, Cerro (mt.) A6

Isiboro (riv.) C5
Iténez (Guaporé) (riv.) C3
Itonamas (riv.) C3
Izozog (swamp) E6
Jara, Cerrito (mt.) F6
Las Yungas (reg.) B5
Lauca (riv.) A6
Lípez, Cordillera de
(range) B8
Liverpool (swamp) D4
Machupo (riv.) C3
Madidi (riv.) A3
Madre de Diós (riv.) A3
Mamoré (riv.) C2
Mandioré (lag.) F6
Manuripi (riv.) B2
Mizque (riv.) C6
Mosetenes, Cordillera de
(range) B5
Negro (riv.) D4
Occidental, Cordillera
(range) A6
Ollagüe (vol.) B7
Oriental, Cordillera (range) C5
Ortón (riv.) B2
Otuquis (riv.) F6
Paraguá (riv.) E4
Paraguay (riv.) F7
Parapetí (riv.) D6
Petas, Las (riv.) F5
Pilaya (riv.) C7
Pilcomayo (riv.) D7
Piray (riv.) D5
Poopó (lake) B6
Pupuya, Nevada (mt.) A4
Puquintica, Nevado (mt.) A6
Rápulo (riv.) C4
Real, Cordillera (range) A5
Rogagua (lake) B3
Rogaguado (lake) C3
Sajama, Nevada (mt.) A6
San Fernando (riv.) F5
San Juan (riv.) C7
San Lorenzo, Serranía
(mts.) E5
San Luis (lake) C3
San Martín (riv.) D3
San Miguel (riv.) D4
San Simón, Serranía
(mts.) D4
Santiago, Serranía de
(mts.) F6
Sécure (riv.) C4
Sillajhuay, Cordillera (mt.) A6
Suches (riv.) A4
Sunsas, Serranía de (mts.) F5
Tahuamanu (riv.) A2
Tarija, Rio Grande de (riv.) C8
Tequeje (riv.) B3
Tijamuchi (riv.) C4
Titicaca (lake) A4
Tocorpuri, Cerros de (mt.) A8
Tucavaca (riv.) F6
Tuichi (riv.) A4
Uberaba (lag.) G5
Uyuni (salt dep.) B7
Yacuma (riv.) B3
Yapacani (riv.) C5
Yata (riv.) C3
Yungas, Las (reg.) B5
Zapaleri, Cerro (mt.) B8

‡Population of canton.

Agriculture, Industry and Resources

DOMINANT LAND USE

- Diversified Tropical Crops (chiefly plantation agriculture)
- Upland Cultivated Areas
- Upland Livestock Grazing, Limited Agriculture
- Extensive Livestock Ranching
- Forests
- Nonagricultural Land

MAJOR MINERAL OCCURRENCES

Ag	Silver	G	Natural Gas	Sb	Antimony
Au	Gold	O	Petroleum	Sn	Tin
Cu	Copper	Pb	Lead	W	Tungsten
Fe	Iron Ore	S	Sulfur	Zn	Zinc

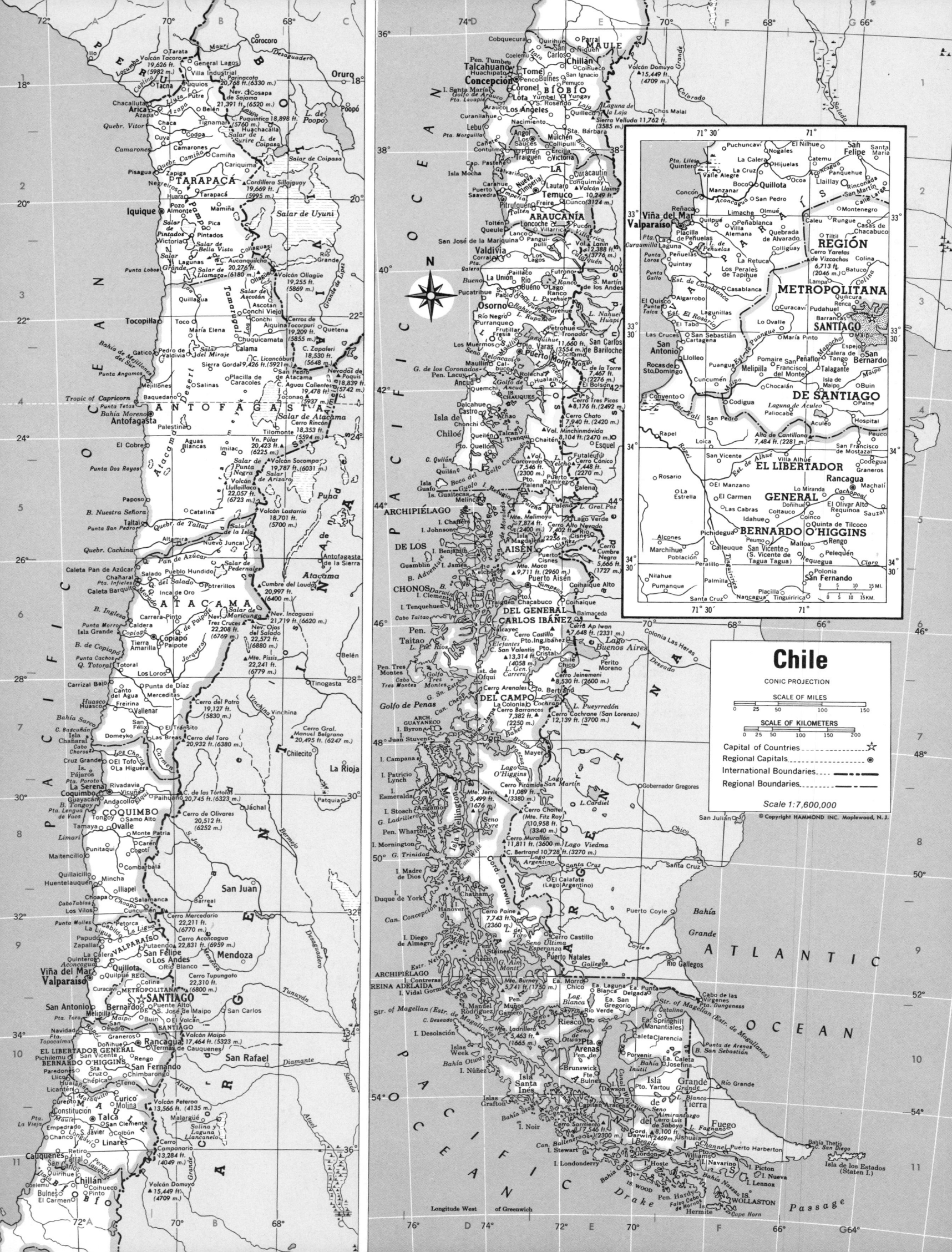
Chile
CONIC PROJECTION
SCALE OF MILES
0 25 50 100 150
SCALE OF KILOMETERS
0 25 50 100 150 200
Capital of Countries
Regional Capitals
International Boundaries
Regional Boundaries
Scale 1:7,600,000
© Copyright HAMMOND INC. Maplewood, N. J.
REGIÓN METROPOLITANA DE SANTIAGO
EL LIBERTADOR GENERAL BERNARDO O'HIGGINS
SANTIAGO
Valparaíso
Viña del Mar
San Antonio
Rancagua
San Fernando
Quillota
San Felipe
Melipilla
Talagante
San Bernardo
Puente Alto
TARAPACÁ
ANTOFAGASTA
ATACAMA
COQUIMBO
VALPARAÍSO
MAULE
BIOBÍO
ARAUCANÍA
LOS LAGOS
AISÉN DEL GENERAL CARLOS IBÁÑEZ DEL CAMPO
MAGALLANES Y ANTÁRTICA CHILENA
PERU
BOLIVIA
ARGENTINA
PACIFIC OCEAN
ATLANTIC OCEAN
Arica
Iquique
Tocopilla
Antofagasta
Calama
Copiapó
La Serena
Coquimbo
Ovalle
Talca
Chillán
Concepción
Talcahuano
Los Ángeles
Temuco
Valdivia
Osorno
Puerto Montt
Castro
Puerto Aisén
Coihaique
Puerto Natales
Punta Arenas
Tropic of Capricorn
Salar de Atacama
Salar de Uyuni
Isla de Chiloé
Golfo de Penas
Str. of Magellan (Estr. de Magallanes)
Tierra del Fuego
Cape Horn
Drake Passage
Mendoza
San Juan
La Rioja
Río Gallegos
Longitude West of Greenwich

Topography

0   100   200 MI.

0   100   200 KM.

AREA 292,257 sq. mi. (756,946 sq. km.)
POPULATION 11,275,440
CAPITAL Santiago
LARGEST CITY Santiago
HIGHEST POINT Ojos del Salado 22,572 ft.
   (6,880 m.)
MONETARY UNIT Chilean escudo
MAJOR LANGUAGE Spanish
MAJOR RELIGION Roman Catholicism

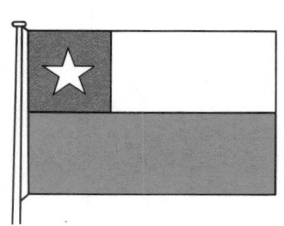

5,000 m.	2,000 m.	1,000 m.	500 m.	200 m.	100 m.	Sea	
16,404 ft.	6,562 ft.	3,281 ft.	1,640 ft.	656 ft.	328 ft.	Level	Below

REGIONS

Aisén del General Carlos
  Ibáñez del Campo
  65,478 . . . . E6
Antofagasta 341,203 . . . . B4
Atacama 183,071 . . . . B6
Bíobío 1,516,552 . . . . E1
Coquimbo 419,178 . . . . A8
El Libertador General
  Bernardo O'Higgins
  584,989 . . . . A10
La Araucanía 692,924 . . . . E2
Los Lagos 843,430 . . . . . D3
Magallanes 132,333 . . . . E10
Maule 723,224 . . . . A11
Santiago, Región
  Metropolitana de (Santiago
  Metropolitan Region)
  4,294,938 . . . . A9
Tarapacá 273,427 . . . . . . B2
Valparaíso 1,204,693 . . . . A9

CITIES and TOWNS

Achao ○11,501 . . . . D4
Aguas Blancas ○203 . . . . B4
Algarrobo ○3,941 . . . . . . F3
Ancud 11,900 . . . . D4
Andacollo 6,000 . . . . . . A8
Angol 42,670 . . . . D1
Antofagasta 125,100 . . . . A4
Arauco 5,400 . . . . D1
Arica 87,700 . . . . A1
Ascotán B3
Barrancas ○184,241 . . . . G3
Belén ○925 . . . . B1
Buin 11,800 . . . . G4
Bulnes 6,900 . . . . E1
Cabildo 5,800 . . . . A9
Calama 45,900 . . . . . . B3
Calbuco ○21,673 . . . . . D4
Caldera ○3,268 . . . . . . A6
Calera de Tango ○6,198 . . G4
Calle Larga ○7,172 . . . . G2
Cañete 7,900 . . . . D2
Carahue ○12,733 . . . . . D2
Cartagena ○7,124 . . . . . F3
Casablanca 5,500 . . . . . F3
Casas de Chacabuco G2
Castro 11,200 . . . . D4
Catalina ○1,637 . . . . . . B5
Catemu ○8,728 . . . . . . G2
Cauquenes 20,200 . . . . . A11
Cerro Castillo ○537 . . . . E9
Cerro Manantiales F10
Chaitén ○4,067 . . . . . . E4
Chañaral ○36,949 . . . . . A6
Chanco ○12,433 . . . . . . A11
Chépica ○11,199 . . . . . . A10
Chillán 128,515 . . . . . . A11
Chimbarongo 5,300 . . . . . A10
Chonchi ○8,911 . . . . . . D4
Chuquicamata 22,100 . . . . B3
Cobquecura ○6,298 . . . . D1
Cochamó ○5,042 . . . . . . E3
Codegua ○6,757 . . . . . . G4
Codpa ○950 . . . . B1
Coelemu 5,400 . . . . D1
Coihaique 32,129 . . . . . . E6
Coihueco ○17,276 . . . . . A11
Coinco ○4,942 . . . . G5
Colbún ○12,924 . . . . . . A11
Colina 7,400 . . . . G3
Collipulli 7,200 . . . . . . E2
Coltauco ○11,857 . . . . . F5
Combarbalá ○17,332 . . . . A8
Concepción 206,226 . . . . D1
Constitución 11,500 . . . . A11
Contulmo ○13,987 . . . . . D2
Copiapó 45,200 . . . . . . B6
Coquimbo 73,953 . . . . . . A8
Coronel 37,300 . . . . . . D1
Corral ○5,533 . . . . D3
Cunco ○18,836 . . . . E2
Curacautín 9,800 . . . . . . E2
Curacaví 5,800 . . . . G3
Curanilahue 13,200 . . . . . D1
Curepto ○13,020 . . . . . . A10
Curicó 41,300 . . . . A10
Dalcahue ○7,084 . . . . . . D4
Domeiko A7
Doñihue ○8,837 . . . . . . G5
El Carmen ○13,226 . . . . . A11
El Monte 7,000 . . . . G4
El Quisco ○2,152 . . . . . . E3
El Tabo ○2,180 . . . . F3
El Tofo A7
Empedrado ○7,887 . . . . . A11
Ercilla ○8,061 . . . . E2
Estancia Caleta
  Josefina ○1,042 . . . . . F10
Estancia Morro Chico ○785 . E9
Estancia San Gregorio
  ○1,156 . . . . E9
Estancia Springhill
  (Cerro Manantiales) F10

Freire ○23,313 . . . . E2
Freirina ○5,523 . . . . A7
Fresia ○15,359 . . . . D3
Frutillar ○12,721 . . . . . . D3
Futaleufú ○2,366 . . . . . . E4
Futrono ○7,109 . . . . E3
Galvarino ○9,495 . . . . . . D2
General Lagos ○810 . . . . B1
Graneros 8,900 . . . . G5
Guayacán A8
Hijuelas ○7,128 . . . . F2
Hualañé ○6,912 . . . . A10
Huara ○1,934 . . . . B2
Huasco ○4,971 . . . . A7
Illapel 12,200 . . . . A8
Inca de Oro 1,406 . . . . . . B6
Iquique 64,500 . . . . A2
Isla de Maipo ○12,903 . . . G4
La Calera 24,600 . . . . . . F2
La Cruz ○8,907 . . . . F2
La Estrella ○3,707 . . . . . F5
Lago Ranco ○12,767 . . . . E3
Lagunas ○5,653 . . . . B3
La Higuera ○6,991 . . . . . A7
La Ligua 7,500 . . . . A9
Lampa ○10,220 . . . . G3
Lanco 5,200 . . . . D2
Las Cabras ○12,119 . . . . F5
La Serena 99,908 . . . . . . A8
La Unión 15,200 . . . . . . D3
Lautaro 11,900 . . . . E2
Lebu 12,500 . . . . D1
Licantén ○6,354 . . . . . . A10
Limache 15,200 . . . . F2
Linares 37,900 . . . . A11
Llay-Llay 9,700 . . . . G2
Loica F4
Loncoche ○17,539 . . . . . D2
Longaví ○15,909 . . . . . . A11
Lonquimay ○9,524 . . . . . E2
Los Andes 23,500 . . . . . B9
Los Ángeles 49,500 . . . . D1
Los Lagos ○14,934 . . . . . D3
Los Muermos ○9,296 . . . . D3
Los Sauces ○7,613 . . . . . D2
Los Vilos ○10,453 . . . . . A9
Lota 48,100 . . . . D1
Machalí 5,800 . . . . G5
Maipú ○117,872 . . . . . . G3
Malloa ○9,742 . . . . G5
Marchigüe ○4,451 . . . . . F5
María Elena 5,900 . . . . . B3
María Pinto ○5,980 . . . . . G3
Maullín ○14,544 . . . . . . D4
Mejillones ○3,333 . . . . . A4
Melipilla 23,900 . . . . . . F4
Mincha ○11,329 . . . . . . A8
Molina 9,400 . . . . A10
Monte Patria ○18,927 . . . A8
Mulchén 13,700 . . . . . . E1
Nacimiento ○17,651 . . . . D1
Nancagua ○11,076 . . . . . F6
Navidad ○6,618 . . . . . . A10
Negreiros ○1,144 . . . . . . B2
Niquén ○13,640 . . . . E1
Nogales ○18,529 . . . . . . F2
Nueva Imperial 8,000 . . . . D2
Olivar Alto ○5,414 . . . . . G5
Ollagüe B3
Olmué ○8,804 . . . . F2
Osorno 68,800 . . . . D3
Ovalle 31,700 . . . . A8
Paihuano ○6,048 . . . . . . B8
Paillaco 5,200 . . . . D3
Paine ○21,876 . . . . G4
Palmilla ○7,965 . . . . F6
Panguipulli 5,700 . . . . . . E2
Panquehue ○4,230 . . . . . G2
Papudo ○2,594 . . . . A9
Paredones ○7,404 . . . . . A10
Parral 17,000 . . . . A11
Pedro de Valdivia 6,200 . . . B4
Pemuco ○7,577 . . . . E1
Peñaflor 15,500 . . . . G4
Penco ○33,962 . . . . D1
Petorca ○8,343 . . . . A9
Peumo ○11,308 . . . . F5
Pica ○1,487 . . . . B2
Pichidegua ○13,550 . . . . F5
Pichilemu ○8,042 . . . . . . A10
Pinto ○8,687 . . . . A11
Pisagua ○1,880 . . . . A2
Pitrufquén 7,800 . . . . . . D2
Placilla ○6,441 . . . . F6
Porvenir ○4,000 . . . . . . E10
Potrerillos 5,800 . . . . . . B6
Pozo Almonte ○1,798 . . . B2
Puchuncaví ○7,542 . . . . . F2
Pudahuel E2
Pueblo Hundido 6,200 . . . B6
Puente Alto 65,100 . . . . . B10
Puerto Aisén 17,848 . . . . E6
Puerto Cisnes ○2,800 . . . E5

Puerto Ingeniero
  Ibáñez ○1,900 . . . . . . E6
Puerto Montt 119,059 . . . . E4
Puerto Natales 17,280 . . . E9
Puerto Quellón ○7,734 . . . D4
Puerto Varas 10,900 . . . . E3
Puerto Williams ○949 . . . F11
Pumanque ○3,137 . . . . . F6
Punitaqui ○16,167 . . . . . A8
Punta Arenas 2,140 . . . . . E10
Purén ○11,604 . . . . D2
Purranque 5,900 . . . . . . D3
Putaendo ○12,806 . . . . . A9
Putre ○855 . . . . B1
Puyehue E3
Queilén ○6,055 . . . . D4
Quemchi ○6,707 . . . . . . D4
Quilicura 8,100 . . . . G3
Quillagua B3
Quilleco ○16,043 . . . . . . E1
Quillota 36,500 . . . . F2
Quilpué 40,600 . . . . F2
Quinta de Tilcoco ○6,513 . . G5
Quintero 9,900 . . . . F2
Quirihue ○11,178 . . . . . . E1
Rancagua 140,589 . . . . . G5
Renca ○67,168 . . . . G3
Rengo 12,400 . . . . G5
Requínoa ○10,730 . . . . . G5
Retiro ○15,146 . . . . A11
Rinconada San Martín
  ○4,118 . . . . G2
Río Blanco B9
Río Bueno 9,600 . . . . . . D3
Río Negro 5,100 . . . . . . D3
Río Verde ○554 . . . . E10
Rocas de Santo
  Domingo ○4,114 . . . . . F4
Rosario ○3,383 . . . . F5
Salamanca ○18,741 . . . . A9
Samo Alto ○5,689 . . . . . A8
San Antonio 46,700 . . . . . F3
San Bernardo ○117,766 . . G4
San Carlos 17,000 . . . . . E1
San Clemente ○23,273 . . . A11
San Felipe 26,100 . . . . . . G2
San Fernando 23,600 . . . . G6
San Francisco de
  Mostazal ○11,439 . . . . G4
San Ignacio ○13,523 . . . . E1
San Javier 10,800 . . . . . . A11
San José de
  Maipo ○9,601 . . . . . . B10
San Pablo ○7,978 . . . . . . D3
San Pedro ○8,255 . . . . . F4
San Pedro de Atacama . . . C4
San Rosendo ○14,337 . . . E1
Santa Bárbara ○14,345 . . . E1
Santa Cruz 8,600 . . . . . . F6
Santa María ○8,162 . . . . . G2
Santiago (cap.) 3,614,947 . G3
Santiago *3,672,374 . . . . . G3
San Vicente F4
San Vicente (San Vicente
  de Tagua Tagua) ○28,333 F5
Sierra Gorda ○8,805 . . . . B4
Talagante 16,500 . . . . . . G4
Talca 133,160 . . . . A11
Talcahuano 148,300 . . . . D1
Taltal 6,400 . . . . A5
Tamaya A8
Tarapacá B2
Temuco 197,232 . . . . . . E2
Teno ○17,675 . . . . A10
Termas de Cauquenes . . . B10
Tierra Amarilla ○7,899 . . . A6
Tiltil ○9,198 . . . . G2
Toco ○8,734 . . . . B3
Toconao C4
Tocopilla 22,000 . . . . . . A3
Tomé 29,600 . . . . D1
Toltén 16,265 . . . . D2
Traiguén 11,400 . . . . D2
Valdivia 115,536 . . . . . . D3
Vallenar 26,800 . . . . A7
Valparaíso 271,580 . . . . . E2

Victoria 16,500 . . . . D2
Vicuña 5,100 . . . . A8
Villa Alemana 29,600 . . . . F2
Villa Alhué ○5,078 . . . . . G4
Villarrica 25,091 . . . . . . E2
Viña del Mar 281,361 . . . . F2
Yumbel ○21,858 . . . . . . E1
Yungay ○10,725 . . . . . . E1
Zapallar ○2,894 . . . . A9
Zapiga B2

OTHER FEATURES

Aconcagua (riv.) F2
Aculeo (lag.) G4
Adventure (bay) D5
Aguas Calientes, Cerro (mt.) C4
Almirantazgo (bay) F11
Almirante Montt (gulf) D9
Ancud (gulf) D4
Angamos (isl.) D8
Angamos (pt.) A4
Ap Iwan, Cerro (mt.) E6
Arauco (gulf) D1
Arenales, Cerro (mt.) D7
Atacama (des.) B4
Atacama, Salar de
  (salt dep.) C4
Aucanquilcha, Cerro (mt.) . B3
Azapa, Quebrada (riv.) . . . B1
Baker (riv.) D7
Ballenero (chan.) E11
Bascuñán (cape) A7
Beagle (chan.) E11
Bella Vista, Salar de
  (salt dep.) B3
Benjamín (isl.) D5
Bío-Bío (riv.) E2
Blanca (lag.) E10
Blanco (lake) F10
Bravo (riv.) D7
Brunswick (pen.) E10
Bueno (riv.) D3
Buenos Aires (lake) E6
Byron (isl.) D7
Cachapoal (riv.) G5
Cachina, Quebrada (riv.) . . A5
Cachos (pt.) A6
Calafquén (lake) E3
Camarones (riv.) A2
Camiña, Quebrada (riv.) . . B2
Campana (riv.) D7
Campanario, Cerro (mt.) . . A10
Capitán Aracena (isl.) E10
Carmen (riv.) B7
Castillo, Cerro (mt.) E6
Catalina (pt.) F10
Chaffers (isl.) D5
Chaltel, Cerro (mt.) E8
Chañaral (isl.) A7
Chatham (isl.) D9
Chauques (isls.) D4
Cheap (chan.) D7
Chiloé (isl.) 119,286 . . . . D4
Choapa (riv.) A9
Chonos (arch.) D6
Choros (cape) A7
Cisnes (riv.) E5
Clarence (isl.) E10
Clemente (isl.) D6
Cochrane (lake) E7
Cochrane, Cerro (mt.) . . . E7
Cockburn (chan.) E11
Concepción (chan.) D9
Cónico, Cerro (mt.) E4
Contreras (isl.) D9
Cook (isl.) E11
Copiapó (bay) A6
Copiapó (riv.) A6
Corcovado (gulf) D4
Corcovado (vol.) D5
Coronados (gulf) D4
Curaumilla (pt.) E2
Darwin (bay) D6
Darwin, Cordillera (mts.) . . D8
Darwin, Cordillera (mts.) . . E11

(continued on following page)

Agriculture, Industry and Resources

DOMINANT LAND USE

Cereals, Livestock

Mediterranean Agriculture (cereals, fruit, livestock)

Pasture Livestock

Extensive Livestock Ranching

Limited Seasonal Grazing

Forests

Nonagricultural Land

MAJOR MINERAL OCCURRENCES

Ag Silver
Au Gold
C   Coal
Cu Copper
Fe Iron Ore
G   Natural Gas
Gp Gypsum

Hg Mercury
Id Iodine
Mn Manganese
Mo Molybdenum
N   Nitrates
Na Salt
O   Petroleum
S   Sulfur

⚡ Water Power   ▨ Major Industrial Areas

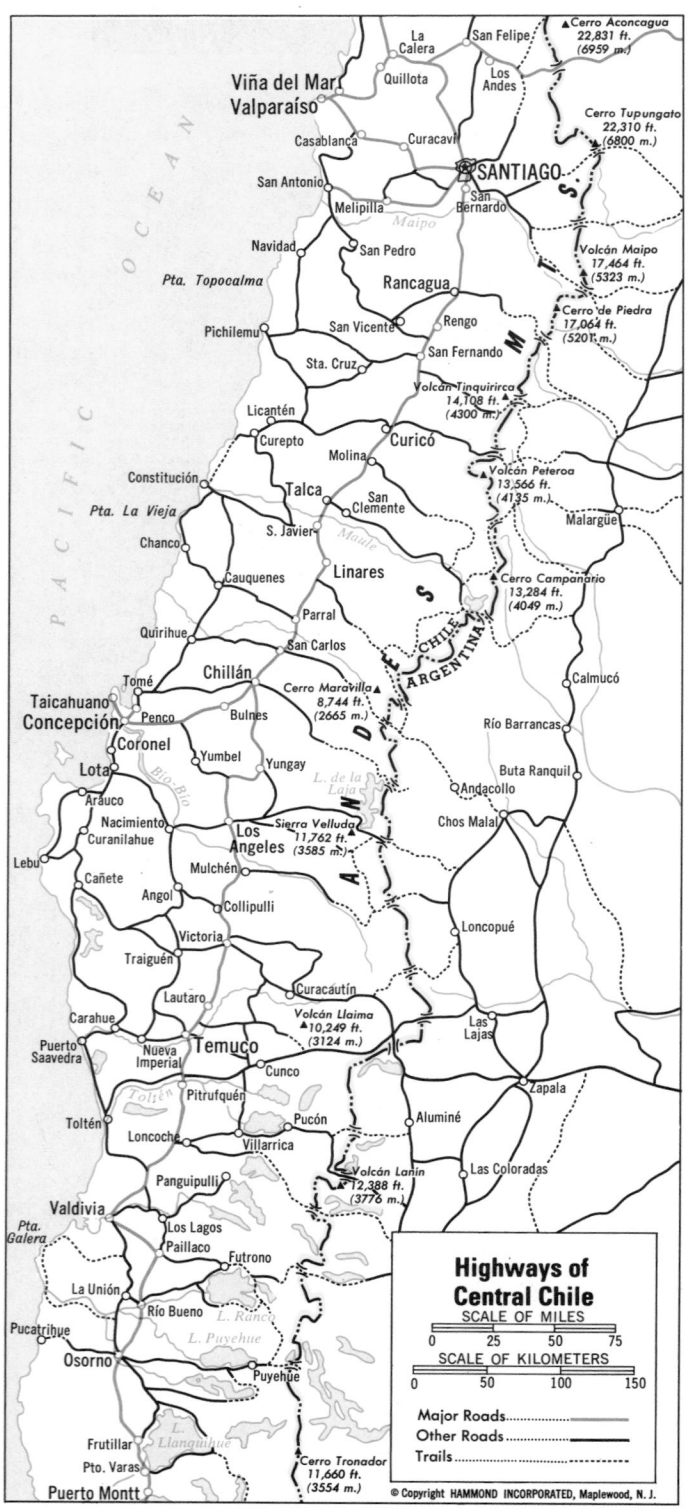

Highways of Central Chile

SCALE OF MILES

0 . . 25 . . 50 . . 75

SCALE OF KILOMETERS

0 . . 50 . . 100 . . 150

Major Roads . . . .
Other Roads . . . .
Trails . . . .

© Copyright HAMMOND INCORPORATED, Maplewood, N.J.

*City and suburbs.
○ Population of commune.

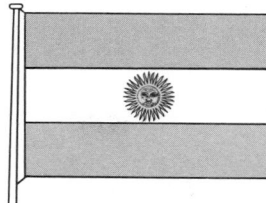

PROVINCES

Buenos Aires 10,796,036 ... D4
Catamarca 206,204 .... C2
Chaco 692,410 .... D2
Chubut 262,196 .... C5
Córdoba 2,407,135 .... D3
Corrientes 657,716 .... E2
Distrito Federal 2,908,001 . H7
Entre Ríos 902,241 .... E3
Formosa 292,479 .... D1
Jujuy 408,514 .... C1
La Pampa 207,132 .... C4
La Rioja 163,342 .... C2
Mendoza 1,187,305 ...... C4
Misiones 579,579 .... F2
Neuquén 241,904 .... C4
Río Negro 383,896 .... C5
Salta 662,369 .... D1
San Juan 469,973 .... C3
San Luis 212,837 .... C3
Santa Cruz 114,479 ..... C6
Santa Fe 2,457,188 ..... D3
Santiago del Estero 652,318 D2
Tierra del Fuego, Antártida,
e Islas del Atlántico
Sur 29,451 .... C7
Tucumán 968,066 .... C2

CITIES and TOWNS

Abra Pampa 2,929 ...... C1
Adolfo Alsina 7,707 ..... D4
Aguaray 4,802 .... D1
Aguilares 20,286 .... C2
Aimogasta 4,640 .... C2
Alberti 6,440 .... G7
Alcorta 5,818 .... F6
Algarrobo del Águila C4
Allen 14,041 .... C4
Alpachiri 1,657 .... D4
Alta Gracia 30,628 ..... D3
Aluminé 1,560 .... B4
Alvear 5,419 .... E2
Ameghino 2,775 ...... D3
Añatuya 15,025 ...... D2
Andalgalá 6,853 ...... C2
Antofagasta de la Sierra . C2
Apóstoles 11,252 ..... E2
Arrecifes 17,719 ..... F7
Arroyo Seco 12,886 ... F6
Ascensión 3,031 ..... F7
Avellaneda 330,654 ... G7
Ayacucho 12,363 .... E4
Azul 43,582 .... E4
Bahía Blanca 220,765 . D4
Bahía Bustamante C6
Bahía Thetis C7
Balcarce 28,985 .... E4
Balnearia 4,531 .... D3
Baradero 20,103 ... G6
Barrancas 3,602 ... F6
Barranqueras E2
Barreal 2,739 ..... C3
Basavilbaso 7,657 . G6
Belén 7,411 ...... C2

Bella Vista, Corrientes
14,229 .... E2
Bella Vista, Tucumán 9,177 . D2
Bell Ville 26,559 ...... D3
Bolívar 16,382 .... D4
Bovril 4,735 .... G5
Bragado 27,101 ...... F7
Buenos Aires (cap.)
2,908,001 .... H7
Buenos Aires *9,927,404 .. H7
Cafayate 5,048 ...... C2
Calafate B7
Calchaquí 5,958 .... F5
Caleta Olivia 20,141 . C6
Camarones C5
Campana 51,498 ... G6
Cañada de Gómez 24,706 . F6
Canals 6,627 ...... D3
Cañuelas 14,831 ... G7
Carcarañá 11,121 .. F6
Carlos Casares 13,286 . F7
Carlos Tejedor 4,421 . D4
Carmen de Areco 7,882 . F7
Carmen de Patagones
13,981 .... D5
Casilda 23,492 .... F6
Castelli 4,507 .... H7
Catamarca 88,432 . C2
Caucete 14,512 ... C3
Ceres 10,743 ..... D2
Coronda 11,554 ... F6
Coronel Brandsen 10,484 . H7
Coronel Dorrego 10,661 .. D4
Coronel Pringles 16,592 .. D4
Coronel Suárez 16,359 ... D4

Chamical 6,333 .... C3
Charadai 1,078 .... D2
Charata 13,070 .... D2
Chascomús 21,864 .... H7
Chepes 4,775 .... C3
Chicoana 1,844 ..... C2
Chilecito 14,010 .... C2
Chivilcoy 43,779 .... F7
Choele-Choel 6,191 .. C4
Chos-Malal 4,823 .. C4
Cinco Saltos 15,094 . C4
Cipolletti 40,123 ... C4
Clorinda 21,008 ... C2
Colón, Buenos Aires 16,070 . F6
Colón, Entre Ríos 11,648 .. G6
Colonia Las Heras 3,176 .. C6
Comandante Fontana 4,468 . D2
Comandante Luis Piedrabuena
2,492 .... C6
Comodoro Rivadavia 96,865 . C6
Concepción 29,359 .... C2
Concepción de
la Sierra 2,778 .... E2
Concepción del
Uruguay 46,065 ...... G6
Concordia 93,618 ...... G5
Constanza 1,313 ...... G6
Córdoba 982,018 ..... D3

Agriculture, Industry and Resources

DOMINANT LAND USE

Wheat, Livestock

Wheat, Corn, Livestock

Diversified Tropical Crops (chiefly plantation agriculture)

Truck Farming, Horticulture, Special Crops

Intensive Livestock Ranching

Upland Livestock Grazing, Limited Agriculture

Extensive Livestock Ranching

Forests

Nonagricultural Land

MAJOR MINERAL OCCURRENCES

Ag Silver
Be Beryl
C   Coal
Cu Copper
Fe Iron Ore
G   Natural Gas
Mn Manganese
Na Salt

O   Petroleum
Pb Lead
S   Sulfur
Sn Tin
U   Uranium
W   Tungsten
Zn Zinc

⚡ Water Power
▨ Major Industrial Areas

AREA 1,072,070 sq. mi. (2,776,661 sq. km.)
POPULATION 28,438,000
CAPITAL Buenos Aires
LARGEST CITY Buenos Aires
HIGHEST POINT Cerro Aconcagua 22,831 ft.
(6,959 m.)
MONETARY UNIT Argentine peso
MAJOR LANGUAGE Spanish
MAJOR RELIGION Roman Catholicism

Coronel Vidal 4,774 ...... E4
Corral de Bustos 8,613 ... D3
Corrientes 179,590 ...... E2
Cosquín 13,929 .... D3
Crespo 10,668 .... F6
Cruz del Eje 23,473 ... C3
Curuzú Cuatiá 24,955 .. G5
Cutral-Có 25,870 ..... C4
Daireaux 8,150 ...... D4
Deán Funes 16,306 .. D3
Diamante 13,464 ... F6
Dolavon 1,778 ..... C5
Dolores 19,307 .... E4
Eduardo Castex 5,397 . D4
El Bolsón 5,001 ... B5
Eldorado 22,821 .. F2
El Maitén 2,350 .. B5
Elortondo 4,939 . F6
El Quebrachal 2,202 . D2
Embarcación 9,016 . D1
Empedrado 4,732 .. E2
Escobar 70,829 ... G7
Esperanza 22,838 . F5
Esquel 17,228 ... B5
Esquina 10,380 . G5
Famatina 1,237 . C2
Federación 7,259 . G5
Felipe Yofré 1,140 . G4
Fernández 6,062 . D2
Fiambalá 1,201 . C2
Firmat 13,588 . F6
Formosa 95,067 . E2
Fortín Olmos 1,101 . F4
Frías 20,901 ... D2
Gaiman 2,651 .. C5
Gálvez 14,711 . F6
General Acha 7,647 . C4
General Alvear, Buenos Aires
5,481 .... F7
General Alvear,
Mendoza 21,250 ... C3
General Arenales 3,332 . F7
General Belgrano 10,909 . G7
General Conesa 3,566 ... C5
General Galarza 3,057 .. C6
General Güemes 15,534 . D1
General José de
San Martín 16,296 ... E2
General Juan Madariaga
13,409 .... E4
General La Madrid 5,154 . D4
General Las Heras 6,005 . G7
General Paz 5,127 .... H7
General Pico 30,180 ... D4
General Ramírez 5,393 . F6
General Roca 38,296 .. C4
General San Martín, Buenos
Aires 384,306 .... G7
General San Martín,
La Pampa 2,168 ... D4
General Viamonte 10,112 . F7
General Villegas 11,307 . D4
Gobernador Crespo 2,972 . F5
Godoy Cruz 141,553 .... C3
Goya 47,357 .... G4
Gualeguay 24,883 .... G6
Gualeguaychú 51,057 .. G6
Guandacol 1,351 .... C2
Hasenkamp 2,804 ... F5
Helvecia 3,927 .... F5
Hernandarias 3,002 . F5
Hernando 8,619 ... D3
Huinca Renancó 7,187 . D3
Humahuaca 3,963 ... C1
Humberto (Humberto
Primo) 4,163 ..... F5
Ibarreta 5,262 ... D2
Ibicuy 3,082 .... G6
Ingeniero Huergo 3,385 . C4
Ingeniero Jacobacci 4,045 . C5
Ingeniero Luiggi 3,002 . D4
Intendente Alvear 3,640 . D4
Itatí 3,269 ...... E2

Ituzaingó 8,687 .... E2
Jáchal 8,832 .... C3
Jesús María 17,594 .... D3
Joaquín V. González 6,054 . D2
Juárez 11,798 ...... E4
Jujuy 124,487 ...... C1
Junín 62,080 ...... F7
Junín de los Andes 5,638 . B4
La Banda 46,994 ... D2
Laboulaye 16,883 . D3
La Carlota 8,614 . D3
La Cruz 4,132 ... E2
La Cumbre 6,110 . C3
La Falda 12,502 . D3
Laguna Paiva 11,129 . F5
Lanús 465,891 ... H7
La Paz, Entre Ríos 14,920 . G5
La Paz, Mendoza 4,604 .. C3
La Plata 560,341 .... H7
Laprida 6,495 ..... D4
La Quiaca 8,289 ... C1
La Rioja 66,826 .. C2
Larroque 3,147 .. F5
Las Flores 18,287 . F7
Las Lomitas 4,047 . D1
Las Palmas 5,061 . E2
Las Parejas 7,430 . F6
Las Rosas 9,725 . F6
Las Varillas 10,605 . D3
La Toma 4,325 .. C3
Lincoln 19,009 . F7
Loberia 8,898 . E4
Lobos 20,798 . G7
Lomas de Zamora 508,620 . G7
Lucas González 3,015 ... G6
Luján 38,919 .... G7
Lules 11,391 ... C2
Maciel 4,066 .. F6
Magdalena 7,135 . H7
Maipú 7,289 .. E4
Malabrigo 3,294 . F4
Malargüe 9,496 . C4
Maquinchao 1,299 . C5
Marcos Juárez 19,827 . D3
Mar del Plata 407,024 . E4
Máximo Paz 3,216 ... F6
Mburucuyá 3,044 .. E2
Médanos 4,511 .. D4
Mendoza 596,796 . C3
Mercedes, Buenos Aires
46,581 .... G7
Mercedes, Corrientes
20,603 ...... G4
Mercedes, San Luis 50,856 . C3
Merlo 293,059 ... G7
Metán 18,928 .. D2
Miramar 15,473 . E4
Monte Caseros 18,247 . G5
Monte Quemado 4,707 . D2
Monteros 15,832 .. C2
Morón 596,769 ... G7
Morteros 11,456 . D3
Navarro 7,176 .. G7
Necochea 50,939 . E4
Neuquén 90,037 . C4
Nogoyá 15,862 .. F6
Ñorquincó B5
Nueve de Julio 26,608 . F7
Oberá 27,311 .... F2
Olavarría 63,686 . D4
Oliva 9,231 .... D3
Palo Santo 3,088 . E2
Paraná 159,581 .. F5
Paso de Los Libres 24,112 . E2
Pedro Luro 3,142 ... D4
Pehuajó 25,613 ... D4
Pellegrini 3,940 .. D4
Pergamino 68,989 . F6
Pico Truncado 9,626 . C6
Pigüé 10,793 ... D4
Pilar 3,805 ... F5
Pirané 9,039 . E2
Plaza Huincul 7,988 . B4

(continued on following page)

(continued)

Posadas 139,941 .... E2
Presidencia de la Plaza 4,904 .... D2
Presidencia Roque Sáenz Peña 49,261 .... D2
Puán 4,148 .... D4
Puerto Deseado 4,017 .... D6
Puerto Harberton C7
Puerto Iguazú 10,250 .... F2
Puerto Madryn 20,709 .... C5
Puerto Rico 8,195 .... D1
Punta Alta 54,375 .... D4
Quequén 11,737 .... E4
Quimili 8,972 .... D2
Quines 3,352 .... C3
Quitilipi 9,937 .... D2
Rafaela 53,132 .... F5
Ramallo 8,248 .... F6
Rauch 8,348 .... E4
Rawson 12,981 .... D5
Reconquista 32,442 .... F4
Recreo 3,502 .... C2
Resistencia 218,438 .... E2
Rinconada C1
Río Colorado 7,361 .... D4
Río Cuarto 110,148 .... D3
Río Gallegos 43,479 .... C7
Río Grande 13,271 .... C7
Río Segundo 12,839 .... D3
Río Tercero 34,735 .... D3
Rivadavia 10,953 .... C3
Rojas 14,247 .... F7
Romang 4,017 .... F4
Roque Pérez 5,434 .... G7
Rosario 954,606 .... F6
Rosario de la Frontera 13,531 .... D2
Rosario de Lerma 9,540 .... C1
Rosario del Tala 9,552 .... G6
Rufino 15,306 .... D3
Saladas 7,345 .... E2
Saladillo 14,806 .... G7
Salliqueló 5,479 .... D4
Salta 260,323 .... C1
Salto 18,462 .... F7
San Antonio de Areco 12,932 .... G7
San Antonio de los Cobres 2,357 .... C1
San Antonio Oeste 8,690 .... C5
San Carlos 7,613 .... F6
San Carlos de Bariloche 48,222 .... B5
San Cayetano 5,960 .... E4
San Cristóbal 13,345 .... F5
San Fernando 128,939 .... G7
San Francisco, Córdoba 58,616 .... D3
San Francisco, San Luis 2,448 .... C3
San Genaro 2,977 .... F6
San Ignacio 3,437 .... E2
San Jaime de la Frontera 2,811 .... G5
San Javier 7,557 .... F5
San José de Feliciano 4,986 .... G5
San Juan 290,479 .... C3
San Julián 4,278 .... C6
San Justo 14,135 .... F5
San Luis 70,632 .... C3
San Martín 29,746 .... C3
San Martín de los Andes 9,507 .... C5
San Miguel del Monte 8,414 .... G7
San Miguel de Tucumán 496,914 .... D2
San Nicolás 96,313 .... F6
San Pedro, Buenos Aires 27,058 .... F6
San Pedro, Jujuy 36,907 .... D1
San Rafael 70,477 .... C3
San Ramón de la Nva. Orán 32,955 .... D1
San Salvador 4,342 .... G5
San Sebastián C7
Santa Cruz 2,353 .... C7
Santa Elena 14,655 .... F5
Santa Fe 287,240 .... F5
Santa Lucía 4,452 .... E2
Santa María 5,380 .... C2
Santa Rosa, Córdoba 4,306 .... D3
Santa Rosa, La Pampa 51,689 .... C4
Santa Rosa, San Luis 2,878 .... C3
Santa Victoria D1
Santiago del Estero 148,357 .... D2
Santo Tomé, Corrientes 14,352 .... E2
Santo Tomé, Santa Fe 35,363 .... F5
Sarmiento 6,313 .... B6
Sauce 4,677 .... G5
Sierra Grande 9,585 .... C5
Suipacha 4,505 .... G7
Sunchales 12,493 .... F5
Suncho Corral 3,837 .... D2
Tafí Viejo 26,625 .... C2
Tandil 78,821 .... E4
Tapalquén 5,356 .... E4
Tartagal 31,367 .... D1
Tigre 199,366 .... G7
Tinogasta 7,829 .... C2
Toay 3,617 .... D4
Tornquist 4,696 .... D4
Tostado 10,492 .... D2
Trelew 52,073 .... C5
Trenque Lauquen 22,504 .... D4
Tres Arroyos 42,118 .... D4
Trevelín 2,935 .... B5
Tunuyán 14,665 .... C3
Urdinarrain 5,472 .... G6
Ushuaia 10,988 .... C7
Valcheta 2,994 .... C5
Vedia 6,273 .... F7
Veinticinco de Mayo 18,936 .... F7
Venado Tuerto 46,775 .... D3
Vera 13,555 .... F5
Verónica 5,657 .... H7
Viale 5,635 .... F5
Vicente López 289,815 .... G7
Victoria 18,883 .... F6
Victorica 3,895 .... C4
Vicuña Mackenna 5,665 .... D3
Viedma 24,338 .... D5
Villa Ángela 25,586 .... D2
Villa Atuel 2,774 .... C3
Villa Cañas 7,303 .... F6
Villa Constitución 36,157 .... F6
Villa del Rosario 10,133 .... D3
Villa Dolores 21,508 .... C3
Villa Elisa 4,106 .... G6
Villa Federal 9,222 .... G5
Villaguay 18,699 .... G5
Villa Guillermina 2,971 .... D2
Villa Huidobro 4,154 .... D3
Villa María 67,490 .... D3
Villa María Grande 4,517 .... F5
Villa Nueva 4,604 .... C3
Villa Ocampo 9,162 .... D2
Villa Regina 14,017 .... C4
Villa San José 6,800 .... G6
Villa San Martín 6,237 .... D2
Vinchina 1,070 .... C2
Zapala 18,293 .... B4
Zárate 65,504 .... G6
Zavalla 3,800 .... F6

OTHER FEATURES

Aconcagua, Cerro (mt.) C3
Andes, Cordillera de los (mts.) C2
Argentino (lake) B7
Arizaro, Salar de (salt dep.) C2
Arrecifes (riv.) G6
Atacama, Puna de (reg.) C2
Atuel (riv.) C4
Bermejo (riv.) E2
Blanca (bay) D4
Brazo Sur, Pilcomayo (riv.) E1
Buenos Aires (lake) B6
Campanario, Cerro (mt.) C4
Chaco Austral (reg.) D2
Chaco Central (reg.) D1
Chico (riv.) C5
Chico (riv.) C6
Chubut (riv.) C5
Colhué Huapi (lake) C6
Colorado (riv.) D4
Cónico, Cerro (mt.) B5
Corrientes (riv.) E2
Coyle (riv.) B7
Delgada (pt.) D5
Desaguadero (riv.) C3
Deseado (riv.) C6
Diamante (riv.) C3
Domuyo (vol.) B4
Dos Bahías (cape)) D5
Dulce (riv.) D2
Dungeness (pt.) C7
El Chocón (res.) C4
Estados, Los (isl.) D7
Fagnano (lake) C7
Famatina, Sierra de (mts.) C2
Feliciano (riv.) G5
Gallegos (riv.) B7
General Manuel Belgrano, Cerro (mt.) C2
Gran Chaco (reg.) D1
Grande (bay) C7
Grande (falls) E3
Grande de Tierra del Fuego (isl.) C7
Gualeguay (riv.) G5
Guayaquilaró (riv.) G5
Iguazú (falls) F2
Iguazú Nat'l Park E2
Lanín (vol.) B4
Lanín Nat'l Park B4
Lechiguanas (isls.) G6
Lennox (isl.) C8
Limay (riv.) C4
Llancanelo, Salina y Laguna (salt lake) C4
Llullaillaco (vol.) C1
Magallenes (Magellan) (str.) C7
Maipo (vol.) C3
Mar Chiquita (lake) D3
Mendoza (riv.) C3
Mercedario, Cerro (mt.) B3
Mogotes (pt.) E4
Montemayor (plat.) C5
Nahuel Huapi (lake) B5
Nahuel Huapi Nat'l Park B5
Negro (riv.) D4
Neuquén (riv.) C4
Ninfas (pt.) D5
Norte (pt.) D5
Nuevo (gulf) D5
Ojos del Salado, Cerro (mt.) C2
Pampa de las Tres Hermanas (plain) C6
Pampas (plain) D4
Paraná (riv.) E2
Patagonia (reg.) C5
Peteroa (vol.) B4
Pilcomayo (riv.) E1
Pissis (mt.) C2
Plata, Río de la (est.) E4
Pueyrredón (lake) B6
Puna de Atacama (reg.) C2
Quinto (riv.) D3
Rincón, Cerro (mt.) C1
Saladillo (riv.) D2
Salado (riv.) C4
Salado (riv.) H7
Salado del Norte (riv.) D2
Salí (riv.) C2
Salto (riv.) F7
Samborombón (bay) E4
San Antonio (cape) E4
San Diego (cape) D7
San Jorge (gulf) C6
San Juan (riv.) C3
San Lorenzo, Cerro (mt.) B6
San Martín (lake) B6
San Matías (gulf) D5
Santa Cruz (riv.) B7
Senguerr (riv.) B6
Staten (Los Estados) (isl.) D7
Tarija (riv.) D1
Tercero (riv.) D3
Teuco (riv.) D1
Tierra del Fuego, Grande de (isl.) C7
Toro, Cerro del (mt.) B2
Tres Puntas (cape) D6
Trinidad (isl.) D4
Tronador (mt.) B5
Tunuyán (riv.) C3
Tupungato, Cerro (mt.) B3
Uruguay (riv.) E3
Valdés (pen.) D5
Viedma (lake) B6
Zapaleri, Cerro (mt.) C1

Topography

0 150 300 MI.
0 150 300 KM.

5,000 m. 16,404 ft. | 2,000 m. 6,562 ft. | 1,000 m. 3,281 ft. | 500 m. 1,640 ft. | 200 m. 656 ft. | 100 m. 328 ft. | Sea Level | Below

Highways of Central Argentina

MILES 0 25 50 75
KILOMETRES 0 50 100 150

Major Roads
Other Roads

FALKLAND ISLANDS

CITIES and TOWNS

Stanley (cap.) 1,050 .... E7

OTHER FEATURES

Adventure (sound) E7
Choiseul (sound) E7
East Falkland (isl.) 1,491 .... E7
Falkland (isls.) D7
Falkland (sound) D7
George (isl.) E7
Jason (isls.) D7
Lively (isl.) E7
Malvinas (Falkland) (isls.) D7
Pebble (isl.) E7
Saunders (isl.) E7
Weddel (isl.) D7
West Falkland (isl.) 322 .... D7

*City and suburbs.

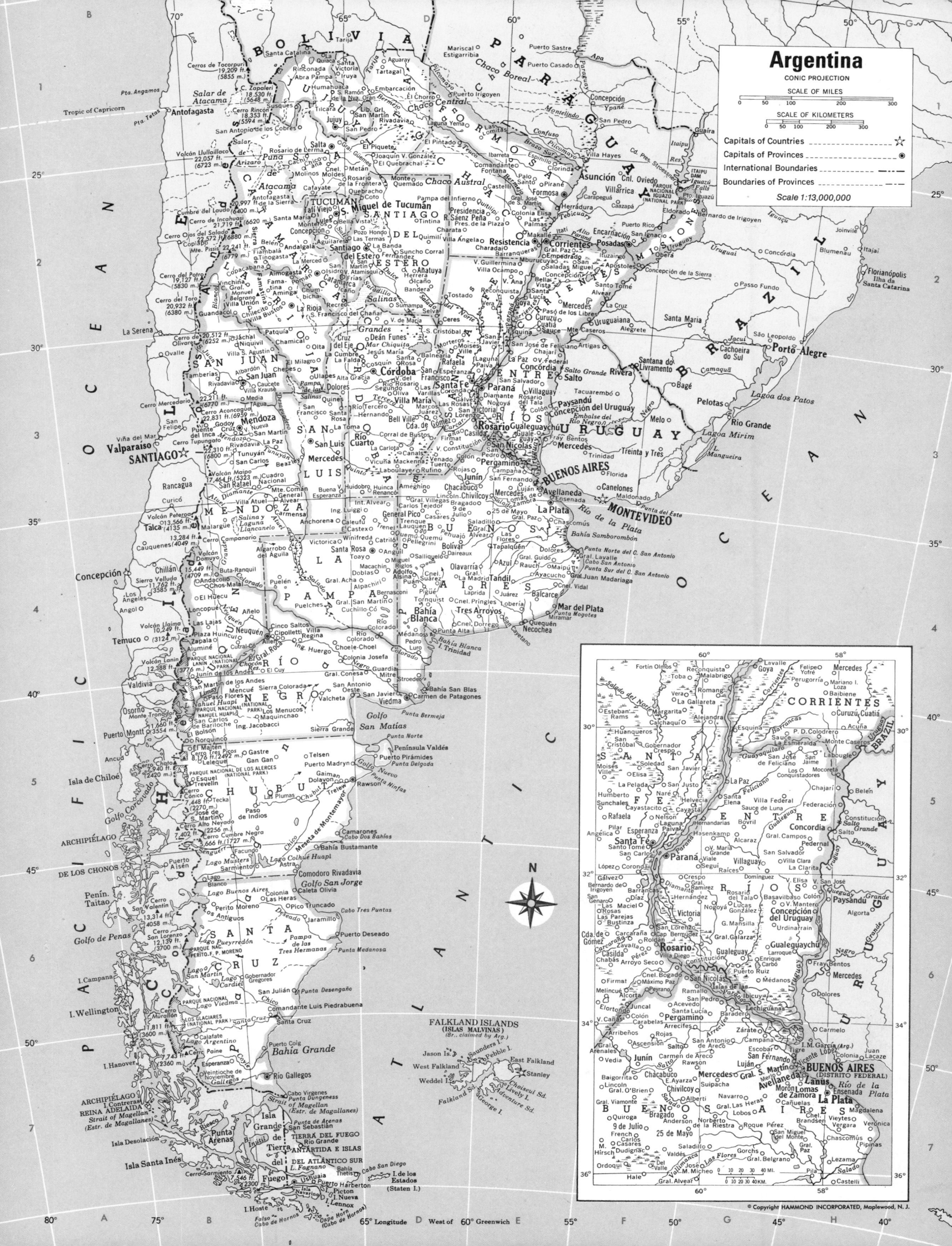

Argentina
CONIC PROJECTION
SCALE OF MILES
0 50 100 200 300
SCALE OF KILOMETERS
0 50 100 200 300
Capitals of Countries
Capitals of Provinces
International Boundaries
Boundaries of Provinces
Scale 1:13,000,000
BOLIVIA
PARAGUAY
URUGUAY
BRAZIL
CHILE
PACIFIC OCEAN
ATLANTIC OCEAN
JUJUY
SALTA
FORMOSA
CHACO
TUCUMÁN
SANTIAGO DEL ESTERO
CATAMARCA
LA RIOJA
SAN JUAN
CÓRDOBA
SANTA FE
CORRIENTES
MISIONES
ENTRE RÍOS
SAN LUIS
MENDOZA
BUENOS AIRES
LA PAMPA
NEUQUÉN
RÍO NEGRO
CHUBUT
SANTA CRUZ
TIERRA DEL FUEGO, ANTÁRTIDA E ISLAS DEL ATLÁNTICO SUR
Tropic of Capricorn
Antofagasta
Asunción
Resistencia
Corrientes
Posadas
S. Miguel de Tucumán
Santiago del Estero
Catamarca
La Rioja
San Juan
Córdoba
Santa Fe
Paraná
Rosario
Mendoza
San Luis
Valparaíso
SANTIAGO
BUENOS AIRES
MONTEVIDEO
La Plata
Santa Rosa
Neuquén
Viedma
Rawson
Río Gallegos
Ushuaia
Porto Alegre
Mar del Plata
Bahía Blanca
Golfo San Matías
Golfo San Jorge
Bahía Grande
Río de la Plata
Strait of Magellan (Estr. de Magallanes)
FALKLAND ISLANDS (ISLAS MALVINAS) (Br., claimed by Arg.)
West Falkland
East Falkland
Stanley
Isla de Chiloé
I. Wellington
Cape Horn (Cabo de Hornos)
I. de los Estados (Staten I.)
65° Longitude West of 60° Greenwich
CORRIENTES
SANTA FE
ENTRE RÍOS
BUENOS AIRES
BUENOS AIRES (DISTRITO FEDERAL)
Concepción del Uruguay
Gualeguaychú
Paysandú
Rosario
Santa Fé
Paraná
0 10 20 30 40 MI.
0 10 20 30 40 KM.
© Copyright HAMMOND INCORPORATED, Maplewood, N. J.

Paraguay

CONIC PROJECTION

SCALE OF MILES
0 20 40 60 80 100 120 140

SCALE OF KILOMETERS
0 20 40 60 80 100 120 140

Capitals of Countries .... ★
Capitals of Departments .... ◉
International Boundaries .... — ·· —
Department Boundaries .... — · —

Scale 1:6,740,000

© Copyright HAMMOND INCORPORATED, Maplewood, N.J.

PARAGUAY

DEPARTMENTS

Alto Paraguay	C2
Alto Paraná	E4
Amambay	D3
Asunción	A4
Boquerón	B3
Caaguazú	D-E4
Caazapá	D-E5
Canendiyu	E4
Central	D4
Chaco	B-C2
Concepción	D3
Cordillera	D4
Guairá	D4
Itapúa	E5
Misiones	D5
Ñeembucú	C-D5
Nueva Asunción	B2
Paraguarí	D4-5
Presidente Hayes	C3
San Pedro	D4-5

CITIES and TOWNS

Abaí 1,507	E4
Acahay 1,937	B5
Alberdi 2,346	D5
Altos 1,441	B4
Antequera 1,281	D4
Aregua 3,941	B4
Arroyos y Esteros 1,253	B4
Asunción (cap.) 387,676	A4
Atyrá 1,427	B4
Ayolas 309	D5
Belén 1,219	D3
Bella Vista 3,101	D3
Bella Vista 1,421	E5
Benjamín Aceval 2,877	C4
Buena Vista 1,353	D5
Caacupé 7,278	B5
Caaguazú 7,950	D4
Caapucú 1,400	B5
Caazapá 3,132	D5
Caballero 1,225	B4
Capiatá 2,827	B4
Capitán Bado 915	E3
Capitán Meza 375	E5
Caraguatay 1,439	B4
Carapeguá 3,416	B5
Carayaí 1,190	C4
Carmen del Paraná 1,980	D5
Cerrito 958	C4
Ciudad Presidente Stroessner 7,085	E4
Concepción 19,392	D3
Coronel Bogado 3,973	D5
Coronel Martínez 1,598	B5
Coronel Oviedo 13,786	D4
Curuguaty 1,112	E4
Desmochados 551	C5
Doctor Cecilio Báez 1,300	D4
Doctor Juan L. Mallorquín 1,913	E4
Doctor Juan Manuel Frutos 1,494	E4
Doctor M. Irala 468	E4
Emboscada 1,222	B4
Encarnación 23,343	E5
Escobar 548	B5
Eusebio Ayala 4,328	B4
Fernando de la Mora 36,834	A4
Filadelfia 1,438	B3
Fram 1,090	E5
Fuerte Olimpo 3,063	C2
General Artigas 3,542	D5
General Elizardo Aquino 1,304	D4
General Eugenio A. Garay 740	A2
Guarambaré 3,640	B5
Hernandarias 3,898	E4
Hohenau 1,121	E5
Horqueta 4,328	D3
Hugo Stroessner 536	C4
Humaitá 938	C5
Isla Pucú 1,766	B4
Isla Umbú 236	C5
Itá 7,041	B5
Itacurubí 1,997	B5
Itacurubí del Rosario 2,467	D4
Itapé 1,376	D5
Itaquyry	E4
Itaugua 3,767	B5
Iturbe 3,413	E5
Jesús 1,495	E5
Juan de Mena 1,027	D4
La Colmena 1,804	B5
Lambaré 31,656	A4
Laureles 435	D5
Lima 1,098	D4
Limpio 2,219	B4
Loreto 1,258	D3
Luque 13,921	B4
Maciel 376	D5
Mariano Roque Alonso 1,492	A4
Mariscal Estigarribia 3,150	B3
Mayor Martínez 324	C5

Mayor Pablo Lagerenza	B1
Mbocayaty 925	C5
Mbuyapey 1,560	E5
Ñacunday 380	E5
Natalicio Talavera 1,228	D4
Nueva Germania 572	D3
Nueva Italia 1,517	B5
Numí 941	B5
Paraguarí 5,036	B5
Paso de Patria 698	C5
Pedro Juan Caballero 21,033	E3
Pilar 12,506	C5
Pirayú 2,698	B5
Piribebuy 4,497	B4
Primero de Marzo 696	B4
Puerto Casado 4,078	C3
Puerto Guaraní 302	C2
Puerto Pinasco 5,477	C3
Puerto Presidente Franco 4,152	E4
Puerto Sastre 160	C2
Quiindy 2,664	B5
Quyquyó 928	B5
Roque González de Santa Cruz 1,375	B5
Rosario 4,165	D4
Salto del Guairá	E3
San Antonio 4,906	A4
San Bernardino 949	B4
San Cosme y Damián 602	D5
San Estanislao 4,753	D4
San Ignacio 6,116	D5
San Joaquín 536	E4
San José 3,102	D5
San Juan Bautista 6,457	D5
San Juan Bautista de Ñeembucú 688	C5
San Juan Nepomuceno 2,974	E5
San Lázaro 1,767	C2
San Lorenzo 11,616	B4
San Miguel 1,030	D5
San Patricio 1,130	D5
San Pedro 3,186	D3
San Pedro del Paraná 2,723	D5
San Salvador 1,393	C5
Santa Elena 1,439	C5
Santa María 793	D5
Santa Rosa 3,736	D5
Santiago 1,265	D5
Sapucaí 1,864	B5
Tacuaras 193	C5
Tacuatí 836	D3
Tavaí 472	D5
Tebicuary MI 183	C5
Tobatí 4,983	B4
Trinidad 837	D5
Unión 1,286	D4
Valenzuela 1,108	B5
Valle Mi 1,318	D3
25 de Diciembre 439	D4
Villa Florida 1,261	C5
Villa Franca 359	C5
Villa Hayes 4,749	A4
Villa Oliva 564	C5
Villarrica 17,687	D4
Villeta 3,156	A5
Yabebyry 797	C5
Yaguarón 3,368	B5
Yataity 1,159	D4
Ybycuí 1,736	B5
Ybytymí 816	B5
Yegros 1,051	D5
Ygatimí 996	E4
Yhú 964	D4
Ypacaraí 5,195	B5
Ypané 1,474	A5
Ypé Jhú 645	D4
Yuty 2,392	D5

OTHER FEATURES

Acaray (riv.)	E4
Alto Paraná (riv.)	D5
Amambay, Cordillera de (mts.)	D3
Apa (riv.)	D3
Aquidabán (riv.)	D3
Chaco Boreal (reg.)	B2-3
Chovoreca (mt.)	C1
Confuso (riv.)	C4
Coronel F. Cabrera (mt.)	B1
González, Riacho (riv.)	C4
Gran Chaco (reg.)	B2-3
Iguazú (falls)	E4
Itaipú (res.)	E4
Jara (hill)	C3
Mbaracayú, Cordillera de (mts.)	E3
Monday (riv.)	E4
Montelindo (riv.)	C3
Mosquito, Riacho (riv.)	C3
Negro (riv.)	C3
Paraguay (riv.)	D4
Pilcomayo (riv.)	C4
Tebicuary (riv.)	C5
Timane (riv.)	B2
Vera (lag.)	D5
Verde (riv.)	C4

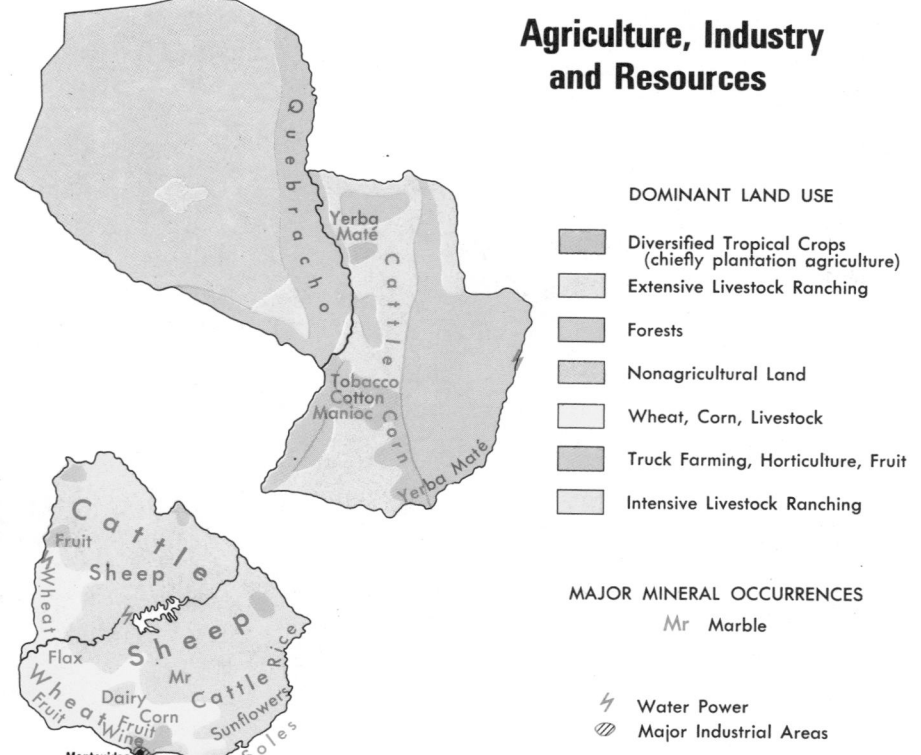

Agriculture, Industry and Resources

DOMINANT LAND USE

- Diversified Tropical Crops (chiefly plantation agriculture)
- Extensive Livestock Ranching
- Forests
- Nonagricultural Land
- Wheat, Corn, Livestock
- Truck Farming, Horticulture, Fruit
- Intensive Livestock Ranching

MAJOR MINERAL OCCURRENCES

Mr Marble

⚡ Water Power

⚙ Major Industrial Areas

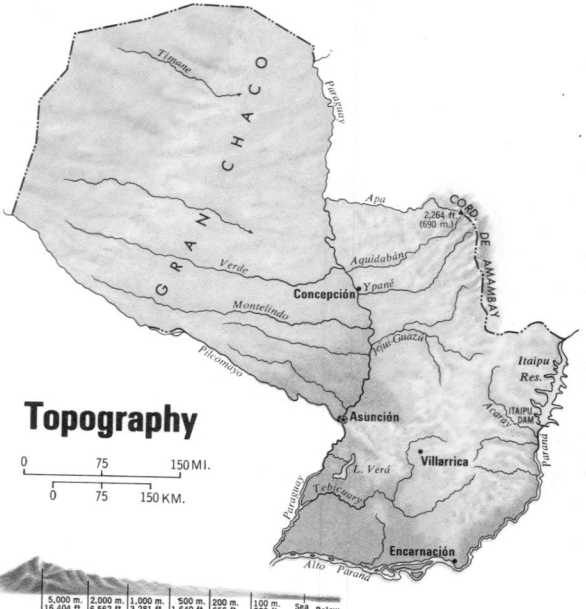

Topography

0   75   150 MI.
0   75   150 KM.

| 5,000 m. 16,404 ft. | 2,000 m. 6,562 ft. | 1,000 m. 3,281 ft. | 500 m. 1,640 ft. | 200 m. 656 ft. | 100 m. 328 ft. | Sea Level Below |

PARAGUAY

AREA 157,047 sq. mi. (406,752 sq. km.)
POPULATION 2,973,000
CAPITAL Asunción
LARGEST CITY Asunción
HIGHEST POINT Amambay Range
  2,264 ft. (690 m.)
MONETARY UNIT guaraní
MAJOR LANGUAGES Spanish, Guaraní
MAJOR RELIGION Roman Catholicism

URUGUAY

AREA 72,172 sq. mi. (186,925 sq. km.)
POPULATION 2,899,000
CAPITAL Montevideo
LARGEST CITY Montevideo
HIGHEST POINT Mirador Nacional 1,644 ft.
  (501 m.)
MONETARY UNIT Uruguayan peso
MAJOR LANGUAGE Spanish
MAJOR RELIGION Roman Catholicism

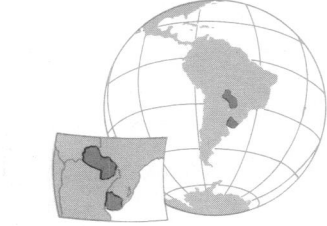

PARAGUAY

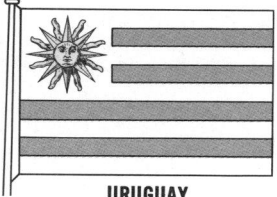

URUGUAY

Topography

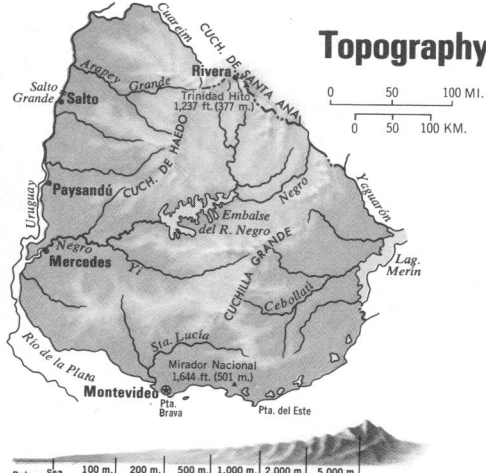

| Below Sea Level | 100 m. 328 ft. | 200 m. 656 ft. | 500 m. 1,640 ft. | 1,000 m. 3,281 ft. | 2,000 m. 6,562 ft. | 5,000 m. 16,404 ft. |

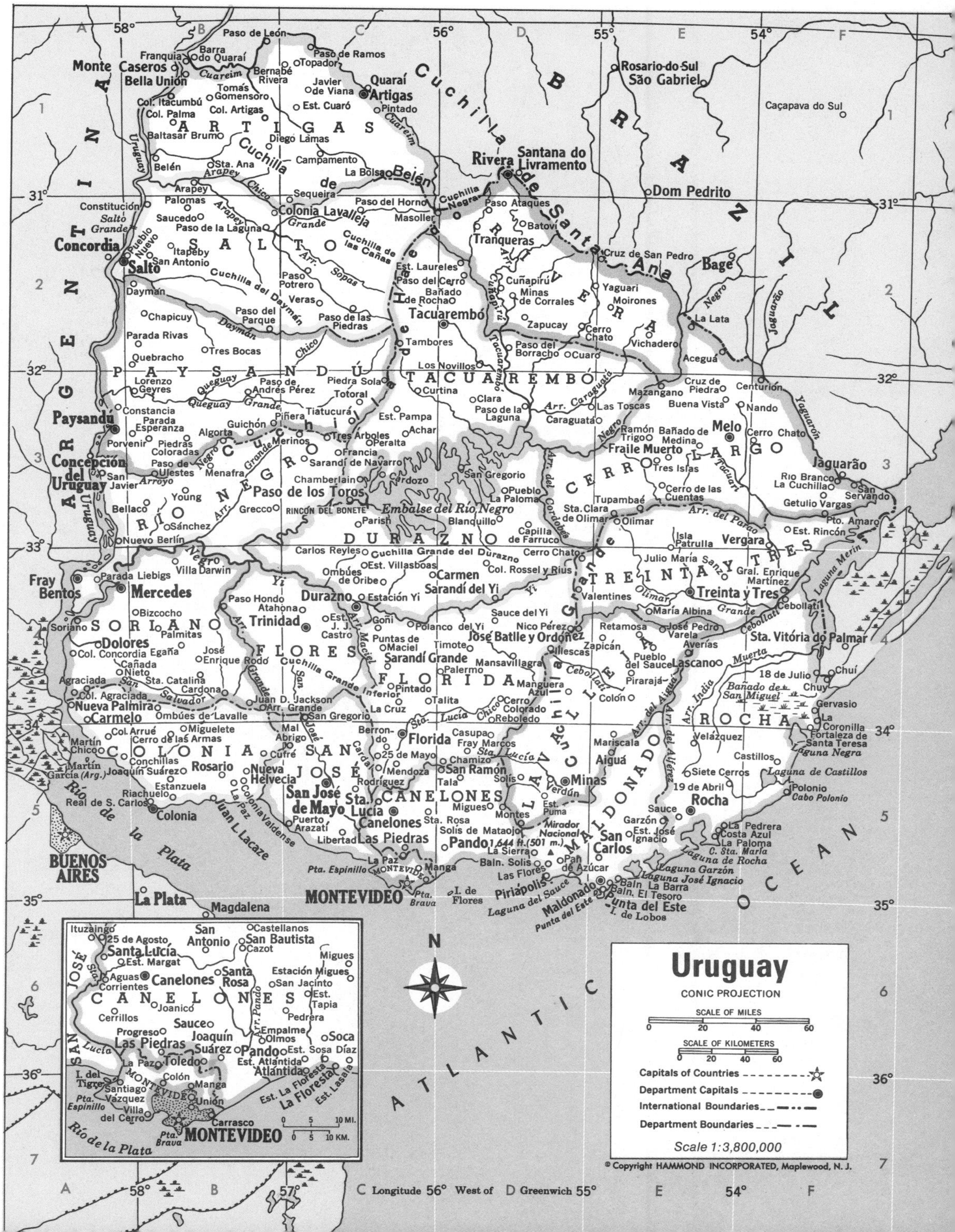

Uruguay

CONIC PROJECTION

SCALE OF MILES

SCALE OF KILOMETERS

Capitals of Countries ....☆
Department Capitals ....●
International Boundaries .....
Department Boundaries ......

Scale 1:3,800,000

® Copyright HAMMOND INCORPORATED, Maplewood, N.J.

North America

LAMBERT AZIMUTHAL EQUAL-AREA PROJECTION

MILES
0 100 200 400 600 800

KILOMETERS
0 100 200 400 600 800

Capitals of Countries .... ⊛
Other Capitals .... ⊙
International Boundaries .... ———
Other Boundaries .... —·—·—

Scale 1:36,600,000

© Copyright HAMMOND INCORPORATED, Maplewood, N.J.

Population Distribution

AREA 9,363,000 sq. mi. (24,250,170 sq. km.)
POPULATION 370,000,000
LARGEST CITY New York
HIGHEST POINT Mt. McKinley 20,320 ft. (6,194 m.)
LOWEST POINT Death Valley -282 ft. (-86 m.)

Vegetation

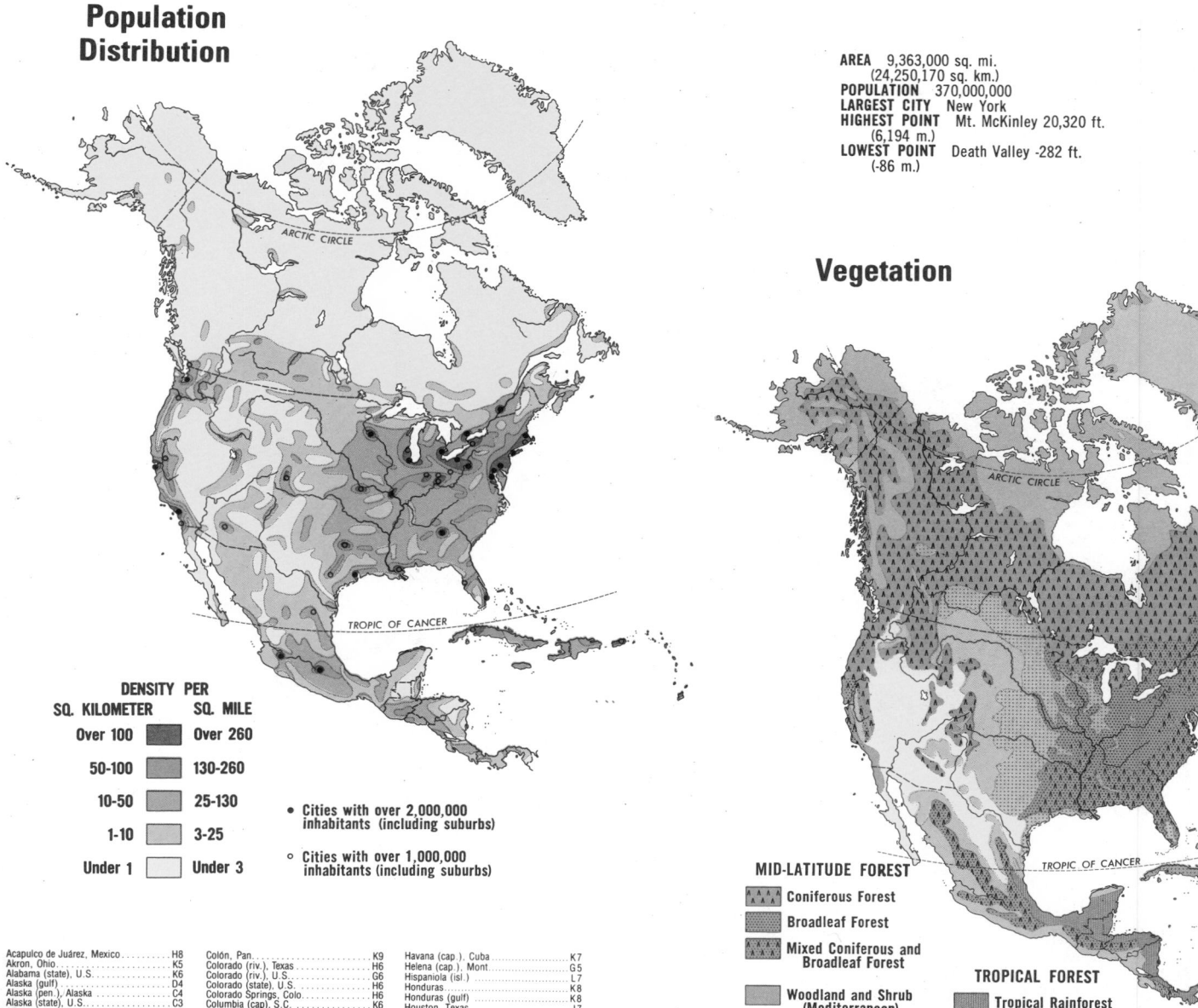

DENSITY PER

SQ. KILOMETER	SQ. MILE
Over 100	Over 260
50-100	130-260
10-50	25-130
1-10	3-25
Under 1	Under 3

• Cities with over 2,000,000 inhabitants (including suburbs)
○ Cities with over 1,000,000 inhabitants (including suburbs)

MID-LATITUDE FOREST
Coniferous Forest
Broadleaf Forest
Mixed Coniferous and Broadleaf Forest
Woodland and Shrub (Mediterranean)

MID-LATITUDE GRASSLAND
Short Grass (Steppe)
Tall Grass (Prairie)

TROPICAL FOREST
Tropical Rainforest
Light Tropical Forest

TROPICAL GRASSLAND
Wooded Savanna

DESERT AND DESERT SHRUB

TUNDRA AND ALPINE

PERMANENT ICE

Average January Temperature

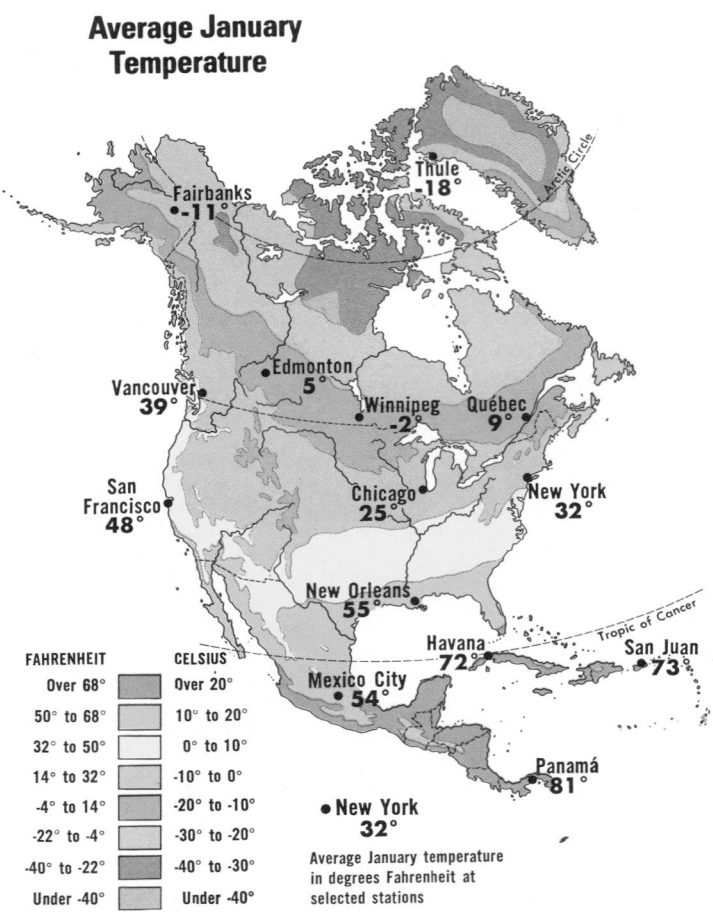

Thule -18°
Fairbanks -11°
Vancouver 39°
Edmonton 5°
Winnipeg -2°
Québec 9°
San Francisco 48°
Chicago 25°
New York 32°
New Orleans 55°
Havana 72°
San Juan 73°
Mexico City 54°
Panamá 81°

FAHRENHEIT	CELSIUS
Over 68°	Over 20°
50° to 68°	10° to 20°
32° to 50°	0° to 10°
14° to 32°	-10° to 0°
-4° to 14°	-20° to -10°
-22° to -4°	-30° to -20°
-40° to -22°	-40° to -30°
Under -40°	Under -40°

● **New York 32°**
Average January temperature in degrees Fahrenheit at selected stations

Average July Temperature

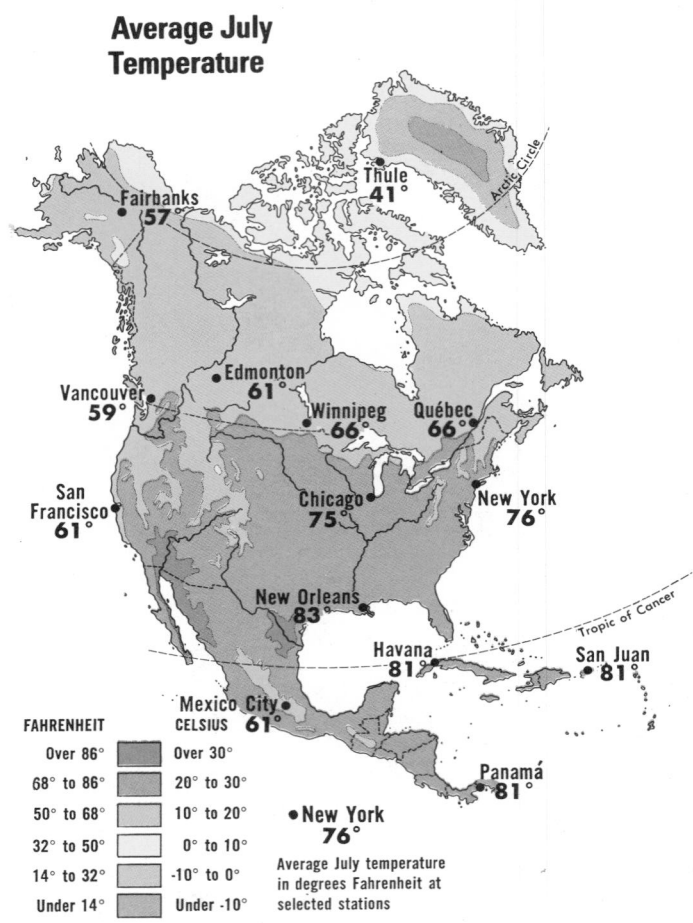

Thule 41°
Fairbanks 57°
Vancouver 59°
Edmonton 61°
Winnipeg 66°
Québec 66°
San Francisco 61°
Chicago 75°
New York 76°
New Orleans 83°
Havana 81°
San Juan 81°
Mexico City 61°
Panamá 81°

FAHRENHEIT	CELSIUS
Over 86°	Over 30°
68° to 86°	20° to 30°
50° to 68°	10° to 20°
32° to 50°	0° to 10°
14° to 32°	-10° to 0°
Under 14°	Under -10°

● **New York 76°**
Average July temperature in degrees Fahrenheit at selected stations

Rainfall

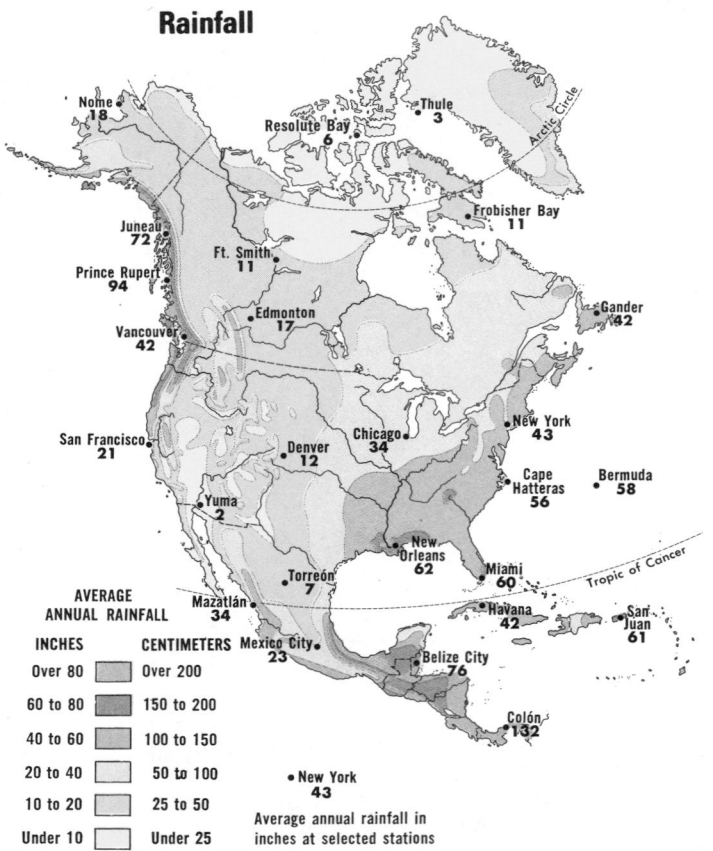

Nome 18
Thule 3
Resolute Bay 6
Frobisher Bay 11
Juneau 72
Ft. Smith 11
Prince Rupert 94
Gander 42
Vancouver 42
Edmonton 17
San Francisco 21
Chicago 34
New York 43
Denver 12
Cape Hatteras 56
Bermuda 58
Yuma 2
New Orleans 62
Miami 60
Torreón 7
Mazatlán 34
Havana 42
San Juan 61
Mexico City 23
Belize City 76
Colón 132

AVERAGE ANNUAL RAINFALL

INCHES	CENTIMETERS
Over 80	Over 200
60 to 80	150 to 200
40 to 60	100 to 150
20 to 40	50 to 100
10 to 20	25 to 50
Under 10	Under 25

● **New York 43**
Average annual rainfall in inches at selected stations

Vegetation/Relief

SCALE OF MILES
0   200   400   600   800   1000

SCALE OF KILOMETERS
0   200   400   600   800   1000

Capitals of Countries..............................⊛
Other Capitals..◉
International Boundaries......................— ·· —
Canals...

Depths in Fathoms

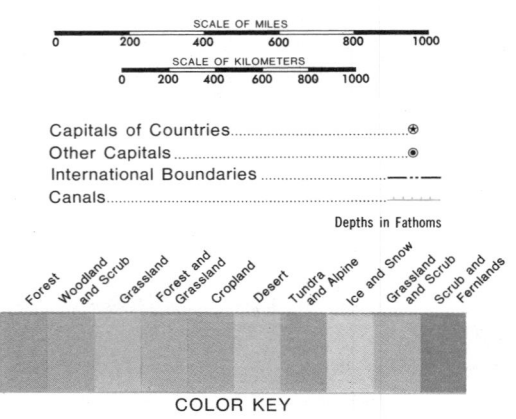

Forest · Woodland and Scrub · Grassland · Forest and Grassland · Cropland · Desert · Tundra and Alpine · Ice and Snow · Grassland and Scrub · Scrub and Fernlands

COLOR KEY

North Pole
A S I A
U.S.S.R.
EAST SIBERIAN SEA
BERING SEA
St. Lawrence I.
Bering Strait
Seward Pen.
Nome
Pt. Barrow
BEAUFORT SEA
ARCTIC OCEAN
Queen Elizabeth Islands
Ellesmere I.
GREENLAND (Den.)
GREENLAND SEA
Denmark Strait
ICELAND
Reykjavík
Brooks Range
Alaska
Yukon
Mt. McKinley 20,320 ft. (6194 m.)
Alaska Range
Fairbanks
Alaska Pen.
Anchorage
Kodiak I.
Gulf of Alaska
Melville I.
Banks I.
Devon I.
Parry Channel
Baffin Bay
Victoria I.
Baffin I.
Davis Strait
Arctic Circle
Nûk
C. Farewell
Inuvik
Dawson
Great Bear L.
Mt. Logan 19,524 ft. (5951 m.)
Whitehorse
Juneau
Mackenzie
Yellowknife
Great Slave L.
Laurentian Plateau
C. Chidley
Ungava Peninsula
Labrador
LABRADOR SEA
Hudson Bay
C A N A D A
L. Athabasca
Peace
Athabasca
Churchill
Nelson
Smallwood Res.
Newfoundland
Gander
St. John's
C. Race
Alexander Arch.
Prince Rupert
Queen Charlotte Is.
Coast Mountains
Rocky Mountains
Fraser
North Saskatchewan
Edmonton
Saskatchewan
South Saskatchewan
Saskatoon
Calgary
Regina
L. Winnipeg
Albany
Eastmain
James Bay
Gulf of St. Lawrence
Cape Breton I.
Vancouver I.
Victoria
Vancouver
Columbia
Seattle
Mt. Rainier 14,410 ft. (4392 m.)
Portland
Winnipeg
Thunder Bay
Missouri
Red
Duluth
L. Superior
Sudbury
Québec
St. Lawrence
Montréal
Ottawa
Saint John
Halifax
C. Mendocino
Cascade Range
Snake
Great Basin
Great Salt Lake
Salt Lake City
Minneapolis
Mississippi
L. Michigan
L. Huron
Toronto
L. Ontario
Boston
C. Cod
Buffalo
Milwaukee
Detroit
L. Erie
Cleveland
New York
San Francisco
Coast Ranges
Sierra Nevada
North Platte
Platte
South Platte
Omaha
Chicago
Pittsburgh
Philadelphia
Columbus
Washington
Indianapolis
Cincinnati
Ohio
Denver
Pikes Peak 14,110 ft. (4301 m.)
Great Plains
Kansas City
Mt. Whitney 14,494 ft. (4418 m.)
Las Vegas
Colorado
Arkansas
U N I T E D   S T A T E S
St. Louis
Wichita
Norfolk
C. Hatteras
Ozark Plateau
Tulsa
Nashville
Mt. Mitchell 6,684 ft. (2037 m.)
Charlotte
Bermuda (U.K.)
Los Angeles
San Diego
Phoenix
Albuquerque
Oklahoma City
Memphis
Tennessee
Appalachian Mts.
Red
Birmingham
Atlanta
Tucson
El Paso
Ciudad Juárez
Rio
Fort Worth
Dallas
Jacksonville
Gulf of California
Lower California
New Orleans
San Antonio
Houston
C. Canaveral
Tampa
Chihuahua
Grande
Corpus Christi
Gulf of Mexico
Miami
BAHAMAS
Nassau
Tropic of Cancer
Culiacán
Monterrey
Sierra Madre Occidental
Sierra Madre Oriental
C. San Lucas
M E X I C O
Tampico
Havana
CUBA
Turks and Caicos Is. (U.K.)
West Indies
DOMINICAN REPUBLIC
Guadalajara
Mérida
Yucatán Pen.
Bay of Campeche
Greater Antilles
Santiago de Cuba
HAITI
Port-au-Prince
Santo Domingo
San Juan
PUERTO RICO
Mexico City
Veracruz
Popocatépetl 17,887 ft. (5452 m.)
JAMAICA
Kingston
CARIBBEAN SEA
Acapulco
BELIZE
NETHERLANDS ANTILLES
Aruba
Curaçao
Bonaire
Willemstad
GUATEMALA
HONDURAS
Tegucigalpa
Guatemala
San Salvador
EL SALVADOR
NICARAGUA
Managua
Barranquilla
Caracas
VENEZUELA
COSTA RICA
San José
Panama Canal
Panamá
PANAMA
Bogotá
COLOMBIA
SOUTH AMERICA
PACIFIC OCEAN
ATLANTIC OCEAN
Longitude 90° West of Greenwich

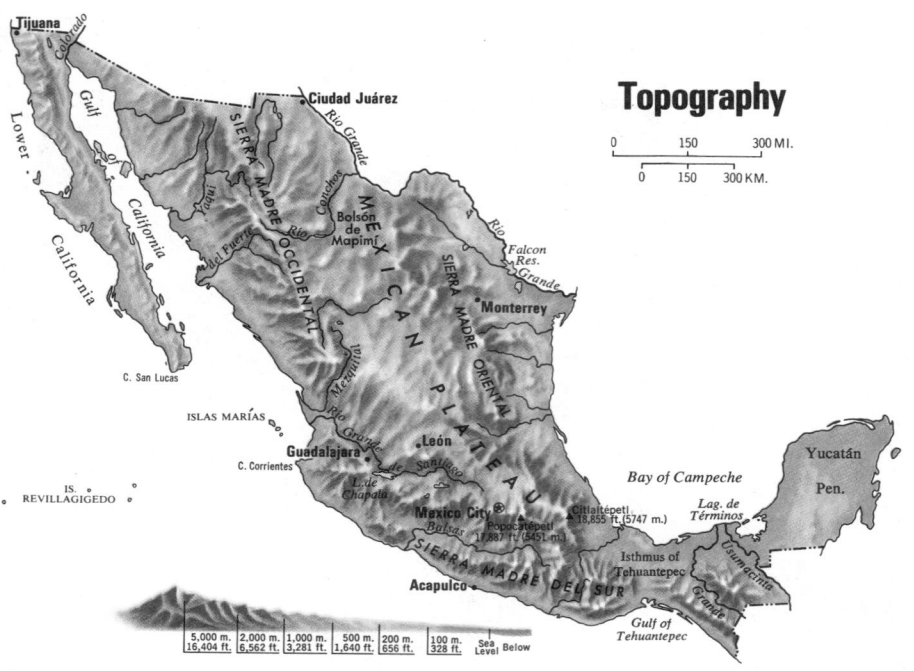

Topography

0   150   300 MI.

0   150   300 KM.

| 5,000 m. 16,404 ft. | 2,000 m. 6,562 ft. | 1,000 m. 3,281 ft. | 500 m. 1,640 ft. | 200 m. 656 ft. | 100 m. 328 ft. | Sea Level Below |

Mexico

CONIC PROJECTION

SCALE OF MILES

0   100   200

SCALE OF KILOMETERS

0   100   200   300

National Capitals .... ☆ State Capitals ....
International Boundaries -- -- -- State Boundaries ....

Scale 1:9,400,000

© Copyright HAMMOND INCORPORATED, Maplewood, N.J.

(continued on following page)

AREA 761,601 sq. mi. (1,972,546 sq. km.)
POPULATION 67,395,826
CAPITAL Mexico City
LARGEST CITY Mexico City
HIGHEST POINT Citlaltépetl 18,855 ft.
 (5,747 m.)
MONETARY UNIT Mexican peso
MAJOR LANGUAGE Spanish
MAJOR RELIGION Roman Catholicism

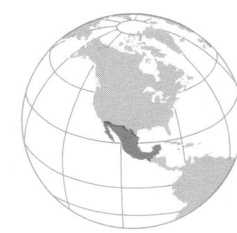

States Indicated by Numbers

1 Tlaxcala   6 Querétaro
2 Morelos   7 Guanajuato
3 Distrito Federal 8 Aguascalientes
4 México   9 Nayarit
5 Hidalgo   10 Colima

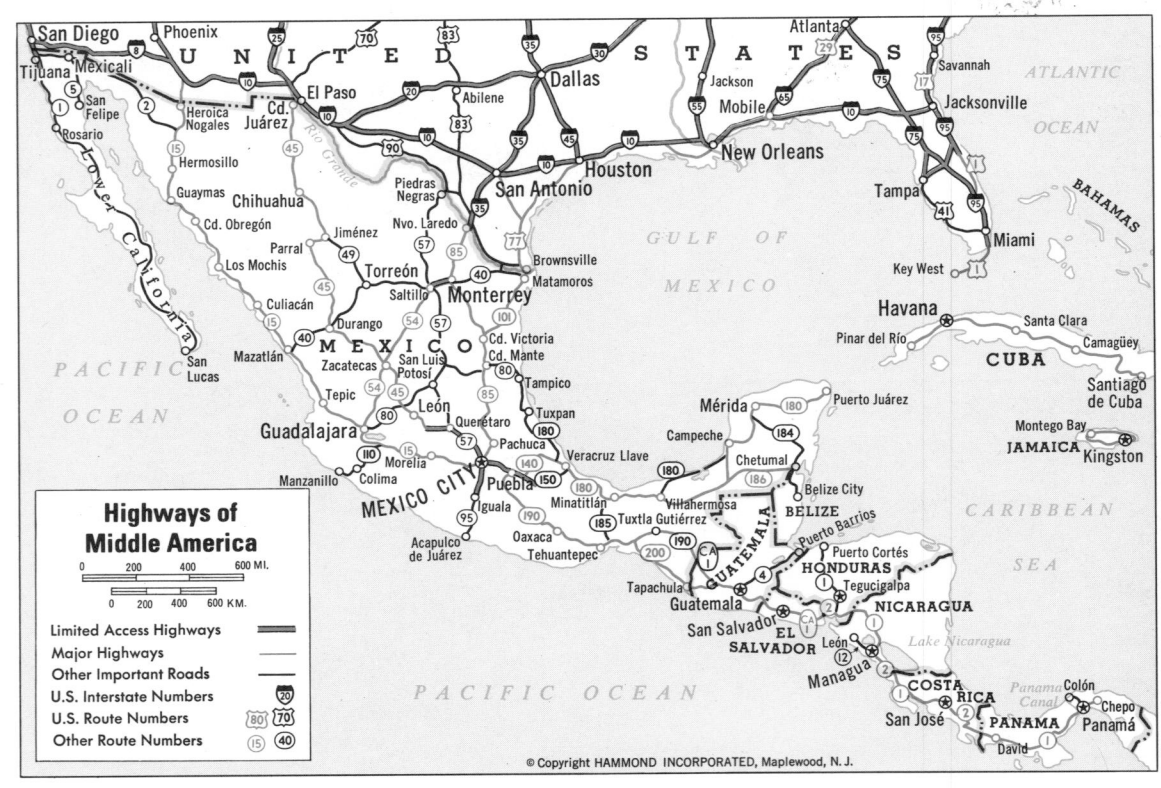

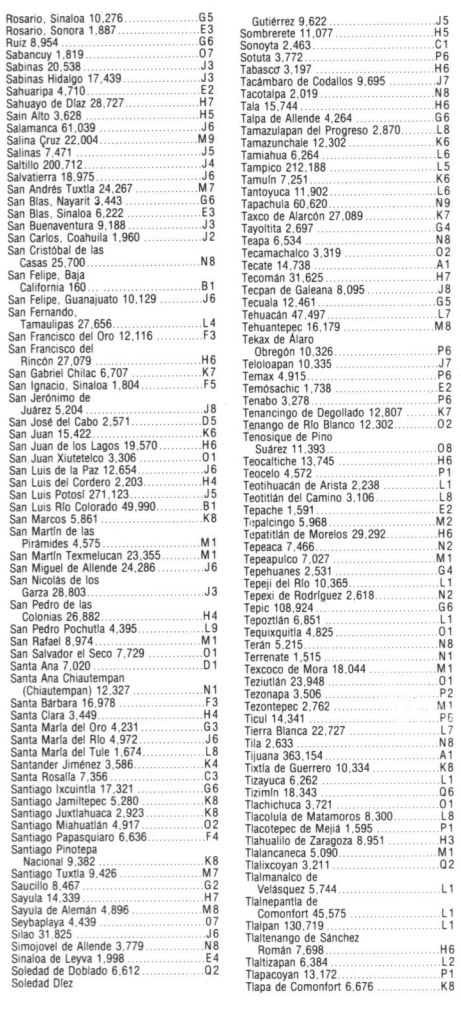

Agriculture, Industry and Resources

DOMINANT LAND USE

- Wheat, Livestock
- Cereals (chiefly corn), Livestock
- Diversified Tropical Cash Crops
- Cotton, Mixed Cereals
- Livestock, Limited Agriculture
- Range Livestock
- Forests
- Nonagricultural Land

MAJOR MINERAL OCCURRENCES

Ag	Silver	G	Natural Gas	O	Petroleum
Au	Gold	Gr	Graphite	Pb	Lead
C	Coal	Hg	Mercury	S	Sulfur
Cu	Copper	Mn	Manganese	Sb	Antimony
F	Fluorspar	Mo	Molybdenum	Sn	Tin
Fe	Iron Ore	Na	Salt	W	Tungsten
				Zn	Zinc

⚡ Water Power

▨ Major Industrial Areas

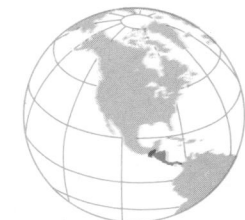

GUATEMALA
AREA 42,042 sq. mi. (108,889 sq. km.)
POPULATION 7,262,419
CAPITAL Guatemala
LARGEST CITY Guatemala
HIGHEST POINT Tajumulco 13,845 ft.
(4,220 m.)
MONETARY UNIT quetzal
MAJOR LANGUAGES Spanish, Quiché
MAJOR RELIGION Roman Catholicism

BELIZE
AREA 8,867 sq. mi. (22,966 sq. km.)
POPULATION 144,857
CAPITAL Belmopan
LARGEST CITY Belize City
HIGHEST POINT Victoria Peak 3,681 ft. (1,122 m.)
MONETARY UNIT Belize dollar
MAJOR LANGUAGES English, Spanish, Mayan
MAJOR RELIGIONS Roman Catholicism, Protestantism

EL SALVADOR
AREA 8,260 sq. mi. (21,393 sq. km.)
POPULATION 4,813,000
CAPITAL San Salvador
LARGEST CITY San Salvador
HIGHEST POINT Santa Ana 7,825 ft.
(2,385 m.)
MONETARY UNIT colón
MAJOR LANGUAGE Spanish
MAJOR RELIGION Roman Catholicism

HONDURAS
AREA 43,277 sq. mi. (112,087 sq. km.)
POPULATION 3,691,000
CAPITAL Tegucigalpa
LARGEST CITY Tegucigalpa
HIGHEST POINT Las Minas 9,347 ft.
(2,849 m.)
MONETARY UNIT lempira
MAJOR LANGUAGE Spanish
MAJOR RELIGION Roman Catholicism

NICARAGUA
AREA 45,698 sq. mi. (118,358 sq. km.)
POPULATION 2,703,000
CAPITAL Managua
LARGEST CITY Managua
HIGHEST POINT Cerro Mocotón 6,913 ft.
(2,107 m.)
MONETARY UNIT córdoba
MAJOR LANGUAGE Spanish
MAJOR RELIGION Roman Catholicism

COSTA RICA
AREA 19,575 sq. mi. (50,700 sq. km.)
POPULATION 2,245,000
CAPITAL San José
LARGEST CITY San José
HIGHEST POINT Chirripó Grande
12,530 ft. (3,819 m.)
MONETARY UNIT colón
MAJOR LANGUAGE Spanish
MAJOR RELIGION Roman Catholicism

PANAMA
AREA 29,761 sq. mi. (77,082 sq. km.)
POPULATION 1,830,175
CAPITAL Panamá
LARGEST CITY Panamá
HIGHEST POINT Vol. Baru 11,401 ft.
(3,475 m.)
MONETARY UNIT balboa
MAJOR LANGUAGE Spanish
MAJOR RELIGION Roman Catholicism

Agriculture, Industry and Resources

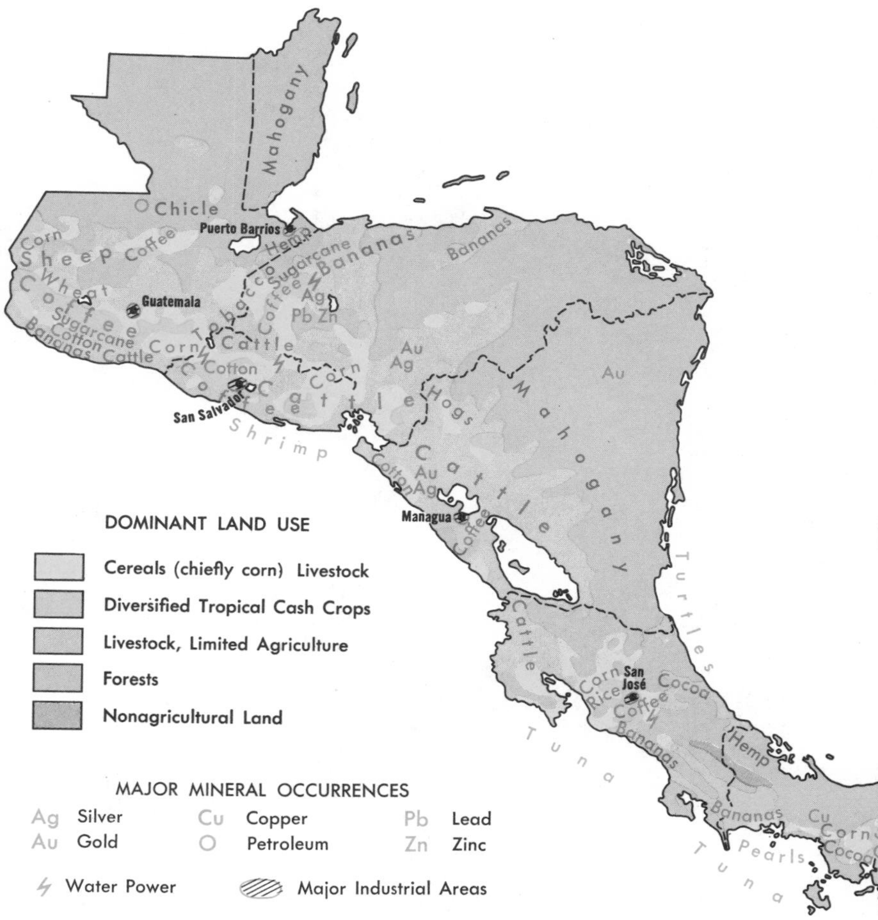

GUATEMALA

HONDURAS

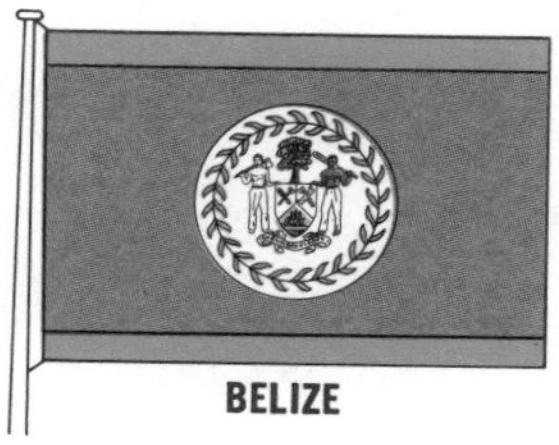

BELIZE

NICARAGUA

EL SALVADOR

COSTA RICA

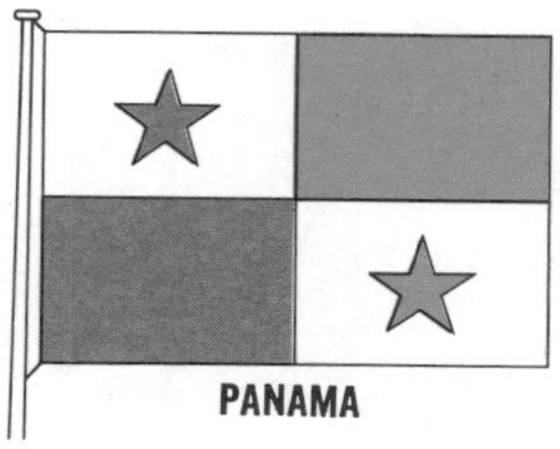

PANAMA

DOMINANT LAND USE

- Cereals (chiefly corn) Livestock
- Diversified Tropical Cash Crops
- Livestock, Limited Agriculture
- Forests
- Nonagricultural Land

MAJOR MINERAL OCCURRENCES

Ag	Silver	Cu	Copper	Pb	Lead
Au	Gold	O	Petroleum	Zn	Zinc

⚡ Water Power   ▨ Major Industrial Areas

(continued on following page)

Central America

CONIC PROJECTION

SCALE OF MILES

0 25 50 100 150

SCALE OF KILOMETERS

0 25 50 100 150

Capitals of Countries .... ☆

International Boundaries ....

Canals ....

Scale 1:5,780,000

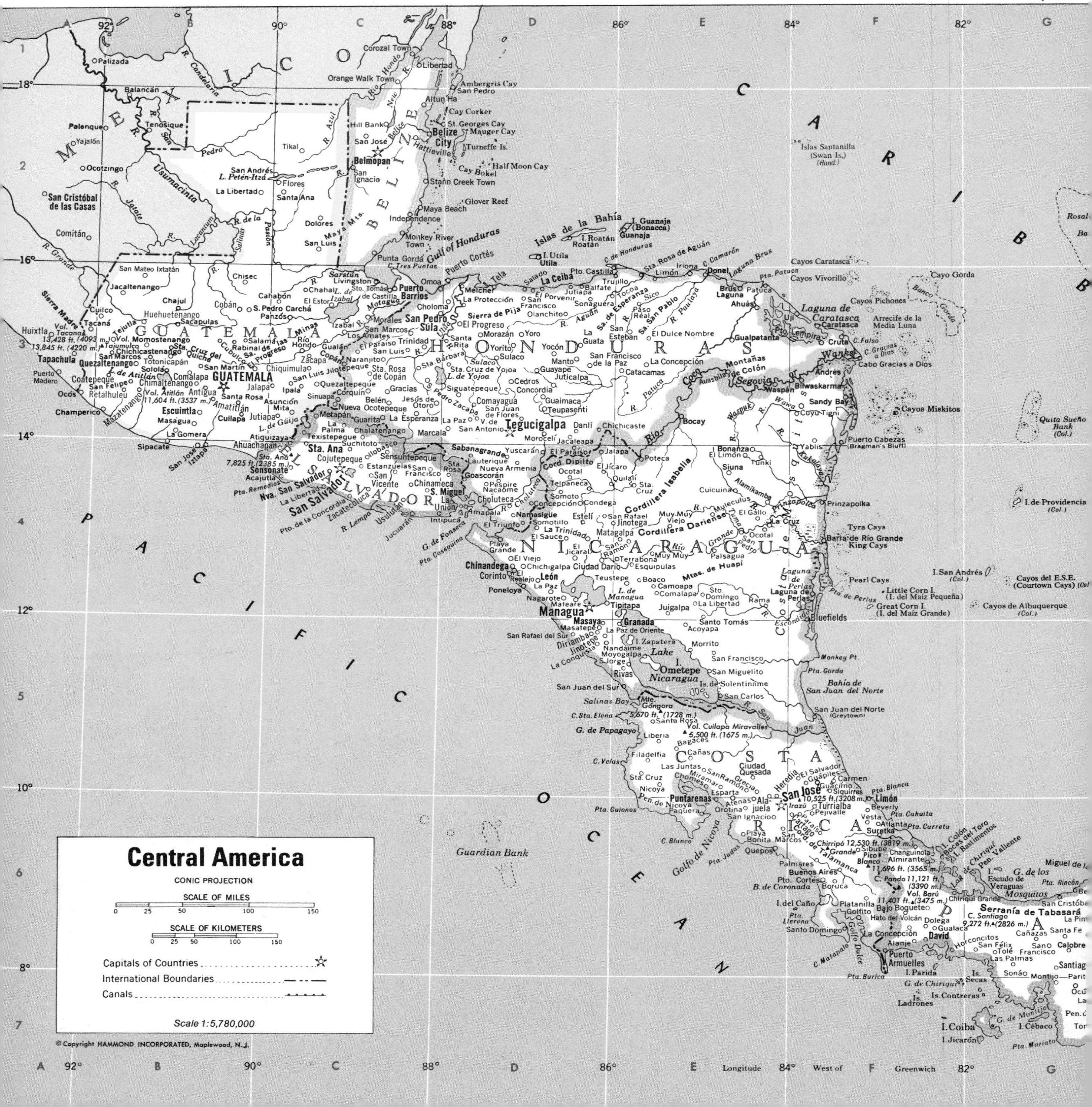

© Copyright HAMMOND INCORPORATED, Maplewood, N.J.

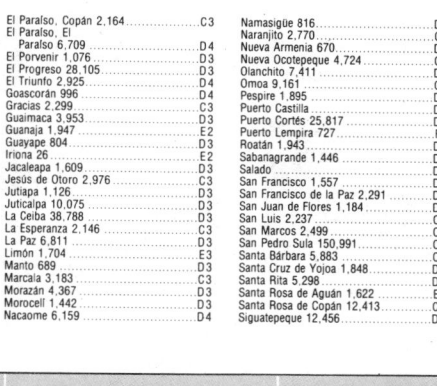

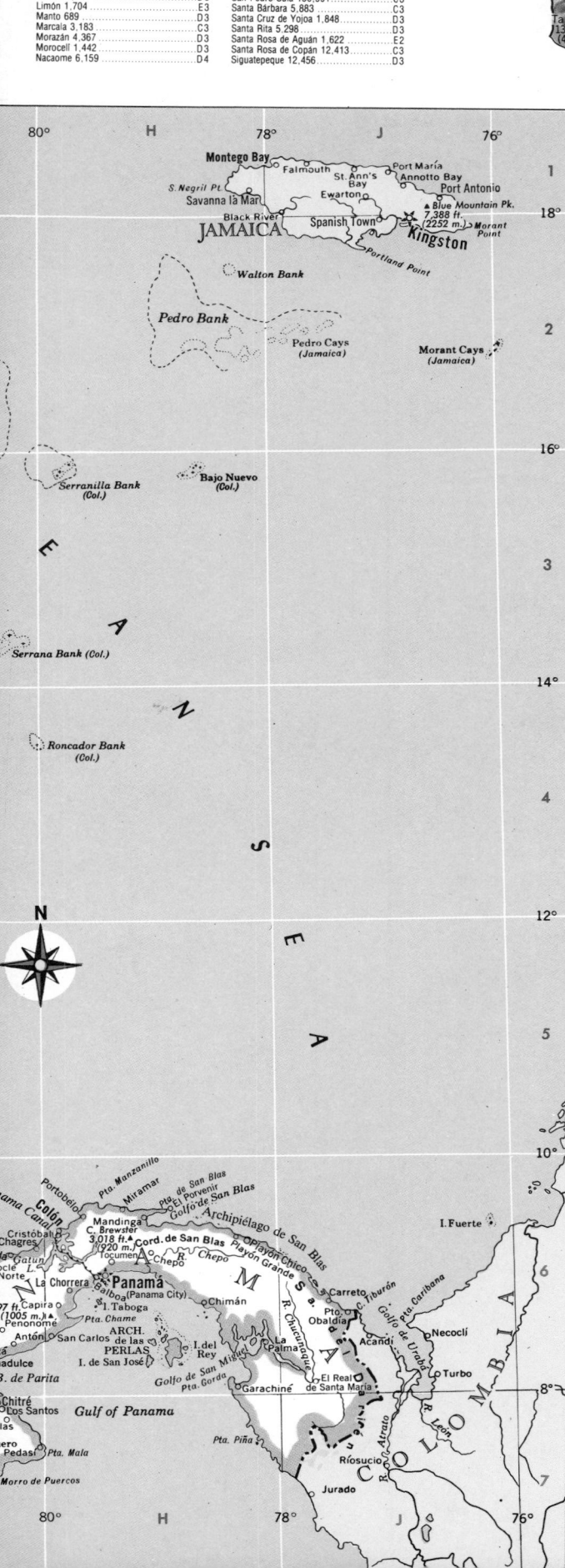

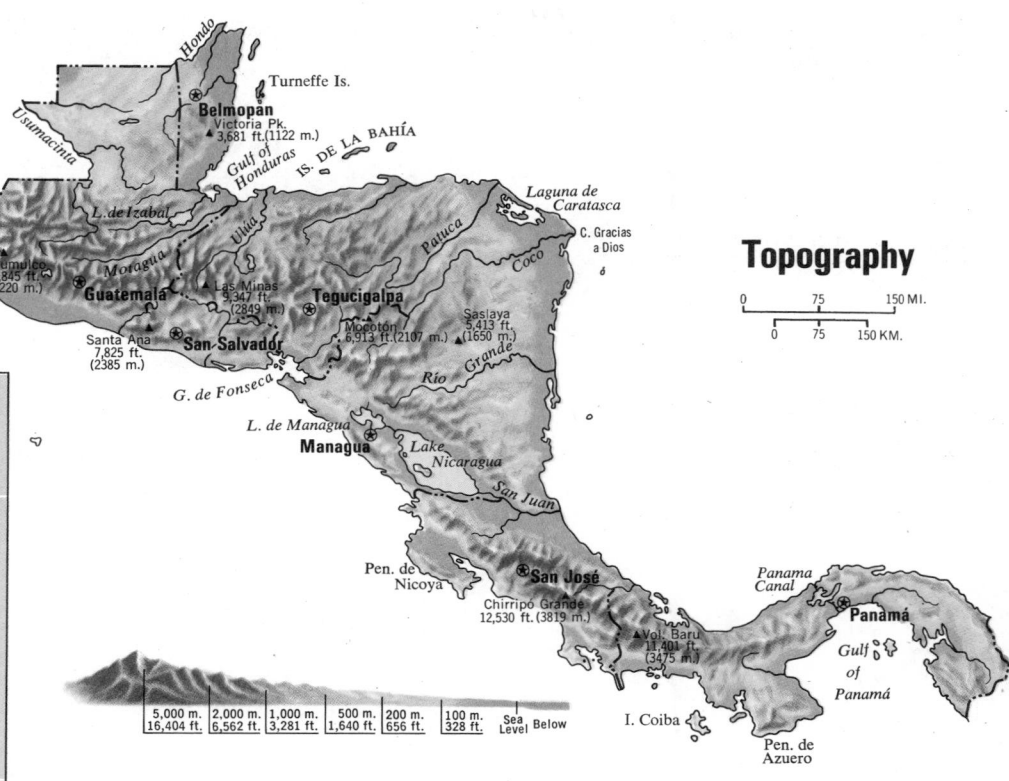

Topography

0   75   150 MI.

0   75   150 KM.

| 5,000 m. 16,404 ft. | 2,000 m. 6,562 ft. | 1,000 m. 3,281 ft. | 500 m. 1,640 ft. | 200 m. 656 ft. | 100 m. 328 ft. | Sea Level | Below |

CUBA

HAITI

DOMINICAN REPUBLIC

JAMAICA

TRINIDAD AND TOBAGO

BARBADOS

GRENADA

BAHAMAS

DOMINICA

ST. LUCIA

ST. VINC. & GRENS.

ANTIGUA AND BARBUDA

CUBA

AREA 44,206 sq. mi. (114,494 sq. km.)
POPULATION 9,706,369
CAPITAL Havana
LARGEST CITY Havana
HIGHEST POINT Pico Turquino
  6,561 ft. (2,000 m.)
MONETARY UNIT Cuban peso
MAJOR LANGUAGE Spanish
MAJOR RELIGION Roman Catholicism

HAITI

AREA 10,694 sq. mi. (27,697 sq. km.)
POPULATION 5,053,792
CAPITAL Port-au-Prince
LARGEST CITY Port-au-Prince
HIGHEST POINT Pic La Selle 8,793 ft. (2,680 m.)
MONETARY UNIT gourde
MAJOR LANGUAGES Creole French, French
MAJOR RELIGION Roman Catholicism

DOMINICAN REPUBLIC

AREA 18,704 sq. mi. (48,443 sq. km.)
POPULATION 5,647,977
CAPITAL Santo Domingo
LARGEST CITY Santo Domingo
HIGHEST POINT Pico Duarte
  10,417 ft. (3,175 m.)
MONETARY UNIT Dominican peso
MAJOR LANGUAGE Spanish
MAJOR RELIGION Roman Catholicism

JAMAICA

AREA 4,411 sq. mi. (11,424 sq. km.)
POPULATION 2,184,000
CAPITAL Kingston
LARGEST CITY Kingston
HIGHEST POINT Blue Mountain Peak
  7,402 ft. (2,256 m.)
MONETARY UNIT Jamaican dollar
MAJOR LANGUAGE English
MAJOR RELIGIONS Protestantism,
  Roman Catholicism

PUERTO RICO

AREA 3,515 sq. mi. (9,104 sq. km.)
POPULATION 3,196,520
CAPITAL San Juan
MONETARY UNIT U.S. dollar
MAJOR LANGUAGES Spanish, English
MAJOR RELIGION Roman Catholicism

NETHERLANDS ANTILLES

AREA 390 sq. mi. (1,010 sq. km.)
POPULATION 246,000
CAPITAL Willemstad
MONETARY UNIT Antilles guilder
MAJOR LANGUAGES Dutch, Papiamento, English
MAJOR RELIGIONS Roman Catholicism,
  Protestantism

BERMUDA

AREA 21 sq. mi. (54 sq. km.)
POPULATION 67,761
CAPITAL Hamilton
MONETARY UNIT Bermuda dollar
MAJOR LANGUAGE English
MAJOR RELIGION Protestantism

ANGUILLA

Anguilla (isl.) 6,519 . . . . F3

ANTIGUA and BARBUDA

Antigua (isl.) 76,213 . . . . G3
Barbuda (isl.) 1,071 . . . . G3
Caribbean (sea) B4
Codrington 1,071 . . . . G3
Falmouth 1,134 . . . . F3
Redonda (isl.) F3
Saint John's (cap.) 21,814 . . . . G3

BAHAMAS

Acklins (isl.) 616 . . . . C2
Andros (isl.) 8,397 . . . . B1
Atwood (Samana) (cay) D2
Berry (isls.) 509 . . . . B1
Biminis, The (isls.) 1,432 . . . . . B1
Caicos (passg.) D2
Cat (isl.) 2,143 . . . . C1
Cay Sal (bank) B2
Crooked (isl.) 517 . . . . D2
Crooked Island (passg.) C1
Eleuthera (isl.) 8,326 . . . . C1
Exuma (cays) C1
Exuma (sound) C2
Flamingo (cay) C2
Freeport 22,301 . . . . B1
Grand Bahama (isl.) 33,102 . . . B1
Great Abaco (isl.) 7,324 . . . . . C1
Great Bahama (bank) B1
Great Exuma (isl.) C2
Great Inagua (isl.) 939 . . . . . . D2
Great Isaac (isl.) B1
Gun (cay) B1
Harbour (isl.) C1
Little Inagua (isl.) D2

Long (cay) 33 . . . . C2
Long (isl.) 3,353 . . . . C2
Mayaguana (isl.) 476 . . . . D2
Mayaguana (passg.) D2
Mira Por Vos (cays) C2
Nassau (cap.) 135,437 . . . . . . C1
New Providence (isl.) 135,437 . . C1
North East Providence (chan.) . . C1
North West Providence (chan.) . . B1
Old Bahama (chan.) B2
Plana (cays) D2
Ragged (cays) 146. . . . . C2
Rum (cay) C2
Samana (cay) D2
San Salvador (isl.) D1
Santarén (chan.) C1
Tongue of the Ocean (chan.) . . . C1
Verde (cay) C2
Watling (San Salvador) (isl.) . . . C1

BARBADOS

Bridgetown (cap.) 7,552 . . . . . G4
Speightstown G4

BERMUDA

Bermuda (isl.) H3
Castle (harb.) H2
Great (sound) G3
Hamilton (cap.) 1,617 . . . . G3
Harrington (sound) G3
Ireland (isl.) G3
North (rapid) H2
Saint Davids (isl.) H2
Saint George 1,647 . . . . H2
Saint George's (isl.) H2
Somerset (isl.) G3

CAYMAN ISLANDS

Bartlett Deep B3
Cayman Brac (isl.) 1,603 . . . . . B3
George Town (cap.) 7,617 . . . . B3
Grand Cayman (isl.) 15,000 . . . B3
Little Cayman (isl.) 74 . . . . B3
Misteriosa (bank) A3

CUBA

Bayamo 109,201 . . . . C2
Camagüey 245,235 . . . . B2
Cienfuegos 107,396 . . . . B2
Florida (str.) B1
Guanabacoa 89,741 . . . . A2
Guantánamo 178,129 . . . . C2
Havana (cap.) 1,924,886 . . . . . A2
Holguín 190,155 . . . . C2
Juventud (Pines) (isl.) 57,879 . . A2
Manzanillo 95,420 . . . . C2
Marianao ○127,563 . . . . A2
Matanzas 103,302 . . . . B2
Pinar del Río 104,598 . . . . A2
San Felipe (cays) A2
Santa Clara 175,113 . . . . B2
Santiago de Cuba 362,432 . . . . C3
Windward (passg.) C3

DOMINICA

Portsmouth 2,329 . . . . G4
Roseau (cap.) 9,968 . . . . G4

DOMINICAN REPUBLIC

La Romana 91,571 . . . . E3
San Francisco de Macorís 64,906 . E3
San Pedro de Macorís 78,562 . . E3
Santiago 278,638 . . . . D3
Santo Domingo (cap.) 1,313,172 . E3

GRENADA

Carriacou (isl.) 6,052 . . . . G4
Gouyave 2,498 . . . . F4
Grenadines (isls.) G4
Saint George's (cap.) 6,463. . . . F5

GUADELOUPE

Basse-Terre (cap.) 13,397 . . . . F4
Saint-Barthélemy (isl.) 3,059 . . F3
Saint Martin (isl.) 8,072 . . . . . F3

HAITI

Cap-Haïtien 64,406 . . . . D3
Gonaïves 34,209 . . . . D3
Port-au-Prince (cap.) 449,831 . . D3
Gonâve (isl.) D3
Jamaica (chan.) C3
Tortuga (isl.) D2

JAMAICA

Blue Mountain (peak) C3
Jamaica (chan.) C3
Kingston (cap.) 106,791 . . . . . C3
Montego Bay 43,521 . . . . B3
Pedro (cays) B3
Savanna-la-Mar 11,759 . . . . . . B3

MARTINIQUE

Fort-de-France (cap.) 96,649 . . . G4
Saint-Pierre 4,923 . . . . G4
Pelée (vol.) G4

MONTSERRAT

Plymouth (cap.) 1,623 . . . . F3

NETHERLANDS ANTILLES

Aruba (isl.) E4
Bonaire (isl.) E4
Curaçao (isl.) E4
Oranjestad 10,100 . . . . D4
Saba (isl.) F3
Saint Eustatius (isl.) F3
Saint Martin (Sint Maarten) (isl.) . F3
Willemstad (cap.) 95,000 . . . . . E4

PUERTO RICO

Bayamón 185,087 . . . . G1
Caguas 87,214 . . . . G1
Culebra (isl.) 1,265 . . . . G1
Mayagüez 82,968 . . . . F1
Mona (passg.) E3
Ponce 161,739 . . . . F1

San Juan (cap.) 424,600 . . . . . G1
Vieques (isl.) 7,662 . . . . G1

SAINT CHRISTOPHER and NEVIS

Basseterre (cap.) 14,725 . . . . . F3
Nevis (isl.) 9,300 . . . . F3
Saint Christopher (isl.) 35,104 . . F3

SAINT LUCIA

Castries (cap.) ●42,770. . . . . . . G4
Vieux Fort ●10,675 . . . . G4

SAINT VINCENT and THE GRENADINES

Bequia (isl.) G4
Georgetown 1,100 . . . . G4
Grenadines (isls.) 8,371 . . . . . . G4
Kingstown (cap.) 17,117 . . . . . G4

TRINIDAD and TOBAGO

Port-of-Spain (cap.) 67,978 . . . . G5
Scarborough 6,057 . . . . G5
Tobago (isl.) 39,695 . . . . G5
Trinidad (isl.) 1,020,130 . . . . . . G5

TURKS and CAICOS ISLANDS

Caicos (isls.) 4,008 . . . . D2
Cockburn Harbour D2
Grand Caicos (isl.) 371 . . . . . . D2
Grand Turk (isl.) 3,146 . . . . . . D2
Providenciales (isl.) 979 . . . . . D2
Turks (isls.) 3,348. . . . . D2

VIRGIN ISLANDS (British)

Anegada (isl.) 89 . . . . H1
Jost Van Dyke (isl.) 135 . . . . . . G1
Road Town (cap.) 2,200 . . . . . . H1
Tortola (isl.) 9,257 . . . . H1
Virgin Gorda (isl.) 1,443 . . . . . . H1

VIRGIN ISLANDS (U.S.)

Charlotte Amalie (cap.) 11,842 . . H1
Christiansted 2,914 . . . . H2
Fredriksted 1,046 . . . . G2
Saint Croix (isl.) 49,725 . . . . . . H2
Saint John (isl.) 2,472 . . . . H1
Saint Thomas (isl.) 44,372 . . . . G1

WEST INDIES

Antilles, Greater (isls.) B2
Antilles, Lesser (isls.) E4
Aves (Bird) (isl.) F4
Hispaniola (isl.) D2
Leeward (isls.) F3
Navassa (isl.) C3
Windward (isls.) G4

● Population of district.
○ Population of municipality.

Topography

0   100   200 MI.
0   100   200 KM.

| Below Sea Level | 100 m. 328 ft. | 200 m. 656 ft. | 500 m. 1,640 ft. | 1,000 m. 3,281 ft. | 2,000 m. 6,562 ft. | 5,000 m. 16,404 ft. |

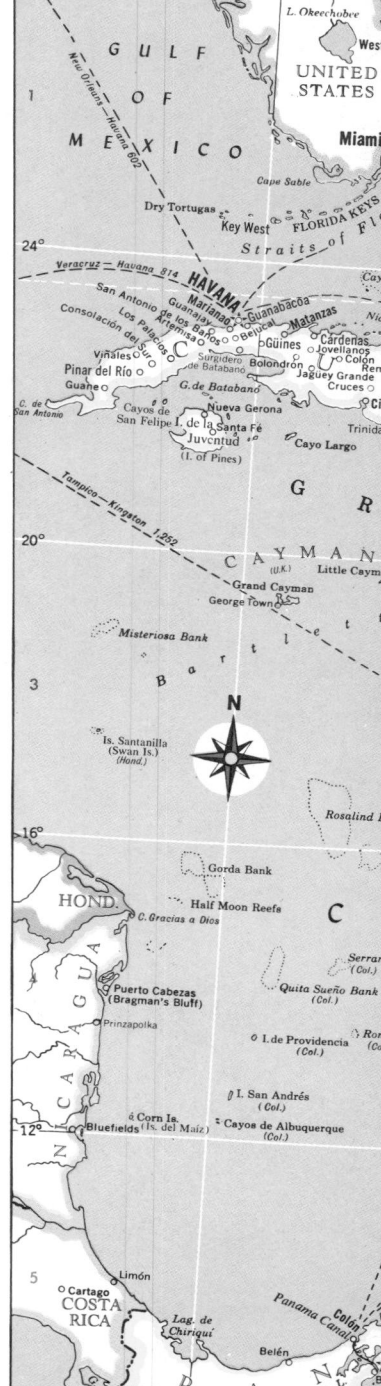

TRINIDAD AND TOBAGO

AREA 1,980 sq. mi. (5,128 sq. km.)
POPULATION 1,067,108
CAPITAL Port of Spain
LARGEST CITY Port of Spain
HIGHEST POINT Mt. Aripo 3,084 ft. (940 m.)
MONETARY UNIT Trinidad and Tobago dollar
MAJOR LANGUAGES English, Hindi
MAJOR RELIGIONS Roman Catholicism, Protestantism, Hinduism, Islam

ST. CHRISTOPHER & NEVIS

BARBADOS

AREA 166 sq. mi. (430 sq. km.)
POPULATION 248,983
CAPITAL Bridgetown
LARGEST CITY Bridgetown
HIGHEST POINT Mt. Hillaby 1,104 ft. (336 m.)
MONETARY UNIT Barbadian dollar
MAJOR LANGUAGE English
MAJOR RELIGION Protestantism

BAHAMAS

AREA 5,382 sq. mi. (13,939 sq. km.)
POPULATION 209,505
CAPITAL Nassau
LARGEST CITY Nassau
HIGHEST POINT Mt. Alvernia 206 ft. (63 m.)
MONETARY UNIT Bahamian dollar
MAJOR LANGUAGE English
MAJOR RELIGIONS Roman Catholicism, Protestantism

GRENADA

AREA 133 sq. mi. (344 sq. km.)
POPULATION 103,103
CAPITAL St. George's
LARGEST CITY St. George's
HIGHEST POINT Mt. St. Catherine 2,757 ft. (840 m.)
MONETARY UNIT East Caribbean dollar
MAJOR LANGUAGES English, French patois
MAJOR RELIGIONS Roman Catholicism, Protestantism

DOMINICA

AREA 290 sq. mi. (751 sq. km.)
POPULATION 74,089
CAPITAL Roseau
HIGHEST POINT Morne Diablotin 4,747 ft. (1,447 m.)
MONETARY UNIT Dominican dollar
MAJOR LANGUAGES English, French patois
MAJOR RELIGIONS Roman Catholicism, Protestantism

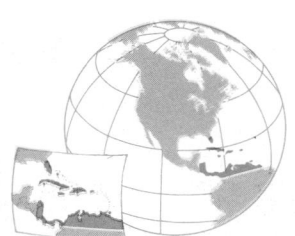

SAINT LUCIA

AREA 238 sq. mi. (616 sq. km.)
POPULATION 115,783
CAPITAL Castries
HIGHEST POINT Mt. Gimie 3,117 ft. (950 m.)
MONETARY UNIT East Caribbean dollar
MAJOR LANGUAGES English, French patois
MAJOR RELIGIONS Roman Catholicism, Protestantism

SAINT VINCENT AND THE GRENADINES

AREA 150 sq. mi. (388 sq. km.)
POPULATION 124,000
CAPITAL Kingstown
HIGHEST POINT Soufrière 4,000 ft. (1,219 m.)
MONETARY UNIT East Caribbean dollar
MAJOR LANGUAGE English
MAJOR RELIGIONS Protestantism, Roman Catholicism

ANTIGUA AND BARBUDA

AREA 171 sq. mi. (443 sq. km.)
POPULATION 75,000
CAPITAL St. John's
HIGHEST POINT Boggy Peak 1,319 ft. (402 m.)
MONETARY UNIT East Caribbean dollar
MAJOR LANGUAGE English
MAJOR RELIGION Protestantism

SAINT CHRISTOPHER & NEVIS

AREA 104 sq. mi. (269 sq. km.)
POPULATION 44,404
CAPITAL Basseterre
HIGHEST POINT Mt. Misery 4,314 ft. (1,315 m.)
MONETARY UNIT East Caribbean dollar
MAJOR LANGUAGE English
MAJOR RELIGIONS Protestantism, Roman Catholicism

The West Indies

CONIC PROJECTION

SCALE OF MILES
0 50 100 150 200

SCALE OF KILOMETERS
0 50 100 200 300

Capitals — — — — — ☆

Scale 1:11,200,000
Distances are given in Nautical Miles

Puerto Rico

Bermuda Islands

© Copyright HAMMOND INCORPORATED, Maplewood, N.J.

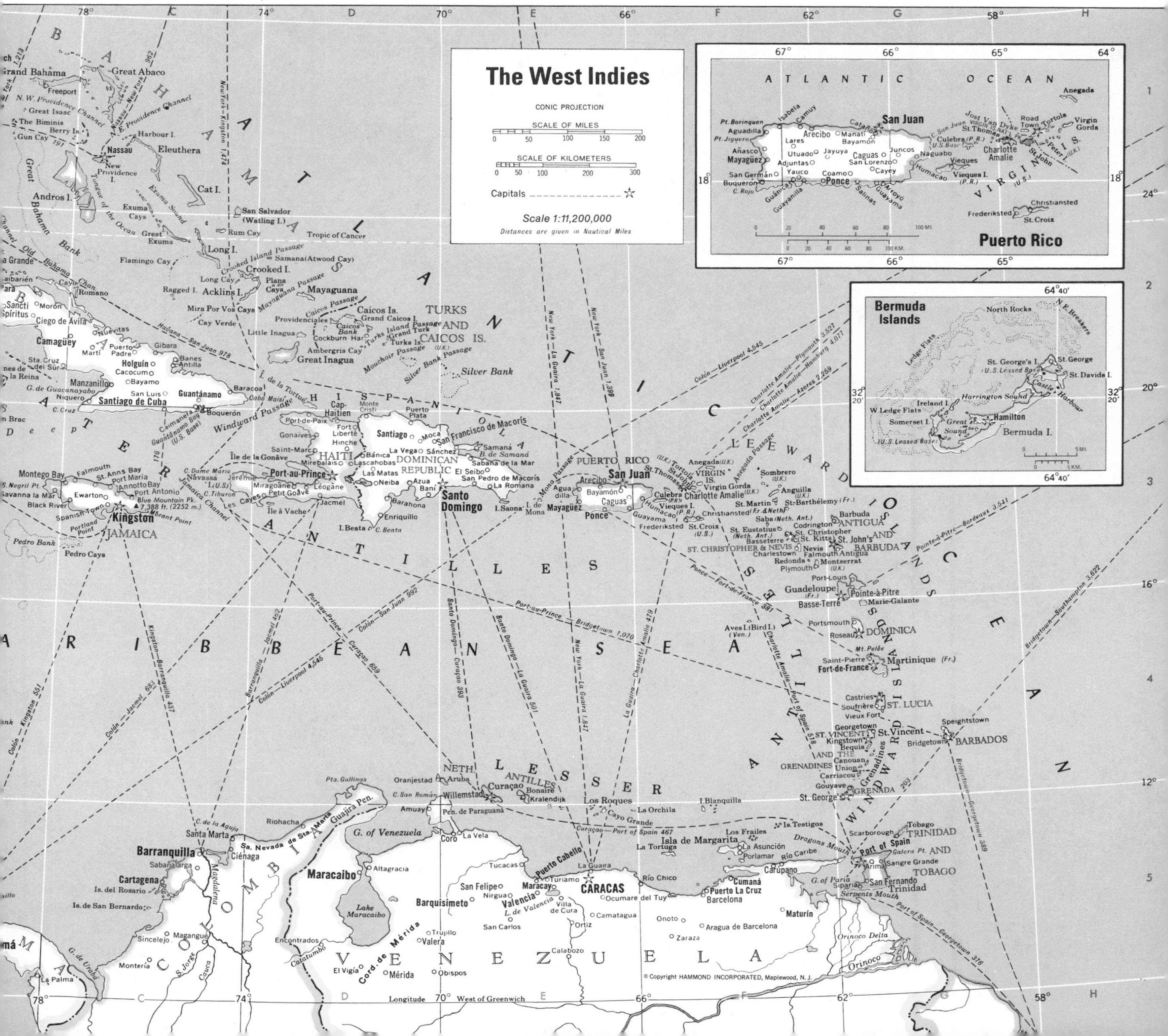

CUBA

PROVINCES

Camagüey 664,566.......G2
Ciego de Ávila 320,961.....F2
Cienfuegos 326,412.......E2
Granma 739,335.......H4
Guantánamo 466,609.....K4
Habana 1,924,886.......C1
Habana, La (Havana)
586,029.......C1
Holguín 911,034.......J3
Juventud (municipio
especial) 57,879.......C2
Las Tunas 436,341.......H3
Matanzas 557,628.......D1
Pinar del Río 640,740.......A2
Sancti Spíritus 399,700.....F2
Santiago de Cuba 909,506...J4
Villa Clara 764,743.......E1

CITIES and TOWNS

Abreus 2,767.......D2
Agramonte 4,603.......D1
Aguada de Pasajeros 20,219 D2
Alacranes 4,959.......D1
Alonso Rojas 1,427.......B2
Alquízar 12,691.......C1
Altagracia 1,722.......G3
Alto Songo-La Maya 25,188 .J4

Amarillas 2,767.......D2
Amazonas 1,066.......F2
Antilla 10,052.......J3
Arroyo Blanco 1,431.......F2
Artemisa 45,689.......B1
Báez 4,178.......D2
Báguanos 12,678.......J3
Bahía Honda 16,901.......B1
Baire 4,879.......H4
Banao 803.......F2
Banes 38,905.......J3
Baracoa 36,702.......K4
Baraguá 12,633.......F2
Bauta 26,826.......C1
Bayamo 109,201.......H4
Bejucal 15,649.......C1
Bolondrón 5,840.......D1
Buenaventura 4,711.......H3
Buenavista 1,303.......F2
Buey Arriba 8,017.......H4
Cabaiguán 36,544.......F2
Cabañas 4,897.......B1
Cabezas 5,262.......C1
Cacocum 14,145.......H3
Caibarién 32,094.......E1
Caimanera 6,664.......J4
Calabazar de Sagua 9,023..E1
Calimete 19,925.......D1
Camagüey 245,235.......G3
Camajuaní 26,653.......E1
Campechuela 20,743.......G4
Canasí 1,637.......C1

Candelaria 10,810.......B1
Cárdenas 65,585.......D1
Cartagena 2,166.......D2
Cascajal 3,530.......E1
Cauto del Embarcadero 949..H4
Cauto el Cristo 1,626.......J3
Central Amancio Rodríguez
22,506.......G3
Central Bolivia 6,301.......G2
Central Brasil 4,904.......G2
Central Cándido González
3,414.......G3
Central Colombia 16,799...G3
Central Frank País 9,066..K3
Central Guatemala 5,584...J3
Central Haití 3,609.......G3
Central Los Reynaldos 3,997 J4
Central Loynaz Echevarría
3,245.......J3
Central Manuel Tames 7,864 K4
Céspedes 6,634.......G2
Chambas 19,877.......F2
Chaparra 8,428.......H3
Cidra 3,567.......D1
Ciego de Ávila 80,010.......F2
Cienfuegos 107,396.......E2
Colón 47,010.......D1
Condado 33,115.......E2
Consolación del Norte 4,681 B1
Consolación del Sur 34,334 .B2
Contramaestre 44,991.......G3
Corralillo 15,822.......D1

Cruces 20,324.......E2
Cueto 23,183.......J3
Cumanayagua 25,338.......E2
Daiquirí.......J4
Delicias 10,562.......H3
Dos Caminos 3,772.......J4
Dos Ríos 1,786.......J4
El Caney 3,921.......J4
El Cobre 3,952.......J4
El Santo 2,473.......E1
Encrucijada 23,029.......E1
Esmeralda 17,205.......G1
Esperanza 9,241.......E2
Florencia 6,979.......F2
Florida 43,881.......G3
Fomento 17,310.......F2
Gaspar 2,682.......F2
Gibara 23,137.......J3
Guáimaro 29,712.......G3
Guanabacoa 89,741.......C1
Guanajay 21,042.......B1
Guane 14,126.......A2
Guantánamo 178,129.......K4
Guaro 3,086.......J4
Guasimal 3,057.......F2
Guayabal 3,703.......G3
Guayos 6,753.......F2
Güines 51,691.......C1
Güira de Melena 19,851...C1
Guisa 15,182.......H4
Herradura 3,762.......B1

Holguín 190,155.......J3
Ignacio Agramonte 1,487...G3
Imías 4,491.......K4
Isabela de Sagua 3,721.....E1
Jagüey Grande 30,205.......D2
Jamaica 5,128.......K4
Jaruco 16,844.......C1
Jatibonico 17,047.......F2
Jíbaro 1,263.......F2
Jiguaní 25,069.......H4
Jobabo 14,899.......H3
Jovellanos 35,043.......D1
La Coloma 3,462.......B2
La Maya-Alto Songo 25,188..J4
Las Martinas 4,511.......A2
Limonar 9,629.......D1
Los Arabos 10,664.......E1
Los Palacios 21,884.......B1
Lugareño 4,396.......G2
Mabay 6,176.......H4
Maceo 2,652.......J4
Majagua 9,110.......F2
Manacas 5,914.......E2
Manatí 11,054.......H3
Manguito 2,739.......D1
Manicaragua 33,900.......E2
Mantua 9,165.......A2
Mapos (Amazonas) 1,066...F2
Manzanillo 95,420.......G4
Marianao ○127,563.......C1
Mariel 24,115.......B1
Martí 11,474.......D1

Matanzas 103,302.......C1
Máximo Gómez, Ciego
de Ávila 5,116.......F2
Máximo Gómez, Matanzas
4,970.......D1
Mayajigua 4,425.......F2
Mayarí 54,699.......J3
Mayarí Arriba 2,302.......J4
Media Luna 13,794.......G4
Mendoza 2,914.......B2
Meneses 4,768.......F2
Minas 17,675.......G2
Minas de Matahambre
14,976.......A1
Moa 28,696.......K3
Morón 40,396.......F2
Nicaro 9,506.......J3
Niquero 15,544.......G4
Nueva Gerona 17,175.......B2
Nuevitas 35,103.......G2
Orozco 4,256.......B1
Palma Soriano 66,222.......J4
Palmira 19,680.......E2
Pedro Betancourt 22,915...D1
Perico 20,633.......D1
Pilón 10,194.......H4
Pinar del Río 104,598.......B2
Placetas 46,038.......E2
Primero Enero 14,807.......F2
Puerto Esperanza 3,499.....A1
Puerto Padre 46,806.......H3
Quemado de Güines 11,208 E1

Rancho Veloz 3,966.......D1
Ranchuelo 34,255.......E2
Regla 38,491.......C1
Remedios 27,722.......E2
Repúbliica Dominicana
2,540.......F2
Río Cauto 19,550.......H4
Rodas 16,350.......E2
Sagua de Tánamo 15,327...K3
Sagua la Grande 52,315....E1
San Andrés 2,127.......H3
San Antonio de los Baños
28,137.......C1
San Cristóbal 30,769.......B1
Sancti Spíritus 79,542.......F2
San Diego de los Baños
1,430.......B1
San Germán 12,362.......J3
San José de las Lajas
37,149.......C1
San José de los Ramos
1,726.......D1
San Juan y Martínez 13,227 B2
San Luis, Pinar del Río
5,677.......B2
San Luis, Santiago de Cuba
32,826.......J4
San Nicolás 12,368.......C1
San Ramón 2,676.......H4
Santa Clara 175,113.......E2
Santa Cruz del Norte
15,239.......C1

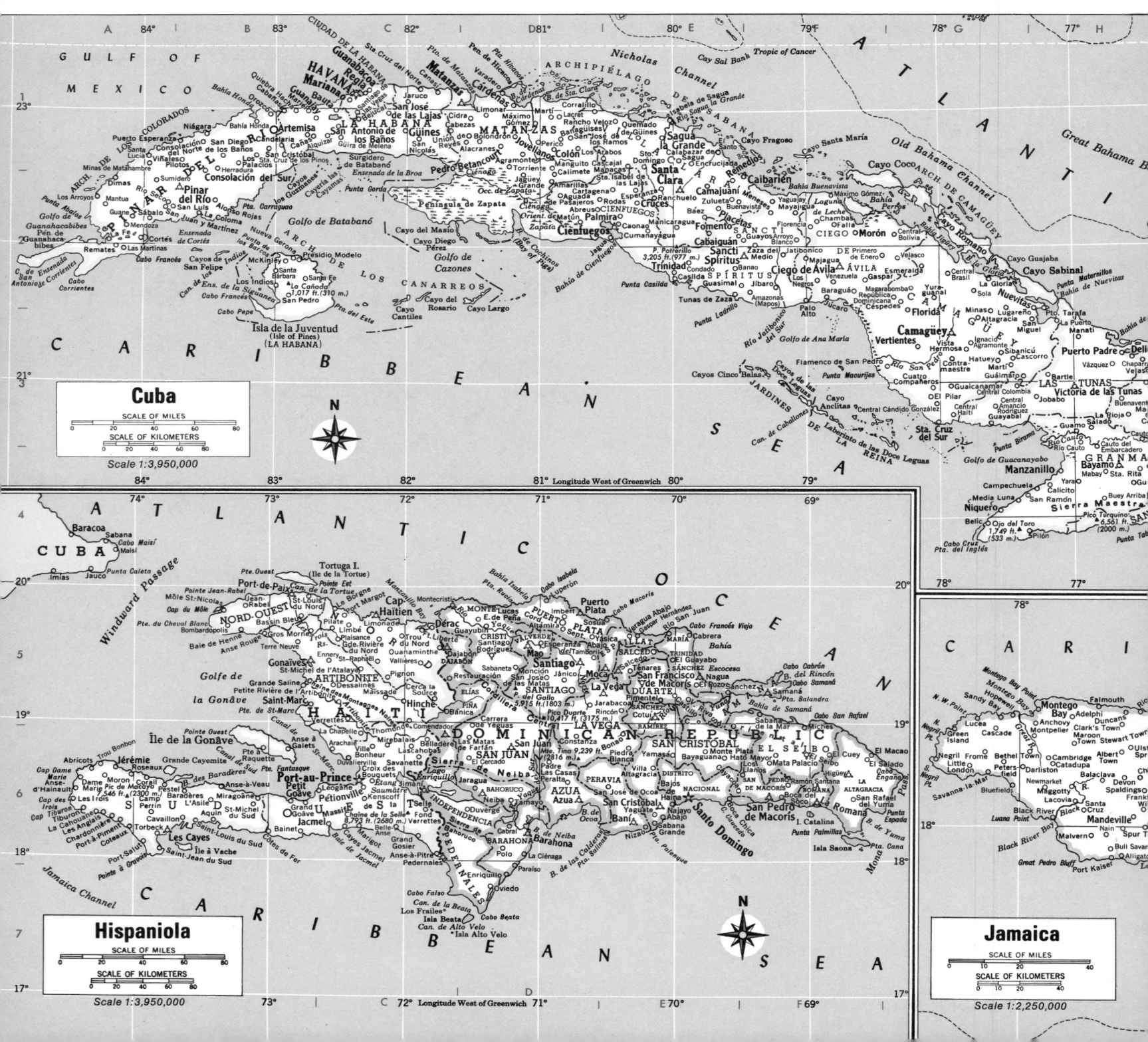

Santa Cruz de los Pinos 3,545 B1
Santa Cruz del Sur 27,142 G3
Santa Fe 3,925 B2
Santa Isabel de las Lajas 7,279 E2
Santa Lucía 3,734 J3
Santa Rita 6,358 H4
Santiago de Cuba 362,432 J4
Santiago de las Vegas 29,325 C1
Santo Domingo 32,950 E1
Sibanicú 14,252 G3
Sola 2,436 G2
Sumidero 980 A2
Surgidero de Batabanó 11,533 C1
Tacajó 4,469 J3
Torriente 1,759 D11
Trinidad 42,080 E2
Unión de Reyes 28,422 C1
Varadero 14,737 D1
Vázquez 3,851 H3
Velasco 5,618 H3
Venezuela 13,744 F2
Vertientes 25,178 G3
Victoria de las Tunas 87,522 H3
Viñales 2,049 A1
Yaguajay 30,720 F2
Yara 238,879 H4
Zaza del Medio 7,495 F2
Zulueta 5,425 E2

OTHER FEATURES

Abalos (pt.) A2
Ana María (gulf) F3
Anclitas (cay) F3
Batabanó (gulf) C2
Birama (pt.) G4
Broa (inlet) C1
Buenavista (bay) F2
Caballones (chan.) F3
Camagüey (arch.) G2
Cantiles (cay) C3
Cárdenas (bay) D1
Carraguao (pt.) B2
Casilda (pt.) E2
Cauto (riv.) H3
Cayamas (cays) C2
Cazones (gulf) C2
Cienfuegos (bay) D2
Cinco Balas (cays) E3
Cochinos (bay) D2
Coco (cay) G1
Corrientes (cape) A2
Corrientes (inlet) A2
Cortés (inlet) B2
Cristal, Sierra del (mts.) J3
Cruz (cape) G4
Diego Pérez (cay) C2
Doce Leguas (cays) F3
Este (pt.) C3
Fragoso (cay) F1
Francés (cape) A2
Gorda (pt.) C2
Gran Piedra (mt.) J4
Guacanayabo (gulf) G4
Guajaba (cay) G2
Guanahacabibes (gulf) A2
Guanahacabibes (pen.) A2
Guantánamo (bay) J4
Guantánamo Bay U.S. Nav. Reserve K4
Guarico (pt.) K3
Guzmanes (cays) B2
Hicacos (pen.) D1
Hicacos (pt.) D1
Honda (bay) B1
Indios (chan.) B2
Inglés (pt.) G4
Jardines de la Reina (arch.) F3
Jatibonico del Sur (riv.) F3
Jigüey (bay) G2
Juventud, Isla de la (Pines) (isl.) 57,879 B3
Laberinto de las Doce Leguas (cays) F3
Ladrillo (pt.) E3
Largo (cay) D2
Leche (lag.) F2
Los Barcos (pt.) B2
Los Canarreos (arch.) C2
Los Colorados (arch.) A1
Lucrecia (cape) J3
Macurijes (pt.) F3
Maestra, Sierra (mts.) H4
Maisí (cape) K4
Mangle (pt.) J3
Masío (cay) C2
Matanzas (bay) D1
Nicholas (chan.) E1
Nipe (bay) J3
Nuevitas (bay) H2
Ojo del Toro (mt.) G4
Old Bahama (chan.) G1
Pepe (cape) B3
Perros (bay) G2
Pigs (Cochinos) (bay) D2
Pines (Isla de la Juventud) (isl.) 7,879 B3
Potrerillo (peak) E2
Quemado (pt.) K4
Romano (cay) G2
Rosario (cay) C2
Sabana (arch.) E1
Sabinal (cay) H2
Sagua la Grande (riv.) E1
San Antonio (cape) A2
San Felipe (cays) B2
San Pedro (riv.) G3
Santa Clara (bay) D1
Santa María (cay) F1
Siguanea (bay) B2
Tabacal (pt.) H4
Toa, Cuchillas de (mts.) K4
Tortuguilla (pt.) K4
Turquino (peak) H4
Zapata (pen.) C2
Zapata Occidental (swamp) D2
Zapata Oriental (swamp) D2

DOMINICAN REPUBLIC

PROVINCES

Azua 142,770 D6
Bahoruco 78,636 D6
Barahona 137,160 D6
Dajabón 57,709 D5
Distrito Nacional 1,550,739 E6
Duarte 235,544 E5
Elías Piña 65,384 C5
El Seibo 157,866 F6
Espaillat 164,017 E5
Independencia 38,768 D6
La Altagracia 100,112 F6
La Romana 109,769 F6
La Vega 385,043 D6
María Trinidad Sánchez 112,629 E5
Monte Cristi 83,407 D5
Pedernales 17,006 D7
Peravia 168,123 E6
Puerto Plata 206,757 D5
Salcedo 99,191 E5
Samaná 65,699 E5
Sánchez Ramírez 126,567 E5
San Cristóbal 446,132 E6
San Juan 239,957 D6
San Pedro de Macorís 152,890 F6
Santiago 550,372 D5
Santiago Rodríguez 55,411 D5
Valverde 100,319 D5

CITIES and TOWNS

Altamira 2,759 D5
Azua 31,481 D6
Bajos de Haina 33,135 E6
Baní 36,705 E6
Barahona 49,334 D6
Bonao 44,486 E6
Cabrera 2,542 E5
Comendador 5,962 C6
Constanza 15,141 D6
Cotuí 16,688 E5
Dajabón 8,808 D5
El Seibo 13,511 F6
Hato Mayor 17,859 F6
Higüey 33,501 F6
Imbert 5,315 D5
Jarabacoa 13,416 E5
Jimaní 3,327 C6
La Romana 91,571 F6
La Vega 52,432 E5
Luperón 2,500 D5
Mao 33,527 D5
Moca 31,176 D5
Monción 3,344 D5
Nagua 20,912 E5
Puerto Plata 45,348 D5
Sabana de la Mar 9,983 F5
Sabaneta 9,170 D5
Samaná 5,023 F5
Sánchez 7,919 E5
San Cristóbal 58,520 E6
San Francisco de Macorís 64,906 E5
San Juan 49,764 D6
San Pedro de Macorís 78,562 F6
Santiago 278,638 D5
Santo Domingo (cap.) 1,313,172 E6
Tenares 4,065 E5
Villa Altagracia 20,890 E6

OTHER FEATURES

Alto Velo (chan.) C7
Alto Velo (isl.) D7
Balandra (pt.) F5
Beata (cape) D7
Beata (chan.) C7
Beata (isl.) C7
Cabrón (cape) F5
Calderas (bay) D6
Cana (pt.) F6
Catalina (isl.) F6
Caucedo (capee) E6
Central, Cordillera (range) D5
Duarte (peak) D5
Engaño (cape) F6
Enriquillo (lake) C6
Escocesa (bay) E5
Espada (pt.) F6
Falso (cape) C7
Francés Viejo (cape) E5
Gallo (mt.) D5
Isabela (bay) D5
Isabela (cape) D5
Los Frailes (isl.) C7
Macorís (cape) E5
Manzanillo (bay) C5
Mona (passg.) F6
Neiba (bay) D6
Neiba, Sierra de (mts.) D6
Ocoa (bay) D6
Oriental, Cordillera (range) F6
Palenque (pt.) E6
Palmillas (pt.) F6
Rincón (bay) F5
Rucia (pt.) D5
Salinas (pt.) E6
Samaná (bay) F5
Samaná (cape) F5
San Rafael (cape) F5
Saona (isl.) F6
Septentrional, Cordillera (range) D5
Tina (mt.) D6
Yaque del Norte (riv.) D5
Yaque del Sur (riv.) D6
Yuma (bay) F6
Yuna (riv.) E5

HAITI

DEPARTMENTS

Artibonite C5
Nord C5
Nord-Ouest B5
Ouest C6
Sud A6

CITIES and TOWNS

Anse-à-Galets 3,623 B6
Anse-d'Hainault 5,220 A6
Aquin 3,820 B6
Cap-Haïtien 64,406 C5
Croix des Bouquets 4,365 C6
Dame Marie 4,320 A6
Dérac 1,300 C5
Dessalines 7,984 C5
Fort Liberté 5,012 C5
Gonaïves 34,209 B5
Grande Rivière du Nord 6,007 C5
Gros Morne 4,739 B5
Hinche 10,070 C5
Jacmel 13,730 C6
Jérémie 18,493 A6
Kenscoff 2,605 C6
Lascahobas 3,805 C6
Léogâne 5,782 C6
Les Cayes 34,090 B6
Limbé 10,476 C5
Miragoâne 4,327 B6
Mirebalais 6,069 C6
Ouanaminthe 7,276 C5
Pétionville 35,333 C6
Petite Rivière de l'Artibonite 10,099 B5
Petit Goâve 7,310 B6
Pignon 4,576 C5
Port-au-Prince (cap.) 449,831 C6
Port-de-Paix 15,540 B5
Saint-Louis du Nord 7,203 B5
Saint-Marc 24,165 B5
Saint-Michel de l'Atalaye 7,559 C5
Saint-Raaphaël 3,889 C5
Trou du Nord 7,637 C5
Verrettes 3,670 C5

OTHER FEATURES

Artibonite (riv.) C5
Baradères (bay) B6
Cheval Blanc (pt.) B5
Dame Marie (cape) A6
Est (pt.) C4
Fantasque (pt.) B6
Gonâve (gulf) B5
Gonâve (isl.) B6
Grande Cayemite (isl.) B6
Gravois (pt.) A7
Irois (cape) A6
Jean-Rabel (pt.) B5
Macaya (mt.) A6
Manzanillo (bay) C5
Môle (cape) B5
Noires (mts.) C5
Ouest (pt.) B4
Ouest (pt.) B6
Saint-Marc (chan.) B6
Saint-Marc (pt.) B5
Saumâtre (lake) C6
Selle (peak) C6
Sud (chan.) B6
Tortue (chan.) C5
Tortue (Tortuga) (isl.) C4
Tortuga (isl.) C4
Trois-Rivières (riv.) B5
Vache (isl.) B6
Windward (passg.) A5

JAMAICA

CITIES and TOWNS

Alley J7
Alligator Pond H6
Anchovy 2,558 H5
Annotto Bay K6
Bamboo 2,971 J6
Bath K6
Black River 2,701 H6
Bog Walk J6
Bowden K6
Browns Town 5,479 J6
Bull Savanna-Junction 5,110 H6
Cambridge 2,449 H6
Catadupa H6
Christiana H6
Discovery Bay 1,814 J5
Falmouth 3,937 H5
Green Island G6
Hope Bay K6
Kingston (cap.) 106,791 K6
Kingston *516,865 J7
Linstead J6
Lucea 3,635 G5
Mandeville 14,421 H6
Maroon Town 2,717 H6
May Pen 26,074 J6
Montego Bay 43,521 H5
Montpelier H6
Morant Bay 7,465 K7
Negril G6
Ocho Rios 5,851 J6
Oracabessa J5
Port Antonio 10,538 K6
Port Kaiser H7
Port Maria 5,259 J6
Port Morant K6
Saint Ann's Bay 7,101 J5
Saint Margaret's Bay K6
Savanna-la-Mar 11,759 G6
Spanish Town 40,731 J6
Williamsfield H6

OTHER FEATURES

Black (riv.) H6
Black River (bay) G6
Blue (mts.) J6
Blue Mountain (peak) K6
Galina (pt.) J6
Grande (riv.) K6
Great (riv.) H6
Great Pedro Bluff (prom.) H6
Long (bay) H7
Luana (pt.) G6
Minho (riv.) J6
Montego (bay) G5
Montego Bay ((pt.) G5
North East (pt.) K6
North Negril (pt.) G6
North West (pt.) G5
Old Harbour (bay) J6
Portland (pt.) J7
Sir John's (peak) K6
South East (pt.) K6
South Negril (pt.) G6

*City and Suburbs.
○ Population of municipality.

LEGEND
Capitals of Countries ☆
Provincial Capitals ⚠
International Boundaries
Provincial Boundaries

© Copyright HAMMOND INCORPORATED, Maplewood, N. J.

Longitude West of Greenwich

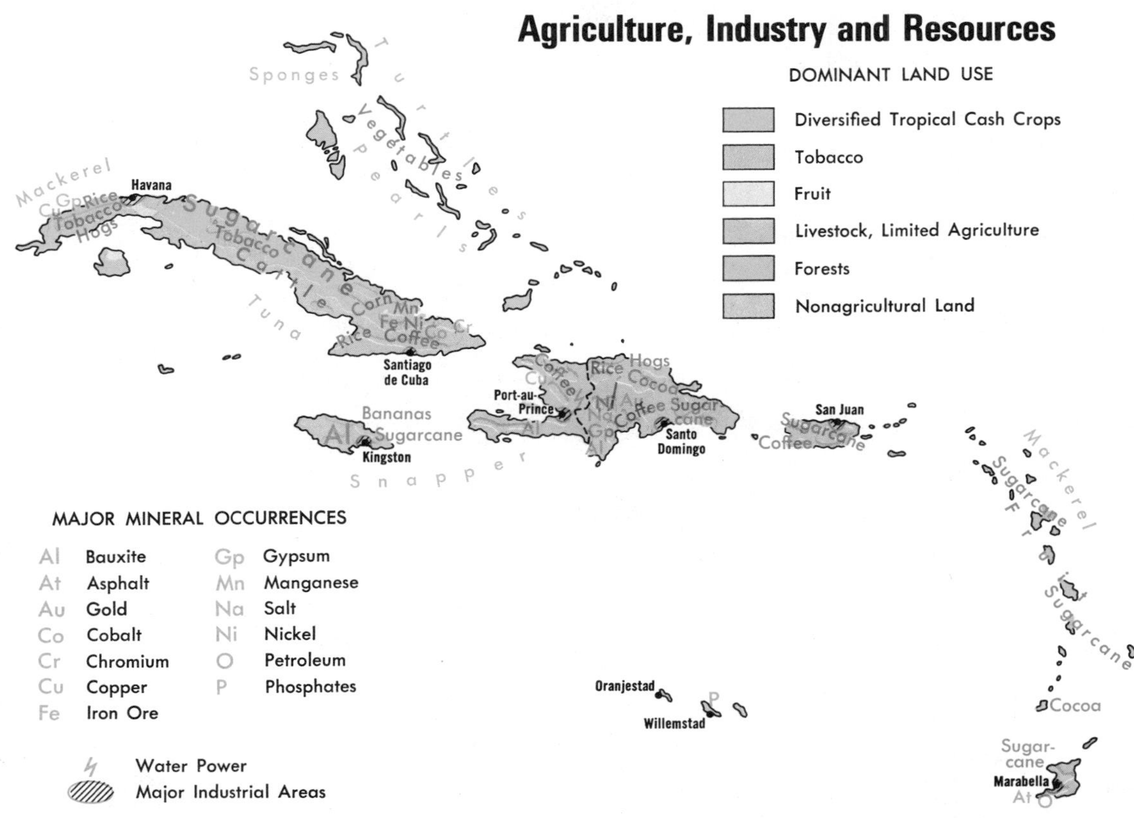
Agriculture, Industry and Resources
DOMINANT LAND USE
Diversified Tropical Cash Crops
Tobacco
Fruit
Livestock, Limited Agriculture
Forests
Nonagricultural Land
MAJOR MINERAL OCCURRENCES
Al Bauxite
At Asphalt
Au Gold
Co Cobalt
Cr Chromium
Cu Copper
Fe Iron Ore
Gp Gypsum
Mn Manganese
Na Salt
Ni Nickel
O Petroleum
P Phosphates
Water Power
Major Industrial Areas
Havana
Santiago de Cuba
Port-au-Prince
Santo Domingo
San Juan
Kingston
Oranjestad
Willemstad
Marabella
Sponges
Vegetables
Turtles
Pearls
Mackerel
Sugarcane
Tobacco
Hogs
Cattle
Tuna
Rice
Coffee
Cocoa
Bananas
Snapper

(continued)

PUERTO RICO

DISTRICTS
Aguadilla A1
Arecibo C1
Bayamón D1
Guayama D2
Humacao E2
Mayagüez B2
Ponce C2
San Juan D1

CITIES and TOWNS
Adjuntas 5,239 B2
Aguada 5,025 A1
Aguadilla 22,039 A1
Aguas Buenas 3,766 E2
Aibonito 9,331 D2
Añasco 5,646 A1
Ángeles ○2,817 B2
Arecibo 48,779 B1
Arroyo 8,435 E3
Bahomamey A1
Bajadero 3,678 C1
Barceloneta 4,502 C1
Barranquitas 3,618 D2
Bayamón 185,087 D1
Boquerón ○3,675 A3
Cabo Rojo 10,292 A2
Caguas 87,214 E2
Caguas †156,819 E2
Camuy 3,834 B1
Carolina 147,835 E1
Cataño 26,243 D1
Cayey 23,305 D2
Ceiba 4,973 F2
Central Aguirre 1,049 D3
Ciales 3,582 C1
Cidra 6,069 D2
Coamo 12,851 D2
Comerío 5,736 D2
Coquí 3,018 D3
Corozal 5,889 D1
Coto Laurel ○5,192 C2
Culebra (Dewey) 938 G1
Dorado 10,203 D1
Ensenada B3
Esperanza 1,130 G2
Fajardo 26,928 F1
Florida 3,641 C1
Guánica 9,628 B3
Guayama 21,097 E3
Guayanilla 6,163 B3
Guaynabo 65,075 D1
Gurabo 7,645 E2
Hatillo 5,019 B1
Hato Rey E1
Hormigüeros 12,031 A2
Humacao 19,147 E2
Isabela 12,087 A1
Isabel Segunda 2,330 G2
Jayuya 3,588 C2
Jobos 4,194 D3
Juana Díaz 10,469 C2
Juncos 7,851 E2
Lajas 4,275 A2
Lares 5,224 B2
Las Piedras 4,857 E2
Levittown 31,613 D1
Loíza 3,932 E1
Loíza Aldea E1
Luquillo 4,531 F1
Manatí 17,347 C1
Maricao 1,390 B2
Mayagüez 82,968 A2
Mayagüez †98,155 A2
Moca 3,960 A1
Naguabo 4,135 F2
Naranjito 2,849 D1
Palmer 1,566 F1
Palo Seco 1,172 D1
Parguera A3
Patillas 3,172 E2
Peñuelas 4,235 B2
Playa de Fajardo F1
Playa de Humacao ○5,573 F2
Ponce 161,739 C3
Ponce †168,272 C3
Puerto Nuevo D1
Puerto Real 2,390 A2
Puerto Real (Playa de Fajardo) F1
Punta Santiago (Playa de Humacao) ○5,573 F2
Quebradillas 3,770 B1
Río Blanco 1,433 F2
Río Grande 12,047 E1
Río Piedras E1
Rosario A2
Sabana Grande 7,435 B2
Sabana Seca 11,431 D1
Salinas 6,220 D3
San Antonio 2,681 A1
San Germán 13,054 A2
San Juan (cap.) 424,600 E1
San Juan †1,081,193 E1
San Lorenzo 8,880 E2
San Sebastián 10,619 B1
Santa Isabel 6,948 C3
Santurce E1
Tallaboa 1,059 B3
Toa Alta 4,427 D1
Toa Baja 1,992 D1
Trujillo Alto 41,141 E1
Utuado 11,113 B2
Vega Alta 10,582 D1
Vega Baja 18,233 D1
Vieques (Isabel Segunda) 2,330 G2
Villalba 3,469 C2
Yabucoa 6,797 E2
Yauco 14,594 B2

OTHER FEATURES
Aguadilla (bay) A1
Algarrobo (pt.) A2
Añasco (bay) A1
Arenas (pt.) F2
Bauta (riv.) C2
Bayamón (riv.) D1
Boquerón (bay) A3
Borinquen (pt.) A1
Cabullones (pt.) C3
Caja de Muertos (isl.) C3
Camuy (riv.) B1
Canovanas (riv.) E1
Caonillas (lake) C2
Carite (lake) E2
Carraízo (lake) E1
Cayey, Sierra de (mts.) D2
Central, Cordillera (range) C2
Cerro Gordo (pt.) D1
Coamo (res.) D3
Coamo (riv.) D3
Culebra (isl.) 1,265 G1
Culebrinas (riv.) A1
Culebrita (isl.) G2
El Toro (mt.) F2
El Yunque (mt.) F1
Este (pt.) G2
Fajardo (riv.) F1
Figuras (pt.) E3
Fosforescente (bay) A3
Grande de Añasco (riv.) B2
Grande de Arecibo (riv.) C1
Grande de Loíza (riv.) E1
Grande de Manatí (riv.) C1
Guajataca (lake) B1
Guanajibo (pt.) A2
Guanajibo (riv.) A2
Guánica (lake) B3
Guaniquilla (pt.) A2
Guayabal (lake) C2
Guayanés (pt.) F2
Guayanés (riv.) E2
Guayanilla (bay) B3
Guayo (lake) B2
Guilarte (mt.) B2
Honda (bay) F2
Jacaguas (riv.) C2
Jaicoa, Cordillera (mts.) B1
Jiguero (pt.) A1
Jobos (bay) D3
Lima (pt.) F2
Luquillo, Sierra de (mts.) E2
Manglillo (pt.) B3
Mayagüez (bay) A2
Miquillo (pt.) F1
Molinos (pt.) G1
Mona (passg.) A2
Negra (pt.) G2
Nigua (riv.) D2
Ola Grande (pt.) D3
Palmas Altas (pt.) C1
Patillas (lake) E2
Petrona (pt.) D3
Pirata (mt.) F2
Plata (riv.) D2
Puerca (pt.) F2
Puerto Medio Mundo (bay) F2
Punta, Cerro de (mt.) C2
Ramey A.F.B. A1
Rincón (bay) D3
Rojo (cape) A3
Roosevelt Road Naval Res. F2
Salinas (pt.) D1
San José (lag.) E1
San Juan, Cabezas de (prom.) F1
San Juan Nat'l Hist. Site D1
Soldado (pt.) G2
Sucia (bay) A3
Tanamá (riv.) B1
Toro, El (mt.) F2
Torrecilla (lag.) E1
Tortuguero (lag.) D1
Tuna (pt.) E3
Vacía Talega (pt.) E1
Vieques (isl.) 7,662 G2
Vieques (passg.) F2
Vieques (sound) G2
Yagüez (riv.) A2
Yauco (lake) B2
Yeguas ((pt.) F3

ANTIGUA

CITIES and TOWNS
All Saints 1,796 E11
Cedar Grove 1,460 E11
Falmouth 1,134 E11
Freetown 1,250 E11
Jennings 1,370 D11
Liberta 2,394 E11
Old Road 1,244 D11
Parham 1,570 E11
Saint John's (cap.) 21,814 E11
Willikies 1,843 E11

OTHER FEATURES
Antigua (isl.) 76,213 E11
Boggy (peak) D11
Boon (pt.) E11
Green (isl.) E11
Guiana (isl.) E11
Long (isl.) E11
Saint John's (harb.) C11
Standfast (pt.) E11
Willoughby (bay) E11

BARBADOS

CITIES and TOWNS
Bathsheba B8
Belleplaine B8
Bridgetown (cap.) 7,552 B9
Carlton B8
Cave Hill B9
Checker Hall B8
Codrington B8
Crab Hill B8
Crane C9
Drax Hall B8
Ellerton B9
Greenland B8
Holetown B8
Kendal B8
Lodge Hill B8
Marchfield B9
Mount Standfast B8
Oistins B9
Rose Hill B8
Rouen B9
Saint Lawrence B9
Saint Martins C9
Scarboro B9
Seawell B9
Six Mens B8
Speightstown B8
Spring Hall B8
Welchman Hall B8

OTHER FEATURES
Carlisle (bay) B9
Hillaby (mt.) B8
Long (bay) B9
North (pt.) B8
Oistins (bay) B9
Pelican (isl.) B9
Ragged (pt.) C8
Sam Lord's Castle C9
South (pt.) B9

DOMINICA

CITIES and TOWNS
Barroui 1,480 E6
Castle Bruce 1,975 F6
Coulihaut 1,735 E6
Delice F7
Grand Bay 3,152 F7
Hampstead E5
La Plaine F6
Mahout 2,095 E6
Marigot 3,183 F6
Petit Soufrière F6
Portsmouth 2,329 E5
Rosalie F6
Roseau (cap.) 9,968 E7
Roseau *16,035 E7
Saint Joseph 2,643 E6
Salybia F6
Soufrière E7
Vieille Case E5
Wesley 2,002 F5

OTHER FEATURES
Capuchin (cape) E5
Carib Reserve F6
Clyde (riv.) F6
Crumpton (pt.) F5
Diablotin, Morne (mt.) E6
Dominica (passg.) E5
Douglas (bay) E5
Grand (bay) F7
Jaquet (pt.) E6
Layou (riv.) E6
Martinique (passg.) E7
Micotrin (mt.) F6
Pagoua (bay) F6
Prince Rupert (bay) E5
Scotts (head) E7
Soufrière (bay) E7
Trois Pitons, Morne (mt.) E6

GRENADA

CITIES and TOWNS
Gouyave 2,498 C8
Grand Roy C8
Grenville 1,723 D8
Hermitage D8
La Taste D8
Marquis D8
Mount Tivoli D8
Saint George's (cap.) 6,463 C9
Saint George's *34,624 C9
Sauteurs 605 D8
Victoria 1,673 D8
Woodford C8

OTHER FEATURES
Bedford (pt.) D8
David (pt.) D8
Great Bacolet (pt.) D8
Green (isl.) D8
Grenville (bay) D8
Gros (pt.) C8
Halifax (harb.) C8
Irvin's (bay) D8
Les Tantes (isls.) D7
Molinière (pt.) C8
Prickly (pt.) C9
Ronde (isl.) D7
Saint Catherine (mt.) D8
Saline (pt.) C9
Sinai (mt.) D8
Telescope (pt.) D8

GUADELOUPE
Total Population 329,017

CITIES and TOWNS
Anse-Bertrand 1,921 A5
Baie-Mahault 5,874 A6
Baillif 3,844 A7
Bananier A7
Basse-Terre (cap.) 13,397 A7
Bouillante 1,821 A6
Bourg-des-Saintes 907 A7
Capesterre 7,541 A7
Ferry A6
Gosier 13,741 B6
Gourbeyre 5,637 A7
Goyave 1,709 A6
Grand-Bourg 3,249 B7
Lamentin 2,319 A6
Les Abymes 51,837 B6
Morne-à-l'Eau 9,457 A6
Moule 9,800 B6
Petit-Bourg 5,097 A6
Petit-Canal 1,581 A6
Pigeon A6
Pointe-à-Pitre 25,151 B6
Pointe-Noire 2,180 A6
Port-Louis 4,517 B5
Saint-Claude 6,755 A7
Sainte-Anne 11,527 B6
Sainte-Marguerite B6
Sainte-Marie A6
Sainte-Rose 4,805 A6
Saint-François 3,141 B6
Trois-Rivières 7,881 A7
Vieux-Fort 1,073 B7
Vieux-Habitants 4,065 A7

OTHER FEATURES
Allègre (pt.) A6
Antigues (pt.) A5
Basse-Terre (isl.) 138,777 A6
Châteaux (pt.) B6
Constant, Morne (hill) B7
Désirade, La (isl.) 1,602 B6
Fajou (isl.) A6
Grand Cul-de-Sac Marin (bay) A6
Grande-Terre (isl.) B6
Grande Vigie (pt.) B5
Grand-Îlet (isl.) A7
Guadeloupe (isl.) 167,896 B6
Guadeloupe (passg.) A5
Guadeloupe Nat'l Park A6
Kahouanne (isl.) A6
Marie-Galante (isl.) 13,757 B7
Nord (pt.) B7
Nord-Est (bay) B6
Petit Cul-de-Sac Marin (bay) A6
Petite-Terre (isls.) B6
Saintes (chan.) A7
Saintes (isls.) 2,901 A7
Salée (riv.) A6
Sans Toucher (mt.) A6
Soufrière (mt.) A7
Terre-de-Bas (isl.) 1,427 A7
Terre-de-Haut (isl.) 1,453 A7
Vieux-Fort (pt.) A7

MARTINIQUE
Total Population 330,220

CITIES and TOWNS
Ajoupa-Bouillon 1,569 C5
Basse-Pointe 2,163 C5
Bellefontaine 818 C6
Case-Pilote 1,776 C6
Ducos 4,429 D6
Fond-Saint-Denis 962 C6
Fort-de-France (cap.) 96,649 C6
Grand' Rivière 1,053 C5
Gros-Morne 1,976 D6
La Trinité 3,380 D6
Le Carbet 2,321 C6
Le François 2,940 D6
Le Lamentin 6,872 D6
Le Lorrain 2,024 D6
Le Marin 2,651 D7
Le Morne-Rouge 2,650 C5
Le Prêcheur 1,350 C5
Le Robert 3,610 D6
Le Saint-Esprit 3,947 D6
Les Trois-Îlets 1,484 D6
Le Vauclin 3,054 D6
Macouba 1,142 C5
Marigot 1,765 D5
Rivière-Pilote 1,587 D7
Rivière-Salée 1,859 D7
Sainte-Luce 1,502 D7
Sainte-Marie 3,966 D5
Saint-Joseph 2,052 D6
Saint-Pierre 4,923 C6
Schoelcher 16,412 C6

OTHER FEATURES
Cabet, Pitons du (mt.) C6
Cabrits (isl.) D7
Caravelle (pen.) D6
Cul-de-Sac du Marin (bay) D7
Diable (pt.) D5
Ferré (cape) E7
Fort-de-France (bay) C6
Galion (bay) D6
Lézarde (riv.) D6
Long (isl.) D6
Lorrain (riv.) D5
Martinique (passg.) C5
Pelée (vol.) C5
Pilote (riv.) D7
Ramiers (isl.) C6
Ramville (isl.) D6
Robert (harb.) D6
Rose (pt.) D6
Saint-Martin (cape) C5
Saint-Pierre (bay) C6
Salines (pt.) D7
Salomon (pt.) C7
Vauclin (mt.) D6

NETHERLANDS ANTILLES

CITIES and TOWNS
Aresji D9
Ascension F8
Bacuna E8
Balashi E10
Boven Bolivia E8
Bubali D10
Bushiribana E10
Dokterstuin F8
Druif D1
Emmastad F9
Entrejo E8
Fontein E8
Fuik G9
Groot Sint Joris G9
Hato G8
Kralendijk (cap.), Bonaire 2,500 E8
Lago E10
Lagoen F8
Montanja di Reij G9
New Port G9
Noord di Salinja E8
Onima E8
Oranjestad (cap.), Aruba 10,100 D10
Otrabanda F9
Patrick F8
Rincon E8
Rooi E8
Santa Barbara G9
Santa Catharina G9
Savaneta E10
Savonet F8
Sint Anna D1
Sint Jan D8
Sint Kruis F8
Sint Martha F8
Sint Michiel F9
Sint Nicolaas E10
Sint Willebrordus F8
Terra Corra E8
Westpunt, Aruba D10
Westpunt, Curaçao F8
Willemstad (cap.) 95,000 F9
Willemstad *130,000 F9

OTHER FEATURES
Aruba (isl.) 55,148 E9
Basora (pt.) E10
Bonaire (isl.) 8,087 E9
Bullen (bay) F8
Caracas (bay) G9
Curaçao (isl.) 145,430 G7
Goto (lake) D8
Jamanota (mt.) E10
Kanon (pt.) G9
Klein Bonaire (isl.) E8
Kudarebe (pt.) D9
Lac (bay) D9
Lacre (pt.) E9
Malmok (mt.) E8
Noord (pt.) D8
Noord (pt.) F8
Paarden (bay) D10
Palm (beach) D10
Pekelmeer (lake) E9
Piscadera (bay) F9
Schottegat (bay) G9
Sint Anna (bay) F9
Sint Christoffel (mt.) F8
Sint Joris (bay) G9
Slag (bay) D8
Vierkant (pt.) E8

SAINT CHRISTOPHER and NEVIS

CITIES and TOWNS
Basseterre (cap.) 14,725 C10
Cayon C10
Charlestown 1,326 C11
Cotton Ground 471 C11
Dieppe Bay C10
Frigate Bay C10
Gingerland D11
Golden Rock C10
Newcastle D11
Old Road Town C10
Sadlers Village C10
Sandy Point 862 C10
Tabernacle C10
Zion Hill D11

OTHER FEATURES
Brimstone (hill) C10
Dogwood (pt.) D11
Fort (pt.) C11
Great Salt (pond) D10
Heldens (pt.) C10
Horse Shoe (pt.) C11
Misery (mt.) C10
Monkey (hill) C10
Narrows, The (str.) D11
Nevis (isl.) 9,300 D11
Nevis (peak) D11
North Friars (bay) D10
Pinney's (beach) D11
Saint Christopher (Saint Kitts) (isl.) 35,104 D10
South Friars (bay) C10

SAINT LUCIA

CITIES and TOWNS
Anse la Raye •5,007 F6
Canaries •2,075 G6
Castries (cap.) •42,770 G6
Choc G5
Choiseul •6,382 F7
Dauphin G5
Dennery •9,654 G6
Gros Islet •10,329 G5
Laborie •6,944 G7
Marigot G6
Marquis G6
Micoud •12,264 G6
Praslin G6
Soufrière •7,456 F6
Vieux Fort •10,675 G7

OTHER FEATURES
Beaumont (pt.) F6
Canaries, Piton (mt.) G6
Cannelles (pt.) G7
Cannelles (riv.) G6
Cap (pt.) G5
Choc (bay) G5
Fond d'Or (bay) G6
Gimie (mt.) G6
Grand Caille (pt.) F6
Grand Cul de Sac (riv.) G6
Gros Islet (bay) G5
Gros Piton (mt.) G6
La Sorcière (mt.) G6
Maria (isls.) G7
Ministre (pt.) G7
Moule-à-Chique (cape) G7
Petit Piton (mt.) G6
Pigeon (isl.) G5
Port Castries (harb.) G6
Port Praslin (bay) G6
Roseau (riv.) G6
Saint Lucia (chan.) G5
Saint Vincent (chan.) G7
Savannes (bay) G7
Sorcière, La (mt.) G6
Soufrière (bay) F6
Vierge (pt.) G6

SAINT VINCENT and THE GRENADINES

CITIES and TOWNS
Barrouallie 1,298 A9
Calliaqua 627 A9
Camden Park A9
Colonarie A9
Georgetown 1,100 A8
Kingstown (cap.) 17,117 A9
Kingstown *23,330 A9
Layou 1,147 A9
Wallibu A8

OTHER FEATURES
Colonarie (pt.) A9
Cumberland (bay) A8
Dark (head) A8
De Volet (pt.) A8
Espagnol (pt.) A8
Greathead (bay) A9
Kingstown (bay) A9
Owia (bay) A8
Porter (pt.) A8
Richmond (peak) A8
Saint Andrew (mt.) A9
Saint Vincent (passg.) A8
Soufrière (mt.) A8
Yambou (head) A9

TRINIDAD and TOBAGO

CITIES and TOWNS
Arima 11,390 B10
Arouca B10
Basse Terre B11
Biche B10
Blanchisseuse B10
California A11
Carapichaima B10
Caroni B10
Cedros A11
Chaguanas 6,122 B10
Chaguaramas A10
Couva 3,635 B10
Cunapo B10
Ecclesville B11
Flanagin Town B10
Fullarton A11
Fyzabad 1,564 A11
Grande Rivière B10
Guaico B10
Guayaguayare B11
La Brea 1,487 A11
Marabella 18,158 A11
Matelot B10
Matura B10
Mayaro 2,638 B11
Moruga B11
Mucurapo A10
Palo Seco A11
Peñal 3,606 B11
Point Fortin 6,538 A11
Port-of-Spain (cap.) 67,978 A10
Princes Town 8,288 B11
Redhead B10
Rio Claro 2,423 B11
Saint Joseph 4,132 B10
Saint Joseph B11
San Fernando 33,490 A11
San Francique A11
Sangre Grande 8,948 B1
San Juan A10
Sans Souci B10
Siparia 5,773 B11
Tabaquite 2,309 B11
Tacarigua B10
Talparo B10
Toco 1,287 B10
Tunapuna 10,251 B10
Upper Manzanilla B1
Valencia B10
Waterloo A10

OTHER FEATURES
Aripo, El Cerro del (mt.) B10
Boca Grande (passg.) A10
Chacachacare (isl.) A10
Chupara (pt.) B10
Cocos (bay) B10
Dragons Mouth (str.) A10
El Tucuche (mt.) B10
Erin (bay) A11
Galeota (pt.) B11
Galera (pt.) C10
Guapo (bay) A11
Guatuaro (pt.) B11
Icacos (pt.) A11
Maracas (bay) C10
Pitch (lake) A11

VIRGIN ISLANDS (Br.)

CITIES and TOWNS
Road Town (cap.) 2,200 D3
West End C4

OTHER FEATURES
Flanagan (passg.) D4
Frenchman (cay) C4
Great Thatch (isl.) C4
Great Tobago (isl.) B3
Jost Van Dyke (isl.) 135 C3
Little Tobago (isl.) B3
Narrows, The (str.) C4
Norman (isl.) D4
Peter (isl.) D4
Road (bay) D3
Sage (mt.) D4
Sir Francis Drake (chan.) D4
Tortola (isl.) 9,257 D3

VIRGIN ISLANDS (U.S.)

CITIES and TOWNS
Bethlehem E4
Canebay E3
Charlotte Amalie (cap.) 11,842 B4
Christiansted 2,914 F4
Cruz Bay 1,928 C4
Diamond F4
Eastend D4
Emmaus C4
Fredensdal F4
Frederiksted 1,046 E4
Grove Place 3,599 E4
Kingshill F4
Longford F4
Negro Bay E4

OTHER FEATURES
Altona (lag.) F4
Annaly (bay) E3
Baron Bluff (prom.) E3
Bordeaux (mt.) C4
Brass (isls.) A4
Buck (isl.) G3
Buck Island (chan.) F3
Buck Island Reef Nat'l Mon. G3
Butler (bay) E4
Caneel (bay) B4
Capella (isls.) B5
Christiansted Nat'l Hist. Site F4
Coral (bay) C4
Crown (mt.) A4
Dutch Cap (cay) A4
Eagle (mt.) E4
East (pt.) G4
Flanagan (passg.) D4
Flat (cays) A4
Grass (pt.) G4
Great (pond) F4
Great Pond (bay) F4
Green (cay) F4
Hams Bluff (prom.) E3
Hans Lollik (isls.) B4
Hassel (isl.) B4
Jersey (bay) B4
Krause Lagoon (chan.) F4
Leeward (passg.) B4
Long (pt.) B4
Long (pt.) E4
Lovango (cay) C4
Magens (bay) B4
Maho (bay) C4
Narrows, The (str.) C4
Nulliberg (mt.) B4
Perseverance (bay) A4
Picara (pt.) B4
Pillsbury (sound) B4
Privateer (pt.) D4
Pull (pt.) F3
Ram (head) C5
Red (pt.) B4
Reef (bay) C4
Saba (isl.) A4
Saint Croix (isl.) 49,725 G4
Saint James (isls.) B4
Saint John (isl.) 2,472 C4
Saint Thomas (harb.) B4
Saint Thomas (isl.) 44,372 A4
Salt (cay) A4
Salt (riv.) F4
Salt River (bay) F3
Sandy (pt.) D4
Savana (isl.) A4
Southwest (cape) E4
Tague (bay) G4
Thatch (cay) B4
Turner Hole (bay) G4
U.S. Nav. Air Sta. A4
Virgin (str.) A4
Virgin Isls. Nat'l Park C4
Water (isl.) A4
Westend Saltpond (lag.) E4

*City and suburbs.
• Population of district.
†Population of met. area.
○ Population of municipality.

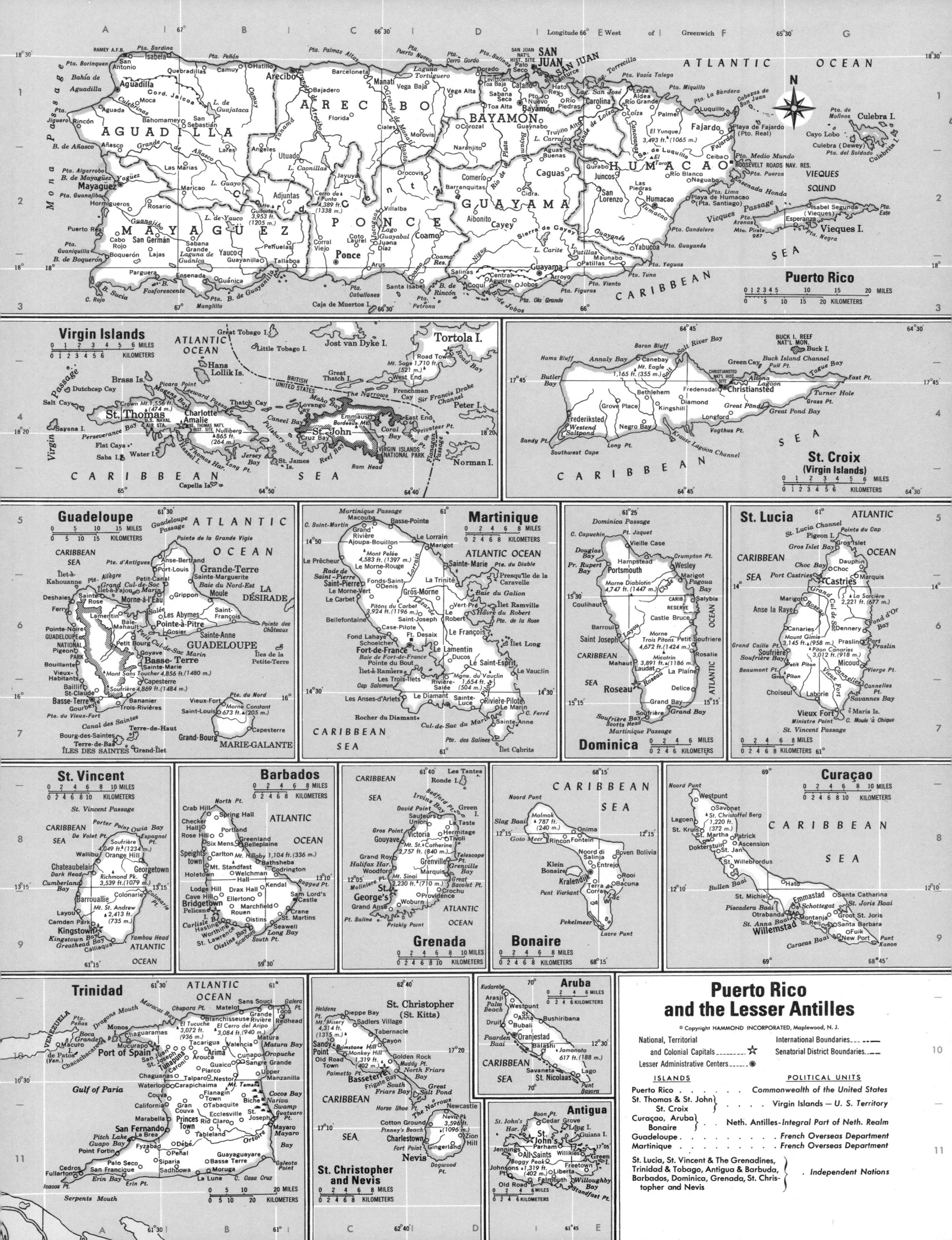

Puerto Rico and the Lesser Antilles

© Copyright HAMMOND INCORPORATED, Maplewood, N. J.

National, Territorial and Colonial Capitals .... ☆
International Boundaries ....
Lesser Administrative Centers .... ◉
Senatorial District Boundaries ....

ISLANDS	POLITICAL UNITS
Puerto Rico	Commonwealth of the United States
St. Thomas & St. John	Virgin Islands – U. S. Territory
St. Croix	
Curaçao, Aruba	Neth. Antilles-Integral Part of Neth. Realm
Bonaire	
Guadeloupe	French Overseas Department
Martinique	French Overseas Department
St. Lucia, St. Vincent & The Grenadines, Trinidad & Tobago, Antigua & Barbuda, Barbados, Dominica, Grenada, St. Christopher and Nevis	Independent Nations

Canada
CONIC PROJECTION

SCALE OF MILES
0 50 100 200 300

SCALE OF KILOMETERS
0 50 100 200 300 400 500

Capitals of Countries .... ☆
Provincial & Territorial Capitals .... △
Administrative Centers .... ◉
International Boundaries .... ▬▬▬
Provincial Boundaries .... ▬ ▬ ▬
Regional Boundaries .... ▬ ▪ ▬ ▪

Scale 1:19,600,000

© Copyright HAMMOND INCORPORATED, Maplewood, N.J.

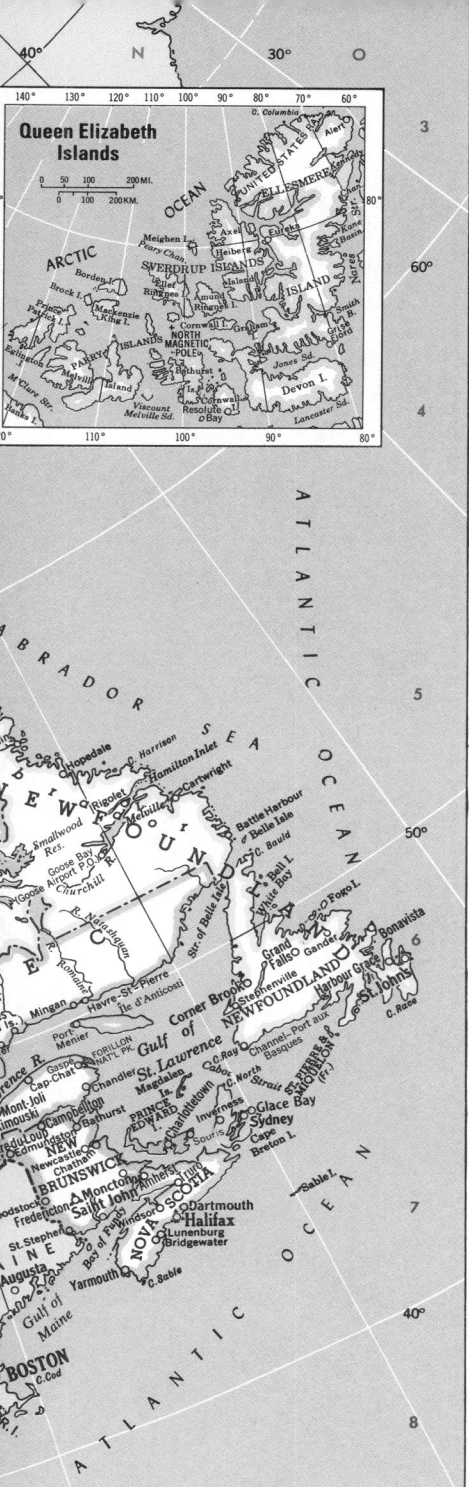

Queen Elizabeth Islands

AREA 3,851,787 sq. mi. (9,976,139 sq. km.)
POPULATION 24,343,181
CAPITAL Ottawa
LARGEST CITY Montréal
HIGHEST POINT Mt. Logan 19,524 ft. (5,951 m.)
MONETARY UNIT Canadian dollar
MAJOR LANGUAGES English, French
MAJOR RELIGIONS Protestantism, Roman Catholicism

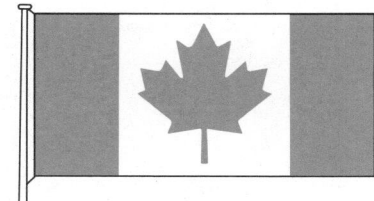

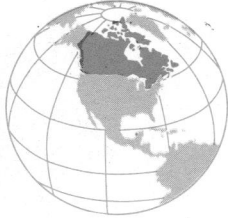

Population Distribution

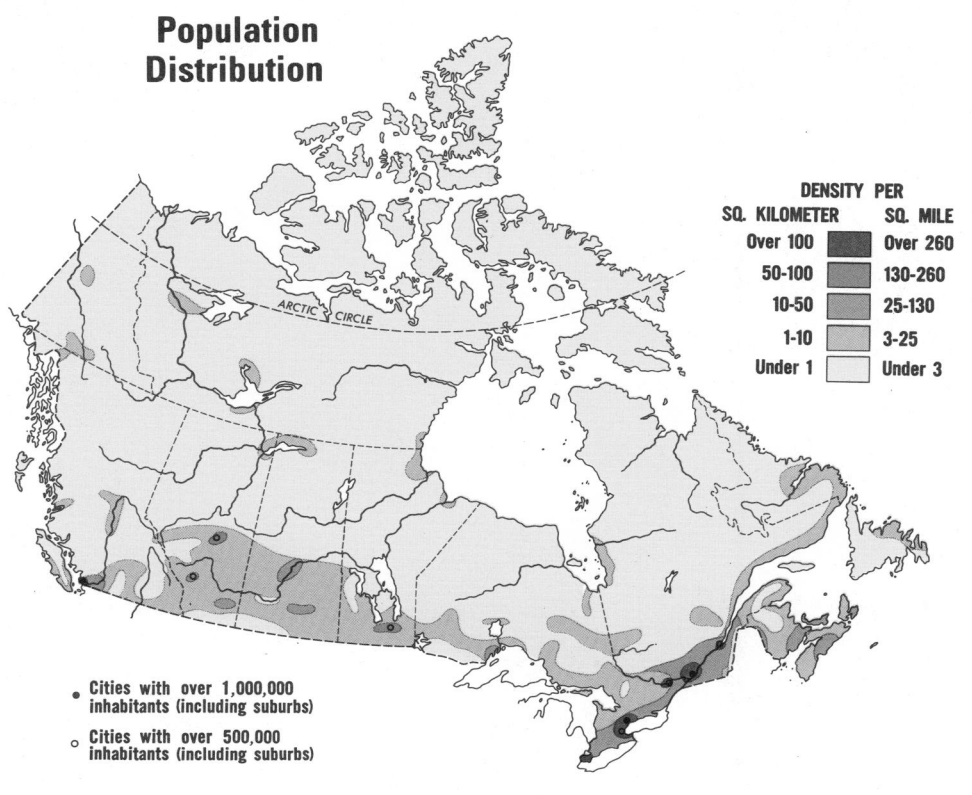

DENSITY PER

SQ. KILOMETER	SQ. MILE
Over 100	Over 260
50-100	130-260
10-50	25-130
1-10	3-25
Under 1	Under 3

● Cities with over 1,000,000 inhabitants (including suburbs)

○ Cities with over 500,000 inhabitants (including suburbs)

Vegetation

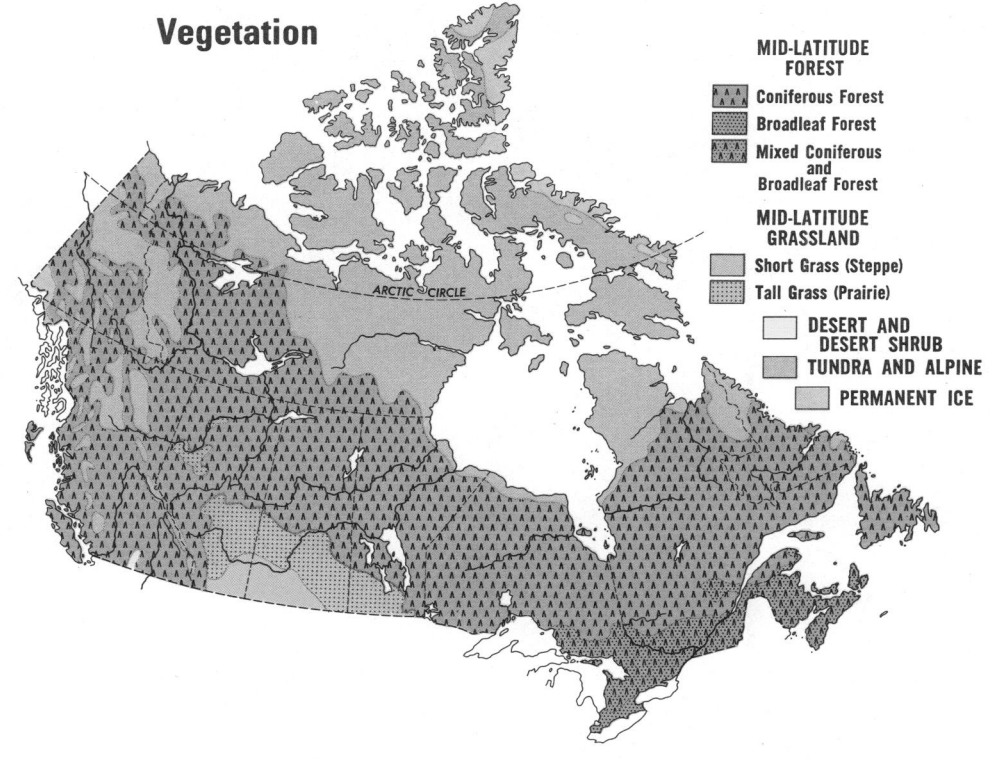

MID-LATITUDE FOREST
Coniferous Forest
Broadleaf Forest
Mixed Coniferous and Broadleaf Forest

MID-LATITUDE GRASSLAND
Short Grass (Steppe)
Tall Grass (Prairie)

DESERT AND DESERT SHRUB
TUNDRA AND ALPINE
PERMANENT ICE

Average January Temperature

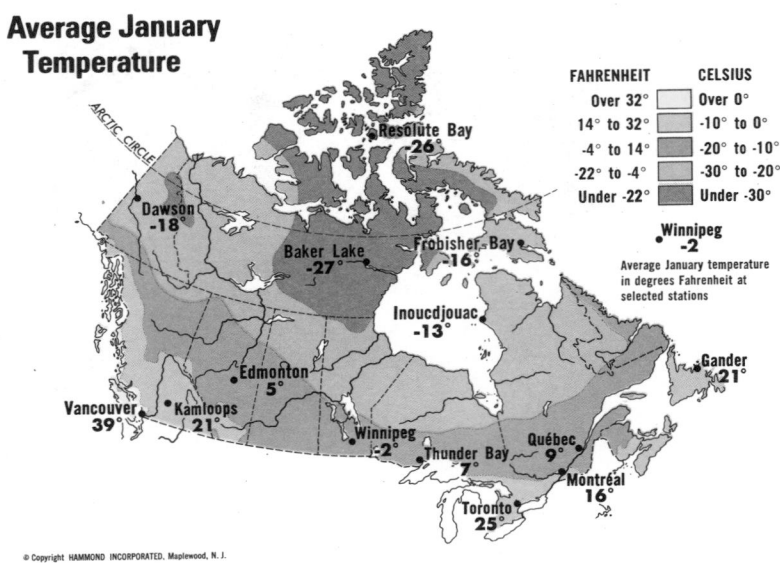

FAHRENHEIT	CELSIUS
Over 32°	Over 0°
14° to 32°	-10° to 0°
-4° to 14°	-20° to -10°
-22° to -4°	-30° to -20°
Under -22°	Under -30°

Winnipeg
-2
Average January temperature in degrees Fahrenheit at selected stations

Resolute Bay -26

Dawson -18°

Baker Lake -27°

Frobisher Bay -16°

Inoucdjouac -13°

Edmonton 5°

Gander 21°

Vancouver 39°

Kamloops 21°

Winnipeg -2°

Thunder Bay 7°

Québec 9°

Montréal 16°

Toronto 25°

© Copyright HAMMOND INCORPORATED, Maplewood, N.J.

Average July Temperature

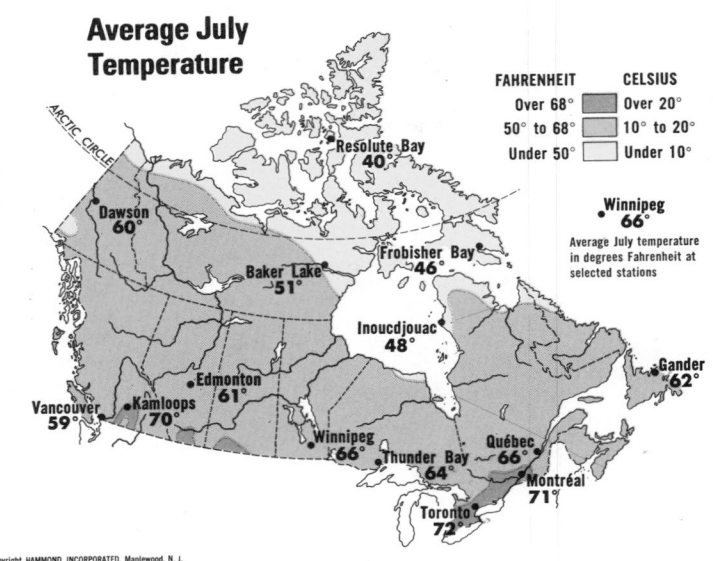

FAHRENHEIT	CELSIUS
Over 68°	Over 20°
50° to 68°	10° to 20°
Under 50°	Under 10°

Winnipeg 66°
Average July temperature in degrees Fahrenheit at selected stations

Resolute Bay 40

Dawson 60°

Baker Lake 51°

Frobisher Bay 46°

Inoucdjouac 48°

Edmonton 61°

Gander 62°

Vancouver 59°

Kamloops 70°

Winnipeg 66°

Thunder Bay 64°

Québec 66°

Montréal 71°

Toronto 72°

© Copyright HAMMOND INCORPORATED, Maplewood, N.J.

Agriculture, Industry and Resources

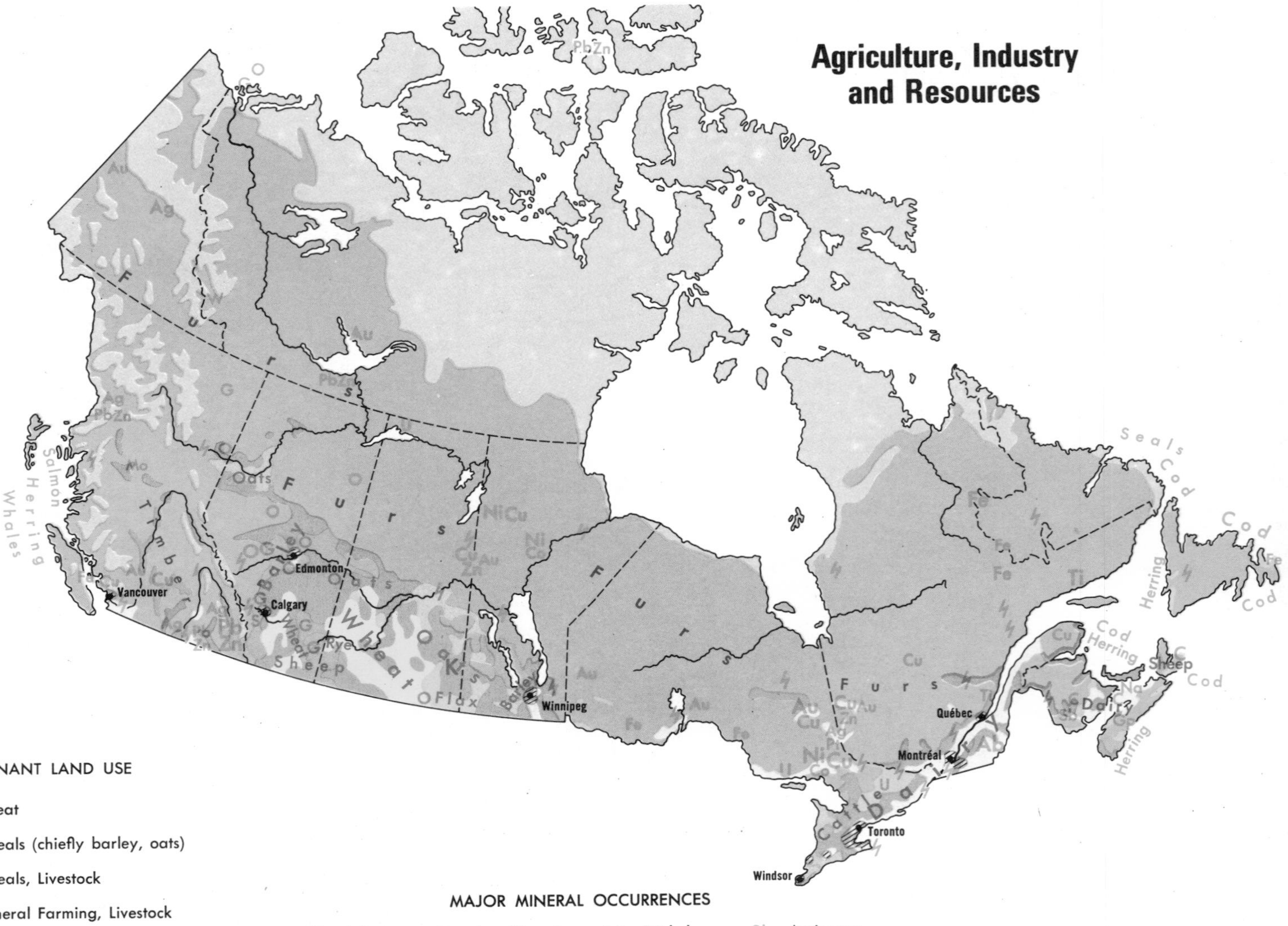

DOMINANT LAND USE

- Wheat
- Cereals (chiefly barley, oats)
- Cereals, Livestock
- General Farming, Livestock
- Dairy
- Fruit, Vegetables
- Pasture Livestock
- Range Livestock
- Forests
- Nonagricultural Land

MAJOR MINERAL OCCURRENCES

Ab	Asbestos	Fe	Iron Ore	Ni	Nickel	Sb	Antimony
Ag	Silver	G	Natural Gas	O	Petroleum	Ti	Titanium
Au	Gold	Gp	Gypsum	Pb	Lead	U	Uranium
C	Coal	K	Potash	Pt	Platinum	W	Tungsten
Co	Cobalt	Mo	Molybdenum	S	Sulfur	Zn	Zinc
Cu	Copper	Na	Salt				

⚡ Water Power

▨ Major Industrial Areas

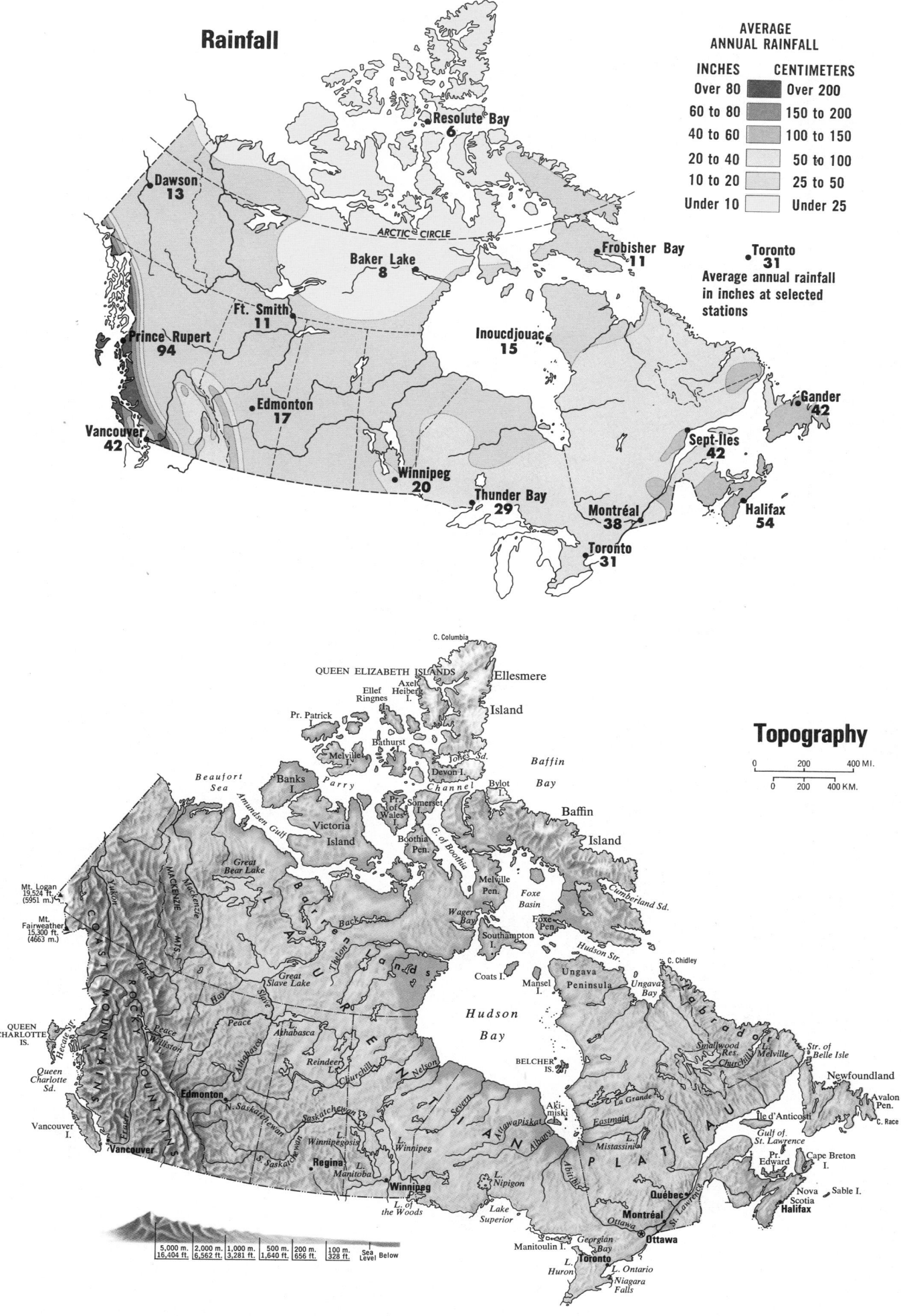

Rainfall

AVERAGE ANNUAL RAINFALL

INCHES	CENTIMETERS
Over 80	Over 200
60 to 80	150 to 200
40 to 60	100 to 150
20 to 40	50 to 100
10 to 20	25 to 50
Under 10	Under 25

Resolute Bay
6

Dawson
13

ARCTIC CIRCLE

Frobisher Bay
11

Toronto
31
Average annual rainfall
in inches at selected
stations

Baker Lake
8

Ft. Smith
11

Inoucdjouac
15

Prince Rupert
94

Gander
42

Edmonton
17

Sept-Îles
42

Vancouver
42

Winnipeg
20

Thunder Bay
29

Halifax
54

Montréal
38

Toronto
31

Topography

0   200   400 MI.
0   200   400 KM.

C. Columbia

QUEEN ELIZABETH ISLANDS   Ellesmere

Axel
Heiberg
I.

Ellef
Ringnes
I.

Island

Pr. Patrick
I.

Bathurst

Baffin

Melville

Jones Sd.

Bay

Beaufort
Sea

Banks
I.

Parry

Devon I.

Bylot
I.

Channel

Pr.
of
Wales

Somerset
I.

Baffin

Victoria
Island

Boothia
Pen.

G. of Boothia

Island

Great
Bear Lake

Cumberland Sd.

Mt. Logan
19,524 ft.
(5951 m.)

Melville
Pen.

Foxe
Basin

Wager
Bay

Mt.
Fairweather
15,300 ft.
(4663 m.)

Amundsen Gulf

MACKENZIE

Back

Southampton
I.

Foxe
Pen.

Hudson Str.

C. Chidley

Great
Slave Lake

Coats I.

Mansel
I.

Ungava
Peninsula

Ungava
Bay

QUEEN
CHARLOTTE
IS.

Peace

Williston
L.

Peace

Athabasca

Reindeer
L.

Churchill

Hudson

Bay

Smallwood
Res.
Churchill

Melville

Queen
Charlotte
Sd.

BELCHER
IS.

Newfoundland

Edmonton

N. Saskatchewan

Nelson

Akimiski
I.

La Grande

Eastmain

Île d'Anticosti

Avalon
Pen.

C. Race

Vancouver
I.

Saskatchewan

Winnipegosis
L.

L.
Winnipeg

Severn

Attawapiskat

Albany

L.
Mistassini

PLATEAU

Gulf of
St. Lawrence

Pr.
Edward

Cape Breton
I.

Vancouver

S. Saskatchewan

Regina

L.
Manitoba

Abitibi

Québec

Nova
Scotia

Sable I.

L.
Nipigon

St. Lawrence

Montréal

Halifax

L. of
the Woods

Lake
Superior

Ottawa

Ottawa

Georgian
Bay

5,000 m.
16,404 ft. | 2,000 m.
6,562 ft. | 1,000 m.
3,281 ft. | 500 m.
1,640 ft. | 200 m.
656 ft. | 100 m.
328 ft. | Sea
Level | Below

Manitoulin I.

Toronto

L. Ontario

L.
Huron

Niagara
Falls

Newfoundland
including Labrador

SCALE

Capitals of Provinces .... ⊛
Provincial Boundaries ....
Provincial Boundary according to
Imperial Privy Council decision, 1927 ....

Scale 1:5,200,000

NEWFOUNDLAND

CITIES and TOWNS

Admiral's Beach 362 . . . . D2
Admiral's Cove 99 . . . . D2
Anchor Point 368 . . . . C3
Aquaforte 200 . . . . D2
Argentia 93 . . . . C2
Arnold's Cove 1,124 . . . . . . C2
Avondale 890 . . . . D2
Badger 1,090 . . . . C4
Badger's Quay-Valleyfield-Pool's Island 1,566 . . . . . . D4
Baie Verte 2,491 . . . . C4
Battle Harbour C3
Bauline 423 . . . . D2
Bay Bulls 1,081 . . . . D2
Bay de Verde 786 . . . . D2
Bay L'Argent 483 . . . . D4
Bay Roberts 4,512 . . . . D2
Bellburns 147 . . . . C3
Belleoram 565 . . . . C4
Bellevue 286 . . . . D2
Bide Arm 339 . . . . C3
Big Pond 167 . . . . D2
Birchy Bay 707 . . . . D4
Bird Cove 400 . . . . C3
Bishop's Falls 4,395 . . . . . . C4
Black Tickle 194 . . . . C3
Blackhead Road 1,855 . . . . . D2
Blaketown 617 . . . . D2
Bloomfield 715 . . . . D2
Bonavista 4,460 . . . . D2
Botwood 4,074 . . . . C4
Branch 462 . . . . D2
Brigus 898 . . . . D2
Broad Cove 198 . . . . D2
Brooklyn 197 . . . . D2
Brownsdale 199 . . . . D2
Buchans 1,655 . . . . C4
Bunyan's Cove 590 . . . . C2
Burgeo 2,504 . . . . C4
Burin 2,904 . . . . C2
Burnt Islands 991 . . . . C4
Burnt Point 260 . . . . D2
Calvert 482 . . . . D2
Campbellton 703 . . . . D4
Cape Broyle 698 . . . . D2
Cape Ray 484 . . . . C4
Caplin Cove 150 . . . . D2
Carbonear 5,335 . . . . D2
Carmanville 966 . . . . D4
Cartwright 658 . . . . C3
Catalina 1,162 . . . . D2
Cavendish 343 . . . . D2
Champney's West 141 . . . . . D2
Chance Cove 498 . . . . D2
Change Islands 580 . . . . . . D4
Channel-Port aux Basques 5,988 . . . . C4
Chapel Arm 689 . . . . D2
Charlottetown 330 . . . . D2
Charlottetown 250 . . . . C3
Churchill Falls 936 . . . . B3
Clarenville 2,878 . . . . C2
Clarke's Beach 1,009 . . . . . D2
Codroy 346 . . . . C4
Colinet 318 . . . . D2
Colliers 819 . . . . D2
Come By Chance 337 . . . . . C2
Conception Harbour 917 . . . D2
Conche 464 . . . . C3
Cook's Harbour 388 . . . . . . C3
Corner Brook 24,339 . . . . . C4
Cow Head 695 . . . . C4
Cox's Cove 980 . . . . C4
Cupids 706 . . . . D2
Daniell's Harbour 614 . . . . . C3
Dark Cove 1,344 . . . . D4
Davis Inlet 240 . . . . B2
Deep Bight 243 . . . . C2
Deer Lake 4,348 . . . . C4
Dildo 877 . . . . D2
Dunville 1,817 . . . . D2
Durrell 1,145 . . . . D4
Eastport 597 . . . . D1
Elliston 527 . . . . D2
Embree 846 . . . . C4
Englee 998 . . . . C3
English Harbour 118 . . . . . . D2
English Harbour West 327 . . C4
Fermeuse 584 . . . . D2
Ferryland 795 . . . . D2
Flat Bay 322 . . . . C4
Flat Rock 808 . . . . D2
Fleur de Lys 616 . . . . C3
Flowers Cove 459 . . . . C3
Fogo 1,105 . . . . D4
Forteau 520 . . . . C3
Fortune 2,473 . . . . C4
Fox Harbour 280 . . . . C3
Fox Harbour 538 . . . . D2
François 219 . . . . C4
Freshwater 1,276 . . . . C2
Freshwater 209 . . . . D2
Gambo 2,932 . . . . D4
Gander 10,404 . . . . D4
Garnish 761 . . . . C4
Gaskiers-Point la Haye 505 . . D2
Gaultois 558 . . . . C4
Georges Brook 356 . . . . D2
Glenwood 1,129 . . . . D4
Glovertown 2,165 . . . . C1
Goobies 185 . . . . D2
Goose Bay-Happy Valley 7,103 . . . . B3
Gooseberry Cove 195 . . . . . C2
Goose Cove 134 . . . . C2
Goose Cove 368 . . . . C3
Goulds 4,242 . . . . D2
Grand Bank 3,901 . . . . C4
Grand Falls 8,765 . . . . C4
Grates Cove 275 . . . . D2
Green Island Cove 222 . . . . C3
Green's Harbour 785 . . . . . D2
Greenspond 423 . . . . D4
Grey River 234 . . . . C4
Gull Island 362 . . . . D2
Hampden 838 . . . . C4
Hant's Harbour 542 . . . . D2
Happy Adventure 352 . . . . . D2
Happy Valley-Goose Bay 7,103 . . . . B3
Harbour Breton 2,464 . . . . . . C4
Harbour Deep 278 . . . . C3
Harbour Grace 2,988 . . . . . . D2
Harbour Main-Chapel Cove-Lakeview 1,303 . . . . D2
Hare Bay 1,520 . . . . D4
Hawke's Bay 553 . . . . C3
Head of Bay d'Espoir 586 . . . C4
Heart's Content 625 . . . . D2
Heart's Delight-Islington 899 D2
Heart's Desire 416 . . . . D2
Heatherton 328 . . . . C4
Hermitage 863 . . . . C4
Hickman's Harbour 479 . . . . D2
Hillview 295 . . . . D2
Hodge's Cove 438 . . . . D2
Holyrood 1,789 . . . . D2
Hopedale 425 . . . . B2
Howley 456 . . . . C4
Isle aux Morts 1,238 . . . . . . C4
Jackson's Arm 623 . . . . C4
Jeffrey's 276 . . . . C4
Jerseyside 641 . . . . B3
Job's Cove 201 . . . . D2
Joe Batt's Arm-Barr'd Islands 1,155 . . . . . D4
Keels 129 . . . . D1
Kelligrews (Foxtrap-Greeleytown-Peachtown-Kelligrews) 2,292 . . . . D2
Kilbride 5,014 . . . . D2
King's Cove 253 . . . . D1
King's Point 825 . . . . C4
Kippens 1,219 . . . . C4
Labrador City 11,538 . . . . . . A3
Lamaline 548 . . . . C4
L'Anse-au-Clair 267 . . . . C3
L'Anse-au-Loup 589 . . . . C3
L'Anse au Meadow 66 . . . . . . C3
La Poile 186 . . . . C4
Lark Harbour 783 . . . . C4
La Scie 1,422 . . . . C4
Lawn 999 . . . . C4
Lethbridge 686 . . . . D2
Lewisporte 3,963 . . . . C4
Little Bay Islands 407 . . . . . . C4
Little Catalina 750 . . . . D2
Little Heart's Ease 467 . . . . . D2
Lodge Bay 124 . . . . C3
Long Harbour-Mount Arlington Heights 660 . . . . D2
Lourdes 932 . . . . C4
Lower Island Cove 415 . . . . . D2
Lumsden 645 . . . . D4
Main Brook 514 . . . . C3
Makkovik 347 . . . . C2
Markland 344 . . . . D2
Mary's Harbour 408 . . . . C3
Marystown 6,299 . . . . D4
McCallum 243 . . . . C4
Melrose 416 . . . . D2
Middle Arm, Green Bay 575 . C4
Millertown 228 . . . . C4
Milltown-Head of Bay d'Espoir 1,376 . . . . C4
Milton 258 . . . . D2
Mobile 171 . . . . D2
Mount Carmel-Mitchell's Brook-St. Catherine's 699 . . . . . . D2
Mount Pearl 11,543 . . . . D2
Musgrave Harbour 1,554 . . . D4
Musgravetown 635 . . . . C2
Nain 938 . . . . B2
New Bonaventure 106 . . . . . . D2
New Chelsea 144 . . . . D2
New Harbour 777 . . . . D2
Newmans Cove 231 . . . . D2
New Perlican 350 . . . . D2
Newtown 511 . . . . D4
Nippers Harbour 259 . . . . . . C4
Norman's Cove-Long Cove 1,152 . . . . D2
Norris Arm 1,216 . . . . C4
Norris Point 1,033 . . . . C4
North Harbour 151 . . . . D2
North River 245 . . . . D2
North West Brook 279 . . . . . C2
North West River 515 . . . . . . B3
O'Donnells 280 . . . . D2
Old Bonaventure 111 . . . . . . D2
Old Perlican 709 . . . . D2
Paradise 2,861 . . . . D2
Parkers Cove 424 . . . . D4
Parson's Pond 605 . . . . C3
Pasadena 2,685 . . . . C4
Patrick's Cove 155 . . . . C2
Perry's Cove 141 . . . . D2
Peterview 1,119 . . . . C4
Petites 108 . . . . C4
Petley 147 . . . . D2
Petty Harbour-Maddox Cove 853 . . . . D2
Picadilly 524 . . . . C4
Pinware River 201 . . . . C3
Placentia 2,204 . . . . C2
Plate Cove 474 . . . . D2
Point La Haye 195 . . . . D2
Point Lance 141 . . . . C2
Point Leamington 848 . . . . . . C4
Point Verde 296 . . . . C2
Pollards Point 502 . . . . C4
Port au Bras 366 . . . . D4
Port au Choix 1,311 . . . . C3
Port au Port 603 . . . . C4
Port Blandford 702 . . . . C2
Port Hope Simpson 581 . . . . C3
Port Kirwan 164 . . . . D2
Port Rexton 489 . . . . D2
Port Saunders 769 . . . . C3
Portugal Cove 2,361 . . . . D2
Portugal Cove South 371 . . . D2
Port Union 671 . . . . D2
Postville 223 . . . . B3
Pouch Cove 1,522 . . . . D2
Princeton 204 . . . . D2
Raleigh 373 . . . . C3
Ramea 1,386 . . . . C4
Red Bay 316 . . . . C3
Red Head Cove 225 . . . . D2
Rencontre East 230 . . . . C4
Renews-Cappahayden 578 . . D2
Rigolet 271 . . . . C3
Riverhead 431 . . . . D2
River of Ponds 304 . . . . C3
Robert's Arm 1,005 . . . . C4
Rocky Harbour 1,273 . . . . C4
Roddickton 1,142 . . . . C3
Rose Blanche-Harbour le Cou 975 . . . . C4
Rushoon 520 . . . . D4
Saint Alban's 1,968 . . . . C4
Saint Andrew's 262 . . . . C4
Saint Anthony 3,107 . . . . C3
Saint Brendan's 468 . . . . D4
Saint Bride's 599 . . . . C2
Saint George's 1,756 . . . . . . C4
St. John's (cap.) 83,770 . . . D2
Saint Joseph's 262 . . . . D2
Saint Lawrence 2,012 . . . . . . C4
Saint Lunaire-Griquet 1,010 . . C3
Saint Mary's 701 . . . . D2
Saint Paul's 454 . . . . C4
Saint Phillips 1,365 . . . . D2
Saint Shotts 239 . . . . D2
Saint Vincent's-Saint Stephens-Peter's River 796 . . . . D2
Sally's Cove 100 . . . . C4
Salmon Cove 786 . . . . D2
Seal Cove 751 . . . . D2
Seal Cove-White Bay 498 . . . C4
Seldom-Little Seldom 560 . . D4
Ship Harbour 265 . . . . D2
Shoal Cove 223 . . . . C3
Shoal Harbour 1,000 . . . . . . C2
South Branch 264 . . . . C4
South Brook, Hall's Bay Dist. 786 . . . . C4
South Brook, Humber Dist. 477 . . . . C4
Southern Harbour 772 . . . . . C2
South River 645 . . . . D2
Spaniard's Bay 2,125 . . . . . . D2
Springdale 3,501 . . . . C4
Stephenville 8,876 . . . . C4
Stephenville Crossing 2,172 . C4
Summerford 1,198 . . . . C4
Summerville 346 . . . . D2
Sunnyside 703 . . . . D2
Sweet Bay 204 . . . . D2
Swift Current 329 . . . . C2
Terrenceville 796 . . . . C4
Tilting 427 . . . . D4
Torbay 3,394 . . . . D2
Tors Cove 355 . . . . D2
Traytown 383 . . . . D1
Trepassey 1,473 . . . . D2
Trinity 522 . . . . D2
Trinity 375 . . . . D4
Trout River 759 . . . . C4
Twillingate 1,506 . . . . C4
Upper Island Cove 2,025 . . . D2
Victoria 1,870 . . . . D2
Wabana 4,254 . . . . D2
Wabush 3,155 . . . . A3
Wesleyville 1,125 . . . . D4
Western Bay 463 . . . . D2
West Saint Modeste 273 . . . . C3
Whitbourne 1,233 . . . . D2
Wild Cove 152 . . . . C3
Windsor 5,747 . . . . C4
Winterton 753 . . . . D2
Witless Bay 907 . . . . D2

OTHER FEATURES

Alexis (riv.) C3
Anguille (cape) C4
Annieopscotch (mts.) C4
Ashuanipi (lake) A3
Ashuanipi (riv.) A3
Atikonak (lake) B3
Attikamagen (lake) A3
Avalon (pen.) D2
Barachois Pond Prov. Park . . C4
Bauld (cape) C3
Bell (isl.) C3
Bell (isl.) D2
Belle Isle (isl.) C3
Belle Isle (str.) C3
Blackhead (bay) D2
Bonavista (bay) D1
Bonavista (cape) D1
Bonne (bay) C4
Branch (riv.) C2
Broyle (cape) D2
Bull Arm (inlet) D2
Burin (pen.) C4
Butter Pot Prov. Park D2
Cabot (str.) B4
Canada (bay) C3
Chidley (cape) B1
Churchill (falls) B3
Churchill (riv.) B3
Cirque (mt.) B2
Clode (sound) D2
Conception (bay) D2
Deep (inlet) B2
Double Mer (lake) C3
Dyke (lake) A3
Eagle (riv.) C3
Espoir (bay) C4
Exploits (riv.) C4
Fogo (isl.) D4
Fortune (bay) C4
Freels (cape) D3
Gander (lake) D4
Gander (riv.) D4
Glover (isl.) C4
Goose (riv.) B3
Grand (lake) B3
Grand (lake) C4
Grates (pt.) D2
Great Colinet (isl.) D2
Grey (isls.) C3
Groais (isl.) C3
Gros Morne (mt.) C4
Gros Morne Nat'l Park C4
Groswater (bay) C3
Hamilton (inlet) C3
Hamilton (sound) D4
Hare (bay) C3
Hawke (hills) D2
Hebron (fjord) B2
Hermitage (bay) C4
Holyrood (bay) D2
Horse (isls.) C3
Horse Chops (head) D2
Humber (riv.) C4
Ingornachoix (bay) C3
Ireland's Eye (isl.) D2
Islands (bay) C4
Kaipokok (bay) B2
Kanairiktok (riv.) B3
Kaumajet (mts.) B2
Kingurutik (mesa) B2
Labrador (reg.) B2
Labrador (sea) C2
La Manche Valley Prov. Park D2
La Poile (bay) C4
Little Mecatina (riv.) B3
Long (isl.) C2
Long (lake) A3
Long (pt.) C4
Long Range (mts.) C4
Main Topsail (mt.) C4
Makkovik (cape) C2
McLelan (str.) B1
Mealy (lake) C3
Meelpaeg (lake) C4
Melville (lake) C3
Menihek (lakes) A3
Merasheen (isl.) C2
Mistaken (pt.) D2
Mistastin (lake) B2
Nachvak (fjord) B2
Naskaupi (riv.) B3
Newfoundland (isl.) C4
Newman (sound) D2
New World (isl.) C4
Norman (cape) C3
North Aulatsivik (isl.) B2
Notre Dame (bay) C4
Okak (bay) B2
Ossokmanuan (res.) B3
Petitsikapau (lake) A3
Pine (cape) D2
Pinware (riv.) C3
Pistolet (bay) C3
Placentia (bay) C2
Ponds (isl.) C3
Port au Port (bay) C4
Port au Port (pen.) C4
Port Manvers (harb.) B2
Race (cape) D2
Ramah (bay) B2
Ramea (isls.) C4
Random (isl.) D2
Random (sound) D2
Ray (cape) C4
Red (isl.) C2
Red Indian (lake) C4
Red Wine (riv.) B3
Rocky (riv.) D2
Round (pond) C4
Saglek (bay) B2
Saint Francis (cape) D2
Saint George (cape) C4
Saint George's (bay) C4
Saint John (bay) C3
Saint John (cape) C3
Saint Lawrence (gulf) B4
Saint Lewis (cape) C3
Saint Mary's (bay) C2
Saint Mary's (cape) C2
Saint Michaels (bay) C3
Salmonier (riv.) D2
Sandwich (bay) C3
Shabogamo (lake) A3
Shoal (bay) D2
Smallwood (res.) B3
Smith (sound) D2
South Aulatsivik (isl.) B2
Spear (cape) D2
Squires Mem. Park C4
Swale (isl.) D1
Terra Nova (riv.) C2
Terra Nova Nat'l Park D2
Territok (cape) B2
Thoresby (mt.) B2
Torbay (pt.) D2
Torngat (mts.) B2
Trespassey (bay) D2
Trinity (bay) D2
Tunungayualok (isl.) B2
Ukasiksalik (isl.) B2
Victoria (lake) C4
White (bay) C3
White Bear (lake) C4
White Handkerchief (cape) . . B2

SAINT PIERRE and MIQUELON

CITIES and TOWNS

Saint-Pierre (cap.) 5,415 . . . C4

OTHER FEATURES

Miquelon (isl.) 626 . . . . C4
Saint Pierre (isl.) 5,415 . . . . C4

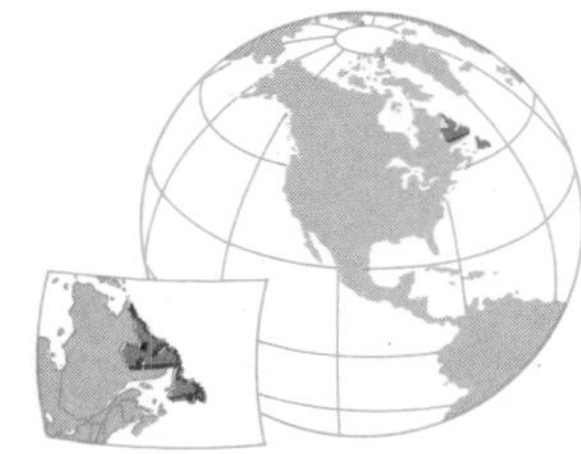

AREA 156,184 sq. mi. (404,517 sq. km.)
POPULATION 567,681
CAPITAL St. John's
LARGEST CITY St. John's
HIGHEST POINT in Torngat Mountains 5,420 ft. (1,652 m.)
SETTLED IN 1610
ADMITTED TO CONFEDERATION 1949
PROVINCIAL FLOWER Pitcher Plant

Agriculture, Industry and Resources

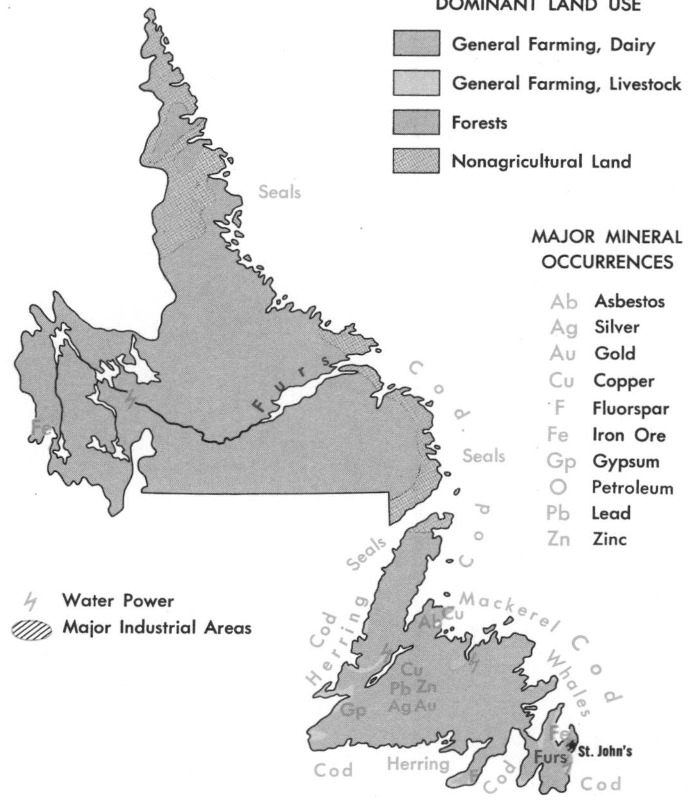

DOMINANT LAND USE
General Farming, Dairy
General Farming, Livestock
Forests
Nonagricultural Land
MAJOR MINERAL OCCURRENCES
Ab Asbestos
Ag Silver
Au Gold
Cu Copper
F Fluorspar
Fe Iron Ore
Gp Gypsum
O Petroleum
Pb Lead
Zn Zinc
Water Power
Major Industrial Areas
Seals
Furs
Cod
Herring
Mackerel
Whales
St. John's

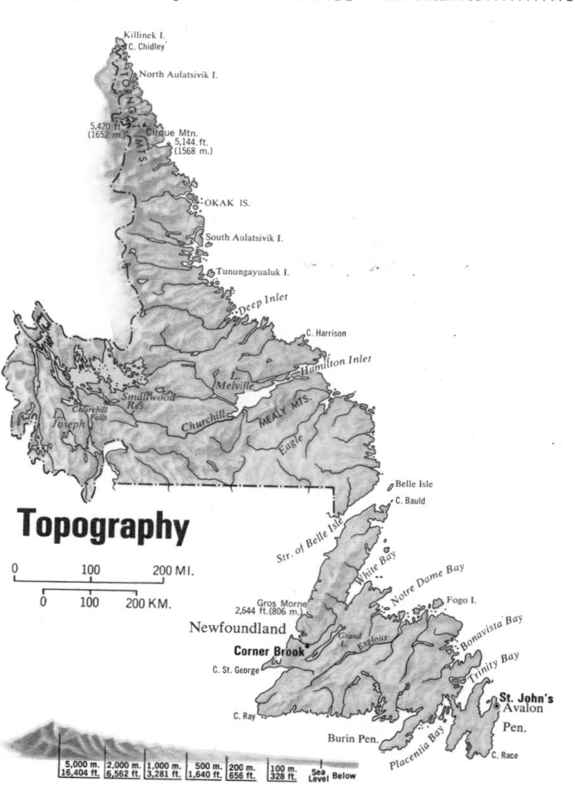

Topography
Killinek I.
C. Chidley
North Aulatsivik I.
OKAK IS.
South Aulatsivik I.
Tunungayualuk I.
Deep Inlet
C. Harrison
Hamilton Inlet
Melville
Smallwood Res.
Churchill
MEALY MTS.
Eagle
Joseph
Belle Isle
C. Bauld
Str. of Belle Isle
White Bay
Notre Dame Bay
Fogo I.
Gros Morne 2,644 ft. (806 m.)
Newfoundland
Corner Brook
C. St. George
Bonavista Bay
Trinity Bay
St. John's
Avalon Pen.
C. Ray
Burin Pen.
Placentia Bay
C. Race
0 100 200 MI.
0 100 200 KM.
5,000 m. 16,404 ft.
2,000 m. 6,562 ft.
1,000 m. 3,281 ft.
500 m. 1,640 ft.
200 m. 656 ft.
100 m. 328 ft.
Sea Level
Below

NOVA SCOTIA

COUNTIES

Annapolis 22,522	C 4
Antigonish 18,110	F 3
Cape Breton 127,035	H 3
Colchester 43,224	E 3
Cumberland 35,231	D 3
Digby 21,689	C 4
Guysborough 12,752	F 3
Halifax 288,126	E 4
Hants 33,121	D 4
Inverness 22,337	G 2
Kings 49,739	D 4
Lunenburg 45,746	D 4
Pictou 50,350	F 3
Queens 13,126	C 4
Richmond 12,284	H 3
Shelburne 17,328	C 5
Victoria 8,432	H 2
Yarmouth 26,290	C 5

CITIES and TOWNS

Alder Point 651	H 2
Aldershot	D 3
Amherst◉ 9,684	D 3
Annapolis Royal◉ 631	C 4
Antigonish◉ 5,205	F 3
Arichat 824	H 3
Aylesford 744	D 3
Baddeck◉ 972	H 2
Barrington Passage 722	C 5
Bear River-Sissiboo 854	C 4
Beaverbank 1,322	E 4
Berwick 1,699	D 4
Bridgetown 1,047	C 4
Bridgewater 6,669	D 4
Brookfield 619	E 3
Brooklyn 1,269	D 4
Cambridge Station 799	D 3
Canning 763	D 3
Canso 1,255	H 3
Centreville 765	D 3
Chéticamp 1,022	G 2

Chester 1,131	D 4
Chester Basin 639	D 4
Church Point 318	B 4
Clark's Harbour 1,059	C 5
Coldbrook Station 617	D 3
Cow Bay 670	E 4
Dartmouth 62,277	E 4
Debert 618	E 3
Digby◉ 2,558	C 4
Dominion 2,856	J 2
Donkin 873	J 2
Ellershouse-Hartville 662	D 4
Elmsdale 1,712	E 4
Enfield 1,510	E 4
Fall River 1,897	E 4
Falmouth 1,110	D 3
Glace Bay 21,466	J 2
Guysborough◉ 496	G 3
Halifax (cap.)◉ 114,594	E 4
Halifax ◈277,727	E 4
Hantsport 1,395	D 3
Herring Cove 1,323	E 4
Hilden 1,262	E 3

Ingonish 471	H 2
Inverness 2,013	G 2
Judique 925	G 3
Kentville◉ 4,974	D 3
Kingston 1,612	D 4
Lakeside 936	E 4
Lantz 1,172	E 4
Liverpool◉ 3,304	D 4
Lockeport 929	C 5
Louisbourg 1,410	J 3
Louisdale 979	G 3
Lower West Pubnico 790	C 5
Lunenburg◉ 3,014	D 4
Mahone Bay 1,228	D 4
Meteghan 890	B 4
Middleton 1,834	C 4
Milford Station 748	E 3
Milton 1,678	D 4
Mount Uniacke 1,145	E 4
Mulgrave 1,099	G 3
Musquodoboit Harbour 936	E 4
New Glasgow 10,464	F 3
New Victoria 1,374	H 2

New Waterford 8,808	J 2
North Sydney 7,820	H 2
Oxford 1,470	E 3
Parrsboro 1,799	D 3
Pictou◉ 4,628	F 3
Porters Lake 893	E 4
Port Hastings 312	G 3
Port Hawkesbury 3,850	G 3
Port Hood 701	G 2
Port Morien 717	J 2
Port Williams 1,227	D 3
Prospect 693	E 4
Pugwash 648	E 3
Reserve Mines 2,472	H 2
River Hébert 835	D 3
Saint Peters 669	H 3
Sandy Point 691	C 5
Scotchtown 2,037	H 2
Sheet Harbour 819	F 4
Shelburne◉ 2,303	C 5
Shubenacadie 984	E 3
Springhill 4,896	D 3
Stellarton 5,435	F 3

Stewiacke 1,174	E 3
Sydney◉ 29,444	H 2
Sydney Mines 8,501	H 2
Terence Bay 960	E 4
Thorburn 1,014	F 3
Three Mile Plains 1,355	D 4
Timberlea 1,159	E 4
Trenton 3,154	F 3
Truro 12,552	E 3
Waterville 687	D 3
Waverley 1,699	E 4
Wedgeport 827	C 5
Western Shore 1,712	D 4
Westmount 3,097	H 2
Westville 4,522	F 3
Wileville 746	D 4
Windsor◉ 3,646	D 3
Wolfville 3,235	D 3
Yarmouth◉ 7,475	B 5

OTHER FEATURES

Advocate (bay)	D 3

Ainslie (lake)	G 2
Amet (sound)	E 3
Andrew (isl.)	H 3
Annapolis (basin)	C 4
Annapolis (riv.)	D 4
Antigonish (harb.)	G 3
Argos (cape)	H 2
Aspy (bay)	H 2
Avon (riv.)	D 3
Baccaro (pt.)	C 5
Baddeck (riv.)	H 2
Barachois (pt.)	H 2
Barren (isl.)	C 5
Barrington (bay)	C 5
Bedford (basin)	E 4
Berry (head)	G 3
Boularderie (isl.)	H 2
Bras d'Or (lake)	H 3
Breton (cape)	J 3
Brier (isl.)	B 4
Canso (cape)	H 3
Canso (isl.)	H 3
Canso (str.)	G 3
Cap d'Or (cape)	D 3

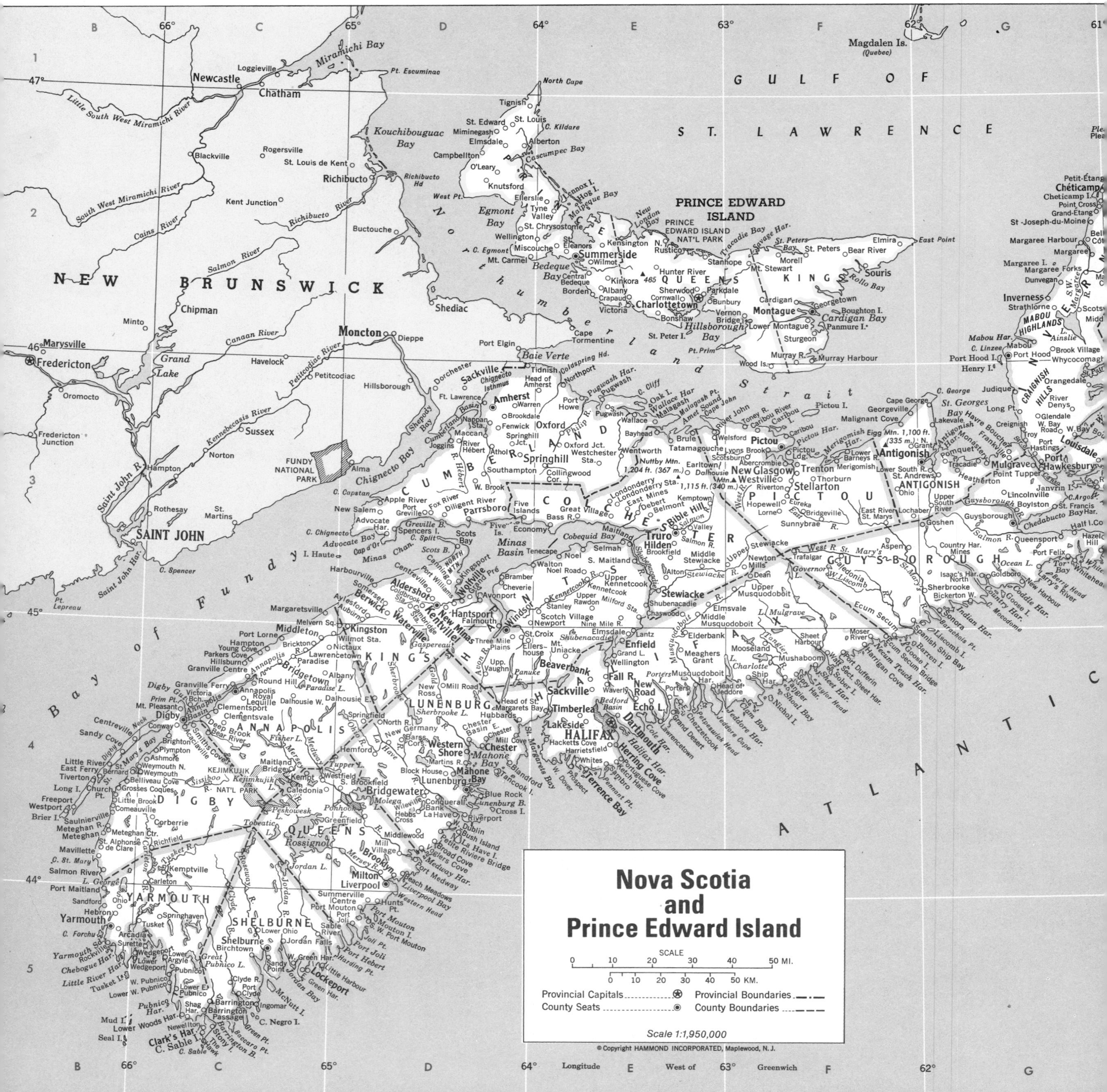

Nova Scotia and Prince Edward Island

SCALE
0   10   20   30   40   50 MI.
0 10 20 30 40 50 KM.

Provincial Capitals .... ⊛   Provincial Boundaries ..─ · ─ ·
County Seats .... ◉   County Boundaries ..── ── ──

Scale 1:1,950,000

© Copyright HAMMOND INCORPORATED, Maplewood, N.J.

⊚County seat.
*Population of metropolitan area.

PRINCE EDWARD ISLAND
AREA 2,184 sq. mi. (5,657 sq. km.)
POPULATION 122,506
CAPITAL Charlottetown
LARGEST CITY Charlottetown
HIGHEST POINT 465 ft. (142 m.)
SETTLED IN 1720
ADMITTED TO CONFEDERATION 1873
PROVINCIAL FLOWER Lady's Slipper

NOVA SCOTIA
AREA 21,425 sq. mi. (55,491 sq. km.)
POPULATION 847,442
CAPITAL Halifax
LARGEST CITY Halifax
HIGHEST POINT Cape Breton Highlands 1,747 ft. (532 m.)
SETTLED IN 1605
ADMITTED TO CONFEDERATION 1867
PROVINCIAL FLOWER Trailing Arbutus or Mayflower

Topography

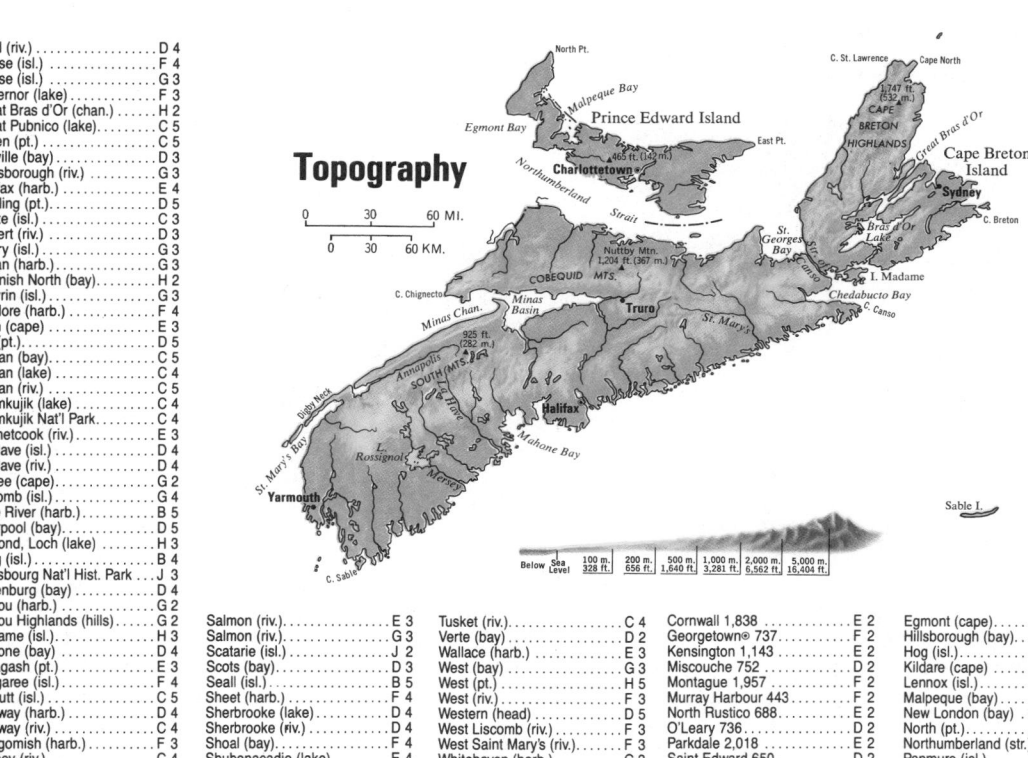

Agriculture, Industry and Resources

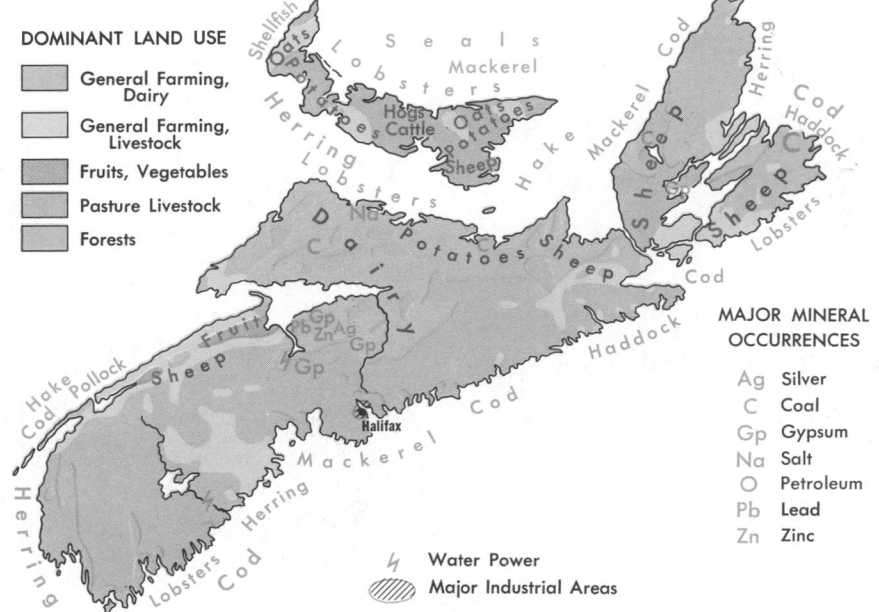

DOMINANT LAND USE

- General Farming, Dairy
- General Farming, Livestock
- Fruits, Vegetables
- Pasture Livestock
- Forests

MAJOR MINERAL OCCURRENCES

- Ag Silver
- C Coal
- Gp Gypsum
- Na Salt
- O Petroleum
- Pb Lead
- Zn Zinc

⚡ Water Power
▨ Major Industrial Areas

COUNTIES

Albert 23,632 . . . . F 3
Carleton 24,659 . . . . C 2
Charlotte 26,571 . . . . C 3
Gloucester 86,156 . . . . E 1
Kent 30,799 . . . . E 2
King's 51,114 . . . . E 3
Madawaska 34,892 . . . . B 1
Northumberland 54,134 . . . . . D 2
Queen's 12,485 . . . . D 3
Restigouche 40,593 . . . . C 1
Saint John 86,148 . . . . D 3
Sunbury 21,012 . . . . C 1
Victoria 20,815 . . . . B 2
Westmorland 107,640 . . . . . . F 2
York 74,213 . . . . C 3

CITIES and TOWNS

Acadie Siding 64 . . . . E 2
Acadieville 176 . . . . E 2
Adamsville 94 . . . . E 2
Albert Mines 120 . . . . F 3
Alcida 174 . . . . E 1
Aldouane 64 . . . . E 2
Allardville 478 . . . . E 1
Alma 329 . . . . F 3
Anagance 114 . . . . E 3
Anse-Bleue 562 . . . . E 1

Apohaqui 341 . . . . E 3
Argyle 63 . . . . C 2
Armstrong Brook 191 . . . . C 2
Aroostook 403 . . . . C 2
Arthurette 178 . . . . C 2
Astle 201 . . . . D 2
Atholville 1,694 . . . . D 1
Aulac 113 . . . . F 3
Back Bay 455 . . . . D 3
Baie-Sainte-Anne 709 . . . . . . F 1
Baie-Verte 175 . . . . F 2
Bairdsville 81 . . . . C 2
Baker Brook 527 . . . . B 1
Balmoral 1,823 . . . . D 1
Barachois 686 . . . . F 2
Barnaby River 38 . . . . E 2
Barnettville 117 . . . . E 2
Bartibog Bridge 122 . . . . F 1
Bas-Caraquet 1,859 . . . . F 1
Bass River 112 . . . . E 2
Bath 794 . . . . C 2
Bathurst⊗ 15,705 . . . . E 1
Bayfield 81 . . . . G 2
Bayside . . . . C 3
Beaubois 211 . . . . D 1
Beaver Brook Station 95 . . . . . E 2
Beaver Harbour 316 . . . . D 3
Beechwood 111 . . . . C 2
Beersville 52 . . . . E 2
Belledune 690 . . . . E 1

Bellefleur 83 . . . . C 1
Bellefond 243 . . . . E 1
Belleisle Creek 145 . . . . E 3
Benjamin River 171 . . . . D 1
Ben Lomond . . . . E 3
Benton 101 . . . . C 3
Beresford 3,652 . . . . E 1
Berry Mills 238 . . . . E 2
Bertrand 1,268 . . . . E 1
Berwick 129 . . . . E 3
Black Point 131 . . . . D 1
Black River 150 . . . . E 3
Blacks Harbour 1,356 . . . . D 3
Blackville 892 . . . . E 2
Blissfield 119 . . . . D 2
Bloomfield Ridge 153 . . . . D 2
Bloomfield Station 62 . . . . E 3
Bocabec 34 . . . . C 3
Boiestown 299 . . . . D 2
Bonny River 153 . . . . D 3
Bosse 193 . . . . B 1
Bourgeois 215 . . . . F 2
Brantville 1,066 . . . . E 1
Breau-Village 293 . . . . F 2
Brest 94 . . . . E 2
Brewers Mills 199 . . . . C 2
Briggs Corner 89 . . . . E 2
Bristol 824 . . . . C 2
Brockway (Lower Brockway-
  Brockway) 97 . . . . C 3

Browns Flat 295 . . . . D 3
Buctouche 2,476 . . . . F 2
Burnsville 156 . . . . E 1
Burton⊗ 291 . . . . D 3
Burtts Corner 484 . . . . D 2
Cambridge-Narrows 433 . . . . . . E 3
Campbellton 9,818 . . . . D 1
Canaan 115 . . . . D 2
Canaan Forks 78 . . . . E 2
Canaan Road 86 . . . . E 2
Canterbury 474 . . . . C 3
Cap-Bateau 417 . . . . F 1
Cap Lumière 262 . . . . F 2
Cap-Pelé 2,199 . . . . F 2
Caraquet 4,315 . . . . F 1
Carlingford 229 . . . . C 2
Carlisle 75 . . . . C 2
Caron Brook 171 . . . . B 1
Carrolls Crossing 119 . . . . D 2
Castalia 145 . . . . D 4
Centre-Saint-Simon (St.
  Simon) 991 . . . . F 1
Centreville 577 . . . . C 2
Chance Harbour 63 . . . . D 3
Charlo 1,603 . . . . D 1
Chatham 6,779 . . . . E 1
Chatham Head . . . . E 2
Chipman 1,829 . . . . E 2

Clair 915 . . . . B 1
Clarendon 80 . . . . D 3
Cliffordvale (Limestone-
  Cliffordvale) 69 . . . . C 2
Clifton 194 . . . . E 1
Coal Branch 90 . . . . E 2
Coal Creek 61 . . . . E 2
Cocagne Cape 278 . . . . F 2
Cocagne-Cocagne Sud 600 . . . . F 2
Codys 125 . . . . E 3
Coldstream 217 . . . . C 2
Coles Island 150 . . . . E 3
College Bridge 536 . . . . F 3
Collette 198 . . . . E 2
Connell 58 . . . . C 2
Connors 96 . . . . B 1
Cork 54 . . . . D 3
Cornhill 111 . . . . E 3
Coughlan 181 . . . . D 2
Cross Creek 192 . . . . D 2
Cumberland Bay 231 . . . . E 3
Dalhousie⊗ 4,958 . . . . D 1
Dalhousie Junction 105 . . . . . . D 1
Darlington 749 . . . . D 1
Daulnay 398 . . . . E 1
Dawsonville 278 . . . . C 1
Debec 200 . . . . C 2
Dieppe 8,511 . . . . F 2
Dipper Harbour 166 . . . . D 3
Doaktown 1,009 . . . . D 2

Dorchester⊗ 1,101 . . . . F 3
Dorchester Crossing 605 . . . . . F 2
Douglastown 1,091 . . . . E 1
Drummond 849 . . . . C 1
Duguayville 337 . . . . E 1
Dumfries 150 . . . . C 3
Dupuis Corner 303 . . . . F 2
Durham Bridge 255 . . . . D 2
East Riverside-Kingshurst
  989 . . . . E 3
Edmundston⊗ 12,044 . . . . B 1
Eel River Bridge 377 . . . . F 1
Eel River Crossing 1,431 . . . . . D 1
Elgin 301 . . . . E 3
Enniskillen 63 . . . . D 3
Escuminac 194 . . . . F 1
Evandale 58 . . . . D 3
Evangeline 356 . . . . F 1
Everett 48 . . . . C 1
Fairfield 250 . . . . E 3
Fairhaven 142 . . . . C 4
Fairisle 415 . . . . E 1
Fairvale 3,960 . . . . E 3
Ferry Road 325 . . . . E 1
Fielding 197 . . . . C 2
Five Fingers 189 . . . . C 1
Flatlands 249 . . . . D 1
Florenceville 709 . . . . C 2
Forest City 25 . . . . C 3
Fosterville 58 . . . . C 3

Four Falls 69 . . . . C 2
Fredericton (cap.)⊗ 43,723 . . . . D 3
Fredericton Junction 711 . . . . . D 3
Gagetown⊗ 618 . . . . D 3
Gardner Creek 56 . . . . E 3
Geary 654 . . . . D 3
Germantown 62 . . . . F 3
Gillespie 96 . . . . C 1
Glassville 147 . . . . C 2
Glencoe 147 . . . . D 1
Glenlivet 284 . . . . D 1
Gloucester Junction 36 . . . . . . E 1
Gondola Point 3,076 . . . . E 3
Grafton 385 . . . . C 2
Grand Bay 3,173 . . . . D 3
Grande-Anse 817 . . . . E 1
Grand Falls 6,203 . . . . C 1
Grand Falls Hill 152 . . . . C 1
Grand Harbour 614 . . . . D 4
Gray Rapids 266 . . . . E 2
Hammondvale 72 . . . . E 3
Hampstead 87 . . . . D 3
Hampton⊗ 3,141 . . . . E 3
Harcourt 127 . . . . E 2
Hardwicke 114 . . . . F 1
Hardwood Ridge 191 . . . . D 2
Hartland 846 . . . . C 2
Harvey, Albert 58 . . . . F 3
Harvey, York 356 . . . . D 3
Hatfield Point 176 . . . . E 3

New Brunswick
SCALE
0 5 10   20   30   40 MI.
0 5 10   20   30   40 KM.
Provincial Capitals . . . . ⊛
County Seats . . . . ⊗
International Boundaries . . . . . .
Provincial Boundaries . . . .
County Boundaries . . . .
Scale 1:1,900,000

© Copyright HAMMOND INCORPORATED, Maplewood, N. J.

AREA

AREA 28,354 sq. mi. (73,437 sq. km.)
POPULATION 696,403
CAPITAL Fredericton
LARGEST CITY Saint John
HIGHEST POINT Mt. Carleton 2,690 ft. (820 m.)
SETTLED IN 1611
ADMITTED TO CONFEDERATION 1867
PROVINCIAL FLOWER Purple Violet

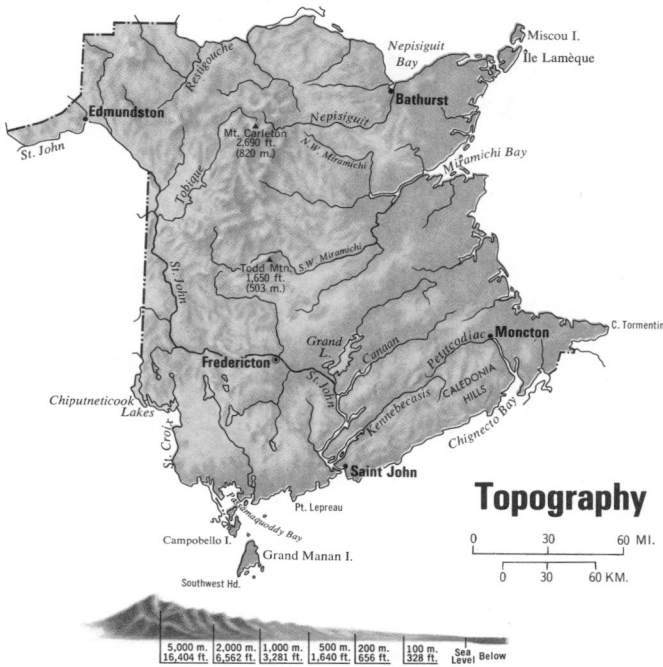

Topography

0   30   60 MI.

0   30   60 KM.

| 5,000 m. 16,404 ft. | 2,000 m. 6,562 ft. | 1,000 m. 3,281 ft. | 500 m. 1,640 ft. | 200 m. 656 ft. | 100 m. 328 ft. | Sea Level | Below |

Agriculture, Industry and Resources

DOMINANT LAND USE

- Cereals, Livestock
- Dairy
- Potatoes
- General Farming, Livestock
- Pasture Livestock
- Forests

MAJOR MINERAL OCCURRENCES

- Ag Silver
- C Coal
- Cu Copper
- Pb Lead
- Sb Antimony
- Zn Zinc
- ⚡ Water Power
- ▨ Major Industrial Areas

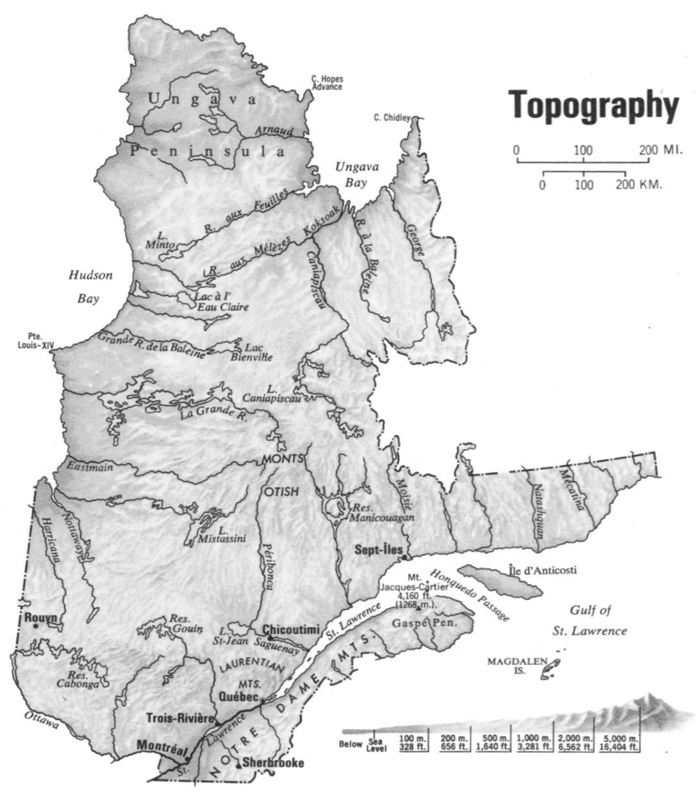

Topography
0 100 200 MI.
0 100 200 KM.
Ungava Peninsula
C. Hopes Advance
C. Chidley
Ungava Bay
Hudson Bay
Pte. Louis-XIV
Grande R. de la Baleine
Lac Bienville
L. Caniapiscau
La Grande R.
MONTS OTISH
L. Mistassini
Res. Manicouagan
Sept-Îles
Île d'Anticosti
Mt. Jacques-Cartier 4,160 ft. (1268 m.)
Gulf of St. Lawrence
Gaspé Pen.
MAGDALEN IS.
Rouyn
Res. Gouin
L. St-Jean
Chicoutimi
Res. Cabonga
Ottawa
Trois-Rivières
Québec
Montréal
Sherbrooke
LAURENTIAN MTS.
NOTRE DAME MTS.
Below Sea Level 100 m. 328 ft. 200 m. 656 ft. 500 m. 1,640 ft. 1,000 m. 3,281 ft. 2,000 m. 6,562 ft. 5,000 m. 16,404 ft.

COUNTIES

Argenteuil 32,454 . . . . C 4
Arthabaska 59,277 . . . . E 4
Bagot 26,840 . . . . E 4
Beauce 73,427 . . . . G 3
Beauharnois 54,034 . . . . C 4
Bellechasse 23,559 . . . . G 3
Berthier 31,096 . . . . C 3
Bonaventure 40,487 . . . . C 2
Brome 17,436 . . . . E 4
Chambly 307,090 . . . . J 4
Champlain 119,595 . . . . E 2
Charlevoix-Est 17,448 . . . . G 2
Charlevoix-Ouest 14,172 . . . . G 2
Châteauguay 59,968 . . . . D 4
Chicoutimi 174,441 . . . . G 1
Compton 20,536 . . . . F 4
Deux-Montagnes 71,252 . . . . C 4
Dorchester 33,949 . . . . G 3
Drummond 69,770 . . . . E 4
Frontenac 26,814 . . . . G 4
Gaspé-Est 41,173 . . . . D 1
Gaspé-Ouest 18,943 . . . . C 1
Gatineau 54,229 . . . . B 3
Hull 131,213 . . . . B 4
Huntingdon 16,953 . . . . C 4
Iberville 23,180 . . . . D 4
Île-de-Montréal 1,760,122 . . . . H 4
Île-Jésus 268,335 . . . . H 4
Joliette 60,384 . . . . C 3
Kamouraska 28,642 . . . . H 2
Labelle 34,395 . . . . B 3
Lac-Saint-Jean-Est 47,891 . . . . F 1
Lac-Saint-Jean-Ouest 62,952 . E 1
Laprairie 105,962 . . . . H 4
L'Assomption 109,705 . . . . D 4
Lévis 94,104 . . . . J 3
L'Islet 22,062 . . . . G 2
Lotbinière 29,653 . . . . F 3
Maskinongé 20,763 . . . . D 3
Matane 29,955 . . . . B 1
Matapédia 23,715 . . . . B 2
Mégantic 57,892 . . . . F 3
Missisquoi 36,161 . . . . D 4
Montcalm 27,557 . . . . C 3
Montmagny 25,622 . . . . G 3
Montmorency No. 1 23,048 . . . F 2
Montmorency No. 2 6,436 . . . G 3
Napierville 13,562 . . . . D 4
Nicolet 33,513 . . . . E 3
Papineau 37,975 . . . . B 4
Pontiac 20,283 . . . . A 3
Portneuf 58,843 . . . . E 3
Québec 458,980 . . . . F 3
Richelieu 53,058 . . . . D 4
Richmond 40,871 . . . . E 4
Rimouski 89,061 . . . . J 1
Rivière-du-Loup 41,250 . . . . H 2
Rouville 42,391 . . . . D 4
Saguenay 115,881 . . . . H 1
Saint-Hyacinthe 55,888 . . . . D 4
Saint-Jean 55,576 . . . . D 4
Saint-Maurice 107,703 . . . . D 3
Shefford 70,733 . . . . E 4
Sherbrooke 115,983 . . . . E 4
Soulanges 15,429 . . . . C 4
Stanstead 38,186 . . . . F 4
Témiscouata 52,570 . . . . J 2
Terrebonne 193,865 . . . . H 4
Vaudreuil 50,043 . . . . C 4
Verchères 63,353 . . . . J 4
Wolfe 15,635 . . . . F 4
Yamaska 14,797 . . . . E 3

CITIES and TOWNS

Acton Vale 4,371 . . . . E 4
Albanel 992 . . . . E 1
Alma◎ 26,322 . . . . F 1
Amqui◎ 4,048 . . . . B 2
Ancienne-Lorette 12,935 . . . . H 3
Angers . . . . B 4
Anjou 37,346 . . . . H 4
Annaville 712 . . . . E 3
Armagh 878 . . . . G 3
Arthabaska◎ 6,827 . . . . F 3
Arvida . . . . F 1
Asbestos 7,967 . . . . F 4
Ascot Corner 847 . . . . F 4
Audet 760 . . . . G 4
Ayer's Cliff◎ 810 . . . . E 4
Aylmer 26,695 . . . . B 4
Baie-Comeau 12,866 . . . . A 1
Baie-d'Urfé 3,674 . . . . G 4
Baie-Saint-Paul◎ 3,961 . . . . G 2
Baie-Trinité 749 . . . . B 1
Beaconsfield 19,613 . . . . H 4
Beauceville 4,302 . . . . G 3
Beauharnois◎ 7,025 . . . . D 4
Beaumont 791 . . . . F 3
Beauport 60,447 . . . . J 3
Beaupré 2,740 . . . . G 2
Bécancour◎ 10,247 . . . . E 3
Bedford◎ 2,832 . . . . E 4
Beebe Plain 1,072 . . . . E 4
Bélair (Val-Bélair) 12,695 . . . . H 3
Beloeil 17,540 . . . . D 4
Bernierville 2,120 . . . . F 3
Berthier-en-Bas 562 . . . . G 3
Berthierville◎ 4,049 . . . . D 3
Bic 2,994 . . . . J 1
Biencourt 824 . . . . J 2
Black Lake 5,148 . . . . F 3
Blainville 14,682 . . . . H 4
Boischatel 3,345 . . . . J 3
Bois-des-Filion 4,943 . . . . H 4
Bolduc 1,565 . . . . G 4
Bonaventure 1,371 . . . . C 2
Boucherville 29,704 . . . . J 4
Bromont 2,731 . . . . E 4
Bromptonville 3,035 . . . . F 4
Brossard 52,232 . . . . H 4
Brownsburg 2,875 . . . . C 4
Buckingham 7,992 . . . . B 4
Cabano 3,291 . . . . J 2
Cacouna 1,160 . . . . H 2
Calumet 729 . . . . C 4
Candiac 8,502 . . . . J 4
Cap-à-l'Aigle 819 . . . . G 2
Cap-Chat 3,464 . . . . B 1
Cap-de-la-Madeleine 32,626 . E 3
Caplan-Rivière Caplan 1,139 . C 2
Cap-Saint-Ignace 1,485 . . . . G 2
Cap-Santé◎ 671 . . . . F 3
Carignan 4,544 . . . . J 4
Carleton 2,710 . . . . C 2
Causapscal 2,501 . . . . B 2
Chambly 12,190 . . . . J 4
Chambord 961 . . . . E 1
Chandler 3,946 . . . . D 2
Charlemagne 4,827 . . . . H 4
Charlesbourg 68,326 . . . . J 3
Charny 8,240 . . . . J 3
Châteauguay 36,928 . . . . H 4
Château-Richer◎ 3,628 . . . . F 3
Chénéville 633 . . . . B 4
Chicoutimi◎ 60,064 . . . . G 1
Chicoutimi-Jonquière *135,172 . . . . G 1
Chute-aux-Outardes 2,280 . . . A 1
Clermont 3,621 . . . . G 2
Coaticook 6,271 . . . . F 4
Coleraine 1,660 . . . . F 4
Compton 728 . . . . F 4
Contrecoeur 5,449 . . . . D 4
Cookshire◎ 1,480 . . . . F 4
Coteau-du-Lac 1,247 . . . . C 4
Coteau-Landing◎ 1,386 . . . . C 4
Côte-Saint-Luc 27,531 . . . . H 4
Courcelles 608 . . . . G 4
Courville . . . . J 3
Cowansville 12,240 . . . . E 4
Crabtree 1,950 . . . . D 4
Danville 2,200 . . . . E 4
Daveluyville 1,257 . . . . E 3
Deauville 942 . . . . E 4
Dégelis 3,477 . . . . J 2
Delisle 4,011 . . . . F 1
Delson 4,935 . . . . H 4
Desbiens 1,541 . . . . E 1
Deschaillons-sur-Saint-Laurent 950 . . . . E 3
Deschambault 977 . . . . E 3
Deschênes . . . . B 4
Deux-Montagnes 9,944 . . . . H 4
Didyme 667 . . . . E 1
Disraëli 3,181 . . . . F 4
Dolbeau 8,766 . . . . E 1
Dollard-des-Ormeaux 39,940 . H 4
Donnacona 5,731 . . . . F 3
Dorion 5,749 . . . . C 4
Dorval 17,727 . . . . H 4
Dosquet 703 . . . . F 3
Douville . . . . D 4
Drummondville◎ 27,347 . . . . E 4
Drummondville-Sud 9,220 . . . . E 4
Dunham 2,887 . . . . E 4
Durham-Sud 1,045 . . . . E 4
East Angus 4,016 . . . . F 4
East Broughton 1,397 . . . . F 3
East Broughton Station 1,302 . F 3
Eastman 612 . . . . E 4
Entrelacs 1,735 . . . . C 3
Farnham 6,498 . . . . E 4
Ferme-Neuve 2,266 . . . . B 3
Forestville 4,271 . . . . H 1
Frampton 684 . . . . G 3
Francoeur 1,422 . . . . F 3
Gaspé 17,261 . . . . D 1
Gatineau 74,988 . . . . B 4
Giffard . . . . J 3
Girardville 1,128 . . . . E 1
Gracefield 869 . . . . A 3
Granby 38,069 . . . . E 4
Grand'Mère 15,442 . . . . E 3
Grande-Rivière 4,420 . . . . D 2
Grandes-Bergeronnes 748 . . . H 1
Grande-Vallée 700 . . . . D 1
Greenfield Park 18,527 . . . . J 4
Grenville 1,417 . . . . C 4
Gros-Morne 672 . . . . C 1
Hampstead 7,598 . . . . H 4
Ham-Sud◎ 62 . . . . F 4
Hauterive 13,995 . . . . A 1
Hébertville 2,515 . . . . F 1
Hébertville-Station 1,442 . . . . F 1
Hemmingford 737 . . . . D 4
Henryville 595 . . . . D 4
Howick 639 . . . . D 4
Hudson 4,414 . . . . C 4
Hull◎ 56,225 . . . . B 4
Huntingdon◎ 3,018 . . . . C 4
Île-Perrot 5,945 . . . . G 4
Iberville◎ 8,587 . . . . D 4
Inverness◎ 329 . . . . F 3
Joliette◎ 16,987 . . . . D 3
Jonquière 60,354 . . . . F 1
Jonquière-Chicoutimi *135,172 . . . . F 1
Kingsey Falls 818 . . . . E 4
Kirkland 10,476 . . . . H 4
Knowlton (Lac-Brome)◎ 4,316 . . . . E 4
La Baie 20,935 . . . . G 1
Labelle 1,534 . . . . C 3
Lac-à-la-Croix 1,017 . . . . F 1
Lac-Alouette-Lac-Brière 1,356 D 4
Lac-au-Saumon 1,332 . . . . B 2
Lac-aux-Sables 838 . . . . E 3
Lac-Beaufort . . . . F 3
Lac-Bouchette 1,703 . . . . E 1
Lac-Carré 717 . . . . C 3
Lac-des-Écorces 766 . . . . B 3
Lac-Drolet 1,120 . . . . G 4
Lac-Etchemin 2,729 . . . . G 3
Lachenaie 8,631 . . . . D 4
Lachine 37,521 . . . . H 4
Lachute◎ 11,729 . . . . C 4
Lac-Mégantic◎ 6,119 . . . . G 4
Lacolle 1,319 . . . . D 4
Lac-Saint-Charles 5,837 . . . . H 3
Lafontaine 4,799 . . . . C 4
La Guadeloupe 1,692 . . . . F 4
La Malbaie◎ 4,030 . . . . G 2
Lambton 1,559 . . . . F 4
L'Annonciation 2,384 . . . . C 3
Lanoraie (Lanoraie-d'Autry) 1,613 . . . . D 4
La Pêche 4,977 . . . . B 4
La Pérade 1,039 . . . . E 3
La Pocatière 4,560 . . . . H 2
La Prairie◎ 10,627 . . . . J 4
La Providence . . . . E 4
Larouche 662 . . . . F 1
La Salle 76,299 . . . . H 4
L'Ascension 1,287 . . . . F 1
L'Assomption◎ 4,844 . . . . D 4
La Station-du-Coteau 892 . . . . C 4
Laterrière 788 . . . . F 1
La Tuque 11,556 . . . . E 2
Laurentides 1,947 . . . . D 4
Laurier-Station 1,123 . . . . F 3
Laurierville 939 . . . . F 3
Lauzon 13,362 . . . . J 3
Laval 268,335 . . . . H 4
Lavaltrie 2,053 . . . . D 4
L'Avenir 1,116 . . . . E 4
Lawrenceville 562 . . . . E 4
Le Moyne 6,137 . . . . J 4
L'Épiphanie 2,971 . . . . D 4
Léry 2,239 . . . . H 4
Lévis 17,895 . . . . J 3
Lennoxville 3,922 . . . . F 4
Les Méchins 803 . . . . B 1
Linière 1,168 . . . . G 3
L'Islet 1,070 . . . . G 2
L'Islet-sur-Mer 774 . . . . G 2
L'Isle-Verte 1,142 . . . . G 1
Longueuil◎ 124,320 . . . . J 4
Loretteville◎ 15,060 . . . . H 3
Lorraine 6,881 . . . . H 4
Louiseville◎ 3,735 . . . . E 3
Luceville 1,524 . . . . J 1
Lyster 830 . . . . F 3
Magog 13,604 . . . . E 4
Maniwaki◎ 5,424 . . . . B 3
Manseau 626 . . . . E 3
Maple Grove 2,009 . . . . H 4
Maria 1,178 . . . . C 2
Marieville◎ 4,877 . . . . D 4
Mascouche 20,345 . . . . H 4
Maskinongé 1,005 . . . . E 3
Masson 4,264 . . . . B 4
Massueville 671 . . . . E 4
Matane◎ 13,612 . . . . B 1
Matapédia 586 . . . . B 2
Melocheville 1,892 . . . . C 4
Mercier 6,352 . . . . H 4
Metabetchouan 3,406 . . . . F 1
Mirabel◎ 14,080 . . . . H 4
Mistassini 6,682 . . . . E 1
Montauban 557 . . . . E 3
Mont-Carmel 807 . . . . H 2
Montcerf 570 . . . . A 3
Montebello 1,229 . . . . B 4
Mont-Joli 6,359 . . . . J 1
Mont-Laurier◎ 8,405 . . . . B 3
Mont-Louis 756 . . . . C 1
Montmagny◎ 12,405 . . . . G 3
Montréal◎ 980,354 . . . . H 4
Montréal *2,828,349 . . . . H 4
Montréal-Est 3,778 . . . . J 4
Montréal-Nord 94,914 . . . . H 4
Mont-Rolland 1,517 . . . . C 4
Mont-Royal 19,247 . . . . H 4
Mont-Saint-Hilaire 10,066 . . . . D 4
Morin Heights 592 . . . . C 4
Murdochville 3,396 . . . . C 1
Nantes 1,167 . . . . F 4

Agriculture, Industry and Resources

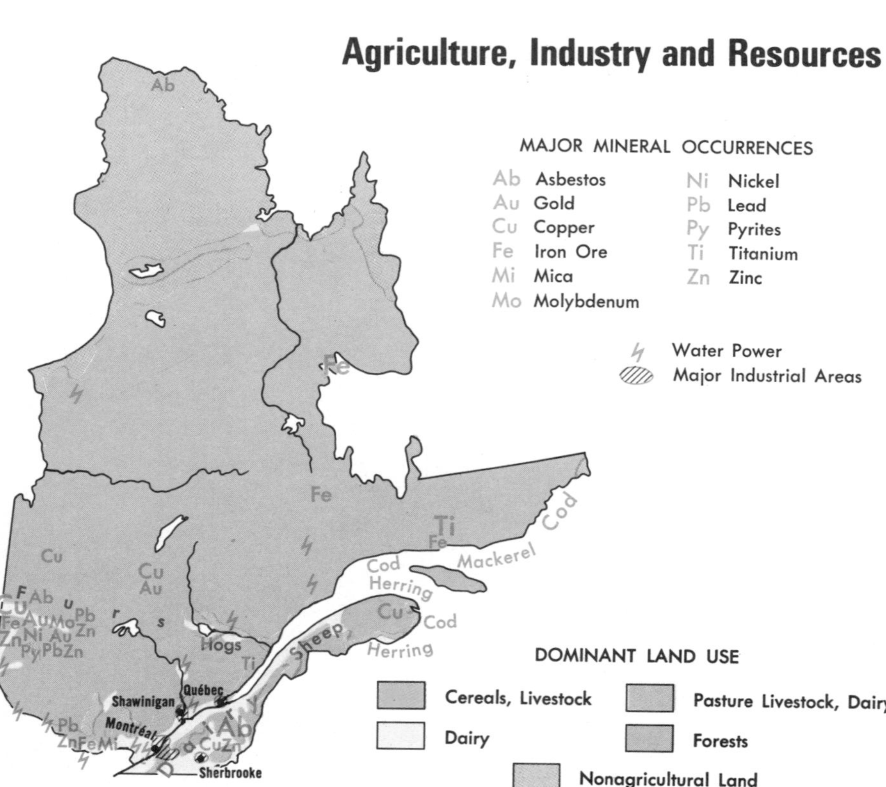

MAJOR MINERAL OCCURRENCES
Ab Asbestos
Au Gold
Cu Copper
Fe Iron Ore
Mi Mica
Mo Molybdenum
Ni Nickel
Pb Lead
Py Pyrites
Ti Titanium
Zn Zinc
Water Power
Major Industrial Areas
DOMINANT LAND USE
Cereals, Livestock
Dairy
Pasture Livestock, Dairy
Forests
Nonagricultural Land
Cod
Mackerel
Herring
Hogs
Sheep
Shawinigan
Québec
Montréal
Sherbrooke

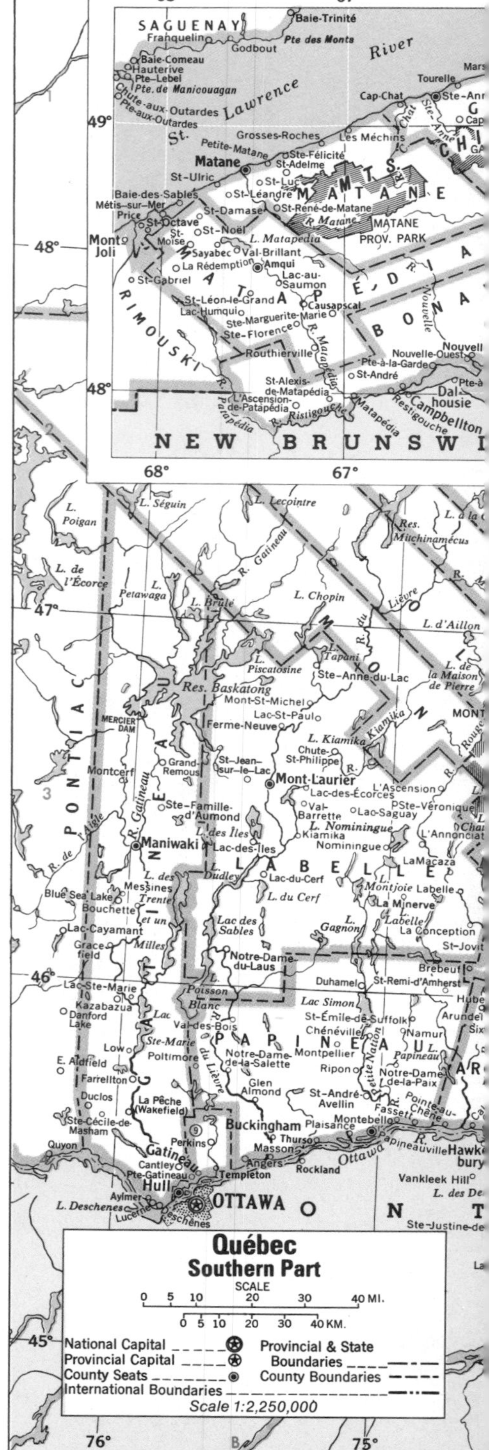

Québec
Southern Part
SCALE
0 5 10 20 30 40 MI.
0 5 10 20 30 40 KM.
National Capital
Provincial Capital
County Seats
International Boundaries
Provincial & State Boundaries
County Boundaries
Scale 1:2,250,000
SAGUENAY
NEW BRUNSWICK
OTTAWA
Hull
Gatineau
Maniwaki
Mont-Laurier
Matane

Napierville⊙ 2,343 ..... D 4
Neuville 996 ..... F 3
New Carlisle⊙ 1,292 ..... D 2
New Richmond 4,257 ..... C 2
Nicolet 4,880 ..... E 3
Nominingue 881 ..... B 3
Normandin 4,041 ..... E 1
North Hatley 689 ..... F 4
Notre-Dame-de-la-Doré 1,064 E 1
Notre-Dame-des-Laurentides H 3
Notre-Dame-des-Prairies
6,150 ..... D 3
Notre-Dame-du-Bon-Conseil
1,089 .....
Notre-Dame-du-Lac⊙ 2,258 .. J 2
Nouvelle 669 ..... C 2
Oka 1,538 ..... C 4
Omerville 1,398 ..... E 4
Ormstown 1,659 ..... D 4
Orsainville H 3
Otis 673 ..... G 1
Otterburn Park 4,268 ..... D 4
Outremont 24,338 ..... H 4
Pabos 1,295 ..... D 2
Pabos-Mills 1,565 ..... D 2
Papineauville 1,481 ..... C 4
Paspébiac 1,914 ..... D 2
Percé⊙ 4,839 ..... D 1
Petit-Cap 1,023 .....
Petite-Matane 1,065 ..... B 1
Petit-Saguenay (Saint-
François-d'Assise) 804 .. J 1
Pierrefonds 38,390 ..... H 4
Pierreville 1,212 ..... E 3

Pincourt 8,750 ..... D 4
Pintendre 1,849 ..... J 3
Plaisance 748 ..... B 4
Plessisville 7,249 ..... F 3
Pohénégamooke 3,702 ..... H 2
Pointe-à-la-Croix 1,481 ..... C 2
Pointe-au-Père 796 ..... J 1
Pointe-au-Pic 1,054 ..... G 2
Pointe-aux-Outardes 1,056 .. A 1
Pointe-aux-Trembles 36,270 .. J 4
Pointe-Calumet 2,935 ..... G 4
Pointe-Claire 24,571 ..... H 4
Pointe-Gatineau ..... B 4
Pointe-Lebel 1,573 ..... A 1
Pont-Rouge 3,580 ..... F 3
Port-Alfred 8,621 ..... G 1
Portneuf 1,333 ..... F 3
Portneuf-sur-Mer (Rivière-
Portneuf-sur-Mer) 1,255 .. H 1
Price 2,273 ..... A 1
Princeville 4,023 ..... F 3
Proulxville 588 ..... E 3
Québec (cap.) 166,474 ..... H 3
Québec⊙ *576,075 ..... H 3
Quyon 744 ..... A 4
Rawdon 2,958 ..... D 3
Repentigny 34,419 ..... J 4
Richelieu 1,832 ..... D 4
Richmond⊙ 3,568 ..... E 4
Rigaud 2,268 ..... C 4
Rimouski⊙ 29,120 ..... J 1
Rimouski-Est 2,506 ..... J 1
Ripon 620 ..... B 4

Rivière-à-Pierre 615 ..... E 3
Rivière-au-Renard 2,211 ..... D 1
Rivière-Bleue 1,690 ..... J 2
Rivière-Bois-Clair 604 ..... F 3
Rivière-du-Loup 13,459 ..... H 2
Rivière-du-Moulin ..... G 1
Rivière-Éternité 659 ..... G 1
Rivière-Portneuf-Portneuf-sur-
Mer 1,255 ..... H 1
Robertsonville 1,987 ..... F 3
Roberval⊙ 11,429 ..... E 1
Rock Island 1,179 ..... E 4
Rosemère 7,778 ..... H 4
Rougemont 972 ..... D 4
Roxboro 6,292 ..... H 4
Roxton Falls 1,245 ..... E 4
Sacré-Cœur-de-Saguenay
1,678 ..... H 1
Saint-Adelme 618 ..... B 1
Saint-Adelphe 1,159 ..... E 3
Saint-Adolphe-d'Howard
1,686 ..... C 4
Saint-Adrien 597 ..... F 4
Saint-Agapville 2,954 ..... F 3
Saint-Aimé-des-Lacs 861 ..... G 2
Saint-Alban 673 ..... E 3
Saint-Alexandre-de-
Kamouraska 1,048 ..... H 2
Saint-Alexis-des-Monts 1,984. D 3
Saint-Amable 2,424 ..... J 4
Saint-Ambroise 3,606 ..... F 1
Saint-Anaclet 1,377 ..... J 1
Saint-André-Avellin 1,312 ..... B 4
Saint-André-Est 1,293 ..... C 4

Saint-Anselme 1,808 ..... F 3
Saint-Antoine 7,012 ..... H 4
Saint-Antonin 941 ..... H 2
Saint-Aubert 884 ..... G 2
Saint-Augustin-de-Québec
2,475 ..... E 3
Saint-Basile-Sud 1,719 ..... F 3
Saint-Basile-le-Grand 7,658 .. J 4
Saint-Benjamin 1,027 .....
Saint-Bernard 585 .....
Saint-Bernard-sur-Mer 711 ... J 4
Saint-Boniface-de-Shawinigan
3,164 ..... D 3
Saint-Bruno 2,580 ..... F 1
Saint-Bruno-de-Montarville
22,880 ..... J 4
Saint-Camille-de-Bellechasse
1,744 ..... G 3
Saint-Casimir 1,133 ..... E 3
Saint-Césaire 2,935 ..... D 4
Saint-Charles 1,019 ..... G 3
Saint-Charles-de-Mandeville
1,392 ..... D 3
Saint-Chrysostome 1,018 ..... D 4
Saint-Côme 660 ..... D 3
Saint-Constant 9,938 ..... H 4
Saint-Cyprien 860 ..... J 2
Saint-Cyrille 1,041 ..... E 4
Saint-Damien-de-Buckland
1,522 ..... G 3
Saint-David 5,380 ..... J 3
Saint-David-de-Falardeau
1,876 ..... F 1
Saint-Denis 861 ..... D 4

Saint-Dominique 2,068 ..... E 4
Saint-Donat-de-Montcalm
1,521 ..... C 3
Sainte-Catherine 1,474 ..... F 3
Sainte-Claire 1,566 ..... G 3
Sainte-Croix 1,814 ..... F 3
Sainte-Adèle 4,675 ..... C 4
Sainte-Agathe 709 ..... F 3
Sainte-Agathe-des-Monts
5,641 ..... C 3
Sainte-Anne-de-Beaupré
3,292 ..... F 2
Sainte-Anne-de-Bellevue
3,981 ..... H 4
Sainte-Anne-des-Monts⊙
6,062 ..... C 1
Saint-Damien-de-Buckland
Sainte-Anne-des-Plaines
4,258 ..... H 4
Sainte-Anne-du-Lac 686 ..... B 3
Sainte-Aurélie 1,045 ..... E 4
Sainte-Blandine 849 ..... J 1

Sainte-Félicité 711 ..... B 1
Sainte-Foy 68,883 ..... H 3
Sainte-Geneviève 2,573 ..... H 4
Sainte-Geneviève-de-
Batiscan⊙ 356 ..... E 3
Sainte-Hélène-de-Bagot
1,328 ..... E 4
Sainte-Hénédine⊙ 639 ..... F 3
Sainte-Julie-de-Verchères
14,243 ..... J 4
Sainte-Julienne⊙ 750 ..... D 3
Sainte-Justine 1,080 ..... G 3
Saint-Elle 639 .....
Saint-Elzéar 743 ..... F 3
Sainte-Marie 8,937 ..... G 3

Sainte-Martine⊙ 2,196 ..... D 4
Saint-Émile 5,216 ..... H 3
Sainte-Monique 705 ..... F 1
Sainte-Pétronille 982 ..... J 3
Sainte-Perpétue-de-L'Islet
1,232 ..... H 2
Saint-Éphrem-de-Tring 973 .. G 3
Saint-Épiphane 647 ..... H 2
Saint-Pudentienne 866 ..... E 4
Sainte-Rosalie 2,862 ..... E 4
Saint-Esprit 1,068 ..... D 4
Sainte-Thérèse 18,750 ..... H 4
Sainte-Thérèse-Ouest
(Boisbriand) 13,471 ..... H 4
Sainte-Thècle 1,703 ..... E 3
Sainte-Étienne-de-Grès 845 .. E 3
Saint-Étienne-de-Lauzon
1,218 ..... J 3

AREA 594,857 sq. mi. (1,540,680 sq. km.)
POPULATION 6,438,403
CAPITAL Québec
LARGEST CITY Montréal
HIGHEST POINT Mont D'Iberville 5,420 ft.
(1,652 m.)
SETTLED IN 1608
ADMITTED TO CONFEDERATION 1867
PROVINCIAL FLOWER White Garden Lily

COUNTIES
indicated by numbers:
1 Iberville D4
2 Napierville D4
3 Rouville E4
4 St-Hyacinthe D4
5 Ile-de-Montréal H4
6 Deux-Montagnes G4
7 Soulanges C4
8 Beauharnois D4
9 Hull B4
10 Ile-Jésus H4
11 Richelieu D4
12 Vaudreuil C4

Internal divisions represent Municipal Counties

© Copyright HAMMOND INCORPORATED, Maplewood, N.J.

Gaspé Peninsula
0 5 10 20 30 40 MI.
0 5 10 20 30 40 KM.

(continued)

Saint-Eustache 29,716 .... H 4
Saint-Fabien 1,361 .... J 1
Saint-Félicien 9,058 .... E 1
Saint-Félix-de-Valois 1,462 ... D 3
Saint-Ferréol-les-Neiges 1,758 .... G 2
Saint-Flavien 734 .... F 3
Saint-François-de-Sales 831 . E 1
Saint-François-du-Lac⊙ 942 .. E 3
Saint-Fulgence 950 .... G 1
Saint-Gabriel 3,161 .... D 3
Saint-Gabriel-de-Rimouski 779 .... J 1
Saint-Gédéon, Frontenac 1,569 .... G 4
Saint-Gédéon, Lac-St-Jean-E. 1,000 .... F 1
Saint-Georges, Beauce 10,342 .... G 3
Saint-Georges, Champlain 3,344 .... E 3
Saint-Georges-Ouest 6,378 .. G 3
Saint-Germain-de-Grantham 1,373 .... E 4
Saint-Gervais 973 .... G 3
Saint-Gilles 912 .... F 3
Saint-Grégoire (Mont-St-Grégoire) 740 .... D 4
Saint-Henri 1,970 .... J 3
Saint-Honoré, Beauce 1,116 .. G 4
Saint-Honoré, Chicoutimi 1,790 .... F 1
Saint-Hubert 60,573 .... J 4
Saint-Hubert-de-Témiscouata 871 .... J 2
Saint-Hyacinthe⊙ 38,246 ..... D 4
Saint-Isidore 811 .... F 3
Saint-Isidore-de-Laprairie 769 D 4
Saint-Jacques 2,152 .... D 4
Saint-Jacques-le-Mineur 1,203 .... H 4
Saint-Jean-Chrysostome 6,930 .... J 3
Saint-Jean-de-Dieu 1,377 .... J 1
Saint-Jean-de-Matha 931 .... D 3
Saint-Jean-Port-Joli⊙ 1,813 .. G 2
Saint-Jean-sur-Richelieu⊙ 35,640 .... D 4
Saint-Jérôme 25,123 .... H 4
Saint-Joachim 1,139 .... G 2
Saint-Joseph-de-Beauce 3,216 .... G 3
Saint-Joseph-de-Sorel 2,545 . D 3
Saint-Jovite 3,841 .... C 3
Saint-Lambert 20,557 .... J 4
Saint-Laurent 65,900 .... H 4
Saint-Lazare 731 .... G 3
Saint-Léonard 79,429 .... H 4
Saint-Léonard-d'Aston 992 ... E 3
Saint-Léon-de-Chicoutimi 749 F 1
Saint-Léon-de-Standon 816 .. G 3
Saint-Léon-le-Grand 722 ..... B 2
Saint-Liboire⊙ 746 .... E 4
Saint-Louis-de-Gonzague 615 .... D 4
Saint-Louis-de-Terrebonne 14,172 .... H 4
Saint-Louis-du-Ha! Ha! 809 .. H 2
Saint-Luc 8,815 .... D 4
Saint-Luc-de-Matane 598 .... B 1
Saint-Marc-des-Carrières 2,822 .... E 3
Saint-Méthode-de-Frontenac 925 .... F 3
Saint-Michel-de-Bellechasse 963 .... G 3
Saint-Michel-des-Saints 1,584 .... D 3
Saint-Nazaire-de-Chicoutimi 962 .... F 1
Saint-Nérée 970 .... G 3
Saint-Nicolas 5,074 .... H 3
Saint-Noël 666 .... B 1
Saint-Odilon 580 .... G 3
Saint-Omer 718 .... C 2
Saint-Ours 625 .... D 4
Saint-Pacôme 1,996 .... G 2
Saint-Pamphile 3,428 .... H 3
Saint-Pascal⊙ 2,763 .... H 2
Saint-Paul-de-Montminy 602 .. G 3
Saint-Paulin 663 .... D 3
Saint-Paul-l'Ermite (Le Gardeur) 8,312 .... J 4
Saint-Philippe-de-Néri 715 ... H 2
Saint-Pie 1,725 .... E 4
Saint-Pierre 5,305 .... H 4
Saint-Pierre-d'Orléans 880 ... G 3
Saint-Polycarpe 602 .... C 4
Saint-Prime 2,522 .... E 1
Saint-Prosper-de-Dorchester 2,150 .... G 3
Saint-Raphaël⊙ 1,346 .... G 3
Saint-Raymond 3,605 .... F 3
Saint-Rédempteur 4,463 ..... J 3
Saint-Régis 1,370 .... C 4
Saint-Rémi 5,146 .... D 4
Saint-Roch-de-l'Achigan 1,160 .... D 4
Saint-Roch-de-Richelieu 1,650 .... D 4
Saint-Romuald-d'Etchemin⊙ 9,849 .... J 3
Saint-Sauveur-des-Monts 2,348 .... C 4
Saint-Siméon 1,152 .... G 2
Saint-Simon 602 .... H 1
Saint-Stanislas 1,443 .... E 3
Saint-Sylvère 1,006 .... E 3
Saint-Timothée 2,113 .... D 4
Saint-Tite 3,031 .... E 3
Saint-Tite-des-Caps 626 ..... G 2
Saint-Ubald 1,605 .... E 3
Saint-Ulric 792 .... B 1
Saint-Urbain-de-Charlevoix 1,079 .... G 2
Saint-Victor 1,104 .... G 3
Saint-Zacharie 1,284 .... G 3
Saint-Zotique 1,774 .... C 4
Sault-au-Mouton 828 .... H 1
Sawyerville 939 .... F 4
Sayabec 1,721 .... B 2
Scotstown 762 .... F 4
Senneville 1,221 .... G 4
Shannon 3,488 .... F 3
Shawbridge 942 .... C 4
Shawinigan 23,011 .... E 3
Shawinigan-Sud 11,325 ...... E 3
Shawville 1,608 .... A 4
Sherbrooke⊙ 74,075 .... E 4
Sherrington 614 .... D 4
Sillery 12,825 .... J 3
Sorel⊙ 20,347 .... D 4
Squatec 1,000 .... J 2
Stanstead Plain 1,093 .... F 4
Sutton 1,599 .... E 4
Tadoussac⊙ 900 .... H 1
Templeton .... B 4
Terrebonne 11,769 .... H 4
Thetford Mines 19,965 .... F 3
Thurso 2,780 .... B 4
Tourelle (Tourelle-Grand-Tourelle) 942 .... C 1
Tourville 659 .... H 2
Tracy 12,843 .... D 3
Tring-Jonction 1,315 .... F 3
Trois-Pistoles 4,445 .... H 1
Trois-Rivières 50,466 .... E 3
Trois-Rivières *111,453 ...... E 3
Trois-Rivières-Ouest 13,107 .. E 3
Upton 926 .... E 4
Val-Barrette 609 .... B 3
Val-Brillant 687 .... B 1
Valcourt 2,601 .... E 4
Val-David 2,336 .... C 3
Vallée-Jonction 1,200 .... G 3
Valleyfield (Salaberry-de-Valleyfield) 29,574 .... C 4
Vanier 10,725 .... J 3
Varennes 8,764 .... J 4
Vaudreuil⊙ 7,608 .... C 4
Verchères⊙ 4,473 .... J 4
Verdun 61,287 .... H 4
Victoriaville 21,838 .... F 3
Villeneuve .... J 3
Warwick 2,847 .... F 4
Waterloo⊙ 4,664 .... E 4
Waterville 1,397 .... F 4
Weedon-Centre 1,263 .... F 4
Westmount 20,480 .... H 4
Wickham 2,043 .... E 4
Windsor 5,233 .... F 4
Wottonville 673 .... F 4
Yamachiche⊙ 1,258 .... E 3

OTHER FEATURES

Alma (isl.) .... F 1
Aylmer (lake) .... F 4
Baskatong (res.) .... B 3
Batiscan (riv.) .... E 2
Bécancour (riv.) .... F 3
Bonaventure (isl.) .... D 1
Bonaventure (riv.) .... C 1
Brome (lake) .... E 4
Brompton (lake) .... E 4
Cascapédia (riv.) .... C 1
Chaleur (bay) .... C 2
Champlain (lake) .... D 4
Chaudière (riv.) .... G 4
Chic-Chocs (mts.) .... C 1
Chicoutimi (riv.) .... F 2
Coudres (isl.) .... G 2
Deschênes (lake) .... A 4
Deux Montagnes (lake) ...... C 4
Ditton (riv.) .... F 4
Forillon Nat'l Park .... D 1
Fort Chambly Nat'l Hist. Park . J 4
Gaspé (bay) .... D 1
Gaspé (cape) .... D 1
Gaspé (pen.) .... D 2
Gaspésie Prov. Park .... C 1
Gatineau (riv.) .... B 3
Îles (lake) .... B 3
Jacques-Cartier (mt.) .... C 1
Jacques-Cartier (riv.) .... F 2
Kénogami (lake) .... F 1
Kiamika (lake) .... B 3
La Maurice Nat'l Park .... D 3
Laurentides Prov. Park .... F 2
Lièvre (riv.) .... B 4
Lièvres (isl.) .... H 2
Maskinongé (riv.) .... D 3
Matane (riv.) .... B 1
Matane Prov. Park .... B 1
Matapédia (riv.) .... B 2
Mégantic (lake) .... G 4
Memphremagog (lake) .... E 4
Mercier (dam) .... A 3
Métabetchouane (riv.) .... F 1
Mille Îles (riv.) .... H 4
Montmorency (riv.) .... F 2
Mont-Tremblant Prov. Park .... C 3
Nicolet (riv.) .... E 3
Nominingue (lake) .... B 3
Nord (riv.) .... C 4
Orléans (isl.) .... F 3
Ottawa (riv.) .... B 4
Ouareau (riv.) .... D 3
Ouelle (riv.) .... H 2
Patapédia (riv.) .... B 2
Péribonca (riv.) .... F 1
Petite Nation (riv.) .... B 4
Prairies (riv.) .... H 4
Rimouski (riv.) .... J 1
Ristigouche (riv.) .... B 2
Saguenay (riv.) .... G 1
Sainte-Anne (riv.) .... F 3
Sainte-Anne (riv.) .... G 2
Saint-François (lake) .... F 4
Saint-François (riv.) .... E 4
Saint-Jean (lake) .... E 1
Saint Lawrence (gulf) .... D 2
Saint Lawrence (riv.) .... H 1
Saint-Louis (lake) .... H 4
Saint-Maurice (riv.) .... E 2
Saint-Pierre (lake) .... E 3
Shawinigan (riv.) .... E 3
Shipshaw (riv.) .... F 1
Soeurs (isl.) .... H 4
Témiscouata (lake) .... H 2
Tremblant (lake) .... C 3
Trente et un Milles (lake) ..... B 3
Verte (isl.) .... H 1
Yamaska (riv.) .... E 4
York (riv.) .... D 1

⊙County seat.
*Population of metropolitan area.

QUÉBEC, NORTHERN

INTERNAL DIVISIONS

Abitibi (county) 93,529 .... B 2
Abitibi (terr.) .... B 3
Berthier (county) 31,096 ..... B 3
Bonaventure (county) 40,487 . D 3
Champlain (county) 119,595 .. C 3
Charlevoix-Est (co.) 17,448 ... C 3
Charlevoix-Ouest (county) 14,172 .... C 3
Chicoutimi (county) 174,441 .. C 2
Gaspé-Est (county) 41,173 ... E 3
Gaspé-Ouest (county) 18,943 D 3
Gatineau (county) 54,229 .... B 3
Joliette (county) 60,384 ...... B 3
Lac-Saint-Jean-Est (county) 47,891 .... C 3
Lac-Saint-Jean-Ouest (county) 62,952 .... C 2
Maskinongé (county) 20,763 . C 3
Matane (county) 29,955 ...... D 3
Matapédia (county) 23,715 ... D 3
Mistassini (terr.) .... B 2
Montcalm (county) 27,557 .... B 3
Montmorency No. I (county) 23,048 .... C 3
Nouveau-Québec (terr.) ...... E 1
Pontiac (county) 20,283 ...... B 3
Portneuf (county) 58,843 ..... C 3
Québec (county) 458,980 .... C 3
Rimouski (county) 69,099 .... D 3
Saguenay (county) 115,881 .. D 2
Saint-Maurice (co.) 107,703 .. C 3
Témiscamingue (co.) 52,570 .. B 3

CITIES and TOWNS

Alma⊙ 26,322 .... C 3
Amos⊙ 9,421 .... B 3
Baie-Comeau 12,866 .... D 3
Baie-du-Poste 1,690 .... C 2
Chicoutimi⊙ 60,064 .... C 3
Gaspé 17,261 .... E 3
Hauterive 13,995 .... D 3
Jonquière 60,354 .... C 3
Lévis 17,895 .... C 3
La Tuque 11,556 .... C 3
Manicouagan .... D 2
Maniwaki⊙ 5,424 .... B 3
Matane⊙ 13,612 .... D 3
Mistassini (Baie-du-Poste) 1,690 .... C 2
Mont-Laurier⊙ 8,405 .... B 3
Montmagny⊙ 12,405 .... C 3
New Carlisle⊙ 781 .... E 3
Nouveau-Comptoir .... B 2
Percé⊙ 4,839 .... E 3
Port-Cartier-Ouest .... D 3
Port-Menier⊙ 275 .... E 3
Povungnituk 745 .... E 1
Québec (cap.)⊙ 166,474 ..... C 3
Rimouski⊙ 29,120 .... D 3
Rivière-au-Tonnerre 480 ...... D 2
Rivière-du-Loup 13,459 ...... D 3
Rouyn 17,224 .... B 3
Sept-Îles 29,262 .... D 2
Seven Islands (Sept-Îles) 29,262 .... D 2
Shawinigan 23,011 .... C 3
Tadoussac 900 .... C 3
Val d'Or 21,371 .... B 3
Ville-Marie 2,651 .... B 3

OTHER FEATURES

Allard (lake) .... E 2
Anticosti (isl.) .... E 3
Baleine, Grand Rivière de la (riv.) .... B 1
Bell (riv.) .... B 3
Betsiamites (riv.) .... C 2
Bienville (lake) .... C 2
Broadback (riv.) .... B 2
Cabonga (res.) .... B 3
Caniapiscau (riv.) .... D 1
Eastmain (riv.) .... B 2
Eau Claire (lake) .... C 1
Feuilles (riv.) .... C 1
Gaspésie Prov. Park .... D 3
George (riv.) .... F 2
Gouin (res.) .... C 3
Grande Rivière, La (riv.) ...... B 2
Honguedo (passage) .... E 3
Hudson (bay) .... A 1
Hudson (str.) .... F 1
Jacques-Cartier (passage) ... E 3
James (bay) .... A 2
Koksoak (riv.) .... D 1
Laurentides Prov. Park .... C 3
Louis-XIV (pt.) .... B 2
Manicouagan (res.) .... D 2
Minto (lake) .... E 2
Mistassibi (riv.) .... C 3
Mistassini (lake) .... C 2
Moisie (riv.) .... D 2
Natashquan (riv.) .... E 2
Nottaway (riv.) .... B 2
Nouveau-Québec (crater) .... F 1
Otish (mts.) .... C 2
Ottawa (riv.) .... B 3
Péribonca (riv.) .... C 3
Plétipi (lake) .... C 2
Saguenay (riv.) .... C 3
Saint-Jean (lake) .... C 3
Saint Lawrence (gulf) .... E 3
Saint Lawrence (riv.) .... D 3
Ungava (pen.) .... E 1

⊙County seat.
*Population of metropolitan area.

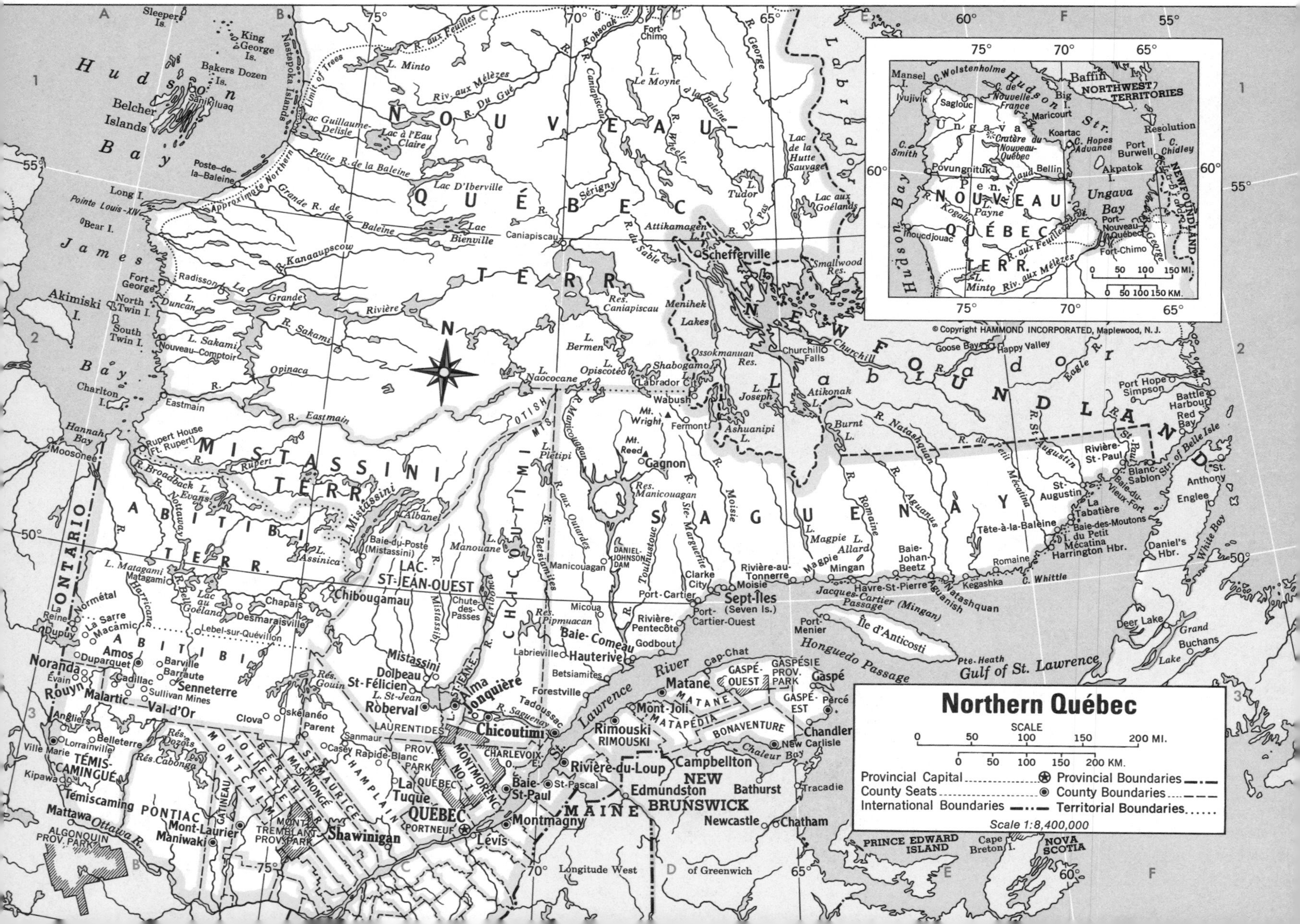
Northern Québec
SCALE
0 50 100 150 200 MI.
0 50 100 150 200 KM.
Provincial Capital
Provincial Boundaries
County Seats
County Boundaries
International Boundaries
Territorial Boundaries
Scale 1:8,400,000
© Copyright HAMMOND INCORPORATED, Maplewood, N. J.
Longitude West of Greenwich
Hudson Bay
James Bay
Belcher Islands
Akimiski I.
N O U V E A U - Q U É B E C T E R R.
MISTASSINI TERR.
ABITIBI TERR.
SAGUENAY
NEWFOUNDLAND
NEW BRUNSWICK
MAINE
ONTARIO
PRINCE EDWARD ISLAND
NOVA SCOTIA
Gulf of St. Lawrence
Honguedo Passage
Île d'Anticosti
Schefferville
Sept-Îles (Seven Is.)
Chicoutimi
Jonquière
Baie-Comeau
Hauterive
Rimouski
Rivière-du-Loup
QUÉBEC
Lévis
Montmagny
Shawinigan
La Tuque
Roberval
Chibougamau
Val-d'Or
Rouyn
Noranda
Amos
Maniwaki
Matane
Gaspé
Fort-Chimo
Gagnon
L. Mistassini
L. Minto
Lac D'Iberville
Caniapiscau
Campbellton
Edmundston
Bathurst
Newcastle
Chatham
Labrador City
Wabush
Churchill Falls

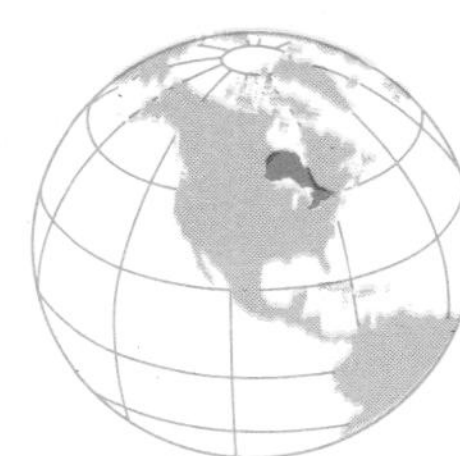

ONTARIO, NORTHERN

INTERNAL DIVISIONS

Algoma (terr. dist.) 133,553 ... D 3
Cochrane (terr. dist.) 96,875 ... D 2
Kenora (terr. dist.) 59,421 ... C 2
Manitoulin (terr. dist.) 11,001 ... D 3
Nipissing (terr. dist.) 80,268 ... E 3
Parry Sound (terr. dist.)
  33,528 ... E 3
Rainy River (terr. dist.) 22,798 B 3
Renfrew (county) 87,484 ... E 3
Sudbury (reg. munic.)
  159,779 ... D 3
Sudbury (terr. dist.) 27,068 ... D 3
Thunder Bay (terr. dist.)
  153,997 ... C 3
Timiskaming (terr. dist.)
  41,288 ... D 3

CITIES and TOWNS

Chalk River 1,010 ... E 3
Elliot Lake 16,723 ... D 3
Fort Albany 482 ... D 2
Fort Frances⊛ 8,906 ... B 3
Kapuskasing 12,014 ... D 3
Kenora⊛ 9,817 ... B 3
Kirkland Lake 12,219 ... D 3
Moose Factory 1,452 ... D 2
Moosonee 1,433 ... D 2
Nickel Centre 12,318 ... D 3
North Bay⊛ 51,268 ... E 3
Pembroke 14,026 ... E 3
Sault Sainte Marie⊛ 82,697 . D 3
Sudbury 91,829 ... D 3
Thunder Bay 112,486 ... C 3
Timmins 46,114 ... D 3
Valley East 20,433 ... D 3

OTHER FEATURES

Abitibi (lake) ... E 3
Abitibi (riv.) ... D 2
Albany (riv.) ... C 2
Algonquin Prov. Park ... E 3
Asheweig (riv.) ... C 2
Attawapiskat (lake) ... C 2
Attawapiskat (riv.) ... C 2
Basswood (lake) ... B 3
Berens (riv.) ... A 2
Big Trout (lake) ... B 2
Black Duck (riv.) ... C 1
Bloodvein (riv.) ... A 2
Caribou (isl.) ... C 3

Cobham (riv.) ... A 2
Eabamet (lake) ... C 2
Ekwan (riv.) ... C 2
English (riv.) ... B 2
Fawn (riv.) ... C 2
Finger (lake) ... B 2
Georgian (bay) ... D 3
Hannah (bay) ... D 2
Henrietta Maria (cape) ... D 1
Hudson (bay) ... D 1
Huron (lake) ... D 3
James (bay) ... D 2
Kapiskau (riv.) ... D 2
Kapuskasing (riv.) ... D 3
Kenogami (riv.) ... D 3
Kesagami (riv.) ... E 2
Lake of the Woods (lake) ... B 3
Lake Superior Prov. Park ... D 3
Little Current (riv.) ... C 3
Long (lake) ... C 3
Manitoulin (isl.) ... D 3
Mattagami (riv.) ... D 3
Michipicoten (isl.) ... C 3
Mille Lacs (lake) ... B 3
Missinaibi (lake) ... D 3
Missinaibi (riv.) ... D 2
Missisa (lake) ... D 2
Nipigon (lake) ... C 3
Nipissing (lake) ... E 3
North (chan.) ... D 3
North Caribou (lake) ... B 2
Nungesser (lake) ... B 2
Ogidaki (mt.) ... D 3
Ogoki (riv.) ... C 2
Opazatika (riv.) ... D 3
Opinnagau (riv.) ... D 2
Otoskwin (riv.) ... B 2
Ottawa (riv.) ... E 3
Pipestone (riv.) ... B 2
Polar Bear Prov. Park ... D 2
Pukaskwa Prov. Park ... C 3
Quetico Prov. Park ... B 3
Rainy (lake) ... B 3
Red (lake) ... B 2
Sachigo (riv.) ... B 2
Saganaga (lake) ... B 3
Saint Ignace (isl.) ... C 3
Saint Joseph (lake) ... B 2
Sandy (lake) ... B 2
Savant (lake) ... B 2
Seine (riv.) ... B 2
Seul (lake) ... B 2
Severn (lake) ... B 2
Severn (riv.) ... B 2
Shamattawa (riv.) ... C 2
Shibogama (lake) ... C 2

Sibley Prov. Park ... C 3
Slate (isls.) ... C 3
Stout (lake) ... B 2
Superior (lake) ... C 3
Sutton (lake) ... D 2
Sutton (riv.) ... D 2
Timagami (lake) ... D 3
Timiskaming (lake) ... E 2
Trout (lake) ... B 2
Wabuk (pt.) ... D 1
Winisk (lake) ... C 2
Winisk (riv.) ... C 2
Winnipeg (riv.) ... A 2
Woods (lake) ... B 3

ONTARIO

INTERNAL DIVISIONS

Algoma (terr. dist.) 133,553 ... J 5
Brant (county) 104,427 ... D 4
Bruce (county) 60,020 ... C 3
Cochrane (terr. dist.) 96,875 ... J 4
Dufferin (county) 31,145 ... D 3
Dundas (county) 18,946 ... J 2
Durham (reg. munic.) 283,639 F 3
Elgin (county) 69,707 ... C 5
Essex (county) 312,467 ... B 5
Frontenac (county) 108,133 ... H 3
Glengarry (county) 20,254 ... K 2
Grenville (county) 27,176 ... J 3
Grey (county) 73,824 ... D 3
Haldimand-Norfolk (reg.
  munic.) 89,456 ... E 5
Haliburton (county) 11,361 ... F 2
Halton (reg. munic.) 253,883 ... E 4
Hamilton-Wentworth (reg.
  munic.) 411,445 ... D 4
Hastings (county) 106,883 ... G 3
Huron (county) 56,127 ... C 4
Kenora (terr. dist.) 59,421 ... G 5
Kent (county) 107,022 ... C 5
Lambton (county) 123,445 ... B 5
Lanark (county) 45,676 ... H 3
Leeds (county) 53,765 ... H 3
Lennox and Addington
  (county) 33,040 ... G 3
Manitoulin (terr. dist.) 11,001 ... D 3
Middlesex (county) 318,184 ... C 4
Muskoka (dist. munic.)
  38,370 ... E 3
Niagara (reg. munic.) 368,288 E 4
Nipissing (terr. dist.) 80,268 ... F 2
Northumberland (county)
  64,966 ... G 3

Ottawa-Carleton (reg. munic.)
  546,849 ... J 2
Oxford (county) 85,920 ... D 4
Parry Sound (terr. dist.)
  33,528 ... D 2
Peel (reg. munic.) 490,731 ... E 4
Perth (county) 66,096 ... C 4
Peterborough (county)
  102,452 ... F 3
Prescott (county) 30,365 ... K 2
Prince Edward (county)
  22,336 ... G 3
Rainy River (terr. dist.) 22,798 G 5
Renfrew (county) 87,484 ... G 2
Russell (county) 22,412 ... J 2
Simcoe (county) 225,071 ... E 3
Stormont (county) 61,927 ... K 2
Sudbury (reg. munic.)
  159,779 ... K 6
Sudbury (terr. dist.) 27,068 ... J 5
Thunder Bay (terr. dist.)
  153,997 ... H 5
Timiskaming (terr. dist.)
  41,288 ... K 5
Toronto (metro. munic.)
  2,137,395 ... K 4
Victoria (county) 47,854 ... F 3
Waterloo (reg. munic.)
  305,496 ... D 4
Wellington (county) 129,432 . D 4
York (reg. munic.) 252,053 ... E 4

CITIES and TOWNS

Ailsa Craig 765 ... C 4
Ajax 25,475 ... E 4
Alban 342 ... D 1
Alexandria 3,271 ... K 2
Alfred 1,057 ... K 2
Alliston 4,712 ... E 3
Almonte 3,855 ... H 2
Alvinston 736 ... B 5
Amherstburg 5,685 ... A 5
Amherst View 6,110 ... H 3
Ancaster 14,428 ... D 4
Angus 3,085 ... E 3
Apsley 264 ... F 2
Arkona 473 ... C 4
Armstrong 378 ... H 4
Arnprior 5,828 ... H 2
Aroland 291 ... H 4
Arthur 1,700 ... D 4
Astorville 340 ... E 1
Athens 948 ... J 3
Atherley 366 ... E 3
Atikokan 4,452 ... G 5

Atwood 723 ... D 4
Aurora 16,267 ... J 3
Avonmore 273 ... K 2
Aylmer 5,254 ... C 5
Ayr 1,295 ... D 4
Ayton 424 ... D 4
Baden 945 ... D 4
Bala 577 ... D 2
Bancroft 2,329 ... G 2
Barrie⊛ 38,423 ... E 3
Barry's Bay 1,216 ... G 2
Batawa 430 ... G 3
Bath 1,071 ... H 3
Bayfield 649 ... C 4
Beachburg 682 ... H 2
Beachville 917 ... D 4
Beardmore 583 ... H 5
Beaverton 1,952 ... E 3
Beeton 1,989 ... E 3
Belle River 3,568 ... B 5
Belleville⊛ 34,881 ... G 3
Belmont 831 ... C 5
Bethany 365 ... F 3
Bewdley 508 ... F 3
Binbrook 306 ... D 4
Blackstock 720 ... F 3
Blenheim 4,044 ... C 5
Blind River 3,444 ... J 5
Bloomfield 718 ... G 4
Blyth 926 ... C 4
Bobcaygeon 1,625 ... F 3
Bonfield 540 ... E 1
Bothwell 915 ... C 5
Bourget 1,057 ... J 2
Bracebridge⊛ 9,063 ... E 2
Bradford 7,370 ... E 3
Braeside 492 ... H 2
Brampton⊛ 149,030 ... J 4
Brantford⊛ 74,315 ... D 4
Bridgenorth 1,633 ... F 3

Brigden 635 ... B 5
Brighton 3,147 ... G 3
Britt 419 ... D 2
Brockville⊛ 19,896 ... J 3
Bruce Mines 635 ... J 5
Brussels 962 ... C 4
Burford 1,461 ... D 4
Burgessville 302 ... D 4
Burk's Falls 922 ... E 2
Burlington 114,853 ... E 4
Cache Bay 665 ... D 1
Caesarea 551 ... F 3
Calabogie 256 ... H 2
Caledon 26,645 ... E 4
Callander 1,158 ... E 1
Cambridge 77,183 ... D 4
Campbellford 3,409 ... G 3
Cannington 1,623 ... E 3
Capreol 3,845 ... K 5
Caramat 265 ... H 5
Cardinal 1,753 ... J 3
Carleton Place 5,626 ... H 2
Carlisle 781 ... D 4
Carlsbad Springs 616 ... J 2
Carp 707 ... H 2
Cartier 590 ... J 5
Casselman 1,675 ... J 2
Castleton 346 ... F 3
Chalk River 1,010 ... G 1
Chapleau 3,243 ... J 5
Charing Cross 443 ... B 5
Chatham⊛ 40,952 ... B 5
Chatsworth 383 ... D 3
Cherry Valley 289 ... G 4
Chesley 1,840 ... C 3
Chesterville 1,430 ... J 2
Chute-à-Blondeau 365 ... K 2
City View ... J 2
Clarence Creek 796 ... J 2
Clarksburg 508 ... D 3

Clifford 645 ... D 4
Clinton 3,081 ... C 4
Cobalt 1,759 ... K 5
Cobden 997 ... H 2
Coboconk 426 ... F 3
Cobourg⊛ 11,385 ... F 4
Cochrane⊛ 4,848 ... K 5
Colborne 1,796 ... G 4
Colchester 711 ... B 6
Coldwater 964 ... E 3
Collingwood 12,064 ... D 3
Comber 667 ... B 5
Consecon 295 ... G 3
Cookstown 918 ... E 3
Cornwall⊛ 46,144 ... K 2
Cottam 404 ... B 5
Courtland 647 ... D 5
Courtright 1,024 ... B 5
Crediton 370 ... C 4
Creemore 1,182 ... D 3
Crysler 540 ... J 2
Cumberland 518 ... J 2
Cumberland Beach-Bramshot-
  Buena Vista 679 ... E 3
Dashwood 426 ... C 4
Deep River 5,095 ... G 1
Delaware 481 ... C 5
Delhi 4,043 ... D 5
Delta 360 ... H 3
Deseronto 1,740 ... G 3
Douglas 303 ... H 2
Drayton 809 ... D 4
Dresden 2,550 ... B 5
Drumbo 476 ... D 4
Dryden 6,640 ... G 4
Dublin 295 ... C 4
Dubreuilville △988 ... J 5
Dundalk 1,250 ... D 3
Dundas 19,586 ... D 4
Dungannon 284 ... C 4
Dunnville 11,353 ... E 5
Durham 2,458 ... D 3
Dutton 1,115 ... C 5
Earlton 1,028 ... K 5
East York 101,974 ... J 4
Echo Bay 786 ... J 5
Eden Mills 318 ... D 4
Eganville 1,245 ... G 2
Egmondville 465 ... C 4
Elgin 327 ... H 3
Elk Lake 526 ... K 5
Elliot Lake 16,723 ... B 1
Elmira 7,063 ... D 4
Elmvale 1,183 ... E 3
Elmwood 364 ... C 3
Elora 2,666 ... D 4
Embro 727 ... C 4
Embrun 1,883 ... J 2
Emeryville-Puce 1,611 ... B 5
Emo 762 ... F 5
Englehart 1,689 ... K 5
Enterprise 357 ... H 3
Erieau 430 ... C 5
Erin 2,313 ... D 4
Espanola 5,836 ... J 5
Essex 6,295 ... B 5
Etobicoke 298,713 ... J 4
Everett 570 ... E 3
Exeter 3,732 ... C 4
Fauquier 561 ... J 5
Fenelon Falls 1,701 ... F 3
Fergus 6,064 ... D 4
Field 462 ... E 1
Finch 353 ... J 2
Fingal 380 ... C 5
Fitzroy Harbour 446 ... H 2
Flesherton 565 ... D 3
Foleyet 426 ... J 5
Fordwich 365 ... C 4
Forest 2,671 ... C 4
Formosa 393 ... C 3
Fort Erie 24,096 ... E 5
Fort Frances⊛ 8,906 ... F 5
Foxboro 597 ... G 3
Frankford 1,919 ... G 3
Fraserdale 303 ... J 5
Freelton 307 ... D 4
Gananoque 4,863 ... H 3
Garden Village 270 ... E 1
Geraldton 2,956 ... H 5
Glencoe 1,694 ... C 5
Glen Miller 639 ... G 3
Glen Robertson 378 ... K 2
Glen Walter 710 ... K 2
Goderich⊛ 7,322 ... C 4
Gogama 652 ... J 5
Goodwood 335 ... E 3
Gore Bay⊛ 777 ... B 2
Gorrie 468 ... C 4
Grafton 409 ... G 4
Grand Bend 680 ... C 4
Grand Valley 1,226 ... D 4
Granton 315 ... C 4
Gravenhurst 8,532 ... E 3
Greely 567 ... J 2
Green Bay 459 ... K 2
Grimsby 15,797 ... E 4
Guelph⊛ 71,207 ... D 4

(continued on following page)

Northern Ontario

SCALE
0 25 50 100 150 200 MI.
0 25 50 100 150 200 KM.

Provincial Capital ... ⊛ Provincial and
County Seats ... ◉ State Boundaries ____
International Boundaries ... County Boundaries ......

Scale 1:8,550,000

© Copyright HAMMOND INCORPORATED, Maplewood, N.J.

Longitude West of Greenwich

OTHER FEATURES

Topography

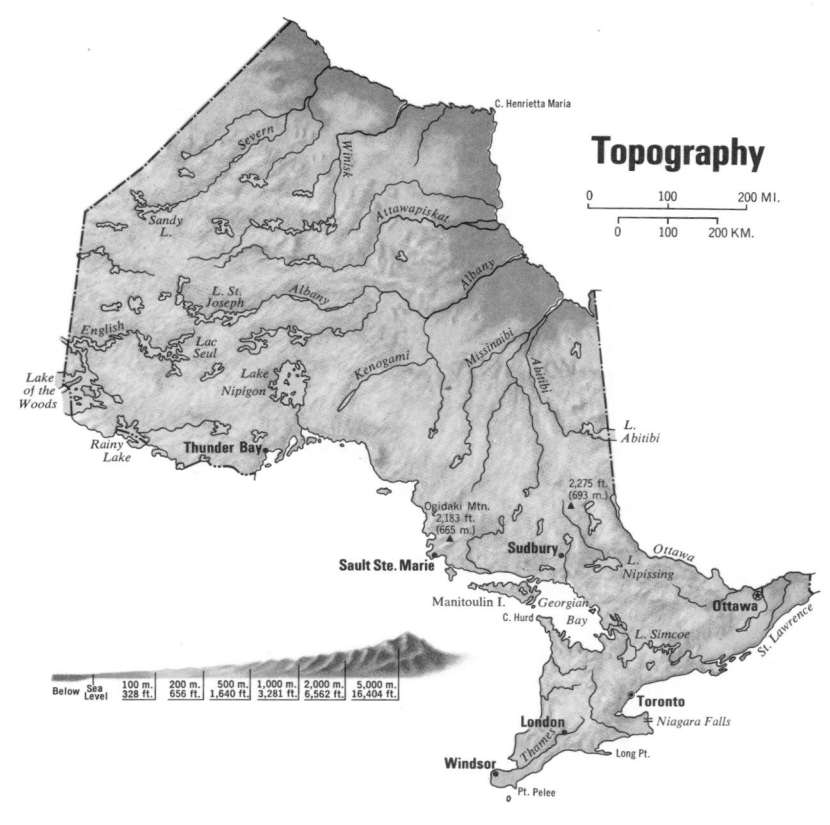

Agriculture, Industry and Resources

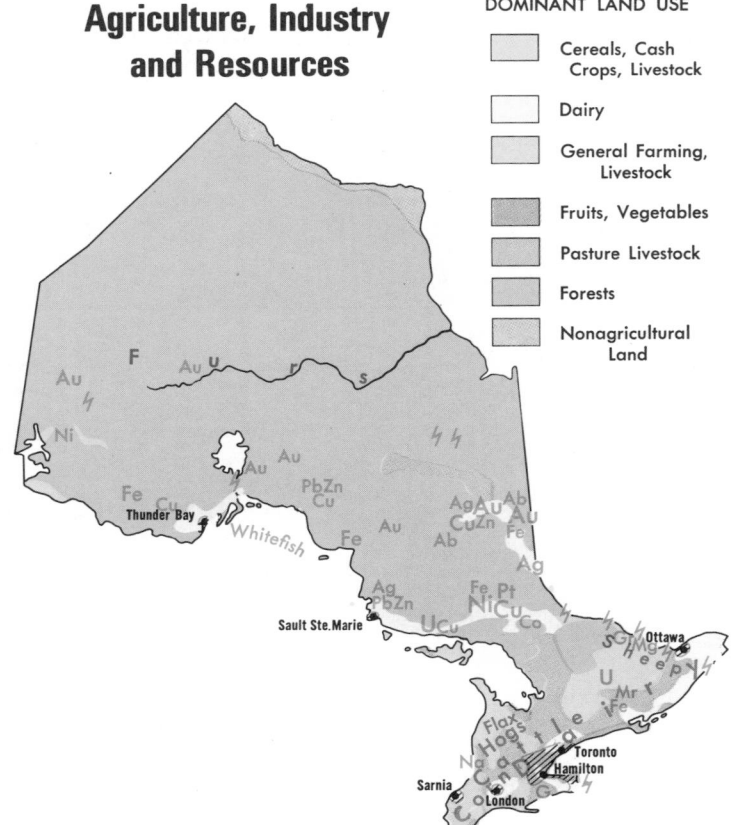

DOMINANT LAND USE

- Cereals, Cash Crops, Livestock
- Dairy
- General Farming, Livestock
- Fruits, Vegetables
- Pasture Livestock
- Forests
- Nonagricultural Land

MAJOR MINERAL OCCURRENCES

Ab	Asbestos	Mg	Magnesium
Ag	Silver	Mr	Marble
Au	Gold	Na	Salt
Co	Cobalt	Ni	Nickel
Cu	Copper	Pb	Lead
Fe	Iron Ore	Pt	Platinum
G	Natural Gas	U	Uranium
Gr	Graphite	Zn	Zinc

⚡ Water Power
▨ Major Industrial Areas

Ontario Southern Part

Scale 1:2,620,000

National Capital ⊛
Provincial Capital ⊛
County Seats ◉
Provincial & State Boundaries
County Boundaries
International Boundaries
Canals

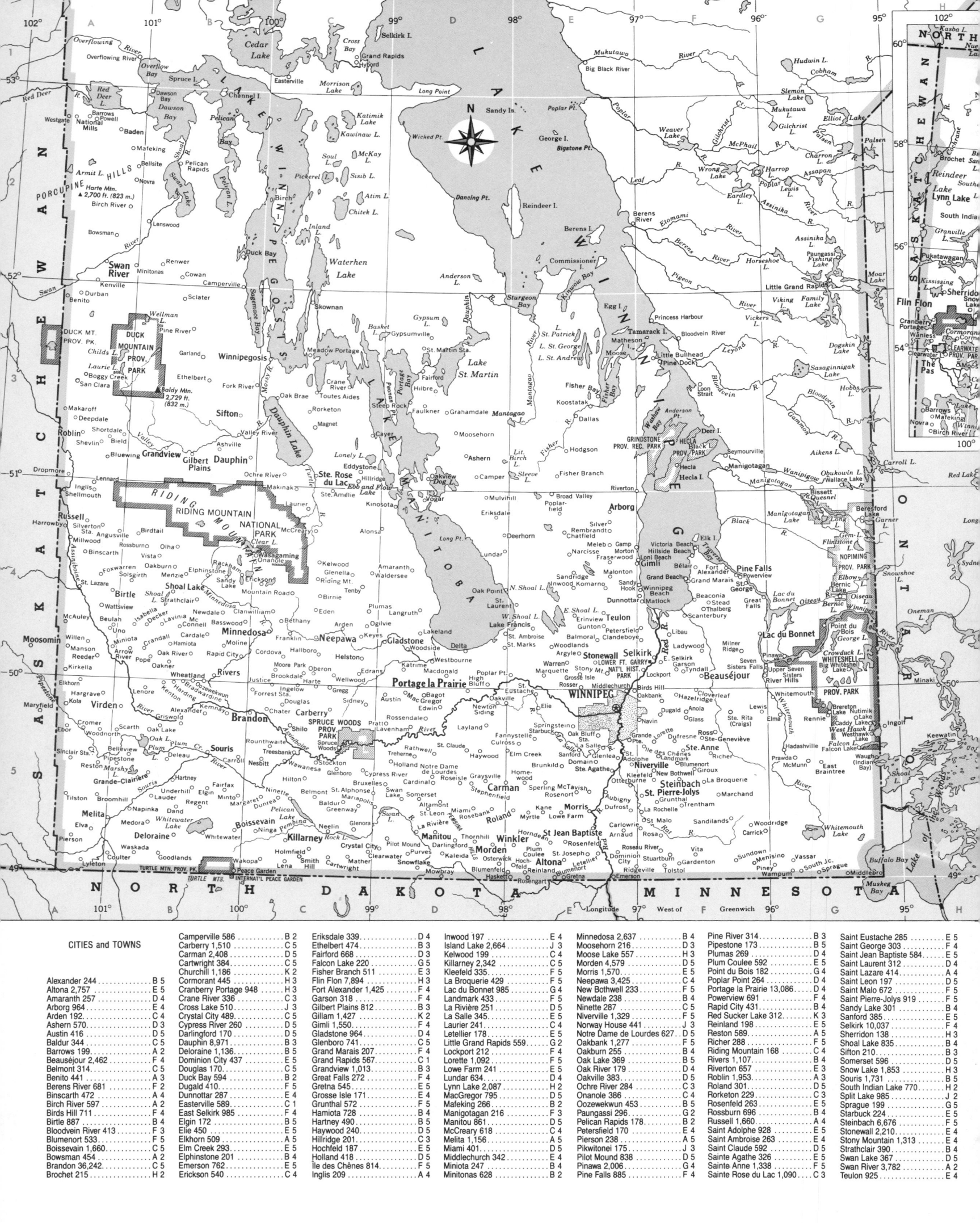

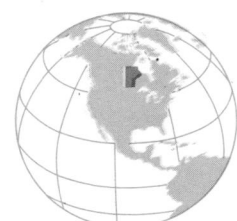

Manitoba
Northern Part

SCALE
0   40   80   120 MI.
0   40   80   120 KM.

Manitoba
Southern Part

SCALE
0 5 10   20   40   60 MI.
0 5 10 20   40   60 KM.

Provincial Capital .... ✪
International Boundaries ─ ∙∙ ─ ∙∙ ─
Provincial Boundaries ─── ∙ ───

Scale 1:2,340,000

© Copyright HAMMOND INCORPORATED, Maplewood, N.J.

The Pas 6,390 .... H 3
Thicket Portage 195 .... J 3
Thompson 14,288............ J 2
Treherne 743 .... D 5
Tyndall 421................ F 4
Virden 2,940 .... A 5
Vita 364 .... F 5
Wabowden 655 .... J 3
Wallace Lake ●2,044 .... G 3
Wanless 193 .... H 3
Warren 459................ E 4
Waskada 239.............. B 5
Wawanesa 492 .... C 5
Whitemouth 320 .... G 5
Whitewater ●856 .... B 5
Winkler 5,046.............. E 5
Winnipeg (cap.) 564,473 ... E 5
Winnipeg *584,842 .... E 5
Winnipeg Beach 565 .... F 4
Winnipegosis 855.......... B 3
Woodlands 185............ E 4
Wooodridge 170 .... G 5
York Landing 229 .... J 2

OTHER FEATURES

Aikens (lake) .... G 3
Anderson (lake)............ D 2
Anderson (pt.) .... F 3
Armit (lake) .... A 2
Assapan (riv.) .... G 2
Assiniboine (riv.) .... C 5
Assinika (lake)............. G 2
Assinika (riv.) .... G 2
Atim (lake) .... C 2
Baldy (mt.) .... B 3
Basket (lake) .... C 3
Beaverhill (lake) .... J 3
Berens (isl.) .... E 2
Berens (riv.) .... F 2
Bernic (lake) .... G 4
Big Sand (lake) .... H 2
Bigstone (lake) .... J 3
Bigstone (pt.) .... E 2
Bigstone (riv.) .... J 3
Birch (isl.) .... C 2
Black (isl.) .... F 3
Black (riv.) .... F 4
Bloodvein (riv.) .... F 3
Bonnet (lake) .... G 4
Buffalo (bay) .... G 5
Burntwood (riv.) .... J 2
Caribou (riv.) .... J 1
Carroll (lake) .... G 3
Cedar (lake) .... B 1
Channel (isl.) .... B 2
Charron (lake) .... G 2
Childs (lake) .... A 3
Chitek (lake) .... C 2
Churchill (cape) .... K 2
Churchill (riv.) .... J 2
Clear (lake) .... C 4
Clearwater Lake Prov. Park .. H 3
Cobham (riv.) .... G 1
Cochrane (riv.) .... H 2
Commissioner (isl.). ...... E 2
Cormorant (lake). .... H 3
Cross (bay) .... C 1
Cross (lake) .... J 3
Crowduck (lake) .... G 4
Dancing (pt.) .... D 2
Dauphin (lake) .... C 3
Dauphin (riv.) .... D 3
Dawson (bay) .... B 2
Dog (lake) .... D 3
Dogskin (lake) .... G 2
Duck Mountain Prov. Park .. B 3
Eardley (lake) .... F 2

East Shoal (lake) .... E 4
Ebb and Flow (lake) .... C 3
Egg (isl.) .... E 3
Elbow (lake) .... G 4
Elk (isl.) .... F 4
Elliot (lake) .... G 2
Etawney (lake) .... J 2
Etomami (riv.) .... F 2
Falcon (lake) .... G 5
Family (lake) .... G 3
Fisher (bay) .... E 3
Fisher (riv.) .... E 3
Fishing (lake) .... G 4
Flintstone (lake) .... G 4
Fox (riv.) .... K 2
Gammon (riv.) .... G 3
Garner (lake) .... G 4
Gem (lake) .... G 4
George (isl.) .... E 2
George (lake) .... G 4
Gilchrist (creek) .... F 2
Gilchrist (lake) .... G 2
Gods (lake) .... K 3
Gods (riv.) .... K 3
Granville (lake) .... H 2
Grass (riv.) .... J 2
Grass River Prov. Park ..... H 3
Grindstone Prov. Rec. Park .. F 3
Gunisao (lake) .... J 3
Gypsum (lake) .... D 3
Harrop (lake) .... G 2
Harte (mt.) .... A 2
Hayes (riv.) .... K 3
Hecla (isl.) .... F 3
Hecla Prov. Park .... F 3
Hobbs (lake) .... G 3
Horseshoe (lake) .... G 2
Hubbart (pt.) .... K 2
Hudson (bay) .... K 2
Hudwin (lake) .... G 1
Inland (lake) .... C 2
International Peace Garden .. B 5
Island (lake) .... K 3
Katimik (lake) .... C 2
Kawinaw (lake) .... C 2
Kinwow (bay) .... E 2
Kississing (lake) .... H 2
Knee (lake) .... J 3
Lake of the Woods (lake). ... H 5
La Salle (riv.) .... E 5
Laurie (lake) .... A 3
Leaf (riv.) .... F 2
Lewis (lake) .... G 2
Leyond (riv.) .... F 3
Little Birch (lake) .... E 3
Lonely (lake) .... C 3
Long (lake) .... G 4
Long (pt.) .... D 1
Long (pt.) .... D 4
Manigotagan (lake) .... G 4

Manigotagan (riv.) .... G 3
Manitoba (lake) .... D 4
Mantagao (riv.) .... E 3
Marshy (lake) .... B 5
McKay (lake) .... C 2
McPhail (riv.) .... F 2
Minnedosa (riv.) .... B 4
Moar (lake) .... G 2
Molson (lake) .... J 3
Moose (isl.) .... E 3
Morrison (lake) .... C 1
Mossy (riv.) .... C 3
Mukutawa (lake) .... G 2
Mukutawa (riv.) .... E 1
Muskeg (bay) .... G 6
Nejanilini (lake) .... J 1
Nelson (riv.) .... J 2
Nopiming Prov. Park ..... G 4
Northern Indian (lake) .... J 2
North Knife (lake) .... J 2
North Seal (riv.) .... H 2
North Shoal (lake). .... E 4
Nueltin (lake) .... H 1
Oak (lake) .... B 5
Obukowin (lake) .... G 3
Oiseau (lake) .... G 4
Oiseau (riv.) .... G 4
Overflow (bay) .... A 1
Overflowing (riv.) .... A 1
Owl (riv.) .... K 2
Oxford (lake) .... J 3
Paint (lake) .... J 2
Palsen (riv.) .... G 2
Pelican (bay) .... B 2
Pelican (lake) .... B 2
Pelican (lake) .... C 5
Pembina (hills) .... D 5
Pembina (riv.) .... C 5
Peonan (pt.) .... D 3
Pickerel (lake) .... C 2
Pigeon (riv.) .... F 2
Pipestone (creek) ...... A 5
Plum (creek) .... B 5
Plum (lake) .... B 5
Poplar (riv.) .... E 2
Porcupine (hills) .... A 2
Portage (bay) .... D 3
Punk (isl.) .... F 3
Quesnel (lake) .... G 4
Rat (riv.) .... F 5
Red (riv.) .... F 4
Red Deer (lake) .... A 2
Red Deer (riv.) .... A 2
Reindeer (isl.) .... E 2
Reindeer (lake) .... H 2
Riding (mt.) .... B 4
Riding Mountain Nat'l Park .. B 4
Rock (lake) .... C 5
Ross (isl.) .... J 3
Sagemace (bay) .... B 3

Saint Andrew (lake) .... E 3
Saint George (lake) .... E 3
Saint Martin (lake) .... D 3
Saint Patrick (lake) ...... E 3
Sale (riv.) .... E 5
Sandy (isls.)............ D 2
Sasaginnigak (lake) ..... G 3
Seal (riv.) .... J 2
Selkirk (isl.) .... C 1
Setting (lake) .... H 3
Shoal (lake) .... G 5
Shoal (riv.) .... B 2
Sipiwesk (lake) .... J 3
Sisib (lake) .... C 2
Sleeve (lake) .... E 3
Slemon (lake) .... G 1
Snowshoe (lake) .... G 4
Soul (lake) .... C 2
Souris (riv.) .... B 5
Southern Indian (lake) .. H 2
South Knife (riv.) ...... J 2
South Seal (riv.) ...... J 2
Split (lake) .... J 2
Spruce (isl.) .... B 1
Spruce Woods Prov. Park .. C 5
Stevenson (lake) ...... J 3
Sturgeon (bay) .... E 3
Swan (lake) .... B 2
Swan (lake) .... D 5
Swan (riv.) .... A 3
Tadoule (lake) .... J 2
Tamarack (isl.) ...... F 3
Tatnam (cape) .... K 2
Traverse (bay) .... F 4
Turtle (mts.) .... B 5
Turtle (riv.) .... C 3
Turtle Mountain Prov. Park .. B 5
Valley (lake) .... B 3
Vickers (lake) .... F 3
Viking (lake) .... G 3
Wanipigow (lake) .... G 3
Washow (bay) .... F 3
Waterhen (lake) ..... C 2
Weaver (lake) .... F 2
Wellman (lake) ...... B 3
West Hawk (lake) .... G 5
West Shoal (lake) .... E 4
Whitemouth (lake). ... G 5
Whitemouth (riv.). .... G 5
Whiteshell Prov. Park .. G 4
Whitewater (lake) .... B 5
Wicked (pt.) .... D 2
Winnipeg (lake) ..... E 2
Winnipeg (riv.) ..... G 4
Winnipegosis (lake) .. C 2
Woods (lake) .... H 5
Wrong (lake) .... F 2

*Population of metropolitan area.
●Population of rural municipality.

AREA 250,999 sq. mi. (650,087 sq. km.)
POPULATION 1,026,241
CAPITAL Winnipeg
LARGEST CITY Winnipeg
HIGHEST POINT Baldy Mtn. 2,729 ft.
    (832 m.)
SETTLED IN 1812
ADMITTED TO CONFEDERATION 1870
PROVINCIAL FLOWER Prairie Crocus

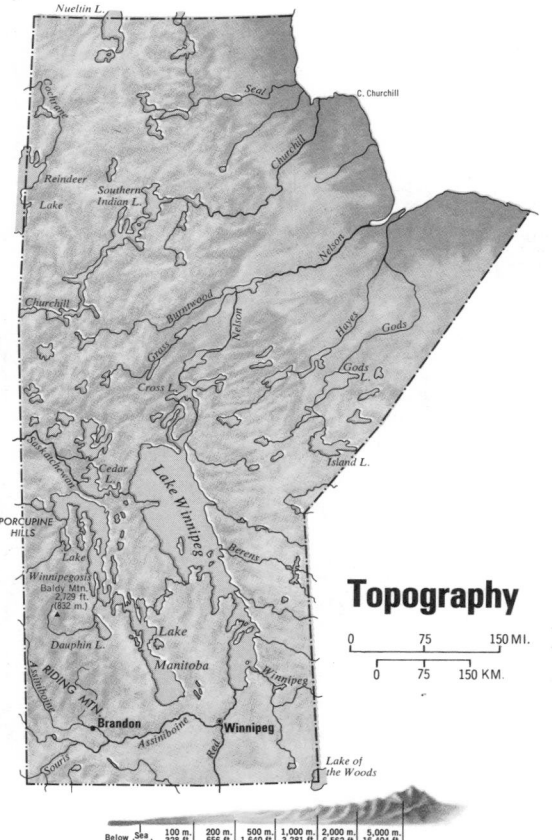

Topography

0   75   150 MI.
0   75   150 KM.

Below 100 m. 200 m. 500 m. 1,000 m. 2,000 m. 5,000 m.
Sea   328 ft. 656 ft. 1,640 ft. 3,281 ft. 6,562 ft. 16,404 ft.
Level

Agriculture, Industry and Resources

DOMINANT LAND USE

Cereals (chiefly barley, oats)
Cereals, Livestock
Dairy
Livestock
Forests
Nonagricultural Land

MAJOR MINERAL OCCURRENCES

Au Gold
Co Cobalt
Cu Copper
Na Salt

Ni Nickel
O   Petroleum
Pb Lead
Pt Platinum
Zn Zinc

⚡ Water Power
▨ Major Industrial Areas

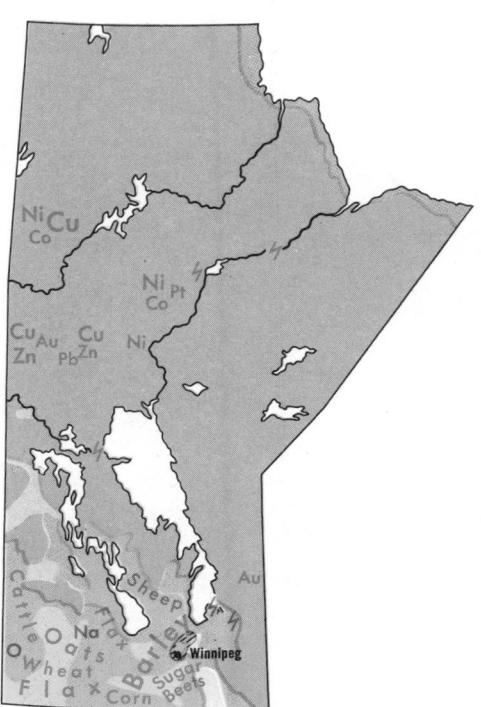

Topography

0   60   120 MI.

0   60   120 KM.

5,000 m. 2,000 m. 1,000 m. 500 m. 200 m. 100 m. Sea
16,404 ft. 6,562 ft. 3,281 ft. 1,640 ft. 656 ft. 328 ft. Level Below

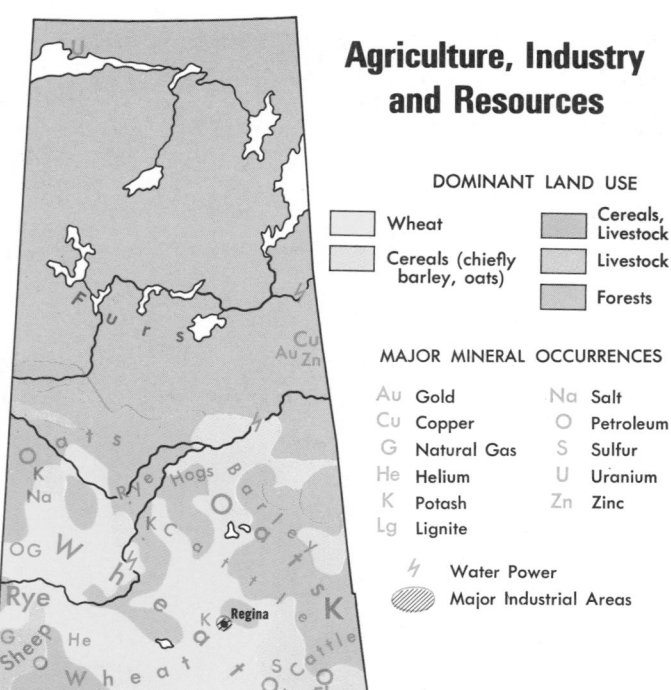

Agriculture, Industry and Resources

DOMINANT LAND USE

- Wheat
- Cereals (chiefly barley, oats)
- Cereals, Livestock
- Livestock
- Forests

MAJOR MINERAL OCCURRENCES

Au Gold
Cu Copper
G Natural Gas
He Helium
K Potash
Lg Lignite

Na Salt
O Petroleum
S Sulfur
U Uranium
Zn Zinc

⚡ Water Power
▨ Major Industrial Areas

Buffalo Pound Prov. Park ..... F 5
Cabri (lake) ..... B 4
Cactus (hills) ..... F 5
Candle (lake) ..... F 2
Cannington Manon Hist. Park . J 6
Canoe (lake) ..... L 3
Carrot (riv.) ..... J 2
Chaplin (lake) ..... E 5
Chipman (riv.) ..... M 2
Chitek (lake) ..... D 2
Churchill (riv.) ..... M 3
Clearwater (riv.) ..... L 3
Cochrane (riv.) ..... N 2
Coteau (hills) ..... D 4
Cowan (lake) ..... D 2
Crane (lake) ..... B 5
Crean (lake) ..... E 1
Cree (lake) ..... L 3
Cree (riv.) ..... M 2
Cumberland (lake) ..... J 1
Cypress (hills) ..... B 6
Cypress (lake) ..... B 6
Cypress Hills Prov. Park ..... B 6
Danielson Prov. Park ..... E 4
Delaronde (lake) ..... E 1
Diefenbaker (lake) ..... E 4
Doré (lake) ..... L 3
Douglas Prov. Park ..... E 4
Duck Lake Hist. Park ..... E 3
Duck Mountain Prov. Park ..... K 4
Eagle (hills) ..... C 3
Eaglehill (creek) ..... D 4
Ear (lake) ..... B 3
Echo Valley Prov. Park ..... G 5
Etomami (riv.) ..... J 3
Eyebrow (lake) ..... E 5
Eyehill (creek) ..... B 3
Fife (lake) ..... E 6
File (hills) ..... H 5
Fir (riv.) ..... J 2
Fond du Lac (riv.) ..... M 2
Forrest (lake) ..... L 3
Fort Battleford Nat'l Hist. Park C 3
Fort Carlton Hist. Park ..... E 3
Fort Pitt Hist. Park ..... B 2
Fort Walsh Nat'l Hist. Park ..... A 6
Foster (riv.) ..... M 3
Frenchman (riv.) ..... C 6
Frobisher (lake) ..... L 3
Gap (creek) ..... B 6
Gardiner (dam) ..... D 4
Geikie (riv.) ..... M 3
Good Spirit (lake) ..... J 4
Goodspirit Lake Prov. Park ..... J 4
Great Sand (hills) ..... B 5
Green (lake) ..... D 1
Greenwater Lake Prov. Park ..... H 3
Haultain (riv.) ..... L 3
Île-à-la-Crosse (lake) ..... L 3
Ironspring (creek) ..... G 3
Jackfish (lake) ..... C 2
Katepwa Prov. Park ..... H 5
Kingsmere (lake) ..... E 1
Kiyiu (lake) ..... C 4
Lac La Ronge Prov. Park ..... M 3
Lanigan (creek) ..... F 4
Last Mountain (lake) ..... F 4
Leaf (lake) ..... J 2
Leech (lake) ..... J 4
Lenore (lake) ..... G 3
Little Manitou (lake) ..... F 4
Lodge (creek) ..... B 6
Long (creek) ..... H 6
Loon (creek) ..... G 4
Makwa (lake) ..... B 1
Makwa (riv.) ..... B 1
Manito (lake) ..... B 3
Maple (creek) ..... B 5
McFarlane (riv.) ..... L 2
Meadow (lake) ..... C 1
Meadow Lake Prov. Park ..... K 4
Meeting (lake) ..... D 2
Midnight (lake) ..... C 2
Ministikwan (lake) ..... B 1
Missouri Coteau (hills) ..... F 5
Montreal (lake) ..... F 1
Moose (mt.) ..... J 6
Moose Jaw (riv.) ..... G 5
Moose Mountain (creek) ..... J 6
Moose Mountain Prov. Park ..... J 6
Mossy (riv.) ..... H 1
Muddy (lake) ..... B 3
Mudjatik (riv.) ..... L 3
Nipawin Prov. Park ..... G 1
North Saskatchewan (riv.) ..... D 3
Notukeu (creek) ..... D 6
Oldman (riv.) ..... L 2
Old Wives (lake) ..... E 5
Opuntia (lake) ..... C 4
Overflowing (riv.) ..... K 2
Pasquia (hills) ..... J 2
Pasquia (riv.) ..... K 2
Pelican (lake) ..... E 5
Peter Pond (lake) ..... L 3
Pheasant (hills) ..... J 5
Pine Lake Prov. Park ..... E 4
Pinto (creek) ..... D 6
Pipestone (creek) ..... K 6
Pipestone (riv.) ..... L 2
Ponass (lakes) ..... H 3
Poplar (riv.) ..... E 6
Porcupine (hills) ..... K 3
Primrose (lake) ..... L 3
Primrose Lake Air Weapons Range ..... L 3
Prince Albert Nat'l Park ..... E 1
Qu'Appelle (riv.) ..... J 5
Quill (lakes) ..... G 4
Red Deer (riv.) ..... A 5
Red Deer (riv.) ..... K 3
Reindeer (lake) ..... N 3
Reindeer (riv.) ..... M 3
Riou (lake) ..... M 2
Rivers (lake) ..... F 6
Ronge, La (lake) ..... M 3
Rowans Ravine Prov. Park ..... F 4
St. Victor Petroglyphs Hist. Park ..... E 6

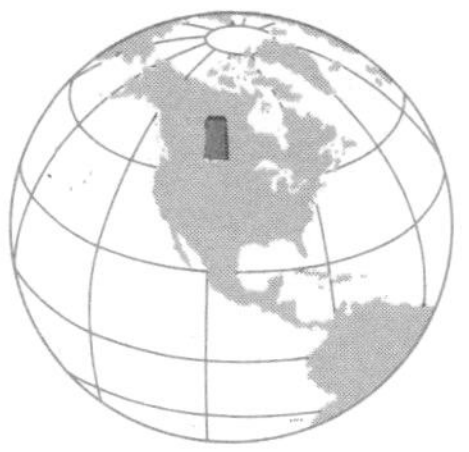

AREA 251,699 sq. mi. (651,900 sq. km.)
POPULATION 968,313
CAPITAL Regina
LARGEST CITY Regina
HIGHEST POINT Cypress Hills 4,567 ft. (1,392 m.)
SETTLED IN 1774
ADMITTED TO CONFEDERATION 1905
PROVINCIAL FLOWER Prairie Lily

Saskatchewan (riv.) ..... H 2
Saskatchewan Landing Prov. Park ..... C 5
Saskeram (riv.) ..... K 2
Scott (lake) ..... M 2
Selwyn (lake) ..... M 2
Souris (riv.) ..... H 6
South Saskatchewan (riv.) ..... C 5
Steele Narrows Hist. Park ..... B 2
Stripe (lake) ..... C 4
Sturgeon (riv.) ..... E 2
Swan (riv.) ..... J 3
Swift Current (creek) ..... D 5
Tazin (lake) ..... L 2
The Battlefords Prov. Park ..... C 2
Thickwood (hills) ..... D 2
Thunder (hills) ..... L 4
Tobin (lake) ..... H 2
Torch (riv.) ..... H 2
Touchwood (hills) ..... G 4
Tramping (lake) ..... C 3
Trout (riv.) ..... L 2
Turtle (lake) ..... C 2
Twelvemile (lake) ..... E 6
Vermilion (hills) ..... E 5
Wapawekka (hills) ..... M 4
Waskana (creek) ..... G 5
Waskesiu (lake) ..... E 2
Wathaman (riv.) ..... M 3
Weed (hills) ..... J 5
White Fox (riv.) ..... G 2
White Gull (creek) ..... G 2
Whiteshore (lake) ..... C 3
Whiteswan (lakes) ..... F 1
William (riv.) ..... L 2
Willow Bunch (lake) ..... F 6
Witchekan (lake) ..... D 2
Wollaston (lake) ..... N 2
Wood (mt.) ..... E 6
Wood (riv.) ..... E 6
Wood Mountain Hist. Park ..... E 6

*Population of metropolitan area.
•Population of rural municipality.

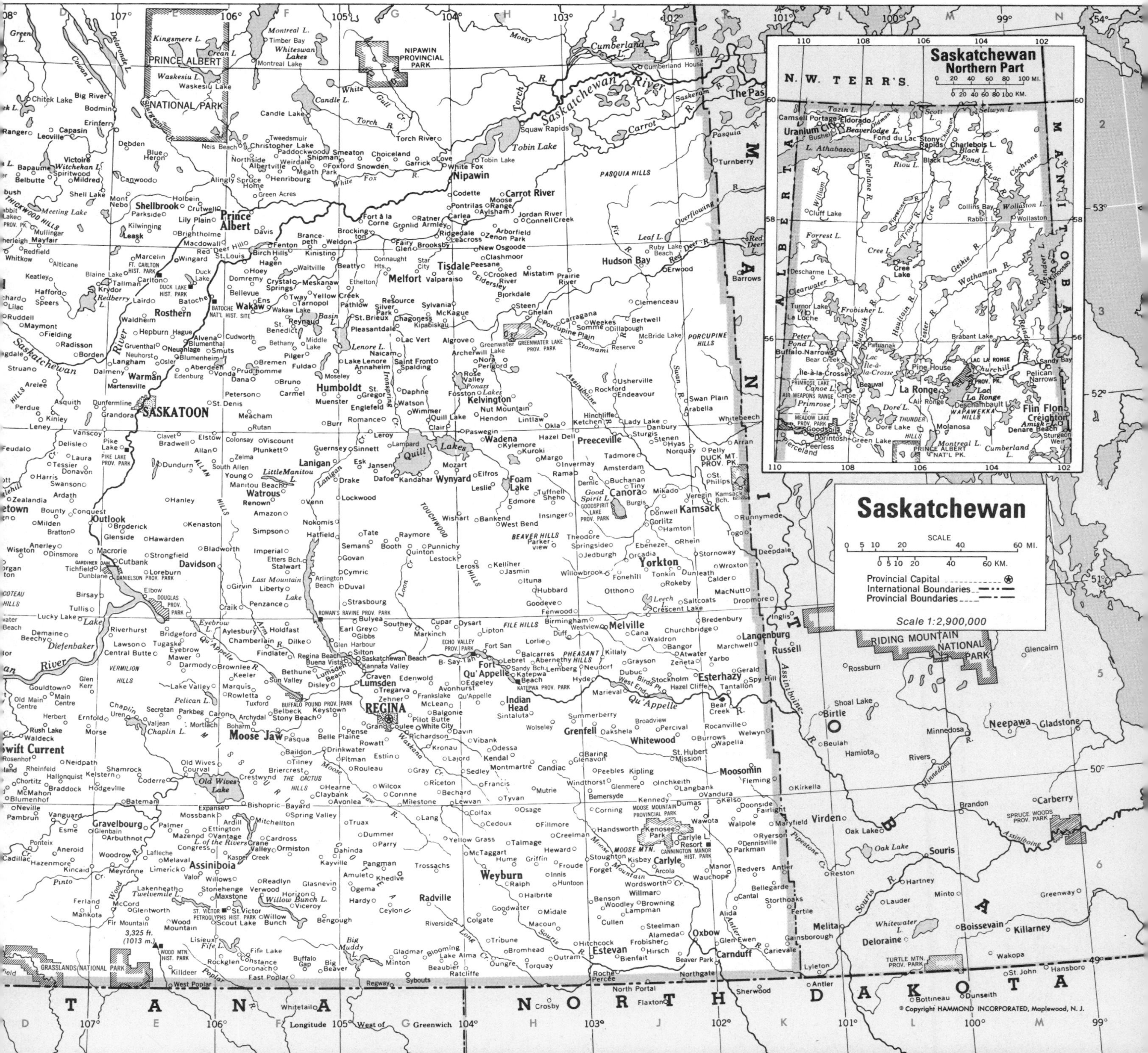
Saskatchewan
SCALE
0 5 10 20 40 60 MI.
0 5 10 20 40 60 KM.
Provincial Capital
International Boundaries
Provincial Boundaries
Scale 1:2,900,000
Saskatchewan Northern Part
Longitude 105° West of Greenwich 104°
© Copyright HAMMOND INCORPORATED, Maplewood, N. J.

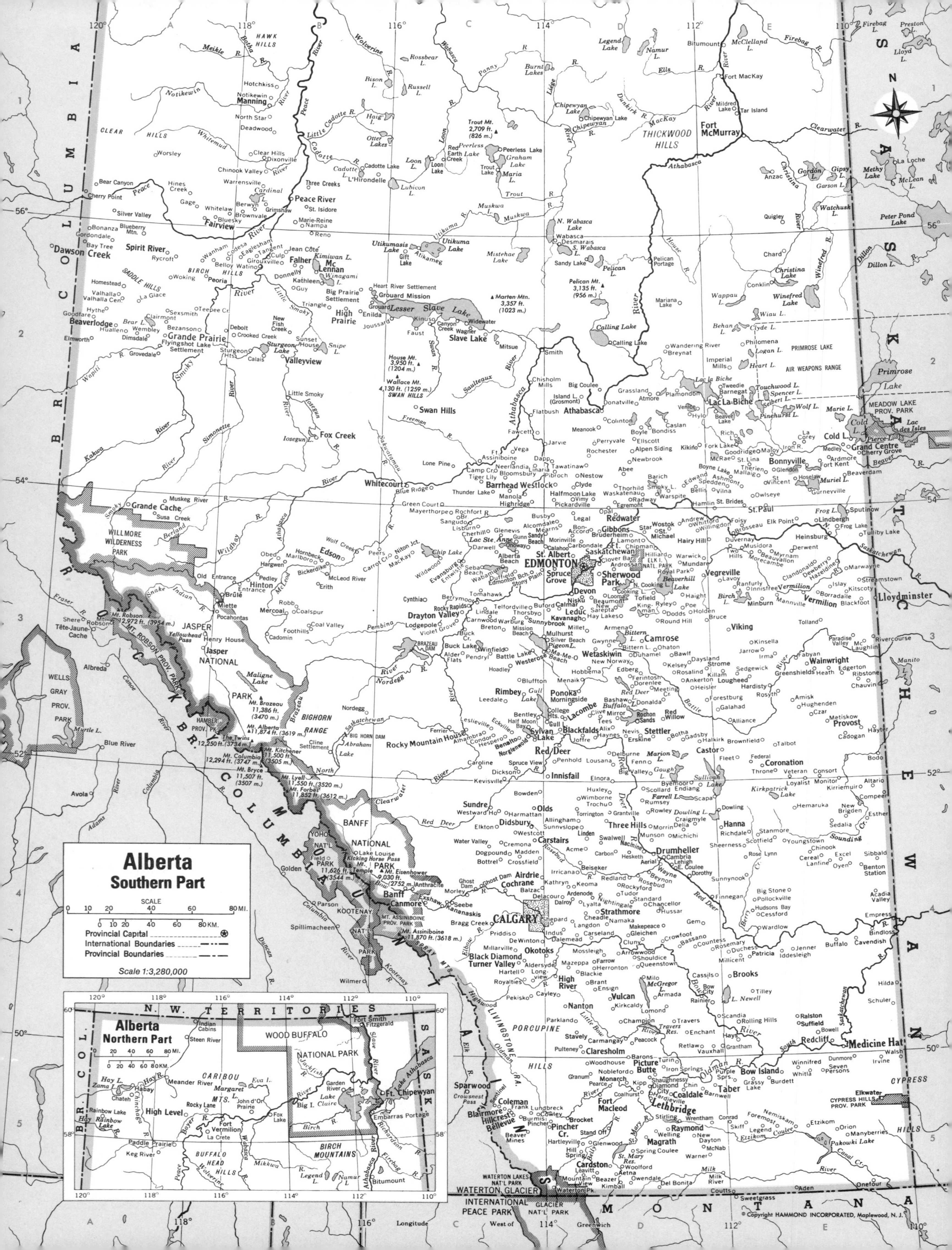

Alberta
Southern Part
SCALE
0 10 20 40 60 80 MI.
0 10 20 40 60 80 KM.
Provincial Capital
International Boundaries
Provincial Boundaries
Scale 1:3,280,000
Alberta
Northern Part
N. W. TERRITORIES
WOOD BUFFALO
NATIONAL PARK
BRITISH COLUMBIA
SASKATCHEWAN
MONTANA
EDMONTON
CALGARY
Red Deer
Lethbridge
Medicine Hat
Fort McMurray
Grande Prairie
Peace River
Lesser Slave Lake
JASPER NATIONAL PARK
BANFF NATIONAL PARK
WATERTON LAKES NAT'L PARK
WATERTON-GLACIER INTERNATIONAL PEACE PARK
Longitude West of Greenwich
© Copyright HAMMOND INCORPORATED, Maplewood, N. J.

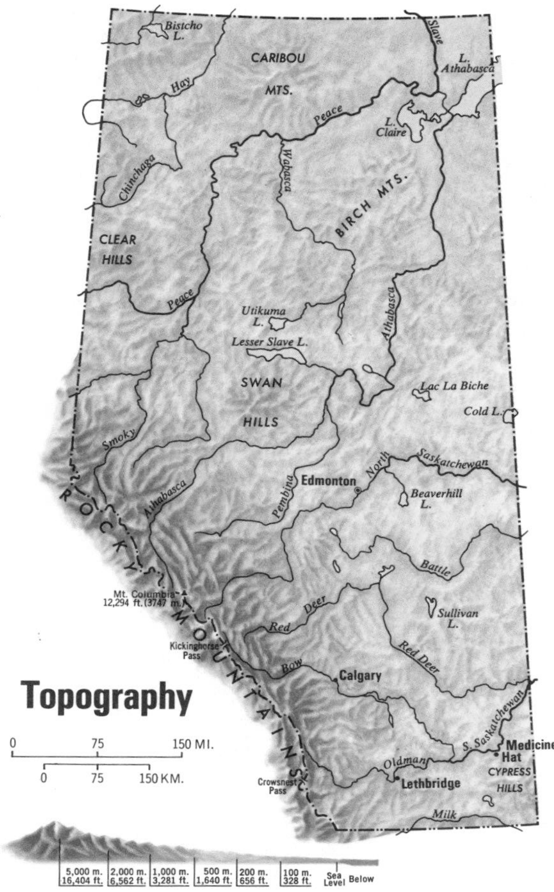
Bistcho L.
CARIBOU MTS.
Slave
L. Athabasca
Hay
Peace
L. Claire
Wabasca
BIRCH MTS.
Chinchaga
CLEAR HILLS
Peace
Utikuma L.
Athabasca
Lesser Slave L.
SWAN HILLS
Lac La Biche
Cold L.
Smoky
Saskatchewan
North
Edmonton
Pembina
Athabasca
Beaverhill L.
Battle
Mt. Columbia 12,294 ft. (3747 m.)
Red Deer
Sullivan L.
Kicking Horse Pass
Bow
Red Deer
Calgary
ROCKY MOUNTAINS
S. Saskatchewan
Medicine Hat
Oldman
Lethbridge
CYPRESS HILLS
Crowsnest Pass
Milk
0 75 150 MI.
0 75 150 KM.
5,000 m. 16,404 ft.
2,000 m. 6,562 ft.
1,000 m. 3,281 ft.
500 m. 1,640 ft.
200 m. 656 ft.
100 m. 328 ft.
Sea Level
Below

Topography

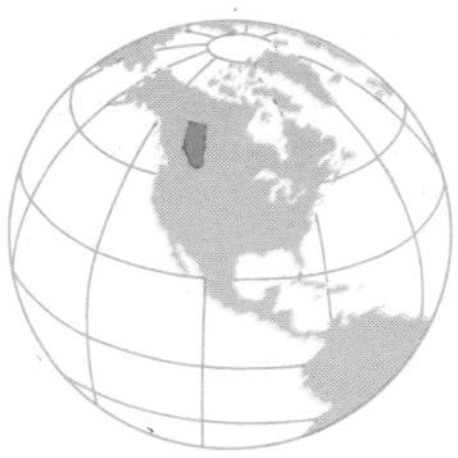

AREA 255,285 sq. mi. (661,185 sq. km.)
POPULATION 2,237,724
CAPITAL Edmonton
LARGEST CITY Edmonton
HIGHEST POINT Mt. Columbia 12,294 ft. (3,747 m.)
SETTLED IN 1861
ADMITTED TO CONFEDERATION 1905
PROVINCIAL FLOWER Wild Rose

CITIES and TOWNS

Acme 457 D 4
Airdrie 8,414 C 4
Alberta Beach 485 C 3
Alix 837 D 3
Andrew 548 D 3
Antler Lake 334 D 3
Ardmore 224 E 2
Arrowwood 156 D 4
Athabasca 1,731 D 2
Banff 4,208 C 4
Barnwell 359 D 5
Barons 315 D 4
Barrhead 3,736 C 2
Bashaw 875 D 3
Bassano 1,200 D 4
Bawlf 350 D 3
Beaumont 2,638 D 3
Beaverlodge 1,937 A 2
Beiseker 580 D 4
Bentley 823 C 3
Berwyn 557 B 1
Big Valley 360 D 3
Black Diamond 1,444 C 4
Blackfalds 1,488 D 3
Blackfoot 220 E 3
Blackie 298 D 4
Bon Accord 1,376 D 3
Bonnyville 4,454 E 2
Bowden 989 C 4
Bow Island 1,491 E 5
Boyle 638 D 2
Bragg Creek 505 C 4
Breton 552 C 3
Brooks 9,421 E 4
Bruce 88 E 3
Bruderheim 1,136 D 3
Burdett 220 E 5
Calgary 592,743 C 4
Calgary *592,743 C 4
Calmar 1,003 D 3
Camrose 12,570 D 3
Canmore 3,484 C 4
Carbon 434 D 4
Cardston 3,267 D 5
Carmangay 266 D 4
Caroline 436 C 3
Carseland 484 D 4
Carstairs 1,587 D 4
Castor 1,123 D 3
Cereal 249 E 4
Champion 339 D 4
Chauvin 298 E 3
Chipman 266 D 3
Clairmont 469 A 2
Claresholm 3,493 D 4
Clive 364 D 3
Clyde 364 D 2
Coaldale 4,579 D 5
Coalhurst 882 D 5
Cochrane 3,544 C 4
Cold Lake 2,110 E 2
College Heights 267 D 3
Consort 632 E 3
Cooking Lake 218 D 3
Coronation 1,309 E 3
Coutts 400 D 5
Cowley 304 D 5
Cremona 382 C 4
Crossfield 1,217 C 4
Daysland 679 D 3
Delburne 574 D 3
Desmarais 260 D 2
Devon 3,885 D 3
Didsbury 3,095 C 4
Donalda 280 D 3
Donnelly 336 B 2
Drayton Valley 5,042 C 3
Drumheller 6,508 D 4
Duchess 429 E 4
East Coulee 218 D 4
Eckville 870 C 3
Edgerton 387 E 3
Edmonton (cap.) 532,246 D 3
Edmonton *657,057 D 3
Edmonton Beach 280 C 3
Edson 5,835 B 3
Elk Point 1,022 E 3
Elnora 249 D 3
Entwistle 462 C 3
Erskine 259 D 3
Evansburg 779 C 3
Exshaw 353 C 4
Fairview 2,869 A 1
Falher 1,102 B 2
Faust 399 C 2
Foremost 568 E 5
Forestburg 924 E 3
Fort Assiniboine 207 C 2
Fort Chipewyan 944 C 5
Fort Macleod 3,139 D 5
Fort McKay 267 E 1
Fort McMurray 31,000 E 1
Fort Saskatchewan 12,169 D 3
Fort Vermilion 752 B 5
Fox Creek 1,978 B 2
Fox Lake 634 B 5
Gibbons 2,276 D 3
Gift Lake 428 C 2
Girouxville 325 B 2
Gleichen 381 D 4
Glendon 430 E 2
Glenwood 259 D 5
Grand Centre 3,146 E 2
Grande Cache 4,523 A 3
Grande Prairie 24,263 A 2
Granum 399 D 5
Grimshaw 2,316 B 1
Grouard Mission 221 C 2
Hanna 2,806 E 4
Hardisty 641 E 3
Hay Lakes 302 D 3
Heisler 212 D 3
High Level 2,194 A 5
High Prairie 2,506 B 2
High River 4,792 D 4
Hines Creek 575 A 1
Hinton 8,342 B 3
Holden 430 D 3
Hughenden 267 E 3
Hythe 639 A 2
Innisfail 5,247 D 3
Innisfree 255 E 3
Irma 474 E 3
Irricana 558 D 4
Irvine 360 E 5
Jasper 3,269 B 3
John d'Or Prairie 437 B 5
Joussard 330 B 2
Killam 1,005 E 3
Kinuso 285 C 2
Kitscoty 497 E 3
Lac La Biche 2,007 E 2
Lacombe 5,591 D 3
La Crete 479 B 5
Lake Louise 355 B 4
Lamont 1,563 D 3
Leduc 12,471 D 3
Legal 1,022 D 3
Lethbridge 54,072 D 5
Linden 407 D 4
Little Buffalo Lake 253 B 1
Lloydminster 8,997 E 3
Longview 301 C 4
Lougheed 226 E 3
Lundbreck 244 C 5
Magrath 1,576 D 5
Manning 1,173 B 1
Mannville 788 E 3
Marlboro 211 B 3
Marwayne 500 E 3
Mayerthorpe 1,475 C 3
McLennan 1,125 B 2
Medicine Hat 40,380 E 4
Milk River 894 D 5
Millet 1,120 D 3
Mirror 507 D 3
Monarch 212 D 5
Morinville 4,657 D 3
Morrin 244 D 4
Mundare 604 D 3
Myrnam 397 E 3
Nacmine 369 D 4
Nampa 334 B 1
Nanton 1,641 D 4
New Norway 291 D 3
New Sarepta 417 D 3
Nobleford 534 D 5
North Calling Lake 234 D 2
Okotoks 3,847 C 4
Olds 4,813 D 4
Onoway 621 C 3
Oyen 975 E 4
Peace River 5,907 B 1
Penhold 1,531 D 3
Picture Butte 1,404 D 5
Pincher Creek 3,757 D 5
Plamondon 259 D 2
Pollockville 19 E 4
Ponoka 5,221 D 3
Provost 1,645 E 3
Rainbow Lake 504 A 5
Ralston 357 E 4
Raymond 2,837 D 5
Redcliff 3,876 E 4
Red Deer 46,393 D 3
Redwater 1,932 D 3
Rimbey 1,685 C 3
Robb 230 B 3
Rockyford 329 D 4
Rocky Mountain House 4,698 C 3
Rosemary 328 E 4
Rycroft 649 A 2
Ryley 483 D 3
Saint Albert 31,996 D 3
Saint Paul 4,884 E 3
Sangudo 398 C 3
Sedgewick 879 E 3
Sexsmith 1,180 A 2
Shaughnessy 270 D 5
Sherwood Park 29,285 D 3
Slave Lake 4,506 C 2
Smith 216 D 2
Smoky Lake 1,074 D 2
Spirit River 1,104 A 2
Spruce Grove 10,326 D 3
Standard 379 D 4
Stavely 504 D 4
Stettler 5,136 D 3
Stirling 688 D 5
Stony Plain 4,839 C 3
Strathmore 2,986 D 4
Strome 281 E 3
Sundre 1,742 C 4
Swan Hills 2,497 C 2
Sylvan Lake 3,779 C 3
Taber 5,988 E 5
Thorhild 576 D 2
Thorsby 737 C 3
Three Hills 1,787 D 4
Tilley 345 E 4
Tofield 1,504 D 3
Trochu 880 D 4
Turner Valley 1,311 C 4
Two Hills 1,193 E 3
Valleyview 2,061 B 2
Vauxhall 1,049 D 4
Vegreville 5,251 E 3
Vermilion 3,766 E 3
Veteran 314 E 3
Viking 1,232 E 3
Vilna 345 E 2
Vulcan 1,489 D 4
Wabamun 662 C 3
Wabasca 701 D 2
Wainwright 4,266 E 3
Warburg 501 C 3
Warner 477 D 5
Waskatenau 290 D 2
Wembley 1,169 A 2
Westlock 4,424 C 2
Wetaskiwin 9,597 D 3
Whitecourt 5,585 C 2
Wildwood 441 C 3
Willingdon 366 E 3
Youngstown 297 E 4

OTHER FEATURES

Abraham (lake) B 3
Alberta (mt.) B 3
Assiniboine (mt.) C 4
Athabasca (lake) C 5
Athabasca (riv.) D 1
Banff Nat'l Park B 4
Battle (riv.) D 3
Bear (lake) A 2
Beaver (riv.) E 2
Beaverhill (lake) D 3
Behan (lake) E 2
Belly (riv.) D 5
Berland (riv.) A 3
Berry (creek) E 4
Biche (lake) E 2
Big (isl.) B 5
Big Horn (dam) B 3
Bighorn (range) B 3
Birch (hills) A 2
Birch (lake) E 3
Birch (mts.) B 5
Birch (riv.) B 5
Bison (lake) B 1
Bittern (lake) D 3
Botha (riv.) B 1
Bow (riv.) D 4
Boyer (riv.) A 5
Brazeau (mt.) B 3
Brazeau (riv.) B 3
Buffalo (lake) D 3
Buffalo Head (hills) B 5
Burnt (lakes) C 1
Cadotte (lake) B 1
Cadotte (riv.) B 1
Calling (lake) D 2
Canal (creek) E 5
Cardinal (lake) B 1
Caribou (mts.) B 5
Chinchaga (riv.) A 5
Chip (lake) C 3
Chipewyan (lake) D 1
Chipewyan (riv.) D 1
Christina (lake) E 2
Christina (riv.) E 1
Claire (lake) B 5
Clear (hills) A 1
Clearwater (riv.) C 4
Clearwater (riv.) E 1
Clyde (lake) E 2
Cold (lake) E 2
Columbia (mt.) B 3
Crowsnest (pass) C 5
Cypress (hills) E 5
Cypress Hills Prov. Park E 5
Dillon (riv.) E 2
Dowling (lake) D 4
Dunkirk (riv.) D 1
Eisenhower (mt.) C 4
Elbow (riv.) C 4
Elk Island Nat'l Park D 3
Ells (riv.) D 1
Etzikom Coulee (riv.) E 5
Eva (lake) B 5
Farrell (lake) D 4
Firebag (riv.) E 1
Forbes (mt.) B 4
Freeman (riv.) C 2
Frog (lake) E 3
Garson (lake) E 1
Gipsy (lake) E 1
Gordon (lake) E 1
Gough (lake) D 3
Graham (lake) C 1
Gull (lake) C 3
Haig (lake) B 1
Hawk (hills) B 1
Hay (lake) A 5
Hay (riv.) A 5
Heart (lake) E 2
Highwood (riv.) C 4
House (mt.) C 2
House (riv.) D 2
Iosegun (lake) B 2
Iosegun (riv.) B 2
Jackfish (riv.) B 5
Jasper Nat'l Park A 3
Kakwa (riv.) A 2
Kickinghorse (pass) B 4
Kimiwan (lake) B 2
Kirkpatrick (lake) E 4
Kitchener (mt.) B 3
Legend (lake) D 1
Lesser Slave (lake) C 2
Liége (riv.) D 1
Little Bow (riv.) D 4
Little Cadotte (riv.) B 1
Little Smoky (riv.) B 2
Livingstone (range) C 4
Logan (lake) E 2
Loon (lake) C 1
Loon (riv.) C 1
Lubicon (lake) C 1
Lyell (mt.) B 4
MacKay (riv.) D 1
Maligne (lake) B 3
Margaret (lake) B 5
Marie (lake) E 2
Marion (lake) D 3
Marten (mt.) C 2
McClelland (lake) E 1
McGregor (lake) D 4
McLeod (riv.) B 3
Meikle (riv.) A 1
Mikkwa (riv.) B 5
Milk (riv.) D 5
Mistehae (lake) C 2
Muriel (lake) E 2
Muskwa (lake) C 1
Muskwa (riv.) C 1
Namur (lake) D 1
Newell (lake) E 4
Nordegg (riv.) C 3
North Saskatchewan (riv.) E 3
North Wabasca (lake) D 1
Notikewin (riv.) A 1
Oldman (riv.) D 5
Otter (lakes) B 1
Pakowki (lake) E 5
Panny (riv.) C 1
Peace (riv.) B 1
Peerless (lake) C 1
Pelican (lake) D 2
Pelican (mts.) D 2
Pembina (riv.) C 3
Pigeon (lake) D 3
Pinehurst (lake) E 2
Porcupine (hills) C 4
Primrose (lake) E 2
Rainbow (lake) A 5
Red Deer (lake) D 3
Red Deer (riv.) D 4
Richardson (riv.) C 5
Rocky (mts.) B-C 4
Rosebud (riv.) D 4
Russell (lake) C 1
Saddle (hills) A 2
Sainte Anne (lake) C 3
Saint Mary (res.) D 5
Saint Mary (riv.) D 5
Saulteaux (riv.) C 2
Seibert (lake) E 2
Simonette (riv.) A 2
Slave (riv.) C 5
Smoky (riv.) A 2
Snake Indian (riv.) A 3
Snipe (lake) B 2
Sounding (creek) E 4
South Saskatchewan (riv.) E 4
South Wabasca (lake) D 2
Spencer (lake) E 2
Spray (mts.) C 4
Sturgeon (lake) B 2
Sullivan (lake) D 3
Swan (hills) C 2
Swan (riv.) C 2
Temple (mt.) B 4
The Twins (mt.) B 3
Thickwood (hills) D 1
Touchwood (lake) E 2
Travers (res.) D 4
Trout (mt.) C 1
Trout (riv.) C 1
Utikuma (lake) C 2
Utikuma (riv.) C 1
Utikumasis (lake) C 2
Vermilion (riv.) E 3
Wabasca (riv.) C 1
Wallace (mt.) C 2
Wapiti (riv.) A 2
Wappau (lake) E 2
Watchusk (lake) E 1
Waterton-Glacier Int'l Peace Park C 5
Waterton Lakes Nat'l Park C 5
Whitemud (riv.) A 1
Wildhay (riv.) B 3
Willmore Wilderness Prov. Park A 3
Winagami (lake) B 2
Winefred (lake) E 2
Winefred (riv.) E 2
Wolf (lake) E 2
Wolverine (riv.) B 1
Wood Buffalo Nat'l Park B 5
Yellowhead (pass) A 3
Zama (lake) A 5

*Population of metropolitan area.

Agriculture, Industry and Resources

DOMINANT LAND USE

- Wheat
- Cereals (chiefly barley, oats)
- Cereals, Livestock
- Dairy
- Pasture Livestock
- Range Livestock
- Forests
- Nonagricultural Land

MAJOR MINERAL OCCURRENCES

- C Coal
- G Natural Gas
- Na Salt
- O Petroleum
- S Sulfur
- Water Power
- Major Industrial Areas

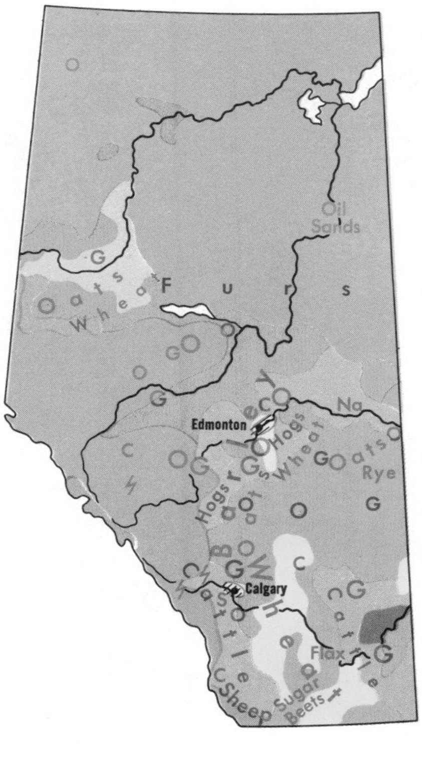
Oil Sands
Furs
Oats
Wheat
Edmonton
Na
Hogs
Wheat
Oats
Rye
Calgary
Cattle
Flax
Sheep
Sugar Beets

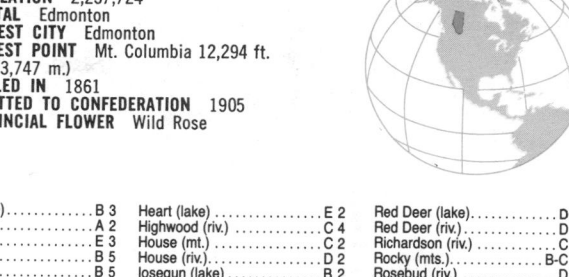

Topography

0   100   200 MI.

0   100   200 KM.

| Below Sea Level | 100 m. 328 ft. | 200 m. 656 ft. | 500 m. 1,640 ft. | 1,000 m. 3,281 ft. | 2,000 m. 6,562 ft. | 5,000 m. 16,404 ft. |

Agriculture, Industry and Resources

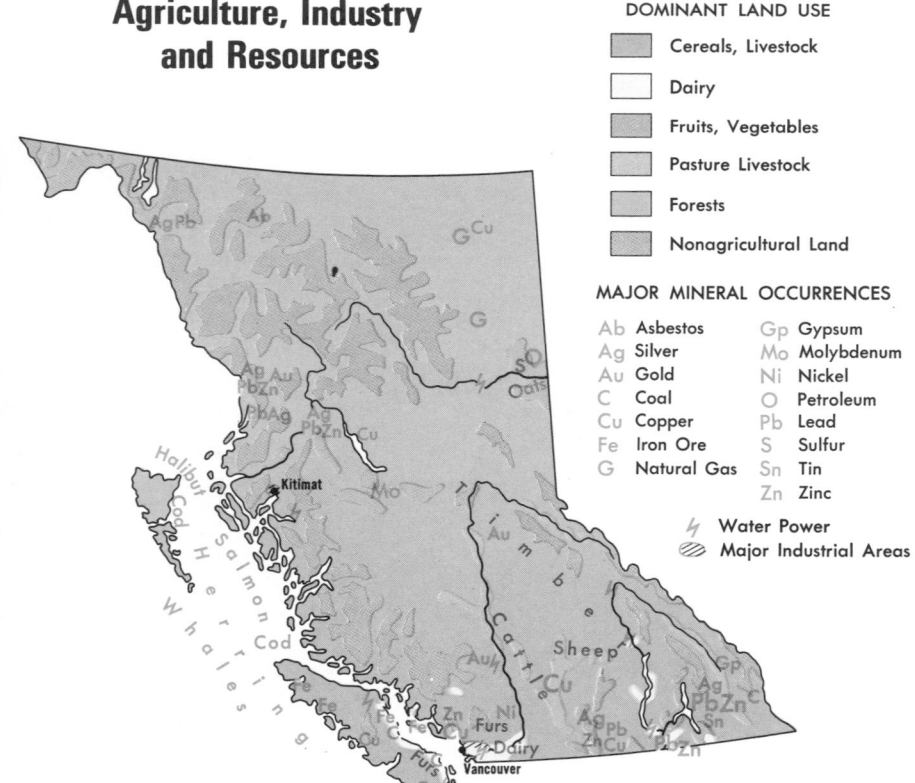

DOMINANT LAND USE

- Cereals, Livestock
- Dairy
- Fruits, Vegetables
- Pasture Livestock
- Forests
- Nonagricultural Land

MAJOR MINERAL OCCURRENCES

Ab	Asbestos	Gp	Gypsum
Ag	Silver	Mo	Molybdenum
Au	Gold	Ni	Nickel
C	Coal	O	Petroleum
Cu	Copper	Pb	Lead
Fe	Iron Ore	S	Sulfur
G	Natural Gas	Sn	Tin
		Zn	Zinc

⚡ Water Power
〰 Major Industrial Areas

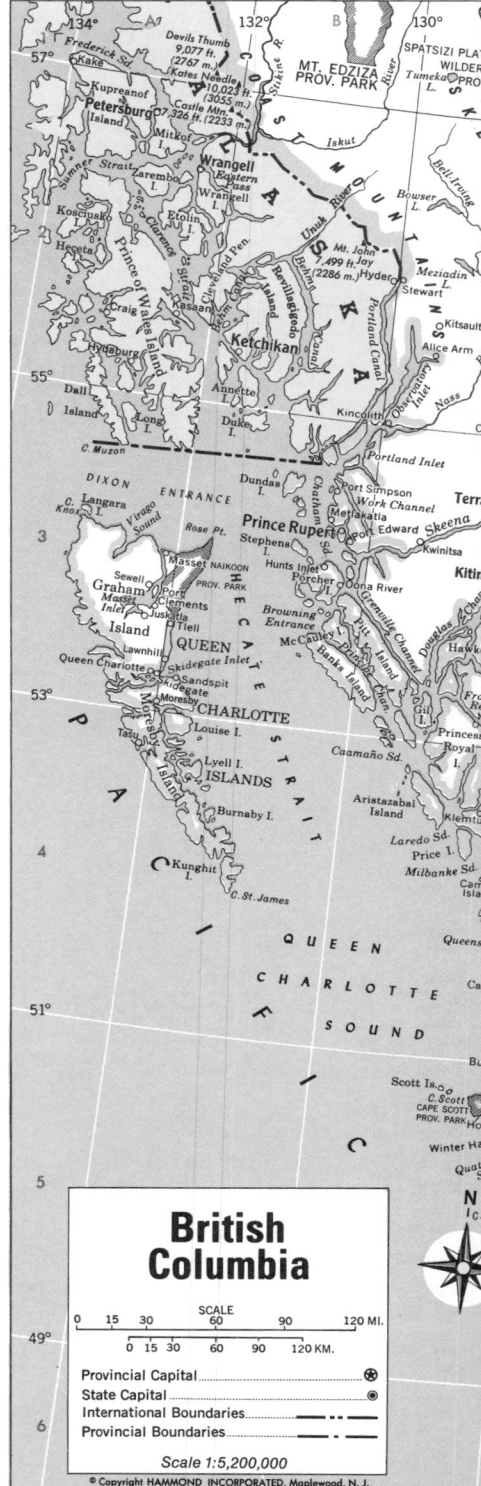

British Columbia

SCALE		
0 15 30 60 90 120 MI.		
0 15 30 60 90 120 KM.		

Provincial Capital ....⊛
State Capital ....◉
International Boundaries ....
Provincial Boundaries ....

Scale 1:5,200,000

© Copyright HAMMOND INCORPORATED, Maplewood, N.J.

AREA 366,253 sq. mi. (948,596 sq. km.)
POPULATION 2,744,467
CAPITAL Victoria
LARGEST CITY Vancouver
HIGHEST POINT Mt. Fairweather 15,300 ft.
  (4,663 m.)
SETTLED IN 1806
ADMITTED TO CONFEDERATION 1871
PROVINCIAL FLOWER Dogwood

*Population of metropolitan area.
○Population of municipality.

NORTHWEST TERRITORIES

Topography

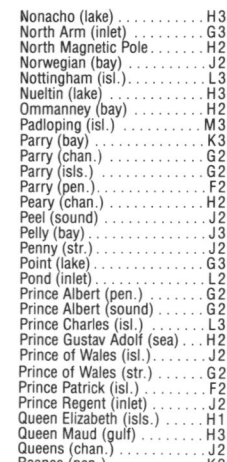

0   200   400 MI.

0   200   400 KM.

5,000 m. 2,000 m. 1,000 m. 500 m. 200 m. 100 m. Sea
16,404 ft. 6,562 ft. 3,281 ft. 1,640 ft. 656 ft. 328 ft. Level
Below

Agriculture, Industry and Resources

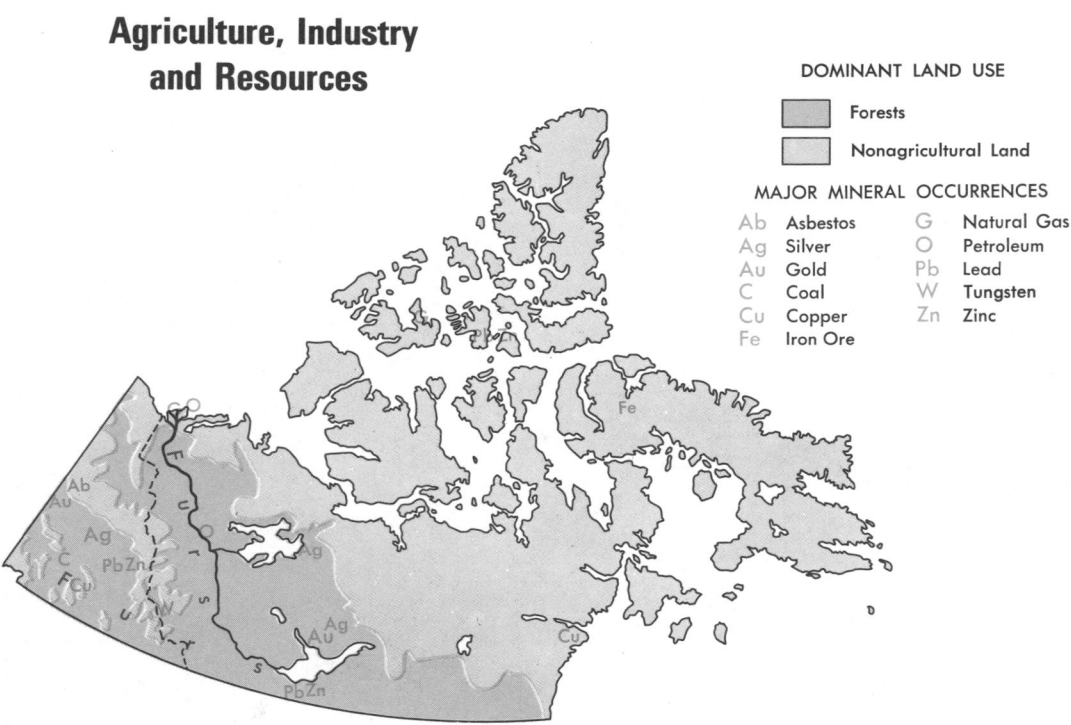

DOMINANT LAND USE

Forests

Nonagricultural Land

MAJOR MINERAL OCCURRENCES

Ab Asbestos   G Natural Gas
Ag Silver   O Petroleum
Au Gold   Pb Lead
C Coal   W Tungsten
Cu Copper   Zn Zinc
Fe Iron Ore

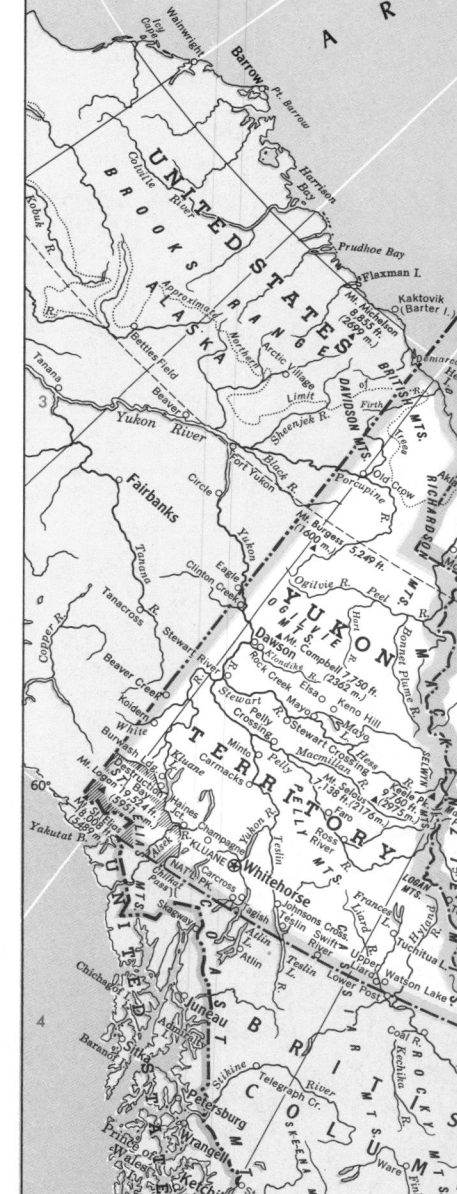

YUKON TERRITORY

AREA 207,075 sq. mi.
(536,324 sq. km.)
POPULATION 23,153
CAPITAL Whitehorse
LARGEST CITY Whitehorse
HIGHEST POINT Mt. Logan 19,524 ft.
(5,951 m.)
SETTLED IN 1897
ADMITTED TO CONFEDERATION 1898
PROVINCIAL FLOWER Fireweed

NORTHWEST TERRITORIES

AREA 1,304,896 sq. mi. (3,379,683 sq. km.)
POPULATION 45,741
CAPITAL Yellowknife
LARGEST CITY Yellowknife
HIGHEST POINT Mt. Sir James MacBrien
9,062 ft. (2,762 m.)
SETTLED IN 1800
ADMITTED TO CONFEDERATION 1870
PROVINCIAL FLOWER Mountain Avens

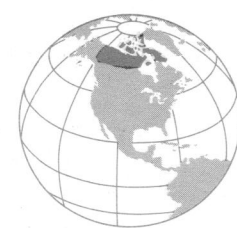

Yukon and Northwest Territories

SCALE
0 50 100   200   300 MI.
0 50 100   200   300 KM.

Territorial Capitals . . . . ⊛
Regional Capitals . . . . ⊙
International Boundaries . . . . —·—·—
Provincial & Territorial Boundaries . . . . —··—··—
Regional Boundaries . . . . —···—···—

Scale 1:14,000,000

All islands in Hudson and James Bay
lie within the Northwest Territories

© Copyright HAMMOND INCORPORATED, Maplewood, N.J.

United States

POLYCONIC PROJECTION

SCALE OF MILES

SCALE OF KILOMETERS

Capitals of Countries .... ☆
State Capitals .... △
International Boundaries ....

Scale 1:17,400,000

© Copyright HAMMOND INCORPORATED, Maplewood, N.J.

AREA 3,623,420 sq. mi.
    (9,384,658 sq. km.)
POPULATION 226,504,825
CAPITAL Washington
LARGEST CITY New York
HIGHEST POINT Mt. McKinley 20,320 ft.
    (6,194 m.)
MONETARY UNIT U.S. dollar
MAJOR LANGUAGE English
MAJOR RELIGIONS Protestantism,
    Roman Catholicism, Judaism

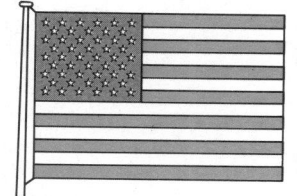
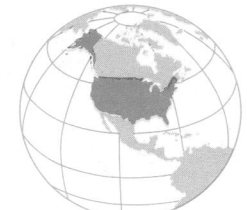

Population Distribution

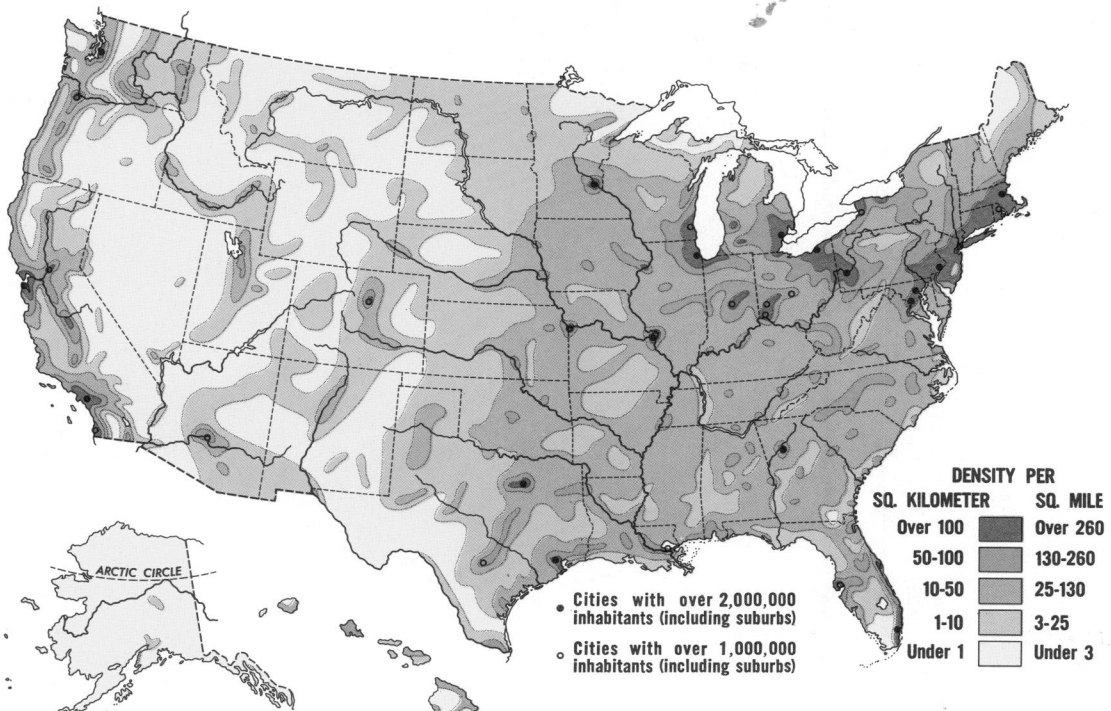

DENSITY PER

SQ. KILOMETER	SQ. MILE
Over 100	Over 260
50-100	130-260
10-50	25-130
1-10	3-25
Under 1	Under 3

• Cities with over 2,000,000 inhabitants (including suburbs)
○ Cities with over 1,000,000 inhabitants (including suburbs)

Vegetation

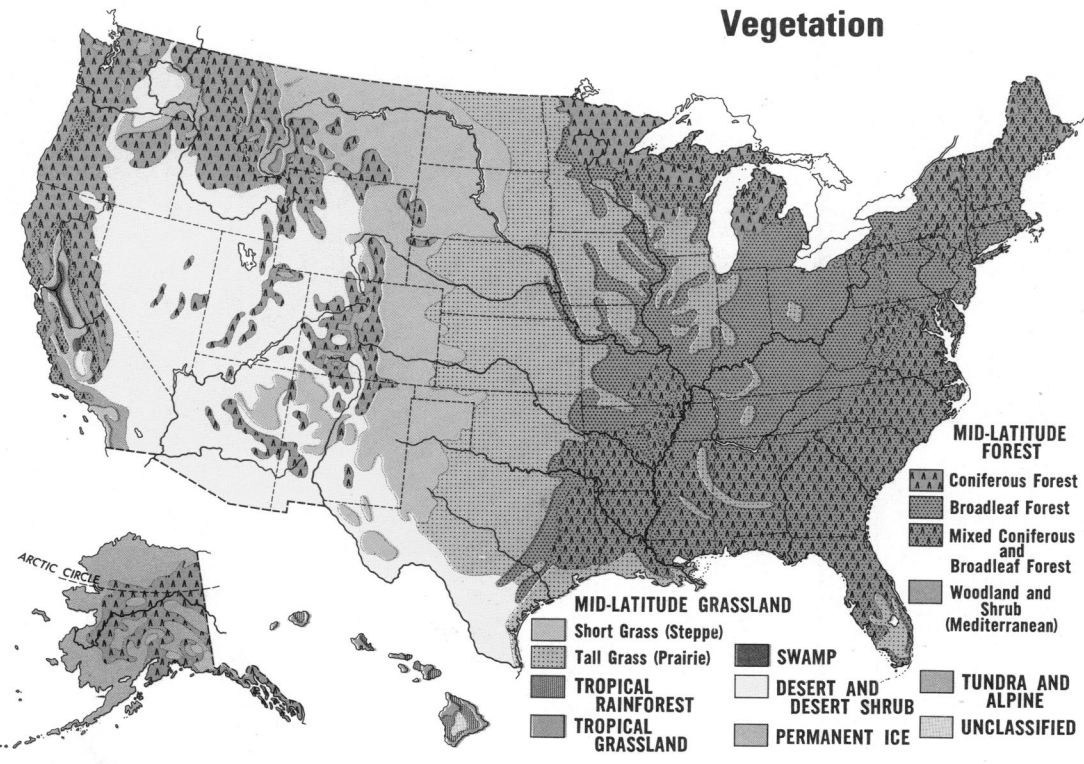

MID-LATITUDE FOREST

- Coniferous Forest
- Broadleaf Forest
- Mixed Coniferous and Broadleaf Forest
- Woodland and Shrub (Mediterranean)

MID-LATITUDE GRASSLAND

- Short Grass (Steppe)
- Tall Grass (Prairie)

TROPICAL RAINFOREST

TROPICAL GRASSLAND

- SWAMP
- DESERT AND DESERT SHRUB
- PERMANENT ICE
- TUNDRA AND ALPINE
- UNCLASSIFIED

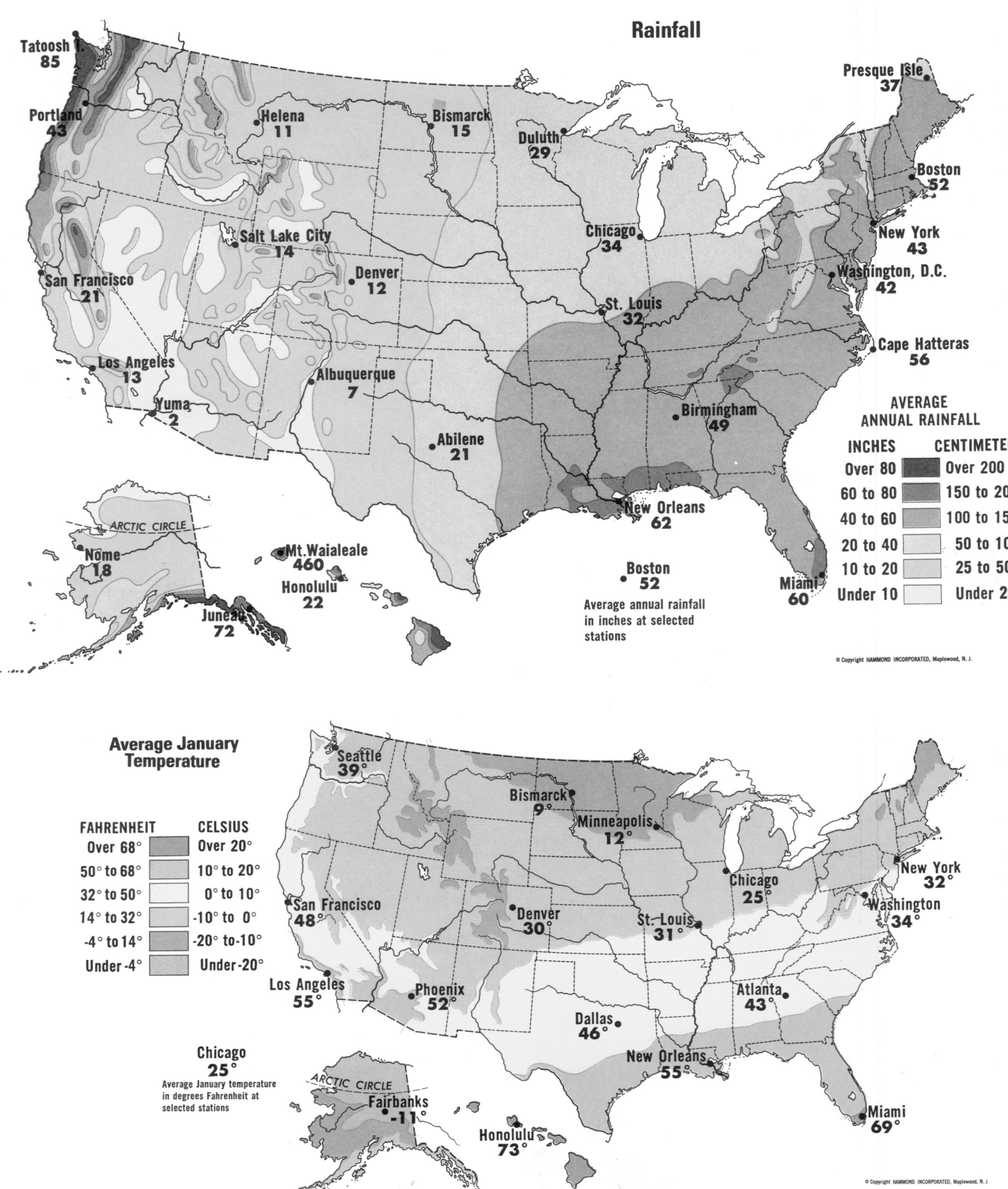

Rainfall

Tatoosh I.
85

Portland
43

Helena
11

Bismarck
15

Duluth
29

Presque Isle
37

Boston
52

Chicago
34

New York
43

Salt Lake City
14

Washington, D.C.
42

San Francisco
21

Denver
12

St. Louis
32

Cape Hatteras
56

Los Angeles
13

Albuquerque
7

Birmingham
49

Yuma
2

Abilene
21

New Orleans
62

ARCTIC CIRCLE

Nome
18

Mt. Waialeale
460

Honolulu
22

Juneau
72

Boston
52

Miami
60

Average annual rainfall in inches at selected stations

AVERAGE ANNUAL RAINFALL

INCHES	CENTIMETER
Over 80	Over 200
60 to 80	150 to 200
40 to 60	100 to 150
20 to 40	50 to 100
10 to 20	25 to 50
Under 10	Under 25

© Copyright HAMMOND INCORPORATED, Maplewood, N.J.

Average January Temperature

FAHRENHEIT	CELSIUS
Over 68°	Over 20°
50° to 68°	10° to 20°
32° to 50°	0° to 10°
14° to 32°	-10° to 0°
-4° to 14°	-20° to -10°
Under -4°	Under -20°

Seattle
39°

Bismarck
9°

Minneapolis
12°

New York
32°

San Francisco
48°

Denver
30°

St. Louis
31°

Chicago
25°

Washington
34°

Los Angeles
55°

Phoenix
52°

Dallas
46°

Atlanta
43°

New Orleans
55°

Miami
69°

Chicago
25°

Average January temperature in degrees Fahrenheit at selected stations

ARCTIC CIRCLE

Fairbanks
-11°

Honolulu
73°

© Copyright HAMMOND INCORPORATED, Maplewood, N.J.

Topography

0   200   400 MI.

0   200   400 KM.

C. Flattery

Seattle

Mt. St. Helens 9,364 ft. (2854 m.)

Mt. Rainier 14,410 ft. (4392 m.)

ROCKY

BITTERROOT RANGE

Snake

COLUMBIA

PLATEAU

Columbia

Missouri

Fort Peck Lake

Yellowstone

Rainy

Lake Superior

Keweenaw Pen.

St. Lawrence

Gulf of Maine

CASCADE RANGE

GREAT

Lake Sakakawea

Red

Lake

Wisconsin

Lake Huron

Lake Michigan

Lake Ontario

L. Champlain

Niagara Falls

Boston

C. Cod

SIERRA NEVADA

Great

Lake Oahe

Missouri

James

Minneapolis

Des Moines

Lake Erie

Detroit **Cleveland**

Lake Ontario

New York

Long Island

Central Valley

Great Salt Lake

Basin

N. Platte

Milwaukee

Chicago

Illinois

Ohio

Washington

Philadelphia

ATLANTIC

PACIFIC OCEAN

San Francisco

COLORADO

Colorado

Denver

Mt. Elbert 14,431 ft. (4399 m.)

Platte

Kansas City

Missouri

St. Louis

Indianapolis

APPALACHIAN MTS.

Chesapeake Bay

Mt. Whitney 14,494 ft. (4418 m.)

Arkansas

OZARK

Ohio

Wabash

Tennessee

C. Hatteras

Pt. Conception

Lake Powell

MOUNTAINS

PLATEAU

Mt. Mitchell 6,684 ft. (2037 m.)

OCEAN

SANTA BARBARA IS.

Mojave Desert

Mead

Grand Canyon

Colorado

PLATEAU

Gila

Canadian

Arkansas

Memphis

Wheeler L.

Savannah

Chattahoochee

ATLANTIC COASTAL MTS.

C. Fear

Los Angeles

Phoenix

Rio Grande

LLANO

Red

Mississippi

Atlanta

San Diego

ESTACADO

Dallas

Pecos

Red

GULF

Jacksonville

EDWARDS PLATEAU

Brazos

COASTAL

PLAIN

ATLANTIC

C. Canaveral

Rio Grande

Colorado

Houston

New Orleans

Mississippi Delta

L. Okeechobee

The Everglades

Miami

Gulf of Mexico

FLORIDA KEYS

ARCTIC OCEAN

0   200   400 MI.

0   200   400 KM.

BROOKS RANGE

Bering Str.

St. Lawrence I.

Yukon

Tanana

Mt. McKinley 20,320 ft. (6194 m.)

Anchorage

Kauai

Oahu

Molokai

Honolulu

HAWAIIAN ISLANDS

Maui

PACIFIC OCEAN

BERING SEA

Alaska Ra.

Gulf of Alaska

Kodiak I.

ALEXANDER ARCHIPELAGO

Aleutian Islands

0   50   100 MI.

0   50   100 KM.

Mauna Kea 13,796 ft. (4205 m.)

Hawaii

5,000 m. 16,404 ft. | 2,000 m. 6,562 ft. | 1,000 m. 3,281 ft. | 500 m. 1,640 ft. | 200 m. 656 ft. | 100 m. 328 ft. | Sea Level | Below

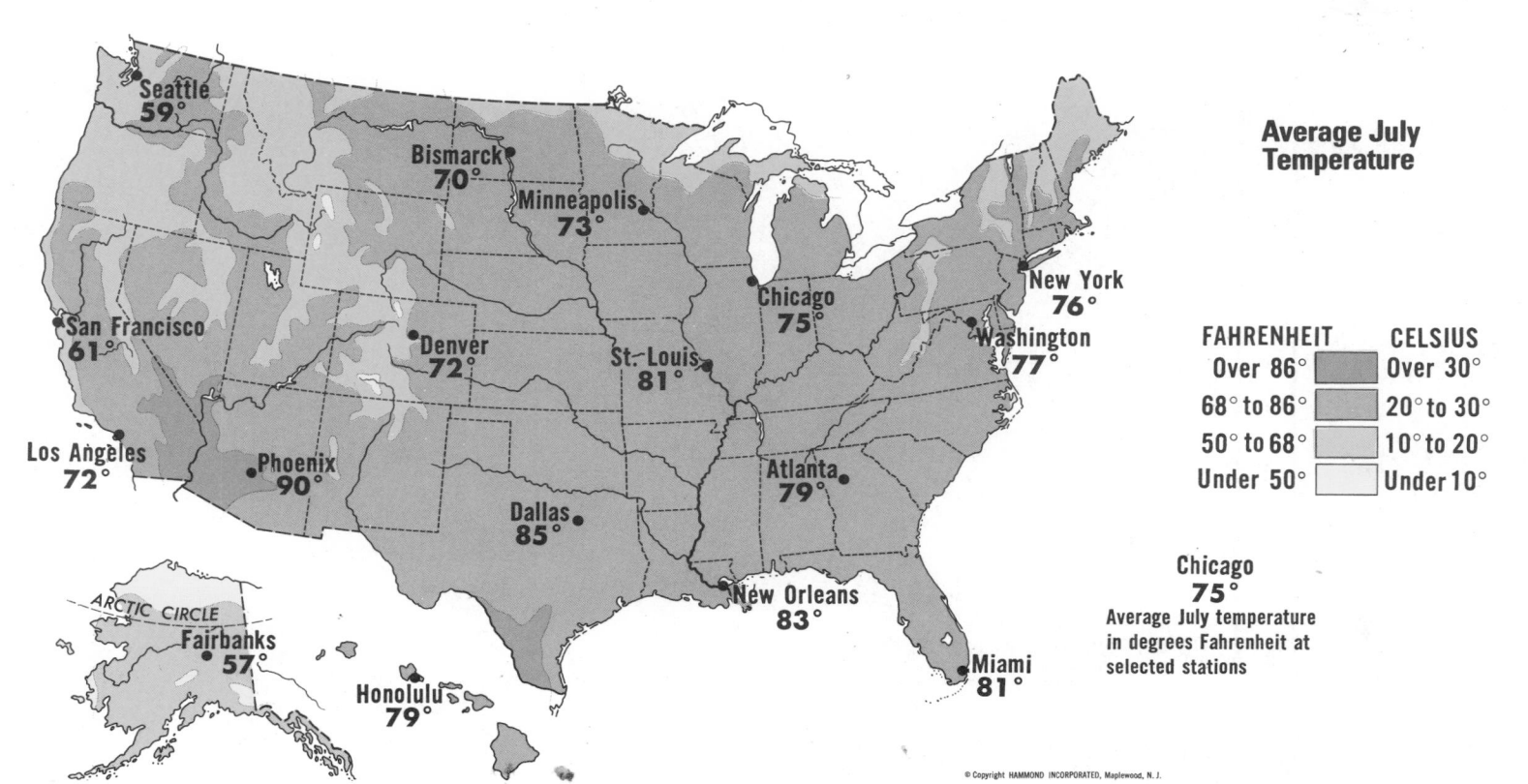

Seattle **59°**

Bismarck **70°**

Minneapolis **73°**

Chicago **75°**

New York **76°**

Average July Temperature

San Francisco **61°**

Denver **72°**

St. Louis **81°**

Washington **77°**

Los Angeles **72°**

Phoenix **90°**

Dallas **85°**

Atlanta **79°**

FAHRENHEIT	CELSIUS
Over 86°	Over 30°
68° to 86°	20° to 30°
50° to 68°	10° to 20°
Under 50°	Under 10°

New Orleans **83°**

ARCTIC CIRCLE

Fairbanks **57°**

Honolulu **79°**

Miami **81°**

Chicago
75°
Average July temperature
in degrees Fahrenheit at
selected stations

United States
Standard Time Zones

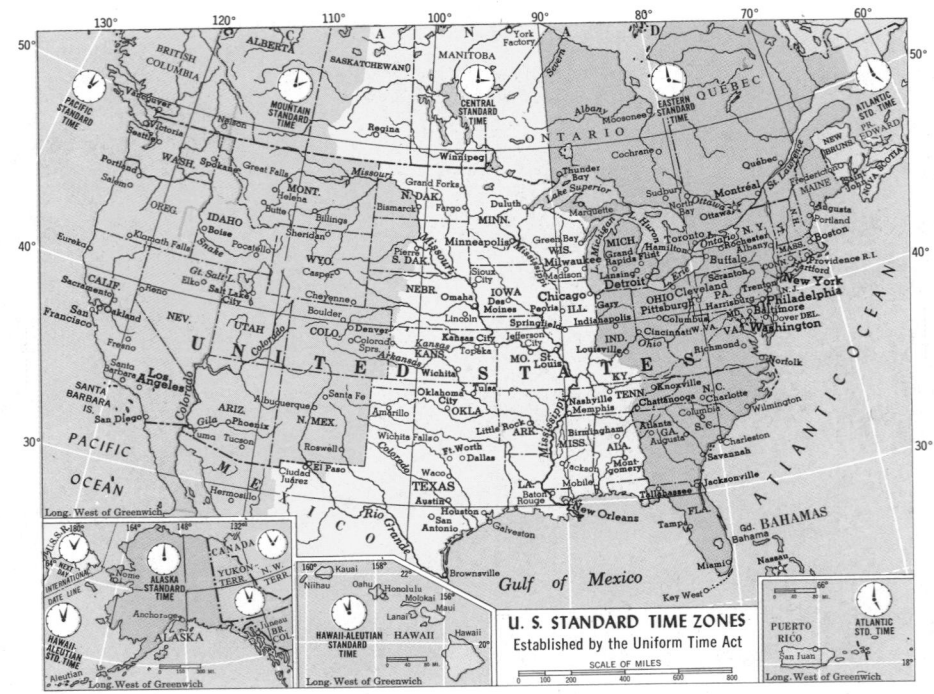

U. S. STANDARD TIME ZONES
Established by the Uniform Time Act

Agriculture, Industry and Resources

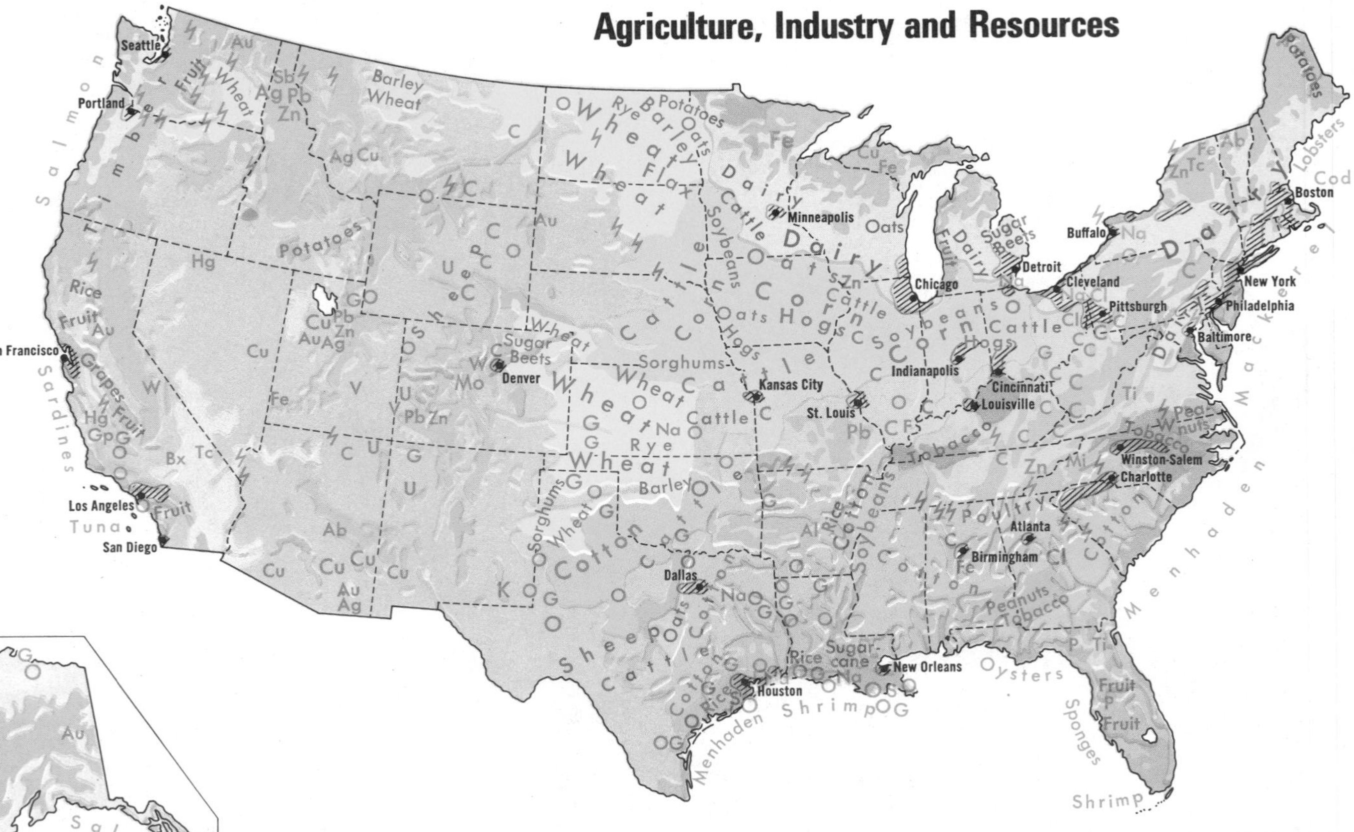

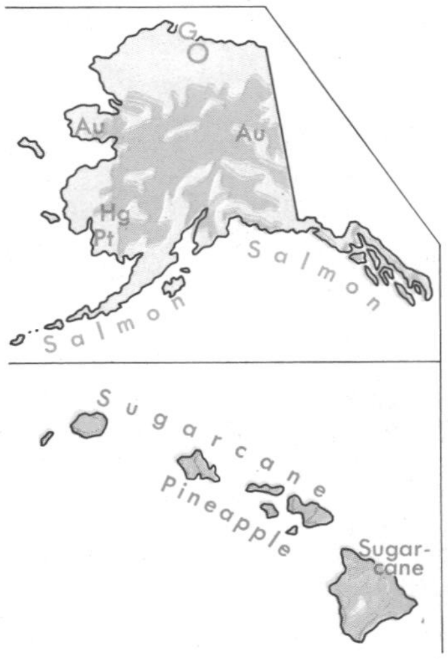

DOMINANT LAND USE

- Wheat and Small Grains
- Feed Grains and Livestock
- Dairy
- General Farming
- Cotton
- Fruit, Truck and Mixed Farming
- Tobacco and General Farming
- Special Crops and General Farming
- Range Livestock
- Forests
- Swampland
- Nonagricultural Land

MAJOR MINERAL OCCURRENCES

Ab	Asbestos	Gp	Gypsum	Sb	Antimony
Ag	Silver	Hg	Mercury	Tc	Talc
Al	Bauxite	K	Potash	Ti	Titanium
Au	Gold	Mi	Mica	U	Uranium
Bx	Borax	Mo	Molybdenum	V	Vanadium
C	Coal	Na	Salt	W	Tungsten
Cl	Clay	O	Petroleum	Zn	Zinc
Cu	Copper	P	Phosphates		
F	Fluorspar	Pb	Lead	⚡	Water Power
Fe	Iron Ore	Pt	Platinum	▨	Major Industrial Areas
G	Natural Gas	S	Sulfur		

AREA 51,705 sq. mi. (133,916 sq. km.)
POPULATION 3,893,888
CAPITAL Montgomery
LARGEST CITY Birmingham
HIGHEST POINT Cheaha Mtn. 2,407 ft. (734 m.)
SETTLED IN 1702
ADMITTED TO UNION December 14, 1819
POPULAR NAME Heart of Dixie; Cotton State;
    Yellowhammer State
STATE FLOWER Camellia
STATE BIRD Yellowhammer

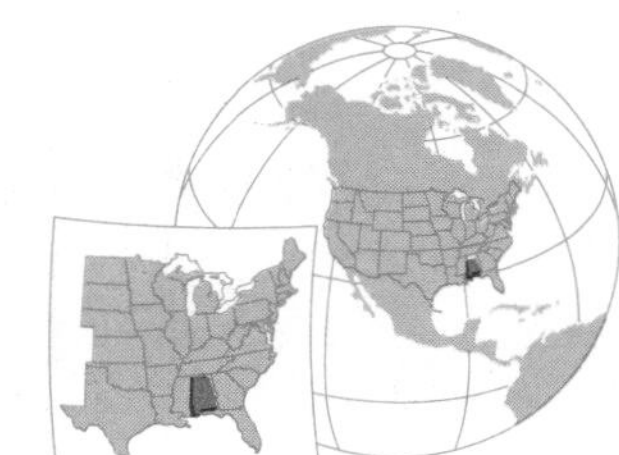

COUNTIES

Autauga 32,259 ....E5
Baldwin 78,556 ....C9
Barbour 24,756 ....H7
Bibb 15,723 ....D5
Blount 36,459 ....E2
Bullock 10,596 ....G6
Butler 21,680 ....E7
Calhoun 119,761 ....G3
Chambers 39,191 ....H5
Cherokee 18,760 ....G2
Chilton 30,612 ....E5
Choctaw 16,839 ....B6
Clarke 27,702 ....C7
Clay 13,703 ....G4
Cleburne 12,595 ....G3
Coffee 38,533 ....G8
Colbert 54,519 ....C1
Conecuh 15,884 ....E8
Coosa 11,377 ....F5
Covington 36,850 ....E7
Crenshaw 14,110 ....F7
Cullman 61,642 ....E2
Dale 47,821 ....G8
Dallas 53,981 ....D6
De Kalb 53,658 ....G2
Elmore 43,390 ....F5
Escambia 38,440 ....D8
Etowah 103,057 ....F2
Fayette 18,809 ....C3
Franklin 28,350 ....C2
Geneva 24,253 ....G8
Greene 11,021 ....C5
Hale 15,604 ....C5
Henry 15,302 ....H7
Houston 74,632 ....H8
Jackson 51,407 ....F1
Jefferson 671,324 ....E3
Lamar 16,453 ....B3
Lauderdale 80,546 ....C1
Lawrence 30,170 ....D1
Lee 76,283 ....H5
Limestone 46,005 ....E1
Lowndes 13,253 ....E6
Macon 26,829 ....G6
Madison 196,966 ....E1
Marengo 25,047 ....C6
Marion 30,041 ....C2
Marshall 65,622 ....F2
Mobile 364,980 ....B9
Monroe 22,651 ....D7
Montgomery 197,038 ....F6
Morgan 90,231 ....E2
Perry 15,012 ....D5
Pickens 21,481 ....B4
Pike 28,050 ....G7
Randolph 20,075 ....H4
Russell 47,356 ....H6
Saint Clair 41,205 ....F3
Shelby 66,298 ....E4
Sumter 16,908 ....B5
Talladega 73,826 ....F4
Tallapoosa 38,676 ....G5
Tuscaloosa 137,541 ....C4
Walker 68,660 ....D3
Washington 16,821 ....B8
Wilcox 14,755 ....D7
Winston 21,953 ....D2

CITIES and TOWNS

Zip Name/Pop. Key

36310 Abbeville⊙ 3,155 ....H7
35440 Abernant 405 ....D4
35005 Adamsville 2,498 ....D3
35540 Addison 746 ....D2
35006 Adger 400 ....D4
35441 Akron 604 ....C5
35007 Alabaster 7,079 ....E4
35950 Albertville 12,039 ....F2
†35115 Aldrich 500 ....E4
35010 Alexander City 13,807 ....G5
36250 Alexandria 600 ....G3
35442 Aliceville 3,207 ....B4
35013 Allgood 387 ....F3
36501 Alma 500 ....C8
35952 Altoona 928 ....F2
36420 Andalusia⊙ 10,415 ....E8
35610 Anderson 405 ....D1
36201 Anniston⊙ 29,523 ....G3
 Anniston‡ 116,936 ....G3
35016 Arab 5,967 ....E2
35805 Ardmore 1,096 ....E1
†35173 Argo 600 ....E3
36311 Ariton 844 ....G7
35033 Arkadelphia 150 ....D3
35541 Arley 276 ....D2
35035 Ashby 500 ....E4
36312 Ashford 2,165 ....H8
36251 Ashland⊙ 2,052 ....G4
35953 Ashville 1,489 ....F3
35611 Athens⊙ 14,558 ....E1
36503 Atmore 8,789 ....C8

35954 Attalla 7,737 ....F2
36830 Auburn 28,471 ....H5
36003 Autaugaville 843 ....E6
†36312 Avon 433 ....H8
36505 Axis 500 ....B9
†36420 Babbie 553 ....F8
35019 Baileyton 396 ....E2
36005 Banks 160 ....G7
36507 Bay Minette⊙ 7,455 ....C9
36509 Bayou La Batre 2,005 ....B10
35543 Bear Creek 353 ....C2
36425 Beatrice 558 ....D7
†35653 Belgreen 500 ....C2
35545 Belk 308 ....C3
36901 Bellamy 700 ....B6
35615 Belle Mina 675 ....E1
36313 Bellwood 400 ....G8
36785 Benton 74 ....E6
35546 Berry 916 ....C3
35020 Bessemer 31,729 ....D4
†36872 Beulah 500 ....H5
36006 Billingsley 106 ....E5
*35201 Birmingham⊙ 284,413 ....D3
 Birmingham‡ 847,360 ....D3
36314 Black 156 ....G8
35031 Blountsville 1,509 ....E2
36201 Blue Mountain 284 ....G3
†36017 Blue Springs 112 ....G7
35957 Boaz 7,151 ....F2
35443 Boligee 164 ....C5
35032 Bon Air 118 ....F4
36511 Bon Secour 850 ....C10
†35120 Branchville 365 ....F3
36009 Brantley 1,151 ....F7
35034 Brent 2,862 ....D5
36426 Brewton⊙ 6,680 ....D8
35740 Bridgeport 2,974 ....G1
35520 Brighton 5,308 ....D4
35548 Brilliant 871 ....C2
35036 Brookside 1,409 ....E3
35444 Brookwood 492 ....D4
36010 Brundidge 3,213 ....G7
36725 Burkville 250 ....E6
36431 Burnt Corn 60 ....D7
36904 Butler⊙ 1,882 ....B6
†36767 Cahaba 75 ....D6
35040 Calera 2,035 ....E4
†36047 Calhoun 950 ....F6
36513 Calvert 600 ....B8
36726 Camden⊙ 2,406 ....D7
36850 Camp Hill 1,628 ....G5
†36502 Canoe 560 ....D8
†36726 Canton Bend 300 ....D6
35549 Carbon Hill 2,452 ....D3
35041 Cardiff 140 ....E3
†36420 Carolina 203 ....E8
35447 Carrollton⊙ 1,104 ....B4
36023 Carrville 820 ....G5
†36548 Carson 400 ....C8
36432 Castleberry 847 ....D8
35959 Cedar Bluff 1,129 ....G2
35960 Centre⊙ 2,351 ....G2
35042 Centreville⊙ 2,504 ....D5
36518 Chatom⊙ 1,122 ....B8
35043 Chelsea 600 ....E4
35616 Cherokee 1,589 ....C1
36611 Chickasaw 7,402 ....B9
35044 Childersburg 5,084 ....F4
36254 Choccolocco 500 ....G3
36905 Choctaw 600 ....B6
36550 Chrysler 500 ....C8
36521 Chunchula 700 ....B9
36522 Citronelle 2,841 ....B8
35045 Clanton⊙ 5,832 ....E5
†36322 Clayhatchee 560 ....G8
36015 Clayton⊙ 1,589 ....G7
35049 Cleveland 487 ....E3
36017 Clio 1,224 ....G7
35449 Coaling 400 ....D4
36523 Coden 600 ....B10
36318 Coffee Springs 339 ....G8
36524 Coffeeville 448 ....B7
35452 Coker 800 ....C4
35961 Collinsville 1,383 ....G2
36319 Columbia 881 ....H8
35051 Columbiana⊙ 2,655 ....E4
36020 Coosada 980 ....F5
35550 Cordova 3,123 ....D3
35453 Cottondale 500 ....C4
36320 Cottonwood 1,352 ....H8
†35172 County Line 199 ....E3
†36467 County Line 124 ....F8
35618 Courtland 456 ....D1
36321 Cowarts 418 ....H8
36435 Coy 950 ....D7
36525 Creola 1,652 ....B9
36906 Cromwell 650 ....B6
35962 Crossville 1,222 ....G2
36907 Cuba 486 ....B6
35055 Cullman⊙ 13,084 ....E2
36852 Cusseta 650 ....H5
36853 Dadeville⊙ 3,263 ....G5

36322 Daleville 4,250 ....G8
36526 Daphne 3,406 ....C9
36528 Dauphin Island 950 ....B10
36256 Daviston 334 ....G4
36731 Dayton 113 ....C6
*35601 Decatur⊙ 42,002 ....D1
36257 De Armanville 350 ....G3
36732 Demopolis 7,678 ....C6
35552 Detroit 326 ....B2
35062 Dora 2,327 ....D3
*36303 Dothan⊙ 48,750 ....H8
35553 Double Springs⊙ 1,057 ....D2
35964 Douglas 116 ....F2
36028 Dozier 494 ....F7
35744 Dutton 276 ....G1
36426 East Brewton 3,012 ....E8
36024 Eclectic 1,124 ....F5
36261 Edwardsville 207 ....H3
36323 Elba⊙ 4,355 ....F8
36530 Elberta 491 ....C10
35554 Eldridge 230 ....C2
35620 Elkmont 429 ....E1
36025 Elmore 600 ....F5
35458 Elrod 746 ....C4
35063 Empire 600 ....D4
36330 Enterprise 18,033 ....G8
35460 Epes 399 ....B5
35461 Ethelsville 95 ....B4
36027 Eufaula 12,097 ....H7
36532 Fairhope 7,286 ....C10
35208 Fairview 450 ....E2
35622 Falkville 1,310 ....E2
36738 Faunsdale 174 ....C6
35555 Fayette⊙ 5,287 ....C3
36855 Five Points 197 ....H4
35966 Flat Rock 750 ....G1
†35601 Flint City 673 ....D1
36441 Flomaton 1,882 ....D8
36442 Florala 2,165 ....F8
*35630 Florence⊙ 37,029 ....C1
 Florence‡ 135,023 ....C1
36535 Foley 4,003 ....C10
35214 Forestdale 10,814 ....E3
36740 Forkland 429 ....C5
36031 Fort Davis 500 ....G6
36032 Fort Deposit 1,519 ....E7
36856 Fort Mitchell 900 ....H6
35967 Fort Payne⊙ 11,485 ....G2
35463 Fosters 400 ....C4
36444 Franklin 133 ....G6
36445 Frisco City 1,424 ....D8
36539 Fruitdale 500 ....B8
36262 Fruithurst 239 ....G3
36446 Fulton 606 ....C7
35068 Fultondale 6,217 ....E3
35771 Fyffe 1,305 ....G2
35464 Gainesville 207 ....B5
35972 Gallant 475 ....F2
36038 Gantt 314 ....E8
35070 Garden City 655 ....E2
35071 Gardendale 7,928 ....E3
35973 Gaylesville 192 ....G2
†35459 Geiger 200 ....B5
36340 Geneva⊙ 4,866 ....G8
36033 Georgiana 1,993 ....E7
35974 Geraldine 911 ....G2
36908 Gilbertown 218 ....B7
35559 Glen Allen 312 ....C3
35905 Glencoe 4,648 ....G3
36034 Glenwood 341 ....F7
†35010 Goldville 89 ....G4
†36024 Good Hope 1,442 ....E2
35072 Goodwater 1,895 ....F4
36466 Gordo 2,112 ....C4
36343 Gordon 362 ....H8
†35580 Gorgas 500 ....D3
36035 Goshen 365 ....F7
†36482 Gosport 500 ....C7
36541 Grand Bay 3,185 ....B10
35747 Grant 632 ....F1
35073 Graysville 2,642 ....D3
35074 Green Pond 750 ....D4
36744 Greensboro⊙ 3,248 ....C5
36037 Greenville⊙ 7,807 ....E7
36350 Grimes 298 ....H8
36651 Grove Hill⊙ 1,912 ....C7
35563 Guin 2,418 ....C3
36542 Gulf Shores 1,349 ....C10
35976 Guntersville⊙ 7,041 ....F2
35748 Gurley 735 ....F1
35563 Gu-Win 266 ....C3
†35553 Hackleburg 883 ....C2
†36319 Haleburg 106 ....H8
35565 Haleyville 5,306 ....C2

35570 Hamilton⊙ 5,093 ....C2
†35989 Hammondville 369 ....G1
35077 Hanceville 2,220 ....E2
36039 Hardaway 600 ....G6
35078 Harpersville 934 ....F4
36344 Hartford 2,647 ....G8
35640 Hartselle 8,858 ....E2
36858 Hatchechubbee 840 ....H6
†35672 Hatton 950 ....D1
35079 Hayden 268 ....E3
36040 Hayneville⊙ 592 ....E6
35750 Hazel Green 1,503 ....E1
36345 Headland 3,327 ....H8
†36558 Healing Springs 100 ....B7
†36420 Heath 354 ....F8
36264 Heflin⊙ 3,014 ....G3
35080 Helena 2,130 ....E4
35978 Henagar 1,188 ....G1
35979 Higdon 925 ....G1
35013 Highland Lake 210 ....F3
35643 Hillsboro 278 ....D1
†36201 Hobson City 1,268 ....G3
35571 Hodges 250 ....C2
35903 Hokes Bluff 3,216 ....G3
35082 Hollins 500 ....F4
35083 Holly Pond 493 ....E2
35752 Hollywood 1,110 ....G1
35209 Homewood 21,412 ....E4
36043 Hope Hull 975 ....F6
†36467 Horn Hill 186 ....F8
35020 Hueytown 13,478 ....D4
*35801 Huntsville⊙ 142,513 ....E1
 Huntsville‡ 308,593 ....E1
36860 Hurtsboro 752 ....H6
35981 Ider 698 ....G1
35210 Irondale 6,510 ....E3
36545 Jackson 6,073 ....C8
36861 Jacksons Gap 800 ....G5
36265 Jacksonville 9,735 ....G3
35501 Jasper⊙ 11,894 ....D3
35085 Jemison 1,828 ....E5
35573 Kansas 267 ....C3
35574 Kennedy 604 ....B3
35645 Killen 747 ....D1
35091 Kimberly 1,043 ....E3
36761 Kinsey 1,239 ....H8
†36301 Kinsey 1,239 ....H8
36453 Kinston 604 ....F7
36862 Lafayette⊙ 3,647 ....H5
†35986 Lakeview 441 ....G1
36863 Lanett 6,897 ....H5
36864 Langdale 2,034 ....H5
†35768 Larkinsville 425 ....F1
36911 Lavaca 500 ....B6
35094 Leeds 8,638 ....E3
35983 Leesburg 116 ....G2
35646 Leighton 1,218 ....D1

36548 Leroy 699 ....B8
35647 Lester 117 ....D1
†36322 Level Plains 867 ....G8
35648 Lexington 884 ....D1
†36420 Libertyville 141 ....F8
35096 Lincoln 2,081 ....F3
†36748 Linden⊙ 2,773 ....C6
36266 Lineville 2,257 ....G4
35020 Lipscomb 3,741 ....E4
36912 Lisman 638 ....B6
†36876 Little Shawmut 2,793 ....H5
†35653 Littleville 1,262 ....C1
35470 Livingston⊙ 3,187 ....B5
36865 Loachapoka 335 ....G5
36455 Lockhart 547 ....F8
35097 Locust Fork 488 ....E3
†35137 Longview 475 ....E4
36048 Louisville 791 ....G7
36751 Lower Peach Tree 926 ....C7
36752 Lowndesboro 207 ....E6
36551 Loxley 804 ....C9
36049 Luverne⊙ 2,639 ....F7
35575 Lynn 554 ....C2
35758 Madison 4,057 ....E1
36348 Madrid 172 ....H8
36555 Magnolia Springs 800 ....C10
36349 Malvern 558 ....G8
36750 Maplesville 754 ....E5
35112 Margaret 757 ....F3
36756 Marion⊙ 4,467 ....D5
35114 Maylene 500 ....E4
35111 McCalla 657 ....E4
36552 McCullogh 500 ....D8
36553 McIntosh 319 ....B8
35456 McKenzie 605 ....E7
†35442 Memphis 95 ....B4
35984 Mentone 476 ....G1
35759 Meridianville 1,403 ....F1
35228 Midfield 6,203 ....E4
36350 Midland City 1,903 ....H8
35501 Midway⊙ 572 ....G7
35085 Midway 500 ....E5
†35150 Mignon 2,054 ....F4
36054 Millbrook 3,101 ....F6
35576 Millport 1,287 ....B3
36558 Millry 956 ....B7
36761 Minter 450 ....E6
*36601 Mobile⊙ 200,452 ....B9
 Mobile‡ 442,819 ....B9
36460 Monroeville⊙ 5,674 ....D7
†35804 Monrovia 441 ....E1
35115 Montevallo 3,965 ....E4
*36101 Montgomery
 (cap.)⊙ 178,857 ....F6
 Montgomery‡ 272,687 ....F6
36559 Montrose 750 ....C9
†35125 Moody 1,840 ....F3
35649 Mooresville 58 ....E1

35116 Morris 623 ....E3
35650 Moulton⊙ 3,197 ....D2
35474 Moundville 1,310 ....C5
†35957 Mountainboro 266 ....F2
35223 Mountain Brook 19,718 ....E4
36560 Mount Vernon 1,038 ....B8
36268 Munford 700 ....F3
35660 Muscle Shoals 8,911 ....C1
36763 Myrtlewood 252 ....C6
36764 Nanafalia 500 ....B6
36303 Napier Field 493 ....H8
35578 Nauvoo 259 ....D3
†35049 Nectar 367 ....E3
36765 Newbern 307 ....C5
36351 New Brockton 1,392 ....G8
35760 New Hope 1,546 ....F1
35761 New Market 680 ....F1
†35050 New Site 340 ....G4
36352 Newton 1,540 ....G8
36353 Newville 814 ....H8
35086 North Johns 243 ....D4
35476 Northport 14,291 ....C4
36866 Notasulga 876 ....G5
35006 Oak Grove 638 ....F4
36766 Oak Hill 63 ....D7
35579 Oakman 770 ....D3
35120 Odenville 724 ....F3
36271 Ohatchee 650 ....G3
35121 Oneonta⊙ 4,824 ....E3
†36467 Onycha 147 ....F8
36801 Opelika⊙ 21,896 ....H5
36467 Opp 7,204 ....F8
36561 Orange Beach 600 ....C10
36767 Orrville 349 ....D6
35763 Owens Cross Roads 804 ....E1
36203 Oxford 8,939 ....G3
36360 Ozark⊙ 13,188 ....G8
35764 Paint Rock 221 ....F1
35580 Parrish 1,583 ....D3
35124 Pelham 6,759 ....E4
35125 Pell City⊙ 6,616 ....F3
36916 Pennington 355 ....B6
36562 Perdido 500 ....C8
36471 Peterman 600 ....D7
36062 Petrey 93 ....F7
36867 Phenix City⊙ 26,928 ....H6
35581 Phil Campbell 1,549 ....C2
†35447 Pickensville 132 ....B4
36272 Piedmont 5,544 ....G3
36371 Pinckard 771 ....G8
36768 Pine Apple 298 ....D7
36769 Pine Hill 510 ....C7
35765 Pisgah 699 ....G1
36758 Plantersville 650 ....E5
35127 Pleasant Grove 7,102 ....D4
36564 Point Clear 1,812 ....C10
†36441 Pollard 144 ....D8

(continued on following page)

Tennessee Valley Region

MILES
0 50 100

Major dams named in red

ILL. Ohio River Owensboro

KENTUCKY

Paducah
BARKLEY
KEN-TUCKY
L. Barkley

L. Cumberland Somerset VA.

Bowling Green

WOLF CREEK
SOUTH HOLSTON
Bristol

Clarksville
OLD HICKORY
Cumberland R.
CHEATHAM
Kentucky Lake
J.P. PRIEST
CENTER HILL
DALE HOLLOW
Norris L.
NORRIS
FT. PATRICK HENRY
WATAUGA
Johnson City
Camden
Nashville
T E N N E S S E E
CHEROKEE
Cherokee L.

Duck R.
GREAT FALLS
MELTON HILL
DOUGLAS
NORTH

Columbia
Savannah
TELLICO
WATTS BAR
FONTANA
CAROLINA

PICKWICK
TIMS FORD
CHICKAMAUGA
HIWASSEE
Asheville

Tennessee R.
Chickamauga L.
APALACHIA

Florence
Wheeler
NICKAJACK
OCOEE
CHATUGE

MISS.
WILSON
WHEELER
Huntsville
Chattanooga
BLUE RIDGE
NOTTELY
SOUTH

Decatur
Tennessee R.
GEORGIA
CAROLINA

A L A B A M A

Eufaula
GUNTERSVILLE
Guntersville L.

height of gates above sea level

WATTS BAR 815 745
FT. LOUDOUN
WHEELER GUNTERSVILLE NICKAJACK CHICKAMAUGA 685 635
WILSON 595 556
PICKWICK 508
KENTUCKY 418
 375 300

0 22 miles above mouth 207 259 275 349 425 471 530 602 650
Paducah Knoxville

TENNESSEE RIVER PROFILE

© C. S. Hammond & Co., Maplewood, N. J.

Agriculture, Industry and Resources

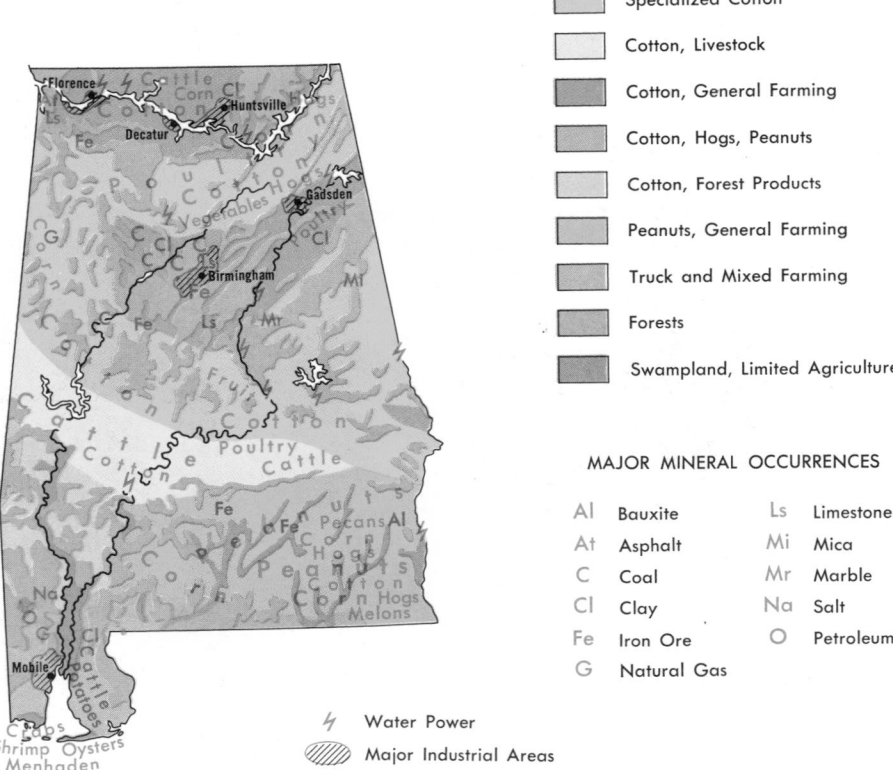

DOMINANT LAND USE

- Specialized Cotton
- Cotton, Livestock
- Cotton, General Farming
- Cotton, Hogs, Peanuts
- Cotton, Forest Products
- Peanuts, General Farming
- Truck and Mixed Farming
- Forests
- Swampland, Limited Agriculture

MAJOR MINERAL OCCURRENCES

Al	Bauxite	Ls	Limestone
At	Asphalt	Mi	Mica
C	Coal	Mr	Marble
Cl	Clay	Na	Salt
Fe	Iron Ore	O	Petroleum
G	Natural Gas		

⚡ Water Power

▨ Major Industrial Areas

Topography

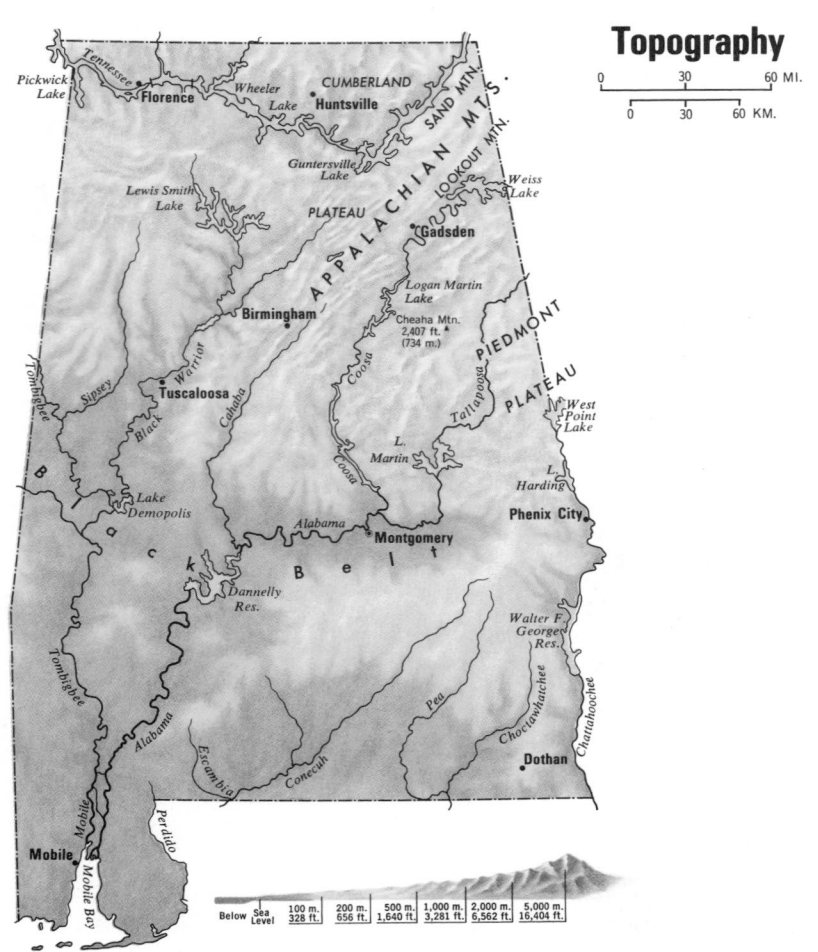

Below Sea Level	100 m. 328 ft.	200 m. 656 ft.	500 m. 1,640 ft.	1,000 m. 3,281 ft.	2,000 m. 6,562 ft.	5,000 m. 16,404 ft.

Topography scale: 0 30 60 MI. / 0 30 60 KM.

Alabama

SCALE

0 5 10 20 30 40 MI.

0 5 10 20 30 40 KM.

State Capitals .... ⊛

County Seats .... ⊙

Major Limited Access Hwys. ————

Scale 1:1,930,000

© Copyright HAMMOND INCORPORATED, Maplewood, N.J.

Agriculture, Industry and Resources

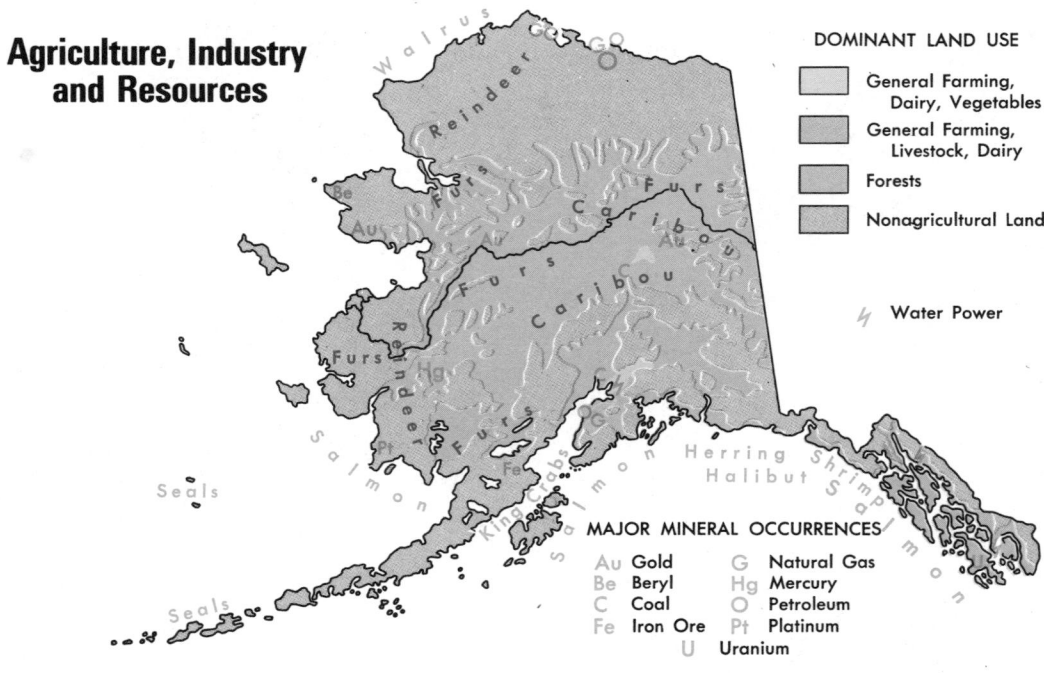

DOMINANT LAND USE

- General Farming, Dairy, Vegetables
- General Farming, Livestock, Dairy
- Forests
- Nonagricultural Land

⚡ Water Power

MAJOR MINERAL OCCURRENCES

Au	Gold	G	Natural Gas
Be	Beryl	Hg	Mercury
C	Coal	O	Petroleum
Fe	Iron Ore	Pt	Platinum
		U	Uranium

Topography

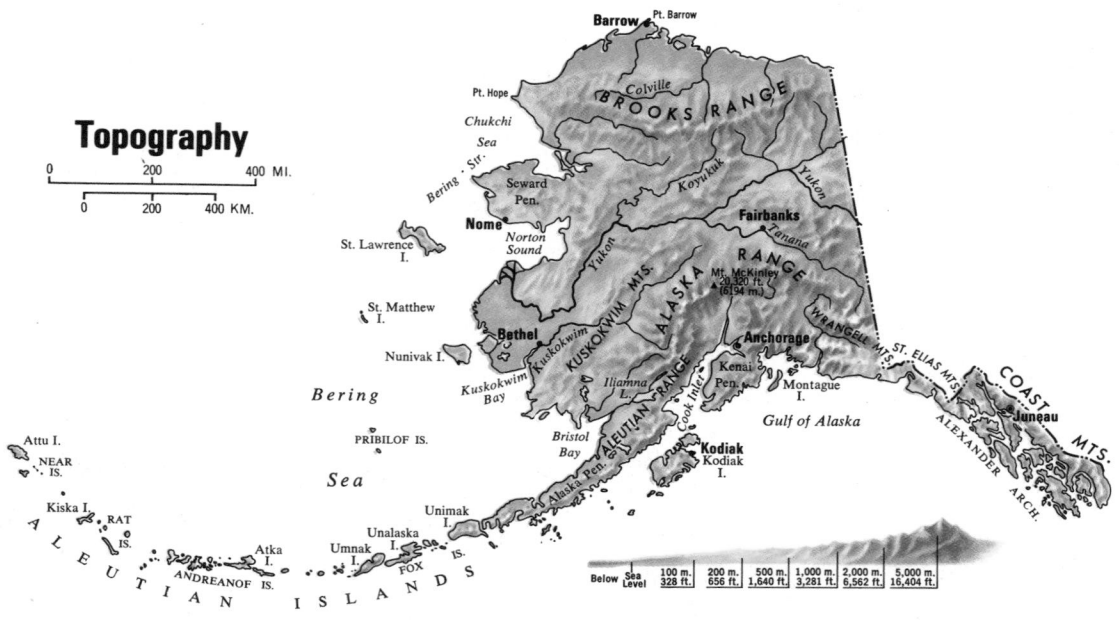

Below Sea Level | 100 m. 328 ft. | 200 m. 656 ft. | 500 m. 1,640 ft. | 1,000 m. 3,281 ft. | 2,000 m. 6,562 ft. | 5,000 m. 16,404 ft.

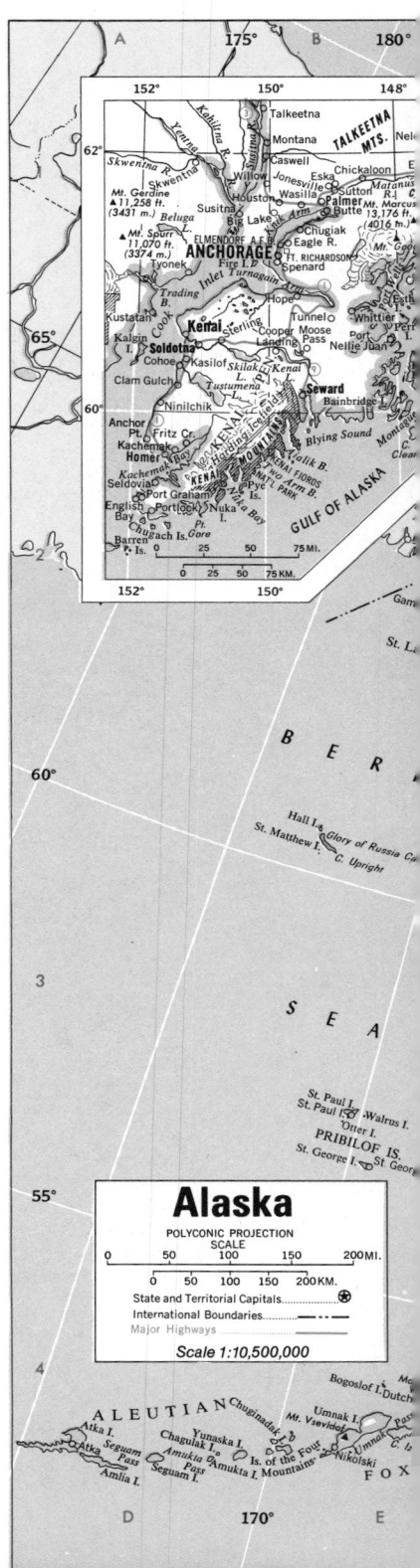

Alaska

POLYCONIC PROJECTION

SCALE

State and Territorial Capitals .... ⊛
International Boundaries .... — · · —
Major Highways ....

Scale 1:10,500,000

McKinley (mt.) H2
Meade (riv.) G1
Mendenhall (cape) E3
Mentasta (pass) K2
Merrill (pass) H2
Michelson (mt.) K1
Middleton (isl.) J3
Misty Fjords Nat'l Mon. N2
Mitkof (isl.) N2
Montague (isl.) D1
Muir (glac.) M1
Mulchatna (riv.) G2
Muzon (cape) M2
Naknek (lake) G3
Near (isls.) H3
Nelson (riv.) E2
Newenham (cape) F3
Noatak (riv.) F1
Norton (bay) F2
Norton (sound) E1
Nowitna (riv.) H2
Nuka (bay) C2
Nunivak (isl.) E3
Nushagak (riv.) G2
Nuyakuk (lake) F3
Ommaney (cape) M2
Otter (isl.) D3
Pastol (bay) F2
Pavlof (isls.) F3
Pavlof (vol.) F3
Philip Smith (mts.) J1
Porcupine (riv.) K1
Port Clarence (inlet) E1
Port Heiden (inlet) G3

Portland Canal (inlet) N2
Port Moller (inlet) F3
Port Wells (inlet) C1
Pribilof (isls.) D3
Prince of Wales (cape) E1
Prince of Wales (isl.) N2
Prince William (sound) D1
Prudhoe (bay) J1
Rat (isls.) K4
Redoubt (vol.) H2
Revillagigedo (chan.) N2
Revillagigedo (isl.) N2
Romanzof (cape) E2
Sagavanirktok (riv.) J1
Saint Elias (cape) K3
Saint Elias (mts.) L2
Saint George (isl.) D3
Saint Lawrence (isl.) D2
Saint Matthew (isl.) D2
Saint Paul (isl.) D3
Salisbury (sound) M1
Sanak (isl.) F4
Sanford (mt.) K2
Schwatka (mts.) G1
Seguam (isl.) D4
Selawik (lake) F1
Semichi (isls.) J3
Semidi (isls.) G3
Semisopochnoi (isl.) K4
Seward (pen.) E1
Seymour (canal) N1
Sheenjek (riv.) K1
Shelikof (str.) H3
Shemya (isl.) J3

Shishaldin (vol.) E4
Shumagin (isls.) G4
Shuyak (isl.) H3
Sitka (sound) M1
Sitka Nat'l Hist. Park M1
Sitkinak (str.) H3
Skilak (lake) C1
Skwentna (riv.) A1
Smith (bay) H1
Spencer (cape) L1
Stephens (passage) N1
Stevenson Entrance (str.) ... H3
Stikine (riv.) N2
Stikine (str.) N2
Stony (riv.) G2
Stuart (isl.) F2
Suemez (isl.) M2
Sumner (str.) M2
Susitna (riv.) B1
Sutwik (isl.) G3
Taku (glac.) N1
Taku (riv.) N1
Talkeetna (mts.) J2
Tanaga (isl.) K4
Tanaga (vol.) K4
Tanana (riv.) J2
Taylor (mts.) G2
Tazlina (lake) D1
Tazlina (riv.) D1
Teshekpuk (lake) H1
Tigalda (isl.) F4
Tikchik (lkes) G2
Togiak (bay) F3
Tugidak (isl.) G3

Turnagain Arm (inlet) B1
Tustumena (lake) C1
Two Arm (bay) C2
Ugashik (lkes) G3
Umnak (isl.) E4
Umnak (passage) E4
Unalaska (isl.) E4
Unga (isl.) F3
Unimak (isl.) E4
Unimak (passage) F4
Utukok (riv.) F1
Valley of Ten Thousand Smokes .G3
Vancouver (mt.) L2
Veniaminof (crater) F3
Vsevidof (vol.) E4
Walrus (isl.) E3
Walrus (isls.) F3
Waring (mts.) G1
West Point (mt.) K2
White (pass) N1
White (riv.) K2
White Mountains Nat'l Rec. Area J1
Witherspoon (mt.) C1
Wrangell (cape) H3
Wrangell (isl.) N2
Wrangell (mts.) K2
Wrangell-St. Elias Nat'l Park . K2
Yakobi (isl.) M1
Yakutat (bay) K3
Yentna (riv.) A1
Yukon (riv.) F2

⊙ Court House
‡ Population of metropolitan area.
† Zip of nearest p.o.
* Multiple zips.

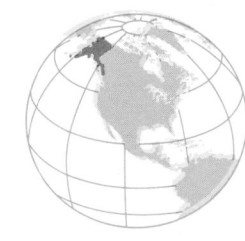

AREA 591,004 sq. mi. (1,530,700 sq. km.)
POPULATION 401,851
CAPITAL Juneau
LARGEST CITY Anchorage
HIGHEST POINT Mt. McKinley 20,320 ft.
(6194 m.)
SETTLED IN 1801
ADMITTED TO UNION January 3, 1959
POPULAR NAME Great Land; Last Frontier
STATE FLOWER Forget-me-not
STATE BIRD Willow Ptarmigan

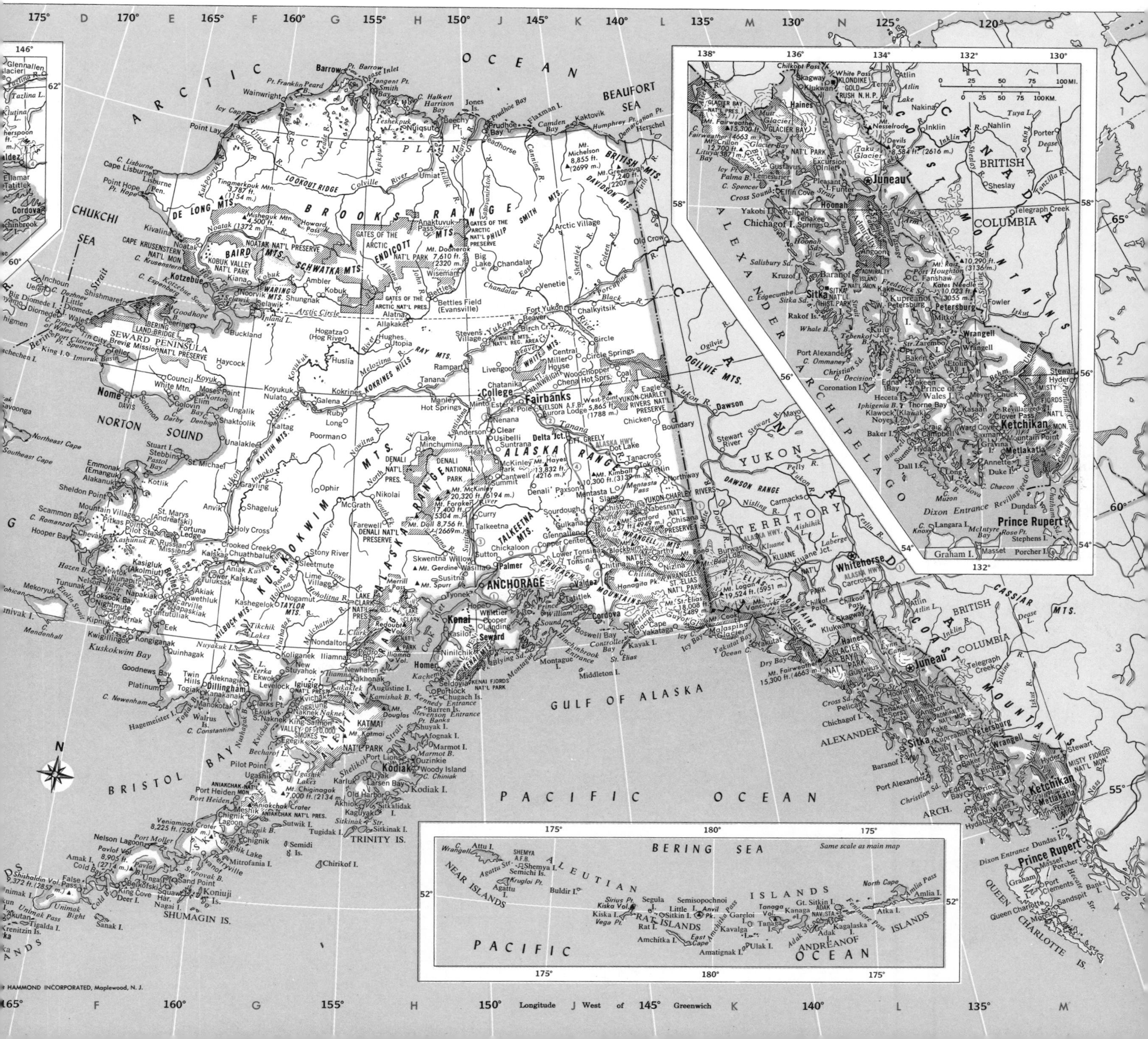

© HAMMOND INCORPORATED, Maplewood, N. J.

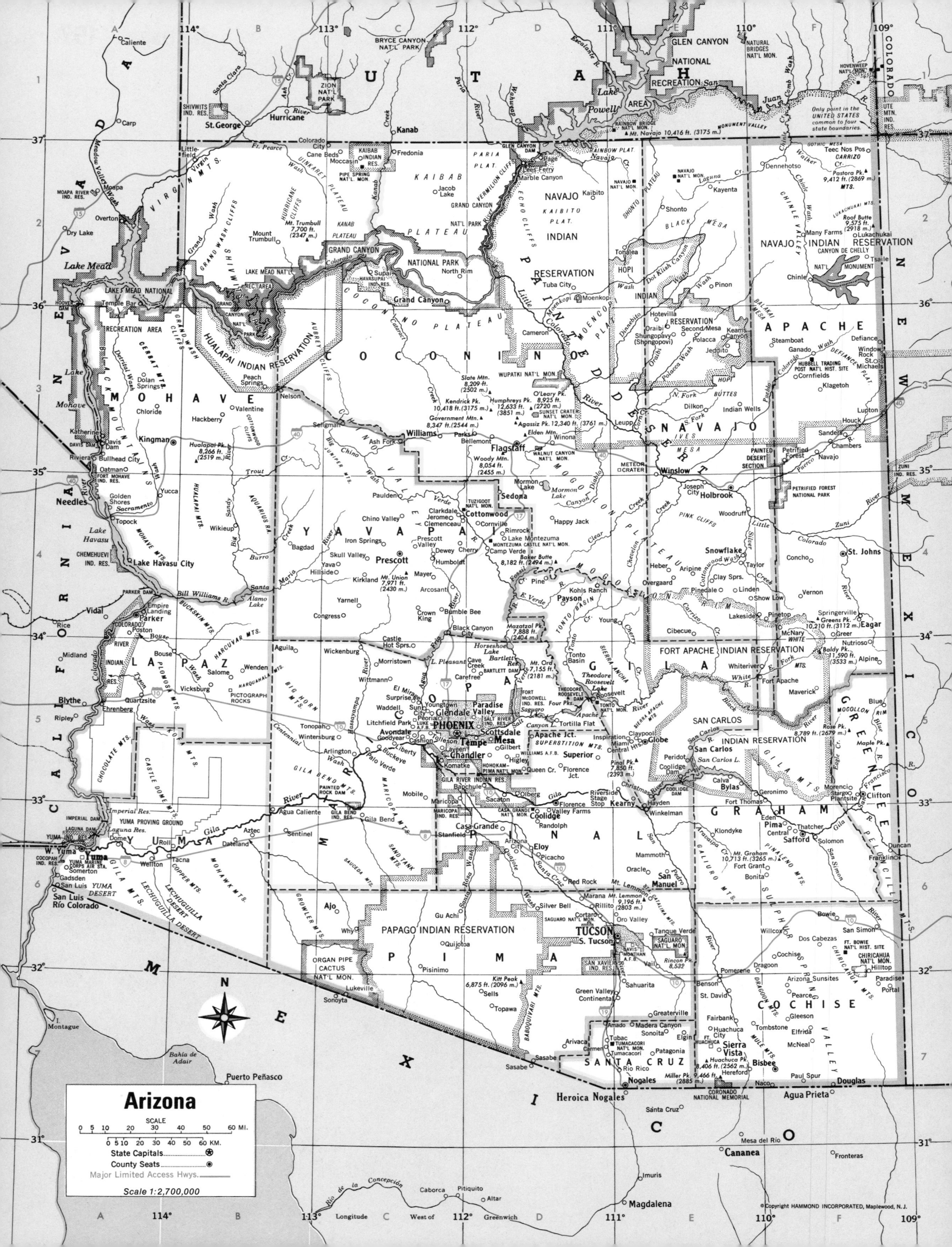

Arizona
SCALE
0 5 10 20 30 40 50 60 MI.
0 5 10 20 30 40 50 60 KM.
State Capitals
County Seats
Major Limited Access Hwys.
Scale 1:2,700,000
©Copyright HAMMOND INCORPORATED, Maplewood, N.J.
114°
113°
112°
111°
110°
109°
37°
36°
35°
34°
33°
32°
31°
Longitude
West of
Greenwich
U T A H
N E V A D A
C A L I F O R N I A
M E X I C O
N E W M E X I C O
COLORADO
Only point in the UNITED STATES common to four state boundaries.
GLEN CANYON NATIONAL RECREATION AREA
Lake Powell
BRYCE CANYON NAT'L PARK
ZION NAT'L PARK
NATURAL BRIDGES NAT'L MON.
HOVENWEEP NAT'L MON.
UTE MTN. IND. RES.
SHIVWITS IND. RES.
RAINBOW BRIDGE NAT'L MON.
Mt. Navajo 10,416 ft. (3175 m.)
MONUMENT VALLEY
Caliente
Carp
St. George
Hurricane
Kanab
Moapa
Overton
Dry Lake
MOAPA RIVER IND. RES.
Lake Mead
LAKE MEAD NATIONAL RECREATION AREA
Temple Bar
HOOVER DAM
Colorado City
Cane Beds
Moccasin
KAIBAB INDIAN RES.
PIPE SPRING NAT'L MON.
Fredonia
Littlefield
Ft. Pearce
KAIBAB PLATEAU
PARIA PLAT.
Jacob Lake
GRAND CANYON NAT'L PARK
KANAB PLATEAU
UINKARET PLATEAU
Mt. Trumbull 7,700 ft. (2347 m.)
Mount Trumbull
GRAND CANYON NATIONAL PARK
North Rim
Supai
HAVASUPAI IND. RES.
Grand Canyon
GRAND WASH CLIFFS
SHIVWITS PLATEAU
VIRGIN MTS.
GLEN CANYON DAM
Page
Lees Ferry
Marble Canyon
VERMILION CLIFFS
ECHO CLIFFS
NAVAJO INDIAN RESERVATION
KAIBITO PLAT.
Kaibito
NAVAJO NAT'L MON.
Kayenta
Shonto
SHONTO PLATEAU
BLACK MESA
Tonalea
HOPI INDIAN RESERVATION
Tuba City
Moenkopi
Hotevilla
Oraibi
Shungopavy (Shongopovi)
Second Mesa
Polacca
Keams Canyon
Jeddito
Pinon
Cameron
PAINTED DESERT
MOENCOPI PLAT.
Teec Nos Pos
CARRIZO
Dennehotso
Pastora Pk. 9,412 ft. (2869 m.)
LUKACHUKAI MTS.
Roof Butte 9,575 ft. (2918 m.)
Lukachukai
Many Farms
CANYON DE CHELLY NAT'L MONUMENT
Tsaile
Chinle
CHINLE VALLEY
A P A C H E
Steamboat
Ganado
Defiance
Window Rock
St. Michaels
HUBBELL TRADING POST NAT'L HIST. SITE
Cornfields
Klagetoh
DEFIANCE PLAT.
Lupton
Houck
Sanders
Chambers
Navajo
Petrified Forest
PAINTED DESERT SECTION
PETRIFIED FOREST NATIONAL PARK
ZUNI IND. RES.
N A V A J O
Dilkon
Indian Wells
Leupp
Winslow
METEOR CRATER
Joseph City
Holbrook
Woodruff
PINK CLIFFS
C O C O N I N O
COCONINO PLATEAU
HUALAPAI INDIAN RESERVATION
AUBREY CLIFFS
Peach Springs
WUPATKI NAT'L MON.
SUNSET CRATER NAT'L MON.
Slate Mtn. 8,209 ft. (2502 m.)
Kendrick Pk. 10,418 ft. (3175 m.)
Humphreys Pk. 12,633 ft. (3851 m.)
O'Leary Pk. 8,925 ft. (2720 m.)
Agassiz Pk. 12,340 ft. (3761 m.)
Government Mtn. 8,347 ft. (2544 m.)
Elden Mtn.
Winona
Flagstaff
WALNUT CANYON NAT'L MON.
Woody Mtn. 8,054 ft. (2455 m.)
Bellemont
Parks
Williams
Ash Fork
Seligman
Nelson
Mormon Lake
Sedona
M O H A V E
Dolan Springs
CERBAT MTS.
Chloride
Valentine
Hackberry
Kingman
Hualapai Pk. 8,266 ft. (2519 m.)
Katherine
DAVIS DAM
Davis Dam
Riviera
Bullhead City
Oatman
FORT MOHAVE IND. RES.
Needles
Golden Shores
Topock
Yucca
Lake Havasu
CHEMEHUEVI IND. RES.
Lake Havasu City
HUALAPAI MTS.
MOHAVE MTS.
Wikieup
Y A V A P A I
Paulden
Chino Valley
Clarkdale
Jerome
Clemenceau
Cottonwood
TUZIGOOT NAT'L MON.
Cornville
Rimrock
Lake Montezuma
MONTEZUMA CASTLE NAT'L MON.
Camp Verde
Prescott Valley
Prescott
Iron Springs
Bagdad
Skull Valley
Yava
Hillside
Kirkland
Dewey
Humboldt
Cherry
Mayer
Mt. Union 7,971 ft. (2430 m.)
Arcosanti
Yarnell
Congress
Crown King
Bumble Bee
Black Canyon City
Happy Jack
Baker Butte 8,182 ft. (2494 m.)
MOGOLLON PLATEAU
Pine
Payson
Kohls Ranch
Heber
Aripine
Overgaard
Snowflake
Taylor
Clay Sprs.
Pinedale
Linden
Show Low
Concho
St. Johns
Vernon
Lakeside
Pinetop
Springerville
Eagar
Greens Pk. 10,210 ft. (3112 m.)
Greer
McNary
Nutrioso
Alpine
Cibecue
FORT APACHE INDIAN RESERVATION
Whiteriver
Fort Apache
Maverick
Baldy Pk. 11,590 ft. (3533 m.)
Young
Mazatzal Pk. 7,888 ft. (2404 m.)
Horseshoe Lake
Bartlett Res.
Mt. Ord 7,155 ft. (2181 m.)
Tonto Basin
Theodore Roosevelt Lake
Roosevelt
TONTO NAT'L MON.
Four Pks.
SIERRA ANCHA
Castle Hot Sprs.
Wickenburg
Aguila
Morristown
Wittmann
Cave Creek
Carefree
BARTLETT DAM
L. Pleasant
El Mirage
Surprise
Youngtown
Sun City
Peoria
Glendale
Paradise Valley
Waddell
Litchfield Park
LUKE A.F.B.
PHOENIX
Scottsdale
SALT RIVER IND. RES.
FORT McDOWELL IND. RES.
Avondale
Goodyear
Cashion
Tolleson
Tempe
Mesa
Gilbert
Laveen
Chandler
Komatke
Higley
WILLIAMS A.F.B.
Queen Cr.
Apache Jct.
SUPERSTITION MTS.
Canyon L.
Tortilla Flat
Tonopah
Wintersburg
Arlington
Buckeye
Liberty
Palo Verde
Mobile
HOHOKAM-PIMA NAT'L MON.
GILA RIVER INDIAN RES.
Bapchule
Sacaton
Maricopa
Olberg
Superior
Florence Jct.
Inspiration
Claypool
Miami
Central Hts.
Globe
Pinal Pk. 7,850 ft. (2393 m.)
Florence
Valley Farms
Coolidge
Randolph
Riverside Stage Stop
Kearny
Hayden
Winkelman
Peridot
San Carlos
San Carlos L.
Coolidge Dam
SAN CARLOS INDIAN RESERVATION
Calva
Bylas
Geronimo
Fort Thomas
G R A H A M
Eden
Pima
Central
Safford
Thatcher
Solomon
Klondyke
Mt. Graham 10,713 ft. (3265 m.)
Fort Grant
Bonita
GREENLEE
Rose Pk. 8,789 ft. (2679 m.)
Maple Pk.
Morenci
Stargo
Plantsite
Clifton
Duncan
Franklin
Blue
Mohave
Parker
PARKER DAM
Empire Landing
Poston
COLORADO RIVER INDIAN RES.
Bouse
L A P A Z
Salome
Wenden
Vicksburg
Quartzsite
Ehrenberg
Blythe
Ripley
Vidal
Rice
Midland
PICTOGRAPH ROCKS
HARCUVAR MTS.
BUCKSKIN MTS.
PLOMOSA MTS.
KOFA MTS.
CASTLE DOME MTS.
CHOCOLATE MTS.
Imperial Res.
IMPERIAL DAM
LAGUNA DAM
Laguna Res.
YUMA PROVING GROUND
YUMA IND. RES.
Y U M A
Roll
Dome
Dateland
Aztec
Tacna
Wellton
W. Yuma
Yuma
COCOPAH IND. RES.
YUMA MARINE CORPS AIR STA.
Somerton
Gadsden
San Luis
San Luis Río Colorado
YUMA DESERT
LECHUGUILLA DESERT
MOHAWK MTS.
COPPER MTS.
GILA MTS.
Agua Caliente
Sentinel
GILA BEND IND. RES.
Gila Bend
PAINTED ROCK DAM
M A R I C O P A
MARICOPA IND. RES.
Stanfield
Casa Grande
CASA GRANDE NAT'L MON.
P I N A L
Arizona City
Eloy
Picacho
Red Rock
Mammoth
Oracle
San Manuel
Marana
Rillito
Cortaro
Mt. Lemmon 9,196 ft. (2803 m.)
Oro Valley
SANTA CATALINA MTS.
Silver Bell
SAGUARO NAT'L MON.
TUCSON
S. Tucson
DAVIS MONTHAN A.F.B.
SAN XAVIER IND. RES.
Tanque Verde
Vail
Rincon Pk. 8,532
Sahuarita
Green Valley
Continental
Ajo
Why
Gu Achi
PAPAGO INDIAN RESERVATION
Quijotoa
P I M A
ORGAN PIPE CACTUS NAT'L MON.
Pisinimo
Kitt Peak 6,875 ft. (2096 m.)
Sells
Topawa
Lukeville
Sonoyta
GROWLER MTS.
BABOQUIVARI MTS.
Greaterville
Amado
Madera Canyon
Sonoita
Elgin
Arivaca
Tubac
TUMACACORI NAT'L MON.
Tumacacori
Carmen
Patagonia
Sasabe
SANTA CRUZ
Rio Rico
Nogales
Heroica Nogales
Benson
St. David
Pomerene
Dragoon
Fairbank
Huachuca City
FT. HUACHUCA
Sierra Vista
Huachuca Pk. 8,406 ft. (2562 m.)
Miller Pk. 9,466 ft. (2885 m.)
Hereford
CORONADO NATIONAL MEMORIAL
Tombstone
Gleeson
Elfrida
McNeal
Pearce
Sunsites
C O C H I S E
Willcox
Dos Cabezas
Cochise
FT. BOWIE NAT'L HIST. SITE
CHIRICAHUA NAT'L MON.
Hilltop
Paradise
Portal
Bowie
San Simon
Bisbee
Naco
Paul Spur
Douglas
Agua Prieta
SULPHUR SPRINGS VALLEY
DRAGOON MTS.
CHIRICAHUA MTS.
Santa Cruz
Cananea
Mesa del Río
Fronteras
Imuris
Magdalena
Caborca
Pitiquito
Altar
Río de la Concepción
Puerto Peñasco
Bahía de Adair
I. Montague

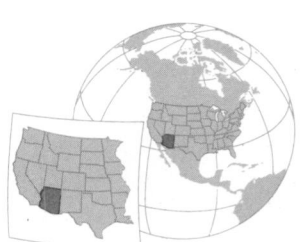

AREA 114,000 sq. mi. (295,260 sq. km.)
POPULATION 2,718,425
CAPITAL Phoenix
LARGEST CITY Phoenix
HIGHEST POINT Humphreys Pk. 12,633 ft.
(3851 m.)
SETTLED IN 1752
ADMITTED TO UNION February 14, 1912
POPULAR NAME Grand Canyon State
STATE FLOWER Saguaro Cactus Blossom
STATE BIRD Cactus Wren

Agriculture, Industry and Resources

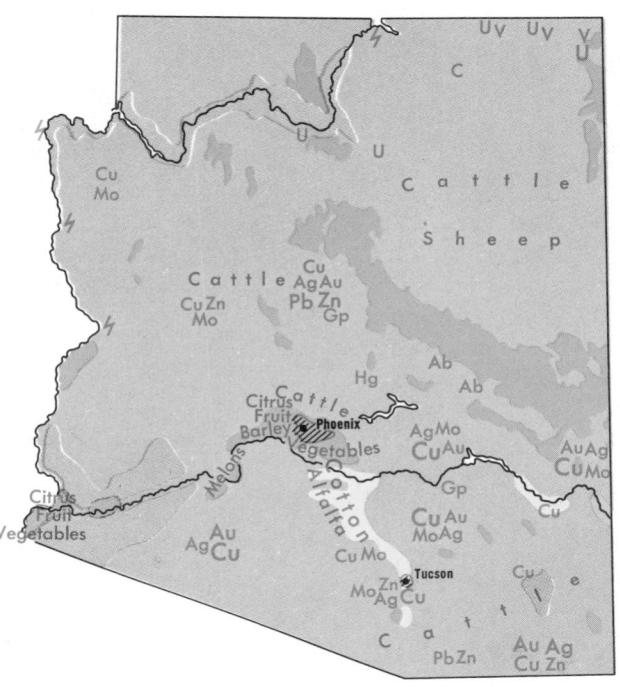

MAJOR MINERAL OCCURRENCES

Ab	Asbestos	Cu	Copper	Pb	Lead
Ag	Silver	Gp	Gypsum	U	Uranium
Au	Gold	Hg	Mercury	V	Vanadium
C	Coal	Mo	Molybdenum	Zn	Zinc

DOMINANT LAND USE

Fruit, Truck and Mixed Farming

Cotton and Alfalfa

General Farming, Livestock, Special Crops

Range Livestock

Forests

Nonagricultural Land

⚡ Water Power

▨ Major Industrial Areas

COUNTIES

Apache 52,108	F3
Cochise 85,686	F7
Coconino 75,008	C3
Gila 37,080	E5
Graham 22,862	E6
Greenlee 11,406	F5
La Paz 13,100	A5
Maricopa 1,509,052	C5
Mohave 55,865	A3
Navajo 67,629	E3
Pima 531,443	D6
Pinal 90,918	D6
Santa Cruz 20,459	E7
Yavapai 68,145	C4
Yuma● 81,800	A6

●1982 official estimate.

CITIES and TOWNS

Zip	Name/Pop.	Key
†85333	Agua Caliente 60	B6
85320	Aguila 900	B5
85321	Ajo 5,189	C6
85920	Alpine 450	F5
85640	Amado 75	D7
85220	Apache Junction 9,935	D5
†85901	Aripine 25	E4
85601	Arivaca 400	D7
85223	Arizona City 825	D6
85625	Arizona Sunsites 825	F7
85322	Arlington 950	C5
86320	Ash Fork 800	C3
85323	Avondale 8,168	C5
†85333	Aztec 20	B6
86321	Bagdad 2,331	B4
85221	Bapchule 400	D5
86015	Bellemont 210	D3
85602	Benson 4,190	E7
85603	Bisbee⊙ 7,154	F7
85324	Black Canyon City 600	C4
85922	Blue 50	F5
†85643	Bonita 20	E6
85325	Bouse 500	A5
85605	Bowie 600	F6
85326	Buckeye 3,434	C5
86430	Bullhead City-Riviera 10,364	A3
†86301	Bumble Bee 15	C4
85530	Bylas 1,175	E5
†85530	Calva 10	E5
86020	Cameron 600	D3
86322	Camp Verde 1,125	D4
†86022	Cane Beds 30	B2
85331	Carefree 986	C5
85640	Carmen 200	D7
85222	Casa Grande 14,971	D6
85329	Cashion 3,014	C5
†85342	Castle Hot Springs 50	C5
85331	Cave Creek 1,589	D5
85531	Central 300	F6
†85501	Central Heights-Midland City 2,791	E5
85502	Chambers 500	F3
85224	Chandler 29,673	D5
†86327	Cherry 20	C4
86503	Chinle 2,815	F2
86323	Chino Valley 2,858	C4
86431	Chloride 225	A3
†85292	Christmas 201	E5
85911	Cibecue 100	E4
86324	Clarkdale 1,512	C4
85532	Claypool 2,362	E5
†85934	Clay Springs 500	E4
†86326	Clemenceau 300	C4
85533	Clifton⊙ 4,245	F5
85606	Cochise 150	F6
86021	Colorado City 350	B2
85924	Concho 100	F4
85332	Congress 800	C4
†85640	Continental 250	D7
85228	Coolidge 6,851	D6
†85542	Coolidge Dam 42	E5
†86505	Cornfields 200	F3
86325	Cornville 425	D4
85230	Cortaro 375	D6
†86326	Cottonwood 4,550	D4
86333	Crown King 100	C4
85333	Dateland 100	B6
†86430	Davis Dam 125	A3
86327	Dewey 100	C4
†86047	Dilkon 90	E3
86441	Dolan Springs 870	A3
†85364	Dome 48	A6
†85643	Dos Cabezas 30	F6
85607	Douglas 13,058	F7
85609	Dragoon 150	F6
85534	Duncan 603	F6
85925	Eagar 2,791	F4
85535	Eden 89	F6
85334	Ehrenburg 93	A5

(continued on following page)

Topography

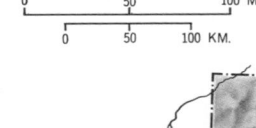

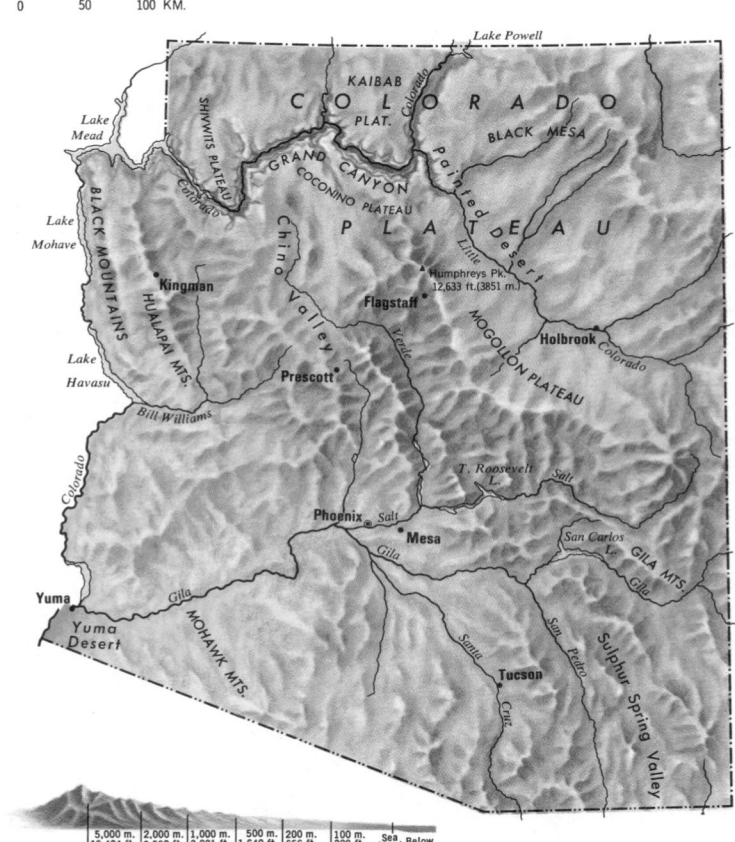

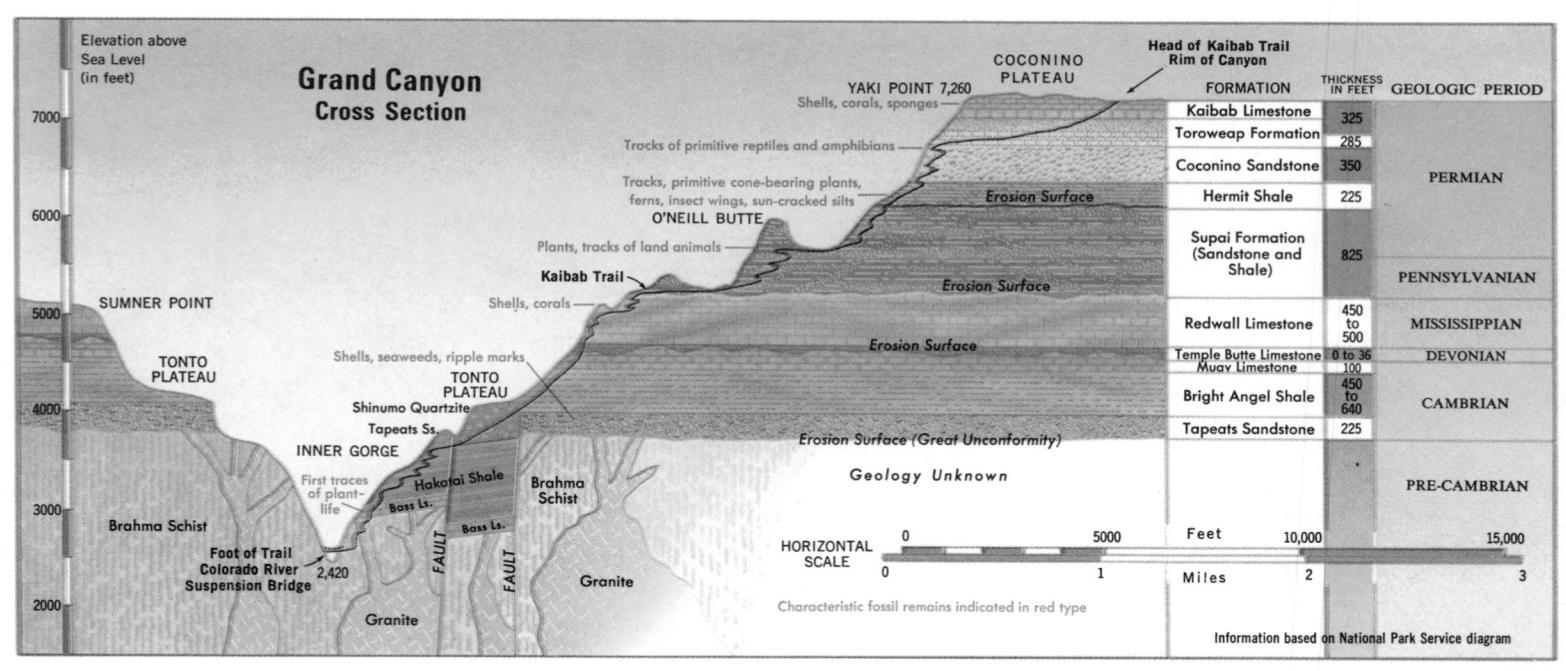

Grand Canyon Cross Section

FORMATION	THICKNESS IN FEET	GEOLOGIC PERIOD
Kaibab Limestone	325	PERMIAN
Toroweap Formation	285	
Coconino Sandstone	350	
Hermit Shale	225	
Supai Formation (Sandstone and Shale)	825	PENNSYLVANIAN
Redwall Limestone	450 to 500	MISSISSIPPIAN
Temple Butte Limestone	0 to 36	DEVONIAN
Muav Limestone	100	
Bright Angel Shale	450 to 640	CAMBRIAN
Tapeats Sandstone	225	
		PRE-CAMBRIAN

Information based on National Park Service diagram

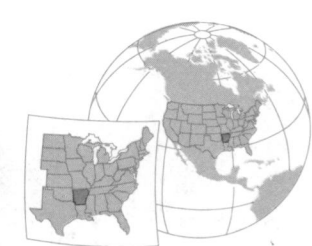

AREA 53,187 sq. mi. (137,754 sq. km.)
POPULATION 2,286,435
CAPITAL Little Rock
LARGEST CITY Little Rock
HIGHEST POINT Magazine Mtn. 2,753 ft. (839 m.)
SETTLED IN 1685
ADMITTED TO UNION June 15, 1836
POPULAR NAME Land of Opportunity
STATE FLOWER Apple Blossom
STATE BIRD Mockingbird

COUNTIES

Arkansas 24,175 ....H5
Ashley 26,538 ....G7
Baxter 27,409 ....F1
Benton 78,115 ....B1
Boone 26,067 ....D1
Bradley 13,803 ....F7
Calhoun 6,079 ....E6
Carroll 16,203 ....C1
Chicot 17,793 ....H7
Clark 23,326 ....D5
Clay 20,616 ....K1
Cleburne 16,909 ....F2
Cleveland 7,868 ....F6
Columbia 26,644 ....D7
Conway 19,505 ....E3
Craighead 63,239 ....J2
Crawford 36,892 ....B2
Crittenden 49,499 ....K3
Cross 20,434 ....J3
Dallas 10,515 ....E6
Desha 19,760 ....H6
Drew 17,910 ....G6
Faulkner 46,192 ....F3
Franklin 14,705 ....C2
Fulton 9,975 ....G1
Garland 70,531 ....D4
Grant 13,008 ....F5
Greene 30,744 ....J1
Hempstead 23,635 ....C6
Hot Spring 26,819 ....E5
Howard 13,459 ....C5
Independence 30,147 ....G2
Izard 10,768 ....G1
Jackson 21,646 ....H2
Jefferson 90,718 ....G5
Johnson 17,423 ....C2
Lafayette 10,213 ....C7
Lawrence 18,447 ....H1
Lee 15,539 ....J4
Lincoln 13,369 ....G6
Little River 13,952 ....B6
Logan 20,144 ....C3
Lonoke 34,518 ....G4
Madison 11,373 ....C1
Marion 11,334 ....E1
Miller 37,766 ....C7
Mississippi 59,517 ....K2
Monroe 14,052 ....H4
Montgomery 7,771 ....C4
Nevada 11,097 ....D6
Newton 7,756 ....D2
Ouachita 30,541 ....E6
Perry 7,266 ....E4
Phillips 34,772 ....J5
Pike 10,373 ....C5
Poinsett 27,032 ....J2
Polk 17,007 ....B5
Pope 39,021 ....D3
Prairie 10,140 ....G4
Pulaski 340,613 ....F4
Randolph 16,834 ....H1
Saint Francis 30,858 ....J3
Saline 53,161 ....E4
Scott 9,685 ....B4
Searcy 8,847 ....E2
Sebastian 95,172 ....B3
Sevier 14,060 ....B6
Sharp 14,607 ....G1
Stone 9,022 ....F2
Union 48,573 ....E7
Van Buren 13,357 ....E2
Washington 100,494 ....B2
White 50,835 ....G3
Woodruff 11,222 ....H3
Yell 17,026 ....D3

CITIES and TOWNS

Zip   Name/Pop.   Key

72001 Adona 230 ....E3
72002 Alexander 223 ....F4
72410 Alicia 246 ....H2
72820 Alix 225 ....C3
†72046 Allport 295 ....G4
72921 Alma 2,755 ....B3
72003 Almyra 294 ....H5
72004 Altheimer 1,231 ....G5
72821 Altus 441 ....C3
72005 Amagon 126 ....H2
71921 Amity 859 ....D5
71922 Antoine 194 ....D5
71923 Arkadelphia⊙ 10,005 ....D5
†1630 Arkansas City⊙ 668 ....H6
72310 Armorel 500 ....L2
71822 Ashdown⊙ 4,218 ....B6
72513 Ash Flat⊙ 524 ....G1
72823 Atkins 3,002 ....E3
72311 Aubrey 267 ....J4
72006 Augusta⊙ 3,496 ....H3
72007 Austin 269 ....G4
72711 Avoca 256 ....B1
72010 Bald Knob 2,756 ....G3
71631 Banks 216 ....F6
72922 Barber 35 ....B3
72923 Barling 3,761 ....B3
72313 Bassett 243 ....K2
72924 Bates 35 ....B4
72501 Batesville⊙ 8,263 ....G2
72411 Bay 1,605 ....J2
71720 Bearden 1,191 ....E6
72613 Beaver 35 ....C1
72012 Beebe 3,599 ....G3
72014 Beedeville 183 ....H3
†72712 Bella Vista 2,589 ....B1
†72601 Bellefonte 393 ....D1
72824 Belleville 571 ....D3
71823 Ben Lomond 155 ....B6
72015 Benton⊙ 17,717 ....E4
72712 Bentonville⊙ 8,756 ....B1
72615 Bergman 320 ....E1
72616 Berryville⊙ 2,966 ....C1
†72764 Bethel Heights 296 ....B1
72016 Bigelow 373 ....E3
72617 Big Flat 150 ....F1
72413 Biggers 363 ....J1
72017 Biscoe 486 ....H4
72414 Black Oak 309 ....K2
72415 Black Rock 848 ....H1
71960 Black Springs 92 ....C5
65611 Blue Eye 43 ....D1
72826 Blue Mountain 112 ....C3
71722 Bluff City 292 ....D6
72315 Blytheville⊙ 23,844 ....L2
†71858 Bodcaw 197 ....D6
†72901 Bonanza 553 ....B3
72416 Bono 967 ....J2
72927 Booneville⊙ 3,718 ....C3
72020 Bradford 950 ....G3
71826 Bradley 790 ....C7
72928 Branch 353 ....C3
72021 Brinkley 4,909 ....H4
72417 Brookland 840 ....J2
72022 Bryant 2,682 ....F4
71827 Buckner 436 ....D7
72619 Bull Shoals 1,312 ....E1
72321 Burdette 328 ....L2
72023 Cabot 4,806 ....F4
72322 Caldwell 283 ....J3
71828 Cale 110 ....D6
72519 Calico Rock 1,046 ....F1
71724 Calion 638 ....E7
72201 Cammack Village 920 ....E4
†72473 Campbell Station 297 ....H2
72419 Caraway 1,165 ....K2
72024 Carlisle 2,567 ....G4
71725 Carthage 568 ....E5
72025 Casa 179 ....D3
72421 Cash 285 ....J2
72026 Casscoe 297 ....H4
†72951 Caulksville 234 ....C3
72521 Cave City 1,634 ....G2
72718 Cave Springs 429 ....B1
72932 Cedarville 375 ....B2
72719 Centerton 425 ....B1
72829 Centerville 300 ....D3
†72923 Central City 339 ....B3
72933 Charleston⊙ 1,748 ....B3
†72525 Cherokee Village-Hidden
          Valley 4,058 ....G1
72324 Cherry Valley 729 ....J3
72934 Chester 139 ....B2
71726 Chidester 342 ....D6
72029 Clarendon⊙ 2,361 ....H4
72325 Clarkedale 300 ....K3
72830 Clarksville⊙ 5,237 ....D3
72031 Clinton⊙ 1,284 ....F2
72476 College City 432 ....J1
72326 Colt 378 ....J3
71831 Columbus 265 ....C6
72523 Concord 234 ....G2
72032 Conway⊙ 20,375 ....F3
72524 Cord 250 ....H2
72422 Corning⊙ 3,650 ....J1
72626 Cotter 920 ....E1
72036 Cotton Plant 1,323 ....H3
71937 Cove 391 ....B5
72037 Coy 183 ....G4
72327 Crawfordsville 685 ....K3
71635 Crossett 6,706 ....G7
71728 Curtis 300 ....D6
72526 Cushman 556 ....G2
†71950 Daisy 177 ....C5
72039 Damascus 307 ....F3
72833 Danville⊙ 1,698 ....D3
72834 Dardanelle⊙ 3,621 ....D3
72424 Datto 112 ....J1
72722 Decatur 1,013 ....A1
72425 Delaplaine 161 ....J1
71940 Delight 431 ....C5
72426 Dell 310 ....K2
†72821 Denning 238 ....C3
71832 De Queen⊙ 4,594 ....B5
71638 Dermott 4,731 ....H7
72040 Des Arc⊙ 2,001 ....G4
72041 De Valls Bluff⊙ 738 ....H4
72042 De Witt⊙ 3,928 ....H5

72644 Diamond City 650 ....E1
72043 Diaz 1,192 ....H2
71833 Dierks 1,249 ....B5
71941 Donaldson 300 ....E5
72837 Dover 948 ....D3
71639 Dumas 6,091 ....H6
72935 Dyer 608 ....B3
72330 Dyess 446 ....K2
72331 Earle 3,517 ....K3
71701 East Camden 632 ....E6
72332 Edmondson 344 ....K3
72333 Elaine 991 ....J5
71730 El Dorado⊙ 25,270 ....E7
72727 Elkins 579 ....C1
72728 Elm Springs 781 ....B1
71740 Emerson 444 ....D7
71835 Emmet 475 ....D6
72046 England 3,081 ....G4
72047 Enola 186 ....F3
71640 Eudora 3,840 ....H7
72632 Eureka Springs⊙ 1,989 ....C1
72532 Evening Shade 397 ....G1
72633 Everton 134 ....E1
72730 Farmington 1,283 ....B1
72701 Fayetteville⊙ 36,608 ....B1
          Fayetteville-Springdale
          07 ....B1
†71747 Felsenthal 220 ....F7
72429 Fisher 302 ....J2
72634 Flippin 1,072 ....E1
71742 Fordyce⊙ 5,175 ....F6
71836 Foreman 1,377 ....B6
72335 Forrest City⊙ 13,803 ....J3
*72901 Fort Smith⊙ 71,626 ....B3
          Fort Smith‡ 203,269 ....B3
71837 Fouke 614 ....C7
71642 Fountain Hill 352 ....G7
†72016 Fourche 51 ....E4
72536 Franklin 253 ....G1
72017 Fredonia (Biscoe) 486 ....H4
71942 Friendship 163 ....E5
71838 Fulton 326 ....C6
72732 Garfield 187 ....C1
71839 Garland 660 ....C7
72052 Garner 216 ....G3
72635 Gassville 859 ....F1
72733 Gateway 75 ....B1
71840 Genoa 350 ....C7
72734 Gentry 1,468 ....A1
72636 Gilbert 43 ....E2
72055 Gillett 927 ....H5
71841 Gilham 252 ....B5
72339 Gilmore 503 ....K3
71943 Glenwood 1,402 ....C5
72340 Goodwin 225 ....J4
†72315 Gosnell 3,215 ....K2
71643 Gould 1,671 ....G6
71644 Grady 488 ....G5
71944 Grannis 349 ....B5
72838 Gravelly 300 ....C4
72736 Gravette 1,218 ....B1
72058 Greenbrier 1,423 ....F3
72638 Green Forest 1,609 ....D1
72737 Greenland 622 ....B1
72430 Greenway 317 ....K1
72936 Greenwood⊙ 3,317 ....B3
†72067 Greers Ferry 558 ....F2
72060 Griffithville 254 ....G3
72431 Grubbs 546 ....H2
72540 Guion 177 ....G2
†71923 Gum Springs 255 ....D5
71743 Gurdon 2,707 ....D6
72061 Guy 209 ....F3
72937 Hackett 505 ....B3
71638 Halley H6
71646 Hamburg⊙ 3,394 ....G7
71744 Hampton⊙ 1,627 ....F6
72542 Hardy 643 ....H1
72745 Harrell 302 ....F7
72432 Harrisburg⊙ 1,921 ....J2
72601 Harrison⊙ 9,567 ....D1
72938 Hartford 613 ....B3
72840 Hartman 517 ....C3
†72015 Haskell 1,074 ....E4
71945 Hatfield 410 ....B5
72842 Havana 352 ....D3
72341 Haynes 359 ....J4
72064 Hazen 1,636 ....G4
72543 Heber Springs⊙ 4,589 ....G2
72843 Hector 449 ....E3
72342 Helena⊙ 9,598 ....J4
72065 Hensley 500 ....F4
71647 Hermitage 378 ....F7
72347 Hickory Ridge 478 ....J3
72067 Higden 45 ....F2
72068 Higginson 333 ....G3
†72734 Highfill 92 ....B1
72738 Hindsville C1
72069 Holly Grove 754 ....H4
†72958 Hon 250 ....B4
71801 Hope⊙ 10,290 ....C6
71842 Horatio 989 ....B3
72512 Horseshoe Bend 1,909 ....G1
71901 Hot Springs National
          Park⊙ 35,781 ....D4
72070 Houston 183 ....E3

(continued on following page)

Agriculture, Industry and Resources

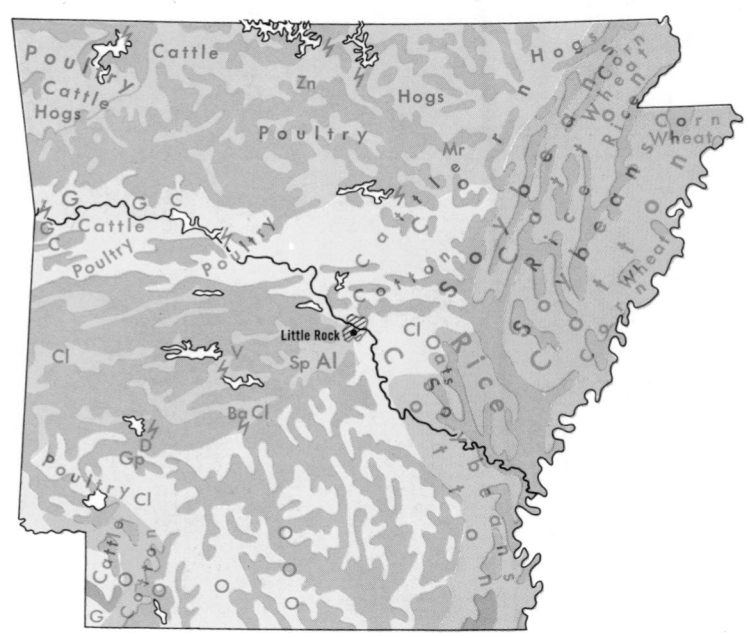

DOMINANT LAND USE

Fruit and Mixed Farming

Specialized Cotton

Cotton, General Farming

Rice, General Farming

General Farming, Livestock, Truck Farming, Cotton

Forests

Swampland, Limited Agriculture

MAJOR MINERAL OCCURRENCES

Al Bauxite
Ba Barite
C Coal
Cl Clay
D Diamonds
G Natural Gas

Gp Gypsum
Mr Marble
O Petroleum
Sp Soapstone
V Vanadium
Zn Zinc

⚡ Water Power   ▨ Major Industrial Areas

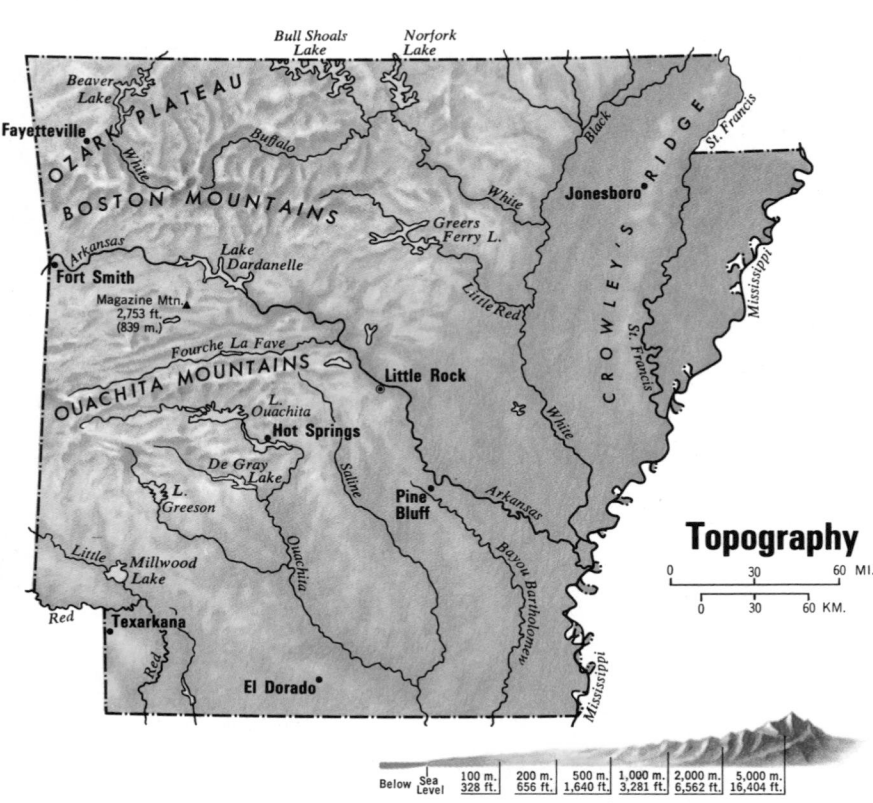

Topography

0 .... 30 .... 60 MI.

0 .... 30 .... 60 KM.

Below Sea Level | 100 m. 328 ft. | 200 m. 656 ft. | 500 m. 1,640 ft. | 1,000 m. 3,281 ft. | 2,000 m. 6,562 ft. | 5,000 m. 16,404 ft.

71764 Stephens 1,366 .... E7	72770 Tontitown 615 .... B1
72159 Steprock 600 .... G3	72167 Traskwood 459 .... E5
72469 Strawberry 280 .... H2	72472 Trumann 6,405 .... J2
71765 Strong 785 .... F7	72168 Tucker 375 .... G5
72160 Stuttgart⊙ 10,941 .... H4	72473 Tuckerman 2,078 .... H2
72865 Subiaco 744 .... C3	†72015 Tull 281 .... E5
72470 Success 223 .... J1	72169 Tupelo 248 .... H3
72579 Sulphur Rock 316 .... H2	72384 Turrell 1,041 .... K3
72768 Sulphur Springs 496 .... B1	72386 Tyronza 777 .... K3
72677 Summit 506 .... E1	72170 Ulm 201 .... H4
72471 Swifton 859 .... H2	72955 Uniontown 600 .... B2
71861 Taylor 657 .... D7	71768 Urbana 500 .... D1
75502 Texarkana⊙ 21,459 .... C7	72682 Valley Springs 190 .... D1
Texarkana‡ 127,019 .... C7	72956 Van Buren⊙ 12,020 .... C3
71766 Thornton 711 .... F6	71972 Vandervoort 98 .... B5
72166 Tichnor 350 .... H5	72370 Victoria 175 .... K2
71670 Tillar 280 .... H6	72173 Vilonia 736 .... F3
71767 Tinsman 112 .... F6	†72002 Vimy Ridge 600 .... F4
71851 Tollette 407 .... C6	72583 Viola 362 .... G1

72433 Hoxie 2,961 .... H1	72365 Marked Tree 3,201 .... K2	†71801 Patmos 88 .... C7
72348 Hughes 1,919 .... J4	72443 Marmaduke 1,168 .... K1	72123 Patterson 567 .... H3
72072 Humnoke 442 .... G4	72650 Marshall 1,595 .... E2	72453 Peach Orchard 243 .... J1
72073 Humphrey 872 .... G5	72366 Marvell 1,724 .... J4	71964 Pearcy 400 .... D5
72074 Hunter 170 .... H3	72106 Mayflower 1,381 .... F4	72751 Pea Ridge 1,488 .... B1
72940 Huntington 662 .... B3	72444 Maynard 381 .... J1	†72104 Perla 149 .... E5
72740 Huntsville⊙ 1,394 .... C1	71847 McCaskill 87 .... C6	72125 Perry 254 .... E3
71747 Huttig 976 .... F7	72101 McCrory 1,942 .... H3	71801 Perrytown 282 .... C6
72434 Imboden 661 .... H1	72441 McDougal 239 .... K1	72126 Perryville⊙ 1,058 .... E3
72075 Jacksonport 288 .... H2	71654 McGehee 5,671 .... H6	72454 Piggott⊙ 3,762 .... K1
72076 Jacksonville 27,589 .... F4	71752 McNeil 725 .... D7	*71601 Pine Bluff⊙ 56,636 .... F5
†72501 Jamestown G2	72102 McRae 641 .... G3	Pine Bluff‡ 90,718 .... F5
72641 Jasper⊙ 519 .... D1	72556 Melbourne⊙ 1,619 .... G1	†72847 Piney 2,283 .... D3
72079 Jefferson 250 .... F5	72367 Mellwood 250 .... H5	72857 Plainview 752 .... D4
71650 Jerome 54 .... G7	71953 Mena⊙ 5,154 .... B4	72568 Pleasant Plains 267 .... G2
72080 Jerusalem 300 .... E3	72107 Menifee 368 .... E3	72127 Plumerville 785 .... E3
71949 Jessieville 350 .... D4	72945 Midland 286 .... B3	72455 Pocahontas⊙ 5,995 .... H1
72741 Johnson 375 .... B1	71851 Mineral Springs 936 .... C6	72374 Poplar Grove 300 .... J4
72350 Joiner 725 .... K3	72445 Minturn 169 .... H2	72457 Portia 480 .... H1
72401 Jonesboro⊙ 31,530 .... J2	†71639 Mitchellville 618 .... H6	71663 Portland 701 .... H7
72081 Judsonia 2,025 .... G3	72447 Monette 1,165 .... K2	72858 Pottsville 564 .... D3
71749 Junction City 813 .... E7	72108 Monroe 250 .... H4	72458 Powhatan 49 .... H1
72351 Keiser 962 .... K2	71655 Monticello⊙ 8,259 .... G6	72128 Poyen 329 .... E5
72082 Kensett 1,751 .... G3	71658 Montrose 641 .... H7	72753 Prairie Grove 1,708 .... B2
72083 Keo 208 .... G4	72368 Moro 327 .... H4	72129 Prattsville 317 .... F5
†72956 Kibler 798 .... B3	72110 Morrilton⊙ 7,355 .... E3	71857 Prescott⊙ 4,103 .... D6
71652 Kingsland 320 .... F6	71659 Moscow 325 .... G5	72672 Pyatt 217 .... E1
71950 Kirby 800 .... C5	72946 Mountainburg 595 .... B2	72131 Quitman 556 .... F3
72435 Knobel 503 .... J1	72653 Mountain Home⊙ 8,066 .... F1	72951 Ratcliff 197 .... C3
72845 Knoxville 264 .... D3	71956 Mountain Pine 1,068 .... D4	†72333 Ratio 250 .... J5
72436 Lafe 215 .... J1	72560 Mountain View⊙ 2,147 .... F2	72459 Ravenden 338 .... H1
72437 Lake City⊙ 1,842 .... K2	71758 Mount Holly 250 .... E7	72460 Ravenden Springs 230 .... H1
72642 Lakeview 512 .... E1	71957 Mount Ida⊙ 1,023 .... C4	71726 Reader 127 .... D6
†72389 Lake View 609 .... J5	72561 Mount Pleasant 438 .... G2	72461 Rector 2,336 .... K1
71653 Lake Village⊙ 3,088 .... H7	72111 Mount Vernon 157 .... F3	72132 Redfield 745 .... F5
72846 Lamar 708 .... D3	72947 Mulberry 1,444 .... B2	71670 Reed 395 .... H6
72941 Lavaca 1,092 .... B3	71958 Murfreesboro⊙ 1,883 .... C5	72462 Reyno 521 .... J1
71750 Lawson 250 .... F7	71852 Nashville⊙ 4,554 .... C6	71665 Rison⊙ 1,325 .... F6
72438 Leachville 1,882 .... K2	72562 Newark 1,128 .... H2	†72104 Rockport 231 .... E5
72644 Lead Hill 247 .... D1	72851 New Blaine 200 .... D3	72134 Roe 136 .... H4
72084 Leola 481 .... E5	71959 Newhope 300 .... C5	72756 Rogers 17,429 .... B1
72354 Lepanto 1,964 .... K2	72112 Newport⊙ 8,339 .... H2	†72355 Rondo 330 .... J4
72645 Leslie 501 .... E2	72461 Nimmons 112 .... K1	72137 Rose Bud 202 .... F3
72085 Letona 231 .... G3	†71601 Noble Lake 250 .... G5	71858 Rosston 274 .... D6
71845 Lewisville⊙ 1,476 .... C7	72658 Norfork 399 .... F1	72952 Rudy 79 .... B2
72355 Lexa 500 .... J4	71960 Norman 539 .... C4	72139 Russell 232 .... G3
72744 Lincoln 1,422 .... B2	71759 Norphlet 756 .... E7	72801 Russellville⊙ 14,031 .... D3
†72712 Little Flock 663 .... B1	†72801 Norristown 625 .... D3	72140 Saint Charles 199 .... H5
*72201 Little Rock	71635 North Crossett 3,513 .... G7	72464 Saint Francis 266 .... K1
(cap.)⊙ 158,461 .... F4	*72114 North Little Rock 64,288 .... F4	72760 Saint Paul 198 .... C2
Little Rock-North Little	72660 Oak Grove 265 .... C1	72576 Salem⊙ 1,424 .... G1
Rock‡ 393,494 .... F4	†71801 Oakhaven 72 .... C6	†72658 Salesville 406 .... F1
71846 Lockesburg 616 .... B6	71961 Oden 184 .... C4	72863 Scranton 244 .... C3
72847 London 859 .... D3	71853 Ogden 334 .... B6	72143 Searcy⊙ 13,612 .... G3
72086 Lonoke⊙ 4,128 .... G4	72564 Oil Trough 280 .... G2	72465 Sedgwick 205 .... J2
72087 Lonsdale 117 .... E4	72449 O'Kean 291 .... J1	†72103 Shannon Hills 1,656 .... F4
71751 Louann 282 .... E7	71962 Okolona 200 .... D5	72150 Sheridan⊙ 3,042 .... F5
72745 Lowell 1,078 .... B1	72853 Ola 1,121 .... D4	72152 Sherrill 161 .... F5
†72856 Lurton 38 .... D2	72662 Omaha 191 .... D1	72116 Sherwood 10,406 .... F4
72358 Luxora 1,739 .... K2	†72110 Oppelo 486 .... E3	72153 Shirley 354 .... F2
72440 Lynn 345 .... H2	72370 Osceola⊙ 8,881 .... K2	72577 Sidney 270 .... G1
72359 Madison 1,238 .... J4	72565 Oxford 520 .... G1	72761 Siloam Springs 7,940 .... B1
72943 Magazine 799 .... C3	71855 Ozan 111 .... C6	71762 Smackover 2,453 .... E7
72553 Magness 196 .... H2	72949 Ozark⊙ 3,597 .... C3	72466 Smithville 113 .... H1
71753 Magnolia⊙ 11,909 .... D7	72372 Palestine 976 .... J4	†71658 Snyder 700 .... G7
72104 Malvern⊙ 10,163 .... E5	72121 Pangburn 673 .... G3	71763 Sparkman 622 .... E6
72554 Mammoth Spring 1,158 .... G1	72450 Paragould⊙ 15,248 .... J1	72764 Springdale 23,458 .... B1
72442 Manila 2,553 .... K2	72855 Paris⊙ 3,991 .... C3	Springdale-Fayetteville‡
72944 Mansfield 1,000 .... B3	71661 Parkdale 471 .... H7	177,850 .... B1
72360 Marianna⊙ 6,220 .... J4	72373 Parkin 2,035 .... J3	71860 Stamps 2,859 .... D7
†72395 Marie 287 .... K2	72950 Parks 600 .... B4	71667 Star City⊙ 2,066 .... G6
72364 Marion⊙ 2,996 .... K3		

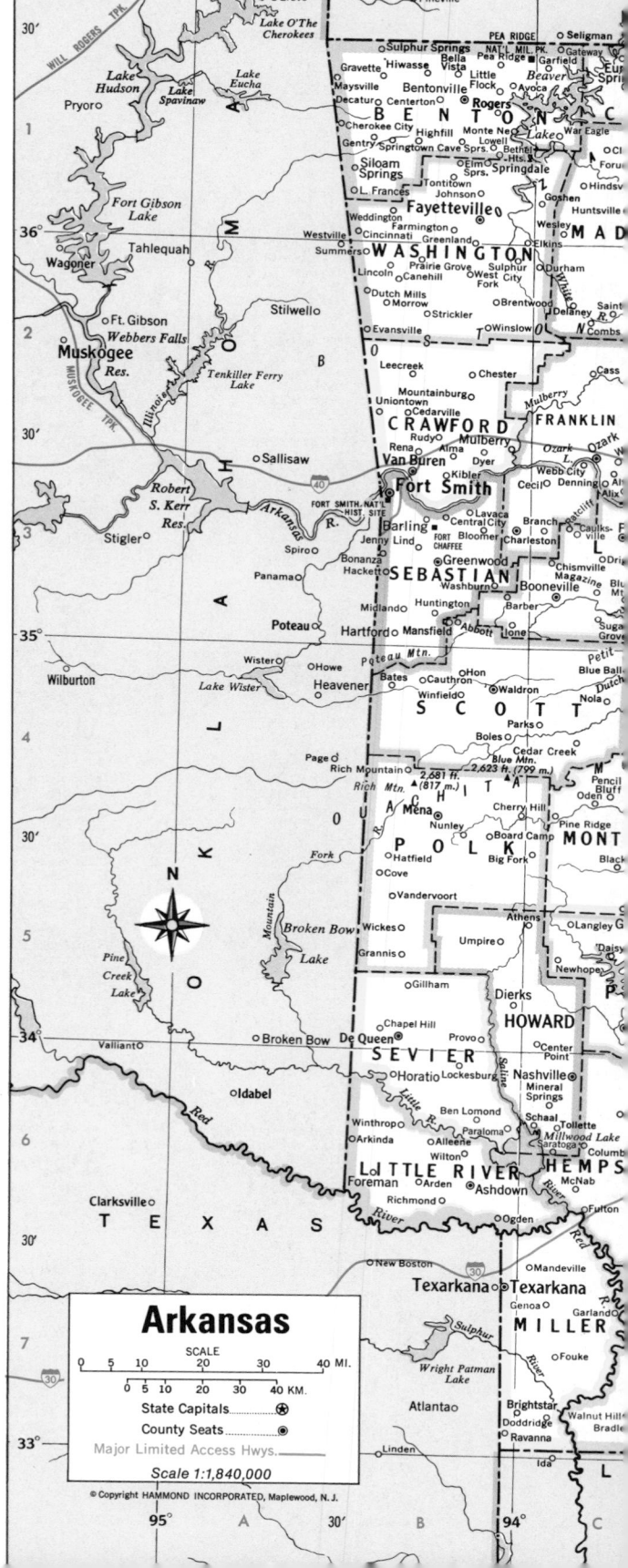

Arkansas

SCALE

0 5 10 .... 20 .... 30 .... 40 MI.

0 5 10 .... 20 .... 30 .... 40 KM.

State Capitals .... ✪

County Seats .... ⊙

Major Limited Access Hwys. _____

Scale 1:1,840,000

© Copyright HAMMOND INCORPORATED, Maplewood, N.J.

California

SCALE

State Capitals .... ⊛
County Seats .... ◉
Canals
Major Limited Access Hwys.

Scale 1 : 4,400,000

San Francisco and Vicinity

Sacramento and Vicinity

Los Angeles and Vicinity

© Copyright HAMMOND INCORPORATED, Maplewood, N.J.

AREA 158,706 sq. mi. (411,049 sq. km.)
POPULATION 23,667,565
CAPITAL Sacramento
LARGEST CITY Los Angeles
HIGHEST POINT Mt. Whitney 14,494 ft. (4418 m.)
SETTLED IN 1769
ADMITTED TO UNION September 9, 1850
POPULAR NAME Golden State
STATE FLOWER Golden Poppy
STATE BIRD California Valley Quail

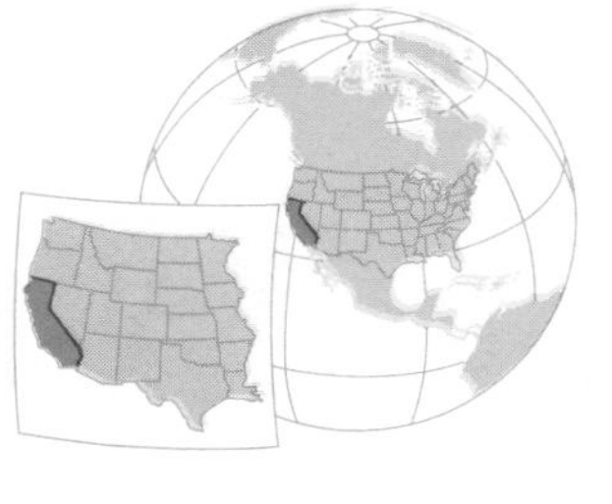

COUNTIES

Alameda 1,105,379 D6
Alpine 1,097 F5
Amador 19,314 E5
Butte 143,851 D4
Calaveras 20,710 E5
Colusa 12,791 C4
Contra Costa 656,380 D6
Del Norte 18,217 B2
El Dorado 85,812 E5
Fresno 514,229 E7
Glenn 21,350 C4
Humboldt 108,514 B3
Imperial 92,110 K10
Inyo 17,895 H7
Kern 403,089 G8
Kings 73,738 G8
Lake 36,366 C4
Lassen 21,661 E3
Los Angeles 7,477,503 G9
Madera 63,116 F6
Marin 222,592 C5
Mariposa 11,108 E6
Mendocino 66,738 B4
Merced 134,558 E6
Modoc 8,610 E2
Mono 8,577 F5
Monterey 290,444 D7
Napa 99,199 C5
Nevada 51,645 E4
Orange 1,932,709 H10
Placer 117,247 E4
Plumas 17,340 E4
Riverside 663,199 J10
Sacramento 783,381 D5
San Benito 25,005 D7
San Bernardino 895,016 J9
San Diego 1,861,846 J10
San Francisco (city county) 678,974 J2
San Joaquin 347,342 D6
San Luis Obispo 155,435 E8
San Mateo 587,329 J3
Santa Barbara 298,694 E9
Santa Clara 1,295,071 D6
Santa Cruz 188,141 C6
Shasta 115,715 C3
Sierra 3,073 E4
Siskiyou 39,732 C2
Solano 235,203 D5
Sonoma 299,681 C5
Stanislaus 265,900 D6
Sutter 52,246 D4
Tehama 38,888 C3
Trinity 11,858 B3
Tulare 245,738 G7
Tuolumne 33,928 F5
Ventura 529,174 F9
Yolo 113,374 D5
Yuba 49,733 D4

CITIES and TOWNS

Zip	Name/Pop.	Key
94501	Alameda 63,852	J2
94507	Alamo 8,505	K2
94706	Albany 15,130	J2
*91801	Alhambra 64,615	C10
92001	Alpine 5,368	J11
91001	Altadena 40,983	C10
96101	Alturas⊙ 3,025	E2
†95116	Alum Rock 16,890	L3
*92801	Anaheim 219,494	D11
	Anaheim-Santa Ana-Garden Grove‡ 1,931,570	D11
96007	Anderson 7,381	C3
95222	Angels Camp 2,302	E5
94508	Angwin 3,526	C5
94509	Antioch 42,683	L1
92307	Apple Valley 14,305	H9
95003	Aptos 7,039	K4
91006	Arcadia 45,994	C10
95521	Arcata 12,850	A3
95825	Arden-Arcade 87,570	B8
93420	Arroyo Grande 11,290	E8
90701	Artesia 14,301	C11
93203	Arvin 6,863	G8
†94577	Ashland 13,983	K2
95413	Asti 75	C5
93422	Atascadero 16,232	E8
94025	Atherton 7,797	K3
95301	Atwater 17,530	E6
95603	Auburn⊙ 7,540	C8
90704	Avalon 2,022	G10
93204	Avenal 4,137	E8
91702	Azusa 29,380	D10
*93301	Bakersfield⊙ 105,735	G8
	Bakersfield‡ 403,089	G8
91706	Baldwin Park 50,554	D10
92220	Banning 14,020	J10
92311	Barstow 17,690	H9
†93402	Baywood Park-Los Osos 10,933	E8
92223	Beaumont 6,818	J10
90201	Bell 25,450	C11
90706	Bellflower 53,441	C11
90201	Bell Gardens 34,117	C11
94002	Belmont 24,505	J3
94510	Benicia 15,376	K1
95005	Ben Lomond 7,238	K4
*94701	Berkeley 103,328	J2
*90210	Beverly Hills 32,367	B10
92315	Big Bear Lake	J9
93920	Big Sur 500	D7
93514	Bishop 3,333	G6
92316	Bloomington 18,888	E10
92225	Blythe 6,805	L10
94923	Bodega Bay 800	B5
93516	Boron 2,040	H8
92004	Borrego Springs 1,405	J10
95006	Boulder Creek 5,662	J4
92227	Brawley 14,946	K11
92621	Brea 27,913	D11
94513	Brentwood 4,434	L2
93517	Bridgeport⊙ 525	F5
94005	Brisbane 2,969	J2
95605	Broderick-Bryte 10,194	B8
*90622	Buena Park 64,165	D11
*91501	Burbank 84,625	C10
94010	Burlingame 26,173	J2
96013	Burney 3,187	D3
92231	Calexico 14,412	K11
93505	California City 2,743	H8
94515	Calistoga 3,879	C5
93745	Calwa 6,640	F7
93010	Camarillo 37,797	F9
95008	Campbell 26,910	K3
*91303	Canoga Park	B10
92624	Capistrano Beach 6,168	H10
95010	Capitola 9,095	K4
92007	Cardiff-by-the-Sea 10,054	H10
92008	Carlsbad 35,490	H10
93923	Carmel 4,707	D7
93924	Carmel Valley 4,013	D7
95608	Carmichael 43,108	C8
93013	Carpinteria 10,835	F9
90745	Carson 81,221	C11
94546	Castro Valley 44,011	K2
95012	Castroville 4,396	D7
92234	Cathedral City 4,130	J10
96019	Central Valley 3,424	C3
95307	Ceres 13,281	D6
†90701	Cerritos 53,020	C11
†94541	Cherryland 9,425	K2
95926	Chico 26,603	D4
	Chico‡ 143,851	D4
†93555	China Lake 4,275	H8
95309	Chinese Camp 150	E6
91710	Chino 40,165	D10
93610	Chowchilla 5,122	E6
*92010	Chula Vista 83,927	J11
95610	Citrus Heights 85,911	C8
91711	Claremont 30,950	D10
95425	Cloverdale 3,989	B5
93612	Clovis 33,021	F7
92236	Coachella 9,129	J10
93210	Coalinga 6,593	E7
95713	Colfax 981	E4
92324	Colton 15,201	E10
95932	Colusa⊙ 4,075	C4
90040	Commerce 10,509	C10
*90220	Compton 81,286	C11
*94520	Concord 103,255	K1
93212	Corcoran 6,454	F7
96021	Corning 4,745	C4
91720	Corona 37,791	E11
92118	Coronado 18,790	H11
94925	Corte Madera 8,074	J2
*92626	Costa Mesa 82,562	D11
94928	Cotati 3,346	C5
*91722	Covina 33,751	D10
95531	Crescent City⊙ 3,075	A2
92325	Crestline 6,715	H9
90201	Cudahy 17,984	C11
90230	Culver City 38,139	B10
95014	Cupertino 34,265	K3
93615	Cutler 3,149	F7
90630	Cypress 40,391	D11
*94014	Daly City 78,519	H2
92629	Dana Point 10,602	H10
94526	Danville 26,446	K2
95616	Davis 36,640	B8
93215	Delano 16,491	F8
95315	Delhi 2,832	E6
92014	Del Mar 5,017	H11
92240	Desert Hot Springs 5,941	J9
93618	Dinuba 9,907	F7
95620	Dixon 7,541	B9
93620	Dos Palos 3,121	E6
*90240	Downey 82,602	C11
95936	Downieville⊙ 500	E4
91010	Duarte 16,766	D10
94566	Dublin 13,496	K2
93219	Earlimart 4,578	F8
90022	East Los Angeles 100,017	C10
*92020	El Cajon 73,892	J11
92243	El Centro⊙ 23,996	K11
94530	El Cerrito 22,731	J2
95630	El Dorado Hills 3,453	C8
94018	El Granada 3,582	H3
95624	Elk Grove 10,959	B9
*91731	El Monte 79,494	D10
†93030	El Rio 5,674	F9
90245	El Segundo 13,752	B11
92630	El Toro 38,153	E11
94608	Emeryville 3,714	J2
92024	Encinitas 10,796	H10
91316	Encino	B10
95320	Escalon 3,127	E6
*92025	Escondido 64,355	J10
95501	Eureka⊙ 24,153	A3
93221	Exeter 5,606	F7
94930	Fairfax 7,391	H1
94533	Fairfield⊙ 58,099	K1
95628	Fair Oaks 22,602	C8
92028	Fallbrook 14,041	H10
93223	Farmersville 5,544	F7
95018	Felton 4,564	K4
93015	Fillmore 9,602	G9
93622	Firebaugh 3,740	E7
95828	Florin 16,523	B8
95630	Folsom 11,003	C8
92335	Fontana 37,107	E10
†93268	Ford City 3,392	F8
95437	Fort Bragg 5,019	B4
†95421	Fort Ross 30	B5
95540	Fortuna 7,591	A3
94404	Foster City 23,287	J2
92708	Fountain Valley 55,080	D11
95019	Freedom 6,416	L4
*94536	Fremont 131,945	K3
*93706	Fresno⊙ 217,289	F7
	Fresno‡ 515,013	F7
*92631	Fullerton 102,034	D11
95632	Galt 5,514	C9
*90747	Gardena 45,165	C11
*92640	Garden Grove 123,307	D11
95020	Gilroy 21,641	D6
92509	Glen Avon Heights 8,444	E10
*91201	Glendale 139,060	C10
91740	Glendora 38,500	D10
93926	Gonzales 2,891	D7
91344	Granada Hills	B10
92324	Grand Terrace 8,498	E10
95945	Grass Valley 6,697	D4
93308	Greenacres 5,381	F8
93927	Greenfield 4,181	D7
95948	Gridley 3,982	D4
93433	Grover City 8,827	E8
93434	Guadalupe 3,629	E9
95322	Gustine 3,142	D6
94019	Half Moon Bay 7,282	H3
93230	Hanford⊙ 20,958	F7
90250	Hawthorne 56,447	C11
*94541	Hayward 94,342	K2
95448	Healdsburg 7,217	B5
92343	Hemet 22,454	H10
94547	Hercules 5,963	J1
90254	Hermosa Beach 18,070	B11
92345	Hesperia 13,540	H9
92346	Highland 10,908	H9
94010	Hillsborough 10,372	J2
95023	Hollister⊙ 11,488	D7
90028	Hollywood	C10
92250	Holtville 4,399	K11
†91720	Home Gardens 5,783	E11
95326	Hughson 2,943	E6
*92646	Huntington Beach 170,505	C11
90255	Huntington Park 46,223	C11
92251	Imperial 3,451	K11
92032	Imperial Beach 22,689	H11
93526	Independence⊙ 748	H7
92201	Indio 21,611	J10
*90301	Inglewood 94,245	B11
92713	Irvine 62,134	D11
95642	Jackson⊙ 2,331	C9
†94701	Kensington 5,342	J2
93600	Kerman 4,002	E7
93930	King City 5,495	D7
93631	Kingsburg 5,115	F7
91011	La Cañada 20,153	C10
91214	La Crescenta-Montrose 16,531	C10
94549	Lafayette 20,879	K2
*92651	Laguna Beach 17,901	G10
92653	Laguna Hills 33,600	D11
92677	Laguna Niguel 12,237	H10
90631	La Habra 45,232	D11
92037	La Jolla	H11
92352	Lake Arrowhead 6,272	H9
92330	Lake Elsinore 5,982	F11
93240	Lake Isabella 3,428	G8
95453	Lakeport⊙ 3,675	C4
*90712	Lakewood 74,654	C11
92041	La Mesa 50,308	H11
90638	La Mirada 40,986	D11
93241	Lamont 9,616	G8
93534	Lancaster 48,027	G9
*91744	La Puente 30,882	D10
94939	Larkspur 11,064	H1
95330	Lathrop 3,717	D6
91750	La Verne 23,508	D10
90260	Lawndale 23,460	B11
92045	Lemon Grove 20,780	J11
93245	Lemoore 8,832	F7
†92311	Lenwood 2,974	H9
92024	Leucadia 9,478	H10
95648	Lincoln 4,132	B8
†95901	Linda 10,225	D4
93247	Lindsay 6,924	F7
95953	Live Oak 3,103	D4
†95073	Live Oak 11,482	K4
94550	Livermore 48,349	L2
95334	Livingston 5,326	E6
95240	Lodi 35,221	C9
92354	Loma Linda 10,694	F10
90717	Lomita 18,807	C11
93436	Lompoc 26,267	E9
*90801	Long Beach 361,334	C11
90720	Los Alamitos 11,529	D11
94022	Los Altos 25,769	K3
94022	Los Altos Hills 7,421	J3
*90001	Los Angeles⊙ 2,966,850	C10
	Los Angeles-Long Beach‡ 7,477,657	C10
93635	Los Banos 10,341	E6
95030	Los Gatos 26,906	K4
†93402	Los Osos-Baywood Park 10,933	E8
90262	Lynwood 48,548	C11
93637	Madera⊙ 21,732	E7
90265	Malibu	B10
93546	Mammoth Lakes 3,929	G6
90266	Manhattan Beach 31,542	B11
95336	Manteca 24,925	D6
93933	Marina 20,647	D7
95338	Mariposa⊙ 1,150	F6
94553	Martinez⊙ 22,582	K1
95901	Marysville⊙ 9,898	D4
90201	Maywood 21,810	C10
93250	McFarland 5,151	F8
93023	Meiners Oaks-Mira Monte 9,512	F9
93640	Mendota 5,038	E7
94025	Menlo Park 26,369	J3
95340	Merced⊙ 36,499	E6
94030	Millbrae 20,058	J2
94941	Mill Valley 12,967	H2
95035	Milpitas 37,820	L3
91752	Mira Loma 8,707	E10
92691	Mission Viejo 50,666	D11
*95350	Modesto⊙ 106,602	D6
	Modesto‡ 265,902	D6
93501	Mojave 2,886	G8
91016	Monrovia 30,531	D10
91763	Montclair 22,628	D10
90640	Montebello 52,929	C10
93940	Monterey 27,558	D7
91754	Monterey Park 54,338	C10
95030	Monte Sereno 3,434	K4
91214	Montrose-La Crescenta 16,531	C10
93021	Moorpark 4,030	G9
94556	Moraga 15,014	K2
95037	Morgan Hill 17,060	L4
93442	Morro Bay 9,064	D8
*94042	Mountain View 58,655	K3
96067	Mount Shasta 2,837	C5
92405	Muscoy 6,188	E10
94558	Napa⊙ 50,879	C5
92050	National City 48,772	J11
92363	Needles 4,120	L9
95959	Nevada City⊙ 2,431	D4
94560	Newark 32,126	K3
91321	Newhall 12,029	G9
95360	Newman 2,785	D6
*92660	Newport Beach 62,556	D11
93444	Nipomo 5,247	E8
91760	Norco 21,126	E11
95660	North Highlands 37,825	B8
*91601	North Hollywood	B10
90650	Norwalk 85,286	C11
94947	Novato 43,916	H1
95361	Oakdale 8,474	E6
*94601	Oakland⊙ 339,337	J2
93022	Oak View 4,671	F9
93445	Oceano 4,478	E8
92054	Oceanside 76,698	H10
93308	Oildale 23,382	F8
93023	Ojai 6,816	F9
*91761	Ontario 88,820	D10
†95060	Opal Cliffs 5,041	K4
*92666	Orange 91,450	D11
93646	Orange Cove 4,026	F7
94563	Orinda 16,825	J2
95963	Orland 4,031	C4
93647	Orosi 4,076	F7
95965	Oroville⊙ 8,683	D4
93030	Oxnard 108,195	F9
	Oxnard-Simi Valley-Ventura‡ 529,899	F9
94553	Pacheco-Vine Hill 6,129	K1
94044	Pacifica 36,866	H2
93950	Pacific Grove 15,755	C7
93550	Palmdale 12,277	G9
92260	Palm Desert 11,801	J10
92262	Palm Springs 32,366	J10
*94301	Palo Alto 55,225	K3
90274	Palos Verdes Estates 14,376	B11
95969	Paradise 22,571	D4
90723	Paramount 36,407	C11
93648	Parlier 2,902	F7
*91101	Pasadena 118,072	C10
93446	Paso Robles 9,163	E8
95363	Patterson 3,908	D6
93953	Pebble Beach	C7
92370	Perris 6,827	F11
94952	Petaluma 33,834	H1
90660	Pico Rivera 53,387	C10
94611	Piedmont 10,498	J2
94564	Pinole 14,253	J1
93449	Pismo Beach 5,364	E8
94565	Pittsburg 33,034	L1
92670	Placentia 35,041	D11
95667	Placerville⊙ 6,739	C8
94523	Pleasant Hill 25,124	K2
94566	Pleasanton 35,160	L2
*91766	Pomona 92,742	D10
93257	Porterville 19,707	G7
93041	Port Hueneme 17,803	F9
94025	Portola Valley 3,939	J3
92064	Poway 32,263	J11
93534	Quartz Hill 7,421	G9
95971	Quincy⊙ 4,451	E4
92065	Ramona 8,173	J10
95670	Rancho Cordova 42,881	C8
91730	Rancho Cucamonga 55,250	E10
92270	Rancho Mirage 6,281	J10
90274	Rancho Palos Verdes 36,577	B11
92067	Rancho Santa Fe 4,014	H10
96080	Red Bluff⊙ 9,490	C3
96001	Redding⊙ 41,995	C3
	Redding○	80
92373	Redlands 43,619	H9
*90277	Redondo Beach 57,102	B11
*94061	Redwood City⊙ 54,951	J3
93654	Reedley 11,071	F7
92376	Rialto 37,474	E10
*94801	Richmond 74,676	J1
93555	Ridgecrest 15,929	H8
95562	Rio Dell 2,687	A3
95673	Rio Linda 7,359	B8
94571	Rio Vista 3,142	L1
95366	Ripon 3,509	D6
95367	Riverbank 5,695	E6
*92501	Riverside⊙ 170,591	E11
	Riverside-San Bernardino-Ontario‡ 1,557,080	E11
95677	Rocklin 7,344	B8
94572	Rodeo 8,286	J1
94928	Rohnert Park 22,965	C5
90274	Rolling Hills 2,049	B11
90274	Rolling Hills Estates 7,701	B11
91770	Rosemead 42,604	C10
95678	Roseville 24,347	B8
94957	Ross 2,801	H1
92509	Rubidoux 17,048	E10

(continued on following page)

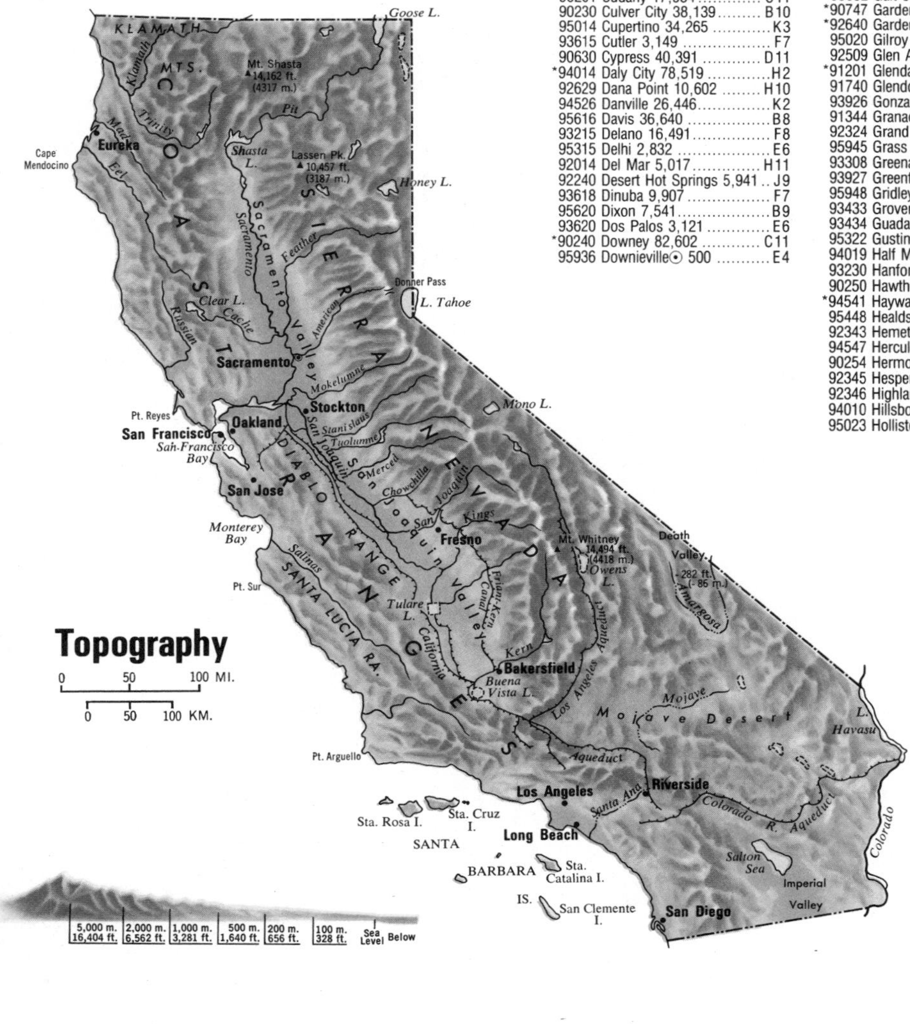

KLAMATH
MTS.
Goose L.
Mt. Shasta 14,162 ft. (4317 m.)
Pit
Trinity
Klamath
Eureka
Mad
Eel
Cape Mendocino
Shasta L.
Lassen Pk. 10,457 ft. (3187 m.)
Honey L.
COAST
Sacramento
Feather
SIERRA
Donner Pass
L. Tahoe
Clear L.
Cache
Russian
American
Sacramento
Pt. Reyes
San Francisco
Oakland
Stockton
San Francisco Bay
Mokelumne
Stanislaus
Tuolumne
Mono L.
San Jose
DIABLO
Merced
Chowchilla
San Joaquin
NEVADA
Monterey Bay
Salinas
Fresno
Kings
RANGE
Pt. Sur
SANTA LUCIA RA.
Mt. Whitney 14,494 ft. (4418 m.)
Owens L.
Death Valley
-282 ft. (-86 m.)
Amargosa
Tulare L.
California Aqueduct
Kern
Bakersfield
Buena Vista L.
Los Angeles Aqueduct
Mojave
Mojave Desert
L. Havasu
Pt. Arguello
Aqueduct
Los Angeles
Riverside
Santa Ana
Colorado R. Aqueduct
Colorado
Sta. Rosa I.
Sta. Cruz I.
Long Beach
SANTA BARBARA IS.
Sta. Catalina I.
San Clemente I.
Salton Sea
Imperial Valley
San Diego
Topography
0 50 100 MI.
0 50 100 KM.
5,000 m. 16,404 ft.
2,000 m. 6,562 ft.
1,000 m. 3,281 ft.
500 m. 1,640 ft.
200 m. 656 ft.
100 m. 328 ft.
Sea Level
Below

Agriculture, Industry and Resources

DOMINANT LAND USE

Wheat, Small Grains

Specialized Dairy

Fruit and Mixed Farming

Fruit, Truck and Mixed Farming

General Farming, Livestock, Special Crops

Cotton, Alfalfa

Potatoes, General Farming

Range Livestock

Forests

Urban Areas

Nonagricultural Land

MAJOR MINERAL OCCURRENCES

Ab	Asbestos	Lt	Lithium
Ag	Silver	Mg	Magnesium
Au	Gold	Mo	Molybdenum
Bx	Borax	Mr	Marble
Cl	Clay	Na	Salt
Cu	Copper	O	Petroleum
Fe	Iron Ore	Pb	Lead
G	Natural Gas	Pt	Platinum
Gp	Gypsum	Tc	Talc
Hg	Mercury	W	Tungsten
K	Potash	Zn	Zinc

⚡ Water Power

Major Industrial Areas

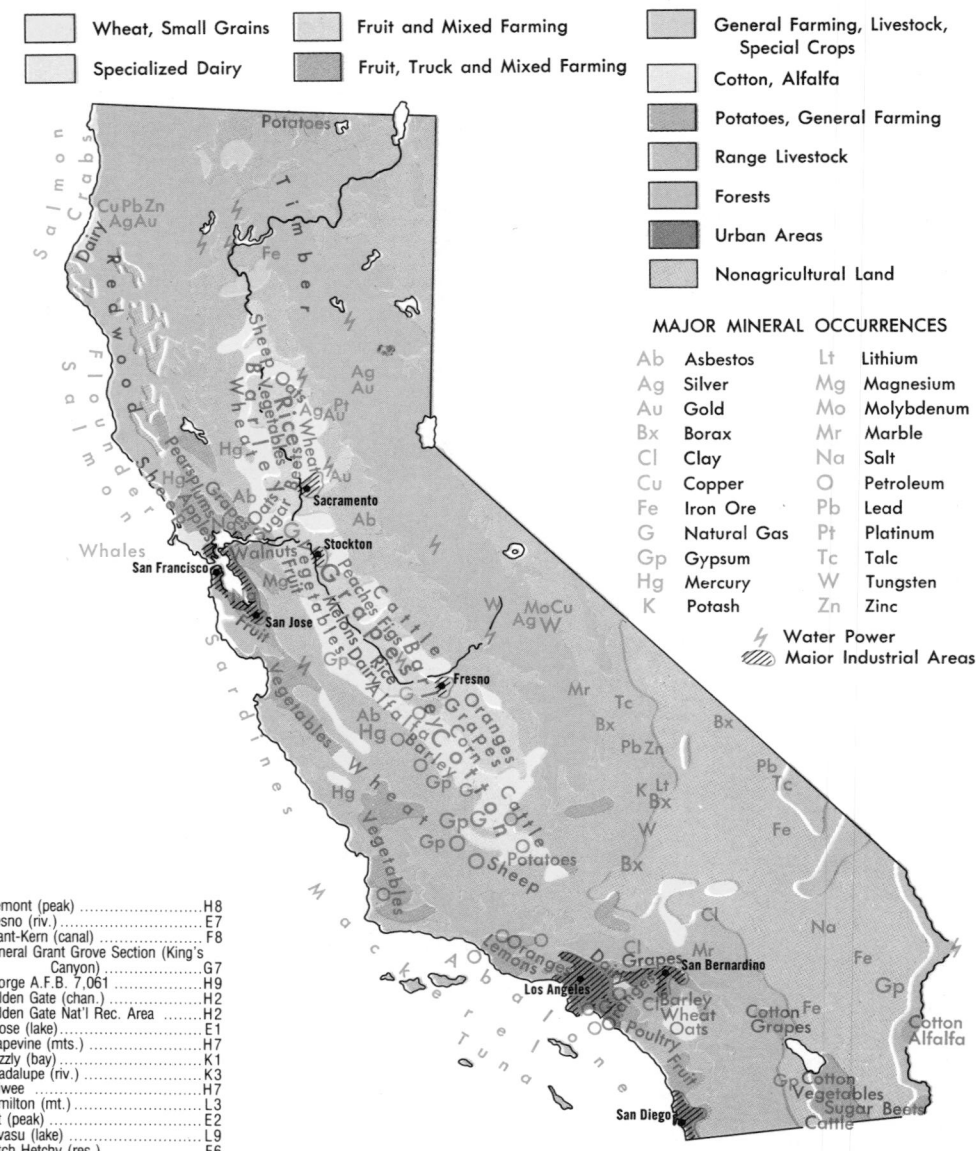

AREA 104,091 sq. mi. (269,596 sq. km.)
POPULATION 2,889,735
CAPITAL Denver
LARGEST CITY Denver
HIGHEST POINT Mt. Elbert 14,433 ft. (4399 m.)
SETTLED IN 1858
ADMITTED TO UNION August 1, 1876
POPULAR NAME Centennial State
STATE FLOWER Rocky Mountain Columbine
STATE BIRD Lark Bunting

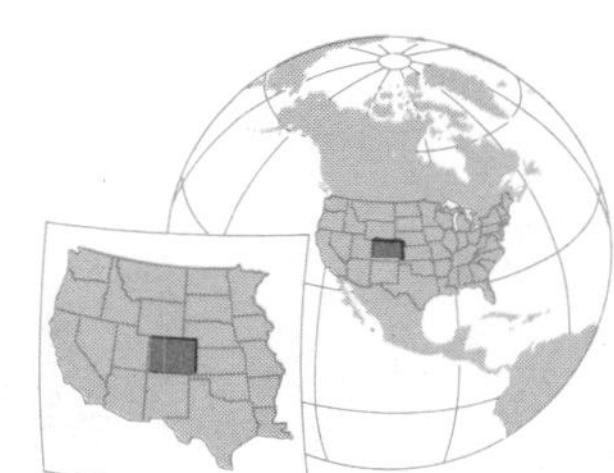

COUNTIES

Adams 245,944 .... L3
Alamosa 11,799 .... H7
Arapahoe 293,621 .... L3
Archuleta 3,664 .... E8
Baca 5,419 .... O8
Bent 5,945 .... N7
Boulder 189,625 .... J2
Chaffee 13,227 .... G5
Cheyenne 2,153 .... O5
Clear Creek 7,308 .... H3
Conejos 7,794 .... G8
Costilla 3,071 .... J8
Crowley 2,988 .... M6
Custer 1,528 .... J6
Delta 21,225 .... D5
Denver 492,365 .... K3
Dolores 1,658 .... C7
Douglas 25,153 .... K4
Eagle 13,320 .... F3
Elbert 6,850 .... L4
El Paso 309,424 .... K5
Fremont 28,676 .... J5
Garfield 22,514 .... C3
Gilpin 2,441 .... H3
Grand 7,475 .... G2
Gunnison 10,689 .... E5
Hinsdale 408 .... E7
Huerfano 6,440 .... K7
Jackson 1,863 .... G1
Jefferson 371,741 .... J3
Kiowa 1,936 .... O6
Kit Carson 7,599 .... O4
Lake 8,830 .... G4
La Plata 27,195 .... D8
Larimer 149,184 .... H1
Las Animas 14,897 .... L8
Lincoln 4,663 .... M5
Logan 19,800 .... N1
Mesa 81,530 .... B5
Mineral 804 .... F7
Moffat 13,133 .... C1
Montezuma 16,510 .... B8
Montrose 24,352 .... C6
Morgan 22,513 .... M2
Otero 22,567 .... M7
Ouray 1,925 .... D6
Park 5,333 .... H4
Phillips 4,542 .... P1
Pitkin 10,338 .... F4
Prowers 13,070 .... P7
Pueblo 125,972 .... K6
Rio Blanco 6,255 .... C3
Rio Grande 10,511 .... G7
Routt 13,404 .... E1
Saguache 3,935 .... G6
San Juan 833 .... D7
San Miguel 3,192 .... C6
Sedgwick 3,266 .... P1
Summit 8,848 .... G3
Teller 8,034 .... J5
Washington 5,304 .... N3
Weld 123,438 .... L1
Washington 5,304 .... N3
Weld 123,438 .... L1
Yuma 9,682 .... P2

CITIES and TOWNS

Zip *Name/Pop.* *Key*

80101 Agate 90 .... M4
81020 Aguilar 624 .... K8
80720 Akron⊙ 1,716 .... N2
81101 Alamosa⊙ 6,830 .... H8
80510 Allenspark 200 .... J2
80420 Alma 132 .... G4
81210 Almont 135 .... F5
80721 Amherst 85 .... P1
80801 Anton 55 .... N3
81120 Antonito 1,103 .... H8
80802 Arapahoe 300 .... P5
81021 Arlington 37 .... N6
80804 Arriba 236 .... N4
†81323 Arriola 56 .... B8
*80001 Arvada 84,576 .... J3
81611 Aspen⊙ 3,678 .... F4
80722 Atwood 100 .... N1
80610 Ault 1,056 .... K1
*80010 Aurora 158,588 .... K3
81410 Austin D5
81620 Avon 640 .... F3
81022 Avondale 750 .... L6
80421 Bailey 150 .... H4
†80624 Barnesville 20 .... L2
81621 Basalt 529 .... E4
81122 Bayfield 724 .... D8
81411 Bedrock 45 .... B6
†80758 Beecher Island 5 .... P3
80512 Bellvue 250 .... J1
80102 Bennett 942 .... L3
80513 Berthoud 2,362 .... J2
†80438 Berthoud Pass 40 .... H3
80805 Bethune 149 .... P4
81023 Beulah 650 .... K6
80908 Black Forest 3,372 .... K4
80422 Black Hawk 232 .... J3
81123 Blanca 252 .... H8
†80424 Blue River 230 .... G4
†81155 Bonanza 8 .... G6
81024 Boncarbo 200 .... K8
80423 Bond 65 .... F3
81025 Boone 431 .... L6
*80301 Boulder⊙ 76,685 .... J2
†81428 Bowie 18 .... D5
80821 Boyero 12 .... N5
81026 Brandon 30 .... P6
81027 Branson 73 .... M8
80424 Breckenridge⊙ 818 .... G4
80611 Briggsdale 85 .... L1
80601 Brighton⊙ 12,773 .... K3
81028 Bristol 200 .... P6
†81212 Brookside 178 .... J6
80020 Broomfield 20,730 .... J3
80723 Brush 4,082 .... M2
†80742 Buckingham 5 .... L1
81211 Buena Vista 2,075 .... G5
80425 Buffalo Creek 150 .... J4
80807 Burlington⊙ 3,107 .... P4
80426 Burns 100 .... F3
80103 Byers 490 .... L3
81320 Cahone 200 .... B7
80808 Calhan 541 .... L4
81029 Campo 185 .... O8
81212 Canon City⊙ 13,037 .... J6
81124 Capulin 600 .... G8
81623 Carbondale 2,084 .... E4
80612 Carr 49 .... K1
80909 Cascade 950 .... K5
80104 Castle Rock⊙ 3,921 .... K4
81413 Cedaredge 1,184 .... D5
81125 Center 1,630 .... G7
80427 Central City⊙ 329 .... J3
81126 Chama 239 .... J8
81030 Cheraw 233 .... N6
80810 Cheyenne Wells⊙ 950 .... P5
81127 Chimney Rock 76 .... E8
81031 Chivington 20 .... O6
81128 Chromo 115 .... F8
81220 Cimarron 50 .... D6
80428 Clark 20 .... F1
81520 Clifton 5,223 .... C4
80429 Climax 975 .... G4
81221 Coal Creek 190 .... J6
81222 Coaldale 153 .... H6
80430 Coalmont 50 .... F1
81032 Cokedale 90 .... K8
81624 Collbran 344 .... C4
†81401 Colona 54 .... D6
81019 Colorado City 411 .... K6
*80901 Colorado Springs⊙ 214,821 .... K5
Colorado Springs‡ 317,458 .... K5
†80428 Columbine 12 .... E1
80022 Commerce City 16,234 .... K3
80432 Como 30 .... H4
81129 Conejos⊙ 200 .... G8
80812 Cope 110 .... O3
†80611 Cornish 15 .... L2
81321 Cortez⊙ 7,095 .... B8
81223 Cotopaxi 250 .... H6
80434 Cowdrey 80 .... G1
81625 Craig⊙ 8,133 .... D2
81415 Crawford 268 .... D5
81130 Creede⊙ 610 .... E7
81224 Crested Butte 959 .... E5
81131 Crestone 54 .... H7
80813 Cripple Creek⊙ 655 .... J5
80726 Crook 177 .... O1
81033 Crowley 192 .... M6
81055 Cuchara 43 .... J8
80514 Dacono 2,321 .... K2
†80728 Dailey 20 .... O1
81630 De Beque 279 .... C4
†80135 Deckers 4 .... J4
80105 Deer Trail 463 .... M3
†81059 Delhi 10 .... M7
81132 Del Norte⊙ 1,709 .... G7
81416 Delta⊙ 3,931 .... D5
*80201 Denver (cap.)⊙ 492,365 .... K3
Denver‡ 1,619,921 .... K3
†81054 Deora 2 .... O7
80435 Dillon 337 .... H3
81610 Dinosaur 313 .... B2
80814 Divide 700 .... J5
81323 Dolores 802 .... C8
81324 Dove Creek⊙ 826 .... A7
†81239 Doyleville 75 .... F6
80515 Drake 300 .... J2
81301 Durango⊙ 11,649 .... D8
81036 Eads⊙ 878 .... O6
81631 Eagle⊙ 950 .... F3
80615 Eaton 1,932 .... K1
80727 Eckley 262 .... P2
80214 Edgewater 4,766 .... J3
81632 Edwards 250 .... F3
81325 Egnar 50 .... B7
80106 Elbert 200 .... L4
†80466 Eldora 100 .... H3
80107 Elizabeth 789 .... K4
81633 Elk Springs 18 .... C2
80438 Empire 423 .... H3
†80110 Englewood 30,021 .... K3
80516 Erie 1,254 .... K2
80517 Estes Park 2,703 .... J2
†81433 Eureka 25 .... D7
80620 Evans 5,063 .... K2
80439 Evergreen 6,376 .... J3
80440 Fairplay⊙ 421 .... H4
81037 Farisita 116 .... J7
†80221 Federal Heights 7,846 .... J3
80520 Firestone 1,204 .... K2
†80810 Firstview 6 .... O5
80815 Flagler 550 .... N4
80728 Fleming 388 .... O1
81226 Florence 2,987 .... J6
80816 Florissant 130 .... J5
80521 Fort Collins⊙ 65,092 .... J1
Fort Collins‡ 149,184 .... J1
81133 Fort Garland 700 .... J8
80621 Fort Lupton 4,251 .... K2
81038 Fort Lyon 500 .... N6
80701 Fort Morgan⊙ 8,768 .... M2
80817 Fountain 8,324 .... K5
81039 Fowler 1,227 .... L6
80441 Foxton 12 .... J4
80116 Franktown 200 .... K4
80442 Fraser 470 .... H3
80530 Frederick 855 .... K2
80820 Freshwater (Guffey) 24 .... H5
80443 Frisco 1,221 .... G3
81521 Fruita 2,810 .... B4
80622 Galeton 200 .... K1
81134 Garcia 75 .... J8
81040 Gardner 100 .... J7
81227 Garfield 30 .... G5
81522 Gateway 350 .... B5
80818 Genoa 165 .... N4
80444 Georgetown⊙ 830 .... H3
80623 Gilcrest 1,025 .... K2
80624 Gill 250 .... L2
81634 Gilman 160 .... G3
81523 Glade Park 100 .... B5
†80485 Glendevey 50 .... H1
80532 Glen Haven 110 .... H2
81601 Glenwood Springs⊙ 4,637 .... E4
80401 Golden⊙ 12,237 .... J3
†80653 Goodrich 85 .... M2
†80480 Gould 12 .... G2
81041 Granada 557 .... P6
80446 Granby 963 .... H2
81501 Grand Junction⊙ 27,956 .... B4
80447 Grand Lake 382 .... H2
81228 Granite 47 .... G4
80448 Grant 50 .... H4
80631 Greeley⊙ 53,006 .... K2
Greeley‡ 123,438 .... K2
†80118 Greenland 21 .... K4
80819 Green Mountain Falls 607 .... K5
†81640 Greystone 2 .... B1
80729 Grover 158 .... L1
80820 Guffey 24 .... H5
81042 Gulnare 6 .... K8
81230 Gunnison⊙ 5,785 .... E5
81637 Gypsum 743 .... F3
80730 Hale 4 .... P3
81638 Hamilton 100 .... D2
81043 Hartman 122 .... P6
80449 Hartsel 69 .... H4
81044 Hasty 150 .... O6
81045 Haswell 126 .... N6
80731 Haxtun 1,014 .... O1
81639 Hayden 1,720 .... E2
80732 Hereford 50 .... L1
81326 Hesperus 250 .... C8
80733 Hillrose 213 .... N2
81232 Hillside 79 .... H6
81046 Hoehne 400 .... L8
81047 Holly 969 .... P6
80734 Holyoke⊙ 2,092 .... P1
81136 Hooper 71 .... H7
81419 Hotchkiss 849 .... D5
80451 Hot Sulphur Springs⊙ 405 .... H2
81233 Howard 200 .... H6
80641 Hoyt 60 .... L2
80642 Hudson 698 .... K2
80821 Hugo⊙ 776 .... N4
80533 Hygiene 450 .... J2
80452 Idaho Springs 2,077 .... H3
80735 Idalia 125 .... P3
81137 Ignacio 667 .... D8
80736 Iliff 218 .... N1
80455 Jamestown 223 .... J2
†81082 Jansen 267 .... K8
81138 Jaroso 50 .... H8
80456 Jefferson 50 .... H4
80822 Joes 100 .... O3
80534 Johnstown 1,535 .... K2
80737 Julesburg⊙ 1,528 .... P1
80823 Karval 51 .... N5
80643 Keenesburg 541 .... L2
†80729 Keota 4 .... L1
80644 Kersey 913 .... L2
81049 Kim 100 .... N8
80117 Kiowa⊙ 206 .... L4
80824 Kirk 30 .... P3
80825 Kit Carson 278 .... O5
80459 Kremmling 1,296 .... G2
†80832 Kutch 2 .... M5
80026 Lafayette 8,935 .... K3
†81132 La Garita 10 .... G7
80739 Laird 105 .... P2
81140 La Jara 858 .... H8
81050 La Junta⊙ 8,388 .... M7
81235 Lake City⊙ 206 .... E6
80827 Lake George 500 .... J5
80215 Lakewood 113,808 .... J3
81052 Lamar⊙ 7,713 .... O6
80535 Laporte 950 .... J1
80118 Larkspur 141 .... K4
80645 La Salle 1,929 .... K2
81054 Las Animas⊙ 2,818 .... N6
†81151 Lasauces 150 .... H8
†81153 Lavalley 237 .... J8
81055 La Veta 611 .... J8
†80452 Lawson 108 .... H3
†81625 Lay 40 .... D2
81420 Lazear 60 .... D5
80461 Leadville⊙ 3,879 .... G4
†81323 Lebanon 50 .... B8
81327 Lewis 150 .... B8
80828 Limon 1,805 .... M4
†81212 Lincoln Park 2,984 .... J6
80740 Lindon 60 .... N3
*80120 Littleton⊙ 28,631 .... K3
80536 Livermore 150 .... J1
†80601 Lochbuie 895 .... K2
†80701 Log Lane Village 709 .... M2
81524 Loma 265 .... B4
80501 Longmont 42,942 .... J2
†80135 Longview 10 .... J4
80027 Louisville 5,593 .... J3
80131 Louviers 300 .... K4
80537 Loveland 30,244 .... J2
80646 Lucerne 135 .... K2
†81054 Lycan 4 .... P7
80540 Lyons 1,137 .... J2
81525 Mack 380 .... B4
81421 Maher 75 .... D5
†80461 Malta 200 .... G4
81141 Manassa 945 .... H8
81328 Mancos 870 .... C8
80829 Manitou Springs 4,475 .... J5
81058 Manzanola 459 .... M6
†81623 Marble 30 .... E4
81329 Marvel 176 .... C8
80541 Masonville 200 .... J2
†80649 Masters 50 .... L2
80830 Matheson 120 .... M4
81640 Maybell 130 .... C2
81057 McClave 125 .... O6
80463 McCoy 62 .... F3
80542 Mead 356 .... K2
81641 Meeker⊙ 2,356 .... D2
81642 Meredith 47 .... F4
80741 Merino 255 .... N2
81005 Mesa 120 .... C4
81330 Mesa Verde National Park 45 .... C8
81142 Mesita 70 .... H8
80543 Milliken 1,506 .... K2
80477 Milner 196 .... F2
81645 Minturn 1,060 .... G3

(continued on following page)

Agriculture, Industry and Resources

DOMINANT LAND USE

- Specialized Wheat
- Wheat, Range Livestock
- Wheat, Grain Sorghums, Range Livestock
- Dry Beans, General Farming
- Sugar Beets, Dry Beans, Livestock, General Farming
- Fruit, Mixed Farming
- General Farming, Livestock, Special Crops
- Range Livestock
- Forests
- Urban Areas
- Nonagricultural Land

MAJOR MINERAL OCCURRENCES

Ag	Silver	Mi	Mica
Au	Gold	Mo	Molybdenum
Be	Beryl	Mr	Marble
C	Coal	O	Petroleum
Cl	Clay	Pb	Lead
Cu	Copper	U	Uranium
F	Fluorspar	V	Vanadium
Fe	Iron Ore	W	Tungsten
G	Natural Gas	Zn	Zinc

Water Power
Major Industrial Areas

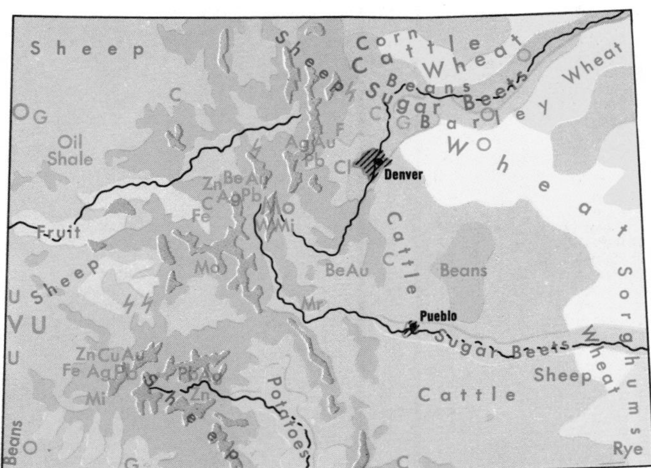

Topography

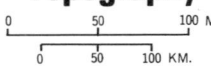

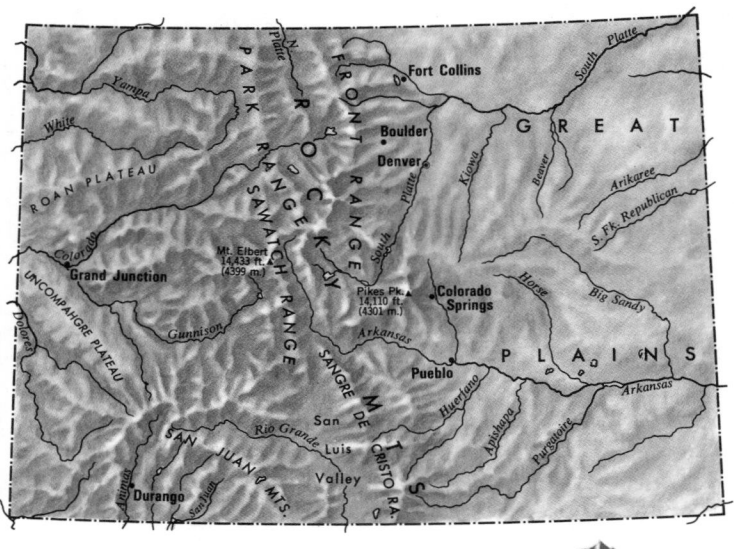

Below Sea Level — 100 m. 328 ft. | 200 m. 656 ft. | 500 m. 1,640 ft. | 1,000 m. 3,281 ft. | 2,000 m. 6,562 ft. | 5,000 m. 16,404 ft.

81646 Molina 200 .... D4	80473 Rand 50 .... G2	81334 Towaoc 300 .... B8	Bent's Old Fort Nat'l Hist.
81144 Monte Vista 3,902 .... G7	81648 Rangely 2,113 .... B2	80180 Towner 61 .... P6	Site M6
†80435 Montezuma 6 .... H3	80742 Raymer (New Raymer) 80 .M1	81081 Trinchera 30 .... M8	Big Grizzly (creek) G1
81401 Montrose⊙ 8,722 .... D6	81649 Red Cliff 409 .... G4	81082 Trinidad⊙ 9,663 .... L8	Big Sandy (creek) N4
80132 Monument 690 .... K4	80545 Red Feather Lakes 150 .... H1	†80864 Truckton 10 .... L5	Big Thompson (riv.) H2
80465 Morrison 478 .... J3	†81326 Red Mesa 100 .... C8	81251 Twin Lakes 40 .... G4	Bijou (creek) L3
81146 Mosca 100 .... H7	81623 Redstone 115 .... E4	81436 Two Buttes 84 .... P7	Black Canyon of the Gunnison Nat'l
81236 Nathrop 150 .... H5	81431 Redvale 300 .... B6	81436 Uravan 500 .... B6	Mon. D5
81422 Naturita 819 .... B6	81066 Red Wing 200 .... J7	†81064 Utleyville 2 .... O8	Black Squirrel (creek) L5
80466 Nederland 1,212 .... H3	81332 Rico 76 .... C7	81657 Vail 2,261 .... G4	Blanca (peak) H7
81647 New Castle 563 .... E3	81432 Ridgway 369 .... D6	†81064 Valdez 12 .... K8	Blue (mt.) B2
80742 New Raymer 80 .... M1	81650 Rifle 3,215 .... D3	80755 Vernon 50 .... P3	Blue (riv.) G3
†81054 Ninaview 2 .... N7	81650 Rio Blanco 4 .... C3	81087 Vilas 118 .... P8	Blue Mesa (res.) E5
80544 Niwot 500 .... J2	81244 Rockvale 338 .... J6	81155 Villa Grove 37 .... G6	Bonny (res.) P3
†81022 North Avondale 110 .... L6	81067 Rocky Ford 4,804 .... M6	81088 Villegreen 6 .... M8	Box Elder (creek) K4
80233 Northglenn 29,847 .... K3	80652 Roggen 100 .... L2	81001 Vineland 100 .... K6	Cache la Poudre (riv.) H1
†81050 North La Junta 1,076 .... N7	81148 Romeo 308 .... G8	80548 Virginia Dale 2 .... J1	Cameron (peak) H1
81423 Norwood 478 .... C6	80833 Rush 40 .... L5	80861 Vona 94 .... O4	Camp Hale G4
81424 Nucla 1,027 .... B6	81069 Rye 232 .... K7	†81130 Wagon Wheel Gap 20 .... F7	Carbon (peak) E5
80648 Nunn 295 .... K1	81149 Saguache⊙ 656 .... G6	80480 Walden⊙ 947 .... G1	Castle (peak) F5
80467 Oak Creek 929 .... F2	†81236 Saint Elmo 75 .... G5	81089 Walsenburg⊙ 3,945 .... K7	Cebolla (peak) E6
81237 Ohio 100 .... F5	81201 Salida⊙ 44,870 .... H6	81090 Walsh 884 .... P8	Chacuaco (creek) M8
81425 Olathe 1,262 .... D5	81150 San Acacio 50 .... J8	80481 Ward 129 .... H2	Cheesman (lake) J4
81062 Olney Springs 253 .... M6	81151 Sanford 687 .... H8	80653 Weldona 200 .... M2	Clay (creek) O7
81426 Ophir 38 .... D7	†81069 San Isabel 8 .... K7	80549 Wellington 1,215 .... K1	Cochetopa (creek) F6
80649 Orchard 79 .... L2	81152 San Luis⊙ 842 .... J8	81252 Westcliffe⊙ 324 .... H6	Colorado (riv.) A5
†81501 Orchard Mesa 4,876 .... C4	81153 San Pablo 150 .... J8	†80135 Westcreek 2 .... J4	Colorado Nat'l Mon. B4
81063 Ordway⊙ 1,135 .... M6	81248 Sargents 31 .... F6	80030 Westminster 50,211 .... J3	Conejos (peak) G8
†81120 Ortiz 163 .... H8	†81430 Sawpit 41 .... D7	81091 Weston 150 .... K8	Conejos (riv.) G8
80743 Otis 534 .... O2	80911 Security-Widefield 18,768 .... K5	81253 Wetmore 150 .... J6	Crestone (peak) H7
81427 Ouray⊙ 684 .... D6	80135 Sedalia 200 .... K4	80033 Wheat Ridge 30,293 .... J3	Crow (creek) L1
80744 Ovid 439 .... P1	80749 Sedgwick 258 .... O1	81527 Whitewater 300 .... C5	Culebra (creek) H8
80745 Padroni 100 .... N1	81070 Segundo 200 .... K8	80654 Wiggins 531 .... L2	Culebra (peak) J8
†81147 Pagosa Junction 15 .... F8	80834 Seibert 180 .... O4	80862 Wild Horse 13 .... N5	Curecanti Nat'l Rec. Area F6
†81147 Pagosa Springs⊙ 1,331 .... E8	80546 Severance 102 .... K1	81092 Wiley 425 .... O6	Del Norte (peak) F7
81526 Palisade 1,551 .... C4	80135 Shawnee 100 .... H4	†81226 Williamsburg 72 .... J6	De Weese (plat.) J6
80133 Palmer Lake 1,130 .... J4	†80110 Sheridan 5,377 .... J3	80550 Windsor 4,277 .... J2	Dinosaur Nat'l Mon. B2
80746 Paoli 81 .... P1	81071 Sheridan Lake 87 .... P6	80482 Winter Park 480 .... H3	Disappointment (creek) B7
81428 Paonia 1,425 .... D5	81652 Silt 923 .... D4	81655 Wolcott 30 .... F3	Dolores (riv.) B5
81635 Parachute 338 .... C4	81249 Silver Cliff 280 .... H6	80863 Woodland Park 2,634 .... J4	Douglas (creek) B3
81429 Paradox 250 .... B6	80476 Silver Plume 140 .... H3	80757 Woodrow 24 .... M3	Eagle (riv.) E3
†81212 Parkdale 21 .... H6	80498 Silverthorne 989 .... G3	81656 Woody Creek 400 .... F4	Elbert (mt.) G4
80134 Parker 200 .... K4	81433 Silverton⊙ 794 .... D7	80758 Wray⊙ 2,131 .... P2	El Diente (peak) C7
81239 Parlin 100 .... F6	80835 Simla 494 .... M4	80483 Yampa 472 .... F2	Eleven Mile Canyon (res.) H5
80468 Parshall 80 .... G2	81653 Slater 10 .... E1	81335 Yellow Jacket 115 .... B7	Elk (riv.) F1
80747 Peetz 220 .... N1	81654 Snowmass 999 .... E4	80864 Yoder 25 .... L5	Empire (res.) L2
81240 Penrose 500 .... K6	80750 Snyder 200 .... M2	80759 Yuma 2,824 .... O2	Ent A.F.B. K5
80831 Peyton 250 .... K4	81434 Somerset 200 .... E5		Ethel (mt.) F1
80469 Phippsburg 300 .... F2	81154 South Fork 500 .... F7	OTHER FEATURES	Evans (mt.) H3
80650 Pierce 878 .... K1	81073 Springfield⊙ 1,657 .... O8		Florissant Fossil Beds Nat'l
80470 Pine 100 .... J4	81074 Starkville 127 .... L8	Adams (mt.) H6	Mon. J5
80471 Pinecliffe 375 .... J3	80477 Steamboat Springs⊙ 5,098 .... F2	Adobe Creek (res.) N6	Fort Carson 19,399 .... K5
†81001 Pinon 50 .... K6	80751 Sterling⊙ 11,385 .... N1	Air Force Academy 8,655 .... K5	Fountain (creek) K5
81241 Pitkin 75 .... F5	80754 Stoneham 35 .... M1	Alamosa (creek) G8	Frenchman (creek) P1
81430 Placerville 50 .... D6	81075 Stonington 27 .... P8	Alva B. Adams (tunnel) H2	Frenchman, North Fork (creek) O1
†81624 Plateau City 35 .... D4	80136 Strasburg 1,005 .... L3	Animas (riv.) D8	Frenchman, South Fork (creek) O1
†80743 Platner 30 .... N2	80836 Stratton 705 .... O4	Antero (mt.) G5	Front (range) H1
80651 Platteville 1,662 .... K2	81076 Sugar City 306 .... M6	Antero (res.) H5	Gore (range) G3
81331 Pleasant View 300 .... B7	†81640 Sunbeam 19 .... C1	Antora (peak) G6	Graham (peak) E8
81242 Poncha Springs 321 .... G6	80027 Superior 208 .... J3	Apishapa (riv.) L8	Granby (lake) H2
†81226 Portland 17 .... K6	81077 Swink 668 .... M7	Arapaho Nat'l Rec. Area G2	Great Sand Dunes Nat'l Mon. H7
81427 Portland K6	80478 Tabernash 250 .... H3	Arapahoe (peak) H2	Green (riv.) A2
81243 Powderhorn 100 .... E6	81435 Telluride⊙ 1,047 .... D7	Arikaree (riv.) O3	Green Mountain (res.) G3
81064 Pritchett 183 .... O8	†80461 Tennessee Pass 5 .... G4	Arkansas (riv.) P6	Gunnison (riv.) C5
†80736 Proctor 25 .... N1	81250 Texas Creek 80 .... H6	Arkansas Divide (mts.) L4	Gunnison (tunnel) C5
81065 Pryor 50 .... K8	†81082 Thatcher 50 .... L7	Baker (mt.) H2	Gunnison, North Fork (riv.) D5
*81001 Pueblo⊙ 101,686 .... K6	80229 Thornton 40,343 .... K3	Bald (mt.) H4	Hale, Camp G4
Pueblo‡ 125,972 .... K6	†81137 Tiffany 24 .... D8	Bear (creek) P8	Handies (peak) E7
80472 Radium 22 .... G3	80547 Timnath 185 .... J2	Beaver (creek) M3	Harvard (mt.) G5
80832 Ramah 119 .... L4	†81034 Timpas 25 .... M7	Bennett (peak) G7	Hermosa (peak) D7
80473 Rand 50 .... G2	†81210 Tincup 8 .... F5		Hesperus (mt.) C8
81648 Rangely 2,113 .... B2	80479 Toponas 55 .... F2		Holy Cross (mt.) F4

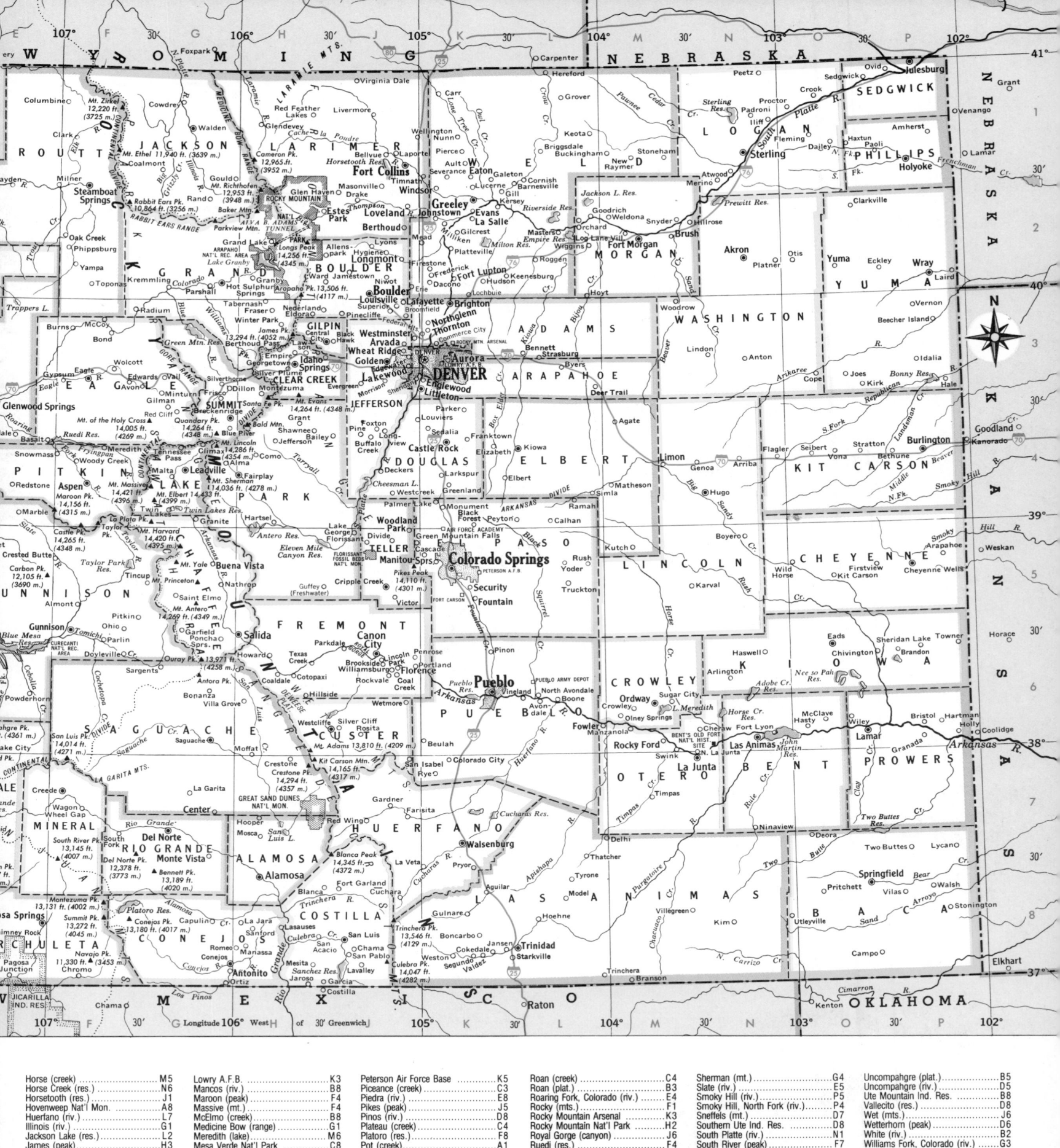

Connecticut

SCALE

0   5   10   15 MI.

0   5   10   15 KM.

State Capitals .... ✪
Major Limited Access Hwys. ———
Scale 1:610,000

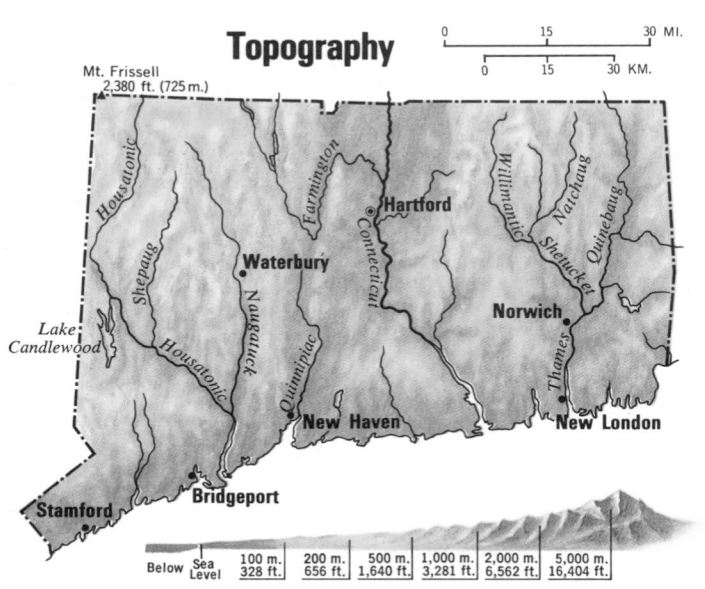

Topography

Mt. Frissell
2,380 ft. (725 m.)

0   15   30 MI.

0   15   30 KM.

Below Sea Level	100 m. 328 ft.	200 m. 656 ft.	500 m. 1,640 ft.	1,000 m. 3,281 ft.	2,000 m. 6,562 ft.	5,000 m. 16,404 ft.

COUNTIES

Fairfield 807,143 ....B3
Hartford 807,766 ....D1
Litchfield 156,769 ....B1
Middlesex 129,017 ....E3
New Haven 761,337 ....D3
New London 238,409 ....G2
Tolland 114,823 ....F1
Windham 92,312 ....H1

CITIES and TOWNS

Zip	Name/Pop.	Key
06230	Abington 600	G1
06231	Amston 900	F2
06232	Andover○ 2,144	F2
06401	Ansonia 19,039	C3
06278	Ashford○ 3,221	G1
06278	Ashford P.O.	
	(Warrenville) 500	G1
†06241	Attawaugan 400	H1
06001	Avon○ 11,201	D1
06001	Avon 1,434	D1
06233	Ballouville 800	H1
06330	Baltic	G2
06750	Bantam 860	B2
†06063	Barkhamsted 2,935	D1
†06423	Bashan 90	F2
06403	Beacon Falls○ 3,995	C3
06037	Berlin 15,121	E2
†06501	Bethany○ 4,330	C3
06801	Bethel○ 16,004	B3
06801	Bethel 8,755	B3
06751	Bethlehem○ 2,573	C2
06751	Bethlehem 1,762	C2
06002	Bloomfield 18,608	E1
06112	Blue Hills	E1
06040	Bolton○ 3,951	F1
06404	Botsford 400	C3
06405	Branford○ 23,363	D3
06405	Branford 5,438	D3
*06601	Bridgeport 142,546	C4
	Bridgeport‡ 395,455	C4
06752	Bridgewater○ 1,563	B2
06010	Bristol 57,370	D2
	Bristol‡ 73,762	D2
06016	Broad Brook	E1
06804	Brookfield○ 12,872	B3
06234	Brooklyn○ 5,691	H1
06013	Burlington○ 5,660	D1
06830	Byram	A4
06018	Canaan○ 1,002	B1
06018	Canaan 1,160	B1
†06897	Cannondale 400	B4
06331	Canterbury○ 3,426	H2
06019	Canton○ 7,635	D1
06019	Canton 1,680	D1
06409	Centerbrook 800	F3
06332	Central Village 950	H2
06235	Chaplin○ 1,793	G1
06410	Cheshire○ 21,788	D2
06410	Cheshire 5,722	D2
06412	Chester○ 3,068	F3
06412	Chester 1,388	F3
06413	Clinton○ 11,195	E3
06413	Clinton 3,168	E3
06414	Cobalt 700	E2
06415	Colchester○ 7,761	F2
06415	Colchester 3,190	F2
06021	Colebrook○ 1,221	C1
06022	Collinsville 2,555	D1
06237	Columbia○ 3,386	F2
06753	Cornwall○ 1,288	B1
06807	Cos Cob	A4
06238	Coventry○ 8,895	F1
06416	Cromwell○ 10,265	E2
06810	Danbury 60,470	B3
	Danbury‡ 146,405	B3
06239	Danielson 4,553	H1
06820	Darien○ 18,892	B4
06241	Dayville	H1
06417	Deep River○ 3,994	F3
06417	Deep River 2,495	F3
06418	Derby 12,346	C3
06422	Durham○ 5,143	E3
06422	Durham 2,641	E3
06023	East Berlin 950	E2
06239	East Brooklyn 1,251	H1
06024	East Canaan 800	B1
06242	Eastford○ 1,028	G1
06025	East Glastonbury 300	E2
06026	East Granby○ 4,102	E1
06423	East Haddam○ 5,621	F3
06424	East Hampton○ 8,572	E2

AREA 5,018 sq. mi. (12,997 sq. km.)
POPULATION 3,107,576
CAPITAL Hartford
LARGEST CITY Bridgeport
HIGHEST POINT Mt. Frissell (S. Slope) 2,380 ft. (725 m.)
SETTLED IN 1635
ADMITTED TO UNION January 9, 1788
POPULAR NAME Constitution State; Nutmeg State
STATE FLOWER Mountain Laurel
STATE BIRD Robin

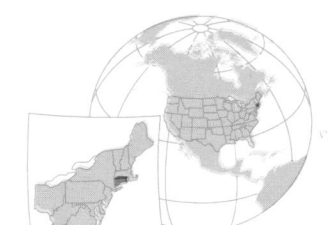

06351 Lisbon○ 3,279	G2
06759 Litchfield○ 7,605	C2
06759 Litchfield 1,489	C2
†06378 Lords Point 500	H3
06443 Madison 14,031	E3
06443 Madison 2,069	E3
06040 Manchester○ 49,761	E1
06040 Manchester 31,058	E1
†06250 Mansfield○ 20,634	F1
06250 Mansfield Center 1,043	G1
06777 Marble Dale 300	B2
06444 Marion 900	D2
06447 Marlborough○ 4,746	F2
06447 Marlborough 1,039	F2
†06382 Massapeag 350	G3
06252 Mechanicsville 425	H1
06450 Meriden 57,118	D2
Meriden‡ 57,118	D2
06762 Middlebury○ 5,995	C2
06455 Middlefield○ 3,796	E2
06456 Middle Haddam 325	E2
06457 Middletown 39,040	E2
06460 Milford 49,101	C4
06467 Milldale 975	D2
†06759 Milton 600	C1
06468 Monroe 14,010	C3
06468 Monroe P.O. (Stepney)	B3
06353 Montville 16,455	G3
06353 Montville 1,711	G3
06469 Moodus 1,179	F2
06354 Moosup 3,308	H2
06763 Morris○ 1,899	C2
06355 Mystic 2,333	H3
06770 Naugatuck 26,456	C3
*06050 New Britain 73,840	E2
New Britain‡ 142,241	E2
06840 New Canaan○ 17,931	B4
06810 New Fairfield○ 11,260	A3
06057 New Hartford○ 4,884	C1
06057 New Hartford 1,310	C1
*06501 New Haven 126,109	D3
New Haven-West	
Haven‡ 417,592	D3
06111 Newington○ 28,841	E2
06320 New London 28,842	G3
New London-Norwich‡	
248,554	G3
06776 New Milford○ 19,420	B2
06776 New Milford 5,186	B2
06777 New Preston 1,209	B2
06470 Newtown○ 19,107	B3
06470 Newtown 2,022	B3
06357 Niantic 3,151	G3
06340 Noank 1,406	G3
06058 Norfolk○ 2,156	C1
06471 North Branford○ 11,554	E3
06778 Northfield 600	C2
06254 North Franklin 500	G2
06060 North Granby 900	D1
06255 North Grosvenor	
Dale 1,856	H1
†06437 North Guilford	E3
06473 North Haven○ 22,080	D3
06359 North Stonington○ 4,219	H3
06256 North Windham 200	G1
*06850 Norwalk 77,767	B4
06360 Norwich 38,074	G2
06370 Oakdale 608	G3
06779 Oakville 8,737	C2
06371 Old Lyme 6,159	F3

06372 Old Mystic 600	H3
06475 Old Saybrook○ 9,287	F3
06475 Old Saybrook 1,857	F3
06373 Oneco 550	H2
06477 Orange○ 13,237	C3
06483 Oxford○ 6,634	C3
06379 Pawcatuck 5,216	H3
06781 Pequabuck 642	C2
06601 Pine Meadow 400	D1
†06405 Pine Orchard 300	D3
06374 Plainfield 12,774	H2
06374 Plainfield 2,799	H2
06062 Plainville 16,401	D2
06063 Pleasant Valley 300	C1
†06385 Pleasure Beach 1,356	G3
06782 Plymouth○ 10,732	C2
06258 Pomfret○ 2,775	H1
†06340 Poquonock Bridge 2,549	G3
06480 Portland○ 8,383	E2
06480 Portland 5,914	E2
06712 Prospect○ 6,807	D2
06260 Putnam○ 8,580	H1
06260 Putnam 6,855	H1
06375 Quaker Hill 2,052	G3
06262 Quinebaug 1,088	H1
06875 Redding○ 7,272	B3
06876 Redding Ridge 550	B3
06877 Ridgefield○ 20,120	B3
06877 Ridgefield 6,066	B3
06065 Riverton 250	D1
06481 Rockfall 900	E2
†06066 Rockville	F1
06067 Rocky Hill 14,559	E2
06263 Rogers 650	H1
06783 Roxbury○ 1,468	B2
†06415 Salem○ 2,335	F3
06068 Salisbury○ 3,896	B1
06264 Scotland○ 1,072	G2
06483 Seymour○ 13,434	C3
06069 Sharon○ 2,623	B1
06484 Shelton 31,314	C3
06784 Sherman○ 2,281	B2
06070 Simsbury○ 21,161	D1
06070 Simsbury 5,488	D1
06071 Somers○ 8,473	F1
06071 Somers 1,643	F1
06072 Somersville 750	F1
06487 South Britain 390	B3
06488 Southbury○ 14,156	C3
†06238 South Coventry	
(Coventry) 3,769	F1
06073 South Glastonbury	E2
06489 Southington○ 36,879	D2
06785 South Kent 450	B2
06265 South Willington 450	F1
06266 South Windham 1,399	G1
06074 South Windsor○ 17,198	E1
06267 South Woodstock 1,319	G1
06075 Stafford○ 9,268	F1
06076 Stafford Springs 3,392	F1
06077 Staffordville 500	G1
*06901 Stamford 102,453	A4
Stamford‡ 198,854	A4
†06468 Stepney	B3
06377 Sterling○ 1,791	H2
06491 Stevenson 300	C3
06378 Stonington○ 16,220	H3
06378 Stonington 1,228	H3
06268 Storrs 11,394	F1
06497 Stratford○ 50,541	C4

06078 Suffield○ 9,294	E1
06078 Suffield 1,122	E1
06079 Taconic 400	B1
06380 Taftville	G2
06081 Tariffville 1,324	D1
06786 Terryville 5,234	C2
06787 Thomaston○ 6,276	C2
06277 Thompson○ 8,141	H1
†06082 Thompsonville	E1
06084 Tolland○ 9,694	F1
06790 Torrington 30,987	C1
06611 Trumbull○ 32,989	C4
06382 Uncasville 1,597	G3
†06076 Union 546	G1
06066 Vernon○ 27,974	F1
06383 Versailles 540	G2
06384 Voluntown○ 1,637	H2
06492 Wallingford○ 37,274	D3
06492 Wallingford 17,821	D3
06754 Warren○ 1,027	B2
†06278 Warrenville 500	G1
06793 Washington○ 3,657	B2
06794 Washington Depot 900	B2
*06701 Waterbury 103,266	C2
Waterbury‡ 228,178	C2
06385 Waterford○ 17,843	G3
06385 Waterford 2,736	G3
06795 Watertown○ 19,489	C2
06089 Weatogue 2,249	D1
06498 Westbrook○ 5,216	F3
06498 Westbrook 2,035	F3
06796 West Cornwall 425	B1
06090 West Granby 567	D1
06107 West Hartford○ 61,301	D1
06516 West Haven 53,184	D3
06388 West Mystic 3,364	H3
06883 Weston○ 8,284	B4
06880 Westport○ 25,290	B4
06896 West Redding 500	B3
06092 West Simsbury 2,140	D1
06109 Wethersfield○ 26,013	E2
06517 Whitneyville	D3
06226 Willimantic 14,652	G2
†06279 Willington○ 4,694	F1
06897 Wilton○ 15,351	B4
06094 Winchester○ 10,841	C1
06094 Winchester Center 350	C1
06280 Windham○ 21,062	G2
06095 Windsor○ 25,204	E1
06095 Windsor 17,517	E1
06096 Windsor Locks○ 12,190	E1
06097 Windsorville 450	E1
06098 Winsted 8,092	C1
†06417 Winthrop 750	E3
06716 Wolcott○ 13,008	D2
†06515 Woodbridge○ 7,761	D3
06798 Woodbury○ 6,942	C2
06798 Woodbury 1,290	C2
†06460 Woodmont 1,797	D4
06281 Woodstock○ 5,117	H1

OTHER FEATURES

Aspetuck (res.)	B4
Bantam (lake)	C2
Barkhamsted (res.)	D1
Bear (mt.)	B1
Byram (riv.)	A4
Candlewood (lake)	A2
Coast Guard Academy	G3

Colebrook River (lake)	C1
Congamond (lkes)	E1
Connecticut (riv.)	E2
Dennis (hill)	C1
Easton (res.)	B3
Eight Mile (riv.)	F3
Farmington (riv.)	D1
French (riv.)	H1
Frissell (mt.)	B1
Gaillard (lake)	D3
Gardner (lake)	G2
Hammonasset (pt.)	E3
Hammonasset (res.)	E3
Haystack (mt.)	C1
Highland (lake)	C1
Hockanum (riv.)	E1
Hop (riv.)	F1
Housatonic (riv.)	C3
Lillinonah (lake)	B3
Little (riv.)	G2
Long Island (sound)	C4
Mad (riv.)	C1
Mashapaug (lake)	G1
Mason (isl.)	H3
Mattabesset (riv.)	E2
Mianus (riv.)	A4
Mohawk (mt.)	B1
Moosup (riv.)	H2
Mount Hope (riv.)	G1
Mudge (pond)	B1
Mystic (riv.)	H3
Natchaug (riv.)	G1
Naugatuck (riv.)	C3
Nepaug (res.)	D1
Niantic (riv.)	G3
Norwalk (riv.)	B4
Pachaug (pond)	H2
Pawcatuck (riv.)	H3
Pequabuck (riv.)	C2
Pequonnock (riv.)	C4
Pocotopaug (lake)	E2
Quaddick (res.)	H1
Quinebaug (riv.)	G2
Quinnipiac (riv.)	D3
Rippowam (riv.)	A4
Sachem (head)	E4
Salmon (brook)	D1
Salmon (riv.)	F2
Saugatuck (res.)	B3
Scantic (riv.)	E1
Shenipsit (lake)	F1
Shepaug (riv.)	B2
Shetucket (riv.)	G2
Silvermine (riv.)	B4
Spectacle (lkes)	B2
Still (riv.)	B3
Still (riv.)	C1
Talcott (range)	D1
Thames (riv.)	G3
Thomaston (res.)	C2
Titicus (riv.)	A3
Trap Falls (res.)	C3
Twin (lkes)	B1
Wamgumbaug (lake)	F1
Waramaug (lake)	B2
West Rock Ridge (hills)	D3
Willimantic (riv.)	F1
Wononskopomuc (lake)	B1
Yantic (riv.)	G2

‡Population of metropolitan area.
○Population of town or township.
† Zip of nearest p.o.   * Multiple zips.

06424 East Hampton 2,152	E2
06108 East Hartford 52,563	E1
06027 East Hartland 900	D1
06512 East Haven○ 25,028	D3
06243 East Killingly 900	H1
06333 East Lyme 13,870	G3
†06763 East Morris 800	C2
06612 Easton○ 5,962	B4
†06088 East Windsor○ 8,925	E1
06028 East Windsor Hill 500	E1
06244 East Woodstock 400	H1
06029 Ellington○ 9,711	F1
06082 Enfield○ 42,695	E1
06082 Enfield 8,151	E1
06426 Essex○ 5,078	F3
06426 Essex 2,501	F3
06245 Fabyan 600	H1
06430 Fairfield○ 54,849	B4
06031 Falls Village 600	B1
06032 Farmington○ 16,407	D2
06334 Fitchville 400	G2
†06254 Franklin○ 1,592	G2
06335 Gales Ferry 1,191	G3
06755 Gaylordsville 960	A2
06829 Georgetown 1,834	B4
06336 Gilman 350	G2
06337 Glasgo 450	H2
06033 Glastonbury 24,327	E2
06033 Glastonbury 7,049	E2
06756 Goshen○ 1,706	C1
06339 Ledyard○ 13,735	G3
06035 Granby 7,956	D1
06035 Granby 1,912	D1

06830 Greenwich○ 59,578	A4
06246 Grosvenor Dale 700	H1
06340 Groton○ 41,062	G3
06340 Groton 10,086	G3
06437 Guilford○ 17,375	E3
06437 Guilford 2,555	E3
06438 Haddam○ 6,383	E3
06439 Hadlyme 450	F3
06514 Hamden○ 51,071	D3
06247 Hampton○ 1,322	G1
06350 Hanover 500	G2
*06101 Hartford (cap.) 136,392	E1
Hartford‡ 726,114	E1
†06091 Hartland○ 1,416	D1
06791 Harwinton○ 4,889	C1
06791 Harwinton 3,293	C1
06440 Hawleyville 600	B3
06082 Hazardville 5,436	E1
06248 Hebron○ 5,453	F2
06441 Higganum 1,660	E2
†06040 Highland Park 500	F1
06351 Jewett City 3,294	H2
06335 Kensington 7,502	D2
06757 Kent○ 2,505	B2
†06241 Killingly○ 14,519	H1
†06413 Killingworth○ 3,976	E3
06424 Lake Pocotopaug 2,137	F2
06758 Lakeside 350	B2
06249 Lebanon○ 4,762	G2
06339 Ledyard○ 13,735	G3
†06437 Leetes Island 500	E3
†06039 Lime Rock 350	B1

Agriculture, Industry and Resources

DOMINANT LAND USE

- Specialized Dairy
- Dairy, Poultry, Mixed Farming
- Forests
- Urban Areas

MAJOR MINERAL OCCURRENCES

Cl Clay   Mi Mica

Major Industrial Areas

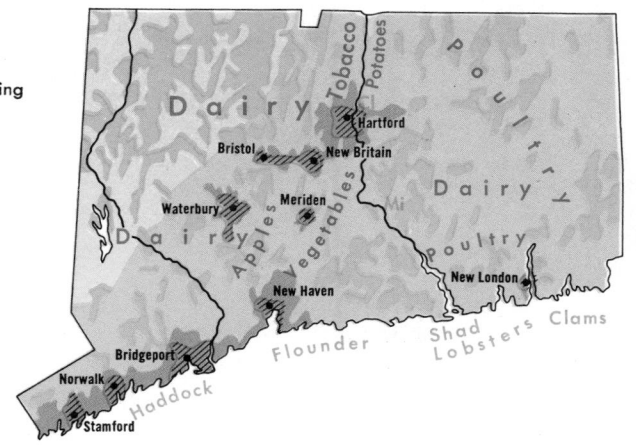

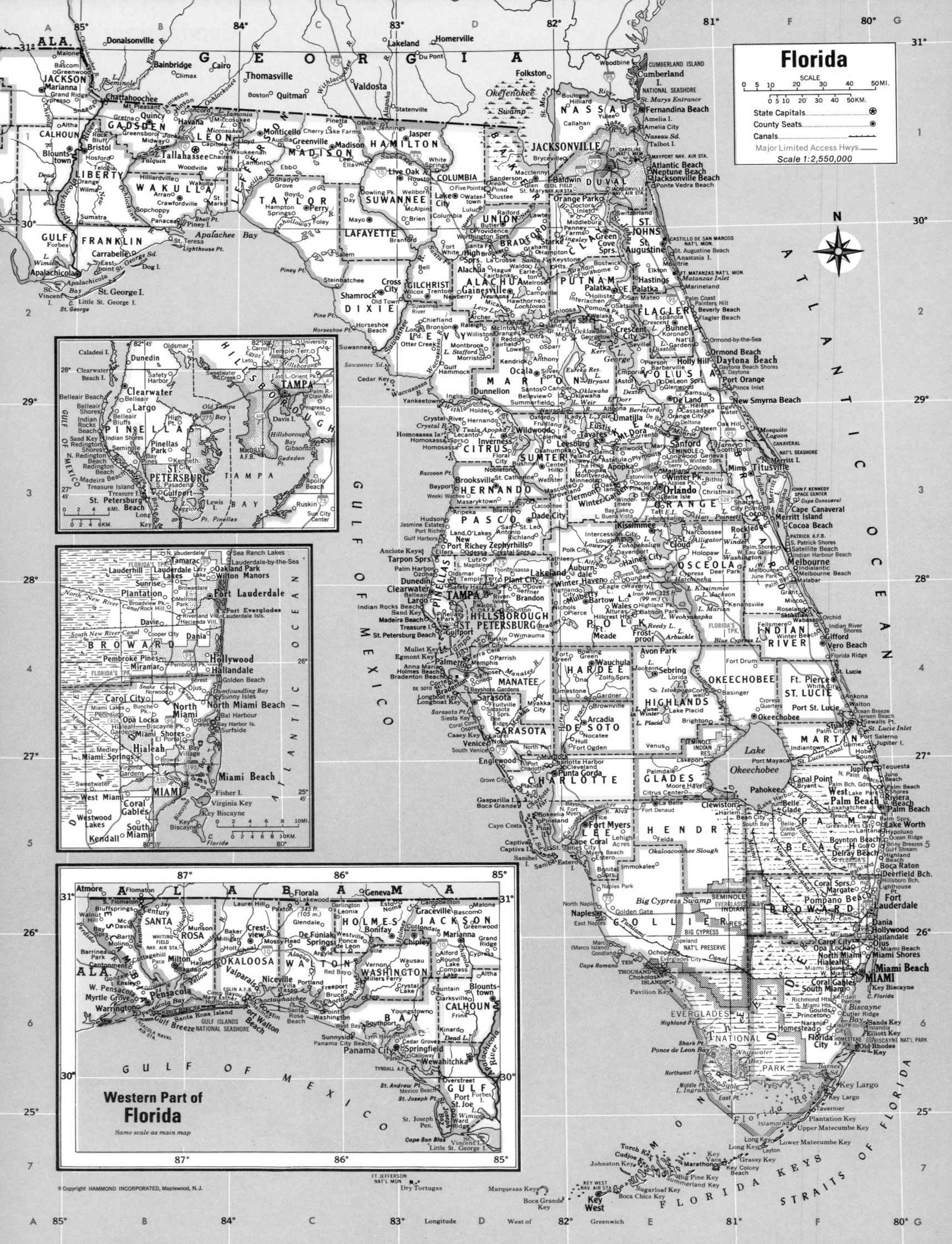
Florida
SCALE
0 5 10 20 30 40 50 MI.
0 5 10 20 30 40 50 KM.
State Capitals
County Seats
Canals
Major Limited Access Hwys.
Scale 1:2,550,000
GEORGIA
ALA.
ATLANTIC OCEAN
GULF OF MEXICO
STRAITS OF FLORIDA
FLORIDA KEYS
Lake Okeechobee
EVERGLADES NATIONAL PARK
Big Cypress Swamp
Okefenokee Swamp
Apalachee Bay
Tallahassee
Jacksonville
Tampa
St. Petersburg
Orlando
Miami
Miami Beach
Fort Lauderdale
Key West
Western Part of Florida
Same scale as main map
ALABAMA
GULF OF MEXICO
Longitude West of Greenwich
© Copyright HAMMOND INCORPORATED, Maplewood, N.J.

AREA 58,664 sq. mi. (151,940 sq. km.)
POPULATION 9,746,342
CAPITAL Tallahassee
LARGEST CITY Jacksonville
HIGHEST POINT (Walton County) 345 ft. (105 m.)
SETTLED IN 1565
ADMITTED TO UNION March 3, 1845
POPULAR NAME Sunshine State; Peninsula State
STATE FLOWER Orange Blossom
STATE BIRD Mockingbird

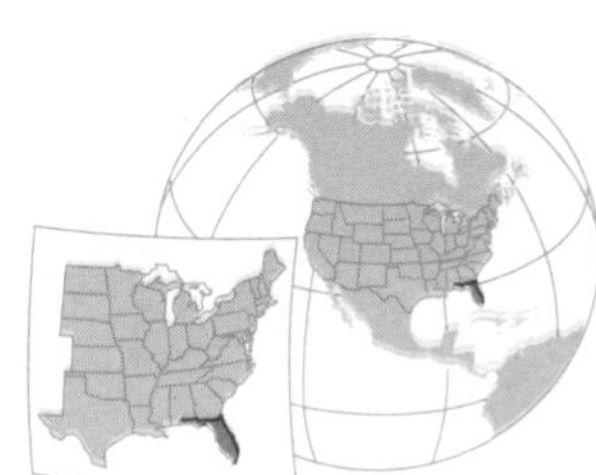

Topography

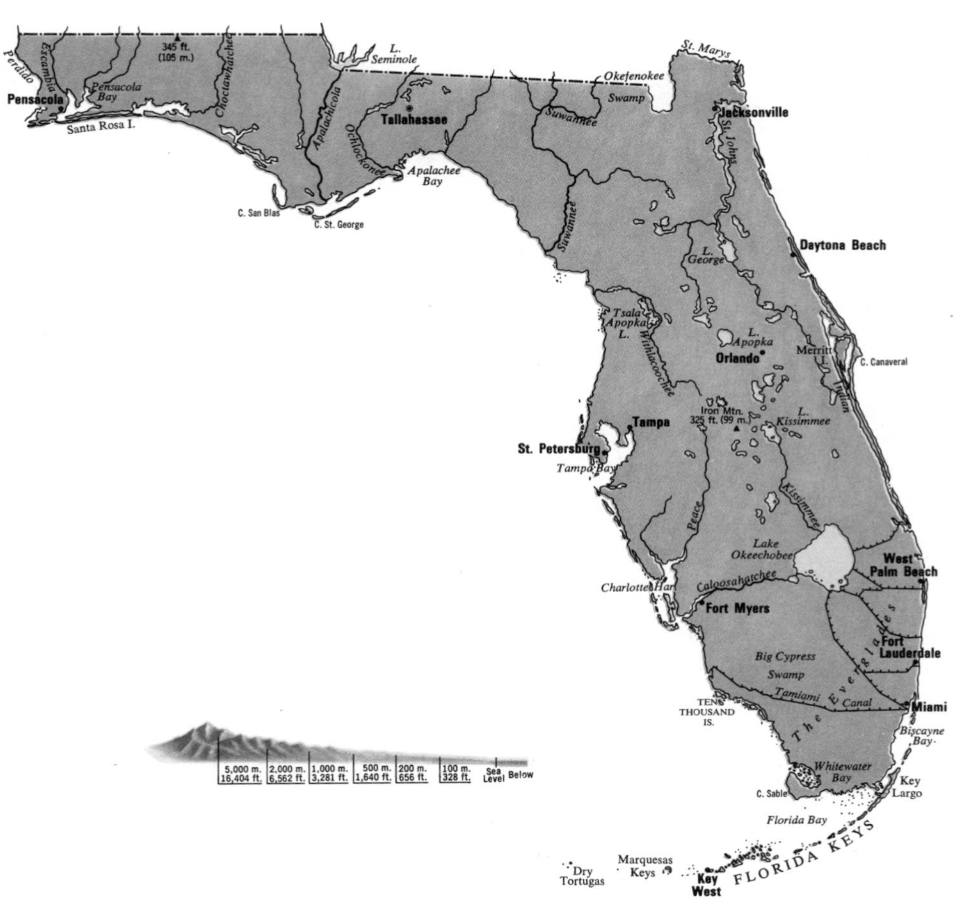

0 50 100 MI.
0 50 100 KM.
Perdido
Escambia
Pensacola
Pensacola Bay
Santa Rosa I.
Choctawhatchee
345 ft. (105 m.)
Apalachicola
Ochlockonee
L. Seminole
Tallahassee
Apalachee Bay
C. San Blas
C. St. George
St. Marys
Okefenokee Swamp
Suwannee
Jacksonville
St. Johns
L. George
Daytona Beach
Tsala Apopka L.
Withlacoochee
L. Apopka
Orlando
Merritt I.
C. Canaveral
Indian
Iron Mtn. 325 ft. (99 m.)
L. Kissimmee
Tampa
St. Petersburg
Tampa Bay
Peace
Kissimmee
Lake Okeechobee
West Palm Beach
Charlotte Har.
Caloosahatchee
Fort Myers
Fort Lauderdale
Big Cypress Swamp
The Everglades
Tamiami Canal
Miami
TEN THOUSAND IS.
Biscayne Bay
Whitewater Bay
C. Sable
Key Largo
Florida Bay
FLORIDA KEYS
Marquesas Keys
Dry Tortugas
Key West
5,000 m. 16,404 ft.
2,000 m. 6,562 ft.
1,000 m. 3,281 ft.
500 m. 1,640 ft.
200 m. 656 ft.
100 m. 328 ft.
Sea Level
Below

COUNTIES

Alachua 151,348 D2
Baker 15,289 D1
Bay 97,740 C6
Bradford 20,023 D2
Brevard 272,959 F3
Broward 101,820 F5
Calhoun 9,294 D6
Charlotte 58,460 E5
Citrus 54,703 D3
Clay 67,052 E2
Collier 85,791 E5
Columbia 35,399 D1
Dade 1,625,781 F6
De Soto 19,039 E4
Dixie 7,751 C2
Duval 571,003 E1
Escambia 233,794 B6
Flagler 10,913 E2
Franklin 7,661 B2
Gadsden 41,565 B1
Gilchrist 5,767 D2
Glades 5,992 E5
Gulf 10,658 D7
Hamilton 8,761 D1
Hardee 19,379 E4
Hendry 18,599 E5
Hernando 44,4693
Highlands 47,526 E4
Hillsborough 646,960 D4
Holmes 14,723 C5
Indian River 59,896 F4
Jackson 39,154 D5
Jefferson 10,703 C1
Lafayette 4,035 C2
Lake 104,870 E3
Lee 205,266 E5
Leon 148,655 B1
Levy 19,870 D2
Liberty 4,260 B1
Madison 14,894 C1
Manatee 148,442 D4
Marion 122,488 D2
Martin 64,014 F4
Monroe 63,188 E7
Nassau 32,894 E1
Okaloosa 109,920 C6
Okeechobee 20,264 F4
Orange 471,016 E3
Osceola 49,287 E3
Palm Beach 576,863 F5
Pasco 193,643 D3
Pinellas 728,531 D4
Polk 321,652 E4
Putnam 50,549 E2
Saint Johns 51,303 E2
Saint Lucie 87,182 F4
Santa Rosa 55,988 B6
Sarasota 202,251 D4
Seminole 179,752 E3
Sumter 24,272 D3
Suwannee 22,287 C1
Taylor 16,532 C1
Union 10,166 D1
Volusia 258,762 E2
Wakulla 10,887 B1
Walton 21,300 C6
Washington 14,509 C6

CITIES and TOWNS

Zip *Name/Pop.* *Key*

32615 Alachua 3,561 D2
32420 Alford 548 D6
32701 Altamonte Springs 22,028 E3
32421 Altha 478 A1
33820 Alturas 900 E4
33501 Anna Maria 1,537 D4
32320 Apalachicola⊙ 2,565 A2
33570 Apollo Beach 4,014 C3
32703 Apopka 6,019 E3
33821 Arcadia⊙ 6,002 E4
32618 Archer 1,230 D2
33502 Aripeka 450 D3
32705 Astatula 755 E3
32233 Atlantic Beach 7,847 E1
33823 Auburndale 6,501 E3
33825 Avon Park 8,026 E4
32807 Azalea Park 8,301 E3
32530 Bagdad 1,479 B6
32234 Baldwin 1,526 E1
†33101 Bal Harbour 2,973 C4
33830 Bartow⊙ 14,780 E4
32423 Bascom 134 A1
†33101 Bay Harbor Islands 4,869 B4
†32786 Bay Lake 74 E3
33504 Bay Pines 5,757 B3
33507 Bayshore Gardens 14,945 D4
†33578 Bee Ridge 3,313 D4
32619 Bell 227 D2
33540 Belleair 3,673 B2
†33540 Belleair Beach 1,643 B2
33540 Belleair Bluffs 2,522 B3
†33540 Belleair Shores 80 B3
33430 Belle Glade 16,535 F5
†33430 Belle Glade Camp 1,645 F5
†32801 Belle Isle 2,848 E3
32620 Belleview 1,913 D2
†32036 Beverly Beach 217 E2
33152 Biscayne Park 3,088 B4
†32801 Bithlo 3,143 E3
32424 Blountstown⊙ 2,632 A1
33921 Boca Grande 900 D5
*33432 Boca Raton 49,505 F5
32425 Bonifay⊙ 2,534 C5
33923 Bonita Springs 5,435 E5
33834 Bowling Green 2,310 E4
*33435 Boynton Beach 35,624 F5
*33506 Bradenton⊙ 30,170 D4
Bradenton‡ 148,442 D4
33510 Bradenton Beach 1,595 D4
33835 Bradley 1,108 D4
33511 Brandon 41,826 D4
32008 Branford 622 D2
†33435 Briny Breezes 387 G5
32321 Bristol⊙ 1,044 B1
†33314 Broadview Park 6,022 B4
32621 Bronson⊙ 853 D2
32622 Brooker 429 D2
33512 Brooksville⊙ 5,582 D3
†33311 Browardale 7,409 B4
32010 Bunnell⊙ 1,816 E2
33513 Bushnell⊙ 983 D3
32011 Callahan 869 E1
32401 Calloway 7,154 D6
32426 Campbellton 336 D5
32624 Candler 275 E2
32920 Cape Canaveral 5,733 F3
33904 Cape Coral 32,103 E5
33055 Carol City 47,349 B4
Carrabelle 1,304 B2
32427 Caryville 633 C6
32707 Casselberry 15,247 E3
†32401 Cedar Grove 1,104 D6
32625 Cedar Key 700 C2
33514 Center Hill 751 D3
32535 Century 495 B5
†33950 Charlotte Harbor 2,084 E5
32324 Chattahoochee 5,332 B1
32626 Chiefland 1,986 D2
32428 Chipley⊙ 3,330 D6
†32548 Cinco Bayou 202 B6
*33515 Clearwater⊙ 85,528 B2
32711 Clermont 5,461 E3
†33950 Cleveland 2,417 E5
33440 Clewiston 5,219 E5
32922 Cocoa 16,096 F3
32931 Cocoa Beach 10,926 F3
†33060 Coconut Creek 6,288 F5
33521 Coleman 1,022 D3
33328 Cooper City 10,140 B4
†33559 Coral Cove 2,042 D4
33134 Coral Gables 43,241 B5
33060 Coral Springs 37,349 F5
33522 Cortez 3,821 D4
32431 Cottondale 1,056 D6
32327 Crawfordville⊙ 1,110 B1
32012 Crescent City 1,722 E2
32536 Crestview⊙ 7,617 C6
32628 Cross City⊙ 2,154 C2
32629 Crystal River 2,778 D3
33157 Cutler Ridge 20,886 F6
33880 Cypress Gardens 8,043 E3
†33472 Cypress Quarters 1,479 F4
33525 Dade City⊙ 4,923 D3
33004 Dania 11,811 B4
33837 Davenport 1,509 E3
33314 Davie 20,877 B4
*32014 Daytona Beach 54,176 F2
Daytona Beach‡ 258,762 F2
32016 Daytona Beach Shores 1,324 F2
32713 De Bary 4,980 E3
33441 Deerfield Beach 39,193 F5
32433 De Funiak Springs⊙ 5,563 C6
32720 De Land⊙ 15,354 E2
32028 De Leon Springs 1,669 E2
*33444 Delray Beach 34,325 F5
32725 Deltona 15,710 E3
32541 Destin 3,672 C6
33527 Dover 2,354 D4
33838 Dundee 2,227 E3
33528 Dunedin 30,203 B2
32630 Dunnellon 1,427 D2
33839 Eagle Lake 1,678 E4
†33601 East Lake-Orient Park 5,612 C2
†33940 East Naples 12,127 E5
32031 East Palatka 1,613 E2
32328 Eastpoint 1,246 B2
32751 Eatonville 2,185 E3
32437 Ebro 233 C6
32032 Edgewater 6,726 F3
†32801 Edgewood 1,034 E3
†33614 Egypt Lake 11,932 C2
33531 Elfers 11,396 D3
†33101 El Portal 1,819 B4
33533 Englewood 9,633 D5
32504 Ensley 14,422 B6
32425 Esto 304 C5
32726 Eustis 9,453 E3
33929 Everglades City 524 E6
32634 Fairfield 450 D2
†32693 Fanning Springs (Suwannee Riv.) 314 D2
32948 Fellsmere 1,161 F4
32034 Fernandina Beach⊙ 7,224 E1
32922 Five Points 1,691 D1
32036 Flagler Beach 2,208 E2
32636 Floral City 1,181 D3
33034 Florida City 6,174 F6
†32960 Florida Ridge 4,988 F4
†33472 Fort Drum 70 F4
*33301 Fort Lauderdale⊙ 153,279 C4
Fort Lauderdale-Hollywood‡ 1,014,043 C4
33841 Fort Meade 5,546 E4
*33901 Fort Myers⊙ 36,638 E5
Fort Myers-Cape Coral‡ 205,266 E5
33931 Fort Myers Beach 5,753 E5
33842 Fort Ogden 900 E4
*33450 Fort Pierce⊙ 33,802 F4
32548 Fort Walton Beach 20,829 C6
Fort Walton Beach‡ 109,920 C6
32038 Fort White 386 D2
32438 Fountain 900 D6
32439 Freeport 669 C6
33843 Frostproof 2,995 E4
32731 Fruitland Park 2,259 D3
33578 Fruitville 3,070 D4
*32601 Gainesville⊙ 81,371 D2
Gainesville‡ 151,348 D2
32732 Geneva 1,120 E3
33534 Gibsonton 7,219 C3
32960 Gifford 6,240 F4
32040 Glen Saint Mary 462 D1
†33160 Golden Beach 612 C4
33999 Golden Gate 4,327 E5
†33444 Golf 110 F5
32560 Gonzalez 6,084 B6
33933 Goodland 600 E6
†32502 Goulding 5,352 B6
33170 Goulds 7,078 F6
32440 Graceville 2,918 D5
32442 Grand Ridge 591 A1
33463 Greenacres City 8,843 F5
32043 Green Cove Springs⊙ 4,154 E2
32330 Greensboro 562 B1
32331 Greenville 1,096 C1
32443 Greenwood 577 A1
32332 Gretna 1,448 B1
33533 Grove City 1,932 D5
32736 Groveland 1,992 E3
32561 Gulf Breeze 5,478 B6
33737 Gulfport 11,180 B3
†33444 Gulf Stream 475 F5
†33301 Hacienda Village 126 B4
33844 Haines City 10,799 E3
33009 Hallandale 36,517 B4
32044 Hampton 466 D2
33440 Harlem 2,669 F5
32045 Hastings 636 E2
32333 Havana 2,782 B1
32640 Hawthorne 1,303 D2
32642 Hernando 1,653 D3
*33010 Hialeah 145,254 B4
†33010 Hialeah Gardens 2,700 B4
33431 Highland Beach 2,030 F5
33846 Highland City 1,555 E4
32401 Highland Park 184 E4
32643 High Springs 2,491 D2
32405 Hiland Park 4,763 C6
†33827 Hillcrest Heights 177 E4
32046 Hilliard 1,869 E1
†33060 Hillsboro Beach 1,554 F5
33455 Hobe Sound 6,822 F4
32047 Hollister 980 E2
32017 Holly Hill 9,953 E2
*33020 Hollywood 121,323 B4
33509 Holmes Beach 4,023 D4
*33030 Homestead 20,668 F6
32646 Homosassa 1,426 D3
32648 Horseshoe Beach 304 C2
32334 Hosford 750 B1
32737 Howey In The Hills 626 E3
33568 Hudson 5,799 D3
†33460 Hypoluxo 573 F5
33934 Immokalee 11,038 E5
32903 Indialantic 2,883 F3
†33139 Indian Creek 103 B4
†32901 Indian Harbour Beach 5,967 F3
32960 Indian River Shores 1,254 F4
33535 Indian Rocks Beach 3,717 B3
†33535 Indian Shores 984 B3
33456 Indiantown 3,383 F4
32649 Inglis 1,173 D2
32048 Interlachen 848 E2
32650 Inverness⊙ 4,095 D3
33036 Islamorada 1,441 F7
†33101 Islandia 12 F6
*32201 Jacksonville⊙ 540,920 E1
Jacksonville‡ 737,519 E1
32250 Jacksonville Beach 15,462 E1
†33568 Jasmine Estates 11,995 D3
32052 Jasper⊙ 2,093 D1
32565 Jay 633 B5
32053 Jennings 749 C1
33457 Jensen Beach 6,639 F4
†32901 June Park 4,051 F3
†33404 Juno Beach 1,142 F5
33458 Jupiter 9,868 F5
†33455 Jupiter Island 364 F4
33849 Kathleen 1,866 D3
33156 Kendall 73,758 B5
33709 Kenneth City 4,344 B3
33149 Key Biscayne 6,313 B5
33051 Key Colony Beach 977 F7
33037 Key Largo 7,447 F6
32656 Keystone Heights 1,056 E2
33040 Key West⊙ 24,382 E7
32741 Kissimmee⊙ 15,487 E3
33935 La Belle⊙ 2,287 E5
33537 Lacoochee 1,720 D3
32658 La Crosse 170 D2
32659 Lady Lake 1,193 E3
33850 Lake Alfred 3,134 E3
†32830 Lake Buena Vista 98 E3
32054 Lake Butler⊙ 1,830 D1
†33601 Lake Carroll 13,012 C2
32055 Lake City⊙ 9,257 D1
32744 Lake Helen 2,047 E3
*33801 Lakeland 47,406 D3
Lakeland-Winter Haven‡ 321,652 D3
†33612 Lake Magdalene 13,331 D3
32746 Lake Mary 2,853 E3
33403 Lake Park 6,909 F5
33852 Lake Placid 963 E4
33853 Lake Wales 8,466 E4
*33460 Lake Worth 27,048 G5
33539 Land O'Lakes 4,515 D3
33462 Lantana 8,048 F5
*33540 Largo 58,977 B3
33308 Lauderdale-by-the-Sea 2,639 C3
†33313 Lauderdale Lakes 25,426 B3
33313 Lauderhill 37,271 B3
33545 Laurel 6,368 D4
32567 Laurel Hill 610 C5
32058 Lawtey 692 D1
†33050 Layton 88 F7
†33301 Lazy Lake 31 B3
32059 Lee 297 C1
32748 Leesburg 13,191 E3
33936 Lehigh Acres 9,604 E5
33033 Leisure City 17,905 F6
†33614 Leto 9,003 C2
33064 Lighthouse Point 11,488 F5
32060 Live Oak⊙ 6,732 D1
32662 Lochloosa 450 E2
33548 Longboat Key 4,843 D4
32750 Longwood 10,029 E3
33549 Lutz 5,555 D3
32444 Lynn Haven 6,239 C6
32063 Macclenny⊙ 3,851 D1

(continued on following page)

33738 Madeira Beach 4,520 ....B3
32340 Madison⊙ 3,487 ....C1
32751 Maitland 8,763 ....E3
32950 Malabar 1,118 ....F3
32445 Malone 897 ....A1
33550 Mango 6,493 ....D4
33050 Marathon 7,568 ....E7
33937 Marco (Marco Island) 4,679 ....E6
33063 Margate 35,900 ....F5
32446 Marianna⊙ 7,006 ....A1
†32084 Marineland 31 ....E2
32569 Mary Esther 3,530 ....B6
32753 Mascotte 1,112 ....E3
32066 Mayo⊙ 891 ....C1
32664 McIntosh 404 ....D2
†33101 Medley 537 ....B4
*32901 Melbourne 46,536 ....F3
Melbourne-Titusville-Cocoa‡ 272,959 ....F3
32951 Melbourne Beach 2,713 ....F3
†33301 Melrose Park 5,672 ....B4
†33561 Memphis 5,501 ....D4
32952 Merritt Island 30,708 ....F3
32410 Mexico Beach 632 ....D6
*33101 Miami⊙ 346,931 ....B5
Miami‡ 1,625,979 ....B5
33139 Miami Beach 96,298 ....C5
†33101 Miami Lakes 9,809 ....B4
33153 Miami Shores 9,244 ....B4
33166 Miami Springs 12,350 ....B5
32667 Micanopy 737 ....D2
†32960 Micco 3,585 ....F4
32343 Midway 950 ....B1
32570 Milton⊙ 7,206 ....B6
32754 Mims 7,583 ....F3
32755 Minneola 851 ....E3
33023 Miramar 32,813 ....B4
32577 Molino 1,456 ....B6
32344 Monticello⊙ 2,994 ....C1
32756 Montverde 397 ....E3
33471 Moore Haven⊙ 1,250 ....E5
32757 Mount Dora 5,883 ....E3
33860 Mulberry 2,932 ....E4
33938 Murdock 272 ....D4
32506 Myrtle Grove 14,238 ....B6
*33940 Naples⊙ 17,581 ....E5
†33940 Naples Park 5,438 ....E5
33032 Naranja 10,381 ....F6
32233 Neptune Beach 5,248 ....E1
32669 Newberry 1,826 ....D2
*33552 New Port Richey 11,196 ...D3
32069 New Smyrna Beach 13,557 F2
32578 Niceville 8,543 ....C6
33555 Nokomis 3,108 ....D4
32452 Noma 113 ....C5
†33169 Norland 19,471 ....B4
33141 North Bay Village 4,920 ....B4

33903 North Fort Myers 22,808 ...E5
†33063 North Lauderdale 18,653 ...B3
33161 North Miami 42,566 ....B4
33161 North Miami Beach 36,481 C4
33940 North Naples 7,950 ....E5
33403 North Palm Beach 11,344 ..F5
33595 North Port 6,205 ....D4
†33708 North Redington Beach 1,156 ....B3
32759 Oak Hill 938 ....F3
32760 Oakland 658 ....E3
33334 Oakland Park 23,035 ....B3
*32670 Ocala⊙ 37,170 ....D2
Ocala‡ 122,488 ....D2
†33457 Ocean Breeze Park 469 ......F4
33444 Ocean Ridge 1,355 ....F5
32761 Ocoee 7,803 ....E3
33163 Ojus 17,344 ....B4
32762 Okahumpka 900 ....D3
33472 Okeechobee⊙ 4,225 ....F4
33557 Oldsmar 2,608 ....B2
33558 Oneco 6,417 ....D4
33054 Opa Locka 14,460 ....B4
32763 Orange City 2,795 ....E3
32073 Orange Park 8,766 ....E1
†32970 Orchid 42 ....F4
*32801 Orlando⊙ 128,291 ....E3
Orlando‡ 700,699 ....E3
32074 Ormond Beach 21,378 ......E2
32074 Ormond-by-the-Sea 7,665 .E2
33559 Osprey 1,660 ....D4
32683 Otter Creek 167 ....D2
32765 Oviedo 3,074 ....E3
32570 Pace 5,006 ....B6
33476 Pahokee 6,346 ....F5
†32036 Painters Hill 40 ....E2
32077 Palatka⊙ 10,175 ....E2
32905 Palm Bay 18,560 ....F3
33480 Palm Beach 9,729 ....G4
†33403 Palm Beach Gardens 14,407 ....F5
†33404 Palm Beach Shores 1,232 .G5
33490 Palm City 2,177 ....F4
32037 Palm Coast 2,837 ....E2
33561 Palmetto 8,637 ....D4
33563 Palm Harbor 5,215 ....D3
33619 Palm River-Clair Mel 14,447 ....C3
†32901 Palm Shores 77 ....F3
33460 Palm Springs 8,166 ....F5
*32401 Panama City⊙ 33,346 ......C6
Panama City‡ 97,740 ......C6
32407 Panama City Beach 2,148 ..C6
32401 Parker 4,298 ....C6
†33441 Parkland 545 ....F5
32538 Paxton 659 ....C5
†33023 Pembroke Park 4,783 ......B4
33024 Pembroke Pines 35,776 ....B4

32079 Penney Farms 630 ....E2
†33010 Pennsuco 15 ....B4
*32501 Pensacola⊙ 57,619 ....B6
Pensacola‡ 289,782 ....B6
33157 Perrine 16,129 ....F6
32347 Perry⊙ 8,254 ....C1
32080 Pierson 1,085 ....E2
32808 Pine Hills 35,771 ....E3
33565 Pinellas Park 32,811 ....B3
33317 Plantation 48,653 ....B4
33566 Plant City 17,064 ....D3
33868 Polk City 576 ....E3
32081 Pomona Park 791 ....E2
*33060 Pompano Beach 52,618 ....F5
32455 Ponce de Leon 454 ....C6
†32019 Ponce Inlet 1,003 ....F2
33952 Port Charlotte 25,770 ......D5
32019 Port Orange 18,756 ....F2
33568 Port Richey 2,165 ....D3
32456 Port Saint Joe 4,027 ....D6
33452 Port Saint Lucie 14,690 ....F4
33492 Port Salerno 4,511 ....F4
33032 Princeton 10,381 ....F6
*33950 Punta Gorda⊙ 6,797 ....E5
32351 Quincy⊙ 8,591 ....B1
32083 Raiford 259 ....D1
32686 Reddick 657 ....D2
33708 Redington Beach 1,708 ....B3
†33708 Redington Shores 2,142 ...B3
†33158 Richmond Heights 8,577 ...F6
†33301 Riverland 5,919 ....B4
33404 Riviera Beach 26,489 ....G5
32955 Rockledge 11,877 ....F3
32957 Roseland 1,607 ....F4
33570 Ruskin 5,117 ....C3
33572 Safety Harbor 6,461 ....B2
32084 Saint Augustine⊙ 11,985 ..E2
32084 Saint Augustine Beach 1,289 ....E2
32769 Saint Cloud 7,840 ....E3
33956 Saint James City 1,298 ....D5
33574 Saint Leo 917 ....D3
33452 Saint Lucie 593 ....F4
32355 Saint Marks 286 ....B1
*33701 Saint Petersburg 238,647 ..B3
33736 Saint Petersburg Beach 9,354 ....B3
†33508 Samoset 5,747 ....D4
†32069 Samsula 1,971 ....E2
33576 San Antonio 529 ....D3
32771 Sanford⊙ 23,176 ....E3
33957 Sanibel 3,363 ....D5
*33577 Sarasota⊙ 48,868 ....D4
Sarasota‡ 202,251 ....D4
†33577 Sarasota Springs 13,860 ...D4
32935 Satellite Beach 9,163 ....F3
32775 Scottsmoor 900 ....F3
†33301 Sea Ranch Lakes 584 ......C3

32958 Sebastian 2,831 ....F4
33870 Sebring⊙ 8,736 ....E4
33584 Seffner 6,493 ....D4
33542 Seminole 4,586 ....B3
†33457 Sewalls Point 1,187 ....F4
32579 Shalimar 390 ....C6
32959 Sharpes 4,149 ....F3
32688 Silver Springs 1,082 ....D2
32460 Sneads 1,690 ....B1
32358 Sopchoppy 444 ....B1
33493 South Bay 3,886 ....F5
32021 South Daytona 11,252 ......F2
33143 South Miami 10,944 ....B5
†33157 South Miami Heights 23,559 ....F6
33707 South Pasadena 4,188 ......B3
†32901 South Patrick Shores 9,816 ....F3
†32401 Southport 1,992 ....C6
33452 South Port Saint Lucie (Port Saint Lucie 14,690 ......F4
33595 South Venice 8,075 ....D4
32690 Sparr 902 ....D2
32401 Springfield 7,220 ....D6
32091 Starke⊙ 5,306 ....D2
33494 Stuart⊙ 9,467 ....F4
33586 Sun City D4
†33570 Sun City Center 5,605 ......C3
†33450 Sunland Gardens F4
33160 Sunny Isles 12,564 ....C4
33313 Sunrise 39,681 ....B4
33154 Surfside 3,763 ....B4
32692 Suwannee (Fanning Sprs.) 314 ....C2
†33144 Sweetwater 8,251 ....B5
†32043 Switzerland 3,906 ....E1
32809 Taft 900 ....E3
*32301 Tallahassee (cap.)⊙ 81,548 ....B1
Tallahassee‡ 159,542 ....B1
†33321 Tamarac 29,376 ....B3
*33601 Tampa⊙ 271,523 ....C2
Tampa-Saint Petersburg‡ 1,569,492 ..C2
*33589 Tarpon Springs 13,251 ......D3
32778 Tavares⊙ 4,103 ....E3
33070 Tavernier 1,834 ....F6
33617 Temple Terrace 11,097 ......C2
33458 Tequesta 3,685 ....F5
33905 Tice 6,645 ....E5
32780 Titusville⊙ 31,910 ....F3
33740 Treasure Island 6,316 ......B3
32693 Trenton⊙ 1,131 ....D2
32784 Umatilla 1,872 ....E3
33620 University 24,514 ....C2
32580 Valparaiso 6,142 ....C6
*33595 Venice 12,153 ....D4
32462 Vernon 885 ....C6

32960 Vero Beach⊙ 16,176 ......F4
†33166 Virginia Gardens 2,098 ....B5
32970 Wabasso 2,157 ....F4
†32327 Wakulla 225 ....B1
32694 Waldo 993 ....D2
†32456 Ward Ridge 104 ....D6
32507 Warrington 15,792 ....B6
†32055 Watertown 3,804 ....D1
33873 Wauchula⊙ 2,986 ....E4
32463 Wausau 347 ....D6
33877 Waverly 1,208 ....E4
33597 Webster 856 ....D3
†33512 Weeki Wachee 8 ....D3
32093 Welaka 492 ....E2
32935 West Eau Gallie 2,591 ......F3
†32901 West Melbourne 5,078 ......F3
†33101 West Miami 6,076 ....B5
*33401 West Palm Beach⊙ 63,305 F5
West Palm Beach-Boca Raton‡ 573,125 ....F5
†32502 West Pensacola 24,371 ....B6
32464 Westville 343 ....C6
†33165 Westwood Lakes 11,478 ...B5
32465 Wewahitchka⊙ 1,742 ....D6
†32465 White City 4,110 ....F4
32096 White Springs 781 ....D1
32785 Wildwood 2,665 ....D3
32696 Williston 2,240 ....D2
33334 Wilton Manors 12,742 ......B3
33598 Wimauma 1,477 ....D4
32786 Windermere 1,302 ....E3
33880 Winter Haven 21,119 ......E3
*32789 Winter Park 22,339 ....E3
†32801 Winter Springs 10,475 ......E3
32362 Woodville 1,768 ....B1
32697 Worthington Springs 220 ..D2
32698 Yankeetown 600 ....D2
32097 Yulee 3,168 ....E1
32798 Zellwood 1,760 ....E3
33599 Zephyrhills 5,742 ....D3
33890 Zolfo Springs 1,495 ....E4

OTHER FEATURES

Alapaha (riv.) C1
Alligator (lake) E3
Amelia (isl.) E1
Anastasia (isl.) E2
Anclote (keys) D3
Apalachee (bay) B2
Apalachicola (bay) B2
Apalachicola (riv.) A1
Apopka (lake) E3
Arbuckle (lake) E4
Aucilla (riv.) C1
Banana (riv.) F3
Beresford (lake) E3
Big Cypress (swamp) E5
Big Cypress Nat'l Preserve E5
Biscayne (bay) F6
Biscayne (key) B5
Biscayne Nat'l Park F6
Blackwater (riv.) B6
Blue Cypress (lake) F4
Boca Chica (key) E7
Boca Ciega (bay) B3
Boca Grande (key) D7
Bryant (lake) E2
Caloosahatchee (riv.) E5
Captiva (isl.) D5
Casey (key) D4
Castillo de San Marcos Nat'l Mon. E2
Cecil Field Naval Air Sta. E1
Charlotte (harb.) D5
Chattahoochee (riv.) B1
Chipola (riv.) D6
Choctawhatchee (riv.) C6
Crescent (lake) E2
Cumberland Island Nat'l Seashore E1
Cypress (lake) E3
De Soto Nat'l Mem. D4
Dead (lake) D6
Dexter (lake) E2
Dog (isl.) B2
Dorr (lake) E2
Dry Tortugas (keys) D7
Dumfoundling (bay) C4
East (pt.) E6
Eglin A.F.B. 7,574 ....C6
Egmont (key) D4
Elliott (key) F6
Escambia (riv.) B6
Estero (isl.) E5
Eureka (res.) E2
Everglades, The (swamp) F6
Everglades Nat'l Park F6
Fenholloway (riv.) C1
Florida (bay) F6
Florida (cape) F6
Florida (keys) E7
Florida (strs) F7
Fort Caroline Nat'l Mem. E1
Fort Jefferson Nat'l Mon. C7
Fort Matanzas Nat'l Mon. E2
Gasparilla (isl.) D5
George (lake) E2
Grassy (key) F7
Gulf Island Nat'l Seashore B6
Harney (lake) F3
Hart (lake) E3
Hillsborough (bay) C3
Hillsborough (canal) F5
Hillsborough (riv.) C2
Homosassa (isls.) D3
Homestead A.F.B. 7,594 ....F6
Iamonia (lake) B1
Indian (riv.) F3
Iron (mt.) E4
Istokpoga (lake) E4
Jackson (lake) B1
Jackson (lake) E4
Jacksonville Naval Air Sta. E1
John F. Kennedy Space Center F3
June in Winter (lake) E4
Kennedy (Canaveral) (cape) F3

Kerr (lake) E2
Key Largo (key) F6
Key Vaca (key) E7
Key West Naval Air Sta. E7
Kissimmee (lake) E4
Kissimmee (riv.) E4
Largo (key) F6
Levy (lake) D2
Lochloosa (lake) D2
Long (key) B3
Long (key) F7
Longboat (key) D4
Lower Matecumbe (key) F7
Lowery (lake) E3
MacDill A.F.B. C3
Manatee (riv.) D4
Marco (isl.) E6
Marian (lake) E4
Marquesas (keys) D7
Matanzas (inlet) E2
Mayport Naval Air Sta. E1
McCoy A.F.B. E3
Merritt (isl.) F3
Mexico (gulf) C4
Miami (canal) F5
Miami (riv.) B5
Miccosukee (lake) B1
Monroe (lake) E3
Mosquito (lag.) F3
Mullet (key) D4
Myakka (riv.) D4
Nassau (riv.) E1
Nassau (sound) E1
New (riv.) B1
New (riv.) D1
Newnans (lake) D2
North Merritt (isl.) F3
North New River (canal) F5
Ochlockonee (riv.) B1
Okaloacoochee Slough (swamp) E5
Okeechobee (lake) F5
Okefenokee (swamp) D1
Oklawaha (riv.) E2
Old Rhodes (key) F6
Old Tampa (bay) B3
Olustee (riv.) D1
Orange (lake) D2
Patrick A.F.B. 2,843 ....F3
Peace (riv.) E4
Pensacola (bay) B6
Pensacola Naval Air Sta. B6
Perdido (riv.) B6
Pine (isl.) D5
Pine Island (sound) D5
Pine Log (creek) C6
Pinellas (pt.) C3
Piney (isl.) B1
Piney (pt.) C2
Placid (lake) E4
Plantation (key) F7
Poinsett (lake) F3
Ponce de Leon (bay) E6
Port Everglades (harb.) C4
Port Tampa (harb.) B3
Reedy (lake) E4
Romano (cape) E6
Sable (cape) E6
Saint Andrew (pt.) D6
Saint George (cape) A2
Saint George (isl.) B2
Saint George (sound) B2
Saint Johns (riv.) E2
Saint Joseph (bay) D6
Saint Joseph (pt.) D6
Saint Lucie (canal) F4
Saint Lucie (inlet) F4
Saint Marys (riv.) D1
Saint Marys Entrance (inlet) E1
Saint Vincent (isl.) D7
San Blas (cape) D7
Sand (key) B3
Sands (key) F6
Sanibel (isl.) D5
Santa Fe (lake) D2
Santa Fe (riv.) D2
Santa Rosa (isl.) B6
Santa Rosa (sound) B6
Sarasota (pt.) D4
Seminole (lake) B1
Seminole Ind. Res. E4
Seminole Ind. Res. F5
Shark (pt.) E6
Shoal (riv.) C6
Snake Creek (canal) B4
South New River (canal) F5
Stafford (lake) D2
Sugarloaf (key) E7
Suwannee (riv.) C2
Suwannee (sound) C2
Talbot (isl.) E1
Talquin (lake) B1
Tamiami (canal) E6
Tampa (bay) D4
Ten Thousand (isls.) E6
Torch (key) E7
Treasure (isl.) B3
Tsala Apopka (lake) D3
Tyndall A.F.B. 4,542 ....C6
Upper Matecumbe (key) F7
Vaca (key) E7
Virginia (key) B5
Waccasassa (bay) D2
Waccasassa (riv.) D2
Washington (lake) F3
Weir (lake) E2
Weohyakapka (lake) E4
West Palm Beach (canal) F5
Whitewater (bay) F6
Whiting Field Naval Air Sta. B6
Wimico (lake) A2
Winder (lake) F3
Withlacoochee (riv.) C1
Withlacoochee (riv.) D2
Yale (lake) E3
Yellow (riv.) B6

⊙County seat.
‡Population of metropolitan area.
† Zip of nearest p.o. * Multiple zips.

Agriculture, Industry and Resources

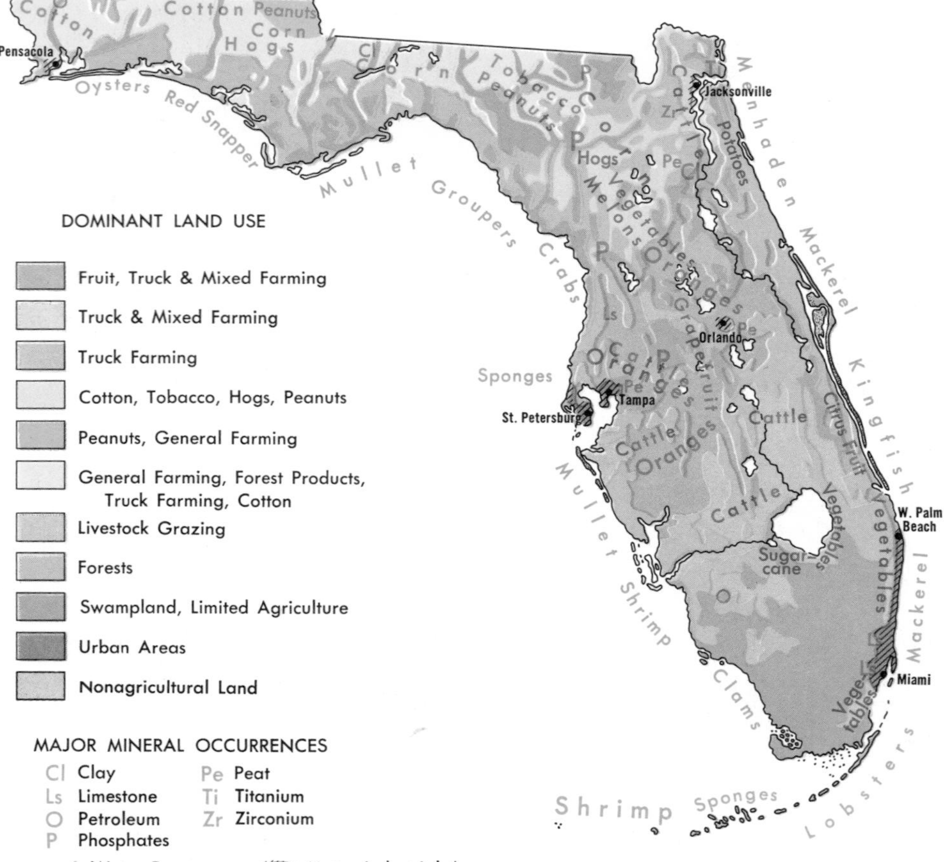

Pensacola
Jacksonville
Orlando
Tampa
St. Petersburg
W. Palm Beach
Miami
Cotton
Peanuts
Corn
Hogs
Tobacco
Oysters
Red Snapper
Mullet
Groupers
Crabs
Sponges
Potatoes
Menhaden
Mackerel
Kingfish
Citrus Fruit
Vegetables
Cattle
Oranges
Melons
Sugar-cane
Shrimp
Clams
Lobsters
DOMINANT LAND USE
Fruit, Truck & Mixed Farming
Truck & Mixed Farming
Truck Farming
Cotton, Tobacco, Hogs, Peanuts
Peanuts, General Farming
General Farming, Forest Products, Truck Farming, Cotton
Livestock Grazing
Forests
Swampland, Limited Agriculture
Urban Areas
Nonagricultural Land
MAJOR MINERAL OCCURRENCES
Cl Clay
Ls Limestone
O Petroleum
P Phosphates
Pe Peat
Ti Titanium
Zr Zirconium
Water Power
Major Industrial Areas

AREA 58,910 sq. mi. (152,577 sq. km.)
POPULATION 5,463,105
CAPITAL Atlanta
LARGEST CITY Atlanta
HIGHEST POINT Brasstown Bald 4,784 ft.
(1458 m.)
SETTLED IN 1733
ADMITTED TO UNION January 2, 1788
POPULAR NAME Empire State of the South;
Peach State
STATE FLOWER Cherokee Rose
STATE BIRD Brown Thrasher

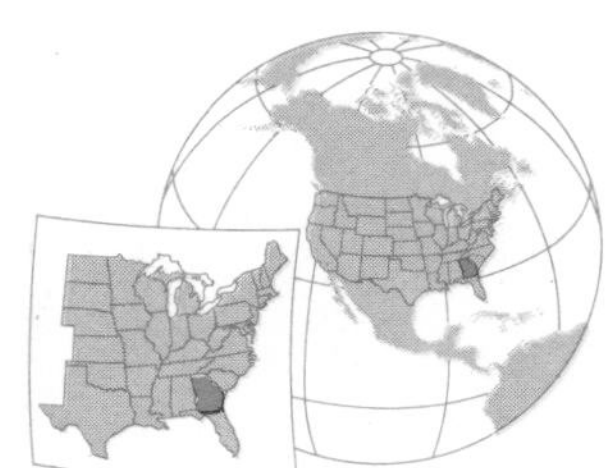

COUNTIES

Appling 15,565	H7
Atkinson 6,141	G8
Bacon 9,379	G7
Baker 3,808	D8
Baldwin 34,686	F4
Banks 8,702	E2
Barrow 21,293	E2
Bartow 40,760	C2
Ben Hill 16,000	F7
Berrien 13,525	F8
Bibb 151,085	E5
Bleckley 10,767	F6
Brantley 8,701	J8
Brooks 15,255	E9
Bryan 10,175	K6
Bulloch 35,785	J6
Burke 19,349	J4
Butts 13,665	E4
Calhoun 5,717	C7
Camden 13,371	J9
Candler 7,518	H6
Carroll 56,346	B3
Catoosa 36,991	B1
Charlton 7,343	H9
Chatham 202,226	K6
Chattahoochee 21,732	C6
Chattooga 21,956	B1
Cherokee 51,699	D2
Clarke 74,498	F3
Clay 3,553	B7
Clayton 150,357	D3
Clinch 6,660	G9
Cobb 297,694	C3
Coffee 26,894	G8
Colquitt 35,376	E8
Columbia 40,118	H3
Cook 13,490	F8
Coweta 39,268	C4
Crawford 7,684	E5
Crisp 19,489	E7
Dade 12,318	A1
Dawson 4,774	D2
De Kalb 483,024	D3
Decatur 25,495	C9
Dodge 16,955	F6
Dooly 10,826	E6
Dougherty 100,978	D7
Douglas 54,573	C3
Early 13,158	C8
Echols 2,297	G9
Effingham 18,327	K6
Elbert 18,758	G2
Emanuel 20,795	H5
Evans 8,428	J6
Fannin 14,748	D1
Fayette 29,043	C4
Floyd 79,800	B2
Forsyth 27,958	D2
Franklin 15,185	F2
Fulton 589,904	D3
Gilmer 11,110	D1
Glascock 2,382	G4
Glynn 54,981	J8
Gordon 30,070	C2
Grady 19,845	D9
Greene 11,391	F3
Gwinnett 166,903	D2
Habersham 25,020	E1
Hall 75,649	E2
Hancock 9,466	G4
Haralson 18,422	B3
Harris 15,464	C5
Hart 18,585	G2
Heard 6,520	B4
Henry 36,309	D4
Houston 77,605	E6
Irwin 8,988	F7
Jackson 25,343	E2
Jasper 7,553	E4
Jeff Davis 11,473	G7
Jefferson 18,403	H4
Jenkins 8,841	J5
Johnson 8,660	G5
Jones 16,579	E5
Lamar 12,215	D4
Lanier 5,654	F8
Laurens 36,990	G6
Lee 11,684	D7
Liberty 37,583	J7
Lincoln 6,949	H3
Long 4,524	J7
Lowndes 67,972	F9
Lumpkin 10,762	D2
Macon 14,003	D6
Madison 17,747	F2
Marion 5,297	C6
McDuffie 18,546	H4
McIntosh 8,046	K7
Meriwether 21,229	C4
Miller 7,038	C8
Mitchell 21,114	D8
Monroe 14,610	E4
Montgomery 7,011	G6
Morgan 11,572	F3
Murray 19,685	C1
Muscogee 170,108	C6
Newton 34,489	E3
Oconee 12,427	F3
Oglethorpe 8,929	F3
Paulding 26,042	C3
Peach 19,151	E5
Pickens 11,652	D2
Pierce 11,897	H8
Pike 8,937	D4
Polk 32,386	B3
Pulaski 8,950	E6
Putnam 10,295	F4
Quitman 2,357	B7
Rabun 10,466	F1
Randolph 9,599	C7
Richmond 181,629	H4
Rockdale 36,747	D3
Schley 3,433	D6
Screven 14,043	J5
Seminole 9,057	C9
Spalding 47,899	D4
Stephens 21,763	F1
Stewart 5,896	C6
Sumter 29,360	D6
Talbot 6,536	C5
Taliaferro 2,032	G3
Tattnall 18,134	J6
Taylor 7,902	D5
Telfair 11,445	G7
Terrell 12,017	D7
Thomas 38,098	E9
Tift 32,862	E7
Toombs 22,592	H6
Towns 5,638	E1
Treutlen 6,087	G6
Troup 50,003	B4
Turner 9,510	E7
Twiggs 9,354	F5
Union 9,390	E1
Upson 25,998	D5
Walker 56,470	B1
Walton 31,211	E3
Ware 37,180	H8
Warren 6,583	G4
Washington 18,842	G4
Wayne 20,750	J7
Webster 2,341	C6
Wheeler 5,155	G6
White 10,120	E1
Whitfield 65,780	B1
Wilcox 7,682	F7
Wilkes 10,951	G3
Wilkinson 10,368	F5
Worth 18,064	E8

CITIES and TOWNS

Zip	Name/Pop.	Key
31001	Abbeville⊙ 985	F7
30101	Acworth 3,648	C2
30103	Adairsville 1,739	C2
31620	Adel⊙ 5,592	F8
31002	Adrian 756	G5
30410	Ailey 579	G6
30411	Alamo⊙ 993	G6
31622	Alapaha 771	F8
*31701	Albany⊙ 74,550	D7
	Albany‡ 112,456	D7
†30204	Aldora 139	D4
31301	Allenhurst 606	J7
31003	Allentown 321	F5
31510	Alma⊙ 3,819	G7
30201	Alpharetta 3,128	D2
30412	Alston 111	H6
30510	Alto 618	E2
†30161	Alto Park	B2
31512	Ambrose 360	G7
31709	Americus⊙ 16,120	D6
31711	Andersonville 267	D6
30802	Appling⊙ 150	H3
31712	Arabi 376	E7
30104	Aragon 855	B2
†30549	Arcade 223	E2
†31520	Arco	J8
31623	Argyle 206	G8
31713	Arlington 1,572	C8
30619	Arnoldsville 187	F3
31714	Ashburn⊙ 4,766	E7
*30601	Athens⊙ 42,549	F3
	Athens‡ 130,015	F3
*30301	Atlanta (cap.)⊙ 425,022	K1
	Atlanta‡ 2,029,618	K1
31715	Attapulgus 623	D9
30203	Auburn 692	E2
*30901	Augusta⊙ 47,532	J4
	Augusta‡ 327,372	J4
30001	Austell 3,939	J1
†30557	Avalon 200	F1
30803	Avera 248	G4
30002	Avondale Estates 1,313	L1
31716	Baconton 763	D8
31717	Bainbridge⊙ 10,553	C9
30511	Baldwin 1,080	E2
30107	Ball Ground 640	D2
30204	Barnesville⊙ 4,887	D4
31625	Barney 146	E8
30413	Bartow 357	G5
31720	Barwick 413	E9
31513	Baxley⊙ 3,586	H7
†31554	Beach	G8
30414	Bellville 173	H6
31721	Benevolence 138	C7
†30136	Berkeley Lake 503	D3
31722	Berlin 538	E8
30620	Bethlehem 281	E3
†31901	Bibb City 667	B5
30621	Bishop 172	F3
31516	Blackshear⊙ 3,222	H8
30512	Blairsville⊙ 530	E1
31723	Blakely⊙ 5,880	C8
30513	Blue Ridge⊙ 1,376	D1
31724	Bluffton 132	C7
30805	Blythe 367	H4
30622	Bogart 819	E3
31626	Boston 1,441	E9
30623	Bostwick 357	E3
30108	Bowdon 1,743	B3
30516	Bowersville 318	G2
30624	Bowman 890	G2
30517	Braselton 308	E2
†30153	Braswell 282	C3
30110	Bremen 3,966	B3
31725	Brinson 274	C9
31726	Bronwood 524	D7
30415	Brooklet 1,035	J6
30205	Brooks 199	D4
31519	Broxton 1,117	G7
31520	Brunswick⊙ 17,605	K8
30113	Buchanan⊙ 1,019	B3
30625	Buckhead 219	F3
31803	Buena Vista⊙ 1,544	C6
30518	Buford 6,578	D2
31006	Butler⊙ 1,959	D5
31007	Byromville 567	E6
31008	Byron 1,661	E5
31009	Cadwell 353	G6
31728	Cairo⊙ 8,777	D9
30701	Calhoun⊙ 5,335	C1
30807	Camak 283	G4
31730	Camilla⊙ 5,414	D8
30520	Canon 704	F2
30114	Canton⊙ 3,601	C2
30203	Carl 239	E3
30627	Carlton 291	F2
30521	Carnesville⊙ 465	F2
30117	Carrollton⊙ 14,078	C3
30120	Cartersville⊙ 9,247	C2
30124	Cave Spring 883	B2
31627	Cecil 280	F8
30125	Cedartown⊙ 8,619	B2
†30601	Center 330	F2
31028	Centerville 2,622	E5
†30217	Centralhatchee 240	B4
†31816	Chalybeate Springs 265	C5
30341	Chamblee 7,137	K1
30705	Chatsworth⊙ 2,493	C1
31011	Chauncey 350	F6
31012	Chester 409	F6
30707	Chickamauga 2,232	B1
30523	Clarkesville⊙ 1,348	F1
30021	Clarkston 4,539	L1
30417	Claxton⊙ 2,694	J6
30525	Clayton⊙ 1,838	F1
30527	Clermont 300	E2
30528	Cleveland⊙ 1,578	E1
31734	Climax 407	D9
31735	Cobb	E7
30420	Cobbtown 494	H6
31014	Cochran⊙ 5,121	F6
30710	Cohutta 407	C1
30628	Colbert 498	F2
31736	Coleman 164	C7
30337	College Park 24,632	K2
30421	Collins 639	H6
31737	Colquitt⊙ 2,065	C8
*31901	Columbus⊙ 169,441	C6
	Columbus‡ 239,196	C6
30629	Comer 930	F2
30529	Commerce 4,092	E2
30206	Concord 317	D4
*30207	Conyers⊙ 6,567	D3
31738	Coolidge 736	E8
31015	Cordele⊙ 11,184	E7
30531	Cornelia 3,203	E1
31739	Cotton 122	D8
30209	Covington⊙ 10,586	E3
30711	Crandall	C1
30630	Crawford 498	F3
30631	Crawfordville⊙ 594	G3
†31771	Crosland	E8
31016	Culloden 281	D5
30130	Cumming⊙ 2,094	D2
31805	Cusseta⊙ 1,218	C6
31740	Cuthbert⊙ 4,340	C7
30211	Dacula 1,577	E3
31015	Daisy 174	J6
30132	Dallas⊙ 2,440	C3
30720	Dalton⊙ 20,743	C1
31741	Damascus 403	C8
30633	Danielsville⊙ 354	F2
31017	Danville 529	F5
31305	Darien⊙ 1,731	K8
31601	Dasher 659	F9
31018	Davisboro 433	G5
31742	Dawson⊙ 5,699	D7
30534	Dawsonville⊙ 342	D2
30808	Dearing 539	H4
*30030	Decatur⊙ 18,404	K1
†31501	Deenwood	H8
31082	Deepstep 120	G4
30535	Demorest 1,130	F1
31532	Denton 286	G7
31743	De Soto 248	D7
31019	Dexter 527	G6
30537	Dillard 238	F1
31629	Dixie 259	F9
†31520	Dock Junction (Arco)	J8
31744	Doerun 1,062	E8
31745	Donalsonville⊙ 3,320	C8
30134	Doraville 7,414	K1
31533	Douglas⊙ 10,980	G7
*30133	Douglasville⊙ 7,641	C3
31021	Dublin⊙ 16,083	G5
31022	Dudley 425	F5
30136	Duluth 2,956	D2
31630	Du Pont 267	G9
†31830	Durand 206	C5
31021	East Dublin 2,916	G5
30539	East Ellijay 469	C1

(continued on following page)

Agriculture, Industry and Resources

DOMINANT LAND USE

- Specialized Cotton
- Cotton, General Farming
- Cotton, Tobacco, Hogs, Peanuts
- Peanuts, General Farming
- General Farming, Livestock, Fruit, Tobacco
- General Farming, Forest Products, Cotton, Truck Farming
- Forests
- Swampland, Limited Agriculture
- Urban Areas

MAJOR MINERAL OCCURRENCES

Al	Bauxite
Ba	Barite
C	Coal
Cl	Clay
Fe	Iron Ore
Gn	Granite
Mi	Mica
Mn	Manganese
Mr	Marble
Sl	Slate
Tc	Talc
Ti	Titanium

⚡ Water Power   ▨ Major Industrial Areas

(continued)

†31046 East Juliette E4
31023 Eastman⊙ 5,330 F6
†30263 East Newnan C4
30344 East Point 37,486 K2
†30677 Eastville E3
31024 Eatonton⊙ 4,833 F4
31307 Eden 990 K6
31746 Edison 1,128 C7
30635 Elberton⊙ 5,686 G2
31806 Ellaville⊙ 1,684 D6
31747 Ellenton 277 E8
31807 Ellerslie 700 C5
30540 Ellijay⊙ 1,507 C1
30137 Emerson 1,110 C2
31749 Enigma 574 F8
†30217 Ephesus 184 B4
30724 Eton 301 C1
†30120 Euharlee 477 C2
30809 Evans H3
30212 Experiment D4
30213 Fairburn 3,466 J2
30139 Fairmount 842 C2
30214 Fayetteville⊙ 2,715 C4
†31071 Finleyson 101 F6
31750 Fitzgerald⊙ 10,187 F7
†31313 Flemington 440 K7
30216 Flovilla 458 E4
30542 Flowery Branch 755 E2
31537 Folkston⊙ 2,243 H9
30050 Forest Park 18,782 K2
31029 Forsyth⊙ 4,624 E4
31751 Fort Gaines⊙ 1,260 C7
30742 Fort Oglethorpe 5,443 B1
31030 Fort Valley⊙ 9,000 E5
30217 Franklin⊙ 711 B4
30639 Franklin Springs 797 F2
31753 Funston 337 E8
30501 Gainesville⊙ 15,280 E2
31408 Garden City 6,895 K6
30425 Garfield 222 H5
30218 Gay 175 C4
31810 Geneva 232 C5
31754 Georgetown⊙ 935 B7
30810 Gibson⊙ 730 G4
30426 Girard 225 J4
30427 Glennville 4,144 J7
30428 Glenwood 824 L1
30641 Good Hope 200 E3
31031 Gordon 2,768 F5
30220 Grantville 1,110 C4
31032 Gray⊙ 2,145 F4
30221 Grayson 464 E3
30726 Graysville 193 B1
30642 Greensboro⊙ 2,985 F3
30222 Greenville⊙ 1,213 C4
30223 Griffin⊙ 20,728 D4
30813 Grovetown 3,491 H4
31312 Guyton 749 K6
31033 Haddock 800 F4
30429 Hagan 880 J6

31632 Hahira 1,534 F9
31811 Hamilton⊙ 506 C5
30228 Hampton 2,059 D4
30354 Hapeville 6,166 K2
30229 Haralson 123 C4
31034 Hardwick F4
30814 Harlem 1,485 H4
31035 Harrison 456 G5
30643 Hartwell⊙ 4,855 G2
31036 Hawkinsville⊙ 4,372 E6
31539 Hazlehurst⊙ 4,249 G7
30545 Helen 265 E1
31037 Helena 1,390 G6
30815 Hephzibah 1,452 H4
30546 Hiawassee⊙ 491 E1
†30410 Higgston 152 G6
30467 Hilltonia 515 J5
31313 Hinesville⊙ 11,309 J7
30141 Hiram 711 C3
31542 Hoboken 514 H8
30230 Hogansville 3,362 C4
30142 Holly Springs 687 D2
†31537 Homeland 683 H9
30547 Homer⊙ 734 F2
31634 Homerville⊙ 3,112 G8
30548 Hoschton 490 E2
30646 Hull 188 F2
31041 Ideal 619 D6
30647 Ila 287 F2
†30705 Industrial City 1,054 C1
31759 Iron City 367 C8
31042 Irwinton⊙ 841 F5
†31031 Ivey 455 F5
30233 Jackson⊙ 4,133 E4
31544 Jacksonville 206 G7
31761 Jakin 194 C8
30143 Jasper⊙ 1,556 D2
30549 Jefferson⊙ 1,820 F2
31044 Jeffersonville⊙ 1,473 F5
30234 Jenkinsburg 360 E4
30235 Jersey 201 E3
31545 Jesup⊙ 9,418 J7
30236 Jonesboro⊙ 4,132 D4
31812 Junction City 254 C5
30144 Kennesaw 5,095 C2
31548 Kingsland 2,008 J9
30145 Kingston 733 C2
31049 Kite 328 G5
31050 Knoxville⊙ 75 E5
30728 La Fayette⊙ 6,517 B1
30240 La Grange⊙ 24,204 B4
30252 Lake 2,963 D3
31635 Lakeland⊙ 2,647 F8
31636 Lake Park 448 F9
30553 Lavonia 2,024 F2
30245 Lawrenceville⊙ 8,928 D3
31762 Leary 783 C8
30146 Lebanon 800 D2
31763 Leesburg⊙ 1,301 D7
31637 Lenox 965 F8

31764 Leslie 470 D7
30648 Lexington⊙ 278 F3
30247 Lilburn 3,765 D3
31051 Lilly 202 E6
†30286 Lincoln Park D5
30817 Lincolnton⊙ 1,406 G3
30147 Lindale B2
†30728 Linwood 417 B1
30058 Lithonia 2,637 D3
30248 Locust Grove 1,479 D4
30249 Loganville 1,841 E3
30433 Lollie G6
†30230 Lone Oak 119 C4
†30741 Lookout Mountain 1,505 B1
30434 Louisville⊙ 2,823 H4
30250 Lovejoy 205 D4
31316 Ludowici⊙ 1,286 J7
30554 Lula 857 E2
31549 Lumber City 1,426 G7
31815 Lumpkin⊙ 1,335 C6
30251 Luthersville 597 C4
30730 Lyerly 482 B2
30436 Lyons⊙ 4,203 H6
30059 Mableton J1
*31201 Macon⊙ 116,860 E5
Macon‡ 254,623 E5
30650 Madison⊙ 2,954 F3
30438 Manassas 116 H6
31816 Manchester 4,796 C5
30255 Mansfield 435 E4
*30060 Marietta⊙ 30,805 J1
31057 Marshallville 1,540 D6
30557 Martin 305 F2
30671 Maxeys 205 F3
30558 Maysville 619 E2
30555 McCaysville 1,219 D1
30253 McDonough⊙ 2,778 D4
31054 McIntyre 386 F5
31055 McRae⊙ 3,409 G6
30256 Meansville 303 D4
30040 Mechanicsville L1
31765 Meigs 1,231 D8
30731 Menlo 611 B2
†31792 Metcalf E9
30439 Metter⊙ 3,531 H6
30441 Midville 670 H5
31320 Midway 457 K7
31060 Milan 1,115 G6
31061 Milledgeville⊙ 12,176 F4
30442 Millen⊙ 3,988 J5
30257 Milner 320 D4
30207 Milstead D3
30559 Mineral Bluff 130 D1
30820 Mitchell 214 G4
30258 Molena 379 D4
30655 Monroe⊙ 8,854 E3
31063 Montezuma 4,830 E6
31064 Monticello⊙ 2,382 E4
31065 Montrose 170 F5
30259 Moreland 358 C4

31766 Morgan⊙ 364 C7
30560 Morganton 263 D1
30260 Morrow 3,791 K2
31638 Morven 471 E9
31768 Moultrie⊙ 15,708 E8
30562 Mountain City 701 F1
†30075 Mountain Park 378 D2
30563 Mount Airy 670 F1
30149 Mount Berry B2
30445 Mount Vernon⊙ 1,737 G6
30261 Mountville 168 C4
30150 Mount Zion 445 B3
31553 Nahunta⊙ 951 H8
31639 Nashville⊙ 4,831 F8
31641 Naylor 228 F9
30151 Nelson 562 D2
30262 Newborn 391 E3
30446 Newington 402 J5
30263 Newnan⊙ 11,449 C4
31770 Newton⊙ 711 D8
31554 Nicholls 1,114 G7
30565 Nicholson 491 F2
*30071 Norcross 3,317 D3
31771 Norman Park 757 E8
†30645 North High Shoals 256 F3
30821 Norwood 306 G4
30448 Nunez 168 H5
31772 Oakfield 113 E7
30732 Oakman 150 C1
31903 Oak Park 256 H6
30566 Oakwood 723 E2
31773 Ochlocknee 627 E9
31774 Ocilla⊙ 3,436 F7
31067 Oconee 306 G5
†30222 Odessadale 142 C5
31555 Odum 401 H7
31406 Oglethorpe⊙ 1,305 D6
30449 Oliver 239 J5
31821 Omaha 169 C6
31775 Omega 996 E8
30266 Orchard Hill 162 D4
30267 Oxford 1,750 E3
30268 Palmetto 2,086 C3
31777 Parrott 222 D7
31557 Patterson 763 H8
31778 Pavo 830 E9
†31201 Payne 196 E5
30269 Peachtree City 6,429 C4
31642 Pearson⊙ 1,827 G8
31779 Pelham 4,306 D8
31321 Pembroke⊙ 1,400 J6
30567 Pendergrass 302 E2
31069 Perry⊙ 9,453 E6
†31794 Phillipsburg E8
31070 Pinehurst 431 E6
30072 Pine Lake 901 D3
31822 Pine Mountain 984 C5
†31312 Pineora 387 K6
†31728 Pine Park D9
31071 Pineview 564 F6

31072 Pitts 384 E7
31073 Plainfield 128 F6
31780 Plains 651 D6
30733 Plainville 281 C2
31322 Pooler 2,543 K6
30450 Portal 694 J5
30270 Porterdale 1,451 E3
31407 Port Wentworth 3,947 K6
31781 Poulan 818 E8
30073 Powder Springs 3,381 C3
31824 Preston⊙ 429 C6
30451 Pulaski 257 J6
31643 Quitman⊙ 5,188 E9
30734 Ranger 171 C2
31645 Ray City 658 F8
30660 Rayle 177 G3
31783 Rebecca 272 E7
30453 Reidsville⊙ 2,296 H6
31601 Remerton 443 F9
31075 Rentz 337 G6
†30518 Rest Haven 231 E2
31076 Reynolds 1,298 D5
31077 Rhine 590 F7
31323 Riceboro 216 K7
31825 Richland 1,802 C6
31324 Richmond Hill 1,177 K7
†31018 Riddleville 154 G5
31326 Rincon 1,988 K6
30736 Ringgold⊙ 1,821 B1
*30274 Riverdale 7,121 K2
†31768 Riverside 99 E8
†30759 Riverside B2
31078 Roberta 859 D5
31079 Rochelle 1,626 F7
30153 Rockmart 3,645 B2
30455 Rocky Ford 223 J5
30161 Rome⊙ 29,654 B2
30170 Roopville 229 B4
30741 Rossville 3,851 B1
*30075 Roswell 23,337 D2
30662 Royston 2,404 F2
†30680 Russell 378 E3
30663 Rutledge 694 E3
31558 Saint Marys 3,596 J9
31522 Saint Simons Island K8
31784 Sale City 336 D8
31082 Sandersville⊙ 6,137 G5
†20436 Santa Claus 167 H6
30456 Sardis 1,180 J5
30275 Sargent 800 C4
31785 Sasser 407 D7
*31401 Savannah⊙ 141,634 L6
Savannah‡ 230,728 L6
31083 Scotland 222 G6
31095 Scott 139 G5
31560 Screven 872 H7
30276 Senoia 900 C4
31084 Seville 209 E7
31085 Shady Dale 155 E4
30172 Shannon B2
30664 Sharon 140 G3
30277 Sharpsburg 194 C4
31786 Shellman 1,254 C7
31826 Shiloh 392 C5
30665 Siloam 446 F3
31787 Smithville 867 D7
30080 Smyrna 20,312 K1
30278 Snellville 8,514 D3
30279 Social Circle 2,591 E3
30457 Soperton⊙ 2,981 G6
31647 Sparks 1,353 F8
31087 Sparta⊙ 1,754 F4
31329 Springfield⊙ 1,075 K6
†30705 Spring Place 246 C1
30823 Stapleton 388 H4
31648 Statenville⊙ 700 G9
30458 Statesboro⊙ 14,866 J6
30666 Statham 1,101 E3
30464 Stillmore 527 H6
30281 Stockbridge 2,103 D3
*30083 Stone Mountain 4,867 D3
†30518 Sugar Hill 2,473 E2
30746 Sugar Valley C1
30466 Summertown 215 H5
30747 Summerville⊙ 4,878 B2
31789 Sumner 213 E7
30284 Sunny Side 338 D4
31563 Surrency 368 H7
30174 Suwanee 1,026 D2
30401 Swainsboro⊙ 7,602 H5
31790 Sycamore 474 E7
30467 Sylvania⊙ 3,352 J5
31791 Sylvester⊙ 5,860 E7
31827 Talbotton⊙ 1,140 C5
30176 Tallapoosa 2,647 B3
30573 Tallulah Falls 162 F1
30575 Talmo E2
30470 Tarrytown 145 H6
30178 Taylorsville 266 C2
30179 Temple 1,520 B3
31089 Tennille 1,709 G5
30285 The Rock 78 D5
30286 Thomaston⊙ 9,682 D5
31792 Thomasville⊙ 18,463 E9
30824 Thomson⊙ 7,001 H4
†31404 Thunderbolt 2,165 K6
31794 Tifton⊙ 13,749 F8
30576 Tiger 299 F1
30668 Tignall 733 G3
30577 Toccoa⊙ 9,104 F1
31090 Toomsboro 673 F5
30752 Trenton⊙ 1,636 A1
30753 Trion 1,732 B1
30755 Tunnel Hill 867 C1
30289 Turin 260 C4
30471 Twin City 1,402 H5
31328 Tybee Island 2,240 L6
30290 Tyrone 1,038 C4
31795 Ty Ty 618 E8
31091 Unadilla 1,566 E6
30291 Union City 4,780 J2
30669 Union Point 1,750 F3
†31794 Unionville F8
30473 Uvalda 646 H6
31601 Valdosta⊙ 37,596 F9
30672 Vanna F2
†30153 Van Wert 303 B3

30756 Varnell 288 C1
†31401 Vernonburg 178 K7
30474 Vidalia 10,393 H6
†30830 Vidette H4
31092 Vienna⊙ 2,886 E6
30180 Villa Rica 3,420 C3
30182 Waco 471 B3
30477 Wadley 2,438 H5
30183 Waleska 450 D2
†30209 Walnut Grove 387 E3
31333 Walthourville 905 J7
31830 Warm Springs 425 C5
31093 Warner Robins 39,893 E5
30828 Warrenton⊙ 2,172 G4
31796 Warwick 488 E7
30673 Washington⊙ 4,662 G3
30677 Watkinsville⊙ 1,240 E3
31831 Waverly Hall 913 C5
31501 Waycross⊙ 19,371 H8
30830 Waynesboro⊙ 5,760 J4
31832 Weston 109 C7
31833 West Point 4,294 B5
31797 Whigham 507 D9
30184 White 501 C2
31568 White Oak 450 J8
30678 White Plains 231 F4
30185 Whitesburg 775 B4
31650 Willacoochee 1,166 G8
30292 Williamson 250 D4
31410 Wilmington Island L7
30680 Winder⊙ 6,705 E3
31406 Windsor Forest K7
30683 Winterville 621 F3
31569 Woodbine⊙ 910 J9
30293 Woodbury 1,738 C5
31836 Woodland 664 D5
30188 Woodstock 2,699 D2
30670 Woodville 455 F3
30833 Wrens 2,415 H4
31096 Wrightsville⊙ 2,526 G5
31097 Yatesville 390 D5
30582 Young Harris 687 E1
30295 Zebulon⊙ 995 D4

OTHER FEATURES

Alapaha (riv.) F7
Allatoona (lake) C2
Altamaha (riv.) H7
Andersonville Nat'l Hist. Site D6
Atlanta Nav. Air Sta. J1
Banks (lake) F9
Bartletts Ferry (dam) B5
Blackshear (lake) E7
Blue Ridge (mts.) D1
Brasstown Bald (mt.) E1
Burton (lake) E1
Carters (lake) C1
Chattahoochee (riv.) B8
Chattahoochee River Nat'l Rec. Area K1
Chattooga (riv.) A2
Chattooga (riv.) F1
Chatuge (lake) E1
Chickamauga and Chattanooga Nat'l Mil. Park B1
Clark Hill (lake) H3
Coosa (riv.) A2
Coosawattee (riv.) C1
Cumberland (isl.) K9
Cumberland Island Nat'l Seashore K9
Dobbins A.F.B. J1
Doboy (sound) K8
Etowah (riv.) C2
Eufaula (Walter F. George Res.) (lake) B7
Flint (riv.) D8
Fort Benning B6
Fort Frederica Nat'l Mon. K8
Fort Gordon H4
Fort McPherson K1
Fort Pulaski Nat'l Mon. L6
Fort Stewart J7
Goat Rock (lake) B5
Harding (lake) B5
Hartwell (lake) G2
Jekyll (isl.) K8
Kennesaw Mtn. Nat'l Battlefield Park J1
Lawson A.A.F. B6
Martin Luther King, Jr., Nat'l Hist. Site K1
Moody A.F.B. F9
Nottely (lake) D1
Ochlockonee (riv.) C10
Ocmulgee (riv.) E5
Ocmulgee Nat'l Mon. F5
Oconee (riv.) F5
Ogeechee (riv.) J5
Okefenokee (swamp) H9
Oliver (lake) B5
Oostanaula (riv.) B2
Ossabaw (sound) K7
Rabun (lake) E1
Robins A.F.B. F5
Saint Andrew (sound) K9
Saint Catherines (isl.) K7
Saint Marys (riv.) J9
Saint Simons K8
Sapelo (isl.) K8
Satilla (riv.) G8
Savannah (riv.) K5
Sea (isls.) K9
Seminole (lake) B9
Sidney Lanier (lake) D2
Sinclair (lake) F4
Skidaway (isl.) L7
Springer (mt.) D1
Suwannee (riv.) G10
Tugaloo (riv.) F1
Walter F. George (res.) B7
Wassaw (sound) L7
Weiss (lake) A2
West Point (lake) B4

⊙County seat.
‡Population of metropolitan area.
† Zip of nearest p.o. * Multiple zips.

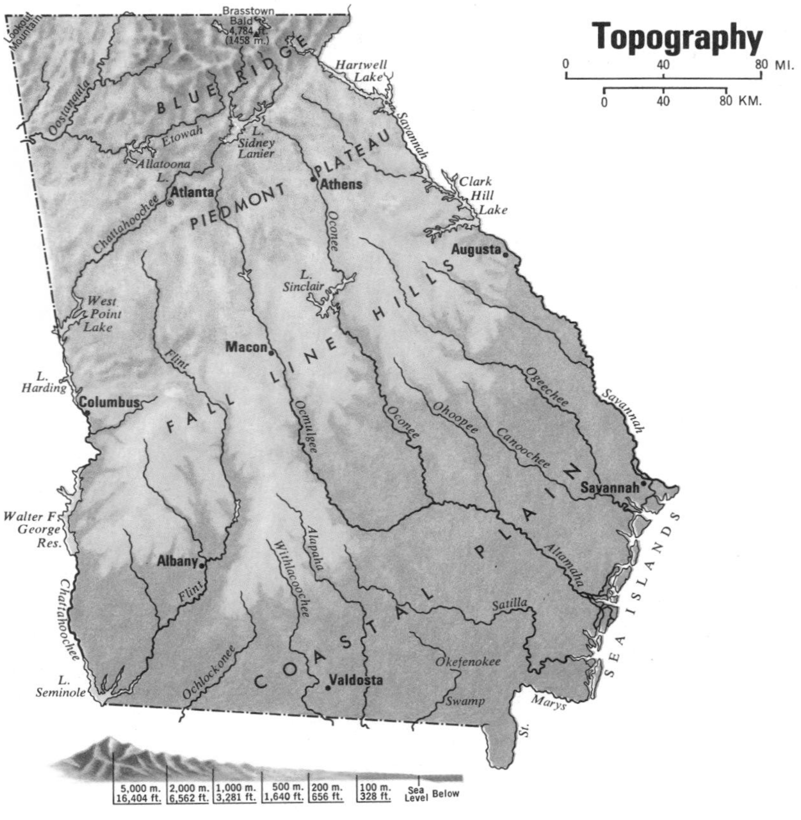

Topography
0 40 80 MI.
0 40 80 KM.
Brasstown Bald 4,784 ft. (1458 m.)
Lookout Mountain
BLUE RIDGE
Hartwell Lake
Oostanaula
Etowah
L. Sidney Lanier
Allatoona L.
Atlanta
PIEDMONT
PLATEAU
Athens
Savannah
Clark Hill Lake
Augusta
Chattahoochee
Oconee
L. Sinclair
West Point Lake
Macon
FALL LINE HILLS
Flint
L. Harding
Columbus
Ocmulgee
Ogeechee
Ohoopee
Oconee
Canoochee
Savannah
Walter F. George Res.
Albany
Flint
Alapaha
Withlacoochee
COASTAL PLAIN
Altamaha
SEA ISLANDS
Satilla
Chattahoochee
Ochlockonee
Valdosta
Okefenokee Swamp
St. Marys
L. Seminole
5,000 m. 16,404 ft.
2,000 m. 6,562 ft.
1,000 m. 3,281 ft.
500 m. 1,640 ft.
200 m. 656 ft.
100 m. 328 ft.
Sea Level
Below

Georgia

SCALE
0 5 10   20   30   40 MI.
0 5 10   20   30   40 KM.

⊛	State Capitals
◉	County Seats
—	Major Limited Access Hwys.

© Copyright HAMMOND INCORPORATED, Maplewood, N.J.

Scale 1:2,210,000

COUNTIES

Hawaii 92,053 .... K7
Honolulu 762,565 .... D3
Kalawao 144 .... G1
Kauai 39,082 .... A1
Maui 70,847 .... J1

CITIES and TOWNS

Zip   Name/Pop.   Key

96701 Aiea 32,879 .... B3
96821 Aina Haina F2
    Ala Moana 96,820 .... C4
96703 Anahola 915 .... C1
†96706 Barbers Point 1,373 .. E2
96704 Captain Cook 2,008 ... G5
96705 Eleele 580 .... C2
96706 Ewa 2,637 .... A4
96706 Ewa Beach 14,369 ..... A4
†96701 Foster Village B3
96714 Haena 200 .... C1
96708 Haiku 619 .... J2
96710 Hakalau J4
†96711 Halawa, Hawaii 50 ..... G3
96748 Halawa, Molokai 15 .... H1
†96701 Halawa Heights B3
96712 Haleiwa 2,412 .... E1
†96718 Halfway House 150 ...... H6
96787 Haliimaile 741 .... J2
†96713 Hamoa 35 .... K2
96713 Hana 643 .... K2
96714 Hanalei 483 .... C1
96715 Hanamaulu 3,227 .... C1
96716 Hanapepe 1,417 .... C2
96717 Hauula 2,997 .... E1
96825 Hawaii Kai F2
96718 Hawaii Nat'l Park 250 .. J6
96719 Hawi 795 .... G3
96824 Hickam Housing 4,425 . B4
96720 Hilo⊙ 35,269 .... J5
96725 Holualoa 1,243 .... G5
96726 Honaunau 950 .... G6
96727 Honokaa 1,936 .... H4
96761 Honokahua 309 .... H1
96728 Honomu 559 .... J4
96729 Hoolehua G1
†96706 Iroquois Point 3,915 ... A4
96730 Kaaawa 959 .... F1
†96761 Kaanapali 541 .... H2
†96793 Kahakuloa 75 .... J1
†96744 Kahaluu 2,925 .... E2
96731 Kahuku 935 .... E1
96732 Kahului 12,978 .... J2
96740 Kailua (Kailua Kona),
    Hawaii 4,751 .... F5
96734 Kailua, Oahu 35,812 ... F2

96740 Kailua Kona 4,751 .... F5
96750 Kainaliu 512 .... G5
†96741 Kalaheo 2,500 .... C2
96742 Kalaupapa⊙ 170 .... G1
†96754 Kalihiwai 40 .... C1
96748 Kaluaaha 20 .... H1
†96748 Kamalo 60 .... H1
96743 Kamuela 1,179 .... G3
96744 Kaneohe 29,919 .... F2
96746 Kapaa 4,467 .... D1
96755 Kapaau 612 .... G3
96817 Kapalama C4
96747 Kaumakani 888 .... C2
96748 Kaunakakai 2,231 .... G1
96708 Kaupakulua 600 .... K2
96743 Kawaihae 40 .... G4
96712 Kawailoa 200 .... E1
96749 Keaau 775 .... J5
96750 Kealakekua 1,033 .... G5
96751 Kealia, Kauai 300 .... D1
96708 Keanae 280 .... K2
96752 Kekaha 3,260 .... C2
96753 Kihei 5,644 .... J2
96754 Kilauea 895 .... C1
96713 Kipahulu 75 .... K2
96713 Koali 60 .... K2
†96755 Kohala (Kapaau) 612 ... G3
96708 Kokomo 500 .... K2
96756 Koloa 1,457 .... C2

†96756 Koloa Landing C2
96757 Kualapuu 502 .... G1
†96775 Kukaiau 75 .... H4
96727 Kukuihaele 332 .... H3
96790 Kula 800 .... J2
96759 Kunia 550 .... E2
96760 Kurtistown 900 .... J5
96761 Lahaina 6,095 .... H2
96762 Laie 4,643 .... E1
96763 Lanai City 2,092 .... H2
96764 Laupahoehoe 500 .... J4
96765 Lawai 950 .... C2
96766 Lihue⊙ 4,000 .... C2
†96779 Lower Paia 1,500 .... J1
96719 Mahukona 2 .... G3
96790 Maili 5,026 .... D2
96792 Makaha 6,582 .... D2
96706 Makakilo 7,691 .... E2
96768 Makawao 2,900 .... K2
96769 Makaweli 500 .... B2
96751 Makena 100 .... J2
96822 Makiki C4
96770 Maunaloa 633 .... G1
96744 Maunawili 5,239 .... F2
96789 Mililani Town 21,365 ... E2
96828 Moiliili C4
96734 Mokapu 11,615 .... F2
96771 Mountainview 540 .... J5
96772 Naalehu 1,168 .... H7
†96713 Nahiku 50 .... K2

96792 Nanakuli 8,185 .... D2
†96761 Napili-Honokowai 2,446 . H1
96773 Ninole 75 .... J4
96781 Onomea 10 .... J4
96704 Ookala 401 .... J4
96775 Paauhau 350 .... H4
96776 Paauilo 755 .... J4
96777 Pahala 1,619 .... H6
96778 Pahoa 923 .... J5
96779 Paia J2
96780 Papaaloa J4
96781 Papaikou 1,567 .... J5
†96781 Paukaa 544 .... J5
96708 Pauwela 468 .... K2
†96708 Peahi 308 .... K2
96782 Pearl City 42,575 .... B3
96783 Pepeekeo J4
96714 Princeville 500 .... C1
96766 Puhi 991 .... C2
96788 Pukalani 3,950 .... J2
†96748 Pukoo 50 .... H1
†96713 Puuiki 75 .... K2
96784 Puunene 572 .... J2
†96801 Puunui C4
96786 Schofield Barracks 18,851 . E2
96779 Spreckelsville 350 ...... J1
†96708 Ulumalu 201 .... K2
96776 Umikoa 25 .... H4
96785 Volcano 400 .... J6

96786 Wahiawa 16,911 .... E2
†96788 Waiakoa J2
96816 Waialae D4
†96731 Waialee 50 .... E1
96748 Waialua, Molokai 30 .... H1
96791 Waialua, Oahu 4,051 ... E1
96792 Waianae 7,941 .... D2
†96793 Waihee 413 .... J2
96793 Waikapu 698 .... J2
96815 Waikiki C4
†96748 Wailau 20 .... H1
†96710 Wailea, Hawaii 150 ..... J4
96790 Wailea, Maui 1,124 ..... J2
96746 Wailua 1,587 .... C1
96793 Wailuku⊙ 10,260 .... J2
96795 Waimanalo 3,562 .... F2
96795 Waimanalo Bch. 4,161 . F2
96743 Waimea (Kamuela),
    Hawaii 1,179 .... G3
96796 Waimea, Kauai 1,569 ... B2
†96720 Wainaku 1,045 .... J5
96714 Wainiha 175 .... C1
96797 Waipahu 29,139 .... A3
†96786 Waipio Acres 4,091 ..... E2
†96786 Whitmore Village 2,318 . E1

OTHER FEATURES

Alalakeiki (chan.) J3
Alenuihaha (chan.) E7

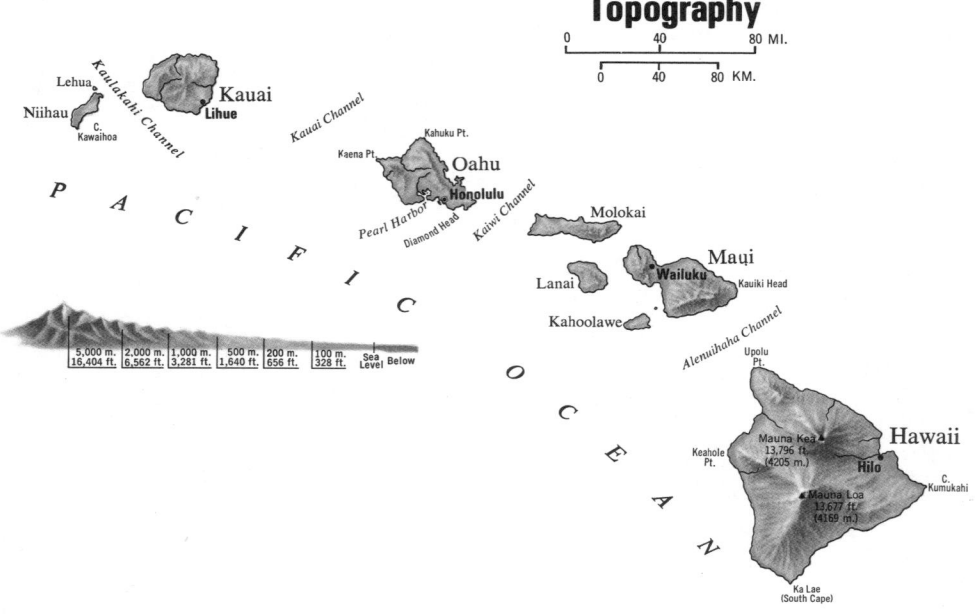

Topography

Agriculture, Industry and Resources

DOMINANT LAND USE

Diversified Tropical Cash Crops

Livestock Grazing

Forests

Urban Areas

Nonagricultural Land

Major Industrial Areas

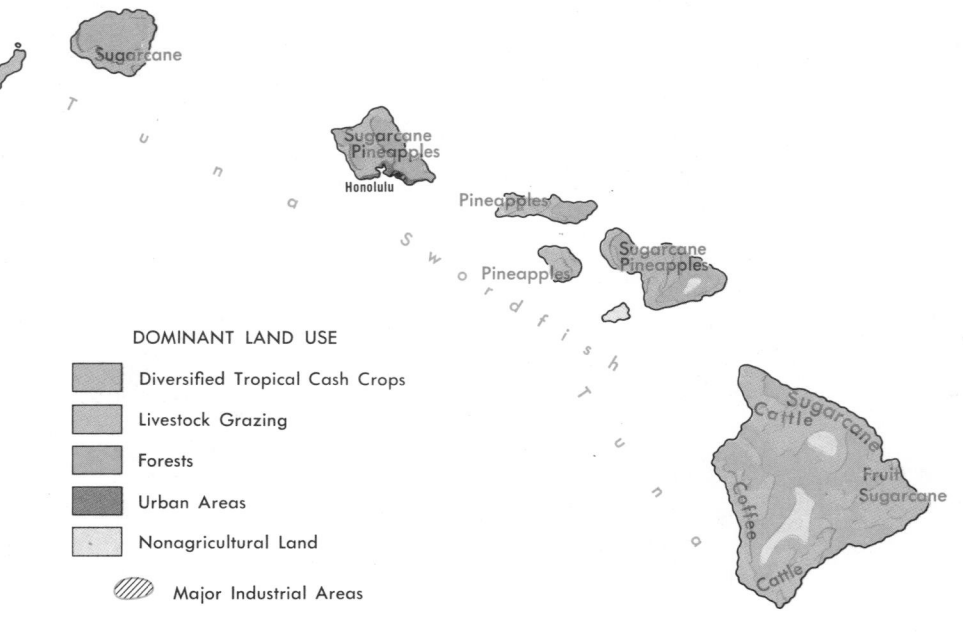

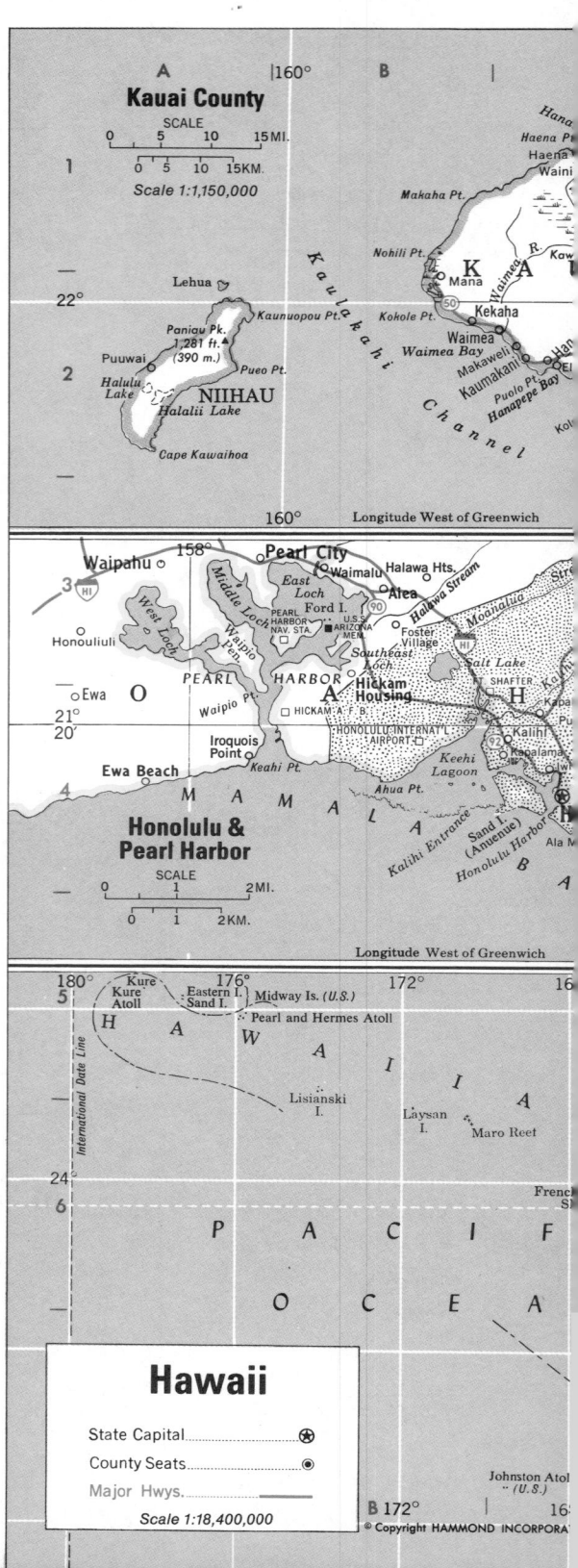

Kauai County

SCALE
0 5 10 15 MI.
0 5 10 15KM.
Scale 1:1,150,000

Honolulu & Pearl Harbor

SCALE
0 1 2MI.
0 1 2KM.

Hawaii

State Capital .... ⊛
County Seats .... ⊙
Major Hwys. _____

Scale 1:18,400,000

© Copyright HAMMOND INCORPORA

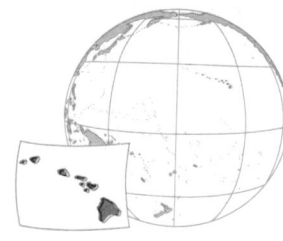

AREA 6,471 sq. mi. (16,760 sq. km.)
POPULATION 964,691
CAPITAL Honolulu
LARGEST CITY Honolulu
HIGHEST POINT — Mauna Kea 13,796 ft. (4205 m.)
SETTLED IN —
ADMITTED TO UNION August 21, 1959
POPULAR NAME Aloha State
STATE FLOWER Hibiscus
STATE BIRD Nene (Hawaiian Goose)

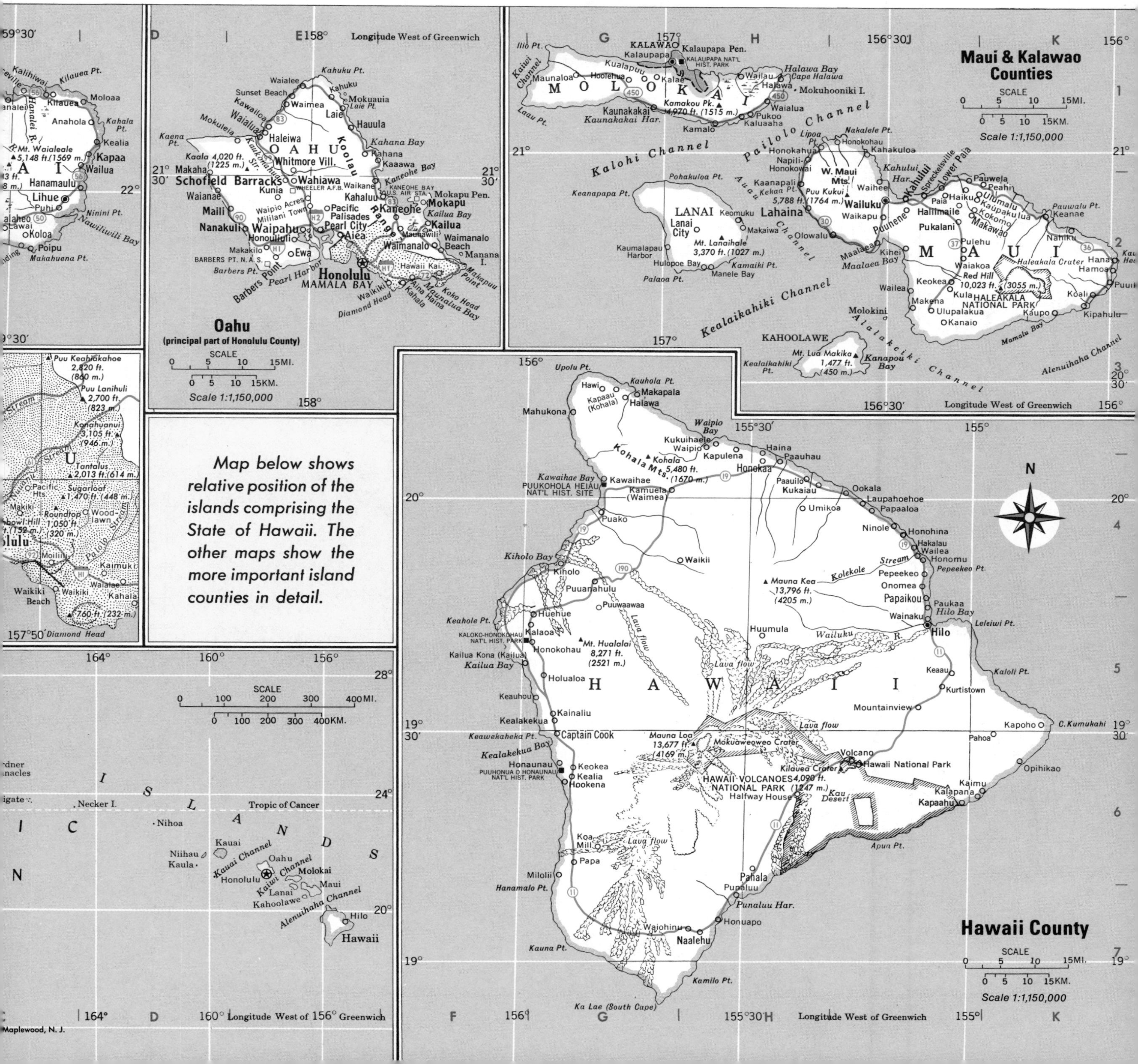

Oahu
(principal part of Honolulu County)

SCALE
0 5 10 15MI.
0 5 10 15KM.
Scale 1:1,150,000

Map below shows relative position of the islands comprising the State of Hawaii. The other maps show the more important island counties in detail.

SCALE
0 100 200 300 400MI.
0 100 200 300 400KM.

Maui & Kalawao Counties

SCALE
0 5 10 15MI.
0 5 10 15KM.
Scale 1:1,150,000

Hawaii County

SCALE
0 5 10 15MI.
0 5 10 15KM.
Scale 1:1,150,000

Maplewood, N.J.

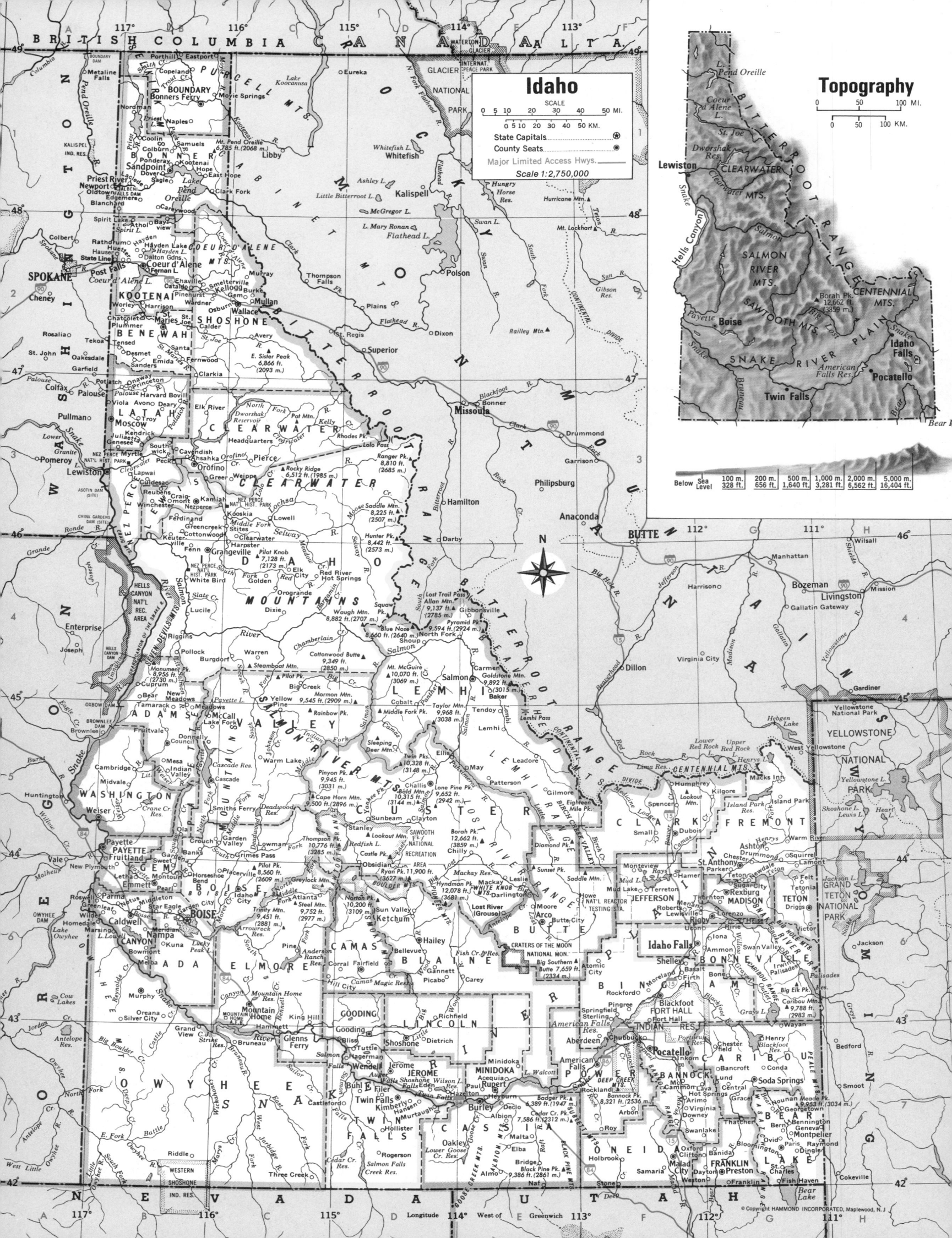

Idaho
SCALE
0 5 10 20 30 40 50 MI.
0 5 10 20 30 40 50 KM.
State Capitals
County Seats
Major Limited Access Hwys.
Scale 1:2,750,000
Topography
0 50 100 MI.
0 50 100 KM.
Below Sea Level
100 m. 328 ft.
200 m. 656 ft.
500 m. 1,640 ft.
1,000 m. 3,281 ft.
2,000 m. 6,562 ft.
5,000 m. 16,404 ft.
L. Pend Oreille
Coeur d'Alene L.
St. Joe
Dworshak Res.
Lewiston
CLEARWATER
MTS.
Clearwater
Salmon
Hells Canyon
SALMON RIVER MTS.
BITTERROOT RANGE
Borah Pk. 12,662 ft. (3859 m.)
CENTENNIAL MTS.
SAWTOOTH MTS.
Payette
Boise
Big Lost
SNAKE RIVER PLAIN
Snake
Idaho Falls
American Falls Res.
Pocatello
Twin Falls
Bruneau
Bear
BRITISH COLUMBIA
CANADA
ALTA.
WASHINGTON
OREGON
NEVADA
UTAH
MONTANA
WYOMING
BOUNDARY
BONNER
KOOTENAI
BENEWAH
SHOSHONE
LATAH
CLEARWATER
NEZ PERCE
LEWIS
IDAHO
ADAMS
VALLEY
WASHINGTON
PAYETTE
GEM
BOISE
CANYON
ADA
ELMORE
CAMAS
BLAINE
CUSTER
LEMHI
BUTTE
CLARK
FREMONT
JEFFERSON
MADISON
TETON
BONNEVILLE
BINGHAM
CARIBOU
BEAR LAKE
FRANKLIN
ONEIDA
POWER
BANNOCK
CASSIA
MINIDOKA
LINCOLN
GOODING
JEROME
TWIN FALLS
OWYHEE
PURCELL MTS.
CABINET MTS.
COEUR D'ALENE MTS.
BITTERROOT RANGE
CLEARWATER MOUNTAINS
SALMON RIVER MTS.
LOST RIVER RANGE
LEMHI RANGE
BEAVERHEAD MTS.
CENTENNIAL MTS.
SAWTOOTH NATIONAL RECREATION AREA
CRATERS OF THE MOON NATIONAL MON.
YELLOWSTONE NATIONAL PARK
GRAND TETON NATIONAL PARK
GLACIER NATIONAL PARK
HELLS CANYON NAT'L REC. AREA
FORT HALL INDIAN RES.
Bonners Ferry
Sandpoint
Coeur d'Alene
Wallace
Kellogg
St. Maries
Moscow
Lewiston
Orofino
Grangeville
Salmon
Challis
McCall
Cascade
Weiser
Payette
Emmett
Caldwell
Nampa
Boise
Mountain Home
Fairfield
Hailey
Ketchum
Arco
Idaho Falls
Blackfoot
Pocatello
Rexburg
Rigby
St. Anthony
Driggs
Soda Springs
Preston
Malad City
Montpelier
Paris
American Falls
Rupert
Burley
Twin Falls
Jerome
Gooding
Shoshone
Murphy
Spokane
Missoula
Butte
Bozeman
Kalispell
Borah Pk. 12,662 ft. (3859 m.)
Longitude 114° West of Greenwich
© Copyright HAMMOND INCORPORATED, Maplewood, N.J.

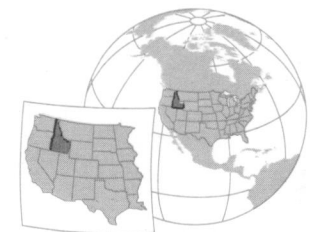

AREA 83,564 sq. mi. (216,431 sq. km.)
POPULATION 944,038
CAPITAL Boise
LARGEST CITY Boise
HIGHEST POINT Borah Pk. 12,662 ft. (3859 m.)
SETTLED IN 1842
ADMITTED TO UNION July 3, 1890
POPULAR NAME Gem State
STATE FLOWER Syringa
STATE BIRD Mountain Bluebird

COUNTIES

Ada 173,036	B6
Adams 3,347	B5
Bannock 65,421	F7
Bear Lake 6,931	G7
Benewah 8,292	B2
Bingham 36,489	F6
Blaine 9,841	D6
Boise 2,999	C6
Bonner 24,163	B1
Bonneville 65,980	G6
Boundary 7,289	B1
Butte 3,342	E6
Camas 818	D6
Canyon 83,756	B6
Caribou 8,695	G7
Cassia 19,427	E7
Clark 798	F5
Clearwater 10,390	C3
Custer 3,385	D5
Elmore 21,565	C6
Franklin 8,895	G7
Fremont 10,813	G5
Gem 11,972	B6
Gooding 11,874	D6
Idaho 14,769	C4
Jefferson 15,304	F6
Jerome 14,840	D7
Kootenai 59,770	B2
Latah 28,749	B3
Lemhi 7,460	D4
Lewis 4,118	B3
Lincoln 3,436	D6
Madison 19,480	G6
Minidoka 19,718	E7
Nez Perce 33,220	B3
Oneida 3,258	F7
Owyhee 8,272	B7
Payette 15,825	B5
Power 6,844	F7
Shoshone 19,226	B2
Teton 2,897	G6
Twin Falls 52,927	D7
Valley 5,604	C5
Washington 8,803	B5

CITIES and TOWNS

Zip	Name/Pop.	Key
83210	Aberdeen 1,528	F7
83350	Acequia 100	E7
83311	Albion 286	E7
83211	American Falls⊙ 3,626	E7
†83401	Ammon 4,669	G6
83213	Arco⊙ 1,241	E6
83314	Arimo 338	F7
83420	Ashton 1,219	G5
83801	Athol 312	B2
83217	Bancroft 505	G7
83218	Basalt 414	F6
83313	Bellevue 1,016	D6
83221	Blackfoot⊙ 10,065	F6
83314	Bliss 208	D7
83223	Bloomington 212	G7
*83701	Boise (cap.)⊙ 102,160	B6
	Boise‡ 173,036	B6
83805	Bonners Ferry⊙ 1,906	B1
83806	Bovill 289	B3
83316	Buhl 3,629	D7
83318	Burley⊙ 8,761	E7
83213	Butte City 93	E6
83605	Caldwell⊙ 17,699	B6
83610	Cambridge 428	B5
83611	Cascade⊙ 945	C5
83321	Castleford 191	C7
83226	Challis⊙ 758	D5
†83851	Chatcolet 181	B2
83202	Chubbuck 7,052	F7
83811	Clark Fork 449	B1
83227	Clayton 43	D5
83228	Clifton 208	F7
83814	Coeur d'Alene⊙ 20,054	B2
83522	Cottonwood 941	B3
83612	Council⊙ 917	B5
83523	Craigmont 556	B3
†83622	Crouch 69	B5
83524	Culdesac 261	B3
†83814	Dalton Gardens 1,795	B2
83232	Dayton 368	F7
83823	Deary 539	B3
83323	Declo 276	E7
83324	Dietrich 101	D7
83615	Donnelly 139	B5
83234	Downey 645	F7
83422	Driggs⊙ 727	G6
83423	Dubois⊙ 413	F5
83616	Eagle 2,620	B6
†83836	East Hope 258	B1
83325	Eden 355	D7
83827	Elk River 265	B3
83617	Emmett⊙ 4,605	B6
83327	Fairfield⊙ 404	D6
83526	Ferdinand 144	B3
†83814	Fernan Lake 178	B2
83328	Filer 1,645	D7
83236	Firth 460	F6
83203	Fort Hall 750	F6
83237	Franklin 423	G7
83619	Fruitland 2,456	B6
†83704	Garden City 4,571	B6
83832	Genesee 791	B3
83239	Georgetown 544	G7
83623	Glenns Ferry 1,374	C7
83330	Gooding⊙ 2,949	D7
83241	Grace 1,216	G7
83624	Grand View 366	B7
83530	Grangeville⊙ 3,666	B3
83626	Greenleaf 663	B6
83332	Hagerman 602	D7
83333	Hailey⊙ 2,109	D6
83425	Hamer 93	F6
83334	Hansen 1,078	D7
83833	Harrison 260	B2
†83854	Hauser 305	A2
†83835	Hayden 2,586	B2
83835	Hayden Lake 273	B2
83335	Hazelton 496	E7
83336	Heyburn 2,889	E7
†83301	Hollister 167	D7
83628	Homedale 2,078	A6
83836	Hope 106	B1
83629	Horseshoe Bend 700	B6
†83854	Huetter 65	B2
83631	Idaho City⊙ 300	C6
*83401	Idaho Falls⊙ 39,590	F6
83245	Inkom 830	F7
83427	Iona 1,072	G6
83428	Irwin 113	G6
83429	Island Park 154	G5
83338	Jerome⊙ 6,891	D7
83535	Juliaetta 522	B3
83536	Kamiah 1,478	B3
83837	Kellogg 3,417	B2
83537	Kendrick 395	B3
83340	Ketchum 2,200	D6
83341	Kimberly 2,307	D7
83539	Kooskia 784	C3
83840	Kootenai 280	B1
83634	Kuna 1,767	B6
83540	Lapwai 1,043	B3
83246	Lava Hot Springs 467	F7
83464	Leadore 114	E5
83501	Lewiston⊙ 27,986	A3
83431	Lewisville 502	F6
83251	Mackay 541	E6
83252	Malad City⊙ 1,915	F7
83342	Malta 196	E7
83639	Marsing 786	B6
83638	McCall 2,188	C5
83250	McCammon 770	F7
83641	Melba 276	B6
83434	Menan 605	F6
83642	Meridian 6,658	B6
83644	Middleton 1,901	B6
83645	Midvale 205	B5
83343	Minidoka 101	E7
83254	Montpelier 3,107	G7
83255	Moore 210	E6
83843	Moscow⊙ 16,513	B3
83647	Mountain Home⊙ 7,540	C6
83845	Moyie Springs 386	B1
†83450	Mud Lake 243	F6
83846	Mullan 1,269	C2
83650	Murphy⊙ 200	B6
83344	Murtaugh 114	D7
83651	Nampa 25,112	B6
83436	Newdale 329	G6
83654	New Meadows 576	B4
83655	New Plymouth 1,186	B6
83543	Nezperce⊙ 517	B3
83656	Notus 437	B6
83346	Oakley 663	D7
†99156	Oldtown 257	A1
†83855	Onaway 254	B3
83544	Orofino⊙ 3,711	B3
83849	Osburn 2,220	B2
†83263	Oxford 66	F7
83261	Paris⊙ 707	G7
83438	Parker 262	G6
83660	Parma 1,820	B6
83347	Paul 940	E7
83661	Payette⊙ 5,448	B5
83545	Peck 209	B3
83546	Pierce 1,060	C3
83850	Pinehurst 2,183	B2
83851	Plummer 634	B2
*83201	Pocatello⊙ 46,340	F7
83852	Ponderay 399	B1
83854	Post Falls 5,736	A2
83857	Potlatch 819	A3
83855	Preston⊙ 3,759	G7
83856	Priest River 1,639	A1
83858	Rathdrum 1,369	A2
83548	Reubens 87	B3
83440	Rexburg⊙ 11,559	G6
83349	Richfield 357	D6
83442	Rigby⊙ 2,624	F6
83549	Riggins 527	B4
83443	Ririe 555	G6

83444	Roberts 466	F6
83271	Rockland 283	F7
83350	Rupert⊙ 5,476	E7
83445	Saint Anthony⊙ 3,212	G6
83272	Saint Charles 211	G7
83861	Saint Maries⊙ 2,794	B2
83467	Salmon⊙ 3,308	D4
83864	Sandpoint⊙ 4,460	B1
83274	Shelley 3,300	F6
83352	Shoshone⊙ 1,242	D7
†83650	Silver City 1	B6
83868	Smelterville 776	B2
83276	Soda Springs⊙ 4,051	G7
83869	Spirit Lake 834	A2
83278	Stanley 99	D5
83552	Stites 253	C3
83448	Sugar City 1,022	G6
83353	Sun Valley 545	D6
83449	Swan Valley 135	G6
83870	Tensed 113	B2
83451	Teton 559	G6
83452	Tetonia 191	G6
83871	Troy 820	B3
83301	Twin Falls⊙ 26,209	D7
83454	Ucon 833	F6
83455	Victor 323	G6
83873	Wallace⊙ 1,736	C2
83553	Weippe 534	C3
83672	Weiser⊙ 4,771	B5
83355	Wendell 1,974	D7
83286	Weston 310	F7
83554	White Bird 154	B4
83676	Wilder 1,260	A6
83555	Winchester 343	B3
83876	Worley 206	B2

OTHER FEATURES

Albeni Falls (dam)	B1
Albion (mts.)	E7
Allan (mt.)	D4
American Falls (res.)	F6
Anderson Ranch (res.)	C6
Antelope (creek)	E6
Arrowrock (res.)	C6
Auger (falls)	D7
Badger (peak)	E7
Bald (mt.)	D5
Bannock (creek)	F7
Bannock (peak)	F7
Bannock (range)	F7
Bargamin (creek)	C4
Battle (creek)	B7
Bear (lake)	G7
Bear (riv.)	G7
Beaver (creek)	F5
Beaverhead (mts.)	E4
Big (creek)	C4
Big Boulder (creek)	B7
Big Elk (peak)	G6
Big Hole (mts.)	G6
Big Lost (riv.)	E6
Big Southern (butte)	E6
Big Wood (riv.)	D6
Birch (creek)	F5
Birch Creek (valley)	E5
Bitterroot (range)	D3
Blackfoot (res.)	G7
Black Pine (mts.)	E7
Blue Nose (mt.)	D4
Boise (mts.)	B6
Boise (riv.)	B6
Borah (peak)	E5
Boulder (mts.)	D6
Brownlee (dam)	B5
Bruneau (riv.)	C7
Camas (creek)	D5
Camas (creek)	D6
Camas (creek)	F5
Canyon (creek)	C6
Cape Horn (mt.)	C5
Caribou (mt.)	G6
Caribou (range)	G6
Cascade (res.)	C5
Castle (creek)	B7
Castle (peak)	D5
Cedar Creek (peak)	E7
Cedar Creek (res.)	D7
Centennial (mts.)	F5
Clearwater (mts.)	C3
Clearwater (riv.)	B3
Coeur d'Alene (lake)	B2
Coeur d'Alene (mts.)	B2
Coeur d'Alene (riv.)	B2
Cottonwood (butte)	C4
Craig (mts.)	B4
Crane Creek (res.)	B5
Craters of the Moon Nat'l Mon.	E6
Deadwood (res.)	C5
Deep (creek)	B7
Deep (creek)	F7
Deep Creek (mts.)	F7
Diamond (peak)	E5
Dworshak (res.)	C3
East Sister (peak)	C2

Eighteen Mile (peak)	E5
Fish Creek (res.)	E6
Fort Hall Ind. Res.	F6
Goldstone (mt.)	E4
Goose (creek)	E7
Goose Creek (mts.)	D7
Grand Canyon of the Snake River (canyon)	B4
Grays (lake)	G6
Grays Lake Outlet (creek)	G6
Greylock (mt.)	C6
Hayden (mt.)	D4
Hells (canyon)	B4
Hells Canyon Nat'l Rec. Area	B4
Henrys (lake)	G5
Henrys Fork, Snake (riv.)	G5
Hunter (peak)	D3
Hyndman (peak)	D6
Indian (creek)	C5
Island Park (res.)	G5
Jarbidge (riv.)	C7
Johnson (creek)	C5
Jordan (creek)	A7
Kootenai (riv.)	C1
Lemhi (riv.)	E5
Lemhi (range)	E5
Lemhi (riv.)	E5
Little Lost (riv.)	E5
Little Owyhee (riv.)	B7
Little Salmon (riv.)	B4
Little Weiser (riv.)	B5
Little Wood (riv.)	D6
Lochsa (riv.)	C3
Lolo (creek)	C3
Lolo (pass)	D3
Lone Pine (peak)	D5
Lookout (mt.)	D5
Lookout (mt.)	F5
Lost River (range)	E5
Lost Trail (pass)	E4
Lowell (lake)	B6
Lower Goose Creek (res.)	D7
Lower Granite (lake)	A3
Lucky Peak (lake)	B6
Mackay (res.)	E6
Magic (res.)	D6
Malad (riv.)	F7
Marsh (creek)	F7
McGuire (mt.)	D4
Meade (peak)	G7
Meadow (creek)	C4
Medicine Lodge (creek)	F5

Middle Fork (peak)	D5
Monument (peak)	B4
Moose (creek)	D3
Mores (creek)	C6
Mormon (mt.)	D4
Mountain Home (res.)	C6
Mountain Home A.F.B. 6,403	C6
Moyie (riv.)	B1
Mud (lake)	F6
National Reactor Testing Sta.	F6
Nez Perce Nat'l Hist. Park	B-C3
North Fork (riv.)	B7
Norton (peak)	D6
Orofino (creek)	C3
Owyhee (mts.)	B6
Owyhee, East Fork (riv.)	B7
Oxbow (dam)	B5
Pack (riv.)	B1
Pahsimeroi (riv.)	E5
Palisades (res.)	G6
Palouse (riv.)	B3
Panther (creek)	D4
Payette (lake)	C4
Payette (mts.)	B5
Payette (riv.)	B6
Peale (mt.)	G7
Pend Oreille (lake)	B1
Pend Oreille (mt.)	B1
Pend Oreille (riv.)	A1
Pilot (peak)	C4
Pilot (peak)	C6
Pilot Knob (mt.)	C4
Pinyon (peak)	C5
Pioneer (mts.)	D6
Portneuf (res.)	F7
Pot (mt.)	C3
Potlatch (riv.)	B3
Priest (lake)	B1
Priest (riv.)	B1
Purcell (mts.)	B1
Pyramid (peak)	E4
Raft (riv.)	E7
Rainbow (mt.)	C4
Ranger (peak)	D3
Rays (lake)	F6
Red (riv.)	C4
Redfish (lake)	D5
Reynolds (peak)	B6
Rhodes (peak)	D3
Rocky (mts.)	D1
Rocky Ridge (mt.)	C3

Ryan (peak)	D6
Saddle (mt.)	D3
Saddle (mt.)	F6
Sailor (creek)	C7
Saint Joe (riv.)	B2
Saint Maries (riv.)	B2
Salmon (falls)	C7
Salmon (riv.)	B4
Salmon Falls (creek)	D7
Salmon Falls Creek (res.)	D7
Salmon River (mts.)	C5
Sawtooth (range)	C6
Sawtooth Nat'l Rec. Area	D5
Secesh (riv.)	C4
Selkirk (mts.)	B1
Selway (riv.)	C3
Seven Devils (mts.)	B4
Shoshone (falls)	D7
Sleeping Deer (mt.)	D5
Smith (creek)	B1
Smoky (mts.)	D6
Snake (riv.)	A3
Snake River (plain)	D7
Snake River (range)	G6
Spirit (lake)	B2
Squaw (creek)	B5
Squaw (peak)	D4
Steamboat (mt.)	C4
Steel (mt.)	C6
Strike, C.J. (res.)	C7
Sublett (mts.)	E7
Sunset (peak)	E6
Taylor (mt.)	D5
Teton (riv.)	G6
Thompson (peak)	C5
Trinity (mts.)	C6
Trout (creek)	B1
Twin (falls)	D7
Twin Peaks (mt.)	D5
Walcott (lake)	E7
Wasatch (range)	G7
Waugh (mt.)	D4
Weiser (riv.)	B5
Western Shoshone Ind. Res.	B7
White Knob (mts.)	E6
Wickahoney (creek)	C7
Willow (creek)	G6
Wilson Lake (res.)	D7
Yankee Fork, Salmon (riv.)	D5
Yellowstone Nat'l Park	G5

⊙County seat.
‡Population of metropolitan area.
† Zip of nearest p.o.
* Multiple zips.

Agriculture, Industry and Resources

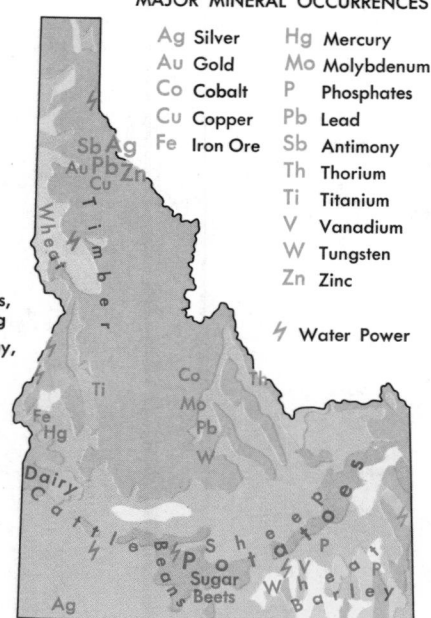

DOMINANT LAND USE

■ Wheat, General Farming
■ Wheat, Peas
■ Specialized Dairy
■ Potatoes, Beans, Sugar Beets, Livestock, General Farming
■ General Farming, Dairy, Hay, Sugar Beets
■ General Farming, Livestock, Special Crops
■ General Farming, Dairy, Range Livestock
■ Range Livestock
■ Forests

MAJOR MINERAL OCCURRENCES

Ag	Silver	Hg	Mercury
Au	Gold	Mo	Molybdenum
Co	Cobalt	P	Phosphates
Cu	Copper	Pb	Lead
Fe	Iron Ore	Sb	Antimony
		Th	Thorium
		Ti	Titanium
		V	Vanadium
		W	Tungsten
		Zn	Zinc

⚡ Water Power

Illinois

SCALE

0 5 10 20 30 40 MI.

0 5 10 20 30 40 KM.

State Capitals ⊛

County Seats ◉

Canals

Major Limited Access Hwys.

Scale 1:2,160,000

St. Louis

Chicago and Vicinity

AREA 56,345 sq. mi. (145,934 sq. km.)
POPULATION 11,426,596
CAPITAL Springfield
LARGEST CITY Chicago
HIGHEST POINT Charles Mound 1,235 ft. (376 m.)
SETTLED IN 1720
ADMITTED TO UNION December 3, 1818
POPULAR NAME Prairie State; Land of Lincoln
STATE FLOWER Native Violet
STATE BIRD Cardinal

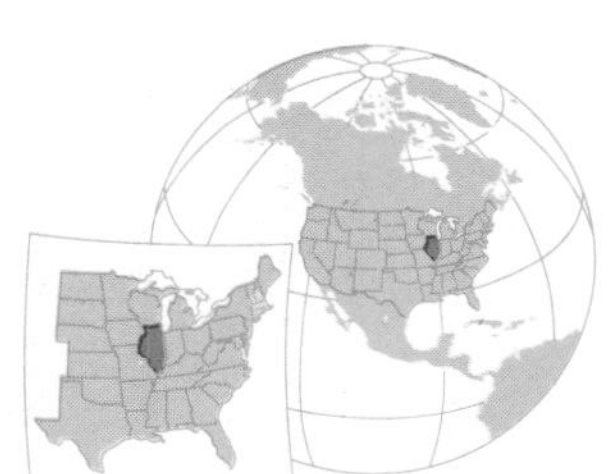

COUNTIES

Adams 71,622 ..... B4
Alexander 12,264 ..... D6
Bond 16,224 ..... D5
Boone 28,630 ..... E1
Brown 5,411 ..... C4
Bureau 39,114 ..... D2
Calhoun 5,867 ..... C4
Carroll 18,779 ..... D1
Cass 15,084 ..... C4
Champaign 168,392 ..... E3
Christian 36,446 ..... D4
Clark 16,913 ..... F4
Clay 15,283 ..... E5
Clinton 32,617 ..... D5
Coles 52,260 ..... E4
Cook 5,253,655 ..... F2
Crawford 20,818 ..... F4
Cumberland 11,062 ..... E4
De Kalb 74,624 ..... E2
De Witt 18,108 ..... E3
Douglas 19,774 ..... E4
Du Page 658,835 ..... E2
Edgar 21,725 ..... F4
Edwards 7,961 ..... E5
Effingham 30,944 ..... E4
Fayette 22,167 ..... D4
Ford 15,265 ..... E3
Franklin 43,201 ..... E5
Fulton 43,687 ..... C3
Gallatin 7,590 ..... E6
Greene 16,661 ..... C4
Grundy 30,582 ..... E2
Hamilton 9,172 ..... E5
Hancock 23,877 ..... B3
Hardin 5,383 ..... E6
Henderson 9,114 ..... C3
Henry 57,968 ..... C2
Iroquois 32,976 ..... F3
Jackson 61,522 ..... D6
Jasper 11,318 ..... E4
Jefferson 36,354 ..... E5
Jersey 20,538 ..... C4
Jo Daviess 23,520 ..... C1
Johnson 9,624 ..... E6
Kane 278,405 ..... E2
Kankakee 102,926 ..... F2
Kendall 37,202 ..... E2
Knox 61,607 ..... C3
Lake 440,372 ..... E1
La Salle 112,033 ..... E2
Lawrence 17,807 ..... F5
Lee 36,328 ..... D2
Livingston 41,381 ..... E3
Logan 31,802 ..... D3
Macon 131,375 ..... E4
Macoupin 49,384 ..... D4
Madison 247,691 ..... D5
Marion 43,523 ..... E5
Marshall 14,479 ..... D2
Mason 19,492 ..... D3
Massac 14,990 ..... E6
McDonough 37,467 ..... C3
McHenry 147,897 ..... E1
McLean 119,149 ..... E3
Menard 11,700 ..... D3
Mercer 19,286 ..... C2
Monroe 20,117 ..... C5
Montgomery 31,686 ..... D4
Morgan 37,502 ..... C4
Moultrie 14,546 ..... E4
Ogle 46,338 ..... D1
Peoria 200,466 ..... D3
Perry 21,714 ..... D5
Piatt 16,581 ..... E4
Pike 18,896 ..... C4
Pope 4,404 ..... E6
Pulaski 8,840 ..... D6
Putnam 6,085 ..... D2
Randolph 35,652 ..... D5
Richland 17,587 ..... E5
Rock Island 165,968 ..... C2
Saint Clair 267,531 ..... D5
Saline 28,448 ..... E6
Sangamon 176,089 ..... D4
Schuyler 8,365 ..... C3
Scott 6,142 ..... C4
Shelby 23,923 ..... E4
Stark 7,389 ..... D2
Stephenson 49,536 ..... D1
Tazewell 132,078 ..... D3
Union 17,765 ..... D6
Vermilion 95,222 ..... F3
Wabash 13,713 ..... F5
Warren 21,943 ..... C3
Washington 15,472 ..... D5
Wayne 18,059 ..... E5
White 17,864 ..... E5
Whiteside 65,970 ..... D2
Will 324,460 ..... F2
Williamson 56,538 ..... E6
Winnebago 250,884 ..... D1
Woodford 33,320 ..... D3

CITIES and TOWNS

Zip *Name/Pop.* *Key*

61410 Abingdon 4,210 ..... C3
60101 Addison 29,826 ..... B5
61230 Albany 1,014 ..... C2
62806 Albion⊙ 2,285 ..... E5
61231 Aledo⊙ 3,881 ..... C2
61412 Alexis 1,076 ..... C2
60102 Algonquin 5,834 ..... E1
62207 Alorton 2,237 ..... B2
61413 Alpha 815 ..... C2
†60658 Alsip 17,134 ..... B6
62411 Altamont 2,389 ..... E4
62002 Alton 34,171 ..... A2
61310 Amboy 2,377 ..... D2
61232 Andalusia 1,238 ..... C2
62906 Anna 5,408 ..... D6
61234 Annawan 908 ..... C2
60002 Antioch 4,419 ..... E1
61910 Arcola 2,714 ..... E4
62501 Argenta 994 ..... E4
*60004 Arlington Heights 66,116 ... B5
61911 Arthur 2,122 ..... E4
60911 Ashkum 735 ..... E3
62612 Ashland 1,351 ..... C4
62808 Ashley 658 ..... D5
61912 Ashmore 883 ..... F4
61006 Ashton 1,140 ..... D2
62510 Assumption 1,283 ..... E4
61501 Astoria 1,370 ..... C3
62613 Athens 1,371 ..... D4
61235 Atkinson 1,138 ..... C2
61723 Atlanta 1,807 ..... D3
61913 Atwood 1,464 ..... E4
62615 Auburn 3,616 ..... D4
62311 Augusta 764 ..... C3
*60504 Aurora 81,293 ..... E2
62907 Ava 811 ..... D6
62216 Aviston 846 ..... D5
61415 Avon 1,019 ..... C3
†60015 Bannockburn 1,316 ..... B5
60010 Barrington 9,029 ..... A5
†60010 Barrington Hills 3,631 ..... A5
62312 Barry 1,487 ..... B4
60103 Bartlett 13,254 ..... A5
61607 Bartonville 6,137 ..... D3
60510 Batavia 12,574 ..... E2
62618 Beardstown 6,338 ..... C3
62219 Beckemeyer 1,119 ..... D5
60401 Beecher 2,024 ..... F2
*62220 Belleville⊙ 41,580 ..... B3
60104 Bellwood 19,811 ..... B5
61008 Belvidere⊙ 15,176 ..... E1
61813 Bement 1,770 ..... E4
62009 Benld 1,638 ..... D4
60106 Bensenville 16,124 ..... B5
62812 Benton⊙ 7,778 ..... E6
60162 Berkeley 5,467 ..... B5
60402 Berwyn 46,849 ..... B6
62010 Bethalto 8,630 ..... B2
61914 Bethany 1,550 ..... E4
61420 Blandinsville 886 ..... C3
60108 Bloomingdale 12,659 ..... A5
61701 Bloomington⊙ 44,189 ..... D3
Bloomington-Normal‡ 119,149 ..... D3
60406 Blue Island 21,855 ..... B6
62513 Blue Mound 1,338 ..... D4
62621 Bluffs 821 ..... C4
60439 Bolingbrook 37,261 ..... A6
60914 Bourbonnais 13,280 ..... F2
60407 Braceville 721 ..... E2
61421 Bradford 924 ..... D2
60915 Bradley 11,008 ..... F2
60408 Braidwood 3,429 ..... E2
62230 Breese 3,516 ..... D5
62417 Bridgeport 2,281 ..... F5
60455 Bridgeview 14,155 ..... B6
62012 Brighton 2,364 ..... C4
61517 Brimfield 890 ..... D3
60153 Broadview 8,618 ..... B6
60513 Brookfield 19,395 ..... B6
†62059 Brooklyn (Lovejoy) 1,233 .. A2
62910 Brookport 1,128 ..... E6
61314 Buda 668 ..... D2
†60090 Buffalo Grove 22,230 ..... B5
62014 Bunker Hill 1,700 ..... D4
60459 Burbank 28,462 ..... B6
†60601 Burnham 4,030 ..... C6
†60558 Burr Ridge 3,833 ..... B6
61422 Bushnell 3,811 ..... C3
61010 Byron 2,035 ..... D1
62206 Cahokia 18,904 ..... A3
62914 Cairo⊙ 5,931 ..... D6
60409 Calumet City 39,697 ..... C6
†60643 Calumet Park 8,788 ..... C6
62915 Cambria 1,090 ..... D6
61238 Cambridge⊙ 2,217 ..... C2
62320 Camp Point 1,285 ..... B3
61520 Canton 14,626 ..... C3
61239 Carbon Cliff 1,578 ..... C2
62901 Carbondale 26,414 ..... D6
62626 Carlinville⊙ 5,439 ..... D4
62231 Carlyle⊙ 3,388 ..... D5
62821 Carmi⊙ 6,264 ..... E5
†60187 Carol Stream 15,472 ..... A5
60110 Carpentersville 23,272 ..... E1
62917 Carrier Mills 2,268 ..... E6
62016 Carrollton⊙ 2,816 ..... C4
62918 Carterville 3,445 ..... D6
62321 Carthage⊙ 2,978 ..... B3
60013 Cary 6,640 ..... E1
62420 Casey 3,026 ..... F4
62232 Caseyville 4,308 ..... B2
61817 Catlin 2,226 ..... F3
61013 Cedarville 766 ..... D1
†62801 Central City 1,505 ..... D5
62801 Centralia 15,126 ..... D5
62206 Centreville 9,747 ..... B3
61818 Cerro Gordo 1,553 ..... E4
61820 Champaign 58,133 ..... E3
Champaign-Urbana-Rantoul‡ 168,392 ..... E3
62627 Chandlerville 842 ..... C3
60410 Channahon 3,734 ..... E2
61920 Charleston⊙ 19,355 ..... E4
62629 Chatham 5,597 ..... D4
60921 Chatsworth 1,187 ..... E3
60922 Chebanse 1,191 ..... F3
61726 Chenoa 1,847 ..... E3
61016 Cherry Valley 946 ..... D1
62233 Chester⊙ 8,401 ..... D6
*60601 Chicago⊙ 3,005,072 ..... C5
Chicago‡ 7,102,328 ..... C5
60411 Chicago Heights 37,026 ..... C6
60415 Chicago Ridge 13,473 ..... B6
61523 Chillicothe 6,176 ..... D3
61924 Chrisman 1,413 ..... F4
62822 Christopher 3,086 ..... D6
60650 Cicero 61,232 ..... B5
60924 Cissna Park 825 ..... F3
60514 Clarendon Hills 6,870 ..... B6
62824 Clay City 1,038 ..... E5
62324 Clayton 889 ..... B3
60927 Clifton 1,390 ..... F3
61727 Clinton⊙ 8,014 ..... E3
60416 Coal City 3,028 ..... E2
61240 Coal Valley 3,800 ..... C2
62920 Cobden 1,210 ..... D6
62017 Coffeen 842 ..... D4
62326 Colchester 1,729 ..... C3
61728 Colfax 920 ..... E3
62234 Collinsville 19,613 ..... B2
61241 Colona 2,172 ..... C2
62236 Columbia 4,269 ..... C5
60112 Cortland 1,019 ..... E2
62018 Cottage Hills B2
62237 Coulterville 1,118 ..... D5
†60525 Countryside 6,538 ..... B6
62922 Creal Springs 845 ..... E6
60431 Crest Hill 9,252 ..... E2
†60445 Crestwood 10,852 ..... B6
60417 Crete 5,417 ..... F2
61611 Creve Coeur 6,851 ..... D3
62827 Crossville 944 ..... F5
60014 Crystal Lake 18,590 ..... E1
61427 Cuba 1,648 ..... C3
62330 Dallas City 1,408 ..... B3
61320 Dalzell 824 ..... D2
61732 Danvers 921 ..... D3
61832 Danville⊙ 38,985 ..... F3
†60559 Darien 14,536 ..... B6
*62521 Decatur⊙ 94,081 ..... E4
Decatur‡ 131,375 ..... E4
60015 Deerfield 17,430 ..... B5
†60010 Deer Park 1,368 ..... A5
60115 De Kalb 33,099 ..... E2
61734 Delavan 1,973 ..... D3
61322 Depue 1,873 ..... D2
62924 De Soto 1,589 ..... D6
*60016 Des Plaines 53,568 ..... B5
62530 Divernon 1,081 ..... D4
†60469 Dixmoor 4,175 ..... C6
61021 Dixon⊙ 15,701 ..... D2
60419 Dolton 24,766 ..... C6
62926 Dongola 886 ..... D6
60515 Downers Grove 42,572 ..... A6
60118 Dundee (East and West Dundee) 6,169 ..... E1
61525 Dunlap 824 ..... D3
62239 Dupo 3,039 ..... A3
62832 Du Quoin 6,594 ..... D5
61024 Durand 1,073 ..... D1
60420 Dwight 4,146 ..... E2
60518 Earlville 1,382 ..... E2
62024 East Alton 7,096 ..... A2
†60411 East Chicago Heights 5,347 ..... C6
61025 East Dubuque 2,194 ..... C1
†60118 East Dundee (Dundee) 2,618 ..... E1
61430 East Galesburg 928 ..... C3
†60429 East Hazelcrest 1,362 ..... C6
61244 East Moline 20,907 ..... C2
61611 East Peoria 22,385 ..... D3
*62201 East Saint Louis 55,200 ..... A2
62531 Edinburg 1,231 ..... D4
62025 Edwardsville⊙ 12,480 ..... B2
62401 Effingham⊙ 11,270 ..... E4
60119 Elburn 1,224 ..... E2
62930 Eldorado 5,198 ..... E6
60120 Elgin 63,981 ..... E1
61028 Elizabeth 772 ..... C1
62931 Elizabethtown⊙ 478 ..... E6
60007 Elk Grove Village 28,907 ... B5
62932 Elkville 973 ..... D6
60126 Elmhurst 44,276 ..... B5
61529 Elmwood 2,117 ..... D3
60635 Elmwood Park 24,016 ..... B5
61738 El Paso 2,676 ..... D3
62028 Elsah 990 ..... C5
60421 Elwood 814 ..... E2
62933 Energy 1,138 ..... E6
62835 Enfield 890 ..... E5
62934 Equality 831 ..... E6
61250 Erie 1,725 ..... C2
61530 Eureka⊙ 4,306 ..... D3
*60201 Evanston 73,706 ..... B5
62242 Evansville 863 ..... D5
60642 Evergreen Park 22,260 ..... B6
61739 Fairbury 3,544 ..... E3
62837 Fairfield⊙ 5,954 ..... E5
†62201 Fairmont City 2,313 ..... B2
61841 Fairmount 851 ..... F3
62208 Fairview Heights 12,414 ..... B3
61842 Farmer City 2,252 ..... E3
61531 Farmington 3,118 ..... C3
62534 Findlay 868 ..... E4
61843 Fisher 1,572 ..... E3
61740 Flanagan 978 ..... E3
62839 Flora 5,379 ..... E5
60422 Flossmoor 8,423 ..... B6
60130 Forest Park 15,177 ..... B5
†60402 Forest View 764 ..... B6
61741 Forrest 1,246 ..... E3
61030 Forreston 1,384 ..... D1
60020 Fox Lake 6,831 ..... A4
60021 Fox River Grove 2,515 ..... A5
60423 Frankfort 4,357 ..... B6
61031 Franklin Grove 965 ..... D2
60131 Franklin Park 17,507 ..... B5
62243 Freeburg 2,989 ..... D5
61032 Freeport⊙ 26,266 ..... D1
61252 Fulton 3,936 ..... C2
62935 Galatia 1,042 ..... E6
61036 Galena⊙ 3,876 ..... C1
61401 Galesburg⊙ 35,305 ..... C3
61434 Galva 3,185 ..... D2
60424 Gardner 1,322 ..... E2
61254 Geneseo 6,373 ..... C2
60134 Geneva⊙ 9,881 ..... E2
60135 Genoa 3,276 ..... E1
61846 Georgetown 4,220 ..... F4
62245 Germantown 1,191 ..... D5
60936 Gibson City 3,498 ..... E3
61847 Gifford 848 ..... E3
62033 Gillespie 3,740 ..... D4
60938 Gilman 1,913 ..... E3
62640 Girard 2,246 ..... D4
61533 Glasford 1,201 ..... D3
62034 Glen Carbon 5,197 ..... B2
60022 Glencoe 9,200 ..... B5
†60108 Glendale Heights 23,163 ... A5
60137 Glen Ellyn 23,717 ..... A5
60025 Glenview 32,060 ..... B5
60425 Glenwood 10,538 ..... C6
62035 Godfrey A2
62938 Golconda⊙ 960 ..... E6
62939 Goreville 978 ..... E6
62037 Grafton 1,024 ..... C5
62942 Grand Tower 748 ..... D6
†62701 Grandview 1,794 ..... D4
62040 Granite City 36,815 ..... A2
60940 Grant Park 1,038 ..... F2
61326 Granville 1,537 ..... D2
60030 Grayslake 5,260 ..... B4
62844 Grayville 2,313 ..... B4
62044 Greenfield 1,090 ..... C4
†60048 Green Oaks 1,415 ..... B4
†61241 Green Rock 3,324 ..... C2
62428 Greenup 1,655 ..... E4
61534 Green Valley 768 ..... D3
62642 Greenview 830 ..... D3
62246 Greenville⊙ 5,271 ..... D5
61744 Gridley 1,246 ..... E3
62340 Griggsville 1,301 ..... C4
60031 Gurnee 7,179 ..... B4
62341 Hamilton 3,509 ..... B3
60140 Hampshire 1,735 ..... E1
61256 Hampton 1,873 ..... C2
61536 Hanna City 1,361 ..... D3
61041 Hanover 1,069 ..... C1
60103 Hanover Park 28,719 ..... A5
62047 Hardin⊙ 1,107 ..... C4
62946 Harrisburg⊙ 10,410 ..... E6
62537 Harristown 1,456 ..... D4
62048 Hartford 1,887 ..... A2
60033 Harvard 5,126 ..... E1
60426 Harvey 35,810 ..... B6
60656 Harwood Heights 8,228 ..... B5
62644 Havana⊙ 4,277 ..... D3
†60047 Hawthorn Woods 1,658 ..... B5
60429 Hazel Crest 13,973 ..... B6
60034 Hebron 786 ..... E1
†61832 Hegeler 1,853 ..... F3
61327 Hennepin⊙ 716 ..... D2
61537 Henry 2,740 ..... D2
62948 Herrin 10,708 ..... E6
60941 Herscher 1,214 ..... E2
61745 Heyworth 1,598 ..... E3
60457 Hickory Hills 13,778 ..... B6
62249 Highland 7,122 ..... D5
60035 Highland Park 30,611 ..... B5
60040 Highwood 5,452 ..... B5
62049 Hillsboro⊙ 4,408 ..... D4
60162 Hillside 8,279 ..... B5
60520 Hinckley 1,447 ..... E2
60521 Hinsdale 16,726 ..... B6
60525 Hodgkins 2,005 ..... B6
60195 Hoffman Estates 37,272 ..... A5
61849 Homer 1,279 ..... F3
60456 Hometown 5,324 ..... B6
60430 Homewood 19,724 ..... B6
60942 Hoopeston 6,411 ..... F3
61747 Hohedale 913 ..... D3
61748 Hudson 929 ..... E3

(continued on following page)

Topography

0 40 80 MI.
0 40 80 KM.

5,000 m. 16,404 ft. | 2,000 m. 6,562 ft. | 1,000 m. 3,281 ft. | 500 m. 1,640 ft. | 200 m. 656 ft. | 100 m. 328 ft. | Sea Level | Below

Agriculture, Industry and Resources

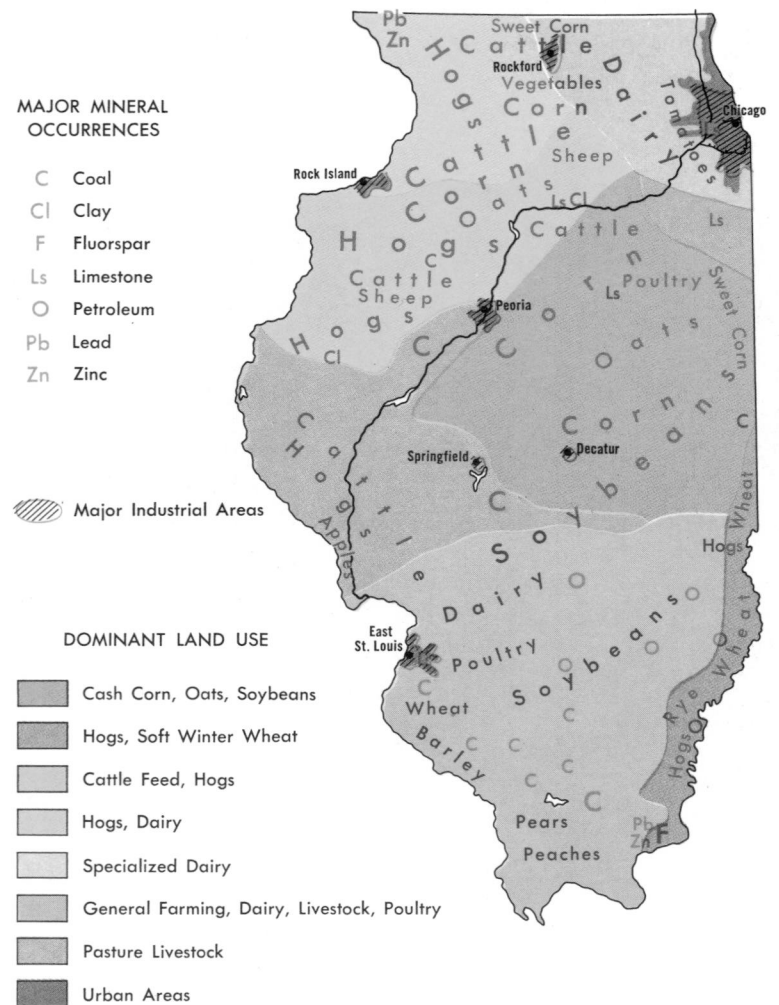

MAJOR MINERAL OCCURRENCES

C	Coal
Cl	Clay
F	Fluorspar
Ls	Limestone
O	Petroleum
Pb	Lead
Zn	Zinc

Major Industrial Areas

DOMINANT LAND USE

Cash Corn, Oats, Soybeans

Hogs, Soft Winter Wheat

Cattle Feed, Hogs

Hogs, Dairy

Specialized Dairy

General Farming, Dairy, Livestock, Poultry

Pasture Livestock

Urban Areas

AREA 36,185 sq. mi. (93,719 sq. km.)
POPULATION 5,490,260
CAPITAL Indianapolis
LARGEST CITY Indianapolis
HIGHEST POINT 1,257 ft. (383 m.) (Wayne County)
SETTLED IN 1730
ADMITTED TO UNION December 11, 1816
POPULAR NAME Hoosier State
STATE FLOWER Peony
STATE BIRD Cardinal

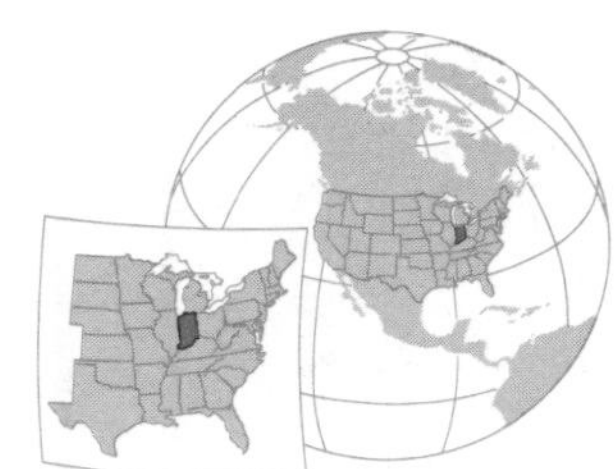

COUNTIES

Adams 29,619 H3
Allen 294,335 G2
Bartholomew 65,088 F6
Benton 10,218 C3
Blackford 15,570 G4
Boone 36,446 E4
Brown 12,377 E6
Carroll 19,722 D3
Cass 40,936 E3
Clark 88,838 F8
Clay 24,862 C6
Clinton 31,545 E4
Crawford 9,820 E8
Daviess 27,836 C7
Dearborn 34,291 H6
Decatur 23,841 G6
De Kalb 33,606 H2
Delaware 128,587 G4
Dubois 34,238 D8
Elkhart 137,330 F1
Fayette 28,272 G5
Floyd 61,169 F8
Fountain 19,033 C4
Franklin 19,612 G6
Fulton 19,335 E2
Gibson 33,156 B8
Grant 80,934 F3
Greene 30,416 D6
Hamilton 82,027 E4
Hancock 43,939 F5
Harrison 27,276 E8
Hendricks 69,804 D5
Henry 53,336 G5
Howard 86,896 E4
Huntington 35,596 G3
Jackson 36,523 E7
Jasper 26,138 C2
Jay 23,239 G4
Jefferson 30,419 G7
Jennings 22,854 F7
Johnson 77,240 E6
Knox 41,838 C7
Kosciusko 59,555 F2
Lagrange 25,550 G1
Lake 522,965 C2
LaPorte 108,632 D1
Lawrence 4,272 E7
Madison 139,336 F4
Marion 765,233 E5
Marshall 39,155 E2
Martin 11,001 D7
Miami 39,820 E3
Monroe 98,785 D6
Montgomery 35,501 D4
Morgan 51,999 E6
Newton 14,844 C3
Noble 35,443 G2
Ohio 5,114 H7
Orange 18,677 E7
Owen 15,841 D6
Parke 16,372 C5
Perry 19,346 D8
Pike 13,465 C8
Porter 119,816 C2
Posey 26,414 B8
Pulaski 13,258 D2
Putnam 29,163 D5
Randolph 29,997 G4
Ripley 24,398 G6
Rush 19,604 G5
Saint Joseph 241,617 E1
Scott 20,422 F7
Shelby 39,887 F5
Spencer 19,361 C9
Starke 21,997 D2
Steuben 24,694 G1
Sullivan 21,107 C6
Switzerland 7,153 G7
Tippecanoe 121,702 D4
Tipton 16,819 E4
Union 6,860 H5
Vanderburgh 167,515 B8
Vermillion 18,229 C5
Vigo 112,385 C6
Wabash 36,640 F3
Warren 8,976 C4
Warrick 41,474 C8
Washington 21,932 E7
Wayne 76,058 G5
Wells 25,401 G3
White 23,867 D3
Whitley 26,215 F2

CITIES and TOWNS

Zip *Name/Pop.* *Key*

47240 Adams 250 F6
†46947 Adamsboro 325 E3
46102 Advance 559 D5
46910 Akron 1,045 E2
47320 Albany 2,625 G4
46701 Albion⊙ 1,637 G2
†47283 Alert 102 F6
46001 Alexandria 6,028 F4
†46738 Altona 263 G2
47917 Ambia 274 C4
46911 Amboy 450 F3
†46131 Amity 200 E6
46103 Amo 444 D5
*46011 Anderson⊙ 64,695 F4
Anderson‡ 139,336 F4
†47024 Andersonville 225 G5
46702 Andrews 1,243 F3
46703 Angola⊙ 5,486 G1
46030 Arcadia 1,801 E4
46704 Arcola 300 G2
†46624 Ardmore 800 E1
46501 Argos 1,547 E2
46104 Arlington 500 F5
46705 Ashley 841 G1
46031 Atlanta 657 E4
47918 Attica 3,841 C4
46502 Atwood 300 F2
46706 Auburn⊙ 8,122 G2
47001 Aurora 3,816 H6
47102 Austin 4,857 F7
46710 Avilla 1,272 G2
47420 Avoca 400 D7
46105 Bainbridge 644 D5
46106 Bargersville 1,647 E5
47006 Batesville 4,152 G6
47920 Battle Ground 812 D3
47421 Bedford⊙ 14,410 E7
46107 Beech Grove 13,196 E5
†46526 Benton 220 F2
46711 Berne 3,300 H3
†46111 Bethany 127 E5
46301 Beverly Shores 864 C1
47512 Bicknell 4,713 C7
46713 Bippus 300 F3
47513 Birdseye 533 D8
†46406 Black Oak C1
47831 Blanford 500 B5
47138 Blocher 400 F7
47424 Bloomfield⊙ 2,705 D6
47832 Bloomingdale 409 C5
47401 Bloomington⊙ 52,044 D6
Bloomington‡ 98,387 D6
†47360 Blountsville 213 G4
†46176 Blue Ridge 219 F5
46714 Bluffton⊙ 8,705 G3
46110 Boggstown 200 F5
46302 Boone Grove 220 C2
47601 Boonville⊙ 6,300 C8
47106 Borden 384 F8
47324 Boston 189 H5
47921 Boswell 810 C3
46504 Bourbon 1,522 E2
47833 Bowling Green 200 D6
47107 Bradford 350 E8
47834 Brazil⊙ 7,852 C5
46506 Bremen 3,565 E2
47836 Bridgeton 250 C5
†45030 Bright 450 H6
46720 Brimfield 292 G2
46913 Bringhurst 275 E3
46507 Bristol 1,203 F1
47922 Brook 926 C3
46111 Brooklyn 889 E5
†47250 Brooksburg 132 G7
47923 Brookston 1,701 D3
47012 Brookville⊙ 2,874 G6
46112 Brownsburg 6,242 E5
47220 Brownstown⊙ 2,704 F7
47325 Brownsville 250 H5
47516 Bruceville 646 C7
47326 Bryant 277 G3
47924 Buck Creek 225 D4
47647 Buckskin 200 C8
47925 Buffalo 500 D3
46914 Bunker Hill 984 E3
46508 Burket 260 F2
46915 Burlington 680 E4
47926 Burnettsville 496 D3
47222 Burney 300 F6
†46401 Burns Harbor 920 C1
46916 Burrows 250 E3
46721 Butler 2,509 H2
47223 Butlerville 300 F6
†46371 Byron 200 C5
†47362 Cadiz 180 G5
47327 Cambridge City 2,407 G5
46917 Camden 618 D3
47108 Campbellsburg 695 E7
47224 Canaan 90 G7
47519 Cannelburg 152 C7
47520 Cannelton⊙ 2,373 D9
47837 Carbon 307 C5
47838 Carlisle 717 C7
46032 Carmel 18,272 E5
46114 Cartersburg 300 E5
46115 Carthage 886 F5
47927 Cates 125 C4
47928 Cayuga 1,258 C5
47016 Cedar Grove 217 H6
46303 Cedar Lake 8,754 C2
47521 Celestine 150 D8
†47842 Centenary 150 B5
†46901 Center 310 E4
47840 Centerpoint 242 C6
46116 Centerton 250 E5
47330 Centerville 2,284 H5
47929 Chalmers 554 D3
47610 Chandler 3,043 C8
47111 Charlestown 5,596 F8
46117 Charlottesville 300 F5
†47138 Chelsea 200 F7
46017 Chesterfield 2,701 F4
46304 Chesterton 8,531 D1
47611 Chrisney 537 C8
46723 Churubusco 1,638 G2
46034 Cicero 2,557 E4
47225 Clarksburg 300 G6
47930 Clarks Hill 653 D4
47130 Clarksville 15,164 F8
47841 Clay City 883 C6
46510 Claypool 464 F2
46118 Clayton 703 D5
47426 Clear Creek 200 E6
†46737 Clear Lake 301 H1
47226 Clifford 310 F6
47842 Clinton 5,267 C5
46120 Cloverdale 1,357 D5
†47834 Cloverland 175 C6
47427 Coal City 225 D6
47845 Coalmont 450 C6
46121 Coatesville 474 D5
47931 Colburn 300 D3
46035 Colfax 823 D4
47978 Collegeville 1,059 C3
46725 Columbia City⊙ 5,091 G2
47201 Columbus⊙ 30,614 E6
47331 Connersville⊙ 17,023 G5
46919 Converse 1,279 F3
47228 Cortland 175 F7
46730 Corunna 304 G2
47112 Corydon⊙ 2,724 E8
47932 Covington⊙ 2,883 C4
†47302 Cowan 428 G4
47114 Crandall 176 E8
47522 Crane D7
47933 Crawfordsville⊙ 13,325 D4
46732 Cromwell 458 F2
47229 Crothersville 1,747 F7
46307 Crown Point⊙ 16,455 C2
46511 Culver 1,601 E2
46229 Cumberland 3,375 E5
47612 Cynthiana 874 B8
47523 Dale 1,693 D8
47334 Daleville F4
47847 Dana 803 C5
46122 Danville⊙ 4,220 D5
47940 Darlington 811 D4
47618 Darmstadt 1,280 B8
47941 Dayton 781 D4
46733 Decatur⊙ 8,649 H3
47524 Decker 256 B7
†46917 Deer Creek 250 E3
46923 Delphi⊙ 3,042 D3
46310 Demotte 2,559 C2
46926 Denver 589 E3
47230 Deputy 200 F7
47302 Desoto 385 G4
47018 Dillsboro 1,038 G6
46513 Donaldson 320 E2
†47118 Doolittle Mills 200 D8
47335 Dublin 979 G5
47525 Dubois 550 D8
47848 Dugger 1,118 C6
†46304 Dune Acres 291 C1
47336 Dunkirk 3,180 G4
†46514 Dunlap 5,397 F1
47337 Dunreith 184 F5
47231 Dupont 392 G7
46311 Dyer 9,555 C1
†46074 Eagletown 306 E4
47942 Earl Park 469 C3
46312 East Chicago 39,786 C1
47019 East Enterprise 250 H7
†47370 East Germantown (Pershing) 438 G5
47338 Eaton 1,804 G4
47116 Eckerty 108 D8
47339 Economy 237 G5
†46011 Edgewood 2,215 F4
46124 Edinburgh 4,856 E6
47528 Edwardsport 459 C7
†47150 Edwardsville 700 F8
47613 Elberfeld 640 C8
47117 Elizabeth 178 F8
47232 Elizabethtown 603 F6
46514 Elkhart 41,305 F1
Elkhart‡ 137,330 F1
47429 Ellettsville 3,328 D6
47529 Elnora 756 C7
†47018 Elrod 200 G6
†47901 Elston 500 D4
46036 Elwood 10,867 F4
46125 Eminence 200 D5
47118 English⊙ 633 E8
46524 Etna Green 522 E2
†47928 Eugene 400 B5
*47701 Evansville⊙ 130,496 C9
Evansville‡ 309,408 C9
†47331 Everton 500 G5
46126 Fairland 950 F5
46928 Fairmount 3,286 F4
†47842 Fairview Park 1,545 C5
47850 Farmersburg 1,240 C6
47340 Farmland 1,560 G4
†47421 Fayetteville 180 D7
47532 Ferdinand 2,192 D8
46128 Fillmore 550 D5
46129 Finly 400 F5
46038 Fishers 2,008 E5
47234 Flat Rock 323 F6
46929 Flora 2,303 E3
47119 Floyds Knobs 500 F8
47851 Fontanet 325 C5
46039 Forest 400 E4
47648 Fort Branch 2,504 B8
46040 Fortville 2,787 F5
*46801 Fort Wayne⊙ 172,028 G2
Fort Wayne‡ 382,961 G2
47341 Fountain City 839 H5
46130 Fountaintown 225 F5
47944 Fowler⊙ 2,319 C3
46930 Fowlerton 300 F4
47946 Francesville 944 D3
47649 Francisco 612 B8
46041 Frankfort⊙ 15,168 E4
46131 Franklin⊙ 11,563 E6
46044 Frankton 2,080 F4
47120 Fredericksburg 233 E8
47431 Freedom 100 D6
47535 Freelandville 600 C7
47235 Freetown 600 E7
46737 Fremont 1,180 H1
47432 French Lick 2,265 D7
46931 Fulton 393 E3
†47119 Galena 1,186 F8
46932 Galveston 1,822 E3
46738 Garrett 4,751 G2
*46401 Gary 151,953 C1
Gary-Hammond-East Chicago‡ 642,781 C1
46933 Gas City 6,370 F4
47342 Gaston 1,150 G4
46740 Geneva 1,430 H3
47537 Gentryville 299 C8
47122 Georgetown 1,494 F8
46133 Glenwood 370 G5
†47567 Glezen 300 C8
46045 Goldsmith 235 E4

(continued on following page)

Agriculture, Industry and Resources

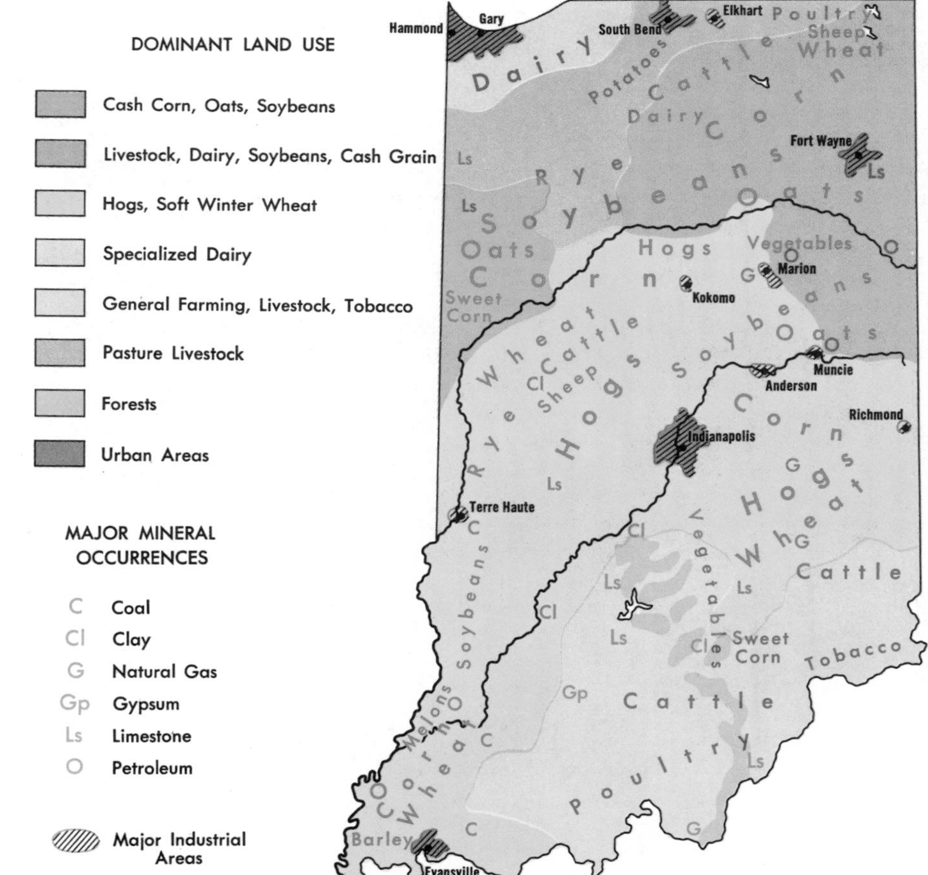

DOMINANT LAND USE
Cash Corn, Oats, Soybeans
Livestock, Dairy, Soybeans, Cash Grain
Hogs, Soft Winter Wheat
Specialized Dairy
General Farming, Livestock, Tobacco
Pasture Livestock
Forests
Urban Areas
MAJOR MINERAL OCCURRENCES
C Coal
Cl Clay
G Natural Gas
Gp Gypsum
Ls Limestone
O Petroleum
Major Industrial Areas
Hammond
Gary
South Bend
Elkhart
Fort Wayne
Marion
Kokomo
Muncie
Anderson
Richmond
Indianapolis
Terre Haute
Evansville
Poultry
Sheep
Wheat
Dairy
Potatoes
Cattle
Corn
Rye
Soybeans
Oats
Hogs
Vegetables
Sweet Corn
Tobacco
Melons
Barley

47948 Goodland 1,200 C3
46526 Goshen⊙ 19,665 F1
47433 Gosport 729 D6
46741 Grabill 658 H2
47615 Grandview 670 C9
46530 Granger 350 E1
46135 Greencastle⊙ 8,403 D5
†47025 Greendale 3,795 H6
46140 Greenfield⊙ 11,299 F5
47344 Greensboro 175 G5
47240 Greensburg⊙ 9,254 G6
47345 Greens Fork 426 H5
46936 Greentown 2,265 E4
47124 Greenville 537 F8
46142 Greenwood 19,327 E5
47616 Griffin 192 B8
46319 Griffith 17,026 C1
46144 Gwynneville 250 F5
47346 Hagerstown 1,950 G5
46742 Hamilton 587 H1
46532 Hamlet 738 D2
*46320 Hammond 93,714 B1
46340 Hanna 550 D2
47243 Hanover 4,054 F7
47125 Hardinsburg 298 E8
46743 Harlan 840 H2
47853 Harmony 613 C5
47434 Harrodsburg 400 D6
47348 Hartford City⊙ 7,622 G4
47244 Hartsville 379 F6
47617 Hatfield 800 C9
47639 Haubstadt 1,389 B8
†47546 Haysville 600 D8
47640 Hazleton 368 B8
46341 Hebron 2,696 C2
47436 Heltonville 400 E7
46937 Hemlock 300 F4
47126 Henryville 1,132 F7
46322 Highland 25,935 B1
47949 Hillsboro 561 C4
47854 Hillsdale 500 C5
46745 Hoagland 600 H3
46342 Hobart 22,987 C1
46047 Hobbs 200 F4
47541 Holland 683 C8
47023 Holton 487 G6
46146 Homer 235 F5
47246 Hope 2,185 F6
†46069 Hortonville 240 E4
46746 Howe 800 G1
46747 Hudson 447 G1
46552 Hudson Lake 1,347 D1
46748 Huntertown 1,265 G2
47542 Huntingburg 5,376 D8
46750 Huntington⊙ 16,202 G3
†46064 Huntsville 120 G4
47437 Huron 250 D7
47855 Hymera 1,054 C6
47950 Idaville 655 D3
*46201 Indianapolis (cap.)⊙ 700,807 E5
Indianapolis‡ 1,166,929 E5
†46601 Indian Village 151 E1
46048 Ingalls 909 F5
47545 Ireland 600 C8
46147 Jamestown 924 D5
47438 Jasonville 2,497 C6
47546 Jasper⊙ 9,097 D8
47130 Jeffersonville⊙ 21,220 F8
†47565 Johnson 100 B8
†46074 Jolietville 300 E4
46938 Jonesboro 2,279 F4
47247 Jonesville 213 F6
46049 Kempton 410 E4
46755 Kendallville 7,299 G2
47351 Kennard 441 G5
47951 Kentland⊙ 1,936 C3
46939 Kewanna 711 E2
46759 Keystone 204 G3
46760 Kimmell 250 F2
47952 Kingman 566 C5
46345 Kingsbury 329 D1
46346 Kingsford Heights 1,618 D2
46050 Kirklin 662 E4
46148 Knightstown 2,325 F5
47857 Knightsville 763 C5
46534 Knox⊙ 3,674 D2
46901 Kokomo⊙ 47,808 E4
Kokomo‡ 103,715 E4
†46574 Koontz Lake 1,436 D2
46347 Kouts 1,619 C2
46348 La Crosse 713 D2
47954 Ladoga 1,151 D5
*47901 Lafayette⊙ 43,011 D4
Lafayette-West Lafayette‡ 121,702 D4
46940 La Fontaine 946 F3
46761 Lagrange⊙ 2,164 F1
46941 Lagro 549 F3
†46157 Lake Hart 231 E5
†46703 Lake James 400 H1
46943 Laketon 500 F3
46349 Lake Village 900 C2
46536 Lakeville 629 E1
46944 Landess 150 F3
47136 Lanesville 570 E8
46763 Laotto 361 G2
46537 Lapaz 651 E2
46051 Lapel 1,881 F4
46350 LaPorte⊙ 21,796 D1
46764 Larwill 286 F2
47024 Laurel 819 G6
46226 Lawrence 25,591 E5
47025 Lawrenceburg⊙ 4,403 H6
47137 Leavenworth 356 E8
46052 Lebanon⊙ 11,456 D4
46538 Leesburg 629 F2
46945 Leiters Ford 280 E2
46765 Leo 500 G2
47551 Leopold 175 D8
46355 Leroy 400 C2
†47240 Letts 247 F6
47352 Lewisville 577 G5
47138 Lexington F7
47353 Liberty⊙ 1,844 H5
46766 Liberty Center 275 G3
46946 Liberty Mills 200 F2
46767 Ligonier 3,134 F2
47955 Linden 700 D4
46769 Linn Grove 175 H3
47441 Linton 6,315 C6
†46755 Lisbon 200 G2
47139 Little York 150 F7
46149 Lizton 456 D5
46947 Logansport⊙ 17,731 E3
†46360 Long Beach 2,262 D1
47553 Loogootee 3,100 D7
47354 Losantville 306 G4
46356 Lowell 5,827 C2
46950 Lucerne 135 E3
†46601 Lydick E1
†47874 Lyford 400 C5
47355 Lynn 1,250 H4
47619 Lynnville 566 C8
47443 Lyons 782 C7
46951 Macy 282 E3
47250 Madison⊙ 12,472 G7
47555 Magnet 75 D8
†47001 Manchester 250 H6
46150 Manilla 350 F5
†47872 Mansfield 200 C5
†47443 Marco 150 C7
47140 Marengo 892 E8
47556 Mariah Hill 300 D8
†46176 Marietta 234 F6
46952 Marion⊙ 35,874 F3
46770 Markle 975 G3
46056 Markleville 427 F5
47859 Marshall 413 C5
46151 Martinsville⊙ 11,311 D6
46957 Matthews 745 F4
46154 Maxwell 300 F5
46055 McCordsville 600 F5
47860 Mecca 482 C5
47957 Medaryville 731 D2
47260 Medora 853 E7
47958 Mellott 294 C4
47143 Memphis 300 F8
46539 Mentone 973 E2
47861 Merom 360 B6
46410 Merrillville 27,677 C2
47030 Metamora 350 G6
†46703 Metz 200 H1
46958 Mexico 850 E3
46959 Miami 350 E3
†49117 Michiana Shores 464 D1
46360 Michigan City 36,850 C1
46057 Michigantown 453 E4
46540 Middlebury 1,665 F1
47356 Middletown 2,978 F4
47445 Midland 250 C6
47031 Milan 1,566 G6
46542 Milford 1,153 F2
†47240 Milford 177 F6
46543 Millersburg 809 F1
47261 Millhousen 214 G6
47145 Milltown 1,006 E8
†47362 Millville 275 G5
46156 Milroy 750 G6
47357 Milton 729 G5
46544 Mishawaka 40,201 E1
47446 Mitchell 4,641 E7
47358 Modoc 243 G4
46771 Mongo 225 G1
47959 Monon 1,540 D3
46772 Monroe 739 H3
47557 Monroe City 569 C7
46773 Monroeville 1,372 H3
46157 Monrovia 800 E5
46960 Monterey 236 D2
47862 Montezuma 1,352 C5
47558 Montgomery 390 C7
47960 Monticello⊙ 5,162 D3
47962 Montmorenci 300 D4
47359 Montpelier 1,995 G3
47360 Mooreland 479 G5
47032 Moores Hill 566 G6
46158 Mooresville 5,349 E5
46160 Morgantown 897 E6
47963 Morocco 1,348 C3
47033 Morris 350 G6
46161 Morristown 989 F5
†47327 Mount Auburn 192 G5
47964 Mount Ayr 207 C3
47361 Mount Summit 357 G4
47620 Mount Vernon⊙ 7,656 B9
46058 Mulberry 1,225 D4
*47302 Muncie⊙ 77,216 G4
Muncie‡ G4
46321 Munster 20,671 B1
47147 Nabb 150 F7
47034 Napoleon 246 G6
46550 Nappanee 4,694 F2
47448 Nashville⊙ 705 E6
†47421 Needmore 200 E7
47150 New Albany⊙ 37,103 F8
47449 Newberry 246 C7
47630 Newburgh 2,906 C9
46552 New Carlisle 1,439 E1
47362 New Castle⊙ 20,056 G5
†46342 New Chicago 3,284 C1
47863 New Goshen 500 B5
47631 New Harmony 945 B8
46774 New Haven 6,714 H2
47366 New Lisbon 300 G5
†46979 New London 200 E4
47965 New Market 608 D5
46163 New Palestine 749 F5
46553 New Paris 1,062 F2
†47165 New Pekin 1,125 F7
47263 New Point 296 G6
47966 Newport⊙ 704 C5
†47106 New Providence (Borden) 384 F8
47967 New Richmond 403 D4
47968 New Ross 306 D5
†46173 New Salem 200 G5
47161 New Salisbury 350 E8
47632 Newtonville 136 D8
47969 Newtown 277 C4
47035 New Trenton 200 H6
47162 New Washington 800 F7
46961 New Waverly 162 E3
46184 New Whiteland 4,502 E5
†46122 New Winchester 180 D5
46060 Noblesville⊙ 12,056 F4
46366 North Judson 1,653 D2
46554 North Liberty 1,211 E1
46962 North Manchester 5,998 F3
46165 North Salem 581 D5
47805 North Terre Haute C5
47265 North Vernon 5,768 F6
46555 North Webster 709 F2
†47960 Norway 300 D3
46556 Notre Dame E1
†47331 Nulltown 235 G5
46965 Oakford 325 E4
47660 Oakland City 3,301 C8
47561 Oaktown 776 C7
47367 Oakville 220 G4
47562 Odon 1,463 C7
†46401 Ogden Dunes 1,489 C1
47036 Oldenburg 770 G6
47451 Oolitic 1,495 E7
†47343 Orange 200 G5
46063 Orestes 539 F4
46776 Orland 424 G1
47452 Orleans 2,161 D7
46561 Osceola 1,990 E1
47037 Osgood 1,554 G6
46777 Ossian 1,945 G3
46367 Otis 250 D1
47163 Otisco 425 F7
47970 Otterbein 1,118 C4
47564 Otwell 600 C8
47453 Owensburg 785 D7
47665 Owensville 1,261 B8
47971 Oxford 1,327 C3
†46508 Palestine 800 F2
47164 Palmyra 692 E8
47454 Paoli⊙ 3,637 E7
46166 Paragon 538 D6
47368 Parker City 1,414 G4
47666 Patoka 832 B8
47455 Patricksburg 250 D6
47038 Patriot 265 H7
47865 Paxton 200 C6
47165 Pekin 950 E7
46064 Pendleton 2,130 F5
47369 Pennville 805 G4
†46011 Perkinsville 175 F4
47974 Perrysville 532 C4
47370 Pershing 438 G5
†46975 Pershing 425 E2
46970 Peru⊙ 13,764 E3
47567 Petersburg⊙ 2,987 C7
46778 Petroleum 212 G3
46562 Pierceton 1,086 F2
47866 Pimento 150 C6
†46350 Pine Lake 1,676 D1
47975 Pine Village 257 C4
46167 Pittsboro 891 D5
†46923 Pittsburg 175 D3
46168 Plainfield 9,191 E5
47568 Plainville 556 C7
46779 Pleasant Lake 800 H1
46563 Plymouth⊙ 7,693 E2
47868 Poland 230 C6
46781 Poneto 250 G3
46368 Portage 27,409 C1
46304 Porter 2,988 C1
47371 Portland⊙ 7,074 H4
47633 Poseyville 1,247 B8
†46360 Pottawattamie Park 284 C1
47869 Prairie Creek 275 C6
47870 Prairieton 200 B6
46782 Preble 150 H3
†46164 Princes Lakes 937 E6
47670 Princeton⊙ 8,976 B8
46170 Putnamville 250 D5
47456 Quincy 250 D6
47573 Ragsdale 135 C7
46737 Ray 200 H1
†47274 Reddington 400 F6
46171 Reelsville 210 D5
47977 Remington 1,268 C3
47978 Rensselaer⊙ 4,944 C3
47980 Reynolds 632 D3
47634 Richland 500 C9
47374 Richmond⊙ 41,349 H5
47380 Ridgeville 933 G4
47871 Riley 269 C6
47040 Rising Sun⊙ 2,478 H7
46172 Roachdale 958 D5
46974 Roann 548 F3
46783 Roanoke 891 G3
46975 Rochester⊙ 5,050 E2
46977 Rockfield 300 D3
47635 Rockport⊙ 2,590 C9
47872 Rockville⊙ 2,785 C5
46371 Rolling Prairie 550 D1
47574 Rome 50 D9
46784 Rome City 1,319 G1
47981 Romney 250 D4
47874 Rosedale 744 C5
†46601 Roseland 832 E1
†46310 Roselawn 200 C2
46065 Rossville 1,148 D4
46978 Royal Center 908 E3
†47302 Royerton 300 G4
46173 Rushville⊙ 6,113 G5
46175 Russellville 376 D5
46975 Russiaville 973 E4
47575 Saint Anthony 470 D8
47875 Saint Bernice 500 C5
46785 Saint Joe 546 H2
46383 Saint John 3,974 C2
46373 Saint Leon 515 H6
47876 Saint Mary-of-the-Woods 920 B6
†46556 Saint Marys E1
47577 Saint Meinrad 910 D8
47272 Saint Paul 976 F6
†47012 Saint Peter 175 H6
†47620 Saint Philip 400 B9
†47638 Saint Wendel 250 B8
47167 Salem⊙ 5,290 E7
47578 Sandborn 576 C7
†47401 Sanders 65 E6
46374 San Pierre 325 D2
47579 Santa Claus 514 D8
47382 Saratoga 338 H4
†47283 Sardinia 133 F6
46375 Schererville 13,209 C2
46376 Schneider 364 C2
47580 Schnellville 250 D8
47273 Scipio 200 F6
46066 Scircleville 125 E4
47170 Scottsburg⊙ 5,068 F7
47878 Seelyville 1,374 C6
47172 Sellersburg 3,211 F8
47383 Selma 1,056 G4
47274 Seymour 15,050 F7
46068 Sharpsville 617 E4
47879 Shelburn 1,259 C6
46377 Shelby 700 C2
46176 Shelbyville⊙ 14,989 F6
47880 Shepardsville 325 B5
46069 Sheridan 2,200 E4
†47338 Shideler 275 G4
46565 Shipshewana 466 F1
47384 Shirley 919 F5
†46797 Shirley City (Woodburn) 1,002 H2
47581 Shoals⊙ 967 D7
46566 Sidney 194 F2
46982 Silver Lake 576 F2
46983 Sims 250 F3
†46142 Smith Valley E5
47458 Smithville 500 D6
46984 Somerset 350 F3
47683 Somerville 340 C8
*46601 South Bend⊙ 109,727 E1
South Bend‡ 280,772 E1
46786 South Milford 270 G1
†46201 Southport 2,266 E5
46787 South Whitley 1,575 F2
†47355 Spartanburg 201 H4
47172 Speed 800 F8
46224 Speedway 12,641 E5
†47808 Spelterville 200 C5
47460 Spencer⊙ 2,732 D6
46788 Spencerville 400 G2
47385 Spiceland 940 F5
†47374 Spring Grove 469 H5
†46140 Spring Lake 236 F5
47386 Springport 221 G4
47462 Springville 279 D7
47584 Spurgeon 250 C8
47463 Stanford 200 D6
46985 Star City 351 D3
47982 State Line 233 C4
47881 Staunton 607 C6
47585 Stendal 175 C8
47636 Stewartsville 225 B8
46180 Stilesville 350 D5
46351 Stillwell 225 D1
47464 Stinesville 227 D6
47983 Stockwell 310 D4
47387 Straughn 331 G5
46789 Stroh 350 G1
47882 Sullivan⊙ 4,774 C6
47388 Sulphur Springs 345 G4
46379 Sumava Resorts 300 C2
46070 Summitville 1,085 F4
47041 Sunman 924 G6
46987 Sweetser 944 F3
47465 Switz City 300 C6
46567 Syracuse 2,579 F2
47280 Taylorsville 1,247 F6
47586 Tell City 8,704 D9
47637 Tennyson 331 C8
*47801 Terre Haute⊙ 61,125 C6
Terre Haute‡ 176,583 C6
46381 Thayer 350 C2
46071 Thorntown 1,468 D4
†46975 Tiosa 100 E2
46570 Tippecanoe 320 E2
46072 Tipton⊙ 5,004 E4
46571 Topeka 876 F1
†46360 Town of Pines 962 D1
46181 Trafalgar 466 E6
†46360 Trail Creek 2,581 D1
†46725 Tri Lakes 1,356 G2
47588 Troy 550 D9
46988 Twelve Mile 240 E3
46572 Tyner 245 E2
47177 Underwood 550 F7
47390 Union City 3,908 H4
46791 Uniondale 303 G3
46382 Union Mills 650 D2
47468 Unionville 225 E6
47884 Universal 428 C5
46989 Upland 3,335 F4
46990 Urbana 400 F3
†47130 Utica 501 F8
47281 Vallonia 550 E7
46383 Valparaiso⊙ 22,247 C2
46991 Van Buren 935 F3
47987 Veedersburg 2,261 C4
47590 Velpen 375 C8
47282 Vernon⊙ 329 F7
47042 Versailles⊙ 1,560 G6
47043 Vevay⊙ 1,343 G7
†47441 Vicksburg 175 C6
†47170 Vienna 175 F7
47591 Vincennes⊙ 20,857 C7
46992 Wabash⊙ 12,985 F3
47638 Wadesville 450 B8
46573 Wakarusa 1,281 F1
46182 Waldron 850 F6
†47201 Walesboro 214 F6
46574 Walkerton 2,051 E2
†46802 Wallen 945 G2
46994 Walton 1,202 E3
46390 Wanatah 879 D2
46792 Warren 1,254 G3
46580 Warsaw⊙ 10,647 F2
47501 Washington⊙ 11,325 C7
46793 Waterloo 1,951 G2
†47130 Watson 200 F8
47989 Waveland 559 D5
46794 Wawaka 320 F2
47990 Waynetown 915 C4
47392 Webster 350 H5
47469 West Baden Springs 796 D7
†47353 West College Corner 614 H5
46074 Westfield 2,783 E4

Topography

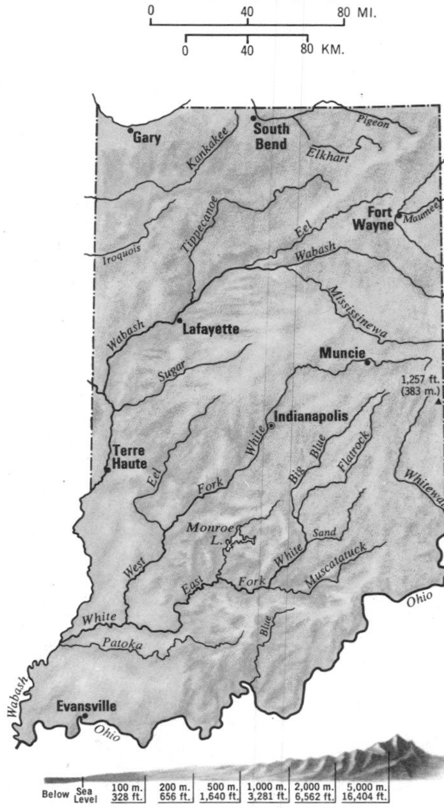

†45030 West Harrison 328 H6
47906 West Lafayette 21,247 D4
47991 West Lebanon 946 C4
46995 West Middleton 327 E4
47596 Westphalia 300 C7
47992 Westpoint 375 C4
47283 Westport 1,450 F6
47885 West Terre Haute 2,806 B6
46391 Westville 2,887 D1
46392 Wheatfield 755 C2
47597 Wheatland 532 C7
46393 Wheeler 540 C1
†47342 Wheeling 180 G4
46184 Whiteland 1,956 E5
46075 Whitestown 497 E5
46394 Whiting 5,630 C1
46186 Wilkinson 493 F5
47470 Williams 350 D7
47993 Williamsport⊙ 1,747 C4
46996 Winamac⊙ 2,370 D2
47394 Winchester⊙ 5,659 G4
46076 Windfall 911 F4
47994 Wingate 373 C4
46590 Winona Lake 2,827 F2
47598 Winslow 1,017 C8
47995 Wolcott 923 C3
46795 Wolcottville 890 G1
46796 Wolflake 230 F2
46797 Woodburn 1,002 H2
†46624 Woodland 400 E1
47471 Worthington 1,574 C6
46595 Wyatt 250 E1
†47630 Yankeetown 250 C9
46798 Yoder 250 G3
47396 Yorktown 3,945 G4
46998 Young America 259 E3
†47808 Youngstown 350 C6
46799 Zanesville 575 G3
46077 Zionsville 3,948 E5

OTHER FEATURES

Anderson (riv.) D8
Bass (lake) D2
Beanblossom (creek) D6
Big (creek) B8
Big Blue (riv.) F5
Big Pine (creek) C3
Big Raccoon (creek) C5
Big Walnut (creek) D5
Blue (riv.) E8
Brookville (lake) G6
Buck (creek) E8
Busseron (creek) C7
Camp (creek) E6
Cedar (creek) G2
Clifty (creek) F6
Coal (creek) C4
Crooked (creek) D2
Cypress (pond) B8
Deer (creek) E3
Deer (creek) D5
Eagle (creek) E4
Eel (riv.) C6
Eel (riv.) F3
Elkhart (riv.) F1
Fawn (riv.) G1
Flatrock (creek) F5
Fort Benjamin Harrison E5
Freeman (lake) D3
Geist (res.) F5
George Rogers Clark Nat'l Hist. Park B7
Graham (creek) F7
Grissom A.F.B. 4,676 E3
Huntington (lake) F3
Indian (creek) E8
Indian (creek) D6
Indiana Dunes Nat'l Lakeshore C1
Iroquois (riv.) B3
Jefferson Proving Ground G7
Kankakee (riv.) C2
Lemon (lake) E6
Lincoln Boyhood Nat'l Mem. C8
Little (riv.) G3
Little Elkhart (riv.) F1
Little Pigeon (creek) C9
Little Vermilion (riv.) B5
Lost (riv.) D7
Maria (creek) C7
Maumee (riv.) H2
Maxinkuckee (lake) E2
Michigan (lake) C1
Mill (creek) D5
Mississinewa (lake) F3
Mississinewa (riv.) F3
Monroe (lake) E6
Morse (res.) E4
Muscatatuck (riv.) E7
Ohio (riv.) B9
Patoka (riv.) C8
Pigeon (creek) C8
Pigeon (riv.) F1
Pipe (creek) F4
Prairie (creek) C7
Richland (creek) D6
Saint Joseph (riv.) E1
Saint Joseph (riv.) H2
Saint Marys (lake) H3
Saint Marys (riv.) H3
Salamonie (lake) F3
Salamonie (riv.) G4
Salt (creek) E6
Sand (creek) F6
Shafer (lake) D3
Silver (creek) F8
Sugar (creek) C5
Sugar (creek) F5
Sugar (creek) B3
Tippecanoe (riv.) E2
Vermilion (riv.) B4
Vernon Fork (creek) F7
Wabash (riv.) B7
Wawasee (lake) F2
White (riv.) B8
White, East Fork (riv.) C7
White, West Fork (riv.) C7
Whitewater (riv.) H6
Wildcat (creek) E4

⊙County seat.
‡Population of metropolitan area.
† Zip of nearest p.o. * Multiple zips.

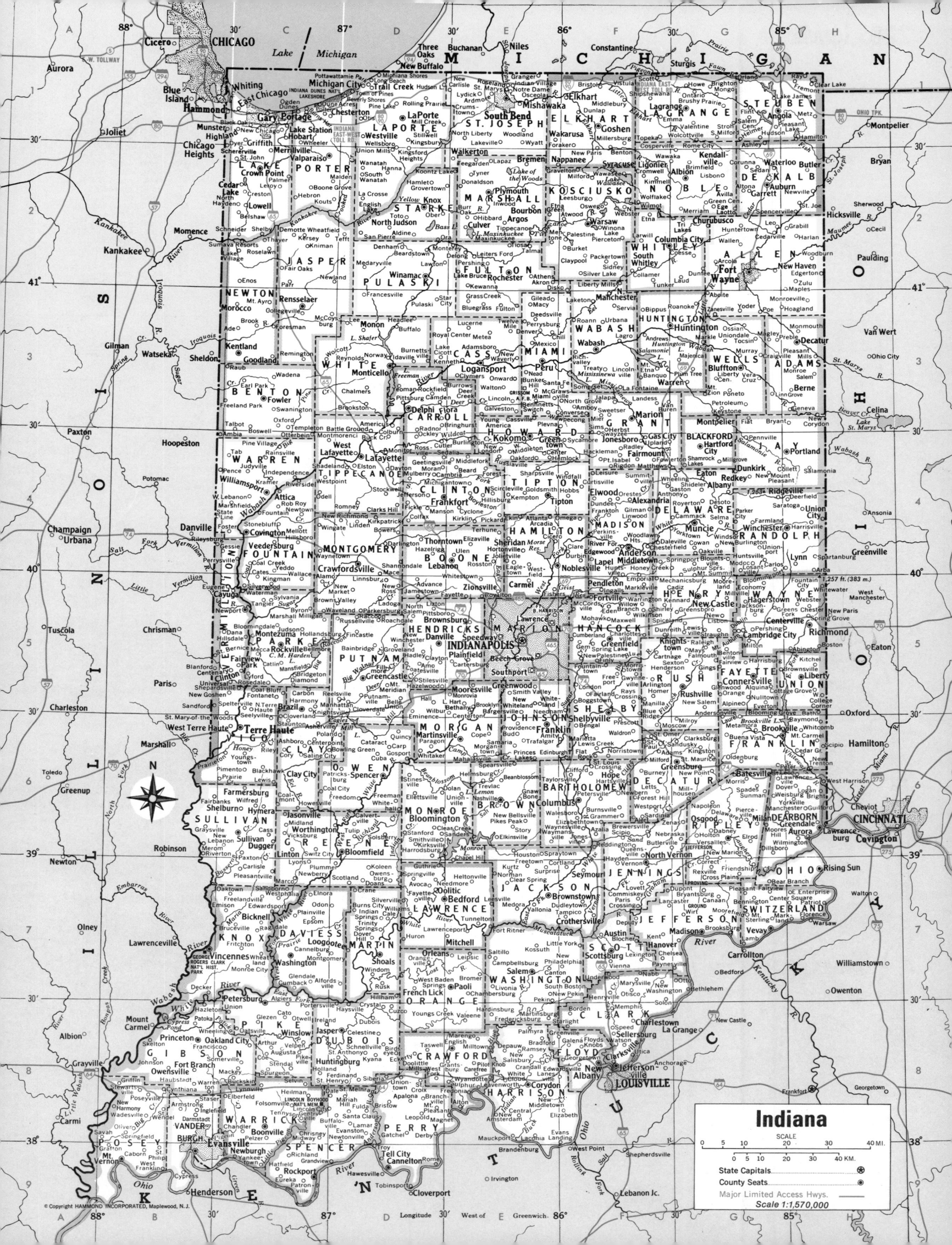

Indiana
SCALE
0 5 10 20 30 40 MI.
0 5 10 20 30 40 KM.
State Capitals
County Seats
Major Limited Access Hwys.
Scale 1:1,570,000
© Copyright HAMMOND INCORPORATED, Maplewood, N.J.
Longitude 30' West of Greenwich 86°
MICHIGAN
ILLINOIS
OHIO
KENTUCKY
Lake Michigan
CHICAGO
INDIANAPOLIS
LOUISVILLE
CINCINNATI
LAKE
PORTER
LAPORTE
ST. JOSEPH
ELKHART
LAGRANGE
STEUBEN
NOBLE
DE KALB
KOSCIUSKO
MARSHALL
STARKE
JASPER
NEWTON
PULASKI
FULTON
WHITLEY
ALLEN
WABASH
MIAMI
CASS
WHITE
BENTON
CARROLL
HUNTINGTON
WELLS
ADAMS
GRANT
BLACKFORD
JAY
HOWARD
TIPTON
CLINTON
TIPPECANOE
WARREN
FOUNTAIN
MONTGOMERY
BOONE
HAMILTON
MADISON
DELAWARE
RANDOLPH
HENRY
WAYNE
HANCOCK
MARION
HENDRICKS
PUTNAM
PARKE
VERMILLION
VIGO
CLAY
OWEN
MORGAN
JOHNSON
SHELBY
RUSH
FAYETTE
UNION
FRANKLIN
DECATUR
BARTHOLOMEW
BROWN
MONROE
GREENE
SULLIVAN
KNOX
DAVIESS
MARTIN
LAWRENCE
JACKSON
JENNINGS
RIPLEY
DEARBORN
OHIO
SWITZERLAND
JEFFERSON
SCOTT
WASHINGTON
ORANGE
DUBOIS
PIKE
GIBSON
POSEY
VANDERBURGH
WARRICK
SPENCER
PERRY
CRAWFORD
HARRISON
FLOYD
CLARK

COUNTIES

Adair 9,509	E6	
Adams 5,731	D6	
Allamakee 15,108	L2	
Appanoose 15,511	H7	
Audubon 8,559	D5	
Benton 23,649	J4	
Black Hawk 137,961	J4	
Boone 26,184	F5	
Bremer 24,820	J3	
Buchanan 22,900	K4	
Buena Vista 20,774	C3	
Butler 17,668	H3	
Calhoun 13,542	D4	
Carroll 22,951	D4	
Cass 16,932	D5	
Cedar 18,635	L5	
Cerro Gordo 48,458	G2	
Cherokee 16,238	B3	
Chickasaw 15,437	J2	
Clarke 8,612	F6	
Clay 19,576	C2	
Clayton 21,098	L3	

Clinton 57,122	M5	
Crawford 18,935	C4	
Dallas 29,513	E5	
Davis 9,104	J7	
Decatur 9,794	F7	
Delaware 18,933	L4	
Des Moines 46,203	L7	
Dickinson 15,629	C2	
Dubuque 93,745	M4	
Emmet 13,336	D2	
Fayette 25,488	K3	
Floyd 19,597	H2	
Franklin 13,036	G3	
Fremont 9,401	B7	
Greene 12,119	E5	
Grundy 14,366	H4	
Guthrie 11,983	D5	
Hamilton 17,862	F4	
Hancock 13,833	F2	
Hardin 21,776	G4	
Harrison 16,348	B5	
Henry 18,890	K6	
Howard 11,114	J2	
Humboldt 12,246	E3	

Ida 8,908	C4	
Iowa 15,429	J5	
Jackson 22,503	M4	
Jasper 36,425	G5	
Jefferson 16,316	K6	
Johnson 81,717	K5	
Jones 20,401	L4	
Keokuk 12,921	J6	
Kossuth 21,891	E2	
Lee 43,106	L7	
Linn 169,775	K4	
Louisa 12,055	L6	
Lucas 10,313	G6	
Lyon 12,896	A2	
Madison 12,597	E6	
Mahaska 22,867	H6	
Marion 29,669	G6	
Marshall 41,652	G4	
Mills 13,406	B6	
Mitchell 12,329	H2	
Monona 11,692	B4	
Monroe 9,209	H7	
Montgomery 13,413	C6	
Muscatine 40,436	L5	

O'Brien 16,972	B2	
Osceola 8,371	B2	
Page 19,063	C7	
Palo Alto 12,721	D2	
Plymouth 24,743	A3	
Pocahontas 11,369	D3	
Polk 303,170	F5	
Pottawattamie 86,561	B6	
Poweshiek 19,306	H5	
Ringgold 6,112	E7	
Sac 14,118	C4	
Scott 160,022	M5	
Shelby 15,043	C5	
Sioux 30,813	A2	
Story 72,326	G4	
Tama 19,533	H4	
Taylor 8,353	D7	
Union 13,858	E7	
Van Buren 8,626	K7	
Wapello 40,241	J6	
Warren 34,878	F6	
Washington 20,141	K6	
Wayne 8,199	G7	
Webster 45,953	E4	

Winnebago 13,010	F2	
Winneshiek 21,876	K2	
Woodbury 100,884	B4	
Worth 9,075	G2	
Wright 16,319	F3	

CITIES and TOWNS

Zip	Name/Pop.	Key
50601	Ackley 1,900	G3
50002	Adair 883	D6
50003	Adel⊙ 2,846	E5
50830	Afton 885	E6
52530	Agency 657	J7
52201	Ainsworth 547	K6
51001	Akron 1,517	A3
50510	Albert City 818	C3
52531	Albia⊙ 4,184	H6
50005	Albion 739	G4
50006	Alden 739	G4
50511	Algona⊙ 6,289	E2
50007	Alleman 307	F5
50008	Allerton 670	G7

Zip	Name/Pop.	Key
50602	Allison⊙ 1,132	H3
51002	Alta 1,720	C3
50603	Alta Vista 314	J2
51003	Alton 986	A3
50009	Altoona 5,764	G5
51230	Alvord 246	A2
52203	Amana 300	K5
50010	Ames 45,775	F4
52205	Anamosa⊙ 4,958	L4
52030	Andrew 349	M4
50020	Anita 1,153	D6
51004	Anthon 687	B4
50604	Aplington 1,027	H3
51430	Arcadia 454	C4
50606	Arlington 498	K3
50514	Armstrong 1,055	D2
51331	Arnolds Park 1,051	C2
50005	Arthur 288	C4
51431	Arthur 288	C4
50022	Ashton 441	B2
51232	Ashton 441	B2
52720	Atalissa 360	L5
52206	Atkins 678	K4
†52001	Asbury 2,017	M4
50022	Atlantic⊙ 7,789	D6

AREA 56,275 sq. mi. (145,752 sq. km.)
POPULATION 2,913,808
CAPITAL Des Moines
LARGEST CITY Des Moines
HIGHEST POINT (Osceola Co.) 1670 ft.
(509 m.)
SETTLED IN 1788
ADMITTED TO UNION December 28, 1846
POPULAR NAME Hawkeye State
STATE FLOWER Wild Rose
STATE BIRD Eastern Goldfinch

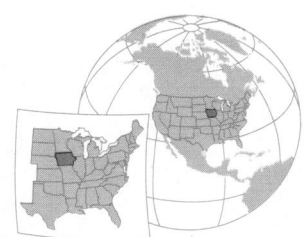

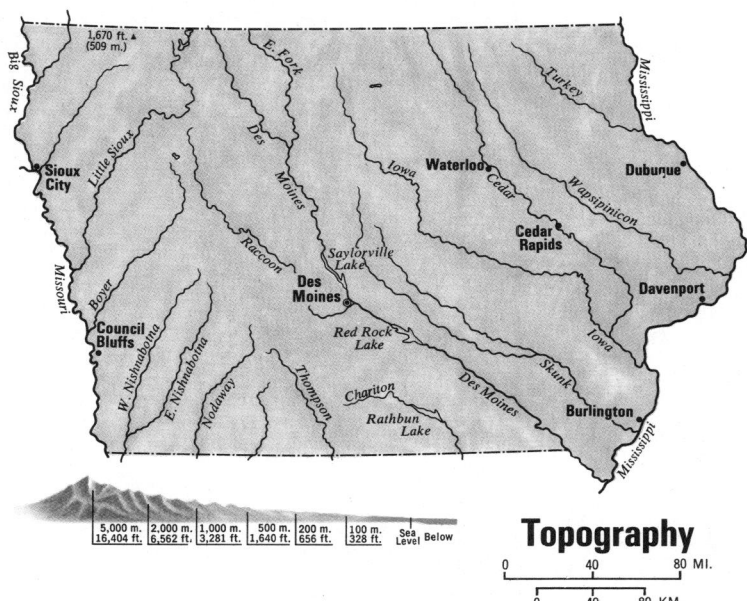

Topography

Agriculture, Industry and Resources

DOMINANT LAND USE

Cattle Feed, Hogs
Cash Corn, Oats, Soybeans
Hogs, Dairy
Livestock, Cash Grain
Dairy, Livestock
Pasture Livestock

MAJOR MINERAL OCCURRENCES

C Coal
Cl Clay
Gp Gypsum
Ls Limestone

Water Power
Major Industrial Areas

51535 Griswold 1,176 ... C6
50638 Grundy Center⊙ 2,880 ... H4
50115 Guthrie Center⊙ 1,713 ... D5
52052 Guttenberg 2,428 ... L3
51640 Hamburg 1,597 ... B7
50441 Hampton⊙ 4,630 ... G3
51536 Hancock 254 ... C6
50544 Harcourt 347 ... E4
51537 Harlan⊙ 5,357 ... C5
52146 Harpers Ferry 258 ... L2
50118 Hartford 761 ... G6
51346 Hartley 1,700 ... C2
50119 Harvey 275 ... H6
50546 Havelock 279 ... D3
51023 Hawarden 2,722 ... A2
52147 Hawkeye 512 ... J3
50641 Hazleton 877 ... K3
52563 Hedrick 847 ... J6
51541 Henderson 236 ... B6
52233 Hiawatha 4,825 ... K4
52235 Hills 547 ... K5
52630 Hillsboro 208 ... K7
51024 Hinton 659 ... A3
50642 Holland 278 ... H4
51025 Holstein 1,477 ... B4
52053 Holy Cross 310 ... L3
52237 Hopkinton 774 ... L4
51026 Hornick 239 ... A4
51238 Hospers 655 ... B2
50122 Hubbard 852 ... G4
50643 Hudson 2,267 ... H4
51239 Hull 1,714 ... A2
50548 Humboldt 4,794 ... E3
50123 Humeston 671 ... G7
50124 Huxley 1,884 ... F5
51445 Ida Grove⊙ 2,285 ... B4
50644 Independence⊙ 6,392 ... K4
50125 Indianola⊙ 10,843 ... F6
51240 Inwood 755 ... A2
50645 Ionia 350 ... J2
52240 Iowa City⊙ 50,508 ... L5
Iowa City⊙‡ 81,717 ... L5
50126 Iowa Falls 6,174 ... G3
51027 Ireton 588 ... A3
51446 Irwin 427 ... C5
50128 Jamaica 275 ... E5
50647 Janesville 840 ... J3
50129 Jefferson⊙ 4,854 ... E4
50648 Jesup 2,343 ... J4
50130 Jewell 1,145 ... F4
50131 Johnston 2,617 ... F5
52247 Kalona 1,862 ... K6
50447 Kanawha 756 ... F3
50133 Kellerton 278 ... E7
50134 Kelley 237 ... F5
50135 Kellogg 654 ... H5
50448 Kensett 360 ... G2
52632 Keokuk⊙ 13,536 ... L8
52565 Keosauqua⊙ 1,003 ... J7
52248 Keota 1,034 ... K6
50136 Keswick 300 ... J6
52249 Keystone 618 ... J5
51543 Kimballton 362 ... D5
51028 Kingsley 1,209 ... A3
51448 Kiron 317 ... C4
50449 Klemme 620 ... F3
50138 Knoxville⊙ 8,143 ... G6
50139 Lacona 376 ... G6
52251 Ladora 289 ... J5
51449 Lake City 2,006 ... D4
50450 Lake Mills 2,281 ... F2
51347 Lake Park 1,123 ... C2
50588 Lakeside 589 ... C3
51450 Lake View 1,291 ... C4
50451 Lakota 330 ... E2
50140 Lamoni 2,705 ... E7
50650 Lamont 554 ... K3
52054 La Motte 322 ... M4
52151 Lansing 1,181 ... L2
50651 La Porte City 2,324 ... J4
51241 Larchwood 701 ... A2
50452 Latimer 441 ... G3
50141 Laurel 278 ... H5
50554 Laurens 1,606 ... D3
52154 Lawler 534 ... J2
51030 Lawton 447 ... A4
52753 Le Claire 2,899 ... N5
50142 Le Grand 921 ... H5
50557 Lehigh 654 ... E4
50453 Leland 274 ... F2
51031 Le Mars⊙ 8,276 ... A3
50851 Lenox 1,338 ... D7
50144 Leon⊙ 2,094 ... F7
51242 Lester 274 ... A2
52754 Letts 473 ... L6
51544 Lewis 497 ... C6
52567 Libertyville 281 ... K7
52155 Lime Springs 476 ... J2
50146 Linden 264 ... E5
50147 Lineville 319 ... G7
52253 Lisbon 1,458 ... L5
50148 Liscomb 296 ... H4
51243 Little Rock 490 ... B2
51545 Little Sioux 251 ... B5
50558 Livermore 490 ... E3
52635 Lockridge 271 ... K7
51546 Logan⊙ 1,540 ... B5
51453 Lohrville 521 ... D4
52755 Lone Tree 1,014 ... L6
52756 Long Grove 596 ... M5
50149 Lorimor 405 ... E6
52254 Lost Nation 524 ... M5
50150 Lovilia 637 ... H6
52255 Lowden 717 ... L5
52757 Low Moor 346 ... N5
52156 Luana 246 ... K2
50151 Lucas 292 ... G6
50560 Lu Verne 418 ... E3
52056 Luxemburg 271 ... L3
50153 Lynnville 406 ... H5
50561 Lytton 377 ... D4
51549 Macedonia 279 ... C6
50156 Madrid 2,281 ... F5
50157 Malcom 418 ... H5
50562 Mallard 407 ... D3
51551 Malvern 1,244 ... B7
52057 Manchester⊙ 4,942 ... L3
51454 Manilla 1,020 ... C5
50456 Manly 1,496 ... G2
51455 Manning 1,609 ... C5
50563 Manson 1,924 ... D3
51034 Mapleton 1,495 ... B4
52060 Maquoketa⊙ 6,313 ... M4
50565 Marathon 442 ... C3
50653 Marble Rock 419 ... H3
51035 Marcus 1,206 ... B3
52301 Marengo⊙ 2,308 ... J5
52302 Marion 19,474 ... K4
52158 Marquette 528 ... L2
50158 Marshalltown⊙ 26,938 ... G4
52305 Martelle 316 ... L4
50160 Martensdale 438 ... F6
50401 Mason City⊙ 30,144 ... G2
50853 Massena 518 ... D6
51036 Maurice 288 ... A3
50161 Maxwell 783 ... G5
50655 Maynard 561 ... K3
50154 McCallsburg 304 ... G4
52758 McCausland 381 ... M5
52157 McGregor 945 ... L2
52306 Mechanicsville 1,166 ... L5
52637 Mediapolis 1,685 ... L6
50162 Melbourne 732 ... G5
50163 Melcher 953 ... G6
51350 Melvin 277 ... B2
50164 Menlo 410 ... E5
51037 Meriden 233 ... B3
51038 Merrill 737 ... A3
50457 Meservey 324 ... G3
52307 Middle 335 ... K5
52638 Middletown 487 ... L7
52064 Miles 398 ... N4
51351 Milford 2,076 ... C2
50166 Milo 778 ... G6
52570 Milton 567 ... J7
50167 Minburn 390 ... E5
51553 Minden 419 ... C6
50168 Mingo 303 ... G5
51555 Missouri Valley 3,107 ... B5
50169 Mitchellville 1,530 ... G5
51556 Modale 373 ... B5
51557 Mondamin 423 ... B5
52159 Monona 1,530 ... L2
50170 Monroe 1,875 ... G5
50171 Montezuma⊙ 1,485 ... H5
52310 Monticello 3,641 ... L4
50173 Montour 387 ... H5
52759 Montpelier 250 ... M6
52639 Montrose 1,038 ... L7
51558 Moorhead 264 ... B5
50566 Moorland 257 ... E4
52571 Moravia 706 ... H7
52640 Morning Sun 959 ... L6
52760 Moscow 350 ... L5
52572 Moulton 762 ... H7
50854 Mount Ayr⊙ 1,938 ... E7
52641 Mount Pleasant⊙ 7,322 ... L7
52314 Mount Vernon 3,325 ... K5
51039 Moville 1,273 ... A4
50174 Murray 703 ... F6
52761 Muscatine⊙ 23,467 ... L6
52574 Mystic 665 ... H7
50658 Nashua 1,846 ... J3
51559 Neola 839 ... B6
50201 Nevada⊙ 5,912 ... G5
52160 New Albin 609 ... L2
50568 Newell 913 ... D3
52315 Newhall 899 ... K5
50660 New Hartford 764 ... H3
52645 New London 2,043 ... L7
51646 New Market 554 ... D7
50206 New Providence 249 ... G4
50207 New Sharon 1,225 ... H6
50208 Newton⊙ 15,292 ... H5
52065 New Vienna 430 ... L3
50210 New Virginia 512 ... F6
52766 Nichols 375 ... L6
50458 Nora Springs 1,572 ... H2
52316 North English 990 ... J5
52317 North Liberty 2,046 ... K5
50459 Northwood⊙ 2,193 ... G2
50211 Norwalk 2,676 ... F6
52318 Norway 633 ... K5
52319 Oakdale 300 ... K5
51560 Oakland 1,552 ... C6
52646 Oakville 470 ... L6
51354 Ocheyedan 599 ... B2
51458 Odebolt 1,299 ... C4
50662 Oelwein 7,564 ... K3
50212 Ogden 1,953 ... E4
51355 Okoboji 559 ... C2
52320 Olin 735 ... L5
52576 Ollie 232 ... J6
51040 Onawa⊙ 3,283 ... A4
51041 Orange City⊙ 4,588 ... A2
50858 Orient 416 ... E6
†51360 Orleans 546 ... C2
50461 Osage⊙ 3,718 ... H2
50213 Osceola⊙ 3,750 ... F6
52577 Oskaloosa⊙ 10,984 ... H6
52161 Ossian 829 ... K2
50569 Otho 692 ... E4
52501 Ottumwa⊙ 27,381 ... J6
52322 Oxford 676 ... K5
52323 Oxford Junction 600 ... M4
51561 Pacific Junction 511 ... B6
50571 Palmer 288 ... D3
52324 Palo 529 ... K4
51562 Panama 229 ... B5
50216 Panora 1,211 ... E5
50665 Parkersburg 1,968 ... H3
52325 Parnell 234 ... J5
50217 Paton 291 ... E4
51046 Paullina 1,224 ... B3
50219 Pella 8,349 ... H6
50220 Perry 7,053 ... E5
50221 Pershing 325 ... G6
51563 Persia 355 ... B5
51047 Peterson 470 ... C3
51048 Pierson 408 ... B3
51564 Pisgah 307 ... B5
50666 Plainfield 469 ... J3
50225 Pleasantville 1,531 ... G6
50464 Plymouth 463 ... G2
50574 Pocahontas⊙ 2,352 ... D3
50226 Polk City 1,658 ... F5
50575 Pomeroy 895 ... D3
51565 Portsmouth 240 ... C5
52162 Postville 1,475 ... K2
50228 Prairie City 1,278 ... G5
50859 Prescott 349 ... D6
52069 Preston 1,120 ... N4
Primghar⊙ 1,050 ... B2
52768 Princeton 965 ... N5
52163 Protivin 368 ... J2
52584 Pulaski 267 ... J7
52326 Quasqueton 599 ... K4
51049 Quimby 424 ... B3
50230 Radcliffe 593 ... G4
50465 Rake 283 ... F2
50667 Raymond 655 ... J4
50668 Readlyn 858 ... J3
50232 Reasnor 277 ... G5
50233 Redfield 959 ... E5
51566 Red Oak⊙ 6,810 ... C6
50669 Reinbeck 1,808 ... H4
50576 Rembrandt 291 ... C3
51050 Remsen 1,592 ... B3
50577 Renwick 410 ... E3
50234 Rhodes 367 ... G5
50466 Riceville 919 ... H2
52585 Richland 600 ... K6
52165 Ridgeway 308 ... K2
50578 Ringsted 557 ... D2
50235 Rippey 304 ... E5
†52722 Riverdale 462 ... N5
52327 Riverside 826 ... K6
51650 Riverton 342 ... B7
52328 Robins 726 ... K4
50468 Rockford 1,012 ... H2
51246 Rock Rapids⊙ 2,693 ... A2
51247 Rock Valley 2,706 ... A2
50469 Rockwell 1,039 ... G3
50579 Rockwell City⊙ 2,276 ... D4
50236 Roland 1,005 ... F4
50581 Rolfe 796 ... D3
50470 Rowan 259 ... F3
52329 Rowley 275 ... K4
51357 Royal 522 ... C2
50471 Rudd 460 ... H2
50237 Runnells 377 ... G5
50238 Russell 593 ... G7
51358 Ruthven 769 ... D2
52330 Ryan 390 ... K4
52070 Sabula 824 ... N4
50583 Sac City⊙ 3,000 ... C4
†52001 Sageville 291 ... M3
50472 Saint Ansgar 1,100 ... H2
50240 Saint Charles 507 ... F6
52649 Salem 463 ... K7
51052 Salix 429 ... A4
51248 Sanborn 1,398 ... B2
51053 Schaller 832 ... C4
51461 Schleswig 868 ... B4
51462 Scranton 748 ... D4
51054 Sergeant Bluff 2,416 ... A4
52590 Seymour 1,036 ... G7
50475 Sheffield 1,224 ... G3
51570 Shelby 665 ... C5
50243 Sheldahl 315 ... F5
51201 Sheldon 5,003 ... B2
50670 Shell Rock 1,478 ... H3
52332 Shellsburg 771 ... K4
51601 Shenandoah 6,274 ... C7
†52401 Shueyville 287 ... K5
51249 Sibley⊙ 3,051 ... B2
51652 Sidney⊙ 1,308 ... B7
52591 Sigourney⊙ 2,330 ... J6
51571 Silver City 291 ... B6
51250 Sioux Center 4,588 ... A2
*51101 Sioux City⊙ 82,003 ... A3
Sioux City‡ 117,457 ... A3
50585 Sioux Rapids 897 ... C3
50244 Slater 1,312 ... F5
51055 Sloan 978 ... A4
51056 Smithland 282 ... B4
51572 Soldier 257 ... B5
52333 Solon 969 ... L5
51301 Spencer⊙ 11,726 ... C2
52168 Spillville 415 ... J2
51360 Spirit Lake⊙ 3,976 ... C2
52336 Springville 1,165 ... L4
50476 Stacyville 538 ... H2
50246 Stanhope 492 ... F4
51573 Stanton 747 ... C7
52337 Stanwood 705 ... L5
50247 State Center 1,292 ... G5
50672 Steamboat Rock 387 ... G4
52651 Stockport 272 ... K7
52769 Stockton 240 ... M5
50588 Storm Lake⊙ 8,814 ... C3
50248 Story City 2,762 ... F4
50249 Stratford 806 ... F4
52076 Strawberry Point 1,463 ... K3
50250 Stuart 1,650 ... E6
50251 Sully 828 ... H5
50674 Sumner 2,335 ... J3
51058 Sutherland 897 ... B3
50590 Swea City 813 ... E2
52338 Swisher 654 ... K5
51653 Tabor 1,088 ... B7
52339 Tama 2,968 ... H5
51463 Templeton 319 ... D5
51364 Terril 420 ... C2
50478 Thompson 668 ... F2
50479 Thornton 442 ... G3
52340 Tiffin 413 ... K5
52772 Tipton⊙ 3,055 ... L5
50480 Titonka 607 ... E2
52342 Toledo⊙ 2,445 ... H4
50675 Traer 1,703 ... J4
51575 Treynor 981 ... B6
50676 Tripoli 1,280 ... J3
50257 Truro 407 ... F6
51576 Underwood 448 ... B6
50258 Union 515 ... G4
†52240 University Heights 1,069 ... K5
52595 University Park 645 ... H6
52345 Urbana 574 ... K4
50322 Urbandale 17,869 ... F5
51060 Ute 479 ... B4
51465 Vail 490 ... C4
52346 Van Horne 682 ... J4
50261 Van Meter 747 ... E5
50262 Van Wert 245 ... F7
50482 Ventura 614 ... F2
52347 Victor 1,046 ... J5
50864 Villisca 1,434 ... C7
52349 Vinton⊙ 5,040 ... J4
52077 Volga 310 ... L3
52169 Wadena 230 ... K3
†51360 Wahpeton 372 ... C2
52773 Walcott 1,425 ... M5
52351 Walford 285 ... K5
52352 Walker 733 ... K4
51365 Wallingford 256 ... D2
51466 Wall Lake 892 ... C4
51577 Walnut 897 ... C6
52653 Wapello⊙ 2,011 ... L6
52353 Washington⊙ 6,584 ... K6
51061 Washta 320 ... B3
*50701 Waterloo⊙ 75,985 ... J4
Waterloo-Cedar Falls‡ 137,961 ... J4
52171 Waucoma 308 ... J2
50263 Waukee 2,227 ... F5
52172 Waukon⊙ 3,983 ... L2
50677 Waverly⊙ 8,444 ... J3
52654 Wayland 720 ... K6
52356 Wellman 1,125 ... K6
50680 Wellsburg 761 ... H4
50483 Wesley 598 ... E2
50597 West Bend 941 ... D3
52358 West Branch 1,867 ... L5
52655 West Burlington 3,371 ... L7
50318 West Des Moines 21,894 ... F5
50681 Westgate 263 ... K3
52776 West Liberty 2,723 ... L5
†51351 West Okoboji 435 ... C2
52656 West Point 1,133 ... K7
51467 Westside 387 ... C4
52175 West Union⊙ 2,783 ... K3
50268 What Cheer 803 ... J6
52777 Wheatland 840 ... M5
51063 Whiting 734 ... A4
50598 Whittemore 647 ... E2
50271 Williams 410 ... F3
52361 Williamsburg 2,033 ... J5
52778 Wilton 2,502 ... M5
50311 Windsor Heights 5,474 ... F5
52659 Winfield 1,042 ... L6
50273 Winterset⊙ 4,021 ... E6
50682 Winthrop 767 ... K4
50484 Woden 287 ... F2
51579 Woodbine 1,463 ... B5
50276 Woodward 1,212 ... E5
50599 Woolstock 235 ... F3
52078 Worthington 432 ... L4
52362 Wyoming 702 ... L4
50277 Yale 299 ... E5
50278 Zearing 630 ... G4

OTHER FEATURES

Big Sioux (riv.) ... A3
Boyer (riv.) ... B5
Cedar (riv.) ... K4
Chariton (riv.) ... G7
Clear (lake) ... G2
Eagle (lake) ... F2
East Nishnabotna (riv.) ... C6
Effigy Mounds Nat'l Mon. ... L2
Five Island (lake) ... D2
Floyd (riv.) ... A3
Herbert Hoover Nat'l Hist. Site ... L5
Iowa (riv.) ... H4
Little Sioux (riv.) ... B3
Lost Island (lake) ... D2
Mississippi (riv.) ... L7
Missouri (riv.) ... A4
Nodaway (riv.) ... D7
Palo Alto (lake) ... D2
Platte (riv.) ... D8
Raccoon (riv.) ... D4
Rathbun (lake) ... G7
Red Rock (lake) ... G6
Rock (riv.) ... A2
Sac and Fox Ind. Res. ... H5
Saylorville (lake) ... F5
Skunk (riv.) ... K6
Spirit (lake) ... C2
Storm (lake) ... C3
Thompson (riv.) ... E7
Trumbull (lake) ... C2
Turkey (riv.) ... K2
Upper Iowa (riv.) ... K2
Wapsipinicon (riv.) ... J3
West Nishnabotna (riv.) ... C6

⊙County seat.
‡Population of metropolitan area.
† Zip of nearest p.o. * Multiple zips.

COUNTIES

Allen 15,654 G4
Anderson 8,749 G3
Atchison 18,397 G2
Barber 6,548 D4
Barton 31,343 D3
Bourbon 15,969 H4
Brown 11,955 G2
Butler 44,782 F4
Chase 3,309 F3
Chautauqua 5,016 F4
Cherokee 22,304 H4
Cheyenne 3,678 A2
Clark 2,599 C4
Clay 9,802 E2
Cloud 12,494 E2
Coffey 9,370 G3
Comanche 2,554 C4
Cowley 36,824 F4
Crawford 37,916 H4
Decatur 4,509 B2
Dickinson 20,175 E3
Doniphan 9,268 G2
Douglas 67,640 G3
Edwards 4,271 C4
Elk 3,918 F4
Ellis 26,098 C3
Ellsworth 6,640 D3
Finney 23,825 B3
Ford 24,315 C4
Franklin 22,062 G3
Geary 29,852 F3
Gove 3,726 B3
Graham 3,995 C2
Grant 6,977 A4
Gray 5,138 B4
Greeley 1,845 A3
Greenwood 8,764 F4
Hamilton 2,514 A3
Harper 7,778 D4
Harvey 30,531 E3
Haskell 3,814 B4
Hodgeman 2,269 C3
Jackson 11,644 G2
Jefferson 15,207 G2
Jewell 5,241 D2
Johnson 270,269 H3
Kearny 3,435 A3
Kingman 8,960 D4
Kiowa 4,046 C4
Labette 25,682 G4
Lane 2,472 B3
Leavenworth 54,809 G2
Lincoln 4,145 D2
Linn 8,234 H3
Logan 3,478 A3
Lyon 35,108 F3
Marion 13,522 E3
Marshall 12,787 F2
McPherson 26,855 E3
Meade 4,788 B4
Miami 21,618 H3
Mitchell 8,117 D2
Montgomery 42,281 G4
Morris 6,419 F3
Morton 3,454 A4
Nemaha 11,211 F2
Neosho 18,967 G4
Ness 4,498 C3
Norton 6,689 C2
Osage 15,319 G3
Osborne 5,959 D2
Ottawa 5,971 E2
Pawnee 8,065 C3
Phillips 7,406 C2
Pottawatomie 14,782 F2
Pratt 10,275 D4
Rawlins 4,105 A2
Reno 64,983 D4
Republic 7,569 E2
Rice 11,900 D3
Riley 63,505 F2
Rooks 7,006 C2
Rush 4,516 C3
Russell 8,868 D3
Saline 48,905 E3
Scott 5,782 B3
Sedgwick 367,088 E4
Seward 17,071 B4
Shawnee 154,916 G2
Sheridan 3,544 B2
Sherman 7,759 A2
Smith 5,947 D2
Stafford 5,694 D3
Stanton 2,339 A4
Stevens 4,736 A4
Sumner 24,928 E4
Thomas 8,451 A2
Trego 4,165 C3
Wabaunsee 6,867 F3
Wallace 2,045 A3
Washington 8,543 E2
Wichita 3,041 A3
Wilson 12,128 G4
Woodson 4,600 G4
Wyandotte 172,335 H2

CITIES and TOWNS

Zip Name/Pop. Key

67510 Abbyville 123 D4
67410 Abilene⊙ 6,572 E3
66830 Admire 158 F3
66930 Agenda 106 E2
67621 Agra 321 C2
67511 Albert 236 C3
67512 Alden 214 D3
67513 Alexander 116 C3
66833 Allen 205 F3
66401 Alma⊙ 925 F2
67622 Almena 517 C2
67330 Altamont 1,054 G4
66834 Alta Vista 430 F3
67623 Alton 135 D2
66710 Altoona 564 G4
66835 Americus 915 F3
67001 Andale 538 E4
67002 Andover 2,801 E4
67003 Anthony⊙ 2,661 D4
66711 Arcadia 460 H4
67004 Argonia 587 E4
67005 Arkansas City 13,201 E4
67514 Arlington 631 D4
66712 Arma 1,676 H4
67831 Ashland⊙ 1,096 C4
67416 Assaria 414 E3
66002 Atchison⊙ 11,407 G2
66932 Athol 90 D2
67008 Atlanta 256 F4
67009 Attica 730 D4
67730 Atwood⊙ 1,665 B2
66402 Auburn 890 G3
67010 Augusta 6,968 F4
67417 Aurora 130 E2
66403 Axtell 470 F2
66404 Baileyville 130 F2
66006 Baldwin City 2,829 G3
67418 Barnard 163 D2
66933 Barnes 257 F2
67332 Bartlett 163 G4
66007 Basehor 1,483 G2
†66749 Bassett 31 G4
66713 Baxter Springs 4,730 H4
67516 Bazine 385 C3
66406 Beattie 316 F2
67013 Belle Plaine 1,706 E4
66935 Belleville⊙ 2,805 E2
67420 Beloit⊙ 4,367 D2
67519 Belpre 154 C4
66407 Belvue 212 F2
66714 Benedict 111 G4
67422 Bennington 579 E2
67016 Bentley 311 E4
67017 Benton 609 E4
66408 Bern 220 F2
67423 Beverly 171 E2
67731 Bird City 546 A2
67520 Bison 279 C3
66010 Blue Mound 319 H3
66411 Blue Rapids 1,280 F2
67018 Bluff City 95 E4
67625 Bogue 197 C2
66012 Bonner Springs 6,266 H2
67732 Brewster 327 A2
66716 Bronson 414 H4
67425 Brookville 259 E3
67521 Brownell 92 C3
67834 Bucklin 786 C4
66717 Buffalo 386 G4
67522 Buhler 1,188 E3
67626 Bunker Hill 124 D3
67019 Burden 518 F4
67523 Burdett 275 C3
66413 Burlingame 1,239 G3
66839 Burlington⊙ 2,901 G3
66840 Burns 224 F3
66936 Burr Oak 366 D2
67020 Burrton 976 E3
66841 Bushong 62 F3
67427 Bushton 388 D3
67021 Byers 47 D4
67022 Caldwell 1,401 E4
67023 Cambridge 113 F4
67333 Caney 2,284 G4
67428 Canton 926 E3
66414 Carbondale 1,518 G3
67429 Carlton 49 E3
66842 Cassoday 122 F3
67430 Cawker City 640 D2
67628 Cedar 53 D2
66843 Cedar Point 66 F3
67024 Cedar Vale 848 F4
66415 Centralia 486 F2
66720 Chanute 10,506 G4
67431 Chapman 1,255 E3
67524 Chase 753 D3
67334 Chautauqua 156 F4
67025 Cheney 1,404 E4
66724 Cherokee 775 H4
67335 Cherryvale 2,769 G4
67336 Chetopa 1,751 G4
67835 Cimarron⊙ 1,491 B4
66416 Circleville 164 G2
67525 Claflin 764 D3
67432 Clay Center⊙ 4,948 E2
67629 Clayton 102 B2
67026 Clearwater 1,684 E4
66937 Clifton 695 E2
67027 Climax 81 F4
66938 Clyde 909 E2
67028 Coats 153 D4
67337 Coffeyville 15,185 G4
67701 Colby⊙ 5,544 A2
67029 Coldwater⊙ 989 C4
67631 Collyer 151 B2
66015 Colony 474 G3
66725 Columbus⊙ 3,426 H4
67030 Colwich 935 E4
66901 Concordia⊙ 6,847 E2
67031 Conway Springs 1,313 E4
67836 Coolidge 82 A3
67837 Copeland 323 B4
66417 Corning 158 F2
66845 Cottonwood Falls⊙ 954 F3
66846 Council Grove⊙ 2,381 F3
66939 Courtland 377 E2
66727 Coyville 98 G4
66940 Cuba 286 E2
†67124 Cullison 154 D4
67435 Culver 167 E3
67035 Cunningham 540 D4
67632 Damar 204 C2
67036 Danville 71 E4
67340 Dearing 475 G4
67838 Deerfield 538 A4
66418 Delia 181 G2
67436 Delphos 570 E2
66419 Denison 231 G2
66017 Denton 156 G2
67037 Derby 9,786 E4
66018 De Soto 2,061 H3
67038 Dexter 366 F4
67839 Dighton⊙ 1,390 B3

AREA 82,277 sq. mi. (213,097 sq. km.)
POPULATION 2,364,236
CAPITAL Topeka
LARGEST CITY Wichita
HIGHEST POINT Mt. Sunflower 4,039 ft. (1231 m.)
SETTLED IN 1831
ADMITTED TO UNION January 29, 1861
POPULAR NAME Sunflower State
STATE FLOWER Sunflower
STATE BIRD Western Meadowlark

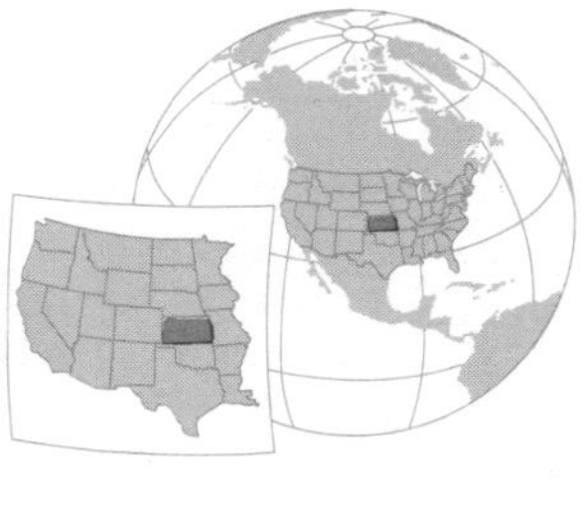

Agriculture, Industry and Resources

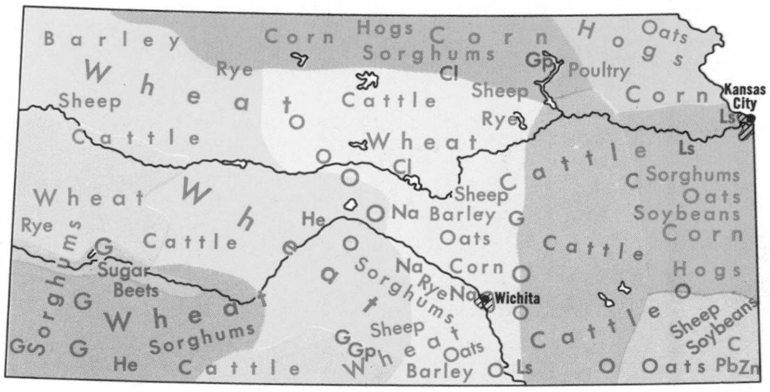

DOMINANT LAND USE

- Specialized Wheat
- Wheat, General Farming
- Wheat, Range Livestock
- Wheat, Grain Sorghums, Range Livestock
- Cattle Feed, Hogs
- Livestock, Cash Grain
- Livestock, Cash Grain, Dairy
- General Farming, Livestock, Cash Grain
- General Farming, Livestock, Special Crops
- Range Livestock

MAJOR MINERAL OCCURRENCES

C	Coal	Ls	Limestone
Cl	Clay	Na	Salt
G	Natural Gas	O	Petroleum
Gp	Gypsum	Pb	Lead
He	Helium	Zn	Zinc

Major Industrial Areas

67801 Dodge City⊙ 18,001 B4
67634 Dorrance 220 D3
67039 Douglass 1,450 F4
67437 Downs 1,324 D2
67635 Dresden 84 B2
66848 Dunlap 82 F3
67438 Durham 130 E3
66849 Dwight 320 F3
†66720 Earlton 79 G4
†67201 Eastborough 854 E4
66020 Easton 460 G2
66021 Edgerton 1,214 H3
67636 Edmond 56 C2
67342 Edna 537 G4
66113 Edwardsville 3,364 H2
66023 Effingham 634 G2
67041 Elbing 175 E3
67042 El Dorado⊙ 10,510 F4
†67361 Elgin 139 F4
67344 Elk City 404 G4
67345 Elk Falls 151 F4
67950 Elkhart⊙ 2,243 A4
67526 Ellinwood 2,508 D3
67637 Ellis 2,062 C3
67439 Ellsworth⊙ 2,465 D3
66850 Elmdale 109 F3
66732 Elsmore 104 G4
66024 Elwood 1,275 H2
66422 Emmett 223 F2
66801 Emporia⊙ 25,287 F3
67840 Englewood 111 C4
67841 Ensign 209 B4
67441 Enterprise 839 E3
66733 Erie⊙ 1,415 G4
66941 Esbon 234 D2
66423 Eskridge 603 F3
66025 Eudora 2,934 G3
67045 Eureka⊙ 3,425 F4
66424 Everest 331 G2
66425 Fairview 258 G2
†66101 Fairway 4,619 H2
67047 Fall River 173 G4
66851 Florence 729 E3
66026 Fontana 173 H3
67842 Ford 272 C4
66942 Formoso 166 D2
67843 Fort Dodge 400 C4
66027 Fort Leavenworth H2
66701 Fort Scott⊙ 8,893 H4
67844 Fowler 592 B4
66427 Frankfort 1,038 F2
66735 Franklin 400 H4
66736 Fredonia⊙ 3,047 G4
67049 Freeport 12 E4
66762 Frontenac 2,586 H4
66738 Fulton 194 H4
66739 Galena 3,587 H4
66740 Galesburg 181 G4
67443 Galva 651 E3
67846 Garden City⊙ 18,256 B4
67050 Garden Plain 775 E4
66030 Gardner 2,392 H3
67529 Garfield 277 C3
66032 Garnett⊙ 3,310 G3
66742 Gas 543 G4
67638 Gaylord 203 D2
67734 Gem 101 B2
67444 Geneseo 496 D3
67051 Geuda Springs 217 E4
66743 Girard⊙ 2,888 H4
67639 Glade 131 C2
67445 Glasco 710 E2
67446 Glen Elder 491 D2
67052 Goddard 1,427 E4
67053 Goessel 421 E3
66428 Goff 196 G2
67735 Goodland⊙ 5,708 A2
67640 Gorham 355 D3
67736 Gove⊙ 148 B3
67737 Grainfield 417 B2
†66441 Grandview Plaza 1,189 F2
66429 Grantville 220 G2
67530 Great Bend⊙ 16,608 D3
66033 Greeley 405 G3
67447 Green 155 E2
66943 Greenleaf 462 E2
67054 Greensburg⊙ 1,885 C4
67346 Grenola 335 F4
66852 Gridley 404 G3
67738 Grinnell 410 B2
67448 Gypsum 423 E3
66944 Haddam 239 E2
67056 Halstead 1,994 E4
66853 Hamilton 363 F4
66945 Hanover 802 F2
67849 Hanston 257 C3
67057 Hardtner 336 D4
67058 Harper 1,823 D4
66854 Hartford 551 F3
66431 Harveyville 280 F3
67347 Havana 169 G4
67543 Haven 1,125 E4
66432 Havensville 183 F2
67059 Haviland 770 C4

(continued on following page)

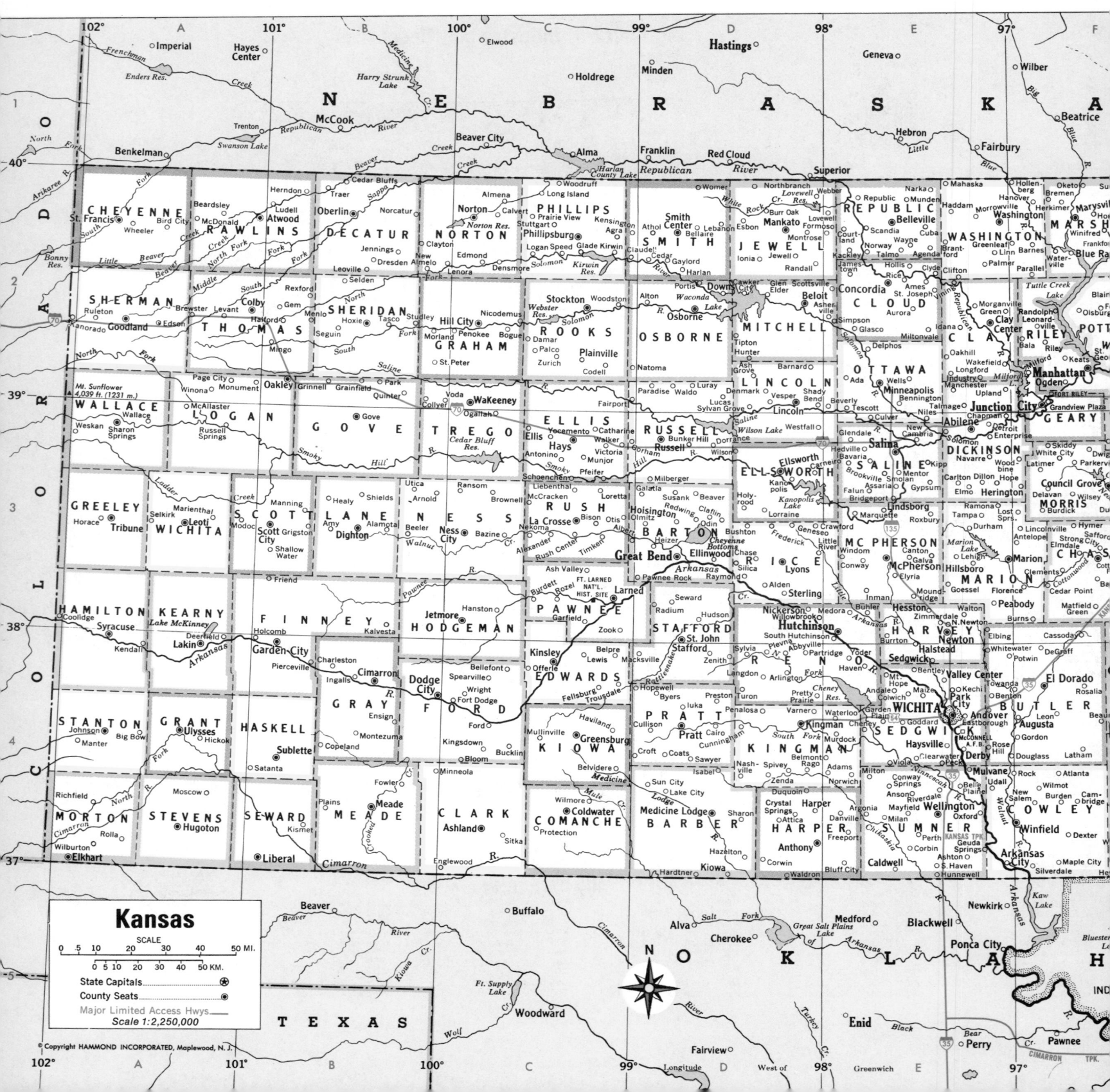

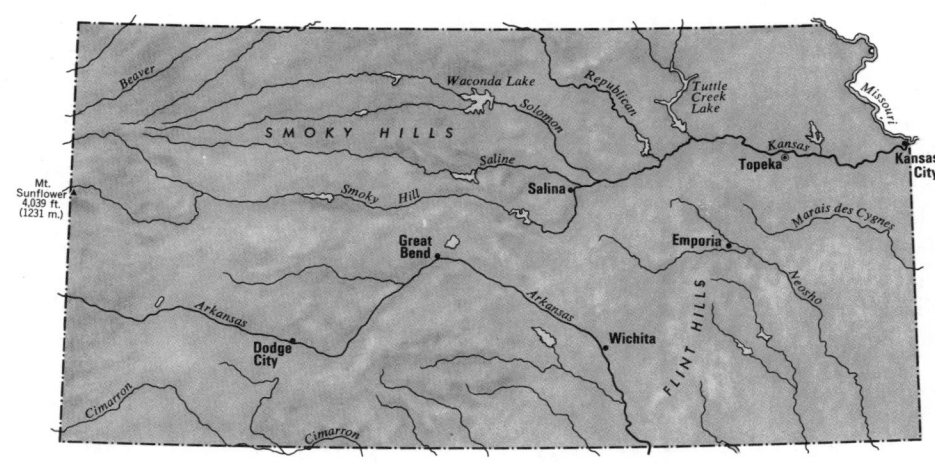

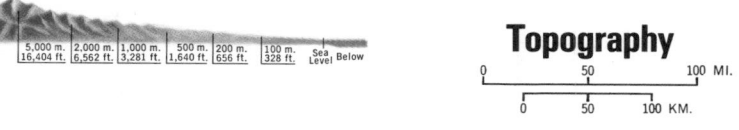

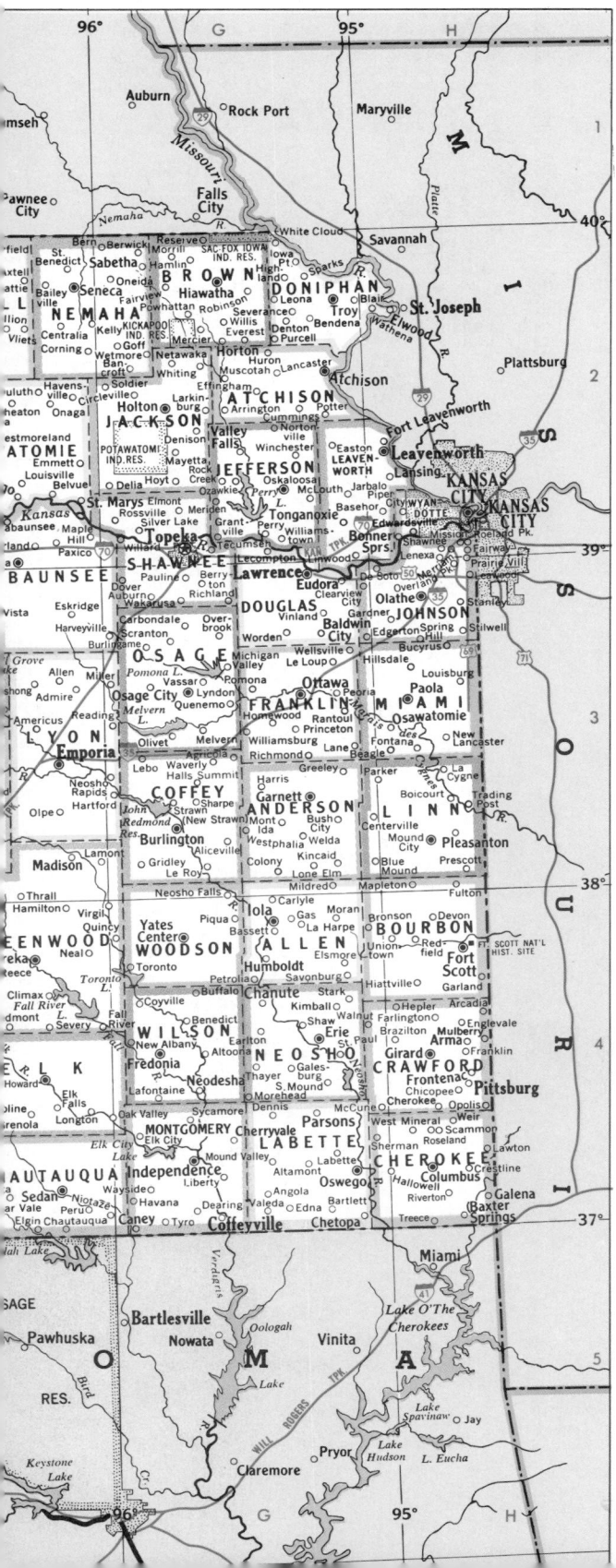

Topography

0 50 100 MI.
0 50 100 KM.

OTHER FEATURES

⊙County seat.
‡Population of metropolitan area.
† Zip of nearest p.o.
* Multiple zips.

KENTUCKY

COUNTIES

Adair 15,233 ..... L6
Allen 14,128 ..... J7
Anderson 12,567 ..... M5
Ballard 8,798 ..... C6
Barren 34,009 ..... K7
Bath 10,025 ..... O4
Bell 34,330 ..... O7
Boone 45,842 ..... M3
Bourbon 19,405 ..... N4
Boyd 55,513 ..... R4
Boyle 25,066 ..... M5
Bracken 7,738 ..... N3
Breathitt 17,004 ..... P5
Breckinridge 16,861 ..... H5
Bullitt 43,346 ..... K5
Butler 11,064 ..... H6
Caldwell 13,473 ..... F6
Calloway 30,031 ..... E7
Campbell 83,317 ..... N3
Carlisle 5,487 ..... C7
Carroll 9,270 ..... L3
Carter 25,060 ..... P4
Casey 14,818 ..... M6
Christian 66,878 ..... F7
Clark 28,322 ..... N4
Clay 22,752 ..... O6
Clinton 9,321 ..... L7
Crittenden 9,207 ..... E6
Cumberland 7,289 ..... L7
Daviess 85,949 ..... G5
Edmonson 9,962 ..... J6
Elliott 6,908 ..... P4
Estill 14,495 ..... O5
Fayette 204,165 ..... N4
Fleming 12,323 ..... O4
Floyd 48,764 ..... R5
Franklin 41,830 ..... M4
Fulton 8,971 ..... C7
Gallatin 4,842 ..... M3
Garrard 10,853 ..... M5
Grant 13,308 ..... M3
Graves 34,049 ..... D7
Grayson 20,854 ..... J5
Green 11,043 ..... K6
Greenup 39,132 ..... R3
Hancock 7,742 ..... H5
Hardin 88,917 ..... K5
Harlan 41,889 ..... P7
Harrison 15,166 ..... N4
Hart 15,402 ..... K6
Henderson 40,849 ..... F5
Henry 12,740 ..... L4
Hickman 6,065 ..... C7
Hopkins 46,174 ..... F6
Jackson 11,996 ..... N6
Jefferson 684,565 ..... K4
Jessamine 26,065 ..... M5
Johnson 24,432 ..... R5
Kenton 137,058 ..... M3
Knott 17,940 ..... R6
Knox 30,239 ..... O7
Larue 11,922 ..... K5
Laurel 38,982 ..... N6
Lawrence 14,121 ..... R4
Lee 7,754 ..... O5
Leslie 14,882 ..... P6
Letcher 30,687 ..... R6
Lewis 14,545 ..... P3
Lincoln 19,053 ..... M6
Livingston 9,219 ..... E6
Logan 24,138 ..... H7
Lyon 6,490 ..... E6
Madison 53,352 ..... N5
Magoffin 13,515 ..... P5
Marion 17,910 ..... L5
Marshall 25,637 ..... E7
Martin 13,925 ..... R5
Mason 17,765 ..... O3
McCracken 61,310 ..... D6
McCreary 15,634 ..... N7
McLean 10,090 ..... G5
Meade 22,854 ..... J5
Menifee 5,117 ..... O5
Mercer 19,011 ..... M5
Metcalfe 9,484 ..... K7
Monroe 12,353 ..... K7
Montgomery 20,046 ..... O4
Morgan 12,103 ..... P5
Muhlenberg 32,238 ..... G6
Nelson 27,584 ..... K5
Nicholas 7,157 ..... N4
Ohio 21,765 ..... H6
Oldham 27,795 ..... L4
Owen 8,924 ..... M3
Owsley 5,709 ..... O6
Pendleton 10,989 ..... N3
Perry 33,763 ..... P6
Pike 81,123 ..... S6
Powell 11,101 ..... O5
Pulaski 45,803 ..... M6
Robertson 2,265 ..... N3
Rockcastle 13,973 ..... N6
Rowan 19,049 ..... P4
Russell 13,708 ..... L7
Scott 21,813 ..... M4
Shelby 23,328 ..... L4
Simpson 14,673 ..... H7
Spencer 5,929 ..... L4
Taylor 21,178 ..... L6
Todd 11,874 ..... G7
Trigg 9,384 ..... F7
Trimble 6,253 ..... L3
Union 17,821 ..... F5
Warren 71,828 ..... H6
Washington 10,764 ..... L5
Wayne 17,022 ..... M7
Webster 14,832 ..... F5
Whitley 33,396 ..... N7
Wolfe 6,698 ..... O5
Woodford 17,778 ..... M4

CITIES and TOWNS

Zip *Name/Pop.* *Key*

42202 Adairville 1,105 ..... H7
42602 Albany⊙ 2,083 ..... L7
41001 Alexandria⊙ 4,735 ..... N3
41601 Allen 338 ..... R5
42204 Allensville 170 ..... G7
40223 Anchorage 1,726 ..... L2
41101 Ashland 27,064 ..... R4
Ashland-Huntington‡ 311,350 ..... R4
42206 Auburn 1,467 ..... H7
†40201 Audubon Park 1,571 ..... J2
41002 Augusta 1,455 ..... N3
41602 Auxier 900 ..... R5
†40222 Bancroft 725 ..... K1
41603 Banner 950 ..... R5
†40201 Barbourmeade 1,038 ..... K1
40906 Barbourville⊙ 3,333 ..... O7
40004 Bardstown⊙ 6,155 ..... L5
42023 Bardwell⊙ 988 ..... D7
42024 Barlow 746 ..... D6
41311 Beattyville⊙ 1,068 ..... O5
42320 Beaver Dam 3,185 ..... H6
40006 Bedford⊙ 835 ..... L3
40359 Beechwood Village 1,462 ..... K2
†40201 Bellemeade 918 ..... L2
41073 Bellevue 7,678 ..... S1
40807 Benham 936 ..... R7
42025 Benton⊙ 3,700 ..... E7
40403 Berea 8,226 ..... N5
41003 Berry 287 ..... N3
41605 Betsy Layne 975 ..... R5
41124 Blaine 358 ..... R4
40008 Bloomfield 954 ..... L5
†40201 Blue Ridge Manor 465 ..... L2
42713 Bonnieville 372 ..... K6
†40403 Boone 300 ..... N5
41314 Booneville⊙ 191 ..... O6
42101 Bowling Green⊙ 40,450 ..... H7
40009 Bradfordsville 331 ..... L6
40108 Brandenburg⊙ 1,831 ..... J4
†42025 Briensburg E7
†40201 Broadfields 311 ..... K2
40409 Brodhead 686 ..... N6
†41016 Bromley 844 ..... S2
40109 Brooks 1,344 ..... K4
41004 Brooksville⊙ 680 ..... N3
†40201 Brownsboro Farm 790 ..... L1
42210 Brownsville⊙ 674 ..... J6
40218 Buechel 6,709 ..... K2
40310 Burgin 1,008 ..... M5
42717 Burkesville⊙ 2,051 ..... L7
41005 Burlington⊙ 500 ..... R2
42519 Burnside 775 ..... M6
41006 Butler 663 ..... N3
42211 Cadiz⊙ 1,661 ..... F7
42327 Calhoun⊙ 1,080 ..... G5
41007 California 135 ..... N3
42029 Calvert City 2,388 ..... E6
†40337 Camargo 1,301 ..... K4
40011 Campbellsburg 714 ..... L3
42718 Campbellsville⊙ 8,715 ..... L6
41301 Campton⊙ 486 ..... O5
42721 Caneyville 642 ..... J6
40311 Carlisle⊙ 1,757 ..... N4
41008 Carrollton⊙ 3,967 ..... L3
42030 Carrsville 99 ..... E6
†42459 Caseyville 43 ..... E5
41129 Catlettsburg⊙ 3,005 ..... R4
42127 Cave City 2,098 ..... K6
†41522 Cedarville 81 ..... S6
42328 Centertown 462 ..... G6
42330 Central City 5,214 ..... G6
42726 Clarkson 666 ..... J6
42404 Clay 1,356 ..... F6
40312 Clay City 1,276 ..... O5
40313 Clearfield 1,250 ..... P4
42031 Clinton⊙ 1,720 ..... D7
40111 Cloverport 1,585 ..... H5
†41501 Coal Run 348 ..... R5
41076 Cold Spring 2,117 ..... T2
42728 Columbia⊙ 3,710 ..... L6
42032 Columbus 296 ..... C7
41729 Combs 900 ..... P6
41131 Concord 67 ..... P3
40701 Corbin 8,075 ..... N7
41010 Corinth 258 ..... M3
42406 Corydon 874 ..... F5
*41011 Covington 49,563 ..... S2
40419 Crab Orchard 843 ..... M6
†41016 Crescent Springs 1,951 ..... R2
†41076 Crestview 528 ..... S2
†41017 Crestview Hills 1,408 ..... R2
40014 Crestwood 531 ..... L4
41030 Crittenden 597 ..... M3
42217 Crofton 823 ..... G6
40823 Cumberland 3,712 ..... R6
41031 Cynthiana⊙ 5,881 ..... N4
40422 Danville⊙ 12,942 ..... M5
42408 Dawson Springs 3,275 ..... F6
41074 Dayton 6,979 ..... T1
†40201 Devondale 1,164 ..... K2
42036 Dexter E7
42409 Dixon⊙ 533 ..... F5
†40243 Douglass Hills 4,384 ..... L2
41034 Dover 305 ..... O3
42337 Drakesboro 798 ..... H6
41035 Dry Ridge 1,250 ..... M3
42037 Dycusburg 64 ..... E6
42410 Earlington 2,011 ..... F6
42038 Eddyville⊙ 1,949 ..... E6
†41017 Edgewood 7,230 ..... S2
42129 Edmonton⊙ 1,401 ..... K7
40117 Ekron 239 ..... J5
42701 Elizabethtown⊙ 15,380 ..... K5
41522 Elkhorn City 1,446 ..... S6
42220 Elkton⊙ 1,815 ..... G7
†41018 Elsmere 7,203 ..... R2
40019 Eminence 2,260 ..... L4
40826 Eolia 875 ..... R6
41018 Erlanger 14,433 ..... R2
40827 Essie 650 ..... P6
42567 Eubank 207 ..... M6
40828 Evarts 1,234 ..... P7
41039 Ewing 144 ..... O4
40118 Fairdale 7,315 ..... K4
40020 Fairfield 169 ..... L5
†41101 Fairview 198 ..... S2
41040 Falmouth⊙ 2,482 ..... N3
41524 Fedscreek 950 ..... S6
42533 Ferguson 1,009 ..... M6
†40222 Fincastle 804 ..... L1
41139 Flatwoods 8,354 ..... R4
41816 Fleming-Neon 1,195 ..... R6
41041 Flemingsburg⊙ 2,835 ..... O4
41042 Florence 15,586 ..... R2
42343 Fordsville 561 ..... H5
41527 Forest Hills 502 ..... L2
40121 Fort Knox 31,055 ..... K5
41017 Fort Mitchell 7,297 ..... S2
41075 Fort Thomas 16,012 ..... S2
†41011 Fort Wright 4,481 ..... S2
41043 Foster 80 ..... N3
42133 Fountain Run 340 ..... K7
40601 Frankfort (cap.)⊙ 25,973 ..... M4
42134 Franklin⊙ 7,738 ..... J7
42411 Fredonia 535 ..... E6
40322 Frenchburg⊙ 550 ..... O5
†41175 Fullerton 950 ..... P3
42041 Fulton 3,137 ..... D7
42140 Gamaliel 456 ..... K7
40324 Georgetown⊙ 10,972 ..... M4
41044 Germantown 347 ..... O3
41045 Ghent 439 ..... L3
42044 Gilbertsville E7
42141 Glasgow⊙ 12,958 ..... J7
41046 Glencoe 354 ..... M3
†40222 Glenview 212 ..... K1
†40222 Goose Creek 394 ..... L1
42045 Grand Rivers 428 ..... E7
†41005 Grant 150 ..... M3
40327 Gratz 124 ..... M4
†40201 Graymoor 1,167 ..... K1
41143 Grayson⊙ 3,423 ..... R4
42743 Greensburg⊙ 2,377 ..... K6
41144 Greenup⊙ 1,386 ..... R3
42345 Greenville⊙ 4,631 ..... G6
42234 Guthrie 1,361 ..... G7
42413 Hanson 485 ..... G6
42048 Hardin 545 ..... E7
40143 Hardinsburg⊙ 2,211 ..... H5
41531 Hardy 900 ..... S5
40831 Harlan⊙ 3,024 ..... P7
40330 Harrodsburg⊙ 7,265 ..... M5
42347 Hartford⊙ 2,512 ..... H6
42348 Hawesville⊙ 1,036 ..... H5
41701 Hazard⊙ 5,371 ..... P6
42049 Hazel 465 ..... E7
40949 Heidrick 400 ..... O7
42420 Henderson⊙ 24,834 ..... F5
42050 Hickman⊙ 2,894 ..... C7
42051 Hickory D7
41076 Highland Heights 4,435 ..... T2
41822 Hindman⊙ 876 ..... R6
42152 Hiseville 349 ..... K6
42748 Hodgenville⊙ 2,531 ..... K5
†40228 Hollow Creek 1,023 ..... K4
†41018 Hopeful Heights R2
42240 Hopkinsville⊙ 27,318 ..... F7
42749 Horse Cave 2,045 ..... K6
†40201 Houston Acres 608 ..... K2
40437 Hustonville 339 ..... M6
41749 Hyden⊙ 488 ..... P6
41051 Independence⊙ 7,998 ..... M3
†40201 Indian Hills 787 ..... K1
41224 Inez⊙ 413 ..... S5
40336 Irvine⊙ 2,889 ..... O5
40146 Irvington 1,409 ..... J5
42350 Island 532 ..... G6
41642 Ivel 850 ..... R5
41339 Jackson⊙ 2,651 ..... P5
42629 Jamestown⊙ 1,441 ..... L7
40299 Jeffersontown 15,795 ..... L2
40337 Jeffersonville 1,528 ..... O5
41537 Jenkins 3,271 ..... R6
40440 Junction City 2,045 ..... M5
40737 Keavy 900 ..... N6
†41011 Kenton Vale 145 ..... S2
42053 Kevil 382 ..... D6
†40201 Kingsley 464 ..... K2
42055 Kuttawa 560 ..... E6
42056 La Center 1,044 ..... C6
41643 Lackey R6
42254 La Fayette 160 ..... F7
40031 La Grange⊙ 2,971 ..... L4
†41017 Lakeside Park 3,038 ..... R2
40444 Lancaster⊙ 3,365 ..... M5
40342 Lawrenceburg⊙ 5,167 ..... M4
40033 Lebanon⊙ 6,590 ..... L5
40150 Lebanon Junction 1,581 ..... K5
42754 Leitchfield⊙ 4,533 ..... J6
42256 Lewisburg 972 ..... G6
42351 Lewisport 1,832 ..... H5
*40501 Lexington⊙ 204,165 ..... N4
Lexington‡ 318,136 ..... N4
42539 Liberty⊙ 2,206 ..... M6
42352 Livermore 1,672 ..... G5
40445 Livingston 334 ..... N6
40036 Lockport 84 ..... M4
40741 London⊙ 4,002 ..... N6
42001 Lone Oak 443 ..... D6
40037 Loretto 954 ..... L5
41230 Louisa⊙ 1,832 ..... R4
*40201 Louisville⊙ 298,840 ..... J2
Louisville‡ 906,240 ..... J2
40854 Loyall 1,210 ..... P7
41016 Ludlow 4,959 ..... S2
40855 Lynch 1,614 ..... R7
†40201 Lynnview 1,157 ..... K4
40040 Mackville 229 ..... L5
42431 Madisonville⊙ 16,979 ..... F6
40962 Manchester⊙ 1,838 ..... O6
42064 Marion⊙ 3,392 ..... E6
41649 Martin 827 ..... R5
42066 Mayfield⊙ 10,705 ..... D7
41056 Maysville⊙ 7,983 ..... O3
41543 McAndrews 975 ..... S5
42354 McHenry 582 ..... H6
40447 McKee⊙ 759 ..... O6
41835 McRoberts 1,106 ..... R6
†40201 Meadow Vale 1,008 ..... L1
41059 Melbourne 628 ..... T2
†41060 Mentor 169 ..... N3
40965 Middlesboro 12,251 ..... O7
40243 Middletown 414 ..... L2
40347 Midway 1,445 ..... M4
40348 Millersburg 987 ..... N4
40045 Milton 718 ..... L3
†40201 Minor Lane Heights 1,882 ..... K4
†40359 Monterey 186 ..... M4
42633 Monticello⊙ 5,677 ..... M7
†40223 Moorland 513 ..... L2
40351 Morehead⊙ 7,789 ..... P4
42437 Morganfield⊙ 3,781 ..... E5
42261 Morgantown⊙ 2,000 ..... H6
42440 Mortons Gap 1,201 ..... F6
41064 Mount Olivet⊙ 346 ..... N3
†40437 Mount Salem 50 ..... M6
40353 Mount Sterling⊙ 5,820 ..... N4
40456 Mount Vernon⊙ 2,334 ..... N6
40047 Mount Washington 3,997 ..... K4
41548 Mouthcard 900 ..... S6
40155 Muldraugh 1,752 ..... J5
42765 Munfordville⊙ 1,783 ..... J6
42071 Murray⊙ 14,248 ..... E7
42441 Nebo 269 ..... F6
41840 Neon-Fleming 1,195 ..... R6
40050 New Castle⊙ 832 ..... L4
40051 New Haven 926 ..... K5
*41071 Newport 21,587 ..... S2
40356 Nicholasville⊙ 10,319 ..... N5
†40201 Northfield 906 ..... K1
40357 North Middletown 637 ..... N4
42442 Nortonville 1,336 ..... G6
42262 Oak Grove 2,088 ..... G7
42159 Oakland 264 ..... J6
41238 Oil Springs 900 ..... P5
40219 Okolona 20,039 ..... K4
41164 Olive Hill 2,539 ..... P4
42301 Owensboro⊙ 54,450 ..... G5
Owensboro‡ 85,949 ..... G5
40359 Owenton⊙ 1,341 ..... M3
40360 Owingsville⊙ 1,419 ..... O4
42001 Paducah⊙ 29,315 ..... D6
41240 Paintsville⊙ 3,815 ..... R5
40361 Paris⊙ 7,935 ..... N4
42160 Park City 614 ..... J6
†41011 Park Hills 3,500 ..... S2
†40201 Parkway Village 754 ..... J2
42266 Pembroke 636 ..... G7
40468 Perryville 841 ..... M5
40056 Pewee Valley 982 ..... L4
41553 Phelps 1,126 ..... S6
41501 Pikeville⊙ 4,756 ..... S6
42635 Pine Knot 1,389 ..... M7
40977 Pineville⊙ 2,599 ..... O7
†40201 Plantation 969 ..... K1
40258 Pleasure Ridge Park 27,332 ..... J4
40057 Pleasureville 837 ..... L4
†42101 Plum Springs 393 ..... J7
42367 Powderly 848 ..... G6
41653 Prestonsburg⊙ 4,011 ..... R5
†41008 Prestonville 205 ..... L3
42445 Princeton⊙ 7,073 ..... F6
40059 Prospect 1,981 ..... K4
42450 Providence 4,434 ..... F6
41169 Raceland 1,970 ..... R3
40160 Radcliff 14,519 ..... K5
40472 Ravenna 793 ..... O5
40475 Richmond⊙ 21,705 ..... N5
†40222 Riverwood 435 ..... K1
42273 Rochester 289 ..... H6

Agriculture, Industry and Resources

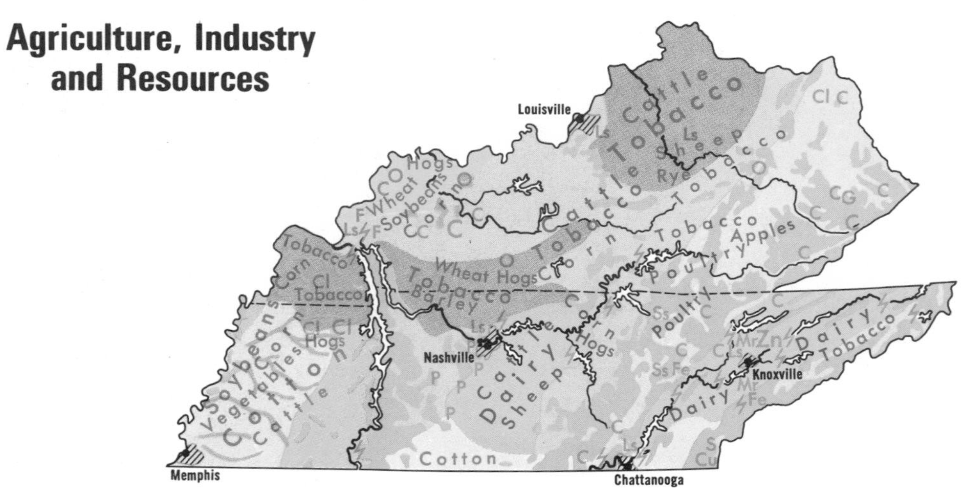

DOMINANT LAND USE

- Hogs, Soft Winter Wheat
- Tobacco, General Farming
- General Farming, Livestock, Tobacco
- General Farming, Livestock, Dairy
- General Farming, Livestock, Fruit, Tobacco
- Specialized Cotton
- Cotton, General Farming
- Cotton, Livestock
- Forests
- Swampland, Limited Agriculture

MAJOR MINERAL OCCURRENCES

C	Coal	G	Natural Gas	P	Phosphates
Cl	Clay	Ls	Limestone	S	Pyrites
Cu	Copper	Mr	Marble	Ss	Sandstone
F	Fluorspar	O	Petroleum	Zn	Zinc
Fe	Iron Ore				

Water Power — Major Industrial Areas

KENTUCKY

AREA 40,409 sq. mi. (104,659 sq. km.)
POPULATION 3,660,257
CAPITAL Frankfort
LARGEST CITY Louisville
HIGHEST POINT Black Mtn. 4,145 ft. (1263 m.)
SETTLED IN 1774
ADMITTED TO UNION June 1, 1792
POPULAR NAME Bluegrass State
STATE FLOWER Goldenrod
STATE BIRD Cardinal

TENNESSEE

AREA 42,144 sq. mi. (109,153 sq. km.)
POPULATION 4,591,120
CAPITAL Nashville
LARGEST CITY Memphis
HIGHEST POINT Clingmans Dome 6,643 ft. (2025 m.)
SETTLED IN 1757
ADMITTED TO UNION June 1, 1796
POPULAR NAME Volunteer State
STATE FLOWER Iris
STATE BIRD Mockingbird

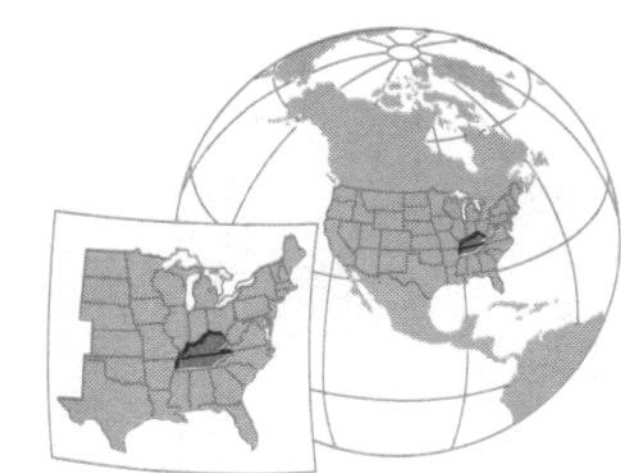

42369 Rockport 511 H6
†40201 Rolling Fields 731 K2
†40201 Rolling Hills 1,122 L1
41169 Russell 3,824 R3
42642 Russell Springs 1,831 L6
42276 Russellville⊙ 7,520 H7
†41015 Ryland Heights 252 M3
42372 Sacramento 538 G6
40370 Sadieville 253 M4
42453 Saint Charles 405 F6
40207 Saint Matthews 13,519 K2
†40201 Saint Regis Park 1,735 K2
42078 Salem 833 E6
40371 Salt Lick 347 O4
41465 Salyersville⊙ 1,352 P5
41083 Sanders 332 M3
41171 Sandy Hook⊙ 627 P4
41056 Sardis 198 O3
42553 Science Hill 655 M6
42164 Scottsville⊙ 4,278 J7
42455 Sebree 1,516 F5
†40201 Seneca Gardens 748 K2
40983 Sextons Creek 975 O6
40374 Sharpsburg 339 O4
40065 Shelbyville⊙ 5,329 L4
40165 Shepherdsville⊙ 4,454 K4
40216 Shively 16,819 K4
41085 Silver Grove 1,260 T2
40067 Simpsonville 642 L4
42456 Slaughters 269 F6
41764 Smilax 987 P6
40068 Smithfield 137 L4
42081 Smithland⊙ 512 E6
42171 Smiths Grove 767 J6
42501 Somerset⊙ 10,649 M6
42776 Sonora 416 K5
42374 South Carrollton 262 G6
41071 Southgate 2,833 T2
41174 South Portsmouth 900 P3
41175 South Shore 1,525 R3
25661 South Williamson 1,016 S5
41086 Sparta 192 M3
42458 Spottsville 914 G5
40069 Springfield⊙ 3,179 L5
†40201 Springlee 498 K2
40379 Stamping Ground 562 M4
40484 Stanford⊙ 2,764 M5
40380 Stanton⊙ 2,691 O5
42647 Stearns 1,557 N7
41567 Stone 900 S5
†40201 Strathmoor Village 466 J2
42459 Sturgis 2,293 F5
†41011 Taylor Mill 4,509 S2
40071 Taylorsville⊙ 801 L4
†40222 Thornhill 233 K1
41189 Tollesboro 808 O3
42167 Tompkinsville⊙ 4,366 K7
42286 Trenton 465 G7
41091 Union 601 M3
42461 Uniontown 1,169 F5
42784 Upton 731 K6
40272 Valley Station 24,474 K4
41179 Vanceburg⊙ 1,939 P3
41265 Van Lear 2,035 R5
†40828 Verda 1,133 P7
40383 Versailles⊙ 6,427 M4
41773 Vicco 456 P6
†41017 Villa Hills 4,402 R2
40175 Vine Grove 3,583 K5
†41063 Visalia 198 N3
40873 Wallins Creek 459 O7
41094 Walton 1,651 M3
41095 Warsaw⊙ 1,328 M3
41096 Washington 624 O3
42085 Water Valley 395 D7
42462 Waverly 434 F5
41666 Wayland 601 R6
41667 Weeksbury 850 R6
†40201 Wellington 653 K2
†40218 West Buechel 1,205 K2
41472 West Liberty⊙ 1,381 P5
40177 West Point 1,339 J4
†42501 West Somerset 850 M6
41101 Westwood 5,973 R4
†40207 Westwood 826 L1
42463 Wheatcroft 325 F5
41669 Wheelwright 865 R6
41390 Whick 280 P6
42464 White Plains 859 G6
41858 Whitesburg⊙ 1,525 R6
42378 Whitesville 788 H5
42653 Whitley City⊙ 1,683 N7
42087 Wickliffe⊙ 1,034 C7
†41071 Wilders 633 S2
40769 Williamsburg⊙ 5,560 N7
41097 Williamstown⊙ 2,502 M3
40078 Willisburg 235 L5
40390 Wilmore 3,787 M5
40391 Winchester⊙ 15,216 N5
†40201 Windy Hills 2,214 K1
42088 Wingo 606 D7
40771 Woodbine 900 N7
42170 Woodburn 330 J7
†40201 Woodland Hills 839 L2
†42001 Woodlawn-Oakdale 4,722 D6
†41071 Woodlawn 331 T2
†40201 Woodlawn Park 1,052 K2
41183 Worthington 1,948 R3
41098 Worthville 272 L3
41144 Wurtland 1,301 R3

OTHER FEATURES

Abraham Lincoln Birthplace Nat'l Hist. Site K5
Barkley (dam) E6
Barkley (lake) F7
Barren (riv.) H6
Barren River (lake) J7
Beech Fork (riv.) L5
Big Sandy (riv.) R4
Black (mt.) R7
Buckhorn (lake) O6
Chaplin (riv.) L5
Clarks, East Fork (riv.) E7
Cove Run (lake) O4
Cumberland (lake) M7
Cumberland (mt.) P7
Cumberland (riv.) K8
Cumberland Gap Nat'l Hist. Park P7
Dale Hollow (lake) L7
Dewey (lake) R5
Dix (riv.) M5
Drakes (creek) J7
Dry (creek) R3
Eagle (creek) M3
Fishtrap (lake) S6
Fort Campbell G7
Grayson (lake) P4
Green (riv.) G6
Green River (lake) L6
Herrington (lake) M5
Hinkston (creek) N4
Kentucky (dam) E7
Kentucky (lake) E8
Kentucky (riv.) M3
Land Between The Lakes Rec. Area E7
Laurel River (lake) N6
Lexington Blue Grass Army Depot N5
Licking (riv.) N3
Mammoth Cave Nat'l Park J6
Mayfield (creek) C7
Mississippi (riv.) A10
Mud (riv.) H7
Nolin (lake) K6
Nolin (riv.) J6
Obion (creek) C7
Ohio (riv.) F5
Paint Lick (riv.) M5
Panther (creek) G5
Pine (mt.) O7
Pond (riv.) G6
Red (riv.) O5
Red (riv.) G7
Rockcastle (riv.) N6
Rolling Fork (riv.) L5
Rough (riv.) H5
Rough River (lake) J5
Salt (riv.) K5
Tennessee (riv.) D6
Tradewater (riv.) F6
Tug Fork (riv.) S5

TENNESSEE

COUNTIES

Anderson 67,346 N8
Bedford 27,916 J9
Benton 14,901 E8
Bledsoe 9,478 L9
Blount 77,770 O9
Bradley 67,547 M10
Campbell 34,923 N8
Cannon 10,234 J9
Carroll 28,285 E9
Carter 50,205 S8
Cheatham 21,616 G8
Chester 12,727 D10
Claiborne 24,595 O8
Clay 7,676 K7
Cocke 28,792 P9
Coffee 38,311 J9
Crockett 14,941 C9
Cumberland 28,676 L9
Davidson 477,811 H8
Decatur 10,857 E9
De Kalb 13,589 K9
Dickson 30,037 G8
Dyer 34,663 C8
Fayette 25,305 C10
Fentress 14,826 M8
Franklin 31,983 J10
Gibson 49,467 D9
Giles 24,625 G10
Grainger 16,751 O8
Greene 54,422 R8
Grundy 13,787 K10
Hamblen 49,300 P8
Hamilton 287,740 L10
Hancock 6,887 P7
Hardeman 23,873 C10
Hardin 22,280 E10
Hawkins 43,751 P8
Haywood 20,318 C9
Henderson 21,390 E9
Henry 28,656 E8
Hickman 15,151 G9
Houston 6,871 F8
Humphreys 15,957 F8
Jackson 9,398 K8
Jefferson 31,284 P8
Johnson 13,745 T7
Knox 319,694 O9
Lake 7,455 B8
Lauderdale 24,555 B9
Lawrence 34,110 G10
Lewis 9,700 F9
Lincoln 26,483 H10
Loudon 28,553 N9
Macon 15,700 J7
Madison 74,546 D9
Marion 24,416 K10
Marshall 19,698 H10
Maury 51,095 G9
McMinn 41,878 M10
McNairy 22,525 D10
Meigs 7,431 M9
Monroe 28,700 N10
Montgomery 83,342 G8
Moore 4,510 J10
Morgan 16,604 M8
Obion 32,781 C8
Overton 17,575 L8
Perry 6,111 F9
Pickett 4,358 M7
Polk 13,602 N10
Putnam 47,690 K8
Rhea 24,235 M9
Roane 48,425 M9
Robertson 37,021 H7
Rutherford 84,058 J9
Scott 19,259 M8
Sequatchie 8,605 L10
Sevier 41,418 O9
Shelby 777,113 B10
Smith 14,935 J8
Stewart 8,665 F7
Sullivan 143,968 S7
Sumner 85,790 H8
Tipton 32,930 B9
Trousdale 6,137 J8
Unicoi 16,362 S8
Union 11,707 O8
Van Buren 4,728 L9
Warren 32,653 K9
Washington 88,755 R8
Wayne 13,946 F10
Weakley 32,896 D8
White 19,567 L9
Williamson 58,108 H9
Wilson 56,064 J8

CITIES and TOWNS

Zip Name/Pop. Key

†38301 Adair 70 D9
37010 Adams 600 G7
38310 Adamsville 1,453 E10
38001 Alamo⊙ 2,615 C9
37701 Alcoa 6,870 N9
37012 Alexandria 689 J8
38501 Algood 2,406 K8
38504 Allardt 654 M8
37301 Altamont⊙ 679 K10
38449 Ardmore 835 H10
38002 Arlington 1,778 B10
37015 Ashland City⊙ 2,329 G8
37303 Athens⊙ 12,080 M10
38004 Atoka 691 B10
38220 Atwood 1,143 D9
37016 Auburntown 204 J9
37743 Baileyton 333 R8
†37650 Banner Hill 2,913 R8
38134 Bartlett 17,170 B10
38544 Baxter 1,411 K8
37305 Beersheba Springs 643 K10
37020 Bell Buckle 450 J9
37205 Belle Meade 3,182 H8
38006 Bells 1,571 C9
37307 Benton⊙ 1,115 M10
†37201 Berry Hill 1,113 H8
†37027 Berry's Chapel 2,703 H9
38315 Bethel Springs 873 D10
38221 Big Sandy 650 E8
37709 Blaine 1,147 O8
37660 Bloomingdale 12,088 R7
37617 Blountville⊙ 2,554 S7
37618 Bluff City 1,121 S8
38008 Bolivar⊙ 6,597 C10
38010 Braden 293 B10
38316 Bradford 1,146 D8
37027 Brentwood 9,431 H8
37710 Briceville 850 N8
38011 Brighton 976 B10
37620 Bristol 23,986 S7
38012 Brownsville⊙ 9,307 C9
38317 Bruceton 1,579 E8
37711 Bulls Gap 821 P8
38015 Burlison 386 B9
37029 Burns 777 G8
38549 Byrdstown⊙ 884 L7
37309 Calhoun 590 M10
38320 Camden⊙ 3,279 E8
37030 Carthage⊙ 2,672 K8
37714 Caryville 2,039 N8
37032 Cedar Hill 420 H7
38551 Celina⊙ 1,580 K7
†37110 Centertown 300 K9
37033 Centerville⊙ 2,824 G9
37034 Chapel Hill 861 H9
37310 Charleston 756 M10
37036 Charlotte⊙ 788 G8
*37401 Chattanooga⊙ 169,558 K10
Chattanooga‡ 426,540 K10
37642 Church Hill 4,110 R7
38324 Clarksburg 400 E9
37040 Clarksville⊙ 54,777 G7
Clarksville‡ 150,220 G7
37311 Cleveland⊙ 26,415 M10
38425 Clifton 773 F10
37716 Clinton⊙ 5,245 N8
37313 Coalmont 625 K10
37315 Collegedale 4,607 M10
38017 Collierville 7,839 B10
38450 Collinwood 1,064 F10
37663 Colonial Heights 6,744 R8
38401 Columbia⊙ 26,571 G9
37720 Concord 8,569 N9
38501 Cookeville⊙ 20,535 L8
37317 Copperhill 418 N10
37047 Cornersville 722 H10
38224 Cottage Grove 117 E8
38326 Counce 975 E10
38019 Covington⊙ 6,065 B9
37318 Cowan 1,790 K10
37723 Crab Orchard 1,065 M9
37049 Cross Plains 655 H7
38555 Crossville⊙ 6,394 L9
37050 Cumberland City 276 F8
37724 Cumberland Gap 263 O8
37725 Dandridge⊙ 1,383 O8
37321 Dayton⊙ 5,913 L9
37322 Decatur⊙ 1,069 M9
38329 Decaturville⊙ 1,004 E9
37324 Decherd 2,233 J10
38391 Denmark 51 D9
37055 Dickson 7,040 G8
37058 Dover⊙ 1,197 F8
37059 Dowelltown 341 K8
38559 Doyle 344 K9
38225 Dresden⊙ 2,256 D8
37326 Ducktown 583 N10
37327 Dunlap⊙ 3,681 L10
38330 Dyer 2,419 D8
38024 Dyersburg⊙ 15,856 C8
†37801 Eagleton Village 5,331 O9
37060 Eagleville 444 H9
37412 East Ridge 21,236 L11
†38367 Eastview 552 D10
37643 Elizabethton⊙ 12,431 S8
38455 Elkton 540 H10
38029 Ellendale 850 B10
37329 Englewood 1,840 M10
38332 Enville 287 E10
37061 Erin⊙ 1,614 F8
37650 Erwin⊙ 4,739 S8
37330 Estill Springs 1,324 J10
38456 Ethridge 548 G10
37331 Etowah 3,758 M10
37062 Fairview 3,648 G9
37656 Fall Branch 1,340 R8
37334 Fayetteville⊙ 7,559 H10
38334 Finger 245 D10
38030 Finley 1,014 B8
†37201 Forest Hills 4,516 H8
37064 Franklin⊙ 12,407 H9
38034 Friendship 763 C9
37737 Friendsville 694 N9
38337 Gadsden 683 D9
38562 Gainesboro⊙ 1,119 K8
37066 Gallatin⊙ 17,191 H8
38036 Gallaway 804 B10
†38019 Garland 301 B9
38037 Gates 729 C9
37738 Gatlinburg 3,210 O9
38138 Germantown 21,482 B10
38338 Gibson 458 D9
†38015 Gilt Edge 142 B9
38229 Gleason 1,335 D8
37072 Goodlettsville 8,327 H8
38563 Gordonsville 893 K8
38039 Grand Junction 360 C10
37338 Graysville 1,380 L10
37742 Greenback 546 N9
37073 Greenbrier 3,180 H8
37743 Greeneville⊙ 14,097 R8
38230 Greenfield 2,109 D8
37339 Gruetli 910 K10
38040 Halls 2,444 C9
37658 Hampton 2,236 S8
37748 Harriman 8,303 M9
37341 Harrison 6,206 L10
37752 Harrogate-Shawanee 2,530 O8
37074 Hartsville⊙ 2,674 J8
38340 Henderson⊙ 4,449 D10
37075 Hendersonville 26,561 H8
38041 Henning 638 B9
38231 Henry 295 E8
38042 Hickory Valley 252 C10
38462 Hohenwald⊙ 3,922 F9
38342 Hollow Rock 955 E8
38232 Hornbeak 452 C8
38044 Hornsby 401 D10
38343 Humboldt 10,209 D9
38344 Huntingdon⊙ 3,962 E8
37345 Huntland 983 J10
37756 Huntsville⊙ 519 N8
37078 Hurricane Mills 850 F9
38463 Iron City 482 F10
37757 Jacksboro⊙ 1,722 N8
38301 Jackson⊙ 49,131 D9
38556 Jamestown⊙ 2,364 M8
37347 Jasper⊙ 2,633 K10
37760 Jefferson City 5,612 P8
37762 Jellico 2,798 N7
37601 Johnson City 39,753 S8
Johnson City-Kingsport-Bristol‡ 433,638 S8
37659 Jonesboro⊙ 2,829 R8
37921 Karns 1,173 N9
38233 Kenton 1,551 C8
†37347 Kimball 1,220 K10
*37660 Kingsport 32,027 R7
37763 Kingston⊙ 4,441 N9
37082 Kingston Springs 1,017 G8
*37901 Knoxville⊙ 175,045 O9
Knoxville‡ 476,517 O9
37083 Lafayette⊙ 3,808 J7
37766 La Follette 8,198 N8
38046 La Grange 185 C10
37769 Lake City 2,335 N8
†38134 Lakeland 612 B10
†37379 Lakesite 651 L10
†37138 Lakewood 2,325 H8
37086 La Vergne 5,495 H9
38464 Lawrenceburg⊙ 10,184 G10
37087 Lebanon⊙ 11,872 J8
37771 Lenoir City 5,446 N9
37091 Lewisburg⊙ 8,760 H10
38351 Lexington⊙ 5,934 E9
37095 Liberty 365 K8
37096 Linden⊙ 1,087 F9
38570 Livingston⊙ 3,372 L8
37097 Lobelville 993 F9
37350 Lookout Mountain 1,886 L11
38469 Loretto 1,612 G10
37774 Loudon⊙ 3,943 N9
37779 Luttrell 962 O8
37352 Lynchburg⊙ 668 J10
38472 Lynnville 383 G10
37354 Madisonville⊙ 2,884 N9
37355 Manchester⊙ 7,250 J10
38237 Martin 8,898 D8
37801 Maryville⊙ 17,480 O9
37806 Mascot 2,203 O8
38049 Mason 471 B10
38050 Maury City 989 C9
37807 Maynardville⊙ 924 O8
37101 McEwen 1,352 F8
38201 McKenzie 5,405 E8
38235 McLemoresville 311 D9
37110 McMinnville⊙ 10,683 K9
38355 Medina 687 D9
38356 Medon 169 D10
*38101 Memphis⊙ 646,174 B10
Memphis‡ 912,887 B10
38357 Michie 530 E10
38052 Middleton 596 D10
38358 Milan 8,083 D9
38359 Milledgeville 392 E10
38053 Millington 20,236 B10
38473 Minor Hill 564 G10
37119 Mitchellville 209 J7
37356 Monteagle 1,126 K10
38574 Monterey 2,610 L8
37357 Morrison 587 K9
†37660 Morrison City 2,032 R7
37814 Morristown⊙ 19,683 P8
38057 Moscow 499 C10
37818 Mosheim 1,539 R8
37683 Mountain City⊙ 2,125 T8
37642 Mount Carmel 3,764 R8
37122 Mount Juliet 2,879 H8
38474 Mount Pleasant 3,375 G9
38058 Munford 2,336 B10
37130 Murfreesboro⊙ 32,845 J9
*37201 Nashville (cap.)⊙ 455,651 H8
Nashville-Davidson‡ 850,505 H8
38059 Newbern 2,794 C8
†37380 New Hope 681 K11
37134 New Johnsonville 1,824 E8
37820 New Market 1,216 O8
37821 Newport⊙ 7,580 P9
37825 New Tazewell 1,677 O8
37826 Niota 765 M9
37360 Normandy 118 J10
37828 Norris 1,374 N8
37829 Oakdale 323 M9
†37201 Oak Hill 4,609 H8
38060 Oakland 472 B10
37830 Oak Ridge 27,662 N8
38240 Obion 1,282 C8
37840 Oliver Springs 3,659 N8
37841 Oneida 3,717 N7
37363 Ooltewah 950 M10
†37660 Orebank 1,284 R7
37141 Orlinda 382 H7
35740 Orme 181 K10
37365 Palmer 1,027 K10
38242 Paris⊙ 10,728 E8
37843 Parrottsville 118 P8
38363 Parsons 2,422 E9
37143 Pegram 1,081 H8
37144 Petersburg 681 H10
37845 Petros 1,286 M8
37846 Philadelphia 507 M9
37863 Pigeon Forge 1,822 O9
37367 Pikeville⊙ 2,085 L9
†38017 Piperton 746 B10
†37738 Pittman Center 488 P9
38578 Pleasant Hill 371 L9
37148 Portland 4,030 H7
37849 Powell 7,220 N8
†37397 Powells Crossroads 918 L10
38478 Pulaski⊙ 7,184 G10
38251 Puryear 624 E8
38367 Ramer 429 D10
37415 Red Bank 13,299 L10
37150 Red Boiling Springs 1,173 K7
†37641 Rheatown R8
†37380 Richard City 87 K11
38080 Ridgely 1,932 B8
†37401 Ridgeside 417 L10
37152 Ridgetop 1,225 H8
38063 Ripley⊙ 6,366 B9
38253 Rives 386 C8
37687 Roan Mountain 1,108 S8
37853 Rockford 567 O9
37854 Rockwood 5,767 M9
37857 Rogersville⊙ 4,368 P8
38053 Rosemark 950 B10
38066 Rossville 379 B10
37860 Russellville 1,069 P8
38369 Rutherford 1,378 C8
37861 Rutledge⊙ 1,058 P8
38481 Saint Joseph 897 G10
37373 Sale Creek 900 L10
38370 Saltillo 434 E10
38254 Samburg 465 C8
38371 Sardis 301 E10
38067 Saulsbury 156 C10
38372 Savannah⊙ 6,992 E10
38374 Scotts Hill 668 E10
38375 Selmer⊙ 3,979 D10
37862 Sevierville⊙ 4,556 P9
37375 Sewanee 2,298 K10
38255 Sharon 1,134 D8
37160 Shelbyville⊙ 13,530 H10
37376 Sherwood 900 K10
37377 Signal Mountain 5,818 L10
38377 Silerton 100 D10
37165 Slayden 69 G8
37166 Smithville⊙ 3,839 K9
37167 Smyrna 8,839 H9
37869 Sneedville⊙ 1,110 P7
37319 Soddy-Daisy 8,388 L10
38068 Somerville⊙ 2,264 C10
†37030 South Carthage 1,004 K8
†37311 South Cleveland 4,360 M10
†37716 South Clinton 1,671 N8
†42041 South Fulton 2,735 D8
37380 South Pittsburg 3,636 K10
37171 Southside 800 G8
38583 Sparta⊙ 4,864 K9
38585 Spencer⊙ 1,126 L9
37381 Spring City 1,951 M9
37172 Springfield⊙ 10,814 H8
37174 Spring Hill 989 H9
38069 Stanton 540 C10
38379 Stantonville 271 E10
†37660 Sullivan Gardens 2,513 R8
38483 Summertown 850 G10
37873 Surgoinsville 1,536 R8
37874 Sweetwater 4,725 N9
37877 Talbott 975 P8
37879 Tazewell⊙ 2,090 O8
37385 Tellico Plains 698 N10
37178 Tennessee Ridge 1,325 F8
38079 Tiptonville⊙ 2,438 B8
38381 Toone 355 D10
37882 Townsend 351 O9
37387 Tracy City 1,356 K10
38382 Trenton⊙ 4,601 D9
38258 Trezevant 921 D8
38259 Trimble 722 C8
38260 Troy 1,093 C8
37388 Tullahoma 15,800 J10
37743 Tusculum 1,242 R8
38261 Union City⊙ 10,436 C8
37181 Vanleer 401 G8
†37397 Victoria 800 K10
37394 Viola 149 K9

(continued on following page)

Topography

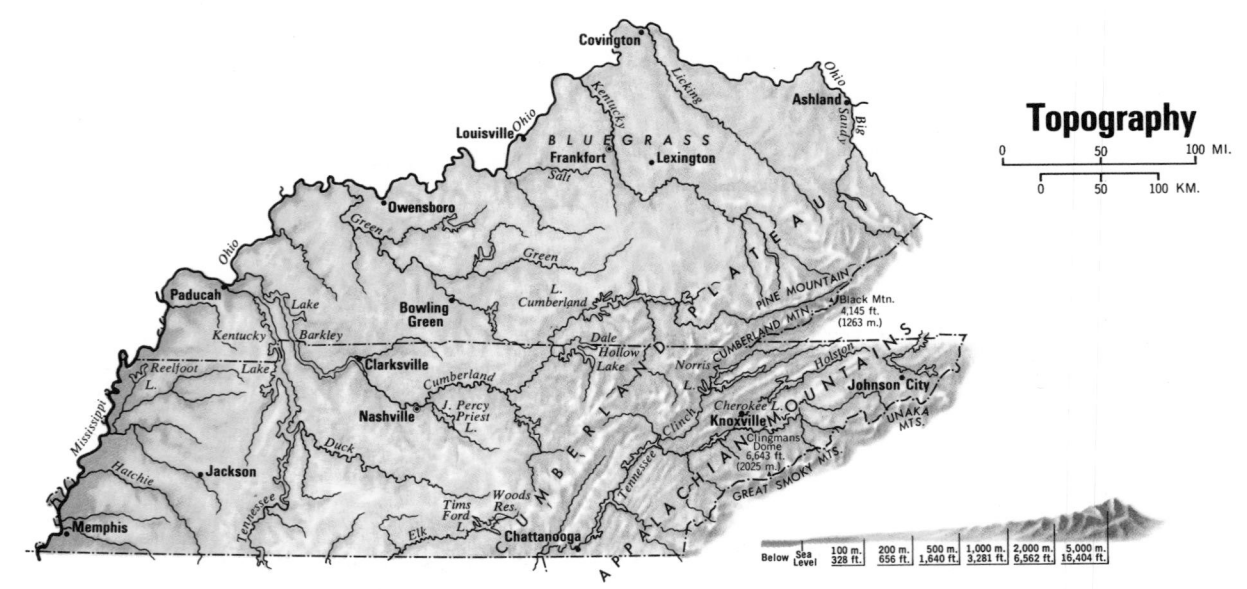

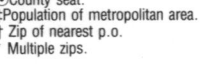

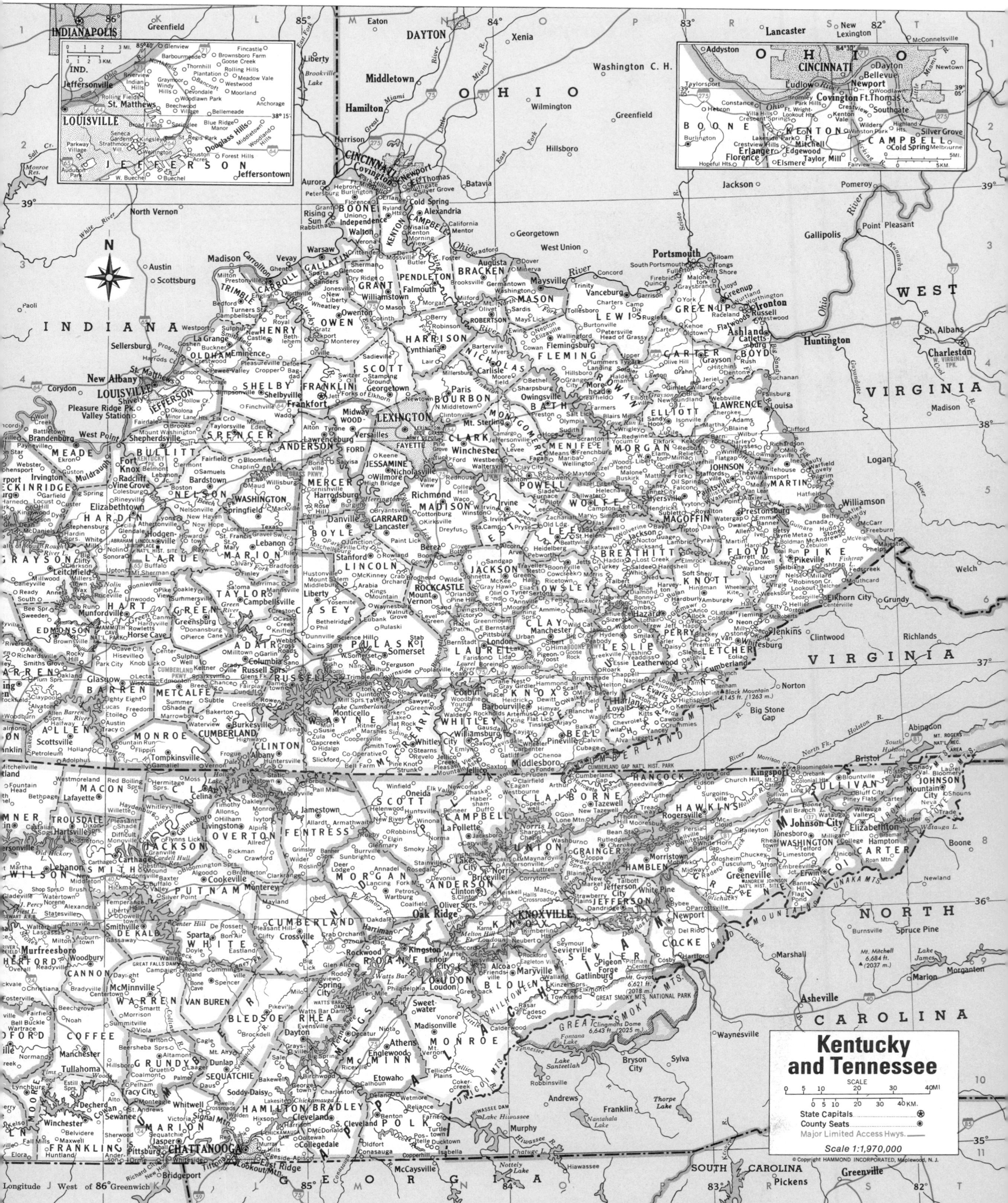
Kentucky and Tennessee
SCALE
0 5 10 20 30 40 MI.
0 5 10 20 30 40 KM.
State Capitals
County Seats
Major Limited Access Hwys.
Scale 1:1,970,000
© Copyright HAMMOND INCORPORATED, Maplewood, N. J.
INDIANA
OHIO
WEST VIRGINIA
VIRGINIA
NORTH CAROLINA
SOUTH CAROLINA
GEORGIA
Longitude West of 86° Greenwich

Topography

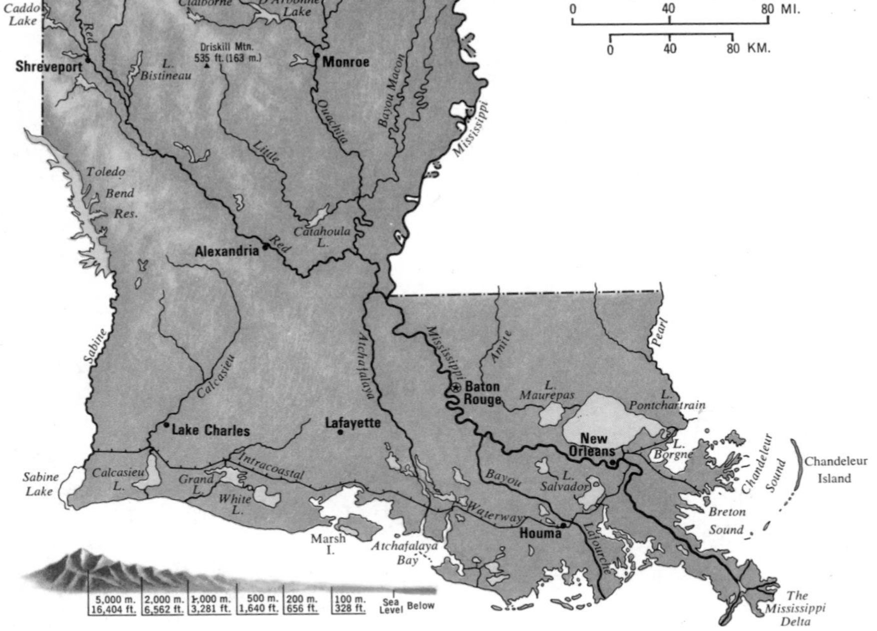

PARISHES

Name/Pop.	Key
Acadia 56,427	F6
Allen 21,390	E5
Ascension 50,068	J6
Assumption 22,084	H7
Avoyelles 41,393	G4
Beauregard 29,692	D5
Bienville 16,387	D2
Bossier 80,721	C1
Caddo 252,358	C1
Calcasieu 167,223	D6
Caldwell 10,761	F2
Cameron 9,336	D7
Catahoula 12,287	G3
Claiborne 17,095	D1
Concordia 22,981	G4
De Soto 25,727	C2
East Baton Rouge 366,191	K1
East Carroll 11,772	H1
East Feliciana 19,015	H5
Evangeline 33,343	F5
Franklin 24,141	G2
Grant 16,703	E3
Iberia 63,752	G7
Iberville 32,159	H6
Jackson 17,321	E2
Jefferson 454,592	K7
Jefferson Davis 32,168	E6
Lafayette 150,017	F6
Lafourche 82,483	K7
La Salle 17,004	F3
Lincoln 39,763	E1
Livingston 58,806	L2
Madison 15,975	H2
Morehouse 34,803	G1
Natchitoches 39,863	D3
Orleans 557,515	L6
Ouachita 139,241	F2
Plaquemines 26,049	L8
Pointe Coupee 24,045	G5
Rapides 135,282	E4
Red River 10,433	D2
Richland 22,187	G2
Sabine 25,280	C3
Saint Bernard 64,097	L7
Saint Charles 37,259	K7
Saint Helena 9,827	J5
Saint James 21,495	L3
Saint John the Baptist 31,924	M3
Saint Landry 84,128	F5
Saint Martin 40,214	G6
Saint Mary 64,253	H7
Saint Tammany 110,869	L6
Tangipahoa 80,698	K5
Tensas 8,525	H2
Terrebonne 94,393	J8
Union 21,167	F1
Vermilion 48,458	F7
Vernon 53,475	D4
Washington 44,207	K5
Webster 43,631	D1
West Baton Rouge 19,086	H6
West Carroll 12,922	H1
West Feliciana 12,186	H5
Winn 17,253	E3

CITIES and TOWNS

Zip	*Name/Pop.*	*Key*
70510	Abbeville⊙ 12,391	F7
70420	Abita Springs 1,072	L6
71316	Acme 235	G4
70710	Addis 1,320	J2
71401	Aimwell 55	G3
70421	Akers 150	N2
70711	Albany 857	M1
71301	Alexandria⊙ 51,565	E4
	Alexandria‡ 151,985	E4
†70458	Alton 500	L6
70340	Amelia 3,617	H7
70422	Amite⊙ 4,301	K5
71403	Anacoco 820	D4
70426	Angie 311	L5
70712	Angola 600	G5
70032	Arabi 10,248	P4
71001	Arcadia⊙ 3,403	E1
71218	Archibald 425	G2
70512	Arnaudville 1,679	G6
71002	Ashland 307	D2
71003	Athens 419	E1
71404	Atlanta 127	E3
70513	Avery Island 500	G7
70714	Baker 12,865	K1
70514	Baldwin 2,644	H7
71405	Ball 3,405	F4
†70401	Baptist 150	M1
70036	Barataria 1,123	K7
70515	Basile 2,635	E5
71219	Baskin 286	G2
71220	Bastrop⊙ 15,527	G1
70715	Batchelor 500	G5
*70801	Baton Rouge (cap.)⊙ 219,419	K2
	Baton Rouge‡ 493,973	K2
†70360	Bayou Cane 15,723	J7
†70380	Bayou Vista 5,805	H7
71004	Belcher 436	C1
70630	Bell City 400	D6
70037	Belle Chasse 5,412	O4
71406	Belmont 350	C3
71407	Bentley 120	E3
71006	Benton⊙ 1,864	C1
†70558	Bermuda 50	D3
71222	Bernice 1,956	E1
70342	Berwick 4,466	H7
71007	Bethany 300	B2
71008	Bienville 249	D2
71009	Blanchard 1,128	C1
70427	Bogalusa 16,976	L5
†71064	Bolinger 200	C1
71223	Bonita 503	G1
71320	Bordelonville 350	G4
*71111	Bossier City 50,817	C1
70343	Bourg 2,073	J7
71409	Boyce 1,198	E4
70040	Braithwaite 350	P4
70516	Branch 200	F6
70517	Breaux Bridge 5,922	G6
70718	Brittany 475	L3
70518	Broussard 2,923	F6
70719	Brusly 1,762	J2
71014	Bryceland 94	E2
71321	Buckeye 280	F4
71322	Bunkie 5,364	F5
70041	Buras-Triumph 4,137	L8
70519	Cade 175	G6
71225	Calhoun 350	F2
71410	Calvin 263	E3
70631	Cameron⊙ 1,736	D7
71411	Campti 1,069	D3
†70584	Cankton 303	F6
70520	Carencro 3,712	G6
70042	Carlisle 975	L7
70721	Carville 1,037	K3
71015	Caspiana 50	C2
71016	Castor 195	D2
70522	Centerville 600	H7
70043	Chalmette⊙ 33,847	P4
†70767	Chamberlin 20	J1
71324	Chase 200	G2
70524	Chataignier 431	F5
71226	Chatham 714	F2
70344	Chauvin 3,338	J8
71325	Cheneyville 865	F4
71412	Chopin 175	E4
71227	Choudrant 809	F1
70525	Church Point 4,599	F6
71414	Clarence 612	E3
71415	Clarks 931	F2
71326	Clayton 1,204	H3
70722	Clinton⊙ 1,919	J5
71416	Cloutierville 100	E3
71417	Colfax⊙ 1,680	E3
71229	Collinston 439	G1
71418	Columbia⊙ 687	F2
70723	Convent⊙ 400	L3
71419	Converse 449	C3
†71107	Cooper Road	C1
71327	Cottonport 1,911	F5
71018	Cotton Valley 1,445	D1
71019	Coushatta⊙ 2,084	D2
70433	Covington⊙ 7,892	K5
†70510	Cow Island 200	F7
†70656	Cravens 200	E5
71020	Creston 135	E3
70526	Crowley⊙ 16,036	F6
71230	Crowville 400	G2
71021	Cullen 1,869	D1
70345	Cut Off 5,049	K7
71420	Cypress 55	D3
70046	Davant 600	L7
70528	Delcambre 2,216	G7
71232	Delhi 3,290	H2
71233	Delta 295	J2
70726	Denham Springs 8,563	L2
70633	De Quincy 3,966	D6
70634	De Ridder⊙ 11,057	D5
71421	Derry 75	E3
70030	Des Allemands 2,920	N4
70047	Destrehan 2,382	N4
†71055	Dixie Inn 453	D1
71422	Dodson 469	E2
70346	Donaldsonville⊙ 7,901	K3
70352	Donner 500	J7
71234	Downsville 213	F1
71023	Doyline 801	D1
70637	Dry Creek 300	D5
71423	Dry Prong 526	E3
71235	Dubach 1,161	E1
71024	Dubberly 421	D1
70353	Dulac 675	J8
71236	Dunn 225	G2
70728	Duplessis 500	K2
70529	Duson 1,253	F6
†71247	East Hodge 439	E2
71025	East Point 100	D2
71330	Echo 525	F4
70049	Edgard⊙ 400	M3
†71019	Edgefield 312	D2
71331	Effie 300	F4
70638	Elizabeth 454	E5
71424	Elmer 200	E4
71051	Elm Grove 100	C2
70532	Elton 1,450	E6
71425	Enterprise 375	G3
71332	Eola 47	F5
71237	Epps 672	G1
70533	Erath 2,133	F7
71238	Eros 158	F2
70534	Estherwood 691	F6
70730	Ethel 250	H5
70535	Eunice 12,479	F6
70639	Evans 500	D5
71333	Evergreen 272	F5
71240	Fairbanks 300	F1
71241	Farmerville⊙ 3,768	F1
70640	Fenton 491	E6

(continued)

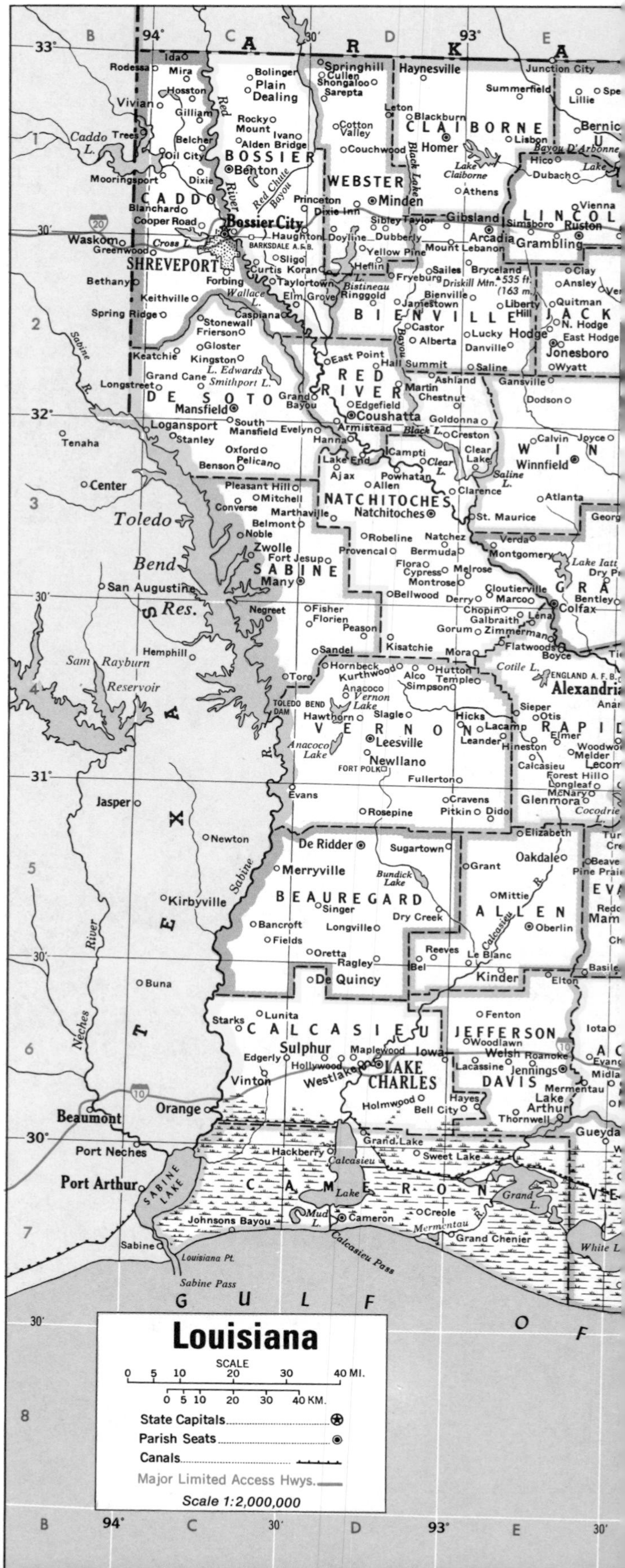

AREA 47,752 sq. mi. (123,678 sq. km.)
POPULATION 4,206,312
CAPITAL Baton Rouge
LARGEST CITY New Orleans
HIGHEST POINT Driskill Mtn. 535 ft. (163 m.)
SETTLED IN 1699
ADMITTED TO UNION April 30, 1812
POPULAR NAME Pelican State
STATE FLOWER Magnolia
STATE BIRD Eastern Brown Pelican

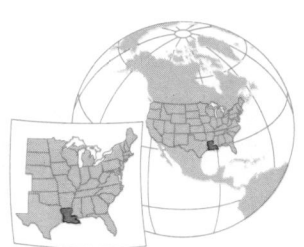

New Orleans, Baton Rouge and Vicinity

© Copyright HAMMOND INCORPORATED, Maplewood, N.J.

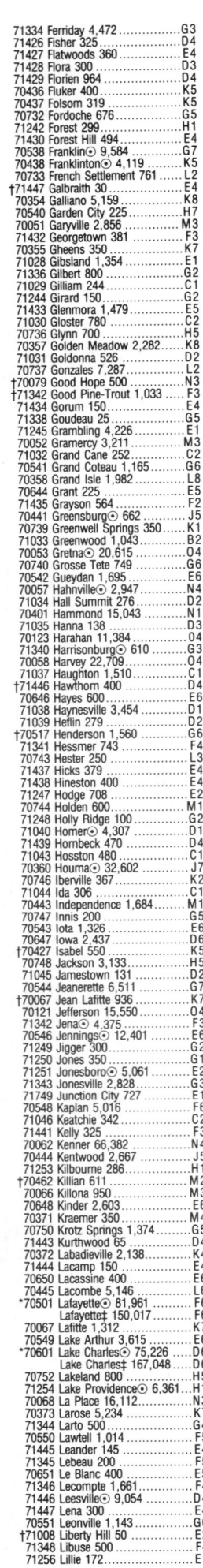

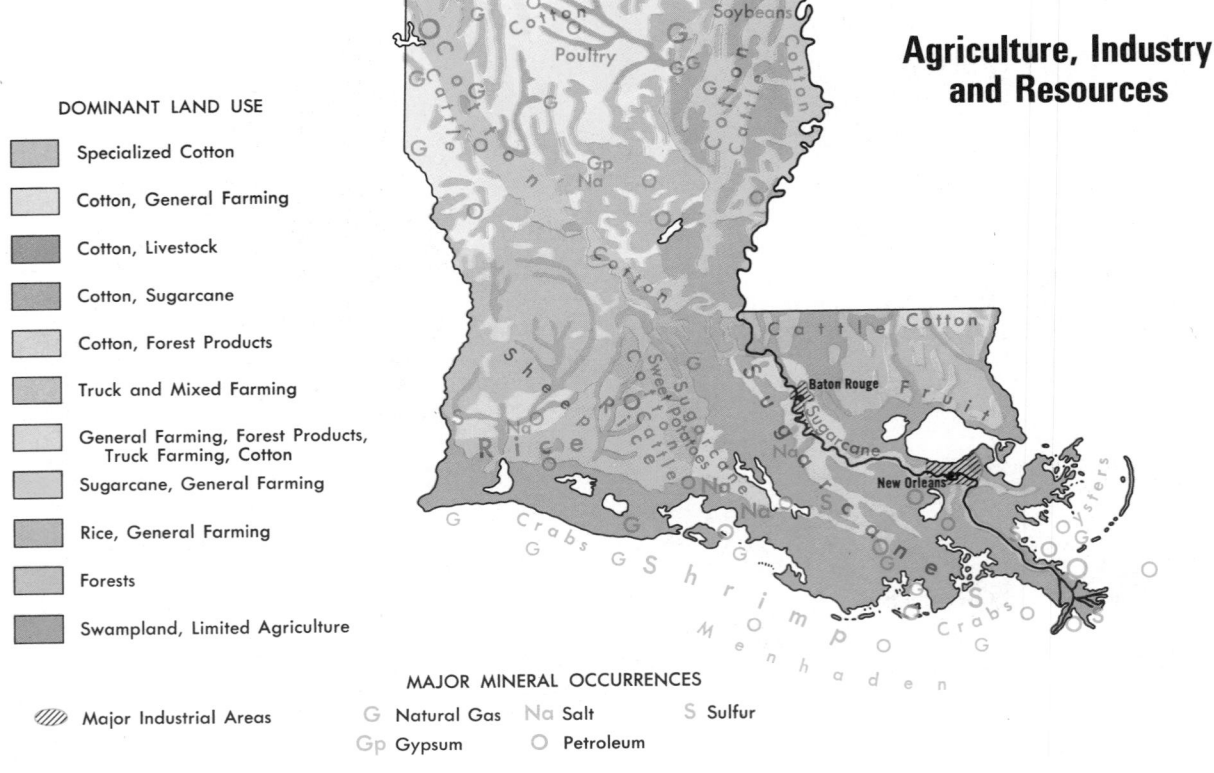

Agriculture, Industry and Resources

DOMINANT LAND USE

- Specialized Cotton
- Cotton, General Farming
- Cotton, Livestock
- Cotton, Sugarcane
- Cotton, Forest Products
- Truck and Mixed Farming
- General Farming, Forest Products, Truck Farming, Cotton
- Sugarcane, General Farming
- Rice, General Farming
- Forests
- Swampland, Limited Agriculture

///// Major Industrial Areas

MAJOR MINERAL OCCURRENCES

G Natural Gas   Na Salt   S Sulfur
Gp Gypsum   O Petroleum

AREA 33,265 sq. mi. (86,156 sq. km.)
POPULATION 1,125,027
CAPITAL Augusta
LARGEST CITY Portland
HIGHEST POINT Katahdin 5,268 ft. (1606 m.)
SETTLED IN 1624
ADMITTED TO UNION March 15, 1820
POPULAR NAME Pine Tree State
STATE FLOWER White Pine Cone & Tassel
STATE BIRD Chickadee

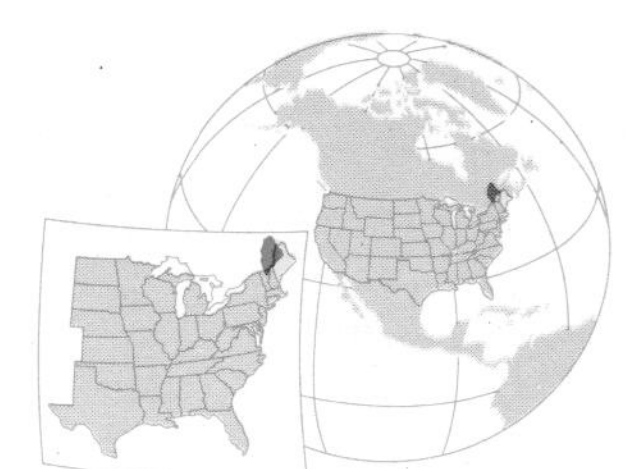

COUNTIES

Androscoggin 99,657 .... C7
Aroostook 91,331 .... F2
Cumberland 215,789 .... C8
Franklin 27,098 .... B5
Hancock 41,781 .... G6
Kennebec 109,889 .... D7
Knox 32,941 .... E7
Lincoln 25,691 .... D7
Oxford 48,968 .... B7
Penobscot 137,015 .... F5
Piscataquis 17,634 .... E4
Sagadahoc 28,795 .... D7
Somerset 45,028 .... C4
Waldo 28,414 .... E6
Washington 34,963 .... H6
York 139,666 .... B9

CITIES and TOWNS

Zip *Name/Pop.* *Key*

04406 Abbot Village○ 576 .... D5
04001 Acton○ 1,228 .... B8
04606 Addison○ 1,061 .... H6
†04610 Alexander○ 385 .... H5
04002 Alfred○ 1,890 .... B9
†04774 Allagash○ 448 .... F1
†04938 Allens Mills 100 .... C6
04535 Alna○ 425 .... D7
†04468 Alton○ 468 .... F5
†04408 Amherst○ 203 .... G6
04216 Andover○ 850 .... B6
04911 Anson○ 2,226 .... D6
†04862 Appleton○ 818 .... E7
†04468 Argyle 225 .... F5
04732 Ashland○ 1,865 .... G2
04607 Ashville 36 .... G7
04912 Athens○ 802 .... D6
†04426 Atkinson○ 306 .... E5
04608 Atlantic 120 .... G7
04210 Auburn⊙ 23,128 .... C7
04330 Augusta (cap.)⊙ 21,819 ... D7
04408 Aurora○ 110 .... G6
04003 Bailey Island 500 .... C8
†04497 Bancroft○ 61 .... H4
04401 Bangor⊙ 31,643 .... F6
Bangor‡ 83,919 .... F6
04609 Bar Harbor○ 4,124 .... G7
04609 Bar Harbor 2,685 .... G7
†04619 Baring○ 308 .... J5
04004 Bar Mills 800 .... C8
04653 Bass Harbor 450 .... G7
04530 Bath⊙ 10,246 .... D8
†04915 Bayside F7
04611 Beals○ 695 .... H7
†04622 Beddington○ 36 .... H6
04915 Belfast⊙ 6,243 .... F7
04917 Belgrade○ 2,043 .... D7
†04915 Belmont○ 520 .... E7
04733 Benedicta○ 225 .... G4
†04937 Benton○ 2,188 .... D6
03901 Berwick○ 4,149 .... B9
03901 Berwick 2,378 .... B9
04217 Bethel○ 2,340 .... B7
04005 Biddeford 19,638 .... B9
04920 Bingham○ 1,184 .... D5
04920 Bingham 1,074 .... D5
04613 Birch Harbor 300 .... H7
04734 Blaine○ 922 .... H2
04734 Blaine-Mars Hill 1,921 ...... H2
04614 Blue Hill○ 1,644 .... F7
04615 Blue Hill Falls 135 .... F7
04537 Boothbay○ 2,308 .... D8
04538 Boothbay Harbor 2,207 ..... D8
04008 Bowdoinham○ 1,828 .... D7
†04481 Bowerbank○ 27 .... E5
04410 Bradford○ 888 .... F5
†04410 Bradford Center 105 .... F5
04411 Bradley○ 1,149 .... F6
04412 Brewer 9,017 .... F6
04735 Bridgewater○ 742 .... H3
04009 Bridgton○ 3,528 .... B7
04009 Bridgton 1,639 .... B7
†04990 Brighton○ 74 .... D5
04539 Bristol○ 2,095 .... D8
04616 Brooklin○ 619 .... F7
04921 Brooks○ 804 .... E6
04617 Brooksville○ 753 .... F7
04413 Brookton 175 .... H4
04010 Brownfield○ 767 .... B8
04414 Brownville○ 1,545 .... E5
04011 Brunswick○ 17,366 .... C8
04011 Brunswick 10,990 .... C8
04219 Bryant Pond 600 .... B7
†04232 Buckfield○ 1,333 .... C7
04618 Bucks Harbor 300 .... J6
04416 Bucksport○ 4,345 .... F6
04416 Bucksport 2,853 .... F6
04540 Burkettville 120 .... E7
04417 Burlington○ 322 .... G5
04922 Burnham○ 951 .... E6
†04093 Buxton○ 5,775 .... C8
†04275 Byron○ 114 .... B6
04619 Calais 4,262 .... J5
04923 Cambridge○ 445 .... E5
04843 Camden○ 4,584 .... F7
04843 Camden 3,743 .... F7
04924 Canaan○ 1,189 .... D6
04221 Canton○ 831 .... C7
03902 Cape Neddick 850 .... B9
04014 Cape Porpoise 500 .... C9
04736 Caribou 9,916 .... G2
04419 Carmel○ 1,695 .... E6
†04947 Carrabassett Valley○ 107 ... C5
†04487 Carroll○ 175 .... G5
†04224 Carthage○ 438 .... C6
†04465 Cary○ 229 .... H4
04015 Casco○ 2,243 .... B7
04421 Castine○ 1,304 .... F7
†04941 Center Montville 16 .... E7
†04623 Centerville○ 28 .... H6
†04757 Chapman○ 406 .... G2
04422 Charleston○ 1,037 .... F5
†04666 Charlotte○ 300 .... J5
04017 Chebeague Island 900 ...... C8
†04345 Chelsea○ 2,522 .... D7
04622 Cherryfield○ 983 .... H6
†04458 Chester○ 434 .... F5
†04938 Chesterville○ 869 .... C6
†04478 Chesuncook 6 .... D3
04926 China○ 2,918 .... E7
†04239 Chisholm 1,796 .... C7
†04428 Clifton○ 462 .... G6
04927 Clinton○ 2,696 .... D6
04927 Clinton 1,305 .... D6
†04623 Columbia○ 275 .... H6
04623 Columbia Falls○ 517 .... H6
†04638 Cooper○ 105 .... H6
04624 Corea 375 .... H7
04928 Corinna○ 1,887 .... E6
04020 Cornish○ 1,047 .... B8
†04976 Cornville○ 838 .... D6
04625 Cranberry Isles○ 198 .... G7
†04610 Crawford○ 86 .... H5
†04015 Crescent Lake 325 .... C7
†04851 Criehaven 5 .... F8
04738 Crouseville 450 .... G2
†04747 Crystal○ 349 .... G4
04021 Cumberland Center○ 5,284 . C8
04021 Cumberland Center 2,015 .. C8
04563 Cushing○ 795 .... E7
04626 Cutler○ 726 .... J6
04543 Damariscotta○ 1,493 .... E7
04543 Damariscotta-Newcastle
1,411 .... E7
04424 Danforth○ 826 .... H4
†04622 Deblois○ 44 .... H6
†04429 Dedham○ 841 .... F6
04627 Deer Isle○ 1,492 .... F7
04022 Denmark○ 672 .... B8
04628 Dennysville○ 296 .... J6
04929 Detroit○ 744 .... E6
04930 Dexter○ 4,286 .... E5
04930 Dexter 3,118 .... E5
04224 Dixfield○ 2,389 .... C6
04224 Dixfield 1,725 .... C6
04932 Dixmont○ 812 .... E6
04426 Dover-Foxcroft○ 4,323 ...... E5
04426 Dover-Foxcroft⊙ 2,974 ...... E5
†04426 Dover South Mills 54 .... E5
04342 Dresden○ 998 .... D7
†04747 Dyer Brook○ 275 .... G3
04739 Eagle Lake○ 1,019 .... F1
04226 East Andover 250 .... B6
04544 East Boothbay 800 .... D8
04427 East Corinth 525 .... F5
04227 East Dixfield 250 .... C6
04429 East Holden 600 .... F6
04027 East Lebanon 950 .... B9
04228 East Livermore 500 .... C7
04630 East Machias○ 1,233 .... J6
04430 East Millinocket○ 2,372 ...... F4
04430 East Millinocket 2,361 ...... F4
04740 Easton○ 1,305 .... H2
04028 East Parsonfield 400 .... B8
04229 East Peru 200 .... C7
†04210 East Poland 200 .... C7
04631 Eastport 1,982 .... K6
04231 East Stoneham 300 .... B7
†04607 East Sullivan 495 .... G6
†04220 East Sumner 120 .... C7
†04862 East Union 75 .... E7
†04428 Eddington○ 1,769 .... F6
†04556 Edgecomb○ 841 .... D8
03903 Eliot○ 4,948 .... B9
04605 Ellsworth⊙ 5,179 .... F6
04031 Emery Mills 100 .... B8
04433 Enfield○ 1,397 .... F5
04434 Etna○ 758 .... E6
04936 Eustis○ 582 .... B5
04435 Exeter○ 823 .... E6
†04938 Fairbanks 400 .... C6
04937 Fairfield○ 6,113 .... D6
04937 Fairfield 3,169 .... D6
04105 Falmouth○ 6,853 .... C8
04105 Falmouth 1,655 .... C8
†04345 Farmingdale○ 2,535 .... D7
†04345 Farmingdale 2,014 .... D7
04938 Farmington○ 6,730 .... C6
04938 Farmington⊙ 3,583 .... C6
04940 Farmington Falls 500 .... C6
†04349 Fayette○ 812 .... C7
04546 Five Islands 225 .... D8
04742 Fort Fairfield○ 4,376 .... H2
04742 Fort Fairfield 2,282 .... H2
04743 Fort Kent○ 4,826 .... F1
04743 Fort Kent 2,375 .... F1
04744 Fort Kent Mills 200 .... F1
04438 Frankfort○ 783 .... F6
04634 Franklin○ 979 .... G6
04941 Freedom○ 458 .... E7
04032 Freeport○ 5,863 .... C8
04032 Freeport 1,906 .... C8
04635 Frenchboro○ 43 .... G7
04745 Frenchville○ 1,450 .... G1
04547 Friendship○ 1,000 .... E7
04037 Fryeburg○ 2,715 .... A7
04037 Fryeburg 1,644 .... A7
04345 Gardiner 6,485 .... D7
04939 Garland○ 718 .... E5
04548 Georgetown○ 735 .... D8
†04217 Gilead○ 191 .... B7
†04401 Glenburn○ 2,319 .... F6
04846 Glen Cove 250 .... E7
04038 Gorham○ 10,101 .... C8
04038 Gorham 4,052 .... C8
†04607 Gouldsboro○ 1,574 .... H7
04746 Grand Isle○ 719 .... G1
04637 Grand Lake Stream○ 198 ... H5
04039 Gray○ 4,344 .... C8
†04408 Great Pond○ 45 .... G6
04236 Greene○ 3,037 .... C7
04441 Greenville○ 1,839 .... D5
04441 Greenville 1,640 .... D5
04442 Greenville Junction 650 ..... D5
04443 Guilford○ 1,793 .... E5
04443 Guilford 1,235 .... E5
04347 Hallowell 2,502 .... D7
†04785 Hamlin○ 340 .... H1
04444 Hampden○ 5,250 .... F6
04444 Hampden 3,538 .... F6
04445 Hampden Highlands 950 ... F6
04640 Hancock○ 1,409 .... G6
04237 Hanover○ 256 .... B7
04942 Harmony○ 755 .... D6
†04011 Harpswell○ 3,796 .... D8
04643 Harrington○ 859 .... H6
04040 Harrison○ 1,667 .... B7
†04221 Hartford○ 480 .... C7
04943 Hartland○ 1,669 .... D6
04943 Hartland 1,041 .... D6
04446 Haynesville○ 169 .... G4
04238 Hebron○ 665 .... C7
†04401 Hermon○ 3,170 .... F6
04944 Hinckley 140 .... D6
04041 Hiram○ 1,067 .... B8
†04730 Hodgdon○ 1,084 .... H3
04042 Hollis Center○ 2,892 .... B8
04847 Hope○ 730 .... E7
04730 Houlton○ 6,766 .... H3
04730 Houlton⊙ 5,730 .... H3
04448 Howland○ 1,602 .... F5
04448 Howland 1,502 .... F5
04449 Hudson○ 797 .... F5
04644 Hulls Cove 200 .... G7
04747 Island Falls○ 981 .... G3
04645 Isle Au Haut○ 57 .... F7
04848 Islesboro○ 521 .... F7
04945 Jackman○ 1,003 .... C4
†04630 Jacksonville 200 .... J6
04239 Jay○ 5,080 .... C7
04348 Jefferson○ 1,616 .... D7
04648 Jonesboro○ 553 .... J6
04649 Jonesport○ 1,512 .... H6
04649 Jonesport 1,050 .... H6
04450 Kenduskeag○ 1,210 .... E6
04043 Kennebunk○ 6,621 .... B9
04043 Kennebunk 3,294 .... B9
†04043 Kennebunk Beach 200 ...... C9
04046 Kennebunkport○ 2,952 ...... C9
04046 Kennebunkport 1,685 .... C9
04349 Kents Hill 300 .... D7
04947 Kingfield○ 1,083 .... C6
04451 Kingman 281 .... G4
†04990 Kingsbury○ 4 .... D5
03904 Kittery○ 9,314 .... B9
03904 Kittery 5,465 .... B9
03905 Kittery Point 1,260 .... B9
†04986 Knox○ 558 .... E6
04453 La Grange○ 509 .... F5
†04463 Lake View○ 20 .... F5
†04605 Lamoine○ 953 .... G7
04455 Lee○ 688 .... G5
†04263 Leeds○ 1,463 .... C7
04456 Levant○ 1,117 .... F6
04240 Lewiston 40,481 .... C7
Lewiston-Auburn‡ 72,378 . C7
04949 Liberty○ 694 .... E7
04749 Lille 300 .... G1
04048 Limerick○ 1,356 .... B8
04750 Limestone○ 8,719 .... H2
04750 Limestone 1,334 .... H2
04049 Limington○ 2,203 .... B8
04457 Lincoln○ 5,066 .... G5
04457 Lincoln 3,524 .... G5
04849 Lincolnville○ 1,414 .... E7
04850 Lincolnville Center 200 ...... E7
†04730 Linneus○ 752 .... H3
04250 Lisbon○ 8,769 .... C7
04250 Lisbon-Lisbon
Center 1,865 .... C7
04252 Lisbon Falls 4,370 .... D7
04350 Litchfield○ 1,954 .... D7
†04627 Little Deer Isle 475 .... F7
04082 Little Falls-South
Windham 1,366 .... C8
†04760 Littleton○ 1,009 .... H3
04253 Livermore○ 1,826 .... C7
04254 Livermore Falls○ 3,572 ..... C7
04254 Livermore Falls 2,441 ...... C7
04255 Locke Mills 600 .... B7
04051 Lovell○ 767 .... B7
†04433 Lowell○ 194 .... F5
04652 Lubec○ 2,045 .... K6
†04730 Ludlow○ 403 .... G3
04654 Machias○ 2,458 .... J6
04654 Machias⊙ 1,277 .... J6
04655 Machiasport○ 1,108 .... H6
†04451 Macwahoc○ 126 .... G4
04756 Madawaska○ 5,282 .... G1
04756 Madawaska 4,165 .... G1
04950 Madison○ 4,367 .... D6
04950 Madison 2,788 .... D6
†04966 Madrid○ 178 .... B6
†04942 Mainstream 100 .... D6
04351 Manchester○ 1,949 .... D7
04757 Mapleton○ 1,895 .... G2
04758 Mars Hill○ 1,892 .... H2
04758 Mars Hill-Blaine 1,921 ...... H2
04759 Masardis○ 328 .... G3
04851 Matinicus 66 .... F8
04459 Mattawamkeag○ 1,000 ...... G5
04256 Mechanic Falls○ 2,616 ...... C7
04256 Mechanic Falls 2,198 .... C7
04657 Meddybemps○ 110 .... J5
†04453 Medford○ 163 .... F5
†04453 Medford Center 100 .... F5
04460 Medway○ 1,871 .... G4
04957 Mercer○ 448 .... D6
04257 Mexico○ 3,698 .... B6
04257 Mexico 3,207 .... B6
†04216 Middledam 10 .... B6
04658 Milbridge○ 1,306 .... H6
04461 Milford○ 2,160 .... F6
04461 Milford 1,688 .... F6
04462 Millinocket○ 7,567 .... F4

(continued on following page)

Agriculture, Industry and Resources

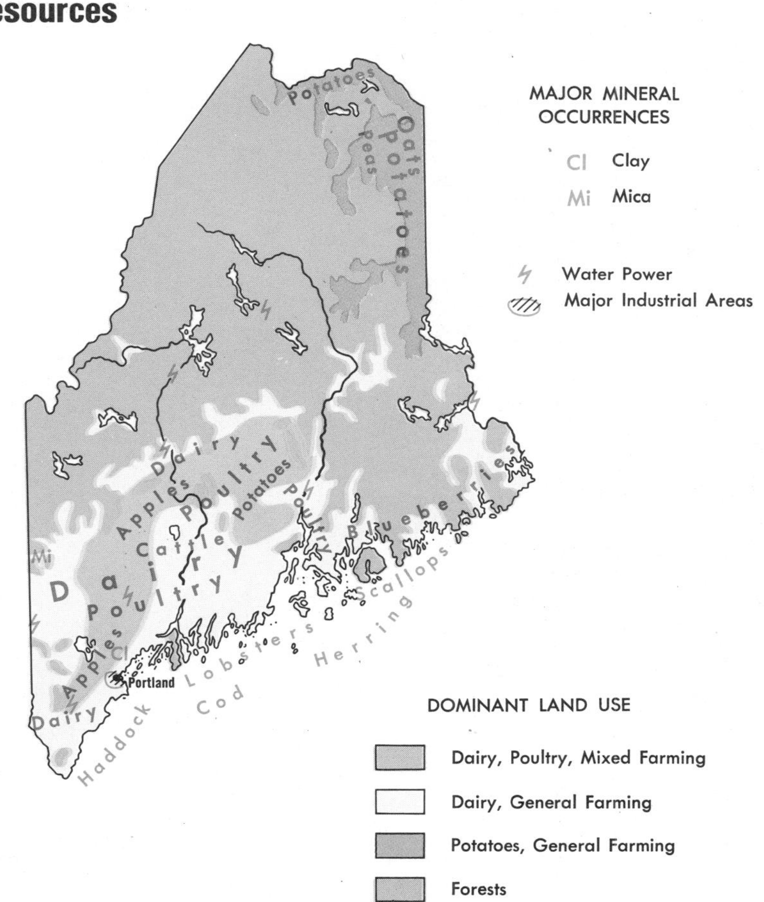

Potatoes
Oats
Peas
Potatoes
Dairy
Poultry
Potatoes
Apples
Cattle
Dairy
Poultry
Blueberries
Scallops
Lobsters
Herring
Cod
Haddock
Portland
Apples
Dairy
Mi
Cl
MAJOR MINERAL OCCURRENCES
Cl Clay
Mi Mica
Water Power
Major Industrial Areas
DOMINANT LAND USE
Dairy, Poultry, Mixed Farming
Dairy, General Farming
Potatoes, General Farming
Forests

04463 Milo○ 2,624 .... F5
04463 Milo 2,255 .... F5
04258 Minot○ 1,631 .... C7
04659 Minturn 150 .... G7
†04776 Monarda 100 .... G4
04852 Monhegan○ 109 .... E8
04259 Monmouth○ 2,888 .... D7
04951 Monroe○ 657 .... E6
04464 Monson○ 804 .... E5
04760 Monticello○ 950 .... H3
†04941 Montville○ 631 .... E7
04054 Moody 500 .... B9
†04478 Moosehead 6 .... D4
†04945 Moose River○ 252 .... C4
04952 Morrill○ 506 .... E7
04660 Mount Desert○ 2,063 .... G7
04352 Mount Vernon○ 1,021 .... D7
04055 Naples○ 1,833 .... B8
04554 Newagen 100 .... D8
†04445 Newburgh○ 1,228 .... F6
04553 Newcastle○ 1,227 .... D7
04553 Newcastle-Damariscotta 1,411 .... E7
04056 Newfield○ 644 .... B8
04260 New Gloucester○ 3,180 .... C8
04554 New Harbor 850 .... E8
04761 New Limerick○ 513 .... G3
04953 Newport○ 2,755 .... E6
04953 Newport 1,748 .... E6
04954 New Portland○ 651 .... C6
04261 Newry○ 235 .... B6
04955 New Sharon○ 969 .... C6
04762 New Sweden○ 737 .... G2
04956 New Vineyard○ 607 .... C6
04555 Nobleboro○ 1,154 .... D7
†04462 Norcross 13 .... F4
04957 Norridgewock○ 2,552 .... D6
04957 Norridgewock 1,318 .... D6
04958 North Anson 950 .... D6
03906 North Berwick○ 2,878 .... B9
03906 North Berwick 1,436 .... B9
04057 North Bridgton 300 .... B7
†04938 North Chesterville 50 .... C6
†04441 North East Carry 2 .... D4
04662 Northeast Harbor 800 .... G7
†04654 Northfield○ 88 .... H6
04853 North Haven○ 373 .... F7
04262 North Jay 800 .... C6
†04254 North Livermore 250 .... C7
04961 North New Portland 500 .... C6
†04476 North Penobscot 246 .... F7
†04849 Northport○ 958 .... E7
†04274 North Raymond 225 .... C8
04266 North Turner 350 .... C7
04962 North Vassalboro 950 .... D7
04267 North Waterford 390 .... B7
04062 North Windham 5,492 .... C8
†04219 North Woodstock 75 .... B7
†04096 North Yarmouth○ 1,919 .... C8
04268 Norway○ 4,042 .... B7
04268 Norway 2,653 .... B7
†04268 Norway Lake 75 .... B7
04763 Oakfield○ 847 .... G3
04963 Oakland○ 5,162 .... D6
04963 Oakland 3,387 .... D6
04063 Ocean Park 200 .... C9
03907 Ogunquit 1,492 .... B9
04064 Old Orchard Beach○ 6,291 .... C9
04064 Old Orchard Beach 6,023 .... C9
04468 Old Town 8,422 .... F6
04964 Oquossoc 150 .... B6
04471 Orient○ 97 .... H4
04472 Orland○ 1,645 .... F6
04473 Orono○ 10,578 .... F6
04473 Orono 9,891 .... F6
04474 Orrington○ 3,244 .... F6
04066 Orrs Island 600 .... D8
†04270 Otisfield○ 897 .... B7
04665 Otter Creek 260 .... G7
04854 Owls Head○ 1,633 .... F7
04764 Oxbow○ 84 .... G3
04270 Oxford○ 3,143 .... B7
04354 Palermo○ 760 .... E7
04965 Palmyra○ 1,485 .... E6
04271 Paris○ 4,168 .... B7
†04443 Parkman○ 621 .... D5
04475 Passadumkeag○ 430 .... F5
04765 Patten○ 1,368 .... F4
04765 Patten 1,057 .... F4
04558 Pemaquid 200 .... E8
04666 Pembroke○ 920 .... J6
04476 Penobscot○ 1,104 .... F7
04766 Perham○ 437 .... G2
04667 Perry○ 737 .... J6
04272 Peru○ 1,564 .... C6
04966 Phillips○ 1,092 .... C6
04562 Phippsburg○ 1,527 .... D8
04967 Pittsfield○ 4,125 .... E6
04967 Pittsfield 3,117 .... E6
†04345 Pittston○ 2,267 .... D7
04767 Plaisted 125 .... F1
†04925 Pleasant Pond 18 .... D5
04969 Plymouth○ 811 .... E6
04273 Poland○ 3,578 .... C7
04562 Popham Beach 40 .... D8
04768 Portage○ 562 .... G2
04855 Port Clyde 400 .... E8
04068 Porter○ 1,222 .... B8
*04101 Portland⊙ 61,572 .... C8
Portland‡ 183,625 .... C8
04069 Pownal○ 1,189 .... C8
†04487 Prentiss○ 205 .... G5
04769 Presque Isle 11,172 .... H2
04668 Princeton○ 994 .... H5
†04981 Prospect○ 511 .... F6
04669 Prospect Harbor 445 .... H7
04770 Quimby 50 .... F2
†04345 Randolph○ 1,834 .... D7
04970 Rangeley○ 1,023 .... B6
04071 Raymond○ 2,251 .... B8
04355 Readfield○ 1,943 .... D7
04357 Richmond○ 2,627 .... D7
04357 Richmond 1,578 .... D7
†04262 Riley 50 .... C6
†04930 Ripley○ 439 .... E5
04671 Robbinston○ 492 .... J5
†04734 Robinsons 160 .... H3
04841 Rockland⊙ 7,919 .... E7
04856 Rockport○ 2,749 .... E7
04478 Rockwood 265 .... D4
†04957 Rome○ 627 .... D6
†04654 Roque Bluffs○ 244 .... H6
04564 Round Pond 400 .... E8
04275 Roxbury○ 373 .... B6
04276 Rumford○ 8,240 .... B6
04276 Rumford 6,256 .... B6
04279 Rumford Point 320 .... B6
04280 Sabattus○ 3,081 .... C7
04280 Sabattus 1,234 .... C7
04072 Saco 12,921 .... C8
04772 Saint Agatha○ 1,035 .... G1
04971 Saint Albans○ 1,400 .... E6
04773 Saint David 915 .... G1
04774 Saint Francis○ 839 .... E1
04857 Saint George○ 1,948 .... E7
†04743 Saint John○ 322 .... F1
†04983 Salem 125 .... C6
†04009 Sandy Creek 132 .... B7
04972 Sandy Point 350 .... F7
04073 Sanford○ 18,020 .... B9
04073 Sanford 10,268 .... B9
04479 Sangerville○ 1,219 .... E5
†04417 Saponac 8 .... G5
04074 Scarborough○ 11,347 .... C8
04074 Scarborough 2,280 .... C8
04674 Seal Cove 215 .... G7
04675 Seal Harbor 500 .... G7
04973 Searsmont○ 782 .... E7
04974 Searsport○ 2,309 .... F7
04974 Searsport 1,348 .... F7
04075 Sebago Lake 800 .... B8
04481 Sebec○ 469 .... E5
04484 Seboeis○ 53 .... F5
†04478 Seboomook 3 .... D4
04676 Sedgwick○ 795 .... F7
04076 Shapleigh○ 1,370 .... B8
04975 Shawmut 500 .... D6
04775 Sheridan 300 .... F2
†04777 Sherman○ 1,021 .... G4
04777 Sherman Station 650 .... F4
04485 Shirley Mills○ 242 .... D5
†04330 Sidney○ 2,052 .... D7
04779 Sinclair 264 .... G1
04976 Skowhegan○ 8,098 .... D6
04976 Skowhegan⊙ 6,517 .... D6
04567 Small Point 22 .... D8
04978 Smithfield○ 748 .... D6
04780 Smyrna Mills○ 354 .... G3
04979 Solon○ 827 .... D6
†04341 Somerville○ 377 .... D7
†04660 Somesville (Mount Desert) 150 .... G7
04677 Sorrento○ 276 .... G7
03908 South Berwick○ 4,046 .... B9
†04009 South Bridgton 373 .... B8
04568 South Bristol○ 800 .... D8
04077 South Casco 750 .... B8
†03903 South Eliot 1,681 .... B9
†04928 South Exeter 100 .... E6
04080 South Hiram 350 .... B8
†04862 South Hope 200 .... E7
†04453 South La Grange 150 .... F5
†04259 South Monmouth 400 .... D7
04281 South Paris⊙ 2,128 .... C7
†04538 Southport○ 598 .... D8
04106 South Portland 22,712 .... C8
04858 South Thomaston○ 1,064 .... E7
†04864 South Union 50 .... E7
04081 South Waterford 300 .... B7
04679 Southwest Harbor○ 1,855 .... G7
04679 Southwest Harbor 1,052 .... G7
04082 South Windham (Little Falls-South Windham 1,366 .... C8
04487 Springfield○ 443 .... G5
04083 Springvale 2,940 .... B9
04782 Stacyville○ 554 .... F4
04084 Standish○ 5,946 .... B8
†04980 Starks○ 440 .... D6
04488 Stetson○ 618 .... E6
04680 Steuben○ 970 .... H6
04489 Stillwater 700 .... F6
04783 Stockholm○ 319 .... G1
04981 Stockton Springs○ 1,230 .... F7
04681 Stonington○ 1,273 .... F7
†04058 Stow○ 186 .... A7
04982 Stratton 600 .... B5
04983 Strong○ 1,506 .... C6
†04689 Sullivan○ 967 .... G6
†04292 Sumner○ 613 .... C7
04232 Sumner-East Sumner C7
04683 Sunset 165 .... F7
†04627 Sunshine 100 .... G7
04684 Surry○ 894 .... F7
04685 Swans Island○ 337 .... G7
†04915 Swanville○ 873 .... E6
†04040 Sweden○ 163 .... B7
04984 Temple○ 518 .... C6
04860 Tenants Harbor 900 .... E8
04861 Thomaston○ 2,900 .... E7
04861 Thomaston 2,348 .... E7
04986 Thorndike○ 603 .... E6
04490 Topsfield○ 240 .... H5
04086 Topsham○ 6,431 .... D8
04086 Topsham 4,657 .... D8
†04653 Tremont○ 1,222 .... G7
†04605 Trenton○ 718 .... G7
04571 Trevett 400 .... D8
04987 Troy○ 701 .... E6
04282 Turner○ 3,539 .... C7
04862 Union○ 1,569 .... E7
04988 Unity○ 1,431 .... E6
†04293 Upper Dam 2 .... B6
04784 Upper Frenchville 405 .... G1
04261 Upton○ 65 .... B6
04785 Van Buren○ 3,557 .... G1
04785 Van Buren 3,282 .... G1
04491 Vanceboro○ 256 .... J4
04989 Vassalboro○ 3,410 .... D7
04401 Veazie○ 1,610 .... F6
04360 Vienna○ 454 .... D6
04863 Vinalhaven○ 1,211 .... F7
04492 Waite○ 130 .... H5
†04915 Waldo○ 495 .... E7
04572 Waldoboro○ 3,985 .... E7
04572 Waldoboro 1,195 .... E7
†04605 Waltham○ 186 .... G6
04864 Warren○ 2,566 .... E7
04786 Washburn○ 2,028 .... G2
04786 Washburn 1,221 .... G2
04574 Washington○ 954 .... E7
04087 Waterboro○ 2,943 .... B8
04088 Waterford○ 951 .... B7
04901 Waterville 17,779 .... D6
04284 Wayne○ 680 .... D7
04285 Weld○ 435 .... C6
04990 Wellington○ 287 .... D5
04090 Wells○ 8,211 .... B9
04686 Wesley○ 140 .... H6
†04530 West Bath○ 1,309 .... D8
04092 Westbrook 14,976 .... C8
04493 West Enfield 609 .... F5
04787 Westfield○ 647 .... G2
†04649 West Jonesport 400 .... H6
04094 West Kennebunk 750 .... B9
†04938 West Mills 75 .... C6
04288 West Minot 400 .... C7
04095 West Newfield 300 .... B8
04424 Weston○ 155 .... H4
04289 West Paris○ 1,390 .... B7
04290 West Peru 700 .... C7
04291 West Poland 250 .... C7
04074 West Scarborough 500 .... C8
04690 West Tremont 250 .... G7
04362 Whitefield○ 1,606 .... D7
04691 Whiting○ 335 .... J6
04692 Whitneyville○ 264 .... H6
†04443 Willimantic○ 164 .... E5
04293 Wilsons Mills 50 .... B6
04294 Wilton○ 4,382 .... C6
04294 Wilton 2,262 .... C6
04363 Windsor○ 1,702 .... D7
04495 Winn○ 503 .... G5
†04901 Winslow○ 8,057 .... D6
†04901 Winslow 5,903 .... D6
04693 Winter Harbor○ 1,120 .... G7
04496 Winterport○ 2,675 .... F6
04496 Winterport 1,126 .... F6
04788 Winterville○ 235 .... F2
04364 Winthrop○ 5,889 .... C7
04364 Winthrop 3,264 .... C7
04578 Wiscasset○ 2,832 .... D7
04694 Woodland○ 1,363 .... H5
04579 Woolwich○ 2,156 .... D8
04497 Wytopitlock 130 .... G4
04096 Yarmouth○ 6,585 .... C8
04096 Yarmouth 2,981 .... C8
03909 York○ 8,465 .... B9
03909 York 4,530 .... B9
03910 York Beach 900 .... B9
03911 York Harbor 950 .... B9

OTHER FEATURES

Abraham (mt.) C5
Acadia Nat'l Park G7
Allagash (lake) D3
Allagash (riv.) E2
Androscoggin (riv.) C7
Aroostook (riv.) G2
Atteam (pond) C4
Baker (lake) D3
Baskahegan (lake) H5
Bear (riv.) B6
Big (brook) E2
Big (lake) H5
Big Black (riv.) D2
Bigelow (bight) C9
Big Spencer (mt.) E4
Black (pond) D3
Blue (mt.) C6
Blue Hill (bay) G7
Bog (lake) H6
Brassua (lake) D4
Casco (bay) C8
Cathance (lake) J6
Caucomgomoc (lake) D3
Center (pond) E5
Chamberlain (lake) E3
Chemquasabamticook (lake) D3
Chesuncook (lake) E3
Chiputneticook (lakes) H4
Clayton (lake) D2
Clifford (lake) H5
Cold Stream (pond) G5
Crawford (lake) H5
Cross (isl.) J6
Cross (lake) G1
Cupsuptic (riv.) B5
Dead (riv.) C5
Deer (isl.) F7
Duck (isls.) G7
Eagle (lake) E3
Eagle (lake) F1
East Machias (riv.) H6
East Musquash (lake) H5
Elizabeth (cape) C8
Ellis (pond) B6
Ellis (riv.) B6
Embden (pond) D6
Endless (lake) F5
Englishman (bay) J6
Eskutassis (pond) G5
Fifth (lake) H5
Fish (riv.) F2
Fish River (lake) F2
Flagstaff (lake) C5
Fourth (lake) H5
Frenchman (bay) G7
Gardner (lake) J6
Georges (isls.) E8
Graham (lake) G6
Grand (lake) H4
Grand Falls (lake) H5
Grand Lake Seboeis (lake) F3
Grand Manan (chan.) K6
Great Moose (lake) D6
Great Wass (isl.) J7
Green (isl.) F8
Harrington (lake) E4
Haut (isl.) G7
Indian Pond (lake) D4
Islesboro (isl.) F7
Jo-Mary (lakes) E4
Katahdin (mt.) F4
Kennebec (riv.) D7
Kezar (lake) B7
Kezar (pond) B7
Kingsbury (pond) D5
Little Black (riv.) E1
Little Madawaska (riv.) G2
Lobster (lake) E4
Long (lake) B7
Long (lake) E2
Long (lake) G1
Long (pond) C4
Long (pond) D6
Long (pond) E5
Long Falls (dam) C5
Longfellow (mts.) B6
Loon (lake) D3
Loring A.F.B. 6,572 .... H2
Lower Roach (pond) E4
Lower Sysladobsis (lake) G5
Machias (bay) J6
Machias (riv.) F2
Machias (riv.) H6
Machias Seal (isl.) J7
Madagascal (pond) G5
Marshall (isl.) G7
Matinicus Rock (isl.) F8
Mattamiscontis (lake) F4
Mattawamkeag (lake) G4
Mattawamkeag (riv.) G4
Meddybemps (lake) J5
Metinic (isl.) E8
Millinocket (lake) F4
Millinocket (lake) F3
Molunkus (lake) G4
Monhegan (isl.) E8
Moose (pond) B7
Moose (riv.) D4
Moosehead (lake) D4
Mooseleuk (stream) F2
Mooselookmeguntic (lake) B6
Mopang (lake) H6
Mount Desert (isl.) G7
Mount Desert Rock (isl.) G8
Moxie (lake) D5
Munsungan (lake) E3
Muscongus (bay) E8
Musquacook (lakes) E2
Nahmakanta (lake) E4
Nicatous (lake) G5
Nollesemic (lake) F4
Old (stream) H6
Onawa (lake) E5
Parlin (pond) C4
Parmachenee (lake) B5
Passamaquoddy (bay) J5
Passamaquoddy Ind. Res. J6
Pemadumcook (lake) E4
Penobscot (bay) F7
Penobscot (lake) C4
Penobscot (riv.) F5
Penobscot Ind. Res. F6
Pierce (pond) C5
Piscataqua (riv.) B9
Piscataquis (riv.) E5
Pleasant (lake) E3
Pleasant (lake) G3
Pleasant (lake) H5
Pleasant (riv.) H6
Pocomoonshine (lake) H5
Portage (lake) F2
Presque Isle A.F.B. G2
Priestly (lake) E2
Pushaw (lake) F6
Ragged (isl.) F8
Ragged (lake) E4
Rainbow (lake) E4
Rangeley (lake) B6
Richardson (lakes) B6
Rocky (lake) J6
Round (pond) E2
Rowe (lake) F2
Saco (riv.) B8
Saint Croix (riv.) J5
Saint Croix Isl. Nat'l Mon. J5
Saint Francis (riv.) E1
Saint Froid (lake) F2
Saint John (pond) D3
Saint John (riv.) G1
Salmon Falls (riv.) B9
Sandy (riv.) C6
Schoodic (lake) F5
Scraggly (lake) F3
Scraggly (lake) H5
Seal (isl.) F8
Sebago (lake) B8
Sebasticook (lake) E6
Seboeis (lake) F5
Seboeis (riv.) F3
Seboomook (lake) D4
Shallow (lake) E3
Small (cape) D8
Sourdnahunk (lake) F3
Spencer (pond) D4
Spencer (stream) C5
Spider (lake) E3
Squa Pan (lake) G2
Square (lake) G1
Sunday (riv.) B6
Swift (riv.) B6
Sysladobsis, Lower (lake) G5
Third (lake) H5
Twin (lakes) F4
Umbagog (lake) A6
Umcalcus (lake) G3
Umsaskis (lake) E2
Union, West Branch (riv.) G6
Vinalhaven (isl.) F7
Wassataquoik (stream) F4
Webb (lake) C6
Webster (brook) E3
West Grand (lake) H5
West Musquash (lake) H5
West Quoddy (head) K6
Wilson E5
Winnecook (lake) E6
Wooden Ball (isl.) F8
Wyman (lake) C5
Wytopitlock (lake) G4

⊙County seat.
‡Population of metropolitan area.
○Population of town or township.
† Zip of nearest p.o.
* Multiple zips.

Topography

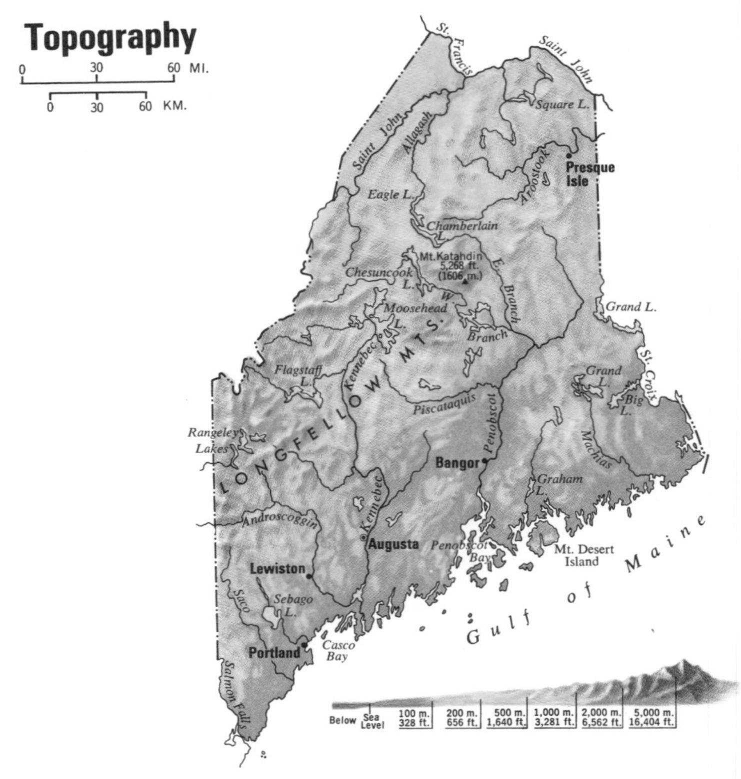

0 30 60 MI.
0 30 60 KM.
St. Francis
Saint John
Square L.
Allagash
Saint John
Aroostook
Presque Isle
Eagle L.
Chamberlain
Mt. Katahdin 5,268 ft. (1606 m.)
Chesuncook L.
Moosehead L.
E. Branch
W. Branch
Grand L.
Flagstaff L.
Kennebec
LONGFELLOW MTS.
Grand L.
St. Croix
Big L.
Piscataquis
Penobscot
Rangeley Lakes
Bangor
Machias
Graham L.
Androscoggin
Kennebec
Augusta
Penobscot Bay
Mt. Desert Island
Lewiston
Gulf of Maine
Sebago L.
Saco
Portland
Casco Bay
Salmon Falls
Below Sea Level
100 m. 328 ft.
200 m. 656 ft.
500 m. 1,640 ft.
1,000 m. 3,281 ft.
2,000 m. 6,562 ft.
5,000 m. 16,404 ft.

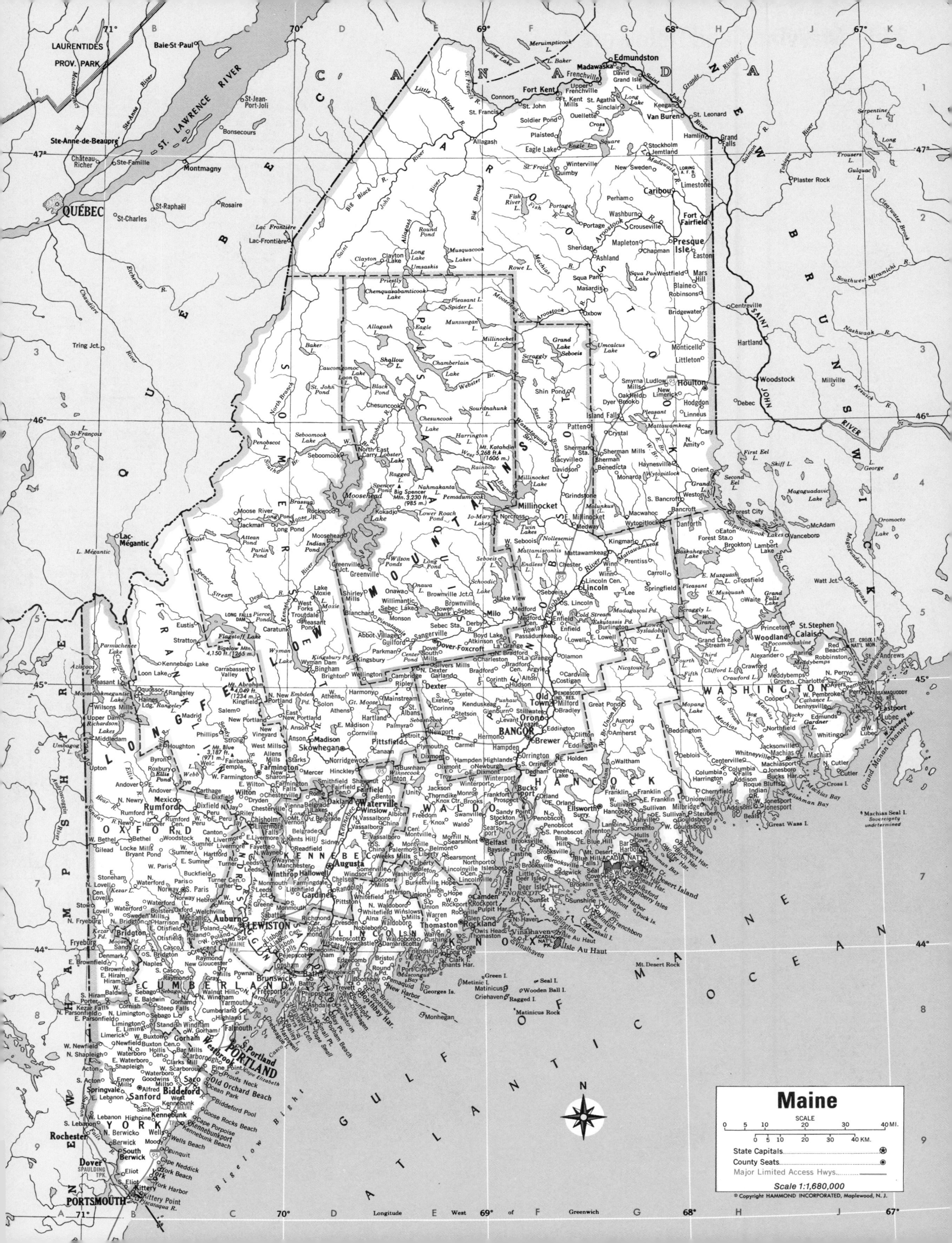

Maine
SCALE
0 5 10 20 30 40 MI.
0 5 10 20 30 40 KM.
State Capitals
County Seats
Major Limited Access Hwys.
Scale 1:1,680,000
© Copyright HAMMOND INCORPORATED, Maplewood, N. J.
Longitude West 69° of Greenwich
ATLANTIC OCEAN
GULF OF MAINE
Bigelow Bight
CANADA
QUEBEC
NEW BRUNSWICK
NEW HAMPSHIRE
ST. LAWRENCE RIVER
LAURENTIDES PROV. PARK
QUÉBEC
Edmundston
Fort Kent
Madawaska
Caribou
Presque Isle
Houlton
Millinocket
Mt. Katahdin 5,268 ft. (1606 m.)
Moosehead L.
BANGOR
Augusta
Waterville
LEWISTON
Auburn
PORTLAND
Biddeford
Saco
Rockland
Ellsworth
Bar Harbor
Calais
Eastport
Machias
Kittery
PORTSMOUTH
AROOSTOOK
PISCATAQUIS
PENOBSCOT
SOMERSET
FRANKLIN
OXFORD
ANDROSCOGGIN
KENNEBEC
WALDO
HANCOCK
WASHINGTON
KNOX
LINCOLN
SAGADAHOC
CUMBERLAND
YORK
LONGFELLOW MOUNTAINS
PENOBSCOT BAY
ACADIA NAT'L PK.
Mt. Desert Island
Isle Au Haut
Monhegan
Matinicus Rock
Machias Seal I. Sovereignty undetermined
Grand Manan Channel

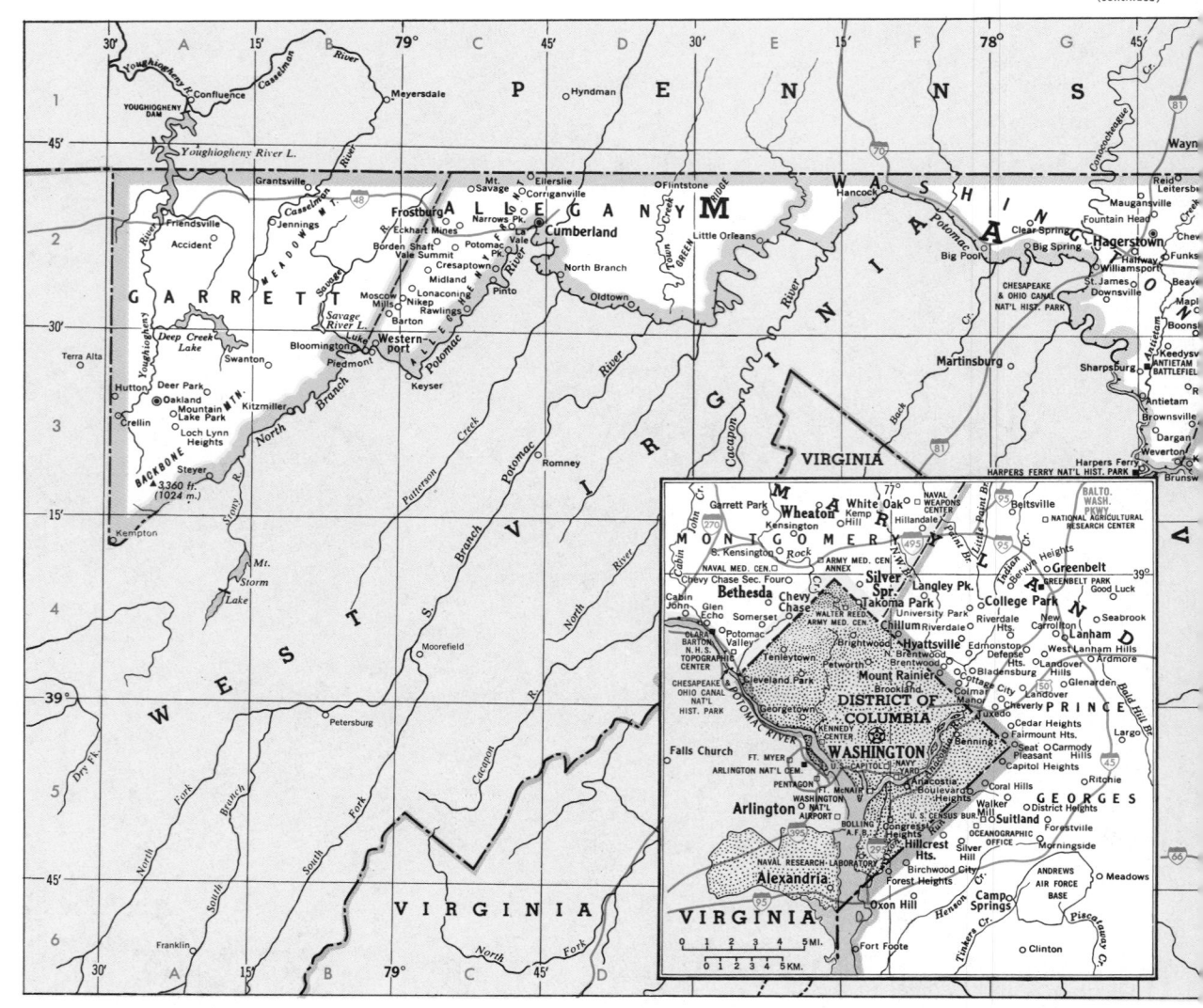

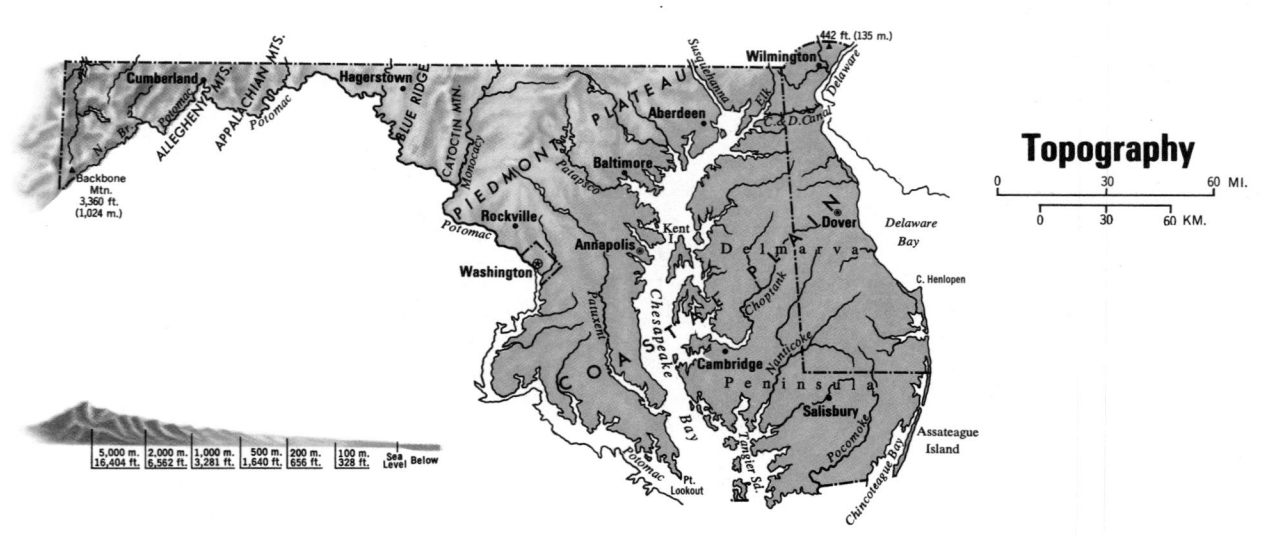

Topography

0 .... 30 .... 60 MI.

0 .... 30 .... 60 KM.

5,000 m. / 16,404 ft. 2,000 m. / 6,562 ft. 1,000 m. / 3,281 ft. 500 m. / 1,640 ft. 200 m. / 656 ft. 100 m. / 328 ft. Sea Level Below

MARYLAND

AREA 10,460 sq. mi. (27,091 sq. km.)
POPULATION 4,216,975
CAPITAL Annapolis
LARGEST CITY Baltimore
HIGHEST POINT Backbone Mtn. 3,360 ft. (1024 m.)
SETTLED IN 1634
ADMITTED TO UNION April 28, 1788
POPULAR NAME Old Line State; Free State
STATE FLOWER Black-eyed Susan
STATE BIRD Baltimore Oriole

DELAWARE

AREA 2,044 sq. mi. (5,294 sq. km.)
POPULATION 594,317
CAPITAL Dover
LARGEST CITY Wilmington
HIGHEST POINT Ebright Road 442 ft. (135 m.)
SETTLED IN 1627
ADMITTED TO UNION December 7, 1787
POPULAR NAME First State; Diamond State
STATE FLOWER Peach Blossom
STATE BIRD Blue Hen Chicken

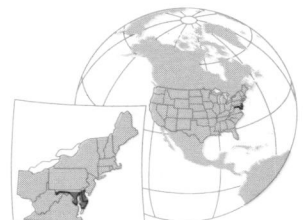

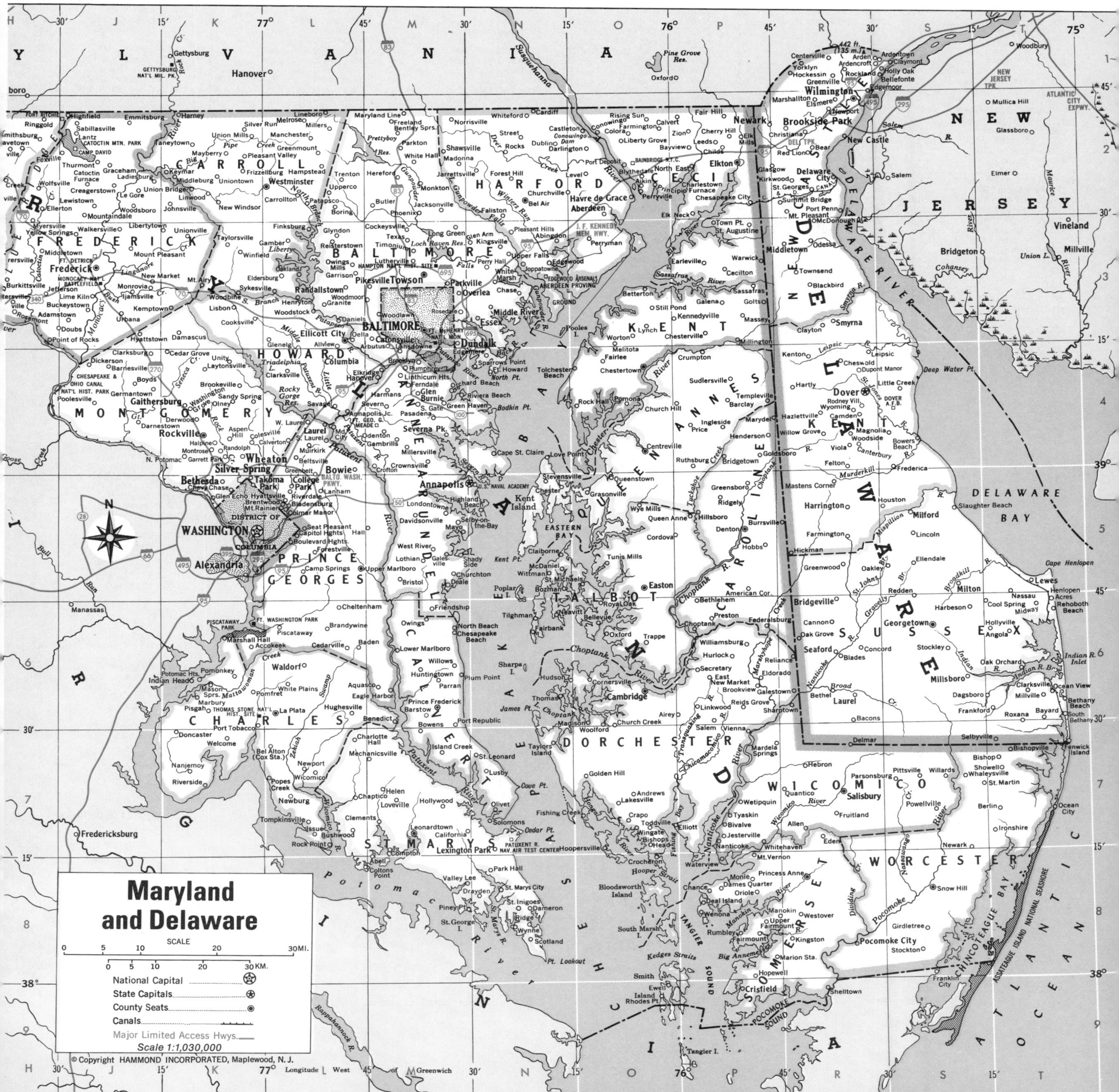

Maryland and Delaware

SCALE

0 5 10   20   30 MI.

0 5 10   20   30 KM.

National Capital .... ⊛
State Capitals .... ⊛
County Seats .... ◉
Canals

Major Limited Access Hwys.
Scale 1:1,030,000

© Copyright HAMMOND INCORPORATED, Maplewood, N.J.

21701 Lewistown 600 J2
20653 Lexington Park 10,361 M7
21762 Libertytown 400 J3
21090 Linthicum Heights 7,457 M4
21766 Little Orleans 600 E2
†21550 Loch Lynn Heights 503 A3
21539 Lonaconing 1,420 C2
†21035 Londontowne 6,052 M4
21092 Long Green 1,626 M3
20656 Loveville 600 M7
21540 Luke 329 B3
21093 Lutherville-Timonium 16,871 M3
21648 Madison 350 O6
21102 Manchester 1,830 L2
20658 Marbury 1,189 K6
21837 Mardela Springs 320 P7
21838 Marion Station 400 R8
†20616 Marshall Hall 325 K6
21649 Marydel 152 P4
†21113 Maryland City 6,949 L4
21767 Maugansville 1,707 H2
21106 Mayo 2,795 M5
20659 Mechanicsville 784 M7
21220 Middle River 26,756 N3
21769 Middletown 1,748 J3
21542 Midland 601 C2
21108 Millersville 380 M4
21651 Millington 546 P3
†20028 Morningside 1,395 G5
†21701 Mountaindale 400 J2
21550 Mountain Lake Park 1,597 A3
21771 Mount Airy 2,450 K3
†21701 Mount Pleasant 400 J3
20822 Mount Rainier 7,361 F4
21545 Mount Savage 1,640 C2
†21853 Mount Vernon 900 P8
†20705 Muirkirk 950 L4
21773 Myersville 432 H3
21840 Nanticoke 450 P7
†21502 Narrows Park-La Vale 5,523 C2
21841 Newark 900 S7
20664 Newburg 550 L7
20784 New Carrollton 12,632 G4
21774 New Market 306 J3
21776 New Windsor 799 K2
20831 North Beach 1,504 N6
†20722 North Brentwood 580 F4
21901 North East 1,469 P2
†20854 North Potomac K4
21550 Oakland⊙ 1,994 A3
†21784 Oakland 2,242 L3
21842 Ocean City 4,946 T7
21113 Odenton 13,270 M4
†21228 Oella 600 L3
20832 Olney 13,026 K4
21206 Overlea 12,965 N3
20836 Owings 700 M6
21117 Owings Mills 9,526 L3
21654 Oxford 754 O6
20745 Oxon Hill 36,267 F6
20667 Park Hall 775 N8
21234 Parkville 35,159 M3
21122 Pasadena 7,439 M4
21128 Perry Hall 13,455 N3
21130 Perryman 1,819 O3
21903 Perryville 2,018 O2
21208 Pikesville 22,555 M3
20674 Piney Point 950 M8
†20735 Piscataway 500 L6
20640 Pisgah 650 K6
21850 Pittsville 519 S7
†21087 Pleasant Hills 2,790 N3
21851 Pocomoke City 3,558 R8
20675 Pomfret 600 L6
†20640 Pomonkey 410 K6
20837 Poolesville 3,428 J4
21904 Port Deposit 664 O2
20677 Port Tobacco 40 K6
20640 Potomac Heights 2,456 K6
†21502 Potomac Park-Bowling Green 2,275 C2
21852 Powellville 400 S7
21655 Preston 498 P6
20678 Prince Frederick⊙ 1,805 M6
21853 Princess Anne⊙ 1,499 P8
†21090 Pumphrey 5,666 M4
21657 Queen Anne 259 O5
21658 Queenstown 491 O5
21133 Randallstown 25,927 L3
21557 Rawlings 500 C2
21136 Reisterstown 19,385 L3
20680 Ridge 550 N8
21660 Ridgely 933 P5
21911 Rising Sun 1,160 O2
†20027 Ritchie 950 G5
†20840 Riverdale Heights G4
†21061 Riviera Beach 8,812 N4
21661 Rock Hall 1,511 O4
†21084 Rocks 450 N2
*20850 Rockville⊙ 43,811 K4
21779 Rohrersville 525 H3
21237 Rosedale 19,956 M3
†21758 Rosemont 305 H3
21662 Royal Oak 600 O6
21780 Sabillasville 450 J2
20684 Saint Inigoes 750 N8
21663 Saint Michaels 1,301 N5
21801 Salisbury⊙ 16,429 R7
20860 Sandy Spring-Ashton 2,659 K4
20863 Savage-Guilford 2,928 L4
20687 Scotland 475 N8
20801 Seabrook-Lanham 15,814 G4
20027 Seat Pleasant 5,217 G5
21664 Secretary 487 P6
†21037 Selby-on-the-Bay 3,125 N5
21144 Severn 20,147 M4
21146 Severna Park 21,253 M4
20867 Shady Side 2,877 M5
21782 Sharpsburg 721 G3
21851 Sharptown 654 R6
20023 Silver Hill-Suitland 32,164 F5
†21157 Silver Run 350 K2
*20901 Silver Spring 72,893 F4
21783 Smithsburg 833 H2
21863 Snow Hill⊙ 2,192 S8
†20015 Somerset 1,101 E4
†21113 South Gate 24,185 M4
†20795 South Kensington 9,344 E4
†20810 South Laurel 18,034 L4
21219 Sparrows Point N4
21666 Stevensville 500 N5
21667 Still Pond 350 O3
21864 Stockton 400 S8
21668 Sudlersville 443 P4
†20746 Suitland-Silver Hill 32,164 F5
21784 Sykesville 1,712 K3
20912 Takoma Park 16,231 F4
21787 Taneytown 2,618 K2
21669 Taylors Island 400 N7
21670 Templeville 96 P4
21788 Thurmont 2,934 J2
21671 Tilghman 979 N6
21093 Timonium-Lutherville 16,871 M3
21672 Toddville 500 O7
21204 Towson⊙ 51,083 M3
21673 Trappe 739 O6
†20780 Tuxedo 500 G5
21791 Union Bridge 927 K2
†20740 University Park 2,536 F4
21155 Upperco 500 L2
21867 Upper Fairmount 500 P8
21156 Upper Falls 550 N3
20870 Upper Marlboro⊙ 828 M5
20692 Valley Lee 600 M8
21869 Vienna 300 P7
20601 Waldorf 9,782 L6
†20023 Walker Mill 10,651 F5
21793 Walkersville 2,212 J3
21912 Warwick 550 P3
20880 Washington Grove 527 K4
20693 Welcome 438 K7
21562 Westernport 2,706 B3
†20784 West Lanham Hills 350 G4
21157 Westminster⊙ 8,808 L2
21871 Westover 450 R8
20902 Wheaton-Glenmont 48,598 E3
21160 Whiteford 500 N2
21161 White Hall 360 M2
21162 White Marsh 500 N3
†20901 White Oak 13,700 F3
20695 White Plains 5,167 L6
21874 Willards 540 S7
21795 Williamsport 2,153 G2
21676 Wittman 544 N5
21797 Woodbine 872 K3
21798 Woodsboro 506 J2
21163 Woodstock 700 L3
21677 Woolford 330 O7
21679 Wye Mills 315 O5
†20680 Wynne 450 N8
†21701 Yellow Springs 940 H3

OTHER FEATURES

Aberdeen Proving Ground 5,722 N3
Allegheny Front (mts.) C2
Andrews A.F.B. 10,064 G5
Antietam (creek) H2
Antietam Nat'l Battlefield H3
Army Chemical Center O3
Back (riv.) N4
Backbone (mt.) A3
Bainbridge N.T.C. O2
Bald Hill Branch (riv.) G4
Big Annemessex (riv.) P8
Big Pipe (creek) K2
Bloodsworth (isl.) O8
Blue Ridge (mts.) H3
Bodkin (pt.) N4
Bush (creek) J3
Cabin John (creek) E4
Camp David J2
Casselman (riv.) B2
Catoctin (creek) H3
Catoctin Mt. Park J2
Cedar (pt.) N7
Census Bureau F5
Chesapeake (bay) N7
Chesapeake and Delaware (canal) R2
Chesapeake and Ohio Canal Nat'l Hist. Park J4
Chester (riv.) O4
Chicamacomico (riv.) P7
Chincoteague (bay) S8
Choptank (riv.) O6
Clara Barton Nat'l Hist. Site E4
Conococheague (creek) G1
Conowingo (dam) O2
Cove (pt.) N7
Deep Creek (lake) A3
Deer (creek) N2
Dividing (creek) R8
Eastern (bay) N5
Elk (riv.) P3
Fishing (bay) O7
Fort Detrick J3
Fort George G. Meade 14,083 L4
Fort McHenry Nat'l Mon. M3
Fort Ritchie 1,754 H2
Fort Washington Park L6
Great Seneca (creek) J4
Greenbelt Park G4
Green Ridge (mts.) E2
Gunpowder (riv.) N3
Gunpowder Falls (creek) M2
Hampton Nat'l Hist. Site M3
Harpers Ferry Nat'l Hist. Park G3
Henson (creek) F6
Honga (riv.) O7
Hooper (str.) O8
Indian (creek) G4
James (pt.) N6
Kedges (strs) O8
Kent (isl.) N5
Kent (pt.) N5
Liberty (lake) L3
Linganore (creek) J3
Little Choptank (riv.) N6
Little Gunpowder Falls (creek) M2
Little Paint Branch (riv.) F4
Little Patuxent (riv.) L4
Loch Raven (res.) M3
Lookout (pt.) N8
Manokin (riv.) P8
Marshyhope (creek) P6
Mattawoman (creek) K6
Meadow (mt.) B2
Middle Patuxent (riv.) L3
Monocacy (riv.) J3
Monocacy Nat'l Battlefield J3
Nanticoke (riv.) P7
Nassawango (creek) S8
National Agricultural Research Center G3
Naval Academy, U.S. 5,367 N5
Naval Medical Center E4
Naval Weapons Center F3
North (pt.) N4
Oceanographic Office F5
Oxon Run (riv.) F5
Paint Branch (riv.) F4
Patapsco (riv.) M4
Patuxent (riv.) M7
Patuxent River Nav. Air Test Ctr. N7
Piscataway (creek) G6
Piscataway Park K6
Pocomoke (riv.) S8
Pocomoke (sound) P9
Pooles (isl.) O3
Poplar (isl.) N5
Potomac (riv.) M8
Prettyboy (res.) M2
Rock (creek) K4
Rocky Gorge (res.) L4
Saint George (isl.) M8
Saint Marys (riv.) N8
Sassafras (riv.) P3
Savage (riv.) B2
Savage River (lake) B2
Severn (riv.) N4
Sharps (isl.) N6
Smith (isl.) O8
South Marsh (isl.) O8
Susquehanna (riv.) N1
Tangier (sound) P8
Thomas Stone Nat'l Hist. Site K6
Tinkers (creek) F6
Topographic Center E4
Town (creek) E2
Transquaking (riv.) P7
Triadelphia (lake) L4
Tuckahoe (creek) P5
Walter Reed Army Med. Ctr. Annex E4
Wicomico (riv.) L7
Wicomico (riv.) R7
Winters Run (creek) N2
Youghiogheny (riv.) A3
Youghiogheny River (lake) A2
Zekiah Swamp (riv.) L7

DELAWARE

COUNTIES

Kent 98,219 R4
New Castle 398,115 R2
Sussex 97,983 S6

CITIES and TOWNS

Zip *Name/Pop.* *Key*

†19801 Arden 516 R1
†19810 Ardencroft 267 R1
†19810 Ardentown 307 S1
19809 Bellefonte 1,279 S1
19930 Bethany Beach 330 T6
19931 Bethel 197 R6
†19973 Blades 664 R6
†19962 Bowers Beach 198 S4
19993 Bridgeville 1,238 R6
19711 Brookside 15,255 R2
19934 Camden 1,757 R4
†19801 Centerville 800 R1
19936 Cheswold 269 R4
†19711 Christiana 500 R2
19937 Clarksville 350 T6
19703 Claymont 10,022 S1
19938 Clayton 1,216 R3
19930 Dagsboro 344 S6
19706 Delaware City 1,858 R2
19940 Delmar 948 R7
19901 Dover (cap.)⊙ 23,507 R4
†19901 Dupont Manor 1,059 R4
†19801 Edgemoor 7,397 S1
19941 Ellendale 361 S5
†19801 Elsmere 6,493 R2
19942 Farmington 141 R5
19943 Felton 547 R4
19944 Fenwick Island 114 T7
19945 Frankford 828 S6
19946 Frederica 864 S4
19947 Georgetown⊙ 1,710 S6
†19711 Glasgow 350 R2
19950 Greenwood 578 R5
19952 Harrington 2,405 R5
†19971 Henlopen Acres 176 T6
19707 Hockessin 950 R1
†19801 Holly Oak S1
19954 Houston 357 S5
19955 Kenton 243 R4
19708 Kirkwood 350 R2
19956 Laurel 3,052 R6
†19901 Leipsic 228 S4
19958 Lewes 2,197 T5
19960 Lincoln 757 S5
19961 Little Creek 230 S4
19962 Magnolia 197 R4
19709 Middletown 2,946 R3
19963 Milford 5,366 S5
19966 Millsboro 1,233 S6
19967 Millville 178 T6
19968 Milton 1,359 S5
19711 Newark 25,247 P2
19720 New Castle 4,907 R2
19804 Newport 1,167 R2
†19966 Oak Orchard 350 T6
19970 Ocean View 495 T6
19730 Odessa 384 R3
19971 Rehoboth Beach 1,730 T6
19901 Rodney Village 1,753 R4
19733 Saint Georges 450 R2
19973 Seaford 5,256 R6
19975 Selbyville 1,251 S7
†19963 Slaughter Beach 121 S5
19977 Smyrna 4,750 R3
†19930 South Bethany 115 T6
19734 Townsend 386 R3
19979 Viola 167 R4
*19801 Wilmington⊙ 70,195 R2
Wilmington‡ 524,108 R2
19980 Woodside 248 R4
19934 Wyoming 960 R4
19736 Yorklyn 600 R1

OTHER FEATURES

Broad (creek) R6
Broadkill (riv.) S5
Chesapeake and Delaware (canal) R2
Choptank (riv.) P5
Deep Water (pt.) S4
Delaware (bay) T5
Delaware (riv.) R3
Dover A.F.B. 4,391 S4
Henlopen (cape) T5
Indian (riv.) S6
Indian River (bay) T6
Indian River (inlet) T6
Leipsic (riv.) R4
Mispillion (riv.) S5
Murderkill (riv.) R5
Nanticoke (riv.) R6
Saint Jones (riv.) R4
Smyrna (res.) R3

DISTRICT OF COLUMBIA

CITIES and TOWNS

Zip *Name/Pop.* *Key*

20007 Georgetown E5
*20001 Washington, D.C. (cap.), U.S. 638,432 F5
Washington‡ 3,060,240 F5

OTHER FEATURES

Anacostia (riv.) F5
Bolling A.F.B. E5
Fort Lesley J. McNair E5
Kennedy Center A5
Naval Yard F5
U.S. Capitol F5
Walter Reed Army Med. Ctr. E4

⊙County seat.
‡Population of metropolitan area.
† Zip of nearest p.o.
* Multiple zips.

Agriculture, Industry and Resources

DOMINANT LAND USE

- Dairy, General Farming
- Fruit and Mixed Farming
- Truck and Mixed Farming
- Tobacco, General Farming
- Forests
- Swampland, Limited Agriculture
- Urban Areas

MAJOR MINERAL OCCURRENCES

- C Coal
- Cl Clay
- G Natural Gas
- Ls Limestone

Water Power

Major Industrial Areas

MASSACHUSETTS

AREA 8,284 sq. mi. (21,456 sq. km.)
POPULATION 5,737,037
CAPITAL Boston
LARGEST CITY Boston
HIGHEST POINT Mt. Greylock 3,491 ft. (1064 m.)
SETTLED IN 1620
ADMITTED TO UNION February 6, 1788
POPULAR NAME Bay State; Old Colony
STATE FLOWER Mayflower
STATE BIRD Chickadee

RHODE ISLAND

AREA 1,212 sq. mi. (3,139 sq. km.)
POPULATION 947,154
CAPITAL Providence
LARGEST CITY Providence
HIGHEST POINT Jerimoth Hill 812 ft. (247 m.)
SETTLED IN 1636
ADMITTED TO UNION May 29, 1790
POPULAR NAME Little Rhody; Ocean State
STATE FLOWER Violet
STATE BIRD Rhode Island Red

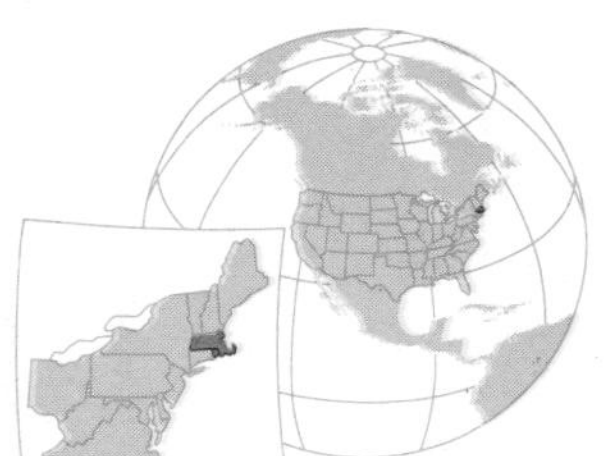

Agriculture, Industry and Resources

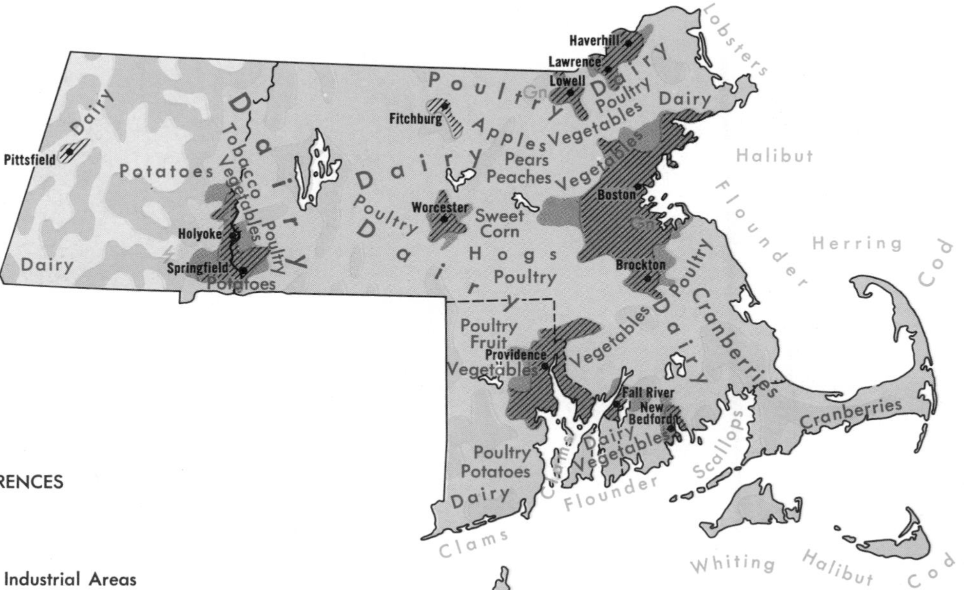

DOMINANT LAND USE

Specialized Dairy
Dairy, Poultry, Mixed Farming
Forests
Urban Areas

MAJOR MINERAL OCCURRENCES

Gn Granite

Water Power
Major Industrial Areas

MASSACHUSETTS

COUNTIES

Barnstable 147,925 N6
Berkshire 145,110 B3
Bristol 474,641 K5
Dukes 8,942 M7
Essex 633,632 L2
Franklin 64,317 D2
Hampden 443,018 D4
Hampshire 138,813 D3
Middlesex 1,367,034 J3
Nantucket 5,087 O7
Norfolk 606,587 K4
Plymouth 405,437 L5
Suffolk 650,142 K3
Worcester 646,352 G3

CITIES and TOWNS

Zip *Name/Pop.* *Key*

02351 Abington○ 13,517 L4
01720 Acton○ 17,544 J3
02743 Acushnet○ 8,704 L6
01220 Adams○ 10,381 B2
01220 Adams 6,857 B2
01001 Agawam○ 26,271 D4
†01261 Alford○ 394 A4
01913 Amesbury○ 13,971 L1
01913 Amesbury 12,236 L1
01002 Amherst○ 33,229 E3
01002 Amherst 17,773 E3
01810 Andover○ 26,370 K2
01810 Andover 8,445 K2
02174 Arlington○ 48,219 C6
01430 Ashburnham○ 4,075 G2
01430 Ashburnham 900 G2
01431 Ashby○ 2,311 G2
01330 Ashfield○ 1,458 C2
01721 Ashland○ 9,165 J3
01331 Athol○ 10,634 F2
01331 Athol 8,708 F2
02703 Attleboro 34,196 J5
01501 Auburn○ 14,845 G4
02322 Avon○ 5,026 K4
*01432 Ayer○ 6,993 H2
*01432 Ayer 3,165 H2
01436 Baldwinville 1,709 F2
02630 Barnstable○ 30,898 N6
02630 Barnstable⊙ 2,033 N6
01005 Barre○ 4,102 F3
01005 Barre 1,136 F3
01223 Becket○ 1,339 B3
01730 Bedford○ 13,067 B6
01007 Belchertown○ 8,339 E3
01007 Belchertown 2,531 E3
02019 Bellingham○ 14,300 J4
02019 Bellingham 4,454 J4
02178 Belmont○ 26,100 C6
†02780 Berkley○ 2,731 K5
01503 Berlin○ 2,215 H3
01337 Bernardston○ 1,750 D2
01915 Beverly 37,655 E5
01821 Billerica○ 36,727 J2
01504 Blackstone○ 6,570 H4
01008 Blandford○ 1,038 C4
01740 Bolton○ 2,530 H3
01009 Bondsville 1,906 E4
*02101 Boston (cap.)⊙ 562,994 D7
Boston‡ 2,763,357 D7
02532 Bourne○ 13,874 M6
02532 Bourne 2,678 M6
01719 Boxborough○ 3,126 H3
01921 Boxford○ 5,374 L2
01921 Boxford 1,841 L2
01505 Boylston○ 3,470 H3
02184 Braintree○ 36,337 D8
02020 Brant Rock-Ocean Bluff 4,055 M4
02631 Brewster○ 5,226 O5
02631 Brewster 1,744 O5
02324 Bridgewater○ 17,202 K5
02324 Bridgewater 6,781 K5
01010 Brimfield○ 2,318 F4
*02401 Brockton 95,172 K4
Brockton‡ 169,374 K4
01506 Brookfield○ 2,397 F4
01506 Brookfield 1,037 F4
02146 Brookline○ 55,062 C7
01338 Buckland○ 1,864 C2
01803 Burlington○ 23,486 C5
02532 Buzzards Bay 3,375 M5
02138 Cambridge⊙ 95,322 C7
02021 Canton○ 18,182 C8
01741 Carlisle○ 3,306 J2
02330 Carver○ 6,988 M5
02632 Centerville 3,640 N6
01339 Charlemont○ 1,149 C2
01507 Charlton○ 6,719 F4
02633 Chatham○ 6,071 P6
02633 Chatham 1,922 P6
01824 Chelmsford○ 31,174 J2
02150 Chelsea 25,431 D6
01225 Cheshire○ 3,124 B2
01011 Chester○ 1,123 C3
01012 Chesterfield○ 1,000 C3
*01013 Chicopee 55,112 D4
02535 Chilmark○ 489 M7
†02054 Clicquot-Millis 3,777 A8
01510 Clinton○ 12,771 H3
01778 Cochituate 6,126 A7
02025 Cohasset○ 7,174 F7
01340 Colrain○ 1,552 D2
01742 Concord○ 16,293 B6
01341 Conway○ 1,213 D2
†01772 Cordaville 1,384 H3
01026 Cummington○ 657 C3
01226 Dalton○ 6,797 B3
01923 Danvers○ 24,100 D5
02714 Dartmouth○ 23,966 K6
02026 Dedham⊙○ 25,298 C7
01342 Deerfield○ 4,517 D2
02638 Dennis○ 12,360 O5
02639 Dennis Port 2,570 O6
02715 Dighton○ 5,352 K5
†02122 Dorchester D7
†01516 Douglas○ 3,730 H4
02030 Dover○ 4,703 B7
02030 Dover 2,051 B7
01826 Dracut○ 21,249 J2
01570 Dudley○ 8,717 G4
01827 Dunstable○ 1,671 J2
02332 Duxbury○ 11,807 M4
02332 Duxbury 1,685 M4
02333 East Bridgewater○ 9,945 L4
01515 East Brookfield○ 1,955 G4
01515 East Brookfield 1,443 G4
01516 East Douglas 1,683 G4
02536 East Falmouth (Teaticket) 5,181 M6
02642 Eastham○ 3,472 O5
01027 Easthampton○ 15,580 D3
01028 East Longmeadow○ 12,905 E4
02334 Easton○ 16,623 K4
01437 East Pepperell 2,212 H2
02539 Edgartown○ 2,204 M7
02539 Edgartown⊙ 1,138 M7
01344 Erving○ 1,326 E2
01929 Essex○ 2,998 L2
01929 Essex 1,490 L2
02149 Everett 37,195 D6
02719 Fairhaven○ 15,759 L6
*02720 Fall River 92,574 K6
Fall River‡ 176,831 K6
*02540 Falmouth○ 23,640 M6
*02540 Falmouth 5,720 M6
01518 Fiskdale 1,859 F4
01420 Fitchburg⊙ 39,580 G2
Fitchburg-Leominster‡ 99,957 G2
†01247 Florida○ 730 B2
02035 Foxboro○ 14,148 J4
02035 Foxboro 5,697 J4
01701 Framingham○ 65,113 A7
02038 Franklin○ 18,217 J4
02038 Franklin 9,296 J4
01440 Gardner 17,900 G2
†02535 Gay Head○ 220 L7
01833 Georgetown○ 5,687 L2
01031 Gilbertville 1,029 F3
†01376 Gill○ 1,259 D2
01930 Gloucester 27,768 M2
01032 Goshen○ 651 C3
01519 Grafton○ 11,238 H4
01033 Granby○ 5,380 E3
01033 Granby 1,302 E3
01034 Granville○ 1,204 C4
01230 Great Barrington○ 7,405 A4
01230 Great Barrington 3,150 A4
01301 Greenfield○ 18,436 D2
01301 Greenfield⊙ 14,198 D2
02041 Green Harbor 2,002 M4
01450 Groton○ 6,154 H2
01450 Groton 1,264 H2
01830 Groveland○ 5,040 L1
01035 Hadley○ 4,125 D3
02338 Halifax○ 5,513 L5
01936 Hamilton○ 6,960 L2
01036 Hampden○ 4,745 E4
01237 Hancock○ 643 A2
02339 Hanover○ 11,358 L4
02341 Hanson○ 8,617 L4
02341 Hanson 2,120 L4
01037 Hardwick○ 2,272 F3
01451 Harvard○ 12,170 H2
02645 Harwich○ 8,971 O6
02645 Harwich 4,399 O6
01038 Hatfield○ 3,045 D3
01038 Hatfield 1,251 D3
01830 Haverhill 46,865 K1
01346 Heath○ 482 C2
02043 Hingham○ 20,339 E8
02043 Hingham 5,742 E8
01235 Hinsdale○ 1,707 B3
02343 Holbrook○ 11,140 D8
01520 Holden○ 13,336 G3
†01550 Holland○ 1,589 F4
01746 Holliston○ 12,622 A8
01040 Holyoke 44,678 D4
01747 Hopedale○ 3,905 H4
01747 Hopedale 2,810 H4
01748 Hopkinton○ 7,114 J4
01748 Hopkinton 2,542 J4
01236 Housatonic 1,314 A3
01452 Hubbardston○ 1,797 F3
01749 Hudson○ 16,408 H3
01749 Hudson 14,156 H3
02045 Hull○ 9,714 E7
01050 Huntington○ 1,804 C4
02601 Hyannis 9,118 N6
01938 Ipswich○ 11,158 L2
01938 Ipswich 4,548 L2
02364 Kingston○ 7,362 M5
02364 Kingston 4,405 M5
02346 Lakeville○ 5,931 L5
02346 Lakeville 1,948 L5
01523 Lancaster○ 6,334 H3
01237 Lanesboro○ 3,131 A2
*01840 Lawrence⊙ 63,175 K2
Lawrence-Haverhill‡ 281,981 K2
01238 Lee○ 6,247 B3
01238 Lee 2,140 B3
01524 Leicester○ 9,446 G4
01240 Lenox○ 6,523 A3
01240 Lenox 2,668 A3
01453 Leominster 34,508 G2
01054 Leverett○ 1,471 E3
02173 Lexington○ 29,479 B6
†01301 Leyden○ 498 D2
01773 Lincoln○ 7,098 B6
01460 Littleton○ 6,970 H2
†01460 Littleton Common 3,109 J2
01106 Longmeadow○ 16,301 D4
*01850 Lowell⊙ 92,418 J2
Lowell‡ 233,410 J2
01056 Ludlow○ 18,150 E4
01462 Lunenburg○ 8,405 H2
01462 Lunenburg 1,789 H2
*01901 Lynn 78,471 D6
01940 Lynnfield○ 11,267 D5
02148 Malden 53,386 D6
01944 Manchester○ 5,424 F5
02048 Mansfield○ 13,453 J4
02048 Mansfield 6,786 J4
01945 Marblehead○ 20,126 E7
02738 Marion○ 3,932 L6
02738 Marion 1,438 L6
01752 Marlborough 30,617 H3
02050 Marshfield○ 20,916 M4
02050 Marshfield 4,421 M4
02051 Marshfield Hills 2,308 M4
02649 Mashpee○ 3,700 M6
02739 Mattapoisett○ 5,597 L6
02739 Mattapoisett 3,159 L6
01754 Maynard○ 9,590 J3
02052 Medfield○ 10,220 B8
02052 Medfield 6,108 B8
02155 Medford 58,076 C6
02053 Medway○ 8,447 J4
02176 Melrose 30,055 D6
01756 Mendon○ 3,108 H4
01860 Merrimac○ 4,451 L1
01844 Methuen○ 36,701 K2
02346 Middleboro○ 16,404 L5
02346 Middleboro 7,012 L5
01243 Middlefield○ 385 B3
01949 Middleton○ 4,135 K2
01757 Milford○ 23,390 H4
01757 Milford 21,730 H4
01527 Millbury○ 11,808 H4
01349 Millers Falls 1,101 E2
02054 Millis○ 6,908 A8
02054 Millis-Clicquot 3,777 A8
01529 Millville○ 1,693 H4
02186 Milton○ 25,860 D7
01057 Monson○ 7,315 E4
01057 Monson 2,167 E4
01351 Montague○ 8,011 E2
01245 Monterey○ 818 B4
†12517 Mount Washington○ 93 A4
01908 Nahant○ 3,947 E6
02554 Nantucket○ 5,087 O7
02554 Nantucket⊙ 3,229 O7
01760 Natick○ 29,461 A7
02192 Needham○ 27,901 B7
*02740 New Bedford⊙ 98,478 K6
New Bedford‡ 169,425 K6
01531 New Braintree○ 671 F3
01950 Newbury○ 4,529 L1
01950 Newburyport⊙ 15,900 L1
†01230 New Marlborough○ 1,160 B4
01355 New Salem○ 688 E2
†02158 Newton 83,622 C7
02056 Norfolk○ 6,363 J4
01247 North Adams 18,063 B2
01059 North Amherst 5,616 E3
01060 Northampton⊙ 29,286 D3
01845 North Andover○ 20,129 K2
*02760 North Attleboro○ 21,095 J5
01532 Northborough○ 10,568 H3
01532 Northborough 5,670 H3
01534 Northbridge○ 12,246 H4
01535 North Brookfield○ 4,150 F3
01535 North Brookfield 2,543 F3
02764 North Dighton 1,174 K5
02651 North Eastham 1,318 O5
01360 Northfield○ 2,386 E2
01360 Northfield 1,182 E2
02358 North Pembroke 2,215 M4
02360 North Plymouth 3,250 L5
01864 North Reading○ 11,455 C5
02060 North Scituate 5,221 F8
02766 Norton○ 12,690 K5
02766 Norton 2,035 K5
02061 Norwell○ 9,182 F8
02062 Norwood○ 29,711 B8
02557 Oak Bluffs○ 1,984 M7
02557 Oak Bluffs 1,124 M7
01068 Oakham○ 994 F3
02065 Ocean Bluff-Brant Rock 4,055 M4
†01566 Old Sturbridge Village 500 F4
02558 Onset 1,493 M6
01364 Orange○ 6,844 E2
01364 Orange 3,942 E2
02653 Orleans○ 5,306 O5
02653 Orleans 1,811 O5
02655 Osterville 1,799 N6
01253 Otis○ 963 B4
01540 Oxford○ 11,680 G4
01540 Oxford 6,369 G4
01069 Palmer○ 11,389 E4
01069 Palmer 3,854 E4
01612 Paxton○ 3,762 G3
01960 Peabody 45,976 E5
†01002 Pelham○ 1,112 E3
02359 Pembroke○ 13,487 L4
01463 Pepperell○ 8,061 H2
01463 Pepperell 2,076 H2
01366 Petersham○ 1,024 F3
†01331 Phillipston○ 953 F2
01866 Pinehurst 6,588 B5
01201 Pittsfield⊙ 51,974 A3
Pittsfield‡ 90,505 A3
01070 Plainfield○ 425 C2
02762 Plainville○ 5,857 J4
02360 Plymouth○ 35,913 M5
02360 Plymouth⊙ 7,232 M5
02367 Plympton○ 1,974 L5
01541 Princeton○ 2,425 G3
02657 Provincetown○ 3,536 O4
02657 Provincetown 3,372 O4
02169 Quincy 84,743 D7
02368 Randolph○ 28,218 D8
02767 Raynham○ 9,085 K5
02768 Raynham Center 3,776 K5
01867 Reading○ 22,678 C5
02769 Rehoboth○ 7,570 K5
02151 Revere 42,423 D6

(continued on following page)

01266 West Stockbridge○ 1,280 ..A3
02575 West Tisbury○ 1,010........M7
01587 West Upton-Upton 2,184..H4
02576 West Wareham 1,837....L5
02090 Westwood○ 13,212.........B8
02673 West Yarmouth 3,852....N6
02188 Weymouth 55,601.........E6
01093 Whately○ 1,341..........D3
01588 Whitinsville 5,379........H4
02382 Whitman○ 13,534..........L4
01095 Wilbraham○ 2,237.........E4
01095 Wilbraham 3,379..........E4
01096 Williamsburg○ 2,237......E4
01267 Williamstown 8,741.......B2
01267 Williamstown 4,798.......B2
01887 Wilmington 17,471........C5
01475 Winchendon○ 7,019.......F2
01475 Winchendon 4,030........F2
01890 Winchester○ 20,701......C6
01270 Windsor○ 598............B2

02152 Winthrop○ 19,294..........D6
01801 Woburn 36,626............C6
02543 Woods Hole 1,080.........M6
*01601 Worcester○ 161,799.....H3
　　　　Worcester‡ 372,940.....H3
01098 Worthington○ 932.........C3
02093 Wrentham 7,580...........J4
　　　　Yarmouth 18,449..........O6
02675 Yarmouth Port 2,490......N6

OTHER FEATURES

Adams Nat'l Hist. Site D7
Agawam (riv.)..................M5
Allerton (pt.)..................E7
Ann (cape)......................M2
Ashmere (lake).................B3
Assabet (riv.)..................H3
Assawompset (pond)..............L5
Bachelor (brook)................D3

Berkshire (hills)...............B4
Big (pond).......................B4
Bigelow (bight).................M1
Blackstone (riv.)................G3
Blue (hills).....................C8
Boston (bay).....................E6
Boston (harb.)..................D7
Boston Nat'l Hist. Park D6
Brewster (isls.)................E7
Buel (lake)......................A4
Buzzards (bay)...................L7
Cambridge (res.)................B6
Cape Cod (bay)..................N5
Cape Cod (canal)................N5
Cape Cod Nat'l Seashore P5
Chappaquiddick (isl.)...........N7
Charles (riv.)..................C7
Chicopee (riv.).................D4
Cobble Mountain (res.)..........C4
Cochituate (lake)...............A7
Cod (cape)......................O4
Concord (riv.)...................J2
Congamond (lkes.)................D4
Connecticut (riv.)..............D2
Cuttyhunk (isl.)................L7
Deer (isl.)......................E7
Deerfield (riv.)................C2
East (pt.)......................E6
East Chop (pt.).................M7
Eastern (pt.)...................M2
Elizabeth (isl.)................L7
Everett (mt.)...................A4
Falls (riv.)....................D2
Fort Rodman.....................L6
Fresh (pond)....................C6
Gammon (pt.)....................N6
Gay Head (prom.)................L7
Grace (mt.).....................E2
Great (pt.).....................O7
Green (riv.)....................B2
Greylock (mt.)..................B2
Gurnet (pt.)....................M4
Hingham (bay)...................E7
Holyoke (range).................D3
Hoosac (mts.)...................B2
Hoosic (riv.)...................A1
Housatonic (riv.)...............A4
Ipswich (riv.)..................L2
John F. Kennedy Nat'l Hist.
　　Site.......................C7
Knightville (res.)..............C3
Laurence G. Hanscom Field B6
Little (riv.)...................C4
Logan Internat'l Airport E7
Long (isl.).....................E7
Long (pt.)......................O4
Long (pond).....................L5
Lowell Nat'l Hist. Park J2
Maine (gulf)....................M2
Manhan (riv.)...................D4
Manomet (pt.)...................N5
Marblehead (neck)...............F6
Martha's Vineyard (isl.)........M7
Massachusetts (bay).............M4
Merrimack (riv.)................K1
Mill (riv.).....................C3
Mill (riv.).....................D3
Millers (riv.)...................F2
Minute Man Nat'l Hist. Park B6
Mishaum (pt.)...................L6
Monomonac (lake)................G2
Monomoy (isl.)..................O6
Monomoy (pt.)...................O6
Mount Hope (bay)................K6
Muskeget (chan.)................N7
Muskeget (isl.).................N7
Mystic (lake)...................C6
Mystic (riv.)...................C6
Nahant (bay)....................E6
Nantucket (isl.)................O8
Nantucket (sound)...............N6
Nashawena (isl.)................L7
Nashua (riv.)...................H3
Naushon (isl.)..................L7
Neponset (riv.).................C8
Nomans Land (isl.)..............L7
Nonamesset (isl.)...............M6
North (riv.)....................D2
North (riv.)....................L4
Onota (lake)....................A3
Otis (res.).....................B4

Otis A.F.B. M6
Pasque (isl.)...................L7
Plum (isl.).....................L2
Plymouth (bay)..................M5
Poge (cape).....................N7
Pontoosuc (lake)................A3
Quabbin (res.)..................E3
Quaboag (riv.)..................F4
Quincy (bay)....................D7
Quinebaug (riv.)................F4
Race (pt.)......................N4
Salem Maritime Nat'l Hist.
　　Site.......................E5
Saugus Iron Works Nat'l Hist.
　　Site.......................D6
Shawshine (riv.)................K2
Silver (lake)...................L4
South (riv.)....................D2
Springfield Armory Nat'l Hist.
　　Site.......................D4
Squibnocket (pt.)...............M7
Stillwater (riv.)...............G3
Sudbury (res.)..................H3
Sudbury (riv.)..................A6
Swift (riv.)....................E4
Taconic (mts.)..................A2
Taunton (riv.)..................K5
Thompson (isl.).................D7
Toby (mt.)......................E3
Tom (mt.).......................D4
Tuckernuck (isl.)...............N7
Vineyard (sound)................L7
Wachusett (mt.).................G3
Wachusett (res.)................G3
Walden (pond)...................A6
Ware (riv.).....................F3
Watuppa (pond)..................K6
Webster (lake)..................G4
Wellfleet (harb.)...............O5
West (riv.).....................H4
West Branch, Farmington
　　(riv.)......................B4
West Chop (pt.).................M7
Westfield (riv.)................C3
Westover A.F.B. D4
Weweantic (riv.)................L5
Whitman (riv.)..................G2
Winter I. Coast Guard Air Sta. .E5

RHODE ISLAND

COUNTIES

Bristol 46,942....................J6
Kent 154,163.....................H6
Newport 81,383...................K6
Providence 571,349...............H5
Washington 93,317................H7

CITIES and TOWNS

Zip	Name/Pop.	Key

02804 Ashaway 1,747.............G7
02806 Barrington○ 16,174........J6
02807 Block Island 620..........H8
02808 Bradford 1,354............H7
02809 Bristol○ 20,128..........J6
02863 Central Falls 16,995......J5
02816 Coventry○ 27,065.........H6
02910 Cranston 71,992...........J5
02818 East Greenwich○⊙ 10,211 H6
02914 East Providence 50,980 ...J5

02822 Exeter○ 4,453............H6
02825 Foster○ 3,370............H5
02828 Greenville 7,516.........H5
02830 Harrisville 1,224........H5
02832 Hope Valley 1,414........H6
02833 Hopkinton○ 6,406.........H7
02835 Jamestown○ 4,040.........J6
02835 Jamestown 2,156..........J6
02881 Kingston 5,479...........J7
02837 Little Compton○ 3,085....K6
02840 Middletown○ 17,216.......J6
02882 Narragansett○ 12,088.....J7
02882 Narragansett 3,342.......J7
02840 Newport○⊙ 29,259.........J7
†02807 New Shoreham (Block
　　　　Island) 620.............H8
02852 North Kingstown○
　　　　21,938..................J6
02908 North Providence○
　　　　29,188..................J5
02859 Pascoag 3,807............H5
*02860 Pawtucket 71,204........J5
02883 Peace
　　　　Dale-Wakefield 6,474 ...J7
02871 Portsmouth○ 14,257.......J6
*02901 Providence
　　　　(cap.)⊙ 156,804........H5
　　　　Providence-Warwick-
　　　　Pawtucket‡ 919,216......H5
02878 Tiverton○ 13,526.........K6
02878 Tiverton 7,653...........K6
†02864 Valley Falls 10,892......J5
*02879 Wakefield-Peace
　　　　Dale 6,474..............J7
02885 Warren○ 10,640...........J6
*02886 Warwick 87,123..........J6
02891 Westerly○ 18,580.........G7
02891 Westerly○ 14,093.........G7
02893 West Warwick 27,026 .....H6
02895 Woonsocket○ 45,914 ......J4

OTHER FEATURES

Black Rock (pt.) H8
Block (isl.)....................H8
Block Island (sound)............H8
Brenton (pt.)...................J7
Conanicut (isl.)................J6
Dickens (pt.)...................H8
Durfee (hill)...................G5
Grace (pt.).....................H8
Jerimoth (hill).................G5
Judith (pt.)....................J7
Mount Hope (bay)................K6
Narragansett (bay)..............J6
Noyes (pt.).....................H7
Pawcatuck (riv.)................G7
Prudence (isl.).................J6
Rhode Island (isl.).............J6
Rhode Island (sound)............J7
Roger Williams Nat'l Mem. J5
Sakonnet (pt.)..................K7
Sakonnet (riv.).................K7
Sandy (pt.).....................H8
Scituate (res.).................H5
Stillwater (res.)...............C2
Touro Synagogue Nat'l Hist.
　　Site.......................J7
Watch Hill (pt.)................G7

⊙County seat (Shire town).
‡Population of metropolitan area.
○Population of town or township.
† Zip of nearest p.o. * Multiple zips.

Massachusetts and Rhode Island

SCALE
0　5　10　15　20 MI.
0　5　10　15　20 KM.

State Capitals...............⊛
County Seats (Shire Towns)...⊙
Canals.......................
Major Limited Access Hwys....

Scale 1:970,000

© Copyright HAMMOND INCORPORATED, Maplewood, N.J.

Topography

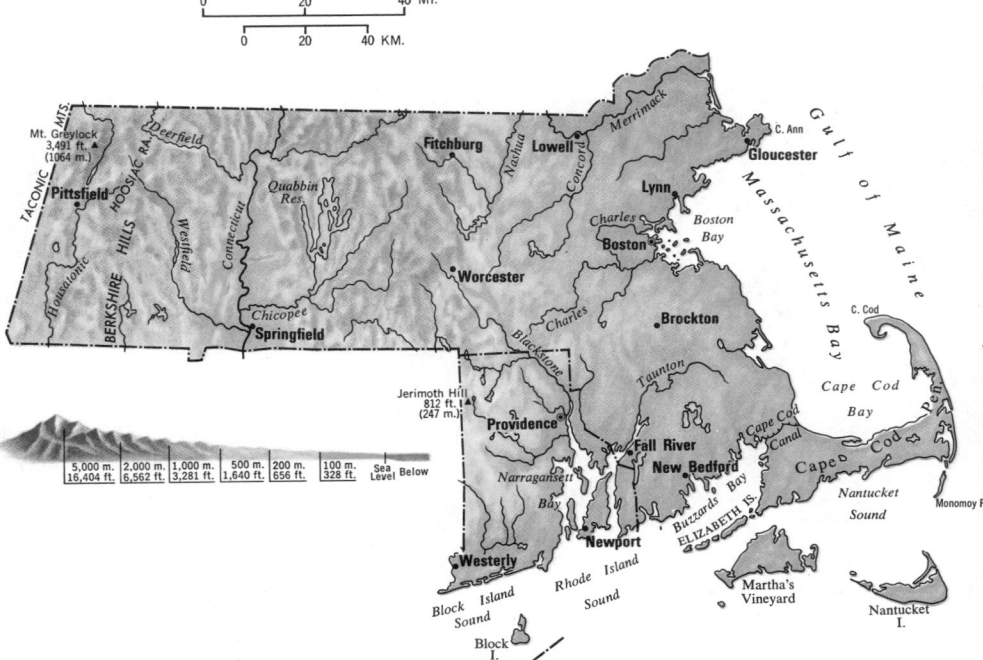

0　20　40 MI.
0　20　40 KM.

| 5,000 m.
16,404 ft. | 2,000 m.
6,562 ft. | 1,000 m.
3,281 ft. | 500 m.
1,640 ft. | 200 m.
656 ft. | 100 m.
328 ft. | Sea
Level | Below |

Michigan

SCALE
0 5 10 20 30 40 50 MI.
0 5 10 20 30 40 50 KM.

State Capitals .... ✹
County Seats .... ◉
Canals ....
Major Limited Access Hwys. ....

Scale 1:2,360,000

Same scale as main map.

ISLE ROYALE NATIONAL PARK
Siskiwit Bay
L. Superior
Same scale as main map

© Copyright HAMMOND INCORPORATED, Maplewood, N.J.

AREA 58,527 sq. mi. (151,585 sq. km.)
POPULATION 9,262,078
CAPITAL Lansing
LARGEST CITY Detroit
HIGHEST POINT Mt. Curwood 1,980 ft. (604 m.)
SETTLED IN 1650
ADMITTED TO UNION January 26, 1837
POPULAR NAME Wolverine State
STATE FLOWER Apple Blossom
STATE BIRD Robin

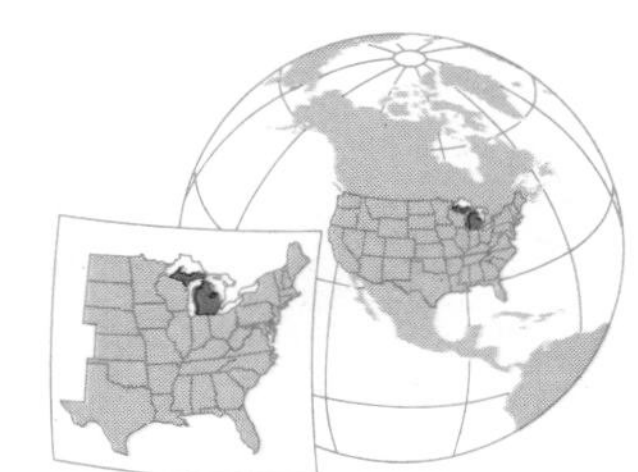

Topography

0 50 100 MI.
0 50 100 KM.

Below Sea Level 100 m. 328 ft. 200 m. 656 ft. 500 m. 1,640 ft. 1,000 m. 3,281 ft. 2,000 m. 6,562 ft. 5,000 m. 16,404 ft.

COUNTIES

Alcona 9,740 F4
Alger 9,225 C2
Allegan 81,555 D6
Alpena 32,315 F4
Antrim 16,194 D3
Arenac 14,706 F4
Baraga 8,484 A2
Barry 45,781 D6
Bay 119,881 E5
Benzie 11,205 C4
Berrien 171,276 C7
Branch 40,188 D7
Calhoun 141,557 D6
Cass 49,499 C7
Charlevoix 19,907 D3
Cheboygan 20,649 E3
Chippewa 29,029 E2
Clare 23,822 E5
Clinton 55,893 E6
Crawford 9,465 E4
Delta 38,947 C2
Dickinson 25,341 B2
Eaton 88,337 E6
Emmet 22,992 E3
Genesee 450,449 F5
Gladwin 19,957 E4
Gogebic 19,686 F2
Grand Traverse 54,899 D4
Gratiot 40,448 E5
Hillsdale 42,071 E7
Houghton 37,872 G1
Huron 36,459 F5
Ingham 275,520 E6
Ionia 51,815 D6
Iosco 28,349 F4
Iron 13,635 G2
Isabella 54,110 E5
Jackson 151,495 E6
Kalamazoo 212,378 D6
Kalkaska 10,952 D4
Kent 444,506 D5
Keweenaw 1,963 A1
Lake 7,711 D5
Lapeer 70,038 F5
Leelanau 14,007 D4
Lenawee 89,948 E7
Livingston 100,289 F6
Luce 6,659 D2
Mackinac 10,178 D2
Macomb 694,600 G6
Manistee 23,019 C4
Marquette 74,101 B2
Mason 26,365 C4
Mecosta 36,961 D5
Menominee 26,201 B3
Midland 73,578 E5
Missaukee 10,009 D4
Monroe 134,659 F7
Montcalm 47,555 D5
Montmorency 7,492 E3
Muskegon 157,589 C5
Newaygo 34,917 D5
Oakland 1,011,793 F6
Oceana 22,002 C5
Ogemaw 16,436 E4
Ontonagon 9,861 F1
Osceola 18,928 D5
Oscoda 6,858 E4
Otsego 14,993 E3
Ottawa 157,174 C6
Presque Isle 14,267 F3
Roscommon 16,374 E4
Saginaw 228,059 E5
Saint Clair 138,802 G6
Saint Joseph 56,083 D7
Sanilac 40,789 G5
Schoolcraft 8,575 C2
Shiawassee 71,140 E6
Tuscola 56,961 F5
Van Buren 66,814 C6
Washtenaw 264,748 F6
Wayne 2,337,891 F6
Wexford 25,102 D4

CITIES and TOWNS

Zip Name/Pop. Key

49220 Addison 655 E7
49221 Adrian⊙ 21,186 F7
48701 Akron 538 F5
†48763 Alabaster 46 F4
49224 Albion 11,059 E6
48001 Algonac 4,412 G6
49010 Allegan⊙ 4,576 D6
48101 Allen Park 34,196 B7
48801 Alma 9,652 E5
48003 Almont 1,857 F6
49707 Alpena⊙ 12,214 F3
*48103 Ann Arbor⊙ 107,966 F6
Ann Arbor‡ 264,748 F6
48005 Armada 1,392 G6
48806 Ashley 570 E5
49011 Athens 960 D6
49709 Atlanta⊙ 475 E3
48611 Auburn 1,921 F5
48703 Au Gres 768 F4
49012 Augusta 913 D6
†48750 Au Sable 1,240 F4
48413 Bad Axe⊙ 3,184 G5
49304 Baldwin⊙ 674 D5
48414 Bancroft 618 E6
49013 Bangor 2,001 C6
49908 Baraga 1,055 G1
49101 Baroda 627 C7
*49014 Battle Creek 35,724 D6
Battle Creek‡ 187,338 D6
48706 Bay City⊙ 41,593 F5
Bay City‡ 119,881 F5
48612 Beaverton 1,025 E5
†49423 Beechwood 2,333 C6
48809 Belding 5,634 D5
49615 Bellaire⊙ 1,063 D4
48111 Belleville 3,366 F6
49021 Bellevue 1,289 E6
49022 Benton Harbor 14,707 C6
Benton Harbor‡ 171,276 C6
†49022 Benton Heights 6,787 C6
48072 Berkley 18,637 B6
49103 Berrien Springs 2,042 C7
49911 Bessemer⊙ 2,553 F2
49617 Beulah⊙ 454 C4
†48010 Beverly Hills 11,598 B6
49307 Big Rapids⊙ 14,361 D5
48415 Birch Run 1,196 F5
*48008 Birmingham 21,689 B6
49228 Blissfield 3,107 F7
48013 Bloomfield Hills 3,985 B6
49026 Bloomingdale 537 C6
49712 Boyne City 3,348 E3
48615 Breckenridge 1,495 E5
49106 Bridgman 2,235 C7
48116 Brighton 4,268 F6
49229 Britton 693 F6
49028 Bronson 2,271 D7
49230 Brooklyn 1,110 E6
48416 Brown City 1,163 G5
49107 Buchanan 5,142 C7
49030 Burr Oak 853 D7
48507 Burton 29,976 F6
48418 Byron 689 E6
49601 Cadillac⊙ 10,199 D4
49316 Caledonia 722 D6
49913 Calumet 1,013 A1
48014 Capac 1,377 G5
48117 Carleton 2,786 F6
48723 Caro⊙ 4,317 F5
48724 Carrollton 7,482 E5
48811 Carson City 1,229 E5
48419 Carsonville 622 G5
48725 Caseville 851 F5
49915 Caspian 1,038 G2
48726 Cass City 2,258 F5
49031 Cassopolis⊙ 1,933 C7
49319 Cedar Springs 2,615 D5
49233 Cement City 539 E6
48015 Center Line 9,293 B6
49622 Central Lake 895 D3
49032 Centreville⊙ 1,202 D7
49720 Charlevoix⊙ 3,296 D3
48813 Charlotte⊙ 8,251 E6
49721 Cheboygan⊙ 5,106 E3
48118 Chelsea 3,816 E6
48616 Chesaning 2,656 E5
48617 Clare 3,300 E5
48016 Clarkston 968 F6
48017 Clawson 15,103 B6
49034 Climax 619 D6
49236 Clinton 2,342 F6
48420 Clio 2,669 F5
49036 Coldwater⊙ 9,461 D7
48618 Coleman 1,429 E5
49038 Coloma 1,833 C6
49040 Colon 1,190 D7
48421 Columbiaville 953 F5
49041 Comstock○ 11,162 D6
49237 Concord 900 E6
49042 Constantine 1,680 D7
49404 Coopersville 2,889 C5
48817 Corunna⊙ 3,206 E6
48422 Croswell 2,073 G5
49920 Crystal Falls⊙ 1,965 A2
49508 Cutlerville 8,256 D6
48423 Davison 6,087 F5
*48120 Dearborn 90,660 B7
48127 Dearborn Heights 67,706 B7
49045 Decatur 1,915 C6
48427 Deckerville 887 G5
49238 Deerfield 957 F7
*48201 Detroit⊙ 1,203,339 B7
Detroit‡ 4,352,762 B7
†48161 Detroit Beach 2,112 F7
48820 De Witt 3,165 E6
48130 Dexter 1,524 F6
48821 Dimondale 1,008 E6
49406 Douglas 948 C6
49047 Dowagiac 6,307 D6
48020 Drayton Plains F6
49726 Drummond Island○ 746 F3
48428 Dryden 650 F6
48131 Dundee 2,575 F7
48429 Durand 4,241 E6
49924 Eagle River⊙ 20 A1
48021 East Detroit 38,280 B6
†49506 East Grand Rapids 10,914 D6
49727 East Jordan 2,185 D3
†49801 East Kingsford A3
48823 East Lansing 51,392 E6
48730 East Tawas 2,584 F4
†49001 Eastwood 7,186 D6
48827 Eaton Rapids 4,510 E6
49111 Eau Claire 573 C6
48229 Ecorse 14,447 B7
48829 Edmore 1,176 E5
49112 Edwardsburg 1,135 C7
49628 Elberta 556 C4
49629 Elk Rapids 1,504 D4
48731 Elkton 953 F5
48831 Elsie 1,022 E5
49829 Escanaba⊙ 14,355 C3
48732 Essexville 4,378 F5
49631 Evart 1,945 D5
48733 Fairgrove 691 F5
49022 Fair Plain 8,289 C6
*48024 Farmington 11,022 F6
48024 Farmington Hills 58,056 F6
48622 Farwell 804 E5
49408 Fennville 934 C6
48430 Fenton 8,098 F6
48220 Ferndale 26,227 B6
49409 Ferrysburg 2,440 C5
48134 Flat Rock 6,853 F6
*48501 Flint⊙ 159,611 F5
Flint‡ 521,589 F5
48433 Flushing 8,624 F5
48835 Fowler 1,021 E5
48836 Fowlerville 2,289 F6
48734 Frankenmuth 3,753 F5
49635 Frankfort 1,603 C4
48025 Franklin 2,864 B6
48026 Fraser 14,560 B6
48623 Freeland 1,364 E5
49412 Fremont 3,672 D5
49415 Fruitport 1,143 C5
49053 Galesburg 1,822 D6
49113 Galien 692 C7
48135 Garden City 35,640 F6
49735 Gaylord⊙ 3,011 E3
48173 Gibraltar 4,458 F6
49837 Gladstone 4,533 C3
48624 Gladwin⊙ 2,479 E5
49055 Gobles 816 D6
48438 Goodrich 795 F6
48439 Grand Blanc 6,848 F6
49417 Grand Haven⊙ 11,763 C5
48837 Grand Ledge 6,920 E6
*49501 Grand Rapids⊙ 181,843 D5
Grand Rapids‡ 601,680 D5
49418 Grandville 12,412 D6
49327 Grant 683 D5
49240 Grass Lake 962 E6
49738 Grayling⊙ 1,792 E4
48838 Greenville 8,019 D5
48138 Grosse Ile 9,320 B7
48236 Grosse Pointe 5,901 B7
†48236 Grosse Pointe Farms 10,551 B6
†48236 Grosse Pointe Park 13,639 B7
†48236 Grosse Pointe Shores 3,122 B6
†48236 Grosse Pointe Woods 18,886 B6
49841 Gwinn 1,408 B2
48212 Hamtramck 21,300 B6
49930 Hancock 5,122 G1
48441 Harbor Beach 2,000 G5
49740 Harbor Springs 1,567 D3
48225 Harper Woods 16,361 B6
48625 Harrison⊙ 1,700 E4
48740 Harrisville⊙ 559 F4
49420 Hart⊙ 1,888 C5
49057 Hartford 2,493 C6
48840 Haslett 7,025 E6
49058 Hastings⊙ 6,418 D6
48030 Hazel Park 20,914 B6
48626 Hemlock 1,362 E5
49421 Hesperia 876 D5
48203 Highland Park 27,909 B6
49242 Hillsdale⊙ 7,432 E7
49423 Holland 26,281 C6
48842 Holt 10,097 E6
49245 Homer 1,791 E6
49931 Houghton⊙ 7,512 G1
48629 Houghton Lake 2,449 E4
48630 Houghton Lake Heights E4
49329 Howard City 1,118 D5
48843 Howell⊙ 6,976 E6
49934 Hubbell 1,278 A1
49247 Hudson 2,545 E7
49426 Hudsonville 4,844 D6
48444 Imlay City 2,495 F5
48141 Inkster 35,190 B7
49643 Interlochen 600 D4
48846 Ionia⊙ 5,920 D6
49801 Iron Mountain⊙ 8,341 B3
49935 Iron River 2,426 G2
49938 Ironwood 7,741 F2
49849 Ishpeming 7,538 B2
48847 Ithaca⊙ 2,950 E5
*49201 Jackson⊙ 39,739 E6
Jackson‡ 151,495 E6
49428 Jenison 16,330 D6
49250 Jonesville 2,172 E6
*49001 Kalamazoo⊙ 79,722 D6
Kalamazoo-Portage‡ 279,192 D6
49646 Kalkaska⊙ 1,654 D4
48030 Keego Harbor 3,083 F6
49330 Kent City 860 D5
49508 Kentwood 30,438 D6
48445 Kinde 600 G5
49801 Kingsford 5,290 A3
49649 Kingsley 664 D4
48848 Laingsburg 1,145 E6
49651 Lake City⊙ 843 D4
49945 Lake Linden 1,181 A1
†49039 Lake Michigan Beach 2,001 C6
48849 Lake Odessa 2,171 D6
48035 Lake Orion 2,907 F6
48850 Lakeview 1,139 D5
†49440 Lakewood Club 695 C5
48144 Lambertville 6,341 F7
49946 L'Anse⊙ 2,500 G1
*48901 Lansing (cap.) 130,414 E6
Lansing-East Lansing‡ 468,482 E6
48446 Lapeer⊙ 6,198 F5
49913 Laurium 2,678 A1
49064 Lawrence 903 C6
49065 Lawton 1,558 D6
49654 Leland⊙ 776 D3
48449 Lennon 600 E5
49251 Leslie 2,110 E6
48450 Lexington 765 G5
48742 Lincoln 361 F4
48146 Lincoln Park 45,105 B7
48451 Linden 2,174 F6
49252 Litchfield 1,353 E6
*48150 Livonia 104,814 F6
49331 Lowell 3,707 D6
49431 Ludington⊙ 8,937 C5

(continued on following page)

48157 Luna Pier 1,443............F7
48851 Lyons 708..................E6
49757 Mackinac Island 479.......E3
49701 Mackinaw City 820.........E3
48071 Madison Heights 35,375...B6
49659 Mancelona 1,432...........E4
48158 Manchester 1,686..........F6
49660 Manistee⊙ 7,566..........C4
49854 Manistique⊙ 3,962........C3
49663 Manton 1,212..............D4
48853 Maple Rapids 683..........E5
49067 Marcellus 1,134...........D6
48039 Marine City 4,414.........G6
49665 Marion 816................D4
48453 Marlette 1,761............F5
49855 Marquette⊙ 23,288........B2
49068 Marshall⊙ 7,201..........E6
49070 Martin 447................D6
48040 Marysville 7,345..........G6
48854 Mason⊙ 6,019.............E6
49071 Mattawan 2,143............D6
48744 Mayville 958..............F5
49657 McBain 519................D4
48122 Melvindale 12,322.........B7
48041 Memphis 1,171.............F5
49072 Mendon 951................D7
49858 Menominee⊙ 10,099........B3
48637 Merrill 851...............E5
48455 Metamora 552..............F5
49254 Michigan Center 5,244.....E6
49333 Middleville 1,797.........D6
48640 Midland⊙ 37,250..........E5
48160 Milan 4,182...............E6
48042 Milford 5,041.............F6
48746 Millington 1,237..........F5
48647 Mio⊙ 975.................E4
48161 Monroe⊙ 23,531..........F7
49437 Montague 2,332............C5
48457 Montrose 1,706............F5
49256 Morenci 2,110.............E7
49336 Morley 507................D5
48857 Morrice 733...............E5
48043 Mount Clemens⊙ 18,806....B6
48458 Mount Morris 3,246........F5
48858 Mount Pleasant⊙ 23,746...E5
48860 Muir 698..................D5
48861 Mulliken 550..............E6
49862 Munising⊙ 3,083..........C2
*49440 Muskegon⊙ 40,823.......C5
   Muskegon-Norton Shores-
   Muskegon Heights‡
   179,591....................C5
49444 Muskegon Heights 14,611..C5
49261 Napoleon 1,400............E6
49073 Nashville 1,628...........D6
49866 Negaunee 5,189............B2
49337 Newaygo 1,271.............D5
48047 New Baltimore 5,439.......G6
49868 Newberry⊙ 2,120.........D2
48164 New Boston 1,200..........F6
49117 New Buffalo 2,821.........C7
48048 New Haven 1,871...........G6
48460 New Lothrop 646...........F5

49120 Niles 13,115..............C7
49262 North Adams 565...........E7
48461 North Branch 896..........F5
49445 North Muskegon 4,024.....C5
49670 Northport 611.............D3
48167 Northville 5,698..........F6
†49441 Norton Shores 22,025....C5
49870 Norway 2,919..............B3
48050 Novi 22,525...............F6
48237 Oak Park 31,537...........B6
48864 Okemos 8,882..............E6
49265 Onaway 1,084..............E3
49675 Onekama 582...............C4
49265 Onsted 670................E6
49953 Ontonagon⊙ 2,182........F1
48033 Orchard Lake 1,798........F6
48462 Ortonville 1,190..........F6
48750 Oscoda 2,431..............F4
48463 Otisville 682.............F5
49078 Otsego 3,802..............D6
48866 Ovid 1,712................E5
48051 Oxford 2,746..............F6
48867 Owosso 16,455.............E5
49004 Parchment 1,817...........D6
49269 Parma 873.................E6
49079 Paw Paw 3,211.............D6
†49038 Paw Paw Lake 4,193......C6
48052 Pearl Beach 3,430.........G6
48466 Peck 606..................G5
49769 Pellston 565..............E3
49449 Pentwater 1,165...........C5
48872 Perry 2,051...............E6
49270 Petersburg 1,222..........F7
49750 Petoskey⊙ 6,097.........E3
48755 Pigeon 1,247..............F5
49169 Pinckney 1,390............F6
48650 Pinconning 1,430..........F5
49080 Plainwell 3,751...........D6
48069 Pleasant Ridge 3,217......B6
*48170 Plymouth 9,986...........F6
*48053 Pontiac⊙ 76,715.........F6
49081 Portage 38,157............D6
48467 Port Austin 839...........F4
48060 Port Huron⊙ 33,981......G6
48875 Portland 3,963............E6
49769 Port Sanilac 598..........G5
49776 Posen 270.................F3
48876 Potterville 1,502.........E6
49082 Quincy 1,569..............E7
49959 Ramsay....................F2
49451 Ravenna 951...............D5
49274 Reading 1,203.............E7
49677 Reed City⊙ 2,221........D5
48757 Reese 1,645...............F5
48062 Richmond 3,536............G6
48218 River Rouge 12,912........B7
48192 Riverview 14,569..........B7
48063 Rochester 7,203...........F6
49341 Rockford 3,324............D5
48173 Rockwood 3,346............F6
49779 Rogers City⊙ 3,923......F3
48065 Romeo 3,509...............F6

48174 Romulus 24,857............F6
49444 Roosevelt Park 4,015.....C5
48653 Roscommon⊙ 834..........E4
48654 Rose City 661.............E4
48066 Roseville 54,311..........B6
49452 Rothbury 522..............C5
*48067 Royal Oak 70,893.........B6
*48601 Saginaw⊙ 77,508.........F5
   Saginaw‡ 228,059..........F5
48655 Saint Charles 2,276.......E5
48079 Saint Clair 4,780.........G6
*48080 Saint Clair Shores 76,210.B6
49781 Saint Ignace⊙ 2,632.....E3
48879 Saint Johns⊙ 7,376......E5
49085 Saint Joseph⊙ 9,622.....C6
48880 Saint Louis 4,107.........E5
48176 Saline 6,483..............F6
48471 Sandusky⊙ 2,216........G5
48881 Saranac 1,421.............D6
49453 Saugatuck 1,079...........C6
49783 Sault Sainte
   Marie⊙ 14,448............E2
49087 Schoolcraft 1,359.........D6
49454 Scottville 1,241..........C5
48759 Sebewaing 2,046...........F5
49455 Shelby 1,624..............C5
48883 Shepherd 1,534............E5
48884 Sheridan 664..............D5
†49085 Shoreham 742.............C6
*49125 Shorewood 1,735...........C7
*48034 Southfield 75,568.........F6
48195 Southgate 32,058..........F6
49090 South Haven 5,943.........C6
48178 South Lyon 5,214..........F6
†48161 South Monroe 4,232.......F7
49963 South Range 861...........G1
48179 South Rockwood 1,353.....F7
†48060 South Sparling 1,718.....G6
49345 Sparta 3,373..............D5
49283 Spring Arbor 2,101........E6
49015 Springfield 5,917.........D6
49456 Spring Lake 2,731.........C5
49284 Springport 675............E6
49964 Stambaugh 1,442...........G2
48658 Standish⊙ 1,264.........F5
48888 Stanton⊙ 1,315..........D5
49887 Stephenson 967............B3
48659 Sterling 457..............E4
48077 Sterling Heights 108,999..B6
49127 Stevensville 1,268........C6
49285 Stockbridge 1,213.........E6
49091 Sturgis 9,468.............D7
48890 Sunfield 591..............D6
49682 Suttons Bay 504...........D3
48473 Swartz Creek 5,013........F6
†48053 Sylvan Lake 1,949........F6
48763 Tawas City⊙ 1,967.......F4
48180 Taylor 77,568.............B7
49286 Tecumseh 7,320............E7
49092 Tekonsha 755..............E6
48128 Three Oaks 1,774..........C7
49093 Three Rivers 7,015........D7

49684 Traverse City⊙ 15,516...D4
48183 Trenton 22,762............B7
*48084 Troy 67,102...............B6
48475 Ubly 862..................G5
49094 Union City 1,667..........D6
49129 Union Pier 1,039..........C7
48767 Unionville 578............F5
*48087 Utica 5,282...............F6
49095 Vandalia 447..............D7
49795 Vanderbilt 525............E3
48768 Vassar 2,727..............F5
49096 Vermontville 832..........E6
48476 Vernon 1,008..............F6
49097 Vicksburg 2,224...........D6
49968 Wakefield 2,591...........F2
49288 Waldron 570...............E7
49504 Walker 15,088.............D6
48088 Walled Lake 4,748.........F6
*48089 Warren 161,134............B6
49098 Watervliet 1,867..........C6
49348 Wayland 2,023.............D6
48184 Wayne 21,159..............F6
48892 Webberville 1,535.........E6
49894 Wells.....................B3
48661 West Branch⊙ 1,785......E4
48185 Westland 84,603...........F6
48894 Westphalia 896............E6
49349 White Cloud⊙ 1,101......D5
49461 Whitehall 2,856...........C5
49099 White Pigeon 1,478........D7
49971 White Pine 1,142..........F1
48189 Whitmore Lake 2,920.......F6
48770 Whittemore 438............F4
48895 Williamston 2,981.........E6
48096 Wixom 6,705...............F6
†49440 Wolf Lake 3,876..........C5
49799 Wolverine 364.............E3
†48183 Woodhaven 10,902.........F6
48897 Woodland 431..............D6
48192 Wyandotte 34,006..........B7
49509 Wyoming 59,616............D6
48097 Yale 1,814................G5
48197 Ypsilanti 24,031..........F6
49464 Zeeland 4,764.............D6
†48601 Zilwaukee 2,201..........F5

OTHER FEATURES

Abbaye (pt.)....................B2
Au Sable (pt.)..................C2
Au Sable (pt.)..................F4
Au Sable (riv.).................E4
Au Train (bay)..................C2
Bad (riv.)......................E5
Barques (pt.)...................C3
Beaver (isl.)...................D3
Beaver (lake)...................F4
Belle (riv.)....................G6
Bete Grise (bay)................B1
Betsy (riv.)....................D2
Big Bay (pt.)...................B2
Big Bay de Noc (bay)............C3
Big Iron (riv.).................F1

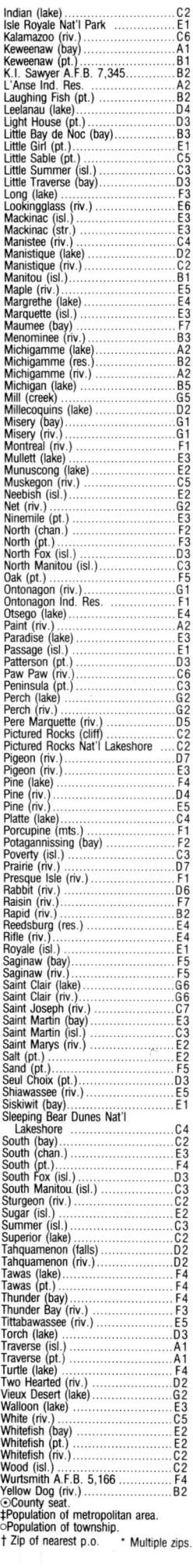

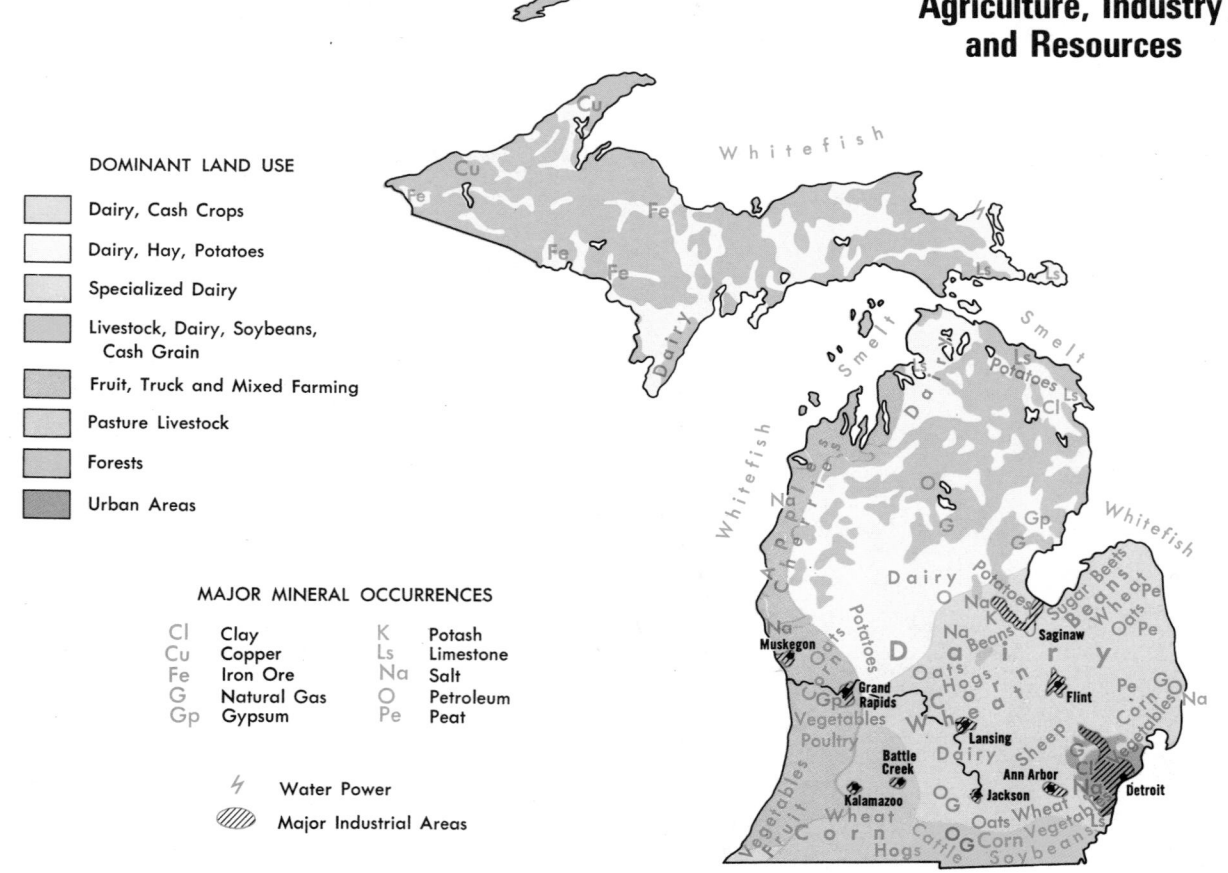

Agriculture, Industry and Resources

DOMINANT LAND USE

Dairy, Cash Crops

Dairy, Hay, Potatoes

Specialized Dairy

Livestock, Dairy, Soybeans, Cash Grain

Fruit, Truck and Mixed Farming

Pasture Livestock

Forests

Urban Areas

MAJOR MINERAL OCCURRENCES

Cl   Clay   K   Potash
Cu   Copper   Ls   Limestone
Fe   Iron Ore   Na   Salt
G   Natural Gas   O   Petroleum
Gp   Gypsum   Pe   Peat

⚡   Water Power

▨   Major Industrial Areas

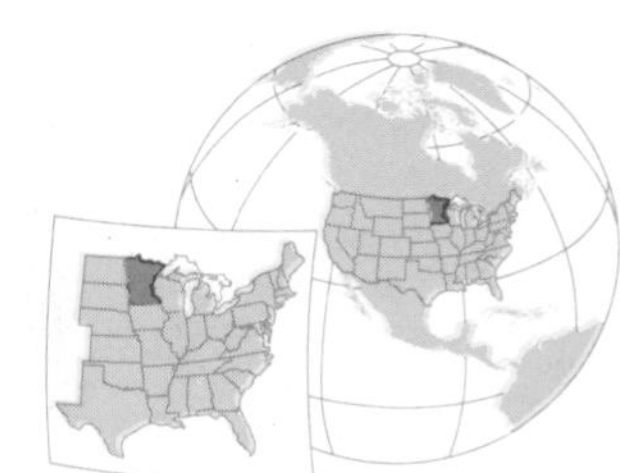

AREA 84,402 sq. mi. (218,601 sq. km.)
POPULATION 4,075,970
CAPITAL St. Paul
LARGEST CITY Minneapolis
HIGHEST POINT Eagle Mtn. 2,301 ft. (701 m.)
SETTLED IN 1805
ADMITTED TO UNION May 11, 1858
POPULAR NAME North Star State; Gopher State
STATE FLOWER Pink & White Lady's-Slipper
STATE BIRD Common Loon

COUNTIES

Name/Pop.	Key
Aitkin 13,404	E4
Anoka 195,998	E5
Becker 29,336	C4
Beltrami 30,982	C2
Benton 25,187	D5
Big Stone 7,716	B5
Blue Earth 52,314	D6
Brown 28,645	D6
Carlton 29,936	F4
Carver 37,046	E6
Cass 21,050	D4
Chippewa 14,941	C5
Chisago 25,717	F5
Clay 49,327	B4
Clearwater 8,761	C3
Cook 4,092	H3
Cottonwood 14,854	C6
Crow Wing 41,722	D4
Dakota 194,279	E6
Dodge 14,773	F7
Douglas 27,839	C5
Faribault 19,714	D7
Fillmore 21,930	F7
Freeborn 36,329	E7
Goodhue 38,749	F6
Grant 7,171	B5
Hennepin 941,411	E5
Houston 18,382	G7
Hubbard 14,098	D3
Isanti 23,600	E5
Itasca 43,069	E3
Jackson 13,690	C7
Kanabec 12,161	E5
Kandiyohi 36,763	C5
Kittson 6,672	B2
Koochiching 17,571	E2
Lac qui Parle 10,592	B6
Lake 13,043	G3
Lake of the Woods 3,764	D2
Le Sueur 23,434	E6
Lincoln 8,207	B6
Lyon 25,207	C6
Mahnomen 5,535	C3
Marshall 13,027	B2
Martin 24,687	D7
McLeod 29,657	D6
Meeker 20,594	D5
Mille Lacs 18,430	E5
Morrison 29,311	D4
Mower 40,390	F7
Murray 11,507	C6
Nicollet 26,929	D6
Nobles 21,840	C7
Norman 9,379	B3
Olmsted 92,006	F7
Otter Tail 51,937	C4
Pennington 15,258	B2
Pine 19,871	F4
Pipestone 11,690	B6
Polk 34,844	B3
Pope 11,657	C5
Ramsey 459,784	E5
Red Lake 5,471	B3
Redwood 19,341	C6
Renville 20,401	C6
Rice 46,087	E6
Rock 10,703	B7
Roseau 12,574	C2
Saint Louis 222,229	F3
Scott 43,784	E6
Sherburne 29,908	E5
Sibley 15,448	D6
Stearns 108,161	D5
Steele 30,328	E7
Stevens 11,322	B5
Swift 12,920	C5
Todd 24,991	D4
Traverse 5,542	B5
Wabasha 19,335	F6
Wadena 14,192	D4
Waseca 18,448	E6
Washington 113,571	F5
Watonwan 12,361	D7
Wilkin 8,454	B4
Winona 46,256	G6
Wright 58,681	D5
Yellow Medicine 13,653	B6

CITIES and TOWNS

Zip	Name/Pop.	Key
56510	Ada⊙ 1,971	B3
55909	Adams 797	F7
56110	Adrian 1,336	C7
55001	Afton 2,550	F6
56430	Ah-Gwah-Ching 400	D3
56431	Aitkin⊙ 1,770	E4
56433	Akeley 486	D3
56307	Albany 1,569	D5
56207	Alberta 145	B5
56007	Albert Lea⊙ 19,200	E7
55301	Albertville 564	E5
56009	Alden 687	E7
56308	Alexandria⊙ 7,608	C5
56111	Alpha 180	D7
55910	Altura 354	G6
56710	Alvarado 385	B2
56010	Amboy 606	D7
†55303	Andover 9,387	E5
55302	Annandale 1,568	D5
55303	Anoka⊙ 15,634	E5
56208	Appleton 1,842	C5
†55124	Apple Valley 21,818	G6
56713	Argyle 741	B2
55307	Arlington 1,779	D6
56309	Ashby 486	C4
55704	Askov 350	F4
56209	Atwater 1,128	D5
56511	Audubon 383	C4
55705	Aurora 2,670	F3
55912	Austin⊙ 23,020	E7
56114	Avoca 201	C7
56310	Avon 804	D5
55706	Babbitt 2,435	G3
56435	Backus 255	D4
56714	Badger 320	B2
56621	Bagley⊙ 1,321	C3
56115	Balaton 752	C6
56514	Barnesville 2,207	B4
55707	Barnum 464	F4
56311	Barrett 388	B5
56515	Battle Lake 708	C4
56623	Baudette⊙ 1,170	D2
†56401	Baxter 2,625	D4
55003	Bayport 2,932	F5
56211	Beardsley 344	B5
55601	Beaver Bay 283	G3
56116	Beaver Creek 260	B7
55308	Becker 601	E5
56312	Belgrade 805	C5
†55027	Bellechester 220	F6
56011	Belle Plaine 2,754	E6
56212	Bellingham 290	B5
56214	Belview 438	C6
56601	Bemidji⊙ 10,949	D3
56626	Bena 153	D3
56215	Benson⊙ 3,656	C5
56437	Bertha 510	C4
55005	Bethel 272	E5
56117	Bigelow 249	C7
56627	Big Falls 490	E2
56628	Bigfork 457	E3
55309	Big Lake 2,210	E5
56118	Bingham Lake 222	C7
55310	Bird Island 1,372	D6
55708	Biwabik 1,428	F3
56630	Blackduck 653	D3
†55433	Blaine 28,558	G5
56216	Blomkest 200	D6
55917	Blooming Prairie 1,969	E7
55420	Bloomington 81,831	G6
56013	Blue Earth⊙ 4,132	D7
56518	Bluffton 206	C4
56519	Borup 160	B3
55709	Bovey 813	E3
56314	Bowlus 276	D5
56218	Boyd 329	C6
55006	Braham 1,015	E5
56401	Brainerd⊙ 11,489	D4
†55056	Branch 1,866	F5
56315	Brandon 473	C5
56520	Breckenridge⊙ 3,909	B4
†56472	Breezy Point 384	D4
56119	Brewster 559	C7
56014	Bricelyn 487	E7
55429	Brooklyn Center 31,230	G5
†55444	Brooklyn Park 43,332	G5
56715	Brooks 173	B3
56316	Brooten 647	C5
56438	Browerville 693	D4
55918	Brownsdale 691	F7
56219	Browns Valley 887	B5
55919	Brownsville 418	G7
55312	Brownton 697	D6
56317	Buckman 171	D5
55313	Buffalo⊙ 4,560	E5
55314	Buffalo Lake 782	D6
55713	Buhl 1,284	F3
55337	Burnsville 35,674	E6
56318	Burtrum 177	D5
56120	Butterfield 634	D7
55920	Byron 1,715	F6
55921	Caledonia⊙ 2,691	G7
56521	Callaway 238	C3
55716	Calumet 469	E3
55008	Cambridge⊙ 3,287	E5
56522	Campbell 286	B4
56220	Canby 2,143	B6
55009	Cannon Falls 2,653	F6
55922	Canton 386	F7
56319	Carlos 364	C5
55718	Carlton⊙ 862	F4
55315	Carver 642	E6
56633	Cass Lake 1,001	D3
55012	Center City⊙ 458	F5
†55038	Centerville 734	E5
56121	Ceylon 543	D7
55316	Champlin 9,006	G5
56122	Chandler 344	C7
55317	Chanhassen 6,359	F6
55318	Chaska⊙ 8,346	F6
55923	Chatfield 2,055	F7
55013	Chisago City 1,634	E5
55719	Chisholm 5,930	E3
56221	Chokio 559	B5
55014	Circle Pines 3,321	G5
56222	Clara City 1,574	C6
55924	Claremont 591	E6
56440	Clarissa 663	C4
56223	Clarkfield 1,171	C6
56016	Clarks Grove 620	E7
56634	Clearbrook 579	C3
55319	Clear Lake 266	E5
55320	Clearwater 379	D5
56224	Clements 227	D6
56017	Cleveland 699	E6
56523	Climax 273	B3
56225	Clinton 622	B5
56226	Clontarf 196	C5
55720	Cloquet 11,142	F4
†55068	Coates 207	E6
55321	Cokato 2,056	D5
56320	Cold Spring 2,294	D5
55722	Coleraine 1,116	E3
55322	Cologne 545	E6
55421	Columbia Heights 20,029	G5
56019	Comfrey 548	D6
56020	Conger 183	E7
55723	Cook 800	F3
55433	Coon Rapids 35,826	G5
†55340	Corcoran 4,252	F5
56228	Cosmos 571	D6
55016	Cottage Grove 18,994	F6
56229	Cottonwood 924	C6
56021	Courtland 399	D6
55726	Cromwell 229	F4
56716	Crookston⊙ 8,628	B3
56441	Crosby 2,218	D4
56442	Crosslake 1,064	E4
†55428	Crystal 25,543	G5
55429	Crystal Bay (Orono) 6,845	F5
56123	Currie 359	C6
56323	Cyrus 334	C5
55925	Dakota 350	G7
56324	Dalton 248	C4
56230	Danube 590	C6
56231	Danvers 152	C5
56022	Darfur 139	D6
55324	Darwin 282	D5
55325	Dassel 1,066	D5
56232	Dawson 1,901	B6
55327	Dayton 4,070	E5
55391	Deephaven 3,716	G5
56527	Deer Creek 392	C4
56636	Deer River 907	E3
56444	Deerwood 580	E4
56233	De Graff 179	C5
55328	Delano 2,480	E5
56023	Delavan 262	D7
†55110	Dellwood 751	F5
56528	Dent 167	C4
56501	Detroit Lakes⊙ 7,106	C4
55926	Dexter 279	F7
56529	Dilworth 2,585	B4
55927	Dodge Center 1,816	F6
56235	Donnelly 317	B5
55929	Dover 312	F7
*55801	Duluth⊙ 92,811	F4
	Duluth-Superior‡ 266,650	F4
56236	Dumont 173	B5
55019	Dundas 422	E6
56127	Dunnell 216	D7
55111	Eagan 20,700	G6
56446	Eagle Bend 593	D4
56024	Eagle Lake 1,470	E6
†55005	East Bethel 6,626	E5
56721	East Grand Forks 8,537	B3
†56401	East Gull Lake 586	D4
56025	Easton 283	E7
56237	Echo 334	C6
55344	Eden Prairie 16,263	G6
55329	Eden Valley 763	D5
56128	Edgerton 1,123	B7
55424	Edina 46,073	G5
55931	Eitzen 226	G7
†55910	Elba 198	F6
56531	Elbow Lake⊙ 1,358	B5
55932	Elgin 667	F6
56533	Elizabeth 195	B4
55020	Elko 274	E6
55330	Elk River⊙ 6,785	E5
56026	Ellendale 555	E7
56129	Ellsworth 629	C7
56027	Elmore 882	D7
56325	Elrosa 214	C5
55731	Ely 4,820	G3
56028	Elysian 454	E6
56447	Emily 588	E4
56029	Emmons 465	E7
56534	Erhard 194	B4
56535	Erskine 585	B3
56326	Evansville 571	C4
55734	Eveleth 5,042	F3
55331	Excelsior 2,523	E6
55934	Eyota 1,244	F7
55332	Fairfax 1,405	D6
56031	Fairmont⊙ 11,506	D7
55113	Falcon Heights 5,291	G5
55021	Faribault⊙ 16,241	E6
55024	Farmington 4,370	E6
56641	Federal Dam 192	D3
56536	Felton 264	B3
56537	Fergus Falls⊙ 12,519	B4
56540	Fertile 869	B3
56448	Fifty Lakes 263	D4
55735	Finlayson 202	F4
56723	Fisher 453	B3
56328	Flensburg 256	D5
55736	Floodwood 648	E4
56329	Foley⊙ 1,606	D5
†56308	Forada 191	C5
55025	Forest Lake 4,596	F5
56330	Foreston 283	E5
56542	Fosston 1,599	C3
55935	Fountain 327	F7
56543	Foxhome 161	B4
55333	Franklin 512	D6
56544	Frazee 1,284	C4
56032	Freeborn 323	E7
56331	Freeport 563	D5
55432	Fridley 30,228	G5
56033	Frost 293	D7
56131	Fulda 1,308	C7
56332	Garfield 284	C5
56450	Garrison 174	E4
56132	Garvin 172	C6
56545	Gary 241	B3
55334	Gaylord⊙ 1,933	D6
56035	Geneva 417	E7
56239	Ghent 356	C6
55335	Gibbon 787	D6
55741	Gilbert 2,721	F3
56333	Gilman 156	E5
55336	Glencoe⊙ 4,396	D6
56036	Glenville 851	E7
56334	Glenwood⊙ 2,523	C5
56547	Glyndon 882	B4
55427	Golden Valley 22,775	G5
56644	Gonvick 362	C3
55027	Goodhue 657	F6
56725	Goodridge 191	C2
56037	Good Thunder 560	D6
55027	Goodview 2,567	G6
56240	Graceville 780	B5
56039	Granada 377	D7
55604	Grand Marais⊙ 1,289	G2
55936	Grand Meadow 965	F7
55744	Grand Rapids⊙ 7,934	E3
56241	Granite Falls⊙ 3,451	C6
55030	Grasston 123	E5
56726	Greenbush 817	B2
†55373	Greenfield 1,391	F5
55338	Green Isle 357	E6
56335	Greenwald 259	D5
56336	Grey Eagle 338	D5
56243	Grove City 596	D5
56727	Grygla 216	C2
56452	Hackensack 285	D4
56728	Hallock⊙ 1,405	A2
56548	Halstad 690	B3
55339	Hamburg 475	D6
55340	Hamel 2,623	F5
55304	Ham Lake 7,832	E5
55938	Hammond 178	F6
55031	Hampton 299	E6
56244	Hancock 877	C5
56245	Hanley Falls 265	C6
55341	Hanover 647	E5
56041	Hanska 429	D6
56134	Hardwick 279	B7
55939	Harmony 1,133	F7
55032	Harris 678	F5
56042	Hartland 322	E7
55033	Hastings⊙ 12,827	F6
56549	Hawley 1,634	B4
55940	Hayfield 1,243	F7
56043	Hayward 294	E7
55342	Hector 1,252	D6
56044	Henderson 739	E6
56136	Hendricks 737	B6
56550	Hendrum 336	B3
56551	Henning 832	C4
56248	Herman 600	B5
†55811	Hermantown 6,759	F4
56137	Heron Lake 783	C7
56453	Hewitt 299	C4
55746	Hibbing 21,193	F3
55748	Hill City 533	E4
56138	Hills 598	B7
55037	Hinckley 963	E4
56552	Hitterdal 253	B4

(continued on following page)

Agriculture, Industry and Resources

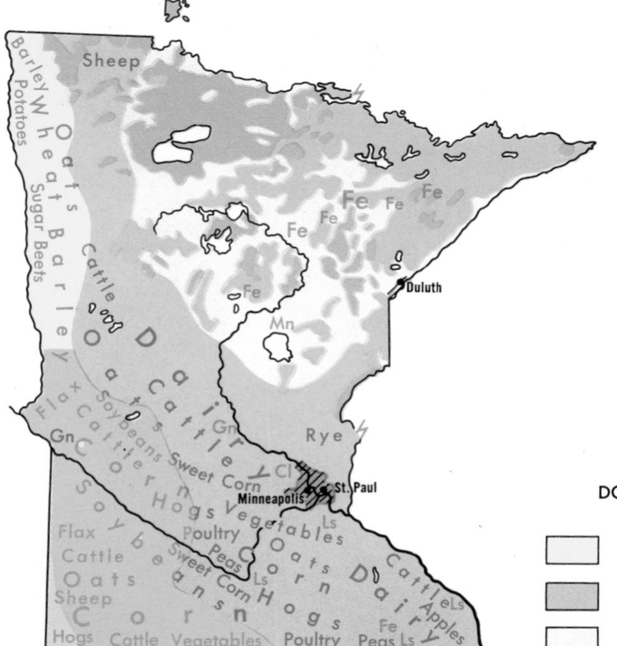

MAJOR MINERAL OCCURRENCES

Cl Clay
Fe Iron Ore
Gn Granite
Ls Limestone
Mn Manganese

Water Power
Major Industrial Areas

DOMINANT LAND USE

Wheat, General Farming
Dairy, Livestock
Dairy, Hay, Potatoes
Cattle Feed, Hogs
Livestock, Cash Grain
Forests
Swampland, Limited Agriculture
Urban Areas

56339 Hoffman 631 C5
55941 Hokah 686 G7
56340 Holdingford 635 D5
56139 Holland 234 B6
56045 Hollandale 290 E7
56249 Holloway 142 C5
55343 Hopkins 15,336 G5
55943 Houston 1,057 G7
55349 Howard Lake 1,240 D5
55750 Hoyt Lakes 3,186 F3
55038 Hugo 3,771 E5
55350 Hutchinson 9,244 D6
†55359 Independence 2,640 F5
56649 International Falls⊙ 5,611 E2
55075 Inver Grove Heights 17,171 E6
56141 Iona 248 C7
56455 Ironton 537 D4
55040 Isanti 858 E5
56342 Isle 573 E4
56142 Ivanhoe⊙ 761 B6
56143 Jackson⊙ 3,797 C7
56048 Janesville 1,897 E6
56144 Jasper 731 B7
56145 Jeffers 437 C6
56456 Jenkins 219 D4
55352 Jordan 2,663 E6
56251 Kandiyohi 447 D5
56732 Karlstad 934 B2
56050 Kasota 739 D6
55944 Kasson 2,827 F6
55753 Keewatin 1,443 E3
56650 Kelliher 324 D3
55945 Kellogg 440 G6
55754 Kelly Lake 900 F3
56733 Kennedy 405 B2
56343 Kensington 331 C5
55946 Kenyon 1,529 E6
56252 Kerkhoven 761 C5
56051 Kiester 670 E7
56052 Kilkenny 177 E6
55353 Kimball 651 D5
55758 Kinney 447 F3
55947 La Crescent 3,674 G7
56054 Lafayette 507 D6
56149 Lake Benton 869 B6
56734 Lake Bronson 298 B2
55041 Lake City 4,505 F6
56055 Lake Crystal 2,078 D6
55042 Lake Elmo 5,296 F6
56150 Lakefield 1,845 C7
†55398 Lake Fremont (Zimmerman) 1,074 E5
55043 Lakeland 1,812 F6
56253 Lake Lillian 329 C6
56554 Lake Park 716 B4
†55043 Lake Saint Croix Beach 1,176 F6
†56401 Lake Shore 583 D4
55044 Lakeville 14,790 E6
56151 Lake Wilson 380 B7
56152 Lamberton 1,032 C6
56735 Lancaster 368 B2
55949 Lanesboro 923 G7
56461 Laporte 160 D3
†55744 La Prairie 536 E3
56344 Lastrup 150 D4
†55101 Lauderdale 1,985 G5
56057 Le Center⊙ 1,967 E6
55951 Le Roy 930 F7
55354 Lester Prairie 1,229 D6
56058 Le Sueur 3,763 E6
55952 Lewiston 1,226 G7
56060 Lewisville 273 D7
†55014 Lexington 2,150 G5
†55050 Lilydale 417 G5
55045 Lindstrom 1,972 F5
†55038 Lino Lakes 4,966 G5
56155 Lismore 276 B7
55355 Litchfield⊙ 5,904 D5
56345 Little Falls⊙ 7,250 D5
56653 Littlefork 918 E2
†56334 Long Beach 263 C5
55356 Long Lake 1,747 F5
56347 Long Prairie⊙ 2,859 D5
56655 Longville 191 D4
55046 Lonsdale 1,160 E6
55357 Loretto 297 F5
56349 Lowry 283 C5
56255 Lucan 262 C6
56156 Luverne⊙ 4,568 B7
55953 Lyle 576 F7
56157 Lynd 304 C6
55954 Mabel 861 G7
56062 Madelia 2,130 D6
56256 Madison⊙ 2,212 B5
56063 Madison Lake 592 E6
56158 Magnolia 234 B7
56557 Mahnomen⊙ 1,283 C3
55115 Mahtomedi 3,851 F5
56001 Mankato⊙ 28,651 E6
55955 Mantorville⊙ 705 F6
†55369 Maple Grove 20,525 G5
55358 Maple Lake 1,132 D5
55359 Maple Plain 1,421 F5
56065 Mapleton 1,516 E7
†55912 Mapleview 253 E7
55109 Maplewood 26,990 G5
55764 Marble 757 E3
56257 Marietta 279 B5
55047 Marine on Saint Croix 543 F5
56258 Marshall⊙ 11,161 C6
55360 Mayer 388 E6
56260 Maynard 428 C6
55956 Mazeppa 680 F6
55760 McGregor 447 E4
56556 McIntosh 681 C3
55761 McKinley 230 F3
55049 Medford 775 E6
55441 Medicine Lake 419 G5
†55340 Medina (Hamel) 2,623 F5
†56352 Meire Grove 174 C5
56352 Melrose 2,409 D5
56464 Menahga 980 C4
55050 Mendota 219 G5
†55050 Mendota Heights 7,288 G6
56736 Mentor 219 B3
56737 Middle River 349 B2
†55033 Miesville 179 F6
56262 Milan 417 C5
55957 Millville 186 F6
56263 Milroy 242 C6
56354 Miltona 187 C4
*55401 Minneapolis⊙ 370,951 G5
Minneapolis-Saint Paul‡ 2,114,256 G5
56264 Minneota 1,470 C6
55959 Minnesota City 265 G6
56068 Minnesota Lake 744 E7
55343 Minnetonka 38,683 G5
†55364 Minnetrista 3,236 F5
56265 Montevideo⊙ 5,845 C6
56069 Montgomery 2,349 E6
55362 Monticello 2,830 E5
55363 Montrose 762 E5
56560 Moorhead⊙ 29,998 B4
Moorhead-Fargo‡ 137,574 B4
55767 Moose Lake 1,408 F4
55051 Mora⊙ 2,890 E5
56266 Morgan 975 D6
56267 Morris⊙ 5,367 C5
55052 Morristown 639 E6
56270 Morton 549 C6
56466 Motley 444 D4
55364 Mound 9,280 E6
†55112 Mounds View 12,593 G5
55768 Mountain Iron 4,134 F3
56159 Mountain Lake 2,277 D7
56271 Murdock 343 C5
55769 Nashwauk 1,419 E3
56355 Nelson 209 C5
55053 Nerstrand 255 E6
56467 Nevis 332 D4
55366 New Auburn 331 D6
55112 New Brighton 23,269 G5
56738 Newfolden 384 B2
55367 New Germany 347 E6
†55428 New Hope 23,087 G5
56273 New London 812 C5
55054 New Market 286 E6
56356 New Munich 302 D5
55055 Newport 3,323 F6
56071 New Prague 2,952 E6
56072 New Richland 1,263 E7
56073 New Ulm⊙ 13,755 D6
56567 New York Mills 972 C4
56074 Nicollet 709 D6
56568 Nielsville 145 B3
56468 Nisswa 1,407 D4
55056 North Branch 1,597 F5
55057 Northfield 12,562 E6
56001 North Mankato 9,145 D6
†55101 North Oaks 2,846 G5
56661 Northome 312 D3
56275 North Redwood 206 D6
56075 Northrop 269 D7
55109 North Saint Paul 11,921 G5
55368 Norwood 1,219 E6
†55109 Oakdale 12,123 E5
56276 Odessa 177 B5
56160 Odin 134 D7
56569 Ogema 215 C3
56358 Ogilvie 423 E5
56161 Okabena 263 C7
56742 Oklee 536 C3
56277 Olivia⊙ 2,802 C6
56359 Onamia 691 E4
56162 Ormsby 181 D7
†55323 Orono 6,845 F5
55960 Oronoco 574 F6
55771 Orr 294 F2
56278 Ortonville⊙ 2,550 B5
56360 Osakis 1,355 C5
56744 Oslo 379 A2
55369 Osseo 2,974 G5
55961 Ostrander 293 F7
56571 Ottertail 239 C4
55060 Owatonna⊙ 18,632 E6
56469 Palisade 155 E4
56361 Parkers Prairie 917 C4
56470 Park Rapids⊙ 2,976 D4
56362 Paynesville 2,140 D5
56363 Pease 174 E5
†56472 Pelican Lakes (Breezy Point) 384 D4
56572 Pelican Rapids 1,867 B4
56078 Pemberton 208 E7
56279 Pennock 410 C5
56472 Pequot Lakes 681 D4
56573 Perham 2,086 C4
55962 Peterson 291 G7
†56364 Pierz 1,018 D5
56473 Pillager 341 D4
55063 Pine City⊙ 2,489 F5
55963 Pine Island 1,986 F6
56474 Pine River 881 D4
56164 Pipestone⊙ 4,887 B7
55964 Plainview 2,416 F6
55370 Plato 390 D6
56748 Plummer 353 B3
†55441 Plymouth 31,615 G5
56280 Porter 211 B6
55965 Preston⊙ 1,478 F7
55371 Princeton 3,146 E5
56281 Prinsburg 557 C6
55372 Prior Lake 7,284 E6
55810 Proctor 3,180 F4
55967 Racine 285 F7
56475 Randall 527 D4
55065 Randolph 351 E6
56668 Ranier 237 E2
56282 Raymond 723 C5
56750 Red Lake Falls⊙ 1,732 B3
55066 Red Wing⊙ 13,736 F6
56283 Redwood Falls⊙ 5,210 C6
56672 Remer 396 E3
56284 Renville 1,493 C6
56166 Revere 158 C6
56367 Rice 499 D5
55423 Richfield 37,851 G6
56368 Richmond 867 D5
55422 Robbinsdale 14,422 G5
55901 Rochester⊙ 57,890 F6
Rochester‡ 91,971 F6
55067 Rock Creek 890 F5
55373 Rockford 2,408 F5
56369 Rockville 597 D5
55374 Rogers 652 E5
55969 Rollingstone 528 G6
56371 Roscoe 154 D5
56751 Roseau⊙ 2,272 C2
55970 Rose Creek 371 F7
55068 Rosemount 5,083 E6
55113 Roseville 35,820 G5
56579 Rothsay 476 B4
56167 Round Lake 480 C7
56373 Royalton 660 D5
55069 Rush City 1,198 F5
55971 Rushford 1,478 G7
56168 Rushmore 387 C7
56169 Russell 412 C6
56170 Ruthton 328 B6
55778 Rutledge 185 F4
56580 Sabin 446 B4
56285 Sacred Heart 666 C6
55414 Saint Anthony 7,981 G5
55375 Saint Bonifacius 857 F5
55972 Saint Charles 2,184 F7
56080 Saint Clair 655 E6
56301 Saint Cloud⊙ 42,566 D5
Saint Cloud‡ 163,256 D5
55070 Saint Francis 1,184 E5
56554 Saint Hilaire 388 B2
56081 Saint James⊙ 4,346 D7
56374 Saint Joseph 2,994 D5
55426 Saint Louis Park 42,931 G5
56376 Saint Martin 220 D5
55376 Saint Michael 1,519 E5
*55101 Saint Paul (cap.)⊙ 270,230 G6
Saint Paul-Minneapolis‡ 2,114,256 G5
55071 Saint Paul Park 4,864 G6
56082 Saint Peter⊙ 9,056 E6
56375 Saint Stephen 453 D5
56755 Saint Vincent 141 A2
56083 Sanborn 518 C6
55072 Sandstone 1,594 F4
56377 Sartell 3,427 D5
56378 Sauk Centre 3,709 C5
56379 Sauk Rapids 5,793 D5
55337 Savage 3,954 G6
†55720 Scanlon 1,050 F4
56477 Sebeka 774 C4
55074 Shafer 180 F5
55379 Shakopee⊙ 9,941 F6
56581 Shelly 276 B3
56171 Sherburn 1,275 D7
56676 Shevlin 193 C3
†55112 Shoreview 17,300 G5
†55331 Shorewood 4,646 F5
55614 Silver Bay 2,917 G3
55381 Silver Lake 698 D6
†56001 Skyline 399 D6
56172 Slayton⊙ 2,420 C7
56085 Sleepy Eye 3,581 D6
†56345 Sobieski 219 D5
55382 South Haven 205 D5
56679 South International Falls 2,806 E2
55075 South Saint Paul 21,235 G6
56288 Spicer 909 C5
56087 Springfield 2,303 C6
55974 Spring Grove 1,275 G7
†55432 Spring Lake Park 6,477 E5
55384 Spring Park 1,465 F5
55975 Spring Valley 2,616 F7
56681 Squaw Lake 162 D3
55079 Stacy 996 E5
56479 Staples 2,887 D4
56381 Starbuck 1,224 C5
56173 Steen 153 B7
56757 Stephen 898 A2
55385 Stewart 616 D6
55976 Stewartville 3,925 F7
55082 Stillwater⊙ 12,290 F5
55988 Stockton 517 G6
56174 Storden 341 C6
56758 Strandquist 136 B2
55783 Sturgeon Lake 222 F4
†55075 Sunfish Lake 344 E6
56382 Swanville 295 D5
55786 Taconite 331 E3
56291 Taunton 177 B6
55084 Taylors Falls 623 F5
56683 Tenstrike 159 D3
56701 Thief River Falls⊙ 9,105 B2
†56319 Thomson 152 F4
†55331 Tonka Bay 1,354 F5
55790 Tower 640 F3
56175 Tracy 2,478 C6
56176 Trimont 805 D7
56088 Truman 1,392 D7
56089 Twin Lakes 210 E7
56584 Twin Valley 907 B3
55616 Two Harbors⊙ 4,039 G3
56178 Tyler 1,353 B6
56585 Ulen 514 B3
56586 Underwood 332 C4
56384 Upsala 400 D5
55979 Utica 249 G7
†55101 Vadnais Heights 5,111 G5
56587 Vergas 287 C4
55085 Vermillion 438 F6
56481 Verndale 504 C4
56090 Vernon Center 365 D7
56292 Vesta 360 C6
55386 Victoria 1,425 F6
56385 Villard 275 C5
55792 Virginia 11,056 F3
55981 Wabasha⊙ 2,372 G6
56293 Wabasso 745 C6
55387 Waconia 2,638 E6
56482 Wadena⊙ 4,699 C4
56386 Wahkon 271 E4
56387 Waite Park 3,496 D5
56091 Waldorf 249 E7
56484 Walker⊙ 970 D3
56180 Walnut Grove 753 C6
55982 Waltham 176 F7
55983 Wanamingo 717 F6
55743 Warba 150 E3
56762 Warren⊙ 2,105 B2
56763 Warroad 1,216 C2
56093 Waseca⊙ 8,219 E6
55388 Watertown 1,818 E6
56096 Waterville 1,717 E6
55389 Watkins 757 D5
56295 Watson 238 C5
56589 Waubun 390 C3
55390 Waverly 470 E5
55391 Wayzata 3,621 G5
56181 Welcome 855 D7
56097 Wells 2,777 E7
56590 Wendell 216 B4
56183 Westbrook 978 C6
55985 West Concord 762 F6
55118 West Saint Paul 18,527 G5
56296 Wheaton⊙ 1,969 B5
55110 White Bear Lake 22,538 G5
55090 Willernie 654 G5
56686 Williams 217 D2
56201 Willmar⊙ 15,895 C5
55795 Willow River 303 F4
56185 Wilmont 380 C7
56687 Wilton 176 C3
56101 Windom⊙ 4,666 C7
56592 Winger 200 B3
56098 Winnebago 1,869 D7
55987 Winona⊙ 25,075 G6
55395 Winsted 1,522 D6
55396 Winthrop 1,376 D6
55796 Winton 276 G3
56594 Wolverton 177 B4
†55798 Woodbury 10,297 F6
56297 Wood Lake 420 C6
56186 Woodstock 180 B7
56187 Worthington⊙ 10,243 C7
55797 Wrenshall 333 F4
55798 Wright 162 E4
55990 Wykoff 482 F7
55092 Wyoming 1,559 F5
55397 Young America 1,237 E6
55398 Zimmerman 1,074 E5
55991 Zumbro Falls 208 F6
55992 Zumbrota 2,129 F6

OTHER FEATURES

Ash (riv.) F2
Bald Eagle (lake) G3
Basswood (lake) G2
Battle (riv.) D3
Baudette (riv.) D2
Bear (riv.) E3
Bemidji (lake) D3
Benton (lake) B6
Big Fork (riv.) E2
Big Sandy (lake) E4
Big Stone (lake) B5
Birch (lake) G3
Black (riv.) D2
Blue Earth (riv.) D7
Bois de Sioux (riv.) B4
Bowstring (lake) E3
Buffalo (riv.) B4
Burntside (lake) F3
Cass (lake) D3
Cedar (riv.) F7
Chippewa (riv.) C5
Christina (lake) C4
Clearwater (riv.) C3
Cloquet (riv.) F4
Cobb (riv.) E7
Cottonwood (riv.) C6
Crooked (creek) F4
Crooked (lake) G2
Crow (riv.) F5
Crow Wing (riv.) D4
Cuyuna (range) D4
Dead (lake) C4
Deer (lake) E3
Des Moines (riv.) C7
Eagle (mt.) G2
East Swan (riv.) F3
Elbow (lake) C3
Emily (lake) C5
Fond du Lac Ind. Res. F4
Grand Portage Ind. Res. G2
Grand Portage Nat'l Mon. G2
Green (lake) D5
Greenwood (lake) G3
Gull (lake) D4
Heron (lake) C7
Hill (riv.) C3
Independence (lake) F5
Isabella (lake) G3
Itasca (lake) C3
Kabetogama (lake) E2
Kanaranzi (creek) C7
Kettle (riv.) F4
Knife (lake) G2
La Croix (lake) F2
Lac qui Parle (lake) C5
Lac qui Parle (riv.) B6
Lake of the Woods (lake) D1
Leaf (riv.) C4
Leech (lake) D3
Leech Lake Ind. Res. D3
Lida (lake) C4
Little Fork (riv.) E2
Little Rock (creek) C7
Long (lake) D4
Long (lake) F3
Long Prairie (riv.) D4
Lost (riv.) C3
Lower Red (lake) C3
Maple (lake) B3
Maple (riv.) E7
Marsh (lake) B5
Mary (lake) C5
Mesabi (range) E3
Middle (riv.) B2
Mille Lac Ind. Res. E4
Mille Lacs (lake) E4
Miltona (lake) C4
Minneapolis-Saint Paul Airport G5
Minnesota (riv.) E6
Minnetonka (lake) F5
Minnewaska (lake) C5
Misquah (hills) F2
Mississippi (riv.) D4
Moose (riv.) C2
Mud (lake) C2
Mud (riv.) C2
Muskeg (bay) C2
Mustinka (riv.) B5
Nemadji (riv.) F4
Nett (lake) E2
Nett Lake Ind. Res. E2
North (lake) F1
Otter Tail (lake) C4
Otter Tail (riv.) B4
Partridge (riv.) G3
Pelican (lake) C4
Pelican (lake) D4
Pelican (lake) F2
Pelican (riv.) B4
Pelican (riv.) F2
Pepin (lake) F6
Pigeon (riv.) G2
Pike (riv.) F3
Pipestone Nat'l Mon. B6
Pokegama (lake) E3
Pomme de Terre (riv.) C5
Poplar (riv.) C3
Prairie (riv.) E3
Rainy (lake) E2
Rainy (riv.) D2
Rapid (riv.) D2
Redeye (riv.) C4
Red Lake (riv.) B2
Red Lake Ind. Res. C2
Red River of the North (riv.) A2
Redwood (riv.) C6
Reno (lake) C5
Rice (lake) E4
Rock (riv.) B7
Root (riv.) G7
Roseau (riv.) B2
Rum (riv.) E5
Saganaga (lake) H2
Saint Croix (riv.) F5
Saint Louis (riv.) F4
Sand (creek) F6
Sand Hill (riv.) B3
Sarah (lake) F5
Schoolcraft (riv.) C3
Shakopee (creek) C5
Shell (riv.) C4
Shetek (lake) C6
Sleepy Eye (creek) C6
Snake (riv.) A2
Snake (riv.) E4
South Fowl (lake) G1
Star (lake) C4
Sturgeon (riv.) F3
Superior (lake) G3
Swan (lake) D6
Tamarac (riv.) A2
Tamarack (riv.) D2
Thief (lake) C2
Thief (riv.) B2
Traverse (lake) B5
Trout (lake) F2
Two Rivers (riv.) A1
Upper Red (lake) D2
Vermilion (lake) F3
Vermilion (range) F3
Vermilion (riv.) F2
Voyageurs Nat'l Park F2
Wabatawangang (lake) D3
West Swan (riv.) F3
White Earth Ind. Res. C3
Whiteface (riv.) F3
Whitefish (lake) D4
White Iron (lake) G3
Wild Rice (lake) F4
Wild Rice (riv.) B3
Willow (riv.) E3
Winnibigoshish (lake) D3
Woods (lake) D1
Zumbro (riv.) F6

⊙County seat.
‡Population of metropolitan area.
† Zip of nearest p.o. * Multiple zips.

Topography

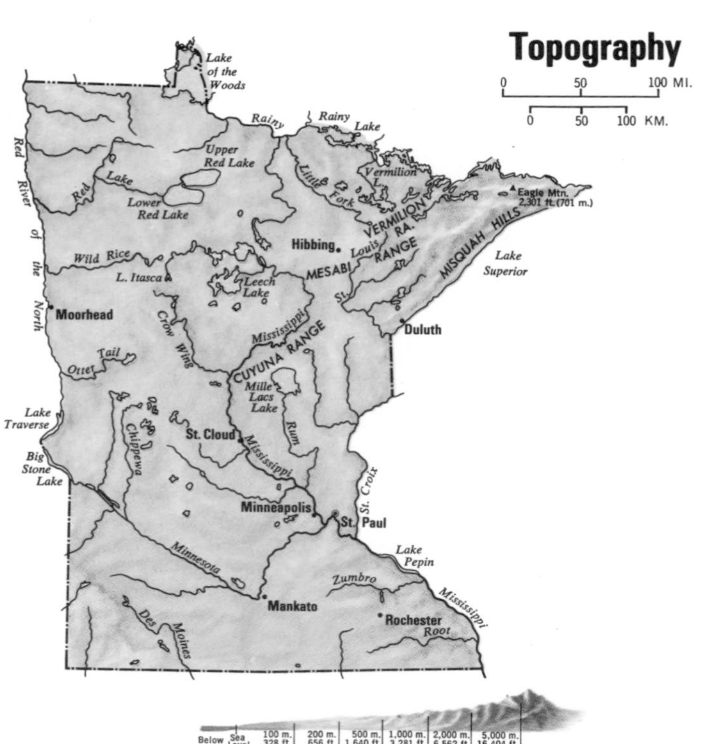
0 50 100 MI.
0 50 100 KM.
Lake of the Woods
Rainy
Rainy Lake
Upper Red Lake
Red Lake
Lower Red Lake
Red River of the North
Little Fork
Vermilion
Eagle Mtn. 2,301 ft. (701 m.)
VERMILION RA.
MISQUAH HILLS
Hibbing
MESABI RANGE
Louis
Lake Superior
Wild Rice
L. Itasca
Leech Lake
Moorhead
Crow Wing
Mississippi
Duluth
Otter Tail
CUYUNA RANGE
Mille Lacs Lake
Rum
Lake Traverse
St. Cloud
Chippewa
Big Stone Lake
Minneapolis
St. Croix
St. Paul
Lake Pepin
Minnesota
Zumbro
Mississippi
Mankato
Rochester
Root
Des Moines
Below Sea Level
100 m. 328 ft.
200 m. 656 ft.
500 m. 1,640 ft.
1,000 m. 3,281 ft.
2,000 m. 6,562 ft.
5,000 m. 16,404 ft.

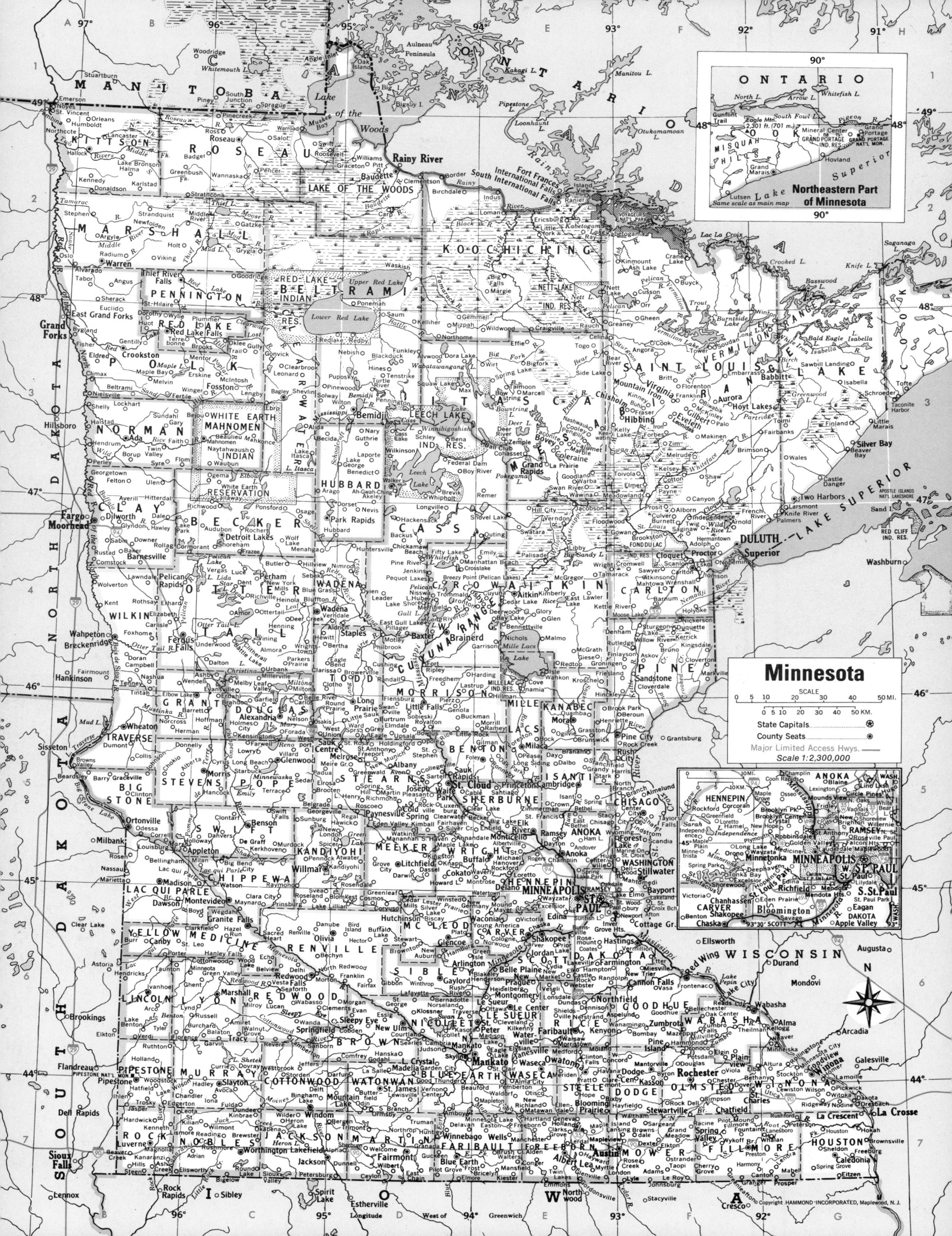

Minnesota
SCALE
0 5 10 20 30 40 50 MI.
0 5 10 20 30 40 50 KM.
State Capitals
County Seats
Major Limited Access Hwys.
Scale 1:2,300,000
Northeastern Part of Minnesota
Same scale as main map
ONTARIO
MANITOBA
NORTH DAKOTA
SOUTH DAKOTA
IOWA
WISCONSIN
LAKE SUPERIOR
Lake of the Woods
Upper Red Lake
Lower Red Lake
Mille Lacs Lake
KITTSON
ROSEAU
LAKE OF THE WOODS
MARSHALL
PENNINGTON
RED LAKE
POLK
BELTRAMI
KOOCHICHING
CLEARWATER
NORMAN
MAHNOMEN
ITASCA
SAINT LOUIS
LAKE
COOK
HUBBARD
CLAY
BECKER
CASS
WADENA
OTTER TAIL
WILKIN
CROW WING
AITKIN
CARLTON
PINE
TODD
MORRISON
MILLE LACS
KANABEC
GRANT
DOUGLAS
TRAVERSE
STEVENS
POPE
BIG STONE
STEARNS
BENTON
SHERBURNE
ISANTI
CHISAGO
ANOKA
SWIFT
KANDIYOHI
MEEKER
WRIGHT
HENNEPIN
RAMSEY
WASHINGTON
CHIPPEWA
LAC QUI PARLE
YELLOW MEDICINE
RENVILLE
MC LEOD
CARVER
SCOTT
DAKOTA
LINCOLN
LYON
REDWOOD
SIBLEY
NICOLLET
LE SUEUR
RICE
GOODHUE
WABASHA
BROWN
PIPESTONE
MURRAY
COTTONWOOD
WATONWAN
BLUE EARTH
WASECA
STEELE
DODGE
OLMSTED
WINONA
ROCK
NOBLES
JACKSON
MARTIN
FARIBAULT
FREEBORN
MOWER
FILLMORE
HOUSTON
MINNEAPOLIS
ST. PAUL
DULUTH
© Copyright HAMMOND INCORPORATED, Maplewood, N. J.

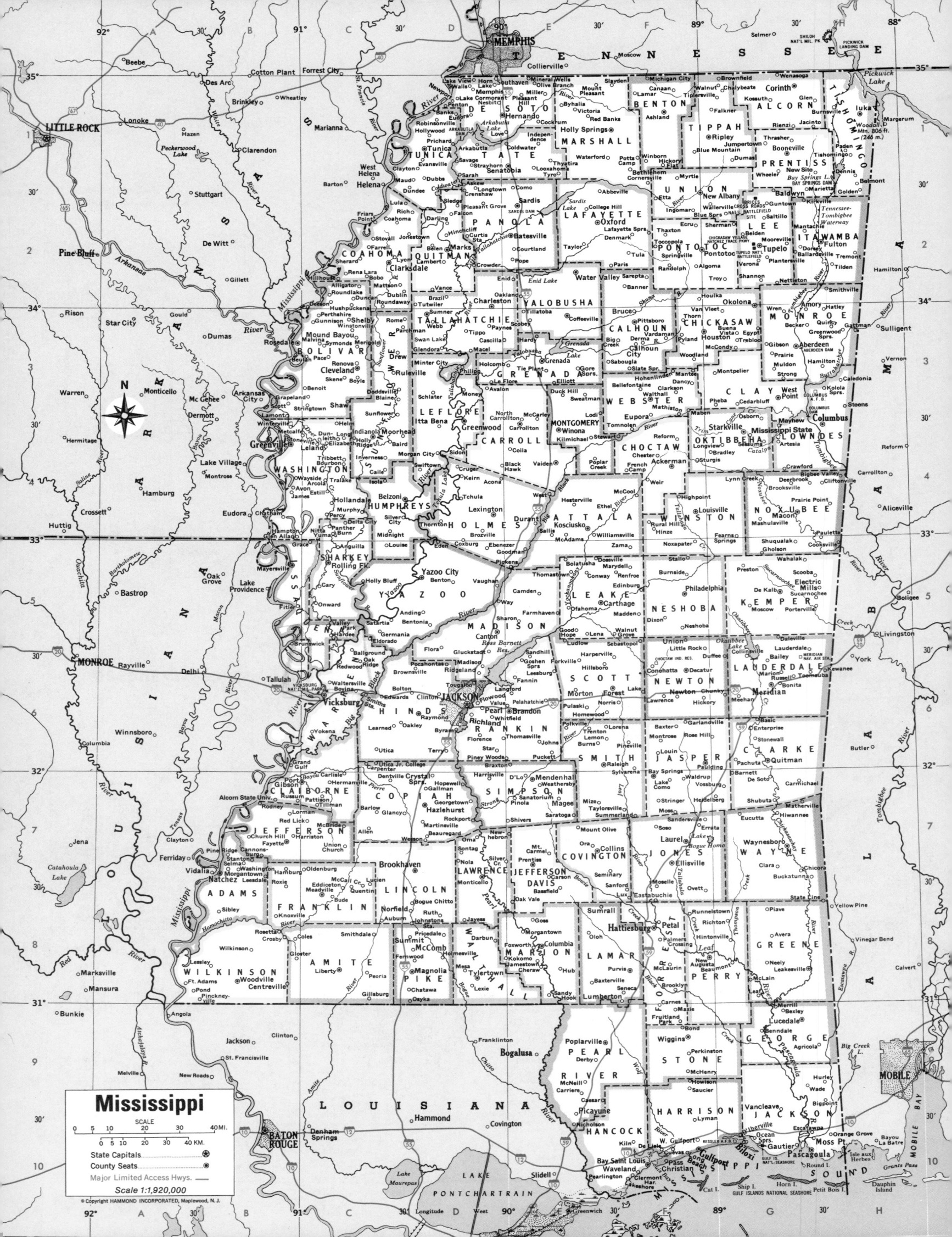

Mississippi

SCALE

0 5 10 20 30 40 MI.

0 5 10 20 30 40 KM.

State Capitals .... ⊛

County Seats .... ◉

Major Limited Access Hwys. ——————

Scale 1:1,920,000

© Copyright HAMMOND INCORPORATED, Maplewood, N.J.

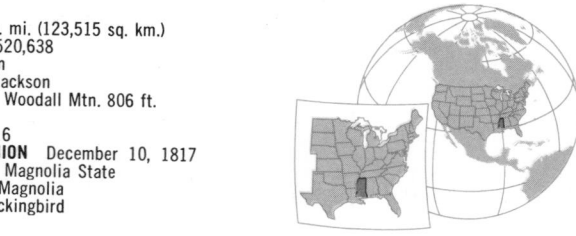

AREA 47,689 sq. mi. (123,515 sq. km.)
POPULATION 2,520,638
CAPITAL Jackson
LARGEST CITY Jackson
HIGHEST POINT Woodall Mtn. 806 ft. (246 m.)
SETTLED IN 1716
ADMITTED TO UNION December 10, 1817
POPULAR NAME Magnolia State
STATE FLOWER Magnolia
STATE BIRD Mockingbird

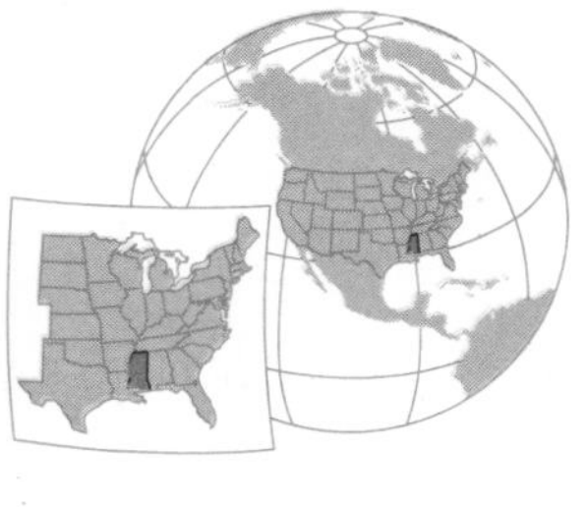

Topography

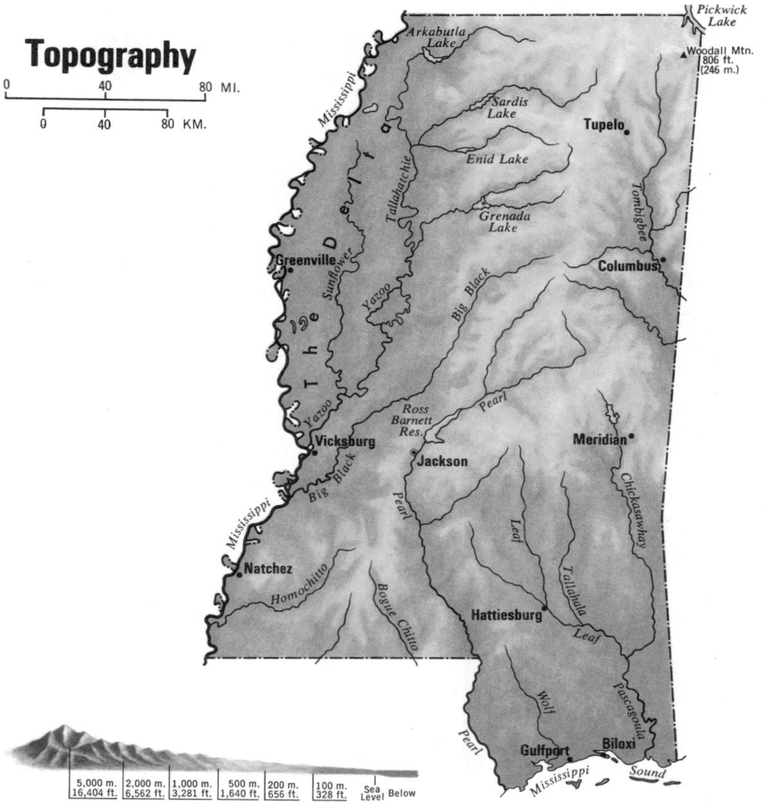

0 40 80 MI.
0 40 80 KM.
Pickwick Lake
Woodall Mtn. 806 ft. (246 m.)
Arkabutla Lake
Mississippi
Sardis Lake
Tupelo
Enid Lake
Tallahatchie
Tombigbee
Grenada Lake
Greenville
Columbus
Sunflower
Yazoo
Big Black
The Delta
Ross Barnett Res.
Pearl
Vicksburg
Jackson
Meridian
Chickasawhay
Natchez
Homochitto
Bogue Chitto
Leaf
Tallahala
Hattiesburg
Wolf
Pascagoula
Gulfport
Biloxi
Mississippi Sound
5,000 m. 16,404 ft.
2,000 m. 6,562 ft.
1,000 m. 3,281 ft.
500 m. 1,640 ft.
200 m. 656 ft.
100 m. 328 ft.
Sea Level
Below

COUNTIES

Adams 38,035 ... B8
Alcorn 33,036 ... G1
Amite 13,369 ... C8
Attala 19,865 ... E4
Benton 8,153 ... F1
Bolivar 45,965 ... C3
Calhoun 15,664 ... F3
Carroll 9,776 ... E4
Chickasaw 17,853 ... G3
Choctaw 8,996 ... F4
Claiborne 12,279 ... C7
Clarke 16,945 ... G6
Clay 21,082 ... G3
Coahoma 36,918 ... C2
Copiah 26,503 ... D7
Covington 15,927 ... E7
De Soto 53,930 ... E1
Forrest 66,018 ... F8
Franklin 8,208 ... C8
George 15,297 ... G9
Greene 9,827 ... G8
Grenada 21,043 ... E3
Hancock 24,537 ... E10
Harrison 157,665 ... F10
Hinds 250,998 ... D6
Holmes 22,970 ... D4
Humphreys 13,931 ... C4
Issaquena 2,513 ... B5
Itawamba 20,518 ... H2
Jackson 118,015 ... G9
Jasper 17,265 ... F6
Jefferson 9,181 ... B7
Jefferson Davis 13,846 ... E7
Jones 61,912 ... F7
Kemper 10,148 ... G5
Lafayette 31,030 ... E2
Lamar 23,821 ... E8
Lauderdale 77,285 ... G6
Lawrence 12,518 ... D7
Leake 18,790 ... E5
Lee 57,061 ... G2
Leflore 41,525 ... D3
Lincoln 30,174 ... D8
Lowndes 57,304 ... H4
Madison 41,613 ... D5
Marion 25,708 ... E8
Marshall 29,296 ... E1
Monroe 36,404 ... H3
Montgomery 13,366 ... E4
Neshoba 23,789 ... F5
Newton 19,944 ... F6
Noxubee 13,212 ... G4
Oktibbeha 36,018 ... G4
Panola 28,164 ... E2
Pearl River 33,795 ... E9
Perry 9,864 ... G8
Pike 36,173 ... D8
Pontotoc 20,918 ... F2
Prentiss 24,025 ... G1
Quitman 12,636 ... D2
Rankin 69,427 ... E6
Scott 24,556 ... E6
Sharkey 7,964 ... C5
Simpson 23,441 ... E7
Smith 15,077 ... E6
Stone 9,716 ... F9
Sunflower 34,844 ... C3
Tallahatchie 17,157 ... D3
Tate 20,119 ... E1
Tippah 18,739 ... G1
Tishomingo 18,434 ... H1
Tunica 9,652 ... D1
Union 21,741 ... F2
Walthall 13,761 ... D8
Warren 51,627 ... C6
Washington 72,344 ... C4
Wayne 19,135 ... G7
Webster 10,300 ... F3
Wilkinson 10,021 ... B8
Winston 19,474 ... F4
Yalobusha 13,139 ... E2
Yazoo 27,349 ... D5

CITIES and TOWNS

Zip *Name/Pop.* *Key*

38601 Abbeville 448 ... F2
39730 Aberdeen⊙ 7,184 ... H3
39735 Ackerman⊙ 1,567 ... F4
39096 Alcorn State University ... B7
38820 Algoma 175 ... G2
†39083 Allen 15 ... C7
38720 Alligator 256 ... C2
38821 Amory 7,307 ... H3
38721 Anguilla 950 ... C5
38722 Arcola 588 ... C4
38602 Arkabutla 400 ... D1
39736 Artesia 526 ... G4
38603 Ashland⊙ 532 ... F1
38604 Askew 300 ... D1
†39664 Auburn 500 ... C8
38912 Avalon 100 ... D3
38723 Avon 400 ... B4
39320 Bailey 320 ... G6
38724 Baird 150 ... C4
38824 Baldwyn 3,427 ... G2
†39156 Ballground 30 ... C5
38913 Banner 120 ... F2
†39083 Barlow 20 ... C7
†39330 Basic 60 ... G6
39421 Bassfield 325 ... E8
38606 Batesville⊙ 4,692 ... E2
†39343 Baxter 75 ... F6
†39455 Baxterville 100 ... E8
39520 Bay Saint Louis⊙ 7,891 ... F10
39422 Bay Springs⊙ 1,884 ... F7
39423 Beaumont 1,112 ... G8
†39191 Beauregard 185 ... D7
38825 Becker 350 ... G3
38826 Belden 241 ... G2
38609 Belen 400 ... D2
39737 Bellefontaine 400 ... F3
38827 Belmont 1,420 ... H1
39038 Belzoni⊙ 2,982 ... C4
†39450 Benndale 500 ... G9
38725 Benoit 499 ... C3
39039 Benton 350 ... D5
39040 Bentonia 518 ... D5
†38659 Bethlehem 210 ... F1
38726 Beulah 431 ... B3
39738 Bigbee Valley 370 ... H4
38914 Big Creek 146 ... F3
†39567 Bigpoint 350 ... H9
*39530 Biloxi 49,311 ... G10
Biloxi-Gulfport‡ 191,918 ... G10
†38917 Black Hawk 41 ... E4
38727 Blaine 75 ... C3
38610 Blue Mountain 867 ... G1
38828 Blue Springs 131 ... G2
†38614 Bobo 200 ... C2
39629 Bogue Chitto 575 ... D8
39041 Bolton 664 ... D6
39550 Bond 350 ... F9
†39301 Bonita 300 ... G6
38829 Booneville⊙ 6,199 ... G1
†38756 Bourbon 200 ... C4
†39180 Bovina 50 ... C6
38730 Boyle 888 ... C3
39042 Brandon⊙ 9,626 ... E6
39044 Braxton 172 ... D6
38963 Brazil 229 ... D2
39601 Brookhaven⊙ 10,800 ... C7
39425 Brooklyn 450 ... F8
39739 Brooksville 1,038 ... G4
†38683 Brownfield 125 ... G1
38915 Bruce 2,208 ... F3
39322 Buckatunna 500 ... G7
39630 Bude 1,092 ... C8
38833 Burnsville 889 ... H1
38611 Byhalia 757 ... E1
†39205 Byram 250 ... D6
†38754 Caile 30 ... C4
39740 Caledonia 497 ... H3
38916 Calhoun City 2,033 ... F3
39045 Camden 150 ... E5
38612 Canaan 200 ... F1
39046 Canton⊙ 11,116 ... D5
39049 Carlisle 425 ... C7
†39360 Carmichael 75 ... G7
39050 Carpenter 200 ... C6
39426 Carriere 900 ... E9
38917 Carrollton⊙ 338 ... E4
39427 Carson 400 ... E7
39051 Carthage⊙ 3,453 ... E5
39054 Cary 470 ... C5
38920 Cascilla 230 ... D3
39741 Cedarbluff 175 ... G3
39631 Centreville 1,844 ... B8
38684 Chalybeate 350 ... G1
38921 Charleston⊙ 2,878 ... D2
39632 Chatawa 300 ... D8
38731 Chatham 150 ... B4
39323 Chunky 277 ... G6
39055 Church Hill 350 ... B7
39324 Clara 275 ... G7
38614 Clarksdale⊙ 21,137 ... D2
39551 Clermont Harbor 550 ... F10
38732 Cleveland⊙ 14,524 ... C3
39056 Clinton 14,660 ... D6
38617 Coahoma 350 ... C2
†38632 Cockrum 150 ... E1
38922 Coffeeville⊙ 1,129 ... E3
38923 Coila 75 ... E4
38618 Coldwater 1,505 ... E1
†39638 Coles 150 ... C8
†38655 College Hill 150 ... E2
39428 Collins⊙ 2,131 ... E7
39325 Collinsville 700 ... G6
39429 Columbia⊙ 7,733 ... E8
39701 Columbus⊙ 27,383 ... H3
38619 Como 1,378 ... E1
39057 Conehatta 200 ... F6
†39051 Conway 25 ... E5
38834 Corinth⊙ 13,839 ... G1
†38659 Cornersville 65 ... F1
38620 Courtland 381 ... E2
†39095 Coxburg 300 ... D5
39743 Crawford 495 ... G4
38621 Crenshaw 1,019 ... D2
39633 Crosby 349 ... B8
38622 Crowder 789 ... D2
38924 Cruger 540 ... D4
39059 Crystal Springs 4,902 ... D7
†38606 Curtis Station 350 ... D2
39326 Daleville 210 ... G5
†39643 Darbun 100 ... D8
38623 Darling 275 ... D2
39327 Decatur⊙ 1,148 ... F6
†39739 Deerbrook 30 ... G4
39328 De Kalb⊙ 1,159 ... G5
†39571 De Lisle 450 ... F10
39061 Delta City 310 ... C4
†38655 Denmark 40 ... F2
38838 Dennis 150 ... H1
†39059 Dentville 175 ... C7
†39470 Derby 298 ... E9
38839 Derma 793 ... F3
†39532 D'Iberville 13,369 ... G10
39062 D'Lo 463 ... E7
38736 Doddsville 232 ... C3
38737 Drew 2,528 ... C3
38739 Dublin 100 ... C2
38925 Duck Hill 706 ... E3
†39337 Duffee 175 ... G6
38625 Dumas 312 ... G1
38740 Duncan 501 ... C2
38626 Dundee 600 ... D1
39063 Durant 2,889 ... E4
39436 Eastabuchie 200 ... F8
39064 Ebenezer 200 ... D5
38841 Ecru 687 ... F2
39634 Eddiceton 65 ... C8
39065 Eden 150 ... D5
39066 Edwards 1,515 ... C6
†39156 Eldorado 20 ... C5
39329 Electric Mills 100 ... G5
38742 Elizabeth 500 ... C4
38926 Elliott 200 ... E3
39437 Ellisville⊙ 4,652 ... F7
38927 Enid ... E2
39330 Enterprise 607 ... G6
†39440 Errata 85 ... F7
39552 Escatawpa 5,367 ... G10
39067 Ethel 486 ... F4
38627 Etta 75 ... F2
39744 Eupora 2,048 ... F3
†38676 Evansville 60 ... D1
38628 Falcon 260 ... D2
38629 Falkner 251 ... G1
38630 Farrell 300 ... C2
39069 Fayette⊙ 2,033 ... B7
39635 Fernwood 500 ... D8
39070 Fitler 175 ... B5
39071 Flora 1,507 ... D5
39073 Florence 1,111 ... D6
†39201 Flowood 943 ... D6
39074 Forest⊙ 5,229 ... F6
39076 Forkville 185 ... E6
39636 Fort Adams 75 ... B8
39483 Foxworth 800 ... E8
39745 French Camp 306 ... F4
38631 Friars Point 1,400 ... C2
39577 Fruitland Park 75 ... F9
38843 Fulton⊙ 3,238 ... H2
39077 Gallman ... D7
38844 Gattman 151 ... H3
39553 Gautier 8,917 ... G10
39078 Georgetown 343 ... D7
†39354 Gholson 50 ... G5
†39083 Glancy 25 ... C7
38846 Glen 100 ... H1
38744 Glen Allan 650 ... B4
38928 Glendora 220 ... D3
39638 Gloster 1,726 ... B8
†39110 Gluckstadt 150 ... D5
38847 Golden 292 ... H2
39079 Goodman 1,285 ... E5
38929 Gore Springs 125 ... E3
38745 Grace 325 ... C5
†38725 Grapeland 200 ... B3
38701 Greenville⊙ 40,613 ... B4
38930 Greenwood⊙ 20,115 ... D4
38848 Greenwood Springs 170 ... H3
38901 Grenada⊙ 12,641 ... E3
*39501 Gulfport⊙ 39,676 ... F10
38746 Gunnison 708 ... C3
38849 Guntown 359 ... G2
†39661 Hamburg 150 ... B7
39746 Hamilton 500 ... H3
†38901 Hardy 45 ... E3
39080 Harperville 200 ... E6
39081 Harriston 500 ... C7
39082 Harrisville 500 ... D7
†38821 Hatley 497 ... H3
39401 Hattiesburg⊙ 40,829 ... F8
39083 Hazlehurst⊙ 4,437 ... D7
39439 Heidelberg 1,098 ... F7
39086 Hermanville 750 ... C7
38632 Hernando⊙ 2,969 ... E1
†39192 Hesterville 25 ... E4
39332 Hickory 670 ... F6
38633 Hickory Flat 458 ... F1
39087 Hillsboro 800 ... E6
†38646 Hinchcliff 60 ... D2
†39462 Hintonville 300 ... F8
†39108 Hinze 30 ... F4
†39751 Hohenlinden 96 ... F3
38940 Holcomb 50 ... D3
38748 Hollandale 4,336 ... C4
39088 Holly Bluff 700 ... C5
38749 Holly Ridge 350 ... C4
38635 Holly Springs⊙ 7,285 ... E1
†38676 Hollywood 80 ... D1
†39648 Holmesville 50 ... D8
38637 Horn Lake 4,326 ... D1
38850 Houlka 710 ... G2
38851 Houston⊙ 3,747 ... G3
†39574 Howison 300 ... F9
†39429 Hub 80 ... E8
39555 Hurley 500 ... H9
†38774 Hushpuckena 60 ... C2
38638 Independence 150 ... E1
38751 Indianola⊙ 8,221 ... C4
†38652 Ingomar 150 ... F2
38753 Inverness 1,034 ... C4
38754 Isola 834 ... C4
38941 Itta Bena 2,904 ... D4
38852 Iuka⊙ 2,846 ... H1
†38865 Jacinto 65 ... H1
*39201 Jackson (cap.)⊙ 202,895 ... D6
Jackson‡ 320,425 ... D6
39641 Jayess 200 ... D8
38639 Jonestown 1,231 ... D2
†38829 Jumpertown 472 ... G1
†38924 Keirn 3 ... D4
†39364 Kewanee 250 ... H6
39747 Kilmichael 906 ... E4
39556 Kiln 800 ... F10
†39661 Knoxville 65 ... B8
39643 Kokomo 250 ... E8
†39740 Kolola Springs 100 ... H3
39090 Kosciusko⊙ 7,415 ... E4
38834 Kossuth 190 ... G1
38640 Lafayette Springs 80 ... F2
39092 Lake 524 ... F6
38641 Lake Cormorant 300 ... D1
39558 Lakeshore 550 ... F10
38642 Lamar 200 ... F1
38643 Lambert 1,624 ... D2
38755 Lamont 400 ... B3
39335 Lauderdale 600 ... G5
39440 Laurel⊙ 21,897 ... F7
39336 Lawrence 250 ... F6
39450 Leaf 250 ... G8
39451 Leakesville⊙ 1,120 ... G8
39093 Learned 113 ... C6
38756 Leland 6,667 ... C4
39094 Lena 231 ... E5
†39667 Lexie 40 ... D8
39095 Lexington⊙ 2,628 ... D4
39645 Liberty⊙ 669 ... C8
39337 Little Rock 70 ... F5
39560 Long Beach 7,967 ... F10
†39759 Longview 800 ... G4
39096 Lorman 350 ... B7
39338 Louin 338 ... F6
39097 Louise 400 ... C5
39339 Louisville⊙ 7,323 ... G4
†38632 Love 50 ... D1
39452 Lucedale⊙ 2,429 ... G9
39646 Lucien 75 ... C7
39098 Ludlow 350 ... E5
38644 Lula 394 ... C2
39455 Lumberton 2,217 ... E8
†39501 Lyman 500 ... F10
†39739 Lynn Creek 20 ... G4
38645 Lyon 531 ... D2
39750 Maben 855 ... F3
39341 Macon⊙ 2,396 ... G4
39109 Madden 450 ... F5
39110 Madison 2,241 ... D6
39111 Magee 3,497 ... E7
39652 Magnolia⊙ 2,461 ... D8
†38769 Malvina 100 ... C3
38855 Mantachie 732 ... H2
39751 Mantee 158 ... F3
38856 Marietta 298 ... H2
39342 Marion 771 ... G6
38646 Marks⊙ 2,260 ... D2
†39083 Martinsville 30 ... D7
†39051 Marydell 99 ... F5
39752 Mathiston 632 ... F3
38758 Mattson 200 ... C2
†39458 Maxie 233 ... F9
39113 Mayersville⊙ 378 ... B5
39753 Mayhew 150 ... G4
39107 McAdams 350 ... E4
†39144 McBride 2 ... C7
39647 McCall Creek 250 ... C7
38943 McCarley 250 ... E3
39648 McComb 12,331 ... D8
38854 McCondy 150 ... G3
39108 McCool 203 ... F4
39561 McHenry 660 ... F9
39456 McLain 688 ... G8
39457 McNeill 800 ... E9
39653 Meadville⊙ 575 ... C8
39114 Mendenhall⊙ 2,533 ... E7
39301 Meridian⊙ 46,577 ... G6
38759 Merigold 574 ... C3
†39667 Mesa 30 ... D8
38760 Metcalfe 952 ... B4
38647 Michigan City 350 ... F1
39115 Midnight 500 ... C4
38648 Mineral Wells 250 ... E1
38944 Minter City 150 ... D3
39762 Mississippi State ... G4
39116 Mize 363 ... E7
38945 Money 350 ... D3
39654 Monticello⊙ 1,834 ... D7
39754 Montpelier 175 ... G3
†39338 Montrose 120 ... F6
38857 Mooreville 200 ... G2
38761 Moorhead 2,358 ... C4
38946 Morgan City 319 ... D4
39484 Morgantown 325 ... E8
†39120 Morgantown 3,445 ... B7
39117 Morton 3,303 ... E6
†39328 Moscow 30 ... G5
39460 Moselle 525 ... F8
39460 Moss 65 ... F7
39563 Moss Point 18,998 ... G10
38762 Mound Bayou 2,917 ... C3
†39474 Mount Carmel 30 ... E7
39119 Mount Olive 993 ... E7
38649 Mount Pleasant 250 ... E1
38650 Myrtle 402 ... F1
39120 Natchez⊙ 22,015 ... B7
39461 Neely 270 ... G8
38651 Nesbit 366 ... D1
39365 Neshoba 250 ... F5
38858 Nettleton 1,911 ... G2
38652 New Albany⊙ 7,072 ... G2
39462 New Augusta⊙ 589 ... F8
39140 Newhebron 470 ... D7
38850 New Houlka (Houlka) 710 ... G2
38859 New Site 100 ... H1
39345 Newton 3,708 ... F6
39463 Nicholson 400 ... E10
38763 Nitta Yuma 150 ... C4
†39629 Norfield 75 ... C8
38947 North Carrollton 859 ... E3
39346 Noxapater 516 ... F5
38948 Oakland 540 ... E2
†39154 Oakley 133 ... D6
39656 Oak Vale ... E8
39564 Ocean Springs 14,504 ... G10
39141 Ofahoma 350 ... E5
38860 Okolona⊙ 3,409 ... G2
38654 Olive Branch 2,067 ... E1
†39482 Oloh 93 ... E8
†39654 Oma 200 ... D7
†39501 Orange Grove 13,476 ... H10
39657 Osyka 581 ... D8
39464 Ovett 600 ... F8
38655 Oxford⊙ 9,882 ... F2
38764 Pace 519 ... C3
39347 Pachuta 256 ... G6
38861 Paden 119 ... H1
†39401 Palmers Crossing 2,765 ... F8
38765 Panther Burn 300 ... C4
38738 Parchman 200 ... D3
38949 Paris 253 ... F2
39567 Pascagoula⊙ 29,318 ... G10
Pascagoula-Moss Point‡ 118,015 ... G10
39571 Pass Christian 5,014 ... F10
39144 Pattison 540 ... C7
39348 Paulding⊙ 630 ... F6
39349 Paulette 230 ... H4
†38920 Paynes 100 ... D3
39028 Pearl 18,580 ... D6
39572 Pearlington 500 ... E10
39145 Pelahatchie 1,445 ... E6
39573 Perkinston 950 ... F9
†38746 Perthshire 25 ... C3
39465 Petal 8,476 ... F8
39755 Pheba 280 ... G3
39350 Philadelphia⊙ 6,434 ... F5
38950 Philipp 975 ... D3
†39476 Piave 150 ... G8
39466 Picayune 10,361 ... E9
39146 Pickens 1,386 ... E5
39148 Piney Woods 450 ... D6
39149 Pinola ... E7

(continued on following page)

Mississippi-
Missouri
River System

MILES
0   100   200   300

Navigable Waterways
over 9 feet deep
Major River Ports..........⊙

© Copyright HAMMOND INCORPORATED.

Agriculture, Industry and Resources

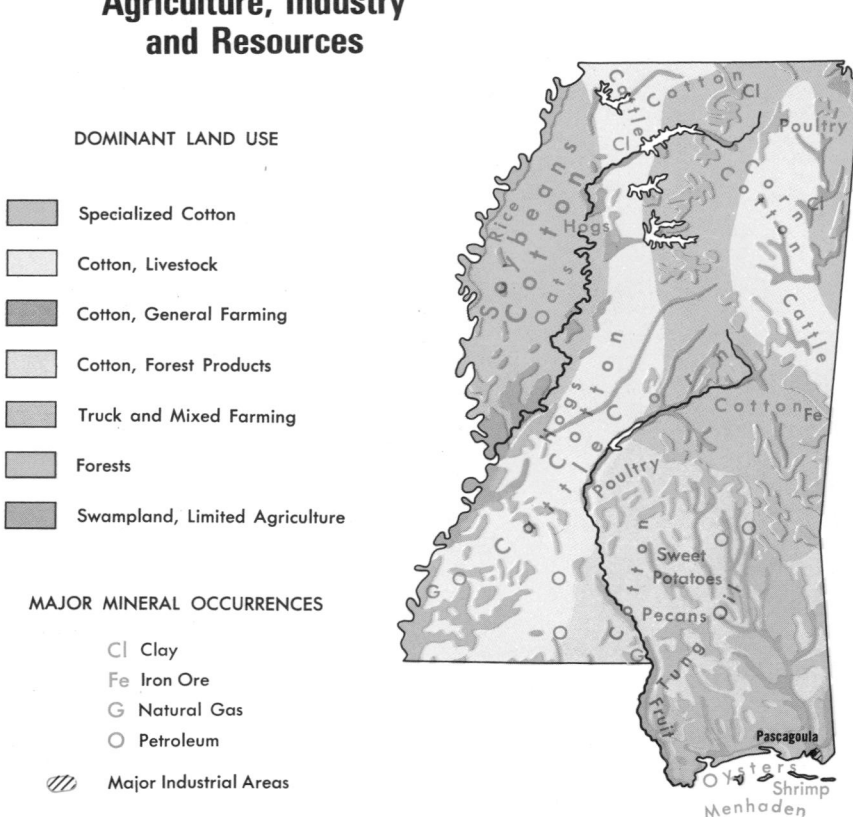

DOMINANT LAND USE

Specialized Cotton

Cotton, Livestock

Cotton, General Farming

Cotton, Forest Products

Truck and Mixed Farming

Forests

Swampland, Limited Agriculture

MAJOR MINERAL OCCURRENCES

Cl   Clay

Fe   Iron Ore

G   Natural Gas

O   Petroleum

///   Major Industrial Areas

AREA 69,697 sq. mi. (180,515 sq. km.)
POPULATION 4,916,759
CAPITAL Jefferson City
LARGEST CITY St. Louis
HIGHEST POINT Taum Sauk Mtn. 1,772 ft. (540 m.)
SETTLED IN 1764
ADMITTED TO UNION August 10, 1821
POPULAR NAME Show Me State
STATE FLOWER Hawthorn
STATE BIRD Bluebird

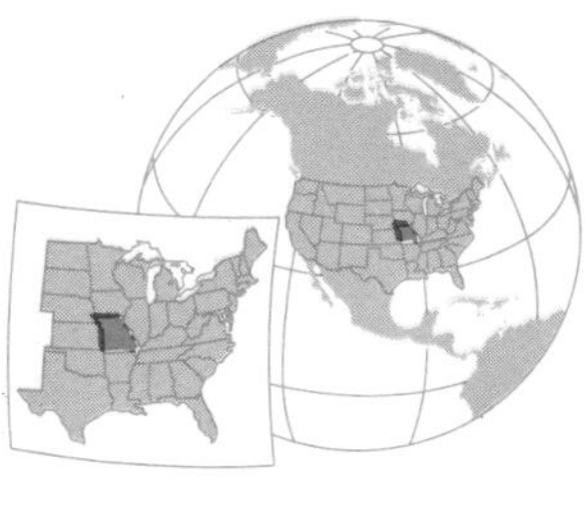

COUNTIES

Adair 24,870 G2
Andrew 13,980 C3
Atchison 8,605 B2
Audrain 26,458 J4
Barry 24,408 E9
Barton 11,292 D7
Bates 15,873 D6
Benton 12,183 F6
Bollinger 10,301 M8
Boone 100,376 H4
Buchanan 87,888 C3
Butler 37,693 M9
Caldwell 8,660 E3
Callaway 32,252 J5
Camden 20,017 G6
Cape Girardeau 58,837 N8
Carroll 12,131 F4
Carter 5,428 L9
Cass 51,029 D5
Cedar 11,894 E7
Chariton 10,489 F3
Christian 22,402 F9
Clark 8,493 J2
Clay 136,488 D4
Clinton 15,916 D3
Cole 56,663 H6
Cooper 14,643 G5
Crawford 18,300 K7
Dade 7,383 E8
Dallas 12,096 F7
Daviess 8,905 E3
De Kalb 8,222 D3
Dent 14,517 J7
Douglas 11,594 G9
Dunklin 36,324 M10
Franklin 71,233 K6
Gasconade 13,181 J6
Gentry 7,887 D2
Greene 185,302 F8
Grundy 11,959 E2
Harrison 9,890 E2
Henry 19,672 E6
Hickory 6,367 F7
Holt 6,882 B2
Howard 10,008 G4
Howell 28,807 J9
Iron 11,084 L7
Jackson 629,266 R5
Jasper 86,958 D8
Jefferson 146,183 L6
Johnson 39,059 E5
Knox 5,508 H2
Laclede 24,323 G7
Lafayette 29,925 E4
Lawrence 28,973 E8
Lewis 10,901 J2
Lincoln 22,193 L4
Linn 15,495 F3
Livingston 15,739 E3
Macon 16,313 G3
Madison 10,725 M8
Maries 7,551 J6
Marion 28,638 J3
McDonald 14,917 D9
Mercer 4,685 E2
Miller 18,532 H6
Mississippi 15,726 O9
Moniteau 12,068 G5
Monroe 9,716 H3
Montgomery 11,537 K5
Morgan 13,807 G6
New Madrid 22,945 N9
Newton 40,555 D9
Nodaway 21,996 C2
Oregon 10,238 K9
Osage 12,014 J6
Ozark 7,961 H9
Pemiscot 24,987 N10
Perry 16,784 N7
Pettis 36,378 F5
Phelps 33,633 J7
Pike 17,568 K4
Platte 46,341 C4
Polk 18,822 F7
Pulaski 42,011 H7
Putnam 6,092 F2
Ralls 8,984 J3
Randolph 25,460 G3
Ray 21,378 E4
Reynolds 7,230 L8
Ripley 12,458 L9
Saint Charles 144,107 M2
Saint Clair 8,622 E6
Sainte Genevieve 15,180 M7
Saint Francois 42,600 M7
Saint Louis 973,896 O3
Saint Louis (city county) 453,085 P3
Saline 24,919 F4
Schuyler 4,979 G2
Scotland 5,415 H2
Scott 39,647 N8
Shannon 7,885 K8
Shelby 7,826 H3
Stoddard 29,009 N9
Stone 15,587 F9
Sullivan 7,434 F2
Taney 20,467 F9
Texas 21,070 J8
Vernon 19,806 D7
Warren 14,900 K5
Washington 17,983 L7
Wayne 11,277 L8
Webster 20,414 G8
Worth 3,008 D2
Wright 16,188 H8

CITIES and TOWNS

Zip *Name/Pop.* *Key*

64720 Adrian 1,484 D6
63730 Advance 1,054 N8
63123 Affton 23,181 P4
64401 Agency 419 C3
64830 Alba 474 D8
64402 Albany⊙ 2,152 D2
63430 Alexandria 417 K2
64001 Alma 445 E4
65606 Alton⊙ 721 K9
64421 Amazonia 314 C3
64723 Amsterdam 231 D6
64831 Anderson 1,237 D9
63620 Annapolis 370 L8
63820 Anniston 320 O9
64724 Appleton City 1,257 D6
63821 Arbyrd 704 M10
63621 Arcadia 683 L7
64725 Archie 753 D5
65230 Armstrong 360 G4
63010 Arnold 19,141 M6
65604 Ash Grove 1,157 E8
65010 Ashland 1,021 H5
63530 Atlanta 441 H3
63332 Augusta 308 L5
65605 Aurora 6,437 E9
65231 Auxvasse 858 J4
65608 Ava⊙ 2,761 G9
64010 Avondale 612 P5
63011 Ballwin 12,656 N3
64011 Bates City 199 E5
†65619 Battlefield 1,227 F8
†63101 Bella Villa 758 R4
63735 Bell City 539 N8
65013 Belle 1,233 J6
†63137 Bellefontaine Neighbors 12,082 R2
63333 Bellflower 403 K4
†63101 Bel-Nor 2,047 P2
†63101 Bel-Ridge 3,682 P2
64012 Belton 12,708 C5
63736 Benton⊙ 674 O8
63134 Berkeley 15,922 P2
63822 Bernie 1,975 M9
63823 Bertrand 688 O9
64424 Bethany⊙ 3,095 E2
63532 Bevier 733 G3
65610 Billings 911 F8
65438 Birch Tree 622 K9
63624 Bismarck 1,625 L7
65321 Blackburn 314 F4
†63031 Black Jack 5,293 R1
65014 Bland 662 J6
63825 Bloomfield⊙ 1,795 M9
63627 Bloomsdale 397 M6
64015 Blue Springs 25,927 R6
†64101 Blue Summit R5
65613 Bolivar⊙ 5,919 F7
63628 Bonne Terre 3,797 L7
65233 Boonville⊙ 6,959 G5
64723 Bosworth 394 F4
65441 Bourbon 1,259 K6
63334 Bowling Green⊙ 3,022 K4
65616 Branson 2,550 F9
63533 Brashear 332 H2
64624 Braymer 986 E3
64625 Breckenridge 523 E3
†63114 Breckenridge Hills 5,666 O2
63144 Brentwood 8,209 P3
63044 Bridgeton 18,445 O2
†63044 Bridgeton Terrace 334 O2
64628 Brookfield 5,555 F3
64630 Browning 368 F2
65236 Brunswick 1,272 F4
64631 Bucklin 713 G3
64016 Buckner 2,848 R5
65622 Buffalo⊙ 2,217 F7
65237 Bunceton 419 G5
63629 Bunker 673 K8
64428 Burlington Junction 657 B2
64730 Butler⊙ 4,107 D6
65689 Cabool 2,090 H8
64632 Cainsville 496 E2
65239 Cairo 315 H4
65323 Calhoun 427 E6
65018 California⊙ 3,381 H5
63534 Callao 326 G3
†63101 Calverton Park 1,717 P2
65020 Camdenton⊙ 2,303 G6
64429 Cameron 4,519 D3
63933 Campbell 2,134 M10
63828 Canalou 369 N9
63435 Canton 2,435 J2
63701 Cape Girardeau 34,361 O8
63829 Cardwell 831 M10
64834 Carl Junction 3,937 C8
64633 Carrollton⊙ 4,700 E4
64835 Carterville 1,973 D8
64836 Carthage⊙ 11,104 D8
63830 Caruthersville⊙ 7,958 N10
65625 Cassville⊙ 2,091 E9
65022 Cedar City 427 H5
63436 Center 669 J3
65023 Centertown 304 H5
63633 Centerville⊙ 241 L8
65240 Centralia 3,537 H4
63740 Chaffee 3,241 N8
65024 Chamois 546 J5
†63101 Charlack 1,537 P2
63834 Charleston⊙ 5,230 O9
64733 Chilhowee 349 E5
64601 Chillicothe⊙ 9,089 E3
63437 Clarence 1,147 H3
65243 Clark 304 H4
65025 Clarksburg 352 G5
†63017 Clarkson Valley 1,435 N3
63336 Clarksville 585 K4
63837 Clarkton 1,228 M10
†64119 Claycomo 1,671 P5
63105 Clayton⊙ 14,273 P3
64734 Cleveland 485 C5
65631 Clever 551 F8
64735 Clinton⊙ 8,366 E6
65325 Cole Camp 1,022 F6
65201 Columbia⊙ 62,061 H5
Columbia‡ 100,376 H5
†63128 Concord 20,896 P4
64020 Concordia 2,129 E5
65632 Conway 601 G7
†63101 Cool Valley 2,084 P2
63839 Cooter 479 N10
64021 Corder 483 E4
†64501 Country Club Village 1,234 C3
64437 Craig 379 B2
65633 Crane 1,185 E9
64739 Creighton 301 D6
†63126 Crestwood 12,815 O3
63141 Creve Coeur 11,757 O2
65452 Crocker 979 H7
63019 Crystal City 3,618 M6
†63101 Crystal Lake Park 496 O3
65453 Cuba 2,120 K6
63339 Curryville 323 K4
64439 Dearborn 547 C3
64740 Deepwater 475 E6
64440 De Kalb 245 C3
†63135 Dellwood 6,200 R2
63744 Delta 524 N8
63636 Des Arc 237 L8
63601 Desloge 3,481 M7
63020 De Soto 5,993 L6
63131 Des Peres 8,254 O3
63841 Dexter 7,043 N9
64840 Diamond 766 D9
65459 Dixon 1,402 H6
63935 Doniphan⊙ 1,921 L9
†65550 Doolittle 701 J7
63536 Downing 462 H2
64742 Drexel 908 C6
64841 Duenweg 703 D8
†64801 Duquesne 1,252 D8
64442 Eagleville 364 D2
64443 Easton 313 C3
63845 East Prairie 3,713 O9
64444 Edgerton 584 C3
63537 Edina⊙ 1,520 H2
†63101 Edmundson 1,374 O2
65026 Eldon 4,342 G6
64744 El Dorado Springs 3,868 E7
63638 Ellington 1,215 L8
†63011 Ellisville 6,233 M3
63937 Ellsinore 362 L9
63343 Elsberry 1,272 L4
63639 Elvins 1,548 L7
65466 Eminence⊙ 614 K8
63344 Eolia 401 L4
63846 Essex 545 N9
†63601 Esther 1,038 M7
63025 Eureka 3,862 M4
65646 Everton 317 E8
63440 Ewing 400 J2
64024 Excelsior Springs 10,424 R4
65647 Exeter 588 D9
64446 Fairfax 835 B2
65648 Fair Grove 863 F8
65649 Fair Play 384 E7
63345 Farber 503 J4
63640 Farmington⊙ 8,270 M7
65248 Fayette⊙ 2,983 G4
63026 Fenton 2,417 O4
63135 Ferguson 24,740 P2
64163 Ferrelview 447 O4
63028 Festus 7,574 M6
64449 Fillmore 265 C2
63940 Fisk 450 M9
63601 Flat River 4,443 M7
*63031 Florissant 55,372 P1
65652 Fordland 569 G8
64451 Forest City 387 B3
65653 Forsyth⊙ 1,010 F9
63441 Frankford 443 K4
63645 Fredericktown⊙ 4,036 M7
65035 Freeburg 554 J6
64746 Freeman 485 C5
†63101 Frontenac 3,654 O3
65251 Fulton⊙ 11,046 J5
65655 Gainesville⊙ 707 G9
65656 Galena⊙ 423 F9
64640 Gallatin⊙ 2,063 E3
64641 Galt 323 F2
64747 Garden City 1,021 D5
63037 Gerald 921 K6
63848 Gideon 1,240 N10
64642 Gilman City 414 D2
64118 Gladstone 24,990 P5
65254 Glasgow 1,336 G4
†64068 Glenaire 541 R5
63122 Glendale 6,035 P3
64748 Golden City 900 D8
63843 Goodman 1,030 C9
63543 Gorin H2
64454 Gower 1,276 C3
64029 Grain Valley 1,327 S6
64844 Granby 1,908 D9
64030 Grandview 24,502 P6
64456 Grant City⊙ 1,068 D2
†63155 Grantwood Village 1,002 O4
65037 Gravois Mills G6
63545 Green City 719 F2
65661 Greenfield⊙ 1,394 E8
65332 Green Ridge 488 F5
63546 Greentop 538 H2
63944 Greenville⊙ 393 M8
64034 Greenwood 1,315 R6
64643 Hale 529 F3
65255 Hallsville 624 H4
64644 Hamilton 1,582 E3
†63101 Hanley Hills 2,439 P2
63401 Hannibal 18,811 K3
64035 Hardin 688 E4
64701 Harrisonville⊙ 6,372 D5
65667 Hartville⊙ 576 G8
63945 Harviell M9
63349 Hawk Point 386 K5
63851 Hayti 3,964 N10
†63851 Hayti Heights 1,023 N10
†63736 Haywood City 425 N9
*63042 Hazelwood 12,935 P2
64036 Henrietta 424 E4
63048 Herculaneum 2,293 M6
65041 Hermann⊙ 2,695 K5
65668 Hermitage⊙ 384 F7
65257 Higbee 817 H4
64037 Higginsville 4,595 E4
63350 High Hill 254 K5
63050 Hillsboro⊙ 1,508 L6
†63101 Hillsdale 2,247 R2
63852 Holcomb 632 N10
64040 Holden 2,195 E5
63853 Holland 295 N10
65672 Hollister 1,439 F9
64048 Holt 276 D4
65043 Holts Summit 2,540 H5
†63879 Homestown 306 N10
64461 Hopkins 634 C1
63855 Hornersville 704 M10
65483 Houston⊙ 2,157 J8
65333 Houstonia 327 F5
†64152 Houston Lake 280 O5
†63869 Howardville 536 N9
65674 Humansville 907 E7
64752 Hume 315 C6
63443 Hunnewell 235 J3
†63101 Huntleigh 428 O3
65259 Huntsville⊙ 1,657 H4
63547 Hurdland 227 H2
65486 Iberia 852 H6
63754 Illmo 1,368 O8

(continued on following page)

Agriculture, Industry and Resources

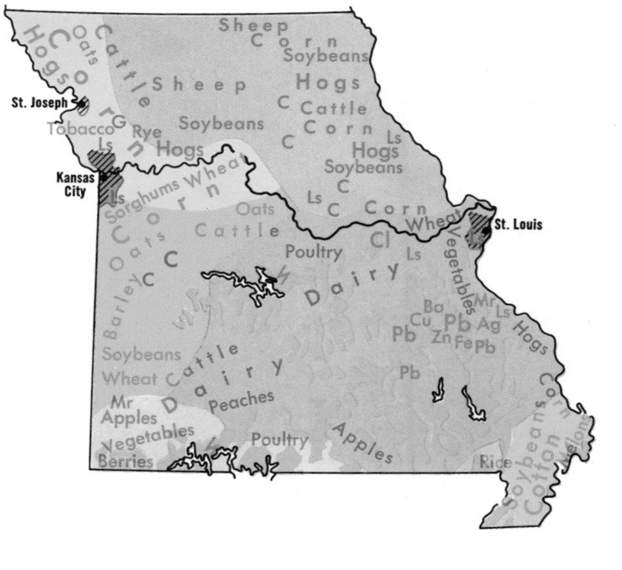

DOMINANT LAND USE

- Cattle Feed, Hogs
- Livestock, Cash Grain, Dairy
- Pasture Livestock
- Specialized Cotton
- General Farming, Dairy, Livestock, Poultry
- General Farming, Livestock, Truck Farming, Cotton
- Fruit and Mixed Farming
- Forests
- Urban Areas

MAJOR MINERAL OCCURRENCES

Ag	Silver	G	Natural Gas
Ba	Barite	Ls	Limestone
C	Coal	Mr	Marble
Cl	Clay	Pb	Lead
Cu	Copper	Zn	Zinc
Fe	Iron Ore		

Water Power — Major Industrial Areas

(continued)

*64050 Independence⊙ 111,806 ... R5
63648 Irondale 349 ... L7
†64801 Iron Gates 314 ... C8
63650 Ironton⊙ 1,743 ... L7
63755 Jackson⊙ 7,827 ... N8
64648 Jamesport 651 ... E3
65046 Jamestown 317 ... G5
64755 Jasper 1,012 ... D8
65101 Jefferson City (cap.)⊙ 33,619 ... H5
63136 Jennings 17,026 ... R2
63351 Jonesburg 614 ... K5
64801 Joplin 39,023 ... C8
Joplin‡ 127,513 ... C8
†63645 Junction City 238 ... M7
63445 Kahoka⊙ 2,101 ... J2
*64101 Kansas City 448,159 ... P5
Kansas City‡ 1,327,020 ... P5
64060 Kearney 1,433 ... D4
63758 Kelso 455 ... O8
63857 Kennett⊙ 10,145 ... M10
65261 Keytesville⊙ 689 ... G4
64649 Kidder 265 ... D3
65686 Kimberling City 1,285 ... F9
64463 King City 1,063 ... D2
64650 Kingston⊙ 280 ... E3
64061 Kingsville 365 ... D5
63140 Kinloch 4,455 ... P2
63501 Kirksville⊙ 17,167 ... H2
63122 Kirkwood 27,987 ... O3
65336 Knob Noster 2,040 ... E5
63446 Knox City 281 ... H2
63447 La Belle 845 ... J2
64651 Laclede 445 ... F3
63352 Laddonia 726 ... J4
†63124 Ladue 9,376 ... P3
63448 La Grange 1,217 ... K2
64063 Lake Lotawana 1,875 ... R6
65049 Lake Ozark 427 ... G6
†63336 Lake Saint Louis 3,843 ... N2
†63101 Lakeshire 1,593 ... P4
†64015 Lake Tapawingo 925 ... R6
†64152 Lake Waukomis 1,050 ... P5
64034 Lake Winnebago 681 ... R6
64759 Lamar⊙ 4,053 ... D8
65337 La Monte 1,054 ... F5
64847 Lanagan 440 ... C9
63548 Lancaster⊙ 855 ... H1
63549 La Plata 1,423 ... H2
64652 Laredo 340 ... E2
64760 Latour 84 ... D5
64062 Lawson 1,688 ... D4
†63640 Leadington 238 ... M7
63653 Leadwood 1,371 ... L7
65535 Leasburg 304 ... K6
65536 Lebanon⊙ 9,507 ... G7
64063 Lee's Summit 28,741 ... R6
64761 Leeton 604 ... E5
63125 Lemay 35,424 ... R4
64066 Levasy 235 ... S5
63452 Lewistown 502 ... J2
64067 Lexington⊙ 5,063 ... E4
64762 Liberal 701 ... D7
64068 Liberty⊙ 16,251 ... R5
65542 Licking 1,272 ... J8
63862 Lilbourn 1,463 ... N9
65338 Lincoln 819 ... F6
65051 Linn⊙ 1,211 ... J5
65052 Linn Creek 242 ... G6
64653 Linneus⊙ 421 ... F3
65682 Lockwood 971 ... E8
64070 Lone Jack 420 ... S6
63353 Louisiana 4,261 ... K4
64763 Lowry City 676 ... E6

63762 Lutesville 865 ... M8
63552 Macon⊙ 5,680 ... H3
65263 Madison 656 ... H4
64466 Maitland 415 ... B2
63863 Malden 6,096 ... M9
65339 Malta Bend 292 ... F4
63011 Manchester 6,191 ... O3
65704 Mansfield 1,423 ... G8
63143 Maplewood 10,960 ... P3
63764 Marble Hill⊙ 601 ... N8
64658 Marceline 2,938 ... F3
65705 Marionville 1,920 ... E8
†63101 Marlborough 2,012 ... P3
63655 Marquand 397 ... M8
65340 Marshall⊙ 12,781 ... F4
65706 Marshfield⊙ 3,871 ... G8
63866 Marston 742 ... N9
63357 Marthasville 543 ... L5
65264 Martinsburg 309 ... J4
63043 Maryland Heights 5,676 ... O2
64468 Maryville⊙ 9,558 ... C2
63857 Matthews 547 ... N9
64469 Maysville⊙ 1,187 ... D3
64071 Mayview 291 ... E4
64659 Meadville 416 ... F3
63555 Memphis⊙ 2,105 ... H2
64660 Mendon 252 ... F3
64661 Mercer 442 ... F2
65058 Meta 336 ... H6
65265 Mexico⊙ 12,276 ... J4
63359 Middletown 268 ... J4
63556 Milan⊙ 1,947 ... F2
65707 Miller 795 ... E8
63952 Mill Spring 257 ... L8
64769 Mindenmines 318 ... C8
†63801 Miner 1,182 ... N9
63660 Mineral Point 358 ... L7
64072 Missouri City 343 ... R5
65270 Moberly 13,418 ... G4
65059 Mokane 293 ... J5
†63101 Moline Acres 2,774 ... R2
65708 Monett 6,148 ... E9
63456 Monroe City 2,557 ... J3
63361 Montgomery City⊙ 2,101 ... K5
63457 Monticello⊙ 134 ... J2
64770 Montrose 498 ... E6
63868 Morehouse 1,220 ... N9
63767 Morley 745 ... N8
65710 Morrisville 331 ... F8
64073 Mosby 284 ... R4
63362 Moscow Mills 484 ... K5
64470 Mound City 1,447 ... B2
65711 Mountain Grove 3,974 ... H8
65548 Mountain View 1,664 ... J8
64665 Mount Moriah 162 ... E2
65712 Mount Vernon⊙ 3,341 ... E8
†63088 Murphy 8,121 ... O4
64074 Napoleon 271 ... E4
63953 Naylor 602 ... L9
63954 Neelyville 474 ... M9
65347 Nelson 248 ... F4
64850 Neosho⊙ 9,493 ... D9
64772 Nevada⊙ 9,044 ... D7
65063 New Bloomfield 519 ... J5
65550 Newburg 743 ... J7
63558 New Cambria 246 ... G3
63363 New Florence 731 ... K5
65274 New Franklin 1,228 ... G4
†63736 New Hamburg ... O8
64471 New Hampton 358 ... D2
63068 New Haven 1,581 ... K5
63459 New London⊙ 1,161 ... K3
63869 New Madrid⊙ 3,204 ... O9
65713 Niangua 376 ... G8

65714 Nixa 2,662 ... F8
64854 Noel 1,161 ... D9
64668 Norborne 931 ... E4
63121 Normandy 5,174 ... R2
64116 North Kansas City 4,507 ... P5
†64152 Northmoor 506 ... P5
65717 Norwood 391 ... H8
63559 Novinger 626 ... G2
64075 Oak Grove 4,067 ... S6
†63080 Oak Grove 386 ... K6
†63101 Oakland 1,728 ... P3
63769 Oak Ridge 252 ... N7
†64116 Oakview 497 ... P5
63401 Oakwood 227 ... P5
64076 Odessa 3,088 ... E5
63366 O'Fallon 8,677 ... L5
63369 Old Monroe 272 ... L5
63124 Olivette 7,985 ... O2
63050 Olympian Village 774 ... M6
63771 Oran 1,266 ... N8
64473 Oregon⊙ 901 ... B2
64855 Oronogo 525 ... D8
64077 Orrick 922 ... D4
65065 Osage Beach 1,992 ... G6
64474 Osborn 381 ... D3
64776 Osceola⊙ 841 ... E6
65348 Otterville 472 ... G5
63114 Overland 19,620 ... O2
65066 Owensville 2,241 ... K6
65721 Ozark⊙ 2,980 ... F8
63069 Pacific 4,410 ... L5
†63101 Pagedale 4,542 ... P2
63461 Palmyra⊙ 3,469 ... J3
65275 Paris⊙ 1,598 ... J4
64152 Parkville 1,997 ... O5
64130 Parkway 254 ... L6
63870 Parma 1,081 ... N9
64670 Pattonsburg 502 ... D2
64078 Peculiar 1,571 ... D5
63462 Perry 836 ... J4
63775 Perryville⊙ 7,343 ... N7
63070 Pevely 2,732 ... M6
64476 Pickering 215 ... C2
63957 Piedmont 2,359 ... L8
65723 Pierce City 1,391 ... E8
65276 Pilot Grove 745 ... G5
63663 Pilot Knob 722 ... L7
†63120 Pine Lawn 6,662 ... R2
64856 Pineville⊙ 504 ... D9
64079 Platte City⊙ 2,114 ... C4
†64152 Platte Woods 467 ... O5
64477 Plattsburg⊙ 2,095 ... D3
64080 Pleasant Hill 3,301 ... D5
65725 Pleasant Hope 354 ... F8
†64836 Pleasant Valley 1,545 ... R5
64671 Polo 583 ... D3
63901 Poplar Bluff⊙ 17,139 ... L9
63373 Portage Des Sioux 488 ... M5
63873 Portageville 3,470 ... N10
63664 Potosi⊙ 2,528 ... L7
65068 Prairie Home 279 ... G5
64673 Princeton⊙ 1,264 ... E2
64857 Purcell 322 ... D8
64674 Purdin 243 ... F3
65734 Purdy 928 ... E9
63960 Puxico 833 ... M9
63561 Queen City 783 ... H2
63961 Qulin 545 ... M9
†64101 Randolph 91 ... P5
64479 Ravenwood 436 ... C2
65555 Raymondville 388 ... J8
64083 Raymore 3,154 ... D5
64133 Raytown 31,759 ... P6
65737 Reeds Spring 461 ... F9

65738 Republic 4,485 ... E8
64779 Rich Hill 1,471 ... D6
65556 Richland 1,922 ... H7
64085 Richmond⊙ 5,499 ... D4
63117 Richmond Heights 11,516 ... P3
64481 Ridgeway 516 ... D2
63874 Risco 446 ... N9
†63601 Rivermines 414 ... L7
64168 Riverside 3,206 ... O5
†63101 Riverview 3,367 ... R2
65279 Rocheport 272 ... H5
65740 Rockaway Beach 292 ... F9
†63119 Rock Hill 5,702 ... P3
64482 Rock Port⊙ 1,511 ... B2
64780 Rockville 281 ... D6
65742 Rogersville 741 ... G8
65401 Rolla⊙ 13,303 ... J7
63091 Rosebud 326 ... K6
64483 Rosendale 223 ... C2
64484 Rushville 271 ... B3
65074 Russellville 667 ... H6
64864 Saginaw 293 ... C8

63074 Saint Ann 15,523 ... O2
63301 Saint Charles⊙ 37,379 ... N1
63077 Saint Clair 3,485 ... K6
63670 Sainte Genevieve⊙ 4,481 ... M6
65075 Saint Elizabeth 312 ... H6
†63101 Saint George 1,545 ... P4
65559 Saint James 3,328 ... J6
63114 Saint John 7,854 ... P2
*64501 Saint Joseph⊙ 76,691 ... C3
Saint Joseph‡ 101,868 ... C3
*63101 Saint Louis⊙ 453,085 ... R3
Saint Louis‡ 2,355,276 ... R3
†65101 Saint Martins 739 ... H5
63673 Saint Marys 565 ... M7
63366 Saint Paul 607 ... L5
63376 Saint Peters 15,700 ... M1
65583 Saint Robert 1,735 ... H7
65560 Salem⊙ 4,454 ... J7
65281 Salisbury 1,975 ... G4
63126 Sappington 11,388 ... O4
64862 Sarcoxie 1,381 ... D8
64485 Savannah⊙ 4,184 ... C3

64783 Schell City 327 ... D6
63780 Scott City 3,262 ... O8
65301 Sedalia⊙ 20,927 ... F5
65745 Seligman 508 ... D9
63876 Senath 1,728 ... M10
64865 Seneca 1,853 ... C9
65746 Seymour 1,535 ... G8
63468 Shelbina 2,169 ... H3
63469 Shelbyville⊙ 645 ... H3
64784 Sheldon 491 ... D7
†63101 Shrewsbury 5,077 ... P3
64088 Sibley 382 ... S5
63801 Sikeston 17,431 ... N9
63377 Silex 287 ... K4
64487 Skidmore 437 ... B2
65349 Slater 2,492 ... G4
65350 Smithton 559 ... F5
64089 Smithville 1,873 ... D4
64863 South West City 516 ... D9
†63138 Spanish Lake 20,632 ... R1
65753 Sparta 743 ... F9
64679 Spickard 389 ... F2

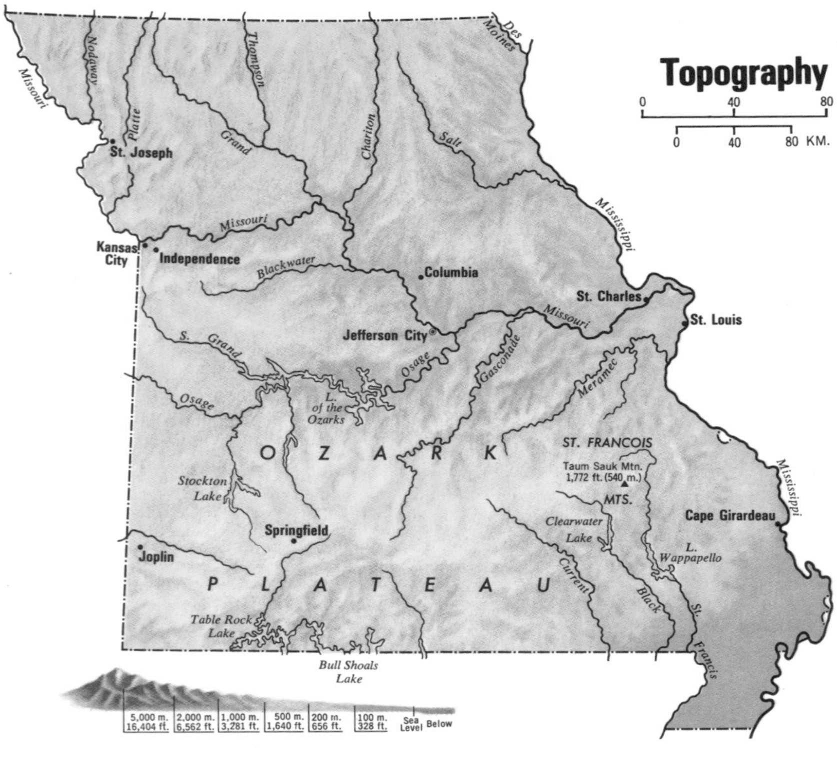

Topography
0 40 80 MI.
0 40 80 KM.
St. Joseph
Kansas City
Independence
Columbia
St. Charles
St. Louis
Jefferson City
Springfield
Joplin
Cape Girardeau
O Z A R K
P L A T E A U
ST. FRANCOIS MTS.
Taum Sauk Mtn. 1,772 ft. (540 m.)
Missouri
Mississippi
Osage
Grand
Chariton
Salt
Blackwater
Gasconade
Meramec
Current
Black
St. Francis
L. of the Ozarks
Stockton Lake
Table Rock Lake
Bull Shoals Lake
Clearwater Lake
L. Wappapello
5,000 m. 16,404 ft.
2,000 m. 6,562 ft.
1,000 m. 3,281 ft.
500 m. 1,640 ft.
200 m. 656 ft.
100 m. 328 ft.
Sea Level
Below

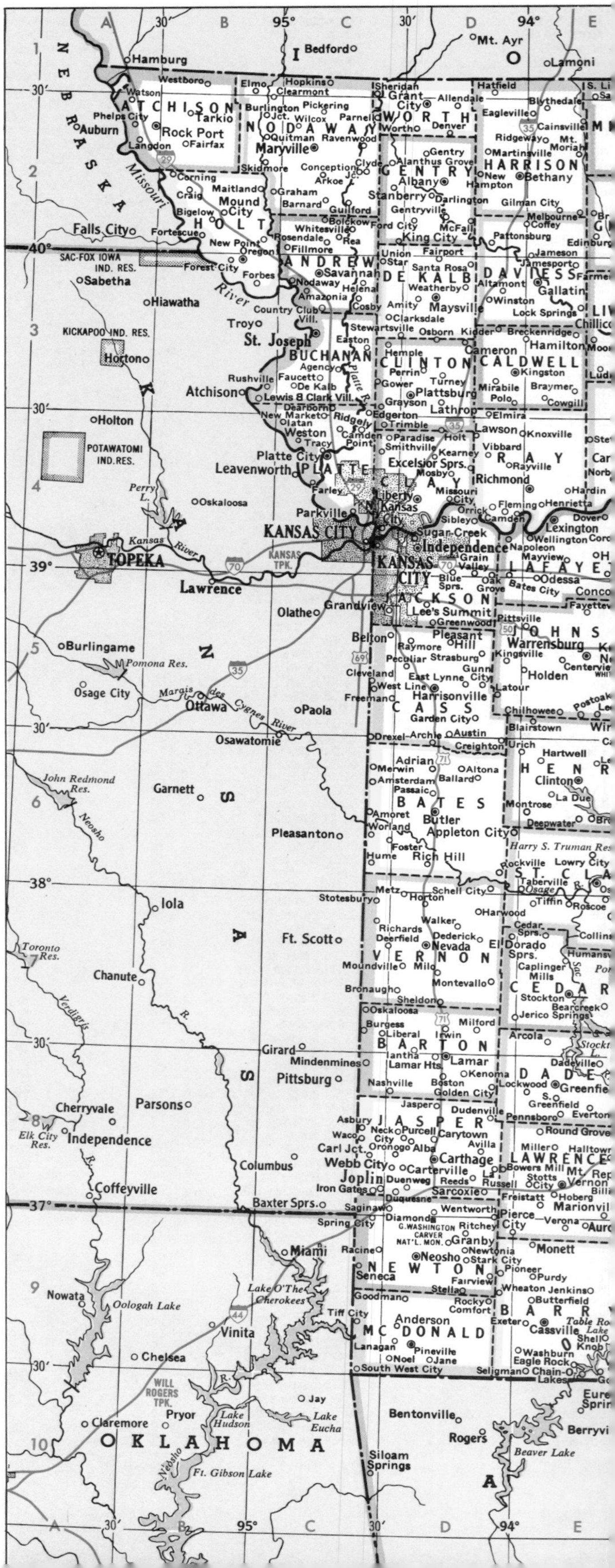

N E B R A S K A
K A N S A S
O K L A H O M A
TOPEKA
KANSAS CITY
Independence
St. Joseph
Lawrence
Leavenworth
Atchison
Joplin
Falls City
Ottawa
Olathe
Coffeyville
Miami
Vinita

*65801 Springfield⊙ 133,116 .... F8
Springfield‡ 207,704 .... F8
64489 Stanberry 1,387 .... C2
63877 Steele 2,419 .... N10
65565 Steelville⊙ 1,470 .... K7
64490 Stewartsville 832 .... C3
65785 Stockton⊙ 1,432 .... E7
65567 Stoutland 286 .... G7
65078 Stover 1,041 .... G6
65757 Strafford 1,121 .... F8
65284 Sturgeon 901 .... H4
64054 Sugar Creek 4,305 .... R5
63080 Sullivan 5,461 .... K6
65571 Summersville 551 .... J8
†63101 Sunset Hills 4,363 .... O4
65351 Sweet Springs 1,694 .... F5
65759 Taneyville 300 .... F9
†65101 Taos 759 .... H5
64491 Tarkio 2,375 .... B2
†64063 Tarsney Lakes 329 .... R6
65791 Thayer 2,211 .... J9
†63025 Times Beach 2,041 .... N4
65081 Tipton 2,155 .... G5
†63101 Town and Country 3,187 .... O3
64079 Tracy 310 .... C4
64683 Trenton⊙ 6,811 .... E2
63379 Troy⊙ 2,624 .... L5
65082 Tuscumbia⊙ 241 .... H6
†63088 Twin Oaks 426 .... N3
63084 Union⊙ 5,506 .... L6
64494 Union Star 423 .... C2
63565 Unionville⊙ 2,178 .... G2
63130 University City 42,738 .... P3
65767 Urbana 329 .... F7
64788 Urich 509 .... E6
63088 Valley Park 3,232 .... O3
63965 Van Buren⊙ 850 .... L8
63382 Vandalia 3,170 .... J4
63784 Vanduser 320 .... N9
†63101 Velda 1,988 .... P2
65769 Verona 592 .... E9
65084 Versailles⊙ 2,406 .... G6
65566 Viburnum 836 .... K7
†63020 Victoria 375 .... M6
65582 Vienna⊙ 514 .... H6
†63101 Vinita Park 2,283 .... P2
64790 Walker 325 .... D7
65770 Walnut Grove 504 .... F8
†65101 Wardsville 535 .... H6
64093 Warrensburg⊙ 13,807 .... E5
63383 Warrenton⊙ 3,219 .... K5
65355 Warsaw⊙ 1,494 .... F6
†63101 Warson Woods 2,127 .... O3
63090 Washington 9,251 .... K5
64096 Waverly 941 .... E4
63472 Wayland 498 .... J2
65583 Waynesville⊙ 2,879 .... H7
†64152 Weatherby Lake 1,446 .... O5
65774 Weaubleau 464 .... F7
64870 Webb City 7,309 .... C8
63119 Webster Groves 23,097 .... P3
64097 Wellington 780 .... E4
63112 Wellston 4,495 .... R2
63384 Wellsville 1,546 .... K4
63385 Wentzville 3,193 .... L5
64498 Westboro 188 .... B1
64098 Weston 1,440 .... C4
65775 West Plains⊙ 7,741 .... J9
†63101 Westwood 319 .... O3
65779 Wheatland 364 .... F7
64874 Wheaton 548 .... E9
64688 Wheeling 379 .... F3
†63101 Wilbur Park 564 .... P3
65781 Willard 1,799 .... F8
63977 Williamsville 418 .... L9
65793 Willow Springs 2,215 .... H9
†63834 Wilson City 309 .... O9
†63435 Winchester 2,237 .... N3
65360 Windsor 3,058 .... E5
63389 Winfield 592 .... L5
65588 Winona 1,050 .... K8
64689 Winston 246 .... D3
†64024 Woods Heights 747 .... S4
†63101 Woodson Terrace 4,788 .... P2
63390 Wright City 1,179 .... K5
63474 Wyaconda 359 .... J2
63882 Wyatt 441 .... O9

OTHER FEATURES

Bagnell (dam) G6
Big (riv.) L6
Black (riv.) L10
Bull Shoals (lake) G10
Chariton (riv.) G1
Clearwater (lake) L8
Cuivre (riv.) N2
Current (riv.) K8
Des Moines (riv.) J1
Fort Leonard Wood 21,262 .... H7
Gasconade (riv.) H7
George Washington Carver Nat'l Mon. D9
Grand (riv.) F3
Jefferson Nat'l Expansion Mem. Nat'l His R3
Lake City Arsenal R5
Meramec (riv.) N3
Mississippi (riv.) L4
Missouri (riv.) H5
Norfork (lake) H10
Osage (riv.) E6
Ozark (plat.) F9
Ozark Nat'l Scenic Riverways K8
Ozarks, Lake of the (lake) F6
Platte (riv.) C3
Pomme de Terre (lake) E7
Richards Gebaur A.F.B. 4,305 .... P6
Sac (riv.) E7
Saint Francis (riv.) M9
Salt (riv.) J3
Stockton (lake) E7
Table Rock (res.) E9
Taneycomo (lake) F9
Taum Sauk (mt.) L7
Wappapello (lake) L8
White (riv.) G10
Whiteman A.F.B. E5
Wilson's Creek Nat'l Battlefield F8

⊙County seat.
‡Population of metropolitan area.
† Zip of nearest p.o. * Multiple zips.

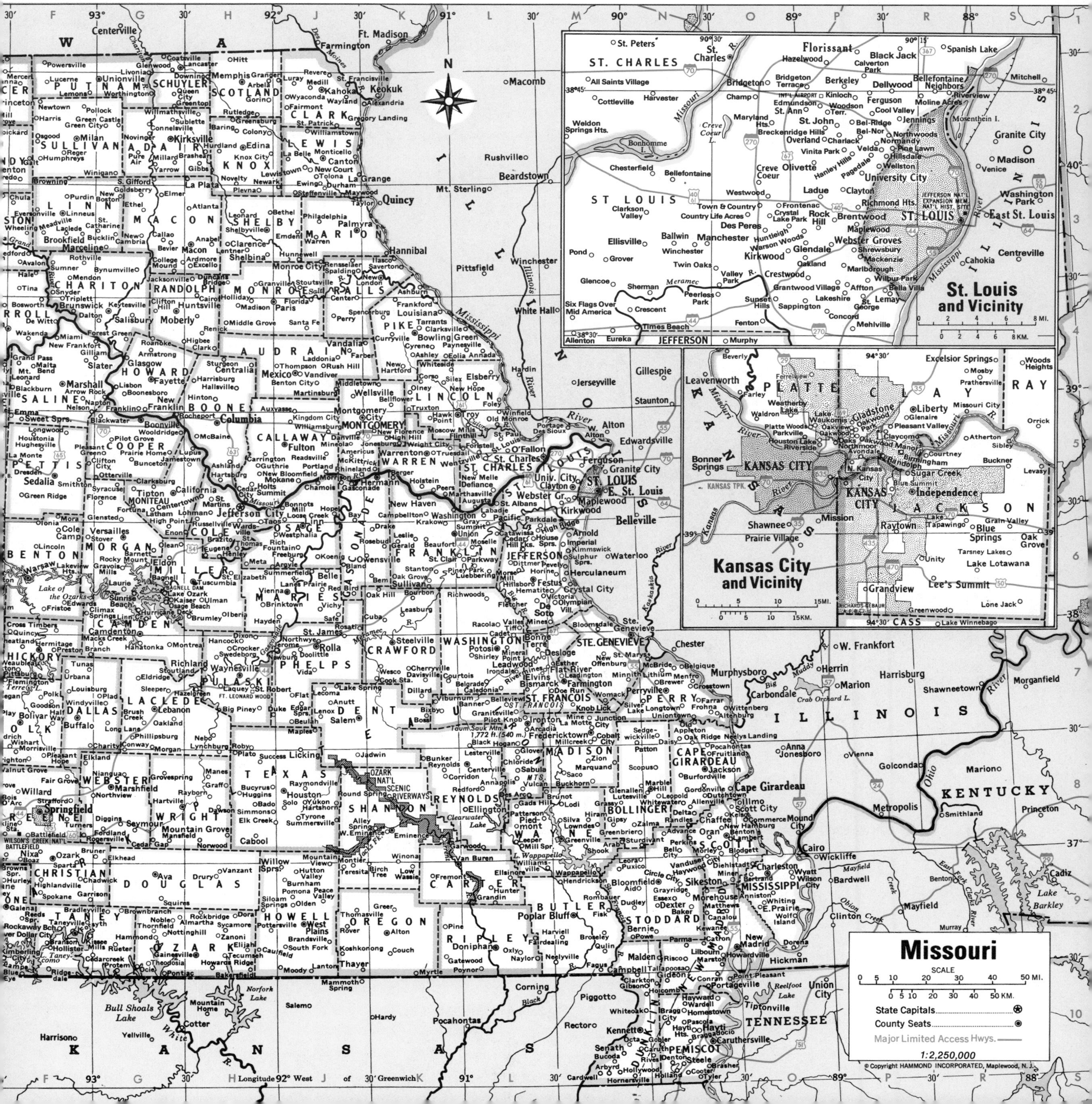

Agriculture, Industry and Resources

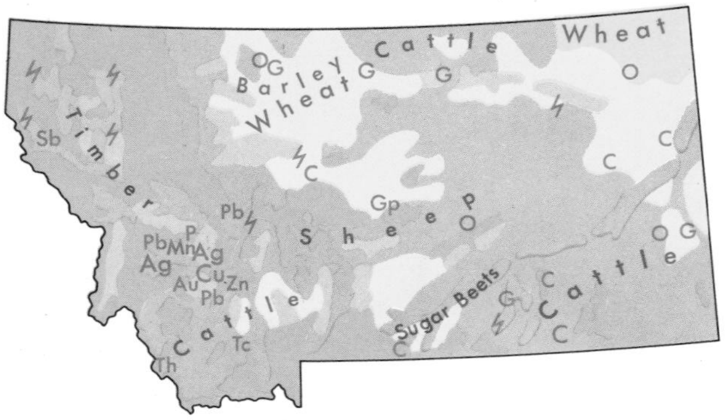
Wheat
Cattle
Barley
Wheat
Timber
Sb
Sheep
Cattle
Sugar Beets
Cattle
Pb
Ag
Au
Cu
Zn
Gp
P
O
G
C
Th
Tc

DOMINANT LAND USE

- Specialized Wheat
- Wheat, Range Livestock
- General Farming, Dairy, Range Livestock
- General Farming, Livestock, Special Crops
- Range Livestock
- Sugar Beets, Beans, Livestock, General Farming
- Forests

MAJOR MINERAL OCCURRENCES

Ag	Silver	O	Petroleum
Au	Gold	P	Phosphates
C	Coal	Pb	Lead
Cu	Copper	Sb	Antimony
G	Natural Gas	Tc	Talc
Gp	Gypsum	Th	Thorium
Mn	Manganese	Zn	Zinc

ϟ Water Power

COUNTIES

Beaverhead 8,186	C5
Big Horn 11,096	J5
Blaine 6,999	G2
Broadwater 3,267	E4
Carbon 8,099	G5
Carter 1,799	M5
Cascade 80,696	E3
Chouteau 6,092	F3
Custer 13,109	L4
Daniels 2,835	L2
Dawson 11,805	M3
Deer Lodge 12,518	C5
Fallon 3,763	M4
Fergus 13,076	G3
Flathead 51,966	B2
Gallatin 42,865	E5
Garfield 1,656	J3
Glacier 10,628	C2
Golden Valley 1,026	G4
Granite 2,700	C4
Hill 17,985	F2
Jefferson 7,029	D4
Judith Basin 2,646	F4
Lake 19,056	B3
Lewis and Clark 43,039	D3
Liberty 2,329	E2
Lincoln 17,752	A2
Madison 5,448	D5
McCone 2,702	L3
Meagher 2,154	F4
Mineral 3,675	B3
Missoula 76,016	C3
Musselshell 4,428	H4
Park 12,869	F5
Petroleum 655	H3
Phillips 5,367	J2
Pondera 6,731	D2
Powder River 2,520	L5
Powell 6,958	D4
Prairie 1,836	L4
Ravalli 22,493	B4
Richland 12,243	M3
Roosevelt 10,467	L2
Rosebud 9,899	K4
Sanders 8,675	A3
Sheridan 5,414	M2
Silver Bow 38,092	D5
Stillwater 5,598	G5
Sweet Grass 3,216	G5
Teton 6,491	D3
Toole 5,559	E2
Treasure 981	J4
Valley 10,250	K2
Wheatland 2,359	G4
Wibaux 1,476	M4
Yellowstone 108,035	H4
Yellowstone Nat'l Park 275	F6

CITIES and TOWNS

Zip	Name/Pop.	Key
59001	Absarokee 830	G5
59820	Alberton 368	B3
59710	Alder 120	D5
†59741	Amsterdam 130	E5
59711	Anaconda-Deer Lodge County⊙ 12,518	C4
59312	Angela 50	K4
59211	Antelope 83	M2
59821	Arlee 200	B3
59003	Ashland 600	K5
59410	Augusta 497	D3
59713	Avon 125	D4
59411	Babb 150	C2
59212	Bainville 245	M2
59313	Baker⊙ 2,354	M4
59006	Ballantine 380	J5
†59725	Bannack 2	C5
59613	Basin 350	D4
59007	Bearcreek 61	G5
59008	Belfry 300	H5
59714	Belgrade 2,336	E5
59412	Belt 825	E3
59314	Biddle 28	L5
59910	Big Arm 250	B3
59911	Bigfork 1,080	C2
59520	Big Sandy 835	G2
59011	Big Timber⊙ 1,690	G5
*59101	Billings⊙ 66,842	H5
	Billings‡ 108,035	H5
59012	Birney 100	K5
59414	Black Eagle 1,500	E3
59415	Blackfoot 100	D2
59823	Bonner-West Riverside 1,742	C4
59632	Boulder⊙ 1,441	E4
59521	Box Elder 300	F2
59715	Bozeman⊙ 21,645	E5
59416	Brady 450	E2
59014	Bridger 724	H5
59317	Broadus⊙ 712	L5
59015	Broadview 120	H4
59213	Brockton 374	M2
59417	Browning 1,226	C2
59016	Busby 700	J5
59701	Butte-Silver Bow County⊙ 37,205	D5
59720	Cameron 150	E5
59633	Canyon Creek 100	D4
†59347	Cartersville 115	K4
59421	Cascade 773	E3
59824	Charlo 250	B3
59522	Chester⊙ 963	E2
59523	Chinook⊙ 1,660	G2
59422	Choteau⊙ 1,798	D3
59215	Circle⊙ 931	L3
59634	Clancy 550	E4
59018	Clyde Park 283	F5
†59351	Coalwood 2	L5
59322	Cohagen 12	K3
59323	Colstrip 1,476	K5
59912	Columbia Falls 3,112	B2
59019	Columbus⊙ 1,439	G5
59826	Condon 300	C3
59827	Conner 420	B5
59425	Conrad⊙ 3,074	D2
59020	Cooke City 120	G5
59913	Coram 450	C2
59828	Corvallis 500	C4
59217	Crane 163	M3
59022	Crow Agency 975	J5
59218	Culbertson 887	M2
59024	Custer 300	J4
59427	Cut Bank⊙ 3,688	D2
59829	Darby 581	B4
59914	Dayton 140	B3
59830	De Borgia 300	A3
59025	Decker 150	K5
59722	Deer Lodge⊙ 4,023	D4
59430	Denton 356	G3

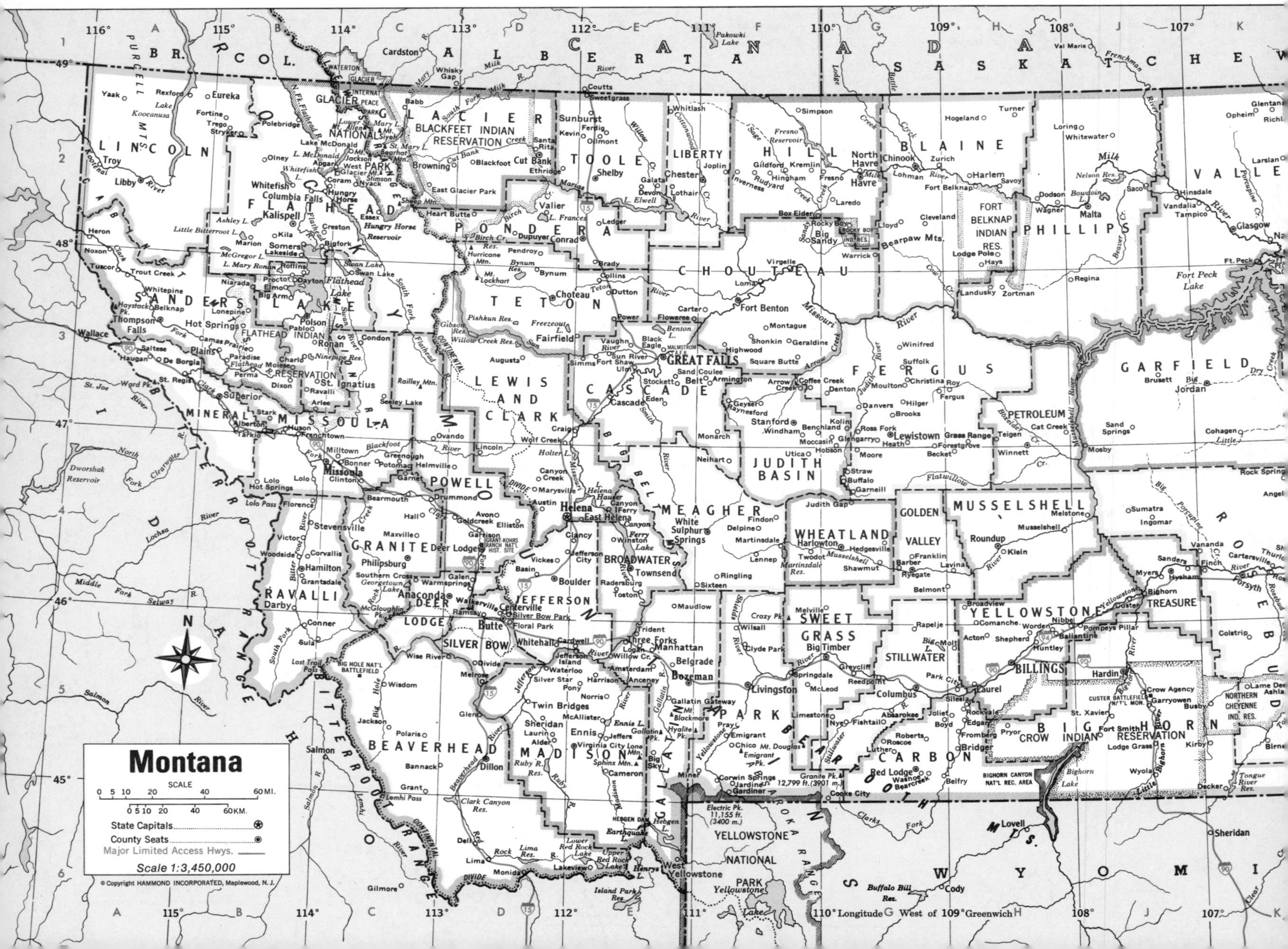
BRITISH COLUMBIA
ALBERTA
SASKATCHEWAN
CANADA
LINCOLN
FLATHEAD
GLACIER
TOOLE
LIBERTY
HILL
BLAINE
PHILLIPS
VALLEY
SANDERS
LAKE
PONDERA
TETON
CHOUTEAU
FERGUS
GARFIELD
MINERAL
MISSOULA
LEWIS AND CLARK
CASCADE
JUDITH BASIN
PETROLEUM
POWELL
MEAGHER
WHEATLAND
GOLDEN VALLEY
MUSSELSHELL
GRANITE
RAVALLI
DEER LODGE
JEFFERSON
BROADWATER
SILVER BOW
SWEET GRASS
STILLWATER
YELLOWSTONE
TREASURE
BEAVERHEAD
MADISON
GALLATIN
PARK
CARBON
BIG HORN
IDAHO
WYOMING
BITTERROOT RANGE
GLACIER NATIONAL PARK
BLACKFEET INDIAN RESERVATION
FLATHEAD INDIAN RESERVATION
FORT BELKNAP INDIAN RES.
CROW INDIAN RESERVATION
YELLOWSTONE NATIONAL PARK
GREAT FALLS
Helena
BILLINGS
Butte
Missoula
Bozeman
Kalispell
Havre
Lewistown
Livingston
Fort Peck Lake
Montana
SCALE
State Capitals
County Seats
Major Limited Access Hwys.
Scale 1:3,450,000
© Copyright HAMMOND INCORPORATED, Maplewood, N. J.
110° Longitude West of 109° Greenwich

Topography

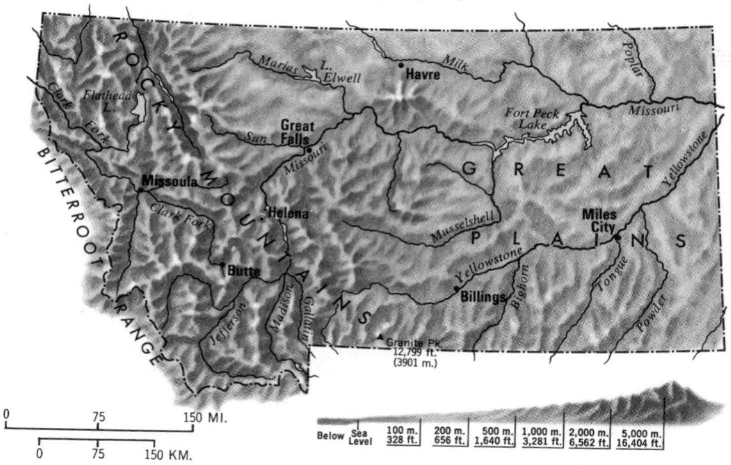
ROCKY MOUNTAINS
BITTERROOT RANGE
GREAT PLAINS
Marias
L. Elwell
Havre
Milk
Poplar
Missouri
Fort Peck Lake
Flathead L.
Clark Fork
Great Falls
Sun
Missoula
Helena
Musselshell
Miles City
Yellowstone
Butte
Billings
Bighorn
Tongue
Powder
Jefferson
Madison
Gallatin
Granite Pk. 12,799 ft. (3901 m.)
0 75 150 MI.
0 75 150 KM.
Below Sea Level
100 m. 328 ft.
200 m. 656 ft.
500 m. 1,640 ft.
1,000 m. 3,281 ft.
2,000 m. 6,562 ft.
5,000 m. 16,404 ft.

AREA 147,046 sq. mi. (380,849 sq. km.)
POPULATION 786,690
CAPITAL Helena
LARGEST CITY Billings
HIGHEST POINT Granite Pk. 12,799 ft. (3901 m.)
SETTLED IN 1809
ADMITTED TO UNION November 8, 1889
POPULAR NAME Treasure State; Big Sky Country
STATE FLOWER Bitterroot
STATE BIRD Western Meadowlark

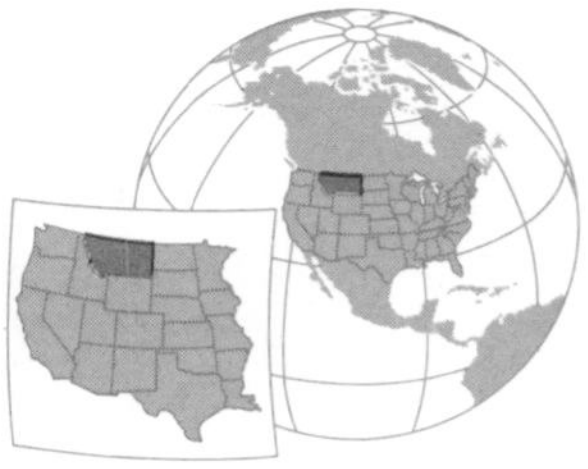

59725 Dillon⊙ 3,976 .... D5
59727 Divide 275 .... D5
59831 Dixon 550 .... B3
59524 Dodson 158 .... H2
59832 Drummond 414 .... D4
59432 Dupuyer 105 .... D2
59433 Dutton 359 .... E3
59434 East Glacier Park 475 .... C2
59635 East Helena 1,647 .... E4
59026 Edgar 220 .... H5
59324 Ekalaka⊙ 620 .... M5
59728 Elliston 250 .... D4
59915 Elmo 250 .... B3
59729 Ennis 660 .... E5
59917 Eureka 1,119 .... B2
59436 Fairfield 650 .... D3
59221 Fairview 1,366 .... M3
59326 Fallon 225 .... L4
59222 Flaxville 142 .... L2
59833 Florence 700 .... B4
59441 Forestgrove 100 .... H3
59327 Forsyth⊙ 2,553 .... K4
†59526 Fort Belknap 185 .... H2
59442 Fort Benton⊙ 1,693 .... F3
59918 Fortine 250 .... A2
59223 Fort Peck 456 .... K2
59443 Fort Shaw 200 .... E3
†59075 Fort Smith 300 .... J5
59225 Frazer 200 .... K2
59834 Frenchtown 300 .... B3
59226 Froid 323 .... M2
59029 Fromberg 469 .... H5
59444 Galata 100 .... E2
59730 Gallatin Gateway 600 .... E5
59030 Gardiner 600 .... F5
59731 Garrison 300 .... D4
59031 Garryowen 200 .... J5
59446 Geraldine 305 .... F3
59447 Geyser 125 .... F3
59525 Gildford 250 .... F2
59230 Glasgow⊙ 4,455 .... K2
59330 Glendive⊙ 5,978 .... M3
59733 Goldcreek 100 .... D4
59835 Grantsdale 500 .... B4
59032 Grass Range 139 .... H3
59401 Great Falls⊙ 56,725 .... E3
Great Falls‡ 80,696 .... E3
59836 Greenough 120 .... C4
59837 Hall 130 .... C4
59840 Hamilton⊙ 2,661 .... B4
59034 Hardin⊙ 3,300 .... J5
59526 Harlem 1,023 .... H2
59036 Harlowton⊙ 1,181 .... F4
59735 Harrison 94 .... E5
59842 Haugan 90 .... A3
59501 Havre⊙ 10,891 .... G2
59527 Hays 400 .... H2
59448 Heart Butte 300 .... C2
59601 Helena (cap.)⊙ 23,938 .... E4
59843 Helmville 250 .... C4
59450 Highwood 150 .... F3
59528 Hingham 186 .... F2
59241 Hinsdale 260 .... K2
59452 Hobson 261 .... G4
59845 Hot Springs 601 .... B3
59919 Hungry Horse 700 .... C2
59037 Huntley 250 .... H5
59846 Huson 97 .... B3
59038 Hysham⊙ 449 .... J4
59530 Inverness 150 .... F2
59336 Ismay 31 .... M4
59736 Jackson 210 .... C5
59638 Jefferson City 162 .... E4
59041 Joliet 580 .... G5
59531 Joplin 300 .... F2
59337 Jordan⊙ 485 .... J3
59453 Judith Gap 213 .... G4
59901 Kalispell⊙ 10,648 .... B2
59454 Kevin 208 .... D2
59920 Kila 350 .... B2
59338 Kinsey 100 .... L4
†59072 Klein 250 .... H4
59532 Kremlin 304 .... F2
59922 Lakeside 663 .... B2
59243 Lambert 203 .... M3
59043 Lame Deer 460 .... K5
59044 Laurel 5,481 .... H5
59046 Lavina 164 .... H4
59457 Lewistown⊙ 7,104 .... G3
59923 Libby⊙ 2,748 .... A2
59739 Lima 272 .... D6
59639 Lincoln 473 .... D4
59047 Livingston⊙ 6,994 .... F5
59050 Lodge Grass 771 .... J5
†59524 Lodge Pole 292 .... H2
59847 Lolo 2,418 .... B4
†59847 Lolo Hot Springs 25 .... B4
59460 Loma 200 .... F3
59225 Lustre 25 .... K2
59538 Malta⊙ 2,367 .... J2
59741 Manhattan 988 .... E5
59925 Marion 450 .... B2
59052 McLeod 150 .... G5
59247 Medicine Lake 408 .... M2
59743 Melrose 350 .... D5
59054 Melstone 238 .... H4
59055 Melville 100 .... F4
59301 Miles City⊙ 9,602 .... L4
59851 Milltown 300 .... C4
*59801 Missoula⊙ 33,388 .... C4
59463 Monarch 120 .... F3
59464 Moore 229 .... G4
59059 Musselshell 117 .... H4
59248 Nashua 495 .... K2
59465 Neihart 91 .... F4
†59501 North Havre 1,230 .... G2
59853 Noxon 800 .... A3
59927 Olney 200 .... B2
59250 Opheim 210 .... K2
59252 Outlook 122 .... M2
59854 Ovando 300 .... C3
59855 Pablo 500 .... B3
59856 Paradise 400 .... B3
59063 Park City 800 .... H5
59253 Peerless 110 .... L2
59467 Pendroy 100 .... D2
59858 Philipsburg⊙ 1,138 .... C4
59859 Plains 1,116 .... B3
59254 Plentywood⊙ 2,476 .... M2
59344 Plevna 191 .... M4
59860 Polson⊙ 2,798 .... B3
59064 Pompeys Pillar 300 .... J5
59747 Pony 130 .... E5
59255 Poplar 995 .... L2
59468 Power 159 .... E3
59929 Proctor 150 .... B3
59066 Pryor 146 .... H5
59641 Radersburg 104 .... E4
59863 Ravalli 150 .... B3
59068 Red Lodge⊙ 1,896 .... G5
59069 Reedpoint 160 .... G5
59258 Reserve 80 .... M2
59930 Rexford 130 .... A2
59259 Richey 417 .... L3
59642 Ringling 102 .... F4
59070 Roberts 312 .... G5
59931 Rollins 200 .... B3
59864 Ronan 1,530 .... C3
59347 Rosebud 259 .... K4
59072 Roundup⊙ 2,119 .... H4
59471 Roy 200 .... H3
59540 Rudyard 450 .... F2
59074 Ryegate⊙ 273 .... G4
59261 Saco 252 .... J2
59865 Saint Ignatius 877 .... C3
59866 Saint Regis 500 .... A3
59075 Saint Xavier 200 .... J5
59867 Saltese 90 .... A3
59472 Sand Coulee 600 .... E3
59473 Santa Rita 120 .... D2
59262 Savage 300 .... M3
59263 Scobey⊙ 1,382 .... L2
59868 Seeley Lake 900 .... C3
59474 Shelby⊙ 3,142 .... E2
59079 Shepherd 200 .... H5
59749 Sheridan 646 .... D5
59270 Sidney⊙ 5,726 .... M3
59751 Silver Star 125 .... D5
59477 Simms 200 .... E3
59932 Somers 700 .... B2
59479 Stanford⊙ 595 .... F3
59870 Stevensville 1,207 .... C4
59480 Stockett 500 .... E3
59933 Stryker 96 .... B2
59871 Sula 200 .... B5
59482 Sunburst 476 .... E2
59483 Sun River 300 .... E3
59872 Superior⊙ 1,054 .... B3
59911 Swan Lake 100 .... C3
59484 Sweetgrass 250 .... E2
59349 Terry⊙ 929 .... L4
59873 Thompson Falls⊙ 1,478 .... A3
59752 Three Forks 1,247 .... E5
59644 Townsend⊙ 1,587 .... E4
59874 Trout Creek 300 .... A3
59935 Troy 1,088 .... A2
59542 Turner 150 .... H2
59754 Twin Bridges 437 .... D5
59085 Twodot 285 .... F4
59485 Ulm 450 .... E3
59486 Valier 640 .... D2
59487 Vaughn 2,270 .... E3
59875 Victor 700 .... B4
59755 Virginia City⊙ 192 .... E5
59351 Volborg 125 .... L5
59701 Walkerville 887 .... D4
59756 Warmsprings 500 .... D4
59275 Westby 291 .... M2
59936 West Glacier 150 .... C2
59758 West Yellowstone 735 .... E6
59937 Whitefish 3,703 .... B2
59759 Whitehall 1,030 .... D5
59645 White Sulphur Springs⊙ 1,302 .... E4
59276 Whitetail 150 .... L2
59544 Whitewater 100 .... J2
59353 Wibaux⊙ 782 .... M3
59760 Willow Creek 150 .... E5
59086 Wilsall 250 .... F5
59489 Winifred 155 .... G3
59087 Winnett⊙ 207 .... H4
59647 Winston 120 .... E4
59761 Wisdom 140 .... C5
59762 Wise River 150 .... C5
59648 Wolf Creek 500 .... D3
59201 Wolf Point⊙ 3,074 .... L2
59088 Worden 600 .... H5
59089 Wyola 350 .... J5

OTHER FEATURES

Absaroka (range) F5
Allen (mt.) C2
Arrow (creek) F3
Ashley (lake) B2
Battle (creek) G1
Bearhat (mt.) C2
Bearpaw (mts.) G2
Beartooth (mts.) G5
Beaver (creek) J2
Beaverhead (riv.) D5
Benton (lake) E3
Big (lake) G5
Big Belt (mts.) E4
Big Dry (creek) K3
Big Hole (riv.) C5
Big Hole Nat'l Battlefield C5
Bighorn (lake) H5
Bighorn (riv.) J5
Bighorn Canyon Nat'l Rec. Area H5
Big Muddy (riv.) M2
Big Porcupine (creek) J4
Birch (creek) D2
Birch Creek (res.) D2
Bitterroot (range) B4
Bitterroot (riv.) B4
Blackfeet Ind. Res. D2
Blackfoot (riv.) C4
Blackmore (mt.) F5
Bowdoin (lake) J2
Boxelder (creek) H3
Boxelder (creek) M5
Bynum (res.) D2
Cabinet (mts.) A2
Canyon Ferry (lake) E4
Clark Canyon (res.) D6
Clark Fork (riv.) A3
Clarks Fork, Yellowstone (riv.) G6
Cottonwood (creek) E2
Cow (creek) G2
Crazy (peak) F4
Crow Ind. Res. H5
Custer Battlefield Nat'l Mon. J5
Cut Bank (creek) D2
Douglas (mt.) F5
Earthquake (lake) E6
Electric (peak) F6
Elwell (lake) E2
Emigrant (peak) F5
Ennis (lake) E5
Flathead (lake) C3
Flathead (riv.) B2
Flathead, North Fork (riv.) B2
Flathead, South Fork (riv.) C3
Flathead Ind. Res. B3
Flatwillow (creek) H4
Fort Belknap Ind. Res. H2
Fort Peck (lake) K3
Fort Union Trading Post Nat'l Hist. Site N2
Frances (lake) D2
Freezeout (lake) D3
Frenchman (riv.) J1
Fresno (res.) F2
Gallatin (peak) E5
Gallatin (riv.) E5
Georgetown (lake) C4
Gibson (res.) D3
Glacier Nat'l Park C2
Granite (peak) F5
Grant-Kohrs Ranch Nat'l Hist. Site D4
Hauser (lake) E4
Haystack (peak) A3
Hebgen (lake) E6
Helena (lake) E4
Holter (lake) D4
Hungry Horse (res.) C2
Hurricane (mt.) D2
Hyalite (peak) E5
Jackson (mt.) C2
Jefferson (riv.) D5
Judith (riv.) G3
Koocanusa (lake) A2
Kootenai (riv.) A2
Lemhi (pass) C6
Lewis (range) C2
Lima (res.) D6
Little Bighorn (riv.) J5
Little Bitterroot (lake) B2
Little Dry (creek) K3
Little Missouri (riv.) M5
Lockhart (mt.) D3
Lodge (creek) G1
Lolo (pass) B4
Lone (mt.) E5
Lost Trail (pass) B5
Lower Red Rock (lake) E6
Lower Saint Mary (lake) C2
Madison (riv.) E5
Malmstrom A.F.B. 6,675 .... E3
Marias (riv.) D2
Martinsdale (res.) F4
Mary Ronan (lake) B3
McDonald (lake) B2
McGloughlin (peak) C4
McGregor (lake) B3
Medicine (lake) M2
Milk (riv.) J2
Mission (range) C3
Missouri (riv.) L3
Musselshell (riv.) J3
Nelson (res.) J2
Ninepipe (res.) C3
Northern Cheyenne Indian Reservation K5
O'Fallon (creek) L4
Pishkun (res.) D3
Poplar (riv.) L2
Porcupine (creek) K2
Powder (riv.) L4
Purcell (mts.) A2
Railley (mt.) C3
Red Rock (lkes) E6
Red Rock (riv.) D6
Redwater (riv.) L3
Rock (creek) C4
Rocky (mts.) D4
Rocky Boy's Ind. Res. G2
Rosebud (creek) K4
Ruby (riv.) D5
Ruby River (res.) D5
Sage (creek) F2
Saint Mary (lake) C2
Saint Mary (riv.) C1
Sandy (creek) F2
Sheep (mt.) C2
Shields (riv.) F4
Siyeh (mt.) C2
Smith (riv.) E3
Sphinx (mt.) E5
Stillwater (riv.) G5
Stimson (mt.) C2
Sun (riv.) D3
Swan (lake) C3
Teton (riv.) E3
Tongue (riv.) K5
Upper Red Rock (lake) E6
Ward (peak) A3
Waterton-Glacier Int'l Peace Park C2
Whitefish (lake) B2
Willow (creek) E2
Willow Creek (res.) D3
Yellowstone (riv.) M3
Yellowstone National Park F6

⊙County seat.
‡Population of metropolitan area.
† Zip or nearest p.o. * Multiple zips.

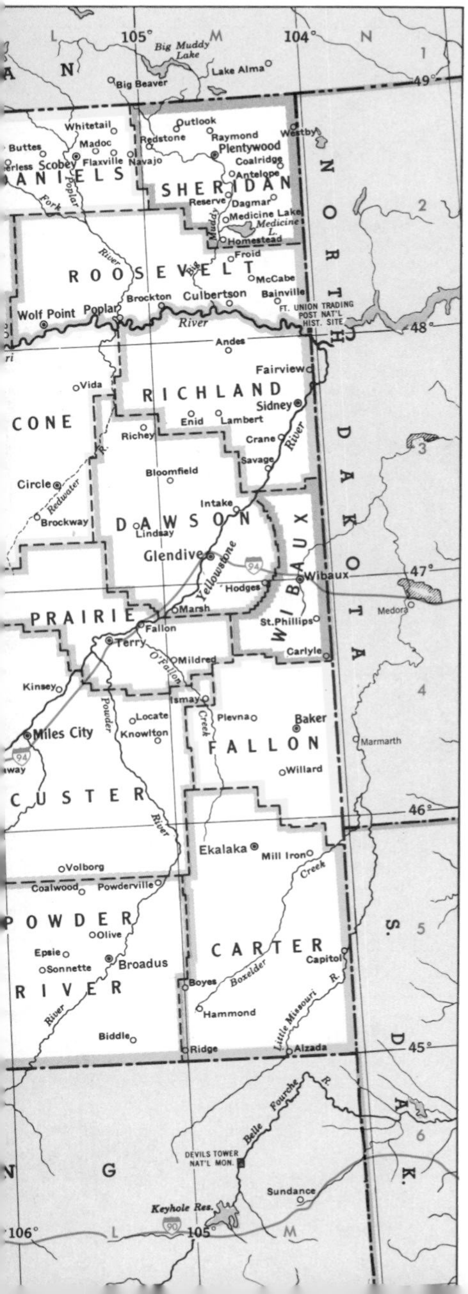
SHERIDAN
ROOSEVELT
RICHLAND
DAWSON
WIBAUX
PRAIRIE
FALLON
CUSTER
CARTER
POWDER RIVER
NORTH DAKOTA
Plentywood
Wolf Point
Culbertson
Sidney
Glendive
Wibaux
Terry
Miles City
Baker
Ekalaka
Broadus
Medicine Lake
Fairview
Circle
Richey
Lambert
Savage
Fallon
Ismay
Plevna
Alzada
Capitol
Hammond
Biddle
Volborg
Powderville
Yellowstone
Missouri
Little Missouri R.
DEVILS TOWER NAT'L MON.
Sundance
Keyhole Res.
105°
104°
106°
49°
48°
47°
46°
45°

COUNTIES

Adams 30,656 .... F4
Antelope 8,675 .... F2
Arthur 513 .... C3
Banner 918 .... A3
Blaine 867 .... E3
Boone 7,391 .... F3
Box Butte 13,696 .... A2
Boyd 3,331 .... F2
Brown 4,377 .... E2
Buffalo 34,797 .... E4
Burt 8,813 .... H3
Butler 9,330 .... G3
Cass 20,297 .... H4
Cedar 11,375 .... G2
Chase 4,758 .... C4
Cherry 6,758 .... C2
Cheyenne 10,057 .... A3
Clay 8,106 .... F4
Colfax 9,890 .... G3
Cuming 11,664 .... H3
Custer 13,877 .... E3
Dakota 16,573 .... H2
Dawes 9,609 .... A2
Dawson 22,304 .... E4
Deuel 2,462 .... B3
Dixon 7,137 .... H2
Dodge 35,847 .... H3
Douglas 397,038 .... H3
Dundy 2,861 .... C4
Fillmore 7,920 .... G4
Franklin 4,377 .... F4
Frontier 3,647 .... D4
Furnas 6,486 .... E4
Gage 24,456 .... H4
Garden 2,802 .... B3
Garfield 2,363 .... F3
Gosper 2,140 .... E4
Grant 877 .... C3
Greeley 3,462 .... F3
Hall 47,690 .... F4
Hamilton 9,301 .... F4
Harlan 4,292 .... E4
Hayes 1,356 .... C4
Hitchcock 4,079 .... C4
Holt 13,552 .... F2
Hooker 990 .... C3
Howard 6,773 .... F3
Jefferson 9,817 .... G4
Johnson 5,285 .... H4
Kearney 7,053 .... F4
Keith 9,364 .... C3
Keya Paha 1,301 .... E2
Kimball 4,882 .... A3
Knox 11,457 .... G2
Lancaster 192,884 .... H4
Lincoln 36,455 .... D4
Logan 983 .... D3
Loup 859 .... E3
Madison 31,382 .... G3
McPherson 593 .... C3
Merrick 8,945 .... F3
Morrill 6,085 .... A3
Nance 4,740 .... F3
Nemaha 8,367 .... J4
Nuckolls 6,726 .... F4
Otoe 15,183 .... H4
Pawnee 3,937 .... H4
Perkins 3,637 .... C4
Phelps 9,769 .... E4
Pierce 8,481 .... G2
Platte 28,852 .... G3
Polk 6,320 .... G3
Red Willow 12,615 .... D4
Richardson 11,315 .... J4
Rock 2,383 .... E2
Saline 13,131 .... G4
Sarpy 86,015 .... H3
Saunders 18,716 .... H3
Scotts Bluff 38,344 .... A3
Seward 15,789 .... G4
Sheridan 7,544 .... B2
Sherman 4,226 .... F3
Sioux 1,845 .... A2
Stanton 6,549 .... G3
Thayer 7,582 .... G4
Thomas 973 .... D3
Thurston 7,186 .... H2
Valley 5,633 .... E3
Washington 15,508 .... H3
Wayne 9,858 .... G2
Webster 4,858 .... F4
Wheeler 1,060 .... F3
York 14,798 .... G4

CITIES and TOWNS

Zip *Name/Pop.* *Key*

68301 Adams 395 .... H4
69210 Ainsworth⊙ 2,256 .... D2
68620 Albion⊙ 1,997 .... F3
68810 Alda 601 .... F4
68710 Allen 390 .... H2
69301 Alliance⊙ 9,920 .... A2
68920 Alma⊙ 1,369 .... E4
68304 Alvo 144 .... H4
68812 Amherst 269 .... E4
68814 Ansley 644 .... E3
68922 Arapahoe 1,107 .... E4
68815 Arcadia 412 .... F3
68002 Arlington 1,117 .... H3
69120 Arnold 813 .... D3
69121 Arthur⊙ 124 .... C3
68003 Ashland 2,274 .... H3
68713 Atkinson 1,521 .... E2
68305 Auburn⊙ 3,482 .... J4
68818 Aurora⊙ 3,717 .... F4
68924 Axtell 602 .... E4
68004 Bancroft 552 .... H2
68622 Bartlett⊙ 144 .... F3
69020 Bartley 342 .... D4
68714 Bassett⊙ 1,009 .... E2
68715 Battle Creek 948 .... G3
69334 Bayard 1,435 .... A3
68310 Beatrice⊙ 12,891 .... H4
68926 Beaver City⊙ 775 .... E4
68313 Beaver Crossing 458 .... G4
68716 Beemer 853 .... H3
68005 Bellevue 21,813 .... J3
68624 Bellwood 407 .... G3
69021 Benkelman⊙ 1,235 .... C4
68317 Bennet 523 .... H4
68007 Bennington 631 .... H3
68927 Bertrand 775 .... E4
69122 Big Springs 505 .... B3
68928 Bladen 298 .... F4
68008 Blair⊙ 6,418 .... H3
68718 Bloomfield 1,393 .... G2
68930 Blue Hill 883 .... F4
68318 Blue Springs 521 .... H4
68010 Boys Town 622 .... H3
68319 Bradshaw 373 .... G4
69123 Brady 377 .... D3
68821 Brewster⊙ 46 .... D3
69336 Bridgeport⊙ 1,668 .... A3
68822 Broken Bow⊙ 3,979 .... E3
69127 Brule 438 .... C3
68322 Bruning 330 .... G4
68823 Burwell⊙ 1,383 .... E3
68722 Butte⊙ 529 .... F2
68824 Cairo 737 .... F3
68825 Callaway 579 .... D3
69022 Cambridge 1,206 .... D4
68932 Campbell 441 .... F4
68015 Cedar Bluffs 632 .... H3
68016 Cedar Creek 311 .... H3
68627 Cedar Rapids 447 .... F3
68724 Center⊙ 123 .... G2
68826 Central City⊙ 3,083 .... F3
68017 Ceresco 836 .... H3
69337 Chadron⊙ 5,933 .... B2
68725 Chambers 390 .... F2
68827 Chapman 349 .... F3
69129 Chappell⊙ 1,095 .... B3
68327 Chester 435 .... G4
68628 Clarks 445 .... G3
68629 Clarkson 817 .... G3
68328 Clatonia 273 .... H4
68933 Clay Center⊙ 962 .... F4
68726 Clearwater 409 .... F2
†69343 Clinton 80 .... B2
68727 Coleridge 673 .... G2
68601 Columbus⊙ 17,328 .... G3
68329 Cook 341 .... H4
68331 Cortland 403 .... H4
69130 Cozad 4,453 .... E4
69339 Crawford 1,315 .... A2
68729 Creighton 1,341 .... G2
68333 Crete 4,872 .... G4
68730 Crofton 948 .... G2
69024 Culbertson 767 .... C4
69025 Curtis 1,014 .... D4
68731 Dakota City⊙ 1,440 .... H2
69131 Dalton 345 .... B3
68831 Dannebrog 356 .... F3
68335 Davenport 445 .... G4
68632 David City⊙ 2,514 .... G3
68020 Decatur 723 .... H2
68340 Deshler 997 .... G4
68341 De Witt 642 .... G4
68342 Diller 311 .... H4
69133 Dix 275 .... A3
68633 Dodge 815 .... H3
68832 Doniphan 696 .... F4
68343 Dorchester 611 .... G4
68634 Duncan 410 .... G3
68347 Eagle 832 .... H4
68935 Edgar 705 .... F4
68636 Elgin 807 .... F3
68022 Elkhorn 1,344 .... H3
68836 Elm Creek 862 .... E4
68349 Elmwood 598 .... H4
68937 Elwood⊙ 716 .... E4
68733 Emerson 874 .... H2
68350 Endicott 198 .... G4
69028 Eustis 460 .... D4
68735 Ewing 520 .... F2
68351 Exeter 807 .... G4
68352 Fairbury⊙ 4,885 .... G4
68938 Fairfield 543 .... G4
68354 Fairmont 767 .... G4
68355 Falls City⊙ 5,374 .... J4
69029 Farnam 268 .... D4
68358 Firth 384 .... H4
68023 Fort Calhoun 641 .... J3
68939 Franklin⊙ 1,167 .... E4
68025 Fremont⊙ 23,979 .... H3
68359 Friend 1,079 .... G4
68638 Fullerton⊙ 1,506 .... F3
68361 Geneva⊙ 2,400 .... G4
68640 Genoa 1,090 .... G3
69341 Gering⊙ 7,760 .... A3
68840 Gibbon 1,531 .... F4
68841 Giltner 400 .... F4
68941 Glenvil 363 .... F4
69343 Gordon 2,167 .... B2
69138 Gothenburg 3,479 .... D4
68801 Grand Island⊙ 33,180 .... F4
69140 Grant⊙ 1,270 .... C4
68842 Greeley⊙ 597 .... F3
68366 Greenwood 587 .... H3
68367 Gresham 320 .... G3
68028 Gretna 1,609 .... H3
68942 Guide Rock 344 .... F4
68738 Hadar 286 .... G2
68368 Hallam 290 .... H4
68843 Hampton 419 .... G4
69346 Harrison⊙ 361 .... A2
68739 Hartington⊙ 1,730 .... G2
68944 Harvard 1,217 .... F4
68901 Hastings⊙ 23,045 .... F4
69032 Hayes Center⊙ 231 .... C4
69347 Hay Springs 794 .... B2
68370 Hebron⊙ 1,906 .... G4
69348 Hemingford 1,023 .... A2
68371 Henderson 1,072 .... G4
68029 Herman 340 .... H3
69143 Hershey 633 .... D3
68372 Hickman 687 .... H4
68947 Hildreth 394 .... E4
68948 Holbrook 297 .... D4
68949 Holdrege⊙ 5,624 .... E4
68030 Homer 564 .... H2
68031 Hooper 932 .... H3
68740 Hoskins 306 .... G2
68641 Howells 677 .... H3
68376 Humboldt 1,176 .... J4
68642 Humphrey 799 .... G3
69350 Hyannis⊙ 336 .... C3
69033 Imperial⊙ 1,941 .... C4
69034 Indianola 856 .... D4
68743 Jackson 287 .... H2
68378 Johnson 341 .... J4
68955 Juniata 703 .... F4
68847 Kearney⊙ 21,158 .... E4
68956 Kenesaw 854 .... F4
68034 Kennard 372 .... H3
69145 Kimball⊙ 3,120 .... A3
69035 Lamar 60 .... C4
68745 Laurel 1,031 .... G2
†68046 La Vista 9,588 .... J3
68957 Lawrence 350 .... F4
68643 Leigh 509 .... G3
69147 Lewellen 368 .... B3
68850 Lexington⊙ 7,040 .... E4
*68501 Lincoln (cap.)⊙ 171,932 .... H4
Lincoln‡ 192,884 .... H4
68644 Lindsay 383 .... G3
69149 Lodgepole 413 .... B3
69217 Long Pine 521 .... E2
68958 Loomis 447 .... E4
68037 Louisville 1,022 .... H3
68853 Loup City⊙ 1,368 .... E3
69352 Lyman 551 .... A3
68746 Lynch 357 .... F2
68038 Lyons 1,214 .... H3
68748 Madison⊙ 1,950 .... G3
69150 Madrid 284 .... C4
68402 Malcolm 355 .... H4
68854 Marquette 303 .... G4
69151 Maxwell 410 .... D3
69038 Maywood 332 .... D4
69001 McCook⊙ 8,404 .... D4
68401 McCool Junction 404 .... G4
68041 Mead 506 .... H3
68752 Meadow Grove 400 .... G2
68856 Merna 389 .... E3
68405 Milford 2,108 .... H4
68406 Milligan 332 .... G4
69356 Minatare 969 .... A3
68959 Minden⊙ 2,939 .... F4
69357 Mitchell 1,956 .... A3
68647 Monroe 294 .... G3
69358 Morrill 1,097 .... A3
69152 Mullen⊙ 720 .... C2
68409 Murray 465 .... J4
68410 Nebraska City⊙ 7,127 .... J4
68413 Nehawka 270 .... H4
68756 Neligh⊙ 1,893 .... G2
68961 Nelson⊙ 733 .... F4
68757 Newcastle 348 .... H2
68758 Newman Grove 930 .... G3
68760 Niobrara 419 .... G2
68962 Nora 24 .... G4
68701 Norfolk 19,449 .... G2
68649 North Bend 1,368 .... H3
68859 North Loup 405 .... F3
69101 North Platte⊙ 24,509 .... D3
68761 Oakdale 410 .... F2
68045 Oakland 1,393 .... H3
68415 Odell 322 .... H4
69153 Ogallala⊙ 5,638 .... C3
*68101 Omaha⊙ 313,911 .... J3
Omaha‡ 570,399 .... J3
68763 O'Neill⊙ 4,049 .... F2
68764 Orchard 482 .... F2
68862 Ord⊙ 2,658 .... F3
68966 Orleans 527 .... E4
68651 Osceola⊙ 975 .... G3
69154 Oshkosh⊙ 1,057 .... B3
68765 Osmond 871 .... G2
68863 Overton 633 .... E4
68967 Oxford 1,109 .... E4
69040 Palisade 401 .... C4
68864 Palmer 487 .... F3
68418 Palmyra 512 .... H4
68046 Papillion⊙ 6,399 .... J3
68420 Pawnee City⊙ 1,156 .... H4
69155 Paxton 568 .... C3
68047 Pender⊙ 1,318 .... H2
68421 Peru 998 .... J4
68652 Petersburg 381 .... G3
68865 Phillips 405 .... F4
68767 Pierce⊙ 1,535 .... G2
68768 Pilger 400 .... G2
68769 Plainview 1,483 .... G2
68653 Platte Center 367 .... G3
68048 Plattsmouth⊙ 6,295 .... J3
68866 Pleasanton 349 .... E4
68424 Plymouth 506 .... G4
68654 Polk 440 .... G3
68770 Ponca⊙ 1,057 .... H2
68867 Poole F4
69156 Potter 369 .... A3
68050 Prague 285 .... H3
68127 Ralston 5,143 .... J3
68771 Randolph 1,106 .... G2
68869 Ravenna 1,296 .... F4
68970 Red Cloud⊙ 1,300 .... F4
68658 Rising City 392 .... G3
69360 Rushville⊙ 1,217 .... B2
68660 Saint Edward 891 .... G3
68873 Saint Paul⊙ 2,094 .... F3
†68760 Santee 388 .... G2
68874 Sargent 828 .... E3
68661 Schuyler⊙ 4,151 .... G3
68875 Scotia 349 .... F3
69361 Scottsbluff 14,156 .... A3
68057 Scribner 1,011 .... H3
68434 Seward⊙ 5,713 .... H4
68662 Shelby 724 .... G3
68876 Shelton 1,046 .... F4
68436 Shickley 413 .... G4
69162 Sidney⊙ 6,010 .... B3
68663 Silver Creek 496 .... G3
68664 Snyder 387 .... H3
68776 South Sioux City 9,339 .... H2
68665 Spalding 645 .... F3
68777 Spencer 596 .... F2
68059 Springfield 782 .... H3
68778 Springview⊙ 326 .... E2
68779 Stanton⊙ 1,603 .... G3
68439 Staplehurst 306 .... G4
69163 Stapleton⊙ 340 .... D3
68442 Stella 289 .... J4
68443 Sterling 526 .... H4
69042 Stockville⊙ 45 .... D4
69043 Stratton 499 .... C4
68666 Stromsburg 1,290 .... G3
68780 Stuart 641 .... E2
68978 Superior 2,502 .... F4
69165 Sutherland 1,238 .... C3
68979 Sutton 1,416 .... G4
68446 Syracuse 1,638 .... H4
68447 Table Rock 393 .... H4

Agriculture, Industry and Resources

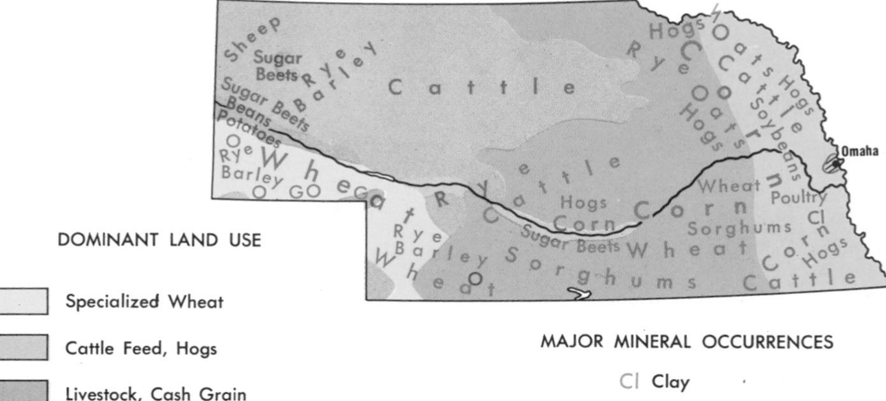

Sheep
Sugar Beets
Rye
Barley
Cattle
Hogs
Oats
Corn
Soybeans
Sugar Beets
Beans
Potatoes
Wheat
GO
Omaha
Poultry
Cl
Sorghums

DOMINANT LAND USE

Specialized Wheat

Cattle Feed, Hogs

Livestock, Cash Grain

General Farming, Livestock, Special Crops

Sugar Beets, Dry Beans, Livestock, General Farming

Range Livestock

MAJOR MINERAL OCCURRENCES

Cl Clay

G Natural Gas

O Petroleum

Water Power

Major Industrial Areas

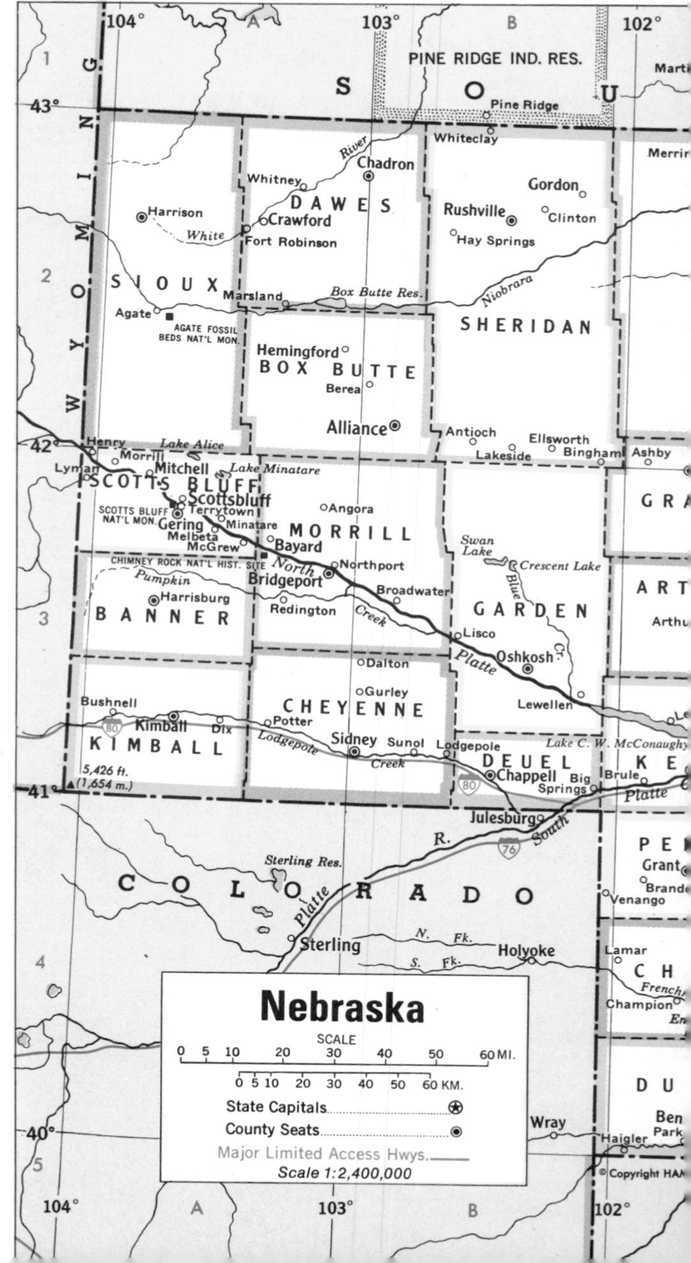

104°
103°
102°
43°
42°
41°
40°
PINE RIDGE IND. RES.
Pine Ridge
Whiteclay
Chadron
Whitney
DAWES
Crawford
Fort Robinson
Harrison
Rushville
Gordon
Clinton
Hay Springs
SIOUX
Marsland
Box Butte Res.
Niobrara
Agate
AGATE FOSSIL BEDS NAT'L MON.
SHERIDAN
Hemingford
BOX BUTTE
Berea
Alliance
WYOMING
Henry
Lake Alice
Morrill
Mitchell
Lake Minatare
Lyman
SCOTTS BLUFF
Scottsbluff
Terrytown
SCOTTS BLUFF NAT'L MON.
Gering
Minatare
Melbeta
McGrew
Angora
MORRILL
Bayard
CHIMNEY ROCK NAT'L HIST. SITE
Pumpkin
Northport
Bridgeport
Broadwater
Harrisburg
BANNER
Redington
Antioch
Ellsworth
Lakeside
Bingham
Ashby
Swan Lake
Crescent Lake
GARDEN
Lisco
Oshkosh
Dalton
Gurley
CHEYENNE
Bushnell
Kimball
Dix
Potter
KIMBALL
Sidney
Sunol
Lodgepole
Lodgepole Creek
Lewellen
DEUEL
Chappell
Big Springs
Brule
5,426 ft. (1,654 m.)
Julesburg
Sterling Res.
COLORADO
Sterling
N. Fk.
S. Fk.
Holyoke
Lamar
Grant
Venango
Wray
Haigler
Nebraska
SCALE
0 5 10 20 30 40 50 60 MI.
0 5 10 20 30 40 50 60 KM.
State Capitals
County Seats
Major Limited Access Hwys.
Scale 1:2,400,000
© Copyright HA

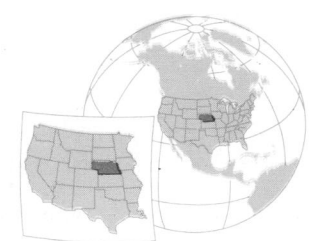

AREA 77,355 sq. mi. (200,349 sq. km.)
POPULATION 1,569,825
CAPITAL Lincoln
LARGEST CITY Omaha
HIGHEST POINT (Kimball Co.) 5,246 ft. (1654 m.)
SETTLED IN 1847
ADMITTED TO UNION March 1, 1867
POPULAR NAME Cornhusker State
STATE FLOWER Goldenrod
STATE BIRD Western Meadowlark

Topography

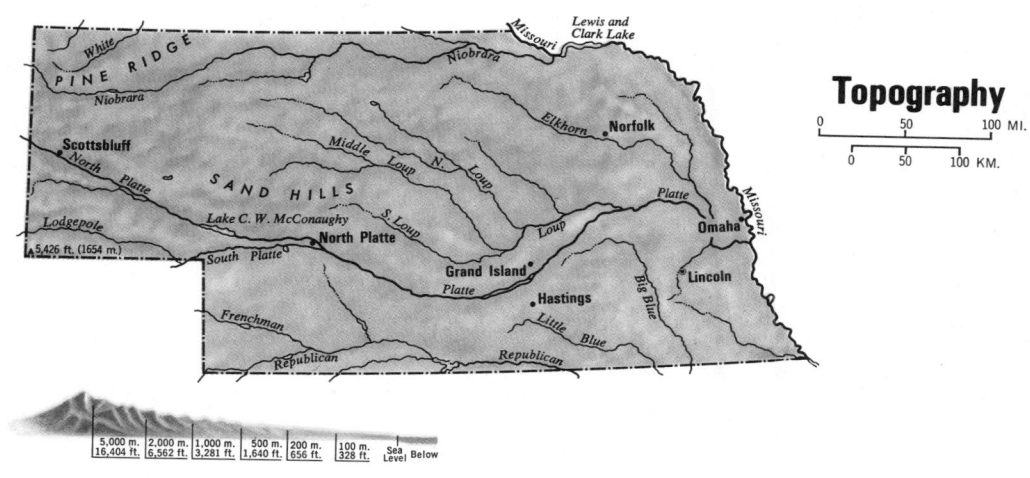

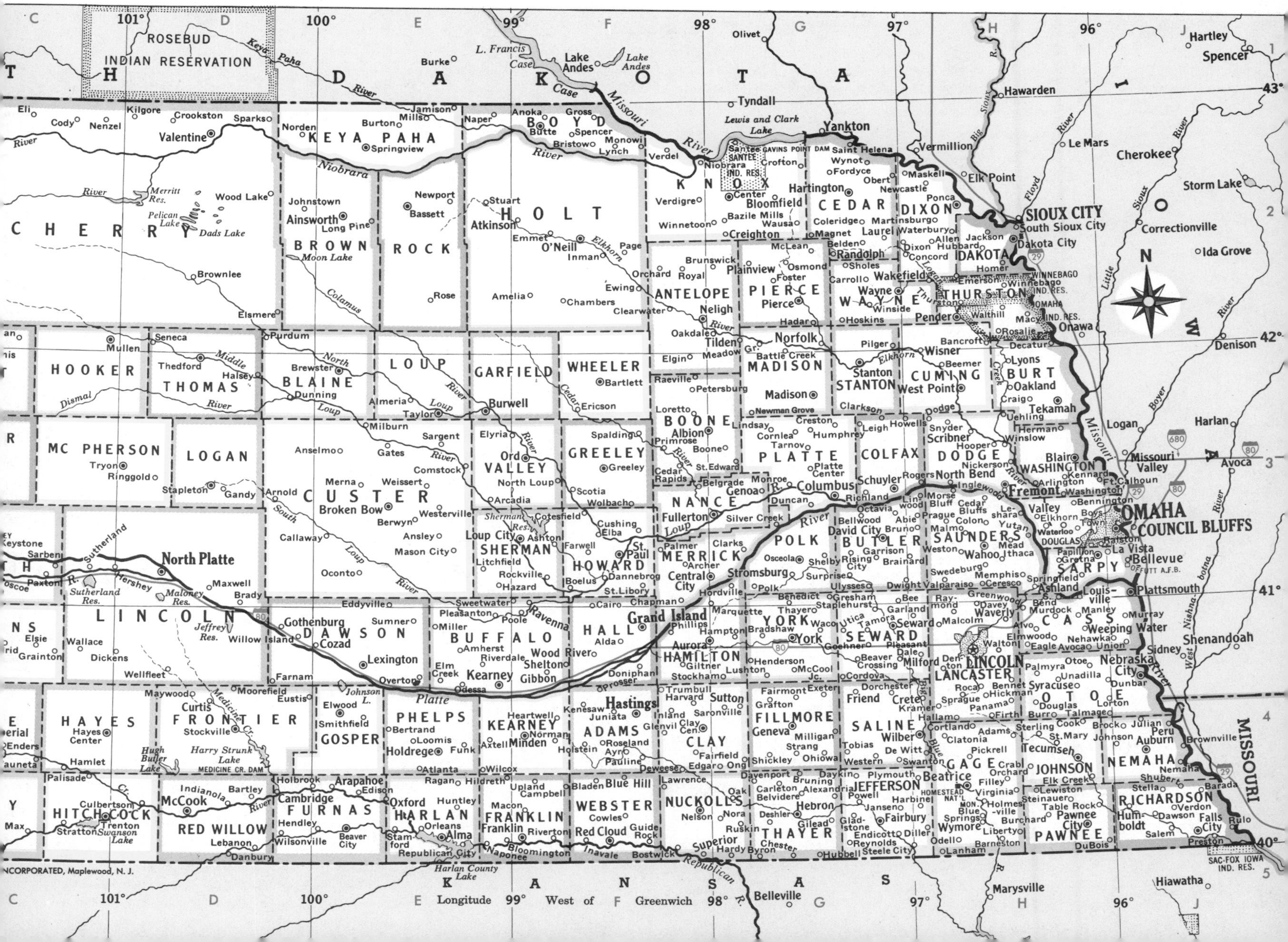

Nevada
SCALE
0 5 10 20 30 40 50 60 MI.
0 5 10 20 30 40 50 60 KM.
State Capitals
County Seats
Major Limited Access Hwys.
Scale 1:2,740,000
© Copyright HAMMOND INCORPORATED, Maplewood, N. J.
Longitude West of Greenwich
120° 119° 118° 117° 116° 115° 114°
42° 41° 40° 39° 38° 37° 36°
O R E G O N
I D A H O
U T A H
A R I Z O N A
C A L I F O R N I A
W A S H O E
H U M B O L D T
E L K O
P E R S H I N G
L A N D E R
E U R E K A
C H U R C H I L L
W H I T E P I N E
S T O R E Y
L Y O N
D O U G L A S
M I N E R A L
N Y E
E S M E R A L D A
L I N C O L N
C L A R K
Carson City
RENO
Sparks
Winnemucca
Elko
Lovelock
Fallon
Yerington
Minden
Gardnerville
Hawthorne
Babbitt
Tonopah
Goldfield
Austin
Eureka
Ely
East Ely
McGill
Pioche
Caliente
Panaca
Battle Mountain
Carlin
Wells
LAS VEGAS
North Las Vegas
Henderson
Boulder City
Sunrise Manor
Winchester
Paradise Valley
Virginia City
Gold Hill
Silver City
Dayton
Truckee
Lake Tahoe
Pyramid Lake
Walker L.
Lake Mead
Lake Mohave
GREAT SALT LAKE DESERT
NELLIS AIR FORCE RANGE AND NUCLEAR TESTING SITE
DEATH VALLEY NATIONAL MONUMENT
YOSEMITE NATIONAL PARK
KINGS CANYON NAT'L PARK
SEQUOIA NATIONAL PARK
LAKE MEAD NATIONAL RECREATION AREA
HOOVER DAM
DAVIS DAM
FRESNO
Madera
Hanford
Visalia
Tulare
Porterville
Mariposa
Bishop
Independence
Mojave
Trona
Kingman
Wendover
Jackpot
Owyhee
Mountain City
Denio
McDermitt
Gerlach
Nixon
Wadsworth
Fernley
Hazen
Mina
Luning
Gabbs
Manhattan
Round Mountain
Beatty
Rhyolite (Ghost Town)
Mercury
Indian Springs
Pahrump
Goodsprings
Searchlight
Mesquite
Bunkerville
Overton
Logandale
Glendale
Moapa
Alamo
Hiko
Wheeler Pk. 13,063 ft. (3982 m.)
Boundary Pk. 13,143 ft. (4006 m.)
Charleston Pk. 11,919 ft. (3633 m.)
Mt. Whitney 14,494 ft. (4418 m.)
Arc Dome 11,775 ft. (3589 m.)
Humboldt R.
Walker R.
Carson R.
Truckee R.
Virgin R.
White R.
Colorado R.

AREA 110,561 sq. mi. (286,353 sq. km.)
POPULATION 800,493
CAPITAL Carson City
LARGEST CITY Las Vegas
HIGHEST POINT Boundary Pk. 13,143 ft. (4006 m.)
SETTLED IN 1850
ADMITTED TO UNION October 31, 1864
POPULAR NAME Silver State; Sagebrush State
STATE FLOWER Sagebrush
STATE BIRD Mountain Bluebird

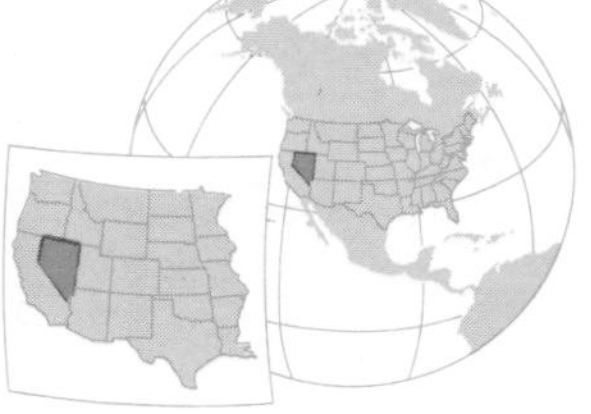

Agriculture, Industry and Resources

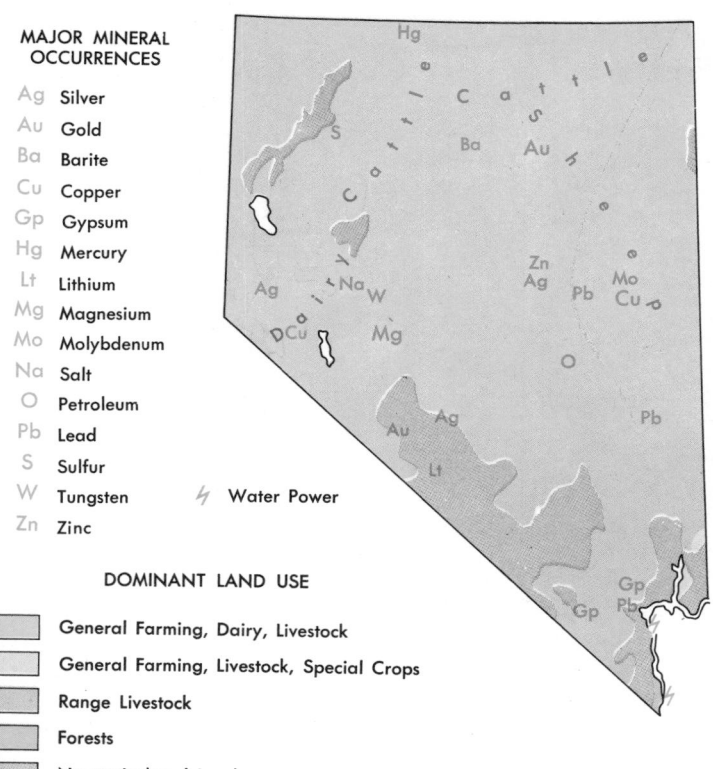

MAJOR MINERAL OCCURRENCES

- Ag Silver
- Au Gold
- Ba Barite
- Cu Copper
- Gp Gypsum
- Hg Mercury
- Lt Lithium
- Mg Magnesium
- Mo Molybdenum
- Na Salt
- O Petroleum
- Pb Lead
- S Sulfur
- W Tungsten
- Zn Zinc
- Water Power

DOMINANT LAND USE

- General Farming, Dairy, Livestock
- General Farming, Livestock, Special Crops
- Range Livestock
- Forests
- Nonagricultural Land

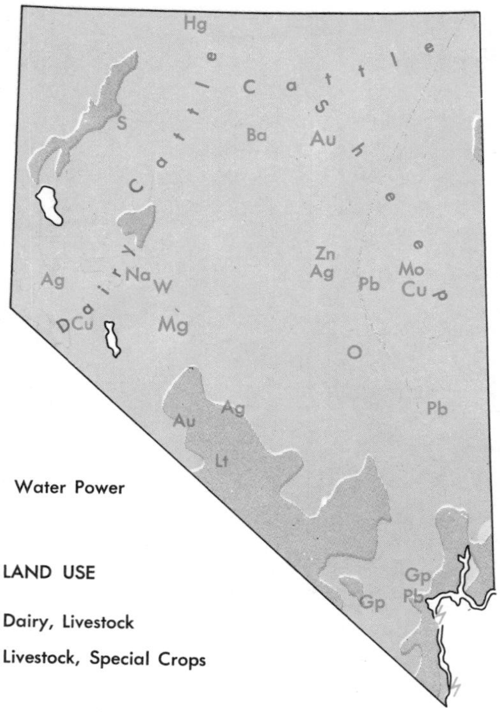

Hg
Cattle
Dairy Cattle
Sheep
S
Ba
Au
Zn
Ag
Mo
Cu
Pb
Na
W
Mg
O
Au
Ag
Lt
Gp

Topography

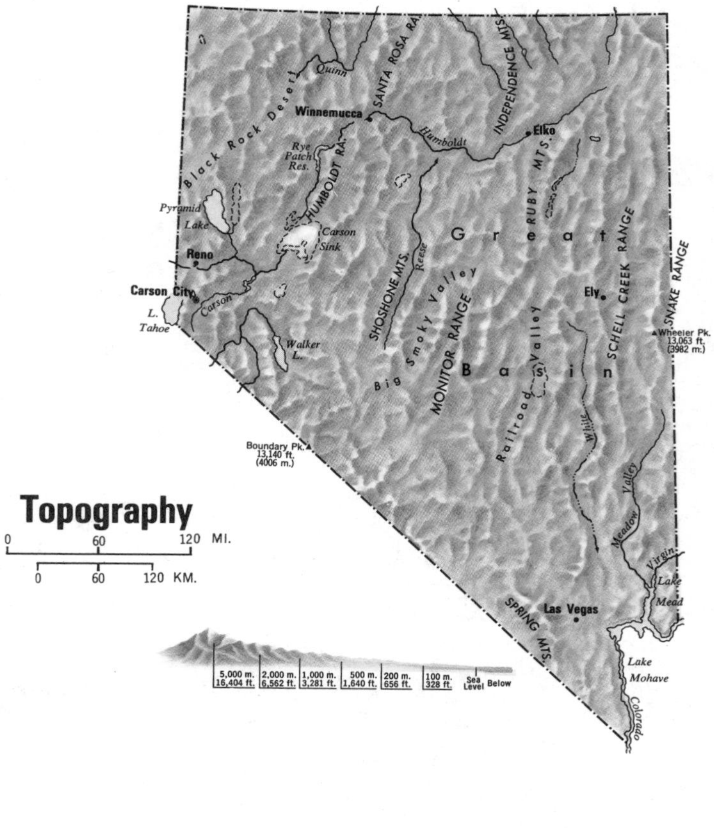

Quinn
SANTA ROSA RA.
INDEPENDENCE MTS.
Black Rock Desert
Winnemucca
Humboldt
Elko
Rye Patch Res.
HUMBOLDT RA.
RUBY MTS.
Pyramid Lake
Carson Sink
Great Basin
Reno
SHOSHONE MTS.
Reese
Big Smoky Valley
SCHELL CREEK RANGE
SNAKE RANGE
Ely
Carson City
Carson
L. Tahoe
Walker L.
MONITOR RANGE
Railroad Valley
White
Wheeler Pk. 13,063 ft. (3982 m.)
Boundary Pk. 13,140 ft. (4006 m.)
Meadow Valley
Virgin
Lake Mead
SPRING MTS.
Las Vegas
Lake Mohave
Colorado
0 60 120 MI.
0 60 120 KM.
5,000 m. 16,404 ft.
2,000 m. 6,562 ft.
1,000 m. 3,281 ft.
500 m. 1,640 ft.
200 m. 656 ft.
100 m. 328 ft.
Sea Level
Below

COUNTIES

Carson City (city) 32,022 .... B3
Churchill 13,917 .... C3
Clark 463,087 .... F6
Douglas 19,421 .... B4
Elko 17,269 .... F1
Esmeralda 777 .... D5
Eureka 1,198 .... E3
Humboldt 9,434 .... C1
Lander 4,076 .... D3
Lincoln 3,732 .... F5
Lyon 13,594 .... B3
Mineral 6,217 .... C4
Nye 9,048 .... E4
Pershing 3,408 .... C2
Storey 1,503 .... B3
Washoe 193,623 .... B2
White Pine 8,167 .... F3

CITIES and TOWNS

Zip *Name/Pop.* *Key*

89001 Alamo 300 .... F5
89310 Austin 300 .... E3
89416 Babbitt C4
89311 Baker 140 .... G3
89820 Battle Mountain⊙ 2,749 .... E2
89003 Beatty 600 .... E6
89821 Beowawe 77 .... E2
†89508 Black Springs 180 .... B3
89005 Boulder City 9,590 .... G7
89007 Bunkerville 300 .... G6
89008 Caliente 982 .... G5
89822 Carlin 1,232 .... E2
†89008 Carp 30 .... G5
89701 Carson City (cap.) 32,022 .... B3
†89043 Caselton G5
†89301 Cherry Creek 80 .... G3
89402 Crystal Bay 6,225 .... A3
89403 Dayton 350 .... B3
89823 Deeth 125 .... F1
89404 Denio 35 .... C1
89314 Duckwater 80 .... F4
89010 Dyer 56 .... C5
89315 East Ely G3
89112 East Las Vegas 6,449 .... F6
89801 Elko⊙ 8,758 .... F2
89301 Ely⊙ 4,882 .... G3
89316 Eureka⊙ 300 .... E3
89406 Fallon⊙ 4,262 .... C3
89408 Fernley 750 .... B3
89409 Gabbs 811 .... D4
89410 Gardnerville 1,610 .... B4
89411 Genoa 254 .... B4
89412 Gerlach 400 .... B2
89413 Glenbrook 800 .... B3
89414 Golconda 275 .... D2
89013 Goldfield⊙ 500 .... D5
89019 Goodsprings 80 .... F7
89824 Halleck 68 .... F2
89415 Hawthorne⊙ 3,741 .... C4
89417 Hazen 76 .... C3
89015 Henderson 24,363 .... G6
89017 Hiko 210 .... F5
†89418 Humboldt 14 .... C2
89418 Imlay 250 .... C2
89018 Indian Springs 500 .... F6
†89310 Ione 20 .... D4
†89834 Jack Creek E1
89825 Jackpot 400 .... G1
89826 Jarbidge 11 .... F1
89019 Jean 125 .... F7
89828 Lamoille 100 .... F2
*89101 Las Vegas⊙ 164,674 .... F6
Las Vegas‡ 461,816 .... F6
89829 Lee 125 .... F2
89021 Logandale 410 .... G6
89419 Lovelock⊙ 1,680 .... C2
89317 Lund 380 .... F4
89420 Luning 90 .... C4
89022 Manhattan 93 .... E4
†89447 Mason 200 .... B4
89421 McDermitt 240 .... D1
89318 McGill 1,419 .... G3
89023 Mercury 900 .... E6
89024 Mesquite 500 .... G6
89422 Mina 450 .... C4
89423 Minden⊙ 1,029 .... B4
89025 Moapa 275 .... G6
89830 Montello 100 .... G1
89831 Mountain City 100 .... F1
†89046 Nelson 75 .... G7
89424 Nixon 400 .... B3
89030 North Las Vegas 42,739 .... F6
89425 Orovada 200 .... D1
89040 Overton 1,111 .... G6
89041 Pahrump 400 .... E6
89042 Panaca 650 .... G5
89119 Paradise Valley 84,818 .... F6
89426 Paradise Valley 115 .... D1
89043 Pioche⊙ 850 .... G5
*89501 Reno⊙ 100,756 .... B3
Reno‡ 193,623 .... B3
†89003 Rhyolite (Ghost Town) 8 .... E6
89045 Round Mountain 400 .... E4
89833 Ruby Valley 150 .... F2
89319 Ruth 455 .... F3
89427 Schurz 800 .... C4
89046 Searchlight 500 .... F7
89428 Silver City 150 .... B3
89047 Silverpeak 100 .... D5
89430 Smith 200 .... B4
89431 Sparks 40,780 .... B3
†89406 Stillwater 150 .... C3
†89445 Sulphur C2
†89110 Sunrise Manor 44,155 .... F6
†89431 Sun Valley 8,822 .... B3
†89835 Thousand Springs G1
89049 Tonopah⊙ 1,952 .... D4
89834 Tuscarora 24 .... E1
89438 Valmy 200 .... D2
89121 Vegas Creek G6
89440 Virginia City⊙ 750 .... B3
89442 Wadsworth 400 .... B3
89443 Weed Heights 8 .... B4
89444 Wellington 505 .... B4
89835 Wells 1,218 .... G1
†89109 Winchester 19,728 .... F6
89445 Winnemucca⊙ 4,140 .... D2
89447 Yerington⊙ 2,021 .... B4
89448 Zephyr Cove 1,316 .... A3

OTHER FEATURES

Alkali (lake) B1
Antelope (range) E3
Arc Dome (mt.) D4
Arrow Canyon (range) G6
Beaver Creek Fork, Humboldt (riv.) F1
Belted (range) E5
Berlin (mt.) D4
Big (mt.) B1
Big Smoky (valley) D4
Bishop (creek) F1
Black Rock (des.) B2
Black Rock (range) B1
Boundary (peak) C5
Buffalo (creek) B2
Butte (mts.) F3
Cactus (range) E5
Carson (lake) C3
Carson (riv.) B3
Carson (sink) C3
Cedar (mt.) D4
Charleston (peak) F6
Clan Alpine (mts.) D3
Columbus Salt (marsh) C4
Cortez (mts.) E2
Crescent (valley) E2
Davis (dam) G7
Death Valley Nat'l Mon. E6
Delamar (mts.) G5
Desatoya (mts.) D3
Desert (range) F6
Desert (valley) C1
Devil's Hole (Death Valley Nat'l Mon.) E6
Division (peak) B1
Duck (creek) G3
East (range) D2
East Walker (riv.) B4
Egan (range) G4
Ely (range) G4
Emigrant (peak) C5
Excelsior (mts.) C4
Fallon Ind. Res. C3
Fallon Nav. Air Sta. C3
Fish Creek (mts.) D2
Fort McDermitt Ind. Res. D1
Fort Mohave Ind. Res. G7
Franklin (lake) F2
Frenchman Flat (basin) F6
Gillis (range) C4
Golden Gate (range) F5
Goshute (mts.) G2
Goshute Ind. Res. G3
Granite (peak) B2
Granite (range) B2
Grant (range) F4
Great Salt Lake (des.) H2
High Rock (creek) B1
Highland (peak) G5
Hoover (dam) G7
Hot Creek (range) E4
Hot Creek (valley) E4
Humboldt (range) C2
Humboldt (riv.) E2
Humboldt (sink) C2
Humboldt Salt (marsh) D3
Huntington (creek) F2
Independence (mts.) E1
Jackson (mts.) C1
Job (peak) C3
Kawich (peak) E5
Kawich (range) E5
Kelley (creek) D1
Kings (riv.) C1
Lahontan (res.) B3
Lake Mead Nat'l Rec. Area G6
Las Vegas (range) F6
Lehman Caves Nat'l Mon. G4
Little Humboldt (riv.) D1
Little Smoky (valley) E4
Lone (mt.) D4
Long (valley) B1
Marys (riv.) F1
Mason (peak) F1
Massacre (lake) B1
Mead (lake) G6
Meadow Valley Wash (riv.) G5
Moapa River Ind. Res. G6
Mohave (lake) G7
Monitor (range) E4
Monte Cristo (range) D4
Mormon (mts.) G5
Muddy (mts.) G6
Nellis A.F.B. 7,476 .... F6
Nellis Air Force Range and Nuclear Testing Site E5
Nelson (creek) G2
New Pass (range) D3
Nightingale (mts.) B2
Owyhee (riv.) E1
Pahranagat (range) F5
Pahrock (range) F5
Pah-rum (peak) B2
Pahrump (valley) F6
Pahute (mesa) E5
Pancake (range) F4
Pequop (mts.) G2
Pilot (peak) C4
Pine (creek) E2
Pine Forest (range) C1
Pintwater (range) F6
Piper (peak) D5
Potosi (mt.) F7
Pyramid (lake) B2
Pyramid Lake Ind. Res. B2
Quinn (riv.) D1
Quinn Canyon (range) F4
Railroad (valley) F4
Reese (riv.) D3
Reveille (peak) E5
Reveille (range) E4
Ruby (lake) F2
Ruby (mts.) F2
Rye Patch (res.) C2
Sand Springs (salt flat) C3
Santa Rosa (range) D1
Schell Creek (range) G3
Sheep (range) F6
Shoshone (mt.) E6
Shoshone (mts.) D3
Shoshone (range) E2
Silver Peak (range) D5
Simpson Park (mts.) E3
Smith Creek (valley) D3
Smoke Creek (des.) B2
Snake (mts.) F1
Snake (range) G3
Snow Water (lake) G2
Sonoma (range) D2
Specter (range) E6
Spotted (range) F6
Spring (creek) D2
Spring (mts.) F6
Spring (valley) G3
Stillwater (range) C3
Sulphur Spring (range) E3
Summit (lake) C1
Summit Lake Ind. Res. B1
Table (mt.) C3
Tahoe (lake) B3
Thousand Spring (creek) G1
Timber (mt.) F4
Timber (mt.) E5
Timpahute (range) F5
Toana (range) G2
Toiyabe (range) D3
Topaz (lake) B4
Toquima (range) E4
Trident (peak) C1
Trinity (range) C2
Truckee (riv.) B3
Tule (des.) G5
Tuscarora (mts.) E1
Virgin (mts.) G6
Virgin (peak) G6
Virgin (riv.) G6
Virginia (range) B3
Walker (lake) C4
Walker (riv.) C3
Walker River Ind. Res. C3
Washoe (lake) B3
Wassuk (range) C4
Western Shoshone Ind. Res. E1
Wheeler (peak) G4
White (riv.) F4
White Pine (range) F3
Wild Horse (res.) E1
Winnemucca (lake) B2
Winnemucca Ind. Res. D2
Yerington Ind. Res. B3
Yucca Flat (basin) E6

⊙County seat.
‡Population of metropolitan area.
† Zip of nearest p.o.
* Multiple zips.

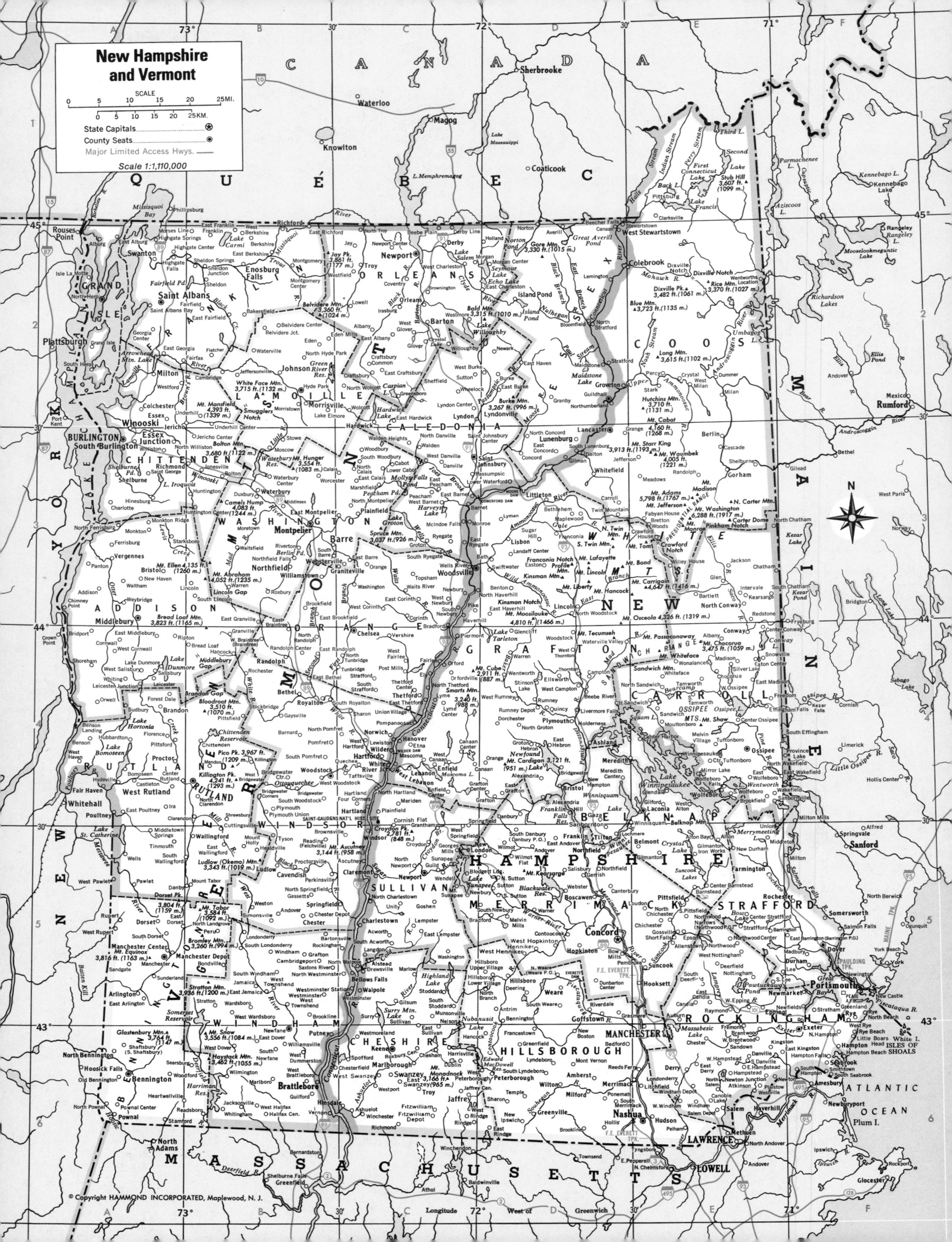

New Hampshire and Vermont
SCALE
0 5 10 15 20 25 MI.
0 5 10 15 20 25 KM.
State Capitals
County Seats
Major Limited Access Hwys.
Scale 1:1,110,000
CANADA
QUÉBEC
NEW YORK
MAINE
MASSACHUSETTS
ATLANTIC OCEAN
VERMONT
NEW HAMPSHIRE
GRAND ISLE
FRANKLIN
ORLEANS
ESSEX
LAMOILLE
CALEDONIA
CHITTENDEN
WASHINGTON
ADDISON
ORANGE
RUTLAND
WINDSOR
BENNINGTON
WINDHAM
COOS
GRAFTON
CARROLL
BELKNAP
SULLIVAN
MERRIMACK
STRAFFORD
CHESHIRE
HILLSBOROUGH
ROCKINGHAM
WHITE MTS.
LAKE CHAMPLAIN
Sherbrooke
Magog
Waterloo
Knowlton
Coaticook
L. Memphremagog
Plattsburgh
BURLINGTON
South Burlington
Montpelier
Barre
Saint Albans
Newport
Rutland
Bennington
Brattleboro
Concord
MANCHESTER
Nashua
Portsmouth
Keene
Laconia
Lebanon
Claremont
Dover
Berlin
Lancaster
Rumford
Sanford
LAWRENCE
LOWELL
Haverhill
Newburyport
Lake Winnipesaukee
Mt. Washington 6,288 ft. (1917 m.)
Mt. Mansfield 4,393 ft. (1339 m.)
N
ISLES OF SHOALS
Longitude 72° West of Greenwich
45°
44°
43°
73°
72°
71°
© Copyright HAMMOND INCORPORATED, Maplewood, N. J.

NEW HAMPSHIRE

AREA 9,279 sq. mi. (24,033 sq. km.)
POPULATION 920,610
CAPITAL Concord
LARGEST CITY Manchester
HIGHEST POINT Mt. Washington 6,288 ft.
(1917 m.)
SETTLED IN 1623
ADMITTED TO UNION June 21, 1788
POPULAR NAME Granite State
STATE FLOWER Purple Lilac
STATE BIRD Purple Finch

VERMONT

AREA 9,614 sq. mi. (24,900 sq. km.)
POPULATION 511,456
CAPITAL Montpelier
LARGEST CITY Burlington
HIGHEST POINT Mt. Mansfield 4,393 ft. (1339 m.)
SETTLED IN 1764
ADMITTED TO UNION March 4, 1791
POPULAR NAME Green Mountain State
STATE FLOWER Red Clover
STATE BIRD Hermit Thrush

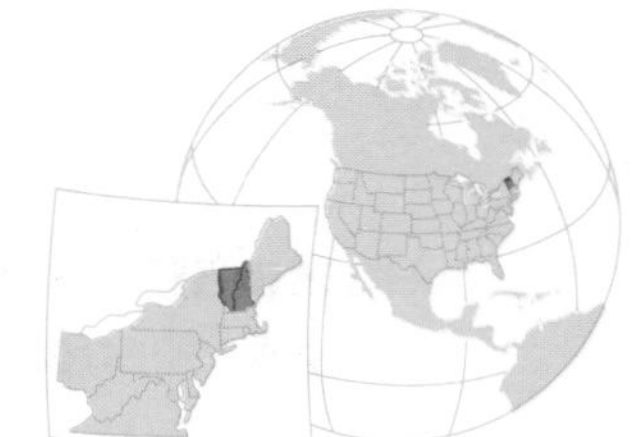

NEW HAMPSHIRE

COUNTIES

Belknap 42,884 .... D4
Carroll 27,931 .... E4
Cheshire 62,116 .... C6
Coos 35,147 .... E2
Grafton 65,806 .... D4
Hillsborough 276,608 .... D6
Merrimack 98,302 .... D5
Rockingham 190,345 .... E5
Strafford 85,408 .... E5
Sullivan 36,063 .... C5

CITIES and TOWNS

Zip	Name/Pop.	Key
03601 Acworth○ 590 .... C5
†03864 Albany○ 383 .... E4
†03222 Alexandria○ 706 .... D4
†03275 Allenstown○ 4,398 .... E5
03602 Alstead○ 1,461 .... C5
03809 Alton○ 2,440 .... E5
03810 Alton Bay 500 .... E5
03031 Amherst○ 8,243 .... D6
03216 Andover○ 1,587 .... D5
03440 Antrim○ 2,208 .... D5
03440 Antrim 1,142 .... D5
03217 Ashland○ 1,807 .... D4
03217 Ashland 1,479 .... D4
03441 Ashuelot 810 .... C6
03032 Auburn○ 2,883 .... E5
03218 Barnstead○ 2,292 .... E5
†03825 Barrington○ 4,404 .... F5
03812 Bartlett○ 1,566 .... E3
03740 Bath○ 761 .... D3
03102 Bedford○ 9,481 .... D6
03220 Belmont○ 4,026 .... E5
03442 Bennington○ 890 .... D5
†03785 Benton○ 333 .... D3
03570 Berlin○ 13,084 .... E3
03574 Bethlehem○ 1,784 .... D3
03301 Boscawen○ 3,435 .... D5
03221 Bradford○ 1,115 .... D5
†03833 Brentwood○ 2,004 .... E6
†03222 Bridgewater○ 606 .... D4
03222 Bristol○ 2,198 .... D4
03222 Bristol 1,258 .... D4
†03872 Brookfield○ 385 .... E4
03033 Brookline○ 1,766 .... D6
03223 Campton○ 1,694 .... D4
03741 Canaan○ 2,456 .... C4
03034 Candia○ 2,989 .... E5
03224 Canterbury○ 1,410 ...... D5
†03595 Carroll○ 647 .... D3
03813 Center Conway 558 ...... E4
03226 Center Harbor○ 808 ..... E4
03814 Center Ossipee 800 ...... E4
03603 Charlestown○ 4,417 ..... C5
03603 Charlestown 1,294 .... C5
†04037 Chatham○ 189 .... E3
03036 Chester○ 2,006 .... E6
03443 Chesterfield○ 2,561 ..... C6
†03258 Chichester○ 1,492 ...... E5
03817 Chocorua 575 .... E4
03743 Claremont○ 14,557 ...... C5
†05902 Clarksville○ 262 .... E1
03301 Concord (cap.)⊙ 30,400 .. D5
03229 Contoocook○ 1,499 ..... D5
03818 Conway○ 7,158 .... E4
03818 Conway 1,781 .... E4
03746 Cornish Flat 450 .... C4
†03753 Croydon○ 457 .... C5
†03598 Dalton○ 672 .... D3
03230 Danbury○ 804 .... D4
03819 Danville○ 1,318 .... E6
03037 Deerfield○ 1,979 .... E5
†03244 Deering○ 1,041 .... D5
03038 Derry○ 18,875 .... E6
03038 Derry 12,248 .... E6
†03266 Dorchester○ 244 ...... D4
03820 Dover⊙ 22,377 .... F5
03444 Dublin○ 1,303 .... C6
†03588 Dummer○ 390 .... E2
†03301 Dunbarton○ 1,174 .... D5
03824 Durham○ 10,652 .... F5
03824 Durham 8,448 .... F5
03231 East Andover 500 ...... D5
03826 East Hampstead 900 ... E6
03827 East Kingston○ 1,135 .. F6
†03580 Easton○ 124 .... D3
03446 East Swanzey 500 ...... C6
03832 Eaton (Eaton Center) 256 . E4
†03264 Ellsworth○ 53 .... D4
03748 Enfield○ 3,175 .... C4
03748 Enfield 1,581 .... C4
03042 Epping○ 3,460 .... E5
03042 Epping 1,384 .... E5
03234 Epsom○ 2,743 .... E5
03579 Errol○ 313 .... E2
03750 Etna 550 .... C4
03833 Exeter○ 11,024 .... F6

03833 Exeter⊙ 8,947 .... F6
03835 Farmington○ 4,630 ...... E5
03835 Farmington 3,284 .... E5
03447 Fitzwilliam○ 1,795 ...... C6
03043 Francestown○ 830 ...... D6
03580 Franconia○ 743 .... D3
03235 Franklin 7,901 .... D5
03836 Freedom○ 720 .... E4
03044 Fremont○ 1,333 .... E6
†03246 Gilford○ 4,841 .... E4
03237 Gilmanton○ 1,941 ..... E5
03448 Gilsum○ 652 .... C5
03838 Glen 600 .... E3
03045 Goffstown○ 11,315 .... D5
03581 Gorham○ 3,322 .... E3
03581 Gorham 2,180 .... E3
03752 Goshen○ 549 .... C5
03240 Grafton○ 739 .... D4
03753 Grantham○ 704 .... C5
03047 Greenfield○ 972 ...... D6
03840 Greenland○ 2,129 .... F5
03048 Greenville○ 1,988 .... D6
03048 Greenville 1,447 ...... D6
†03241 Groton○ 255 .... D4
03582 Groveton○ 1,389 .... D2
03754 Guild 500 .... C5
03841 Hampstead○ 3,785 .. E6
03842 Hampton○ 10,493 ... F6
03842 Hampton 6,779 ...... F6
03844 Hampton Falls○ 1,372 . F6
03449 Hancock○ 1,193 ..... C6
03755 Hanover○ 9,119 ..... C4
03755 Hanover 6,861 .... C4
03450 Harrisville○ 860 ..... C6
03765 Haverhill○ 3,445 .... C3
03241 Hebron○ 349 .... D4
03242 Henniker○ 3,246 ... D5
03242 Henniker 1,538 ..... D5
03243 Hill○ 736 .... D4
03244 Hillsboro○ 3,437 ... D5
03244 Hillsboro 1,797 .... D5
03451 Hinsdale○ 3,631 ... C6
03451 Hinsdale 1,546 .... C6
03245 Holderness○ 1,586 . D4
03049 Hollis○ 4,679 ...... D6
03106 Hooksett○ 7,303 .. E5
03106 Hooksett 1,868 ... E5
03301 Hopkinton○ 3,861 . D5
03051 Hudson○ 14,022 .. E6
03051 Hudson 6,248 ..... E6
03845 Intervale 725 ...... E3
03846 Jackson○ 642 .... E3
03452 Jaffrey○ 4,349 ... C6
03452 Jaffrey 2,684 ..... C6
03583 Jefferson○ 803 .. D3
03431 Keene⊙ 21,449 .. C6
03848 Kingston○ 4,111 . E6
03246 Laconia⊙ 15,575 . E4
03584 Lancaster○ 3,401 . D3
03584 Lancaster⊙ 2,134 . D3
†03585 Landaff○ 266 ... D3
†03602 Langdon○ 437 .. C5
03766 Lebanon 11,134 . C4
†03857 Lee○ 2,111 .... F5
03606 Lempster○ 637 . C5
03251 Lincoln○ 1,313 . D3
03585 Lisbon○ 1,517 . D3
03585 Lisbon 1,151 ... D3
03053 Litchfield○ 4,150 . E6
03561 Littleton○ 5,558 . D3
03561 Littleton 4,480 .. D3
03301 Loudon○ 2,454 . E5
†03585 Lyman○ 281 ... D3
03768 Lyme○ 1,289 .. C4
†03082 Lyndeborough○ 1,070 . D6
†03820 Madbury○ 987 . F5
03849 Madison○ 1,051 . E4
*03101 Manchester 90,936 . E6
Manchester† 160,767 . E6
03455 Marlborough○ 1,846 . C6
03455 Marlborough 1,184 . C6
03456 Marlow○ 542 ..... C5
03850 Melvin Village 450 . E4
03253 Meredith○ 4,646 . D4
03253 Meredith 1,202 .. D4
03770 Meriden○ 803 ... C4
03054 Merrimack○ 15,406 . D6
03588 Milano○ 1,013 .. E2
03055 Milford○ 8,685 . D6
03055 Milford 6,269 ... D6
03851 Milton○ 2,438 . F5
03852 Milton Mills 450 . F4
03771 Monroe○ 619 .. C3
03057 Mont Vernon○ 1,444 . D6
03254 Moultonboro○ 2,206 . E4
03060 Nashua⊙ 67,865 . D6
Nashua† 114,221 . D6
†03457 Nelson○ 442 . C6
03070 New Boston○ 1,928 . D6
03255 Newbury○ 961 .. C5
03854 New Castle○ 936 . F5
03855 New Durham○ 1,183 . E5
03856 Newfields○ 817 . F5
03256 New Hampton○ 1,249 . D4

†03801 Newington○ 716 ...... F5
03071 New Ipswich○ 2,433 . D6
03257 New London○ 2,935 . D5
03257 New London 1,335 .. D5
03857 Newmarket○ 4,290 . F5
03857 Newmarket 3,749 ... F5
03773 Newport○ 6,229 ..... C5
03773 Newport⊙ 4,388 .... C5
03858 Newton○ 3,068 ..... E6
03859 Newton Junction 450 . E6
03860 North Conway 2,104 . E3
†03276 Northfield○ 3,051 .. D5
†03276 Northfield-Tilton 2,574 . D5
03862 North Hampton○ 3,425 . F6
03590 North Stratford 600 . D2
†03582 Northumberland○ 2,520 . D2
03261 Northwood○ 2,175 . E5
03262 North Woodstock 750 . D3
03290 Nottingham○ 1,952 . E5
†03741 Orange○ 197 ...... D4
03777 Orford○ 928 .... C4
03864 Ossipee○ 2,465 ... E4
03076 Pelham○ 8,090 .... E6
†03275 Pembroke○ 4,861 . E5
03458 Peterborough○ 4,895 . D6
03458 Peterborough 2,568 . D6
03779 Piermont○ 507 ... C4
03592 Pittsburg○ 780 ... E1
03263 Pittsfield○ 2,889 . E5
03263 Pittsfield 1,584 .. E5
03781 Plainfield○ 1,749 . C4
03865 Plaistow○ 5,609 . E6
03264 Plymouth○ 5,094 . D4
03264 Plymouth 3,628 .. D4
03801 Portsmouth 26,254 . F5
Portsmouth-Dover-Rochester†
163,880 .... F5
03593 Randolph○ 274 .. E3
03077 Raymond○ 5,453 . E5
03077 Raymond 1,192 .. E5
†03470 Richmond○ 518 . C6
03461 Rindge○ 3,375 .. C6
03867 Rochester 21,560 . E5
†03431 Roxbury○ 190 .. C6
03266 Rumney○ 1,212 . D4
03870 Rye○ 4,508 .... F5
03871 Rye Beach 600 . F6
03079 Salem 24,124 .. E6
03268 Salisbury○ 781 . D5
03269 Sanbornton○ 1,679 . D5
03872 Sanbornville○ 750 . F4
03873 Sandown○ 2,057 . E6
03270 Sandwich○ 905 . E4
03874 Seabrook○ 5,917 . F6
†03458 Sharon○ 184 ... D6
†03581 Shelburne○ 318 . E3
03878 Somersworth 10,350 . F5
†01913 South Hampton○ 660 . F6
03462 Spofford 750 .. C6
†03284 Springfield○ 532 . C4
†03582 Stark○ 470 .... E2
†03576 Stewartstown○ 943 . E2
03464 Stoddard○ 482 . C6
03884 Strafford○ 1,663 . E5
†03590 Stratford○ 989 . D2
03885 Stratham○ 2,507 . F5
03585 Sugar Hill 397 . D3
†03445 Sullivan○ 585 . C5
†03782 Sunapee○ 2,312 . C5
03275 Suncook 4,698 . D5
03431 Surry○ 656 .... C6
†03260 Sutton○ 1,091 . D5
†03431 Swanzey○ 5,183 . C6
03886 Tamworth○ 1,672 . E4
03084 Temple○ 692 .. D6
†03285 Thornton○ 952 . D4
03276 Tilton○ 3,387 . D5
03276 Tilton-Northfield 2,574 . D5
03465 Troy○ 2,131 ... C6
03465 Troy 1,318 .... C6
†03816 Tuftonboro○ 1,500 . E4
03595 Twin Mountain 500 . D3
†03743 Unity○ 1,092 . C5
†03872 Wakefield○ 2,237 . F4
03608 Walpole○ 3,188 . C5
03278 Warner○ 1,963 . D5
03279 Warren○ 650 .. D4
03280 Washington○ 411 . C5
03223 Waterville Valley○ 180 . D4
03281 Weare○ 3,232 . D5
†03301 Webster○ 1,095 . D5
03282 Wentworth○ 527 . D4
†03579 Wentworths Location○ 49 . E2
†03242 West Henniker 500 . D5
03784 West Lebanon○ 1,195 . C4
03467 Westmoreland○ 1,531 . C5
03597 West Stewartstown 700 . E2
03469 West Swanzey 1,022 . C6
03865 Westville 750 . E6
03598 Whitefield○ 1,681 . D3
03598 Whitefield 1,005 . D3
†03287 Wilmot○ 725 . D5
03287 Wilmot Flat 450 . D5
03086 Wilton○ 2,669 . D6
03086 Wilton 1,310 .. D6
03470 Winchester○ 3,465 . C6

03470 Winchester 1,732 ...... C6
03087 Windham○ 5,664 ..... E6
03289 Winnisquam 500 ..... E5
03894 Wolfeboro○ 3,968 .... E4
03894 Wolfeboro 2,271 ...... E4
03896 Wolfeboro Falls 600 .. E4
03293 Woodstock○ 1,008 ... D4
03785 Woodsville○ 1,195 .... C3

OTHER FEATURES

Adams (mt.) E3
Ammonoosuc (riv.) D3
Androscoggin (riv.) E2
Ashuelot (riv.) C6
Back (lake) E1
Baker (riv.) D4
Bearcamp (riv.) E4
Beaver (brook) E6
Belknap (mt.) E5
Blackwater (res.) D5
Blue (mt.) E2
Bond (mt.) E3
Bow (lake) E5
Cabot (mt.) E2
Cannon (mt.) D3
Cardigan (mt.) D4
Carrigain (mt.) E3
Carter Dome (mt.) E3
Chocorua (mt.) E4
Cocheco (riv.) E5
Cold (riv.) C5
Comerford (dam) D3
Connecticut (riv.) B6

Contoocook (riv.) D6
Conway (lake) E4
Crawford Notch (pass) . E3
Croydon (peak) C5
Croydon Branch, Sugar (riv.) . C5
Crystal (lake) E4
Cube (mt.) D4
Dixville (peak) E2
Dixville Notch (pass) .. E2
Edward MacDowell (res.) . D6
Ellis (riv.) E3
Everett (dam) D5
Exeter (riv.) E6
First Connecticut (lake) . E1
Francis (lake) E1
Franconia Notch (pass) . D3
Franklin Falls (res.) .. D4
Gale (riv.) D3
Great (bay) F5
Halls (stream) E1
Hancock (mt.) D3
Highland (lake) E5
Hutchins (mt.) E2
Indian (stream) E1
Jefferson (mt.) D5
Kearsarge (mt.) D5
Kinsman (mt.) D3
Kinsman Notch (pass) . D3
Lafayette (mt.) D3
Lamprey (riv.) E5
Liberty (mt.) D3
Lincoln (mt.) D3
Long (mt.) E2
Mad (riv.) D4

Madison (mt.) E3
Mascoma (lake) C4
Massabesic (lake) E6
Merrimack (riv.) D5
Merrymeeting (lake) .. E5
Mohawk (riv.) E2
Monadnock (mt.) C6
Monroe (mt.) E3
Moore (dam) D3
Moore (res.) D3
Moosilauke (mt.) ... D3
Nash (stream) E2
Newfound (lake) ... D4
North Carter (mt.) . E3
North Twin (mt.) .. D3
Nubanusit (lake) .. C5
Osceola (mt.) E3
Ossipee (lake) ... E4
Ossipee (mts.) .. E4
Ossipee (riv.) ... F4
Passaconaway (mt.) . E4
Pawtuckaway (pond) . E5
Pease A.F.B. F5
Pemigewasset (riv.) . D4
Perry (stream) E1
Pine (riv.) E4
Pinkham Notch (pass) . E3
Piscataqua (riv.) .. F5
Piscataquog (riv.) . D5
Presidential (range) . E3
Rice (riv.) E2
Saco (riv.) E3
Saint-Gaudens Nat'l Hist. Site . B4
Salmon Falls (riv.) . F5

(continued on following page)

Topography

(Scale) 0 20 40 MI.
0 20 40 KM.

Elevation scale: 5,000 m. 16,404 ft. | 2,000 m. 6,562 ft. | 1,000 m. 3,281 ft. | 500 m. 1,640 ft. | 200 m. 656 ft. | 100 m. 328 ft. | Sea Level | Below

Agriculture, Industry and Resources

DOMINANT LAND USE

- Specialized Dairy
- Dairy, General Farming
- Dairy, Poultry, Mixed Farming
- Forests
- Water Power
- Major Industrial Areas

MAJOR MINERAL OCCURRENCES

- Ab Asbestos
- Be Beryl
- Gn Granite
- Mi Mica
- Mr Marble
- Sl Slate
- Tc Talc
- Th Thorium

Sandwich (mt.) E4
Sandwich (range) E4
Second (lake) E1
Shaw (mt.) E4
Shoals (isls.) F6
Smarts (mt.) C4
Souhegan (riv.) D6
South Twin (mt.) D3
Squam (lake) E4
Starr King (mt.) E3
Stub Hill (mt.) E1
Sugar (riv.) C5
Sunapee (lake) C5
Suncook (lkes) E5
Suncook (riv.) E5
Surry Mountain (lake) C5
Tarleton (lake) D4
Tecumseh (mt.) D4
Third (lake) E1
Tom (mt.) E3
Umbagog (lake) E2
Upper Ammonoosuc (riv.) E2
Warner (riv.) D5
Washington (mt.) E3
Waumbek (mt.) E3
Wentworth (lake) E4
White (isl.) F6
White (mts.) E3
Whiteface (mt.) E4
Wild Ammonoosuc (riv.) D3
Wilder (dam) C4
Winnipesaukee (lake) E4
Winnipesaukee (riv.) D5
Winnisquam (lake) D4

VERMONT

COUNTIES

Addison 29,406 A3
Bennington 33,345 A6
Caledonia 25,808 C2
Chittenden 115,534 A3
Essex 6,313 D2
Franklin 34,788 B2
Grand Isle 4,613 A2
Lamoille 16,767 B2
Orange 22,739 C3
Orleans 23,440 C2
Rutland 58,347 A4
Washington 52,393 B3
Windham 36,933 B5
Windsor 51,030 B4

CITIES and TOWNS

Zip Name/Pop. Key
05820 Albany○ 705 C2
05440 Alburg○ 1,352 A2
05440 Alburg 496 A2
†05143 Andover○ 350 B5
05250 Arlington○ 2,184 A5
05250 Arlington 1,309 A5
05441 Bakersfield○ 852 B2
05031 Barnard○ 790 B4
05821 Barnet○ 1,338 C3
05641 Barre 9,824 C3
05641 Barre○ 7,090 C3
05822 Barton○ 2,990 C2
05822 Barton 1,062 C2
05823 Beebe Plain 500 C2
05902 Beecher Falls 950 D2
05101 Bellows Falls 3,456 C5
05442 Belvidere○ 218 B2
05201 Bennington○ 15,815 A6
05201 Bennington⊙ 9,349 A6
05731 Benson○ 739 A4
†05476 Berkshire○ 1,116 B2
05032 Bethel○ 1,715 B4
05032 Bethel 1,016 B4
†03590 Bloomfield○ 188 D2
†05466 Bolton○ 715 B3
05732 Bomoseen 700 A4
05340 Bondville 500 B5
05033 Bradford○ 2,191 C3
05033 Bradford 831 C3
†05669 Braintree○ 1,065 B4
05733 Brandon○ 4,194 A4
05733 Brandon 1,925 A4
05301 Brattleboro○ 11,886 B6
05301 Brattleboro 8,596 B6
05034 Bridgewater○ 867 B4
05734 Bridport○ 997 A4
05443 Bristol○ 3,293 A3
05443 Bristol 1,793 A3
05036 Brookfield○ 959 B3
†05345 Brookline○ 310 B5
†05860 Brownington○ 708 C2
†05871 Burke○ 1,385 D2
05401 Burlington⊙ 37,712 A3
Burlington‡ 114,070 A3
05647 Cabot○ 958 C3
05647 Cabot 259 C3
05648 Calais○ 1,207 B3
05444 Cambridge○ 2,019 B2
05444 Cambridge 217 B2
05903 Canaan○ 1,196 D2
05735 Castleton○ 3,637 A4
05142 Cavendish○ 1,355 B5
05736 Center Rutland 465 A4
05445 Charlotte○ 2,561 A3
05038 Chelsea 1,091 C4
05143 Chester○ 2,791 B5
05143 Chester-Chester Depot 1,267 B5
05737 Chittenden○ 927 B4
†05759 Clarendon○ 2,372 A4
05446 Colchester○ 12,629 A2
05824 Concord○ 1,125 D3
05039 Corinth○ 904 C3
†05753 Cornwall○ 993 A4
05825 Coventry○ 674 C2
05826 Craftsbury○ 844 C2
05739 Danby○ 992 A5
05828 Danville○ 1,705 C3
05829 Derby○ 4,222 C2
05829 Derby (Derby Center) 598 C2
05830 Derby Line 874 C2
05251 Dorset○ 1,648 A5
†05676 Duxbury○ 877 B3
05252 East Arlington 600 A5
05649 East Barre-Graniteville 2,172 C3
05253 East Dorset 550 A5
05837 East Haven○ 280 D2
05740 East Middlebury 550 A4
05651 East Montpelier○ 2,205 B3
05741 East Poultney 450 A4
05742 East Wallingford 500 B5
05652 Eden○ 612 B2
05450 Enosburg Falls 1,207 B2
05451 Essex○ 14,392 A2
05452 Essex Junction 7,033 A3
05454 Fairfax○ 1,805 B2
05455 Fairfield○ 1,493 B2
05743 Fair Haven○ 2,819 A4
05743 Fair Haven 2,363 A4
05045 Fairlee○ 770 C4
05456 Ferrisburg○ 2,117 A3
†05444 Fletcher○ 626 B2
05745 Forest Dale 500 A4
05457 Franklin○ 1,006 B2
†05478 Georgia○ 2,818 A2
05904 Gilman 600 D3
05839 Glover○ 843 C2
05146 Grafton○ 604 B5
05840 Granby○ 70 D2
05458 Grand Isle○ 1,238 A2
05654 Graniteville-East Barre 2,172 C3
05747 Granville○ 288 B4
05841 Greensboro○ 677 C2
05046 Groton○ 667 C3
05905 Guildhall 202 D2
†05301 Guilford○ 1,532 B6
†05358 Halifax○ 488 B6
05748 Hancock○ 334 B4
05843 Hardwick○ 2,613 C2
05843 Hardwick 1,476 C2
05047 Hartford○ 7,963 C4
05048 Hartland○ 2,396 C4
†05459 Highgate○ 2,493 B2
05461 Hinesburg○ 2,690 A3
†05830 Holland○ 473 D2
05749 Hubbardton○ 490 A4
05462 Huntington○ 1,161 B3
05655 Hyde Park○ 2,021 B2
05655 Hyde Park⊙ 475 B2
05750 Hydeville 500 A4
†05777 Ira○ 354 A4
05845 Irasburg○ 870 C2
05846 Island Pond 1,216 D2
05463 Isle La Motte○ 393 A2
05342 Jacksonville 252 B6
05343 Jamaica○ 681 B5
†05859 Jay○ 302 C2
05464 Jeffersonville 491 B2
05465 Jericho○ 3,575 A2
05465 Jericho 1,340 A2
05656 Johnson○ 2,581 B2
05656 Johnson 1,393 B2
05751 Killington 700 B4
†05752 Leicester○ 803 A4
†03576 Lemington○ 108 D2
†05443 Lincoln○ 870 B3
05148 Londonderry○ 1,510 B5
05847 Lowell○ 573 C2
05149 Ludlow○ 2,414 B5
05149 Ludlow 1,352 B5
05906 Lunenburg○ 1,138 D3
05849 Lyndon○ 4,924 C2
05850 Lyndon Center C2
05851 Lyndonville 1,401 C2
†05905 Maidstone○ 100 D2
05254 Manchester○ 3,261 A5
05254 Manchester⊙ 563 A5
05255 Manchester Center 1,719 A5
05344 Marlboro○ 695 B6
05658 Marshfield○ 1,267 C3
05658 Marshfield 301 C3
†05701 Mendon○ 1,056 B4
05753 Middlebury○ 7,574 A3
05753 Middlebury⊙ 5,591 A3
†05602 Middlesex○ 1,235 B3
05757 Middletown Springs○ 603 A5
05468 Milton○ 6,829 A2
05468 Milton 1,411 A2
05469 Monkton○ 1,201 A3
05470 Montgomery○ 681 B2
05471 Montgomery Center 400 B2
05602 Montpelier (cap.)⊙ 8,241 B3
05660 Moretown○ 1,221 B3
05853 Morgan○ 460 D2
†05661 Morristown○ 4,448 B2
05661 Morrisville 2,074 B2
05758 Mount Holly○ 938 B5
†05739 Mount Tabor○ 211 B5
†05871 Newark○ 280 D2
05051 Newbury○ 1,699 C3
05051 Newbury 425 C3
05345 Newfane○ 1,129 B6
05345 Newfane⊙ 119 B6
05472 New Haven○ 1,217 A3
05855 Newport○ 1,319 C2
05855 Newport⊙ 4,756 C2
05257 North Bennington 1,685 A6
05663 Northfield○ 5,435 B3
05663 Northfield 2,033 B3
05664 Northfield Falls 600 B3
05052 North Hartland 500 C4
05474 North Hero 442 A2
05665 North Hyde Park 450 B2
05053 North Pomfret 400 B4
05260 North Pownal 700 A6
05150 North Springfield B5
05859 North Troy 717 C2
†05101 North Westminster 310 B5
05907 Norton○ 184 D2
05055 Norwich○ 2,398 C4
†05201 Old Bennington 353 A6
†05649 Orange○ 752 C3
05860 Orleans 983 C2
05760 Orwell○ 901 A4
†05491 Panton○ 537 A3
05761 Pawlet○ 1,244 A5
05862 Peacham○ 531 C3
05151 Perkinsville 187 B5
05152 Peru○ 312 B5
05762 Pittsfield○ 396 B4
05763 Pittsford○ 2,590 A4
05763 Pittsford 666 A4
05667 Plainfield○ 1,249 C3
05667 Plainfield 599 C3
05056 Plymouth○ 405 B4
†05067 Pomfret○ 856 B4
05058 Post Mills 500 C4
05764 Poultney○ 3,196 A4
05764 Poultney 1,554 A4
05261 Pownal○ 3,269 A6
05765 Proctor○ 1,998 A4
05153 Proctorsville 481 B5
05346 Putney○ 1,850 B6
05059 Quechee 900 C4
05060 Randolph○ 4,689 B4
05060 Randolph 2,217 B4
05062 Reading○ 647 B5
05350 Readsboro○ 638 B6
05350 Readsboro 402 B6
05476 Richford○ 2,206 B2
05476 Richford 1,471 B2
05477 Richmond○ 3,159 A3
05477 Richmond 865 A3
05766 Ripton○ 327 A4
05767 Rochester○ 1,054 B4
†05101 Rockingham○ 5,538 B5
05669 Roxbury○ 452 B3
†05068 Royalton○ 2,100 B4
05768 Rupert○ 605 A5
05701 Rutland○ 3,300 B4
05701 Rutland⊙ 18,436 B4
05042 Ryegate○ 1,000 C3
05478 Saint Albans○ 3,555 A2
05478 Saint Albans⊙ 7,308 A2
†05401 Saint George○ 677 A2
05819 Saint Johnsbury○ 7,938 D3
05819 Saint Johnsbury⊙ 7,150 D3
05863 Saint Johnsbury Center 400 D3
05769 Salisbury○ 881 A4
†05250 Sandgate○ 234 A5
05154 Saxtons River 593 B5
†05363 Searsburg○ 72 A6
05262 Shaftsbury○ 3,001 A6
05065 Sharon○ 828 C4
05866 Sheffield○ 435 C2
05482 Shelburne○ 5,000 A3
05483 Sheldon○ 1,618 B2
05770 Shoreham○ 972 A4
†05738 Shrewsbury○ 866 B4
05670 South Barre 1,301 B3
05401 South Burlington 10,679 A3
05486 South Hero○ 1,188 A2
05155 South Londonderry 500 B5
05068 South Royalton 700 C4
05069 South Ryegate 400 C3
05156 Springfield○ 10,190 B5
05156 Springfield 5,603 B5
05352 Stamford○ 773 A6
05487 Starksboro○ 1,336 A3
05772 Stockbridge○ 508 B4
05672 Stowe○ 2,991 B3
05672 Stowe 531 B3
05072 Strafford○ 731 C4
†05360 Stratton○ 122 B5
†05733 Sudbury○ 380 A4
†05250 Sunderland○ 768 A5
05867 Sutton○ 667 C2
05488 Swanton○ 5,141 A2
05488 Swanton 2,520 A2
05074 Thetford○ 2,188 C4
†05773 Tinmouth○ 406 A5
05076 Topsham○ 767 C3
05353 Townshend○ 849 B5
05868 Troy○ 1,498 C2
05077 Tunbridge○ 925 C4
05489 Underhill○ 2,172 B2
05490 Underhill Center 575 B2
05491 Vergennes 2,273 A3
05354 Vernon○ 1,175 B6
05079 Vershire○ 442 C4
05673 Waitsfield○ 1,300 B3
†05873 Walden○ 575 C3
05773 Wallingford○ 1,893 B5
05773 Wallingford 1,141 B5
†05491 Waltham○ 394 A3
05355 Wardsboro○ 505 B5
05674 Warren○ 956 B3
05675 Washington○ 855 C3
05676 Waterbury○ 4,465 B3
05676 Waterbury 1,892 B3
05492 Waterville○ 470 B2
05678 Websterville 700 B3
05774 Wells○ 815 A5
05081 Wells River 396 C3
05301 West Brattleboro 2,795 B6
05871 West Burke 338 C2
05356 West Dover 550 B6
05083 West Fairlee○ 427 C4
05874 Westfield○ 418 C2
05494 Westford○ 1,413 A2
05875 West Glover C2
†05743 West Haven○ 253 A4
05158 Westminster○ 2,493 C5
05158 Westminster 319 C5
†05860 Westmore○ 257 C2
05161 Weston○ 627 B5
05777 West Rutland○ 2,351 A4
05777 West Rutland 2,169 A4
05359 West Townshend 500 B5
†05753 Weybridge○ 667 A3
†05851 Wheelock○ 444 C2
05001 White River Junction 2,582 C4
05778 Whiting○ 379 A4
05361 Whitingham○ 1,043 B6
05088 Wilder 1,461 C4
05679 Williamstown○ 2,284 B3
05495 Williston○ 3,843 A3
05363 Wilmington○ 1,808 B6
†05359 Windham○ 223 B5
05089 Windsor○ 4,084 C5
05089 Windsor 3,478 C5
05404 Winooski 6,318 A2
05680 Wolcott○ 986 C2
05681 Woodbury○ 573 C3
†05201 Woodford○ 314 A6
05091 Woodstock○ 3,214 B4
05091 Woodstock⊙ 1,178 B4
05682 Worcester○ 727 B3

OTHER FEATURES

Abraham (mt.) B3
Arrowhead Mountain (lake) A2
Ascutney (mt.) C5
Bald (mt.) D2
Barton (riv.) C2
Batten Kill (riv.) A5
Belvidere (mt.) B2
Black (riv.) B5
Black (riv.) C2
Bloodroot (mt.) B4
Bolton (mt.) B3
Bomoseen (lake) A4
Brandon Gap (pass) B4
Bread Loaf (mt.) A3
Bromley (mt.) B5
Brown's (riv.) A2
Burke (mt.) D2
Camels Hump (mt.) B3
Carmi (lake) B2
Caspian (lake) C2
Champlain (lake) A2
Chittenden (res.) B4
Clyde (riv.) C2
Comerford (dam) D3
Connecticut (riv.) C4
Crystal (lake) C2
Dorset (peak) A5
Dunmore (lake) A4
Echo (lake) D2
Ellen (mt.) B3
Equinox (mt.) A5
Fairfield (pond) A2
Glastenbury (mt.) A6
Gore (mt.) D2
Green (mts.) B4
Green River (res.) B2
Groton (lake) C3
Hardwick (lake) C2
Harriman (res.) B6
Harveys (lake) C3
Haystack (mt.) B6
Hoosic (riv.) A6
Hortonia (lake) A4
Hunger (mt.) B3
Iroquois (lake) A3
Island (pond) D2
Jay (peak) B2
Joes (brook) C3
Killington (peak) B4
Lamoille (riv.) A2
Lewis (creek) A3
Lincoln Gap (pass) B3
Little (riv.) B3
Mad (riv.) B3
Maidstone (lake) D2
Mansfield (mt.) B2
Memphremagog (lake) C1
Mettawee (riv.) A5
Middlebury Gap (pass) B4
Mill (riv.) B4
Missisquoi (riv.) B2
Mollys Falls (pond) C3
Moore (dam) D3
Moore (res.) D3
Moose (riv.) D2
Norton (pond) D2
Nulhegan (riv.) D2
Ottauquechee (riv.) B4
Otter (creek) A3
Passumpsic (riv.) D2
Pico (peak) B4
Poultney (riv.) A4
Saint Catherine (lake) A5
Salem (lake) C2
Seymour (lake) D2
Shelburne (pond) A3
Smugglers Notch (pass) B2
Snow (mt.) B6
Somerset (res.) A5
Spruce (mt.) C3
Stratton (mt.) B5
Tabor (mt.) B5
Trout (riv.) B2
Waits (riv.) C3
Waterbury (res.) B3
Wells (riv.) C3
West (riv.) B5
White (riv.) C4
White Face (mt.) B2
Wilder (dam) C4
Willoughby (lake) D2
Winooski (riv.) B3

⊙County seat.
‡Population of metropolitan area.
○Population of town or township.
† Zip of nearest p.o. * Multiple zips.

AREA 7,787 sq. mi. (20,168 sq. km.)
POPULATION 7,364,823
CAPITAL Trenton
LARGEST CITY Newark
HIGHEST POINT High Point 1,803 ft. (550 m.)
SETTLED IN 1617
ADMITTED TO UNION December 18, 1787
POPULAR NAME Garden State
STATE FLOWER Purple Violet
STATE BIRD Eastern Goldfinch

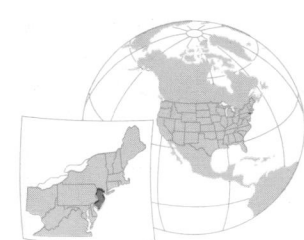

Agriculture, Industry and Resources

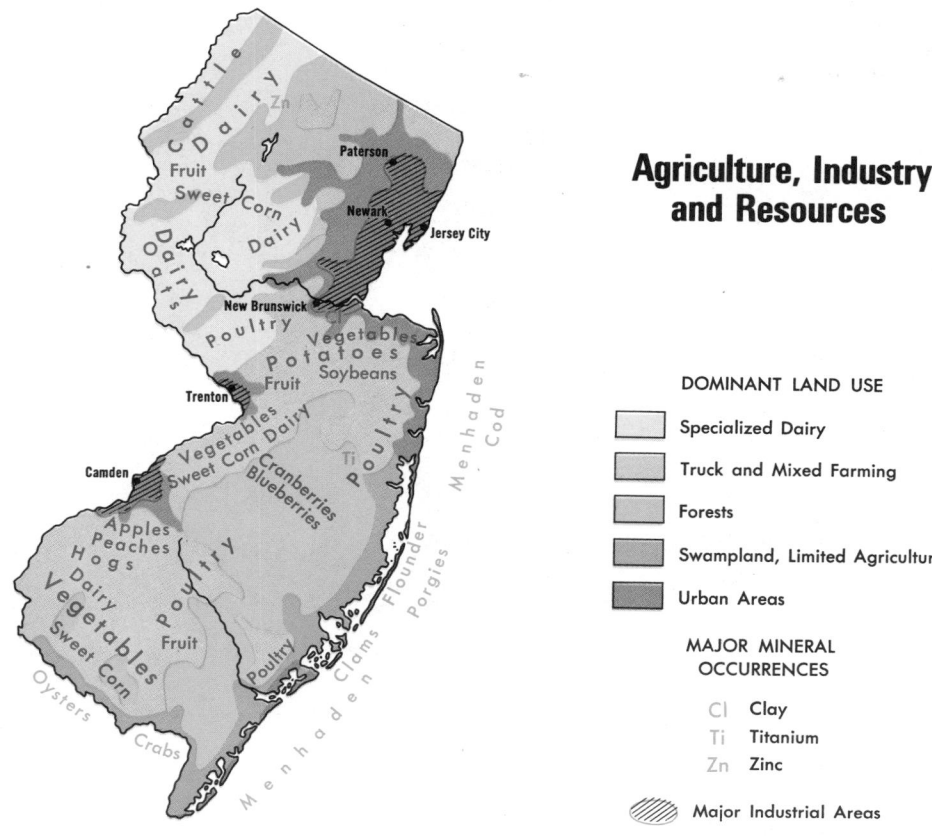

DOMINANT LAND USE

Specialized Dairy

Truck and Mixed Farming

Forests

Swampland, Limited Agriculture

Urban Areas

MAJOR MINERAL OCCURRENCES

Cl Clay
Ti Titanium
Zn Zinc

Major Industrial Areas

The Urban Northeast

Urbanized Areas
• Places with more than 10,000 inhabitants
• Places with 5,000-10,000 inhabitants
· Places with 2,500-5,000 inhabitants

© Copyright HAMMOND INCORPORATED, Maplewood, N. J.

COUNTIES

County	Pop.	Key
Atlantic	194,119	D5
Bergen	845,385	E2
Burlington	362,542	D4
Camden	471,650	D4
Cape May	82,266	D5
Cumberland	132,866	C5
Essex	851,116	E2
Gloucester	199,917	C4
Hudson	556,972	E2
Hunterdon	87,361	D2
Mercer	307,863	D3
Middlesex	595,893	E3
Monmouth	503,173	E3
Morris	407,630	D2
Ocean	346,038	E4
Passaic	447,585	E1
Salem	64,676	C4
Somerset	203,129	D2
Sussex	116,119	D1
Union	504,094	E2
Warren	84,429	C2

CITIES and TOWNS

Zip	Name/Pop.	Key
08201	Absecon 6,859	D5
07820	Allamuchy 600	D2
07401	Allendale 5,901	B1
07711	Allenhurst 912	F3
08501	Allentown 1,962	D3
08720	Allenwood	E3
08001	Alloway 1,370	C4
08865	Alpha 2,644	C2
07620	Alpine 1,549	C1
07821	Andover 892	D2
08801	Annandale 1,040	D2
07712	Asbury Park 17,015	F3
	Asbury Park-Long Branch‡ 503,173	F3
†08033	Ashland	B3
08004	Atco	D4
*08401	Atlantic City 40,199	E5
	Atlantic City‡ 194,119	E5
07716	Atlantic Highlands 4,950	F3
08106	Audubon 9,533	B3
†08106	Audubon Park 1,274	B3
08202	Avalon 2,162	D5
07001	Avenel	E2
07717	Avon By The Sea 2,337	E3
08005	Barnegat 1,012	E4
08006	Barnegat Light 619	E4
08007	Barrington 7,418	B3
07920	Basking Ridge	D2
08742	Bay Head 1,340	E3
07002	Bayonne 65,047	B2
08008	Beach Haven 1,714	E4
08722	Beachwood 7,687	E4
07921	Bedminster○ 2,469	D2
08502	Belle Mead	D3
07109	Belleville 35,367	B2
08031	Bellmawr 13,721	B3
07719	Belmar 6,771	E3
07823	Belvidere○ 2,475	C2
07621	Bergenfield 25,568	C1
07922	Berkeley Heights○ 12,549	E2
08009	Berlin 5,786	D4
07924	Bernardsville 6,715	D2
08010	Beverly 2,919	D3
08012	Blackwood 5,219	C4
07825	Blairstown○ 4,360	C2
07003	Bloomfield 47,792	B2
07403	Bloomingdale 7,867	E1
08804	Bloomsbury 864	C2
07603	Bogota 8,344	B2
07005	Boonton 8,620	E2
08505	Bordentown 4,441	D3
08805	Bound Brook 9,710	D2
07720	Bradley Beach 4,772	F3
07826	Branchville 870	D1
08723	Breton Woods	E3
08723	Brick 53,629	E3
08014	Bridgeport 750	C4
08302	Bridgeton○ 18,795	C5
08807	Bridgewater○ 29,175	D2
08730	Brielle 4,068	E3
08203	Brigantine 8,318	E5
08030	Brooklawn 2,133	B3
08015	Browns Mills 10,568	D4
07828	Budd Lake 6,523	D2
08310	Buena 3,642	D4
08016	Burlington 10,246	D3
07405	Butler 7,616	E2
07006	Caldwell 7,624	B2
07830	Califon 1,023	D2
*08101	Camden○ 84,910	B3
†08701	Candlewood 6,750	E3
08204	Cape May 4,853	D6
08210	Cape May Court House○ 3,597	D5
07072	Carlstadt 6,166	B2
08069	Carneys Point 7,574	C4
07008	Carteret 20,598	E2
07009	Cedar Grove○ 12,600	B2
†08723	Cedarwood Park	E3

Zip	Name/Pop.	Key
07928	Chatham 8,537	E2
08019	Chatsworth 700	D4
08879	Cheesequake	E3
*08034	Cherry Hill○ 68,785	B3
†08089	Chesilhurst 1,590	D4
07930	Chester 1,433	D2
†08505	Chesterfield○ 3,867	D3
†08077	Cinnaminson○ 16,072	B3
07066	Clark 16,699	A3
08020	Clarksboro	C4
08510	Clarksburg 800	E3
08312	Clayton 6,013	C4
08021	Clementon 5,764	D4
07010	Cliffside Park 21,464	C2
07721	Cliffwood	E3
*07011	Clifton 74,388	B2
08809	Clinton 1,910	D2
07624	Closter 8,164	C1
08108	Collingswood 15,838	B3
08213	Cologne 800	D4
07832	Columbia 600	C2
08022	Columbus 800	D3
07961	Convent Station	E2
†08270	Corbin City 254	D5
†07821	Cranberry Lake 500	D2
08512	Cranbury 1,255	E3
07016	Cranford○ 24,573	E2
07626	Cresskill 7,609	C1
08515	Crosswicks 265	D3
07723	Deal 1,952	F3
08023	Deepwater 800	C4
08110	Delair	B3
08075	Delanco 3,730	D3
08075	Delran 14,811	B3
07627	Demarest 4,963	C1
08214	Dennisville 890	D5
07834	Denville○ 14,380	E2
08096	Deptford○ 23,473	B4
08317	Dorothy 900	D5
07801	Dover 14,681	D2
07628	Dumont 18,334	C1
08812	Dunellen 6,593	E2
08816	East Brunswick○ 37,711	E3
07936	East Hanover○ 9,319	E2
07734	East Keansburg	E3
08873	East Millstone 950	D3
†07100	East Newark 1,923	B2
*07017	East Orange 77,690	B2
07073	East Rutherford 7,849	B2
07724	Eatontown 12,703	E3
07020	Edgewater 4,628	C2
†08010	Edgewater Park○ 9,273	D3
*08817	Edison○ 70,193	E2
08215	Egg Harbor City 4,618	D4
07740	Elberon	F3
*07201	Elizabeth⊙ 106,201	B2
08318	Elmer 1,569	C4
†07407	Elmwood Park 18,377	B2
08217	Elwood 1,538	D4
07630	Emerson 7,793	B1
*07631	Englewood 23,701	C2
07632	Englewood Cliffs 5,698	C2
07726	Englishtown 976	E3
07021	Essex Fells 2,363	B2
08319	Estell Manor 848	D5
08025	Ewan 610	C4
07006	Fairfield○ 7,987	A2
07701	Fair Haven 5,679	E3
07410	Fair Lawn 32,229	B1
08320	Fairton 1,107	C5
07022	Fairview 10,519	C2
07023	Fanwood 7,767	E2
07931	Far Hills 677	D2
07727	Farmingdale 1,348	E3
†08505	Fieldsboro 597	D3
07836	Flanders	D2
08822	Flemington○ 4,132	D2
08518	Florence-Roebling 7,677	D3
07932	Florham Park 9,359	E2
†08037	Folsom 1,892	D4
08863	Fords	E2
08731	Forked River 900	E4
07024	Fort Lee 32,449	C2
07416	Franklin 4,486	D1
07417	Franklin Lakes 8,769	B1
†08823	Franklin Park○ 31,358	D3
08322	Franklinville	C4
07728	Freehold○ 10,020	E3
08825	Frenchtown 1,573	C2
07026	Garfield 26,803	B2
07027	Garwood 4,752	E2
08026	Gibbsboro 2,510	B4
08027	Gibbstown	C4
†08753	Gilford Park 6,528	E4
07933	Gillette	E2
08028	Glassboro 14,574	C4
08029	Glendora 5,632	B4
08826	Glen Gardner 834	D2
07028	Glen Ridge 7,855	B2
07452	Glen Rock 11,497	B1
08030	Gloucester City 13,121	B3
07435	Green Pond 800	E1
07935	Green Village 800	D2
08323	Greenwich○ 973	C5
08032	Grenloch 700	C4

(continued on following page)

07093 Guttenberg 7,340 .... C2
*07601 Hackensack⊙ 36,039 ...... B2
07840 Hackettstown 8,850 .... D2
08033 Haddonfield 12,337 .... B3
08035 Haddon Heights 8,361 ...... B3
08036 Hainesport○ 3,236 .... D4
07508 Haledon 6,607 .... B1
07419 Hamburg 1,832 .... D1
08690 Hamilton Square-
Mercerville 25,446 .... D3
08037 Hammonton 12,298 .... D4
08827 Hampton 1,614 .... D2
07640 Harrington Park 4,532 ...... C1
07029 Harrison 12,242 .... B2
†08057 Hartford 650 .... D4
08008 Harvey Cedars 363 .... E4
07604 Hasbrouck Heights 12,166 . B2
07641 Haworth 3,509 .... C1
07506 Hawthorne 18,200 .... B2
07730 Hazlet 23,013 .... E3
08828 Helmetta 955 .... E3
07421 Hewitt 950 .... E1
08829 High Bridge 3,435 .... D2
07422 Highland Lakes 2,888 .... E1
08904 Highland Park 13,396 .... D2
07732 Highlands 5,187 .... F3
08520 Hightstown 4,581 .... D3
07642 Hillsdale 10,495 .... B1
07205 Hillside○ 21,440 .... B2
†08083 Hi-Nella 1,250 .... B4
07030 Hoboken 42,460 .... C2
07423 Ho Ho Kus 4,129 .... B1
07733 Holmdel○ 8,447 .... E3
07843 Hopatcong 15,531 .... D2
07844 Hope 310 .... D2
08525 Hopewell 2,001 .... D3
07731 Howell○ 25,065 .... E3
†07712 Interlaken 1,037 .... E3
07845 Ironia D2
07111 Irvington 61,493 .... B2
08830 Iselin E2
08732 Island Heights 1,575 .... E4
08527 Jackson○ 25,644 .... E3
08831 Jamesburg 4,114 .... E3
*07301 Jersey City⊙ 223,532 ...... B2
Jersey City‡ 556,972 .... B2
07734 Keansburg 10,613 .... E3
07032 Kearny 35,735 .... B2
08824 Kendall Park 7,419 .... D3
07033 Kenilworth 8,221 .... E2
07735 Keyport 7,413 .... E3
08528 Kingston D3
07405 Kinnelon 7,770 .... E2
07848 Lafayette 900 .... D1
07034 Lake Hiawatha E2
07849 Lake Hopatcong D2
08733 Lakehurst 2,908 .... E3
†07871 Lake Mohawk 8,498 .... D1
08701 Lakewood 22,863 .... E3
08530 Lambertville 4,044 .... D3
07850 Landing D2
08734 Lanoka Harbor E4
08021 Laurel Springs 2,249 .... B4
08879 Laurence Harbor 6,737 ..... E3
08735 Lavallette 2,072 .... E4
08045 Lawnside 3,042 .... B3
08648 Lawrenceville 19,724 .... D3
08833 Lebanon 820 .... D2
07852 Ledgewood D2
08327 Leesburg 700 .... D5
07737 Leonardo E3
07605 Leonia 8,027 .... C2
07938 Liberty Corner D2
07035 Lincoln Park 8,806 .... A1
07738 Lincroft E3
07036 Linden 37,836 .... A3
08021 Lindenwold 18,196 .... B4
08221 Linwood 6,144 .... D5
07424 Little Falls○ 11,496 .... B2
07643 Little Ferry 9,399 .... B2
07739 Little Silver 5,548 .... F3
07039 Livingston○ 28,040 .... E2
07644 Lodi 23,956 .... B2
07740 Long Branch 29,819 .... F3
Long Branch-Asbury Park‡
503,173 .... F3
08403 Longport 1,249 .... D5
07853 Long Valley 1,682 .... D2
08048 Lumberton 600 .... D4
07071 Lyndhurst○ 20,326 .... B2
07939 Lyons D2
07940 Madison 15,357 .... E2
08049 Magnolia 4,881 .... B3
07430 Mahwah○ 12,127 .... E1
08328 Malaga 950 .... C4
08050 Manahawkin 1,469 .... E4
08736 Manasquan 5,354 .... E3
08738 Mantoloking 433 .... E3
08051 Mantua○ 9,193 .... C4
08835 Manville 11,278 .... D2
08052 Maple Shade○ 20,525 .... B3
07040 Maplewood○ 22,950 .... E2
08402 Margate City 9,179 .... E5
07746 Marlboro○ 17,560 .... E3
08053 Marlton 9,411 .... D4
08223 Marmora 650 .... D5
08836 Martinsville D2
07747 Matawan 8,837 .... E3
08330 Mays Landing⊙ 2,054 .... D5
07607 Maywood 9,895 .... B2
07428 McAfee 800 .... D1
†08232 McKee City 950 .... D5
08055 Medford D4
08055 Medford Lakes 4,958 .... D4
07945 Mendham 4,899 .... D2
08837 Menlo Park E2
08619 Mercerville-Hamilton
Square 25,446 .... D3
08109 Merchantville 3,972 .... B3
08840 Metuchen 13,762 .... E2
08846 Middlesex 13,480 .... E2
07748 Middletown○ 62,574 .... E3
07432 Midland Park 7,381 .... B1
08848 Milford 1,368 .... C2
07041 Millburn○ 19,543 .... E2
07946 Millington 975 .... D2
†08876 Millstone 530 .... D2

08850 Milltown 7,136 .... E3
08332 Millville 24,815 .... C5
†07801 Mine Hill○ 3,325 .... D2
08342 Mizpah 900 .... D5
07750 Monmouth Beach 3,318 .... F3
08852 Monmouth Junction 2,579 . D3
07434 Monroe○ 15,858 .... E3
*07042 Montclair 38,321 .... B2
07645 Montvale 7,318 .... B1
07045 Montville○ 14,290 .... E2
†07070 Moonachie 2,706 .... B2
08057 Moorestown 13,695 .... B3
07950 Morris Plains 5,305 .... D2
07960 Morristown⊙ 16,614 .... D2
07046 Mountain Lakes 4,153 ...... E2
07092 Mountainside 7,118 .... E2
07856 Mount Arlington 4,251 ...... D2
08059 Mount Ephraim 4,863 .... B3
07970 Mount Freedom D2
08060 Mount Holly 10,818 .... D4
†08054 Mount Laurel○ 17,614 .... D4
†07828 Mount Olive○ 18,748 .... D2
08061 Mount Royal 900 .... C4
08062 Mullica Hill 1,050 .... C4
08087 Mystic Islands 4,929 .... E4
08063 National Park 3,552 .... B3
07752 Navesink E3
07753 Neptune○ 28,366 .... E3
07753 Neptune City 5,276 .... E3
07857 Netcong 3,557 .... D2
*07101 Newark⊙ 329,248 .... B2
Newark‡ 1,965,304 .... B2
*08901 New Brunswick⊙ 41,442 .. E3
New Brunswick-Perth
Amboy-Sayreville‡
595,893 .... E3
08533 New Egypt 2,111 .... E3
08344 Newfield 1,563 .... D4
07435 Newfoundland 900 .... D1
08224 New Gretna 800 .... E4
07646 New Milford 16,876 .... B1
07974 New Providence 12,426 ..... E2
07860 Newton⊙ 7,748 .... D1
08346 Newtonville 950 .... D4
07976 New Vernon D2
07032 North Arlington 16,587 ...... B2
07047 North Bergen○ 47,019 .... B2
08876 North Branch 610 .... D2
08902 North Brunswick○ 22,220 .. D3
†07006 North Caldwell 5,832 .... B2
08204 North Cape May 4,029 .... C6
08225 Northfield 7,795 .... D5
07508 North Haledon 8,177 .... B1
07060 North Plainfield 19,108 ...... E2
07647 Northvale 5,046 .... F1
08260 North Wildwood 4,714 .... D6
07648 Norwood 4,413 .... C1
07110 Nutley 28,998 .... B2
07755 Oakhurst E3
07436 Oakland 13,443 .... B1
08107 Oaklyn 4,223 .... B3
08226 Ocean City 13,949 .... D5
08740 Ocean Gate 1,385 .... E4
07756 Ocean Grove F3
07757 Oceanport 5,888 .... F3
07439 Ogdensburg 2,737 .... D1
08857 Old Bridge 21,815 .... E3
07675 Old Tappan 4,168 .... C1
07649 Oradell 8,658 .... B1
*07050 Orange 31,136 .... B2
08723 Osbornsville E3
07863 Oxford 1,587 .... C2
07470 Packanack Lake B1
07650 Palisades Park 13,732 .... C2
08065 Palmyra 7,085 .... B3
07652 Paramus 26,474 .... B1
07656 Park Ridge 8,515 .... B1
07054 Parsippany-Troy
Hills○ 49,868 .... E2
07055 Passaic 52,463 .... E2
*07501 Paterson⊙ 137,970 .... B2
Paterson-Clifton-Passaic‡
447,585 .... B2
08066 Paulsboro 6,944 .... C4
07977 Peapack-Gladstone 2,038 .. D2
08067 Pedricktown C4
08068 Pemberton 1,198 .... D4
08534 Pennington 2,109 .... D3
08110 Pennsauken○ 33,775 .... B3
08069 Penns Grove 5,760 .... C4
08070 Pennsville 12,467 .... C4
07440 Pequannock○ 13,776 .... B1
*08861 Perth Amboy 38,951 .... E2
08865 Phillipsburg 16,647 .... C2
08741 Pine Beach 1,796 .... E4
07058 Pine Brook E2
08021 Pine Hill 8,684 .... D4
08854 Piscataway○ 42,223 .... D2
08071 Pitman 9,744 .... C4
*07060 Plainfield 45,555 .... E2
08536 Plainsboro D3
08232 Pleasantville 13,435 .... D5
08742 Point Pleasant 17,747 .... E3
08742 Point Pleasant Beach
5,415 .... E3
08240 Pomona 2,358 .... D5
07442 Pompton Lakes 10,660 .... A1
07444 Pompton Plains B1
07758 Port Monmouth E3
†07850 Port Morris 616 .... D2
07865 Port Murray 250 .... D2
08349 Port Norris 1,730 .... C5
08241 Port Republic 837 .... D4
08540 Princeton 12,035 .... D3
08550 Princeton Junction 2,419 .... D3
†07885 Prospect Park 5,142 .... B1
08072 Quinton 750 .... C4
*07065 Rahway 26,723 .... E2
†08054 Ramblewood 6,475 .... D4
07446 Ramsey 12,899 .... B1
†07801 Randolph○ 17,828 .... D2
08869 Raritan 6,128 .... D2
07701 Red Bank 12,031 .... E3
07657 Ridgefield 10,294 .... B2
07660 Ridgefield Park 12,738 .... B2
*07450 Ridgewood 25,208 .... B1
08551 Ringoes 682 .... D3

07456 Ringwood 12,625 .... E1
08242 Rio Grande 2,016 .... D5
07457 Riverdale 2,530 .... A1
07661 River Edge 11,111 .... B1
08075 Riverside○ 7,941 .... B3
08077 Riverton 3,068 .... B3
07675 River Vale○ 9,489 .... B1
07662 Rochelle Park○ 5,603 .... B2
07866 Rockaway 6,852 .... D2
07647 Rockleigh 192 .... C1
08553 Rocky Hill 717 .... D3
08554 Roebling-Florence 7,677 ..... D3
08555 Roosevelt 835 .... E3
07068 Roseland 5,330 .... A2
07203 Roselle 20,641 .... B2
07204 Roselle Park 13,377 .... A2
08352 Rosenhayn 950 .... C5
†07876 Roxbury○ 18,878 .... D2
07760 Rumson 7,623 .... F3
08078 Runnemede 9,461 .... B3
*07070 Rutherford 19,068 .... B2
07662 Saddle Brook○ 14,084 .... B1
07458 Saddle River 2,763 .... B1
08079 Salem⊙ 6,959 .... C4
08872 Sayreville 29,969 .... E3
07076 Scotch Plains○ 20,774 .... E2
07760 Sea Bright 1,812 .... F3
08302 Seabrook 1,411 .... C5
08750 Sea Girt 2,650 .... E3
08243 Sea Isle City 2,644 .... D5
08751 Seaside Heights 1,802 .... E4
08752 Seaside Park 1,795 .... E4
07094 Secaucus 13,719 .... B2
07077 Sewaren E2
08080 Sewell C4
08353 Shiloh 604 .... C5
08008 Ship Bottom 1,427 .... E4
07078 Short Hills E2
07701 Shrewsbury 2,962 .... E3
08081 Sicklerville D4
08558 Skillman D3
08201 Smithville 70 .... E5
08083 Somerdale 5,900 .... B4
08244 Somers Point 10,330 .... D5
08876 Somerville⊙ 11,973 .... D2
08879 South Amboy 8,322 .... E3
†07719 South Belmar 1,566 .... E3
08880 South Bound Brook 4,331 ...... E2
†08852 South Brunswick○ 17,127 .... E3
07079 South Orange○ 15,864 .... A2
07080 South Plainfield 20,521 .... E2
08882 South River 14,361 .... E3
08753 South Toms River 3,954 .... E4
07871 Sparta○ 13,333 .... D1
08884 Spotswood 7,840 .... E3
07081 Springfield○ 13,955 .... E2
07762 Spring Lake 4,215 .... F3
†07762 Spring Lake Heights 5,424 ...... E3
07874 Stanhope 3,638 .... D2
08886 Stewartsville 950 .... C2
07980 Stirling E2
07460 Stockholm D1
08559 Stockton 643 .... D3
08247 Stone Harbor 1,187 .... D5
08084 Stratford 8,005 .... B4
†07747 Strathmore E3
07876 Succasunna 10,931 .... D2
07901 Summit 21,071 .... E2
08008 Surf City 1,571 .... E4
07461 Sussex 2,418 .... D1
08085 Swedesboro 2,031 .... C4
07878 Tabor E2
07666 Teaneck○ 39,007 .... B2
07670 Tenafly 13,552 .... C1
07608 Teterboro 19 .... B2
08086 Thorofare B4
08887 Three Bridges 750 .... D2
07724 Tinton Falls 7,740 .... E3
08753 Toms River⊙ 7,465 .... E4
07512 Totowa 11,448 .... B1
07082 Towaco E2
*08601 Trenton (cap.)⊙ 92,124 .... D3
Trenton‡ 307,863 .... D3
08087 Tuckerton 2,472 .... E4
07083 Union○ 50,184 .... A2
07735 Union Beach 6,354 .... E3
07087 Union City 55,593 .... C2
†07421 Upper Greenwood
Lake 2,734 .... E1
†07458 Upper Saddle River 7,958 .... B1
08406 Ventnor City 11,704 .... E5
07462 Vernon 800 .... E1
07044 Verona 14,166 .... B2
08251 Villas 5,909 .... D5
08088 Vincentown 900 .... D4
08360 Vineland 53,753 .... C5
Vineland-Millville-Bridgeton‡
132,866 .... C5
†08043 Voorhees○ 12,919 .... B3
07463 Waldwick 10,802 .... B1
07719 Wall○ 18,952 .... E3
07057 Wallington 10,741 .... B2
†07712 Wanamassa E3
07465 Wanaque 10,025 .... B1
08758 Waretown 1,175 .... E4
†07060 Warren○ 9,805 .... D2
07882 Washington 6,429 .... D2
07060 Watchung 5,290 .... E2
07470 Wayne○ 46,474 .... A1
07087 Weehawken○ 13,168 .... C2
08090 Wenonah 2,303 .... C4
07006 West Caldwell 11,407 .... A2
†08204 West Cape May 1,091 .... D6
08092 West Creek 827 .... E4
†08086 West Deptford○ 18,002 .... B3
*07090 Westfield 30,447 .... E2
07764 West Long Branch 7,380 .... F3
07480 West Milford 950 .... E1
08108 Westmont 15,875 .... B3
07093 West New York 39,194 .... C2
07052 West Orange 39,510 .... A2
07424 West Paterson 11,293 .... B2
08628 West Trenton D3
08093 Westville 4,786 .... B3
†08260 West Wildwood 360 .... D6
07675 Westwood 10,714 .... B1
07885 Wharton 5,485 .... D2

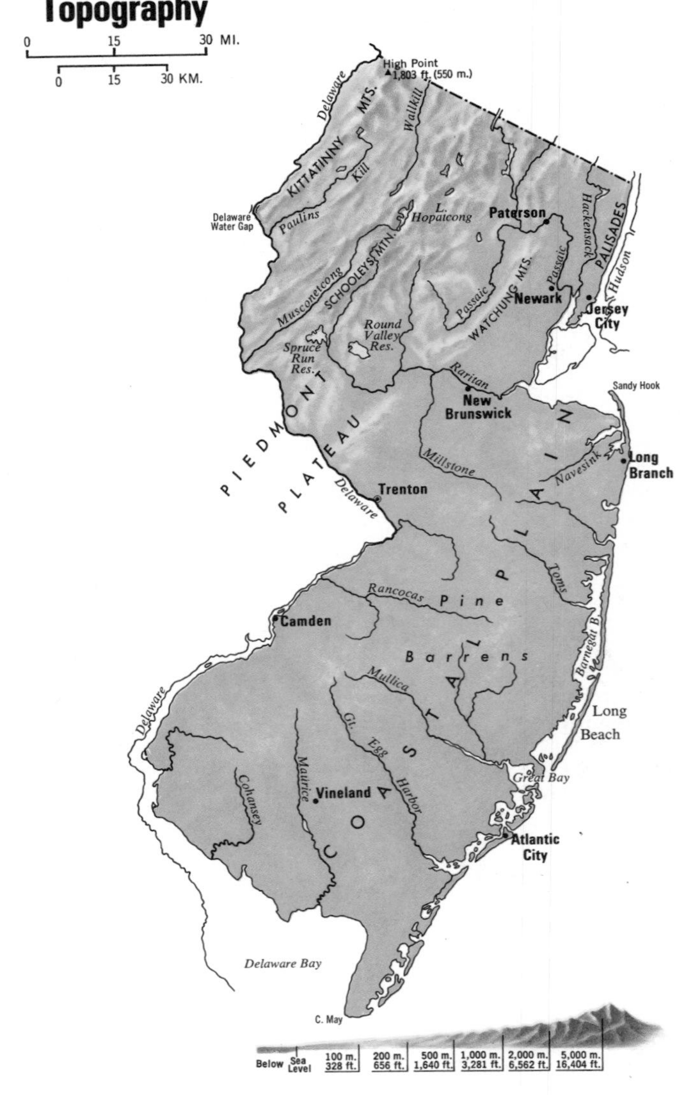

07981 Whippany E2
08889 White House Station D2
†07866 White Meadow Lake 8,429 D2
08252 Whitesboro 1,583 .... D5
07765 Wickatunk 950 .... E3
08260 Wildwood 4,913 .... D6
08260 Wildwood Crest 4,149 .... D6
08094 Williamstown 5,768 .... D4
08046 Willingboro○ 39,912 .... D3
†07036 Winfield○ 1,785 .... B2
08270 Woodbine 2,809 .... D5
07095 Woodbridge○ 90,074 .... E2
08096 Woodbury⊙ 10,353 .... B4
08097 Woodbury Heights 3,460 .... B4
07675 Woodcliff Lake 5,644 .... B1
†08107 Wood-Lynne 2,578 .... B3
†07885 Woodport D2
07075 Wood-Ridge 7,929 .... B2
08098 Woodstown 3,250 .... C4
08562 Wrightstown 3,031 .... D3
07481 Wyckoff○ 15,500 .... B1
08620 Yardville 9,414 .... D3

OTHER FEATURES

Absecon (inlet) E5
Alloways (creek) C4
Arthur Kill (str.) B3
Atlantic Highlands (ridge) E3
Barnegat (bay) E4
Batsto (riv.) D4
Bayonne Military Ocean Terminal .. B2
Beach Haven (inlet) E4
Beaver (brook) D2
Ben Davis (pt.) C5
Big Flat (brook) D1
Big Timber (creek) C4
Boonton (res.) E2
Brigantine (inlet) E5
Budd (lake) D2
Canistear (res.) E1
Cedar (creek) E4
Clinton (res.) E1
Cohansey (riv.) C5
Cold Spring (inlet) D6
Cooper (riv.) B3
Corson (inlet) D5
Crosswicks (creek) D3
Culvers (lake) D1
Delaware (bay) C5
Delaware (riv.) D3
Delaware Water Gap Nat'l Rec.
Area C1
Earle Naval Weapons Sta. E3
Echo (lake) E1
Edison Nat'l Hist. Site A2
Egg Island (pt.) C5
Fort Dix 14,297 .... D3
Fort Hancock F3
Fort Monmouth E3
Gateway Nat'l Rec. Area E2
Great (bay) E4
Great Egg Harbor (inlet) E5
Greenwood (lake) E1
Hackensack (riv.) C1
Hereford (inlet) D5
High Point (mt.) D1
Hopatcong (lake) D2
Hudson (riv.) C1
Island (beach) E4
Kill Van Kull (str.) B2
Kittatinny (mts.) D1
Lakehurst Naval Air Engineering
Center E3
Lamington (riv.) D2
Landing (creek) D4
Little Egg (harb.) E4
Lockatong (creek) C3
Long (beach) E4
Long Beach (isl.) E4
Lower New York (bay) E2
Manasquan (riv.) E3
Manumuskin (riv.) D5
Maurice (riv.) C4
May (cape) C6
McGuire A.F.B. 7,853 .... D3
Metedeconk (riv.) E3
Mill (creek) E4
Millstone (riv.) D3
Mohawk (lake) D1
Morristown Nat'l Hist. Park D2
Mullica (riv.) D4
Musconetcong (riv.) C2
Navesink (riv.) E3
Newark (bay) B2
Oak Ridge (res.) D1
Oldmans (creek) C4
Oradell (res.) B1
Oswego (riv.) E4
Owassa (lake) D1
Palisades C1
Passaic (riv.) E2
Paulins Kill (riv.) D1
Pennsauken (creek) B3
Pequest (riv.) D2
Picatinny Arsenal D2
Pohatcong (creek) C2
Pompton (lake) B1
Raccoon (creek) C4
Ramapo (riv.) E1
Rancocas (creek) D3
Raritan (bay) E3
Raritan (riv.) D2
Ridgeway Branch, Toms (riv.) .. E3
Round Valley (res.) D2
Saddle (riv.) B1
Salem (riv.) C4
Sandy Hook (spit) F3
Shoal Branch, Wading (riv.) D4
Spruce Run (res.) D2
Statue of Liberty Nat'l Mon. B2
Stony (brook) D3
Stow (creek) C5
Swartswood (lake) D1
Tappan (lake) C1
The Narrows (str.) E2
Toms (riv.) E3
Townsend (inlet) D5
Tuckahoe (riv.) D5
Union (lake) C5
Upper New York (bay) B2
Wading (riv.) D4
Wallkill (riv.) D1
Wanaque (res.) E1
Wawayanda (lake) E1

⊙County seat.
‡Population of metropolitan area.
○Population of town or township.
† Zip of nearest p.o. * Multiple zips.

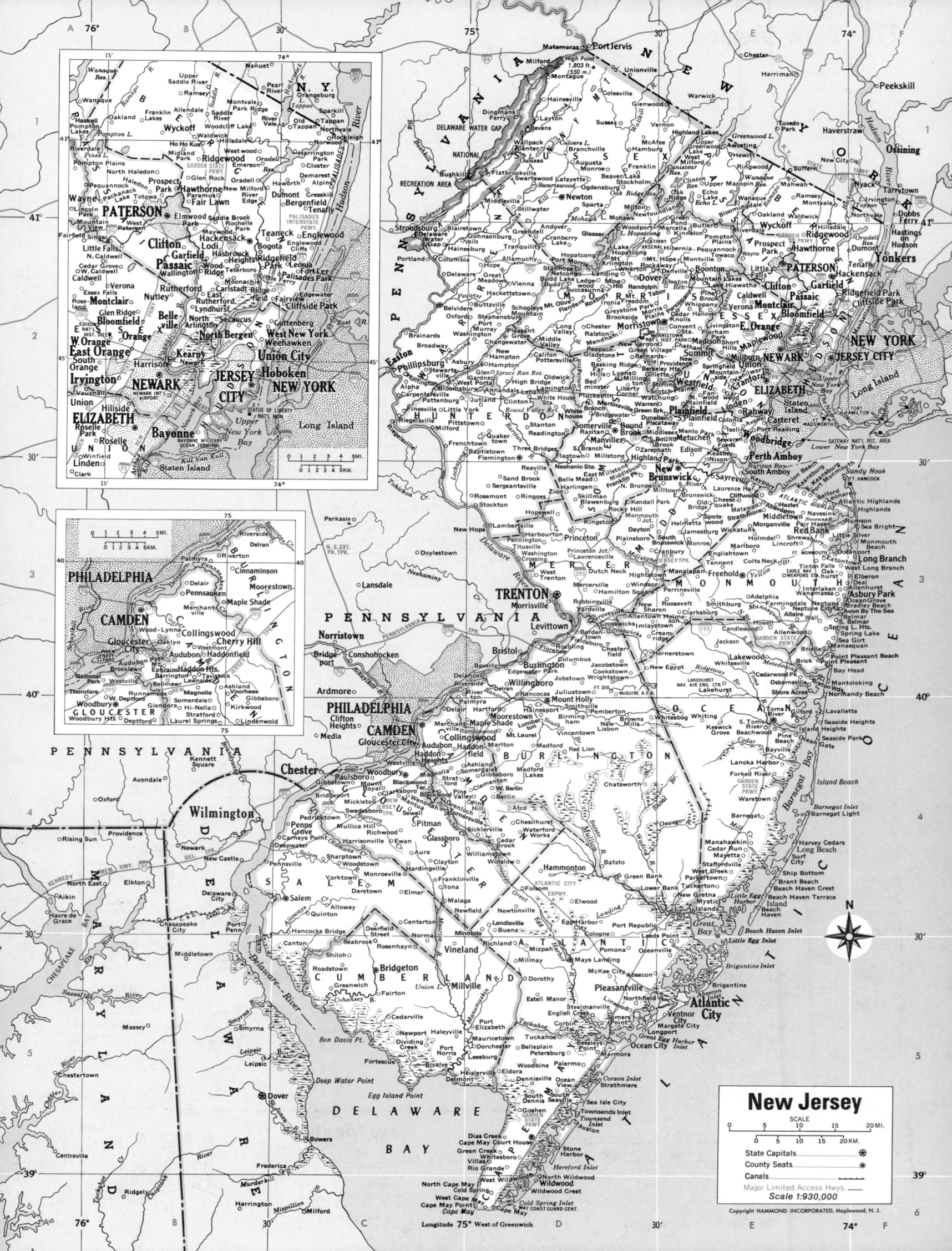
New Jersey
SCALE
0 5 10 15 20 MI.
0 5 10 15 20 KM.
State Capitals
County Seats
Canals
Major Limited Access Hwys.
Scale 1:930,000
Copyright HAMMOND INCORPORATED, Maplewood, N. J.
Longitude 75° West of Greenwich
PENNSYLVANIA
NEW YORK
DELAWARE
MARYLAND
ATLANTIC OCEAN
DELAWARE BAY
TRENTON
NEWARK
JERSEY CITY
PATERSON
ELIZABETH
CAMDEN
PHILADELPHIA
Atlantic City

COUNTIES

Bernalillo 419,700 .... C4
Catron 2,720 .... A4
Chaves 51,103 .... E5
Cibola B3
Colfax 13,667 .... E2
Curry 42,019 .... F4
De Baca 2,454 .... E4
Dona Ana 96,340 .... C6
Eddy 47,855 .... E6
Grant 26,204 .... A5
Guadalupe 4,496 .... E4
Harding 1,090 .... F3
Hidalgo 6,049 .... A7
Lea 55,993 .... F6
Lincoln 10,997 .... D5
Los Alamos 17,599 .... C3
Luna 15,585 .... B6
McKinley 56,449 .... A3
Mora 4,205 .... E3
Otero 44,665 .... D6
Quay 10,577 .... F3
Rio Arriba 29,282 .... B2
Roosevelt 15,695 .... F4
Sandoval 34,799 .... C3
San Juan 81,433 .... A2
San Miguel 22,751 .... D3
Santa Fe 75,360 .... C3
Sierra 8,454 .... B5
Socorro 12,566 .... C5
Taos 19,456 .... D2
Torrance 7,491 .... D4
Union 4,725 .... F2
Valencia 61,115 .... C4

CITIES and TOWNS

Zip *Name/Pop.* *Key*

87510 Abiquiu 500 .... C2
†87034 Acoma 150 .... B4
†87034 Acomita (Pueblo of Acoma) 975 .... B3
88310 Alamogordo⊙ 24,024 .... C6
*87101 Albuquerque⊙ 331,767 .... C3
Albuquerque‡ 454,499 .... C3
87511 Alcalde 975 .... C2
87001 Algodones 195 .... C3
88312 Alto 285 .... D5
87512 Amalia 200 .... D2
88021 Anthony 3,285 .... C6
87711 Anton Chico 400 .... D3
87930 Arrey 367 .... B6
87513 Arroyo Hondo 400 .... D2
87514 Arroyo Seco 500 .... D2
88210 Artesia 10,385 .... E6
87410 Aztec⊙ 5,512 .... B2
88023 Bayard 3,036 .... A6
87002 Belen 5,617 .... C4
88314 Bent 294 .... D5
88024 Berino 600 .... C6
87004 Bernalillo⊙ 3,012 .... C3
87412 Blanco 200 .... B2
87413 Bloomfield 4,881 .... A2
87005 Bluewater 300 .... A3
87006 Bosque (Bosque Farms) 3,353 .... C4
87712 Buena Vista 178 .... D3
87515 Canjilon 380 .... C2
87516 Canones 300 .... C2
88316 Capitan 762 .... D5
88414 Capulin 100 .... F2
88220 Carlsbad⊙ 25,496 .... E6
88301 Carrizozo⊙ 1,222 .... D5
87007 Casa Blanca 560 .... B4
88113 Causey 81 .... F5
87518 Cebolla 100 .... C2
87008 Cedar Crest 600 .... C3
†87410 Cedar Hill 145 .... B2
88026 Central 1,968 .... A6
87010 Cerrillos 500 .... D3
87519 Cerro 400 .... D2
87713 Chacon 310 .... D2
87520 Chama 1,090 .... C2
88027 Chamberino 700 .... C6
87521 Chamisal 642 .... D2
87522 Chimayo 1,993 .... D3
87714 Cimarron 888 .... E2
88415 Clayton⊙ 2,968 .... F2
87715 Cleveland 450 .... D2
88028 Cliff 600 .... A6
88317 Cloudcroft 521 .... D6
88101 Clovis⊙ 31,194 .... F4
†87041 Cochiti 983 .... C3
88029 Columbus 414 .... B7
88416 Conchas Dam 240 .... E3
87523 Cordova 750 .... D2
88318 Corona 236 .... D4
87048 Corrales 2,791 .... C3
87524 Costilla 400 .... D2
87313 Crownpoint 1,134 .... A3
†86504 Crystal 200 .... A2
87013 Cuba 609 .... B2
87014 Cubero 300 .... B3
87821 Datil 150 .... B4
88030 Deming⊙ 9,964 .... B6
87933 Derry 175 .... B6
88418 Des Moines 178 .... F2
88230 Dexter 882 .... E5
87527 Dixon 800 .... D2
88032 Dona Ana 800 .... C6

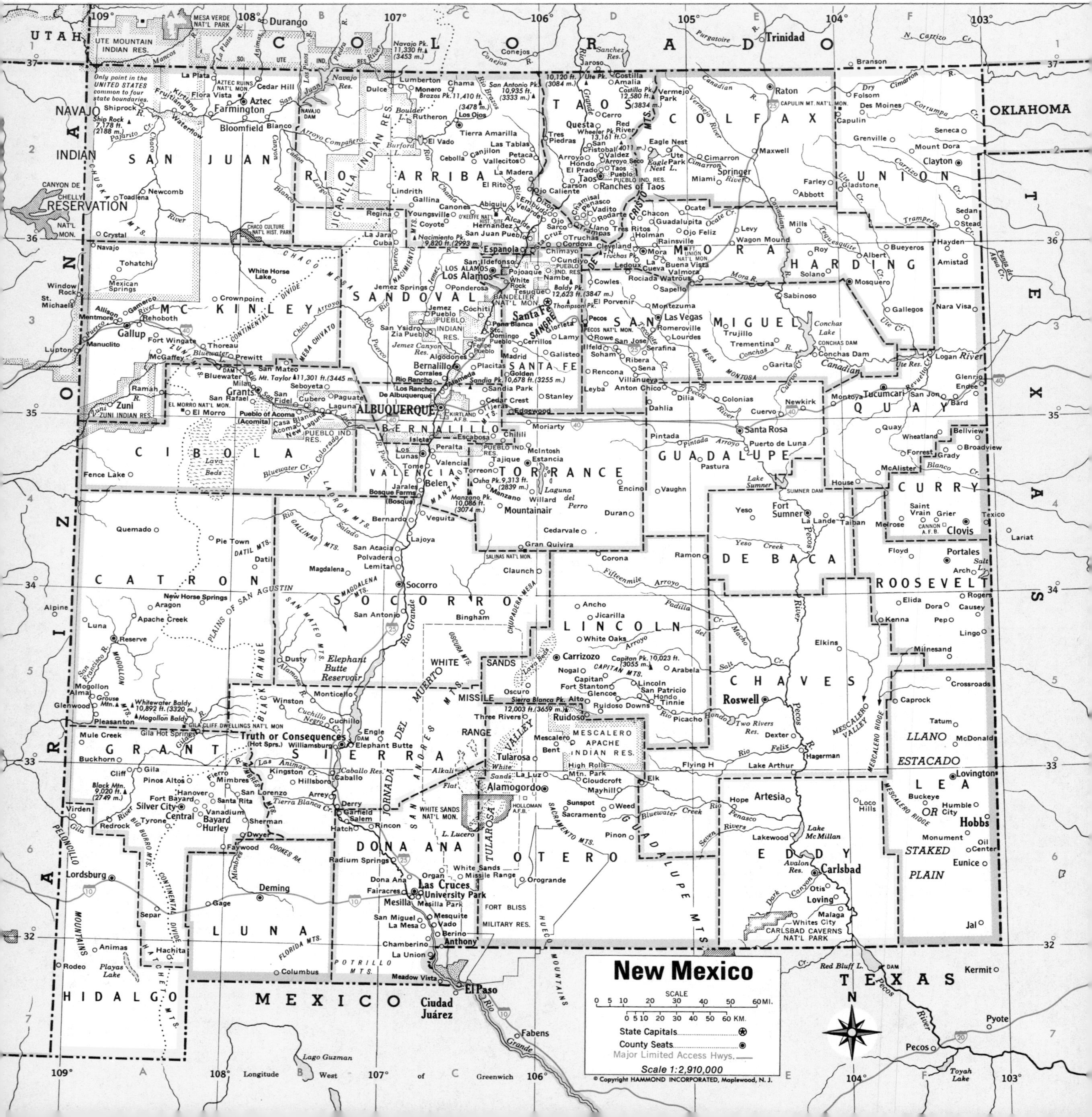

88115 Dora 168 F5
87528 Dulce 1,648 B2
87718 Eagle Nest 202 D2
88116 Elida 202 F5
87529 El Prado 200 D2
87530 El Rito 475 C2
87531 Embudo 400 C2
88321 Encino 155 D4
87532 Espanola 6,803 C3
87016 Estancia⊙ 830 D4
87532 Eunice 2,970 F6
88033 Fairacres 700 C6
87401 Farmington 31,222 A2
†88041 Fierro 200 A6
87415 Flora Vista 500 A2
88118 Floyd 146 F4
88419 Folsom 73 F2
88036 Fort Bayard 400 A6
88323 Fort Stanton 80 D5
88119 Fort Sumner⊙ 1,421 E4
87316 Fort Wingate 800 A3
87416 Fruitland 800 A2
†87540 Galisteo 125 D3
87017 Gallina 420 C2
87301 Gallup⊙ 18,167 A3
87317 Gamerco 800 A3
87936 Garfield 600 B6
88038 Gila 350 A6
88324 Glencoe 125 D5
88039 Glenwood 220 A5
87535 Glorieta 300 D3
88120 Grady 122 F4
87020 Grants 11,439 B3
88424 Grenville 39 F2
87722 Guadalupita 300 D2
88232 Hagerman 936 E5
88041 Hanover 300 A6
87937 Hatch 1,028 B6
87537 Hernandez 500 C2
88325 High Rolls-Mountain Park 555 D5
88042 Hillsboro 175 B6
88240 Hobbs 29,153 F6
87723 Holman 400 D2
88336 Hondo 425 D5
88250 Hope 111 E6
87901 Hot Springs (Truth or Consequences)⊙ 5,219 B5
88121 House 117 F4
88043 Hurley 1,616 A6
87022 Isleta 1,246 C4
88252 Jal 2,675 F6
87023 Jarales 700 C4
87024 Jemez Pueblo 1,503 C3
87025 Jemez Springs 316 C3
87417 Kirtland 2,358 A2
87026 Laguna 900 B3
87027 La Jara 210 B2
88253 Lake Arthur 327 E5
88337 La Luz 1,194 C6
87539 La Madera 200 C2
88044 La Mesa 900 C6
87418 La Plata 150 A2
88001 Las Cruces⊙ 45,086 C6
Las Cruces‡ 96,340 C6
87701 Las Vegas⊙ 14,322 D3
87725 Ledoux 300 D3
87823 Lemitar 800 B4
88338 Lincoln 100 D5
87543 Llano 325 D2
88255 Loco Hills 375 F6
88426 Logan 735 F3
88045 Lordsburg⊙ 3,195 A6
87544 Los Alamos⊙ 11,039 C3
87031 Los Lunas⊙ 3,525 C4
†87101 Los Ranchos De Albuquerque 2,702 C3
88256 Loving 1,355 E6
88260 Lovington⊙ 9,727 F6
87547 Lumberton 175 C2
87824 Luna 200 A5
87825 Magdalena 1,022 B4
88263 Malaga 300 E6
87728 Maxwell 316 E2
88339 Mayhill 300 D6
†79901 Meadow Vista 3,377 C7
88124 Melrose 649 F4
87319 Mentmore 315 A3
88340 Mescalero 1,259 D5
88046 Mesilla 2,029 C6
88047 Mesilla Park C6
88048 Mesquite 500 C6
87320 Mexican Springs 150 A3
87729 Miami 112 E2
87021 Milan 3,747 B3
88049 Mimbres 300 B6
87731 Montezuma 250 D3
87939 Monticello 125 B5
88265 Monument 300 F6
87732 Mora⊙ D3
87035 Moriarty 1,276 D4
87733 Mosquero⊙ 197 F3
87036 Mountainair 1,170 C4
†87501 Nambe 1,017 D3
88430 Nara Visa 250 F3
87328 Navajo 920 A3
†87325 Newcomb 500 A2
87038 New Laguna 250 B4
88266 Oil Center 236 F6
87549 Ojo Caliente 600 D2
87735 Ojo Feliz 133 E2
87550 Ojo Sarco 380 D2
88052 Organ 300 C6
87040 Paguate 500 B3
87552 Pecos 885 D3
87041 Pena Blanca 700 C3
87553 Penasco 860 D2
87042 Peralta 400 C4
88343 Picacho 100 D5
88053 Pinos Altos 250 A6
87044 Ponderosa 300 C3
88130 Portales⊙ 9,940 F4
87045 Prewitt 300 B3
88432 Puerto de Luna 175 E4
87829 Quemado 450 A4
87556 Questa 1,202 D2
88054 Radium Springs 150 B6
87736 Rainsville 350 D2
87321 Ramah 574 A3
87557 Ranches of Taos 1,411 D2
87740 Raton⊙ 8,225 E2
87558 Red River 332 D2
87322 Rehoboth 200 A3
87830 Reserve⊙ 439 A5
87560 Ribera 84 D3
87940 Rincon 300 C6
87124 Rio Rancho 9,985 C3
87561 Rodarte 650 D2
88201 Roswell⊙ 39,676 E5
87562 Rowe 290 D3
87743 Roy 381 E3
88345 Ruidoso 4,260 D5
88346 Ruidoso Downs 949 D5
87941 Salem 400 B6
87831 San Acacia 286 B4
87832 San Antonio 359 B5
87564 San Cristobal 350 D2
87047 Sandia Park 450 C3
†87001 San Felipe Pueblo 1,465 C3
†87501 San Ildefonso 232 C3
88434 San Jon 341 F3
87565 San Jose 150 D3
87566 San Juan Pueblo 870 C2
88041 San Lorenzo 200 B6
87050 San Mateo 200 B3
88058 San Miguel 400 C6
88348 San Patricio 300 D5
87051 San Rafael 300 A3
87567 Santa Cruz 754 D2
87501 Santa Fe (cap.)⊙ 48,953 C3
†88041 Santa Rita 600 B6
88435 Santa Rosa⊙ 2,469 E4
87052 Santo Domingo Pueblo 2,082 C3
87053 San Ysidro 199 C3
87745 Sapello 600 D3
87055 Seboyeta 125 B3
87568 Sena 150 D3
87569 Serafina 225 D3
87420 Shiprock 7,237 A2
88061 Silver City⊙ 9,887 A6
87801 Socorro⊙ 7,173 C4
†87565 Soham 104 D3
87747 Springer 1,657 E2
87057 Tajique 145 C4
87571 Taos⊙ 3,369 D2
†87571 Taos Pueblo 900 D2
88267 Tatum 896 F5
87574 Tesuque 1,014 C3
88135 Texico 958 F4
87323 Thoreau 1,099 A3
87575 Tierra Amarilla⊙ 850 C2
87059 Tijeras 311 C3
87324 Toadlena 200 A2
87325 Tohatchi 1,011 A3
87060 Tome 500 C4
87577 Tres Piedras 200 D2
87578 Truchas 275 D2
†87701 Trujillo 148 E3
87901 Truth or Consequences⊙ 5,219 B5
88401 Tucumcari⊙ 6,765 F3
88352 Tularosa 2,536 C5
88003 University Park 4,353 C6
87579 Vadito 400 D2
88072 Vado 325 C6
87580 Valdez 300 D2
†87031 Valencia 500 C4
87581 Vallecitos 450 C2
88073 Vanadium 150 A6
88353 Vaughn 737 D4
87582 Velarde 950 C2
87583 Villanueva 500 D3
†88055 Virden 246 A6
87752 Wagon Mound 416 E2
87421 Waterflow 475 A2
87753 Watrous 175 D3
87544 White Rock 6,560 C3
88002 White Sands Missile Range 3,120 C6
87063 Willard 166 D4
87942 Williamsburg 433 B5
88136 Yeso 200 E4
87064 Youngsville 125 C2
†87053 Zia Pueblo 500 C3
87327 Zuni 5,551 A3

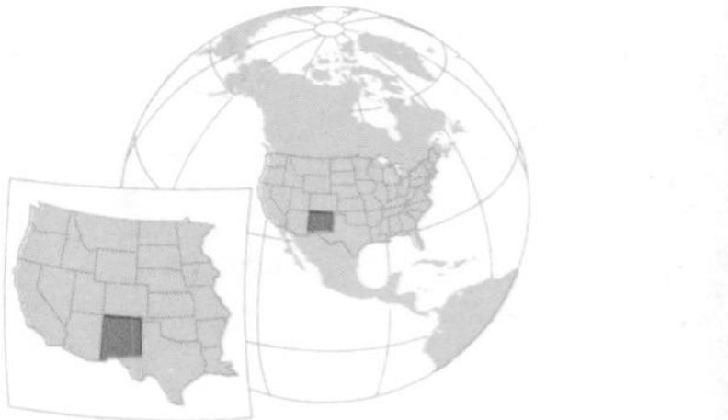

AREA 121,593 sq. mi. (314,926 sq. km.)
POPULATION 1,302,981
CAPITAL Santa Fe
LARGEST CITY Albuquerque
HIGHEST POINT Wheeler Pk. 13,161 ft. (4011 m.)
SETTLED IN 1605
ADMITTED TO UNION January 6, 1912
POPULAR NAME Land of Enchantment
STATE FLOWER Yucca
STATE BIRD Road Runner

OTHER FEATURES

Abiquiu (res.) C2
Alamosa (riv.) B5
Animas (riv.) B1
Avalon (res.) E6
Aztec Ruins Nat'l Mon. A2
Baldy (peak) D3
Bandelier Nat'l Mon. C3
Big Burro (mts.) A6
Black (mt.) A6
Black (range) B5
Blanco (creek) F4
Bluewater (creek) B4
Bluewater (creek) D6
Bluewater (lake) A3
Boulder (lake) C2
Brazos (peak) C2
Burford (lake) C2
Caballo (res.) B6
Canadian (riv.) F3
Cannon A.F.B. 3,798 F4
Canyon Blanco (creek) B2
Capitan (mts.) D5
Capitan (peak) D5
Capulin Mountain Nat'l Mon. E2
Carlsbad Caverns Nat'l Park E6
Carrizo (creek) F2
Chaco (mesa) B3
Chaco (riv.) A2
Chaco Culture Nat'l Hist. Park B2
Chico Arroyo (creek) B3
Chivato (mesa) B3
Chupadera (mesa) C5
Chuska (mts.) A2
Cimarron (riv.) E2
Colorado, Arroyo (riv.) B4
Compañero, Arroyo (creek) B2
Conchas (lake) E3
Conchas (riv.) E3
Cookes (range) B6
Corrumpa (creek) F2
Costilla (peak) D2
Cuchillo Negro (creek) B5
Cuervo (creek) E3
Dark Canyon (creek) E6
Datil (mts.) B4
Dry Cimarron (riv.) F2
Eagle Nest (lake) D2
Elephant Butte (res.) B5
El Morro Nat'l Mon. A3
El Rito (riv.) C2
Fifteenmile Arroyo (creek) D4
Florida (mts.) B7
Fort Bliss Mil. Res. C6
Fort Union Nat'l Mon. E3
Gallinas (mts.) B4
Gallinas (riv.) E3
Gila (riv.) A6
Gila Cliff Dwellings Nat'l Mon. A5
Grouse (mt.) A5
Guadalupe (mts.) D6
Hatchet (mts.) A7
Holloman A.F.B. 7,245 C6
Hueco (mts.) D6
Jemez (riv.) C3
Jemez Canyon (res.) C3
Jicarilla Ind. Res. B2
Jornada del Muerto (valley) C5
Kirtland A.F.B. C3
Ladron (mts.) B4
La Plata (riv.) A1
Largo, Cañon (creek) B2
Las Animas (creek) B5
Llano Estacado (Staked) (plain) F5
Lucero (lake) C6
Macho, Arroyo del (creek) D5
Magdalena (mts.) B4
Manzano (mts.) C4
Manzano (peak) C4
McMillan (lake) E6
Mescalero (ridge) F6
Mescalero (valley) F5
Mescalero Apache Ind. Res. D5
Mimbres (mts.) B6
Mimbres (riv.) B6
Mogollon (mts.) A5
Mogollon Baldy (peak) A5
Montosa (mesa) E3
Mora (riv.) E3
Nacimiento (mts.) C3
Nacimiento (peak) C2
Navajo (res.) B2
Navajo Ind. Res. A2
North Truchas (peak) D3
Ocate (creek) E2
O'Keeffe Nat'l Hist. Site C2
Oscura (mts.) C5
Osha (peak) C4
Padilla (creek) D5
Pajarito (creek) A2
Pecos (riv.) E5
Pecos Nat'l Mon. D3
Peloncillo (mts.) A6
Perro (mts.) D4
Pinos, Rio de los (riv.) B2
Pintada Arroyo (creek) E4
Playas (lake) A7
Potrillo (mts.) B7
Pueblo Ind. Res. B4
Pueblo Ind. Res. D3
Pueblo Ind. Res. C4
Pueblo Ind. Res. D2
Puerco (riv.) A3
Red Bluff (lake) E7
Revuelto (creek) F3
Rio Brazos (riv.) C2
Rio Chama (riv.) C2
Rio Felix (riv.) E5
Rio Grande (riv.) C5
Rio Hondo (riv.) E5
Rio Penasco (riv.) E6
Rio Puerco (riv.) C4
Rio Salado (riv.) B4
Rocky (mts.) C1
Sacramento (mts.) D6
Salinas Nat'l Mon. C4
Salt (creek) E5
Salt (lake) F4
San Agustin (plains) B5
San Andres (mts.) C6
San Antonio (peak) C2
Sandia (peak) C3
San Francisco (riv.) A5
Sangre de Cristo (mts.) D3
San Jose (riv.) B3
San Juan (riv.) B2
San Mateo (mts.) B5
Seven Rivers (riv.) E6
Ship Rock (peak) A2
Sierra Blanca (peak) C5
Staked (Llano Estacado) (plain) F5
Sumner (lake) E4
Taylor (mt.) B3
Tecolote (creek) D3
Tequesquite (creek) E2
Thompson (peak) D3
Tierra Blanca (creek) B6
Tramperos (creek) F2
Tularosa (valley) C6
Ute (creek) F3
Ute (peak) D2
Ute (res.) F3
Ute Mountain Ind. Res. A1
Vermejo (riv.) E2
Wheeler (peak) D2
White Sands (des.) C5
White Sands Missile Range C5
White Sands Nat'l Mon. C6
Whitewater Baldy (mt.) A5
Wingate Army Depot A3
Yeso (creek) E4
Zuni (mts.) A3
Zuni (riv.) A3
Zuni Ind. Res. A3

⊙County seat.
‡Population of metropolitan area.
† Zip of nearest p.o. * Multiple zips.

Topography

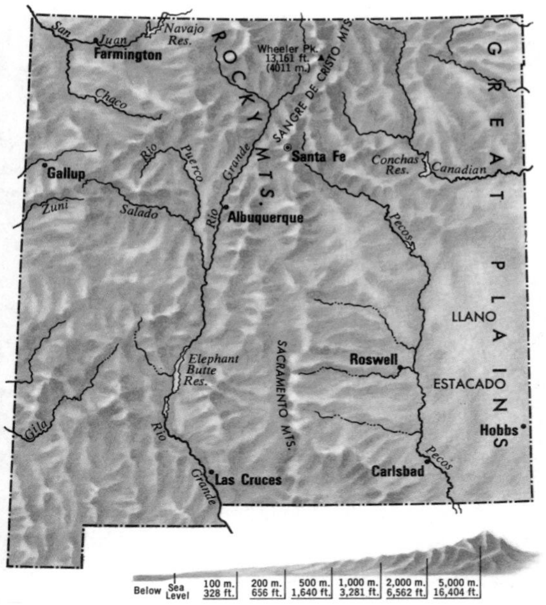

Agriculture, Industry and Resources

DOMINANT LAND USE

- Wheat, Grain Sorghums, Range Livestock
- General Farming, Livestock, Special Crops
- General Farming, Livestock, Cash Grain
- Dry Beans, General Farming
- Cotton, Forest Products
- Range Livestock
- Forests
- Nonagricultural Land

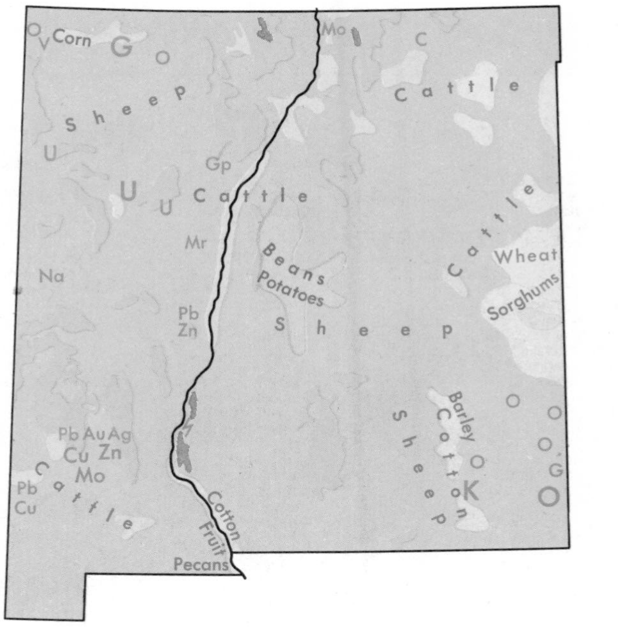

MAJOR MINERAL OCCURRENCES

Ag	Silver	Gp	Gypsum			U	Uranium		
Au	Gold	K	Potash			V	Vanadium	ϟ	Water Power
C	Coal	Mo	Molybdenum	O	Petroleum	Zn	Zinc		
Cu	Copper	Mr	Marble	Pb	Lead				
G	Natural Gas	Na	Salt						

New York

SCALE
0 5 10 20 30 40 MI.
0 5 10 20 30 40 KM.

State Capitals............⊛
County Seats.............⊙
Canals....................
Major Limited Access Hwys. ____

Scale 1:1,920,000

COUNTIES

Albany 285,909	M5
Allegany 51,742	D6
Bronx 1,168,972	N9
Broome 213,648	J6
Cattaraugus 85,697	C6
Cayuga 79,894	G4
Chautauqua 146,925	B6
Chemung 97,656	G6
Chenango 49,344	J6
Clinton 80,750	N1
Columbia 59,487	N6
Cortland 48,820	H5
Delaware 46,824	K6
Dutchess 245,055	N7
Erie 1,015,472	C5
Essex 36,176	N2
Franklin 44,929	M1
Fulton 55,153	M4
Genesee 59,400	D4
Greene 40,861	M6
Hamilton 5,034	L3
Herkimer 66,714	L4
Jefferson 88,151	J2
Kings 2,230,936	N9
Lewis 25,035	K3
Livingston 57,006	E5
Madison 65,150	J5
Monroe 702,238	E4
Montgomery 53,439	M5
Nassau 1,321,582	N9
New York 1,428,285	C4
Niagara 227,354	C4
Oneida 253,466	J4
Onondaga 463,920	H5
Ontario 88,909	F5

Orange 259,603	M8
Orleans 38,496	D4
Oswego 113,901	H4
Otsego 59,075	K5
Putnam 77,193	N8
Queens 1,891,325	N9
Rensselaer 151,966	O5
Richmond 352,121	M9
Rockland 259,530	M8
Saint Lawrence 114,254	K2
Saratoga 153,759	N4
Schenectady 149,946	M5
Schoharie 29,710	M5
Schuyler 17,686	G6
Seneca 33,733	G5
Steuben 99,217	F6
Suffolk 1,284,231	P9
Sullivan 65,155	L7
Tioga 49,812	H6
Tompkins 87,085	H6
Ulster 158,158	M7
Warren 54,854	O4
Washington 54,795	O4
Wayne 84,581	F4
Westchester 866,599	N8
Wyoming 39,895	D5
Yates 21,459	F5

CITIES and TOWNS

Zip	Name/Pop.	Key
13605	Adams 1,701	J3
14801	Addison 2,028	F6
14001	Akron 2,971	C4
†12201	Albany (cap.)⊙ 101,727	N5
	Albany-Schenectady-Troy‡	
	795,019	N5
14411	Albion⊙ 4,897	D4

14004	Alden 2,488	C5
13607	Alexandria Bay 1,265	J2
14802	Alfred 4,967	E6
14706	Allegany 2,078	C6
12009	Altamont 1,292	M5
11930	Amagansett 2,188	R9
11701	Amityville 9,076	O9
12010	Amsterdam 21,872	M5
14006	Angola 2,292	C5
14009	Arcade 2,052	D5
10502	Ardsley 4,183	O6
12603	Arlington 11,305	N7
12015	Athens 1,738	N6
11509	Atlantic Beach 1,775	P7
14011	Attica 2,659	D5
13021	Auburn⊙ 32,548	G5
13026	Aurora 926	G5
12018	Averill Park 1,337	O5
14414	Avon 3,006	E5
11702	Babylon 12,388	O9
13733	Bainbridge 1,603	J6
11510	Baldwin 31,630	R7
13027	Baldwinsville 6,446	H4
12020	Ballston Spa⊙ 4,711	N5
†12550	Balmville 2,919	M7
14020	Batavia⊙ 16,703	D5
14810	Bath⊙ 6,042	F6
11705	Bayport 9,282	O9
11706	Bay Shore 10,784	O9
11709	Bayville 7,034	R6
12508	Beacon 12,937	N7
11710	Bellmore 18,106	R7
11713	Bellport 2,809	P9
14813	Belmont⊙ 1,024	E6
11714	Bethpage 16,840	R7
14814	Big Flats 2,892	G6
*13901	Binghamton⊙ 55,860	J6
	Binghamton‡ 301,336	J6

13612	Black River 1,384	J3
14219	Blasdell 3,288	C5
14715	Bolivar 1,345	D6
13309	Boonville 2,344	K4
13613	Brasher	
	Falls-Winthrop 1,454	L1
11717	Brentwood 44,321	O9
11932	Bridgehampton 1,941	R9
†12524	Brinckerhoff 3,030	N7
12025	Broadalbin 1,415	M4
14420	Brockport 9,776	D4
14716	Brocton 1,416	B6
*10401	Bronx	
	(borough)⊙ 1,168,972	N9
10708	Bronxville 6,267	O7
*11201	Brooklyn	
	(borough)⊙ 2,230,936	N9
†11545	Brookville 3,290	R6
10511	Buchanan 2,041	N8
*14201	Buffalo⊙ 357,870	B5
	Buffalo‡ 1,242,573	B5
12413	Cairo 1,281	M6
14423	Caledonia 2,188	E5
12816	Cambridge 1,820	O4
13316	Camden 2,667	J4
13031	Camillus 1,298	H4
13317	Canajoharie 2,412	L5
14424	Canandaigua⊙ 10,419	F5
13032	Canastota 4,773	J4
14823	Caneseo 2,679	C5
13617	Canton⊙ 7,055	K1
10512	Carmel⊙ 27,948	N8
13619	Carthage 3,643	J3
12033	Castleton-on-Hudson 1,627	N5
12414	Catskill⊙ 4,718	M6
†14850	Cayuga Heights 3,170	H6

13035	Cazenovia 2,599	J5
11516	Cedarhurst 6,162	P7
14720	Celoron 1,405	B6
11720	Centereach 30,136	O9
11934	Center Moriches 5,703	P9
11722	Central Islip 19,734	O9
13036	Central Square 1,418	H4
10917	Central Valley 1,705	M8
12919	Champlain 1,410	N1
12037	Chatham 2,001	N6
14225	Cheektowaga 92,145	C5
10918	Chester 1,910	M8
13037	Chittenango 4,290	J4
14428	Churchville 1,399	E4
14031	Clarence 18,146	C5
13624	Clayton 1,816	H2
†12118	Clifton Park⊙ 23,989	N5
14432	Clifton Springs 2,039	F4
13323	Clinton 2,107	K4
14433	Clyde 2,491	G4
12043	Cobleskill 5,272	L5
12047	Cohoes 18,144	N5
10516	Cold Spring 2,161	N8
11724	Cold Spring Harbor 5,336	R6
†12201	Colonie 8,869	N5
11725	Commack 34,719	O9
13326	Cooperstown⊙ 2,342	L5
11726	Copiague 20,132	O9
12822	Corinth 2,702	N4
14830	Corning 12,953	F6
12518	Cornwall On Hudson 3,164	M8
13045	Cortland⊙ 20,138	H5
12051	Coxsackie 2,786	N6
10520	Croton-on-Hudson 6,889	N8
14727	Cuba 1,739	D6
11935	Cutchogue-New	
	Suffolk 2,788	P8
12929	Dannemora 3,770	N1

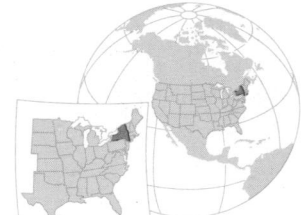

AREA 49,108 sq. mi. (127,190 sq. km.)
POPULATION 17,558,072
CAPITAL Albany
LARGEST CITY New York
HIGHEST POINT Mt. Marcy 5,344 ft. (1629 m.)
SETTLED IN 1614
ADMITTED TO UNION July 26, 1788
POPULAR NAME Empire State
STATE FLOWER Rose
STATE BIRD Bluebird

Topography

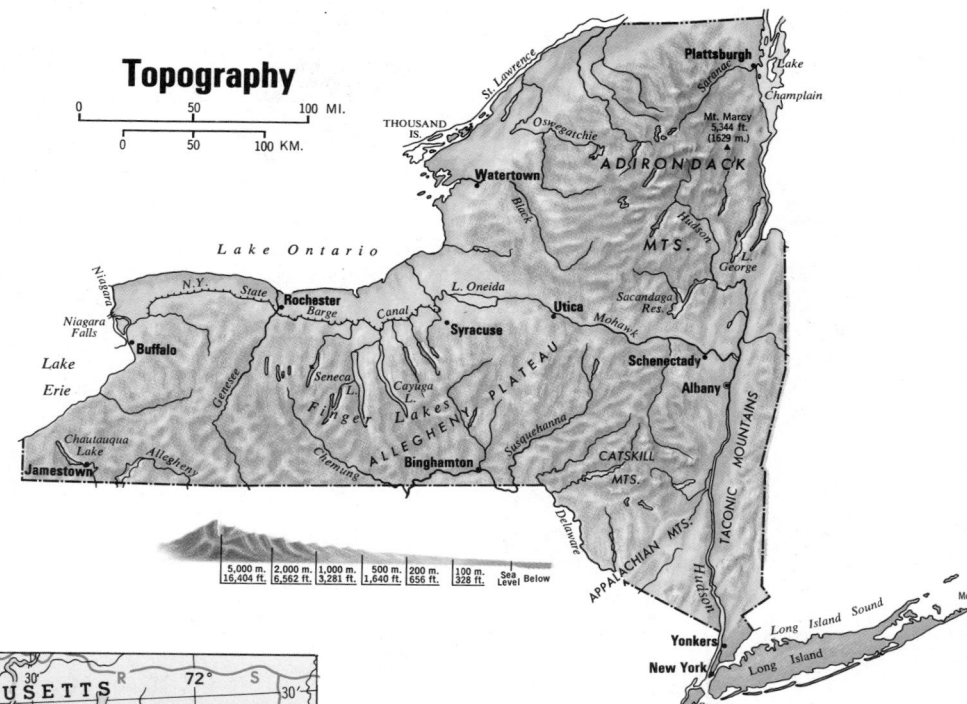

0   50   100 MI.
0   50   100 KM.

| 5,000 m. 16,404 ft. | 2,000 m. 6,562 ft. | 1,000 m. 3,281 ft. | 500 m. 1,640 ft. | 200 m. 656 ft. | 100 m. 328 ft. | Sea Level | Below |

© Copyright HAMMOND INCORPORATED, Maplewood, N.J.

14437 Dansville 4,979 .... E5	14456 Geneva 15,133 .... G5	
11729 Deer Park 30,394 .... O9	11542 Glen Cove 24,618 .... R6	
13753 Delhi⊙ 3,374 .... L6	12801 Glens Falls 15,897 .... N4	
12054 Delmar 8,423 .... N5	Glens Falls‡ 109,649 .... N4	
14043 Depew 19,819 .... C5	12078 Gloversville 17,836 .... M4	
13754 Deposit 1,897 .... K6	10526 Golden's Bridge 1,367 .... N8	
13214 DeWitt 9,024 .... H4	10924 Goshen⊙ 4,874 .... M8	
11746 Dix Hills 26,693 .... O9	13642 Gouverneur 4,285 .... K2	
10522 Dobbs Ferry 10,053 .... O6	14070 Gowanda 2,713 .... B6	
13329 Dolgeville 2,602 .... L4	12832 Granville 2,696 .... O4	
12522 Dover Plains 1,753 .... O7	*11020 Great Neck 9,168 .... P6	
14837 Dundee 1,556 .... F5	14616 Greece 16,177 .... E4	
14048 Dunkirk 15,310 .... B5	13778 Greene 1,747 .... J6	
14052 East Aurora 6,803 .... C5	12183 Green Island 2,696 .... N5	
10709 Eastchester 20,305 .... P6	11944 Greenport 2,273 .... P8	
11937 East Hampton 1,886 .... R9	12834 Greenwich 1,955 .... O4	
†11576 East Hills 7,160 .... R7	10925 Greenwood Lake 2,809 .... M8	
11554 East Meadow 39,317 .... R7	13073 Groton 2,313 .... H5	
11731 East Northport 20,187 .... O9	12835 Hadley-Lake Luzerne 1,988 N4	
14445 East Rochester 7,596 .... F4	12086 Hagaman 1,331 .... M5	
11518 East Rockaway 10,917 .... R7	14075 Hamburg 10,582 .... C5	
13057 East Syracuse 3,412 .... H4	13346 Hamilton 3,725 .... J5	
14057 Eden 3,000 .... C5	11946 Hampton Bays 7,256 .... R9	
14058 Elba 750 .... D4	13783 Hancock 1,526 .... K7	
12932 Elizabethtown⊙ 659 .... N2	10528 Harrison 23,046 .... P6	
12428 Ellenville 4,405 .... M7	10530 Hartsdale 10,216 .... P6	
14059 Elma 2,459 .... C5	10706 Hastings On Hudson 8,573 O6	
*14901 Elmira⊙ 35,327 .... G6	11787 Hauppauge 20,960 .... O9	
Elmira‡ 97,656 .... G6	10927 Haverstraw 8,800 .... M8	
14903 Elmira Heights 4,279 .... G6	10532 Hawthorne 5,010 .... O6	
11003 Elmont 27,592 .... P7	*11550 Hempstead 40,404 .... R7	
10523 Elmsford 3,361 .... O6	13350 Herkimer⊙ 8,383 .... L4	
11731 Elwood 11,847 .... O9	11557 Hewlett 6,986 .... P7	
13760 Endicott 14,457 .... H6	†11557 Hewlett Harbor 1,331 .... P7	
13760 Endwell 11,706 .... H6	11801 Hicksville 43,245 .... R7	
14450 Fairport 5,970 .... F4	12528 Highland 3,967 .... M7	
†12601 Fairview 5,582 .... N7	10928 Highland Falls 4,187 .... M8	
14733 Falconer 2,778 .... B6	10931 Hillburn 926 .... M8	
11735 Farmingdale 7,946 .... R7	†10977 Hillcrest 5,733 .... K8	
13066 Fayetteville 4,709 .... J4	14468 Hilton 4,151 .... E4	
†12801 Fernwood 3,640 .... N4	14080 Holland 1,347 .... C5	
12524 Fishkill 1,555 .... N7	14470 Holley 1,882 .... D4	
†11901 Flanders-Riverside 5,400 .... P9	13077 Homer 3,635 .... H5	
*11001 Floral Park 16,805 .... P7	14472 Honeoye Falls 2,410 .... F5	
10921 Florida 1,947 .... M8	12090 Hoosick Falls 3,609 .... O5	
12068 Fonda⊙ 1,006 .... M5	12533 Hopewell Junction 1,754 .... N7	
12937 Fort Covington⊙ 1,804 .... M1	14843 Hornell 10,234 .... E6	
12828 Fort Edward 3,561 .... O4	14845 Horseheads 7,348 .... G6	
13339 Fort Plain 2,555 .... L5	14744 Houghton 1,604 .... D6	
13340 Frankfort 2,995 .... K4	12534 Hudson⊙ 7,986 .... N6	
11010 Franklin Square 29,051 .... R7	12839 Hudson Falls⊙ 7,419 .... O4	
14737 Franklinville 1,887 .... D6	11743 Huntington 21,727 .... R6	
14063 Fredonia 11,126 .... B6	11746 Huntington Station 28,769 R6	
11520 Freeport 38,272 .... R7	12443 Hurley 4,892 .... M7	
14738 Frewsburg 1,908 .... B6	12538 Hyde Park 2,550 .... N6	
14739 Friendship 1,461 .... D6	13357 Ilion 9,450 .... K5	
13069 Fulton 13,312 .... H4	11696 Inwood 8,228 .... P7	
11530 Garden City 22,927 .... R7	14617 Irondequoit 57,648 .... E4	
14067 Gasport 1,339 .... C4	10533 Irvington 5,774 .... O6	
14454 Geneseo⊙ 6,746 .... E5	11558 Island Park 4,847 .... R7	

(continued on following page)

11751 Islip 13,438 .... O9
14850 Ithaca⊙ 28,732 .... G6
*11401 Jamaica⊙ N9
14701 Jamestown 35,775 .... B6
11753 Jericho 12,739 .... R6
13790 Johnson City 17,126 .... J6
12095 Johnstown⊙ 9,360 .... M4
13080 Jordan 1,371 .... H4
12944 Keeseville 2,025 .... O2
14271 Kenmore 18,474 .... C5
12446 Kerhonkson 1,646 .... M7
12106 Kinderhook 1,377 .... N6
11754 Kings Park 16,131 .... O9
11024 Kings Point 5,234 .... P6
12401 Kingston⊙ 24,481 .... M7
14218 Lackawanna 22,701 .... B5
10512 Lake Carmel 7,295 .... N8
†14006 Lake Erie Beach 4,625 .... B5
12845 Lake George⊙ 1,047 .... N4
12449 Lake Katrine 2,011 .... M7
12846 Lake Luzerne-Hadley 1,988 N4
12946 Lake Placid 2,490 .... N2
12108 Lake Pleasant⊙ 700 .... M4
11040 Lake Success 2,396 .... P7
14750 Lakewood 3,941 .... B6
14086 Lancaster 13,056 .... C5
14882 Lansing 3,039 .... H5
10538 Larchmont 6,308 .... P7
12110 Latham 11,182 .... N5
†11560 Lattingtown 1,749 .... R6
11559 Lawrence 6,175 .... P7
14482 Le Roy 4,900 .... E5
11756 Levittown 57,045 .... R7
14092 Lewiston 3,326 .... B4
12754 Liberty 4,293 .... L7
14485 Lima 2,025 .... E5
11757 Lindenhurst 26,919 .... O9
13365 Little Falls 6,156 .... L4
14755 Little Valley⊙ 1,203 .... C6
13088 Liverpool 2,849 .... H4
12758 Livingston Manor 1,436 .... L7
†11743 Lloyd Harbor 3,405 .... R6
14094 Lockport⊙ 24,844 .... C4
†11791 Locust Grove 9,670 .... R6
11561 Long Beach 34,073 .... R7
13367 Lowville⊙ 3,364 .... J3
11563 Lynbrook 20,424 .... P7
14489 Lyons⊙ 4,160 .... F4
14502 Macedon 1,400 .... F4
10541 Mahopac 7,681 .... N8
12953 Malone⊙ 7,668 .... M1
11565 Malverne 9,262 .... R7
10543 Mamaroneck 17,616 .... P7
14504 Manchester 1,698 .... F5
11030 Manhasset 8,485 .... P7
*10001 Manhattan (borough) 1,428,285 .... M9
13104 Manlius 5,241 .... J5
13108 Marcellus 1,870 .... H5
12542 Marlboro 2,275 .... M7
11758 Massapequa 24,454 .... R7
11762 Massapequa Park 19,779 .... R7
13662 Massena 12,851 .... L1
11950 Mastic Beach 8,318 .... P9
11952 Mattituck 3,923 .... P9
12543 Maybrook 2,007 .... M8
14757 Mayville⊙ 1,626 .... A6
12118 Mechanicville 5,500 .... N5
14103 Medina 6,392 .... D4
†13021 Melrose Park 2,171 .... G5
11746 Melville 8,139 .... O9
†12201 Menands 4,012 .... N5
11566 Merrick 24,478 .... R7
13114 Mexico 1,621 .... H4
12122 Middleburgh 1,358 .... M5
12550 Middle Hope 3,229 .... M7
14105 Middleport 1,995 .... C4
10940 Middletown 21,454 .... L8
†12020 Milton 2,063 .... N4
11501 Mineola⊙ 20,757 .... R7
13115 Minetto 1,629 .... H4
12956 Mineville-Witherbee 1,925 .... O2
13116 Minoa 3,640 .... H4
13407 Mohawk 2,956 .... L4
10950 Monroe 5,996 .... M8
10952 Monsey 12,380 .... J8
12549 Montgomery 2,316 .... M7
12701 Monticello⊙ 6,306 .... L7
14865 Montour Falls 1,791 .... G6
13118 Moravia 1,582 .... H5
12962 Morrisonville 1,721 .... N1
13408 Morrisville 2,707 .... J5
10549 Mount Kisco 8,025 .... N8
14510 Mount Morris 3,039 .... E5
*10550 Mount Vernon 66,713 .... O7
10954 Nanuet 12,578 .... K8
12123 Nassau 1,285 .... N5
Nassau-Suffolk‡ 2,605,813 R7
14513 Newark 10,017 .... G4
13411 New Berlin 1,392 .... K5
12550 Newburgh 23,438 .... M7
Newburgh-Middletown‡ 259,603 .... M7
10956 New City⊙ 35,859 .... K8
14108 Newfane 3,120 .... C4
13413 New Hartford 2,313 .... K4
11040 New Hyde Park 9,801 .... P7
12561 New Paltz 4,938 .... M7
*10801 New Rochelle 70,794 .... P7
†10901 New Square 1,750 .... K8
12550 New Windsor 7,812 .... N8
*10001 New York⊙ 7,071,639 .... M9
New York‡ 9,119,737 .... M9
13417 New York Mills 3,549 .... K4
*14301 Niagara Falls 71,384 .... C4
†12301 Niskayuna 5,223 .... N5
13667 Norfolk 1,599 .... K1
14110 North Boston 2,743 .... C5
14111 North Collins 1,496 .... C5
11768 Northport 7,651 .... O9
13212 North Syracuse 7,970 .... H4
10591 North Tarrytown 7,994 .... O6
14120 North Tonawanda 35,760 .... C4
12134 Northville 1,304 .... M4
13815 Norwich⊙ 8,082 .... J5
13668 Norwood 1,902 .... L1
10960 Nyack 6,428 .... K8

14125 Oakfield 1,791 .... D4
11572 Oceanside 33,639 .... R7
13669 Ogdensburg 12,375 .... K1
14126 Olcott 1,571 .... C4
14760 Olean 18,207 .... D6
13421 Oneida 10,810 .... J4
13820 Oneonta 14,933 .... K6
14127 Orchard Park 3,671 .... C5
13424 Oriskany 1,680 .... K4
10562 Ossining 20,196 .... N8
13126 Oswego⊙ 19,793 .... G4
14521 Ovid⊙ 666 .... G5
13827 Owego⊙ 4,364 .... H6
13830 Oxford 1,765 .... J6
11771 Oyster Bay 6,497 .... R6
14870 Painted Post 2,196 .... F6
14522 Palmyra 3,729 .... F4
11772 Patchogue 11,291 .... P9
12564 Pawling 1,996 .... N7
10965 Pearl River 15,893 .... K8
10566 Peekskill 18,236 .... N8
10803 Pelham 6,848 .... O7
†10803 Pelham Manor 6,130 .... O7
14527 Penn Yan⊙ 5,242 .... F5
14530 Perry 4,198 .... D5
12972 Peru 1,716 .... N1
14532 Phelps 2,004 .... F5
12565 Philmont 1,539 .... N6
13135 Phoenix 2,357 .... H4
10968 Piermont 2,269 .... K8
12567 Pine Plains 1,303 .... N7
14534 Pittsford 1,568 .... E4
11803 Plainview 28,037 .... R7
12901 Plattsburgh⊙ 21,057 .... O1
10570 Pleasantville 6,749 .... N8
13140 Port Byron 1,400 .... G4
10573 Port Chester 23,565 .... P7
†13901 Port Dickinson 1,974 .... J6
12466 Port Ewen 2,813 .... N7
12974 Port Henry 1,450 .... O2
11777 Port Jefferson 6,731 .... P9
12771 Port Jervis 8,699 .... L8
11050 Port Washington 14,521 .... R6
13676 Potsdam 10,635 .... K1
*12601 Poughkeepsie⊙ 29,757 .... N7
Poughkeepsie‡ 245,055 .... N7
14873 Prattsburg○ 1,657 .... F5
13142 Pulaski 2,415 .... H3
10579 Putnam Valley○ 8,994 .... N8
*11101 Queens (borough) 1,891,325 .... N9
14772 Randolph 1,398 .... C6
14131 Ransomville 1,401 .... C4
12143 Ravena 3,091 .... N6
12571 Red Hook 1,692 .... N7
†12601 Red Oaks Mill 5,236 .... N7
12144 Rensselaer 9,047 .... N5
12572 Rhinebeck 2,542 .... N7
13439 Richfield Springs 1,561 .... K5
*10301 Richmond (Staten Island) (borough) 352,121 .... M9
11901 Riverhead⊙ 6,339 .... P9
*14601 Rochester⊙ 241,741 .... E4
Rochester‡ 971,879 .... E4
*11570 Rockville Centre 25,412 .... R7
13440 Rome 43,826 .... J4
11575 Roosevelt 14,109 .... R7
11576 Roslyn 2,134 .... R6
12979 Rouses Point 2,266 .... O1
10580 Rye 15,083 .... P6
11963 Sag Harbor 2,581 .... R8
11780 Saint James 12,122 .... O9
13452 Saint Johnsville 1,974 .... L5
14779 Salamanca 6,890 .... C6
†13132 Sand Ridge 1,293 .... H4
†11050 Sands Point 2,742 .... P6
12983 Saranac Lake 5,578 .... M2
12866 Saratoga Springs 23,906 .... N4
12477 Saugerties 3,882 .... M6
13146 Savannah○ 1,905 .... G4
11782 Sayville 12,013 .... O9
10583 Scarsdale 17,650 .... P6
*12301 Schenectady⊙ 67,972 .... M5
12157 Schoharie⊙ 1,016 .... M5
12871 Schuylerville 1,256 .... N4
12302 Scotia 7,280 .... N5
14546 Scottsville 1,789 .... E4
11579 Sea Cliff 5,364 .... R6
11783 Seaford 16,117 .... R7
13148 Seneca Falls 7,466 .... G5
13460 Sherburne 1,561 .... K5
13461 Sherrill 2,830 .... J4
14548 Shortsville 1,669 .... F5
13838 Sidney 4,861 .... K6
14136 Silver Creek 3,088 .... B5
13152 Skaneateles 2,789 .... H5
†14201 Sloan 4,529 .... C5
10974 Sloatsburg 3,154 .... M8
11787 Smithtown 30,906 .... O9
14551 Sodus 1,790 .... G4
14555 Sodus Point 1,334 .... G4
13209 Solvay 7,140 .... H4
11968 Southampton 4,000 .... R9
12779 South Fallsburg 2,196 .... L7
†12801 South Glens Falls 3,714 .... N4
†10960 South Nyack 3,602 .... K8
11971 Southold 4,770 .... P8
†14901 Southport 8,329 .... G6
14559 Spencerport 3,424 .... E4
10977 Spring Valley 20,537 .... K8
14141 Springville 4,285 .... C5
*10301 Staten Island (borough) 352,121 .... M9
12170 Stillwater 1,572 .... N5
11790 Stony Brook 16,155 .... O9
10980 Stony Point 8,686 .... M8
12172 Stottville 1,387 .... N6
10901 Suffern 10,794 .... J8
11791 Syosset 9,818 .... R6
*13201 Syracuse⊙ 170,105 .... H4
Syracuse‡ 642,375 .... H4
10983 Tappan 8,267 .... K8
10591 Tarrytown 10,648 .... O6
†11020 Thomaston 2,684 .... P7
12883 Ticonderoga 2,938 .... N3
12486 Tillson 1,529 .... M7
14150 Tonawanda 18,693 .... B4

*12180 Troy⊙ 56,638 .... N5
14886 Trumansburg 1,722 .... G5
10707 Tuckahoe 6,076 .... O7
12986 Tupper Lake 4,478 .... M2
13849 Unadilla 1,367 .... K6
11553 Uniondale 20,016 .... R7
*13501 Utica⊙ 75,632 .... K4
Utica-Rome‡ 320,180 .... K4
12184 Valatie 1,492 .... N6
10989 Valley Cottage 8,214 .... K8
*11580 Valley Stream 35,769 .... P7
13850 Vestal○ 27,238 .... H6
14564 Victor 2,370 .... F5
†10901 Viola 5,340 .... J8
12186 Voorheesville 3,320 .... M5
12586 Walden 5,659 .... M7
12589 Wallkill 2,064 .... M7
13856 Walton 3,329 .... K6
13163 Wampsville⊙ 569 .... J4
11793 Wantagh 19,817 .... R7
12590 Wappingers Falls 5,110 .... N7
12885 Warrensburg 2,834 .... N3
14569 Warsaw⊙ 3,619 .... D5
10990 Warwick 4,320 .... M8
10992 Washingtonville 2,380 .... M8
12188 Waterford 2,405 .... N5
13165 Waterloo⊙ 5,303 .... G5
13601 Watertown⊙ 27,861 .... J3
13480 Waterville 1,672 .... K5
12189 Watervliet 11,354 .... N5
14891 Watkins Glen⊙ 2,440 .... G6
14892 Waverly 4,738 .... G7
14572 Wayland 1,846 .... E5
14580 Webster 5,499 .... F4
13166 Weedsport 1,952 .... G4
14895 Wellsville 5,769 .... E6
11590 Westbury 13,871 .... R7
†13619 West Carthage 1,824 .... J3
†14901 West Elmira 5,485 .... G6
14787 Westfield 3,446 .... A6
†12801 West Glens Falls 5,331 .... N4
11977 Westhampton 2,774 .... P9
11978 Westhampton Beach 1,629 P9
12491 West Hurley 2,382 .... M6
10994 West Nyack 8,553 .... K8
14788 Westons Mills 1,837 .... D6
10996 West Point 8,105 .... M8
11796 West Sayville 8,185 .... O9
14224 West Seneca 51,210 .... C5
12887 Whitehall 3,241 .... O3
*10601 White Plains⊙ 46,999 .... P6
13492 Whitesboro 4,460 .... K4
14588 Willard 1,339 .... G5
14589 Williamson 1,768 .... F4
14221 Williamsville 6,017 .... C5
11596 Williston Park 8,216 .... R7
13865 Windsor 1,155 .... J6

13697 Winthrop-Brasher Falls 1,454 .... L1
12998 Witherbee-Mineville 1,925 .... N2
14590 Wolcott 1,496 .... G4
11598 Woodmere 17,205 .... P7
12498 Woodstock 2,280 .... M6
12790 Wurtsboro 1,128 .... L7
11798 Wyandanch 13,215 .... N9
*10701 Yonkers 195,351 .... O6
10598 Yorktown Heights 7,696 .... N8
13495 Yorkville 3,115 .... K4
14174 Youngstown 2,191 .... C4

OTHER FEATURES

Adirondack (mts.) M3
Algonquin (peak) M2
Allegany Ind. Res. 1,243 .... C6
Allegheny (res.) C7
Allegheny (riv.) C6
Ashokan (res.) M7
Ausable (riv.) N2
Batten Kill (riv.) O4
Beaver (riv.) K3
Big Moose (lake) L3
Black (lake) J1
Black (riv.) K3
Block Island (sound) S8
Blue Mountain (lake) M3
Bonaparte (lake) K2
Brandreth (lake) L3
Brant (lake) N3
Brookhaven Nat'l Lab. P9
Butterfield (lake) J2
Canandaigua (lake) F5
Canisteo (riv.) F6
Cannonsville (res.) K6
Catskill (mts.) L6
Cattaraugus (creek) C6
Cattaraugus Ind. Res. 1,994 .... C5
Cayuga (lake) G5
Champlain (lake) O1
Chateaugay, Upper (lake) M1
Chautauqua (lake) A6
Chazy (lake) N1
Chenango (riv.) J6
Cohocton (riv.) F6
Conesus (lake) E5
Conewango (creek) B6
Cranberry (lake) L2
Deer (riv.) J3
Deer (riv.) L1
Delaware (riv.) K7
East (riv.) N9
Erie (lake) A5
Fire Island Nat'l Seashore P9
Fishers (isl.) S8

Forked (lake) L3
Fort Drum J2
Fort Niagara C4
Fort Stanwix Nat'l Mon. J4
Fulton Chain (lkes) K3
Galloo (isl.) H3
Gardiners (bay) R8
Gardiners (isl.) R8
Gateway Nat'l Rec. Area M9
Genesee (riv.) E5
George (lake) N4
Grand (isl.) B5
Grass (riv.) K1
Great Sacandaga (lake) M4
Great South (bay) O9
Great South (beach) O9
Greenwood (lake) M8
Grenadier (isl.) H2
Griffiss A.F.B. K4
Haystack (mt.) N2
Hemlock (lake) E5
Hinckley (res.) K4
Honeoye (lake) F5
Honnedaga (lake) L3
Hudson (riv.) N7
Hunter (mt.) M6
Indian (lake) M3
Jones (beach) R7
Keuka (lake) F5
Lila (lake) L2
Little Tupper (lake) L2
Long (isl.) P9
Long (lake) M2
Long Island (sound) P9
Manhattan (isl.) M9
Marcy (mt.) N2
Martin Van Buren Nat'l Hist. Site N6
Meacham (lake) M1
Mohawk (riv.) L5
Montauk (pt.) S8
Moose (riv.) K3
Neversink (res.) L7
New York State Barge (canal) C4
Niagara (riv.) B4
Oil Spring Ind. Res. 6 .... D6
Oneida (lake) J4
Onondaga Ind. Res. 596 .... H5
Ontario (lake) F3
Orient (pt.) R8
Oswegatchie (riv.) K2
Oswego (riv.) H4
Otisco (lake) H5
Otsego (lake) L5
Otselic (riv.) J5
Owasco (lake) G5
Peconic (bay) R9

Peninsula (pt.) H3
Pepacton (res.) L6
Piseco (lake) M4
Placid (lake) N2
Plattsburgh A.F.B. 5,905 .... N1
Pleasant (lake) M4
Plum (isl.) R8
Poosepatuck Ind. Res. 203 .... P9
Raquette (lake) L3
Rondout (res.) M7
Round (lake) L2
Sacandaga (lake) L3
Sackets (harb.) H3
Sagamore Hill Nat'l Hist. Site R6
Saint Lawrence (lake) K1
Saint Lawrence (riv.) J2
Saint Regis (riv.) L1
Saint Regis Ind. Res. 1,802 .... M1
Salmon (res.) J3
Salmon (riv.) H3
Salmon (riv.) M1
Saranac (lkes) M2
Saranac (riv.) N1
Saratoga (lake) N4
Saratoga Nat'l Hist. Park N4
Schoharie (res.) M6
Schroon (lake) N3
Seneca (lake) G5
Seneca (riv.) G5
Shelter (isl.) R8
Shinnecock Ind. Res. 297 .... R9
Silver (lake) N1
Skaneateles (lake) H5
Skylight (mt.) M2
Slide (mt.) L6
Staten (isl.) M9
Statue of Liberty Nat'l Mon. M9
Stony (isl.) H3
Stony (pt.) H3
Susquehanna (riv.) H6
Thousand (isls.) H2
Tioughnioga (riv.) H6
Titus (lake) M1
Tomhannock (res.) O5
Tonawanda Ind. Res. 467 .... D4
Toronto (res.) L7
Tupper (lake) M2
Tuscarora Ind. Res. 921 .... B4
Unadilla (riv.) K5
Upper Chateaugay (lake) M1
Valcour (isl.) N1
Wallkill (riv.) L8
Whiteface (mt.) N2
Whitney Point (lake) J6
Woodhull (lake) L3

⊙County seat.
‡Population of metropolitan area.
○Population of town or township.
† Zip of nearest p.o. * Multiple zips.

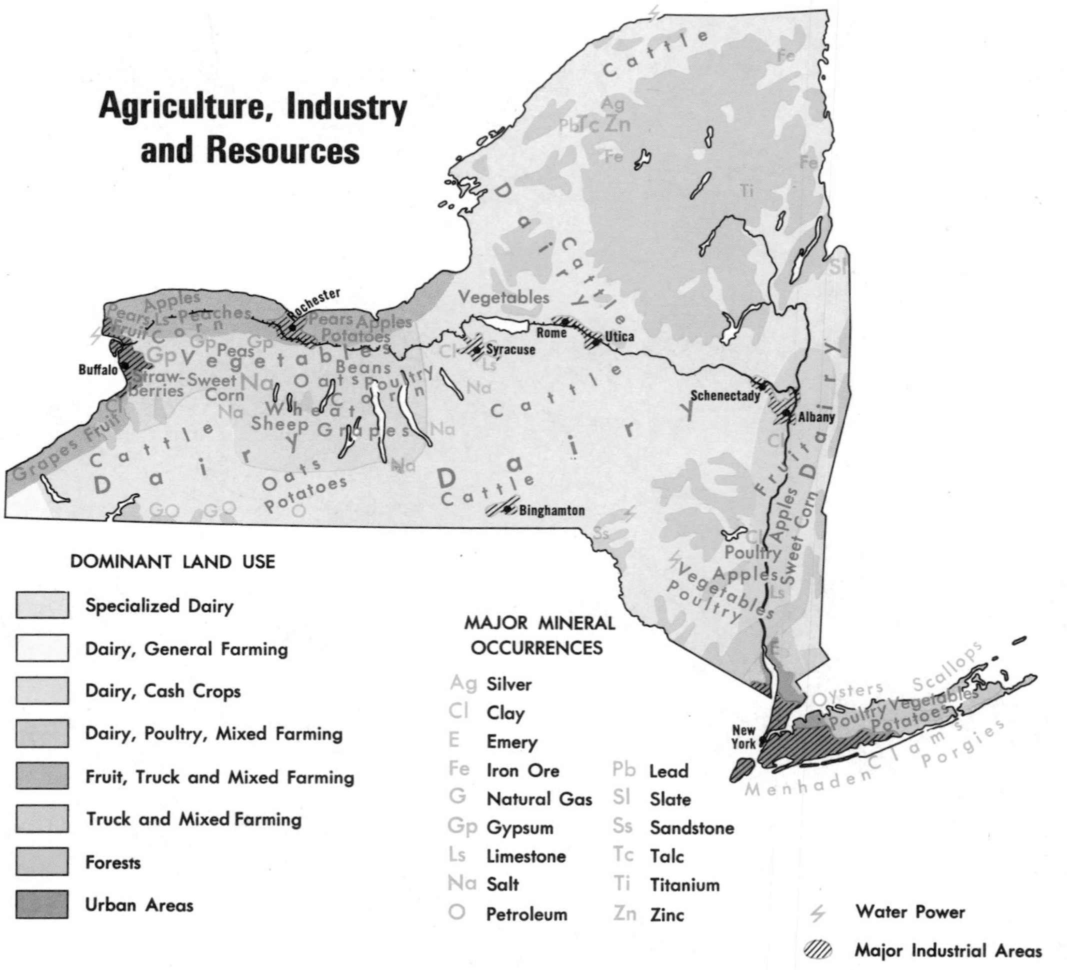

Agriculture, Industry and Resources

DOMINANT LAND USE

- Specialized Dairy
- Dairy, General Farming
- Dairy, Cash Crops
- Dairy, Poultry, Mixed Farming
- Fruit, Truck and Mixed Farming
- Truck and Mixed Farming
- Forests
- Urban Areas

MAJOR MINERAL OCCURRENCES

Ag	Silver		
Cl	Clay		
E	Emery		
Fe	Iron Ore	Pb	Lead
G	Natural Gas	Sl	Slate
Gp	Gypsum	Ss	Sandstone
Ls	Limestone	Tc	Talc
Na	Salt	Ti	Titanium
O	Petroleum	Zn	Zinc

Water Power

Major Industrial Areas

AREA 52,669 sq. mi. (136,413 sq. km.)
POPULATION 5,881,813
CAPITAL Raleigh
LARGEST CITY Charlotte
HIGHEST POINT Mt. Mitchell 6,684 ft. (2037 m.)
SETTLED IN 1650
ADMITTED TO UNION November 21, 1789
POPULAR NAME Tarheel State
STATE FLOWER Flowering Dogwood
STATE BIRD Cardinal

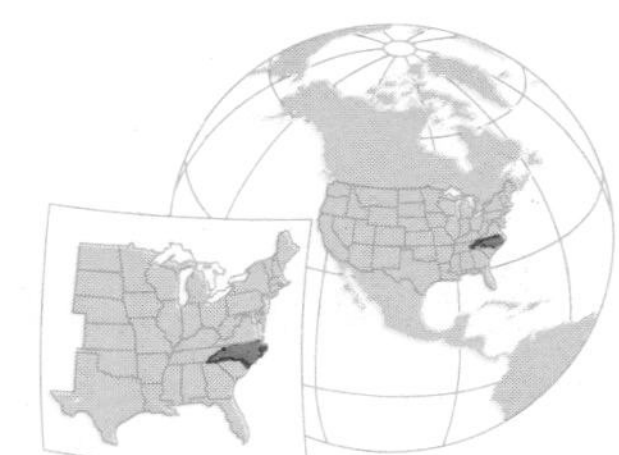

Great Smoky Mountains

MILES
0 5 10 15

Cosby
TENN.
N.C.
Little Pigeon R.
W. Fk. Little Pigeon R.
Pigeon R.
Gatlinburg
Mt. Guyot 6,621 ft. (2018 m.)
CHILHOWEE MTN.
Little R.
Townsend
COVE MTN.
Mt. Le Conte ▲6,593 ft. (2010 m.)
BALSAM MOUNTAIN
HUGHES RIDGE
NATIONAL PARK
Newfound Gap
Chilhowee
HANNAH MTN.
Clingmans Dome 6,643 ft. (2025 m.)
Gregory Bald 4,948 ft. (1508 m.)
WELCH RIDGE
CHEROKEE INDIAN RES.
Waynesville
Little R.
Fontana Dam
Tennessee R.
Tapoco
TENN. N.C.
Fontana Lake
Bryson City
Tuckasegee R.
PLOTT BALSAMS
CHEOAH MTS.
Sylva

© HAMMOND INCORPORATED

COUNTIES

Alamance 99,319 .... L3
Alexander 24,999 .... G3
Alleghany 9,587 .... G1
Anson 25,649 .... J4
Ashe 22,325 .... F2
Avery 14,409 .... F2
Beaufort 40,355 .... R4
Bertie 21,024 .... P2
Bladen 30,491 .... M5
Brunswick 35,777 .... N6
Buncombe 160,934 .... D3
Burke 72,504 .... F3
Cabárrus 85,895 .... H4
Caldwell 67,746 .... F3
Camden 5,829 .... S2
Carteret 41,092 .... R5
Caswell 20,705 .... L2
Catawba 105,208 .... G3
Chatham 33,415 .... L3
Cherokee 18,933 .... A4
Chowan 12,558 .... R2
Clay 6,619 .... B4
Cleveland 83,435 .... F4
Columbus 51,037 .... M6
Craven 71,043 .... P4
Cumberland 247,160 .... M4
Currituck 11,089 .... S2
Dare 13,377 .... T3
Davidson 113,162 .... J3
Davie 24,599 .... H3
Duplin 40,952 .... O5
Durham 152,785 .... M3
Edgecombe 55,988 .... O3
Forsyth 243,683 .... J2
Franklin 30,055 .... N2
Gaston 162,568 .... G4
Gates 8,875 .... R2
Graham 7,217 .... B4
Granville 34,043 .... M2
Greene 16,117 .... O3
Guilford 317,154 .... K3
Halifax 55,286 .... O2
Harnett 59,570 .... M4
Haywood 46,495 .... C3
Henderson 58,580 .... D4
Hertford 23,368 .... P2
Hoke 20,383 .... L4
Hyde 5,873 .... S3
Iredell 82,538 .... H3
Jackson 25,811 .... C4
Johnston 70,599 .... N4
Jones 9,705 .... P4
Lee 36,718 .... L4
Lenoir 59,819 .... O4
Lincoln 42,372 .... G3
Macon 20,178 .... B4
Madison 16,827 .... D3
Martin 25,948 .... P3
McDowell 35,135 .... E3
Mecklenburg 404,270 .... H4
Mitchell 14,428 .... E2
Montgomery 22,469 .... K4
Moore 50,505 .... L4
Nash 67,153 .... O2
New Hanover 103,471 .... O6
Northampton 22,584 .... P2
Onslow 112,784 .... P5
Orange 77,055 .... L2
Pamlico 10,398 .... R4
Pasquotank 28,462 .... S2
Pender 22,215 .... O5
Perquimans 9,486 .... S2
Person 29,164 .... M2
Pitt 90,146 .... P3
Polk 12,984 .... E4
Randolph 91,728 .... K3
Richmond 45,481 .... K4
Robeson 101,610 .... L5
Rockingham 83,426 .... K2
Rowan 99,186 .... H3
Rutherford 53,787 .... E4
Sampson 49,687 .... N4
Scotland 32,273 .... L5
Stanly 48,517 .... J4
Stokes 33,086 .... J2
Surry 59,449 .... H2
Swain 10,283 .... B3
Transylvania 23,417 .... D4
Tyrrell 3,975 .... S3
Union 70,380 .... H4
Vance 36,748 .... N2
Wake 301,327 .... M3
Warren 16,232 .... N2
Washington 14,801 .... R3
Watauga 31,666 .... F2
Wayne 97,054 .... N4
Wilkes 58,657 .... G2
Wilson 63,132 .... O3
Yadkin 28,439 .... H2
Yancey 14,934 .... E3

CITIES and TOWNS

Zip *Name/Pop.* *Key*

28315 Aberdeen 1,945 .... L4
27910 Ahoskie 4,887 .... P2
27201 Alamance 320 .... K2
28001 Albemarle⊙ 15,110 .... J4
†28043 Alexander Mills 643 .... F4
28509 Alliance 616 .... R4
28702 Almond 140 .... B4
28901 Andrews 1,621 .... B4
27501 Angier 1,709 .... M4
28007 Ansonville 794 .... J4
27502 Apex 2,847 .... M3
28510 Arapahoe 467 .... R4
27263 Archdale 5,326 .... K3
†28642 Arlington 872 .... H2
28420 Ash 150 .... N6
27203 Asheboro⊙ 15,252 .... K3
*28801 Asheville⊙ 53,583 .... D3
Asheville‡ 177,761 .... D3
†27983 Askewville 227 .... R2
28421 Atkinson 298 .... N5
28512 Atlantic Beach 941 .... R5
27805 Aulander 1,214 .... P2
27806 Aurora 698 .... R4
28318 Autryville 228 .... M4
27915 Avon 500 .... U4
28513 Ayden 4,361 .... P4
27916 Aydlett 205 .... T2
28009 Badin 1,514 .... J4
27807 Bailey 685 .... N3
28705 Bakersville⊙ 373 .... E2
28706 Balfour 1,772 .... E4
28707 Balsam 200 .... C4
28604 Banner Elk 1,087 .... F2
†27030 Bannertown 1,028 .... H1
27008 Barber 155 .... H3
†28739 Barker Heights 1,267 .... D4
28710 Bat Cave 450 .... E4
27808 Bath 207 .... R4
27809 Battleboro 632 .... O2
28515 Bayboro⊙ 759 .... R4
†27892 Beargrass 82 .... P3
28516 Beaufort⊙ 3,826 .... R5
27810 Belhaven 2,430 .... R3
27811 Bellarthur 350 .... O3
28012 Belmont 4,607 .... H4
†28451 Belville 102 .... N6
†28090 Belwood 613 .... F4
27208 Bennett 254 .... K3
27504 Benson 2,792 .... N4
28016 Bessemer City 4,787 .... G4
27812 Bethel 1,825 .... P3
28518 Beulaville 1,060 .... O5
†28803 Biltmore Forest 1,499 .... E3
27209 Biscoe 1,334 .... K4
27813 Black Creek 523 .... O3
28711 Black Mountain 4,083 .... E3
28320 Bladenboro 1,428 .... M5
27212 Blanch 200 .... L2
28605 Blowing Rock 1,337 .... F2
28092 Boger City 2,252 .... G4
28461 Boiling Spring Lakes 998 .... N7
28017 Boling Springs 2,381 .... F4
28422 Bolivia⊙ 252 .... N6
28423 Bolton 563 .... N6
27213 Bonlee 300 .... L3
28606 Boomer 250 .... G2
28607 Boone⊙ 10,191 .... F2
27011 Boonville 1,028 .... H2
28322 Bowdens 200 .... N4
28712 Brevard⊙ 5,323 .... D4
28519 Bridgeton 461 .... R4
27505 Broadway 908 .... L4
†28601 Brookford 467 .... G3
28424 Brunswick 223 .... M6
28713 Bryson City⊙ 1,556 .... C4
27506 Buies Creek 1,939 .... M4
27507 Bullock 525 .... M2
27508 Bunn 505 .... N3
28425 Burgaw⊙ 1,738 .... N5
27215 Burlington 37,266 .... K2
Burlington‡ 99,136 .... F2
28714 Burnsville⊙ 1,452 .... E3
27509 Butner 4,240 .... M2
27312 Bynum 350 .... L3
†29566 Calabash 128 .... M7
28325 Calypso 689 .... N4
27921 Camden⊙ 300 .... S2
28326 Cameron 225 .... L4
27229 Candor 868 .... K4
28716 Canton 4,631 .... D3
†28584 Cape Carteret 944 .... P5
28428 Carolina Beach 2,000 .... O6
27510 Carrboro 7,336 .... L3
28327 Carthage⊙ 925 .... K4
27511 Cary 21,763 .... M3
28020 Casar 346 .... F3
28717 Cashiers 553 .... C4
27816 Castalia 358 .... O2
28429 Castle Hayne 1,087 .... O6
†28461 Caswell Beach 110 .... N7
28609 Catawba 509 .... G3
27230 Cedar Falls 400 .... K3
27231 Cedar Grove 250 .... L2
28520 Cedar Island 310 .... S5
†27549 Centerville 135 .... N2
28430 Cerro Gordo 295 .... M6
28431 Chadbourn 1,975 .... M6
†28445 Chadwick Acres 15 .... P6
27514 Chapel Hill 32,421 .... L3
*28201 Charlotte⊙ 314,447 .... H4
Charlotte-Gastonia‡ 637,218 .... H4
28021 Cherryville 4,844 .... G4
28023 China Grove 2,081 .... H3
28521 Chinquapin 280 .... O5
27817 Chocowinity 644 .... P4
28610 Claremont 880 .... G3
28433 Clarkton 664 .... M6
27520 Clayton 4,091 .... N3
27012 Clemmons 7,401 .... J2
27013 Cleveland 595 .... H3
28328 Clinton⊙ 7,552 .... N5
28721 Clyde 1,008 .... D3
27521 Coats 1,385 .... M4
27922 Cofield 465 .... R2
27924 Colerain 284 .... R2
27925 Columbia⊙ 758 .... S3
28722 Columbus⊙ 727 .... E4
28522 Comfort 325 .... O5
27818 Como 89 .... P1
28025 Concord⊙ 16,942 .... H4
27819 Conetoe 215 .... O3
28613 Conover 4,245 .... G3
27820 Conway 678 .... P2
27014 Cooleemee 1,448 .... H3
28031 Cornelius 1,460 .... H4
27927 Corolla 158 .... T2
28523 Cove City 500 .... P4
28032 Cramerton 1,869 .... G4
27522 Creedmoor 1,641 .... M2
27928 Creswell 426 .... S3
27852 Crisp 435 .... O3
28616 Crossnore 297 .... F2
28331 Cumberland 400 .... M5
27237 Cumnock 200 .... L3
27929 Currituck⊙ 700 .... T2
28034 Dallas 3,340 .... G4
27016 Danbury⊙ 140 .... J2
28036 Davidson 3,241 .... H4
28524 Davis 612 .... R5
27239 Denton 949 .... J3
28725 Dillsboro 179 .... C4
27017 Dobson⊙ 1,222 .... H2
†27801 Dortches 885 .... O2
28526 Dover 600 .... P4
28619 Drexel 1,392 .... F3
28332 Dublin 477 .... M5
28334 Dunn 8,962 .... M4
*27701 Durham⊙ 100,538 .... M2
Durham-Raleigh‡ 530,673 .... M2
27242 Eagle Springs 280 .... K4
28038 Earl 206 .... F4
†28434 East Arcadia 461 .... N6
27018 East Bend 602 .... H2
28726 East Flat Rock 3,365 .... E4
†28723 East Laport 150 .... C4
28352 East Laurinburg 536 .... L5
†28752 East Marion 1,851 .... F3
28039 East Spencer 2,150 .... J3
27288 Eden 15,672 .... K1
27932 Edenton⊙ 5,357 .... R2
27909 Elizabeth City⊙ 14,004 .... S2
28337 Elizabethtown⊙ 3,551 .... M5
28621 Elkin 2,858 .... H2
28622 Elk Park 535 .... E2
28040 Ellenboro 560 .... F4
28338 Ellerbe 1,415 .... K4
27822 Elm City 1,561 .... O3
27244 Elon College 2,873 .... L2
†28557 Emerald Isle 865 .... P5
27823 Enfield 2,995 .... O2
28728 Enka 5,567 .... D3
28339 Erwin 2,828 .... M4
27247 Ether 425 .... K4
27935 Eure 300 .... R2
27830 Eureka 303 .... O3
27825 Everetts 213 .... P3
28438 Evergreen 310 .... M6
28439 Fair Bluff 1,095 .... M6
27826 Fairfield 900 .... S3
28340 Fairmont 2,658 .... L6
28730 Fairview 1,122 .... D3
28341 Faison 636 .... N4
28041 Faith 552 .... J3

(continued on following page)

Agriculture, Industry and Resources

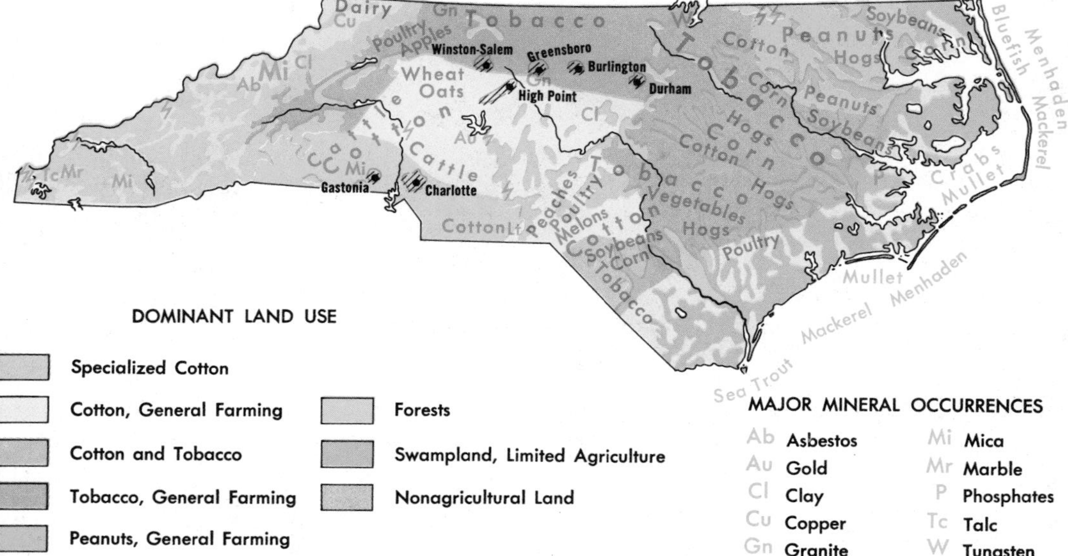
Dairy
Tobacco
Poultry
Apples
Winston-Salem
Greensboro
Burlington
Durham
High Point
Wheat
Oats
Cotton
Peanuts
Hogs
Soybeans
Corn
Bluefish
Menhaden
Mackerel
Cattle
Gastonia
Charlotte
Peaches
Melons
Vegetables
Crabs
Mullet
Sea Trout
DOMINANT LAND USE
Specialized Cotton
Cotton, General Farming
Cotton and Tobacco
Tobacco, General Farming
Peanuts, General Farming
General Farming, Livestock, Fruit, Tobacco
General Farming, Truck Farming, Tobacco, Livestock
Forests
Swampland, Limited Agriculture
Nonagricultural Land
Water Power
Major Industrial Areas
MAJOR MINERAL OCCURRENCES
Ab Asbestos
Au Gold
Cl Clay
Cu Copper
Gn Granite
Lt Lithium
Mi Mica
Mr Marble
P Phosphates
Tc Talc
W Tungsten

Topography

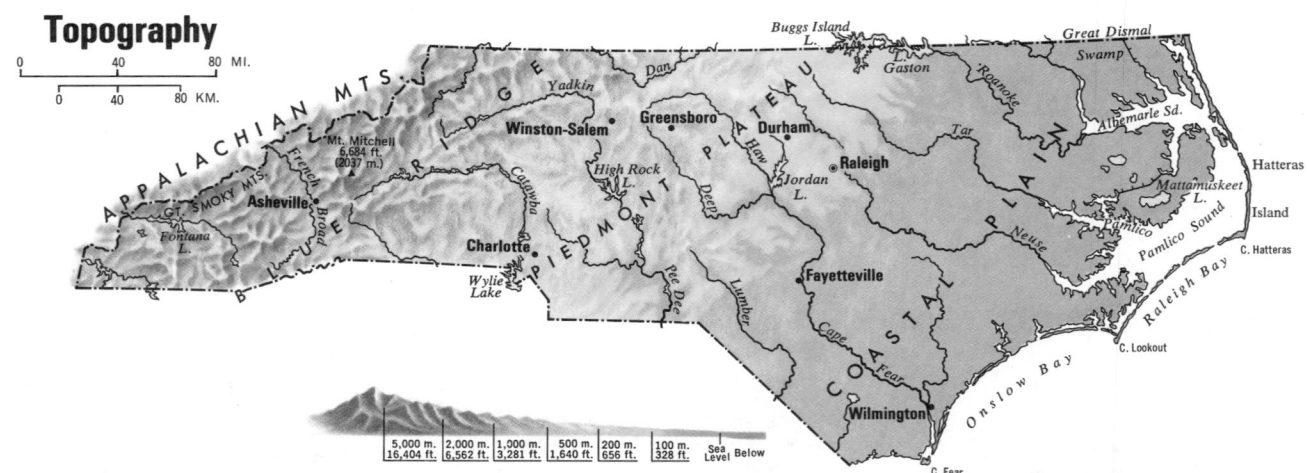

| 5,000 m. 16,404 ft. | 2,000 m. 6,562 ft. | 1,000 m. 3,281 ft. | 500 m. 1,640 ft. | 200 m. 656 ft. | 100 m. 328 ft. | Sea Level | Below |

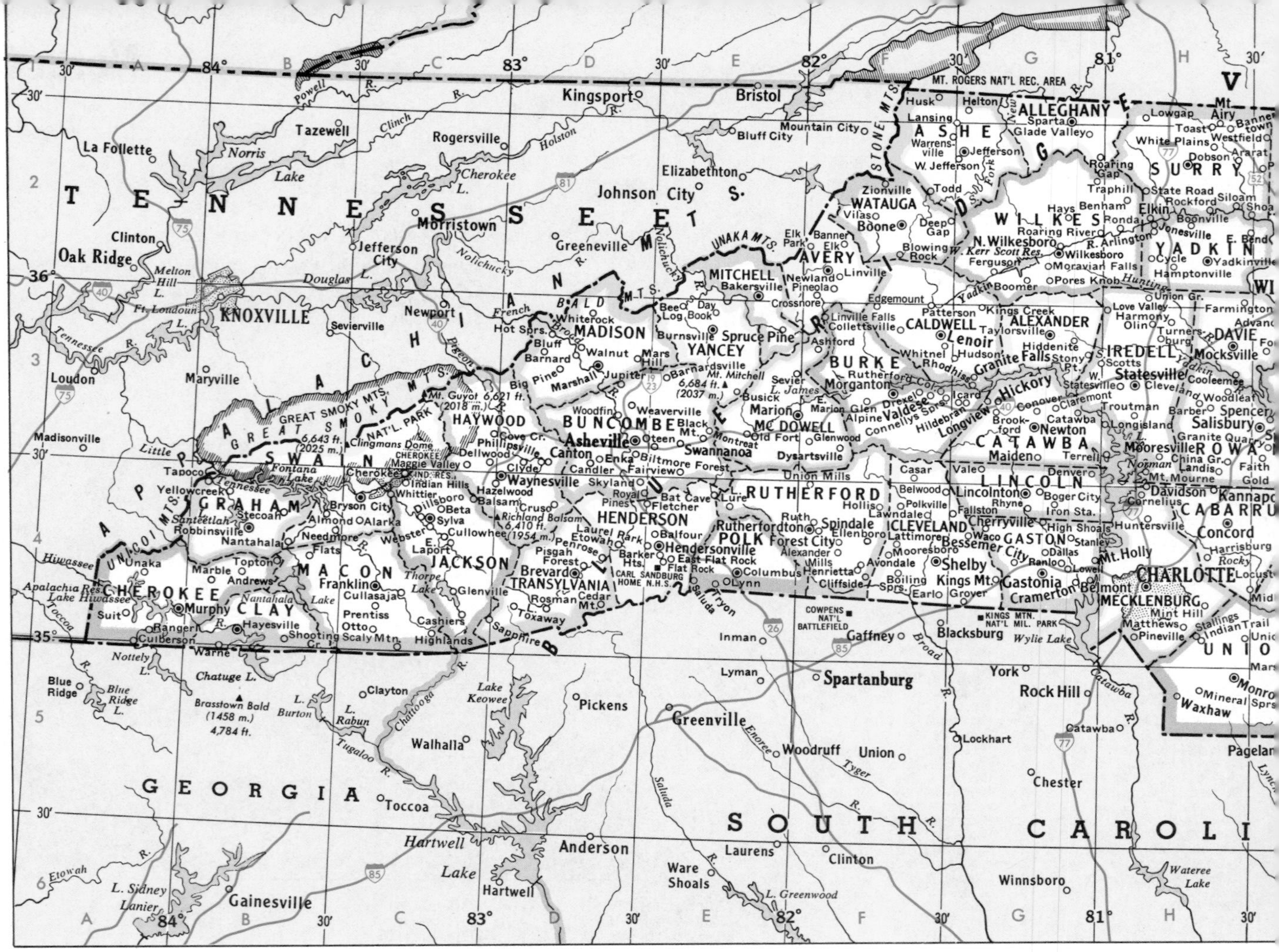

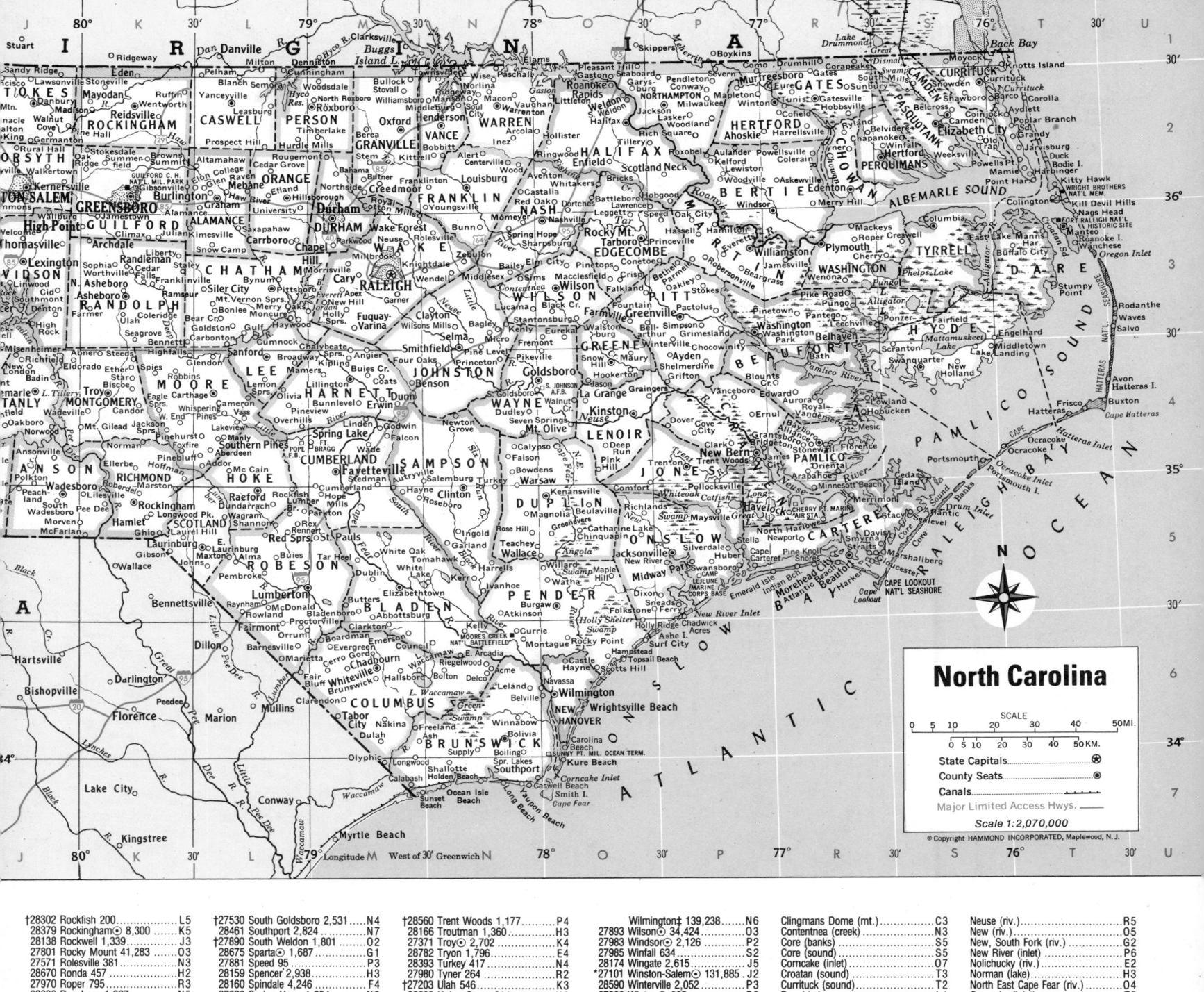

North Carolina

SCALE
0 5 10 20 30 40 50 MI.
0 5 10 20 30 40 50 KM.

State Capitals........................⊛
County Seats.........................◉
Canals..............................
Major Limited Access Hwys._____

Scale 1:2,070,000

© Copyright HAMMOND INCORPORATED, Maplewood, N.J.

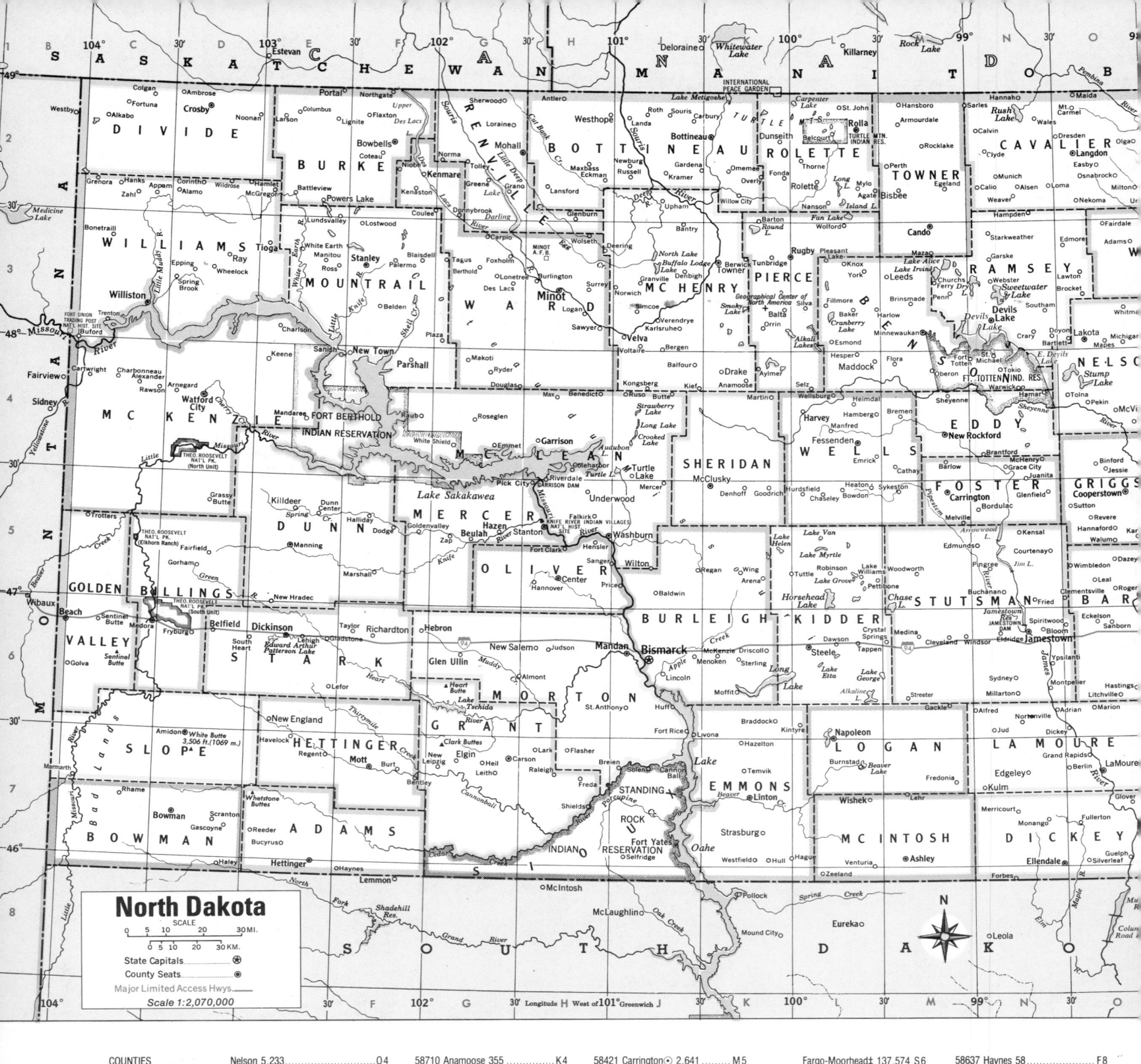

North Dakota

SCALE

0 5 10   20   30 MI.

0 5 10   20   30 KM.

⊛ State Capitals

◉ County Seats

Major Limited Access Hwys.

Scale 1:2,070,000

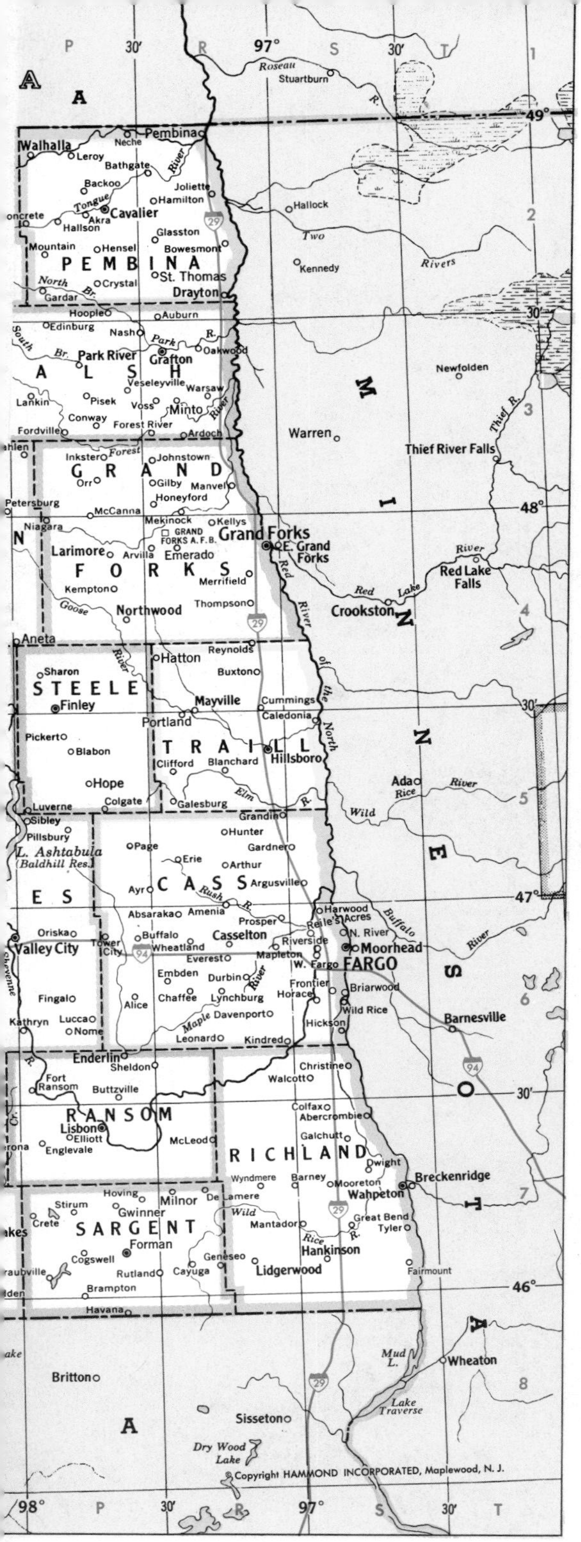

Walhalla
Pembina
Cavalier
PEMBINA
Drayton
WALSH
Park River
Grafton
Minto
Warren
Thief River Falls
GRAND FORKS
Grand Forks
E. Grand Forks
Larimore
Northwood
Crookston
Red Lake Falls
STEELE
Finley
Mayville
TRAILL
Hillsboro
Portland
Hope
CASS
Casselton
Valley City
Moorhead
FARGO
West Fargo
Barnesville
Enderlin
RANSOM
Lisbon
RICHLAND
Wahpeton
Breckenridge
SARGENT
Forman
Milnor
Lidgerwood
Hankinson
Wheaton
Sisseton
Britton
Copyright HAMMOND INCORPORATED, Maplewood, N. J.

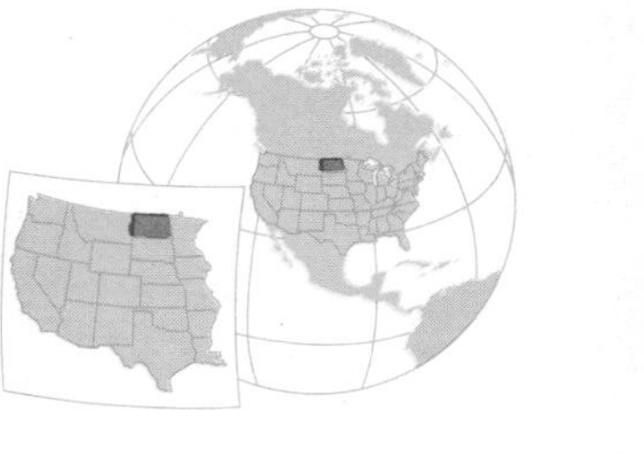

AREA 70,702 sq. mi. (183,118 sq. km.)
POPULATION 652,717
CAPITAL Bismarck
LARGEST CITY Fargo
HIGHEST POINT White Butte 3,506 ft. (1069 m.)
SETTLED IN 1780
ADMITTED TO UNION November 2, 1889
POPULAR NAME Flickertail State; Sioux State
STATE FLOWER Wild Prairie Rose
STATE BIRD Western Meadowlark

†58501 Lincoln 656 .... J6
58552 Linton⊙ 1,561 .... K7
58054 Lisbon⊙ 2,283 .... P7
58461 Litchville 251 .... O6
58056 Luverne 65 .... P5
58348 Maddock 677 .... L4
58554 Mandan⊙ 15,513 .... J6
58642 Manning⊙ 75 .... E5
58058 Mantador 76 .... R7
58256 Manvel 308 .... R3
58059 Mapleton 306 .... R6
58643 Marmarth 190 .... B7
58759 Max 317 .... H4
58257 Mayville 2,255 .... R4
58463 McClusky⊙ 658 .... K4
58254 McVille 626 .... O4
58467 Medina 521 .... M6
58645 Medora⊙ 94 .... C6
58259 Michigan 502 .... O3
58060 Milnor 716 .... R7
58351 Minnewaukan⊙ 461 .... M3
58701 Minot⊙ 32,843 .... H3
58261 Minto 592 .... R3
58761 Mohall⊙ 1,049 .... G2
58471 Monango 59 .... N7
58472 Montpelier 96 .... N6
58646 Mott⊙ 1,315 .... F7
58352 Munich 300 .... N2
58561 Napoleon⊙ 1,103 .... L6
58265 Neche 471 .... P2
58647 New England 825 .... E6
58562 New Leipzig 352 .... G7
58356 New Rockford⊙ 1,791 .... N4
58563 New Salem 1,081 .... G6
58763 New Town 1,335 .... F4
58266 Niagara 76 .... P4
58062 Nome 67 .... P6
58765 Noonan 283 .... D2
†58102 North River 65 .... S6
58267 Northwood 1,240 .... P4
58474 Oakes 2,112 .... O7
58063 Oriska 125 .... P6
58064 Page 329 .... P5
58769 Palermo 97 .... F3
58270 Park River 1,844 .... P3
58770 Parshall 1,059 .... F4
58271 Pembina 673 .... R2
58476 Pingree 88 .... N5
58772 Portal 238 .... E2
58274 Portland 627 .... R5
58773 Powers Lake 466 .... E2
58849 Ray 766 .... D3
58649 Reeder 355 .... E7
58477 Regan 71 .... K5
58650 Regent 297 .... E7
58275 Reynolds 309 .... R4
58651 Rhame 222 .... C7
58652 Richardton 699 .... F6
†58078 Riverside 465 .... S6
58365 Rocklake 287 .... M2
58479 Rogers 68 .... O5
58366 Rolette 667 .... L2
58367 Rolla⊙ 1,538 .... L2
58368 Rugby⊙ 3,335 .... L3
58067 Rutland 250 .... P7
58369 Saint John 401 .... L2
58276 Saint Thomas 528 .... R2
58780 Sanish E4
58781 Sawyer 417 .... H3
58653 Scranton 415 .... D7
58568 Selfridge 273 .... J7
58654 Sentinel Butte 86 .... C6
58068 Sheldon 173 .... P6
58782 Sherwood 294 .... G2
58374 Sheyenne 307 .... M4
58655 South Heart 294 .... D6
58850 Spring Brook 52 .... D3
58784 Stanley⊙ 1,631 .... F3
58571 Stanton⊙ 623 .... H5
58482 Steele⊙ 796 .... L6
58573 Strasburg 623 .... K7
58483 Streeter 264 .... M6
58785 Surrey 999 .... H3
58487 Tappen 271 .... L6
58656 Taylor 239 .... F6
58278 Thompson 785 .... R4
58852 Tioga 1,597 .... E3
58380 Tolna 241 .... O4
58071 Tower City 293 .... P6
58788 Towner⊙ 867 .... K3
58575 Turtle Lake 802 .... J4
58576 Underwood 1,329 .... H5
58072 Valley City⊙ 7,774 .... P6
58790 Velva 1,101 .... J3
58792 Voltaire 65 .... J3
58075 Wahpeton⊙ 9,064 .... S7
58281 Wales 74 .... N2
58282 Walhalla 1,429 .... P2
58577 Washburn⊙ 1,767 .... J5
58854 Watford City⊙ 2,119 .... D4
58078 West Fargo 10,099 .... S6
58793 Westhope 741 .... H2
58794 White Earth 98 .... E3
58795 Wildrose 214 .... D2
58801 Williston⊙ 13,336 .... C3
58384 Willow City 329 .... K2
58579 Wilton 950 .... J5
58492 Wimbledon 330 .... O5
58495 Wishek 1,345 .... L7
58385 Wolford 76 .... L3
58081 Wyndmere 550 .... R7
58386 York 69 .... L3
58580 Zap 511 .... G5
58581 Zeeland 253 .... L8

OTHER FEATURES

Alkali (lkes) L3
Alkaline (lake) L6
Apple (creek) J6
Arrowwood (lake) N5
Ashtabula (lake) P5
Audubon (lake) H4
Bad Lands (reg.) C7
Baldhill (Ashtabula) (res.) P5
Bear (creek) O7
Beaver (creek) B5
Beaver (creek) K7
Beaver (lake) L7
Buffalo Lodge (lake) J3
Cannonball (riv.) G7
Carpenter (lake) L2
Cedar (creek) G7
Chase (lake) M5
Cherry (creek) D4
Clark (buttes) G7
Coteau du Missouri (plain) G3
Cranberry (lake) L3
Crooked (lake) J4
Cut Bank (creek) H2
Darling (lake) G2
Deep (riv.) J1
Des Lacs (riv.) G3
Devils (lake) N3
Dry (lake) M3
East Devils (lake) N4
Egg (creek) H3
Elm (riv.) N8
Elm (riv.) R5
Etta (lake) L6
Fan (lake) L2
Forest (riv.) P3
Fort Berthold Ind. Res. E4
Fort Totten Ind. Res. N4
Fort Union Trading Post Nat'l Hist. Site B3
Garrison (dam) H5
George (lake) L6
Goose (riv.) P4
Grand, North Fork (riv.) E8
Grand Forks A.F.B. 9,390 .... R4
Green (riv.) D5
Grove (lake) L5
Heart (butte) G6
Heart (riv.) F6
Helen (lake) K5
Horsehead (lake) L5
International Peace Garden K1
Irvine (lake) M3
Island (lake) L2
James (riv.) N6
Jamestown (res.) N6
Jim (lake) N5
Knife (riv.) G5
Knife R. Indian Villages Nat'l Hist. Site H5
Little Deep (creek) G2
Little Knife (riv.) F3
Little Missouri (riv.) D4
Little Muddy (riv.) C3
Long (lake) J4
Long (lake) K6
Long (lake) L2
Maple (riv.) O8
Maple (riv.) R6
Metigoshe (lake) K2
Minot A.F.B. 9,880 .... H3
Missouri (riv.) H5
Muddy (creek) G6
Myrtle (lake) L5
North (lake) J3
Oahe (lake) J7
Oak (creek) J8
Park (riv.) R3
Patterson, Edward A. (lake) E6
Pembina (riv.) O1
Pipestem (riv.) M5
Porcupine (creek) J7
Red River of the North (riv.) S4
Round (lake) K3
Rush (lake) N2
Rush (riv.) R5
Sakakawea (lake) G5
Sentinel (butte) C6
Shell (creek) F3
Sheyenne (riv.) O6
Smoky (lake) K3
Souris (riv.) J2
Spring (creek) E5
Standing Rock Ind. Res. J7
Strawberry (lake) J4
Stump (lake) O4
Sweetwater (lake) N3
Theodore Roosevelt Nat'l Mem. Park C5, D4, D6
Thirty Mile (creek) F6
Tongue (riv.) P2
Tschida (lake) G6
Turtle (lake) H4
Turtle (mts.) K2
Turtle Mountain Ind. Res. L2
Upper Des Lacs (lake) F2
Van (lake) L5
Whetstone (buttes) E7
White (butte) D7
White Butte (mt.) D7
White Earth (riv.) E3
Wild Rice (riv.) R7
Yellowstone (riv.) B4

⊙County seat.
‡Population of metropolitan area.
† Zip of nearest p.o.
* Multiple zips.

Topography

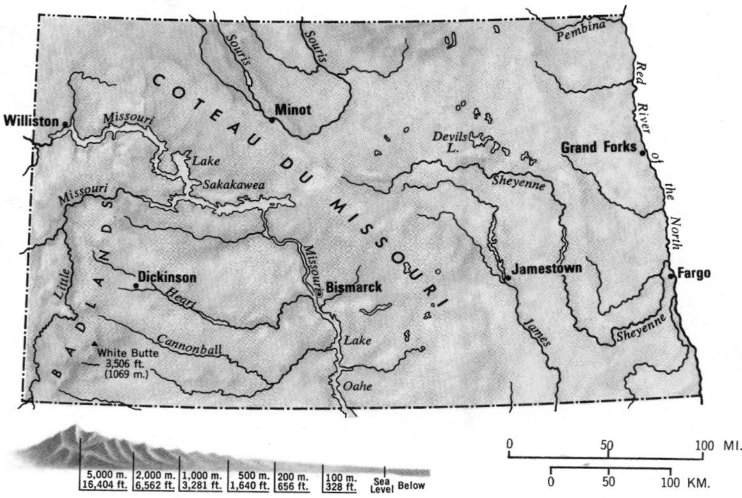

COTEAU DU MISSOURI
Williston
Minot
Grand Forks
Devils L.
Lake Sakakawea
Missouri
Souris
Pembina
Red River of the North
Sheyenne
Dickinson
Bismarck
Jamestown
Fargo
Heart
Cannonball
James
Oahe
Little Missouri
BADLANDS
White Butte 3,506 ft. (1069 m.)
5,000 m. 16,404 ft.
2,000 m. 6,562 ft.
1,000 m. 3,281 ft.
500 m. 1,640 ft.
200 m. 656 ft.
100 m. 328 ft.
Sea Level
Below
0 50 100 MI.
0 50 100 KM.

Agriculture, Industry and Resources

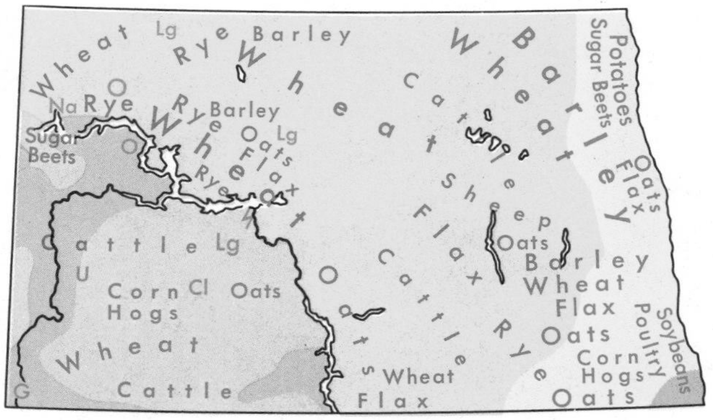

Wheat
Rye
Barley
Sugar Beets
Potatoes
Oats
Flax
Cattle
Sheep
Corn
Hogs
Poultry
Soybeans
Lg
Na
Cl

DOMINANT LAND USE

- Specialized Wheat
- Wheat, General Farming
- Wheat, Range Livestock
- Livestock, Cash Grain
- Sugar Beets, Dry Beans, Livestock, General Farming
- Range Livestock
- Water Power

MAJOR MINERAL OCCURRENCES

- Cl Clay
- G Natural Gas
- Lg Lignite
- Na Salt
- O Petroleum
- U Uranium

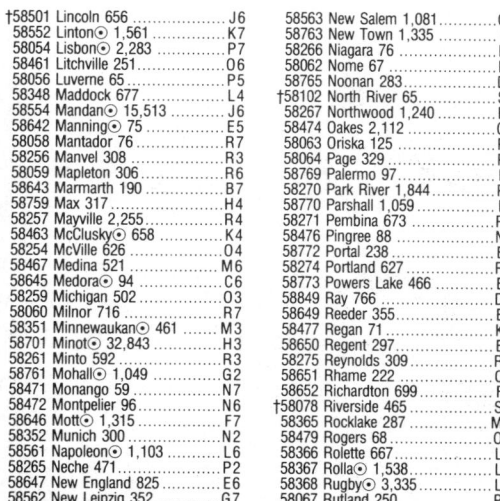

Ohio

SCALE

0 5 10 20 30 40 MI.

0 5 10 20 30 40 KM.

State Capitals .... ⊛

County Seats .... ◉

Major Limited Access Hwys. _____

Scale 1:1,800,000

© Copyright HAMMOND INCORPORATED, Maplewood, N.J.

Topography

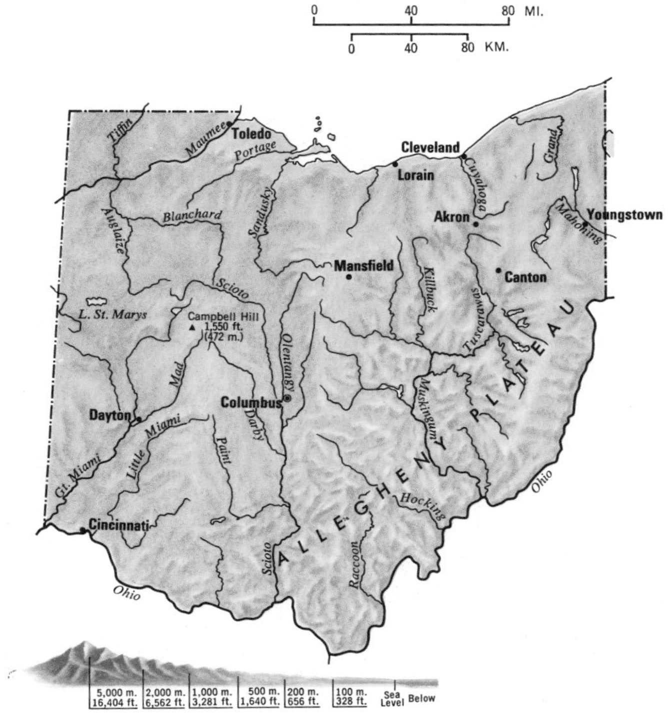

0
40
80 MI.
0
40
80 KM.
Tiffin
Maumee
Toledo
Portage
Cleveland
Lorain
Cuyahoga
Grand
Youngstown
Mahoning
Akron
Blanchard
Auglaize
Sandusky
Mansfield
Canton
Scioto
Killbuck
Tuscarawas
L. St. Marys
Campbell Hill
1,550 ft.
(472 m.)
Olentangy
Mad
Columbus
Muskingum
PLATEAU
Dayton
Miami
Little
Darby
Paint
Gt. Miami
ALLEGHENY
Hocking
Ohio
Cincinnati
Scioto
Raccoon
Ohio
5,000 m. 16,404 ft.
2,000 m. 6,562 ft.
1,000 m. 3,281 ft.
500 m. 1,640 ft.
200 m. 656 ft.
100 m. 328 ft.
Sea Level
Below

AREA 41,330 sq. mi. (107,045 sq. km.)
POPULATION 10,797,624
CAPITAL Columbus
LARGEST CITY Cleveland
HIGHEST POINT Campbell Hill 1,550 ft. (472 m.)
SETTLED IN 1788
ADMITTED TO UNION March 1, 1803
POPULAR NAME Buckeye State
STATE FLOWER Scarlet Carnation
STATE BIRD Cardinal

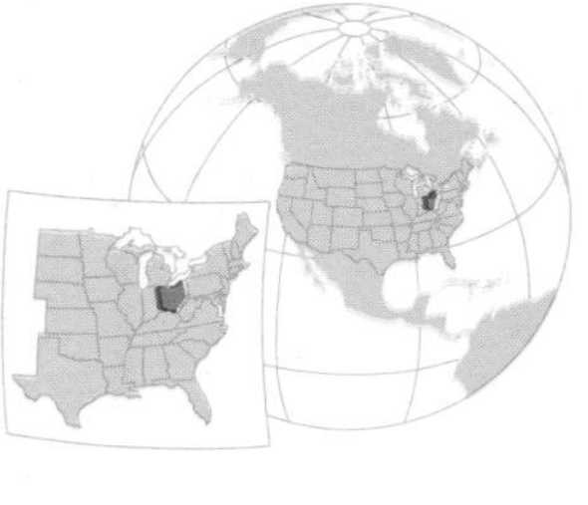

COUNTIES

Name/Pop.	Key
Adams 24,328	D8
Allen 112,241	B4
Ashland 46,178	F4
Ashtabula 104,215	J2
Athens 56,399	F7
Auglaize 42,554	B4
Belmont 82,569	J5
Brown 31,920	C8
Butler 258,787	A7
Carroll 25,598	H4
Champaign 33,649	C5
Clark 150,236	C6
Clermont 128,483	B7
Clinton 34,603	C7
Columbiana 113,572	J4
Coshocton 36,024	G5
Crawford 50,075	E4
Cuyahoga 1,498,400	G3
Darke 55,096	A5
Defiance 39,987	A3
Delaware 53,840	D5
Erie 79,655	E3
Fairfield 93,678	E6
Fayette 27,467	D6
Franklin 869,126	E5
Fulton 37,751	B2
Gallia 30,098	F8
Geauga 74,474	H3
Greene 129,769	C6
Guernsey 42,024	H5
Hamilton 873,224	A7
Hancock 64,581	C3
Hardin 32,719	C4
Harrison 18,152	H5
Henry 28,383	B3
Highland 33,477	C7
Hocking 24,304	F6
Holmes 29,416	G4
Huron 54,608	E3
Jackson 30,592	E7
Jefferson 91,564	J5
Knox 46,304	F5
Lake 212,801	H2
Lawrence 63,849	E8
Licking 120,981	F5
Logan 39,155	C5
Lorain 274,909	F3
Lucas 471,741	C2
Madison 33,004	D6
Mahoning 289,487	J4
Marion 67,974	D4
Medina 113,150	G3
Meigs 23,641	F7
Mercer 38,334	A4
Miami 90,381	B5
Monroe 17,382	H6
Montgomery 571,697	B6
Morgan 14,241	G6
Morrow 26,480	E4
Muskingum 83,340	G5
Noble 11,310	G6
Ottawa 40,076	D2
Paulding 21,302	A3
Perry 31,032	F6
Pickaway 43,662	D6
Pike 22,802	D7
Portage 135,856	H3
Preble 38,223	A6
Putnam 32,991	B3
Richland 131,205	E4
Ross 65,004	D7
Sandusky 63,267	D3
Scioto 84,545	D8
Seneca 61,901	D3
Shelby 43,089	B5
Stark 378,823	H4
Summit 524,472	G3
Trumbull 241,863	J3
Tuscarawas 84,614	H5
Union 29,536	D5
Van Wert 30,458	A4
Vinton 11,584	E7
Warren 99,276	B7
Washington 64,266	H7
Wayne 97,408	G4
Williams 36,369	A2
Wood 107,372	C3
Wyandot 22,651	D4

CITIES and TOWNS

Zip	Name/Pop.	Key
45101	Aberdeen 1,566	C8
45810	Ada 5,669	C4
45001	Addyston 1,195	B9
43101	Adelphi 472	E7
43901	Adena 1,062	J5
*44301	Akron⊙ 237,177	G3
	Akron‡ 660,328	G3
45710	Albany 905	F7
43001	Alexandria 489	E5
45812	Alger 992	C4
44601	Alliance 24,315	H4
43102	Amanda 720	E6
†45201	Amberley 3,442	C9
45102	Amelia 1,108	D10
44001	Amherst 10,638	F3
43903	Amsterdam 783	J5
44003	Andover 1,205	J2
45302	Anna 1,038	B5
45303	Ansonia 1,267	A5
45813	Antwerp 1,765	A3
44606	Apple Creek 741	G4
44804	Arcadia 580	D3
45304	Arcanum 2,002	A6
43502	Archbold 3,318	B2
45814	Arlington 1,187	C4
†45201	Arlington Heights 1,082	C9
44805	Ashland⊙ 20,326	F4
43003	Ashley 1,057	E5
44004	Ashtabula 23,449	J2
43103	Ashville 2,046	E6
45701	Athens⊙ 19,743	F7
44807	Attica 865	E3
44201	Atwater 975	H3
44202	Aurora 8,177	H3
44010	Austinburg 900	J2
44515	Austintown 33,636	J3
44011	Avon 7,241	F3
44012	Avon Lake 13,222	F2
†43512	Ayersville 950	B3
†44805	Bailey Lakes 397	F4
45612	Bainbridge 1,042	D7
43804	Baltic 563	G5
43105	Baltimore 2,689	E6
44203	Barberton 29,751	G4
43713	Barnesville 4,633	H6
43905	Barton 1,039	J5
45103	Batavia⊙ 1,896	B7
†44870	Bay View 804	E3
44140	Bay Village 17,846	G9
44608	Beach City 1,083	G4
44122	Beachwood 9,983	J9
43716	Beallsville 601	J6
45808	Beaverdam 492	C4
44146	Bedford 15,056	H9
†44146	Bedford Heights 13,214	J9
43906	Bellaire 8,241	J5
45305	Bellbrook 5,174	C6
43310	Belle Center 930	C4
43311	Bellefontaine⊙ 11,888	C5
44811	Bellevue 8,187	E3
44813	Bellville 1,714	E4
43718	Belmont 714	J5
44609	Beloit 1,093	J4
45714	Belpre 7,193	G7
44017	Berea 19,567	G10
43908	Bergholz 914	J4
44814	Berlin Heights 756	F3
45106	Bethel 2,231	B8
43719	Bethesda 1,429	H5
44815	Bettsville 752	D3
45715	Beverly 1,471	G6
43209	Bexley 13,405	E6
45107	Blanchester 3,202	B7
44817	Bloomdale 744	D3
43106	Bloomingburg 869	D6
44818	Bloomville 1,019	D3
†45242	Blue Ash 9,506	C9
45817	Bluffton 3,310	C4
44512	Boardman 39,161	J3
44612	Bolivar 989	G4
†44264	Boston Heights 781	J10
45306	Botkins 1,372	B5
44695	Bowerston 487	H5
43402	Bowling Green⊙ 25,728	C3
45308	Bradford 2,166	B5
43406	Bradner 1,175	C3
44211	Brady Lake 470	H3
†44101	Bratenahl 1,485	H9
44141	Brecksville 10,132	H10
43107	Bremen 1,432	F6
44613	Brewster 2,321	G4
43912	Bridgeport 2,642	J5
†45211	Bridgetown 11,460	B9
43913	Brilliant 1,751	J5
†44240	Brimfield 3,161	H3
44402	Bristolville 900	J3
†44141	Broadview Heights 10,920	H10
44403	Brookfield 1,527	J3
44144	Brooklyn 12,342	H9
†44131	Brooklyn Heights 1,653	H9
44142	Brook Park 26,195	G9
†43912	Brookside 887	J5
45309	Brookville 4,322	B6
44212	Brunswick 28,104	G3
43506	Bryan⊙ 7,879	A3
45716	Buchtel 585	F7
43008	Buckeye Lake	F6
44820	Bucyrus⊙ 13,433	E4
†45680	Burlington 900	F9
44021	Burton 1,401	H3
44822	Butler 991	F4
43723	Byesville 2,572	G6
43907	Cadiz⊙ 4,058	J5
45820	Cairo 596	B4
43920	Calcutta 1,121	J4
43724	Caldwell⊙ 1,935	G6
43314	Caledonia 759	D4
43725	Cambridge⊙ 13,573	G5
45311	Camden 1,971	A6
44405	Campbell 11,619	J3
45111	Camp Dennison 625	D9
44614	Canal Fulton 3,481	H4
43110	Canal Winchester 2,749	E6
44406	Canfield 5,535	J3
*44701	Canton⊙ 93,077	H4
	Canton‡ 404,421	H4
43315	Cardington 1,665	E5
43316	Carey 3,674	D4
45005	Carlisle 4,276	B6
43112	Carroll 641	E6
44615	Carrollton⊙ 3,065	J4
44824	Castalia 973	E3
45314	Cedarville 2,799	C6
45822	Celina⊙ 9,137	A4
43011	Centerburg 1,275	E5
45459	Centerville 18,886	B6
44022	Chagrin Falls 4,335	J9
†45631	Chambersburg	F8
44024	Chardon⊙ 4,434	H2
45719	Chauncey 1,050	F7
†45202	Cherry Grove 850	C10
45619	Chesapeake 1,370	E9
44026	Chesterland 2,301	H2
†45211	Cheviot 9,888	B9
45601	Chillicothe⊙ 23,420	E7
45389	Christiansburg 593	C5
*45201	Cincinnati⊙ 385,457	B9
	Cincinnati‡ 1,401,403	B9
43113	Circleville⊙ 11,700	D6
43915	Clarington 558	J6
43115	Clarksburg 483	D7
45113	Clarksville 525	C7
45315	Clayton 752	B6
*44101	Cleveland⊙ 573,822	H9
	Cleveland‡ 1,898,720	H9
44118	Cleveland Heights 56,438	H9
45002	Cleves 2,094	B9
44216	Clinton 1,277	G4
43410	Clyde 5,489	E3
†45638	Coal Grove 2,602	E9
45621	Coalton 639	E7
45828	Coldwater 4,220	A5
†44034	Colebrook 700	J2
44028	Columbia Station 518	G10
44408	Columbiana 4,987	J4
*43201	Columbus (cap.)⊙ 565,032	E6
	Columbus‡ 1,093,293	E6
45830	Columbus Grove 2,313	B4
43811	Conesville 451	G5
44030	Conneaut 13,835	J2
45831	Continental 1,179	B3
45832	Convoy 1,140	A4
45723	Coolville 649	G7
43730	Corning 789	F6
44410	Cortland 5,011	J3
43812	Coshocton⊙ 13,405	G5
†45238	Covedale 5,830	B10
45318	Covington 2,610	B5
†44429	Craig Beach 1,657	H3
44827	Crestline 5,406	E4
44217	Creston 1,828	G3
45806	Cridersville 1,843	B4
43731	Crooksville 2,766	F6
45623	Crown City 513	F8
†45341	Crystal Lakes 1,463	C6
*44221	Cuyahoga Falls 43,890	G3
†44101	Cuyahoga Heights 739	H9
43413	Cygnet 646	C3
44618	Dalton 1,357	G4
43014	Danville 1,127	F5
†43123	Darbydale 825	D6
*45401	Dayton⊙ 193,444	B6
	Dayton‡ 830,070	B6
44411	Deerfield 800	H3
45236	Deer Park 6,745	C9
43512	Defiance⊙ 16,810	B3
43318	Degraff 1,358	C5
43015	Delaware⊙ 18,780	E5
45833	Delphos 7,314	B4
43515	Delta 2,831	B2
44621	Dennison 3,398	H5
†45202	Dent 800	B9
43516	Deshler 1,870	C3
45750	Devola 2,708	H7
43917	Dillonvale 912	J5
44622	Dover 11,782	G4
44230	Doylestown 2,493	G4
43821	Dresden 1,646	G5
43017	Dublin 3,855	D5
43734	Duncan Falls 900	G6
45836	Dunkirk 954	C4
44730	East Canton 1,721	H4
44112	East Cleveland 36,957	H9
†44094	Eastlake 22,104	J8
43920	East Liverpool 16,687	J4
44413	East Palestine 5,306	J4
44626	East Sparta 868	H4
45320	Eaton⊙ 6,839	A6
†44035	Eaton Estates 1,806	G3
43517	Edgerton 1,813	A3
†44004	Edgewood 3,099	J2
43320	Edison 504	E4
43518	Edon 947	A2
45321	Eldorado 509	A6
45807	Elida 1,349	B4
43416	Elmore 1,271	D3
45216	Elmwood Place 2,840	B9
*44035	Elyria⊙ 57,538	F3
45322	Englewood 11,329	B6
45323	Enon 2,597	C6
44117	Euclid 59,999	J9
†45201	Evendale 1,954	C9
45042	Excello 900	B7
45324	Fairborn 29,702	B6
†45201	Fairfax 2,222	C9
45014	Fairfield 30,777	A7
44313	Fairlawn 6,100	G3
44077	Fairport Harbor 3,357	H2
44126	Fairview Park 19,311	G9
45325	Farmersville 950	A6
43521	Fayette 1,222	B2
45120	Felicity 929	B8
45840	Findlay⊙ 35,594	C3
45326	Fletcher 498	B5
43977	Flushing 1,266	J5
45843	Forest 1,633	C4
45405	Forest Park 18,675	B9
45230	Forestville 950	C10
45844	Fort Jennings 538	B4
45845	Fort Loramie 977	B5
†45426	Fort McKinley	B6
45846	Fort Recovery 1,370	A5
†45801	Fort Shawnee 4,541	B4
44830	Fostoria 15,743	D3
45628	Frankfort 1,008	D7
45005	Franklin 10,711	B6
45629	Franklin Furnace 1,093	E8
43822	Frazeysburg 1,025	F5
44627	Fredericksburg 511	G4
43019	Fredericktown 2,299	F5
43973	Freeport 525	H5
43420	Fremont⊙ 17,834	D3
45630	Friendship 900	D8
43230	Gahanna 18,001	E5
44833	Galion 12,391	E4
45631	Gallipolis⊙ 5,576	F8
43022	Gambier 2,056	F5
44125	Garfield Heights 34,938	J9
44231	Garrettsville 1,769	H3
44040	Gates Mills 2,236	J9
44041	Geneva 6,655	J2
44043	Geneva-on-the-Lake 1,634	H2
43430	Genoa 2,213	D2
45121	Georgetown⊙ 3,467	C8
45327	Germantown 5,015	B6
45328	Gettysburg 545	A5
43431	Gibsonburg 2,479	D3
44420	Girard 12,517	J3
45848	Glandorf 746	B3
45246	Glendale 2,368	C9
†44139	Glenwillow 492	J10
45732	Glouster 2,211	F6
44629	Gnadenhutten 1,320	G5
†45201	Golf Manor 4,317	C9
45122	Goshen	B7
44044	Grafton 2,231	F3
43522	Grand Rapids 962	C3
44045	Grand River 412	H2
†43212	Grandview Heights 7,420	D6
43023	Granville 3,851	E5
45330	Gratis 809	A6
43322	Green Camp 475	D4
45123	Greenfield 5,150	D7
45218	Greenhills 4,927	B9
44232	Greensburg 950	G4
44836	Green Springs 1,568	E3
44630	Greentown 300	H4
45331	Greenville⊙ 12,999	A5
44837	Greenwich 1,458	E3
43123	Grove City 16,816	D6
43125	Groveport 3,286	E6
45849	Grover Hill 486	B3
45634	Hamden 1,010	F7
45130	Hamersville 688	C8
*45011	Hamilton⊙ 63,189	A7
	Hamilton-Middletown‡ 258,787	A7
43524	Hamler 625	B3
43931	Hannibal 550	J6
†43055	Hanover 926	F5
43126	Harrisburg 363	D6
45030	Harrison 5,855	A9
45850	Harrod 506	C4
†44085	Hartsgrove 200	J2
44632	Hartville 1,772	H4
43525	Haskins 568	C3
43127	Haydenville 395	F7
44838	Hayesville 518	F4
43055	Heath 6,969	F5
43025	Hebron 2,035	E6
43526	Hicksville 3,929	A3
†44143	Highland Heights 5,739	J9
43026	Hilliard 8,008	D5
45133	Hillsboro⊙ 6,356	C7
44234	Hiram 1,360	H3
43527	Holgate 1,315	B3
43528	Holland 1,048	C2
45033	Hooven 550	A9
43976	Hopedale 857	J5
44425	Hubbard 9,245	J3
45424	Huber Heights 35,480	B6
44236	Hudson 4,615	H3
†44022	Hunting Valley 786	J9
44839	Huron 7,123	E3
44131	Independence 6,607	H9
†45201	Indian Hill 5,521	C9
43932	Irondale 535	J4
45638	Ironton⊙ 14,290	E8
45640	Jackson⊙ 6,675	E7
45334	Jackson Center 1,310	B5
45740	Jacksonville 651	F7
45335	Jamestown 1,702	C6
44047	Jefferson⊙ 2,952	J2
†43162	Jefferson (West Jefferson) 4,448	D6
43128	Jeffersonville 1,252	C6
44840	Jeromesville 582	F4
43437	Jerry City 512	C3
43986	Jewett 972	H5
43031	Johnstown 3,158	E5
43748	Junction City 754	F6
45853	Kalida 1,019	B4
44240	Kent 26,164	H3
43326	Kenton⊙ 8,605	C4
45429	Kettering 61,186	B6
44637	Killbuck 937	G5
45034	Kings Mills 500	B7
45644	Kingston 1,208	E7
44048	Kingsville	J2
44428	Kinsman 900	J3
43033	Kirkersville 626	E6
†44094	Kirtland 5,969	H2
43951	Lafferty 855	H5
44050	Lagrange 1,258	F3
44250	Lakemore 2,744	H3
43440	Lakeside 850	E2
43331	Lakeview 1,089	C4
44107	Lakewood 61,963	G9
43130	Lancaster⊙ 34,953	E6
43934	Lansing 950	J5
43332	La Rue 861	D4
43135	Laurelville 591	E7
†45501	Lawrenceville 307	C6
45036	Lebanon⊙ 9,636	B7
45135	Leesburg 1,019	D7
44431	Leetonia 2,121	J4
45856	Leipsic 2,171	C3
45338	Lewisburg 1,450	A6
44904	Lexington 3,823	E4
43532	Liberty Center 1,111	B3
*45801	Lima⊙ 47,381	B4
	Lima‡ 218,244	B4
†45201	Lincoln Heights 5,259	C9
43442	Lindsey 571	D3
44432	Lisbon⊙ 3,159	J4
44253	Litchfield 650	F3
43136	Lithopolis 652	E6
45742	Little Hocking 800	G7
45215	Lockland 4,292	C9
44254	Lodi 2,942	F3
43138	Logan⊙ 6,557	F6
43140	London⊙ 6,958	C6
*44052	Lorain 75,416	F3
	Lorain-Elyria‡ 274,909	F3
†44481	Lordstown 3,280	J3
44842	Loudonville 2,945	F4
44641	Louisville 7,996	H4
45140	Loveland 9,106	D9
45744	Lowell 729	H6
44436	Lowellville 1,558	J3
44843	Lucas 753	F4
45648	Lucasville 3,349	E8
43443	Luckey 895	D3
45142	Lynchburg 1,205	C7
44124	Lyndhurst 18,092	J9
43533	Lyons 596	B2
44056	Macedonia 6,571	J10
†45202	Mack	B9
45243	Madeira 9,341	C9
44057	Madison 2,291	H2
44643	Magnolia 986	H4
43758	Malta 956	G6
44644	Malvern 1,032	H4
45144	Manchester 2,313	C8
*44901	Mansfield⊙ 53,927	F4
	Mansfield‡ 131,205	F4
44255	Mantua 1,041	H3
44137	Maple Heights 29,735	H9
†43440	Marblehead 679	E2
45860	Maria Stein 950	A5

(continued on following page)

Agriculture, Industry and Resources

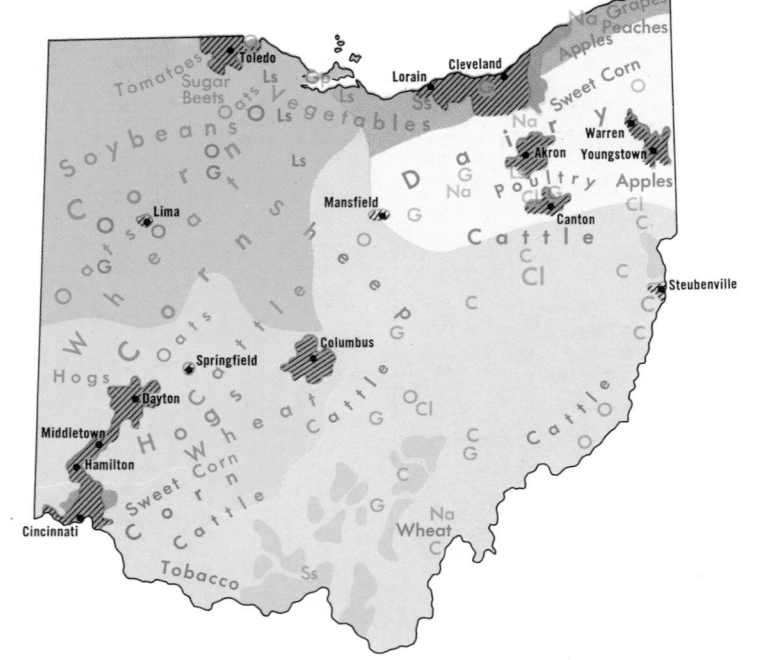

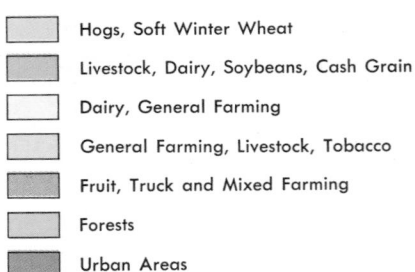

DOMINANT LAND USE

- Hogs, Soft Winter Wheat
- Livestock, Dairy, Soybeans, Cash Grain
- Dairy, General Farming
- General Farming, Livestock, Tobacco
- Fruit, Truck and Mixed Farming
- Forests
- Urban Areas

MAJOR MINERAL OCCURRENCES

- C   Coal
- Cl Clay
- G   Natural Gas
- Gp Gypsum
- Ls Limestone
- Na Salt
- O   Petroleum
- Ss Sandstone

Major Industrial Areas

OTHER FEATURES

⊙County seat.
‡Population of metropolitan area.
† Zip of nearest p.o.   * Multiple zips.

AREA 69,956 sq. mi. (181,186 sq. km.)
POPULATION 3,025,290
CAPITAL Oklahoma City
LARGEST CITY Oklahoma City
HIGHEST POINT Black Mesa 4,973 ft. (1516 m.)
SETTLED IN 1889
ADMITTED TO UNION November 16, 1907
POPULAR NAME Sooner State
STATE FLOWER Mistletoe
STATE BIRD Scissor-tailed Flycatcher

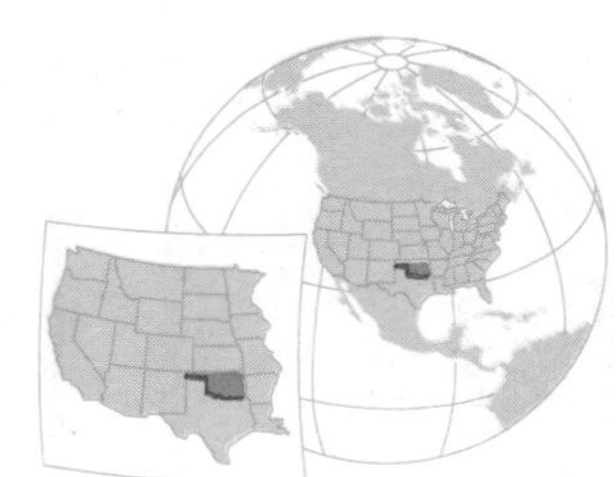

COUNTIES

Adair 18,575 ..... S3
Alfalfa 7,077 ..... K1
Atoka 12,748 ..... O6
Beaver 6,806 ..... E1
Beckham 19,243 ..... G4
Blaine 13,443 ..... K3
Bryan 30,535 ..... O7
Caddo 30,905 ..... K4
Canadian 56,452 ..... K3
Carter 43,610 ..... M6
Cherokee 30,684 ..... R3
Choctaw 17,203 ..... P6
Cimarron 3,648 ..... A1
Cleveland 133,173 ..... M4
Coal 6,041 ..... O5
Comanche 112,456 ..... K5
Cotton 7,338 ..... K6
Craig 15,014 ..... R1
Creek 59,016 ..... O3
Custer 25,995 ..... H3
Delaware 23,946 ..... S2
Dewey 5,922 ..... H2
Ellis 5,596 ..... G2
Garfield 62,820 ..... L2
Garvin 27,856 ..... M5
Grady 39,490 ..... L5
Grant 6,518 ..... L1
Greer 7,028 ..... G5
Harmon 4,519 ..... G5
Harper 4,715 ..... G1
Haskell 11,010 ..... R4
Hughes 14,338 ..... O4
Jackson 30,356 ..... H5
Jefferson 8,183 ..... L6
Johnston 10,356 ..... N6
Kay 49,852 ..... M1
Kingfisher 14,187 ..... L3
Kiowa 12,711 ..... J5
Latimer 9,840 ..... R5
Le Flore 40,698 ..... S5
Lincoln 26,601 ..... N3
Logan 26,881 ..... M3
Love 7,469 ..... M7
Major 8,772 ..... K2
Marshall 10,550 ..... N6
Mayes 32,261 ..... R2
McClain 20,291 ..... L5
McCurtain 36,151 ..... S6
McIntosh 15,562 ..... P4
Murray 12,147 ..... M6
Muskogee 66,939 ..... R3
Noble 11,573 ..... M2
Nowata 11,486 ..... P1
Okfuskee 11,125 ..... O3
Oklahoma 568,933 ..... M3
Okmulgee 39,169 ..... P3
Osage 39,327 ..... O1
Ottawa 32,870 ..... S1
Pawnee 15,310 ..... N2
Payne 62,435 ..... N2
Pittsburg 40,524 ..... P5
Pontotoc 32,598 ..... N5
Pottawatomie 55,239 ..... N4
Pushmataha 11,773 ..... R6
Roger Mills 4,799 ..... G3
Rogers 46,436 ..... P2
Seminole 27,473 ..... N4
Sequoyah 30,749 ..... S3
Stephens 43,419 ..... L6
Texas 17,727 ..... C1
Tillman 12,398 ..... J6
Tulsa 470,593 ..... P2
Wagoner 41,801 ..... P3
Washington 48,113 ..... P1
Washita 13,798 ..... J4
Woods 10,923 ..... J1
Woodward 21,172 ..... H2

CITIES and TOWNS

Zip *Name/Pop.* *Key*

74720 Achille 480 ..... O7
74820 Ada⊙ 15,902 ..... N5
74330 Adair 508 ..... R2
73901 Adams 150 ..... D1
73520 Addington 141 ..... L6
74331 Afton 1,174 ..... S1
74824 Agra 354 ..... N3
74721 Albany 65 ..... O7
73001 Albert 100 ..... K4
74521 Albion 165 ..... R5
74522 Alderson 366 ..... P5
73002 Alex 769 ..... L5
73716 Aline 313 ..... K1
74825 Allen 998 ..... O5
73521 Altus⊙ 23,101 ..... H5
73717 Alva⊙ 6,416 ..... J1
73004 Amber 416 ..... L4
73718 Ames 314 ..... K2
73719 Amorita 66 ..... K1
73005 Anadarko⊙ 6,378 ..... K4
74523 Antlers⊙ 2,989 ..... P6
73006 Apache 1,560 ..... K5
73620 Arapaho⊙ 851 ..... H3
73401 Ardmore⊙ 23,689 ..... M6
74901 Arkoma 2,175 ..... T4
73832 Arnett⊙ 714 ..... G2
74826 Asher 659 ..... N5
74524 Ashland 72 ..... O5
74525 Atoka⊙ 3,409 ..... O6
74827 Atwood 225 ..... O5
74001 Avant 461 ..... O2
†73860 Avard 51 ..... J1
73930 Baker 70 ..... D1
74002 Barnsdall 1,501 ..... O1
†74965 Baron 300 ..... S3
74003 Bartlesville⊙ 34,568 ..... O1
74722 Battiest 250 ..... S6
73932 Beaver⊙ 1,939 ..... F1
74421 Beggs 1,428 ..... P3
†74966 Bengal 300 ..... R5
74723 Bennington 302 ..... P7
74331 Bernice 318 ..... S1
73622 Bessie 245 ..... H4
73008 Bethany 22,130 ..... L3
74724 Bethel 350 ..... S6
†74801 Bethel Acres 2,314 ..... M4
74332 Big Cabin 252 ..... R1
74630 Billings 632 ..... M1
73009 Binger 791 ..... K4
73720 Bison 103 ..... L2
74058 Blackburn 114 ..... N2
74631 Blackwell 8,400 ..... M1
73526 Blair 1,092 ..... H5
73010 Blanchard 1,688 ..... L4
74528 Blanco 215 ..... P5
74529 Blocker 135 ..... P4
†74701 Blue 150 ..... O7
74333 Bluejacket 247 ..... R1
73933 Boise City⊙ 1,761 ..... B1
74726 Bokchito 628 ..... O6
74930 Bokoshe 556 ..... S4
74829 Boley 423 ..... O4
74727 Boswell 702 ..... P6
74830 Bowlegs 522 ..... N4
74009 Bowring 115 ..... O1
74422 Boynton 518 ..... P3
73011 Bradley 284 ..... L5
74423 Braggs 351 ..... R3
74632 Braman 355 ..... M1
73012 Bray 591 ..... L5
73721 Breckinridge 261 ..... L2
†73047 Bridgeport 115 ..... K3
74010 Bristow 4,702 ..... O3
74012 Broken Arrow 35,761 ..... P2
74728 Broken Bow 3,965 ..... S7
74530 Bromide 180 ..... N6
†74873 Brooksville 46 ..... M4
†74437 Bryant 74 ..... P4
73834 Buffalo⊙ 1,381 ..... G1
74931 Bunch 64 ..... S3
74633 Burbank 161 ..... N1
73722 Burlington 206 ..... K1
73430 Burneyville 150 ..... M7
73624 Burns Flat 2,431 ..... H4
73625 Butler 388 ..... H3
74831 Byars 353 ..... N5
†74820 Byng 833 ..... N5
73723 Byron 67 ..... K1
73527 Cache 1,661 ..... J5
74729 Caddo 923 ..... O6
74730 Calera 1,390 ..... O7
73014 Calumet 469 ..... K3
74531 Calvin 315 ..... O5
73835 Camargo 264 ..... H2
74932 Cameron 365 ..... T4
74425 Canadian 279 ..... P4
74533 Caney 147 ..... O6
73724 Canton 854 ..... J2
73626 Canute 676 ..... H4
73725 Capron 54 ..... J1
74335 Cardin 500 ..... S1
73726 Carmen 516 ..... J1
73015 Carnegie 2,016 ..... J4
74832 Carney 622 ..... N3
73727 Carrier 259 ..... K2
73627 Carter 367 ..... H4
74934 Cartersville 79 ..... S4
73016 Cashion 547 ..... L3
74833 Castle 130 ..... O4
74015 Catoosa 1,561 ..... P2
73017 Cement 884 ..... K5
74534 Centrahoma 166 ..... O5
74834 Chandler⊙ 2,926 ..... N3
73528 Chattanooga 403 ..... J6
74426 Checotah 3,454 ..... R4
74016 Chelsea 1,754 ..... P1
73728 Cherokee⊙ 2,105 ..... K1
73838 Chester 104 ..... J2
73628 Cheyenne⊙ 1,207 ..... G3
73018 Chickasha⊙ 15,828 ..... L4
74635 Chilocco 400 ..... M1
73020 Choctaw 7,520 ..... M3
74337 Chouteau 1,559 ..... R2
†74965 Christie 375 ..... S3
73111 Cimarron L3
74017 Claremore⊙ 12,085 ..... R2
74535 Clarita 72 ..... O6
74536 Clayton 833 ..... R5
74835 Clearview 250 ..... O4
73729 Cleo Springs 514 ..... K2
74020 Cleveland 2,972 ..... O2
73601 Clinton 8,796 ..... H3
74538 Coalgate⊙ 2,001 ..... O5
74733 Colbert 1,122 ..... O7
74338 Colcord 530 ..... S2
†73010 Cole 309 ..... L5
73432 Coleman 200 ..... O6
74021 Collinsville 3,556 ..... P2
73021 Colony 185 ..... J4
73529 Comanche 1,937 ..... L6
74339 Commerce 2,556 ..... R1
73022 Concho 300 ..... L3
†73041 Cooperton 31 ..... J5
74022 Copan 960 ..... P1
73632 Cordell⊙ 3,301 ..... H4
73024 Corn 542 ..... J4
†73456 Cornish 115 ..... L6
74428 Council Hill 141 ..... P3
73025 Countyline 550 ..... L6
73730 Covington 715 ..... L2
74429 Coweta 4,554 ..... P3
†74934 Cowlington 546 ..... S4
73027 Coyle 345 ..... M3
73638 Crawford 53 ..... G3
73028 Crescent 1,651 ..... L3
74837 Cromwell 337 ..... N4
74430 Crowder 431 ..... P4
†73446 Cumberland 100 ..... N6
74023 Cushing 7,720 ..... N3
73639 Custer City 530 ..... J3
73029 Cyril 1,220 ..... K5
73731 Dacoma 226 ..... J1
74838 Dale 160 ..... M4
74026 Davenport 974 ..... N3
73530 Davidson 501 ..... J6
73030 Davis 2,782 ..... M5
74636 Deer Creek 174 ..... L1
74027 Delaware 544 ..... P1
73115 Del City 28,523 ..... L4
74028 Depew 682 ..... O3
73531 Devol 186 ..... J6
74431 Dewar 1,048 ..... P4
74029 Dewey 3,545 ..... P1
73031 Dibble 348 ..... L4
†73401 Dickson 996 ..... M6
73641 Dill City 649 ..... H4
74340 Disney 464 ..... S2
73032 Dougherty 210 ..... M6
73733 Douglas 89 ..... L2
74341 Douthat 30 ..... S1
73734 Dover 570 ..... L3
73735 Drummond 482 ..... L2
74030 Drumright 3,162 ..... N3
73533 Duncan⊙ 22,517 ..... L5
74701 Durant⊙ 11,972 ..... O6
73642 Durham 30 ..... G3
74839 Dustin 498 ..... O4
74734 Eagletown 650 ..... S6
73033 Eakly 452 ..... K4
74840 Earlsboro 266 ..... N4
†73532 East Duke 484 ..... H5
73034 Edmond 34,637 ..... M3
73537 Eldorado 688 ..... G6
73538 Elgin 1,003 ..... K5
73644 Elk City 9,579 ..... G4
73539 Elmer 131 ..... H6
73035 Elmore City 582 ..... M5
73935 Elmwood 300 ..... F1
73036 El Reno⊙ 15,486 ..... K3
†73529 Empire City 13 ..... L6
73701 Enid⊙ 50,363 ..... L2
73645 Erick 1,375 ..... G4
74342 Eucha 210 ..... S2
74432 Eufaula⊙ 3,159 ..... P4
74637 Fairfax 1,949 ..... N1
74343 Fairland 1,073 ..... S1
73736 Fairmont 419 ..... L2
†74080 Fair Oaks 346 ..... P2
73737 Fairview⊙ 3,370 ..... J2
†74881 Fallis 22 ..... M3
74935 Fanshawe 416 ..... S5
73840 Fargo 409 ..... G2
73540 Faxon 140 ..... J6
73646 Fay 140 ..... J3
73937 Felt 120 ..... A1
74543 Finley 350 ..... R6
74842 Fittstown 500 ..... N5
74843 Fitzhugh 150 ..... N5
†73569 Fleetwood 12 ..... L7
73541 Fletcher 1,074 ..... K5
74652 Foraker 34 ..... Q1
†73101 Forest Park 1,148 ..... M3
73938 Forgan 611 ..... E1
73038 Fort Cobb 760 ..... K4
74434 Fort Gibson 2,477 ..... R3
73841 Fort Supply 559 ..... G1
74735 Fort Towson 789 ..... R7
73647 Foss 188 ..... H4
73039 Foster 100 ..... M5
73435 Fox 400 ..... M6
74031 Foyil 191 ..... R2
74844 Francis 365 ..... N5
73542 Frederick⊙ 6,153 ..... H6
73842 Freedom 339 ..... H1
73843 Gage 667 ..... G2
74936 Gans 346 ..... S4
73738 Garber 1,215 ..... M2
74736 Garvin 162 ..... S7
73844 Gate 146 ..... F1
73040 Geary 1,700 ..... K3
73436 Gene Autry 178 ..... N6
73543 Geronimo 726 ..... K6
†74531 Gerty 149 ..... O5
74032 Glencoe 490 ..... M2
74033 Glenpool 2,706 ..... P3
74737 Golden 300 ..... S6
†73093 Goldsby 603 ..... L4
73739 Goltry 305 ..... K1
†74740 Goodwater 240 ..... S7
73939 Goodwell 1,186 ..... C1
74435 Gore 445 ..... R3
73041 Gotebo 457 ..... J4
73544 Gould 318 ..... G5
74545 Gowen 75 ..... R5
73042 Gracemont 503 ..... K4
73545 Grady 85 ..... L6
73437 Graham 200 ..... M6
†74652 Grainola 67 ..... N1
73546 Grandfield 1,445 ..... J6
†74349 Grand Lake Towne 36 ..... S1
73547 Granite 1,617 ..... H5
†74437 Grayson 150 ..... P3
73043 Greenfield 233 ..... K3
74344 Grove 3,378 ..... S1
73044 Guthrie⊙ 10,312 ..... M3
73942 Guymon⊙ 8,492 ..... D1
74546 Haileyville 832 ..... P5
74034 Hallett 186 ..... N2
†73069 Hall Park 577 ..... M4
73650 Hammon 866 ..... H3
74845 Hanna 157 ..... P4
74846 Harden City 250 ..... N5
73944 Hardesty 243 ..... D1
73832 Harmon 27 ..... G2
73045 Harrah 2,897 ..... M4
†74740 Harris 192 ..... S7
74547 Hartshorne 2,380 ..... R5
74436 Haskell 1,953 ..... P3
73548 Hastings 246 ..... K6
74740 Haworth 341 ..... S7
73549 Headrick 223 ..... H5
73438 Healdton 3,769 ..... M6
74937 Heavener 2,776 ..... S5
73741 Helena 710 ..... K1
74741 Hendrix 106 ..... O7
73046 Hennepin 300 ..... M5
73742 Hennessey 2,287 ..... L2
74437 Henryetta 6,432 ..... O4
†73086 Hickory 95 ..... N5
73743 Hillsdale 110 ..... K1
73047 Hinton 1,432 ..... K4
73744 Hitchcock 172 ..... K3
74438 Hitchita 126 ..... P3
73651 Hobart⊙ 4,735 ..... J5
74439 Hoffman 407 ..... P4
74848 Holdenville⊙ 5,469 ..... O4
73550 Hollis⊙ 2,958 ..... G5
73551 Hollister 82 ..... J6
74035 Hominy 3,130 ..... O2
74549 Honobia 80 ..... R5
73945 Hooker 1,788 ..... D1
†74366 Hoot Owl 3 ..... R2
73746 Hopeton 42 ..... J1
74940 Howe 562 ..... S5
74440 Hoyt 160 ..... R4
74743 Hugo⊙ 7,172 ..... P7
74441 Hulbert 633 ..... R3
74640 Hunter 276 ..... L1
73048 Hydro 938 ..... J3
74745 Idabel⊙ 7,622 ..... S7
73552 Indiahoma 364 ..... J5
74442 Indianola 254 ..... P4
74036 Inola 1,550 ..... P2
73747 Isabella 113 ..... K2
74346 Jay⊙ 2,100 ..... S2
†73759 Jefferson 92 ..... L1
74037 Jenks 5,876 ..... P2
74038 Jennings 395 ..... N2
73749 Jet 352 ..... K1
73049 Jones 2,270 ..... M3
74347 Kansas 491 ..... S2
74641 Kaw City 283 ..... N1
74039 Kellyville 960 ..... O3

(continued on following page)

Agriculture, Industry and Resources

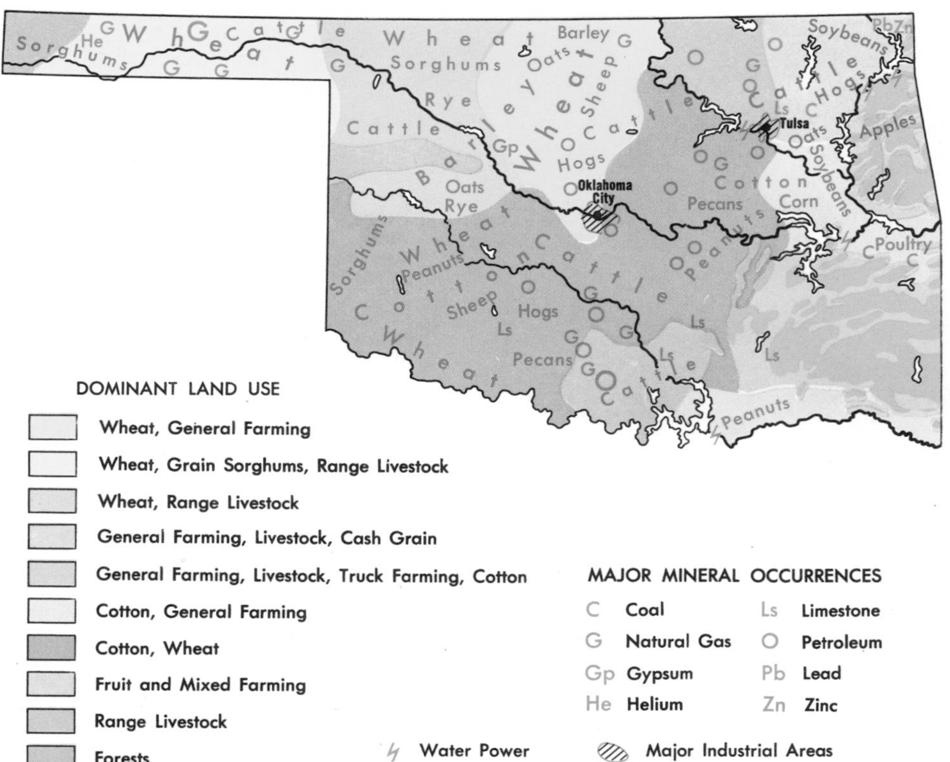

Wheat
Barley
Sorghums
Oats
Rye
Cattle
Sheep
Hogs
Soybeans
Tulsa
Apples
Oklahoma City
Cotton
Pecans
Corn
Peanuts
Poultry
DOMINANT LAND USE
Wheat, General Farming
Wheat, Grain Sorghums, Range Livestock
Wheat, Range Livestock
General Farming, Livestock, Cash Grain
General Farming, Livestock, Truck Farming, Cotton
Cotton, General Farming
Cotton, Wheat
Fruit and Mixed Farming
Range Livestock
Forests
MAJOR MINERAL OCCURRENCES
C Coal
G Natural Gas
Gp Gypsum
He Helium
Ls Limestone
O Petroleum
Pb Lead
Zn Zinc
Water Power
Major Industrial Areas

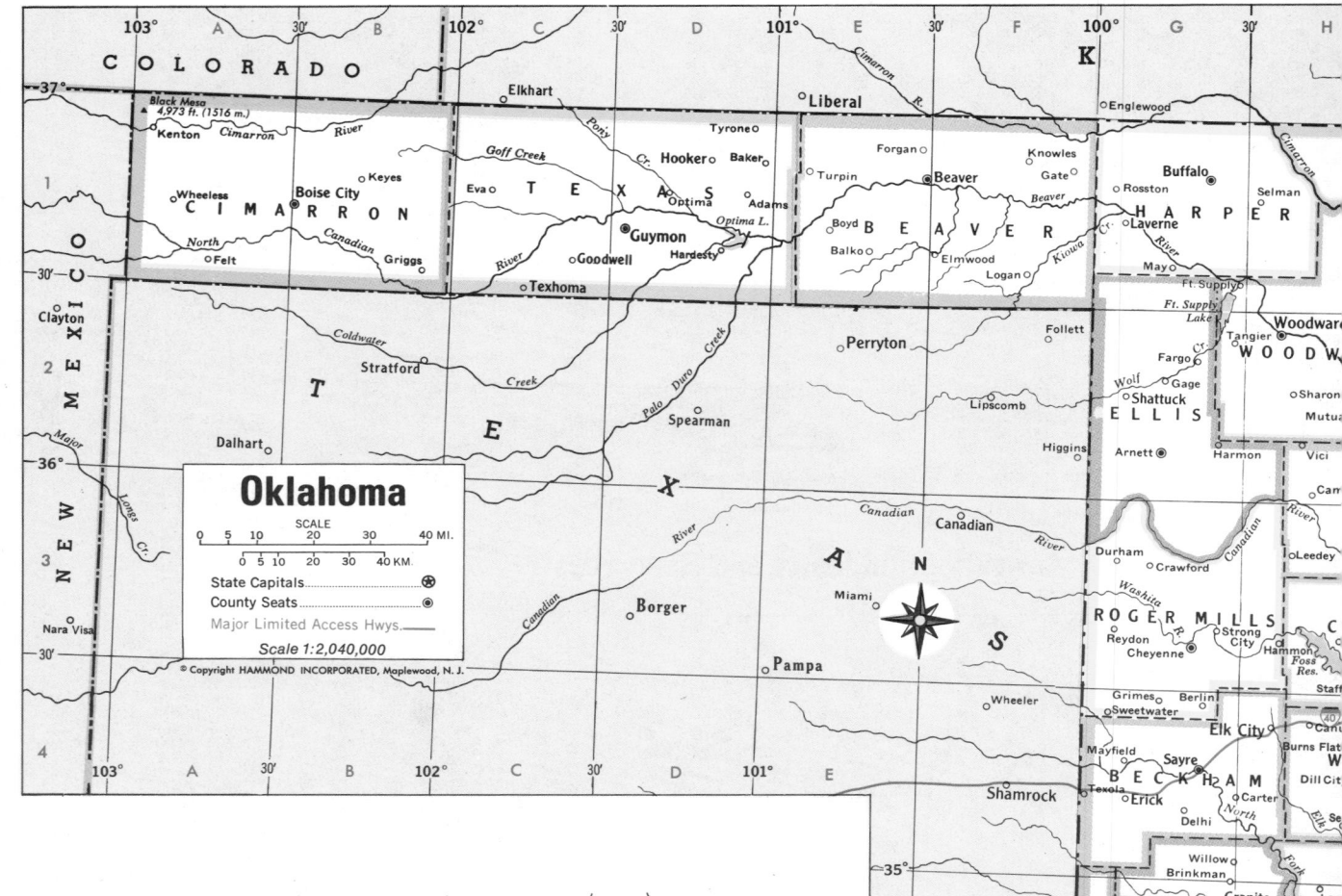

Oklahoma
SCALE
0 5 10 20 30 40 MI.
0 5 10 20 30 40 KM.
State Capitals
County Seats
Major Limited Access Hwys.
Scale 1:2,040,000
© Copyright HAMMOND INCORPORATED, Maplewood, N. J.
COLORADO
NEW MEXICO
TEXAS
CIMARRON
TEXAS
BEAVER
HARPER
ELLIS
ROGER MILLS
BECKHAM
Boise City
Guymon
Beaver
Buffalo
Black Mesa 4,973 ft. (1516 m.)
Kenton
Keyes
Goodwell
Hooker
Texhoma
Arnett
Cheyenne
Sayre
Elk City
Perryton
Dalhart
Spearman
Borger
Pampa
Canadian

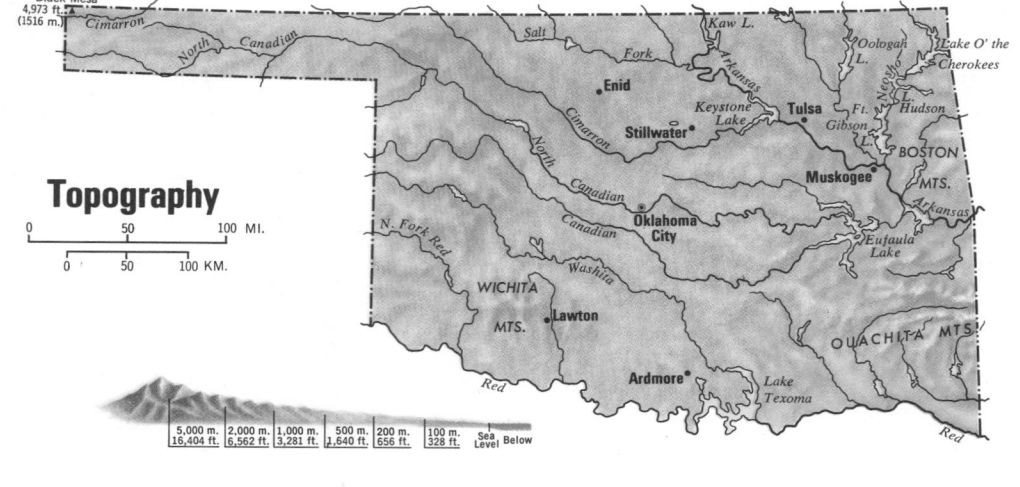

Topography
0 50 100 MI.
0 50 100 KM.
Black Mesa 4,973 ft. (1516 m.)
Enid
Stillwater
Tulsa
Muskogee
Oklahoma City
Lawton
Ardmore
Kaw L.
Keystone Lake
Eufaula Lake
Lake Texoma
Lake O' the Cherokees
WICHITA MTS.
OUACHITA MTS.
BOSTON MTS.
5,000 m. 16,404 ft.
2,000 m. 6,562 ft.
1,000 m. 3,281 ft.
500 m. 1,640 ft.
200 m. 656 ft.
100 m. 328 ft.
Sea Level
Below

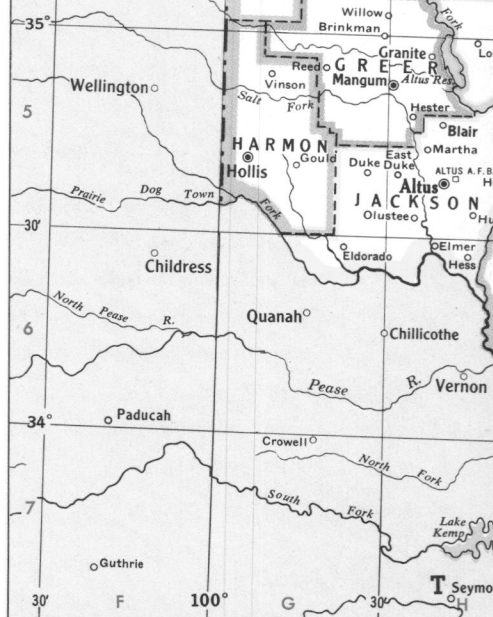

GREER
HARMON
JACKSON
Mangum
Hollis
Altus
Wellington
Childress
Quanah
Chillicothe
Vernon
Paducah
Guthrie

COUNTIES

Baker 16,134 ....K3
Benton 68,211 ....D3
Clackamas 241,911 ....D1
Clatsop 32,489 ....D2
Columbia 35,646 ....D2
Coos 64,047 ....C4
Crook 13,091 ....G3
Curry 16,992 ....C5
Deschutes 62,142 ....F4
Douglas 93,748 ....D4
Gilliam 2,057 ....G2
Grant 8,210 ....J3
Harney 8,314 ....H4
Hood River 15,835 ....F2
Jackson 132,456 ....E5
Jefferson 11,599 ....F3
Josephine 58,855 ....D5
Klamath 59,117 ....F5
Lake 7,532 ....G5
Lane 275,226 ....E4
Lincoln 35,264 ....D3
Linn 89,495 ....E3

Malheur 26,896 ....K4
Marion 204,692 ....E3
Morrow 7,519 ....H2
Multnomah 562,640 ....E2
Polk 45,203 ....D3
Sherman 2,172 ....G2
Tillamook 21,164 ....D2
Umatilla 58,861 ....J2
Union 23,921 ....K2
Wallowa 7,273 ....K2
Wasco 21,732 ....F2
Washington 245,860 ......D2
Wheeler 1,513 ....G3
Yamhill 55,332 ....D2

CITIES and TOWNS

Zip   Name/Pop.   Key

†97330 Adair Village 589 ...D3
97810 Adams 240 ....J2
97620 Adel 24 ....H5
97901 Adrian 162 ....K4
†97365 Agate Beach 975 ....C3
97406 Agness 150 ....C5
97321 Albany⊙ 26,678 ......D3
97407 Allegany 300 ....D4
97005 Aloha 28,353 ....A2
97409 Alvadore 800 ....D3
97101 Amity 1,092 ....D2
97001 Antelope 39 ....G3
97530 Applegate 150 ....D5
97458 Arago 200 ....C4
97812 Arlington 521 ....G2
97520 Ashland 14,943 ......E5
97103 Astoria⊙ 9,998 ......D1
97813 Athena 965 ....J2
97325 Aumsville 1,432 .....E3
97002 Aurora 523 ....B2
†97617 Austin 19 ....J3
97814 Baker⊙ 9,471 ....K3
†97378 Ballston 120 ....D2
97411 Bandon 2,311 ....C4
97106 Banks 489 ....A1
†97013 Barlow 105 ....B2

†97009 Barton 100 ....B2
†97136 Bar View 170 ....C2
†97420 Barview 1,462 ......C4
97817 Bates 56 ....J3
97107 Bay City 986 ....D2
97621 Beatty 350 ....F5
97108 Beaver 350 ....D2
97004 Beavercreek 708 ....B2
97005 Beaverton 30,582 ...A2
†97701 Bend⊙ 17,263 ......F3
†97058 Biggs 50 ....G2
97412 Blachly 80 ....D3
97108 Blaine 38 ....D2
97326 Blodgett 100 ....D3
97413 Blue River 318 .....E3
97622 Bly 800 ....F5
97818 Boardman 1,261 .....H2
97623 Bonanza 270 ....F5
97008 Bonneville 80 ......F2
97009 Boring 150 ....B2
97010 Bridal Veil 20 .....E2
†97458 Bridge 200 ....D4
†97136 Brighton 150 ......C2
97001 Brightwood 200 .....E2

97414 Broadbent 400 ......C4
97903 Brogan 130 ....K3
97415 Brookings 3,384 ....C5
97524 Brownsboro 150 .....E5
97327 Brownsville 1,261 ..E3
†97351 Buena Vista 130 ...D3
†97720 Burns⊙ 3,579 .....H4
97522 Butte Falls 428 ....E5
†97002 Butteville 20 .....A2
97109 Buxton 350 ....D2
97416 Camas Valley 750 ...D4
97730 Camp Sherman 350 ...F3
†97493 Canary 23 ....D4
97013 Canby 7,659 ....B2
97110 Cannon Beach 1,187 .D2
97820 Canyon City⊙ 639 ..J3
97417 Canyonville 1,288 ..D5
97111 Carlton 1,302 ......D2
97014 Cascade Locks 838 ..E2
97329 Cascadia 250 ....E3
97523 Cave Junction 1,023 .D5
97821 Cayuse 200 ....J2

97225 Cedar Hills 9,619 ..A2
97005 Cedar Mill 900 .....A2
†97058 Celilo 50 ....G2
97502 Central Point 6,357 .D5
97420 Charleston 500 .....C4
97306 Chemawa 400 ....A3
97731 Chemult 800 ....F4
†97058 Chenoweth 2,820 ...C4
†97119 Cherry Grove 350 ..D2
†97055 Cherryville 75 ....E2
97419 Cheshire 300 ....D3
97624 Chiloquin 778 ......F5
97015 Clackamas B2
97016 Clatskanie 1,648 ...D1
97112 Cloverdale 260 .....D2
97401 Coburg 699 ....E3
97017 Colton 305 ....B3
97018 Columbia City 678 ..D2
97823 Condon⊙ 783 ....G2
97420 Coos Bay 14,424 ....C4
97423 Coquille⊙ 4,481 ...C4
97113 Cornelius 4,462 ....A2
97330 Corvallis⊙ 40,960 .D3
97424 Cottage Grove 7,148 .D4

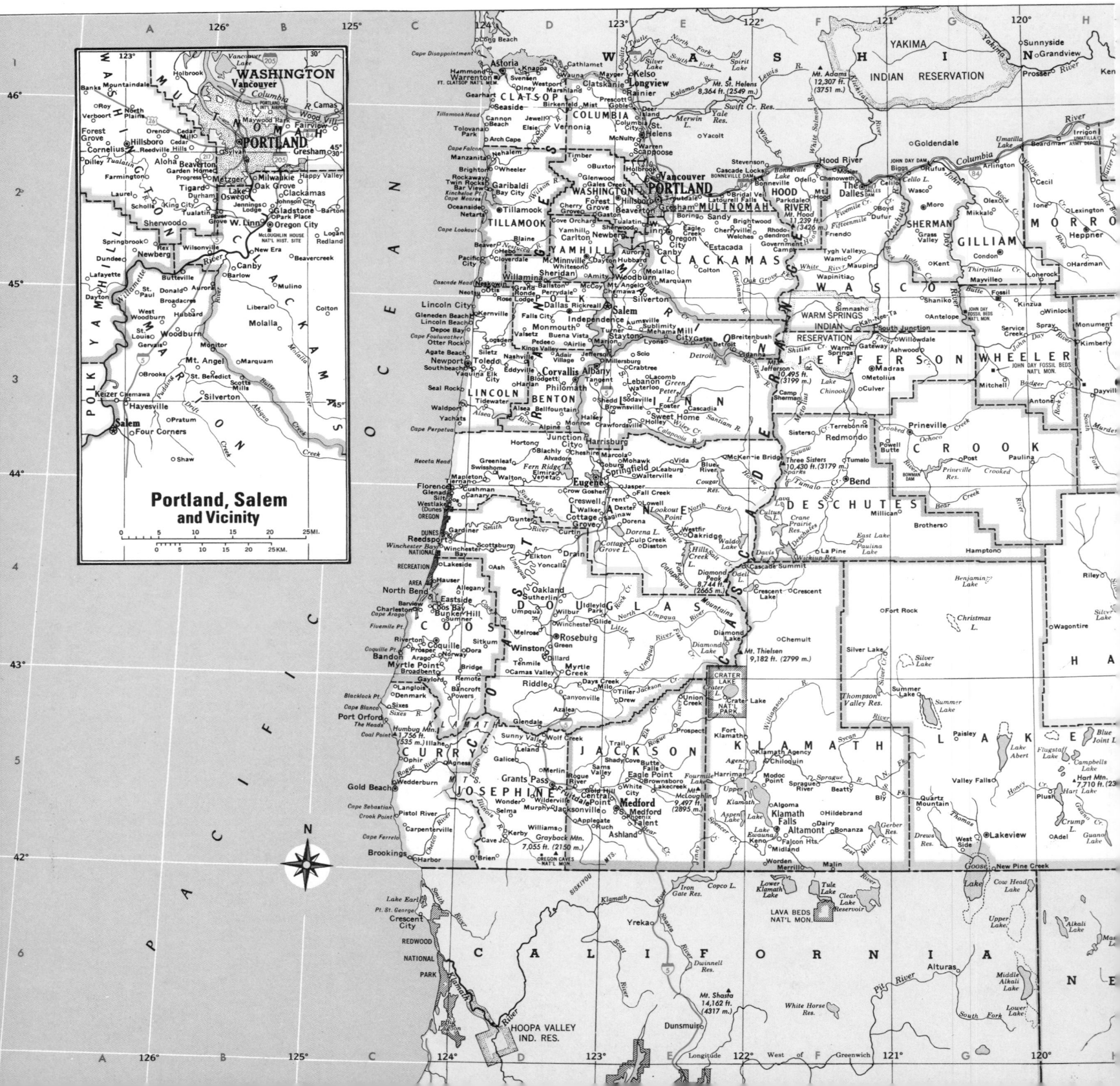

Portland, Salem and Vicinity

AREA 97,073 sq. mi. (251,419 sq. km.)
POPULATION 2,633,149
CAPITAL Salem
LARGEST CITY Portland
HIGHEST POINT Mt. Hood 11,239 ft. (3426 m.)
SETTLED IN 1810
ADMITTED TO UNION February 14, 1859
POPULAR NAME Beaver State
STATE FLOWER Oregon Grape
STATE BIRD Western Meadowlark

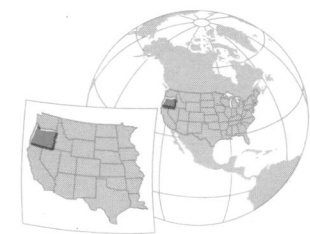

Topography

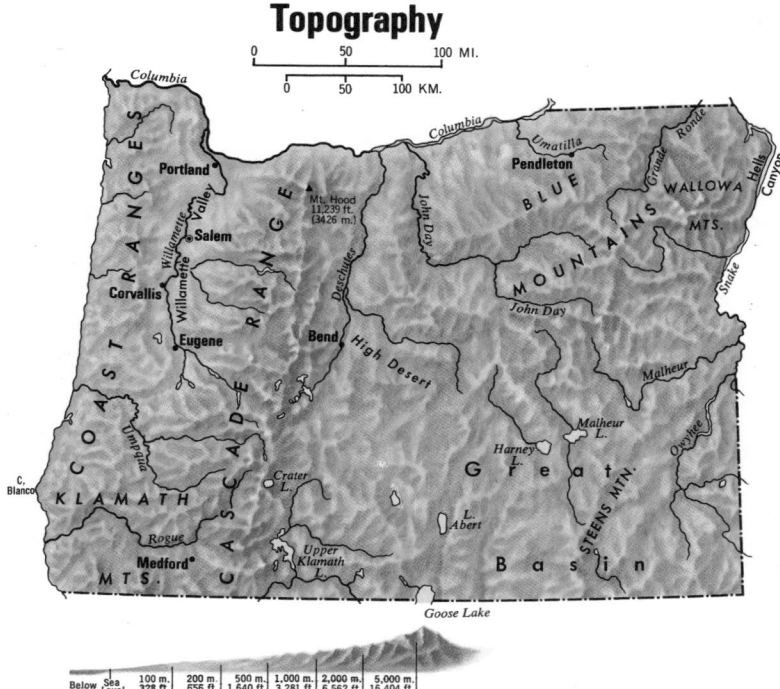

Below Sea Level	100 m. 328 ft.	200 m. 656 ft.	500 m. 1,640 ft.	1,000 m. 3,281 ft.	2,000 m. 6,562 ft.	5,000 m. 16,404 ft.

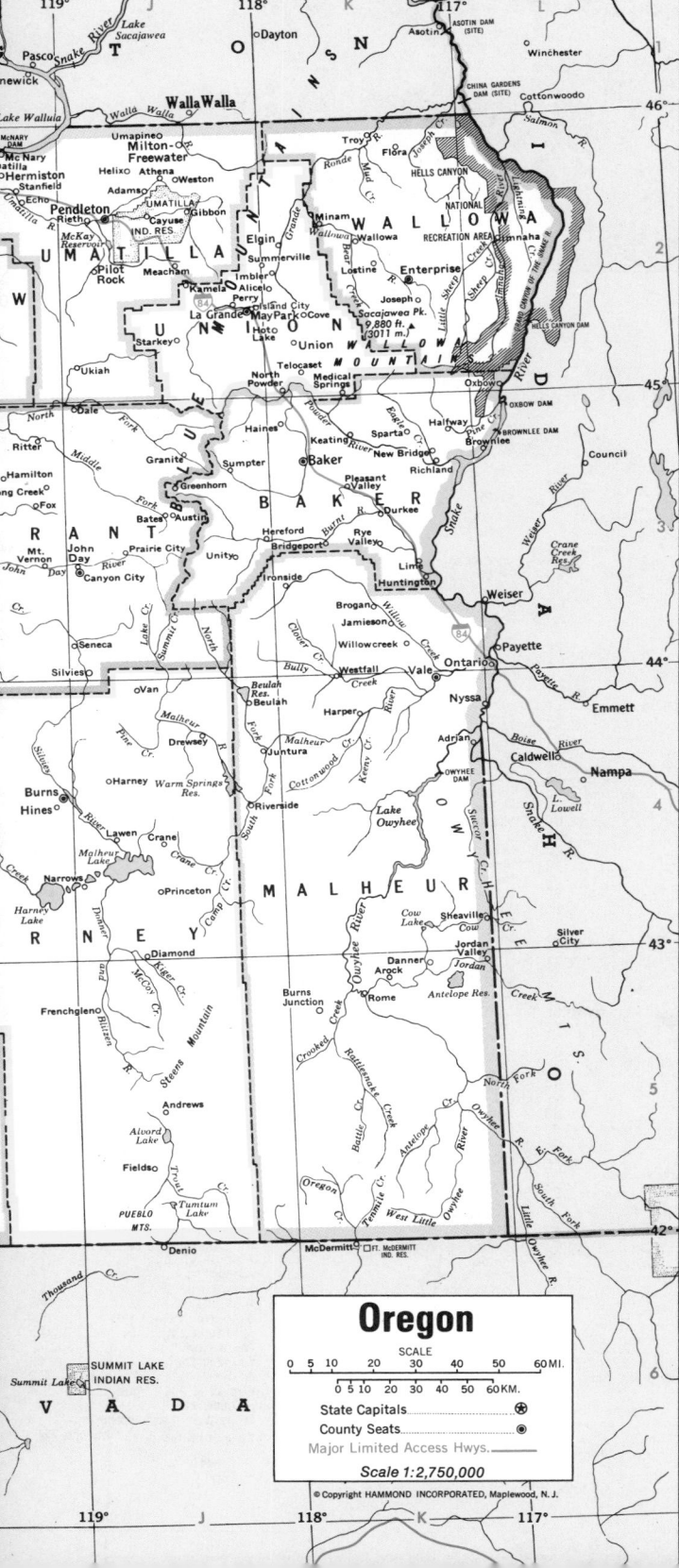

Oregon

SCALE
0 5 10 20 30 40 50 60 MI.
0 5 10 20 30 40 50 60 KM.

State Capitals ⊛
County Seats ⊙
Major Limited Access Hwys.

Scale 1:2,750,000

© Copyright HAMMOND INCORPORATED, Maplewood, N.J.

(continued on following page)

Agriculture, Industry and Resources

DOMINANT LAND USE

☐	Specialized Wheat
☐	Wheat, Peas
☐	Specialized Dairy
☐	Dairy, Poultry, Mixed Farming
☐	Fruit and Mixed Farming
☐	Potatoes, General Farming
☐	General Farming, Dairy, Hay, Sugar Beets
☐	General Farming, Livestock, Special Crops
☐	Range Livestock
☐	Forests
☐	Nonagricultural Land

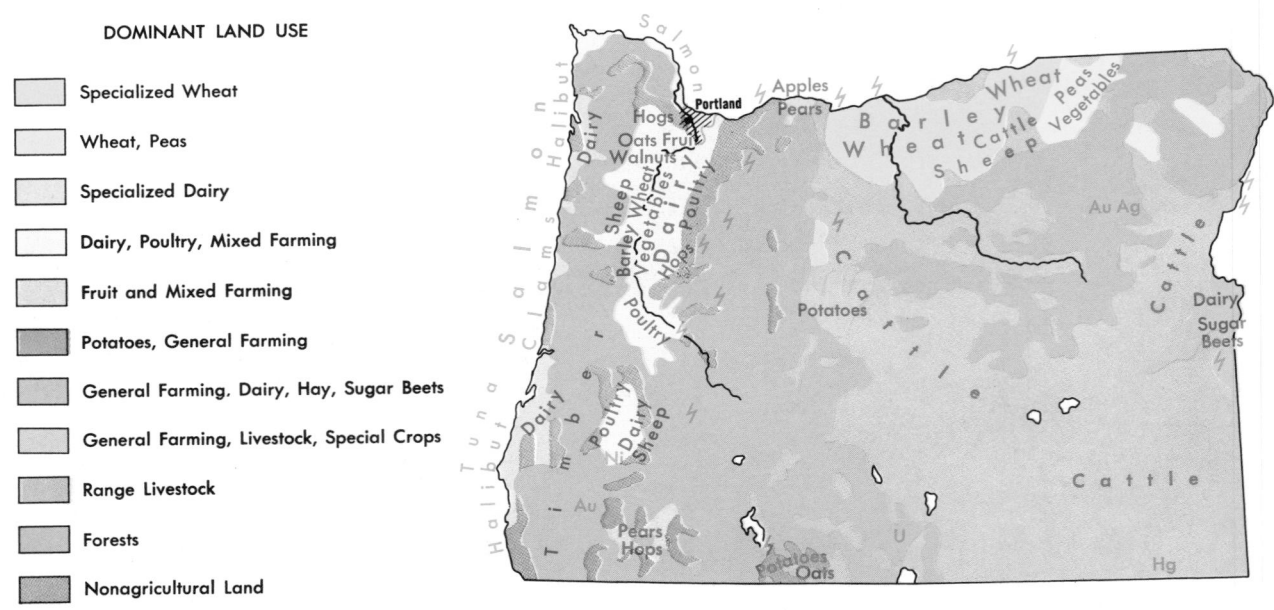

MAJOR MINERAL OCCURRENCES

Ag Silver   Hg Mercury   ⚡ Water Power

Au Gold   Ni Nickel   ▨ Major Industrial Areas

U Uranium

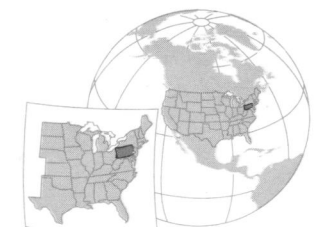

DOMINANT LAND USE

- Specialized Dairy
- Dairy, General Farming
- Fruit and Mixed Farming
- Fruit, Truck and Mixed Farming
- General Farming, Livestock, Tobacco
- General Farming, Livestock, Fruit, Tobacco
- Forests
- Urban Areas

AREA 45,308 sq. mi. (117,348 sq. km.)
POPULATION 11,863,895
CAPITAL Harrisburg
LARGEST CITY Philadelphia
HIGHEST POINT Mt. Davis 3,213 ft. (979 m.)
SETTLED IN 1682
ADMITTED TO UNION December 12, 1787
POPULAR NAME Keystone State
STATE FLOWER Mountain Laurel
STATE BIRD Ruffed Grouse

MAJOR MINERAL OCCURRENCES

C	Coal	G	Natural Gas	Sl	Slate
Cl	Clay	Ls	Limestone	Ss	Sandstone
Co	Cobalt	O	Petroleum	Zn	Zinc
Fe	Iron Ore				

⚡ Water Power
▨ Major Industrial Areas

Agriculture, Industry and Resources

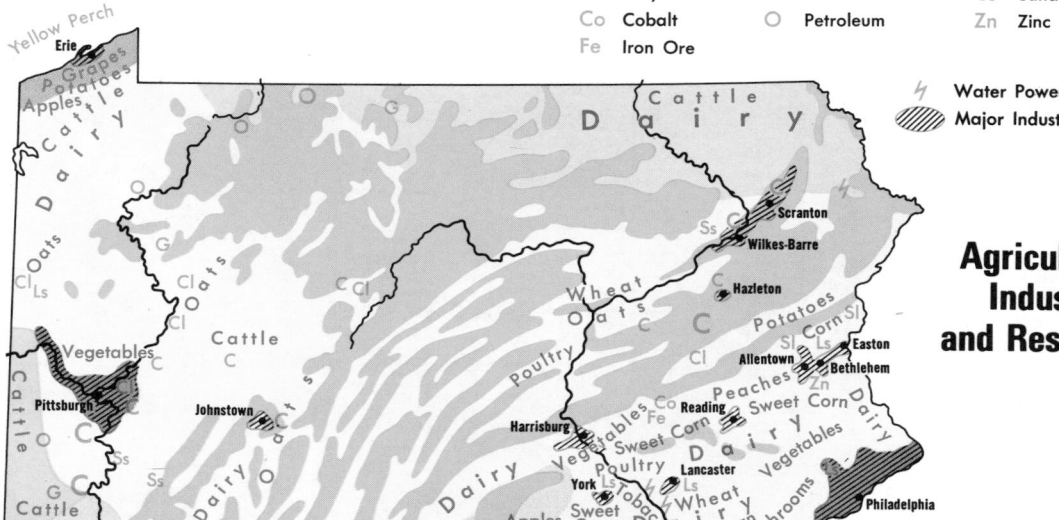

(continued on following page)

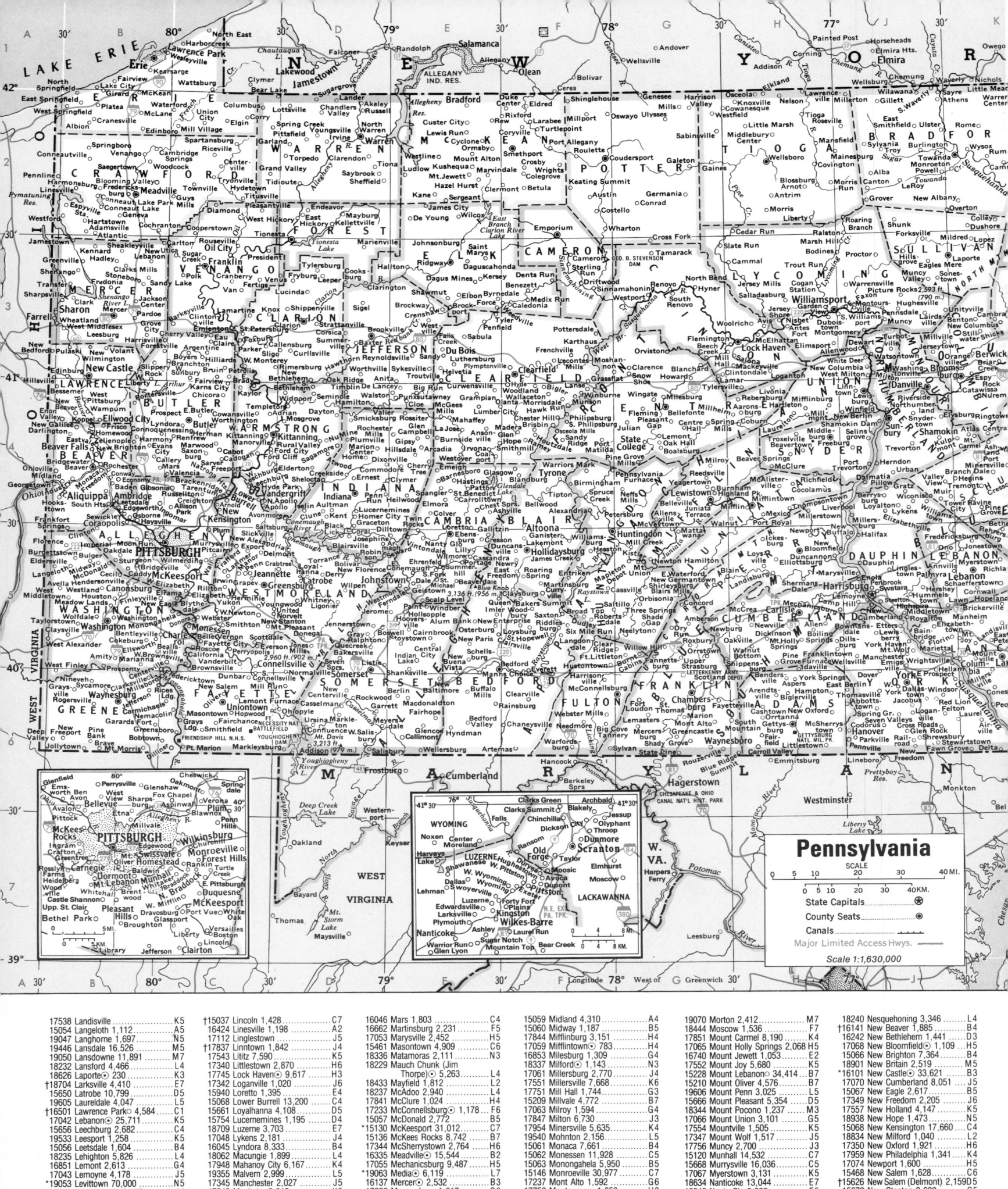

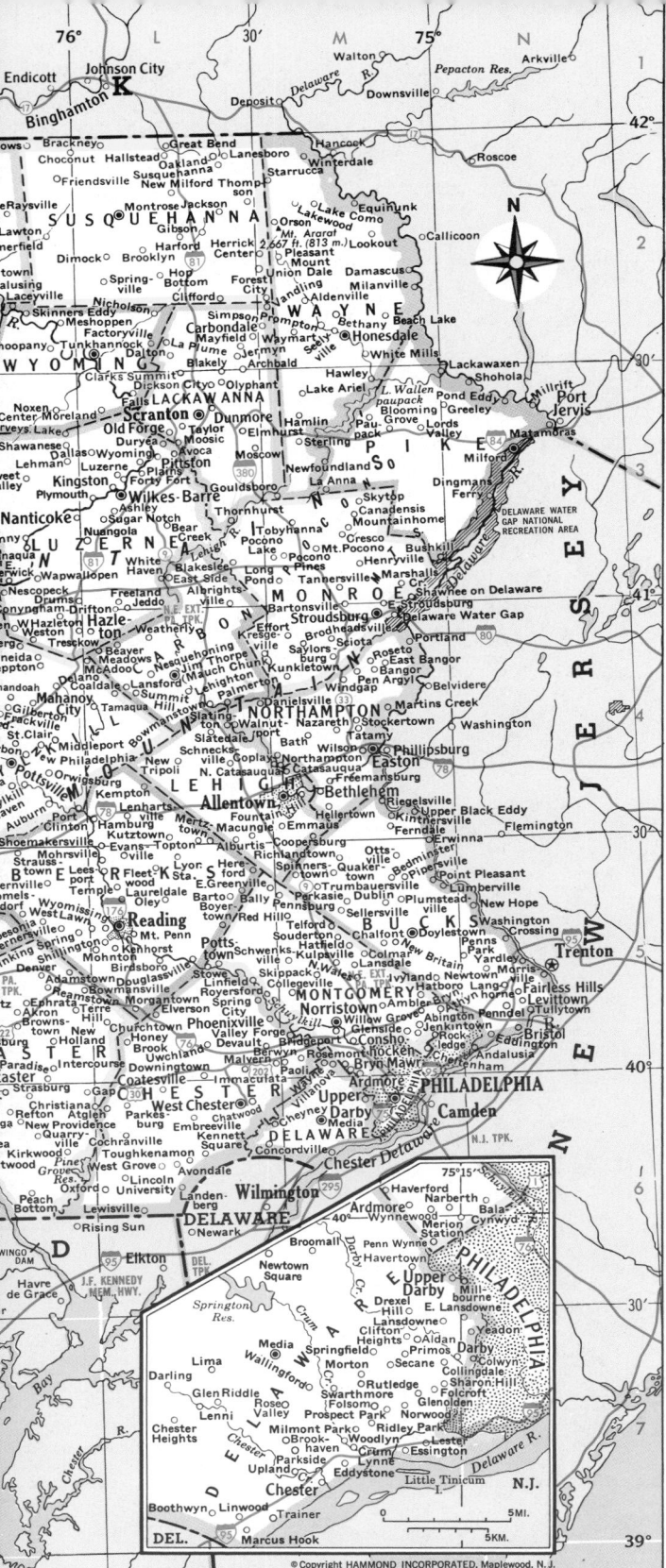

16823 Pleasant Gap 1,859	....G4	
15236 Pleasant Hills 9,676	....B7	
16341 Pleasantville 1,099	....C2	
15239 Plum 25,390	....C5	
18651 Plymouth 7,605	....E7	
15474 Point Marion 1,642	....C6	
16342 Polk 1,884	....C3	
15946 Portage 3,510	....E5	
16743 Port Allegany 2,593	....F2	
17965 Port Carbon 2,576	....K4	
†15133 Port Vue 5,316	....C7	
19464 Pottstown 22,729	....L5	
17901 Pottsville⊙ 18,195	....K4	
19076 Prospect Park 6,593	....M7	
15767 Punxsutawney 7,479	....E4	
17566 Quarryville 1,558	....K6	
†15104 Rankin 2,892	....C7	
*19601 Reading⊙ 78,686	....L5	
Reading‡ 312,509	....L5	
17567 Reamstown 1,308	....K5	
18076 Red Hill 1,727	....L5	
17356 Red Lion 5,824	....J6	
17084 Reedsville 1,023	....G4	
17764 Renovo 1,812	....G3	
15851 Reynoldsville 3,016	....D3	
17087 Richland 1,470	....K5	
18955 Richlandtown 1,180	....M5	
15853 Ridgway⊙ 5,604	....E3	
19078 Ridley Park 7,889	....M7	
18077 Riegelsville 993	....M4	
16248 Rimersburg 1,096	....D3	
17868 Riverside 2,266	....J4	
16673 Roaring Spring 2,962	....F5	
19551 Robesonia 1,748	....K5	
15074 Rochester 4,759	....B4	
15477 Roscoe 1,123	....C5	
18013 Roseto 1,484	....M4	
†19101 Rockledge 2,538	....M5	
15557 Rockwood 1,058	....D6	
*19065 Rose Valley 1,038	....L7	
17250 Rouzerville 1,371	....G6	
19468 Royersford 4,243	....L5	
16249 Rural Valley 1,033	....D4	
15076 Russellton 1,878	....C4	
17970 Saint Clair 4,037	....K4	
15857 Saint Marys 6,417	....E3	
15951 Saint Michael 1,445	....E5	
15681 Saltsburg 964	....C4	
*15801 Sandy 1,835	....E4	
16056 Saxonburg 1,336	....C4	
*15963 Scalp Level 1,186	....E5	
19473 Schwenksville 1,041	....L5	
15683 Scottdale 5,833	....C5	
*18501 Scranton⊙ 88,117	....F7	
Scranton (Northeast Pa.)‡ 640,396	....F7	
17870 Selinsgrove 5,227	....J4	
18960 Sellersville 3,143	....M5	
15143 Sewickley 4,778	....B4	
17872 Shamokin 10,357	....J4	
17876 Shamokin Dam 1,622	....J4	
16146 Sharon 19,057	....B3	
Sharon‡ 128,299	....B3	
19079 Sharon Hill 6,221	....N7	
15215 Sharpsburg 4,351	....B6	
16150 Sharpsville 5,375	....A3	
16347 Sheffield 1,471	....D2	
17976 Shenandoah 7,589	....K4	
18655 Shickshinny 1,192	....K3	
19607 Shillington 5,601	....K5	
16748 Shillington 1,310	....F2	
17257 Shippensburg 5,261	....H5	
19555 Shoemakersville 1,391	....K4	
17361 Shrewsbury 2,688	....J6	
19608 Sinking Spring 2,617	....K5	
18080 Slatington 4,277	....L4	
15684 Slickville.1,178	....C5	
16057 Slippery Rock 3,047	....B3	
16749 Smethport⊙ 1,797	....F2	
15478 Smithfield 1,084	....C6	
15501 Somerset⊙ 6,474	....D6	
18964 Souderton 6,657	....M5	
15425 South Connellsville 2,296	....C6	
15956 South Fork 1,401	....E5	
†18840 South Waverly 1,176	....J2	

17701 South Williamsport 6,581	..J3	
15775 Spangler 2,399	....E4	
19475 Spring City 3,389	....L5	
15144 Springdale 4,418	....C6	
19064 Springfield 25,326	....M7	
17362 Spring Grove 1,832	....J6	
16801 State College 36,130	....G4	
State College‡ 112,760	....G4	
17263 State Line 1,253	....G6	
17113 Steelton 6,484	....J5	
17363 Stewartstown 1,072	....K6	
16153 Stoneboro 1,177	....B3	
19464 Stowe 3,860	....L5	
17579 Strasburg 1,999	....K6	
18360 Stroudsburg⊙ 5,148	....M4	
15082 Sturgeon 1,312	....B5	
†16323 Sugar Creek 5,954	....C3	
18706 Sugar Notch 1,191	....E7	
18250 Summit Hill 3,418	....L4	
17801 Sunbury⊙ 12,292	....J4	
18847 Susquehanna 1,994	....L2	
19081 Swarthmore 5,950	....M7	
†17111 Swatara⊙ 18,796	....J5	
15218 Swissvale 11,345	....C7	
18704 Swoyersville 5,795	....E7	
15865 Sykesville 1,537	....E3	
18252 Tamaqua 8,843	....L4	
15084 Tarentum 6,419	....C4	
18517 Taylor 7,246	....F7	
18969 Telford 3,507	....M5	
19560 Temple 1,486	....L5	
17581 Terre Hill 1,217	....L5	
18512 Throop 4,166	....F7	
16351 Tidioute 844	....D2	
16353 Tionesta⊙ 659	....C2	
16684 Tipton 1,348	....F4	
16354 Titusville 6,884	....C2	
19562 Topton 1,555	....L5	
19374 Toughkenamon 1,111	....L6	
18848 Towanda⊙ 3,526	....J2	
17980 Tower City 1,667	....J4	
15085 Trafford 3,662	....C5	
19013 Trainer 2,056	....L7	
17981 Tremont 1,796	....K4	
18254 Tresckow 1,128	....K4	
17881 Trevorton 2,192	....J4	
16947 Troy 1,381	....J2	
19007 Tullytown 2,277	....N5	
18657 Tunkhannock⊙ 2,144	....L2	
15145 Turtle Creek 6,959	....C7	
16686 Tyrone 6,346	....F4	
16438 Union City 3,623	....C2	
15401 Uniontown⊙ 14,510	....C6	
*19082 Upper Darby⊙ 84,054	....M6	
15241 Upper Saint Claire⊙ 19,023	B7	
19481 Valley Forge 400	....L5	
17983 Valley View 1,722	....J4	
15690 Vandergrift 6,823	....D4	
15147 Verona 3,179	....C6	
15132 Versailles 2,150	....C7	
19085 Villanova 1	....M6	
18088 Walnutport 2,007	....L4	
16365 Warren⊙ 12,146	....D2	
15301 Washington⊙ 18,363	....B5	
16441 Waterford 1,568	....B2	
17777 Watsontown 2,366	....J3	
19087 Wayne	....M6	
17268 Waynesboro 9,726	....G6	
15370 Waynesburg⊙ 4,482	....B6	
18255 Weatherly 2,891	....L4	
16901 Wellsboro⊙ 3,805	....H2	
19565 Wernersville 1,811	....K5	
16510 Wesleyville 3,998	....C1	
15417 West Brownsville 1,433	..C5	
19380 West Chester⊙ 17,435	..L6	
16950 Westfield 1,268	....H2	
18201 West Hazleton 4,871	....K4	
*16201 West Kittanning 1,591	..C4	
†15656 West Leechburg 1,395	..C4	
16159 West Middlesex 1,064	..B3	
15122 West Mifflin 26,279	....C7	
†15905 Westmont 6,113	....D5	
15089 West Newton 3,387	....C5	
16160 West Pittsburg 1,133	....B4	
18643 West Pittston 5,980	....F7	
15229 West View 7,648	....B6	

18644 West Wyoming 3,288	....E7	
†17401 West York 4,526	....J6	
15120 Whitaker 1,615	....C7	
†15234 Whitehall 15,206	....B7	
18661 White Haven 1,921	....L3	
15131 White Oak 9,480	....C7	
17097 Wiconisco 1,321	....J4	
*18701 Wilkes-Barre⊙ 51,551	..F7	
15221 Wilkinsburg 23,669	....C7	
16693 Williamsburg 1,400	....F5	
17701 Williamsport⊙ 33,401	..H3	
Williamsport‡ 118,416	..H3	
17098 Williamstown 1,664	....J4	
19090 Willow Grove	....M5	
15148 Windber 2,421	....C5	
15025 Wilson 7,564	....M4	
15963 Windber 5,585	....E5	
18091 Windgap 2,651	....M4	
19567 Womelsdorf 1,827	....K5	
19094 Woodlyn	....M7	
17368 Wrightsville 2,365	....J5	
18644 Wyoming 3,655	....F7	
19610 Wyomissing 6,551	....K5	
19067 Yardley 2,533	....N5	
19050 Yeadon 11,727	....N7	
17099 Yeagertown 1,305	....G4	
*17401 York⊙ 44,619	....J6	
York‡ 381,255	....J6	
16371 Youngsville 2,006	....D2	
15697 Youngwood 3,749	....D5	
16063 Zelienople 3,502	....B4	

OTHER FEATURES

Allegheny (res.)	....E2	
Allegheny (riv.)	....D2	
Allegheny Front (mts.)	....E5	
Appalachian (mts.)	....H4	
Ararat (mt.)	....M2	
Arthur (lake)	....C4	
Beaver (riv.)	....B4	
Blue (mt.)	....G5	
Blue Knob (mt.)	....E5	
Casselman (riv.)	....D6	
Clarion (riv.)	....D3	
Conemaugh (riv.)	....D5	
Conemaugh River (lake)	..D4	
Conewango (creek)	....D1	
Davis (mt.)	....D6	
Delaware (riv.)	....N3	
Delaware Water Gap Nat'l Rec. Area	..N3	
Erie (lake)	....B1	
Fort Necessity Nat'l Battlefield	..C6	
George B. Stevenson (dam)	..G3	
Gettysburg Nat'l Mil. Park	..H6	
Glendale (lake)	....F4	
Juniata (riv.)	....G5	
Laurel Hill (mt.)	....D5	
Lehigh (riv.)	....L3	
Letterkenny Army Depot	..G6	
Licking (creek)	....F6	
Little Tinicum (isl.)	....M7	
Lycoming (creek)	....H3	
Monongahela (riv.)	....C6	
North (mt.)	....K3	
Ohio (riv.)	....A4	
Oil (creek)	....C2	
Pine (creek)	....H2	
Pine Grove (res.)	....K6	
Pocono (mts.)	....L4	
Pymatuning (res.)	....A2	
Redbank (creek)	....E3	
Schuylkill (riv.)	....M5	
Shenango River (lake)	..B3	
Sinnemahoning (creek)	..F3	
South (mt.)	....H6	
Susquehanna (riv.)	....H1	
Tioga (riv.)	....H1	
Tionesta (lake)	....D3	
Towanda (creek)	....J2	
Tuscarora (riv.)	....G5	
Wallenpaupack (lake)	..M3	
Youghiogheny River (riv.)	..D6	

⊙County seat.
‡Population of metropolitan area.
⊙Population of town or township.
† Zip of nearest p.o. * Multiple zips.

18067 Northampton 8,240	....M4	
15673 North Apollo 1,487	....D4	
15104 North Braddock 8,711	..C7	
†18032 North Catasauqua 2,554	...L4	
16428 North East 4,568	....C1	
17857 Northumberland 3,636	..J4	
19454 North Wales 3,391	....M5	
†16365 North Warren 1,232	..D2	
15674 Norvelt 2,541	....D5	
19074 Norwood 6,647	....M7	
15071 Oakdale 1,955	....B5	
15072 Oakmont 7,039	....C4	
†15059 Ohioville 4,217	....B4	
16301 Oil City 13,881	....C3	
18518 Old Forge 9,304	....F7	
15472 Oliver 3,777	....C6	
18447 Olyphant 5,204	....F7	
17961 Orwigsburg 2,700	....K4	
16666 Osceola Mills 1,466	....F4	
19363 Oxford 3,633	....K6	
15963 Paint 1,177	....E5	
18071 Palmerton 5,455	....L4	
17078 Palmyra 7,228	....J5	
19301 Paoli 5,277	....M5	

17562 Paradise 1,107	....K5	
19365 Parkesburg 2,578	....L6	
†19013 Parkside 2,464	....M7	
17331 Parkville 5,009	....J6	
16668 Patton 2,441	....E4	
18072 Pen Argyl 3,388	....M4	
17103 Penbrook 3,006	....J5	
19047 Penndel 2,703	....N5	
18073 Pennsburg 2,339	....M5	
17331 Pennville 1,398	....J6	
†19151 Penn Wynne	....M6	
18944 Perkasie 5,241	....M5	
15473 Perryopolis 2,139	....C5	
*19101 Philadelphia⊙ 1,688,210	..N6	
Philadelphia‡ 4,716,818	..N6	
16866 Philipsburg 3,533	....F4	
19460 Phoenixville 14,165	....L5	
17963 Pine Grove 2,244	....K4	
16868 Pine Grove Mills 1,030	..G4	
15140 Pitcairn 4,175	....C5	
*15201 Pittsburgh⊙ 423,938	..B7	
Pittsburgh‡ 2,263,894	..B7	
*18640 Pittston 9,930	....F7	
†18701 Plains 5,455	....F7	

Topography

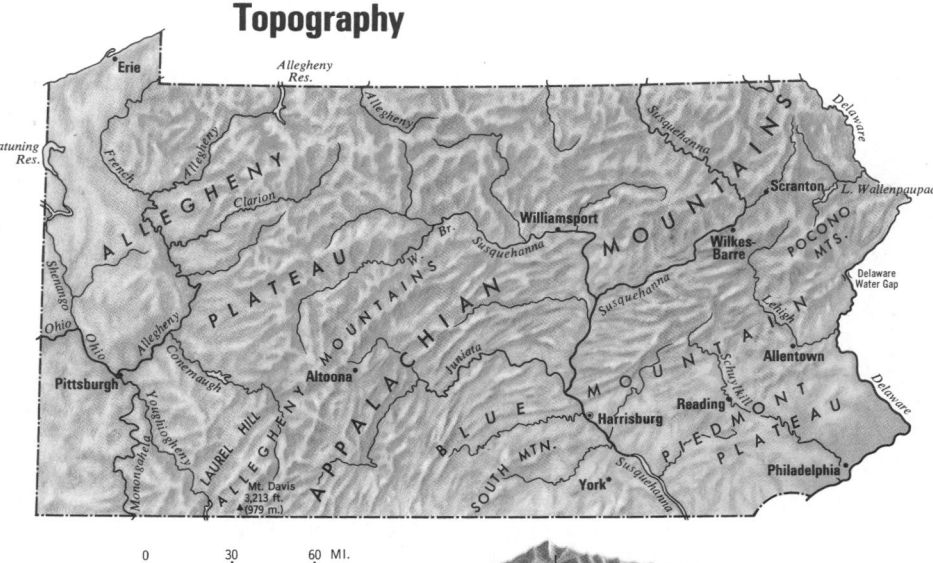

5,000 m. 16,404 ft.	2,000 m. 6,562 ft.	1,000 m. 3,281 ft.	500 m. 1,640 ft.	200 m. 656 ft.	100 m. 328 ft.	Sea Level	Below

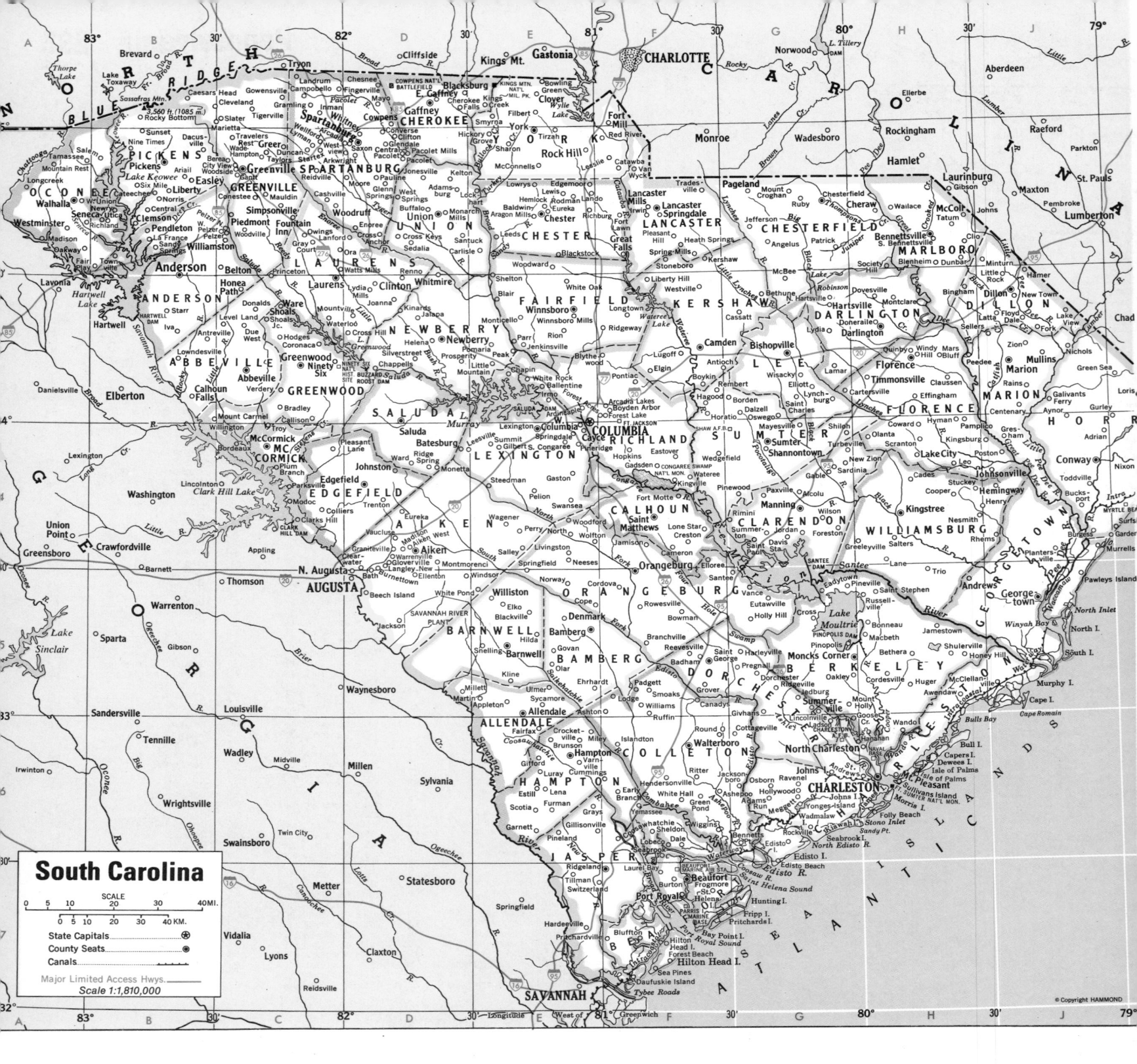

South Carolina

SCALE
0 5 10   20   30   40MI.
0 5 10   20   30   40 KM.

State Capitals .... ⊛
County Seats .... ⊙
Canals ....
Major Limited Access Hwys. ....
Scale 1:1,810,000

© Copyright HAMMOND

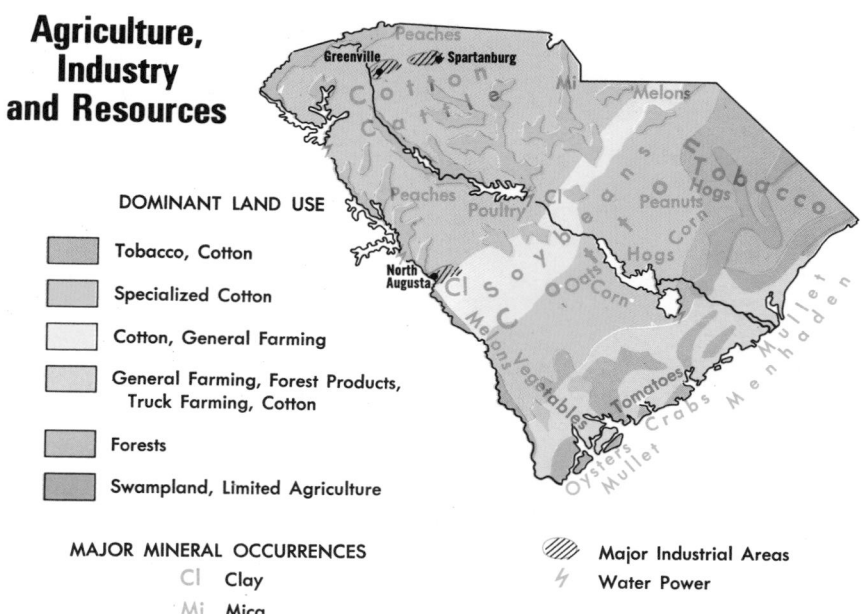

Agriculture, Industry and Resources

DOMINANT LAND USE

- Tobacco, Cotton
- Specialized Cotton
- Cotton, General Farming
- General Farming, Forest Products, Truck Farming, Cotton
- Forests
- Swampland, Limited Agriculture

MAJOR MINERAL OCCURRENCES

Cl Clay
Mi Mica

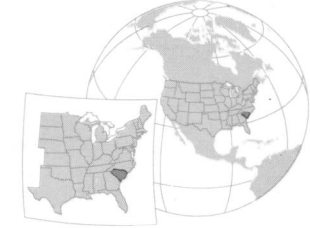

Major Industrial Areas
Water Power

AREA 31,113 sq. mi. (80,583 sq. km.)
POPULATION 3,121,833
CAPITAL Columbia
LARGEST CITY Columbia
HIGHEST POINT Sassafras Mtn. 3,560 ft. (1085 m.)
SETTLED IN 1670
ADMITTED TO UNION May 23, 1788
POPULAR NAME Palmetto State
STATE FLOWER Carolina (Yellow) Jessamine
STATE BIRD Carolina Wren

†29720 Lancaster Mills 2,096 ...... F2
29356 Landrum 2,141 .... C1
29564 Lane 554 .... H5
29834 Langley 1,714 .... D4
29565 Latta 1,804 .... J3
29902 Laurel Bay 5,238 .... F7
29360 Laurens⊙ 10,587 .... C3
29070 Leesville 2,296 .... E4
†29730 Lesslie 1,102 .... E2
29072 Lexington⊙ 2,131 .... E4
29657 Liberty 3,167 .... B2
†29483 Lincolnville 808 .... G6
29075 Little Mountain 282 .... E3
29076 Livingston 166 .... E4
29364 Lockhart 85 .... E2
29082 Lodge 145 .... F5
29569 Loris 2,193 .... K3
29659 Lowndesville 197 .... B3
†29706 Lowrys 225 .... E2
29078 Lugoff 2,939 .... F3
29932 Luray 149 .... E6
29325 Lydia Mills 925 .... D3
29365 Lyman 1,067 .... C2
29080 Lynchburg 534 .... G3
†29829 Madison 1,150 .... D4
29102 Manning⊙ 4,746 .... G4
29661 Marietta-Slater 1,834 .... C1
29571 Marion⊙ 7,700 .... J3
29662 Mauldin 8,143 .... C2
29104 Mayesville 663 .... G4
29101 McBee 774 .... G3
29458 McClellanville 436 .... H5
29570 McColl 2,677 .... H2
29726 McConnells 171 .... E2
29835 McCormick⊙ 1,725 ...... C4
29460 Meggett 249 .... G6
†29379 Monarch Mills 2,353 ... D2
29461 Moncks Corner⊙ 3,699 . G5
29105 Monetta 167 .... D4
29840 Mount Carmel 182 .... C3
29727 Mount Croghan 146 ..... G2
29464 Mount Pleasant 14,209 . H6
29574 Mullins 6,068 .... J3
29576 Murrells Inlet 2,410 ..... K4
29577 Myrtle Beach 18,446 .... K4
29107 Neeses 557 .... E4
29108 Newberry⊙ 9,866 .... D3
29809 New Ellenton 2,628 ..... D5
†29536 New Town 950 .... J3
29581 Nichols 606 .... J3
29666 Ninety Six 2,249 .... C3
29667 Norris 903 .... B2
29112 North 1,304 .... E4
29841 North Augusta 13,593 ... C5
29406 North Charleston 62,534 . G6
†29550 North Hartsville 2,650 .. G3
29582 North Myrtle Beach 3,960. K4
29113 Norway 518 .... E4
29114 Olanta 699 .... H4
29843 Olar 381 .... E5
29115 Orangeburg⊙ 14,933 ... F4
29372 Pacolet 1,556 .... D2
29373 Pacolet Mills 1,051 ...... D2
29728 Pageland 2,720 .... G2
29583 Pamplico 1,213 .... H4
29844 Parksville 157 .... C4
29584 Patrick 375 .... G2
29102 Paxville 244 .... G4
29122 Peak 82 .... E3
29123 Pelion 213 .... E4
29669 Pelzer 130 .... B2
29670 Pendleton 3,154 .... B2
29124 Perry 273 .... E4
29671 Pickens⊙ 3,199 .... B2
29673 Piedmont 2,992 .... C2
29934 Pineland 800 .... E6
†29169 Pineridge 1,287 .... E4
29468 Pineville 900 .... H5
29125 Pinewood 689 .... G4
29469 Pinopolis 788 .... G5
29845 Plum Branch 73 .... C4
29126 Pomaria 271 .... E3
29935 Port Royal 2,977 .... F7
29127 Prosperity 803 .... D3
29501 Quinby 952 .... H3
29470 Ravenel 1,655 .... G6

29471 Reevesville 241 .... F5
29729 Richburg 269 .... E2
29936 Ridgeland⊙ 1,143 .... F7
29129 Ridge Spring 969 .... D4
29472 Ridgeville 603 .... G5
29130 Ridgeway 343 .... F3
29730 Rock Hill 35,344 .... E2
    Rock Hill‡ 106,720 .... E2
29133 Rowesville 388 .... F5
29741 Ruby 256 .... G2
29407 Saint Andrews 9,908 ..... G6
29477 Saint George⊙ 2,134 .... F5
29135 Saint Matthews⊙ 2,496 . F4
29479 Saint Stephen 1,850 ..... H5
29676 Salem 194 .... A2
29137 Salley 584 .... E4
29138 Saluda⊙ 2,752 .... D4
29142 Santee 612 .... F5
†29301 Saxon 4,383 .... D2
29939 Scotia 72 .... E6
29591 Scranton 861 .... H4
29592 Sellers 348 .... H3
29678 Seneca 7,436 .... A2
29742 Sharon 323 .... E2
29145 Silverstreet 200 .... D3
29681 Simpsonville 9,037 ...... C2
29682 Six Mile 470 .... B2
29683 Slater-Marietta 1,834 ... C1
29481 Smoaks 165 .... F5
29743 Smyrna 47 .... E1
†29812 Snelling 111 .... E4
29593 Society Hill 848 .... H2
†29512 South Bennettsville 1,065 . H2
†29169 South Congaree 2,113 ... E4
*29301 Spartanburg⊙ 43,826 .. C1
29169 Springdale 2,985 .... E4
†29720 Springdale 2,570 .... F2
29146 Springfield 604 .... E4
†29067 Spring Mills 1,419 ...... F2
29684 Starr 241 .... B3
29377 Startex 1,006 .... C2
29554 Stuckey 222 .... H4
29482 Sullivans Island 1,867 .. H6
29148 Summerton 1,173 .... G4
29483 Summerville 6,706 ...... G5
†29054 Summit 172 .... E4
29150 Sumter⊙ 24,890 .... G4
29577 Surfside Beach 2,522 ... K4
29160 Swansea 888 .... E4
29846 Sycamore 261 .... E5
29594 Tatum 101 .... H2
29687 Taylors 15,801 .... C2
29688 Tigerville 975 .... C1
29161 Timmonsville 2,112 ..... H3
29690 Travelers Rest 3,017 ... C2
29847 Trenton 404 .... D4
29848 Troy 705 .... C4
29162 Turbeville 549 .... G4
29849 Ulmer 91 .... E5
29379 Union⊙ 10,523 .... D2
†29678 Utica 1,501 .... B2
29163 Vance 89 .... G5
29944 Varnville 2,498 .... E6
29607 Wade-Hampton 20,180 . C2
29164 Wagener 903 .... E4
29691 Walhalla⊙ 3,977 .... A2
29488 Walterboro⊙ 6,209 .... F6
29166 Ward 98 .... D4
29692 Ware Shoals 2,370 ..... C3
29851 Warrenville 1,029 ...... D4
29384 Waterloo 200 .... C3
†29360 Watts Mills 1,324 ...... D2
29385 Wellford 2,143 .... C2
29169 West Columbia 10,409 . E4
29693 Westminster 3,114 ..... A2
29669 West Pelzer 944 .... B2
29696 West Union 300 .... B2
†29301 Westview 1,999 .... C2
29178 Whitmire 2,038 .... D3
29303 Whitney 4,052 .... D1
29493 Williams 205 .... F5
29697 Williamston 4,310 ...... B2
29853 Williston 3,173 .... E5
29856 Windsor 55 .... E5
†29501 Windy Hill 1,622 .... H3
29180 Winnsboro⊙ 2,919 ..... E3

†29180 Winnsboro Mills 1,890 ... E3
†29112 Woodford 206 .... E4
29388 Woodruff 5,171 .... D2
29945 Yemassee 789 .... F6
29745 York⊙ 6,412 .... E1

OTHER FEATURES

Ashepoo (riv.) F6
Ashley (riv.) G6
Bay Point (isl.) F7
Beaufort Marine Air Sta. F7
Big Black (creek) G2
Black (riv.) H4
Blue Ridge (mts.) B1
Broad (riv.) E2
Broad (riv.) F7
Buck (creek) J3
Bull (isl.) H6
Bullock (creek) E2
Bulls (bay) H6
Bush (riv.) D3
Cape (isl.) J5
Capers (isl.) H6
Catawba (riv.) F2
Catfish (creek) J3
Charleston A.F.B. G6
Chattooga (riv.) A2
Clark Hill (dam) C4
Clark Hill (lake) C4
Combahee (riv.) F6
Congaree (riv.) F4
Congaree Nat'l Mon. E4
Cooper (riv.) H6
Coosaw (riv.) G7
Coosawhatchie (riv.) E6
Cowpens Nat'l Battlefield D1
Crooked (creek) H2
Deep (creek) B2
Dewees (isl.) H6
Donaldson A.F.B. C2

Edisto (isl.) G6
Edisto (riv.) G7
Enoree (riv.) C2
Fort Jackson F4
Fort Sumter Nat'l Mon. H6
Four Hole Swamp (creek) F5
Fripp (isl.) G7
Great Pee Dee (riv.) J4
Greenwood (lake) D3
Hartwell (dam) B3
Hartwell (lake) A3
Hilton Head (isl.) F7
Hunting (isl.) G7
Intracoastal Waterway H5
James (isl.) H6
Johns (isl.) G6
Juniper (creek) H2
Keowee (lake) B2
Keowee (riv.) B2
Kiawah (isl.) G6
Kings Mountain Nat'l Mil. Park . E1
Little (riv.) C3
Little (riv.) D3
Little Lynches (riv.) G3
Little Pee Dee (riv.) J4
Little River (inlet) L4
Lumber (riv.) J3
Lynches (riv.) H3
Marion (lake) G4
Morris (isl.) H6
Moultrie (lake) G5
Murphy (isl.) J5
Murray (lake) D4
Myrtle Beach A.F.B. K4
Naval Base H6
New (riv.) E6
Ninety Six Nat'l Hist. Site ... C3
North (inlet) J5
North (isl.) J5
North Edisto (riv.) G6
Pacolet (riv.) D1
Palms, Isle of (isl.) H6

Parris Island Marine Base F7
Pee Dee (riv.) H2
Pinopolis (dam) G5
Pocotaligo (riv.) G4
Port Royal (sound) F7
Pritchards (isl.) G7
Reedy (riv.) C2
Robinson (lake) G3
Romain (cape) J6
Saint Helena (isl.) F7
Saint Helena (sound) G7
Salkehatchie (riv.) E5
Saluda (riv.) D3
Sandy (pt.) H6
Sandy (riv.) E2
Santee (dam) G4
Santee (riv.) H5
Sassafras (mt.) B1
Savannah (riv.) E6
Savannah River Plant D5
Sea (isls.) G7
Seabrook (isl.) G6
Seneca (riv.) B2
Shaw A.F.B. 6,939 .... F4
South (isl.) J5
Stevens (creek) C4
Stono (inlet) H6
Thompsons (creek) G2
Tugaloo (riv.) A2
Turkey (creek) E2
Tybee Roads (chan.) F7
Tyger (riv.) D2
Waccamaw (riv.) J5
Wadmalaw (isl.) G6
Wando (riv.) H6
Wateree (lake) F3
Wateree (riv.) F3
Winyah (bay) J5
Wylie (lake) E1

⊙County seat.
‡Population of metropolitan area.
† Zip of nearest p.o. * Multiple zips.

29554 Hemingway 853 .... J4
†29706 Hemlock (Eureka) 1,627 .. E2
29717 Hickory Grove 344 .... E2
29813 Hilda 355 .... E5
29928 Hilton Head Island 11,344 . F7
29653 Hodges 154 .... C3
29059 Holly Hill 1,785 .... G5
29449 Hollywood 729 .... G6
29654 Honea Path 4,114 .... C3
29349 Inman 1,554 .... C1
29063 Irmo 3,957 .... E3
†29720 Irwin 1,373 .... F2
29451 Isle of Palms 3,421 ...... H6
29655 Iva 1,369 .... B3
29831 Jackson 1,771 .... D5
29453 Jamestown 193 .... H5
†29483 Jedburg 900 .... G5
29718 Jefferson 651 .... G2
29351 Joanna 1,839 .... D3
29555 Jonesville 1,421 .... J4
29832 Johnston 2,624 .... D4
29353 Jonesville 1,201 .... D2
29067 Kershaw 1,993 .... G2
29556 Kingstree⊙ 4,147 ...... H4
29814 Kline 315 .... E5
29456 Ladson 13,246 .... G6
29560 Lake City 6,731 .... H4
29563 Lake View 939 .... J3
29069 Lamar 1,333 .... G3
29720 Lancaster⊙ 9,703 .... F2

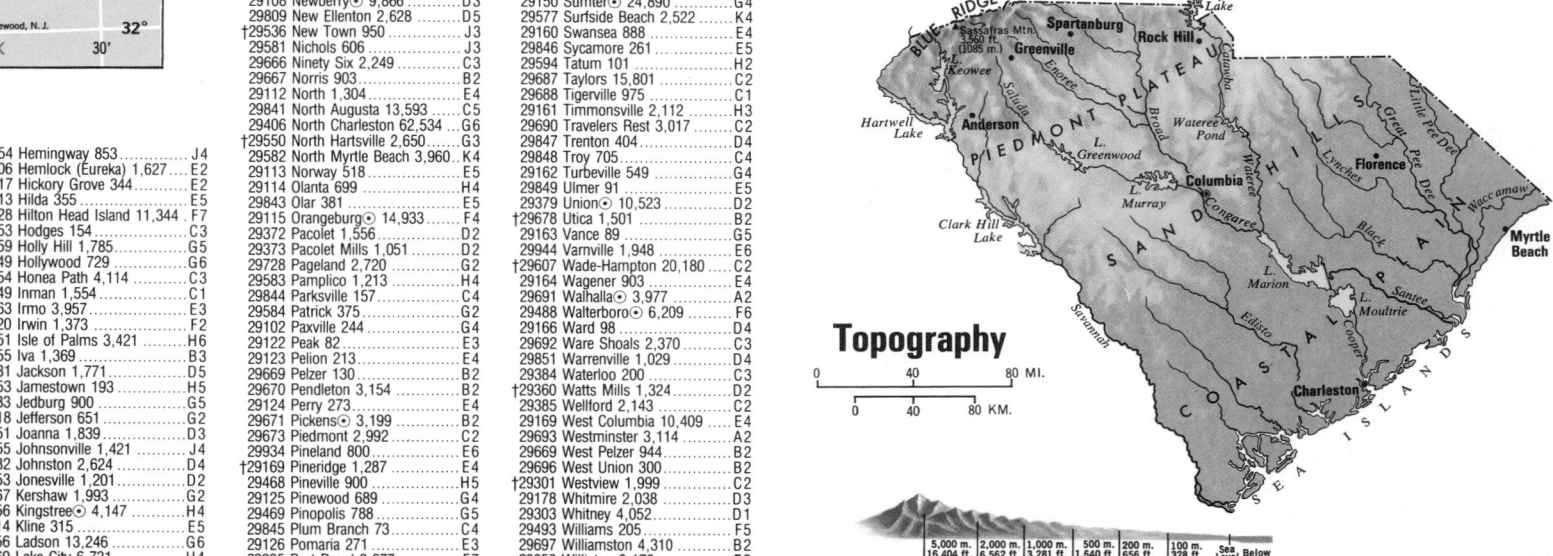

Topography

0 ____ 40 ____ 80 MI.
0 ____ 40 ____ 80 KM.

| 5,000 m. | 2,000 m. | 1,000 m. | 500 m. | 200 m. | 100 m. | Sea | Below |
| 16,404 ft. | 6,562 ft. | 3,281 ft. | 1,640 ft. | 656 ft. | 328 ft. | Level | |

COUNTIES

Aurora 3,628 .... M6
Beadle 19,195 .... N5
Bennett 3,044 .... F7
Bon Homme 8,059 .... O7
Brookings 24,332 .... R5
Brown 36,962 .... N2
Brule 5,245 .... L6
Buffalo 1,795 .... L5
Butte 8,372 .... B4
Campbell 2,243 .... J2
Charles Mix 9,680 .... M7
Clark 4,894 .... O4
Clay 13,689 .... P8
Codington 20,885 .... P4
Corson 5,196 .... G2
Custer 6,000 .... B6
Davison 17,820 .... N6
Day 8,133 .... O3

Deuel 5,289 .... R4
Dewey 5,366 .... G3
Douglas 4,181 .... N7
Edmunds 5,159 .... L3
Fall River 8,439 .... B7
Faulk 3,327 .... L3
Grant 9,013 .... R3
Gregory 6,015 .... L7
Haakon 2,794 .... F5
Hamlin 5,261 .... P4
Hand 4,948 .... L4
Hanson 3,415 .... O6
Harding 1,700 .... B2
Hughes 14,220 .... J5
Hutchinson 9,350 .... O7
Hyde 2,069 .... K4
Jackson 3,437 .... F6
Jerauld 2,929 .... M5
Jones 1,463 .... H6
Kingsbury 6,679 .... O5
Lake 10,724 .... P5
Lawrence 18,339 .... B5
Lincoln 13,942 .... R7

Lyman 3,864 .... J6
Marshall 5,404 .... O2
McCook 6,444 .... P6
McPherson 4,027 .... L2
Meade 20,717 .... D5
Mellette 2,249 .... H6
Miner 3,739 .... O5
Minnehaha 109,435 .... R6
Moody 6,692 .... R5
Pennington 70,361 .... C6
Perkins 4,700 .... D3
Potter 3,674 .... J3
Roberts 10,911 .... P2
Sanborn 3,213 .... N5
Shannon 11,323 .... D7
Spink 9,201 .... N4
Stanley 2,533 .... H5
Sully 1,990 .... J4
Todd 7,328 .... H7
Tripp 7,268 .... K7
Turner 9,255 .... P7
Union 10,938 .... R8
Walworth 7,011 .... J3

Yankton 18,952 .... P7
Ziebach 2,308 .... F4

CITIES and TOWNS

Zip	Name/Pop.	Key
57401	Aberdeen⊙ 25,851	M3
57310	Academy 10	M7
57520	Agar 139	J4
57420	Akaska 49	J3
57714	Allen 300	F7
57312	Alpena 288	N5
57211	Altamont 58	R4
57001	Alcester 885	R7
57311	Alexandria⊙ 588	O6
57421	Amherst 75	O2
57422	Andover 139	O3
57715	Ardmore 16	B7
57212	Arlington 991	P5
57313	Armour⊙ 819	N7
57423	Artas 43	K2
57314	Artesian 227	O6
57424	Ashton 154	N3
57213	Astoria 154	S4
57425	Athol 38	M3
57002	Aurora 507	R5
57315	Avon 576	N8
57214	Badger 99	P5
57003	Baltic 679	R6
57316	Bancroft 41	O4
57426	Barnard 65	N2
57716	Batesland 163	E7
57427	Bath 175	N3
57717	Belle Fourche⊙ 4,692	B4
57521	Belvidere 80	G6
57215	Bemis 37	R4
57004	Beresford 1,865	R7
57216	Big Stone City 672	S3
57421	Bijou Hills 75	L6
†57310	Bijou Hills 12	L6
57620	Bison⊙ 457	E2
57718	Black Hawk 1,608	C5
57522	Blunt 424	J4
57317	Bonesteel 358	M7
57428	Bowdle 644	K3
57719	Box Elder 3,186	D5
57217	Bradley 135	O3
57005	Brandon 2,589	R6
57218	Brandt 129	R4
57429	Brentford 91	N3
57319	Bridgewater 653	P6
57219	Bristol 445	O3
57430	Britton⊙ 1,590	O2
†57350	Broadland 49	N4
57006	Brookings⊙ 14,951	R5
57220	Bruce 254	R5
57221	Bryant 388	P4
57720	Buffalo⊙ 453	B2
57722	Buffalo Gap 186	C6
57621	Bullhead 400	G2
57010	Burbank 92	R8
57523	Burke⊙ 859	L7
†57276	Bushnell 76	R5
57222	Butler 22	O3
57724	Camp Crook 100	B2
57012	Canistota 626	P6
57321	Canova 194	O6
57013	Canton⊙ 2,886	R7
57725	Caputa 50	D5

(continued on following page)

AREA 77,116 sq. mi. (199,730 sq. km.)
POPULATION 690,768
CAPITAL Pierre
LARGEST CITY Sioux Falls
HIGHEST POINT Harney Pk. 7,242 ft. (2207 m.)
SETTLED IN 1856
ADMITTED TO UNION November 2, 1889
POPULAR NAME Coyote State; Sunshine State
STATE FLOWER Pasqueflower
STATE BIRD Ring-necked Pheasant

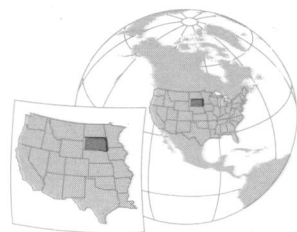

Topography

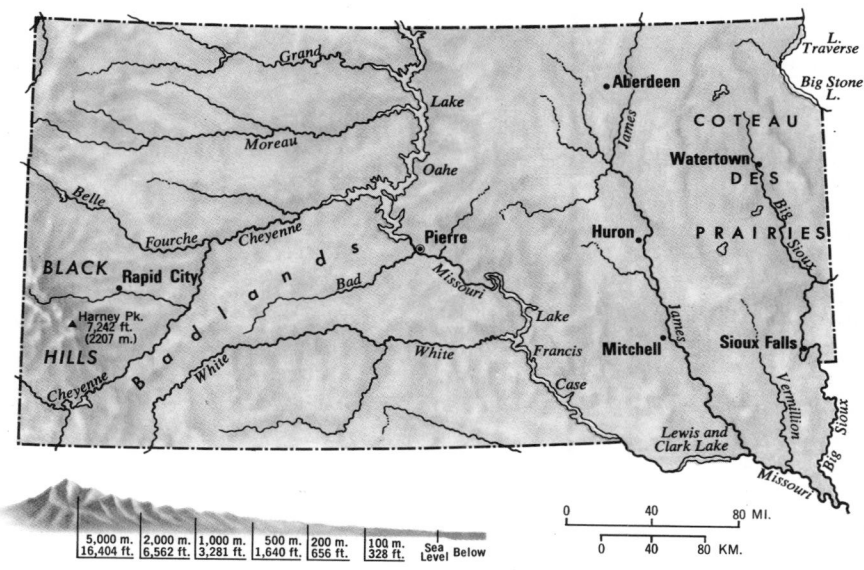

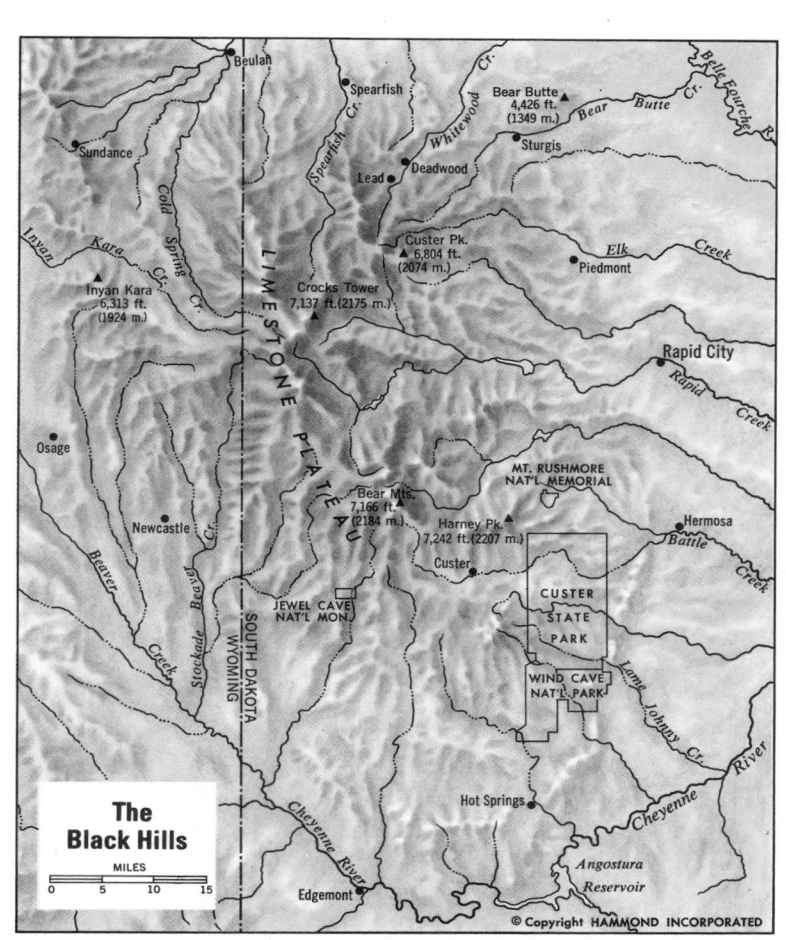

The Black Hills

MILES
0 5 10 15

© Copyright HAMMOND INCORPORATED

Agriculture, Industry and Resources

DOMINANT LAND USE

- Specialized Wheat
- Wheat, General Farming
- Wheat, Range Livestock
- Cattle Feed, Hogs
- Livestock, Cash Grain
- General Farming, Livestock, Special Crops
- Range Livestock
- Forests

⚡ Water Power

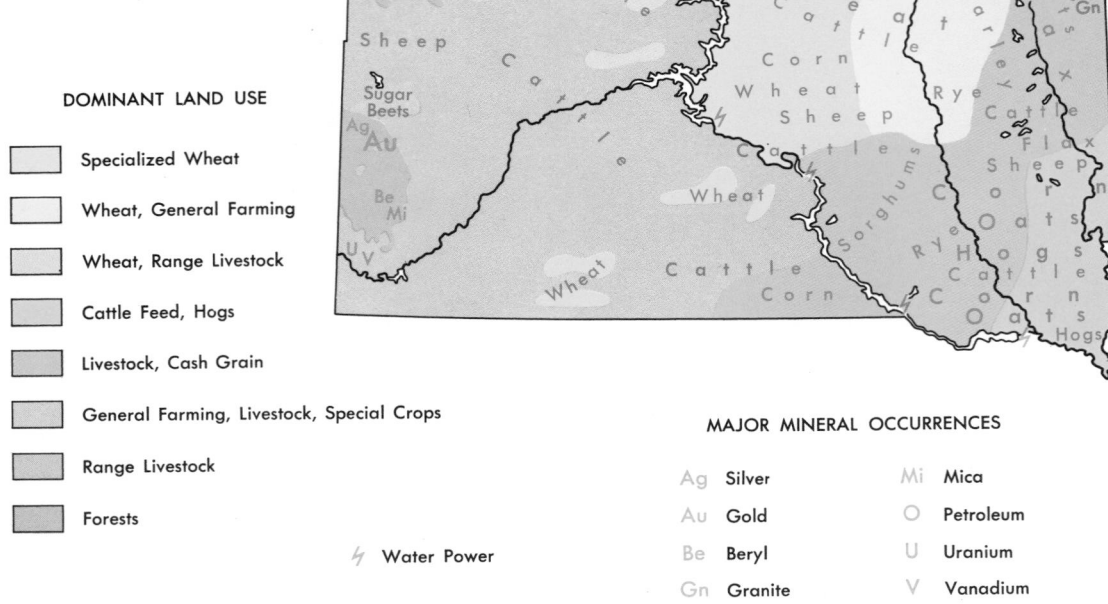

MAJOR MINERAL OCCURRENCES

Ag	Silver	Mi	Mica
Au	Gold	O	Petroleum
Be	Beryl	U	Uranium
Gn	Granite	V	Vanadium

AREA 266,807 sq. mi. (691,030 sq. km.)
POPULATION 14,229,288
CAPITAL Austin
LARGEST CITY Houston
HIGHEST POINT Guadalupe Pk. 8,749 ft. (2667 m.)
SETTLED IN 1686
ADMITTED TO UNION December 29, 1845
POPULAR NAME Lone Star State
STATE FLOWER Bluebonnet
STATE BIRD Mockingbird

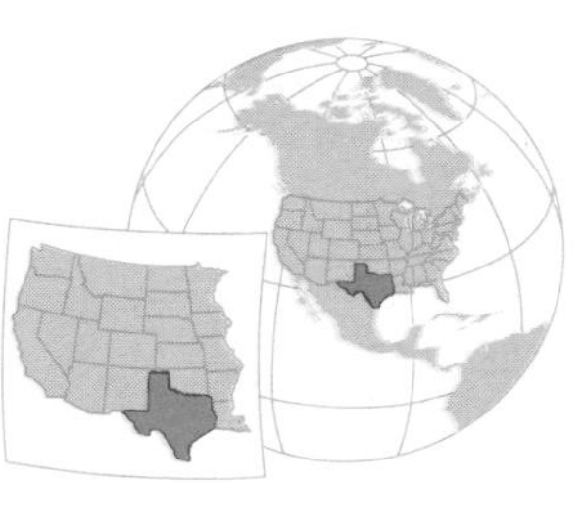

COUNTIES

Anderson 38,381 J6
Andrews 13,323 B5
Angelina 64,172 K6
Aransas 14,260 H10
Archer 7,266 F4
Armstrong 1,994 C3
Atascosa 25,055 F9
Austin 17,726 H8
Bailey 8,168 B3
Bandera 7,084 E8
Bastrop 24,726 G7
Baylor 4,919 E4
Bee 26,030 G9
Bell 157,820 G6
Bexar 988,798 F8
Blanco 4,681 F8
Borden 859 C5
Bosque 13,401 G6
Bowie 75,301 K4
Brazoria 169,587 J8
Brazos 93,588 H7
Brewster 7,573 A8
Briscoe 2,579 C3
Brooks 8,428 F11
Brown 33,057 F6
Burleson 12,313 H7
Burnet 17,803 F7
Caldwell 23,637 G8
Calhoun 19,574 H9
Callahan 10,992 E5
Cameron 209,727 G11
Camp 9,275 K5
Carson 6,672 C2
Cass 29,430 K4
Castro 10,556 B3
Chambers 18,538 K8
Cherokee 38,127 J6
Childress 6,950 D3
Clay 9,582 F4
Cochran 4,825 B4
Coke 3,196 D6
Coleman 10,439 E6
Collin 144,576 H4
Collingsworth 4,648 D3
Colorado 18,823 H8
Comal 36,446 F8
Comanche 12,617 F5
Concho 2,915 E6
Cooke 27,656 G4
Coryell 56,767 G6
Cottle 2,947 D3
Crane 4,600 B6
Crockett 4,608 C7
Crosby 8,859 C4
Culberson 3,315 C11
Dallam 6,531 B1
Dallas 1,556,390 H5
Dawson 16,184 C5
Deaf Smith 21,165 B3
Delta 4,839 J4
Denton 143,126 G4
De Witt 18,903 G9
Dickens 3,539 D4
Dimmit 11,367 E9
Donley 4,075 D2
Duval 12,517 F10
Eastland 19,480 F5
Ector 115,374 B6
Edwards 2,033 D7
Ellis 59,743 H5
El Paso 479,899 A10
Erath 22,560 F5
Falls 17,946 H6
Fannin 24,285 H4
Fayette 18,832 H8
Fisher 5,891 D5
Floyd 9,834 C3
Foard 2,158 E3
Fort Bend 130,846 J8
Franklin 6,893 J4
Freestone 14,830 H6
Frio 13,785 E9
Gaines 13,150 B5
Galveston 195,940 K8
Garza 5,336 C4
Gillespie 13,532 F7
Glasscock 1,304 C6
Goliad 5,193 G9
Gonzales 15,949 G8
Gray 26,386 D2
Grayson 89,796 H4
Gregg 99,495 K5
Grimes 13,580 J7
Guadalupe 46,708 G8
Hale 37,592 C3
Hall 5,594 D3
Hamilton 8,297 F6
Hansford 6,209 C1
Hardeman 6,368 E3
Hardin 40,721 K7
Harris 2,409,547 J8
Harrison 52,265 K5
Hartley 3,987 B2
Haskell 7,725 E4
Hays 40,594 F7
Hemphill 5,304 D2
Henderson 42,606 J5
Hidalgo 283,323 F11
Hill 25,024 G5
Hockley 23,230 B4
Hood 17,714 G5
Hopkins 25,247 J4
Houston 22,299 J6
Howard 33,142 C5
Hudspeth 2,728 B10
Hunt 55,248 H4
Hutchinson 26,304 C2
Irion 1,386 C6
Jack 7,408 F4
Jackson 13,352 H9
Jasper 30,781 K7
Jeff Davis 1,647 C11
Jefferson 250,938 K8
Jim Hogg 5,168 F11
Jim Wells 36,498 F10
Johnson 67,649 G5
Jones 17,268 E5
Karnes 13,593 G9
Kaufman 39,029 H5
Kendall 10,635 F8
Kenedy 543 G11
Kent 1,145 D4
Kerr 28,780 E7
Kimble 4,063 E7
King 425 D4
Kinney 2,279 D8
Kleberg 33,358 G10
Knox 5,329 E4
Lamar 42,156 J4
Lamb 18,669 B3
Lampasas 12,005 F6
La Salle 5,514 E9
Lavaca 19,004 H8
Lee 10,952 H7
Leon 9,594 J6
Liberty 47,088 K7
Limestone 20,224 H6
Lipscomb 3,766 D1
Live Oak 9,606 F9
Llano 10,144 F7
Loving 91 A6
Lubbock 211,651 C4
Lynn 8,605 C4
Madison 10,649 J6
Marion 10,360 K5
Martin 4,684 C5
Mason 3,683 E7
Matagorda 37,828 H9
Maverick 31,398 D9
McCulloch 8,735 E6
McLennan 170,755 G6
McMullen 789 F9
Medina 23,164 E8
Menard 2,346 E7
Midland 82,636 B6
Milam 22,732 H7
Mills 4,477 F6
Mitchell 9,088 D5
Montague 17,410 G4
Montgomery 128,487 J7
Moore 16,575 C2
Morris 14,629 K4
Motley 1,950 D3
Nacogdoches 46,786 K6
Navarro 35,323 H5
Newton 13,254 L7
Nolan 17,359 D5
Nueces 268,215 G10
Ochiltree 9,588 D1
Oldham 2,283 B2
Orange 83,838 L7
Palo Pinto 24,062 F5
Panola 20,724 K5
Parker 44,609 G5
Parmer 11,038 B3
Pecos 14,618 B7
Polk 24,407 K7
Potter 98,637 C2
Presidio 5,188 C12
Rains 4,839 J5
Randall 75,062 C2
Reagan 4,135 C6
Real 2,469 E8
Red River 16,101 J4
Reeves 15,801 D11
Refugio 9,289 G9
Roberts 1,187 D2
Robertson 14,653 H6
Rockwall 14,528 H5
Runnels 11,872 E6
Rusk 41,382 K5
Sabine 8,702 L6
San Augustine 8,785 K6
San Jacinto 11,434 J7
San Patricio 58,013 G10
San Saba 6,204 F6
Schleicher 2,820 D7
Scurry 18,192 D5
Shackelford 3,915 E5
Shelby 23,084 K6
Sherman 3,174 C1
Smith 128,366 J5
Somervell 4,154 G5
Starr 27,266 F11
Stephens 9,926 F5
Sterling 1,206 C6
Stonewall 2,406 D4
Sutton 5,130 D7
Swisher 9,723 C3
Tarrant 860,880 G5
Taylor 110,932 E5
Terrell 1,595 B7
Terry 14,581 B4
Throckmorton 2,053 E4
Titus 21,442 K4
Tom Green 84,784 D6
Travis 419,573 G7
Trinity 9,450 J6
Tyler 16,223 K7
Upshur 28,595 K5
Upton 4,619 B6
Uvalde 22,441 E8
Val Verde 35,910 C8
Van Zandt 31,426 J5
Victoria 68,807 H9
Walker 41,789 J7
Waller 19,798 J8
Ward 13,976 A6
Washington 21,998 H7
Webb 99,258 E10
Wharton 40,242 H8
Wheeler 7,137 D2
Wichita 121,082 F3
Wilbarger 15,931 E3
Willacy 17,495 G11
Williamson 76,507 G7
Wilson 16,756 F8
Winkler 9,944 A6
Wise 26,575 G4
Wood 24,697 J5
Yoakum 8,299 B4
Young 19,083 F4
Zapata 6,628 E11
Zavala 11,666 E9

CITIES and TOWNS

Zip	Name/Pop.	Key
*79601	Abilene⊙ 98,315	E5
	Abilene‡ 139,192	E5
78516	Alamo 5,831	F11
78209	Alamo Heights 6,252	K10
76430	Albany⊙ 2,450	E5
78332	Alice⊙ 20,961	F10
75002	Allen 8,314	H1
79830	Alpine⊙ 5,465	D12
77511	Alvin 16,515	J3
*79101	Amarillo⊙ 149,230	C2
	Amarillo‡ 173,699	C2
77514	Anahuac⊙ 1,840	K8
77830	Anderson⊙ 500	J7
79714	Andrews⊙ 11,061	B5
77515	Angleton⊙ 13,929	J8
79501	Anson⊙ 2,831	E5
78336	Aransas Pass 7,173	G10
76351	Archer City⊙ 1,862	F4
*76010	Arlington 160,123	F2
79502	Aspermont⊙ 1,357	D4
75751	Athens⊙ 10,197	J5
75551	Atlanta 6,272	K4
*78701	Austin (cap.)⊙ 345,496	G7
	Austin‡ 536,450	G7
76020	Azle 5,822	E2
77518	Bacliff 4,851	K2
79504	Baird⊙ 1,696	E5
75180	Balch Springs 13,746	H2
†78201	Balcones Heights 2,511	J10
76821	Ballinger⊙ 4,207	E6
78003	Bandera⊙ 947	F8
77532	Barrett 3,183	K1
78602	Bastrop⊙ 3,789	G7
77414	Bay City⊙ 17,837	H9
77520	Baytown 56,923	L2
*77701	Beaumont⊙ 118,102	K7
	Beaumont-Port Arthur-Orange‡ 375,497	K7
76021	Bedford 20,821	F2
78102	Beeville⊙ 14,574	G9
77401	Bellaire 14,950	J2
76704	Bellmead 7,569	H6
77418	Bellville⊙ 2,860	H8
76513	Belton⊙ 10,660	G7
76126	Benbrook 13,579	E2
79505	Benjamin⊙ 257	E4
76932	Big Lake⊙ 3,404	C6
79720	Big Spring⊙ 24,804	C5
78006	Boerne⊙ 3,229	J10
75418	Bonham⊙ 7,338	H4
79007	Borger 15,837	C2
75557	Boston⊙ 400	K4
76230	Bowie 5,610	G4
78832	Brackettville⊙ 1,676	D8
76825	Brady⊙ 5,969	E6
77422	Brazoria 3,025	J9
76024	Breckenridge⊙ 6,921	F5
77833	Brenham⊙ 10,966	H7
77611	Bridge City 7,667	L7
79316	Brownfield⊙ 10,387	B4
*78520	Brownsville⊙ 84,997	G12
	Brownsville-Harlingen-San Benito‡ 209,680	G12
76801	Brownwood⊙ 19,396	F6
77801	Bryan⊙ 44,337	H7
	Bryan-College Station‡ 93,588	H7
76354	Burkburnett 10,668	F3
76028	Burleson 11,734	F3
78611	Burnet⊙ 3,410	F7
77836	Caldwell⊙ 2,953	H7
76520	Cameron⊙ 5,721	H7
79014	Canadian⊙ 3,491	D2
75103	Canton⊙ 2,845	J5
79015	Canyon⊙ 10,724	C3
78834	Carrizo Springs⊙ 6,886	E9
*75006	Carrollton 40,595	G2
75633	Carthage⊙ 6,447	K5
†78213	Castle Hills 4,773	J10
75104	Cedar Hill 6,849	G3
75935	Center⊙ 5,827	K6
75833	Centerville⊙ 799	H6
77530	Channelview 17,471	K1
79018	Channing⊙ 304	B2
79201	Childress⊙ 5,817	D3
76437	Cisco 4,517	E5
79226	Clarendon⊙ 2,220	C3
75426	Clarksville⊙ 4,917	K4
79019	Claude⊙ 1,112	C2
†77565	Clear Lake Shores 755	K2
76031	Cleburne⊙ 19,218	G5
77327	Cleveland 5,977	K7
77531	Clute 9,577	J9
77331	Coldspring⊙ 569	J7
76834	Coleman⊙ 5,960	E6
77840	College Station 37,272	H7
76034	Colleyville 6,700	F2
79512	Colorado City⊙ 5,405	C5
78934	Columbus⊙ 3,923	H8
76442	Comanche⊙ 4,075	F6
75428	Commerce 8,136	J4
*77301	Conroe⊙ 18,034	J7
78109	Converse 5,150	K11
75432	Cooper⊙ 2,338	J4
76522	Copperas Cove 19,469	G6
*78401	Corpus Christi⊙ 231,999	G10
	Corpus Christi‡ 326,228	G10
75110	Corsicana⊙ 21,712	H5
78014	Cotulla⊙ 3,912	E9
79731	Crane⊙ 3,622	B6
75835	Crockett⊙ 7,405	J6
79322	Crosbyton⊙ 2,289	C4
79227	Crowell⊙ 1,509	E4
76036	Crowley 5,852	E3
78839	Crystal City⊙ 8,334	E9
77954	Cuero⊙ 7,124	G8
75638	Daingerfield⊙ 3,030	K4
79022	Dalhart⊙ 6,854	B1
*75201	Dallas⊙ 904,078	G2
	Dallas-Ft. Worth‡ 2,974,878	G2
77535	Dayton 4,908	J7
76234	Decatur⊙ 4,104	G4
77536	Deer Park 22,648	K2
76444	De Leon 2,478	F5
78840	Del Rio⊙ 30,034	D8
75020	Denison 23,884	H4
76201	Denton⊙ 48,063	G4

(continued on following page)

DOMINANT LAND USE

- Wheat, Grain Sorghums, Range Livestock
- Cotton, Wheat
- Specialized Cotton
- Cotton, General Farming
- Cotton, Forest Products
- Cotton, Range Livestock
- Rice, General Farming
- Peanuts, General Farming
- General Farming, Livestock, Cash Grain
- General Farming, Forest Products, Truck Farming, Cotton
- Fruit, Truck and Mixed Farming
- Range Livestock
- Forests
- Swampland, Limited Agriculture
- Nonagricultural Land
- Urban Areas

MAJOR MINERAL OCCURRENCES

At	Asphalt	He	Helium
Cl	Clay	Ls	Limestone
Fe	Iron Ore	Na	Salt
G	Natural Gas	O	Petroleum
Gn	Granite	S	Sulfur
Gp	Gypsum	Tc	Talc
Gr	Graphite	U	Uranium

Water Power
Major Industrial Areas

Agriculture, Industry and Resources

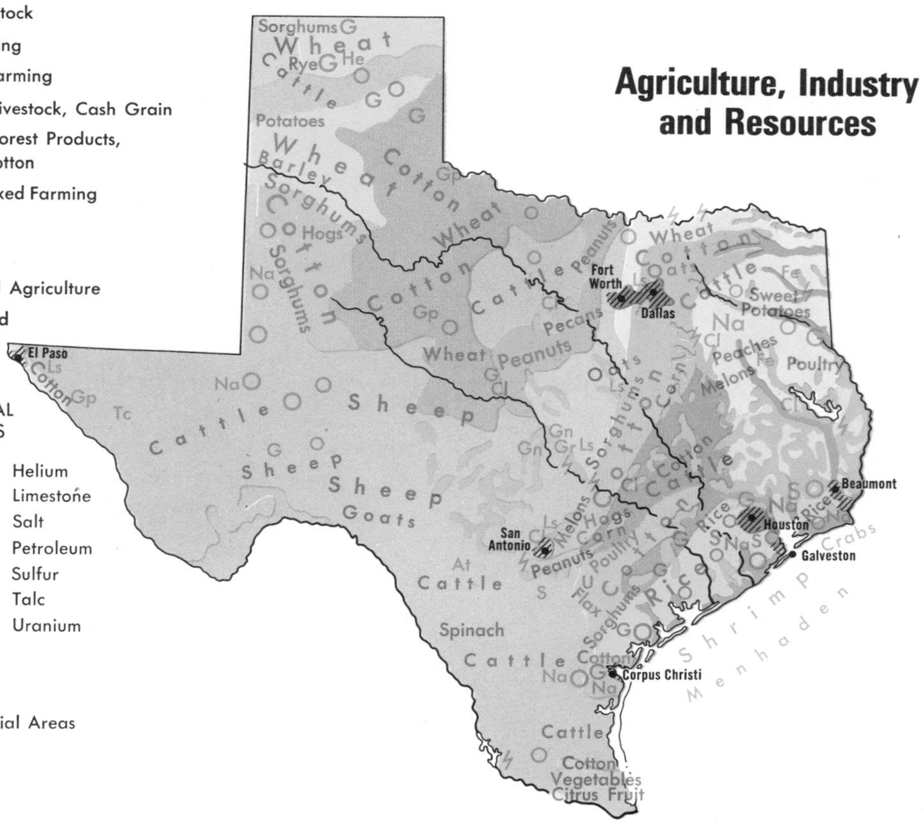

(continued)

79323 Denver City 4,704 .... B4
75115 De Soto 15,538 .... G3
78016 Devine 3,756 .... E8
75941 Diboll 5,227 .... K6
79229 Dickens⊙ 409 .... D4
77539 Dickinson 7,505 .... K3
79027 Dimmitt⊙ 5,019 .... B3
78537 Donna 9,952 .... F11
79029 Dumas⊙ 12,194 .... C2
75116 Duncanville 27,781 .... G3
78852 Eagle Pass⊙ 21,407 .... D9
76448 Eastland⊙ 3,747 .... F5
78539 Edinburg⊙ 24,075 .... F11
77957 Edna⊙ 5,650 .... H9
77437 El Campo 10,462 .... H8
76936 Eldorado⊙ 2,061 .... D7
78621 Elgin 4,535 .... G7
*79901 El Paso⊙ 425,259 .... A10
El Paso‡ 479,899 .... A10
78543 Elsa 5,061 .... G11
75440 Emory⊙ 813 .... J5
75119 Ennis 12,110 .... H5
76039 Euless 24,002 .... F2
76140 Everman 5,387 .... F3
79838 Fabens 4,285 .... B10
75840 Fairfield⊙ 3,505 .... H6
78355 Falfurrias⊙ 6,103 .... F10
75234 Farmers Branch 24,863 .... G2
79325 Farwell⊙ 1,354 .... A3
78114 Floresville⊙ 4,381 .... K11
†75067 Flower Mound 4,402 .... F1
79235 Floydada⊙ 4,193 .... C3
†76119 Forest Hill 11,684 .... F2
79734 Fort Davis⊙ 900 .... D11
79735 Fort Stockton⊙ 8,688 ...... A7
*76101 Fort Worth⊙ 385,164 ...... F2
77856 Franklin⊙ 1,349 .... H7
78624 Fredericksburg⊙ 6,412 ..... E7
76842 Fredonia 50 .... E7
77541 Freeport 13,444 .... J9
77546 Friendswood 10,719 .... J2
79035 Friona 3,809 .... B3
75034 Frisco 3,499 .... H4
79738 Gail⊙ 171 .... C5
76240 Gainesville⊙ 14,081 .... G4
77547 Galena Park 9,879 .... J1
*77550 Galveston⊙ 61,902 .... L3
Galveston-Texas
City‡ 195,940 .... L3
79739 Garden City⊙ 350 .... C6
*75040 Garland 138,857 .... H2
76528 Gatesville⊙ 6,260 .... G6
78626 Georgetown⊙ 9,468 .... G7
78022 George West⊙ 2,627 .... F9
78942 Giddings⊙ 3,950 .... H7
75644 Gilmer⊙ 5,167 .... J5
75647 Gladewater 6,548 .... K5
76043 Glen Rose⊙ 2,075 .... G5
76844 Goldthwaite⊙ 1,783 .... F6
77963 Goliad⊙ 1,990 .... G9
78629 Gonzales⊙ 7,152 .... G8
76046 Graham⊙ 9,170 .... F4
76048 Granbury⊙ 3,332 .... G5
*75050 Grand Prairie 71,462 ..... G2
76051 Grapevine 11,801 .... F2
75401 Greenville⊙ 22,161 .... H4
76642 Groesbeck⊙ 3,373 .... H6
77619 Groves 17,090 .... L8
75845 Groveton⊙ 1,262 .... J7
79236 Guthrie⊙ 170 .... D4
77964 Hallettsville⊙ 2,865 ...... G8
76117 Haltom City 29,014 .... F2
76531 Hamilton⊙ 3,189 .... G6
78550 Harlingen 43,543 .... G11
79521 Haskell⊙ 3,782 .... E4
77859 Hearne 5,418 .... H7
78361 Hebbronville⊙ 4,684 ...... F10
75948 Hemphill⊙ 1,353 .... L6
77445 Hempstead⊙ 3,456 .... J7
75652 Henderson⊙ 11,473 .... K5
76365 Henrietta⊙ 3,149 .... F4
79045 Hereford⊙ 15,853 .... B3
†75201 Highland Park 8,909 ...... G2
77562 Highlands 6,467 .... K1
76645 Hillsboro⊙ 7,397 .... G5
77563 Hitchcock 6,655 .... K3
78861 Hondo⊙ 6,057 .... E8
*77001 Houston⊙ 1,595,138 .... J2
Houston‡ 2,905,350 .... J2
*77338 Humble 6,729 .... J7
†77001 Hunters Creek
Village 4,215 .... J1
77340 Huntsville⊙ 23,936 .... J7
76053 Hurst 31,420 .... F2
76367 Iowa Park 6,184 .... F4
*75061 Irving 109,943 .... G2
77029 Jacinto City 8,953 .... J1
76056 Jacksboro⊙ 4,000 .... F4
75766 Jacksonville 12,264 ...... J5
75951 Jasper⊙ 6,959 .... L7
79528 Jayton⊙ 638 .... D4
75657 Jefferson⊙ 2,643 .... K5
†77001 Jersey Village 4,084 ..... J1
78636 Johnson City⊙ 872 .... F7
78026 Jourdanton⊙ 2,743 .... F9
76849 Junction⊙ 2,593 .... E7
78118 Karnes City⊙ 3,296 .... G9
77450 Katy 5,660 .... J8
75142 Kaufman⊙ 4,658 .... H5
76248 Keller 4,156 .... F2
78119 Kenedy 4,356 .... G9
79745 Kermit⊙ 8,015 .... B6
78028 Kerrville⊙ 15,276 .... E7
75662 Kilgore 11,006 .... K5
76541 Killeen 46,296 .... G6
Killeen-Temple‡ 214,656 ... G6
78363 Kingsville⊙ 28,808 .... G10
†78109 Kirby 6,435 .... K11
77625 Kountze⊙ 2,716 .... K7
78945 La Grange⊙ 3,768 .... G8
77566 Lake Jackson 19,102 ...... J8
76135 Lake Worth 4,394 .... E2
77568 La Marque 15,372 .... K3
79331 Lamesa⊙ 11,790 .... C5
76550 Lampasas⊙ 6,165 .... F6
*75146 Lancaster 14,807 .... G3
77571 La Porte 14,062 .... K2

*78040 Laredo⊙ 91,449 .... E10
Laredo‡ 99,258 .... E10
77573 League City 16,578 .... K2
78873 Leakey⊙ 468 .... E8
†78201 Leon Valley 9,088 .... J10
79336 Levelland⊙ 13,809 .... B4
*75067 Lewisville 24,273 .... G1
77575 Liberty⊙ 7,945 .... K7
75563 Linden⊙ 2,443 .... K4
79056 Lipscomb⊙ 52 .... D1
79339 Littlefield⊙ 7,409 .... B4
†78201 Live Oak 8,183 .... K10
77351 Livingston⊙ 4,928 .... K7
78643 Llano⊙ 3,071 .... F7
78644 Lockhart⊙ 7,953 .... G8
79241 Lockney 2,334 .... C3
*75601 Longview⊙ 62,762 .... K5
Longview-Marshall‡
151,752 .... K5
*79401 Lubbock⊙ 173,979 .... C4
Lubbock‡ 211,651 .... C4
75901 Lufkin⊙ 28,562 .... K6
78648 Luling 5,039 .... G8
77864 Madisonville⊙ 3,660 ...... J7
76063 Mansfield 8,092 .... F3
77578 Manvel 3,549 .... J3
79843 Marfa⊙ 2,466 .... C12
76661 Marlin⊙ 7,099 .... H6
75670 Marshall⊙ 24,921 .... K5
76856 Mason⊙ 2,153 .... E7
79244 Matador⊙ 1,052 .... D3
78368 Mathis 5,667 .... G9
78501 McAllen 66,281 .... F11
McAllen-Pharr-Edinburg‡
283,229 .... F11
76657 McGregor 4,513 .... G6
75069 McKinney⊙ 16,256 .... H4
†77520 McNair K1
79245 Memphis⊙ 3,352 .... D3
76859 Menard⊙ 1,697 .... E7
79754 Mentone⊙ 50 .... D10
78570 Mercedes 11,851 .... F12
76665 Meridian⊙ 1,330 .... G6
76941 Mertzon⊙ 687 .... C6
*75149 Mesquite 67,053 .... H2
76667 Mexia 7,094 .... H6
79059 Miami⊙ 813 .... D2
*79701 Midland⊙ 70,525 .... C6
Midland‡ 82,636 .... C6
76065 Midlothian 3,219 .... G5
75773 Mineola 4,346 .... J5
76067 Mineral Wells 14,468 .... F5
78572 Mission 22,653 .... F11
77459 Missouri City 24,533 .... J2
79756 Monahans⊙ 8,397 .... B6
76251 Montague⊙ 1,253 .... G4
79346 Morton⊙ 2,674 .... B4
75455 Mount Pleasant⊙ 11,003 .. K4
75457 Mount Vernon⊙ 2,025 ..... J4
79347 Muleshoe⊙ 4,842 .... B3
75961 Nacogdoches⊙ 27,149 ..... J6
†77598 Nassau Bay 4,526 .... K2
77868 Navasota 5,971 .... J7
77627 Nederland 16,855 .... K8
75570 New Boston 4,628 .... K4
78130 New Braunfels⊙ 22,402 . K10
75966 Newton⊙ 1,620 .... L7
76118 North Richland
Hills 30,592 .... F2
79760 Odessa⊙ 90,027 .... B6
Odessa‡ 115,374 .... B6
76374 Olney 4,060 .... F4
77630 Orange⊙ 23,628 .... L7
76943 Ozona⊙ 3,766 .... C7
79248 Paducah⊙ 2,216 .... D4
76866 Paint Rock⊙ 256 .... E6
77465 Palacios 4,667 .... H9
75801 Palestine⊙ 15,948 .... J6
76072 Palo Pinto⊙ 350 .... F5
79065 Pampa⊙ 21,396 .... D2
79068 Panhandle⊙ 2,226 .... C2
75460 Paris⊙ 25,498 .... J4
*77501 Pasadena 112,560 .... J2
77581 Pearland 13,248 .... J2
78061 Pearsall⊙ 7,383 .... E9
79772 Pecos⊙ 12,855 .... D10
79070 Perryton⊙ 7,991 .... D1
78577 Pharr 21,381 .... F11
75686 Pittsburg⊙ 4,245 .... J4
79355 Plains⊙ 1,457 .... B4
79072 Plainview⊙ 22,187 ...... C3
75074 Plano 72,331 .... G1
78064 Pleasanton 6,346 .... F9
77640 Port Arthur 61,251 ..... K8
78578 Port Isabel 3,769 ...... G11
78374 Portland 12,023 .... G10
77979 Port Lavaca⊙ 10,911 ..... H9
77651 Port Neches 13,944 ...... K7
79356 Post⊙ 3,961 .... C4
78065 Poteet 3,086 .... F8
77445 Prairie View 3,993 ...... J7
79845 Presidio 1,723 .... C12
79252 Quanah⊙ 3,890 .... E3
76470 Ranger 3,142 .... F5
79778 Rankin⊙ 1,216 .... B6
78580 Raymondville⊙ 9,493 .... G11
78377 Refugio⊙ 3,898 .... G9
75080 Richardson 72,496 ...... G2
76118 Richland Hills 7,977 .... F2
77469 Richmond⊙ 9,692 .... J8
78582 Rio Grande City⊙ 8,930 .. F11
77019 River Oaks 6,890 .... E2
76945 Robert Lee⊙ 1,202 ...... D6
78380 Robstown 12,100 .... G10
79543 Roby⊙ 814 .... D5
76567 Rockdale 5,611 .... G7
78382 Rockport⊙ 3,686 .... H9
78880 Rocksprings⊙ 1,317 ..... D8
75087 Rockwall⊙ 5,939 .... H5
78584 Roma-Los Saenz 3,384 .... E11
77471 Rosenberg 17,995 .... J8
78664 Round Rock 12,740 ...... G7
75088 Rowlett 7,522 .... H2
75785 Rusk⊙ 4,681 .... J6
76179 Saginaw 5,736 .... E2
*76901 San Angelo⊙ 73,240 ..... D6
San Angelo‡ 84,784 .... D6

Topography

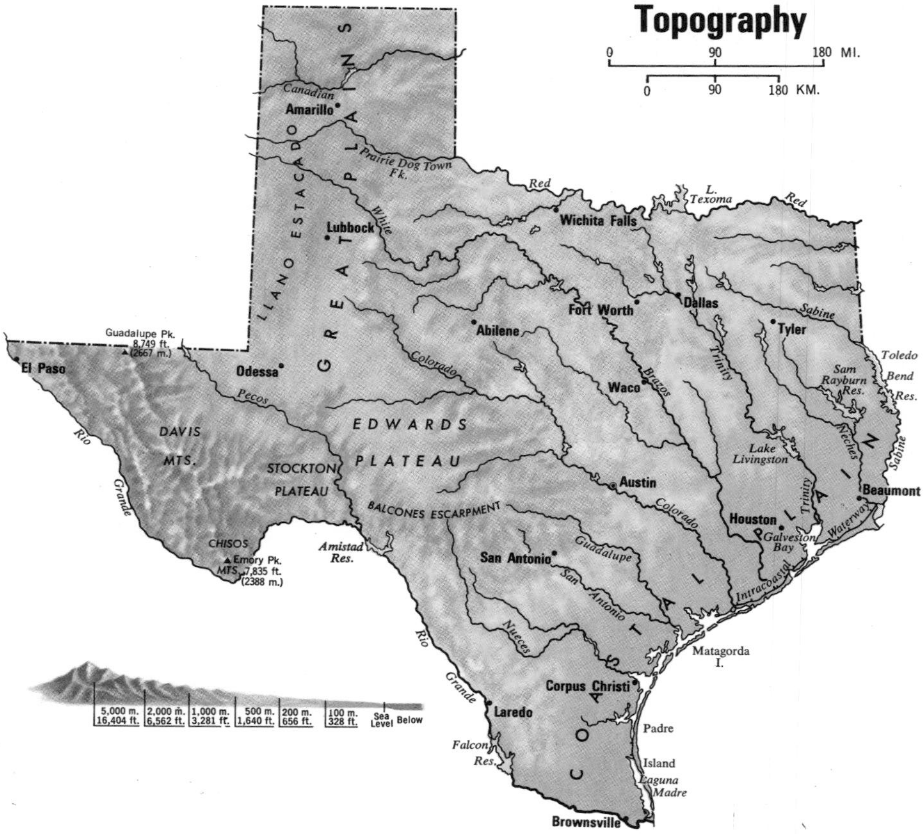
Topography
0 90 180 MI.
0 90 180 KM.
Canadian
Amarillo
Prairie Dog Town Fk.
LLANO ESTACADO
GREAT PLAINS
Lubbock
White
Red
L. Texoma
Red
Wichita Falls
Fort Worth
Dallas
Sabine
Tyler
Abilene
Guadalupe Pk. 8,749 ft. (2667 m.)
El Paso
Odessa
Colorado
Toledo Bend Res.
Sam Rayburn Res.
Waco
Brazos
Trinity
Pecos
EDWARDS PLATEAU
DAVIS MTS.
Rio Grande
STOCKTON PLATEAU
Lake Livingston
Neches
Sabine
Austin
Beaumont
BALCONES ESCARPMENT
Colorado
Trinity
Houston
Galveston Bay
Waterway
CHISOS MTS.
Emory Pk. 7,835 ft. (2388 m.)
Amistad Res.
San Antonio
Guadalupe
San Antonio
Intracoastal
COASTAL PLAIN
Nueces
Rio Grande
Matagorda I.
5,000 m. 16,404 ft.
2,000 m. 6,562 ft.
1,000 m. 3,281 ft.
500 m. 1,640 ft.
200 m. 656 ft.
100 m. 328 ft.
Sea Level
Below
Corpus Christi
Laredo
Padre Island
Falcon Res.
Laguna Madre
Brownsville

*78201 San Antonio⊙ 786,023 .... J11
San Antonio‡ 1,071,954 .. J11
75972 San Augustine⊙ 2,930 ..... K6
78586 San Benito 17,988 .... G12
79848 Sanderson⊙ 1,241 .... B7
78384 San Diego⊙ 5,225 .... F10
76266 Sanger 2,574 .... G4
78589 San Juan 7,608 .... F11
78666 San Marcos⊙ 23,420 .... F8
76877 San Saba⊙ 2,847 .... F6
†76101 Sansom Park Village 3,921 E2
†77510 Santa Fe 6,172 .... K3
78385 Sarita⊙ 200 .... G10
78154 Schertz 7,262 .... K10
77586 Seabrook 4,670 .... K2
75159 Seagoville 7,304 .... H3
77474 Sealy 3,875 .... H8
78155 Seguin⊙ 17,854 .... G8
79360 Seminole⊙ 6,080 .... B5
†78357 Seven Sisters 2 .... F9
76380 Seymour⊙ 3,657 .... E4
75090 Sherman⊙ 30,413 .... H4
Sherman-Denison‡ 89,796 H4
79851 Sierra Blanca⊙ 800 ...... B11
77656 Silsbee 7,684 .... K7
79257 Silverton⊙ 918 .... C3
78387 Sinton⊙ 6,044 .... G9
79364 Slaton 6,804 .... C4
78957 Smithville 3,470 .... G7
79549 Snyder⊙ 12,705 .... D5
76950 Sonora⊙ 3,856 .... D7
77587 South Houston 13,293 ..... J2
79081 Spearman⊙ 3,413 .... C1
*77373 Spring J7
†77001 Spring Valley 3,353 ...... J1
77477 Stafford 4,755 .... J2
79553 Stamford 4,542 .... E5
79782 Stanton⊙ 2,314 .... C5
76401 Stephenville⊙ 11,881 ..... F5
76951 Sterling City⊙ 915 .... D6
79083 Stinnett⊙ 2,222 .... C2
79084 Stratford⊙ 1,917 .... C1
77478 Sugar Land 8,826 .... J8
75482 Sulphur Springs⊙ 12,804 . J4
77480 Sweeny 3,538 .... J8
79556 Sweetwater⊙ 12,242 ..... D5
78390 Taft 3,686 .... G9
79373 Tahoka⊙ 3,262 .... C4
76574 Taylor 10,619 .... G7
†77586 Taylor Lake Village 3,669 .. K2
75860 Teague 3,390 .... H6
76501 Temple 42,354 .... G6
79852 Terlingua 100 .... D12
75160 Terrell 13,269 .... H5
†78201 Terrell Hills 4,644 ...... K11
*75501 Texarkana 31,271 .... L4
Texarkana, Tex.-Texarkana,
Ark.‡ 27,019 .... L4
77590 Texas City 41,403 .... K3
73949 Texhoma 358 .... C1
The Colony 11,586 .... G1
76083 Throckmorton⊙ 1,174 ..... F4
78072 Tilden⊙ 450 .... F9
77375 Tomball 3,996 .... J7
75862 Trinity 2,620 .... J7
79088 Tulia⊙ 5,033 .... C3
*75701 Tyler⊙ 70,508 .... J5
Tyler‡ 128,366 .... J5
78148 Universal City 10,720 ..... K10
†75205 University Park 22,254 ..... G2
78801 Uvalde⊙ 14,178 .... E8
75095 Van Alstyne 1,860 .... H4

79855 Van Horn⊙ 2,772 .... C11
79092 Vega⊙ 900 .... B2
76384 Vernon⊙ 12,695 .... E3
77901 Victoria⊙ 50,695 .... H9
Victoria‡ 68,807 .... H9
77662 Vidor 11,834 .... L7
*76701 Waco⊙ 101,261 .... G6
Waco‡ 170,755 .... G6
75501 Wake Village 3,865 ..... K4
75165 Waxahachie⊙ 14,624 .... H5
76086 Weatherford⊙ 12,049 .... G5
79095 Wellington⊙ 3,043 ...... D3
78596 Weslaco 19,331 .... F11
77486 West Columbia 4,109 .... J8
77630 West Orange 4,610 ...... L7
†77005 West University
Place 12,010 .... J2
†76101 Westworth 3,651 .... E2
77488 Wharton⊙ 9,033 .... J8
79096 Wheeler⊙ 1,584 .... D2
75693 White Oak 4,415 .... K5
76273 Whitesboro 3,197 .... H4
76108 White Settlement 13,508 ... E2
*76301 Wichita Falls⊙ 94,201 ..... F4
Wichita Falls‡ 130,664 ..... F4
†78201 Windcrest 5,332 .... K11
75494 Winnsboro 3,458 .... J5
79567 Winters 3,061 .... E6
75979 Woodville⊙ 2,821 .... K7
75098 Wylie 3,152 .... H1
78076 Zapata⊙ 3,831 .... E11

OTHER FEATURES

Amistad (res.) C8
Amistad Nat'l Rec. Area D8
Angelina (riv.) K6
Apache (mts.) C11
Aransas (passage) H10
Arlington (lake) F2
Baffin (bay) G10
Balcones Escarpment (plat.) ... E8
Beals (creek) C5
Benbrook (lake) E3
Bergstrom A.F.B. G7
Big Bend Nat'l Park A8
Bolivar (pen.) K8
Brazos (riv.) H7
Brownwood (lake) E6
Buchanan (lake) F7
Buck (creek) D3
Caddo (lake) L5
Canadian (riv.) D1
Carrizo (creek) A1
Carswell A.F.B. E2
Cathedral (mt.) D12
Cavallo (passage) H9
Cedar (lake) B5
Cerro Alto (mt.) B10
Chamizal Nat'l Mem. A10
Chase N.A.S. G9
Chinati (mts.) C12
Chinati (peak) C12
Chisos (mts.) A8
Cibolo (creek) K11
Clear Fork, Brazos (riv.) D5
Coldwater (creek) B1
Colorado (riv.) F7
Copano (bay) G9
Corpus Christi (lake) F9

Corpus Christi N.A.S. G10
Cottonwood Draw (dry riv.) C10
Davis (mts.) C11
Deep (creek) C5
Delaware (creek) C10
Delaware (mts.) C10
Denison (dam) H4
Devils (riv.) D7
Diablo, Sierra (mts.) C10
Double Mountain Fork, Brazos
(riv.) C4
Dyess A.F.B. D5
Eagle (peak) C11
Eagle Mountain (lake) E2
Edwards (plat.) C7
Elephant (mt.) D12
Ellington A.F.B. K2
Elm Fork, Trinity (riv.) G2
Emory (peak) A8
Falcon (res.) E11
Finlay (mts.) B10
Fort Bliss 12,687 .... A10
Fort Davis Nat'l Hist. Site D11
Fort Hood 31,250 .... G6
Frio (riv.) E8
Galveston (bay) L2
Galveston (isl.) K8
Glass (mts.) A7
Goodfellow A.F.B. D6
Grapevine (lake) F2
Guadalupe (mts.) C10
Guadalupe (peak) B10
Guadalupe (riv.) G8
Guadalupe Mts. Nat'l Park C10
Houston (lake) J8
Houston Ship (chan.) K2
Howard (creek) C7
Hubbard Creek (lake) F5
Hueco (mts.) B10
Intracoastal Waterway J9
Johnson Draw (dry riv.) C7
Kelly A.F.B. J11
Kemp (lake) E4
Kingsville N.A.S. G10
Kiowa (creek) D1
Lackland A.F.B. 14,459 ...... J11
Lake Meredith Nat'l Rec. Area C2
Lampasas (riv.) G6
Laughlin A.F.B. 2,994 .... D8
Lavon (lake) H1
Leon (riv.) F6
Livermore (mt.) C11
Livingston (lake) K7
Llano (riv.) D7
Llano Estacado (plain) B4
Locke (mt.) D11
Los Olmos (creek) F10
Los Olmos (creek) F11
Lyndon B. Johnson Nat'l Hist.
Site F7
Lyndon B. Johnson Space Ctr. K2
Madre (lag.) G11
Maravillas (creek) A7
Matagorda (bay) H9
Matagorda (isl.) H9
Matagorda (pen.) J9
Matagorda Isl. Bombing and Gunnery
Range H9
Medina (lake) E8
Medina (riv.) J11
Mexico (gulf) K9
Middle Concho (riv.) C6

Mountain Creek (lake) G2
Mustang (creek) A1
Mustang (isl.) G10
Mustang Draw (dry riv.) B5
Navasota (riv.) H7
Navidad (riv.) H8
Neches (riv.) K6
North Concho (riv.) C6
North Pease (riv.) D3
Nueces (riv.) F9
Padre (isl.) G10
Padre Island Nat'l Seashore G11
Palo Duro (creek) B2
Palo Duro (creek) C1
Pease (riv.) D3
Pecos (riv.) C7
Pedernales (riv.) F7
Possum Kingdom (lake) F5
Prairie Dog Town Fork, Red (riv.) ... C3
Quitman (mts.) B11
Red (riv.) F3
Red Bluff (lake) A6
Reese A.F.B. 1,934 .... B4
Rio Grande (riv.) D9
Rita Blanca (creek) B2
Sabine (riv.) L7
Salt Fork, Red (riv.) D3
Sam Rayburn (res.) K6
San Antonio (bay) H9
San Antonio (mt.) B10
San Antonio Missions Nat'l Hist.
Park J11
San Francisco (creek) B8
San Luis (passage) K8
San Martine Draw (dry riv.) C11
San Saba (riv.) D7
Santa Isabel (creek) E10
Santiago (mts.) A8
Santiago (peak) D12
Sheppard A.F.B. F3
Sierra Diablo (mts.) C10
Sierra Vieja (mts.) C11
Staked (Llano Estacado) (plain) B4
Stamford (lake) E4
Stockton (plat.) B7
Sulphur (riv.) J4
Sulphur Draw (dry riv.) B4
Sulphur Springs (creek) B4
Tenmile (creek) G3
Terlingua (creek) D12
Texoma (lake) H3
Tierra Blanca (creek) B3
Toledo Bend (res.) L6
Toyah (creek) D11
Toyah (lake) A6
Travis (lake) G7
Trinity (bay) L2
Trinity (riv.) H5
Trinity, West Fork (riv.) ... G2
Trujillo (creek) A2
Vieja, Sierra (mts.) C11
Walnut (creek) F3
Washita (riv.) D2
West (bay) K3
White (riv.) C3
White River (lake) C4
White Rock (creek) G2
Wichita (riv.) F4
Wolf (creek) D1
Worth (lake) E2
⊙County seat.
‡Population of metropolitan area.
† Zip of nearest p.o. * Multiple zips.

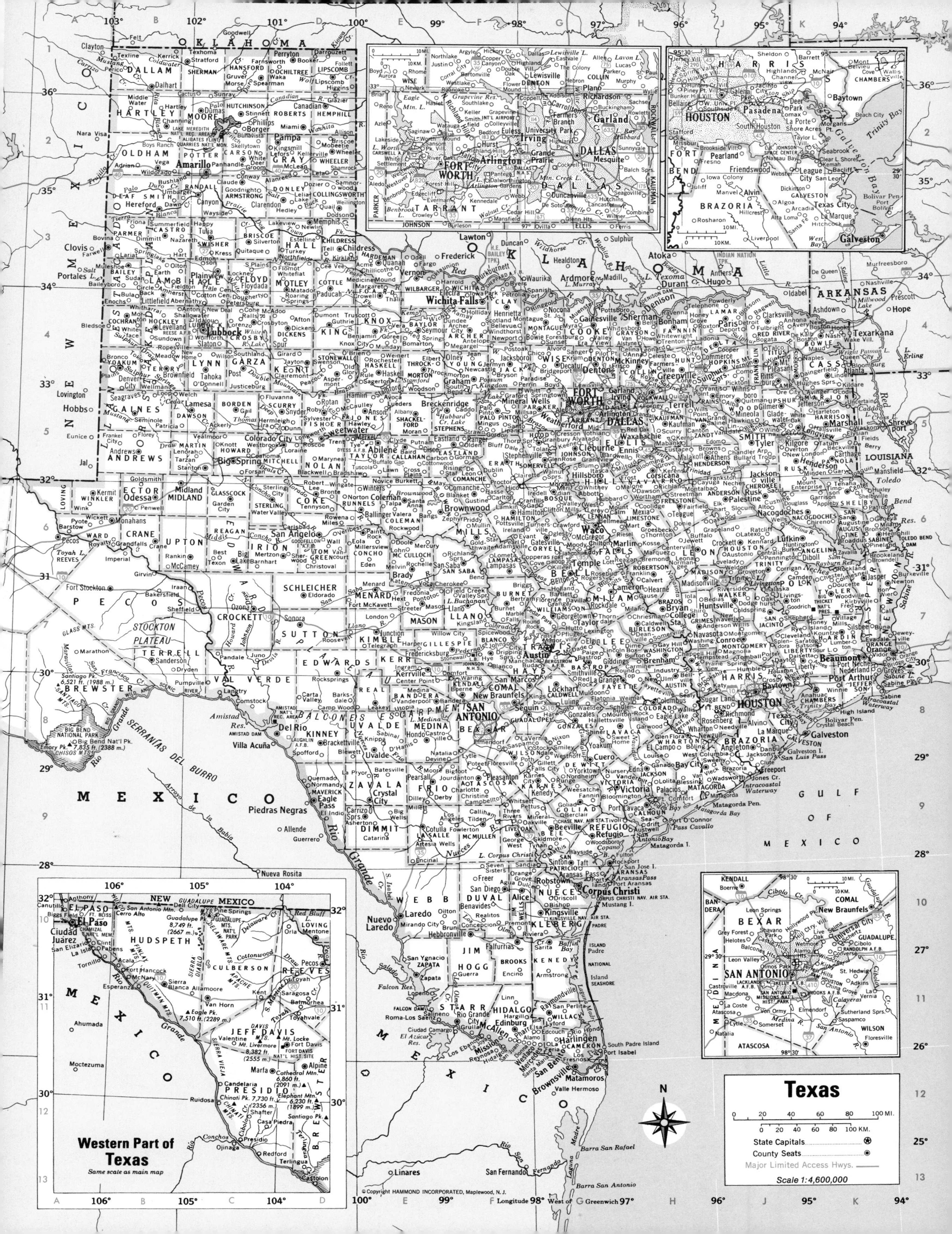

Texas
0 20 40 60 80 100 MI.
0 20 40 60 80 100 KM.
State Capitals
County Seats
Major Limited Access Hwys.
Scale 1:4,600,000
Western Part of
Texas
Same scale as main map
© Copyright HAMMOND INCORPORATED, Maplewood, N. J.
Longitude 98° West of Greenwich 97°
OKLAHOMA
NEW MEXICO
ARKANSAS
LOUISIANA
MEXICO
GULF OF MEXICO
HOUSTON
DALLAS
FORT WORTH
SAN ANTONIO

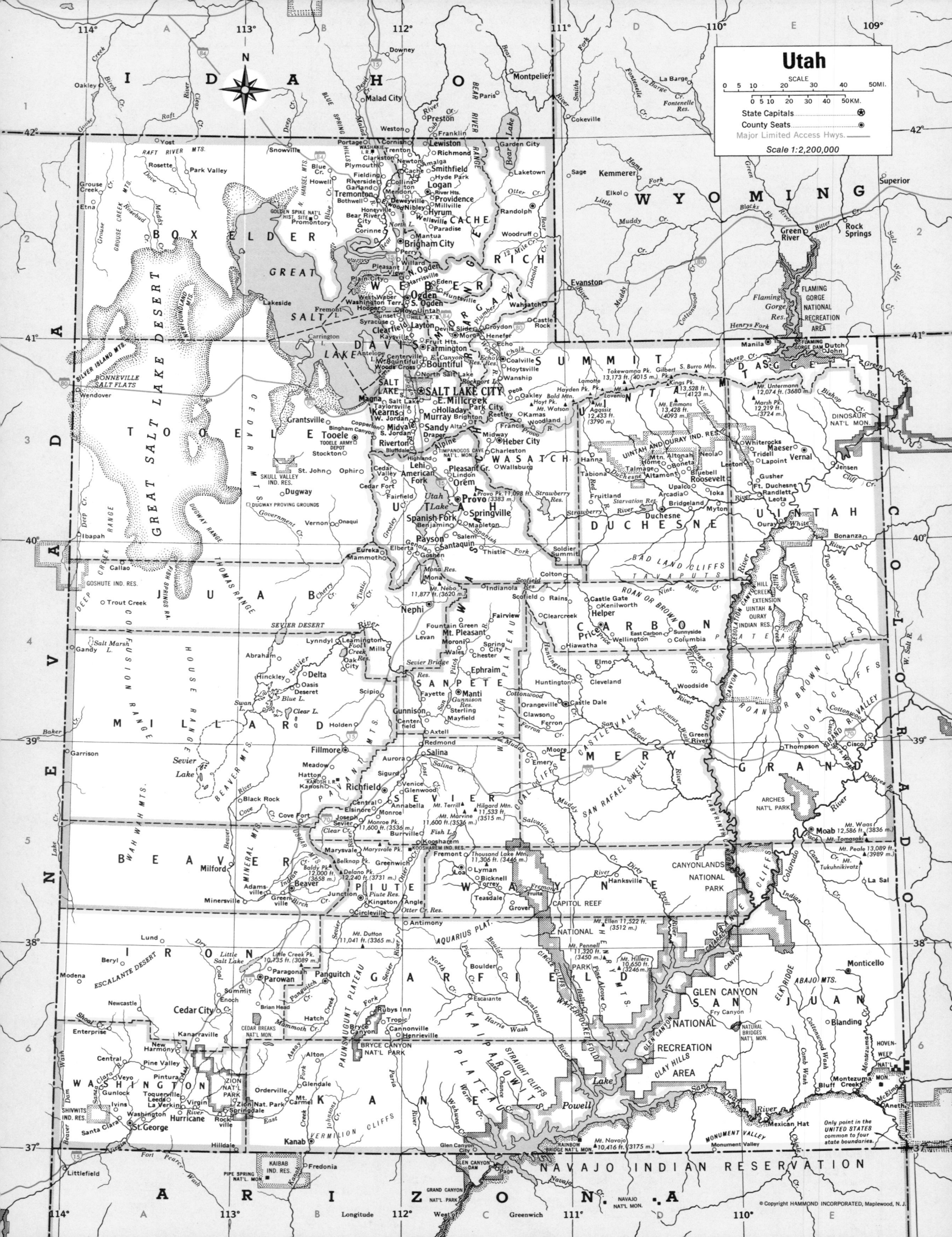

Utah
SCALE
0 5 10 20 30 40 50MI.
0 5 10 20 30 40 50KM.
State Capitals
County Seats
Major Limited Access Hwys.
Scale 1:2,200,000
I D A H O
W Y O M I N G
N E V A D A
A R I Z O N A
C O L O R A D O
BOX ELDER
CACHE
RICH
WEBER
MORGAN
DAVIS
SUMMIT
DAGGETT
SALT LAKE
TOOELE
WASATCH
UTAH
DUCHESNE
UINTAH
JUAB
CARBON
SANPETE
MILLARD
EMERY
GRAND
SEVIER
BEAVER
PIUTE
WAYNE
IRON
GARFIELD
SAN JUAN
WASHINGTON
KANE
GREAT SALT LAKE
GREAT SALT LAKE DESERT
SALT LAKE CITY
Ogden
Logan
Provo
Orem
Brigham City
Tooele
Nephi
Price
Vernal
Moab
Richfield
Beaver
Cedar City
St. George
Kanab
Monticello
Parowan
Manti
Fillmore
FLAMING GORGE NATIONAL RECREATION AREA
ARCHES NAT'L PARK
CANYONLANDS NATIONAL PARK
CAPITOL REEF NATIONAL PARK
GLEN CANYON NATIONAL RECREATION AREA
BRYCE CANYON NAT'L PARK
ZION NAT'L PARK
CEDAR BREAKS NAT'L MON.
NAVAJO INDIAN RESERVATION
Only point in the UNITED STATES common to four state boundaries.
Longitude West of Greenwich
© Copyright HAMMOND INCORPORATED, Maplewood, N.J.

AREA 84,899 sq. mi. (219,888 sq. km.)
POPULATION 1,461,037
CAPITAL Salt Lake City
LARGEST CITY Salt Lake City
HIGHEST POINT Kings Pk. 13,528 ft. (4123 m.)
SETTLED IN 1847
ADMITTED TO UNION January 4, 1896
POPULAR NAME Beehive State
STATE FLOWER Sego Lily
STATE BIRD Sea Gull

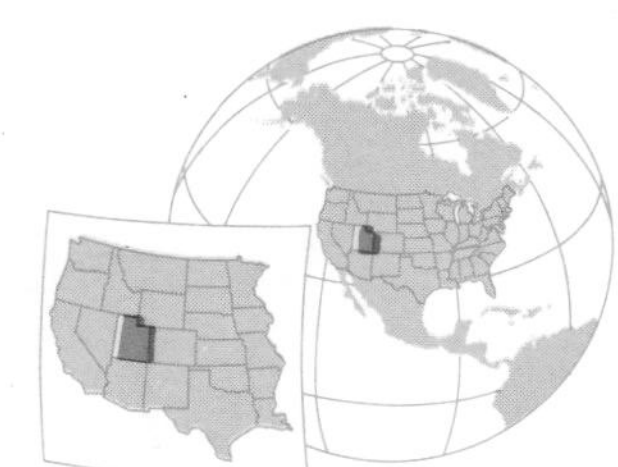

COUNTIES

Beaver 4,378 ..... A5
Box Elder 33,222 ..... A2
Cache 57,176 ..... C2
Carbon 22,179 ..... D4
Daggett 769 ..... E3
Davis 146,540 ..... B3
Duchesne 12,565 ..... D3
Emery 11,451 ..... D4
Garfield 3,673 ..... C6
Grand 8,241 ..... E5
Iron 17,349 ..... A6
Juab 5,530 ..... A4
Kane 4,024 ..... B6
Millard 8,970 ..... A4
Morgan 4,917 ..... C2
Piute 1,329 ..... B5
Rich 2,100 ..... C2
Salt Lake 619,066 ..... B3
San Juan 12,253 ..... E6
Sanpete 14,620 ..... C4
Sevier 14,727 ..... C5
Summit 10,198 ..... D3
Tooele 26,033 ..... A3
Uintah 20,506 ..... E3
Utah 218,106 ..... C3
Wasatch 8,523 ..... C3
Washington 26,065 ..... A6
Wayne 1,911 ..... C5
Weber 144,616 ..... B2

CITIES and TOWNS

Zip *Name/Pop.* *Key*

†84003 Alpine 2,649 ..... C3
84003 American Fork 12,693 ..... C3
84713 Beaver⊙ 1,792 ..... B5
84511 Blanding 3,118 ..... E6
†84065 Bluffdale 1,300 ..... B3
84010 Bountiful 32,877 ..... C3
84302 Brigham City⊙ 15,596 ..... C2
†84101 Brighton 150 ..... C3
84513 Castle Dale⊙ 1,910 ..... D4
84720 Cedar City 10,972 ..... A6
84014 Centerville 8,069 ..... C3
84015 Clearfield 17,982 ..... B2
84017 Coalville⊙ 1,031 ..... C3
84624 Delta 1,930 ..... B4
84020 Draper 5,521 ..... C3
84021 Duchesne⊙ 1,677 ..... D3
84022 Dugway 1,646 ..... B3
84520 East Carbon 1,942 ..... D4
84109 East Millcreek 24,150 ..... C3
84627 Ephraim 2,810 ..... C4
84025 Farmington⊙ 4,691 ..... C3
84523 Ferron 1,718 ..... C4
84631 Fillmore⊙ 2,083 ..... B5
†84037 Fruit Heights 2,728 ..... C2
84312 Garland 1,405 ..... B2
84029 Grantsville 4,419 ..... B3
84525 Green River 1,048 ..... D4
84634 Gunnison 1,255 ..... C4
†84401 Harrisville 1,371 ..... C2
84032 Heber City⊙ 4,362 ..... C3
84526 Helper 2,724 ..... D4
†84043 Highland 2,435 ..... C3
†84767 Hilldale 1,009 ..... A6
84117 Holladay 22,189 ..... C3
84528 Huntington 2,316 ..... C4
84737 Hurricane 2,361 ..... A6
84318 Hyde Park 1,495 ..... C2
84319 Hyrum 3,952 ..... C2
84740 Junction⊙ 151 ..... B5
84036 Kamas 1,064 ..... C3
84741 Kanab⊙ 2,148 ..... B6
84037 Kaysville 9,811 ..... B2
84118 Kearns 21,353 ..... B3
84745 La Verkin 1,174 ..... A6
84041 Layton 22,862 ..... C2
84043 Lehi 6,848 ..... C3
84320 Lewiston 1,438 ..... C2
†84062 Lindon 2,796 ..... C3
84747 Loa⊙ 364 ..... C5
84321 Logan⊙ 26,844 ..... C2
†84078 Maeser 2,216 ..... E3
84044 Magna 13,138 ..... B3
84046 Manila⊙ 272 ..... E3
84642 Manti⊙ 2,080 ..... C4
†84663 Mapleton 2,726 ..... C3
84531 Mexican Hat 250 ..... E6
84047 Midvale 10,146 ..... B3
84049 Midway 1,194 ..... C3
84751 Milford 1,293 ..... A5
84532 Moab⊙ 5,333 ..... E5
84754 Monroe 1,476 ..... B5
84535 Monticello⊙ 1,929 ..... E6
84050 Morgan⊙ 1,896 ..... C2
84646 Moroni 1,086 ..... C4
84647 Mount Pleasant 2,049 ..... C4
84107 Murray 25,750 ..... C3
84648 Nephi⊙ 3,285 ..... C4
†84321 Nibley 1,036 ..... C2
†84404 North Ogden 9,309 ..... C2
†84010 North Salt Lake 5,548 ..... C3
*84401 Ogden⊙ 64,407 ..... C2
Ogden-Salt Lake City‡ 936,255 ..... C4
84537 Orangeville 1,309 ..... C4
84057 Orem 52,399 ..... C3
Orem-Provo‡ 218,106 ..... C3
84759 Panguitch⊙ 1,343 ..... B6
84060 Park City 2,823 ..... C3
84761 Parowan⊙ 1,836 ..... B6
84651 Payson 8,246 ..... C3
†84302 Perry 1,084 ..... C2
†84401 Plain City 2,379 ..... B2
84062 Pleasant Grove 10,833 ..... C3
†84401 Pleasant View 3,983 ..... B2
84501 Price⊙ 9,086 ..... D4
84332 Providence 2,675 ..... C2
84601 Provo⊙ 74,108 ..... C3
Provo-Orem‡ 218,106 ..... C3
84064 Randolph⊙ 659 ..... C2
84701 Richfield⊙ 5,482 ..... B5
84333 Richmond 1,705 ..... C2
†84321 River Heights 1,211 ..... C2
84065 Riverton 7,293 ..... B3
84066 Roosevelt 3,842 ..... D3
84067 Roy 19,694 ..... C2
Saint George⊙ 11,350 ..... A6
84653 Salem 2,233 ..... C3
84654 Salina 1,992 ..... C5
*84101 Salt Lake City (cap)⊙ 163,697 ..... C3
Salt Lake City-Ogden‡ 936,255 ..... C3
*84070 Sandy 52,210 ..... C3
84765 Santa Clara 1,091 ..... A6
84655 Santaquin 2,175 ..... C4
84335 Smithfield 4,993 ..... C2
†84065 South Jordan 7,492 ..... B3
†84403 South Ogden 11,366 ..... C2
84115 South Salt Lake 9,884 ..... C3
84660 Spanish Fork 9,825 ..... C3
84663 Springville 12,101 ..... C3
†84015 Sunset 5,733 ..... B2
†84041 Syracuse 3,702 ..... B2
†84101 Taylorsville 17,448 ..... B3
84074 Tooele⊙ 14,335 ..... B3
84337 Tremonton 3,464 ..... B2
84078 Vernal⊙ 6,600 ..... E3
84780 Washington 3,092 ..... A6
†84403 Washington Terrace 8,212 ..... B2
84542 Wellington 1,406 ..... D4
84339 Wellsville 1,952 ..... C2
84083 Wendover 1,099 ..... A3
†84087 West Bountiful 3,556 ..... B3
84084 West Jordan 27,192 ..... B3
84340 Willard 1,241 ..... C2
84087 Woods Cross 4,263 ..... B3

OTHER FEATURES

Abajo (mts.) E6
Agassiz (mt.) D3
Antelope (isl.) B3
Aquarius (plat.) C5
Arches Nat'l Park E5
Assay (creek) B6
Bad Land (cliffs) D4
Baldy (peak) B5
Bear (lake) C2
Bear (riv.) B2
Beaver (mts.) A5
Beaver (riv.) A5
Beaver Dam Wash (creek) A6
Birch (creek) B5
Blue (creek) B2
Bonneville (salt flats) A3
Book (cliffs) E4
Brown (Roan) (cliffs) E4
Bryce Canyon Nat'l Park B6
Canyonlands Nat'l Park D5
Capitol Reef Nat'l Park C5
Castle (valley) D4
Cedar (mts.) B3
Cedar Breaks Nat'l Mon. B6
Chalk (creek) C3
Chinle (creek) E6
Clear (lake) B4
Cliff (creek) E3
Coal (cliffs) C5
Colorado (riv.) E5
Confusion (range) A4
Cottonwood (creek) C4
Cub (creek) C1
Deep (creek) B1
Deep Creek (range) A4
Delano (peak) B5
Desolation (canyon) E4
Dinosaur Nat'l Mon. E3
Dirty Devil (riv.) D5
Dolores (riv.) E5
Dry Coal (creek) A6
Duchesne (riv.) D3
Dugway (range) A3
Dugway Proving Grounds B3
Dutton (mt.) B5
East Canyon (res.) C3
Echo (res.) C3
Elk (ridge) E6
Ellen (mt.) D5
Emmons (mt.) D3
Escalante (des.) A6
Escalante (riv.) C6
Fish (lake) C5
Fish Springs (range) A4
Flaming Gorge (res.) E3
Flaming Gorge Nat'l Rec. Area E2
Fool Creek (res.) B4
Fremont (isl.) B2
Fremont (riv.) C5
Glen Canyon Nat'l Rec. Area D6
Golden Spike Nat'l Hist. Site B2
Goshute Ind. Res. A4
Government (creek) B3
Gray (canyon) D4
Great Salt (lake) B2
Great Salt Lake (des.) A3
Greeley (creek) B3
Green (riv.) D4
Grouse (creek) A2
Grouse Creek (mts.) A2
Gunnison (res.) C4
Henry (mts.) D6
Hilgard (mt.) C5
Hill (creek) E4
Hill A.F.B. C2
Hill Creek Ext., Uintah and Ouray Ind. Res. E4
Hillers (mt.) D6
House (range) A4
Hovenweep Nat'l Mon. E6
Huntington (creek) C4
Indian (creek) B5
Jordan (riv.) C3
Kaiparowits (plat.) C6
Kanab (creek) B7
Kanosh Ind. Res. B5
Kings (peak) D3
Koosharem Ind. Res. C5
Little Creek (peak) B6
Little Salt (lake) A6
Malad (riv.) B1
Marsh (peak) E3
Marvine (mt.) C5
Mineral (mts.) B5
Mona (res.) C4
Monroe (peak) B5
Montezuma (creek) E6
Monument (valley) D6
Muddy (creek) C4
Natural Bridges Nat'l Mon. E6
Navajo (mt.) D6
Navajo Ind. Res. D7
Nebo (mt.) C4
Newfoundland (mts.) A2
Nine Mile (creek) D4
North (lake) B2
Orange (cliffs) D5
Otter (creek) C5
Otter Creek (res.) C5
Paria (riv.) B6
Paunsaugunt (plat.) B6
Pavant (mts.) B5
Peale (mt.) E5
Pennell (mt.) D6
Piute (res.) B5
Plumber (creek) C2
Powell (lake) D6
Price (riv.) D4
Provo (peak) C3
Provo (riv.) C3
Raft River (mts.) A2
Rainbow Bridge Nat'l Mon. C6
Roan (cliffs) E4
Rockport (lake) C3
Salvation (creek) C5
San Juan (riv.) D6
San Pitch (riv.) C4
San Rafael (riv.) D4
San Rafael Swell (mts.) D5
Santa Clara (riv.) A6
Sevier (des.) B4
Sevier (lake) A5
Sevier (riv.) B4
Sevier Bridge (res.) C4
Shivwits Ind. Res. A6
Silver Island (mts.) A3
Skull Valley Ind. Res. B3
Spanish Fork (riv.) C3
Strait (cliffs) C6
Strawberry (res.) C3
Strawberry (riv.) D3
Swan (lake) B4
Tavaputs (plat.) D4
Thomas (range) A4
Thousand Lake (mt.) C5
Timpanogos Cave Nat'l Mon. C3
Tokewamna (peak) D3
Tooele Army Depot B3
Two Water (creek) E4
Uinta (mts.) D3
Uinta (riv.) D3
Uintah and Ouray Ind. Res. D3
Utah (lake) C3
Virgin (riv.) A6
Waas (mt.) E5
Wah Wah (mts.) A5
Wahweap (creek) C6
Wasatch (range) C3
Washakie Ind. Res. B2
Waterpocket Fold (cliffs) D6
Weber (riv.) C3
White (riv.) E3
Willow (creek) E4
Zion Nat'l Park A6

⊙County seat.
‡Population of metropolitan area.
† Zip of nearest p.o.
* Multiple zips.

Agriculture, Industry and Resources

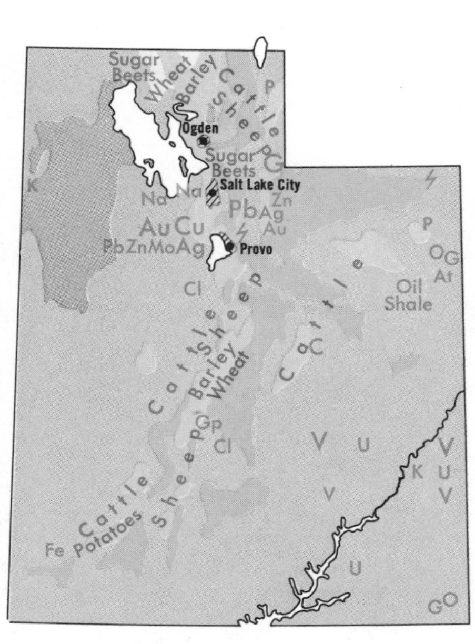
Sugar Beets
Wheat
Barley
Cattle
Sheep
P
Ogden
Sugar Beets
Salt Lake City
K
Na
Na
Pb Ag
Zn
Au
AuCu
PbZnMoAg
Provo
P
OG
At
Oil Shale
Cl
Cattle
Sheep
Barley
Wheat
Cattle
Gp
Cl
V
U
K
U
V
Cattle
Sheep
Potatoes
Fe
U
GO

DOMINANT LAND USE

Wheat, General Farming
General Farming, Livestock, Special Crops
Range Livestock
Forests
Nonagricultural Land

MAJOR MINERAL OCCURRENCES

Ag	Silver	Fe	Iron Ore	O	Petroleum
At	Asphalt	G	Natural Gas	P	Phosphates
Au	Gold	Gp	Gypsum	Pb	Lead
C	Coal	K	Potash	U	Uranium
Cl	Clay	Mo	Molybdenum	V	Vanadium
Cu	Copper	Na	Salt	Zn	Zinc

Water Power
Major Industrial Areas

Topography

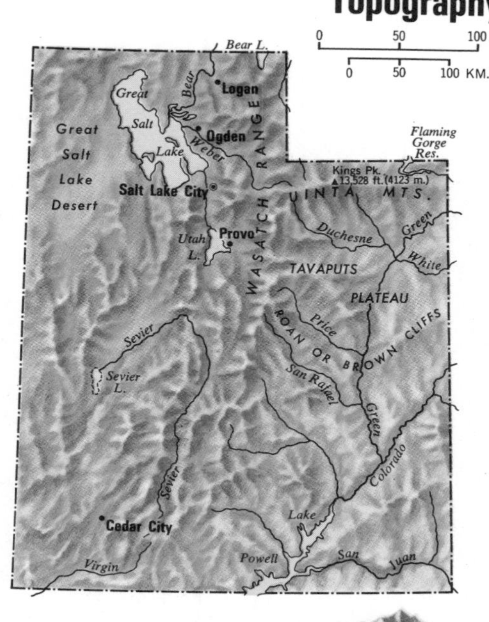
0 50 100 MI.
0 50 100 KM.
Bear L.
Logan
Great
Bear
Salt
Ogden
Lake
Weber
Great
Salt
Lake
Desert
Salt Lake City
Flaming Gorge Res.
Kings Pk. 13,528 ft. (4123 m.)
UINTA MTS.
WASATCH RANGE
Utah L.
Provo
Duchesne
Green
White
TAVAPUTS
PLATEAU
Price
ROAN OR BROWN CLIFFS
Sevier
Sevier L.
San Rafael
Green
Colorado
Sevier
Cedar City
Lake
Powell
San Juan
Virgin

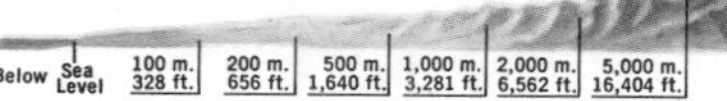
Below Sea Level
100 m. 328 ft.
200 m. 656 ft.
500 m. 1,640 ft.
1,000 m. 3,281 ft.
2,000 m. 6,562 ft.
5,000 m. 16,404 ft.

Topography

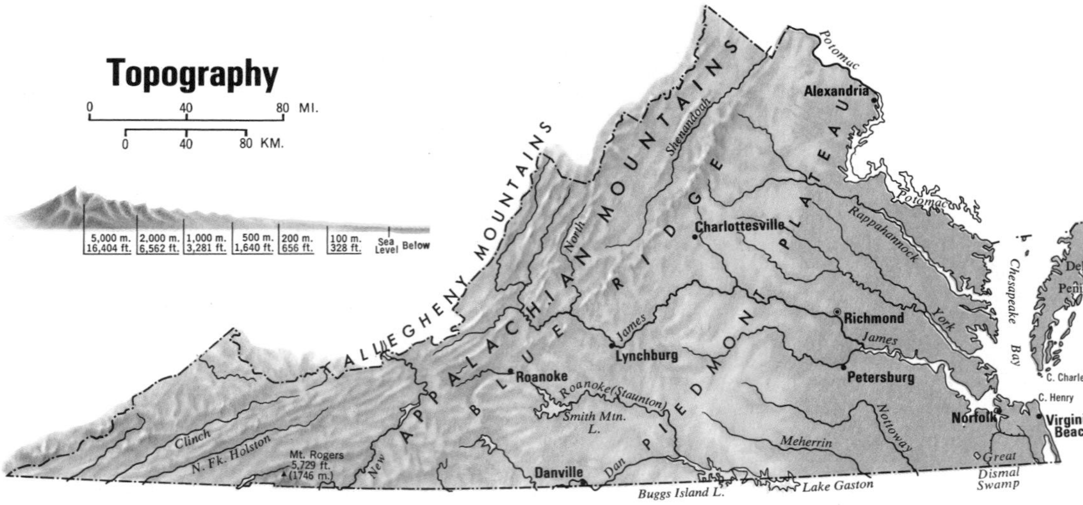

COUNTIES

Accomack 31,268 .... S5
Albemarle 55,783 .... L5
Alleghany 14,333 .... H5
Amelia 8,405 .... M6
Amherst 29,122 .... K5
Appomattox 11,971 .... L6
Arlington 152,599 .... S2
Augusta 53,732 .... K4
Bath 5,860 .... J4
Bedford 34,927 .... J6
Bland 6,349 .... F6
Botetourt 23,270 .... J5
Brunswick 15,632 .... N7
Buchanan 37,989 .... D6
Buckingham 11,751 .... L5
Campbell 45,424 .... K6
Caroline 17,904 .... O4
Carroll 27,270 .... G7
Charles City 6,692 .... O6
Charlotte 12,266 .... L6
Chesterfield 141,372 .... N6
Clarke 9,965 .... M2
Craig 3,948 .... H6
Culpeper 22,620 .... M3
Cumberland 7,881 .... M6
Dickenson 19,806 .... D6
Dinwiddie 22,602 .... N6
Essex 8,864 .... P5
Fairfax 596,901 .... O3
Fauquier 35,889 .... N3
Floyd 11,563 .... H7
Fluvanna 10,244 .... M5
Franklin 35,740 .... J6
Frederick 34,150 .... M2
Giles 17,810 .... G6
Gloucester 20,107 .... P6
Goochland 11,761 .... N5
Grayson 16,579 .... F7
Greene 7,625 .... M4
Greensville 10,903 .... N7
Halifax 30,599 .... L7
Hanover 50,398 .... N5
Henrico 180,735 .... O6
Henry 57,654 .... J7
Highland 2,937 .... J4
Isle of Wight 21,603 .... P7
James City 22,763 .... P6
King and Queen 5,968 .... P5
King George 10,543 .... O4
King William 9,334 .... O5
Lancaster 10,129 .... R5
Lee 25,956 .... B7
Loudoun 57,427 .... N2
Louisa 17,825 .... N5
Lunenburg 12,124 .... M7
Madison 10,232 .... M4
Mathews 7,995 .... R6
Mecklenburg 29,444 .... M7
Middlesex 7,719 .... R5
Montgomery 63,516 .... H6
Nelson 12,204 .... L5
New Kent 8,781 .... P5
Northampton 14,625 .... S6
Northumberland 9,828 .... R5
Nottoway 14,666 .... M6
Orange 18,063 .... M4
Page 19,401 .... M3
Patrick 17,647 .... H7
Pittsylvania 66,147 .... K7
Powhatan 13,062 .... N5
Prince Edward 16,456 .... M6
Prince George 25,733 .... O6
Prince William 144,703 .... O3
Pulaski 35,229 .... G6
Rappahannock 6,093 .... M3
Richmond 6,952 .... P5
Roanoke 72,945 .... H6
Rockbridge 17,911 .... K5
Rockingham 57,038 .... L4
Russell 31,761 .... D7
Scott 25,068 .... C7
Shenandoah 27,559 .... L3
Smyth 33,366 .... E7
Southampton 18,731 .... O7
Spotsylvania 34,435 .... N4
Stafford 40,470 .... O4
Surry 6,046 .... P6
Sussex 10,874 .... O7
Tazewell 50,511 .... E6
Warren 21,200 .... M3
Washington 46,487 .... D7
Westmoreland 14,041 .... P4
Wise 43,863 .... C6
Wythe 25,522 .... F7
York 35,463 .... P6

CITIES and TOWNS

Zip *Name/Pop.* *Key*

24210 Abingdon⊙ 4,318 .... D7
23301 Accomac⊙ 522 .... S5
23001 Achilles 525 .... R6
22920 Afton 350 .... L4
23821 Alberta 394 .... N7
*22301 Alexandria (I.C.) 103,217 .. S3
24310 Allisonia 325 .... G7
24517 Altavista 3,849 .... K6
24520 Alton 500 .... K7
23002 Amelia Court House⊙ 500. N6
24521 Amherst⊙ 1,135 .... K5
24601 Amonate 350 .... E6
22003 Annandale 49,524 .... S3
24216 Appalachia 2,418 .... C7
24522 Appomattox⊙ 1,345 .... L6
24053 Ararat 500 .... G7
*22201 Arlington⊙ 152,599 .... T3
22922 Arrington 500 .... L5
23004 Arvonia 500 .... M5
22011 Ashburn 345 .... O2
23005 Ashland 4,640 .... N5
24311 Atkins 1,352 .... F7
24411 Augusta Springs 600 .... K4
24312 Austinville 750 .... F7
24054 Axton 540 .... J7
22041 Bailey's Crossroads 12,564 .... S3
24230 Banner 327 .... D7
22923 Barboursville 600 .... M4
24055 Bassett 2,034 .... J7
24314 Bastian 600 .... F6
22924 Batesville 575 .... L5
23015 Beaverdam 500 .... N5
24523 Bedford (I.C.)⊙ 5,991 .... J6
23306 Belle Haven 589 .... S5
24218 Ben Hur 400 .... B7
22610 Bentonville 500 .... M3
22611 Berryville⊙ 1,752 .... M2
24526 Big Island 500 .... K5
24603 Big Rock 900 .... D6
24219 Big Stone Gap 4,748 .... C7
24220 Birchleaf 650 .... D6
23307 Birdsnest 736 .... S6
24604 Bishop 600 .... E6
24060 Blacksburg 30,638 .... H6
23824 Blackstone 3,624 .... N6
24527 Blairs 500 .... K7
24315 Bland⊙ 950 .... F6
23308 Bloxom 407 .... S5
24605 Bluefield 5,946 .... F6
24064 Blue Ridge 2,347 .... J6
24606 Boissevain 975 .... F6
23235 Bon Air 16,224 .... N5
24065 Boones Mill 344 .... J6
22713 Boston 400 .... M3
22427 Bowling Green⊙ 665 .... O4
22620 Boyce 401 .... M2
23917 Boydton⊙ 486 .... M7
23827 Boykins 791 .... O7
22714 Brandy Station 400 .... N4
24607 Breaks 550 .... D6
22812 Bridgewater 3,289 .... K4
24201 Bristol (I.C.) 19,042 .... D7
24316 Broadford 500 .... E7
22815 Broadway 1,234 .... L3
23920 Brodnax 492 .... N7
22430 Brooke 245 .... O4
24528 Brookneal 1,454 .... L6
24415 Brownsburg 300 .... K5
22610 Browntown 300 .... M3
22622 Brucetown 250 .... M2
24066 Buchanan 1,205 .... J5
23921 Buckingham⊙ 200 .... L5
24416 Buena Vista (I.C.) 6,717 .... K5
24529 Buffalo Junction 300 .... L7
22015 Burke 33,835 .... R3
24608 Burkes Garden 267 .... F6
23922 Burkeville 606 .... M6
22435 Callao 500 .... P5
24067 Callaway 225 .... H7
22016 Calverton 500 .... N3
23310 Cape Charles 1,512 .... R6
23313 Capeville 325 .... R6
23829 Capron 238 .... O7
23315 Carrsville 300 .... P7
23830 Carson 500 .... O6
22017 Casanova 370 .... N3
24069 Cascade 835 .... J7
24224 Castlewood 2,420 .... D7
24070 Catawba 350 .... H6
22019 Catlett 500 .... N3
24609 Cedar Bluff 1,550 .... E6
22437 Center Cross 360 .... P5
†22401 Chancellorsville 40 .... N4
22021 Chantilly 12,259 .... O3
23030 Charles City⊙ 5 .... O6
23923 Charlotte Court House⊙ 568 .... L6
*22901 Charlottesville (I.C.)⊙ 39,916 .... M4
Charlottesville‡ 113,568 ... M4
23924 Chase City 2,749 .... M7
24531 Chatham⊙ 1,390 .... K7
23316 Cheriton 695 .... R6
*23320 Chesapeake (I.C.) 114,486 .... R7
23831 Chester 11,728 .... O6
23832 Chesterfield⊙ 950 .... N6
22623 Chester Gap 400 .... M3
24319 Chilhowie 1,269 .... E7
23336 Chincoteague 1,607 .... T5
24073 Christiansburg⊙ 10,345 .... H6
23032 Church View 200 .... P5
23899 Claremont 380 .... P6
23927 Clarksville 1,468 .... L7
†23061 Clay Bank 200 .... P6
†23139 Clayville 200 .... N6
22624 Clear Brook 300 .... M2
24225 Cleveland 360 .... D7
24422 Clifton Forge (I.C.) 5,046 .... J5
24321 Clinchburg 250 .... E7
24226 Clinchco 900 .... D6
24244 Clinchport 89 .... C7
24228 Clintwood⊙ 1,369 .... D6
24534 Clover 215 .... L7
24077 Cloverdale 850 .... J6
24535 Cluster Springs 350 .... L7
23035 Cobbs Creek 700 .... R6
24230 Coeburn 2,625 .... D7
24536 Coleman Falls 250 .... K6
†24450 Collierstown 300 .... J5
24078 Collinsville 7,517 .... J7
22443 Colonial Beach 2,474 .... P4
23834 Colonial Heights (I.C.) 16,509 .... O6
23038 Columbia 111 .... M5
24538 Concord 500 .... K6
23837 Courtland⊙ 976 .... O7
22931 Covesville 475 .... L5
24426 Covington (I.C.)⊙ 9,063 .... H5
24430 Craigsville 845 .... J4
23930 Crewe 2,325 .... M6
24431 Crimora 450 .... L4
24322 Cripple Creek 200 .... F7
24323 Crockett 200 .... F7
22932 Crozet 2,553 .... L4
23039 Crozier 300 .... N5
24539 Crystal Hill 475 .... L7
23934 Cullen 725 .... L6
22701 Culpeper⊙ 6,621 .... M4
23040 Cumberland⊙ 300 .... M6
22448 Dahlgren 950 .... O4
22193 Dale City 33,127 .... O3
24083 Daleville 450 .... J6
24236 Damascus 1,330 .... E7
24237 Dante 1,083 .... D7
*24540 Danville (I.C.) 45,642 .... J7
Danville‡ 111,789 .... J7

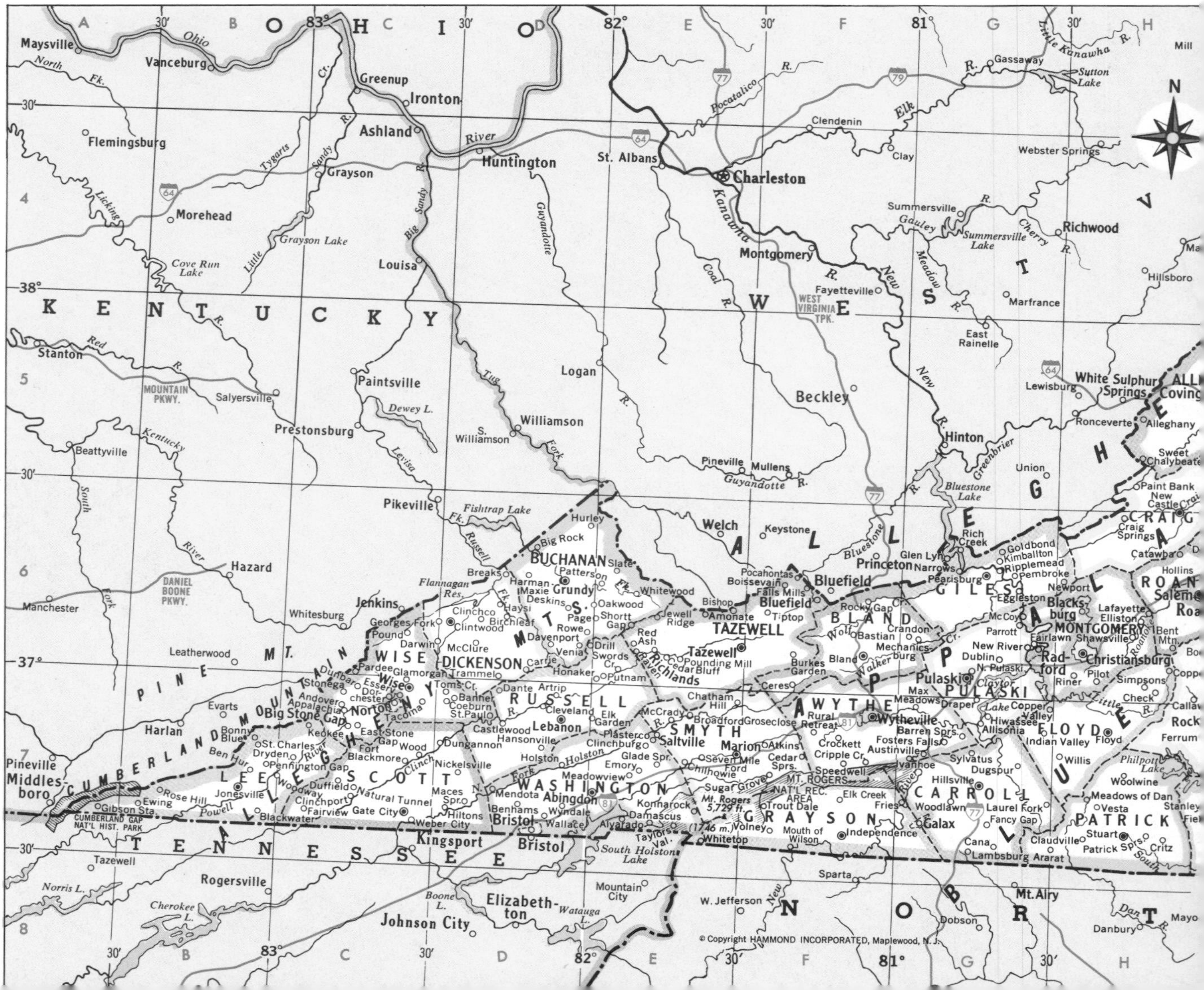

24239 Davenport 230 .... D6
22821 Dayton 1,017 .... L4
24432 Deerfield 500 .... K4
23043 Deltaville 1,082 .... R5
23839 Dendron 307 .... P6
†24520 Denniston 200 .... L7
23936 Dillwyn 637 .... M5
23841 Dinwiddie⊙ 500 .... N6
23842 Disputanta 800 .... O6
23937 Drakes Branch 617 .... L7
23844 Drewryville 200 .... O7
24243 Dryden 400 .... B7
24549 Dry Fork 200 .... K7
24084 Dublin 2,368 .... G6
24244 Duffield 148 .... C7
22026 Dumfries 3,214 .... O3
23938 Dundas 200 .... M7
24245 Dungannon 339 .... D7
22027 Dunn Loring 6,077 .... S2
22454 Dunnsville 800 .... P5
24085 Eagle Rock 750 .... J5
22936 Earlysville 210 .... M4
24246 East Stone Gap 240 .... C7
23347 Eastville⊙ 238 .... R6
23845 Ebony 400 .... N7
22824 Edinburg 752 .... M3
24086 Eggleston 350 .... G6
22827 Elkton 1,520 .... L4
24087 Elliston-Lafayette 1,172 .... H6
24327 Emory-Meadowview 2,292 .... E7
23847 Emporia (I.C.)⊙ 4,840 .... N7
22937 Esmont 950 .... L5
24274 Esserville 750 .... G2
23803 Ettrick 4,890 .... O6
23939 Evergreen 300 .... L6
24248 Ewing 800 .... B7
23350 Exmore 1,300 .... S5
22030 Fairfax (I.C.)⊙ 19,390 .... R3
22039 Fairfax Station R3
24435 Fairfield 465 .... K5
24141 Fairlawn 1,794 .... G6
*22040 Falls Church (I.C.) 9,515 .... S2
24613 Falls Mills 800 .... F6
22401 Falmouth 3,271 .... O4
24328 Fancy Gap 200 .... G7
23901 Farmville⊙ 6,067 .... M6
24088 Ferrum 200 .... H7
24089 Fieldale 1,190 .... H7
24090 Fincastle⊙ 282 .... J6
22939 Fishersville 975 .... K4
22627 Flint Hill 750 .... M3
24091 Floyd⊙ 411 .... H7
24551 Forest 497 .... K6
23055 Fork Union 350 .... M5
24437 Fort Defiance 600 .... L4
22578 Foxwells 400 .... R5
22310 Franconia 8,476 .... S3
23851 Franklin (I.C.) 7,308 .... P7
23354 Franktown 500 .... S6
*22401 Fredericksburg (I.C.) 15,322 .... N4
24330 Fries 758 .... F7
22630 Front Royal⊙ 11,126 .... M3
22065 Gainesville 600 .... N3
24333 Galax (I.C.) 6,524 .... G7
22463 Garrisonville 200 .... N4
24251 Gate City⊙ 2,494 .... C7
†24228 Georges Fork 200 .... C6
24340 Glade Spring 1,722 .... E7
24554 Gladys 500 .... K6
24555 Glasgow 1,259 .... K5
23060 Glen Allen 6,202 .... N5
24093 Glen Lyn 235 .... G6
†24541 Glenwood 2,276 .... K7
23061 Gloucester⊙ 1,545 .... P6
23062 Gloucester Point 5,841 .... R6
24094 Goldbond 250 .... G6
22720 Goldvein 500 .... N4
23063 Goochland⊙ 800 .... N5
24556 Goode 200 .... K6
22942 Gordonsville 1,421 .... M4
22637 Gore 500 .... M2
24439 Goshen 134 .... K5
23692 Grafton 500 .... P6
23356 Greenbackville 300 .... T5
23942 Green Bay 500 .... M6
23357 Greenbush 200 .... S5
24440 Greenville 400 .... K5
22943 Greenwood 800 .... L4
24557 Gretna 1,255 .... K7
24441 Grottoes 1,369 .... L4
†22306 Groveton 18,860 .... T3
24614 Grundy⊙ 1,699 .... D6
23066 Gwynn 205 .... R5
22469 Hague 425 .... P4
24558 Halifax⊙ 772 .... L7
23359 Hallwood 243 .... S5
22068 Hamilton 598 .... N2
23943 Hampden-Sydney 1,011 .... L6
*23601 Hampton (I.C.) 122,617 .... R6
23069 Hanover⊙ 500 .... O5
23389 Harborton 200 .... S5
24101 Hardy 325 .... J6
24618 Harman-Maxie 650 .... D6
22801 Harrisonburg (I.C.)⊙ 19,671 .... K4
23071 Hartfield 700 .... R5
22069 Haymarket 230 .... N3
22472 Haynesville 500 .... P5
24256 Haysi 371 .... D6
22473 Heathsville⊙ 300 .... P5
24102 Henry 300 .... J7
*22070 Herndon 11,449 .... O3
23075 Highland Springs 12,146 .... O5
22132 Hillsboro 115 .... N2
24343 Hillsville⊙ 2,123 .... G7
24258 Hiltons 300 .... D7
24347 Hiwassee 250 .... G7
24020 Hollins College 12,295 .... H6
24260 Honaker 1,475 .... D6
23860 Hopewell (I.C.) 23,397 .... O6
23395 Horntown 400 .... T5
24445 Hot Springs 300 .... J4
24104 Huddleston 200 .... K6

(continued on following page)

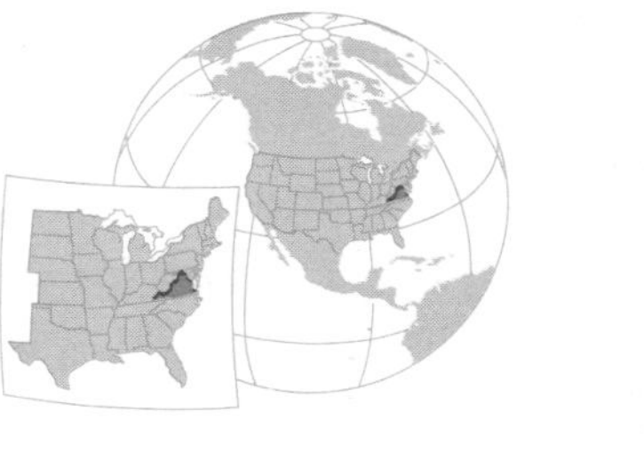

AREA 40,767 sq. mi. (105,587 sq. km.)
POPULATION 5,346,818
CAPITAL Richmond
LARGEST CITY Norfolk
HIGHEST POINT Mt. Rogers 5,729 ft. (1746 m.)
SETTLED IN 1607
ADMITTED TO UNION June 26, 1788
POPULAR NAME Old Dominion
STATE FLOWER Dogwood
STATE BIRD Cardinal

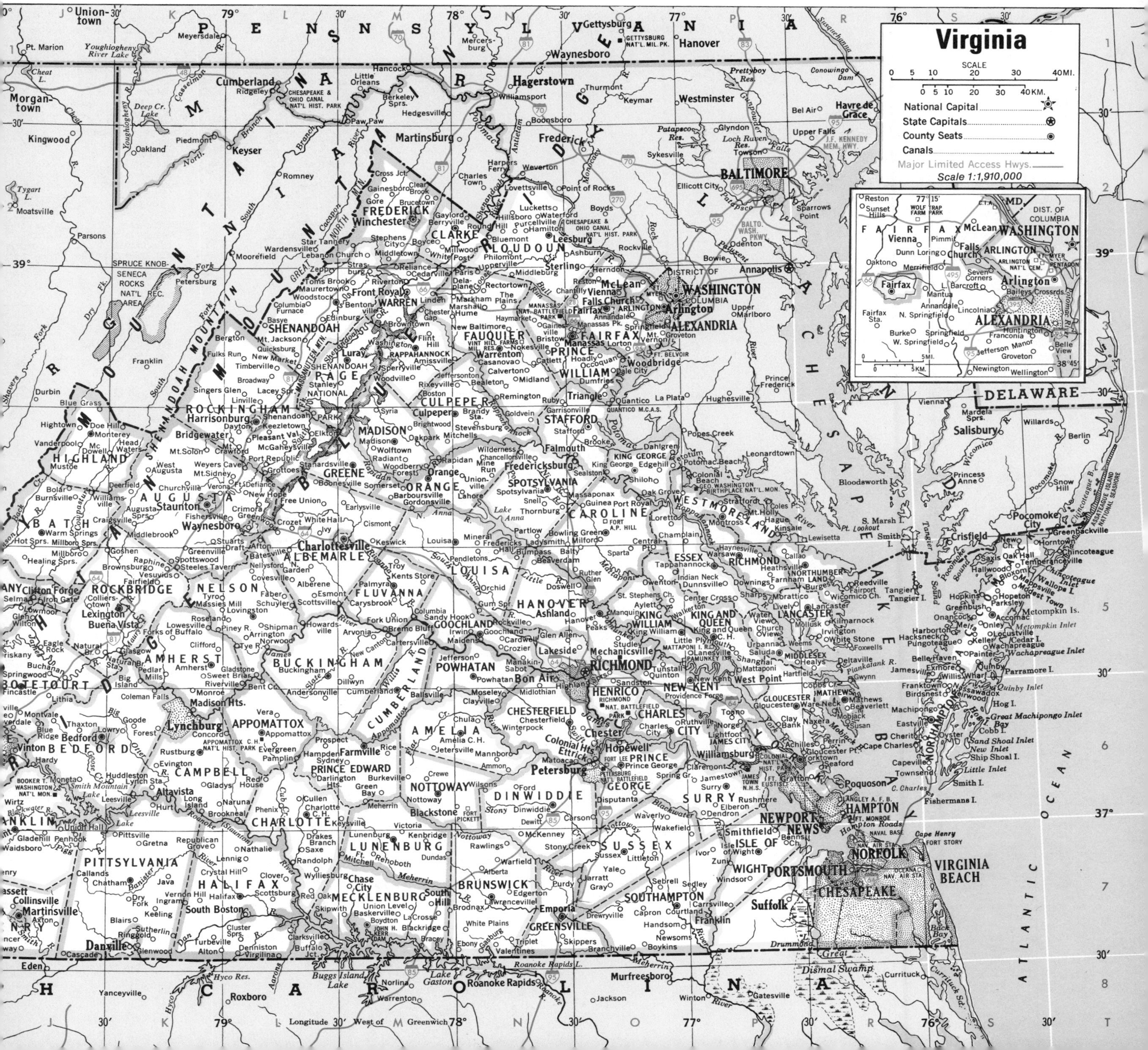

Agriculture, Industry and Resources

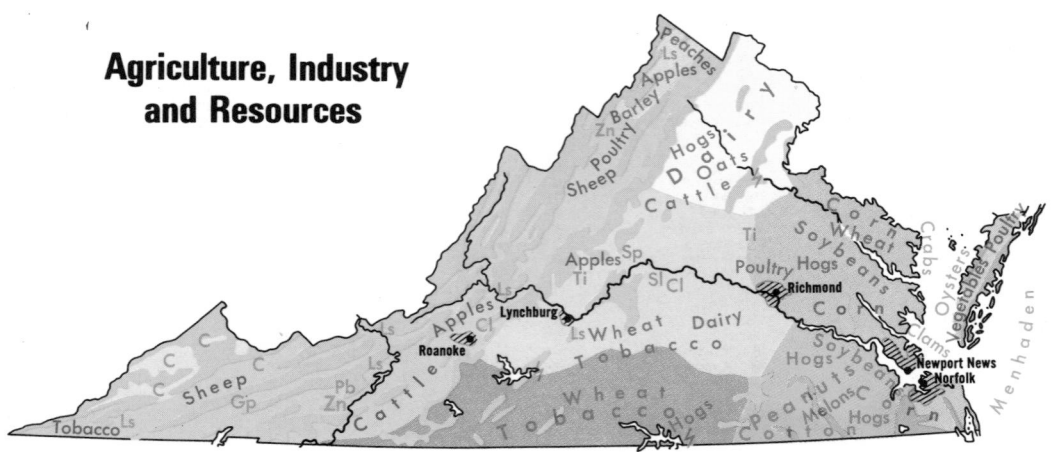

MAJOR MINERAL OCCURRENCES

C	Coal	Sl	Slate	⚡	Water Power
Cl	Clay	Sp	Soapstone	▨	Major Industrial Areas
Gp	Gypsum	Ti	Titanium		
Ls	Limestone	Zn	Zinc		
Pb	Lead				

DOMINANT LAND USE

- Dairy, General Farming
- General Farming, Livestock, Dairy
- General Farming, Livestock, Tobacco
- General Farming, Livestock, Fruit, Tobacco
- General Farming, Truck Farming, Tobacco, Livestock
- Tobacco, General Farming
- Peanuts, General Farming
- Fruit and Mixed Farming
- Truck and Mixed Farming
- Forests
- Swampland, Limited Agriculture

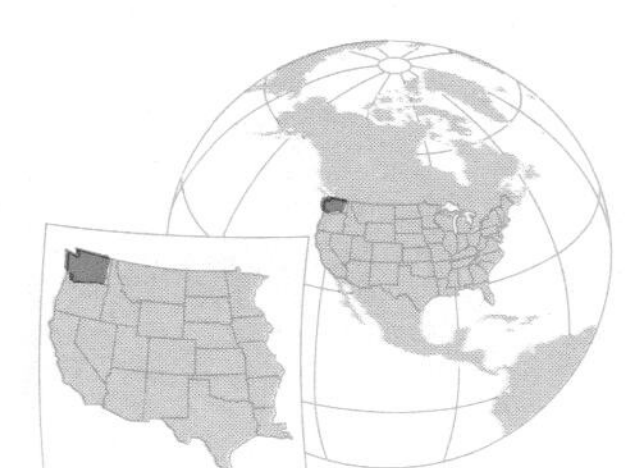

AREA 68,139 sq. mi. (176,480 sq. km.)
POPULATION 4,132,180
CAPITAL Olympia
LARGEST CITY Seattle
HIGHEST POINT Mt. Rainier 14,410 ft. (4392 m.)
SETTLED IN 1811
ADMITTED TO UNION November 11, 1889
POPULAR NAME Evergreen State
STATE FLOWER Western Rhododendron
STATE BIRD Willow Goldfinch

COUNTIES

Adams 13,267	G3
Asotin 16,823	H4
Benton 109,444	F4
Chelan 45,061	E3
Clallam 51,648	B2
Clark 192,227	C5
Columbia 4,057	H4
Cowlitz 79,548	C4
Douglas 22,144	F3
Ferry 5,811	G2
Franklin 35,025	G4
Garfield 2,468	H4
Grant 48,522	F3
Grays Harbor 66,314	B3
Island 44,048	C2
Jefferson 15,965	B3
King 1,269,749	D3
Kitsap 147,152	C3
Kittitas 24,877	E3
Klickitat 15,822	E5
Lewis 56,028	C4
Lincoln 9,604	G3
Mason 31,184	B3
Okanogan 30,639	F2
Pacific 17,237	B4
Pend Oreille 8,580	H2
Pierce 485,667	C3
San Juan 7,838	C2
Skagit 64,138	D2
Skamania 7,919	D5

Snohomish 337,720	D2
Spokane 341,835	H3
Stevens 28,979	H2
Thurston 124,264	C4
Wahkiakum 3,832	B4
Walla Walla 47,435	G4
Whatcom 106,701	D2
Whitman 40,103	H4
Yakima 172,508	E4

CITIES and TOWNS

Zip	Name/Pop.	Key
98520	Aberdeen 18,739	B3
98220	Acme 500	C2
99001	Airway Heights 1,730	H3
99102	Albion 631	H4
†98328	Alder 300	C4
98002	Algona 1,467	C3
98524	Allyn 850	C3
99103	Almira 330	G3
98526	Amanda Park 495	A3
98601	Amboy 480	C5
98221	Anacortes 9,013	C2
98603	Ariel 386	C5
98223	Arlington 3,282	C2
98304	Ashford 300	C4
99402	Asotin⊙ 943	H4
98002	Auburn 26,417	C3
98110	Bainbridge Island-Winslow (Winslow) 2,196	A2
98604	Battle Ground 2,774	C5

†98004	Beaux Arts Village 328	B2
98305	Beaver 450	A2
98528	Belfair 500	C3
*98004	Bellevue 73,903	B2
98225	Bellingham⊙ 45,794	C2
	Bellingham‡ 106,701	C2
99320	Benton City 1,980	F4
98605	Bingen 644	D5
98010	Black Diamond 1,170	D3
98230	Blaine 2,363	C2
†98390	Bonney Lake 5,328	C3
98011	Bothell 7,943	B1
98310	Bremerton 36,208	A2
	Bremerton‡ 146,609	A2
98812	Brewster 1,337	F2
98813	Bridgeport 1,174	F3
†98036	Brier 2,915	C3
98320	Brinnon 500	B3
†98101	Bryn Mawr-Skyway 11,754	B2
98321	Buckley 3,143	C3
98530	Bucoda 519	C4
98921	Buena 590	E4
98166	Burien 23,189	A2
98233	Burlington 3,894	C2
98013	Burton 650	C3
98607	Camas 5,681	C5
98323	Carbonado 456	D3
98324	Carlsborg 500	B2
98814	Carlton 410	F2
98014	Carnation 913	D3
98610	Carson 500	D5
98815	Cashmere 2,240	E3

98611	Castle Rock 2,162	B4
98612	Cathlamet⊙ 635	B4
98531	Centralia 11,555	C4
98520	Central Park 2,709	B3
98532	Chehalis⊙ 6,100	C4
98816	Chelan 2,802	E3
99004	Cheney 7,630	H3
99109	Chewelah 1,888	H2
98614	Chinook 928	B4
98326	Clallam Bay 600	A2
99403	Clarkston 6,903	H4
98235	Clearlake 750	C2
98922	Cle Elum 1,773	E3
98236	Clinton 900	C3
†98004	Clyde Hill 3,229	B2
98055	Coalfield 500	B2
99111	Colfax⊙ 2,780	H4
99324	College Place 5,771	G4
99113	Colton 307	H4
†98632	Columbia Heights 2,515	C4
98114	Colville⊙ 4,510	H2
98819	Conconully 157	F2
98237	Concrete 592	D2
99326	Connell 1,981	G4
98535	Copalis Beach 600	A3
98536	Copalis Crossing 500	B3
98537	Cosmopolis 1,575	B4
99115	Coulee City 510	F3
99116	Coulee Dam 1,412	G3
98239	Coupeville⊙ 1,006	C2
99117	Creston 309	G3
99119	Cusick 246	H2

98240	Custer 300	C2
98617	Dallesport 600	D5
98241	Darrington 1,064	D2
99122	Davenport⊙ 1,559	G3
98243	Deer Harbor 400	B2
99006	Deer Park 2,140	H3
98188	Des Moines 7,378	B2
99213	Dishman 10,169	H3
98326	Dixie 210	G4
99329		
98821	Dryden 500	E3
†98382	Dungeness 675	B2
98327	Du Pont 559	C3
98019	Duvall 729	D3
98245	Eastsound 800	B2
98801	East Wenatchee 1,640	E3
98328	Eatonville 998	C4
98020	Edmonds 27,679	C3
99123	Electric City 927	F3
98926	Ellensburg⊙ 11,752	E3
98541	Elma 2,720	B4
99124	Elmer City 312	G2
99125	Endicott 290	H4
†98310	Enetai 2,638	A2
98822	Entiat 445	E3
98022	Enumclaw 5,427	D3
98823	Ephrata⊙ 5,359	F3
†98310	Erlands Point 1,254	A2
*98201	Everett⊙ 54,413	C3
98247	Everson 898	C2
99012	Fairfield 582	H3
†98901	Fairview-Sumach 2,788	E4
98024	Fall City 1,528	D3
99128	Farmington 176	H3
98248	Ferndale 3,855	C2
98424	Fife 1,823	C3
98466	Fircrest 5,477	C3
†98531	Fords Prairie 2,582	B4
98331	Forks 3,060	A3
99014	Four Lakes 500	H3
98250	Friday Harbor⊙ 1,200	B2
†98901	Fruitvale 3,967	E4
99130	Garfield 599	H3
†99362	Garrett 1,134	G4
98824	George 261	F3
98335	Gig Harbor 2,429	C3
98336	Glenoma 500	C4
98619	Glenwood 626	D4
98251	Gold Bar 794	D3
98620	Goldendale⊙ 3,575	E5
98337	Gorst 750	C3
99133	Grand Coulee 1,180	G3
98930	Grandview 5,615	F4
98932	Granger 1,812	E4
98252	Granite Falls 911	D2
98547	Grayland 750	A4
98621	Grays River 350	B4
98253	Greenbank 600	C2
98339	Hadlock-Irondale 1,752	C2
98255	Hamilton 268	D2
†98366	Harper 300	A2
98933	Harrah 343	E4
99134	Harrington 507	G3
99135	Hartline 165	F3
99332	Hatton 81	G4
98025	Hobart 500	D3
98548	Hoodsport 500	B3
98550	Hoquiam 9,719	A3
†98004	Hunts Point 480	B2
98624	Ilwaco 604	A4
98256	Index 147	D3
98342	Indianola 800	A1
99139	Ione 594	H2
98027	Issaquah 5,536	C3
98343	Joyce 375	B2
98033	Juanita 17,232	B1
99335	Kahlotus 203	G4
98625	Kalama 1,216	C4
98344	Kapowsin 500	C4
98626	Kelso⊙ 11,129	C4
98028	Kenmore 7,281	B1
99336	Kennewick 34,397	F4
98031	Kent 23,152	C3
99141	Kettle Falls 1,087	H2
98345	Keyport 900	A2
98346	Kingston 950	C3
98033	Kirkland 18,779	B2
98934	Kittitas 782	E4
98628	Klickitat 750	D5
†98832	Krupp (Marlin) 83	F3
98629	La Center 439	C5
98503	Lacey 13,940	C3
98257	La Conner 633	C2
99143	Lacrosse 373	H4
†98101	Lake Forest Park 2,485	B1
98258	Lake Stevens 1,660	C3
98260	Langley 650	C2
98350	La Push 500	A3
99017	Lamont 101	H3
98018	Latah 155	H3
98826	Leavenworth 1,522	E3
99019	Liberty Lake 1,599	J3
98555	Lilliwaup 75	B3
99341	Lind 567	G4
98556	Littlerock 850	B4
98631	Long Beach 1,199	A4

98351	Longbranch 640	C3
98632	Longview 31,052	B4
99148	Loon Lake 500	H2
98262	Lummi Island 675	C2
98635	Lyle 580	D5
98263	Lyman 285	D2
98264	Lynden 4,022	C2
98036	Lynnwood 22,641	C3
98935	Mabton 1,248	E4
99149	Malden 200	H3
98829	Malott 350	F2
98353	Manchester 400	A2
98830	Mansfield 315	F3
98266	Maple Falls 300	D2
98038	Maple Valley 900	C3
99151	Marcus 174	H2
98268	Marietta-Alderwood 2,324	C2
98832	Marlin 83	F3
98270	Marysville 5,080	C2
99344	Mattawa 299	F4
98557	McCleary 1,419	B3
99022	Medical Lake 3,600	H3
98039	Medina 3,220	B2
98040	Mercer Island (city) 21,522	B2
99343	Mesa 278	G4
99152	Metaline 190	H2
99153	Metaline Falls 296	H2
98043	Mountlake Terrace 16,534	B1
98354	Milton 3,162	C3
98355	Mineral 550	C4
98562	Moclips 500	A3
98836	Monitor 650	E3
98272	Monroe 2,869	D3
98563	Montesano⊙ 3,247	B4
98356	Morton 1,264	C4
98837	Moses Lake 10,629	F3
98564	Mossyrock 463	C4
98043	Mountlake Terrace 16,534	B1
98273	Mount Vernon⊙ 13,009	C2
98936	Moxee City 687	E4
98275	Mukilteo 1,426	C3
98937	Naches 644	E4
98565	Napavine 611	C4
98638	Naselle 500	B4
†98310	Navy Yard City 2,594	A2
98357	Neah Bay 800	A2
98283	Newhalem 350	D2
99156	Newport⊙ 1,665	H2
†98501	Nisqually 500	C3
98276	Nooksack 429	C2
98358	Nordland 706	C2
†98100	Normandy Park 4,268	A2
98045	North Bend 1,701	D3
98639	North Bonneville 394	C5
99157	Northport 368	H2
99158	Oakesdale 444	H3
98277	Oak Harbor 12,271	C2
98568	Oakville 537	B4
98569	Ocean City 350	A3
98640	Ocean Park 918	A4
98551	Ocean Shores 1,692	A3
†98520	Ocosta 369	B4
99159	Odessa 1,009	G3
98840	Okanogan⊙ 2,302	F2
98359	Olalla 500	A2
*98501	Olympia (cap.)⊙ 27,447	C3
	Olympia‡ 124,264	C3
98841	Omak 4,007	F2
98570	Onalaska 600	C4
99214	Opportunity 21,241	H3
98662	Orchards 8,828	C5
98844	Oroville 1,483	F2
98360	Orting 1,787	C3
99344	Othello 4,454	F4
99027	Otis Orchards-East Farms 4,597	H3
98938	Outlook 300	E4
98047	Pacific 2,261	C3
98571	Pacific Beach 900	A3
98361	Packwood 800	D4
99161	Palouse 1,005	H4
98939	Parker 500	E4
98444	Parkland 23,355	C3
99301	Pasco⊙ 18,425	F4
98846	Pateros 555	E2
98572	Pe Ell 617	B4
98847	Peshastin 500	E3
98281	Point Roberts 500	B2
99347	Pomeroy⊙ 1,716	H4
98362	Port Angeles⊙ 17,311	B2
†98101	Port Blakely 600	A2
98366	Port Orchard⊙ 4,787	A2
98368	Port Townsend⊙ 6,067	C2
†98584	Potlach 100	B3
98370	Poulsbo 3,453	A1
98348	Prescott 341	G4
98050	Preston 500	D3
99350	Prosser⊙ 3,896	F4
99163	Pullman 23,579	H4
98371	Puyallup 18,251	C3
98376	Quilcene 900	B3
98575	Quinault 450	B3
98848	Quincy 3,525	F3
98576	Rainier 891	C4

(continued on following page)

Agriculture, Industry and Resources

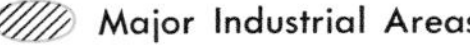

DOMINANT LAND USE

- Specialized Wheat
- Wheat, Peas
- Dairy, Poultry, Mixed Farming
- Fruit and Mixed Farming
- General Farming, Dairy, Range Livestock
- General Farming, Livestock, Special Crops
- Range Livestock
- Forests
- Urban Areas
- Nonagricultural Land

MAJOR MINERAL OCCURRENCES

Ag	Silver	Mr	Marble
Au	Gold	Pb	Lead
C	Coal	Tc	Talc
Cl	Clay	U	Uranium
Cu	Copper	W	Tungsten
Gp	Gypsum	Zn	Zinc
Mg	Magnesium		

⚡ Water Power

▨ Major Industrial Areas

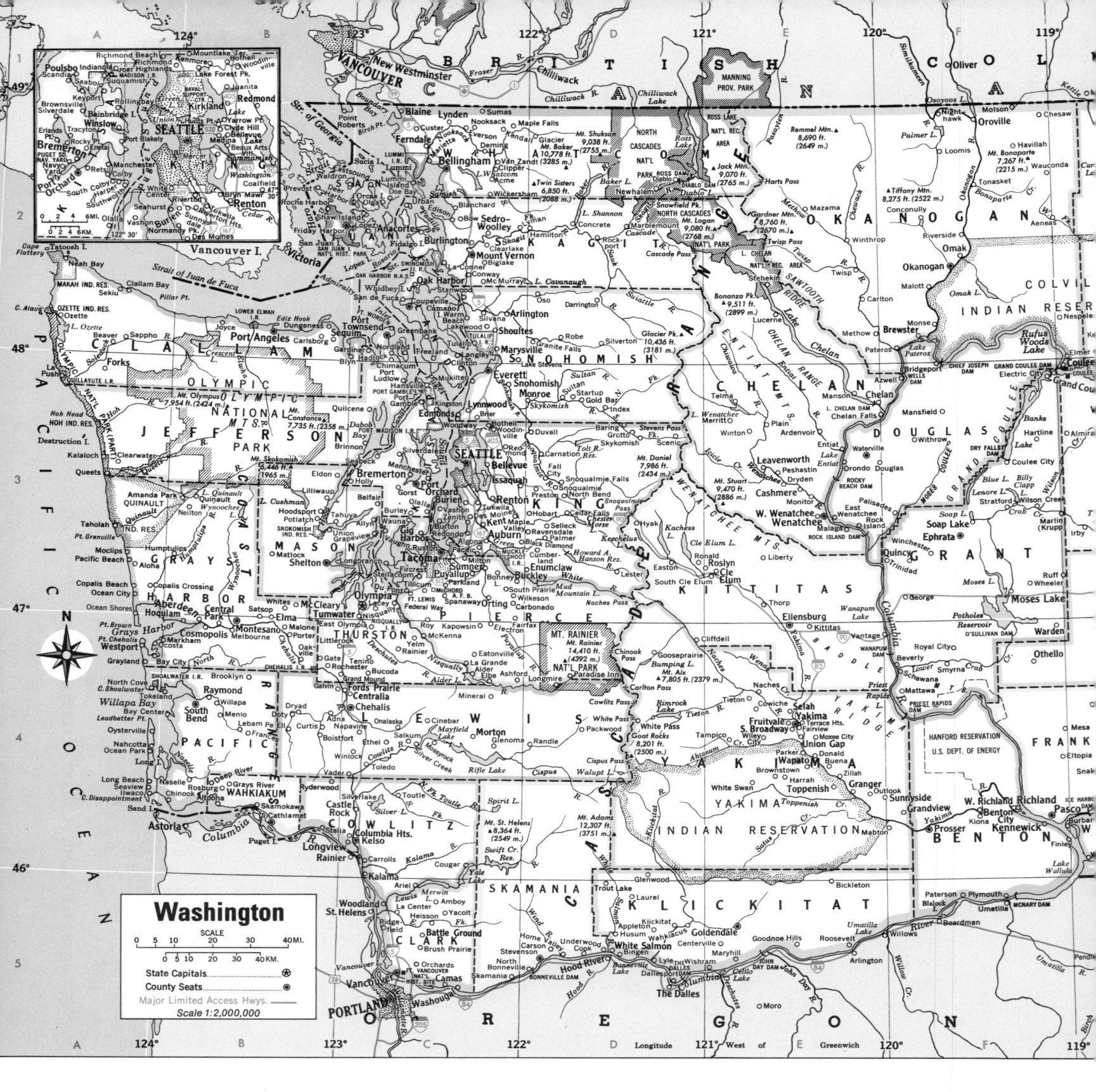

Washington

SCALE
0 5 10 20 30 40MI.
0 5 10 20 30 40KM.

State Capitals.............................⊛
County Seats..............................◉
Major Limited Access Hwys._____
Scale 1:2,000,000

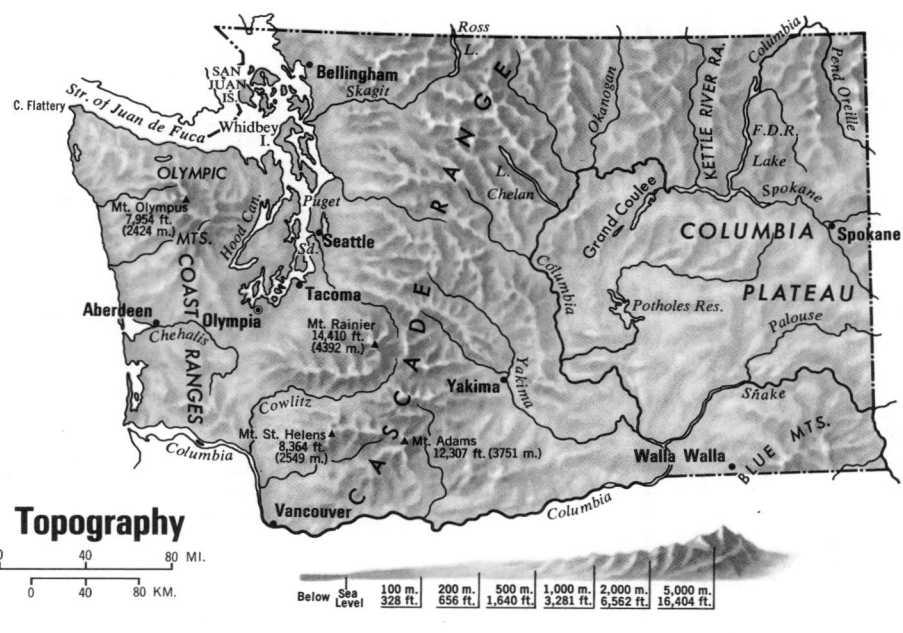

Topography

0 — 40 — 80 MI.
0 — 40 — 80 KM.

Below Sea Level	100 m. 328 ft.	200 m. 656 ft.	500 m. 1,640 ft.	1,000 m. 3,281 ft.	2,000 m. 6,562 ft.	5,000 m. 16,404 ft.

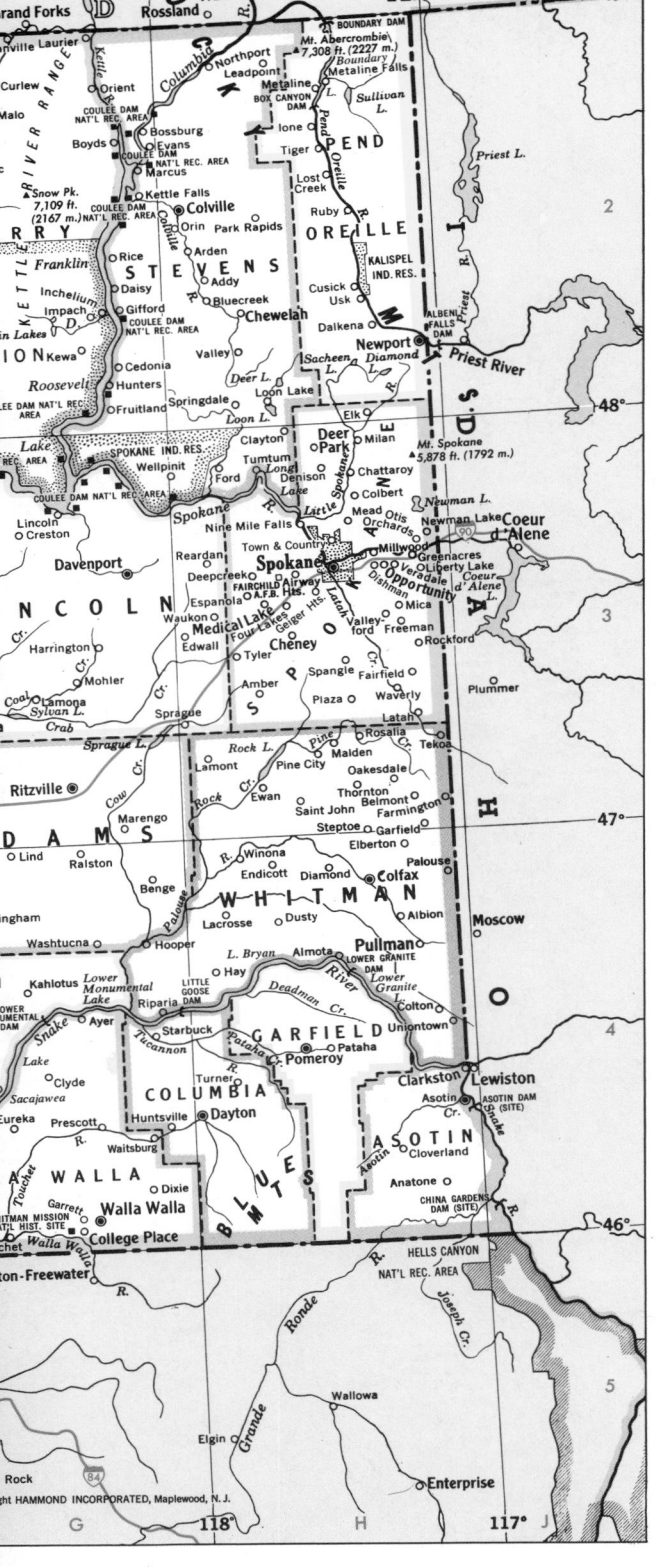

Right HAMMOND INCORPORATED, Maplewood, N.J.

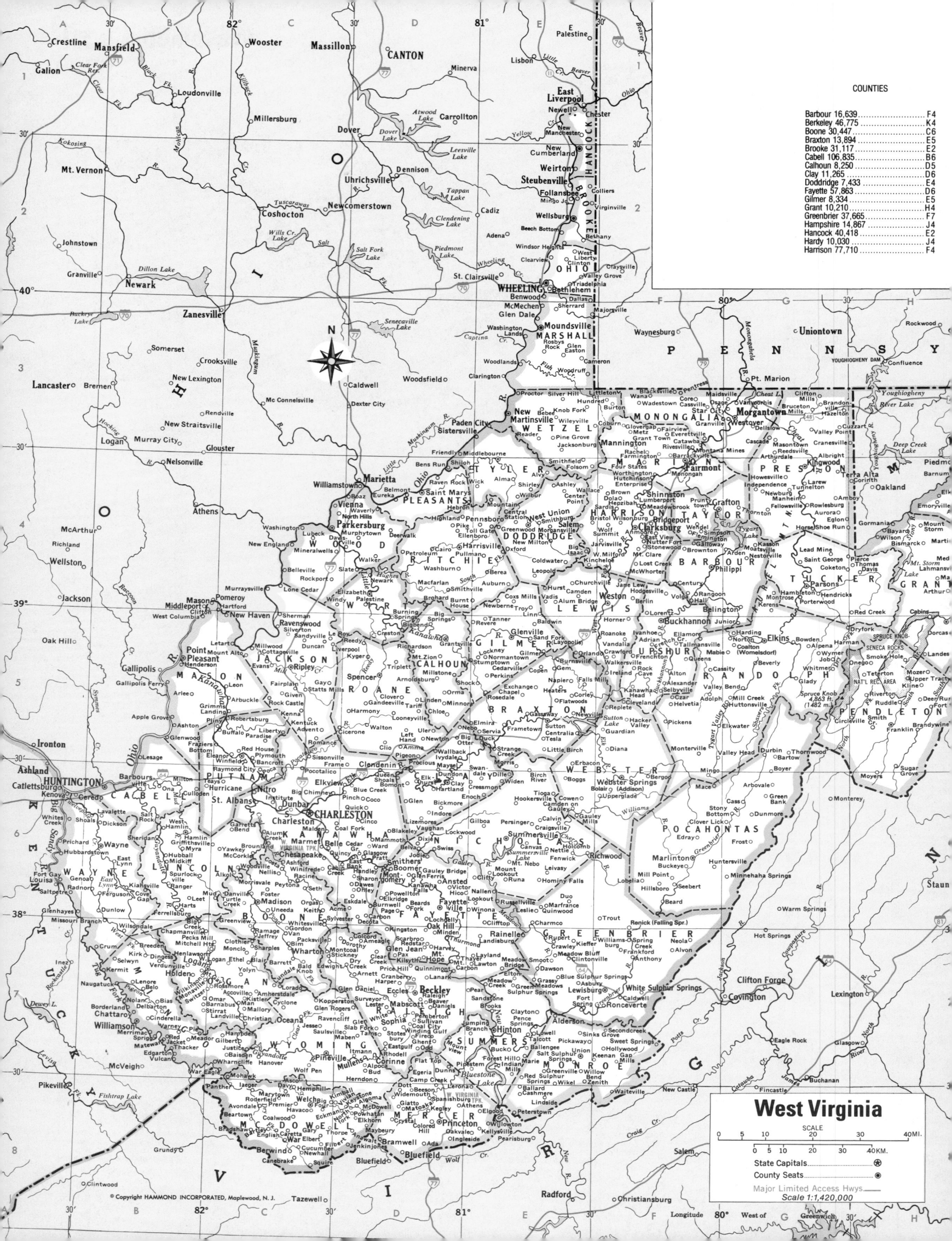

West Virginia

State Capitals ⊛
County Seats ⊙
Major Limited Access Hwys.
Scale 1:1,420,000

SCALE
0 5 10   20   30   40 MI.
0 5 10   20   30   40 KM.

® Copyright HAMMOND INCORPORATED, Maplewood, N.J.

Jackson 25,794 ... C5
Jefferson 30,302 ... L4
Kanawha 231,414 ... C6
Lewis 18,813 ... E4
Lincoln 23,675 ... B6
Logan 50,679 ... C7
Marion 65,789 ... F4
Marshall 41,608 ... E3
Mason 27,045 ... B5
McDowell 49,899 ... C8
Mercer 73,942 ... D8
Mineral 27,234 ... J4
Mingo 37,336 ... B7
Monongalia 75,024 ... F3
Monroe 12,873 ... E7
Morgan 10,711 ... K3
Nicholas 28,126 ... E6
Ohio 61,389 ... E2
Pendleton 7,910 ... H5
Pleasants 8,236 ... D4
Pocahontas 9,919 ... F6
Preston 30,460 ... G4
Putnam 38,181 ... C6
Raleigh 86,821 ... D7
Randolph 28,734 ... G5
Ritchie 11,442 ... D4
Roane 15,952 ... D5
Summers 15,875 ... E7
Taylor 16,584 ... F4
Tucker 8,675 ... F4
Tyler 11,320 ... E4
Upshur 23,427 ... F5
Wayne 46,021 ... B6
Webster 12,245 ... F6
Wetzel 21,874 ... E3
Wirt 4,922 ... D4
Wood 93,648 ... D4
Wyoming 35,993 ... C7

AREA 24,231 sq. mi. (62,758 sq. km.)
POPULATION 1,950,279
CAPITAL Charleston
LARGEST CITY Charleston
HIGHEST POINT Spruce Knob 4,863 ft. (1482 m.)
SETTLED IN 1774
ADMITTED TO UNION June 20, 1863
POPULAR NAME Mountain State
STATE FLOWER Big Rhododendron
STATE BIRD Cardinal

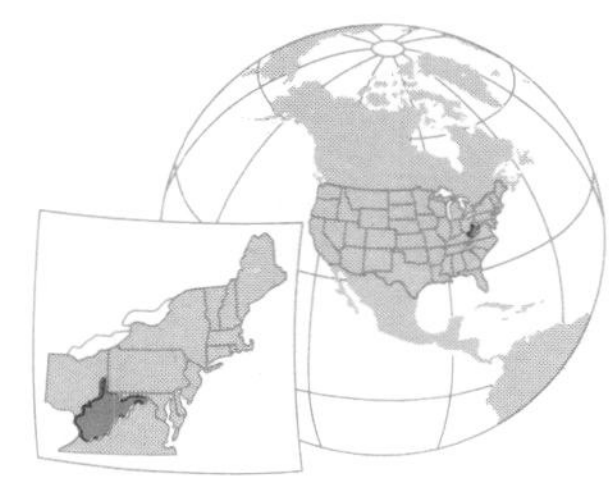

CITIES and TOWNS

Zip	Name/Pop.	Key
25606	Accoville 975	C7
†26288	Addison (Webster Springs)⊙ 939	F6
26210	Adrian 510	F5
26519	Albright 357	G3
24910	Alderson 1,375	E7
24807	Algoma 200	D8
25501	Alkol 500	C6
26320	Alma 197	E4
24710	Alpoca 200	D7
26321	Alum Bridge 150	E4
25003	Alum Creek 900	C6
26322	Alvy 150	E4
25004	Ameagle 230	D7
25607	Amherstdale 1,075	C7
25005	Amma 200	D5
24808	Anawalt 652	D8
26323	Anmoore 865	F4
25812	Ansted 1,952	D6
25502	Apple Grove 900	B5
24915	Arbovale 610	G6
26816	Arthur 350	H4
26520	Arthurdale 1,063	G3
24916	Asbury 280	E7
24809	Asco 175	C8
25009	Ashford 400	C6
25503	Ashton 259	B5
24712	Athens 1,147	E8
26325	Auburn 116	E4
26704	Augusta 750	J4
26705	Aurora 250	G4
24811	Avondale 250	C8
25608	Baisden 500	C7
26801	Baker 200	J4
25410	Bakerton 125	L4
25010	Bald Knob 356	C7
26326	Baldwin 92	E5
25011	Bancroft 528	C5
25504	Barboursville 2,871	B6
25609	Barnabus 750	C7
26559	Barrackville 1,815	F3
25013	Barrett 950	C7
24813	Bartley 900	C8
24920	Bartow 500	G5
†25411	Bath (Berkeley Springs) 789	K3
26707	Bayard 540	H4
25014	Beards Fork 400	D6
25813	Beaver (Glen Hedrick) 1,122	D7
25801	Beckley⊙ 20,492	D7
26030	Beech Bottom 507	E2
24714	Beeson 300	D8
26250	Belington 2,038	F4
25015	Belle 1,621	C6
26133	Belleville 105	C4
26134	Belmont 887	D4
26656	Belva 275	D6
26135	Bens Run 85	D4
26031	Benwood 1,994	E2
26298	Bergoo 220	F6
25411	Berkeley Springs (Bath)⊙ 789	K3
24815	Berwind 615	C8
26032	Bethany 1,336	E2
†26003	Bethlehem 3,045	E2
26253	Beverly 475	G5
25019	Bickmore 300	D6
26136	Bigbend 120	D5
25302	Big Chimney 450	C6
25505	Big Creek 500	B7
26137	Big Springs 485	D5
25021	Bim 500	C7
26610	Birch River 650	E6
26521	Blacksville 248	F3
25022	Blair 800	C7
26817	Bloomery 200	K4
25026	Blue Creek 650	D6
24701	Bluefield 16,060	D8
26288	Bolair 450	F6
†25425	Bolivar 672	L4
25030	Bomont 170	D6
25031	Boomer 1,051	D6
24817	Bradshaw 1,002	C8
24715	Bramwell 989	D8
26523	Brandonville 92	G3
26802	Brandywine 300	H5
25666	Breeden 600	B7
26330	Bridgeport 6,604	F4
26138	Brohard 80	D4
25957	Brooks 196	E7
26334	Brownton 400	F4
26525	Bruceton Mills 296	G3
24924	Buckeye 125	F6
26201	Buckhannon⊙ 6,820	F5
24716	Bud 400	D7
25033	Buffalo 1,034	C5
25413	Bunker Hill 600	K4
26710	Burlington 300	J4
26335	Burnsville 531	E5
26336	Burnt House 175	D4
26562	Burton 200	F3
25035	Cabin Creek 900	C6
26337	Cairo 428	D4
24925	Caldwell 795	F7
26660	Calvin 400	E6
26208	Camden on Gauley 236	E6
26033	Cameron 1,474	E3
24819	Canebrake 300	C8
26662	Canvas 300	E6
26711	Capon Bridge 191	K4
26823	Capon Springs 580	K4
25037	Carbon 300	D6
24821	Caretta 650	C8
24927	Cass 148	G6
26527	Cassville 800	F3
25039	Cedar Grove 1,479	D6
26339	Center Point 250	E4
26612	Centralia 100	E5
26340	Central Station 200	E4
26214	Century 250	F4
25507	Ceredo 2,255	B6
25508	Chapmanville 1,164	B7
*25301	Charleston (cap.)⊙ 63,968	C6
	Charleston‡ 269,595	C6
25414	Charles Town⊙ 2,857	L4
25958	Charmco 800	E6
25667	Chattaroy 1,383	B7
25418	Cherry Run 120	L3
†25301	Chesapeake 2,364	C6
26034	Chester 3,297	E1
26301	Clarksburg⊙ 22,371	F4
25043	Clay⊙ 940	D6
25044	Clear Creek 300	D7
†26003	Clearview 740	E2
25045	Clendenin 1,373	D5
26215	Cleveland 74	F5
25822	Clifftop 100	E6
25237	Clifton 325	B5
24928	Clintonville 250	E7
25046	Clio 300	D5
25047	Clothier 900	C7
25823	Coal City 2,324	D7
25306	Coal Fork 2,775	D6
26257	Coalton 306	G5
24824	Coalwood 650	C8
25048	Colcord 600	D7
26035	Colliers 864	E2
26615	Copen 50	E5
25826	Corinne 900	D7
25051	Costa 250	C6
25239	Cottageville 300	C5
25509	Cove Gap 650	B6
26206	Cowen 723	E6
26342	Coxs Mills 275	E4
26205	Craigsville 1,562	E6
25828	Cranberry 315	D7
24931	Crawley 395	E7
25669	Crum 500	B7
24826	Cucumber 274	C8
25510	Culloden 2,931	B6
24827	Cyclone 500	C7
26036	Dallas 450	E2
25832	Daniels 1,959	D7
25053	Danville 727	C6
†25428	Darkesville 150	L4
26260	Davis 979	H4
24828	Davy 882	C8
25054	Dawes 800	D6
24932	Dawson 300	E7
25670	Delbarton 981	B7
26531	Dellslow 300	G3
26217	Diana 300	F5
26617	Dille 300	E6
25671	Dingess 600	B7
25059	Dixie 985	D6
25060	Dorothy 400	D7
24721	Dott 100	D8
25062	Dry Creek 441	D7
26263	Dryfork 425	H5
25063	Duck 500	E5
25064	Dunbar 9,285	C6
24934	Dunmore 280	G6
26264	Durbin 379	G5
25067	East Bank 1,155	D6
25835	Eastgulf 300	D7
25512	East Lynn 150	B6
†26301	East View 1,222	F4
25836	Eccles 1,162	D7
24829	Eckman 750	C8
25672	Edgarton 415	B7
26716	Eglon 70	G4
24830	Elbert 400	C8
25070	Eleanor 1,282	C5
26143	Elizabeth⊙ 856	D4
26717	Elk Garden 291	H4
26241	Elkins⊙ 8,536	G5
25071	Elkview 1,161	C6
26267	Ellamore 250	F5
26346	Ellenboro 357	D4
25965	Elton 200	E7
24832	English 500	C8
26568	Enterprise 1,110	F4
25075	Eskdale 400	D6
25076	Ethel 450	C7
26144	Eureka 125	D4
25241	Evans 400	C5
26533	Everettville 175	F3
26554	Fairmont 23,863	F4
26570	Fairview 759	F3
†24966	Falling Spring (Renick) 240	F6
26571	Farmington 583	F3
25840	Fayetteville⊙ 2,366	D6
26202	Fenwick 500	E6
24835	Filbert 130	D8
26818	Fisher 500	H4
25841	Flat Top 550	D7
26621	Flatwoods 405	E5
26347	Flemington 452	F4
26037	Follansbee 3,994	E2
26348	Folsom 360	E4
24935	Forest Hill 314	E7
26719	Fort Ashby 1,205	J4
25514	Fort Gay 886	A6
26806	Fort Seybert 200	H5
24936	Fort Spring 250	E7
25081	Foster 500	C6
26572	Four States 500	F4
25071	Frame 76	C5
26623	Frametown 150	E5
26807	Franklin⊙ 780	H5
25082	Fraziers Bottom 250	B5
26219	Frenchton 102	F5
26146	Friendly 242	D3
25515	Gallipolis Ferry 325	B5
26349	Galloway 500	F4
25243	Gandeeville 150	D5
24941	Gap Mills 300	F7
24836	Gary 2,233	C8
26624	Gassaway 1,225	E5
25085	Gauley Bridge 1,177	D6
26240	Gauley Mills 165	E6
25244	Gay 300	C5
25420	Gerrardstown 240	K4
25843	Ghent 500	D7
25621	Gilbert 757	C7
26671	Gilboa 500	E6
26350	Gilmer 110	E5
26268	Glady 175	G5
25086	Glasgow 1,031	D6
25088	Glen 175	D6
26038	Glen Dale 1,875	E3
26039	Glen Easton 100	E3
25090	Glen Ferris 200	D6
25421	Glengary 250	K4
†25813	Glen Hedrick (Beaver) 1,122	D7
25846	Glen Jean	D7
25848	Glen Rogers 500	D7
26351	Glenville⊙ 2,155	E5
25849	Glen White 300	D7
25520	Glenwood 400	B5
†26585	Glovergap 100	F3
25093	Gordon 300	C7
26720	Gormania 100	H4
26354	Grafton⊙ 6,845	G4
26147	Grantsville⊙ 788	D5
26574	Grant Town 987	F3
26534	Granville 992	F3
24943	Grassy Meadows 100	E7
25422	Great Cacapon 750	K3
24944	Green Bank 115	G6
25966	Green Sulphur Springs 225	E7
24945	Greenville 125	E7
26360	Greenwood 750	E4
25095	Grimms Landing 350	B5
26221	Guardian 175	F5
26222	Hacker Valley 440	F5
25423	Halltown 375	L4
26269	Hambleton 403	G4
25523	Hamlin⊙ 1,219	B6
25623	Hampden 300	C7
25424	Hancock 175	K3
25102	Handley 633	D6
†26250	Harding 100	G5
26270	Harman 181	G5
25246	Harmony 600	D5
25851	Harper 400	D7
25425	Harpers Ferry 361	L4
26362	Harrisville⊙ 1,673	E4
25247	Hartford 556	C4
25524	Harts 400	B6
25852	Harvey 300	D7
24841	Havaco 350	C8
26627	Heaters 440	E5
25427	Hedgesville 217	K3
26224	Helvetia 130	F5
24842	Hemphill 700	C8
25106	Henderson 604	B5
26271	Hendricks 390	G4
25624	Henlawson 900	B7
26369	Hepzibah 600	F4
24726	Herndon 500	D7
25854	Hico 750	D6
24946	Hillsboro 276	F6
25951	Hinton⊙ 4,622	E7
25625	Holden 2,036	B7
26372	Horner 125	F5
26769	Horse Shoe Run 500	G4
†25506	Hubball 145	B6
26575	Hundred 485	E3
*25701	Huntington⊙ 63,684	A6
	Huntington-Ashland‡ 311,350	A6
25526	Hurricane 3,751	C6
26273	Huttonsville 242	G5
24844	Iaeger 833	C8
26374	Independence 200	G4
24949	Indian Mills 150	E7
25111	Indore 300	D6
25112	Institute	C6
25428	Inwood 1,159	K4
24847	Itmann 600	D7
25113	Ivydale 800	D5
26377	Jacksonburg 400	E3
26378	Jane Lew 406	F4
25114	Jeffrey 900	C7
24848	Jenkinjones 750	D8
24849	Jesse 400	C7
26674	Jodie 440	D6
25969	Jumping Branch 700	E7
26824	Junction 75	J4

(continued on following page)

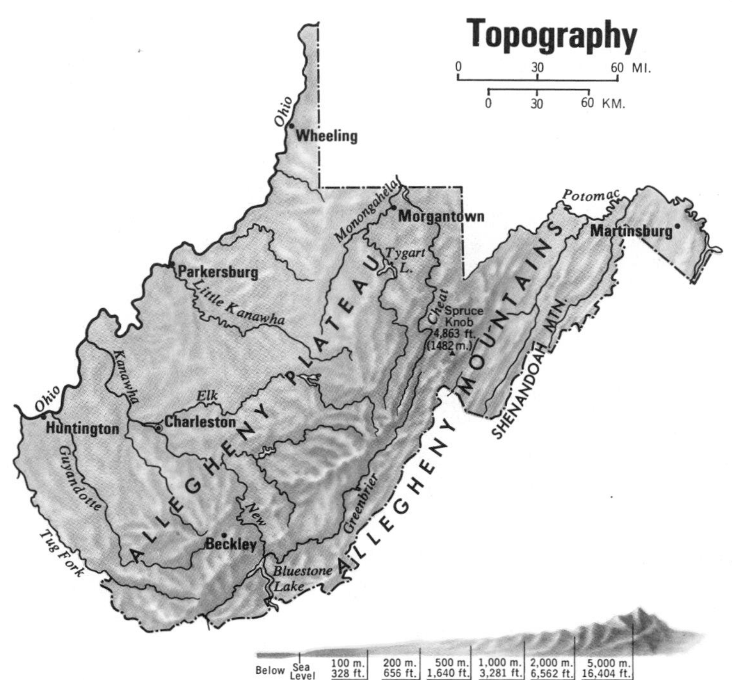
Topography
0 30 60 MI.
0 30 60 KM.
Ohio
Wheeling
Morgantown
Potomac
Martinsburg
Parkersburg
Little Kanawha
Monongahela
Tygart L.
Cheat
Spruce Knob 4,863 ft. (1482 m.)
ALLEGHENY PLATEAU
ALLEGHENY MOUNTAINS
SHENANDOAH MTN.
Kanawha
Elk
Charleston
Huntington
Guyandotte
Tug Fork
New
Greenbrier
Beckley
Bluestone Lake
Below Sea Level
100 m. 328 ft.
200 m. 656 ft.
500 m. 1,640 ft.
1,000 m. 3,281 ft.
2,000 m. 6,562 ft.
5,000 m. 16,404 ft.

Agriculture, Industry and Resources

DOMINANT LAND USE

- Dairy, General Farming
- General Farming, Livestock, Dairy
- General Farming, Livestock, Tobacco
- General Farming, Livestock, Fruit, Tobacco
- Fruit and Mixed Farming
- Forests

MAJOR MINERAL OCCURRENCES

- C Coal
- Cl Clay
- G Natural Gas
- Ls Limestone
- Na Salt
- O Petroleum
- ⚡ Water Power
- Major Industrial Areas

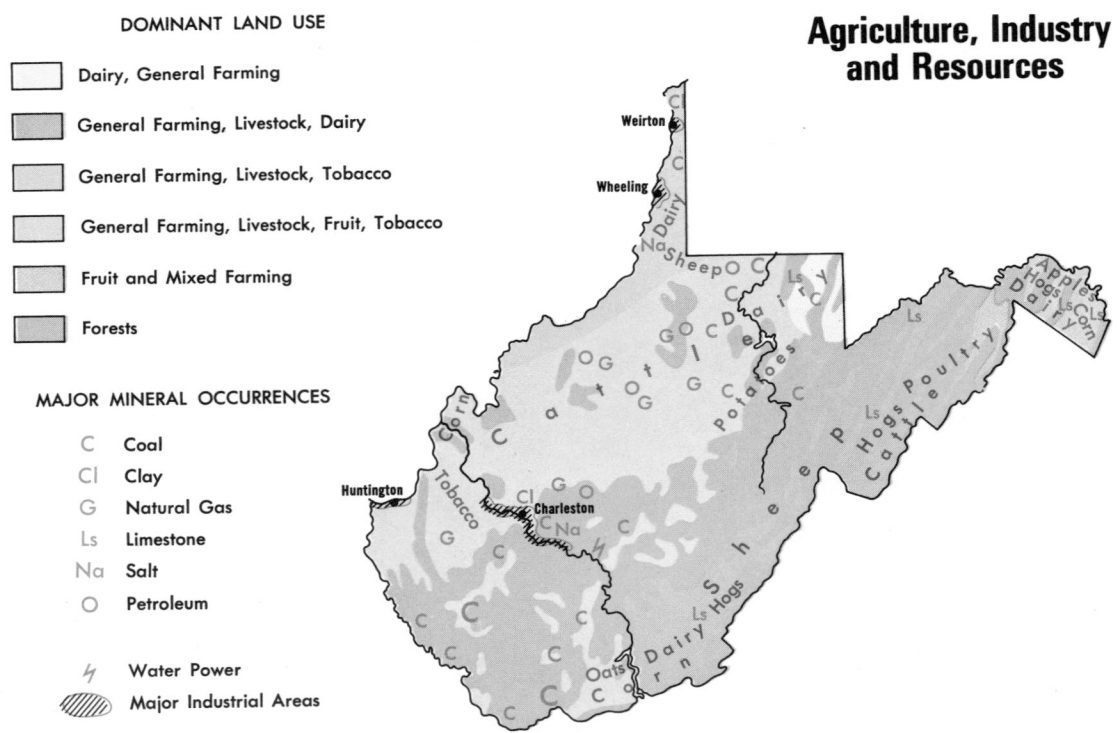

AREA 56,153 sq. mi. (145,436 sq. km.)
POPULATION 4,705,521
CAPITAL Madison
LARGEST CITY Milwaukee
HIGHEST POINT Timms Hill 1,951 ft. (595 m.)
SETTLED IN 1670
ADMITTED TO UNION May 29, 1848
POPULAR NAME Badger State
STATE FLOWER Wood Violet
STATE BIRD Robin

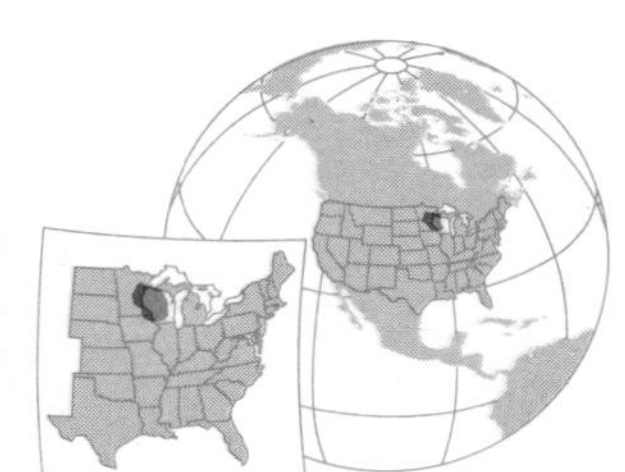

COUNTIES

County	Key
Adams 13,457	G7
Ashland 16,783	E3
Barron 38,730	C5
Bayfield 13,822	D3
Brown 175,280	L7
Buffalo 14,309	C7
Burnett 12,340	B4
Calumet 30,867	K7
Chippewa 52,127	D5
Clark 32,910	E6
Columbia 43,222	H9
Crawford 16,556	E9
Dane 323,545	H9
Dodge 75,064	J9
Door 25,029	M6
Douglas 44,421	C3
Dunn 34,314	C6
Eau Claire 78,805	D6
Florence 4,172	K4
Fond du Lac 88,964	K8
Forest 9,044	J4
Grant 51,736	E10
Green 30,012	G10
Green Lake 18,370	H8
Iowa 19,802	F9
Iron 6,730	F3
Jackson 16,831	E7
Jefferson 66,152	J9
Juneau 21,039	F8
Kenosha 123,137	K10
Kewaunee 19,539	L6
La Crosse 91,056	D8
Lafayette 17,412	F10
Langlade 19,978	H5
Lincoln 26,555	G5
Manitowoc 82,918	L7
Marathon 111,270	G6
Marinette 39,314	K5
Marquette 11,672	H8
Menominee 3,373	J5
Milwaukee 964,988	L9
Monroe 35,074	E8
Oconto 28,947	K6
Oneida 31,216	G4
Outagamie 128,799	K7
Ozaukee 66,981	L9
Pepin 7,477	C6
Pierce 31,149	B6
Polk 32,351	B5
Portage 57,420	G6
Price 15,788	F4
Racine 173,132	K10
Richland 17,476	F9
Rock 139,420	H10
Rusk 15,589	D5
Saint Croix 43,262	B5
Sauk 43,469	G9
Sawyer 12,843	D4
Shawano 35,928	J6
Sheboygan 100,935	L8
Taylor 18,817	E5
Trempealeau 26,158	D7
Vernon 25,642	E8
Vilas 16,535	G3
Walworth 71,507	J10
Washburn 13,174	C4
Washington 84,848	K9
Waukesha 280,080	K9
Waupaca 42,831	J6
Waushara 18,526	H7
Winnebago 131,722	J8
Wood 72,799	F7

CITIES and TOWNS

Zip	*Name/Pop.*	*Key*
54405	Abbotsford 1,901	F6
53910	Adams 1,744	G8
53001	Adell 545	L8
53501	Afton 225	H10
53502	Albany 1,051	G10
†53534	Albion 300	H10
54201	Algoma 3,656	M6
53002	Allenton 915	K9
†54301	Allouez 14,882	L7
54610	Alma⊙ 876	C7
54611	Alma Center 454	E7
54805	Almena 526	B5
54909	Almond 477	G7
54720	Altoona 4,393	C6
54102	Amberg 875	K5
54001	Amery 2,404	B5
54406	Amherst 701	H7
54407	Amherst Junction 225	H7
54408	Aniwa 273	H6
54409	Antigo⊙ 8,653	H5
54911	Appleton⊙ 58,913	J7
	Appleton-Oshkosh‡ 291,325	J7
†54568	Arbor Vitae 900	G4
54612	Arcadia 2,109	D7
53503	Arena 451	G9
54511	Argonne 600	J4
53504	Argyle 720	G10
54721	Arkansaw 400	B6
53911	Arlington 440	H9
54103	Armstrong Creek 615	K4
54410	Arpin 361	G6
53003	Ashippun 750	H1
54806	Ashland⊙ 9,115	E2
54304	Ashwaubenon 14,486	K7
54411	Athens 988	G5
54412	Auburndale 641	F6
54722	Augusta 1,560	D6
†53520	Avon 120	H10
54413	Babcock 250	F7
53801	Bagley 317	D10
54202	Baileys Harbor 250	M5
54002	Baldwin 1,620	B6
54810	Balsam Lake⊙ 749	B5
54921	Bancroft 355	G7
54614	Bangor 1,012	E8
53913	Baraboo⊙ 8,081	G9
†54873	Barnes 225	D3
53507	Barneveld 579	F10
54812	Barron⊙ 2,595	C5
†53001	Batavia 125	K8
54723	Bay City 543	B6
54814	Bayfield 778	E2
†53201	Bayside 4,724	M1
54922	Bear Creek 454	J6
53916	Beaver Dam 14,149	J9
53802	Beetown 150	E10
53004	Belgium 892	L8
†54631	Bell Center 124	E9
53508	Belleville 1,302	G10
53510	Belmont 826	F10
53511	Beloit 35,207	H10
53803	Benton 983	F10
54923	Berlin 5,478	H8
†54410	Bethel 210	F6
†54440	Bevent 200	H6
53103	Big Bend 1,345	K2
54926	Big Falls 107	H6
54817	Birchwood 437	C4
54414	Birnamwood 688	H6
†54494	Biron 698	G7
54106	Black Creek 1,097	K7
53515	Black Earth 1,145	G9
54615	Black River Falls⊙ 3,434	E7
†54541	Blackwell 550	J4
54616	Blair 1,142	D7
53516	Blanchardville 803	G10
54617	Bloom City 167	E8
54724	Bloomer 3,342	D5
53804	Bloomington 743	E10
53517	Blue Mounds 387	G9
53518	Blue River 412	E9
†53581	Boaz 161	E9
†53105	Bohners Lake 1,507	K10
54107	Bonduel 1,160	K6
53805	Boscobel 2,662	E9
54512	Boulder Junction 780	G3
54416	Bowler 339	J6
54725	Boyceville 862	C5
54726	Boyd 660	E6
54203	Branch 300	L7
53919	Brandon 862	J8
54513	Brantwood 500	F4
53920	Briggsville 250	H8
54110	Brillion 2,907	L7
53520	Brodhead 3,153	G10
54417	Brokaw 298	G5
53005	Brookfield 34,035	K1
53521	Brooklyn 627	H10
53209	Brown Deer 12,921	L1
†53105	Brown's Lake 1,648	K3
53006	Brownsville 433	J8
53522	Browntown 284	G10
54819	Bruce 905	D5
54820	Brule 335	C2
54204	Brussels 500	L6
†54622	Buffalo 894	C7
53105	Burlington 8,385	K10
53922	Burnett 260	J9
53007	Butler 2,059	K1
54514	Butternut 438	E3
53009	Byron 40	K8
54821	Cable 227	D3
54727	Cadott 1,247	D6
53923	Cambria 680	H8
53523	Cambridge 844	H9
54822	Cameron 1,115	C5
†53019	Campbellsport 1,740	K8
54618	Camp Douglas 589	F8
53109	Camp Lake 2,060	K10
54823	Canton 100	C5
54928	Caroline 450	J6
53011	Cascade 615	K8
54205	Casco 484	L6
54619	Cashton 827	E8
53806	Cassville 1,270	E10
54620	Cataract 200	E7
54515	Catawba 205	E4
54206	Cato 85	L7
53924	Cazenovia 259	F8
54111	Cecil 445	K6
53012	Cedarburg 9,005	L9
53013	Cedar Grove 1,420	L8
54824	Centuria 711	A5
54621	Chaseburg 279	D8
54419	Chelsea 120	F5
†53029	Chenequa 532	J1
54728	Chetek 1,931	C5
54420	Chili 185	F6
53014	Chilton⊙ 2,965	K7
54729	Chippewa Falls⊙ 12,270	D6
54004	Clayton 425	B5
54005	Clear Lake 899	B5
53015	Cleveland 1,270	L8
53525	Clinton 1,751	J10
54929	Clintonville 4,567	J6
53016	Clyman 317	J9
53526	Cobb 409	F10
54622	Cochrane 512	C7
54421	Colby 1,496	F6
54112	Coleman 852	L5
54730	Colfax 1,149	C6
54930	Coloma 367	H7
53925	Columbus 4,049	H9
54113	Combined Locks 2,573	K7
†53147	Como 1,376	K10
54519	Conover 480	H3
54731	Conrath 86	E5
54623	Coon Valley 758	E8
54732	Cornell 1,583	D5
54827	Cornucopia 250	D2
54520	Crandon⊙ 1,969	H4
54114	Crivitz 1,041	L5
53528	Cross Plains 2,156	G9
53807	Cuba City 2,129	F10
53110	Cudahy 19,547	M2
54829	Cumberland 1,983	C4
54422	Curtiss 127	F6
54006	Cushing 150	A4
54931	Dale 410	J7
54733	Dallas 477	C5
53926	Dalton 300	H8
53529	Dane 518	G9
53114	Darien 1,152	J10
53530	Darlington⊙ 2,300	F10
53531	Deerfield 1,466	H9
54007	Deer Park 232	B5
53532	De Forest 3,367	H9
53018	Delafield 4,083	J1
53115	Delavan 5,684	J10
†53115	Delavan Lake 2,082	J10
†54856	Delta 35	D3
54208	Denmark 1,475	L7
54115	De Pere 14,892	K7
†54663	De Soto 318	D9
†54014	Diamond Bluff 100	A6
53808	Dickeyville 1,156	E10
54625	Dodge 185	D7
53533	Dodgeville⊙ 3,458	F10
54425	Dorchester 613	F5
53118	Dousman 1,153	J1
54734	Downing 242	B5
54735	Downsville 200	C6
53928	Doylestown 294	H9
54009	Dresser 670	A5
54832	Drummond 200	D3
54736	Durand⊙ 2,047	C6
53119	Eagle 1,008	H2
54521	Eagle River⊙ 1,326	H4
54626	Eastman 371	D9
53120	East Troy 2,385	J2
54701	Eau Claire⊙ 51,509	D6
	Eau Claire‡ 130,507	D6
53019	Eden 534	K8
54426	Edgar 1,194	G6
53534	Edgerton 4,335	H10
54209	Egg Harbor 238	M5
54427	Eland 230	H6
54428	Elcho 500	H5
54429	Elderon 191	H6
54932	Eldorado 200	J8
54738	Eleva 593	D6
53020	Elkhart Lake 1,054	L8
53121	Elkhorn⊙ 4,605	J10
54739	Elk Mound 737	C6
54210	Ellison Bay 112	M5
54011	Ellsworth⊙ 2,143	A6
53122	Elm Grove 6,735	K1
54740	Elmwood 885	B6
†53401	Elmwood Park 483	M3
53929	Elroy 1,504	F8
54430	Elton 150	J5
54933	Embarrass 496	J6
53930	Endeavor 335	G8
54211	Ephraim 319	M5
54627	Ettrick 462	D7
53536	Evansville 2,835	H10
54835	Exeland 219	D4
54741	Fairchild 577	D6
53931	Fair Water 310	J8
54742	Fall Creek 1,148	D6
53932	Fall River 850	H9
†54840	Falun 95	A4
54120	Fence 200	K4
53809	Fennimore 2,212	E9
54431	Fenwood 165	F6
54628	Ferryville 227	D9
54524	Fifield 310	F4
54212	Fish Creek 119	M5
54121	Florence⊙ 780	K4
54935	Fond du Lac⊙ 35,863	K8
53125	Fontana 1,764	J10
53537	Footville 794	H10
54123	Forest Junction 140	K7
54213	Forestville 455	L6
53538	Fort Atkinson 9,785	J10
54629	Fountain City 963	C7
54836	Foxboro 360	B2
53933	Fox Lake 1,373	J8
†53117	Fox Point 7,649	M1
54214	Francis Creek 589	L7
53132	Franklin 16,871	L2
54837	Frederic 1,039	B4
53021	Fredonia 1,437	L8
54940	Fremont 510	J7
53934	Friendship⊙ 744	G8
53935	Friesland 267	H8
54630	Galesville 1,239	D7
54631	Gays Mills 627	E9
53127	Genesee Depot 350	J2
54632	Genoa 283	D8
53128	Genoa City 1,202	K11
53022	Germantown 10,729	K1
54124	Gillett 1,356	K6
54433	Gilman 436	E5
54743	Gilmanton 300	C7
54435	Gleason 200	G5
53023	Glenbeulah 423	L8
†53209	Glendale 13,882	M1
54526	Glen Flora 83	E4
53810	Glen Haven 160	E10
54013	Glenwood City 950	B5
54527	Glidden 940	E3
54125	Goodman 875	K4
54838	Gordon 600	C3
53540	Gotham 250	F9
53024	Grafton 8,381	L9
53936	Grand Marsh 725	G8
54839	Grand View 447	D3
54436	Granton 399	E6
54840	Grantsburg⊙ 1,153	A4
53541	Gratiot 280	F10
*54301	Green Bay⊙ 87,899	K6
	Green Bay‡ 175,280	K6
53129	Greendale 16,928	L2
53220	Greenfield 31,467	L2
54941	Green Lake⊙ 1,208	H8
54126	Greenleaf 300	L7
54942	Greenville 900	J7
54437	Greenwood 1,124	E6
54128	Gresham 534	J6
54014	Hager City 110	A6
53130	Hales Corners 7,110	K2
54015	Hammond 991	A6
54943	Hancock 419	G7
54529	Harshaw 87	G4
53027	Hartford 7,046	K9
53029	Hartland 5,559	J1
54440	Hatley 300	H6
54841	Haugen 251	C4
54530	Hawkins 407	E4
54842	Hawthorne 200	C3
54843	Hayward⊙ 1,698	D3
53811	Hazel Green 1,282	F11
54531	Hazelhurst 630	G4
†53538	Hebron 450	J10
53137	Helenville 300	J10
54844	Herbster 100	D2
54441	Hewitt 470	F6
53543	Highland 860	F9
54129	Hilbert 1,176	K7
†54511	Hiles 350	J4

(continued on following page)

Agriculture, Industry and Resources

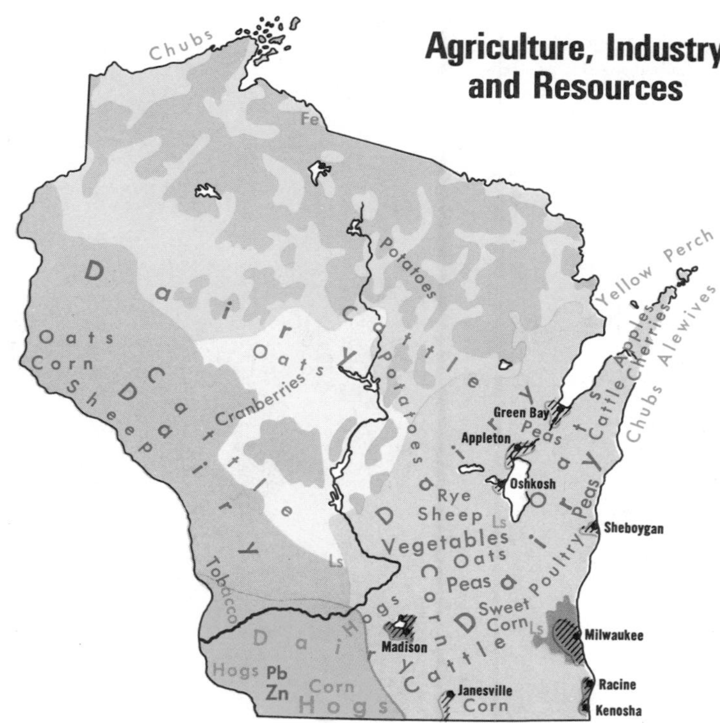
Chubs
Fe
Yellow Perch
Apples
Cherries
Alewives
Chubs
Potatoes
Dairy
Cattle
Oats
Corn
Sheep
Cranberries
Green Bay
Appleton
Peas
Oshkosh
Rye
Sheep
Ls
Vegetables
Oats
Peas
Sweet Corn
Poultry
Sheboygan
Tobacco
Hogs
Madison
Milwaukee
Hogs Pb Zn
Corn
Janesville
Corn
Racine
Kenosha

DOMINANT LAND USE

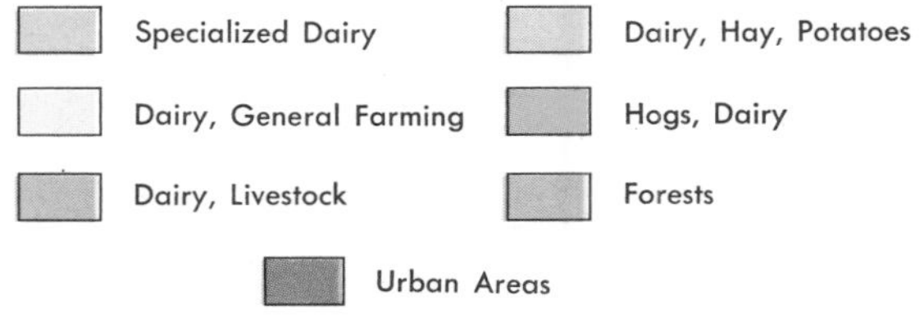
Specialized Dairy
Dairy, Hay, Potatoes
Dairy, General Farming
Hogs, Dairy
Dairy, Livestock
Forests
Urban Areas

MAJOR MINERAL OCCURRENCES

Fe Iron Ore
Pb Lead
Ls Limestone
Zn Zinc

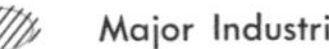 Major Industrial Areas

54634 Hillsboro 1,263 F8
53031 Hingham 250 K8
54635 Hixton 364 E7
54745 Holcombe 200 D5
53544 Hollandale 271 G10
54636 Holmen 2,411 D8
53138 Honey Creek 300 J3
53032 Horicon 3,584 J9
54944 Hortonville 2,016 J7
†55082 Houlton 915 A5
54303 Howard 8,240 K6
53081 Howards Grove-Millersville 1,838 L8
53033 Hubertus 600 K1
54016 Hudson⊙ 5,434 A6
54746 Humbird 190 E6
54534 Hurley⊙ 2,015 F3
53034 Hustisford 874 J9
54637 Hustler 170 F8
54747 Independence 1,180 D7
54945 Iola 957 H6
54536 Iron Belt 300 F3
53035 Iron Ridge 766 K9
54847 Iron River 878 D2
†53941 Ironton 206 F8
53036 Ixonia 525 H1
53037 Jackson 1,817 K9
†54235 Jacksonport 150 M6
53545 Janesville⊙ 51,071 H10
Janesville-Beloit‡ 139,420 H10
53549 Jefferson⊙ 5,647 J10
54748 Jim Falls 100 D5
53038 Johnson Creek 1,136 J9
53550 Juda 500 H10
54443 Junction City 523 G6
53039 Juneau⊙ 2,045 J9
53139 Kansasville 150 L3
54130 Kaukauna 11,310 K7
†53050 Kekoskee 224 J8
54215 Kellnersville 369 L7
54638 Kendall 486 F8
54537 Kennan 194 F5
*53140 Kenosha⊙ 77,685 M3
Kenosha‡ 123,137 M3
54135 Keshena⊙ 980 J6
53040 Kewaskum 2,381 K8
54216 Kewaunee⊙ 2,801 M7
53042 Kiel 3,083 L8
53812 Kieler 800 E10
54136 Kimberly 5,881 K7
53939 Kingston 328 H8
54749 Knapp 419 B6
†54455 Knowlton 127 G6
53044 Kohler 1,651 L8
53147 Krakow 345 K6
54538 Lac du Flambeau 500 G4
†53066 Lac La Belle 289 H1
54601 La Crosse⊙ 48,347 D8
La Crosse‡ 91,056 D8
54848 Ladysmith⊙ 3,826 D5
54639 La Farge 746 E8
53940 Lake Delton 1,158 G8
53147 Lake Geneva 5,612 K10
53551 Lake Mills 3,670 H9
54849 Lake Nebagamon 780 C3
54539 Lake Tomahawk 600 H4
†54494 Lake Wazeecha 2,176 G7
†54729 Lake Wissota 1,788 D6
54138 Lakewood 425 K5
53813 Lancaster⊙ 4,076 E10
54540 Land O'Lakes 786 H3
53046 Lannon 987 K1
53941 La Valle 412 F8
53047 Lebanon 250 H1
54139 Lena 585 K6
†54656 Leon 100 E8
54948 Leopolis 200 J6
54851 Lewis 200 B4
53942 Limeridge 191 F9
53553 Linden 395 F10
54140 Little Chute 7,907 K7
53554 Livingston 642 E10
53555 Lodi 1,959 G9
53943 Loganville 239 F9
†54970 Lohrville 336 H7
53048 Lomira 1,446 J8
53556 Lone Rock 577 F9
54542 Long Lake 150 J4
53557 Lowell 326 J9
54446 Loyal 1,252 E6
54447 Lublin 142 E5
54853 Luck 997 B4
54217 Luxemburg 1,040 L6
53944 Lyndon Station 375 F8
54640 Lynxville 174 D9
53148 Lyons 550 K10
*53701 Madison (cap.)⊙ 170,616 H9
Madison‡ 323,545 H9
54750 Maiden Rock 172 B6
54949 Manawa 1,205 J7
54220 Manitowoc⊙ 32,547 L7
54226 Maplewood 200 M6
54448 Marathon 1,552 G6
54855 Marengo 130 E3
54227 Maribel 363 L7
54143 Marinette⊙ 11,965 L5
54950 Marion 1,348 J6
53946 Markesan 1,446 J8
53947 Marquette 204 H8
53559 Marshall 2,363 H9
54449 Marshfield 18,290 F6
54856 Mason 102 D3
54450 Mattoon 382 J5
53948 Mauston⊙ 3,284 F8
53050 Mayville 4,333 K9
53560 Mazomanie 1,248 G9
53558 McFarland 3,783 H10
54543 McNaughton 450 H4
54451 Medford⊙ 4,035 F5
54546 Mellen 1,046 E3
54642 Melrose 507 E7
54619 Melvina 117 E8
54952 Menasha 14,728 J7
53051 Menomonee Falls 27,845 K1
54751 Menomonie⊙ 12,769 C6
53092 Mequon 16,193 L1
54452 Merrill⊙ 9,578 G5
54754 Merrillan 587 E7
53561 Merrimac 365 G9
53056 Merton 1,045 K1
53562 Middleton 11,848 G9
54857 Mikana 200 C4
54453 Milan 153 F6
†53038 Milford 35 J9
54454 Milladore 250 G6
54643 Millston 110 E7
54858 Milltown 732 B4
53563 Milton 4,092 J10
*53201 Milwaukee⊙ 636,236 M1
Milwaukee‡ 1,397,143 M1
54644 Mindoro 200 D7
53565 Mineral Point 2,259 F10
54548 Minocqua 950 G4
54859 Minong 557 C3
54228 Mishicot 1,503 L7
54755 Mondovi 2,545 C6
54549 Monico 250 H4
53716 Monona 8,809 H9
53566 Monroe⊙ 10,027 G10
53949 Montello⊙ 1,273 H8
53569 Montfort 616 E10
53570 Monticello 1,021 G10
54550 Montreal 887 F3
53571 Morrisonville 375 G9
54455 Mosinee 3,015 G6
54149 Mountain 250 K5
53057 Mount Calvary 585 K8
53816 Mount Hope 197 D10
53572 Mount Horeb 3,251 G10
54645 Mount Sterling 223 D9
†53572 Mount Vernon 138 G10
53149 Mukwonago 4,014 J2
53573 Muscoda 1,331 F9
53150 Muskego 15,277 K2
53058 Nashotah 513 J1
54646 Necedah 773 F7
54956 Neenah 22,432 J7
54456 Neillsville⊙ 2,780 E6
54457 Nekoosa 2,519 G7
54756 Nelson 389 C7
54458 Nelsonville 199 H7
54150 Neopit 1,065 J6
53059 Neosho 575 J9
54960 Neshkoro 386 H8
54551 Newald 375 J4
54757 New Auburn 466 D5
53151 New Berlin 30,529 K2
53060 Newburg 783 K9
†61075 New Diggings 65 F10
54229 New Franken 150 L6
53574 New Glarus 1,763 G10
53061 New Holstein 3,412 K8
53950 New Lisbon 1,390 F8
54961 New London 6,210 J7
54017 New Richmond 4,306 A5
54151 Niagara 2,079 K4
54152 Nichols 267 K6
†53401 North Bay 219 M3
†54935 North Fond du Lac 3,844 J8
53951 North Freedom 616 G9
†54016 North Hudson 2,218 A5
53064 North Lake 400 J1
53217 North Shore 14,930 M1
54648 Norwalk 517 E8
53154 Oak Creek 16,932 M2
54649 Oakdale 150 F8
53065 Oakfield 990 J8
53066 Oconomowoc 9,909 H1
†53066 Oconomowoc Lake 524 H1
54153 Oconto⊙ 4,505 L6
54154 Oconto Falls 2,500 K6
54962 Ogdensburg 214 J7
54459 Ogema 238 F5
53069 Okauchee 3,958 J1
†53555 Okee 250 H9
†54880 Oliver 253 B2
54963 Omro 2,763 J7
54650 Onalaska 9,249 D8
54155 Oneida 900 K7
54651 Ontario 398 E8
53070 Oostburg 1,647 L8
53575 Oregon 3,876 H10
53576 Orfordville 1,143 H10
54020 Osceola 1,581 A5
54901 Oshkosh⊙ 49,620 J8
54758 Osseo 1,474 D6
54460 Owen 998 F6
53952 Oxford 432 H8
53953 Packwaukee 271 G8
†53168 Paddock Lake 2,207 K10
53156 Palmyra 1,515 H2
53954 Pardeeville 1,594 H8
54552 Park Falls 3,192 F4
†54481 Park Ridge 643 H6
53817 Patch Grove 259 D10
53157 Pell Lake 1,826 K10
54553 Pence 234 F3
54759 Pepin 890 B7
54157 Peshtigo 2,807 L5
53072 Pewaukee 4,637 K1
54554 Phelps 950 H3
54555 Phillips⊙ 1,522 E4
54464 Phlox 150 J5
54465 Pickerel 107 J5
54760 Pigeon Falls 338 D7
54466 Pittsville 810 F7
53577 Plain 676 F9
54966 Plainfield 813 G7
†53017 Plat 120 K1
53818 Platteville 9,580 F10
53158 Pleasant Prairie 950 L10
54467 Plover 5,310 G7
54761 Plum City 505 B6
53073 Plymouth 6,027 L8
†54423 Polonia 200 H6
54864 Poplar 569 C2
53901 Portage⊙ 7,896 G8
54469 Port Edwards 2,077 G7
53074 Port Washington⊙ 8,612 L9
54865 Port Wing 290 D2
53820 Potosi 736 E10
54160 Potter 330 K7
54161 Pound 407 L5
53955 Poynette 1,447 G9
54967 Poy Sippi 425 J7
53821 Prairie du Chien⊙ 5,859 D9
53578 Prairie du Sac 2,145 G9
54762 Prairie Farm 387 C5
54556 Prentice 605 F4
54021 Prescott 2,654 A6
54968 Princeton 1,479 H8
54162 Pulaski 1,875 K6
54164 Pulcifer 35 K6
*53401 Racine⊙ 85,725 M3
Racine‡ 173,132 M3
54867 Radisson 280 D4
53956 Randolph 1,691 H8
53075 Random Lake 1,287 K8
†53126 Raymond 300 L2
54652 Readstown 396 E9
54970 Redgranite 976 J7
53959 Reedsburg 5,038 G8
54230 Reedsville 1,134 L7
53579 Reeseville 649 J9
53580 Rewey 233 F10
54501 Rhinelander⊙ 7,873 H4
54470 Rib Lake 945 F5
54868 Rice Lake 7,691 C5
53581 Richland Center⊙ 4,997 F9
54763 Ridgeland 300 B5
53582 Ridgeway 503 F10
53960 Rio 785 H9
54971 Ripon 7,111 J8
54022 River Falls 9,019 A6
†53201 River Hills 1,642 M1
54023 Roberts 833 A6
53167 Rochester 746 K3
†53523 Rockdale 200 J10
53077 Rockfield 200 L1
54653 Rockland 383 D8
53961 Rock Springs 426 F8
†53178 Rome 200 H1
54974 Rosendale 725 J8
54473 Rosholt 520 H6
54474 Rothschild 3,338 G6
†53583 Roxbury 260 G9
54475 Rudolph 392 G7
†54751 Rusk 40 C6
53079 Saint Cloud 560 K8
54024 Saint Croix Falls 1,497 A5
†53207 Saint Francis 10,042 M2
†54601 Saint Joseph Ridge 450 D8
54232 Saint Nazianz 738 L7
54765 Sand Creek 225 C5
53583 Sauk City 2,703 G9
53080 Saukville 3,494 L9
54559 Saxon 375 F3
54977 Scandinavia 292 H7
54476 Schofield 2,226 H6
†54843 Seeley 68 D3
54654 Seneca 235 E9
53584 Sextonville 225 F9
54165 Seymour 2,530 K6
53585 Sharon 1,280 J11
54166 Shawano⊙ 7,013 J6
53081 Sheboygan⊙ 48,085 L8
Sheboygan‡ 100,935 L8
53085 Sheboygan Falls 5,253 L8
54766 Sheldon 292 D5
54871 Shell Lake⊙ 1,135 C4
54169 Sherwood 372 K7
54170 Shiocton 805 K7
53211 Shorewood 14,327 M1
†53701 Shorewood Hills 1,837 G9
53586 Shullsburg 1,484 F10
53170 Silver Lake 1,598 K10
54872 Siren 896 B4
54234 Sister Bay 564 M5
53086 Slinger 1,612 K9
54655 Soldiers Grove 622 E9
54873 Solon Springs 590 C3
54025 Somerset 860 A5
53172 South Milwaukee 21,069 M2
53587 South Wayne 495 G10
54656 Sparta⊙ 6,934 E8
54479 Spencer 1,754 F6
54801 Spooner 2,365 B4
53588 Spring Green 1,265 G9
54767 Spring Valley 982 B6
54768 Stanley 2,095 E6
54026 Star Prairie 420 A5
54480 Stetsonville 487 F5
54657 Steuben 175 E9
54481 Stevens Point⊙ 22,970 G7
54172 Stiles 300 L6
53825 Stitzer 190 E10
53088 Stockbridge 567 K7
54769 Stockholm 104 B7
54658 Stoddard 762 D8
54876 Stone Lake 210 C4
53589 Stoughton 7,589 H10
54484 Stratford 1,385 F6
54770 Strum 944 D6
54235 Sturgeon Bay⊙ 8,847 M6
53177 Sturtevant 4,130 M3
54173 Suamico 900 K6
53178 Sullivan 434 H1
54485 Summit Lake 250 H5
53590 Sun Prairie 12,931 H9
54880 Superior⊙ 29,571 C2
Superior-Duluth‡ 266,650 C2
†54880 Superior Village 580 B2
54174 Suring 581 K5
53089 Sussex 3,482 K1
53090 Taycheedah 350 K8
54659 Taylor 411 E7
†53820 Tennyson 476 E10
53091 Theresa 766 K8
53092 Thiensville 3,341 L1
54771 Thorp 1,635 E6
54562 Three Lakes 950 H4
54486 Tigerton 865 H6
54240 Tisch Mills 315 L7
54660 Tomah 7,204 F8
54487 Tomahawk 3,527 G5
54563 Tony 146 E5
54888 Trego 280 C4
54661 Trempealeau 956 C8
54662 Tunnel City 200 E7
54889 Turtle Lake 762 B5
53181 Twin Lakes 3,474 K11

Topography

0 40 80 MI.
0 40 80 KM.

Below Sea Level | 100 m. 328 ft. | 200 m. 656 ft. | 500 m. 1,640 ft. | 1,000 m. 3,281 ft. | 2,000 m. 6,562 ft. | 5,000 m. 16,404 ft.

54241 Two Rivers 13,354 M7
53962 Union Center 216 F8
53182 Union Grove 3,517 L3
54488 Unity 418 F6
54245 Valders 984 L7
53593 Verona 3,336 G9
54489 Vesper 554 F7
54664 Viola 696 E8
54665 Viroqua⊙ 3,716 D8
54566 Wabeno 800 J5
53093 Waldo 416 L8
53183 Wales 1,992 J1
53184 Walworth 1,607 J10
54666 Warrens 300 E7
53962 Wascott 70 C3
54891 Washburn⊙ 2,080 D2
54246 Washington Island 550 M5
53185 Waterford 2,051 K3
53594 Waterloo 2,393 J9
53094 Watertown 18,113 J9
53021 Waubeka 450 L9
53186 Waukesha⊙ 50,365 K1
53597 Waunakee 3,866 G9
54981 Waupaca⊙ 4,472 H7
53963 Waupun 8,132 J8
54401 Wausau⊙ 32,426 G6
Wausau‡ 111,270 G6
54177 Wausaukee 648 K5
54982 Wautoma⊙ 1,629 H7
53226 Wauwatosa 51,308 L1
53826 Wauzeka 580 E9
†54126 Wayside 140 L7
54893 Webster 610 B4
53214 West Allis 63,982 L1
†53913 West Baraboo 846 G9
53095 West Bend⊙ 21,484 K9
54490 Westboro 750 F5
54667 Westby 1,797 E8
53964 Westfield 1,033 H8
†53201 West Milwaukee 3,535 L1
†54476 Weston 8,775 G6
54669 West Salem 3,276 D8
54983 Weyauwega 1,549 H7
54895 Weyerhaeuser 313 D5
54772 Wheeler 231 C5
54773 Whitehall⊙ 1,530 D7
54491 White Lake 309 J5
54247 Whitelaw 649 L7
53190 Whitewater 11,520 J10
†54481 Whiting 2,050 H7
54984 Wild Rose 741 H7
53191 Williams Bay 1,763 J10
54027 Wilson 155 B6
54670 Wilton 465 F8
54567 Winchester 300 G3
53185 Wind Lake 900 K2
†53401 Wind Point 1,695 M2
53598 Windsor 827 H9
54985 Winnebago 1,433 J8
54986 Winneconne 1,935 J7
54896 Winter 376 E4
53965 Wisconsin Dells 2,521 G8
54494 Wisconsin Rapids⊙ 17,995 G7
54498 Withee 509 E6
54499 Wittenberg 997 H6
53968 Wonewoc 842 F8
53827 Woodman 116 E9
54568 Woodruff 850 G4
54028 Woodville 725 B6
54180 Wrightstown 1,169 K7
54671 Wyeville 163 F7
53969 Wyocena 548 H9
54182 Zachow 135 K6

OTHER FEATURES

Apostle (isls.) F2
Apostle Islands Nat'l Lakeshore E1
Apple (riv.) A5
Bad River Ind. Res. E2
Bardon (lake) C3
Bear (isl.) E1
Beaver Dam (lake) J9
Beulah (lake) J2
Big Eau Pleine (res.) G6
Big Muskego (lake) L2
Big Rib (riv.) G5
Black (riv.) E7
Butternut (lake) J4
Castle Rock (lake) G8
Cat (isl.) E1
Chambers (isl.) M5
Chequamegon (bay) E2
Chetac (lake) D4
Chippewa (lake) D4
Chippewa (riv.) B7
Clam (lake) B4
Clam (riv.) A4
Dells, The (valley) G8
Denoon (lake) K2
Du Bay (lake) G6
Eagle (lake) H2
Eagle (lake) K3
Eau Claire (riv.) D6
Flambeau (riv.) E4
Flambeau Flowage (res.) F3
Fox (riv.) K2
Fox (riv.) K7
General Mitchell Field M2
Geneva (lake) K10
Golden (lake) H1
Green (bay) L6
Grindstone (lake) C4
Holcombe Flowage (res.) D5
Jump (riv.) E5
Kegonsa (lake) H10
Kickapoo (riv.) E9
Koshkonong (lake) H10
La Belle (lake) H1
Lac Court Oreilles Ind. Res. D4
Lac du Flambeau Ind. Res. G3
Long (lake) C4
Madeline (isl.) E2
Mendota (lake) H9
Menominee (riv.) L5
Metonga (lake) J4
Michigan (isl.) F2
Michigan (lake) M9
Mississippi (riv.) D10
Montreal (riv.) F2
Moose (lake) E3
Moose (lake) F3
Nagawicka (lake) J1
Namekagon (lake) D3
Namekagon (riv.) C3
North (lake) J1
Oak (isl.) E2
Oconomowoc (lake) H1
Oconto (riv.) K5
Okauchee (lake) J1
Outer (isl.) F1
Owen (lake) D3
Pecatonica (riv.) H11
Pelican (lake) H4
Pepin (lake) B7
Peshtigo (riv.) K5
Petenwell (lake) G7
Pewaukee (lake) K1
Phantom (lake) J2
Pine (lake) J1
Porte des Morts (str.) N5
Poygan (lake) J7
Puckaway (lake) H8
Red Cedar (riv.) C5
Red Cliff Ind. Res. E2
Rib (mt.) G6
Rock (riv.) J9
Round (lake) F4
Round (lake) D3
Saint Croix (lake) A6
Saint Croix (riv.) A4
Saint Croix Flowage (res.) C3
Saint Louis (riv.) A2
Sand (isl.) D2
Shawano (lake) K6
Shell (lake) C4
Spider (lake) D3
Stockbridge Ind. Res. J6
Stockton (isl.) F2
Sugar (riv.) H10
Sugarbush Hill (mt.) J4
Superior (lake) F1
Thunder (lake) H4
Tichigan (lake) K2
Timms Hill (mt.) F5
Trempealeau (riv.) C7
Trout (lake) G3
Vieux Desert (lake) J3
Washington (isl.) M5
Willow (res.) F4
Wind (lake) K2
Winnebago (lake) K7
Wisconsin (riv.) E9
Wolf (riv.) J5
Yellow (lake) B4
Yellow (riv.) F7

⊙County seat.
‡Population of metropolitan area.
† Zip of nearest p.o. * Multiple zips.

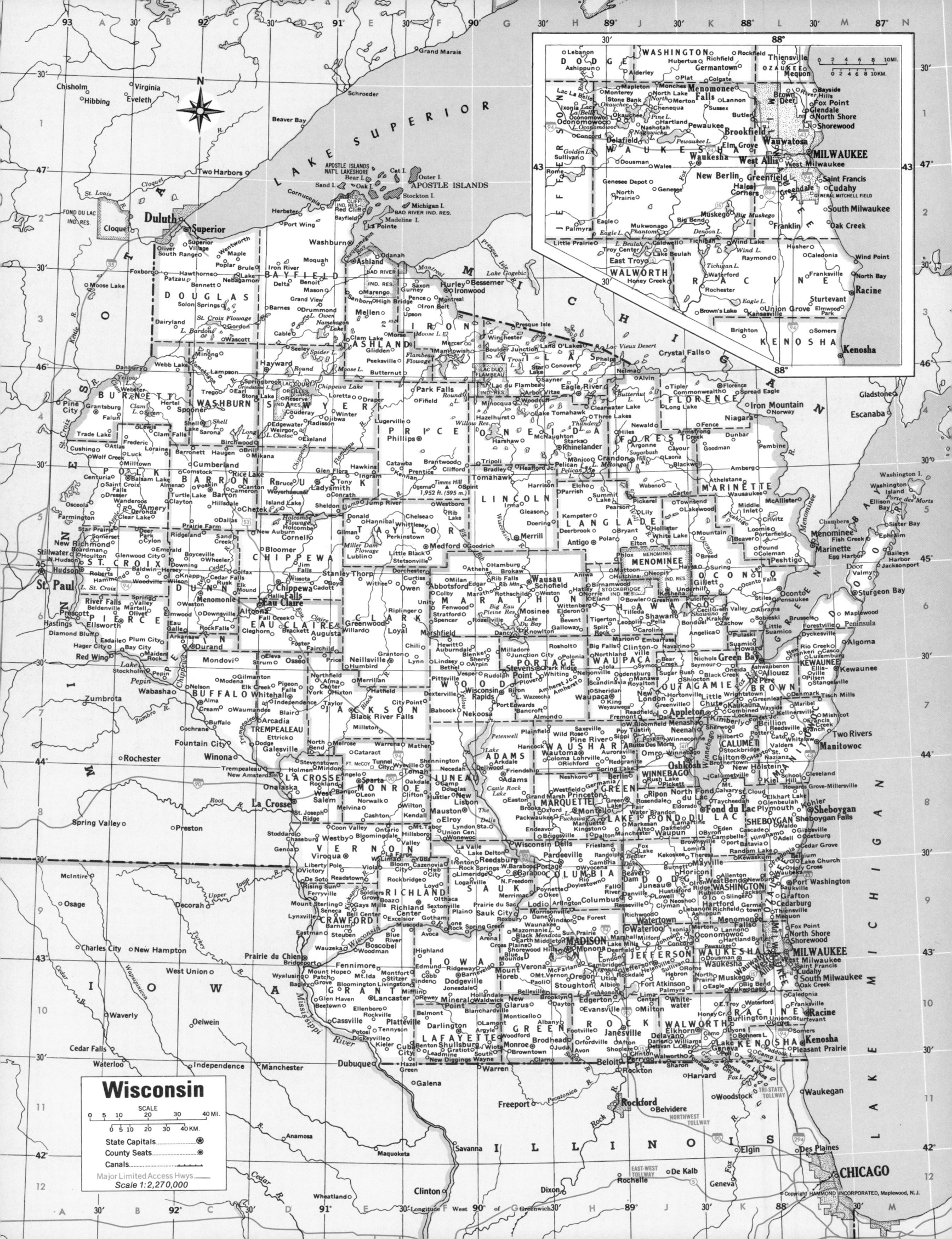

Wisconsin
SCALE
0 5 10 20 30 40 MI.
0 5 10 20 30 40 KM.
State Capitals
County Seats
Canals
Major Limited Access Hwys.
Scale 1:2,270,000
LAKE SUPERIOR
LAKE MICHIGAN
MICHIGAN
MINNESOTA
IOWA
ILLINOIS
GREEN BAY
APOSTLE ISLANDS
DOUGLAS
BAYFIELD
ASHLAND
IRON
VILAS
BURNETT
WASHBURN
SAWYER
PRICE
ONEIDA
FLORENCE
FOREST
POLK
BARRON
RUSK
LINCOLN
LANGLADE
MARINETTE
ST. CROIX
DUNN
CHIPPEWA
TAYLOR
MENOMINEE
OCONTO
PIERCE
PEPIN
EAU CLAIRE
CLARK
MARATHON
SHAWANO
DOOR
KEWAUNEE
BUFFALO
TREMPEALEAU
JACKSON
WOOD
PORTAGE
WAUPACA
OUTAGAMIE
BROWN
LA CROSSE
MONROE
JUNEAU
ADAMS
WAUSHARA
WINNEBAGO
CALUMET
MANITOWOC
VERNON
MARQUETTE
GREEN LAKE
FOND DU LAC
SHEBOYGAN
RICHLAND
SAUK
COLUMBIA
DODGE
WASHINGTON
OZAUKEE
CRAWFORD
GRANT
IOWA
DANE
JEFFERSON
WAUKESHA
MILWAUKEE
LAFAYETTE
GREEN
ROCK
WALWORTH
RACINE
KENOSHA
MADISON
MILWAUKEE
Duluth
Superior
St. Paul
Green Bay
Eau Claire
La Crosse
Oshkosh
Appleton
Wausau
Sheboygan
Racine
Kenosha
Janesville
Rockford
CHICAGO
© Copyright HAMMOND INCORPORATED, Maplewood, N.J.
Longitude West 90° of Greenwich

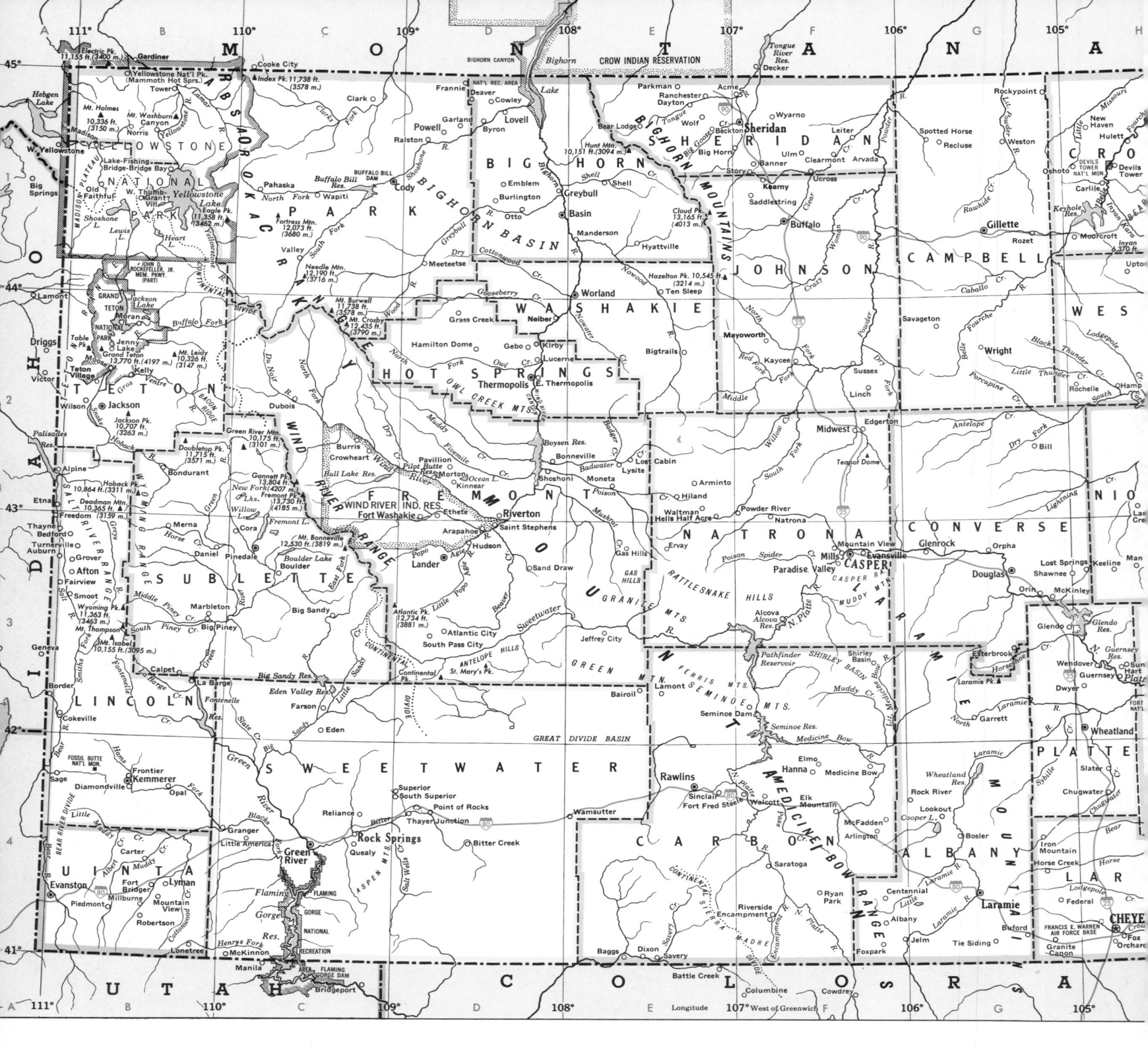

Agriculture, Industry and Resources

DOMINANT LAND USE

- Specialized Wheat
- Specialized Dairy
- General Farming, Livestock, Special Crops
- Sugar Beets, Dry Beans, Livestock, General Farming
- Range Livestock
- Forests
- Nonagricultural Land

MAJOR MINERAL OCCURRENCES

- C   Coal
- Cl   Clay
- Fe   Iron Ore
- G   Natural Gas
- O   Petroleum
- P   Phosphates
- So   Soda Ash
- U   Uranium
- V   Vanadium
- ⚡   Water Power

COUNTIES

County	Pop.	Key
Albany	29,062	G4
Big Horn	11,896	E1
Campbell	24,367	G1
Carbon	21,896	F4
Converse	14,069	G3
Crook	5,308	H1
Fremont	38,992	D2
Goshen	12,040	H4
Hot Springs	5,710	D2
Johnson	6,700	F1
Laramie	68,649	H4
Lincoln	12,177	B3
Natrona	71,856	F3
Niobrara	2,924	H2
Park	21,639	C1
Platte	11,975	H4
Sheridan	25,048	F1
Sublette	4,548	C3
Sweetwater	41,723	D4
Teton	9,355	B2
Uinta	13,021	B4
Washakie	9,496	E2
Weston	7,106	H2

CITIES and TOWNS

Zip	Name/Pop.	Key
83110	Afton 1,481	B3
82050	Albin 128	H4
82620	Alcova 275	F3

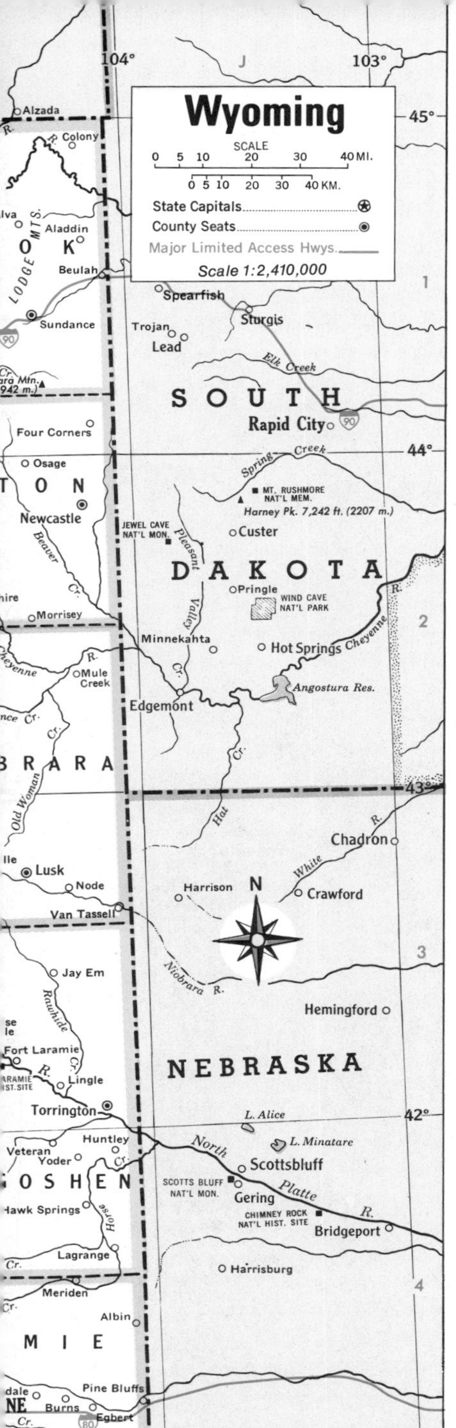

Wyoming
SCALE
0 5 10 20 30 40 MI.
0 5 10 20 30 40 KM.
State Capitals
County Seats
Major Limited Access Hwys.
Scale 1:2,410,000
104°
103°
J
45°
44°
43°
42°
41°
Alzada
Colony
Alva
Aladdin
Beulah
Spearfish
Sundance
Trojan
Lead
Sturgis
Elk Creek
SOUTH
DAKOTA
Rapid City
Four Corners
Osage
Newcastle
JEWEL CAVE NAT'L MON.
MT. RUSHMORE NAT'L MEM.
Harney Pk. 7,242 ft. (2207 m.)
Custer
Pringle
WIND CAVE NAT'L PARK
Morrisey
Minnekahta
Hot Springs
Cheyenne
Mule Creek
Angostura Res.
Edgemont
Chadron
Lusk
Node
Harrison
Crawford
Van Tassell
Jay Em
Niobrara R.
Hemingford
Fort Laramie
Lingle
NEBRASKA
Torrington
L. Alice
L. Minatare
Huntley
Veteran
Yoder
North Platte R.
Scottsbluff
SCOTTS BLUFF NAT'L MON.
Gering
CHIMNEY ROCK NAT'L HIST. SITE
Bridgeport
Hawk Springs
Lagrange
Harrisburg
Meriden
Albin
Pine Bluffs
Burns
Egbert
Carpenter
© Copyright HAMMOND INCORPORATED, Maplewood, N. J.
H
104°

AREA 97,809 sq. mi. (253,325 sq. km.)
POPULATION 469,557
CAPITAL Cheyenne
LARGEST CITY Casper
HIGHEST POINT Gannett Pk. 13,804 ft. (4207 m.)
SETTLED IN 1834
ADMITTED TO UNION July 10, 1890
POPULAR NAME Equality State
STATE FLOWER Indian Paintbrush
STATE BIRD Meadowlark

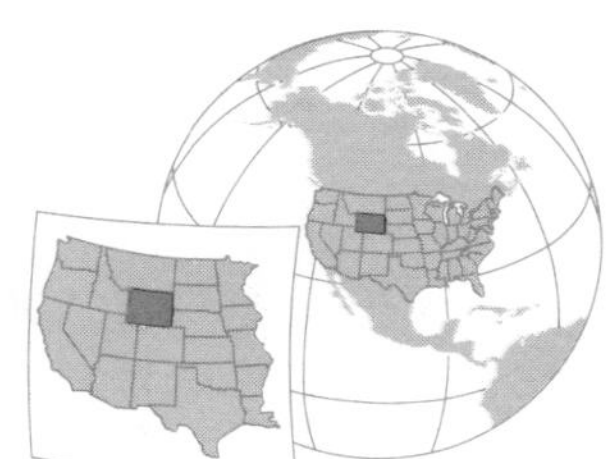

Topography

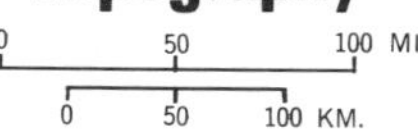

0 50 100 MI.
0 50 100 KM.

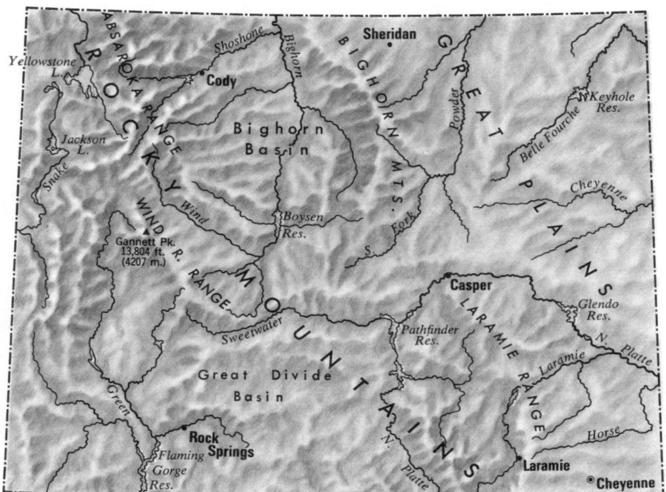

Yellowstone L.
ABSAROKA RANGE
ROCKY
MOUNTAINS
Shoshone
Cody
Sheridan
Bighorn
BIGHORN MTS.
GREAT PLAINS
Powder
Keyhole Res.
Belle Fourche
Cheyenne
Jackson L.
Snake
Bighorn Basin
Wind
Boysen Res.
S. Fork
WIND R. RANGE
Gannett Pk. 13,804 ft. (4207 m.)
Casper
Glendo Res.
N. Platte
Sweetwater
Pathfinder Res.
LARAMIE RANGE
Laramie
Great Divide Basin
Green
Rock Springs
Flaming Gorge Res.
Horse
Laramie
Cheyenne

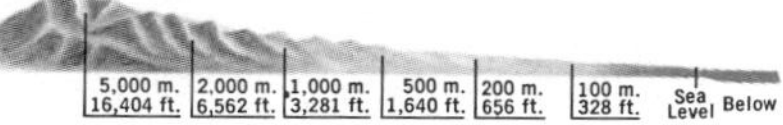

5,000 m. 16,404 ft.
2,000 m. 6,562 ft.
1,000 m. 3,281 ft.
500 m. 1,640 ft.
200 m. 656 ft.
100 m. 328 ft.
Sea Level
Below

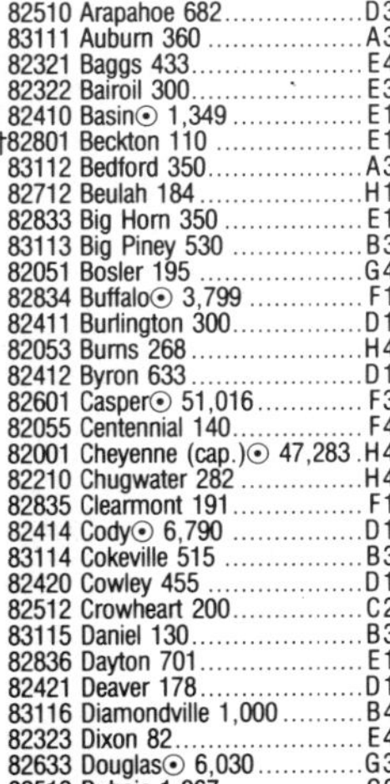
82510 Arapahoe 682 ..... D3
83111 Auburn 360 ..... A3
82321 Baggs 433 ..... E4
82322 Bairoil 300 ..... E3
82410 Basin⊙ 1,349 ..... E1
†82801 Beckton 110 ..... E1
83112 Bedford 350 ..... A3
82712 Beulah 184 ..... H1
82833 Big Horn 350 ..... E1
83113 Big Piney 530 ..... B3
82051 Bosler 195 ..... G4
82834 Buffalo⊙ 3,799 ..... F1
82411 Burlington 300 ..... D1
82053 Burns 268 ..... H4
82412 Byron 633 ..... D1
82601 Casper⊙ 51,016 ..... F3
82055 Centennial 140 ..... F4
82001 Cheyenne (cap.)⊙ 47,283 . H4
82210 Chugwater 282 ..... H4
82835 Clearmont 191 ..... F1
82414 Cody⊙ 6,790 ..... D1
83114 Cokeville 515 ..... B3
82420 Cowley 455 ..... D1
82512 Crowheart 200 ..... C2
83115 Daniel 130 ..... B3
82836 Dayton 701 ..... E1
82421 Deaver 178 ..... D1
83116 Diamondville 1,000 ..... B4
82323 Dixon 82 ..... E4
82633 Douglas⊙ 6,030 ..... G3
82513 Dubois 1,067 ..... C2
†82443 East Thermopolis 359 ..... D2

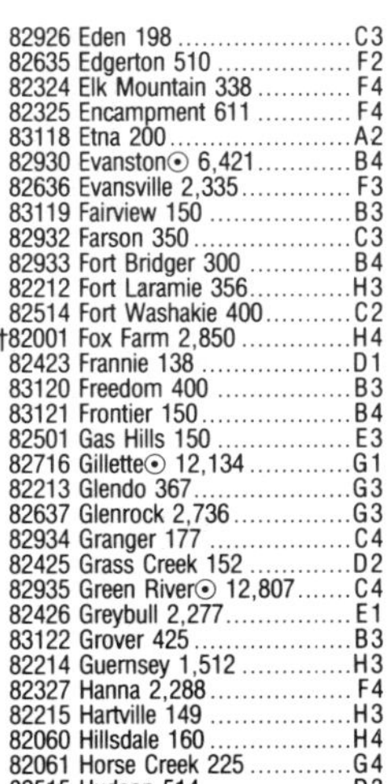
82926 Eden 198 ..... C3
82635 Edgerton 510 ..... F2
82324 Elk Mountain 338 ..... F4
82325 Encampment 611 ..... F4
83118 Etna 200 ..... A2
82930 Evanston⊙ 6,421 ..... B4
82636 Evansville 2,335 ..... F3
83119 Fairview 150 ..... B3
82932 Farson 350 ..... C3
82933 Fort Bridger 300 ..... B4
82212 Fort Laramie 356 ..... H3
82514 Fort Washakie 400 ..... C2
†82001 Fox Farm 2,850 ..... H4
82423 Frannie 138 ..... D1
83120 Freedom 400 ..... B3
83121 Frontier 150 ..... B4
82501 Gas Hills 150 ..... E3
82716 Gillette⊙ 12,134 ..... G1
82213 Glendo 367 ..... G3
82637 Glenrock 2,736 ..... G3
82934 Granger 177 ..... C4
82425 Grass Creek 152 ..... D2
82935 Green River⊙ 12,807 ..... C4
82426 Greybull 2,277 ..... E1
83122 Grover 425 ..... B3
82214 Guernsey 1,512 ..... H3
82327 Hanna 2,288 ..... F4
82215 Hartville 149 ..... H3
82060 Hillsdale 160 ..... H4
82061 Horse Creek 225 ..... G4
82515 Hudson 514 ..... D3
82720 Hulett 291 ..... H1

83001 Jackson⊙ 4,511 ..... B2
82310 Jeffrey City 1,882 ..... E3
82639 Kaycee 271 ..... F2
83011 Kelly 100 ..... B2
83101 Kemmerer⊙ 3,273 ..... B4
82516 Kinnear 145 ..... D2
82430 Kirby 129 ..... D2
83123 La Barge 302 ..... B3
82221 Lagrange 232 ..... H4
82520 Lander⊙ 7,867 ..... D3
82070 Laramie⊙ 24,410 ..... G4
82640 Linch 187 ..... F2
82223 Lingle 475 ..... H3
82929 Little America 175 ..... C4
†82642 Lost Cabin 25 ..... E2
82224 Lost Springs 9 ..... G3
82431 Lovell 2,447 ..... D1
†82443 Lucerne 240 ..... D2
82225 Lusk⊙ 1,650 ..... H3
82937 Lyman 2,284 ..... B4
82642 Lysite 175 ..... E2
†82190 Mammoth Hot Springs
(Yellowstone Nat'l Park 350 ..... B1
82432 Manderson 174 ..... E1
82227 Manville 94 ..... H3
†83113 Marbleton 537 ..... B3
82938 McKinnon 135 ..... C4
82329 Medicine Bow 953 ..... F4
82433 Meeteetse 512 ..... D1
82643 Midwest 638 ..... F2
82644 Mills 2,139 ..... F3
82721 Moorcroft 1,014 ..... H1
83012 Moose 150 ..... B2
83013 Moran 200 ..... B2
†82601 Mountain View F3
82939 Mountain View 628 ..... B4
82701 Newcastle⊙ 3,596 ..... H2
82190 Old Faithful 75 ..... B1
†82001 Orchard Valley 3,327 ..... H4
82723 Osage 500 ..... H2
†82601 Paradise Valley F3
82523 Pavillion 287 ..... D2
82082 Pine Bluffs 1,077 ..... H4
82941 Pinedale⊙ 1,066 ..... C3
82942 Point of Rocks 425 ..... D4
82435 Powell 5,310 ..... D1
82839 Ranchester 655 ..... E1
82301 Rawlins⊙ 11,547 ..... E4
82725 Recluse 225 ..... G1
82943 Reliance 325 ..... C4
†82325 Riverside 55 ..... F4
82501 Riverton 9,247 ..... D2
82944 Robertson 142 ..... B4
82083 Rock River 415 ..... G4
82901 Rock Springs 19,458 ..... C4
82331 Saratoga 2,410 ..... F4
82801 Sheridan⊙ 15,146 ..... F1
82615 Shirley Basin 400 ..... F3
82649 Shoshoni 879 ..... D2
82334 Sinclair 586 ..... E4
83126 Smoot 310 ..... B3
†82945 South Superior 586 ..... D4

82842 Story 637 ..... F1
82729 Sundance⊙ 1,087 ..... H1
82945 Superior 500 ..... D4
82442 Ten Sleep 407 ..... E1
83127 Thayne 256 ..... A3
82443 Thermopolis⊙ 3,852 ..... D2
82240 Torrington⊙ 5,441 ..... H3
82730 Upton 1,193 ..... H1
82242 Van Tassell 10 ..... H3
82335 Walcott 200 ..... F4
82336 Wamsutter 681 ..... E4
82201 Wheatland⊙ 5,816 ..... H3
83014 Wilson 480 ..... B2
82401 Worland⊙ 6,391 ..... E1
82732 Wright 1,117 ..... G2
82190 Yellowstone Nat'l Pk. 350 .. B1
82244 Yoder 110 ..... H4

OTHER FEATURES

Absaroka (range) C1
Antelope (creek) G2
Antelope (hills) D3
Aspen (mts.) C4
Atlantic (peak) D3
Badwater (creek) E2
Bear (creek) H4
Bear (riv.) B4
Bear Lodge (mts.) H1
Bear River Divide (mts.) B4
Beaver (creek) D3
Beaver (creek) H2
Belle Fourche (riv.) H1
Big Goose (creek) E1
Bighorn (basin) D1
Bighorn (lake) D1
Bighorn (mts.) E1
Bighorn (riv.) D1
Bighorn Canyon Nat'l Rec. Area D1
Big Sandy (riv.) C3
Bitter (creek) C4
Blacks Fork, Green (riv.) C4
Black Thunder (creek) G2
Bonneville (mt.) C3
Boysen (res.) D2
Buffalo Bill (dam) C1
Buffalo Bill (res.) C1
Buffalo Fork, Snake (riv.) B2
Burwell (mt.) C2
Caballo (creek) G1
Casper (range) F3
Cheyenne (riv.) H2
Chugwater (creek) H4
Clarks Fork (riv.) C1
Clear (creek) F1
Cloud (peak) E1
Cottonwood (creek) B4
Crazy Woman (creek) F1
Crosby (mt.) C2
Crow (creek) H4
Deadman (mt.) B2
Devils Tower Nat'l Mon. H1

Doubletop (peak) B2
Dry (creek) C2
Dry Cottonwood (creek) D1
Eagle (peak) B1
Fivemile (creek) D2
Flaming Gorge (res.) C4
Flaming Gorge Nat'l Rec. Area C4
Fontenelle (creek) B3
Fontenelle (res.) B3
Fort Laramie Nat'l Hist. Site H3
Fortress (mt.) C1
Fossil Butte Nat'l Mon. B4
Francis E. Warren A.F.B. 3,627 ..... G4
Fremont (lake) C3
Fremont (peak) C2
Gannett (peak) C2
Gas (hills) E3
Glendo (res.) H3
Gooseberry (creek) D1
Grand Teton (mt.) B2
Grand Teton Nat'l Park B2
Granite (mts.) E3
Great Divide (basin) E3
Green (mt.) E3
Green (riv.) C4
Green, East Fork (riv.) C3
Green River (mt.) C2
Greybull (riv.) D1
Greys (riv.) B3
Gros Ventre (riv.) B2
Guernsey (res.) H3
Hams Fork (riv.) B4
Hazelton (peak) E1
Henrys Fork, Green (riv.) C4
Hoback (peak) B2
Hoback (riv.) B2
Holmes (mt.) B1
Horse (creek) H4
Horseshoe (creek) G3
Hunt (mt.) E1
Index (peak) C1
Inyan Kara (creek) H1
Inyan Kara (mt.) H1
Isabel (mt.) B3
Jackson (lake) B2
Jackson (peak) B2
John D. Rockefeller, Jr., Mem.
Pkwy. B1
Keyhole (res.) H1
Lamar (riv.) B1
Lance (creek) H2
Laramie (mts.) G3
Laramie (peak) G3
Laramie (riv.) G4
Leidy (mt.) B2
Lewis (lake) B1
Lightning (creek) G2
Little Missouri (riv.) H1
Little Muddy (creek) B4
Little Powder (riv.) G1
Little Sandy (creek) C3
Little Thunder (creek) G2

Lodgepole (creek) H2
Lodgepole (creek) H4
Madison (plat.) B1
Medicine Bow (range) F4
Medicine Bow (riv.) F3
Middle Piney (creek) B3
Muddy (creek) D2
Muskrat (creek) E2
Needle (mt.) C1
Niobrara (riv.) J3
North Laramie (riv.) G3
North Platte (riv.) H3
Nowater (creek) E2
Nowood (riv.) E1
Owl, North Fork (creek) D2
Owl Creek (mts.) D2
Palisades (res.) A2
Pass (creek) F4
Pathfinder (res.) F3
Poison (creek) E2
Poison Spider (creek) F3
Popo Agie (riv.) D3
Powder (riv.) F2
Rattlesnake (range) E3
Rawhide (creek) G1
Rawhide (creek) H3
Rocky (mts.) C1
Salt (riv.) B3
Salt River (range) B3
Salt Wells (creek) D4
Seminoe (mts.) E3
Seminoe (res.) F3
Shell (creek) E1
Shirley (basin) F3
Shoshone (lake) B1
Shoshone (riv.) D1
Sierra Madre (mts.) E4
Slate (creek) C3
Smiths Fork (riv.) B3
Snake (riv.) B2
South Cheyenne (riv.) H2
South Piney (creek) B3
Sweetwater (riv.) D3
Sybille (creek) G4
Teapot Dome (mt.) F2
Teton (range) B2
Tongue (riv.) E1
Washburn (mt.) B1
Wheatland (res.) G4
Willow (creek) F2
Wind (riv.) C2
Wind River (canyon) D2
Wind River (range) C2
Wind River Ind. Res. C2
Wood (riv.) C2
Wyoming (peak) B3
Wyoming (range) B2
Yellowstone (lake) B1
Yellowstone (riv.) B1
Yellowstone Nat'l Park B1

⊙County seat.
† Zip of nearest p.o. * Multiple zips.

Acquisitions of Territory

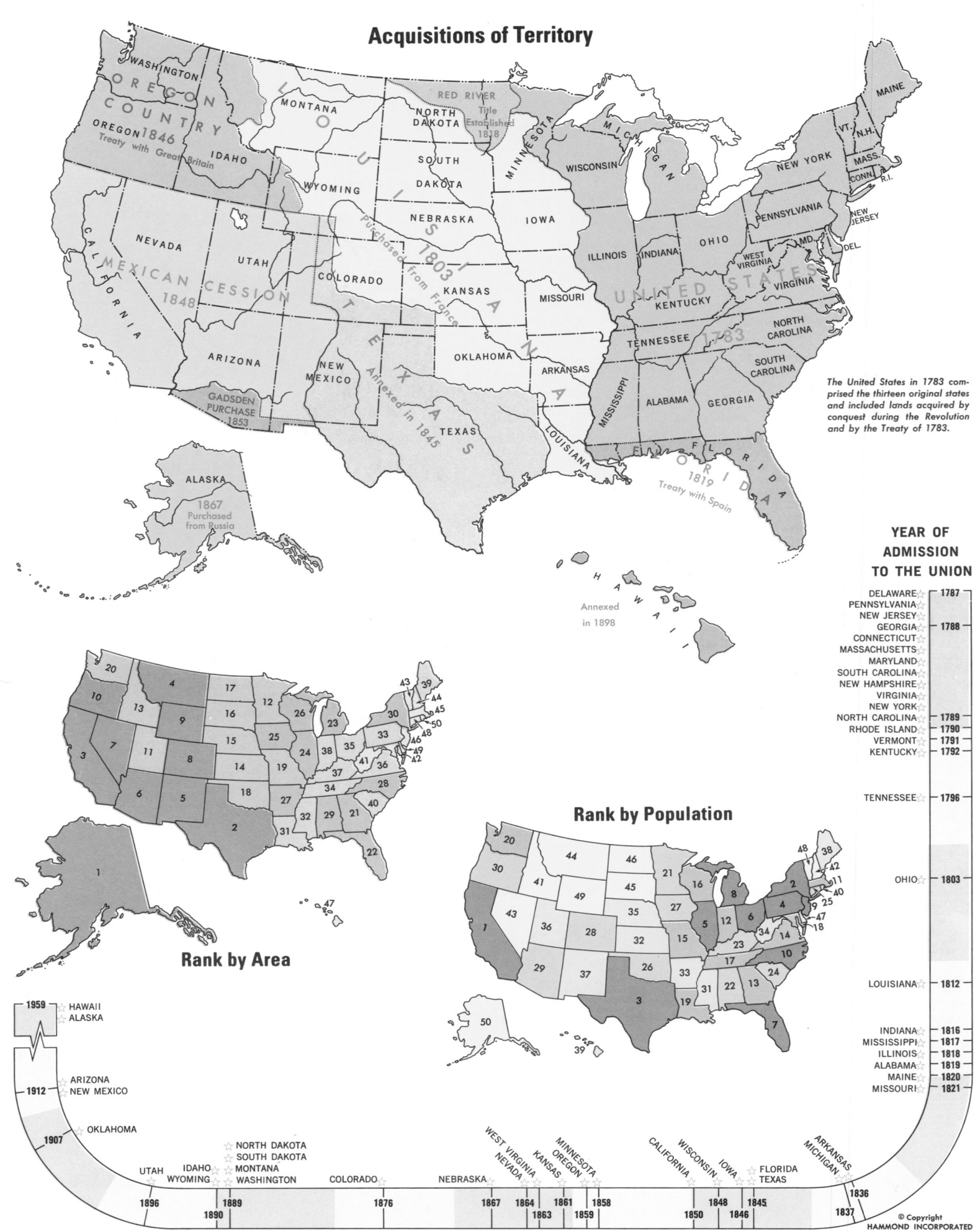

WASHINGTON

OREGON COUNTRY

OREGON 1846
Treaty with Great Britain

IDAHO

MONTANA

NORTH DAKOTA

RED RIVER
Title Established 1818

MINNESOTA

MICHIGAN

MAINE

VT. N.H.

NEW YORK

MASS.
CONN.
R.I.

L O U I S I A N A

WISCONSIN

PENNSYLVANIA

NEW JERSEY

NEVADA

UTAH

WYOMING

SOUTH DAKOTA

NEBRASKA

IOWA

ILLINOIS

INDIANA

OHIO

WEST VIRGINIA

MD.

DEL.

CALIFORNIA

MEXICAN CESSION 1848

COLORADO

Purchased from France 1803

KANSAS

MISSOURI

UNITED STATES

KENTUCKY

VIRGINIA

1783

ARIZONA

NEW MEXICO

Annexed in 1845

OKLAHOMA

ARKANSAS

TENNESSEE

NORTH CAROLINA

SOUTH CAROLINA

GADSDEN PURCHASE 1853

T E X A S

TEXAS

MISSISSIPPI

ALABAMA

GEORGIA

LOUISIANA

ALASKA
1867
Purchased from Russia

F L O R I D A
1819
Treaty with Spain

H A W A I I
Annexed in 1898

The United States in 1783 comprised the thirteen original states and included lands acquired by conquest during the Revolution and by the Treaty of 1783.

YEAR OF ADMISSION TO THE UNION

State	Year
DELAWARE ☆	1787
PENNSYLVANIA ☆	
NEW JERSEY ☆	
GEORGIA ☆	1788
CONNECTICUT ☆	
MASSACHUSETTS ☆	
MARYLAND ☆	
SOUTH CAROLINA ☆	
NEW HAMPSHIRE ☆	
VIRGINIA ☆	
NEW YORK ☆	
NORTH CAROLINA ☆	1789
RHODE ISLAND ☆	1790
VERMONT ☆	1791
KENTUCKY ☆	1792
TENNESSEE ☆	1796
OHIO ☆	1803
LOUISIANA ☆	1812
INDIANA ☆	1816
MISSISSIPPI ☆	1817
ILLINOIS ☆	1818
ALABAMA ☆	1819
MAINE ☆	1820
MISSOURI ☆	1821

Rank by Area

Rank by Population

Year	States
1959	☆ HAWAII, ☆ ALASKA
1912	☆ ARIZONA, ☆ NEW MEXICO
1907	☆ OKLAHOMA
1896	UTAH
1890	WYOMING
1889	☆ NORTH DAKOTA, ☆ SOUTH DAKOTA, ☆ MONTANA, ☆ WASHINGTON
	IDAHO
1876	COLORADO
1867	NEBRASKA
1864	NEVADA
1863	WEST VIRGINIA
1861	KANSAS
1859	OREGON
1858	MINNESOTA
1850	CALIFORNIA
1848	WISCONSIN
1846	IOWA
1845	FLORIDA, TEXAS
1837	MICHIGAN
1836	ARKANSAS

© Copyright
HAMMOND INCORPORATED

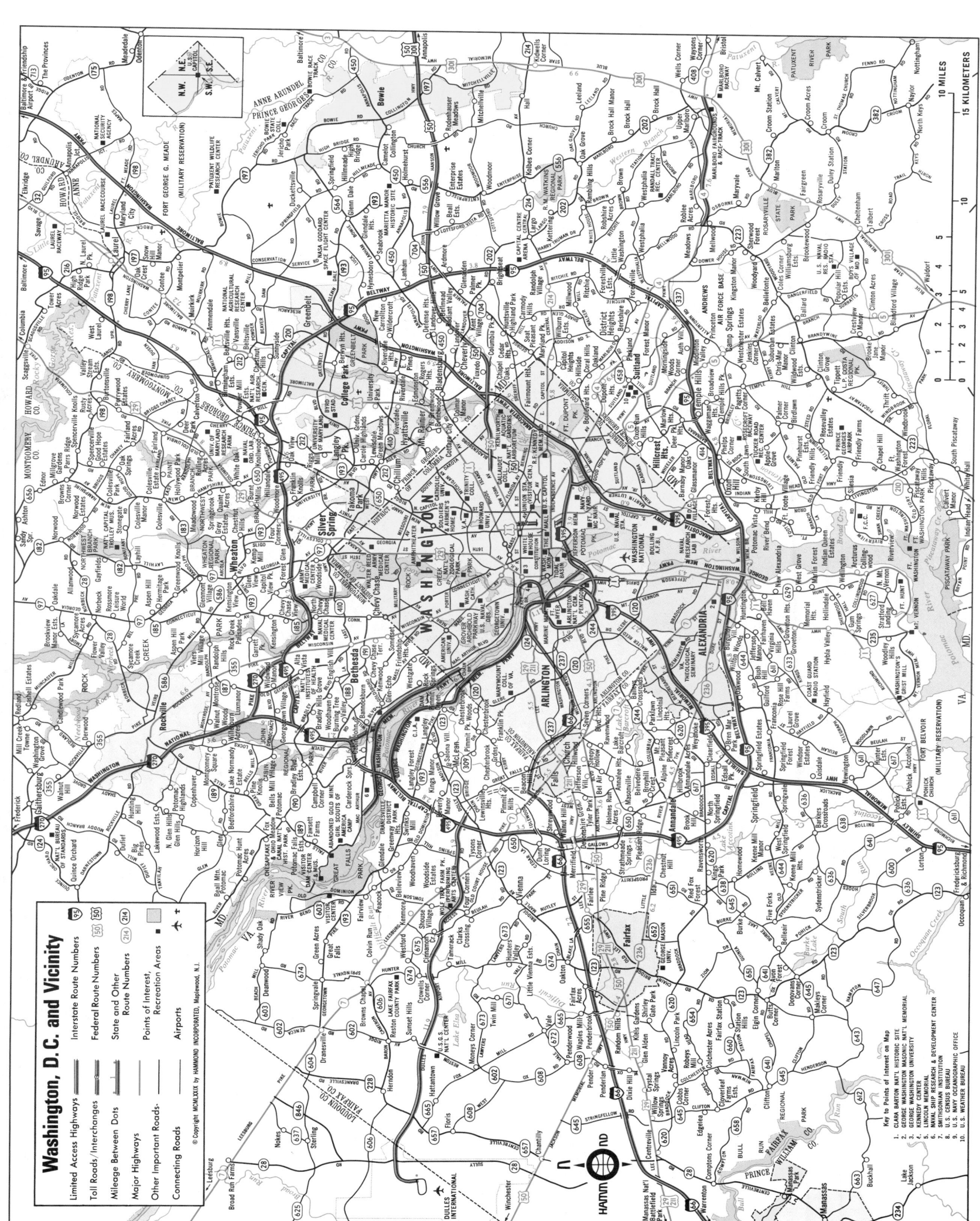

Washington, D.C. and Vicinity

Limited Access Highways

Toll Roads/Interchanges

Mileage Between Dots

Major Highways

Other Important Roads

Connecting Roads

Interstate Route Numbers

Federal Route Numbers

State and Other Route Numbers

Points of Interest, Recreation Areas

Airports

© Copyright MCMLXXIX by HAMMOND INCORPORATED, Maplewood, N.J.

Key to Points of Interest on Map
1. Clara Barton Nat'l Historic Site
2. George Washington Masonic Nat'l Memorial
3. George Washington University
4. Lincoln Memorial
5. Kennedy Center
6. Naval Ship Research & Development Center
7. Smithsonian Institution
8. U.S. Census Bureau
9. Navy Oceanographic Office
10. U.S. Weather Bureau

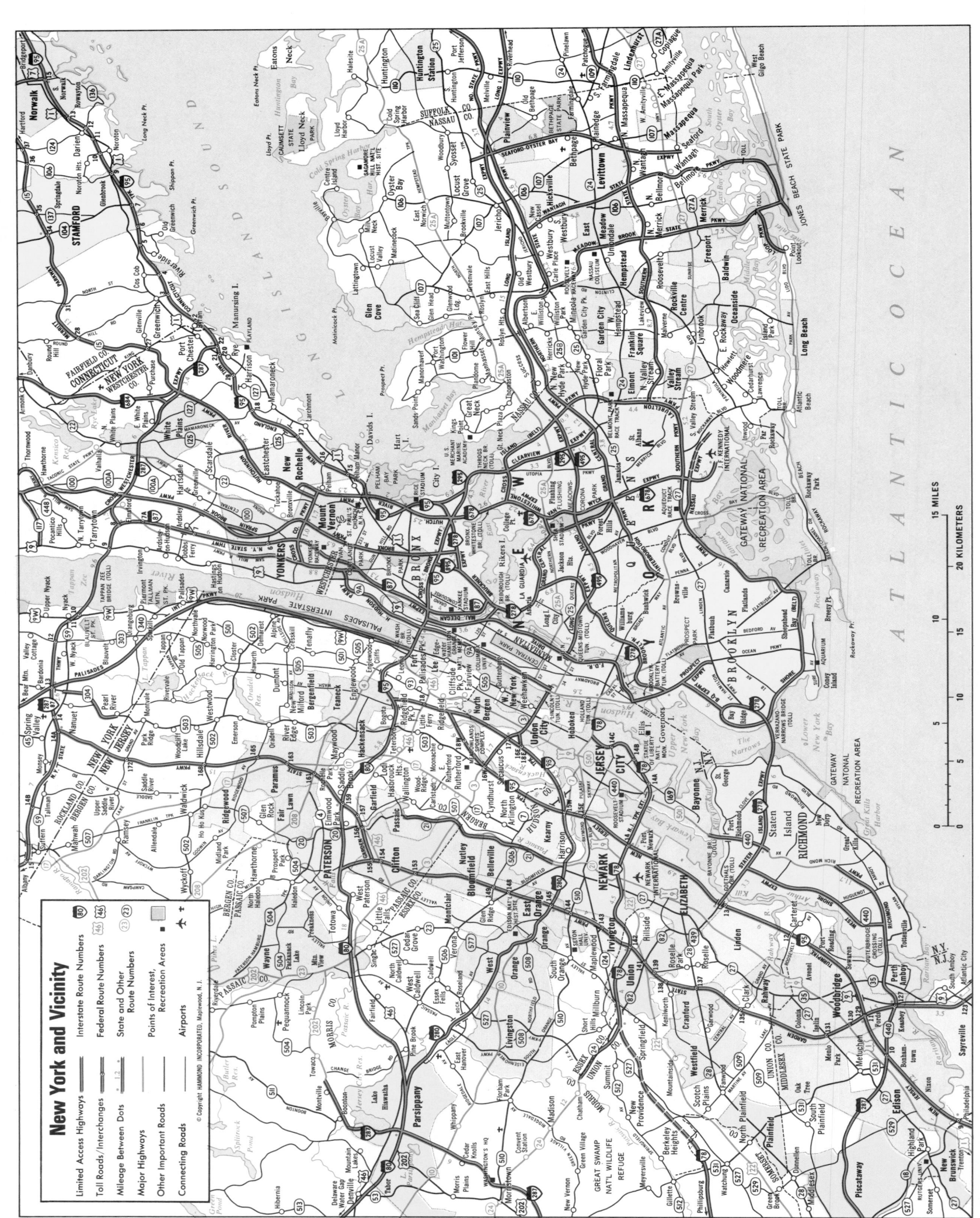

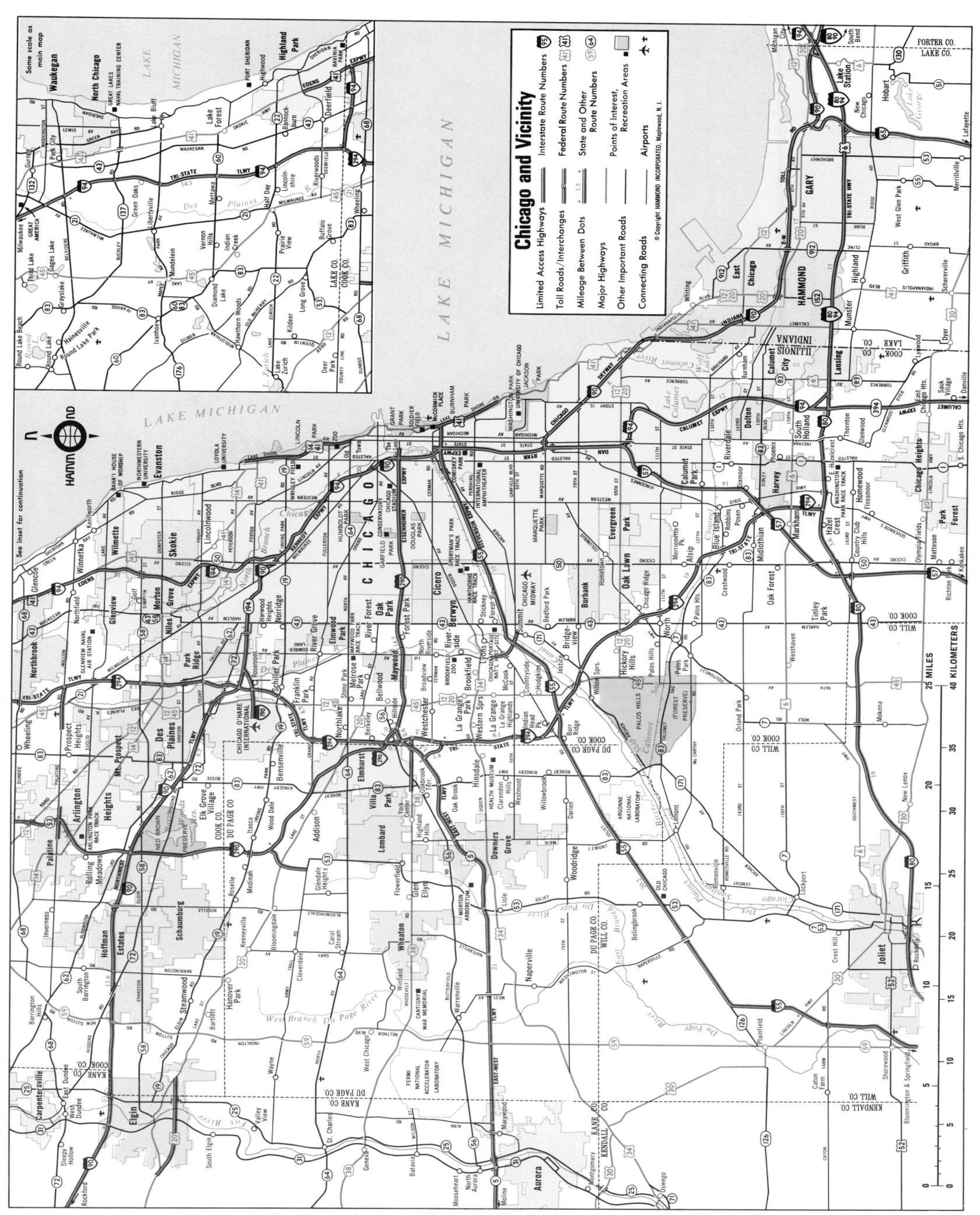

Chicago and Vicinity

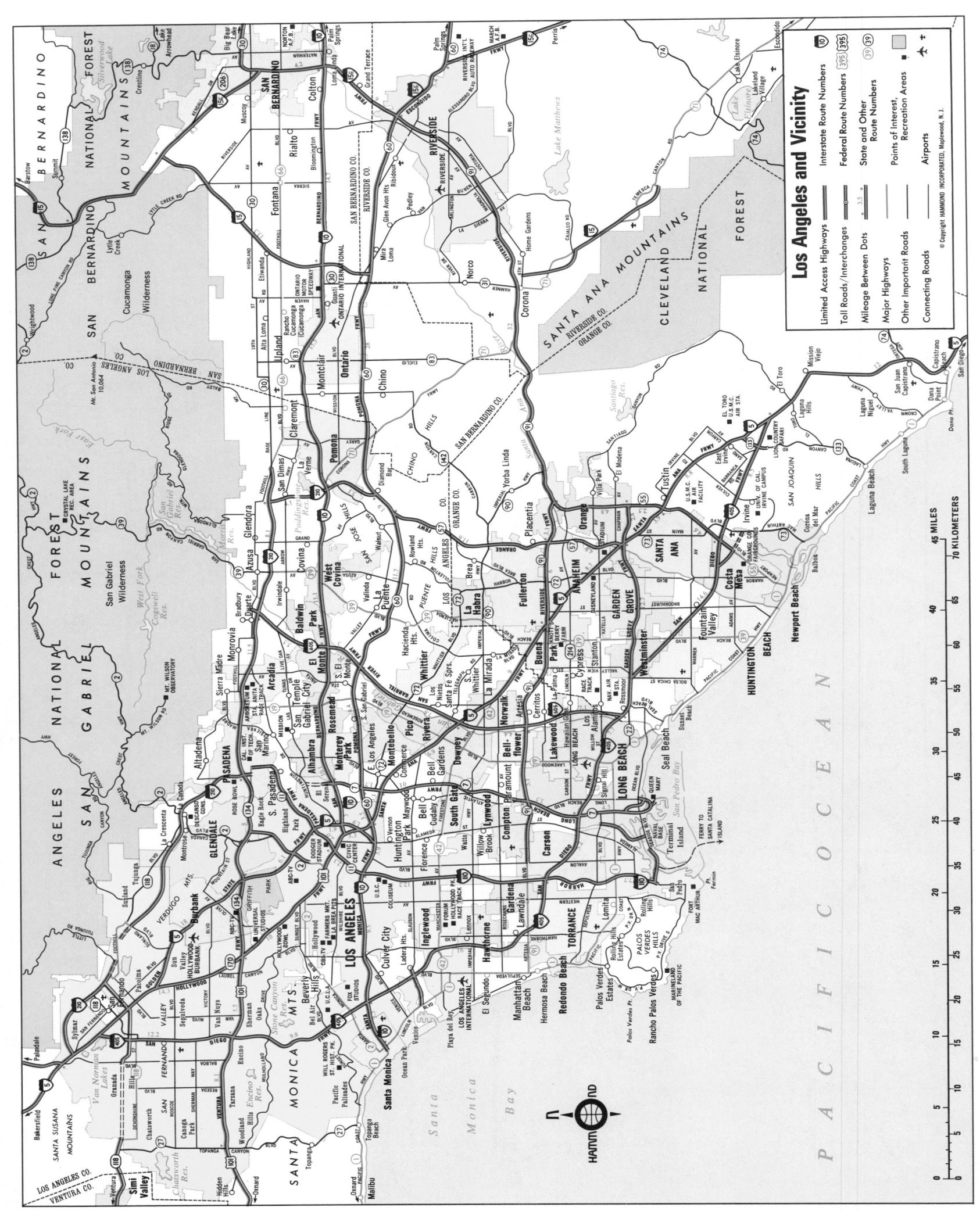

Los Angeles and Vicinity
Limited Access Highways
Toll Roads/Interchanges
Mileage Between Dots
Major Highways
Other Important Roads
Connecting Roads
Interstate Route Numbers
Federal Route Numbers
State and Other Route Numbers
Points of Interest, Recreation Areas
Airports
© Copyright HAMMOND INCORPORATED, Maplewood, N.J.
MILES
KILOMETERS
PACIFIC OCEAN
Santa Monica Bay
ANGELES NATIONAL FOREST
SAN GABRIEL MOUNTAINS
SAN BERNARDINO NATIONAL FOREST
SAN BERNARDINO MOUNTAINS
SANTA ANA MOUNTAINS
CLEVELAND NATIONAL FOREST
SANTA MONICA MTS.
LOS ANGELES
LONG BEACH
PASADENA
GLENDALE
ANAHEIM
SANTA ANA
RIVERSIDE
SAN BERNARDINO
HAMMOND

INDEX OF THE WORLD

Introduction

This index contains a complete alphabetical listing of more than one hundred thousand names shown on all the maps included in this atlas. Names not found in the individual indexes accompanying the maps appear here. The user who is unfamiliar with the location of a country, town, or physical feature, or who is in doubt as to which country, state or province a place belongs will find the answers to his questions in this index. Entries are indexed to all maps or insets showing the place.

The name of the feature sought will be found in its proper alphabetical sequence, followed by the name of the political division in which it is located, the page number of the map on which it will be found, and the key reference necessary for finding its location on the map. After noting the key reference letter-number combination for the place name, turn to the page number indicated. The place name will be found within the square formed by the two lines of latitude and the two lines of longitude which enclose the coordinates—i.e., the marginal letters and numbers. An open circle (○) after the name signifies a township — better known as a town — in the northeastern U.S.

All index entries for cities and towns in the United States are followed by a five-digit postal ZIP code number applying to the community. This useful feature permits the reader to address his mail so that it will be routed and delivered more efficiently and quickly by the U.S. Postal Service. A dagger (†) designates those places that do not possess a post office. The ZIP code number listed in such cases refers to that of the nearest post office. An asterisk (*) marks those larger cities which are divided into multiple ZIP code areas. Using the single ZIP code number listed in such cases will direct your letter to the proper city with dispatch. However, if the precise ZIP code number of the address within the city is needed, it is suggested that the reader refer to the latest National ZIP Code Directory at his local post office. This detailed guide lists every street in a multiple ZIP code city with the proper ZIP code for the street.

Because of limitations of space on the map, place names do not always appear in their complete form on the map. The complete forms are, however, given in the index. Variant spellings of names and alternate names are also given in this index. The alternate form or spelling of the name appears first, followed in parentheses by the name as it appears on the map. Physical features are usually listed under their proper names and not according to their generic terms; that is to say, Rio Negro will be found under Negro and not under Rio Negro. Exceptions are familiar names such as Rio Grande.

The abbreviations for the political division names and geographical features are explained on page XVI of the atlas. In addition, reference can be made to the Gazetteer-Index appearing on pages IX through XIII in which area, population, capital, map reference and population source data may be found for all major political and physical divisions of the world. Population figures for most entries are also included in the comprehensive individual indexes accompanying each map.

A

Aa (riv.), Switzerland 39/F3
Aachen, W. Germany 22/B3
Aadorf, Switzerland 39/G2
Aalen, W. Germany 22/D4
Aalsmeer, Netherlands 27/F4
Aalst, Belgium 27/D7
Aalten, Netherlands 27/K5
Aalter, Belgium 27/C6
Äänekoski, Finland 18/O5
Aarau, Switzerland 39/F2
Aarberg, Switzerland 39/D2
Aarburg, Switzerland 39/E2
Aardenburg, Netherlands 27/C6
Aare (riv.), Switzerland 39/E3
Aargau (canton), Switzerland 39/F2
Aarlen (Arlon), Belgium 27/H9
Aarons (creek), Va. 307/L7
Aaronsburg, Pa. (16820) 294/H4
Aarschot, Belgium 27/F7
Aat (Ath), Belgium 27/D7
Aba, China 77/F5
Aba, Hungary 41/E3
Aba, Nigeria 106/F7
Aba, Nigeria 102/C4
Aba, Zaire 115/F3
Aba as Sa'ud, Saudi Arabia 59/D6
Abacaxis (riv.), Brazil 132/B4
Abadan, Iran 54/F6
Abadan, Iran 66/F5
Abadan, Iran 59/E3
Abadeh, Iran 66/H5
Abadeh, Iran 59/F3
Abadla, Algeria 106/D2
Abádszalók, Hungary 41/F3
Abaeté, Brazil 132/E7
Abaetetuba, Brazil 132/D3
Abaetetuba, Brazil 120/E3
Abagnar (Silinhot), China 77/J3
Abaí, Paraguay 144/E4
Abaiang (atoll), Kiribati 87/H5
'Abaila, Saudi Arabia 59/F5
Abajo (mts.), Utah 304/E6
Abakan, U.S.S.R. 54/L4
Abakan, U.S.S.R. 48/K4
Abala, Congo 115/C4
Abalos (pt.), Cuba 158/A2
Abana, Turkey 63/F2
Abancay, Peru 120/B4
Abancay, Peru 128/F9
Abapó, Bolivia 136/D6
Abaq, China 77/J3
Abarqu, Iran 59/F3
Abarqu, Iran 66/H5
'Abasan, Gaza Strip 65/A5
Abashiri, Japan 81/M1
Abashiri (riv.), Japan 81/M1
Abau, Papua N.G. 85/C7
Abaújszántó, Hungary 41/F2
Abay (riv.), Ethiopia 111/G5
Abay, U.S.S.R. 48/H5
Abaya (lake), Ethiopia 111/G6
Abaza, U.S.S.R. 48/J4
Abbaye (pt.), Mich. 250/B2
Abbe (lake), Djibouti 111/H5
Abbeville, Ala. (36310) 195/H7
Abbeville, France 28/D2
Abbeville, Georgia (31001) 217/F7
Abbeville, La. (70510) 238/F7
Abbeville, Miss. (38601) 256/F2
Abbeville (co.), S.C. 296/B3
Abbeville, S.C. (29620) 296/C3
Abbey, Sask. 181/C5
Abbey (head), Scotland 15/E6
Abbeydorney, Ireland 17/B7
Abbeyfeale, Ireland 10/B4
Abbeyfeale, Ireland 17/C7
Abbeylara, Ireland 17/F4
Abbeyleix, Ireland 17/G6
Abbotsford, Br. Col. 184/L3
Abbotsford, Wis. (54405) 317/F6
Abbott, Ark. (†72944) 202/B3
Abbott, N. Mex. (†87747) 274/E2
Abbott, Texas (76621) 303/G6
Abbottabad, Pakistan 68/C2
Abbottabad, Pakistan 59/K3
Abbottsburg, N.C. (28321) 281/M5
Abbottsford, Georgia (†30240) 217/B4
Abbottstown, Pa. (17301) 294/J6
Abbot Village○, Maine (04406) 243/D5
Abbyville, Kansas (67510) 232/D4
'Abdul 'Aziz, Jebel (mts.), Syria 63/J4
Abdulino, U.S.S.R. 52/H4
Abéché, Chad 102/D3
Abéché, Chad 111/D5
Abee, Alberta 182/D2
Abell, Md. (20606) 245/M8
Abemama (atoll), Kiribati 87/H5
Abengourou, Ivory Coast 106/D7
Abengourou, Ivory Coast 102/B4
Åbenrå, Denmark 18/F9
Åbenrå, Denmark 21/C7
Abeokuta, Niger 106/E7
Abeokuta, Nigeria 102/C4
Aberaeron, Wales 13/C5
Aberaeron, Wales 10/D4
Abercarn, Wales 13/B6
Aberchirder, Scotland 15/F3
Abercorn, Québec 172/E4
Abercorn (Mbala), Zambia 115/F5
Abercrombie, N. Dak. (58001) 282/S7
Abercrombie, Nova Scotia 168/F3
Abercrombie (mt.), Wash. 310/H2
Aberdare, Wales 13/A6
Aberdare, Wales 10/E5
Aberdaron, Wales 13/C5
Aberdeen, Idaho (83210) 220/F7
Aberdeen, Ky. (42201) 237/H6
Aberdeen, Md. (21001) 245/O2
Aberdeen, Miss. (39730) 256/H3
Aberdeen (dam), Miss. 256/H3
Aberdeen○, N.J. (†07747) 273/E3
Aberdeen, N.S. Wales 97/F3
Aberdeen, N.C. (28315) 281/L4
Aberdeen (lake), N.W. Terrs. 187/J3
Aberdeen, Ohio (45101) 284/C8
Aberdeen, Sask. 181/E3
Aberdeen, Scotland 7/D3
Aberdeen, Scotland 15/F3
Aberdeen, Scotland 10/F2
Aberdeen (trad. co.), Scotland 15/B5
Aberdeen, S. Africa 118/C6
Aberdeen, S. Dak. 146/J5
Aberdeen, S. Dak. 188/G1
Aberdeen, S. Dak. (57401) 298/M3
Aberdeen, Wash. 188/B1
Aberdeen, Wash. (98520) 310/B3
Aberdeen Proving Ground, Md. 245/N3
Aberdour, Scotland 15/D1
Aberfeldy, Sask. 181/B2
Aberfeldy, Scotland 10/E2
Aberfeldy, Scotland 15/E4
Aberfoyle, Scotland 15/D4
Abergavenny, Wales 13/B6
Abergavenny, Wales 10/E5
Abergele, Wales 13/D4
Aberlady, Scotland 15/F4
Aberlour, Scotland 15/E3
Abernant, Ala. (35440) 195/D4
Abernathy, Texas (79311) 303/B4
Abernethy, Sask. 181/H5
Abernethy, Scotland 15/E4
Aberporth, Wales 13/C5
Abert (lake), Oreg. 188/C2
Abert (lake), Oreg. 291/G5
Abertillery, Wales 13/B6
Abertillery, Wales 10/E5
Aberystwyth, Wales 13/C5
Aberystwyth, Wales 10/D4
Abez', U.S.S.R. 52/K1
Abha, Saudi Arabia 59/D6
Abha, Saudi Arabia 54/F8
Abhar, Iran 66/F2
Abiad, Ras el (Blanc) (cape), Tunisia 106/G1
Abibe, Serranía de (mts.), Colombia 126/B3
'Abidiya, Sudan 59/B6
Abidjan (cap.), Ivory Coast 2/J5
Abidjan (cap.), Ivory Coast 102/B4
Abidjan (cap.), Ivory Coast 106/D7
Abie, Nebr. (68001) 264/H3
Abilene, Kansas (67410) 232/E3
Abilene, Texas 146/J6
Abilene, Texas (*79601) 303/E5
Abilene, Texas 188/G4
Abingdon, England 10/F5
Abingdon, England 13/F6
Abingdon, Ill. (61410) 222/C3
Abingdon, Iowa (†52533) 229/J6
Abingdon, Md. (21009) 245/N3
Abingdon, Va. (24210) 307/D7
Abingdon Downs, Queensland 95/B3
Abington, Conn. (06230) 210/G1
Abington, Ind. (†47330) 227/H5
Abington○, Mass. (02351) 249/L4
Abington, Pa. (19001) 294/M5
Abington, Scotland 15/E5
Abiqua (creek), Oreg. 291/B3
Abiquiu, N. Mex. (87510) 274/C2
Abiquiu (res.), N. Mex. 274/C2
Abita Springs, La. (70420) 238/L6
Abitibi (riv.), Ont. 162/H5
Abitibi (lake), Ont. 162/H6
Abitibi (lake), Ontario 175/E3
Abitibi (riv.), Ontario 175/D2
Abitibi (riv.), Ontario 177/J5
Abitibi (terr.), Québec 174/B3
Abitibi (county), Québec 174/B2
Abkhaz A.S.S.R., U.S.S.R. 48/E5
Abkhaz A.S.S.R., U.S.S.R. 52/F6
Abminga, S. Australia 94/D2
Abner, N.C. (†27371) 281/K4
Abnûb, Egypt 111/J4
Åbo (Turku), Finland 18/N6
Aboisso, Ivory Coast 106/D7
Aboite, Ind. (†46783) 227/G3
Abomey, Benin 106/E7
Abong-Mbang, Cameroon 115/B3
Abony, Hungary 41/E3
Abor (hills), India 68/G3
Aborlan, Philippines 82/B6
Abou Deïa, Chad 111/C5
Aboyne, Scotland 15/F3
Abqaiq, Saudi Arabia 59/E4
Abra (prov.), Philippines 82/C2
Abra (riv.), Philippines 82/C2
Abraham (lake), Alberta 182/B3
Abraham (mt.), Maine 243/C5
Abraham, Utah (†84635) 304/B4
Abraham (mt.), Vt. 268/B3
Abraham Lincoln Birthplace Nat'l Hist. Site, Ky. 237/K5
Abrams, Wis. (54101) 317/L6
Abrantes, Portugal 33/B3
Abra Pampa, Argentina 143/C1
Abreus, Cuba 158/D2
'Abri, Sudan 111/F3
Abricots, Haiti 158/A6
Abruzzi (reg.), Italy 34/D3
Absaraka, N. Dak. (58002) 282/P6
Absaroka (range), Mont. 262/F5
Absaroka (range), Wyo. 319/C1
Absarokee, Mont. (59001) 262/G5
Absecon, N.J. (08201) 273/D5
Absecon (inlet), N.J. 273/E5
Abu, India 68/C4
Abu 'Arish, Saudi Arabia 59/D6
Abu Dara, Ras (cape), Sudan 59/C5
Abu Dara, Ras (cape), Sudan 111/G3
Abu Deleiq, Sudan 59/B6
Abu Dhabi (cap.), U.A.E. 54/G7
Abu Dhabi (cap.), U.A.E. 59/F5
Abu ed Duhur, Syria 63/G5
Abu Habl, Wadi (dry riv.), Sudan 111/F5
Abu Hadriya, Saudi Arabia 59/E4
Abu Hamed, Sudan 111/F4
Abu Hamed, Sudan 59/B6
Abuja, Niger 106/F7
Abu Kemal, Syria 59/D3
Abu Kemal, Syria 63/J5
Abukuma (riv.), Japan 81/K4
Abu-Mad, Ras (cape), Saudi Arabia 59/C5
Abu Matariq, Sudan 111/E5
Abumombazi, Zaire 115/D3
Abunã (riv.), Bolivia 136/B2
Abunã, Brazil 132/H10
Abunã (riv.), Brazil 132/G10
Abu Qir (bay), Egypt 111/J2
Abu Qurqâs, Egypt 111/J4
Abu Road, India 68/C4
Abu Rujmein, Jebel (mts.), Syria 63/H5
Abu Shagara, Ras (cape), Sudan 111/G3
Abu Shagara, Ras (cape), Sudan 59/C5
Abut (head), N. Zealand 100/B5
Abu Tabari (well), Sudan 111/E4
Abuyog, Philippines 82/E5
Abu Zabad, Sudan 59/A7
Abu Zabad, Sudan 111/E5
Abwong, Sudan 111/F6
Aby (lag.), Ivory Coast 106/D8
Åbybro, Denmark 21/C3
Abydos (ruins), Egypt 111/F2
Abydos (ruins), Turkey 63/B6
Abyei, Sudan 111/E6
Acacías, Colombia 126/D6
Acaciaville, Nova Scotia 168/C4
Academy, S. Dak. (57310) 298/M7
Acadia (par.), La. 238/F6
Acadia Nat'l Park, Maine 243/G7
Acadia Valley, Alberta 182/E4
Acadie Siding, New Bruns. 170/E2
Acadieville, New Bruns. 170/E2
Acahay, Paraguay 144/B5
Acajutla, El Salvador 154/B4
Acala, Mexico 150/N8
Acala, Texas (†79839) 303/B10
Acámbaro, Mexico 150/J7
Acampo, Calif. (95220) 204/C9
Acandí, Colombia 126/B3
Acaponeta, Mexico 150/G5
Acapulco de Juárez, Mexico 146/H8
Acapulco de Juárez, Mexico 150/K8
Acaraí, Serra do (range), Brazil 132/B2
Acarai (mts.), Guyana 131/B5
Acaraú, Brazil 132/F3
Acaray (riv.), Paraguay 144/E4
Acarí, Peru 128/E10
Acarí (riv.), Peru 128/E10
Acarigua, Venezuela 124/D3
Acatlán de Osorio, Mexico 150/K7
Acatzingo de Hidalgo, Mexico 150/N2
Acayucan, Mexico 150/M8
Acchilla, Bolivia 136/C7
Accident, Md. (21520) 245/A2
Accokeek, Md. (20607) 245/L6
Accomac, Va. (23301) 307/S5
Accomack (co.), Va. 307/S5
Accord, Mass. (02018) 249/E8
Accord, N.Y. (12404) 276/M7
Accoville, W. Va. (25606) 312/C7
Accra (cap.), Ghana 102/B4
Accra (cap.), Ghana 106/D7
Accra (cap.), Ghana 2/J5
Accrington, England 10/G1
Accrington, England 13/H1
Aceguá, Uruguay 145/E2
Acequia, Idaho (83350) 220/E7
Acevedo, Argentina 143/F6
Achacachi, Bolivia 136/A5
Achaguas, Venezuela 124/D4
Achalpur, India 68/D4
Achao, Chile 138/D4
Achar, Uruguay 145/C3
Acharacle, Scotland 15/C4
Achégour (well), Niger 106/G5
Achenkirch, Austria 41/A3
Achill (head), Ireland 10/A4
Achill (head), Ireland 17/A4
Achill (isl.), Ireland 10/A4
Achill (isl.), Ireland 17/A4
Achille, Okla. (74720) 288/O7
Achilles, Va. (23001) 307/R6
Achill Sound, Ireland 17/B4
Achiltibuie, Scotland 15/C3
Achinsk, U.S.S.R. 48/K4
Achnasheen, Scotland 10/D2
Achnasheen, Scotland 15/C3
Achourat (well), Mali 106/D4
A'Chralaig (mt.), Scotland 15/C3
Acı (lake), Turkey 63/C4
Acıgöl, Turkey 63/F3
Acıpayam, Turkey 63/C4
Acireale, Italy 34/E6
Ackerly, Texas (79713) 303/C5
Ackerman, Miss. (39735) 256/F4
Ackerville, Ala. (†36778) 195/D6
Ackley, Iowa (50601) 229/G3
Acklins (isl.), Bahamas 146/L7
Acklins (isl.), Bahamas 156/C2
Ackworth, Iowa (50001) 229/G6
Aclare, Ireland 17/D3
Acle, England 13/J5
Acme, Alberta 182/D4
Acme, La. (71316) 238/G4
Acme, Mich. (49610) 250/D4
Acme, N.C. (†28456) 281/N6
Acme, Texas (†79252) 303/E3
Acme, Wash. (98220) 310/C2
Acme, W. Va. (†25122) 312/D6
Acme, Wyo. (82839) 319/E1
Acoaxet, Mass. (†02837) 249/K7
Acobamba, Peru 128/E9
Acolla, Peru 128/E8
Acoma, N. Mex. (†87034) 274/B4
Acomayo, Cusco, Peru 128/G9
Acomayo, Huánuco, Peru 128/E7
Acomita (Pueblo of Acoma), N. Mex. (†87034) 274/B3
Acona, Miss. (†39095) 256/D4
Aconcagua (mt.) 120/C6
Aconcagua, Cerro (mt.), Argentina 143/C3
Aconcagua, Chile 138/A9
Aconcagua (riv.), Chile 138/F2
Aconchi, Mexico 150/D2
Acopiara, Brazil 132/G4
Acora, Peru 128/H11
Acorizal, Brazil 132/C6
Acoyapa, Nicaragua 154/E5
Acqui Terme, Italy 34/B2
Acraman (lake), S. Australia 94/D5
Acre (state), Brazil 132/G10
Acre (riv.), Brazil 132/G10
Acre, Israel 65/C2

Allgäu 327

Alabat (isl.), Philippines 82/D3
Alaca, Turkey 63/F2
Alacahan, Turkey 63/G3
Alaçam, Turkey 63/F2
Alachua (co.), Fla. 212/D2
Alachua, Fla. (32615) 212/D2
Alacrán (reef), Mexico 150/P5
Alacranes, Cuba 158/D1
Aladağ (mt.), Turkey 63/F4
Aladagh, Kuh-i- (mt.), Iran 59/G2
'Aladagh, Kuh-e (mts.), Iran 66/K2
Aladdin, Wyo. (82710) 319/H1
Alaejos, Spain 33/D2
Alagir, U.S.S.R. 52/F6
Alagoa Grande, Brazil 132/H4
Alagoas (state), Brazil 132/G5
Alagoinhas, Brazil 120/F4
Alagoinhas, Brazil 132/G6
Alagón, Spain 33/F2
Alagón (riv.), Spain 33/C2
Alah (riv.), Philippines 82/E7
Al Ahqaf (Bahr es Safi) (des.), Saudi Arabia 59/E6
Al 'Ain, Saudi Arabia 59/C4
Alajuela, C. Rica 154/E6
Alakanuk, Alaska (99554) 196/E2
Alakol' (lake), U.S.S.R. 48/J5
Al 'Ala, Saudi Arabia 59/C4
Alalakeiki (chan.), Hawaii 218/J3
Alalapadu, Suriname 131/C4
Alamagan (isl.), No. Marianas 87/E4
Alamance (co.), N.C. 281/L3
Alamance, N.C. (27201) 281/K2
Alameda (co.), Calif. 204/D6
Alameda, Calif. (94501) 204/J2
Alameda (creek), Calif. 204/K3
Alameda, N. Mex. (87114) 274/C3
Alameda, Sask. 181/J6
Alamikamba, Nicaragua 154/E4
Alamo (lake), Ariz. 198/B4
Alamo (riv.), Calif. 204/K10
Alamo, Georgia (30411) 217/G6
Alamo, Ind. (47916) 227/C5
Alamo, Mexico 150/L6
Alamo, Nev. (89001) 266/F5
Alamo, N. Dak. (58830) 282/D2
Alamo, Tenn. (38001) 237/C9
Alamo, Texas (78516) 303/F11
Ala Moana, Hawaii 218/C4
Alamo-Danville, Calif. (94507) 204/K2
Alamogordo, N. Mex. 188/E4
Alamogordo, N. Mex. (88310) 274/C6
Alamo Heights, Texas (78209) 303/K10
Álamos, Mexico 150/E3
Alamosa (co.), Colo. 208/H7
Alamosa, Colo. (81101) 208/H8
Alamosa (creek), Colo. 208/G8
Alamosa (riv.), N. Mex. 274/B5
Alamota, Kansas (67830) 232/B3
Åland (Ahvenanmaa) (prov.), Finland 18/L6
Åland (isls.), Finland 7/F2
Åland (isls.), Finland 18/L6
Alanje, Panama 154/F6
Alanreed, Texas (79002) 303/D2
Alanson, Mich. (49706) 250/E3
Alanthus Grove, Mo. (†64489) 261/D2
Alanya, Turkey 59/B2
Alanya, Turkey 63/D4
Alaotra (lake), Madagascar 118/H3
Alapaha (riv.), Fla. 212/C1
Alapaha, Georgia (31622) 217/F8
Alapaha (riv.), Georgia 217/F7
Alaqua (creek), Fla. 212/C6
Alarcón (res.), Spain 33/E3
Alarka, N.C. (†28713) 281/C4
Alas (str.), Indonesia 85/F7
Alaşehir, Turkey 63/C3
Alashtar, Iran 66/E4
Alaska (reg.) 4/C17
Alaska 188/C5
Alaska (gulf) 146/D4
ALASKA 196
Alaska (gulf), Alaska 188/D6
Alaska (pen.), Alaska 188/C6
Alaska (range), Alaska 188/C6
Alaska (range), Alaska 146/C3
Alaska (pen.), Alaska 146/C4
Alaska (gulf), Alaska 196/K3
Alaska (pen.), Alaska 196/G3
Alaska (range), Alaska 196/H2
Alaska, Mich. (†49316) 250/D6
Alaska (state), U.S. 2/B2
Alaska (state), U.S. 146/C3
Alaska (range), U.S. 4/C17
Alaska (pen.), U.S. 4/D18
Alaska (gulf), U.S. 4/D17
Alaska Highway, Yukon 187/E3
Alassio, Italy 34/A2
Alatna, Alaska (†99720) 196/H1
Alatna (riv.), Alaska 196/H1
Alatri, Italy 34/D4
Alatyr', U.S.S.R. 52/G4
Al 'Auda, Saudi Arabia 59/E4
Alausí, Ecuador 128/C4
Álava (prov.), Spain 33/E1
Alava (cape), Wash. 188/A1
Alava (cape), Wash. 310/A2
Alaverdi, U.S.S.R. 52/F6
Alavus, Finland 18/N5
Alayor, Spain 33/J3
Al 'Azair, Iraq 66/E5
Alazeya (riv.), U.S.S.R. 48/Q3
Al'Aziziya, Iraq 59/E3
Al 'Aziziya, Iraq 66/D4
Alba, Italy 34/B2
Alba, Mich. (49611) 250/E4
Alba, Mo. (64830) 261/D8
Alba, Pa. (16910) 294/J2
Alba, Texas (75410) 303/J5
Albacete (prov.), Spain 33/E3
Albacete, Spain 7/D5
Albacete, Spain 33/F3
Alba de Tormes, Spain 33/D2
Albaida, Spain 33/F3
Alba Iulia, Romania 45/F2
Albalate del Arzobispo, Spain 33/F2
Alban, Ontario 177/D1
Albanel, Québec 172/E1
Albanel (lake), Québec 174/C2
Albania 2/K3
Albania 7/G4
ALBANIA 45/E5
Albano (lake), Italy 34/F7
Albano Laziale, Italy 34/F7
Albany, Australia 87/B9
Albany, Calif. (94706) 204/J2
Albany, Ga. 146/K6
Albany, Georgia (*31701) 217/D7
Albany, Ill. (61230) 222/C2
Albany, Ind. (47320) 227/G4
Albany, Jamaica 158/J6
Albany, Ky. (42602) 237/L7
Albany, La. (70711) 238/M1
Albany, Minn. (56307) 255/D5
Albany, Mo. (64402) 261/D2
Albany○, N.H. (†03864) 268/E4
Albany (cap.), N.Y. 188/M2
Albany (cap.), N.Y. 146/L5
Albany (co.), N.Y. 276/M5
Albany (cap.), N.Y. (*12201) 276/N5
Albany, N. Zealand 100/B1
Albany, Nova Scotia 168/C4
Albany, Ohio (45710) 284/F7
Albany, Okla. (74721) 288/O7
Albany (riv.), Ont. 146/K4
Albany (riv.), Ont. 162/H5
Albany (riv.), Ontario 175/C2
Albany, Oreg. 188/B2
Albany, Oreg. (97321) 291/D3
Albany, Pr. Edward I. 168/E2
Albany, Texas (76430) 303/E5
Albany, Vt. (05820) 268/C2
Albany○, Vt. (05820) 268/C2
Albany, W. Australia 88/B6
Albany, W. Australia 92/B6
Albany, Wis. (53502) 317/G10
Albany (co.), Wyo. 319/G4
Albany, Wyo. (†82055) 319/F4
Albany Creek, Queensland 88/J2
Albardon, Argentina 143/C3
Albarracín, Spain 33/F2
Albatross (pt.), N. Zealand 100/E3
Albatross (bay), Queensland 88/G2
Albatross (bay), Queensland 95/B2
Albay (prov.), Philippines 82/D4
Albay (gulf), Philippines 82/D4
Albee, S. Dak. (57210) 298/S3
Albemarle (pt.), Ecuador 128/B9
Albemarle (sound), N.C. 188/L3
Albemarle, N.C. (28001) 281/J4
Albemarle (sound), N.C. 281/S2
Albemarle (co.), Va. 307/L5
Albenga, Italy 34/B3
Albeni Falls (dam), Idaho 220/B1
Alberdi, Paraguay 144/D5
Alberene, Va. (†22959) 307/L5
Alberga, S. Australia 94/D2
Alberga, The (riv.), S. Australia 94/D2
Alberga, The (riv.), S. Australia 88/E5
Alberhill, Calif. (†92330) 204/E11
Alberni (inlet), Br. Col. 184/H3
Albers, Ill. (62215) 222/D5
Albert (canal), Belgium 27/F6
Albert, France 28/E2
Albert, Kansas (67511) 232/C3
Albert (co.), New Bruns. 170/F3
Albert, N. Mex. (87733) 274/F3
Albert, N.S. Wales 97/D3
Albert, Okla. (73001) 288/K4
Albert (lake), Québec 172/C3
Albert (Mobuto Sese Seko) (lake), Uganda 115/F3
Albert (creek), Wyo. 319/B4
Albert (Mobuto Sese Seko) (lake), Zaire 115/F3
Alberta (prov.) 162/E5
Alberta (prov.) Canada 146/G4
Alberta, Ala. (36720) 195/D6
ALBERTA 182
Alberta (mt.), Alberta 182/B3
Alberta (mt.), Alta. 162/E5
Alberta, La. (†71016) 238/D2
Alberta, Minn. (56207) 255/B5
Alberta, Va. (23821) 307/N7
Alberta Beach, Alberta 182/C3
Albert City, Iowa (50510) 229/C3
Albert Edward (bay), N.W. Terrs. 187/H3
Albert Head, Br. Col. 184/J4
Alberti, Argentina 143/G7
Albertirsa, Hungary 41/E3
Albert Lea, Minn. (56007) 255/E7
Albert Mines, New Bruns. 170/F3
Alberton, Mont. (59820) 262/B3
Alberton, Pr. Edward I. 168/E2
Alberton, S. Africa 118/H6
Albert Town, Jamaica 158/H6
Albertville, Ala. (35950) 195/F2
Albertville, France 28/G5
Albertville, Minn. (55301) 255/E5
Albertville, Sask. 181/F2
Albeuve, Switzerland 39/D3
Albi, France 28/E6
Albia, Iowa (52531) 229/H6
Albin, Wyo. (82050) 319/H4
Albina, Suriname 131/D3
Albino, Italy 34/B2
Albion, Calif. (95410) 204/B4
Albion, Idaho (83311) 220/E7
Albion (mts.), Idaho 220/E7
Albion, Ill. (62806) 222/E5
Albion, Ind. (46701) 227/G2
Albion, Iowa (50005) 229/H4
Albion○, Maine (04910) 243/E6
Albion, Mich. (49224) 250/E6
Albion, Nebr. (68620) 264/F3
Albion, N.Y. (14411) 276/D4
Albion, Okla. (74521) 288/R5
Albion, Pa. (16401) 294/B2
Albion, R.I. (02802) 249/H5
Albion, Wash. (99102) 310/H4
Albion, Wis. (†53534) 317/H10
Al Birk, Saudi Arabia 59/D6
Albocácer, Spain 33/F2
Alborán (isl.), Spain 7/D5
Alborán (isl.), Spain 33/E5
Ålborg, Denmark 7/F3
Ålborg, Denmark 18/G8
Ålborg (bay), Denmark 21/D4
Alborn, Minn. (55702) 255/F4
Albox, Spain 33/E4
Albreda, Br. Col. 184/H4
Albright, W. Va. (26519) 312/G3
Albrightsville, Pa. (18210) 294/L3
Albristhorn (mt.), Switzerland 39/D4
Albufeira, Portugal 33/B4
Albuñol, Spain 33/E4
Albuquerque (cays), Colombia 126/A10
Albuquerque, N. Mex. 146/H6
Albuquerque, N. Mex. 188/E3
Albuquerque, N. Mex. (*87101) 274/C3
Alburg, Vt. (05440) 268/A2
Alburg○, Vt. (05440) 268/A2
Alburnett, Iowa (52202) 229/K4
Alburquerque, Spain 33/C3
Alburtis, Pa. (18011) 294/L5
Albury, Australia 87/E9
Albury, N. S. Wales 88/H7
Albury, N.S. Wales 97/D5
Albury, N. Zealand 100/C6
Alca, Peru 128/F10
Alcácer do Sal, Portugal 33/B3
Alcalá, Bolivia 136/C6
Alcalá de Chivert, Spain 33/G2
Alcalá de Guadaira, Spain 33/D4
Alcalá de Henares, Spain 33/G4
Alcalá de los Gazules, Spain 33/D4
Alcalá la Real, Spain 33/E4
Alcalde, N. Mex. (87511) 274/C2
Alcamo, Italy 34/D6
Alcanar, Spain 33/G2
Alcañices, Spain 33/C2
Alcañiz, Spain 33/F2
Alcântara, Portugal 33/A1
Alcántara, Spain 33/C3
Alcántara (res.), Spain 33/C3
Alcántarata (res.), Portugal 33/C3
Alcantarilla, Spain 33/F4
Alcaraz, Argentina 143/G5
Alcaraz, Spain 33/E3
Alcaraz, Sierra de (range), Spain 33/E3
Alcatraz (isl.), Calif. 204/J2
Alcaudete, Spain 33/E4
Alcázar de San Juan, Spain 33/E3
Alcester, S. Dak. (57001) 298/R7
Alcida, New Bruns. 170/E1
Alcira, Spain 33/F3
Alco, Ark. (72610) 202/F2
Alco, La. (71402) 238/D4
Alcoa, Tenn. (37701) 237/N9
Alcobaça, Brazil 132/G7
Alcobaça, Portugal 33/B3
Alcolu, S.C. (29001) 296/G4
Alcomdale, Alberta 182/C3
Alcona (co.), Mich. 250/F4
Alcona Beach, Ontario 177/E3
Alcones, Chile 138/F5
Alcony, Ohio (†45373) 284/B5
Alcora, Spain 33/F2
Alcorisa, Spain 33/F2
Alcorn, Ky. (†40447) 237/O5
Alcorn (co.), Miss. 256/G1
Alcorn State University, Miss. (39096) 256/B7
Alcorta, Argentina 143/F6
Alcoutim, Portugal 33/C4
Alcova, Wyo. (82620) 319/F3
Alcova (res.), Wyo. 319/F3
Alcoy, Spain 33/F3
Alcudia (bay), Spain 33/H3
Alda, Nebr. (68810) 264/F4
Aldabra (isls.), Seychelles 102/G5
Aldabra (isls.), Seychelles 118/H1
Aldama, Chihuahua, Mexico 150/G2
Aldama, Tamaulipas, Mexico 150/L5
Aldan, Pa. (†19018) 294/M7
Aldan, U.S.S.R. 54/O4
Aldan (riv.), U.S.S.R. 54/P3
Aldan, U.S.S.R. 48/N4
Aldan (plat.), U.S.S.R. 48/N4
Aldan (riv.), U.S.S.R. 48/O3
Aldeburgh, England 13/J5
Aldeburgh, England 10/G4
Aldeia Carajá, Brazil 132/D6
Aldeia Nova de São Bento, Portugal 33/C4
Alden, Ill. (60001) 222/E1
Alden, Iowa (50006) 229/G4
Alden, Kansas (67512) 232/D3
Alden, Mich. (49612) 250/D4
Alden, Minn. (56009) 255/E7
Alden, N.Y. (14004) 276/C5
Alden Bridge, La. (†71006) 238/C1
Aldenville, Pa. (18401) 294/M2
Alder, Mont. (59710) 262/D5
Alder, Wash. (†98328) 310/C4
Alder (lake), Wash. 310/C4
Alder Creek, N.Y. (13301) 276/K4
Alder Flats, Alberta 182/C3
Alderley, Wis. (†53066) 317/J1
Alderney (isl.), Chan. Is. 10/E6
Alderney (isl.), Chan. Is. 13/E8
Alderpoint, Calif. (95411) 204/B3
Alder Point, Nova Scotia 168/H2
Aldershot, England 10/F5
Aldershot, England 13/G8
Aldershot, Nova Scotia 168/D3
Alderson, Okla. (74522) 288/P5
Alderson, W. Va. (24910) 312/E7
Aldersyde, Alberta 182/C4
Aldine, Ind. (†46366) 227/D2
Aldora, Georgia (†30204) 217/D4
Aldouane, New Bruns. 170/E2
Aldrich, Ala. (†35115) 195/E4
Aldrich, Minn. (56434) 255/C4
Aldrich, Mo. (65601) 261/F7
Aldridge Brownhills, England 10/G3
Aldridge Brownhills, England 13/E5
Aledo, Ill. (61231) 222/C2
Aledo, Texas (76008) 303/E2
Aleg, Mauritania 106/B5
Alegre, Brazil 135/F2
Alegre, Brazil 132/F8
Alegrete, Brazil 132/B10
Alegrete, Brazil 120/D5
'Aleih, Lebanon 63/F6
Alejandra, Argentina 143/F5
Alejandría, Bolivia 136/C3
Alejandro Selkirk (isl.), Chile 120/A6
Aleknagik, Alaska (99555) 196/G3
Aleksandriya, U.S.S.R. 52/D5
Aleksandrov Gay, U.S.S.R. 52/G4
Aleksandrovsk, U.S.S.R. 52/J3
Aleksandrovsk-Sakhalinsky, U.S.S.R. 54/R4
Aleksandrovsk-Sakhalinskiy, U.S.S.R. 48/P5
Aleksandrów Kujawski, Poland 47/D2
Aleksandrów Łódzki, Poland 47/D3
Alekseyevka, U.S.S.R. 48/H4
Alekseyevka, U.S.S.R. 52/E4
Aleksin, U.S.S.R. 52/E4
Aleksinac, Yugoslavia 45/E4
Além Paraíba, Brazil 135/E2
Alençon, France 28/D3
Alenquer, Brazil 132/C3
Alenquer, Brazil 120/D3
Alenuihaha (chan.), Hawaii 218/E7
Aleppo (prov.), Syria 63/G4
Aleppo, Syria 54/E6
Aleppo, Syria 59/C2
Aleppo, Syria 63/G4
Aléria, France 28/B6
Alert, Canada 4/A12
Alert, Ind. (†47283) 227/F6
Alert, N.C. (†27589) 281/N2
Alert, N.W.T. 162/N3
Alert, N.W. Terrs. 187/M1
Alert (pt.), N.W. Terrs. 187/K1
Alert Bay, Br. Col. 184/D5
Alès, France 28/E5
Alessandria (prov.), Italy 34/B2
Alessandria, Italy 34/B2
Ålestrup, Denmark 21/C4
Ålesund, Norway 7/E2
Ålesund, Norway 18/D5
Aletschhorn (mt.), Switzerland 39/F4
Aleutian (isls.), Alaska 188/D6
Aleutian (isls.), Alaska 196/J4
Aleutian (range), Alaska 196/G3
Aleutian (isls.), U.S. 4/D18
Aleutian (isls.), U.S. 2/A3
Alex, Okla. (73002) 288/L5
Alexander (arch.), Alaska 146/E4
Alexander (arch.), Alaska 196/L1
Alexander (isl.) 5/B15
Alexander, Ark. (72002) 202/F4
Alexander (lake), Conn. 210/H1
Alexander, Georgia (30801) 217/J4
Alexander (co.), Ill. 222/D6
Alexander, Ill. (62601) 222/D4
Alexander, Iowa (50420) 229/G3
Alexander, Kansas (67513) 232/C3
Alexander○, Maine (†04610) 243/H5
Alexander, Manitoba 179/B5
Alexander, N.Y. (14005) 276/D5
Alexander (co.), N.C. 281/G3
Alexander, N. Dak. (58831) 282/C4
Alexander (cape), Solomon Is. 86/D2
Alexander (arch.), U.S. 4/D16
Alexander, W. Va. (26218) 312/F5
Alexander Bay, S. Africa 102/D7
Alexander Bay, S. Africa 118/B5
Alexander City, Ala. (35010) 195/G5
Alexander Mills, N.C. (†28043) 281/F4
Alexandra, N. Zealand 100/B6
Alexandra, S. Africa 118/H6
Alexandra, Victoria 97/C5
Alexandra Land (isl.), U.S.S.R. 4/A8
Alexandra Land (isl.), U.S.S.R. 48/E1
Alexandretta (Iskenderun), Turkey 63/G4
Alexandretta (gulf), Turkey 63/F4
Alexandria, Ala. (36250) 195/G3
Alexandria, Br. Col. 184/F4
Alexandria, Egypt 2/L4
Alexandria, Egypt 102/E1
Alexandria, Egypt 59/A3
Alexandria, Egypt 111/J2
Alexandria, Ind. (46001) 227/F4
Alexandria, Jamaica 158/J6
Alexandria, Ky. (41001) 237/N3
Alexandria, La. 146/J6
Alexandria, La. 188/H4
Alexandria, La. (71301) 238/E4
Alexandria, Minn. (56308) 255/C5
Alexandria, Mo. (63430) 261/K2
Alexandria, Nebr. (68303) 264/G4
Alexandria○, N.H. (†03222) 268/D4
Alexandria, North. Terr. 93/E5
Alexandria, Ohio (43001) 284/E5
Alexandria, Ontario 177/K2
Alexandria, Pa. (16611) 294/F4
Alexandria, Romania 45/G3
Alexandria, Scotland 15/A1
Alexandria, Scotland 10/A1
Alexandria, S. Dak. (57311) 298/O6
Alexandria, Tenn. (37012) 237/J8
Alexandria, Va. 188/L3
Alexandria (I.C.), Va. (*22301) 307/S3
Alexandria Bay, N.Y. (13607) 276/J2
Alexandrina (lake), S. Australia 94/F6
Alexandroúpolis, Greece 45/H5
Alexis, Ill. (61412) 222/C2
Alexis (riv.), Newf. 166/C3
Alexis Creek, Br. Col. 184/F4
Aleysk, U.S.S.R. 48/J4
Aleza Lake, Br. Col. 184/G3
Alfalfa (co.), Okla. 288/K1
Alfalfa, Okla. (†73015) 288/J4
Al Falluja, Iraq 59/D3
Al Falluja, Iraq 66/C4
Alfaro, Spain 33/F1
Alfatar, Bulgaria 45/H4
Al Fatha, Iraq 59/D2
Al Fatha, Iraq 66/C3
Alfeld, W. Germany 22/C2
Alfenas, Brazil 135/D2
Alférez (riv.), Uruguay 145/E5
Alford, England 13/H4
Alford, Fla. (32420) 212/D6
Alford○, Mass. (†01261) 249/A4
Alford, Scotland 15/F3
Alford, Scotland 10/E2
Alfordsville, Ind. (†47553) 227/C7
Alfred, Maine (04002) 243/B9
Alfred○, Maine (04002) 243/B9
Alfred, N.Y. (14802) 276/E6
Alfred, N. Dak. (58411) 282/N6
Alfred, Ontario 177/K2
Alfredton, N. Zealand 100/F4
Alfreton, England 13/F4
Alga, U.S.S.R. 48/F5
Ålgård, Norway 18/D7
Algarrobo, Chile 138/F3
Algarrobo (pt.), P. Rico 161/A2
Algarrobo del Águila, Argentina 143/C4
Algeciras, Colombia 126/C6
Algeciras, Spain 33/D4
Algemesí, Spain 33/F3
Alger (co.), Mich. 250/C2
Alger, Mich. (48610) 250/E4
Alger, Ohio (45812) 284/C4
Algeria 2/J4
Algeria 102/C2
ALGERIA 106/D3
Algés, Portugal 33/A1
Algete, Spain 33/G4
Alghero, Italy 34/B4
Algiers (cap.), Algeria 102/C1
Algiers (cap.), Algeria 106/E1
Algiers (cap.), Algeria 2/K4
Algiers, Ind. (†47567) 227/C7
Algoa, Ark. (†72112) 202/H3
Algoa (bay), S. Africa 118/D6
Algoa, Texas (†77511) 303/K3
Algodones, N. Mex. (87001) 274/C3
Algoma, Miss. (38820) 256/G2
Algoma (terr. dist.), Ontario 177/J5
Algoma (terr. dist.), Ontario 175/D3
Algoma, Oreg. (†97601) 291/F5
Algoma, W. Va. (24807) 312/D8
Algoma, Wis. (54201) 317/M6
Algoma Mills, Ontario 177/B1
Algona, Iowa (50511) 229/E2
Algona, Wash. (98002) 310/C3
Algonac, Mich. (48001) 250/G6
Algonquin, Ill. (60102) 222/E1
Algonquin (peak), N.Y. 276/M2
Algonquin Park, Ontario 177/F2
Algonquin Prov. Park, Ontario 177/F2
Algonquin Prov. Park, Ontario 175/E3
Algood, Tenn. (38501) 237/K8
Algorta, Uruguay 145/B3
Algrove, Sask. 181/H3
Alhama de Granada, Spain 33/E4
Alhama de Murcia, Spain 33/F4
Alhambra, Alberta 182/C3
Alhambra, Calif. (*91801) 204/C10
Alhambra, Ill. (62001) 222/D5
Al Hawtah, P.D.R. Yemen 59/E6
Al Hilla, Saudi Arabia 59/E5
Al Hoceima, Morocco 106/D1
Alhos Vedros, Portugal 33/B3
Alhué, Estero de (riv.), Chile 138/F4
Alía, Spain 33/D3
'Aliabad, Kuh-e (mt.), Iran 59/F3
'Aliabad, Kuh-e (mt.), Iran 66/G3
Aliağa, Turkey 63/B3
Alibag, India 68/C5
Alibates Flint Quarries Nat'l Mon., Texas 303/C2
Ali-Bayramly, U.S.S.R. 52/G7
Alibeyköyü, Turkey 63/D6
Alicante (prov.), Spain 33/F3
Alicante, Spain 33/F3
Alicante, Spain 7/D5
Alice (lake), Nebr. 264/A2
Alice, N. Dak. (58003) 282/P6
Alice (lake), N. Dak. 282/M3
Alice, Ontario 177/G2
Alice (chan.), Philippines 82/B8
Alice (riv.), Queensland 95/C4
Alice, Texas (78332) 303/F10
Alice Arm, Br. Col. 184/C2
Alicel, Oreg. (†97824) 291/J2
Alice Springs, Australia 87/D8
Alice Springs, North. Terr. 88/E4
Alice Springs, North. Terr. 93/D7
Aliceville, Ala. (35442) 195/B4
Aliceville (dam), Ala. 195/B4
Aliceville, Kansas (66832) 232/G3
Alicia, Ark. (72410) 202/H2
Alicia (bank), Colombia 126/B8
Alicudi (isl.), Italy 34/E5
Alida, Minn. (†56676) 255/C3
Alida, Sask. 181/K6
Aligarh, India 68/D3
'Ali Gharbi, Iraq 66/E4
Alijó, Portugal 33/C2
Alima (riv.), Congo 115/B4
Alimodian, Philippines 82/D5
Alindao, Cent. Afr. Rep. 115/D2
Aline, Georgia (†30420) 217/H6
Aline, Okla. (73716) 288/K1
Alingly, Sask. 181/E2
Alingsås, Sweden 18/H7
Alipore, India 68/F2
Aliquippa, Pa. (15001) 294/B4
Ali Sabieh, Djibouti 111/H5
'Ali Sharqi, Iraq 66/E4
Aliskerovo, U.S.S.R. 48/R3
Alivérion, Greece 45/G6
Aliwal North, S. Africa 118/D6
Alix, Alberta 182/D3
Alix, Ark. (72820) 202/C3
Aljezur, Portugal 33/B4
Aljojuca, Mexico 150/O1
Aljustrel, Portugal 33/B4
Alkabo, N. Dak. (58832) 282/C2
Alkali (lakes), Calif. 204/E2
Alkali (lake), Nev. 266/B1
Alkali (lakes), N. Dak. 282/L3
Alkali Lake, Br. Col. 184/F4
Alkaline (lake), N. Dak. 282/L6
Alken, Belgium 27/G7
Alkmaar, Netherlands 27/F3
Alkmaardermeer (lake), Netherlands 27/F3
Alkol, W. Va. (25501) 312/C6
Al Kufa, Iraq 66/D4
Al Kumait, Iraq 66/E4
Al Kuwait (cap.), Kuwait 59/E4
Al Kuwait (cap.), Kuwait 54/F7
Allagash○, Maine (†04774) 243/F1
Allagash (lake), Maine 243/D3
Allagash (riv.), Maine 243/E2
Allahabad, India 68/E3
Allahabad, India 54/K7
Allaine (riv.), Switzerland 39/D2
Allaire, N.J. (†07727) 273/E3
Allakaket, Alaska (99720) 196/H1
Allakh-Yun', U.S.S.R. 48/O3
Allamakee (co.), Iowa 229/L2
Allaman, Switzerland 39/B4
All American (canal), Calif. 204/K11
Allamoore, Texas (†79855) 303/C11
Allamuchy, N.J. (07820) 273/D2
Allan (mt.), Idaho 220/D4
Allan, Sask. 181/E4
Allan (hills), Sask. 181/E4
Allanmyo, Burma 72/B3
Allanwater, Ontario 175/C2
Allanwater, Ontario 177/G4
'Allaqi, Wadi (dry riv.), Egypt 111/F3
Allard (lake), Québec 174/E2
Allardt, Tenn. (38504) 237/M8
Allardville, New Bruns. 170/E1
Allariz, Spain 33/C1
Allatoona (lake), Georgia 217/C2
Alle, Switzerland 39/D2
Alleene, Ark. (71820) 202/B6
Allegan (co.), Mich. 250/D6
Allegan, Mich. (49010) 250/D6
Allegany (co.), Md. 245/C2
Allegany (co.), N.Y. 276/D6
Allegany, N.Y. (14706) 276/C6
Allegany, Oreg. (97407) 291/D4
Allegany Ind. Res., N.Y. 276/C6
Alleghany, Calif. (95910) 204/E4
Alleghany (co.), N.C. 281/G1
Alleghany (co.), Va. 307/H5
Alleghany, Va. (†24426) 307/H5
Allegheny (res.), N.Y. 276/C7
Allegheny (riv.), N.Y. 276/C6
Allegheny (co.), Pa. 294/B5
Allegheny (res.), Pa. 294/E2
Allegheny (riv.), Pa. 294/D2
Allegheny (mts.), Va. 307/H5
Allegheny Front (mts.), Md. 245/C2
Allegheny Front (mts.), Pa. 294/E5
Allègre (pt.), Guadeloupe 161/A6
Allegre, Ky. (42203) 237/G7
Alleman, Iowa (50007) 229/F5
Allemands (lake), La. 238/M4
Allen, Ala. (36419) 195/C7
Allen, Argentina 143/C4
Allen (co.), Ind. 227/G2
Allen, Lough (lake), Ireland 10/C3
Allen (lake), Ireland 17/E3
Allen, Bog of (marsh), Ireland 17/H5
Allen (co.), Kansas 232/G4
Allen, Kansas (66833) 232/F3
Allen (co.), Ky. 237/J7
Allen, Ky. (41601) 237/R5
Allen (par.), La. 238/E5
Allen, La. (†71469) 238/D3
Allen, Md. (21810) 245/R7
Allen, Mich. (49227) 250/E7
Allen, Miss. (†39083) 256/C7
Allen (mt.), Mont. 262/C2
Allen, Nebr. (68710) 264/H2
Allen (co.), Ohio 284/B4
Allen, Okla. (74825) 288/O5
Allen, Pa. (†17007) 294/H5
Allen, S. Dak. (57714) 298/F7
Allen, Texas (75002) 303/H1
Allendale, England 13/E3
Allendale, Ill. (62410) 222/F5
Allendale, Mo. (†64456) 261/D2
Allendale, N.J. (07401) 273/B1
Allendale (co.), S.C. 296/E6
Allendale, S.C. (29810) 296/E5
Allende, Coahuila, Mexico 150/J2
Allende, Nuevo León, Mexico 150/J4
Allendorf, Iowa (51330) 229/B2
Allenford, Ontario 177/C3
Allenhurst, Georgia (31301) 217/J7
Allenhurst, N.J. (07711) 273/F3
Allen Park, Mich. (48101) 250/B7
Allens Mills, Maine (†04938) 243/C6
Allenspark, Colo. (80510) 208/J2
Allen Springs, Ky. (†42122) 237/J7
Allenstein (Olsztyn), Poland 47/E2
Allenstown○, N.H. (†03275) 268/E5
Allensville, Ky. (42204) 237/G7
Allensville, Ohio (45611) 284/E7
Allensville, Pa. (17002) 294/G4
Allenton, Mo. (63001) 261/M4
Allenton, R.I. (†02852) 249/H6
Allenton, Wis. (53002) 317/K9
Allentown, Georgia (31003) 217/F5
Allentown, N.J. (08501) 273/D3
Allentown, N.Y. (14707) 276/E6
Allentown, Ohio (†45801) 284/B4
Allentown, Pa. 188/L2
Allentown, Pa. (*18101) 294/L4
Allentsteig, Austria 41/C2
Allenville, Ill. (†61951) 222/E4
Allenville, Mo. (†63740) 261/N8
Allenwood, N.J. (08720) 273/E3
Allenwood, Pa. (17810) 294/H3
Alleppey-Cochin, India 68/D7
Aller (riv.), W. Germany 22/C2
Allerton, Ill. (61810) 222/F4
Allerton, Iowa (50008) 229/G7
Allerton, Mass. (02045) 249/E7
Allerton (pt.), Mass. 249/E7
Alley, Jamaica 158/J7
Alley Spring, Mo. (†65466) 261/J8
Allgäu (reg.), W. Germany 22/D5

328 Allgäu

Allgäu Alps (mts.), Austria 41/A3
Allgood, Ala. (35013) 195/F3
Alliance, Alberta 182/E3
Alliance, Nebr. (69301) 264/A2
Alliance, N.C. (28509) 281/R4
Alliance, Ohio (44601) 284/H4
Al Lidam, Saudi Arabia 59/D5
Allier (dept.), France 28/E4
Allier (riv.), France 28/E5
Alligator (lake), Fla. 212/E3
Alligator (pt.), La. 238/L6
Alligator, Miss. (38720) 256/C2
Alligator (lake), N.C. 281/S3
Alligator (riv.), N.C. 281/S3
Alligator Pond, Jamaica 158/H6
Allingåbro, Denmark 21/D5
Allinge-Sandvig, Denmark 18/J9
Allinge-Sandvig, Denmark 21/F8
Allingham, Alberta 182/D4
Allingtown, Conn. (†06516) 210/D3
Allison, Iowa (50602) 229/H3
Allison, N. Mex. (†87301) 274/A3
Allison, Texas (79003) 303/D2
Allisona, Tenn. (†37046) 237/H9
Allisonia, Va. (24310) 307/G7
Allison Park, Pa. (15101) 294/C4
Alliston, Ontario 177/E3
Al Lith, Saudi Arabia 59/C5
Alloa, Scotland 10/B1
Alloa, Scotland 15/C1
Allock, Ky. (41710) 237/P6
Allons, Tenn. (38541) 237/L8
Allouez, Mich. (49805) 250/A1
Allouez, Wis. (†54301) 317/L7
Allow (riv.), Ireland 17/D7
Alloway, N.J. (08001) 273/C4
Alloways (creek), N.J. 273/C4
Allport, Ark. (†72046) 202/G4
Allred, Tenn. (38542) 237/L8
All Saints, Ant. & Bar. 161/E11
All Saints Village, Mo. (†63376) 261/M2
Allsboro, Ala. (†35616) 195/B1
Allsbrook, S.C. (†29569) 296/K3
Allschwil, Switzerland 39/D1
Allview, Md. (†21043) 245/L3
Allyn, Wash. (98524) 310/C3
Alma, Ala. (36501) 195/C8
Alma, Ark. (72921) 202/B3
Alma, Colo. (80420) 208/G4
Alma, Georgia (31510) 217/G7
Alma, Ill. (62807) 222/E5
Alma, Kansas (66401) 232/F2
Alma, Mich. (48801) 250/E5
Alma, Mo. (64001) 261/E4
Alma, Nebr. (68920) 264/E4
Alma, New Bruns. 170/F3
Alma, N. Mex. (†88039) 274/A5
Alma, N.C. (†28364) 281⅔5
Alma, Ontario 177/D4
Alma, Québec 174/C3
Alma, Québec 172/F1
Alma (isl.), Québec 172/F1
Alma, W. Va. (26320) 312/E4
Alma, Wis. (54610) 317/C7
Alma-Ata, U.S.S.R. 2/N3
Alma-Ata, U.S.S.R. 54/J5
Alma-Ata, U.S.S.R. 48/H5
Alma Center, Wis. (54611) 317/E7
Alma City, Minn. (†56048) 255/E6
Almada, Portugal 33/A1
Almadén, Spain 33/D3
Almagro, Spain 33/E3
Almaguer, Colombia 126/B7
Almanor (lake), Calif. 204/D3
Almansa, Spain 33/F3
Almanza, Spain 33/D1
Almanzor (mt.), Spain 33/D2
Almanzora (riv.), Spain 33/F4
Almartha, Mo. (†65773) 261/H9
Almazán, Spain 33/E2
Almaznyy, U.S.S.R. 48/M3
Almeida, Sierra (mts.), Chile 138/C4
Almeida, Portugal 33/C2
Almeirim, Portugal 33/B3
Almelo, Netherlands 27/K4
Almelund, Minn. (55002) 255/F5
Almena, Kansas (67622) 232/C2
Almena, Wis. (54805) 317/B5
Almenara, Brazil 120/E4
Almendra (res.), Spain 33/C2
Almendralejo, Spain 33/C3
Almere, Netherlands 27/G4
Almeria, Nebr. (68811) 264/E3
Almería (prov.), Spain 33/E4
Almería, Spain 7/D5
Almería, Spain 33/E4
Almería (gulf), Spain 33/E4
Al'met'yevsk, U.S.S.R. 52/H3
Älmhult, Sweden 18/H8
Almira, Wash. (99103) 310/G3
Almirantazgo (bay), Chile 138/F11
Almirante, Panama 154/F6
Almirante Montt (gulf), Chile 138/D9
Almirós, Greece 45/F6
Almo, Idaho (83312) 220/E7
Almo, Ky. (42020) 237/E7
Almodóvar, Portugal 33/B4
Almodóvar del Campo, Spain 33/D3
Almoharín, Spain 33/D3
Almoloya del Río, Mexico 150/K1
Almon, Georgia (†30209) 217/E3
Almond, N.Y. (14804) 276/E6
Almond, N.C. (28702) 281/B4
Almond (riv.), Scotland 15/E4
Almond, Wis. (54909) 317/G7
Almont, Colo. (81210) 208/of5
Almont, Mich. (48003) 250/F6
Almont, N. Dak. (58520) 282/H6
Almonte, Ontario 177/H2
Almonte, Spain 33/C4
Almora, India 68/D3
Almora, Minn. (†56551) 255/C4
Almorox, Spain 33/D2
Almota, Wash. (†99111) 310/H4
Al Muadhdham, Saudi Arabia 59/C4
Almudévar, Spain 33/F1
Almuñécar, Spain 33/E4
Almus, Turkey 63/G2
Al Musaiyib, Iraq 59/D3
Al Musaiyib, Iraq 66/D4
Almyra, Ark. (72003) 202/H5
Alna○, Maine (04535) 243/D7
Alness, Scotland 15/D3
Alness (riv.), Scotland 15/D3
Alnwick, England 10/F3
Alnwick, England 13/F2
Alofi (cap.), Niue 87/K7
Aloha, Oreg. (97005) 291/A2
Aloha, Wash. (98550) 310/A3
Alon, Burma 72/B2
Along, India 68/G3
Alonsa, Manitoba 179/C4
Alonso Rojas, Cuba 158/B2
Alor (isl.), Indonesia 85/G7
Álora, Spain 33/D4
Alor Gajah, Malaysia 72/D7
Alor Setar, Malaysia 72/D6
Alorton, Ill. (62207) 222/B2
Alost (Aalst), Belgium 27/D7
Alotau, Papua N.G. 87/E7
Aloysius (mt.), W. Australia 92/E4
Alpachiri, Argentina 143/D4
Alpaugh, Calif. (93201) 204/F8
Alpena, Ark. (72611) 202/D1
Alpena (co.), Mich. 250/F4
Alpena, Mich. (49707) 250/F3
Alpena, S. Dak. (57312) 298/N5
Alpena, W. Va. (†26254) 312/G5
Alpen Siding, Alberta 182/D2
Alpera, Spain 33/F3
Alpes-de-Haute-Provence (dept.), France 28/G5
Alpes-Maritimes (dept.), France 28/G6
Alpha, Ill. (61413) 222/C2
Alpha, Iowa (52130) 229/K3
Alpha, Ky. (42603) 237/L7
Alpha, Mich. (49902) 250/A2
Alpha, Minn. (56111) 255/D7
Alpha, N.J. (08865) 273/C2
Alpha, Queensland 88/H4
Alpharetta, Georgia (30201) 217/D2
Alphen aan de Rijn, Netherlands 27/F4
Alpiarça, Portugal 33/B3
Alpine, Ala. (35014) 195/F4
Alpine, Ariz. (85920) 198/F5
Alpine, Ark. (†71921) 202/D5
Alpine (co.), Calif. 204/F5
Alpine, Calif. (92001) 204/J11
Alpine, Ind. (†47331) 227/G5
Alpine, Ky. (42519) 237/M7
Alpine, N.J. (07620) 273/C1
Alpine, N.Y. (14805) 276/G6
Alpine, Oreg. (97456) 291/D3
Alpine, Tenn. (38543) 237/L8
Alpine, Texas (79830) 303/D12
Alpine, Utah (†84003) 304/C3
Alpine, Wyo. (83128) 319/B2
Alpirsbach, W. Germany 22/C4
Alpnach, Switzerland 39/F3
Alpoca, W. Va. (24710) 312/D7
Alportel, Portugal 33/C4
Alps (mts.) 7/E4
Alpu, Turkey 63/D3
Al Qa'im, Iraq 66/B3
Al Qaiyara, Iraq 66/C3
Al Qosh, Iraq 66/C2
Alquina, Ind. (†47331) 227/G5
Alquízar, Cuba 158/C1
Al Qurna, Iraq 66/E5
Al Qurna, Iraq 59/E3
Alroy Downs, North. Terr. 93/E5
Als (isl.), Denmark 21/C8
Alsace (trad. prov.), France, 29
Alsager, England 13/E4
Alsager, England 10/G2
Alsask, Sask. 181/B4
Alsatia, La. (†71276) 238/H1
Alsdorf, W. Germany 22/B3
Alsea, Oreg. (97324) 291/D3
Alsea (riv.), Oreg. 291/D3
Alsek (riv.), Alaska 196/L3
Alsek (riv.), Br. Col. 184/H1
Alsek (riv.), Yukon 187/E3
Alsen, N. Dak. (58311) 282/N2
Alsey, Ill. (62610) 222/C4
Alsfeld, W. Germany 22/C3
Alsip, Ill. (†60658) 222/B6
Alsózsolca, Hungary 41/F2
Alstead○, N.H. (03602) 268/C5
Alsten (isl.), Norway 18/H4
Alstfjorden (fjord), Norway 18/G3
Alston, England 13/E3
Alston, Georgia (30412) 217/H6
Alston, Mich. (†49958) 250/G1
Alstonville, N.S. Wales 97/G1
Alta, Iowa (51002) 229/C3
Alta, Norway 18/N2
Alta, Utah (84070) 304/C3
Altadena, Calif. (91001) 204/C10
Altaelv (riv.), Norway 18/N2
Alta Gracia, Argentina 143/D3
Altagracia, Cuba 158/G3
Altagracia, Venezuela 124/C2
Altagracia de Orituco, Venezuela 124/E3
Altai (mts.) 54/K5
Altai (mts.), Mongolia 77/C2
Alta Loma, Calif. (91701) 204/E10
Alta Loma, Texas (77510) 303/K3
Altamachi (riv.), Bolivia 136/B5
Altamaha (riv.), Ga. 188/K4
Altamaha (riv.), Georgia 217/H7
Altamaha (sound), Georgia 217/K8
Altamahaw, N.C. (27202) 281/L2
Altamira, Brazil 132/C3
Altamira, Chile 138/B5
Altamira, Dom. Rep. 158/D5
Altamira, Mexico 150/L5
Altamont, Ill. (62411) 222/E4
Altamont, Kansas (67330) 232/G4
Altamont, Manitoba 179/D5
Altamont, Mo. (64620) 261/D3
Altamont, N.Y. (12009) 276/M5
Altamont, Oreg. (†97601) 291/F5
Altamont, S. Dak. (57211) 298/R4
Altamont, Tenn. (37301) 237/K10
Altamont, Utah (84001) 304/D3
Altamonte Springs, Fla. (32701) 212/E3
Altamura, Italy 34/F4
Altar, Mexico 150/D1
Altario, Alberta 182/E4
Altata, Mexico 150/E4
Alt Aussee, Austria 41/B3
Alta Vista, Iowa (50603) 229/J2
Alta Vista, Kansas (66834) 232/F3
Altavista, Va. (24517) 307/K6
Altay, China 77/C2
Altay, Mongolia 77/E2
Altay (mts.), U.S.S.R. 48/J5
Altdorf, Switzerland 39/G3
Altea, Spain 33/G3
Altena, W. Germany 22/B3
Altenburg, E. Germany 22/E3
Altenburg, Mo. (63732) 261/O7
Altepexi, Mexico 150/L7
Alter do Chão, Portugal 33/C3
Altevatn (lake), Norway 18/L2
Altha, Fla. (32421) 212/A1
Altheim, Austria 41/B2
Altheimer, Ark. (72004) 202/G5
Althofen, Austria 41/C3
Alticane, Sask. 181/D3
Altındağ, Turkey 63/E2
Altınova, Turkey 63/B3
Altınözü, Turkey 63/G4
Altıntaş, Turkey 63/C3
Altiplano (plat.) 120/C4
Altkirch, France 28/G4
Altmar, N.Y. (13302) 276/J3
Altmark (reg.), E. Germany 22/D2
Altmühl (riv.), W. Germany 22/D4
Altnaharra, Scotland 15/D2
Alto, Georgia (30510) 217/E2
Alto, La. (71216) 238/G2
Alto, Mich. (49302) 250/D6
Alto, N. Mex. (88312) 274/D5
Alto, Tenn. (†37324) 237/K10
Alto, Texas (75925) 303/J6
Alto, Wis. (†53963) 317/J8
Alto Araguaia, Brazil 132/C7
Alto Chicapa, Angola 115/C6
Alto Cuale, Angola 115/C5
Alto Cuale, Angola 102/D5
Alto de Cantillana (mt.), Chile 138/G4
Alto Lucero, Mexico 150/P1
Alto Molócuè, Mozambique 118/F3
Alton, Ala. (†35210) 195/E3
Alton, Calif. (†95540) 204/A3
Alton, England 13/G6
Alton, England 10/F5
Alton, Ill. 188/J3
Alton, Ill. (62002) 222/A2
Alton, Ind. (†47137) 227/E8
Alton, Iowa (51003) 229/A3
Alton, Kansas (67623) 232/D2
Alton, Ky. (†40342) 237/M4
Alton, La. (†70458) 238/L6
Alton○, Maine (†04468) 243/F5
Alton, Mo. (65606) 261/K9
Alton○, N.H. (03809) 268/E5
Alton, N.Y. (14413) 276/G4
Alton, Nova Scotia 168/E3
Alton, R.I. (†02894) 249/G7
Alton, Utah (84710) 304/B6
Alton, Va. (24520) 307/K7
Alton, W. Va. (†26210) 312/F5
Altona, Ill. (61414) 222/C2
Altona, Ind. (†46738) 227/G2
Altona, Manitoba 179/E5
Altona, Mich. (†49336) 250/D5
Altona, Mo. (†64720) 261/D6
Altona, N.Y. (12910) 276/N1
Altona, Victoria 97/H5
Altona, Victoria 88/K7
Altona (bay), Victoria 97/H5
Altona (bay), Victoria 88/K7
Altona (lag.), Virgin Is. (U.S.) 161/F4
Altona, W. Germany 22/C2
Altonah, Utah (84002) 304/D3
Alton Bay, N.H. (03810) 268/E5
Alton Downs, S. Australia 94/F2
Alto Nevado, Cerro (mt.), Chile 138/E5
Altoona, Ala. (35952) 195/F2
Altoona, Fla. (32702) 212/E3
Altoona, Iowa (50009) 229/G5
Altoona, Kansas (66710) 232/G4
Altoona, Pa. 188/L2
Altoona, Pa. (*16601) 294/F4
Altoona, Wash. (†98643) 310/B4
Altoona, Wis. (54720) 317/C6
Alto Paraguay (dept.), Paraguay 144/C2
Alto Paraná (dept), Paraguay 144/E4
Alto Paraná (riv.), Paraguay 144/D5
Alto Park, Georgia (†30161) 217/B2
Alto Parnaíba, Brazil 132/E5
Alto Pass, Ill. (62905) 222/D6
Alto Ritacuva (mt.), Colombia 120/B2
Alto Ritacuva (mt.), Colombia 126/D4
Altos, Brazil 132/F4
Altos, Paraguay 144/B4
Alto Seco, Bolivia 136/D6
Alto Songo, Cuba 158/J4
Altotonga, Mexico 150/P1
Altötting, W. Germany 22/E4
Alto Velo (chan.), Dom. Rep. 158/C7
Alto Velo (isl.), Dom. Rep. 158/D7
Altrincham, England 13/H2
Altrincham, England 10/G2
Altro, Ky. (41306) 237/P6
Altstätten, Switzerland 39/J2
Altun Ha, Belize 154/C2
Altun Shan (range), China 54/K6
Altun Shan (range), China 77/C4
Altura, Minn. (55910) 255/G6
Alturas, Calif. (96101) 204/E2
Alturas, Fla. (33820) 212/E4
Altus, Ark. (72821) 202/C3
Altus, Okla. (73521) 288/H5
Altus (res.), Okla. 288/H5
Altus A.F.B., Okla. 288/H5
Alubijid, Philippines 82/E6
Alucra, Turkey 63/H2
Alūksne, U.S.S.R. 53/D2
Alula, Somalia 115/K1
Alula, Somalia 102/H3
Alum Bank, Pa. (15521) 294/E5
Alum Bridge, W. Va. (26321) 312/E4
Alum Creek, W. Va. (25003) 312/C6
Aluminé, Argentina 143/B4
Alum Rock, Calif. (†95116) 204/L3
Alus, Iraq 66/C3
Alushta, U.S.S.R. 52/D6
Alva, Fla. (33920) 212/E5
Alva, Ky. (†40977) 237/P7
Alva (lake), New Bruns. 170/D3
Alva, Okla. (73717) 288/J1
Alva, Scotland 10/B1
Alva, Scotland 15/C1
Alva, Wyo. (82711) 319/H1
Alva B. Adams (tunnel), Colo. 208/H2
Alvada, Ohio (44802) 284/D3
Alvadore, Oreg. (97409) 291/D3
Alvalade, Portugal 33/B4
Alvaneu, Switzerland 39/J3
Alvarado, Mexico 150/M7
Alvarado, Minn. (56710) 255/B2
Alvarado, Texas (76009) 303/G5
Álvaro S. Lima (res.), Brazil 135/B3
Alvaton, Georgia (30202) 217/C4
Alvaton, Ky. (42122) 237/J7
Alvdal, Norway 18/G5
Älvdalen, Sweden 18/J6
Alvear, Argentina 143/E2
Alvena, Sask. 181/E3
Alvesta, Sweden 18/J8
Alvin, Br. Col. 184/L2
Alvin, Ill. (61811) 222/F3
Alvin, Texas (77511) 303/J3
Alvin, Wis. (49936) 317/J4
Alvinston, Ontario 177/B5
Alvito, Portugal 33/B3
Älvkarleby, Sweden 18/K6
Alvo, Nebr. (68304) 264/H4
Alvon, W. Va. (†24986) 312/F7
Alvord, Iowa (51230) 229/A2
Alvord (lake), Oreg. 291/J5
Alvord, Texas (76225) 303/G4
Alvordton, Ohio (43501) 284/A2
Älvsborg (co.), Sweden 18/H7
Älvsbyn, Sweden 18/M4
Alvwood, Minn. (†56630) 255/D3
Alvy, W. Va. (26322) 312/E4
Alwar, India 68/D3
Alxa Shamo (des.), China 77/F4
Alxa Youqi, China 77/F4
Alxa Zuoqi, China 77/F4
Aly, Ark. (†72860) 202/D4
Alyangula, North. Terr. 88/F2
Alyangula, North. Terr. 93/E2
Alyth, Scotland 10/E2
Alyth, Scotland 15/E4
Alytus, U.S.S.R. 53/C3
Alz (riv.), W. Germany 22/E4
Alzada, Mont. (59311) 262/M5
Alzette (riv.), Luxembourg 27/J9
Alzey, W. Germany 22/C4
Amacuro (riv.), Venezuela 124/H4
Amadeus (lake), Australia 87/D8
Amadeus (lake), North. Terr. 88/E4
Amadeus (lake), North. Terr. 93/B8
Amadi, Sudan 111/F6
'Amadiya, Iraq 59/D2
'Amadiya, Iraq 66/C2
Amadjuak, N.W.T. 162/J3
Amadjuak (lake), N.W.T. 162/K3
Amadjuak, N.W. Terrs. 187/L3
Amadjuak (lake), N.W. Terrs. 187/L3
Amado, Ariz. (85640) 198/D7
Amador (co.), Calif. 204/E5
Amadora, Portugal 33/A1
Amador City, Calif. (95601) 204/C9
Amagansett, N.Y. (11930) 276/R9
Amagasaki, Japan 81/H8
Amager (isl.), Denmark 21/F6
Amagi, Japan 81/E7
Amagon, Ark. (72005) 202/H2
Amahai, Indonesia 85/H6
Amak (isl.), Alaska 196/F3
Amakura (riv.), Guyana 131/A2
Amakusa (isls.), Japan 81/D7
Åmål, Sweden 18/H7
Amalfi, Colombia 126/C4
Amalfi, Italy 34/E4
Amalga, Utah (†84335) 304/C2
Amalia, N. Mex. (87512) 274/D2
Amaliás, Greece 45/E7
Amalner, India 68/C4
Amambaí, Brazil 132/C8
Amambaí, Serra de (range), Brazil 132/C7
Amambay, Paraguay 144/D3
Amambay, Cordillera de (mts.), Paraguay 144/D-E3
Amami (isl.), Japan 54/P7
Amami (isls.), Japan 81/N5
Amami-O-Shima (isl.), Japan 81/N5
Amana, Iowa (52203) 229/K5
Amanavén, Colombia 126/G6
Amanda, Ohio (43102) 284/E6
Amanda Park, Wash. (98526) 310/A3
Amanos (mts.), Turkey 63/G4
Amantea, Italy 34/E5
Amanu (atoll), Fr. Poly. 87/N7
Amapá (terr.), Brazil 132/D2
Amapá, Brazil 120/D2
Amapá, Brazil 132/D2
Amapala, Honduras 154/D4
Amapari (riv.), Brazil 132/C2
'Amara, Iraq 66/E5
'Amara, Iraq 59/E3
Amarante, Brazil 132/F4
Amarante, Portugal 33/B2
Amaranth, Manitoba 179/D4
Amarapura, Burma 72/B2
Amareleja, Portugal 33/C3
Amarete, Bolivia 136/A4
Amargosa, Brazil 132/F6
Amargosa (range), Calif. 204/J7
Amargosa (riv.), Calif. 204/J7
Amarillas, Cuba 158/D2
Amarillo, Texas 188/F3
Amarillo, Texas 146/H6
Amarillo, Texas (*79101) 303/C2
Amasa, Mich. (49903) 250/G2
Amasra, Turkey 63/E2
Amasya (prov.), Turkey 63/F2
Amasya, Turkey 59/C1
Amasya, Turkey 63/G2
Amatignak (isl.), Alaska 196/K4
Amatitlán, Guatemala 154/B3
Amatlán de los Reyes, Mexico 150/P2
Amay, Belgium 27/G7
Amazon (riv.) 2/G6
Amazon (riv.), Brazil 120/D3
Amazon (riv.), Brazil 132/C3
Amazon (riv.), Colombia 126/E9
Amazon (riv.), Peru 128/F4
Amazon, Sask. 181/F4
Amazonas (state), Brazil 132/G9
Amazonas (comm.), Colombia 126/D8
Amazonas, Cuba 158/F2
Amazonas (dept.), Peru 128/C5
Amazonas (terr.), Venezuela 124/E5
Amazonia, Mo. (64421) 261/C3
Ambala, India 68/D2
Ambalavao, Madagascar 118/H4
Ambam, Cameroon 115/B3
Ambanja, Madagascar 118/H2
Ambarchik, U.S.S.R. 4/B1
Ambarchik, U.S.S.R. 48/R3
Ambato, Ecuador 120/B3
Ambato, Ecuador 128/C3
Ambato Boeny, Madagascar 118/H3
Ambatofinandrahana, Madagascar 118/H4
Ambatolampy, Madagascar 102/G6
Ambatolampy, Madagascar 118/H3
Ambatomainty, Madagascar 118/H3
Ambatondrazaka, Madagascar 118/H3
Ambatondrazaka, Madagascar 102/G6
Ambelau (isl.), Indonesia 85/H6
Amber, Iowa (†52205) 229/L4
Amber (Bobaomby) (cape), Madagascar 102/G6
Amber (Bobaomby) (cape), Madagascar 118/H2
Amber, Okla. (73004) 288/L4
Amber, Wash. (†99004) 310/H3
Amberg, W. Germany 22/D4
Amberg, Wis. (54102) 317/K5
Ambergris (cay), Belize 154/D1
Ambergris (cay), Turks & Caicos 156/D2
Ambérieu-en-Bugey, France 28/F5
Amberley, N. Zealand 100/D5
Amberley, Ohio (†45201) 284/C9
Amberson, Pa. (17210) 294/G5
Ambert, France 28/E5
Ambia, Ind. (47917) 227/C4
Ambikapur, India 68/E4
Ambil (isl.), Philippines 82/C4
Ambilobe, Madagascar 118/H2
Amble, England 13/F2
Amble, Mich. (†49329) 250/D5
Ambler, Alaska (99786) 196/G1
Ambler, Pa. (19002) 294/M5
Ambo, Peru 128/D8
Amboasary, Madagascar 118/H4
Ambodifototra, Madagascar 118/J3
Ambohimahasoa, Madagascar 118/H4
Amboise, France 28/D4
Ambon (Amboina), Indonesia 85/H6
Ambon, Indonesia 54/O10
Ambositra, Madagascar 102/G7
Ambositra, Madagascar 118/H4
Ambovombe, Madagascar 118/H5
Amboy, Calif. (92304) 204/K9
Amboy, Georgia (†31714) 217/E7
Amboy, Ill. (61310) 222/D2
Amboy, Ind. (46911) 227/F3
Amboy, Minn. (56010) 255/D7
Amboy, Wash. (98601) 310/C5
Amboy, W. Va. (26701) 312/G4
Amboyna (cay), Philippines 85/E4
Ambridge, Pa. (15003) 294/B4
Ambriz, Angola 115/B5
Ambrose, Georgia (31512) 217/G7
Ambrose, N. Dak. (58833) 282/D2
Ambrym (isl.), Vanuatu 87/G7
Ambunti, Papua N.G. 85/B6
Amburgey, Ky. (41801) 237/R6
Amchitka (isl.), Alaska 188/D6
Amchitka (isl.), Alaska 196/K4
Amchitka (passage), Alaska 196/K4
Am-Dam, Chad 111/D5
Amderma, U.S.S.R. 52/K1
Amderma, U.S.S.R. 48/F3
Amdo, China 77/D5
Ameagle, W. Va. (25004) 312/D7
Amealco, Mexico 150/K6
Ameca, Mexico 150/H6
Amecameca de Juárez, Mexico 150/L1
Ameghino, Argentina 143/D3
Amel, Belgium 27/J8
Ameland (isl.), Netherlands 27/H2
Amelia (isl.), Fla. 212/E1
Amelia, Italy 34/D3
Amelia, La. (70340) 238/H7
Amelia, Nebr. (68711) 264/F2
Amelia, Ohio (45102) 284/D10
Amelia (co.), Va. 307/M6
Amelia City, Fla. (†32034) 212/E1
Amelia Court House, Va. (23002) 307/N6
Amenia, N.Y. (12501) 276/N7
Amenia, N. Dak. (58004) 282/R6
America, Ill. (†62996) 222/D6
American (highlands), Ant. 2/N10
American (riv.), Calif. 204/C8
Americana, Brazil 135/C3
American Corner, Md. (†21632) 245/P5
American Falls, Idaho (83211) 220/E7
American Falls (res.), Idaho 188/D2
American Falls (res.), Idaho 220/F6
American Fork, Utah (84003) 304/C3
American Highland 5/B4
American Samoa 2/A6
AMERICAN SAMOA 86/N9
American Samoa 87/J7
Americus, Georgia (31709) 217/D6
Americus, Ind. (†47901) 227/D3
Americus, Kansas (66835) 232/F3
Americus, Mo. (†65069) 261/J5
Amersfoort, Netherlands 27/G4
Amersham, England 13/G7
Amery, Man. 162/G4
Amery, Manitoba 179/J2
Amery, Wis. (54001) 317/B5
Amery Ice Shelf, Ant. 2/N9
Amery Ice Shelf 5/C4
Ames, Iowa (50010) 229/F4
Ames, Kansas (66931) 232/E2
Ames, N.Y. (13317) 276/L5
Ames, Okla. (73718) 288/K2
Ames, Texas (†77575) 303/K7
Amesbury, England 13/F6
Amesbury, Mass. (01913) 249/L1
Amesbury○, Mass. (01913) 249/L1
Amesville, Conn. (†06031) 210/B1
Amesville, Ohio (45711) 284/F7
Amet (sound), Nova Scotia 168/E3
Amfilokhía, Greece 45/E6
Ámfissa, Greece 45/F6
Amga (riv.), U.S.S.R. 48/O3
Amguid, Algeria 106/F3
Amgun' (riv.), U.S.S.R. 48/O4
Amherst, Burma 72/C3
Amherst, Colo. (80721) 208/P1
Amherst○, Maine (†04408) 243/G6
Amherst, Mass. (01002) 249/E3
Amherst○, Mass. (01002) 249/E3
Amherst, Nebr. (68812) 264/E4
Amherst○, N.H. (03031) 268/D6
Amherst, N.Y. (†14226) 276/C4
Amherst, N.S. 162/K6
Amherst, Nova Scotia 168/D3
Amherst, Ohio (44001) 284/F3
Amherst (isl.), Ontario 177/H3
Amherst, S. Dak. (57421) 298/O2
Amherst, Texas (79312) 303/B4
Amherst (co.), Va. 307/K5
Amherst, Va. (24521) 307/K5
Amherst (mt.), W. Australia 92/D2
Amherst, Wis. (54406) 317/H7
Amherstburg, Ontario 177/A5
Amherstdale, W. Va. (25607) 312/C7
Amherst Junction, Wis. (54407) 317/H7
Amherst View, Ontario 177/H3
Amidon, N. Dak. (58620) 282/D7
Amiens, France 7/E4
Amiens, France 28/D3
Amindiri (isl.), India 68/C6
Amindivi (isls.), India 68/C6
Aminga, Argentina 143/C2
Amini (Amindiri) (isl.), India 68/C6
'Amir, Ras (cape), Libya 111/D1
Amiret, Minn. (56112) 255/C6
Amisk, Alberta 182/E3
Amisk (lake), Sask. 181/M4
Amissville, Va. (22002) 307/M3
Amistad (res.) 188/F5
Amistad (res.), Mexico 150/J2
Amistad, N. Mex. (88410) 274/F3
Amistad (dam), Texas 303/C8
Amistad (res.), Texas 303/C8
Amistad Nat'l Rec. Area, Texas 303/D8
Amite, La. (70422) 238/K5
Amite (riv.), La. 238/L2
Amite (co.), Miss. 256/C8
Amite (riv.), Miss. 256/C9
Amity, Ark. (71921) 202/D5
Amity, Georgia (†30817) 217/G3
Amity, Ind. (†46131) 227/E6
Amity, Mo. (†64469) 261/D3
Amity, Oreg. (97101) 291/D2
Amity, Pa. (15311) 294/B5
Amityville, N.Y. (11701) 276/O9
Åmli, Norway 18/F7
Amlia (isl.), Alaska 196/L4
Amlia (passage), Alaska 196/L4
Amlwch, Wales 10/D4
Amlwch, Wales 13/C4
Amma, W. Va. (25005) 312/D5
Amman (dist.), Jordan 65/D4
Amman (cap.), Jordan 54/E6
Amman (cap.), Jordan 65/D4
Amman (cap.), Jordan 59/C3
Ammanford, Wales 13/C6
Ammersee (lake), W. Germany 22/D4
Ammie, Ky. (†40933) 237/O6
Ammon, Idaho (†83401) 220/G6
Ammon, Va. (23822) 307/N6
Ammonoosuc (riv.), N.H. 268/D3
Amnat, Thailand 72/E4
Amo, Ind. (46103) 227/D5
Amol, Iran 59/F2
Amol, Iran 66/H2
Amonate, Va. (24601) 307/E6
Amor, Minn. (†56515) 255/C4
Amora, Portugal 33/A1
Amorbach, W. Germany 22/C4
Amoret, Mo. (64722) 261/C6
Amorgós (isl.), Greece 45/G7
Amorita, Okla. (73719) 288/K1
Amory, Miss. (38821) 256/H3
Amos, Que. 162/J6
Amos, Québec 174/B3
Åmotfors, Sweden 18/H7
Amoy (Xiamen), China 77/J7
Amozoc de Mota, Mexico 150/N2
Ampana, Indonesia 85/G6
Ampanihy, Madagascar 118/G4
Amparo, Brazil 135/C3
Amper (riv.), W. Germany 22/D4
Amphitrite (isls.), China 85/E2
Amposta, Spain 33/G2
Ampthill, England 13/G5
Amqui, Québec 172/B2
'Amran, Yemen Arab Rep. 59/D6
Amravati, India 68/D4
Amreli, India 68/C4
Amriswil, Switzerland 39/H1
'Amrit (ruins), Syria 63/F5
Amritsar, India 54/J6

Antsiranana 329

Amritsar, India 68/C2
Amrum (isl.), W. Germany 22/C1
Amsden, Ohio (44803) 284/D3
Amstelveen, Netherlands 27/B5
Amsterdam (isl.) 2/N7
Amsterdam, Georgia (31734) 217/D9
Amsterdam, Mo. (64723) 261/D6
Amsterdam, Mont. (†59741) 262/E5
Amsterdam (cap.), Netherlands 27/B4
Amsterdam (cap.), Netherlands 7/E3
Amsterdam, N.Y. (12010) 276/M5
Amsterdam, Ohio (43903) 284/J5
Amsterdam, Sask. 181/J4
Amstetten, Austria 41/C2
Amston, Conn. (06231) 210/F2
Am-Timan, Chad 111/D5
Amuay, Venezuela 124/C2
Amudar'ya (riv.) 2/N3
Amudar'ya (riv.), U.S.S.R. 54/H5
Amudar'ya (riv.), U.S.S.R. 48/G5
Amukta (isl.), Alaska 196/D4
Amukta (passage), Alaska 196/D4
Amuku (mts.), Guyana 131/B4
Amulet, Sask. 181/G6
Amund Ringnes (isl.), N.W.T. 162/M3
Amund Ringnes (isl.), N.W. Terrs. 187/J2
Amundsen (sea) 2/D10
Amundsen (bay) 5/C3
Amundsen (sea) 5/B13
Amundsen (gulf), Canada 4/B16
Amundsen (gulf), N.W.T. 162/D1
Amundsen (gulf), N.W.T. 146/F2
Amundsen (gulf), N.W. Terrs. 187/F2
Amundsen-Scott Station 5/A14
Amuntai, Indonesia 85/F6
Amur (riv.) 2/R3
Amur (riv.) 54/P5
Amur (Heilong Jiang) (riv.), China 77/L2
'Amur, Wadi (dry riv.), Sudan 111/G4
Amur (riv.), U.S.S.R. 48/O4
Amurang, Indonesia 85/G5
Amursk, U.S.S.R. 48/O4
Amy, Kansas (†67850) 232/B3
Amya (pass), Burma 72/C4
Amya (pass), Thailand 72/C4
Amyun, Lebanon 63/F5
An, Burma 72/B3
'Ana, Iraq 66/B3
'Ana, Iraq 59/D3
Anaa (atoll), Fr. Poly. 87/M7
Anabar (riv.), U.S.S.R. 48/M2
Anabel, Mo. (63431) 261/H3
Ana Branch, Darling (riv.), N.S. Wales 97/A3
'Anabta, West Bank 65/C3
Anacapa (isl.), Calif. 204/F10
Anaco, Venezuela 124/F3
Anacoco, La. (71403) 238/D4
Anacoco (lake), La. 238/D4
Anaconda, Mont. 188/D1
Anaconda-Deer Lodge County, Mont. (59711) 262/C4
Anacortes, Wash. (98221) 310/C2
Anacostia, D.C. (20020) 245/F5
Anacostia (riv.), D.C. 245/F5
Anadarko, Okla. (73005) 288/K4
Anadia, Portugal 33/B2
Anadolufeneri, Turkey 63/D5
Anadoluhisarı, Turkey 63/D6
Anadyr', U.S.S.R 2/T2
Anadyr', U.S.S.R. 4/C1
Anadyr' (gulf), U.S.S.R. 4/C18
Anadyr' (gulf), U.S.S.R. 54/V3
Anadyr' (riv.), U.S.S.R. 54/U3
Anadyr' (riv.), U.S.S.R. 4/C1
Anadyr', U.S.S.R. 48/S3
Anadyr' (gulf), U.S.S.R. 48/T3
Anadyr' (range), U.S.S.R. 48/S3
Anadyr' (riv.), U.S.S.R. 48/S3
Anadyr' U.S.S.R. 54/U3
Anáfi (isl.), Greece 45/G7
Anagance, New Bruns. 170/E3
Anaheim, Calif. 188/C4
Anaheim, Calif. (*92801) 204/D11
Anahim Lake, Br. Col. 184/E4
Anahola, Hawaii (96703) 218/C1
Anáhuac, Chihuahua, Mexico 150/F2
Anáhuac, Nuevo León, Mexico 150/J3
Anahuac, Texas (77514) 303/K8
Anaï (well), Algeria 106/G4
Anai Mudi (mt.), India 68/D6
'Anaiza, Saudi Arabia 59/D4
'Anaiza, Saudi Arabia 54/F7
Anak, N. Korea 81/B4
Anakapalle, India 68/E5
Anaktalik Brook (riv.), Newf. 166/B2
Anaktuvuk Pass, Alaska (99721) 196/H1
Analalava, Madagascar 118/H2
Ana María (gulf), Cuba 158/F3
Anambas (isls.), Indonesia 85/D5
Anambra (state), Nigeria 106/F7
Anamoose, N. Dak. (58710) 282/K4
Anamosa, Iowa (52205) 229/L4
Anamur, Turkey 63/E4
Anamur (cape), Turkey 59/B2
Anamur (cape), Turkey 63/E5
Anan, Japan 81/G7
Anandale, La. (†71301) 238/F4
Ananea, Bolivia 136/A4
Anantapur, India 68/D6
Anantnag, India 68/D2
Anapa, U.S.S.R. 52/E6
Anápolis, Brazil 132/D7
Anápolis, Brazil 120/E4
Anar, Iran 66/J5
Anar, Iran 59/G3
Anarak, Iran 66/H4
Anarak, Iran 59/F3
Anar Darreh, Afghanistan 59/H3
Anar Darreh, Afghanistan 68/A2
Añasco, P. Rico 161/A1
Añasco, P. Rico 156/F1
Añasco (bay), P. Rico 161/A1
Anastasia (isl.), Fla. 212/E2
Anatahan (isl.), No. Marianas 87/E4
Anatolia (reg.), Turkey 63/D3
Anatone, Wash. (99401) 310/H4
Añatuya, Argentina 143/D2
Anauá (riv.), Brazil 132/B2
Anawalt, W. Va. (24808) 312/D8
Anaye (well), Niger 106/G5
Anbar (gov.), Iraq 66/B4
Ancash (dept.), Peru 128/D7
Ancaster, Ontario 177/D4
Anceney, Mont. (†59741) 262/E5
Ancenis, France 28/C4
Anchieta, Brazil 132/F8
Ancho, N. Mex. (†88301) 274/D5
Anchor, Ill. (61720) 222/E3
Anchorage, Alaska 188/D6
Anchorage, Alaska 146/D3
Anchorage, Alaska (*99501) 196/B1
Anchorage, Ky. (40223) 237/L2
Anchorage, U.S. 2/B2
Anchorage, U.S. 4/D17
Anchorena, Argentina 143/C4
Anchor Point, Alaska (99556) 196/B2
Anchor Point, Newf. 166/C3
Anchorville, Mich. (48004) 250/G6
Anchovy, Jamaica 158/H5
Ancienne-Lorette, Québec 172/H3
Ancitas (cay), Cuba 158/F3
Anclote (keys), Fla. 212/D3
Anco, Ky. (41711) 237/P6
Ancohuma (mt.), Bolivia 120/C4
Ancohuma, Nevada (mt.), Bolivia 136/A4
Ancón, Peru 128/D8
Ancona, Ill. (61311) 222/E2
Ancona (prov.), Italy 34/D3
Ancona, Italy 34/D3
Ancona, Italy 7/F4
Ancón de Sardinas (bay), Colombia 126/A7
Ancón de Sardinas (bay), Ecuador 128/C2
Ancoraimes, Bolivia 136/A4
Ancram, N.Y. (12502) 276/N6
Ancroft, England 13/F2
Ancrum, Scotland 15/F5
Ancud, Chile 120/B7
Ancud, Chile 138/D4
Ancud (gulf), Chile 138/D4
Anda (Anta), China 77/L2
Andacollo, Argentina 143/B4
Andacollo, Chile 138/A8
Andado, North. Terr. 93/D8
Andahuaylas, Peru 128/F9
Andale, Kansas (67001) 232/E4
Andalgalá, Argentina 143/C2
Åndalsnes, Norway 18/F5
Andalusia, Ala. (36420) 195/E8
Andalusia, Ill. (61232) 222/C2
Andalusia, Pa. (†19020) 294/N5
Andalusia (reg.), Spain 33/C4
Andaman (sea) 54/L8
Andaman (sea), Burma 72/B4
Andaman (isls.), India 2/P5
Andaman (isls.), India 54/L8
Andaman (isls.), India 68/G6
Andaman (sea), India 68/G6
Andaman and Nicobar Isls. (terr.), India 68/G6
Andamarca, Bolivia 136/B6
Andamarca, Peru 128/E8
Andamooka, S. Australia 94/E4
Andapa, Madagascar 118/H2
Andaraí, Brazil 132/F6
Andau, Austria 41/D3
Andeer, Switzerland 39/H3
Andelfingen, Switzerland 39/G1
Andenne, Belgium 27/G8
Anderlecht, Belgium 27/B9
Anderlues, Belgium 27/E8
Andermatt, Switzerland 39/G3
Andernach, W. Germany 22/B3
Anderson, Ala. (35610) 195/D1
Anderson, Alaska (†99760) 196/H2
Anderson, Argentina 143/F7
Anderson, Calif. (96007) 204/C3
Anderson, Ind. 188/J2
Anderson, Ind. (*46011) 227/F4
Anderson (riv.), Ind. 227/D8
Anderson, Iowa (†51652) 229/B7
Anderson (co.), Kansas 232/G3
Anderson (co.), Ky. 237/M5
Anderson (lake), Manitoba 179/D2
Anderson (pt.), Manitoba 179/F3
Anderson, Mo. (64831) 261/D9
Anderson (riv.), N.W.T. 162/D2
Anderson (riv.), N.W. Terrs. 187/F3
Anderson, S.C. 188/K4
Anderson (co.), S.C. 296/B2
Anderson, S.C. (*29621) 296/B2
Anderson (bay), Tasmania 99/D2
Anderson (co.), Tenn. 237/N8
Anderson, Tenn. (†37376) 237/K10
Anderson (co.), Texas 303/J6
Anderson, Texas (77830) 303/J7
Anderson Ranch (res.), Idaho 220/C6
Andersonville, Georgia (31711) 217/D6
Andersonville, Ind. (†47024) 227/G5
Andersonville, Tenn. (37705) 237/O8
Andersonville, Va. (23911) 307/L6
Andersonville Nat'l Hist. Site, Georgia 217/D6
Andes (range), 120/B2-6
Andes, Cordillera de los (mts.), Argentina 143/C2
Andes, Cordillera de los (mts.), Chile 138/C5,E
Andes, Colombia 126/C5
Andes, Mont. (†59218) 262/M3
Andes, N.Y. (13731) 276/L6
Andes, Cordillera de los (mts.), Peru 128/F10
Andes (lake), S. Dak. 298/N7
Andheri, India 68/B7
Andhra Pradesh (state), India 68/D5
Andijk, Netherlands 27/G3
Andikíthira (isl.), Greece 45/F8
Andilamena, Madagascar 118/H3
Andimeshk, Iran 66/F4
Anding, Miss. (†39040) 256/D5
Andırın, Turkey 63/G4
Ándissa, Greece 45/H6
Andizhan, U.S.S.R. 54/J5
Andizhan, U.S.S.R. 48/H5
Andkhvoy, Afghanistan 68/A1
Andkhvoy, Afghanistan 59/H2
Andoas Nuevo, Ecuador 128/D4
Andoma, Zaire 115/E3
Andong, S. Korea 81/D5
Andorra 7/E4
ANDORRA 33/G1
Andorra, Spain 33/F2
Andorra la Vella (cap.), Andorra 33/G1
Andover○, Conn. (06232) 210/F2
Andover, England 10/F5
Andover, England 13/F6
Andover, Ill. (61233) 222/C2
Andover, Iowa (52701) 229/N5
Andover, Kansas (67002) 232/E4
Andover, Maine (04216) 243/B6
Andover○, Maine (04216) 243/B6
Andover, Mass. (01810) 249/K2
Andover○, Mass. (01810) 249/K2
Andover, Minn. (†55303) 255/E5
Andover○, N.H. (03216) 268/D5
Andover, N.J. (07821) 273/D2
Andover, N.Y. (14806) 276/E6
Andover, Ohio (44003) 284/J2
Andover, S. Dak. (57422) 298/O3
Andover○, Vt. (†05143) 268/B5
Andover, Va. (24215) 307/C7
Andøya (isl.), Norway 18/J2
Andradas, Brazil 135/C3
Andradina, Brazil 132/D8
Andraitx, Spain 33/H3
Andravídha, Greece 45/E6
Andre (lake), Newf. 166/A3
Andreafski (Saint Marys), Alaska (†99658) 196/F2
Andreanof (isls.), Alaska 196/L4
Andreas (cape), Cyprus 63/F5
Andrelândia, Brazil 135/D2
Andrés, Nicaragua 154/F3
Andrespol, Poland 47/D3
Andrew, Alberta 182/D3
Andrew, Iowa (52030) 229/M4
Andrew, La. (†70548) 238/F6
Andrew (co.), Mo. 261/C3
Andrew (isl.), Nova Scotia 168/H3
Andrew Johnson Nat'l Hist. Site, Tenn. 237/R8
Andrews, (†21626) 245/O7
Andrews, Ind. (46702) 227/F3
Andrews, N.C. (28901) 281/B4
Andrews, Oreg. (†97732) 291/J5
Andrews, S.C. (29510) 296/H5
Andrews (co.), Texas 303/B5
Andrews, Texas (79714) 303/B5
Andrews A.F.B., Md. 245/G5
Andreyevka, U.S.S.R. 52/H4
Andria, Italy 34/F4
Androka, Madagascar 118/G5
Andros (isl.), Bahamas 146/L7
Andros (isl.), Bahamas 156/B1
Ándros, Greece 45/G7
Ándros (isl.), Greece 45/G7
Androscoggin (co.), Maine 243/C7
Androscoggin (riv.), Maine 243/C7
Androscoggin (riv.), N.H. 268/E2
Androth (isl.), India 68/C6
Andrychów, Poland 47/D4
Andsfjorden (fjord), Norway 18/K2
Andújar, Spain 33/D3
Andul, India 68/F2
Andulo, Angola 102/D6
Andulo, Angola 115/C6
Anéfis, Mali 106/E5
Anegada (isl.), Virgin Is. (Br.) 156/H1
Anegada (passage), Virgin Is. (Br.) 156/F3
Aného (Anécho), Togo 106/E7
Aneityum (Anatom) (isl.), Vanuatu 87/H8
'Aneiza, Jebel (mt.), Iraq 66/A4
'Aneiza, Jebel (mt.), Iraq 59/C3
'Aneiza, Jebel (mt.), Jordan 59/C3
'Aneiza, Jebel (mt.), Saudi Arabia 59/C3
Añelo, Argentina 143/C4
Anerley, Sask. 181/D4
Aneroid, Sask. 181/D6
Aneta, N. Dak. (58212) 282/P4
Aneth, Utah (84510) 304/E6
Aneto (peak), Spain 33/G1
Angaki (Quirino), Philippines 82/C2
Angamos (isl.), Chile 138/D8
Angamos (pt.), Chile 138/A4
Angara (riv.), U.S.S.R. 54/L4
Angara (riv.), U.S.S.R. 48/K4
Angarsk, U.S.S.R. 54/M4
Angarsk, U.S.S.R. 48/L4
Angas Downs, North. Terr. 93/C8
Angaston, S. Australia 94/F6
Angaur (isl.), Belau 87/D5
Ånge, Sweden 18/J5
Ange-Gardien, Québec 172/E4
Angel (isl.), Calif. 204/J2
Angel (falls), Venezuela 120/C2
Angel (fall), Venezuela 124/G5
Angela, Mont. (59312) 262/K4
Ángel de la Guarda (isl.), Mexico 150/C2
Angeles, Philippines 82/C3
Ángeles, P. Rico 161/B2
Ängelholm, Sweden 18/H8
Angélica, Argentina 143/E5
Angelica, N.Y. (14709) 276/E6
Angelica, Wis. (†54162) 317/K6
Angelina (co.), Texas 303/K6
Angelina (riv.), Texas 303/K6
Angelo, Wis. (†54656) 317/E8
Angels Camp, Calif. (95222) 204/E5
Angelus, S.C. (†29718) 296/G2
Angerman (riv.), Sweden 7/F2
Ångermanälven (riv.), Sweden 18/K5
Angermünde, E. Germany 22/E2
Angers, France 7/D4
Angers, France 28/C4
Angers, Québec 172/B4
Angicos, Brazil 132/G4
Angie, La. (70426) 238/L5
Angier, N.C. (27501) 281/M4
Angijak (isl.), N.W. Terrs. 187/M3
Angikuni (lake), N.W. Terrs. 187/J3
Angkor Wat (ruins), Cambodia 72/E4
Angle, Utah (†84712) 304/C5
Angle Inlet, Minn. (56711) 255/C1
Anglem (mt.), N. Zealand 100/A7
Anglesey (isl.), Wales 13/C4
Anglesey (isl.), Wales 10/D4
Angleton, Texas (77515) 303/J8
Anglia, Sask. 181/C4
Angliers, Québec 174/B3
Angmagssalik, Greenl. 4/C11
Angmagssalik, Greenland 146/Q3
Ango, Zaire 115/E3
Angoche, Mozambique 118/G3
Angoche, Mozambique 102/G6
Angoche (isl.), Mozambique 118/G3
Angol, Chile 138/D1
Angola 2/K6
Angola 102/D6
ANGOLA 115/C6
Angola, Del. (†19966) 245/T6
Angola, Ind. (46703) 227/G1
Angola, Kansas (67331) 232/G4
Angola, La. (70712) 238/G5
Angola, N.Y. (14006) 276/C5
Angola (swamp), N.C. 281/O5
Angola on the Lake, N.Y. (†14006) 276/B5
Angoon, Alaska (99820) 196/M1
Angora, Minn. (55703) 255/F3
Angora, Nebr. (69331) 264/A3
Angoram, Papua N.G. 85/B6
Angostura (falls), Colombia 120/B2
Angostura (falls), Colombia 126/E6
Angostura, Mexico 150/E4
Angostura (res.), S. Dak. 298/B7
Angoulême, France 28/D5
Angoumois (trad. prov.), France, 29
Angra do Heroísmo (dist.), Portugal 33/C1
Angra do Heroísmo, Portugal 33/C1
Angra dos Reis, Brazil 135/D3
Angren, U.S.S.R. 48/H5
Ang Thong, Thailand 72/C4
Anguil, Argentina 143/D4
Anguilla (isl.) 146/M8
ANGUILLA 156
Anguilla, Anguilla 156/F3
Anguilla, Miss. (38721) 256/C5
Anguillara Sabazia, Italy 34/F6
Anguille (cape), Newf. 166/C4
Angurugu, North. Terr. 93/E3
Angus, Iowa (†50220) 229/E5
Angus, Minn. (56712) 255/B2
Angus, Ontario 177/E3
Angus (trad. prov.), Scotland, 15/B5
Angusville, Manitoba 179/A4
Angwin, Calif. (94508) 204/C5
Anhée, Belgium 27/F8
Anholt, Denmark 21/E4
Anholt (isl.), Denmark 21/E4
Anholt (isl.), Denmark 18/G8
Anhua, China 77/H6
Anhui (Anhwei), China 77/J5
Aniak, Alaska (99557) 196/G2
Aniakchak (vol.), Alaska 196/G3
Aniakchak Nat'l Mon., Alaska 196/G3
Aniakchak Nat'l Preserve, Alaska 196/G3
Anicuns, Brazil 132/D7
Aniene (riv.), Italy 34/F6
Animas (riv.), Colo. 208/D8
Animas, N. Mex. (88020) 274/A7
Animas (riv.), N. Mex. 274/B1
Añimbo, Bolivia 136/C7
Anin, Burma 72/C4
Anin, West Bank 65/C2
Anina, Romania 45/E3
Anita, Iowa (50020) 229/D6
Anita, Pa. (15711) 294/D3
Aniva (cape), U.S.S.R. 48/P5
Aniwa, Wis. (54408) 317/H6
'Anjara, Jordan 65/D3
Anjidiv (Angediva) (isl.), India 68/C6
Anjou (trad. prov.), France, 29
Anjou, Québec 172/H4
Anjouan (isl.), Comoros 102/G6
Anjouan (isl.), Comoros 118/G2
Anju, N. Korea 81/B4
Anjum, Netherlands 27/J2
Ankang, China 77/G5
Ankara (prov.), Turkey 63/E3
Ankara (cap.), Turkey 63/E3
Ankara (cap.), Turkey 2/L4
Ankara (cap.), Turkey 54/E5
Ankara (cap.), Turkey 59/B2
Ankara (riv.), Turkey 63/D3
Ankazoabo, Madagascar 118/G4
Ankeny, Iowa (50021) 229/F5
Anker (riv.), England 10/G3
Ankerton, Alberta 182/D3
Ankhor, Somalia 115/J1
Anking (Anqing), China 77/J5
Anklam, E. Germany 22/E2
Ankober, Ethiopia 111/H6
Ankona, Fla. (†33450) 212/F4
Ankoro, Zaire 115/E5
An Loc (Binh Long), Vietnam 72/E5
Anlu, China 77/H5
Anmoore, W. Va. (26323) 312/F4
Ann (cape), Mass. 249/M2
Anna, Ill. (62906) 222/D6
Anna, Ky. (†42270) 237/J6
Anna, Ohio (45302) 284/B5
Anna, Texas (75003) 303/H4
Anna (lke), Va. 307/N4
Annaba, Algeria 102/C1
Annaba, Algeria 106/F1
Annabella, Utah (84711) 304/B5
Annaberg-Buchholz, E. Germany 22/E3
Anna Creek, S. Australia 94/D3
Annada, Mo. (63330) 261/L4
Annadel, Tenn. (†37770) 237/M8
Annagry, Ireland 17/E1
Annaheim, Sask. 181/G3
Annai, Guyana 131/B4
An Najaf (gov.), Iraq 66/C5
An Najaf, Iraq 59/D3
An Najaf, Iraq 66/D5
An Najaf, Iraq 54/F6
Annalee (riv.), Ireland 17/G3
Annalong, N. Ireland 17/K3
Annaly (bay), Virgin Is. (U.S.) 161/E3
Anna Maria, Fla. (33501) 212/D4
Annan, Scotland 15/E6
Annan, Scotland 10/E3
Annan (riv.), Scotland 15/E5
Annandale, Minn. (55302) 255/D5
Annandale, N.J. (08801) 273/D2
Annandale, Va. (22003) 307/S3
Annandale-on-Hudson, N.Y. (12504) 276/N6
Anna Plains, W. Australia 92/C2
Annapolis, Calif. (95412) 204/B5
Annapolis, Ill. (62413) 222/F4
Annapolis (cap.), Md. (*21401) 245/M5
Annapolis (cap.), Md. 188/L3
Annapolis, Mo. (63620) 261/L8
Annapolis (co.), Nova Scotia 168/C4
Annapolis (basin), Nova Scotia 168/C4
Annapolis (riv.), Nova Scotia 168/C4
Annapolis Junction, Md. (20701) 245/M4
Annapolis Royal, Nova Scotia 168/C4
Annapurna (mt.), Nepal 68/E3
Ann Arbor, Mich. 188/K2
Ann Arbor, Mich. (*48103) 250/F6
Anna Regina, Guyana 131/B2
Annascaul, Ireland 17/B7
An Nasiriya, Iraq 59/E3
An Nasiriya, Iraq 66/D5
Annat, Scotland 15/C3
Annaville, Québec 172/E3
Annawan, Ill. (61234) 222/C2
Annbank Station, Scotland 15/D5
Anne (mt.), Tasmania 99/C4
Anne Arundel (co.), Md. 245/M4
Annecy, France 28/G5
Annemanie, Ala. (36721) 195/D6
Anner (riv.), Ireland 17/F7
Anneta, Ky. (†42754) 237/J6
Annette, Alaska (99920) 196/N2
An Nhon, Vietnam 72/F4
Annieopscotch (mts.), Newf. 166/C4
Anniston, Ala. 188/J4
Anniston, Ala. (36201) 195/G3
Anniston, Mo. (63820) 261/O9
Anniston Army Depot, Ala. 195/F3
Annobon (isl.), Equat. Guinea 102/C5
Annona, Texas (75550) 303/K4
Annonay, France 28/F5
Annotto Bay, Jamaica 156/C3
Annotto Bay, Jamaica 158/K6
Annville, Ky. (40402) 237/O6
Annville, Pa. (17003) 294/J5
Annweiler am Trifels, W. Germany 22/B4
Anoka (co.), Minn. 255/E5
Anoka, Minn. (55303) 255/E5
Anoka, Nebr. (†68722) 264/F2
Anola, Manitoba 179/F5
Ano Nuevo (pt.), Calif. 204/J4
Áno Viánnos, Greece 45/G8
Anóyia, Greece 45/G8
Anqing (Anking), China 77/J5
Ans, Belgium 27/H7
Ansager, Denmark 21/B6
Ansai, China 77/G4
Ansbach, W. Germany 22/D4
Anse à Galets, Haiti 158/B6
Anse-à-Pitre, Haiti 158/C6
Anse-au-Griffon, Québec 172/D1
Anse-aux-Gascons, Québec 172/D2
Anse-à-Veau, Haiti 158/B6
Anse-Bertrand, Guadeloupe 161/A5
Anse-Bleue, New Bruns. 170/E1
Anse Boileau, Seychelles 118/H5
Anse-d'Hainault, Haiti 158/A6
Anse la Raye, St. Lucia 161/F6
Anselmo, Nebr. (68813) 264/E3
Anser Group (isls.), Tasmania 99/C1
Anserma, Colombia 126/B5
Anse Rouge, Haiti 158/B5
Anse Royale, Seychelles 118/H5
Anshan, China 77/K3
Anshan, China 54/O5
Anshun, China 77/G6
Ansley, Ala. (36001) 195/F7
Ansley, La. (†71228) 238/E2
Ansley, Nebr. (68814) 264/E3
Anson, Kansas (†67103) 232/E4
Anson, Maine (04911) 243/D6
Anson○, Maine (04911) 243/D6
Anson (pt.), Norfolk I. 88/K5
Anson (bay), Norfolk I. 88/K5
Anson (co.), N.C. 281/J4
Anson (bay), North. Terr. 88/D2
Anson, Texas (79501) 303/E5
Ansŏng, S. Korea 81/C5
Ansongo, Mali 106/E5
Ansonia, Conn. (06401) 210/C3
Ansonia, Ohio (45303) 284/A5
Ansonville, N.C. (28007) 281/J4
Ansonville, Pa. (†16656) 294/E4
Ansted, W. Va. (25812) 312/D6
Anta, Peru 128/F9
Antabamba, Peru 128/F10
Antakya, Turkey 59/C2
Antakya, Turkey 63/G4
Antalaha, Madagascar 118/J2
Antalaha, Madagascar 102/H6
Antalya (prov.), Turkey 63/D4
Antalya, Turkey 54/D6
Antalya, Turkey 63/D4
Antalya, Turkey 59/B2
Antalya (gulf), Turkey 63/D4
Antalya (gulf), Turkey 59/B2
Antananarivo (prov.), Madagascar 118/H3
Antananarivo (cap.), Madagascar 2/M6
Antananarivo (cap.), Madagascar 102/G6
Antananarivo (cap.), Madagascar 118/H3
Antarctic (pen.), Ant. 2/G9
Antarctic (pen.) 5/C15
Antarctica 2/E11
ANTARCTICA 5
Antarctic Circle 2/A9
An Teallach (mt.), Scotland 15/C3
Antelope (creek), Idaho 220/E6
Antelope, Kansas (66836) 232/F3
Antelope, Mont. (59211) 262/M2
Antelope (co.), Nebr. 264/F2
Antelope (range), Nev. 266/E3
Antelope, Oreg. (97001) 291/G3
Antelope (creek), Oreg. 291/K5
Antelope (res.), Oreg. 291/K5
Antelope, Sask. 181/C5
Antelope (lake), Sask. 181/C5
Antelope (creek), S. Dak. 298/D3
Antelope, Texas (76350) 303/F4
Antelope (isl.), Utah 304/B3
Antelope (creek), Wyo. 319/G2
Antelope (hills), Wyo. 319/D3
Antequera, Paraguay 144/D4
Antequera, Spain 33/D4
Antero (mt.), Colo. 208/G5
Antero (res.), Colo. 208/H5
Antes Fort, Pa. (17720) 294/H3
Anthon, Iowa (51004) 229/B4
Anthony, Fla. (32617) 212/D2
Anthony, Ind. (†47302) 227/G4
Anthony, Kansas (67003) 232/D4
Anthony, N. Mex. (88021) 274/C6
Anthony, R.I. (†02816) 249/H6
Anthony, Texas (88021) 303/A10
Anthony, W. Va. (24914) 312/F7
Anthony Lagoon, North. Terr. 88/E3
Anthony Lagoon, North. Terr. 93/D4
Anthracite, Alberta 182/C4
Anti-Atlas (ranges), Morocco 106/C3
Antibes, France 28/G6
Anticosti (isl.), Que. 146/M5
Anticosti (isl.), Que. 162/K6
Anticosti (isl.), Québec 174/E3
Antietam, Md. (†21782) 245/H3
Antietam (creek), Md. 245/H2
Antietam Nat'l Battlefield, Md. 245/H3
Antigo, Wis. (54409) 317/H5
Antigonish (co.), Nova Scotia 168/F3
Antigonish, Nova Scotia 168/F3
Antigonish (harb.), Nova Scotia 168/G3
Antigua (isl.) 146/M8
ANTIGUA & BARBUDA 156
ANTIGUA & BARBUDA 161
Antigua (isl.), Ant. & Bar. 161/E11
Antigua (isl.), Ant. & Bar. 156/G3
Antigua, Guatemala 154/B3
Antigua (riv.), Mexico 150/Q1
Antigua, Spain 33/B4
Antigues (pt.), Guadeloupe 161/A5
Antiguo Morelos, Mexico 150/K5
Antilla, Cuba 156/C2
Antilla, Cuba 158/J3
Antilles, Greater (isls.), W. Indies 156/B2
Antilles, Lesser (isls.), W. Indies 156/E4
Antimony, Utah (84712) 304/C5
Antioch, Calif. (94509) 204/L1
Antioch, Georgia (†30240) 217/B4
Antioch, Ill. (60002) 222/E1
Antioch, Nebr. (69340) 264/B2
Antioch, Ohio (43710) 284/H6
Antioch, S.C. (†29020) 296/F3
Antioch (Antakya), Turkey 63/G4
Antioch, W. Va. (†26743) 312/H4
Antioquia (dept.), Colombia 126/B4
Antioquia, Colombia 126/B4
Antique (prov.), Philippines 82/D5
Antiquity, Ohio (†45771) 284/G8
Antisana (mt.), Ecuador 128/D3
Anti-Taurus (mts.), Turkey 63/G3
Antler, N. Dak. (58711) 282/H2
Antler, Sask. 181/K6
Antler (riv.), Sask. 181/K6
Antler Lake, Alberta 182/D3
Antlers, Okla. (74523) 288/P6
Antofagasta (reg.), Chile 138/B4
Antofagasta, Chile 120/B5
Antofagasta, Chile 2/F7
Antofagasta, Chile 138/A4
Antofagasta de la Sierra, Argentina 143/C2
Antoine, Ark. (71922) 202/D5
Antoing, Belgium 27/C7
Anton, Colo. (80801) 208/N3
Antón, Panama 154/G6
Anton, Texas (79313) 303/B4
Anton Chico, N. Mex. (87711) 274/D3
Antone, Oreg. (†97750) 291/H3
Antongil (bay), Madagascar 118/J3
Antonina, Brazil 135/B4
Antonino, Kansas (67624) 232/C3
Antonito, Colo. (81120) 208/H8
Antony, France 28/B2
Antora (peak), Colo. 208/G6
Antreville, S.C. (†29620) 296/B3
Antrim (co.), Mich. 250/D3
Antrim, Mich. (†49659) 250/D4
Antrim, N.H. (03440) 268/D5
Antrim○, N.H. (03440) 268/D5
Antrim (dist.), N. Ireland 17/J2
Antrim, N. Ireland 10/C3
Antrim, N. Ireland 17/J2
Antrim, Ohio (†43973) 284/H5
Antrim, Pa. (†16901) 294/H2
Antsalova, Madagascar 118/G3
Antsirabe, Madagascar 102/G7
Antsirabe, Madagascar 118/H3
Antsiranana (prov.), Madagascar 118/H2
Antsiranana, Madagascar 118/H2
Antsiranana, Madagascar 102/G6

330 Antsia

Antsia, U.S.S.R. 53/D2
Antsohihy, Madagascar 118/H2
Antu, China 77/L3
An Tuc (An Khe), Vietnam 72/F4
Antwerp (prov.), Belgium 27/F6
Antwerp, Belgium 7/E3
Antwerp, Belgium 27/E6
Antwerp, N.Y. (13608) 276/J2
Antwerp, Ohio (45813) 284/A3
Antwerpen (Antwerp), Belgium 27/E6
An Uaimh, Ireland 10/C4
An Uaimh, Ireland 17/H4
Anuenue (Sand) (isl.), Hawaii 218/C4
Anuradhapura, Sri Lanka 68/E7
Anutt, Mo. (†65401) 261/J7
Anvik, Alaska (99558) 196/F2
Anvil (peak), Alaska 196/K4
Anxi, China 77/E3
Anxious (bay), S. Australia 94/D5
Anyang, China 77/H4
A'nyêmaqên Shan (mts.), China 77/E5
Anykščiai, U.S.S.R. 53/C3
Anzá, Colombia 126/C4
'Anza, West Bank 65/C3
Anzac, Alberta 182/E1
Anzaldo, Bolivia 136/C5
Anzhero-Sudzhensk, U.S.S.R. 54/K4
Anzhero-Sudzhensk, U.S.S.R. 48/J4
Anzio, Italy 34/D4
Anzoátegui (state), Venezuela 124/F3
Aoiz, Spain 33/F1
Aoji-ri, N. Korea 81/E2
Aomori (pref.), Japan 81/K3
Aomori, Japan 54/R5
Aomori, Japan 81/K3
Ao Paray (riv.), Paraguay 144/A5
Aosta (reg.), Italy 34/A2
Aosta (prov.), Italy 34/A2
Aosta, Italy 34/A2
Aouara, Fr. Guiana 131/E3
Aouinet Bel Egrâ (well), Algeria 106/C3
Aoulef, Algeria 106/E3
Aozou, Chad 111/C3
Apa (riv.), Paraguay 144/D3
Apache (co.), Ariz. 198/F3
Apache (lake), Ariz. 198/D5
Apache, Okla. (73006) 288/K5
Apache (mts.), Texas 303/C11
Apache Creek, N. Mex. (†87830) 274/A5
Apache Junction, Ariz. (85220) 198/D5
Apalachee (bay), Fla. 188/K5
Apalachee (bay), Fla. 212/B2
Apalachee, Georgia (†30650) 217/E3
Apalachia (res.), N.C. 281/A4
Apalachicola, Fla. (32320) 212/A2
Apalachicola (bay), Fla. 212/B2
Apalachicola (riv.), Fla. 212/A1
Apalachin, N.Y. (13732) 276/H6
Apalona, Ind. (†47576) 227/D8
Apan, Mexico 150/M1
Apaporis (riv.), Colombia 126/F8
Aparecida, Brazil 135/D3
Aparri, Philippines 82/C1
Aparri, Philippines 85/G2
Aparurén, Venezuela 124/G5
Apataki (atoll), Fr. Poly. 87/M7
Apatin, Yugoslavia 45/D3
Apatity, U.S.S.R. 52/D1
Apatzingán de la Constitución, Mexico 150/H7
Ape, U.S.S.R. 53/D2
Apeldoorn, Netherlands 27/H4
Apennines (mts.), Italy 7/F4
Apennines, Central (range), Italy 34/D3
Apennines, Northern (range), Italy 34/B2
Apennines, Southern (range), Italy 34/E4
Apere (riv.), Bolivia 136/C4
Apex, N.C. (27502) 281/M3
Apgar, Mont. (†59936) 262/B2
Apia (cap.), W. Samoa 2/A6
Apia (cap.), W. Samoa 87/J7
Apia (cap.), W. Samoa 86/M8
Apiaí, Brazil 135/B4
Apishapa (riv.), Colo. 208/L8
Apison, Tenn. (37302) 237/L10
Ap Iwan, Cerro (mt.), Chile 138/E6
Apizaco, Mexico 150/N1
Aplao, Peru 128/F11
Aplin, Ark. (†72126) 202/E4
Aplington, Iowa (50604) 229/H3
Ap Long Ha, Vietnam 72/F5
Apo (vol.), Philippines 82/E7
Apohaqui, New Bruns. 170/E3
Apolda, E. Germany 22/D3
Apolima (str.), W. Samoa 86/L8
Apollo, Georgia (†31024) 217/F4
Apollo, Pa. (15613) 294/C4
Apollo Bay, Victoria 97/B6
Apollo Beach, Fla. (33570) 212/C3
Apolo, Bolivia 136/A4
Aponguao (riv.), Venezuela 124/H5
Apopka, Fla. (32703) 212/E3
Apopka (lake), Fla. 212/E3
Aporé (riv.), Brazil 132/D7
Apostle (isls.), Wis. 317/F2
Apostle Islands Nat'l Lakeshore, Wis. 317/E1
Apóstoles, Argentina 143/E2
Apoteri, Guyana 131/B3
Appalachia, Va. (24216) 307/C7
Appalachian (mts.) 188/K3
Appalachian (mts.), N.C. 281/D2
Appalachian (mts.), Pa. 294/H4
Appalachian (mts.), Tenn. 237/M10
Appalachian (mts.), U.S. 146/K6
Appalachian (mts.), Va. 307/J5
Appam, N. Dak. (†58830) 282/C2
Appanoose (co.), Iowa 229/H7
Appelscha, Netherlands 27/J3
Appenzell, Ausser Rhoden (canton), 39/H2
Appenzell, Inner Rhoden (canton), Switzerland 39/H2
Appenzell, Switzerland 39/H2
Apperson, Okla. (†74633) 288/N1
Appin, Ontario 177/C5
Appin (dist.), Scotland 15/C4
Appingedam, Netherlands 27/K2
Apple (creek), Ill. 222/C4
Apple (riv.), Ill. 222/C1
Apple (creek), N. Dak. 282/J6
Apple (riv.), Wis. 317/A5
Appleby, England 13/E3
Appleby, England 10/E3
Appleby, Texas (75961) 303/K6
Apple Creek, Ohio (44606) 284/G4
Applecross, Scotland 15/C3
Appledale, Br. Col. 184/J5
Applegate, Calif. (95703) 204/E5
Applegate, Mich. (48401) 250/G5
Applegate, Oreg. (97530) 291/D5
Apple Grove, W. Va. (25502) 312/B5
Apple Hill, Ontario 177/K2
Apple River, Ill. (61001) 222/C1
Apple River, Nova Scotia 168/D3
Apples, Switzerland 39/B3
Appleton, Ark. (72822) 202/E3
Appleton, Maine (†04540) 243/E7
Appleton, Maine (†04862) 243/E7
Appleton, Minn. (56208) 255/C5
Appleton (Old Appleton), Mo. (†63770) 261/N7
Appleton, N.Y. (14008) 276/C4
Appleton, Ontario 177/H2
Appleton, S.C. (†29836) 296/E5
Appleton, Wash. (98602) 310/D5
Appleton, Wis. 188/J2
Appleton, Wis. (54911) 317/J7
Appleton City, Mo. (64724) 261/D6
Apple Valley, Calif. (92307) 204/H9
Apple Valley, Minn. (†55124) 255/G6
Appling (co.), Georgia 217/H7
Appling, Georgia (30802) 217/H3
Appomattox (co.), Va. 307/L6
Appomattox, Va. (24522) 307/L6
Appomattox (riv.), Va. 307/M6
Appomattox Court House Nat'l Hist. Park, Va. 307/K6
Apponaug, R.I. (†02887) 249/J6
Approuague (riv.), Fr. Guiana 131/E4
Apra (harb.), Guam 86/K7
Aprilia, Italy 34/D4
Apsheron (pen.), U.S.S.R. 52/H6
Apsheronsk, U.S.S.R. 52/F6
Apsley, Ontario 177/F3
Apsley, Victoria 97/A5
Apt, France 28/F6
Aptos, Calif. (95003) 204/K4
Apua (pt.), Hawaii 218/J6
Apulia (Puglia) (reg.), Italy 34/F4
Apulia Station, N.Y. (13020) 276/H5
Apure (state), Venezuela 124/D4
Apure (riv.), Venezuela 124/E4
Apurímac (dept.), Peru 128/F10
Apurímac (riv.), Peru 120/B4
Apurímac (riv.), Peru 128/F9
Apurito, Venezuela 124/D4
Ap Vinh Hao, Vietnam 72/F5
Aqaba (gulf) 54/E7
'Aqaba (gulf), Egypt 111/G2
'Aqaba (gulf), Egypt 59/C4
'Aqaba (gulf), Israel 65/D6
'Aqaba, Jordan 65/D6
'Aqaba, Jordan 59/C4
Aqaba (gulf), Jordan 65/D6
'Aqaba (gulf), Saudi Arabia 59/C4
Aqcheh, Afghanistan 68/B1
Aqcheh, Afghanistan 59/J2
Aq Darband, Iran 66/M2
'Aqiq, Sudan 111/G4
'Aqqaba, West Bank 65/C3
Aqqikkol Hu (lake), China 77/C4
'Aqra, Iraq 66/D2
'Aqraba, West Bank 65/C3
Aqsu (Aksu), China 77/B3
Aquades Beach, Sask. 181/C2
Aquaforte, Newf. 166/D2
Aqua Park, Okla. (†74435) 288/R3
Aquarius (range), Ariz. 198/B4
Aquarius (plat.), Utah 304/C5
Aquasco, Md. (20608) 245/L6
Aquia, Peru 128/D8
Aquidabán (riv.), Paraguay 144/D3
Aquidauana, Brazil 120/D5
Aquidauana, Brazil 132/C8
Aquila, Mexico 150/H7
Aquila, Switzerland 39/G3
Aquiles Serdán, Mexico 150/G2
Aquilla, Ohio (†44024) 284/H2
Aquin, Haiti 158/B6
Ara (riv.), Japan 81/O2
Arab, Ala. (35016) 195/E2
'Arab, Shatt-al- (riv.), Iran 59/E4
'Arab, Shatt-al- (riv.), Iran 66/F5
'Arab, Shatt-al- (riv.), Iraq 59/E4
'Arab, Shatt-al- (riv.), Iraq 66/F5
Arab, Mo. (63733) 261/M8
'Araba, Wadi (valley), Israel 65/D5
'Araba, Wadi (valley), Jordan 65/D5
Arabela, N. Mex. (†88351) 274/D5
Arabella, Sask. 181/K3
Arabi, Georgia (31712) 217/E7
'Arabi (isl.), Iran 66/G7
Arabi, La. (70032) 238/P4
Arabia, Ky. (†40437) 237/M6
Arabia, Ohio (†45659) 284/F8
Arabian (sea) 54/H8
Arabian (sea) 2/N5
Arabian (des.), Egypt 111/F2
Arabian (des.), Egypt 59/B4
Arabian (sea), India 68/B5
Arabian (sea), Pakistan 68/B5
Arabian (sea), P.D.R. Yemen 59/H5
Arabopó, Venezuela 124/H5
Araç, Turkey 63/E2
Araca, Bolivia 136/B5
Aracaju, Brazil 120/F4
Aracaju, Brazil 132/G5
Aracataca, Colombia 126/D2
Aracati, Brazil 132/G4
Araçatuba, Brazil 132/D8
Araçatuba, Brazil 135/A2
Araceli, Philippines 82/C5
Aracena, Spain 33/C4
Araçuaí, Brazil 132/F7
Arad, Israel 65/C5
Arad, Romania 7/G4
Arad, Romania 45/E2
Arada, Chad 111/D4
'Aradah, U.A.E. 59/F5
Aradan, Iran 66/H3
Arafat, Jebel (mt.), Saudi Arabia 59/D5
Arafura (sea) 87/D6
Arafura (sea) 2/R6
Arafura (sea) 88/E2
Arafura (sea), Indonesia 85/J8
Arafura (sea), North. Terr. 93/D1
Arago, Minn. (†56470) 255/C3
Arago, Oreg. (97458) 291/C4
Arago (cape), Oreg. 291/C4
Aragon, Georgia (30104) 217/B2
Aragon, N. Mex. (87820) 274/A5
Aragón (reg.), Spain 33/F2
Aragón (riv.), Spain 33/F1
Aragona, Italy 34/D6
Aragua (state), Venezuela 124/E3
Araguacema, Brazil 132/D5
Aragua de Barcelona, Venezuela 124/F3
Aragua de Maturín, Venezuela 124/G3
Araguaia (riv.), Brazil 120/E3
Araguaia (riv.), Brazil 132/D4
Araguaiana, Brazil 132/C6
Araguaína, Brazil 120/E3
Araguari, Brazil 120/E4
Araguari, Brazil 132/D7
Araguari (riv.), Brazil 132/D2
Araioses, Brazil 132/F3
Arak, Algeria 106/E3
Arak, Iran 54/G6
Arak, Iran 59/E3
Arak, Iran 66/F3
Arakan (state), Burma 72/B3
Arakan Yoma (mts.), Burma 72/B3
Araks (riv.) 54/F6
Araks (riv.), Iran 59/E2
Araks (Aras) (riv.), Iran 66/E1
Araks (riv.), Turkey 63/K2
Araks (riv.), U.S.S.R. 7/J5
Araks (riv.), U.S.S.R. 52/G7
Aral (sea), U.S.S.R. 54/G5
Aral (sea), U.S.S.R. 48/F5
Aralık, Turkey 63/L3
Aral Sea (lake), U.S.S.R. 2/M3
Aral'sk, U.S.S.R. 54/H5
Aral'sk, U.S.S.R. 48/G5
Aramac, Queensland 95/C4
Aramberri, Mexico 150/J5
Arampampa, Bolivia 136/B5
Aran (isl.), Ireland 10/B3
Aran (isl.), Ireland 17/D2
Aran (isls.), Ireland 17/B5
Aran (isls.), Ireland 10/B4
Aranda de Duero, Spain 33/E2
Arandas, Mexico 150/H6
Aran Fawddwy (mt.), Wales 13/C5
Arani, Bolivia 136/C5
Aranjuez, Spain 33/E2
Aransas (co.), Texas 303/H10
Aransas (passage), Texas 303/H10
Aransas Pass, Texas (78336) 303/G10
Araoua (mts.), Fr. Guiana 131/E4
Araouane, Mali 106/D5
Araouane, Mali 102/B3
Arapaho, Okla. (73620) 288/H3
Arapahoe (co.), Colo. 208/L3
Arapahoe, Colo. (80802) 208/P5
Arapahoe (peak), Colo. 208/H2
Arapahoe, Nebr. (68922) 264/E4
Arapahoe, N.C. (28510) 281/R4
Arapahoe, Wyo. (82510) 319/D3
Arapaho Nat'l Rec. Area, Colo. 208/G2
Arapey, Uruguay 145/B1
Arapey Chico (riv.), Uruguay 145/B1
Arapey Grande (riv.), Uruguay 145/B2
Arapicos, Ecuador 128/D3
Arapiraca, Brazil 120/F3
Arapkir, Turkey 63/H3
Arapkir, Turkey 59/C2
'Ar'ar, Wadi (dry riv.), Iraq 66/B5
'Ar'ar, Wadi (dry riv.), Iraq 59/D3
'Ar'ar, Wadi (dry riv.), Saudi Arabia 59/D3
Araracuara, Colombia 126/E8
Araracuara, Cerros de (mts.), Colombia 126/E7
Araranguá, Brazil 132/D10
Araraquara, Brazil 132/E8
Araraquara, Brazil 135/B2
Araras, Brazil 135/C3
Ararat, Ala. (†36921) 195/B7
Ararat, N.C. (27007) 281/H2
Ararat (mt.), Pa. 294/M2
Ararat (mt.), Turkey 54/F6
Ararat (mt.), Turkey 63/L3
Ararat (mt.), Turkey 59/D2
Ararat, Victoria 88/G7
Ararat, Victoria 97/B5
Ararat, Va. (24053) 307/G7
Arari, Brazil 132/E3
Araruama (lake), Brazil 135/E3
Aras (Araks) (riv.), Iran 66/E1
Aras (Araks) (riv.), Iran 59/E2
Aratürük (Yiwu), China 77/D3
Arauca (riv.) 120/C2
Arauca (inten.), Colombia 126/E4
Arauca, Colombia 120/B2
Arauca, Colombia 126/E4
Arauca (riv.), Colombia 126/E4
Arauca (riv.), Venezuela 124/E4
Arauco, Chile 138/D1
Arauco (gulf), Chile 138/D1
Arauquita, Colombia 126/E4
Araure, Venezuela 124/D3
Aravaca, Spain 33/F4
Aravaipa (creek), Ariz. 198/E6
Arawa, Papua N.G. 86/C2
Arawe, Papua N.G. 86/B2
Arax (Araks) (riv.), Asia 59/E2
Araxá, Brazil 132/E7
Araya, Venezuela 124/F2
Arba, Ind. (†47355) 227/H4
Arba Mench, Ethiopia 111/G6
Arba Mench, Ethiopia 102/F4
Arbeca, Spain 33/G2
Arbedo-Castione, Switzerland 39/G4
Arbela (Erbil), Iraq 59/D2
Arbela (Erbil), Iraq 66/D2
Arbela, Mo. (63432) 261/H2
Arboga, Sweden 18/J7
Arbois, France 28/F4
Arbon, Idaho (83212) 220/F7
Arbon, Switzerland 39/H1
Arborea, Italy 34/B5
Arborfield, Sask. 181/H2
Arborg, Manitoba 179/E4
Arbor Vitae, Wis. (†54568) 317/G4
Arbovale, W. Va. (24915) 312/G6
Arbrå, Sweden 18/K6
Arbroath, Scotland 15/F4
Arbroath, Scotland 10/E2
Arbroth, La. (†70736) 238/H5
Arbucias, Spain 33/H2
Arbuckle, Calif. (95912) 204/C4
Arbuckle (lake), Fla. 212/E4
Arbuckle, W. Va. (25006) 312/C5
Arbuckles, Lake of the (lake), Okla. 288/M6
Arbuthnot, Sask. 181/E6
Arbutus, Md. (†21227) 245/M4
Arbyrd, Mo. (63821) 261/M10
Arcachon, France 28/C5
Arcachon (bay), France 28/C5
Arcade, Georgia (†30549) 217/E2
Arcade, N.Y. (14009) 276/D5
Arcadia, Calif. (91006) 204/C10
Arcadia, Fla. (33821) 212/E4
Arcadia, Ind. (46030) 227/E4
Arcadia, Iowa (51430) 229/C4
Arcadia, Kansas (66711) 232/H4
Arcadia, La. (71001) 238/E1
Arcadia, Mich. (49613) 250/C4
Arcadia, Mo. (63621) 261/L7
Arcadia, Nebr. (68815) 264/F3
Arcadia, Nova Scotia 168/B5
Arcadia, Ohio (44804) 284/D3
Arcadia, Okla. (73007) 288/M3
Arcadia, Pa. (15712) 294/E4
Arcadia, R.I. (†02832) 249/H6
Arcadia, S.C. (29320) 296/C2
Arcadia, Texas (77517) 303/K3
Arcadia, Utah (†84012) 304/D3
Arcadia, Wis. (54612) 317/D7
Arcadia Lakes, S.C. (†29201) 296/F3
Arcahaie, Haiti 158/C6
Arcanum, Ohio (45304) 284/A6
Arcas (cay), Mexico 150/N6
Arcata, Calif. (95521) 204/A3
Arc Dome (mt.), Nev. 266/D4
Arcelia, Mexico 150/J7
Arch, N. Mex. (†88130) 274/F4
Archambault (lake), Québec 172/C3
Archangel, U.S.S.R. 4/C7
Archangel, U.S.S.R. 2/M2
Archangel, U.S.S.R. 7/J2
Archangel (Arkhangel'sk), U.S.S.R. 48/E3
Archangel (Arkhangel'sk), U.S.S.R. 52/F2
Archbald, Pa. (18403) 294/F6
Archbold, Ohio (43502) 284/B2
Arch Cape, Oreg. (97102) 291/D2
Archdale, N.C. (27263) 281/K3
Archena, Spain 33/F3
Archer, Fla. (32618) 212/D2
Archer, Iowa (51231) 229/B2
Archer, Nebr. (68816) 264/F3
Archer (fiord), N.W. Terrs. 187/M1
Archer (riv.), Queensland 95/B2
Archer (co.), Texas 303/F4
Archer City, Texas (76351) 303/F4
Archerfield, Queensland 88/K3
Archerfield, Queensland 95/D3
Archerwill, Sask. 181/H3
Arches Nat'l Park, Utah 304/E5
Archibald, La. (71218) 238/G2
Archidona, Ecuador 128/D3
Archidona, Spain 33/D4
Archie, La. (†71343) 238/G3
Archie, Mo. (64725) 261/D5
Archiestown, Scotland 15/E3
Archuleta (co.), Colo. 208/E8
Archydal, Sask. 181/F5
Arcis-sur-Aube, France 28/F3
Arckaringa (creek), S. Australia 94/D2
Arco, Georgia (†31520) 217/J8
Arco, Idaho (83213) 220/E6
Arco, Idaho 188/D2
Arco, Minn. (56113) 255/B6
Arcola, Ill. (61910) 222/E4
Arcola, Ind. (46704) 227/G2
Arcola, La. (†70456) 238/K5
Arcola, Miss. (38722) 256/C4
Arcola, Mo. (65603) 261/E7
Arcola, N.C. (27589) 281/N2
Arcola, Sask. 181/J6
Arcopongo, Bolivia 136/B5
Arcosanti, Ariz. (†86333) 198/C4
Arcos de Jalón, Spain 33/E2
Arcos de la Frontera, Spain 33/D4
Arcos de Valdevez, Portugal 33/B2
Arcot, India 68/D6
Arcoverde, Brazil 132/G5
Arctic (ocean) 54/C1
Arctic (ocean) 146/B2
Arctic (plain), Alaska 196/G1
Arctic, R.I. (†02893) 249/J6
Arctic Bay, Canada 4/B14
Arctic Bay, N.W.T. 162/H1
Arctic Bay, N.W. Terrs. 187/K2
Arctic Circle 2/J2
Arctic Ocean 2/B2
Arctic Ocean 4/A15
Arctic Ocean, U.S.S.R. 48/K1
Arctic Red (riv.), N.W. Terrs. 187/E3
Arctic Red River, N.W.T. 162/C2
Arctic Red River, N.W. Terrs. 187/E3
Arctic Village, Alaska (99722) 196/K1
Arda (riv.), Greece 45/G5
Ardabil, Iran 54/F6
Ardabil, Iran 59/E2
Ardabil, Iran 66/F1
Ardagh, Limerick, Ireland 17/C7
Ardagh, Longford, Ireland 17/F4
Ardahan, Turkey 59/D1
Ardahan, Turkey 63/K2
Ardal, Iran 66/G4
Årdal, Norway 18/E7
Årdalstangen, Norway 18/F6
Ardanuç, Turkey 63/K2
Ardara, Ireland 17/E2
Ardath, Sask. 181/D4
Ardavasar, Scotland 15/B3
Ardbeg, Ontario 177/D2
Ardèche (dept.), France 28/F5
Ardee, Ireland 17/H4
Ardee, Ireland 10/C4
Arden, Ark. (†71822) 202/B6
Arden, Del. (†19801) 245/R1
Arden, Denmark 21/C4
Arden, Manitoba 179/C4
Arden, Ontario 177/G3
Arden, Wash. (†99114) 310/H2
Arden, W. Va. (†26405) 312/G4
Arden-Arcade, Calif. (95825) 204/B8
Ardencroft, Del. (†19810) 245/R1
Ardennes (for.), Belgium 27/F9
Ardennes (dept.), France 28/F3
Ardenode, Alberta 182/D4
Ardentown, Del. (†19810) 245/S1
Ardenvoir, Wash. (98811) 310/E3
Ardersier, Scotland 15/E3
Ardeşen, Turkey 63/J2
Ardestan, Iran 59/F3
Ardestan, Iran 66/H4
Ardez, Switzerland 39/K3
Ardfert, Ireland 17/B7
Ardfinnan, Ireland 17/F7
Ardgay, Scotland 15/D3
Ardglass, N. Ireland 17/K3
Ardgour (dist.), Scotland 15/C4
Ardhéa, Greece 45/F5
Ardila (riv.), Spain 33/C3
Ardill, Sask. 181/F6
Ardino, Bulgaria 45/G5
Ardivachar (pt.), Scotland 15/A3
Ardle (riv.), Scotland 15/E4
Ardlethan, N.S. Wales 97/D4
Ardmore, Ala. (35805) 195/E1
Ardmore, Alberta 182/E2
Ardmore, Ind. (†46624) 227/E1
Ardmore, Ireland 17/F8
Ardmore, Md. (†20785) 245/G4
Ardmore, Mo. (†65247) 261/H3
Ardmore, Okla. 188/G4
Ardmore, Okla. (73401) 288/M6
Ardmore, Pa. (19003) 294/M6
Ardmore, S. Dak. (57715) 298/B7
Ardmore, Tenn. (38449) 237/H10
Ardnamurchan (pen.), Scotland 15/B4
Ardnamurchan (pt.), Scotland 15/B4
Ardoch, N. Dak. (58213) 282/R3
Ardon, Switzerland 39/D4
Ardooie, Belgium 27/C7
Ardrahan, Ireland 17/D5
Ardrishaig, Scotland 15/C4
Ardrossan, Alberta 182/D3
Ardrossan, Scotland 10/D3
Ardrossan, Scotland 15/D5
Ards (dist.), N. Ireland 17/K2
Ardsley, N.Y. (10502) 276/O6
Åre, Sweden 18/H5
Arecibo (dist.), P. Rico 161/C1
Arecibo, P. Rico 156/G1
Arecibo, P. Rico 161/B1
Aredale, Iowa (50605) 229/H3
Areguá, Paraguay 144/B4
Areia Branca, Brazil 132/G4
Arelee, Sask. 181/D3
Arena (pt.), Calif. 188/B3
Arena (pt.), Calif. 204/B5
Arena (pt.), Mexico 150/E5
Arena, N. Dak. (58412) 282/K5
Arena (isl.), Philippines 82/C6
Arena, Wis. (53503) 317/G9
Arenac (co.), Mich. 250/F4
Arenales, Cerro (mt.), Chile 138/D7
Arenas (pt.), Argentina 143/C7
Arenas (cay), Mexico 150/O5
Arenas (pt.), P. Rico 161/F2
Arenas de San Pedro, Spain 33/D2
Arendal, Norway 18/F7
Arendjelovac, Yugoslavia 45/E3
Arendonk, Belgium 27/G6
Arendtsville, Pa. (17303) 294/H6
Arenillas, Ecuador 128/B4
Arenys de Mar, Spain 33/H2
Arenzville, Ill. (62611) 222/C4
Areópolis, Greece 45/F7
Arequipa (dept.), Peru 128/F10
Arequipa, Peru 128/G11
Arequipa, Peru 120/B4
Arequipa, Peru 2/F6
Arequipa, Peru 128/72
Aresji, Neth. Ant. 161/D9
Areuse (riv.), Switzerland 39/C3
Arévalo, Spain 33/D2
Areyonga, North. Terr. 88/E4
Areyonga, North. Terr. 93/C8
Arezzo (prov.), Italy 34/C3
Arezzo, Italy 34/C3
Arfa Deh, Iran 66/H3
Arga (riv.), Spain 33/F1
Argadargada, North. Terr. 93/E6
Argalant, Mongolia 77/G3
Argalastí, Greece 45/F6
Argamasilla de Alba, Spain 33/E3
Arganda, Spain 33/G4
Argao, Philippines 82/D6
Argenta, Br. Col. 184/J5
Argenta, Ill. (62501) 222/E4
Argenta, Italy 34/D2
Argentan, France 28/D3
Argentat, France 28/D5
Argenteuil, France 28/A1
Argenteuil (co.), Québec 172/C4
Argentia, Newf. 166/C2
Argentina 2/F7
Argentina 120/C6
ARGENTINA 143
Argentine, Pa. (†16040) 294/C3
Argentino (lake), Argentina 143/B7
Argenton-sur-Creuse, France 28/D4
Argeş (riv.), Romania 45/G3
Argo, Ala. (†35173) 195/E3
Argo, Sudan 111/F4
Argo, Sudan 59/B6
Argolis (gulf), Greece 45/F7
Argonia, Kansas (67004) 232/E4
Argonne, Wis. (54511) 317/J4
Argonne Nat'l Laboratory, Ill. 222/B6
Árgos, Greece 45/F7
Argos, Ind. (46501) 227/E2
Argos (cape), Nova Scotia 168/G3
Argostólion, Greece 45/E6
Arguello (pt.), Calif. 204/E9
Arguin (bay), Mauritania 106/A4
Argun (riv.) 54/N4
Argun' (Ergun He) (riv.), China 77/K1
Argun' (riv.), U.S.S.R. 48/M4
Argungu, Nigeria 106/E6
Argus (range), Calif. 204/H7
Argusville, N. Dak. (58005) 282/R5
Arguvan, Turkey 63/H3
Argyle, Fla. (32422) 212/C6
Argyle, Georgia (31623) 217/G8
Argyle, Iowa (52619) 229/K7
Argyle, Maine (†04468) 243/F5
Argyle, Manitoba 179/E4
Argyle, Mich. (48410) 250/G5
Argyle, Minn. (56713) 255/B2
Argyle, Mo. (65001) 261/J6
Argyle, New Bruns. 170/C2
Argyle, N.Y. (12809) 276/O4
Argyle, Texas (76226) 303/F1
Argyle (lake), W. Australia 88/D3
Argyle (lake), W. Australia 92/E2
Argyle, Wis. (53504) 317/G10
Argyle Downs, W. Australia 92/E2
Argyll (dist.), Scotland 15/C4
Argyll (trad. co.), Scotland 15/B5
Arhangay, Mongolia 77/F2
Arhavi, Turkey 63/J2
Arhli (Arlit), Niger 106/F4
Ar Horqin, China 77/K3
Århus (co.), Denmark 21/D5
Århus, Denmark 7/E3
Århus, Denmark 21/D5
Århus, Denmark 18/F8
Aria, N. Zealand 100/E3
Ariah Park, N.S. Wales 97/D4
Ariail, S.C. (†29640) 296/B2
Ariano Irpino, Italy 34/E4
Ariari (riv.), Colombia 126/D6
Aribinda, Upper Volta 106/D6
Arica, Chile 120/B4
Arica, Chile 138/A1
Arica, Colombia 126/E9
Aricagua, Venezuela 124/C3
Ariccia, Italy 34/F7
Arichat, Nova Scotia 168/H3
Arichuna, Venezuela 124/E4
Arichuna (riv.), Venezuela 124/D4
Arid (cape), W. Australia 88/C6
Arid (cape), W. Australia 92/C6
Ariège (dept.), France 28/D6
Ariel, Wash. (98603) 310/C5
Ariguaní (riv.), Colombia 126/D3
Ariha (Jericho), West Bank 65/C4
Arikaree (riv.), Colo. 208/O3
Arima, Trin. & Tob. 156/G5
Arima, Trin. & Tob. 161/B10
Arimo, Idaho (83214) 220/F7
Arinagour, Scotland 15/B4
Aringa, Uganda 115/F3
Arinos (riv.), Brazil 132/B5
Ario de Rosales, Mexico 150/J7
Arion, Iowa (51520) 229/B5
Aripao, Venezuela 124/F4
Aripeka, Fla. (33502) 212/D3
Aripine, Ariz. (†85901) 198/E4
Aripo, El Cerro del (mt.), Trin. & Tob. 161/B10
Ariporo (riv.), Colombia 126/E4
Aripuanã, Brazil 120/C3
Aripuanã, Brazil 132/A5
Aripuanã (riv.), Brazil 120/D3
Aripuanã (riv.), Brazil 132/A4
Arisaig, Scotland 15/C4
Arisaig (sound), Scotland 15/C4
Arismendi, Venezuela 124/D3
Arispe, Iowa (50831) 229/E7
Aristazabal (isl.), Br. Col. 184/C4
Aritao, Philippines 82/C2
Ariton, Ala. (36311) 195/G7
Arivaca, Ariz. (85601) 198/D7
Arivonimamo, Madagascar 118/H3
Arixang (Wenquan), China 77/B3
Ariza, Spain 33/E2
Arizaro, Salar de (salt dep.), Argentina 143/C2
Arizona 188/D4
ARIZONA 198
Arizona (state), U.S. 146/G6
Arizona City, Ariz. (85223) 198/D6
Arizona Sunsites, Ariz. (85625) 198/F7
Arizpe, Mexico 150/D1
Årjäng, Sweden 18/H7
Arjay, Ky. (40902) 237/O7
Arjeplog, Sweden 18/L3
Arjona, Colombia 126/C2
Arkabutla, Miss. (38602) 256/D1
Arkabutla (dam), Miss. 256/D1
Arkabutla (lake), Miss. 256/D1
Arkadelphia, Ala. (35033) 195/E3
Arkadelphia, Ark. (71923) 202/D5
Arkaig, Loch (lake), Scotland 15/C4
Arkaig, Loch (lake), Scotland 10/D2
Arkalyk, U.S.S.R. 48/G4
Arkansas 188/H3
Arkansas (riv.) 188/H3
ARKANSAS 202
Arkansas (co.), Ark. 202/H5

Atchison 331

Arkansas (riv.), Ark. 202/G5
Arkansas (riv.), Colo. 208/P6
Arkansas (riv.), Kansas 232/D3
Arkansas (riv.), Okla. 288/S4
Arkansas (state), U.S. 146/J6
Arkansas (riv.), U.S. 2/E4
Arkansas (riv.), U.S. 146/J6
Arkansas City, Ark. (71630) 202/H6
Arkansas City, Kans. 188/G3
Arkansas City, Kansas (67005) 232/E4
Arkansas Divide (mts.), Colo. 208/L4
Arkansas Post Nat'l Mem., Ark. 202/H5
Arkansaw, Wis. (54721) 317/B6
Arkdale, Wis. (54613) 317/G7
Arkhángelos, Greece 45/J7
Arkhipo-Osipovka, U.S.S.R. 52/E6
Arkinda, Ark. (71821) 202/B6
Arklow, Ireland 10/C4
Arklow, Ireland 17/J6
Arklow (bank), Ireland 17/K6
Arkoe, Mo. (†64468) 261/C2
Arkoma, Okla. (74901) 288/T4
Arkona (cape), E. Germany 22/E1
Arkona, Ontario 177/C4
Arkport, N.Y. (14807) 276/E6
Arkticheskiy Institut (isls.), U.S.S.R. 48/H2
Arkville, N.Y. (12406) 276/L6
Arkwright, S.C. (†29301) 296/C2
Arlee, Mont. (59821) 262/B3
Arlee, W. Va. (†25106) 312/B5
Arles, France 28/F6
Arley, Ala. (35541) 195/D2
Arlington, Ala. (36722) 195/C6
Arlington, Ariz. (85322) 198/C5
Arlington, Colo. (81021) 208/N6
Arlington, Georgia (31713) 217/C8
Arlington, Ill. (61312) 222/D2
Arlington, Ind. (46104) 227/F5
Arlington, Iowa (50606) 229/K3
Arlington, Kansas (67514) 232/D4
Arlington, Ky. (42021) 237/D7
Arlington○, Mass. (02174) 249/C6
Arlington, Minn. (55307) 255/D6
Arlington, Nebr. (68002) 264/H3
Arlington, N.Y. (12603) 276/N7
Arlington, N.C. (†28642) 281/H2
Arlington, Ohio (45814) 284/C4
Arlington, Oreg. (97812) 291/G2
Arlington, S. Dak. (57212) 298/P5
Arlington, Tenn. (38002) 237/B10
Arlington, Tex. 188/G4
Arlington, Texas (*76010) 303/F2
Arlington (lake), Texas 303/F2
Arlington, Vt. (05250) 268/A5
Arlington○, Vt. (05250) 268/A5
Arlington (co.), Va. 307/S2
Arlington, Va. (*22201) 307/T3
Arlington, Wash. (98223) 310/C2
Arlington, Wis. (53911) 317/H9
Arlington, Wyo. (†82080) 319/F4
Arlington Beach, Sask. 181/F4
Arlington Heights, Ill. (*60004) 222/B5
Arlington Heights, Ohio (†45201) 284/C9
Arlington Nat'l Cemetery, Va. 307/T3
Arlit (Arhli), Niger 106/F4
Arló, Hungary 41/F2
Arlon, Belgium 27/H9
Arltunga, North. Terr. 93/D7
Arm (riv.), Sask. 181/F5
Arma, Kansas (66712) 232/H4
Arma (plat.), Saudi Arabia 59/E4
Armada, Alberta 182/D4
Armada, Mich. (48005) 250/G6
Armadale, Scotland 15/C2
Armadale, Scotland 10/B1
Armagh (dist.), N. Ireland 17/H3
Armagh, N. Ireland 10/C3
Armagh, N. Ireland 17/H3
Armagh, Pa. (15920) 294/E5
Armagh, Québec 172/G3
Armathwaite, Tenn. (38506) 237/M8
Armavir, U.S.S.R. 7/J4
Armavir, U.S.S.R. 48/E5
Armavir, U.S.S.R. 52/F5
Armena, Alberta 182/D3
Armenia, Colombia 120/B2
Armenia, Colombia 126/B5
Armenian S.S.R., U.S.S.R. 7/J4
Armenian S.S.R., U.S.S.R. 52/F6
Armenian S.S.R., U.S.S.R. 48/E6
Armentières, France 28/E2
Armería, Mexico 150/G7
Armero, Colombia 126/C5
Armidale, Australia 87/F9
Armidale, N. S. Wales 88/J6
Armidale, N.S. Wales 97/F2
Armington, Ill. (61721) 222/D3
Armington, Mont. (†59412) 262/F3
Arminto, Wyo. (82630) 319/E2
Armistead, La. (†71019) 238/D3
Armit (lake), Manitoba 179/A2
Armley, Sask. 181/G2
Armona, Calif. (93202) 204/F7
Armorel, Ark. (72310) 202/L2
Armour, S. Dak. (57313) 298/N7
Armourdale, N. Dak. (†58365) 282/M2
Armoy, N. Ireland 17/J1
Armstrong, Br. Col. 184/H5
Armstrong, Ill. (61812) 222/F3
Armstrong, Ind. (†47708) 227/B8
Armstrong, Iowa (50514) 229/D2
Armstrong, Mo. (65230) 261/G4
Armstrong, Ont. 162/H5
Armstrong, Ontario 175/C2
Armstrong, Ontario 177/H4
Armstrong (co.), Pa. 294/D4
Armstrong (co.), Texas 303/C3
Armstrong, Texas (78338) 303/G11
Armstrong Brook, New Bruns. 170/E1
Armstrong Creek, Wis. (54103) 317/K4
Armstrongs Mills, Ohio (43904) 284/J6
Armuchee, Georgia (30105) 217/B2
Army Chemical Center, Md. 245/O3
Army Med. Ctr. Annex (Walter Reed), Md. 245/E4
Arnala, Greece 45/F5
Arnaud, Manitoba 179/E5
Arnaud (riv.), Québec 174/F1
Arnaudville, La. (70512) 238/G6
Arnauti (cape), Cyprus 59/B2
Arnauti (cape), Cyprus 63/E5
Arnavutköy, Turkey 63/D6
Arnedo, Spain 33/E1
Arnegard, N. Dak. (58835) 282/D4
Årnes, Norway 18/G6
Arnett, Okla. (73832) 288/G2
Arnett, W. Va. (25007) 312/D7
Arney (riv.), N. Ireland 17/F3
Arnheim, Mich. (†49958) 250/G1
Arnhem (cape), Australia 87/D7
Arnhem, Netherlands 27/H4
Arnhem (cape), North. Terr. 88/F2
Arnhem (cape), North. Terr. 93/E2
Arnhem Land (reg.), Australia 87/D7
Arnhem Land (reg.), North. Terr. 88/E2
Arnhem Land (reg.), North. Terr. 93/D2
Arnhem Land Aboriginal Reserve, North. Terr. 88/E2
Arnhem Land Aboriginal Res., North. Terr. 93/C2
Arno (riv.), Italy 34/C3
Arno (atoll), Marshall Is. 87/H5
Arnold, Calif. (95223) 204/E5
Arnold, England 13/F4
Arnold, Kansas (67515) 232/B3
Arnold, Mich. (49819) 250/B2
Arnold, Minn. (†55801) 255/F4
Arnold, Mo. (63010) 261/M6
Arnold, Nebr. (69120) 264/D3
Arnold (riv.), North. Terr. 93/D3
Arnold, Pa. (15068) 294/C4
Arnold Mills, R.I. (†02864) 249/J5
Arnoldsburg, W. Va. (25234) 312/D5
Arnold's Cove, Newf. 166/C2
Arnolds Park, Iowa (51331) 229/C2
Arnoldstein, Austria 41/B3
Arnoldsville, Georgia (30619) 217/F3
Arnot, Pa. (16911) 294/H2
Arnøya (isl.), Norway 18/M1
Arnprior, Ontario 177/H2
Arnsberg, W. Germany 22/C3
Arnstadt, E. Germany 22/D3
Årø (isl.), Denmark 21/C7
Aro (riv.), Venezuela 124/F4
Aroa, Venezuela 124/D2
Aroab, Namibia 118/B5
Aroche, Spain 33/C4
Arock, Oreg. (97902) 291/K5
Aroland, Ontario 177/H4
Aroland, Ontario 175/C2
Arolla, Switzerland 39/E4
Arolsen, W. Germany 22/C3
Aroma, Bolivia 136/B6
Aroma, Sudan 111/G4
Aroma Park, Ill. (60910) 222/F2
Aromas, Calif. (95004) 204/D7
Aroostook (co.), Maine 243/F2
Aroostook (riv.), Maine 243/G2
Aroostook, New Bruns. 170/C2
Arorae (atoll), Kiribati 87/H6
Aroroy, Philippines 82/D4
Arosa, Ría de (est.), Spain 33/B1
Arosa, Switzerland 39/J3
Aroser Rothorn (mt.), Switzerland 39/J3
Årøsund, Denmark 21/C7
Arouca, Trin. & Tob. 161/B10
Arp, Georgia (†31783) 217/F7
Arp, Texas (75750) 303/J5
Arpa (riv.), Turkey 63/K2
Arpaçay, Turkey 63/K2
Arpin, Wis. (54410) 317/G6
Arque, Bolivia 136/B5
'Arraba, West Bank 65/C3
'Arrabe, Israel 65/C2
Arrah, India 68/E3
Ar Rahhaliya, Iraq 66/C4
Ar Rahhaliya, Iraq 59/D3
Arraias, Brazil 132/E6
Arran, Fla. (†32327) 212/B1
Arran, Sask. 181/K4
Arran (isl.), Scotland 15/C5
Arran (isl.), Scotland 10/D3
Arras, Br. Col. 184/G2
Arras, France 28/E2
Arrecifal, Colombia 126/F6
Arrecife, Spain 106/B3
Arrecife, Spain 33/C4
Arrecife de la Media Luna (reefs), Honduras 154/F3
Arrecifes, Argentina 143/F7
Arrecifes (riv.), Argentina 143/G6
Arrey, N. Mex. (87930) 274/B6
Arriaga, Mexico 150/N8
Arriba, Colo. (80804) 208/N4
Arribeños, Argentina 143/F7
Arrington, Kansas (†66436) 232/G2
Arrington, Tenn. (37014) 237/H9
Arrington, Va. (22922) 307/L5
Arriola, Colo. (†81323) 208/B8
Arrochar, Scotland 15/D4
Arronches, Portugal 33/C3
Arrow (lake), Ireland 17/E3
Arrow (creek), Mont. 262/F3
Arrow Canyon (range), Nev. 266/G6
Arrow Creek, Mont. (†59424) 262/F3
Arrowhead Mountain (lake), Vt. 268/A2
Arrow River, Manitoba 179/B4
Arrowrock (res.), Idaho 220/C6
Arrow Rock, Mo. (65320) 261/F4
Arrowsmith, Ill. (61722) 222/E3
Arrowtown, N. Zealand 100/B6
Arrowwood, Alberta 182/D4
Arrowwood (lake), N. Dak. 282/N5
Arroyas, Los (lake), Bolivia 136/C3
Arroyo, P. Rico 161/E3
Arroyo, P. Rico 156/G1
Arroyo Blanco, Cuba 158/F2
Arroyo de la Luz, Spain 33/C3
Arroyo del Valle (dry riv.), Calif. 204/L3
Arroyo Grande, Bolivia 136/A2
Arroyo Grande, Calif. (93420) 204/E8
Arroyo Hondo (dry riv.), Calif. 204/L3
Arroyo Hondo, N. Mex. (87513) 274/D2
Arroyo Mocho (dry riv.), Calif. 204/L2
Arroyo Seco, Argentina 143/F6
Arroyo Seco (dry riv.), Calif. 204/K10
Arroyo Seco, N. Mex. (87514) 274/D2
Arroyos y Esteros, Paraguay 144/B4
Ar Rumaila, Iraq 66/E5
Års, Denmark 21/C4
Ars-en-Ré, France 28/C4
Arsen'yev, U.S.S.R. 48/O5
Arsin, Turkey 63/H2
Arslanköy, Turkey 63/F4
Árta, Greece 45/E6
Artá, Spain 33/H3
Artas, S. Dak. (57423) 298/K2
Artawiya, Saudi Arabia 59/E4
Arteaga, Mexico 150/H7
Artem, U.S.S.R. 48/O5
Artemas, Pa. (17211) 294/E6
Artemisa, Cuba 158/B1
Artemisa, Cuba 156/A2
Artemovskiy, U.S.S.R. 48/M4
Artemus, Ky. (40903) 237/O7
Artena, Italy 34/F7
Artesia, Calif. (90701) 204/C11
Artesia, Miss. (39736) 256/G4
Artesia, N. Mex. 188/F4
Artesia, N. Mex. (88210) 274/E6
Artesian, S. Dak. (57314) 298/O6
Artesia Wells, Texas (78001) 303/E9
Arth, Switzerland 39/F2
Arthabaska (co.), Québec 172/E4
Arthabaska, Québec 172/F3
Arthur, Ill. (61911) 222/E4
Arthur, Ind. (†47598) 227/C8
Arthur, Iowa (51431) 229/C4
Arthur (co.), Nebr. 264/C3
Arthur, Nebr. (69121) 264/C3
Arthur (range), N. Zealand 100/D4
Arthur, N. Dak. (58006) 282/R5
Arthur, Ontario 177/D4
Arthur (lake), Pa. 294/C4
Arthur (lake), Tasmania 99/D4
Arthur (range), Tasmania 99/C5
Arthur (riv.), Tasmania 99/B3
Arthur, Tenn. (37707) 237/O7
Arthur (riv.), W. Australia 92/B2
Arthur, W. Va. (26816) 312/H4
Arthurdale, W. Va. (26520) 312/G3
Arthuret, England 13/E2
Arthurette, New Bruns. 170/C2
Arthur Kill (str.), N.J. 273/B3
Arthur's (pass), N. Zealand 100/C5
Arthurstown, Ireland 17/H7
Artibonite (dept.), Haiti 158/C5
Artibonite (riv.), Haiti 158/C5
Artigas (dept.), Uruguay 145/B1
Artigas, Uruguay 145/C1
Artillery (lake), N.W. Terrs. 187/H3
Artland, Sask. 181/B3
Artois, Calif. (95913) 204/C4
Artois (trad. prov.), France 29
Artova, Turkey 63/G2
Artux (Atushi), China 77/A4
Artvin (prov.), Turkey 63/J2
Artvin, Turkey 59/D1
Artvin, Turkey 63/J2
Aru (isls.), Indonesia 85/K7
Aru, Zaire 115/F3
Arua, Uganda 115/F3
Aruba (isl.), Neth. Ant. 161/E9
Aruba (isl.), Neth. Ant. 156/E4
Arucas, Spain 33/B5
Arunachal Pradesh (terr.), India 68/G3
Arundel, England 13/G7
Arundel, England 10/F5
Arundel, Québec 172/C4
Årup, Denmark 21/D7
Aruppukkottai, India 68/D7
'Arura, West Bank 65/C3
Arus, P. Rico 161/C3
Arusha (reg.), Tanzania 115/G4
Arusha, Tanzania 102/F5
Arusha, Tanzania 115/G4
Arusi (prov.), Ethiopia 111/G6
Aruwimi (riv.), Zaire 115/E3
Arva, Ireland 17/F4
Arva, Ontario 177/C4
Arvada, Colo. (*80001) 208/J3
Arvada, Wyo. (82831) 319/F1
Arvayheer, Mongolia 77/F2
Arvel, Ky. (†40447) 237/O5
Arvi, India 68/D4
Arvida, Québec 172/F1
Arvidsjaur, Sweden 18/L4
Arvika, Sweden 18/H7
Arvilla, N. Dak. (58214) 282/P4
Arvin, Calif. (93203) 204/G8
Arvonia, Va. (23004) 307/M5
Arwad (Ruad) (isl.), Syria 63/F5
Arxan, China 77/K2
Arys', U.S.S.R. 48/G5
Arzamas, U.S.S.R. 48/E4
Arzamas, U.S.S.R. 52/F3
Arzúa, Spain 33/B1
As, Belgium 27/H6
Aš, Czech. 41/B1
Aså, Denmark 21/D3
Asaba, Nigeria 106/F7
Asadabad, Iran 66/F3
Asahan (riv.), Indonesia 85/B5
Asahi, Japan 81/K6
Asahi (mt.), Japan 81/J4
Asahikawa, Japan 81/L2
Asahikawa, Japan 54/P5
Asama (mt.), Japan 81/J5
Asansol, India 68/F4
Åsarna, Sweden 18/J5
Asau, W. Samoa 86/L8
Asbest, U.S.S.R. 48/G4
Asbestos, Québec 172/F4
Asbury, Iowa (†52001) 229/M4
Asbury, Mo. (64832) 261/C8
Asbury, N.J. (08802) 273/C2
Asbury, W. Va. (24916) 312/E7
Asbury Park, N.J. (07712) 273/F3
As Busaiya, Iraq 66/E5
Ascención (Añez), Bolivia 136/D4
Ascensión, Argentina 143/F7
Ascension (par.), La. 238/J6
Ascensión, Mexico 150/E1
Ascension, Neth. Ant. 161/F8
Ascension (isl.), St. Helena 102/A5
Ascension (isl.), St. Helena 2/J6
Aschaffenburg, W. Germany 22/C4
Aschendorf, W. Germany 22/B2
Aschersleben, E. Germany 22/D3
Asco, W. Va. (24809) 312/D8
Ascog, Scotland 15/A2
Ascoli Piceno (prov.), Italy 34/D3
Ascoli Piceno, Italy 34/D3
Ascona, Switzerland 39/G4
Ascope, Peru 128/C6
Ascot, Queensland 88/K2
Ascot, Queensland 95/E2
Ascotán, Chile 138/B3
Ascotán, Salar de (salt dep.), Chile 138/B3
Ascot Corner, Québec 172/F4
Ascrib (isls.), Scotland 15/B3
Ascutney, Vt. (05030) 268/C5
Ascutney (mt.), Vt. 268/C5
Åseda, Sweden 18/J8
Åsele, Sweden 18/K4
Asenovgrad, Bulgaria 45/G5
Asèr, Ras (cape), Somalia 2/M5
Asèr, Ras (cape), Somalia 115/K1
Ash (riv.), Minn. 255/F2
Ash, N.C. (28420) 281/N6
Ash, Oreg. (†97473) 291/D4
Ash (creek), Utah 304/A6
'Ashaira, Saudi Arabia 59/D5
Ashanti (reg.), Ghana 102/B4
Ashanti (reg.), Ghana 106/D7
Ashaway, R.I. (02804) 249/G7
Ashboro, Ind. (†47840) 227/C6
Ashburn, Georgia (31714) 217/E7
Ashburn, Mo. (63433) 261/K3
Ashburn, Va. (22011) 307/O2
Ashburnham, Mass. (01430) 249/G2
Ashburnham○, Mass. (01430) 249/G2
Ashburton (riv.), Australia 87/B8
Ashburton, England 13/D7
Ashburton, N. Zealand 100/C5
Ashburton (riv.), W. Australia 88/B4
Ashburton (riv.), W. Australia 92/A3
Ashburton Downs, W. Australia 88/B4
Ashby, Ala. (†35035) 195/E4
Ashby○, Mass. (01431) 249/G2
Ashby, Minn. (56309) 255/C4
Ashby, Nebr. (69333) 264/C2
Ashbyburg, Ky. (†42456) 237/G5
Ash Creek, Minn. (†56173) 255/B7
Ashcroft, Br. Col. 184/G5
Ashdale, Maine (†04565) 243/D8
Ashdod, Israel 65/B4
Ashdot Ya'aqov, Israel 65/D2
Ashdown, Ark. (71822) 202/B6
Ashe (co.), N.C. 281/F2
Ashe (isl.), N.C. 281/P6
Asheboro, N.C. (27203) 281/K3
Ashepoo, S.C. (†29446) 296/G6
Ashepoo (riv.), S.C. 296/F6
Asher, Okla. (74826) 288/N5
Ashern, Manitoba 179/D3
Asherton, Texas (78827) 303/E9
Asherville, Ind. (†47834) 227/C6
Asherville, Kansas (67420) 232/D2
Asheville, N.C. 188/K3
Asheville, N.C. (*28801) 281/D3
Asheweig (riv.), Ontario 175/C2
Ashfield○, Mass. (01330) 249/C2
Ashfield, N. S. Wales 88/K4
Ashfield, N.S. Wales 97/J3
Ash Flat, Ark. (72513) 202/G1
Ashford, Ala. (36312) 195/H8
Ashford○, Conn. (06278) 210/G1
Ashford, England 10/G5
Ashford, England 13/H6
Ashford, Ireland 17/J5
Ashford, N.S. Wales 97/F1
Ashford, N.C. (†28752) 281/F3
Ashford, Wash. (98304) 310/C4
Ashford, W. Va. (25009) 312/C6
Ashford P.O. (Warrenville), Conn. (06278) 210/G1
Ash Fork, Ariz. (86320) 198/C3
Ash Grove, Kansas (†67455) 232/D2
Ash Grove, Mo. (65604) 261/E8
Ashgrove, Queensland 88/K2
Ashhurst, N. Zealand 100/E4
Ashibetsu, Japan 81/L2
Ashikaga, Japan 81/J5
Ashington, England 13/F2
Ashington, England 10/F3
Ashippun, Wis. (53003) 317/H1
Ashiya, Japan 81/H8
Ashizuri (cape), Japan 81/F7
Ashkhabad, U.S.S.R. 54/G6
Ashkhabad, U.S.S.R. 48/F6
Ashkum, Ill. (60911) 222/E3
Ash Lake, Minn. (†55771) 255/F2
Ashland, Ala. (36251) 195/G4
Ashland, Calif. (†94577) 204/K2
Ashland, Georgia (†30521) 217/F2
Ashland, Ill. (62612) 222/C4
Ashland, Kansas (67831) 232/C4
Ashland, Ky. (41101) 237/R4
Ashland, Ky. 188/K3
Ashland, La. (71002) 238/D2
Ashland, Maine (04732) 243/G2
Ashland○, Maine (04732) 243/G2
Ashland○, Mass. (01721) 249/J3
Ashland, Miss. (38603) 256/F1
Ashland, Mo. (65010) 261/H5
Ashland, Mont. (59003) 262/K5
Ashland, Nebr. (68003) 264/H3
Ashland, N.H. (03217) 268/D4
Ashland○, N.H. (03217) 268/D4
Ashland, N.J. (†08033) 273/B3
Ashland, N.Y. (12407) 276/M6
Ashland (co.), Ohio 284/F4
Ashland, Ohio (44805) 284/F4
Ashland, Okla. (74524) 288/O5
Ashland, Oreg. (97520) 291/E5
Ashland, Pa. (17921) 294/K4
Ashland, Va. (23005) 307/N5
Ashland (co.), Wis. 317/E3
Ashland, Wis. (54806) 317/E2
Ashland City, Tenn. (37015) 237/G8
Ashley (co.), Ark. 202/G7
Ashley, Ill. (62808) 222/D5
Ashley, Ind. (46705) 227/G1
Ashley, Mich. (48806) 250/E5
Ashley, Mo. (†63334) 261/K4
Ashley (lake), Mont. 262/B2
Ashley, N.S. Wales 97/E1
Ashley, N. Dak. (58413) 282/M7
Ashley, Ohio (43003) 284/E5
Ashley, Pa. (18706) 294/E7
Ashley (riv.), S.C. 296/G6
Ashley, W. Va. (†26339) 312/E4
Ashley Falls, Mass. (01222) 249/A4
Ashmere (lake), Mass. 249/B3
Ashmont, Alberta 182/E2
Ashmore, Ill. (61912) 222/F4
Ashmore, Nova Scotia 168/C4
Ashmore (isls.), Terr. of Ashmore and Cartier Is. 88/C2
Ashmore and Cartier Is., Terr. of, 88/C2
Ashokan, N.Y. (†12491) 276/M7
Ashokan (res.), N.Y. 276/M7
Ashport, Tenn. (†38063) 237/B9
Ashqelon, Israel 65/A4
Ash Shabicha, Iraq 66/C5
Ashtabula (lake), N. Dak. 282/P5
Ashtabula (co.), Ohio 284/J2
Ashtabula, Ohio (44004) 284/J2
Ashton, Idaho (83420) 220/G5
Ashton, Ill. (61006) 222/D2
Ashton, Iowa (51232) 229/B2
Ashton, Kansas (†67051) 232/E4
Ashton, Mich. (†49677) 250/D5
Ashton, Nebr. (68817) 264/F3
Ashton, R.I. (02864) 249/J5
Ashton, S.C. (†29082) 296/E5
Ashton, S. Dak. (57424) 298/N3
Ashton, W. Va. (25503) 312/B5
Ashton Creek, Br. Col. 184/H5
Ashton-under-Lyne, England 13/H2
Ashton-under-Lyne, England 10/G2
Ashuanipi (lake), Newf. 166/A3
Ashuanipi (riv.), Newf. 166/A3
Ashuanpi, Newf. 166/A3
Ashuelot, N.H. (03441) 268/C6
Ashuelot (riv.), N.H. 268/C6
Ash Valley, Kansas (†67550) 232/C3
Ashville, Ala. (35953) 195/F3
Ashville, Maine (04607) 243/G7
Ashville, Manitoba 179/B3
Ashville, Ohio (43103) 284/E6
Ashville, Pa. (16613) 294/F4
Ashwaubenon, Wis. (54304) 317/K7
Ashwood, Oreg. (97711) 291/G3
'Asi (Orontes) (riv.), Syria 63/G5
Asia 2/P3
Asia (isls.), Indonesia 85/J5
Asid (gulf), Philippines 82/D4
Asidonhoppo, Suriname 131/D4
Asilah, Morocco 106/C1
Asinara (gulf), Italy 34/B4
Asinara (isl.), Italy 34/B4
Asino, U.S.S.R. 48/J4
'Asir (reg.), Saudi Arabia 59/D6
Aşkale, Turkey 63/J3
Askeaton, Ireland 17/D6
Askew, Miss. (38604) 256/D1
Askewville, N.C. (†27983) 281/R2
Askim, Norway 18/E4
Askim, Sweden 18/G8
Aski Mosul, Iraq 66/C2
Askival (mt.), Scotland 15/B4
Askov, Denmark 21/C7
Askov, Minn. (55704) 255/F4
Askvoll, Norway 18/D6
Asmara, Ethiopia 111/G4
Asmara, Ethiopia 59/C6
Asmara, Ethiopia 102/F3
Asnaes, Denmark 21/E6
Åsnen (lake), Sweden 18/J8
Asnières-sur-Seine, France 28/A1
Aso (mt.), Japan 81/E7
Aso National Park, Japan 81/E7
Asosa, Ethiopia 111/F5
Asoteriba, Jebel (mt.), Sudan 111/G3
Asotin (co.), Wash. 310/H4
Asotin, Wash. (99402) 310/H4
Asotin (creek), Wash. 310/H4
Asotin (dam), Wash. 310/J4
Aspang Markt, Austria 41/D3
Aspatria, England 13/D3
Aspe, Spain 33/F3
Aspelund, Minn. (†55946) 255/F6
Aspen, Colo. (81611) 208/F4
Aspen, Nova Scotia 168/F3
Aspen (lake), Oreg. 291/E5
Aspen (mts.), Wyo. 319/C4
Aspen Grove, Br. Col. 184/G5
Aspen Hill, Md. 245/K4
Aspermont, Texas (79502) 303/D4
Aspers, Pa. (17304) 294/H6
Aspetuck, Conn. (†06880) 210/B4
Aspetuck (res.), Conn. 210/B3
Aspetuck (riv.), Conn. 210/B3
Aspinwall, Iowa (51432) 229/C5
Aspinwall, Pa. (15215) 294/C6
Aspiring (mt.), N. Zealand 100/B6
Aspley, Queensland 88/K2
Aspy (bay), Nova Scotia 168/H2
Asquith, Sask. 181/D3
Assab, Ethiopia 59/D7
Assab, Ethiopia 111/H5
Assaba (reg.), Mauritania 106/B5
Assabet (riv.), Mass. 249/H3
Assad, Bahrat (lake), Syria 63/H4
Assakarai (dry riv.), Niger 106/F5
Assale (lake), Ethiopia 111/H5
As Salman, Iraq 59/E3
As Salman, Iraq 66/D5
Assam (state), India 68/G3
Assapan (riv.), Manitoba 179/G2
Assaria, Kansas (67416) 232/E3
Assateague Island Nat'l Seashore, Va. 307/T4
Assawompset (pond), Mass. 249/L5
Assay (creek), Utah 304/B6
Asse, Belgium 27/E7
Asselar (well), Mali 106/D5
Asselle, Ethiopia 102/F4
Asselle, Ethiopia 111/G6
Assen, Netherlands 27/K3
Assenede, Belgium 27/D6
Assens, Århus, Denmark 21/D4
Assens, Fyn, Denmark 21/D7
Assesse, Belgium 27/G8
Assigny (lake), Newf. 166/A3
Assiniboia, Sask. 181/E6
Assiniboine (mt.), Alberta 182/C4
Assiniboine (mt.), Br. Col. 184/K5
Assiniboine (riv.), Manitoba 179/C5
Assiniboine (riv.), Sask. 181/J3
Assinica (lake), Québec 174/C3
Assinika (lake), Manitoba 179/G2
Assinika (riv.), Manitoba 179/G2
Assinippi, Mass. (02339) 249/E8
Assis, Brazil 132/D8
Assis, Brazil 135/A3
Assisi, Italy 34/D3
Assonet, Mass. (02702) 249/K5
Assumption, Ill. (62510) 222/E4
Assumption (par.), La. 238/H7
Assumption, Ohio (†43540) 284/B2
Assumption (isl.), Seychelles 118/H1
Assynt (dist.), Scotland 15/C2
Assynt, Loch (lake), Scotland 15/D2
Assyria, Mich. (†49021) 250/D6
Astara, U.S.S.R. 52/G7
Astatula, Fla. (32705) 212/E3
Asten, Netherlands 27/H6
Asterabad (Gorgan), Iran 59/F2
Asterabad (Gorgan), Iran 66/J2
Asti, Calif. (95413) 204/C5
Asti (prov.), Italy 34/B2
Asti, Italy 34/B2
Astillero, Peru 128/H9
Astipálaia, Greece 45/H7
Astipálaia (isl.), Greece 45/H7
Astle, New Bruns. 170/D2
Aston (bay), N.W. Terrs. 187/J2
Aston-Jonction, Québec 172/E3
Astor, Fla. (32002) 212/E2
Astorga, Spain 33/C1
Astoria, Ill. (61501) 222/C3
Astoria, Oreg. 188/B1
Astoria, Oreg. (97103) 291/D1
Astoria, S. Dak. (57213) 298/S4
Astorville, Ontario 177/E1
Astove (isl.), Seychelles 102/G6
Astove (isl.), Seychelles 118/H2
Astra, Argentina 143/C6
Astrakhan', U.S.S.R. 7/J4
Astrakhan', U.S.S.R. 52/G5
Astrakhan', U.S.S.R. 48/E5
Astray (lake), Newf. 166/A3
Astudillo, Spain 33/D1
Asturias (reg.), Spain 33/C1
Asunción, Bolivia 136/B2
Asuncion (isl.), No. Marianas 87/E4
Asunción, Paraguay 144/A4
Asunción (cap.), Paraguay 2/F7
Asunción (dept.), Paraguay 144/A4
Asunción (cap.), Paraguay 120/D5
Asuncion (passage), Philippines 82/D5
Asunción Mita, Guatemala 154/C3
Asunción Nochixtlán, Mexico 150/L8
Asunta, Bolivia 136/B5
Aswad, Ras al (cape), Saudi Arabia 59/C5
Aswân, Egypt 111/F3
Aswân, Egypt 59/B5
Aswân, Egypt 102/F2
Aswân (dam), Egypt 59/B5
Aswân (dam), Egypt 111/F3
Aswân High (dam), Egypt 102/F2
Aswân High (dam), Egypt 111/F3
Asyût, Egypt 111/J4
Asyût, Egypt 102/F2
Asyût, Egypt 59/B4
Aszód, Hungary 41/E3
Atabapo (riv.), Colombia 126/G6
Atabapo (riv.), Venezuela 124/E6
Atacama, Puna de (reg.), Argentina 143/C2
Atacama (reg.), Chile 138/B6
Atacama (des.), Chile 120/C5
Atacama (des.), Chile 138/B4
Atacama, Salar de (salt dep.), Chile 138/C4
Atafu (atoll), Tokelau Is. 87/J6
Atahona, Uruguay 145/B4
Atakora (mts.), Benin 106/E6
Atakpamé, Togo 106/E7
Atalándi, Greece 45/F6
Atalaya, Peru 128/E8
Atalissa, Iowa (52720) 229/L5
Atambua, Indonesia 85/G7
Atami, Japan 81/J6
Atapirire, Venezuela 124/F3
Atar, Mauritania 106/B4
Atar, Mauritania 102/A2
Ataran (riv.), Burma 72/C4
Atascadero, Calif. (93422) 204/E8
Atascosa (co.), Texas 303/F9
Atascosa, Texas (78002) 303/J11
Atbara (riv.), Ethiopia 111/G4
Atbara, Sudan 111/F4
Atbara, Sudan 59/B6
Atbara, Sudan 102/F3
Atbara (riv.), Sudan 59/C6
Atbara (riv.), Sudan 111/G4
Atbasar, U.S.S.R. 48/G4
Atchafalaya (bay), La. 238/H8
Atchafalaya (riv.), La. 238/G6
Atchison, Kans. 188/G3

332 Atchison

Atchison (co.), Kansas 232/G2
Atchison, Kansas (66002) 232/G2
Atchison (co.), Mo. 261/B2
Atco, N.J. (08004) 273/D4
Ateca, Spain 33/F2
Atén, Bolivia 136/A4
Atenas, C. Rica 154/E6
Atessa, Italy 34/E3
Atglen, Pa. (19310) 294/K6
Ath, Belgium 27/D7
Athabasca (lake) 162/F4
Athabasca, Alberta 182/D2
Athabasca (lake), Alberta 182/C5
Athabasca (riv.), Alberta 182/D1
Athabasca, Alta. 162/E5
Athabasca (riv.), Alta. 162/E4
Athabasca (riv.), Alta. 146/G4
Athabasca (lake), Canada 146/H4
Athabasca (lake), Sask. 181/L2
Athalia, Ohio (†45669) 284/F8
Athalmer, Br. Col. 184/K5
Athboy, Ireland 17/H4
Athea, Ireland 17/C7
Athelstan, Iowa (†50836) 229/D7
Athelstan, Québec 172/C4
Athelstane, Wis. (54104) 317/K5
Athena, Oreg. (97813) 291/J2
Athenry, Ireland 17/D5
Athens, Ala. (35611) 195/E1
Athens, Ark. (†71943) 202/C5
Athens, Ga. 188/K4
Athens, Georgia (*30601) 217/F3
Athens (cap.), Greece 7/G5
Athens (cap.), Greece 45/F7
Athens (cap.), Greece 2/K4
Athens, Greater, Greece 45/F7
Athens, Ill. (62613) 222/D4
Athens, Ind. (46912) 227/E2
Athens, La. (71003) 238/E1
Athens, Maine (04912) 243/D6
Athens○, Maine (04912) 243/D6
Athens, Mich. (49011) 250/D6
Athens, N.Y. (12015) 276/N6
Athens (co.), Ohio 284/F7
Athens, Ohio (45701) 284/F7
Athens, Ontario 177/J3
Athens, Pa. (18810) 294/K2
Athens, Tenn. (37303) 237/M10
Athens, Texas (75751) 303/J5
Athens, W. Va. (24712) 312/E8
Athens, Wis. (54411) 317/G5
Athensville, Ill. (†62082) 222/C4
Atherley, Ontario 177/E3
Atherton, Calif. (94025) 204/K3
Atherton, Mo. (†64050) 261/R5
Atherton, Queensland 95/C3
Atherton, Queensland 88/G3
Athertonville, Ky. (†42748) 237/K5
Athleague, Ireland 17/E4
Athlone, Ireland 10/C4
Athlone, Ireland 17/F5
Athok, Burma 72/B3
Athol, Idaho (83801) 220/B2
Athol, Kansas (66932) 232/D2
Athol, Mass. (01331) 249/F2
Athol○, Mass. (01331) 249/F2
Athol, N.Y. (12810) 276/N4
Athol, N. Zealand 100/B6
Athol, Nova Scotia 168/D3
Athol (dist.), Scotland 15/D4
Athol, S. Dak. (57425) 298/M3
Atholville, New Bruns. 170/D1
Áthos (mt.), Greece 45/G5
Athy, Ireland 17/H6
Athy, Ireland 10/C4
Ati, Chad 111/C5
Ati, Chad 102/D3
Atibaia, Brazil 135/C3
Atico, Peru 128/F11
Atienza, Spain 33/E2
Atikameg, Alberta 182/C2
Atikokan, Ont. 162/G6
Atikokan, Ontario 177/G5
Atikokan, Ontario 175/B3
Atikonak (lake), Newf. 166/B3
Atim (lake), Manitoba 179/C2
Atiquizaya, El Salvador 154/C3
Atitlán (lake), Guatemala 154/B3
Atitlán (vol.), Guatemala 154/B3
Atiu (isl.), Cook Is. 87/L8
Atka, Alaska (99502) 196/D4
Atka, Alaska 188/D6
Atka (isl.), Alaska 196/L4
Atka, U.S.S.R. 48/Q3
Atkarsk, U.S.S.R. 52/G4
Atkins, Ark. (72823) 202/E3
Atkins, Iowa (52206) 229/K4
Atkins, Va. (24311) 307/F7
Atkinson (co.), Georgia 217/G8
Atkinson, Georgia (†31543) 217/J8
Atkinson, Ill. (61235) 222/C2
Atkinson○, Maine (†04426) 243/E5
Atkinson, Minn. (†55718) 255/F4
Atkinson, Nebr. (68713) 264/E2
Atkinson○, N.H. (03811) 268/E6
Atkinson, N.C. (28421) 281/N5
Atkinson (pt.), N.W. Terrs. 187/E2
Atkinson Field, Guyana 131/B2
Atlanta, Ark. (†71740) 202/D7
Atlanta, C. Rica 154/F6
Atlanta (cap.), Ga. 188/K4
Atlanta (cap.), Ga. 146/K6
Atlanta (cap.), Georgia (*30301) 217/K1
Atlanta, Idaho (83601) 220/C6
Atlanta, Ill. (61723) 222/D3
Atlanta, Ind. (46031) 227/E4
Atlanta, Kansas (67008) 232/F4
Atlanta, La. (71404) 238/E3
Atlanta, Mich. (49709) 250/E3
Atlanta, Mo. (63530) 261/H3
Atlanta, Nebr. (68923) 264/E4
Atlanta, N.Y. (14808) 276/F5
Atlanta, Ohio (43104) 284/D6
Atlanta, Texas (75551) 303/K4
Atlanta, U.S. 2/E4
Atlanta Nav. Air Sta., Georgia 217/J1
Atlantic (ocean) 102/B5
Atlantic (ocean) 146/M6
Atlantic, Iowa (50022) 229/D6
Atlantic, Maine (04608) 243/G7
Atlantic (co.), N.J. 273/D5
Atlantic, N.C. (28511) 281/S5
Atlantic, Pa. (16111) 294/B3
Atlantic (peak), Wyo. 319/D3
Atlantic Beach, Fla. (32233) 212/E1
Atlantic Beach, N.Y. (11509) 276/P7
Atlantic Beach, N.C. (28512) 281/R5
Atlantic Beach, S.C. (†29582) 296/K4
Atlantic City, N.J. 188/M3
Atlantic City, N.J. (*08401) 273/E5
Atlantic City, Wyo. (†82520) 319/D3
Atlantic Highlands, N.J. (07716) 273/F3
Atlantic Highlands (ridge), N.J. 273/E3
Atlantic Mine, Mich. (49905) 250/G1
Atlántico (dept.), Colombia 126/C2
Atlantic Ocean 4/D11
Atlantic Ocean 7/C4
Atlantic Ocean, England 13/A7
Atlantic Ocean, Scotland 15/B2
Atlantic Ocean Ocean, Portugal 33/A3
Atlántida, Uruguay 145/B6
Atlas (mts.) 102/B1
Atlas (mts.), Algeria 106/E2
Atlas (mts.), Morocco 106/C2
Atlas, Pa. (17851) 294/K4
Atlas, Wis. (†54853) 317/A4
Atlin, Br. Col. 184/J1
Atlin (lake), Br. Col. 184/J1
Atlit, Israel 65/B2
Atlixco, Mexico 150/M2
Atmore, Ala. (36503) 195/C8
Atmore, Alberta 182/D2
Atnarko, Br. Col. 184/E4
Atocha, Bolivia 136/B7
Atoka (co.), Okla. 288/O6
Atoka, Okla. (74525) 288/O6
Atoka (res.), Okla. 288/P5
Atoka, Tenn. (38004) 237/B10
Atomic City, Idaho (83215) 220/F6
Atotonilco el Alto, Mexico 150/H6
Atoui, Wadi (dry riv.), Mauritania 106/B4
Atoui, Wadi (dry riv.), Western Sahara 106/B4
Atoyac (riv.), Mexico 150/N2
Atoyac (riv.), Mexico 150/O2
Atoyac de Álvarez, Mexico 150/J8
Atrak (Atrek) (riv.), Iran 66/J2
Atrato (riv.), Colombia 126/B4
Atrek (riv.), Iran 59/G2
Atrek (Atrak) (riv.), Iran 66/J2
Atrek (riv.), U.S.S.R. 48/F6
Atri, Italy 34/D3
Atsugi, Japan 81/O2
Atsumi (bay), Japan 81/H6
Attachie, Br. Col. 184/G2
Attala (co.), Miss. 256/E4
Attalens, Switzerland 39/C3
Attalla, Ala. (35954) 195/F2
Attapu, Laos 72/E4
Attapulgus, Georgia (31715) 217/D9
Attawapiskat (riv.), Ont. 146/K4
Attawapiskat (riv.), Ont. 162/H5
Attawapiskat, Ontario 175/D2
Attawapiskat (lake), Ontario 175/C2
Attawapiskat (riv.), Ontario 175/C2
Attawaugan, Conn. (†06241) 210/H1
Atteam (pond), Maine 243/C4
Attebubu, Ghana 106/D7
Atterberry, Ill. (†62675) 222/D3
Atter See (lake), Austria 41/B3
Attert, Belgium 27/H9
Attica, Ind. (47918) 227/C4
Attica, Iowa (†50138) 229/G6
Attica, Kansas (67009) 232/D4
Attica, Mich. (48412) 250/F5
Attica, N.Y. (14011) 276/D5
Attica, Ohio (44807) 284/E3
Attikamagen (lake), Newf. 166/A3
'Attil, West Bank 65/C3
Attleboro, Mass. (02703) 249/J5
Attleboro Falls, Mass. (02763) 249/J5
Attleborough, England 13/H5
Attnang-Puchheim, Austria 41/B2
Attock, Pakistan 68/C2
Attu (isl.), Alaska 188/D6
Attu (isl.), Alaska 196/J3
Attu (isl.), U.S. 4/D1
Attunga, N.S. Wales 97/F2
Atuel (riv.), Argentina 143/C4
Atuntaqui, Ecuador 128/C2
Atuona, Fr. Poly. 87/M7
Atura, Uganda 115/F3
Atushi (Artux), China 77/A4
Åtvidaberg, Sweden 18/K7
Atwater, Calif. (95301) 204/E6
Atwater, Minn. (56209) 255/D5
Atwater, Ohio (44201) 284/H3
Atwater, Sask. 181/J5
Atwood (Samana) (cay), Bahamas 156/D2
Atwood, Colo. (80722) 208/N1
Atwood, Ill. (61913) 222/E4
Atwood, Ind. (46502) 227/F2
Atwood, Kansas (67730) 232/B2
Atwood, Mich. (†49729) 250/D3
Atwood (lake), Ohio 284/H4
Atwood, Okla. (74827) 288/O5
Atwood, Ontario 177/D4
Atwood, Pa. (†16249) 294/D4
Atwood, Tenn. (38220) 237/D9
Atwoodville, Conn. (†06250) 210/G1
Atyrá, Paraguay 144/B4
Au, Switzerland 39/J2
Auasbila, Honduras 154/E3
Auau (chan.), Hawaii 218/H2
Aubagne, France 28/F6
Aubange, Belgium 27/H9
Aube (dept.), France 28/E3
Aube (riv.), France 28/F3
Aubenas, France 28/F5
Auberry, Calif. (93602) 204/F6
Aubervilliers, France 28/B1
Aubigny, Manitoba 179/E5
Aubonne, Switzerland 39/B4
Aubrey (cliffs), Ariz. 198/B3
Aubrey, Ark. (72311) 202/J4
Auburn, Ala. (36830) 195/H5
Auburn, Calif. (95603) 204/C8
Auburn, Georgia (30203) 217/E2
Auburn, Ill. (62615) 222/D4
Auburn, Ind. (46706) 227/G2
Auburn (mt.), Ind. 227/G5
Auburn, Iowa (51433) 229/D4
Auburn, Kansas (66402) 232/G3
Auburn, Ky. (42206) 237/H7
Auburn, Maine (04210) 243/C7
Auburn, Maine 188/M2
Auburn○, Mass. (01501) 249/G4
Auburn, Mich. (48611) 250/F5
Auburn, Miss. (†39664) 256/C8
Auburn, Nebr. (68305) 264/J4
Auburn○, N.H. (03032) 268/E5
Auburn, N. S. Wales 88/K4
Auburn, N.S. Wales 97/J3
Auburn, N.Y. 188/L2
Auburn, N.Y. (13021) 276/G5
Auburn, N. Dak. (†58237) 282/R2
Auburn, Nova Scotia 168/D3
Auburn, Ontario 177/C4
Auburn, Pa. (17922) 294/K4
Auburn, Wash. (98002) 310/C3
Auburn, W. Va. (26325) 312/E4
Auburn, Wyo. (83111) 319/A3
Auburndale, Fla. (33823) 212/E3
Auburndale, Mass. (†02166) 249/B7
Auburndale, Wis. (54412) 317/F6
Auburn Heights, Mich. (48057) 250/F6
Auburntown, Tenn. (37016) 237/J9
Aubusson, France 28/E4
Aucanquilcha, Cerro (mt.), Chile 138/B3
Auce, U.S.S.R. 53/B2
Auch, France 28/D6
Auchenblae, Scotland 15/F4
Auchencairn, Scotland 15/E6
Auchinleck, Scotland 15/D5
Auchterarder, Scotland 10/D2
Auchterarder, Scotland 15/E4
Auchtermuchty, Scotland 15/E4
Aucilla, Fla. (†32344) 212/C1
Aucilla (riv.), Fla. 212/C1
Auckland (isls.), N. Zealand 2/S8
Auckland, N.Zealand 2/T7
Auckland, N. Zealand 100/B1
Auckland, N. Zealand 87/H1
Auclair, Québec 172/J2
Aude (dept.), France 28/E6
Audegle, Somalia 115/J3
Auden, Ontario 177/H4
Auden, Ontario 175/C2
Audenarde (Oudenaarde), Belgium 27/D7
Auderghem, Belgium 27/C9
Audet, Québec 172/G4
Audincourt, France 28/G4
Audrain (co.), Mo. 261/J4
Audubon (co.), Iowa 229/D5
Audubon, Iowa (50025) 229/D5
Audubon, Minn. (56511) 255/C4
Audubon, N.J. (08106) 273/B3
Audubon (lake), N. Dak. 282/H4
Audubon Park, Ky. (†40201) 237/J2
Audubon Park, N.J. (†08106) 273/B3
Aue, E. Germany 22/E3
Auerbach, E. Germany 22/E3
Augathella, Queensland 95/C5
Augathella, Queensland 88/H5
Auger (falls), Idaho 220/D7
Augher, N. Ireland 17/G3
Aughnacloy, N. Ireland 17/H3
Aughrabies (King George's) (falls), S. Africa 118/B5
Aughrim, Ireland 17/J6
Auglaize (co.), Ohio 284/B4
Auglaize (riv.), Ohio 284/B4
Au Gres, Mich. (48703) 250/F4
Augsburg, W. Germany 7/E4
Augsburg, W. Germany 22/D4
Augusta, Ark. (72006) 202/H3
Augusta (cape), Colombia 126/C2
Augusta, Ga. 188/K4
Augusta, Ga. 146/K6
Augusta, Georgia (*30901) 217/J4
Augusta, Ill. (62311) 222/C3
Augusta, Ind. (†47598) 227/C8
Augusta, Iowa (†52658) 229/L7
Augusta, Italy 34/E6
Augusta, Kansas (67010) 232/F4
Augusta, Ky. (41002) 237/N3
Augusta (cap.), Maine 146/M5
Augusta (cap.), Maine (04330) 243/D7
Augusta (cap.), Maine 188/N2
Augusta, Mich. (49012) 250/D6
Augusta, Mo. (63332) 261/L5
Augusta, Mont. (59410) 262/D3
Augusta, N.J. (07822) 273/D1
Augusta, Ohio (44607) 284/J4
Augusta (co.), Va. 307/K4
Augusta, W. Australia 92/A6
Augusta, W. Va. (26704) 312/J4
Augusta, Wis. (54722) 317/D6
Augusta Springs, Va. (24411) 307/K4
Augustenborg, Denmark 21/D8
Augustine (isl.), Alaska 196/H3
Augustów, Poland 47/F2
Augustus (isl.), W. Australia 92/D1
Augustus (mt.), W. Australia 92/B4
Aujila, Libya 102/E2
Aujila, Libya 111/D2
Auki, Solomon Is. 86/E3
Auki, Solomon Is. 87/G6
Aulac, New Bruns. 170/F3
Aulander, N.C. (27805) 281/P2
Auld (lake), W. Australia 88/C4
Auldearn, Scotland 15/E3
Aulencia (riv.), Spain 33/F4
Aullville, Mo. (†64037) 261/E4
Aulnay-sous-Bois, France 28/B1
Ault, Colo. (80610) 208/K1
Ault (peak), Switzerland 39/H3
Aultbea, Scotland 15/C3
Aultman, Pa. (15713) 294/D4
Aumsville, Oreg. (97325) 291/E3
Auning, Denmark 21/D5
Aunis (trad. prov.), France 29
Aur, Pulau (isl.), Malaysia 72/E7
Aura, Mich. (49906) 250/A2
Aura, N.J. (†08028) 273/C4
Aurangabad, Bihar, India 68/E4
Aurangabad, Maharashtra, India 68/D5
Auraria, Georgia (†30534) 217/E1
Auray, France 28/B4
Aurelia, Iowa (51005) 229/C3
Aurès (lag.), Algeria 106/F1
Aurich, W. Germany 22/B2
Aurignac, France 28/D6
Aurillac, France 28/E5
Aurland, Norway 18/E6
Aurora, Ark. (†72740) 202/C2
Aurora, Brazil 132/G4
Aurora, Colo. 188/F3
Aurora, Colo. (*80010) 208/K3
Aurora, Guyana 131/B2
Aurora, Ill. (*60504) 222/E2
Aurora, Ind. (47001) 227/H6
Aurora, Iowa (50607) 229/K3
Aurora, Kansas (67417) 232/E2
Aurora○, Maine (04408) 243/G6
Aurora, Minn. (55705) 255/F3
Aurora, Mo. (65605) 261/E9
Aurora, Nebr. (68818) 264/F4
Aurora, N.Y. (13026) 276/G5
Aurora, N.C. (27806) 281/R4
Aurora, Ohio (44202) 284/H3
Aurora, Ontario 177/J3
Aurora, Oreg. (97002) 291/B2
Aurora, Philippines 82/D4
Aurora (co.), S. Dak. 298/M6
Aurora, S. Dak. (57002) 298/R5
Aurora, Texas (†76078) 303/E1
Aurora, Utah (84620) 304/B5
Aurora, W. Va. (26705) 312/G4
Aurora Lodge, Alaska (†99701) 196/J2
Auroraville, Wis. (†54923) 317/H7
Aus, Namibia 118/B5
Au Sable, Mich. (†48750) 250/F4
Au Sable (pt.), Mich. 250/F4
Au Sable (pt.), Mich. 250/C2
Au Sable (riv.), Mich. 250/E4
Ausable (riv.), N.Y. 276/N2
Au Sable Forks, N.Y. (12912) 276/N2
Auschwitz (Oświęcim), Poland 47/D3
Ausert (well), Western Sahara 106/B4
Auskerry (isl.), Scotland 15/F1
Aust-Agder (co.), Norway 18/E7
Austell, Georgia (30001) 217/J1
Austerlitz (Slavkov), Czech. 41/D2
Austin, Ark. (72007) 202/G4
Austin, Colo. (81410) 208/D5
Austin, Ind. (47102) 227/F7
Austin, Ky. (42123) 237/K7
Austin, Manitoba 179/D5
Austin, Minn. 188/H2
Austin, Minn. (55912) 255/E7
Austin, Mo. (†64725) 261/D5
Austin, Mont. (†59601) 262/D4
Austin, Nev. 188/C3
Austin, Nev. (89310) 266/E3
Austin, Oreg. (†97817) 291/J3
Austin, Pa. (16720) 294/F2
Austin (co.), Texas 303/H8
Austin (cap.), Texas 146/J6
Austin (cap.), Texas (*78701) 303/G7
Austin (cap.), Texas 188/G4
Austin (lake), W. Australia 88/B5
Austin (lake), W. Australia 92/B4
Austinburg, Ohio (44010) 284/J2
Austintown, Ohio (44515) 284/J3
Austinville, Iowa (50608) 229/H3
Austinville, Va. (24312) 307/F7
Austonio, Texas (†75835) 303/J6
Austral (isls.), Fr. Polynesia 2/B7
Austral (isls.), Fr. Poly. 87/L8
Australia 2/R7
Australia 87/C8
AUSTRALIA 88
Australia Aboriginal Reserve, W. Australia 88/D5
Australia Aboriginal Res., W. Australia 92/E4
Australian, Br. Col. 184/F4
Australian Alps (mts.), N.S. Wales 97/D5
Australian Alps (mts.), Victoria 97/D5
Australian Alps (mts.), Victoria 88/H7
Australian Capital Territory, /H7
Australian Capital Terr., Australia 87/F9
AUSTRALIAN CAPITAL TERRITORY 97/E4
Australind, W. Australia 92/A2
Austria 2/K3
Austria 7/F4
AUSTRIA 41
Austwell, Texas (77950) 303/H9
Autauga (co.), Ala. 195/E5
Autaugaville, Ala. (36003) 195/E6
Autlán de Navarro, Mexico 150/G7
Au Train, Mich. (49806) 250/C2
Au Train (bay), Mich. 250/C2
Autreyville, Georgia (†31768) 217/E8
Autryville, N.C. (28318) 281/M4
Autun, France 28/F4
Auvelais, Belgium 27/F8
Auvergne, Ark. (†72112) 202/H2
Auvergne (mts.), France 28/E5
Auvergne (trad. prov.) France 29
Auvergne, North. Terr. 93/B3
Auvergne, Québec 172/F3
Auxerre, France 28/E4
Auxier, Ky. (41602) 237/R5
Auxonne, France 28/F4
Auxvasse, Mo. (65231) 261/J4
Auyantepui (mt.), Venezuela 124/G5
Auyuittuq Nat'l Park, N.W. Terrs. /M3
Auyuittuq Nat'l Park, Que. 162/K2
Ava, Ill. (62907) 222/D6
Ava, Mo. (65608) 261/G9
Ava, N.Y. (13303) 276/K4
Ava, Ohio (43711) 284/G6
Avallon, France 28/E4
Avalon, Calif. (90704) 204/G10
Avalon, Georgia (†30557) 217/F1
Avalon, Miss. (38912) 256/D3
Avalon, Mo. (64621) 261/F3
Avalon (pen.), Newf. 166/D2
Avalon, N.J. (08202) 273/D5
Avalon (res.), N. Mex. 274/E6
Avalon, Pa. (15202) 294/B6
Avanos, Turkey 63/F3
Avans, Georgia (†30752) 217/A1
Avant, Okla. (74001) 288/O2
Avard, Okla. (†73860) 288/J1
Avaré, Brazil 132/D8
Avaré, Brazil 135/B3
Avarua (cap.), Cook Is. 87/L8
Avayalik (isls.), Newf. 166/B1
Avaz, Iran 66/M4
Aveiro (dist.), Portugal 33/B2
Aveiro, Portugal 33/B2
Avej, Iran 66/F3
Avella, Pa. (15312) 294/B5
Avellaneda, Argentina 143/G7
Avellino (prov.), Italy 34/E4
Avellino, Italy 34/E4
Avenal, Calif. (93204) 204/E8
Avenches, Switzerland 39/D3
Avenel, N.J. (07001) 273/E2
Aventon, N.C. (†27891) 281/O2
Avera, Georgia (30803) 217/G4
Avera, Miss. (†39456) 256/G8
Averias, Uruguay 145/E4
Averill, Mich. (†48640) 250/E5
Averill, Minn. (†56547) 255/B4
Averill○, Vt. (05901) 268/D2
Averill Park, N.Y. (12018) 276/O5
Aversa, Italy 34/E4
Avery, Idaho (83802) 220/C2
Avery, Iowa (†52531) 229/H6
Avery (co.), N.C. 281/F2
Avery, Ohio (†44846) 284/E3
Avery, Okla. (†74023) 288/N3
Avery, Texas (75554) 303/K4
Avery Island, La. (70513) 238/G7
Aves (Bird) (isl.), Venezuela 156/F4
Avesnes-sur-Helpe, France 28/F2
Avesta, Sweden 18/J6
Aveyron (dept.), France 28/E5
Avezzano, Italy 34/D3
Aviemore, Scotland 15/E3
Avigliano, Italy 34/E4
Avignon, France 28/F6
Avignon, France 7/E4
Avihayil, Israel 65/B3
Ávila (prov.), Spain 33/D2
Ávila de los Caballeros, Spain 33/D2
Avilés, Spain 33/C1
Avilla, Ind. (46710) 227/G2
Avilla, Mo. (64833) 261/D8
Avinger, Texas (75630) 303/K5
Avion, France 28/E2
Avis, Pa. (17721) 294/H3
Avis, Portugal 33/C3
Aviston, Ill. (62216) 222/D5
Avize, France 28/F3
Avlum, Denmark 21/B5
Avoca, Ark. (72711) 202/B1
Avoca, Ind. (47420) 227/D7
Avoca, Iowa (51521) 229/C6
Avoca, Ireland 17/J6
Avoca, Mich. (48006) 250/G5
Avoca, Minn. (56114) 255/C7
Avoca, Nebr. (68307) 264/H4
Avoca, N.Y. (14809) 276/F6
Avoca, Pa. (18641) 294/F7
Avoca, Tasmania 99/D3
Avoca, Texas (79503) 303/E5
Avoca, Victoria 97/B5
Avoca (riv.), Victoria 97/B5
Avoca, Wis. (53506) 317/F9
Avoch, Scotland 15/D3
Avola, Br. Col. 184/H4
Avola, Italy 34/E6
Avon, Ala. (†36312) 195/H8
Avon, Colo. (81620) 208/F3
Avon, Conn. (06001) 210/D1
Avon○, Conn. (06001) 210/D1
Avon (co.), England 13/E6
Avon (riv.), England 13/F7
Avon (riv.), England 13/F5
Avon (riv.), England 10/E4
Avon, Idaho (†83823) 220/B3
Avon, Ill. (61415) 222/C3
Avon○, Mass. (02322) 249/K4
Avon, Minn. (56310) 255/D5
Avon, Miss. (38723) 256/B4
Avon, Mont. (59713) 262/D4
Avon, N.Y. (14414) 276/E5
Avon, N.C. (27915) 281/U4
Avon (riv.), Nova Scotia 168/D4
Avon, Ohio (44011) 284/F3
Avon (riv.), Scotland 15/C1
Avon (riv.), Scotland 15/E3
Avon, S. Dak. (57315) 298/N8
Avon (riv.), W. Australia 88/B6
Avon (riv.), W. Australia 92/A1
Avon, Wis. (†53520) 317/H10
Avon By The Sea, N.J. (07717) 273/E3
Avondale, Ariz. (85323) 198/C5
Avondale, Colo. (81022) 208/L6
Avondale, Mich. (†49631) 250/D4
Avondale, Mo. (64010) 261/P5
Avondale, Newf. 166/D2
Avondale, N.S. Wales 97/F3
Avondale, N.C. (†28076) 281/F4
Avondale, Pa. (19311) 294/L6
Avondale, W. Va. (24811) 312/C8
Avondale Estates, Georgia (30002) 217/L1
Avon Downs, North. Terr. 88/F4
Avon Downs, North. Terr. 93/E5
Avonhurst, Sask. 181/G5
Avon Lake, Ohio (44012) 284/F2
Avonlea, Sask. 181/G5
Avonmore, Ontario 177/K2
Avonmore, Pa. (15618) 294/C4
Avon Park, Fla. (33825) 212/E4
Avonport, Nova Scotia 168/D3
Avon Water (riv.), Scotland 15/D5
Avoyelles (par.), La. 238/G4
Avranches, France 28/C3
Awa (isl.), Japan 81/J4
Awaji, Japan 81/H8
Awaji (isl.), Japan 81/H8
Awanui, N. Zealand 100/D1
Awareh, Ethiopia 111/H6
Awarua (bay), N. Zealand 100/A6
Awash, Ethiopia 111/H6
Awash (riv.), Ethiopia 111/H5
Awaso, Ghana 106/D7
Awat, China 77/A3
Awatere (riv.), N. Zealand 100/D5
Awbeg (riv.), Ireland 17/D7
Awe, Loch (lake), Scotland 10/D2
Awe, Loch (lake), Scotland 15/C4
Aweil, Sudan 111/E6
Awendaw, S.C. (29429) 296/H5
Awosting, N.J. (†07421) 273/E1
Axe Edge (mt.), England 13/H2
Axel, Netherlands 27/D6
Axel Heiberg (isl.), Canada 4/A14
Axel Heiberg (isl.), N.W.T. 146/J1
Axel Heiberg (isl.), N.W. Terrs. 187/J2
Axel Heiburg (isl.), N.W.T. 162/N3
Axim, Ghana 106/D8
Axis, Ala. (36505) 195/B9
Ax-les-Thermes, France 28/D6
Axminster, England 13/D7
Axminster, England 10/E5
Axochiapan, Mexico 150/M2
Axson, Georgia (31624) 217/G8
Axtell, Kansas (66403) 232/F2
Axtell, Nebr. (68924) 264/E4
Axtell, Utah (84621) 304/C4
Axton, Va. (24054) 307/J7
Axum (Aksum), Ethiopia 111/G5
Ayabaca, Peru 128/C5
Ayabe, Japan 81/G6
Ayacucho, Argentina 143/E4
Ayacucho, Bolivia 136/D5
Ayacucho (dept.), Peru 128/E9
Ayacucho, Peru 128/F9
Ayacucho, Peru 120/B4
Ayaguz, U.S.S.R. 54/K5
Ayaguz, U.S.S.R. 48/J5
Ayakkum Hu (lake), China 77/C4
Ayamonte, Spain 33/C4
Ayan, U.S.S.R. 54/P4
Ayan, U.S.S.R. 48/O4
Ayancık, Turkey 63/F1
Ayapel, Colombia 126/C3
Ayapel, Serranía de (mts.), Colombia 126/C4
Ayaş, Turkey 63/E2
Ayata, Bolivia 136/A4
Ayaviri, Peru 128/G10
Aybak, Afghanistan 68/B1
Aybak, Afghanistan 59/J2
Aybastı, Turkey 63/G2
Aycliffe, England 13/F3
Ayden, N.C. (28513) 281/P4
Aydın (prov.), Turkey 63/B4
Aydin, Turkey 59/A2
Aydın, Turkey 63/B4
Aydıncık, Turkey 63/E4
Aydlett, N.C. (27916) 281/T2
Aydyrlinskiy, U.S.S.R. 52/K4
Ayer, Mass. (*01432) 249/H2
Ayer○, Mass. (*01432) 249/H2
Ayer, Switzerland 39/E4
Ayer, Wash. (†99348) 310/G4
Ayers, Maine (†04666) 243/J6
Ayer's Cliff, Québec 172/E4
Ayers Rock, Mt. Olga Nat'l Park, North. Terr. 88/E5
Ayers Rock (mt.), North. Terr. 88/E5
Ayers Rock Nat'l Park, North. Terr. 93/B8
Ayersville, Ohio (†43512) 284/B3
Ayiá, Greece 45/F6
Áyion Óros (aut. dist.), Greece 45/G5
Áyios Evstrátios (isl.), Greece 45/G6
Áyios Kírikos, Greece 45/H7
Áyios Matthaíos, Greece 45/D6
Áyios Nikólaos, Greece 45/G8
Áyios Yeóryios (cape), Greece 45/G5
Aykhal, U.S.S.R. 48/M3
Aylen (lake), Ontario 177/G2
Aylesbury, England 13/G7
Aylesbury, England 10/F5
Aylesbury, Sask. 181/F5
Aylesford, England 13/J8
Aylesford, Nova Scotia 168/D3
Aylett, Va. (23009) 307/O5
Ayllón, Spain 33/E2
Aylmer, N. Dak. (†58710) 282/K4
Aylmer (lake), N.W. Terrs. 187/H3
Aylmer, Ontario 177/C5
Aylmer, Québec 172/B4
Aylmer (lake), Québec 172/F4
Aylsham, England 13/J5
Aylsham, Sask. 181/H2
Aynor, S.C. (29511) 296/J3
Ayod, Sudan 111/F6
Ayolas, Paraguay 144/D5
Ayon (isl.), U.S.S.R. 48/R2
Ayora, Spain 33/F3
Ayr, Nebr. (68925) 264/F4
Ayr, N. Dak. (58007) 282/P5
Ayr, Ontario 177/D4
Ayr, Queensland 95/C3
Ayr, Queensland 88/H3
Ayr, Scotland 15/D5
Ayr, Scotland 10/D3
Ayr, Heads of (cape), Scotland 15/D5
Ayr (trad. co.), Scotland 15/A5
Ayr (riv.), Scotland 15/D5
Ayrancı, Turkey 63/E4
Ayre (pt.), I. of Man 13/C3
Ayre (pt.), I. of Man 10/D3
Ayrshire, Iowa (50515) 229/D2
Ayton, Ontario 177/D3
Ayton, Scotland 15/F5

Aytos, Bulgaria 45/H4
Ayu (isls.), Indonesia 85/J5
Ayun, Saudi Arabia 59/D4
Ayutla de los Libres, Mexico 150/K8
Ayutthaya (Phra Nakhon Si Ayutthaya), Thailand 72/D4
Ayvacık, Turkey 63/B3
Ayvalık, Turkey 59/A2
Ayvalık, Turkey 63/B3
Aywaille, Belgium 27/H8
Azalea, Oreg. (97410) 291/D5
Azalea Park, Fla. (32807) 212/E3
Azalia, Ind. (†47232) 227/F6
Azalia, Mich. (48110) 250/F6
Azamgarh, India 68/E3
Azángaro, Peru 128/H10
Azángaro (riv.), Peru 128/G10
Azaoua (reg.), Niger 106/E5
Azaouad (reg.), Mali 106/D5
Azaouak (dry riv.), Mali 106/E5
Azapa, Chile 138/A1
Azapa, Quebrada (riv.), Chile 138/B1
Azare, Nigeria 106/G6
Azaz, Syria 63/G4
Azbine (Aïr) (mts.), Niger 106/F5
Azcapotzalco, Mexico 150/L1
Azdavay, Turkey 63/E2
Azemmour, Morocco 106/C2
Azerbaidzhan S.S.R., U.S.S.R. 7/J4
Azerbaidzhan S.S.R., U.S.S.R. 48/E5
Azerbaidzhan S.S.R., U.S.S.R. 52/G6
Azerbaijan, East (prov.), Iran 66/E1
Azerbaijan, West (prov.), Iran 66/D1
Azerbaijan (reg.), Iran 66/D1
Aziscoos (lake), Maine 243/A5
Azle, Texas (76020) 303/E2
Azogues, Ecuador 128/C4
AZORES 33
Azores (isls.), Portugal 2/H4
Azores (isls.), Portugal 33/A2
Azoum, Bahr, Chad 111/D5
Azov (sea), U.S.S.R. 7/H4
Azov, U.S.S.R. 52/E5
Azov (sea), U.S.S.R. 52/E5
Azov (sea), U.S.S.R. 48/D5
Azoyú, Mexico 150/K8
Azpeitia, Spain 33/E1
Azrou, Morocco 106/C2
Aztec, Ariz. (†85333) 198/B6
Aztec, N. Mex. (87410) 274/B2
Aztec Ruins Nat'l Mon., N. Mex. 274/A2
Azua (prov.), Dom. Rep. 158/D6
Azua, Dom. Rep. 156/D3
Azua, Dom. Rep. 158/D6
Azuaga, Spain 33/D3
Azuara, Spain 33/F2
Azuay (prov.), Ecuador 128/C4
Azuero (pen.), Panama 154/G7
Azul, Argentina 143/E4
Azul, Argentina 120/D6
Azul (riv.), Guatemala 154/C2
Azul, Cordillera (mts.), Peru 128/E7
Azurduy, Bolivia 136/C6
Azure (lake), Br. Col. 184/G4
Azusa, Calif. (91702) 204/D10
Azwell, Wash. (†98846) 310/F3
Azzel Mati, Sebkha (lake), Algeria 106/E3
Az Zubair, Iraq 66/E5

B

Ba, Fiji 86/P10
Baa, Indonesia 85/G8
Baaba (isl.), New Caled. 86/G4
Ba'albek, Lebanon 63/G5
Baan Baa, N.S. Wales 97/E2
Baar, Switzerland 39/F2
Baarle-Nassau, Netherlands 27/F6
Baarn, Netherlands 27/G4
Baatsagaan, Mongolia 77/E2
Baba, Ecuador 128/C3
Baba (cape), Turkey 63/D2
Baba (cape), Turkey 63/A3
Babadag, Romania 45/J3
Babadağ, Turkey 63/C4
Babaeski, Turkey 63/B2
Babahoyo, Ecuador 128/C3
Babanusa, Sudan 111/E5
Babar (isl.), Indonesia 85/H7
Babar (isls.), Indonesia 85/H7
Babati, Tanzania 115/G4
Babayevo, U.S.S.R. 52/E3
Babb, Mont. (59411) 262/C2
Babbie, Ala. (†36420) 195/F8
Babbitt, Minn. (55706) 255/G3
Babbitt, Nev. (89416) 266/C4
Babcock, Wis. (54413) 317/F7
Babel (isls.), Tasmania 99/E1
Bab el Mandeb (str.) 102/G3
Bab el Mandeb (str.), Djibouti 111/H5
Babelthuap (isl.), Belau 87/D5
Babia (riv.), Mexico 150/J2
Babil (heads), Iraq 66/D4
Babine (lake), Br. Col. 162/D5
Babine, Br. Col. 184/D2
Babine (lake), Br. Col. 184/E3
Babine (riv.), Br. Col. 184/D2
Babo, Indonesia 85/K7
Babol, Iran 54/G6
Babol, Iran 59/F2
Babol, Iran 66/H2
Babol Sar, Iran 66/H2
Baboquivari (mts.), Ariz. 198/D7
Baboua, Cent. Afr. Rep. 115/C2
Babson Park, Fla. (33827) 212/E4
Babuyan (isls.), Philippines 54/O8
Babuyan (chan.), Philippines 82/A3
Babuyan (isl.), Philippines 82/B2
Babuyan (isls.), Philippines 85/G2
Babuyan (isls.), Philippines 82/A2
Babylon (ruins), Iraq 66/D4
Babylon, N.Y. (*11702) 276/O9
Baca (co.), Colo. 208/O8
Bacabal, Brazil 120/E3
Bacabal, Maranhão, Brazil 132/E4
Bacabal, Pará, Brazil 132/B4
Bacadéhuachi, Mexico 150/E2
Bacalar, Mexico 150/P7
Bacalar (lake), Mexico 150/P7
Bacan (isls.), Indonesia 85/H6
Bacanora, Mexico 150/E2
Bacarra, Philippines 82/C1
Bacău, Romania 7/G4
Bacău, Romania 45/H2
Baccalieu (isl.), Newf. 166/D2
Bac Can, Vietnam 72/E2
Baccaro (pt.), Nova Scotia 168/C5
Bacchus Marsh, Victoria 97/C5
Bacerac, Mexico 150/E1
Bac Giang, Vietnam 72/E2
Bach, Mich. (†48759) 250/F5
Bachaquero, Venezuela 124/C3
Bache (pen.), N.W. Terrs. 187/L2
Bache, Okla. (74526) 288/P5
Bachelor (brook), Mass. 249/D3
Bachiniva, Mexico 150/F2
Bach Long Vi, Dao (isl.), Vietnam 72/F2
Bachu (Maralwexi), China 77/A4
Back (bay), India 68/B7
Back (riv.), Md. 245/N4
Back (lake), N.H. 268/E1
Back (riv.), N.W.T. 146/H3
Back (riv.), N.W.T. 162/G2
Back (riv.), N.W. Terrs. 187/J3
Back (bay), Va. 307/S7
Back (creek), Va. 307/J4
Bačka Topola, Yugoslavia 45/D3
Back Bay, New Bruns. 170/D3
Backbone (mt.), Md. 245/A3
Backnang, W. Germany 22/C4
Backoo, N. Dak. (58215) 282/P2
Backus, Minn. (56435) 255/D4
Backway, The (inlet), Newf. 166/C3
Bac Lieu, Vietnam 72/E5
Bacliff, Texas (77518) 303/K2
Bac Ninh, Vietnam 72/E2
Baco (mt.), Philippines 82/C4
Bacolod, Philippines 85/G3
Bacolod, Philippines 54/O8
Bacolod, Philippines 82/D5
Bacon (co.), Georgia 217/G7
Bacone, Okla. (†74401) 288/R3
Bacon Ridge (mts.), Wyo. 319/B2
Baconton, Del. (†19940) 245/R6
Baconton, Georgia (31716) 217/D8
Bácsalmás, Hungary 41/E3
Bács-Kiskun (co.), Hungary 41/E3
Bácum, Mexico 150/D3
Bacuna, Neth. Ant. 161/E8
Bacup, England 13/H1
Bacup, England 10/G1
Bad (riv.), Mich. 250/E5
Bad (hills), Sask. 181/C4
Bad (lake), Sask. 181/C4
Bad (riv.), S. Dak. 298/G5
Badacsonytomaj, Hungary 41/D3
Badagara, India 68/D6
Bad Aibling, W. Germany 22/D5
Badajoz (prov.), Spain 33/C3
Badajoz, Spain 33/C3
Badalona, Spain 33/H2
Bad Aussee, Austria 41/B3
Bad Axe, Mich. (48413) 250/G5
Bad Berleburg, W. Germany 22/C3
Bad Berneck, W. Germany 22/D3
Bad Bramstedt, W. Germany 22/C2
Bad Brückenau, W. Germany 22/C3
Baddeck, Nova Scotia 168/H2
Baddeck (riv.), Nova Scotia 168/H2
Bad Doberan, E. Germany 22/D1
Bad Driburg, W. Germany 22/C3
Bad Dürkheim, W. Germany 22/C4
Bad Dürrenberg, E. Germany 22/D3
Bad Ems, W. Germany 22/B3
Baden, Austria 41/D2
Baden, Manitoba 179/A2
Baden, Md. (†20613) 245/M6
Baden, Ontario 177/D4
Baden, Pa. (15005) 294/B4
Baden, Switzerland 39/F2
Ba Den, Nui (mt.), Vietnam 72/E5
Baden-Baden, W. Germany 22/C4
Badenoch (dist.), Scotland 15/D4
Badenweiler, W. Germany 22/B5
Baden-Württemberg (state), W. Germany 22/C4
Bad Freienwalde, E. Germany 22/F2
Bad Gandersheim, W. Germany 22/D3
Badgastein, Austria 41/B3
Badger (peak), Idaho 220/E7
Badger, Iowa (50516) 229/E3
Badger, Minn. (56714) 255/B2
Badger, Newf. 166/C4
Badger (creek), Oreg. 291/H3
Badger, S. Dak. (57214) 298/P5
Badger (creek), Wyo. 319/E2
Badger's Quay, Newf. 166/D4
Bad Goisern, Austria 41/B3
Badham, S.C. (†29471) 296/F5
Bad Harzburg, W. Germany 22/D3
Bad Hersfeld, W. Germany 22/C3
Badhoevedorp, Netherlands 27/B5
Bad Hofgastein, Austria 41/B3
Bad Homburg vor der Höhe, W. Germany 22/C3
Bad Honnef, W. Germany 22/B3
Badian, Philippines 82/D6
Badin, N.C. (28009) 281/J4
Badin, Pakistan 68/B4
Badiraguato, Mexico 150/F4
Bad Ischl, Austria 41/B3
Bad Kissingen, W. Germany 22/D3
Bad Kreuznach, W. Germany 22/B4
Bad Land (butte), Utah 304/D4
Bad Lands (reg.), N. Dak. 282/C7
Badlands Nat'l Park, S. Dak. 298/E6
Bad Langensalza, E. Germany 22/D3
Bad Lauterberg im Harz, W. Germany 22/D3
Bad Leonfelden, Austria 41/C2
Bad Liebenwerda, E. Germany 22/E3
Bad Lippspringe, W. Germany 22/C3
Bad Mergentheim, W. Germany 22/C4
Bad Münster-Ebernburg, W. Germany 22/B4
Bad Münstereifel, W. Germany 22/B3
Bad Muskau, E. Germany 22/F3
Bad Nauheim, W. Germany 22/C3
Bad Neuenahr-Ahrweiler, W. Germany 22/B3
Bad Neustadt an der Saale, W. Germany 22/D3
Bado, Mo. (†65447) 261/H8
Bad Oldesloe, W. Germany 22/D2
Ba Don, Vietnam 72/E3
Bad Orb, W. Germany 22/C3
Bad Pyrmont, W. Germany 22/C3
Badr, Saudi Arabia 59/C5
Badra, Iraq 66/D4
Bad Ragaz, Switzerland 39/H2
Bad Reichenhall, W. Germany 22/E5
Bad River Ind. Res., Wis. 317/E2
Bad Sachsa, W. Germany 22/D3
Bad Salzschlirf, W. Germany 22/C3
Bad Salzuflen, W. Germany 22/C2
Bad Salzungen, E. Germany 22/C3
Bad Sankt-Leonhard im Lavanttal, Austria 41/C3
Bad Schwartau, W. Germany 22/D2
Bad Segeberg, W. Germany 22/D2
Bad Tölz, W. Germany 22/D5
Baduen, Somalia 115/J2
Badulla, Sri Lanka 68/E7
Bad Vilbel, W. Germany 22/C3
Bad Waldsee, W. Germany 22/C5
Badwater (creek), Wyo. 319/E2
Bad Wildungen, W. Germany 22/C3
Bad Wimpfen, W. Germany 22/C4
Baelum, Denmark 21/D4
Baena, Spain 33/D4
Baerle-Hertog, Belgium 27/F6
Báez, Cuba 158/E2
Baeza, Ecuador 128/D3
Baeza, Spain 33/E4
Bafa (lake), Turkey 63/B4
Baffin (bay) 4/B13
Baffin (bay) 146/M2
Baffin (isl.), Canada 2/F2
Baffin (isl.), Canada 4/C13
Baffin (bay), Canada 2/F2
Baffin (isl.), N.W.T. 146/L2
Baffin (isl.), N.W.T. 162/J1
Baffin (bay), N.W.T. 162/J1
Baffin (dist.), N.W. Terrs. 187/K2
Baffin (bay), N.W. Terrs. 187/M2
Baffin (isl.), N.W. Terrs. 187/L2
Baffin (bay), Texas 303/G10
Bafia, Cameroon 115/B3
Bafing (riv.), Guinea 106/B6
Bafing (riv.), Mali 106/B6
Bafoulabé, Mali 106/B6
Bafoussam, Cameroon 115/B2
Bafq, Iran 59/G3
Bafq, Iran 66/J5
Bafra, Turkey 59/C1
Bafra, Turkey 63/F2
Bafra (cape), Turkey 59/C1
Bafra (cape), Turkey 63/G2
Baft, Iran 66/K6
Baft, Iran 59/G4
Baga, Nigeria 106/G6
Bagabag, Philippines 82/C2
Bagac, Philippines 82/C3
Bagaces, C. Rica 154/E5
Bagadó, Colombia 126/B5
Bagalkot, India 68/D5
Bagam (well), Niger 106/F5
Bagamoyo, Tanzania 115/G5
Baganga, Philippines 82/F7
Baganian (pen.), Philippines 82/D7
Bagansiapiapi, Indonesia 85/C5
Bagata, Zaire 115/C4
Bagdad, Ariz. (86321) 198/B4
Bagdad, Fla. (32530) 212/B6
Bagdad, Ky. (40003) 237/L4
Bagdad, Tasmania 99/D4
Bagdarin, U.S.S.R. 48/M4
Bagé, Brazil 120/D6
Bagé, Brazil 132/C10
Bagenalstown, Ireland 10/C4
Bagenalstown (Muinebeag), Ireland 17/H6
Bagenkop, Denmark 21/D8
Baggs, Wyo. (82321) 319/E4
Baghbaghu, Iran 66/M3
Baghdad (heads), Iraq 66/D4
Baghdad (cap.), Iraq 59/E3
Baghdad (cap.), Iraq 54/F6
Baghdad (cap.), Iraq 2/M4
Baghdad (cap.), Iraq 66/D4
Bagheria, Italy 34/D5
Baghlan, Afghanistan 54/H6
Baghlan, Afghanistan 59/J2
Baghlan, Afghanistan 68/B1
Baghu, Iran 66/K7
Bağırpaşa Dağı (mt.), Turkey 59/D2
Bağırpaşa Dağı (mt.), Turkey 63/J3
Bagley, Iowa (50026) 229/E5
Bagley, Minn. (56621) 255/C3
Bagley, N.C. (†27542) 281/N3
Bagley, Wis. (53801) 317/D10
Bagnell, Mo. (†65026) 261/G6
Bagnell (dam), Mo. 261/G6
Bagnères-de-Bigorre, France 28/D6
Bagnères-de-Luchon, France 28/D6
Bagnolet, France 28/B2
Bagnols-sur-Cèze, France 28/F5
Bågø (isl.), Denmark 21/C7
Bago, Philippines 82/D5
Bagoé (riv.), Ivory Coast 106/C6
Bagoé (riv.), Mali 106/C6
Bagot, Manitoba 179/D5
Bagot (co.), Québec 172/E4
Bagrax (Bosten Hu) (lake), China 77/C3
Bagua, Peru 128/C5
Báguanos, Cuba 158/J3
Baguio, Philippines 54/N8
Baguio, Philippines 85/G2
Baguio, Philippines 82/C2
Baguirmi (reg.), Chad 111/C5
Bagwell, Texas (75412) 303/J4
Bahama, N.C. (27503) 281/M2
Bahamas 2/F4
Bahamas 146/L7
BAHAMAS 156/C1
Bahariya (oasis), Egypt 111/E2
Bahariya (oasis), Egypt 59/A4
Bahawalnagar, Pakistan 68/C2
Bahawalpur, Pakistan 54/J7
Bahawalpur, Pakistan 68/C3
Bahawalpur, Pakistan 59/K4
Bahçe, Turkey 63/G4
Bahçesaray, Turkey 63/K3
Bahia (state), Brazil 132/F6
Bahia (Salvador), Brazil 132/G6
Bahía (isls.), Honduras 154/D2
Bahía Blanca, Argentina 2/F7
Bahía Blanca, Argentina 143/D4
Bahía Blanca, Argentina 120/C6
Bahía Bustamante, Argentina 143/C6
Bahía de Caráquez, Ecuador 128/B3
Bahía Honda, Cuba 158/B1
Bahía Kino, Mexico 150/C2
Bahía San Blas, Argentina 143/D5
Bahía Thetis, Argentina 143/C7
Bahía Tortugas, Mexico 150/B3
Bahir Dar, Ethiopia 111/G5
Bahomamey, P. Rico 161/A1
Bahoruco (prov.), Dom. Rep. 158/D6
Bahoruco, Sierra de (mts.), Dom. Rep. 158/D6
Bahraich, India 68/E3
Bahrain 54/G7
BAHRAIN 59/F4
Bahramabad (Rafsanjan), Iran 66/K5
Bahr Azoum (riv.), Sudan 111/D5
Bahr el 'Arab (riv.), Sudan 111/E6
Bahr el Ghazal (dry riv.), Chad 111/C5
Bahr El Ghazal (prov.), Sudan 111/E6
Bahr es Safi (des.), Saudi Arabia 59/E6
Bahr ez Zeraf (riv.), Sudan 111/F6
Bahr Yusef (stream), Egypt 111/J4
Baia de Aramă, Romania 45/F3
Baia dos Tigres, Angola 115/B7
Baia Farta, Angola 115/B6
Baia Mare, Romania 45/F2
Baião, Brazil 132/D3
Baibiene, Argentina 143/G4
Baibokoum, Chad 111/C6
Bai Bung, Mui (Ca Mau) (pt.), Vietnam 72/E5
Baicheng (Bay), Xinjiang Uygur, China 77/B3
Baicheng, Jilin, China 77/K2
Baida, Libya 102/E1
Baida, Libya 111/D1
Baidyabati, India 68/F1
Baie-Comeau, Québec 172/A1
Baie-Comeau, Québec 174/D3
Baie de Henne, Haiti 158/B5
Baie-des-Bacons, Québec 172/H1
Baie-des-Moutons, Québec 174/F2
Baie-des-Rochers, Québec 172/H2
Baie-des-Sables, Québec 172/A1
Baie-du-Poste, Québec 174/C2
Baie-d'Urfé, Québec 172/G4
Baie-du-Vieux-Fort, Québec 174/F2
Baie-Johan-Beetz, Québec 174/E2
Baie-Mahault, Guadeloupe 161/A6
Baiersbronn, W. Germany 22/C4
Baie-Sainte-Anne, New Bruns. 170/F1
Baie-Sainte-Catherine, Québec 172/H1
Baie-Saint-Paul, Que. 162/J6
Baie-Saint-Paul, Québec 174/C3
Baie-Saint-Paul, Québec 172/G2
Baie-Trinité, Québec 172/B1
Baie-Verte, New Bruns. 170/F2
Baie Verte, Newf. 166/C4
Baieville, Québec 172/E3
Baigorrita, Argentina 143/F7
Baiji, Iraq 66/C3
Baildon, Sask. 181/F5
Baile Átha Cliath (Dublin) (cap.), Ireland 17/K5
Baile Átha Cliath (Dublin) (cap.), Ireland 10/C4
Băile Herculane, Romania 45/F3
Bailén, Spain 33/E3
Băileşti, Romania 45/F3
Bailey, Colo. (80421) 208/H4
Bailey, Iowa (†50455) 229/H2
Bailey, Mich. (49303) 250/D5
Bailey, Miss. (39320) 256/G6
Bailey, N.C. (27807) 281/N3
Bailey (co.), Texas 303/B3
Baileyboro, Texas (†79371) 303/B3
Bailey Island, Maine (04003) 243/D8
Bailey Lakes, Ohio (†44805) 284/F4
Bailey's Crossroads, Va. (22041) 307/S3
Baileys Harbor, Wis. (54202) 317/M5
Baileyton, Ala. (35019) 195/E2
Baileyton, Tenn. (37743) 237/R8
Baileyville, Conn. (†06455) 210/E2
Baileyville, Ill. (61007) 222/D1
Baileyville, Kansas (66404) 232/F2
Bailieborough, Ireland 17/G4
Bailique (isl.), Brazil 132/D2
Bailivanish, Scotland 15/A3
Baillie (isls.), N.W. Terrs. 187/F2
Baillieston, Scotland 15/B2
Baillif, Guadeloupe 161/A7
Bailundo, Angola 115/C6
Baima, China 77/E5
Bainbridge (isl.), Alaska 196/C1
Bainbridge, Georgia (31717) 217/C9
Bainbridge, Ind. (46105) 227/D5
Bainbridge, N.Y. (13733) 276/J6
Bainbridge (dist.), N. Ireland 17/J3
Bainbridge, Ohio (45612) 284/D7
Bainbridge, Pa. (17502) 294/J5
Bainbridge (isl.), Wash. 310/A2
Bainbridge Island-Winslow (Winslow), Wash. (98110) 310/A2
Bainbridge N.T.C., Md. 245/O2
Bainet, Haiti 158/B6
Baingoin, China 77/D5
Bains, La. (70713) 238/H5
Bainville, Mont. (59212) 262/M2
Baird (inlet), Alaska 196/F2
Baird (mts.), Alaska 196/F1
Baird, Miss. (38724) 256/C4
Baird (pen.), N.W. Terrs. 187/L3
Baird, Texas (79504) 303/E5
Bairdstown, Ohio (†45872) 284/C3
Bairdsville, New Bruns. 170/C2
Baire, Cuba 158/H4
Bairiki (cap.), Kiribati 87/H5
Bairin Zuoqi, China 77/J3
Bairnsdale, Victoria 88/H7
Bairnsdale, Victoria 97/D5
Bairoil, Wyo. (82322) 319/E3
Bais, Philippines 82/D6
Baisden, W. Va. (25608) 312/C7
Baïse (riv.), France 28/D6
Baisha, China 77/G8
Baitadi, Nepal 68/E3
Bait al Faqih, Yemen Arab Rep. 59/D7
Bai Thuong, Vietnam 72/E3
Baixa da Banheira, Portugal 33/B3
Baixoaixo (isl.), Portugal 33/B2
Baixo Guandu, Brazil 132/F7
Baja, Hungary 41/E3
Baja California (state), Mexico 150/B1
Baja California Sur (state), Mexico 150/C3
Bajadero, P. Rico 161/C1
Bajgiran, Iran 66/L2
Bajo Boquete, Panama 154/F6
Bajo Nuevo (shoal), Colombia 126/C8
Bajos de Haina, Dom. Rep. 158/E6
Bajram Curri, Albania 45/D4
Bakala, Cent. Afr. Rep. 115/D2
Bakar, Yugoslavia 45/B3
Bakel, Senegal 106/B6
Baker (isl.), Alaska 196/M2
Baker, Calif. (92309) 204/J8
Baker (riv.), Chile 138/D7
Baker (mt.), Colo. 208/H2
Baker (co.), Fla. 212/D1
Baker, Fla. (32531) 212/C5
Baker (co.), Georgia 217/D8
Baker, Idaho (†83467) 220/E4
Baker, La. (70714) 238/K1
Baker (lake), Maine 243/D3
Baker, Minn. (56513) 255/B4
Baker, Mo. (†63846) 261/N9
Baker, Mont. (59313) 262/M4
Baker, Nev. (89311) 266/G3
Baker (riv.), N.H. 268/D4
Baker, N. Dak. (†58386) 282/L3
Baker (lake), N.W. Terrs. 187/J3
Baker, Okla. (73930) 288/D1
Baker, Oreg. 188/C2
Baker (co.), Oreg. 291/K3
Baker, Oreg. (97814) 291/K3
Baker (isl.), Pacific 87/J5
Baker (creek), Utah 304/A4
Baker (lake), Wash. 310/D2
Baker (mt.), Wash. 310/D2
Baker (riv.), Wash. 310/D2
Baker, W. Va. (26801) 312/J4
Baker Brook, New Bruns. 170/B1
Baker Butte (mt.), Ariz. 198/D4
Baker Hill, Ala. (36004) 195/H7
Baker Lake, N.W.T. 162/G3
Baker Lake, N.W. Terrs. 187/J3
Bakers (isl.), Mass. 249/F5
Bakersfield, Calif. 146/G6
Bakersfield, Calif. 188/C3
Bakersfield, Calif. (*93301) 204/G8
Bakersfield, Mo. (65609) 261/H9
Bakersfield, Texas (†79752) 303/B7
Bakersfield○, Vt. (05441) 268/B2
Bakers Summit, Pa. (16614) 294/F5
Bakersville, Conn. (†06057) 210/C1
Bakersville, N.C. (28705) 281/E2
Bakersville, Ohio (43803) 284/G5
Bakersville, Pa. (†15501) 294/D5
Bakerton, Ky. (42711) 237/L7
Bakerton, W. Va. (25410) 312/L4
Bakerville, Tenn. (†37185) 237/F9
Bakewell, England 10/G2
Bakewell, England 13/J2
Bakewell, Tenn. (37304) 237/L10
Bakharz, Kuhha-ye (mt.), Iran 66/M3
Bakhchisaray, U.S.S.R. 52/D6
Bakhmach, U.S.S.R. 52/D4
Bakhtegan (lake), Iran 66/J6
Bakhtiari (gov.), Iran 66/F4
Bakhun, Kuh-e (mt.), Iran 66/K6
Bakhuys (mts.), Suriname 131/C3
Bakia, Cent. Afr. Rep. 115/E2
Bakırköy, Turkey 63/D6
Baklan, Turkey 63/C4
Bako, Ethiopia 111/G6
Bakony (mts.), Hungary 41/D3
Bakool (prov.), Somalia 115/H3
Bakouma, Cent. Afr. Rep. 115/D2
Bakoy (riv.), Guinea 106/B6
Bakoy (riv.), Mali 106/B6
Bakraband, Kuh-e (mts.), Iran 66/M7
Baktalórántháza, Hungary 41/G2
Baktu (Paektu) (mt.), N. Korea 81/C3
Baku, U.S.S.R. 2/M3
Baku, U.S.S.R. 7/J4
Baku, U.S.S.R. 54/G5
Baku, U.S.S.R. 48/F5
Baku, U.S.S.R. 52/H6
Bala, Kansas (†66531) 232/F2
Bala, Ontario 177/E2
Balâ, Turkey 63/E3
Bala, Wales 13/D5
Bala, Wales 10/E4
Balabac, Philippines 82/A7
Balabac (isl.), Philippines 85/F4
Balabac (isl.), Philippines 82/A7
Balabac (str.), Philippines 85/F4
Balabac (str.), Philippines 82/A7
Balabalagan (isls.), Indonesia 85/F6
Balabio (isl.), New Caled. 86/G4
Balaclava, Jamaica 158/H6
Bala-Cynwyd, Pa. (19004) 294/N6
Balad, Somalia 115/J3
Balaghat, India 68/E4
Balaguer, Spain 33/G2
Balaïtous (mt.), Spain 33/F1
Balakai (mesa), Ariz. 198/F3
Balakhna, U.S.S.R. 52/F3
Balaklava, S. Australia 94/F6
Balaklava, U.S.S.R. 52/D6
Balakovo, U.S.S.R. 7/J3
Balakovo, U.S.S.R. 48/E4
Balakovo, U.S.S.R. 52/G4
Balallan, Scotland 15/B2
Bal'ama, Jordan 65/E3
Balambangan (isl.), Malaysia 85/F4
Balancán de Domínguez, Mexico 150/O8
Balandra (pt.), Dom. Rep. 158/F5
Balanga, Philippines 82/C3
Balangala, Zaire 115/D3
Ba Lang An, Mui (cape), Vietnam 72/F4
Balangiga, Philippines 82/E5
Balao, Ecuador 128/C4
Balashi, Neth. Ant. 161/E10
Balashov, U.S.S.R. 7/J3
Balashov, U.S.S.R. 52/F4
Balashov, U.S.S.R. 48/E4
Balasore, India 68/F4
Balassagyarmat, Hungary 41/E2
Balaton (lake), Hungary 7/F4
Balaton (lake), Hungary 41/D3
Balaton, Minn. (56115) 255/C6
Balatonfüred, Hungary 41/D3
Balatonszentgyörgy, Hungary 41/D3
Balayan (bay), Philippines 82/C4
Balbi (mt.), Papua N.G. 86/C2
Balboa, Panama 154/H6
Balbriggan, Ireland 17/J4
Balbriggan, Ireland 10/C4
Balcarce, Argentina 143/E4
Balcarres, Sask. 181/H5
Balchik, Bulgaria 45/H4
Balch Springs, Texas (75180) 303/H2
Balclutha, N. Zealand 100/B7
Balcones Escarpment (plat.), Texas 303/E8
Balcones Heights, Texas (†78201) 303/J10
Bald (mt.), Colo. 208/H4
Bald (hill), Conn. 210/G1
Bald (mt.), Idaho 220/D5
Bald (mt.), New Bruns. 170/C1
Bald (mts.), N.C. 281/D3
Bald (mts.), Tenn. 237/R9
Bald (mt.), Utah 304/C3
Bald (mt.), Vt. 268/D2
Bald (head), W. Australia 88/B7
Bald (head), W. Australia 92/B6
Bald Eagle (lake), Minn. 255/G3
Baldeggersee (lake), Switzerland 39/F2
Baldhill (Ashtabula) (res.), N. Dak. 282/P5
Bald Hill Branch (riv.), Md. 245/G4
Bald Hills, Queensland 88/K2
Bald Knob, Ark. (72010) 202/G3
Bald Knob, W. Va. (25010) 312/C7
Baldonnel, Br. Col. 184/G2
Baldur, Manitoba 179/C5
Baldwin (co.), Ala. 195/C9
Baldwin, Fla. (32234) 212/E1
Baldwin (co.), Georgia 217/F4
Baldwin, Georgia (30511) 217/E2
Baldwin, Ill. (62217) 222/D5
Baldwin, Iowa (52207) 229/M4
Baldwin, La. (70514) 238/H7
Baldwin, Mich. (49304) 250/D5
Baldwin, N.Y. (11510) 276/R7
Baldwin, N. Dak. (58521) 282/J5
Baldwin, Pa. (†15208) 294/B7
Baldwin, W. Va. (26326) 312/E5
Baldwin, Wis. (54002) 317/B6
Baldwin-Aragon Mills, S.C. (†29706) 296/E2
Baldwin City, Kansas (66006) 232/G3
Baldwin Park, Calif. (91706) 204/D10
Baldwinsville, N.Y. (13027) 276/H4
Baldwinton, Sask. 181/B3
Baldwinville, Mass. (01436) 249/F2
Baldwyn, Miss. (38824) 256/G2
Baldy (peak), Ariz. 198/F5
Baldy (mt.), Manitoba 179/B3
Baldy (peak), N. Mex. 274/D3
Baldy (peak), Utah 304/B5
Bale (prov.), Ethiopia 111/H6
Bale (mt.), Ethiopia 111/G6
Baleares (prov.), Spain 33/H3
Balearic (isls.), Spain 7/E5
Balearic (Baleares) (isls.), Spain 33/H3
Baleine, Grande R. de la (riv.), Que. 162/J4
Baleine, Grand Rivière de la (riv.), Québec 174/B1
Baleine, Petite Rivière de la (riv.), Québec 174/B1
Baleine (riv.), Québec 174/D1
Baleine, R. à la (riv.), Que. 162/K4
Balen, Belgium 27/G6
Baler, Philippines 82/C3
Baler (bay), Philippines 82/C3
Balerna, Switzerland 39/G5
Balerno, Scotland 15/D2
Baleshare (isl.), Scotland 15/A3
Balestrand, Norway 18/E6
Baley, U.S.S.R. 48/M4
Balfate, Honduras 154/D3
Balfour, Br. Col. 184/J5
Balfour, N.C. (28706) 281/E4
Balfour, N. Dak. (58712) 282/J4
Balfron, Scotland 15/B1
Balgonie, Sask. 181/G5
Balhaf, P.D.R. Yemen 59/E7
Bal Harbour, Fla. (†33101) 212/C4
Bali, Cameroon 115/A2
Bali (isl.), Indonesia 54/N10
Bali (isl.), Indonesia 85/F7
Bali (sea), Indonesia 85/E7
Bali (str.), Indonesia 85/E7

334 Baliangao

Baliangao, Philippines 82/D6
Balicuatro (isls.), Philippines 82/E4
Balige, Indonesia 85/B5
Balıkesir (prov.), Turkey 63/B3
Balıkesir, Turkey 63/B3
Balıkesir, Turkey 59/A2
Balikpapan, Indonesia 54/N10
Balikpapan, Indonesia 85/F6
Balık-Uzun (lake), Turkey 63/G2
Balimbing (Bato-Bato), Philippines 82/C8
Baling, Malaysia 72/D6
Balingasag, Philippines 82/E6
Balingen, W. Germany 22/C4
Balintang (chan.), Philippines 82/A2
Balintang (isls.), Philippines 82/A2
Baljennie, Sask. 181/C3
Balk, Netherlands 27/H3
Balkan (mts.) 7/G4
Balkan (mts.), Bulgaria 45/G4
Balkan, Ky. (40804) 237/O7
Balkány, Hungary 41/G3
Balkbrug, Netherlands 27/J3
Balkh, Afghanistan 68/B1
Balkh, Afghanistan 59/J2
Balkhash, U.S.S.R. 54/J5
Balkhash (lake), U.S.S.R. 2/N3
Balkhash (lake), U.S.S.R. 54/J5
Balkhash, U.S.S.R. 48/H5
Balkhash (lake), U.S.S.R. 48/H5
Balko, Okla. (73931) 288/E1
Ball (mt.), Conn. 210/C1
Ball (pond), Conn. 210/A3
Ball, La. (71405) 238/F4
Ball (bay), Norfolk I. 88/L6
Balla, Ireland 17/C4
Balladonia, W. Australia 92/D6
Ballaghaderreen, Ireland 17/E4
Ballaigues, Switzerland 39/B3
Ballantine, Mont. (59006) 262/J5
Ballantrae, Scotland 15/C5
Ballantyne (str.), N.W. Terrs. 187/G2
Ballarat, Australia 87/E9
Ballarat, Victoria 88/G7
Ballarat, Victoria 97/C5
Ballard (co.), Ky. 237/C6
Ballard, Mo. (†64730) 261/D6
Ballard (cape), Newf. 166/D2
Ballard (lake), W. Australia 88/B5
Ballard, W. Va. (24918) 312/E8
Ballardsville, Miss. (†38801) 256/H2
Ballardvale, Mass. (01810) 249/K2
Ballater, Scotland 10/E2
Ballater, Scotland 15/F3
Ball Club, Minn. (†56636) 255/E3
Ballenas (bay), Mexico 150/C3
Ballenero (chan.), Chile 138/E11
Ballengee, W. Va. (†24981) 312/E7
Ballens, Switzerland 39/B3
Ballenstedt, E. Germany 22/D3
Ballentine, S.C. (29002) 296/E3
Balleny (isls.), Ant. 2/S9
Balleny (isls.) 5/C9
Ballerup, Denmark 21/F6
Ballesteros, Philippines 82/C1
Balleza, Mexico 150/F3
Ball Ground, Georgia (30107) 217/D2
Ballground, Miss. (†39156) 256/C5
Ballia, India 68/E3
Ballidu, W. Australia 92/B5
Ballina, Mayo, Ireland 17/C3
Ballina, Tipperary, Ireland 17/E6
Ballina, Ireland 10/B3
Ballina, N.S. Wales 97/G1
Ballinagh, Ireland 17/G4
Ballinakill, Ireland 17/G6
Ballinamore, Ireland 17/F3
Ballinasloe, Ireland 10/B4
Ballinasloe, Ireland 17/E5
Ballincollig-Carrigrohane, Ireland 17/D8
Ballindine, Ireland 17/C4
Ballineen, Ireland 17/D8
Ballingarry, Limerick, Ireland 17/D7
Ballingarry, Tipperary, Ireland 17/F6
Ballinger, Texas (76821) 303/E6
Ballingry, Scotland 15/D1
Ballinlough, Ireland 17/D4
Ballinluig, Scotland 15/E4
Ballinrobe, Ireland 10/B4
Ballinrobe, Ireland 17/C4
Ballinskelligs (bay), Ireland 17/A8
Ballintober, Ireland 17/E4
Ballintra, Ireland 17/E2
Ballisodare, Ireland 17/E3
Ballivor, Ireland 17/H4
Balloch, Highland, Scotland 15/D3
Balloch, Strathclyde, Scotland 15/B1
Ballouville, Conn. (06233) 210/H1
Ballston, Oreg. (†97378) 291/D2
Ballston Spa, N.Y. (12020) 276/N5
Ballsville, Va. (†29139) 307/M6
Balltown, Iowa (†52073) 229/M3
Ballville, Ohio (†43420) 284/D3
Ballwin, Mo. (63011) 261/N3
Bally, India 68/F1
Bally, Pa. (19503) 294/L5
Ballybay, Ireland 17/G3
Ballybofey-Stranorlar, Ireland 17/F2
Ballybunio, Ireland 10/B4
Ballybunion, Ireland 17/B7
Ballycanew, Ireland 17/J6
Ballycarney, Ireland 17/J6
Ballycarry, N. Ireland 17/K2
Ballycastle, Ireland 17/C3
Ballycastle, N. Ireland 10/C3
Ballycastle, N. Ireland 17/J1
Ballyclare, N. Ireland 17/J2
Ballyconnell, Ireland 17/F3
Ballycotton, Ireland 17/F8
Ballycotton (bay), Ireland 17/F8
Ballydehob, Ireland 17/C8
Ballyduff, Ireland 17/B7
Ballygally, N. Ireland 17/K2
Ballygar, Ireland 17/E4
Ballygawley, N. Ireland 17/G3
Ballygeary, Ireland 17/J7
Ballygrant, Scotland 15/B5
Ballyhaise, Ireland 17/G3
Ballyhaunis, Ireland 17/D4
Ballyheige (bay), Ireland 17/B7
Ballyheigue, Ireland 17/B7
Ballyhoura (hills), Ireland 17/E7
Ballyjamesduff, Ireland 17/G4
Ballykelly, N. Ireland 17/G1
Ballylanders, Ireland 17/E7
Ballylongford, Ireland 17/B6
Ballymahon, Ireland 17/F4
Ballymakeery, Ireland 17/C8
Ballymena (dist.), N. Ireland 17/J2
Ballymena, N. Ireland 17/J2
Ballymena, N. Ireland 10/C3
Ballymoney (dist.), N. Ireland 17/J1
Ballymoney, N. Ireland 10/C3
Ballymoney, N. Ireland 17/J1
Ballymore, Ireland 17/F5
Ballymore Eustace, Ireland 17/J5
Ballymote, Ireland 17/D3
Ballymote, Ireland 10/B3
Ballynahinch, N. Ireland 17/J3
Ballynakill (harb.), Ireland 17/A4
Ballyporeen, Ireland 17/E7
Ballyragget, Ireland 17/G6
Ballyroan, Ireland 17/G6
Ballysadare (bay), Ireland 17/D3
Ballyshannon, Ireland 10/B3
Ballyshannon, Ireland 17/E3
Ballyteige (bay), Ireland 17/H7
Ballytore, Ireland 17/H5
Ballywalter, N. Ireland 17/K2
Balmaceda, Chile 138/E6
Balmat, N.Y. (13609) 276/K2
Balmazújváros, Hungary 41/F3
Balmertown, Ontario 175/B2
Balmhorn (mt.), Switzerland 39/E4
Balmoral, Manitoba 179/E4
Balmoral, New Bruns. 170/D1
Balmoral, Queensland 88/K2
Balmoral, Queensland 95/E2
Balmoral, Victoria 97/A5
Balmoral Castle, Scotland 10/
Balmoral Castle, Scotland 15/E3
Balmorhea, Texas (79718) 303/D11
Balmville, N.Y. (†12550) 276/M7
Balnearia, Argentina 143/D3
Balneario El Tesoro, Uruguay 145/E5
Balneario La Barra, Uruguay 145/E5
Balneario Solis, Uruguay 145/D5
Balombo, Angola 115/B6
Balonne (riv.), Queensland 88/H5
Balonne (riv.), Queensland 95/D6
Balotra, India 68/C3
Baloy (mt.), Philippines 82/D5
Balpunga, N.S. Wales 97/A3
Balrampur, India 68/E3
Balranald, N. S. Wales 88/G6
Balranald, N.S. Wales 97/B4
Balş, Romania 45/G3
Balsam, N.C. (28707) 281/C4
Balsam (lake), Ontario 177/F3
Balsam Creek, Ontario 177/E1
Balsam Lake, Wis. (54810) 317/B5
Balsapuerto, Peru 128/D5
Balsas, Brazil 120/E3
Balsas, Brazil 132/E4
Balsas (riv.), Brazil 132/E5
Balsas (riv.), Mexico 146/H8
Balsas (riv.), Mexico 150/J7
Bålsta, Sweden 18/G1
Balsthal, Switzerland 39/E2
Balta, N. Dak. (58313) 282/K3
Baltanás, Spain 33/D2
Baltasar Brum, Uruguay 145/B1
Baltasound, Scotland 15/G2
Baltic (sea) 2/K3
Baltic (sea) 7/F3
Baltic, Conn. (06330) 210/G2
Baltic (sea), Denmark 21/E9
Baltic (sea), E. Germany 22/E1
Baltic (sea), Finland 18/K9
Baltic, Mich. (†49905) 250/G1
Baltic, Ohio (43804) 284/G5
Baltic (sea), Poland 47/B1
Baltic, S. Dak. (57003) 298/R6
Baltic (sea), Sweden 18/K9
Baltic (sea), U.S.S.R. 52/B3
Baltic (sea), U.S.S.R. 48/B4
Baltimore, Ireland 10/B5
Baltimore, Ireland 17/C9
Baltimore (city county), Md. 245/M3
Baltimore (co.), Md. 245/M3
Baltimore, Md. (*21201) 245/M3
Baltimore, Md. 188/L3
Baltimore, Md. 146/L6
Baltimore, Ohio (43105) 284/E6
Baltimore, Ontario 177/F3
Baltinglass, Ireland 17/H6
Baltistan (reg.), Pakistan 68/D1
Baltit, Pakistan 68/C1
Baltiysk, U.S.S.R. 52/A4
Baltra (isl.), Ecuador 128/B9
Baltray, Ireland 17/J4
Baltrum (isl.), W. Germany 22/B2
Balty, Va. (†22546) 307/O5
Baluchistan (reg.), Iran 66/M7
Baluchistan (prov.), Pakistan 68/B3
Baluchistan (reg.), Pakistan 59/J4
Balurghat, India 68/F3
Balvi, U.S.S.R. 53/D2
Balwina Aboriginal Reserve, W. Australia 88/D4
Balwina Aboriginal Res., W. Australia 92/E3
Balya, Turkey 63/B3
Balykshi, U.S.S.R. 48/F5
Balzac, Alberta 182/C4
Balzar, Ecuador 128/C3
Bam, Iran 54/G7
Bam, Iran 66/L6
Bam, Iran 59/G4
Bam, U.S.S.R. 48/N4
Bama, Nigeria 106/G6
Bamako (cap.), Mali 2/J5
Bamako (cap.), Mali 106/C6
Bamako (cap.), Mali 102/B3
Bamba, Mali 106/D5
Bambamarca, Peru 128/C6
Bamban, Philippines 82/C3
Bambari, Cent. Afr. Rep. 102/E4
Bambari, Cent. Afr. Rep. 115/D2
Bamberg (co.), S.C. 296/E5
Bamberg, S.C. (29003) 296/E5
Bamberg, W. Germany 22/D4
Bambesa, Zaire 115/E3
Bambili, Zaire 115/E3
Bambio, Cent. Afr. Rep. 115/C3
Bamble, Norway 18/F7
Bamboo, Jamaica 158/J6
Bamboo Creek, W. Australia 92/C3
Bambuí, Brazil 132/E8
Bambuí, Brazil 135/C2
Bamenda, Cameroon 115/B2
Bamfield, Br. Col. 184/E6
Bamian, Afghanistan 59/J3
Bamian, Afghanistan 68/B2
Bamingui, Cent. Afr. Rep. 115/D2
Bamingui (riv.), Cent. Afr. Rep. 115/C2
Bamoa, Mexico 150/E4
Bampur, Iran 59/H4
Bampur, Iran 66/M7
Bampur (riv.), Iran 66/M7
Bamyili-Beswick, North. Terr. 93/C3
Banaba (isl.), Kiribati 87/G6
Bañado de Medina, Uruguay 145/E3
Bañado de Rocha, Uruguay 145/C2
Banagher, Ireland 17/F5
Banagüises, Cuba 158/D1
Banahao (mt.), Philippines 82/C3
Banalia, Zaire 115/E3
Banam, Cambodia 72/E5
Banamba, Mali 106/C6
Banamba, Mali 102/B3
Banamichi, Mexico 150/D2
Banana (riv.), Fla. 212/F3
Banana, Zaire 115/B5
Bananal (isl.), Brazil 120/D4
Bananal (isl.), Brazil 132/D5
Bananier, Guadeloupe 161/A7
Banao, Cuba 158/F2
Ban Aranyaprathet, Thailand 72/D4
Bânâs, Ras (cape), Egypt 111/G3
Bânâs, Ras (cape), Egypt 59/C5
Banas (riv.), India 68/D3
Banaz, Turkey 63/C3
Banaz (riv.), Turkey 63/C3
Banbar, China 77/E5
Ban Boun Tai, Laos 72/D2
Banbridge, N. Ireland 17/J3
Banbury, England 10/F4
Banbury, England 13/F5
Bancalan (isl.), Philippines 82/A6
Bancannia (lake), N.S. Wales 97/A2
Banchory, Scotland 10/E2
Banchory, Scotland 15/F3
Bancoran (isl.), Philippines 82/B7
Bancroft, Idaho (83217) 220/G7
Bancroft, Iowa (50517) 229/E2
Bancroft, Kansas (†66428) 232/G2
Bancroft, Ky. (†40222) 237/K1
Bancroft, La. (†70653) 238/C5
Bancroft, Maine (†04497) 243/H4
Bancroft○, Maine (†04497) 243/H4
Bancroft, Mich. (48414) 250/E6
Bancroft, Nebr. (68004) 264/H2
Bancroft, Ontario 177/G2
Bancroft, Oreg. (†97458) 291/D5
Bancroft, S. Dak. (57316) 298/O4
Bancroft, W. Va. (25011) 312/C5
Bancroft, Wis. (54921) 317/G7
Bancroft (Chililabombwe), Zambia 115/E6
Banda, Gabon 115/B4
Banda, India 68/D3
Banda (sea), Indonesia 54/O10
Banda (isls.), Indonesia 85/H6
Banda (sea), Indonesia 85/H7
Banda Aceh, Indonesia 85/A4
Banda Aceh, Indonesia 54/L9
Bandai (mt.), Japan 81/K5
Bandai-Asahi National Park, Japan 81/J4
Bandama (riv.), Ivory Coast 106/C7
Bandana, Ky. (42022) 237/D6
Bandanaira, Indonesia 85/H6
Bandar (Machilipatnam), India 68/E5
Bandar 'Abbas, Iran 66/J7
Bandar 'Abbas, Iran 54/G7
Bandar 'Abbas, Iran 59/G4
Bandar-e Deylam, Iran 66/G5
Bandar-e Lengeh, Iran 66/J7
Bandar-e Lengeh, Iran 59/F4
Bandar-e Ma'shur, Iran 66/F5
Bandar-e Pahlavi (Enzeli), Iran 59/E2
Bandar-e Pahlavi (Enzeli), Iran 66/F2
Bandar-e Rig, Iran 59/F4
Bandar-e Rig, Iran 66/G6
Bandar-e Torkaman, Iran 66/H2
Bandar-e Torkaman, Iran 59/F2
Bandar Khomeini, Iran 66/F5
Bandar Khomeini, Iran 59/E3
Bandar Maharani (Muar), Malaysia 72/D7
Bandar Penggaram (Batu Pahat), Malaysia 72/D7
Bandar Seri Begawan, Brunei 85/E4
Bandar Seri Begawan (cap.), Brunei 54/N9
Bandar Shahpur, Iran 66/F5
Bandawe, Malawi 115/F6
Bande, Spain 33/B1
Bandeira (mt.), Brazil 120/E5
Bandeira, Pico da (mt.), Brazil 132/F8
Bandeira (mt.), Brazil 135/E2
Bandelier Nat'l Mon., N. Mex. 274/C3
Bandera, Argentina 143/D2
Bandera (co.), Texas 303/E8
Bandera, Texas (78003) 303/F8
Banderas (bay), Mexico 150/G6
Banderilla, Mexico 150/P1
Bandholm, Denmark 21/E8
Bandiagara, Mali 106/D6
Bandırma, Turkey 59/A1
Bandırma, Turkey 63/B2
Bandon, Ireland 10/B5
Bandon, Ireland 17/D8
Bandon (riv.), Ireland 17/D8
Bandon, Oreg. (97411) 291/C4
Bandra, India 68/B7
Bandundu (prov.), Zaire 115/C4
Bandundu, Zaire 102/D5
Bandundu, Zaire 115/C4
Bandung, Indonesia 54/M10
Bandung, Indonesia 85/H2
Bandy, Va. (24602) 307/E6
Bandya, W. Australia 92/C4
Banes, Cuba 156/C2
Banes, Cuba 158/J3
Banff, Alberta 182/C4
Banff, Alta. 162/E5
Banff, Scotland 15/F3
Banff, Scotland 10/E2
Banff (trad. co.), Scotland 15/A5
Banff Nat'l Park, Alberta 182/B4
Banff Nat'l Park, Alta. 162/E5
Banfora, Upper Volta 106/D6
Bangalore, India 2/N5
Bangalore, India 54/J8
Bangalore, India 68/D6
Bangalow, N.S. Wales 97/G1
Bangar, Philippines 82/C2
Bangassou, Centr. Afr. Rep. 102/E4
Bangassou, Cent. Afr. Rep. 115/D3
Banggai, Indonesia 85/G6
Banggai (arch.), Indonesia 85/G6
Banggi (isl.), Malaysia 85/F4
Bangil, Indonesia 85/K2
Bangka (isl.), Indonesia 54/M10
Bangka (isl.), Indonesia 85/D6
Bangka (str.), Indonesia 85/C6
Bangkalan, Indonesia 85/K2
Bangkok (cap.), Thailand 2/P5
Bangkok (cap.), Thailand 72/D4
Bangkok (cap.), Thailand 54/M8
Bangladesh 2/P4
Bangladesh 54/L7
BANGLADESH 68/G4
Bang Lamung, Thailand 72/D4
Bangong Co (lake), China 77/A5
Bangor, Calif. (95914) 204/D4
Bangor, Maine 146/M5
Bangor, Maine (04401) 243/F6
Bangor, Maine 188/N2
Bangor, Mich. (49013) 250/C6
Bangor, N.Y. (12966) 276/M1
Bangor, N. Ireland 17/K2
Bangor, Pa. (18013) 294/M4
Bangor, Sask. 181/J5
Bangor, Wales 13/C4
Bangor, Wales 10/D4
Bangor, Wis. (54614) 317/E8
Bangs, Texas (76823) 303/E6
Bang Saphan, Thailand 72/C5
Bangued, Philippines 85/G2
Bangued, Philippines 82/C2
Banguezane (mt.), Niger 106/F5
Bangui (cap.), Centr. Afr. Rep. 102/D4
Bangui (cap.), Centr. Afr. Rep. 2/K5
Bangui (cap.), Cent. Afr. Rep. 115/C3
Bangui, Philippines 85/G2
Bangui, Philippines 82/C1
Bangui (bay), Philippines 82/C1
Bangweulu (lake), Zambia 115/F6
Ban Houayxay, Laos 72/D2
Baní, Dom. Rep. 158/E6
Baní, Dom. Rep. 156/D3
Bani (riv.), Mali 106/C6
Bani, Jebel (mts.), Morocco 106/C3
Bani, Philippines 82/B2
Bania, Cent. Afr. Rep. 115/C3
Baniara, Papua N.G. 85/C7
Bánica, Dom. Rep. 156/D3
Bánica, Dom. Rep. 158/D5
Banida, Idaho (†83263) 220/G7
Banister (riv.), Va. 307/K7
Bani Suheila, Gaza Strip 65/A5
Baniyas, Syria 63/F5
Banja Luka, Yugoslavia 7/F4
Banja Luka, Yugoslavia 45/C3
Banjarmasin, Indonesia 54/N10
Banjarmasin, Indonesia 85/E6
Banjul (cap.), Gambia 102/A3
Banjul (cap.), Gambia 106/A6
Banka Banka, North. Terr. 93/C5
Ban Kantang, Thailand 72/C6
Ban Kapong, Thailand 72/C5
Bankass, Mali 106/D6
Bankend, Sask. 181/H4
Ban Kèngkok, Laos 72/E3
Bankfoot, Scotland 15/E4
Bankhead (lake), Ala. 195/D4
Bankhead, Scotland 15/F3
Ban Khlong Yai, Thailand 72/D5
Ban Khon, Laos 72/E4
Banks, Ala. (36005) 195/G7
Banks (pt.), Alaska 196/H3
Banks, Ark. (71631) 202/F6
Banks (isl.), Br. Col. 184/B3
Banks (isl.), Canada 2/C2
Banks (isl.), Canada 4/B16
Banks (bay), Ecuador 128/B9
Banks (co.), Georgia 217/E2
Banks (lake), Georgia 217/F9
Banks, Idaho (83602) 220/B5
Banks, Miss. (†38664) 256/D1
Banks (cape), N. S. Wales 88/L4
Banks (cape), N.S. Wales 97/K4
Banks (pen.), N. Zealand 100/D5
Banks (isl.), N.W.T. 146/F2
Banks (isl.), N.W.T. 162/D1
Banks (isl.), N.W. Terrs. 187/F2
Banks, Oreg. (97106) 291/A1
Banks (isl.), Queensland 88/G2
Banks (isl.), Queensland 95/B1
Banks (str.), Tasmania 88/H8
Banks (str.), Tasmania 99/D2
Banks (isls.), Vanuatu 87/G7
Banks (lake), Wash. 310/F3
Bankston, Ala. (35542) 195/C3
Bankston, Iowa (†52045) 229/L3
Bankstown, N. S. Wales 88/K4
Bankstown, N.S. Wales 97/J3
Ban Kui Nua, Thailand 72/D4
Bankura, India 68/F4
Ban Lahanam, Laos 72/E3
Ban Me Thuot, Vietnam 72/F4
Bann (riv.), Ireland 17/J6
Bann (riv.), N. Ireland 17/H2
Bannack, Mont. (†59725) 262/C5
Banner, Ill. (†61520) 222/D3
Banner, Ky. (41603) 237/R5
Banner, Miss. (38913) 256/F2
Banner, Mo. (†63623) 261/L7
Banner (co.), Nebr. 264/A3
Banner, Va. (24230) 307/D7
Banner, Wyo. (82832) 319/F1
Banner Elk, N.C. (28604) 281/F2
Banner Hill, Tenn. (†37650) 237/R8
Banner Springs, Tenn. (†38556) 237/M8
Bannertown, N.C. (†27030) 281/H1
Ban Ngon, Thailand 72/D3
Banning, Calif. (92220) 204/J10
Banning, Georgia (†30185) 217/C3
Bannister, Mich. (48807) 250/E5
Bannock (co.), Idaho 220/F7
Bannock (creek), Idaho 220/F7
Bannock (peak), Idaho 220/F7
Bannock (range), Idaho 220/F7
Bannockburn, Ill. (†60015) 222/B5
Bannockburn, Ontario 177/G3
Bannockburn, Scotland 15/C1
Bannockburn, Scotland 10/B1
Bannow, Ireland 17/H7
Bannu, Pakistan 59/K3
Bannu, Pakistan 68/C2
Bañolas, Spain 33/H1
Bánovce nad Bebravou, Czech. 41/E2
Ban Pak Phanang, Thailand 72/D5
Banphot Phisai, Thailand 72/C3
Ban Pua, Thailand 72/D3
Banquo, Ind. (†46940) 227/F3
Ban Sattahip, Thailand 72/D4
Bansberia, India 68/F1
Bansha, Ireland 17/E7
Banská Bystrica, Czech. 41/E2
Banská Štiavnica, Czech. 41/E2
Bansko, Bulgaria 45/F5
Banstead, England 13/H8
Banstead, England 10/B6
Bansud, Philippines 82/C4
Banswara, India 68/C4
Bantam, Conn. (06750) 210/B2
Bantam (lake), Conn. 210/C2
Bantam (riv.), Conn. 210/B2
Bantayan, Philippines 82/D5
Bantayan (isl.), Philippines 82/D5
Ban Tha Uthen, Thailand 72/D3
Banton, Philippines 82/D4
Banton (isl.), Philippines 82/D4
Bantry, Ireland 10/B5
Bantry, Ireland 17/C8
Bantry (bay), Ireland 10/A5
Bantry (bay), Ireland 17/B8
Bantry, N. Dak. (58713) 282/J3
Bantul, Indonesia 85/J2
Bañuelo (mt.), Spain 33/D3
Banyak (isls.), Indonesia 85/B5
Banyo, Cameroon 115/B2
Banyo, Queensland 88/K2
Banyumas, Indonesia 85/J2
Banyuwangi, Indonesia 85/L2
Banzare Coast (reg.) 5/C7
Baode, China 77/H4
Baoding (Paoting), China 77/J4
Bao Ha, Vietnam 72/D2
Baoji (Paoki), China 77/G5
Baoji, China 54/M6
Bao Lac, Vietnam 72/E2
Baoshan, China 77/E7
Baoting, China 77/G8
Baotou (Paotow), China 77/G3
Baotou, China 54/M5
Baoulé (riv.), Ivory Coast 106/C6
Baoulé (dry riv.), Mali 106/C6
Baoulé (riv.), Mali 106/C6
Bapaume, Sask. 181/D2
Bapchule, Ariz. (85221) 198/D5
Bapsfontein, S. Africa 118/J6
Baptist, La. (†70401) 238/M1
Baptiste (lake), Ontario 177/G2
Baptistown, N.J. (08803) 273/D2
Baqên, China 77/D5
Ba'quba, Iraq 59/D3
Ba'quba, Iraq 66/D4
Baquedano, Chile 138/A4
Baquerizo Moreno, Ecuador 128/C9
Baqura, Jordan 65/D2
Bar, Yugoslavia 45/D4
Bara, Sudan 111/F5
Bara, Sudan 59/B7
Barabai, Indonesia 85/F6
Barabinsk, U.S.S.R. 48/H4
Baraboo, Wis. (53913) 317/G9
Baracaldo, Spain 33/E1
Barachois, New Bruns. 170/F2
Barachois (pt.), Nova Scotia 168/G4
Barachois, Québec 172/D1
Barachois Pond Prov. Park, Newf. 166/C4
Baracoa, Cuba 158/K4
Baracoa, Cuba 156/C2
Barada, Nebr. (†68457) 264/J4
Baradères, Haiti 158/B6
Baradères (bay), Haiti 158/B6
Baradero, Argentina 143/G6
Baradine, N.S. Wales 97/E2
Baradine (creek), N.S. Wales 97/E2
Baraga (co.), Mich. 250/A2
Baraga, Mich. (49908) 250/G1
Baragoi, Kenya 115/G3
Baraguá, Cuba 158/F2
Baragua, Venezuela 124/D2
Barahona (prov.), Dom. Rep. 158/D6
Barahona, Dom. Rep. 158/D6
Barahona, Dom. Rep. 156/D3
Barajas, Spain 33/F4
Barak, Turkey 63/G4
Baraka (riv.), Ethiopia 111/G4
Baraka (riv.), Sudan 111/G4
Baraka (riv.), Sudan 59/C6
Baraka, Zaire 115/E4
Baraki Barak, Afghanistan 59/J3
Baraki Barak, Afghanistan 68/B2
Baralzon (lake), Manitoba 179/J1
Barama (riv.), Guyana 131/A2
Baramanni, Guyana 131/B2
Baramati, India 68/C5
Baramita, Guyana 131/A2
Baramula, India 68/C2
Baranagar, India 68/F1
Barankwa, Sudan 59/B7
Baranoa, Colombia 126/C2
Baranof (isl.), Alaska 196/M1
Baranovichi, U.S.S.R. 7/G3
Baranovichi, U.S.S.R. 48/C4
Baranovichi, U.S.S.R. 52/C4
Baranya (co.), Hungary 41/E4
Barão de Cocais, Brazil 135/E1
Baras, Philippines 82/E4
Barasat, India 68/F1
Baratang (isl.), India 68/G6
Barataria, La. (70036) 238/K7
Barataria (bay), La. 238/L8
Barataria (passage), La. 238/L8
Barawa (Brava), Somalia 115/H3
Baraya, Colombia 126/C6
Barbacena, Brazil 120/E5
Barbacena, Brazil 135/E2
Barbacena, Brazil 132/F8
Barbacoas, Colombia 126/A7
Barbacoas, Venezuela 124/E3
Barbados 2/G5
Barbados 146/N8
BARBADOS 156/G4
BARBADOS 161/B8
Barbar (isls.), Indonesia 85/J7
Barbas (cape), Western Sahara 106/A4
Barbastro, Spain 33/F1
Barbate (riv.), Spain 33/D4
Barbeau, Mich. (49710) 250/E2
Barbeau (peak), N.W. Terrs. 187/L1
Barber, Ark. (72922) 202/B3
Barber (co.), Kansas 232/D4
Barber, Mont. (†59074) 262/G4
Barber, N.C. (27008) 281/H3
Barbers (pt.), Hawaii 218/E2
Barbers Point, Hawaii (†96706) 218/E2
Barbers Point Nav. Air Sta., Hawaii 218/E2
Barberton, Ohio (4r203) 284/G4
Barberton, S. Africa 118/E5
Barberville, Fla. (32005) 212/E2
Barbezieux-St-Hilaire, France 28/C5
Barbil, India 68/F4
Barbizon, France 28/E3
Barbosa, Colombia 126/D5
Barbour (co.), Ala. 195/H7
Barbour (co.), W. Va. 312/F4
Barbourmeade, Ky. (†40201) 237/K1
Barboursville, Va. (22923) 307/M4
Barboursville, W. Va. (25504) 312/B6
Barbourville, Ky. (40906) 237/O7
Barbuda (isl.) 146/M8
Barbuda (isl.), Ant. & Bar. 156/G3
Barcaldine, Queensland 88/G4
Barcaldine, Queensland 95/C4
Barcaldine, Scotland 15/C4
Barcarrota, Spain 33/C3
Barce (El Marj), Libya 111/D1
Barcellona Pozzo di Gotto, Italy 34/E5
Barcelona (prov.), Spain 33/G2
Barcelona, Spain 7/E4
Barcelona, Spain 33/H2
Barcelona, Venezuela 124/F2
Barcelona, Venezuela 120/C2
Barceloneta, P. Rico 161/C1
Barcelonnette, France 28/G5
Barcelos, Brazil 120/C3
Barcelos, Brazil 132/H9
Barcelos, Portugal 33/B2
Barclay, Md. (21607) 245/P4
Barco, N.C. (27917) 281/T2
Barcoo (creek), Queensland 88/G4
Barcoo (creek), Queensland 95/B5
Barcoo (creek), S. Australia 88/F5
Barcoo (creek), S. Australia 94/F3
Barcos (pt.), Cuba 158/B2
Barcs, Hungary 41/D4
Barczewo, Poland 47/E2
Bard, Calif. (92222) 204/L11
Bard, N. Mex. (88411) 274/F3
Bardai, Chad 111/C3
Bardai, Chad 102/D2
Bardejov, Czech. 41/F2
Bardera, Somalia 115/H3
Bardera, Somalia 102/G4
Bardney, England 13/G4
Bardolph, Ill. (61416) 222/C3
Bardon (lake), Wis. 317/C3
Bardonia, N.Y. (†10954) 276/K8
Bardsey (isl.), Wales 13/C5
Bardstown, Ky. (40004) 237/L5
Barduelv (riv.), Norway 18/L2
Bardwell, Ky. (42023) 237/D7
Bardwell, Texas (75101) 303/H5
Bareilly, India 54/K7
Bareilly, India 68/D3
Barellan, N.S. Wales 97/D4
Bärenhorn (mt.), Switzerland 39/H3
Barents (sea) 2/L2
Barents (sea) 7/J1
Barents (sea) 4/B8
Barents (sea), U.S.S.R. 48/D2
Barents (sea), U.S.S.R. 52/E1
Barentsburg, Norway 18/C2
Barentsøya (isl.), Norway 18/D2
Bäretswil, Switzerland 39/G2
Barfield, Ark. (†72315) 202/L2
Barfleur, France 28/C3
Barfleur (pt.), France 28/C3
Barga, China 77/B5
Bargal, Somalia 115/K1
Bargamin (creek), Idaho 220/C4
Bargersville, Ind. (46106) 227/E5
Bargo, N.S. Wales 97/F4
Bargrax (Bohu), China 77/C3

Baxterville 335

Barham, N.S. Wales 97/C4
Bar Harbor, Maine (04609) 243/G7
Bar Harbor○, Maine (04609) 243/G7
Bari (prov.), Italy 34/F4
Bari, Italy 34/F4
Bari, Italy 7/F4
Bari (prov.), Somalia 115/J1
Baria (riv.), Venezuela 124/E7
Barich, Alberta 182/D2
Barichara, Colombia 126/D4
Barida, Ras (cape), Saudi Arabia 59/C5
Barima (riv.), Guyana 131/B2
Barinas (state), Venezuela 124/D3
Barinas, Venezuela 124/C3
Barinas, Venezuela 120/C2
Baring, Maine (†04619) 243/J5
Baring○, Maine (†04619) 243/J5
Baring, Mo. (63531) 261/H2
Baring (head), N. Zealand 100/B3
Baring (cape), N.W. Terrs. 187/G3
Baring, Sask. 181/J5
Baring, Wash. (98224) 310/D3
Barinitas, Venezuela 124/C3
Baripada, India 68/F4
Bariri, Brazil 135/B3
Bariri (res.), Brazil 135/B3
Bâris, Egypt 111/F3
Barisal, Bangladesh 68/G4
Barisan (mts.), Indonesia 85/C6
Baritbog (riv.), New Bruns. 170/E1
Barito (riv.), Indonesia 85/E6
Bark (lake), Ontario 177/G2
Barkam, China 77/F5
Barker, N.Y. (14012) 276/C4
Barker Heights, N.C. (†28739) 281/D4
Barkeyville, Pa. (†16038) 294/C3
Barkhamsted○, Conn. (†06063) 210/D1
Barkhamsted (res.), Conn. 210/D1
Barkhan, Pakistan 68/B3
Barkhan, Pakistan 59/J4
Barking, England 10/C5
Barking, England 13/H8
Barkley (sound), Br. Col. 184/E6
Barkley (dam), Ky. 237/E6
Barkley (lake), Ky. 237/F7
Barkley (lake), Tenn. 237/F7
Barkly Downs, Queensland 95/A4
Barkly East, S. Africa 118/D6
Barkly Tableland (plat.), Australia 87/D7
Barkly Tableland, North. Terr. 88/F3
Barkly Tableland, North. Terr. 93/D4
Barkly Tableland, Queensland 95/A4
Barkmere, Québec 172/C3
Barkol, China 77/D3
Bark River, Mich. (49807) 250/B3
Barksdale, Texas (78828) 303/D8
Barksdale A.F.B., La. 238/C2
Barlby, England 13/G4
Bar-le-Duc, France 28/F3
Barlee (lake), Australia 87/B8
Barlee (lake), W. Australia 88/B5
Barlee (lake), W. Australia 92/B5
Barletta, Italy 34/F4
Barlinek, Poland 47/B2
Barling, Ark. (72923) 202/B3
Barlow, Br. Col. 184/F3
Barlow, Ky. (42024) 237/D6
Barlow, Miss. (†39083) 256/C7
Barlow, N. Dak. (†58421) 282/M4
Barlow, Ohio (45612) 284/G7
Barlow, Oreg. (†97013) 291/B2
Barlow Bend, Ala. (†36545) 195/C8
Barmedman, N.S. Wales 97/D4
Barmer, India 68/C3
Barmera, S. Australia 94/G6
Bar Mills, Maine (04004) 243/C8
Barmouth, Wales 10/D4
Barmouth, Wales 13/C5
Barna, Ireland 17/C5
Barnabus, W. Va. (25609) 312/C7
Barnaby (riv.), New Bruns. 170/E2
Barnaby River, New Bruns. 170/E2
Barnard, Kansas (67418) 232/D2
Barnard, Mo. (64423) 261/C2
Barnard, N.C. (†28753) 281/D3
Barnard, S. Dak. (57426) 298/N2
Barnard○, Vt. (05031) 268/B4
Barnard Castle, England 13/E3
Barnardsville, N.C. (28709) 281/E3
Barnaul, U.S.S.R. 54/K4
Barnaul, U.S.S.R. 48/J4
Barn Bluff (mt.), Tasmania 99/B3
Barnegat, Alberta 182/E2
Barnegat, N.J. (08005) 273/E4
Barnegat (bay), N.J. 273/E4
Barnegat (inlet), N.J. 273/E4
Barnegat Light, N.J. (08006) 273/E4
Barnes (sound), Fla. 212/F6
Barnes, Kansas (66933) 232/F2
Barnes (co.), N. Dak. 282/O5
Barnes, Wis. (†54873) 317/D3
Barnesboro, Pa. (15714) 294/E4
Barnes City, Iowa (50027) 229/H6
Barnes Corners, N.Y. (13610) 276/J3
Barneston, Nebr. (68309) 264/H4
Barnesville, Colo. (†80624) 208/L2
Barnesville, Georgia (30204) 217/D4
Barnesville, Md. (20703) 245/J4
Barnesville, Minn. (56514) 255/B4
Barnesville, N.C. (28319) 281/L6
Barnesville, Ohio (43713) 284/H6
Barnet, England 13/H7
Barnet, England 10/B5
Barnet○, Vt. (05821) 268/C3
Barnett, Georgia (†30821) 217/G3
Barnett, Miss. (†39347) 256/G7
Barnett, Mo. (65011) 261/G6
Barnettville, New Bruns. 170/E2
Barneveld, Netherlands 27/H4
Barneveld, N.Y. (13304) 276/K4
Barneveld, Wis. (53507) 317/F10
Barneville-Carteret, France 28/C3
Barney, Georgia (31625) 217/E8
Barney, N. Dak. (58008) 282/S7
Barnhart, Texas (76930) 303/C6
Barnhill, Ohio (†44663) 284/H5
Barnoldswick, England 13/H1
Barnrock, Ky. (†41219) 237/R5
Barnsdall, Okla. (74002) 288/O1
Barnsley, England 13/J2
Barnsley, England 10/F4
Barnstable (co.), Mass. 249/N6
Barnstable, Mass. (02630) 249/N6
Barnstable○, Mass. (02630) 249/N6
Barnstaple, England 10/E5
Barnstaple, England 13/D6
Barnstaple (bay), England 10/D5
Barnstaple (bay), England 13/C6
Barnstead○, N.H. (03218) 268/E5
Barnum, Iowa (50518) 229/E3
Barnum, Minn. (55707) 255/F4
Barnum, W. Va. (†26726) 312/H4
Barnum, Wis. (†54631) 317/E9
Barnwell, Ala. (†36532) 195/C10
Barnwell, Alberta 182/D5
Barnwell (co.), S.C. 296/E5
Barnwell, S.C. (29812) 296/E5
Baro (riv.), Ethiopia 111/G6
Baro, Nigeria 106/F7
Baroda (Vadodara), India 68/C4
Baroda, India 54/J7
Baroda, Mich. (49101) 250/C7
Baroghil (pass), Afghanistan 68/C1
Baroghil (pass), Pakistan 68/C1
Baron, Okla. (†74965) 288/S3
Baron Bluff (prom.), Virgin Is. (U.S.) 161/E3
Barons, Alberta 182/D4
Barooga, N.S. Wales 97/C4
Barossa (res.), S. Australia 94/C6
Barotseland (reg.), Zambia 115/D7
Barpeta, India 68/G3
Barqa (Cyrenaica) (reg.), Libya 111/D1
Barques (pt.), Mich. 250/C3
Barquisimeto, Venezuela 124/D2
Barquisimeto, Venezuela 120/C2
Barr, Scotland 15/D5
Barr, Tenn. (†38040) 237/B9
Barra, Brazil 132/F5
Barra (head), Scotland 10/C2
Barra (head), Scotland 15/A4
Barra (isl.), Scotland 15/A4
Barra (isl.), Scotland 10/C2
Barra (isls.), Scotland 10/C2
Barra (sound), Scotland 15/A3
Barraba, N.S. Wales 97/F2
Barra Bonita (res.), Brazil 135/B3
Barrackpore, India 68/F1
Barrackville, W. Va. (26559) 312/F3
Barra de Río Grande, Nicaragua 154/F4
Barra do Bugres, Brazil 132/B6
Barra do Corda, Brazil 132/E4
Barra do Piraí, Brazil 132/E8
Barra do Piraí, Brazil 135/E3
Barra Isles (isls.), Scotland 15/A4
Barra Mansa, Brazil 135/D3
Barranca, Lima, Peru 128/C8
Barranca, Loreto, Peru 128/D5
Barrancabermeja, Colombia 126/C4
Barranca de Upía, Colombia 126/D5
Barrancas, Argentina 143/F6
Barrancas (riv.), Argentina 143/G5
Barrancas, Chile 138/G3
Barrancas, Colombia 126/D2
Barrancas, Barinas, Venezuela 124/C3
Barrancas, Monagas, Venezuela 124/G3
Barranco de Loba, Colombia 126/C3
Barrancos, Cerro (mt.), Chile 138/D7
Barrancos, Portugal 33/C3
Barranqueras, Argentina 143/E2
Barranquilla, Colombia 120/B1
Barranquilla, Colombia 126/C2
Barranquitas, P. Rico 161/D2
Barras (riv.), Bolivia 136/B6
Barras, Brazil 132/F4
Barras, Colombia 126/D8
Barraute, Québec 174/B3
Barre, Mass. (01005) 249/F3
Barre○, Mass. (01005) 249/F3
Barre, Québec 172/G3
Barre, Vt. (05641) 268/C3
Barre○, Vt. (05641) 268/C3
Barreal, Argentina 143/C3
Barreau (pt.), New Bruns. 170/F1
Barre Center, N.Y. (†14411) 276/D4
Barreiras, Brazil 120/E4
Barreiras, Brazil 132/E6
Barreirinha, Brazil 132/B3
Barreirinhas, Brazil 132/F3
Barreiro, Portugal 33/B1
Barreiros, Brazil 132/H5
Barren (isls.), Alaska 196/B2
Barren (isl.), India 68/G6
Barren (co.), Ky. 237/K7
Barren (riv.), Ky. 237/H6
Barren (isls.), Madagascar 118/G3
Barren (isl.), Nova Scotia 168/G4
Barren (cape), Tasmania 99/E2
Barren Plains, Tenn. (†37172) 237/H7
Barren River (lake), Ky. 237/J7
Barren Springs, Va. (24313) 307/G7
Barre Plains, Mass. (†01005) 249/F3
Barrera, Bolivia 136/B3
Barretos, Brazil 132/D8
Barretos, Brazil 135/B2
Barrett, Minn. (56311) 255/B5
Barrett, Texas (77532) 303/K1
Barrett, W. Va. (25013) 312/C7
Barretts, Georgia (†31601) 217/F8
Barrhead, Alberta 182/C2
Barrhead, Scotland 10/A1
Barrhead, Scotland 15/B2
Barrhill, Scotland 15/D5
Barrie, Ontario 177/E3
Barrie (isl.), Ontario 177/B1
Barrière, Br. Col. 184/H4
Barrineau Park, Fla. (†32533) 212/B6
Barrington, Ill. (60010) 222/A5
Barrington○, N.H. (†03825) 268/F5
Barrington, N.J. (08007) 273/B3
Barrington, Nova Scotia 168/C5
Barrington (bay), Nova Scotia 168/C5
Barrington○, R.I. (02806) 249/J6
Barrington, Tasmania 99/C3
Barrington Hills, Ill. (†60010) 222/A5
Barrington P.O. (East Barrington), N.H. (03825) 268/F5
Barrington Passage, Nova Scotia 168/C5
Barrington Tops (mt.), N.S. Wales 97/F2
Barringun, N.S. Wales 97/C1
Barron (co.), Wis. 317/C5
Barron, Wis. (54812) 317/C5
Barronett, Wis. (54813) 317/B4
Barrouallie, St. Vin. & Grens. 161/A9
Barroui, Dominica 161/E6
Barrow, Alaska (99723) 196/G1
Barrow, Alaska 188/C5
Barrow, Alaska 146/C2
Barrow (pt.), Alaska 146/C2
Barrow (pt.), Alaska 196/G1
Barrow (isl.), Australia 87/B8
Barrow (co.), Georgia 217/E2
Barrow (riv.), Ireland 17/H7
Barrow (riv.), Ireland 10/C4
Barrow (str.), N.W.T. 162/G1
Barrow (str.), N.W. Terrs. 187/J2
Barrow (bay), Ontario 177/C2
Barrow, U.S. 4/B17
Barrow (pt.), U.S. 2/B2
Barrow (pt.), U.S. 4/B18
Barrow (isl.), W. Australia 88/A4
Barrow (isl.), W. Australia 92/A3
Barrow Creek, North. Terr. 93/D6
Barrow-in-Furness, England 10/E3
Barrow-in-Furness, England 13/D3
Barrows, Manitoba 179/A2
Barrowsville, Mass. (†02766) 249/K5
Barr Smith (mt.) 5/C5
Barruelo de Santullán, Spain 33/D1
Barry, Ill. (62312) 222/B4
Barry (co.), Mich. 250/D6
Barry, Minn. (56210) 255/B5
Barry (co.), Mo. 261/E9
Barry (mts.), Victoria 97/D5
Barry, Wales 13/B7
Barry, Wales 10/E5
Barry's Bay, Ontario 177/G2
Barryton, Mich. (49305) 250/D5
Barryville, N.Y. (12719) 276/L8
Barsi, India 68/D5
Barsinghausen, W. Germany 22/C2
Barss Corners, Nova Scotia 168/D4
Barstow, Calif. (92311) 204/H9
Barstow, Md. (20610) 245/M6
Barstow, Texas (79719) 303/A6
Bar-sur-Aube, France 28/F3
Bar-sur-Seine, France 28/F3
Bartelso, Ill. (62218) 222/D5
Barterville, Ky. (†40311) 237/N4
Barth, E. Germany 22/E1
Barth, Fla. (†32533) 212/B6
Barthel, Sask. 181/B2
Bartholomew (bayou), Ark. 202/G6
Bartholomew (co.), Ind. 227/F6
Bartibog Bridge, New Bruns. 170/E1
Bartica, Guyana 120/D2
Bartica, Guyana 131/B2
Bartın, Turkey 63/E2
Bartle, Cuba 158/H3
Bartle Frere (mt.), Queensland 88/H3
Bartle Frere (mt.), Queensland 95/C3
Bartlesville, Okla. (74003) 288/O1
Bartlett (dam), Ariz. 198/D5
Bartlett (res.), Ariz. 198/D5
Bartlett, Ill. (60103) 222/A5
Bartlett, Iowa (51655) 229/B7
Bartlett, Kansas (67332) 232/G4
Bartlett, Nebr. (68622) 264/F3
Bartlett○, N.H. (03812) 268/E3
Bartlett, N. Dak. (†58344) 282/N3
Bartlett, Ohio (45713) 284/G7
Bartlett, Tenn. (38134) 237/B10
Bartlett, Texas (76511) 303/G7
Bartlett Deep, Cayman Is. 156/B3
Bartletts Ferry (dam), Ala. 195/H5
Bartletts Ferry (dam), Georgia 217/B5
Bartley, Nebr. (69020) 264/D4
Bartley, W. Va. (24813) 312/C8
Barto, Pa. (19504) 294/L5
Bartolomeu Dias, Mozambique 118/F4
Barton, Ala. (†35616) 195/C1
Barton, Ark. (72312) 202/J4
Barton (co.), Kansas 232/D3
Barton, Md. (21521) 245/B2
Barton (co.), Mo. 261/D7
Barton, N. Dak. (58315) 282/K2
Barton, Ohio (43905) 284/J5
Barton, Oreg. (†97009) 291/B2
Barton, Vt. (05822) 268/C2
Barton○, Vt. (05822) 268/C2
Barton (riv.), Vt. 268/C2
Barton City, Mich. (48705) 250/F4
Barton Hills, Mich. (48105) 250/F6
Bartonsville, Pa. (18321) 294/M4
Bartonsville, Vt. (†05143) 268/B5
Barton-upon-Humber, England 13/G4
Barton-upon-Humber, England 10/F4
Bartonville, Ill. (61607) 222/D3
Bartonville, Texas (†76226) 303/F1
Bartoszyce, Poland 47/E1
Bartow, Fla. (33830) 212/E4
Bartow (co.), Georgia 217/C2
Bartow, Georgia (30413) 217/G5
Bartow, W. Va. (24920) 312/G5
Bartra Antiguo, Peru 128/E4
Bartra Nuevo, Peru 128/E4
Barú (isl.), Colombia 126/C2
Barú (vol.), Panama 154/F6
Baruipur, India 68/F2
Barus, Indonesia 85/B5
Barut, Tanjong (cape), Malaysia 85/E5
Baruun-Urt, Mongolia 77/H2
Barvas, Scotland 10/C1
Barvas, Scotland 15/B2
Barview, Oreg. (†97420) 291/C4
Bar View, Oreg. (†97136) 291/C2
Barville, Québec 174/B3
Barwani, India 68/D4
Barwick, Georgia (31720) 217/E9
Barwick, Ontario 175/B3
Barwick, Ontario 177/F5
Barwon (riv.) 88/H5
Barwon (riv.), N.S. Wales 97/D2
Barysh, U.S.S.R. 52/G4
Baryulgil, N.S. Wales 97/G1
Basalt, Colo. (81621) 208/E4
Basalt, Idaho (83218) 220/F6
Basankusu, Zaire 115/C3
Basavibaso, Argentina 143/G6
Bas-Caraquet, New Bruns. 170/F1
Bascharage, Luxembourg 27/H9
Basco, Ill. (62313) 222/B3
Basco, Philippines 82/A2
Bascom, Fla. (32423) 212/A1
Bascom, Ohio (44809) 284/D3
Bascuñán (cape), Chile 138/A7
Basehor, Kansas (66007) 232/G2
Basel, Switzerland 39/E1
Basel, Switzerland 7/E4
Baselland (canton), Switzerland 39/E2
Baselstadt (canton), Switzerland 39/E1
Basey, Philippines 82/E5
Bashan, Conn. (†06423) 210/F2
Bashan (lake), Conn. 210/F3
Bashaw, Alberta 182/D3
Bashi, Ala. (†36784) 195/C7
Bashi (chan.), China 77/K7
Bashi (chan.), Philippines 82/A1
Bashkir A.S.S.R., U.S.S.R. 48/F4
Bashkir A.S.S.R., U.S.S.R. 52/J4
Basht, Iran 66/G5
Basic, Miss. (†39330) 256/G6
Basilan (prov.), Philippines 82/D7
Basilan, Philippines 82/C7
Basilan (isl.), Philippines 85/G4
Basilan (isl.), Philippines 82/D7
Basilan (str.), Philippines 82/C7
Basildon, England 13/J8
Basildon, England 10/G5
Basile, La. (70515) 238/E5
Basilicata (reg.), Italy 34/F4
Basim, India 68/D4
Basin, Mont. (59613) 262/D4
Basin (lake), Sask. 181/F3
Basin, Wyo. (82410) 319/E1
Basinger, Fla. (†33472) 212/F4
Basingstoke, England 10/F5
Basingstoke, England 13/F6
Basirhat, India 68/F4
Basit (cape), Syria 63/F5
Baskahegan (lake), Maine 243/H5
Başkale, Turkey 63/K3
Baskatong (res.), Que. 162/J6
Baskatong (res.), Québec 172/B3
Baskerville, Va. (23915) 307/M7
Basket (lake), Manitoba 179/C3
Baskett, Ky. (42402) 237/F5
Baskil, Turkey 63/H3
Baskin, La. (71219) 238/G2
Basking Ridge, N.J. (07920) 273/D2
Başmakçı, Turkey 63/C4
Basodino (peak), Switzerland 39/G4
Basoko, Zaire 115/D3
Basom, N.Y. (14013) 276/D4
Basongo, Zaire 115/D4
Basora (pt.), Neth. Ant. 161/E10
Basra (gov.), Iraq 66/E5
Basra, Iraq 2/M4
Basra, Iraq 66/E5
Basra, Iraq 59/E3
Basra, Iraq 54/F6
Bas-Rhin (dept.), France 28/G3
Bass (str.) 88/H7
Bass (str.), Australia 87/E9
Bass (isls.), Fr. Poly. 87/M8
Bass (lake), Ind. 227/D2
Bass (str.), Tasmania 99/C1
Bassano, Alberta 182/D4
Bassano del Grappa, Italy 34/C2
Bassas da India (isl.), Réunion 102/F7
Bassas da India (isl.), Réunion 118/F4
Bassecourt, Switzerland 39/D2
Bassein, Burma 54/L8
Bassein, Burma 72/B3
Bassein, India 68/C5
Basse-Pointe, Martinique 161/C5
Basse-Sambre, Belgium 27/F8
Basse Santa Su, Gambia 106/B6
Basse-Terre (cap.), Guadeloupe 161/A7
Basse-Terre (cap.), Guadeloupe 156/F4
Basse-Terre (isl.), Guadeloupe 161/A6
Basseterre (cap.), St. Chris.-Nevis 161/C10
Basseterre (cap.), St. Chris.-Nevis 156/F3
Basse Terre, Trin. & Tob. 161/B11
Bassett, Ark. (72313) 202/K2
Bassett, Iowa (†50645) 229/J2
Bassett, Kansas (†66749) 232/G4
Bassett, Nebr. (68714) 264/E2
Bassett, Va. (24055) 307/J7
Bassfield, Miss. (39421) 256/E8
Bass Harbor, Maine (04653) 243/G7
Bassikounou, Mauritania 106/C5
Bassin Bleu, Haiti 158/B5
Bass River, New Bruns. 170/E2
Bass River, Nova Scotia 168/E3
Bassum, W. Germany 22/C2
Basswood, Manitoba 179/B4
Basswood (lake), Minn. 255/G2
Basswood (lake), Ontario 175/B3
Båstad, Sweden 18/H8
Bastak, Iran 66/J7
Bastam, Iran 66/J2
Bastar, India 68/E5
Bastelica, France 28/B6
Bastenaken (Bastogne), Belgium 27/H9
Bastia, France 7/E4
Bastia, France 28/B6
Bastian, Va. (24314) 307/F6
Bastimentos (isl.), Panama 154/G6
Bastogne, Belgium 27/H9
Bastrop, La. (71220) 238/G1
Bastrop (co.), Texas 303/G7
Bastrop, Texas (78602) 303/G7
Bastuträsk, Sweden 18/L4
Basye, Va. (22810) 307/L3
Bas-Zaïre (prov.), Zaire 115/B4
Bata, Equat. Guinea 102/C4
Bata, Equat. Guinea 115/B3
Bataan (prov.), Philippines 82/C3
Batabanó (gulf), Cuba 158/C2
Batabanó (gulf), Cuba 156/A2
Batag (isl.), Philippines 82/E4
Batagay, U.S.S.R. 48/O3
Batala, India 68/D2
Batalha, Brazil 132/F3
Batalha, Portugal 33/B3
Batan (isls.), Philippines 54/O7
Batan, Albay (isl.), Philippines 82/E4
Batan, Batanes (isl.), Philippines 82/B2
Batan (isls.), Philippines 85/G1
Batan (isls.), Philippines 82/A2
Batanes (prov.), Philippines 82/A2
Batang, China 77/E5
Batang, China 54/L6
Batang, Indonesia 85/J2
Batangafo, Cent. Afr. Rep. 115/C2
Batangas (prov.), Philippines 82/C4
Batangas, Philippines 82/B4
Batangas, Philippines 85/G3
Batas (isl.), Philippines 82/B5
Bátaszék, Hungary 41/E3
Batatais, Brazil 135/C2
Batavia, Ill. (60510) 222/E2
Batavia (Jakarta) (cap.), Indonesia 85/H1
Batavia, Iowa (52533) 229/J7
Batavia, Mich. (†49036) 250/D7
Batavia, N.Y. (14020) 276/D5
Batavia, Ohio (45103) 284/B7
Batavia, Wis. (†53001) 317/K8
Batawa, Ontario 177/G3
Bataysk, U.S.S.R. 52/E5
Bat Cave, N.C. (28710) 281/E4
Batchelor, La. (70715) 238/G5
Batchelor, North. Terr. 93/B2
Batchtown, Ill. (62006) 222/C4
Batchwana Bay, Ontario 177/J5
Batdambang, Cambodia 54/M8
Batdambang (Battambang), Cambodia 72/D4
Bateman, Sask. 181/E5
Batemans Bay, N.S. Wales 97/F4
Bates, Ark. (72924) 202/B4
Bates, Mich. (†49690) 250/D4
Bates (co.), Mo. 261/D6
Bates (mt.), Norfolk I. 88/L5
Bates, Oreg. (97817) 291/J3
Batesburg, S.C. (29006) 296/D4
Bates City, Mo. (64011) 261/E5
Batesland, S. Dak. (57716) 298/E7
Batesville, Ala. (†36018) 195/H6
Batesville, Ark. (72501) 202/G2
Batesville, Ind. (47006) 227/G6
Batesville, Miss. (38606) 256/E2
Batesville, Ohio (43715) 284/H6
Batesville, Texas (78829) 303/E9
Batesville, Va. (22924) 307/L5
Bath, England 13/E6
Bath, England 10/E5
Bath, Ill. (62617) 222/C3
Bath, Ind. (47010) 227/H5
Bath, Jamaica 158/K6
Bath (co.), Ky. 237/O4
Bath, Maine (04530) 243/D8
Bath, Mich. (48808) 250/E6
Bath, Netherlands 27/E6
Bath, New Bruns. 170/C2
Bath○, N.H. (03740) 268/D3
Bath, N.Y. (14810) 276/F6
Bath, N.C. (27808) 281/R4
Bath, Ontario 177/H3
Bath, Pa. (18014) 294/M4
Bath, S.C. (29816) 296/D5
Bath, S. Dak. (57427) 298/N3
Bath (co.), Va. 307/J4
Bath (Berkeley Springs), W. Va. (†25411) 312/K3
Batha (riv.), Chad 111/C5
Bathgate, N. Dak. (58216) 282/P2
Bathgate, Scotland 15/C2
Bathgate, Scotland 10/C1
Bathsheba, Barbados 161/B8
Bath Springs, Tenn. (38311) 237/E10
Bathurst (isl.), Australia 87/C7
Bathurst (isl.), Canada 4/B14
Bathurst (Banjul) (cap.), Gambia 106/A6
Bathurst, N. Br. 162/K6
Bathurst, New Bruns. 170/E1
Bathurst, N. S. Wales 88/H6
Bathurst, N.S. Wales 97/E3
Bathurst (isl.), North Terr. 88/D2
Bathurst (isl.), North Terr. 93/A1
Bathurst (isl.), N.W.T. 162/F1
Bathurst (isl.), N.W.T. 146/H2
Bathurst (cape), N.W.T. 162/D1
Bathurst (cape), N.W.Terrs. 187/F2
Bathurst (inlet), N.W. Terrs. 187/H3
Bathurst (isl.), N.W. Terrs. 187/H2
Bathurst (harb.), Tasmania 99/C5
Bathurst Inlet, N.W. Terrs. 187/H3
Bathurst Island, North. Terr. 93/B1
Bathurst Island Mission, North. Terr. 88/E2
Bathurst Mines, New Bruns. 170/E1
Batié, Upper Volta 106/D7
Batı Fırat (riv.), Turkey 63/H3
Batin, Wadi al (dry riv.), Iraq 59/E4
Batin, Wadi al (dry riv.), Iraq 66/E6
Batin, Wadi al (dry riv.), Saudi Arabia 59/E4
Batina (reg.), Oman 59/G5
Batini (mt.), Fiji 86/Q10
Batiscan, Québec 172/E3
Batiscan (lake), Québec 172/E2
Batiscan (riv.), Québec 172/E2
Batley, England 13/J1
Batlow, N.S. Wales 97/E4
Batman, Turkey 63/J4
Batna, Algeria 102/C1
Batna, Algeria 106/F1
Bato, Catanduanes, Philippines 82/E4
Bato, Leyte, Philippines 82/E5
Bato-Bato, Philippines 82/C8
Batobato, Philippines 82/E7
Batoche, Sask. 181/E3
Batoche Nat'l Hist. Site, Sask. 181/E3
Baton Rouge (cap.), La. 146/J6
Baton Rouge (cap.), La. 188/H4
Baton Rouge (cap.), La. (*70801) 238/K2
Batopilas, Mexico 150/F3
Batouri, Cameroon 115/B3
Batovi, Uruguay 145/D2
Batrun, Lebanon 63/F5
Bat Shelomo, Israel 65/B2
Batson, Texas (77519) 303/K7
Batsto, N.J. (08037) 273/D4
Batsto (riv.), N.J. 273/D4
Batten Kill (riv.), N.Y. 276/O4
Batten Kill (riv.), Vt. 268/A5
Batterbee (cape), Ant. 2/N9
Batterbee (cape) 5/C3
Bätterkinden, Switzerland 39/E2
Battersea, Ontario 177/H3
Batticaloa, Sri Lanka 68/E7
Battiest, Okla. (74722) 288/S6
Batti Malv (isl.), India 68/G7
Battle (riv.) 162/E5
Battle (riv.), Alberta 182/D3
Battle, England 13/H7
Battle, England 10/G5
Battle (creek), Idaho 220/B7
Battle (riv.), Minn. 255/D3
Battle (creek), Mont. 262/G1
Battle (creek), Oreg. 291/K5
Battle (creek), Sask. 181/B6
Battle (riv.), Sask. 181/B3
Battle (creek), S. Dak. 298/C6
Battleboro, N.C. (27809) 281/O2
Battle Creek, Iowa (51006) 229/B4
Battle Creek, Mich. 188/J2
Battle Creek, Mich. (*49014) 250/D6
Battle Creek, Nebr. (68715) 264/G3
Battlefield, Mo. (†65619) 261/F8
Battleford, Sask. 162/E5
Battleford, Sask. 181/C3
Battle Ground, Ind. (47920) 227/D3
Battle Ground, Wash. (98604) 310/C5
Battle Harbour, Newf. 166/C3
Battle Harbour, Newf. 162/L5
Battle Lake, Alberta 182/C3
Battle Lake, Minn. (56515) 255/C4
Battle Mountain, Nev. (89820) 266/E2
Battles Wharf, Ala. (†36532) 195/C10
Battletown, Ky. (40104) 237/J4
Battleview, N. Dak. (58714) 282/E2
Battock (mt.), Scotland 15/F4
Battonya, Hungary 41/F3
Battrum, Sask. 181/C5
Batu (isls.), Indonesia 85/B6
Batuco, Chile 138/G3
Batu Gajah, Malaysia 72/D6
Batulaki, Philippines 82/E8
Batumi, U.S.S.R. 48/E5
Batumi, U.S.S.R. 52/F6
Batu Pahat, Malaysia 72/D7
Baturaja, Indonesia 85/C6
Baturité, Brazil 132/G4
Batusangkar, Indonesia 85/C6
Bat Yam, Israel 65/B3
Bauang, Philippines 82/C2
Baubau, Indonesia 85/G7
Bauchi (state), Nigeria 106/F6
Bauchi, Nigeria 106/F6
Baudette, Minn. (56623) 255/D2
Baudette (riv.), Minn. 255/D2
Baudh, India 68/E4
Baudó, Serranía de (mts.), Colombia 126/B5
Baudó (riv.), Colombia 126/B5
Baugé, France 28/D4
Bauld (cape), Newf. 166/C3
Bauld (cape), Newf. 162/L5
Bauline, Newf. 166/D2
Baulkham Hills, N. S. Wales 88/K4
Baulkham Hills, N.S. Wales 97/H3
Baulmes, Switzerland 39/C3
Bauma, Switzerland 39/G2
Baumann (fjord), N.W. Terrs. 187/K2
Baume-les-Dames, France 28/G4
Baures, Bolivia 136/D3
Baures (riv.), Bolivia 136/D3
Bauria, India 68/E2
Baurtregaum (mt.), Ireland 17/A7
Bauru, Brazil 120/E5
Bauru, Brazil 135/B3
Bauru, Brazil 132/D8
Bauska, U.S.S.R. 53/B2
Bauta, Cuba 158/C1
Bauta (riv.), P. Rico 161/C2
Bautzen, E. Germany 22/F3
Bauxite, Ark. (72011) 202/F4
Bavaria, Kansas (67419) 232/E3
Bavaria (state), W. Germany 22/D4
Bavarian (for.), W. Germany 22/E4
Bavarian Alps (mts.), Austria 41/A3
Bavarian Alps (range), W. Germany 22/D5
Baviácora, Mexico 150/E2
Bavispe, Mexico 150/E1
Bavispe, Río de (riv.), Mexico 150/E1
Bawean (isl.), Indonesia 85/K1
Bawku, Ghana 106/D6
Bawlf, Alberta 182/D3
Ba Xian, China 77/J4
Baxley, Georgia (31513) 217/H7
Baxoi, China 77/E5
Baxter (co.), Ark. 202/F1
Baxter, Iowa (50028) 229/G5
Baxter, Minn. (†56401) 255/D4
Baxter, Miss. (†39343) 256/F6
Baxter, Pa. (†15829) 294/D3
Baxter, Tenn. (38544) 237/K8
Baxter Springs, Kansas (66713) 232/H4
Baxterville, Miss. (†39455) 256/E8

Bay, Ark. (72411) 202/J2
Bay (Baicheng), China 77/B3
Bay (co.), Fla. 212/C6
Bay (co.), Mich. 250/E5
Bay, Mo. (65041) 261/J5
Bay, Laguna de (lake), Philippines 82/C3
Bay (prov.), Somalia 115/H3
Bayag (Calanasan), Philippines 82/C1
Bayaguana, Dom. Rep. 158/E6
Bayamhongor, Mongolia 77/E2
Bayamo, Cuba 156/C2
Bayamo, Cuba 158/H4
Bayamón (dist.), P. Rico 161/D1
Bayamón, P. Rico 161/D1
Bayamón, P. Rico 156/G1
Bayamón (riv.), P. Rico 161/D1
Bayanbaraat, Mongolia 77/G2
Bayandalay, Mongolia 77/F3
Bayan Dobo Suma, Mongolia 77/G3
Bayang, Philippines 82/E7
Bayangovĭ, Mongolia 77/F3
Bayan Har Shan (range), China 77/E5
Bayanhongor, Mongolia 77/E2
Bayan Mod, China 77/F3
Bayan Obo, China 77/G3
Bayan-Ölgiy, Mongolia 77/C2
Bayan-Öndör, Mongolia 77/E3
Bayan-Uul, Mongolia 77/E2
Bayard, Del. (†19945) 245/T6
Bayard, Iowa (50029) 229/D5
Bayard, Nebr. (69334) 264/A3
Bayard, N. Mex. (88023) 274/A6
Bayard, Sask. 181/F5
Bayard, W. Va. (26707) 312/H4
Bayat, Turkey 63/F2
Baybay, Philippines 82/E5
Baybay, Philippines 85/H3
Bayble, Scotland 15/B2
Bayboro, N.C. (28515) 281/R4
Bay Bulls, Newf. 166/D2
Bayburt, Turkey 59/D1
Bayburt, Turkey 63/J2
Bay Center, Wash. (98527) 310/A4
Bay Chimo, N.W. Terrs. 187/H3
Bay City, Mich. 188/K2
Bay City, Mich. (48706) 250/F5
Bay City, Oreg. (97107) 291/D2
Bay City, Texas (77414) 303/H9
Bay City, Wash. (†98520) 310/B4
Bay City, Wis. (54723) 317/B6
Baydaratа (bay), U.S.S.R. 52/L1
Bay de Verde, Newf. 166/D2
Baydhabo, Somalia 115/H3
Baydhabo, Somalia 102/G4
Baydrag, Mongolia 77/E2
Bay du Vin (riv.), New Bruns. 170/E2
Bayerischer Wald Nat'l Park, W. Germany 22/E4
Bayeux, France 28/C3
Bayfield, Colo. (81122) 208/D8
Bayfield, New Bruns. 170/G2
Bayfield, Ontario 177/C4
Bayfield (sound), Ontario 177/B2
Bayfield (co.), Wis. 317/D3
Bayfield, Wis. (54814) 317/E2
Bayham, Ontario 177/D5
Bay Harbor Islands, Fla. (†33101) 212/B4
Bay Head, N.J. (08742) 273/E3
Bayhead, Nova Scotia 168/E3
Bayındır, Turkey 63/B3
Bayırköy, Turkey 63/B6
Baykal (lake), U.S.S.R. 54/N4
Baykal (lake), U.S.S.R. 2/Q3
Baykal (lake), U.S.S.R. 48/L4
Baykal (mts.), U.S.S.R. 48/L4
Baykan, Turkey 63/J3
Baykit, U.S.S.R. 48/K3
Baykonyr, U.S.S.R. 48/G5
Bay Lake, Fla. (†32786) 212/E3
Bay Lake, Minn. (†56444) 255/E4
Bay L'Argent, Newf. 166/D4
Baylis, Ill. (62314) 222/C4
Baylor (co.), Texas 303/E4
Bay Minette, Ala. (36507) 195/C9
Bay Mission, W. Australia 88/C3
Baynes Lake, Br. Col. 184/K5
Bayombong, Philippines 82/C2
Bayombong, Philippines 85/G2
Bayonne, France 28/C6
Bayonne, N.J. (07002) 273/B2
Bayonne Military Ocean Terminal, N.J. 273/B2
Bayou, Ky. (†42081) 237/E6
Bayou Barbary, La. (†70754) 238/M2
Bayou Bodcau (res.), Ark. 202/C7
Bayou Cane, La. (†70360) 238/J7
Bayou Chicot, La. (†70586) 238/F5
Bayou Current, La. (†71353) 238/G5
Bayou D'Arbonne (lake), La. 238/F1
Bayou Des Arc (riv.), Ark. 202/G3
Bayou Goula, La. (70716) 238/J3
Bayou La Batre, Ala. (36509) 195/B10
Bayou Meto, Ark. (†72160) 202/H5
Bayou Vista, La. (†70380) 238/H7
Bayóvar, Peru 128/B5
Bay Pines, Fla. (33504) 212/B3
Bay Point, Maine (†04548) 243/D8
Bay Point (isl.), S.C. 296/F7
Bayport, Fla. (†33512) 212/D3
Bay Port, Mich. (48720) 250/F5
Bayport, Minn. (55003) 255/F5
Bayport, N.Y. (11705) 276/O9
Bayram-Ali, U.S.S.R. 48/G6
Bayramiç, Turkey 63/B3
Bayreuth, W. Germany 22/D4
Bayrischzell, W. Germany 22/E5
Bay Roberts, Newf. 166/D2
Bays, Ky. (41310) 237/P5
Bays (lake), Ontario 177/F2
Bay Saint Lawrence, Nova Scotia 168/H1
Bay Saint Louis, Miss. (39520) 256/F10
Bayshore, Fla. (†33902) 212/E5
Bayshore, Mich. (49711) 250/D3
Bay Shore, N.Y. (11706) 276/O9
Bayshore Gardens, Fla. (33507) 212/D4
Bayside, Calif. (95524) 204/B3
Bayside, Maine (†04915) 243/F7
Bayside, New Bruns. 170/C3
Bayside, Ontario 177/G3
Bayside, Texas (78340) 303/G9
Bayside, Wis. (†53201) 317/M1
Bay Springs, Fla. (†36502) 212/B6
Bay Springs, Miss. (39422) 256/F7
Bay Springs (dam), Miss. 256/H1
Bay Springs (lake), Miss. 256/H1
Bayston Hill, England 13/E5
Baysville, Ontario 177/E2
Baytown, Texas (77520) 303/L2
Bay Tree, Alberta 182/A2
Bayuca, Spain 33/B1
Bayview, Calif. (†95501) 204/A3
Bayview, Idaho (83803) 220/B2
Bayview, Md. (†21901) 245/P2
Bay View, Mich. (49770) 250/E3
Bay View, N. Zealand 100/F3
Bay View, Ohio (†44870) 284/E3
Bay Village, Ohio (44140) 284/G9
Bayville, N.J. (08721) 273/E4
Bayville, N.Y. (11709) 276/R6
Baywood, La. (†70739) 238/K1
Baywood Park-Los Osos, Calif. (†93402) 204/E8
Baza, Spain 33/E4
Bazaar, Kansas (†66845) 232/F3
Bazaruto, Ilha do (isl.), Mozambique 118/F4
Bazas, France 28/C5
Bazhong, China 77/G5
Bazile Mills, Nebr. (†68729) 264/G2
Bazine, Kansas (67516) 232/C3
Bazman, Iran 66/M7
Bazman, Kuh-e (mt.), Iran 66/H4
Bazman, Kuh-e (mt.), Iran 59/H4
Beach (pond), Conn. 210/H2
Beach, Georgia (†31554) 217/G8
Beach, N. Dak. (58621) 282/C6
Beachburg, Ontario 177/H2
Beach City, Ohio (44608) 284/G4
Beach City, Texas (†77520) 303/L2
Beach Haven, N.J. (08008) 273/E4
Beach Haven (inlet), N.J. 273/E4
Beach Haven Crest, N.J. (†08008) 273/E4
Beach Haven Terrace, N.J. (†08008) 273/E4
Beach Lake, Pa. (18405) 294/M2
Beach Meadows, Nova Scotia 168/D4
Beachport, S. Australia 94/F7
Beachton, Georgia (†31792) 217/D9
Beachville, Ontario 177/D4
Beachwood, N.J. (08722) 273/E4
Beachwood, Ohio (44122) 284/J9
Beachy (head), England 10/G5
Beachy (head), England 13/H7
Beacon, Iowa (52534) 229/H6
Beacon, N.Y. (12508) 276/N7
Beacon, Tenn. (†38363) 237/E9
Beacon Falls○, Conn. (06403) 210/C3
Beaconia, Manitoba 179/F4
Beaconsfield, England 13/G8
Beaconsfield, Iowa (50030) 229/E7
Beaconsfield, Québec 172/H4
Beaconsfield, Tasmania 99/C3
Beadle, Sask. 181/B4
Beadle (co.), S. Dak. 298/N5
Beagle (chan.), Chile 138/E11
Beagle, Kansas (†66064) 232/G3
Beagle (gulf), North. Terr. 93/A2
Beagle, W. Australia 88/C3
Beaglebay Aboriginal Res., W. Australia 92/C2
Beagle Bay Mission, W. Australia 92/C2
Beal (range), Queensland 95/B5
Bealanana, Madagascar 118/H2
Beal City, Mich. (†48858) 250/D5
Beale (cape), Br. Col. 184/E6
Beale A.F.B., Calif. 204/D4
Bealeton, Va. (22712) 307/N3
Beallsville, Ohio (43716) 284/J6
Beallsville, Pa. (15313) 294/C5
Beals, Ky. (†42451) 237/G5
Beals○, Maine (04611) 243/H7
Beals (creek), Texas 303/C5
Beaman, Iowa (50609) 229/H4
Beaminster, England 13/E7
Beanblossom, Ind. (†46160) 227/E6
Beanblossom (creek), Ind. 227/D6
Bean City, Fla. (†33459) 212/F5
Bean Station, Tenn. (37708) 237/P8
Bear (mt.), Alaska 196/K2
Bear (lake), Alberta 182/A2
Bear (lake), Br. Col. 184/D2
Bear (creek), Colo. 208/P8
Bear (hill), Conn. 210/B2
Bear (mt.), Conn. 210/B1
Bear, Del. (19701) 245/R2
Bear, Idaho (83612) 220/B4
Bear (lake), Idaho 220/G7
Bear (riv.), Idaho 220/G7
Bear (isl.), Ireland 17/B8
Bear (riv.), Maine 243/B6
Bear (riv.), Minn. 255/E3
Bear (creek), N. Dak. 282/O7
Bear (isl.), Norway 4/B9
Bear (creek), Oreg. 291/K2
Bear (creek), Oreg. 291/E5
Bear (creek), Oreg. 291/G4
Bear (hills), Sask. 181/C4
Bear (isls.), U.S.S.R. 4/B1
Bear (lake), Utah 304/C2
Bear (riv.), Utah 304/B2
Bear (isl.), Wis. 317/E1
Bear (creek), Wyo. 319/H4
Bear (riv.), Wyo. 319/B4
Bear Branch, Ind. (†47018) 227/G7
Bearcamp (riv.), N.H. 268/E4
Bear Canyon, Alberta 182/A1
Bear Creek, Ala. (35543) 195/C2
Bearcreek, Mo. (†65649) 261/E7
Bearcreek, Mont. (59007) 262/G5
Bear Creek, N.C. (27207) 281/L3
Bear Creek, Pa. (18602) 294/F7
Bear Creek, Sask. 181/K5
Bear Creek, Wis. (54922) 317/J6
Beard, Ind. (†46041) 227/E4
Beard, W. Va. (†24946) 312/F6
Bearden, Ark. (71720) 202/E6
Bearden, Okla. (74859) 288/O4
Beardmore (glac.) 5/A8
Beardmore, Ontario 177/H5
Beardmore, Ontario 175/C3
Beards Fork, W. Va. (25014) 312/D6
Beardsley, Kansas (†67745) 232/A2
Beardsley, Minn. (56211) 255/B5
Beardstown, Ill. (62618) 222/C3
Beardstown, Ind. (†46996) 227/D2
Beardstown, Tenn. (†37097) 237/F9
Beargrass, N.C. (†27892) 281/P3
Bearhat (mt.), Mont. 262/C2
Bear in the Lodge (creek), S. Dak. 298/F6
Bear Island, Ontario 177/K5
Bear Lake, Br. Col. 184/F3
Bear Lake (co.), Idaho 220/G7
Bear Lake, Mich. (49614) 250/C4
Bear Lake, Pa. (16402) 294/C1
Bear Lodge, Wyo. (†82836) 319/E1
Bear Lodge (mts.), Wyo. 319/H1
Bearmouth, Mont. (†59832) 262/C4
Béarn (trad. prov.), France 29
Bearpaw (mts.), Mont. 262/G2
Bear River, Minn. (†55723) 255/E3
Bear River, Nova Scotia 168/C4
Bear River, Pr. Edward I. 168/F2
Bear River (range), Utah 304/C1
Bear River City, Utah (84301) 304/B2
Bear River Divide (mts.), Wyo. 319/B4
Bearsden, Scotland 15/B2
Bearskin Lake, Ontario 175/B2
Bear Spring, Tenn. (†37058) 237/F8
Beartooth (mts.), Mont. 262/G5
Beartown, W. Va. (†24817) 312/C8
Beas de Segura, Spain 33/E3
Beason, Ill. (62512) 222/D3
Beata (cape), Dom. Rep. 158/D7
Beata (cape), Dom. Rep. 156/D3
Beata (chan.), Dom. Rep. 158/C7
Beata (isl.), Dom. Rep. 158/C7
Beata (isl.), Dom. Rep. 156/D3
Beatenberg, Switzerland 39/E3
Beaton, Br. Col. 184/J5
Beatrice, Ala. (36425) 195/D7
Beatrice, Nebr. 188/G2
Beatrice, Nebr. (68310) 264/H4
Beatrice (cape), North. Terr. 88/F2
Beatrice (cape), North. Terr. 93/E3
Beattie, Kansas (66406) 232/F2
Beattock, Scotland 15/E5
Beatton (riv.), Br. Col. 184/G1
Beatton River, Br. Col. 184/G1
Beatty, Nev. (89003) 266/E6
Beatty, Oreg. (97621) 291/F5
Beatty, Sask. 181/G3
Beattyville, Ky. (41311) 237/O5
Beau (lake), Québec 172/H2
Beaubier, Sask. 181/G6
Beaubois, New Bruns. 170/E1
Beaucaire, France 28/F6
Beauce (co.), Québec 172/G3
Beauceville, Québec 172/G3
Beaucoup, Ill. (†62263) 222/D5
Beaudesert, Queensland 95/E6
Beauford, Minn. (†56037) 255/D7
Beaufort (sea) 4/B16
Beaufort (sea) 146/D2
Beaufort (sea), Alaska 196/K1
Beaufort, Malaysia 85/F4
Beaufort, Mo. (65013) 261/K6
Beaufort (co.), N.C. 281/R4
Beaufort, N.C. (28516) 281/R5
Beaufort (sea), N.W. Terrs. 162/C1
Beaufort (sea), N.W. Terrs. 187/D2
Beaufort (co.), S.C. 296/F7
Beaufort, S.C. (29902) 296/F7
Beaufort, Victoria 97/B5
Beaufort (sea), Yukon 187/E2
Beaufort Marine Air Sta., S.C. 296/F7
Beaufort West, S. Africa 118/C6
Beauharnois (co.), Québec 172/C4
Beauharnois, Québec 172/D4
Beaulac, Québec 172/F4
Beaulieu, Minn. (†56557) 255/C3
Beauly, Scotland 10/D2
Beauly, Scotland 15/D3
Beauly (riv.), Scotland 15/D3
Beaumaris (bay), Victoria 97/J6
Beaumaris (bay), Victoria 88/L8
Beaumaris, Wales 13/C4
Beaumaris, Wales 10/D4
Beaumont, Alberta 182/D3
Beaumont, Belgium 27/E8
Beaumont, Calif. (92223) 204/J10
Beaumont, Kansas (67012) 232/F4
Beaumont, Miss. (39423) 256/G8
Beaumont, N. Zealand 100/B6
Beaumont, Québec 172/F3
Beaumont (pt.), St. Lucia 161/F6
Beaumont, Texas 146/J6
Beaumont, Texas 188/H4
Beaumont, Texas (*77701) 303/K7
Beaune, France 28/F4
Beauport, Québec 172/J3
Beaupré, Québec 172/G2
Beauraing, Belgium 27/F8
Beauregard (par.), La. 238/D5
Beauregard, Miss. (†39191) 256/D7
Beauséjour, Manitoba 179/F4
Beauty, Ky. (41203) 237/S5
Beauty Point, Tasmania 99/C3
Beauvais, France 28/E3
Beauval, Sask. 181/L3
Beauvallon, Alberta 182/E3
Beaux Arts Village, Wash. (†98004) 310/B2
Beaver (riv.) 162/F5
Beaver, Alaska (99724) 196/J1
Beaver (creek), Alaska 196/J1
Beaver (riv.), Alberta 182/E2
Beaver, Ark. (72613) 202/C1
Beaver (lake), Ark. 202/C1
Beaver (creek), Colo. 208/M3
Beaver (creek), Idaho 220/F5
Beaver, Iowa (50031) 229/E4
Beaver, Kansas (67517) 232/D3
Beaver (creek), Kansas 232/A2
Beaver, La. (†71463) 238/E5
Beaver (isl.), Mich. 250/D3
Beaver (lake), Mich. 250/F4
Beaver (creek), Mont. 262/J2
Beaver (creek), Nebr. 264/D5
Beaver (riv.), Newf. 166/B3
Beaver (brook), N.H. 268/E6
Beaver (brook), N.J. 273/C2
Beaver (riv.), N.Y. 276/K3
Beaver (creek), N. Dak. 282/K7
Beaver (creek), N. Dak. 282/B5
Beaver (lake), N. Dak. 282/L7
Beaver, Ohio (45613) 284/E7
Beaver (co.), Okla. 288/E1
Beaver, Okla. (73932) 288/F1
Beaver (creek), Okla. 288/K6
Beaver (riv.), Okla. 288/F1
Beaver, Oreg. (97108) 291/D2
Beaver (co.), Pa. 294/B4
Beaver, Pa. (15009) 294/B4
Beaver (riv.), Pa. 294/B4
Beaver (hills), Sask. 181/H4
Beaver (riv.), Sask. 181/L4
Beaver (creek), S. Dak. 298/A6
Beaver (co.), Utah 304/A5
Beaver, Utah (84713) 304/B5
Beaver (mts.), Utah 304/A5
Beaver (riv.), Utah 304/A5
Beaver, Wash. (98305) 310/A2
Beaver (Glen Hedrick), W. Va. (25813) 312/D7
Beaver, Wis. (54105) 317/K5
Beaver (creek), Wyo. 319/H2
Beaver (creek), Wyo. 319/D3
Beaverbank, Nova Scotia 168/E4
Beaver Bay, Minn. (55601) 255/G3
Beaver Brook Station, New Bruns. 170/E1
Beaver City, Nebr. (68926) 264/E4
Beaver Cove, Br. Col. 184/D5
Beaver Creek, Md. (†21740) 245/H2
Beaver Creek, Minn. (56116) 255/B7
Beavercreek, Ohio (†45690) 284/C6
Beavercreek, Oreg. (97004) 291/B2
Beaver Creek, Yukon 187/D3
Beaver Creek Fork, Humboldt (riv.), Nev. 266/F1
Beaver Crossing, Nebr. (68313) 264/G4
Beaverdale, Pa. (15921) 294/E5
Beaverdam, Alberta 182/E2
Beaver Dam, Ky. (42320) 237/H6
Beaverdam, Ohio (45808) 284/C4
Beaverdam, Va. (23015) 307/N5
Beaver Dam, Wis. (53916) 317/J9
Beaver Dam (lake), Wis. 317/J9
Beaver Dams, N.Y. (14812) 276/F6
Beaver Dam Wash (creek), Utah 304/A6
Beaverdell, Br. Col. 184/H5
Beaver Falls, N.Y. (13305) 276/K3
Beaver Falls, Pa. (15010) 294/B4
Beaver Harbour, New Bruns. 170/D3
Beaverhead (mts.), Idaho 220/E4
Beaverhead (co.), Mont. 262/C5
Beaverhead (riv.), Mont. 262/D5
Beaverhill (lake), Alberta 182/D3
Beaverhill (lake), Manitoba 179/J3
Beaver Lake, Alberta 182/E2
Beaver Lake, N.J. (†07416) 273/D1
Beaverlett, Va. (23016) 307/R6
Beaverlodge, Alberta 182/A2
Beaverlodge (lake), Sask. 181/L2
Beaver Meadows, Pa. (18216) 294/L4
Beaver Mines, Alberta 182/C5
Beaver Park, Sask. 181/J6
Beaver River, N.Y. (13306) 276/L3
Beaver River Flow (lake), N.Y. 276/K3
Beaver Springs, Pa. (17812) 294/H4
Beaverton, Ala. (35544) 195/B3
Beaverton, Mich. (48612) 250/E5
Beaverton, Ontario 177/E3
Beaverton, Oreg. (97005) 291/A2
Beavertown, Pa. (17813) 294/H4
Beaverville, Ill. (60912) 222/F3
Beawar, India 68/C3
Beazer, Alberta 182/D5
Beazley, Argentina 143/C3
Bebedouro, Brazil 132/D8
Bebedouro, Brazil 135/B2
Bebee, W. Va. (†26155) 312/E3
Bebington, England 10/F2
Bebington, England 13/G2
Bebra, W. Germany 22/C3
Bécancour, Québec 172/E3
Bécancour (riv.), Québec 172/F3
Beccles, England 13/J5
Beccles, England 10/G4
Bečej, Yugoslavia 45/E3
Becerreá, Spain 33/C1
Béchar, Algeria 102/B1
Béchar, Algeria 106/D2
Bechar (pt.), W. Australia 88/A3
Bechard, Sask. 181/G5
Becharof (lake), Alaska 196/G3
Bechyn, Minn. (†56275) 255/C6
Bechyně, Czech. 41/C2
Becida, Minn. (56625) 255/C3
Beckemeyer, Ill. (62219) 222/D5
Becker (co.), Minn. 255/C4
Becker, Minn. (55308) 255/E5
Becker, Miss. (38825) 256/G3
Becket○, Mass. (01223) 249/B3
Becket, Mont. (†59441) 262/G4
Beckham (co.), Okla. 288/G4
Beckley, W. Va. (25801) 312/D7
Beckton, Wyo. (†82801) 319/E1
Beckville, Texas (75631) 303/K5
Beckwourth, Calif. (96129) 204/E4
Bečva (riv.), Czech. 41/E2
Bedale, England 13/F3
Bédarieux, France 28/E6
Beddington○, Maine (†04622) 243/H6
Beddouza, Ras (cape), Morocco 106/C2
Bedele, Ethiopia 111/G6
Bedeque (bay), Pr. Edward I. 168/E2
Bedessa, Ethiopia 111/H6
Bedford, England 10/F4
Bedford, England 13/G5
Bedford (pt.), Grenada 161/D8
Bedford, Ind. (47421) 227/E7
Bedford, Iowa (50833) 229/D7
Bedford, Ky. (40006) 237/L3
Bedford○, Mass. (01730) 249/B6
Bedford, Mich. (49020) 250/D6
Bedford, Mo. (†64643) 261/F3
Bedford○, N.H. (03102) 268/D6
Bedford (basin), Nova Scotia 168/E4
Bedford, Ohio (44146) 284/H9
Bedford (co.), Pa. 294/E6
Bedford, Pa. (15522) 294/F5
Bedford, Québec 172/E4
Bedford (co.), Tenn. 237/J9
Bedford, Texas (76021) 303/F2
Bedford (co.), Va. 307/J6
Bedford (I.C.), Va. (24523) 307/J6
Bedford, Wyo. (83112) 319/A3
Bedford Heights, Ohio (†44146) 284/J9
Bedford Hills, N.Y. (10507) 276/N8
Bedford Park, Ill. (†60601) 222/B6
Bedfordshire (co.), England 13/G5
Bedford Valley, Pa. (†15522) 294/E6
Bedias, Texas (77831) 303/J7
Bedington, W. Va. (†25401) 312/L3
Bedlington, England 13/F2
Bedlington, England 10/E3
Bedminster○, N.J. (07921) 273/D2
Bedminster, Pa. (18910) 294/M5
Bedouaram (well), Niger 106/G5
Bedourie, Queensland 95/A5
Bedourie, Queensland 88/F4
Bedretto, Switzerland 39/G4
Bedrock, Colo. (81411) 208/B6
Bedsted, Denmark 21/B4
Bedwas and Machen, Wales 13/B6
Bedwellty, Wales 13/B6
Bedworth, England 13/F5
Bedworth, England 10/F4
Będzin, Poland 47/B3
Bee, Nebr. (68314) 264/H3
Bee (co.), Texas 303/G9
Beebe, Ark. (72012) 202/G3
Beebe Plain, Québec 172/E4
Beebe Plain, Vt. (05823) 268/C2
Beebe River, N.H. (03219) 268/D4
Bee Branch, Ark. (72013) 202/F3
Beech Bluff, Tenn. (38313) 237/D9
Beech Bottom, W. Va. (26030) 312/E2
Beech Creek, Ky. (42321) 237/G6
Beech Creek, Pa. (16822) 294/G3
Beecher, Ill. (60401) 222/F2
Beecher City, Ill. (62414) 222/E4
Beecher Falls, Vt. (05902) 268/D2
Beecher Island, Colo. (†80758) 208/P3
Beech Fork (riv.), Ky. 237/L5
Beech Grove, Ind. (46107) 227/E5
Beech Grove, Ky. (42322) 237/G5
Beechgrove, Tenn. (37018) 237/J9
Beech Island, S.C. (29842) 296/D5
Beechwood, Mass. (02025) 249/F8
Beechwood, Mich. (†49423) 250/C6
Beechwood, New Bruns. 170/C2
Beechwood, N.S. Wales 97/G2
Beechwood Village, Ky. (40359) 237/K2
Beechworth, Victoria 97/D5
Beechy, Sask. 181/D5
Beechy Point, Alaska (†99723) 196/H1
Beedeville, Ark. (72014) 202/H3
Beekman, La. (†71220) 238/G1
Beeler, Kansas (67518) 232/B3
Bee Log, N.C. (†28714) 281/E3
Beemer, Nebr. (68716) 264/H3
Beenleigh, Queensland 88/J5
Beer Ef'e (well), Israel 65/C5
Be'eri, Israel 65/A5
Bee Ridge, Fla. (†33578) 212/D4
Be'er Menuha, Israel 65/D5
Beernem, Belgium 27/C6
Be'er Ora, Israel 65/D5
Beersheba (Be'er Sheva), Israel 65/B5
Beersheba Springs, Tenn. (37305) 237/K10
Beer Sheva' (dry riv.), Israel 65/B5
Beersville, New Bruns. 170/E2
Be'er Tuveya, Israel 65/B4
Beeskow, E. Germany 22/F2
Beesleys Point, N.J. (†08226) 273/D5
Beeson, W. Va. (24714) 312/D8
Bee Spring, Ky. (42207) 237/J6
Beeston and Stapleford, England 13/F5
Beeton, Ontario 177/E3
Beetown, Wis. (53802) 317/E10
Beeville, Texas (78102) 303/G9
Befale, Zaire 115/D3
Befandriana, Madagascar 118/H3
Beg (lake), N. Ireland 17/J2
Bega, N.S. Wales 88/J7
Bega, N.S. Wales 97/E5
Begemdir (prov.), Ethiopia 111/G5
Beger, Mongolia 77/E2
Beggs, Okla. (74421) 288/P3
Begnins, Switzerland 39/B4
Béhague (pt.), Fr. Guiana 131/F3
Behan (lake), Alberta 182/E2
Behbehan, Iran 66/G5
Behistun (ruins), Iran 66/E3
Behm Canal (inlet), Alaska 196/N2
Behshahr, Iran 66/H2
Bei'an (Pehan), China 77/L2
Beica, Ethiopia 111/F6
Beihai (Pakhoi), China 77/G7
Beijing (Peking) (cap.), Peoples Rep. of China 54/N5
Beijing (Peking) (cap.), Peoples Rep. of China 77/J3
Beilen, Netherlands 27/K3
Beinn a Ghlo (mt.), Scotland 15/E4
Beinn Bhan (mt.), Scotland 15/C3
Beinn Bheigeir (mt.), Scotland 15/B5
Beinn Dearg (mt.), Scotland 15/D3
Beinn Dearg (mt.), Scotland 15/E4
Beinn Dhorain (mt.), Scotland 15/E2
Beinn Dorain (mt.), Scotland 15/D4
Beinn Eighe (mt.), Scotland 15/C3
Beinwil am See, Switzerland 39/F2
Beira, Mozambique 118/F3
Beira, Mozambique 102/F7
Beira, Somalia 115/J2
Beirne, Ark. (71721) 202/D6
Beirut (cap.), Lebanon 54/E6
Beirut (cap.), Lebanon 59/C3
Beirut (cap.), Lebanon 63/F6
Beiseker, Alberta 182/D4
Beishan, China 77/E3
Beitbridge, Zimbabwe 118/E4
Beit Fajjar, West Bank 65/C4
Beit Guvrin, Israel 65/B4
Beith, Scotland 10/A1
Beith, Scotland 15/D5
Beit Hanina, West Bank 65/C4
Beit Hanun, Gaza Strip 65/A4
Beit Jala, West Bank 65/C4
Beit Lahm (Bethlehem), West Bank 65/C4
Beit Nuba, West Bank 65/C4
Beit Sahur, West Bank 65/C4
Beiuș, Romania 45/F2
Beja (dist.), Portugal 33/C3
Beja, Portugal 33/C3
Béja, Tunisia 106/F1
Bejaïa, Algeria 106/F1
Bejaïa, Algeria 102/C1
Béjar, Spain 33/D2
Bejestan, Iran 59/G3
Bejestan, Iran 66/K3
Bejhi (riv.), Pakistan 68/B3
Bejou, Minn. (56516) 255/B3
Bejucal, Cuba 158/C1
Bejucal, Cuba 156/A2
Bekasi, Indonesia 85/H2
Békés (co.), Hungary 41/F3
Békés, Hungary 41/F3
Békéscsaba, Hungary 41/F3
Bekily, Madagascar 118/G4
Bekwai, Ghana 106/D7
Bel, La. (†70658) 238/D6
Bela, Pakistan 68/B3
Bela, Pakistan 59/J4
Bélabo, Cameroon 115/B3
Bela Crkva, Yugoslavia 45/E3
Bélair, Manitoba 179/F4
Bel Air, Md. (21014) 245/N2
Bélair, Québec 172/H3
Bel Alton, Md. (20611) 245/L7
Belas, Portugal 33/A1
Belau (Palau) 87/D5
Bela Vista, Angola 115/C6
Bela Vista, Brazil 120/D5
Bela Vista, Mato Grosso, Brazil 132/C8
Bela Vista, Rondônia, Brazil 132/H10
Bela Vista, Mozambique 118/E5
Bela Vista de Goiás, Brazil 132/D7
Belawan, Indonesia 85/B5
Belaya (riv.), U.S.S.R. 7/K3
Belaya (riv.), U.S.S.R. 52/H3
Belaya Tserkov', U.S.S.R. 52/C5
Belbeck, Sask. 181/F5
Belbutte, Sask. 181/D2
Bełchatów, Poland 47/D3
Belcher, Ky. (41513) 237/S6
Belcher, La. (71004) 238/C1
Belcher (isls.), N.W.T. 146/K4
Belcher (isl.), N.W.T. 162/H4
Belcher (chan.), N.W. Terrs. 187/J2
Belcheragh, Afghanistan 68/B1
Belcheragh, Afghanistan 59/J2
Belchertown, Mass. (01007) 249/E3
Belchertown○, Mass. (01007) 249/E3
Belchite, Spain 33/F2
Belcourt, N. Dak. (58316) 282/L2
Belcross, N.C. (†27921) 281/S2
Belden, Calif. (95915) 204/D3
Belden, Miss. (38826) 256/G2
Belden, Nebr. 264/G2
Belden, N. Dak. (58715) 282/F3
Beldenville, Wis. (54003) 317/A6
Belding, Mich. (48809) 250/D5
Belebey, U.S.S.R. 52/H4
Belém, Brazil 2/G6
Belém, Brazil 120/E3
Belém, Brazil 132/E3
Belém, Portugal 33/A1
Belén, Argentina 143/C2
Belén, Chile 138/B1
Belén, Honduras 154/C3
Belen, Miss. (38609) 256/D2
Belen, N. Mex. (87002) 274/C4
Belén, Panama 154/G6
Belén, Paraguay 144/D3
Belén, Uruguay 145/B1
Belén (range), Uruguay 145/C1
Belén de los Andaquíes, Colombia 126/C7
Belep (isls.), New Caled. 87/G7
Belet Weyne, Somalia 115/J3
Belet Weyne, Somalia 102/G4
Belev, U.S.S.R. 52/E4
Belfair, Wash. (98528) 310/C3
Belfast, Maine (04915) 243/F7
Belfast, N.Y. (14711) 276/D6
Belfast (cap.), N. Ireland 7/D3
Belfast (dist.), N. Ireland 17/J2
Belfast (cap.), N. Ireland 10/D3
Belfast (cap.), N. Ireland 17/J2
Belfast (inlet), N. Ireland 17/K2
Belfast, Tenn. (37019) 237/H10
Belfast Lough (inlet), N. Ireland 10/D3
Belfaux, Switzerland 39/D3
Belfield, N. Dak. (58622) 282/D6
Belford, England 13/F2
Belford, N.J. (07718) 273/E3
Belfort (terr.), France 28/G4
Belfort, France 28/G4
Belfry, Ky. (41514) 237/S5
Belfry, Mont. (59008) 262/H5
Belgaum, India 68/C5
Belgique, Mo. (†63775) 261/N7
Belgium 2/K3
Belgium 7/E3

Bering 337

BELGIUM 27
Belgium, Ill. (†61883) 222/F3
Belgium, Wis. (53004) 317/L8
Belgorod, U.S.S.R. 7/H3
Belgorod, U.S.S.R. 52/E4
Belgorod, U.S.S.R. 48/D4
Belgorod-Dnestrovskiy, U.S.S.R. 52/D5
Belgrade, Maine (04917) 243/D7
Belgrade○, Maine (04917) 243/D7
Belgrade, Minn. (56312) 255/C5
Belgrade, Mo. (63622) 261/L7
Belgrade, Mont. (59714) 262/E5
Belgrade, Nebr. (68623) 264/G3
Belgrade (cap.), Yugoslavia 7/G4
Belgrade (cap.), Yugoslavia 2/K3
Belgrade (cap.), Yugoslavia 45/E3
Belgrade Lakes, Maine (04918) 243/D6
Belgrave, Ontario 177/C4
Belgrave Heights, Victoria 97/J5
Belgrave South, Victoria 97/K5
Belgreen, Ala. (†35653) 195/C2
Belhaven, N.C. (27810) 281/R3
Belic, Cuba 158/G4
Belice (riv.), Italy 34/D6
Beli Manastir, Yugoslavia 45/D3
Belington, W. Va. (26250) 312/F4
Belitung (Billiton) (isl.), Indonesia 85/D6
Belize 2/E5
Belize 146/K8
BELIZE 154/C2
Belize (riv.), Belize 154/C2
Belize City, Belize 154/C2
Bélizon, Fr. Guiana 131/E3
Belk, Ala. (35545) 195/C3
Belknap, Ill. (†62995) 222/E6
Belknap, Iowa (†52537) 229/J7
Belknap, Mont. (†59874) 262/A3
Belknap (co.), N.H. 268/D4
Belknap (mt.), N.H. 268/E5
Belknap (peak), Utah 304/B5
Belkofski, Alaska (†99612) 196/F3
Bell, Calif. (90201) 204/C11
Bell, Fla. (32619) 212/D2
Bell (co.), Ky. 237/O7
Bell (isl.), Newf. 166/D2
Bell (isl.), Newf. 166/C3
Bell (isl.), Newf. 162/L5
Bell (pen.), N.W. Terrs. 187/K3
Bell (riv.), Que. 162/J6
Bell (riv.), Québec 174/B3
Bell (co.), Texas 303/G6
Bella Bella, Br. Col. 184/D4
Bellac, France 28/D4
Bellaco, Uruguay 145/B3
Bella Coola, Br. Col. 184/D4
Bella Coola (riv.), Br. Col. 184/D4
Belladère, Haiti 158/C6
Bella Flor, Bolivia 136/A2
Bellaghy, N. Ireland 17/H2
Bellagio, Italy 34/B2
Bellaire, Kansas (66934) 232/D2
Bellaire, Mich. (49615) 250/D4
Bellaire, Ohio (43906) 284/J5
Bellaire, Texas (77401) 303/J2
Bellamy, Ala. (36901) 195/B6
Bellarmin, Québec 172/G4
Bellarthur, N.C. (27811) 281/O3
Bellary, India 68/D5
Bellata, N.S. Wales 97/E1
Bella Unión, Uruguay 145/B1
Bella Villa, Mo. (†63101) 261/R4
Bella Vista, Corrientes, Argentina 143/E2
Bella Vista, Tucumán, Argentina 143/D2
Bella Vista, Ark. (†72712) 202/B1
Bella Vista, Bolivia 136/E3
Bella Vista, Salar de (salt dep.), Chile 138/B3
Bella Vista, Paraguay 144/D3
Bella Vista, Paraguay 144/E5
Bellavista, Peru 128/C5
Bell Bay, Tasmania 99/C3
Bellbird-Cessnock, N.S. Wales 97/F3
Bellbrook, Ohio (45305) 284/C6
Bell Buckle, Tenn. (37020) 237/J9
Bellburns, Newf. 166/C3
Bell Center, Wis. (†54631) 317/E9
Bell City, La. (70630) 238/D6
Bell City, Mo. (63735) 261/N8
Belle (riv.), Mich. 250/G6
Belle, Mo. (65013) 261/J6
Belle, W. Va. (25015) 312/C6
Belleair, Fla. (33540) 212/B2
Belleair Beach, Fla. (†33540) 212/B2
Belleair Bluffs, Fla. (33540) 212/B3
Belleair Shores, Fla. (†33540) 212/B3
Belle-Anse, Haiti 158/C6
Belle Center, Ohio (43310) 284/C4
Belle Chasse, La. (70037) 238/O4
Bellechasse (co.), Québec 172/G3
Bellechester, Minn. (†55027) 255/F6
Belle Côte, Nova Scotia 168/G2
Belle D'Eau, La. (†71330) 238/F4
Belledune, New Bruns. 170/E1
Belleek, N. Ireland 17/E3
Bellefleur, New Bruns. 170/C1
Bellefond, New Bruns. 170/E1
Bellefont, Kansas (†67876) 232/C4
Bellefontaine, Martinique 161/C6
Bellefontaine, Miss. (39737) 256/F3
Bellefontaine, Mo. (†63017) 261/N2
Bellefontaine, Ohio (43311) 284/C5
Bellefontaine Neighbors, Mo. (†63137) 261/R2
Bellefonte, Ark. (†72601) 202/D1
Bellefonte, Del. (19809) 245/S1
Bellefonte, Pa. (16823) 294/G4
Belle Fourche (riv.) 188/F2
Belle Fourche, S. Dak. (57717) 298/B4
Belle Fourche (res.), S. Dak. 298/B4
Belle Fourche (riv.), S. Dak. 298/C4
Belle Fourche (riv.), Wyo. 319/H1
Bellegarde, Sask. 181/K6
Belle Glade, Fla. (33430) 212/F5
Belle Glade Camp, Fla. (†33430) 212/F5
Belle Haven, Va. (23306) 307/S5
Belle-Île (isl.), France 28/B4
Belle Isle (str.), Canada 146/N5
Belle Isle (str.), Canada 2/G3
Belle Isle, Fla. (†32801) 212/E3
Belleisle (bay), New Bruns. 170/E3
Belle Isle (isl.), Newf. 166/C3
Belle Isle (str.), Newf. 166/C3
Belle Isle (str.), Newf. 162/L5
Belleisle Creek, New Bruns. 170/E3
Belle-Marche, Nova Scotia 168/H2
Belle Mead, N.J. (08502) 273/D3
Bellemeade, Ky. (†40201) 237/K2
Belle Meade, Tenn. (37205) 237/H8
Belle Mina, Ala. (35615) 195/E1
Bellemont, Ariz. (86015) 198/D3
Belleoram, Newf. 166/C4
Belleplain, N.J. (†08270) 273/D5
Belleplaine, Barbados 161/B8
Belle Plaine, Iowa (52208) 229/J5
Belle Plaine, Kansas (67013) 232/E4
Belle Plaine, Minn. (56011) 255/E6
Belle Plaine, Sask. 181/F5
Belle Prairie City, Ill. (†62828) 222/E5
Belle Rive, Ill. (62810) 222/E5
Belle River, Minn. (†56319) 255/C5
Belle River, Ontario 177/B5
Belle Rose, La. (70341) 238/K3
Bellerose, N.Y. (11426) 276/P7
Belle Terre, N.Y. (†11777) 276/O9
Belleterre, Québec 174/B3
Belle Union, Ind. (†46121) 227/D5
Belle Valley, Ohio (43717) 284/G6
Belle Vernon, Pa. (15012) 294/C5
Belleview, Fla. (32620) 212/D2
Belleview, Manitoba 179/B5
Belleview, Mo. (63623) 261/L7
Belle View, Va. (22307) 307/T3
Belleville, Ark. (72824) 202/D3
Belleville, Fla. (†31636) 212/C1
Belleville, France 28/F4
Belleville, Ill. 188/J3
Belleville, Ill. (*62220) 222/B3
Belleville, Kansas (66935) 232/E2
Belleville, Mich. (48111) 250/F6
Belleville, N.J. (07109) 273/B2
Belleville, N.Y. (13611) 276/H3
Belleville, Ontario 177/G3
Belleville, Pa. (17004) 294/G4
Belleville, W. Va. (26133) 312/C4
Belleville, Wis. (53508) 317/G10
Bellevue, Alberta 182/C5
Bellevue, Idaho (83313) 220/D6
Bellevue, Iowa (52031) 229/M4
Bellevue, Ky. (†41073) 237/S1
Bellevue, Md. (†21662) 245/O6
Bellevue, Mich. (49021) 250/E6
Bellevue, Nebr. (68005) 264/J3
Bellevue, Newf. 166/D2
Bellevue, Ohio (44811) 284/E3
Bellevue, Pa. (15202) 294/B6
Bellevue, Sask. 181/F3
Bellevue, Texas (76228) 303/F4
Bellevue, Wash. (*98004) 310/B2
Belley, France 28/F5
Bell Farm, Ky. (†42647) 237/M7
Bellflower, Calif. (90706) 204/C11
Bellflower, Ill. (61724) 222/E3
Bellflower, Mo. (63333) 261/K4
Bellfountain, Oreg. (†97456) 291/D3
Bell Gardens, Calif. (90201) 204/C11
Bellin, Que. 162/J3
Bellin, Québec 174/F1
Bellingen, N.S. Wales 97/G2
Bellingham, England 13/E2
Bellingham, Mass. (02019) 249/J4
Bellingham○, Mass. (02019) 249/J4
Bellingham, Minn. (56212) 255/B5
Bellingham, Wash. 188/B1
Bellingham, Wash. (98225) 310/C2
Bellingham, Wash. 310/80
Bellingshausen (sea), Ant. 2/E9
Bellingshausen (sea) 5/C14
Bellinzona, Switzerland 39/H4
Bell-Irving (riv.), Br. Col. 184/C2
Bellis, Alberta 182/D2
Belliveau Cove, Nova Scotia 168/B4
Bellmawr, N.J. (08031) 273/B3
Bellmead, Texas (76704) 303/H6
Bellmont, Ill. (62811) 222/F5
Bellmore, Ind. (47830) 227/C5
Bellmore, N.Y. (11710) 276/R7
Bello, Colombia 126/C4
Bello, Colombia 120/B2
Bellona (reefs), New Caled. 87/G8
Bellona (isl.), Solomon Is. 86/D3
Bellot (str.), N.W.T. 162/G1
Bellot (str.), N.W. Terrs. 187/J2
Bellows Falls, Vt. (05101) 268/C5
Belloy, Alberta 182/A2
Bellport, N.Y. (11713) 276/P9
Bell Rock, N.W. Terrs. 187/G3
Bell Rock (isl.), Scotland 15/F4
Bells, Tenn. (38006) 237/C9
Bells, Texas (75414) 303/H4
Bellsbank, Scotland 15/D5
Bellshill, Scotland 15/C2
Bellsite, Manitoba 179/B2
Bellsund, Norway 18/C2
Belluno (prov.), Italy 34/D1
Belluno, Italy 34/D1
Bellview, Ala. (†36452) 195/D7
Bellview, N. Mex. (88111) 274/F4
Bell Ville, Argentina 143/D3
Bell Ville, Argentina 120/C6
Bellville, Georgia (30414) 217/H6
Bellville, Ohio (44813) 284/E4
Bellville, S. Africa 118/F6
Bellville, Texas (77418) 303/H8
Bellvue, Colo. (80512) 208/J1
Bellwald, Switzerland 39/F4
Bellwood, Ala. (36313) 195/G8
Bellwood, Ill. (60104) 222/B5
Bellwood, La. (†71468) 238/D3
Bellwood, Nebr. (68624) 264/G3
Bellwood, Pa. (16617) 294/F4
Belly (riv.), Alberta 182/D5
Belmar, N.J. (07719) 273/E3
Bélmez, Spain 33/D3
Belmond, Iowa (50421) 229/F3
Belmont, Ala. (†35450) 195/C5
Belmont, Calif. (94002) 204/J3
Belmont, Georgia (†30501) 217/E2
Belmont, Kansas (67014) 232/D4
Belmont, Ky. (40105) 237/K5
Belmont, La. (71406) 238/C3
Belmont○, Maine (†04915) 243/E7
Belmont, Manitoba 179/C5
Belmont○, Mass. (02178) 249/C6
Belmont, Miss. (38827) 256/H1
Belmont, Mont. (†59046) 262/G4
Belmont○, N.H. (03220) 268/E5
Belmont, N.Y. (14813) 276/E6
Belmont, N. Zealand 100/B2
Belmont, N.C. (28012) 281/H4
Belmont, Nova Scotia 168/E3
Belmont (co.), Ohio 284/J5
Belmont, Ohio (43718) 284/J5
Belmont, Ontario 177/C5
Belmont, Wash. (99104) 310/H3
Belmont, W. Va. (26134) 312/D4
Belmont, Wis. (53510) 317/F10
Belmonte, Brazil 132/G6
Belmonte, Portugal 33/C2
Belmonte, Spain 33/E3
Belmopán (cap.), Belize 146/K8
Belmopán (cap.), Belize 154/C2
Belmore, N.S. Wales 97/J3
Belmore, Ohio (45815) 284/B3
Belmullet, Ireland 17/B3
Bel-Nor, Mo. (†63101) 261/P2
Belo, W. Va. (†25661) 312/B7
Beloeil, Belgium 27/D7
Beloeil, Québec 172/D4
Belogorsk, U.S.S.R. 54/O4
Belogorsk, U.S.S.R. 48/N4
Belogradchik, Bulgaria 45/F4
Belo Horizonte, Brazil 2/G6
Belo Horizonte, Brazil 120/E4
Belo Horizonte, Brazil 132/F7
Belo Horizonte, Brazil 135/D1
Beloit, Ala. (†36759) 195/D6
Beloit, Kansas (67420) 232/D2
Beloit, Ohio (44609) 284/J4
Beloit, Wis. 188/J2
Beloit, Wis. (53511) 317/H10
Belomorsk, U.S.S.R. 48/D3
Belomorsk, U.S.S.R. 52/D2
Belorado, Spain 33/E1
Belorechensk, U.S.S.R. 52/E6
Beloretsk, U.S.S.R. 52/J4
Beloretsk, U.S.S.R. 48/F4
Belo-Tsiribihina, Madagascar 118/G3
Belovo, U.S.S.R. 48/J4
Beloye (lake), U.S.S.R. 48/D3
Beloye (lake), U.S.S.R. 52/E2
Belozersk, U.S.S.R. 52/E3
Belp, Switzerland 39/D3
Belpre, Kansas (67519) 232/C4
Belpre, Ohio (45714) 284/G7
Bel-Ridge, Mo. (†63101) 261/P2
Belshaw, Ind. (†46356) 227/C2
Belt, Mont. (59412) 262/E3
Belted (range), Nev. 266/E5
Belterra, Brazil 132/C3
Belton, Ky. (42324) 237/H6
Belton, Mo. (64012) 261/C5
Belton, S.C. (29627) 296/C2
Belton, Texas (76513) 303/G7
Beltra (lake), Ireland 17/C4
Beltrami (co.), Minn. 255/C2
Beltrami, Minn. (56517) 255/B3
Beltsville, Md. (20705) 245/G3
Bel'tsy, U.S.S.R. 7/G4
Bel'tsy, U.S.S.R. 52/C5
Belturbet, Ireland 17/G3
Beluga (lake), Alaska 196/B1
Belumut, Gunong (mt.), Malaysia 72/D7
Belush'ya Guba, U.S.S.R. 4/B7
Belush'ya Guba, U.S.S.R. 52/H1
Belva, W. Va. (26656) 312/D6
Belvedere, Calif. (94920) 204/H2
Belvedere, Georgia (†30032) 217/L1
Belvidere, Ill. (61008) 222/E1
Belvidere, Kansas (67015) 232/C4
Belvidere, Nebr. (68315) 264/G4
Belvidere, N.J. (07823) 273/C2
Belvidere, N.C. (27919) 281/S2
Belvidere, S. Dak. (57521) 298/G6
Belvidere, Tenn. (37306) 237/J10
Belvidere○, Vt. (05442) 268/B2
Belvidere (mt.), Vt. 268/B2
Belvidere Center, Vt. (05442) 268/B2
Belvidere Junction, Vt. (†05492) 268/B2
Belview, Minn. (56214) 255/C5
Belville, N.C. (†28451) 281/N6
Belvue, Kansas (66407) 232/F2
Belwood, N.C. (†28090) 281/F4
Belwood, Ontario 177/D4
Belyando (riv.), Queensland 88/H4
Belyando (riv.), Queensland 95/C4
Belyy (isl.), U.S.S.R. 4/B6
Belyy (isl.), U.S.S.R. 48/G2
Belzoni, Miss. (39038) 256/C4
Belzoni, Okla. (†74523) 288/R6
Belzyce, Poland 47/F3
Bem, Mo. (†65066) 261/K6
Bembe, Angola 115/B5
Bemboka, N.S. Wales 97/E5
Bement, Ill. (61813) 222/E4
Bemersyde, Sask. 181/J5
Bemidji, Minn. (56601) 255/D3
Bemidji (lake), Minn. 255/D3
Bemis, S. Dak. (57215) 298/R4
Bemiss, Georgia (†31601) 217/F9
Bemmel, Netherlands 27/H5
Bemus Point, N.Y. (14712) 276/B6
Bena, Minn. (56626) 255/D3
Benabarre, Spain 33/G1
Bena-Dibele, Zaire 115/D4
Ben Alder (mt.), Scotland 15/D4
Benalla, Victoria 97/D5
Benalto, Alberta 182/C3
Benanee, N.S. Wales 97/B4
Benares (Varanasi), India 68/E3
Benavente, Spain 33/D1
Benavides, Texas (78341) 303/F10
Ben Avon, Pa. (†15202) 294/B6
Ben Avon (mt.), Scotland 15/E3
Ben Barvas (mt.), Scotland 15/B2
Benbecula (isl.), Scotland 15/A3
Benbecula (isl.), Scotland 10/C2
Benbrook, Texas (76126) 303/E2
Benbrook (lake), Texas 303/E3
Benchland, Mont. (†59462) 262/F3
Ben Cruachan (mt.), Scotland 15/C4
Bencubbin, W. Australia 92/B5
Bend, Oreg. 188/B2
Bend, Oreg. (97701) 291/F3
Bend, Texas (76824) 303/F7
Ben Dash (hill), Ireland 17/C6
Ben Davis (pt.), N.J. 273/C5
Bendel (state), Nigeria 106/F7
Bendemeer, N.S. Wales 97/F2
Bendena, Kansas (66008) 232/G2
Bender Beila, Somalia 115/K2
Bender Beila, Somalia 102/G4
Bender Cassim (Bosaso), Somalia 115/J1
Bendersville, Pa. (17306) 294/H6
Bendery, U.S.S.R. 52/C5
Bendigo, Australia 87/E9
Bendigo, Victoria 88/G7
Bendigo, Victoria 97/C5
Bendoc, Victoria 97/E5
Bendon, Mich. (†49643) 250/D4
Bendorf, W. Germany 22/B3
Bene Beraq, Israel 65/B3
Benedict (pond), Conn. 210/C1
Benedict, Kansas (66714) 232/G4
Benedict, Md. (20612) 245/M6
Benedict, Minn. (56436) 255/D3
Benedict, Nebr. (68316) 264/G3
Benedict (mt.), Newf. 166/C3
Benedict, N. Dak. (58716) 282/H4
Benedicta○, Maine (04733) 243/G4
Beneditinos, Brazil 132/F4
Benenitra, Madagascar 118/H4
Benešov, Czech. 41/C2
Benevelan, Loch (lake), Scotland 15/D3
Benevento (prov.), Italy 34/E4
Benevento, Italy 34/E4
Benevolence, Georgia (31721) 217/C7
Benewah (co.), Idaho 220/B2
Benezett, Pa. (15821) 294/F3
Benfica, Portugal 33/A1
Benfleet, England 13/J8
Benga, Mozambique 118/E3
Bengal (bay) 54/K8
Bengal, Bay of (sea), Bangladesh 68/F5
Bengal, Bay of (sea) 2/P5
Bengal, Bay of (sea), Burma 72/B3
Bengal, Bay of (sea), India 68/F5
Bengal, Ind. (†46131) 227/F6
Bengal, Okla. (†74966) 288/R5
Ben Gardane, Tunisia 106/G2
Bengbis, Cameroon 115/B3
Bengbu (Pengpu), China 77/J5
Benge, Wash. (99105) 310/G4
Benggala (str.), Indonesia 85/A4
Benghazi, Libya 2/L4
Benghazi, Libya 102/D1
Benghazi (cap.), Libya 111/C1
Ben Ghnema, Jebel (mts.), Libya 111/C2
Bengkalis, Indonesia 85/C5
Bengkayang, Indonesia 85/E5
Bengkulu, Indonesia 85/C6
Bengo (dist.), Angola 115/B5
Bengough, Sask. 181/F6
Ben Griam More (mt.), Scotland 15/D2
Bengtsfors, Sweden 18/H7
Benguela (dist.), Angola 115/B6
Benguela, Angola 115/B6
Benguela, Angola 102/D6
Ben Guerdane (well), Mauritania 106/B3
Benguet (prov.), Philippines 82/C2
Benha, Egypt 111/J3
Benham, Ky. (40807) 237/R7
Benham, N.C. (†28621) 281/G2
Benhams, Va. (†24201) 307/D7
Ben Hee (mt.), Scotland 15/D2
Ben Hill (co.), Georgia 217/F7
Ben Hope (mt.), Scotland 15/D2
Ben Horn (mt.), Scotland 15/D2
Ben Hur, Va. (24218) 307/B7
Beni, El (dept.), Bolivia 136/C3
Beni (riv.), Bolivia 120/C4
Beni (riv.), Bolivia 136/B2
Beni, Zaire 115/E3
Beni Abbès, Algeria 106/D2
Benicarló, Spain 33/G2
Benicia, Calif. (94510) 204/K1
Benicito (riv.), Bolivia 136/C3
Beni Mazar, Egypt 111/J4
Beni Mellal, Morocco 106/C2
Beni Mellal, Morocco 102/B1
Benin 2/K5
Benin 102/C4
BENIN 106/E7
Benin (bight), Benin 106/E8
Benin (bight), Ghana 106/E8
Benin (bight), Nigeria 106/E8
Benin (bight), Togo 106/E8
Benin City, Nigeria 106/F7
Benin City, Nigeria 102/C4
Beni Ounif, Algeria 106/D2
Beni Saf, Algeria 106/D1
Beni Suef, Egypt 111/J3
Beni Suef, Egypt 102/E2
Beni Suef, Egypt 59/B4
Benito, Manitoba 179/A3
Beni Ulid, Libya 111/B1
Benjamín (isl.), Chile 138/D5
Benjamin, New Bruns. 170/D1
Benjamin (lake), Oreg. 291/G4
Benjamin, Texas (79505) 303/E4
Benjamin, Utah (†84660) 304/C3
Benjamín Aceval, Paraguay 144/C4
Benjamin Constant, Brazil 132/G9
Benjamin Constant, Brazil 120/B3
Benjamín Hill, Mexico 150/D1
Benkelman, Nebr. (69021) 264/C4
Ben Kilbreck (mt.), Scotland 15/D2
Ben Lawers (mt.), Scotland 15/D4
Benld, Ill. (62009) 222/D4
Ben Lomond, Ark. (71823) 202/B6
Ben Lomond, Calif. (95005) 204/K4
Ben Lomond, New Bruns. 170/E3
Ben Lomond (mt.), Scotland 15/D4
Ben Loyal (mt.), Scotland 15/D2
Ben Lui (mt.), Scotland 15/D4
Ben Macdhui (mt.), Scotland 15/E3
Ben Mhor (mt.), Scotland 15/A3
Ben More (mt.), Scotland 15/D4
Ben More (mt.), Scotland 15/B4
Ben More Assynt (mt.), Scotland 15/D2
Bennan (head), Scotland 15/C5
Bennane (head), Scotland 15/C5
Benndale, Miss. (†39450) 256/G9
Bennet, Nebr. (68317) 264/H4
Bennett, Br. Col. 184/J1
Bennett, W.A.C. (dam), Br. Col. 184/F2
Bennett, Colo. (80102) 208/L3
Bennett (peak), Colo. 208/G7
Bennett (creek), Idaho 220/C6
Bennett, Iowa (52721) 229/L5
Bennett, N.C. (27208) 281/K3
Bennett (lake), North. Terr. 93/B7
Bennett (co.), S. Dak. 298/F7
Bennett, Wis. (54815) 317/C3
Bennettsbridge, Ireland 17/G6
Bennetts Point, S.C. (†29446) 296/G6
Bennetts Switch, Ind. (†46901) 227/E3
Bennettsville, S.C. (29512) 296/H2
Bennettville, Minn. (†56431) 255/E4
Ben Nevis (mt.), Scotland 7/D3
Ben Nevis (mt.), Scotland 15/D4
Ben Nevis (mt.), Scotland 10/D2
Benning, D.C. (20019) 245/F5
Bennington, Idaho (†83254) 220/G7
Bennington, Ind. (47011) 227/G7
Bennington, Kansas (67422) 232/E2
Bennington, Nebr. (68007) 264/H3
Bennington○, N.H. (03442) 268/D5
Bennington, Okla. (74723) 288/P7
Bennington (co.), Vt. 268/A6
Bennington, Vt. (05201) 268/A6
Bennington○, Vt. (05201) 268/A6
Benns Church, Va. (†23430) 307/P7
Benoit, Miss. (38725) 256/C3
Benoit, Wis. (54816) 317/D3
Benom, Gunong (mt.), Malaysia 72/D7
Benoni, S. Africa 118/J6
Bensenville, Ill. (60106) 222/B5
Bensheim, W. Germany 22/C4
Benson, Ariz. (85602) 198/E7
Benson, Ill. (61516) 222/D3
Benson, La. (†71419) 238/C3
Benson, Minn. (56215) 255/C5
Benson, N.C. (27504) 281/N4
Benson (co.), N. Dak. 282/M3
Benson (Hollsopple), Pa. (15935) 294/E5
Benson, Sask. 181/J6
Benson○, Vt. (05731) 268/A4
Benson Landing, Vt. (†05731) 268/A4
Bens Run, W. Va. (26135) 312/D4
Bent (co.), Colo. 208/N7
Bent, N. Mex. (88314) 274/D5
Bent Creek, Va. (†24553) 307/L5
Benteng, Indonesia 85/F7
Bentham, England 13/E3
Bentheim, W. Germany 22/B2
Bentinck (isl.), Burma 72/C5
Bentinck (isl.), Queensland 88/F3
Bentinck (isl.), Queensland 95/A3
Bentiu, Sudan 111/E6
Bentley, Alberta 182/C3
Bentley, Ill. (†62321) 222/B3
Bentley, Iowa (†51559) 229/B6
Bentley, Kansas (67016) 232/E4
Bentley, La. (71407) 238/E3
Bentley, Mich. (48613) 250/E5
Bentley, N. Dak. (58522) 282/F7
Bentley, Okla. (†74525) 288/O6
Bentley Springs, Md. (21019) 245/M2
Bentleyville, Ohio (†44022) 284/J9
Bentleyville, Pa. (15314) 294/B5
Bentley with Arksey, England 13/F4
Bent Mountain, Va. (24059) 307/H6
Bento Gonçalves, Brazil 132/C10
Benton, Ala. (36785) 195/E6
Benton, Alberta 182/E4
Benton (co.), Ark. 202/B1
Benton, Ark. (72015) 202/E4
Benton, Calif. (93512) 204/G6
Benton, Ill. (62812) 222/E6
Benton (co.), Ind. 227/C3
Benton, Ind. (†46526) 227/F2
Benton (co.), Iowa 229/J4
Benton, Iowa (50835) 229/E7
Benton, Kansas (67017) 232/E4
Benton, Ky. (42025) 237/E7
Benton, La. (71006) 238/C1
Benton○, Maine (†04937) 243/D6
Benton (co.), Minn. 255/D5
Benton, Minn. (†55322) 255/F6
Benton (lake), Minn. 255/B6
Benton (co.), Miss. 256/F1
Benton, Miss. (39039) 256/D5
Benton (co.), Mo. 261/F6
Benton, Mo. (63736) 261/O8
Benton (lake), Mont. 262/E3
Benton, New Bruns. 170/C3
Benton○, N.H. (†03785) 268/D3
Benton, Ohio (44654) 284/G4
Benton (co.), Oreg. 291/D3
Benton, Pa. (17814) 294/K3
Benton (co.), Tenn. 237/E8
Benton, Tenn. (37307) 237/M10
Benton (co.), Wash. 310/F4
Benton, Wis. (53803) 317/F10
Benton City, Mo. (65232) 261/J4
Benton City, Wash. (99320) 310/F4
Bentong, Malaysia 72/D7
Benton Harbor, Mich. (49022) 250/C6
Benton Heights, Mich. (†49022) 250/C6
Bentonia, Miss. (39040) 256/D5
Benton Ridge, Ohio (45816) 284/C4
Bentonsport, Iowa (†52565) 229/K7
Bentonville, Ark. (72712) 202/B1
Bentonville, Ind. (47322) 227/G5
Bentonville, Ohio (45105) 284/C8
Bentonville, Va. (22610) 307/M3
Bent's Old Fort Nat'l Hist. Site, Colo. 208/M6
Benué (riv.), Cameroon 115/A2
Benue (state), Nigeria 106/F7
Benue (riv.), Nigeria 102/C4
Benue (riv.), Nigeria 106/F7
Ben Vorlich (mt.), Scotland 15/D4
Ben Vrackie (mt.), Scotland 15/E4
Benwee (head), Ireland 17/B3
Benwood, W. Va. (26031) 312/E2
Ben Wyvis (mt.), Scotland 15/D3
Benxi (Penki), China 77/K3
Benxi, China 54/O5
Benzie (co.), Mich. 250/C4
Benzonia, Mich. (49616) 250/D4
Beo, Indonesia 85/H5
Beograd (Belgrade) (cap.), Yugoslavia 45/E3
Beowawe, Nev. (89821) 266/E2
Beppu, Japan 81/E7
Bequia (isl.), St. Vin. & Grens. 156/G4
Beragh, N. Ireland 17/G2
Berar (reg.), India 68/D4
Berat, Albania 45/D5
Berau (bay), Indonesia 85/J6
Berber, Sudan 111/F4
Berber, Sudan 59/B6
Berber, Sudan 102/F3
Berbera, Somalia 115/J1
Berbera, Somalia 102/G3
Berberati, Cent. Afr. Rep. 102/D4
Berberati, Cent. Afr. Rep. 115/C3
Berbice (riv.), Guyana 131/B3
Berchem, Belgium 27/F6
Berchem-Sainte-Agathe, Belgium 27/B9
Bercher, Switzerland 39/C3
Berchtesgaden, W. Germany 22/E5
Berck, France 28/D2
Berclair, Texas (78107) 303/G9
Berdichev, U.S.S.R. 48/C5
Berdichev, U.S.S.R. 52/C5
Berdsk, U.S.S.R. 48/J4
Berdyansk, U.S.S.R. 7/H4
Berdyansk, U.S.S.R. 52/E5
Berea, Ky. (40403) 237/N5
Berea, Nebr. (†69301) 264/A2
Berea, N.C. (†27565) 281/M2
Berea, Ohio (44017) 284/G10
Berea, S.C. (29611) 296/C2
Berea, Spain 33/C1
Berea, W. Va. (26327) 312/E4
Bereda, Somalia 115/K1
Bereda, Somalia 102/H3
Beregovo, U.S.S.R. 52/B5
Berekum, Ghana 106/D7
Berenguela, Bolivia 136/A5
Berenice (ruins), Egypt 111/F3
Berens (riv.), Man. 162/G5
Berens (isl.), Manitoba 179/E2
Berens (riv.), Manitoba 179/F2
Berens (riv.), Ontario 175/A2
Berens River, Man. 162/G5
Berens River, Manitoba 179/F2
Beresford (lake), Fla. 212/E3
Beresford, New Bruns. 170/E1
Beresford, S. Dak. (57004) 298/R7
Beresford Lake, Manitoba 179/G4
Berești Tîrg, Romania 45/H2
Berettyó (riv.), Hungary 41/F3
Berettyóújfalu, Hungary 41/F3
Berezina (riv.), U.S.S.R. 52/C4
Bereznik, U.S.S.R. 52/F2
Berezniki, U.S.S.R. 7/K3
Berezniki, U.S.S.R. 48/F4
Berezniki, U.S.S.R. 52/J3
Berezovo, U.S.S.R. 48/G3
Berg, Norway 18/K2
Berg, Switzerland 39/H1
Berga, Algeria 106/E3
Berga, Spain 33/G1
Bergama, Turkey 63/B3
Bergama, Turkey 59/A2
Bergamo (prov.), Italy 34/B2
Bergamo, Italy 34/B2
Bergeijk, Netherlands 27/G6
Bergen (Mons), Belgium 27/E8
Bergen, E. Germany 22/E1
Bergen, Minn. (†56101) 255/D7
Bergen, Netherlands 27/F3
Bergen (co.), N.J. 273/E2
Bergen, N.Y. (14416) 276/E4
Bergen, N. Dak. (58792) 282/J3
Bergen, Norway 18/D6
Bergen, Norway 7/E2
Berg en Dal, Suriname 131/D3
Bergenfield, N.J. (07621) 273/C1
Bergen op Zoom, Netherlands 27/E5
Berger, Mo. (63014) 261/K5
Bergerac, France 28/D5
Bergholz, Ohio (43908) 284/J4
Bergisch Gladbach, W. Germany 22/B3
Bergland, Mich. (49910) 250/F1
Bergman, Ark. (72615) 202/E1
Bergoo, W. Va. (26298) 312/F6
Bergos (riv.), Turkey 63/C6
Bergshamra, Sweden 18/L7
Bergsjö, Sweden 18/K5
Bergstrom A.F.B., Texas 303/G7
Bergton, Va. (22811) 307/L3
Berguent, Morocco 106/D2
Bergum, Netherlands 27/H2
Bergumermeer (lake), Netherlands 27/J2
Bergün-Bravuogn, Switzerland 39/J3
Berhala (str.), Indonesia 85/C6
Berhampore, India 68/F4
Berhampur, India 68/F5
Berhida, Hungary 41/E3
Bering (sea) 2/A3

Blandburg 339

Big Spencer (mt.), Maine 243/E4
Big Spring, Georgia (†30240) 217/C5
Big Spring, Ky. (40106) 237/J5
Big Spring, Md. (21722) 245/G2
Big Spring, Tenn. (37323) 237/M10
Big Spring, Texas 188/F4
Big Spring, Texas (79720) 303/C5
Big Springs, Nebr. (69122) 264/B3
Big Springs, S. Dak. (†57001) 298/S8
Big Springs, W. Va. (26137) 312/D5
Big Star (lake), Mich. 250/C5
Bigstick (lake), Sask. 181/B5
Big Stone, Alberta 182/E4
Bigstone (lake), Manitoba 179/J3
Bigstone (pt.), Manitoba 179/E2
Bigstone (riv.), Manitoba 179/J3
Big Stone (co.), Minn. 255/B5
Big Stone (lake), Minn. 255/B5
Big Stone (lake), S. Dak. 298/R3
Big Stone City, S. Dak. (57216) 298/S3
Big Stone Gap, Va. (24219) 307/C7
Big Sur, Calif. (93920) 204/D7
Big Thicket Nat'l Preserve, Texas 303/K7
Big Thompson (riv.), Colo. 208/H2
Big Timber, Mont. (59011) 262/G5
Big Timber (creek), N.J. 273/C4
Big Tracadie (riv.), New Bruns. 170/E1
Bigtrails, Wyo. (†82442) 319/E2
Big Trout (lake), Ontario 177/F2
Big Trout (lake), Ontario 175/B2
Big Trout Lake, Ontario 175/C2
Big Valley, Alberta 182/D3
Big Walnut (creek), Ind. 227/D5
Big Walnut (creek), Ohio 284/E5
Big Wells, Texas (78830) 303/E9
Big Whiteshell Lake, Manitoba 179/G4
Big Wood (riv.), Idaho 220/D6
Bihać, Yugoslavia 45/B3
Bihar (state), India 68/F4
Bihar, India 68/F3
Biharamulo, Tanzania 115/F4
Biharkeresztes, Hungary 41/F3
Biharnagybajom, Hungary 41/F3
Bijagós (isls.), Guinea-Biss. 106/A6
Bijagós (isls.), Guinea-Biss. 102/A3
Bijapur, Karnataka, India 68/D5
Bijapur, Madhya Pradesh, India 68/E5
Bijar, Iran 66/E3
Bijeljina, Yugoslavia 45/D3
Bijelo Polje, Yugoslavia 45/D4
Bijiang, China 77/E6
Bijie, China 77/G6
Bijnor, India 68/D3
Bijou (creek), Colo. 208/L3
Bijou Hills, S. Dak. (†57310) 298/L6
Bikaner, India 54/J7
Bikaner, India 68/C3
Bikar (atoll), Marshall Is. 87/H4
Bikin, U.S.S.R. 48/O5
Bikini (atoll), Marshall Is. 87/G4
Bikoro, Zaire 115/C4
Bikoro, Zaire 102/D5
Bilaspur, India 68/E4
Bilauktaung (range), Burma 72/C4
Bilauktaung (range), Thailand 72/C4
Bilbao, Spain 33/E1
Bilbao, Spain 7/D4
Bileća, Yugoslavia 45/D4
Bilecik (prov.), Turkey 63/D2
Bilecik, Turkey 59/A1
Bilecik, Turkey 63/D2
Biłgoraj, Poland 47/F3
Bilibino, U.S.S.R. 4/C1
Bilibino, U.S.S.R. 48/R3
Bilin, Burma 72/C3
Bílina, Czech. 41/B1
Biliran (isl.), Philippines 82/E5
Bill, Wyo. (82631) 319/G2
Billate (riv.), Ethiopia 111/G6
Billerica◯, Mass. (01821) 249/J2
Billings (lake), Conn. 210/H2
Billings, Mo. (65610) 261/F8
Billings, Mont. 146/H5
Billings, Mont. 188/E1
Billings, Mont. (*59101) 262/H5
Billings (co.), N. Dak. 282/D5
Billings, Okla. (74630) 288/M1
Billingsgate (isl.), Mass. 249/O5
Billingshurst, England 13/G6
Billingsley, Ala. (36006) 195/E5
Billiton (isl.), Indonesia 54/M10
Billiton (isl.), Indonesia 85/D6
Bill Williams (riv.), Ariz. 198/B4
Billy Clapp (lake), Wash. 310/F3
Bilma, Niger 102/D3
Bilma, Niger 106/G5
Biloela, Queensland 88/J4
Biloela, Queensland 95/D5
Biloku, Guyana 131/B5
Biloxi, Miss. 146/K6
Biloxi, Miss. 188/J4
Biloxi, Miss. (*39530) 256/G10
Biltine, Chad 111/D5
Biltine, Chad 102/D3
Biltmore Forest, N.C. (†28803) 281/E3
Bilwaskarma, Nicaragua 154/F3
Bilzen, Belgium 27/G7
Bim, W. Va. (25021) 312/C7
Biminis, The (isls.), Bahamas 156/B1
Bina-Itawa, India 68/D4
Binalbagan, Philippines 82/D5
Binalong, N.S. Wales 97/E4
Binboğa (mts.), Turkey 63/G3
Binbrook, Ontario 177/E4
Binche, Belgium 27/E8
Binda, N.S. Wales 97/E4
Bindloss, Alberta 182/E4
Bindoon, W. Australia 92/B1
Bindura, Zimbabwe 118/E3
Binéfar, Spain 33/G2
Binevenagh (mt.), N. Ireland 17/H1
Binford, N. Dak. (58416) 282/O4
Binga (mt.), Mozambique 118/E3
Bingara, N.S. Wales 97/F1
Bingen, Wash. (98605) 310/D5
Bingen, W. Germany 22/B4
Binger, Okla. (73009) 288/K4
Bingerville, Ivory Coast 106/D7
Bingham (co.), Idaho 220/F6
Bingham, Ill. (62011) 222/D4
Bingham, Maine (04920) 243/D5
Bingham◯, Maine (04920) 243/D5
Bingham, Nebr. (69335) 264/B2
Bingham, N. Mex. (87815) 274/C5
Bingham, S.C. (†29565) 296/H3
Bingham Lake, Minn. (56118) 255/C7
Binghamton, N.Y. 188/L2
Binghamton, N.Y. (*13901) 276/J6
Bingöl (prov.), Turkey 63/J3
Bingöl (Çapakçur), Turkey 63/J3
Bingöl Dağları (mts.), Turkey 63/J3
Binhai, China 77/K5
Binh Long (An Loc), Vietnam 72/E5
Binh Son, Vietnam 72/F4
Binjai, Indonesia 85/B5
Binn, Switzerland 39/F4
Binnaway, N.S. Wales 97/E2
Binningen, Switzerland 39/D1
Binongko (isl.), Indonesia 85/G7
Binscarth, Manitoba 179/A4
Bintan (isl.), Indonesia 85/C5
Bintuhan, Indonesia 85/C6
Bintulu, Malaysia 85/E5
Binyamina, Israel 65/B2
Binyang, China 77/G7
Biobío (reg.), Chile 138/E1
Bío-Bío (riv.), Chile 138/E2
Biograd, Yugoslavia 45/B4
Bioko (isl.), Equat. Guinea 102/C4
Bioko (terr.), Equat. Guinea 115/A3
Bioko (isl.), Equat. Guinea 115/A3
Biola, Calif. (93606) 204/E7
Bippus, Ind. (46713) 227/F3
Bir, India 68/D5
Bira, U.S.S.R. 48/O5
Birag, Kuh-e (mts.), Iran 66/M7
Bir 'Ali, P.D.R. Yemen 59/E7
Birama (pt.), Cuba 158/G4
Birao, Cent. Afr. Rep. 115/D1
Biratnagar, Nepal 68/F3
Biratori, Japan 81/L2
Bir Bala, Iran 66/L8
Bir Bala, Iran 59/G4
Bircao, Somalia 115/H4
Birch (creek), Alaska 196/J1
Birch (hills), Alberta 182/A2
Birch (lake), Alberta 182/E3
Birch (mts.), Alberta 182/B5
Birch (riv.), Alberta 182/B5
Birch (creek), Idaho 220/F5
Birch (isl.), Manitoba 179/C2
Birch (lake), Minn. 255/G3
Birch (creek), Mont. 262/D2
Birch (lake), Sask. 181/C2
Birch (creek), Utah 304/B5
Birch (pt.), Wash. 310/C2
Birch Creek, Alaska (†99740) 196/J1
Birch Creek (valley), Idaho 220/E5
Birch Creek (res.), Mont. 262/D2
Birchdale, Minn. (56629) 255/D2
Birch Harbor, Maine (04613) 243/H7
Birch Hills, Sask. 181/F3
Birchip, Victoria 97/B4
Birch Island, Br. Col. 184/H4
Birchleaf, Va. (24220) 307/D6
Birch River, Manitoba 179/A2
Birch River, W. Va. (26610) 312/E6
Birch Run, Mich. (48415) 250/F5
Birchtown, Nova Scotia 168/C5
Birch Tree, Mo. (65438) 261/K9
Birchwood, Md. (†20021) 245/F5
Birchwood, Tenn. (37308) 237/M10
Birchwood, Wis. (54817) 317/C4
Birchy Bay, Newf. 166/D4
Bird (isl.), La. 238/M8
Bird (creek), Okla. 288/O1
Bird City, Kansas (67731) 232/A2
Bird Cove, Newf. 166/C3
Bird Island, Minn. (55310) 255/D6
Birds, Ill. (62415) 222/F5
Birdsboro, Pa. (19508) 294/L5
Birdseye, Ind. (47513) 227/D8
Birds Hill, Manitoba 179/F4
Birdsnest, Va. (23307) 307/S6
Birdsong, Ark. (†72386) 202/K3
Birdsville, Ky. (†42081) 237/D6
Birdsville, Queensland 88/F5
Birdsville, Queensland 95/A5
Birdtail, Manitoba 179/B4
Birdum, North. Terr. 93/C3
Birdwood, S. Australia 94/C7
Birecik, Turkey 63/H4
Bir el Khzaim (well), Mauritania 106/C4
Bireuen, Indonesia 85/B4
Bir Ganduz (well), Western Sahara 106/A4
Birganj, Nepal 68/F3
Bir Hakeim (ruins), Libya 111/D1
Birigui, Brazil 135/A2
Birjand, Iran 66/L4
Birjand, Iran 59/G3
Birjand, Iran 54/G6
Birken, Br. Col. 184/F5
Birkenfeld, Oreg. (97016) 291/D1
Birkenfeld, W. Germany 22/B4
Birkenhead, England 13/G2
Birkenhead, England 10/F2
Birkenhead, N. Zealand 100/B1
Birkenhead Lake Prov. Park, Br. Col. 184/F5
Birkerød, Denmark 21/F6
Birket Qârûn (lake), Egypt 111/J3
Bir Ksaib Ounane (well), Mali 106/C4
Birksgate (range), S. Australia 94/A2
Bîrlad, Romania 45/H2
Bîrlad (riv.), Romania 45/H2
Birmingham, Ala. 146/K6
Birmingham, Ala. 188/J4
Birmingham, Ala. 195/D3
Birmingham, England 7/D3
Birmingham, England 10/G3
Birmingham, England 13/F5
Birmingham, Iowa (52535) 229/K7
Birmingham, Mich. (*48008) 250/B6
Birmingham, Mo. (†64068) 261/R5
Birmingham, N.J. (08011) 273/D4
Birmingham, Ohio (44816) 284/F3
Birmingham, Pa. (†16686) 294/F4
Birmingham, Sask. 181/H5
Birmitrapur, India 68/E4
Bir Mogreïn, Mauritania 106/B3
Birnam, Scotland 15/E4
Birnamwood, Wis. (54414) 317/H6
Birney, Mont. (59012) 262/K5
Birnie, Manitoba 179/C4
Birnin Kebbi, Nigeria 106/E6
Birni-N'Konni, Niger 106/E6
Birni-N'Konni, Niger 102/C3
Bir Nzaran (well), Western Sahara 106/B4
Birobidzhan, U.S.S.R. 54/O5
Birobidzhan, U.S.S.R. 48/O5
Biron, Wis. (†54494) 317/G7
Bir Ounane (well), Mali 106/D4
Birqin, West Bank 65/C3
Birr, Ireland 17/F5
Birr, Ireland 10/B4
Birregurra, Victoria 97/B6
Birrie (riv.), N. S. Wales 88/H5
Birrie (riv.), N.S. Wales 97/D1
Birrimbah, North. Terr. 93/C3
Birrindudu, North. Terr. 93/A5
Birriwa, N.S. Wales 97/E3
Birs (riv.), Switzerland 39/D2
Birsay, Sask. 181/D4
Birsk, U.S.S.R. 52/J3
Birta, Ark. (†72853) 202/D3
Bir Taba, Egypt 59/B4
Bir Taba (well), Egypt 111/F2
Birtle, Manitoba 179/B4
Biru, China 77/D5
Biruaca, Venezuela 124/E4
Biruni, U.S.S.R. 48/G5
Biržai, U.S.S.R. 53/C2
Bir Zeit, West Bank 65/C4
Bisbee, Ariz. 188/E4
Bisbee, Ariz. (85603) 198/F7
Bisbee, N. Dak. (58317) 282/M2
Biscarrosse (lake), France 28/C5
Biscay (bay) 2/J3
Biscay (bay) 7/D4
Biscay (bay), France 28/B5
Biscay, Minn. (†55336) 255/D6
Biscay (bay), Spain 33/E1
Biscay Bay (riv.), Newf. 166/D2
Biscayne (bay), Fla. 212/F6
Biscayne (key), Fla. 212/B5
Biscayne Nat'l Park, Fla. 212/F6
Biscayne Park, Fla. (33152) 212/B4
Bisceglie, Italy 34/F4
Bischofshofen, Austria 41/B3
Bischofswerda, E. Germany 22/F3
Bischofszell, Switzerland 39/H1
Biscoe (isls.) 5/C15
Biscoe, Ark. (72017) 202/H4
Biscoe, N.C. (27209) 281/K4
Biscotasing, Ontario 177/J5
Biscotasing, Ontario 175/D3
Biscucuy, Venezuela 124/D3
Bisha, Saudi Arabia 59/D5
Bisha, Wadi (dry riv.), Saudi Arabia 59/D5
Bishiara (well), Libya 111/D3
Bisho (cap.), Ciskei, S. Africa 102/E8
Bishop, Calif. (93514) 204/G6
Bishop, Georgia (30621) 217/F3
Bishop, Md. (†21813) 245/S7
Bishop (creek), Nev. 266/F1
Bishop, Texas (78343) 303/G10
Bishop (creek), Utah 304/E3
Bishop, Va. (24604) 307/E6
Bishop Auckland, England 10/E3
Bishop Auckland, England 13/E3
Bishopbriggs, Scotland 15/B2
Bishop Hill, Ill. (61419) 222/C2
Bishopric, Sask. 181/F5
Bishop's Falls, Newf. 166/C4
Bishops Head, Md. (21611) 245/O7
Bishops Mitre (mt.), Newf. 166/B2
Bishop's Stortford, England 10/G5
Bishop's Stortford, England 13/H6
Bishopton, Québec 172/F4
Bishopton, Scotland 15/B2
Bishopville, Md. (21813) 245/T7
Bishopville, S.C. (29010) 296/G3
Bishri, Jebel el (mts.), Syria 63/H5
Biskra, Algeria 106/F2
Biskra, Algeria 102/C1
Biskupiec, Poland 47/E2
Bislig, Philippines 85/H4
Bislig, Philippines 82/F6
Bismarck, Ark. (71929) 202/D5
Bismarck, Ill. (61814) 222/F3
Bismarck, Mo. (63624) 261/L7
Bismarck (cap.), N. Dak. 146/H5
Bismarck (cap.), N. Dak. 188/G1
Bismarck (cap.), N. Dak. (58501) 282/J6
Bismarck (arch.), Papua N.G. 87/E6
Bismarck (arch.), Papua N.G. 86/B1
Bismarck (sea), Papua N.G. 86/B1
Bismarck (arch.), Papua N.G. 2/S6
Bismarck, W. Va. (†26739) 312/H4
Bismil, Turkey 63/J4
Bison (lake), Alberta 182/B1
Bison, Kansas (67520) 232/C3
Bison, Okla. (73720) 288/L2
Bison, S. Dak. (57620) 298/E2
Bispgården, Sweden 18/K5
Bissau (cap.), Guinea-Biss. 106/A6
Bissau (cap.), Guinea-Biss. 102/A3
Bissett, Manitoba 179/G4
Bistineau (lake), La. 238/D2
Bistrita, Romania 45/G2
Bita (riv.), Colombia 126/F5
Bitagron, Suriname 131/C3
Bitam, Gabon 115/B3
Bitburg, W. Germany 22/B4
Bitely, Mich. (49309) 250/D5
Bithlo, Fla. (†32801) 212/E3
Bitkine, Chad 111/C5
Bitlis (prov.), Turkey 63/J3
Bitlis, Turkey 63/J3
Bitlis, Turkey 59/D2
Bitola, Yugoslavia 45/E5
Bitola, Yugoslavia 7/G4
Bitonto, Italy 34/F4
Bitter (lakes), Egypt 111/K3
Bitter (lake), Sask. 181/B5
Bitter (creek), Wyo. 319/C4
Bitter Creek, Wyo. (†82901) 319/D4
Bitterfeld, E. Germany 22/E3
Bitterfontein, S. Africa 118/B6
Bittern (lake), Alberta 182/D3
Bittern Lake, Alberta 182/D3
Bitterroot (range) 188/D1
Bitterroot (range), Idaho 220/D3
Bitterroot (range), Mont. 262/B4
Bitterroot (riv.), Mont. 262/B4
Bitterroot (range), U.S. 146/G5
Bitti, Italy 34/B4
Bitumount, Alberta 182/E1
Bitung, Indonesia 85/H5
Biu, Nigeria 106/G6
Biu (plat.), Nigeria 106/G6
Bivalve, Md. (21814) 245/P7
Bivalve, N.J. (08301) 273/C5
Bivolari, Romania 45/H2
Biwa (lake), Japan 81/H6
Biwabik, Minn. (55708) 255/F3
Bixby, Minn. (†55334) 255/E7
Bixby, Mo. (65439) 261/K7
Bixby, Okla. (74008) 288/P3
Biyang, China 77/H5
Biysk, U.S.S.R. 54/K4
Biysk, U.S.S.R. 48/J4
Bizcocho, Uruguay 145/B4
Bizerte, Tunisia 106/F1
Bizerte, Tunisia 102/C1
Bjargtangar (pt.), Iceland 21/A1
Bjelovar, Yugoslavia 45/C3
Bjerringbro, Denmark 21/C5
Bjorkdale, Sask. 181/H3
Bjørnafjorden (fjord), Norway 18/D6
Bjorne (pen.), N.W. Terrs. 187/K2
Bjørnøya (isl.), Norway 18/D3
Blabon, N. Dak. (†58046) 282/P5
Blachly, Oreg. (97412) 291/D3
Black (sea) 2/L3
Black (sea) 54/E5
Black (sea) 7/H4
Black, Ala. (36314) 195/G8
Black (riv.), Alaska 196/K1
Black (mesa), Ariz. 198/E2
Black (mts.), Ariz. 198/A3
Black (riv.), Ariz. 198/E5
Black (riv.), Ark. 202/H2
Black (sea), Bulgaria 45/J4
Black (pond), Conn. 210/G1
Black (pt.), Conn. 210/G3
Black (mts.), England 13/D6
Black (creek), Fla. 212/E1
Black (head), Ireland 17/C5
Black (riv.), Jamaica 158/H6
Black (mt.), Ky. 237/R7
Black (lake), La. 238/D3
Black (pond), Maine 243/D3
Black (isl.), Manitoba 179/F3
Black (riv.), Manitoba 179/F4
Black (lake), Mich. 250/E3
Black (riv.), Mich. 250/E3
Black (riv.), Mich. 250/G5
Black (riv.), Minn. 255/D2
Black (creek), Miss. 256/F8
Black, Mo. (63625) 261/L7
Black (riv.), Mo. 261/L10
Black (mt.), N. Mex. 274/A6
Black (range), N. Mex. 274/B5
Black (lake), N.Y. 276/J1
Black (riv.), N.Y. 276/K3
Black (riv.), N.C. 281/N5
Black (riv.), Ohio 284/F3
Black (riv.), Ontario 177/E3
Black (sea), Romania 45/J4
Black (lake), Sask. 181/M2
Black (riv.), S.C. 296/H4
Black (sea), Turkey 63/E1
Black (sea), U.S.S.R. 48/D5
Black (sea), U.S.S.R. 52/D6
Black (creek), Vt. 268/B2
Black (riv.), Vt. 268/C2
Black (riv.), Vt. 268/B5
Black (riv.), Vietnam 72/D2
Black (mts.), Wales 13/D6
Black (for.), W. Germany 22/C4
Black (riv.), Wis. 317/E7
Black (riv.), Yukon 187/D3
Blackall, Australia 87/E8
Blackall, Queensland 88/H4
Blackall, Queensland 95/C5
Black Bear (creek), Okla. 288/M2
Blackberry (riv.), Conn. 210/B1
Blackbird, Del. (†19734) 245/R3
Blackbourne (pt.), Norfolk I. 88/L6
Black Branch, Nulhegan (riv.), Vt. 268/D2
Blackburn (mt.), Alaska 196/K2
Blackburn, England 13/H1
Blackburn, England 10/G1
Blackburn, La. (†71038) 238/D1
Blackburn, Mo. (65321) 261/F4
Blackburn, Okla. (74058) 288/N2
Blackburn, Ontario 177/J2
Blackburn, Scotland 15/C2
Black Butte (lake), Calif. 204/C4
Black Canyon City, Ariz. (85324) 198/C4
Black Canyon of the Gunnison Nat'l Mon., Colo. 208/D5
Black Creek, Br. Col. 184/E5
Black Creek, N.C. (27813) 281/O3
Black Creek, Wis. (54106) 317/K7
Black Diamond, Alberta 182/C4
Black Diamond, Wash. (98010) 310/D3
Blackduck, Minn. (56630) 255/D3
Black Duck (riv.), Ontario 175/C1
Black Eagle, Mont. (59414) 262/E3
Black Earth, Wis. (53515) 317/G9
Black Elster (riv.), E. Germany 22/E3
Blackey, Ky. (41804) 237/R6
Blackfalds, Alberta 182/D3
Blackfeet Ind. Res., Mont. 262/D2
Blackfoot, Alberta 182/E3
Blackfoot, Idaho (83221) 220/F6
Blackfoot (res.), Idaho 220/G7
Blackfoot (riv.), Idaho 220/G6
Blackfoot, Mont. (59415) 262/D2
Blackfoot (riv.), Mont. 262/C4
Blackford (co.), Ind. 227/G4
Blackford, Ky. (42403) 237/F6
Blackford, Scotland 15/E4
Black Forest, Colo. (80908) 208/K4
Blackfork, Ohio (45615) 284/E8
Black Fork, Mohican (riv.), Ohio 284/F4
Blackgum, Okla. (†74962) 288/S3
Black Hall, Conn. (†06371) 210/F3
Black Hawk, Colo. (80422) 208/J3
Blackhawk, Ind. (†47866) 227/C6
Black Hawk (co.), Iowa 229/J4
Black Hawk, Miss. (†38917) 256/E4
Black Hawk, S. Dak. (57718) 298/C5
Blackhead (bay), Newf. 166/D2
Blackhead Road, Newf. 166/D2
Black Hills (mts.) 188/F2
Black Hills (mts.), S. Dak. 298/B5
Blackie, Alberta 182/D4
Black Isle (pen.), Scotland 15/D3
Black Jack, Mo. (†63031) 261/R1
Black Lake (bayou), La. 238/D1
Black Lake, Québec 172/F3
Black Lake, Sask. 181/M2
Blackledge (riv.), Conn. 210/F2
Black Lick, Pa. (15716) 294/D4
Blacklock (pt.), Oreg. 291/C5
Black Mesa (mt.), Okla. 288/A1
Blackmore (mt.), Mont. 262/F5
Black Mountain, N.C. (28711) 281/E3
Black Oak, Ark. (72414) 202/K2
Black Oak, Ind. (†46406) 227/C1
Black Pine (mts.), Idaho 220/E7
Black Pine (peak), Idaho 220/E7
Black Pine (creek), S. Dak. 298/G6
Black Point, Calif. (†94947) 204/J1
Black Point, Conn. (†06357) 210/G3
Black Point, New Bruns. 170/D1
Blackpool, England 13/G1
Blackpool, England 10/F1
Blackridge, Va. (23916) 307/M7
Black River, Jamaica 158/H6
Black River, Jamaica 156/B3
Black River (bay), Jamaica 158/G6
Black River, Mich. (48721) 250/F4
Black River, New Bruns. 170/E3
Black River (pond), Newf. 166/C2
Black River, N.Y. (13612) 276/J3
Black River Bridge, New Bruns. 170/E2
Black River Falls, Wis. (54615) 317/E7
Black Rock, Ark. (72415) 202/H1
Black Rock (des.), Nev. 266/B2
Black Rock (range), Nev. 266/B1
Black Rock (pt.), R.I. 249/H8
Black Rock, Utah (†84751) 304/B5
Blacksburg, S.C. (29702) 296/D1
Blacksburg, Va. (24060) 307/H6
Blacks Fork, Green (riv.), Wyo. 319/C4
Blacks Harbour, New Bruns. 170/D3
Blackshear, Georgia (31516) 217/H8
Blackshear (lake), Georgia 217/E7
Blacksher, Ala. (†36507) 195/C8
Blacksod (bay), Ireland 17/A3
Black Springs, Ark. (†71960) 202/C5
Black Springs, Nev. (†89508) 266/B3
Black Squirrel (creek), Colo. 208/L5
Blackstairs (mt.), Ireland 17/H6
Blackstock, Ontario 177/F3
Blackstock, S.C. (29014) 296/E2
Blackstone◯, Mass. (01504) 249/H4
Blackstone (riv.), Mass. 249/G3
Blackstone, Va. (23824) 307/N6
Blacksville, W. Va. (26521) 312/F3
Black Thunder (creek), Wyo. 319/G2
Black Tickle, Newf. 166/C3
Blackton, Ark. (†72069) 202/H4
Blacktown, N. S. Wales 88/K4
Blacktown, N.S. Wales 97/H3
Blackville, New Bruns. 170/E2
Blackville, S.C. (29817) 296/E5
Black Volta (riv.) 102/B3
Black Volta (riv.), Ghana 106/D6
Black Volta (riv.), Ivory Coast 106/D6
Black Volta (riv.), Upper Volta 106/D6
Black Warrior (riv.), Ala. 195/C5
Blackwater (riv.), England 13/H6
Blackwater (riv.), Fla. 212/B6
Blackwater, Ireland 17/J7
Blackwater (riv.), Ireland 10/B4
Blackwater (riv.), Ireland 17/D7
Blackwater (riv.), Ireland 17/H4
Blackwater, Mo. (65322) 261/G5
Blackwater (res.), N.H. 268/D5
Blackwater (riv.), N. Ireland 17/H3
Blackwater, Queensland 95/D4
Blackwater, Queensland 88/H4
Blackwater (res.), Scotland 15/D4
Blackwater, Va. (24221) 307/B7
Blackwater (riv.), Va. 307/J6
Blackwater (riv.), Va. 307/O6
Blackwell, Ark. (72019) 202/E3
Blackwell (brook), Conn. 210/H1
Blackwell, Okla. (74631) 288/M1
Blackwell, Texas (79506) 303/D5
Blackwell, Wis. (†54541) 317/J4
Blackwood (Ngunju) (cape), Indonesia 85/F8
Blackwood, N.J. (08012) 273/C4
Blackwood Terrace, N.J. (†08096) 273/C4
Bladen, Nebr. (68928) 264/F4
Bladen (co.), N.C. 281/M5
Bladenboro, N.C. (28320) 281/M5
Bladensburg, Md. (20710) 245/G4
Bladensburg, Ohio (43005) 284/F5
Blades, Del. (†19973) 245/R6
Bladon Springs, Ala. (36902) 195/B7
Bladworth, Sask. 181/E4
Blaeberry, Br. Col. 184/J4
Blaenavon, Wales 13/B6
Blagodarnoye, U.S.S.R. 52/F5
Blagoevgrad, Bulgaria 45/F5
Blagoveshchensk, U.S.S.R. 54/O4
Blagoveshchensk, U.S.S.R. 48/N4
Blagoveshchensk, U.S.S.R. 52/J4
Blain, France 28/C4
Blain, Pa. (17006) 294/H5
Blaine, Georgia (†30175) 217/C1
Blaine (co.), Idaho 220/D6
Blaine, Kansas (66410) 232/F2
Blaine, Ky. (41124) 237/R4
Blaine◯, Maine (04734) 243/H2
Blaine, Mich. (†48032) 250/G5
Blaine, Minn. (†55433) 255/G5
Blaine, Miss. (38727) 256/C3
Blaine (co.), Mont. 262/G2
Blaine (co.), Nebr. 264/E3
Blaine, Ohio (43909) 284/J5
Blaine (co.), Okla. 288/K3
Blaine, Oreg. (†97108) 291/D2
Blaine, Tenn. (37709) 237/O8
Blaine, Wash. (98230) 310/C2
Blaine Lake, Sask. 181/D3
Blaine-Mars Hill, Maine (04734) 243/H2
Blainville, Québec 172/H4
Blair, Kansas (†66090) 232/H2
Blair, Nebr. (68008) 264/H3
Blair, Okla. (73526) 288/H5
Blair (co.), Pa. 294/F4
Blair, S.C. (29015) 296/E3
Blair, W. Va. (25022) 312/C7
Blair, Wis. (54616) 317/D7
Blair Athol, Queensland 95/C4
Blair Atholl, Scotland 10/E2
Blair Atholl, Scotland 15/E4
Blairgowrie and Rattray, Scotland 15/E4
Blairgowrie and Rattray, Scotland 10/E2
Blairmore, Alberta 182/C5
Blairs, Va. (24527) 307/K7
Blairsburg, Iowa (50034) 229/F4
Blairsden, Calif. (96103) 204/E4
Blairs Mills, Ky. (41402) 237/P4
Blairs Mills, Pa. (17213) 294/G5
Blairstown, Iowa (52209) 229/J5
Blairstown, Mo. (64726) 261/E5
Blairstown◯, N.J. (07825) 273/C2
Blairsville, Georgia (30512) 217/E1
Blairsville, Pa. (15717) 294/D5
Blaisdell, N. Dak. (58720) 282/F3
Blaj, Romania 45/F2
Blake (pt.), Mich. 250/E1
Blakeley, Minn. (†56011) 255/E6
Blakeley, W. Va. (†25160) 312/D6
Blakely, Georgia (31723) 217/C8
Blakely, Pa. (18447) 294/F6
Blakesburg, Iowa (52536) 229/H7
Blakeslee, Ohio (43505) 284/A2
Blakeslee, Pa. (18610) 294/L3
Blaketown, Newf. 166/D2
Blalock, Ala. (†36773) 195/D6
Blalock, Georgia (†30525) 217/E1
Blalock (isl.), Wash. 310/F5
Blanc (cape) 2/J4
Blanc (mt.), France 7/E4
Blanc (mt.), France 28/G5
Blanc (mt.), Italy 34/A2
Blanc (cape), Mauritania 102/A2
Blanc (cape), Mauritania 106/A4
Blanc (cape), Tunisia 106/G1
Blanc (cape), Western Sahara 106/A4
Blanca (bay), Argentina 120/C6
Blanca (bay), Argentina 143/D4
Blanca (lag.), Chile 138/E10
Blanca (peak), Colo. 188/F3
Blanca, Colo. (81123) 208/H8
Blanca (peak), Colo. 208/H7
Blanca (pt.), C. Rica 154/F5
Blanca, Cordillera (mts.), Peru 128/D7
Blanch, N.C. (27212) 281/L2
Blanchard, Idaho (83804) 220/A1
Blanchard, Iowa (51630) 229/C7
Blanchard, La. (71009) 238/C1
Blanchard◯, Maine (†04406) 243/D5
Blanchard, Mich. (49310) 250/D5
Blanchard, N. Dak. (58009) 282/R5
Blanchard (riv.), Ohio 284/C4
Blanchard, Okla. (73010) 288/L4
Blanchard, Pa. (16826) 294/G3
Blanchard, Wash. (†98232) 310/C2
Blanchardstown, Ireland 17/H5
Blanchardville, Wis. (53516) 317/G10
Blanche, Ky. (†40902) 237/O7
Blanche (riv.), Québec 172/E2
Blanche (lake), S. Australia 88/F5
Blanche (lake), S. Australia 94/F3
Blanche, Tenn. (†38488) 237/H10
Blanche (lake), W. Australia 88/C4
Blanche Marie (fall), Suriname 131/C3
Blanchester, Ohio (45107) 284/B7
Blanchisseuse, Trin. & Tob. 161/B10
Blanco (riv.), Argentina 143/C2
Blanco (riv.), Bolivia 136/D4
Blanco (lake), Chile 138/F10
Blanco (cape), C. Rica 154/E6
Blanco (peak), C. Rica 154/F6
Blanco (riv.), Mexico 150/Q2
Blanco, N. Mex. (87412) 274/B2
Blanco (creek), N. Mex. 274/F4
Blanco, Okla. (74528) 288/P5
Blanco (cape), Oreg. 188/A2
Blanco (cape), Oreg. 291/C5
Blanco (cape), Peru 128/B5
Blanco (riv.), Peru 128/F6
Blanco (co.), Texas 303/F8
Blanco, Texas (78606) 303/F7
Blanc-Sablon, Québec 174/F2
Bland, Mo. (65014) 261/J6
Bland (co.), Va. 307/F6
Bland, Va. (24315) 307/F6
Blandburg, Pa. (16619) 294/F4

Caltagirone 345

Butler (co.), Ala. 195/E7
Butler, Ala. (36904) 195/B6
Butler, Georgia (31006) 217/D5
Butler, Ill. (62015) 222/D4
Butler, Ind. (46721) 227/H2
Butler (co.), Iowa 229/H3
Butler (co.), Kansas 232/F4
Butler (co.), Ky. 237/H6
Butler, Ky. (41006) 237/N3
Butler, Md. (21023) 245/M2
Butler, Minn. (†56567) 255/C4
Butler (co.), Mo. 261/M9
Butler, Mo. (64730) 261/D6
Butler (co.), Nebr. 264/G3
Butler, N.J. (07405) 273/E2
Butler (co.), Ohio 284/A7
Butler, Ohio (44822) 284/F4
Butler, Okla. (73625) 288/H3
Butler (co.), Pa. 294/C4
Butler, Pa. (16001) 294/C4
Butler, S. Dak. (57222) 298/O3
Butler, Tenn. (37640) 237/T8
Butler (bay), Virgin Is. (U.S.) 161/E4
Butler, Wis. (53007) 317/K1
Butler Springs, Ala. (†36030) 195/E7
Butlerville, Ark. (†72176) 202/G4
Butlerville, Ind. (47223) 227/F6
Butlerville, Ohio (†45162) 284/B7
Butner, N.C. (27509) 281/M2
Bütschelegg (mt.), Switzerland 39/D3
Bütschwil, Switzerland 39/H2
Buttahatchee (riv.), Ala. 195/B3
Buttahatchee (riv.), Miss. 256/H3
Butte (co.), Calif. 204/D4
Butte (co.), Idaho 220/E6
Butte, Mont. 146/G5
Butte, Mont. 188/D1
Butte, Nebr. (68722) 264/F2
Butte (mts.), Nev. 266/F3
Butte, N. Dak. (58723) 282/J4
Butte (creek), Oreg. 291/G2
Butte (creek), Oreg. 291/B3
Butte (co.), S. Dak. 298/B4
Butte City, Calif. (95920) 204/C4
Butte City, Idaho (83213) 220/E6
Butte Des Morts, Wis. (†54901) 317/J7
Butte Falls, Oreg. (97522) 291/E5
Butter (creek), Oreg. 291/H2
Butterfield, Ark. (†72104) 202/E5
Butterfield, Minn. (56120) 255/D7
Butterfield, Mo. (65623) 261/E9
Butterfield (lake), N.Y. 276/J2
Butternut, Mich. (†48811) 250/E5
Butternut, Wis. (54514) 317/E3
Butternut (lake), Wis. 317/J4
Butter Pot Prov. Park, Newf. 166/D2
Butters, N.C. (28324) 281/M5
Butterworth, Malaysia 72/D6
Butterworth (Gcuwa), S. Africa 118/D6
Buttes, Switzerland 39/C3
Butte-Silver Bow County, Mont. (59701) 262/D5
Buttevant, Ireland 17/D7
Butteville, Oreg. (†97002) 291/A2
Butt of Lewis (prom.), Scotland 15/B2
Button (isls.), N.W. Terrs. 187/M3
Buttonwillow, Calif. (93206) 204/F8
Butts (co.), Georgia 217/E4
Buttzville, N.J. (07829) 273/D2
Buttzville, N. Dak. (†58054) 282/P6
Butuan, Philippines 82/E6
Butuan, Philippines 85/H4
Butuan, Philippines 54/O9
Butuan (bay), Philippines 82/E6
Butumi, U.S.S.R. 7/J4
Butung (isl.), Indonesia 54/O10
Butung (isl.), Indonesia 85/G6
Buturlinovka, U.S.S.R. 52/F4
Butzbach, W. Germany 22/C3
Bützow, E. Germany 22/E2
Buxtehude, W. Germany 22/C2
Buxton, England 10/G2
Buxton, England 13/J2
Buxton○, Maine (†04093) 243/C8
Buxton, N.C. (27920) 281/U4
Buxton, N. Dak. (58218) 282/R4
Buxton, Oreg. (97109) 291/D2
Buxton Center, Maine (†04093) 243/B8
Buy, U.S.S.R. 52/F3
Buyck, Minn. (55771) 255/F2
Buynaksk, U.S.S.R. 52/G6
Büyükada, Turkey 63/D6
Büyük Ağrı (Ararat) (mt.), Turkey 63/L3
Büyük Ağrı (Ararat) (mt.), Turkey 59/D2
Büyükanafarta, Turkey 63/B6
Büyükdere, Turkey 63/D5
Büyük Hasan Dağı, Turkey 63/E3
Büyük Menderes (riv.), Turkey 59/A2
Buzău, Romania 45/H3
Buzău (riv.), Romania 45/H3
Buzeima (well), Libya 111/D3
Buziaş, Romania 45/E3
Buzios (cape), Brazil 135/F3
Buzuluk, U.S.S.R. 52/H4
Buzuluk, U.S.S.R. 48/F4
Buzzard Roost (dam), S.C. 296/D3
Buzzards (bay), Mass. 249/L7
Buzzards Bay, Mass. (02532) 249/M5
Byala, Bulgaria 45/G4
Byala Slatina, Bulgaria 45/F4
Byam Martin (chan.), N.W. Terrs. 187/H2
Byam Martin (isl.), N.W. Terrs. 187/H2
Byars, Okla. (74831) 288/N5
Bybee, Tenn. (37713) 237/P8
Bydgoszcz (prov.), Poland 47/C2
Bydgoszcz, Poland 47/C2
Bydgoszcz, Poland 7/F3
Byemoor, Alberta 182/D4
Byers, Colo. (80103) 208/L3
Byers, Kansas (67021) 232/D4
Byers, Texas (76357) 303/F3
Byesville, Ohio (43723) 284/G6
Byfield, Mass. (01922) 249/L1
Byford, W. Australia 88/B2
Bygland, Minn. (†56723) 255/B3
Bygland, Norway 18/F7
Byhalia, Miss. (38611) 256/E1
Bykhov, U.S.S.R. 52/C4
Bylas, Ariz. (85530) 198/E5
Bylot (isl.), N.W.T. 146/L2
Bylot (isl.), N.W.T. 162/J1
Bylot (isl.), N.W. Terrs. 187/L2
Byng, Okla. (†74820) 288/N5
Byng Inlet, Ontario 177/D2
Byng Inlet, Ontario 175/D3
Bynum, Mont. (59419) 262/D3
Bynum (res.), Mont. 262/D2
Bynum, N.C. (27312) 281/L3
Bynumville, Mo. (†65281) 261/G3
Byram, Conn. (06830) 210/A4
Byram (pt.), Conn. 210/A4
Byram (riv.), Conn. 210/A4
Byram, Miss. (†39205) 256/D6
Byrd Station 5/A12
Byrdstown, Tenn. (38549) 237/L7
Byrnedale, Pa. (15827) 294/E3
Byrock, N.S. Wales 97/D2
Byromville, Georgia (31007) 217/E6
Byron, Calif. (94514) 204/L2
Byron (isl.), Chile 138/D7
Byron, Georgia (31008) 217/E5
Byron, Ill. (61010) 222/D1
Byron, Ind. (†46371) 227/C5
Byron, Maine (†04275) 243/B6
Byron○, Maine (†04275) 243/B6
Byron, Mich. (48418) 250/E6
Byron, Minn. (55920) 255/F6
Byron, Nebr. (68325) 264/G4
Byron (bay), Newf. 166/C3
Byron (cape), N. S. Wales 88/J5
Byron (cape), N.S. Wales 97/G1
Byron, N.Y. (14422) 276/D4
Byron, Okla. (73723) 288/K1
Byron (lake), S. Dak. 298/N4
Byron, Wis. (53009) 317/K8
Byron, Wyo. (82412) 319/D1
Byron Bay, N.S. Wales 97/G1
Byron Center, Mich. (49315) 250/D6
Byrum, Denmark 21/E3
Byskeälv (riv.), Sweden 18/L4
Bystřice nad Pernštejnem, Czech. 41/D2
Bystřice pod Hostýnem, Czech. 41/D2
Bystrzyca Kłodzka, Poland 47/C3
Bytča, Czech. 41/E2
Bytom, Poland 47/A3
Bytów, Poland 47/C1

C

Caacupé, Paraguay 144/B5
Caaguazú (dept.), Paraguay 144/D-E4
Caaguazú, Paraguay 144/D4
Caála, Angola 115/C6
Caamaño (sound), Br. Col. 184/C4
Caapucú, Paraguay 144/D5
Caatingas (for.), Brazil 120/E3
Caazapá (dept.), Paraguay 144/D-E5
Caazapá, Paraguay 144/D5
Caba, Philippines 82/C2
Cabadbaran, Philippines 82/E6
Cabaiguán, Cuba 158/E2
Cabalasan (mt.), Philippines 82/E5
Caballero, Paraguay 144/B5
Caballo, N. Mex. (87931) 274/B6
Caballo (res.), N. Mex. 274/B6
Caballo (creek), Wyo. 319/G1
Caballococha, Peru 128/G4
Caballones (chan.), Cuba 158/F3
Cabana, Peru 128/C7
Cabañaquinta, Spain 33/D1
Cabañas, Cuba 158/B1
Cabanatuan, Philippines 54/O8
Cabanatuan, Philippines 82/C3
Cabanatuan, Philippines 85/G2
Cabanes, Spain 33/F2
Cabano, Québec 172/J2
Cabarroguis, Philippines 82/C2
Cabarrus (co.), N.C. 281/H4
Cabazon, Calif. (92230) 204/J10
Cabbage Tree (creek), Queensland 95/D2
Cabedelo, Brazil 132/H4
Cabell (co.), W. Va. 312/B6
Cabery, Ill. (60919) 222/E3
Cabet, Pitons du (mt.), Martinique 161/C6
Cabeza del Buey, Spain 33/D3
Cabezas, Bolivia 136/D6
Cabezas, Cuba 158/D1
Cabildo, Chile 138/A9
Cabimas, Venezuela 120/B1
Cabimas, Venezuela 124/C2
Cabin Creek, W. Va. (25035) 312/C6
Cabinda (dist.), Angola 115/B5
Cabinda, Angola 115/B5
Cabinda, Angola 102/D5
Cabinet (mts.), Mont. 262/A2
Cabin John (creek), Md. 245/E4
Cabin John-Brookmont, Md. (20731) 245/E4
Cabins, W. Va. (26855) 312/H4
Cable, Minn. (†56301) 255/D5
Cable, Ohio (43009) 284/C5
Cable, Wis. (54821) 317/D3
Cabo Blanco, Peru 128/B5
Cabo Delgado (prov.), Mozambique 118/F2
Cabo Frio, Brazil 132/F8
Cabo Frio, Brazil 135/F3
Cabo Gracias a Dios, Nicaragua 154/F3
Cabonga (res.), Québec 174/B3
Cabool, Mo. (65689) 261/H8
Cabora Bassa (dam), Mozambique 118/E3
Caborn, Ind. (†47620) 227/B9
Cabo Rojo, P. Rico 161/A2
Cabo San Lucas, Mexico 150/E5
Cabot (str.) 162/K6
Cabot, Ark. (72023) 202/F4
Cabot (str.), Canada 146/N5
Cabot (lake), Newf. 166/B2
Cabot (str.), Newf. 166/B4
Cabot (mt.), N.H. 268/E2
Cabot (head), Ontario 177/C2
Cabot, Pa. (16023) 294/C4
Cabot, Vt. (05647) 268/C3
Cabot○, Vt. (05647) 268/C3
Cabo Vírgenes, Argentina 143/C7
Cabra, Spain 33/D4
Cabra de Santo Cristo, Spain 33/E4
Cabral, Dom. Rep. 158/D6
Cabral (lag.), Paraguay 144/A5
Cabrera, Dom. Rep. 158/E5
Cabrera (isl.), Spain 33/H3
Cabri, Sask. 181/C5
Cabri (lake), Sask. 181/B4
Cabrillo Nat'l Mon., Calif. 204/H11
Cabrits (isl.), Martinique 161/D7
Cabrón (cape), Dom. Rep. 158/F5
Cabruta, Venezuela 124/E4
Cabudare, Venezuela 124/D3
Cabugao, Philippines 82/C2
Cabulauan (isls.), Philippines 82/C5
Cabullones (pt.), P. Rico 161/C3
Caburai (mt.), Guyana 131/A3
Cabure, Venezuela 124/D2
Caçador, Brazil 132/D9
Cacahoatán, Mexico 150/N9
Čačak, Yugoslavia 45/E4
Caçapava, Brazil 135/D3
Caçapava do Sul, Brazil 132/C10
Cacapon (riv.), W. Va. 312/J4
Cáceres (lag.), Bolivia 136/G6
Cáceres, Brazil 132/B7
Cáceres, Brazil 120/D4
Cáceres, Colombia 126/C4
Cáceres (prov.), Spain 33/C3
Cáceres, Spain 33/C3
Cáceres, Spain 7/D5
Cachapoal (riv.), Chile 138/G5
Cache (riv.), Ark. 202/H3
Cache (riv.), Ill. 222/D6
Cache, Okla. (73527) 288/J5
Cache (creek), Okla. 288/K6
Cache (co.), Utah 304/C2
Cache Bay, Ontario 177/D1
Cache Creek, Br. Col. 184/G5
Cache Junction, Utah (84304) 304/C2
Cache la Poudre (riv.), Colo. 208/H1
Cacheu, Guinea-Biss. 106/A6
Cachi, Argentina 143/C2
Cachina, Quebrada (riv.), Chile 138/A5
Cachipo, Venezuela 124/G3
Cachoeira, Brazil 132/G6
Cachoeira de Itapemirim, Brazil 120/E5
Cachoeira do Arari, Brazil 132/D3
Cachoeira do Sul, Brazil 132/C10
Cachoeira do Sul, Brazil 120/D6
Cachoeiro de Itapemirim, Brazil 132/G8
Cachorras, Colombia 126/D8
Cachos (pt.), Chile 138/A6
Cachuela Esperanza, Bolivia 136/C2
Cachuma (lake), Calif. 204/F9
Cacocum, Cuba 158/H3
Cacocum, Cuba 156/C2
Cacolo, Angola 115/C6
Caconda, Angola 115/B6
Cacouna, Québec 172/H2
Cactus (range), Nev. 266/E5
Cactus (hills), Sask. 181/F5
Cactus, Texas (79013) 303/B1
Cactus Lake, Sask. 181/B3
Cacuri, Venezuela 124/F5
Cacuso, Angola 115/C5
Čadca, Czech. 41/E2
Caddo (riv.), Ark. 202/D5
Caddo (par.), La. 238/C1
Caddo (lake), La. 238/B1
Caddo (co.), Okla. 288/K4
Caddo, Okla. (74729) 288/O6
Caddo, Texas (76029) 303/F5
Caddo (lake), Texas 303/L5
Caddo Gap, Ark. (71935) 202/C5
Caddo Valley, Ark. (†71923) 202/D5
Caddy Lake, Manitoba 179/G5
Cade, La. (70519) 238/G6
Cadereyta Jiménez, Mexico 150/K4
Cades, S.C. (29518) 296/H4
Cades, Tenn. (†38358) 237/D9
Cades Cove, Tenn. (†37882) 237/O9
Cadet, Mo. (63630) 261/L6
Cadibarrawirracanna (lake), S. Australia 94/D3
Cadillac, Mich. (49601) 250/D4
Cadillac, Québec 174/B3
Cadillac, Sask. 181/D6
Cadiz, Calif. (92319) 204/K9
Cadiz (lake), Calif. 204/K9
Cadiz, Ind. (†47362) 227/G5
Cadiz, Ky. (42211) 237/F7
Cadiz, Ohio (43907) 284/J5
Cadiz, Philippines 82/D5
Cádiz (prov.), Spain 33/D4
Cádiz, Spain 33/C4
Cádiz, Spain 7/D5
Cádiz (gulf), Spain 33/C4
Cádizadiz (gulf), Portugal 33/C4
Cadogan, Alberta 182/E3
Cadogan○, Pa. (16212) 294/C4
Cadomin, Alberta 182/B3
Cadott, Wis. (54727) 317/D6
Cadotte (lake), Alberta 182/B1
Cadotte (riv.), Alberta 182/B1
Cadotte Lake, Alberta 182/B1
Cadron (creek), Ark. 202/F3
Caduruan (pt.), Philippines 82/D5
Cadwell, Georgia (31009) 217/G6
Cadyville, N.Y. (12918) 276/N1
Caen, France 28/C3
Caen, France 7/E4
Caerleon, Wales 13/B6
Caernarfon, Wales 13/C4
Caernarfon, Wales 10/D4
Caernarfon (bay), Wales 13/C4
Caernarfon (bay), Wales 10/D4
Caerphilly, Wales 13/B6
Caerphilly, Wales 10/E5
Caesar, Miss. (†39466) 256/E9
Caesarea, Ontario 177/F3
Caesars Head, S.C. (†29635) 296/B1
Caeté, Brazil 135/E1
Caetité, Brazil 132/F6
Cafayate, Argentina 143/C2
Cafelândia, Brazil 135/B2
Cagayan (prov.), Philippines 82/C1
Cagayan (isls.), Philippines 82/C6
Cagayan (isls.), Philippines 85/F4
Cagayan (riv.), Philippines 82/C2
Cagayancillo, Philippines 82/C6
Cagayan de Oro, Philippines 82/E6
Cagayan de Oro, Philippines 85/G4
Cagayan Sulu (isl.), Philippines 85/F4
Cagayan Sulu (isl.), Philippines 82/B7
Cagle, Tenn. (†37327) 237/L10
Cagles Mill (lake), Ind. 227/D6
Cagli, Italy 34/D3
Cagliari (prov.), Italy 34/B5
Cagliari, Italy 7/E5
Cagliari, Italy 34/B5
Cagliari (gulf), Italy 34/B5
Cagua (vol.), Philippines 82/D1
Cagua, Venezuela 124/E2
Caguán (riv.), Colombia 126/C7
Caguas, P. Rico 161/E2
Caguas, P. Rico 156/G1
Caha (mts.), Ireland 17/B8
Cahaba, Ala. (†36767) 195/D6
Cahaba (riv.), Ala. 195/D5
Cahabón, Guatemala 154/C3
Cahir, Ireland 10/B4
Cahir, Ireland 17/F7
Cahirciveen, Ireland 17/A8
Cahirciveen, Ireland 10/A5
Cahokia, Ill. (62206) 222/A3
Cahone, Colo. (81320) 208/B7
Cahore (pt.), Ireland 17/J6
Cahors, France 28/D5
Cahuapanas, Peru 128/D5
Cahuilla Ind. Res., Calif. 204/J10
Cahuinari (riv.), Colombia 126/E8
Cahuita (pt.), C. Rica 154/F6
Caiapônia, Brazil 132/C7
Caibarién, Cuba 158/F2
Caibarién, Cuba 156/B2
Caibiran, Philippines 82/E5
Caicara, Venezuela 124/G3
Caicara de Orinoco, Venezuela 124/E4
Caicedonia, Colombia 126/C5
Caicó, Brazil 120/F3
Caicó, Brazil 132/G4
Caicos (passage), Bahamas 156/D2
Caicos (bank), Turks & Caicos 156/D2
Caicos (isls.), Turks & Caicos 156/D2
Caicos (passage), Turks & Caicos 156/D2
Caile, Miss. (†38754) 256/C4
Cailloma, Peru 128/G10
Caillou (bay), La. 238/J8
Caimanera, Cuba 158/J4
Caimanera, Cuba 156/C3
Cain (creek), S. Dak. 298/N5
Cainde, Angola 115/B7
Cains (riv.), New Bruns. 170/D2
Cains Store, Ky. (42520) 237/M6
Cainsville, Mo. (64632) 261/E2
Cainsville, Tenn. (†37085) 237/J9
Caird Coast (reg.) 5/B17
Cairnbaan, Scotland 15/C4
Cairnbrook, Pa. (15924) 294/E5
Cairndow, Scotland 15/D4
Cairn Gorm (mt.), Scotland 15/E3
Cairngorm (mts.), Scotland 15/E3
Cairnryan, Scotland 15/D6
Cairns, Australia 87/E7
Cairns, Queensland 95/C3
Cairns, Queensland 88/H3
Cairnsmore (mt.), Scotland 15/D5
Cairn Toul (mt.), Scotland 15/E3
Cairo (cap.), Egypt 102/F2
Cairo (cap.), Egypt 111/J3
Cairo (cap.), Egypt 2/L4
Cairo, Egypt 59/B4
Cairo, Georgia (31728) 217/D9
Cairo, Ill. 188/J3
Cairo, Ill. (62914) 222/D6
Cairo, Kansas (†67035) 232/D4
Cairo, Mo. (65239) 261/H4
Cairo, Nebr. (68824) 264/F3
Cairo, N.Y. (12413) 276/M6
Cairo, Ohio (45820) 284/B4
Cairo, Okla. (†74538) 288/O5
Cairo, W. Va. (26337) 312/D4
Caissie (pt.), New Bruns. 170/F2
Caister-on-Sea, England 13/J5
Caistor, England 13/G4
Caithness (trad. co.), Scotland 15/B4
Caiundo, Angola 102/D6
Caiundo, Angola 115/C7
Caiza, Bolivia 136/C7
Cajabamba, Ecuador 128/C3
Cajabamba, Peru 128/C6
Cajacay, Peru 128/D8
Caja de Muertos (isl.), P. Rico 161/C3
Cajamarca (dept.), Peru 128/C6
Cajamarca, Peru 128/C6
Cajamarca, Peru 120/B3
Cajatambo, Peru 128/D8
Cajazeiras, Brazil 132/G4
Cajidiocan, Philippines 82/D4
Cajuata, Bolivia 136/B5
Cajuru, Brazil 135/C2
Čakovec, Yugoslavia 45/C2
Çal, Turkey 63/C3
Çala, Turkey 63/K2
Calabar, Nigeria 102/D4
Calabar, Nigeria 106/F7
Calabash, N.C. (†29566) 281/M7
Calabazar de Sagua, Cuba 158/E1
Calabogie, Ontario 177/H2
Calabozo, Venezuela 124/E3
Calabria (reg.), Italy 34/F5
Cala Burras (pt.), Spain 33/D4
Calaceite, Spain 33/G2
Calacoto, Bolivia 136/A5
Caladesi (isl.), Fla. 212/B2
Calafat, Romania 45/F3
Calafate, Argentina 143/B7
Calafquén (lake), Chile 138/E3
Calagnaan (isl.), Philippines 82/D5
Calagua (isls.), Philippines 82/D3
Calahoo, Alberta 182/D3
Calahorra, Spain 33/E1
Calais, Alberta 182/B2
Calais, France 28/D2
Calais, France 7/E3
Calais (Dover) (str.), France 28/D2
Calais, Maine 188/N1
Calais, Maine (04619) 243/J5
Calais○, Vt. (05648) 268/B3
Calama, Brazil 132/H10
Calama, Chile 120/C5
Calama, Chile 138/B3
Calamar, Bolívar, Colombia 126/C2
Calamar, Vaupés, Colombia 126/D7
Calamarca, Bolivia 136/A5
Calamba, Laguna, Philippines 82/C3
Calamba, Misamis Occ., Philippines 82/D6
Calamian Group (isls.), Philippines 85/F3
Calamian Group (isls.), Philippines 82/B4
Calamine, Ark. (72418) 202/H1
Calamocha, Spain 33/F2
Calamus, Iowa (52729) 229/M5
Calanasan, Philippines 82/C1
Calancasca (riv.), Switzerland 39/H4
Calanda, Spain 33/F2
Calang, Indonesia 85/B5
Calansho, Serir (des.), Libya 111/D2
Calansho Sand Sea (des.), Libya 111/D2
Calapan, Philippines 82/C4
Calapan, Philippines 85/G3
Calapooia (riv.), Oreg. 291/E3
Calapooya (mts.), Oreg. 291/E4
Călăraşi, Romania 45/H3
Calarcá, Colombia 126/C5
Calasparra, Spain 33/F3
Calatayud, Spain 33/F2
Calatorao, Spain 33/F2
Calauag, Philippines 82/D4
Calaveras (co.), Calif. 204/E5
Calaveras (res.), Calif. 204/L3
Calaveras (lake), Texas 303/K11
Calavite (cape), Philippines 82/C4
Calayan, Philippines 82/A2
Calayan (isl.), Philippines 82/A2
Calbayog, Philippines 82/E4
Calbe, E. Germany 22/D3
Calbuco, Chile 138/D4
Calca, Peru 128/G9
Calcasieu (par.), La. 238/D6
Calcasieu, La. (71433) 238/E4
Calcasieu (lake), La. 238/D7
Calcasieu (passage), La. 238/D7
Calcasieu (riv.), La. 238/E5
Calceta, Ecuador 128/C3
Calchaquí, Argentina 143/F5
Calcis, Ala. (†35178) 195/F4
Calcutta, India 68/F2
Calcutta, India 54/K7
Calcutta, India 2/P4
Calcutta, Ohio (43920) 284/J4
Calcutta, Suriname 131/C3
Caldas (dept.), Colombia 126/C5
Caldas da Rainha, Portugal 33/B3
Caldas Novas, Brazil 132/D7
Calder, Idaho (83808) 220/B2
Calder, Sask. 181/K4
Calder, Loch (lake), Scotland 15/E2
Caldera, Chile 120/B5
Caldera, Chile 138/A6
Calderas (bay), Dom. Rep. 158/D6
Calderas, Venezuela 124/C3
Calderwood, Tenn. (†37801) 237/N9
Caldicot, Wales 13/E6
Çaldıran, Turkey 63/K3
Caldwell, Ark. (72322) 202/J3
Caldwell, Idaho (83605) 220/B6
Caldwell, Idaho 188/C2
Caldwell, Kansas (67022) 232/E4
Caldwell (co.), Ky. 237/F6
Caldwell (par.), La. 238/F2
Caldwell (co.), Mo. 261/E3
Caldwell, N.J. (07006) 273/B2
Caldwell (co.), N.C. 281/F3
Caldwell, Ohio (43724) 284/G6
Caldwell (co.), Texas 303/G8
Caldwell, Texas (77836) 303/H7
Caldwell, W. Va. (24925) 312/F7
Caldwell, Wis. (†53149) 317/J2
Caldy (isl.), Wales 13/C6
Cale, Ark. (71828) 202/D6
Cale, Ind. (†47544) 227/D7
Caledon, N. Ireland 17/H3
Caledon, Ontario 177/E4
Caledon, S. Africa 118/B7
Caledonia, Ill. (61011) 222/E1
Caledonia, Mich. (49316) 250/D6
Caledonia, Minn. (55921) 255/G7
Caledonia, Miss. (39740) 256/H3
Caledonia, Mo. (63631) 261/L7
Caledonia, N.Y. (14423) 276/E5
Caledonia, N. Dak. (58219) 282/S5
Caledonia, Guysborough, Nova Scotia 168/F3
Caledonia, Queens, Nova Scotia 168/C4
Caledonia, Ohio (43314) 284/D4
Caledonia, Pa. (†15868) 294/F3
Caledonia (co.), Vt. 268/C2
Caledonia, Wis. (53108) 317/L2
Caledonian (canal), Scotland 15/D3
Calella, Spain 33/H2
Calenzana, France 28/B6
Calera, Ala. (35040) 195/E4
Calera, Okla. (74730) 288/O7
Calera de Tango, Chile 138/G4
Caleta Barquito, Chile 138/A6
Caleta Clarencia, Chile 138/E10
Caleta Olivia, Argentina 143/C6
Caleta Olivia, Argentina 120/C7
Caleta Pan de Azúcar, Chile 138/A5
Caleu, Chile 138/G2
Caleufú, Argentina 143/C4
Calexico, Calif. (92231) 204/K11
Calf of Man (isl.), I. of Man 13/C3
Calfsound, Scotland 15/F1
Calgary, Alberta 182/C4
Calgary, Alta. 162/E5
Calgary (cap.), Alta.. 146/G4
Calgary, Canada 2/D3
Calhan, Colo. (80808) 208/L4
Calheta, Portugal 33/A2
Calhoun (co.), Ala. 195/G3
Calhoun, Ala. (†36047) 195/F6
Calhoun (co.), Ark. 202/E6
Calhoun (co.), Fla. 212/D6
Calhoun (co.), Georgia 217/C7
Calhoun, Georgia (30701) 217/C1
Calhoun (co.), Ill. 222/C4
Calhoun, Ill. (62419) 222/E5
Calhoun (co.), Iowa 229/D4
Calhoun, Ky. (42327) 237/G5
Calhoun, La. (71225) 238/F2
Calhoun (co.), Mich. 250/D6
Calhoun (co.), Miss. 256/F3
Calhoun, Mo. (65323) 261/E6
Calhoun (co.), S.C. 296/F4
Calhoun, Tenn. (37309) 237/M10
Calhoun (co.), Texas 303/H9
Calhoun (co.), W. Va. 312/D5
Calhoun City, Miss. (38916) 256/F3
Calhoun Falls, S.C. (29628) 296/B3
Cali, Colombia 126/B6
Cali, Colombia 120/B2
Calicito, Cuba 158/H4
Calicoan (isl.), Philippines 82/E5
Calico Rock, Ark. (72519) 202/F1
Calicut (Kozhikode), India 68/D6
Caliente, Nev. (89008) 266/G5
Califon, N.J. (07830) 273/D2
California 188/B3
CALIFORNIA 204
California, Ky. (41007) 237/N3
California, Md. (20619) 245/M7
California (gulf), Mexico 146/G7
California (gulf), Mexico 150/D3
California, Mo. (65018) 261/H5
California, Pa. (15419) 294/C5
California, Trin. & Tob. 161/A11
California (state), U.S. 146/G6
California Aqueduct, Calif. 204/E7
California City, Calif. (93505) 204/H8
California Hot Springs, Calif. (93207) 204/G8
California Junction, Iowa (†51555) 229/B5
Calimete, Cuba 158/D1
Calio, N. Dak. (58322) 282/N2
Calion, Ark. (71724) 202/E7
Calipatria, Calif. (92233) 204/K10
Calistoga, Calif. (94515) 204/C5
Calixa-Lavallée, Québec 172/J4
Calkiní, Mexico 150/O6
Çalköy, Turkey 63/C3
Call, Texas (75933) 303/L7
Callabonna (lake), S. Australia 88/G5
Callabonna (lake), S. Australia 94/F3
Callafo, Ethiopia 111/H6
Callahan, Calif. (96014) 204/C2
Callahan, Fla. (32011) 212/E1
Callahan (co.), Texas 303/E5
Callalli, Peru 128/G10
Callan, Ireland 17/G7
Callan, Ireland 10/C4
Callander, Ont. 162/H6
Callander, Ontario 177/E1
Callander, Scotland 10/D2
Callander, Scotland 15/D4
Callands, Va. (24530) 307/J7
Callantsoog, Netherlands 27/F3
Callao, Mo. (63534) 261/G3
Callao (prov.), Peru 128/D9
Callao, Peru 128/D9
Callao, Peru 2/F6
Callao, Peru 120/B4
Callao, Utah (†84034) 304/A4
Callao, Va. (22435) 307/P5
Callapa, Bolivia 136/A5
Callaway, Minn. (56521) 255/C3
Callaway (co.), Mo. 261/J5
Callaway, Nebr. (68825) 264/D3
Callaway, Va. (24067) 307/H7
Calle Larga, Chile 138/G2
Callender, Iowa (50523) 229/E4
Callensburg, Pa. (16213) 294/D3
Callery, Pa. (16024) 294/C4
Calleuque, Chile 138/F5
Calliaqua, St. Vin. & Grens. 161/A9
Callicoon, N.Y. (12723) 276/K7
Callicoon Center, N.Y. (12724) 276/L7
Callihan, Texas (78007) 303/F9
Callimont, Pa. (†15552) 294/E6
Calling (lake), Alberta 182/D2
Callis, Somalia 115/J2
Callison, S.C. (29819) 296/C3
Callosa de Ensarriá, Spain 33/G3
Calloway, Fla. (32401) 212/D6
Calloway (co.), Ky. 237/E7
Calmar, Alberta 182/D3
Calmar, Iowa (52132) 229/K2
Calmer, Ark. (†71665) 202/F6
Calnali, Mexico 150/K6
Calne, England 13/F6
Calobre, Panama 154/G6
Caloosahatchee (riv.), Fla. 212/E5
Caloundra, Queensland 88/J5
Caloundra, Queensland 95/E5
Čalovo, Czech. 41/D3
Calpella, Calif. (95418) 204/B4
Calpet, Wyo. (†83123) 319/B3
Calpulálpan, Mexico 150/M1
Calstock, England 13/C7
Caltagirone, Italy 34/E6

346 Caltanissetta

Caltanissetta (prov.), Italy 34/D6
Caltanissetta, Italy 34/D6
Caluire-et-Cuire, France 28/F5
Calulo, Angola 115/C6
Calumet (lake), Ill. 222/C6
Calumet, Iowa (51009) 229/B3
Calumet, La. (†70538) 238/H7
Calumet, Mich. 188/J1
Calumet, Mich. (49913) 250/A1
Calumet, Minn. (55716) 255/E3
Calumet, Okla. (73014) 288/K3
Calumet, Québec 172/C4
Calumet (co.), Wis. 317/K7
Calumet City, Ill. (60409) 222/C6
Calumet Park, Ill. (†60643) 222/C6
Calumetville, Wis. (†53049) 317/K8
Caluquembe, Angola 102/D6
Caluquembe, Angola 115/B6
Calva, Ariz. (†85530) 198/E5
Calvados (dept.), France 28/C3
Calvary, Georgia (31729) 217/D9
Calvary, Ky. (†40033) 237/L6
Calvert, Ala. (36513) 195/B8
Calvert (isl.), Br. Col. 184/C4
Calvert, Kansas (†67622) 232/C2
Calvert (co.), Md. 245/M6
Calvert, Md. (†21911) 245/O2
Calvert, Newf. 166/D2
Calvert, Texas (77837) 303/H7
Calvert City, Ky. (42029) 237/E6
Calvert Hills, North. Terr. 93/E4
Calverton, Md. (†20705) 245/L4
Calverton, Va. (22016) 307/N3
Calverton Park, Mo. (†63101) 261/P2
Calvertville, Ind. (†47424) 227/D6
Calvi, France 28/B6
Calvillo, Mexico 150/H6
Calvin, Ky. (40813) 237/O7
Calvin, La. (71410) 238/E3
Calvin, N. Dak. (58323) 282/N2
Calvin, Okla. (74531) 288/O5
Calvin, W. Va. (26660) 312/E6
Calvinia, S. Africa 102/E8
Calvinia, S. Africa 118/B6
Calwa, Calif. (93745) 204/F7
Calypso, N.C. (28325) 281/N4
Calzada de Calatrava, Spain 33/E3
Camabatela, Angola 115/C5
Camacho, Bolivia 136/C7
Camacupa, Angola 115/C6
Camaguán, Venezuela 124/E3
Camagüey (prov.), Cuba 158/G2
Camagüey, Cuba 158/G3
Camagüey, Cuba 146/L7
Camagüey, Cuba 156/B2
Camagüey (arch.), Cuba 158/G2
Camaiore, Italy 34/C3
Camajuaní, Cuba 158/E2
Camak, Georgia (30807) 217/G4
Camaná, Peru 128/F11
Camanche (res.), Calif. 204/C9
Camanche, Iowa (52730) 229/N5
Camano (isl.), Wash. 310/C2
Camanongue, Angola 115/D6
Camanongue, Angola 102/E6
Camaquã, Brazil 132/C10
Câmara de Lobos, Portugal 33/A2
Çamardı, Turkey 63/F4
Camargo, Bolivia 136/C7
Camargo, Ill. (61919) 222/E4
Camargo, Ky. (†40337) 237/K4
Camargo, Okla. (73835) 288/H2
Camarillo, Calif. (93010) 204/F9
Camarines Norte (prov.), Philippines 82/D3
Camarines Sur (prov.), Philippines 82/D4
Camarón (cape), Honduras 154/E2
Camarones, Argentina 143/C5
Camarones, Chile 138/B2
Camarones (riv.), Chile 138/A2
Camas (co.), Idaho 220/D6
Camas (creek), Idaho 220/D6
Camas (creek), Idaho 220/F5
Camas (creek), Idaho 220/D5
Camas, Wash. (98607) 310/C5
Camas Prairie, Mont. (†59857) 262/B3
Camas Valley, Oreg. (97416) 291/D4
Camatagua, Venezuela 124/E3
Camatindi, Bolivia 136/D7
Ca Mau (Mui Bai Bung) (pt.), Vietnam 72/E5
Cambará, Brazil 135/A3
Cambará, Brazil 132/D8
Cambay, India 68/C4
Cambay (gulf), India 54/J7
Cambay (gulf), India 68/C4
Camberwell, Victoria 88/L7
Camberwell, Victoria 97/J5
Cambodia 2/Q5
Cambodia 54/M8
CAMBODIA (KAMPUCHEA) 72
Camborne-Redruth, England 10/D5
Camborne-Redruth, England 13/B7
Cambra, Pa. (18611) 294/K3
Cambrai, France 28/E2
Cambria, Alberta 182/D4
Cambria, Calif. (93428) 204/D8
Cambria, Ill. (62915) 222/D6
Cambria, Ind. (†46041) 227/D4
Cambria, Iowa (†50060) 229/G7
Cambria, Mich. (†49242) 250/E7
Cambria, Minn. (†56073) 255/D6
Cambria (co.), Pa. 294/E4
Cambria, Wis. (53923) 317/H8
Cambrian (mts.), Wales 13/D5
Cambridge, England 13/G5
Cambridge, England 10/G4
Cambridge, Idaho (83610) 220/B5
Cambridge, Ill. (61238) 222/C2
Cambridge, Iowa (50046) 229/G5
Cambridge, Jamaica 158/H6
Cambridge, Kansas (67023) 232/F4
Cambridge○, Maine (04923) 243/E5
Cambridge, Md. (21613) 245/O6
Cambridge, Mass. (02138) 249/C7
Cambridge (res.), Mass. 249/B6
Cambridge, Minn. (55008) 255/E5
Cambridge, Nebr. (69022) 264/D4
Cambridge, N.Y. (12816) 276/O4
Cambridge, N. Zealand 100/E2
Cambridge, Ohio (43725) 284/G5
Cambridge, Ontario 177/D4
Cambridge, Tasmania 99/D4
Cambridge, Vt. (05444) 268/B2
Cambridge○, Vt. (05444) 268/B2
Cambridge, Wis. (53523) 317/H9
Cambridge Bay, Canada 4/B15
Cambridge Bay, N.W.T. 162/F2
Cambridge Bay, N.W. Terrs. 187/H3
Cambridge City, Ind. (47327) 227/G5
Cambridge-Narrows, New Bruns. 170/E3
Cambridgeport, Vt. (05141) 268/B5
Cambridgeshire (co.), England 13/G5
Cambridge Springs, Pa. (16403) 294/C2
Cambridge Station, Nova Scotia 168/D3
Cambuí, Brazil 135/C3
Cambulo, Angola 115/D5
Cambulo, Angola 102/E5
Cambuslang, Scotland 15/B2
Camden, Ala. (36726) 195/D7
Camden (bay), Alaska 196/K1
Camden, Ark. (71701) 202/E6
Camden, Del. (19934) 245/R4
Camden, England 13/H8
Camden, England 10/B5
Camden (co.), Georgia 217/J9
Camden, Ill. (62319) 222/C3
Camden, Ind. (46917) 227/D3
Camden, Maine (04843) 243/F7
Camden○, Maine (04843) 243/F7
Camden, Mich. (49232) 250/E7
Camden, Miss. (39045) 256/E5
Camden (co.), Mo. 261/G6
Camden, Mo. (64017) 261/D4
Camden, N.J. 188/M3
Camden (co.), N.J. 273/D4
Camden, N.J. (*08101) 273/B3
Camden, N.S. Wales 97/F4
Camden, N.Y. (13316) 276/J4
Camden (co.), N.C. 281/S2
Camden, N.C. (27921) 281/S2
Camden, Ohio (45311) 284/A6
Camden, S.C. (29020) 296/F3
Camden, Tenn. (38320) 237/E8
Camden, Texas (75934) 303/K7
Camden, W. Va. (26338) 312/E4
Camden Haven, N.S. Wales 97/G2
Camden on Gauley, W. Va. (26208) 312/E6
Camden Park, St. Vin. & Grens. 161/A9
Camden Point, Mo. (64018) 261/C4
Camdenton, Mo. (65020) 261/G6
Cameia, Angola 115/D6
Camelford, England 13/C7
Çameli, Turkey 63/C4
Camels Hump (mt.), Vt. 268/B3
Camerino, Italy 34/D3
Cameron, Ariz. (86020) 198/D3
Cameron (peak), Colo. 208/H1
Cameron, Ill. (61423) 222/C3
Cameron (par.), La. 238/D7
Cameron, La. (70631) 238/D7
Cameron, Mo. (64429) 261/D3
Cameron, Mont. (59720) 262/E5
Cameron, N.Y. (14819) 276/F6
Cameron (mts.), N. Zealand 100/A7
Cameron, N.C. (28326) 281/L4
Cameron (isl.), N.W. Terrs. 187/H2
Cameron, Ohio (43914) 284/J6
Cameron, Okla. (74932) 288/T4
Cameron (co.), Pa. 294/F3
Cameron, Pa. (†15834) 294/F3
Cameron, S.C. (29030) 296/F4
Cameron (co.), Texas 303/G11
Cameron, Texas (76520) 303/H7
Cameron, W. Va. (26033) 312/E3
Cameron, Wis. (54822) 317/C5
Cameron Falls, Ontario 177/H5
Cameron Highlands, Malaysia 72/D6
Cameroon 2/K5
Cameroon 102/D4
CAMEROON 115/B2
Cameroon (mt.), Cameroon 102/C4
Cameroon (mt.), Cameroon 115/A3
Camerota, Italy 34/E4
Cametá, Brazil 132/D3
Camiguin (prov.), Philippines 82/E6
Camiguin, Cagayan (isl.), Philippines 82/B3
Camiguin, Camiguin (isl.), Philippines 82/E6
Camiling, Philippines 82/C3
Camilla, Georgia (31730) 217/D8
Camillus, N.Y. (13031) 276/H4
Camiña, Chile 138/B2
Camiña, Quebrada (riv.), Chile 138/B2
Caminha, Portugal 33/B2
Camino, Calif. (95709) 204/E5
Camiri, Bolivia 120/C5
Camiri, Bolivia 136/D7
Camlachie, Ontario 177/B4
Çamlıdere, Turkey 63/E2
Cammack, Ind. (†47302) 227/G4
Cammack Village, Ark. (†72201) 202/E4
Cammal, Pa. (17723) 294/H3
Camoapa, Nicaragua 154/E4
Camocim, Brazil 132/F3
Camolin, Ireland 17/J6
Camooweal, Queensland 88/F3
Camooweal, Queensland 95/A3
Camopi, Fr. Guiana 131/E4
Camopi (riv.), Fr. Guiana 131/E4
Camorta (isl.), India 68/G7
Camoruco, Colombia 126/E4
Camotes (isls.), Philippines 82/E5
Camotes (sea), Philippines 82/E5
Camp (creek), Georgia 217/J2
Camp (creek), Ind. 227/E6
Camp (creek), Oreg. 291/J4
Camp (co.), Texas 303/K5
Campaign, Tenn. (38550) 237/K9
Campamento, Uruguay 145/C1
Campana, Argentina 143/G6
Campana (isl.), Chile 120/B7
Campana (isl.), Chile 138/D7
Campanario, Cerro (mt.), Argentina 143/C4
Campanario, Cerro (mt.), Chile 138/A10
Campanario, Spain 33/D3
Campanha, Brazil 135/D2
Campania, Georgia (†30814) 217/H4
Campania (reg.), Italy 34/E4
Campaspe (riv.), Victoria 97/C5
Campbell, Ala. (36727) 195/C7
Campbell, Alaska (†99901) 196/M2
Campbell, Calif. (95008) 204/K3
Campbell (co.), Ky. 237/N3
Campbell, Minn. (56522) 255/B4
Campbell, Mo. (63933) 261/M9
Campbell, Nebr. (68932) 264/F4
Campbell, N.Y. (14821) 276/F6
Campbell (cape), N. Zealand 100/E4
Campbell, Ohio (44405) 284/J3
Campbell (hill), Ohio 284/C5
Campbell (co.), S. Dak. 298/J2
Campbell (co.), Tenn. 237/N8
Campbell (co.), Va. 307/K6
Campbell (co.), Wyo. 319/G1
Campbell (mt.), Yukon 187/E3
Campbellford, Ontario 177/G3
Campbell Hall, N.Y. (10916) 276/M8
Campbell Hill, Ill. (62916) 222/D6
Campbell Island, Br. Col. 184/C4
Campbellpore, Pakistan 68/C2
Campbell River, Br. Col. 184/E5
Campbells (lake), Oreg. 291/H5
Campbellsburg, Ind. (47108) 227/E7
Campbellsburg, Ky. (40011) 237/L3
Campbellsport, Wis. (†53019) 317/K8
Campbell Station, Ark. (†72473) 202/H2
Campbellsville, Ky. (42718) 237/L6
Campbellton, Fla. (32426) 212/D5
Campbellton, Mo. (†63068) 261/K5
Campbellton, N. Br. 162/K6
Campbellton, N. Br. 146/M5
Campbellton, New Bruns. 170/D1
Campbellton, Newf. 166/D4
Campbellton, Pr. Edward I. 168/D2
Campbellton, Texas (78008) 303/F9
Campbelltown, N.S. Wales 97/F4
Campbelltown, S. Australia 88/E8
Campbelltown, S. Australia 94/B7
Campbell Town, Tasmania 99/D3
Campbeltown, Scotland 15/C5
Campbeltown, Scotland 10/C3
Camp Creek, Alberta 182/C2
Camp Creek, W. Va. (25820) 312/D7
Camp Crook, S. Dak. (57724) 298/B2
Camp David, Md. 245/J2
Camp Dennison, Ohio (45111) 284/D9
Camp Dix, Ky. (41127) 237/P3
Camp Douglas, Wis. (54618) 317/F8
Campeche (state), Mexico 150/O7
Campeche, Mexico 146/J8
Campeche, Mexico 150/O7
Campeche (bay), Mexico 146/J7
Campeche (bank), Mexico 150/O6
Campeche (bay), Mexico 150/N7
Campechuela, Cuba 158/G4
Camper, Manitoba 179/D3
Camperdown, Victoria 97/C6
Camperville, Manitoba 179/B2
Camp Grove, Ill. (61424) 222/D2
Camp Hale, Colo. 208/G4
Camp Hill, Ala. (36850) 195/G5
Camp Hill, Pa. (17011) 294/H5
Camp Hill, Queensland 88/K3
Camp Hill, Queensland 95/E3
Campiglia Marittima, Italy 34/C3
Campile, Ireland 17/H7
Campillo de Altobuey, Spain 33/F3
Campillos, Spain 33/D4
Campina Grande, Brazil 120/F3
Campina Grande, Brazil 132/G4
Campinas, Brazil 120/E5
Campinas, Brazil 135/C3
Campinas, Brazil 132/E8
Campina Verde, Brazil 135/B1
Campina Verde, Brazil 132/D7
Camp Lake, Wis. (53109) 317/K10
Camp Lejeune Marine Corps Base, N.C. 281/P5
Campli, Italy 34/D3
Camp Morton, Manitoba 179/E4
Camp Nelson, Calif. (93208) 204/G7
Campo, Calif. (92006) 204/J11
Campo, Cameroon 115/B3
Campo, Colo. (81029) 208/O8
Campoalegre, Colombia 126/C6
Campobasso (prov.), Italy 34/E4
Campobasso, Italy 34/E4
Campobello (isl.), New Bruns. 170/D4
Campobello, S.C. (29322) 296/C1
Campo Belo, Brazil 132/E8
Campo Belo, Brazil 135/D2
Campo Claro, Venezuela 124/G2
Campo de Criptana, Spain 33/E3
Campo de la Cruz, Colombia 126/C2
Campo Florido, Brazil 135/B1
Campo Formoso, Brazil 132/F5
Campo Grande, Brazil 120/D5
Campo Grande, Brazil 132/8
Campo Ind. Res., Calif. 204/J11
Campo Largo, Brazil 135/B4
Campo Maior, Brazil 132/F4
Campo Maior, Portugal 33/C3
Campos, Brazil 132/F8
Campos, Brazil 135/F2
Campos, Brazil 120/E5
Campos (reg.), Brazil 120/E4
Campos Altos, Brazil 135/C1
Campo Seco, Calif. (95226) 204/D9
Campo Tencia (peak), Switzerland 39/G4
Campo Tures, Italy 34/C1
Camp Pendleton, Calif. 204/H10
Camp Perrin, Haiti 158/A6
Camp Point, Ill. (62320) 222/B3
Camp Robinson, Ontario 177/G4
Camp Robinson, Ontario 175/B2
Camp Sherman, Oreg. (97730) 291/F3
Camp Springs, Md. (20748) 245/G6
Campti, La. (71411) 238/D3
Campton, Georgia (†30655) 217/E3
Campton, Ky. (41301) 237/O5
Campton○, N.H. (03223) 268/D4
Camptown, Pa. (18815) 294/K2
Campus, Ill. (60920) 222/E2
Camp Verde, Ariz. (86322) 198/D4
Campville, Fla. (†32640) 212/D2
Camp Wood, Texas (78833) 303/D8
Cam Ranh, Vietnam 72/F5
Cam Ranh, Vinh (bay), Vietnam 72/F5
Camrose, Alberta 182/D3
Camrose, Alta. 162/E5
Camsell (riv.), N.W. Terrs. 187/G3
Camsell Portage, Sask. 181/L2
Camuy, P. Rico 161/B1
Camuy, P. Rico 156/F1
Camuy (riv.), P. Rico 161/B1
Çan, Turkey 63/B2
Čaňa, Czech. 41/F2
Cana (pt.), Dom. Rep. 158/F6
Cana, Sask. 181/J5
Cana, Va. (24317) 307/G7
Canaan, Conn. (06018) 210/B1
Canaan○, Conn. (06018) 210/B1
Canaan (mt.), Conn. 210/B1
Canaan, Ind. (47224) 227/G7
Canaan○, Maine (04924) 243/D6
Canaan, Miss. (38612) 256/F1
Canaan, New Bruns. 170/E2
Canaan (riv.), New Bruns. 170/E2
Canaan○, N.H. (03741) 268/C4
Canaan, N.Y. (12029) 276/O6
Canaan○, Vt. (05903) 268/D2
Canaan Center, N.H. (†03741) 268/C4
Canaan Forks, 170/E2
Canaan Road, New Bruns. 170/E2
Canada 2/D3
Canada 4/C13
Canada 146/G4
CANADA 163
Cañada, La (mt.), Cuba 158/B2
Canada, Ky. (41519) 237/S5
Canada (bay), Newf. 166/C3
Cañada de Gómez, Argentina 143/F6
Cañada Nieto, Uruguay 145/B4
Canadensis, Pa. (18325) 294/M3
Canadian (riv.) 188/F3
Canadian (riv.), N. Mex. 274/F3
Canadian (co.), Okla. 288/K3
Canadian, Okla. (74425) 288/P4
Canadian (riv.), Okla. 288/O4
Canadian, Texas (79014) 303/D2
Canadian (riv.), Texas 303/D1
Canadian (riv.), U.S. 146/H6
Canadian City, Okla. (†73064) 288/L4
Canadice (lake), N.Y. 276/F5
Canadys, S.C. (29433) 296/F5
Canagua (riv.), Venezuela 124/C3
Canajoharie, N.Y. (13317) 276/L5
Çanakkale (prov.), Turkey 63/B2
Çanakkale, Turkey 63/B6
Çanakkale, Turkey 59/A2
Çanakkale Boğazı (Dardanelles) (str.), Turkey 63/B6
Çanakkale Boğazı (str.), Turkey 59/A2
Canal (creek), Alberta 182/E5
Canala, New Caled. 86/G4
Canala (bay), New Caled. 86/H4
Canal Flats, Br. Col. 184/K5
Canal Fulton, Ohio (44614) 284/H4
Canalou, Mo. (63828) 261/N9
Canal Point, Fla. (33438) 212/F5
Canals, Argentina 143/D3
Canal Winchester, Ohio (43110) 284/E6
Canandaigua, N.Y. (14424) 276/F5
Canandaigua (lake), N.Y. 276/F5
Cananea, Mexico 150/D1
Cananéia, Brazil 132/E9
Cananéia, Brazil 135/C4
Canannova, Cuba 158/K3
Cañar (prov.), Ecuador 128/C4
Cañar, Ecuador 128/C4
Canaries, St. Lucia 161/G6
Canaries, Piton (mt.), St. Lucia 161/G6
Canarreos, Los (arch.), Cuba 158/C2
Canary, Oreg. (†97493) 291/D4
Canary (isls.), Spain 102/A2
Canary (isls.), Spain 2/H4
Canary (isls.), Spain 33/B4
Canary (isls.), Spain 106/A3
Cañas, C. Rica 154/E5
Cañas, Cuba 158/B1
Cañas (range), Uruguay 145/C2
Canaseraga, N.Y. (14822) 276/E6
Cañasgordas, Colombia 126/B4
Canasí, Cuba 158/C1
Canastota, N.Y. (13032) 276/J4
Canatlán, Mexico 150/G4
Canaveral (cape), Fla. 146/L7
Canaveral (Kennedy) (cape), Fla. 188/L5
Canaveral (cape), U.S. 2/F4
Canavieiras, Brazil 132/G6
Cañazas, Panama 154/G6
Canbelego, N.S. Wales 97/D2
Canberra (cap.), Australia 87/F9
Canberra (cap.), Australia 2/S7
Canberra (cap.), Australia, Aust. Cap. Terr. 97/E4
Canby, Calif. (96015) 204/E2
Canby, Minn. (56220) 255/B6
Canby, Oreg. (97013) 291/B2
Cancún, Mexico 150/Q6
Candala, Somalia 115/J1
Candarave, Peru 128/G11
Çandarlı (gulf), Turkey 63/B3
Candás, Spain 33/D1
Candéias, Brazil 120/F4
Candela, Mexico 150/J3
Candelaria, Bolivia 136/F5
Candelaria (riv.), Bolivia 136/F5
Candelaria, Cuba 158/B1
Candelaria, Mexico 150/O7
Candelaria (riv.), Mexico 150/O8
Candelaria, Philippines 82/B3
Candelaria, Texas (†79843) 303/C12
Candelaria, Venezuela 124/F4
Candeleda, Spain 33/D2
Candelero (pt.), P. Rico 161/F2
Candelo, N.S. Wales 97/E5
Candia (Iráklion), Greece 45/G8
Candia○, N.H. (03034) 268/E5
Candiac, Québec 172/J4
Candiac, Sask. 181/H5
Cândido Mendes, Brazil 132/E3
Çandır, Turkey 63/F3
Candle (lake), Sask. 181/F2
Candle Lake, Sask. 181/F2
Candler, Fla. (32624) 212/E2
Candler (co.), Georgia 217/H6
Candler, N.C. (28715) 281/D3
Candlewood (lake), Conn. 210/A2
Candlewood, N.J. (†08701) 273/E3
Cando, N. Dak. (58324) 282/M3
Cando, Sask. 181/C3
Candon, Philippines 82/C2
Candor, N.Y. (13743) 276/H6
Candor, N.C. (27229) 281/K4
Cane (creek), Utah 304/E5
Canea (Khaniá), Greece 45/G8
Caneadea, N.Y. (14717) 276/D6
Canebay, Virgin Is. (U.S.) 161/E3
Cane Beds, Ariz. (†86022) 198/B2
Canebrake, W. Va. (24819) 312/C8
Caneel (bay), Virgin Is. (U.S.) 161/B4
Canehill, Ark. (72717) 202/B2
Canelones (dept.), Uruguay 145/D5
Canelones, Uruguay 120/D6
Canelones, Uruguay 145/B6
Canelos, Ecuador 128/D3
Canendiyu (dept.), Paraguay 144/E4
Cañete (riv.), 128/D9
Cañete, Chile 138/D2
Cañete, Spain 33/F2
Cane Valley, Ky. (42720) 237/L6
Caney, Kansas (67333) 232/G4
Caney, Ky. (41407) 237/P5
Caney, Okla. (74533) 288/O6
Caney (riv.), Okla. 288/O1
Caney Fork (riv.), Tenn. 237/L9
Caneyville, Ky. (42721) 237/J6
Canfield, Ark. (71829) 202/C7
Canfield, Ohio (44406) 284/J3
Canford, Br. Col. 184/G5
Cangallo, Peru 128/E9
Cangamba, Angola 115/C6
Cangas, Spain 33/B1
Cangas de Narcea, Spain 33/C1
Cangas de Onís, Spain 33/D1
Canguaretama, Brazil 132/H4
Cangyuan, China 77/E7
Cangzhou (Tsangchow), China 77/J4
Caniapiscau (riv.), Que. 162/K4
Caniapiscau, Québec 174/D1
Caniapiscau (res.), Québec 174/D2
Caniapiscau (riv.), Québec 174/D1
Canicattì, Italy 34/E6
Canigao (chan.), Philippines 82/E5
Canik (mts.), Turkey 63/G2
Caniles, Spain 33/E4
Canim (lake), Br. Col. 184/G4
Canim Lake, Br. Col. 184/G4
Canindé, Brazil 132/G4
Canistear (res.), N.J. 273/E1
Canisteo, N.Y. (14823) 276/E6
Canisteo (riv.), N.Y. 276/F6
Canistota, S. Dak. (57012) 298/P6
Cañitas de Felipe Pescador, Mexico 150/H5
Canjáyar, Spain 33/E4
Canje (riv.), Guyana 131/C2
Canjilon, N. Mex. (87515) 274/C2
Çankaya, Turkey 63/E3
Çankırı (prov.), Turkey 63/E2
Çankırı, Turkey 63/E2
Çankırı, Turkey 59/B1
Cankton, La. (†70584) 238/F6
Canlaon, Philippines 82/D5
Canlaon (peak), Philippines 82/D5
Canmer, Ky. (42722) 237/K6
Canmore, Alberta 182/C4
Canna (isl.), Scotland 10/C2
Canna (isl.), Scotland 15/B3
Canna (sound), Scotland 15/B3
Cannalville, Ohio (†43777) 284/F6
Cannanore, India 68/C6
Cannelburg, Ind. (47519) 227/C7
Cannel City, Ky. (41408) 237/P5
Cannelles (pt.), St. Lucia 161/G7
Cannelles (riv.), St. Lucia 161/G6
Cannelton, Ind. (47520) 227/D9
Cannes, France 28/G6
Cannich, Scotland 15/D3
Canning (riv.), Alaska 196/J1
Canning, Nova Scotia 168/D3
Canning, S. Dak. (†57501) 298/K5
Canning (riv.), W. Australia 88/B3
Canning (res.), W. Australia 88/B2
Canning, W. Australia 92/A1
Cannington, Ontario 177/E3
Cannington Manon Hist. Park, Sask. 181/J6
Cannock, England 10/G2
Cannock, England 13/E5
Cannon, Del. (19935) 245/R6
Cannon (mt.), N.H. 268/D3
Cannon (co.), Tenn. 237/J9
Cannon A.F.B., N. Mex. 274/F4
Cannon Ball, N. Dak. (58528) 282/J7
Cannonball (riv.), N. Dak. 282/G7
Cannon Beach, Oreg. (97110) 291/D2
Cannondale, Conn. (†06897) 210/B4
Cannon Falls, Minn. (55009) 255/F6
Cannonsburg, Miss. (†39120) 256/B7
Cannonsville (res.), N.Y. 276/K6
Cannonville, Utah (84718) 304/B6
Cann River, Victoria 97/E5
Caño (isl.), C. Rica 154/F6
Canoas, Brazil 132/D10
Canoas, Brazil 120/D5
Canobie Lake, N.H. (†03079) 268/E6
Caño Capure (riv.), Venezuela 124/H3
Canoe, Ala. (†36502) 195/D8
Canoe (riv.), Br. Col. 184/H4
Canoe (lake), Sask. 181/L3
Canoe Lake, Sask. 181/L3
Canoe River, Br. Col. 184/H4
Canoga Park, Calif. (*91303) 204/B10
Canoinhas, Brazil 132/D9
Caño Macareo (riv.), Venezuela 124/H3
Caño Mánamo (riv.), Venezuela 124/G3
Canon, Georgia (30520) 217/F2
Canonbie, Scotland 15/F5
Canonchet, R.I. (†02833) 249/H7
Canon City, Colo. (81212) 208/J6
Canones, N. Mex. (87516) 274/C2
Canonsburg, Pa. (15317) 294/B5
Canoochee, Georgia (30416) 217/H5
Canoose Flowage (lake), New Bruns. 170/C3
Canora, Sask. 181/J4
Canosa di Puglia, Italy 34/E4
Canouan (isl.), St. Vin. & Grens. 156/G4
Canova, S. Dak. (57321) 298/O6
Canovanas (riv.), P. Rico 161/E1
Canowindra, N.S. Wales 97/E3
Canquella, Bolivia 136/A7
Cansado, Mauritania 106/A4
Canso, Nova Scotia 168/H3
Canso (cape), Nova Scotia 168/H3
Canso (str.), Nova Scotia 168/G3
Canta, Peru 128/D8
Cantabrian (range), Spain 33/C1
Cantagalo, Brazil 135/E3
Cantal (dept.), France 28/E5
Cantal, Sask. 181/K6
Cantalejo, Spain 33/D2
Cantanhede, Portugal 33/B2
Cantaura, Venezuela 124/F3
Canterbury○, Conn. (06331) 210/H2
Canterbury, Del. (†19943) 245/R4
Canterbury, England 10/G5
Canterbury, England 13/H6
Canterbury, New Bruns. 170/C3
Canterbury○, N.H. (03224) 268/D5
Canterbury, N.S. Wales 88/K4
Canterbury, N.S. Wales 97/J3
Canterbury (bight), N. Zealand 100/D6
Can Tho, Vietnam 72/E5
Can Tho, Vietnam 54/M9
Cantil, Calif. (93519) 204/H8
Cantiles (cay), Cuba 158/C3
Cantillana, Alto de (mt.), Chile 138/G4
Cantley, Québec 172/B4
Canto del Agua, Chile 138/A7
Canto do Buriti, Brazil 132/F5
Canton (Guangzhou), China 77/H7
Canton, China 54/N7
Canton, China 2/Q4
Canton, Conn. (06019) 210/D1
Canton○, Conn. (06019) 210/D1
Canton, Georgia (30114) 217/C2
Canton, Ill. (61520) 222/C3
Canton, Ind. (†47167) 227/E7
Canton, Kansas (67428) 232/E3
Canton, Ky. (42212) 237/F7
Canton (isl.), Kiribati 87/J6
Canton○, Maine (04221) 243/C7
Canton○, Mass. (02021) 249/C8
Canton, Minn. (55922) 255/F7
Canton, Miss. (39046) 256/D5
Canton, Mo. (63435) 261/J2
Canton, N.J. (†08079) 273/C5
Canton, N.Y. (13617) 276/K1
Canton, N.C. (28716) 281/D3
Canton (Hensel), N. Dak. (†58241) 282/P2
Canton, Ohio 188/K2
Canton, Ohio (*44701) 284/H4
Canton, Okla. (73724) 288/J2
Canton (lake), Okla. 288/J2
Canton, Pa. (17724) 294/J2
Canton, S. Dak. (57013) 298/R7
Canton, Texas (75103) 303/J5
Canton, Wis. (54823) 317/C5
Canton-Bégin, Québec 172/F1
Canton Bend, Ala. (†36726) 195/D6
Canton Center, Conn. (06020) 210/D1
Cantonment, Fla. (32533) 212/B6
Canton-Patapédia, Québec 172/B2
Cantoria, Spain 33/E4
Cantrall, Ill. (62625) 222/D4
Cantril, Iowa (52542) 229/J7
Cantù, Italy 34/B2
Cantuar, Sask. 181/C5
Cantwell, Alaska (99729) 196/J2
Canuck, Sask. 181/C6
Cañuelas, Argentina 143/G7
Canumã (riv.), Brazil 132/B4
Canutama, Brazil 132/G9
Canute, Okla. (73626) 288/H4
Canutillo, Texas (79835) 303/A10
Canvas, W. Va. (26662) 312/E6
Canvey Island, England 13/J8
Canvey Island, England 10/G5
Canwood, Sask. 181/E2
Canyon (lake), Ariz. 198/D5
Canyon, Br. Col. 184/J5
Canyon, Calif. (94516) 204/K2
Canyon (co.), Idaho 220/B6
Canyon (creek), Idaho 220/C6
Canyon, Minn. (55717) 255/F3
Canyon, Texas (79015) 303/C3
Canyon, Wyo. (82190) 319/B1
Canyon Blanco (creek), N. Mex. 274/B2
Canyon City, Oreg. (97820) 291/J3
Canyon Creek, Alberta 182/C2
Canyon Creek, Mont. (59633) 262/D4
Canyon de Chelly Nat'l Mon., Ariz. 198/F2
Canyon Ferry, Mont. (†59601) 262/E4
Canyon Ferry (lake), Mont. 262/E4
Canyonlands Nat'l Park, Utah 304/D5
Canyonville, Oreg. (97417) 291/D5
Cao Bang, Vietnam 72/E2
Caol, Scotland 15/C4
Cao Lanh, Vietnam 72/E5
Caonao, Cuba 158/E2
Caonillas (lake), P. Rico 161/C2

352 Chumikan

Chumikan, U.S.S.R. 48/O4
Chumphon, Thailand 72/C5
Chuna (riv.), U.S.S.R. 48/K4
Chunchi, Ecuador 128/C4
Ch'unch'ŏn, S. Korea 81/D5
Chunchula, Ala. (36521) 195/B9
Ch'ungju, S. Korea 81/C5
Chungking (Chongqing), China 77/G6
Chŭngsan, N. Korea 81/B4
Chungshan (Zhongshan), China 77/H7
Chunky, Miss. (39323) 256/G6
Chunya, Tanzania 115/F5
Chunya (riv.), U.S.S.R. 48/K3
Chupaca, Peru 128/E9
Chupadera (mesa), N. Mex. 274/C5
Chupara (pt.), Trin. & Tob. 161/B10
Chuquibamba, Peru 128/F10
Chuquibambilla, Peru 128/F9
Chuquicamata, Chile 138/B3
Chuquichambi, Bolivia 136/B5
Chuquisaca (dept.), Bolivia 136/C6
Chur, Switzerland 39/J3
Churachandpur, India 68/G4
Church, Iowa (†52151) 229/L2
Churchbridge, Sask. 181/J5
Church Creek, Md. (21622) 245/O6
Church Hill, Md. (21623) 245/O4
Church Hill, Miss. (39055) 256/B7
Church Hill, Tenn. (37642) 237/R7
Churchill (riv.) 162/G4
Churchill (pk.), Br. Col. 162/D4
Churchill (peak), Br. Col. 184/L2
Churchill (riv.), Canada 146/J4
Churchill, Man. 146/J4
Churchill, Man. 162/G4
Churchill (cape), Man. 162/G4
Churchill, Manitoba 179/K2
Churchill (cape), Manitoba 179/K2
Churchill (riv.), Manitoba 179/J2
Churchill (co.), Nev. 266/C3
Churchill (falls), Newf. 166/B3
Churchill (riv.), Newf. 166/B3
Churchill, Pa. (†15235) 294/C7
Churchill (riv.), Que. 162/K5
Churchill (riv.), Sask. 181/M3
Churchill, Victoria 97/D6
Churchill Falls, Newf. 166/B3
Churchman (mt.), W. Australia 92/B5
Church Point, La. (70525) 238/F6
Church Point, Nova Scotia 168/B4
Church's Ferry, N. Dak. (58325) 282/M3
Church Stretton, England 13/E5
Churchton, Md. (20733) 245/N5
Churchtown, Pa. (†17555) 294/L5
Church View, Va. (23032) 307/P5
Churchville, Md. (21028) 245/N2
Churchville, N.Y. (14428) 276/E4
Churchville, Va. (24421) 307/K4
Churchville, W. Va. (†26338) 312/E4
Churdan, Iowa (50050) 229/D4
Churfirsten (mt.), Switzerland 39/H2
Churin, Peru 128/D8
Churu, India 68/D3
Churubusco, Ind. (46723) 227/G2
Churubusco, N.Y. (12923) 276/N1
Churuguara, Venezuela 124/D2
Churwalden, Switzerland 39/J3
Chushul, India 68/D2
Chuska (mts.), N. Mex. 274/A2
Chusovoy, U.S.S.R. 52/J3
Chute-à-Blondeau, Ontario 177/K2
Chute-aux-Outardes, Québec 172/A1
Chute-des-Passes, Québec 174/C3
Chute-Saint-Philippe, Québec 172/B3
Chuvash A.S.S.R., U.S.S.R. 48/E4
Chuvash A.S.S.R., U.S.S.R. 52/G3
Chu Xian, China 77/J5
Chuxiong, China 77/F7
Chuy, Uruguay 145/F4
Chvalšiny, Czech. 41/C2
Ciales, P. Rico 161/C1
Ciamis, Indonesia 85/H2
Ciampino, Italy 34/F7
Cianjur, Indonesia 85/H2
Cibecue, Ariz. (85911) 198/E4
Cibola (co.), N. Mex. 274/B3
Cibolo, Texas (78108) 303/K10
Cibolo (creek), Texas 303/K11
Çiçekdagı, Turkey 63/F3
Cicero, Ill. (60650) 222/B5
Cicero, Ind. (46034) 227/E4
Cícero Dantas, Brazil 132/G5
Cicerone, W. Va. (†25243) 312/D5
Ciconsine (lake), Québec 172/D2
Cid, N.C. (†27292) 281/J3
Cide, Turkey 63/E2
Cidlina (riv.), Czech. 41/C1
Cidra, Cuba 158/D1
Cidra, P. Rico 161/D2
Ciechanów (prov.), Poland 47/E2
Ciechanów, Poland 47/E2
Ciechocinek, Poland 47/D2
Ciego de Ávila (prov.), Cuba 158/F2
Ciego de Ávila, Cuba 156/B2
Ciego de Ávila, Cuba 158/F2
Ciempozuelos, Spain 33/F5
Ciénaga, Colombia 120/B1
Ciénaga, Colombia 126/C2
Ciénaga de Oro, Colombia 126/C3
Cienfuegos (prov.), Cuba 158/E2
Cienfuegos, Cuba 156/B2
Cienfuegos, Cuba 146/K7
Cienfuegos, Cuba 158/D2
Cienfuegos (bay), Cuba 158/D2
Cieplice Śląskie-Zdrój, Poland 47/B3
Čierny Balog, Czech. 41/E2
Cieszyn, Poland 47/D4
Cieza, Spain 33/F3
Çifteler, Turkey 63/D3
Cifuentes, Spain 33/E2
Cigánd, Hungary 41/F2
Cihanbeyli, Turkey 63/E3
Cihuatlán, Mexico 150/G7
Cijara (res.), Spain 33/D3
Cijulang, Indonesia 85/H2
Cilacap, Indonesia 85/H2
Çıldır, Turkey 63/K2
Çıldır (lake), Turkey 63/K2
Cilleros, Spain 33/C2
Cilo Dağı (mt.), Turkey 63/K4
Cima, Calif. (92323) 204/K8
Cimahi, Indonesia 85/H2
Cimarron (riv.) 188/G3
Cimarron, Colo. (81220) 208/D6
Cimarron, Kansas (67835) 232/B4
Cimarron (riv.), Kansas 232/B4
Cimarron, N. Mex. (87714) 274/E2
Cimarron (riv.), N. Mex. 274/E2
Cimarron (co.), Okla. 288/A1
Cimarron, Okla. (73111) 288/L3
Cimarron (riv.), Okla. 288/N2
Cimin, Turkey 63/H3
Cimone (mt.), Italy 34/C2
Cîmpeni, Romania 45/F2
Cîmpia Turzii, Romania 45/F2
Cîmpina, Romania 45/H3
Cîmpulung, Romania 45/G3
Cîmpulung Moldovenesc, Romania 45/G2
Cinaruco (riv.), Colombia 126/F4
Cinaruco (riv.), Venezuela 124/D4
Cinca (riv.), Spain 33/G2
Cincinnati, Ark. (†72769) 202/B1
Cincinnati, Iowa (52549) 229/G7
Cincinnati, Ohio 146/K6
Cincinnati, Ohio (*45201) 284/B9
Cincinnati, Ohio 188/K3
Cincinnatus, N.Y. (13040) 276/H5
Cinclare, La. (†70767) 238/J2
Cinco, W. Va. (†25301) 312/D6
Cinco Balas (cays), Cuba 158/E3
Cinco Bayou, Fla. (†32548) 212/B6
Cinco Saltos, Argentina 143/C4
Cinderella, W. Va. (†25661) 312/B7
Cinderford, England 13/E6
Çine, Turkey 63/B4
Cinebar, Wash. (98533) 310/C4
Ciney, Belgium 27/G8
Cinnaminson○, N.J. (†08077) 273/B3
Cintalapa de Figueroa, Mexico 150/N8
Cinto (mt.), France 28/B6
Cipolletti, Argentina 143/C4
Circeo (cape), Italy 34/D4
Circle, Alaska (99733) 196/K1
Circle, Mont. (59215) 262/L3
Circle (butte), Utah 304/C6
Circle Back, Texas (†79371) 303/B3
Circle City, Mo. (†63846) 261/N9
Circle Pines, Minn. (55014) 255/G5
Circle Springs, Alaska (†99730) 196/K1
Circleville, Kansas (66416) 232/G2
Circleville, Ohio (43113) 284/D6
Circleville, Utah (84723) 304/B5
Circleville, W. Va. (26804) 312/H5
Circular (head), Tasmania 99/B2
Cirebon, Indonesia 85/H2
Cirebon, Indonesia 54/M10
Ciremay (mt.), Indonesia 85/H2
Cirencester, England 10/F5
Cirencester, England 13/E6
Cirque (mt.), Newf. 166/B2
Cisco, Georgia (30708) 217/C1
Cisco, Ill. (61830) 222/E3
Cisco, Texas (76437) 303/E5
Cisco, Utah (84515) 304/E5
Cisco Springs Wash (creek), Utah 304/E4
Ciskei (bantustan), S. Africa 102/E8
Cismont, Va. (†22947) 307/M4
Cisnădie, Romania 45/G3
Cisne (isls.), Honduras 154/F2
Cisne, Ill. (62823) 222/E5
Cisneros, Colombia 126/C4
Cisnes (riv.), Chile 138/E5
Cispus (pass), Wash. 310/D4
Cispus (riv.), Wash. 310/D4
Cissna Park, Ill. (60924) 222/F3
Citlaltépetl (mt.), Mexico 150/O2
Citra, Fla. (32627) 212/D2
Citronelle, Ala. (36522) 195/B8
Citrus (co.), Fla. 212/D3
Citrus Center, Fla. (†33471) 212/E5
Citrus Heights, Calif. (95610) 204/C8
Cittadella, Italy 34/C2
Città di Castello, Italy 34/C3
Cittanova, Italy 34/F5
City Mills, Mass. (†02056) 249/J4
City Point, Fla. (†32922) 212/F3
City Point, Wis. (†54466) 317/F7
City View, Ontario 177/J2
City View, S.C. (29611) 296/C2
Ciudad Acuña (Villa Acuña), Mexico 150/J2
Ciudad Altamirano, Mexico 150/J7
Ciudad Bolívar, Venezuela 120/C2
Ciudad Bolívar, Venezuela 124/G3
Ciudad Bolivia, Venezuela 124/C3
Ciudad Camargo, Chihuahua, Mexico 150/G3
Ciudad Camargo, Tamaulipas, Mexico 150/K3
Ciudad Darío, Nicaragua 154/D4
Ciudad del Carmen, Mexico 150/N7
Ciudad Delicias, Mexico 150/G2
Ciudad del Maíz, Mexico 150/K5
Ciudad de Nutrias, Venezuela 124/D3
Ciudad de Río Grande, Mexico 150/H5
Ciudadela, Spain 33/H2
Ciudad Guayana, Venezuela 120/C2
Ciudad Guayana, Venezuela 124/G3
Ciudad Guerrero, Mexico 150/F2
Ciudad Guzmán, Mexico 150/H7
Ciudad Hidalgo, Chiapas, Mexico 150/N9
Ciudad Hidalgo, Michoacán, Mexico 150/J7
Ciudad Juárez, Mexico 146/H6
Ciudad Juárez, Mexico 150/F1
Ciudad Lerdo, Mexico 150/H4
Ciudad Madero, Mexico 150/L5
Ciudad Mante, Mexico 150/K5
Ciudad Mendoza, Mexico 150/O2
Ciudad Miguel Alemán, Mexico 150/K3
Ciudad Obregón, Mexico 146/H7
Ciudad Obregón, Mexico 150/E3
Ciudad Ojeda, Venezuela 120/B2
Ciudad Ojeda, Venezuela 124/C2
Ciudad Piar (co.), Venezuela 124/G4
Ciudad Quesada, C. Rica 154/E5
Ciudad Real (prov.), Spain 33/D3
Ciudad Real, Spain 33/D3
Ciudad Río Bravo, Mexico 150/K4
Ciudad-Rodrigo, Spain 33/C2
Ciudad Satélite, Mexico 150/L1
Ciudad Serdán, Mexico 150/O2
Ciudad Valles, Mexico 150/K5
Ciudad Victoria, Mexico 150/K5
Civa (cape), Turkey 63/G2
Cividale del Friuli, Italy 34/D1
Civitavecchia, Italy 34/C3
Civitella del Tronto, Italy 34/D3
Civray, France 28/D4
Çivril, Turkey 63/C3
Cizre, Turkey 63/K4
Clachan, Scotland 15/C5
Clackamas (co.), Oreg. 291/E2
Clackamas, Oreg. (97015) 291/B2
Clackamas (riv.), Oreg. 291/E2
Clackmannan, Scotland 10/B1
Clackmannan, Scotland 15/C1
Clackmannan (trad. co.), Scotland 15/A5
Clacton, England 13/J6
Clacton, England 10/G5
Claflin, Kansas (67525) 232/D3
Claiborne, Ala. (36434) 195/D7
Claiborne (par.), La. 238/D1
Claiborne (lake), La. 238/E1
Claiborne, Md. (21624) 245/N5
Claiborne (co.), Miss. 256/C7
Claiborne (co.), Tenn. 237/O8
Clair, New Bruns. 170/B1
Clair, Sask. 181/G3
Claire (lake), Alberta 182/B5
Claire (lake), Alta. 162/E4
Claire City, S. Dak. (57224) 298/P2
Clairemont, Texas (†79518) 303/D4
Clair Engle (lake), Calif. 204/C3
Clairette, Texas (†76457) 303/F5
Clairfield, Tenn. (37715) 237/O7
Clairmont, Alberta 182/A2
Clairmont Springs, Ala. (†35160) 195/G4
Clairton, Pa. (15025) 294/C7
Clallam (co.), Wash. 310/B2
Clallam Bay, Wash. (98326) 310/A2
Clam (bay), Nova Scotia 168/F4
Clam (lake), Wis. 317/B4
Clam (riv.), Wis. 317/A4
Clamart, France 28/A2
Clamecy, France 28/E4
Clam Falls, Wis. (54825) 317/B4
Clam Gulch, Alaska (99568) 196/B1
Clam Lake, Wis. (54517) 317/E3
Clan Alpine (mts.), Nev. 266/D3
Clancy, Mont. (59634) 262/E4
Clandeboye, Manitoba 179/E4
Clandeboye, Ontario 177/C4
Clandonald, Alberta 182/E3
Clanton, Ala. (35045) 195/E5
Clanwilliam, Manitoba 179/C4
Clanwilliam, S. Africa 118/B6
Clapperton (isl.), Ontario 177/B1
Clara, Ireland 10/C4
Clara, Ireland 17/F5
Clara, Miss. (39324) 256/G7
Clara, Uruguay 145/D3
Clara Barton Nat'l Hist. Site, Md. 245/E4
Clara City, Minn. (56222) 255/C6
Claravale, North. Terr. 93/B3
Clare, Ill. (60111) 222/E1
Clare, Ind. (†46060) 227/F4
Clare, Iowa (50524) 229/E3
Clare (co.), Ireland 17/D6
Clare (isl.), Ireland 10/A4
Clare (isls.), Ireland 17/A4
Clare (riv.), Ireland 17/D5
Clare (co.), Mich. 250/E5
Clare, Mich. (48617) 250/E5
Clare, N.S. Wales 97/B3
Clare, S. Australia 94/F5
Claregalway, Ireland 17/D5
Claremont, Calif. (91711) 204/D10
Claremont, Ill. (62421) 222/F5
Claremont, Jamaica 158/J6
Claremont, Minn. (55924) 255/E6
Claremont, N.H. (03743) 268/C5
Claremont, N.C. (28610) 281/G3
Claremont, S. Dak. (57432) 298/N2
Claremont, Va. (23899) 307/P6
Claremore, Okla. (74017) 288/R2
Claremorris, Ireland 17/C4
Claremorris, Ireland 10/B4
Clarence (str.), Alaska 196/N2
Clarence (isl.), Chile 120/B8
Clarence (isl.), Chile 138/E10
Clarence, Iowa (52216) 229/M5
Clarence, La. (71414) 238/E3
Clarence, Mo. (63437) 261/H3
Clarence (riv.), N. S. Wales 88/J5
Clarence (riv.), N.S. Wales 97/G1
Clarence○, N.Y. (14031) 276/C5
Clarence (riv.), N. Zealand 100/E5
Clarence (str.), North. Terr. 88/E2
Clarence (str.), North. Terr. 93/B2
Clarence (cape), N.W. Terrs. 187/K2
Clarence (head), N.W. Terrs. 187/L2
Clarence, Pa. (16829) 294/G3
Clarence Bridge, N. Zealand 100/E5
Clarence Creek, Ontario 177/J2
Clarenceville, Québec 172/D4
Clarendon, Ark. (72029) 202/H4
Clarendon, New Bruns. 170/D3
Clarendon, N.C. (28432) 281/M6
Clarendon (lake), Ontario 177/G3
Clarendon, Pa. (16313) 294/D2
Clarendon (co.), S.C. 296/G4
Clarendon, Texas (79226) 303/C3
Clarendon○, Vt. (†05759) 268/A4
Clarendon Hills, Ill. (60514) 222/B6
Clarens, Switzerland 39/C4
Clarenville, Newf. 166/C2
Claresholm, Alberta 182/D4
Clariden (mt.), Switzerland 39/G3
Clarie Coast (reg.) 5/C7
Clarinda, Iowa (51632) 229/C7
Clarines, Venezuela 124/F3
Clarington, Ohio (43915) 284/J6
Clarington, Pa. (15828) 294/D3
Clarion, Iowa (50525) 229/F3
Clarión (isl.), Mexico 150/B7
Clarion, Mich. (†49796) 250/E3
Clarion (co.), Pa. 294/D3
Clarion, Pa. (16214) 294/D3
Clarion (riv.), Pa. 294/D3
Clarion River, East Branch (lake), Pa. 294/E2
Clarissa, Minn. (56440) 255/C4
Clarita, Okla. (74535) 288/O6
Clark (lake), Alaska 196/H2
Clark (co.), Ark. 202/D5
Clark, Colo. (80428) 208/F1
Clark (co.), Idaho 220/F5
Clark (co.), Ill. 222/F4
Clark (co.), Ind. 227/F8
Clark (co.), Kansas 232/C4
Clark (co.), Ky. 237/N4
Clark (co.), Mo. 261/J2
Clark, Mo. (65243) 261/H4
Clark (co.), Nev. 266/F6
Clark○, N.J. (07066) 273/A3
Clark, N.C. (†28560) 281/P4
Clark (buttes), N. Dak. 282/G7
Clark (co.), Ohio 284/C6
Clark, Ohio (43810) 284/G5
Clark (pt.), Ontario 177/C3
Clark, Pa. (16113) 294/B3
Clark (co.), S. Dak. 298/O4
Clark, S. Dak. (57225) 298/O4
Clark (co.), Wash. 310/C5
Clark (co.), Wis. 317/E6
Clark, Wyo. (†59008) 319/C1
Clark Canyon (res.), Mont. 262/D6
Clark Center, Ill. (†62441) 222/F4
Clarkdale, Ariz. (86324) 198/C4
Clarke (co.), Ala. 195/C7
Clarke (co.), Georgia 217/F3
Clarke (co.), Iowa 229/F6
Clarke (co.), Miss. 256/G6
Clarke (range), Queensland 95/C4
Clarke (isl.), Tasmania 99/E2
Clarke (co.), Va. 307/M2
Clarke City, Québec 174/D2
Clarkedale, Ark. (72325) 202/K3
Clarke's Beach, Newf. 166/D2
Clarkesville, Georgia (30523) 217/F1
Clarkfield, Minn. (56223) 255/C6
Clark Fork, Idaho (83811) 220/B1
Clark Fork (riv.), Mont. 188/D1
Clark Fork (riv.), Mont. 262/A3
Clark Hill (lake), Georgia 217/H3
Clark Hill (dam), S.C. 296/C4
Clark Hill (lake), S.C. 296/C4
Clarkia, Idaho (83812) 220/B2
Clark Island, Maine (†04859) 243/E8
Clarklake, Mich. (49234) 250/E6
Clarkrange, Tenn. (38553) 237/L8
Clarks, East Fork (riv.), Ky. 237/E7
Clarks, La. (71415) 238/F2
Clarks, Nebr. (68628) 264/G3
Clarksboro, N.J. (08020) 273/C4
Clarksburg, Calif. (95612) 204/B9
Clarksburg, Ind. (47225) 227/G6
Clarksburg, Md. (20734) 245/J4
Clarksburg, Mo. (65025) 261/G5
Clarksburg, N.J. (08510) 273/E3
Clarksburg, Ohio (43115) 284/D7
Clarksburg, Ontario 177/D3
Clarksburg, Tenn. (38324) 237/E9
Clarksburg, W. Va. 188/K3
Clarksburg, W. Va. (26301) 312/F4
Clarks Corner, Conn. (†06256) 210/G1
Clarksdale, Miss. 188/J4
Clarksdale, Miss. (38614) 256/D2
Clarksdale, Mo. (64430) 261/D3
Clarks Falls, Conn. (†06359) 210/H3
Clarks Fork, Yellowstone (riv.), Mont. 262/G6
Clarks Fork (riv.), Wyo. 319/C1
Clarks Green, Pa. (†18411) 294/F6
Clarks Grove, Minn. (56016) 255/E7
Clark's Harbour, Nova Scotia 168/C5
Clarks Hill, Ind. (47930) 227/D4
Clarks Hill, S.C. (29821) 296/C4
Clarks Mill, Maine (†04847) 243/B8
Clarks Mills, Pa. (16114) 294/B3
Clarkson, Ky. (42726) 237/J6
Clarkson, Miss. (†39752) 256/F3
Clarkson, Nebr. (68629) 264/G3
Clarkson, N.Y. (14430) 276/E4
Clarkson Valley, Mo. (†63017) 261/N3
Clarks Point, Alaska (99569) 196/G3
Clarks Summit, Pa. (18411) 294/F6
Clarkston, Georgia (30021) 217/L1
Clarkston, Mich. (48016) 250/F6
Clarkston, Scotland 15/B2
Clarkston, Utah (84305) 304/B2
Clarkston, Wash. (99403) 310/H4
Clark's Town, Jamaica 158/H6
Clarksville, Ark. (72830) 202/D3
Clarksville, Del. (19937) 245/T6
Clarksville, Fla. (32430) 212/D6
Clarksville, Ind. (47130) 227/F8
Clarksville, Iowa (50619) 229/H3
Clarksville, Md. (21029) 245/L4
Clarksville, Mich. (48815) 250/D6
Clarksville, Mo. (63336) 261/K4
Clarksville○, N.H. (†05902) 268/E1
Clarksville, N.Y. (12041) 276/M5
Clarksville, Ohio (45113) 284/C7
Clarksville (Clark), Pa. (16113) 294/B3
Clarksville, Pa. (15322) 294/B6
Clarksville, Tenn. 188/J3
Clarksville, Tenn. (37040) 237/G7
Clarksville, Texas (75426) 303/K4
Clarksville, Va. (23927) 307/L7
Clarkton, Mo. (63837) 261/M10
Clarkton, N.C. (28433) 281/M6
Clarno, Wis. (†53566) 317/G10
Claro (riv.), Bolivia 136/A3
Claro (riv.), Brazil 132/D7
Claro (riv.), Chile 138/G5
Claro, Switzerland 39/G4
Clashmoor, Sask. 181/H3
Clashmore, Ireland 17/F8
Clatonia, Nebr. (68328) 264/H4
Clatskanie, Oreg. (97016) 291/D1
Clatsop (co.), Oreg. 291/D1
Claud, Ala. (†36024) 195/F5
Claude, Texas (79019) 303/C2
Claudell, Kansas (†66951) 232/C2
Claudville, Va. (24076) 307/H7
Claudy, N. Ireland 17/G2
Claunch, N. Mex. (87011) 274/C4
Claussen, S.C. (†29501) 296/H3
Clausthal-Zellerfeld, W. Germany 22/D3
Claverack-Red Mills, N.Y. (12513) 276/N6
Claveria, Philippines 82/C1
Clavet, Sask. 181/E4
Clawson, Mich. (48017) 250/B6
Clawson, Utah (84516) 304/C4
Claxton, Georgia (30417) 217/J6
Clay (co.), Ala. 195/G4
Clay (co.), Ark. 202/K1
Clay, Calif. (†95638) 204/C9
Clay (creek), Colo. 208/O7
Clay (co.), Fla. 212/E2
Clay (co.), Georgia 217/B7
Clay (co.), Ill. 222/E5
Clay (co.), Ind. 227/C6
Clay (co.), Iowa 229/C2
Clay (co.), Kansas 232/E2
Clay (co.), Ky. 237/O6
Clay, Ky. (42404) 237/F6
Clay, La. (†71270) 238/E2
Clay (co.), Minn. 255/B4
Clay (co.), Miss. 256/G3
Clay (co.), Mo. 261/D4
Clay (co.), Nebr. 264/F4
Clay (co.), N.C. 281/B4
Clay (co.), S. Dak. 298/P8
Clay (co.), Tenn. 237/K7
Clay (co.), Texas 303/F4
Clay (hills), Utah 304/D6
Clay (co.), W. Va. 312/D6
Clay, W. Va. (25043) 312/D6
Claybank, Sask. 181/F5
Clay Bank, Va. (†23061) 307/P6
Clay Center, Kansas (67432) 232/E2
Clay Center, Nebr. (68933) 264/F4
Clay Center, Ohio (43408) 284/D2
Clay City, Ill. (62824) 222/E5
Clay City, Ind. (47841) 227/C6
Clay City, Ky. (40312) 237/O5
Claycomo, Mo. (†64119) 261/P5
Clay Cross, England 13/J2
Claydon, Sask. 181/B6
Clayhatchee, Ala. (†36322) 195/G8
Claymont, Del. (19703) 245/S1
Claymour, Ky. (†42220) 237/G7
Clayoquot (sound), Br. Col. 184/D5
Claypool, Ariz. (85532) 198/E5
Claypool, Ind. (46510) 227/F2
Claypool, Ky. (†42101) 237/J7
Claysburg, Pa. (16625) 294/F5
Clay Springs, Ariz. (†85934) 198/E4
Claysville, Ohio (43729) 284/G6
Claysville, Pa. (15323) 294/B5
Clayton, Ala. (36015) 195/G7
Clayton, Calif. (94517) 204/K2
Clayton, Del. (19938) 245/R3
Clayton (co.), Georgia 217/D3
Clayton, Georgia (30525) 217/F1
Clayton, Idaho (83227) 220/D5
Clayton, Ill. (62324) 222/B3
Clayton, Ind. (46118) 227/D5
Clayton (co.), Iowa 229/L3
Clayton, Iowa (†52049) 229/L3
Clayton, Kansas (67629) 232/B2
Clayton, La. (71326) 238/H3
Clayton (lake), Maine 243/D2
Clayton, Mich. (49235) 250/E7
Clayton, Miss. (†38626) 256/D1
Clayton, Mo. (63105) 261/P3
Clayton, N.J. (08312) 273/C4
Clayton, N. Mex. (88415) 274/F2
Clayton, N.Y. (13624) 276/H2
Clayton, N.C. (27520) 281/N3
Clayton, Ohio (45315) 284/B6
Clayton, Okla. (74536) 288/R5
Clayton, S. Dak. (†57332) 298/O7
Clayton, Victoria 97/J5
Clayton, Wash. (99110) 310/H3
Clayton, W. Va. (†24910) 312/E7
Clayton, Wis. (54004) 317/B5
Clayton Lake, Maine (04018) 243/E2
Claytonville, Ill. (60926) 222/F3
Claytor (lake), Va. 307/G6
Clayville, N.Y. (13322) 276/K5
Clayville, R.I. (02815) 249/H5
Clayville, S. Africa 118/H6
Clayville, Va. (†23139) 307/N6
Clear, Alaska (99704) 196/J2
Clear (cape), Alaska 196/D1
Clear (hills), Alberta 182/A1
Clear (creek), Ariz. 198/D4
Clear (lake), Calif. 188/B3
Clear (lake), Calif. 204/C4
Clear (lake), Iowa 229/G2
Clear (cape), Ireland 7/C3
Clear (cape), Ireland 17/B9
Clear (cape), Ireland 10/B5
Clear (isl.), Ireland 17/C9
Clear (lake), La. 238/D3
Clear (lake), Manitoba 179/C4
Clear (lake), Ontario 177/F3
Clear (lake), Ontario 177/G2
Clear (creek), Utah 304/B5
Clear (lake), Utah 304/B4
Clear (creek), Wyo. 319/F1
Clear Boggy (creek), Okla. 288/O6
Clearbrook, Br. Col. 184/L3
Clearbrook, Minn. (56634) 255/C3
Clear Brook, Va. (22624) 307/M2
Clear Creek, Calif. (†96039) 204/B2
Clear Creek (co.), Colo. 208/H3
Clear Creek, Ind. (47426) 227/E6
Clearcreek, Utah (†84538) 304/C4
Clear Creek, W. Va. (25044) 312/D7
Clearfield, Iowa (50840) 229/D7
Clearfield, Ky. (40313) 237/P4
Clearfield (co.), Pa. 294/F3
Clearfield, Pa. (16830) 294/F3
Clearfield, S. Dak. (57581) 298/K7
Clearfield, Utah (84015) 304/B2
Clear Fork (res.), Ohio 284/E4
Clear Fork, Mohican (riv.), Ohio 284/F4
Clear Fork, Brazos (riv.), Texas 303/D5
Clear Fork, Guyandotte (riv.), W. Va. 312/C7
Clear Hills, Alberta 182/B1
Clearlake, Calif. (95422) 204/C5
Clear Lake (res.), Calif. 204/D2
Clear Lake, Ind. (†46737) 227/H1
Clear Lake, Iowa (50428) 229/G2
Clear Lake, La. (†71414) 238/E3
Clear Lake, Minn. (55319) 255/E5
Clear Lake, S. Dak. (57226) 298/R4
Clearlake, Wash. (98235) 310/C2
Clear Lake, Wis. (54005) 317/B5
Clearlake Oaks, Calif. (95423) 204/C4
Clear Lake Shores, Texas (†77565) 303/K2
Clearmont, Mo. (64431) 261/C1
Clearmont, Wyo. (82835) 319/F1
Clear Ridge, Pa. (†17229) 294/F5
Clear Spring, Ind. (†47220) 227/E7
Clear Spring, Md. (21722) 245/G2
Clearview, Okla. (74835) 288/O4
Clearview, W. Va. (†26003) 312/E2
Clearview City, Kansas (66019) 232/G3
Clearville, Pa. (15535) 294/F6
Clearwater (riv.), Alberta 182/C4
Clearwater (riv.), Alberta 182/E1
Clearwater, Br. Col. 184/G4
Clearwater (lake), Br. Col. 184/G4
Clearwater (riv.), Br. Col. 184/G4
Clearwater, Fla. 188/K5
Clearwater, Fla. (*33515) 212/B2
Clearwater (co.), Idaho 220/C3
Clearwater, Idaho (83521) 220/C3
Clearwater (mts.), Idaho 220/C3
Clearwater (riv.), Idaho 220/B3
Clearwater, Kansas (67026) 232/E4
Clearwater, Manitoba 179/D5
Clearwater (co.), Minn. 255/C3
Clearwater, Minn. (55320) 255/D5
Clearwater (riv.), Minn. 255/C3
Clearwater (lake), Mo. 261/L8
Clearwater, Nebr. (68726) 264/F2
Clearwater (brook), New Bruns. 170/D2
Clearwater (riv.), Sask. 181/L3
Clearwater, S.C. (29822) 296/D4
Clearwater, Wash. (†98331) 310/A3
Clearwater Beach (isl.), Fla. 212/B2
Clearwater Lake, Manitoba 179/H3
Clearwater Lake, Wis. (54518) 317/H4
Clearwater Lake Beach, Sask. 181/D5
Clearwater Lake Prov. Park, Manitoba 179/H3
Cleator Moor, England 13/D3
Cleburne (co.), Ala. 195/G3
Cleburne (co.), Ark. 202/F2
Cleburne, Texas 188/G4
Cleburne, Texas (76031) 303/G5
Cle Elum, Wash. (98922) 310/E3
Cle Elum (lake), Wash. 310/E3
Cleethorpes, England 13/H4
Cleethorpes, England 10/F4
Cleeves, Sask. 181/C2
Cleghorn, Iowa (51014) 229/B3
Cleghorn, Wis. (†54738) 317/C6
Clem, Georgia (†30117) 217/B3
Clemenceau, Ariz. (†86326) 198/C4
Clemenceau, Sask. 181/J3
Clément, Fr. Guiana 131/E4
Clemente (isl.), Chile 138/D6
Clementon, N.J. (08021) 273/D4
Clements, Calif. (95227) 204/C9
Clements, Kansas (66844) 232/F3
Clements, Md. (20624) 245/L7
Clements, Minn. (56224) 255/D6
Clementson, Minn. (56623) 255/D2
Clementsport, Nova Scotia 168/C4
Clementsvale, Nova Scotia 168/C4
Clementsville, N. Dak. (†58492) 282/O5
Clemmons, N.C. (27012) 281/J2
Clemons, Iowa (50051) 229/G4
Clemscot, Okla. (†73437) 288/L6
Clemson, S.C. (29631) 296/B2
Clendenin, W. Va. (25045) 312/D5
Clendening (lake), Ohio 284/H5
Cleopatra Needle (mt.), Philippines 82/B5
Cleora, Okla. (†74331) 288/S1
Cleo Springs, Okla. (73729) 288/K2
Clerf (riv.), Luxembourg 27/J8
Clermont, Fla. (32711) 212/E3
Clermont, France 28/E3
Clermont, Georgia (30527) 217/E2
Clermont, Iowa (52135) 229/K3
Clermont, Ky. (40110) 237/K5
Clermont, N.Y. (†12526) 276/N6
Clermont (co.), Ohio 284/B7
Clermont, Pa. (†16740) 294/E2
Clermont, Québec 172/G2
Clermont, Queensland 88/H4
Clermont, Queensland 95/C4
Clermont-Ferrand, France 7/E4
Clermont-Ferrand, France 28/E5
Clermont Harbor, Miss. (39551) 256/F10
Clervaux, Luxembourg 27/J8
Cleve, S. Australia 88/F6
Cleve, S. Australia 94/E5
Clevedon, England 13/D6
Cleveland, Ala. (35049) 195/E3
Cleveland (co.), Ark. 202/F6
Cleveland, Ark. (72030) 202/E3
Cleveland (co.), England 13/F3
Cleveland (hills), England 13/F3
Cleveland, Fla. (†33950) 212/E5
Cleveland, Georgia (30528) 217/E1
Cleveland, Minn. (56017) 255/E6
Cleveland, Miss. (38732) 256/C3

Coleman 353

Cleveland, Mo. (64734) 261/C5
Cleveland, Mont. (†59523) 262/G2
Cleveland, N. Mex. (87715) 274/D2
Cleveland, N.Y. (13042) 276/J4
Cleveland (co.), N.C. 281/F4
Cleveland, N.C. (27013) 281/H3
Cleveland, N. Dak. (58424) 282/M6
Cleveland, Ohio 188/K2
Cleveland, Ohio (*44101) 284/H9
Cleveland, Ohio 146/K5
Cleveland (co.), Okla. 288/M4
Cleveland, Okla. (74020) 288/O2
Cleveland, S.C. (29635) 296/C1
Cleveland, Tenn. (37311) 237/M10
Cleveland, Texas (77327) 303/K7
Cleveland, Utah (84518) 304/D4
Cleveland, Va. (24225) 307/D7
Cleveland, W. Va. (26215) 312/F5
Cleveland, Wis. (53015) 317/L8
Cleveland Heights, Ohio (44118) 284/H9
Cleveland-Hopkins Mun. Airport, Ohio 284/G9
Clevelândia do Norte, Brazil 132/D2
Cleveland Park, D.C. (20008) 245/E4
Clever, Mo. (65631) 261/F8
Cleves, Iowa (†50601) 229/G4
Cleves, Ohio (45002) 284/B9
Clew (bay), Ireland 17/B4
Clew (bay), Ireland 10/B4
Clewiston, Fla. (33440) 212/E5
Clichy, France 28/B1
Clicquot-Millis, Mass. (†02054) 249/A8
Clifden, Ireland 10/B4
Clifden, Ireland 17/B5
Cliff, N. Mex. (88028) 274/A6
Cliff (cape), Nova Scotia 168/E3
Cliff (creek), Utah 304/E3
Cliffdell, Wash. (†98937) 310/E4
Clifford, Ind. (47226) 227/F6
Clifford, Ky. (41208) 237/S4
Clifford (lake), Maine 243/H5
Clifford, Mich. (48727) 250/F5
Clifford, N. Dak. (58016) 282/R5
Clifford, Ontario 177/D4
Clifford, Pa. (18413) 294/L2
Clifford, Va. (24533) 307/K5
Clifford, Wis. (†54564) 317/F4
Cliffordvale, New Bruns. 170/C2
Cliffside, N.C. (28024) 281/F4
Cliffside Park, N.J. (07010) 273/C2
Clifftop, W. Va. (25822) 312/E6
Cliffwood, N.J. (07721) 273/E3
Clifton, Ariz. (85533) 198/F5
Clifton, Colo. (81520) 208/C4
Clifton, Idaho (83228) 220/F7
Clifton, Ill. (60927) 222/F3
Clifton, Kansas (66937) 232/E2
Clifton, La. (†70438) 238/K5
Clifton○, Maine (†04428) 243/G6
Clifton, New Bruns. 170/E1
Clifton, N.J. (*07011) 273/B2
Clifton, S.C. (29324) 296/D2
Clifton, Tenn. (38425) 237/F10
Clifton, Texas (76634) 303/G6
Clifton, W. Va. (25237) 312/B5
Clifton, Wis. (†54618) 317/F8
Clifton City, Mo. (†65348) 261/G5
Clifton Dartmouth Hardness, England 10/E5
Clifton Dartmouth Hardness, England 13/D7
Clifton Forge (I.C.), Va. (24422) 307/J5
Clifton Heights, Pa. (19018) 294/M7
Clifton Hill, Mo. (65244) 261/G4
Clifton Hills, S. Australia 94/F2
Clifton Mills, W. Va. (†26525) 312/G3
Clifton Park○, N.Y. (†12118) 276/N5
Clifton Springs, N.Y. (14432) 276/F4
Cliftonville, Miss. (†39739) 256/H4
Clifty, Ark. (†72756) 202/C1
Clifty (creek), Ind. 227/F6
Clifty, Ky. (42216) 237/G7
Clifty, Tenn. (†38583) 237/L9
Clifty, W. Va. (†25854) 312/E6
Climax, Colo. (80429) 208/G4
Climax, Georgia (31734) 217/D9
Climax, Kansas (67027) 232/F4
Climax, Ky. (40413) 237/N6
Climax, Mich. (49034) 250/D6
Climax, Minn. (56523) 255/B3
Climax, N.C. (27233) 281/K3
Climax, Sask. 181/C6
Climax Springs, Mo. (65324) 261/G6
Climbing Hill, Iowa (51015) 229/B4
Clinch (co.), Georgia 217/G9
Clinch (riv.), Tenn. 237/N9
Clinch (riv.), Va. 307/C7
Clinchburg, Va. (24321) 307/E7
Clinchco, Va. (24226) 307/D6
Clinchfield, Georgia (31013) 217/E6
Clinchmore, Tenn. (†37714) 237/N8
Clinchport, Va. (24244) 307/C7
Cline Settlement, Alberta 182/B3
Clingmans Dome (mt.), N.C. 281/C3
Clingmans Dome (mt.), Tenn. 237/P10
Clint, Texas (79836) 303/B10
Clinton, Ala. (35448) 195/C5
Clinton, Ark. (72031) 202/F2
Clinton, Br. Col. 184/G4
Clinton, Conn. (06413) 210/E3
Clinton○, Conn. (06413) 210/E3
Clinton (co.), Ill. 222/D5
Clinton, Ill. (61727) 222/E3
Clinton (co.), Ind. 227/E4
Clinton, Ind. (47842) 227/C5
Clinton (co.), Iowa 229/M5
Clinton, Iowa 188/J2
Clinton, Iowa (52732) 229/N5
Clinton (co.), Ky. 237/L7
Clinton, Ky. (42031) 237/D7
Clinton, La. (70722) 238/J5
Clinton, Maine (04927) 243/D6
Clinton○, Maine (04927) 243/D6
Clinton, Md. (20735) 245/G6
Clinton○, Mass. (01510) 249/H3
Clinton (co.), Mich. 250/E6
Clinton, Mich. (49236) 250/F6
Clinton, Minn. (56225) 255/B5
Clinton, Miss. (39056) 256/D6
Clinton (co.), Mo. 261/D3
Clinton, Mo. (64735) 261/E6
Clinton, Mont. (59825) 262/C4
Clinton, Nebr. (†69343) 264/B2
Clinton, N.J. (08809) 273/D2
Clinton (res.), N.J. 273/E1
Clinton (co.), N.Y. 276/N1
Clinton, N.Y. (13323) 276/K4
Clinton, N. Zealand 100/B7
Clinton, N.C. (28328) 281/N5
Clinton (co.), Ohio 284/C7
Clinton, Ohio (44216) 284/G4
Clinton, Okla. (73601) 288/H3
Clinton, Ontario 177/C4
Clinton (co.), Pa. 294/G3
Clinton, Pa. (15026) 294/B5
Clinton, S.C. (29325) 296/D3
Clinton, Tenn. (37716) 237/N8
Clinton, Wash. (98236) 310/C3
Clinton, W. Va. (†26058) 312/E2
Clinton, Wis. (53525) 317/J10
Clinton-Colden (lake), N.W. Terrs. 187/H3
Clinton Corners, N.Y. (12514) 276/N7
Clinton Creek, Yukon 187/D3
Clintondale, N.Y. (12515) 276/M7
Clintondale, Pa. (†17751) 294/H3
Clinton Falls, Minn. (†55060) 255/E6
Clintonville, Conn. (†06473) 210/D3
Clintonville, Ky. (†40361) 237/N4
Clintonville, Pa. (16372) 294/C3
Clintonville, W. Va. (24928) 312/E7
Clintonville, Wis. (54929) 317/J6
Clintwood, Va. (24228) 307/D6
Clio, Ala. (36017) 195/G7
Clio, Iowa (50052) 229/G7
Clio, La. (†70462) 238/M2
Clio, Mich. (48420) 250/F5
Clio, S.C. (29525) 296/H2
Clio, W. Va. (25046) 312/D5
Clipper, Wash. (98244) 310/C2
Clipperton (isl.) 146/H8
Clipperton (isl.) 2/D5
Clisham (mt.), Scotland 15/B3
Clitherall, Minn. (56524) 255/C4
Clitheroe, England 13/H1
Clitheroe, England 10/G1
Clive, Alberta 182/D3
Clive, Iowa (50318) 229/F5
Clive, N. Zealand 100/F3
Cliza, Bolivia 136/C5
Cloan, Sask. 181/C3
Cloates (pt.), W. Australia 92/A3
Clode (sound), Newf. 166/D2
Cloe, Pa. (†15767) 294/E4
Cloghan, Ireland 17/F5
Clogh-Chatsworth, Ireland 17/G6
Clogheen, Ireland 17/F7
Clogher, N. Ireland 17/G3
Clogherhead, Ireland 17/J4
Cloghy, N. Ireland 17/K3
Clonakilty, Ireland 10/B5
Clonakilty, Ireland 17/D8
Clonakilty (bay), Ireland 17/D8
Clonaslee, Ireland 17/F5
Cloncurry, Australia 87/E8
Cloncurry, Queensland 95/B4
Cloncurry, Queensland 88/G4
Cloncurry (riv.), Queensland 95/B4
Clondalkin, Ireland 17/J5
Clonegal, Ireland 17/H6
Clones, Ireland 10/C3
Clones, Ireland 17/G3
Clonfert, Ireland 17/E5
Clonmany, Ireland 17/G1
Clonmel, Ireland 17/F7
Clonmel, Ireland 10/C4
Clonmellon, Ireland 17/H4
Clonroche, Ireland 17/H7
Clontarf, Minn. (56226) 255/C5
Clontuskert, Ireland 17/E4
Cloone, Ireland 17/F4
Cloppenburg, W. Germany 22/B2
Clopton, Ala. (36317) 195/G7
Cloquet, Minn. (55720) 255/F4
Cloquet (riv.), Minn. 255/F4
Cloridorme, Québec 172/D1
Clorinda, Argentina 143/E2
Closeburn, Scotland 15/E5
Closplint, Ky. (40927) 237/P7
Closter, N.J. (07624) 273/C1
Clothier, W. Va. (25047) 312/C7
Clotho, Minn. (†56347) 255/C4
Cloud (co.), Kansas 232/E2
Cloud (peak), Wyo. 319/E1
Cloud Chief, Okla. (†73632) 288/J4
Cloudcroft, N. Mex. (88317) 274/D6
Cloudland, Georgia (30709) 217/A1
Cloudy (bay), N. Zealand 100/E4
Cloudy, Okla. (74537) 288/R6
Cloughjordan, Ireland 17/E6
Cloughmills, N. Ireland 17/J2
Cloutierville, La. (71416) 238/E3
Clova, Québec 174/B3
Clover (creek), Oreg. 291/K3
Clover, S.C. (29710) 296/E1
Clover, Va. (24534) 307/L7
Clover, W. Va. (†25276) 312/D5
Clover Bar, Alberta 182/D3
Clover Bend, Ark. (†72433) 202/H2
Clover Bottom, Ky. (40447) 237/N5
Cloverdale, Ala. (35617) 195/C1
Cloverdale, Calif. (95425) 204/B5
Cloverdale, Ind. (46120) 227/D5
Cloverdale, Minn. (†55037) 255/F4
Cloverdale, Ohio (45827) 284/B3
Cloverdale, Oreg. (97112) 291/D2
Cloverdale, Va. (24077) 307/J6
Cloverland, Ind. (†47834) 227/C6
Cloverland, Wash. (†99402) 310/H4
Cloverleaf, Manitoba 179/F5
Clover Lick, W. Va. (†24979) 312/F6
Clover Pass, Alaska (†99901) 196/N2
Cloverport, Ky. (40111) 237/H5
Cloverton, Minn. (†55048) 255/F4
Clovis, Calif. (93612) 204/F7
Clovis, N.Mex. 188/F4
Clovis, N. Mex. (88101) 274/F4
Clovulin, Scotland 15/C4
Cloyne, Ireland 17/E8
Cloyne, Ontario 177/G3
Cluanie, Loch (lake), Scotland 15/C3
Club (isl.), Ontario 177/C2
Cluff Lake, Sask. 181/L2
Cluj-Napoca, Romania 45/F2
Cluj-Napoca, Romania 7/G4
Clun, England 10/E4
Clun, England 13/D6
Clune, Pa. (15727) 294/D4
Clunes, Victoria 97/B5
Cluny, Alberta 182/D4
Cluny, France 28/F4
Cluses, France 28/G4
Clusone-Fiorine, Italy 34/C2
Cluster Springs, Va. (24535) 307/L7
Clute, Texas (77531) 303/J9
Clutha (riv.), N. Zealand 100/B6
Clutier, Iowa (52217) 229/J4
Clwyd (co.), Wales 13/D4
Clyattville, Georgia (31604) 217/F9
Clyde, Alberta 182/D2
Clyde (lake), Alberta 182/E2
Clyde, Canada 4/B13
Clyde (riv.), Dominica 161/F6
Clyde, Kansas (66938) 232/E2
Clyde, Mo. (64432) 261/C2
Clyde, N.Y. (14433) 276/G4
Clyde, N.C. (28721) 281/D3
Clyde, N. Dak. (†58352) 282/N2
Clyde, N.W.T. 162/J1
Clyde (inlet), N.W.T. 162/K1
Clyde, N.W. Terrs. 187/M2
Clyde (inlet), N.W. Terrs. 187/M2
Clyde (riv.), Nova Scotia 168/C5
Clyde, Ohio (43410) 284/E3
Clyde (firth), Scotland 15/D5
Clyde (firth), Scotland 10/D3
Clyde (riv.), Scotland 10/E3
Clyde (riv.), Scotland 15/D5
Clyde (riv.), Tasmania 99/D4
Clyde, Texas (79510) 303/E5
Clyde (riv.), Vt. 268/C2
Clyde, Wash. (†99348) 310/G4
Clydebank, Scotland 15/B2
Clydebank, Scotland 10/A1
Clyde Hill, Wash. (†98004) 310/B2
Clyde Park, Mont. (59018) 262/F5
Clyde River, Nova Scotia 168/C5
Clyman, Wis. (53016) 317/J9
Clymer, N.Y. (14724) 276/A6
Clymer, Pa. (15728) 294/E4
Clymers, Ind. (†46947) 227/E3
Clyo, Georgia (31303) 217/K6
Cnoc May (mt.), Scotland 15/C5
Coachella, Calif. (92236) 204/J10
Coachella (canal), Calif. 204/K10
Coachford, Ireland 17/D8
Coahoma (co.), Miss. 256/C2
Coahoma, Miss. (38617) 256/C2
Coahoma, Texas (79511) 303/C5
Coahuila (state), Mexico 150/H3
Coakley, Ky. (†42782) 237/K6
Coal (creek), Ind. 227/C4
Coal, Mo. (†64735) 261/E6
Coal (co.), Okla. 288/O5
Coal (pt.), Oreg. 291/C5
Coal (butte), Utah 304/C5
Coal (creek), Wash. 310/G3
Coal (riv.), W. Va. 312/C6
Coal Bluff, Ind. (†47874) 227/C5
Coal Branch, New Bruns. 170/E2
Coalburn, Scotland 15/E5
Coal City, Ill. (60416) 222/E2
Coal City, Ind. (47427) 227/D6
Coal City, W. Va. (25823) 312/D7
Coalcomán de Matamoros, Mexico 150/H7
Coal Creek, Alaska (†99701) 196/K1
Coal Creek, Colo. (81221) 208/J6
Coal Creek, Ind. (†47932) 227/C4
Coal Creek, New Bruns. 170/E2
Coaldale, Alberta 182/D5
Coaldale, Colo. (81222) 208/H6
Coaldale, Nev. (†89049) 266/D4
Coaldale, Pa. (18218) 294/L4
Coaldale (Six Mile Run), Pa. (16679) 294/F5
Coalfield, Tenn. (37719) 237/N8
Coalfield, Wash. (†98055) 310/B2
Coal Fork, W. Va. (25306) 312/D6
Coalgate, Okla. (74538) 288/O5
Coal Grove, Ohio (†45638) 284/E9
Coal Harbour, Br. Col. 184/D5
Coal Hill, Ark. (72832) 202/C3
Coalhurst, Alberta 182/D5
Coaling, Ala. (35449) 195/D4
Coalinga, Calif. (93210) 204/E7
Coalisland, N. Ireland 17/H2
Coalmont, Br. Col. 184/G5
Coalmont, Colo. (80430) 208/F1
Coalmont, Ind. (47845) 227/C6
Coalmont, Tenn. (37313) 237/K10
Coalport, Pa. (16627) 294/E4
Coalridge, Mont. (†59219) 262/M2
Coal Run, Ky. (†41501) 237/R5
Coalspur, Alberta 182/B3
Coalton, Ill. (†62075) 222/D4
Coalton, Ohio (45621) 284/E7
Coalton, W. Va. (26257) 312/G5
Coal Valley, Alberta 182/B3
Coal Valley, Ill. (61240) 222/C2
Coalville, England 13/F5
Coalville, Iowa (†50501) 229/E4
Coalville, Utah (84017) 304/C3
Coalwood, Mont. (†59351) 262/L5
Coalwood, W. Va. (24824) 312/C8
Coambo, Angola 115/C5
Coambo, Angola 102/D5
Coamo, P. Rico 161/D2
Coamo, P. Rico 156/G1
Coamo (res.), P. Rico 161/D3
Coamo (riv.), P. Rico 161/D3
Coari, Brazil 120/C3
Coari, Brazil 132/H9
Coarsegold, Calif. (93614) 204/F6
Coast (mts.) 162/C4
Coast (ranges) 188/B2
Coast (mts.), Alaska 196/N1
Coast (mts.), Br. Col. 146/E4
Coast (mts.), Br. Col. 184/D3
Coast (ranges), Calif. 204/D7
Coast (prov.), Kenya 115/G4
Coast (ranges), Oreg. 291/D5
Coast (ranges), U.S. 146/F5
Coast (ranges), Wash. 310/B3
Coast Guard Academy, Conn. 210/G3
Coatbridge, Scotland 10/B1
Coatbridge, Scotland 15/C2
Coatepec, Mexico 150/P1
Coatepeque, Guatemala 154/A3
Coates, Minn. (†55068) 255/E6
Coatesville, Ind. (46121) 227/D5
Coatesville, Pa. (19320) 294/L5
Coatetelco, Mexico 150/L2
Coaticook, Québec 172/F4
Coatopa, Ala. (35450) 195/B6
Coats, Kansas (67028) 232/D4
Coats, N.C. (27521) 281/M4
Coats (isl.), N.W.T. 162/H3
Coats (isl.), N.W.T. 146/K3
Coats (isl.), N.W. Terrs. 187/K3
Coatsburg, Ill. (62325) 222/B3
Coats Land (reg.), Ant. 2/H10
Coats Land (reg.) 5/B17
Coatsville, Mo. (63535) 261/G1
Coatzacoalcos, Mexico 146/J8
Coatzacoalcos, Mexico 150/M7
Coatzingo, Mexico 150/N2
Cobalt, Conn. (06414) 210/E2
Cobalt, Idaho (83229) 220/D4
Cobalt, Ont. 162/H6
Cobalt, Ontario 177/K5
Cobalt, Ontario 175/D3
Cobalt City, Mo. (†63645) 261/M7
Cobán, Guatemala 154/B3
Cobar, N. S. Wales 88/H6
Cobar, N.S. Wales 97/C2
Cobargo, N.S. Wales 97/E5
Cobb (co.), Georgia 217/C3
Cobb, Georgia (31735) 217/E7
Cobb, Ky. (42405) 237/F6
Cobb (riv.), Minn. 255/E7
Cobb (isl.), Va. 307/S6
Cobb, Wis. (53526) 317/F10
Cobbadah, N.S. Wales 97/F2
Cobble Hill, Br. Col. 184/K3
Cobble Mountain (res.), Mass. 249/C4
Cobbs Creek, Va. (23035) 307/R6
Cobbtown, Georgia (30420) 217/H6
Cobden, Ill. (62920) 222/D6
Cobden, Minn. (†56085) 255/D6
Cobden, Ontario 177/H2
Cobden, Victoria 97/B6
Cobequid (bay), Nova Scotia 168/E3
Cóbh, Ireland 10/B5
Cóbh, Ireland 17/E8
Cobham (riv.), Manitoba 179/G1
Cobham (riv.), Ontario 175/A2
Cobija, Bolivia 136/A2
Cobija, Brazil 120/C4
Coble, Tenn. (†37033) 237/F9
Cobleskill, N.Y. (12043) 276/L5
Coboconk, Ontario 177/F3
Cobourg (pen.), North. Terr. 88/E2
Cobourg (pen.), North. Terr. 93/C1
Cobourg, Ontario 177/F4
Cobquecura, Chile 138/D1
Cobram, Victoria 97/C4
Cobre, Nev. (†89830) 266/G1
Cóbuè, Mozambique 118/F2
Coburg, Iowa (†51566) 229/C7
Coburg (isl.), N.W. Terrs. 187/L2
Coburg, Oreg. (97401) 291/E3
Coburg, Victoria 88/K7
Coburg, Victoria 97/H5
Coburg, W. Germany 22/D3
Coburn, Pa. (16832) 294/H4
Coburn, W. Va. (26562) 312/F3
Coca, Ecuador 128/D3
Cocachacra, Peru 128/G11
Cocagne, New Bruns. 170/F2
Cocagne (isl.), New Bruns. 170/F2
Cocagne (riv.), New Bruns. 170/F2
Cocagne Cape, New Bruns. 170/F2
Cocama, Peru 128/G8
Cocanada (Kakinada), India 68/E5
Cocani, Bolivia 136/B7
Cocapata, Bolivia 136/B5
Cocentaina, Spain 33/F3
Cochabamba (dept.), Bolivia 136/C5
Cochabamba, Bolivia 120/C4
Cochabamba, Bolivia 136/C5
Cochamó, Chile 138/E3
Coche (isl.), Venezuela 124/F2
Cocheco (riv.), N.H. 268/E5
Cochecton, N.Y. (12726) 276/K7
Cochem, W. Germany 22/B3
Cochenour, Ontario 175/B2
Cochetopa (creek), Colo. 208/F6
Cochimbo, Serra do (mts.), Brazil 132/C5
Cochin, Sask. 181/C2
Cochin-Alleppey, India 68/D6
Cochinos (bay), Cuba 158/D2
Cochise (co.), Ariz. 198/F7
Cochise, Ariz. (85606) 198/F6
Cochiti, N. Mex. (†87041) 274/C3
Cochituate, Mass. (01778) 249/A7
Cochituate (lake), Mass. 249/A7
Cochran, Georgia (31014) 217/F6
Cochran (co.), Texas 303/B4
Cochrane, Ala. (†35442) 195/B4
Cochrane, Alberta 182/C4
Cochrane (lake), Chile 138/E7
Cochrane, Cerro (mt.), Chile 138/E7
Cochrane (riv.), Manitoba 179/H2
Cochrane, Ont. 146/K5
Cochrane, Ont. 162/H6
Cochrane (terr. dist.), Ontario 177/J4
Cochrane (terr. dist.), Ontario 175/D2
Cochrane, Ontario 177/K5
Cochrane, Ontario 175/D3
Cochrane (riv.), Sask. 181/N2
Cochrane, Wis. (54622) 317/C7
Cochranton, Pa. (16314) 294/B2
Cochranville, Pa. (19330) 294/L6
Cockburn (chan.), Chile 138/E11
Cockburn (isl.), Ontario 177/A2
Cockburn, S. Australia 94/G5
Cockburn (sound), W. Australia 88/B2
Cockburn Harbour, Turks & Caicos 156/D2
Cockburnspath, Scotland 15/F5
Cocke (co.), Tenn. 237/P9
Cockenoe (isl.), Conn. 210/B4
Cockenzie and Port Seton, Scotland 15/D1
Cockermouth, England 13/D3
Cockermouth, England 10/E3
Cockeysville, Md. (21030) 245/M3
Cockrell Hill, Texas (75211) 303/G2
Cockrum, Miss. (†38632) 256/E1
Coclé del Norte, Panama 154/G6
Coco (chan.), Burma 72/B4
Coco (cay), Cuba 158/G1
Coco (riv.), Honduras 154/E3
Coco (chan.), India 68/G6
Coco (riv.), Nicaragua 154/E3
Coco, W. Va. (†25071) 312/D6
Cocoa, Fla. (32922) 212/F3
Cocoa Beach, Fla. (32931) 212/F3
Cocobeach, Gabon 115/B3
Cocodrie (lake), La. 238/E5
Cocolamus, Pa. (17014) 294/H4
Coconino (co.), Ariz. 198/C3
Coconino (plat.), Ariz. 198/C3
Coconut Creek, Fla. (†33060) 212/F5
Cocopah Ind. Res., Ariz. 198/A6
Cocorit, Mexico 150/E3
Cocos (isls.), Australia 2/P6
Cocos (isls.), Australia 54/L11
Cocos (isl.), C. Rica 146/K9
Cocos (isl.), Guam 86/K7
Cocos (bay), Trin. & Tob. 161/B10
Cocuy, Sierra Nevada del (mts.), Colombia 126/D4
Cod (cape), Mass. 146/M5
Cod (cape), Mass. 188/N2
Cod (cape), Mass. 249/O4
Cod (isl.), Newf. 166/B2
Codajás, Brazil 120/C3
Codajás, Brazil 132/H9
Coddle (harb.), Nova Scotia 168/G3
Codegua, Chile 138/G4
Codell, Kansas (67630) 232/C2
Coden, Ala. (36523) 195/B10
Codera (cape), Venezuela 124/F2
Coderre, Sask. 181/E5
Codesa, Alberta 182/B2
Codes Corner, Ontario 177/H3
Codette, Sask. 181/H2
Codfish (isl.), N. Zealand 100/A7
Codigua, Chile 138/F4
Codington (co.), S. Dak. 298/P4
Codó, Brazil 120/E3
Codó, Brazil 132/E4
Codorus, Pa. (17311) 294/J6
Codpa, Chile 138/B1
Codrington, Ant. & Bar. 156/G3
Codrington, Barbados 161/B8
Codroipo, Italy 34/D2
Codroy, Newf. 166/C4
Cody, Nebr. (69211) 264/C2
Cody, Wyo. (82414) 319/D1
Codys, New Bruns. 170/E3
Coe, Ind. (†47598) 227/C8
Coeburn, Va. (24230) 307/D7
Coe Hill, Ontario 177/G3
Coelemu, Chile 138/D1
Coello, Ill. (62825) 222/D6
Coen, Queensland 88/G2
Coen, Queensland 95/B2
Coeroeni (riv.), Suriname 131/C4
Coesfeld, W. Germany 22/B3
Coesse, Ind. (†46725) 227/G2
Coeur d'Alene, Idaho (83814) 220/B2
Coeur d'Alene, Idaho 188/C1
Coeur d'Alene (lake), Idaho 220/B2
Coeur d'Alene (mts.), Idaho 220/C2
Coeur d'Alene (riv.), Idaho 220/B2
Coevorden, Netherlands 27/K3
Coeymans, N.Y. (12045) 276/N6
Coffee (co.), Ala. 195/G8
Coffee (co.), Georgia 217/G8
Coffee (co.), Tenn. 237/J9
Coffee Creek, Mont. (59424) 262/F3
Coffeen, Ill. (62017) 222/D4
Coffee Springs, Ala. (36318) 195/G8
Coffeeville, Ala. (36524) 195/B7
Coffeeville (dam), Ala. 195/B7
Coffeeville, Miss. (38922) 256/E3
Coffey (co.), Kansas 232/G3
Coffey, Mo. (64636) 261/E2
Coffeyville, Kans. 188/G3
Coffeyville, Kansas (67337) 232/G4
Coffin (bay), S. Australia 94/D6
Coffin Bay (pen.), S. Australia 94/D6
Coffs Harbour, N. S. Wales 88/J6
Coffs Harbour, N.S. Wales 97/G2
Cofield, N.C. (27922) 281/R2
Cogan Station, Pa. (†17728) 294/H3
Cogar, Okla. (†73059) 288/K4
Cogdell, Georgia (31628) 217/G8
Cogealac, Romania 45/J3
Coggon, Iowa (52218) 229/L4
Coghinas (riv.), Italy 34/B4
Coglians (Hohe Warte) (mt.), Austria 41/B3
Cognac, France 28/C5
Cogolludo, Spain 33/E2
Cogotí, Chile 138/A8
Cogswell, N. Dak. (58017) 282/P7
Cogtong, Philippines 82/E6
Cohagen, Mont. (59322) 262/K3
Cohansey (riv.), N.J. 273/C5
Cohasset, Ala. (†36474) 195/E8
Cohasset○, Mass. (02025) 249/F7
Cohasset, Minn. (55721) 255/E3
Cohoctah, Mich. (48816) 250/F6
Cohocton, N.Y. (14826) 276/F5
Cohocton (riv.), N.Y. 276/F6
Cohoe, Alaska (†99669) 196/B1
Cohoes, N.Y. (12047) 276/N5
Cohoni, Bolivia 136/B5
Cohuna, Victoria 97/C4
Cohutta, Georgia (30710) 217/C1
Coiba, Isla de (isl.), Panama 154/F7
Coihaique, Chile 138/E6
Coihaique Alto, Chile 138/E6
Coihueco, Chile 138/A11
Coila, Miss. (38923) 256/E4
Coill Dubh, Ireland 17/H5
Coimbatore, India 54/J8
Coimbatore, India 68/D6
Coimbra (dist.), Portugal 33/B2
Coimbra, Portugal 7/D4
Coimbra, Portugal 33/B2
Coin, Iowa (51636) 229/C7
Coín, Spain 33/D4
Coinco, Chile 138/G5
Coinjock, N.C. (27923) 281/S2
Coipasa, Bolivia 136/A6
Coipasa (lake), Bolivia 136/B6
Coipasa (salt dep.), Bolivia 136/A6
Coire, Loch (lake), Scotland 15/D2
Cojata, Peru 128/H10
Cojedes (state), Venezuela 124/D3
Cojedes (riv.), Venezuela 124/D3
Cojimíes, Ecuador 128/B2
Cojoro, Venezuela 124/C2
Cojutepeque, El Salvador 154/C4
Cokato, Minn. (55321) 255/D5
Coke (co.), Texas 303/D6
Cokeburg, Pa. (15324) 294/B5
Cokedale, Colo. (81032) 208/K8
Coker, Ala. (35452) 195/C4
Cokercreek, Tenn. (37314) 237/N10
Coketon, W. Va. (†26292) 312/G4
Cokeville, Wyo. (83114) 319/B3
Colaba (pt.), India 68/B7
Colac, Victoria 88/G7
Colac, Victoria 97/B6
Colachel, India 68/D7
Colair (lake), India 68/E5
Colamus (riv.), Nebr. 264/E2
Colasay, Peru 128/C5
Colatina, Brazil 120/E4
Colatina, Brazil 132/F7
Colbeck (cape) 5/B10
Colbert (co.), Ala. 195/C1
Colbert, Georgia (30628) 217/F2
Colbert, Okla. (74733) 288/O7
Colbert, Wash. (99005) 310/H3
Colborne, Ontario 177/G4
Colbún, Chile 138/A11
Colburn, Idaho (83865) 220/B1
Colburn, Ind. (47931) 227/D3
Colby, Kansas (67701) 232/A2
Colby, Wash. (†98366) 310/A2
Colby, Wis. (54421) 317/F6
Colcamar, Peru 128/D6
Colchester, Conn. (06415) 210/F2
Colchester○, Conn. (06415) 210/F2
Colchester, England 13/H6
Colchester, England 10/G5
Colchester, Ill. (62326) 222/C3
Colchester (co.), Nova Scotia 168/E3
Colchester, Ontario 177/B6
Colchester○, Vt. (05446) 268/A2
Colcord, Okla. (74338) 288/S2
Colcord, W. Va. (25048) 312/D7
Cold (bay), Alaska 196/F4
Cold (lake), Alberta 182/E2
Cold (riv.), N.H. 268/C5
Cold Bay, Alaska (99571) 196/F3
Cold Brook, N.Y. (13324) 276/L4
Coldbrook Station, Nova Scotia 168/D3
Colden, N.Y. (14033) 276/C5
Coldingham, Scotland 15/F5
Cold Lake, Alberta 182/E2
Cold Spring, Ky. (41076) 237/T2
Cold Spring, Minn. (56320) 255/D5
Cold Spring, N.J. (†08204) 273/D6
Cold Spring (inlet), N.J. 273/D6
Cold Spring, N.Y. (10516) 276/N8
Coldspring (head), Nova Scotia 168/E3
Coldspring, Texas (77331) 303/J7
Cold Spring Harbor, N.Y. (11724) 276/R6
Cold Springs, Okla. (†73564) 288/J5
Coldstream, Br. Col. 184/H5
Cold Stream (pond), Maine 243/G5
Coldstream, New Bruns. 170/C2
Coldstream, Scotland 10/E3
Coldstream, Scotland 15/F5
Coldstream, Victoria 97/K4
Coldwater, Kansas (67029) 232/C4
Coldwater, Mich. (49036) 250/D7
Coldwater, Miss. (38618) 256/E1
Coldwater (riv.), Miss. 256/D1
Coldwater, Ohio (45828) 284/A5
Coldwater, Ontario 177/E3
Coldwater, Tenn. (†37334) 237/H10
Coldwater (creek), Texas 303/B1
Coldwater, W. Va. (†26411) 312/E4
Cole (co.), Mo. 261/H6
Cole (harb.), Nova Scotia 168/E4
Cole, Okla. (†73010) 288/L5
Colebrook○, Conn. (06021) 210/C1
Colebrook, N.H. (03576) 268/E2
Colebrook○, N.H. (03576) 268/E2
Colebrook, Ohio (†44034) 284/J2
Colebrook, Tasmania 99/D4
Colebrook River (lake), Conn. 210/C1
Cole Camp, Mo. (65325) 261/F6
Coleen (riv.), Alaska 196/K1
Colegrove, Pa. (†16749) 294/F2
Coleharbor, N. Dak. (58531) 282/H4
Coleman, Alberta 182/C5
Coleman, Alta. 162/E6
Coleman, Fla. (33521) 212/D3
Coleman, Georgia (31736) 217/C7
Coleman, Mich. (48618) 250/E5
Coleman, Okla. (73432) 288/O6
Coleman (riv.), Queensland 95/B2
Coleman (co.), Texas 303/E6
Coleman, Texas (76834) 303/E6

Cotonou 355

Conroe, Texas (*77301) 303/J7
Conroy, Iowa (52220) 229/J5
Consecon, Ontario 177/G3
Conselheiro Lafaiete, Brazil 135/E2
Conselheiro Lafaiete, Brazil 132/E8
Consett, England 13/H3
Conshohocken, Pa. (19428) 294/M5
Consolación del Norte, Cuba 158/B1
Consolación del Sur, Cuba 158/B2
Consolación del Sur, Cuba 156/A2
Consort, Alberta 182/E3
Constable, N.Y. (12926) 276/M1
Constableville, N.Y. (13325) 276/J3
Constance (lake), Austria 41/A3
Constance, Ky. (41009) 237/R2
Constance, Sask. 181/F6
Constance (lake), Switzerland 39/H1
Constance (mt.), Wash. 310/B3
Constance (lake), W. Germany 22/C5
Constancia, Uruguay 145/B3
Constant, Morne (hill), Guadeloupe 161/B7
Constanța, Romania 7/G4
Constanța, Romania 45/J3
Constantia, N.Y. (13044) 276/H4
Constantia, S. Africa 118/E6
Constantina, Spain 33/D4
Constantine (cape), Alaska 196/G3
Constantine, Algeria 102/C1
Constantine, Algeria 106/F1
Constantine, Mich. (49042) 250/D7
Constanza, Argentina 143/G6
Constanza, Dom. Rep. 158/D6
Constitución, Chile 138/A11
Constitución, Uruguay 145/A2
Constitution, Georgia 217/K2
Constitution, Ohio (45722) 284/G7
Consuegra, Spain 33/E3
Consul, Ala. (†36783) 195/C6
Consul, Sask. 181/B6
Contact, Nev. (†89825) 266/G1
Contamana, Peru 128/E6
Contas (riv.), Brazil 132/F6
Contentnea (creek), N.C. 281/N3
Conthey, Switzerland 39/D4
Continental, Ariz. (†85640) 198/D7
Continental, Ohio (45831) 284/B3
Continental (peak), Wyo. 319/D3
Contla, Mexico 150/N1
Contoocook, N.H. (03229) 268/D5
Contoocook (riv.), N.H. 268/D6
Contra Costa (co.), Calif. 204/D6
Contramaestre, Cuba 158/G3
Contratación, Colombia 126/D4
Contrecoeur, Québec 172/D4
Contreras (isl.), Chile 138/D9
Contreras (isls.), Panama 154/F7
Controller (bay), Alaska 196/J3
Contulmo, Chile 138/D2
Contumazá, Peru 128/C6
Contwoyto (lake), N.W.T. 162/E2
Contwoyto (lake), N.W. Terrs. 187/H3
Convención, Colombia 126/D3
Convent, La. (70723) 238/L3
Convent Station, N.J. (07961) 273/E2
Conversano, Italy 34/F4
Converse (hill), Conn. 210/F1
Converse, Ind. (46919) 227/F3
Converse, La. (71419) 238/C3
Converse, S.C. (29329) 296/D2
Converse, Texas (78109) 303/K11
Converse (co.), Wyo. 319/G3
Convoy, Ireland 17/F2
Convoy, Ohio (45832) 284/A4
Conway (co.), Ark. 202/E3
Conway, Ark. (72032) 202/F3
Conway (lake), Ark. 202/F3
Conway, Iowa (50834) 229/D7
Conway, Kansas (67434) 232/E3
Conway, Ky. (40417) 237/N6
Conway○, Mass. (01341) 249/D2
Conway, Mich. (49722) 250/E3
Conway, Miss. (†39051) 256/E5
Conway, Mo. (65632) 261/G7
Conway, N.H. (03818) 268/E4
Conway○, N.H. (03818) 268/E4
Conway (lake), N.H. 268/E4
Conway, N.C. (27820) 281/P2
Conway, N. Dak. (†58233) 282/P3
Conway, Nova Scotia 168/C4
Conway, Pa. (15027) 294/B4
Conway, S.C. (29526) 296/J4
Conway, Texas (†79068) 303/C2
Conway, Wash. (98238) 310/C2
Conway Springs, Kansas (67031) 232/E4
Conwy, Wales 10/E4
Conwy, Wales 13/D4
Conwy (bay), Wales 13/C4
Conyers, Georgia (*30207) 217/D3
Conyngham, Pa. (18219) 294/K3
Coober Pedy, S. Australia 88/E5
Coober Pedy, S. Australia 94/D3
Cooch Behar, India 68/F3
Coogee, N.S. Wales 97/K3
Cook (isls.) 87/K7
Cook (inlet), Alaska 196/B1
Cook (mt.), Alaska 196/K2
Cook (cape), Br. Col. 184/C5
Cook (bay), Chile 138/E11
Cook (co.), Georgia 217/F8
Cook (co.), Ill. 222/F2
Cook (co.), Minn. 255/H3
Cook, Minn. (55723) 255/F3
Cook, Nebr. (68329) 264/H4
Cook (isls.), N. Zealand 2/B6
Cook (mt.), N. Zealand 87/G10
Cook (str.), N. Zealand 87/H10
Cook (mt.), N. Zealand 100/C5
Cook (str.), N. Zealand 100/E4
Cook, S. Australia 88/E6
Cook, S. Australia 94/B4
Cook (inlet), U.S. 4/D17
Cook (pt.), Victoria 97/H5
Cook (pt.), Victoria 88/K7
Cook, Wash. (98605) 310/D5
Cooke (co.), Texas 303/G4
Cooke City, Mont. (59020) 262/G5
Cookes (range), N. Mex. 274/B6
Cookeville, Tenn. (38501) 237/L8
Cooking Lake, Alberta 182/D3
Cook's (Paopao) (bay), Fr. Poly. 86/S12
Cooks, Mich. (49817) 250/C3
Cooksburg, Pa. (16217) 294/D3
Cooks Falls, N.Y. (12728) 276/K7
Cook's Harbour, Newf. 166/C3
Cookshire, Québec 172/F4
Cooks Mills, Ill. (†61931) 222/E4
Cook Station, Mo. (65449) 261/K7
Cookstown, N.J. (08511) 273/D3
Cookstown (dist.), N. Ireland 17/H2
Cookstown, N. Ireland 10/C3
Cookstown, N. Ireland 17/H2
Cookstown, Ontario 177/E3
Cooksville, Ill. (61730) 222/E3
Cooksville, Md. (21723) 245/K3
Cooksville, Miss. (†39341) 256/H5
Cooktown, Australia 87/E7
Cooktown, Queensland 95/C2
Cooktown, Queensland 88/H3
Cool, Texas (†76086) 303/G5
Coolabah, N.S. Wales 97/D2
Cooladdi, Queensland 95/C5
Cooladdi, Queensland 88/H5
Coolah, N.S. Wales 97/E2
Coolamon, N.S. Wales 97/D4
Coolaney, Ireland 17/D3
Coolatai, N.S. Wales 97/F1
Cooleemee, N.C. (27014) 281/H3
Cooley, Minn. (†55769) 255/E3
Coolgardie, W. Australia 88/C6
Coolgardie, W. Australia 92/C5
Coolgreany, Ireland 17/J6
Coolibah, North. Terr. 93/B3
Coolidge, Ariz. (85228) 198/D6
Coolidge (dam), Ariz. 198/E5
Coolidge, Georgia (31738) 217/E8
Coolidge, Kansas (67836) 232/A3
Coolidge, Texas (76635) 303/H6
Coolidge Dam, Ariz. (†85542) 198/E5
Coolin, Idaho (83821) 220/B1
Cool Spring, Del. (†19951) 245/T6
Cool Valley, Mo. (†63101) 261/P2
Coolville, Ohio (45723) 284/G7
Cooma, N. S. Wales 88/H7
Cooma, N.S. Wales 97/E5
Coombs, Br. Col. 184/H3
Coonabarabran, N.S. Wales 97/E2
Coonamble, N. S. Wales 88/H6
Coonamble, N. S. Wales 97/E2
Coondapoor, India 68/C6
Coon Rapids, Iowa (50058) 229/D5
Coon Rapids, Minn. (55433) 255/G5
Coon Valley, Wis. (54623) 317/E8
Cooper, Ala. (†35045) 195/E5
Cooper (pt.), Calif. 204/D7
Cooper, Iowa (50059) 229/E5
Cooper, Ky. (†42633) 237/M7
Cooper, Maine (†04638) 243/H6
Cooper○, Maine (†04638) 243/H6
Cooper (co.), Mo. 261/G5
Cooper (riv.), N.J. 273/B3
Cooper, S.C. (†29560) 296/H4
Cooper (riv.), S.C. 296/G6
Cooper, Texas (75432) 303/J4
Cooper (lake), Wyo. 319/G4
Co-Operative, Ky. (42610) 237/M7
Cooper City, Fla. (33328) 212/B4
Cooperdale, Ohio (†43842) 284/F5
Cooper Landing, Alaska (99572) 196/C1
Coopers (Barcoo) (creek), Queensland 95/B5
Coopers (Barcoo) (creek), S. Australia 88/G5
Coopers (Barcoo) (creek), S. Australia 94/F3
Coopersburg, Pa. (18036) 294/M5
Coopers Mills, Maine (04341) 243/E7
Coopers Plains, N.Y. (14827) 276/F6
Coopers Plains, Queensland 95/D3
Coopers Plains, Queensland 88/K3
Cooperstown, N.Y. (13326) 276/L5
Cooperstown, N. Dak. (58425) 282/O5
Cooperstown, Pa. (16317) 294/C2
Coopersville, Ky. (42611) 237/M7
Coopersville, Mich. (49404) 250/C5
Cooperton, Okla. (†73041) 288/J5
Coorabie, S. Australia 88/E6
Coorabie, S. Australia 94/B4
Coorong, The (lag.), S. Australia 94/F6
Coorow, W. Australia 92/B5
Coos (co.), N.H. 268/E2
Coos (co.), Oreg. 291/C4
Coos (riv.), Oreg. 291/D4
Coosa (co.), Ala. 195/F5
Coosa (riv.), Ala. 195/F4
Coosa, Georgia (30129) 217/B2
Coosa (riv.), Georgia 217/A2
Coosada, Ala. (36020) 195/F5
Coosaw (riv.), S.C. 296/G7
Coosawattee (riv.), Georgia 217/C1
Coosawhatchie, S.C. (29912) 296/F6
Coosawhatchie (riv.), S.C. 296/E6
Coos Bay, Oreg. 188/A2
Coos Bay, Oreg. (97420) 291/C4
Cootamundra, N. S. Wales 88/H6
Cootamundra, N.S. Wales 97/D4
Cootehill, Ireland 17/G3
Cootehill, Ireland 10/C3
Cooter, Mo. (63839) 261/N10
Copacabana, Argentina 143/C2
Copacabana, Bolivia 136/A5
Copake, N.Y. (12516) 276/N6
Copake Falls, N.Y. (12517) 276/N6
Copala, Mexico 150/K8
Copalis Beach, Wash. (98535) 310/A3
Copalis Crossing, Wash. (98536) 310/B3
Copan, Okla. (74022) 288/P1
Copano (bay), Texas 303/G9
Copco (lake), Calif. 204/C2
Cope, Colo. (80812) 208/O3
Cope, Ind. (†46151) 227/E6
Cope, S.C. (29038) 296/E5
Cope (cape), Spain 33/F4
Copeland, Ala. (†36558) 195/B7
Copeland, Fla. (33926) 212/E6
Copeland, Idaho (†83805) 220/B1
Copeland, Kansas (67837) 232/B4
Copeland (isl.), N. Ireland 17/K2
Copemish, Mich. (49625) 250/D4
Copen, W. Va. (26615) 312/E5
Copenhagen (commune), Denmark 21/F6
Copenhagen (cap.), Denmark 7/F3
Copenhagen (cap.), Denmark 21/F6
Copenhagen (cap.), Denmark 18/G9
Copenhagen, N.Y. (13626) 276/J3
Copere, Bolivia 136/D6
Copiague, N.Y. (11726) 276/O9
Copiah (co.), Miss. 256/D7
Copiapó, Chile 120/B5
Copiapó, Chile 138/B6
Copiapó (bay), Chile 138/A6
Copiapó (riv.), Chile 138/A6
Copinsay (isl.), Scotland 15/F2
Coplay, Pa. (18037) 294/L4
Copley, S. Australia 94/F4
Copmanhurst, N.S. Wales 97/G1
Coporito, Venezuela 124/H3
Coporolo (riv.), Angola 115/B6
Coppell, Texas (75019) 303/G2
Coppename (riv.), Suriname 131/C3
Copper (riv.), Alaska 196/J2
Copper (mts.), Ariz. 198/B6
Copperas Cove, Texas (76522) 303/G6
Copper Canyon, Texas (†76226) 303/F1
Copper Center, Alaska (99573) 196/J2
Copper City, Mich. (49917) 250/A1
Copperfield, W. Australia 88/C5
Copperfield, W. Australia 92/B5
Copper Harbor, Mich. (49918) 250/B1
Copperhill, Tenn. (37317) 237/N10
Copper Hill, Va. (24079) 307/H6
Coppermine, Canada 4/C15
Coppermine, N.W.T. 162/E2
Coppermine (riv.), N.W.T. 162/E2
Coppermine, N.W. Terrs. 187/G3
Coppermine (riv.), N.W. Terrs. 187/G3
Copper Mountain, Br. Col. 184/G5
Copperton, Utah (†84006) 304/B3
Copper Valley, Va. (†24141) 307/G7
Coppet, Switzerland 39/B4
Coppock, Iowa (†52654) 229/K6
Coqên, China 77/C5
Coquet (riv.), England 13/F2
Coquí, P. Rico 161/D3
Coquille, Oreg. (97423) 291/C4
Coquille (pt.), Oreg. 291/C4
Coquimatlán, Mexico 150/G7
Coquimbo (reg.), Chile 138/A8
Coquimbo, Chile 120/B6
Coquimbo, Chile 138/A8
Coquitlam, Br. Col. 184/K3
Cora, Ill. (†62280) 222/D6
Cora, Wyo. (82925) 319/C3
Corabia, Romania 45/G4
Coracora, Peru 128/F10
Corail, Haiti 158/A6
Coraki, N.S. Wales 97/G1
Coral (sea) 87/F7
Coral (sea) 88/H2
Coral (sea) 2/S6
Coral, Mich. (49322) 250/D5
Coral (sea), New Caled. 86/G4
Coral (sea), Papua N.G. 85/B7
Coral, Pa. (15731) 294/D5
Coral (bay), Philippines 82/A6
Coral (sea), Queensland 95/C1
Coral (bay), Virgin Is. (U.S.) 161/C4
Coral Cove, Fla. (†33559) 212/D4
Coral Gables, Fla. (33134) 212/B5
Coral Harbour, N.W.T. 162/H2
Coral Harbour, N.W. Terrs. 187/K3
Coral Hills, Md. (†20027) 245/G5
Coral Sea Islands (terr.), Australia 87/E7
CORAL SEA ISLANDS TERR. 95/C2
Coral Sea Islands Territory, /J3
Coral Springs, Fla. (33060) 212/F5
Coralville, Iowa (52241) 229/K5
Coralville (lake), Iowa 229/K5
Coram, Mont. (59913) 262/C2
Coramba, N.S. Wales 97/G2
Corangamite (lake), Victoria 97/B6
Corantijn (riv.), Suriname 131/C3
Coraopolis, Pa. (15108) 294/B4
Corapeake, N.C. (27926) 281/R1
Corato, Italy 34/F4
Corbeil, Ontario 177/E1
Corberrie, Nova Scotia 168/C4
Corbigny, France 28/E4
Corbin, Kansas (67032) 232/E4
Corbin, Ky. (40701) 237/N7
Corbin City, N.J. (†08270) 273/D5
Corbridge, England 13/E3
Corby, England 13/G5
Corcelles-près-Payerne, Switzerland 39/C3
Corcoran, Calif. (93212) 204/F7
Corcoran, Minn. (†55340) 255/F5
Corcovado (gulf), Chile 120/B7
Corcovado (gulf), Chile 138/D4
Corcovado (vol.), Chile 138/D5
Corcubión, Spain 33/B1
Cord, Ark. (72524) 202/H2
Cordaville, Mass. (†01772) 249/H3
Cordele, Georgia (31015) 217/E7
Cordelia, Calif. (†94585) 204/K1
Cordell, Okla. (73632) 288/H4
Cordell Hull (res.), Tenn. 237/K8
Corder, Mo. (64021) 261/E4
Cordesville, S.C. (29434) 296/H5
Cordillera (dept.), Paraguay 144/D4
Cordillo Grounds, S. Australia 94/G2
Córdoba (prov.), Argentina 143/D3
Córdoba, Argentina 2/F7
Córdoba, Argentina 143/D3
Córdoba, Argentina 120/C6
Córdoba (dept.), Colombia 126/C3
Córdoba, Mexico 150/P2
Córdoba (prov.), Spain 33/D3
Córdoba, Spain 33/D4
Córdoba, Spain 7/D5
Cordobés (riv.), Uruguay 145/D3
Cordova, Ala. (35550) 195/D3
Cordova, Alaska (99574) 196/D1
Cordova, Alaska 188/D6
Cordova, Alaska 146/D3
Cordova (bay), Alaska 196/M2
Cordova, Ill. (61242) 222/C2
Cordova, Manitoba 179/C4
Cordova, Md. (21625) 245/O5
Cordova, Nebr. (68330) 264/G4
Cordova, N. Mex. (87523) 274/D2
Córdova, Peru 128/E10
Cordova, S.C. (29039) 296/F5
Cordova, Tenn. (38018) 237/B10
Cordova, U.S. 4/C17
Cordova Mines, Ontario 177/G3
Core (banks), N.C. 281/S5
Core (sound), N.C. 281/S5
Core, W. Va. (26529) 312/F3
Corea, Maine (04624) 243/H7
Coredó (Humboldt) (bay), Colombia 126/B4
Coree South, N.S. Wales 97/C4
Corella, Spain 33/F1
Corey, La. (†71201) 238/F2
Corfield, Queensland 88/G4
Corfield, Queensland 95/B4
Corfu (Kérkira) (isl.), Greece 45/D6
Corfu, N.Y. (14036) 276/D5
Corgémont, Switzerland 39/D2
Cori, Italy 34/F7
Coria, Spain 33/C3
Coria del Río, Spain 33/C4
Corigliano Calabro, Italy 34/F5
Corinda, Queensland 88/K3
Corinda, Queensland 95/A3
Corinda, Queensland 95/D3
Coringa (islets), Australia 87/F7
Coringa (isls.), Coral Sea Is. Terr. 88/H3
Corinna○, Maine (04928) 243/E6
Corinne, Okla. (†74751) 288/R6
Corinne, Sask. 181/G5
Corinne, Utah (84307) 304/B2
Corinne, W. Va. (25826) 312/D7
Corinth, Ark. (†72833) 202/C3
Corinth, Georgia (†30230) 217/B4
Corinth, Greece 45/F7
Corinth (gulf), Greece 45/F6
Corinth, Ky. (41010) 237/M3
Corinth, Miss. (38834) 256/G1
Corinth, N.Y. (12822) 276/N4
Corinth, N. Dak. (†58830) 282/D2
Corinth○, Vt. (05039) 268/C3
Corinth, W. Va. (26713) 312/H4
Corinto, Brazil 132/E7
Corinto, Colombia 126/B6
Corinto, Nicaragua 154/D4
Coriole, Somalia 115/H3
Coripata, Bolivia 136/B5
Corisco (isl.), Equat. Guinea 115/A3
Cork (co.), Ireland 17/D7
Cork, Ireland 7/D3
Cork, Ireland 10/B5
Cork, Ireland 17/E8
Cork (harb.), Ireland 17/E8
Cork (harb.), Ireland 10/B5
Cork, New Bruns. 170/D3
Corker (cay), Belize 154/D2
Corleone, Italy 34/D6
Corley, W. Va. (26616) 312/E5
Çorlu, Turkey 63/B2
Cormorant, Manitoba 179/H3
Cormorant (lake), Manitoba 179/H3
Cormorant, Minn. (†56572) 255/B4
Corn (creek), Ariz. 198/E3
Corn, Okla. (73024) 288/J4
Cornaca, Bolivia 136/C7
Corncake (inlet), N.C. 281/O7
Cornelia, Georgia (30531) 217/E1
Cornélio Procópio, Brazil 132/D8
Cornelius, N.C. (28031) 281/H4
Cornelius, Oreg. (97113) 291/A2
Cornell, Ill. (61319) 222/E3
Cornell, Mich. (49818) 250/B3
Cornell, Wis. (54732) 317/D5
Corner (inlet), Victoria 97/D6
Corner Brook, Newf. 166/C4
Corner Brook, Newf. 162/K6
Cornerstone, Ark. (†72004) 202/G5
Cornersville, Md. (†21613) 245/O6
Cornersville, Miss. (†38659) 256/F1
Cornersville, Tenn. (37047) 237/H10
Cornerville, Ark. (†71667) 202/G6
Cornettes de Bise (mts.), Switzerland 39/C4
Cornfield (pt.), Conn. 210/F3
Cornfields, Ariz. (†86505) 198/F3
Cornhill, New Bruns. 170/E3
Cornhill, Scotland 15/F3
Corning, Ark. (72422) 202/J1
Corning, Calif. (96021) 204/C4
Corning, Iowa (50841) 229/D7
Corning, Kansas (66417) 232/F2
Corning, Mo. (64435) 261/B2
Corning, N.Y. (14830) 276/F6
Corning, Ohio (43730) 284/F6
Corning, Sask. 181/J6
Cornish, Colo. (†80611) 208/L2
Cornish○, Maine (04020) 243/B8
Cornish, Okla. (†73456) 288/L6
Cornish, Utah (84308) 304/B2
Cornish Flat, N.H. (03746) 268/C4
Cornishville, Ky. (40314) 237/M5
Cornland, Ill. (62519) 222/D4
Cornlea, Nebr. (68630) 264/G3
Corno (mt.), Italy 34/D3
Cornucopia, Wis. (54827) 317/D2
Cornville, Ariz. (86325) 198/D4
Cornville○, Maine (†04976) 243/D6
Cornwall○, Conn. (06753) 210/B1
Cornwall (co.), England 13/C7
Cornwall (cape), England 13/B7
Cornwall (isl.), N.W.T. 162/M3
Cornwall (isl.), N.W. Terrs. 187/J2
Cornwall, Ont. 162/J7
Cornwall, Ontario 177/K2
Cornwall, Pa. (17016) 294/K5
Cornwall, Pr. Edward I. 168/E2
Cornwall, Tasmania 99/E3
Cornwall○, Vt. (†05753) 268/A4
Cornwall Bridge, Conn. (06754) 210/B1
Cornwall Center, Conn. (†06796) 210/B1
Cornwall Hollow, Conn. (†06031) 210/B
Cornwallis (isl.), N.W.T. 162/F1
Cornwallis (isl.), N.W. Terrs. 187/J2
Cornwall On Hudson, N.Y. (12518) 276/M8
Cornwell, Fla. (33836) 212/E4
Coro, Venezuela 124/D2
Coro, Venezuela 120/C1
Coroatá, Brazil 132/F3
Corocoro, Bolivia 120/C4
Corocoro, Bolivia 136/A5
Corofin, Ireland 17/C6
Coroico, Bolivia 136/B5
Corolla, N.C. (27927) 281/T2
Coromandel, Brazil 132/E7
Coromandel, N. Zealand 100/E2
Coromandel (pen.), N. Zealand 100/F2
Coromandel (range), N. Zealand 100/E2
Coromandel Coast (reg.), India 68/E6
Coron, Philippines 82/C4
Coron (isl.), Philippines 82/C5
Corona, Ala. (†35546) 195/C3
Corona, Calif. (91720) 204/E11
Corona, N. Mex. (88318) 274/D4
Corona, S. Dak. (57227) 298/R3
Coronaca, S.C. (†29646) 296/C3
Coronach, Sask. 181/F6
Coronada (bay), C. Rica 154/F6
Coronado, Calif. (92118) 204/H11
Coronado (pt.), Philippines 82/C7
Coronado Nat'l Memorial, Ariz. 198/E7
Coronados (gulf), Chile 138/D4
Coronation (isl.), Alaska 196/M2
Coronation, Alberta 182/E3
Coronation (isl.) 5/C16
Coronation (gulf), N.W.T. 162/E2
Coronation (gulf), N.W. Terrs. 187/G3
Coronda, Argentina 143/F6
Coronel, Chile 138/D1
Coronel, Chile 120/B6
Coronel Bogado, Argentina 143/F6
Coronel Bogado, Paraguay 144/D5
Coronel Brandsen, Argentina 143/H7
Coronel Dorrego, Argentina 143/D4
Coronel F. Gabrera, Bolivia 136/E6
Coronel F. Cabrera (mt.), Paraguay 144/B1
Coronel Martínez, Paraguay 144/B5
Coronel Moldes, Argentina 143/C2
Coronel Oviedo, Paraguay 144/C5
Coronel Pringles, Argentina 143/D4
Coronel Suárez, Argentina 143/D4
Coronel Vidal, Argentina 143/E4
Corongo, Peru 128/D7
Coronie (dist.), Suriname 131/C3
Coropuna, Nudo (mt.), Peru 128/F10
Corororoke, Victoria 97/B6
Çorovodë, Albania 45/E5
Corowa, N.S. Wales 97/D4
Corozal, Colombia 126/C3
Corozal, P. Rico 161/D1
Corozal Town, Belize 154/C1
Corozo Pando, Venezuela 124/E3
Corpach, Scotland 15/C4
Corpus Christi, Texas 188/G5
Corpus Christi, Texas 146/J7
Corpus Christi, Texas (*78401) 303/G10
Corpus Christi (bay), Texas 188/G5
Corpus Christi (lake), Texas 303/F9
Corpus Christi N.A.S., Texas 303/G10
Corque, Bolivia 136/B6
Corquín, Honduras 154/C3
Corral, Chile 138/D3
Corral, Idaho (83322) 220/D6
Corral City, Texas (†76226) 303/F1
Corral de Almaguer, Spain 33/E3
Corral de Bustos, Argentina 143/D3
Corrales, N. Mex. (87048) 274/C3
Corralillo, Cuba 158/D1
Corralitos, Calif. (†95076) 204/L4
Corral Viejo, P. Rico 161/C2
Correct, Ind. (†47042) 227/G7
Correctionville, Iowa (51016) 229/B4
Correggio, Italy 34/C2
Corregidor (isl.), Philippines 82/C3
Correll, Minn. (56227) 255/B5
Corrente, Brazil 132/E5
Corrente (riv.), Brazil 132/E6
Correntina, Brazil 132/E6
Corrèze (dept.), France 28/D5
Corrib (lake), Ireland 17/C5
Corrib, Lough (lake), Ireland 10/B4
Corridon, Mo. (†63633) 261/L8
Corrie, Scotland 15/C5
Corrientes (prov.), Argentina 143/E2
Corrientes, Argentina 143/E2
Corrients, Argentina 120/D5
Corrientes (riv.), Argentina 143/E2
Corrientes (cape), Colombia 120/B2
Corrientes (cape), Colombia 126/B5
Corrientes (cape), Cuba 158/A2
Corrientes (inlet), Cuba 158/A2
Corrientes (cape), Mexico 146/H7
Corrientes (cape), Mexico 150/F6
Corrientes (riv.), Peru 128/E4
Corrigan, Texas (75939) 303/K7
Corriganville, Md. (21524) 245/C2
Corrigin, W. Australia 92/B6
Corriverton, Guyana 131/C3
Corrumpa (creek), N. Mex. 274/F2
Corry, Pa. (16407) 294/C2
Corryong, Victoria 97/D5
Corryton, Tenn. (37721) 237/O8
Corse (cape), France 28/B6
Corse du Sud (dept.), France 28/B6
Corserine (mt.), Scotland 15/D5
Corsewall (pt.), Scotland 15/C5
Corsham, England 13/E6
Corsica (isl.), France 7/E4
Corsica (isl.), France 28/B6
Corsica, Pa. (15829) 294/D3
Corsica, S. Dak. (57328) 298/N7
Corsicana, Texas 188/G4
Corsicana, Texas (75110) 303/H5
Corso, Mo. (63377) 261/K4
Corson (inlet), N.J. 273/D5
Corson (co.), S. Dak. 298/G2
Corson, S. Dak. (57019) 298/R6
Cortaro, Ariz. (85230) 198/D6
Corte, France 28/B6
Corte Madera, Calif. (94925) 204/J2
Cortés, Cuba 158/A2
Cortés (inlet), Cuba 158/B2
Cortez, Colo. (81321) 208/B8
Cortez, Fla. (33522) 212/D4
Cortez (mts.), Nev. 266/E2
Cortina d'Ampezzo, Italy 34/D1
Cortland, Ill. (60112) 222/E2
Cortland, Ind. (47228) 227/F7
Cortland, Nebr. (68331) 264/H4
Cortland (co.), N.Y. 276/H5
Cortland, N.Y. (13045) 276/H5
Cortland, Ohio (44410) 284/J3
Cortona, Italy 34/C3
Coruche, Portugal 33/B3
Çoruh (riv.), Turkey 59/D1
Çoruh (riv.), Turkey 63/J2
Çorum (prov.), Turkey 63/F2
Çorum, Turkey 59/B1
Çorum, Turkey 63/F2
Çorum (riv.), Turkey 63/F2
Corumbá, Brazil 120/D4
Corumbá, Brazil 132/B7
Corunna, Ind. (46730) 227/G2
Corunna, Mich. (48817) 250/E6
Corunna, Ontario 177/B5
Corvallis, Mont. (59828) 262/C4
Corvallis, Oreg. 188/B2
Corvallis, Oreg. (97330) 291/D3
Corvo (isl.), Portugal 33/A1
Corvuso, Minn. (†56228) 255/D6
Corwen, Wales 10/E4
Corwen, Wales 13/D5
Corwin, Kansas (†67061) 232/D4
Corwin, Ohio (†45068) 284/B6
Corwin Springs, Mont. (59021) 262/F5
Corwith, Iowa (50430) 229/F3
Cory, Ind. (47846) 227/C6
Corydon, Ind. (47112) 227/E8
Corydon, Iowa (50060) 229/G7
Corydon, Ky. (42406) 237/F5
Coryell (co.), Texas 303/G6
Coryville, Pa. (†16731) 294/F2
Corzoneso, Switzerland 39/G4
Cosalá, Mexico 150/F4
Cosamaloapan de Carpio, Mexico 150/M7
Cosapa, Bolivia 136/A6
Cosautlán de Carvajal, Mexico 150/P1
Cosby, Mo. (64436) 261/C3
Cosby, Tenn. (37722) 237/P9
Cos Cob, Conn. (06807) 210/A4
Coscomatepec de Bravo, Mexico 150/P2
Cosegüina (pt.), Nicaragua 154/D4
Cosenza (prov.), Italy 34/F5
Cosenza, Italy 34/F5
Cosenza, Italy 7/F5
Coshocton (co.), Ohio 284/G5
Coshocton, Ohio (43812) 284/G5
Cosine, Sask. 181/A3
Cosío, Mexico 150/H5
Cosmoledo (isls.), Seychelles 102/G5
Cosmoledo (isls.), Seychelles 118/H1
Cosmo Newbery Aboriginal Reserve, W. Australia 88/C5
Cosmo Newbery Aboriginal Res., W. Australia 92/C5
Cosmopolis, Wash. (98537) 310/B4
Cosmos, Minn. (56228) 255/D6
Cosne-Cours-sur-Loire, France 28/E4
Cosperville, Ind. (†46794) 227/F1
Cosquín, Argentina 143/D3
Cossonay, Switzerland 39/B3
Costa, W. Va. (25051) 312/C6
Costa Azul, Uruguay 145/E5
Costa Brava (reg.), Spain 33/H2
Costa da Caparica, Portugal 33/A1
Costa de Sola (Costa del Sol) (reg.), Spain 33/D4
Costa Mesa, Calif. (*92626) 204/D11
Costa Rica 2/E5
Costa Rica 146/K8
Costa Rica, Bolivia 136/A2
COSTA RICA 154/E5
Costa Rica, Mexico 150/F4
Costa Smeralda (reg.), Italy 34/B4
Costa Verde (reg.), Italy 34/B5
Costello, Pa. (†16720) 294/G2
Costessey, England 13/J5
Costești, Romania 45/G3
Costigan, Maine (04423) 243/F5
Costilla (co.), Colo. 208/J8
Costilla, N. Mex. (87524) 274/D2
Costilla (peak), N. Mex. 274/D2
Cosumnes (riv.), Calif. 204/C9
Coswig, Dresden, E. Germany 22/E3
Coswig, Halle, E. Germany 22/E3
Cotabato, Philippines 85/G4
Cotabato, Philippines 82/D7
Cotacajes (riv.), Bolivia 136/B5
Cotagaita, Bolivia 136/C7
Cotahuasi, Peru 128/F10
Cotati, Calif. (94928) 204/C5
Coteau, N. Dak. (58728) 282/F2
Coteau (hills), Sask. 181/D4
Coteau-du-Lac, Québec 172/C4
Coteau du Missouri (plain), N. Dak. 282/G3
Coteau-Landing, Québec 172/C4
Coteaux, Haiti 158/A6
Côte-d'Or (dept.), France 28/F4
Côte-d'Or (mts.), France 28/F4
Cotentin (pen.), France 28/C3
Côte-Saint-Luc, Québec 172/H4
Côtes de Fer, Haiti 158/B6
Côtes-du-Nord (dept.), France 28/B3
Cotesfield, Nebr. (68829) 264/F3
Cotija de la Paz, Mexico 150/H7
Cotile (lake), La. 238/E4
Coto, Argentina 143/D2
Cotoca, Bolivia 136/D5
Coto Laurel, P. Rico 161/C2
Cotonou, Benin 102/C4

Cyrenaica 357

Crossgar, N. Ireland 17/K3
Crosshaven, Ireland 17/E8
Crosshill, Scotland 15/D5
Cross Hill, S.C. (29332) 296/D3
Cross Junction, Va. (22625) 307/M2
Cross Keys, S.C. (†29379) 296/D2
Cross Lake, Manitoba 179/J3
Crosslake, Minn. (56442) 255/E4
Crossley (mt.), N. Zealand 100/D5
Crossmaglen, N. Ireland 17/H3
Crossmichael, Scotland 15/D6
Crossmolina, Ireland 17/C3
Crossnore, N.C. (28616) 281/F2
Cross Plains, Ind. (47017) 227/G7
Cross Plains, Tenn. (37049) 237/H7
Cross Plains, Texas (76443) 303/E5
Cross Plains, Wis. (53528) 317/G9
Cross River (state), Nigeria 106/F7
Cross Roads, Calif. (†92242) 204/L9
Crossroads, N. Mex. (88114) 274/F5
Cross Roads, Pa. (†17322) 294/J6
Cross Timbers, Mo. (65634) 261/F6
Crosstown, Mo. (†63775) 261/N7
Cross Village, Mich. (49723) 250/D3
Crossville, Ala. (35962) 195/G2
Crossville, Ill. (62827) 222/F5
Crossville, Tenn. (38555) 237/L9
Crosswicks, N.J. (08515) 273/D3
Crosswicks (creek), N.J. 273/D3
Croswell, Mich. (48422) 250/G5
Crotch (lake), Ontario 177/H3
Crothersville, Ind. (47229) 227/F7
Croton (Hartford), Ohio (43013) 284/E5
Crotone, Italy 34/F5
Croton Falls, N.Y. (10519) 276/N8
Croton-on-Hudson, N.Y. (10520) 276/N8
Crouch, Idaho (†83622) 220/B5
Crouseville, Maine (04738) 243/G2
Crow (creek), Colo. 208/L1
Crow (riv.), Minn. 255/F5
Crow, Oreg. (†97401) 291/D4
Crow (creek), S. Dak. 298/A4
Crow (creek), Wyo. 319/H4
Crow Agency, Mont. (59022) 262/J5
Crowborough, England 13/H6
Crow Creek Ind. Res., S. Dak. 298/L5
Crowder, Miss. (38622) 256/D2
Crowder, Okla. (74430) 288/P4
Crowduck (lake), Manitoba 179/G4
Crowdy (head), N.S. Wales 97/G2
Crowell, Texas (79227) 303/E4
Crowfoot, Alberta 182/D4
Crowheart, Wyo. (82512) 319/C2
Crow Ind. Res., Mont. 262/H5
Crowl (creek), N.S. Wales 97/C2
Crow Lake, S. Dak. (†57382) 298/M6
Crowle, England 13/G4
Crowley (lake), Calif. 204/G6
Crowley (co.), Colo. 208/M6
Crowley, Colo. (81033) 208/M6
Crowley, La. (70526) 238/F6
Crowley, Texas (76036) 303/E3
Crowley Lake, Calif. (93546) 204/G6
Crowley's Ridge (mt.), Ark. 202/J2
Crown, Minn. (†55005) 255/E5
Crown (mt.), Virgin Is. (U.S.) 161/A4
Crown City, Ohio (45623) 284/F8
Crown King, Ariz. (86333) 198/C4
Crown Point, Ind. (46307) 227/C2
Crownpoint, N. Mex. (87313) 274/A3
Crown Point, N.Y. (12928) 276/N3
Crown Prince Frederik (isl.), N.W. Terrs. 187/K3
Crownsville, Md. (21032) 245/M4
Crows Landing, Calif. (95313) 204/D6
Crowsnest (pass), Alberta 182/C5
Crowsnest, Br. Col. 184/K5
Crowsnest (pass), Br. Col. 184/K5
Crowville, La. (71230) 238/G2
Crow Wing (co.), Minn. 255/D4
Crow Wing (riv.), Minn. 255/D4
Croydon, England 13/H8
Croydon, England 10/B6
Croydon○, N.H. (†03753) 268/C5
Croydon (peak), N.H. 268/C5
Croydon, Queensland 88/G3
Croydon, Queensland 95/B3
Croydon, Utah (84018) 304/C2
Croydon, Victoria 88/M7
Croydon, Victoria 97/K5
Croydon Branch, Sugar (riv.), N.H. 268/C5
Crozet (isls.) 2/M8
Crozet, Va. (22932) 307/L4
Crozier (chan.), N.W. Terrs. 187/G2
Crozier, Va. (23039) 307/N5
Cruces, Cuba 158/E2
Cruces, Cuba 156/B2
Cruden Bay, Scotland 15/G3
Cruger, Miss. (38924) 256/D4
Cruillas, Mexico 150/K4
Crum (creek), Pa. 294/M7
Crum, W. Va. (25669) 312/B7
Crumlin, N. Ireland 17/J2
Crum Lynne, Pa. (19022) 294/M7
Crummies, Ky. (40821) 237/P7
Crump, Mich. (†48634) 250/E5
Crump (lake), Oreg. 291/H5
Crump, Tenn. (38327) 237/E10
Crumpton (pt.), Dominica 161/F5
Crumpton, Md. (21628) 245/P4
Crumrod, Ark. (72328) 202/H5
Crumstown, Ind. (†46554) 227/E1
Crusheen, Ireland 17/D6
Cruso, N.C. (†28716) 281/D4
Cruta, Honduras 154/F3
Crutchfield, Ky. (42034) 237/D7
Crutwell, Sask. 181/E2
Cruz (cape), Cuba 156/C3
Cruz (cape), Cuba 158/G4
Cruz Alta, Brazil 120/D5
Cruz Alta, Brazil 132/C10
Cruz Bay, Virgin Is. (U.S.) 161/C4
Cruz del Eje, Argentina 143/C3
Cruz del Eje, Argentina 120/C6
Cruz de Piedra, Uruguay 145/E3
Cruz de San Pedro, Uruguay 145/E2
Cruzeiro, Brazil 135/D3
Cruzeiro do Sol, Brazil 120/B3
Cruzeiro do Sul, Brazil 132/G10
Cruz Grande, Chile 138/A7
Crysler, Ontario 177/J2
Crystal (mts.), Congo 115/B4
Crystal (lake), Conn. 210/F1
Crystal (pond), Conn. 210/G1
Crystal (bay), Fla. 212/D3
Crystal (mts.), Gabon 115/B4
Crystal, Ind. (†47527) 227/D8
Crystal○, Maine (†04747) 243/G4
Crystal, Mich. (48818) 250/E5
Crystal (lake), Mich. 250/C4
Crystal, Minn. (†55428) 255/G5
Crystal, N.H. (†03591) 268/E2
Crystal (lake), N.H. 268/E5
Crystal, N. Mex. (†86504) 274/A2
Crystal, N. Dak. (58222) 282/P2
Crystal (lake), Vt. 268/C2
Crystal, W. Va. (†24747) 312/D8
Crystal Bay (Orono), Minn. (55323) 255/F5
Crystal Bay, Nev. (89402) 266/A3
Crystal Beach, Texas (77650) 303/K8
Crystal Brook, S. Australia 94/E5
Crystal City, Manitoba 179/C5
Crystal City, Mo. (63019) 261/M6
Crystal City, Texas (78839) 303/E9
Crystal Falls, Mich. (49920) 250/A2
Crystal Falls, Ontario 177/E1
Crystal Hill, Va. (24539) 307/L7
Crystal Lake, Conn. (†06066) 210/F1
Crystal Lake, Fla. (†32463) 212/D6
Crystal Lake, Ill. (60014) 222/E1
Crystal Lake, Iowa (50432) 229/F2
Crystal Lake Park, Mo. (†63101) 261/O3
Crystal Lakes, Ohio (†45341) 284/C6
Crystal River, Fla. (32629) 212/D3
Crystal Springs, Ark. (†71968) 202/D5
Crystal Springs (res.), Calif. 204/J3
Crystal Springs, Fla. (33524) 212/D3
Crystal Springs, Georgia (†30105) 217/B2
Crystal Springs, Kansas (†67058) 232/D4
Crystal Springs, Miss. (39059) 256/D7
Crystal Springs, N. Dak. (58427) 282/L6
Crystal Springs, Sask. 181/F3
Crystal Valley, Mich. (†49420) 250/C5
Csabrendek, Hungary 41/D3
Csákvár, Hungary 41/E3
Csanádpalota, Hungary 41/F3
Csenger, Hungary 41/G3
Csepel, Hungary 41/E3
Csepelsziget (isl.), Hungary 41/E3
Csepreg, Hungary 41/D3
Csongrád (co.), Hungary 41/F3
Csongrád, Hungary 41/E3
Csorna, Hungary 41/D3
Csorvás, Hungary 41/F3
Csurgó, Hungary 41/D3
Ctesiphon (ruins), Iraq 66/D4
Cúa, Venezuela 124/E2
Cuadro Nacional, Argentina 143/C3
Cuamba, Mozambique 118/F2
Cuando (riv.), Angola 115/C7
Cuando (riv.), Zambia 115/D7
Cuando Cubango (dist.), Angola 115/C7
Cuangar, Angola 115/C7
Cuango (riv.) 102/D5
Cuango, Angola 115/C5
Cuango (riv.), Angola 115/C5
Cuanza (riv.), Angola 102/D6
Cuanza (riv.), Angola 115/C5
Cuanza-Norte (dist.), Angola 115/B5
Cuanza-Sul (dist.), Angola 115/C6
Cuao (riv.), Venezuela 124/E5
Cua Rao, Vietnam 72/E3
Cuareim (riv.), Uruguay 145/B1
Cuaró, Uruguay 145/D2
Cuatrociénagas de Carranza, Mexico 150/H3
Cuatro Compañeros, Cuba 158/G3
Cuatro Ojos, Bolivia 136/D5
Cuauhtémoc, Mexico 150/F2
Cuautepec de Hinojosa, Mexico 150/K6
Cuautitlán de Romero Rubio, Mexico 150/L1
Cuautla Morelos, Mexico 150/L2
Cub (creek), Utah 304/C1
Cub (creek), Va. 307/L6
Cuba 2/E4
Cuba 146/L7
Cuba, Ala. (36907) 195/B6
CUBA 156/B2
CUBA 158
Cuba, Ill. (61427) 222/C3
Cuba, Ind. (†47460) 227/D6
Cuba, Kansas (66940) 232/E2
Cuba, Mo. (65453) 261/K6
Cuba, N. Mex. (87013) 274/B2
Cuba, N.Y. (14727) 276/D6
Cuba (chan.), N. Zealand 100/D7
Cuba, Ohio (45114) 284/C7
Cuba, Portugal 33/C3
Cuba City, Wis. (53807) 317/F10
Cubage, Ky. (40822) 237/O7
Cubagua (isl.), Venezuela 124/F2
Cuballing, W. Australia 92/B2
Cubango (riv.), Angola 102/D6
Cubango (riv.), Angola 115/C7
Cubango (riv.), Namibia 118/B3
Cubatão, Brazil 135/C3
Cube (mt.), N.H. 268/D4
Cubero, N. Mex. (87014) 274/B3
Cubiro, Venezuela 124/D3
Cub Run, Ky. (42729) 237/J6
Çubuk, Turkey 63/E2
Cubulco, Guatemala 154/B3
Cuchara, Colo. (81055) 208/J8
Cuchi, Angola 115/C6
Cuchi, Angola 102/D6
Cuchillo, N. Mex. (87932) 274/B5
Cuchillo-Có, Argentina 143/D4
Cuchillo Negro (creek), N. Mex. 274/B5
Cuchivero, Venezuela 124/F4
Cuchivero (riv.), Venezuela 124/F4
Cuckfield, England 13/G6
Cuckfield, England 10/F5
Cucumber, W. Va. (24826) 312/C8
Cúcuta, Colombia 126/D4
Cúcuta, Colombia 120/B2
Cudahy, Calif. (90201) 204/C5
Cudahy, Wis. (53110) 317/M2
Cudal, N.S. Wales 97/E3
Cuddalore, India 68/E6
Cuddapah, India 68/D6
Cuddeback (lake), Calif. 204/H8
Cuddy, Pa. (15031) 294/B5
Cudgewa, Victoria 97/D5
Cudillero, Spain 33/C1
Cudjoe (key), Fla. 212/E7
Cudrefin, Switzerland 39/D3
Cudworth, Sask. 181/F3
Cue, W. Australia 88/B5
Cue, W. Australia 92/B4
Cuéllar, Spain 33/D2
Cuéllar-Baza, Spain 33/E4
Cuemaní (riv.), Colombia 126/D7
Cuenca, Ecuador 120/B3
Cuenca, Ecuador 128/C4
Cuenca (prov.), Spain 33/E2
Cuenca, Spain 33/E2
Cuenca, Sierra de (range), Spain 33/F3
Cuencamé de Ceniceros, Mexico 150/H4
Cuernavaca, Mexico 150/L2
Cuero, Texas (77954) 303/G8
Cuervo, N. Mex. (88417) 274/E3
Cuervo (creek), N. Mex. 274/E3
Cueto, Cuba 158/J3
Cuevas, Miss. (†39571) 256/F10
Cuevas del Almanzora, Spain 33/F4
Cuevas de Vinromá, Spain 33/F2
Cuevo, Bolivia 136/D7
Cufré, Uruguay 145/B5
Cuiabá, Brazil 120/D4
Cuiabá, Brazil 132/C6
Cuiabá (riv.), Brazil 132/B7
Cuicatlán, Mexico 150/L8
Cuicuina, Nicaragua 154/E4
Cuilapa, Guatemala 154/B3
Cuilapa Miravalles (vol.), C. Rica 154/E5
Cuilcagh (mt.), Ireland 17/F3
Cuilco, Guatemala 154/B3
Cuillin (hills), Scotland 15/B3
Cuillin (sound), Scotland 10/C2
Cuillin (sound), Scotland 15/B3
Cuilo, Angola 115/C5
Cuitlahuac, Mexico 150/P2
Cuito (riv.), Angola 115/C7
Cuito-Cuanavale, Angola 115/C7
Cuitzeo (lake), Mexico 150/J7
Cuivre (riv.), Mo. 261/N2
Cujmir, Romania 45/F3
Cukmantl, Czech. 41/D1
Çukur, Turkey 63/F3
Çukurca, Turkey 63/K4
Culaba, Philippines 82/E5
Cu Lao, Hon (isls.), Vietnam 72/F5
Culberson, N.C. (28903) 281/A4
Culberson (co.), Texas 303/C11
Culbertson, Mont. (59218) 262/M2
Culbertson, Nebr. (69024) 264/C4
Culcairn, N.S. Wales 97/D4
Culdaff, Ireland 17/G1
Culdaff (bay), Ireland 17/G1
Culdesac, Idaho (83524) 220/B3
Cul-de-Sac du Marin (bay), Martinique 161/D7
Culebra (creek), Colo. 208/H8
Culebra (peak), Colo. 208/J8
Culebra, P. Rico 161/G1
Culebra (isl.), P. Rico 161/G1
Culebra (isl.), P. Rico 156/G1
Culebras, Peru 128/C7
Culebrinas (riv.), P. Rico 161/A1
Culebrita (isl.), P. Rico 161/G2
Culemborg, Netherlands 27/G5
Culgoa (riv.), N.S. Wales 97/D1
Culgoa (riv.), Queensland 95/C6
Culiacán, Mexico 150/F4
Culiacán, Mexico 146/H7
Culion, Philippines 82/C5
Culion (isl.), Philippines 82/B5
Cullasaja, N.C. (†28734) 281/C4
Cullburra-Orient Point, N.S. Wales 97/F4
Cullen, La. (71021) 238/D1
Cullen, Sask. 181/J6
Cullen, Scotland 15/F3
Cullen, Va. (23934) 307/L6
Cullen Bullen, N.S. Wales 97/F3
Culleoka, Tenn. (38451) 237/G10
Cullera, Spain 33/F3
Cullin (lake), Ireland 17/C4
Cullison, Kansas (†67124) 232/D4
Cullman (co.), Ala. 195/E2
Cullman, Ala. (35055) 195/E2
Culloden, Georgia (31016) 217/D5
Culloden, W. Va. (25510) 312/B6
Cullom, Ill. (60929) 222/E3
Cullomburg, Ala. (36920) 195/B7
Cullompton, England 13/D7
Cullowhee, N.C. (28723) 281/C4
Cully, Switzerland 39/C4
Cullybackey, N. Ireland 17/J2
Culotte (lake), Québec 172/C2
Culp, Alberta 182/B2
Culp Creek, Oreg. (97427) 291/E4
Culpeper (co.), Va. 307/M3
Culpeper, Va. (22701) 307/M4
Culpepper (isl.), Ecuador 128/B8
Culpina, Bolivia 136/C7
Culross, Manitoba 179/E5
Culross, Scotland 10/B1
Culross, Scotland 15/C1
Culta, Bolivia 136/B6
Cults, Scotland 15/F3
Cultus (lake), Oreg. 291/F4
Cultus Lake, Br. Col. 184/M3
Culuene (riv.), Brazil 132/C6
Culver, Ind. (46511) 227/E2
Culver, Kansas (67435) 232/E3
Culver, Minn. (55727) 255/F4
Culver, Oreg. (97734) 291/F3
Culver (pt.), W. Australia 88/D6
Culver (pt.), W. Australia 92/D6
Culver City, Calif. (90230) 204/B10
Culverden, N. Zealand 100/D5
Culvers (lake), N.J. 273/D1
Culverton, Georgia (†31087) 217/G4
Cuma, Angola 115/B6
Cumaná, Venezuela 120/C2
Cumaná, Venezuela 124/F2
Cumanacoa, Venezuela 124/F2
Cumanayagua, Cuba 158/E2
Cumaria, Peru 128/F7
Cumback, Ind. (†47501) 227/C7
Cumbal, Colombia 126/B7
Cumberland (riv.) 188/J3
Cumberland (plat.), Ala. 195/F1
Cumberland, Br. Col. 184/E5
Cumberland (sound), Canada 4/C13
Cumberland (isl.), Georgia 217/K9
Cumberland (co.), Ill. 222/E4
Cumberland, Ind. (46229) 227/E5
Cumberland, Iowa (50843) 229/D6
Cumberland (co.), Ky. 237/L7
Cumberland, Ky. (40823) 237/R6
Cumberland (lake), Ky. 237/M7
Cumberland (mt.), Ky. 237/P7
Cumberland (riv.), Ky. 237/K8
Cumberland (co.), Maine 243/C8
Cumberland, Md. (21502) 245/D2
Cumberland, Md. 245/80
Cumberland, Md. 188/L3
Cumberland (basin), New Bruns. 170/F3
Cumberland (co.), N.J. 273/C5
Cumberland (co.), N.C. 281/M4
Cumberland, N.C. (28331) 281/M5
Cumberland (pen.), N.W.T. 162/K2
Cumberland (pen.), N.W. Terrs. 187/M3
Cumberland (sound), N.W.T. 146/N3
Cumberland (sound), N.W.T. 162/K2
Cumberland (sound), N.W. Terrs. 187/M3
Cumberland (co.), Nova Scotia 168/D3
Cumberland (basin), Nova Scotia 168/D3
Cumberland, Ohio (43732) 284/G6
Cumberland, Okla. (†73446) 288/N6
Cumberland, Ontario 177/J2
Cumberland (co.), Pa. 294/H5
Cumberland (isls.), Queensland 88/H4
Cumberland (isls.), Queensland 95/D4
Cumberland (bay), St. Vin. & Grens. 161/A8
Cumberland (lake), Sask. 181/J1
Cumberland (co.), Tenn. 237/L9
Cumberland (plat.), Tenn. 237/L9
Cumberland (riv.), Tenn. 237/K8
Cumberland (co.), Va. 307/M6
Cumberland, Va. (23040) 307/M6
Cumberland (mt.), Va. 307/B7
Cumberland, Wash. (†98022) 310/D3
Cumberland, Wis. (54829) 317/C4
Cumberland Bay, New Bruns. 170/E2
Cumberland Beach, Ontario 177/E3
Cumberland Center, Maine (04021) 243/C8
Cumberland Center○, Maine (04021) 243/C8
Cumberland City, Tenn. (37050) 237/F8
Cumberland Furnace, Tenn. (37051) 237/G8
Cumberland Gap, Tenn. (37724) 237/O8
Cumberland Gap Nat'l Hist. Park, Ky. 237/P7
Cumberland Gap Nat'l Hist. Park, Tenn. 237/O7
Cumberland Gap Nat'l Hist. Park, Va. 307/A7
Cumberland House, Sask. 181/J2
Cumberland Island Nat'l Seashore, Georgia 217/K9
Cumbernauld, Scotland 15/C1
Cumbre del Laudo (mt.), Argentina 143/C2
Cumbre Negra, Cerro (mt.), Argentina 143/C5
Cumbre Negra, Cerro (mt.), Chile 138/E5
Cumbria (co.), England 13/D3
Cumbrian (mts.), England 13/D3
Cumbum, India 68/D5
Cumby, Texas (75433) 303/J4
Cuming (co.), Nebr. 264/H3
Cummaquid, Mass. (02637) 249/N6
Cumming, Georgia (30130) 217/D2
Cumming, Iowa (50061) 229/F6
Cummings, Kansas (66016) 232/G2
Cummings, N. Dak. (58223) 282/S4
Cummings, S.C. (†29944) 296/E6
Cummingsville, Tenn. (†38583) 237/L9
Cummington○, Mass. (01026) 249/C3
Cummins, S. Australia 94/D6
Cumnock, N.S. Wales 97/E3
Cumnock, N.C. (27237) 281/L3
Cumnock and Holmhead, Scotland 10/D3
Cumnock and Holmhead, Scotland 15/D5
Cumpas, Mexico 150/E1
Çumra, Turkey 63/E4
Cuñapirú, Uruguay 145/D2
Cuñapirú, Arroyo (riv.), Uruguay 145/D2
Cunapo, Trin. & Tob. 161/B10
Cuñare, Colombia 126/D7
Cunaviche, Venezuela 124/E4
Cunco, Chile 138/E2
Cuncumén, Coquimbo, Chile 138/A9
Cuncumén, Santiago, Chile 138/F4
Cundeelee Aboriginal Reserve, W. Australia 88/C6
Cundeelee Aboriginal Res., W. Australia 92/C5
Cunderdin, W. Australia 92/B5
Cundiff, Ky. (42730) 237/L7
Cundinamarca (dept.), Colombia 126/C5
Cundiyo, N. Mex. (87522) 274/D3
Cunduacán, Mexico 150/N7
Cundys Harbor, Maine (04011) 243/D8
Cunene (riv.) 102/D6
Cunene (dist.), Angola 115/C7
Cunene (dam), Angola 115/B7
Cunene (riv.), Angola 115/B7
Cuneo (prov.), Italy 34/A2
Cuneo, Italy 34/A2
Çüngüş, Turkey 63/H3
Cunnamulla, Australia 87/E8
Cunnamulla, Queensland 95/C5
Cunnamulla, Queensland 88/H5
Cunningham, Kansas (67035) 232/D4
Cunningham, Ky. (42035) 237/D7
Cunningham, N.C. (†27343) 281/L1
Cunningham, Tenn. (37052) 237/G8
Cunningham, Wash. (99327) 310/G4
Cuorgnè, Italy 34/A2
Cupar, Sask. 181/G5
Cupar, Scotland 15/E4
Cupar, Scotland 10/E2
Cupertino, Calif. (95014) 204/K3
Cupica (gulf), Colombia 126/B4
Cupids, Newf. 166/D2
Ćuprija, Yugoslavia 45/E4
Cuprum, Idaho (†83612) 220/B4
Cupsuptic (riv.), Maine 243/B5
Cuquenán (riv.), Venezuela 124/H5
Cuquiari (riv.), Colombia 126/E7
Curaçá, Brazil 132/G5
Curaçao (isl.), Neth. Ant. 161/G7
Curaçao (isl.), Neth. Ant. 156/E4
Curacautín, Chile 138/E2
Curacaví, Chile 138/G3
Curahuara de Carangas, Bolivia 136/A5
Curahuara de Pacajes, Bolivia 136/A5
Curanilahue, Chile 138/D1
Curaray (riv.), Ecuador 128/D3
Curaumilla (pt.), Chile 138/F3
Curdsville, Ky. (42334) 237/G5
Curecanti Nat'l Rec. Area, Colo. 208/F6
Curepipe, Mauritius 118/G5
Curepto, Chile 138/A10
Curiapo, Venezuela 124/H3
Curiche, Bolivia 136/D6
Curicó, Chile 120/B6
Curicó, Chile 138/A10
Curieuse (isl.), Seychelles 118/H5
Curitiba, Brazil 132/D9
Curitiba, Brazil 120/F5
Curitiba, Brazil 135/B4
Curlew, Iowa (50527) 229/D3
Curlew (isls.), La. 238/M7
Curlew, Wash. (99118) 310/G2
Curlew (lake), Wash. 310/G2
Curlewis, N.S. Wales 97/F2
Curllsville, Pa. (16221) 294/D3
Curnamona, S. Australia 94/F4
Curragh, The, Ireland 17/H5
Curragh, The (racecourse), Ireland 10/C4
Currais Novos, Brazil 132/G4
Curran, Ill. (62632) 222/D4
Curran, Mich. (48728) 250/F4
Currant, Nev. (†89314) 266/F4
Currawilla, Queensland 95/B5
Current (riv.), Ark. 202/J1
Current (riv.), Mo. 261/K8
Currie, Minn. (56123) 255/C6
Currie, Nev. (†89301) 266/G2
Currie, N.C. (28435) 281/N6
Currie, Scotland 15/D2
Currie, Tasmania 99/A1
Currituck (co.), N.C. 281/S2
Currituck, N.C. (27929) 281/T2
Currituck (sound), N.C. 281/T2
Curry, Alaska (†99676) 196/J2
Curry (co.), N. Mex. 274/F4
Curry (co.), Oreg. 291/C5
Curryville, Mo. (63339) 261/K4
Curryville, Pa. (16631) 294/F5
Curtea de Argeş, Romania 45/G3
Curtice, Ohio (43412) 284/D2
Curtin, Oreg. (97428) 291/D4
Curtina, Uruguay 145/C3
Curtis, Ark. (71728) 202/D6
Curtis, La. (†71101) 238/C2
Curtis, Mich. (49820) 250/D2
Curtis, Nebr. (69025) 264/D4
Curtis, Okla. (†73852) 288/H2
Curtis (isl.), Queensland 88/J4
Curtis (isl.), Queensland 95/D4
Curtis, Wash. (98538) 310/B4
Curtis Group (isls.), Tasmania 99/C1
Curtiss, Wis. (54422) 317/F6
Curtis Station, Miss. (†38606) 256/D2
Curtisville, Ind. (†46036) 227/F4
Curuá (riv.), Brazil 132/C4
Curuçá, Brazil 132/E3
Curuguaty, Paraguay 144/E4
Curup, Indonesia 85/C6
Cururú, Bolivia 136/D4
Cururupu, Brazil 132/E3
Curutú (riv.), Venezuela 124/G5
Curuzú Cuatiá, Argentina 143/G5
Curuzú Cuatiá, Argentina 120/D5
Curve, Tenn. (†38063) 237/B9
Curvelo, Brazil 132/E7
Curwensville, Pa. (16833) 294/E4
Curwood (mt.), Mich. 250/A2
Cusachón (isl.), Colombia 126/D1
Cusco, Peru 120/B4
Cusco (dept.), Peru 128/F9
Cusco (Cuzco), Peru 128/F9
Cushendall, N. Ireland 17/J1
Cushing, Iowa (51018) 229/B4
Cushing○, Maine (04563) 243/E7
Cushing, Minn. (56443) 255/D4
Cushing, Nebr. (†68873) 264/F3
Cushing, Okla. (74023) 288/N3
Cushing, Texas (75760) 303/J6
Cushing, Wis. (54006) 317/A4
Cushman, Ark. (72526) 202/G2
Cushman, Mass. (01002) 249/D3
Cushman, Oreg. (†97439) 291/D4
Cushman (lake), Wash. 310/B3
Cusiana (riv.), Colombia 126/D5
Cusick, Wash. (99119) 310/H2
Cuslett, Newf. 166/C2
Cusset, France 28/E4
Cusseta, Ala. (36852) 195/H5
Cusseta, Georgia (31805) 217/C6
Cusson, Minn. (†55771) 255/F2
Custar, Ohio (43511) 284/C3
Custer (co.), Colo. 208/J6
Custer (co.), Idaho 220/D5
Custer, Ky. (40115) 237/J5
Custer, Mich. (49405) 250/C5
Custer (co.), Mont. 262/L4
Custer, Mont. (59024) 262/J4
Custer (co.), Nebr. 264/E3
Custer (co.), Okla. 288/H3
Custer (co.), S. Dak. 298/B6
Custer, S. Dak. (57730) 298/B6
Custer, Wash. (98240) 310/C2
Custer Battlefield Nat'l Mon., Mont. 262/J5
Custer City, Okla. (73639) 288/J3
Custer City, Pa. (16725) 294/E2
Custer Park, Ill. (60418) 222/E2
Cut Bank, Mont. (59427) 262/D2
Cut Bank (creek), Mont. 262/D2
Cut Bank (creek), N. Dak. 282/H2
Cutbank, Sask. 181/E4
Cutchogue-New Suffolk, N.Y. (11935) 276/P8
Cutervo, Peru 128/C6
Cuthbert, Georgia (31740) 217/C7
Cut Knife, Sask. 181/B3
Cutler, Calif. (93615) 204/F7
Cutler, Ill. (62238) 222/D5
Cutler, Ind. (46920) 227/D4
Cutler, Maine (04626) 243/J6
Cutler○, Maine (04626) 243/J6
Cutler, Ohio (45724) 284/G7
Cutler Ridge, Fla. (33157) 212/F6
Cutlerville, Mich. (49508) 250/D6
Cut Off, La. (70345) 238/K7
Cutra (lake), Ireland 17/D5
Cutral-Có, Argentina 143/C4
Cutshin, Ky. (41732) 237/P6
Cuttaburra (creek), N.S. Wales 97/C1
Cuttack, India 54/K7
Cuttack, India 68/F4
Cutten, Calif. (95534) 204/A3
Cuttingsville, Vt. (05738) 268/B4
Cuttyhunk, Mass. (02713) 249/L7
Cuttyhunk (isl.), Mass. 249/L7
Cuvier (isl.), N. Zealand 100/E2
Cuvier (cape), W. Australia 88/A4
Cuvier (cape), W. Australia 92/A4
Cuvo (riv.), Angola 115/B6
Cuxhaven, W. Germany 22/C2
Cuya, Chile 138/B2
Cuyabeno, Ecuador 128/E3
Cuyahoga (co.), Ohio 284/G3
Cuyahoga (riv.), Ohio 284/H10
Cuyahoga Falls, Ohio (*44221) 284/G3
Cuyahoga Heights, Ohio (†44101) 284/H9
Cuyama, Calif. (93214) 204/F9
Cuyama (riv.), Calif. 204/E8
Cuyapaipe Ind. Res., Calif. 204/J11
Cuyk, Netherlands 27/H5
Cuylerville, N.Y. (†14481) 276/E5
Cuyo, Philippines 82/C5
Cuyo (isl.), Philippines 82/C5
Cuyo (isls.), Philippines 82/C5
Cuyo (isls.), Philippines 85/G3
Cuyocuyo, Peru 128/H10
Cuyo East (passage), Philippines 82/C5
Cuyo West (passage), Philippines 82/C5
Cuyuna, Minn. (†56444) 255/E4
Cuyuna (range), Minn. 255/D4
Cuyuni (riv.) 120/C2
Cuyuni (riv.), Guyana 131/B2
Cuyuni (riv.), Venezuela 124/H4
Cuyu Tigni, Nicaragua 154/F3
Cuzco, Ind. (†47432) 227/D8
Cuzzart, W. Va. (26530) 312/H3
Čvrsnica (mt.), Yugoslavia 45/C4
Cwmamman, Wales 13/D6
Cwmbran, Wales 13/B6
Cyangugu, Rwanda 115/E4
Cyclades (isls.), Greece 45/G7
Cycle, N.C. (27015) 281/H2
Cyclone, Ind. (†46041) 227/E4
Cyclone, Pa. (16726) 294/E2
Cyclone, W. Va. (24827) 312/C7
Cygnet, Ohio (43413) 284/C3
Cygnet, Tasmania 99/C5
Cylinder, Iowa (50528) 229/D2
Cylon, Wis. (†54017) 317/B5
Cymric, Sask. 181/G4
Cynthia, Alberta 182/C3
Cynthiana, Ind. (47612) 227/B8
Cynthiana, Ky. (41031) 237/N4
Cynthiana, Ohio (45624) 284/D7
Cypert, Ark. (†72366) 202/J5
Cypress, Ala. (35454) 195/C5
Cypress (hills), Alberta 182/E5
Cypress (bayou), Ark. 202/F3
Cypress, Calif. (90630) 204/D11
Cypress, Fla. (32432) 212/A1
Cypress (lake), Fla. 212/E3
Cypress, Ill. (62923) 222/D6
Cypress, Ind. (†47708) 227/B9
Cypress (pond), Ind. 227/B8
Cypress, La. (71420) 238/D3
Cypress (hills), Sask. 181/B6
Cypress (lake), Sask. 181/B6
Cypress Gardens, Fla. (33880) 212/E3
Cypress Hills Prov. Park, Alberta 182/E5
Cypress Hills Prov. Park, Sask. 181/B6
Cypress Inn, Tenn. (38452) 237/F10
Cypress Prov. Park, Br. Col. 184/K3
Cypress Quarters, Fla. (†33472) 212/F4
Cypress River, Manitoba 179/D5
Cyprus 2/L4
Cyprus 54/E6
CYPRUS 59/B2
CYPRUS 63/E5
Cyrenaica (reg.), Libya 102/E1
Cyrenaica (reg.), Libya 111/D1

358 Cyrene

Cyrene (Shahat), Libya 111/D1
Cyrene, Mo. (†63334) 261/K4
Cyril, Okla. (73029) 288/K5
Cyrus, Minn. (56323) 255/C5
Czar, Alberta 182/E3
Czar, W. Va. (†26224) 312/F5
Czarna Białostocka, Poland 47/F2
Czarnków, Poland 47/C2
Czechoslovakia 2/K3
Czechoslovakia 7/F4
CZECHOSLOVAKIA 41
Czechowice-Dziedzice, Poland 47/D4
Czech Socialist Rep., Czech. 41/B1
Czeladź, Poland 47/B4
Czersk, Poland 47/D2
Częstochowa (prov.), Poland 47/D3
Częstochowa, Poland 47/D3
Częstochwa, Poland 7/F3
Człuchów, Poland 47/C2

D

Da'an (Talai), China 77/K2
Daaquam, Québec 172/H3
Dabajuro, Venezuela 124/C2
Dabakala, Ivory Coast 106/D7
Dabas, Hungary 41/E3
Daba Shan (range), China 77/G5
Dabeiba, Colombia 126/B4
Dabhoi, India 68/C4
Dabney, Ind. (†47023) 227/G6
Dabob (bay), Wash. 310/C3
Dabola, Guinea 106/B6
Dabou, Ivory Coast 106/D7
Daboya, Ghana 106/D7
Dąbrowa Górnicza, Poland 47/B3
Dąbrowa Tarnowska, Poland 47/E3
Dăbuleni, Romania 45/F4
Dacca (cap.), Bangladesh 54/L7
Dacca (cap.), Bangladesh 68/G4
Dachau, W. Germany 22/D4
Dačice, Czech. 41/C2
Dac Lac, Cao Nguyen (plat.), Vietnam 72/F4
Dacoma, Okla. (73731) 288/J1
Dacono, Colo. (80514) 208/K2
Dacre, Ontario 177/G2
Dacula, Georgia (30211) 217/E3
Dacusville, S.C. (†29640) 296/B2
Dadanawa, Guyana 131/B4
Daday, Turkey 63/E2
Dade (co.), Fla. 212/F6
Dade (co.), Georgia 217/A1
Dade (co.), Mo. 261/E8
Dade City, Fla. (33525) 212/D3
Dadeville, Ala. (36853) 195/G5
Dadeville, Mo. (65635) 261/E8
Dadra and Nagar Haveli (terr.), India 68/C4
Dads (lake), Nebr. 264/D2
Dadu, Pakistan 68/B3
Dadu, Pakistan 59/J4
Dăeni, Romania 45/J3
Daer (res.), Scotland 15/E5
Daet, Philippines 85/G3
Daet, Philippines 82/D3
Dafang, China 77/G6
Dafna, Israel 65/D1
Dafoe, Sask. 181/G4
Dafter, Mich. (49724) 250/E2
Dagabur, Ethiopia 111/H6
Dagana, Senegal 106/A5
Dagda, U.S.S.R. 53/D2
Dagelet (Ullŭng) (isl.), S. Korea 81/E5
Dagestan A.S.S.R., U.S.S.R. 48/E5
Dagestan A.S.S.R., U.S.S.R. 52/G6
Dagestanskiye Ogni, U.S.S.R. 52/G6
Daggett, Calif. (92327) 204/H9
Daggett, Mich. (49821) 250/B3
Daggett (co.), Utah 304/E3
Dagmar, Mont. (59219) 262/M2
Dagö (Hiiumaa) (isl.), U.S.S.R. 52/B3
Dagsboro, Del. (19930) 245/S6
Dagua, Colombia 126/B6
Daguan, China 77/F6
D'Aguilar (range), Tasmania 99/B4
Dagupan, Philippines 82/C2
Daguscahonda, Pa. (†15853) 294/E3
Dagus Mines, Pa. (15831) 294/E3
Dahab, Egypt 111/F2
Dahana (des.), Saudi Arabia 54/F7
Dahana (des.), Saudi Arabia 59/E4
Dahinda, Ill. (61428) 222/C3
Dahinda, Sask. 181/G6
Da Hingan Ling (Great Khingan) (range), China 54/O5
Da Hingan Ling (range), China 77/J3
Dahlak (arch.), Ethiopia 111/H4
Dahlak (arch.), Ethiopia 59/D6
Dahlak (isl.), Ethiopia 59/D6
Dahlak (isl.), Ethiopia 111/H4
Dahlem, W. Germany 22/E4
Dahlen, N. Dak. (58224) 282/P3
Dahlgren, Ill. (62828) 222/E5
Dahlgren, Va. (22448) 307/O4
Dahlia, N. Mex. (†87711) 274/D3
Dahlonega, Georgia (30533) 217/D1
Dahme, E. Germany 22/E3
Dai (mt.), Japan 81/F6
Dailekh, Nepal 68/E3
Dailey, Colo. (†80728) 208/O1
Dailly, Scotland 15/D5
Daimanji (mt.), Japan 81/F5
Daimiel, Spain 33/E3
Daingean, Ireland 17/G5
Daingerfield, Texas (75638) 303/K4
Daio (cape), Japan 81/H6
Daiquirí, Cuba 158/J4
Daireaux, Argentina 143/D4
Dairût, Egypt 111/J4
Dairy, Oreg. (97625) 291/F5
Dairy Flat-Redvale, N. Zealand 100/B1
Dairyland, Wis. (†54830) 317/B3
Daisen-Oki National Park, Japan 81/F6
Daisetsu (mt.), Japan 81/L2
Daisetsu-Zan National Park, Japan 81/L2
Daisetta, Texas (77533) 303/K7
Daisy, Ark. (†71950) 202/C5
Daisy, Georgia (30423) 217/J6
Daisy, Ky. (41733) 237/P6
Daisy, Mo. (63743) 261/N7
Daisy, Okla. (74540) 288/P5
Daisy, Wash. (†99167) 310/G2
Daito, Japan 81/J8
Daito (isls.), Japan 54/P7
Dajabón (prov.), Dom. Rep. 158/D5
Dajabón, Dom. Rep. 158/D5
Dajarra, Queensland 88/F4
Dajarra, Queensland 95/A4
Dakar (cap.), Senegal 2/J5
Dakar (cap.), Senegal 102/A3
Dakar (cap.), Senegal 106/A6
Dakhla (oasis), Egypt 111/E2
Dakhla (oasis), Egypt 59/A4
Dakhla, W. Sahara 102/A2
Dakhla, Western Sahara 106/A4
Dakoro, Niger 106/F6
Dakota, Georgia (†31714) 217/E7
Dakota, Ill. (61018) 222/D1
Dakota (co.), Minn. 255/E6
Dakota, Minn. (55925) 255/G7
Dakota (co.), Nebr. 264/H2
Dakota City, Iowa (50529) 229/E3
Dakota City, Nebr. (68731) 264/H2
Dal (riv.), Sweden 7/F2
Dala, Angola 115/D6
Dalaba, Guinea 106/B6
Dalälven (riv.), Sweden 18/K6
Dalaman (riv.), Turkey 63/C4
Dalandzadgad, Mongolia 77/G3
Dalanganem (isls.), Philippines 82/C5
Dalark, Ark. (†71923) 202/E5
Da Lat, Vietnam 72/F5
Dalavich, Scotland 15/C4
Dalbandin, Pakistan 68/A3
Dalbandin, Pakistan 59/H4
Dalbeattie, Scotland 10/E3
Dalbeattie, Scotland 15/E6
Dalbo, Minn. (55017) 255/E5
Dalby, Queensland 95/D5
Dalby, Queensland 88/J5
Dalby, Sweden 18/H6
Dalcahue, Chile 138/D4
Dalcour, La. (†70040) 238/P4
Dale (co.), Ala. 195/G8
Dale, Ill. (62829) 222/E6
Dale, Ind. (47523) 227/D8
Dale, Minn. (†56549) 255/B4
Dale, Norway 18/E6
Dale, Okla. (74838) 288/M4
Dale, Oreg. (97880) 291/J3
Dale, Pa. (†15901) 294/E5
Dale, S.C. (29914) 296/F6
Dale (mt.), W. Australia 88/B2
Dale (mt.), W. Australia 92/B1
Dale, Wis. (54931) 317/J7
Dale City, Va. (22193) 307/O3
Dale Hollow (lake), Ky. 237/L7
Dale Hollow (lake), Tenn. 237/L7
Dalemead, Alberta 182/D4
Dalen, Netherlands 27/K3
Daleside, S. Africa 118/H7
Daleville, Ala. (36322) 195/G8
Daleville, Ind. (47334) 227/F4
Daleville, Miss. (39326) 256/G5
Daleville, Va. (24083) 307/J6
Dale West, W. Australia 92/B2
Dalhart, Texas (79022) 303/B1
Dalhousie, New Bruns. 170/D1
Dalhousie (cape), N.W. Terrs. 187/E2
Dalhousie (mt.), Nova Scotia 168/E3
Dalhousie East, Nova Scotia 168/D4
Dalhousie Junction, New Bruns. 170/D1
Dalhousie West, Nova Scotia 168/C4
Dali, China 77/E6
Dalías, Spain 33/E4
Daliburgh, Scotland 15/A3
Dalizi, China 77/L3
Dalkeith, Ontario 177/K2
Dalkeith, Scotland 10/C1
Dalkeith, Scotland 15/D2
Dalkena, Wash. (†99156) 310/H2
Dall (isl.), Alaska 196/M2
Dall (mt.), Alaska 196/H2
Dallam (co.), Texas 303/B1
Dallas (co.), Ala. 195/D6
Dallas (co.), Ark. 202/E6
Dallas, Georgia (30132) 217/C3
Dallas (co.), Iowa 229/E5
Dallas, Iowa (50062) 229/G6
Dallas, Manitoba 179/E3
Dallas (co.), Mo. 261/F7
Dallas, N.C. (28034) 281/G4
Dallas, Oreg. (97338) 291/D3
Dallas, Pa. (18612) 294/E7
Dallas, Scotland 15/E3
Dallas, S. Dak. (57529) 298/K7
Dallas (co.), Texas 303/H5
Dallas, Texas (*75201) 303/G2
Dallas, Texas 188/G4
Dallas, Texas 146/J6
Dallas, U.S. 2/E4
Dallas, W. Va. (26036) 312/E2
Dallas, Wis. (54733) 317/C5
Dallas Center, Iowa (50063) 229/E5
Dallas City, Ill. (62330) 222/B3
Dallas Naval Air Sta., Texas 303/G2
Dallastown, Pa. (17313) 294/J6
Dalles, The, Oreg. (97058) 291/F2
Dalles, The (dam), Oreg. 291/F2
Dalles, The (dam), Wash. 310/D5
Dallesport, Wash. (98617) 310/D5
Dallol, Ethiopia 111/G5
Dallol Bosso (dry riv.), Niger 106/E6
Dalmaj, Hor (lake), Iraq 66/D4
Dalmally, Scotland 10/D2
Dalmally, Scotland 15/D4
Dalmatia, Pa. (17017) 294/J4
Dalmatia (reg.), Yugoslavia 45/C4
Dalmellington, Scotland 15/D5
Dalmellington, Scotland 10/D3
Dalmeny, Sask. 181/E3
Dal'negorsk, U.S.S.R. 48/O5
Dal'nerechensk, U.S.S.R. 48/O5
Daloa, Ivory Coast 106/C7
Daloa, Ivory Coast 102/B4
Dalroy, Alberta 182/D4
Dalry, Scotland 10/A1
Dalry, Scotland 15/D5
Dalrymple, Scotland 15/D5
Dalton, Ark. (72423) 202/H1
Dalton, Georgia (30720) 217/C1
Dalton, Ky. (†42445) 237/F6
Dalton○, Mass. (01226) 249/B3
Dalton, Mich. (†49445) 250/C5
Dalton, Minn. (56324) 255/C4
Dalton, Mo. (65246) 261/F4
Dalton, Nebr. (69131) 264/B3
Dalton○, N.H. (†03598) 268/D3
Dalton, N.Y. (14836) 276/E5
Dalton, N.C. (†27043) 281/J2
Dalton, Ohio (44618) 284/G4
Dalton, Pa. (18414) 294/L2
Dalton, Wis. (53926) 317/H8
Dalton City, Ill. (61925) 222/E4
Daltonganj, India 68/E4
Dalton Gardens, Idaho (†83814) 220/B2
Dalton-in-Furness, England 13/D3
Dalupiri (isl.), Philippines 82/A3
Dalwallinu, W. Australia 88/B6
Dalwallinu, W. Australia 92/B5
Dalwhinnie, Scotland 15/D4
Dalworthington Gardens, Texas (†76101) 303/F2
Daly (cape) 5/C4
Daly (riv.), North. Terr. 88/E2
Daly (riv.), North. Terr. 93/B2
Daly (bay), N.W. Terrs. 187/K3
Dalyat al-Karmel, Israel 65/B2
Daly City, Calif. (*94014) 204/H2
Daly River, North. Terr. 88/E2
Daly River, North. Terr. 93/B2
Daly River Aboriginal Reserve, North. Terr. 88/D2
Daly River Aboriginal Res., North. Terr. 93/A2
Dalyup, W. Australia 92/C6
Daly Waters, Australia 87/D7
Daly Waters, North. Terr. 88/E3
Daly Waters, North. Terr. 93/C4
Dalzell, Ill. (61320) 222/D2
Dalzell, S.C. (29040) 296/G3
Dam, Saudi Arabia 59/D5
Daman (dist.), India 68/C4
Damanhur, Egypt 111/J3
Damanhur, Egypt 59/A3
Damar (isl.), Indonesia 85/H7
Damar (isls.), Indonesia 85/H7
Damar, Kansas (67632) 232/C2
Damara, Cent. Afr. Rep. 115/C2
Damaraland (reg.), Namibia 118/B4
Damariscotta○, Maine (04543) 243/E7
Damariscotta-Newcastle, Maine (04543) 243/E7
Damascus, Ark. (72039) 202/F3
Damascus, Georgia (31741) 217/C8
Damascus, Md. (20750) 245/K3
Damascus, Ohio (44619) 284/J4
Damascus, Pa. (18415) 294/M2
Damascus (prov.), Syria 63/G6
Damascus (cap.), Syria 59/C3
Damascus (cap.), Syria 54/E6
Damascus (cap.), Syria 63/G6
Damascus, Va. (24236) 307/E7
Damavand, Iran 66/H3
Damavand (mt.), Iran 54/G6
Damavand (mt.), Iran 59/F2
Damavend (Demavend) (mt.), Iran 66/G3
Damazin (Ed Damazin), Sudan 111/F5
Damba, Angola 115/B5
Dam Doi, Vietnam 72/E5
Dame Marie, Haiti 158/A6
Dame Marie (cape), Haiti 158/A6
Dame Marie (cape), Haiti 156/C3
Dameron, Md. (20628) 245/N8
Dames Ferry, Georgia (†31046) 217/E4
Dames Quarter, Md. (21820) 245/P8
Damghan, Iran 59/F2
Damghan, Iran 66/J2
Damh, Loch (lake), Scotland 15/C3
Damietta, Egypt 102/F1
Damietta, Egypt 111/J3
Damietta, Egypt 59/B3
Damiya, Jordan 65/D3
Dammam, Saudi Arabia 59/F4
Dammastock (mt.), Switzerland 39/F3
Damme, Belgium 27/C6
Damodar (riv.), India 68/F4
Damoh, India 68/D4
Damongo, Ghana 106/D7
Dampier (str.), Indonesia 85/J6
Dampier (str.), Papua N.G. 86/B2
Dampier (str.), Papua N.G. 85/C7
Dampier, W. Australia 88/B4
Dampier (arch.), W. Australia 88/B4
Dampier, W. Australia 92/B3
Dampier (arch.), W. Australia 92/B3
Dampier Downs, W. Australia 92/C2
Dampier Land (reg.), W. Australia 88/C3
Dampier Land (reg.), W. Australia 92/C2
Damqut, P.D.R. Yemen 59/F6
Damvant, Switzerland 39/C2
Dan, Israel 65/D1
Dan (riv.), N.C. 281/L1
Dan (riv.), Va. 307/K7
Dana, Ill. (61321) 222/E3
Dana, Ind. (47847) 227/C5
Dana, Iowa (50064) 229/E4
Dana, Jordan 65/E5
Dana, Sask. 181/F3
Danakil (reg.), Ethiopia 111/H5
Danané, Ivory Coast 106/C7
Da Nang, Vietnam 72/E3
Da Nang, Vietnam 54/M8
Da Nang, Mui (cape), Vietnam 72/F3
Danao, Philippines 82/D5
Dana Point, Calif. (92629) 204/H10
Danba, China 77/F5
Danburg, Georgia (30668) 217/G3
Danbury, Conn. (06810) 210/B3
Danbury, Iowa (51019) 229/B4
Danbury, Nebr. (69026) 264/D4
Danbury○, N.H. (03230) 268/D4
Danbury, N.C. (27016) 281/J2
Danbury, Sask. 181/J4
Danbury, Texas (77534) 303/J8
Danbury, Wis. (54830) 317/B3
Danbury P.O. (South Danbury), N.H. (03230) 268/D5
Danby (lake), Calif. 204/K9
Danby○, Vt. (05739) 268/A5
Dancing (pt.), Manitoba 179/D2
Dancy, Ala. (†35442) 195/B4
Dancy, Miss. (†39751) 256/F3
Dancy, Wis. (†54455) 317/G6
Dancyville, Tenn. (†38069) 237/C10
Dand, Manitoba 179/B5
Dandaragan, W. Australia 88/B6
Dandaragan, W. Australia 92/A5
Dandenong, Victoria 97/K5
Dandenong, Victoria 88/M7
Dandenong (creek), Victoria 97/K5
Dandenong (mt.), Victoria 97/K5
Dandenong (creek), Victoria 88/M7
Danderyd, Sweden 18/H1
Dandong (Tantung), China 77/K3
Dandong, China 54/O5
Dandridge, Tenn. (37725) 237/O8
Dane (riv.), England 13/H2
Dane (co.), Wis. 317/H9
Dane, Wis. (53529) 317/G9
Daneborg, Greenl. 4/B10
Danford Lake, Québec 172/A4
Danforth, Ill. (60930) 222/E3
Danforth, Maine (04424) 243/H4
Danforth○, Maine (04424) 243/H4
Danger (Pukapuka) (atoll), Cook Is. 87/K7
Dangila, Ethiopia 111/G5
Dangrek (mts.), Cambodia 72/D4
Dangrek (Dong Rak) (mts.), Thailand 72/D4
Dangriga (Stann Creek), Belize 153/C2
Dania, Fla. (33004) 212/B4
Daniel (mt.), Wash. 310/D3
Daniel, Wyo. (83115) 319/B3
Daniel Boone, Ky. (†42442) 237/G6
Daniel-Johnson (dam), Québec 174/D2
Daniels, Md. (†21043) 245/L3
Daniels (co.), Mont. 262/L2
Daniels, W. Va. (25832) 312/D7
Daniel's Harbour, Newf. 166/C3
Danielson, Conn. (06239) 210/H1
Danielson Prov. Park, Sask. 181/E4
Danielstown, Guyana 131/B2
Danielsville, Georgia (30633) 217/F2
Danielsville, Pa. (18038) 294/M4
Danilov, U.S.S.R. 52/E3
Dankov, U.S.S.R. 52/E4
Danlí, Honduras 154/D3
Danmarkshavn, Greenl. 4/B10
Dannebrog, Nebr. (68831) 264/F3
Dannelly (res.), Ala. 195/D6
Dannemora, N.Y. (12929) 276/N1
Dannemora, Sweden 18/K6
Dannenberg, W. Germany 22/D2
Danner, Oreg. (†97910) 291/K5
Dannevirke, N. Zealand 100/F4
Dan Sai, Thailand 72/D3
Dansville, Mich. (48819) 250/E6
Dansville, N.Y. (14437) 276/E5
Dante (Hafun), Somalia 115/K1
Dante, S. Dak. (57329) 298/N7
Dante, Va. (24237) 307/D7
Danube (riv.) 7/G4
Danube (riv.), Austria 41/C2
Danube (riv.), Bulgaria 45/H4
Danube (riv.), Czech. 41/C2
Danube (riv.), Hungary 41/E3
Danube, Minn. (56230) 255/C6
Danube (delta), Romania 45/J3
Danube (riv.), Romania 45/H4
Danube (riv.), W. Germany 22/C4
Danube (riv.), Yugoslavia 45/E3
Danubyu, Burma 72/B3
Danvers, Ill. (61732) 222/D3
Danvers○, Mass. (01923) 249/D5
Danvers, Minn. (56231) 255/C5
Danvers, Mont. (59429) 262/G3
Danversport, Mass. (†01923) 249/E5
Danville, Ala. (35619) 195/D2
Danville, Ark. (72833) 202/D3
Danville, Calif. (94526) 204/K2
Danville, Georgia (31017) 217/F5
Danville, Ill. 188/J3
Danville, Ill. (61832) 222/F3
Danville, Ind. (46122) 227/D5
Danville, Iowa (52623) 229/L7
Danville, Kansas (67036) 232/E4
Danville, Ky. (40422) 237/M5
Danville, La. (†71008) 238/E2
Danville, Mo. (†63361) 261/J5
Danville○, N.H. (03819) 268/E6
Danville, Ohio (43014) 284/F5
Danville, Pa. (17821) 294/J4
Danville, Québec 172/E4
Danville○, Vt. (05828) 268/C3
Danville, Va. 188/L3
Danville, Va. 146/L6
Danville (I.C.), Va. (*24540) 307/J7
Danville, Wash. (99121) 310/G2
Danville, W. Va. (25053) 312/C6
Danville, Wis. (†53925) 317/J9
Dan Xian, China 77/G8
Danzig (Gdańsk), Poland 47/D1
Danzig (Gdańsk) (gulf), Poland 47/D1
Daocheng, China 77/F6
Dao Xian, China 77/H6
Dapa, Philippines 82/E6
Dapaong, Togo 106/E6
Daphne, Ala. (36526) 195/C9
Daphne, Sask. 181/G3
Dapitan, Philippines 82/D6
Dapoli, India 68/C5
Dapp, Alberta 182/C2
Da Qaidam, China 77/E4
Darab, Iran 59/G4
Darab, Iran 66/J7
Darabani, Romania 45/H1
Dar al Hamra, Saudi Arabia 59/C4
Daram (isl.), Philippines 82/E5
Daran, Iran 66/G4
Darbandikhan (dam), Iraq 66/D3
Darbhanga, India 68/F3
Darbun, Miss. (†39643) 256/D8
Darby (cape), Alaska 196/F2
Darby, Mont. (59829) 262/B4
Darby (creek), Ohio 284/D5
Darby, Pa. (19023) 294/M7
Darby (creek), Pa. 294/M6
Darby, Victoria 97/D6
Darbydale, Ohio (†43123) 284/D6
Darbyville, Ohio (†43164) 284/D6
D'Arcy, Br. Col. 184/F5
D'Arcy, Sask. 181/C4
Dardanelle, Ark. (72834) 202/D3
Dardanelle (lake), Ark. 202/D3
Dardanelles (str.), Turkey 7/G5
Dardanelles (str.), Turkey 59/A2
Dardanelles (str.), Turkey 63/B6
Darden, Tenn. (38328) 237/E9
Dare (co.), N.C. 281/T3
Dar-el-Beida (Casablanca), Morocco 106/C2
Darende, Turkey 63/G3
Dar es Salaam (cap.), Tanzania 102/F5
Dar es Salaam (cap.), Tanzania 2/M6
Dar es Salaam (cap.), Tanzania 115/G5
Dareton, N.S. Wales 97/B4
Daretown, N.J. (†08318) 273/C4
Darfur, Minn. (56022) 255/D6
Darfur, Northern (prov.), Sudan 111/D5
Darfur, Southern (prov.), Sudan 111/E5
Dargan, Md. (†25425) 245/H3
Dargaville, N. Zealand 100/D1
Dar Hamid (reg.), Sudan 111/F5
Darham Mumingan Lianheqi, China 77/H3
Darhan (Darkhan), Mongolia 77/G2
Darien○, Conn. (06820) 210/B4
Darien, Georgia (31305) 217/K8
Darien, Ill. (†60559) 222/B6
Darien, N.Y. (†14040) 276/D5
Darién (mts.), Panama 154/J6
Darien, Wis. (53114) 317/J10
Darien Center, N.Y. (14040) 276/D5
Dariense, Cordillera (range), Nicaragua 154/E4
Darjeeling, India 68/F3
Dark (head), St. Vin. & Grens. 161/A8
Darkan, W. Australia 92/B2
Dark Canyon (creek), N. Mex. 274/E6
Dark Cove, Newf. 166/D4
Darke (co.), Ohio 284/A5
Darkesville, W. Va. (†25428) 312/L4
Darkin (riv.), W. Australia 88/B2
Darlag, China 77/E5
Darling (river), Australia 87/E9
Darling, Miss. (38623) 256/D2
Darling (riv.), N.S. Wales 88/G6
Darling (riv.), N.S. Wales 97/B3
Darling (lake), N. Dak. 282/G2
Darling, Pa. (†19063) 294/L7
Darling (range), W. Australia 88/B6
Darling (range), W. Australia 92/A1
Darling Downs, Queensland 95/D5
Darlingford, Manitoba 179/D5
Darlington, Ala. (36730) 195/D7
Darlington, England 10/F3
Darlington, England 13/F3
Darlington, Fla. (†32464) 212/C5
Darlington, Idaho (83231) 220/E6
Darlington, Ind. (47940) 227/D4
Darlington, La. (†70441) 238/J5
Darlington, Md. (21034) 245/N2
Darlington, Mo. (64438) 261/D2
Darlington, New Bruns. 170/D1
Darlington, Pa. (16115) 294/A4
Darlington (co.), S.C. 296/H3
Darlington, S.C. (29532) 296/H3
Darlington, Wis. (53530) 317/F10
Darlington Heights, Va. (23935) 307/L6
Darlington Point, N.S. Wales 97/C4
Darliston, Jamaica 158/H6
Darłowo, Poland 47/C1
Dar Masalit (reg.), Sudan 111/D5
Darmody, Sask. 181/E5
Darmstadt, Ill. (†62255) 222/D5
Darmstadt, Ind. (†47618) 227/B8
Darmstadt, W. Germany 22/C4
Darnell, La. (71231) 238/G1
Darnestown, Md. (†20760) 245/J4
Darnick, N.S. Wales 97/B3
Darnley (cape) 5/C4
Darnley (bay), N.W. Terrs. 187/F3
Daroca, Spain 33/F2
Darra, Queensland 88/K3
Darreh Gaz, Iran 66/L2
Darrington, Wash. (98241) 310/D2
Dar Rounga (reg.), Cent. Afr. Rep. 115/D2
Darrouzett, Texas (79024) 303/D1
Darrow, La. (70725) 238/K3
Darrtown, Ohio (†45056) 284/A7
Darsser Ort (pt.), E. Germany 22/E1
Dart (cape) 5/B12
Dart (riv.), England 13/D7
D'Artagnan, Québec 172/J3
Dartford, England 13/J8
Dartford, England 10/C5
Dartmoor, Victoria 97/A5
Dartmoor National Park, England 13/C7
Dartmouth (Clifton Dartmouth Hardness), England 10/E5
Dartmouth (Clifton Dartmouth Hardness), England 13/D7
Dartmouth○, Mass. (02714) 249/K6
Dartmouth, N.S. 162/K7
Dartmouth, Nova Scotia 168/E4
Dartmouth (riv.), Québec 172/D1
Darton, England 13/J2
Dartuch (cape), Spain 33/H3
Daru, Papua N.G. 87/E6
Daru, Papua N.G. 85/B7
Daruvar, Yugoslavia 45/C3
Darvel, Scotland 15/D5
Darwell, Alberta 182/C3
Darwen, England 10/G1
Darwen, England 13/H1
Darwin, Australia 2/R6
Darwin, Australia 87/D7
Darwin, Calif. (93522) 204/H7
Darwin (bay), Chile 138/D6
Darwin, Cordillera (mts.), Chile 138/D8
Darwin, Cordillera (mts.), Chile 138/E11
Darwin (Culpepper) (isl.), Ecuador 128/B8
Darwin, Ill. (†62477) 222/F4
Darwin, Minn. (55324) 255/D5
Darwin (cap.), North. Terr. 88/E2
Darwin (cap.), North. Terr. 93/B2
Darwin, Okla. (†74523) 288/P6
Das (isl.), U.A.E. 59/F4
Dash, Ben (hill), Ireland 17/C6
Dashan, Ras (mt.), Ethiopia 59/C7
Dashbalbar, Mongolia 77/H2
Dasher, Georgia (31601) 217/F9
Dashinchilen, Mongolia 77/F2
Dasht (riv.), Pakistan 68/A3
Dasht (riv.), Pakistan 59/H4
Dashtiari, Iran 66/M8
Dashtiari, Iran 59/H4
Dashwood, Br. Col. 184/H3
Dashwood, Ontario 177/C4
Dasol (bay), Philippines 82/B3
Dassel, Minn. (55325) 255/D5
Datça, Turkey 63/B4
Dateland, Ariz. (85333) 198/B6
Datia, India 68/D3
Datil, N. Mex. (87821) 274/B4
Datil (mts.), N. Mex. 274/B4
Datong, Qinghai, China 77/F4
Datong (Tatung), Shanxi, China 77/H3
Datto, Ark. (72424) 202/J1
Datu Piang, Philippines 82/E7
Daua (riv.), Kenya 115/H3
Daufuskie Island, S.C. (29915) 296/F7
Daugava (Western Dvina) (riv.), U.S.S.R. 53/D2
Daugavpils, U.S.S.R. 7/G3
Daugavpils, U.S.S.R. 53/D3
Daugavpils, U.S.S.R. 48/C4
Daugavpils, U.S.S.R. 52/C3
Daule, Ecuador 128/B3
Daulnay, New Bruns. 170/E1
Daun, W. Germany 22/B3
Daung Kyun (isl.), Burma 72/C4
Dauphin, Man. 162/F5
Dauphin, Manitoba 179/B3
Dauphin (lake), Manitoba 179/C3
Dauphin (riv.), Manitoba 179/D3
Dauphin (cape), Nova Scotia 168/H2
Dauphin (co.), Pa. 294/J5
Dauphin, Pa. (17018) 294/J5
Dauphin, St. Lucia 161/G5
Dauphiné (trad. prov.), France 29
Dauphin Island, Ala. (36528) 195/B10
Daus, Tenn. (†37327) 237/L10
Davangere, India 68/D6
Davant, La. (70046) 238/L7
Davao, Philippines 85/H4
Davao, Philippines 54/O9
Davao, Philippines 2/R5
Davao, Philippines 82/E7
Davao (gulf), Philippines 82/E7
Davao (gulf), Philippines 85/H4
Davao del Norte (prov.), Philippines 82/E7
Davao del Sur (prov.), Philippines 82/E7
Davao Oriental (prov.), Philippines 82/F7
Daveluyville, Québec 172/E3
Davenport, Calif. (95017) 204/K4
Davenport, Fla. (33837) 212/E3
Davenport, Iowa (*52801) 229/M5
Davenport, Iowa 188/H2
Davenport, Nebr. (68335) 264/G4
Davenport, N.Y. (13750) 276/L6
Davenport, N. Dak. (58021) 282/R6
Davenport (mt.), North. Terr. 93/B7
Davenport, Okla. (74026) 288/N3
Davenport, Va. (24239) 307/D6
Davenport, Wash. (99122) 310/G3
Daventry, England 13/F5
Davey, Nebr. (68336) 264/H4
Davey (riv.), Tasmania 99/B4
David (pt.), Grenada 161/D8
David, Ky. (41616) 237/R5
David, Panama 154/F6
David City, Nebr. (68632) 264/G3
Davidson (mts.), Alaska 196/K1
Davidson, Maine (†04782) 243/F4
Davidson (co.), N.C. 281/J3
Davidson, N.C. (28036) 281/H4
Davidson, Okla. (73530) 288/J6
Davidson, Sask. 181/E4
Davidson (co.), Tenn. 237/H8
Davidson (mts.), Yukon 187/D3
Davidsonville, Md. (21035) 245/M5
Davie, Fla. (33314) 212/B4
Davie (co.), N.C. 281/H3
Daviess (co.), Ind. 227/C7
Daviess (co.), Ky. 237/G5
Daviess (co.), Mo. 261/E3
Davik, Norway 18/D6
Davilla, Texas (76523) 303/G7
Davin, Sask. 181/H5
Daviot, Scotland 15/D3
Davis (str.) 2/G2
Davis (str.) 146/N3
Davis (str.) 4/C12
Davis (sea) 5/C5
Davis (dam), Ariz. 198/A3
Davis, Calif. (95616) 204/B8
Davis (isl.), Fla. 212/C3
Davis, Ill. (61019) 222/D1

Dent d'Hérens 359

Davis (co.), Iowa 229/J7
Davis (dam), Nev. 266/G7
Davis, N.C. (28524) 281/R5
Davis (str.), N.W.T. 162/K1
Davis (str.), N.W. Terrs. 187/M3
Davis, Okla. (73030) 288/M5
Davis (lake), Oreg. 291/F4
Davis (mt.), Pa. 294/D6
Davis, Sask. 181/F2
Davis, S. Dak. (57021) 298/P7
Davis (mts.), Texas 303/C11
Davis (co.), Utah 304/B3
Davis, W. Va. (26260) 312/H4
Davisboro, Georgia (31018) 217/G5
Davis City, Iowa (50065) 229/F7
Davis Cove, Newf. 166/D4
Davis Creek, Calif. (96108) 204/E2
Davis Dam, Ariz. (†86430) 198/A3
Davis Inlet, Newf. 166/B2
Davis Junction, Ill. (61020) 222/D1
Davis-Monthan A.F.B., Ariz. 198/E6
Davison, Mich. (48423) 250/F5
Davison (co.), S. Dak. 298/N6
Davis Station 5/C4
Davis Station, S.C. (29041) 296/G4
Daviston, Ala. (36256) 195/G4
Davisville, Mo. (65456) 261/K7
Davisville, R.I. (02854) 249/H6
Davisville, W. Va. (26142) 312/C4
Davlekanovo, U.S.S.R. 52/H4
Davos, Switzerland 39/J3
Davos (valley), Switzerland 39/J3
Davy, W. Va. (24828) 312/C8
Dawa (riv.), Ethiopia 111/G7
Dawasir, Hadhb (range), Saudi Arabia 59/D5
Dawasir, Wadi (dry riv.), Saudi Arabia 59/E5
Dawes (co.), Nebr. 264/A2
Dawes, W. Va. (25054) 312/D6
Dawlish, England 13/D7
Dawn, Mo. (64638) 261/E3
Dawn, Texas (79025) 303/B3
Dawna (range), Burma 72/C3
Dawson, Ala. (35963) 195/G2
Dawson, Canada 4/C16
Dawson (isl.), Chile 138/E10
Dawson (co.), Georgia 217/D2
Dawson, Georgia (31742) 217/D7
Dawson, Ill. (62520) 222/D4
Dawson, Iowa (50066) 229/E5
Dawson (bay), Manitoba 179/B2
Dawson, Minn. (56232) 255/B6
Dawson, Mo. (†65548) 261/H8
Dawson (co.), Mont. 262/M3
Dawson (co.), Nebr. 264/E4
Dawson, Nebr. (68337) 264/J4
Dawson, N. Dak. (58428) 282/L6
Dawson (inlet), N.W. Terrs. 187/J3
Dawson (riv.), Queensland 88/H4
Dawson (riv.), Queensland 95/D5
Dawson (co.), Texas 303/C5
Dawson, Texas (76639) 303/H6
Dawson, W. Va. (24932) 312/E7
Dawson, Yukon 146/E3
Dawson, Yukon 162/C3
Dawson, Yukon 187/E3
Dawson Bay, Manitoba 179/B2
Dawson Creek, Br. Col. 146/F4
Dawson Creek, Br. Col. 162/D4
Dawson Creek, Br. Col. 184/G2
Dawson Springs, Ky. (42408) 237/F6
Dawsonville, Georgia (30534) 217/D2
Dawsonville, New Bruns. 170/C1
Dawu, China 77/H5
Dawu, China 77/F5
Dax, France 28/C6
Da Xian, China 77/G5
Day, Fla. (32013) 212/C1
Day, Minn. (†55006) 255/E5
Day (co.), S. Dak. 298/O3
Day Book, N.C. (†28714) 281/E3
Daykin, Nebr. (68338) 264/G4
Daylesford, Victoria 97/C5
Daylight, Tenn. (†37110) 237/K9
Daymán, Uruguay 145/B2
Daymán (range), Uruguay 145/B2
Daymán (riv.), Uruguay 145/B2
Dayong, China 77/H6
Days Creek, Oreg. (97429) 291/D5
Daysland, Alberta 182/D3
Daysville, Ky. (†42276) 237/G7
Dayton, Ala. (36731) 195/C6
Dayton, Idaho (83232) 220/F7
Dayton, Ill. (†61350) 222/E2
Dayton, Ind. (47941) 227/D4
Dayton, Iowa (50530) 229/E4
Dayton, Ky. (41074) 237/T1
Dayton, Mich. (†49113) 250/C7
Dayton, Minn. (55327) 255/E5
Dayton, Mont. (59914) 262/B3
Dayton, Nev. (89403) 266/B3
Dayton, N.J. (08810) 273/D3
Dayton, N.Y. (4041) 276/C6
Dayton, Ohio (*45401) 284/B6
Dayton, Ohio 146/K6
Dayton, Ohio 188/K3
Dayton, Oreg. (97114) 291/A3
Dayton, Pa. (16222) 294/D4
Dayton, Tenn. (37321) 237/L9
Dayton, Texas (77535) 303/J7
Dayton, Va. (22821) 307/L4
Dayton, Wash. (99328) 310/H4
Dayton, Wis. (†53508) 317/H10
Dayton, Wyo. (82836) 319/E1
Daytona Beach, Fla. 188/K5
Daytona Beach, Fla. 146/K7
Daytona Beach, Fla. (*32014) 212/F2
Daytona Beach Shores, Fla. (32016) 212/F2
Dayu, China 77/H6
Dayville, Conn. (06241) 210/H1
Dayville, Oreg. (97825) 291/H3
Dazey, N. Dak. (58429) 282/O5
Dazhai, China 77/H4
Dazkırı, Turkey 63/D4
De Aar, S. Africa 118/C6
Dead (lake), Fla. 212/D6
Dead (sea), Israel 65/C4
Dead (sea), Israel 59/C3
Dead (sea), Jordan 59/C3
Dead (sea), Jordan 65/C4
Dead (riv.), Maine 243/C5
Dead (riv.), Mich. 250/B2
Dead (lake), Minn. 255/C4
Dead (sea), West Bank 59/C3
Deadhorse, Alaska (†99723) 196/J1
Deadman (creek), Wash. 310/H4
Deadman (mt.), Wyo. 319/B2
Deadwood, Alberta 182/B1
Deadwood (res.), Idaho 220/C5
Deadwood (riv.), Idaho 220/C5
Deadwood, S. Dak. (57732) 298/B5
Deaf Smith (co.), Texas 303/B3
Deal, England 13/J6
Deal, England 10/G5
Deal, N.J. (07723) 273/F3
Deal (isl.), Tasmania 99/D1
Deale, Md. (20751) 245/M5
Deal Island, Md. (21821) 245/P8
Dean (chan.), Br. Col. 184/D4
Dean (riv.), Br. Col. 184/D4
Dean, Nova Scotia 168/F3
Deán Funes, Argentina 143/D3
Deanville, Texas (77852) 303/H7
Dearborn (co.), Ind. 227/H6
Dearborn, Mich. (*48120) 250/B7
Dearborn, Mo. (64439) 261/C3
Dearborn Heights, Mich. (48127) 250/B7
Dearing, Georgia (30808) 217/H4
Dearing, Kansas (67340) 232/G4
De Armanville, Ala. (36257) 195/G3
Dearne, England 13/K2
Deary, Idaho (83823) 220/B3
Dease (inlet), Alaska 196/H1
Dease (lake), Br. Col. 184/K2
Dease (riv.), Br. Col. 184/K2
Dease (str.), N.W.T. 146/G3
Dease (str.), N.W.T. 162/F2
Dease (str.), N.W. Terrs. 187/H3
Dease Arm (inlet), N.W. Terrs. 187/F3
Death (valley), Calif. 204/H7
Death Valley (depr.), Calif. 188/C3
Death Valley, Calif. (92328) 204/J7
Death Valley Junction, Calif. (92328) 204/J7
Death Valley Nat'l Mon., Calif. 204/H7
Death Valley Nat'l Mon., Nev. 266/E6
Deatsville, Ala. (36022) 195/F5
Deauville, France 28/C3
Deauville, Québec 172/E4
Deaver, Wyo. (82421) 319/D1
Deavertown, Ohio (†43731) 284/G6
De Baca (co.), N. Mex. 274/E4
Deba Habe, Nigeria 106/G6
Debar, Yugoslavia 45/E5
De Bary, Fla. (32713) 212/E3
Debden, Sask. 181/E2
Débé, Trin. & Tob. 161/B11
Debec, New Bruns. 170/C2
De Beque, Colo. (81630) 208/C4
De Berry, Texas (75639) 303/L5
Debert, Nova Scotia 168/E3
Dębica, Poland 47/E3
De Bilt, Netherlands 27/G4
Dęblin, Poland 47/E3
Deblois○, Maine (†04622) 243/H6
Dębno, Poland 47/B2
Debo (lake), Mali 106/D5
Debolt, Alberta 182/B2
De Borgia, Mont. (59830) 262/A3
Debra Birhan, Ethiopia 111/G6
Debra Markos, Ethiopia 111/G5
Debra Markos, Ethiopia 102/F3
Debra Tabor, Ethiopia 111/G5
Debrecen, Hungary 41/F3
Debrecen, Hungary 7/G4
Decatur, Ala. (*35601) 195/D1
Decatur, Ark. (72722) 202/A1
Decatur (co.), Georgia 217/C9
Decatur, Georgia (*30030) 217/K1
Decatur, Ill. 188/J3
Decatur, Ill. 146/K6
Decatur, Ill. (*62521) 222/E4
Decatur (co.), Ind. 227/G6
Decatur, Ind. (46733) 227/H3
Decatur (co.), Iowa 229/F7
Decatur, Iowa (50067) 229/F7
Decatur (co.), Kansas 232/B2
Decatur, Mich. (49045) 250/C6
Decatur, Miss. (39327) 256/F6
Decatur, Nebr. (68020) 264/H2
Decatur, Ohio (45115) 284/C8
Decatur (co.), Tenn. 237/E9
Decatur, Tenn. (37322) 237/M9
Decatur, Texas (76234) 303/G4
Decaturville, Tenn. (38329) 237/E9
Decazeville, France 28/E5
Deccan (plat.), India 68/D6
Decherd, Tenn. (37324) 237/J10
Děčín, Czech. 41/C1
Decision (cape), Alaska 196/M2
Decize, France 28/E4
Decker, Ind. (47524) 227/B7
Decker, Manitoba 179/B4
Decker, Mich. (48426) 250/F5
Decker, Mont. (59025) 262/K5
Decker Lake, Br. Col. 184/E3
Deckers, Colo. (†80135) 208/J4
Deckerville, Ark. (†72386) 202/K3
Deckerville, Mich. (48427) 250/G5
Declo, Idaho (83323) 220/E7
Decorah, Iowa (52101) 229/K2
Decota, W. Va. (†25122) 312/D6
Decoy, Ky. (41321) 237/P5
Dededo, Guam 86/K6
Dedegül Dağı (mt.), Turkey 63/D4
Dedemsvaart, Netherlands 27/J3
Dederick, Mo. (†64744) 261/D7
Dedham, Iowa (51440) 229/D5
Dedham, Maine (†04429) 243/F6
Dedham○, Maine (†04429) 243/F6
Dedham, Mass. (02026) 249/C7
Dédougou, Upper Volta 106/D6
Dedza, Malawi 115/F6
Dee (riv.), England 13/D4
Dee (riv.), England 10/E4
Dee (riv.), Ireland 17/H4
Dee (riv.), Scotland 15/D5
Dee (riv.), Scotland 15/F3
Dee (riv.), Scotland 10/E2
Dee (riv.), Tasmania 99/C4
Dee (riv.), Wales 10/E4
Dee (riv.), Wales 13/D4
Deedsville, Ind. (46921) 227/E3
Deel (riv.), Ireland 17/C3
Deel (riv.), Ireland 17/G4
Deel (riv.), Ireland 17/D7
Deele (riv.), Ireland 17/F2
Deenwood, Georgia (†31501) 217/H8
Deep (creek), Idaho 220/F7
Deep (creek), Idaho 220/B7
Deep (inlet), Newf. 166/B2
Deep (riv.), N.C. 281/K3
Deep (riv.), N. Dak. 282/J1
Deep (creek), S.C. 296/B2
Deep (creek), Texas 303/C5
Deep (creek), Utah 304/B1
Deep (creek), Utah 304/A3
Deep Bight, Newf. 166/C2
Deep Brook, Nova Scotia 168/C4
Deep Creek (mts.), Idaho 220/F7
Deep Creek (lake), Md. 245/A3
Deep Creek (range), Utah 304/A4
Deepcreek, Wash. (†99010) 310/H3
Deepdale, Manitoba 179/A3
Deep Fork, North Canadian (riv.), Okla. 288/N3
Deep Gap, N.C. (28618) 281/F2
Deephaven, Minn. (55391) 255/G5
Deeping Saint James, England 13/G5
Deep River, Conn. (06417) 210/F3
Deep River○, Conn. (06417) 210/F3
Deep River (res.), Conn. 210/F2
Deep River, Iowa (52222) 229/J5
Deep River, Ontario 177/G1
Deep River, Ontario 175/E3
Deep River, Wash. (†98638) 310/B4
Deep Run, N.C. (28525) 281/O4
Deep Springs, Calif. (†93513) 204/H6
Deepstep, Georgia (31082) 217/G4
Deep Valley, Pa. (†15352) 294/A6
Deep Water (pt.), Del. 245/S4
Deepwater, Mo. (64740) 261/E6
Deepwater, N.J. (08023) 273/C4
Deepwater, N.S. Wales 97/F1
Deer (isl.), Alaska 196/F4
Deer, Ark. (72628) 202/D2
Deer (creek), Ind. 227/D5
Deer (creek), Ind. 227/E3
Deer (isl.), Maine 243/F7
Deer (creek), Md. 245/N2
Deer (isl.), Mass. 249/E7
Deer (riv.), Mich. 250/A2
Deer (lake), Minn. 255/E3
Deer (creek), Miss. 256/C4
Deer (isl.), New Bruns. 170/D4
Deer (harb.), Newf. 166/D2
Deer (riv.), N.Y. 276/L1
Deer (riv.), N.Y. 276/J3
Deer (creek), Ohio 284/D6
Deer (lake), Wash. 310/H2
Deerbrook, Miss. (†39739) 256/G4
Deerbrook, Wis. (54424) 317/H5
Deer Creek, Ill. (61733) 222/D3
Deer Creek, Ind. (†46917) 227/E3
Deer Creek, Minn. (56527) 255/C4
Deer Creek (lake), Ohio 284/D6
Deer Creek, Okla. (74636) 288/L1
Deerfield, Ill. (60015) 222/B5
Deerfield, Ind. (†47380) 227/H4
Deerfield, Kansas (67838) 232/A4
Deerfield○, Mass. (01342) 249/D2
Deerfield (riv.), Mass. 249/C2
Deerfield, Mich. (49238) 250/F7
Deerfield, Mo. (64741) 261/D7
Deerfield○, N.H. (03037) 268/E5
Deerfield, Ohio (44411) 284/H3
Deerfield (riv.), Vt. 268/B6
Deerfield, Va. (24432) 307/K4
Deerfield, Wis. (53531) 317/H9
Deerfield Beach, Fla. (33441) 212/F5
Deerfield Street, N.J. (08313) 273/C4
Deerford, La. (†70791) 238/K1
Deer Grove, Ill. (61243) 222/D2
Deer Harbor, Wash. (98243) 310/B2
Deerhorn, Manitoba 179/E4
Deering, Alaska (99736) 196/F1
Deering○, N.H. (†03244) 268/D5
Deering, N. Dak. (58731) 282/J3
Deer Island, Oreg. (97054) 291/E2
Deer Isle, Maine (04627) 243/F7
Deer Isle○, Maine (04627) 243/F7
Deer Lake, Newf. 166/C4
Deer Lake, Ontario 175/B2
Deer Lodge (co.), Mont. 262/C5
Deer Lodge, Mont. (59722) 262/D4
Deer Lodge, Tenn. (37726) 237/M8
Deer Park, Ala. (36529) 195/B8
Deer Park, Calif. (94576) 204/C5
Deer Park, Fla. (†32901) 212/F3
Deer Park, Ill. (†60010) 222/A5
Deer Park, Md. (21550) 245/A3
Deer Park, N.Y. (11729) 276/O9
Deer Park, Ohio (45236) 284/C9
Deer Park, Texas (77536) 303/K2
Deer Park, Wash. (99006) 310/H3
Deer Park, Wis. (54007) 317/B5
Deer River, Minn. (56636) 255/E3
Deer River, N.Y. (13627) 276/J3
Deer Run, W. Va. (†26807) 312/H5
Deersville, Ohio (44693) 284/H5
Deerton, Mich. (49822) 250/B2
Deer Trail, Colo. (80105) 208/M3
Deerwalk, W. Va. (†26180) 312/D4
Deerwood, Minn. (56444) 255/E4
Deesa, India 68/C4
Deeson, Miss. (†38740) 256/C2
Deeth, Nev. (89823) 266/F1
Dee Why, N. S. Wales 88/L4
Dee Why, N.S. Wales 97/K3
Defense Heights, Md. (†20784) 245/G4
Deferiet, N.Y. (13628) 276/J2
Defiance (plat.), Ariz. 198/F3
Defiance, Iowa (51527) 229/C5
Defiance, Mo. (63341) 261/L5
Defiance (co.), Ohio 284/A3
Defiance, Ohio (43512) 284/B3
De Fluessen (lake), Netherlands 27/G3
Defoe, Ky. (40017) 237/L4
Deford, Mich. (48729) 250/F5
De Forest, Wis. (53532) 317/H9
Defoy, Québec 172/E3
De Funiak Springs, Fla. (32433) 212/C6
Dégelis, Québec 172/J2
Degema, Nigeria 106/F8
Degersheim, Switzerland 39/H2
Deggendorf, W. Germany 22/E4
De Graff, Kansas (†66840) 232/F4
De Graff, Minn. (56233) 255/C5
DeGraff, Ohio (43318) 284/C5
Degrasse, N.Y. (13629) 276/L2
De Gray (lake), Ark. 202/D5
De Grey, W. Australia 88/B4
De Grey, W. Australia 92/B3
De Grey (riv.), W. Australia 88/C4
De Grey (riv.), W. Australia 92/B3
De Haan, Belgium 27/C6
Deh Bid, Iran 66/H5
Dehdez, Iran 66/G5
Deheq, Iran 66/G4
Dehiwala-Mt. Lavinia, Sri Lanka 68/D7
Dehkhvareqan, Iran 66/D2
Dehlco, La. (†71269) 238/G2
De Honte (bay), Netherlands 27/D6
Dehra Dun, India 68/D2
Dehua, China 77/J6
Deim Zubeir, Sudan 111/E6
Deinze, Belgium 27/C7
Deir Abu Sa'id, Jordan 65/D3
Deir Ballut, West Bank 65/C3
Deir el Balah, Gaza Strip 65/A5
Deir ez Zor (prov.), Syria 63/H5
Deir ez Zor, Syria 63/H5
Deir ez Zor, Syria 59/C2
Deir Sharaf, West Bank 65/C3
Dej, Romania 45/F2
De Kalb (co.), Ala. 195/G2
De Kalb (co.), Georgia 217/D3
De Kalb (co.), Ill. 222/E2
De Kalb, Ill. (60115) 222/E2
De Kalb (co.), Ind. 227/H2
De Kalb, Miss. (39328) 256/G5
De Kalb (co.), Mo. 261/D3
De Kalb, Mo. (64440) 261/C3
De Kalb (co.), Tenn. 237/K9
De Kalb, Texas (75559) 303/K4
De Kalb Junction, N.Y. (13630) 276/K2
Dekese, Zaire 115/D4
Dekoa, Cent. Afr. Rep. 115/C2
De Koog, Netherlands 27/F2
De Koven, Ky. (†42459) 237/E5
Dela, Okla. (†74523) 288/P6
Delacour, Alberta 182/D4
Delacroix, La. (†70085) 238/L7
Delafield, Ill. (†62859) 222/E5
Delafield, Wis. (53018) 317/J1
Delagoa (bay), Mozambique 118/E5
Delair, N.J. (08110) 273/B3
Delamar (mts.), Nev. 266/G5
De Lamere, N. Dak. (58022) 282/R7
DeLancey, Pa. (15733) 294/D4
Delanco○, N.J. (08075) 273/D3
De Land, Fla. (32720) 212/E2
De Land, Ill. (61839) 222/E3
Delaney, Ark. (†72727) 202/C2
Delano, Calif. (93215) 204/F8
Delano, Minn. (55328) 255/E5
Delano, Pa. (18220) 294/K4
Delano, Tenn. (37325) 237/M10
Delano (peak), Utah 304/B5
Delanson, N.Y. (12053) 276/M5
Delaplaine, Ark. (72425) 202/J1
Delaplane, Va. (22025) 307/N3
Delaram, Afghanistan 59/H3
Delaram, Afghanistan 68/A2
Delaronde (lake), Sask. 181/E1
Delavan, Ill. (61734) 222/D3
Delavan, Kansas (66847) 232/F3
Delavan, Minn. (56023) 255/D7
Delavan, Wis. (53115) 317/J10
Delavan Lake, Wis. (†53115) 317/J10
Delaware 188/L3
Delaware (bay) 188/M3
Delaware, Ark. (72835) 202/D3
DELAWARE 245
Delaware (bay), Del. 245/T5
Delaware (riv.), Del. 245/R3
Delaware (co.), Ind. 227/G4
Delaware, Ind. (†47037) 227/G6
Delaware (co.), Iowa 229/L4
Delaware, Iowa (52036) 229/L4
Delaware, N.J. (07833) 273/C2
Delaware (bay), N.J. 273/C5
Delaware (riv.), N.J. 273/D3
Delaware (co.), N.Y. 276/K6
Delaware (riv.), N.Y. 276/K7
Delaware (co.), Ohio 284/D5
Delaware, Ohio (43015) 284/E5
Delaware (lake), Ohio 284/E5
Delaware (co.), Okla. 288/S2
Delaware, Okla. (74027) 288/P1
Delaware, Ontario 177/C5
Delaware (co.), Pa. 294/M6
Delaware (riv.), Pa. 294/N3
Delaware (creek), Texas 303/C10
Delaware (mts.), Texas 303/C10
Delaware (state), U.S. 146/L6
Delaware City, Del. (19706) 245/R2
Delaware Water Gap Nat'l Rec. Area, N.J. 273/C1
Delaware Water Gap, Pa. (18327) 294/M4
Delaware Water Gap Nat'l Rec. Area, Pa. 294/N3
Delbarton, W. Va. (25670) 312/B7
Del Bonita, Alberta 182/D5
Delburne, Alberta 182/D3
Delcambre, La. (70528) 238/G7
Del City, Okla. (73115) 288/L4
Delco, N.C. (28436) 281/N6
Deldoul, Algeria 106/E3
Deleau, Manitoba 179/B5
Delegate, N.S. Wales 97/E5
Delémont, Switzerland 39/D2
De Leon, Texas (76444) 303/F5
De Leon Springs, Fla. (32028) 212/E2
Delevan, N.Y. (14042) 276/D6
Delfi, Greece 45/F6
Delft, Minn. (56124) 255/C7
Delft, Netherlands 27/E4
Delfzijl, Netherlands 27/K2
Delgada (pt.), Argentina 143/D5
Delgada (pt.), Calif. 204/A3
Delgada (pt.), Mexico 150/L7
Delgado (cape), Mozambique 102/G6
Delgado (cape), Mozambique 118/G2
Delgado Chalbaud, Cerro (mt.), Venezuela 124/G6
Delgertsogt, Mongolia 77/G2
Delgo, Sudan 111/F3
Delhi, Calif. (95315) 204/E6
Delhi, Colo. (†81059) 208/M7
Delhi, Ill. (†62052) 222/C4
Delhi (terr.), India 68/D3
Delhi, India 68/D3
Delhi, India 54/J7
Delhi, India 2/N4
Delhi, Iowa (52223) 229/L4
Delhi, La. (71232) 238/H2
Delhi, Minn. (56234) 255/C6
Delhi, N.Y. (13753) 276/L6
Delhi, Okla. (†73662) 288/G4
Delhi, Ontario 177/D5
Delia, Alberta 182/D4
Delia, Kansas (66418) 232/G2
Delice, Dominica 161/F7
Delice, Turkey 63/E3
Delice (riv.), Turkey 63/F3
Délices, Fr. Guiana 131/E3
Delicias, Cuba 158/H3
Delicias, Venezuela 124/B4
Delight, Ark. (71940) 202/C5
Delijan, Iran 66/G4
Delingha, China 77/E4
De Lisle, Miss. (†39571) 256/F10
Delisle, Québec 172/F1
Delisle, Sask. 181/D4
Delitzsch, E. Germany 22/E3
Dell, Ark. (72426) 202/K2
Dell, Mont. (59724) 262/D6
Dell City, Texas (79837) 303/C10
Dell Rapids, S. Dak. (57022) 298/R6
Dellrose, Tenn. (38453) 237/H10
Dellroy, Ohio (44620) 284/H4
Dells, The (valley), Wis. 317/G8
Dellslow, W. Va. (26531) 312/G3
Dellwood, Minn. (†55110) 255/F5
Dellwood, Mo. (†63135) 261/R2
Dellwood, N.C. (†28786) 281/C3
Dellwood, Wis. (53927) 317/G7
Dellys, Algeria 106/E1
Delmar, Ala. (35551) 195/C2
Del Mar, Calif. (92014) 204/H11
Delmar, Del. (19940) 245/R7
Delmar, Iowa (52037) 229/M4
Delmar, Md. (21875) 245/R7
Delmar, N.Y. (12054) 276/N5
Delmas, Sask. 181/C3
Delmas, S. Africa 118/J6
Delmenhorst, W. Germany 22/C2
Delmont, N.J. (08314) 273/C5
Delmont, Pa. (15626) 294/D5
Delmont, S. Dak. (57330) 298/N7
Del Norte (co.), Calif. 204/B2
Del Norte, Colo. (81132) 208/G7
Del Norte (peak), Colo. 208/F7
Deloit, Iowa (51441) 229/C4
DeLong (mts.), Alaska 196/F1
De Long, Ill. (†61436) 222/C3
Delong, Ind. (46922) 227/E2
Deloraine, Man. 162/G6
Deloraine, Manitoba 179/B5
Deloraine, Tasmania 99/C3
Delorme (lake), Québec 174/C2
Deloro, Ontario 177/G3
Delphi, Ind. (46923) 227/D3
Delphia, Ky. (41735) 237/P6
Delphos, Iowa (50844) 229/E7
Delphos, Kansas (67436) 232/E2
Delphos, Ohio (45833) 284/B4
Delpine, Mont. (†59053) 262/F4
Delran○, N.J. (08075) 273/B3
Delray Beach, Fla. (*33444) 212/F5
Del Rey Oaks, Calif. (93940) 204/D7
Del Rio, Tenn. (37727) 237/P9
Del Rio, Texas 188/F5
Del Rio, Texas 146/H7
Del Rio, Texas (78840) 303/D8
Del Rosa, Calif. (92404) 204/E10
Delson, Québec 172/H4
Delta, Ala. (36258) 195/G4
Delta, Br. Col. 184/K3
Delta (co.), Colo. 208/D5
Delta, Colo. (81416) 208/D5
Delta, Iowa (52550) 229/J6
Delta, La. (71233) 238/J2
Delta, Manitoba 179/D4
Delta (co.), Mich. 250/C2
Delta, Mo. (63744) 261/N8
Delta, Ohio (43515) 284/B2
Delta, Ontario 177/H3
Delta, Pa. (17314) 294/K6
Delta (co.), Texas 303/J4
Delta, Utah (84624) 304/B4
Delta, Wis. (†54856) 317/D3
Delta Amacuro (terr.), Venezuela 124/H3
Delta City, Miss. (39061) 256/C4
Delta Junction, Alaska (99737) 196/J2
Deltaville, Va. (23043) 307/R5
Delton, Mich. (49046) 250/D6
Deltona, Fla. (32725) 212/E3
Delungra, N.S. Wales 97/F1
Del Valle, Argentina 143/F7
Del Valle (lake), Calif. 204/L3
Delvin, Ireland 17/G4
Delvinákion, Greece 45/E6
Delvinë, Albania 45/D6
Delwin, Mich. (†48858) 250/E5
Demaine, Sask. 181/D5
Demak, Indonesia 85/J2
Demanda, Sierra de la (range), Spain 33/E1
Demarcation (pt.), Alaska 196/K1
Demarest, N.J. (07627) 273/C1
Demavend (Damavend) (mt.), Iran 66/G3
Demba, Zaire 115/D5
Dembidollo, Ethiopia 111/F6
Demchok, India 68/D2
Demerara (riv.), Guyana 131/B3
Demidov, U.S.S.R. 52/D3
Deming, N. Mex. (88030) 274/B6
Deming, Wash. (98244) 310/C2
Demini (riv.), Brazil 132/H8
Demirci, Turkey 63/C3
Demirkent, Turkey 63/E4
Demirköy, Turkey 63/B2
Demir Qapu, Syria 63/J4
Demmin, E. Germany 22/E2
Democracia, Venezuela 124/E6
Demopolis, Ala. (36732) 195/C6
Demopolis (dam), Ala. 195/C5
Demopolis (lake), Ala. 195/C5
Demorest, Georgia (30535) 217/F1
De Mossville, Ky. (41033) 237/N3
Demotte, Ind. (46310) 227/C2
Dempo (mt.), Indonesia 85/C6
Dempster, S. Dak. (57230) 298/R4
Demster, N.Y. (†13126) 276/H3
Demta, Indonesia 85/L6
Denain, France 28/E2
Denali, Alaska (†99729) 196/J2
Denali Nat'l Park, Alaska 196/H2
Denali Nat'l Preserve, Alaska 196/H2
Denare Beach, Sask. 181/M4
Denau, U.S.S.R. 48/G6
Denbigh (cape), Alaska 196/F2
Denbigh, N. Dak. (58732) 282/J3
Denbigh, Ontario 177/G2
Denbigh, Wales 13/D4
Denbigh, Wales 10/E4
Den Burg, Netherlands 27/F2
Denby, S. Dak. (57733) 298/E7
Denby Dale, England 13/J2
Den Chai, Thailand 72/C3
Dender (riv.), Belgium 27/D7
Denderleeuw, Belgium 27/E7
Dendermonde, Belgium 27/E6
Dendron, Va. (23839) 307/P6
Denekamp, Netherlands 27/L4
Denezhkin Kamen' (mt.), U.S.S.R. 52/J2
Dengkou, China 77/G3
Dêngqên, China 77/E5
Denham, Ind. (46925) 227/D2
Denham, Minn. (55728) 255/F4
Denham, W. Australia 92/A4
Denham Springs, La. (70726) 238/L2
Den Helder, Netherlands 27/F3
Denhoff, N. Dak. (58430) 282/K5
Denholm, Sask. 181/C3
Denholm, Scotland 15/F5
Denia, Spain 33/G3
Deniliquin, N. S. Wales 88/G7
Deniliquin, N.S. Wales 97/C4
Denio, Nev. (89404) 266/C1
Denison, Iowa (51442) 229/C4
Denison, Kansas (66419) 232/G2
Denison (dam), Okla. 288/O7
Denison (range), Tasmania 99/C4
Denison, Texas 188/G4
Denison, Texas (75020) 303/H4
Denison (dam), Texas 303/H4
Denison, Wash. (†99006) 310/H3
Denizli (prov.), Turkey 63/C4
Denizli, Turkey 63/C4
Denizli, Turkey 59/A2
Denman, N.S. Wales 97/F3
Denman Island, Br. Col. 184/H2
Denmark 2/K3
Denmark 7/E3
Denmark (strait) 4/C11
Denmark (str.) 146/S3
Denmark (str.) 7/B2
DENMARK 18/D9
DENMARK 21/E6
Denmark, Iowa (52624) 229/L7
Denmark, Kansas (†67455) 232/D2
Denmark○, Maine (04022) 243/B8
Denmark, Miss. (†38655) 256/F2
Denmark (bay), N.W. Terrs. 187/H2
Denmark, Oreg. (†97450) 291/C5
Denmark, S.C. (29042) 296/E5
Denmark, Tenn. (38391) 237/D9
Denmark, W. Australia 88/B7
Denmark, W. Australia 92/B6
Denmark, Wis. (54208) 317/L7
Dennard, Ark. (72629) 202/E2
Dennehotso, Ariz. (86535) 198/F2
Dennery, St. Lucia 161/G6
Denning, Ark. (†72821) 202/C3
Dennis (hill), Conn. 210/C1
Dennis, Kansas (67341) 232/G4
Dennis○, Mass. (02638) 249/O5
Dennis, Miss. (38838) 256/H1
Dennis (head), Scotland 15/F1
Dennison, Minn. (55018) 255/E6
Dennison, Ohio (44621) 284/H5
Dennis Port, Mass. (02639) 249/O6
Denniston, Va. (†24520) 307/L7
Dennisville, N.J. (08214) 273/D5
Dennisville, Sask. 181/K6
Denny and Dunipace, Scotland 10/B1
Denny and Dunipace, Scotland 15/C1
Dennysville○, Maine (04628) 243/J6
Den Oever, Netherlands 27/G3
Denoon (lake), Wis. 317/K2
Denpasar, Indonesia 85/E7
Densmore, Kansas (67633) 232/C2
Dent, Minn. (56528) 255/C4
Dent (co.), Mo. 261/J7
Dent, Ohio (†45202) 284/B9
Dent Blanche (mt.), Switzerland 39/E4
Dent de Lys (mt.), Switzerland 39/D4
Dent de Ruth (mt.), Switzerland 39/D3
Dent d'Hérens (mt.), Switzerland 39/E5

362 Dovre

Dovre, Norway 18/F6
Dovrefjell (hills), Norway 18/F5
Dow (Xau) (lake), Botswana 118/C4
Dow, Ill. (62022) 222/C4
Dow, Okla. (†74547) 288/P5
Dowa, Malawi 115/F6
Dowagiac, Mich. (49047) 250/D6
Dow City, Iowa (51528) 229/B5
Dowell, Ill. (62927) 222/D6
Dowelltown, Tenn. (37059) 237/K8
Dowlatabad, Afghanistan 59/H3
Dowlatabad, Afghanistan 68/A2
Dowlatabad, Kerman, Iran 66/K6
Dowlatabad, Khorasan, Iran 66/M2
Dowlat Yar, Afghanistan 59/J3
Dowlat Yar, Afghanistan 68/B2
Dowling, Alberta 182/E4
Dowling (lake), Alberta 182/D4
Dowling, Mich. (49050) 250/D6
Dowling Park, Fla. (32060) 212/C1
Down (dist.), N. Ireland 17/K3
Downe, Sask. 181/C4
Downer, Minn. (†56514) 255/B4
Downers Grove, Ill. (60515) 222/A6
Downey, Calif. (*90240) 204/C11
Downey, Idaho (83234) 220/F7
Downey, Iowa (†52358) 229/L5
Downfall (creek), Queensland 95/D2
Downham Market, England 13/H5
Downham Market, England 10/G4
Downieville, Calif. (95936) 204/E4
Downing, Mo. (63536) 261/H2
Downing, Wis. (54734) 317/B5
Downings, Va. (†22460) 307/P5
Downingtown, Pa. (19335) 294/L5
Downpatrick (head), Ireland 17/C3
Downpatrick, N. Ireland 10/C3
Downpatrick, N. Ireland 17/K3
Downs, Ill. (61736) 222/E3
Downs, Kansas (67437) 232/D2
Downsville, La. (71234) 238/F1
Downsville, Md. (†21795) 245/G2
Downsville, N.Y. (13755) 276/L6
Downsville, Wis. (54735) 317/C6
Downton, England 13/F6
Dows, Iowa (50071) 229/F3
Dowshi, Afghanistan 59/J2
Dowshi, Afghanistan 68/B1
Doyle, Calif. (96109) 204/E3
Doyle, Georgia (†31803) 217/D6
Doyle, Tenn. (38559) 237/K9
Doylestown, Ohio (44230) 284/G4
Doylestown, Pa. (18901) 294/M5
Doylestown, Wis. (53928) 317/H9
Doyleville, Colo. (†81239) 208/F6
Doyline, La. (71023) 238/D1
Doyon, N. Dak. (58328) 282/O3
Dozen (isls.), Japan 81/F5
Dozier, Ala. (36028) 195/F7
Dozier, Texas (†79079) 303/D2
Dozois (res.), Québec 174/B3
Dra, Wadi (dry riv.), Morocco 106/C3
Drachten, Netherlands 27/J2
Dracut○, Mass. (01826) 249/J2
Drăgănești Olt, Romania 45/G3
Drăgășani, Romania 45/F3
Dragonera (isl.), Spain 33/H3
Dragons Mouth (str.), Trin. & Tob. 156/F5
Dragons Mouth (str.), Trin. & Tob. 161/A10
Dragons Mouth (str.), Venezuela 124/H2
Dragoon, Ariz. (85609) 198/F6
Dragoon (mts.), Ariz. 198/F7
Draguignan, France 28/G6
Drain, Oreg. (97435) 291/D4
Drake (passage) 2/F8
Drake (passage) 5/C15
Drake (passage), Chile 138/E11
Drake, Colo. (80515) 208/J2
Drake, Mo. (†65066) 261/K6
Drake, N. Dak. (58736) 282/K4
Drake, Sask. 181/G4
Drakensberg (range), Lesotho 118/D6
Drakensberg (range), S. Africa 118/D6
Drakensberg (range), Swaziland 118/D6
Drakes (creek), Ky. 237/J7
Drakesboro, Ky. (42337) 237/H6
Drakes Branch, Va. (23937) 307/L7
Drakesville, Iowa (52552) 229/J7
Draketown, Georgia (†30179) 217/B3
Dráma, Greece 45/F5
Drammen, Norway 7/E3
Drammen, Norway 18/C4
Drance (riv.), Switzerland 39/D4
Drancy, France 28/B1
Drang, Ia (riv.), Cambodia 72/E4
Draper, S. Dak. (57531) 298/J6
Draper, Utah (84020) 304/C3
Draper, Va. (24324) 307/G7
Draper, Wis. (†54852) 317/E4
Draperstown, N. Ireland 17/H2
Draperstown, N. Ireland 10/C3
Drasco, Ark. (72530) 202/G2
Drau (riv.), Austria 41/C3
Drava (riv.) 7/F4
Dráva (riv.), Hungary 41/D3
Drava (riv.), Yugoslavia 45/C3
Dravosburg, Pa. (15034) 294/C7
Drawsko Pomorskie, Poland 47/B2
Drax Hall, Barbados 161/B8
Drayden, Md. (20630) 245/N8
Drayton, N. Dak. (58225) 282/R2
Drayton, Ontario 177/D4
Drayton Plains, Mich. (48020) 250/F6
Drayton Valley, Alberta 182/C3
Drenthe (prov.), Netherlands 27/K3
Dresbach, Minn. (55930) 255/G7
Dresden, E. Germany 7/F3
Dresden (dist.), E. Germany 22/E3
Dresden, E. Germany 22/E3
Dresden, Kansas (67635) 232/B2
Dresden○, Maine (04342) 243/D7
Dresden, Mo. (†65301) 261/F5
Dresden, N.Y. (14441) 276/F5
Dresden, N. Dak. (†58249) 282/O2
Dresden, Ohio (43821) 284/G5
Dresden, Ontario 177/B5
Dresden, Tenn. (38225) 237/D8
Dresden Station, N.Y. (†12887) 276/O3
Dresser, Wis. (54009) 317/A5
Dreux, France 28/D3
Drew (co.), Ark. 202/G6
Drew, Miss. (38737) 256/C3
Drew, Oreg. (†97484) 291/E5
Drewry, Ala. (†36460) 195/D8
Drewryville, Va. (23844) 307/O7
Drews (res.), Oreg. 291/G5
Drewsey, Oreg. (97904) 291/J4
Drewsville, N.H. (03604) 268/C5
Drexel, Mo. (64742) 261/C6
Drexel, N.C. (28619) 281/F3
Drexel Hill, Pa. (19026) 294/M6
Dreyfus, Ky. (40426) 237/N5
Drezdenko, Poland 47/B2
Driebergen, Netherlands 27/G4
Driffield, England 13/G3
Driffield, England 10/F4
Drift (creek), Oreg. 291/B3
Drifton, Pa. (18221) 294/L3
Driftwood, Okla. (†73722) 288/K1
Driftwood, Pa. (15832) 294/F3
Driggs, Ark. (†72943) 202/C3
Driggs, Idaho (83422) 220/G6
Drill, Va. (†24260) 307/E6
Drimoleague, Ireland 17/C8
Drin (riv.), Albania 45/E4
Drina (riv.), Yugoslavia 45/D3
Drinkwater, Sask. 181/F5
Dripping Springs, Texas (78620) 303/F7
Driscoll, N. Dak. (58532) 282/K6
Driscoll, Texas (78351) 303/G10
Drishane, Ireland 17/C7
Driskill (mt.), La. 238/E2
Drøbak, Norway 18/D4
Drobeta-Turnu Severin, Romania 45/F3
Drogenbos, Belgium 27/B10
Drogheda, Ireland 17/J4
Drogheda, Ireland 10/C4
Drogobych, U.S.S.R. 52/B5
Drogobych, U.S.S.R. 48/C5
Droichead Nua, Ireland 10/C4
Droichead Nua, Ireland 17/H5
Droitwich, England 13/E5
Dromahair, Ireland 17/E3
Drome (dept.), France 28/F5
Drome (riv.), France 28/F5
Dromore, Bainbridge, N. Ireland 17/J3
Dromore, Omagh, N. Ireland 17/G3
Dromore West, Ireland 17/D3
Dronfield, England 13/J2
Drongan, Scotland 15/D5
Dronne (riv.), France 28/D5
Dronninglund, Denmark 21/D3
Dronten (prov.), Netherlands 27/H4
Dronten, Netherlands 27/H3
Dropmore, Manitoba 179/A3
Drouin, Victoria 97/C6
Druid, Sask. 181/C4
Druif, Neth. Ant. 161/D10
Drum (hills), Ireland 17/F7
Drum (bay), La. 238/M7
Drum (inlet), N.C. 281/S5
Drumaness, N. Ireland 17/K3
Drumbeg, Scotland 15/C2
Drumbo, Ontario 177/D4
Drumcar, Ireland 17/J4
Drumconrath, Ireland 17/H4
Drumheller, Alberta 182/D4
Drumheller, Alta. 162/E5
Drumhill, N.C. (†27937) 281/R1
Drumkeerin, Ireland 17/E3
Drumlish, Ireland 17/F4
Drummond, Idaho (†83420) 220/G5
Drummond (isl.), Mich. 250/F2
Drummond, Mont. (59832) 262/D4
Drummond, New Bruns. 170/C1
Drummond (mt.), North. Terr. 93/E5
Drummond, Okla. (73735) 288/L2
Drummond (co.), Québec 172/E4
Drummond (range), Queensland 88/H4
Drummond (range), Queensland 95/C5
Drummond (lake), Va. 307/P7
Drummond, Wis. (54832) 317/D3
Drummond Island, Mich. (49726) 250/F3
Drummonds, Tenn. (38023) 237/A10
Drummondville, Québec 172/E4
Drummondville-Nord, Québec 172/E4
Drummondville-Sud, Québec 172/E4
Drummore, Scotland 15/D6
Drummoyne, N. S. Wales 88/K4
Drummoyne, N.S. Wales 97/J3
Drumnadrochit, Scotland 15/D3
Drumquin, N. Ireland 17/G3
Drumright, Okla. (74030) 288/N3
Drums, Pa. (18222) 294/K3
Drumshanbo, Ireland 17/E3
Drury, Mo. (65638) 261/H9
Druskininkai, U.S.S.R. 53/C3
Druten, Netherlands 27/H5
Druz, Jebel ed (mts.), Syria 63/G6
Druzhba, U.S.S.R. 48/J5
Druzhina, U.S.S.R. 48/P3
Drvar, Yugoslavia 45/C3
Dry (bay), Alaska 196/L3
Dry (creek), Ky. 237/R3
Dry (lake), N. Dak. 282/M3
Dry (riv.), North. Terr. 88/E3
Dry (riv.), North. Terr. 93/C3
Dry (creek), S. Dak. 298/G4
Dry (lake), S. Dak. 298/P3
Dry (creek), Wyo. 319/C2
Dryad, Wash. (†98532) 310/B4
Dryanovo, Bulgaria 45/G4
Dry Branch, Georgia (31020) 217/F5
Dry Cimarron (riv.), N. Mex. 274/F2
Dry Coal (creek), Utah 304/A6
Dry Cottonwood (creek), Wyo. 319/D1
Dry Creek, La. (70637) 238/D5
Dry Creek, W. Va. (25062) 312/D7
Dryden, Ark. (†72401) 202/J2
Dryden, Maine (04225) 243/C6
Dryden, Mich. (48428) 250/F6
Dryden, N.Y. (13053) 276/H6
Dryden, Ontario 177/G4
Dryden, Ontario 175/B3
Dryden, Texas (78851) 303/C7
Dryden, Va. (24243) 307/B7
Dryden, Wash. (98821) 310/E3
Dry Falls (dam), Wash. 310/F3
Dry Fork, Va. (24549) 307/K7
Dryfork, W. Va. (26263) 312/H5
Dry Fork (riv.), W. Va. 312/G5
Dry Fork (riv.), W. Va. 312/C8
Dry Fork, Cheyenne (riv.), Wyo. 319/G2
Dry Fork, Powder (riv.), Wyo. 319/F2
Dry Lake, Nev. (†89040) 266/G6
Drymen, Scotland 15/B1
Dry Mills, Maine (†04039) 243/C8
Dry Prong, La. (71423) 238/E3
Dry Ridge, Ky. (41035) 237/M3
Dry Run, Pa. (17220) 294/G5
Drysdale (riv.), W. Australia 88/D3
Drysdale (riv.), W. Australia 92/D1
Dry Tortugas (keys), Fla. 212/D7
Drytown, Calif. (95699) 204/C8
Dry Wood (lake), S. Dak. 298/P2
Dschang, Cameroon 115/A2
Duaca, Venezuela 124/D2
Duaringa, Queensland 95/D4
Duart, Ontario 177/C5
Duarte, Calif. (91010) 204/D10
Duarte (prov.), Dom. Rep. 158/E5
Duarte (peak), Dom. Rep. 158/D5
Dubach, La. (71235) 238/E1
Dubai, U.A.E. 59/F4
Dubawnt (lake), N.W.T. 162/F3
Dubawnt (lake), N.W.T. 146/H3
Dubawnt (lake), N.W. Terrs. 187/H3
Dubawnt (riv.), N.W.T. 162/F3
Dubawnt (riv.), N.W. Terrs. 187/H3
Du Bay (lake), Wis. 317/G6
Dubberly, La. (71024) 238/D1
Dubbo, N. S. Wales 88/H6
Dubbo, N.S. Wales 97/E3
Dubbs, Miss. (†38626) 256/D1
Dübendorf, Switzerland 39/G2
Dublin, Calif. (94566) 204/K2
Dublin, Georgia (31021) 217/G5
Dublin, Ind. (47335) 227/G5
Dublin (co.), Ireland 17/J5
Dublin (cap.), Ireland 7/D3
Dublin (cap.), Ireland 17/K5
Dublin (cap.), Ireland 10/C4
Dublin (bay), Ireland 10/C4
Dublin (bay), Ireland 17/J5
Dublin, Ky. (†42039) 237/D7
Dublin, Md. (†21154) 245/N2
Dublin, Mich. (†49689) 250/D4
Dublin, Miss. (38739) 256/C2
Dublin○, N.H. (03444) 268/C6
Dublin, N.C. (28332) 281/M5
Dublin, Ohio (43017) 284/D5
Dublin, Ontario 177/C4
Dublin, Pa. (18917) 294/M5
Dublin, Texas (76446) 303/F5
Dublin, Va. (24084) 307/G6
Dubna, U.S.S.R. 52/E4
Dubna, U.S.S.R. 52/E3
Dubnica nad Váhom, Czech. 41/E2
Dubno, U.S.S.R. 52/C4
Dubois, Idaho (83423) 220/F5
Dubois, Ill. (62831) 222/D5
Dubois (co.), Ind. 227/D8
Dubois, Ind. (47525) 227/D8
Du Bois, Nebr. (68345) 264/H4
DuBois, Pa. (15801) 294/E3
Dubois, Wyo. (82513) 319/C2
Duboistown, Pa. (†17701) 294/H3
Dubréka, Guinea 106/B7
Dubreuilville, Ontario 177/J5
Dubrovnik, Yugoslavia 45/C4
Dubrueilville, Ontario 175/D3
Dubuc, Sask. 181/J5
Dubuque (co.), Iowa 229/M4
Dubuque, Iowa 188/H2
Dubuque, Iowa (52001) 229/M3
Duchcov, Czech. 41/B1
Duchesne (co.), Utah 304/D3
Duchesne, Utah (84021) 304/D3
Duchesne (riv.), Utah 304/D3
Duchess, Alberta 182/E4
Duchess, Queensland 88/F4
Duchess, Queensland 95/A4
Ducie (isl.), Pitcairn Is. 87/O8
Duck (isls.), Maine 243/G7
Duck (lake), Mich. 250/F4
Duck (creek), Nev. 266/G3
Duck, N.C. (†27949) 281/T2
Duck (creek), Ohio 284/H6
Duck (isl.), Ontario 177/H4
Duck (isls.), Ontario 177/A2
Duck (riv.), Tenn. 237/F9
Duck, W. Va. (25063) 312/E5
Duck Bay, Manitoba 179/B2
Duck Hill, Miss. (38925) 256/E3
Duck Lake, Sask. 181/E3
Duck Lake Hist. Park, Sask. 181/E3
Duck Lake Post, Manitoba 179/J2
Duck Mountain Prov. Park, Manitoba 179/B3
Duck Mountain Prov. Park, Sask. 181/K4
Duck River, Tenn. (38454) 237/G9
Ducktown, Georgia (†30130) 217/D2
Ducktown, Tenn. (37326) 237/N10
Duckwater, Nev. (89314) 266/F4
Duclos, Québec 172/A4
Ducor, Calif. (93218) 204/G8
Ducos, Martinique 161/D6
Dudelange, Luxembourg 27/J10
Dudenville, Mo. (†64748) 261/D8
Duderstadt, W. Germany 22/D3
Dudhi, India 68/E4
Dudignac, Argentina 143/F7
Düdingen, Switzerland 39/D3
Dudinka, U.S.S.R. 54/K3
Dudinka, U.S.S.R. 4/B5
Dudinka, U.S.S.R. 48/J3
Dudley, England 13/E5
Dudley, England 10/G3
Dudley, Georgia (31022) 217/F5
Dudley○, Mass. (01570) 249/G4
Dudley, Mo. (63936) 261/M9
Dudley, N.C. (28333) 281/N4
Dudley, Pa. (16634) 294/F5
Dudley (lake), Québec 172/B3
Dudleytown, Ind. (†47274) 227/F7
Dudváh (riv.), Czech. 41/D2
Dudweiler, W. Germany 22/B4
Dueñas, Spain 33/D2
Duenweg, Mo. (64841) 261/D8
Duero (Douro) (riv.), Spain 33/C2
Due West, S.C. (29639) 296/C3
Duff, Sask. 181/H5
Duff, Tenn. (37729) 237/N8
Duffee, Miss. (†39337) 256/G6
Duffel, Belgium 27/F6
Dufferin (county), Ontario 177/D3
Duffield, Alberta 182/C3
Duffield, Va. (24244) 307/C7
Dufftown, Scotland 10/E2
Dufftown, Scotland 15/E3
Dufourspitze (mt.), Switzerland 39/E5
Dufresne, Manitoba 179/F5
Dufrost, Manitoba 179/E5
Dufur, Oreg. (97021) 291/F2
Dugald, Manitoba 179/F5
Dugger, Ind. (47848) 227/C6
Dugi Otok (isl.), Yugoslavia 45/B3
Dugspur, Va. (24325) 307/G7
Duguayville, New Bruns. 170/E1
Du Gué (riv.), Québec 174/C1
Dugway, Utah (84022) 304/B3
Dugway (range), Utah 304/A3
Dugway Proving Grounds, Utah 304/B3
Duhamel, Alberta 182/D3
Duhamel, Québec 172/B3
Duich, Loch (inlet), Scotland 15/C3
Duida, Cerro (mt.), Venezuela 124/F6
Duifken (pt.), Queensland 88/G2
Duifken (pt.), Queensland 95/B2
Duiker (pt.), S. Africa 118/E6
Duinain (riv.), Scotland 15/B3
Duirinish (dist.), Scotland 15/B3
Duisburg, W. Germany 22/B3
Duitama, Colombia 126/D5
Duiveland (isl.), Netherlands 27/D5
Duivendrecht, Netherlands 27/C5
Duke, Ala. (†36279) 195/G3
Duke (isl.), Alaska 196/N2
Duke, Mo. (65461) 261/H7
Duke, Okla. (73532) 288/G5
Duke Center, Pa. (16729) 294/F2
Dukedom, Tenn. (38226) 237/D8
Duke of Gloucester (isls.), Fr. Poly. 87/M8
Dukes (co.), Mass. 249/M7
Dukes, Mich. (†49885) 250/B2
Dukhan, Qatar 59/F4
Duki, Pakistan 68/B2
Dukla (pass), Czech. 41/F2
Dukla (pass), Poland 47/E4
Dukou, China 77/F6
Dulac, La. (70353) 238/J8
Dulah, N.C. (†28463) 281/M6
Dulan, China 77/E4
Dulce (riv.), Argentina 143/D2
Dulce (gulf), C. Rica 154/F6
Dulce, N. Mex. (87528) 274/B2
Duleek, Ireland 17/J4
Dulgalakh (riv.), U.S.S.R. 48/O3
Dülmen, W. Germany 22/B3
Dulunguin (pt.), Philippines 82/C7
Duluth, Georgia (30136) 217/D2
Duluth, Kansas (66421) 232/F2
Duluth, Minn. 146/J5
Duluth, Minn. 188/H1
Duluth, Minn. (*55801) 255/F4
Dulverton, England 13/D6
Duma, Syria 63/G6
Duma, West Bank 65/C3
Dumagasa (pt.), Philippines 82/C7
Dumaguete, Philippines 82/D6
Dumaguete, Philippines 85/G4
Dumanquilas (bay), Philippines 82/D7
Dumaran (isl.), Philippines 85/G3
Dumaran (isl.), Philippines 82/C5
Dumaresq (riv.), N.S. Wales 97/F1
Dumas, Ark. (71639) 202/H6
Dumas, Miss. (38625) 256/G1
Dumas, Sask. 181/J6
Dumas, Texas (79029) 303/C2
Dumbarton, New Bruns. 170/C3
Dumbarton, Scotland 10/A1
Dumbarton, Scotland 15/B1
Dum Dum, India 68/F1
Dume (pt.), Calif. 204/G10
Dumeir, Syria 63/G6
Dumfoundling (bay), Fla. 212/C4
Dumfries, New Bruns. 170/C3
Dumfries, Scotland 15/E5
Dumfries, Scotland 10/E3
Dumfries (trad. co.), Scotland, 15/B5
Dumfries, Va. (22026) 307/O3
Dumfries and Galloway (reg.), Scotland 15/E5
Dumlu, Turkey 63/J2
Dummer○, N.H. (†03588) 268/E2
Dummer, Sask. 181/G6
Dümmersee (lake), W. Germany 22/C2
Dumont, Iowa (50625) 229/H3
Dumont, Minn. (56236) 255/B5
Dumont, N.J. (07628) 273/C1
Dumont, Texas (79232) 303/D4
Dumont d'Urville Station 5/C7
Dumyât (Damietta), Egypt 111/J3
Dumyat (Damietta), Egypt 59/B3
Dun (isl.), Scotland 15/A2
Duna (Danube) (riv.), Hungary 41/E3
Dunaff (head), Ireland 17/F1
Dunaföldvár, Hungary 41/E3
Dunaharaszti, Hungary 41/E3
Dunajec (riv.), Czech. 41/F2
Dunajec (riv.), Poland 47/E4
Dunajská Streda, Czech. 41/D3
Dunakeszi, Hungary 41/E3
Dunalley, Tasmania 99/D4
Dunany (pt.), Ireland 17/J4
Dunaszekcső, Hungary 41/E3
Dunaújváros, Hungary 41/E3
Dunav (Danube) (riv.), Bulgaria 45/H4
Dunavecse, Hungary 41/E3
Dunbar, Iowa (†50158) 229/H5
Dunbar, Nebr. (68346) 264/J4
Dunbar, Okla. (†74557) 288/P6
Dunbar, Pa. (15431) 294/C6
Dunbar, Scotland 10/E2
Dunbar, Scotland 15/F4
Dunbar, S.C. (†29525) 296/H2
Dunbar, W. Va. (25064) 312/C6
Dunbar, Wis. (54119) 317/K4
Dunbarton○, N.H. (†03301) 268/D5
Dunbarton (trad. co.), Scotland 15/A5
Dunbarton Center, N.H. (†03301) 268/D5
Dunbeath, Scotland 15/E2
Dunbeg, Scotland 15/C4
Dunblane, Sask. 181/D4
Dunblane, Scotland 15/E4
Dunblane, Scotland 10/D2
Dunbridge, Ohio (43414) 284/C3
Duncan, Ariz. (85534) 198/F6
Duncan, Br. Col. 184/J3
Duncan (riv.), Br. Col. 184/J5
Duncan (isls.), China 85/E2
Duncan, Ill. (†61559) 222/D3
Duncan (passage), India 68/G6
Duncan, Miss. (38740) 256/C2
Duncan, Nebr. (68634) 264/G3
Duncan, Okla. (73533) 288/L5
Duncan (lake), Québec 174/B2
Duncan, S.C. (29334) 296/C2
Duncan, W. Va. (25240) 312/C5
Duncan Falls, Ohio (43734) 284/G6
Duncannon, Ireland 17/H7
Duncannon, Pa. (17020) 294/H5
Duncans, Jamaica 158/H5
Duncans Bridge, Mo. (†63437) 261/H3
Duncansby (head), Scotland 15/F2
Duncansby (head), Scotland 10/E1
Duncansville, Pa. (16635) 294/F5
Duncanville, Ala. (35456) 195/D4
Duncanville, Texas (75116) 303/G3
Dunchurch, Ontario 177/E2
Duncombe, Iowa (50532) 229/E4
Duncombe (bay), Norfolk I. 88/L5
Dundaga, U.S.S.R. 53/B2
Dundalk, Ireland 17/H3
Dundalk, Ireland 10/C4
Dundalk (bay), Ireland 10/C4
Dundalk (bay), Ireland 17/J4
Dundalk, Md. (21222) 245/N3
Dundalk, Ontario 177/D3
Dundarrach, N.C. (†28386) 281/L5
Dundas (isl.), Br. Col. 184/B3
Dundas, Greenl. 4/B13
Dundas, Greenland 146/M2
Dundas, Ill. (62425) 222/E5
Dundas, Minn. (55019) 255/E6
Dundas (str.), North. Terr. 88/E2
Dundas (str.), North. Terr. 93/B1
Dundas (pen.), N.W. Terrs. 187/G2
Dundas, Ohio (45625) 284/E7
Dundas (county), Ontario 177/J2
Dundas, Ontario 177/E2
Dundas, Va. (23938) 307/M7
Dundas (lake), W. Australia 88/C6
Dundas (lake), W. Australia 92/C6
Dundee, Fla. (33838) 212/E3
Dundee (East and West Dundee), Ill. (60118) 222/E1
Dundee, Ind. (†47348) 227/F4
Dundee, Iowa (52038) 229/L3
Dundee, Ky. (42338) 237/H5
Dundee, Mich. (48131) 250/F7
Dundee, Minn. (56126) 255/C7
Dundee, Miss. (38626) 256/D1
Dundee, N.Y. (14837) 276/F5
Dundee, Oreg. (97115) 291/A2
Dundee, Scotland 7/D3
Dundee, Scotland 15/F4
Dundee, Scotland 10/E2
Dundee, S. Africa 118/E5
Dundee, Texas (76358) 303/F4
Dundgovĭ, Mongolia 77/G2
Dundon, W. Va. (†25043) 312/D6
Dundonald, Scotland 15/D5
Dundrum, N. Ireland 17/K3
Dundrum (bay), N. Ireland 17/K3
Dundurn, Sask. 181/E4
Dundy (co.), Nebr. 264/C4
Dune Acres, Ind. (†46304) 227/C1
Dunedin, Fla. (33528) 212/B2
Dunedin, N. Zealand 2/T8
Dunedin, N. Zealand 100/C6
Dunedoo, N.S. Wales 97/E3
Dunellen, N.J. (08812) 273/D2
Dunes (Westlake), Oreg. (†97493) 291/C4
Dunfanaghy, Ireland 17/F1
Dunfee, Ind. (†46802) 227/G2
Dunfermline, Ill. (61524) 222/D3
Dunfermline, Sask. 181/D3
Dunfermline, Scotland 15/D1
Dunfermline, Scotland 10/C1
Dungalear Station, N.S. Wales 97/D1
Dungannon (dist.), N. Ireland 17/H3
Dungannon, N. Ireland 17/H3
Dungannon, Ontario 177/C4
Dungannon, Va. (24245) 307/D7
Dungarpur, India 68/C4
Dungarvan, Ireland 10/C4
Dungarvan, Ireland 17/F7
Dungarvan (harb.), Ireland 10/C4
Dungarvan (harb.), Ireland 17/G7
Dungarvon (riv.), New Bruns. 170/D2
Dungeness (pt.), Argentina 143/C7
Dungeness (pt.), Chile 138/F10
Dungeness (prom.), England 13/J7
Dungeness (prom.), England 10/G5
Dungeness, Wash. (†98382) 310/B2
Dungiven, N. Ireland 17/H2
Dungloe, Ireland 17/E2
Dungog, N.S. Wales 97/F3
Dungu, Zaire 115/E3
Dungunab, Sudan 59/C5
Dungunab, Sudan 111/G3
Dunham, Québec 172/E4
Dunhua (Tunhwa), China 77/L3
Dunhuang, China 77/E3
Dunkeld, Queensland 95/D5
Dunkeld, Scotland 15/E4
Dunkeld, Victoria 97/B5
Dunkellin (riv.), Ireland 17/D5
Dunkerton, Iowa (50626) 229/J3
Dunkery (hill), England 13/D6
Dunkineely, Ireland 17/E2
Dunkirk (riv.), Alberta 182/D1
Dunkirk (Dunkerque), France 28/E2
Dunkirk, France 28/E2
Dunkirk, Ind. (47336) 227/G4
Dunkirk, N.Y. (14048) 276/B5
Dunkirk, Ohio (45836) 284/C4
Dunkley, Br. Col. 184/F3
Dunklin (co.), Mo. 261/M10
Dunkwa, Ghana 106/D7
Dún Laoghaire, Ireland 10/D4
Dún Laoghaire, Ireland 17/K5
Dunlap, Ill. (61525) 222/D3
Dunlap, Ind. (†46514) 227/F1
Dunlap, Iowa (51529) 229/B5
Dunlap, Kansas (66848) 232/F3
Dunlap, Tenn. (37327) 237/L10
Dunlavin, Ireland 17/H5
Dunleath, Sask. 181/K4
Dunleer, Ireland 17/J4
Dunleith, Miss. (†38756) 256/C4
Dunlow, W. Va. (25511) 312/B6
Dunloy, N. Ireland 17/J1
Dunmanus (bay), Ireland 17/B8
Dunmanway, Ireland 17/C8
Dunmanway, Ireland 10/B5
Dunmor, Ky. (42339) 237/G6
Dunmore, Alberta 182/E5
Dunmore, Ireland 17/D4
Dunmore, Pa. (18512) 294/F7
Dunmore (lake), Vt. 268/A4
Dunmore, W. Va. (24934) 312/G6
Dunmore East, Ireland 17/G7
Dunn, La. (71236) 238/G2
Dunn, N.C. (28334) 281/M4
Dunn (co.), N. Dak. 282/E5
Dunn, Texas (79516) 303/D5
Dunn (co.), Wis. 317/C6
Dunnamanagh, N. Ireland 17/G2
Dunn Center, N. Dak. (58626) 282/E5
Dunnegan, Mo. (65640) 261/E7
Dunnell, Minn. (56127) 255/D7
Dunnellon, Fla. (32630) 212/D2
Dunnet, Scotland 15/E2
Dunnet (bay), Scotland 15/E2
Dunnet (head), Scotland 10/E1
Dunnet (head), Scotland 15/E2
Dunnigan, Calif. (95937) 204/C5
Dunning, Nebr. (68833) 264/D3
Dunning, Scotland 15/E4
Dunn Loring, Va. (22027) 307/S2
Dunnottar, Manitoba 179/E4
Dunnottar, S. Africa 118/J6
Dunns, W. Va. (†25841) 312/D7
Dunnsville, Va. (22454) 307/P5
Dunnville, Ky. (42528) 237/M6
Dunnville, Ontario 177/E5
Du Noir (riv.), Wyo. 319/C2
Dunolly, Victoria 97/B5
Dunoon, Scotland 15/A2
Dunoon, Scotland 10/A1
Dunphy, Nev. (†89821) 266/E2
Dunragit, Scotland 15/D6
Dunrea, Manitoba 179/C5
Dunreith, Ind. (47337) 227/F5
Duns, Scotland 10/E3
Duns, Scotland 15/F5
Dunscore, Scotland 15/E5
Dunseith, N. Dak. (58329) 282/K2
Dunshaughlin, Ireland 17/H5
Dunsmuir, Calif. (96025) 204/C2
Dunstable, England 10/F5
Dunstable, England 13/G6
Dunstable○, Mass. (01827) 249/J2
Dunster, Br. Col. 184/G3
Duntochter, Scotland 15/B2
Dunure, Scotland 15/D5
Dunvegan, Nova Scotia 168/F4
Dunvegan, Scotland 15/B3
Dunvegan, Loch (inlet), Scotland 15/B3
Dunville, Newf. 166/D2
Dunwoody, Georgia (†30338) 217/K1
Duo, W. Va. (†25984) 312/E6
Duolun, China 77/J3
Duong Dong, Vietnam 72/D5
Du Page (co.), Ill. 222/E2
Du Page, East Branch (riv.), Ill. 222/A6
Du Page, West Branch (riv.), Ill. 222/A6
Du Page (riv.), Ill. 222/E2
Duparquet, Québec 174/B3
Duperow, Sask. 181/C4
Duplessis, La. (70728) 238/K2
Duplin (co.), N.C. 281/O5
Dupo, Ill. (62239) 222/A3
Du Pont, Georgia (31630) 217/G9
Dupont, Ind. (47231) 227/G7
Dupont, Ohio (45837) 284/B3
Dupont, Pa. (18641) 294/F7
Du Pont, Wash. (98327) 310/C3
Dupont Manor, Del. (†19901) 245/R4
Dupree, S. Dak. (57623) 298/F3
Dupuis Corner, New Bruns. 170/F2
Dupuy, Québec 174/B3
Dupuyer, Mont. (59432) 262/D2
Duque de Bragança, Angola 115/C5
Duque de Caxias, Brazil 135/E3
Duque de York (isl.), Chile 138/C9
Duquesne, Mo. (†64801) 261/D8
Duquesne, Pa. (15110) 294/C7
Duquette, Minn. (55729) 255/F4
Du Quoin, Ill. (62832) 222/D5
Duquoin, Kansas (†67058) 232/D4
Dura, West Bank 65/C4
Durack (range), W. Australia 88/D3
Durağan, Turkey 63/F2
Duran, N. Mex. (88319) 274/D4
Durance (riv.), France 28/F6

Eastsound 363

Durand, Georgia (†31830) 217/C5
Durand, Ill. (61024) 222/D1
Durand, Mich. (48429) 250/E6
Durand, Wis. (54736) 317/C6
Durango, Colo. 188/E3
Durango, Colo. (81301) 208/D8
Durango, Iowa (52039) 229/M3
Durango (state), Mexico 150/G4
Durango, Mexico 146/H7
Durango, Mexico 150/G4
Durango, Spain 33/E1
Duranillin, W. Australia 92/B2
Durant, Iowa (52747) 229/M5
Durant, Miss. (39063) 256/E4
Durant, Okla. 188/G4
Durant, Okla. (74701) 288/O6
Duratón (riv.), Spain 33/E2
Durazno (dept.), Uruguay 145/C3
Durazno, Uruguay 145/C4
Durazno, Grande del (range), Uruguay 145/D4
Durban, Manitoba 179/A3
Durban, S. Africa 2/L7
Durban, S. Africa 102/F7
Durban, S. Africa 118/E5
Durbanville, S. Africa 118/F6
Durbe, U.S.S.R. 53/A2
Durbin, Ind. (†46060) 227/F4
Durbin, N. Dak. (58023) 282/R6
Durbin, W. Va. (26264) 312/G5
Durbuy, Belgium 27/H8
Düren, W. Germany 22/B3
Durfee (hill), R.I. 249/G5
Durg, India 68/E4
Durgapur, India 68/F4
Durgerdam, Netherlands 27/C4
Durham, Ark. (†72701) 202/C2
Durham, Calif. (95938) 204/D4
Durham, Conn. (06422) 210/E3
Durham○, Conn. (06422) 210/E3
Durham (co.), England 13/F3
Durham, England 13/J3
Durham, England 10/F3
Durham, Kansas (67438) 232/E3
Durham, Mo. (63438) 261/J3
Durham, N.H. (03824) 268/F5
Durham○, N.H. (03824) 268/F5
Durham (pt.), N. Zealand 100/D7
Durham, N.C. 188/L3
Durham (co.), N.C. 281/M3
Durham, N.C. (*27701) 281/M2
Durham, Okla. (73642) 288/G3
Durham (reg. munic.), Ontario 177/F3
Durham, Ontario 177/D3
Durham, Oreg. (†97233) 291/A2
Durham Bridge, New Bruns. 170/D2
Durham Center, Conn. (†06422) 210/E3
Durham Downs, Queensland 95/B5
Durham-Sud, Québec 172/E4
Durhamville, N.Y. (13054) 276/J4
Duri, N.S. Wales 97/F3
Durkee, Oreg. (97905) 291/K3
Durness, Scotland 15/D2
Durnford (pt.), Western Sahara 106/A4
Dürnten, Switzerland 39/G2
Duror, Scotland 15/C4
Durrell, Newf. 166/D4
Dürrenroth, Switzerland 39/E2
Durrës (Durazzo), Albania 45/D5
Durrës, Albania 7/F4
Durrington, England 13/F6
Durrow, Laoighis, Ireland 17/G6
Durrow, Offaly, Ireland 17/F5
Dursey (isl.), Ireland 17/A8
Dursunbey, Turkey 63/C3
Duruh, Iran 59/H3
Duruh, Iran 66/M4
D'Urville (isl.), N. Zealand 100/D4
Duryea, Pa. (18642) 294/F7
Dusa Marreb, Somalia 115/J2
Dûsh, Egypt 59/B5
Dûsh, Egypt 111/F3
Dushan, China 77/G6
Dushanbe, U.S.S.R. 54/H6
Dushanbe, U.S.S.R. 2/N4
Dushanbe, U.S.S.R. 48/G6
Dushore, Pa. (18614) 294/K2
Dusky (sound), N. Zealand 100/A6
Duson, La. (70529) 238/F6
Düsseldorf, W. Germany 7/E3
Düsseldorf, W. Germany 22/B3
Dustin, Okla. (74839) 288/O4
Dusty, N. Mex. (87934) 274/B5
Dusty, Wash. (†99143) 310/H4
Dutch (creek), Ark. 202/C4
Dutch Cap (cay), Virgin Is. (U.S.) 161/A4
Dutchess (co.), N.Y. 276/N7
Dutch Flat, Calif. (95714) 204/E4
Dutch Harbor, Alaska (†99685) 196/E4
Dutch John, Utah (84023) 304/E3
Dutch Mills, Ark. (†72744) 202/B2
Dutch Neck, N.J. (†08550) 273/D3
Dutchtown, Mo. (63745) 261/N8
Dutton, Ala. (35744) 195/G1
Dutton, Ark. (†72760) 202/C2
Dutton (mt.), Conn. 210/C1
Dutton, Mont. (59433) 262/E3
Dutton, Ontario 177/C5
Dutton (mt.), Utah 304/B5
Duval (co.), Fla. 212/E1
Duval, Sask. 181/G4
Duval (co.), Texas 303/F10
Duvalierville, Haiti 158/C6
Duvall, Wash. (98019) 310/D3
Duvergé, Dom. Rep. 158/D6
Duvernay, Alberta 182/E3
Duwadami, Saudi Arabia 59/D5
Duxbury (pt.), Calif. 204/H2
Duxbury, Mass. (02332) 249/M4
Duxbury○, Mass. (02332) 249/M4
Duxbury○, Vt. (†05676) 268/B3
Duyun (Tuyün), China 77/G6
Düzce, Turkey 63/D2
Duzdab (Zahedan), Iran 66/M6
Dvina, (bay), U.S.S.R. 52/E2
Dvina, Northern (riv.), U.S.S.R. 4/C7
Dvina, Northern (riv.), U.S.S.R. 7/J2
Dvina, Northern (riv.), U.S.S.R. 48/E3
Dvina, Northern (riv.), U.S.S.R. 52/F2
Dvina, Western (riv.) U.S.S.R. 53/C2
Dvina, Western (riv.), U.S.S.R. 48/C4
Dvina, Western (riv.), U.S.S.R. 52/C3
Dvina, Western (riv.), U.S.S.R. 7/G3
Dvinsk (Daugavpils), U.S.S.R. 52/C3
Dvory nad Žitavou, Czech. 41/E3
Dvůr Králové nad Labem, Austria 41/C1
Dwale, Ky. (41621) 237/R5
Dwarka, India 68/B4
Dwellingup, W. Australia 92/B2
Dwight, Ill. (60420) 222/E2
Dwight, Kansas (66849) 232/F3
Dwight, Nebr. (68635) 264/G3
Dwight, N. Dak. (58024) 282/S7
Dwight, Ontario 177/F2
Dworshak (res.), Idaho 220/C3
Dwyer, N. Mex. (†88034) 274/B6
Dwyer, Wyo. (82211) 319/G3
Dyas, Ala. (†36507) 195/C9
Dyat'kovo, U.S.S.R. 52/D4
Dybvad, Denmark 21/D3
Dyce, Scotland 15/F3
Dyckesville, Wis. (†54217) 317/L6
Dycusburg, Ky. (42037) 237/E6
Dyer, Ark. (72935) 202/B3
Dyer, Ind. (46311) 227/C1
Dyer, Ky. (†40115) 237/J5
Dyer, Nev. (89010) 266/C5
Dyer (cape), N.W.T. 162/K2
Dyer (cape), N.W. Terrs. 187/M3
Dyer (co.), Tenn. 237/C8
Dyer, Tenn. (38330) 237/D8
Dyer Brook○, Maine (†04747) 243/G3
Dyersburg, Tenn. (38024) 237/C8
Dyersville, Iowa (52040) 229/L3
Dyess, Ark. (72330) 202/K2
Dyess A.F.B., Texas 303/D5
Dyfed, Wales 13/C6
Dyje (riv.), Czech. 41/D2
Dyke (lake), Newf. 166/A3
Dykh-Tau (mt.), U.S.S.R. 52/F6
Dyle (riv.), Belgium 27/F7
Dysart, Iowa (52224) 229/J4
Dysart, Sask. 181/H5
Dysartsville, N.C. (†28761) 281/F3
Dzamîn Üüd, Mongolia 77/H3
Dzaoudzi (cap.), Comoros 118/H2
Dzavhan, Mongolia 77/E2
Dzavhan Gol (riv.), Mongolia 77/D2
Dzerzhinsk, U.S.S.R. 7/J3
Dzerzhinsk, U.S.S.R. 48/E4
Dzerzhinsk, U.S.S.R. 52/F3
Dzhalal-Abad, U.S.S.R. 48/H5
Dzhalilabad, U.S.S.R. 52/G7
Dzhalinda, U.S.S.R. 48/N4
Dzhambul, U.S.S.R. 54/J5
Dzhambul, U.S.S.R. 48/H5
Dzhankoy, U.S.S.R. 52/D5
Dzhelinda, U.S.S.R. 48/M2
Dzhetygara, U.S.S.R. 48/G4
Dzhezkazgan, U.S.S.R. 54/H5
Dzhezkazgan, U.S.S.R. 48/G5
Dzhugdzhur (range), U.S.S.R. 54/P4
Dzhugdzhur (range), U.S.S.R. 48/O4
Dzhul'fa, U.S.S.R. 52/G7
Dzhusaly, U.S.S.R. 48/G5
Działdowo, Poland 47/E2
Dzibalchén, Mexico 150/P7
Dzibichaltún (ruin), Mexico 150/P6
Dzidzantún, Mexico 150/P6
Dzierżoniów, Poland 47/C3
Dzilam de Bravo, Mexico 150/P6
Dzitbalché, Mexico 150/P6
Dzurh, Mongolia 77/E2
Dzüünharaa, Mongolia 77/G2
Dzuunmod, Mongolia 77/G2

E

Eabamet (lake), Ontario 175/C2
Eads, Colo. (81036) 208/O6
Eads, Tenn. (38028) 237/B10
Eadytown, S.C. (†29468) 296/G5
Eagan, Minn. (55111) 255/G6
Eagan, Tenn. (37730) 237/O7
Eagar, Ariz. (85925) 198/F4
Eagarville, Ill. (†62033) 222/D4
Eagle, Alaska 188/D5
Eagle, Alaska (99738) 196/K2
Eagle (creek), Ariz. 198/F5
Eagle (lake), Calif. 204/E3
Eagle (peak), Calif. 204/E2
Eagle (co.), Colo. 208/F3
Eagle, Colo. (81631) 208/F3
Eagle (riv.), Colo. 208/E3
Eagle, Idaho (83616) 220/B6
Eagle (creek), Ind. 227/E4
Eagle (lake), Iowa 229/F2
Eagle (creek), Ky. 237/M3
Eagle (lake), Maine 243/F1
Eagle (lake), Maine 243/E3
Eagle, Mich. (48822) 250/E6
Eagle (mt.), Minn. 255/G2
Eagle, Nebr. (68347) 264/H4
Eagle (riv.), Newf. 166/C3
Eagle, Ontario 177/C5
Eagle (lake), Ontario 177/F5
Eagle (lake), Ontario 177/E2
Eagle (creek), Oreg. 291/K3
Eagle (hills), Sask. 181/C3
Eagle (peak), Texas 303/C11
Eagle (mt.), Virgin Is. (U.S.) 161/E4
Eagle, Wis. (53119) 317/H2
Eagle (lake), Wis. 317/H2
Eagle (lake), Wis. 317/K3
Eagle (peak), Wyo. 319/B1
Eagle Bay, N.Y. (13331) 276/L3
Eagle Bend, Minn. (56446) 255/D4
Eagle Bridge, N.Y. (12057) 276/O5
Eagle Butte, S. Dak. (57625) 298/G4
Eagle City, Okla. (73658) 288/J3
Eagle Crags (mt.), Calif. 204/J8
Eagle Creek, Oreg. (97022) 291/E2
Eagle Grove, Iowa (50533) 229/F3
Eagle Harbor, Md. (†20608) 245/M6
Eagle Harbor, Mich. (49951) 250/A1
Eaglehawk, Victoria 97/C5
Eaglehill (creek), Sask. 181/D4
Eagle Lake, Fla. (33839) 212/E4
Eagle Lake, Maine (04739) 243/F1
Eagle Lake○, Maine (04739) 243/F1
Eagle Lake, Minn. (56024) 255/E6
Eagle Lake, Ontario 177/F2
Eagle Lake, Texas (77434) 303/H8
Eagle Mills, Ark. (71729) 202/E6
Eagle Mountain, Calif. (92241) 204/K10
Eagle Mountain (lake), Texas 303/E2
Eagle Nest, N. Mex. (87718) 274/D2
Eagle Nest (lake), N. Mex. 274/D2
Eagle Pass, Texas (78852) 303/D9
Eagle Point, Oreg. (97524) 291/E5
Eagle River, Alaska (99577) 196/C1
Eagle River, Mich. (49924) 250/A1
Eagle River, Wis. (54521) 317/H4
Eagle Rock, Mo. (65641) 261/E9
Eagle Rock, Va. (24085) 307/J5
Eaglesfield, Scotland 15/E5
Eaglesham, Alberta 182/B2
Eaglesham, Scotland 15/D5
Eagles Mere, Pa. (17731) 294/J3
Eagle Springs, N.C. (27242) 281/K4
Eagleton Village, Tenn. (†37801) 237/O9
Eagletown, Ind. (†46074) 227/E4
Eagletown, Okla. (74734) 288/S6
Eagleville, Calif. (96110) 204/E2
Eagleville, Conn. (†06268) 210/F1
Eagleville, Mo. (64442) 261/D2
Eagleville, Tenn. (37060) 237/H9
Eakly, Okla. (73033) 288/K4
Ealing, England 13/H8
Ealing, England 10/B5
Ear (lake), Sask. 181/B3
Earby, England 13/H1
Eardley (lake), Manitoba 179/F2
Ear Falls, Ontario 175/B2
Earl (lake), Calif. 204/A2
Earl, N.C. (28038) 281/F4
Earl, Wis. (54833) 317/C4
Earle, Ark. (72331) 202/K3
Earle Naval Weapons Sta., N.J. 273/E3
Earleton, Fla. (32631) 212/D2
Earleville, Md. (21919) 245/P3
Earl Grey, Sask. 181/G5
Earlham, Iowa (50072) 229/E6
Earlimart, Calif. (93219) 204/F8
Earling, Iowa (51530) 229/C5
Earlington, Ky. (42410) 237/F6
Earl Park, Ind. (47942) 227/C3
Earlsboro, Okla. (74840) 288/N4
Earlston, Scotland 15/F5
Earlton, Kansas (†66720) 232/G4
Earlton, Ontario 177/K5
Earltown, Nova Scotia 168/E3
Earlville, Ill. (60518) 222/E2
Earlville, Iowa (52041) 229/L4
Earlville, N.Y. (13332) 276/J5
Early (co.), Georgia 217/C8
Early, Iowa (50535) 229/C4
Early Branch, S.C. (29916) 296/F6
Earlysville, Va. (22936) 307/M4
Earn, Loch (lake), Scotland 15/D4
Earn (riv.), Scotland 15/E4
Earnslaw (mt.), N. Zealand 100/B6
Earp, Calif. (92242) 204/L9
Earth, Texas (79031) 303/B3
Earthquake (lake), Mont. 262/E6
Easby, N. Dak. (†58249) 282/O2
Easington, England 13/J3
Easingwold, England 13/F3
Eask (lake), Ireland 17/E2
Easky, Ireland 17/D3
Easley, S.C. (29640) 296/B2
East (cape), Alaska 196/K4
East (riv.), Conn. 210/E3
East (pt.), Fla. 212/E6
East (bay), La. 238/M8
East (pt.), Mass. 249/E6
East (range), Nev. 266/D2
East (pt.), N.S. Wales 97/J2
East (riv.), N.Y. 276/N9
East (cape), N. Zealand 87/H9
East (cape), N. Zealand 100/G2
East (bay), Nova Scotia 168/H3
East (riv.), Nova Scotia 168/F3
East (lake), Oreg. 291/F4
East (pt.), Pr. Edward I. 168/G2
East (Dezhnev) (cape), U.S.S.R. 4/C18
East (pt.), Virgin Is. (U.S.) 161/G4
Eastaboga, Ala. (36260) 195/F3
Eastabuchie, Miss. (39436) 256/F8
East Albany, Vt. (†05820) 268/C2
East Alburg, Vt. (†05440) 268/A2
East Aldfield, Québec 172/A4
East Alligator (riv.), North. Terr. 93/C2
East Alton, Ill. (62024) 222/A2
East Andover, Maine (04226) 243/B6
East Andover, N.H. (03231) 268/D5
East Angus, Québec 172/F4
East Arcadia, N.C. (†28434) 281/N6
East Arlington, Vt. (05252) 268/A5
East Arrow Park, Br. Col. 184/J5
East Aspetuck (riv.), Conn. 210/B2
East Aurora, N.Y. (14052) 276/C5
East Baldwin, Maine (04024) 243/B8
East Bangor, Pa. (18013) 294/M4
East Bank, W. Va. (25067) 312/D6
East Barnet, Vt. (†05821) 268/C3
East Barre-Graniteville, Vt. (05649) 268/C3
East Barrington, N.H. (03825) 268/F5
East Baton Rouge (par.), La. 238/K1
East Bay, Nova Scotia 168/H2
East Bay (hills), Nova Scotia 168/H3
East Bend, N.C. (27018) 281/H2
East Berbice-Corantyne (dist.), Guyana 131/C3
East Berkshire, Vt. (05447) 268/B2
East Berlin, Conn. (06023) 210/E2
East Berlin, Pa. (17316) 294/J6
East Bernard, Texas (77435) 303/H8
East Bernstadt, Ky. (40729) 237/N6
East Berwick, Pa. (†18603) 294/K3
East Bethany, N.Y. (14054) 276/D5
East Bethel, Minn. (†55005) 255/E5
East Bethel, Vt. (†05032) 268/B4
East Bloomfield, N.Y. (14443) 276/E5
East Blue Hill, Maine (04629) 243/G7
East Blythe, Calif. (†92225) 204/L10
East Boothbay, Maine (04544) 243/D8
Eastborough, Kansas (†67201) 232/E4
Eastbourne, England 13/H7
Eastbourne, England 10/G5
Eastbourne, N. Zealand 100/B3
East Brady, Pa. (16028) 294/C3
East Braintree, Manitoba 179/G5
East Braintree, Mass. (†02184) 249/D8
East Braintree, Vt. (†05060) 268/B3
East Branch, N.Y. (13756) 276/K7
East Branch, Rocky (riv.), Ohio 284/G10
East Brewster, Mass. (†02631) 249/O5
East Brewton, Ala. (36426) 195/E8
East Bridgewater○, Mass. (02333) 249/L4
East Brisbane, Queensland 88/K3
East Brisbane, Queensland 95/E3
East Brookfield, Mass. (01515) 249/G4
East Brookfield○, Mass. (01515) 249/G4
East Brookfield, Vt. (†05036) 268/C3
East Brooklyn, Conn. (†06239) 210/H1
East Broughton, Québec 172/F3
East Broughton Station, Québec 172/F3
East Brownfield, Maine (†04010) 243/B8
East Brunswick○, N.J. (08816) 273/E3
East Burke, Vt. (05832) 268/D2
East Butler, Pa. (16029) 294/C4
East Calais, Vt. (05650) 268/C3
East Calder, Scotland 15/D2
East Camden, Ark. (71701) 202/E6
East Canaan, Conn. (06024) 210/B1
East Candia, N.H. (03040) 268/E5
East Canton, Ohio (44730) 284/H4
East Canyon (res.), Utah 304/C3
East Cape Girardeau, Ill. (†62957) 222/D6
East Carbon, Utah (84520) 304/D4
East Carondelet, Ill. (62240) 222/A3
East Carroll (par.), La. 238/H1
East Chain, Minn. (†56031) 255/D7
East Charleston, Vt. (05833) 268/D2
Eastchester, N.Y. (10709) 276/P6
East Chester, Nova Scotia 168/D4
East Chevington, England 13/F2
East Chezzetcook, Nova Scotia 168/E4
East Chicago, Ind. (46312) 227/C1
East Chicago Heights, Ill. (†60411) 222/C6
East China (sea) 54/O7
East China (sea), China 77/L6
East China (sea), Japan 81/C8
East China (sea), S. Korea 81/C8
East Chop (pt.), Mass. 249/M7
East Claridon, Ohio (44033) 284/H2
East Cleveland, Ohio (44112) 284/H9
East Coast Bays, N. Zealand 100/B1
East Concord, Vt. (†05906) 268/D3
East Conemaugh, Pa. (15909) 294/E5
East Corinth, Maine (04427) 243/F5
East Corinth, Vt. (05040) 268/C3
East Cote Blanche (bay), La. 238/G7
East Coulée, Alberta 182/D4
East Craftsbury, Vt. (05826) 268/C2
East Dedham, Mass. (02026) 249/C8
East Demerara-West Coast Berbice (dist.), Guyana 131/C2
East Dennis, Mass. (02641) 249/O5
East Dereham, England 13/H5
East Dereham, England 10/G4
East Derry, N.H. (03041) 268/E6
East Detroit, Mich. (48021) 250/B6
East Devils (lake), N. Dak. 282/N4
East Dixfield, Maine (04227) 243/C6
East Dixmont, Maine (†04932) 243/E6
East Dorset, Vt. (05253) 268/A5
East Douglas, Mass. (01516) 249/G4
East Dover, Vt. (05341) 268/B6
East Dublin, Georgia (31021) 217/G5
East Dubuque, Ill. (61025) 222/C1
East Duke, Okla. (†73532) 288/H5
East Dundee (Dundee), Ill. (†60118) 222/E1
East Durham, N.Y. (12423) 276/M6
East Eddington, Maine (04428) 243/F6
East Ellijay, Georgia (30539) 217/C1
East Ely, Nev. 266/G3
Eastend, Sask. 181/C6
Eastend, Virgin Is. (U.S.) 161/D4
East Enterprise, Ind. (47019) 227/H7
Easter (isl.), Chile 87/Q8
Easter (isl.), Chile 2/D7
Eastern (pt.), Conn. 210/G3
Eastern (Arabian) (des.), Egypt 111/F2
Eastern (prov.), Kenya 115/G4
Eastern (bay), Md. 245/N5
Eastern (pt.), Mass. 249/M2
Eastern (creek), N.S. Wales 97/H3
Eastern Channel (str.), Japan 81/D7
Eastern Ghats (mts.), India 68/D6
Eastern Samar (prov.), Philippines 82/E5
Eastern Scheldt (est.), Netherlands 27/D5
Eastern Taurus (mts.), Turkey 63/J3
Eastern Wolf (isl.), New Bruns. 170/D4
Easterville, Manitoba 179/C1
East Fairfield, Vt. (05448) 268/B2
East Falkland (isl.), 143/E7
East Falkland (isl.), Falk. Is. 120/D8
East Falmouth (Teaticket), Mass. (02536) 249/M6
East Farnham, Québec 172/E4
East Faxon, Pa. (†17701) 294/J3
East Feliciana (par.), La. 238/H5
East Ferry, Nova Scotia 168/B4
East Flanders (prov.), Belgium 27/D7
East Flat Rock, N.C. (28726) 281/E4
Eastford○, Conn. (06242) 210/G1
East Fork, Little Miami (riv.), Ohio 284/C7
East Fork, Green (riv.), Wyo. 319/C3
East Foxboro, Mass. (†02035) 249/K4
East Franklin, Maine (†04634) 243/G6
East Franklin, Vt. (†05457) 268/B2
East Freedom, Pa. (16637) 294/E5
East Freetown, Mass. (02717) 249/L5
East Friesland (reg.), W. Germany 22/B2
East Frisian (isls.), W. Germany 22/B2
East Gaffney, S.C. (†29340) 296/D1
East Galesburg, Ill. (61430) 222/C3
Eastgate, Nev. (†89406) 266/D3
East Georgia, Vt. (†05455) 268/A2
East Germantown (Pershing), Ind. (†47370) 227/G5
East Germany 7/F3
EAST GERMANY 22
East Gillespie, Ill. (†62033) 222/D4
East Glacier Park, Mont. (59434) 262/C2
East Glastonbury, Conn. (06025) 210/E2
East Grafton, N.H. (†03240) 268/D4
East Granby○, Conn. (06026) 210/E1
East Grand Forks, Minn. (56721) 255/B3
East Grand Rapids, Mich. (†49506) 250/D6
East Granville, Vt. (†05669) 268/B3
East Greenbush, N.Y. (12061) 276/N5
East Green Harbour, Nova Scotia 168/C5
East Greenville, Ohio (†44666) 284/G4
East Greenville, Pa. (18041) 294/L5
East Greenwich, R.I. (02818) 249/H6
East Grinstead, England 10/G5
East Grinstead, England 13/G6
Eastgulf, W. Va. (25835) 312/D7
East Gull Lake, Minn. (†56401) 255/D4
East Haddam○, Conn. (06423) 210/F3
Eastham○, Mass. (02642) 249/O5
East Hampstead, N.H. (03826) 268/E6
East Hampton, Conn. (06424) 210/E2
East Hampton○, Conn. (06424) 210/E2
Easthampton○, Mass. (01027) 249/D3
East Hampton, N.Y. (11937) 276/R9
East Hanover○, N.J. (07936) 273/E2
East Hardin, Ill. (†62031) 222/C4
East Hardwick, Vt. (05836) 268/C2
East Hartford○, Conn. (06108) 210/E1
East Hartland, Conn. (06027) 210/D1
East Harwich, Mass. (†02645) 249/O6
East Haven○, Conn. (06512) 210/D3
East Haven○, Vt. (05837) 268/D2
East Haverhill, N.H. (†03780) 268/D3
East Hazelcrest, Ill. (†60429) 222/C6
East Hebron, N.H. (03232) 268/D4
East Helena, Mont. (59635) 262/E4
East Hereford, Québec 172/F4
East Herkimer, N.Y. 276/L4
East Hickory, Pa. (16321) 294/D2
East Hills, N.Y. (†11576) 276/R7
East Hiram, Maine (†04041) 243/B8
East Hodge, La. (†71247) 238/E2
East Holden, Maine (04429) 243/F6
East Hope, Idaho (†83836) 220/B1
East Jackson, Maine (†04986) 243/E6
East Jamaica, Vt. (†05343) 268/B5
East Jordan, Mich. (49727) 250/D3
East Juliette, Georgia (†31046) 217/E4
East Keansburg, N.J. (07734) 273/E3
East Kelowna, Br. Col. 184/H5
East Kent, Conn. (†06785) 210/B2
East Kilbride, Scotland 15/B2
East Killingly, Conn. (06243) 210/H1
East Kingsford, Mich. (†49801) 250/A3
East Kingston○, N.H. (03827) 268/F6
East Knox, Maine (†04921) 243/E7
East Korea (bay), N. Korea 81/D4
East Lake, Mich. (49626) 250/C4
East Lake, Minn. (†55760) 255/E4
East Lake, N.C. (27931) 281/S3
Eastlake, Ohio (†44094) 284/J8
East Lake-Orient Park, Fla. (†33601) 212/C2
Eastland, Tenn. (†38583) 237/L9
Eastland (co.), Texas 303/F5
Eastland, Texas (76448) 303/F5
East Lansdowne, Pa. (†19050) 294/M7
East Lansing, Mich. (48823) 250/E6
East Laport, N.C. (†28723) 281/C4
East Las Vegas, Nev. (89112) 266/F6
East Laurinburg, N.C. (28352) 281/L5
East Lebanon, Maine (04027) 243/B9
East Lee, Mass. (†01238) 249/B3
Eastleigh, England 13/F7
Eastleigh, England 10/F5
East Lempster, N.H. (03605) 268/C5
East Limington, Maine (†04049) 243/B8
East Linton, Scotland 15/F5
East Litchfield, Conn. (†06759) 210/C1
East Livermore, Maine (04228) 243/C7
East Liverpool, Ohio (43920) 284/J4
East Loch (inlet), Hawaii 218/B3
East Loch Tarbert (inlet), Scotland 15/B3
East London, S. Africa 102/E8
East London, S. Africa 118/D6
East Longmeadow○, Mass. (01028) 249/E4
East Los Angeles, Calif. (90022) 204/C10
East Lowell, Maine (†04433) 243/G5
East Lyme○, Conn. (06333) 210/G3
East Lynn, Ill. (60932) 222/F3
East Lynn, W. Va. (25512) 312/B6
East Lynn (lake), W. Va. 312/B6
East Lynne, Mo. (64743) 261/D5
East Machias, Maine (04630) 243/J6
East Machias○, Maine (04630) 243/J6
East Machias (riv.), Maine 243/H6
East Madison, Maine (†04950) 243/D6
East Madison, N.H. (†03849) 268/E4
Eastmain, Que. 162/J5
Eastmain (riv.), Que. 146/L4
Eastmain (riv.), Que. 162/J5
Eastmain, Québec 174/B2
Eastmain (riv.), Québec 174/B2
Eastman, Georgia (31023) 217/F6
Eastman, Québec 172/E4
Eastman, Wis. (54626) 317/D9
East Marion, N.C. (†28752) 281/F3
East Meadow, N.Y. (11554) 276/R7
East Meredith, N.Y. (13757) 276/L6
East Middlebury, Vt. (05740) 268/A4
East Millcreek, Utah (84109) 304/C3
East Millinocket, Maine (04430) 243/F4
East Millinocket○, Maine (04430) 243/F4
East Millstone, N.J. (08873) 273/D3
East Milton, Mass. (†02186) 249/D7
East Mines, Nova Scotia 168/E3
East Moline, Ill. (61244) 222/C2
East Montpelier○, Vt. (05651) 268/B3
East Moriches, N.Y. (11940) 276/P9
East Morris, Conn. (†06763) 210/C2
East Murton, England 13/J3
East Musquash (lake), Maine 243/H5
East Naples, Fla. (†33940) 212/E5
East Newark, N.J. (†07100) 273/B2
East New Market, Md. (21631) 245/P6
East Newnan, Georgia (†30263) 217/C4
East New Portland, Maine (†04954) 243/D6
East Nishnabotna (riv.), Iowa 229/C6
East Northfield, Mass. (†01360) 249/E2
East Northport, N.Y. (11731) 276/O9
East Norton, Mass. (†02766) 249/K5
East Norwalk, Conn. (†06856) 210/B4
East Olympia, Wash. (98540) 310/B4
Easton, Calif. (93706) 204/F7
Easton○, Conn. (06612) 210/B4
Easton (res.), Conn. 210/B3
Easton, Ill. (62633) 222/D3
Easton, Kansas (66020) 232/G2
Easton, La. (†70586) 238/F5
Easton○, Maine (04740) 243/H2
Easton, Md. (21601) 245/O5
Easton○, Mass. (02334) 249/K4
Easton, Minn. (56025) 255/E7
Easton, Mo. (64443) 261/C3
Easton○, N.H. (†03580) 268/D3
Easton, Pa. (18042) 294/M4
Easton, Wash. (98925) 310/D3
Easton, Wis. (†53936) 317/G8
Eastondale, Mass. (†02375) 249/K4
East Orange, N.J. (*07017) 273/B2
East Orland, Maine (04431) 243/F6
East Orleans, Mass. (02643) 249/P5
East Otis, Mass. (01029) 249/B4
East Otisfield, Maine (†04270) 243/B7
East Otto, N.Y. (14729) 276/C6
Eastover, S.C. (29044) 296/F4
East Palatka, Fla. (32031) 212/E2
East Palestine, Ohio (44413) 284/J4
East Park (res.), Calif. 204/C4
East Parsonfield, Maine (04028) 243/B8
East Peacham, Vt. (†05821) 268/C3
East Pembroke, Mass. (†02359) 249/M4
East Pembroke, N.Y. (14056) 276/D5
East Peoria, Ill. (61611) 222/D3
East Pepperell, Mass. (01437) 249/H2
East Peru (Peru), Iowa (†50222) 229/F6
East Peru, Maine (04229) 243/C7
East Petersburg, Pa. (17520) 294/K5
East Pleasant Plain, Iowa (†52540) 229/K6
Eastpoint, Fla. (32328) 212/B2
East Point, Georgia (30344) 217/K2
East Point, Ky. (41216) 237/R5
East Point, La. (71025) 238/D2
East Poland, Maine (†04210) 243/C7
East Poplar, Sask. 181/F6
Eastport, Idaho (83826) 220/B1
Eastport, Maine 188/N2
Eastport, Maine (04631) 243/K6
Eastport, Mich. (49627) 250/D3
Eastport, Newf. 166/D1
Eastport, N.Y. (11941) 276/P9
East Poultney, Vt. (05741) 268/A4
East Prairie, Mo. (63845) 261/O9
East Preston, England 13/G7
East Prospect, Pa. (17317) 294/J6
East Providence, R.I. (02914) 249/J5
East Putnam, Conn. (†06260) 210/H1
East Randolph, N.Y. (14730) 276/C6
East Randolph, Vt. (05041) 268/B4
East Retford, England 13/G4
East Retford, England 10/F4
East Richford, Vt. (†05476) 268/B2
East Ridge, Tenn. (37412) 237/L11
Eastriggs, Scotland 15/E5
East Rindge, N.H. (†03461) 268/D6
East River, Conn. (†06443) 210/E3
East River Saint Marys, Nova Scotia 168/F3
East Riverside-Kingshurst, New Bruns. 170/E3
East Rochester, N.Y. (14445) 276/F4
East Rochester, Ohio (44625) 284/H4
East Rockaway, N.Y. (11518) 276/R7
East Rutherford, N.J. (07073) 273/B2
Eastry, England 13/J6
East Ryegate, Vt. (05042) 268/C3
East Saint Louis, Ill. 188/J3
East Saint Louis, Ill. (*62201) 222/A2
East Sandwich, Mass. (02537) 249/N6
East Saugus, Mass. (†01906) 249/D6
East Sebago, Maine (04029) 243/B8
East Selkirk, Manitoba 179/F4
East Shoal (lake), Manitoba 179/E4
East Siberian (sea), U.S.S.R. 4/B1
East Siberian (sea), U.S.S.R. 54/T2
East Siberian (sea), U.S.S.R. 48/S2
Eastside, Oreg. (97420) 291/C4
East Side, Pa. (18634) 294/L3
East Sister (peak), Idaho 220/C2
East Sister (isl.), Tasmania 99/E1
East Smithfield, Pa. (18817) 294/J2
Eastsound, Wash. (98245) 310/B2

364 East Sparta

East Sparta, Ohio (44626) 284/H4
East Spencer, N.C. (28039) 281/J3
East Springfield, N.Y. (13333) 276/L5
East Springfield, Pa. (16411) 294/A2
East Stone Gap, Va. (24246) 307/C7
East Stoneham, Maine (04231) 243/B7
East Stroudsburg, Pa. (18301) 294/M4
East Sullivan, Maine (†04607) 243/G6
East Sullivan, N.H. (03445) 268/C6
East Sumner, Maine (†04220) 243/C7
East Sussex (co.), England 13/H7
East Swan (riv.), Minn. 255/F3
East Swanzey, N.H. (03446) 268/C6
East Syracuse, N.Y. (13057) 276/H4
East Tawas, Mich. (48730) 250/F4
East Templeton, Mass. (01438) 249/G2
East Thermopolis, Wyo. (†82443) 319/D2
East Thetford, Vt. (05043) 268/C4
East Thompson, Conn. (†06255) 210/H1
East Tintic (creek), Utah 304/B4
East Tohopekaliga (lake), Fla. 212/E3
East Troy, Wis. (53120) 317/J2
East Union, Maine (†04862) 243/E7
Eastvale, Pa. (†15010) 294/B4
Eastvale, Texas (†75067) 303/G1
East Vassalboro, Maine (04935) 243/D7
East Verde (riv.), Ariz. 198/D4
Eastview, Tenn. (†38367) 237/D10
East View, W. Va. (†26301) 312/F4
East Village, Conn. (†06468) 210/C3
Eastville, Georgia (†30677) 217/E3
Eastville, Va. (23347) 307/R6
East Wakefield, N.H. (03830) 268/E4
East Walker (riv.), Nev. 266/B4
East Wallingford, Vt. (05742) 268/B5
East Walpole, Mass. (02032) 249/C8
East Wareham, Mass. (02538) 249/M5
East Washington, Pa. (†15301) 294/B5
East Waterboro, Maine (04030) 243/B8
East Waterford, Pa. (17021) 294/G5
East Wenatchee, Wash. (98801) 310/E3
East Weymouth, Mass. (†02189) 249/E8
East Whately, Mass. (†01373) 249/D3
East Williamson, N.Y. (14449) 276/F4
East Willington, Conn. (†06279) 210/G1
East Wilton, Maine (04234) 243/C6
East Windsor○, Conn. (†06088) 210/E1
East Windsor Hill, Conn. (06028) 210/E1
East Winn, Maine (†04495) 243/G5
East Wolfeboro, N.H. (†03894) 268/E4
Eastwood, Mich. (†49001) 250/D6
Eastwood, N.S. Wales 88/K4
Eastwood, N.S. Wales 97/J3
Eastwood, Ontario 177/D4
East Woodstock, Conn. (06244) 210/H1
East Worcester, N.Y. (12064) 276/L5
East York, Ontario 177/J4
Eaton, Colo. (80615) 208/K1
Eaton, Ill. (†62454) 222/F4
Eaton, Ind. (47338) 227/G4
Eaton, Maine (†04424) 243/H4
Eaton (co.), Mich. 250/E6
Eaton (Eaton Center)○, N.H. (03832) 268/E4
Eaton, N.Y. (13334) 276/J5
Eaton, Ohio (45320) 284/A6
Eaton, Tenn. (38331) 237/C9
Eaton Center, N.H. (03832) 268/E4
Eaton Estates, Ohio (†44035) 284/G3
Eatonia, Sask. 181/B4
Eaton Rapids, Mich. (48827) 250/E6
Eatonton, Georgia (31024) 217/F4
Eatontown, N.J. (07724) 273/E3
Eatonville, Fla. (32751) 212/E3
Eatonville, Wash. (98328) 310/C4
Eau Claire, Mich. (49111) 250/C6
Eau Claire, Pa. (16030) 294/C3
Eau Claire, Lac à l' (lake), Que. 162/J4
Eau Claire (lake), Québec 174/C1
Eau Claire, Wis. 188/H2
Eau Claire (co.), Wis. 317/D6
Eau Claire, Wis. (54701) 317/D6
Eau Claire (riv.), Wis. 317/D6
Eau Galle, Wis. (54737) 317/B6
Eauripik (atoll), Micronesia 87/E5
Ebal (mt.), Jordan 65/C3
Ebano, Mexico 150/K5
Ebb, Fla. (†32331) 212/C1
Ebb and Flow (lake), Manitoba 179/C3
Ebbw Vale, Wales 13/B6
Ebbw Vale, Wales 10/E5
Ebeltoft, Denmark 21/D5
Ebeltoft, Denmark 18/G8
Ebenezer, Miss. (39064) 256/D5
Ebenezer, Sask. 181/J4
Ebenfurth, Austria 41/D3
Eben Junction, Mich. (49825) 250/B2
Ebensburg, Pa. (15931) 294/E5
Ebensee, Austria 41/B3
Eberbach, W. Germany 22/C4
Ebersbach, E. Germany 22/F3
Eberswalde-Finow, E. Germany 22/E2
Ebetsu, Japan 81/K2
Ebingen, W. Germany 22/C4
Ebinur Hu (lake), China 77/B2
Ebnat-Kappel, Switzerland 39/H2
Eboli, Italy 34/E4
Ebolowa, Cameroon 102/D4
Ebolowa, Cameroon 115/B3
Ebon (atoll), Marshall Is. 87/G5
Ebony, Va. (23845) 307/N7
Ebor, Manitoba 179/A5
Ebrach, W. Germany 22/D4
Ebrié (lag.), Ivory Coast 106/D8
Ebro, Fla. (32437) 212/C6
Ebro, Minn. (†56621) 255/C3
Ebro (riv.), Spain 7/D4
Ebro (riv.), Spain 33/G2
Ecatepec de Morelos, Mexico 150/L1
Ecaussinnes, Belgium 27/E7
Ecclefechan, Scotland 15/E5
Eccles, W. Va. (25836) 312/D7
Ecclesville, Trin. & Tob. 161/B11
Eceabat, Turkey 63/B6
Echallens, Switzerland 39/C3
Echarate, Peru 128/F9
Echeconnee, Georgia (†31008) 217/E5
Echmiadzin, U.S.S.R. 52/F6
Echo, Ala. (†36360) 195/G8
Echo (cliffs), Ariz. 198/D2
Echo, La. (71330) 238/F4
Echo, Minn. (56237) 255/C6
Echo (lake), N.J. 273/E1
Echo, Oreg. (97826) 291/H2
Echo (lake), Tasmania 99/C4
Echo, Utah (84024) 304/C3
Echo (res.), Utah 304/C3
Echo (lake), Vt. 268/D2
Echo Bay, Ontario 177/J5
Echo Bay, Ontario 175/D3
Echola, Ala. (35457) 195/C4
Echo Lake, N.J. (†07435) 273/E1
Echo Lake, Nova Scotia 168/E4
Echols (co.), Georgia 217/G9
Echols, Ky. (42340) 237/H6
Echo Valley Prov. Park, Sask. 181/G5
Echt, Netherlands 27/H6
Echternach, Luxembourg 27/J9
Echuca, Victoria 97/C5
Echuca, Victoria 88/G7
Écija, Spain 33/D4
Eck, Loch (lake), Scotland 15/A1
Eckelson, N. Dak. (58432) 282/O6
Eckerman, Mich. (49728) 250/E2
Eckernförde, W. Germany 22/D1
Eckerty, Ind. (47116) 227/D8
Eckhart Mines, Md. (21528) 245/C2
Eckley, Colo. (80727) 208/P2
Eckman, N. Dak. (†58760) 282/H2
Eckman, W. Va. (24829) 312/C8
Eckville, Alberta 182/C3
Eclectic, Ala. (36024) 195/F5
Eclipse (harb.), Newf. 166/B2
Eclipse (sound), N.W. Terrs. 187/L2
Economy, Ind. (47339) 227/G5
Economy, Nova Scotia 168/D3
Economy, Pa. (†15005) 294/B4
Écorce (lake), Québec 172/A2
Écorces (riv.), Québec 172/F1
Ecorse, Mich. (48229) 250/B7
Écrins, Les (mt.), France 28/G5
Ecru, Miss. (38841) 256/F2
Ector (co.), Texas 303/B6
Ecuador 2/D6
Ecuador 120/B3
ECUADOR 128
Ecublens, Switzerland 39/B3
Ecum Secum, Nova Scotia 168/F3
Ecum Secum Bridge, Nova Scotia 168/F4
Edam, Sask. 181/C2
Edam-Volendam, Netherlands 27/G4
Eday (isl.), Scotland 10/E1
Eday (isl.), Scotland 15/F1
Edberg, Alberta 182/D3
Edcouch, Texas (78538) 303/G11
Edd, Ethiopia 111/H5
Edd, Ethiopia 59/D7
Ed Da'ein, Sudan 111/E5
Ed Damazin, Sudan 111/F5
Ed Damer, Sudan 111/F4
Ed Damer, Sudan 59/B6
Ed Damer, Sudan 102/F3
Ed Debba, Sudan 111/F4
Ed Debba, Sudan 59/B6
Edderton, Scotland 15/D3
Eddiceton, Miss. (39634) 256/C8
Eddington, Maine (†04428) 243/F6
Eddington○, Maine (†04428) 243/F6
Eddington, Pa. (19020) 294/N5
Eddleston, Scotland 15/E5
Eddontenajon, Br. Col. 184/K2
Eddrachillis (bay), Scotland 15/C2
Ed Dueim, Sudan 59/B7
Ed Dueim, Sudan 111/F5
Ed Dueim, Sudan 102/F3
Eddy (co.), N. Mex. 274/E6
Eddy (co.), N. Dak. 282/N4
Eddy, Texas (76524) 303/G6
Eddystone (rocks), England 13/C7
Eddystone (rocks), England 10/D5
Eddystone, Manitoba 179/C3
Eddystone, Pa. (†19013) 294/M7
Eddystone (pt.), Tasmania 88/H8
Eddystone (pt.), Tasmania 99/E2
Eddyville, Ill. (62928) 222/E6
Eddyville, Iowa (52553) 229/H6
Eddyville, Ky. (42038) 237/E6
Eddyville, Nebr. (68834) 264/E3
Eddyville, Oreg. (97343) 291/D3
Ede, Netherlands 27/H4
Ede, Nigeria 106/E7
Edéa, Cameroon 115/B3
Edelény, Hungary 41/F2
Edelstein, Ill. (61526) 222/D3
Eden, Ariz. (85535) 198/F6
Edén, Ecuador 128/E3
Eden (riv.), England 13/E3
Eden (riv.), England 10/E3
Eden, Georgia (31307) 217/K6
Eden, Idaho (83325) 220/D7
Eden, Ind. (†46140) 227/F5
Eden, Manitoba 179/C4
Eden, Md. (21822) 245/R7
Eden, Miss. (39065) 256/D5
Eden, Mont. (†59401) 262/E3
Eden, N.S. Wales 97/E5
Eden, N.Y. (14057) 276/C5
Eden, N.C. (27288) 281/K1
Eden (riv.), Scotland 15/F4
Eden, S. Dak. (57232) 298/P2
Eden, Texas (76837) 303/E6
Eden, Utah (84310) 304/C2
Eden○, Vt. (05652) 268/B2
Eden, Wis. (53019) 317/K8
Eden, Wyo. (82926) 319/C3
Edenburg, Sask. 181/E3
Edenburg, S. Africa 118/D5
Edendale, S. Africa 118/D5
Edenderry, Ireland 10/C4
Edenderry, Ireland 17/G5
Edenhope, Victoria 97/A5
Eden Mills, Ontario 177/D4
Eden Mills, Vt. (05653) 268/C2
Eden Prairie, Minn. (55344) 255/G6
Edenton, N.C. (27932) 281/R2
Edenton, Ohio (†45122) 284/C7
Edenvale, S. Africa 118/H6
Eden Valley, Minn. (55329) 255/D5
Eden Valley (res.), Wyo. 319/C3
Edenville, Mich. (48620) 250/E5
Edenwold, Sask. 181/G5
Eder (res.), W. Germany 22/C3
Eder (riv.), W. Germany 22/C3
Ederney and Kesh, N. Ireland 17/F2
Edgar (co.), Ill. 222/F4
Edgar, Mont. (59026) 262/H5
Edgar, Nebr. (68935) 264/F4
Edgar, Wis. (54426) 317/G6
Edgard, La. (70049) 238/M3
Edgar Springs, Mo. (65462) 261/J7
Edgarton, W. Va. (25672) 312/B7
Edgartown, Mass. (02539) 249/M7
Edgartown○, Mass. (02539) 249/M7
Edge (isl.), Norway 4/B8
Edgecliff, Texas (†76101) 303/E2
Edgecomb○, Maine (†04556) 243/D8
Edgecombe (co.), N.C. 281/O3
Edgecumbe (cape), Alaska 196/L1
Edgecumbe, N. Zealand 100/F2
Edgefield, La. (†71019) 238/D2
Edgefield (co.), S.C. 296/D4
Edgefield, S.C. (29824) 296/C4
Edge Hill, Georgia (†30810) 217/G4
Edgehill, Va. (†22485) 307/O4
Edgeley, N. Dak. (58433) 282/N7
Edgeley, Sask. 181/H5
Edgell (isl.), N.W. Terrs. 187/M3
Edgemere, Idaho (†83856) 220/B1
Edgemere, Md. (†21219) 245/N4
Edgemont, Ark. (72044) 202/F2
Edgemont, S. Dak. (57735) 298/B7
Edgemoor, Del. (†19801) 245/S1
Edgemoor, S.C. (29712) 296/E2
Edgemount, N.C. (28645) 281/F2
Edgeøya (isl.), Norway 18/E2
Edgerly, La. (†70668) 238/C6
Edgerton, Alberta 182/E3
Edgerton, Ind. (†46797) 227/H2
Edgerton, Kansas (66021) 232/H3
Edgerton, Minn. (56128) 255/B7
Edgerton, Mo. (64444) 261/C3
Edgerton, Ohio (43517) 284/A3
Edgerton, Va. (†23868) 307/N7
Edgerton, Wis. (53534) 317/H10
Edgerton, Wyo. (82635) 319/F2
Edgewater, Br. Col. 184/J5
Edgewater, Colo. (80214) 208/J3
Edgewater, Fla. (32032) 212/F3
Edgewater, N.J. (07020) 273/C2
Edgewater, Wis. (54834) 317/D4
Edgewater Park○, N.J. (†08010) 273/D3
Edgewood, Br. Col. 184/H5
Edgewood, Calif. (96094) 204/C2
Edgewood, Fla. (†32801) 212/E3
Edgewood, Ill. (62426) 222/E5
Edgewood, Ind. (†46011) 227/F4
Edgewood, Iowa (52042) 229/K3
Edgewood, Ky. (†41017) 237/S2
Edgewood, Md. (21040) 245/N3
Edgewood, N. Mex. (87015) 274/C3
Edgewood, Ohio (†44004) 284/J2
Edgewood, Pa. (†15218) 294/B7
Edgeworth, Pa. (†15143) 294/B4
Edgington, Ill. (†61284) 222/C2
Édhessa, Greece 45/F5
Edievale, N. Zealand 100/B6
Edina, Minn. (55424) 255/G5
Edina, Mo. (63537) 261/H2
Edinboro, Pa. (16412) 294/B2
Edinburg, Ill. (62531) 222/D4
Edinburg, Miss. (†39051) 256/F5
Edinburg, Mo. (†64683) 261/E2
Edinburg, N. Dak. (58227) 282/P3
Edinburg, Pa. (16116) 294/B3
Edinburg, Texas (78539) 303/F11
Edinburg, Va. (22824) 307/M3
Edinburgh, Ind. (46124) 227/E6
Edinburgh (cap.), Scotland 7/D3
Edinburgh (cap.), Scotland 15/D1
Edinburgh (cap.), Scotland 10/C1
Edingen (Enghien), Belgium 27/D7
Edirne (prov.), Turkey 63/B2
Edirne, Turkey 7/G4
Edirne, Turkey 63/B2
Edirne, Turkey 59/A1
Edison, Calif. (93220) 204/G8
Edison (lake), Calif. 204/F6
Edison, Georgia (31746) 217/C7
Edison, Nebr. (68936) 264/E4
Edison○, N.J. (*08817) 273/E2
Edison, Ohio (43320) 284/E4
Edison, Wash. (98246) 310/C2
Edison Nat'l Hist. Site, N.J. 273/A2
Edisto (isl.), S.C. 296/G6
Edisto (riv.), S.C. 296/G7
Edisto Beach, S.C. (†29438) 296/G7
Edisto Island, S.C. (29438) 296/G6
Edith, Georgia (†31631) 217/G9
Edithburgh, S. Australia 94/E6
Ediz Hook (pen.), Wash. 310/B2
Edjeleh, Algeria 106/F3
Edmeston, N.Y. (13335) 276/K5
Edmond, Kansas (67636) 232/C2
Edmond, Okla. (73034) 288/M3
Edmonds, Wash. (98020) 310/C3
Edmondson, Ark. (72332) 202/K3
Edmondt, Fr. Guiana 131/E3
Edmonson (co.), Ky. 237/J6
Edmonson, Texas (79032) 303/C3
Edmonston, Md. (†20781) 245/F4
Edmonton (cap.), Alberta 182/D3
Edmonton, Alta. 146/G4
Edmonton (cap.), Alta. 162/E5
Edmonton, Canada 2/D3
Edmonton, Ky. (42129) 237/K7
Edmonton Beach, Alberta 182/C3
Edmore, Mich. (48829) 250/E5
Edmore, N. Dak. (58330) 282/O3
Edmore, Sask. 181/H4
Edmund, Wis. (†53533) 317/F9
Edmunds, Maine (†04628) 243/J6
Edmunds, N. Dak. (†58746) 282/M5
Edmunds (co.), S. Dak. 298/L3
Edmundson, Mo. (†63101) 261/O2
Edmundston, N. Br. 162/K6
Edmundston, New Bruns. 170/B1
Edna, Ala. (†36922) 195/B6
Edna, Iowa (†51246) 229/A2
Edna, Kansas (67342) 232/G4
Edna, Texas (77957) 303/H9
Edna Bay, Alaska (†99901) 196/M2
Edo (riv.), Japan 81/P2
Edolo, Italy 34/C1
Edom, Texas (†75656) 303/J5
Edon, Ohio (43518) 284/A2
Édouard (lake), Québec 172/E2
Edrans, Manitoba 179/C4
Edray, W. Va. (†24954) 312/F6
Edremit, Turkey 63/B3
Edremit, Turkey 59/A2
Edremit (gulf), Turkey 63/B3
Edri, Libya 111/B2
Edsbyn, Sweden 18/J6
Edson, Alberta 182/B3
Edson, Alta. 162/E5
Edson, Kansas (67733) 232/A2
Eduardo Castex, Argentina 143/D4
Edwall, Wash. (99008) 310/H3
Edwand, Alberta 182/D2
Edward (lake) 102/E5
Edward, N.C. (27821) 281/R4
Edward (lake), Uganda 115/E4
Edward (lake), Zaire 115/E4
Edward MacDowell (res.), N.H. 268/D6
Edwards, Colo. (81632) 208/F3
Edwards (co.), Ill. 222/E5
Edwards, Ill. (61528) 222/D3
Edwards (riv.), Ill. 222/C2
Edwards (co.), Kansas 232/C4
Edwards (lake), La. 238/C2
Edwards, Miss. (39066) 256/C6
Edwards, Mo. (65326) 261/F6
Edwards, N.Y. (13635) 276/K2
Edwards (co.), Texas 303/D7
Edwards (plat.), Texas 303/C7
Edwards A.F.B., Calif. 204/H9
Edwardsburg, Mich. (49112) 250/C7
Edwardsport, Ind. (47528) 227/C7
Edwardsville, Ala. (36261) 195/H3
Edwardsville, Ill. (62025) 222/B2
Edwardsville, Ind. (†47150) 227/F8
Edwardsville, Kansas (66113) 232/H2
Edwardsville, Pa. (18704) 294/E7
Edward VII (pen.) 5/B11
Edward VIII (bay) 5/C4
Edwight, W. Va. (†25189) 312/C7
Edwin, Ala. (†36317) 195/H7
Edwin, Manitoba 179/D5
Edzell, Scotland 15/F4
Eefde, Netherlands 27/J4
Eek, Alaska (99578) 196/F2
Eeklo, Belgium 27/D6
Eel (riv.), Calif. 204/B4
Eel (riv.), Ind. 227/C6
Eel (riv.), Ind. 227/F3
Eel River Bridge, New Bruns. 170/F1
Eel River Crossing, New Bruns. 170/D1
Eems (riv.), Netherlands 27/K2
Eersterivier, S. Africa 118/F6
Efate (isl.), Vanuatu 87/G7
Eferding, Austria 41/B2
Effie, La. (71331) 238/F4
Effie, Minn. (56639) 255/E3
Effigy Mounds Nat'l Mon., Iowa 229/L2
Effingham (co.), Georgia 217/K6
Effingham (co.), Ill. 222/E4
Effingham, Ill. (62401) 222/E4
Effingham, Kansas (66023) 232/G2
Effingham, S.C. (29541) 296/H3
Effingham Falls, N.H. (†03814) 268/E4
Effort, Pa. (18330) 294/M4
Efland, N.C. (27243) 281/L2
Eflâni, Turkey 63/E2
Egadi (isls.), Italy 34/C6
Egan, Ill. (61026) 222/D1
Egan (range), Nev. 266/G4
Egan, S. Dak. (57024) 298/R6
Egaña, Uruguay 145/B4
Eganville, Ontario 177/G2
Egbert, Wyo. (†82053) 319/H4
Ege, Ind. (†46763) 227/G2
Egegik, Alaska (99579) 196/G3
Egeland, N. Dak. (58331) 282/M2
Eger, Hungary 41/F3
Egeria, W. Va. (†25902) 312/D7
Egernsund, Denmark 21/C8
Egerton (mt.), W. Australia 92/B4
Egg (isl.), Manitoba 179/E3
Egg (creek), N. Dak. 282/H3
Egg, Switzerland 39/G2
Eggenburg, Austria 41/C2
Eggertsville, N.Y. (†14226) 276/C5
Egg Harbor, Wis. (54209) 317/M5
Egg Harbor City, N.J. (08215) 273/D4
Egg Island (pt.), N.J. 273/C5
Eggiwil, Switzerland 39/E3
Egg Lagoon, Tasmania 99/A1
Eggleston, Va. (24086) 307/G6
Egham, England 13/G8
Egham, England 10/B5
Éghezée, Belgium 27/F7
Egilsay (isl.), Scotland 15/F1
Eglin A.F.B., Fla. 212/C6
Eglington (isl.), N.W.T. 162/L3
Eglinton (cape), N.W. Terrs. 187/M2
Eglinton (isl.), N.W. Terrs. 187/F2
Eglisau, Switzerland 39/G1
Eglon, W. Va. (26716) 312/G4
Egmond aan Zee, Netherlands 27/E3
Egmondville, Ontario 177/C4
Egmont (key), Fla. 212/D4
Egmont (cape), N. Zealand 100/D3
Egmont (mt.), N. Zealand 100/D3
Egmont (cape), Nova Scotia 168/H2
Egmont (bay), Pr. Edward I. 168/D2
Egmont (cape), Pr. Edward I. 168/D2
Egnach, Switzerland 39/H1
Egnar, Colo. (81325) 208/B7
Egremont, Alberta 182/D2
Egremont, England 13/D3
Eğridir, Turkey 63/D4
Eğridir (lake), Turkey 59/B2
Eğridir (lake), Turkey 63/D4
Egtved, Denmark 21/C6
Egvekinot, U.S.S.R. 48/S3
Egyek, Hungary 41/F3
Egypt 2/L4
Egypt 102/E2
EGYPT 111/E2
EGYPT 59/A4
Egypt, Georgia (†31329) 217/K6
Egypt, Miss. (†38860) 256/G3
Egypt Lake, Fla. (†33614) 212/C2
Eha Amufu, Nigeria 106/F7
Ehime (pref.), Japan 81/F7
Ehingen, W. Germany 22/C4
Ehrenberg (range), North. Terr. 93/B7
Ehrenburg, Ariz. (85334) 198/A5
Ehrenfeld, Pa. (†15956) 294/E5
Ehrhardt, S.C. (29081) 296/E5
Ehrwald, Austria 41/A3
Eiao (isl.), Fr. Poly. 87/M6
Eibar, Spain 33/E1
Eichstätt, W. Germany 22/D4
Eider (riv.), W. Germany 22/C1
Eidfjord, Norway 18/E6
Eidsfoss, Norway 18/C4
Eidson, Tenn. (37731) 237/P7
Eidsvold, Queensland 95/D5
Eidsvoll, Norway 18/G6
Eielson A.F.B., Alaska 196/J2
Eigenbrakel (Braine-l'Alleud), Belgium 27/E7
Eigersund, Norway 18/D7
Eigg (mt.), Nova Scotia 168/F3
Eigg (isl.), Scotland 15/B4
Eigg (isl.), Scotland 10/C2
Eigg (sound), Scotland 15/B4
Eight Degree (chan.), India 68/C7
Eighteen Mile (peak), Idaho 220/E5
Eight Mile (brook), Conn. 210/C3
Eight Mile (riv.), Conn. 210/F3
Eights Coast (reg.) 5/B14
Eighty Eight, Ky. (42130) 237/K7
Eighty Mile (beach), W. Australia 88/C3
Eighty Mile (beach), W. Australia 92/C2
Eijerlandsche Gat (str.), Netherlands 27/F2
Eil, Loch (lake), Scotland 15/C4
Eil, Somalia 115/J2
Eildon, Victoria 97/C5
Eildon (lake), Victoria 97/C5
Eileen, Ill. (†60416) 222/E2
Eileen (lake), N.W.T. 162/F3
Eilenburg, E. Germany 22/E3
Eilerts de Haan (mts.), Suriname 131/C4
Eina, Norway 18/G6
Einbeck, W. Germany 22/C3
Eindhoven, Netherlands 27/G6
'Ein Gedi, Israel 65/C5
'Ein Harod, Israel 65/C2
'Ein Netafim (well), Israel 65/D5
Einsiedeln, Switzerland 39/G2
Eirunepé, Brazil 132/G10
Eirunepé, Brazil 120/B3
Eisenach, E. Germany 22/D3
Eisenberg, E. Germany 22/D3
Eisenerz, Austria 41/C3
Eisenhower (mt.), Alberta 182/C4
Eisenhüttenstadt, E. Germany 22/F2
Eisenkappel-Vellach, Austria 41/C3
Eisenstadt, Austria 41/D3
Eiserfeld, W. Germany 22/C3
Eishort, Loch (inlet), Scotland 15/B3
Eisleben, E. Germany 22/D3
Eisling (mts.), Luxembourg 27/H9
Eitzen, Minn. (55931) 255/G7
Ejby, Denmark 21/C7
Ejea de los Caballeros, Spain 33/F1
Ejido, Venezuela 124/C3
Ejin, China 77/F3
Ejin Horo, China 77/G4
Ejutla de Crespo, Mexico 150/L8
Ekalaka, Mont. (59324) 262/M5
Ekenäs, Finland 18/N6
Ekeren, Belgium 27/E6
Eketahuna, N. Zealand 100/E4
Ekibastuz, U.S.S.R. 48/H4
Ekibin, Queensland 88/K3
Ekimchan, U.S.S.R. 48/O4
Ekin, Ind. (†46072) 227/E4
Ekonk, Conn. (†06384) 210/H2
Ekron, Ky. (40117) 237/J5
Eksjö, Sweden 18/J8
Ekuk, Alaska (†99569) 196/G3
Ekwan (riv.), Ont. 162/H5
Ekwan (riv.), Ontario 175/C2
Ekwok, Alaska (99580) 196/G3
El Aaiún (Laayoune), Morocco 102/A2
El Aaiún (Laayoune), Western Sahara 106/B3
El Abbasiya, Sudan 111/F5
El Abiar, Libya 111/D1
El Abiod Sidi Cheikh, Algeria 106/E2
El Agheila, Libya 111/C1
Elaine, Ark. (72333) 202/J5
El 'Al, Jordan 65/D4
El 'Alamein, Egypt 111/E1
El 'Alamein, Egypt 59/A3
El Almacén, Venezuela 124/G4
El Amparo de Apure, Venezuela 124/C4
Elams, N.C. (†23919) 281/O1
Elamton, Ky. (41420) 237/P5
Elamville, Ala. (†36311) 195/G7
Eland, Wis. (54427) 317/H6
El Ángel, Ecuador 128/C2
El Arahal, Spain 33/D4
El 'Arish, Egypt 59/B3
El 'Arish, Egypt 111/F1
El Asiento, Bolivia 136/B6
El Asnam, Algeria 106/E1
El Asnam, Algeria 102/C1
Elassón, Greece 45/F6
Elat, Israel 65/D6
Elath (Elat), Israel 65/D6
Elath, Israel 59/B4
El Athale (Itala), Somalia 115/J3
Elato (atoll), Micronesia 87/E5
El 'Atrun (oasis), Sudan 111/E4
El 'Auja, Israel 65/D5
Elâzığ (prov.), Turkey 63/H3
Elâzığ, Turkey 59/C2
Elâzığ, Turkey 63/H3
El Azizia, Libya 111/B1
El Azúcar (res.), Mexico 150/K3
Elba, Ala. (36323) 195/F8
Elba, Idaho (83326) 220/E7
Elba (isl.), Italy 7/E4
Elba (isl.), Italy 34/C3
Elba, Minn. (†55910) 255/F6
Elba, Nebr. (68835) 264/F3
Elba, N.Y. (14058) 276/D4
Elba, Ohio (45728) 284/H6
El Bab, Syria 63/G4
El Balqa (dist.), Jordan 65/D4
El Banco, Colombia 126/D3
El Barco, Spain 33/C1
El Barco de Ávila, Spain 33/D2
El Bardi, Libya 111/D1
El Barkat, Libya 111/B3
Elbasan, Albania 45/E5
El Baúl, Venezuela 124/D3
El Bawiti, Egypt 111/E2
El Bawiti, Egypt 102/E2
El Bawiti, Egypt 59/A4
El Bayadh, Algeria 106/E2
El Bayadh, Algeria 102/C1
Elbe (riv.) 7/F3
Elbe (riv.), E. Germany 22/D2
Elbe, Wash. (98330) 310/C4
Elbe (riv.), W. Germany 22/C2
El Beida, Yemen Arab Rep. 59/E7
El Beni (dept.), Bolivia 136/C3
Elberfeld, Ind. (47613) 227/C8
Elberon, Iowa (52225) 229/J4
Elberon, N.J. (07740) 273/F3
Elberon, Va. (23846) 307/P6
Elbert (mt.), Colo. 188/E3
Elbert (co.), Colo. 208/L4
Elbert, Colo. (80106) 208/L4
Elbert (mt.), Colo. 208/G4
Elbert (co.), Georgia 217/G2
Elbert, Texas (76359) 303/E4
Elbert, W. Va. (24830) 312/C8
Elberta, Ala. (36530) 195/C10
Elberta, Georgia (†31093) 217/E5
Elberta, Mich. (49628) 250/C4
Elberta, Utah (84626) 304/B4
Elberton, Georgia (30635) 217/G2
Elberton, Wash. (†99130) 310/H4
Elbeuf, France 28/D3
Elbing, Kansas (67041) 232/E3
Elbing (Elbląg), Poland 47/D1
El Bira, West Bank 65/C4
Elbistan, Turkey 63/G3
Elbląg (prov.), Poland 47/D1
Elbląg, Poland 47/D1
Elbląg, Poland 7/F3
El Bolsón, Argentina 143/B5
Elbon, Pa. (†15823) 294/E3
El Bonillo, Spain 33/E3
El Boquerón (pass), Peru 128/E7
El Borma, Tunisia 106/F2
Elbow (riv.), Alberta 182/C4
Elbow (lake), Manitoba 179/G4
Elbow (lake), Minn. 255/C3
Elbow, Sask. 181/E4
Elbow Lake, Minn. (56531) 255/B5
Elbridge, N.Y. (13060) 276/G5
Elbridge, Tenn. (38227) 237/C8
El'brus (mt.), U.S.S.R. 7/J4
El'brus (mt.), U.S.S.R. 52/F6
El Buheyrat (prov.), Sudan 111/E6
El Bur, Somalia 115/J3
Elburg, Netherlands 27/H4
El Burgo de Osma, Spain 33/E2
Elburn, Ill. (60119) 222/E2
Elburz (mts.), Iran 59/F2
Elburz (mts.), Iran 66/G2
El Cajon, Calif. (*92020) 204/J11
El Callao, Venezuela 124/G4
El Calvario, Venezuela 124/E3
El Campo, Texas (77437) 303/H8
El Caney, Cuba 158/J4
El Carmen, El Beni, Bolivia 136/D3
El Carmen, Santa Cruz, Bolivia 136/F6
El Carmen, Ñuble, Chile 138/A11
El Carmen, O'Higgins, Chile 138/F5
El Carmen, Chocó, Colombia 126/B5
El Carmen, Nariño, Colombia 126/A6
El Carmen, Norte de Santander, Colombia 126/D3
El Carmen de Bolívar, Colombia 126/C3
El Carre, Ethiopia 111/H6
El Centro, Calif. 188/C4
El Centro, Calif. (92243) 204/K11
El Centro, Colombia 126/D4
El Cercado, Dom. Rep. 158/D6
El Cerrito, Calif. (94530) 204/J2
El Cerrito, Colombia 126/B6
El Cerro, Bolivia 136/E5
El Chaparro, Venezuela 124/F3
Elche, Spain 33/F3
Elche de la Sierra, Spain 33/E3
Elcho (isl.), North. Terr. 93/D1
Elcho, Wis. (54428) 317/H5
El Chocón (res.), Argentina 143/C4
Elcho Island Mission, North. Terr. 93/D1
El Choro, Bolivia 136/B6
El Chorro, Argentina 143/D1
Elco, Ill. (62929) 222/D6
El Cobre, Chile 138/A4
El Cobre, Cuba 158/J4
El Cocuy, Colombia 126/D4
El Convento, Chile 138/F4
El Corazón, Ecuador 128/C3
El Cristo, Venezuela 124/G4
El Cuey, Dom. Rep. 158/F6
El Cuy, Argentina 143/C4
Elda, Spain 33/F3
El Dara, Ill. (†62312) 222/B4

Fairhaven 367

Espada (pt.), Colombia 126/E1
Espada (pt.), Dom. Rep. 158/F6
Espagnol (pt.), St. Vin. & Grens. 161/A8
Espaillat (prov.), Dom. Rep. 158/E5
Espalion, France 28/E5
Española (isl.), Ecuador 128/C10
Espanola, Fla. (†32010) 212/E2
Espanola, N. Mex. (87532) 274/C3
Espanola, Ontario 177/J5
Espanola, Ontario 175/D3
Espanola, Wash. (†99022) 310/H3
Esparta, C. Rica 154/E5
Esparto, Calif. (95627) 204/C5
Espejo, Chile 138/G3
Espejo, Spain 33/D4
Espelkamp, W. Germany 22/C2
Espenberg (cape), Alaska 196/F1
Esperança, Brazil 132/G4
Esperance, Australia 87/C9
Esperance, N.Y. (12066) 276/M5
Esperance, W. Australia 88/C6
Esperance, W. Australia 92/C6
Esperance (bay), W. Australia 92/C6
Esperanza, Argentina 143/F5
Esperanza, Br. Col. 184/D5
Esperanza, Cuba 158/E2
Esperanza, Dom. Rep. 158/D5
Esperanza (mts.), Honduras 154/E3
Esperanza, Puebla, Mexico 150/O2
Esperanza, Sonora, Mexico 150/E3
Esperanza, Peru 128/G7
Esperanza, P. Rico 161/G2
Esperanza, Texas (†79841) 303/B11
Esperanza, Venezuela 124/E6
Espichel (cape), Portugal 33/B3
Espigão Mestre (Geral de Goiás) (range), Brazil 132/E6
Espinal, Colombia 126/C5
Espinhaço (mts.), Brazil 120/E4
Espinhaço, Serra do (range), Brazil 132/F7
Espinho, Portugal 33/B2
Espinillo, Argentina 143/E2
Espinillo (pt.), Uruguay 145/A7
Espino, Venezuela 124/F3
Espírito Santo (state), Brazil 132/F7
Espírito Santo (state), Brazil 135/F2
Espíritu Santo (isl.), Mexico 150/D4
Espiritu Santo (cape), Philippines 85/H3
Espiritu Santo (cape), Philippines 82/E4
Espiritu Santo (isl.), Vanuatu 87/G7
Espita, Mexico 150/Q6
Espiye, Turkey 63/H2
Esplanada, Brazil 132/G5
Espluga de Francolí, Spain 33/G2
Espoir (bay), Newf. 166/C4
Espoo, Finland 18/O6
Esposende, Portugal 33/B2
Esprit-Saint, Québec 172/J1
Espungabera, Mozambique 118/E4
Espy, Pa. (17815) 294/K4
Espyville Station, Pa. (16414) 294/B2
Esqueda, Mexico 150/E1
Esquel, Argentina 143/B5
Esquel, Argentina 120/B7
Esquimalt, Br. Col. 184/K4
Esquina, Argentina 143/G5
Esquipulas, Nicaragua 154/E4
Es Sahab, Jordan 65/E4
Es Salt, Jordan 65/D3
Es Salt, Jordan 59/C3
Essaouira, Morocco 106/B2
Essaouira, Morocco 102/A1
Essé, Cameroon 115/B3
Essen, Belgium 27/F6
Essen, W. Germany 7/E3
Essen, W. Germany 22/B3
Essendon, Victoria 88/K7
Essendon, Victoria 97/H5
Essequibo (riv.), Guyana 120/D2
Essequibo (riv.), Guyana 131/B3
Esserville, Va. (24274) 307/G2
Essex, Calif. (92332) 204/K9
Essex, Conn. (06426) 210/F3
Essex○, Conn. (06426) 210/F3
Essex (co.), England 13/H6
Essex, Ill. (60935) 222/E2
Essex, Iowa (51638) 229/C7
Essex, Md. (21221) 245/N3
Essex (co.), Mass. 249/L2
Essex, Mass. (01929) 249/L2
Essex○, Mass. (01929) 249/L2
Essex, Mo. (63846) 261/N9
Essex, Mont. (59916) 262/C2
Essex (co.), N.J. 273/E2
Essex (co.), N.Y. 276/N2
Essex, N.Y. (12936) 276/O2
Essex (county), Ontario 177/B5
Essex, Ontario 177/B5
Essex (co.), Vt. 268/D2
Essex○, Vt. (05451) 268/A2
Essex (co.), Va. 307/P5
Essex Fells, N.J. (07021) 273/B2
Essex Junction, Vt. (05452) 268/A3
Essexville, Mich. (48732) 250/F5
Es Sidr, Libya 111/C1
Essie, Ky. (40827) 237/P6
Essig, Minn. (56030) 255/D6
Essington, Pa. (19029) 294/M7
Esslingen am Neckar, W. Germany 22/C4
Essonne (dept.), France 28/E3
Es Sukhna, Jordan 65/E3
Es Sukhne, Syria 59/C3
Es Sukhne, Syria 63/H5
Es Suki, Sudan 59/B7
Es Suweida (prov.), Syria 63/G6
Es Suweida, Syria 59/C3
Es Suweida, Syria 63/G6
Est (pt.), Haiti 158/C4
Est (lake), Québec 172/H2
Estacada, Oreg. (97023) 291/E2
Estaca de Vares (pt.), Spain 33/C1
Estación Atlántida, Uruguay 145/B6
Estación Cuaró, Uruguay 145/C1
Estación J.J. Castro, Uruguay 145/C4
Estación José Ignacio, Uruguay 145/E5
Estación La Floresta, Uruguay 145/C7
Estación Lasala, Uruguay 145/C7
Estación Laureles, Uruguay 145/C2
Estación Margat, Uruguay 145/B6
Estación Migues, Uruguay 145/C6
Estación Pampa, Uruguay 145/C3
Estación Puma, Uruguay 145/D5
Estación Rincón, Uruguay 145/F3
Estación Sosa Díaz, Uruguay 145/C6
Estación Tapia, Uruguay 145/C6
Estación Villasboas, Uruguay 145/C4
Estación Yí, Uruguay 145/C4
Estados (isl.), Argentina 120/C8
Estados, Los (isl.), Argentina 143/D7
Estahbanat, Iran 59/F4
Estahbanat, Iran 66/J6
Estaire, Ontario 177/D1
Estampuis, Belgium 27/C7
Estância, Brazil 132/G5
Estância, Brazil 120/F4
Estancia, N. Mex. (87016) 274/D4
Estancia Caleta Josefina, Chile 138/F10
Estancia Laguna Blanca, Chile 138/E9
Estancia Morro Chico, Chile 138/E9
Estancia Punta Delgada, Chile 138/E9
Estancia San Gregorio, Chile 138/E9
Estancia Springhill (Cerro Manantiales), Chile 138/F10
Estanzuela, Uruguay 145/B5
Estanzuelas, El Salvador 154/C4
Estarca, Bolivia 136/C7
Estats (peak), Spain 33/G1
Estavayer-le-Lac, Switzerland 39/C3
Estcourt, S. Africa 118/D5
Este (pt.), Cuba 158/C3
Este, Italy 34/C2
Este (pt.), P. Rico 161/G2
Este (pt.), Uruguay 120/D6
Este (pt.), Uruguay 145/D6
Esteban Rams, Argentina 143/F5
Esteli, Nicaragua 154/D4
Estella, Spain 33/E1
Estelline, S. Dak. (57234) 298/R4
Estelline, Texas (79233) 303/D3
Estell Manor, N.J. (08319) 273/D5
Estepa, Spain 33/D4
Estepona, Spain 33/D4
Ester, Alaska (99725) 196/J2
Esterbrook, Wyo. (†82633) 319/G3
Estérel, Québec 172/C3
Esterhazy, Sask. 181/K5
Estero (bay), Calif. 204/D8
Estero (pt.), Calif. 204/D8
Estero, Fla. (33928) 212/E5
Estero (isl.), Fla. 212/E5
Estes Park, Colo. (80517) 208/J2
Este Sudeste (cays), Colombia 126/A10
Estevan, Sask. 162/F6
Estevan, Sask. 181/J6
Estevan Point, Br. Col. 184/D5
Estey, Mich. (†48652) 250/E5
Esther (isl.), Alaska 196/C1
Esther, Alberta 182/E4
Esther, La. (†70510) 238/F7
Esther, Mo. (†63601) 261/M7
Estherville, Iowa (51334) 229/D2
Estherwood, La. (70534) 238/F6
Estill (co.), Ky. 237/O5
Estill, Miss. (†38748) 256/C4
Estill, S.C. (29918) 296/E6
Estillfork, Ala. (35745) 195/F1
Estill Springs, Tenn. (37330) 237/J10
Estlin, Sask. 181/G5
Esto, Fla. (32425) 212/C5
Eston, England 13/F3
Eston, Sask. 162/F5
Eston, Sask. 181/C4
ESTONIA 53
Estonian S.S.R., U.S.S.R. 7/G3
Estonian S.S.R., U.S.S.R. 48/C4
Estonian S.S.R, U.S.S.R. 52/C3
Estoril, Portugal 33/B3
Estral Beach, Mich. (†48166) 250/F7
Estreito (res.), Brazil 135/C2
Estrela, Serra da (mts.), Portugal 33/C2
Estrella (riv.), Calif. 204/E8
Estremadura (reg.), Spain 33/C3
Estremoz, Portugal 33/C3
Estrondo, Serra do (range), Brazil 132/D4
Estuary, Sask. 181/B5
Esztergom, Hungary 41/E3
Etadunna, S. Australia 94/F3
Etalle, Belgium 27/H9
Étampes, France 28/E3
Étaples, France 28/D2
Etawah, India 68/D3
Etawney (lake), Manitoba 179/J2
Etchojoa, Mexico 150/E3
Ethan, S. Dak. (57334) 298/N6
Ethel, Ark. (72048) 202/H5
Ethel (mt.), Colo. 208/F1
Ethel, La. (70730) 238/H5
Ethel, Miss. (39067) 256/F4
Ethel, Mo. (63539) 261/G3
Ethel, Ontario 177/C4
Ethel, Wash. (98542) 310/C4
Ethel, W. Va. (25076) 312/C7
Ethelbert, Manitoba 179/B3
Ethel Creek, W. Australia 92/C3
Ethelsville, Ala. (35461) 195/B4
Ethelton, Sask. 181/G3
Ether, N.C. (27247) 281/K4
Ethete, Wyo. (82520) 319/D2
Ethiopia 2/L5
Ethiopia 102/F4
ETHIOPIA 59/C7
ETHIOPIA 111/G5
Ethridge, Mont. (59435) 262/D2
Ethridge, Tenn. (38456) 237/G10
Etive, Loch (inlet), Scotland 15/C4
Etiwanda, Calif. (91739) 204/E10
Etna, Calif. (96027) 204/C2
Etna, Ind. (†46725) 227/F2
Etna (vol.), Italy 7/F5
Etna (vol.), Italy 34/E6
Etna○, Maine (04434) 243/E6
Etna, N.H. (03750) 268/C4
Etna, Ohio (43018) 284/E6
Etna, Pa. (15223) 294/B6
Etna, Utah (†84313) 304/A2
Etna, Wyo. (83118) 319/A2
Etna Green, Ind. (46524) 227/E2
Etobicoke, Ontario 177/J4
Etoile, Ky. (42131) 237/K7
Etoile, Zaire 115/E6
Etolin (isl.), Alaska 196/N2
Etolin (str.), Alaska 196/E2
Etomami (riv.), Manitoba 179/F2
Etomami (riv.), Sask. 181/J3
Eton, England 10/F5
Eton, England 13/G8
Eton, Georgia (30724) 217/C1
Etosha Pan (salt pan), Namibia 118/B3
Etosha Salt Pan, Namibia 102/D6
Etoumbi, Congo 115/B3
Etowah (co.), Ala. 195/F2
Etowah, Ark. (72428) 202/K2
Etowah (riv.), Georgia 217/C2
Etowah, N.C. (28729) 281/D4
Etowah, Tenn. (37331) 237/M10
Étretat, France 28/D3
Etta, Miss. (38627) 256/F2
Etta (lake), N. Dak. 282/L6
Et Tafila, Jordan 65/E5
Et Taiyiba, Jordan 65/D2
Ettelbruck, Luxembourg 27/J9
Et Tell el Abyad, Syria 63/H4
Etten-Leur, Netherlands 27/F5
Etter, Minn. (†55033) 255/F6
Etterbeek, Belgium 27/B9
Etters, Pa. (17319) 294/J5
Etters Beach, Sask. 181/F4
Ettington, Sask. 181/F6
Ettlingen, W. Germany 22/C4
Ettrick, Scotland 15/E5
Ettrick, Va. (23803) 307/O6
Ettrick, Wis. (54627) 317/D7
Ettrick Pen (mt.), Scotland 15/E5
Etty, Ky. (41523) 237/R6
Etzatlán, Mexico 150/G6
Etzikom, Alberta 182/E5
Etzikom Coulee (riv.), Alberta 182/E5
Eu, France 28/D3
Euabalong, N.S. Wales 97/D3
Eubank, Ky. (42567) 237/M6
Euboea (Évvoia) (isl.), Greece 45/G6
Eucha, Okla. (74342) 288/S2
Eucha (lake), Okla. 288/S2
Eucla, W. Australia 92/E5
Euclid, Minn. (56722) 255/B3
Euclid, Ohio (44117) 284/J9
Eucumbene (lake), N.S. Wales 97/E5
Eudora, Miss. (†39360) 256/G7
Eudora, Ark. (71640) 202/H7
Eudora, Kansas (66025) 232/G3
Eudora, Miss. (†38632) 256/D1
Eudora, Mo. (65645) 261/E7
Eufaula, Ala. (36027) 195/H7
Eufaula (Walter F. George Res.) (lake), Ala 195/H7
Eufaula (Walter F. George Res.) (lake), Georgia 217/B7
Eufaula (res.), Ohio 284/L4
Eufaula, Okla. (74432) 288/P4
Eufaula (lake), Okla. 288/P4
Eugene, Ind. (†47928) 227/B5
Eugene, Mo. (65032) 261/H6
Eugene, Oreg. 188/B2
Eugene, Oreg. 146/F5
Eugene, Oreg. (*97401) 291/D3
Eugene O'Neill Nat'l Hist. Site, Calif. 204/K2
Eugowra, N.S. Wales 97/E3
Euharlee, Georgia (†30120) 217/C2
Euless, Texas (76039) 303/F2
Eulo, Queensland 95/C6
Eulonia, Georgia (†31331) 217/K7
Eumungerie, N.S. Wales 97/E2
Eunice, La. (70535) 238/F6
Eunice, N. Mex. (88231) 274/F6
Eunola, Ala. (†36340) 195/G8
Eupen, Belgium 27/J7
Euphrates (riv.) 54/F6
Euphrates (riv.), Iran 59/E3
Euphrates (riv.), Iraq 59/E3
Euphrates (riv.), Iraq 66/D4
Euphrates (riv.), Syria 59/E3
Euphrates (El Furat) (riv.), Syria 63/H4
Euphrates (Fırat) (riv.), Turkey 63/G4
Eupora, Miss. (39744) 256/F3
Eure (dept.), France 28/D3
Eure (riv.), France 28/D3
Eure, N.C. (27935) 281/R2
Eure-et-Loir (dept.), France 28/D3
Eureka, Calif. 188/B2
Eureka, Calif. 146/F5
Eureka, Calif. (95501) 204/A3
Eureka, Canada 4/A14
Eureka, Colo. (†81433) 208/D7
Eureka (res.), Fla. 212/E2
Eureka, Ill. (61530) 222/D3
Eureka, Ind. (†47635) 227/C9
Eureka, Kansas (67045) 232/F4
Eureka, Mo. (63025) 261/M4
Eureka, Mont. (59917) 262/B2
Eureka (co.), Nev. 266/E3
Eureka, Nev. (89316) 266/E3
Eureka, N.C. (27830) 281/O3
Eureka, N.W.T. 146/K2
Eureka, N.W.T. 162/N3
Eureka, N.W. Terrs. 187/K2
Eureka (sound), N.W. Terrs. 187/K2
Eureka, Nova Scotia 168/F3
Eureka, S.C. (†29706) 296/E2
Eureka, S.C. (†29847) 296/D4
Eureka, S. Dak. (57437) 298/K2
Eureka, Utah (84628) 304/B4
Eureka, Wash. (†99348) 310/G4
Eureka, W. Va. (26144) 312/D4
Eureka Lodge, Alaska (†99588) 196/C1
Eureka Springs, Ark. (72632) 202/C1
Euroa, Victoria 97/C5
Europa (pt.), Gibraltar 33/D4
Europa (isl.), Réunion 102/G7
Europa (isl.), Réunion 118/G4
Europe 2/K3
Europoort, Netherlands 27/E5
Eusebio Ayala, Paraguay 144/B4
Euskirchen, W. Germany 22/B3
Eustace, Texas (75124) 303/H5
Eustis, Fla. (32726) 212/E3
Eustis, Maine (04936) 243/B5
Eustis○, Maine (04936) 243/B5
Eustis, Nebr. (69028) 264/D4
Euston, N.S. Wales 97/B4
Eutaw, Ala. (35462) 195/C5
Eutawville, S.C. (29048) 296/G5
Eutin, W. Germany 22/D1
Eutsuk (lake), Br. Col. 184/D3
Eva, Ala. (35621) 195/E2
Eva (lake), Alberta 182/B5
Eva, La. (†71354) 238/G4
Eva, Okla. (†73949) 288/C1
Eva, Tenn. (38333) 237/E8
Evadale, Texas (77615) 303/L7
Eva Downs, North. Terr. 93/D5
Évain, Québec 174/B3
Evan, Minn. (56238) 255/D6
Evan (lake), Québec 174/B2
Evandale, New Bruns. 170/D3
Evandale, Tasmania 99/D3
Evangeline (par.), La. 238/F5
Evangeline, La. (70537) 238/F6
Evangeline, New Bruns. 170/F1
Evans, Colo. (80620) 208/K2
Evans (mt.), Colo. 208/H3
Evans (co.), Georgia 217/J6
Evans, Georgia (30809) 217/H3
Evans, La. (70639) 238/D5
Evans (head), N.S. Wales 97/G1
Evans (str.), N.W.T. 162/H3
Evans (str.), N.W. Terrs. 187/K3
Evans, Wash. (99126) 310/H2
Evans, W. Va. (25241) 312/C5
Evansburg, Alberta 182/C3
Evans Center, N.Y. (†14006) 276/B5
Evans City, Pa. (16033) 294/B4
Evansdale, Iowa (50707) 229/J4
Evans Head, N.S. Wales 97/G1
Evans Mills, N.Y. (13637) 276/J2
Evansport, Ohio (43519) 284/B3
Evanston, Ill. (*60201) 222/B5
Evanston, Ind. (47531) 227/D8
Evanston, Wyo. 188/D2
Evanston, Wyo. (82930) 319/B4
Evansville (Bettles Field), Alaska (†99726) 196/H1
Evansville, Ark. (72729) 202/B2
Evansville, Ill. (62242) 222/D5
Evansville, Ind. 188/J3
Evansville, Ind. 146/K6
Evansville, Ind. (*47701) 227/C9
Evansville, Minn. (56326) 255/C4
Evansville, Miss. (†38676) 256/D1
Evansville, Pa. (19521) 294/L5
Evansville, Wis. (53536) 317/H10
Evansville, Wyo. (82636) 319/F3
Evant, Texas (76525) 303/G6
Evanton, Scotland 15/D3
Evart, Mich. (49631) 250/D5
Evarts, Ky. (40828) 237/P7
Evaton, S. Africa 118/H7
Evaz, Iran 66/J7
Eveleth, Minn. (55734) 255/F3
Evelyn, La. (†71052) 238/D3
Evendale, Ohio (†45201) 284/C9
Evening Shade, Ark. (72532) 202/G1
Evenki Aut. Okr., U.S.S.R. 48/K3
Evensk, U.S.S.R. 4/C1
Evensk, U.S.S.R. 48/Q3
Evensville, Tenn. (37332) 237/M9
Even Yehuda, Israel 65/B3
Everard (lake), S. Australia 88/E6
Everard (lake), S. Australia 94/D4
Everard (ranges), S. Australia 94/C2
Evere, Belgium 27/C9
Everest (mt.) 54/K7
Everest (mt.), China 77/C6
Everest, Kansas (66424) 232/G2
Everest (mt.), Nepal 68/F3
Everest, N. Dak. (†58023) 282/R6
Everett, Georgia (31536) 217/J8
Everett, Mass. (02149) 249/D6
Everett (mt.), Mass. 249/A4
Everett, New Bruns. 170/C1
Everett (dam), N.H. 268/D5
Everett (mts.), N.W. Terrs. 187/M3
Everett, Ontario 177/E3
Everett, Pa. (15537) 294/F5
Everett, Wash. 188/B1
Everett, Wash. (*98201) 310/C3
Everetts, N.C. (27825) 281/P3
Everettville, W. Va. (26533) 312/F3
Evergem, Belgium 27/D6
Everglades, The (swamp), Fla. 212/F6
Everglades, The (swamp), Fla. 188/K5
Everglades City, Fla. (33929) 212/E6
Everglades Nat'l Park, Fla. 212/F6
Evergreen, Ala. (36401) 195/E8
Evergreen, Colo. (80439) 208/J3
Evergreen, La. (71333) 238/F5
Evergreen, N.C. (28438) 281/M6
Evergreen, Va. (23939) 307/L6
Evergreen Park, Ill. (60642) 222/B6
Everly, Iowa (51338) 229/C2
Everman, Texas (76140) 303/F3
Everson, Pa. (15631) 294/C5
Everson, Wash. (98247) 310/C2
Eversonville, Mo. (†64688) 261/F3
Everton, Ark. (72633) 202/E1
Everton, Ind. (†47331) 227/G5
Everton, Mo. (65646) 261/E8
Evesham, England 10/E4
Evesham, England 13/F5
Evesham, Sask. 181/B3
Evington, Va. (24550) 307/K6
Evolène, Switzerland 39/D4
Évora (dist.), Portugal 33/C3
Évora, Portugal 7/D5
Évora, Portugal 33/C3
Évreux, France 28/D3
Évros (riv.), Greece 45/H5
Évry, France 28/E3
Évvoia (isl.), Greece 7/G5
Évvoia (isl.), Greece 45/G6
Ewa, Hawaii (96706) 218/A4
Ewab (Kai) (isls.), Indonesia 85/J7
Ewa Beach, Hawaii (96706) 218/A4
Ewan, N.J. (08025) 273/C4
Ewan, Wash. (99127) 310/H3
Ewaninga, North. Terr. 93/D7
Ewart, Iowa (†50171) 229/H5
Ewarton, Jamaica 156/C3
Ewarton, Jamaica 158/J6
Ewauna (lake), Oreg. 291/F5
Ewe, Loch (inlet), Scotland 15/C3
Ewell, Md. (21824) 245/O9
Ewen, Mich. (49925) 250/F2
Ewing, Ill. (62836) 222/E5
Ewing, Ky. (41039) 237/O4
Ewing, Mo. (63440) 261/J2
Ewing, Nebr. (68735) 264/F2
Ewing (mt.), North. Terr. 93/E7
Ewing, Va. (24248) 307/B7
Ewington, Ohio (45627) 284/F8
Ewo, Congo 115/B4
Exaltación, Bolivia 136/C3
Excel, Ala. (36439) 195/D8
Excel, Alberta 182/E4
Excello, Mo. (65247) 261/H3
Excello, Ohio (45042) 284/B7
Excelsior, Minn. (55331) 255/E6
Excelsior (mts.), Nev. 266/C4
Excelsior, Wis. (†53518) 317/E9
Excelsior Springs, Mo. (64024) 261/R4
Exchange, W. Va. (26619) 312/E5
Excursion Inlet, Alaska (†99826) 196/M1
Exe (riv.), England 13/D7
Exe (riv.), England 10/E5
Executive Committee (range) 5/B12
Exeland, Wis. (54835) 317/D4
Exeter, Calif. (93221) 204/F7
Exeter, Conn. (†06249) 210/F2
Exeter, England 13/D7
Exeter, England 10/E5
Exeter, Ill. (†62694) 222/C4
Exeter, Maine (04435) 243/E6
Exeter○, Maine (04435) 243/E6
Exeter, Mo. (65647) 261/D9
Exeter, Nebr. (68351) 264/G4
Exeter, N.H. (03833) 268/F6
Exeter○, N.H. (03833) 268/F6
Exeter (riv.), N.H. 268/E6
Exeter (sound), N.W. Terrs. 187/M3
Exeter, Ontario 177/C4
Exeter○, R.I. (02822) 249/H6
Exeter, Tasmania 99/C3
Exira, Iowa (50076) 229/D5
Exline, Iowa (52555) 229/H7
Exminster, England 13/D7
Exmoor National Park, England 13/D6
Exmore, Va. (23350) 307/S5
Exmouth, England 13/D7
Exmouth, England 10/E5
Exmouth, W. Australia 88/A4
Exmouth (gulf), W. Australia 88/A4
Exmouth, W. Australia 92/A3
Exmouth (gulf), W. Australia 92/A3
Expanse, Sask. 181/E6
Experiment, Georgia (30212) 217/D4
Exploits (riv.), Newf. 166/C4
Export, Pa. (15632) 294/C5
Exshaw, Alberta 182/C4
Extension, Br. Col. 184/J3
Extension, La. (71239) 238/G3
Exu, Brazil 132/G4
Exuma (cays), Bahamas 156/C1
Exuma (sound), Bahamas 156/C1
Eyasi (lake), Tanzania 115/F4
Eye, England 10/G4
Eye, England 13/J5
Eye (pen.), Scotland 15/B2
Eyebrow, Sask. 181/E5
Eyebrow (lake), Sask. 181/E5
Eyehill (creek), Sask. 181/B3
Eyemouth, Scotland 15/F5
Eyemouth, Scotland 10/F3
Eynesil, Turkey 63/H2
Eynhallow (sound), Scotland 15/E1
Eynort, Loch (inlet), Scotland 15/A3
Eyota, Minn. (55934) 255/F7
Eyre (lake), Australia 87/D8
Eyre (bay), Chile 138/D8
Eyre (mts.), N. Zealand 100/B6
Eyre (riv.), Queensland 88/F5
Eyre (lake), S. Australia 88/F5
Eyre (pen.), S. Australia 88/F6
Eyre (pen.), S. Australia 94/D5
Eyre, W. Australia 92/D6
Eyrecourt, Ireland 17/E5
Eyre North (lake), S. Australia 94/E3
Eyre South (lake), S. Australia 94/E3
Eysturoy (isl.), Denmark 21/B3
Eyüp, Turkey 63/D6
Ezel, Ky. (41425) 237/P5
Ezequiel Montes, Mexico 150/K6
Ezibider, Turkey 63/H2
Ezine, Turkey 63/B3
Ezna, Iran 66/F4
Ez Zababida, West Bank 65/C3
Ez Zarqa', Jordan 65/E3
Ez Zuetina, Libya 111/D1

F

Faaa, Fr. Poly. 86/S13
Fabens, Texas (79838) 303/B10
Faber (lake), N.W. Terrs. 187/G3
Faber, Va. (22938) 307/L5
Fabius, Ala. (35965) 195/G1
Fabius, N.Y. (13063) 276/J5
Fåborg, Denmark 21/D7
Fåborg, Denmark 18/G9
Fabriano, Italy 34/D3
Fabyan, Alberta 182/E3
Fabyan, Conn. (06245) 210/H1
Fabyan House, N.H. (†03595) 268/E3
Facatativá, Colombia 126/C5
Faceville, Georgia (†31717) 217/C9
Fachi, Niger 106/G5
Fackler, Ala. (35746) 195/G1
Factoryville, Pa. (18419) 294/L2
Facundo, Argentina 143/C6
Fada, Chad 111/D4
Fada-N'Gourma, Upper Volta 106/E6
Fadd, Hungary 41/E3
Faddeyevskiy (isl.), U.S.S.R. 4/B2
Faddeyevskiy (isl.), U.S.S.R. 48/P2
Faden, Newf. 166/A3
Faenza, Italy 34/D2
Faerøe (isls.), Den. 4/C10
Faerøe (isls.), Denmark 7/D2
Faerøe (isls.), Denmark 21/B2
FAERØE ISLANDS, Denmark 21/B2
Faerøe Islands, Denmark 21/B2
Fafan (riv.), Ethiopia 111/H6
Fafe, Portugal 33/B2
Fagan, Ky. (†40322) 237/O5
Făgăraș, Romania 45/G3
Fagernes, Norway 18/F6
Fagersta, Sweden 18/J6
Fagnano (lake), Argentina 143/C7
Fagnano (lake), Chile 138/F11
Faguibine (lake), Mali 106/D5
Fagundes, Brazil 132/C4
Fagus, Mo. (63938) 261/M9
Fahan, Ireland 17/G1
Fahrej (Iranshahr), Iran 66/M7
Fahrej (Iranshahr), Iran 59/H4
Faial (isl.), Portugal 33/B1
Faid, Saudi Arabia 59/D4
Faido, Switzerland 39/G4
Fainaven (mt.), Scotland 15/D2
Fair (head), N. Ireland 17/J1
Fair (isl.), Scotland 10/F1
Fairacres, N. Mex. (88033) 274/C6
Fairbank, Ariz. (85612) 198/E7
Fairbank, Iowa (50629) 229/K3
Fairbank, Md. (†21671) 245/N6
Fairbanks, Alaska 146/D3
Fairbanks, Alaska (99701) 196/J2
Fairbanks, Alaska 188/D5
Fairbanks, Fla. (†32601) 212/D2
Fairbanks, Ind. (47849) 227/B6
Fairbanks, La. (71240) 238/F1
Fairbanks, Maine (†04938) 243/C6
Fairbanks, Minn. (†55602) 255/G3
Fairbanks, U.S. 4/C17
Fairbanks, U.S. 2/C2
Fair Bluff, N.C. (28439) 281/M6
Fairborn, Ohio (45324) 284/B6
Fairburn, Georgia (30213) 217/J2
Fairburn, S. Dak. (57738) 298/C6
Fairbury, Ill. (61739) 222/E3
Fairbury, Nebr. (68352) 264/G4
Fairchance, Pa. (15436) 294/C6
Fairchild, Wis. (54741) 317/D6
Fairchild A.F.B., Wash. 310/H3
Fairdale, Ill. (†60146) 222/E1
Fairdale, Ky. (40118) 237/K4
Fairdale, N. Dak. (58229) 282/O3
Fairdealing, Mo. (63939) 261/L9
Fairfax, Ala. (36854) 195/H5
Fairfax, Calif. (94930) 204/H1
Fairfax, Iowa (52228) 229/K5
Fairfax, Manitoba 179/B5
Fairfax, Minn. (55332) 255/D6
Fairfax, Mo. (64446) 261/B2
Fairfax, Ohio (†45201) 284/C9
Fairfax, Okla. (74637) 288/N1
Fairfax, S.C. (29827) 296/E6
Fairfax, S. Dak. (57335) 298/M7
Fairfax○, Vt. (05454) 268/B2
Fairfax (co.), Va. 307/O3
Fairfax (I.C.), Va. (22030) 307/R3
Fairfax, Wash. (†98323) 310/C4
Fairfax Station, Va. (22039) 307/R3
Fairfield, Ala. (35064) 195/E4
Fairfield, Calif. (94533) 204/K1
Fairfield (co.), Conn. 210/B3
Fairfield○, Conn. (06430) 210/B4
Fairfield, Fla. (32634) 212/D2
Fairfield, Idaho (83327) 220/D6
Fairfield, Ill. (62837) 222/E5
Fairfield, Iowa (52556) 229/J6
Fairfield, Ky. (40020) 237/L5
Fairfield, Maine (04937) 243/D6
Fairfield○, Maine (04937) 243/D6
Fairfield, Mont. (59436) 262/D3
Fairfield, Nebr. (68938) 264/G4
Fairfield, New Bruns. 170/E3
Fairfield○, N.J. (07006) 273/A2
Fairfield, N.S. Wales 88/K4
Fairfield, N.S. Wales 97/H3
Fairfield, N. Zealand 100/C6
Fairfield, N.C. (27826) 281/S3
Fairfield, N. Dak. (58627) 282/D5
Fairfield (co.), Ohio 284/E6
Fairfield, Ohio (45014) 284/A7
Fairfield, Pa. (17320) 294/H6
Fairfield (co.), S.C. 296/E3
Fairfield, Tenn. (†37183) 237/J9
Fairfield, Texas (75840) 303/H6
Fairfield, Utah (†84013) 304/B3
Fairfield○, Vt. (05455) 268/B2
Fairfield (pond), Vt. 268/A2
Fairfield, Va. (24435) 307/K5
Fairfield, Wash. (99012) 310/H3
Fairfield Center, Maine (†04937) 243/D6
Fairford, Ala. (†36553) 195/B8
Fairford, Manitoba 179/D3
Fairgrange, Ill. (†61920) 222/E4
Fairgrove, Mich. (48733) 250/F5
Fair Grove, Mo. (65648) 261/F8W
Fair Harbour, Br. Col. 184/D5
Fairhaven○, Mass. (02719) 249/L6
Fair Haven, Mich. (48023) 250/G6
Fairhaven, Minn. (†55382) 255/D5
Fairhaven, New Bruns. 170/C4

370 Fontainebleau

Fontainebleau, France 28/E3
Fontainebleau, Québec 172/F4
Fontana, Calif. (92335) 204/E10
Fontana, Kansas (66026) 232/H3
Fontana (lake), N.C. 281/B4
Fontana, Wis. (53125) 317/J10
Fontanelle, Iowa (50846) 229/E6
Fontanet, Ind. (47851) 227/C5
Fontas (riv.), Br. Col. 184/M2
Fonte Boa, Brazil 132/G9
Fontein, Neth. Ant. 161/E8
Fontenay-le-Comte, France 28/C4
Fontenay-sous-Bois, France 28/C2
Fonteneau (lake), Newf. 166/B3
Fontenelle, Québec 172/D1
Fontenelle (creek), Wyo. 319/B3
Fontenelle (res.), Wyo. 319/B3
Fontibón, Colombia 126/C5
Fontur (prom.), Iceland 7/C2
Fontur (pt.), Iceland 21/D1
Fonyód, Hungary 41/D3
Foochow (Fuzhou), China 77/J6
Fool Creek (res.), Utah 304/B4
Foosland, Ill. (61845) 222/E3
Foothills, Alberta 182/B3
Footscray, Victoria 97/H5
Footscray, Victoria 88/K7
Footville, Ohio (†44084) 284/J2
Footville, Wis. (53537) 317/H10
Foping, China 77/G5
Forada, Minn. (†56308) 255/C5
Foraker (mt.), Alaska 196/H2
Foraker, Ind. (46525) 227/F1
Foraker, Ohio (†45812) 284/C4
Foraker, Okla. (74652) 288/O1
Forbach, France 28/G3
Forbes (mt.), Alberta 182/B4
Forbes (mt.), Br. Col. 184/J4
Forbes (isl.), Fla. 212/D6
Forbes, Minn. (55738) 255/F3
Forbes, Mo. (†64473) 261/B3
Forbes, N.S. Wales 88/H6
Forbes, N.S. Wales 97/E3
Forbes, N. Dak. (58439) 282/N8
Forbes (lake), Québec 172/C3
Forbing, La. (71106) 238/C2
Forbus, Tenn. (38561) 237/M7
Forcados, Nigeria 106/E7
Forcalquier, France 28/F6
Force, Pa. (15841) 294/E3
Forchheim, W. Germany 22/D4
Forchu (bay), Nova Scotia 168/H3
Forchu (cape), Nova Scotia 168/B5
Ford, England 13/F2
Ford (isl.), Hawaii 218/B3
Ford (co.), Ill. 222/E3
Ford (co.), Kansas 232/C4
Ford, Kansas (67842) 232/C4
Ford, Ky. (40320) 237/N5
Ford (riv.), Mich. 250/B2
Ford (cape), North. Terr. 88/D2
Ford (cape), North. Terr. 93/A2
Ford, Va. (23850) 307/N6
Ford, Wash. (99013) 310/H3
Ford City, Calif. (†93268) 204/F8
Ford City, Mo. (†64463) 261/C2
Ford City, Pa. (16226) 294/D4
Ford Cliff, Pa. (16228) 294/D4
Fordland, Mo. (65652) 261/G8
Fordoche, La. (70732) 238/G5
Ford Ranges (mts.) 5/B11
Fords, N.J. (08863) 273/E2
Ford's Bridge, N.S. Wales 97/C1
Fords Prairie, Wash. (†98531) 310/B4
Fordsville, Ky. (42343) 237/H5
Fordville, N. Dak. (58231) 282/P3
Fordwich, Ontario 177/C4
Fordyce, Ark. (71742) 202/F6
Fordyce, Nebr. (68736) 264/G2
Forécariah, Guinea 106/B7
Foreman, Ark. (71836) 202/B6
Foremost, Alberta 182/E5
Foresman, Ind. (†47922) 227/C3
Forest, Belgium 27/B9
Forest, Ind. (46039) 227/E4
Forest, La. (71242) 238/H1
Forest, Miss. (39074) 256/F6
Forest (riv.), N. Dak. 282/P3
Forest, Ohio (45843) 284/C4
Forest, Ontario 177/C4
Forest (co.), Pa. 294/D2
Forest, Va. (24551) 307/K6
Forest (co.), Wis. 317/J4
Forest Acres, S.C. (29206) 296/E3
Forest Beach, S.C. (†29928) 296/F7
Forestburg, Alberta 182/E3
Forestburg, S. Dak. (57338) 298/N5
Forestburg, Texas (76239) 303/G4
Forest City, Ill. (61532) 222/D3
Forest City, Iowa (50436) 229/F2
Forest City, Maine (04413) 243/H4
Forest City, Mo. (64451) 261/B3
Forest City, New Bruns. 170/C3
Forest City, N.C. (28043) 281/E4
Forest City, Pa. (18421) 294/L2
Forestdale, Ala. (35214) 195/E3
Forestdale, R.I. (02824) 249/H5
Forest Dale, Vt. (05745) 268/A4
Forester, Mich. (†48419) 250/G5
Foresters Falls, Ontario 177/H2
Forest Glen, Georgia (†31001) 217/F7
Forest Green, Mo. (†65281) 261/G4
Forest Grove, Br. Col. 184/G4
Forestgrove, Mont. (59441) 262/H3
Forest Grove, Oreg. (97116) 291/A2
Forest Heights, Md. (†20001) 245/F5
Foresthill, Calif. (†95703) 204/E4
Forest Hill, Ind. (†47240) 227/F6
Forest Hill, La. (71430) 238/E4
Forest Hill, Md. (21050) 245/N2
Forest Hill, N.S. Wales 97/D4
Forest Hill, Texas (†76119) 303/F2
Forest Hill, W. Va. (24935) 312/E7
Forest Hills, Ky. (41527) 237/L2
Forest Hills, Pa. (†15221) 294/C7
Forest Hills, Tenn. (†37201) 237/H8
Forest Home, Ala. (36030) 195/E7
Forest Homes, Ill. (†62018) 222/B2
Forestier (cape), Tasmania 99/E4
Forestier (pen.), Tasmania 99/E4
Forest Junction, Wis. (54123) 317/K7
Forest Knolls-Lagunitas, Calif. (94933) 204/H1
Forest Lake, Mich. (49832) 250/C2
Forest Lake, Minn. (55025) 255/F5
Foreston, Minn. (56330) 255/E5
Foreston, S.C. (†29102) 296/G4
Forest Park, Georgia (30050) 217/K2
Forest Park, Ill. (60130) 222/B5
Forest Park, Ohio (45405) 284/B9
Forest Park, Okla. (†73101) 288/M3
Forestport, N.Y. (13338) 276/K4
Forest River, N. Dak. (58233) 282/P3
Forest Station, Maine (†04413) 243/H4
Forest View, Ill. (†60402) 222/B6
Forestville, Conn. (†06010) 210/D2
Forestville, Md. (†20028) 245/G5
Forestville, Mich. (48434) 250/G5
Forestville, N.Y. (14062) 276/B6
Forestville, Ohio (45230) 284/C10
Forestville, Pa. (16035) 294/B3
Forestville, Québec 172/H1
Forestville, Québec 174/D3
Forestville, Wis. (54213) 317/L6
Forez (mts.), France 28/E5
Forfar, Scotland 10/E2
Forfar, Scotland 15/F4
Forgan, Okla. (73938) 288/E1
Forgan, Sask. 181/D4
Forget, Sask. 181/J6
Forge Village, Mass. (01828) 249/H2
Forillon Nat'l Park, Que. 162/K6
Forillon Nat'l Park, Québec 172/D1
Foristell, Mo. (63348) 261/L5
Fork, N.C. (†27028) 281/J3
Fork, S.C. (29543) 296/J3
Forked (lake), N.Y. 276/L3
Forked Deer (riv.), Tenn. 237/C9
Forked Deer, Middle Fork (riv.), Tenn. 237/C9
Forked Deer, North Fork (riv.), Tenn. 237/C8
Forked Deer, South Fork (riv.), Tenn. 237/C9
Forked River, N.J. (08731) 273/E4
Fork Lake, Alberta 182/E2
Forkland, Ala. (36740) 195/C5
Fork Mountain, Tenn. (†37728) 237/N8
Fork River, Manitoba 179/B3
Forks, Wash. (98331) 310/A3
Forks of Buffalo, Va. (†24521) 307/K5
Forks of Elkhorn, Ky. (†40601) 237/M4
Forks of Salmon, Calif. (96031) 204/B2
Forksville, Pa. (18616) 294/J3
Fork Union, Va. (23055) 307/M5
Forkville, Miss. (39076) 256/E6
Forlì (prov.), Italy 34/D2
Forlì, Italy 34/D2
Forman, N. Dak. (58032) 282/P7
Formartine (dist.), Scotland 15/F3
Formby, England 13/G2
Formby, England 10/F2
Formby (head), England 13/G2
Formentera (isl.), Spain 33/G3
Formentor (cape), Spain 33/H2
Formia, Italy 34/D4
Formiga, Brazil 135/D2
Formiga, Brazil 132/E8
Formosa (prov.), Argentina 143/D1
Formosa, Argentina 143/E2
Formosa, Argentina 120/D5
Formosa, Ark. (†72031) 202/E3
Formosa, Brazil 132/E6
Formosa, Serra (range), Brazil 132/C5
Formosa (Taiwan) (isl.), China 2/R4
Formosa (Taiwan) (isl.), China 77/K7
Formosa (Taiwan) (str.), China 77/J7
Formosa (bay), Kenya 115/H4
Formosa, Ontario 177/C3
Formosa, Paraguay 144/C5
Formoso, Kansas (66942) 232/D2
Forney, Ala. (†30124) 195/H2
Forney, Texas (75126) 303/H5
Forres, Scotland 10/E2
Forres, Scotland 15/E3
Forrest, Ill. (61741) 222/E3
Forrest (co.), Miss. 256/F8
Forrest, N. Mex. (†88401) 274/F4
Forrest (lake), Sask. 181/L3
Forrest, W. Australia 88/D6
Forrest (lakes), W. Australia 88/D5
Forrest, W. Australia 92/D5
Forrest City, Ark. (72335) 202/J3
Forreston, Ill. (61030) 222/D1
Forrest River Aboriginal Res., W. Australia 92/D1
Forrest River Mission, W. Australia 92/D1
Forrest Station, Manitoba 179/C5
Forsan, Texas (79733) 303/C5
Forsayth, Queensland 95/B3
Forsayth, Queensland 88/G3
Forshaga, Sweden 18/H7
Forssa, Finland 18/N6
Forst, E. Germany 22/F3
Forster-Tuncurry, N.S. Wales 97/G3
Forsyth (co.), Georgia 217/D2
Forsyth, Georgia (31029) 217/E4
Forsyth, Ill. (62535) 222/D4
Forsyth, Mo. (65653) 261/F9
Forsyth, Mont. (59327) 262/K4
Forsyth (co.), N.C. 281/J2
Fort (pt.), St. Chris.-Nevis 161/C11
Fort (mt.), Switzerland 39/D4
Fort A.P. Hill, Va. 307/O4
Fort Adams, Miss. (39636) 256/B8
Fort à la Corne, Sask. 181/G2
Fort Albany, Ont. 146/K4
Fort Albany, Ont. 162/H5
Fort Albany, Ontario 175/D2
Fort Alexander, Manitoba 179/F4
Fortaleza, Bolivia 136/C1
Fortaleza, Bolivia 136/B3
Fortaleza, Brazil 132/G3
Fortaleza, Brazil 120/F3
Fortaleza, Brazil 2/H6
Fortaleza de Santa Teresa, Uruguay 145/F5
Fort Ann, N.Y. (12827) 276/N4
Fort Apache, Ariz. (85926) 198/F5
Fort Apache Ind. Res., Ariz. 198/E5
Fort Ashby, W. Va. (26719) 312/J4
Fort Assiniboine, Alberta 182/C2
Fort Atkinson, Iowa (52144) 229/J2
Fort Atkinson, Wis. (53538) 317/J10
Fort Augustus, Scotland 10/D2
Fort Augustus, Scotland 15/D3
Fort Battleford Nat'l Hist. Park, Sask. 181/C3
Fort Bayard, N. Mex. (88036) 274/A6
Fort Beaufort, S. Africa 118/D6
Fort Beauséjour Nat'l Hist. Park, New Bruns 170/F3
Fort Belknap, Mont. (†59526) 262/H2
Fort Belknap Ind. Res., Mont. 262/H2
Fort Belvoir, Va. 307/O3
Fort Bend (co.), Texas 303/J8
Fort Benjamin Harrison, Ind. 227/E5
Fort Benning, Georgia 217/B6
Fort Benton, Mont. (59442) 262/F3
Fort Berthold Ind. Res., N. Dak. 282/E4
Fort Bidwell, Calif. (96112) 204/E2
Fort Bidwell Ind. Res., Calif. 204/E2
Fort Blackmore, Va. (24250) 307/C7
Fort Bliss, Texas 303/A10
Fort Bliss Mil. Res., N. Mex. 274/C6
Fort Bowie Nat'l Hist. Site, Ariz. 198/F6
Fort Bragg, Calif. (95437) 204/B4
Fort Bragg, N.C. 281/M4
Fort Branch, Ind. (47648) 227/B8
Fort Bridger, Wyo. (82933) 319/B4
Fort Calhoun, Nebr. (68023) 264/J3
Fort Campbell, Ky. 237/G7
Fort Campbell, Tenn. 237/G7
Fort Carlton Hist. Park, Sask. 181/E3
Fort Caroline Nat'l Mem., Fla. 212/E1
Fort Carson, Colo. 208/K5
Fort Chaffee, Ark. 202/B3
Fort Chambly Nat'l Hist. Park, Québec 172/J4
Fort-Chimo, Que. 162/K4
Fort-Chimo, Québec 174/F2
Fort Chipewyan, Alberta 182/C5
Fort Chipewyan, Alta 162/E4
Fort Chipewyan, Alta. 146/G4
Fort Churchill, Manitoba 179/K2
Fort Clark, N. Dak. (†58571) 282/H5
Fort Clatsop Nat'l Mem., Oreg. 291/C1
Fort Cobb, Okla. (73038) 288/K4
Fort Cobb (res.), Okla. 288/J4
Fort Collins, Colo. 146/H6
Fort Collins, Colo. 188/E2
Fort Collins, Colo. (80521) 208/J1
Fort Covington○, N.Y. (12937) 276/M1
Fort-Dauphin (Faradofay), Madagascar 118/H5
Fort Davis, Ala. (36031) 195/G6
Fort Davis, Alaska 196/E2
Fort Davis, Texas (79734) 303/D11
Fort Davis Nat'l Hist. Site, Texas 303/D11
Fort Defiance, Ariz. (86504) 198/F3
Fort Defiance, Va. (24437) 307/L4
Fort-de-France (cap.), Martinique 161/C6
Fort-de-France (cap.), Martinique 156/G4
Fort-de-France (bay), Martinique 161/C6
Fort Denaud, Fla. (†33935) 212/E5
Fort Deposit, Ala. (36032) 195/E7
Fort-Desaix, Martinique 161/D6
Fort Detrick, Md. 245/J3
Fort Devens, Mass. 249/H2
Fort Dick, Calif. (95531) 204/A2
Fort Dix, N.J. 273/D3
Fort Dodge, Iowa (50501) 229/E3
Fort Dodge, Iowa 188/H2
Fort Dodge, Kansas (67843) 232/C4
Fort Donelson Nat'l Mil. Park, Tenn. 237/F8
Fort Drum, Fla. (†33472) 212/F4
Fort Drum, N.Y. 276/J2
Fort Duchesne, Utah (84026) 304/E3
Forteau, Newf. 166/C3
Fort Edward, N.Y. (12828) 276/O4
Forte República, Angola 115/C5
Forte República, Angola 102/D5
Fort Erie, Ontario 177/E5
Fortescue, Mo. (64452) 261/B2
Fortescue, N.J. (08321) 273/C5
Fortescue (riv.), W. Australia 88/B4
Fortescue (riv.), W. Australia 92/B3
Fort Eustis, Va. 307/P6
Fort Fairfield, Maine (04742) 243/H2
Fort Fairfield○, Maine (04742) 243/H2
Fort Foote, Md. (†20022) 245/F6
Fort-Foureau (Kousseri), Cameroon 115/B1
Fort Frances, Ont. 162/G6
Fort Frances, Ontario 177/F5
Fort Frances, Ontario 175/B3
Fort Franklin, N.W.T. 162/D3
Fort Franklin, N.W. Terrs. 187/F3
Fort Fraser, Br. Col. 184/E3
Fort Frederica Nat'l Mon., Georgia 217/K8
Fort Fred Steele, Wyo. (†82301) 319/E4
Fort Gaines, Ala. 195/B10
Fort Gaines, Georgia (31751) 217/C7
Fort Garland, Colo. (81133) 208/J8
Fort Gay, W. Va. (25514) 312/A6
Fort-George, Que. 146/K4
Fort-George, Que. 162/J5
Fort-George, Québec 174/B2
Fort George G. Meade, Md. 245/L4
Fort Gibson, Okla. (74434) 288/R3
Fort Gibson (lake), Okla. 288/R2
Fort Good Hope, N.W.T. 162/D2
Fort Good Hope, N.W. Terrs. 187/F3
Fort Gordon, Georgia 217/H4
Fort-Gouraud (Fdérik), Mauritania 106/B4
Fort Grant, Ariz. (85643) 198/E6
Fort Greely, Alaska 196/J2
Fort Green, Fla. (33834) 212/E4
Forth, Scotland 15/C2
Forth (firth), Scotland 10/E2
Forth (firth), Scotland 15/F4
Forth (riv.), Scotland 15/B1
Forth (riv.), Scotland 10/C1
Forth, Tasmania 99/C3
Forth (riv.), Tasmania 99/C3
Fort Hall, Idaho (83203) 220/F6
Fort Hall, Kenya 115/G4
Fort Hall Ind. Res., Idaho 220/F6
Fort Hancock, N.J. 273/F3
Fort Hancock, Texas (79839) 303/B11
Forth and Clyde (canal), Scotland 10/B1
Forth and Clyde (canal), Scotland 15/B2
Fort Hertz (Putao), Burma 72/C1
Fort Hood, Texas 303/G6
Fort Howard, Md. (21052) 245/N4
Fort Huachuca, Ariz. 198/E7
Fort Hunter Liggett, Calif. 204/D8
Fortierville, Québec 172/F3
Fortín 10 de Octubre, Paraguay 144/A2
Fortín Ávalos Sánchez, Paraguay 144/C3
Fortín Boquerón, Paraguay 144/C3
Fortín Buenos Aires, Paraguay 144/B3
Fortín Campero, Bolivia 136/C8
Fortín Capitán Escobar, Paraguay 144/B3
Fortín Carlos Antonio López (Pitiantuta), Paraguay 144/C2
Fortín Casanillo, Paraguay 144/C3
Fortín Coronel Bogado, Paraguay 144/C2
Fortín Coronel Sánchez, Paraguay 144/C1
Fortín de las Flores, Mexico 150/P2
Fort Independence Ind. Res., Calif. 204/G7
Fortine, Mont. (59918) 262/A2
Fortín Falcon, Paraguay 144/C3
Fortín Florida, Paraguay 144/C2
Fortín Galpón, Paraguay 144/C1
Fortín General Bruguez, Paraguay 144/C4
Fortín General Caballero, Paraguay 144/C4
Fortín General Delgado, Paraguay 144/B4
Fortín General Díaz, Paraguay 144/B3
Fortín Guaraní, Paraguay 144/C3
Fortín Hernandarias, Paraguay 144/A2
Fortín Infante Rivarola, Paraguay 144/A2
Fortín Isla Poi, Paraguay 144/C3
Fortín Lagerenza i, Paraguay 144/B2
Fortín Madrejón, Paraguay 144/B2
Fortín Max Paredes, Bolivia 136/F6
Fortín Mayor Alberto Gardel, Paraguay 144/A3
Fortín Mayor Rodríguez, Paraguay 144/B3
Fortín Mutum, Bolivia 136/F6
Fortín Nueva Asunción (Picuiba), Paraguay 144/B2
Fortín Olmos, Argentina 143/F4
Fortín Palmar de las Islas, Paraguay 144/B1
Fortín Pilcomayo, Paraguay 144/B3
Fortín Presidente Ayala, Paraguay 144/C3
Fortín Presidente Cardozo, Paraguay 144/B5
Fortín Ravelo, Bolivia 136/E6
Fortín Santiago Rodríguez, Paraguay 144/A2
Fortín Suárez Arana, Bolivia 136/F6
Fortín Teniente Américo Picco, Paraguay 144/C1
Fortín Teniente E. Ochoa, Paraguay 144/B2
Fortín Teniente Esteban Martínez, Paraguay 144/C3
Fortín Teniente Gabino Mendoza, Paraguay 144/B2
Fortín Teniente Juan E. López, Paraguay 144/B2
Fortín Teniente Martínez, Paraguay 144/C2
Fortín Teniente Montenía, Paraguay 144/B3
Fortín Teniente Primero Anselmo Escobar, Paraguay 144/A3
Fortín Teniente Primero M. Cabello, Paraguay 144/B3
Fortín Teniente Primero Ramiro Espínola, Paraguay 144/B2
Fortín Toledo, Paraguay 144/B3
Fortín Torres, Paraguay 144/C2
Fortín Vanguardia, Bolivia 136/F6
Fortín Zalazar, Paraguay 144/C3
Fort Jackson, N.Y. (12938) 276/L1
Fort Jackson, S.C. 296/F4
Fort Jefferson Nat'l Mon., Fla. 212/C7
Fort Jennings, Ohio (45844) 284/B4
Fort Jesup, La. (†71449) 238/C3
Fort Johnson, N.Y. (12070) 276/M5
Fort Jones, Calif. (96032) 204/C2
Fort Kent, Alberta 182/E2
Fort Kent, Maine (04743) 243/F1
Fort Kent○, Maine (04743) 243/F1
Fort Kent Mills, Maine (04744) 243/F1
Fort Klamath, Oreg. (97626) 291/E5
Fort Knox, Ky. (40121) 237/K5
Fort Lallemand, Algeria 106/F2
Fort Lamar, Georgia (†30633) 217/F2
Fort Langley, Br. Col. 184/L3
Fort Laramie, Wyo. (82212) 319/H3
Fort Laramie Nat'l Hist. Site, Wyo. 319/H3
Fort Larned Nat'l Hist. Site, Kansas 232/C3
Fort Lauderdale, Fla. 188/K5
Fort Lauderdale, Fla. (*33301) 212/C4
Fort Lawn, S.C. (29714) 296/F2
Fort Lawrence, Nova Scotia 168/D3
Fort Leavenworth, Kansas (66027) 232/H2
Fort Lee, N.J. (07024) 273/C2
Fort Lee, Va. 307/O6
Fort Leonard Wood, Mo. 261/H7
Fort Lesley J. McNair, D.C. 245/E5
Fort Lewis, Wash. 310/C3
Fort Liard, N.W.T. 146/F3
Fort Liard, N.W.T. 162/D3
Fort Liard, N.W. Terrs. 187/F3
Fort Liberté, Haiti 156/D3
Fort Liberté, Haiti 158/C5
Fort Littleton, Pa. (17223) 294/F5
Fort Loramie, Ohio (45845) 284/B5
Fort Loudon, Pa. (17224) 294/G6
Fort Loudoun (lake), Tenn. 237/N9
Fort Lupton, Colo. (80621) 208/K2
Fort Lyon, Colo. (81038) 208/N6
Fort MacArthur, Calif. 204/C11
Fort Mackay, Alta. 162/E4
Fort Macleod, Alberta 182/D5
Fort Macleod, Alta. 162/E6
Fort MacMahon, Algeria 106/E3
Fort Madison, Iowa 188/H2
Fort Madison, Iowa (52627) 229/L7
Fort Matanzas Nat'l Mon., Fla. 212/E2
Fort McClellan Mil. Res., Ala. 195/G3
Fort McCoy, Fla. (32637) 212/E2
Fort McCoy, Wis. 317/E7
Fort McDermitt Ind. Res., Nev. 266/D1
Fort McDowell Ind. Res., Ariz. 198/D5
Fort McHenry Nat'l Mon., Md. 245/M3
Fort McKavett, Texas (76841) 303/E7
Fort McKay, Alberta 182/E1
Fort McKinley, Ohio (†45426) 284/B6
Fort McMurray, Alberta 182/E1
Fort McMurray, Alta. 146/G4
Fort McMurray, Alta. 162/E4
Fort McPherson, Georgia 217/K1
Fort McPherson, N.W.T. 146/E3
Fort McPherson, N.W.T. 162/C2
Fort McPherson, N.W. Terrs. 187/E3
Fort Meade, Fla. (33841) 212/E4
Fort Meade, Uruguay (57741) 298/C5
Fort Mill, S.C. (29715) 296/F1
Fort Miribel, Algeria 106/E3
Fort Mitchell, Ala. (36856) 195/H6
Fort Mitchell, Ky. (41017) 237/S2
Fort Mitchell, Va. (23941) 307/M7
Fort Mohave Ind. Res., Ariz. 198/A4
Fort Mohave Ind. Res., Calif. 204/L9
Fort Mohave Ind. Res., Nev. 266/G7
Fort Monmouth, N.J. 273/E3
Fort Monroe, Va. 307/R6
Fort Morgan, Ala. 195/C10
Fort Morgan, Colo. (80701) 208/M2
Fort Motte, S.C. (29050) 296/F4
Fort Myer, Va. 307/T2
Fort Myers, Fla. 188/K5
Fort Myers, Fla. (*33901) 212/E5
Fort Myers Beach, Fla. (33931) 212/E5
Fort Necessity, La. (71243) 238/G2
Fort Necessity Nat'l Battlefield, Pa. 294/C6
Fort Nelson, Br. Col. 146/F4
Fort Nelson, Br. Col. 162/D4
Fort Nelson, Br. Col. 184/M2
Fort Nelson (riv.), Br. Col. 184/M2
Fort Niagara, N.Y. 276/C4
Fort Norman, N.W.T. 162/D3
Fort Norman, N.W.T. 146/F3
Fort Norman, N.W. Terrs. 187/F3
Fort Ogden, Fla. (33842) 212/E4
Fort Oglethorpe, Georgia (30742) 217/B1
Fort Ord, Calif. 204/D7
Fort Payne, Ala. (35967) 195/G2
Fort Pearce Wash (dry riv.), Ariz. 198/B2
Fort Pearce Wash (creek), Utah 304/A6
Fort Peck, Mont. (59223) 262/K2
Fort Peck (dam), Mont. 262/K3
Fort Peck (lake), Mont. 262/K3
Fort Peck (lake), Mont. 146/H5
Fort Peck (lake), Mont. 188/E1
Fort Pickett, Va. 307/N6
Fort Pierce, Fla. 188/K5
Fort Pierce, Fla. (*33450) 212/F4
Fort Pierre, S. Dak. (57532) 298/H5
Fort Pillow, Tenn. (38032) 237/B9
Fort Pitt Hist. Park, Sask. 181/B2
Fort Plain, N.Y. (13339) 276/L5
Fort Point Nat'l Hist. Site, Calif. 204/J2
Fort Polk, La. 238/D4
Fort Portal, Uganda 115/F3
Fort Providence, N.W.T. 162/E3
Fort Providence, N.W. Terrs. 187/G3
Fort Pulaski Nat'l Mon., Georgia 217/L6
Fort Qu'Appelle, Sask. 181/H5
Fort Raleigh Nat'l Hist. Site, N.C. 281/T3
Fort Randall (dam), S. Dak. 298/N7
Fort Ransom, N. Dak. (58033) 282/P6
Fort Recovery, Ohio (45846) 284/A5
Fort Resolution, N.W.T. 146/G3
Fort Resolution, N.W.T. 162/E3
Fort Resolution, N.W. Terrs. 187/G3
Fortress (mt.), Wyo. 319/C1
Fort Rice, N. Dak. (58537) 282/J6
Fort Richardson, Alaska 196/C1
Fort Riley-Camp Whiteside, Kansas 232/F2
Fort Ripley, Minn. (56449) 255/D4
Fort Ritchie, Md. 245/H2
Fort Ritner, Ind. (47430) 227/E7
Fort Robinson, Nebr. (†69339) 264/A2
Fort Rock, Oreg. (97735) 291/G4
Fort Rodman, Mass. 249/L6
Fortrose, Scotland 10/D2
Fortrose, Scotland 15/D3
Fort Rosebery (Mansa), Zambia 115/E6
Fort Ross, Calif. (†95421) 204/B5
Fort Rucker, Ala. 195/G8
Fort-Rupert, Que. 146/L4
Fort Rupert (Rupert House), Québec 174/B2
Fort Saint James, Br. Col. 162/D5
Fort Saint James, Br. Col. 184/E3
Fort Saint John, Br. Col. 162/D4
Fort Saint John, Br. Col. 184/G2
Fort Sam Houston, Texas 303/K11
Fort San, Sask. 181/H5
Fort Sandeman, Pakistan 68/B2
Fort Sandeman, Pakistan 59/J3
Fort Saskatchewan, Alberta 182/D3
Fort Saskatchewan, Alta. 162/E5
Fort Scott, Kans. 188/H3
Fort Scott, Kansas (66701) 232/H4
Fort Seneca, Ohio (44829) 284/D3
Fort Severn, Ontario 175/C1
Fort Seward, Calif. (†95440) 204/B3
Fort Seybert, W. Va. (26806) 312/H5
Fort Shafter, Hawaii 218/C3
Fort Shaw, Mont. (59443) 262/E3
Fort Shawnee, Ohio (†45801) 284/B4
Fort Sheridan, Ill. 222/B5
Fort-Shevchenko, U.S.S.R. 48/F5
Fort Sill, Okla. 288/K5
Fort Simpson, Canada 4/C15
Fort Simpson, N.W.T. 146/F3
Fort Simpson, N.W.T. 162/D3
Fort Simpson, N.W. Terrs. 187/F3
Fort Smith, Ark. 188/H3
Fort Smith, Ark. 146/J6
Fort Smith, Ark. (*72901) 202/B3
Fort Smith, Mont. (†59075) 262/J5
Fort Smith, N.W.T. 146/G3
Fort Smith, N.W.T. 162/E3
Fort Smith (dist.), N.W. Terrs. 187/G3
Fort Smith, N.W. Terrs. 187/G4
Fort Smith Nat'l Hist. Site, Ark. 202/B3
Fort Spring, W. Va. (24936) 312/E7
Fort Stanton, N. Mex. (88323) 274/D5
Fort Stanwix Nat'l Mon., N.Y. 276/J4
Fort Steele, Br. Col. 184/K5
Fort Stewart, Georgia 217/J7
Fort Stewart, Ontario 177/G2
Fort Stockton, Texas (79735) 303/A7
Fort Story, Va. 307/S7
Fort Sumner, N. Mex. (88119) 274/E4
Fort Sumter Nat'l Mon., S.C. 296/H6
Fort Supply, Okla. (73841) 288/G1
Fort Supply (lake), Okla. 288/G1
Fort Tarat, Algeria 106/F3
Fort Thomas, Ariz. (85536) 198/E5
Fort Thomas, Ky. (41075) 237/S2
Fort Thompson, S. Dak. (57339) 298/L5
Fort Ticonderoga, N.Y. (†12883) 276/O3
Fort Totten, N. Dak. (58335) 282/M4
Fort Totten Ind. Res., N. Dak. 282/N4
Fort Towson, Okla. (74735) 288/R7
Fortuna, Calif. (95540) 204/A3
Fortuna, Mo. (65034) 261/G5
Fortuna, N. Dak. (58844) 282/C2
Fortuna, Spain 33/F3
Fortuna Ledge, Alaska (99585) 196/F2
Fortune, Newf. 166/C4
Fortune (bay), Newf. 166/C4
Fort Union Nat'l Mon., N. Mex. 274/E3
Fort Union Trading Post Nat'l Hist. Site, Mont. 262/N2
Fort Union Trading Post Nat'l Hist. Site, N. Dak. 282/B3
Fort Valley, Georgia (31030) 217/E5
Fort Vancouver Nat'l Hist. Site, Wash. 310/C5
Fort Vermilion, Alberta 182/B5
Fort Vermilion, Alta. 162/E4
Fort Vermilion, Alta. 146/G4
Fort Victoria, Zimbabwe 102/F7
Fort Victoria, Zimbabwe 118/E4
Fortville, Ind. (46040) 227/F5
Fort Wainwright, Alaska 196/J1
Fort Walsh Nat'l Hist. Park, Sask. 181/A6
Fort Walton Beach, Fla. (32548) 212/C6
Fort Washakie, Wyo. (82514) 319/C2
Fort Washington, Md. (†20744) 245/L6
Fort Washington Park, Md. 245/L6
Fort Wayne, Ind. 188/J2
Fort Wayne, Ind. (*46801) 227/G2
Fort Wellington, Guyana 131/C2
Fort White, Fla. (32038) 212/D2
Fort William, Scotland 10/D2
Fort William, Scotland 15/C4
Fort Wingate, N. Mex. (87316) 274/A3
Fort Worden, Wash. 310/C2
Fort Worth, Texas 146/J6
Fort Worth, Texas (*76101) 303/F2
Fort Worth, Texas 188/G4
Fort Wright, Ky. (†41011) 237/S2
Fort Yates, N. Dak. (58538) 282/J7
Forty Fort, Pa. (18704) 294/F7
Forty Mile (pt.), Mich. 250/F3
Fort Yukon, Alaska 146/D3
Fort Yukon, Alaska (99740) 196/J1
Fort Yukon, Alaska 188/D5
Fort Yukon, U.S. 4/C17
Forum, Ark. (†72740) 202/C1
Fosforescente (bay), P. Rico 161/A3
Foshan (Fatshan), China 77/H7
Fosheim (pen.), N.W. Terrs. 187/K1
Foss, Okla. (73647) 288/H4
Foss (res.), Okla. 288/H3
Fossano, Italy 34/A2
Fosses-La-Ville, Belgium 27/F8
Fossil (creek), Ariz. 198/D4
Fossil, Oreg. (97830) 291/G2
Fossil Butte Nat'l Mon., Wyo. 319/B4
Fossombrone, Italy 34/D3
Fosston, Minn. (56542) 255/C3
Fosston, Sask. 181/H3
Foster, Ind. (†47932) 227/C4
Foster, Ky. (41043) 237/N3
Foster, Mo. (64745) 261/D6
Foster, Nebr. (68737) 264/G2
Foster (co.), N. Dak. 282/N5
Foster, Okla. (73039) 288/M5
Foster, Oreg. (97345) 291/E3
Foster○, R.I. (02825) 249/H5

Front 371

Foster (riv.), Sask. 181/M3
Foster (creek), S. Dak. 298/N4
Foster, W. Va. (25081) 312/C6
Foster, Wis. (†54758) 317/D6
Foster Center (Foster P.O.), R.I. (†02825) 249/H5
Foster City, Calif. (94404) 204/J2
Foster City, Mich. (49834) 250/B3
Fosters, Ala. (35463) 195/C4
Fosters, Mich. (†48415) 250/F5
Fosters Falls, Va. (24329) 307/G7
Fosterton, Sask. 181/C5
Foster Village, Hawaii (†96701) 218/B3
Fosterville, New Bruns. 170/C3
Fosterville, Tenn. (37063) 237/J9
Fostoria, Ala. (†36737) 195/E6
Fostoria, Iowa (51340) 229/C2
Fostoria, Kansas (66426) 232/F2
Fostoria, Mich. (48435) 250/F5
Fostoria, Ohio (44830) 284/D3
Fougamou, Gabon 115/A4
Fougères, France 28/C3
Fouke, Ark. (71837) 202/C7
Foul (bay), Egypt 111/G3
Foul (sound), Ireland 17/B5
Foula (isl.), Scotland 15/F2
Foula (isl.), Scotland 10/G1
Foules, La. (†71326) 238/G3
Foulness Island (pen.), England 13/J6
Foulpointe, Madagascar 118/H3
Foulweather (cape), Oreg. 291/C3
Foulwind (cape), N. Zealand 100/C4
Foumban, Cameroon 115/B2
Foumban, Cameroon 102/D4
Fountain, Ala. (36460) 195/D7
Fountain, Colo. (80817) 208/K5
Fountain (creek), Colo. 208/K5
Fountain, Fla. (32438) 212/D6
Fountain (co.), Ind. 227/C4
Fountain, Ind. (†47918) 227/C4
Fountain, Mich. (49410) 250/C4
Fountain, Minn. (55935) 255/F7
Fountain, N.C. (27829) 281/O3
Fountain City, Ind. (47341) 227/H5
Fountain City, Wis. (54629) 317/C7
Fountain Green, Ill. (†62321) 222/C3
Fountain Green, Utah (84632) 304/C4
Fountain Head, Md. (†21740) 245/G2
Fountain Head, Tenn. (†37148) 237/J7
Fountain Hill, Ark. (71642) 202/G7
Fountain Hill, Pa. (†18015) 294/L4
Fountain Inn, S.C. (29644) 296/C2
Fountain Run, Ky. (42133) 237/K7
Fountaintown, Ind. (46130) 227/F5
Fountain Valley, Calif. (92708) 204/D11
Four (peaks), Newf. 166/B2
Four Buttes, Mont. (59224) 262/L2
Fourche, Ariz. (†72016) 202/D4
Fourche LaFave (riv.), Ark. 202/D4
Four Corners, Oreg. (97301) 291/A3
Four Corners, Wyo. (82715) 319/H1
Four Falls, New Bruns. 170/C2
Four Hole Swamp (creek), S.C. 296/F5
Four Lakes, Wash. (99014) 310/H3
Fourmies, France 28/F2
Four Mile (riv.), Conn. 210/F3
Fourmile (lake), Oreg. 291/E5
Four Mountains (isls.), Alaska 196/E4
Fournier (cape), N. Zealand 100/E7
Fournier, Ontario 177/K2
Four Oaks, N.C. (27524) 281/M4
Four Paths, Jamaica 158/J6
Four Peaks (mt.), Ariz. 198/D5
Four States, W. Va. (26572) 312/F4
Fourteen Mile (pt.), Mich. 250/F1
Fourth (lake), Maine 243/H5
Fourth Cataract, Sudan 111/F4
Fourth Cataract, Sudan 59/B6
Fourth Cataract (dam), Sudan 102/F3
Foveaux (str.), N. Zealand 87/G10
Foveaux (str.), N. Zealand 100/A7
Fowler, Calif. (93625) 204/F7
Fowler, Colo. (81039) 208/L6
Fowler, Ill. (62338) 222/B3
Fowler, Ind. (47944) 227/C3
Fowler, Kansas (67844) 232/B4
Fowler, Mich. (48835) 250/E5
Fowlerton, Ind. (46930) 227/F4
Fowlerton, Texas (78021) 303/F9
Fowlerville, Mich. (48836) 250/F6
Fowlkes, Tenn. (38033) 237/C9
Fowlstown, Georgia (31752) 217/D9
Fowman, Iran 66/F2
Fowyang (Fuyang), China 77/J5
Fox (isls.), Alaska 196/E4
Fox, Ark. (72051) 202/F2
Fox (lake), Ill. 222/A4
Fox (riv.), Ill. 222/E5
Fox (riv.), Ill. 222/E2
Fox (riv.), Manitoba 179/K2
Fox, Mich. (†49813) 250/B3
Fox (isl.), New Bruns. 170/F1
Fox, Okla. (73435) 288/M6
Fox, Oreg. (97831) 291/H3
Fox (riv.), Wis. 317/K7
Fox (riv.), Wis. 317/K2
Foxboro, Mass. (02035) 249/J4
Foxboro○, Mass. (02035) 249/J4
Foxboro, Ontario 177/G3
Foxboro, Wis. (54836) 317/B2
Foxburg, Pa. (16036) 294/C3
Fox Chapel, Pa. (†15238) 294/C6
Fox Creek, Alberta 182/B2
Foxe (basin), Canada 4/C13
Foxe (basin), N.W.T. 146/L3
Foxe (basin), N.W.T. 162/J2
Foxe (basin), N.W. Terrs. 187/L3
Foxe (chan.), N.W.T. 162/H2
Foxe (chan.), N.W.T. 146/K3
Foxe (chan.), N.W. Terrs. 187/K3
Foxe (pen.), N.W.T. 146/L3
Foxe (pen.), N.W.T. 162/J3
Foxe (pen.), N.W. Terrs. 187/L3
Fox Farm, Wyo. (†82001) 319/H4
Foxfire, N.C. (†28373) 281/K4
Foxford, Ireland 17/C4
Foxford, Sask. 181/F2
Fox Glacier, N. Zealand 100/B5
Fox Harbour, Newf. 166/D2
Fox Harbour, Newf. 166/C3
Foxholm, N. Dak. (58738) 282/G3
Foxhome, Minn. (56543) 255/B4
Fox Lake, Alberta 182/B5
Fox Lake, Ill. (60020) 222/A4
Fox Lake, Wis. (53933) 317/J8
Foxon, Conn. (†06512) 210/D3
Foxpark, Wyo. (82057) 319/F4
Fox Point, Wis. (†53117) 317/M1
Fox River, Nova Scotia 168/D3
Fox River Grove, Ill. (60021) 222/A5
Foxton, Colo. (80441) 208/J4
Foxton, N. Zealand 100/E4
Fox Valley, Sask. 181/B5
Foxville, Md. (†21760) 245/H2
Foxwarren, Manitoba 179/A4
Foxwells, Va. (22578) 307/R5
Foxworth, Miss. (39483) 256/E8
Foyers, Scotland 15/D3
Foyil, Okla. (74031) 288/R2
Foyle (inlet), Ireland 17/G1
Foyle, Lough (inlet), Ireland 10/C3
Foyle (riv.), Ireland 17/G2
Foyle, Lough (inlet), N. Ireland 10/C3
Foyle (inlet), N. Ireland 17/G1
Foyle (riv.), N. Ireland 17/G2
Foynes, Ireland 10/B4
Foynes, Ireland 17/C6
Foz do Breu, Brazil 132/F10
Foz do Cunene, Angola 115/B7
Foz do Iguaçu, Brazil 132/C9
Frackville, Pa. (17931) 294/K4
Fraga, Spain 33/G2
Fragoso (cay), Cuba 158/F1
Fraile Muerto, Uruguay 145/E3
Frailes, Los (isl.), Dom. Rep. 158/C7
Fram, Paraguay 144/E5
Framboise, Nova Scotia 168/H3
Framboise Cove (bay), Nova Scotia 168/H3
Frame, W. Va. (25071) 312/C5
Frameries, Belgium 27/D8
Frametown, W. Va. (26623) 312/E5
Framingham○, Mass. (01701) 249/A7
Framingham Center, Mass. (01701) 249/J3
Framlingham, England 13/J5
Frampton, Québec 172/G3
Franca, Brazil 135/C2
Franca, Brazil 132/E8
Francavilla Fontana, Italy 34/F4
France 2/J3
France 7/E4
FRANCE 28
Francés (cape), Cuba 158/B2
Francés (cape), Cuba 158/A2
Frances (lake), Mont. 262/D2
Frances, Wash. (†98577) 310/B4
Frances (lake), Yukon 187/E3
Francestown○, N.H. (03043) 268/D6
Francés Viejo (cape), Dom. Rep. 158/E5
Francesville, Ind. (47946) 227/D3
Franceville, Gabon 115/B4
Franche Comté (trad. prov.), France 29
Francia, Uruguay 145/C3
Francis (lake), N.H. 268/E1
Francis, Okla. (74844) 288/N5
Francis, Sask. 181/H5
Francis, Utah (†84036) 304/C3
Francis Case (lake), S. Dak. 188/F2
Francis Case (lake), S. Dak. 146/J5
Francis Case (lake), S. Dak. 298/L7
Francisco, Ala. (†37345) 195/F1
Francisco, Ind. (47649) 227/B8
Francisco, N.C. (†27053) 281/J2
Francisco de Orellana, Peru 128/F4
Francisco I. Madero, Mexico 150/H4
Francis Creek, Wis. (54214) 317/L7
Francis E. Warren A.F.B., Wyo. 319/G4
Francistown, Botswana 118/D4
Francoeur, Québec 172/F3
Francois (lake), Br. Col. 162/D5
François (lake), Br. Col. 184/D3
François, Newf. 166/C4
François Lake, Br. Col. 184/D3
Franconia○, N.H. (03580) 268/D3
Franconia, Va. (22310) 307/S3
Franconian Jura (range), W. Germany 22/D4
Franconia Notch (pass), N.H. 268/D3
Franeker, Netherlands 27/H2
Frank, Alberta 182/C5
Frankel City, Texas (79737) 303/B5
Frankenberg-Eder, W. Germany 22/C3
Frankenmarkt, Austria 41/B3
Frankenmuth, Mich. (48734) 250/F5
Frankenthal, W. Germany 22/C4
Frankenwald (for.), W. Germany 22/D3
Frankewing, Tenn. (38459) 237/H10
Frankfield, Jamaica 158/H6
Frankford, Del. (19945) 245/S6
Frankford (Kilcormac), Ireland 17/F5
Frankford, Mo. (63441) 261/K4
Frankford, Ontario 177/G3
Frankford, W. Va. (24938) 312/F7
Frankfort, Ala. (†35653) 195/C1
Frankfort, Ill. (60423) 222/B6
Frankfort, Ind. (46041) 227/E4
Frankfort, Kansas (66427) 232/F2
Frankfort (cap.), Ky. (40601) 237/M4
Frankfort (cap.), Ky. 188/K3
Frankfort (cap.), Ky. 146/K6
Frankfort○, Maine (04438) 243/F6
Frankfort, Mich. (49635) 250/C4
Frankfort, N.Y. (13340) 276/K4
Frankfort, Ohio (45628) 284/D7
Frankfort, S. Dak. (57440) 298/N4
Frankfort Springs, Pa. (†15050) 294/A4
Frankfurt (dist.), E. Germany 22/F2
Frankfurt, W. Germany 7/E3
Frankfurt am Main, W. Germany 22/C3
Frankfurt an der Oder, E. Germany 22/F2
Frankland (cape), Tasmania 99/D1
Frankland (range), Tasmania 99/B4
Franklin (co.), Ala. 195/C2
Franklin, Ala. (36444) 195/G6
Franklin (pt.), Alaska 196/G1
Franklin, Ariz. (85534) 198/F6
Franklin (co.), Ark. 202/C2
Franklin, Ark. (72536) 202/G1
Franklin○, Conn. (†06254) 210/G2
Franklin (co.), Fla. 212/B2
Franklin (co.), Georgia 217/F2
Franklin, Georgia (30217) 217/B4
Franklin (co.), Idaho 220/G7
Franklin, Idaho (83237) 220/G7
Franklin (co.), Ill. 222/E5
Franklin, Ill. (62638) 222/C4
Franklin (co.), Ind. 227/G6
Franklin, Ind. (46131) 227/E6
Franklin (co.), Iowa 229/G3
Franklin, Iowa (†52625) 229/L7
Franklin (co.), Kansas 232/G3
Franklin, Kansas (66735) 232/H4
Franklin (co.), Ky. 237/M4
Franklin, Ky. (42134) 237/J7
Franklin (par.), La. 238/G2
Franklin, La. (70538) 238/G7
Franklin (co.), Maine 243/B5
Franklin, Maine (04634) 243/G6
Franklin○, Maine (04634) 243/G6
Franklin, Manitoba 179/C4
Franklin (co.), Mass. 249/D2
Franklin, Mass. (02038) 249/J4
Franklin○, Mass. (02038) 249/J4
Franklin, Mich. (48025) 250/B6
Franklin, Minn. (†55792) 255/F3
Franklin, Minn. (55333) 255/D6
Franklin (co.), Miss. 256/C8
Franklin (co.), Mo. 261/K6
Franklin, Mo. (65250) 261/G4
Franklin, Mont. (†59074) 262/G4
Franklin (co.), Nebr. 264/F4
Franklin, Nebr. (68939) 264/E4
Franklin (lake), Nev. 266/F2
Franklin, N.H. (03235) 268/D5
Franklin, N.J. (07416) 273/D1
Franklin (co.), N.Y. 276/M1
Franklin, N.Y. (13775) 276/K6
Franklin (co.), N.C. 281/N2
Franklin, N.C. (28734) 281/C4
Franklin (dist.), N.W.T. 162/H1
Franklin (bay), N.W.Terrs. 187/F2
Franklin (lake), N.W. Terrs. 187/J3
Franklin (mts.), N.W. Terrs. 187/F3
Franklin (str.), N.W. T. 162/G1
Franklin (str.), N.W. Terrs. 187/J2
Franklin (co.), Ohio 284/E5
Franklin, Ohio (45005) 284/B6
Franklin (co.), Pa. 294/G6
Franklin, Pa. (16323) 294/C3
Franklin, S. Dak. (†57042) 298/P6
Franklin, Tasmania 99/C5
Franklin (riv.), Tasmania 99/B4
Franklin (co.), Tenn. 237/J10
Franklin, Tenn. (37064) 237/H9
Franklin (co.), Texas 303/J4
Franklin, Texas (77856) 303/H7
Franklin (co.), Vt. 268/B2
Franklin○, Vt. (05457) 268/B2
Franklin (co.), Va. 307/J6
Franklin (I.C.), Va. (23851) 307/P7
Franklin (co.), Wash. 310/G4
Franklin, W. Va. (26807) 312/H5
Franklin, Wis. (53132) 317/L2
Franklin D. Roosevelt (lake), Wash. 310/G2
Franklin Falls (res.), N.H. 268/D4
Franklin Furnace, Ohio (45629) 284/E8
Franklin Grove, Ill. (61031) 222/D2
Franklin Lakes, N.J. (07417) 273/B1
Franklin Park, Ill. (60131) 222/B5
Franklin Park○, N.J. (†08823) 273/D3
Franklin River, Br. Col. 184/H3
Franklin Springs, Georgia (30639) 217/F2
Franklin Square, N.Y. (11010) 276/R7
Franklinton, La. (70438) 238/K5
Franklinton, N.C. (27525) 281/N2
Franklintown, Pa. (17323) 294/H5
Franklinville, N.J. (08322) 273/C4
Franklinville, N.Y. (14737) 276/D6
Franklinville, N.C. (27248) 281/K3
Franks (pond), Newf. 166/D2
Frankslake, Sask. 181/G5
Frankston, Texas (75763) 303/J5
Franksville, Wis. (53126) 317/M3
Frankton, Ind. (46044) 227/F4
Franktown, Colo. (80116) 208/K4
Franktown, Ontario 177/H2
Franktown, Va. (23354) 307/S6
Frankville, Ala. (36538) 195/B7
Frankville, Iowa (†52162) 229/K2
Frankville, Nova Scotia 168/G3
Frankville, Ontario 177/J2
Frannie, Wyo. (82423) 319/D1
Franquelin, Québec 172/B1
Franquia, Uruguay 145/B1
Franschhoek, S. Africa 118/F6
Fransfontein, Namibia 118/A4
Františkovy Lázně, Czech. 41/B1
Franz, Ontario 177/J5
Franz, Ontario 175/D3
Franz Josef Land (isls.), U.S.S.R. 2/L1
Franz Josef Land (isls.), U.S.S.R. 4/A7
Franz Josef Land (isls.), U.S.S.R. 48/F1
Frascati, Italy 34/F7
Fraser (isl.), Australia 87/F8
Fraser (riv.), Br. Col. 146/F4
Fraser (riv.), Br. Col. 162/D5
Fraser (lake), Br. Col. 184/E3
Fraser (riv.), Br. Col. 184/F4
Fraser, Colo. (80442) 208/H3
Fraser, Iowa (†50036) 229/E4
Fraser, Mich. (48026) 250/B6
Fraser, Minn. (†55719) 255/F3
Fraser (riv.), Newf. 166/B2
Fraser (isl.), Queensland 88/J4
Fraser (isl.), Queensland 95/E5
Fraserburgh, Scotland 15/G3
Fraserburgh, Scotland 10/E2
Fraserdale, Ontario 175/D3
Fraserdale, Ontario 177/J5
Fraser Lake, Br. Col. 184/E3
Fraser Mills, Br. Col. 184/K3
Fraser Reach (chan.), Br. Col. 184/C3
Frasertown, N. Zealand 100/F3
Fraserwood, Manitoba 179/E4
Frasnes-lez Anvaing, Belgium 27/D7
Frauenfeld, Switzerland 39/G1
Frauenkirchen, Austria 41/D3
Fray Benito, Cuba 158/J3
Fray Bentos, Uruguay 145/A4
Fray Marcos, Uruguay 145/D5
Frazee, Minn. (56544) 255/C4
Frazer, Mont. (59225) 262/K2
Frazeysburg, Ohio (43822) 284/F5
Frazier Park, Calif. (93225) 204/F9
Fraziers Bottom, W. Va. (25082) 312/B5
Frechen, W. Germany 22/B3
Fred, Texas (77616) 303/K7
Freda, N. Dak. (†58569) 282/H7
Fredensborg, Denmark 21/F6
Fredensdal, Virgin Is. (U.S.) 161/F4
Frederic, Mich. (49733) 250/E4
Frederic, Wis. (54837) 317/B4
Frederica, Del. (19946) 245/S4
Fredericia, Denmark 21/C6
Fredericia, Denmark 18/F9
Frederick (sound), Alaska 196/N1
Frederick, Colo. (80530) 208/K2
Frederick, Ill. (62639) 222/C3
Frederick, Kansas (†67444) 232/D3
Frederick (co.), Md. 245/J3
Frederick, Md. (21701) 245/J3
Frederick, Okla. (73542) 288/H6
Frederick, S. Dak. (57441) 298/N2
Frederick (co.), Va. 307/M2
Fredericksburg, Ind. (47120) 227/E8
Fredericksburg, Iowa (50630) 229/J3
Fredericksburg, Ohio (44627) 284/G4
Fredericksburg, Pa. (17026) 294/J5
Fredericksburg, Pa. (†16335) 294/B2
Fredericksburg, Texas (78624) 303/E7
Fredericksburg (I.C.), Va. (*22401) 307/N4
Fredericks Hall, Va. (†23117) 307/N4
Frederickton, N.S. Wales 97/G2
Fredericktown, Mo. (63645) 261/M7
Fredericktown, Ohio (43019) 284/F5
Fredericktown, Pa. (15333) 294/C6
Fredericton, N. Br. 146/M5
Fredericton, N. Br. 162/K6
Fredericton (cap.), New Bruns. 170/D3
Fredericton Junction, New Bruns. 170/D3
Frederika, Iowa (50631) 229/J3
Frederik Hendrik (Kolepom) (isl.), Indonesia 85/K7
Frederiksberg (commune), Denmark 21/F6
Frederiksberg, Denmark 21/F6
Frederiksborg (co.), Denmark 21/E5
Frederikshåb, Greenl. 4/C12
Frederikshåb, Greenland 146/N3
Frederikshavn, Denmark 18/G8
Frederikshavn, Denmark 21/D3
Frederikssund, Denmark 21/E6
Frederiksted, Virgin Is. (U.S.) 161/E4
Frederiksted, Virgin Is. (U.S.) 156/G2
Frederiksvaerk, Denmark 21/E6
Frederiksvaerk, Denmark 18/G8
Frederik Willem IV (falls), Suriname 131/C4
Fredonia, Ala. (†31833) 195/H5
Fredonia, Ariz. (86022) 198/C2
Fredonia (Biscoe), Ark. (72017) 202/H4
Fredonia, Ind. (†47137) 227/E8
Fredonia, Iowa (†52738) 229/L6
Fredonia, Kansas (66736) 232/G4
Fredonia, Ky. (42411) 237/E6
Fredonia, N.Y. (14063) 276/B6
Fredonia, N. Dak. (58440) 282/M7
Fredonia, Pa. (16124) 294/B3
Fredonia, Texas (76842) 303/E7
Fredonia, Wis. (53021) 317/L8
Fredric, Iowa (†52531) 229/H6
Fredrika, Sweden 18/L4
Fredrikstad, Norway 18/D4
Freeborn (co.), Minn. 255/E7
Freeborn, Minn. (56032) 255/E7
Freeburg, Ill. (62243) 222/D5
Freeburg, Minn. (†55921) 255/G7
Freeburg, Mo. (65035) 261/J6
Freeburg, Pa. (17827) 294/H4
Freeburn, Ky. (41528) 237/S5
Freedhem, Minn. (†56345) 255/D4
Freedom, Calif. (95019) 204/L4
Freedom, Ind. (47431) 227/D6
Freedom, Ky. (†42157) 237/K7
Freedom○, Maine (04941) 243/E7
Freedom○, N.H. (03836) 268/E4
Freedom, Okla. (73842) 288/H1
Freedom, Pa. (15042) 294/B4
Freedom, Wyo. (83120) 319/B3
Freehold, N.J. (07728) 273/E3
Freehold, N.Y. (12431) 276/N6
Freel (peak), Calif. 204/F5
Freeland, Md. (21053) 245/M2
Freeland, Mich. (48623) 250/E5
Freeland, N.C. (28440) 281/N6
Freeland, Pa. (18224) 294/L3
Freeland, Wash. (98249) 310/C2
Freeland Park, Ind. (†47944) 227/C3
Freelandville, Ind. (47535) 227/C7
Freels (cape), Newf. 166/D3
Freelton, Ontario 177/D4
Freeman (riv.), Alberta 182/C2
Freeman, Ind. (†47460) 227/D6
Freeman (lake), Ind. 227/D3
Freeman, Mo. (64746) 261/C5
Freeman, S. Dak. (57029) 298/O7
Freeman, Wash. (99015) 310/H3
Freemansburg, Pa. (†18017) 294/M4
Freemanville, Ala. (†36502) 195/D8
Free Mason (isls.), La. 238/M7
Freemont, Calif. 188/B3
Freemont, Sask. 181/B3
Freeport, Bahamas 156/H1
Freeport, Fla. (32439) 212/C6
Freeport, Ill. 188/J2
Freeport, Ill. (61032) 222/D1
Freeport, Ind. (†46161) 227/F5
Freeport, Kansas (67049) 232/E4
Freeport, Maine (04032) 243/C8
Freeport○, Maine (04032) 243/C8
Freeport, Mich. (49325) 250/D6
Freeport, Minn. (56331) 255/D5
Freeport, N.Y. (11520) 276/R7
Freeport, Nova Scotia 168/B4
Freeport, Ohio (43973) 284/H5
Freeport, Pa. (16229) 294/C4
Freeport, Texas (77541) 303/J9
Freer, Texas (78357) 303/F10
Free Soil, Mich. (49411) 250/C4
Freestone (co.), Texas 303/H6
Freetown, Ant. & Bar. 161/E11
Freetown, Ind. (47235) 227/E7
Freetown, N.Y. (†11937) 276/R9
Freetown (cap.), S. Leone 102/A4
Freetown (cap.), S. Leone 106/B7
Free Union, Va. (22940) 307/L4
Freeville, N.Y. (13068) 276/H5
Freezeout (lake), Mont. 262/D3
Fregenal de la Sierra, Spain 33/C3
Fregene, Italy 34/F6
Freiberg, E. Germany 22/E3
Freiburg, W. Germany 7/E4
Freiburg im Breisgau, W. Germany 22/B5
Freidberg, Austria 41/D3
Freienbach, Switzerland 39/G2
Freire, Chile 138/E2
Freirina, Chile 138/A7
Freising, W. Germany 22/D4
Freistadt, Austria 41/C2
Freistatt, Mo. (65654) 261/E8
Freital, E. Germany 22/E3
Freixo de Espada à Cinta, Portugal 33/C2
Fréjus, France 28/G6
Fréjus (pass), France 28/G5
Fréjus (pass), Italy 34/A2
Frelighsburg, Québec 172/E4
Fremantle, Australia 2/Q7
Fremantle, Australia 87/B9
Fremantle, W. Australia 88/B6
Fremantle, W. Australia 92/A1
Fremington, England 13/C6
Fremont, Calif. (*94536) 204/K3
Fremont (peak), Calif. 204/H8
Fremont (co.), Colo. 208/J5
Fremont (co.), Idaho 220/G5
Fremont, Ind. (46737) 227/H1
Fremont (co.), Iowa 229/B7
Fremont, Iowa (52561) 229/H6
Fremont, Mich. (49412) 250/D5
Fremont, Mo. (63941) 261/K9
Fremont, Nebr. 188/G2
Fremont, Nebr. (68025) 264/H3
Fremont○, N.H. (03044) 268/E6
Fremont, N.C. (27830) 281/N3
Fremont, Ohio (43420) 284/D3
Fremont, Utah (84727) 304/C5
Fremont (isl.), Utah 304/B2
Fremont (riv.), Utah 304/C5
Fremont, Wis. (54940) 317/J7
Fremont (co.), Wyo. 319/D2
Fremont (lake), Wyo. 319/C3
Fremont (peak), Wyo. 319/C2
French, Argentina 143/F7
French (riv.), Conn. 210/H1
French (riv.), Ontario 177/D1
French (creek), Pa. 294/C2
French (creek), S. Dak. 298/C6
French (isl.), Victoria 97/C6
Frenchboro○, Maine (04635) 243/G7
French Broad (riv.), N.C. 281/D3
French Broad (riv.), Tenn. 237/R9
Frenchburg, Ky. (40322) 237/O5
French Camp, Miss. (39745) 256/F4
French Creek, W. Va. (26218) 312/F5
French Frigate (shoal), Hawaii 188/F6
French Frigate (shoals), Hawaii 87/K3
French Frigate (shoals), Hawaii 218/C6
Frenchglen, Oreg. (97736) 291/H5
French Guiana 2/G5
French Guiana 120/D2
FRENCH GUIANA 131/E3
French Lick, Ind. (47432) 227/D7
Frenchman (creek), Colo. 208/P1
Frenchman (bay), Maine 243/G7
Frenchman (riv.), Mont. 188/E1
Frenchman (riv.), Mont. 262/J1
Frenchman (creek), Nebr. 264/C4
Frenchman (riv.), Sask. 181/C6
Frenchman (cay), Virgin Is. (Br.) 161/C4
Frenchman Butte, Sask. 181/B2
Frenchman Flat (basin), Nev. 266/F6
Frenchmans Cap (mt.), Tasmania 99/B4
Frenchmans Island, Newf. 166/C3
Frenchpark, Ireland 17/E4
French Polynesia 87/L8
French River, Minn. (†55801) 255/G4
French River, Ontario 177/D1
French Settlement, La. (70733) 238/L2
Frenchton, W. Va. (26219) 312/F5
Frenchtown, Mont. (59834) 262/B3
Frenchtown, N.J. (08825) 273/C2
Frenchville, Maine (04745) 243/G1
Frenchville○, Maine (04745) 243/G1
Frenchville, Pa. (16836) 294/F3
Frenštát pod Radhoštěm, Czech. 41/E2
Fresco, Ivory Coast 106/C7
Fresh (pond), Mass. 249/C6
Freshford, Ireland 17/G6
Freshwater, Calif. (†95501) 204/B3
Freshwater (Guffey), Colo. (80820) 208/H5
Freshwater, England 13/F7
Freshwater, Newf. 166/D2
Fresia, Chile 138/D3
Fresillo, Mexico 146/H7
Fresnillo de González Echeverría, Mexico 150/H5
Fresno (co.), Calif. 204/E7
Fresno, Calif. 146/G6
Fresno, Calif. 188/C3
Fresno, Calif. (*93706) 204/F7
Fresno (riv.), Calif. 204/E7
Fresno, Colombia 126/C5
Fresno, Mont. (†59532) 262/G2
Fresno (res.), Mont. 262/F2
Fresno, Texas (77545) 303/J2
Freudenstadt, W. Germany 22/C4
Frew, Ky. (41744) 237/P6
Frewena, North. Terr. 93/D5
Frewsburg, N.Y. (14738) 276/B6
Freycinet (pen.), Tasmania 99/E4
Fria, Guinea 106/B6
Fria (cape), Namibia 102/D6
Fria (cape), Namibia 118/A3
Friant, Calif. (93626) 204/F7
Friant-Kern (canal), Calif. 204/F8
Friars Point, Miss. (38631) 256/C2
Frias, Argentina 143/D2
Fribourg (canton), Switzerland 39/D3
Fribourg, Switzerland 39/D3
Frick, Switzerland 39/E1
Friday Harbor, Wash. (98250) 310/B2
Fridley, Minn. (55432) 255/G5
Fried, N. Dak. (†58401) 282/N5
Friedberg, W. Germany 22/C3
Friedland, E. Germany 22/E2
Friedrichshafen, W. Germany 22/C5
Friedrichstadt, W. Germany 22/C1
Friend, Kansas (67845) 232/B3
Friend, Nebr. (68359) 264/G4
Friend, Oreg. (97021) 291/F2
Friendly, W. Va. (26146) 312/D3
Friendship, Ark. (71942) 202/E5
Friendship, Ind. (47021) 227/G7
Friendship, Maine (04547) 243/E7
Friendship○, Maine (04547) 243/E7
Friendship, Md. (20758) 245/M6
Friendship, N.Y. (14739) 276/D6
Friendship, Ohio (45630) 284/D8
Friendship, Tenn. (38034) 237/C9
Friendship, Wis. (53934) 317/G8
Friendship Hill Nat'l Hist. Site, Pa. 294/C6
Friendsville, Ill. (†62863) 222/F5
Friendsville, Md. (21531) 245/A2
Friendsville, Pa. (18818) 294/L2
Friendsville, Tenn. (37737) 237/N9
Friendswood, Texas (77546) 303/J2
Frienisberg (mt.), Switzerland 39/D2
Frierson, La. (71027) 238/C2
Fries, Va. (24330) 307/F7
Friesach, Austria 41/C3
Friesche Gat (chan.), Netherlands 27/J2
Friesland, Minn. (†55037) 255/E4
Friesland (prov.), Netherlands 27/H2
Friesland, Wis. (53935) 317/H8
Frigate (isl.), Seychelles 118/J5
Frigate Bay, St. Chris.-Nevis 161/C10
Frimley and Camberley, England 13/G8
Frink, Fla. (†32430) 212/D6
Frinton and Walton, England 10/G5
Frinton and Walton, England 13/J6
Frio (cape), Brazil 120/E5
Frio (cape), Brazil 135/F3
Frio (co.), Texas 303/E9
Frio (riv.), Texas 303/E8
Friockheim, Scotland 15/F4
Friol, Spain 33/C1
Friona, Texas (79035) 303/B3
Fripp (isl.), S.C. 296/G7
Frisches Haff (lag.), Poland 47/D1
Frisco, Colo. (80443) 208/G3
Frisco, N.C. (27936) 281/T4
Frisco, Pa. (†16117) 294/B4
Frisco, Texas (75034) 303/H4
Frisco City, Ala. (36445) 195/D8
Frisian (isls.) 7/E3
Frisian, North (isls.), Denmark 21/B7
Frisian, West (isls.), Netherlands 27/G2
Frisian, East (isls.), W. Germany 22/B2
Frisian, North (isls.), W. Germany 22/B1
Frissell (mt.), Conn. 210/B1
Fristoe, Mo. (†65355) 261/F6
Fritch, Texas (79036) 303/C2
Fritchton, Ind. (†47591) 227/C7
Fritz Creek, Alaska (†99603) 196/B2
Fritzlar, W. Germany 22/C3
Friuli-Venezia Giulia (reg.), Italy 34/D1
Frizzellburg, Md. (†21157) 245/K2
Frobisher (bay), N.W.T. 162/K3
Frobisher (bay), N.W. Terrs. 187/M3
Frobisher, Sask. 181/J6
Frobisher (lake), Sask. 181/L3
Frobisher Bay, N.W.T. 162/K3
Frobisher Bay, N.W. Terrs. 187/M3
Froelich, Iowa (†52047) 229/L2
Frog (lake), Alberta 182/E3
Frog Lake, Alberta 182/E3
Frogmore, S.C. (29920) 296/F7
Frogue, Ky. (†42714) 237/L7
Frohavet (bay), Norway 18/F5
Frohna, Mo. (63748) 261/N7
Frohnleiten, Austria 41/C3
Froid, Mont. (59226) 262/M2
Froidchapelle, Belgium 27/E8
Frolovo, U.S.S.R. 48/E5
Frolovo, U.S.S.R. 52/F5
Fromberg, Mont. (59029) 262/H5
Frome (lake), Australia 87/E9
Frome, England 10/E5
Frome, England 13/E6
Frome, Jamaica 158/G6
Frome (lake), S. Australia 88/G6
Frome (lake), S. Australia 94/G4
Front (range), Colo. 208/H1

372 Fronteira

Fronteira, Portugal 33/C3
Fronteiras, Brazil 132/F4
Frontenac, Kansas (66762) 232/H4
Frontenac, Minn. (55026) 255/F6
Frontenac, Mo. (†63101) 261/O3
Frontenac (county), Ontario 177/H3
Frontenac (co.), Québec 172/G4
Frontera, Mexico 150/N7
Frontier, Mich. (49239) 250/E7
Frontier (co.), Nebr. 264/D4
Frontier, N. Dak. (†58102) 282/S6
Frontier, Sask. 181/C6
Frontier, Wyo. (83121) 319/B4
Front Royal, Va. (22630) 307/M3
Frosinone (prov.), Italy 34/D4
Frosinone, Italy 34/D4
Frösö, Sweden 18/J5
Frost, La. (†70753) 238/L2
Frost, Minn. (56033) 255/D7
Frost, Texas (76641) 303/H5
Frost, W. Va. (†24954) 312/G6
Frostburg, Md. (21532) 245/C2
Frostproof, Fla. (33843) 212/E4
Froude, Sask. 181/H6
Frövi, Sweden 18/J7
Frøya (isl.), Norway 18/F5
Frozen (str.), N.W.T. 162/H2
Frozen (str.), N.W. Terrs. 187/K3
Fruita, Colo. (81521) 208/B4
Fruita, Utah (†84775) 304/C5
Fruitdale, Ala. (36539) 195/B8
Fruitdale, S. Dak. (57742) 298/B4
Fruitdale-Harbeck, Oreg. (†97526) 291/D5
Fruitgrove, Queensland 88/K3
Fruit Heights, Utah (†84037) 304/C2
Fruithurst, Ala. (36262) 195/G3
Fruitland, Idaho (83619) 220/B6
Fruitland, Iowa (52749) 229/L6
Fruitland, Md. (21826) 245/R7
Fruitland, Mo. (†63755) 261/N8
Fruitland, N. Mex. (87416) 274/A2
Fruitland, Tenn. (†38343) 237/D9
Fruitland, Utah (84027) 304/D3
Fruitland, Wash. (99129) 310/G2
Fruitland Park, Fla. (32731) 212/D3
Fruitland Park, Miss. (39577) 256/F9
Fruitport, Mich. (49415) 250/C5
Fruitvale, Br. Col. 184/J5
Fruitvale, Idaho (83620) 220/B5
Fruitvale, Tenn. (38336) 237/C9
Fruitvale, Wash. (†98901) 310/E4
Fruitville, Fla. (33578) 212/D4
Frunze, U.S.S.R. 54/J5
Frunze, U.S.S.R. 48/H5
Frutal, Brazil 135/B2
Frutigen, Switzerland 39/E3
Frutillar, Chile 138/D3
Fry, Georgia (37317) 217/D1
Fryburg, N. Dak. (†58622) 282/D6
Fryburg, Ohio (†45895) 284/B4
Fryburg, Pa. (16326) 294/D3
Fry Canyon, Utah (†84511) 304/D6
Frýdek-Místek, Czech. 41/E2
Frýdlant nad Ostravicí, Czech. 41/E2
Frýdlant v. Čechách, Czech. 41/C1
Frye, Maine (04235) 243/B6
Fryeburg, La. (†71039) 238/D2
Fryeburg, Maine (04037) 243/A7
Fryeburg○, Maine (04037) 243/A7
Fu'an, China 77/K6
Fuchu, Hiroshima, Japan 81/F6
Fuchu, Tokyo, Japan 81/O2
Fuding, China 77/K6
Fuengirola, Spain 33/D4
Fuensalida, Spain 33/D2
Fuente-Álamo, Spain 33/F4
Fuente de Cantos, Spain 33/C3
Fuentelapeña, Spain 33/D2
Fuente Obejuna, Spain 33/D3
Fuenterrabía, Spain 33/E1
Fuentesaúco, Spain 33/D2
Fuentes de Andalucía, Spain 33/D4
Fuentes de Oñoro, Spain 33/C2
Fuerte (isl.), Colombia 126/B3
Fuerte (riv.), Mexico 150/E3
Fuerte Bulnes, Chile 138/E10
Fuerte Olimpo, Argentina 120/D5
Fuerte Olimpo, Paraguay 144/C2
Fuerteventura (isl.), Spain 102/A2
Fuerteventura (isl.), Spain 106/B3
Fuerteventura (isl.), Spain 33/C4
Fuga (isl.), Philippines 82/A3
Fuglebjerg, Denmark 21/E7
Fugu, China 77/H4
Fuhai (Burultokay), China 77/C2
Fuik, Neth. Ant. 161/G9
Fujairah, U.A.E. 59/G4
Fuji, Japan 81/J6
Fuji (mt.), Japan 81/J6
Fuji (riv.), Japan 81/J6
Fujian (Fukien), China 77/J6
Fujieda, Japan 81/J6
Fuji-Hakone-Izu National Park, Japan 81/H6
Fujin, China 77/M2
Fujisawa, Japan 81/O3
Fukagawa, Japan 81/L2
Fukang, China 77/C3
Fukuchiyama, Japan 81/G6
Fukue, Japan 81/D7
Fukui (pref.), Japan 81/G5
Fukui, Japan 81/G5
Fukuoka (pref.), Japan 81/D7
Fukuoka, Japan 54/O6
Fukuoka, Japan 81/D7
Fukushima (pref.), Japan 81/K5
Fukushima, Japan 81/K5
Fukuyama, Japan 81/F6
Fulbourn, England 13/H5
Fulbright, Texas (75436) 303/J4
Fulda, Ind. (47536) 227/D8
Fulda, Minn. (56131) 255/C7
Fulda, Sask. 181/F3
Fulda, W. Germany 22/C3
Fulda (riv.), W. Germany 22/C3
Fulford, England 13/F4
Fulford Harbour, Br. Col. 184/K3
Fuling, China 77/G6
Fulks Run, Va. (22830) 307/L3
Fullarton, Trin. & Tob. 161/A11
Fullerton, Calif. (*92631) 204/D11
Fullerton, Ky. (†41175) 237/P3
Fullerton, La. (70642) 238/D4
Fullerton, Nebr. (68638) 264/F3
Fullerton, N. Dak. (58441) 282/O7
Fully, Switzerland 39/D4
Fulnek, Czech. 41/D2
Fulpmes, Austria 41/A3
Fulton, Ala. (36446) 195/C7
Fulton (co.), Ark. 202/G1
Fulton, Ark. (71838) 202/C6
Fulton (co.), Georgia 217/D3
Fulton (co.), Ill. 222/C3
Fulton, Ill. (61252) 222/C2
Fulton (co.), Ind. 227/E2
Fulton, Ind. (46931) 227/E3
Fulton, Iowa (†52060) 229/M4
Fulton, Kansas (66738) 232/H4
Fulton (co.), Ky. 237/C7
Fulton, Ky. (42041) 237/D7
Fulton, Mich. (49052) 250/D6
Fulton, Miss. (38843) 256/H2
Fulton, Mo. (65251) 261/J5
Fulton (co.), N.Y. 276/M4
Fulton, N.Y. (13069) 276/H4
Fulton (co.), Ohio 284/B2
Fulton, Ohio (43321) 284/E5
Fulton (co.), Pa. 294/F6
Fulton, S. Dak. (57340) 298/O6
Fulton, Tenn. (†38041) 237/B9
Fulton, Texas (78358) 303/H9
Fulton Chain (lakes), N.Y. 276/K3
Fultondale, Ala. (35068) 195/E3
Fultonham, Ohio (43738) 284/F6
Fultonville, N.Y. (12072) 276/M5
Fults, Ill. (62244) 222/C5
Fulwood, England 10/G1
Fulwood, England 13/G1
Funabashi, Japan 81/P2
Funafuti (atoll), Tuvalu 87/H6
Funchal (cap.), Madeira, Port. 102/A1
Funchal (dist.), Portugal 33/A2
Funchal (cap.), Madeira, Portugal 106/A2
Funchal, Portugal 33/A2
Fundación, Colombia 126/C2
Fundão, Portugal 33/C2
Fundy (bay) 162/K7
Fundy (bay), New Bruns. 170/E3
Fundy (bay), Nova Scotia 168/C3
Fundy Nat'l Park, New Bruns. 170/E3
Funhalouro, Mozambique 118/E4
Funing, China 77/K5
Funk, Nebr. (68940) 264/E4
Funk (isl.), Newf. 166/D4
Funkley, Minn. (†56630) 255/D3
Funkstown, Md. (21734) 245/H2
Funston, Georgia (31753) 217/E8
Funter, Alaska (†99801) 196/M1
Funtua, Nigeria 106/F6
Fuping, China 77/H4
Fuquay-Varina, N.C. (27526) 281/M3
Furancungo, Mozambique 118/E2
Furka (pass), Switzerland 39/F3
Furman, Ala. (36741) 195/E6
Furman, S.C. (29921) 296/E6
Furmanov, U.S.S.R. 52/F3
Furnace, Ky. (†40472) 237/O5
Furnace, Mass. (†01031) 249/F3
Furnace, Scotland 15/C4
Furnas (res.), Brazil 120/E5
Furnas (dam), Brazil 135/C2
Furnas (co.), Nebr. 264/E4
Furneaux Group (isls.), Australia 87/E9
Furneaux Group (isls.), Tasmania 88/H8
Furneaux Group (isls.), Tasmania 99/E1
Furnes (Veurne), Belgium 27/B6
Furness, Sask. 181/B2
Furry Creek, Br. Col. 184/K2
Fürstenberg, E. Germany 22/E2
Fürstenfeld, Austria 41/C3
Fürstenfeldbruck, W. Germany 22/D4
Fürstenwalde, E. Germany 22/F2
Fürth, W. Germany 22/D4
Furth im Wald, W. Germany 22/E4
Furukawa, Japan 81/K4
Fury and Hecla (str.), N.W.T. 162/H2
Fury and Hecla (str.), N.W. Terrs. 187/K3
Fusagasugá, Colombia 126/C5
Fushun, China 77/K3
Fushun, China 54/O5
Fusilier, Sask. 181/B4
Fusin (Fuxin), China 77/K3
Fusingchen (Simao), China 77/F7
Fusio, Switzerland 39/G4
Fusong, China 77/L3
Füssen, W. Germany 22/D5
Futa Jallon (mts.), Guinea 106/B6
Futaleufú, Chile 138/E4
Futrono, Chile 138/E3
Futuna (Hoorn) (isls.), Wallis and Futuna 87/J7
Fu Xian, Liaoning, China 77/K4
Fu Xian, Shaanxi, China 77/G4
Fuxin (Fusin), China 77/K3
Fuxin, China 54/O5
Fuyang (Fowyang), China 77/J5
Fuyu, Heilongjiang, China 77/K2
Fuyu, Jilin, China 77/L2
Fuyuan, Heilongjiang, China 77/M2
Fuyuan, Yunnan, China 77/F6
Fuyun, China 77/C2
Füzesabony, Hungary 41/F3
Füzesgyarmat, Hungary 41/F3
Fuzhou (Foochow), Fujian, China 77/J6
Fuzhou, Jiangxi, China 77/J6
Fuzhou, China 2/R4
Fuzhou, China 54/N7
Fyffe, Ala. (35971) 195/G2
Fylingdales, England 13/G3
Fyn (co.), Denmark 21/D7
Fyn (isl.), Denmark 21/D7
Fyn (isl.), Denmark 18/G9
Fyne, Loch (inlet), Scotland 10/D2
Fyne, Loch (inlet), Scotland 15/C5
Fyns Hoved (pt.), Denmark 21/D6
Fyvie, Scotland 15/F3
Fyzabad, Trin. & Tob. 161/A11

G

Gaastra, Mich. (49927) 250/G2
Gabarus, Nova Scotia 168/H3
Gabarus (bay), Nova Scotia 168/H3
Gabarus (cape), Nova Scotia 168/J3
Gabbettville, Georgia (†30240) 217/B5
Gabbs, Nev. (89409) 266/D4
Gabela, Angola 115/B6
Gabès, Tunisia 106/F2
Gabès, Tunisia 102/D1
Gabès (gulf), Tunisia 106/G2
Gabgaba, Wadi (dry riv.), Sudan 111/F3
Gable, S.C. (29051) 296/G4
Gabon 2/K6
Gabon 102/D4
GABON 115/B4
Gaborone (cap.), Botswana 2/L7
Gaborone (cap.), Botswana 118/D4
Gaborone (cap.), Botswana 102/E7
Gabras, Sudan 111/E5
Gabredarre, Ethiopia 111/H6
Gabriel (str.), N.W. Terrs. 187/M3
Gabrik (riv.), Iran 66/L7
Gabriola, Br. Col. 184/J3
Gabrovo, Bulgaria 45/G4
Gachalá, Colombia 126/D5
Gach Saran, Iran 59/F3
Gach Saran, Iran 66/G5
Gackle, N. Dak. (58442) 282/M6
Gacko, Yugoslavia 45/D4
Gadag-Betgeri, India 68/D5
Gäddede, Sweden 18/J4
Gadê, China 77/E5
Gadebusch, E. Germany 22/D2
Gadmen, Switzerland 39/F3
Gadsby, Alberta 182/D3
Gadsden, Ala. 188/J4
Gadsden, Ala. (*35901) 195/G2
Gadsden, Ariz. (85336) 198/A6
Gadsden (co.), Fla. 212/B1
Gadsden, S.C. (29052) 296/F4
Gadsden, Tenn. (38337) 237/D9
Gads Hill, Mo. (†63957) 261/L8
Gadston (pt.), Fla. 212/C3
Gadwal, India 68/D5
Gadyach, U.S.S.R. 52/D4
Găeşti, Romania 45/G3
Gaeta, Italy 34/D4
Gaeta (gulf), Italy 34/D4
Gaferut (isl.), Micronesia 87/E5
Gaffney, S.C. (29340) 296/D1
Gafsa, Tunisia 106/F2
Gagarin, U.S.S.R. 52/D3
Gage, Alberta 182/A1
Gage (co.), Nebr. 264/H4
Gage, N. Mex. (†88030) 274/A6
Gage, Okla. (73843) 288/G2
Gagetown, Mich. (48735) 250/F5
Gagetown, New Bruns. 170/D3
Gaggenau, W. Germany 22/C4
Gagnoa, Ivory Coast 102/B4
Gagnoa, Ivory Coast 106/C7
Gagnon, Que. 162/K5
Gagnon, Québec 174/D2
Gagnon (lake), Québec 172/B3
Gagny, France 28/C1
Gagra, U.S.S.R. 52/E6
Gahanna, Ohio (43230) 284/E5
Gaiba (lag.), Bolivia 136/F5
Gail, Saudi Arabia 59/E5
Gail, Texas (79738) 303/C5
Gaillac, France 28/D6
Gaillard (lake), Conn. 210/D3
Gaillard, Georgia (†31078) 217/D5
Gaima, Papua N.G. 85/B7
Gaiman, Argentina 143/C5
Gaines, Mich. (48436) 250/F6
Gaines, Pa. (16921) 294/G2
Gaines (co.), Texas 303/B5
Gainesboro, Tenn. (38562) 237/K8
Gainesboro, Va. (†22601) 307/M2
Gainestown, Ala. (36540) 195/C8
Gainesville, Ala. (35464) 195/B5
Gainesville (dam), Ala. 195/B5
Gainesville, Fla. 188/K5
Gainesville, Fla. (*32601) 212/D2
Gainesville, Georgia (30501) 217/E2
Gainesville, Mo. (65655) 261/G9
Gainesville, N.Y. (14066) 276/D5
Gainesville, Texas (76240) 303/G4
Gainesville, Va. (22065) 307/N3
Gainsborough, England 10/F4
Gainsborough, England 13/G4
Gainsborough, Sask. 181/K6
Gairdner (lake), Australia 87/D9
Gairdner (lake), S. Australia 88/F6
Gairdner (lake), S. Australia 94/D4
Gairloch, Scotland 15/C3
Gairloch, Loch (inlet), Scotland 15/C3
Gais, Switzerland 39/H2
Gaithersburg, Md. (20760) 245/K4
Gajdel, Czech. 41/E2
Gakona, Alaska (99586) 196/K2
Galadi, Ethiopia 111/J6
Galahad, Alberta 182/E3
Galana (riv.), Kenya 115/G4
Galand, Iran 66/J2
Galanta, Czech. 41/D2
Galápagos (isls.), Ecuador 2/E6
Galápagos (isls.), Ecuador 128/C8
Galashiels, Scotland 10/E3
Galashiels, Scotland 15/F5
Galata, Mont. (59444) 262/E2
Galata, Turkey 63/C6
Galaţi, Romania 7/G4
Galaţi, Romania 45/H3
Galatia, Ill. (62935) 222/E6
Galatia, Kansas (†67567) 232/D3
Galatina, Italy 34/G4
Galatone, Italy 34/F4
Galax (I.C.), Va. (24333) 307/G7
Galbally, Ireland 17/E7
Galbraith, La. (†71447) 238/E4
Galcaio, Somalia 102/G4
Galcaio, Somalia 115/J2
Galchutt, N. Dak. (58034) 282/S7
Gale, Ill. (62936) 222/D6
Gale (riv.), N.H. 268/D3
Galeana, Chihuahua, Mexico 150/F1
Galeana, Nuevo León, Mexico 150/J4
Galela, Indonesia 85/H5
Galen, Mont. (†59722) 262/D4
Galena, Alaska (99741) 196/G2
Galena, Ill. (61036) 222/C1
Galena, Ind. (†47119) 227/F8
Galena, Kansas (66739) 232/H4
Galena, Md. (21635) 245/P3
Galena, Mo. (65656) 261/F9
Galena, Ohio (43021) 284/E5
Galena Park, Texas (77547) 303/J1
Galeota (pt.), Trin. & Tob. 161/B11
Galera (pt.), Chile 138/D3
Galera (pt.), Ecuador 128/B2
Galera (pt.), Trin. & Tob. 161/C10
Galera (pt.), Trin. & Tob. 156/G5
Galesburg, Ill. 188/H2
Galesburg, Ill. (61401) 222/C3
Galesburg, Kansas (66740) 232/G4
Galesburg, Mich. (49053) 250/D6
Galesburg, N. Dak. (58035) 282/R5
Gales Creek, Oreg. (97117) 291/D2
Gales Ferry, Conn. (06335) 210/G3
Galestown, Md. (†19973) 245/P6
Galesville, Md. (20765) 245/M5
Galesville, Wis. (54630) 317/D7
Galeton, Colo. (80622) 208/K1
Galeton, Pa. (16922) 294/G2
Galetta, Ontario 177/H2
Galgenberg (hill), Netherlands 27/H4
Galguduud (prov.), Somalia 115/J2
Galiano, Br. Col. 184/K3
Galiano (isl.), Br. Col. 184/K3
Galice, Oreg. (†97532) 291/D5
Galich, U.S.S.R. 52/F3
Galicia (reg.), Spain 33/B1
Galien, Mich. (49113) 250/C7
Galilee, Sea of (lake), Israel 59/C3
Galilee, Sea of (Tiberias) (lake), Israel 65/D2
Galilee (reg.), Israel 65/C2
Galilee (lake), Queensland 95/C4
Galina (pt.), Jamaica 158/J6
Galion (bay), Martinique 161/D6
Galion, Ohio (44833) 284/E4
Galisteo, N. Mex. (†87540) 274/D3
Galiuro (mts.), Ariz. 198/E6
Galivants Ferry, S.C. (29544) 296/J3
Gallabat, Sudan 111/G5
Gallan (head), Scotland 15/A2
Gallant, Ala. (35972) 195/F2
Gallarate, Italy 34/B2
Gallatin (co.), Ill. 222/E6
Gallatin (co.), Ky. 237/M3
Gallatin, Mo. (64640) 261/E3
Gallatin (co.), Mont. 262/E5
Gallatin (peak), Mont. 262/E5
Gallatin (riv.), Mont. 262/E5
Gallatin, Tenn. (37066) 237/H8
Gallatin Gateway, Mont. (59730) 262/E5
Gallaway, Tenn. (38036) 237/B10
Galle, Sri Lanka 54/J9
Galle, Sri Lanka 68/D7
Gallegos (riv.), Argentina 143/B7
Gallegos, N. Mex. (†87733) 274/F3
Galley (head), Ireland 17/D9
Gallia (co.), Ohio 284/F8
Galliano, La. (70354) 238/K8
Gallina, N. Mex. (87017) 274/C2
Gallinas (pt.), Colombia 120/B1
Gallinas (pt.), Colombia 126/E1
Gallinas (mts.), N. Mex. 274/B4
Gallinas (riv.), N. Mex. 274/E3
Gallion, Ala. (36742) 195/C6
Gallion, La. (†71223) 238/G1
Gallipoli, Italy 34/F4
Gallipoli, Turkey 59/A1
Gallipoli, Turkey 63/C5
Gallipolis, Ohio (45631) 284/F8
Gallipolis Ferry, W. Va. (25515) 312/B5
Gallitzin, Pa. (16641) 294/E4
Gällivare, Sweden 18/M3
Gallman, Miss. (39077) 256/D7
Gallo (pt.), Chile 138/E3
Gallo (mt.), Dom. Rep. 158/D5
Gällö, Sweden 18/J5
Galloo (isl.), N.Y. 276/H3
Galloway, Ark. (†72114) 202/F4
Galloway, Br. Col. 184/K5
Galloway (dist.), Scotland 15/D5
Galloway, Mull of (prom.), Scotland 15/D6
Galloway, Mull of (prom.), Scotland 10/D3
Galloway, W. Va. (26349) 312/F4
Galloway, Wis. (54432) 317/H6
Gallup, N. Mex. 188/E3
Gallup, N. Mex. (87301) 274/A3
Gallur, Spain 33/F2
Galole, Kenya 115/G4
Gal'on, Israel 65/B4
Galston, Scotland 10/D3
Galston, Scotland 15/D5
Galt, Calif. (95632) 204/C9
Galt, Iowa (50101) 229/F3
Galt, Mo. (64641) 261/F2
Galtee (mts.), Ireland 17/E7
Galtymore (mt.), Ireland 17/E7
Galva, Ill. (61434) 222/D2
Galva, Iowa (51020) 229/C3
Galva, Kansas (67443) 232/E3
Galván (mt.), Paraguay 144/C3
Galvarino, Chile 138/D2
Galveston, Ind. (46932) 227/E3
Galveston (co.), Texas 303/K8
Galveston, Texas 146/J7
Galveston, Texas 188/H5
Galveston, Texas (*77550) 303/L3
Galveston (bay), Texas 188/H5
Galveston (bay), Texas 303/L2
Galveston (isl.), Texas 303/K8
Gálvez, Argentina 143/F6
Galvez, La. (†70769) 238/L2
Gálvez, Spain 33/D3
Galvin, Wash. (98544) 310/B4
Galway (co.), Ireland 17/D5
Galway, Ireland 17/C5
Galway, Ireland 7/D3
Galway, Ireland 10/B4
Galway (bay), Ireland 17/C5
Galway (bay), Ireland 10/B4
Galway, N.Y. (12074) 276/N4
Gamaliel, Ky. (42140) 237/K7
Gamarra, Colombia 126/D3
Gamas Ab (riv.), Iran 66/E3
Gamay, Philippines 82/E4
Gamay (bay), Philippines 82/E4
Gamba, China 77/C6
Gambaga, Ghana 106/D6
Gambela, Ethiopia 111/F6
Gambell, Alaska (99742) 196/D2
Gamber, Md. (†21048) 245/L3
Gambia 2/J5
Gambia 102/A3
GAMBIA 106/A6
Gambia (riv.), Gambia 106/B6
Gambia (riv.), Senegal 106/B6
Gambier (isls.), Fr. Poly. 87/N8
Gambier, Ohio (43022) 284/F5
Gambo, Newf. 166/D4
Gamboma, Congo 115/C4
Gambos, Angola 115/B6
Gambrills, Md. (21054) 245/M4
Gamerco, N. Mex. (87317) 274/A3
Gaming, Austria 41/C3
Gamleby, Sweden 18/J8
Gammon (riv.), Manitoba 179/G3
Gammon (pt.), Mass. 249/N6
Gampel, Switzerland 39/E4
Gamu-Gofa (prov.), Ethiopia 111/G6
Gamvik, Norway 18/Q1
Ganado, Ariz. (86505) 198/F3
Ganado, Texas (77962) 303/H8
Ganale Dorya (riv.), Ethiopia 111/H6
Gananoque, Ontario 177/H3
Ganassi, Philippines 82/D7
Ganaveh, Iran 66/G6
Ganda, Angola 115/B6
Gandajika, Zaire 115/D5
Gandara, Philippines 82/E4
Gándara, Spain 33/C1
Gandava, Pakistan 68/B3
Gandava, Pakistan 59/J4
Gandeeville, W. Va. (25243) 312/D5
Gander, Newf. 166/D4
Gander (lake), Newf. 166/D4
Gander (riv.), Newf. 166/D4
Gander, Newf. 162/L6
Gandesa, Spain 33/G2
Gandhinagar, India 68/C4
Gandía, Spain 33/F3
Gandy, Nebr. (†69163) 264/D3
Gandy, Utah (†84728) 304/A4
Gandzha (Kirovabad), U.S.S.R. 52/G6
Ganga (Ganges) (riv.), India 68/F3
Gan Gan, Argentina 143/C5
Ganganagar, India 68/C3
Gangapur, India 68/D3
Gangara, Niger 106/F6
Gangaw, Burma 72/B2
Gangca, China 77/F4
Gangdisê Shan (range), China 77/B5
Ganges (riv.) 54/K7
Ganges (riv.) 2/P4
Ganges, Mouths of the (delta), Bangladesh 68/F3
Ganges (riv.), Bangladesh 68/F3
Ganges, Br. Col. 184/K3
Ganges, Mouths of the (delta), India 68/F4
Ganges (riv.), India 68/F3
Gangtok, India 68/F3
Gan He (riv.), China 77/K2
Gani, Indonesia 85/H6
Ganister, Pa. (†16693) 294/F5
Ganmain, N.S. Wales 97/D4
Gann (Brinkhaven), Ohio (†43006) 284/F5
Gannat, France 28/E4
Gannett, Idaho (†83313) 220/D6
Gannett (peak), Wyo. 188/D2
Gannett (peak), Wyo. 319/C2
Gannvalley, S. Dak. (57341) 298/L5
Ganquan, China 77/H4
Gans, Okla. (74936) 288/S4
Gänserndorf, Austria 41/D2
Gansevoort, N.Y. (12831) 276/N4
Ganshoren, Belgium 27/B9
Gansu (Kansu), China 77/E3
Gansville, La. (†71422) 238/E2
Gantt, Ala. (36038) 195/E8
Gantt, S.C. (†29609) 296/C2
Ganzhou (Kanchow), China 77/H6
Gao (mt.), Cent. Afr. Rep. 115/C2
Gao, Mali 102/C3
Gao, Mali 106/E5
Gao'an, China 77/H6
Gaolan, China 77/F4
Gaotai, China 77/E4
Gaoua, Upper Volta 106/D6
Gaoual, Guinea 106/B6
Gaoyou Hu (lake), China 77/J5
Gap, France 28/G5
Gap, Pa. (17527) 294/L6
Gap (creek), Sask. 181/B6
Gapan, Philippines 82/C3
Gapcreek, Ky. (†42603) 237/M7
Gap Mills, W. Va. (24941) 312/F7
Gar, China 77/B5
Gara (lake), Ireland 17/D4
Gara, Lough (lake), Ireland 10/B4
Garachiné, Panama 154/H6
Garad, Somalia 115/J2
Garadice (lake), Ireland 17/F3
Garah, N.S. Wales 97/E1
Garamba Nat'l Park, Zaire 115/E3
Garanhuns, Brazil 120/F3
Garanhuns, Brazil 132/G5
Garards Fort, Pa. (15334) 294/B6
Garbahaarrey, Somalia 115/H3
Garba Tula, Kenya 115/G3
Garber, Iowa (52048) 229/L3
Garber, Okla. (73738) 288/M2
Garberville, Calif. (95440) 204/B3
Garbosh, Kuh-e (mt.), Iran 66/G4
Garbsen, W. Germany 22/C2
Garça, Brazil 135/B3
Garcia, Colo. (81134) 208/J8
García de Sola (res.), Spain 33/D3
Garcitas, Venezuela 124/C3
Gard (dept.), France 28/F6
Gard (riv.), France 28/F5
Garda (lake), Italy 34/C2
Gardanne, France 28/F6
Gardar, N. Dak. (58234) 282/P2
Gardelegen, E. Germany 22/D2
Garden, Mich. (49835) 250/C3
Garden (isl.), Mich. 250/D3
Garden (pen.), Mich. 250/C3
Garden (co.), Nebr. 264/B3
Garden (isl.), W. Australia 88/A2
Garden (isl.), W. Australia 92/A1
Gardena, Calif. (*90747) 204/C11
Gardena, Idaho (†83629) 220/B5
Gardena, N. Dak. (58739) 282/J2
Garden City, Ala. (35070) 195/E2
Garden City, Georgia (31408) 217/K6
Garden City, Idaho (†83704) 220/B6
Garden City, Iowa (50102) 229/G4
Garden City, Kans. 188/F3
Garden City, Kansas (67846) 232/B4
Garden City, La. (70540) 238/H7
Garden City, Mich. (48135) 250/F6
Garden City, Minn. (56034) 255/D6
Garden City, Mo. (64747) 261/D5
Garden City, N.Y. (11530) 276/R7
Garden City, S. Dak. (57236) 298/O4
Garden City, Texas (79739) 303/C6
Garden City, Utah (84028) 304/C2
Garden City Beach, S.C. (29576) 296/K4
Gardendale, Ala. (35071) 195/E3
Garden Grove, Calif. (*92640) 204/D11
Garden Grove, Iowa (50103) 229/F7
Garden Home-Whitford, Oreg. (97223) 291/A2
Garden Island (bay), La. 238/M8
Garden Plain, Kansas (67050) 232/E4
Garden Prairie, Ill. (61038) 222/E1
Garden Reach, India 68/F2
Garden River, Alberta 182/B5
Gardenstown, Scotland 15/F3
Gardenton, Manitoba 179/F5
Garden Valley, Idaho (83622) 220/C5
Garden View, Pa. (†17701) 294/H3
Garden Village, Ontario 177/E1
Gardez, Afghanistan 59/J3
Gardez, Afghanistan 68/B2
Gardi, Georgia (†31545) 217/J7
Gardiner, Maine (04345) 243/D7
Gardiner, Mont. (59030) 262/F5
Gardiner, Oreg. (97441) 291/C4
Gardiner (dam), Sask. 181/D4
Gardiner, Wash. (98334) 310/B2
Gardiners (bay), N.Y. 276/R8
Gardiners (isl.), N.Y. 276/R8
Gardner (canal), Br. Col. 184/C3
Gardner, Colo. (81040) 208/J7
Gardner (lake), Conn. 210/G2
Gardner, Fla. (†33890) 212/E4
Gardner, Ill. (60424) 222/E2
Gardner, Kansas (66030) 232/H3
Gardner (isl.), Kiribati 87/J6
Gardner (lake), Maine 243/J6
Gardner, Mass. (01440) 249/G2
Gardner, N. Dak. (58036) 282/R5
Gardner, Tenn. (†38237) 237/D8
Gardner (mt.), Wash. 310/A2
Gardner Creek, New Bruns. 170/E3
Gardner Pinnacles (isls.), Hawaii 87/K3
Gardner Pinnacles (isls.), Hawaii 188/F6
Gardner Pinnacles (isls.), Hawaii 218/C6
Gardnerville, Nev. (89410) 266/B4
Gardo, Somalia 115/J2
Gardula, Ethiopia 111/G6
Gare Loch (inlet), Scotland 15/A1
Garelochhead, Scotland 15/A1
Garelochhead, Scotland 10/A1
Gareloi (isl.), Alaska 196/K4
Garessio, Italy 34/A2
Garfield, Ark. (72732) 202/C1
Garfield (co.), Colo. 208/C3
Garfield, Colo. (81227) 208/G5
Garfield, Georgia (30425) 217/H5
Garfield, Kansas (67529) 232/C3
Garfield, Ky. (40140) 237/J5
Garfield, Minn. (56332) 255/C5
Garfield (co.), Mont. 262/J3
Garfield (co.), Nebr. 264/F3
Garfield, N.J. (07026) 273/B2
Garfield, N. Mex. (87936) 274/B6
Garfield (co.), Okla. 288/L2
Garfield (co.), Utah 304/C6
Garfield (co.), Wash. 310/H4
Garfield, Wash. (99130) 310/H3
Garfield Heights, Ohio (44125) 284/J9
Gargaliánoi, Greece 45/E7
Gargunnock, Scotland 15/B1
Garibaldi, Br. Col. 184/F5
Garibaldi, Oreg. (97118) 291/D2
Garibaldi Prov. Park, Br. Col. 184/F5
Garies, S. Africa 118/B6
Garioch (dist.), Scotland 15/F3
Garissa, Kenya 115/G4
Garita, N. Mex. (88421) 274/E3
Garland, Ala. (†36456) 195/E7
Garland (co.), Ark. 202/D4

Ghemines 373

Garland, Ark. (71839) 202/C7
Garland, Kansas (66741) 232/H4
Garland, Maine (04939) 243/E5
Garland○, Maine (04939) 243/E5
Garland, Manitoba 179/B3
Garland, Nebr. (68360) 264/G4
Garland, N.C. (28441) 281/N5
Garland, Pa. (16416) 294/C2
Garland, Tenn. (†38019) 237/B9
Garland, Tex. 188/G4
Garland, Texas (*75040) 303/H2
Garland, Utah (84312) 304/B2
Garland, Wyo. (†82435) 319/D1
Garlandville, Miss. (†39345) 256/F6
Garlieston, Scotland 15/D6
Garlin, Ky. (†42728) 237/L6
Garmisch-Partenkirchen, W. Germany 22/D5
Garmouth, Scotland 15/E3
Garmsar, Iran 59/F2
Garmsar, Iran 66/H3
Garnavillo, Iowa (52049) 229/L3
Garneill, Mont. (59445) 262/G4
Garner, Ark. (72052) 202/G3
Garner, Iowa (50438) 229/F2
Garner (lake), Manitoba 179/G4
Garner, N.C. (27529) 281/M3
Garnet, Mich. (†49762) 250/D2
Garnet, Mont. (†59832) 262/C4
Garnet (bay), N.W. Terrs. 187/L3
Garnett, Kansas (66032) 232/G3
Garnett, S.C. (29922) 296/E6
Garnish, Newf. 166/C4
Garoe, Somalia 115/J2
Garonne (riv.), France 7/D4
Garonne (riv.), France 28/C5
Garoua, Cameroon 102/D4
Garoua, Cameroon 115/B2
Garrabost, Scotland 15/B2
Garrard (co.), Ky. 237/M5
Garretson, S. Dak. (57030) 298/S6
Garrett, Ill. (†61913) 222/E4
Garrett, Ind. (46738) 227/G2
Garrett, Ky. (41630) 237/R6
Garrett (co.), Md. 245/A2
Garrett, Pa. (15542) 294/D6
Garrett, Wash. (†99362) 310/G4
Garrett, Wyo. (82058) 319/G3
Garrett Park, Md. (20766) 245/E3
Garretts Bend, W. Va. (†25523) 312/C6
Garrettsville, Ohio (44231) 284/H3
Garrick, Sask. 181/G2
Garrison, Iowa (52229) 229/J4
Garrison, Ky. (41141) 237/P3
Garrison, Md. (21055) 245/L3
Garrison, Minn. (56450) 255/E4
Garrison, Mo. (65657) 261/F9
Garrison, Mont. (59731) 262/D4
Garrison, Nebr. (68632) 264/G3
Garrison, N.Y. (10524) 276/N8
Garrison, N. Dak. (58540) 282/H4
Garrison (dam), N. Dak. 282/H5
Garrison, Texas (75946) 303/K6
Garrison, Utah (84728) 304/A5
Garrisonville, Va. (22463) 307/N4
Garron (pt.), N. Ireland 17/K1
Garrovillas, Spain 33/C3
Garry (lake), Canada 4/C14
Garry (lake), N.W.T. 162/G2
Garry (lake), N.W. Terrs. 187/H3
Garry, Loch (lake), Scotland 15/D3
Garry (riv.), Scotland 15/D3
Garryowen, Mont. (59031) 262/J5
Garsen, Kenya 115/G4
Garske, N. Dak. (†58382) 282/N3
Garson (lake), Alberta 182/E1
Garson, Manitoba 179/F4
Garstang, England 13/G1
Gartan (lake), Ireland 17/F2
Gartmore, Scotland 15/B1
Garulia, India 68/F1
Garut, Indonesia 85/H2
Garvagh, N. Ireland 17/H2
Garvan (isls.), Ireland 17/G1
Garvin, Minn. (56132) 255/C6
Garvin (co.), Okla. 288/M5
Garvin, Okla. (74736) 288/S7
Garwin, Iowa (50632) 229/H4
Garwolin, Poland 47/E3
Garwood, Mo. (†63965) 261/L8
Garwood, N.J. (07027) 273/E2
Garwood, Texas (77442) 303/H8
Gary, Ind. 146/K5
Gary, Ind. 188/J2
Gary, Ind. (*46401) 227/C1
Gary, Minn. (56545) 255/B3
Gary, S. Dak. (57237) 298/S4
Gary, Texas (75643) 303/K5
Gary, W. Va. (24836) 312/C8
Garyarsa (Gartok), China 77/B5
Garyarsa, China 54/K6
Garysburg, N.C. (27831) 281/O2
Garyville, La. (70051) 238/M3
Garza (co.), Texas 303/C4
Garzê, China 77/F5
Garzón, Colombia 126/C6
Garzón, Uruguay 145/E5
Garzón (lag.), Uruguay 145/E5
Gas, Kansas (66742) 232/G4
Gas (hills), Wyo. 319/E3
Gasan-Kuli, U.S.S.R. 48/F6
Gasburg, Va. (23857) 307/N7
Gas City, Ind. (46933) 227/F4
Gasconade (co.), Mo. 261/J6
Gasconade, Mo. (65036) 261/J5
Gasconade (riv.), Mo. 261/H7
Gascony (trad. prov.), France 29
Gascoyne (riv.), Australia 87/B8
Gascoyne, N. Dak. (58629) 282/D7
Gascoyne (riv.), W. Australia 88/A4
Gascoyne (riv.), W. Australia 92/B4
Gascoyne Junction, W. Australia 92/A4
Gash (Mareb) (riv.), Ethiopia 59/C7
Gash (riv.), Sudan 59/C6
Gashaka, Nigeria 106/G7
Gas Hills, Wyo. (82501) 319/E3
Gash Mareb (riv.), Ethiopia 111/G5
Gasht, Iran 66/M7
Gasker (isl.), Scotland 15/A3
Gaskiers, Newf. 166/D2
Gasmata, Papua N.G. 86/B2
Gaspar, Cuba 158/F2
Gaspar Hernández, Dom. Rep. 158/E5
Gasparilla (isl.), Fla. 212/D5
Gaspé, Que. 162/K6
Gaspé, Québec 172/D1
Gaspé, Québec 174/E3
Gaspé (bay), Québec 172/D1
Gaspé (cape), Québec 172/D1
Gaspé (pen.), Québec 172/D2
Gaspé-Est (county), Québec 174/E3
Gaspé-Est (co.), Québec 172/D1
Gaspé-Ouest (co.), Québec 172/C1
Gaspé-Ouest (county), Québec 174/D3
Gaspereau (riv.), New Bruns. 170/D2
Gaspereau (lake), Nova Scotia 168/D4
Gaspésie Prov. Park, Québec 174/D3
Gaspésie Prov. Park, Québec 172/C1
Gasport, N.Y. (14067) 276/C4
Gasque, Ala. (†36542) 195/C10
Gassan (mt.), Japan 81/J4
Gassaway, Tenn. (†37095) 237/K9
Gassaway, W. Va. (26624) 312/E5
Gassetts, Vt. (†05144) 268/B5
Gassville, Ark. (72635) 202/F1
Gaston, Ind. (47342) 227/G4
Gaston (co.), N.C. 281/G4
Gaston, N.C. (27832) 281/O1
Gaston (res.), N.C. 281/O2
Gaston, Oreg. (97119) 291/D2
Gaston, S.C. (29053) 296/E4
Gaston (lake), Va. 307/M8
Gastonburg, Ala. (†36728) 195/C6
Gastonia, N.C. 188/K3
Gastonia, N.C. (28052) 281/G4
Gastre, Argentina 143/C5
Gat, Israel 65/B4
Gata (cape), Cyprus 59/B3
Gata (cape), Cyprus 63/E5
Gata (cape), Spain 33/F4
Gata (mts.), Spain 33/C2
Gatchel, Ind. (†47586) 227/D8
Gatchina, U.S.S.R. 52/C3
Gate, Okla. (73844) 288/F1
Gate, Wash. (†98579) 310/B4
Gate City, Va. (24251) 307/C7
Gatehouse of Fleet, Scotland 10/E3
Gatehouse of Fleet, Scotland 15/D6
Gates, Nebr. (68839) 264/E3
Gates (co.), N.C. 281/R2
Gates, N.C. (27937) 281/R2
Gates, Oreg. (97346) 291/E3
Gates, Tenn. (38037) 237/C9
Gateshead, England 10/F3
Gateshead, England 13/J3
Gateshead (isl.), N.W. Terrs. 187/J2
Gates Mills, Ohio (44040) 284/J9
Gates of the Arctic Nat'l Park, Alaska 196/H1
Gates of the Arctic Nat'l Preserve, Alaska 196/H1
Gatesville, N.C. (27938) 281/R2
Gatesville, Texas (76528) 303/G6
Gateswood, Ala. (†36507) 195/C9
Gateway, Ark. (72733) 202/B1
Gateway, Colo. (81522) 208/B5
Gateway, Oreg. (†97741) 291/F3
Gateway Nat'l Rec. Area, N.J. 273/E2
Gateway Nat'l Rec. Area, N.Y. 276/M9
Gatewood, Mo. (63942) 261/K9
Gatico, Chile 138/A4
Gatineau (co.), Québec 172/B3
Gatineau (county), Québec 174/B3
Gatineau, Québec 172/B4
Gatineau (riv.), Québec 172/B3
Gatliff, Ky. (†40769) 237/O7
Gatlinburg, Tenn. (37738) 237/O9
Gatooma, Zimbabwe 118/D3
Gatooma, Zimbabwe 102/E6
Gatow, W. Germany 22/E4
Gatteville-le-Phare, France 28/C3
Gattman, Miss. (38844) 256/H3
Gatton, Queensland 88/J5
Gatton, Queensland 95/E5
Gatun (lake), Panama 154/G6
Gatzke, Minn. (56724) 255/C2
Gaucín, Spain 33/D4
Gauhati, India 68/G3
Gauhati, India 54/L7
Gauja (riv.), U.S.S.R. 53/C2
Gauley (riv.), W. Va. 312/D6
Gauley Bridge, W. Va. (25085) 312/D6
Gauley Mills, W. Va. (26240) 312/E6
Gaultois, Newf. 166/C4
Gausdale, Ky. (40906) 237/N7
Gause, Texas (77857) 303/H7
Gaussberg (mt.) 5/C5
Gautier, Miss. (39553) 256/G10
Gavater, Iran 59/H5
Gavater, Iran 66/M8
Gávdhos (isl.), Greece 45/F8
Gave de Pau (riv.), France 28/C6
Gavião, Portugal 33/C3
Gavins Point (dam), Nebr. 264/G2
Gavins Point (dam), S. Dak. 298/P8
Gaviota, Calif. (†93017) 204/E9
Gavkhuni (lake), Iran 59/F3
Gavkhuni (marsh), Iran 66/H4
Gävle, Sweden 7/F2
Gävle, Sweden 18/K6
Gävleborg (co.), Sweden 18/K6
Gawai, Burma 72/C1
Gawler, S. Australia 88/F6
Gawler (ranges), S. Australia 88/F6
Gawler, S. Australia 94/B6
Gawler (ranges), S. Australia 94/E5
Gawler (riv.), S. Australia 94/B6
Gay, Georgia (30218) 217/C4
Gay, Mich. (49928) 250/A1
Gay, U.S.S.R. 52/J4
Gay, W. Va. (25244) 312/C5
Gaya, India 68/F4
Gaya, Niger 106/E6
Gay Head, Mass. (†02535) 249/L7
Gay Head○, Mass. (†02535) 249/L7
Gay Head (prom.), Mass. 249/L7
Gay Hill, Texas (†77833) 303/H7
Gayle, Jamaica 158/J6
Gaylesville, Ala. (35973) 195/G2
Gaylord, Kansas (67638) 232/D2
Gaylord, Mich. (49735) 250/E3
Gaylord, Minn. (55334) 255/D6
Gaylord, Oreg. (97458) 291/C5
Gaylord, Va. (†22611) 307/M2
Gaylordsville, Conn. (06755) 210/A2
Gayndah, Queensland 95/D5
Gayndah, Queensland 88/J5
Gayny, U.S.S.R. 52/H2
Gays, Ill. (61928) 222/E4
Gaysin, U.S.S.R. 52/C5
Gays Mills, Wis. (54631) 317/E9
Gaysport, Ohio (†43720) 284/G6
Gaysville, Vt. (05746) 268/B4
Gayville, S. Dak. (57031) 298/P8
Gaza, Cent. Afr. Rep. 115/C3
Gaza, Egypt 59/B3
Gaza, Gaza Strip 65/A5
Gaza, Iowa (†51245) 229/B2
Gaza (prov.), Mozambique 118/E4
Gaza, N.H. (†03269) 268/D4
GAZA STRIP 59/B3
Gaza Strip 65/A5
Gazelle, Calif. (96034) 204/C2
Gazelle (pen.), Papua N.G. 86/B2
Gaziantep (prov.), Turkey 63/G4
Gaziantep, Turkey 54/E6
Gaziantep, Turkey 63/G4
Gaziantep, Turkey 59/C2
Gazik, Iran 66/L4
Gazipaşa, Turkey 63/E4
Gbarnga, Liberia 106/C7
Gbarnga, Liberia 102/B4
Gbogo, Nigeria 106/F7
Gcuwa, S. Africa 118/D6
Gdańsk (prov.), Poland 47/D1
Gdańsk, Poland 7/F3
Gdańsk, Poland 47/D1
Gdov, U.S.S.R. 52/C3
Gdynia, Poland 7/F3
Gdynia, Poland 47/D1
Gearhart, Oreg. (97138) 291/C1
Geary (co.), Kansas 232/F3
Geary, New Bruns. 170/D3
Geary, Okla. (73040) 288/K3
Geashill, Ireland 17/G5
Geauga (co.), Ohio 284/H3
Gebe (isl.), Indonesia 85/H6
Gebeit Mine, Sudan 111/G3
Gebo, Wyo. (†82430) 319/D2
Gebze, Turkey 63/C2
Gedaref, Sudan 111/G5
Gedaref, Sudan 59/C7
Gedaref, Sudan 102/F3
Geddes, S. Dak. (57342) 298/M7
Gede (mt.), Indonesia 85/H2
Gedera, Israel 65/B4
Gedi (ruins), Kenya 115/G4
Gedinne, Belgium 27/F9
Gediz, Turkey 63/C3
Gediz (riv.), Turkey 63/C3
Gedo, Ethiopia 111/G6
Gedo (prov.), Somalia 115/H3
Gedser, Denmark 21/F8
Gedser Odde (pt.), Denmark 21/E8
Gedsted, Denmark 21/C4
Geebung, Queensland 88/K2
Geebung, Queensland 95/E2
Geel, Belgium 27/F6
Geelong, Victoria 88/L7
Geelong, Victoria 97/C6
Geelong West, Victoria 88/G7
Geelong West, Victoria 97/C6
Geelvink (Cenderawasih) (bay), Indonesia 85/K6
Geelvink (chan.), W. Australia 88/A5
Geelvink (chan.), W. Australia 92/A5
Geertruidenberg, Netherlands 27/F5
Geesthacht, W. Germany 22/D2
Geetingsville, Ind. (†46041) 227/D4
Geeveston, Tasmania 99/C5
Geff, Ill. (62842) 222/E5
Gê'gyai, China 77/B5
Geh, Iran 59/H4
Geh, Iran 66/L7
Gehua, Papua N.G. 85/C8
Geidam, Nigeria 106/G6
Geiger, Ala. (†35459) 195/B5
Geiger Heights, Wash. (†99219) 310/H3
Geikie (riv.), Sask. 181/M3
Geilo, Norway 18/F6
Geiranger, Norway 18/E5
Geislingen an der Steige, W. Germany 22/C4
Geismar, La. (70734) 238/K3
Geist (res.), Ind. 227/F5
Geistown, Pa. (15904) 294/E5
Geita, Tanzania 115/F4
Gejiu (Kokiu), China 77/F7
Gejiu, China 54/M7
Gela, Italy 34/E6
Gelang, Tanjong (pt.), Malaysia 72/D6
Geldenaken (Jodoigne), Belgium 27/F7
Gelderland (prov.), Netherlands 27/H4
Geldermalsen, Netherlands 27/G5
Geldern, W. Germany 22/B3
Geldrop, Netherlands 27/H6
Geleen, Netherlands 27/H7
Gelendzhik, U.S.S.R. 52/E6
Gelgia (riv.), Switzerland 39/J3
Gelibolu (Gallipoli), Turkey 63/C5
Gelidonya (cape), Turkey 59/B2
Gelidonya (cape), Turkey 63/D4
Gelligaer, Wales 13/A6
Gelnhausen, W. Germany 22/C3
Gelnica, Czech. 41/F2
Gelså (riv.), Denmark 21/C7
Gelsenkirchen, W. Germany 22/B3
Gelsted, Denmark 21/C7
Gelterkinden, Switzerland 39/E2
Gem, Alberta 182/D4
Gem (co.), Idaho 220/B6
Gem, Idaho (†83873) 220/C2
Gem, Ind. (†46140) 227/F5
Gem, Kansas (67734) 232/B2
Gem (lake), Manitoba 179/G4
Gem, W. Va. (26625) 312/E5
Gemas, Malaysia 72/D7
Gembloux-sur-Orneau, Belgium 27/F7
Gemena, Zaire 115/D3
Gemena, Zaire 102/E4
Gemerek, Turkey 63/G3
Gemert, Netherlands 27/H5
Gemlik, Turkey 63/C2
Gemmell, Minn. (†56660) 255/D3
Gemona, Italy 34/D1
Gemsa, Egypt 111/F2
Genç, Turkey 63/J3
Gendringen, Netherlands 27/J5
Gene Autry, Okla. (73436) 288/N6
Genemuiden, Netherlands 27/H3
General Acha, Argentina 143/C4
General Alvear, Buenos Aires, Argentina 143/F7
General Alvear, Mendoza, Argentina 143/C3
General Arenales, Argentina 143/F7
General Artigas, Paraguay 144/D5
General Belgrano, Argentina 143/G7
General Bravo, Mexico 150/K4
General Campos, Argentina 143/G5
General Cepeda, Mexico 150/J4
General Conesa, Argentina 143/C5
General Elizardo Aquino, Paraguay 144/D4
General Enrique Martínez, Uruguay 145/F4
General Eugenio A. Garay, Paraguay 144/A2
General Galarza, Argentina 143/C6
General Grant Grove Section (King's Canyon), Calif. 204/G7
General Güemes, Argentina 143/D1
General Guido, Argentina 143/E4
General José de San Martín, Argentina 143/E2
General Juan Madariaga, Argentina 143/E4
General Lagos, Chile 138/B1
General La Madrid, Argentina 143/D4
General Las Heras, Argentina 143/G7
General Lavalle, Argentina 143/E4
General Manuel Belgrano, Cerro (mt.), Argentina 143/C2
General Mitchell Field, Wis. 317/M2
General O'Brien, Argentina 143/F7
General Paz, Argentina 143/E2
General Paz, Argentina 143/H7
General Paz (lake), Chile 138/E5
General Pico, Argentina 143/D4
General Ramírez, Argentina 143/F6
General Roca, Argentina 143/C4
General Saavedra, Bolivia 136/D5
General San Martín, Argentina 143/D4
General San Martín, Argentina 143/G4
General Santos, Philippines 82/E7
General Terán, Mexico 150/K4
General Tinio, Philippines 82/C3
General-Toshevo, Bulgaria 45/H4
General Viamonte, Argentina 143/F7
General Villegas, Argentina 143/D4
Generoso (mt.), Switzerland 39/H5
Genesee, Idaho (83832) 220/B3
Genesee (co.), Mich. 250/F5
Genesee (co.), N.Y. 276/D4
Genesee (riv.), N.Y. 276/E6
Genesee, Pa. (16923) 294/G2
Genesee, Wis. (†53127) 317/J2
Genesee Depot, Wis. (53127) 317/J2
Geneseo, Ill. (61254) 222/C2
Geneseo, Kansas (67444) 232/D3
Geneseo, N.Y. (14454) 276/E5
Geneseo, N. Dak. (58037) 282/R7
Geneva (lake) 7/E4
Geneva (co.), Ala. 195/G8
Geneva, Ala. (36340) 195/G8
Geneva, Fla. (32732) 212/E3
Geneva (lake), France 28/G4
Geneva, Georgia (31810) 217/C5
Geneva, Idaho (83238) 220/G7
Geneva, Ill. (60134) 222/E2
Geneva, Ind. (46740) 227/H3
Geneva, Iowa (50633) 229/G3
Geneva, Ky. (†42406) 237/F5
Geneva, Minn. (56035) 255/E7
Geneva, Nebr. (68361) 264/G4
Geneva, N.Y. (14456) 276/G5
Geneva, Ohio (44041) 284/J2
Geneva, Pa. (16316) 294/B2
Geneva (Genève) (canton), Switzerland 39/B4
Geneva (Genève), Switzerland 39/B4
Geneva, Switzerland 7/E4
Geneva (lake), Switzerland 39/C4
Geneva, Texas (75947) 303/L6
Geneva (lake), Wis. 317/K10
Geneva-on-the-Lake, Ohio (44043) 284/J2
Genezin, Turkey 63/F3
Genichesk, U.S.S.R. 52/E5
Genil (riv.), Spain 33/D4
Genk, Belgium 27/H7
Gennargentu, Monti del (mt.), Italy 34/B5
Gennep, Netherlands 27/H5
Gennevilliers, France 28/B1
Genoa, Ark. (71840) 202/C7
Genoa, Colo. (80818) 208/N4
Genoa, Ill. (60135) 222/E1
Genoa (prov.), Italy 34/B2
Genoa, Italy 7/E4
Genoa, Italy 34/B2
Genoa (gulf), Italy 34/B2
Genoa, Nebr. (68640) 264/G3
Genoa, Nev. (89411) 266/B4
Genoa, N.Y. (13071) 276/G5
Genoa, Ohio (43430) 284/D2
Genoa, W. Va. (25517) 312/A6
Genoa, Wis. (54632) 317/D8
Genoa City, Wis. (53128) 317/K11
Genola, Minn. (†56364) 255/D5
Genola, Utah (†84655) 304/C4
Genova (Genoa), Italy 34/B2
Genovesa (isl.), Ecuador 128/C9
Gent (Ghent), Belgium 27/D6
Genthin, E. Germany 22/E2
Gentilly, France 28/B2
Gentilly, Minn. (†56716) 255/B3
Genting, Indonesia 85/D5
Gentofte, Denmark 21/F6
Gentry, Ark. (72734) 202/A1
Gentry (co.), Mo. 261/D2
Gentry, Mo. (64453) 261/D2
Gentryville, Ind. (47537) 227/C8
Gentryville, Mo. (†64402) 261/D2
Genzano di Roma, Italy 34/F7
Geographe (chan.), W. Australia 88/A4
Geographe (bay), W. Australia 92/A6
Geographe (chan.), W. Australia 92/A4
Geographical Center of North America, N. Dak. 282/K3
Geographical Center of U.S., S. Dak. 298/B4
George (isl.), 143/E7
George (lake), Fla. 212/E2
George, Iowa (51237) 229/B2
George (isl.), Manitoba 179/E2
George (lake), Manitoba 179/G4
George (co.), Miss. 256/G9
George (isl.), Newf. 166/C3
George (lake), N.S. Wales 97/E4
George (lake), N.Y. 276/N4
George (sound), N. Zealand 100/A6
George (lake), N. Dak. 282/L6
George (cape), Nova Scotia 168/G3
George (lake), Nova Scotia 168/B5
George (riv.), Que. 162/K4
George (riv.), Que. 146/M4
George (riv.), Québec 174/F2
George, S. Africa 118/C6
George (lake), Uganda 115/F4
George, Wash. (98824) 310/F3
George A.F.B., Calif. 204/H9
George B. Stevenson (dam), Pa. 294/G3
George Land (isl.), U.S.S.R. 4/B7
George Land (isl.), U.S.S.R. 48/E1
George Rogers Clark Nat'l Hist. Park, Ind. 227/B7
Georges (isls.), Maine 243/E8
Georges (riv.), N. S. Wales 88/K4
Georges (riv.), N.S. Wales 97/H4
Georges Brook, Newf. 166/D2
George's Cove, Newf. 166/C3
Georges Fork, Va. (†24228) 307/C6
Georges Mills, N.H. (03751) 268/C5
Georgetown, Ark. (72054) 202/G3
Georgetown, Calif. (95634) 204/E5
George Town (cap.), Cayman Is. 156/B3
Georgetown, Colo. (80444) 208/H3
Georgetown, Conn. (06829) 210/B4
Georgetown, Del. (19947) 245/S6
Georgetown, D.C. (20007) 245/E5
Georgetown, Fla. (32039) 212/E2
Georgetown, Gambia 106/A6
Georgetown, Georgia (31754) 217/B7
Georgetown (cap.), Guyana 2/G5
Georgetown (cap.), Guyana 131/C2
Georgetown (cap.), Guyana 120/D2
Georgetown, Idaho (83239) 220/G7
Georgetown, Ill. (61846) 222/F4
Georgetown, Ind. (47122) 227/F8
Georgetown, Ky. (40324) 237/M4
Georgetown, La. (71432) 238/F3
Georgetown, Maine (04548) 243/D8
Georgetown○, Maine (04548) 243/D8
George Town (Pinang), Malaysia 72/C6
George Town, Malaysia 54/M9
Georgetown, Mass. (01833) 249/L2
Georgetown○, Mass. (01833) 249/L2
Georgetown, Minn. (56546) 255/B3
Georgetown, Miss. (39078) 256/D7
Georgetown (lake), Mont. 262/C4
Georgetown, Ohio (45121) 284/C8
Georgetown, Pa. (15043) 294/A4
Georgetown, Pr. Edward I. 168/F2
Georgetown, Queensland 88/G3
Georgetown, Queensland 95/B3
Georgetown, St. Vin. & Grens. 161/A8
Georgetown, St. Vin. & Grens. 156/G4
Georgetown (co.), S.C. 296/J5
Georgetown, S.C. 188/L4
Georgetown, S.C. (29440) 296/J5
George Town, Tasmania 99/C3
George Town, Tasmania 88/H8
Georgetown, Tenn. (37336) 237/L10
Georgetown, Texas (78626) 303/G7
George V Coast (reg.) 5/C8
Georgeville, Minn. (†56312) 255/C5
Georgeville, Nova Scotia 168/F3
George Washington Carver Nat'l Mon., Mo. 261/D9
George Washington Birthplace Nat'l Mon., Va. 307/P4
George West, Texas (78022) 303/F9
Georgia 188/K4
GEORGIA 217
Georgia (str.), Br. Col. 184/J3
Georgia (state), U.S. 146/K6
Georgia○, Vt. (†05478) 268/A2
Georgia (str.), Wash. 310/B2
Georgia Center, Vt. (†05478) 268/A2
Georgian (bay), Ont. 162/H6
Georgian (bay), Ontario 177/D2
Georgian (bay), Ontario 175/D3
Georgiana, Ala. (36033) 195/E7
Georgian Bay Is. Nat'l Park, Ontario 177/C2D3
Georgian S.S.R., U.S.S.R. 7/J4
Georgian S.S.R., U.S.S.R. 52/F6
Georgian S.S.R., U.S.S.R. 48/D5
Georgiaville, R.I. (†02917) 249/H5
Georgina (riv.), North. Terr. 93/E6
Georgina (isl.), Ontario 177/E3
Georgina (riv.), Queensland 88/F4
Georgina (riv.), Queensland 95/A4
Georgiu-Dezh, U.S.S.R. 52/E4
Georgsmarienhütte, W. Germany 22/B2
Gera (dist.), E. Germany 22/D3
Gera, E. Germany 22/E3
Geraardsbergen, Belgium 27/D7
Gerald, Mo. (63037) 261/K6
Gerald, Sask. 181/K5
Geral de Goiás, Serra (range), Brazil 132/E6
Geraldine, Ala. (35974) 195/G2
Geraldine, Mont. (59446) 262/F3
Geraldine, N. Zealand 100/C6
Geraldton, Australia 87/B8
Geraldton, Ont. 162/H6
Geraldton, Ontario 177/H5
Geraldton, Ontario 175/C3
Geraldton, W. Australia 88/A5
Geraldton, W. Australia 92/A5
Gerar (dry riv.), Israel 65/B5
Gerber, Calif. (96035) 204/C3
Gerber (res.), Oreg. 291/F5
Gercüş, Turkey 63/J4
Gerdine (mt.), Alaska 196/A1
Gerede, Turkey 63/E2
Gereshk, Afghanistan 59/H3
Gereshk, Afghanistan 68/A2
Geretsried, W. Germany 22/D5
Gérgal, Spain 33/E4
Gerger, Turkey 63/H3
Gerik, Malaysia 72/D6
Gering, Nebr. (69341) 264/A3
Gerlach, Nev. (89412) 266/B2
Gerlachovka (mt.), Czech. 41/E2
Gerlogubi, Ethiopia 111/H6
Germania, Miss. (†39162) 256/C5
Germania, Pa. (16922) 294/G2
Germania, Wis. (†54968) 317/H8
Germano, Ohio (†43825) 284/J5
Germansen (lake), Br. Col. 184/E2
Germansen Landing, Br. Col. 184/E2
Germanton, N.C. (27019) 281/J2
Germantown, Ill. (62245) 222/D5
Germantown, Ky. (41044) 237/O3
Germantown, Md. (20767) 245/J4
Germantown, New Bruns. 170/F3
Germantown, N.Y. (12526) 276/N6
Germantown, Ohio (45327) 284/B6
Germantown, Tenn. (38138) 237/B10
Germantown, Wis. (53022) 317/K1
German Valley, Ill. (61039) 222/D1
Germany (East) 2/K3
Germany (West) 2/K3
GERMANY, EAST 22/E2
GERMANY, WEST 22
Germencik, Turkey 63/B4
Germersheim, W. Germany 22/C4
Germfask, Mich. (49836) 250/C2
Germiston, S. Africa 102/E7
Germiston, S. Africa 118/H6
Gerofit, Israel 65/D5
Gerolstein, W. Germany 22/B3
Gerona (prov.), Spain 33/H1
Gerona, Spain 33/H2
Geronimo, Ariz. (†85536) 198/F5
Geronimo, Okla. (73543) 288/K6
Gerpinnes, Belgium 27/F8
Gerpir (cape), Iceland 21/D1
Gerra, Switzerland 39/G4
Gerrardstown, W. Va. (25420) 312/K4
Gerringong, N.S. Wales 97/F4
Gerrish, N.H. (†03301) 268/D5
Gerry, N.Y. (14740) 276/B6
Gers (dept.), France 28/D6
Gers (riv.), France 28/D6
Gersau, Switzerland 39/G2
Gersfeld, W. Germany 22/C3
Gerster, Mo. (†64776) 261/E7
Gerty, Okla. (†74531) 288/O5
Gervais, Oreg. (97026) 291/A3
Gervasio, Uruguay 145/F4
Gêrzê, China 77/B5
Gerze, Turkey 63/F2
Geser, Indonesia 85/J6
Gesher, Israel 65/E2
Gesher Haziv, Israel 65/C1
Gessie, Ind. (†47974) 227/C4
Getafe, Spain 33/F4
Getaway, Ohio (†45675) 284/F9
Gettysburg, Ohio (45328) 284/A5
Gettysburg, Pa. (17325) 294/H6
Gettysburg, S. Dak. (57442) 298/K3
Gettysburg Nat'l Mil. Park, Pa. 294/H6
Getulio Vargas, Uruguay 145/F3
Getz Ice Shelf 5/B13
Geuda Springs, Kansas (67051) 232/E4
Geurie, N.S. Wales 97/E3
Gevar'am, Israel 65/B4
Gevaş, Turkey 63/K3
Gevgelija, Yugoslavia 45/F5
Gex, France 28/G4
Geyser, Mont. (59447) 262/F3
Geyserville, Calif. (95441) 204/B5
Geyve, Turkey 63/D2
Gezira, El (reg.), Sudan 111/F5
Ghabaghib, Syria 63/H5
Ghadames, Libya 102/D2
Ghadames, Libya 111/A2
Ghaghra (riv.), India 68/E3
Ghaida, P.D.R. Yemen 59/F6
Ghalla, Wadi el (dry riv.), Sudan 111/E5
Ghana 2/J5
Ghana 102/B4
GHANA 106/D7
Ghanzi, Botswana 118/C4
Ghard Abu Muharik (des.), Egypt 111/J4
Ghardaïa, Algeria 106/E2
Ghardaïa, Algeria 102/C1
Gharian, Libya 102/D1
Gharian, Libya 111/B1
Gharib, Jebel (mt.), Egypt 59/B4
Ghat, Libya 102/D2
Ghat, Libya 111/B3
Ghat Kopar, India 68/B7
Ghazaouet, Algeria 106/D2
Ghaziabad, India 68/D3
Ghazipur, India 68/E3
Ghazni, Afghanistan 68/B2
Ghazni, Afghanistan 59/J3
Ghea (riv.), India 68/F1
Gheen, Minn. (55740) 255/F3
Gheens, La. (70355) 238/K7
Ghemines, Libya 111/C1

Gramercy 375

Gobabis, Namibia 118/B4
Gobabis, Namibia 102/D7
Gobernador Crespo, Argentina 143/F5
Gobernador Gregores, Argentina 143/C6
Gobernador Mansilla, Argentina 143/G6
Gobi (des.) 54/M5
Gobi (des.), China 77/G3
Gobi (des.), Mongolia 77/G3
Goble, Oreg. (97048) 291/E1
Gobler, Mo. (63849) 261/N10
Gobles, Mich. (49055) 250/D6
Gobo, Japan 81/G7
Gobwen, Somalia 115/H4
Goch, W. Germany 22/B3
Go Cong, Vietnam 72/E5
Godahl, Minn. (†56081) 255/D6
Godalming, England 13/G8
Godalming, England 10/F5
Godavari (riv.), India 54/J8
Godavari (riv.), India 68/D5
Godbout, Québec 174/D3
Godbout, Québec 172/B1
Goddard, Kansas (67052) 232/E4
Godech, Bulgaria 45/F4
Goderich, Ontario 177/C4
Godfrey, Georgia (30650) 217/F4
Godfrey, Ill. (62035) 222/A2
Godhavn, Greenl. 4/C12
Godhavn, Greenland 146/N3
Godhra, India 68/C4
Gödöllő, Hungary 41/E3
Godoy Cruz, Argentina 143/C3
Gods (lake), Man. 162/G5
Gods (lake), Manitoba 179/K3
Gods (riv.), Man. 162/G4
Gods (riv.), Manitoba 179/K3
Gods Mercy (bay), N.W. Terrs. 187/K3
Gods River, Manitoba 179/K3
Godthåb (Nûk) (cap.), Greenl. 4/C12
Godthåb (Nûk) (cap.), Greenland 2/G2
Godthåb (Nûk) (cap.), Greenland 146/N3
Godwin, N.C. (28344) 281/M4
Godwin Austen (K2) (mt.), Pakistan 68/D1
Godwinsville, Georgia (†31023) 217/F6
Goehner, Nebr. (68364) 264/G4
Goéland (lake), Québec 174/B3
Goélands (lake), Québec 174/E1
Goeree (isl.), Netherlands 27/D5
Goes, Netherlands 27/D6
Goessel, Kansas (67053) 232/E3
Goetzville, Mich. (49736) 250/E2
Goff, Kansas (66428) 232/G2
Goff (creek), Okla. 288/C1
Goffstown◯, N.H. (03045) 268/D5
Gogama, Ontario 175/D3
Gogama, Ontario 177/J5
Gogebic (co.), Mich. 250/F2
Gogebic (lake), Mich. 250/F2
Göggingen, W. Germany 22/D4
Gogrial, Sudan 111/E6
Goi, Ben (bay), Vietnam 72/F4
Goiana, Brazil 132/H4
Goiandira, Brazil 132/E7
Goiânia, Brazil 132/D7
Goiânia, Brazil 120/D4
Goiás (state), Brazil 132/D6
Goiás, Brazil 132/D6
Goiás, Brazil 120/D4
Goil, Loch (lake), Scotland 15/A1
Goin, Tenn. (†37825) 237/O8
Goirle, Netherlands 27/G5
Góis, Portugal 33/B2
Gojjam (prov.), Ethiopia 111/G5
Gökçe, Turkey 63/B2
Gökçeada (isl.), Turkey 59/A1
Gökçeada (isl.), Turkey 63/A2
Gökırmak (riv.), Turkey 63/F2
Göksu (riv.), Turkey 63/E4
Göksun, Turkey 63/G3
Gokteik, Burma 72/C2
Gol, Norway 18/F6
Gola (isl.), Ireland 17/E1
Golan Heights (reg.), West Bank 65/D1
Gölbaşı, Turkey 63/G4
Golborne, England 13/G2
Gol'chikha, U.S.S.R. 48/J2
Golconda, Ill. (62938) 222/E6
Golconda (ruins), India 68/D5
Golconda, Nev. (89414) 266/D2
Gölcük, Turkey 63/C2
Golčův Jeníkov, Czech. 41/C2
Gold (riv.), Nova Scotia 168/D4
Goldap, Poland 47/F1
Gold Bar, Wash. (98251) 310/D3
Gold Beach, Oreg. (97444) 291/C5
Goldbond, Va. (24094) 307/G6
Goldboro, Nova Scotia 168/G3
Gold Bridge, Br. Col. 184/F5
Gold Coast (reg.), Ghana 106/D8
Gold Coast, Queensland 95/E6
Gold Coast, Queensland 88/J5
Goldcreek, Mont. (59733) 262/D4
Golden, Br. Col. 184/J4
Golden, Colo. (80401) 208/J3
Golden, Idaho (†83530) 220/C4
Golden, Ill. g)62339) 222/B3
Golden, Ireland 17/F7
Golden, Miss. (38847) 256/H2
Golden, Mo. (65658) 261/E9
Golden, N. Mex. (†87047) 274/C3
Golden (bay), N. Zealand 100/D4
Golden, Okla. (74737) 288/S6
Golden (lake), Ontario 177/G2
Golden (lake), Wis. 317/H1
Golden Beach, Fla. (†33160) 212/C4
Golden City, Mo. (64748) 261/D8
Goldendale, Wash. (98620) 310/E5
Golden Ears Prov. Park, Br. Col. 184/L2
Golden Gate (chan.), Calif. 188/B3
Golden Gate (chan.), Calif. 204/H2
Golden Gate, Fla. (33999) 212/E5
Golden Gate, Ill. (62843) 222/E5
Golden Gate (range), Nev. 266/F5
Golden Gate Nat'l Rec. Area, Calif. 204/H2
Golden Grove, Jamaica 158/K6
Golden Hill, Md. (†21622) 245/O7
Golden Lake, Ontario 177/G2
Golden Meadow, La. (70357) 238/K8
Golden Prairie, Sask. 181/B5
Golden Rock, St. Chris.-Nevis 161/C10
Golden's Bridge, N.Y. (10526) 276/N8
Golden Shores, Ariz. (†86436) 198/A4
Golden Spike Nat'l Hist. Site, Utah 304/B2
Golden Vale (plain), Ireland 17/E7
Golden Valley, Minn. (55427) 255/G5
Golden Valley (co.), Mont. 262/G4
Golden Valley (co.), N. Dak. 282/C5
Goldenvalley, N. Dak. (58541) 282/F5
Golden Valley, Ontario 177/E2
Goldfield, Iowa (50542) 229/F3
Goldfield, Nev. 188/C3
Goldfield, Nev. (89013) 266/D5
Gold Hill, Ala. (†36879) 195/G5
Gold Hill, Nev. (†89440) 266/B3
Gold Hill, N.C. (28071) 281/J3
Gold Hill, Oreg. (97525) 291/D5
Goldonna, La. (71031) 238/D2
Gold Point, Nev. (†89013) 266/D5
Gold River, Br. Col. 184/D5
Goldsberry, Mo. (†63539) 261/G3
Goldsboro, Md. (21636) 245/P4
Goldsboro, N.C. 188/L3
Goldsboro, N.C. (27530) 281/O4
Goldsboro (Etters), Pa. (17319) 294/J5
Goldsby, Okla. (†73093) 288/L4
Goldsmith, Ind. (46045) 227/E4
Goldsmith, Texas (79741) 303/B5
Goldston, N.C. (27252) 281/L3
Goldstone (mt.), Idaho 220/E4
Goldsworthy, W. Australia 88/C4
Goldsworthy, W. Australia 92/B3
Goldthwaite, Texas (76844) 303/F6
Goldvein, Va. (22720) 307/N4
Goldville, Ala. (†35010) 195/G4
Göle, Turkey 63/K2
Goleniów, Poland 47/B2
Goleta, Calif. (93117) 204/F9
Golf, Fla. (†33444) 212/F5
Golf, Ill. (60029) 222/B5
Golfito, C. Rica 154/F6
Golf Manor, Ohio (†45201) 284/C9
Golfo Santa Clara, Mexico 150/B1
Gölhisar, Turkey 63/C4
Goliad (co.), Texas 303/G9
Goliad, Texas (77963) 303/G9
Gölköy, Turkey 63/G2
Golling an der Salzach, Austria 41/B3
Gölmarmara, Turkey 63/C3
Golmud (Golmo), China 77/D4
Golmud, China 54/L6
Golo (riv.), France 28/B6
Golo (isl.), Philippines 82/C4
Golovin, Alaska (99762) 196/F2
Golpayegan, Iran 59/F3
Golpayegan, Iran 66/G4
Gölpazarı, Turkey 63/D2
Golshan (Tabas), Iran 66/K4
Golspie, Scotland 15/E3
Goltry, Okla. (73739) 288/K1
Golts, Md. (21637) 245/P3
Golub-Dobrzyn, Poland 47/D2
Golungo Alto, Angola 115/B5
Golva, N. Dak. (58632) 282/C6
Goma, Zaire 115/E4
Goma, Zaire 102/E5
Gombari, Zaire 115/E3
Gombe, Nigeria 106/G6
Gomel', U.S.S.R. 7/H3
Gomel', U.S.S.R. 48/D4
Gomel', U.S.S.R. 52/D4
Gomer, Ohio (45809) 284/B4
Gomera (isl.), Spain 106/A3
Gomera (isl.), Spain 33/B5
Gometra (isl.), Scotland 15/B4
Gomez, Fla. (†33455) 212/F4
Gómez Farías, Mexico 150/F2
Gómez Palacio, Mexico 150/G4
Gomishan, Iran 66/J2
Goms (valley), Switzerland 39/F4
Gona, Papua N.G. 85/C7
Gonabad, Iran 59/G3
Gonabad, Iran 66/L3
Gonaïves, Haiti 158/B5
Gonaïves, Haiti 156/D3
Gonâve (gulf), Haiti 158/B5
Gonâve (isl.), Haiti 158/B6
Gonâve (isl.), Haiti 156/D3
Gonbad-e Kavus, Iran 66/J2
Gonbadli, Iran 66/M2
Gönc, Hungary 41/F2
Gonda, India 68/E3
Gondal, India 68/C4
Gondar, Ethiopia 102/F3
Gondar, Ethiopia 59/C7
Gondar, Ethiopia 111/G5
Gondia, India 68/E4
Gondola Point, New Bruns. 170/D3
Gondomar, Portugal 33/B2
Gönen, Turkey 63/B2
Gonggar, China 77/D6
Gongga Shan (mt.), China 77/F6
Gonghe, China 77/E4
Gongliu, China 77/B3
Gongola (state), Nigeria 106/G7
Gongola (riv.), Nigeria 106/G6
Gongolgan, N.S. Wales 97/D2
Góngora (mt.), C. Rica 154/E5
Goñi, Uruguay 145/C4
Gonjo, China 77/E5
Gonvick, Minn. (56644) 255/C3
Gonzaga, Philippines 82/D1
Gonzales, Calif. (93926) 204/D7
Gonzales, La. (70737) 238/L2
Gonzales (co.), Texas 303/G8
Gonzales, Texas (78629) 303/G8
Gonzalez, Fla. (32560) 212/B6
González, Mexico 150/K5
González, Riacho (riv.), Paraguay 144/C3
Goobies, Newf. 166/D2
Goochland (co.), Va. 307/N5
Goochland, Va. (23063) 307/N5
Goodbee, La. (†70433) 238/K6
Goode (mt.), Alaska 196/C1
Goode, Va. (24556) 307/K6
Goodell, Iowa (50439) 229/F3
Goodenough (cape) 5/C7
Gooderham, Ontario 177/F3
Goodeve, Sask. 181/H4
Goodfare, Alberta 182/A2
Goodfellow A.F.B., Texas 303/D6
Goodfield, Ill. (61742) 222/D3
Good Harbor (bay), Mich. 250/D3
Good Hart, Mich. (49737) 250/D3
Good Hope, Ala. (†36024) 195/E2
Goodhope (bay), Alaska 196/F1
Good Hope, Georgia (30641) 217/E3
Good Hope, Ill. (61438) 222/C3
Good Hope, La. (†70079) 238/N3
Good Hope, Miss. (†39094) 256/E5
Good Hope, Ohio (43121) 284/D7
Good Hope (cape), S. Africa 102/D8
Good Hope (cape), S. Africa 2/K7
Good Hope (cape), S. Africa 118/E7
Goodhue (co.), Minn. 255/F6
Goodhue, Minn. (55027) 255/F6
Gooding (co.), Idaho 220/D6
Gooding, Idaho (83330) 220/D7
Goodland, Fla. (33933) 212/E6
Goodland, Ind. (47948) 227/C3
Goodland, Kansas (67735) 232/A2
Goodland, Minn. (55742) 255/E3
Goodlands, Manitoba 179/B5
Goodlettsville, Tenn. (37072) 237/H8
Goodlow, Br. Col. 184/G2
Good Luck, Md. (†20715) 245/G4
Goodman, Miss. (39079) 256/E5
Goodman, Mo. (63843) 261/C9
Goodman, Wis. (54125) 317/K4
Goodnews Bay, Alaska (99589) 196/F3
Goodnight, Texas (†79226) 303/C3
Goodnoe Hills, Wash. (†99356) 310/E5
Goodooga, N.S. Wales 97/D1
Good Pine, La. (†71342) 238/F3
Goodrich, Colo. (†80653) 208/M2
Goodrich, Mich. (48438) 250/F6
Goodrich, N. Dak. (58444) 282/K5
Goodrich, Texas (77335) 303/K7
Goodrich, Wis. (†54451) 317/G5
Goodridge, Alberta 182/E2
Goodridge, Minn. (56725) 255/C2
Goodsoil, Sask. 181/L4
Goodson, Mo. (65659) 261/F7
Good Spirit (lake), Sask. 181/J4
Goodspirit Lake Prov. Park, Sask. 181/J4
Goodspring, Tenn. (38460) 237/G10
Goodsprings, Ala. (35560) 195/D3
Goodsprings, Nev. (89019) 266/F7
Good Thunder, Minn. (56037) 255/D6
Goodview, Minn. (55027) 255/G6
Goodwater, Ala. (35072) 195/F4
Goodwater, Okla. (†74740) 288/S7
Goodwater, Sask. 181/H6
Goodway, Ala. (36449) 195/D8
Goodwell, Okla. (73939) 288/C1
Goodwin, Ark. (72340) 202/J4
Goodwin, S. Dak. (57238) 298/R4
Goodwins Mills, Maine (†04005) 243/B8
Goodwood, Ontario 177/E3
Goodwood, S. Africa 118/F6
Goodyear, Ariz. (85323) 198/C5
Gooik, Belgium 27/E7
Goole, England 10/F4
Goole, England 13/G4
Goolgowi, N.S. Wales 97/C3
Gooloogong, N.S. Wales 97/E3
Goomalling, W. Australia 88/B6
Goomalling, W. Australia 92/B1
Goombalie, N.S. Wales 97/C1
Goondiwindi, Queensland 88/H5
Goondiwindi, Queensland 95/D6
Goor, Netherlands 27/K4
Goose (lake) 188/B2
Goose (lake), Calif. 204/E1
Goose (creek), Idaho 220/E7
Goose (riv.), Newf. 166/B3
Goose (riv.), N. Dak. 282/P4
Goose (isl.), Nova Scotia 168/F4
Goose (isl.), Nova Scotia 168/G3
Goose (lake), Oreg. 291/G5
Goose (creek), Va. 307/J6
Goose (creek), Va. 307/N3
Goose Airport P.O. (Goose Bay), Newf. 162/K5
Goose Bay, Newf. 162/K5
Goose Bay, Newf. 146/M4
Goose Bay-Happy Valley, Newf. 166/B3
Gooseberry (creek), Wyo. 319/D1
Gooseberry Cove, Newf. 166/C2
Goose Cove, Newf. 166/C2
Goose Cove, Newf. 166/C3
Goose Cove, Nova Scotia 168/H2
Goose Creek (mts.), Idaho 220/E7
Goose Creek, Ky. (†40222) 237/L1
Goose Creek, S.C. (29445) 296/H6
Goose Lake, Iowa (52750) 229/N5
Gooseprairie, Wash. (†98937) 310/D4
Goose Rock, Ky. (40944) 237/O6
Goose Rocks Beach, Maine (†04046) 243/C9
Göppingen, W. Germany 22/C4
Góra, Poland 47/C3
Gorakhpur, India 68/E3
Gorchs, Argentina 143/G7
Gorda (pt.), Cuba 158/C2
Gorda (bank), Honduras 154/F3
Gorda (cay), Honduras 154/F3
Gorda (pt.), Nicaragua 154/F5
Gorda (pt.), Panama 154/H6
Gördes, Turkey 63/C3
Gordevio, Switzerland 39/G4
Gørding, Denmark 21/B7
Gordo, Ala. (35466) 195/C4
Gordola, Switzerland 39/G4
Gordon, Ala. (36343) 195/H8
Gordon (lake), Alberta 182/E1
Gordon (riv.), Br. Col. 184/H3
Gordon (isl.), Chile 138/E11
Gordon (co.), Georgia 217/C2
Gordon, Georgia (31031) 217/F5
Gordon, Kansas (†67010) 232/F4
Gordon, Nebr. (69343) 264/B2
Gordon, Ohio (45329) 284/B6
Gordon, Scotland 15/F5
Gordon, Tasmania 99/G5
Gordon (lake), Tasmania 99/C4
Gordon (riv.), Tasmania 99/B4
Gordon, Texas (76543) 303/F5
Gordon, W. Va. (25093) 312/C7
Gordon, Wis. (54838) 317/C3
Gordondale, Alberta 182/A2
Gordon Downs, W. Australia 92/E2
Gordon's Bay, S. Africa 118/F7
Gordonsburg, Tenn. (†38462) 237/F9
Gordonsville, Ala. (†36040) 195/E6
Gordonsville, Minn. (†56036) 255/E7
Gordonsville, Tenn. (38563) 237/K8
Gordonsville, Va. (22942) 307/M4
Gordonvale, Queensland 88/H3
Gordonvale, Queensland 95/C3
Gordonville, Mo. (63752) 261/N8
Gore (pt.), Alaska 196/C2
Goré, Chad 111/C6
Gore (range), Colo. 208/G3
Gore, Ethiopia 111/G6
Gore, Ethiopia 102/F4
Gore, N. Zealand 100/B7
Gore, Ohio (†43188) 284/F6
Gore, Okla. (74435) 288/R3
Gore (mt.), Vt. 268/D2
Gore, Va. (22637) 307/M2
Gore Bay, Ontario 177/B2
Gorebridge, Scotland 10/C1
Gorebridge, Scotland 15/D2
Goree, Texas (76363) 303/E4
Goregaon, India 68/B7
Görele, Turkey 63/H2
Gore Springs, Miss. (38929) 256/E3
Goreville, Ill. (62939) 222/E6
Gorey, Chan. Is. 13/F8
Gorey, Ireland 17/J6
Gorey, Ireland 10/C4
Gorgan, Iran 54/G6
Gorgan, Iran 59/F2
Gorgan (Gurgan), Iran 66/J2
Gorgan (riv.), Iran 66/J2
Gorgan (riv.), Iran 59/F2
Gorgas, Ala. (†35580) 195/D3
Gorgol (reg.), Mauritania 106/B5
Gorgona (isl.), Colombia 126/A6
Gorgona (isl.), Italy 34/B3
Gorham, Ill. (62940) 222/D6
Gorham, Kansas (67640) 232/D3
Gorham, Maine (04038) 243/C8
Gorham◯, Maine (04038) 243/C8
Gorham, N.H. (03581) 268/E3
Gorham◯, N.H. (03581) 268/E3
Gorham, N.Y. (14461) 276/F5
Gorham, N. Dak. (†58627) 282/D5
Gori, U.S.S.R. 52/F6
Gorin, Mo. (63543) 261/H2
Gorinchem, Netherlands 27/G5
Gorizia (prov.), Italy 34/D2
Gorizia, Italy 34/D2
Gorki, U.S.S.R. 52/D4
Gor'kiy, U.S.S.R. 2/M3
Gor'kiy, U.S.S.R. 7/J3
Gor'kiy, U.S.S.R. 48/E4
Gor'kiy, U.S.S.R. 52/F3
Gørlev, Denmark 21/E7
Gorlice, Poland 47/E4
Görlitz, E. Germany 22/F3
Görlitz, E. Germany 7/F3
Gorlitz, Sask. 181/J4
Gorlovka, U.S.S.R. 7/H4
Gorlovka, U.S.S.R. 52/E5
Gorman, Calif. (93243) 204/G9
Gorman, Tenn. (†37101) 237/F8
Gorman, Texas (76454) 303/F5
Gormania, W. Va. (26720) 312/H4
Gormanston, Ireland 17/J4
Gormanston, Tasmania 99/B4
Gorna Oryakhovitsa, Bulgaria 45/G4
Gornji Milanovac, Yugoslavia 45/D3
Gornji Vakuf, Yugoslavia 45/C4
Gorno-Altay Aut. Obl., U.S.S.R. 48/J4
Gorno-Altaysk, U.S.S.R. 48/J4
Gorno-Badakhshan Aut. Obl., U.S.S.R. 48/H6
Gornyak, U.S.S.R. 48/J4
Gorodets, U.S.S.R. 52/F3
Gorodok, U.S.S.R. 52/D3
Goroka, Papua N.G. 85/B7
Goroke, Victoria 97/A5
Gorong (isl.), Indonesia 85/J6
Gorong (isls.), Indonesia 85/J6
Gorongosa Nat'l Park, Mozambique 118/E3
Gorontalo, Indonesia 85/G5
Gorrahei, Ethiopia 111/H6
Gorredijk, Netherlands 27/J2
Gorrie, Ontario 177/C4
Gorst, Wash. (98337) 310/C3
Gort, Ireland 10/B4
Gort, Ireland 17/D5
Gortin, N. Ireland 17/G2
Gorum, La. (71434) 238/E4
Gorumna (isl.), Ireland 17/B5
Goryn' (riv.), U.S.S.R. 52/C4
Gorzów (prov.), Poland 47/B2
Gorzów Wielkopolski, Poland 47/B2
Gorzów Wielkopolski, Poland 7/F3
Göschenen, Switzerland 39/G3
Gose, Japan 81/J8
Gosen, Japan 81/J5
Goshen, Ala. (36035) 195/F7
Goshen, Ark. (72735) 202/C1
Goshen, Calif. (93227) 204/F7
Goshen◯, Conn. (06756) 210/C1
Goshen (pt.), Conn. 210/G3
Goshen, Ind. (46526) 227/F1
Goshen, Ky. (40026) 237/K4
Goshen◯, Mass. (01032) 249/C3
Goshen◯, N.H. (03752) 268/C5
Goshen, N.J. (08218) 273/D5
Goshen, N.Y. (10924) 276/M8
Goshen, Nova Scotia 168/G3
Goshen, Ohio (45122) 284/B7
Goshen, Oreg. (97401) 291/D4
Goshen, Utah (84633) 304/C4
Goshen, Va. (24439) 307/K5
Goshen (co.), Wyo. 319/H4
Goshen Springs, Miss. (†39042) 256/E6
Goshogawara, Japan 81/K3
Goshute (mts.), Nev. 266/G2
Goshute Ind. Res., Nev. 266/G3
Goshute Ind. Res., Utah 304/A4
Gosier, Guadeloupe 161/B6
Goslar, W. Germany 22/D3
Gosnell, Ark. (†72315) 202/K2
Gosper (co.), Nebr. 264/E4
Gospić, Yugoslavia 45/B3
Gosport, Ala. (†36482) 195/C7
Gosport, England 13/F7
Gosport, England 10/F5
Gosport, Ind. (47433) 227/D6
Goss, Miss. (†39429) 256/E8
Gossau, Switzerland 39/H2
Gossville, N.H. (†03234) 268/E5
Gostivar, Yugoslavia 45/E5
Gostyń, Poland 47/C3
Gostynin, Poland 47/D2
Göta (canal), Sweden 18/J7
Göta (riv.), Sweden 18/H7
Gotebo, Okla. (73041) 288/J4
Göteborg, Sweden 7/F3
Göteborg, Sweden 18/G8
Göteborg och Bohus (co.), Sweden 18/G7
Gotha, E. Germany 22/D3
Gotham, Wis. (53540) 317/F9
Gothenburg, Nebr. (69138) 264/D4
Gothic (mesa), Ariz. 198/F2
Gotland (co.), Sweden 18/L8
Gotland (isl.), Sweden 7/F3
Gotland (isl.), Sweden 18/L8
Goto (isls.), Japan 81/D7
Goto (lake), Neth. Ant. 161/D8
Gotse Delchev, Bulgaria 45/F5
Gotska Sandön (isl.), Sweden 18/L7
Gotsu, Japan 81/F6
Göttingen, W. Germany 22/D3
Gottwaldov, Czech. 41/D2
Götzis, Austria 41/A3
Goubere, Cent. Afr. Rep. 115/E2
Gouda, Netherlands 27/F4
Goudeau, La. (71338) 238/G5
Gough (lake), Alberta 182/D3
Gough, Georgia (30811) 217/H4
Gough (isl.), St. Helena 2/J8
Gouin (res.), Que. 162/J6
Gouin (res.), Québec 174/C3
Goulburn, N.S. Wales 88/J6
Goulburn, N.S. Wales 97/E4
Goulburn (isls.), North. Terr. 88/E2
Goulburn (isls.), North. Terr. 93/C1
Goulburn (riv.), Victoria 97/C5
Goulburn Island, North. Terr. 93/C1
Gould, Ark. (71643) 202/G6
Gould, Colo. (†80480) 208/G2
Gould, Okla. (73544) 288/G5
Gould, Québec 172/F4
Gould City, Mich. (49838) 250/D2
Goulding, Fla. (†32502) 212/B6
Goulds, Fla. (33170) 212/F6
Goulds, Newf. 166/D2
Gouldsboro, Maine (†04607) 243/H7
Gouldsboro◯, Maine (†04607) 243/H7
Gouldsboro, Pa. (18424) 294/L3
Gouldtown, Sask. 181/D5
Goulmima, Morocco 106/C2
Goumbou, Mali 106/C6
Gounamitz (riv.), New Bruns. 170/C1
Goundam, Mali 106/D5
Goundam, Mali 102/B3
Gourara (oasis), Algeria 106/E3
Gourbeyre, Guadeloupe 161/A7
Gourdon, France 28/D5
Gouré, Niger 106/G6
Gourma-Rharous, Mali 106/D5
Gournay-en-Bray, France 28/D3
Gouro, Chad 111/C4
Gourock, Scotland 10/A1
Gourock, Scotland 15/A1
Gouveia, Portugal 33/C2
Gouverneur, N.Y. (13642) 276/K2
Gouvy, Belgium 27/H8
Gouyave, Grenada 161/C8
Gouyave, Grenada 156/F4
Govan, Sask. 181/G4
Govan, S.C. (†29843) 296/E5
Gove (co.), Kansas 232/B3
Gove, Kansas (67736) 232/B3
Gove (Nhulunbuy), North. Terr. 93/E2
Govena (cape), U.S.S.R. 48/R4
Govenlock, Sask. 181/B6
Governador Valadares, Brazil 132/F7
Governador Valadares, Brazil 120/E4
Government (mt.), Ariz. 198/C3
Government (peak), Mich. 250/F1
Government (creek), Utah 304/B3
Government Camp, Oreg. (97028) 291/F2
Governor (lake), Nova Scotia 168/F3
Govĭ-Altay, Mongolia 77/E3
Gowan, Minn. (†55736) 255/F4
Gowanda, N.Y. (14070) 276/B6
Gowd-e Zerreh (depr.), Afghanistan 59/H4
Gowen, Mich. (49326) 250/D5
Gowen, Okla. (74545) 288/R5
Gowensville, S.C. (†29356) 296/C1
Gower, Mo. (64454) 261/C3
Gower (isl.), N.S. Wales 97/J2
Gower (mt.), N.S. Wales 97/J2
Gower (pen.), Wales 13/C6
Gowna (lake), Ireland 17/G4
Gowran, Ireland 17/G6
Gowrie, Iowa (50543) 229/E4
Gowrie Park, Tasmania 99/C3
Goya, Argentina 120/D5
Goya, Argentina 143/G4
Goyave, Guadeloupe 161/A6
Goyder (riv.), North. Terr. 93/D2
Goyders (lag.), S. Australia 94/F2
Göynücek, Turkey 63/F2
Göynük, Turkey 63/D2
Goz Beïda, Chad 111/D5
Gozo (isl.), Malta 34/E6
Goz Regeb, Sudan 111/G4
Graaff-Reinet, S. Africa 118/C6
Graal-Müritz, E. Germany 22/E1
Graauw, Netherlands 27/E6
Grabill, Ind. (46741) 227/H2
Grabouw, S. Africa 118/F7
Grabs, Switzerland 39/H2
Gračac, Yugoslavia 45/B3
Gračanica, Yugoslavia 45/D3
Grace, Idaho (83241) 220/G7
Grace (mt.), Mass. 249/E2
Grace, Miss. (38745) 256/C5
Grace (pt.), R.I. 249/H8
Grace City, N. Dak. (58445) 282/N4
Gracefield, Québec 172/A3
Graceham, Md. (†21788) 245/J2
Gracemont, Okla. (73042) 288/K4
Graceton, Minn. (†56686) 255/D2
Graceton, Pa. (15743) 294/D4
Graceville, Fla. (32440) 212/D5
Graceville, Minn. (56240) 255/B5
Graceville, Queensland 88/K3
Gracewood, Georgia (30812) 217/H4
Gracey, Ky. (42232) 237/F7
Grächen, Switzerland 39/E4
Gracias, Honduras 154/C3
Gracias a Dios (cape), Nic. 146/K8
Gracias a Dios (cape), Nicaragua 154/F3
Graciosa (isl.), Portugal 33/C1
Gradačac, Yugoslavia 45/D3
Gradaús, Brazil 120/D3
Gradaús, Brazil 132/D4
Gradaús, Serra dos (range), Brazil 132/D4
Grado, Spain 33/D1
Grady, Ala. (36036) 195/F7
Grady, Ark. (71644) 202/G5
Grady (co.), Georgia 217/D9
Grady (isl.), Newf. 166/C3
Grady, N. Mex. (88120) 274/F4
Grady (co.), Okla. 288/L5
Grady, Okla. (73545) 288/L6
Gradyville, Ky. (42742) 237/L6
Graeagle, Calif. (96103) 204/E4
Graested, Denmark 21/F5
Graettinger, Iowa (51342) 229/D2
Graf, Iowa (†52039) 229/M3
Grafenau, W. Germany 22/E4
Grafenwöhr, W. Germany 22/D4
Graff, Mo. (65660) 261/H8
Graff-Reinet, S. Africa 102/E8
Graford, Texas (76045) 303/F5
Grafton, Australia 87/F8
Grafton (isls.), Chile 138/D10
Grafton, Ill. (62037) 222/C5
Grafton, Ind. (†47620) 227/B9
Grafton, Iowa (50440) 229/G2
Grafton◯, Mass. (01519) 249/H4
Grafton, Nebr. (68365) 264/G4
Grafton, New Bruns. 170/C2
Grafton (co.), N.H. 268/D4
Grafton◯, N.H. (03240) 268/D4
Grafton, N.S. Wales 88/J5
Grafton, N.S. Wales 97/G1
Grafton, N.Y. (12082) 276/N5
Grafton, N. Dak. (58237) 282/R3
Grafton, Ohio (44044) 284/F3
Grafton, Ontario 177/G4
Grafton◯, Vt. (05146) 268/B5
Grafton, Va. (23692) 307/P6
Grafton, W. Va. (26354) 312/G4
Grafton, Wis. (53024) 317/L9
Grafton Center, N.H. (†03240) 268/D4
Graham, Ala. (36263) 195/H4
Graham (lake), Alberta 182/C1
Graham (co.), Ariz. 198/E6
Graham (mt.), Ariz. 198/F6
Graham (isl.), Br. Col. 184/A3
Graham (peak), Colo. 208/E8
Graham, Fla. (32042) 212/D2
Graham, Georgia (†31513) 217/H7
Graham (creek), Ind. 227/F7
Graham (co.), Kansas 232/C2
Graham, Ky. (42344) 237/G6
Graham (lake), Maine 243/G6
Graham, Mo. (64455) 261/C2
Graham (co.), N.C. 281/B4
Graham, N.C. (27253) 281/L2
Graham (isl.), N.W.T. 162/M3
Graham (isl.), N.W. Terrs. 187/J2
Graham, Okla. (73437) 288/M6
Graham, Ontario 175/B3
Graham, Ontario 177/G5
Graham, Texas (76046) 303/F4
Graham Bell (isl.), U.S.S.R. 4/A6
Graham Bell (isl.), U.S.S.R. 48/G1
Grahamdale, Manitoba 179/D3
Graham Land (reg.), Ant. 2/G9
Graham Land (reg.) 5/C15
Graham Reach (chan.), Br. Col. 184/C3
Grahamstown, S. Africa 102/E8
Grahamstown, S. Africa 118/D6
Grahamsville, N.Y. (12740) 276/L7
Grahn, Ky. (41142) 237/P4
Graian Alps (range), France 28/G5
Graian Alps (range), Italy 34/A2
Graiguenamanagh-Tinnahinch, Ireland 17/H6
Grain Coast (reg.), Liberia 106/B8
Grainfield, Kansas (67737) 232/B2
Grainger (co.), Tenn. 237/O8
Graingers, N.C. (†28501) 281/O4
Grainola, Okla. (†74652) 288/N1
Grainton, Nebr. (69169) 264/C4
Grain Valley, Mo. (64029) 261/S6
Grajaú, Brazil 132/E4
Grajaú (riv.), Brazil 132/E4
Grajewo, Poland 47/F2
Gram, Denmark 21/C7
Gramalote, Colombia 126/D4
Gramat, France 28/D5
Grambling, La. (71245) 238/E1
Gramercy, La. (70052) 238/M3

Guadalupe Bravo 377

Great Torrington, England 10/D5
Great Torrington, England 13/C7
Great Valley, N.Y. (14741) 276/C6
Great Victoria (des.) 88/D5
Great Victoria (desert), Australia 87/C8
Great Victoria (des.), S. Australia 94/B3
Great Victoria (des.), W. Australia 92/D5
Great Village, Nova Scotia 168/E3
Great Wall (ruins), China 54/N5
Great Wall (ruins), China 77/G4,J
Great Wass (isl.), Maine 243/J7
Great Western Tiers (mts.), Tasmania 99/C3
Great Yarmouth, England 13/J5
Great Yarmouth, England 10/G4
Great Zab (riv.), Iraq 66/C2
Grecco, Uruguay 145/B3
Grecia, C. Rica 154/E5
Greco (cape), Cyprus 63/F5
Gredos, Sierra de (range), Spain 33/D2
Greece 2/L4
Greece 7/G5
GREECE 45/F6
Greece, N.Y. (14616) 276/E4
Greeley, Colo. 188/F2
Greeley, Colo. (80631) 208/K2
Greeley, Iowa (52050) 229/L3
Greeley (co.), Kansas 232/A3
Greeley, Kansas (66033) 232/G3
Greeley (co.), Nebr. 264/F3
Greeley, Nebr. (68842) 264/F3
Greeley, Pa. (18425) 294/N3
Greeley (creek), Utah 304/B3
Greeleyville, S.C. (29056) 296/H4
Greely (fjord), N.W. Terrs. 187/K1
Greely, Ontario 177/J2
Green (bay) 188/J1
Green (riv.) 188/D3
Green (isl.), Ant. & Bar. 161/E11
Green (riv.), Colo. 208/A2
Green (isl.), Grenada 161/D8
Green (riv.), Ill. 222/D2
Green, Kansas (67447) 232/E2
Green (co.), Ky. 237/K6
Green (riv.), Ky. 237/G6
Green (isl.), Maine 243/F8
Green (riv.), Mass. 249/B2
Green, Mich. (†49953) 250/F1
Green (bay), Mich. 250/B4
Green (lake), Minn. 255/D5
Green (riv.), New Bruns. 170/B1
Green (cape), N.S. Wales 97/F5
Green (swamp), N.C. 281/N6
Green (riv.), N. Dak. 282/D5
Green (pt.), Nova Scotia 168/C5
Green (isl.), Ontario 177/A2
Green, Oreg. (†97470) 291/D4
Green (isls.), Papua N.G. 86/C2
Green (lake), Sask. 181/D1
Green (riv.), Tenn. 237/F10
Green (riv.), U.S. 146/H6
Green (riv.), Utah 304/D4
Green (mts.), Vt. 268/B4
Green (cay), Virgin Is. (U.S.) 161/F4
Green (lake), Wash. 310/A2
Green (riv.), Wash. 310/C3
Green (co.), Wis. 317/G10
Green (bay), Wis. 317/L6
Green (mt.), Wyo. 319/E3
Green (riv.), Wyo. 319/C4
Greenacres, Calif. (93308) 204/F8
Green Acres, Sask. 181/F2
Greenacres, Wash. (99016) 310/J3
Greenacres City, Fla. (33463) 212/F5
Greenan, Sask. 181/C4
Greenback, Tenn. (37742) 237/N9
Greenbackville, Va. (23356) 307/T5
Green Bank, N.J. (†08215) 273/D4
Greenbank, Wash. (98253) 310/C2
Green Bank, W. Va. (24944) 312/G6
Green Bay, N. Zealand 100/B1
Green Bay, Va. (23942) 307/M6
Green Bay, Wis. 188/J2
Green Bay, Wis. 146/J5
Green Bay, Wis. (*54301) 317/K6
Greenbelt, Md. (20770) 245/G4
Greenbelt Park, Md. 245/G4
Greenbrier, Ala. (†35758) 195/E1
Greenbrier, Ark. (72058) 202/F3
Greenbrier, Mo. (†63730) 261/M8
Greenbrier, Tenn. (37073) 237/H8
Greenbrier (co.), W. Va. 312/F7
Greenbrier (riv.), W. Va. 312/F6
Green Brook, N.J. (08812) 273/D2
Greenbush, Mass. (02040) 249/F8
Greenbush, Mich. (48738) 250/F4
Greenbush, Minn. (56726) 255/B2
Greenbush, Va. (23357) 307/S5
Green Camp, Ohio (43322) 284/D4
Greencastle, Ind. (46135) 227/D5
Greencastle, Ireland 17/H1
Green Castle, Mo. (63544) 261/G2
Greencastle, Pa. (17225) 294/G6
Green Center, Ind. (†46701) 227/G2
Green City, Mo. (63545) 261/F2
Green Court, Alberta 182/C2
Green Cove Springs, Fla. (32043) 212/E2
Greencreek, Idaho (83533) 220/B3
Green Creek, N.J. (08219) 273/D5
Greendale, Ind. (†47025) 227/H6
Greendale, Wis. (53129) 317/L2
Greendell, N.J. (07839) 273/D2
Greene (co.), Ala. 195/C5
Greene (co.), Ark. 202/J1
Greene (co.), Georgia 217/F3
Greene (co.), Ill. 222/C4
Greene (co.), Ind. 227/D6
Greene (co.), Iowa 229/E5
Greene, Iowa (50636) 229/H3
Greene○, Maine (04236) 243/C7
Greene (co.), Miss. 256/G8
Greene (co.), Mo. 261/F8
Greene (co.), N.Y. 276/M6
Greene, N.Y. (13778) 276/J6
Greene (co.), N.C. 281/O3
Greene, N. Dak. (†58787) 282/G2
Greene (co.), Ohio 284/C6
Greene (co.), Pa. 294/B6
Greene, R.I. (02827) 249/G6
Greene (co.), Tenn. 237/R8
Greene (co.), Va. 307/M4
Greenevers, N.C. (†28521) 281/O5
Greeneville, Tenn. (37743) 237/R8
Greenfield, Calif. (93927) 204/D7
Greenfield, Ill. (62044) 222/C4
Greenfield, Ind. (46140) 227/F5
Greenfield, Iowa (50849) 229/D6
Greenfield, Mass. (01301) 249/D2
Greenfield○, Mass. (01301) 249/D2
Greenfield, Minn. (†55373) 255/F5
Greenfield, Mo. (65661) 261/E8
Greenfield○, N.H. (03047) 268/D6
Greenfield, Nova Scotia 168/D4
Greenfield, Ohio (45123) 284/D7
Greenfield, Okla. (73043) 288/K3
Greenfield, S. Dak. (†57010) 298/R8
Greenfield, Tenn. (38230) 237/D8
Greenfield, Wis. (53220) 317/L2
Greenfield Hill, Conn. (†06430) 210/B4
Greenfield Park, Québec 172/J4
Greenford, Ohio (44422) 284/J4
Green Forest, Ark. (72638) 202/D1
Green Hall, Ky. (41328) 237/O6
Green Harbor, Mass. (02041) 249/M4
Green Haven, Md. (21122) 245/M4
Greenhills, Ohio (45218) 284/B9
Greenhorn, Oreg. (†97877) 291/J3
Green Island, Iowa (52051) 229/N4
Green Island, Jamaica 158/G6
Green Island, N.Y. (12183) 276/N5
Green Island, N. Zealand 100/C7
Greenisland, N. Ireland 17/K2
Green Island (bay), Philippines 82/B5
Green Island Cove, Newf. 166/C3
Green Isle, Minn. (55338) 255/E6
Green Lake, Maine (†04429) 243/F6
Green Lake, Sask. 181/L4
Green Lake (co.), Wis. 317/H8
Green Lake, Wis. (54941) 317/H8
Greenland 2/G2
Greenland 4/B12
Greenland 146/P2
Greenland (sea) 146/T2
Greenland (sea) 4/B10
Greenland, Ark. (72737) 202/B1
Greenland, Barbados 161/B8
Greenland, Colo. (†80118) 208/K4
Greenland, Mich. (49929) 250/G1
Greenland○, N.H. (03840) 268/F5
Greenlaw, Scotland 15/F5
Greenleaf, Idaho (83626) 220/B6
Greenleaf, Kansas (66943) 232/E2
Greenleaf, Minn. (†55355) 255/D6
Greenleaf, Oreg. (97445) 291/D3
Greenleaf, Wis. (54126) 317/L7
Greenleafton, Minn. (†55965) 255/F7
Greenlee (co.), Ariz. 198/F5
Green Lowther (mt.), Scotland 15/E5
Greenmount, Ky. (†40741) 237/N6
Greenmount, Md. (†21074) 245/L2
Green Mountain (res.), Colo. 208/G3
Green Mountain, Iowa (50637) 229/H4
Green Mountain, N.C. (28740) 281/E3
Green Mountain Falls, Colo. (80819) 208/K5
Green Oaks, Ill. (†60048) 222/B4
Greenock, Scotland 10/A1
Greenock, Scotland 15/A2
Greenore, Ireland 17/J4
Greenore (pt.), Ireland 17/J7
Greenough (mt.), Alaska 196/K1
Greenough, Georgia (†31716) 217/D8
Greenough, Mont. (59836) 262/C4
Green Peter (lake), Oreg. 291/E3
Green Pond, Ala. (35074) 195/D4
Green Pond, N.J. (07435) 273/E1
Green Pond, S.C. (29446) 296/F6
Greenport, N.Y. (11944) 276/P8
Green Ridge (mts.), 245/E2
Green Ridge, Mo. (65332) 261/F5
Green River (lake), Ky. 237/L6
Green River, Utah (84525) 304/D4
Green River (res.), Vt. 268/B2
Green River, Wyo. 188/E2
Green River, Wyo. (82935) 319/C4
Green River (mt.), Wyo. 319/C2
Green Rock, Ill. (†61241) 222/C2
Greens (peak), Ariz. 198/F4
Greensboro, Ala. (36744) 195/C5
Greensboro, Fla. (32330) 212/B1
Greensboro, Georgia (30642) 217/F3
Greensboro, Ind. (47344) 227/G5
Greensboro, Md. (21639) 245/P5
Greensboro, N.C. 146/L6
Greensboro, N.C. 188/K3
Greensboro, N.C. (*27401) 281/K2
Greensboro, Pa. (15338) 294/B6
Greensboro○, Vt. (05841) 268/C2
Greensburg, Ind. (47240) 227/G6
Greensburg, Kansas (67054) 232/C4
Greensburg, Ky. (42743) 237/K6
Greensburg, La. (70441) 238/J5
Greensburg, Mo. (†63531) 261/H2
Greensburg, Ohio (44232) 284/G4
Greensburg, Pa. (15601) 294/D5
Green Sea, S.C. (29545) 296/J3
Greens Farms, Conn. (06436) 210/B4
Greens Fork, Ind. (47345) 227/H5
Greens Harbour, Newf. 166/D2
Greenshields, Alberta 182/E3
Greenslopes, Queensland 88/K3
Greenslopes, Queensland 95/E3
Greenspond, Newf. 166/D4
Green Springs, Ohio (44836) 284/E3
Greenstone (pt.), Scotland 15/C3
Greenstreet, Sask. 181/A2
Green Sulphur Springs, W. Va. (25966) 312/E7
Greensville (co.), Va. 307/N7
Greentop, Mo. (63546) 261/H2
Greentown, Ind. (46936) 227/E4
Greentown, Ohio (44630) 284/H4
Greentree, Pa. (15242) 294/B7
Greenup, Ill. (62428) 222/E4
Greenup (co.), Ky. 237/R3
Greenup, Ky. (41144) 237/R3
Greenvale, Queensland 95/C3
Green Valley, Ariz. (85614) 198/D7
Green Valley, Ill. (61534) 222/D3
Green Valley, Minn. (†56258) 255/C6
Green Valley, Ontario 177/K2
Green Valley, Wis. (54127) 317/K6
Greenview, Calif. (96037) 204/B2
Greenview, Ill. (62642) 222/D3
Greenview, W. Va. (†25166) 312/C6
Green Village, N.J. (07935) 273/D2
Greenville, Ala. (36037) 195/E7
Greenville, Calif. (95947) 204/E3
Greenville, Del. (19807) 245/R1
Greenville, Fla. (32331) 212/C1
Greenville, Georgia (30222) 217/C4
Greenville, Ill. (62246) 222/D5
Greenville, Ind. (47124) 227/F8
Greenville, Iowa (51343) 229/C3
Greenville, Ky. (42345) 237/G6
Greenville, Liberia 106/C8
Greenville, Maine (04441) 243/D5
Greenville○, Maine (04441) 243/D5
Greenville, Mich. (48838) 250/D5
Greenville, Miss. 146/J6
Greenville, Miss. 188/H4
Greenville, Miss. (38701) 256/B4
Greenville, Mo. (63944) 261/M8
Greenville, N.H. (03048) 268/D6
Greenville○, N.H. (03048) 268/D6
Greenville, N.C. (27834) 281/P3
Greenville, Ohio (45331) 284/A5
Greenville, Pa. (16125) 294/B3
Greenville, R.I. (02828) 249/H5
Greenville, S.C. 146/K6
Greenville, S.C. 188/K4
Greenville (co.), S.C. 296/C2
Greenville, S.C. (*29601) 296/C2
Greenville, Texas 188/G4
Greenville, Texas (75401) 303/H4
Greenville, Utah (84731) 304/B5
Greenville, Va. (24440) 307/K5
Greenville, W. Va. (24945) 312/E7
Greenville, Wis. (54942) 317/J7
Greenville Junction, Maine (04442) 243/D5
Greenwald, Minn. (56335) 255/D5
Greenwater Lake, Sask. 181/H3
Greenwater Lake Prov. Park, Sask. 181/H3
Greenway, Ark. (72430) 202/K1
Greenway, Manitoba 179/C5
Greenway, S. Dak. (†57437) 298/K2
Greenwell Springs, La. (70739) 238/K1
Greenwich○, Conn. (06830) 210/A4
Greenwich (pt.), Conn. 210/A4
Greenwich, England 13/H8
Greenwich, England 10/B5
Greenwich (Kapingamarangi) (atoll), Micronesia 87/F5
Greenwich○, N.J. (08323) 273/C5
Greenwich, N.Y. (12834) 276/O4
Greenwich, Ohio (44837) 284/E3
Greenwich, Utah (84732) 304/B5
Greenwood, Ark. (72936) 202/B3
Greenwood, Br. Col. 184/H5
Greenwood, Calif. (95635) 204/E5
Greenwood, Del. (19950) 245/R5
Greenwood, Fla. (32443) 212/A1
Greenwood, Ind. (46142) 227/E5
Greenwood (co.), Kansas 232/F4
Greenwood, Ky. (†42634) 237/N7
Greenwood, La. (71033) 238/B2
Greenwood, Mass. (01880) 249/D6
Greenwood (lake), Minn. 255/G3
Greenwood, Miss. (38930) 256/D4
Greenwood, Mo. (64034) 261/R6
Greenwood, Nebr. (68366) 264/H3
Greenwood (lake), N.J. 273/E1
Greenwood, N.Y. (14839) 276/E6
Greenwood (lake), N.Y. 276/M8
Greenwood, S.C. 188/K4
Greenwood (co.), S.C. 296/C3
Greenwood, S.C. (29646) 296/C3
Greenwood (lake), S.C. 296/D3
Greenwood, S. Dak. (†57380) 298/N8
Greenwood, Va. (22943) 307/L4
Greenwood, W. Va. (26360) 312/E4
Greenwood, Wis. (54437) 317/E6
Greenwood Lake, N.Y. (10925) 276/M8
Greenwood Springs, Miss. (38848) 256/H3
Greer, Ariz. (85927) 198/F4
Greer, Idaho (†83544) 220/B3
Greer, Mo. (†65606) 261/K9
Greer, Ohio (†44628) 284/F4
Greer (co.), Okla. 288/G5
Greer, S.C. (29651) 296/C2
Greers Ferry, Ark. (†72067) 202/F2
Greers Ferry (lake), Ark. 202/G2
Greeson (lake), Ark. 202/C5
Gregg (co.), Texas 303/K5
Greggs, Georgia (†31620) 217/F8
Gregory, Ark. (72059) 202/H3
Gregory, Mich. (48137) 250/E6
Gregory (range), Queensland 95/B3
Gregory (riv.), Queensland 88/F3
Gregory (riv.), Queensland 95/A3
Gregory (lake), S. Australia 88/F5
Gregory (lake), S. Australia 94/F3
Gregory (co.), S. Dak. 298/L7
Gregory, S. Dak. (57533) 298/L7
Gregory (lake), W. Australia 92/C4
Gregory Landing, Mo. (†63345) 261/K2
Gregory's (sound), Ireland 17/B5
Greian (head), Scotland 15/A3
Greifensee (lake), Switzerland 39/G2
Greifswald, E. Germany 22/E1
Grein, Austria 41/C2
Greina (pass), Switzerland 39/G3
Greiz, E. Germany 22/E3
Grelton, Ohio (43523) 284/C3
Gremikha, U.S.S.R. 52/E1
Gremyachinsk, U.S.S.R. 52/J3
Grenå, Denmark 21/D5
Grenå, Denmark 18/G8
Grenada 2/F5
Grenada 146/M8
Grenada, Calif. (96038) 204/C2
GRENADA 161/D9
GRENADA 156/G4
Grenada (isl.), Grenada 156/G4
Grenada (co.), Miss. 256/E3
Grenada, Miss. (38901) 256/E3
Grenada (lake), Miss. 256/E3
Grenadier (isl.), N.Y. 276/H2
Grenadines (isls.), Grenada 156/G4
Grenadines (isls.), St. Vin. & Grens. 156/G4
Grenchen, Switzerland 39/D2
Grenfell, N.S. Wales 97/E3
Grenfell, Sask. 181/J5
Grenloch, N.J. (08032) 273/C4
Grenoble, France 7/E4
Grenoble, France 28/F5
Grenola, Kansas (67346) 232/F4
Grenora, N. Dak. (58845) 282/C2
Grenville (chan.), Br. Col. 184/C3
Grenville, Grenada 161/D8
Grenville (bay), Grenada 161/D8
Grenville, N. Mex. (88424) 274/F2
Grenville (county), Ontario 177/J3
Grenville, Québec 172/C4
Grenville (cape), Queensland 88/G2
Grenville (cape), Queensland 95/B1
Grenville, S. Dak. (57239) 298/O3
Grenville (pt.), Wash. 310/A3
Gresham, Nebr. (68367) 264/G3
Gresham, Oreg. (97030) 291/B2
Gresham, S.C. (29546) 296/J4
Gresham, Wis. (54128) 317/J6
Greshamville, Georgia (†30650) 217/F3
Gresik, Indonesia 85/K2
Gresston, Georgia (†31023) 217/F6
Greta-Branxton, N.S. Wales 97/F3
Greta East, N.S. Wales 97/F3
Gretna, Fla. (32332) 212/B1
Gretna, La. (70053) 238/O4
Gretna, Manitoba 179/E5
Gretna, Nebr. (68028) 264/H3
Gretna, Scotland 10/E3
Gretna, Scotland 15/E5
Gretna, Tasmania 99/D4
Gretna, Va. (24557) 307/K7
Grevelingen (str.), Netherlands 27/E5
Greven, W. Germany 22/B2
Grevená, Greece 45/E5
Grevenbroich, W. Germany 22/B3
Grevenmacher, Luxembourg 27/J9
Grevesmühlen, E. Germany 22/D2
Greville (bay), Nova Scotia 168/D3
Grey (isls.), Newf. 166/C3
Grey (riv.), N. Zealand 100/C5
Grey (cape), North. Terr. 88/F2
Grey (cape), North. Terr. 93/E2
Grey (county), Ontario 177/D3
Grey (range), Queensland 88/G5
Grey (range), Queensland 95/B5
Grey Abbey, N. Ireland 17/K2
Greybull, Wyo. (82426) 319/E1
Greybull (riv.), Wyo. 319/D1
Greycliff, Mont. (59033) 262/G5
Grey Eagle, Minn. (56336) 255/D5
Grey Forest, Texas (†78201) 303/J10
Grey Islands, Newf. 166/C3
Greylock (mt.), Idaho 220/C6
Greylock (mt.), Mass. 249/B2
Greymouth, N. Zealand 100/C5
Greymouth, N. Zealand 87/G10
Grey River, Newf. 166/C4
Greys (riv.), Wyo. 319/B3
Greystone, Colo. (†81640) 208/B1
Greystone, Conn. (†06786) 210/C2
Greystone Park, N.J. (07950) 273/D2
Greystones-Delgany, Ireland 10/D4
Greystones-Delgany, Ireland 17/K5
Greytown, N. Zealand 100/E4
Greytown (San Juan del Norte), Nicaragua 154/F5
Greytown, S. Africa 118/E5
Grez-Doiceau, Belgium 27/F7
Gribbles Settlement, North. Terr. 93/B1
Gridley, Calif. (95948) 204/D4
Gridley (mt.), Conn. 210/B1
Gridley, Ill. (61744) 222/E3
Gridley, Kansas (66852) 232/G3
Gridone (mt.), Switzerland 39/G4
Griend (isl.), Netherlands 27/G2
Grier, N. Mex. (†88101) 274/F4
Gries am Brenner, Austria 41/A3
Griesheim, W. Germany 22/C4
Grieskirchen, Austria 41/B2
Griffin, Georgia (30223) 217/D4
Griffin, Ind. (47616) 227/B8
Griffin, Sask. 181/H6
Griffiss A.F.B., N.Y. 276/K4
Griffith, Ind. (46319) 227/C1
Griffith, N. S. 88/H6
Griffith, N.S. Wales 97/C4
Griffith (isl.), Ontario 177/D3
Griffithsville, W. Va. (25521) 312/B6
Griffithville, Ark. (72060) 202/G3
Grifton, N.C. (28530) 281/P4
Griggs (co.), N. Dak. 282/O5
Griggs, Okla. (†73949) 288/B1
Griggsville, Ill. (62340) 222/C4
Grigston, Kansas (†67871) 232/B3
Grijalva (riv.), Mexico 150/N7
Grim (cape), Tasmania 99/A2
Grimari, Cent. Afr. Rep. 115/C2
Grimbergen, Belgium 27/E7
Grimes, Ala. (†36350) 195/H8
Grimes, Calif. (95950) 204/C4
Grimes, Iowa (50111) 229/F5
Grimes, Okla. (†73628) 288/G4
Grimes (co.), Texas 303/J7
Grimesland, N.C. (27837) 281/P3
Griminish, Scotland 15/A3
Grimma, E. Germany 22/E3
Grimmen, E. Germany 22/E1
Grimms Landing, W. Va. (25095) 312/B5
Grimsby, England 13/G4
Grimsby, England 10/F4
Grimsby, Ontario 177/E4
Grimsel (pass), Switzerland 39/F3
Grímsey (isl.), Iceland 21/C1
Grimshaw, Alberta 182/B1
Grimsley, Tenn. (38565) 237/L2
Grimstad, Norway 18/F7
Grindelwald, Switzerland 39/E3
Grindrod, Br. Col. 184/H5
Grindsted, Denmark 21/B6
Grindstone, Maine (†04460) 243/F4
Grindstone (isl.), New Bruns. 170/F3
Grindstone (lake), Wis. 317/C4
Grind Stone City, Mich. (48467) 250/G4
Grindstone Prov. Rec. Park, Manitoba 179/F3
Grinnell, Iowa (50112) 229/H5
Grinnell, Kansas (67738) 232/B2
Grinnell (pen.), N.W. Terrs. 187/J2
Grippon, Guadeloupe 161/B6
Griqualand West (reg.), S. Africa 118/C5
Griquatown, S. Africa 118/C5
Grise Fiord, Canada 4/B13
Grise Fiord, N.W.T. 162/H1
Grise Fiord, N.W. Terrs. 187/K2
Gris-Nez (cape), France 28/D2
Grisons (Graubünden) (elec. div.), Switzerland 39/H3
Grissom A.F.B., Ind. 227/E3
Griswold, Iowa (51535) 229/C6
Griswold, Manitoba 179/B5
Griswoldville, Mass. (01345) 249/D2
Grīva, U.S.S.R. 53/D3
Grizzly (bay), Calif. 204/K1
Grizzly Flats, Calif. (95636) 204/E5
Groais (isl.), Newf. 166/C3
Grobiņa, U.S.S.R. 53/A2
Grodno, U.S.S.R. 7/G3
Grodno, U.S.S.R. 48/C4
Grodno, U.S.S.R. 52/B4
Grodzisk Mazowiecki, Poland 47/E2
Grodzisk Wielkopolski, Poland 47/C2
Groenlo, Netherlands 27/K4
Groesbeck, Ohio (45239) 284/B9
Groesbeck, Texas (76642) 303/H6
Groesbeek, Netherlands 27/H5
Groix (isl.), France 28/B4
Grójec, Poland 47/E3
Grömitz, W. Germany 22/D1
Gronau, W. Germany 22/B2
Grondines, Québec 172/E3
Grong, Norway 18/H4
Grong Grong, N.S. Wales 97/D4
Groningen, Minn. (†55072) 255/E4
Groningen (prov.), Netherlands 27/K2
Groningen, Netherlands 27/K2
Groningen, Suriname 131/D2
Groninger Wad (sound), Netherlands 27/J2
Gronlid, Sask. 181/G2
Grønnedal, Greenl. 4/C12
Grono, Switzerland 39/H4
Groom, Texas (79039) 303/C2
Groomsport, N. Ireland 17/K2
Groot-Drakenstein, S. Africa 118/F6
Groote (isl.), North. Terr. 88/F2
Groote (riv.), S. Africa 118/C6
Groote Eylandt (isl.), Australia 87/D7
Groote Eylandt (isl.), North. Terr. 93/E3
Groote IJ Polder, Netherlands 27/B4
Grootfontein, Namibia 118/B3
Groot Sint Joris, Neth. Ant. 161/G9
Gros (pt.), Grenada 161/C8
Gros Islet, St. Lucia 161/G5
Gros Islet (bay), St. Lucia 161/G5
Grosmont (Island Lake), Alberta 182/D2
Gros Morne, Haiti 158/B5
Gros-Morne, Martinique 161/D6
Gros Morne (mt.), Newf. 166/C4
Gros-Morne, Québec 172/C1
Gros Morne Nat'l Park, Newf. 166/C4
Gros Piton (mt.), St. Lucia 161/G6
Gross, Nebr. (†68719) 264/F2
Grosse Ile, Mich. (48138) 250/B7
Grosse Isle, Manitoba 179/E4
Gross Emme (riv.), Switzerland 39/E2
Grossenbrode, W. Germany 22/D1
Grossenhain, E. Germany 22/E3
Grosse Pointe, Mich. (48236) 250/B7
Grosse Pointe Farms, Mich. (†48236) 250/B6
Grosse Pointe Park, Mich. (†48236) 250/B7
Grosse Pointe Shores, Mich. (†48236) 250/B6
Grosse Pointe Woods, Mich. (†48236) 250/B6
Grosser Arber (mt.), W. Germany 22/E4
Grosser Peilstein (mt.), Austria 41/C2
Grosses Coques, Nova Scotia 168/B4
Grosses-Roches, Québec 172/B1
Grosse Tete, La. (70740) 238/G6
Grosseto (prov.), Italy 34/C3
Grosseto, Italy 34/C3
Grossglockner (mt.), Austria 41/B3
Gross Litzner (mt.), Switzerland 39/K3
Grossräschen, E. Germany 22/E3
Grosssiegharts, Austria 41/C2
Grosswangen, Switzerland 39/F2
Grosvenor Dale, Conn. (06246) 210/H1
Gros Ventre (riv.), Wyo. 319/B2
Groswater (bay), Newf. 166/C3
Groton, Conn. (06340) 210/G3
Groton○, Conn. (06340) 210/G3
Groton, Mass. (01450) 249/H2
Groton○, Mass. (01450) 249/H2
Groton○, N.H. (†03241) 268/D4
Groton, N.Y. (13073) 276/H5
Groton, S. Dak. (57445) 298/N3
Groton○, Vt. (05046) 268/C3
Groton (lake), Vt. 268/C3
Groton Long (pt.), Conn. 210/H3
Groton Long Point, Conn. (†06340) 210/G3
Grottaferrata, Italy 34/F7
Grottaglie, Italy 34/F4
Grotto, Wash. (98288) 310/D3
Grottoes, Va. (24441) 307/L4
Grouard, Alberta 182/B2
Grouard Mission, Alberta 182/C2
Grouard Mission, Alta. 162/E4
Groundhog (riv.), Ontario 175/D3
Grouse (Lost River), Idaho (†83255) 220/E6
Grouse (mt.), N. Mex. 274/A5
Grouse (creek), Utah 304/A2
Grouse Creek, Utah (84313) 304/A2
Grouse Creek (mts.), Utah 304/A2
Grouw, Netherlands 27/H2
Grovania, Georgia (†31036) 217/E6
Grove, Maine (04638) 243/J5
Grove (lake), N. Dak. 282/L5
Grove, Okla. (74344) 288/S1
Grove Beach, Conn. (†06413) 210/E3
Grove Center, Ky. (†42437) 237/F5
Grove City, Fla. (33533) 212/D5
Grove City, Minn. (56243) 255/D5
Grove City, Ohio (43123) 284/D6
Grove City, Pa. (16127) 294/B3
Grovedale, Alberta 182/A2
Grove Hill, Ala. (36451) 195/C7
Groveland, Calif. (95321) 204/E6
Groveland, Fla. (32736) 212/E3
Groveland, Georgia (†31321) 217/J6
Groveland, Ind. (†46121) 227/D5
Groveland○, Mass. (01830) 249/L1
Groveland, N.Y. (14462) 276/E5
Groveoak, Ala. (35975) 195/F2
Grove Place, Virgin Is. (U.S.) 161/E4
Groveport, Ohio (43125) 284/E6
Grover, Colo. (80729) 208/L1
Grover, Mo. (63040) 261/M3
Grover, N.C. (28073) 281/G4
Grover, Pa. (17735) 294/J2
Grover, S.C. (29447) 296/F5
Grover, S. Dak. (†57201) 298/P4
Grover, Utah (†84773) 304/C5
Grover, Wyo. (83122) 319/B3
Grover City, Calif. (93433) 204/E8
Grover Hill, Ohio (45849) 284/B3
Grovertown, Ind. (46531) 227/D2
Groves, Texas (77619) 303/L8
Grovespring, Mo. (65662) 261/G8
Groveton, N.H. (03582) 268/D2
Groveton, Texas (75845) 303/J7
Groveton, Va. (†22306) 307/T3
Grovetown, Georgia (30813) 217/H4
Groveville, N.J. (†08601) 273/D3
Growler (mts.), Ariz. 198/B6
Groznyy, U.S.S.R. 7/J4
Groznyy, U.S.S.R. 48/E5
Groznyy, U.S.S.R. 52/G6
Grubbs, Ark. (72431) 202/H2
Grubišno Polje, Yugoslavia 45/C3
Grudovo, Bulgaria 45/H4
Grudziądz, Poland 47/D2
Gruenthal, Sask. 181/E3
Gruetli, Tenn. (37339) 237/K10
Gruinard (bay), Scotland 15/C3
Grulla, Texas (78548) 303/F11
Grünberg (Zielona Góra), Poland 47/B3
Grünburg, Austria 41/C3
Grundy (co.), Ill. 222/E2
Grundy (co.), Iowa 229/H4
Grundy (co.), Mo. 261/E2
Grundy (co.), Tenn. 237/K10
Grundy, Va. (24614) 307/D6
Grundy Center, Iowa (50638) 229/H4
Grunthal, Manitoba 179/F5
Gruver, Iowa (51344) 229/D2
Gruver, Texas (79040) 303/C1
Gruyères, Switzerland 39/D3
Gryazi, U.S.S.R. 52/F4
Gryazovets, U.S.S.R. 52/F3
Gryfice, Poland 47/B2
Gryfino, Poland 47/B2
Grygla, Minn. (56727) 255/C2
Gryon, Switzerland 39/D4
Grytviken 5/D17
Gstaad, Switzerland 39/D4
Gsteig, Switzerland 39/D4
Guacamaya, Colombia 126/C6
Guacamayo, Colombia 126/F6
Guacanayabo (gulf), Cuba 156/C2
Guacanayabo (gulf), Cuba 158/G4
Guacara, Venezuela 124/D2
Guachara, Venezuela 124/D4
Gu Achi, Ariz. (†85634) 198/C6
Guácimo, C. Rica 154/F5
Guacuí, Brazil 135/F2
Guadalajara, Mexico 2/D5
Guadalajara, Mexico 150/H6
Guadalajara, Mexico 146/H7
Guadalajara (prov.), Spain 33/E2
Guadalajara, Spain 33/E2
Guadalcanal (isl.), Solomon Is. 87/F7
Guadalcanal (isl.), Solomon Is. 86/D3
Guadalcanal, Spain 33/D3
Guadalimar (riv.), Spain 33/E3
Guadalupe (isl.), Mexico 146/G7
Guadalquivir (riv.), Spain 7/D5
Guadalquivir (riv.), Spain 33/C4
Guadalupe, Potosí, Bolivia 136/B7
Guadalupe, Santa Cruz, Bolivia 136/C6
Guadalupe, Calif. (93434) 204/E9
Guadalupe (riv.), Calif. 204/K3
Guadalupe, Nuevo León, Mexico 150/K4
Guadalupe, Zacatecas, Mexico 150/H5
Guadalupe (co.), N. Mex. 274/E4
Guadalupe (mts.), N. Mex. 274/D6
Guadalupe, Peru 128/E9
Guadalupe, Spain 33/D3
Guadalupe, Sierra de (range), Spain 33/D3
Guadalupe (co.), Texas 303/G8
Guadalupe (mts.), Texas 303/C10
Guadalupe (peak), Texas 303/B10
Guadalupe (riv.), Texas 303/G8
Guadalupe Bravo, Mexico 150/F1

378 Guadalupe

Guadalupe Mts. Nat'l Park, Texas 303/C10
Guadalupe Victoria, Durango, Mexico 150/H4
Guadalupe Victoria, Puebla, Mexico 150/O1
Guadalupe y Calvo, Mexico 150/F3
Guadalupita, N. Mex. (87722) 274/D2
Guadarrama, Sierra de (range), Spain 33/E2
Guadarrama (riv.), Spain 33/F4
Guadarrama, Venezuela 124/D3
Guadeloupe (isl.) 146/M8
GUADELOUPE 161/A5
GUADELOUPE 156/F3
Guadeloupe (isl.), Guadeloupe 161/B6
Guadeloupe (isl.), Guadeloupe 156/F3
Guadeloupe (passage), Guadeloupe 161/A5
Guadeloupe Nat'l Park, Guadeloupe 161/A6
Guadiana (riv.) 7/D5
Guadiana (riv.), Portugal 33/C4
Guadiana (riv.), Spain 33/D3
Guadix, Spain 33/E4
Guafo (gulf), Chile 138/D5
Guafo (isl.), Chile 138/D5
Guage, Ky. (41329) 237/P5
Guaicanamar, Cuba 158/G3
Guaico, Trin. & Tob. 161/B10
Guaimaca, Honduras 154/D3
Guáimaro, Cuba 158/G3
Guaina, Venezuela 124/G5
Guainía (riv.) 120/C2
Guainía (comm.), Colombia 126/F6
Guainía (riv.), Colombia 126/F6
Guainía (riv.), Venezuela 124/E6
Guaira (dept.), Paraguay 144/D4
Guairá (falls), Paraguay 144/E4
Guaitecas (isls.), Chile 138/D5
Guajaba (cay), Cuba 158/G2
Guajará-Mirim, Brazil 132/H10
Guajará-Mirim, Brazil 120/C4
Guajataca (lake), P. Rico 161/B1
Guajira (pen.) 120/B1
Guajira, La (dept.), Colombia 126/D2
Guajira (pen.), Colombia 126/E1
Gualaca, Panama 154/F6
Gualaceo, Ecuador 128/C4
Gualala, Calif. (95445) 204/B5
Gualán, Guatemala 154/C3
Gualaquiza, Ecuador 128/C4
Guale, Ecuador 128/B3
Gualeguay, Argentina 143/G6
Gualeguay (riv.), Argentina 143/G5
Gualeguaychú, Argentina 143/G6
Gualpatanta, Honduras 154/E3
Guam (isl.) 87/E4
GUAM 86/K7
Guam (isl.), U.S. 2/S5
Guamal, Magdalena, Colombia 126/C3
Guamal, Meta, Colombia 126/D6
Guamblin (isl.), Chile 138/D5
Guamo, Cuba 158/H3
Guamote, Ecuador 128/C4
Guampí, Sierra de (mts.), Venezuela 124/F4
Guamúchil, Mexico 150/E4
Guana, Venezuela 124/G5
Guanabacoa, Cuba 158/C1
Guanabacoa, Cuba 156/B2
Guanabara (bay), Brazil 135/E3
Guanacevi, Mexico 150/G4
Guanahacabibes (gulf), Cuba 158/A2
Guanahacabibes (pen.), Cuba 158/A2
Guanaja, Honduras 154/E2
Guanaja (isl.), Honduras 154/E2
Guanajay, Cuba 158/B1
Guanajay, Cuba 156/A2
Guanajibo (pt.), P. Rico 161/A2
Guanajibo (riv.), P. Rico 161/A2
Guanajuato (state), Mexico 150/J6
Guanajuato, Mexico 150/J6
Guanambi, Brazil 120/E4
Guañape (isls.), Peru 128/C7
Guanare, Venezuela 124/D3
Guanare (riv.), Venezuela 124/D3
Guanare Viejo (riv.), Venezuela 124/D3
Guanarito, Venezuela 124/D3
Guandacol, Argentina 143/C2
Guane, Cuba 158/A2
Guane, Cuba 156/A2
Guangdong (Kwangtung) (prov.), China 77/H7
Guangnam, China 77/G7
Guangshan, China 77/J5
Guangxi Zhuangzu (Kwangsi Chuang Aut. Reg.), China 77/G7
Guangyuan, China 77/G5
Guangze, China 77/J6
Guangzhou (Canton), China 77/H7
Guangzhou (Canton), China 54/N7
Guánica, P. Rico 161/B3
Guánica, P. Rico 156/F1
Guánica (lake), P. Rico 161/B3
Guanipa (riv.), Venezuela 124/G3
Guaniquilla (pt.), P. Rico 161/A2
Guano, Ecuador 128/C3
Guano (creek), Oreg. 291/H5
Guano (lake), Oreg. 291/H5
Guanoco, Venezuela 124/G2
Guanta, Venezuela 124/F2
Guantánamo (prov.), Cuba 158/K4
Guantánamo, Cuba 146/L7
Guantánamo, Cuba 158/K4
Guantánamo, Cuba 156/C2
Guantánamo (bay), Cuba 158/J4
Guantánamo (bay), Cuba 156/C3
Guantánamo Bay U.S. Nav. Reserve, Cuba 158/K4
Guan Xian, China 77/F5
Guape, Colombia 126/D6
Guapí, Colombia 126/B6
Guapi (bay), Colombia 126/A6
Guápiles, C. Rica 154/F5
Guapo (bay), Trin. & Tob. 161/A11
Guaporé (riv.) 120/C4
Guaporé (riv.), Bolivia 136/C3
Guaporé (riv.), Brazil 132/H10
Guaqui, Bolivia 136/A5
Guarambaré, Paraguay 144/B5
Guaranda, Ecuador 128/C3
Guarapuava, Brazil 132/C9
Guaratinguetá, Brazil 135/D3
Guaratinguetá, Brazil 132/E8
Guarda (dist.), Portugal 33/C2
Guarda, Portugal 33/C2
Guardatinajas, Venezuela 124/E3
Guardiagrele, Italy 34/E3
Guardia Mitre, Argentina 143/D5
Guardian (bank), C. Rica 154/D6
Guardian, W. Va. (26221) 312/F5
Guareña, Spain 33/C3
Guarenésia, Brazil 135/C2
Guarero, Venezuela 124/B2
Guarico (pt.), Cuba 158/K3
Guárico (state), Venezuela 124/E3
Guarico, Venezuela 124/D3
Guárico (res.), Venezuela 124/E3
Guárico (riv.), Venezuela 124/E3
Guariquén, Venezuela 124/G2
Guarita, Honduras 154/C3
Guaro, Cuba 158/J3
Guarujá, Brazil 135/C4
Guarulhos, Brazil 135/C3
Guasave, Mexico 150/E4
Guasdualito, Venezuela 124/C4
Guasimal, Cuba 158/E2
Guasimal, Venezuela 124/D4
Guasipati, Venezuela 124/H4
Guastalla, Italy 34/C2
Guatemala 2/D5
Guatemala 146/J8
Guatemala (cap.), Guat. 146/J8
GUATEMALA 154/B3
Guatemala (cap.), Guatemala 154/B3
Guateque, Colombia 126/D5
Guatuaro (pt.), Trin. & Tob. 161/B11
Guaviare (riv.), Colombia 120/B2
Guaviare (riv.), Colombia 126/F6
Guaxupé, Brazil 135/C2
Guayabal, Cuba 158/G3
Guayabal (lake), P. Rico 161/C2
Guayabal, Amazonas, Venezuela 124/E6
Guayabal, Guárico, Venezuela 124/E3
Guayabero (riv.), Colombia 126/D6
Guayacán, Chile 138/A8
Guayaguayare, Trin. & Tob. 161/B11
Guayama (dist.), P. Rico 161/D2
Guayama, P. Rico 161/E3
Guayama, P. Rico 156/G1
Guayaneco (arch.), Chile 138/D7
Guayanés (pt.), P. Rico 161/F2
Guayanés (riv.), P. Rico 161/E2
Guayanilla, P. Rico 161/B3
Guayanilla, P. Rico 156/F1
Guayanilla (bay), P. Rico 161/B3
Guayape, Honduras 154/D3
Guayapo, Serranía (mts.), Venezuela 124/E5
Guayaquil, Ecuador 2/E6
Guayaquil, Ecuador 128/B4
Guayaquil, Ecuador 120/A3
Guayaquil (gulf), Ecuador 120/A3
Guayaquil (gulf), Ecuador 128/B4
Guayaquilaró (riv.), Argentina 143/G5
Guayaramerín, Bolivia 136/C2
Guayas (prov.), Ecuador 128/B4
Guayas (riv.), Ecuador 128/C4
Guaymas, Mexico 146/G7
Guaymas, Mexico 150/D3
Guaynabo, P. Rico 161/D1
Guayo (lake), P. Rico 161/B2
Guayos, Cuba 158/F2
Guayubín, Dom. Rep. 158/D5
Guazú-cuá, Paraguay 144/D5
Gubakha, U.S.S.R. 48/F4
Gubakha, U.S.S.R. 52/J3
Guban (reg.), Somalia 115/H1
Gubat, Philippines 82/E4
Gubbio, Italy 34/D3
Guben (Wilhelm-Pieck-Stadt), E. Germany 22/F3
Guben (Gubin), Poland 47/B3
Gubin, Poland 47/B3
Gubkin, U.S.S.R. 52/E4
Guckeen, Minn. (†56013) 255/D7
Gúdar, Sierra de (range), Spain 33/F2
Gudauta, U.S.S.R. 52/F6
Gudenå (riv.), Denmark 21/C5
Gudermes, U.S.S.R. 52/G6
Güdül, Turkey 63/E2
Gudur, India 68/D6
Guebwiller, France 28/G4
Guéckédou, Guinea 106/B7
Guelma, Algeria 106/F1
Guelph, N. Dak. (58447) 282/O7
Guelph, Ont. 162/H7
Guelph, Ontario 177/D4
Guelta de Zemmur (well), Western Sahara 106/B3
Guemar, Algeria 102/C1
Guemar, Algeria 106/F2
Güémez, Mexico 150/K5
Güeppí, Peru 128/E3
Guerara, Algeria 106/E2
Güere (riv.), Venezuela 124/F3
Guéréda, Chad 111/D5
Guéret, France 28/D4
Guerneville, Calif. (95446) 204/B5
Guernica y Luno, Spain 33/E1
Guernsey (isl.), Chan. Is. 13/E8
Guernsey (isl.), Chan. Is. 10/E6
Guernsey, Iowa (50172) 229/J5
Guernsey (co.), Ohio 284/H5
Guernsey, Sask. 181/F4
Guernsey, Wyo. (82214) 319/H3
Guernsey (res.), Wyo. 319/H3
Guerra, Texas (78360) 303/F11
Guerrero (state), Mexico 150/J8
Guerzim, Algeria 106/D3
Gueydan, La. (70542) 238/E6
Guffey, Colo. (80820) 208/H5
Gugerd, Kuh-e (mts.), Iran 66/H3
Guggisberg, Switzerland 39/D3
Gughe (mt.), Ethiopia 111/G6
Guiana (isl.), Ant. & Bar. 161/E11
Guiana Highlands (plat.) 120/C2
Guichi, China 77/J5
Guichón, Uruguay 145/B3
Guidder, Cameroon 115/B2
Guide, China 77/F4
Guide Rock, Nebr. (68942) 264/F4
Guidonia, Italy 34/F6
Guiglo, Ivory Coast 106/C7
Guihulngan, Philippines 82/D5
Güija (lake), El Salvador 154/C3
Güija (lake), Guatemala 154/C3
Guija, Mozambique 118/E4
Guijuelo, Spain 33/D2
Guilarte (mt.), P. Rico 161/B2
Guild, N.H. (03754) 268/C5
Guildford, England 13/G8
Guildford, England 10/F5
Guildford Junction, Tasmania 99/B3
Guildhall, Vt. (05905) 268/D2
Guilford, Conn. (06437) 210/E3
Guilford○, Conn. (06437) 210/E3
Guilford, Ind. (47022) 227/H6
Guilford, Maine (04443) 243/E5
Guilford○, Maine (04443) 243/E5
Guilford, Mo. (64457) 261/C2
Guilford, N.Y. (13780) 276/J6
Guilford (co.), N.C. 281/K3
Guilford○, Vt. (†05301) 268/B6
Guilin (Kweilin), China 77/G6
Guilin, China 54/N7
Guillaume-Delisle (lake), Québec 174/B1
Guimarães, Brazil 132/E3
Guimarães, Portugal 33/B2
Guimaras (isl.), Philippines 82/D5
Guimaras (str.), Philippines 82/D5
Guimba, Philippines 82/C3
Guin, Ala. (35563) 195/C3
Guinan, China 77/F4
Guinda, Calif. (95637) 204/C5
Guinea 2/J5
Guinea 102/A3
GUINEA 106/B6
Guinea (gulf) 2/K5
Guinea (gulf) 102/C4
Guinea (gulf), Benin 106/E8
Guinea (gulf), Ghana 106/E8
Guinea (gulf), Guinea-Biss. 106/E8
Guinea (gulf), Ivory Coast 106/E8
Guinea (gulf), Nigeria 106/E8
Guinea (gulf), Togo 106/E8
Guinea, Va. (†22580) 307/O4
Guinea-Bissau 2/H5
Guinea-Bissau 102/A3
GUINEA-BISSAU 106/A6
Güines, Cuba 158/C1
Güines, Cuba 156/B2
Guingamp, France 28/B3
Guion, Ark. (72540) 202/G2
Guiones (pt.), C. Rica 154/E6
Guiping, China 77/G7
Guipúzcoa (prov.), Spain 33/E1
Güira de Melena, Cuba 158/C1
Guiratinga, Brazil 132/C7
Guir Hamada (des.), Algeria 106/D2
Güiria, Venezuela 124/G2
Guisa, Cuba 158/H4
Guisanbourg, Fr. Guiana 131/F3
Guisborough, England 13/F3
Guise, France 28/E3
Guitiriz, Spain 33/C1
Guiuan, Philippines 82/E5
Guixi, China 77/J6
Gui Xian, China 77/G7
Guiyang (Kweiyang), Guizhou, China 77/G6
Guiyang, Hunan, China 77/H6
Guiyang, China 54/M7
Guizhou (Kweichow) (prov.), China 77/G6
Gujarat (state), India 68/C4
Gujranwala, Pakistan 59/K3
Gujranwala, Pakistan 68/C2
Gujrat, Pakistan 59/K3
Gujrat, Pakistan 68/C2
Gukovo, U.S.S.R. 52/F5
Gulang, China 77/F4
Gulargambone, N.S. Wales 97/E2
Gulbarga, India 68/D5
Gulbene, U.S.S.R. 53/D2
Gulch (cape), Newf. 166/B2
Gulen, Norway 18/D6
Gulf (co.), Fla. 212/D7
Gulf, N.C. (27256) 281/L3
Gulf Breeze, Fla. (32561) 212/B6
Gulf Crest, Ala. (†36521) 195/B8
Gulf Hammock, Fla. (32639) 212/D2
Gulf Harbors, Fla. (†33552) 212/D3
Gulf Island Nat'l Seashore, Fla. 212/B6
Gulf Islands Nat'l Seashore, Miss. 256/G10
Gulfport, Fla. (33737) 212/B3
Gulf Port, Ill. (†52601) 222/B3
Gulfport, Miss. 188/J4
Gulfport, Miss. (*39501) 256/F10
Gulf Shores, Ala. (36542) 195/C10
Gulf Stream, Fla. (†33444) 212/F5
Gulgong, N.S. Wales 97/E3
Gulian, China 77/K1
Gulin, China 77/G6
Gulistan, 48/G5
Gulja (Yining), China 77/B3
Gulkana, Alaska (†99586) 196/J2
Gull (lake), Alberta 182/C3
Gull (lake), Minn. 255/D4
Gull (isl.), Newf. 166/D2
Gullane, Scotland 15/F4
Gull Bay, Ontario 177/H5
Gull Bay, Ontario 175/C3
Gullfoot (lake), Ontario 177/F3
Gull Island, Newf. 166/D2
Gull Island (pt.), Newf. 166/D2
Gulliver, Mich. (49840) 250/D2
Gull Lake, Alberta 182/D3
Gull Lake, Sask. 181/C5
Gully, Minn. (56646) 255/C3
Gülnar, Turkey 63/E4
Gulnare, Colo. (81042) 208/K8
Gulnare, Ky. (41530) 237/S5
Gulquac (lake), New Bruns. 170/D2
Gulquac (riv.), New Bruns. 170/C2
Gülşehir, Turkey 63/F3
Gulu, Uganda 115/F3
Gulvain (mt.), Scotland 15/C4
Guma (Pishan), China 77/A4
Gumaca, Philippines 82/D4
Gumare, Botswana 118/C3
Gumbranch, Georgia (†31313) 217/J7
Gumel, Nigeria 106/F6
Gumeracha, S. Australia 94/C7
Gumma (pref.), Japan 81/J5
Gummersbach, W. Germany 22/B3
Gummi, Nigeria 106/F6
Gum Spring, Va. (23065) 307/N5
Gum Springs, Ark. (†71923) 202/D5
Gümüş, Turkey 63/F2
Gümüşhacıköy, Turkey 63/F2
Gümüşhane (prov.), Turkey 63/H2
Gümüşhane, Turkey 59/C1
Gümüşhane, Turkey 63/H2
Gun (cay), Bahamas 156/B1
Gun (lake), Mich. 250/D6
Guna, India 68/D4
Gunbower, Victoria 97/C4
Gundagai, N.S. Wales 97/D4
Gunderbooka (ranges), N.S. Wales 97/C2
Gündoğmuş, Turkey 63/D4
Güney, Turkey 63/C3
Gunflint Trail, Minn. (†55604) 255/F1
Gungu, Zaire 115/C5
Gunisao (lake), Manitoba 179/J3
Gunlock, Utah (84733) 304/A6
Gunn, Alberta 182/C3
Gunna (isl.), Scotland 15/B4
Gunnbjørn (mt.), Greenl. 4/C11
Gunn City, Mo. (†64760) 261/D5
Gunnedah, N. S. Wales 88/H6
Gunnedah, N.S. Wales 97/F2
Gunning, N.S. Wales 97/E4
Gunnison (co.), Colo. 208/E5
Gunnison, Colo. (81230) 208/E5
Gunnison (riv.), Colo. 208/C5
Gunnison (tunnel), Colo. 208/D6
Gunnison, Miss. (38746) 256/C3
Gunnison, Utah (84634) 304/C4
Gunnison (res.), Utah 304/C4
Gunnworth, Sask. 181/C4
Gunpowder (riv.), Md. 245/N3
Gunpowder, Queensland 95/A3
Gunpowder, Queensland 88/F3
Gunpowder Falls (creek), Md. 245/M2
Guntakal, India 68/D5
Gunter, Ontario 177/G3
Gunter, Oreg. (†97436) 291/D4
Gunter Air Force Base, Ala. 195/F6
Guntersville, Ala. (35976) 195/F2
Guntersville (dam), Ala. 195/F2
Guntersville (lake), Ala. 195/F2
Gunton, Manitoba 179/E4
Guntown, Miss. (38849) 256/G2
Guntur, India 54/K8
Guntur, India 68/D5
Gunungapi (isl.), Indonesia 85/H7
Günzburg, W. Germany 22/D4
Gunzenhausen, W. Germany 22/D4
Gurabo, P. Rico 161/E2
Gurais, India 68/D2
Gurdon, Ark. (71743) 202/D6
Gurgan (Gorgan), Iran 66/J2
Gurguéia (riv.), Brazil 132/E5
Guri, Venezuela 124/G4
Guri (dam), Venezuela 120/C2
Guri (res.), Venezuela 120/C2
Guri (res.), Venezuela 124/G4
Gurk, Austria 41/C3
Gurla Mandhada (mt.), China 77/B5
Gurley, Ala. (35748) 195/F1
Gurley, La. (†70730) 238/H5
Gurley, Nebr. (69141) 264/B3
Gurley, N.S. Wales 97/E1
Gurley, S.C. (†29569) 296/J3
Gurleyville, Conn. (†06268) 210/G1
Gurnee, Ill. (60031) 222/B4
Gurnet (pt.), Mass. 249/M4
Gurney, Wis. (54528) 317/F3
Gurneyville, Alberta 182/E2
Guro, Mozambique 118/E3
Gürpınar, Turkey 63/K3
Gurteen, Ireland 17/D3
Gurtnellen, Switzerland 39/G3
Gürün, Turkey 63/G3
Gurupá, Brazil 132/D3
Gurupi, Brazil 132/D5
Gurupi, Brazil 120/E4
Gurupi, Serra do (range), Brazil 132/E4
Gurupi (riv.), Brazil 132/E3
Gur'yev, U.S.S.R. 54/G5
Gur'yev, U.S.S.R. 48/F5
Gusau, Nigeria 106/F6
Gusau, Nigeria 102/C3
Gusher, Utah (84030) 304/E3
Gusinje, Yugoslavia 45/D4
Gusinoozersk, U.S.S.R. 48/L4
Gus'-Khrustal'nyy, U.S.S.R. 52/F3
Güssing, Austria 41/D3
Gustavo Díaz Ordaz, Mexico 150/K3
Gustavus, Alaska (99826) 196/M1
Gustavus, Ohio (†44417) 284/J3
Gustine, Calif. (95322) 204/D6
Gustine, Texas (76455) 303/F6
Guston, Ky. (40142) 237/J5
Güstrow, E. Germany 22/E2
Gütersloh, W. Germany 22/C3
Guthrie, Ind. (†47421) 227/D7
Guthrie (co.), Iowa 229/D5
Guthrie, Ky. (42234) 237/G7
Guthrie, Minn. (56451) 255/D3
Guthrie, Mo. (†65063) 261/H5
Guthrie, Okla. 188/G3
Guthrie, Okla. (73044) 288/M3
Guthrie, Texas (79236) 303/D4
Guthrie Center, Iowa (50115) 229/D5
Gutiérrez Zamora, Mexico 150/L6
Guttannen, Switzerland 39/F3
Guttenberg, Iowa (52052) 229/L3
Guttenberg, N.J. (07093) 273/C2
Guttingen, Switzerland 39/H1
Gu-Win, Ala. (†35563) 195/C3
Guy, Alberta 182/B2
Guy, Ark. (72061) 202/F3
Guyana 2/G5
Guyana 120/D2
GUYANA 131/B3
Guyandotte (riv.), W. Va. 312/B6
Guyang, China 77/G3
Guymon, Okla. (73942) 288/D1
Guyot (glac.), Alaska 196/K2
Guyot (mt.), N.C. 281/C3
Guyot (mt.), Tenn. 237/P9
Guyra, N.S. Wales 97/F2
Guys, Tenn. (38339) 237/D10
Guysborough (co.), Nova Scotia 168/F3
Guysborough, Nova Scotia 168/G3
Guysborough (riv.), Nova Scotia 168/G3
Guys Mills, Pa. (16327) 294/C2
Guysville, Ohio (45735) 284/G7
Guyton, Georgia (31312) 217/K6
Guyuan, China 77/G4
Guzmán (lake), Mexico 150/F1
Guzmán Blanco, Venezuela 124/E6
Guzmanes (cays), Cuba 158/B2
Gwa, Burma 72/B3
Gwaai, Zimbabwe 118/D3
Gwabegar, N.S. Wales 97/E2
Gwadabawa, Nigeria 106/F6
Gwadar, Pakistan 59/H5
Gwadar, Pakistan 68/A4
Gwalior, India 54/J7
Gwalior, India 68/D3
Gwanda, Zimbabwe 118/D4
Gwda (riv.), Poland 47/C2
Gweebarra (bay), Ireland 17/D2
Gweebarra (riv.), Ireland 17/E2
Gwelo, (Gweru) Zimbabwe 118/D3
Gwelo, Zimbabwe 102/F6
Gwent, Wales 13/D6
Gwersyllt, Wales 13/E4
Gwinn, Mich. (49841) 250/B2
Gwinner, N. Dak. (58040) 282/P7
Gwinnett (co.), Georgia 217/D2
Gwydir (riv.), N.S. Wales 97/E1
Gwynedd, Wales 13/C4
Gwynn, Va. (23066) 307/R5
Gwynne, Alberta 182/D3
Gwynneville, Ind. (46144) 227/F5
Gyaca, China 77/D6
Gyangzê, China 77/C6
Gyaring Co (lake), China 77/C5
Gyaring Hu (lake), China 77/E5
Gyasikan, Ghana 106/D7
Gyda (pen.), U.S.S.R. 54/J2
Gyda (pen.), U.S.S.R. 4/C6
Gyda, U.S.S.R. 48/H2
Gyda (pen.), U.S.S.R. 48/H2
Gydan (Kolyma) (range), U.S.S.R. 48/Q3
Gyirong, China 77/B6
Gylling, Denmark 21/D6
Gympie, Australia 87/F8
Gympie, Queensland 88/J5
Gympie, Queensland 95/E5
Gyobingauk, Burma 72/C3
Gyoma, Hungary 41/F3
Gyöngyös, Hungary 41/E3
Gyönk, Hungary 41/E3
Győr, Hungary 7/F4
Győr, Hungary 41/D3
Győr-Sopron (co.), Hungary 41/D3
Gypsum, Colo. (81637) 208/F3
Gypsum, Kansas (67448) 232/E3
Gypsum (lake), Manitoba 179/D3
Gypsum, Ohio (43433) 284/E2
Gypsumville, Manitoba 179/D3
Gyrfalcon (isls.), N.W. Terrs. 187/M4
Gyula, Hungary 41/F3

H

Haacht, Belgium 27/F7
Haag, Austria 41/C2
Haakon (co.), S. Dak. 298/F5
Haamstede, Netherlands 27/D5
Ha'apai Group (isls.), Tonga 87/J8
Haapajärvi, Finland 18/O5
Haapamäki, Finland 18/O5
Haapsalu, U.S.S.R. 53/B1
Haar, W. Germany 22/D4
Haarlem, Netherlands 27/F4
Haarlemmermeer (Hoofddorp), Netherlands 27/F4
Haarlemmermeer Polder, Netherlands 27/B5
Haast, N. Zealand 100/B5
Haast (pass), N. Zealand 100/B6
Haast (riv.), N. Zealand 100/B5
Haasts Bluff, North. Terr. 88/E4
Haasts Bluff, North. Terr. 93/B7
Haasts Bluff Aboriginal Reserve, North. Terr. 88/E5
Haasts Bluff Aboriginal Res., North. Terr. 93/B7
Hab (riv.), Pakistan 68/B3
Hab (riv.), Pakistan 59/J4
Habahe, China 77/C2
Habana, La (Havana) (prov.), Cuba 158/C1
Habana, Cuba 158/C1
Habay, Alberta 182/A5
Habay, Belgium 27/H9
Habban, P.D.R. Yemen 59/E7
Habbaniya, Iraq 59/D3
Habbaniya, Iraq 66/C4
Habbaniya, Hor al (lake), Iraq 66/C4
Habersham (co.), Georgia 217/E1
Habersham, Georgia (30544) 217/F1
Habersham, Tenn. (†37766) 237/N8
Habiganj, Bangladesh 68/G4
Habikino, Japan 81/J8
Habomai (isls.), Japan 81/N2
Habonim, Israel 65/B2
Haboro, Japan 81/K1
Hachenburg, W. Germany 22/B3
Hachinohe, Japan 81/K3
Hachioji, Japan 81/O2
Hachiro (lag.), Japan 81/J3
Hachita, N. Mex. (88040) 274/A7
Hacıbektaş, Turkey 63/F3
Hacienda Village, Fla. (†33301) 212/B4
Hacılar, Turkey 63/F3
Hack (mt.), S. Australia 94/F4
Hackberry, Ariz. (86411) 198/B3
Hackberry, La. (70645) 238/D7
Hackensack, Minn. (56452) 255/D4
Hackensack, N.J. (*07601) 273/B2
Hackensack (riv.), N.J. 273/C1
Hacker Valley, W. Va. (26222) 312/F5
Hacketstown, Ireland 17/H6
Hackett, Ark. (72937) 202/B3
Hacketts Cove, Nova Scotia 168/E4
Hackettstown, N.J. (07840) 273/D2
Hackleburg, Ala. (35564) 195/C2
Hackleman, Ind. (†46928) 227/F4
Hackney, England 13/H8
Hackney, England 10/B5
Hacksneck, Va. (23358) 307/S5
Hacoda, Ala. (†36442) 195/F8
Hadano, Japan 81/O3
Hadar, Nebr. (68738) 264/G2
Hadarba, Ras (cape), Sudan 111/G3
Hadashville, Manitoba 179/G5
Hadd, Ras al (cape), Oman 59/G5
Hadd, Ras al (cape), Oman 54/H7
Haddam○, Conn. (06438) 210/E3
Haddam, Kansas (66944) 232/E2
Haddam Neck, Conn. (†06424) 210/E2
Haddar, Saudi Arabia 59/E5
Haddington, Scotland 10/E3
Haddington, Scotland 15/F5
Haddix, Ky. (41331) 237/P6
Haddock, Georgia (31033) 217/F4
Haddonfield, N.J. (08033) 273/B3
Haddon Heights, N.J. (08035) 273/B3
Hadejia, Nigeria 106/G6
Hadejia (riv.), Nigeria 106/F6
Hadensville, Ky. (†42234) 237/G7
Hadera, Israel 65/B3
Hadera (dry riv.), Israel 65/B3
Haderslev, Denmark 21/C7
Haderslev, Denmark 18/F9
Hadhar, Iraq 66/C3
Hadhramaut (reg.), P.D.R. Yemen 54/F8
Hadhramaut (dist.), P.D.R. Yemen 59/E7
Hadhramaut, Wadi (dry riv.), P.D.R. Yemen 59/F7
Hadibu, P.D.R. Yemen 54/G8
Hadibu, P.D.R. Yemen 59/F7
Hadım, Turkey 63/E4
Haditha, Iraq 66/C3
Haditha, Iraq 59/D3
Hadiya, Saudi Arabia 59/C4
Hadleigh, England 13/H5
Hadley, Ind. (†46122) 227/D5
Hadley, Ky. (42235) 237/H6
Hadley○, Mass. (01035) 249/D3
Hadley, Minn. (56133) 255/C7
Hadley (bay), N.W. Terrs. 187/H2
Hadley, Pa. (16130) 294/B3
Hadley-Lake Luzerne, N.Y. (12835) 276/N4
Hadlock-Irondale, Wash. (98339) 310/C2
Hadlyme, Conn. (06439) 210/F3
Hadselfjorden (fjord), Norway 18/J2
Hadspen, Tasmania 99/D3
Hadsten, Denmark 21/C5
Hadsund, Denmark 21/D4
Haedo (range), Uruguay 145/C2
Haeju, N. Korea 81/B4
Haena, Hawaii (†96714) 218/C1
Haena (pt.), Hawaii 218/C1
Hafar al Batin, Saudi Arabia 59/E4
Haffe, Syria 63/G5
Hafford, Sask. 181/D3
Hafik, Turkey 63/G3
Haflong, India 68/G3
Hafnarfjördhur, Iceland 21/B2
Haft Gel, Iran 66/F5
Hafun, Somalia 115/K1
Hafun, Ras (cape), Somalia 115/K1
Hagaman, N.Y. (12086) 276/M5
Hagan, Georgia (30429) 217/J6
Hagar, Ontario 177/D1
Hagari (riv.), India 68/D6
Hagarstown, Ill. (62247) 222/D5
Hagarville, Ark. (72839) 202/D2
Hagemeister (isl.), Alaska 196/F3
Hagen, Sask. 181/F3
Hagen, W. Germany 22/B3
Hagenow, E. Germany 22/D2
Hagensborg, Br. Col. 184/D4
Hager City, Wis. (54014) 317/A6
Hagerman, Idaho (83332) 220/D7
Hagerman, N. Mex. (88232) 274/E5
Hagerstown, Ind. (47346) 227/G5
Hagerstown, Md. (21740) 245/G2
Hagerstown, Md. 188/L3
Hagfors, Sweden 18/H6
Hagi, Japan 81/E6
Ha Giang, Vietnam 72/E2
Hagley, Tasmania 99/C3
Hagood, S.C. (†29128) 296/F3
Hags (head), Ireland 17/B6
Hague, Fla. (†32601) 212/D2
Hague (cape), France 28/C3
Hague, The (cap.), Netherlands 7/E3
Hague, The (cap.), Netherlands 27/E4
Hague, N.Y. (12836) 276/N3
Hague, N. Dak. (58542) 282/L7
Hague, Sask. 181/E3
Hague, Va. (22469) 307/P4
Haguenau, France 28/G3
Haha (isl.), Japan 87/E3
Haha (isl.), Japan 81/M3
Ha! Ha! (lake), Qué. 172/G1

Hardesty 379

Ha! Ha! (riv.) Qué. 172/G1
Hahatonka, Mo. (†65020) 261/G7
Hahira, Georgia (31632) 217/F9
Hahndorf, S. Australia 94/C8
Hahnville, La. (70057) 238/N4
Hai, Iraq 59/E3
Hai, Iraq 66/E4
Haifa (dist.), Israel 65/C2
Haifa, Israel 65/B2
Haifa, Israel 59/B3
Haifa (bay), Israel 65/C2
Haifeng, China 77/J7
Haig (lake), Alberta 182/B1
Haight, Alberta 182/D3
Haigler, Nebr. (69030) 264/C4
Haikang, China 77/G7
Haikou (Hoihow), China 77/H7
Haikou, China 54/N8
Haiku, Hawaii (96708) 218/J2
Hail, Saudi Arabia 54/F7
Hail, Saudi Arabia 59/D4
Hailar, China 77/J2
Hailar He (riv.), China 77/K2
Haile, La. (†71260) 238/F1
Hailesboro, N.Y. (13645) 276/K2
Hailey, Idaho (83333) 220/D6
Haileybury, Ontario 177/K5
Haileybury, Ontario 175/D3
Haileyville, Okla. (74546) 288/P5
Hailong, China 77/L3
Hailsham, England 13/H7
Hailun, China 77/L2
Hailuoto, Finland 18/O4
Hailuoto (isl.), Finland 18/O4
Haina, Hawaii (96727) 218/H3
Hainan (isl.), China 2/Q5
Hainan (isl.), China 54/N8
Hainan (isl.), China 77/H8
Hainaut (prov.), Belgium 27/D7
Hainburg an der Donau, Austria 41/D2
Haines, Alaska (99827) 196/M1
Haines, Oreg. (97833) 291/J3
Hainesburg, N.J. (†07832) 273/C2
Haines City, Fla. (33844) 212/E3
Haines Junction, Yukon 187/E3
Haines Landing, Maine (†04964) 243/B6
Hainesport○, N.J. (08036) 273/D4
Hainesville, Ill. (†60030) 222/A4
Hainesville, N.J. (†07826) 273/D1
Hainfeld, Austria 41/C2
Haiphong, Vietnam 54/M7
Hairy Hill, Alberta 182/D3
Haiti 2/F5
Haiti 146/L8
HAITI 158
HAITI 156/D3
Haiwee, Calif. 204/H7
Haiya Junction, Sudan 59/C6
Haiya Junction, Sudan 111/G4
Haiyan, China 77/F4
Haiyang, China 77/K4
Haiyuan, China 77/G4
Hajara, Al (plain), Iraq 66/D5
Hajarain, P.D.R. Yemen 59/E6
Hajdú-Bihar (co.), Hungary 41/F3
Hajdúböszörmény, Hungary 41/F3
Hajdúdorog, Hungary 41/F3
Hajdúhadház, Hungary 41/F3
Hajdúnánás, Hungary 41/F3
Hajdúsámson, Hungary 41/F3
Hajdúszoboszló, Hungary 41/F3
Haji Ibraham (mt.), Iraq 66/D2
Hajja, Yemen Arab Rep. 59/D6
Hajnowka, Poland 47/F2
Hajós, Hungary 41/E3
Haka, Burma 72/B2
Hakalau, Hawaii (96710) 218/J4
Hakkâri (prov.), Turkey 63/K4
Hakkâri (Çöelemerik), Turkey 63/K4
Hakkâri (mts.), Turkey 63/K4
Hakken (mt.), Japan 81/H6
Hakodate, Japan 81/K3
Hakodate, Japan 54/R5
Haku (mt.), Japan 81/H5
Hakui, Japan 81/H5
Hakusan National Park, Japan 81/H5
Hal (Halle), Belgium 27/E7
Halabja, Iraq 66/D3
Halachó, Mexico 150/O6
Halaib, Sudan 59/C5
Halaib, Sudan 111/G3
Halalii (lake), Hawaii 218/A2
Halaula, Hawaii 188/G5
Halawa, Hawaii, Hawaii (†96711) 218/G3
Halawa, Molokai, Hawaii (†96748) 218/H1
Halawa (bay), Hawaii 218/H1
Halawa (cape), Hawaii 218/H1
Halawa (stream), Hawaii 218/B3
Halawa Heights, Hawaii (†96701) 218/B3
Halberstadt, E. Germany 22/D3
Halbrite, Sask. 181/H6
Halbur, Iowa (51444) 229/D4
Halcon (mt.), Philippines 82/C4
Halcyon Dale, Georgia (†30467) 217/J5
Haldane, Ill. (†61030) 222/D1
Haldeman, Ky. (40329) 237/P4
Halden, Norway 18/G7
Haldensleben, E. Germany 22/D2
Haldimand, Ontario 177/E5
Haldimand-Norfolk (reg. munic.), Ontario 177/E5
Hale (co.), Ala. 195/C5
Hale, Argentina 143/F7
Hale, Colo. (80730) 208/P3
Hale, Camp, Colo. 208/G4
Hale, England 13/H2
Hale, Iowa (52230) 229/L4
Hale, Mich. (48739) 250/F4
Hale, Mo. (64643) 261/F3
Hale (riv.), North. Terr. 93/D8
Hale (co.), Texas 303/C3
Hale (mt.), W. Australia 92/B4
Haleakala (crater), Hawaii 218/K2
Haleakala Nat'l Park, Hawaii 218/K2
Haleb (Aleppo), Syria 59/C2
Haleb (Aleppo), Syria 63/G4
Haleburg, Ala. (†36319) 195/H8
Hale Center, Texas (79041) 303/C3
Haledon, N.J. (07508) 273/B1
Haleiwa, Hawaii (96712) 218/E1
Halen, Belgium 27/G7
Hales Corners, Wis. (53130) 317/K2
Halesowen, England 13/E5
Halesowen, England 10/G3
Hales Point, Tenn. (†38040) 237/B9
Halesworth, England 13/J5
Haley, N. Dak. (†58629) 282/D8
Haley Station, Ontario 177/H2
Haleyville, Ala. (35565) 195/C2
Haleyville, N.J. (†08349) 273/C5
Half Assini, Ghana 106/D8
Halfeti, Turkey 63/H4
Half Island Cove, Nova Scotia 168/G3
Half Moon (cay), Belize 154/D2
Halfmoon Bay, Alberta 182/C3
Halfmoon Bay, Br. Col. 184/J2
Half Moon Bay, Calif. (94019) 204/H3
Half Moon Bay (Oban), N. Zealand 100/B7
Half Moon Lake, Alberta 182/D2
Halford, Kansas (†67701) 232/B2
Halfway (riv.), Br. Col. 184/F2
Halfway, Ky. (42150) 237/J7
Halfway, Md. (†21740) 245/G2
Half Way, Mo. (65663) 261/F7
Halfway, Oreg. (97834) 291/K3
Halfway House, Hawaii (†96718) 218/H6
Halfway House, S. Africa 118/H6
Halfweg, Netherlands 27/B4
Halhul, West Bank 65/C4
Haliburton (county), Ontario 177/F2
Haliburton, Ontario 177/F2
Haliburton (lake), Ontario 177/F2
Halileli, Turkey 63/B6
Halifax, Canada 2/F3
Halifax, England 13/J1
Halifax, England 10/G1
Halifax (harb.), Grenada 161/C8
Halifax○, Mass. (02338) 249/L5
Halifax (co.), N.C. 281/O2
Halifax, N.C. (27839) 281/O2
Halifax (co.), Nova Scotia 168/E4
Halifax (cap.), N.S. 162/K7
Halifax (cap.), N.S. 146/M5
Halifax (cap.), Nova Scotia 168/E4
Halifax (harb.), Nova Scotia 168/E4
Halifax, Pa. (17032) 294/J5
Halifax (bay), Queensland 88/H3
Halifax (bay), Queensland 95/C3
Halifax○, Vt. (†05358) 268/B6
Halifax (co.), Va. 307/L7
Halifax, Va. (24558) 307/L7
Halifax Center, Vt. (†05358) 268/B6
Haliimaile, Hawaii (96787) 218/J2
Halil (riv.), Iran 59/G4
Halin, Somalia 115/J2
Halkett (cape), Alaska 196/H1
Halkirk, Alberta 182/D3
Halkirk, Scotland 10/E1
Halkirk, Scotland 15/E2
Hall (isl.), Alaska 196/D2
Hall (co.), Georgia 217/E2
Hall, Ind. (†46157) 227/D5
Hall, Ky. (†41840) 237/R6
Hall, Md. (†20716) 245/L5
Hall (isls.), Micronesia 87/F5
Hall, Mont. (59837) 262/C4
Hall (co.), Nebr. 264/F4
Hall (basin), N.W. Terrs. 187/M1
Hall (lake), N.W. Terrs. 187/K3
Hall (pen.), N.W.T. 162/K3
Hall (pen.), N.W. Terrs. 187/M3
Hall (riv.), Québec 172/C2
Hall (co.), Texas 303/D3
Hall, W. Va. (†26201) 312/F4
Halla (mt.), S. Korea 81/C7
Hallam, Nebr. (68368) 264/H4
Hallam, Victoria 97/K5
Halland (co.), Sweden 18/H8
Hallandale, Fla. (33009) 212/B4
Hallandale (isls.), Scotland 15/E2
Hallaniya (isl.), P.D.R. Yemen 59/G6
Hallau, Switzerland 39/F1
Hall Beach, N.W. Terrs. 187/K3
Hallboro, Manitoba 179/C4
Halle, Belgium 27/E7
Halle, E. Germany 7/F3
Halle (dist.), E. Germany 22/D3
Halle, E. Germany 22/D3
Halleck, Nev. (89824) 266/F2
Hällefors, Sweden 18/J7
Hallein, Austria 41/B3
Halle-Neustadt, E. Germany 22/D3
Hallett, Okla. (74034) 288/N2
Hallettsville, Texas (77964) 303/G8
Halley, Ark. (†71638) 202/H6
Halliday, N. Dak. (58636) 282/F5
Hallie, Wis. (†54729) 317/D6
Halligen (isls.), W. Germany 22/C1
Hall Meadow (brook), Conn. 210/C1
Hallock, Minn. (56728) 255/A2
Hallonquist, Sask. 181/D5
Hallowell, Kansas (66744) 232/H4
Hallowell, Maine (04347) 243/D7
Hall Park, Okla. (†73069) 288/M4
Halls (stream), N.H. 268/E1
Halls, Tenn. (38040) 237/C9
Halls (creek), Utah 304/D6
Hallsberg, Sweden 18/J7
Hallsboro, N.C. (28442) 281/M6
Halls Creek, Australia 87/C7
Halls Creek, W. Australia 88/D3
Halls Creek, W. Australia 92/D2
Halls Crossroads, Tenn. (37918) 237/O8
Hallson, N. Dak. (†58230) 282/P2
Halls Summit, Kansas (†66871) 232/G3
Hallstahammar, Sweden 18/K7
Hallstatt, Austria 41/B3
Hallstavik, Sweden 18/L6
Hallstead, Pa. (18822) 294/L2
Hall Summit, La. (71034) 238/D2
Hallsville, Ill. (†61727) 222/E3
Hallsville, Mo. (65255) 261/H4
Hallsville, Ohio (45633) 284/E7
Hallsville, Texas (75650) 303/K5
Hallton, Pa. (†15860) 294/E3
Halltown, Mo. (65664) 261/E8
Halltown, W. Va. (25423) 312/L4
Hallum, Netherlands 27/H2
Hallwilersee (lake), Switzerland 39/F2
Hallwood, Va. (23359) 307/S5
Halma, Minn. (56729) 255/B2
Halmahera (isl.), Indonesia 54/O9
Halmahera (isl.), Indonesia 85/H5
Halmahera (sea), Indonesia 85/H5
Halmstad, Sweden 18/H8
Halpine, Md. (†20852) 245/K4
Halq el Oued, Tunisia 106/G1
Hals, Denmark 21/D3
Halsell, Ala. (†36912) 195/B6
Halsey, Nebr. (69142) 264/D3
Halsey, Oreg. (97348) 291/D3
Halstad, Minn. (56548) 255/B3
Halstead, England 13/H6
Halstead, England 10/G5
Halstead, Kansas (67056) 232/E4
Haltdalen, Norway 18/G5
Haltemprice, England 13/G4
Haltemprice, England 10/F4
Haltern, W. Germany 22/B3
Haltiatunturi (mt.), Finland 18/M2
Haltom City, Texas (76117) 303/F2
Halton (reg. munic.), Ontario 177/E4
Halton Hills, Ontario 177/E4
Haltwhistle, England 13/E2
Halulu (lake), Hawaii 218/A2
Ham, Chad 111/C5
Ham, France 28/E3
Hama (prov.), Syria 63/G5
Hama, Syria 63/G5
Hama, Syria 59/C2
Hamada, Jebel (mt.), Egypt 59/B5
Hamada, Japan 81/E6
Hamadan (gov.), Iran 66/F3
Hamadan, Iran 66/F3
Hamadan, Iran 59/E3
Hamadan, Iran 54/F6
Hamamatsu, Japan 54/P6
Hamamatsu, Japan 81/H6
Hamar, N. Dak. (58336) 282/N4
Hamar, Norway 18/G6
Hamar, Saudi Arabia 59/E5
Hambantota, Sri Lanka 68/E7
Hamberg, N. Dak. (58337) 282/L4
Hamber Prov. Park, Br. Col. 184/H4
Hamblen (co.), Tenn. 237/P8
Hambleton, W. Va. (26269) 312/G4
Hamburg, Ark. (71646) 202/G7
Hamburg, Conn. (†06371) 210/F3
Hamburg, Ill. (62045) 222/C4
Hamburg, Iowa (51640) 229/B7
Hamburg, Mich. (48139) 250/F6
Hamburg, Minn. (55339) 255/D6
Hamburg, Miss. (†39661) 256/B7
Hamburg, N.J. (07419) 273/D1
Hamburg, N.Y. (14075) 276/C5
Hamburg, Pa. (19526) 294/L4
Hamburg, W. Germany 7/F3
Hamburg (state), W. Germany 22/D2
Hamburg, W. Germany 22/D2
Hamburg, Wis. (54438) 317/G5
Hamda, Saudi Arabia 59/D6
Hamden○, Conn. (06514) 210/D3
Hamden, N.Y. (13782) 276/K6
Hamden, Ohio (45634) 284/F7
Häme (prov.), Finland 18/O6
Hämeenlinna, Finland 18/O6
Hamel, Ill. (62046) 222/B2
Hamel, Minn. (55340) 255/F5
Hamel, Québec 172/G3
Hamelin Pool, W. Australia 88/A5
Hamelin Pool, W. Australia 92/A4
Hameln, W. Germany 22/C2
Hamer, Idaho (83425) 220/F6
Hamer, S.C. (29547) 296/J3
Hamersley (range), W. Australia 88/B4
Hamersley (range), W. Australia 92/B3
Hamersville, Ohio (45130) 284/C8
Hamhŭng, N. Korea 81/C4
Hami (Kumul), China 77/D3
Hami, China 54/L5
Hamill, S. Dak. (57534) 298/K6
Hamilton, Ala. (35570) 195/C2
Hamilton (lake), Ark. 202/D5
Hamilton (cap.), Bermuda 156/G3
Hamilton (mt.), Calif. 204/L3
Hamilton, Colo. (81638) 208/D2
Hamilton (co.), Fla. 212/D1
Hamilton, Georgia (31811) 217/C5
Hamilton (co.), Ill. 222/E5
Hamilton, Ill. (62341) 222/B3
Hamilton (co.), Ind. 227/E4
Hamilton, Ind. (46742) 227/H1
Hamilton (co.), Iowa 229/F4
Hamilton, Iowa (50116) 229/H6
Hamilton (co.), Kansas 232/A3
Hamilton, Kansas (66853) 232/F4
Hamilton○, Mass. (01936) 249/L2
Hamilton, Mich. (49419) 250/C6
Hamilton (co.), Minn. 256/H3
Hamilton, Miss. (39746) 256/H3
Hamilton, Mo. (64644) 261/E3
Hamilton, Mont. (59840) 262/B4
Hamilton (co.), Nebr. 264/F4
Hamilton (inlet), Newf. 166/C3
Hamilton (inlet), Newf. 146/N4
Hamilton (inlet), Newf. 162/L5
Hamilton (sound), Newf. 166/D4
Hamilton (co.), N.Y. 276/L3
Hamilton, N.Y. (13346) 276/J5
Hamilton, N. Zealand 100/E2
Hamilton, N.C. (27840) 281/P3
Hamilton, N. Dak. (58238) 282/R2
Hamilton (co.), Ohio 284/A7
Hamilton, Ohio 188/K3
Hamilton, Ohio (*45011) 284/A7
Hamilton, Ont. 146/K5
Hamilton, Ont. 162/H7
Hamilton, Ontario 177/E4
Hamilton, Oreg. (†97856) 291/H3
Hamilton, Pa. (15744) 294/D4
Hamilton (riv.), Queensland 95/B4
Hamilton, R.I. (†02852) 249/J6
Hamilton, Scotland 15/C2
Hamilton, Scotland 10/B1
Hamilton, The (riv.), S. Australia 94/D2
Hamilton, The (riv.), S. Australia 88/E5
Hamilton, Tasmania 99/C4
Hamilton (co.), Tenn. 237/L10
Hamilton (co.), Texas 303/F6
Hamilton, Texas (76531) 303/G6
Hamilton, Victoria 88/G7
Hamilton, Victoria 97/B5
Hamilton, Va. (22068) 307/N2
Hamilton, Wash. (98255) 310/D2
Hamilton City, Calif. (95951) 204/C4
Hamilton Dome, Wyo. (82427) 319/D2
Hamilton Square-Mercerville, N.J. (08690) 273/D3
Hamilton-Wentworth (reg. munic.), Ontario 177/D4
Hamina, Finland 18/P6
Hamiota, Manitoba 179/B4
Ham Lake, Minn. (55304) 255/E5
Hamler, Ohio (43524) 284/B3
Hamlet, Ind. (46532) 227/D2
Hamlet, Nebr. (69031) 264/C4
Hamlet, N.Y. (†14138) 276/B6
Hamlet, N.C. (28345) 281/K5
Hamlet, N. Dak. (†58795) 282/E2
Hamlet, Ohio (†45102) 284/B8
Hamletsburg, Ill. (62944) 222/E6
Hamlin, Alberta 182/D2
Hamlin, Iowa (50117) 229/D5
Hamlin, Kansas (†66434) 232/G2
Hamlin, Ky. (42046) 237/E7
Hamlin○, Maine (†04785) 243/H1
Hamlin (lake), Mich. 250/C4
Hamlin, N.Y. (14464) 276/E4
Hamlin, Pa. (18427) 294/M3
Hamlin, Sask. 181/C3
Hamlin (co.), S. Dak. 298/P4
Hamlin, Texas (79520) 303/E5
Hamlin, W. Va. (25523) 312/B6
Hamm, W. Germany 22/B3
Hammamet (gulf), Tunisia 106/G1
Hammar, Hor al (lake), Iraq 66/E5
Hammarstrand, Sweden 18/J5
Hamme, Belgium 27/E6
Hammel, Denmark 21/C5
Hammelburg, W. Germany 22/C3
Hammer, S. Dak. (†57255) 298/R2
Hammerdal, Sweden 18/J5
Hammerfest, Norway 4/B9
Hammerfest, Norway 18/N1
Hammerfest, Norway 7/E1
Hammersmith, England 10/B5
Hammersmith, England 13/H8
Hammerum, Denmark 21/C5
Hammett, Idaho (83627) 220/C7
Hammon, Okla. (73650) 288/H3
Hammonasset (pt.), Conn. 210/E3
Hammonasset (res.), Conn. 210/E3
Hammonasset (riv.), Conn. 210/E3
Hammond, Ill. (61929) 222/E4
Hammond, Ind. (*46320) 227/B1
Hammond, Ky. (†40935) 237/O7
Hammond, La. (70401) 238/N1
Hammond, Minn. (55938) 255/F6
Hammond, Mo. (†65762) 261/G9
Hammond, Mont. (59332) 262/M5
Hammond (riv.), New Bruns. 170/E3
Hammond, N.Y. (13646) 276/J2
Hammond, Oreg. (97121) 291/C1
Hammond, Wis. (54015) 317/A6
Hammondsport, N.Y. (14840) 276/F6
Hammondsville, Ohio (43930) 284/J4
Hammondvale, New Bruns. 170/E3
Hammondville, Ala. (†35989) 195/G1
Hammonton, N.J. (08037) 273/D4
Hamnavoe, Scotland 15/G2
Ham-Nord, Québec 172/F4
Hamoa, Hawaii (†96713) 218/K2
Hamois, Belgium 27/G8
Hamont-Achel, Belgium 27/H6
Hampden, Maine (04444) 243/F6
Hampden○, Maine (04444) 243/F6
Hampden (co.), Mass. 249/D4
Hampden○, Mass. (01036) 249/E4
Hampden, Newf. 166/C4
Hampden, N. Zealand 100/C6
Hampden, N. Dak. (58338) 282/N2
Hampden, W. Va. (25623) 312/C7
Hampden Highlands, Maine (04445) 243/F6
Hampden-Sydney, Va. (23943) 307/L6
Hampshire (co.), England 13/F6
Hampshire, Ill. (60140) 222/E1
Hampshire (co.), Mass. 249/D3
Hampshire, Tenn. (38461) 237/G9
Hampshire (co.), W. Va. 312/J4
Hampshire, Wyo. (†82701) 319/H2
Hampstead, Dominica 161/E5
Hampstead, Md. (21074) 245/L2
Hampstead, New Bruns. 170/D3
Hampstead○, N.H. (03841) 268/E6
Hampstead, N.C. (28443) 281/O6
Hampstead, Québec 172/H4
Hampton, Ark. (71744) 202/F6
Hampton○, Conn. (06247) 210/G1
Hampton, Fla. (32044) 212/D2
Hampton, Georgia (30228) 217/D4
Hampton, Ill. (61256) 222/C2
Hampton, Iowa (50441) 229/G3
Hampton, Ky. (42047) 237/E6
Hampton, Minn. (55031) 255/E6
Hampton, Miss. (†38744) 256/B4
Hampton, Nebr. (68843) 264/G4
Hampton, New Bruns. 170/E3
Hampton, N.H. (03842) 268/F6
Hampton○, N.H. (03842) 268/F6
Hampton, N.J. (08827) 273/D2
Hampton, N.Y. (12837) 276/O3
Hampton, Nova Scotia 168/C4
Hampton, Oreg. (†97712) 291/G4
Hampton, Pa. (†17350) 294/H6
Hampton (co.), S.C. 296/E6
Hampton, S.C. (29924) 296/E6
Hampton, Tenn. (37658) 237/S8
Hampton (I.C.), Va. (*23601) 307/R6
Hampton Bays, N.Y. (11946) 276/R9
Hampton Beach, N.H. (03842) 268/F6
Hampton Falls○, N.H. (03844) 268/F6
Hampton Nat'l Hist. Site, Md. 245/M3
Hampton Park, Victoria 97/K6
Hampton Park, Victoria 88/M8
Hampton Roads (est.), Va. 307/R7
Hampton Springs, Fla. (†32347) 212/C1
Hamptonville, N.C. (27020) 281/H2
Hamrat esh Sheikh, Sudan 111/E5
Hamrin, Jabal (mts.), Iraq 66/D3
Hams Bluff (prom.), Virgin Is. (U.S.) 161/E3
Hams Fork (riv.), Wyo. 319/B4
Ham-Sud, Québec 172/F4
Hamton, Sask. 181/J4
Hamtramck, Mich. (48212) 250/B6
Hamur, Turkey 63/K3
Han (riv.), China 54/N6
Han (riv.), S. Korea 81/C5
Hana, Hawaii 188/F5
Hana, Hawaii (96713) 218/K2
Hanac, Turkey 63/K2
Hanaford (Logan), Ill. (†62856) 222/E6
Hanagita (peak), Alaska 196/K2
Hanahan, S.C. (29410) 296/H6
Hanakiya, Saudi Arabia 59/D5
Hanalei, Hawaii (96714) 218/C1
Hanalei (bay), Hawaii 218/C1
Hanalei (riv.), Hawaii 218/C1
Hanamaki, Japan 81/K4
Hanamalo (pt.), Hawaii 218/F7
Hanamaulu, Hawaii (96715) 218/C1
Hanapepe, Hawaii (96716) 218/C2
Hanapepe (bay), Hawaii 218/C2
Hanau, W. Germany 22/C3
Hanbogd, Mongolia 77/G3
Hanceville, Ala. (35077) 195/E2
Hancheng, China 77/H4
Hanchung (Hanzhong), China 77/G5
Hancock, Conn. (†06786) 210/C2
Hancock (co.), Georgia 217/G4
Hancock (co.), Ill. 222/B3
Hancock (co.), Ind. 227/F5
Hancock (co.), Iowa 229/F2
Hancock, Iowa (51536) 229/C6
Hancock (co.), Ky. 237/H5
Hancock (co.), Maine 243/G6
Hancock○, Maine (04640) 243/G6
Hancock, Md. (21750) 245/F2
Hancock○, Mass. (01237) 249/A2
Hancock, Mich. (49930) 250/G1
Hancock, Minn. (56244) 255/C5
Hancock (co.), Miss. 256/E10
Hancock, Mo. (†65452) 261/H7
Hancock○, N.H. (03449) 268/C6
Hancock (mt.), N.H. 268/D3
Hancock, N.Y. (13783) 276/K7
Hancock (co.), Ohio 284/C3
Hancock (co.), Tenn. 237/P7
Hancock○, Vt. (05748) 268/B4
Hancock (co.), W. Va. 312/E2
Hancock, W. Va. (25424) 312/K3
Hancock, Wis. (54943) 317/G7
Hancocks Bridge, N.J. (08038) 273/C4
Hand (co.), S. Dak. 298/L4
Handa (isl.), Scotland 15/C2
Handan (Hantan), China 77/H4
Handan, China 54/N6
Handel, Sask. 181/C3
Handeni, Tanzania 115/G5
Handies (peak), Colo. 208/E7
Handley, W. Va. (25102) 312/D6
Handlová, Czech. 41/E2
Handsom, Va. (23859) 307/O7
Handsworth, Sask. 181/J6
Haney, Br. Col. 184/L3
Hanford, Calif. (93230) 204/F7
Hanford Reservation, Wash. 310/F4
Hangayn Nuruu (mts.), Mongolia 77/E2
Hangchow (Hangzhou), China 77/J5
Hanggin, China 77/G4
Hanging Rock, Ohio (45635) 284/E8
Hangklip (cape), S. Africa 118/F7
Hangö, Finland 18/N7
Hangöudd (prom.), Finland 18/N7
Hangzhou (Hangchow), China 77/J5
Hangzhou, China 54/N6
Hangzhou Wan (bay), China 77/K5
Hanh, Mongolia 77/F1
Hani, Turkey 63/J3
Haniqra, Rosh (cape), Israel 65/C1
Hanish (isls.), Yemen Arab Rep. 59/D7
Hankinson, N. Dak. (58041) 282/S7
Hanko (Hangö), Finland 18/N7
Hanks, N. Dak. (†58856) 282/C2
Hanksville, Utah (84734) 304/D5
Hanle, India 68/D2
Hanley, Sask. 181/E4
Hanley Falls, Minn. (56245) 255/C6
Hanley Hills, Mo. (†63101) 261/P2
Hanlontown, Iowa (50444) 229/G2
Hanmer, N. Zealand 100/D5
Hann (mt.), W. Australia 92/D1
Hanna, Alberta 182/E4
Hanna, Alta. 162/E5
Hanna, Ind. (46340) 227/D2
Hanna, La. (71035) 238/D3
Hanna, Okla. (74845) 288/P4
Hanna, Utah (84031) 304/D3
Hanna, Wyo. (82327) 319/F4
Hanna City, Ill. (61536) 222/D3
Hannaford, N. Dak. (58448) 282/O5
Hannah, N. Dak. (58239) 282/N2
Hannah (bay), Ontario 175/D2
Hannawa Falls, N.Y. (13647) 276/L1
Hannibal, Mo. (63401) 261/K3
Hannibal, Mo. 188/H3
Hannibal, N.Y. (13074) 276/G4
Hannibal, Ohio (43931) 284/J6
Hannibal, Wis. (54439) 317/E5
Hanno, Japan 81/O2
Hannover, N. Dak. (58543) 282/H5
Hannover, W. Germany 7/E3
Hannover, W. Germany 22/C2
Hannuit (Hannut), Belgium 27/G7
Hannut, Belgium 27/G7
Hanöbukten (bay), Sweden 18/J9
Hanoi (cap.), Vietnam 2/Q4
Hanoi (cap.), Vietnam 54/M7
Hanover (isl.), Chile 120/B8
Hanover (isl.), Chile 138/D9
Hanover, Conn. (06350) 210/G2
Hanover, Ill. (61041) 222/C1
Hanover, Ind. (47243) 227/F7
Hanover, Kansas (66945) 232/F2
Hanover○, Maine (04237) 243/B7
Hanover, Md. (21201) 245/M4
Hanover○, Mass. (02339) 249/L4
Hanover, Mich. (49241) 250/E6
Hanover, Minn. (55341) 255/E5
Hanover, N.H. (03755) 268/C4
Hanover○, N.H. (03755) 268/C4
Hanover, N. Mex. (88041) 274/A6
Hanover, Ohio (†43055) 284/F5
Hanover, Ontario 177/C3
Hanover, Pa. (17331) 294/J6
Hanover (co.), Va. 307/N5
Hanover, Va. (23069) 307/O5
Hanover, W. Va. (24839) 312/C7
Hanover Park, Ill. (60103) 222/A5
Hanoverton, Ohio (44423) 284/J4
Hansboro, N. Dak. (58339) 282/M2
Hansell, Iowa (50640) 229/G3
Hansen, Idaho (83334) 220/D7
Hansford (co.), Texas 303/C1
Han Shui (riv.), China 77/H5
Hanska, Minn. (56041) 255/D6
Hans Lollik (isls.), Virgin Is. (U.S.) 161/B4
Hanson, Ky. (42413) 237/G6
Hanson, Mass. (02341) 249/L4
Hanson○, Mass. (02341) 249/L4
Hanson (bay), N. Zealand 100/E7
Hanson (riv.), North. Terr. 93/C6
Hanson, Okla. (†74955) 288/S4
Hanson (co.), S. Dak. 298/O6
Hansonville, Va. (†24266) 307/D7
Hanstholm, Denmark 21/B3
Hanston, Kansas (67849) 232/C3
Hansville, Wash. (98340) 310/C3
Hantan (Handan), China 77/H4
Hants (co.), Nova Scotia 168/D4
Hant's Harbour, Newf. 166/D2
Hantsport, Nova Scotia 168/D3
Hantzsch (riv.), N.W. Terrs. 187/L3
Hanumangarh, India 68/C3
Hanwood, N.S. Wales 97/C4
Hanyuan, China 77/F6
Hanzhong (Hanchung), China 77/G5
Hao (atoll), Fr. Poly. 87/N7
Haouach, Wadi (dry riv.), Chad 111/C4
Haparanda, Sweden 18/N4
Hapeville, Georgia (30354) 217/K2
Happy, Ky. (41746) 237/P6
Happy, Texas (79042) 303/C3
Happy Adventure, Newf. 166/D2
Happy Camp, Calif. (96039) 204/B2
Happy Jack, Ariz. (86024) 198/D4
Happy Jack, La. (†70083) 238/L7
Happy Valley, Oreg. (†97222) 291/B2
Happy Valley-Goose Bay, Newf. 166/B3
Haql, Saudi Arabia 59/C4
Harad, Saudi Arabia 59/E5
Harads, Sweden 18/M3
Harahan, La. (70123) 238/O4
Haraja, Saudi Arabia 59/D6
Haralson (co.), Georgia 217/B3
Haralson, Georgia (30229) 217/C4
Haramachi, Japan 81/K5
Harar (prov.), Ethiopia 111/H6
Harar, Ethiopia 111/H6
Harar, Ethiopia 102/G4
Harardera, Somalia 115/J3
Harare (Salisbury) (cap.), Zimbabwe 102/E6
Haraz, Chad 111/C5
Harbel, Liberia 106/B7
Harbeson, Del. (19951) 245/S6
Harbin, China 77/L2
Harbin, China 2/R3
Harbin, China 54/O5
Harbine, Nebr. (†68377) 264/G4
Harbinger, N.C. (27941) 281/T2
Harboør, Denmark 21/B4
Harbor, Oreg. (97415) 291/C5
Harbor Beach, Mich. (48441) 250/G5
Harbor City, Calif. (90710) 204/C11
Harborcreek, Pa. (16421) 294/C1
Harbor Springs, Mich. (49740) 250/D3
Harborton, Va. (23389) 307/S5
Harbor View, Ohio (43434) 284/C2
Harbour (isl.), Bahamas 156/C1
Harbour Breton, Newf. 166/C4
Harbour Deep, Newf. 166/C3
Harbour Grace, Newf. 166/D2
Harbour Grace, Newf. 162/L6
Harbour Main, Newf. 166/D2
Harbourton, N.J. (†08530) 273/D3
Harbourville, Nova Scotia 168/D3
Harburg-Wilhelmsburg, W. Germany 22/C2
Hårby, Denmark 21/D7
Harco, Ill. (†62935) 222/E6
Harcourt, Iowa (50544) 229/E4
Harcourt, New Bruns. 170/E2
Harcourt, Ontario 177/F2
Harcuvar (mts.), Ariz. 198/B5
Harda, India 68/D4
Hardangerfjord (fjord), Norway 18/D7
Hardangerfjorden (fjord), Norway 7/E3
Hardangervidda (plat.), Norway 18/E6
Hardaway, Ala. (36039) 195/G6
Hardburly, Ky. (41747) 237/P6
Hardee (co.), Fla. 212/E4
Hardee, Miss. (†39177) 256/C5
Hardeeville, S.C. (29927) 296/E7
Hardeman (co.), Tenn. 237/C10
Hardeman (co.), Texas 303/E3
Hardenberg, Netherlands 27/J3
Harden City, Okla. (74846) 288/N5
Harderwijk, Netherlands 27/H4
Hardesty, Okla. (73944) 288/D1

380 Hardieville

Hardieville, Alberta 182/D5
Hardin (co.), Ill. 222/E6
Hardin, Ill. (62047) 222/C4
Hardin (co.), Iowa 229/G4
Hardin (co.), Ky. 237/K5
Hardin, Ky. (42048) 237/E7
Hardin, Mo. (64035) 261/E4
Hardin, Mont. (59034) 262/J5
Hardin (co.), Ohio 284/C4
Hardin (co.), Tenn. 237/E10
Hardin (co.), Texas 303/K7
Harding (lake), Ala. 195/H5
Harding (lake), Georgia 217/B5
Harding, Manitoba 179/B5
Harding, Minn. (56364) 255/E4
Harding (co.), N. Mex. 274/F3
Harding (pt.), Nova Scotia 168/D5
Harding (co.), S. Dak. 298/B2
Harding, W. Va. (†26250) 312/G5
Harding Icefield, Alaska 196/C2
Hardingville, N.J. (†08343) 273/C4
Hardinsburg, Ind. (47125) 227/E8
Hardinsburg, Ky. (40143) 237/H5
Hardin Springs, Ky. (†42712) 237/J5
Hardinville, Ill. (†62449) 222/F5
Hardinxveld-Giessendam, Netherlands 27/G5
Hardisty, Alberta 182/E3
Hardisty (lake), N.W. Terrs. 187/G3
Hardman, Oreg. (†97836) 291/H2
Hardoi, India 68/E3
Hardshell, Ky. (41348) 237/P6
Hardt (mts.), W. Germany 22/C4
Hardtner, Kansas (67057) 232/D4
Hardwar, India 68/D2
Hardwick (Midway-Hardwick), Georgia (31034) 217/F4
Hardwick○, Mass. (01037) 249/F3
Hardwick, Minn. (56134) 255/B7
Hardwick, Vt. (05843) 268/C2
Hardwick○, Vt. (05843) 268/C2
Hardwick (lake), Vt. 268/C2
Hardwicke, New Bruns. 170/E1
Hardwicke Island, Br. Col. 184/E5
Hardwood Ridge, New Bruns. 170/D2
Hardy, Ark. (72542) 202/H1
Hardy (pen.), Chile 138/F11
Hardy, Iowa (50545) 229/E3
Hardy, Ky. (41531) 237/S5
Hardy, Miss. (†38901) 256/E3
Hardy, Nebr. (68943) 264/G4
Hardy, Okla. (†74641) 288/N1
Hardy, Sask. 181/G6
Hardy, Va. (24101) 307/J6
Hardy (co.), W. Va. 312/J4
Hardyville, Ky. (42746) 237/K6
Hare (bay), Newf. 166/C3
Hare (fjord), N.W. Terrs. 187/K1
Hare Bay, Newf. 166/D4
Harelbeke, Belgium 27/C7
Harfleur, France 28/D3
Harford (co.), Md. 245/N2
Harford, N.Y. (13784) 276/H6
Harford, Pa. (18823) 294/L2
Hargeysa, Somalia 115/H2
Hargeysa, Somalia 102/G4
Hargill, Texas (78549) 303/F11
Hargrave, Manitoba 179/A5
Hargwen, Alberta 182/B3
Har Hu (lake), China 77/E4
Hari (riv.), Indonesia 85/C6
Harib, Yemen Arab Rep. 59/E7
Haricha Hamada (des.), Mali 106/D4
Harim, Syria 63/G4
Harima (sea), Japan 81/G6
Harima, Jordan 65/D2
Haringey, England 10/B5
Haringey, England 13/H8
Haringvliet (str.), Netherlands 27/E5
Hariq, Saudi Arabia 59/E5
Harirud (riv.), Afghanistan 68/A1
Harirud (riv.), Afghanistan 59/H3
Hari Rud (riv.), Iran 66/M3
Haris, West Bank 65/C3
Harjavalta, Finland 18/M6
Harjo, Okla. (†74854) 288/N4
Harkaway, Victoria 97/K5
Harkers Island, N.C. (28531) 281/R5
Harkiko, Ethiopia 111/G4
Harlan, Ind. (46743) 227/H2
Harlan, Iowa (51537) 229/C5
Harlan, Kansas (67641) 232/D2
Harlan (co.), Ky. 237/P7
Harlan, Ky. (40831) 237/P7
Harlan (co.), Nebr. 264/F4
Harlan, Oreg. (†97343) 291/D3
Harlan County (lake), Nebr. 264/E5
Harlech, Wales 10/E4
Harlech, Wales 13/C5
Harlem, Fla. (33440) 212/F5
Harlem, Georgia (30814) 217/H4
Harlem, Mont. (59526) 262/H2
Harlem Springs, Ohio (44631) 284/J4
Harleston, England 13/J5
Harleton, Texas (75651) 303/K5
Hårlev, Denmark 21/F7
Harleyville, S.C. (29448) 296/G5
Harlingen, Netherlands 27/G2
Harlingen, N.J. (†08502) 273/D3
Harlingen, Texas (78550) 303/G11
Harlingen, Texas 188/G5
Harlow, England 13/H7
Harlow, N. Dak. (58340) 282/M3
Harlowton, Mont. (59036) 262/F4
Harman, W. Va. (26270) 312/G5
Harman-Maxie, Va. (24618) 307/D6
Harmans, Md. (21077) 245/M4
Harmattan, Alberta 182/C4
Harmon, Ill. (61042) 222/D2
Harmon (co.), Okla. 288/G5
Harmon, Okla. (73832) 288/G2
Harmonsburg, Pa. (16422) 294/B2
Harmony, Ark. (†72830) 202/D2
Harmony, Ind. (47853) 227/C5
Harmony, Maine (04942) 243/D6
Harmony○, Maine (04942) 243/D6
Harmony, Minn. (55939) 255/F7
Harmony, N.C. (28634) 281/H3
Harmony, Pa. (16037) 294/B4
Harmony, R.I. (02829) 249/H5
Harmony, W. Va. (25246) 312/D5
Harms, Tenn. (†37334) 237/H10
Harned, Ky. (40144) 237/J5
Harnett (co.), N.C. 281/M4
Harney (lake), Fla. 212/F3
Harney, Md. (†21787) 245/K2
Harney (co.), Oreg. 291/H4
Harney (lake), Oreg. 188/C2
Harney, Oreg. (†97720) 291/J4
Harney (lake), Oreg. 291/H4
Harney (peak), S. Dak. 298/B6
Härnösand, Sweden 18/L5
Haro, Spain 33/E1
Haro (str.), Wash. 310/B2
Harold, Fla. (32563) 212/B6
Harold, Ky. (41635) 237/R5
Harp (lake), Newf. 166/B2
Harper, Ill. (†61030) 222/D1
Harper, Iowa (52231) 229/J6
Harper (co.), Kansas 232/D4
Harper, Kansas (67058) 232/D4
Harper, Liberia 106/C8
Harper, Liberia 102/B4
Harper (co.), Okla. 288/G1
Harper, Oreg. (97906) 291/K4
Harper, Texas (78631) 303/E7
Harper, Wash. (†98366) 310/A2
Harper, W. Va. (25851) 312/D7
Harpers Ferry, Iowa (52146) 229/L2
Harpers Ferry, W. Va. (25425) 312/L4
Harpers Ferry Nat'l Hist. Park, Md. 245/G3
Harpers Ferry Nat'l Hist. Park, W. Va. 312/L4
Harpersville, Ala. (35078) 195/F4
Harperville, Miss. (39080) 256/E6
Harper Woods, Mich. (48225) 250/B6
Harpeth (riv.), Tenn. 237/G8
Harpster, Idaho (†83521) 220/C4
Harpster, Ohio (43323) 284/D4
Harpswell○, Maine (†04011) 243/D8
Harpswell Center, Maine (†04011) 243/D8
Harpursville, N.Y. (13787) 276/J6
Harput, Turkey 63/H3
Harquahala (mts.), Ariz. 198/B5
Harrah, Okla. (73045) 288/M4
Harrah, Wash. (98933) 310/E4
Harran, Turkey 63/H4
Harrell, Ark. (71745) 202/F7
Harrells, N.C. (28444) 281/N5
Harrellsville, N.C. (27942) 281/R2
Harricana (riv.), Québec 174/B3
Harriet, Ark. (72939) 202/E2
Harrietsfield, Nova Scotia 168/E4
Harrietta, Mich. (49638) 250/D4
Harriettsville, Ohio (†45745) 284/H6
Harrigan Cove, Nova Scotia 168/F4
Harriman, N.Y. (10926) 276/M8
Harriman, Oreg. (†97601) 291/E5
Harriman, Tenn. (37748) 237/M9
Harriman (res.), Vt. 268/B6
Harrington (sound), Bermuda 156/G3
Harrington, Del. (19952) 245/R5
Harrington○, Maine (04643) 243/H6
Harrington (lake), Maine 243/E4
Harrington, N.S. Wales 97/G2
Harrington, S. Dak. (†57551) 298/G7
Harrington, Wash. (99134) 310/G3
Harrington Harbour, Québec 174/F2
Harrington Park, N.J. (07640) 273/C1
Harris, Calif. (†95440) 204/B3
Harris (co.), Georgia 217/C5
Harris, Iowa (51345) 229/C2
Harris, Kansas (†66032) 232/G3
Harris, Mich. (49845) 250/B3
Harris, Minn. (55032) 255/F5
Harris, Mo. (64645) 261/F2
Harris, Okla. (†74740) 288/S7
Harris, Sask. 181/D4
Harris (dist.), Scotland 15/B3
Harris (dist.), Scotland 10/C2
Harris (sound), Scotland 15/A3
Harris (sound), Scotland 10/C2
Harris (lake), S. Australia 94/D4
Harris, Tenn. (†38261) 237/C8
Harris (co.), Texas 303/J8
Harrisburg, Ark. (72432) 202/J2
Harrisburg, Ill. (62946) 222/E6
Harrisburg, Ind. (†47331) 227/G5
Harrisburg, Mo. (65256) 261/H4
Harrisburg, Nebr. (69345) 264/A3
Harrisburg, N.C. (28075) 281/H4
Harrisburg, Ohio (43126) 284/D6
Harrisburg, Oreg. (97446) 291/D3
Harrisburg (cap.), Pa. 188/L2
Harrisburg (cap.), Pa. 146/L5
Harrisburg (cap.), Pa. (*17101) 294/H5
Harrisburg, S. Dak. (57032) 298/R7
Harrismith, S. Africa 118/D5
Harrison (bay), Alaska 196/H1
Harrison, Ark. (72601) 202/D1
Harrison (lake), Br. Col. 184/M2
Harrison, Georgia (31035) 217/G5
Harrison, Idaho (83833) 220/B2
Harrison, Ill. (†61072) 222/D1
Harrison (co.), Ind. 227/E8
Harrison (co.), Iowa 229/B5
Harrison (co.), Ky. 237/N4
Harrison○, Maine (04040) 243/B7
Harrison, Mich. (48625) 250/E4
Harrison (co.), Miss. 256/F10
Harrison (co.), Mo. 261/E2
Harrison, Mont. (59735) 262/E5
Harrison, Nebr. (69346) 264/A2
Harrison (cape), Newf. 166/C3
Harrison (cape), Newf. 162/L5
Harrison, N.J. (07029) 273/B2
Harrison, N.Y. (10528) 276/P6
Harrison (co.), Ohio 284/H5
Harrison, Ohio (45030) 284/A9
Harrison, S. Dak. (57344) 298/M7
Harrison, Tenn. (37341) 237/L10
Harrison (co.), Texas 303/K5
Harrison (co.), W. Va. 312/F4
Harrison, Wis. (†54435) 317/G5
Harrisonburg, La. (71340) 238/G3
Harrisonburg (I.C.), Va. (22801) 307/K4
Harrison Hot Springs, Br. Col. 184/M3
Harrison Valley, Pa. (16927) 294/G2
Harrisonville, Ill. (†62295) 222/C5
Harrisonville, Mo. (64701) 261/D5
Harrisonville, N.J. (08039) 273/C4
Harrisonville, Ohio (†45769) 284/F7
Harrisonville, Pa. (17228) 294/F6
Harriston, Miss. (39081) 256/C7
Harriston, Ontario 177/D4
Harristown, Ill. (62537) 222/D4
Harrisville, Ind. (†47390) 227/H4
Harrisville, Mich. (48740) 250/F4
Harrisville, Miss. (39082) 256/D7
Harrisville○, N.H. (03450) 268/C6
Harrisville, N.Y. (13648) 276/K2
Harrisville, Ohio (43974) 284/J5
Harrisville, Pa. (16038) 294/B3
Harrisville, R.I. (02830) 249/H5
Harrisville, Utah (†84401) 304/C2
Harrisville, W. Va. (26362) 312/E4
Harris Wash (creek), Utah 304/C6
Harrod, Ohio (45850) 284/C4
Harrodsburg, Ind. (47434) 227/D6
Harrodsburg, Ky. (40330) 237/M5
Harrods Creek, Ky. (40027) 237/K4
Harrogate, Br. Col. 184/J5
Harrogate, England 13/J1
Harrogate, England 10/F4
Harrogate-Shawanee, Tenn. (37752) 237/O8
Harrold, S. Dak. (57536) 298/K4
Harrold, Texas (76364) 303/F3
Harrop (lake), Manitoba 179/G2
Harrow, England 13/G8
Harrow, England 10/B5
Harrow, Ontario 177/B5
Harrow, Victoria 97/A5
Harrowby, Manitoba 179/A4
Harrowsmith, Ontario 177/H3
Harry Strunk (lake), Nebr. 264/D4
Harsens Island, Mich. (48028) 250/G6
Harshaw, Wis. (54529) 317/G4
Harstad, Norway 18/K2
Hart (lake), Fla. 212/E3
Hart (co.), Georgia 217/G2
Hart (co.), Ky. 237/K6
Hart, Mich. (49420) 250/C5
Hart (lake), Oreg. 291/H5
Hart (mt.), Oreg. 291/H5
Hart, Texas (79043) 303/B3
Hart (riv.), Yukon 187/E3
Hartbees (riv.), S. Africa 118/C5
Hartberg, Austria 41/C3
Harte, Manitoba 179/C4
Harte (mt.), Manitoba 179/A2
Hartell, Alberta 182/C4
Hartfield, Va. (23071) 307/R5
Hartford, Ala. (36344) 195/G8
Hartford, Ark. (72938) 202/B3
Hartford (co.), Conn. 210/D1
Hartford (cap.), Conn. 146/L5
Hartford (cap.), Conn. 188/M2
Hartford (cap.), Conn. (*06101) 210/E1
Hartford, Ill. (62048) 222/A2
Hartford, Iowa (50118) 229/G6
Hartford, Kansas (66854) 232/F3
Hartford, Ky. (42347) 237/H6
Hartford○, Maine (†04221) 243/C7
Hartford, Mich. (49057) 250/C6
Hartford, N.J. (†08057) 273/D4
Hartford, N.Y. (12838) 276/O4
Hartford, Ohio (†43013) 284/E5
Hartford, Ohio (44424) 284/J3
Hartford, S. Dak. (57033) 298/P6
Hartford, Tenn. (37753) 237/P9
Hartford○, Vt. (05047) 268/C4
Hartford, W. Va. (25247) 312/C4
Hartford, Wis. (53027) 317/K9
Hartford City, Ind. (47348) 227/G4
Harthill, Scotland 15/C2
Hartington, Nebr. (68739) 264/G2
Hartington, Ontario 177/H3
Hartland○, Conn. (†06091) 210/D1
Hartland, England 13/C7
Hartland (pt.), England 13/C6
Hartland (pt.), England 10/D5
Hartland, Maine (04943) 243/D6
Hartland○, Maine (04943) 243/D6
Hartland, Mich. (48029) 250/F6
Hartland, Minn. (56042) 255/E7
Hartland, New Bruns. 170/C2
Hartland○, Vt. (05048) 288/C4
Hartland, W. Va. (†25043) 312/D6
Hartland, Wis. (53029) 317/J1
Hartland Four Corners, Vt. (05049) 268/C4
Hartlepool, England 10/F3
Hartlepool, England 13/F3
Hartleton, Pa. (17829) 294/H4
Hartley, Iowa (51346) 229/C2
Hartley (co.), Texas 303/B2
Hartley, Texas (79044) 303/B2
Hartley, Zimbabwe 118/E3
Hartleyville, Alberta 182/D5
Hartline, Wash. (99135) 310/F3
Hartly, Del. (19953) 245/R4
Hartman, Ark. (72840) 202/C3
Hartman, Colo. (81043) 208/P6
Hartney, Manitoba 179/B5
Harts (pass), Wash. 310/E2
Harts, W. Va. (25524) 312/B6
Hartsburg, Ill. (62643) 222/D3
Hartsburg, Mo. (65039) 261/H5
Hartsdale, N.Y. (10530) 276/P6
Hartsel, Colo. (80449) 208/H4
Hartselle, Ala. (35640) 195/E2
Hartsfield, Georgia (31756) 217/E8
Hartsgrove, Ohio (†44085) 284/J2
Hartshorn, Mo. (65479) 261/J8
Hartshorne, Okla. (74547) 288/R5
Harts Range, North. Terr. 88/F4
Harts Range, North. Terr. 93/D7
Hartstown, Pa. (16131) 294/B2
Hartsville, Ind. (47244) 227/F6
Hartsville, Mass. (†01230) 249/B4
Hartsville, S.C. (29550) 296/G3
Hartsville, Tenn. (37074) 237/J8
Hartville, Mo. (65667) 261/G8
Hartville, Ohio (44632) 284/H4
Hartville, Wyo. (82215) 319/H3
Hartwell, Georgia (30643) 217/G2
Hartwell (dam), Georgia 217/G2
Hartwell (lake), Georgia 217/G2
Hartwell, Mo. (†64788) 261/E6
Hartwell (dam), S.C. 296/B3
Hartwell (lake), S.C. 296/A3
Hartwick, Iowa (52232) 229/J5
Hartwick, N.Y. (13348) 276/K5
Hartz (mt.), Tasmania 99/C5
Harug el Asued, El (mts.), Libya 111/C2
Haruniye, Turkey 63/G4
Har Us Nuur (lake), Mongolia 77/D2
Harvard (mt.), Colo. 208/G5
Harvard, Idaho (83834) 220/B3
Harvard, Ill. (60033) 222/E1
Harvard, Iowa (†50008) 229/G7
Harvard○, Mass. (01451) 249/H2
Harvard, Nebr. (68944) 264/F4
Harvel, Ill. (62538) 222/D4
Harvest, Ala. (35749) 195/E1
Harvester, Mo. (63303) 261/N2
Harvey, Ill. (60426) 222/B6
Harvey, Iowa (50119) 229/H6
Harvey (co.), Kansas 232/E3
Harvey, La. (70058) 238/O4
Harvey, Albert, New Bruns. 170/F3
Harvey, York, New Bruns. 170/D3
Harvey (lake), New Bruns. 170/C3
Harvey (mt.), New Bruns. 170/D3
Harvey, N. Dak. (58341) 282/L4
Harvey, W. Australia 88/B6
Harvey, W. Australia 92/A2
Harvey, W. Va. (25852) 312/D7
Harvey Cedars, N.J. (08008) 273/E4
Harveys (lake), Vt. 268/C3
Harveysburg, Ohio (45032) 284/C7
Harveys Lake, Pa. (18618) 294/E7
Harveyton, Ky. (†41718) 237/P6
Harveyville, Kansas (66431) 232/F3
Harviell, Mo. (63945) 261/M9
Harwich, England 13/J6
Harwich, England 10/G5
Harwich, Mass. (02645) 249/O6
Harwich○, Mass. (02645) 249/O6
Harwich Port, Mass. (02646) 249/O6
Harwinton, Conn. (06791) 210/C1
Harwinton○, Conn. (06791) 210/C1
Harwood, Mo. (64750) 261/D7
Harwood, N. Dak. (58042) 282/S6
Harwood, Ontario 177/F3
Harwood, Texas (78632) 303/G8
Harwood Heights, Ill. (60656) 222/B5
Harwood Island, N.S. Wales 97/G1
Harworth, England 13/F4
Haryana (state), India 68/D3
Harz (mts.), E. Germany 22/D3
Harz (mts.), W. Germany 22/D3
Harzgerode, E. Germany 22/D3
Hasa, Wadi el (dry riv.), Jordan 65/E5
Hasan Dağı, Büyük (mt.), Turkey 63/E3
Hasbrouck Heights, N.J. (07604) 273/B2
Hase (riv.), W. Germany 22/B2
Haseke (prov.), Syria 63/J4
Haselünne, W. Germany 22/B2
Hasenkamp, Argentina 143/F5
Hashtpar, Iran 66/F2
Haskeir (isl.), Scotland 15/A3
Haskell, Ark. (†72015) 202/E4
Haskell (co.), Kansas 232/B4
Haskell, N.J. (07420) 273/A1
Haskell (co.), Okla. 288/R4
Haskell, Okla. (74436) 288/P3
Haskell (co.), Texas 303/E4
Haskell, Texas (79521) 303/E4
Haskett, Manitoba 179/D5
Haskins, Iowa (†52201) 229/K6
Haskins, Ohio (43525) 284/C3
Haslach an der Mühl, Austria 41/C2
Hasle, Denmark 21/F8
Haslemere, England 13/G6
Haslemere, England 10/F5
Haslet, Texas (76052) 303/E2
Haslett, Mich. (48840) 250/E6
Haslev, Denmark 21/E7
Haslingden, England 13/H1
Hassa, Turkey 63/G4
Hassan, India 68/D6
Hassayampa (riv.), Ariz. 198/C5
Hasse, Texas (76456) 303/F6
Hassel (sound), N.W. Terrs. 187/J2
Hassel (isl.), Virgin Is. (U.S.) 161/B4
Hassell, N.C. (27841) 281/P3
Hasselt, Belgium 27/G7
Hasselt, Netherlands 27/J3
Hassfurt, W. Germany 22/D3
Hassi Messaoud, Algeria 106/F2
Hassi R'Mel, Algeria 106/E2
Hässleholm, Sweden 18/H8
Hassloch, W. Germany 22/C4
Haster, Scotland 15/E2
Hastière, Belgium 27/F8
Hastings, England 10/G5
Hastings, England 13/H7
Hastings, Fla. (32045) 212/E2
Hastings, Iowa (51540) 229/C6
Hastings, Mich. (49058) 250/D6
Hastings, Minn. (55033) 255/F6
Hastings, Nebr. 188/G2
Hastings, Nebr. (68901) 264/F4
Hastings, N. Zealand 100/F3
Hastings, N. Dak. (†58049) 282/O6
Hastings, Okla. (73548) 288/K6
Hastings (county), Ontario 177/G3
Hastings, Ontario 177/G3
Hastings, Pa. (16646) 294/E4
Hastings On Hudson, N.Y. (10706) 276/O6
Hasty, Ark. (72640) 202/D1
Hasty, Colo. (81044) 208/O6
Hasvik, Norway 18/M1
Haswell, Colo. (81045) 208/N6
Hat (peak), Calif. 204/E1
Hat (creek), S. Dak. 298/B7
Hatay (prov.), Turkey 63/G4
Hatay (Antakya), Turkey 63/G4
Hatboro, Pa. (19040) 294/M5
Hatch, N. Mex. (87937) 274/B6
Hatch, Utah (84735) 304/B6
Hatchechubbee, Ala. (36858) 195/H6
Hatcher, Georgia (†31754) 217/B7
Hatches Creek, North. Terr. 88/F4
Hatches Creek, North. Terr. 93/D6
Hatchet (mts.), N. Mex. 274/A7
Hatchett (pt.), Conn. 210/G3
Hatchie (riv.), Tenn. 237/B9
Hatchineha (lake), Fla. 212/E3
Hațeg, Romania 45/F3
Hatfield, Ark. (71945) 202/B5
Hatfield, England 13/H7
Hatfield, Ind. (47617) 227/C9
Hatfield, Ky. (†41514) 237/S5
Hatfield, Mass. (01038) 249/D3
Hatfield○, Mass. (01038) 249/D3
Hatfield, Minn. (56135) 255/B7
Hatfield, Mo. (64458) 261/D1
Hatfield, N.S. Wales 97/B3
Hatfield, Pa. (19440) 294/M5
Hatfield, Sask. 181/F4
Hatfield, Wis. (†54754) 317/E7
Hatfield Point, New Bruns. 170/E3
Hatgal, Mongolia 77/E1
Hathaway, Mont. (59333) 262/K4
Hatherleigh, Sask. 181/C2
Hathras, India 68/D3
Hatiba, Ras (cape), Saudi Arabia 59/C5
Ha Tien, Vietnam 72/E5
Hatillo, P. Rico 161/B1
Ha Tinh, Vietnam 72/E3
Hatira (mt.), Israel 65/B6
Hatley, Miss. (†38821) 256/H3
Hatley, Québec 172/F4
Hatley, Wis. (54440) 317/H6
Hato, Neth. Ant. 161/G8
Hato del Volcán, Panama 154/F6
Hato Mayor, Dom. Rep. 158/F6
Hato Rey, P. Rico 161/E1
Hatseva, Israel 65/D5
Hattem, Netherlands 27/H4
Hatteras (cape), N.C. 146/L6
Hatteras (cape), N.C. 188/M3
Hatteras, N.C. (27943) 281/T4
Hatteras (cape), N.C. 281/U4
Hatteras (inlet), N.C. 281/T4
Hatteras (isl.), N.C. 281/U4
Hatteras (cape), U.S. 2/F4
Hattiesburg, Miss. 188/H4
Hattiesburg, Miss. (39401) 256/F8
Hattieville, Ark. (72063) 202/E3
Hattieville, Belize 154/C2
Hatton, Ala. (†35672) 195/D1
Hatton, N. Dak. (58240) 282/R4
Hatton, Sask. 181/B5
Hatton, Scotland 15/G3
Hatton, Utah (†84637) 304/B5
Hatton, Wash. (99332) 310/G4
Hatuey, Cuba 158/G3
Hatvan, Hungary 41/E3
Hat Yai, Thailand 72/C6
Hatzic, Br. Col. 184/L3
Hau Bon, Vietnam 72/E4
Haubstadt, Ind. (47639) 227/B8
Haud (reg.), Ethiopia 111/J6
Haud (plat.), Somalia 115/J2
Haugan, Mont. (59842) 262/A3
Hauge, Norway 18/F7
Haugen, Wis. (54841) 317/C4
Haugesund, Norway 7/E3
Haugesund, Norway 18/D7
Haughton, La. (71037) 238/C1
Hauhungaroa (range), N. Zealand 100/E3
Haukivesi (lake), Finland 18/Q5
Haultain (riv.), Sask. 181/L3
Haunstetten, W. Germany 22/D4
Hauppauge, N.Y. (11787) 276/O9
Haura, P.D.R. Yemen 59/E7
Hauraki (gulf), N. Zealand 100/C1
Hauran, Wadi (dry riv.), Iraq 59/D3
Hauran, Wadi (dry riv.), Iraq 66/B4
Hauroko (lake), N. Zealand 100/A6
Hauru (pt.), Fr. Poly. 86/S12
Hauser, Idaho (†83854) 220/A2
Hauser (lake), Mont. 262/E4
Hauser, Oreg. (†97459) 291/C4
Hausstock (mt.), Switzerland 39/H3
Haut (isl.), Maine 243/G7
Haute (isl.), Nova Scotia 168/C3
Haute-Corse (dept.), France 28/B6
Haute-Garonne (dept.), France 28/D6
Haute-Loire (dept.), France 28/E5
Haute-Marne (dept.), France 28/F3
Hauterive, Québec 172/A1
Hauterive, Québec 174/D3
Hautes-Alpes (dept.), France 28/G5
Haute-Saône (dept.), France 28/G4
Haute-Savoie (dept.), France 28/G5
Hautes-Pyrénées (dept.), France 28/D6
Haute-Vienne (dept.), France 28/D5
Hautmont, France 28/F2
Haut-Rhin (dept.), France 28/G4
Hauts-de-Seine (dept.), France 28/A2
Haut-Zaïre (prov.), Zaire 115/E3
Hauula, Hawaii (96717) 218/E1
Havaco, W. Va. (24841) 312/C8
Havana, Ala. (35467) 195/C5
Havana, Ark. (72842) 202/D3
Havana (cap.), Cuba 156/A2
Havana (cap.), Cuba 2/E4
Havana (cap.), Cuba 146/K7
Havana (cap.), Cuba 158/C1
Havana, Fla. (32333) 212/B1
Havana, Ill. (62644) 222/D3
Havana, Kansas (67347) 232/G4
Havana, Minn. (†55060) 255/E6
Havana, N. Dak. (58043) 282/P8
Havana, Ohio (†44890) 284/E3
Havannah (chan.), New Caled. 86/H5
Havant and Waterloo, England 13/G7
Havasu (lake) 188/D4
Havasu (lake), Ariz. 198/A4
Havasu (lake), Calif. 204/L9
Havasu (lake), U.S. 146/G6
Havasupai Ind. Res., Ariz. 198/C2
Havdrup, Denmark 21/F6
Havel (riv.), E. Germany 22/E2
Havelange, Belgium 27/G8
Havelberg, E. Germany 22/D2
Havelock, Iowa (50546) 229/D3
Havelock, New Bruns. 170/E3
Havelock, N. Zealand 100/D4
Havelock, N.C. (28532) 281/P5
Havelock, N. Dak. (†58647) 282/E7
Havelock, Ontario 177/G3
Havelock North, N. Zealand 100/F3
Haven, Kansas (67543) 232/E4
Havensville, Kansas (66432) 232/F2
Haverford○, Pa. (19041) 294/M6
Haverfordwest, Wales 10/D5
Haverfordwest, Wales 13/B6
Haverhill, England 13/H5
Haverhill, Iowa (50120) 229/H5
Haverhill, Mass. (01830) 249/K1
Haverhill○, N.H. (03765) 268/C3
Haverhill, Ohio (45636) 284/E8
Havering, England 10/C5
Havering, England 13/J8
Haverstraw, N.Y. (10927) 276/M8
Havertown, Pa. (19083) 294/M6
Haviland, Kansas (67059) 232/C4
Haviland, Ohio (45851) 284/A3
Havillah, Wash. (†98855) 310/F2
Havířov, Czech. 41/E2
Havlíčkův Brod, Czech. 41/C2
Havran, Turkey 63/B3
Havre, Mont. 146/G5
Havre, Mont. 188/E1
Havre, Mont. (59501) 262/G2
Havre Boucher, Nova Scotia 168/G3
Havre de Grace, Md. (21078) 245/O2
Havre-Saint-Pierre, Québec 174/E2
Havre-St-Pierre, Que. 162/K5
Havsa, Turkey 63/B2
Havza, Turkey 63/F2
Haw (riv.), N.C. 281/K2
Hawaii 188/F5
HAWAII 218
Hawaii (co.), Hawaii 218/K7
Hawaii (isl.), Hawaii 87/L4
Hawaii (isl.), Hawaii 188/F6
Hawaii (isl.), Hawaii 218/H5
Hawaii (state), U.S. 2/B4
Hawaii (state), U.S. 87/K4
Hawaiian (isls.) 87/J3
Hawaii Kai, Hawaii (96825) 218/F2
Hawaii Nat'l Park, Hawaii (96718) 218/J6
Hawaii Volcanoes Nat'l Park, Hawaii 218/H6
Hawara, Jordan 65/D2
Hawarden, Iowa (51023) 229/A2
Hawarden, N. Zealand 100/D5
Hawarden, Sask. 181/E4
Hawarden, Wales 13/G2
Hawea (lake), N. Zealand 100/B6
Hawera, N. Zealand 100/E3
Hawes, England 13/E3
Hawesville, Ky. (42348) 237/H5
Hawi, Hawaii (96719) 218/G3
Hawick, Minn. (56246) 255/D5
Hawick, Scotland 10/E3
Hawick, Scotland 15/F5
Hawk (hills), Alberta 182/B1
Hawke (hills), Newf. 166/D2
Hawke (isl.), Newf. 166/C3
Hawke (riv.), Newf. 166/C3
Hawke (bay), N. Zealand 100/F3
Hawker, S. Australia 88/F6
Hawker, S. Australia 94/F4
Hawke's Bay, Newf. 166/C3
Hawkesbury (isl.), Br. Col. 184/C3
Hawkesbury, Ontario 177/K2
Hawkestone, Ontario 177/E3
Hawkeye, Iowa (52147) 229/J3
Hawkins, Mich. (†49677) 250/D5
Hawkins (co.), Tenn. 237/P8
Hawkins, Texas (75765) 303/J5
Hawkins, Wis. (54530) 317/E4
Hawkinsville, Georgia (31036) 217/E6
Hawk Junction, Ontario 175/D3
Hawk Junction, Ontario 177/J5
Hawk Point, Mo. (63349) 261/K5
Hawk Run, Pa. (16840) 294/F4
Hawks, Mich. (49743) 250/F3
Hawk Springs, Wyo. (82217) 319/H4
Hawley, Minn. (56549) 255/B4
Hawley, Pa. (18428) 294/M3
Hawley, Texas (79525) 303/E5
Hawleyville, Conn. (06440) 210/B3
Haworth, N.J. (07641) 273/C1
Haworth, Okla. (74740) 288/S7
Hawston, S. Africa 118/G7
Hawthorn, La. (†71446) 238/D4
Hawthorn, Pa. (16230) 294/D3
Hawthorn, Victoria 97/J5
Hawthorne, Calif. (90250) 204/C11
Hawthorne, Fla. (32640) 212/D2
Hawthorne, Nev. (89415) 266/C4
Hawthorne, N.J. (07507) 273/B2
Hawthorne, N.Y. (10532) 276/O6
Hawthorne, Victoria 88/L7
Hawthorne, Wis. (54842) 317/C3
Hawthorn Woods, Ill. (†60047) 222/B5
Haxby, England 13/F3
Haxtun, Colo. (80731) 208/O1
Hay (riv.) 162/E4
Hay (lake), Alberta 182/A5
Hay (riv.), Alberta 182/A5
Hay (riv.), Canada 146/G4
Hay, N.S. Wales 88/H6
Hay, N.S. Wales 97/C4
Hay (dry riv.), North. Terr. 88/F4
Hay (cape), North. Terr. 93/A3
Hay (dry riv.), North. Terr. 93/E7
Hay (lake), Ontario 177/F2

Hérouxville 381

Hay, Wales 10/E4
Hay, Wales 13/D5
Hay, Wash. (99136) 310/H4
Hayama, Japan 81/O3
Hayange, France 28/F3
Haycock, Alaska (†99762) 196/F1
Hayden, Ala. (35079) 195/E3
Hayden, Ariz. (85235) 198/E5
Hayden, Colo. (81639) 208/E2
Hayden, Idaho (†83835) 220/B2
Hayden (lake), Idaho 220/B2
Hayden, Ind. (47245) 227/F7
Hayden, Mo. (†65459) 261/H6
Hayden, N. Mex. (†88410) 274/F3
Hayden (peak), Utah 304/C3
Haydenburg, Tenn. (†38588) 237/K8
Hayden Lake, Idaho (83835) 220/B2
Haydenville, Mass. (01039) 249/C3
Haydenville, Ohio (43127) 284/F7
Hayes (mt.), Alaska 196/J2
Hayes (pen.), Greenl. 4/B13
Hayes, Jamaica 158/J6
Hayes, La. (70646) 238/E6
Hayes (riv.), Man. 162/G4
Hayes (riv.), Manitoba 179/K3
Hayes (co.), Nebr. 264/C4
Hayes (riv.), N.W. Terrs. 187/J3
Hayes, S. Dak. (57537) 298/H5
Hayes, Wis. (†54174) 317/J5
Hayes Center, Nebr. (69032) 264/C4
Hayesville, Iowa (52562) 229/J6
Hayesville, New Bruns. 170/D2
Hayesville, N.C. (28904) 281/B4
Hayesville, Ohio (44838) 284/F4
Hayesville, Oreg. (†97301) 291/A3
Hayfield, Iowa (50445) 229/F2
Hayfield, Minn. (55940) 255/F7
Hayfork, Calif. (96041) 204/B3
Hay Fork, Trinity (riv.), Calif. 204/B3
Hay Lakes, Alberta 182/D3
Hayle, England 13/B7
Haylow, Georgia (†31648) 217/G9
Haymana, Turkey 63/E3
Haymarket, Va. (22069) 307/N3
Hayne, N.C. (†28318) 281/M5
Haynes, Alberta 182/D3
Haynes, Ark. (72341) 202/J4
Haynes, N. Dak. (58637) 282/F8
Haynesville, La. (71038) 238/D1
Haynesville○, Maine (04446) 243/G4
Haynesville, Va. (22472) 307/P5
Hayneville, Ala. (36040) 195/E6
Hayrabolu, Turkey 63/B2
Hay River, N.W.T. 162/E3
Hay River, N.W.T. 146/G3
Hay River, N.W. Terrs. 187/G3
Hays, Alberta 182/E4
Hays, Kansas (67601) 232/C3
Hays, Mont. (59527) 262/H2
Hays, N.C. (28635) 281/G2
Hays (co.), Texas 303/F7
Haysi, Va. (24256) 307/D6
Hay Springs, Nebr. (69347) 264/B2
Haystack (mt.), Conn. 210/C1
Haystack (peak), Mont. 262/A3
Haystack (mt.), N.Y. 276/N2
Haystack (mt.), Vt. 268/B6
Haysville, Ind. (†47546) 227/D8
Haysville, Kansas (67060) 232/E4
Haysville, Pa. (†15143) 294/B4
Hayter, Alberta 182/E3
Hayti, Mo. (63851) 261/N10
Hayti, S. Dak. (57241) 298/P4
Hayti Heights, Mo. (†63851) 261/N10
Hayton, Wis. (†53014) 317/K7
Hayward, Calif. (*94541) 204/K2
Hayward (lake), Conn. 210/F2
Hayward, Minn. (56043) 255/E7
Hayward, Mo. (†63873) 261/N10
Hayward, Wis. (54843) 317/D3
Haywards-Manor Park, N. Zealand 100/B2
Haywood, Manitoba 179/D5
Haywood (co.), N.C. 281/C3
Haywood, N.C. (†27559) 281/L3
Haywood, Okla. (74548) 288/P5
Haywood (co.), Tenn. 237/C9
Haywood City, Mo. (†63736) 261/N9
Hazar (lake), Turkey 63/H3
Hazaran, Kuh-e (mt.), Iran 66/K6
Hazard, Ky. (41701) 237/P6
Hazard, Nebr. (68844) 264/F3
Hazardville, Conn. (06082) 210/E1
Hazaribagh, India 68/F4
Hazar Qadam, Afghanistan 59/J3
Hazar Qadam, Afghanistan 68/B2
Hazebrouck, France 28/E2
Hazel, Ky. (42049) 237/E7
Hazel, S. Dak. (57242) 298/P4
Hazel Cliffe, Sask. 181/J5
Hazel Crest, Ill. (60429) 222/B6
Hazeldean, New Bruns. 170/C2
Hazel Dell, Ill. (62430) 222/E4
Hazel Dell, Sask. 181/H4
Hazeldine, Alberta 182/E3
Hazel Green, Ala. (35750) 195/E1
Hazel Green, Ky. (41332) 237/O5
Hazelgreen, Mo. (†65556) 261/H7
Hazel Green, Wis. (53811) 317/F11
Hazel Grove and Bramhall, England 13/H2
Hazel Hill, Nova Scotia 168/G3
Hazelhurst, Ill. (†61064) 222/D2
Hazel Hurst, Pa. (16733) 294/E2
Hazelhurst, Wis. (54531) 317/G4
Hazel Park, Mich. (48030) 250/B6
Hazel Patch, Ky. (†40729) 237/N6
Hazelridge, Manitoba 179/F5
Hazelrigg, Ind. (†46052) 227/D4
Hazel Run, Minn. (56247) 255/C6
Hazelton, Br. Col. 162/D5
Hazelton, Br. Col. 184/D2
Hazelton (mts.), Br. Col. 184/C2
Hazelton, Idaho (83335) 220/E7
Hazelton, Kansas (67061) 232/D4
Hazelton, N. Dak. (58544) 282/K7
Hazelton, W. Va. (26535) 312*G3
Hazelton (peak), Wyo. 319/E1
Hazelwood, Ind. (†46118) 227/D5
Hazelwood, Mo. (*63042) 261/P2
Hazelwood, N.C. (28738) 281/C4
Hazen (bay), Alaska 196/E2
Hazen, Ark. (72064) 202/G4
Hazen, Nev. (89417) 266/C3
Hazen, N. Dak. (58545) 282/G5
Hazen (lake), N.W. Terrs. 187/L1
Hazen (str.), N.W. Terrs. 187/G2
Hazenmore, Sask. 181/D6
Hazerim, Israel 65/B5
Hazlehurst, Georgia (31539) 217/G7
Hazlehurst, Miss. (39083) 256/D7
Hazlet, N.J. (07730) 273/E3
Hazlet, Sask. 181/C5
Hazleton, Ind. (47640) 227/B8
Hazleton, Iowa (50641) 229/K3
Hazleton, Pa. (18201) 294/L4
Hazlett (lake), W. Australia 88/D4
Hazlettville, Del. (†19953) 245/R4
Hazor Hagelilit, Israel 65/D2
Hazro, Turkey 63/J3
Heacham, England 13/H5
Headford, Ireland 17/C5
Headland, Ala. (36345) 195/H8
Headlee, Ind. (†47960) 227/D3
Head of Amherst, Nova Scotia 168/E3
Head of Bay d'Espoir, Newf. 166/C4
Head of Bight (bay), S. Australia 94/B4
Head of Grassy, Ky. (41145) 237/P4
Head of Island, La. (†70462) 238/L2
Head of Jeddore, Nova Scotia 168/E4
Head of Millstream, New Bruns. 170/E3
Head of Saint Margarets Bay, Nova Scotia 168/E4
Headquarters, Idaho (83534) 220/C3
Headrick, Okla. (73549) 288/H5
Heads, The (prom.), Oreg. 291/C5
Heads of Ayr (cape), Scotland 15/D5
Head Waters, Va. (24442) 307/K4
Heafford Junction, Wis. (54532) 317/G4
Healdsburg, Calif. (95448) 204/B5
Healdton, Okla. (73438) 288/M6
Healdville, Vt. (05147) 268/B5
Healesville, Victoria 97/C5
Healing Springs, Ala. (†36558) 195/B7
Healing Springs, Va. (†24445) 307/J5
Healy, Alaska (99743) 196/H2
Healy, Kansas (67850) 232/B3
Healys, Va. (†23071) 307/R5
Heanor, England 13/F4
Heard (isl.), Australia 2/N8
Heard (co.), Georgia 217/B4
Hearne, Sask. 181/F5
Hearne, Texas (77859) 303/H7
Hearst (isl.) 5/B16
Hearst, Ont. 162/H6
Hearst, Ontario 177/J5
Hearst, Ontario 175/D3
Heart (lake), Alberta 182/E2
Heart (butte), N. Dak. 282/G6
Heart (riv.), N. Dak. 282/F6
Heart (lake), Wyo. 319/B1
Heart Butte, Mont. (59448) 262/C2
Heart River Settlement, Alberta 182/B2
Heart's Content, Newf. 166/D2
Heart's Delight, Newf. 166/D2
Heart's Desire, Newf. 166/D2
Hearts Hill, Sask. 181/B3
Heartwell, Nebr. (68945) 264/F4
Heartwellville, Vt. (†05350) 268/A6
Heaters, W. Va. (26627) 312/E5
Heath, Ala. (†36420) 195/F8
Heath, Alberta 182/E3
Heath (riv.), Bolivia 136/A3
Heath○, Mass. (01346) 249/C2
Heath, Mont. (†59457) 262/G3
Heath, Ohio (43055) 284/F5
Heath (riv.), Peru 128/H9
Heath (pt.), Québec 174/E3
Heathcote, Victoria 97/C5
Heatherton, Newf. 166/C4
Heatherton, Nova Scotia 168/G3
Heathhall, Scotland 15/E5
Heath Springs, S.C. (29058) 296/F2
Heath Steele, New Bruns. 170/D1
Heathsville, Va. (22473) 307/P5
Heaton, N. Dak. (58450) 282/L5
Heavener, Okla. (74937) 288/S5
Hebbardsville, Ky. (†42420) 237/G5
Hebbronville, Texas (78361) 303/F10
Hebbs Cross, Nova Scotia 168/D4
Hebburn, England 13/J3
Hebei (Hopei) (prov.), China 77/J4
Hebel, Queensland 95/C6
Heber, Ariz. (85928) 198/E4
Heber, Calif. (92249) 204/K11
Heber City, Utah (84032) 304/C3
Heber Springs, Ark. (72543) 202/G2
Hebert, La. (71436) 238/G2
Hébert (riv.), Nova Scotia 168/D3
Hébertville, Québec 172/F1
Hébertville-Station, Québec 172/F1
Hebgen (dam), Mont. 262/E6
Hebgen (lake), Mont. 262/E6
Hebi, China 77/H4
Hebo, Oreg. (97122) 291/D2
Hebrides, Inner (isls.), Scotland 10/C2
Hebrides, Inner (isls.), Scotland 15/B4
Hebrides, Outer (isls.), Scotland 10/C2
Hebrides, Outer (isls.), Scotland 15/A3
Hebrides (sea), Scotland 15/B3
Hebrides (sea), Scotland 10/C2
Hebron○, Conn. (06248) 210/F2
Hebron, Ill. (60034) 222/E1
Hebron, Ind. (46341) 227/C2
Hebron, Ky. (41048) 237/R2
Hebron○, Maine (04238) 243/C7
Hebron, Md. (21830) 245/R7
Hebron, Nebr. (68370) 264/G4
Hebron, Newf. 146/M4
Hebron, Newf. 162/K4
Hebron (fjord), Newf. 166/B2
Hebron○, N.H. (03241) 268/D4
Hebron, N. Dak. (58638) 282/G6
Hebron, Nova Scotia 168/B5
Hebron, Ohio (43025) 284/E6
Hebron, Texas (†75067) 303/G1
Hebron, West Bank 65/C4
Hebron, West Bank 59/C3
Hebron, W. Va. (26368) 312/D4
Hebron, Wis. (†53538) 317/J10
Hecate (str.), Br. Col. 162/C5
Hecate (str.), Br. Col. 146/E4
Hecate (str.), Br. Col. 184/B3
Hecelchakán, Mexico 150/O6
Heceta (isl.), Alaska 196/M2
Heceta (head), Oreg. 291/C3
Hechi, China 77/G7
Hechingen, W. Germany 22/C4
Hechuan (Hochwan), China 77/G5
Hecker, Ill. (62248) 222/D5
Hecla, Manitoba 179/F3
Hecla (isl.), Manitoba 179/F3
Hecla, S. Dak. (57446) 298/N2
Hecla Prov. Park, Manitoba 179/F3
Hector, Ark. (72843) 202/E3
Hector, Minn. (55342) 255/D6
Hector, N.Y. (14841) 276/G5
Hede, Sweden 18/H5
Hedemora, Sweden 18/K6
Hedenäset, Sweden 18/N3
Hedensted, Denmark 21/C6
Hedgesville, Mont. (†59078) 262/G4
Hedgesville, W. Va. (25427) 312/K3
Hedley, Br. Col. 184/G5
Hedley, Texas (79237) 303/D3
Hedmark (co.), Norway 18/G6
Hedon, England 13/G4
Hedrick, Iowa (52563) 229/J6
Hedville, Kansas (†67401) 232/E3
Hedwig Village, Texas (†77001) 303/H1
Heemskerk, Netherlands 27/F3
Heemstede, Netherlands 27/F4
Heer, Netherlands 27/H7
Heerde, Netherlands 27/H4
Heerenveen, Netherlands 27/H3
Heerhugowaard, Netherlands 27/F3
Heerlen, Netherlands 27/J7
Heesch, Netherlands 27/G5
Hefei (Hofei), China 77/J5
Hefei, China 54/N6
Heffley Creek, Br. Col. 184/G5
Heflin, Ala. (36264) 195/G3
Heflin, La. (71039) 238/D2
Hegang (Hokang), China 77/L2
Hegang, China 54/O5
Hegau (reg.), W. Germany 22/C5
Hegeler, Ill. (†61832) 222/F3
Hegins, Pa. (17938) 294/K4
Heiban, Sudan 111/F5
Heiberger, Ala. (†36756) 195/D5
Heide, W. Germany 22/C1
Heidelberg, Ky. (41333) 237/O5
Heidelberg, Minn. (†56071) 255/E6
Heidelberg, Miss. (39439) 256/F7
Heidelberg, Pa. (15106) 294/B7
Heidelberg, S. Africa 118/J7
Heidelberg, Victoria 97/J5
Heidelberg, Victoria 88/L7
Heidelberg, W. Germany 22/C4
Heiden, Switzerland 39/H2
Heidenau, E. Germany 22/E3
Heidenheim an der Brenz, W. Germany 22/D4
Heidenreichstein, Austria 41/C2
Heidrick, Ky. (40949) 237/O7
Heihe (Aihui) (Aigun), China 77/L1
Heijo (P'yŏngyang) (cap.), N. Korea 81/C4
Heil, N. Dak. (58546) 282/G7
Heilbron, S. Africa 118/D5
Heilbronn, W. Germany 22/C4
Heiligenblut, Austria 41/B3
Heiligenhafen, W. Germany 22/D1
Heiligenstadt, E. Germany 22/D3
Heilman, Ind. (†47523) 227/C8
Heilongjiang (Heilungkiang) (prov.), China 77/K2
Heilong Jiang (Amur) (riv.), China 77/L2
Heiloo, Netherlands 27/F3
Heilwood, Pa. (15745) 294/E4
Heimberg, Switzerland 39/E3
Heimdal, N. Dak. (58342) 282/L4
Heinola, Finland 18/P6
Heinola, Minn. (†56567) 255/C4
Heinsburg, Alberta 182/E3
Heinze Chaung (bay), Burma 72/C4
Heise, Idaho (†83443) 220/G6
Heiskell, Tenn. (37754) 237/O8
Heisler, Alberta 182/D3
Heislerville, N.J. (08324) 273/D5
Heisson, Wash. (98622) 310/C5
Heist-Knokke, Belgium 27/C6
Heist-op-den-Berg, Belgium 27/F6
Heizer, Kansas (†67530) 232/D3
Hejaz (reg.), Saudi Arabia 59/C4
Hejian, China 77/J4
Hejing, China 77/C3
Hekimhan, Turkey 63/G3
Hekla (mt.), Iceland 4/C11
Hekla (mt.), Iceland 7/C2
Hekla (vol.), Iceland 21/B1
Hekou, China 77/F7
Hel, Poland 47/D1
Hel (pen.), Poland 47/D1
Helan, China 77/G4
Heldens (pt.), St. Chris.-Nevis 161/C10
Helechawa, Ky. (41334) 237/P5
Helen, Georgia (30545) 217/E1
Helen, Md. (20635) 245/M7
Helen (lake), N. Dak. 282/K5
Helena, Ala. (35080) 195/E4
Helena, Ark. (72342) 202/J4
Helena, Calif. (96042) 204/B3
Helena, Georgia (31037) 217/G6
Helena, Mo. (64459) 261/C3
Helena (cap.), Mont. 146/G5
Helena (cap.), Mont. 188/D1
Helena (cap.), Mont. (59601) 262/E4
Helena (lake), Mont. 262/E4
Helena, N.Y. (13649) 276/L1
Helena, Ohio (43435) 284/D3
Helena, Okla. (73741) 288/K1
Helena, S.C. (†29108) 296/D3
Helensburgh, N.S. Wales 97/F4
Helensburgh, Scotland 10/A1
Helensburgh, Scotland 15/A1
Helen Springs, North. Terr. 93/C5
Helensville, N. Zealand 100/B1
Helenville, Wis. (53137) 317/J10
Helenwood, Tenn. (37755) 237/M8
Helez, Israel 65/B4
Helgoland (bay), W. Germany 22/C1
Helgoland (isl.), W. Germany 22/B1
Heliopolis, Egypt 111/J3
Helix, Oreg. (97835) 291/J2
Hellam, Pa. (17406) 294/J6
Hell Canyon (creek), S. Dak. 298/B6
Hellebaek, Denmark 21/F5
Hellendoorn, Netherlands 27/J4
Hellertown, Pa. (18055) 294/M4
Helles (cape), Turkey 63/B6
Hellevoetsluis, Netherlands 27/E5
Hellier, Ky. (41534) 237/S6
Hellín, Spain 33/F3
Hells (canyon), Idaho 220/B4
Hells Canyon (dam), Idaho 220/B4
Hells Canyon (dam), Oreg. 291/L2
Hells Canyon Nat'l Rec. Area, Idaho 220/B4
Hells Canyon Nat'l Rec. Area, Oreg. 291/K2
Hells Canyon Nat'l Rec. Area, Wash. 310/H5
Hells Half Acre, Wyo. (82601) 319/E2
Hell-Ville, Madagascar 102/G6
Hell-Ville, Madagascar 118/H2
Helm, Miss. (†38756) 256/C4
Helmand (riv.), Afghanistan 54/H6
Helmand (riv.), Afghanistan 59/J3
Helmand (riv.), Afghanistan 68/B2
Helmand (Sistan, Daryacheh-ye) (lake), Iran 66/M5
Helmer, Ind. (46744) 227/G1
Helmetta, N.J. (08828) 273/E3
Helmond, Netherlands 27/H6
Helmsburg, Ind. (47435) 227/E6
Helmsdale, Scotland 10/E1
Helmsdale, Scotland 15/E2
Helmsdale (riv.), Scotland 15/E2
Helmsley, England 13/G3
Helmstedt, W. Germany 22/D2
Helmville, Mont. (59843) 262/C4
Helotes, Texas (78023) 303/J10
Helper, Utah (84526) 304/D4
Helsenhorn (mt.), Switzerland 39/F4
Helsingborg, Sweden 18/H8
Helsingborg, Sweden 7/F3
Helsinge, Denmark 21/F6
Helsingør, Denmark 21/F6
Helsingør, Denmark 18/H8
Helsinki (cap.), Finland 18/O6
Helsinki (cap.), Finland 7/G2
Helsinki (cap.), Finland 2/L2
Helston, England 13/B7
Helston, England 10/D5
Helston, Manitoba 179/C4
Helton, Ky. (40840) 237/P7
Helton, N.C. (†28631) 281/G1
Heltonville, Ind. (47436) 227/E7
Helvecia, Argentina 143/F5
Helvetia, Pa. (†15848) 294/E3
Helvetia, W. Va. (26224) 312/F5
Helvick (head), Ireland 17/G7
Helwân, Egypt 59/B4
Helwân, Egypt 111/J3
Hemar (dry riv.), Israel 65/C5
Hemaruka, Alberta 182/E4
Hematite, Mo. (63047) 261/L6
Hemel Hempstead, England 10/F5
Hemel Hempstead, England 13/G7
Hemet, Calif. (92343) 204/H10
Hemford, Nova Scotia 168/D4
Hemingford, Nebr. (69348) 264/A2
Hemingway, S.C. (29554) 296/J4
Hemlock, Ind. (46937) 227/F4
Hemlock, Mich. (48626) 250/E5
Hemlock, N.Y. (14466) 276/E5
Hemlock (lake), N.Y. 276/E5
Hemlock, Ohio (43743) 284/F6
Hemlock (Eureka), S.C. (†29706) 296/E2
Hemlock Grove, Ohio (45738) 284/F7
Hemmingford, Québec 172/D4
Hemnes, Norway 18/J3
Hemphill (co.), Texas 303/D2
Hemphill, Texas (75948) 303/L6
Hemphill, W. Va. (24842) 312/C8
Hemple, Mo. (†64490) 261/D3
Hempstead (co.), Ark. 202/C6
Hempstead, N.Y. (*11550) 276/R7
Hempstead, Texas (77445) 303/J7
Hemse, Sweden 18/L8
Henagar, Ala. (35978) 195/G1
Henan (Honan) (prov.), China 77/H5
Henan, China 77/F5
Hen and Chickens (isls.), N. Zealand 100/E1
Henares (riv.), Spain 33/G4
Henbury, North. Terr. 93/C8
Hendaye, France 28/C6
Hendek, Turkey 63/D2
Henderson, Ala. (†36035) 195/F7
Henderson (co.), Ill. 222/C3
Henderson, Ill. (61439) 222/C2
Henderson (riv.), Ill. 222/C2
Henderson, Ind. (†46173) 227/F5
Henderson, Iowa (51541) 229/B6
Henderson (co.), Ky. 237/F5
Henderson, Ky. (42420) 237/F5
Henderson, La. (†70517) 238/G6
Henderson, Md. (21640) 245/P4
Henderson, Minn. (56044) 255/E6
Henderson, Nebr. (68371) 264/G4
Henderson, Nev. (89015) 266/G6
Henderson, N.Y. (13650) 276/H3
Henderson, N. Zealand 100/B1
Henderson (co.), N.C. 281/D4
Henderson, N.C. (27536) 281/N2
Henderson (isl.), Pitcairn Is. 87/O8
Henderson (co.), Tenn. 237/E9
Henderson, Tenn. (38340) 237/D10
Henderson (co.), Texas 303/J5
Henderson, Texas (75652) 303/K5
Henderson, W. Va. (25106) 312/B5
Hendersonville, N.C. (28739) 281/E4
Hendersonville, Pa. (15339) 294/B5
Hendersonville, S.C. (†29945) 296/F6
Hendersonville, Tenn. (37075) 237/H8
Hendley, Nebr. (68946) 264/D4
Hendon, Sask. 181/H3
Hendorabi (isl.), Iran 66/H7
Hendra, Queensland 88/K2
Hendricks (co.), Ind. 227/D5
Hendricks, Ky. (41441) 237/P5
Hendricks, Minn. (56136) 255/B6
Hendricks, W. Va. (26271) 312/G4
Hendrickson, Mo. (†63967) 261/M9
Hendrix, Okla. (74741) 288/O7
Hendrix Lake, Br. Col. 184/G4
Hendrum, Minn. (56550) 255/B3
Hendry (co.), Fla. 212/E5
Hendrysburg, Ohio (43744) 284/H5
Henefer, Utah (84033) 304/C2
Hengchun, China 77/K7
Hengduan Shan (mts.), China 77/E6
Hengelo, Gelderland, Netherlands 27/J4
Hengelo, Overijssel, Netherlands 27/K4
Hengshan, China 77/G4
Hengshui, China 77/J4
Heng Xian, China 77/G7
Hengyang, China 77/H6
Hengyang, China 54/N7
Henik (lakes), N.W. Terrs. 187/J3
Hénin-Beaumont, France 28/E2
Henjam (isl.), Iran 66/J7
Henlawson, W. Va. (25624) 312/B7
Henley, Mo. (65040) 261/H6
Henley and Grange, S. Australia 88/D8
Henley Harbour, Newf. 166/C3
Henley on Klip, S. Africa 118/H7
Henley-on-Thames, England 13/G8
Henlopen (cape), Del. 245/T5
Henlopen Acres, Del. (†19971) 245/T6
Henne, Denmark 21/B6
Hennebont, France 28/B4
Hennef, W. Germany 22/B3
Hennepin, Ill. (61327) 222/D2
Hennepin (co.), Minn. 255/E5
Hennepin, Okla. (73046) 288/M5
Hennessey, Okla. (73742) 288/L2
Hennigsdorf bei Berlin, E. Germany 22/E3
Henniker, N.H. (03242) 268/D5
Henniker○, N.H. (03242) 268/D5
Henning, Ill. (61848) 222/F3
Henning, Minn. (56551) 255/C4
Henning, Tenn. (38041) 237/B9
Henribourg, Sask. 181/F3
Henrico (co.), Va. 307/O6
Henrietta, Mo. (64036) 261/E4
Henrietta, N.Y. (14467) 276/E4
Henrietta, N.C. (28076) 281/F4
Henrietta, Texas (76365) 303/F4
Henrietta Maria (cape), Ont. 162/H4
Henrietta Maria (cape), Ontario 175/D1
Henriette, Minn. (55036) 255/E5
Henrieville, Utah (84736) 304/C6
Henry (co.), Ala. 195/H7
Henry (co.), Georgia 217/D4
Henry, Idaho (†83230) 220/G7
Henry (co.), Ill. 222/C2
Henry, Ill. (61537) 222/D2
Henry (co.), Ind. 227/G5
Henry (co.), Iowa 229/K6
Henry (co.), Ky. 237/L4
Henry (co.), Mo. 261/E6
Henry, Nebr. (69349) 264/A2
Henry (isl.), Nova Scotia 168/G3
Henry (co.), Ohio 284/B3
Henry, S.C. (†29554) 296/J4
Henry, S. Dak. (57243) 298/P4
Henry (co.), Tenn. 237/E8
Henry, Tenn. (38231) 237/E8
Henry (mts.), Utah 304/D6
Henry (co.), Va. 307/J7
Henry, Va. (24102) 307/J7
Henry (cape), Va. 307/R7
Henryetta, Okla. (74437) 288/O4
Henry House, Alberta 182/B3
Henry Kater (cape), N.W. Terrs. 187/M3
Henrys (lake), Idaho 220/G5
Henrys Fork, Snake (riv.), Idaho 220/G5
Henrys Fork, Green (riv.), Wyo. 319/C4
Henryton, Md. (21080) 245/L3
Henryville, Ind. (47126) 227/F7
Henryville, Pa. (18332) 294/M3
Henryville, Québec 172/D4
Henryville, Tenn. (†38483) 237/G10
Hensall, Ontario 177/C4
Hensel, N. Dak. (58241) 282/P2
Henshaw, Ky. (†42459) 237/F5
Hensies, Belgium 27/D8
Hensler, N. Dak. (58547) 282/H5
Hensley, Ark. (72065) 202/F4
Henson (creek), Md. 245/F6
Hentiy, Mongolia 77/H2
Henty, N.S. Wales 97/D4
Henzada, Burma 72/B3
Henzada, Burma 54/L8
Hepburn, Iowa (†51632) 229/C7
Hepburn, Ohio (†43326) 284/D4
Hepburn, Sask. 181/E3
Hephzibah, Georgia (30815) 217/H4
Hepler, Kansas (66746) 232/H4
Heppner, Oreg. (97836) 291/H2
Hepu (Hoppo), China 77/G7
Hepworth, Ontario 177/C3
Hepzibah, W. Va. (26369) 312/F4
Hequ, China 77/H4
Herald, Calif. (95638) 204/C9
Heralds (cays), 95/D3
Herat, Afghanistan 54/H6
Herat, Afghanistan 59/H3
Herat, Afghanistan 68/A2
Hérault (dept.), France 28/E6
Hérault (riv.), France 28/E6
Herbert, Ala. (†36401) 195/E8
Herbert (riv.), Queensland 88/H3
Herbert, Sask. 181/D5
Herbert Hoover Nat'l Hist. Site, Iowa 229/L5
Herbes (isl.), Ala. 195/B10
Herbeumont, Belgium 27/G9
Herb Lake, Manitoba 179/H3
Herborn, W. Germany 22/C3
Herbst, Ind. (†46952) 227/F3
Herbster, Wis. (54844) 317/D2
Herceg Novi, Yugoslavia 45/D4
Herchmer, Man. 162/G4
Herchmer, Manitoba 179/K2
Herculaneum, Mo. (63048) 261/M6
Hercules, Calif. (94547) 204/J1
Herd, Okla. (†74056) 288/O1
Heredia, C. Rica 154/E5
Hereford, Ariz. (85615) 198/E7
Hereford, Colo. (80732) 208/L1
Hereford, England 13/E5
Hereford, England 10/E4
Hereford, Md. (†21111) 245/M2
Hereford (inlet), N.J. 273/D5
Hereford, Oreg. (97837) 291/K3
Hereford, Pa. (18056) 294/L5
Hereford, S. Dak. (57743) 298/D5
Hereford, Texas (79045) 303/B3
Hereford and Worcester (co.), England 13/E5
Hérémence, Switzerland 39/D4
Herencia, Spain 33/E3
Herentals, Belgium 27/F6
Heretaunga-Pinehaven, N. Zealand 100/C2
Herford, W. Germany 22/C2
Hergiswil, Switzerland 39/F3
Héricourt, France 28/G4
Heringsdorf, E. Germany 22/F1
Herington, Kansas (67449) 232/E3
Heriot Bay, Br. Col. 184/E5
Herisau, Switzerland 39/H2
Herkimer, Kansas (66433) 232/F2
Herkimer (co.), N.Y. 276/L4
Herkimer, N.Y. (13350) 276/L4
Herlen Gol (Kerulen) (riv.), Mongolia 77/H2
Herlong, Calif. (96113) 204/E3
Herm (isl.), Chan. Is. 13/E8
Hermagor-Preseggersee, Austria 41/B3
Herman, Mich. (†49946) 250/A2
Herman, Minn. (56248) 255/B5
Herman, Nebr. (68029) 264/H3
Herman, Pa. (16039) 294/C4
Herman (lake), S. Dak. 298/P5
Herma Ness (prom.), Scotland 15/G2
Hermann, Mo. (65041) 261/K5
Hermannsburg, North. Terr. 88/E4
Hermannsburg, North. Terr. 93/C7
Hermansverk, Norway 18/E6
Hermansville, Mich. (49847) 250/B3
Hermantown, Minn. (†55811) 255/F4
Hermanus, S. Africa 118/C7
Hermanville, Miss. (39086) 256/C7
Hermidale, N.S. Wales 97/C2
Hermil, Lebanon 63/G5
Herminie, Pa. (15637) 294/C5
Hermiston, Oreg. (97838) 291/H2
Hermitage, Ark. (71647) 202/F7
Hermitage, Grenada 161/D8
Hermitage, Mo. (65668) 261/F7
Hermitage, Newf. 166/C4
Hermitage (bay), Newf. 166/C4
Hermitage Springs, Tenn. (†37150) 237/K7
Hermite (isls.), Chile 138/F11
Hermleigh, Texas (79526) 303/D5
Hermon, Ill. (†61458) 222/C3
Hermon○, Maine (†04401) 243/F6
Hermon, N.Y. (13652) 276/K2
Hermon (mt.), Syria 63/F6
Hermosa (peak), Colo. 208/D7
Hermosa, S. Dak. (57744) 298/C6
Hermosa Beach, Calif. (90254) 204/B11
Hermosillo, Mexico 146/G7
Hermosillo, Mexico 150/D2
Hermsdorf, W. Germany 22/E3
Hernád (riv.), Hungary 41/F2
Hernandarias, Argentina 143/F5
Hernandarias, Paraguay 144/E4
Hernández, Argentina 143/F6
Hernandez, N. Mex. (87537) 274/C2
Hernando, Argentina 143/D3
Hernando (co.), Fla. 212/D3
Hernando, Fla. (32642) 212/D3
Hernando, Miss. (38632) 256/E1
Herndon, Georgia (†30442) 217/H5
Herndon, Iowa (†50128) 229/E5
Herndon, Kansas (67739) 232/B2
Herndon, Ky. (42236) 237/G7
Herndon, Pa. (17830) 294/J4
Herndon, Va. (*22070) 307/O3
Herndon, W. Va. (24726) 312/D7
Herne, Belgium 27/E7
Herne, W. Germany 22/B3
Herning, Denmark 18/F8
Herning, Denmark 21/B5
Herod, Georgia (†31742) 217/D7
Herod, Ill. (62947) 222/E6
Heroica Caborca, Mexico 150/C1
Heroica Nogales, Mexico 150/D1
Heron (lake), Minn. 255/C7
Heron, Mont. (59844) 262/A2
Heron (isl.), New Bruns. 170/D1
Heron Bay, Ontario 177/H5
Heron Bay, Ontario 175/C3
Heron Lake, Minn. (56137) 255/C7
Hérouxville, Québec 172/E3

Horwich 383

Hogarth (mt.), North. Terr. 93/E6
Hogatza, Alaska (99744) 196/G1
Hogeland, Mont. (59529) 262/H2
Hog Island (bay), Va. 307/S6
Hog River (Hogatza), Alaska (99744) 196/G1
Hogshead (pt.), Conn. 210/E3
Högyész, Hungary 41/E3
Hoh (head), Wash. 310/A3
Hoh (riv.), Wash. 310/A3
Hohenau, Paraguay 144/E5
Hohenau an der March, Austria 41/D2
Hohenberg, Austria 41/C3
Hohenems, Austria 41/A3
Hohenlinden, Miss. (†39751) 256/F3
Hohen Neuendorf, E. Germany 22/E2
Hohen Solms, La. (†70788) 238/K3
Hohenstollen (mt.), Switzerland 39/F3
Hohenwald, Tenn. (38462) 237/F9
Hohe Tauern (range), Austria 41/B3
Hohe Venn (plat.), Belgium 27/H8
Hohe Warte (mt.), Austria 41/B3
Hohhot (Huhehot), China 77/H3
Hohhot, China 54/N5
Hoh Ind. Res., Wash. 310/A3
Hohokam Pima Nat'l Mon., Ariz. 198/D5
Ho Ho Kus, N.J. (07423) 273/B1
Hoholitna (riv.), Alaska 196/G2
Hoh Xil Shan (mts.), China 77/C4
Hoi An, Vietnam 72/F4
Hoihow (Haikou), China 77/H7
Hoima, Uganda 115/F3
Hoisington, Kansas (67544) 232/D3
Hoi Xuan, Vietnam 72/E2
Højer, Denmark 21/B8
Højslev, Denmark 21/C4
Hokah, Minn. (55941) 255/G7
Hokang (Hegang), China 77/L2
Hoke (co.), N.C. 281/L4
Hokes Bluff, Ala. (35903) 195/G3
Hokianga (harb.), N. Zealand 100/D1
Hokitika, N. Zealand 100/C5
Hokkaido (pref.), Japan 81/K2
Hokkaido (isl.), Japan 2/S3
Hokkaido (isl.), Japan 54/R5
Hokkaido (isl.), Japan 81/L2
Holabird, S. Dak. (57540) 298/K4
Holbaek, Denmark 21/E6
Holbaek, Denmark 18/G9
Holbeach, England 10/F4
Holbeach, England 13/H5
Holbein, Sask. 181/E2
Holberg, Br. Col. 184/C5
Holbrook, Ariz. (86025) 198/E4
Holbrook, Idaho (83243) 220/F7
Holbrook, Iowa (†52325) 229/K5
Holbrook○, Mass. (02343) 249/D8
Holbrook, Nebr. (68948) 264/D4
Holbrook, N.S. Wales 97/D4
Holbrook, Oreg. (†97208) 291/A1
Holcomb, Ill. (61043) 222/D1
Holcomb, Kansas (67851) 232/B3
Holcomb, Miss. (38940) 256/D3
Holcomb, Mo. (63852) 261/N10
Holcomb, N.Y. (14469) 276/F5
Holcomb, W. Va. (26262) 312/E6
Holcombe, Wis. (54745) 317/D5
Holcombe Flowage (res.), Wis. 317/D5
Holden, Alberta 182/D3
Holden, La. (70744) 238/M1
Holden○, Mass. (01520) 249/G3
Holden, Mo. (64040) 261/E5
Holden, Utah (84636) 304/B4
Holden, W. Va. (25625) 312/B7
Holden Beach, N.C. (28462) 281/N7
Holdenville, Okla. (74848) 288/O4
Holder, Fla. (32645) 212/D3
Holderness (pen.), England 13/G4
Holderness○, N.H. (03245) 268/D4
Holdfast, Sask. 181/F5
Holdingford, Minn. (56340) 255/D5
Holdrege, Nebr. (68949) 264/E4
Holeby, Denmark 21/E8
Hølen, Norway 18/D4
Holešov, Czech. 41/D2
Holetown, Barbados 161/B8
Holgate, Ohio (43527) 284/B3
Holguín (prov.), Cuba 158/J3
Holguín, Cuba 146/L7
Holguín, Cuba 158/J3
Holguín, Cuba 156/C2
Holíč, Czech. 41/D2
Holice, Czech. 41/C1
Holiday Hills, Ill. (†60050) 222/A4
Holijsloot, Netherlands 27/C4
Holitna (riv.), Alaska 196/G2
Hollabrunn, Austria 41/D2
Holladay, Tenn. (38341) 237/E9
Holladay, Utah (84117) 304/C3
Hollam's Bird (isl.), Namibia 118/A4
Holland, Georgia (†30730) 217/B2
Holland, Ind. (47541) 227/C8
Holland, Iowa (50642) 229/H4
Holland, Ky. (42153) 237/J7
Holland, Manitoba 179/D5
Holland○, Mass. (†01550) 249/F4
Holland, Mich. (49423) 250/C6
Holland, Minn. (56139) 255/B6
Holland, Mo. (63853) 261/N10
Holland, N.Y. (14080) 276/C5
Holland, Ohio (43528) 284/C2
Holland, Texas (76534) 303/G7
Holland○, Vt. (†05830) 268/D2
Hollandale, Minn. (56045) 255/E7
Hollandale, Miss. (38748) 256/C4
Hollandale, Wis. (53544) 317/G10
Holland Centre, Ontario 177/D3
Hollandia (Jayapura), Indonesia 85/K6
Holland Landing, Ontario 177/E3
Holland Park, Queensland 88/K3
Holland Park, Queensland 95/E3
Holland Patent, N.Y. (13354) 276/K4
Hollandsburg, Ind. (†47872) 227/C5
Hollandstoun, Scotland 15/F1
Hollansburg, Ohio (45332) 284/A5
Hollenbeck (riv.), Conn. 210/B1
Hollenberg, Kansas (66946) 232/F2
Holley, N.Y. (14470) 276/D4
Holley, Oreg. (†97386) 291/E3
Hollick-Kenyon (plat.) 5/B13
Holliday, Mo. (65258) 261/H3
Holliday, Texas (76366) 303/F4
Hollidaysburg, Pa. (16648) 294/F5
Hollins, Ala. (35082) 195/F4
Hollins College, Va. (24020) 307/H6
Hollis, Ark. (†72857) 202/D4
Hollis, Kansas (†66901) 232/E2
Hollis○, N.H. (03049) 268/D6
Hollis, N.C. (†28040) 281/F4
Hollis, Okla. (73550) 288/G5
Hollis Center○, Maine (04042) 243/B8
Hollister, Calif. (95023) 204/D7
Hollister, Fla. (32047) 212/E2
Hollister, Idaho (†83301) 220/D7
Hollister, Mo. (65672) 261/F9
Hollister, N.C. (27844) 281/O2
Hollister, Okla. (73551) 288/J6
Hollister, Wis. (†54491) 317/J5
Holliston○, Mass. (01746) 249/A8
Holloman A.F.B., N. Mex. 274/C6
Holloway, Minn. (56249) 255/C5
Holloway, Ohio (43985) 284/H5
Hollowayville, Ill. (†61356) 222/D2
Hollow Creek, Ky. (†40228) 237/K4
Hollow Rock, Tenn. (38342) 237/E8
Hollsopple, Pa. (15935) 294/E5
Hollum, Netherlands 27/H2
Holly, Colo. (81047) 208/P6
Holly, Mich. (48442) 250/F6
Holly, Wash. (†98310) 310/C3
Holly Bluff, Miss. (39088) 256/C5
Holly Grove, Ark. (72069) 202/H4
Holly Hill, Fla. (32017) 212/E2
Holly Hill, S.C. (29059) 296/G5
Holly Oak, Del. (†19801) 245/S1
Holly Pond, Ala. (35083) 195/E2
Holly Ridge, La. (71248) 238/G2
Holly Ridge, Miss. (38749) 256/C4
Holly Ridge, N.C. (28445) 281/O6
Holly Shelter (swamp), N.C. 281/O6
Holly Springs, Ark. (71746) 202/E6
Holly Springs, Georgia (30142) 217/D2
Holly Springs, Miss. (38635) 256/E1
Holly Springs, N.C. (27540) 281/M3
Hollytree, Ala. (35751) 195/F1
Hollyville, Del. (†19951) 245/T6
Hollywood, Ala. (35752) 195/G1
Hollywood, Ark. (†71923) 202/D5
Hollywood, Calif. (90028) 204/C10
Hollywood, Fla. 188/K5
Hollywood, Fla. (*33020) 212/B4
Hollywood, Georgia (30523) 217/E1
Hollywood, La. (†70663) 238/D6
Hollywood, Md. (20636) 245/M7
Hollywood, Miss. (†38676) 256/D1
Hollywood, Mo. (†63821) 261/M10
Hollywood, S.C. (29449) 296/G6
Hollywood, W. Va. (†24983) 312/F7
Hollywood Park, Texas (†78201) 303/K10
Holman, N. Mex. (87723) 274/D2
Holman (isl.), N.W.T. 162/D1
Holman Island, Canada 4/B15
Holman Island, N.W. Terrs. 187/G2
Holmdel○, N.J. (07733) 273/E3
Holmen, Wis. (54636) 317/D8
Holmes (reef), 95/C3
Holmes (reef), Coral Sea Is. Terr. 88/H3
Holmes (co.), Fla. 212/C5
Holmes (creek), Fla. 212/D5
Holmes, Iowa (†50525) 229/F3
Holmes (co.), Miss. 256/D4
Holmes (co.), Ohio 284/G4
Holmes (mt.), Wyo. 319/B1
Holmes Beach, Fla. (33509) 212/D4
Holmes City, Minn. (56341) 255/C5
Holmeson, N.J. (†08526) 273/E3
Holmestrand, Norway 18/C4
Holmesville, Miss. (†39648) 256/D8
Holmesville, Nebr. (68374) 264/H4
Holmesville, New Bruns. 170/C2
Holmesville, Ohio (44633) 284/G4
Holmesville, Ontario 177/C4
Holmfield, Manitoba 179/C5
Holmfirth, England 13/J2
Holmquist, S. Dak. (†57274) 298/O3
Holmsbu, Norway 18/D4
Holmsund, Sweden 18/M5
Holmwood, La. (†70647) 238/D6
Holon, Israel 65/B3
Holopaw, Fla. (†32901) 212/E3
Holroyd, N.S. Wales 97/H3
Holroyd (riv.), Queensland 95/B2
Holstebro, Denmark 18/F8
Holstebro, Denmark 21/B5
Holsted, Denmark 21/B6
Holstein, Iowa (51025) 229/B4
Holstein, Mo. (†63378) 261/K5
Holstein, Nebr. (68950) 264/F4
Holstein, Ontario 177/D3
Holsteinsborg, Greenl. 4/C12
Holston (riv.), Tenn. 237/O8
Holston, Va. (†24210) 307/D7
Holston, North Fork (riv.), Va. 307/D7
Holston Valley, Tenn. (†37620) 237/S7
Holsworthy, England 10/D5
Holsworthy, England 13/C7
Holt, Ala. (35404) 195/D4
Holt (dam), Ala. 195/D4
Holt, Calif. (95234) 204/D6
Holt, England 13/J5
Holt, Fla. (32564) 212/C6
Holt, Mich. (48842) 250/E6
Holt, Minn. (†56738) 255/B2
Holt (co.), Mo. 261/B2
Holt, Mo. (64048) 261/D4
Holt (co.), Nebr. 264/F2
Holte, Denmark 21/F6
Holter (lake), Mont. 262/D4
Holtland, Tenn. (†37034) 237/H9
Holton, Ind. (47023) 227/G6
Holton, Kansas (66436) 232/G2
Holton, La. (†70422) 238/K5
Holton, Mich. (49425) 250/C5
Holton, Newf. 166/C3
Holts Summit, Mo. (65043) 261/H5
Holtville, Ala. (†36022) 195/F5
Holtville, Calif. (92250) 204/K11
Holtville, New Bruns. 170/D2
Holtwood, Pa. (17532) 294/K6
Holualoa, Hawaii (96725) 218/G5
Holualoa, Hawaii 188/F6
Holwerd, Netherlands 27/H2
Holy (isl.), England 13/F2
Holy (isl.), England 10/F3
Holy (isl.), Scotland 15/C5
Holy (isl.), Wales 10/D4
Holy (isl.), Wales 13/C4
Holy City, Calif. (95026) 204/K4
Holy Cross, Alaska (99602) 196/G2
Holy Cross (mt.), Colo. 208/F4
Holy Cross, Iowa (52053) 229/L3
Holycross, Ireland 17/F6
Holy Cross, Wis. (†53004) 317/L9
Holyhead, Wales 10/D4
Holyhead, Wales 13/C4
Holy Loch (inlet), Scotland 15/A1
Holyoke, Colo. (80734) 208/P1
Holyoke, Mass. (01040) 249/D4
Holyoke (range), Mass. 249/D3
Holyoke, Minn. (55749) 255/F4
Holyrood, Kansas (67450) 232/D3
Holyrood, Newf. 166/D2
Holyrood (bay), Newf. 166/D2
Holyrood (pond), Newf. 166/D2
Holyroyd, N. S. Wales 88/K4
Holy Trinity, Ala. (36859) 195/H6
Holywell, Wales 13/G2
Holywood, N. Ireland 17/K2
Holzminden, W. Germany 22/C3
Homalin, Burma 72/B1
Homathko (riv.), Br. Col. 184/E4
Homayunshahr, Iran 66/G4
Hombori, Mali 106/D5
Hombori (mts.), Mali 106/D5
Homburg, W. Germany 22/B4
Home (bay) 162/K2
Home, Kansas (66438) 232/F2
Home (isl.), Newf. 166/B1
Home (bay), N.W. Terrs. 187/M3
Home, Pa. (15747) 294/D4
Homedale, Idaho (83628) 220/A6
Home Gardens, Calif. (†91720) 204/E11
Home Hill, Queensland 88/H3
Home Hill, Queensland 95/C3
Homeland, Calif. (92348) 204/H10
Homeland, Georgia (†31537) 217/H9
Home Place, La. (†70083) 238/L8
Homer, Alaska (99603) 196/B2
Homer, Georgia (30547) 217/F2
Homer, Ill. (61849) 222/F3
Homer, Ind. (46146) 227/F5
Homer, Ky. (†42276) 237/H7
Homer, La. (71040) 238/D1
Homer, Mich. (49245) 250/E6
Homer, Minn. (55942) 255/G6
Homer, Nebr. (68030) 264/H2
Homer, N.Y. (13077) 276/H5
Homer, Ohio (43027) 284/E5
Homer City, Pa. (15748) 294/D4
Homerville, Georgia (31634) 217/G8
Homerville, Ohio (44235) 284/F3
Homestead, Fla. (*33030) 212/F6
Homestead, Iowa (52236) 229/K5
Homestead, Mont. (59242) 262/M2
Homestead, Okla. (†73763) 288/K2
Homestead, Pa. (15120) 294/B7
Homestead, Queensland 95/C4
Homestead A.F.B., Fla. 212/F6
Homestead Nat'l Mon., Nebr. 264/H4
Homestown, Mo. (†63879) 261/N10
Hometown, Ill. (60456) 222/B6
Home Valley, Wash. (†98648) 310/D5
Homewood, Ala. (35209) 195/E4
Homewood, Calif. (95718) 204/E4
Homewood, Ill. (60430) 222/B6
Homewood, Kansas (†66095) 232/G3
Homewood, Manitoba 179/E5
Homewood, Miss. (†39152) 256/E6
Homewood, Pa. (15208) 294/B4
Homeworth, Ohio (44634) 284/J4
Hominy, Okla. (74035) 288/O2
Hominy Falls, W. Va. (†26651) 312/E6
Homochitto (riv.), Miss. 256/B8
Homoine, Mozambique 118/E4
Homonhon (isl.), Philippines 82/E5
Homosassa, Fla. (32646) 212/D3
Homosassa (isls.), Fla. 212/D3
Homosassa Springs, Fla. (32647) 212/D3
Homra, Hamada el (des.), Libya 111/B2
Homs, Libya 102/D1
Homs, Libya 111/B1
Homs (prov.), Syria 63/G5
Homs, Syria 59/C3
Homs, Syria 63/G5
Homs, Syria 54/E6
Hon, Ark. (†72958) 202/B4
Hon, Libya 102/D2
Hon, Libya 111/C2
Honaker, Va. (24260) 307/D6
Honan (Henan) (prov.), China 77/H5
Honaunau, Hawaii (96726) 218/G6
Honavar, India 68/C6
Honaz Dağı (mt.), Turkey 63/C4
Hon Chong, Vietnam 72/E5
Honda, Colombia 126/C5
Honda (bay), Cuba 158/B1
Honda (bay), Philippines 82/B6
Honda (bay), P. Rico 161/F2
Hondo (riv.), Belize 154/C1
Hondo, Japan 81/E7
Hondo (riv.), Mexico 150/P7
Hondo, N. Mex. (88336) 274/D5
Hondo, Texas (78861) 303/E8
Hondsrug (hills), Netherlands 27/K3
Honduras 2/E5
Honduras 146/K8
HONDURAS 154
Honduras (gulf) 146/K8
Honduras (gulf), Belize 154/D2
Honduras (gulf), Guatemala 154/D2
Honduras (cape), Honduras 154/E2
Honduras (gulf), Honduras 154/D2
Honea Path, S.C. (29654) 296/C3
Honegg (mt.), Switzerland 39/E3
Honeoye, N.Y. (14471) 276/F5
Honeoye (lake), N.Y. 276/F5
Honeoye Falls, N.Y. (14472) 276/F5
Honesdale, Pa. (18431) 294/M2
Honey (lake), Calif. 204/E3
Honey (creek), Ind. 227/C6
Honey (creek), Oreg. 291/G5
Honey Brook, Pa. (19344) 294/L5
Honey Creek, Ind. (†47356) 227/F4
Honey Creek, Iowa (51542) 229/B6
Honey Creek, Wis. (53138) 317/J3
Honeydale, New Bruns. 170/C3
Honeyford, N. Dak. (†58242) 282/R3
Honey Grove, Texas (75446) 303/J4
Honey Harbour, Ontario 177/E3
Honey Hill, S.C. (†29479) 296/H5
Honey Island, Texas (†77625) 303/K7
Honeymoon Bay, Br. Col. 184/J3
Honeyville, Utah (84314) 304/B2
Honeywood, Ontario 177/D3
Honfleur, France 28/D3
Honfleur, Québec 172/G3
Høng, Denmark 21/E7
Honga (riv.), Md. 245/O7
Hon Gai, Vietnam 72/E2
Hongch'ŏn, S. Korea 81/D5
Hong Kong 54/N7
Hong Kong 2/Q4
HONG KONG 77
Hongliahe, China 77/E3
Hongor, Mongolia 77/H2
Hongshui He (riv.), China 77/G7
Hongsŏng, S. Korea 81/C5
Hongtong, China 77/H4
Honguedo (passage), Québec 174/E3
Hongwŏn, N. Korea 81/C3
Hongze Hu (lake), China 77/J5
Honiara (cap.), Solomon Is. 86/D3
Honiara (cap.), Solomon Is. 87/F6
Honiton, England 10/E5
Honiton, England 13/D7
Honjo, Japan 81/J4
Honnedaga (lake), N.Y. 276/L3
Honnelles, Belgium 27/D8
Honningsvag, Norway 18/O1
Honobia, Okla. (74549) 288/R5
Honohina, Hawaii (†96710) 218/J4
Honokaa, Hawaii 188/G5
Honokaa, Hawaii (96727) 218/H4
Honokahua, Hawaii (†96761) 218/H1
Honokohau, Hawaii, Hawaii (†96740) 218/G5
Honokohau, Maui, Hawaii (†96725) 218/J1
Honolulu (co.), Hawaii 218/D3
Honolulu (cap.), Hawaii 87/L3
Honolulu (cap.), Hawaii 188/F5
Honolulu (cap.), Hawaii (*96801) 218/C4
Honolulu (harb.), Hawaii 218/C4
Honolulu, U.S. 2/B5
Honolulu Int'l Airport, Hawaii 218/B4
Honomu, Hawaii (96728) 218/J4
Honor, Mich. (49640) 250/D4
Honoraville, Ala. (36042) 195/F7
Honouliuli, Hawaii (†96706) 218/A3
Honshu (isl.), Japan 2/S4
Honshu (isl.), Japan 54/P6
Honshu (isl.), Japan 81/J5
Honuapo, Hawaii (†96772) 218/H7
Hood, Calif. (95639) 204/B9
Hood (riv.), N.W. Terrs. 187/G3
Hood (mt.), Oreg. 291/F2
Hood (riv.), Oreg. 291/F2
Hood (co.), Texas 303/G5
Hood (canal), Wash. 310/B3
Hood River (co.), Oreg. 291/F2
Hood River, Oreg. (97031) 291/F2
Hoodsport, Wash. (98548) 310/B3
Hoofddorp (Haarlemmermeer), Netherlands 27/F4
Hoogeveen, Netherlands 27/J3
Hoogezand-Sappemeer, Netherlands 27/K2
Hooghly (riv.), India 68/F2
Hooghly-Chinsura, India 68/F1
Hoogkarspel, Netherlands 27/G3
Hoogstraten, Belgium 27/F6
Hook (head), Ireland 17/H7
Hook (isl.), Queensland 88/H4
Hook (isl.), Queensland 95/D4
Hookena, Hawaii (†96704) 218/G6
Hooker (co.), Nebr. 264/C3
Hooker, Okla. (73945) 288/D1
Hooker Creek, North. Terr. 88/E3
Hooker Creek, North. Terr. 93/B5
Hooker Creek Aboriginal Reserve, North. Terr. 88/E3
Hookersville, W. Va. (†26651) 312/E6
Hookerton, N.C. (28538) 281/O4
Hook of Holland, Netherlands 27/D4
Hooks, Texas (75561) 303/K4
Hooksett, N.H. (03106) 268/E5
Hooksett○, N.H. (03106) 268/E5
Hookstown, Pa. (15050) 294/B4
Hoolehua, Hawaii 188/F5
Hoolehua, Hawaii (96729) 218/G1
Hoonah, Alaska (99829) 196/M1
Hoonah (sound), Alaska 196/M1
Hoopa, Calif. (95546) 204/B2
Hoopa Valley Ind. Res., Calif. 204/A2
Hooper, Colo. (81136) 208/H7
Hooper (str.), Md. 245/O8
Hooper, Nebr. (68031) 264/H3
Hooper, Utah (84315) 304/B2
Hooper, Wash. (99333) 310/G4
Hooper Bay, Alaska (99604) 196/E2
Hooper Bay, Alaska 188/C5
Hoopersville, Md. (21642) 245/O7
Hoopeston, Ill. (60942) 222/F3
Hoople, N. Dak. (58243) 282/P2
Hooppole, Ill. (61258) 222/D2
Hoorn, Netherlands 27/G3
Hoorn (isls.), Wallis and Futuna 87/J7
Hoosac (mts.), Mass. 249/B2
Hoosac Tunnel, Mass. (†01339) 249/C2
Hoosic (riv.), Mass. 249/A1
Hoosic (riv.), Vt. 268/A6
Hoosick Falls, N.Y. (12090) 276/O5
Hoosier, Sask. 181/B4
Hoot Owl, Okla. (†74366) 288/R2
Hooven, Ohio (45033) 284/A9
Hoover, Ala. (†35216) 195/E4
Hoover (dam), Ariz. 198/A2
Hoover (dam), Nev. 266/G7
Hoover (res.), Ohio 284/E5
Hoover, S. Dak. (†57760) 298/C3
Hooversville, Pa. (15936) 294/E5
Hop (riv.), Conn. 210/F1
Hopa, Turkey 63/J2
Hopatcong, N.J. (07843) 273/D2
Hopatcong (lake), N.J. 273/D2
Hop Bottom, Pa. (18824) 294/L2
Hope, Alaska (99605) 196/C1
Hope (pt.), Alaska 196/E1
Hope (bay) 5/C16
Hope, Ark. (71801) 202/C6
Hope, Br. Col. 162/D6
Hope, Br. Col. 184/M3
Hope, Idaho (83836) 220/B1
Hope, Ind. (47246) 227/F6
Hope, Kansas (67451) 232/E3
Hope, Ky. (40334) 237/O4
Hope, Maine (04847) 243/E7
Hope○, Maine (04847) 243/E7
Hope, Mich. (48628) 250/E5
Hope, Minn. (56045) 255/E7
Hope, Mo. (†65061) 261/J5
Hope (lake), Newf. 166/B3
Hope, N.J. (07844) 273/D2
Hope, N. Mex. (88250) 274/E6
Hope, N. Dak. (58046) 282/P5
Hope (isl.), Norway 4/B8
Hope, R.I. (02831) 249/H6
Hope, Loch (lake), Scotland 15/D2
Hope Bay, Jamaica 158/K6
Hopedale, Ill. (61747) 222/D3
Hopedale, Mass. (01747) 249/H4
Hopedale○, Mass. (01747) 249/H4
Hopedale, Newf. 166/B2
Hopedale, Newf. 162/L4
Hopedale, Newf. 146/N4
Hopedale, Ohio (43976) 284/J5
Hopeful Heights, Ky. (†41018) 237/R2
Hope Hull, Ala. (36043) 195/F6
Hopei (Hebei) (prov.), China 77/J4
Hopeland, Pa. (17533) 294/K5
Hopelchén, Mexico 150/P7
Hopeman, Scotland 15/E3
Hope Mills, N.C. (28348) 281/M5
Hopen (isl.), Norway 18/E2
Hopes Advance (cape), Québec 174/F1
Hopeton, Okla. (73746) 288/J1
Hopeton, Va. (†23421) 307/S5
Hopetoun, Victoria 97/B4
Hopetoun, W. Australia 92/C6
Hopetown, Québec 172/D2
Hopetown, S. Africa 118/C5
Hopetown, W. Australia 88/C6
Hope Valley, R.I. (02832) 249/H6
Hope Valley (res.), S. Australia 88/E7
Hopeville, Iowa (†50174) 229/F7
Hopewell, Ala. (†36264) 195/H3
Hopewell, Jamaica 158/G5
Hopewell, Kansas (†67557) 232/D4
Hopewell, Md. (†21817) 245/P8
Hopewell, Miss. (†39059) 256/D7
Hopewell, N.J. (08525) 273/D3
Hopewell (isls.), N.W. Terrs. 187/L4
Hopewell, Nova Scotia 168/F3
Hopewell, Ohio (43746) 284/F6
Hopewell, Pa. (16650) 294/F5
Hopewell (I.C.), Va. (23860) 307/O6
Hopewell Cape, New Bruns. 170/F3
Hopewell Hill, New Bruns. 170/F3
Hopewell Junction, N.Y. (12533) 276/N7
Hopfgarten in Nordtirol, Austria 41/B3
Hopi (buttes), Ariz. 198/E3
Hopi Ind. Res., Ariz. 198/E2
Hopkins (co.), Ky. 237/F6
Hopkins, Mich. (49328) 250/D6
Hopkins, Minn. (55343) 255/G5
Hopkins, Mo. (64461) 261/C1
Hopkins (lake), North. Terr. 93/A8
Hopkins, S.C. (29061) 296/F4
Hopkins (co.), Texas 303/J4
Hopkins (riv.), Victoria 97/B5
Hopkins, Va. (†23421) 307/S5
Hopkins (lake), W. Australia 88/D4
Hopkins (lake), W. Australia 92/E4
Hopkinsville, Ky. (42240) 237/F7
Hopkinton, Iowa (52237) 229/L4
Hopkinton, Mass. (01748) 249/J4
Hopkinton○, Mass. (01748) 249/J4
Hopkinton○, N.H. (03301) 268/D5
Hopkinton, N.Y. (12940) 276/L1
Hopkinton○, R.I. (02833) 249/H7
Hopland, Calif. (95449) 204/B5
Hoppo (Hepu), China 77/G7
Hop River, Conn. (†06237) 210/F2
Hopwood, Pa. (15445) 294/C6
Hoquiam, Wash. 188/B1
Hoquiam, Wash. (98550) 310/A3
Horace, Kansas (†67879) 232/A3
Horace, N. Dak. (58047) 282/S6
Horasan, Turkey 63/K2
Horatio, Ark. (71842) 202/B3
Horatio, S.C. (29062) 296/F3
Horažďovice, Czech. 41/B2
Horche, Spain 33/E2
Horconcitos, Panama 154/F6
Hordaland (co.), Norway 18/E6
Horden, England 13/J4
Hordio, Somalia 115/K1
Hordville, Nebr. (68846) 264/G3
Horgen, Switzerland 39/G2
Hořice v Podkrkonoší, Czech. 41/C1
Horicon, Wis. (53032) 317/J9
Horine, Mo. (†63070) 261/M6
Horizon, Sask. 181/F6
Horley, England 13/H8
Hormigüeros, P. Rico 161/A2
Hormoz, Iran 66/J7
Hormoz (isl.), Iran 66/K7
Hormozgan (prov.), Iran 66/J7
Hormuz (str.), Iran 59/G4
Hormuz (str.), Iran 66/K7
Hormuz (str.), Oman 59/G4
Horn (cape) 2/F8
Horn, Austria 41/C2
Horn (cape), Chile 120/C8
Horn (cape), Chile 138/F11
Horn (cape), Iceland 7/B2
Horn (cape), Iceland 21/B1
Horn (head), Ireland 17/E1
Horn (isl.), Miss. 256/G10
Horn (mts.), N.W. Terrs. 187/G3
Horn (riv.), N.W. Terrs. 187/G3
Hornád (riv.), Czech. 41/F2
Hornaday (riv.), N.W. Terrs. 187/F3
Hornafjördhur (fjord), Iceland 21/D1
Horná Štubňa, Czech. 41/E2
Horn-Bad Meinberg, W. Germany 22/C3
Hornbeak, Tenn. (38232) 237/C8
Hornbeck, Alberta 182/B3
Hornbeck, La. (71439) 238/D4
Hornbrook, Calif. (96044) 204/C2
Hornby, N. Zealand 100/D5
Hornby (bay), N.W. Terrs. 187/G3
Hornby Island, Br. Col. 184/H2
Horncastle, England 13/G4
Horncastle, England 10/F4
Horndean, Manitoba 179/E5
Hörnefors, Sweden 18/L5
Hornell, N.Y. (14843) 276/E6
Hornepayne, Ontario 175/C3
Hornepayne, Ontario 177/J5
Horner, W. Va. (26372) 312/F5
Hornerstown, N.J. (†08514) 273/E3
Hornersville, Mo. (63855) 261/M10
Horn Hill, Ala. (†36467) 195/F8
Horní Benešov, Czech. 41/D2
Hornick, Iowa (51026) 229/A4
Horní Libina, Czech. 41/D2
Hornings Mills, Ontario 177/D3
Hornitos, Calif. (95325) 204/E6
Horn Lake, Miss. (38637) 256/D1
Hörnli (mt.), Switzerland 39/G2
Hornos, Falso (cape), Chile 138/F11
Hornsby, N. S. Wales 88/K3
Hornsby, N.S. Wales 97/J3
Hornsby, Tenn. (38044) 237/D10
Hornsea, England 13/G4
Hornsea, England 10/F4
Hornslandet (pen.), Sweden 18/K6
Hornslet, Denmark 21/D5
Horns Road, Nova Scotia 168/H2
Hornsund (bay), Norway 18/C2
Horntown, Va. (23395) 307/T5
Hořovice, Czech. 41/C2
Horqin Youyi Qianqi (Ulanhot), China 77/K2
Horqueta, Paraguay 144/D3
Horry (co.), S.C. 296/J4
Horse (lake), Calif. 204/E3
Horse (creek), Colo. 208/M5
Horse (creek), Fla. 212/E4
Horse (isls.), Newf. 166/C3
Horse (creek), Oreg. 291/F3
Horse (creek), Wyo. 319/H4
Horse (creek), Wyo. 319/B3
Horse Branch, Ky. (42349) 237/H6
Horse Cave, Ky. (42749) 237/K6
Horse Chops (head), Newf. 166/D2
Horse Creek, Calif. (96045) 204/C2
Horse Creek (res.), Colo. 208/N6
Horse Creek, Wyo. (82061) 319/G4
Horsefly, Br. Col. 184/G4
Horsefly (lake), Br. Col. 184/G4
Horsehead (lake), N. Dak. 282/L5
Horsehead (creek), S. Dak. 298/C7
Horseheads, N.Y. (14845) 276/G6
Horsens, Denmark 18/F9
Horsens, Denmark 21/C6
Horsens (fjord), Denmark 21/D6
Horseshoe (lake), Ariz. 198/D5
Horseshoe (pt.), Fla. 212/C2
Horseshoe (lake), Manitoba 179/G2
Horse Shoe (pt.), St. Chris.-Nevis 161/C11
Horseshoe (creek), Wyo. 319/G3
Horseshoe Beach, Fla. (32648) 212/C2
Horseshoe Bend, Ark. (72512) 202/G1
Horseshoe Bend, Idaho (83629) 220/B6
Horseshoe Bend Nat'l Mil. Park, Ala. 195/G5
Horseshoe Lake, Ontario 177/E2
Horse Shoe Run, W. Va. (26769) 312/G4
Horsetooth (res.), Colo. 208/J1
Horsham, England 10/F5
Horsham, England 13/G6
Horsham, Sask. 181/B5
Horsham, Victoria 97/B5
Horsham, Victoria 88/G7
Hørsholm, Denmark 21/F6
Horšovský Týn, Czech. 41/B2
Horst, Netherlands 27/H6
Horta (dist.), Portugal 33/A1
Horta, Portugal 33/B1
Hortaleza, Spain 33/G4
Horten, Norway 18/D4
Hortense, Georgia (31543) 217/J8
Hortensfjord (fjord), Norway 18/G4
Horton, Ala. (35980) 195/F2
Horton, Iowa (†50677) 229/J3
Horton, Kansas (66439) 232/G2
Horton, Mich. (49246) 250/E6
Horton, Mo. (64751) 261/D7
Horton (riv.), N.S. Wales 97/F2
Horton (riv.), N.W. Terrs. 187/F3
Horton, Oreg. (97448) 291/D3
Horton Bay, Mich. (†49712) 250/D3
Hortonia (lake), Vt. 268/A4
Hortonville, Ind. (†46069) 227/E4
Hortonville, Mass. (†02777) 249/K5
Hortonville, Wis. (54944) 317/J7
Hørve, Denmark 21/E6
Horwich, England 10/G2
Horwich, England 13/G2

384 Hoschton

Hoschton, Georgia (30548) 217/E2
Hoselaw, Alberta 182/E2
Hosenofu (well), Libya 111/D3
Hosford, Fla. (32334) 212/B1
Hoshab, Pakistan 68/A3
Hoshab, Pakistan 59/H4
Hoshangabad, India 68/D4
Hoskins, Nebr. (68740) 264/G2
Hosmer, Br. Col. 184/K5
Hosmer, S. Dak. (57448) 298/L2
Hospental, Switzerland 39/F3
Hospers, Iowa (51238) 229/B2
Hospet, India 68/D5
Hospital, Chile 138/G4
Hospital, Ireland 17/E7
Hospitalet, Spain 33/H2
Hosseina, Ethiopia 111/G6
Hosston, La. (71043) 238/C1
Hoste (isl.), Chile 120/B8
Hoste (isl.), Chile 138/F11
Hostinné, Czech. 41/C1
Hoswick, Scotland 15/G2
Hot, Thailand 72/C3
Hotan, China 77/B4
Hotan, China 54/K6
Hotan He (riv.), China 77/B4
Hotchkiss, Alberta 182/B1
Hotchkiss, Colo. (81419) 208/D5
Hotchkissville, Conn. (†06798) 210/C2
Hot Creek (range), Nev. 266/E4
Hot Creek (valley), Nev. 266/E4
Hotevilla, Ariz. (86030) 198/E3
Hotham (inlet), Alaska 196/F1
Hoting, Sweden 18/K4
Hot Lake, Oreg. (†97850) 291/K2
Hot Spring (co.), Ark. 202/E5
Hot Springs, Mont. (59845) 262/B3
Hot Springs (Truth or Consequences), N. Mex. (8790 274/B5
Hot Springs, N.C. (28743) 281/D3
Hot Springs, S. Dak. 188/F2
Hot Springs, S. Dak. (57747) 298/C7
Hot Springs, Va. (24445) 307/J4
Hot Springs (co.), Wyo. 319/D2
Hot Springs Cove, Br. Col. 184/D5
Hot Springs National Park, Ark. 188/H4
Hot Springs National Park, Ark. (71901) 202/D4
Hot Springs Nat'l Park, Ark. 202/D4
Hot Sulphur Springs, Colo. (80451) 208/H2
Hottah (lake), N.W.T. 162/E2
Hottah (lake), N.W. Terrs. 187/G3
Hottentot (bay), Namibia 118/A5
Hotton, Belgium 27/G8
Hou, Nam (riv.), Laos 72/D2
Houck, Ariz. (86506) 198/F3
Houcktown, Ohio (†45840) 284/C4
Houffalize, Belgium 27/H8
Houghton, Iowa (52631) 229/K7
Houghton, Maine (†04275) 243/B6
Houghton, Mich. 188/J1
Houghton (co.), Mich. 250/G1
Houghton, Mich. (49931) 250/G1
Houghton (lake), Mich. 250/E4
Houghton, N.Y. (14744) 276/D6
Houghton, S. Dak. (57449) 298/N2
Houghton Lake, Mich. (48629) 250/E4
Houghton Lake Heights, Mich. (48630) 250/E4
Houghton-le-Spring, England 13/J3
Houhoek, S. Africa 118/F7
Houlka, Miss. (38850) 256/G2
Houlton, Maine 188/N1
Houlton, Maine (04730) 243/H3
Houlton◯, Maine (04730) 243/H3
Houlton, Wis. (†55082) 317/A5
Houma, China 77/H4
Houma, La. (70360) 238/J7
Houndé, Upper Volta 106/D6
Hounslow, England 13/G8
Hounslow, England 10/B5
Hourn, Loch (inlet), Scotland 15/C3
Housatonic (riv.), Conn. 210/C3
Housatonic, Mass. (01236) 249/A3
Housatonic (riv.), Mass. 249/A4
House (mt.), Alberta 182/C2
House (riv.), Alberta 182/D2
House, N. Mex. (88121) 274/F4
House (range), Utah 304/A4
House Springs, Mo. (63051) 261/L6
Houston (co.), Ala. 195/H8
Houston, Ala. (35572) 195/D2
Houston, Alaska (†99687) 196/B1
Houston, Ark. (72070) 202/E3
Houston, Br. Col. 184/D3
Houston, Del. (19954) 245/S5
Houston, Fla. (†32060) 212/D1
Houston (co.), Georgia 217/E6
Houston, Ind. (†47235) 227/E6
Houston (co.), Minn. 255/G7
Houston, Minn. (55943) 255/G7
Houston, Miss. (38851) 256/G3
Houston, Mo. (65483) 261/J8
Houston, Ohio (45333) 284/B5
Houston, Pa. (15342) 294/B5
Houston (co.), Tenn. 237/F8
Houston (co.), Texas 303/J6
Houston, Texas (*77001) 303/J2
Houston, Texas 188/G5
Houston, Texas 146/J7
Houston (lake), Texas 303/J8
Houston, U.S. 2/E4
Houston Acres, Ky. (†40201) 237/K2
Houstonia, Mo. (65333) 261/F5
Houston Lake, Mo. (†64152) 261/O5
Houston Ship (chan.), Texas 303/K2
Hout (bay), S. Africa 118/E6
Houtbaai, S. Africa 118/E6
Houtman Abrolhos (isls.), W. Australia 88/A5
Houtman Abrolhos (isls.), W. Australia 92/A5
Houtrak Polder, Netherlands 27/A4
Houtzdale, Pa. (16651) 294/F4
Hov, Denmark 21/D6
Hovd, Mongolia 77/D2
Hovd (Kobdo, Jirgalanta), Mongolia 77/D2
Hovd, Mongolia 54/L5
Hovd Gol (riv.), Mongolia 77/D2
Hove, England 13/G7
Hove, England 10/F5
Hoven, S. Dak. (57450) 298/K3
Hovenweep Nat'l Mon., Colo. 208/A8
Hovenweep Nat'l Mon., Utah 304/E6
Hoveyzeh, Iran 66/F5
Hoving, N. Dak. (†58060) 282/P7
Hovland, Minn. (55606) 255/G2
Hövsgöl, Mongolia 77/E1
Hövsgöl Nuur (lake), Mongolia 77/F1
Howar, Wadi (dry riv.), Sudan 111/E4
Howard (pass), Alaska 196/G1
Howard (co.), Ark. 202/C5
Howard, Colo. (81233) 208/H6
Howard, Georgia (31039) 217/D5
Howard (co.), Ind. 227/E4
Howard (co.), Iowa 229/J2
Howard, Kansas (67349) 232/F4
Howard (co.), Md. 245/L4
Howard (co.), Mo. 261/G4
Howard (co.), Nebr. 264/F3
Howard, New Bruns. 170/E2
Howard, Ohio (43028) 284/F5
Howard, Pa. (16841) 294/G3
Howard, S. Dak. (57349) 298/P5
Howard (co.), Texas 303/C5
Howard (creek), Texas 303/C7
Howard, Wis. (54303) 317/K6
Howard A. Hanson (res.), Wash. 310/D3
Howard City, Mich. (49329) 250/D5
Howard City (Boelus), Nebr. (68820) 264/F3
Howard Lake, Minn. (55349) 255/D5
Howards Grove-Millersville, Wis. (53081) 317/L8
Howards Ridge, Mo. (†65655) 261/H9
Howardstown, Ky. (40028) 237/K5
Howardsville, Va. (24562) 307/L5
Howardville, Mo. (†63869) 261/N9
Howden, England 13/G4
Howe (cape), Australia 87/F9
Howe (sound), Br. Col. 184/K2
Howe, Idaho (83244) 220/F6
Howe, Ind. (46746) 227/G1
Howe (cape), N. S. Wales 88/J7
Howe (cape), N. S. Wales 97/F5
Howe, Okla. (74940) 288/S5
Howe, Texas (75059) 303/H4
Howell, Ark. (72071) 202/H3
Howell, Georgia (†31636) 217/F9
Howell, Mich. (48843) 250/E6
Howell (co.), Mo. 261/J9
Howell◯, N.J. (07731) 273/E3
Howell, Tenn. (†37334) 237/H10
Howell, Utah (84316) 304/B2
Howells, Nebr. (68641) 264/H3
Howes, S. Dak. (57748) 298/E4
Howesville, Ind. (†47438) 227/C6
Howesville, W. Va. (†26444) 312/G4
Howey In The Hills, Fla. (32737) 212/E3
Howick, N. Zealand 100/C1
Howick, Québec 172/D4
Howick, S. Africa 118/E5
Howison, Miss. (†39574) 256/F9
Howland, Maine (04448) 243/F5
Howland◯, Maine (04448) 243/F5
Howland (isl.), Pacific 87/J5
Howland Ridge, New Bruns. 170/C2
Howley, Newf. 166/C4
Howlong, N.S. Wales 97/D4
Howrah, India 68/F2
Howrah, India 54/K7
Howser, Br. Col. 184/J5
Hoxeyville, Mich. (49641) 250/D4
Hoxie, Ark. (72433) 202/H1
Hoxie, Kansas (67740) 232/B2
Höxter, W. Germany 22/C3
Hoxud, China 77/C3
Hoy (isl.), Scotland 15/E2
Hoy (isl.), Scotland 10/E1
Hoy (sound), Scotland 15/E2
Hoyerswerda, E. Germany 22/F3
Hoylake, England 13/G2
Hoylake, England 10/F2
Hoyland Nether, England 13/J2
Hoyleton, Ill. (62803) 222/D5
Hoyos, Spain 33/C2
Hoyran (lake), Turkey 63/D3
Hoyt, Colo. (80641) 208/L2
Hoyt, Kansas (66440) 232/G2
Hoyt, New Bruns. 170/D3
Hoyt, Okla. (74440) 288/R4
Hoyt (peak), Utah 304/C3
Hoyt Lakes, Minn. (55750) 255/F3
Hoytsville, Utah (†84017) 304/C3
Hoytville, Ohio (43529) 284/C3
Hozat, Turkey 59/C2
Hozat, Turkey 63/H3
Hradec Králové, Czech. 41/C1
Hranice, Czech. 41/D2
Hrinova, Czech. 41/E2
Hron (riv.), Czech. 41/E2
Hronov, Czech. 41/D1
Hrubieszów, Poland 47/F3
Hrušovany, Czech. 41/D2
Hsewi, Burma 72/C2
Hsipaw, Burma 72/C2
Hsüchang (Xuchang), China 77/H5
Htawgaw, Burma 72/C1
Huacaraje, Bolivia 136/D3
Huacareta, Bolivia 136/C7
Huacaya, Bolivia 136/D7
Huachacalla, Bolivia 136/A6
Huachi, Bolivia 136/D4
Huachi, China 77/G4
Huachipato, Chile 138/D1
Huacho, Peru 120/B4
Huacho, Peru 128/D8
Huachuca (peak), Ariz. 198/E7
Huachuca City, Ariz. (85616) 198/E7
Huacrachuco, Peru 128/D7
Huade, China 77/H3
Huadian, China 77/L3
Hua Hin, Thailand 72/D4
Huahine (isl.), Fr. Poly. 87/L7
Huaibei, China 77/J5
Huaibin, China 77/H5
Huaide (Hwaiteh), China 77/K3
Huaiji, China 77/H7
Huainan, China 77/J5
Huainan, China 54/N6
Huairen, China 77/H4
Huajuapan de León, Mexico 150/L8
Hualaihué, Chile 138/E4
Hualalai (mt.), Hawaii 218/G5
Hualañé, Chile 138/A10
Hualapai (mts.), Ariz. 198/B4
Hualapai (peak), Ariz. 198/B3
Hualapai Ind. Res., Ariz. 198/B3
Hualgayoc, Peru 128/C6
Hualien, China 77/K7
Hualla, Peru 128/F9
Huallaga (riv.), Peru 120/B3
Huallaga (riv.), Peru 128/D5
Huallanca, Ancash, Peru 128/D7
Huallanca, Huánuco, Peru 128/D7
Huallen, Alberta 182/A2
Huamachuco, Peru 128/D6
Huamantla, Mexico 150/N1
Huambo (dist.), Angola 115/C6
Huambo, Angola 102/D6
Huambo, Angola 115/C6
Huambo, Angola 2/K6
Huanaqui, Bolivia 136/A7
Huanay, Bolivia 136/B4
Huancabamba, Peru 128/C5
Huancané, Bolivia 136/B6
Huancané, Peru 128/H10
Huancapi, Peru 128/E9
Huancavelica (dept.), Peru 128/E9
Huancavelica, Peru 120/B4
Huancavelica, Peru 128/E9
Huancayo, Peru 128/E9
Huancayo, Pru 120/B4
Huanchaca, Bolivia 136/B7
Huanchaca, Cerro (mt.), Bolivia 136/B7
Huanchaca, Serranía de (mts.), Bolivia 136/E4
Huanchaco, Peru 128/C7
Huanggang, China 77/J5
Huang He (riv.), China 2/Q4
Huang He (Hwang Ho) (riv.), China 54/N6
Huang He (Ma Qu) (riv.), China 77/F5
Huang He (Yellow) (riv.), China 77/J4
Huangling, China 77/G4
Huangliu, China 77/G8
Huangshi, China 77/J5
Huangzhong, China 77/F4
Huanqueros, Argentina 143/F5
Huanta, Peru 128/E9
Huánuco (dept.), Peru 128/D7
Huánuco, Peru 128/E7
Huánuco, Peru 120/B3
Huanuni, Bolivia 136/B6
Huanuni, Bolivia 120/C4
Huan Xian, China 77/G4
Huapai, N. Zealand 100/B1
Huapí (mts.), Nicaragua 154/E4
Huaquechula, Mexico 150/M2
Huara, Chile 138/B2
Huaral, Peru 128/D8
Huaráz, Peru 128/D7
Huaráz, Peru 120/B3
Huari, Bolivia 136/B6
Huari, Peru 128/D7
Huariaca, Peru 128/E8
Huarina, Bolivia 136/A5
Huarmey, Peru 128/C8
Huarochirí, Peru 128/D9
Huarocondo, Peru 128/F9
Huásabas, Mexico 150/E2
Huasaga (riv.), Peru 128/D4
Huascarán (mt.), Peru 120/B3
Huascarán (mt.), Peru 128/D7
Huasco, Chile 138/A7
Huasco (riv.), Chile 138/A7
Huatabampo, Mexico 150/D3
Huatunas (lag.), Bolivia 136/B3
Huatusco de Chicuellar, Mexico 150/P2
Huauchinango, Mexico 150/L6
Huaura, Peru 128/D8
Huautla de Jiménez, Mexico 150/L7
Huayabamba (riv.), Peru 128/D6
Huaylas, Peru 128/C7
Huayllas, Bolivia 136/C6
Hub, Miss. (†39429) 256/E8
Hubball, W. Va. (†25506) 312/B6
Hubbard, Iowa (50122) 229/G4
Hubbard (lake), Mich. 250/F4
Hubbard (co.), Minn. 255/D3
Hubbard, Minn. (†56470) 255/D4
Hubbard, Nebr. (68741) 264/H2
Hubbard, Ohio (44425) 284/J3
Hubbard, Oreg. (97032) 291/A3
Hubbard, Sask. 181/H4
Hubbard, Texas (76648) 303/H6
Hubbard Creek (lake), Texas 303/F5
Hubbard Lake, Mich. (49747) 250/F4
Hubbards, Nova Scotia 168/D4
Hubbardston◯, Mass. (01452) 249/F3
Hubbardston, Mich. (48845) 250/E5
Hubbardstown, W. Va. (†25555) 312/A6
Hubbardsville, N.Y. (13355) 276/J5
Hubbardton◯, Vt. (05749) 268/A4
Hubbart (pt.), Manitoba 179/K2
Hubbell, Mich. (49934) 250/A1
Hubbell, Nebr. (68375) 264/G4
Hubbell Trading Post Nat'l Hist. Site, Ariz. 198/F3
Hub City, Wis. (†53581) 317/F9
Hubei (Hupei) (prov.), China 77/H5
Huberdeau, Québec 172/C4
Huber Heights, Ohio (45424) 284/B6
Hubert, N.C. (28539) 281/P5
Hubertus, Wis. (53033) 317/K1
Hubli-Dharwar, India 68/C5
Hubli-Dharwar, India 54/J8
Huch'ang, N. Korea 81/C3
Hückelhoven, W. Germany 22/B3
Hucknall, England 13/F4
Huddersfield, England 10/G2
Huddersfield, England 13/J2
Huddinge, Sweden 18/H1
Huddleston, Va. (24104) 307/K6
Huddy, Ky. (41535) 237/S5
Hudiksvall, Sweden 18/K6
Hudson (bay) 162/H3
Hudson (str.) 162/J3
Hudson (bay), Canada 2/E3
Hudson (str.), Canada 146/L3
Hudson (bay), Canada 146/K3
Hudson, Colo. (80642) 208/K2
Hudson, Fla. (33568) 212/D3
Hudson, Ill. (61748) 222/E3
Hudson, Ind. (46747) 227/G1
Hudson, Iowa (50643) 229/H4
Hudson, Kansas (67545) 232/D3
Hudson, Ky. (40145) 237/J5
Hudson◯, Maine (04449) 243/F5
Hudson (bay), Manitoba 179/K2
Hudson, Md. (†21613) 245/N6
Hudson, Mass. (01749) 249/H3
Hudson◯, Mass. (01749) 249/H3
Hudson, Mich. (49247) 250/E7
Hudson, N.H. (03051) 268/E6
Hudson◯, N.H. (03051) 268/E6
Hudson (co.), N.J. 273/E2
Hudson (riv.), N.J. 273/C1
Hudson, N.Y. (12534) 276/N6
Hudson (riv.), N.Y. 276/N7
Hudson, N.C. (28638) 281/G3
Hudson (bay), N.W. Terrs. 187/K3
Hudson (str.), N.W. Terrs. 187/L3
Hudson, Ohio (44236) 284/H3
Hudson (lake), Okla. 288/R2
Hudson, Ontario 175/B2
Hudson, Ontario 177/G4
Hudson (bay), Ontario 175/D1
Hudson, Québec 172/C4
Hudson (bay), Québec 174/A1
Hudson (str.), Québec 174/F1
Hudson, S. Dak. (57034) 298/R7
Hudson, Wis. (54016) 317/A6
Hudson, Wyo. (82515) 319/D3
Hudson Bay, Sask. 181/J3
Hudson Falls, N.Y. (12839) 276/O4
Hudson Hope, Br. Col. 184/F2
Hudson Lake, Ind. (46552) 227/D1
Hudsons Bay, Alberta 182/E4
Hudsonville, Mich. (49426) 250/D6
Hudspeth (co.), Texas 303/B10
Hudwin (lake), Manitoba 179/G1
Hue, Vietnam 54/M8
Hue, Vietnam 72/E3
Hueco (mts.), N. Mex. 274/D6
Hueco (mts.), Texas 303/B10
Huedin, Romania 45/F2
Huehue, Hawaii (†96740) 218/G5
Huehuetenango, Guatemala 154/B3
Huehuetlán el Chico, Mexico 150/M2
Huejotzingo, Mexico 150/M1
Huejutla, Mexico 150/K6
Huelma, Spain 33/E4
Huelva (prov.), Spain 33/C4
Huelva, Spain 33/C4
Huelva, Spain 7/D5
Huelva (riv.), Spain 33/C4
Huentelauquén, Chile 138/A8
Huercal-Overa, Spain 33/F4
Huerfano (co.), Colo. 208/K7
Huerfano (riv.), Colo. 208/L7
Huesca (prov.), Spain 33/F1
Huesca, Spain 33/F1
Huéscar, Spain 33/E4
Huetamo, Mexico 150/J7
Huete, Spain 33/E2
Hueffer, Idaho (†83854) 220/B2
Huey, Ill. (62252) 222/D5
Hueyotlipan de Hidalgo, Mexico 150/M1
Hueytown, Ala. (35020) 195/D4
Huff, N. Dak. (58555) 282/J6
Huffman, Ark. (†72315) 202/L2
Huffton, S. Dak. (†57432) 298/N2
Huger, S.C. (29450) 296/H5
Huggins, Mo. (65484) 261/H8
Hugh Butler (lake), Nebr. 264/D4
Hughenden, Alberta 182/E3
Hughenden, Australia 87/E8
Hughenden, Queensland 88/G4
Hughenden, Queensland 95/B4
Hughes, Alaska (99745) 196/H1
Hughes, Ark. (72348) 202/J4
Hughes (co.), Okla. 288/O4
Hughes, S. Australia 94/A4
Hughes (co.), S. Dak. 298/J5
Hughes (riv.), W. Va. 312/D4
Hughes Springs, Texas (75656) 303/K5
Hughestown, Pa. (†18640) 294/F7
Hugheston, Md. (20637) 245/L6
Hughesville, Mo. (65334) 261/F5
Hughesville, Pa. (17737) 294/J3
Hughson, Calif. (95326) 204/E6
Hughton, Sask. 181/D4
Hugh Town, England 13/A8
Hugo, Colo. (80821) 208/N4
Hugo, Minn. (55038) 255/E5
Hugo, Okla. (74743) 288/P7
Hugo (lake), Okla. 288/R6
Hugo Stroessner, Paraguay 144/C4
Hugoton, Kansas (67951) 232/A4
Huhehot (Hohhot), China 77/H3
Huiarau (range), N. Zealand 100/F3
Hüich'ŏn, N. Korea 81/C3
Huila (dist.), Angola 115/B7
Huila (dept.), Colombia 126/C6
Huila (mt.), Colombia 120/B2
Huila, Nevado del (mt.), Colombia 126/C6
Huimanguillo, Mexico 150/N8
Huimin, China 77/J4
Huinca Renancó, Argentina 143/D3
Huining, China 77/G4
Huissen, Netherlands 27/H5
Huitzilán, Mexico 150/O1
Huitzuco de los Figueroa, Mexico 150/K7
Huixcolotla, Mexico 150/N2
Huixtepec, Mexico 150/L8
Huixtla, Mexico 150/N9
Huize, China 77/F6
Huizen, Netherlands 27/G4
Huizhou, China 77/H7
Hulaco, Ala. (†35087) 195/E2
Hulah (lake), Kansas 232/F5
Hulah, Okla. (†67333) 288/O1
Hulah (lake), Okla. 288/O1
Hulan, China 77/L2
Hulbert, Mich. (49748) 250/D2
Hulbert, Okla. (74441) 288/R3
Hulberton, N.Y. (14473) 276/D4
Hulett, Wyo. (82720) 319/H1
Hulin, China 77/M2
Hull, England 7/E3
Hull, England 10/F4
Hull, England 13/G4
Hull, Fla. (†33842) 212/E4
Hull, Georgia (30646) 217/F2
Hull, Ill. (62343) 222/B4
Hull, Iowa (51239) 229/A2
Hull (isl.), Kiribati 87/J6
Hull◯, Mass. (02045) 249/E7
Hull, N. Dak. (†58542) 282/K7
Hull, Que. 162/J6
Hull (co.), Québec 172/B4
Hull, Québec 172/B4
Hulls Cove, Maine (04644) 243/G7
Hulopee (bay), Hawaii 218/G2
Hulopoe Bay, Hawaii (†96763) 218/H2
Hulst, Netherlands 27/E6
Hultsfred, Sweden 18/K8
Hulun Nur (lake), China 77/J2
Huma, China 77/L1
Humacao (dist.), P. Rico 161/E2
Humacao, P. Rico 161/E2
Humacao, P. Rico 156/G1
Humacao (riv.), P. Rico 161/E2
Huma He (riv.), China 77/K1
Humahuaca, Argentina 143/C1
Humaitá, Bolivia 136/B2
Humaitá, Brazil 132/H10
Humaitá, Brazil 120/C3
Humaitá, Brazil 132/G10
Humaitá, Paraguay 144/C5
Humansdorp, S. Africa 118/C6
Humansville, Mo. (65674) 261/E7
Humarock, Mass. (02047) 249/M4
Humber (riv.), England 13/G4
Humber (riv.), England 10/G4
Humber (riv.), Newf. 166/C4
Humber (riv.), Ontario 177/J3
Humberside (co.), England 13/G4
Humberto, Argentina 143/F5
Humbird, Wis. (54746) 317/E6
Humble, Texas (*77338) 303/J7
Humble City, N. Mex. (†88240) 274/F6
Humboldt, Ariz. (86329) 198/C4
Humboldt (co.), Calif. 204/B3
Humboldt (bay), Calif. 204/A3
Humboldt (bay), Colombia 126/B4
Humboldt, Ill. (61931) 222/E4
Humboldt (co.), Iowa 229/E3
Humboldt, Iowa (50548) 229/E3
Humboldt, Kansas (66748) 232/G4
Humboldt, Minn. (56731) 255/A2
Humboldt, Nebr. (68376) 264/J4
Humboldt (co.), Nev. 266/C1
Humboldt, Nev. (†89418) 266/C2
Humboldt (range), Nev. 266/C2
Humboldt (riv.), Nev. 188/C2
Humboldt (riv.), Nev. 266/E2
Humboldt (sink), Nev. 266/C2
Humboldt (mt.), New Caled. 86/H4
Humboldt, Sask. 162/F5
Humboldt, Sask. 181/F3
Humboldt, S. Dak. (57035) 298/P6
Humboldt, Tenn. (38343) 237/D9
Humboldt Salt (marsh), Nev. 266/D3
Humbug (mt.), Oreg. 291/C5
Hume, Ill. (61932) 222/F4
Hume, Mo. (64752) 261/C6
Hume (res.), N.S. Wales 97/D4
Hume, N.Y. (14745) 276/D5
Hume, Sask. 181/H6
Hume (lake), Victoria 97/D4
Hume, Va. (22639) 307/N3
Humenné, Czech. 41/G2
Humeston, Iowa (50123) 229/G7
Humlum, Denmark 21/B4
Hummelstown, Pa. (17036) 294/J5
Hummock (isl.), Tasmania 99/D2
Humnoke, Ark. (72072) 202/G4
Humphrey (pt.), Alaska 196/K1
Humphrey, Ark. (72073) 202/G5
Humphrey, Idaho (†83446) 220/F5
Humphrey, Nebr. (68642) 264/G3
Humphreys (peak), Ariz. 198/D3
Humphreys, La. (†70356) 238/J7
Humphreys (co.), Miss. 256/C4
Humphreys, Mo. (64646) 261/F2
Humphreys, Okla. (†73521) 288/H5
Humphreys (co.), Tenn. 237/F8
Humpolec, Czech. 41/C2
Humptulips, Wash. (98552) 310/A3
Humptulips (riv.), Wash. 310/B3
Humpty Doo, North. Terr. 93/B2
Húnaflói (bay), Iceland 7/B2
Húnaflói (bay), Iceland 21/B1
Hunan (prov.), China 77/H6
Hunchun, China 77/M3
Hundested, Denmark 21/E6
Hundred, W. Va. (26575) 312/E3
Hunedoara, Romania 7/G4
Hunedoara, Romania 45/F3
Hünfeld, W. Germany 22/C3
Hungary 2/K3
Hungary 7/F4
HUNGARY 41
Hunger (mt.), Vt. 268/B3
Hungerford, Queensland 95/B6
Hŭngnam, N. Korea 54/O6
Hungry Horse, Mont. (59919) 262/C2
Hungry Horse (res.), Mont. 262/C2
Hungtow (isl.), China 77/K7
Hunjiang, China 77/L3
Hunmanby, England 13/G3
Hunnewell, Kansas (†67140) 232/E4
Hunnewell, Mo. (63443) 261/J3
Hunse (riv.), Netherlands 27/K3
Hunsrück (mts.), W. Germany 22/B4
Hunstanton, England 13/H5
Hunstanton, England 10/G4
Hunt, Ill. (†62480) 222/E4
Hunt (co.), Texas 303/H4
Hunt (mt.), Wyo. 319/E1
Hunte (riv.), W. Germany 22/C2
Hunter, Ark. (72074) 202/H3
Hunter (isl.), Br. Col. 184/C4
Hunter (peak), Idaho 220/D3
Hunter, Kansas (67452) 232/D2
Hunter, Mo. (†63943) 261/L9
Hunter (riv.), N.S. Wales 97/F3
Hunter, N.Y. (12442) 276/M6
Hunter (mt.), N.Y. 276/M6
Hunter (mts.), N. Zealand 100/A6
Hunter, N. Dak. (58048) 282/R5
Hunter, Okla. (74640) 288/L1
Hunter (isls.), Tasmania 88/G8
Hunter (isl.), Tasmania 99/A2
Hunter (isls.), Tasmania 99/B2
Hunterdon (co.), N.J. 273/D2
Hunter River, Pr. Edward I. 168/E2
Hunters, Wash. (99137) 310/G2
Hunters Creek Village, Texas (†77001) 303/J1
Hunters Hill, N. S. Wales 88/K4
Hunters Hill, N.S. Wales 97/J3
Huntersville, Ky. (†42602) 237/L7
Huntersville, Minn. (†56464) 255/D4
Huntersville, N.C. (28078) 281/H4
Huntersville, W. Va. (†24954) 312/G6
Huntertown, Ind. (46748) 227/G2
Hunterville, N. Zealand 100/E3
Hunting (riv.), N.C. 281/H2
Hunting (isl.), S.C. 296/G7
Huntingburg, Ind. (47542) 227/D8
Huntingdon, Br. Col. 184/L3
Huntingdon (isl.), Newf. 166/C3
Huntingdon (co.), Pa. 294/F5
Huntingdon, Pa. (16652) 294/G5
Huntingdon (co.), Québec 172/C4
Huntingdon, Québec 172/C4
Huntingdon, Tenn. (38344) 237/E8
Huntingdon and Godmanchester, England 13/G5
Huntingdon and Godmanchester, England 10/F4
Huntington, Ark. (72940) 202/B3
Huntington, Conn. (†06484) 210/C3
Huntington, England 13/G3
Huntington (co.), Ind. 227/G3
Huntington, Ind. (46750) 227/G3
Huntington (lake), Ind. 227/F3
Huntington, Iowa (†51334) 229/D2
Huntington◯, Mass. (01050) 249/C4
Huntington (creek), Nev. 266/F2
Huntington, N.J. (†08865) 273/C2
Huntington, N.Y. (11743) 276/R6
Huntington, Oreg. (97907) 291/K3
Huntington, Texas (75949) 303/K6
Huntington, Utah (84528) 304/C4
Huntington (creek), Utah 304/C4
Huntington◯, Vt. (05462) 268/B3
Huntington, Va. (†22301) 307/S3
Huntington, W. Va. 188/K3
Huntington, W. Va. (*25701) 312/A6
Huntington Beach, Calif. (*92646) 204/C11
Huntington Center, Vt. (†05462) 268/B3
Huntington Park, Calif. (90255) 204/C11
Huntington Station, N.Y. (11746) 276/R6
Huntingtown, Md. (20639) 245/M6
Hunting Valley, Ohio (†44022) 284/J9
Huntland, Tenn. (37345) 237/J10
Huntleigh, Mo. (†63101) 261/O3
Huntley, Ill. (60142) 222/E1
Huntley, Minn. (56047) 255/D7
Huntley, Mont. (59037) 262/H5
Huntley, Nebr. (68951) 264/E4
Huntley, Wyo. (82218) 319/H4
Huntly, N. Zealand 100/E2
Huntly, Scotland 10/E2
Huntly, Scotland 15/F3
Huntoon, Sask. 181/H6
Huntsburg, Ohio (44046) 284/H2
Hunts Inlet, Br. Col. 184/B3
Hunts Point, Nova Scotia 168/D5
Hunts Point, Wash. (†98004) 310/B2
Huntsville, Ala. 188/J4
Huntsville, Ala. (*35801) 195/E1
Huntsville, Ark. (72740) 202/C1
Huntsville, Conn. (†06031) 210/B1
Huntsville, Ind. (†47358) 227/F4
Huntsville, Ind. (†46064) 227/G4
Huntsville, Ky. (42251) 237/H6
Huntsville, Mo. (65259) 261/H4
Huntsville, Ohio (43324) 284/C5
Huntsville, Ontario 177/E2
Huntsville, Ontario 175/E3
Huntsville, Tenn. (37756) 237/N8
Huntsville, Texas (77340) 303/J7
Huntsville, Utah (84317) 304/C2
Huntsville, Wash. (†99328) 310/G4
Hunucmá, Mexico 150/O6
Hunza (Baltit), Pakistan 68/C1
Huocheng, China 77/B3
Huon (isls.), New Caled. 87/G7
Huon (gulf), Papua N.G. 87/E6
Huon (gulf), Papua N.G. 85/C7
Huon (pen.), Papua N.G. 86/A2
Huon (riv.), Tasmania 99/C5
Huong Khe, Vietnam 72/E3
Huonville-Ranelagh, Tasmania 99/C5
Huoshan, China 77/J5
Huot, Minn. (†56716) 255/B3
Huo Xian, China 77/H4
Hupei (Hubei) (prov.), China 77/H5
Hurbanovo, Czech. 41/E3
Hurd (cape), Ontario 177/C2
Hurdland, Mo. (63547) 261/H2
Hurdle Mills, N.C. (27541) 281/L2
Hurdsfield, N. Dak. (58451) 282/L5

386 Indianola

Indianola, Miss. (38751) 256/C4
Indianola, Nebr. (69034) 264/D4
Indianola, Okla. (74442) 288/P4
Indianola, Utah (†84629) 304/C4
Indianola, Wash. (98342) 310/A1
Indian Pond (lake), Maine 243/D4
Indian River (bay), Del. 245/T6
Indian River (inlet), Del. 245/T6
Indian River (co.), Fla. 212/F4
Indian River, Maine (†04649) 243/H6
Indian River, Mich. (49749) 250/E3
Indian River, Ontario 177/F3
Indian River Shores, Fla. (32960) 212/F4
Indian Rocks Beach, Fla. (33535) 212/B3
Indian Shores, Fla. (†33535) 212/B3
Indian Springs, Georgia (30231) 217/E4
Indian Springs, Ind. (47544) 227/D7
Indian Springs, Nev. (89018) 266/F6
Indiantown, Fla. (33456) 212/F4
Indian Trail, N.C. (28079) 281/H4
Indian Valley, Idaho (83632) 220/B5
Indian Valley, Va. (24105) 307/G7
Indian Village, Ind. (†46601) 227/E1
Indian Village, La. (†70764) 238/H6
Indian Wells, Ariz. (86031) 198/E3
Indian Wells, Calif. (†92260) 204/J10
Indiga, U.S.S.R. 48/E3
Indiga, U.S.S.R. 52/G1
Indigirka, U.S.S.R. 54/R3
Indigirka (riv.), U.S.S.R. 4/C2
Indigirka (riv.), U.S.S.R. 48/P3
Indigo (crek), Oreg. 291/D5
Indio, Calif. (92201) 204/J10
Indios (chan.), Cuba 158/B2
Indispensable (str.), Solomon Is. 86/E3
Indochina (reg.), Vietnam 72/D2
Indonesia 2/Q6
Indonesia 54/M10
INDONESIA 85
Indooroopilly, Queensland 95/D3
Indooroopilly, Queensland 88/K3
Indore, India 68/D4
Indore, India 54/J7
Indore, W. Va. (25111) 312/D6
Indramayu, Indonesia 85/H2
Indramayu (pt.), Indonesia 85/H1
Indravati (riv.), India 68/E5
Indre (dept.), France 28/D4
Indre (riv.), France 28/D4
Indre-et-Loire (dept.), France 28/D4
Indus (riv.) 2/N4
Indus (riv.) 54/H7
Indus, Alberta 182/D4
Indus (riv.), India 68/B3
Indus, Minn. (†56629) 255/E2
Indus, Mouths of the (delta), Pakistan 68/B4
Indus (riv.), Pakistan 59/J4
Indus (riv.), Pakistan 68/B3
Industrial City, Georgia (†30705) 217/C1
Industry, Ill. (61440) 222/C3
Industry, Kansas (†67410) 232/E2
Industry, Pa. (15052) 294/B4
Industry, Texas (78944) 303/H7
Inebolu, Turkey 59/B1
Inebolu, Turkey 63/E2
Inegöl, Turkey 63/C2
In Eker, Algeria 106/F4
Ineu, Romania 45/E2
Inez, Ky. (41224) 237/S5
Inez, N.C. (27589) 281/N2
Inezgane, Morocco 106/C2
In Ezzane (well), Algeria 106/G4
Infanta, Philippines 82/C3
Infieles (pt.), Chile 138/A6
Infiesto, Spain 33/D1
In-Gall, Niger 106/F5
Ingalls, Ark. (71648) 202/F7
Ingalls (mt.), Calif. 204/E3
Ingalls, Ind. (46048) 227/F5
Ingalls, Kansas (67853) 232/B4
Ingalls, Mich. (49848) 250/B3
Ingavi, Bolivia 136/B2
Ingelmunster, Belgium 27/C7
Ingelow, Manitoba 179/C5
Ingenbohl, Switzerland 39/G2
Ingende, Zaire 115/C4
Ingende, Zaire 102/D5
Ingeniero Huergo, Argentina 143/C4
Ingeniero Jacobacci, Argentina 143/C5
Ingeniero Luiggi, Argentina 143/D4
Ingeniero Montero Hoyos (Tocomechi), Bolivia 136/D5
Ingersoll, Ontario 177/C4
Ingham (co.), Mich. 250/E6
Ingham, Queensland 88/H3
Ingham, Queensland 95/C3
Inglefield, Ind. (47618) 227/B8
Inglés (pt.), Cuba 158/G4
Inglesa (bay), Chile 138/A6
Ingleside, Md. (21644) 245/P4
Ingleside, Ontario 177/J2
Ingleside, W. Va. (†24740) 312/E8
Inglewood, Calif. (*90301) 204/B11
Inglewood, Nebr. (†68025) 264/H3
Inglewood, N. Zealand 100/E3
Inglewood, Victoria 97/B5
Inglis, Fla. (32649) 212/D2
Inglis, Manitoba 179/A4
Ingold, N.C. (28446) 281/N5
Ingoldsby, Ontario 177/F3
Ingolstadt, W. Germany 22/D4
Ingomar, Miss. (†38652) 256/F2
Ingomar, Mont. (59039) 262/J4
Ingomar, Nova Scotia 168/C5
Ingomar, Pa. (15127) 294/C4
Ingonish, Nova Scotia 168/H2
Ingonish Beach, Nova Scotia 168/H2
Ingonish North (bay), Nova Scotia 168/H2
Ingornachoix (bay), Newf. 166/C3
Ingraham (lake), Fla. 212/E6
Ingraham, Ill. (62434) 222/E5
Ingram, Pa. (†15205) 294/B7
Ingram, Texas (78025) 303/E7
Ingram, Va. (24564) 307/K7
Ingram, Wis. (†54530) 317/E5
Ingre, Bolivia 136/D7
In Guezzam, Algeria 106/F5
Ingwavuma, S. Africa 118/E5
Inhambane (prov.), Mozambique 118/E4
Inhambane, Mozambique 118/F4
Inhambane, Mozambique 102/F7
Inhaminga, Mozambique 118/F3
Inharrime, Mozambique 118/F4
Inharrime, Mozambique 102/F7
Inhumas, Brazil 132/D7
Iniesta, Spain 33/F3
Inini, Fr. Guiana 131/E4
Inini (riv.), Fr. Guiana 131/E4
Inírida, Colombia 120/C2
Inírida, Colombia 126/F6
Inírida (riv.), Colombia 126/F6
Inishannon, Ireland 17/D8
Inishbofin (isl.), Ireland 17/A4
Inishbofin (isl.), Ireland 10/A4
Inishbofin (isl.), Ireland 17/E1
Inisheer (isl.), Ireland 17/B5
Inishmaan (isl.), Ireland 17/C5
Inishmore (isl.), Ireland 17/B5
Inishmurray (isl.), Ireland 17/D3
Inishowen (head), Ireland 17/H1
Inishowen (pen.), Ireland 17/G1
Inishshark (isl.), Ireland 17/A4
Inishtrahull (isl.), Ireland 17/G1
Inishtrahull (sound), Ireland 17/G1
Inishturk (isl.), Ireland 10/A4
Inishturk (isls.), Ireland 17/A4
Inistioge, Ireland 17/G7
Injune, Queensland 95/D5
Injune, Queensland 88/H5
Inkerman, New Bruns. 170/F1
Inklin (riv.), Br. Col. 184/J2
Inkom, Idaho (83245) 220/F7
Inkster, Mich. (48141) 250/B7
Inkster, N. Dak. (58244) 282/P3
Inland (lake), Ala. 195/E3
Inland (lake), Alaska 196/G1
Inland (lake), Manitoba 179/C2
Inland, Nebr. (68954) 264/F4
Inle (lake), Burma 72/C2
Inlet, N.Y. (13360) 276/L3
Inman, Georgia (30232) 217/D4
Inman, Kansas (67546) 232/E3
Inman, Nebr. (68742) 264/F2
Inman, S.C. (29349) 296/C1
Inn (riv.), Austria 41/B2
Inn (riv.), Switzerland 39/K3
Inn (riv.), W. Germany 22/E4
Innamincka, S. Australia 94/G2
Innellan, Scotland 15/A2
Inner (sound), Scotland 10/D2
Inner (sound), Scotland 15/C3
Inner Hebrides (isls.), Scotland 15/B4
Innerkip, Ontario 177/D4
Innerleithen, Scotland 10/E3
Innerleithen, Scotland 15/E5
Inner Mongolia (reg.), China 54/N5
Inner Mongolia (reg.), China 77/H3
Inner Mongolian Aut. Reg. (Nei Monggol), China 77/H3
Innertkirchen, Switzerland 39/F3
Innes (lake), N.S. Wales 97/G2
Innis, La. (70747) 238/G5
Inniscrone, Ireland 17/C3
Innisfail, Alberta 182/D3
Innisfail, Queensland 95/C3
Innisfail, Queensland 88/H3
Innisfree, Alberta 182/E3
Innisville, Ontario 177/H2
Innoko (riv.), Alaska 196/G2
Innsbruck, Austria 7/F4
Innsbruck, Austria 41/A3
Inny (riv.), Ireland 17/F4
Inny (riv.), Ireland 17/A8
Inola, Okla. (74036) 288/P2
Inongo, Zaire 115/C4
Inönü, Turkey 63/D3
Inoucdjouac, Que. 162/H4
Inoucdjouac, Québec 174/E1
Inowrocław, Poland 47/D2
Inquisivi, Bolivia 136/B5
In Rhar, Algeria 106/E3
Ins, Switzerland 39/D2
In Salah, Algeria 106/E3
In Salah, Algeria 102/C2
Insch, Scotland 15/F3
Insein, Burma 72/C3
Inset, Norway 18/G5
Insinger, Sask. 181/H4
Inspiration, Ariz. (85537) 198/D5
Institute, W. Va. (25112) 312/C6
Instow, Sask. 181/C6
Inta, U.S.S.R. 7/K2
Inta, U.S.S.R. 52/K1
Inta, U.S.S.R. 48/G3
Intake, Mont. (†59330) 262/M3
Intelewa, Suriname 131/D4
Intendente Alvear, Argentina 143/D4
Intepe, Turkey 63/B6
Intercession City, Fla. (33848) 212/E3
Intercourse, Pa. (17534) 294/K5
Interior, S. Dak. (57750) 298/F6
Interlachen, Fla. (32048) 212/E2
Interlaken, Mass. (†01266) 249/A3
Interlaken, N.J. (†07712) 273/E3
Interlaken, N.Y. (14847) 276/G5
Interlaken, Switzerland 39/E3
Interlochen, Mich. (49643) 250/D4
International Airport, Georgia 217/K2
International Airport, Mo. 261/P2
International Airport (Dallas-Ft. Worth), Texas 303/F2
International Falls, Minn. 188/H1
International Falls, Minn. (56649) 255/E2
International Peace Garden, Manitoba 179/B5
International Peace Garden, N. Dak. 282/K1
Intervale, N.H. (03845) 268/E3
Interview (isl.), India 68/G6
Inthanon, Doi (mt.), Thailand 72/C3
Intipucá, El Salvador 154/D4
Intracoastal Waterway, S.C. 296/H5
Intracoastal Waterway, Texas 303/J9
Intragna, Switzerland 39/G4
Intutu, Peru 128/E4
Inubo (cape), Japan 81/K6
Inútil (bay), Chile 138/E10
Inuvik, Canada 4/C16
Inuvik, N.W.T. 146/E3
Inuvik, N.W.T. 162/C2
Inuvik (dist.), N.W. Terrs. 187/F3
Inuvik, N.W. Terrs. 187/E3
Inver (bay), Ireland 17/E2
Inveraray, Scotland 10/D2
Inveraray, Scotland 15/C4
Inverbervie, Scotland 10/E2
Inverbervie, Scotland 15/F4
Invercargill, N. Zealand 100/B7
Invercassley, Scotland 15/D3
Inverell, N. S. Wales 88/J5
Inverell, N.S. Wales 97/F1
Invergarry, Scotland 15/D3
Invergordon, Scotland 10/D2
Invergordon, Scotland 15/D3
Invergowrie, Scotland 15/E4
Inver Grove Heights, Minn. (55075) 255/E6
Inverhuron, Ontario 177/C3
Inverie, Scotland 15/C3
Inverkeilor, Scotland 15/F4
Inverkeithing, Scotland 15/D1
Inverkeithing, Scotland 10/C1
Inverloch, Victoria 97/C6
Invermay, Ontario 177/C3
Invermay, Sask. 181/J4
Invermere, Br. Col. 184/J5
Invermoriston, Scotland 15/D3
Inverness, Ala. (†36089) 195/G6
Inverness, Calif. (94937) 204/B5
Inverness, Fla. (32650) 212/D3
Inverness, Ill. (†60067) 222/A5
Inverness, Miss. (38753) 256/C4
Inverness, Mont. (59530) 262/F2
Inverness, N.S. 162/K6
Inverness (co.), Nova Scotia 168/G2
Inverness, Nova Scotia 168/G2
Inverness, Québec 172/F3
Inverness, Scotland 15/D3
Inverness, Scotland 7/D3
Inverness, Scotland 10/D2
Inverness, (trad. co.), Scotland, 15/A5
Inverurie, Scotland 15/F3
Inverurie, Scotland 10/E2
Inverway, North. Terr. 93/A4
Investigator (shoal), Philippines 85/E4
Investigator (str.), S. Australia 88/F7
Investigator (str.), S. Australia 94/E6
Investigator Group (isls.), S. Australia 88/E6
Investigator Group (isls.), S. Australia 94/D5
Inwood, Ind. (46533) 227/E2
Inwood, Iowa (51240) 229/A2
Inwood, Manitoba 179/E4
Inwood, N.Y. (11696) 276/P7
Inwood, Ontario 177/C5
Inwood, W. Va. (25428) 312/K4
Inyanga, Zimbabwe 118/E3
Inyan Kara (creek), Wyo. 319/H1
Inyan Kara (mt.), Wyo. 319/H1
Inyo (co.), Calif. 204/H7
Inyo (mts.), Calif. 204/G6
Inyokern, Calif. (93527) 204/H8
Inza, U.S.S.R. 52/G4
Inzana (lake), Br. Col. 184/E3
Ioánnina, Greece 7/G4
Ioánnina, Greece 45/E6
Ioco, Br. Col. 184/K3
Ioka, Utah (†84052) 304/D3
Iola, Ill. (62847) 222/E5
Iola, Kansas (66749) 232/G4
Iola, Texas (77861) 303/H7
Iola, Wis. (54945) 317/H6
Iolotan', U.S.S.R. 48/G6
Ioma, Papua N.G. 85/C7
Iona, Angola 115/B7
Iona, Idaho (83427) 220/G6
Iona, Minn. (56141) 255/C7
Iona (isls.), Newf. 166/C2
Iona, N.J. (†08322) 273/C4
Iona, Nova Scotia 168/H3
Iona, Ontario 177/C5
Iona (isl.), Scotland 15/B4
Iona (isl.), Scotland 10/C2
Iona, S. Dak. (57542) 298/L6
Ione, Ark. (†72927) 202/B3
Ione, Calif. (95640) 204/C9
Ione, Nev. (†89310) 266/D4
Ione, Oreg. (97843) 291/H2
Ione, Wash. (99139) 310/H2
Ionia, Iowa (50645) 229/J2
Ionia, Kansas (66947) 232/D2
Ionia (co.), Mich. 250/D6
Ionia, Mich. (48846) 250/D6
Ionia, Mo. (65335) 261/F6
Ionian (sea) 7/F5
Ionian (isls.), Greece 7/F5
Ionian (sea), Greece 45/D7
Ionian (sea), Italy 34/F6
Ionian Islands (reg.), Greece 45/D6
Íos, Greece 45/G7
Íos (isl.), Greece 45/G7
Iosco (co.), Mich. 250/F4
Iosegun (lake), Alberta 182/B2
Iosegun (riv.), Alberta 182/B2
Iota, La. (70543) 238/E6
Iowa 188/H2
IOWA 229
Iowa (co.), Iowa 229/J5
Iowa (riv.), Iowa 188/H2
Iowa (riv.), Iowa 229/H4
Iowa, La. (70647) 238/D6
Iowa (state), U.S. 146/J5
Iowa (co.), Wis. 317/F9
Iowa City, Iowa 188/H2
Iowa City, Iowa (52240) 229/L5
Iowa Colony, Texas (†77583) 303/J2
Iowa Falls, Iowa (50126) 229/G3
Iowa Park, Texas (76367) 303/F4
Iowa Point, Kansas (†66035) 232/G2
Ipala, Guatemala 154/C3
Ipameri, Brazil 132/E7
Ipanema, Brazil 135/F1
Iparia, Peru 128/E7
Ipatovo, U.S.S.R. 52/F5
Ipava, Ill. (61441) 222/C3
Ipel' (riv.), Czech. 41/E2
Iphigenia (bay), Alaska 196/M2
Ipiales, Colombia 126/B7
Ipil, Philippines 82/D7
Ipin (Yibin), China 77/F6
Ipoh, Malaysia 54/M9
Ipoh, Malaysia 72/D6
Ipoly (riv.), Hungary 41/E2
Iporá, Brazil 120/D4
Ipperwash Prov. Park, Ontario 177/C4
Ippy, Cent. Afr. Rep. 115/D2
Ipsala, Turkey 63/B2
Ipsile, Turkey 63/G2
Ipswich, Australia 87/F8
Ipswich, England 13/J5
Ipswich, England 10/G4
Ipswich, Mass. (01938) 249/L2
Ipswich○, Mass. (01938) 249/L2
Ipswich (riv.), Mass. 249/L2
Ipswich, Queensland 88/J3
Ipswich, Queensland 95/E5
Ipswich, S. Dak. (57451) 298/L3
Ipu, Brazil 132/F4
Iquique, Chile 120/B5
Iquique, Chile 138/A2
Iquitos, Peru 120/B3
Iquitos, Peru 128/F4
Ira, Iowa (50127) 229/G5
Ira, N.Y. (†13033) 276/G4
Ira, Texas (79527) 303/C5
Ira○, Vt. (†05777) 268/A4
Iraan, Texas (79744) 303/B7
Iracoubo, Fr. Guiana 131/E3
Iraël', U.S.S.R. 52/H2
Iráklion, Greece 45/G8
Iráklion, Greece 7/G5
Iran 2/M4
Iran 54/G7
IRAN 66
IRAN 59/F3
Iran (mts.), Malaysia 85/E5
Iranshahr, Iran 66/M7
Iranshahr, Iran 59/H4
Irapa, Venezuela 124/G2
Irapuato, Mexico 150/J6
Iraq 2/M4
Iraq 54/F6
IRAQ 59/D3
IRAQ 66
Irasburg○, Vt. (05845) 268/C2
Irati, Brazil 132/D9
Irati, Brazil 135/A4
Irawan, Philippines 82/B6
Irazú (mt.), C. Rica 154/F6
Irbid, Jordan 65/D2
Irby, Wash. (99159) 310/G3
Irecê, Brazil 120/E4
Iredell (co.), N.C. 281/H3
Iredell, Texas (76649) 303/G6
Ireland 2/J3
Ireland 7/D3
Ireland (isl.), Bermuda 156/G3
Ireland, Ind. (47545) 227/C8
IRELAND 17
IRELAND 10/B4
IRELAND, NORTHERN 10, 17
Ireland, Texas (76536) 303/F6
Ireland, W. Va. (26376) 312/F5
Ireland's Eye (isl.), Ireland 17/K5
Ireland's Eye (isl.), Newf. 166/D2
Irene, S. Africa 118/H6
Irene, S. Dak. (57037) 298/P7
Ireng (riv.), Guyana 131/B3
Ireton, Iowa (51027) 229/A3
Irharhar, Wadi (dry riv.), Algeria 106/F3
Iri, S. Korea 81/C6
Irian Jaya (reg.), Indonesia 2/R6
Irian Jaya (reg.), Indonesia 85/J6
Iriba, Chad 111/D4
Iriga, Philippines 82/D4
Iringa (reg.), Tanzania 115/G5
Iringa, Tanzania 102/F5
Iringa, Tanzania 115/G5
Iriomote (isl.), Japan 81/K7
Irion (co.), Texas 303/C6
Iriona, Honduras 154/E2
Iriri (riv.), Brazil 132/C4
Irish (sea) 7/D3
Irish (sea), England 13/B4
Irish (sea), England 10/D4
Irish (sea), Ireland 10/D4
Irish (sea), Ireland 17/K4
Irish (sea), I. of Man 13/B4
Irish (sea), Wales 13/B4
Irish (sea), Wales 10/D4
Irishtown, New Bruns. 170/F2
Irishtown, Tasmania 99/B2
Irish Vale, Nova Scotia 168/H3
Irkutsk, U.S.S.R. 2/Q3
Irkutsk, U.S.S.R. 54/M4
Irkutsk, U.S.S.R. 48/L4
Irma, Alberta 182/E3
Irma, Wis. (54442) 317/G5
Irmo, S.C. (29063) 296/E3
Iro (cape), Japan 81/J6
Irois (cape), Haiti 158/A6
Iron (mt.), Fla. 212/E4
Iron (co.), Mich. 250/G2
Iron, Minn. (55751) 255/F3
Iron (co.), Mo. 261/L7
Iron (mts.), Tenn. 237/S8
Iron (co.), Utah 304/A6
Iron (co.), Wis. 317/F3
Iron Belt, Wis. (54536) 317/F3
Ironbound (isls.), Newf. 166/C2
Iron Bridge, Ontario 177/A1
Iron City, Georgia (31759) 217/C8
Iron City, Tenn. (38463) 237/F10
Irondale, Ala. (35210) 195/E3
Irondale, Mo. (63648) 261/L7
Irondale, Ohio (43932) 284/J4
Irondequoit, N.Y. (14617) 276/E4
Iron Gate (res.), Calif. 204/C2
Iron Gate, Va. (24448) 307/J5
Iron Gates, Mo. (†64801) 261/C8
Ironia, N.J. (07845) 273/D2
Iron Knob, S. Australia 88/F6
Iron Knob, S. Australia 94/E5
Iron Mountain, Mich. (49801) 250/B3
Iron Mountain, Wyo. (82062) 319/G4
Iron Range, Queensland 95/B2
Iron Ridge, Wis. (53035) 317/K9
Iron River, Alberta 182/E2
Iron River, Mich. (49935) 250/G2
Iron River, Wis. (54847) 317/D2
Irons, Mich. (49644) 250/D4
Ironshire, Md. (†21811) 245/T7
Ironside, Oreg. (97908) 291/K3
Ironspring (creek), Sask. 181/G3
Iron Springs, Alberta 182/D5
Iron Springs, Ariz. (86330) 198/C4
Iron Station, N.C. (28080) 281/G4
Ironton, Minn. (56455) 255/D4
Ironton, Mo. (63650) 261/L7
Ironton, Ohio (45638) 284/E8
Ironton, Wis. (†53941) 317/F8
Ironwood, Mich. (49938) 250/F2
Iroquois (co.), Ill. 222/F3
Iroquois, Ill. (60945) 222/F3
Iroquois (riv.), Ill. 222/F3
Iroquois (riv.), Ind. 227/B3
Iroquois, Ontario 177/J3
Iroquois, S. Dak. (57353) 298/O5
Iroquois (lake), Vt. 268/A3
Iroquois Falls, Ont. 162/H6
Iroquois Falls, Ontario 175/D3
Iroquois Falls, Ontario 177/J5
Iroquois Point, Hawaii (†96706) 218/A4
'Irqa, P.D.R. Yemen 59/E7
Irrara (creek), N.S. Wales 97/C1
Irrawaddy (div.), Burma 72/B3
Irrawaddy, Mouths of the (delta), Burma 72/B4
Irrawaddy (riv.), Burma 54/L7
Irrawaddy (riv.), Burma 72/B3
Irricana, Alberta 182/D4
Irrigon, Oreg. (97844) 291/H2
Irtysh (riv.), U.S.S.R. 54/J4
Irtysh (riv.), U.S.S.R. 48/H4
Irumu, Zaire 115/E3
Irún, Spain 33/F1
Irupana, Bolivia 136/B5
Iruya, Argentina 143/D1
Irvine, Alberta 182/E5
Irvine, Calif. (92713) 204/D11
Irvine, Ky. (40336) 237/O5
Irvine (lake), N. Dak. 282/M3
Irvine, Pa. (16329) 294/D2
Irvine, Scotland 15/D5
Irvine, Scotland 10/D3
Irvinestown, N. Ireland 17/F3
Irving, Ill. (62051) 222/D4
Irving, Iowa (†52225) 229/J5
Irving, N.Y. (14081) 276/B5
Irving, Texas (*75061) 303/G2
Irvington, Ala. (36544) 195/B9
Irvington, Ill. (62848) 222/D5
Irvington, Iowa (50550) 229/E3
Irvington, Ky. (40146) 237/J5
Irvington, N.J. (07111) 273/B2
Irvington, N.Y. (10533) 276/O6
Irvington, Va. (22480) 307/R5
Irvin's (bay), Grenada 161/D8
Irvona, Pa. (16656) 294/E4
Irwin (co.), Georgia 217/F7
Irwin, Idaho (83428) 220/G6
Irwin, Iowa (51446) 229/C5
Irwin, Mo. (64754) 261/D7
Irwin, Ohio (43029) 284/D5
Irwin, Pa. (15642) 294/C5
Irwin, S.C. (†29720) 296/F2
Irwin, Va. (23063) 307/N5
Irwin, W. Australia 88/A5
Irwinton, Georgia (31042) 217/F5
Irwinville, Georgia (31760) 217/F7
Isa, Nigeria 106/F6
Isaac (lake), Br. Col. 184/G3
Isaacs (riv.), Queensland 88/H4
Isaacs (riv.), Queensland 95/D4
Isaac's Harbour North, Nova Scotia 168/G3
Isabel (bay), Ecuador 128/B9
Isabel, Kansas (67065) 232/D4
Isabel, La. (†70427) 238/K5
Isabel, S. Dak. (57633) 298/G3
Isabel (mt.), Wyo. 319/B3
Isabela (bay), Dom. Rep. 158/D5
Isabela (cape), Dom. Rep. 158/D5
Isabela (isl.), Ecuador 128/B9
Isabela (prov.), Philippines 82/C2
Isabela, Philippines 82/C7
Isabela, P. Rico 156/F1
Isabela, P. Rico 161/A1
Isabela de Sagua, Cuba 158/E1
Isabelia, Cordillera (range), Nicaragua 154/E4
Isabella (lake), Calif. 204/G8
Isabella, Manitoba 179/B4
Isabella (co.), Mich. 250/E5
Isabella, Mich. (†49878) 250/C3
Isabella, Minn. (55607) 255/G3
Isabella (lake), Minn. 255/G3
Isabella (riv.), Minn. 255/G3
Isabella (bay), N.W. Terrs. 187/M3
Isabella, Okla. (73747) 288/K2
Isabella, Tenn. (37346) 237/N10
Isabel Segunda, P. Rico 161/G2
Isaccea, Romania 45/J3
Isachsen, Canada 4/B15
Isachsen, N.W. Terrs. 187/H2
Isachsen (cape), N.W. Terrs. 187/H2
Isachsens, N.W.T. 146/H2
Ísafjördhardjúp (fjord), Iceland 21/A1
Ísafjördhur, Iceland 7/B2
Ísafjördhur, Iceland 21/B1
Isahaya, Japan 81/D7
Isana (riv.), Colombia 126/F7
Isangi, Zaire 115/D3
Isanti (co.), Minn. 255/E5
Isanti, Minn. (55040) 255/E5
Isar (riv.), W. Germany 22/E4
Isarog (mt.), Philippines 82/D4
Isbell, Ala. (†35653) 195/C2
Iscar, Spain 33/D2
Ischia (isl.), Italy 34/D4
Ischua, N.Y. (14746) 276/D6
Iscuandé, Colombia 126/A6
Ise, Japan 81/H6
Ise (bay), Japan 81/H6
Isefjord (fjord), Denmark 21/E6
Iselin, N.J. (08830) 273/E2
Iselin, Pa. (†15681) 294/D4
Isenthal, Switzerland 39/F3
Iseo (lake), Italy 34/C2
Isère (dept.), France 28/F5
Isère (riv.), France 28/F5
Iserlohn, W. Germany 22/B3
Isernia (prov.), Italy 34/E4
Isernia, Italy 34/E4
Ise-Shima National Park, Japan 81/H6
Iseyin, Nigeria 106/E7
Isfahan (prov.), Iran 66/H4
Isfahan, Iran 54/G6
Isfahan, Iran 66/G4
Isfahan, Iran 59/F3
Isfjorden (fjord), Norway 18/C2
Isham, Sask. 181/C4
Isherton, Guyana 131/B4
Ishigaki, Japan 81/L7
Ishigaki (isl.), Japan 81/L7
Ishige, Japan 81/P2
Ishikari (bay), Japan 81/K2
Ishikari (riv.), Japan 81/L2
Ishikawa (pref.), Japan 81/H5
Ishim (riv.), U.S.S.R. 54/H4
Ishim, U.S.S.R. 48/H4
Ishim (riv.), U.S.S.R. 48/G4
Ishimbay, U.S.S.R. 52/J4
Ishinomaki, Japan 81/K4
Ishioka, Japan 81/K5
Ishizuchi (mt.), Japan 81/F7
Ishpeming, Mich. (49849) 250/B2
Isiboro (riv.), Bolivia 136/C5
Isil'kul', U.S.S.R. 48/H4
Isimu, Indonesia 85/G5
Isiolo, Kenya 115/G3
Isiro, Zaire 102/E4
Isiro, Zaire 115/E3
Isisford, Queensland 88/G4
Isisford, Queensland 95/C5
Iskenderun, Turkey 59/C2
Iskenderun, Turkey 63/G4
Iskilip, Turkey 63/F2
Iskŭr (riv.), Bulgaria 45/G4
Iskut (riv.), Br. Col. 184/B2
Isla, Salar de la (salt dep.), Chile 138/B5
Isla, Veracruz, Mexico 150/M7
Isla (riv.), Scotland 15/E4
Isla Cristina, Spain 33/C4
Isla de Aguada, Mexico 150/O7
Isla de Maipo, Chile 138/G4
Islâhiye, Turkey 63/G4
Isla Holbox, Mexico 150/Q6
Islamabad (cap.), Pakistan 68/C2
Islamabad (cap.), Pakistan 2/N4
Islamabad (cap.), Pakistan 54/J6
Islamabad (cap.), Pakistan 59/K3
Islamabad District, Pakistan 68/C2
Islamorada, Fla. (33036) 212/F7
Isla Mujeres, Mexico 150/Q6
Island, Ky. (42350) 237/G6
Island (lake), Man. 162/G5
Island (lake), Manitoba 179/K3
Island (beach), N. J. 273/E4
Island (lake), N. Dak. 282/L2
Island (bay), Philippines 82/B6
Island (lag.), S. Australia 94/E4
Island (pond), Vt. 268/D2
Island (co.), Wash. 310/C2
Island City, Oreg. (97851) 291/K2
Island Creek, Md. (†20685) 245/M7
Island Falls○, Maine (04747) 243/G3
Island Falls, Ontario 175/D3
Island Grove, Fla. (32654) 212/D2
Island Heights, N.J. (08732) 273/E4
Islandia, Fla. (†33101) 212/F6
Island Lake, Ill. (60042) 222/A4
Island Lake, Manitoba 179/J3
Island Lake, Wis. (†54757) 317/D5
Island Park, Idaho (83429) 220/G5
Island Park (res.), Idaho 220/G5
Island Park, N.Y. (11558) 276/R7
Island Park, R.I. (†02871) 249/J6
Island Pond, Vt. (05846) 268/D2
Islands (bay), Newf. 166/C4
Islands (bay), Newf. 166/C2
Islands (bay), N. Zealand 100/E1
Islandton, S.C. (29929) 296/F6
Island View, Minn. (†56649) 255/E2
Island View, New Bruns. 170/D3
Isla Patrulla, Uruguay 145/E3
Isla Pucú, Paraguay 144/B4
Isla Umbú, Paraguay 144/C5
Isla Vista, Calif. (93117) 204/E9
Islay, Alberta 182/E3
Islay (isl.), Scotland 15/B5
Islay (isl.), Scotland 10/C3
Islay (sound), Scotland 15/C5
Isle (riv.), France 28/D5
Isle, Minn. (56342) 255/E4
Isle Au Haut○, Maine (04645) 243/F7
Isle-aux-Coudres, Québec 172/G2
Isle-aux-Grues, Québec 172/G2
Isle aux Morts, Newf. 166/C4
Isle La Motte○, Vt. (05463) 268/A2
Isle of Hope, Georgia (†31406) 217/K7
ISLE OF MAN 13/C3
ISLE OF MAN 10/D3

Kamienna Góra 389

Jones Creek, Texas (†77541) 303/J9
Jonesdale, Wis. (†53565) 317/F10
Jones Mills, Ark. (72105) 202/E5
Jones Mills, Pa. (15646) 294/D5
Jonesport, Maine (04649) 243/H6
Jonesport○, Maine (04649) 243/H6
Jones Springs, W. Va. (25427) 312/K4
Jonestown, Miss. (38639) 256/D2
Jonestown, Pa. (17038) 294/K5
Jonesville, Alaska (†99674) 196/B1
Jonesville, Ind. (47247) 227/F6
Jonesville, Ky. (41052) 237/M3
Jonesville, La. (71343) 238/G3
Jonesville, Mich. (49250) 250/E6
Jonesville, N.C. (28642) 281/H2
Jonesville, S.C. (29353) 296/D2
Jonesville, Vt. (05466) 268/B3
Jonesville, Va. (24263) 307/B7
Jonglei, Sudan 111/F6
Joniškis, U.S.S.R. 53/B2
Jönköping (co.), Sweden 18/H8
Jönköping, Sweden 18/H8
Jönköping, Sweden 7/F3
Jonquière, Que. 162/J6
Jonquière, Québec 172/F1
Jonquière, Québec 174/C3
Jonuta, Mexico 150/N7
Jonzac, France 28/C5
Joplin, Mo. (64801) 261/C8
Joplin, Mo. 146/J6
Joplin, Mo. 188/H3
Joplin, Mont. (59531) 262/F2
Joppa, Ala. (35087) 195/E2
Joppa, Ill. (62953) 222/E6
Joppa, Tenn. (†37861) 237/O8
Joppatowne, Md. (†21085) 245/N3
Jorat (mt.), Switzerland 39/C3
Jordan 2/L4
Jordan 54/E6
JORDAN 59/C3
Jordan (dam), Ala. 195/F5
Jordan (lake), Ala. 195/F5
Jordan, (creek) Idaho 220/A7
Jordan, Iowa (†50036) 229/F4
Jordan (riv.), Israel 65/D3
Jordan (riv.), Jordan 65/D3
Jordan, Minn. (55352) 255/E6
Jordan, Mont. (59337) 262/J3
Jordan, N.Y. (13080) 276/H4
Jordan, B. Everett (lake), N.C. 281/M3
Jordan (bay), Nova Scotia 168/C5
Jordan (lake), Nova Scotia 168/C4
Jordan (riv.), Nova Scotia 168/C5
Jordan (creek), Oreg. 291/K5
Jordan, S.C. (†29102) 296/G4
Jordan (riv.), Utah 304/C3
Jordan Falls, Nova Scotia 168/C5
Jordan River, Sask. 181/H2
Jordan Valley, Oreg. (97910) 291/K5
Jorge Montt (isl.), Chile 138/D9
Jorhat, India 68/G3
Jorm, Afghanistan 68/C1
Jorm, Afghanistan 59/K2
Jörn, Sweden 18/M4
Jornada del Muerto (valley), N. Mex. 274/C5
Jorquera (riv.), Chile 138/B6
Jõrva-Jaani, U.S.S.R. 53/D1
Jos, Nigeria 106/F7
Jos, Nigeria 102/C4
Jos (plat.), Nigeria 106/F7
Jose Abad Santos, Philippines 82/E8
José Agustín Palacios, Bolivia 136/B3
José Batlle y Ordóñez, Uruguay 145/D4
José Cardel, Mexico 150/Q1
José de San Martín, Argentina 143/B5
José Enrique Rodó, Uruguay 145/B4
José Ignacio (lag.), Uruguay 145/E5
José M. Micheo, Argentina 143/G7
Jose Panganiban, Philippines 82/D3
José Pedro Varela, Uruguay 145/E4
Joseph (lake), Newf. 166/B3
Joseph (lake), Ontario 177/E2
Joseph, Oreg. (97846) 291/K2
Joseph (creek), Oreg. 291/K2
Joseph, Utah (84739) 304/B5
Joseph Bonaparte (gulf) 88/D2
Joseph Bonaparte (gulf), Australia 87/C7
Joseph Bonaparte (gulf), North. Terr. 93/A3
Joseph Bonaparte (gulf), W. Australia 92/E1
Joseph City, Ariz. (86032) 198/E4
Josephine, Ala. (†36530) 195/C10
Josephine (co.), Oreg. 291/D5
Josephine, Pa. (15750) 294/D5
Joshinetsu-Kogen National Park, Japan 81/J5
Joshua (pt.), Conn. 210/E4
Joshua Tree, Calif. (92252) 204/J9
Joshua Tree Nat'l Mon., Calif. 204/J10
Jostedal, Norway 18/E6
Jostedalsbreen (glac.), Norway 18/E6
Jost Van Dyke (isl.), Virgin Is. (Br.) 161/C3
Jost Van Dyke (isl.), Virgin Is. (Br.) 156/G1
Joubert, S. Dak. (†57344) 298/M7
Jourdanton, Texas (78026) 303/F9
Joure, Netherlands 27/H3
Joussard, Alberta 182/B2
Joux (lake), Switzerland 39/B3
Jovellanos, Cuba 156/B2
Jovellanos, Cuba 158/D1
Joveyn (riv.), Iran 66/K2
Joy, Ill. (61260) 222/C2
Joy, Ky. (†42047) 237/E6
Joyce, La. (71440) 238/E3
Joyce, Wash. (98343) 310/B2
Joyce's Country (dist.), Ireland 17/B4
Joyo, Japan 81/J7
Juab (co.), Utah 304/A4
Juana Díaz, P. Rico 161/C2
Juan Aldama, Mexico 150/H4
Juan D. Jackson, Uruguay 145/C4
Juan de Fuca (str.) 146/F5
Juan de Fuca (str.), Br. Col. 162/D6
Juan de Fuca (str.), Br. Col. 184/J4
Juan de Fuca (str.), Wash. 188/A1
Juan de Fuca (str.), Wash. 310/A2
Juan de Mena, Paraguay 144/D4
Juan de Nova (isl.), Réunion 102/G6
Juan de Nova (isl.), Réunion 118/G3
Juan Fernández (isls.), Chile 2/E7
Juan Fernández (isls.), Chile 120/B6
Juangriego, Venezuela 124/G2
Juani (isl.), Tanzania 115/G5
Juanita, N. Dak. (58453) 282/N4
Juanita, Wash. (98033) 310/B1
Juanjuí, Peru 128/D6
Juan L. Lacaze, Uruguay 145/B5
Juan Stuven (isl.), Chile 138/D7
Juárez, Argentina 143/D4
Juárez, Mexico 150/J3
Juazeiro, Brazil 132/G5
Juàzeiro, Brazil 120/E3
Juazeiro do Norte, Brazil 132/F4
Juàzeiro do Norte, Brazil 120/F3
Juba, Sudan 111/F7
Juba, Sudan 102/F4
Jubail, Saudi Arabia 59/F4
Jubba, Saudi Arabia 59/D4
Jubbada Hoose (prov.), Somalia 115/H3
Jubbulpore (Jabalpur), India 68/D4
Jubilee (lake), W. Australia 88/D5
Juby (cape), Morocco 106/B3
Júcar (riv.), Spain 7/D5
Júcar (riv.), Spain 33/F3
Júcaro, Cuba 158/F2
Juchipila, Mexico 150/H6
Juchique de Ferrer, Mexico 150/Q1
Juchitán de Zaragoza, Mexico 150/M8
Jucuarán, El Salvador 154/C4
Jud, N. Dak. (58454) 282/N6
Juda, Wis. (53550) 317/H10
Judaea (reg.), Israel 65/B5
Judaea (reg.), Jordan 65/C4
Judas (pt.), C. Rica 154/E6
Judenburg, Austria 41/C3
Judibana, Venezuela 124/C2
Judique, Nova Scotia 168/G3
Judith (riv.), Mont. 262/G3
Judith (pt.), R.I. 249/J7
Judith Basin (co.), Mont. 262/F4
Judith Gap, Mont. (59453) 262/G4
Judson, Ind. (47856) 227/C5
Judson, Minn. (†56055) 255/D6
Judson, N. Dak. (†58563) 282/H6
Judsonia, Ark. (72081) 202/G3
Judyville, Ind. (†47993) 227/C4
Juelsminde, Denmark 21/D6
Juhu, India 68/B7
Juichin (Ruijin), China 77/J6
Juigalpa, Nicaragua 154/E4
Juist (isl.), W. Germany 22/B2
Juiz de Fora, Brazil 120/E5
Juiz de Fora, Brazil 135/E2
Juiz de Fora, Brazil 132/F8
Jujuy (prov.), Argentina 143/C1
Jujuy, Argentina 143/C1
Jujuy, Argentina 120/C5
Jukskei (riv.), S. Africa 118/H6
Julesburg, Colo. (80737) 208/P1
Juli, Peru 128/H11
Juliaca, Peru 120/B4
Juliaca, Peru 128/G10
Julia Creek, Queensland 88/G4
Julia Creek, Queensland 95/B4
Juliaetta, Idaho (83535) 220/B3
Julian, Calif. (92036) 204/J10
Julian, Nebr. (68379) 264/J4
Julian, N.C. (27283) 281/K3
Julian, Pa. (16844) 294/G4
Julian Alps (range), Italy 34/D1
Julianatop (mt.), Suriname 131/C4
Julianehåb, Greenl. 4/D12
Julianehåb, Greenland 2/G2
Julianehåb, Greenland 146/P3
Jülich, W. Germany 22/B3
Juliette, Georgia (31046) 217/E4
Juliff, Texas (†77583) 303/J3
Julio María Sanz, Uruguay 145/E4
Juliustown, N.J. (08042) 273/D3
Jullundur, India 68/D2
Jumbilla, Peru 128/C5
Jumbo, Okla. (†74523) 288/P6
Jumilla, Spain 33/F3
Jumla, Nepal 68/E3
Jumna (riv.), India 68/E3
Jump (riv.), Wis. 317/E5
Jumpertown, Miss. (†38829) 256/G1
Jumping Branch, W. Va. (25969) 312/E7
Jump River, Wis. (54434) 317/E5
Junagadh, India 68/B4
Junaina, Saudi Arabia 59/D5
Juncal, Argentina 143/F6
Juncos, P. Rico 161/E2
Juncos, P. Rico 156/G1
Junction, Ill. (62954) 222/E6
Junction, Texas (76849) 303/E7
Junction, Utah (84740) 304/B5
Junction, W. Va. (26824) 312/J4
Junction City, Ark. (71749) 202/E7
Junction City, Georgia (31812) 217/C5
Junction City, Ill. (†61601) 222/D5
Junction City, Kansas (66441) 232/E2
Junction City, Ky. (40440) 237/M5
Junction City, La. (71749) 238/E1
Junction City, Mo. (†63645) 261/M7
Junction City, Ohio (43748) 284/F6
Junction City, Oreg. (97448) 291/D3
Junction City, Wis. (54443) 317/G6
Jundah, Queensland 95/B5
Jundah, Queensland 88/G4
Jundiaí, Brazil 135/C3
Jundiaí, Brazil 132/E8
Juneau, Alaska 146/E4
Juneau (cap.), Alaska 188/E6
Juneau (cap.), Alaska (99801) 196/N1
Juneau, U.S. 4/D16
Juneau, U.S. 2/C3
Juneau (co.), Wis. 317/F8
Juneau, Wis. (53039) 317/J9
Juneda, Spain 33/G2
Junee, N.S. Wales 97/D4
June in Winter (lake), Fla. 212/E4
June Lake, Calif. (93529) 204/G6
June Park, Fla. (†32901) 212/F3
Jungar, China 77/H4
Jungfrau (mt.), Switzerland 39/E3
Jungfraujoch, Switzerland 39/E3
Junggar Pendi (desert basin), China 77/C2
Junglei (prov.), Sudan 111/F6
Juniata, Nebr. (68955) 264/F4
Juniata (co.), Pa. 294/H4
Juniata (riv.), Pa. 294/G5
Juniata Terrace, Pa. (†17044) 294/G4
Junín, Argentina 143/F7
Junín, Argentina 120/C6
Junín (dept.), Peru 128/E8
Junín, Peru 128/E8
Junín (lake), Peru 128/E8
Junín de los Andes, Argentina 143/B4
Junior, W. Va. (26275) 312/G5
Juniper (mts.), Ariz. 198/C3
Juniper (mt.), Colo. 208/C1
Juniper, Georgia (31801) 217/C6
Juniper, New Bruns. 170/C2
Juniper (creek), S.C. 296/H2
Junius, S. Dak. (†57042) 298/P6
Juniye, Lebanon 63/F5
Junlian, China 77/F6
Juno, Georgia (30534) 217/D2
Juno, North. Terr. 93/C5
Juno, Tenn. (†38351) 237/E9
Juno, Texas (76943) 303/C7
Juno Beach, Fla. (†33404) 212/F5
Junosuando, Sweden 18/N3
Juntura, Oreg. (97911) 291/K4
Jun Xian, China 77/H5
Juojärvi (lake), Finland 18/Q5
Jupiter, Fla. (33458) 212/F5
Jupiter, N.C. (28787) 281/D3
Jupiter Island, Fla. (†33455) 212/F4
Juquiá, Brazil 135/C4
Jur (riv.), Sudan 111/E6
Jura (dept.), France 28/F4
Jura (mts.), France 28/F4
Jura (isl.), Scotland 10/D3
Jura (isl.), Scotland 15/C5
Jura (sound), Scotland 15/C5
Jura (sound), Scotland 10/D3
Jura (canton), Switzerland /D2
Jura (mts.), Switzerland 39/B3
Juradó, Colombia 126/B4
Jurbarkas, U.S.S.R. 53/B3
Jurmala, U.S.S.R. 53/B2
Jurmala, U.S.S.R. 52/B3
Jurong, Singapore 72/E6
Juruá (riv.), Brazil 120/C3
Juruá (riv.), Brazil 132/G10
Juruá (riv.), Peru 128/F7
Juruena, Brazil 132/B6
Juruena (riv.), Brazil 120/D4
Juruena (riv.), Brazil 132/B5
Juruti, Brazil 132/B3
Jusepín, Venezuela 124/G3
Juskatla, Br. Col. 184/A3
Jussy, Switzerland 39/B4
Justice, Ill. (†60458) 222/B6
Justice, Manitoba 179/C4
Justice, W. Va. (24851) 312/C7
Justiceburg, Texas (79330) 303/C5
Justin, Texas (76247) 303/F1
Justus, Ohio (†44662) 284/G4
Jutaí (riv.), Brazil 132/G9
Jüterbog, E. Germany 22/E3
Jutiapa, Guatemala 154/B3
Jutiapa, Honduras 154/D3
Juticalpa, Honduras 154/D3
Jutland (pen.), Denmark 21/C5
Jutland (pen.), Denmark 18/F9
Jutland, N.J. (08809) 273/D2
Juuka, Finland 18/Q5
Juventud (municipio especial), Cuba 158/C2
Juventud (isl.), Cuba 146/K7
Juventud, Isla de la (Pines), Cuba 158/B3
Juventud (Pines) (isl.), Cuba 156/A2
Juwara, Oman 59/G6
Ju Xian, China 77/J4
Juye, China 77/J4
Jyderup, Denmark 21/E6
Jylland (Jutland) (pen.), Denmark 21/C5
Jyske Ås (hills), Denmark 21/D3
Jyväskylä, Finland 7/G2
Jyväskylä, Finland 18/O5

K

K2 (mt.) 54/J6
K2 (mt.), Pakistan 68/D1
Kaaawa, Hawaii (96730) 218/F1
Kaabong, Uganda 115/F3
Kaala (mt.), Hawaii 218/D1
Kaanapali, Hawaii (†96761) 218/H2
Kaba (Habahe), China 77/C2
Kaba, Hungary 41/F2
Kabacan, Philippines 82/E7
Kabaena (isl.), Indonesia 85/G7
Kabala, S. Leone 106/B7
Kabale, Uganda 115/E4
Kabalo, Zaire 115/E5
Kabambare, Zaire 115/E4
Kabardin-Balkar A.S.S.R., U.S.S.R. 48/E5
Kabardin-Balkar A.S.S.R., U.S.S.R. 52/F6
Kabare, Zaire 115/E4
Kabarega Nat'l Park, Uganda 115/F3
Kabasalan, Philippines 82/D7
Kabba, Nigeria 106/F7
Kabetogama, Minn. (†56669) 255/F2
Kabetogama (lake), Minn. 255/E2
Kabinakagami (riv.), Ontario 177/J5
Kabin Buri, Thailand 72/D4
Kabinda, Zaire 115/D5
Kabir Kuh (mts.), Iran 66/E4
Kabompo, Zambia 115/D6
Kabompo (riv.), Zambia 115/D6
Kabong, Malaysia 85/E5
Kabongo, Zaire 115/E5
Kabud Gonbad, Iran 66/L2
Kabul (cap.), Afghanistan 68/B2
Kabul (cap.), Afghanistan 59/J3
Kabul (cap.), Afghanistan 54/H6
Kabul (cap.), Afghanistan 2/N4
Kabul (riv.), Afghanistan 68/C2
Kabul (riv.), Afghanistan 59/K3
Kabul (riv.), Pakistan 68/C2
Kabunda, Zaire 115/E6
Kabwe, Zambia 102/E6
Kabwe, Zambia 115/E6
Kabylia (reg.), Algeria 106/E1
Kachemak, Alaska (†99663) 196/B2
Kachemak (bay), Alaska 196/B2
Kachess (lake), Wash. 310/D3
Kachin (state), Burma 72/C1
Kachug, U.S.S.R. 48/L4
Kaçkar Daği (mt.), Turkey 63/J2
Kackley, Kansas (†66948) 232/E2
Kadaň, Czech. 41/B1
Kadan Kyun (isl.), Burma 72/C4
Kadavu (Kandavu) (isl.), Fiji 87/H7
Kadayanallur, India 68/D7
Kadei (riv.), Cameroon 115/C3
Kadei (riv.), Cent. Afr. Rep. 115/C3
Kadei (riv.), Congo 115/C3
Kadıköy, Turkey 63/D6
Kadina, S. Australia 88/F6
Kadina, S. Australia 94/F5
Kadınhanı, Turkey 63/E3
Kadiolo, Mali 106/C6
Kadiri, India 68/D6
Kadirli, Turkey 63/F4
Kadiyevka (Stakhanov), U.S.S.R. 52/E5
Kadmat (isl.), India 68/C6
Kadoka, S. Dak. (57543) 298/F6
Kadoma, Japan 81/J7
Kadoma (Gatooma), Zimbabwe 118/D3
Kadugli, Sudan 111/E5
Kadugli, Sudan 102/E3
Kaduna (state), Nigeria 106/F6
Kaduna, Nigeria 102/C3
Kaduna, Nigeria 106/F6
Kaduna (riv.), Nigeria 106/F7
Kadzherom, U.S.S.R. 52/J2
Kaech'ŏn, N. Korea 81/B4
Kaédi, Mauritania 106/B5
Kaédi, Mauritania 102/A3
Kaélé, Cameroon 115/B1
Kaena (pt.), Hawaii 218/D1
Kaeo, N. Zealand 100/D1
Kaesŏng, N. Korea 81/C4
Kaf, Saudi Arabia 59/C3
Kafan, U.S.S.R. 52/G7
Kafar Kanna, Israel 65/C2
Kaffa (prov.), Ethiopia 111/G6
Kaffrine, Senegal 106/A6
Kafia Kingi, Sudan 111/D6
Kafirévs (cape), Greece 45/G6
Kafr Yasif, Israel 65/C2
Kafue, Zambia 115/E7
Kafue (riv.), Zambia 115/E7
Kafue Nat'l Park, Zambia 115/E6
Kaga, Japan 81/H5
Kaga Bandoro, Cent. Afr. Rep. 115/C2
Kagalaska (isl.), Alaska 196/L4
Kagan, U.S.S.R. 48/G6
Kagawa (pref.), Japan 81/G6
Kagawong, Ontario 177/B2
Kagawong (lake), Ontario 177/B2
Kagera Nat'l Park, Rwanda 115/F4
Kağıthane, Turkey 63/D6
Kağızman, Turkey 63/K2
Kagoshima (pref.), Japan 81/E8
Kagoshima, Japan 81/E8
Kagoshima, Japan 54/O6
Kagoshima (bay), Japan 81/E8
Kagul, U.S.S.R. 52/C5
Kaguyak, Alaska (†99608) 196/H3
Kahakuloa, Hawaii (†96793) 218/J1
Kahala, Hawaii (†96801) 218/D5
Kahala (pt.), Hawaii 218/D1
Kahaluu, Hawaii (†96744) 218/E2
Kahama, Tanzania 115/F4
Kahana, Hawaii (†96717) 218/F1
Kahana (bay), Hawaii 218/F1
Kahayan (riv.), Indonesia 85/E6
Kahemba, Zaire 115/C5
Kahiltna (riv.), Alaska 196/B1
Kahlotus, Wash. (99335) 310/G4
Kah-Nee-Ta, Oreg. (†97761) 291/F3
Kahoka, Mo. (63445) 261/J2
Kahoolawe (isl.), Hawaii 188/F5
Kahoolawe (isl.), Hawaii 87/L4
Kahoolawe (isl.), Hawaii 218/H3
Kahouanne (isl.), Guadeloupe 161/A6
Kahramanmaraş (prov.), Turkey 63/G4
Kâhta, Turkey 63/H4
Kahuku, Hawaii (96731) 218/E1
Kahuku, Hawaii 188/F5
Kahuku (pt.), Hawaii 218/E1
Kahului, Hawaii (96732) 218/J2
Kahului, Hawaii 188/F5
Kahului (harb.), Hawaii 218/J1
Kai (isls.), Indonesia 85/J7
Kaiama, Nigeria 106/E7
Kaiapit, Papua N.G. 85/B7
Kaiapoi, N. Zealand 100/D5
Kaibab (plat.), Ariz. 198/C2
Kaibab Ind. Res., Ariz. 198/C2
Kaibito, Ariz. (86053) 198/D2
Kaibito (plat.), Ariz. 198/D2
Kaieteur (fall), Guyana 131/B3
Kaifeng, China 77/H5
Kaifeng, China 54/N6
Kaikohe, N. Zealand 100/D1
Kaikoura, N. Zealand 100/D5
Kaikoura (pen.), N. Zealand 100/E5
Kaikoura (range), N. Zealand 100/D5
Kaili, China 77/G6
Kailu, China 77/K3
Kailua (Kailua Kona), Hawaii, Hawaii (96740) 218/F5
Kailua, Oahu, Hawaii (96734) 218/F2
Kailua (bay), Hawaii 218/F2
Kailua (bay), Hawaii 218/F5
Kailua Kona, Hawaii (96740) 218/F5
Kaimana, Indonesia 85/J6
Kaimanawa (range), N. Zealand 100/E3
Kaimu, Hawaii (†96778) 218/J6
Kaimuki, Hawaii (96816) 218/D4
Kainaliu, Hawaii (†96750) 218/G5
Kainaliu, Hawaii 188/F6
Kainan (bay) 5/B10
Kaingaroa, N. Zealand 100/E7
Kainji (res.), Nigeria 106/E6
Kaipara (harb.), N. Zealand 100/D2
Kaipara (riv.), N. Zealand 100/A1
Kaiparowits (plat.), Utah 304/C6
Kaipokok (bay), Newf. 166/B2
Kaipokok (riv.), Newf. 166/B3
Kairouan, Tunisia 106/F1
Kairuku, Papua N.G. 85/B7
Kaiser, Mo. (65047) 261/G6
Kaiseregg (mt.), Switzerland 39/D3
Kaiserslautern, W. Germany 22/B4
Kaiserstuhl (mt.), W. Germany 22/B4
Kaitaia, N. Zealand 100/D1
Kaitangata, N. Zealand 100/C7
Kaitumälv (riv.), Sweden 18/M3
Kaiwi (chan.), Hawaii 218/E6
Kaiyuan, Liaoning, China 77/K3
Kaiyuan, Yunnan, China 77/F7
Kaiyuh (mts.), Alaska 196/G2
Kaizuka, Japan 81/H8
Kajaani, Finland 7/G2
Kajaani, Finland 18/P4
Kajabbi, Queensland 88/G3
Kajabbi, Queensland 95/A4
Kajiado, Kenya 115/G4
Kajok, Sudan 111/E6
Kaka, Cent. Afr. Rep. 115/E2
Kaka, Sudan 111/F5
Kakabeka Falls, Ontario 177/G5
Kakabeka Falls, Ontario 175/B3
Kakamega, Kenya 115/F3
Kake, Alaska (99830) 196/M1
Kakhk, Iran 66/L3
Kakhonak, Alaska (†99647) 196/H3
Kakhovka, U.S.S.R. 52/D5
Kakhovka (res.), U.S.S.R. 48/D5
Kakhovka (res.), U.S.S.R. 52/D5
Kakinada, India 54/K8
Kakinada, India 68/E5
Kakisa, N.W. Terrs. 187/G3
Kakkiviak (cape), Newf. 166/B1
Kakogawa, Japan 81/G6
Kaktovik, Alaska (99747) 196/K1
Kakwa (riv.), Alberta 182/A2
Kalaa-Kebira, Tunisia 106/F1
Kalabahi, Indonesia 85/G7
Kalabo, Zambia 115/D6
Kalach, U.S.S.R. 52/F4
Kalachinsk, U.S.S.R. 48/H4
Kalach-na-Donu, U.S.S.R. 52/F5
Kaladan (riv.), Burma 72/B2
Kaladar, Ontario 177/H3
Kalae, Hawaii (†96757) 218/G1
Ka Lae (cape), Hawaii 218/G7
Kalahari (des.) 102/E7
Kalahari (des.), Botswana 118/C4
Kalahari (des.), Namibia 118/C4
Kalahari Gemsbok Nat'l Park, S. Africa 118/C5
Kalaheo, Hawaii (96741) 218/C2
Kalajoki, Finland 18/N4
Kalajoki (riv.), Finland 18/O4
Kalakan, U.S.S.R. 48/M4
Kalaloch, Wash. (†98331) 310/A3
Kalam, Pakistan 68/C1
Kalama, Wash. (98625) 310/C4
Kalama (riv.), Wash. 310/C4
Kalámai, Greece 7/G5
Kalámai, Greece 45/F7
Kalamazoo, Mich. 188/J2
Kalamazoo (co.), Mich. 250/D6
Kalamazoo, Mich. (*49001) 250/D6
Kalamazoo (riv.), Mich. 250/C6
Kalambo (falls), Tanzania 115/F5
Kalambo (falls), Zambia 115/F5
Kalamo, Mich. (†49096) 250/D6
Kalampáka, Greece 45/E6
Kalamunda, W. Australia 88/B2
Kalan, Turkey 63/H3
Kalao (isl.), Indonesia 85/G7
Kalaoa, Hawaii (†96740) 218/G5
Kalaotoa (isl.), Indonesia 85/G5
Kalapana, Hawaii (†96778) 218/J6
Kalasin, Thailand 72/D3
Kalat (Qalat), Afghanistan 68/B2
Kalat (Qalat), Afghanistan 59/J3
Kalat, Pakistan 54/H7
Kalat, Pakistan 59/J4
Kalat, Pakistan 68/B3
Kalâtdlit-Nunât (Greenland) 4/B12
Kalâtdlit-Nunât (Greenland) 146/P2
Kalaupapa, Hawaii (96742) 218/G1
Kalaupapa (pen.), Hawaii 218/H1
Kalaupapa Nat'l Hist. Park, Hawaii 218/H1
Kalávrita, Greece 45/F6
Kalawao (co.), Hawaii 218/G1
Kalbarri, W. Australia 92/A4
Kale, Turkey 63/C4
Kalecik, Turkey 63/E2
Kaleden, Br. Col. 184/H5
Kalegauk (isl.), Burma 72/C4
Kalehe, Zaire 115/E4
Kaleida, Manitoba 179/D5
Kalemie, Zaire 115/E5
Kalemie, Zaire 102/E5
Kalemyo, Burma 72/B2
Kaleva, Mich. (49645) 250/C4
Kalevala, U.S.S.R. 52/D1
Kalewa, Burma 72/B2
Kalgan (Zhangjiakou), China 77/J3
Kalgin (isl.), Alaska 196/B1
Kalgoorlie, Australia 2/R7
Kalgoorlie, W. Australia 88/C6
Kalgoorlie, W. Australia 92/C5
Kalgoorlie-Boulder, W. Australia 92/C5
Kaliakra (cape), Bulgaria 45/J4
Kalianda, Indonesia 85/D7
Kalibo, Philippines 82/D5
Kalida, Ohio (45853) 284/B4
Kalihi, Hawaii (†96801) 218/C4
Kalihi (stream), Hawaii 218/C3
Kalihi Entrance (str.), Hawaii 218/B4
Kalihiwai, Hawaii (†96754) 218/C1
Kalima, Zaire 115/E4
Kalimantan (reg.), Indonesia 85/E5
Kálimnos, Greece 45/H7
Kálimnos (isl.), Greece 45/H7
Kalinga, Queensland 88/K2
Kalinga-Apayao (prov.), Philippines 82/C1
Kalinin, U.S.S.R. 7/H3
Kalinin, U.S.S.R. 48/D4
Kalinin, U.S.S.R. 52/E3
Kaliningrad, U.S.S.R. 7/G3
Kaliningrad, U.S.S.R. 48/B4
Kaliningrad, Kaliningrad, U.S.S.R. 52/B4
Kaliningrad, Moscow Oblast, U.S.S.R. 52/E3
Kalininsk, U.S.S.R. 52/F4
Kalinkovichi, U.S.S.R. 52/C4
Kalispel Ind. Res., Wash. 310/H2
Kalispell, Mont. 188/C1
Kalispell, Mont. (59901) 262/B2
Kalisz (prov.), Poland 47/D3
Kalisz, Poland 7/F3
Kalisz, Poland 47/D3
Kaliua, Tanzania 115/F5
Kalix, Sweden 18/N4
Kalixälv (riv.), Sweden 18/N3
Kalkaska (co.), Mich. 250/D4
Kalkaska, Mich. (49646) 250/D4
Kalkfeld, Namibia 118/B4
Kalkfontein, Botswana 118/C4
Kallaste, U.S.S.R. 53/D1
Kallavesi (lake), Finland 18/P5
Kallsjö (lake), Sweden 18/H5
Kalmalo, Nigeria 106/F6
Kalmar (co.), Sweden 18/K8
Kalmar, Sweden 7/F3
Kalmar, Sweden 18/K8
Kalmarsund (sound), Sweden 18/K8
Kalmthout, Belgium 27/F6
Kalmuck A.S.S.R., U.S.S.R. 52/F5
Kalmuck A.S.S.R., U.S.S.R. 48/E5
Kalmunai, Sri Lanka 68/E7
Kalmykovo, U.S.S.R. 48/F5
Kalo, Iowa (†50569) 229/E4
Kalocsa, Hungary 41/E3
Kalohi (chan.), Hawaii 218/G1
Kaloko-Honokohau Nat'l Hist. Park, Hawaii 218/F6
Kaloli (pt.), Hawaii 218/K5
Kalomo, Zambia 115/E7
Kalona, Iowa (52247) 229/K6
Kalpeni (isl.), India 68/C7
Kalpin, China 77/A3
Kalskag, Alaska (99607) 196/F2
Kaltag, Alaska (99748) 196/G2
Kaltbrunn, Switzerland 39/H2
Kaluaaha, Hawaii (†96748) 218/H1
Kaluga, U.S.S.R. 7/H3
Kaluga, U.S.S.R. 48/D4
Kaluga, U.S.S.R. 52/E4
Kalumburu Mission, W. Australia 88/D2
Kalumburu Mission, W. Australia 92/D1
Kalundborg, Denmark 21/D6
Kalundborg, Denmark 18/G9
Kalush, U.S.S.R. 52/B5
Kalutara, Sri Lanka 68/D7
Kalvarija, U.S.S.R. 53/B3
Kalvesta, Kansas (67856) 232/B3
Kalyan, India 68/C5
Kama, Burma 72/B3
Kama (res.), U.S.S.R. 52/J3
Kama (riv.), U.S.S.R. 7/K3
Kama (riv.), U.S.S.R. 52/H2
Kama, Zaire 115/E4
Kamaiki (pt.), Hawaii 218/H2
Kamaing, Burma 72/C1
Kamaishi, Japan 81/L4
Kamakou (peak), Hawaii 218/H1
Kamakura, Japan 81/O3
Kamakusa, Guyana 131/A3
Kamalino, Hawaii (†96769) 218/A2
Kamalo, Hawaii (†96748) 218/H1
Kaman, Turkey 63/E3
Kamaniskeg (lake), Ontario 177/G2
Kamanjab, Namibia 118/A3
Kamaran (isl.), P.D.R. Yemen 59/D6
Kamarang, Guyana 131/A3
Kamarhati, India 68/F1
Kamaria (falls), Guyana 131/B2
Kamas, Utah (84036) 304/C3
Kamay, Texas (76369) 303/F4
Kambalda, W. Australia 88/C6
Kambalda, W. Australia 92/C5
Kambia, S. Leone 106/B7
Kambove, Zaire 115/E6
Kambove, Zaire 102/E6
Kamchatka (pen.), U.S.S.R. 54/S4
Kamchatka (pen.), U.S.S.R. 2/T3
Kamchatka (pen.), U.S.S.R. 48/Q4
Kamela, Oreg. (†97859) 291/J2
Kamenets-Podol'skiy, U.S.S.R. 52/C5
Kamenice, Czech. 41/C2
Kamenjak (cape), Yugoslavia 45/A3
Kamenka, Archangel, U.S.S.R. 52/F1
Kamenka, Penza, U.S.S.R. 52/F4
Kamen'-na-Obi, U.S.S.R. 48/H4
Kamenskoye, U.S.S.R. 48/R3
Kamensk-Shakhtinskiy, U.S.S.R. 52/F5
Kamensk-Ural'skiy, U.S.S.R. 48/G4
Kamenz, E. Germany 22/F3
Kameoka, Japan 81/J7
Kames, Scotland 15/C5
Kamet (mt.), India 68/D2
Kamiah, Idaho (83536) 220/B3
Kamienna Góra, Poland 47/B3

Lake Chelan 395

Kutina, Yugoslavia 45/C3
Kutná Hora, Czech. 41/C2
Kutno, Poland 47/D2
Kutoarjo, Indonesia 85/J2
Kuttawa, Ky. (42055) 237/E6
Küttigen, Switzerland 39/F2
Kutu, Zaire 115/C4
Kutum, Sudan 111/D5
Kúty, Czech. 41/D2
Kutztown, Pa. (19530) 294/L4
Kuusamo, Finland 18/Q4
Kuusamojärvi (lake), Finland 18/Q4
Kuusankoski, Finland 18/P6
Kuvandyk, U.S.S.R. 52/J4
Kuwait 2/M4
Kuwait 54/F7
KUWAIT 59/E4
Kuybyshev, U.S.S.R. 2/M3
Kuybyshev, U.S.S.R. 7/K3
Kuybyshev, U.S.S.R. 48/F4
Kuybyshev, U.S.S.R. 52/H4
Kuybyshev, U.S.S.R. 48/H4
Kuybyshev (res.), U.S.S.R. 7/K3
Kuybyshev (res.), U.S.S.R. 48/F4
Kuybyshev (res.), U.S.S.R. 52/G4
Kuyto (lake), U.S.S.R. 52/D2
Kuytun, China 77/C3
Kuyucak, Turkey 63/C4
Kuyuwini (riv.), Guyana 131/B4
Kuznetsk, U.S.S.R. 52/G4
Kuzomen', U.S.S.R. 52/E1
Kvaenangen (fjord), Norway 18/N2
Kvaerndrup, Denmark 21/D7
Kvaløy (isl.), Norway 18/K2
Kvaløya (isl.), Norway 18/O1
Kvarner (gulf), Yugoslavia 45/B3
Kvichak, Alaska (†99625) 196/G3
Kvichak (bay), Alaska 196/G3
Kvikkjokk, Sweden 18/K3
Kvinnherad, Norway 18/E6
Kvissleby, Sweden 18/K5
Kviteseid, Norway 18/F7
Kwa (riv.), Zaire 115/C4
Kwai (Mae Nam Khwae Noi) (riv.), Thailand 72/C4
Kwajalein (atoll), Marshall Is. 87/G5
Kwakoegron, Suriname 131/D3
Kwakwani, Guyana 131/C3
Kwale, Kenya 102/F5
Kwale, Kenya 115/G4
Kwamouth, Zaire 115/C4
Kwangchow (Canton), China 77/H7
Kwangju, S. Korea 54/O6
Kwangju, S. Korea 81/C6
Kwango (riv.), Zaire 115/C5
Kwangsi Chuang Aut. Reg. (Guangxi Zhuangzu), China 77/G7
Kwangtung (Guangdong) (prov.), China 77/H7
Kwanmo (mt.), N. Korea 81/D3
Kwara (state), Nigeria 106/E7
Kweichow (Guizhou) (prov.), China 77/G6
Kweilin (Guilin), China 77/G6
Kweisui (Hohhot), China 77/H3
Kweiyang (Guiyang), China 77/G6
Kwekwe (Que Que), Zimbabwe 118/D3
Kwethluk, Alaska (99621) 196/F2
Kwidzin, Poland 47/D2
Kwigillingok, Alaska (99622) 196/F3
Kwilu (riv.), Angola 115/C5
Kwilu (riv.), Zaire 115/C5
Kwinana New Town, W. Australia 88/B2
Kwinana New Town, W. Australia 92/A1
Kwinitsa, Br. Col. 184/C3
Kwitaro (riv.), Guyana 131/B4
Kyabé, Chad 111/C6
Kyabram, Victoria 97/C5
Kyaikto, Burma 72/C3
Kya-in Seikkyi, Burma 72/C3
Kyakhta, U.S.S.R. 54/M4
Kyakhta, U.S.S.R. 48/L4
Kyalite, N.S. Wales 97/B4
Kyana, Ind. (47549) 227/D8
Kyancutta, S. Australia 94/D5
Kyangin, Burma 72/B3
Kyaukme, Burma 72/C2
Kyaukpadaung, Burma 72/B2
Kyaukpyu, Burma 72/B3
Kyaukse, Burma 72/C2
Kybartai, U.S.S.R. 53/B3
Kyeburn, N. Zealand 100/C6
Kyger, Ohio (†45620) 284/F8
Kyger, W. Va. (†25270) 312/D5
Kyjov, Czech. 41/D2
Kyle, Sask. 181/C5
Kyle, S. Dak. (57752) 298/E7
Kyle, Texas (78640) 303/G8
Kyleakin, Scotland 15/C3
Kylemore, Sask. 181/H4
Kyle of Lochalsh, Scotland 15/C3
Kyle of Tongue (inlet), Scotland 15/D2
Kyles Ford, Tenn. (37765) 237/R7
Kylestrome, Scotland 15/D2
Kymi (prov.), Finland 18/Q6
Kyneton, Victoria 97/C5
Kynšperk, Czech. 41/B1
Kynuna, Queensland 95/B4
Kyogle, N.S. Wales 97/G1
Kyonan, Japan 81/O3
Kyŏnghŭng, N. Korea 81/E2
Kyŏngju, S. Korea 81/D6
Kyoto (pref.), Japan 81/J7
Kyoto, Japan 54/P6
Kyoto, Japan 81/J7
Kyrenia, Cyprus 63/E5
Kyritz, E. Germany 22/E2
Kysucké Nové Mesto, Czech. 41/E2
Kythrea, Cyprus 63/E5
Kyuquot, Br. Col. 184/D5
Kyuquot (sound), Br. Col. 184/D5
Kyushu (isl.), Japan 2/R4
Kyushu (isl.), Japan 54/P6
Kyushu (isl.), Japan 81/E7
Kyustendil, Bulgaria 45/F4
Kyusyur, U.S.S.R. 48/N2
Kywebwe, Burma 72/C3
Kyzyl, U.S.S.R. 48/K4
Kyzyl (riv.), U.S.S.R. 54/L4
Kyzyl-Kum (des.), U.S.S.R. 48/G5
Kzyl-Orda, U.S.S.R. 54/H5
Kzyl-Orda, U.S.S.R. 48/G5

L

Laa an der Thaya, Austria 41/D2
La Aduana, Venezuela 124/D3
Laager, Tenn. (37349) 237/K10
La Aguja (cape), Colombia 126/C2
Laakirchen, Austria 41/B3
La Almunia de Doña Godina, Spain 33/F2
La Altagracia (prov.), Dom. Rep. 158/F6
La Anna, Pa. (†18326) 294/M3
La Antigua Veracruz, Mexico 150/Q1
La Araucanía (reg.), Chile 138/E2
La Asunción, Venezuela 124/G2
Laau (pt.), Hawaii 218/G1
Laax, Switzerland 39/H3
Laayoune, W. Sahara 102/A2
Laayoune, Western Sahara 106/B3
Labadie, Mo. (63055) 261/L5
Labadieville, La. (70372) 238/K4
La Baie, Québec 172/G1
La Baie-de-Shawinigan, Québec 172/E3
La Banda, Argentina 143/D2
La Bandera (pt.), P. Rico 161/F1
La Bañeza, Spain 33/C1
La Barca, Mexico 150/H6
La Barge, Wyo. (83123) 319/B3
La Barge (creek), Wyo. 319/B3
La Barra de Navidad, Mexico 150/G7
Labasheeda, Ireland 17/C6
La Baule-Escoublac, France 28/B4
L'Abbaye, Switzerland 39/B3
Labe (riv.), Czech. 41/C1
Labé, Guinea 106/B6
La Bella (lag.), Paraguay 144/B4
La Belle, Fla. (33935) 212/E5
La Belle, Mo. (63447) 261/J2
Labelle (co.), Québec 172/B3
Labelle, Québec 172/C3
Labelle (lake), Québec 172/C3
La Belle (lake), Wis. 317/H1
Laberge (lake), Yukon 162/C3
Laberinto de las Doce Leguas (cays), Cuba 158/F3
La Berra (mt.), Switzerland 39/D3
Labette (co.), Kansas 232/G4
Labette, Kansas (67350) 232/G4
Labinsk, U.S.S.R. 52/F6
La Bisbal, Spain 33/H1
La Blanquilla (isl.), Venezuela 124/F2
Labo, Philippines 82/D3
Labo (mt.), Philippines 82/D3
La Bolsa, Uruguay 145/C1
La Bolt, S. Dak. (57246) 298/R3
La Bonita, Ecuador 128/D2
La Boquilla (res.), Mexico 150/G3
Laborec (riv.), Czech. 41/F2
Laborie, St. Lucia 161/G7
La Bostonnais, Québec 172/E2
Labougle, Argentina 143/G5
Laboulaye, Argentina 143/D3
Labrador (sea) 146/N4
Labrador (sea) 162/L4
Labrador (reg.), Canada 2/G3
Labrador (sea), Newf. 166/C2
Labrador (reg.), Newf. 166/B2
Labrador (reg.), Newf. 146/M4
Labrador (reg.), Newf. 162/K4
Labrador City, Newf. 166/A3
La Branche, Mich. (†49873) 250/B3
Lábrea, Brazil 132/G10
La Brea, Trin. & Tob. 161/A11
Labrieville, Québec 174/C3
La Broquerie, Manitoba 179/F5
Labuan, Malaysia 85/E4
Labuan (isl.), Malaysia 85/E4
Labuha, Indonesia 85/H6
Labuhan, Indonesia 85/G2
Labuk (bay), Malaysia 85/F4
Labutta, Burma 72/B3
Labyrinth (canyon), Utah 304/D5
Labytnangi, U.S.S.R. 48/G3
Lac (bay), Neth. Ant. 161/D9
Lac-à-Beauce, Québec 172/E2
Lacadena, Sask. 181/C5
Lacadie, Québec 172/J4
La Cahouane, Haiti 158/A6
Lac-à-la-Croix, Québec 172/F1
La Calera, Chile 138/F2
Lac-Alouette, Québec 172/D4
Lacamp, La. (71444) 238/E4
La Canada, Calif. (91011) 204/C10
Lacanau (lake), France 28/C5
La Canoa, Venezuela 124/G3
Lacantum (riv.), Mexico 150/O8
La Capilla, 136/C8
La Carlota, Argentina 143/D3
La Carlota, Philippines 82/D5
La Carlota, Spain 33/D4
La Carolina, Spain 33/E3
Lacassine, La. (70650) 238/E6
Lac-au-Saumon, Québec 172/B2
Lac-aux-Sables, Québec 172/E3
Lac Baker, New Bruns. 170/B1
Lac-Beauport, Québec 172/F3
Lac-Bouchette, Québec 172/E1
Laccadive (isls.), India 54/H8
Laccadive (isls.), India 68/C6
Lac-Carré, Québec 172/C3
Lac-Cayamant, Québec 172/A3
Lac-Chat, Québec 172/E2
Lac Court Oreilles Ind. Res., Wis. 317/D4
Lac de Gras (lake), N.W. Terrs. 187/G3
Lac-Delage, Québec 172/H3
Lac-des-Aigles, Québec 172/J2
Lac des Arcs, Alberta 182/C4
Lac-des-Écorces, Québec 172/B3
Lac-des-Îles, Québec 172/B3
Lac-Drolet, Québec 172/G4
Lac-du-Bonnet, Manitoba 179/G4
Lac-du-Cerf, Québec 172/B3
Lac du Flambeau, Wis. (54538) 317/G4
Lac du Flambeau Ind. Res., Wis. 317/G3
Lac-Édouard, Québec 172/E2
La Ceiba, Hond. 146/K8
La Ceiba, Honduras 154/D3
La Ceiba, Apure, Venezuela 124/C4
La Ceiba, Trujillo, Venezuela 124/C3
La Center, Ky. (42056) 237/C6
La Center, Wash. (98629) 310/C5
Lacepede (bay), S. Australia 88/F7
Lacepede (bay), S. Australia 94/F7
Lacepede (isls.), W. Australia 92/C2
Lacepede (range), W. Australia 88/D3
La Cerbatana, Serranía de (mts.), Venezuela 124/E4
Lac-Etchemin, Québec 172/G3
Lacey, Ark. (†71655) 202/G7
Lacey, Wash. (98503) 310/C3
Lacey Spring, Va. (22833) 307/L3
Laceys Spring, Ala. (35754) 195/E1
Laceyville, Pa. (18623) 294/K2
Lac-Frontière, Québec 172/H3
Lac Giao (Ban Me Thuot), Vietnam 72/E4
Lacha (lake), U.S.S.R. 52/E2
La Chapelle, Haiti 158/C5
La Charité-sur-Loire, France 28/E4
La Châtre, France 28/D4
La Chaux-de-Fonds, Switzerland 39/C2
Lachay (pt.), Peru 128/D8
Lachen, Switzerland 39/G2
Lachenaie, Québec 172/D4
Lachine, Mich. (49753) 250/F3
Lachine, Québec 172/H4
Lachlan (range), N.S. Wales 97/C3
Lachlan (riv.), N. W. Wales 88/G6
Lachlan (riv.), N.S. Wales 97/C3
La Chorrera, Colombia 126/D8
La Chorrera, Panama 154/H6
Lac-Humqui, Québec 172/B2
Lachute, Québec 172/C4
La Ciénaga, Dom. Rep. 158/D6
La Ciotat, France 28/F6
Lackawanna, N.Y. (14218) 276/B5
Lackawanna (co.), Pa. 294/L3
Lackawaxen, Pa. (18435) 294/N3
Lackey, Ky. (41643) 237/R6
Lackland A.F.B., Texas 303/J11
Lac La Belle, Wis. (†53066) 317/H1
Lac La Biche, Alberta 182/E2
Lac La Biche, Alta. 162/E5
Lac La Hache, Br. Col. 184/G4
Lac la Martre, N.W. Terrs. 187/G3
La Clarita, Argentina 143/G5
Lac La Ronge Prov. Park, Sask. 181/M3
Laclede, Idaho (83841) 220/B1
La Clede, Ill. (62437) 222/E5
Laclede (co.), Mo. 261/G7
Laclede, Mo. (64651) 261/F3
Lac-Mégantic, Québec 172/G4
Lacolle, Québec 172/D4
La Colmena, Paraguay 144/B5
La Coloma, Cuba 158/B2
La Colonia, Chile 138/D7
Lacomb, Oreg. (†97355) 291/E3
Lacombe, Alberta 182/D3
Lacombe, Alta. 162/E5
Lacombe, La. (70445) 238/L6
Lacon, Ill. (61540) 222/D2
Lacona, Iowa (50139) 229/G6
Lacona, N.Y. (13083) 276/J3
La Concepción, Honduras 154/E3
La Concepción, Panama 154/F6
La Concepción, Venezuela 124/C2
La Concepción, Venezuela 124/B2
La Conception, Québec 172/C3
La Concordia, Mexico 150/N9
Laconia, Ind. (47135) 227/E8
Laconia, N.H. (03246) 268/E4
Laconia, Tenn. (38045) 237/C10
La Conner, Wash. (98257) 310/C2
La Conquista, Nicaragua 154/D5
Lacoochee, Fla. (33537) 212/D3
La Corey, Alberta 182/E2
La Coronilla, Uruguay 145/F4
La Coruña (prov.), Spain 33/B1
La Coruña, Spain 33/B1
La Coruña, Spain 7/D4
La Coste, Texas (78039) 303/J11
La Courneuve, France 28/B1
Lacovia, Jamaica 158/H6
Lac Pelletier, Sask. 181/C6
Lac-Poulin, Québec 172/G3
Lac qui Parle (co.), Minn. 255/B6
Lac qui Parle, Minn. (†56265) 255/B5
Lac qui Parle (lake), Minn. 255/C5
Lac qui Parle (riv.), Minn. 255/B6
Lacre (pt.), Neth. Ant. 161/E9
La Crescent, Minn. (55947) 255/G7
La Crescenta-Montrose, Calif. (91214) 204/C10
La Crete, Alberta 182/B5
La Croche, Québec 172/E2
La Croix (lake), Minn. 255/F2
La Crosse, Fla. (32658) 212/D2
La Crosse, Georgia (†31806) 217/D6
La Crosse, Ind. (46348) 227/D2
La Crosse, Kansas (67548) 232/C3
La Crosse, Va. (23950) 307/M7
Lacrosse, Wash. (99143) 310/H4
La Crosse (co.), Wis. 317/D8
La Crosse, Wis. 146/J5
La Crosse, Wis. 188/H2
La Crosse, Wis. (54601) 317/D8
La Cruz, Argentina 143/E2
La Cruz, Chile 138/F2
La Cruz, Colombia 126/B7
La Cruz, Chihuahua, Mexico 150/G3
La Cruz, Sinaloa, Mexico 150/F5
La Cruz, Nicaragua 154/E4
La Cruz, Uruguay 145/C4
Lac-Saguay, Québec 172/B3
Lac-Saint-Charles, Québec 172/H3
Lac-Sainte-Marie, Québec 172/A4
Lac-Saint-Jean-Est (co.), Québec 172/F1
Lac-Saint-Jean-Est (county), Québec 174/C3
Lac-Saint-Jean-Ouest (co.), Québec 172/E1
Lac-Saint-Jean-Ouest (county), Québec 174/C2
Lac-Saint-Joseph, Québec 172/F3
Lac-Saint-Paul, Québec 172/B3
Lac-Sergent, Québec 172/F3
Lac Seul, Ontario 175/B2
La Cuchilla, Uruguay 145/F3
La Cueva, N. Mex. (†87712) 274/D3
La Cumbre, Argentina 143/C3
La Cure, Switzerland 39/B4
Lacuy (pen.), Chile 138/D4
Lac Vert, Sask. 181/G3
La Cygne, Kansas (66040) 232/H3
Ladakh (reg.), India 68/D2
Ladd, Ill. (61329) 222/D2
Ladder (creek), Kansas 232/A3
Ladder (hills), Scotland 15/E3
Laddonia, Mo. (63352) 261/J4
La Decharge, Québec 172/F1
Ladelle, Ark. (†71655) 202/G7
Ladgasht (Qila Ladgasht), Pakistan 68/A3
Ladhar Bheinn (mt.), Scotland 15/C3
Ladiesburg, Md. (21759) 245/J2
La Digue (isl.), Seychelles 118/J5
Lâdik, Turkey 63/G2
Ladispoli, Italy 34/E6
Ladiz, Iran 66/M6
Ladner, S. Dak. (†57720) 298/B2
Lado, Sudan 111/F6
Ladoga, Ind. (47954) 227/D5
Ladoga (lake), U.S.S.R. 7/H2
Ladoga (lake), U.S.S.R. 48/D3
Ladoga (lake), U.S.S.R. 52/D2
La Dôle (mt.), Switzerland 39/B4
Ladonia, Texas (75449) 303/J4
Ladora, Iowa (52251) 229/J5
La Dorada, Colombia 126/C5
Ladrillero (gulf), Chile 138/C8
Ladrillero (mt.), Chile 138/E10
Ladrillo (pt.), Cuba 158/E3
Ladron (mts.), N. Mex. 274/B4
Ladrones (isls.), Panama 154/F7
Ladson, S.C. (29456) 296/G6
La Due, Mo. (†64735) 261/E6
Ladue, Mo. (†63124) 261/P3
La Durantaye, Québec 172/G3
Lady (pond), Newf. 166/D2
Lady Ann (str.), N.W. Terrs. 187/K2
Ladybank, Scotland 15/E4
Lady Barron, Tasmania 99/E2
Ladybrand, S. Africa 118/D5
Lady Franklin (bay), N.W. Terrs. 187/M1
Lady Franklin (isl.), N.W. Terrs. 187/M3
Lady Lake, Fla. (32659) 212/E3
Lady Lake, Sask. 181/J3
Lady's Island Lake (inlet), Ireland 17/J7
Ladysmith, Br. Col. 184/J3
Ladysmith, S. Africa 102/F7
Ladysmith, S. Africa 118/D5
Ladysmith, Va. (22501) 307/N4
Ladysmith, Wis. (54848) 317/D5
Ladywood, Manitoba 179/F4
Lae, Papua N.G. 85/B7
Lae, Papua N.G. 86/A2
Lae, Papua N.G. 87/E6
Lae, Thailand 72/D3
Laem Chong Phra (cape), Thailand 72/C5
Laem Pho (cape), Thailand 72/D6
Laem Talumphuk (cape), Thailand 72/D5
Laerdal, Norway 18/E6
La Esmeralda, Argentina 143/G5
La Esmeralda, Bolivia 136/D8
La Esmeralda, Venezuela 124/F6
Laesø (isl.), Denmark 18/G8
Laesø (isl.), Denmark 21/D3
La Esperanza, Argentina 143/B7
La Esperanza, Bolivia 136/D4
La Esperanza, Honduras 154/C3
La Esperanza, Venezuela 124/H3
La Estrada, Spain 33/B1
La Estrella, Chile 138/F5
La Estrelleta (prov.), Dom. Rep. 158/C5
La Falda, Argentina 143/D3
La Farge, Wis. (54639) 317/E8
La Fargeville, N.Y. (13656) 276/J2
Lafayette, Ala. (36862) 195/H5
Lafayette (co.), Ark. 202/C7
Lafayette, Calif. (94549) 204/K2
Lafayette, Colo. (80026) 208/K3
Lafayette (co.), Fla. 212/C2
La Fayette, Georgia (30728) 217/B1
La Fayette, Ill. (61449) 222/C2
Lafayette, Ind. 188/J2
Lafayette, Ind. (*47901) 227/D4
La Fayette, Ky. (42254) 237/F7
Lafayette (par.), La. 238/F6
Lafayette, La. (*70501) 238/F6
Lafayette, Minn. (56054) 255/D6
Lafayette (co.), Miss. 256/E2
Lafayette (co.), Mo. 261/E4
Lafayette (mt.), N.H. 268/D3
Lafayette, N.J. (07848) 273/D1
La Fayette, N.Y. (13084) 276/H5
Lafayette, Ohio (45854) 284/C4
Lafayette, Oreg. (97127) 291/A2
La Fayette, R.I. (†02852) 249/H6
Lafayette, Tenn. (37083) 237/J7
Lafayette (co.), Wis. 317/F10
Lafayette-Elliston, Va. (24108) 307/H6
Lafayette Springs, Miss. (38640) 256/F2
Lafe, Ark. (72436) 202/J1
La Fe, Cuba 158/A2
La Feria, Texas (78559) 303/G11
La Ferté-Macé, France 28/C3
Lafferty, Ohio (43951) 284/H5
Lafia, Nigeria 106/F7
Lafiagi, Nigeria 106/F7
Lafitte, La. (70067) 238/K7
La Flèche, France 28/C4
Lafleche, Sask. 181/E6
La Floresta, Uruguay 145/C7
Lafnitz (riv.), Austria 41/D3
La Follette, Tenn. (37766) 237/N8
La Fontaine, Ind. (46940) 227/F3
Lafontaine, Kansas (66750) 232/G4
Lafontaine, Québec 172/C4
Lafourche (par.), La. 238/K7
Lafourche, La. (†70301) 238/J7
Lafourche (bayou), La. 238/K8
La France, S.C. (29656) 296/B2
La Fría, Venezuela 124/B3
Laful, India 68/G7
Lagacéville, New Bruns. 170/E1
La Gallareta, Argentina 143/F5
Lagan (riv.), N. Ireland 17/K2
Lagarfljót (stream), Iceland 21/C1
La Garita, Colo. (†81132) 208/G7
La Garita (mts.), Colo. 208/F7
Lagawe, Philippines 82/C2
Lagayan, Philippines 82/C2
Lage, W. Germany 22/C3
Lågen (riv.), Norway 18/G6
Lages, Brazil 132/D9
Lages, Brazil 120/D5
Laggan, Scotland 15/D3
Laggan, Scotland 10/D2
Laggan (bay), Scotland 15/B5
Laggan, Loch (lake), Scotland 15/D4
Laghouat, Algeria 106/E2
Laghouat, Algeria 102/C1
Laghy, Ireland 17/E2
La Gineta, Spain 33/E3
Lagkadia, Greece 45/E7
La Glace, Alberta 182/A2
La Gloria, Colombia 126/D3
La Gloria, Cuba 158/G2
Lago, Neth. Ant. 161/E10
Lagoa, Portugal 33/B4
Lagoa da Prata, Brazil 135/D2
Lagoa Dourada, Brazil 135/D2
Lago Blanco, Argentina 143/B6
Lagoen, Neth. Ant. 161/F8
La Goleta, Colombia 126/B3
La Gomera, Guatemala 154/B3
Lagonegro, Italy 34/E4
Lagonoy (gulf), Philippines 82/E4
Lagoon (lake), S. Australia 88/F6
Lago Ranco, Chile 138/E3
Lagos (state), Nigeria 106/E7
Lagos (cap.), Nigeria 2/K5
Lagos (cap.), Nigeria 102/C4
Lagos (cap.), Nigeria 106/E7
Lagos, Portugal 33/B4
Lagos de Moreno, Mexico 150/J6
Lagosta (Lastovo) (isl.), Yugoslavia 45/C4
La Goulette (Halq el Oued), Tunisia 106/G1
Lago Verde, Chile 138/E5
La Grand-Combe, France 28/E5
La Grande, Oreg. 188/C1
La Grande, Oreg. (97850) 291/J2
La Grande, Wash. (98348) 310/C4
La Grand Rivière (riv.), Que. 162/J5
La Grange, Ark. (72352) 202/J4
La Grange, Australia 87/C7
La Grange, Calif. (95329) 204/E6
La Grange, Ga. 188/K4
La Grange, Georgia (30240) 217/B4
La Grange, Ill. (60525) 222/B6
Lagrange (co.), Ind. 227/G1
Lagrange, Ind. (46761) 227/F1
La Grange, Ky. (40031) 237/L4
La Grange, Maine (04453) 243/F5
La Grange○, Maine (04453) 243/F5
La Grange, Mo. (63448) 261/K2
La Grange, N.C. (28551) 281/O4
Lagrange, Ohio (44050) 284/F3
La Grange, Tenn. (38046) 237/C10
La Grange, Texas (78945) 303/G8
La Grange, W. Australia 92/C2
Lagrange, Wyo. (82221) 319/H4
La Grange Park, Ill. (60525) 222/B5
La Granja (San Ildefonso), Spain 33/E2
La Gran Sabana (plain), Venezuela 124/G5
La Grita, Venezuela 124/C3
Lagro, Ind. (46941) 227/F3
La Grue (bayou), Ark. 202/H5
La Guadeloupe, Québec 172/F4
La Guaira, Venezuela 124/E2
La Guaira, Venezuela 120/C1
La Guajira (dept.), Colombia 126/D2
La Guardia, Bolivia 136/D5
La Guardia, Spain 33/B2
Laguardia, Spain 33/E1
La Guata, Honduras 154/D3
Laguna (creek), Ariz. 198/E2
Laguna (dam), Ariz. 198/A6
Laguna (res.), Ariz. 198/A6
Laguna, Brazil 132/D10
Laguna (res.), Calif. 204/L11
Laguna, N. Mex. (87026) 274/B3
Laguna (prov.), Philippines 82/C3
Laguna Beach, Calif. (*92651) 204/G10
Laguna de Perlas, Nicaragua 154/F4
Laguna Hills, Calif. (92653) 204/D11
Laguna Niguel, Calif. (92677) 204/H10
Laguna Paiva, Argentina 143/F5
Lagunas, Chile 138/B3
Lagunas, Peru 128/E5
Laguna Yema, Argentina 143/D1
Lagunetas, Venezuela 124/C3
Lagunillas, Bolivia 136/D6
Lagunillas, Chile 138/F3
Lagunillas, Venezuela 124/C2
Lagunitas-Forest Knolls, Calif. (94938) 204/H1
La Habra, Calif. (90631) 204/D11
Lahad Datu, Malaysia 85/F5
Lahaina, Hawaii (96761) 218/H2
Lahaina, Hawaii 188/F5
Laham, Indonesia 85/F5
Lahan, Nong (lake), Thailand 72/D3
La Harpe, Ill. (61450) 222/C3
La Harpe, Kansas (66751) 232/G4
Lahat, Indonesia 85/C6
La Have, Nova Scotia 168/D4
La Have (isl.), Nova Scotia 168/D4
La Have (riv.), Nova Scotia 168/D4
Lahej, P.D.R. Yemen 59/E7
La Higuera, Chile 138/A7
Lahijan, Iran 66/G2
Lahinch, Ireland 17/C6
Lahmansville, W. Va. (26731) 312/H4
Lahn, W. Germany 22/C3
Lahn (riv.), W. Germany 22/C3
Lahnstein, W. Germany 22/B3
Laholm, Sweden 18/H8
Lahoma, Okla. (73754) 288/K2
La Honda, Calif. (94020) 204/J3
Lahontan (res.), Nev. 266/B3
Lahore, Pakistan 59/K3
Lahore, Pakistan 68/C2
Lahore, Pakistan 54/J6
Lahore, Va. (22502) 307/N4
La Horqueta, Venezuela 124/G3
Lahr, W. Germany 22/B4
Lahri, Pakistan 68/B3
Lahti, Finland 7/G2
Lahti, Finland 18/O6
La Huaca, Peru 128/B5
La Huerta, Mexico 150/G7
Laï, Chad 111/C6
Laï, Chad 102/D4
Lai Chau, Vietnam 72/D2
Laidlaw, Br. Col. 184/M3
Laidon, Loch (lake), Scotland 15/D4
Laie, Hawaii (96762) 218/E1
Laie (pt.), Hawaii 218/E1
L'Aigle, France 28/D3
Lai-hka, Burma 72/C2
Laila, Saudi Arabia 59/E5
Lailan, Iraq 66/D3
La Inglesa, Venezuela 124/G3
Laings, Ohio (43752) 284/J6
Laingsburg, Mich. (48848) 250/E6
Lainioälv (riv.), Sweden 18/N3
Lair, Ky. (†41031) 237/N4
Laird, Colo. (80739) 208/P2
Laird, Sask. 181/E3
Lairdsville, Pa. (17742) 294/J3
Lairg, Scotland 10/D1
Lairg, Scotland 15/D2
Lais, Philippines 82/E7
Laisamis, Kenya 115/G3
La Isla, Texas (†79838) 303/A10
Laiwui, Indonesia 85/H6
Laiyang, China 77/K4
Laja (riv.), Chile 138/E1
La Jalca, Peru 128/D6
La Jara, Colo. (81140) 208/H8
La Jara, N. Mex. (87027) 274/B2
Lajas, P. Rico 161/A2
Lajes do Pico, Portugal 33/B1
Lajinha, Brazil 135/F2
La Jolla, Calif. (92037) 204/H11
La Jolla Ind. Res., Calif. 204/J10
Lajord, Sask. 181/G5
La Jose, Pa. (15753) 294/E4
Lajosmizse, Hungary 41/E3
La Joya, Bolivia 136/B5
Lajoya, N. Mex. (87028) 274/C4
La Joya, Peru 128/G11
La Joya, Texas (78560) 303/F11
La Junta, Colo. 188/F3
La Junta, Colo. (81050) 208/M7
Lak Dera (dry riv.), Kenya 115/H3
Lak Dera (dry riv.), Somalia 115/H3
Lake (co.), Calif. 204/C4
Lake (co.), Colo. 208/G4
Lake (co.), Fla. 212/E3
Lake (co.), Ill. 222/E1
Lake (co.), Ind. 227/C2
Lake, Ky. (†40741) 237/O6
Lake (co.), Mich. 250/D5
Lake, Mich. (48632) 250/E5
Lake (co.), Minn. 255/G3
Lake, Miss. (39092) 256/F6
Lake (co.), Mont. 262/B3
Lake (co.), Ohio 284/H2
Lake (co.), Oreg. 291/G5
Lake (creek), Oreg. 291/J3
Lake (co.), S. Dak. 298/P5
Lake (riv.), Tasmania 99/D3
Lake (co.), Tenn. 237/B8
Lake (creek), Utah 304/A5
Lake (creek), Wash. 310/G3
Lake Alfred, Fla. (33850) 212/E3
Lake Alma, Sask. 181/G6
Lake Alpine, Calif. (†95223) 204/F5
Lake Andes, S. Dak. (57356) 298/M7
Lake Ann, Mich. (49650) 250/D4
Lake Ariel, Pa. (18436) 294/M3
Lake Arrowhead, Calif. (92352) 204/H9
Lake Arthur, La. (70549) 238/E6
Lake Arthur, N. Mex. (88253) 274/E5
Lake Arthur, N.S. Wales 97/D4
Lake Barcroft, Va. (†22041) 307/S3
Lake Barrington, Ill. (†60010) 222/A5
Lake Benton, Minn. (56149) 255/B6
Lake Beulah, Wis. (†53120) 317/J2
Lake Bluff, Ill. (60044) 222/B4
Lake Boga, Victoria 97/B4
Lake Bolac, Victoria 97/B5
Lake Bronson, Minn. (56734) 255/B2
Lake Bruce, Ind. (†46939) 227/E2
Lake Buena Vista, Fla. (†32830) 212/E3
Lake Butler, Fla. (32054) 212/D1
Lake Butte Des Morts (Butte Des Morts), Wis. (†54901) 317/J7
Lake Cargelligo, N.S. Wales 97/D3
Lake Carmel, N.Y. (10512) 276/N8
Lake Carroll, Fla. (†33601) 212/C2
Lake Catherine, Ill. (†60002) 222/E1
Lake Charles, La. 188/H4
Lake Charles, La. (*70601) 238/D6
Lake Chelan Nat'l Rec. Area, Wash. 310/E2

Lingshan 399

Leti (isls.), Indonesia 85/H7
Leticia, Colombia 126/F10
Leticia, Colombia 120/B3
L'Etivaz, Switzerland 39/D4
Letka, U.S.S.R. 52/H3
Leto, Fla. (†33614) 212/C2
Letohatchee, Ala. (36047) 195/E6
Leton, La. (†71072) 238/D1
Letona, Ark. (72085) 202/G3
Letong, Indonesia 85/D5
Le Touquet-Paris-Plage, France 28/D2
Letpadan, Burma 72/C3
Le Tréport, France 28/D2
Letsôk-aw Kyun (isl.), Burma 72/C5
Lette, N.S. Wales 97/B4
Letterkenny, Ireland 10/B3
Letterkenny, Ireland 17/F2
Letterkenny Army Depot, Pa. 294/G6
Lettermullan (isl.), Ireland 17/B5
Letts, Ind. (†47240) 227/F6
Letts, Iowa (52754) 229/L6
Lettsworth, La. (70753) 238/G5
Leucadia, Calif. (92024) 204/H10
Leucate (mts.), France 28/E6
Leuchars, Scotland 15/F4
Leuk, Switzerland 39/E4
Leukerbad, Switzerland 39/E4
Leupp, Ariz. (86035) 198/E3
Leurbost, Scotland 15/B2
Leuser (mt.), Indonesia 85/B5
Leuven, Belgium 27/F7
Leuze-en-Hainaut, Belgium 27/D7
Levádhia, Greece 45/F6
Levallois-Perret, France 28/A1
Levan, Utah (84639) 304/C4
Levanger, Norway 18/G5
Levant, Kansas (67743) 232/A2
Levant○, Maine (04456) 243/F6
Levanzo (isl.), Italy 34/D5
Levasy, Mo. (64066) 261/S5
Le Vauclin, Martinique 161/D6
Levee, Ky. (†40337) 237/O5
Level, Md. (†21078) 245/O2
Level Green, Ky. (†40456) 237/N6
Level Land, S.C. (†29655) 296/C3
Levelland, Texas (79336) 303/B4
Levelock, Alaska (99625) 196/G3
Level Plains, Ala. (†36322) 195/G8
Levels, W. Va. (25431) 312/J4
Leven, Scotland 10/E2
Leven, Scotland 15/F4
Leven, Loch (inlet), Scotland 15/D4
Leven (lake), Scotland 15/E4
Leven (riv.), Tasmania 99/B3
Leveque (cape), Australia 87/C7
L'Eveque (cape), N. Zealand 100/D7
Lévêque (cape), W. Australia 88/C3
Lévêque (cape), W. Australia 92/C2
Leverburgh, Scotland 15/B3
Le Verdon-sur-Mer, France 28/C5
Leverett○, Mass. (01054) 249/E3
Levering, Mich. (49755) 250/E3
Leverkusen, W. Germany 22/B3
Levesque, New Bruns. 170/C1
Levice, Czech. 41/E2
Levick (mt.) 5/B8
Levie, France 28/B7
Le Vigan, France 28/E5
Levin, N. Zealand 100/E4
Lévis (co.), Québec 172/J3
Lévis, Québec 172/J3
Lévis, Québec 174/C3
Levisa Fork (riv.), Va. 307/C5
Levítha (isl.), Greece 45/H7
Levittown, N.Y. (11756) 276/R7
Levittown, Pa. (*19053) 294/N5
Levittown, P. Rico 161/D1
Levkás, Greece 45/E6
Levkás (isl.), Greece 45/E6
Levoča, Czech. 41/F2
Lévrier (bay), Mauritania 106/A4
Levuka, Fiji 87/H7
Levukaa, Fiji 86/Q10
Levy (co.), Fla. 212/D2
Levy (lake), Fla. 212/D2
Levy, N. Mex. (†87752) 274/E2
Lewe, Burma 72/B3
Lewellen, Nebr. (69147) 264/B3
Lewes, Del. (19958) 245/T5
Lewes, England 13/H7
Lewes, England 10/G5
Lewis, Colo. (81327) 208/B8
Lewis (isl.), Fla. 212/B3
Lewis (co.), Idaho 220/B3
Lewis, Ind. (47858) 227/C6
Lewis, Iowa (51544) 229/C6
Lewis, Kansas (67552) 232/C4
Lewis (co.), Ky. 237/P3
Lewis, Manitoba 179/F5
Lewis (lake), Manitoba 179/G2
Lewis (co.), Mo. 261/J2
Lewis, Mo. (†64735) 261/E6
Lewis (range), Mont. 262/C2
Lewis (co.), N.Y. 276/K3
Lewis, N.Y. (12950) 276/N2
Lewis (dist.), Scotland 15/B2
Lewis (dist.), Scotland 10/C1
Lewis, Butt of (prom.), Scotland 15/B2
Lewis, Butt of (prom.), Scotland 10/C1
Lewis, S.C. (†29706) 296/E2
Lewis (co.), Tenn. 237/F9
Lewis (creek), Vt. 268/A3
Lewis (co.), Wash. 310/C4
Lewis (riv.), Wash. 310/C5
Lewis (co.), W. Va. 312/E4
Lewis, Wis. (54851) 317/B4
Lewis (lake), Wyo. 319/B1
Lewis and Clark (co.), Mont. 262/D3
Lewis and Clark (lake), Nebr. 264/G2
Lewis and Clark (lake), S. Dak. 298/O8
Lewis and Clark Village, Mo. (†64484) 261/C3
Lewisberry, Pa. (17339) 294/J5
Lewisburg, Ky. (42256) 237/G6
Lewisburg, La. (†70525) 238/F6
Lewisburg, Ohio (45338) 284/A6
Lewisburg, Pa. (17837) 294/J4
Lewisburg, Tenn. (37091) 237/H10
Lewisburg, W. Va. (24901) 312/E7
Lewis Center, Ohio (43035) 284/D5
Lewis Creek, Ind. (†47234) 227/F6
Lewisetta, Va. (22505) 307/R4
Lewisham, England 10/B5
Lewisham, England 13/H8
Lewis Hill (mt.), Newf. 166/C4
Lewisport, Ky. (42351) 237/H5
Lewisporte, Newf. 166/C4
Lewis Run, Pa. (16738) 294/E2
Lewis Smith (dam), Ala. 195/D3
Lewis Smith (lake), Ala. 195/D2
Lewiston, Calif. (96052) 204/C3
Lewiston, Idaho 188/C1
Lewiston, Idaho (83501) 220/A3
Lewiston, Maine 188/N2
Lewiston, Maine (04240) 243/C7
Lewiston, Mich. (49756) 250/E4
Lewiston, Minn. (55952) 255/G7
Lewiston, Nebr. (68380) 264/H4
Lewiston, N.Y. (14092) 276/B4
Lewiston, N.C. (27849) 281/P2
Lewiston, Utah (84320) 304/C2
Lewiston, Vt. (†05055) 268/C4
Lewistown, Ill. (61542) 222/C3
Lewistown, Md. (21701) 245/J2
Lewistown, Mo. (63452) 261/J2
Lewistown, Mont. (59457) 262/G3
Lewistown, Ohio (43333) 284/C5
Lewistown, Pa. (17044) 294/G4
Lewisville, Ark. (71845) 202/C7
Lewisville, Idaho (83431) 220/F6
Lewisville, Ind. (47352) 227/G5
Lewisville, Minn. (56060) 255/D7
Lewisville, Ohio (43754) 284/H6
Lewisville (Ulysses), Pa. (16948) 294/G2
Lewisville, Pa. (19351) 294/L6
Lewisville, Texas (*75067) 303/G1
Lewisville (lake), Texas 303/G1
Lewvan, Sask. 181/H5
Lexa, Ark. (72355) 202/J4
Lexie, Miss. (†39667) 256/D8
Lexington, Ala. (35648) 195/D1
Lexington, Ark. (†72153) 202/F2
Lexington, Georgia (30648) 217/F3
Lexington, Ill. (61753) 222/E3
Lexington, Ind. (47138) 227/F7
Lexington, Ky. (*40501) 237/N4
Lexington, Ky. 146/K6
Lexington, Ky. 188/K3
Lexington○, Mass. (02173) 249/B6
Lexington, Mich. (48450) 250/G5
Lexington, Minn. (†55014) 255/G5
Lexington, Miss. (39095) 256/D4
Lexington, Mo. (64067) 261/E4
Lexington, Nebr. (68850) 264/E4
Lexington, N.Y. (12452) 276/M6
Lexington, N.C. (27292) 281/J3
Lexington, Ohio (44904) 284/E4
Lexington, Okla. (73051) 288/M4
Lexington, Oreg. (97839) 291/H2
Lexington (co.), S.C. 296/E4
Lexington, S.C. (29072) 296/E4
Lexington, Tenn. (38351) 237/E9
Lexington, Texas (78947) 303/G7
Lexington (I.C.), Va. (24450) 307/J5
Lexington Blue Grass Army Depot, Ky. 237/N5
Lexington Park, Md. (20653) 245/M7
Lexsy, Georgia (†30401) 217/H6
Leyba, N. Mex. (87542) 274/D3
Leyburn, England 13/F3
Leyden○, Mass. (†01301) 249/D2
Leye, China 77/G7
Leyland, England 13/G1
Leyland, England 10/F1
Leyond (riv.), Manitoba 179/F3
Leysin, Switzerland 39/C4
Leyte (prov.), Philippines 82/E5
Leyte (isl.), Philippines 54/O8
Leyte (gulf), Philippines 82/E5
Leyte (isl.), Philippines 85/H3
Leyte (isl.), Philippines 82/E5
Lezajsk, Poland 47/F3
Lezama, Argentina 143/H7
Lézarde (riv.), Martinique 161/D6
Lezhë, Albania 45/D5
Lézignan-Corbières, France 28/E6
Lezuza, Spain 33/E3
L'gov, U.S.S.R. 52/E4
Lhanbryde, Scotland 15/E3
Lhari, China 77/D5
Lhasa, China 77/D6
Lhasa, China 2/P4
Lhasa, China 54/L7
Lhazê (Lhatse), China 77/C6
Lhazhong, China 77/C5
Lhokseumawe, Indonesia 85/B4
Lhorong, China 77/E5
Lhozhag, China 77/D6
Lhünzê, China 77/D6
Lhünzhub, China 77/D5
Liancheng, China 77/J6
Lianga, Philippines 82/E6
Lianga (bay), Philippines 82/F6
Lianping, China 77/H7
Lian Xian, China 77/H7
Lianyungang (Lienyünkang), China 77/J5
Lianyunggang, China 54/N6
Liao (riv.), China 54/O5
Liaodong Bandao (pen.), China 77/K3
Liao He (riv.), China 77/K3
Liaoning (prov.), China 77/K3
Liaoyang, China 77/K3
Liaoyuan, China 77/K3
Liard (riv.) 162/D3
Liard (riv.), Br. Col. 184/L2
Liard (riv.), Canada 146/F3
Liard (riv.), N.W. Terrs. 187/F4
Liard (riv.), Yukon 187/E3
Liard River, Br. Col. 184/L2
Libáň, Czech. 41/C1
Líbano, Colombia 126/C5
Libau, Manitoba 179/F4
Libby, Minn. (†55760) 255/E4
Libby, Mont. (59923) 262/A2
Libenge, Zaire 115/C3
Liberal, Kansas (67901) 232/B4
Liberal, Mo. (64762) 261/D7
Liberal, Oreg. (†97042) 291/B3
Liberdade, Brazil 135/D3
Liberec, Czech. 41/C1
Liberia 2/J5
Liberia 102/B4
LIBERIA 106/C7
Liberia, C. Rica 154/E5
Liberta, Ant. & Bar. 161/E11
Libertad, Belize 154/C1
Libertad, Uruguay 145/C5
Libertad, Barinas, Venezuela 124/D3
Libertad, Cojedes, Venezuela 124/D3
Liberty, Ariz. (†85326) 198/C5
Liberty (co.), Fla. 212/B1
Liberty (co.), Georgia 217/J7
Liberty, Ill. (62347) 222/B4
Liberty, Ind. (47353) 227/H5
Liberty, Kansas (67351) 232/G4
Liberty, Ky. (42539) 237/M6
Liberty, Maine (04949) 243/E7
Liberty○, Maine (04949) 243/E7
Liberty (lake), Md. 245/L3
Liberty, Miss. (39645) 256/C8
Liberty, Mo. (64068) 261/R5
Liberty (co.), Mont. 262/E2
Liberty, Nebr. (68381) 264/H4
Liberty (mt.), N.H. 268/D3
Liberty, N.Y. (12754) 276/L7
Liberty, N.C. (27298) 281/K3
Liberty, Pa. (16930) 294/H2
Liberty, Pa. (†15100) 294/C7
Liberty, Sask. 181/F4
Liberty, S.C. (29657) 296/B2
Liberty, Tenn. (37095) 237/K8
Liberty (co.), Texas 303/K7
Liberty, Texas (77575) 303/K7
Liberty, Wash. (†98922) 310/E3
Liberty, W. Va. (25124) 312/C5
Liberty Center, Ind. (46766) 227/G3
Liberty Center, Iowa (50145) 229/F6
Liberty Center, Ohio (43532) 284/B3
Liberty Corner, N.J. (07938) 273/D2
Liberty Grove, Md. (†21918) 245/O2
Liberty Hill, Conn. (†06249) 210/G2
Liberty Hill, La. (†71008) 238/E2
Liberty Hill, S.C. (29074) 296/F3
Liberty Lake, Wash. (99019) 310/J3
Liberty Mills, Ind. (46946) 227/F2
Liberty Pole, Wis. (†54665) 317/D8
Libertytown, Md. (21762) 245/J3
Libertyville, Ala. (†36420) 195/F8
Libertyville, Ill. (60048) 222/B4
Libertyville, Iowa (52567) 229/K7
Libiaz, Poland 47/D4
Libin, Belgium 27/G9
Libochovice, Czech. 41/B1
Libon, Philippines 82/D4
Libong, Ko (isl.), Thailand 72/C6
Libourne, France 28/C5
Libramont-Chevigny, Belgium 27/G9
Library, Pa. (15129) 294/B7
Libres, Mexico 150/O1
Libreville (cap.), Gabon 2/K6
Libreville (cap.), Gabon 115/A3
Libreville (cap.), Gabon 102/C4
Libuse, La. (71348) 238/F4
Libya 2/K4
Libya 102/D2
LIBYA 111/B2
Libyan (des.) 102/E2
Libyan (des.), Egypt 111/E2
Libyan (plat.), Egypt 111/E1
Libyan (des.), Libya 111/D2
Libyan (plat.), Libya 111/D1
Libyan (des.), Sudan 111/E3
Licancábur, Cerro (mt.), Chile 138/B4
Licantén, Chile 138/A10
Licata, Italy 34/D6
Lice, Turkey 63/J3
Lichfield, England 13/F5
Lichfield, England 10/G2
Lichinga, Mozambique 102/F6
Lichinga, Mozambique 118/F2
Lichtenberg, E. Germany 22/F4
Lichtenfels, W. Germany 22/D3
Lichtenrade, W. Germany 22/F4
Lichterfelde, W. Germany 22/E4
Lichtervelde, Belgium 27/C6
Lick (creek), Tenn. 237/R8
Lick Creek, Ill. (†62912) 222/D6
Licking, North Fork (riv.), Ky. 237/O3
Licking, South Fork (riv.), Ky. 237/N3
Licking (riv.), Ky. 237/N3
Licking, Mo. (65542) 261/J8
Licking (co.), Ohio 284/F5
Licking (riv.), Ohio 284/F5
Licking (creek), Pa. 294/F6
Licosa (cape), Italy 34/E4
Lida, Ky. (†40741) 237/O6
Lida (lake), Minn. 255/C4
Lida, U.S.S.R. 52/C4
Lidcombe, N.S. Wales 97/J3
Liddel Water (riv.), Scotland 15/F5
Lidderdale, Iowa (51452) 229/D4
Liddes, Switzerland 39/D5
Liddon (gulf), N.W. Terrs. 187/G4
Lidgerwood, N. Dak. (58053) 282/R7
Lidice, Czech. 41/C1
Lidingö, Sweden 18/H1
Lidköping, Sweden 18/H7
Lido di Ostia, Italy 34/F7
Lido di Venezia, Italy 34/D2
Lidzbark, Poland 47/D2
Lidzbark Warmiński, Poland 47/E1
Liebenthal, Kansas (67553) 232/C3
Liebenthal, Sask. 181/B5
Liechtensteig, Switzerland 39/H2
Liechtenstein 7/F4
LIECHTENSTEIN 39/J2
Liedekerke, Belgium 27/D7
Liége (riv.), Alberta 182/D1
Liège (prov.), Belgium 27/H7
Liège, Belgium 7/E3
Liège, Belgium 27/H7
Liegnitz (Legnica), Poland 47/C3
Lieksa, Finland 18/R5
Lienyünkang (Lianyungang), China 77/J5
Lienz, Austria 41/B3
Liepāja, U.S.S.R. 7/F3
Liepāja, U.S.S.R. 53/A2
Liepāja, U.S.S.R. 48/B4
Liepāja, U.S.S.R. 52/B3
Lier, Belgium 27/F6
Lierneux, Belgium 27/H8
Lierre (Lier), Belgium 27/F6
Liestal, Switzerland 39/E2
Liévin, France 28/E2
Lièvre (riv.), Québec 172/B4
Lièvres (isl.), Québec 172/H2
Liezen, Austria 41/C3
Liffey (riv.), Ireland 17/H5
Liffey (riv.), Ireland 10/C4
Lifford, Ireland 10/C3
Lifford, Ireland 17/F2
Lifu (isl.), New Caled. 87/G8
Lifu (isl.), New Caled. 86/H4
Ligao, Philippines 82/D4
Ligatne, U.S.S.R. 53/C2
Liggett, Ky. (†40831) 237/P7
Lightfoot, Va. (23090) 307/P6
Lighthouse (pt.), Fla. 212/B2
Light House (pt.), Mich. 250/D3
Lighthouse Point, Fla. (33064) 212/F5
Lightning (creek), Oreg. 291/L2
Lightning (creek), Wyo. 319/G2
Lightning Ridge, N.S. Wales 97/E1
Lightsville, Ohio (†45362) 284/A5
Lignite, N. Dak. (58752) 282/F2
Ligon, Ky. (41646) 237/R6
Ligonha (riv.), Mozambique 118/F3
Ligonier, Ind. (46767) 227/F2
Ligonier, Pa. (15658) 294/D5
Liguria (reg.), Italy 34/B2
Ligurian (sea), Italy 34/B3
Lihir Group (isls.), Papua N.G. 86/C1
Lihou (cays), Coral Sea Is. Terr. 88/J3
Lihue, Hawaii (96766) 218/C2
Lihue, Hawaii 188/E5
Lihula, U.S.S.R. 53/C1
Lijiang, China 77/F6
Likasi, Panda-, Zaire 115/E6
Likati, Zaire 115/D3
Likely, Br. Col. 184/G4
Likely, Calif. (96116) 204/E2
Likhoslavl', U.S.S.R. 52/E3
Likouala (riv.), Congo 115/C3
Lila (lake), N.Y. 276/L2
Lilac, Sask. 181/D3
Lilbourn, Mo. (63862) 261/N9
Lilburn, Georgia (30247) 217/D3
Lileah, Tasmania 99/B2
L'Île-Rousse, France 28/B6
Liles (pt.), Chile 138/F2
Lilesville, N.C. (28091) 281/K5
Lilienfeld, Austria 41/C3
Lille, France 7/E3
Lille, France 28/E2
Lille, Maine (04749) 243/G1
Lilleå (riv.), Denmark 21/C5
Lille Baelt (chan.), Denmark 21/C7
Lillehammer, Norway 18/F6
Lillesand, Norway 18/F7
Lillestrøm, Norway 18/E3
Lillian, Ala. (36549) 195/D10
Lillie, La. (71256) 238/E1
Lilliesleaf, Scotland 15/F5
Lillington, N.C. (27546) 281/M4
Lillinonah (lake), Conn. 210/B3
Lilliwaup, Wash. (98555) 310/B3
Lillo, Spain 33/E3
Lillooet, Br. Col. 162/D5
Lillooet, Br. Col. 184/G5
Lillooet (riv.), Br. Col. 184/F5
Lilly, Georgia (31051) 217/E6
Lilly, Ill. (†61755) 222/D3
Lilly, Pa. (15938) 294/E5
Lilly Chapel, Ohio (†43162) 284/D6
Lillydale, Victoria 97/J4
Lilongwe (cap.), Malawi 2/L6
Lilongwe (cap.), Malawi 102/F6
Lilongwe (cap.), Malawi 115/F6
Liloy, Philippines 82/D6
Lily, Ky. (40740) 237/N6
Lily, S. Dak. (57250) 298/O3
Lily, Wis. (54445) 317/J5
Lilydale, Minn. (†55050) 255/G5
Lily Dale, N.Y. (14752) 276/B6
Lilydale, Tasmania 99/D3
Lily Plain, Sask. 181/E2
Lim (fjord), Denmark 18/E8
Lim (riv.), Yugoslavia 45/D4
Lima, Ill. (62348) 222/B3
Lima (isls.), Indonesia 85/F7
Lima, Pulau (isl.), Malaysia 72/F6
Lima, Mont. (59739) 262/D6
Lima (res.), Mont. 262/D6
Lima, N.Y. (14485) 276/E5
Lima, Ohio (*45801) 284/B4
Lima, Ohio 188/K2
Lima (New Lima), Okla. (†74858) 288/D4
Lima, Paraguay 144/D3
Lima, Pa. (†19037) 294/L7
Lima (dept.), Peru 128/D8
Lima (cap.), Peru 2/F6
Lima (cap.), Peru 120/B4
Lima (cap.), Peru 128/D8
Lima (riv.), Portugal 33/B2
Lima (pt.), P. Rico 161/F2
Lima Center, Wis. (†53190) 317/J10
Limache, Chile 138/F2
Lima Duarte, Brazil 135/E2
Limal, Bolivia 136/C8
Limanowa, Poland 47/E4
Limarí (riv.), Chile 138/A8
Limasawa (isl.), Philippines 82/E6
Limassol, Cyprus 59/B3
Limassol, Cyprus 63/E5
Limavady (dist.), N. Ireland 17/H1
Limavady, N. Ireland 10/C3
Limavady, N. Ireland 17/H1
Limaville, Ohio (44640) 284/H4
Limay (riv.), Argentina 120/C6
Limay (riv.), Argentina 143/C4
Limbach-Oberfrohna, E. Germany 22/E3
Limbani, Peru 128/H10
Limbaži, U.S.S.R. 53/C2
Limbé, Haiti 158/C5
Limbourg, Belgium 27/J7
Limbunya, North. Terr. 93/B4
Limburg (prov.), Belgium 27/G7
Limburg (Limbourg), Belgium 27/J7
Limburg (prov.), Netherlands 27/H6
Limburg an der Lahn, W. Germany 22/C3
Lime, Oreg. (†97907) 291/K3
Limedsforsen, Sweden 18/H6
Limeira, Brazil 132/E8
Limeira, Brazil 135/C3
Lime Kiln, Md. (†21701) 245/J3
Limekilns, Scotland 15/D1
Limenária, Greece 45/G5
Limerick (co.), Ireland 17/D7
Limerick, Ireland 17/D6
Limerick, Ireland 10/B4
Limerick, Ireland 7/D3
Limerick○, Maine (04048) 243/B8
Limerick, Sask. 181/E6
Limeridge, Wis. (53942) 317/F9
Lime Rock, Conn. (†06039) 210/B1
Lime Springs, Iowa (52155) 229/J2
Limestone (co.), Ala. 195/E1
Limestone, Ark. (72628) 202/D2
Limestone, Fla. (†33865) 212/E4
Limestone, Maine (04750) 243/H2
Limestone○, Maine (04750) 243/H2
Limestone, Mont. (†59028) 262/F5
Limestone, N.Y. (14753) 276/C6
Limestone, Tenn. (37681) 237/R8
Limestone (co.), Texas 303/H6
Lime Village, Alaska (†99673) 196/G2
Limfjorden (fjord), Denmark 21/D4
Limfjorden (fjord), Denmark 21/A4
Limington, Maine (04049) 243/B8
Limington○, Maine (04049) 243/B8
Limmat (riv.), Switzerland 39/F2
Limmen (bight), North. Terr. 88/F2
Limmen (bight), North. Terr. 93/D3
Limmen Bight (riv.), North. Terr. 88/F3
Limmen Bight (riv.), North. Terr. 93/D4
Límni, Greece 45/F6
Límnos (isl.), Greece 45/G6
Limoeiro, Brazil 132/H4
Limoeiro do Norte, Brazil 132/G4
Limoges, France 7/E4
Limoges, France 28/D5
Limoges, Ontario 177/J2
Limon, Colo. (80828) 208/M4
Limón, C. Rica 146/K8
Limón, C. Rica 154/F6
Limón, Honduras 154/E3
Limonade, Haiti 158/C5
Limonar, Cuba 158/D1
Limoquije, Bolivia 136/C4
Limousin (trad. prov.), France, 29
Limousin (reg.), France 28/D5
Limoux, France 28/E6
Limpio, Paraguay 144/B4
Limpopo (riv.) 102/E7
Limpopo (riv.), Botswana 118/D4
Limpopo (riv.), Mozambique 118/E4
Limpopo (riv.), S. Africa 118/D4
Lim Rock, Ala. (†35776) 195/F1
Linapacan (isl.), Philippines 82/B5
Linapacan (str.), Philippines 82/B5
Linard (peak), Switzerland 39/K3
Linares, Chile 138/A11
Linares, Chile 120/B6
Linares, Mexico 150/K4
Linares, Spain 33/E3
Linares, Spain 7/D5
Linaria, Alberta 182/C2
Lincang, China 77/E7
Linch, Wyo. (82640) 319/F2
Lincklaen, N.Y. (†13052) 276/J5
Lincoln (sea) 146/M1
Lincoln (sea) 4/A12
Lincoln, Ala. (35096) 195/F3
Lincoln, Argentina 143/F7
Lincoln (co.), Ark. 202/G6
Lincoln, Ark. (72744) 202/B2
Lincoln, Calif. (95648) 204/B8
Lincoln (isl.), China 85/E2
Lincoln (co.), Colo. 208/M5
Lincoln (mt.), Colo. 208/G4
Lincoln, Del. (19960) 245/S5
Lincoln, England 13/G4
Lincoln, England 10/F4
Lincoln (co.), Georgia 217/H3
Lincoln (co.), Idaho 220/D6
Lincoln, Ill. (62656) 222/D3
Lincoln, Ind. (†46994) 227/E3
Lincoln, Iowa (50652) 229/H4
Lincoln (co.), Kansas 232/D2
Lincoln, Kansas (67455) 232/D2
Lincoln (co.), Ky. 237/M6
Lincoln (par.), La. 238/E1
Lincoln (co.), Maine 243/D7
Lincoln, Maine (04457) 243/G5
Lincoln○, Maine (04457) 243/G5
Lincoln○, Mass. (01773) 249/B6
Lincoln, Mich. (48742) 250/F4
Lincoln (co.), Minn. 255/B6
Lincoln (co.), Miss. 256/D8
Lincoln (co.), Mo. 261/L4
Lincoln, Mo. (65338) 261/F6
Lincoln (co.), Mont. 262/A2
Lincoln, Mont. (59639) 262/D4
Lincoln (co.), Nebr. 264/D4
Lincoln (cap.), Nebr. 146/J5
Lincoln (cap.), Nebr. 188/G2
Lincoln (cap.), Nebr. (*68501) 264/H4
Lincoln (co.), Nev. 266/F5
Lincoln○, N.H. (03251) 268/D3
Lincoln (mt.), N.H. 268/D3
Lincoln (co.), N. Mex. 274/D5
Lincoln, N. Mex. (88338) 274/D5
Lincoln (co.), N.C. 281/G3
Lincoln, N. Dak. (†58501) 282/J6
Lincoln (sea), N.W. Terrs. 187/M1
Lincoln (co.), Okla. 288/N3
Lincoln, Ontario 177/E4
Lincoln (co.), Oreg. 291/D3
Lincoln, Pa. (†15037) 294/C7
Lincoln (co.), S. Dak. 298/R7
Lincoln (co.), Tenn. 237/H10
Lincoln, Texas (78948) 303/H7
Lincoln (creek), Utah 30r/C2
Lincoln○, Vt. (†05443) 268/B3
Lincoln (co.), Wash. 310/G3
Lincoln, Wash. (99147) 310/G3
Lincoln (co.), W. Va. 312/B6
Lincoln (co.), Wis. 317/G5
Lincoln (co.), Wyo. 319/B3
Lincoln Beach, Oreg. (†97341) 291/C3
Lincoln Boyhood Nat'l Mem., Ind. 227/C8
Lincoln Center, Maine (04458) 243/G5
Lincoln Center, Mass. (01773) 249/B6
Lincoln City, Ind. (47552) 227/C8
Lincoln City, Oreg. (97367) 291/C3
Lincoln Gap (pass), Vt. 268/B3
Lincoln Heights, Ohio (†45201) 284/C9
Lincolnia, Va. (†22313) 307/S3
Lincoln Park, Colo. (†81212) 208/J6
Lincoln Park, Georgia (†30286) 217/D5
Lincoln Park, Mich. (48146) 250/B7
Lincoln Park, N.J. (07035) 273/A1
Lincolnshire (co.), England 13/G4
Lincolnshire, Ill. (†60015) 222/B5
Lincolnton, Georgia (30817) 217/G3
Lincolnton, N.C. (28092) 281/G4
Lincoln University, Pa. (19352) 294/L6
Lincolnville, Ind. (†46992) 227/F3
Lincolnville, Kansas (66858) 232/F3
Lincolnville, Maine (04849) 243/E7
Lincolnville○, Maine (04849) 243/E7
Lincolnville, Nova Scotia 168/G3
Lincolnville, S.C. (†29483) 296/G6
Lincolnville Center, Maine (04850) 243/E7
Lincoln Wolds (hills), England 13/G4
Lincolnwood, Ill. (†60645) 222/B5
Lincroft, N.J. (07738) 273/E3
L'Incudine (mt.), France 28/B7
Lind, Wash. (99341) 310/G4
Linda, Calif. (†95901) 204/D4
Lindale, Alberta 182/C3
Lindale, Georgia (30147) 217/B2
Lindale, Texas (75771) 303/J5
Lindau, W. Germany 22/C5
Lindberg, Alberta 182/E3
Linden, Ala. (36748) 195/C6
Linden, Alberta 182/D4
Linden, Ariz. (†85901) 198/E4
Linden, Calif. (95236) 204/D5
Linden, Guyana 131/L2
Linden, Ind. (47955) 227/D4
Linden, Iowa (50146) 229/E5
Linden, Mich. (48451) 250/F6
Linden, N.J. (07036) 273/A3
Linden, N.C. (28356) 281/M4
Linden (mts.), Switzerland 39/F2
Linden, Tenn. (37096) 237/F9
Linden, Texas (75563) 303/K4
Linden, Va. (22642) 307/M3
Linden, W. Va. (25256) 312/D5
Linden, Wis. (53553) 317/F10
Linden Beach, Ontario 177/B6
Lindenhurst, Ill. (†60046) 222/B4
Lindenhurst, N.Y. (11757) 276/O9
Lindenwold, N.J. (08021) 273/B4
Lindenwood, Ill. (61049) 222/D1
Lindesberg, Sweden 18/J7
Lindesnes (cape), Norway 7/E3
Lindesnes (cape), Norway 18/E8
Lindi (reg.), Tanzania 115/G5
Lindi, Tanzania 102/F5
Lindi, Tanzania 115/G5
Lindi (riv.), Zaire 115/E3
Lindisfarne (Holy) (dist.), England 13/F2
Lindisfarne (Holy) (isl.), England 10/F3
Lindley, N.Y. (14858) 276/F6
Lindon, Colo. (80740) 208/N3
Lindon, Utah (†84062) 304/C3
Líndos, Greece 45/J7
Lindrith, N. Mex. (87029) 274/C2
Lindsay, Calif. (93247) 204/F7
Lindsay, La. (†70748) 238/H5
Lindsay, Mont. (59339) 262/L3
Lindsay, Nebr. (68644) 264/G3
Lindsay, Okla. (73052) 288/L5
Lindsay, Ontario 177/F3
Lindsborg, Kansas (67456) 232/E3
Lindsey, Ohio (43442) 284/D3
Lindsey, Wis. (†54449) 317/F6
Lindside, W. Va. (24951) 312/E8
Lindstrom, Minn. (55045) 255/F5
Line (isls.) 2/B6
Line (isls.), Pacific 87/K5
Lineboro, Md. (21088) 245/L2
Linesville, Pa. (16424) 294/A2
Lineville, Ala. (36266) 195/G4
Lineville, Iowa (50147) 229/G7
Linfen, China 77/H4
Linfield, Pa. (19468) 294/L5
Linganore (creek), Md. 245/J3
Lingao, China 77/G8
Lingayen, Philippines 85/F2
Lingayen, Philippines 82/C2
Lingayen (gulf), Philippines 82/C2
Lingen, W. Germany 22/B2
Lingga (arch.), Indonesia 85/D5
Lingga (isl.), Indonesia 85/D6
Lingle, Wyo. (82223) 319/H3
Linglestown, Pa. (17112) 294/J5
Lingling, China 77/H6
Lingo, N. Mex. (88123) 274/F5
Lingqui, China 77/H4
Lingshan, China 77/G7

Magaguadavic 403

Lutsen, Minn. (55612) 255/F2
Lutsk, U.S.S.R. 7/G3
Lutsk, U.S.S.R. 52/B4
Lutsk, U.S.S.R. 48/C4
Luttrell, Tenn. (37779) 237/O8
Lutts, Tenn. (38471) 237/F10
Lutz, Fla. (33549) 212/D3
Lützelflüh, Switzerland 39/E3
Lützow-Holm (bay) 5/C3
Luuq, Somalia 115/H3
Luverne, Ala. (36049) 195/F7
Lu Verne, Iowa (50560) 229/E3
Luvernen Minn. (56156) 255/B7
Luverne, N. Dak. (58056) 282/P5
Luvua (riv.), Zaire 115/E5
Luwingu, Zambia 115/E6
Luwuk, Indonesia 85/G6
Lux, Miss. (†39401) 256/F8
Luxembourg 7/E4
Luxembourg (prov.), Belgium 27/G9
LUXEMBOURG 27/J9
Luxembourg (cap.), Luxembourg 27/J9
Luxemburg, Iowa (52056) 229/L3
Luxemburg, Minn. (†56301) 255/D5
Luxemburg, Wis. (54217) 317/L6
Luxeuil-les-Bains, France 28/G4
Luxi, China 77/E7
Luxi, China 77/F7
Luxor, Egypt 102/F2
Luxor, Egypt 59/B4
Luxor, Egypt 111/F2
Luxora, Ark. (72358) 202/K2
Luz, Brazil 135/D1
Luz (isl.), Chile 138/D6
Luza, U.S.S.R. 52/G2
Luzein, Switzerland 39/J3
Luzern (canton), Switzerland 39/F2
Luzern (Lucerne), Switzerland 39/F2
Luzerne, Iowa (52257) 229/J5
Luzerne, Mich. (48636) 250/E4
Luzerne (co.), Pa. 294/L3
Luzerne, Pa. (18709) 294/E7
Luzhai, China 77/G7
Luzhi, China 77/G6
Luzhou (Luchow), China 77/G6
Luziânia, Brazil 132/E7
Luzilândia, Brazil 132/F3
Lužnice (riv.), Czech. 41/C2
Luzon (isl.), Philippines 2/R5
Luzon (isl.), Philippines 54/O8
Luzon (isl.), Philippines 82/C3
Luzon (isl.), Philippines 85/G2
Luzon (sea), Philippines 82/B4
Luzon (str.), Philippines 82/A2
Luz-Saint-Sauveur, France 28/C6
L'vov, U.S.S.R. 7/G4
L'vov, U.S.S.R. 48/C4
L'vov (Lwów), U.S.S.R. 52/B5
Lyakhov (isls.), U.S.S.R. 4/B3
Lyal (isl.), Ontario 177/C3
Lyallpur (Faisalabad), Pakistan 68/C2
Lyallpur (Faisalabad), Pakistan 59/K3
Lyalta, Alberta 182/D4
Lyatkhovskiye (isls.), U.S.S.R. 48/O2
Lybster, Scotland 10/E1
Lybster, Scotland 15/E2
Lycan, Colo. (†81054) 208/P7
Lycksele, Sweden 18/L4
Lycoming, N.Y. (13093) 276/H3
Lycoming (co.), Pa. 294/H3
Lycoming (creek), Pa. 294/H3
Lydallville, Conn. (†06040) 210/F1
Lydd, England 13/H7
Lydda, Israel 65/B4
Lydenburg, S. Africa 118/E4
Lydia, Minn. (†55352) 255/E6
Lydia, S.C. (29079) 296/G3
Lydia Mills, S.C. (29325) 296/D3
Lydick, Ind. (†46601) 227/E1
Lyell (mt.), Alberta 182/B4
Lyell (isl.), Br. Col. 184/B4
Lyell (mt.), Br. Col. 184/J4
Lyell (mt.), Tasmania 99/B4
Lyerly, Georgia (30730) 217/B2
Lyford, Ind. (†47874) 227/C5
Lyford, Texas (78569) 303/G11
Lykens, Pa. (17048) 294/J4
Lyle, Minn. (55953) 255/F7
Lyle, Wash. (98635) 310/D5
Lyles, Tenn. (37098) 237/G9
Lyleton, Manitoba 179/A5
Lyman, Miss. (†39501) 256/F10
Lyman, Nebr. (69352) 264/A3
Lyman○, N.H. (†03585) 268/D3
Lyman, S.C. (29365) 296/C2
Lyman (co.), S. Dak. 298/J6
Lyman, Utah (84749) 304/C5
Lyman, Wash. (98263) 310/D2
Lyman, Wyo. (82937) 319/B4
Lyme (bay), England 13/D7
Lyme (bay), England 10/E5
Lyme○, N.H. (03768) 268/C4
Lyme Center, N.H. (03769) 268/C4
Lyme Regis, England 13/E7
Lyme Regis, England 10/E5
Lymington, England 10/F5
Lymington, England 13/F7
Lymm, England 13/H2
Lymm, England 10/G2
Lyn, Ontario 177/J3
Lyna (riv.), Poland 47/E1
Lynbrook, N.Y. (11563) 276/P7
Lynch, Ky. (40855) 237/R7
Lynch, Md. (21646) 245/O3
Lynch, Nebr. (68746) 264/F2
Lynchburg, Mo. (65543) 261/H7
Lynchburg, N. Dak. (†58023) 282/R6
Lynchburg, Ohio (45142) 284/C7
Lynchburg, S.C. (29080) 296/G3
Lynchburg, Tenn. (37352) 237/J10
Lynchburg, Va. 188/L3
Lynchburg, Va. 146/K6
Lynchburg (I.C.), Va. (*24501) 307/K6
Lynches (riv.), S.C. 296/H3
Lynch Station, Va. (24571) 307/K6
Lynd, Minn. (56157) 255/C6
Lynd, Queensland 95/C3
Lyndeborough○, N.H. (†03082) 268/D6
Lynden, Ontario 177/D4
Lynden, Wash. (98264) 310/C2
Lyndhurst○, N.J. (07071) 273/B2
Lyndhurst, N.S. Wales 97/E3
Lyndhurst, Ohio (44124) 284/J9
Lyndhurst, Ontario 177/H3
Lyndhurst, S. Australia 88/F6
Lyndhurst, S. Australia 94/E4
Lyndoch, S. Australia 94/C6
Lyndon, Ill. (61261) 222/D2
Lyndon, Kansas (66451) 232/G3
Lyndon, Ohio (45649) 284/D7
Lyndon○, Vt. (05849) 268/C2
Lyndon, W. Australia 92/A3
Lyndon B. Johnson Nat'l Hist. Site, Texas 303/F7
Lyndon B. Johnson Space Ctr., Texas 303/K2
Lyndon Center, Vt. (05850) 268/C2
Lyndon Station, Wis. (53944) 317/F8
Lyndonville, N.Y. (14098) 276/D4
Lyndonville, Vt. (05851) 268/D2
Lyndora, Pa. (16045) 294/B4
Lynedoch, Ontario 177/D5
Lyness, Scotland 15/E2
Lyngby, Denmark 21/F6
Lynhurst, Ontario 177/C5
Lynn, Ala. (35575) 195/C2
Lynn, Ark. (72440) 202/H2
Lynn, Ind. (47355) 227/H4
Lynn, Mass. (*01901) 249/D6
Lynn, N.C. (28750) 281/E4
Lynn (co.), Texas 303/C4
Lynn, Wis. (†54436) 317/F6
Lynn Canal (inlet), Alaska 196/M1
Lynn Center, Ill. (61262) 222/C2
Lynn Creek, Miss. (†39739) 256/G4
Lynndyl, Utah (84640) 304/B4
Lynnfield○, Mass. (01940) 249/D5
Lynnfield Center (Lynnfield P.O.), Mass. (†01940) 249/C5
Lynn Grove, Ky. (42062) 237/E7
Lynn Haven, Fla. (32444) 212/C6
Lynn Lake, Man. 162/G4
Lynn Lake, Man. 146/H4
Lynn Lake, Manitoba 179/H2
Lynnview, Ky. (†40201) 237/K4
Lynnville, Ill. (†62650) 222/C4
Lynnville, Ind. (47619) 227/C8
Lynnville, Iowa (50153) 229/H5
Lynnville, Ky. (42063) 237/D7
Lynnville, Tenn. (38472) 237/G10
Lynnwood, Wash. (98036) 310/C3
Lynton, England 10/E5
Lynton, England 13/D6
Lynwood, Calif. (90262) 204/C11
Lynwood, Ill. (†60411) 222/C6
Lynx (lake), N.W. Terrs. 187/H3
Lynxville, Wis. (54640) 317/D9
Lyon, France 7/E4
Lyon, France 28/F5
Lyon (co.), Iowa 229/A2
Lyon (co.), Kansas 232/F3
Lyon (co.), Ky. 237/E6
Lyon (co.), Minn. 255/C6
Lyon, Miss. (38645) 256/D2
Lyon (co.), Nev. 266/B3
Lyon (inlet), N.W. Terrs. 187/K3
Lyon, Loch (lake), Scotland 15/D4
Lyon (riv.), Scotland 15/D4
Lyon Mountain, N.Y. (12952) 276/N1
Lyonnais (trad. prov.) France 29
Lyons, Colo. (80540) 208/J2
Lyons, Georgia (30436) 217/H6
Lyons, Ill. (60534) 222/B6
Lyons, Ind. (47443) 227/C7
Lyons, Kansas (67554) 232/D3
Lyons, Ky. (†40051) 237/K5
Lyons, Mich. (48851) 250/E6
Lyons, Nebr. (68038) 264/H3
Lyons, N.J. (07939) 273/D2
Lyons, N.Y. (14489) 276/F4
Lyons, Ohio (43533) 284/B2
Lyons, Oreg. (97358) 291/E3
Lyons (Lyon Station), Pa. (19536) 294/L5
Lyons, S. Dak. (57041) 298/R6
Lyons (riv.), W. Australia 88/B4
Lyons (riv.), W. Australia 92/A4
Lyons, Wis. (53148) 317/K10
Lyons Brook, Nova Scotia 168/F3
Lyons Falls, N.Y. (13368) 276/K3
Lyons Plain, Conn. (†06880) 210/B4
Lyon Station, Pa. (19536) 294/L5
Lyra (reef), Papua N.G. 86/C1
Lys (riv.), Belgium 27/B7
Lys (riv.), France 28/E2
Lysaker, Norway 18/D3
Lysá nad Labem, Czech. 41/C1
Lysander, N.Y. (13094) 276/H4
Lysekil, Sweden 18/G7
Lysite, Wyo. (82642) 319/E2
Lyss, Switzerland 39/D2
Lyster, Québec 172/F3
Lys'va, U.S.S.R. 7/K3
Lys'va, U.S.S.R. 48/F4
Lys'va, U.S.S.R. 52/J3
Lytham Saint Anne's, England 13/G1
Lytham Saint Anne's, England 10/F1
Lytle, Texas (78052) 303/J11
Lyttelton, N. Zealand 100/D5
Lytton, Br. Col. 184/G5
Lytton, Iowa (50561) 229/D4
Lyubertsy, U.S.S.R. 52/E3
Lyubotin, U.S.S.R. 52/E4
Lyudinovo, U.S.S.R. 52/D4

M

Ma'ad, Jordan 65/D2
Maalaea, Hawaii (†96753) 218/J2
Maalaea (bay), Hawaii 218/J2
Ma'alot-Tarshiha, Israel 65/C1
Ma'an (dist.), Jordan 65/D5
Ma'an, Jordan 65/E5
Ma'an, Jordan 59/C3
Ma'anshan, China 77/J5
Maarianhamina (Mariehamn), Finland 18/M7
Maarssen, Netherlands 27/F4
Maas (riv.), Netherlands 27/G5
Maasbree, Netherlands 27/H6
Maaseik, Belgium 27/H6
Maasin, Philippines 82/E5
Maasmechelen, Belgium 27/H7
Maassluis, Netherlands 27/E5
Maastricht, Netherlands 27/H7
Maatsuyker (isls.), Tasmania 99/C5
Mababe (depr.), Botswana 118/C3
Mabalane, Mozambique 118/E4
Mabank, Texas (75147) 303/H5
Mabaruma, Guyana 131/B1
Mabay, Cuba 158/H4
Mabel (lake), Br. Col. 184/H5
Mabel, Minn. (55954) 255/G7
Mabelvale, Ark. (72103) 202/F4
Maben, Miss. (39750) 256/F3
Maben, W. Va. (25870) 312/D7
Maberly, Ontario 177/H3
Mabie, W. Va. (26278) 312/F5
Mabille (lake), Newf. 166/B3
Mabini, Philippines 82/E6
Mablethorpe and Sutton, England 13/H4
Mablethorpe and Sutton, England 10/G4
Mableton, Georgia (30059) 217/J1
Mabote, Mozambique 118/E4
Mabou, Nova Scotia 168/G2
Mabou (harb.), Nova Scotia 168/G2
Mabou Highlands (hills), Nova Scotia 168/G2
Mabrouk, Mali 106/D5
Mabscott, W. Va. (25871) 312/D7
Mabton, Wash. (98935) 310/E4
Macá (mt.), Chile 138/D5
Macachín, Argentina 143/D4
Macaé, Brazil 135/F3
Macaé, Brazil 132/F8
Macaíba, Brazil 132/H4
Macajalar (bay), Philippines 82/E6
Macalister, Br. Col. 184/F4
Macaloge, Mozambique 118/F2
MacAlpine (lake), N.W. Terrs. 187/H3
Macamic, Québec 174/B3
Macan (isls.), Indonesia 85/G7
Macanao (pen.), Venezuela 124/F2
Mação, Portugal 33/B3
Macao (Macau) 77
Macapá, Brazil 120/D2
Macapá, Brazil 132/D2
Macará, Ecuador 128/C5
Macaranaima, Colombia 126/E7
Macarena, Serranía de La (mts.), Colombia 126/D6
Macareo Santo Niño, Venezuela 124/H3
Macarthur, Victoria 97/A6
Macas, Ecuador 128/D4
Macassar, S. Africa 118/F6
Macau 54/N7
Macau, Brazil 120/F3
Macau, Brazil 132/G4
MACAU (MACAO) 77
Macau (Macao) (cap.), Macau 77/H7
Macau 2/Q4
Macaúbas, Brazil 132/F6
Macaya (mt.), Haiti 158/A6
Macbeth, S.C. (†29431) 296/H5
Maccan, Nova Scotia 168/D3
Maccarese, Italy 34/F6
Macclenny, Fla. (32063) 212/D1
Maccles (lake), Newf. 166/C1
Macclesfield, England 10/G2
Macclesfield, England 13/H2
Macclesfield, N.C. (27852) 281/O3
Macdiarmid, Ontario 177/H5
MacDill A.F.B., Fla. 212/C3
Macdoel, Calif. (96058) 204/D2
Macdona, Texas (78054) 303/J11
Macdonald, Manitoba 179/D4
Macdonald (lake), North. Terr. 93/B7
Macdonald (lake), W. Australia 88/D4
Macdonald (lake), W. Australia 92/E3
Macdonaldton, Pa. (†15530) 294/E6
Macdonnell (ranges), Australia 87/D8
Macdonnell (ranges), North. Terr. 88/E4
Macdonnell (ranges), North. Terr. 93/C7
Macdowall, Sask. 181/E2
Macduff, Scotland 10/E2
Macduff, Scotland 15/F3
Mace, Ind. (†47933) 227/D4
Mace, W. Va. (†26281) 312/F6
Macedon, N.Y. (14502) 276/F4
Macedonia, Ark. (†71753) 202/D7
Macedonia, Conn. (†06757) 210/A2
Macedonia (reg.), Greece 45/E5
Macedonia, Ill. (62860) 222/E5
Macedonia, Iowa (51549) 229/C6
Macedonia, Ohio (44056) 284/J10
Macedonia (rep.), Yugoslavia 45/E5
Maceió, Brazil 120/F3
Maceió, Brazil 132/H5
Macel, Miss. (†38950) 256/D3
Macenta, Guinea 102/B4
Macenta, Guinea 106/C7
Maceo, Cuba 158/H3
Maceo, Ky. (42355) 237/H5
Macerata (prov.), Italy 34/D3
Macerata, Italy 34/D3
Maces (bay), New Bruns. 170/D3
Maces Bay, New Bruns. 170/D3
Macfarlan, W. Va. (26148) 312/D4
Macfarlane (lake), S. Australia 88/F6
Macfarlane (lake), S. Australia 94/E5
Macgillicuddy's Reeks (mts.), Ireland 17/B7
MacGregor, Manitoba 179/D5
MacGregor's Bay, Ontario 177/G2
Mach, Pakistan 59/J4
Mach, Pakistan 68/B3
Macha, Bolivia 136/B6
Machacamarca, Bolivia 136/B5
Machachi, Ecuador 128/C3
Machado, Brazil 135/C2
Machakos, Kenya 115/G4
Machala, Ecuador 120/B3
Machala, Ecuador 128/B4
Machalí, Chile 138/G5
Machalilla, Ecuador 128/B3
Machaneng, Botswana 118/D4
Machanga, Mozambique 118/F4
Machareti, Bolivia 136/D7
Machattie (lake), Queensland 88/G5
Machattie (lake), Queensland 95/B5
Machaze, Mozambique 118/E4
Machelen, Belgium 27/C9
Macheng, China 77/J5
Machers, The (pen.), Scotland 15/D6
Machias, Maine (04654) 243/J6
Machias○, Maine (04654) 243/J6
Machias (bay), Maine 243/J6
Machias (riv.), Maine 243/H6
Machias (riv.), Maine 243/F2
Machias-Lime Lake, N.Y. (14101) 276/D6
Machiasport, Maine (04655) 243/H6
Machiasport○, Maine (04655) 243/H6
Machias Seal (isl.), Maine 243/J7
Machico, Portugal 33/A2
Machida, Japan 81/O2
Machilipatnam, India 68/E5
Machipongo, Va. (23405) 307/S6
Machiques, Venezuela 124/B3
Macho, Arroyo del (creek), N. Mex. 274/D5
Machrihanish, Scotland 15/C5
Machupicchu, Peru 128/F9
Machupo (riv.), Bolivia 136/C3
Machynlleth, Wales 13/D5
Machynlleth, Wales 10/D4
Macia, Mozambique 118/E4
Maciel, Argentina 143/F6
Maciel, Paraguay 144/D5
Maciel, Arroyo (riv.), Uruguay 145/C4
Macina (depr.), Mali 106/D6
MacIntyre (riv.), N. S. Wales 88/J5
Macintyre (riv.), N.S. Wales 97/E1
Macintyre (riv.), Queensland 95/D6
Mack, Colo. (81525) 208/B4
Mack, Ohio (†45202) 284/B9
MacKay, Alberta 182/C3
MacKay (riv.), Alberta 182/D1
Mackay, Australia 87/F8
Mackay (lake), Australia 87/D8
Mackay, Idaho (83251) 220/E6
Mackay (res.), Idaho 220/E6
Mackay (lake), North. Terr. 88/D4
Mackay (lake), North. Terr. 93/A7
MacKay (lake), N.W. Terrs. 187/G3
Mackay, Queensland 88/H4
Mackay, Queensland 95/D4
Mackay (lake), W. Australia 92/E3
Mackenzie (bay) 5/C4
Mackenzie, Br. Col. 184/F2
Mackenzie, Br. Col. 184/F2
Mackenzie (bay), Canada 4/B16
Mackenzie (mts.), Canada 4/C16
Mackenzie (mts.), Canada 146/E3
Mackenzie (riv.), Canada 2/C2
Mackenzie (riv.), Canada 4/C16
Mackenzie, Mo. (†63101) 261/P3
Mackenzie (dist.), N.W.T. 162/E3
Mackenzie (bay), N.W. Terrs. 187/E3
Mackenzie (mts.), N.W. Terrs. 187/E3
Mackenzie (riv.), N.W.T. 162/C2
Mackenzie (riv.), N.W.T. 146/F3
Mackenzie (riv.), N.W. Terrs. 187/F3
Mackenzie (bay), Yukon 162/C2
Mackenzie (bay), Yukon 187/E3
Mackenzie (mts.), Yukon 187/E3
Mackenzie King (isl.), Canada 4/B15
Mackenzie King (isl.), N.W.T. 162/M3
Mackenzie King (isl.), N.W. Terrs. 187/G2
Mackey, Ind. (47654) 227/C8
Mackeys, N.C. (†27970) 281/R3
Mackeyville, Pa. (17750) 294/H3
Mackinac (co.), Mich. 250/D2
Mackinac (isl.), Mich. 250/E3
Mackinac (str.), Mich. 250/E3
Mackinac Island, Mich. (49757) 250/E3
Mackinaw, Ill. (61755) 222/D3
Mackinaw (riv.), Ill. 222/E3
Mackinaw City, Mich. (49701) 250/E3
Macklin, Sask. 181/A3
Macks, Ark. (72113) 202/H2
Macksburg, Iowa (50155) 229/E6
Macksburg, Ohio (45746) 284/G6
Macks Creek, Mo. (65786) 261/G7
Macks Inn, Idaho (83433) 220/G5
Macksville, Kansas (67557) 232/D4
Macksville, N.S. Wales 97/G2
Mackville, Ky. (40040) 237/L5
Maclean, N.S. Wales 97/G1
Maclean (str.), N.W. Terrs. 187/H2
Maclear, S. Africa 118/D6
Maclear (cape), S. Africa 118/F7
Macmillan (pass), N.W. Terrs. 187/F3
Macmillan (pass), Yukon 187/F3
Macmillan (riv.), Yukon 187/E3
Macnean (lake), Ireland 17/F3
Macnean (lake), N. Ireland 17/F3
MacNutt, Sask. 181/K4
Macomb, Ill. (61455) 222/C3
Macomb (co.), Mich. 250/G6
Macomb, Okla. (74852) 288/M4
Macomer, Italy 34/B4
Macomia, Mozambique 118/F2
Macon (co.), Ala. 195/G6
Mâcon, France 28/F4
Macon, Ga. 188/K4
Macon, Ga. 146/K6
Macon (co.), Georgia 217/D6
Macon, Georgia (*31201) 217/E5
Macon (co.), Ill. 222/E4
Macon, Ill. (62544) 222/E4
Macon (bayou), La. 238/H1
Macon, Miss. (39341) 256/G4
Macon (co.), Mo. 261/G3
Macon, Mo. (63552) 261/H3
Macon, Nebr. (†68939) 264/E4
Macon (co.), N.C. 281/B4
Macon, N.C. (27551) 281/N2
Macon, Ohio (†45171) 284/C8
Macon (co.), Tenn. 237/J7
Macon, Tenn. (38048) 237/B10
Macondo, Angola 115/D6
Macorís (cape), Dom. Rep. 158/E5
Macosquin, N. Ireland 17/H1
Macotera, Spain 33/D2
Macouba, Martinique 161/C5
Macoun, Sask. 181/H6
Macoupin (co.), Ill. 222/D4
Macoupin (riv.), Ill. 222/C4
Macouria, Fr. Guiana 131/E3
Macquarie (riv.), N. S. Wales 88/H6
Macquarie (lake), N.S. Wales 97/F3
Macquarie (riv.), N.S. Wales 97/D2
Macquarie (harb.), Tasmania 88/G8
Macquarie (harb.), Tasmania 99/B4
Macquarie (riv.), Tasmania 99/D3
Mac-Robertson Land (reg.) 5/B4
Macroom, Ireland 10/B5
Macroom, Ireland 17/C8
Macrorie, Sask. 181/E4
Mactan (isl.), Philippines 82/E5
Mactaquac (lake), New Bruns. 170/C3
MacTier, Ontario 177/E2
Macumba (riv.), S. Australia 88/F5
Macumba, The (riv.), S. Australia 94/E2
Macungie, Pa. (18062) 294/L4
Macurijes (pt.), Cuba 158/F3
Macuro, Venezuela 124/H2
Macusani, Peru 128/G10
Macuspana, Mexico 150/N8
Macuto, Venezuela 124/E2
Macwahoc○, Maine (†04451) 243/G4
Macy, Ind. (46951) 227/E3
Macy, Nebr. (68039) 264/H2
Mad (riv.), Calif. 204/B3
Mad (riv.), Conn. 210/C2
Mad (riv.), Conn. 210/C1
Mad (riv.), N.H. 268/D4
Mad (riv.), Ohio 284/C6
Mad (riv.), Vt. 268/B3
Ma'daba, Jordan 65/D4
Madadi, Chad 111/D4
Madagascal (pond), Maine 243/G5
Madagascar 2/M6
Madagascar 102/G7
MADAGASCAR 118/H3
Madaket, Mass. (†02554) 249/O7
Madama, Niger 106/G4
Madame (isl.), Nova Scotia 168/H3
Madang, Papua N.G. 85/B7
Madang, Papua N.G. 87/E6
Madaoua, Niger 106/F6
Madaras, Hungary 41/E3
Madaripur, Bangladesh 68/G4
Madauk, Burma 72/C3
Madawaska, Maine (04756) 243/G1
Madawaska○, Maine (04756) 243/G1
Madawaska (co.), New Bruns. 170/B1
Madawaska (riv.), New Bruns. 170/B1
Madawaska, Ontario 177/F2
Madawaska (riv.), Ontario 177/G2
Madawaska (riv.), Québec 172/J2
Madbury○, N.H. (†03820) 268/F5
Maddela, Philippines 82/C2
Madden, Alberta 182/C4
Madden, Miss. (39109) 256/F5
Maddock, N. Dak. (58348) 282/L4
Maddy, Loch (inlet), Scotland 15/A3
Madeira (riv.), Brazil 2/F6
Madeira (riv.), Brazil 120/C3
Madeira (riv.), Brazil 132/A4
Madeira, Ohio (45243) 284/C9
Madeira (isl.), Portugal 33/A2
Madeira (isl.), Portugal 106/A2
Madeira (isls.), Portugal 2/H4
Madeira (isls.), Portugal 102/A1
Madeira (isls.), Portugal 33/A2
Madeira (isls.) Portugal 106/A2
Madeira Beach, Fla. (33738) 212/B3
Madeira Park, Br. Col. 184/J2
Madeleine (cape), Québec 172/D1
Madelia, Minn. (56062) 255/D6
Madeline, Calif. (96119) 204/E2
Madeline (isl.), Wis. 317/E2
Maden, Turkey 63/H3
Madera (co.), Calif. 204/F6
Madera, Calif. (93637) 204/E7
Madera, Mexico 150/F2
Madera, Pa. (16661) 294/F4
Madera Canyon, Ariz. (†85637) 198/E7
Madh, India 68/B7
Madhubani, India 68/F3
Madhya Pradesh (state), India 68/D4
Madidi (riv.), Bolivia 136/A3
Madill, Okla. (73446) 288/N6
Madinat ash Sha'b, P.D.R. Yemen 59/E7
Madinat el-Thawra, Syria 63/H5
Madingo-Kayes, Congo 115/B4
Madingou, Congo 115/B4
Madirovalo, Madagascar 118/H3
Madison (co.), Ala. 195/E1
Madison, Ala. (35758) 195/E1
Madison (co.), Ark. 202/C1
Madison, Ark. (72359) 202/J4
Madison, Calif. (95653) 204/D5
Madison, Conn. (06443) 210/E3
Madison○, Conn. (06443) 210/E3
Madison (co.), Fla. 212/C1
Madison, Fla. (32340) 212/C1
Madison (co.), Georgia 217/F2
Madison, Georgia (30650) 217/F3
Madison (co.), Idaho 220/G6
Madison (co.), Ill. 222/D5
Madison, Ill. (62060) 222/A2
Madison (co.), Ind. 227/F4
Madison, Ind. (47250) 227/G7
Madison (co.), Iowa 229/E6
Madison, Kansas (66860) 232/F3
Madison (co.), Ky. 237/N5
Madison (par.), La. 238/H2
Madison, Maine (04950) 243/D6
Madison○, Maine (04950) 243/D6
Madison, Md. (21648) 245/O6
Madison, Minn. (56256) 255/B5
Madison (co.), Miss. 256/D5
Madison, Miss. (39110) 256/D6
Madison (co.), Mo. 261/M8
Madison, Mo. (65263) 261/H4
Madison (co.), Mont. 262/D5
Madison (riv.), Mont. 262/E5
Madison (co.), Nebr. 264/G3
Madison, Nebr. (68748) 264/G3
Madison○, N.H. (03849) 268/E4
Madison (mt.), N.H. 268/E3
Madison, N.J. (07940) 273/E2
Madison (co.), N.Y. 276/J5
Madison, N.Y. (13402) 276/J5
Madison (co.), N.C. 281/D3
Madison, N.C. (27025) 281/J2
Madison (co.), Ohio 284/D6
Madison, Ohio (44057) 284/H2
Madison, Sask. 181/B4
Madison, S.C. (29693) 296/A2
Madison, S.C. (†29829) 296/D4
Madison, S. Dak. (57042) 298/P6
Madison (lake), S. Dak. 298/P6
Madison (co.), Tenn. 237/D9
Madison (co.), Texas 303/J6
Madison (co.), Va. 307/M4
Madison, Va. (22727) 307/M4
Madison, W. Va. (25130) 312/C6
Madison (cap.), Wis. 146/K5
Madison (cap.), Wis. 188/H2
Madison (cap.), Wis. (*53701) 317/H9
Madison, Wyo. (†82190) 319/B1
Madison (plat.), Wyo. 319/B1
Madisonburg, Ohio (†44691) 284/G4
Madison Heights, Mich. (48071) 250/B6
Madison Heights, Va. (24572) 307/K6
Madison Lake, Minn. (56063) 255/E6
Madisonville, Ky. (42431) 237/F6
Madisonville, La. (70447) 238/K6
Madisonville, Tenn. (37354) 237/N9
Madisonville, Texas (77864) 303/J7
Madiun, Indonesia 85/K2
Madley (mt.), W. Australia 92/D4
Madoc, Mont. (†59222) 262/L2
Madoc, Ontario 177/G3
Mado Gashi, Kenya 115/G3
Madoi, China 77/E4
Madona, U.S.S.R. 53/C2
Madona, U.S.S.R. 52/C3
Madonna, Md. (†21161) 245/M2
Madraka, Ras (cape), Oman 59/G6
Madran, New Bruns. 170/E1
Madras, India 68/E6
Madras, India 54/K8
Madras, India 2/P5
Madras, Oreg. (97741) 291/F3
Madre (lag.), Mexico 150/L4
Madre (lag.), Texas 188/G5
Madre (lag.), Texas 303/G11
Madre de Dios (riv.) 120/C4
Madre de Diós (riv.), Bolivia 136/A3
Madre de Dios (isl.), Chile 120/B8
Madre de Dios (isl.), Chile 138/D8
Madre de Dios (dept.), Peru 128/G8
Madre de Dios, Peru 128/G9
Madre de Dios (riv.), Peru 128/G9
Madre del Sur, Sierra (mts.), Mexico 150/K8
Madre Occidental, Sierra (mts.), Mexico 150/F3
Madre Oriental, Sierra (mts.), Mexico 150/J4
Madrid, Ala. (36348) 195/H8
Madrid, Iowa (50156) 229/F5
Madrid○, Maine (†04966) 243/B6
Madrid, Nebr. (69150) 264/C4
Madrid, N. Mex. (†87010) 274/C3
Madrid, N.Y. (13660) 276/K1
Madrid (prov.), Spain 33/E2
Madrid (cap.), Spain 7/D4
Madrid (cap.), Spain 33/F4
Madrid (cap.), Spain 2/J4
Madridejos, Spain 33/E3
Madrigal de las Altas Torres, Spain 33/D2
Madrigalejo, Spain 33/D3
Madrisahorn (mt.), Switzerland 39/J3
Madroñera, Spain 33/D3
Madsen, Ontario 175/B2
Madugula, India 68/E5
Madura (isl.), Indonesia 54/N10
Madura (isl.), Indonesia 85/K2
Madura (str.), Indonesia 85/K2
Madura, W. Australia 92/D5
Madurai, India 54/J9
Madurai, India 68/D7
Madvar, Kuh-e (mt.), Iran 59/F3
Madvar, Kuh-e (mt.), Iran 66/F3
Maebashi, Japan 81/J5
Mae Hong Son, Thailand 72/C3
Mae Klong, Mae Nam (riv.), Thailand 72/C4
Mael, Norway 18/F6
Maella, Spain 33/G2
Maeser, Utah (†84078) 304/E3
Maesteg, Wales 13/D6
Maestra, Sierra (mts.), Cuba 158/H4
Maevatanana, Madagascar 118/H3
Maeystown, Ill. (62256) 222/C5
Mafeking, Manitoba 179/B2
Mafeking (Mafikeng), S. Africa 118/C5
Mafeteng, Lesotho 118/D5
Maffin (bay), Indonesia 85/K6
Maffra, Victoria 97/D5
Mafia (isl.), Tanzania 102/G5
Mafia (isl.), Tanzania 115/H5
Mafikeng (Mafeking), S. Africa 118/C5
Mafra, Brazil 132/D9
Mafra, Portugal 33/B3
Magadan, U.S.S.R. 2/S3
Magadan, U.S.S.R. 54/R4
Magadan, U.S.S.R. 48/P4
Magadi, Kenya 115/G4
Magadino, Switzerland 39/G4
Magaguadavic, New Bruns. 170/C3
Magaguadavic (lake), New Bruns. 170/C3
Magaguadavic (riv.), New Bruns. 170/C3

Mariano Roque Alonso 405

Mandalgovĭ, Mongolia 77/G2
Mandali, Iraq 66/D4
Mandal-Ovoo, Mongolia 77/F3
Mandalya (gulf), Turkey 63/B4
Mandan, N. Dak. 188/F1
Mandan, N. Dak. (58554) 282/J6
Mandaon, Philippines 82/D4
Mandar (cape), Indonesia 85/F6
Mandaree, N. Dak. (58757) 282/E4
Mandaue, Philippines 82/E5
Mandeb, Bab el (str.), Saudi Arabia 59/D7
Mandeb, Bab el (str.), Yemen Arab Rep. 59/D7
Mandera, Kenya 115/H3
Manderson, S. Dak. (57756) 298/D7
Manderson, Wyo. (82432) 319/E1
Mandeville, Ark. (†75501) 202/C7
Mandeville, Jamaica 158/H6
Mandeville, La. (70448) 238/L6
Mandi, India 68/D2
Mandié, Mozambique 118/E3
Mandimba, Mozambique 118/F2
Mandinga, Panama 154/H6
Mandioré (lag.), Bolivia 136/F6
Mandla, India 68/E4
Mándok, Hungary 41/G2
Mandritsara, Madagascar 118/H3
Mand Rud (riv.), Iran 59/F4
Mand Rud (riv.), Iran 66/G6
Mandsaur, India 68/C4
Mandurah, W. Australia 88/B3
Mandurah, W. Australia 92/A2
Manduria, Italy 34/F4
Mandvi, India 68/B4
Manele (bay), Hawaii 218/H2
Manele Bay, Hawaii (†96763) 218/H2
Manendragarh, India 68/E4
Manes, Mo. (†65711) 261/H8
Manfalût, Egypt 111/J4
Manfalût, Egypt 59/B4
Manfred, N. Dak. (58465) 282/L4
Manfredonia, Italy 34/F4
Manfredonia (gulf), Italy 34/F4
Manga, Brazil 132/E6
Manga, Uruguay 145/B7
Mangai, Zaire 115/C4
Mangaia (isl.), Cook Is. 87/L8
Mangakino, N. Zealand 100/E3
Mangalia, Romania 45/J4
Mangalore, India 54/J8
Mangalore, India 68/C6
Mangareva (isl.), Fr. Poly. 87/N8
Mangaweka, N. Zealand 100/E3
Mangere (isl.), N. Zealand 100/E7
Mangerton (mt.), Ireland 17/C8
Mangham, La. (71259) 238/G2
Mangkalihat (cape), Indonesia 85/F5
Manglaralto, Ecuador 128/B3
Mangle (pt.), Cuba 158/J3
Manglillo (pt.), P. Rico 161/B3
Mangnai, China 77/D4
Mango, Fla. (33550) 212/D4
Mango, Togo 106/E6
Mangochi, Malawi 115/G6
Mangoky (riv.), Madagascar 102/G7
Mangoky (riv.), Madagascar 118/G4
Mangole (isl.), Indonesia 85/H6
Mangonui, N. Zealand 100/D1
Mangoro (riv.), Madagascar 118/H3
Mangotsfield, England 10/E5
Mangotsfield, England 13/E6
Mangrol, India 68/B4
Mangsee (isls.), Philippines 82/A7
Mangualde, Portugal 33/C2
Mangueigne, Chad 111/D5
Mangueira (lag.), Brazil 132/D11
Manguera Azul, Uruguay 145/D4
Mangui, China 77/K1
Manguito, Cuba 158/D1
Mangum, Okla. (73554) 288/G5
Mangyshlak (pen.), U.S.S.R. 48/F5
Manhan (riv.), Mass. 249/D4
Manhasset, N.Y. (11030) 276/P7
Manhattan, Ill. (60442) 222/F2
Manhattan, Ind. (†46171) 227/D5
Manhattan, Kansas (66502) 232/F2
Manhattan, Mont. (59741) 262/E5
Manhattan, Nev. (89022) 266/E4
Manhattan (borough), N.Y. (*10001) 276/M9
Manhattan (isl.), N.Y. 276/M9
Manhattan Beach, Calif. (90266) 204/B11
Manhattan Beach, Minn. (56463) 255/E4
Manhay, Belgium 27/H8
Manheim, Pa. (17545) 294/K5
Manheim, W. Va. (26403) 312/G4
Manhiça, Mozambique 118/E5
Man Hpang, Burma 72/C2
Manhuaçu, Brazil 132/F8
Manhuaçu, Brazil 135/E2
Manhumirim, Brazil 135/E2
Maní, Colombia 126/D5
Maniamba, Mozambique 102/F6
Maniamba, Mozambique 118/F2
Manibridge, Manitoba 179/J2
Manica (prov.), Mozambique 118/E4
Manica, Mozambique 118/E3
Manicani (isl.), Philippines 82/E5
Manicaragua, Cuba 158/E2
Manicoré, Brazil 120/C3
Manicoré, Brazil 132/H9
Manicouagan, Québec 174/D2
Manicouagan (pt.), Québec 172/B1
Manicouagan (res.), Québec 174/D2
Manicouagan (riv.), Que. 162/K5
Manicouagan (riv.), Québec 174/D2
Manifest, La. (†71340) 238/G3
Manifold (cape), Queensland 88/J4
Manifold (cape), Queensland 95/D4
Manigotagan, Manitoba 179/F3
Manigotagan (lake), Manitoba 179/G4
Manigotagan (riv.), Manitoba 179/G3
Manigouche, Québec 174/C3
Manihiki (atoll), Cook Is. 87/K7
Manila, Ala. (†36586) 195/C7
Manila, Ark. (72442) 202/K2
Manila (prov.), Philippines 82/C3
Manila (cap.), Philippines 2/R5
Manila (cap.), Philippines 85/G3
Manila (cap.), Philippines 82/C3
Manila (cap.), Philippines 54/N8
Manila (bay), Philippines 82/C3
Manila, Utah (84046) 304/E3
Manildra, N.S. Wales 97/E3
Manilla, Ind. (46150) 227/F5
Manilla, Iowa (51454) 229/C5
Manilla, N.S. Wales 97/F2
Maningrida, North. Terr. 93/C2
Manipa (str.), Indonesia 85/H6
Manipur (riv.), Burma 72/B2
Manipur (state), India 68/G4
Manisa (prov.), Turkey 63/B3
Manisa, Turkey 63/B3
Manisa, Turkey 59/A2
Manistee, Mich. 188/J2
Manistee (co.), Mich. 250/C4
Manistee, Mich. (49660) 250/C4
Manistee (riv.), Mich. 250/C4
Manistique, Mich. (49854) 250/C3
Manistique (lake), Mich. 250/D2
Manistique (riv.), Mich. 250/C2
Manito, Ill. (61546) 222/D3
Manito (lake), Sask. 181/B3
Manitoba (prov.) 162/G5
Manitoba (prov.), Canada 146/J4
MANITOBA 179
Manitoba (lake), Man. 146/H4
Manitoba (lake), Man. 162/G5
Manitoba (lake), Manitoba 179/D4
Manitou, Ky. (42436) 237/F6
Manitou, Manitoba 179/D5
Manitou (isl.), Mich. 250/B1
Manitou, N. Dak. (†58776) 282/E3
Manitou, Okla. (73555) 288/J5
Manitou (lake), Ontario 177/C2
Manitou (lake), Québec 172/C3
Manitou Beach, Sask. 181/F4
Manitoulin (terr. dist.), Ontario 175/D3
Manitoulin (terr. dist.), Ontario 177/B2
Manitoulin (isl.), Ont. 162/H6
Manitoulin (isl.), Ontario 175/D3
Manitoulin (isl.), Ontario 177/B2
Manitou Springs, Colo. (80829) 208/J5
Manitouwadge, Ontario 177/H5
Manitouwadge, Ontario 175/C3
Manitowaning, Ontario 177/C2
Manitowish, Wis. (†54547) 317/F3
Manitowoc (co.), Wis. 317/L7
Manitowoc, Wis. (54220) 317/L7
Maniwaki, Québec 174/B3
Maniwaki, Québec 172/B3
Manizales, Colombia 126/C5
Manizales, Colombia 120/B2
Manja, Jordan 65/D4
Manja, Madagascar 118/G4
Manjacaze, Mozambique 118/E5
Manjimup, W. Australia 88/B6
Manjimup, W. Australia 92/B6
Mankato, Kansas (66956) 232/D2
Mankato, Minn. 188/H2
Mankato, Minn. (56001) 255/E6
Mankono, Ivory Coast 106/C7
Mankota, Sask. 181/D6
Manley, Nebr. (68403) 264/H4
Manley Hot Springs, Alaska (99756) 196/H2
Manlius, Ill. (61338) 222/D2
Manlius, N.Y. (13104) 276/J5
Manlleu, Spain 33/H1
Manly, Iowa (50456) 229/G2
Manly, N. S. Wales 88/L4
Manly, N.S. Wales 97/K3
Manly, N.C. (†28387) 281/L4
Manly, Queensland 88/L2
Manmad, India 68/C4
Manmanoc (mt.), Philippines 82/C2
Mann (riv.), North. Terr. 93/D2
Manna, Indonesia 85/C6
Mannahill, S. Australia 94/F5
Mannar (gulf) 54/J9
Mannar (gulf), India 68/D7
Mannar, Sri Lanka 68/E7
Mannar (gulf), Sri Lanka 68/D7
Mannargudi, India 68/E6
Mannboro, Va. (23105) 307/N6
Männedorf, Switzerland 39/G2
Mannersdorf am Leithagebirge, Austria 41/D3
Manners Sutton, New Bruns. 170/D3
Mannford, Okla. (74044) 288/O2
Mannheim, W. Germany 7/E4
Mannheim, W. Germany 22/C4
Manning, Alberta 182/B1
Manning, Ark. (71757) 202/E5
Manning, Iowa (51455) 229/C5
Manning, Kansas (†67871) 232/B3
Manning (riv.), N.S. Wales 97/F2
Manning, N. Dak. (58642) 282/E5
Manning (cape), N.W. Terrs. 187/F2
Manning (str.), Solomon Is. 86/D2
Manning, S.C. (29102) 296/G4
Manning Prov. Park, Br. Col. 184/G5
Mannington, Ky. (†42217) 237/G6
Mannington, W. Va. (26582) 312/F3
Männlifluh (mt.), Switzerland 39/E3
Manns Choice, Pa. (15550) 294/E6
Manns Harbor, N.C. (27953) 281/T3
Mannsville, Ky. (42758) 237/L6
Mannsville, N.Y. (13661) 276/H3
Mannsville, Okla. (73447) 288/N6
Mannu (riv.), Italy 34/B5
Mannum, S. Australia 94/F6
Mannville, Alberta 182/E3
Mano (riv.), Liberia 106/B7
Mano (riv.), S. Leone 106/B7
Manoa, Bolivia 136/C1
Manokin, Md. (21836) 245/P8
Manokin (riv.), Md. 245/P8
Manokotak, Alaska (99628) 196/G3
Manokwari, Indonesia 85/J6
Manola, Alberta 182/C2
Manombo, Madagascar 118/G4
Manomet, Mass. (02345) 249/M5
Manomet (pt.), Mass. 249/N5
Manono, Zaire 115/E5
Manono, Zaire 102/E5
Manor, Georgia (31550) 217/G8
Manor, Pa. (15665) 294/C5
Manor, Sask. 181/K6
Manor, Texas (78653) 303/G7
Manorhamilton, Ireland 17/E3
Manori, India 68/B6
Manori (creek), India 68/B7
Manorville, N.Y. (11949) 276/P9
Manorville, Pa. (16238) 294/C4
Manosque, France 28/G6
Manotick, Ontario 177/J2
Manouane, Québec 172/C2
Manouane (lake), Québec 174/C2
Manp'o, N. Korea 81/B3
Manquin, Va. (23106) 307/O5
Manra (Sydney) (isl.), Kiribati 87/K6
Manresa, Spain 33/G2
Mansa, Zambia 115/E6
Mansa, Zambia 102/E6
Mansalay, Philippines 82/C4
Mansavillagra, Uruguay 145/D4
Manseau, Québec 172/E3
Mansel (isl.), N.W.T. 162/H3
Mansel (isl.), N.W.T. 146/K3
Mansel (isl.), N.W. Terrs. 187/K3
Mansel'ka (mts.), U.S.S.R. 52/C1
Mansfield, Ark. (72944) 202/B3
Mansfield○, Conn. (†06250) 210/F1
Mansfield, England 13/K2
Mansfield, England 10/F4
Mansfield, Georgia (30255) 217/E4
Mansfield, Ill. (61854) 222/E3
Mansfield, Ind. (†47872) 227/C5
Mansfield, La. (71052) 238/C2
Mansfield, Mass. (02048) 249/J4
Mansfield○, Mass. (02048) 249/J4
Mansfield, Minn. (†56009) 255/E7
Mansfield, Mo. (65704) 261/G8
Mansfield, Ohio 188/K2
Mansfield, Ohio (*44901) 284/F4
Mansfield, Pa. (16933) 294/H2
Mansfield, S. Dak. (57460) 298/N3
Mansfield, Tenn. (38236) 237/E8
Mansfield, Texas (76063) 303/F3
Mansfield (mt.), Vt. 268/B2
Mansfield, Victoria 97/D5
Mansfield, Wash. (98830) 310/F3
Mansfield Center, Conn. (06250) 210/G1
Mansfield Depot, Conn. (06251) 210/F1
Mansfield Woodhouse, England 13/F4
Mansilla de las Mulas, Spain 33/D1
Manso (riv.), Brazil 132/C6
Manso (riv.), Chile 138/E4
Manson, Ind. (†46041) 227/D4
Manson, Iowa (50563) 229/D3
Manson, Manitoba 179/A4
Manson, N.C. (27553) 281/N2
Manson, Wash. (98831) 310/E3
Manson Creek, Br. Col. 184/E2
Mansonville, Québec 172/E4
Mansura, La. (71350) 238/G4
Manta, Ecuador 128/B3
Manta, Ecuador 120/A3
Manta (bay), Ecuador 128/B3
Mantachie, Miss. (38855) 256/H2
Mantador, N. Dak. (58058) 282/R7
Mantagao (lake), Manitoba 179/E3
Mantagao (riv.), Manitoba 179/E3
Mantalingajan (mt.), Philippines 82/A6
Mantario, Sask. 181/B4
Mantaro (riv.), Peru 128/E8
Mantas (well), Niger 106/E5
Manteca, Calif. (95336) 204/D6
Mantecal, Apure, Venezuela 124/D4
Mantecal, Bolívar, Venezuela 124/F4
Mantee, Miss. (39751) 256/F3
Manteigas, Portugal 33/C2
Manteno, Ill. (60950) 222/F2
Manteo, N.C. (27954) 281/T3
Manter, Kansas (67862) 232/A4
Mantes-la-Jolie, France 28/D3
Manti, Utah (84642) 304/C4
Mantiqueira (range), Brazil 135/D3
Manto, Honduras 154/D3
Mantoloking, N.J. (08738) 273/E3
Manton, Calif. (96059) 204/D3
Manton, Mich. (49663) 250/D4
Manton, R.I. (†02904) 249/J5
Mantorville, Minn. (55955) 255/F6
Mänttä, Finland 18/O6
Mantua, Ala. (35472) 195/C4
Mantua, Cuba 158/A2
Mantua (prov.), Italy 34/C2
Mantua, Italy 34/C2
Mantua○, N.J. (08051) 273/C4
Mantua, Ohio (44255) 284/H3
Mantua, Utah (†84302) 304/C2
Mantua, Va. (†22030) 307/S3
Manturovo, U.S.S.R. 52/F3
Manú, Peru 128/G9
Manú (riv.), Peru 128/G8
Manua (isls.), Amer. Samoa 87/K7
Manuae (atoll), Cook Is. 87/K7
Manuel Benavides, Mexico 150/H2
Manuelito, N. Mex. (†86506) 274/A3
Manuel Rodríguez (isl.), Chile 138/D10
Manuels, New Bruns. 170/F1
Manuels, Newf. 166/D2
Manui (isl.), Indonesia 85/G6
Manukan, Philippines 82/D6
Manukau, N. Zealand 100/C1
Manukau (harb.), N. Zealand 100/B1
Manulla, Ireland 17/C4
Manumuskin (riv.), N.J. 273/D5
Manunui, N. Zealand 100/E3
Manuripi (riv.), Bolivia 136/B2
Manus (isl.), Papua N.G. 87/E6
Manus (isl.), Papua N.G. 86/A1
Manutuke, N. Zealand 100/F3
Manvel, N. Dak. (58256) 282/R3
Manvel, Texas (77578) 303/J3
Manville, N.J. (08835) 273/D2
Manville, R.I. (02838) 249/H5
Manville, Wyo. (82227) 319/H3
Many, La. (71449) 238/C3
Manyara (lake), Tanzania 115/G4
Manyas, Turkey 63/B3
Manyberries, Alberta 182/E5
Manych-Gudilo (lake), U.S.S.R. 52/F5
Many Farms, Ariz. (86538) 198/F2
Manyoni, Tanzania 115/G5
Manzai, Pakistan 59/K3
Manzanar, Chile 138/F2
Manzanares, Spain 33/E3
Manzanares (riv.), Spain 33/F4
Manzanillo, Cuba 158/H4
Manzanillo, Cuba 156/C2
Manzanillo (bay), Dom. Rep. 158/C5
Manzanillo (bay), Haiti 158/C5
Manzanillo, Mexico 150/G7
Manzanillo, Mexico 146/H8
Manzanillo (pt.), Panama 154/H6
Manzanita, Oreg. (97130) 291/C2
Manzanita Ind. Res., Calif. 204/J11
Manzano, N. Mex. (†87016) 274/C4
Manzano (mts.), N. Mex. 274/C4
Manzano (peak), N. Mex. 274/C4
Manzanola, Colo. (81058) 208/M6
Manzhouli (Manchouli), China 77/J2
Manzini, Swaziland 118/E5
Mao, Chad 111/C5
Mao, Dom. Rep. 158/D5
Maoke (mts.), Indonesia 85/K6
Maoming (Mowming), China 77/H7
Mapai, Mozambique 118/E4
Mapararí, Venezuela 124/D2
Mapastepec, Mexico 150/N9
Mapes, N. Dak. (58349) 282/O3
Mapia (isls.), Indonesia 85/J5
Mapimí, Mexico 150/G4
Mapimí (depr.), Mexico 150/G3
Mapire, Venezuela 124/F4
Mapiri, Bolivia 136/B4
Mapiripán, Laguna (lake), Colombia 126/E6
Maple (peak), Ariz. 198/F5
Maple (riv.), Mich. 250/E5
Maple (lake), Minn. 255/B3
Maple (riv.), Minn. 255/E7
Maple (riv.), N. Dak. 282/O8
Maple (riv.), N. Dak. 282/P6
Maple (creek), Sask. 181/B5
Maple (riv.), S. Dak. 298/M1
Maple, Wis. (54854) 317/C2
Maple Bay, Br. Col. 184/K3
Maple Bay, Minn. (†56736) 255/B3
Maple City, Kansas (67102) 232/F4
Maple City, Mich. 250/D4
Maple Creek, Sask. 162/F6
Maple Creek, Sask. 181/B6
Maple Falls, Wash. (98266) 310/D2
Maple Grove, Minn. (†55369) 255/G5
Maple Grove, Ontario 177/F4
Maple Grove, Québec 172/H4
Maple Heights, Ohio (44137) 284/H9
Maple Hill, Iowa (50564) 229/D2
Maple Hill, Kansas (66507) 232/F2
Maple Hill, N.C. (28454) 281/O5
Maple Island, Minn. (†55082) 255/E7
Maple Lake, Minn. (55358) 255/D5
Maple Park, Ill. (60151) 222/E2
Maple Plain, Minn. (55359) 255/F5
Maple Rapids, Mich. (48853) 250/E5
Maple Ridge, Br. Col. 184/L3
Maple River, Iowa (†51401) 229/D4
Maples, Ind. (†46802) 227/H2
Maples, Mo. (†65542) 261/J7
Maple Shade○, N.J. (08052) 273/B3
Maplesville, Ala. (36750) 195/E5
Mapleton, Iowa (51034) 229/B4
Mapleton, Kansas (66754) 232/H3
Mapleton○, Maine (04757) 243/G2
Mapleton, Mich. (†49684) 250/D4
Mapleton, Minn. (56065) 255/E7
Mapleton, N.C. (†27855) 281/P2
Mapleton, N. Dak. (58059) 282/R6
Mapleton, Oreg. (97453) 291/C3
Mapleton (Mapleton Depot), Pa. (17052) 294/F5
Mapleton, Utah (†84663) 304/C3
Mapleton, Wis. (†53066) 317/J1
Mapleton Depot, Pa. (17052) 294/F5
Maple Valley, Wash. (98038) 310/C3
Mapleview, Minn. (†55912) 255/E7
Mapleview, New Bruns. 170/C2
Mapleville, Md. (†21713) 245/H2
Mapleville, R.I. (02839) 249/H5
Maplewood, La. (†70663) 238/D6
Maplewood, Minn. (55109) 255/G5
Maplewood, Mo. (63143) 261/P3
Maplewood, N.H. (†03574) 268/D3
Maplewood○, N.J. (07040) 273/E2
Maplewood, Ohio (45340) 284/B5
Maplewood, Wis. (54226) 317/M6
Mapocho (riv.), Chile 138/G3
Mapoon Mission Station, Queensland 88/G2
Mapoon Mission Station, Queensland 95/B1
Maporal, Venezuela 124/C4
Mapos (Amazones), Cuba 158/F2
Mappsville, Va. (23407) 307/T5
Mapuera (riv.), Brazil 132/B3
Maputo (city) (prov.), Mozambique 118/E5
Maputo (prov.), Mozambique 118/E5
Maputo (cap.), Mozambique 2/L7
Maputo (cap.), Mozambique 118/E5
Maputo (cap.), Mozambique 102/F7
Maqatin (ruins), P.D.R. Yemen 59/E7
Maqên, China 77/F5
Maqna, Saudi Arabia 59/C4
Ma Qu (Huang He) (riv.), China 77/F5
Maquapit (lake), New Bruns. 170/D3
Maqueda (chan.), Philippines 82/D3
Maquela do Zombo, Angola 102/D5
Maquela do Zombo, Angola 115/C5
Maquereau (pt.), Québec 172/D2
Maquinchao, Argentina 143/C5
Maquoketa, Iowa (52060) 229/M4
Maquon, Ill. (61458) 222/C3
Mar (mts.), Brazil 120/E5
Mar (range), Brazil 135/C4
Mar, Serra do (range), Brazil 132/E9
Mar (dist.), Scotland 15/F3
Mara, Guyana 131/C3
Mara (reg.), Tanzania 115/F4
Marabá, Brazil 132/D4
Marabá, Brazil 120/E3
Marabahan, Indonesia 85/E6
Marabella, Trin. & Tob. 161/A11
Maracá (isl.), Brazil 120/E2
Maracá (isl.), Brazil 132/D2
Maracaibo, Venezuela 124/C2
Maracaibo, Venezuela 120/B1
Maracaibo (lake), Venezuela 120/B2
Maracaibo (lake), Venezuela 124/C3
Maracaju, Brazil 132/C8
Maracas (bay), Trin. & Tob. 161/C10
Maracay, Venezuela 124/E2
Maracay, Venezuela 120/C2
Marada, Libya 111/C2
Maradi, Niger 106/F6
Maradi, Niger 102/C3
Maragheh, Iran 59/E2
Maragheh, Iran 66/E2
Maragogipe, Brazil 132/G6
Maraira (pt.), Philippines 82/C1
Marajó (est.), Brazil 120/E2
Marajó (isl.), Brazil 120/E3
Marajó (bay), Brazil 132/E2
Marajó (isl.), Brazil 132/D3
Maralal, Kenya 115/G3
Maralinga, S. Australia 88/E6
Maralwexi (Bachu), China 77/A4
Maramag, Philippines 82/E7
Maramec, Okla. (74045) 288/N2
Marampa, S. Leone 106/B7
Marana, Ariz. (85238) 198/D6
Marand, Iran 59/E2
Marand, Iran 66/D1
Marandellas, Zimbabwe 118/E3
Marang, Malaysia 72/D6
Maranguape, Brazil 132/G3
Maranhão (state), Brazil 132/E4
Maranoa (riv.), Queensland 95/C5
Marañón (riv.), Peru 120/B3
Marañón (riv.), Peru 128/E5
Marapanim, Brazil 132/E3
Maras (mt.), Indonesia 85/D6
Maraş, Turkey 59/C2
Maraş (Kahramanmaraş), Turkey 63/G4
Marathon, Fla. (33050) 212/E7
Marathón, Greece 45/G6
Marathon, Iowa (50565) 229/C3
Marathon, N.Y. (13803) 276/J6
Marathon, Ohio (45145) 284/C7
Marathon, Ont. 162/H6
Marathon, Ontario 177/H5
Marathon, Ontario 175/C3
Marathon, Texas (79842) 303/A7
Marathon (co.), Wis. 317/G6
Marathon, Wis. (54448) 317/G6
Maratua (isl.), Indonesia 85/F5
Maravillas, Bolivia 136/B2
Maravillas (creek), Texas 303/A7
Marawi, Philippines 85/G4
Marawi, Philippines 82/E6
Marbach, Switzerland 39/E3
Marbach am Neckar, W. Germany 22/C4
Marbella, Spain 33/D4
Marble, Ark. (72746) 202/C1
Marble, Colo. (†81623) 208/E4
Marble, Minn. (55764) 255/E3
Marble, N.C. (28905) 281/B4
Marble (isl.), N.W.T. 162/G3
Marble (isl.), N.W. Terrs. 187/J3
Marble Bar, Australia 87/C8
Marble Bar, W. Australia 88/B4
Marble Bar, W. Australia 92/C3
Marble Canyon, Ariz. (86036) 198/D2
Marble Canyon Nat'l Mon., Ariz. 198/D2
Marble City, Okla. (74945) 288/S3
Marble Dale, Conn. (06777) 210/B2
Marble Falls, Texas (78654) 303/F7
Marblehead, Ill. (†62301) 222/B4
Marblehead○, Mass. (01945) 249/E7
Marblehead (neck), Mass. 249/F6
Marblehead, Ohio (†43440) 284/E2
Marble Hill, Georgia (30148) 217/D2
Marble Hill, Mo. (63764) 261/N8
Marblemount, Wash. (98267) 310/D2
Marble Rock, Iowa (50653) 229/H3
Marbleton, Québec 172/F4
Marbleton, Wyo. (†83113) 319/B3
Marble Valley, Ala. (†35150) 195/F4
Marburg an der Lahn, W. Germany 22/C3
Marbury, Ala. (36051) 195/E5
Marbury, Md. (20658) 245/K6
Marcala, Honduras 154/C3
Marcali, Hungary 41/D3
Marcapata, Peru 128/G9
Marcelin, Sask. 181/E3
Marceline, Mo. (64658) 261/F3
Marcell, Minn. (56657) 255/E3
Marcella, Ark. (72555) 202/G2
Marcella, N.J. (†07866) 273/E2
Marcelline, Ill. (†62376) 222/B3
Marcellus, Mich. (49067) 250/D6
Marcellus, N.Y. (13108) 276/H5
Marcelville, New Bruns. 170/E2
March (riv.), Austria 41/D2
March, England 10/G4
March, England 13/H5
March A.F.B., Calif. 204/E11
Marchand, Manitoba 179/F5
Marche, Ark. (†72114) 202/F4
Marche (trad. prov.) France 29
Marche (reg.), Italy 34/D3
Marche-en-Famenne, Belgium 27/G8
Marchegg, Austria 41/D2
Marchena (isl.), Ecuador 128/B9
Marchena, Spain 33/D4
Marchfield, Barbados 161/B9
Marchigüe, Chile 138/F5
Marchin, Belgium 27/G8
Mar Chiquita (lake), Argentina 143/D3
Marchwell, Sask. 181/K5
Marco (Marco Island), Fla. (33937) 212/E6
Marco (isl.), Fla. 212/E6
Marco, Ind. (†47443) 227/C7
Marco, La. (†71447) 238/E3
Marcola, Oreg. (97454) 291/E3
Marcona, Peru 128/E10
Marcos Juárez, Argentina 143/D3
Marcus, Iowa (51035) 229/B3
Marcus (isl.), Japan 87/F3
Marcus, S. Dak. (57757) 298/E4
Marcus, Wash. (99151) 310/H2
Marcus Baker (mt.), Alaska 196/C1
Marcus Hook, Pa. (19061) 294/L7
Marcy, N.Y. (13403) 276/K4
Marcy (mt.), N.Y. 276/N2
Mardan, Pakistan 68/C2
Mardan, Pakistan 59/K3
Mardela Springs, Md. (21837) 245/P7
Mar del Plata, Argentina 143/E4
Mar del Plata, Argentina 120/D6
Mardin (prov.), Turkey 63/J4
Mardin, Turkey 63/J4
Mardin, Turkey 59/D2
Maré (isl.), New Caled. 87/G8
Maré (isl.), New Caled. 86/J4
Mareb (riv.), Ethiopia 59/C7
Marechal Deodoro, Brazil 132/H5
Maree, Loch (lake), Scotland 10/D2
Maree, Loch (lake), Scotland 15/C3
Mareeba, Queensland 95/C3
Mareeba, Queensland 88/G3
Mare Island Navy Yard, Calif. 204/J1
Marengo (co.), Ala. 195/C6
Marengo, Ala. (†36736) 195/C6
Marengo, Ill. (60152) 222/E1
Marengo, Ind. (47140) 227/E8
Marengo, Iowa (52301) 229/J5
Marengo, Ohio (43334) 284/E5
Marengo, Sask. 181/B4
Marengo, Wash. (†99004) 310/G3
Marengo, Wis. (54855) 317/E3
Marenisco, Mich. (49947) 250/F2
Marennes, France 28/C5
Mareth, Tunisia 106/F2
Marettimo (isl.), Italy 34/C6
Marfa, Texas (79843) 303/C12
Marfield, N.S. Wales 97/C3
Marfrance, W. Va. (25975) 312/E6
Margai Caka (lake), China 77/C4
Marganets, U.S.S.R. 52/E5
Margao, India 68/C5
Margaree, Nova Scotia 168/G2
Margaree (isl.), Nova Scotia 168/F4
Margaree Centre, Nova Scotia 168/H2
Margaree Forks, Nova Scotia 168/G2
Margaree Harbour, Nova Scotia 168/G2
Margaree Valley, Nova Scotia 168/H2
Margaret, Ala. (35112) 195/F3
Margaret (lake), Alberta 182/B5
Margaret, Manitoba 179/C5
Margaret, Texas (†79227) 303/E3
Margaret (riv.), W. Australia 88/D3
Margaret River, W. Australia 88/A6
Margaret River, W. Australia 92/A6
Margaret River Station, W. Australia 92/D2
Margaretsville, Nova Scotia 168/C3
Margaretville, N.Y. (12455) 276/L6
Margarita, Argentina 143/F5
Margarita (isl.), Venezuela 120/C1
Margarita (isl.), Venezuela 124/F2
Margate, England 13/J6
Margate, England 10/G5
Margate, Fla. (33063) 212/F5
Margate, S. Africa 118/E6
Margate, Tasmania 99/D4
Margate City, N.J. (08402) 273/E5
Margento, Colombia 126/C4
Margerum, Ala. (†35616) 195/B1
Margherita (Jamama), Somalia 115/H3
Margherita (mt.), Uganda 115/E3
Margherita (mt.), Zaire 102/E4
Margherita (mt.), Zaire 115/E3
Margie, Minn. (56658) 255/E2
Margo, Sask. 181/H4
Margos, Peru 128/D8
Margosatubig, Philippines 82/D7
Margow, Dasht-e (des.), Afghanistan 59/H3
Margow, Dasht-e (des.), Afghanistan 68/A2
Margraten, Netherlands 27/H7
Margret, Georgia (†30536) 217/D1
Margrethe (lake), Mich. 250/E4
Marguerite (bay) 5/C15
Maria (isl.), Fr. Poly. 87/L8
Maria (creek), Ind. 227/C7
Maria, Québec 172/C2
Maria (isls.), St. Lucia 161/G7
Maria (isl.), Tasmania 99/E4
Mari A.S.S.R., U.S.S.R. 52/G3
Mari A.S.S.R., U.S.S.R. 48/E4
María Albina, Uruguay 145/E4
María Cleofas (isl.), Mexico 150/F6
María Elena, Chile 138/B3
Mariager, Denmark 21/D4
Mariager, Denmark 18/G8
Mariager (fjord), Denmark 21/D4
Mariah Hill, Ind. (47556) 227/D8
María Madre (isl.), Mexico 150/F6
María Magdalena (isl.), Mexico 150/F6
Marian (lake), Fla. 212/E4
Marian (lake), N.W. Terrs. 187/G3
Marian, Queensland 88/H4
Marian, Queensland 95/D4
Mariana, Brazil 135/E2
Mariana Lake, Alberta 182/D2
Marianao, Cuba 158/C1
Marianao, Cuba 156/A2
Marianas, Northern 87/E4
Mariana Trench 87/E4
Marianna, Ark. (72360) 202/J4
Marianna, Fla. (32446) 212/A1
Marianna, Pa. (15345) 294/B5
Mariano I. Loza, Argentina 143/G4
Mariano Roque Alonso, Paraguay 144/A4

McKinley 407

Matadi, Zaire 102/D5
Matador, Sask. 181/D5
Matador, Texas (79244) 303/D3
Matagalpa, Nicaragua 154/E4
Matagami, Québec 174/B3
Matagami (lake), Québec 174/B3
Matagorda (co.), Texas 303/H9
Matagorda, Texas (77457) 303/J9
Matagorda (bay), Texas 188/G5
Matagorda (bay), Texas 303/H9
Matagorda (isl.), Texas 303/H9
Matagorda (pen.), Texas 303/J9
Matagorda Isl. Bombing and Gunnery Range, Texas 303/H9
Matakana (isl.), N. Zealand 100/F2
Matala (dam), Angola 115/B6
Matam, Senegal 106/B5
Matamoras, Pa. (18336) 294/N3
Matamoros, Mexico 146/J7
Matamoros, Coahuila, Mexico 150/H4
Matamoros, Tamaulipas, Mexico 150/L4
Matane (co.), Québec 172/B1
Matane (county), Québec 174/D3
Matane, Québec 174/D3
Matane, Québec 172/B1
Matane (riv.), Québec 172/B1
Matane Prov. Park, Québec 172/B1
Matanuska (riv.), Alaska 196/C1
Matanza, Colombia 126/D4
Matanzas (prov.), Cuba 158/D1
Matanzas, Cuba 146/K7
Matanzas, Cuba 158/C1
Matanzas, Cuba 156/B2
Matanzas (bay), Cuba 158/D1
Matanzas (inlet), Fla. 212/E2
Mata Palacio, Dom. Rep. 158/F6
Matapalo (cape), C. Rica 154/F6
Matapan (Tainaron) (cape), Greece 45/F7
Matapédia (county), Québec 174/D3
Matapédia (co.), Québec 172/B2
Matapédia, Québec 172/B2
Matapédia (lake), Québec 172/B1
Matapédia (riv.), Québec 172/B2
Mataquito (riv.), Chile 138/A10
Matara, Sri Lanka 68/E7
Mataram, Indonesia 85/F7
Matarani, Peru 120/B4
Matarani, Peru 128/F11
Mataranka, North. Terr. 93/C3
Matarinao (bay), Philippines 82/E5
Mataró, Spain 33/H2
Matatiele, S. Africa 118/D6
Matatindoc (pt.), Philippines 82/D6
Mataura, N. Zealand 100/B7
Mataura (riv.), N. Zealand 100/B6
Mata Utu (cap.), Wallis and Futuna 87/J7
Matawai, N. Zealand 100/F3
Matawan, Minn. (†56072) 255/E7
Matawan, N.J. (07747) 273/E3
Matawin (lake), Québec 172/C3
Matawin (riv.), Québec 172/D3
Mateare, Nicaragua 154/D4
Mateguá, Bolivia 136/D3
Matehuala, Mexico 150/J5
Matelot, Trin. & Tob. 161/B10
Matera (prov.), Italy 34/F4
Matera, Italy 34/F4
Maternillos (pt.), Cuba 158/H2
Mátészalka, Hungary 41/G3
Matetsi, Zimbabwe 118/D3
Mateur, Tunisia 106/F1
Matewan, W. Va. (25678) 312/B7
Matfield Green, Kansas (66862) 232/F3
Mather, Manitoba 179/C5
Mather, Wis. (54641) 317/F7
Mather A.F.B., Calif. 204/C8
Matherville, Ill. (61263) 222/C2
Matherville, Miss. (†39360) 256/G7
Matheson, Colo. (80830) 208/M4
Matheson, Ontario 177/K5
Matheson Island, Manitoba 179/E3
Mathews, Ala. (36052) 195/F6
Mathews (lake), Calif. 204/E11
Mathews, La. (70375) 238/J7
Mathews (co.), Va. 307/R6
Mathews, Va. (23109) 307/R6
Mathias, W. Va. (26812) 312/J5
Mathinna, Tasmania 99/E3
Mathis, Texas (78368) 303/G9
Mathiston, Miss. (39752) 256/F3
Mathoura, N.S. Wales 97/C4
Mathura, India 68/D3
Mati, Philippines 85/H4
Mati, Philippines 82/F7
Matías Romero, Mexico 150/M8
Matinenda (lake), Ontario 177/B1
Matinicus, Maine (04851) 243/F8
Matinicus Rock (isl.), Maine 243/F8
Matlock, England 10/F4
Matlock, England 13/J2
Matlock, Iowa (51244) 229/A2
Matlock, Wash. (98560) 310/B3
Matoaca, Va. (23803) 307/N6
Matoaka, W. Va. (24736) 312/D8
Matochkin Shar (str.), U.S.S.R. 48/F2
Mato Grosso (state), Brazil 132/B6
Mato Grosso, Brazil 120/D4
Mato Grosso, Brazil 132/B6
Mato Grosso (plat.), Brazil 120/D4
Mato Grosso, Planalto de (plat.), Brazil 132/B6
Mato Grosso do Sul (state), Brazil 132/C7
Matopos, Zimbabwe 118/D4
Matosinhos, Portugal 33/B2
Matoury, Fr. Guiana 131/E3
Mátra (mts.), Hungary 41/E3
Matrah, Oman 54/G7
Matrah, Oman 59/G5
Matrei in Osttirol, Austria 41/B3
Matruh, Egypt 59/A3
Matsqui, Br. Col. 184/L3
Matsu (Mazu) (isl.), China 77/K6
Matsubara, Japan 81/H8
Matsue, Japan 81/F6
Matsumae, Japan 81/J3
Matsumoto, Japan 81/H5
Matsusaka, Japan 81/H6
Matsuto, Japan 81/H5
Matsuyama, Japan 81/F7
Matsuyama, Japan 54/P6
Matt, Switzerland 39/H3
Mattabesset (riv.), Conn. 210/E2
Mattagami (riv.), Ontario 175/D3
Mattagami (riv.), Ontario 177/J5
Mattamiscontis (lake), Maine 243/F4
Mattamuskeet (lake), N.C. 281/S3
Mattapan, Mass. (02126) 249/C7
Mattapoisett, Mass. (02739) 249/L6
Mattapoisett○, Mass. (02739) 249/L6
Mattaponi, Va. (23110) 307/P5
Mattaponi (riv.), Va. 307/O5
Mattaponi Ind. Res., Va. 307/P5
Mattawa, Ont. 162/J6
Mattawa, Ontario 177/F1
Mattawa, Ontario 175/E3
Mattawa, Wash. (99344) 310/F4
Mattawamkeag○, Maine (04459) 243/G5
Mattawamkeag (lake), Maine 243/G4
Mattawamkeag (riv.), Maine 243/G4
Mattawan, Mich. (49071) 250/D6
Mattawana, Pa. (17054) 294/G5
Mattawoman (creek), Md. 245/K6
Matterhorn (mt.), Switzerland 39/E4
Mattersburg, Austria 41/D3
Matteson, Ill. (60443) 222/B6
Matthew, Ky. (41454) 237/P5
Matthews, Georgia (30818) 217/H4
Matthews, Ind. (46957) 227/F4
Matthews, Mo. (63857) 261/N9
Matthews, N.C. (28105) 281/H4
Matthews Ridge, Guyana 131/B2
Mattice, Ontario 175/D3
Mattice, Ontario 177/J5
Mattighofen, Austria 41/B2
Mattituck, N.Y. (11952) 276/P9
Mattoon, Ill. (61938) 222/E4
Mattoon, Wis. (54450) 317/J5
Mattson, Miss. (38758) 256/C2
Matu, Venezuela 124/F4
Matucana, Peru 128/D8
Matuku (isl.), Fiji 86/Q11
Matún, Cuba 158/D2
Matura, Trin. & Tob. 161/B10
Matura (bay), Trin. & Tob. 161/B10
Maturín, Venezuela 120/C2
Maturín, Venezuela 124/G3
Matutum (mt.), Philippines 82/E7
Matutum (mt.), Philippines 85/G4
Matveyev (isl.), U.S.S.R. 52/J1
Mau, India 68/E3
Mauá, Brazil 135/C3
Maúa, Mozambique 118/F2
Maubeuge, France 28/F2
Ma-ubin, Burma 72/B3
Mauch Chunk (Jim Thorpe), Pa. (18229) 294/L4
Mauchline, Scotland 15/D5
Mauckport, Ind. (47142) 227/E8
Maud, Ala. (†35616) 195/B1
Maud, Ky. (40042) 237/L5
Maud, Miss. (†38626) 256/D1
Maud, Ohio (†45069) 284/B7
Maud, Okla. (74854) 288/N4
Maud, Scotland 15/F3
Maud, Texas (75567) 303/K4
Maude, N.S. Wales 97/C4
Maudlow, Mont. (59714) 262/E4
Mauerkirchen, Austria 41/B2
Maués, Brazil 132/B3
Maués, Brazil 120/D3
Maués-Açu (riv.), Brazil 132/B4
Maugansville, Md. (21767) 245/H2
Mauger (cay), Belize 154/D2
Maugerville, New Bruns. 170/D3
Maui (co.), Hawaii 218/J1
Maui (isl.), Hawaii 87/L3
Maui (isl.), Hawaii 188/F5
Maui (isl.), Hawaii 218/J2
Mauk, Georgia (31058) 217/D6
Mauke (isl.), Cook Is. 87/L8
Mauldin, S.C. (29662) 296/C2
Maule (reg.), Chile 138/A11
Maule (riv.), Chile 138/A11
Mauléon-Licharre, France 28/C6
Maullín, Chile 138/D4
Maullín (riv.), Chile 138/D3
Maumakeogh (mt.), Ireland 17/C3
Maumee (riv.), Ind. 227/H2
Maumee (bay), Mich. 250/F7
Maumee, Ohio (43537) 284/C2
Maumee (bay), Ohio 284/D2
Maumee (riv.), Ohio 284/A3
Maumelle (lake), Ark. 202/E4
Maumere, Indonesia 85/G7
Maumturk (mts.), Ireland 17/B5
Maun, Botswana 118/C4
Maunabo, P. Rico 161/E3
Mauna Kea (mt.), Hawaii 87/L4
Mauna Kea (mt.), Hawaii 188/G6
Mauna Kea (mt.), Hawaii 218/H4
Maunaloa, Hawaii (96770) 218/G1
Mauna Loa (mt.), Hawaii 188/G6
Mauna Loa (mt.), Hawaii 218/G6
Maunalua (bay), Hawaii 218/F2
Maunawili, Hawaii (†96744) 218/F2
Maungaturoto, N. Zealand 100/E1
Maungdaw, Burma 72/B2
Maunie, Ill. (62861) 222/E5
Maupin, Oreg. (97037) 291/F2
Maurepas, La. (70449) 238/M2
Maurepas (lake), La. 238/M2
Mauretown, Va. (22644) 307/L3
Mauriac, France 28/E5
Maurice, Iowa (51036) 229/A3
Maurice, La. (70555) 238/F6
Maurice (riv.), N.J. 273/C4
Maurice (lake), S. Australia 88/E5
Maurice (lake), S. Australia 94/B3
Mauricetown, N.J. (08325) 273/D5
Mauricio Hirsch, Argentina 143/F7
Maurine, S. Dak. (†57626) 298/E3
Mauritania 2/J4
Mauritania 102/A3
MAURITANIA 106/B5
Mauritius 2/M6
MAURITIUS 118/G5
Maury, N.C. (28554) 281/O4
Maury (co.), Tenn. 237/G9
Maury (riv.), Va. 307/K5
Maury City, Tenn. (38050) 237/C9
Mauston, Wis. (53948) 317/F8
Mautern in Steiermark, Austria 41/C3
Mauthausen, Austria 41/C2
Mauthen-Kötschach, Austria 41/B3
Mauvoisin (dam), Switzerland 39/D4
Mavaca (riv.), Venezuela 124/F6
Maverick, Ariz. (†85920) 198/F5
Maverick (co.), Texas 303/D9
Mavila, Peru 128/H8
Mavillette, Nova Scotia 168/B4
Mavinga, Angola 115/D7
Mavora (mt.), N. Zealand 100/B6
Mavqi'im, Israel 65/B4
Mawai, Malaysia 72/F5
Mawbanna, Tasmania 99/B2
Mawer, Sask. 181/E5
Mawkmai, Burma 72/C2
Mawlaik, Burma 72/B2
Mawlu, Burma 72/C1
Mawson 5/C4
Max, Minn. (56659) 255/D3
Max, Nebr. (69037) 264/C4
Max, N. Dak. (58759) 282/H4
Maxbass, N. Dak. (58760) 282/H2
Maxcanú, Mexico 150/O6
Maxeys, Georgia (30671) 217/F3
Maxie, La. (†70526) 238/F6
Maxie, Miss. (†39458) 256/F9
Máximo Gómez, Ciego de Ávila, Cuba 158/F2
Máximo Gómez, Matanzas, Cuba 158/D1
Máximo Paz, Argentina 143/F6
Maxinkuckee, Ind. (†46511) 227/E2
Maxinkuckee (lake), Ind. 227/E2
Maxixe, Mozambique 118/F4
Max Meadows, Va. (24360) 307/G6
Maxstone, Sask. 181/F6
Maxton, N.C. (28364) 281/L5
Maxville, Mont. (59858) 262/C4
Maxville, Ontario 177/K2
Maxwell, Calif. (95955) 204/C4
Maxwell, Ind. (46154) 227/F5
Maxwell, Iowa (50161) 229/G5
Maxwell, Nebr. (69151) 264/D3
Maxwell, New Bruns. 170/C3
Maxwell, N. Mex. (87728) 274/E2
Maxwell (bay), N.W. Terrs. 187/K2
Maxwell, Tenn. (†37306) 237/J10
Maxwell Air Force Base, Ala. 195/F6
Maxwelton, Queensland 88/G4
May, Idaho (83253) 220/E5
May (cape), N.J. 188/M3
May (cape), N.J. 273/C6
May, Okla. (73851) 288/G1
May, Isle of (isl.), Scotland 15/F4
May, Texas (76857) 303/F5
Maya (mts.), Belize 154/C2
Maya (riv.), U.S.S.R. 54/P4
Maya (riv.), U.S.S.R. 48/O4
Maya Beach, Belize 154/C2
Mayaguana (isl.), Bahamas 146/L7
Mayaguana (isl.), Bahamas 156/D2
Mayaguana (passage), Bahamas 156/D2
Mayagüez (dist.), P. Rico 161/B2
Mayagüez, P. Rico 161/A2
Mayagüez, P. Rico 156/F1
Mayagüez (bay), P. Rico 161/A2
Mayajigua, Cuba 158/F2
Mayals, Spain 33/G2
Mayarí, Cuba 158/J3
Mayarí Arriba, Cuba 158/J4
Mayaro, Trin. & Tob. 161/B11
Mayaro (bay), Trin. & Tob. 161/B11
Maybee, Mich. (48159) 250/F6
Maybell, Colo. (81640) 208/C2
Mayberry, Md. (†21157) 245/K2
Maybeury, W. Va. (24861) 312/D8
Maybole, Scotland 10/D3
Maybole, Scotland 15/D5
Maybrook, N.Y. (12543) 276/M8
Mayburg, Pa. (†16347) 294/D2
Maydena, Tasmania 99/C4
Mayen, W. Germany 22/B3
Mayenne (dept.), France 28/C3
Mayenne, France 28/C3
Mayenne (riv.), France 28/C4
Mayer, Ariz. (86333) 198/C4
Mayer, Chile 138/E7
Mayer, Minn. (55360) 255/E6
Mayersville, Miss. (39113) 256/B5
Mayerthorpe, Alberta 182/C3
Mayes (co.), Okla. 288/R2
Mayesville, S.C. (29104) 296/G4
Mayetta, Kansas (66509) 232/G2
Mayetta, N.J. (†08092) 273/E4
Mayfair, Sask. 181/D2
Mayfield, Georgia (31087) 217/G4
Mayfield, Kansas (67103) 232/E4
Mayfield, Ky. (42066) 237/D7
Mayfield (creek), Ky. 237/C7
Mayfield, N.Y. (12117) 276/M4
Mayfield, Ohio (44124) 284/J9
Mayfield, Okla. (73656) 288/G4
Mayfield, Pa. (18433) 294/L2
Mayfield, Scotland 15/D2
Mayfield, Utah (84643) 304/C4
Mayfield (lake), Wash. 310/C4
Mayfield Heights, Ohio (44124) 284/J9
Mayflower, Ark. (72106) 202/F4
Mayger, Oreg. (†97016) 291/D1
Mayhew, Miss. (39753) 256/G4
Mayhill, N. Mex. (88339) 274/D6
Maykop, U.S.S.R. 7/H4
Maykop, U.S.S.R. 48/D5
Maykop, U.S.S.R. 52/F6
Mayland, Tenn. (†38555) 237/L8
Maylene, Ala. (35114) 195/E4
Maymont, Sask. 181/D3
Maymyo, Burma 72/C2
Mayna, La. (†71343) 238/G4
Maynard, Ark. (72444) 202/J1
Maynard, Iowa (50655) 229/K3
Maynard○, Mass. (01754) 249/J3
Maynard, Minn. (56260) 255/C6
Maynardville, Tenn. (37807) 237/O8
Mayne, Br. Col. 184/K3
Maynooth, Ireland 17/H5
Maynooth, Ontario 177/G2
Mayo, Canada 4/C16
Mayo, Fla. (32066) 212/C1
Mayo (co.), Ireland 17/C4
Mayo, Md. (21106) 245/M5
Mayo (riv.), Peru 128/D6
Mayo (bay), Philippines 82/F7
Mayo, S.C. (29368) 296/D1
Mayo, Yukon 187/E3
Mayo, Yukon 162/C3
Mayo (lake), Yukon 187/E3
Mayodan, N.C. (27027) 281/K2
Mayon (vol.), Philippines 82/D4
Mayor (isl.), N. Zealand 100/F2
Mayor (cape), Spain 33/E1
Mayor Martínez, Paraguay 144/C5
Mayor Pablo Lagerenza, Paraguay 144/B1
MAYOTTE 118/G2
Mayotte (isl), France 102/G6
Mayoworth, Wyo. (†82639) 319/F2
May Park, Oreg. (†97850) 291/J2
May Pen, Jamaica 158/J6
Mayport Naval Air Sta., Fla. 212/E1
Mayrhofen, Austria 41/A3
Mays, Ind. (46155) 227/G5
Maysan (gov.), Iraq 66/E5
Maysel, W. Va. (25133) 312/D5
Mays Landing, N.J. (08330) 273/D5
Mays Lick, Ky. (41055) 237/O3
Maysville, Ark. (72747) 202/A1
Maysville, Georgia (30558) 217/E2
Maysville, Iowa (†52773) 229/M5
Maysville, Ky. (41056) 237/O3
Maysville, Mo. (64469) 261/D3
Maysville, N.C. (28555) 281/P5
Maysville, Okla. (73057) 288/M5
Maysville, W. Va. (26833) 312/H4
Maytiguid (isl.), Philippines 82/B5
Maytown, Ky. (41455) 237/O5
Mayumba, Gabon 115/A4
Mayuram, India 68/D6
Mayview, Mo. (64071) 261/E4
Mayville, Mich. (48744) 250/F5
Mayville, N.Y. (14757) 276/A6
Mayville, N. Dak. (58257) 282/R4
Mayville, Oreg. (97830) 291/G2
Mayville, Wis. (53050) 317/K9
Maywood, Calif. (90201) 204/C10
Maywood, Ill. (60153) 222/B5
Maywood, Mo. (63454) 261/J3
Maywood, Nebr. (69038) 264/D4
Maywood, N.J. (07607) 273/B2
Maywood Park, Oreg. (97220) 291/B2
Maza, N. Dak. (†58324) 282/M3
Mazabuka, Zambia 115/E7
Mazabuka, Zambia 102/E6
Mazagan (El Jadida), Morocco 106/C2
Mazagão, Brazil 132/D3
Mazama, Wash. (98833) 310/E2
Mazamet, France 28/E6
Mazán, Peru 128/F4
Mazana (lake), Québec 172/C2
Mazana (riv.), Québec 172/C2
Mazandaran (prov.), Iran 66/H2
Mazangano, Uruguay 145/E3
Mazapil, Mexico 150/J4
Mazara del Vallo, Italy 34/D6
Mazar-e Sharif, Afghanistan 59/J2
Mazar-e Sharif, Afghanistan 68/B1
Mazarrón, Spain 33/F4
Mazaruni (riv.), Guyana 131/A2
Mazaruni-Potaro (dist.), Guyana 131/A2
Mazatán, Mexico 150/E2
Mazatenango, Guatemala 154/B3
Mazatlán, Mexico 146/H7
Mazatlán, Mexico 150/F5
Mazatzal (peak), Ariz. 198/D4
Mažeikiai, U.S.S.R. 53/A2
Mazenod, Sask. 181/E6
Mazeppa, Alberta 182/D4
Mazeppa, Minn. (55956) 255/F6
Mazgirt, Turkey 63/H3
Mazıdağı, Turkey 63/J4
Mazie, Okla. (74353) 288/R2
Mazinaw (lake), Ontario 177/G3
Mazirbe, U.S.S.R. 53/B2
Mazocruz, Peru 128/H11
Mazoe (riv.), Mozambique 118/E3
Mazoe, Zimbabwe 118/E3
Mazoe (riv.), Zimbabwe 118/E3
Mazomanie, Wis. (53560) 317/G9
Mazon, Ill. (60444) 222/E2
Mazra', Israel 65/C5
Mazu (Matsu) (isl.), China 77/K6
Mazzarino, Italy 34/E6
Mbabane (cap.), Swaziland 118/E5
Mbabane (cap.), Swaziland 102/F7
Mbaïki, Cent. Afr. Rep. 115/C3
Mbakou (res.), Cameroon 115/B2
Mbala, Zambia 102/F5
Mbala, Zambia 115/F5
Mbale, Uganda 115/F3
Mbale, Uganda 102/F4
Mbalmayo, Cameroon 115/B3
Mbamba Bay, Tanzania 115/G6
Mbandaka, Zaire 115/C3
Mbandaka, Zaire 102/D5
Mbanza Congo, Angola 115/B5
Mbanza-Ngungu, Zaire 102/D5
Mbanza-Ngungu, Zaire 115/C5
Mbaracayú, Cordillera de (mts.), Paraguay 144/E3
Mbarangandu (riv.), Tanzania 115/G5
Mbarara, Uganda 115/F4
Mbemkuru (riv.), Tanzania 115/G5
Mbengga (isl.), Fiji 86/Q11
Mbéré (riv.), Cameroon 115/B2
Mbéré (riv.), Cent. Afr. Rep. 115/B2
Mbéré (riv.), Chad 111/C6
Mbeya (reg.), Tanzania 115/F5
Mbeya, Tanzania 102/F5
Mbeya, Tanzania 115/F5
M'Bigou, Gabon 115/B4
Mbinda, Congo 115/B4
Mbini, Equat. Guinea 115/A3
Mbocayaty, Paraguay 144/C5
M'Bour, Senegal 106/A6
M'Bout, Mauritania 106/B5
Mbres, Cent. Afr. Rep. 115/D2
M'Bridge (riv.), Angola 115/B5
Mbuji-Mayi, Zaire 102/E5
Mbuji-Mayi, Zaire 115/D5
Mbulu, Tanzania 115/G4
Mburucuyá, Argentina 143/E2
Mbuyapey, Paraguay 144/D5
McAdam, New Bruns. 170/C3
McAdams, Miss. (39107) 256/E4
McAdoo, Pa. (18237) 294/L4
McAdoo, Texas (79243) 303/D4
McAfee, N.J. (07428) 273/D1
McAlester, Okla. 188/G4
McAlester, Okla. (74501) 288/P5
McAlester (lake), Okla. 288/P4
McAlister, N. Mex. (88427) 274/F4
McAlisterville, Pa. (17049) 294/H4
McAllaster, Kansas (†67755) 232/A3
McAllen, Texas 188/G5
McAllen, Texas (78501) 303/F11
McAllister, Mont. (59740) 262/E5
McAllister, Wis. (†54177) 317/L5
McAlpin, Fla. (32062) 212/D1
McAndrews, Ky. (41543) 237/S5
McArthur, Calif. (96056) 204/D2
McArthur, Ohio (45651) 284/F7
McArthur River, North. Terr. 88/F3
McAuley, Manitoba 179/A4
McBain, Mich. (49657) 250/D4
McBaine, Mo. (†65201) 261/H5
McBean, Georgia (†30908) 217/J4
McBee, S.C. (29101) 296/G3
McBride, Br. Col. 184/G3
McBride, Miss. (†39144) 256/C7
McBride, Mo. (63776) 261/N7
McBride, Okla. (†74441) 288/N7
McBride Lake, Sask. 181/J3
McBrides, Mich. (48852) 250/D5
McCabe, Mont. (59245) 262/M2
McCain, N.C. (28361) 281/L4
McCall, Idaho (83638) 220/C5
McCall, La. (†70346) 238/K3
McCalla, Ala. (35111) 195/E4
McCall Creek, Miss. (39647) 256/C7
McCallsburg, Iowa (50154) 229/G4
McCallum, Newf. 166/C4
McCamey, Texas (79752) 303/B6
McCammon, Idaho (83250) 220/F7
McCanna, N. Dak. (58253) 282/P3
McCarley, Miss. (38943) 256/E3
McCarr, Ky. (41544) 237/S6
McCarthy, Alaska (†99566) 196/K2
McCaskill, Ark. (71847) 202/C6
McCauley (isl.), Br. Col. 184/B3
McCaulley, Texas (79534) 303/E5
McCausland, Iowa (52758) 229/M5
McCaysville, Georgia (30555) 217/D1
McChord A.F.B., Wash. 310/C3
McClain (co.), Okla. 288/L5
McClave, Colo. (81057) 208/O6
McCleary, Wash. (98557) 310/B3
McClellan A.F.B., Calif. 204/B8
McClelland (lake), Alberta 182/E1
McClelland, Ark. (†72006) 202/H3
McClelland, Iowa (51548) 229/B6
McClellanville, S.C. (29458) 296/H5
McCloud, Calif. (96057) 204/C2
McCloud, Tenn. (†37857) 237/R8
McClure (lake), Calif. 204/E6
McClure, Ill. (62957) 222/D6
McClure, Ohio (43534) 284/C3
McClure, Pa. (17841) 294/H4
McClure, Va. (24269) 307/D6
McClusky, N. Dak. (58463) 282/K4
McColl, S.C. (29570) 296/H2
McComb, Miss. (39648) 256/D8
McComb, Ohio (45858) 284/C3
McConaughy, C. W. (lake), Nebr. 264/C3
McCondy, Miss. (38854) 256/G3
McCone (co.), Mont. 262/L3
McConnell, Ill. (61050) 222/D1
McConnell, Manitoba 179/B4
McConnell, Tenn. (†38237) 237/D8
McConnell A.F.B., Kansas 232/E4
McConnells, S.C. (29726) 296/E2
McConnellsburg, Pa. (17233) 294/F6
McConnellsville, N.Y. (13401) 276/J4
McConnelsville, Ohio (43756) 284/G6
McCook, Nebr. (69001) 264/D4
McCook (co.), S. Dak. 298/P6
McCool, Miss. (39108) 256/F4
McCool Junction, Nebr. (68401) 264/G4
McCord, Sask. 181/E6
McCordsville, Ind. (46055) 227/F5
McCorkle, W. Va. (†25564) 312/C6
McCormick (co.), S.C. 296/C4
McCormick, S.C. (29835) 296/C4
McCoy, Colo. (80463) 208/F3
McCoy (head), New Bruns. 170/E3
McCoy, Oreg. (†97338) 291/D2
McCoy (creek), Oreg. 291/J5
McCoy, Va. (24111) 307/G6
McCoy A.F.B., Fla. 212/E3
McCoysburg, Ind. (†47978) 227/C3
McCracken, Kansas (67556) 232/C3
McCracken (co.), Ky. 237/D6
McCrea, Pa. (†17241) 294/H5
McCreary (co.), Ky. 237/N7
McCreary, Manitoba 179/C4
McCrory, Ark. (72101) 202/H3
McCulloch (co.), Texas 303/E6
McCullom Lake, Ill. (†60050) 222/E1
McCullough, Ala. (36552) 195/D8
McCune, Kansas (66753) 232/G4
McCurtain (co.), Okla. 288/S6
McCurtain, Okla. (74944) 288/R4
McCutchenville, Ohio (44844) 284/D4
McDade, Texas (78650) 303/G7
McDaniel, Md. (21647) 245/N5
McDaniels, Ky. (40152) 237/J5
McDavid, Fla. (32568) 212/B5
McDermitt, Nev. (89421) 266/D1
McDermott, Ohio (45652) 284/D8
McDonald (isls.), Australia 2/N8
McDonald, Kansas (67745) 232/A2
McDonald (co.), Mo. 261/D9
McDonald (lake), Mont. 262/B2
McDonald, N. Mex. (88262) 274/F5
McDonald, N.C. (28340) 281/L5
McDonald, Ohio (44437) 284/J3
McDonald, Pa. (15057) 294/B5
McDonald, Tenn. (37353) 237/M10
McDonalds Corners, Ontario 177/H3
McDonnell, Queensland 95/B1
McDonough (lake), Conn. 210/D1
McDonough, Del. (†19709) 245/R3
McDonough, Georgia (30253) 217/D4
McDonough (co.), Ill. 222/C3
McDonough, N.Y. (13801) 276/J5
McDougal, Ark. (72441) 202/K1
McDougall (lake), New Bruns. 170/D3
McDowell, Ala. (†35450) 195/C5
McDowell, Ky. (41647) 237/R6
McDowell (co.), N.C. 281/E3
McDowell, Va. (24458) 307/J4
McDowell (co.), W. Va. 312/C8
McDowell, W. Va. (24858) 312/D8
McDuffie (co.), Georgia 217/H4
McElhattan, Pa. (17748) 294/H3
McElmo (creek), Colo. 208/B8
McElmo (creek), Utah 304/E6
McEwen, Tenn. (37101) 237/F8
McFadden, Wyo. (82080) 319/F4
McFall, Mo. (64657) 261/D2
McFarlan, N.C. (28102) 281/J5
McFarland, Calif. (93250) 204/F8
McFarland, Kansas (66501) 232/F2
McFarland, Mich. (†49880) 250/B2
McFarland, Wis. (53558) 317/H10
McFarlane (riv.), Sask. 181/L2
McGaffey, N. Mex. (†87316) 274/A3
McGaheysville, Va. (22840) 307/L4
McGee, Sask. 181/C4
McGees Mills, Pa. (15755) 294/E4
McGehee, Ark. (71654) 202/H6
McGill, Nev. (89318) 266/G3
McGivney, New Bruns. 170/D2
McGloughlin (peak), Mont. 262/C4
McGrath, Alaska 188/C5
McGrath, Alaska (99627) 196/H2
McGrath, Minn. (56350) 255/E4
McGraw, N.Y. (13101) 276/H5
McGraw Brook, New Bruns. 170/D2
McGrawsville, Ind. (†46911) 227/E3
McGregor (lake), Alberta 182/D4
McGregor, Br. Col. 184/G3
McGregor (riv.), Br. Col. 184/G3
McGregor, Iowa (52157) 229/L2
McGregor, Minn. (55760) 255/E4
McGregor (lake), Mont. 262/B3
McGregor, N. Dak. (58755) 282/D2
McGregor, Ontario 177/B5
McGregor, Texas (76657) 303/G6
McGrew, Nebr. (69353) 264/A3
McGuffey, Ohio (45859) 284/C4
McGuire (mt.), Idaho 220/D4
McGuire A.F.B., N.J. 273/D3
McHenry (co.), Ill. 222/E1
McHenry, Ill. (60050) 222/E1
McHenry, Ky. (42354) 237/H6
McHenry, Miss. (39561) 256/F9
McHenry (co.), N. Dak. 282/J3
McHenry, N. Dak. (58464) 282/N4
McHenry Shores, Ill. (†60050) 222/E1
Mchinga, Tanzania 115/H5
Mchinji, Malawi 115/F6
McIlwraith (range), Queensland 95/B2
McIndoe Falls, Vt. (05050) 268/C3
McIntire, Iowa (50455) 229/H2
McIntosh, Ala. (36553) 195/B8
McIntosh, Fla. (32664) 212/D2
McIntosh (co.), Georgia 217/K7
McIntosh, Georgia (†31320) 217/K7
McIntosh, Minn. (56556) 255/C3
McIntosh, N. Mex. (87032) 274/D4
McIntosh (co.), N. Dak. 282/L7
McIntosh (co.), Okla. 288/P4
McIntosh, Ontario 177/F4
McIntosh, Ontario 175/B3
McIntosh, S. Dak. (57641) 298/G2
McIntyre, Georgia (31054) 217/F5
McIvor, Mich. (†48748) 250/F4
McKague, Sask. 181/G3
McKamie, Ark. (†71860) 202/C7
McKay (lake), Manitoba 179/C2
McKay (res.), Oreg. 291/J2
McKean (co.), Pa. 294/E2
McKean, Pa. (16426) 294/B2
McKeand (riv.), N.W. Terrs. 187/M3
McKee (creek), Ill. 222/C4
McKee, Ky. (40447) 237/O6
McKee City, N.J. (†08232) 273/D5
McKeesport, Pa. 188/L2
McKeesport, Pa. (*15130) 294/C7
McKees Rocks, Pa. (15136) 294/B7
McKellar, Ontario 177/D2
McKendrick, New Bruns. 170/D1
McKenna, Wash. (98558) 310/C4
McKenney, Va. (23872) 307/N7
McKenzie, Ala. (36456) 195/E7
McKenzie (co.), N. Dak. 282/D4
McKenzie, N. Dak. (58553) 282/K6
McKenzie, South Fork (riv.), Oreg. 291/E3
McKenzie, Tenn. (38201) 237/E8
McKenzie Bridge, Oreg. (97401) 291/E3
McKerrow, Ontario 177/C1
McKinlay, Queensland 95/B4
McKinlay, Queensland 88/G4
McKinley, Ala. (†36743) 195/C6
McKinley (mt.), Alaska 146/C3
McKinley (mt.), Alaska 188/D5
McKinley (mt.), Alaska 196/H2
McKinley, Cuba 158/B2
McKinley, Minn. (55761) 255/F3
McKinley (co.), N. Mex. 274/A3
McKinley (mt.),U.S. 4/C17

408 McKinley

McKinley, Wyo. (†82633) 319/G3
McKinley Park, Alaska (99755) 196/J2
McKinleyville, Calif. (95521) 204/A3
McKinney (lake), Kansas 232/A3
McKinney, Ky. (40448) 237/M6
McKinney, Texas (75069) 303/H4
McKinnon, Georgia (†31545) 217/J8
McKinnon, Tenn. (†37175) 237/F8
McKinnon, Wyo. (82938) 319/C4
McKittrick, Calif. (93251) 204/F8
McKittrick, Mo. (65056) 261/J5
McLain, Miss. (39456) 256/G8
McLane, Pa. (†16426) 294/B2
McLaughlin, Alberta 182/E3
McLaughlin, S. Dak. (57642) 298/H2
McLaurin, Miss. (†39401) 256/F8
McLean (co.), Ill. 222/E3
McLean, Ill. (61754) 222/D3
McLean (co.), Ky. 237/G5
McLean, Nebr. (68747) 264/G2
McLean, N.Y. (13102) 276/H5
McLean (co.), N. Dak. 282/G4
McLean, Sask. 181/G5
McLean, Texas (79057) 303/D2
McLean, Va. (*22101) 307/S2
McLeansboro, Ill. (62859) 222/E5
McLelan (str.), Newf. 166/B1
McLemoresville, Tenn. (38235) 237/D9
McLennan, Alberta 182/B2
McLennan (co.), Texas 303/G6
McLeod (riv.), Alberta 182/B3
McLeod (co.), Minn. 255/D6
McLeod, Mont. (59052) 262/G5
McLeod, N. Dak. (58057) 282/R7
McLeod (bay), N.W. Terrs. 187/G3
McLeod (lake), W. Australia 88/A4
McLeod (lake), W. Australia 92/A4
McLeod Lake, Br. Col. 184/F2
McLeod River, Alberta 182/B3
M'Clintock, Manitoba 179/K2
M'Clintock (chan.), N.W.T. 146/H2
M'Clintock (chan.), N.W.T. 162/F1
M'Clintock (bay), N.W. Terrs. 187/K1
M'Clintock (chan.), N.W. Terrs. 187/H2
McLoud, Okla. (74851) 288/M4
McLoughlin (mt.), Oreg. 291/E5
McLoughlin House Nat'l Hist. Site, Oreg. 291/B2
McLouth, Kansas (66054) 232/G2
McLure, Br. Col. 184/H4
M'Clure (str.), Canada 4/B15
M'Clure (cape), N.W.T. 162/D1
M'Clure (str.), N.W.T. 146/F2
M'Clure (str.), N.W.T. 162/E1
M'Clure (cape), N. W. Terrs. 187/F2
M'Clure (str.), N.W. Terrs. 187/G2
McMahon, Sask. 181/D5
McMechen, W. Va. (26040) 312/E3
McMillan, Mich. (49853) 250/D2
McMillan (lake), N.Mex. 188/F4
McMillan (lake), N. Mex. 274/E6
McMillan, Okla. (73445) 288/M6
McMinn (co.), Tenn. 237/M10
McMinnville, Oreg. (97128) 291/D2
McMinnville, Tenn. (37110) 237/K9
McMorran, Sask. 181/C4
McMullen (co.), Texas 303/F9
McMunn, Manitoba 179/G5
McMurdo (sound), Ant. 2/A10
McMurdo (sound) 5/B9
McMurdo, Br. Col. 184/J4
McMurray, Wash. (†98273) 310/C2
McNab, Alberta 182/D5
McNab, Ark. (†71838) 202/C6
McNabb, Ill. (61335) 222/D2
McNair, Texas (†77520) 303/K1
McNairy (co.), Tenn. 237/D10
McNairy, Tenn. (†38315) 237/D10
McNamee, New Bruns. 170/D2
McNary, Ariz. (85930) 198/F4
McNary, La. (†71433) 238/E5
McNary, Oreg. (97858) 291/H2
McNary (dam), Oreg. 291/H2
McNary, Texas (79839) 303/B11
McNary (dam), Wash. 310/F5
McNaughton, Wis. (54543) 317/H4
McNeal, Ariz. (85617) 198/F7
McNeil, Ark. (71752) 202/D7
McNeill, Miss. (39457) 256/E9
McNulty, Oreg. (†97053) 291/E2
McNutt (isl.), Nova Scotia 168/C5
McPhadyen (riv.), Newf. 166/A3
McPhail (riv.), Manitoba 179/F2
McPherson (co.), Kansas 232/E3
McPherson, Kansas (67460) 232/E3
McPherson (co.), Nebr. 264/C3
McPherson (range), N.S. Wales 97/G1
McPherson (co.), S. Dak. 298/L2
McQuady, Ky. (40153) 237/H5
McRae, Alberta 182/E2
McRae, Ark. (72102) 202/G3
McRae, Georgia (31055) 217/G6
McRoberts, Ky. (41835) 237/R6
McShan, Ala. (35471) 195/B4
McSherrystown, Pa. (17344) 294/H6
McTaggart, Sask. 181/H6
McTavish, Manitoba 179/E5
McTavish Arm (inlet), N.W. Terrs. 187/G3
McVeigh, Ky. (41546) 237/S5
McVeytown, Pa. (17051) 294/G4
McVicar Arm (inlet), N.W. Terrs. 187/F3
McVille, N. Dak. (58254) 282/O4
McWhorter, W. Va. (26401) 312/F4
McWilliams, Ala. (36753) 195/D7
Meacham (lake), N.Y. 276/M1
Meacham, Oreg. (97859) 291/J2
Meacham, Sask. 181/F3
Mead (lake) 188/D3
Mead (lake), Ariz. 198/A2
Mead, Colo. (80542) 208/K2
Mead, Nebr. (68041) 264/H3
Mead (lake), Nev. 266/G6
Mead, Okla. (73449) 288/O7
Mead (lake), U.S. 146/G6
Mead, Wash. (99021) 310/H3
Meade (riv.), Alaska 196/G1
Meade (peak), Idaho 220/G7
Meade (co.), Kansas 232/B4
Meade, Kansas (67864) 232/B4
Meade (co.), Ky. 237/J5
Meade (co.), S. Dak. 298/D5
Meador, W. Va. (†25678) 312/B7
Meadow (creek), Idaho 220/C4
Meadow (mt.), Md. 245/B2
Meadow (lake), Sask. 181/C1
Meadow, S. Dak. (57644) 298/E2
Meadow, Texas (79345) 303/B4
Meadow, Utah (84644) 304/B5
Meadow (riv.), W. Va. 312/E6
Meadow Bluff, W. Va. (24958) 312/E7
Meadow Bridge, W. Va. (25976) 312/E7
Meadowbrook, Ill. (†62010) 222/B2
Meadowbrook, W. Va. (26404) 312/F4
Meadow Creek, W. Va. (25977) 312/E7
Meadow Grove, Nebr. (68752) 264/G2
Meadow Lake, Sask. 181/C1
Meadow Lake Prov. Park, Sask. 181/K4
Meadowlands, Minn. (55765) 255/F3
Meadow Lands, Pa. (15347) 294/B5
Meadow Portage, Manitoba 179/C3
Meadows, Idaho (†83654) 220/B5
Meadows, Ill. (†61726) 222/E3
Meadows, Md. (†20870) 245/G5
Meadows, N.H. (03587) 268/E3
Meadows, S. Australia 94/B8
Meadows of Dan, Va. (24120) 307/H7
Meadow Vale, Ky. (†40201) 237/L1
Meadow Valley, Calif. (95956) 204/D4
Meadow Valley Wash (riv.), Nev. 266/G5
Meadowview-Emory, Va. (24361) 307/D7
Meadow Vista, N. Mex. (†79901) 274/C7
Meadville, Miss. (39653) 256/C8
Meadville, Mo. (64659) 261/F3
Meadville, Pa. 188/L2
Meadville, Pa. (16335) 294/B2
Meaford, Ontario 177/D3
Meagher (co.), Mont. 262/F4
Meaghers Grant, Nova Scotia 168/E4
Meakan (mt.), Japan 81/L2
Mealhada, Portugal 33/B2
Mealy, Ky. (41234) 237/R5
Mealy (lake), Newf. 166/C3
Meander, Tasmania 99/C3
Meander River, Alberta 182/A5
Meanook, Alberta 182/D2
Means, Ky. (40346) 237/O5
Meansville, Georgia (30256) 217/D4
Meares (cape), Oreg. 291/C2
Mearim (riv.), Brazil 132/E4
Mearns, Alberta 182/D3
Mears, Mich. (49436) 250/C5
Meath (co.), Ireland 17/H4
Meathas Truim, Ireland 17/G4
Meath Park, Sask. 181/F2
Meaux, France 28/E3
Mebane, N.C. (27302) 281/L2
Mecca, Calif. (92254) 204/K10
Mecca, Ind. (47860) 227/C5
Mecca (cap.), Saudi Arabia 2/M4
Mecca (cap.), Saudi Arabia 59/C5
Mecca (cap.), Saudi Arabia 54/F7
Mechanic Falls, Maine (04256) 243/C7
Mechanic Falls○, Maine (04256) 243/C7
Mechanicsburg, Ill. (62545) 222/D4
Mechanicsburg, Ind. (†47356) 227/G5
Mechanicsburg, Ohio (43044) 284/D5
Mechanicsburg, Pa. (17055) 294/H5
Mechanicsburg, Va. (†24315) 307/G6
Mechanicstown, Ohio (44651) 284/H4
Mechanicsville, Conn. (06252) 210/H1
Mechanicsville, Georgia (30040) 217/L1
Mechanicsville, Iowa (52306) 229/L5
Mechanicsville, Md. (20659) 245/M7
Mechanicsville, Va. (23111) 307/O5
Mechanicville, N.Y. (12118) 276/N5
Mechelen, Belgium 27/F6
Mecheria, Algeria 106/D2
Mechernich, W. Germany 22/B3
Mecidiye, Turkey 63/B5
Mecitözü, Turkey 63/F2
Mecklenburg (bay), E. Germany 22/D1
Mecklenburg (reg.), E. Germany 22/E2
Mecklenburg, N.Y. (14863) 276/G6
Mecklenburg (co.), N.C. 281/H4
Mecklenburg (co.), Va. 307/M7
Mecklenburg (bay), W. Germany 22/D1
Meckling, S. Dak. (57044) 298/R8
Meconta, Mozambique 118/F3
Mecosta (co.), Mich. 250/D5
Mecosta, Mich. (49332) 250/D5
Mecoya, Bolivia 136/C8
Mecsek (mts.), Hungary 41/D3
Mecúfi, Mozambique 118/G2
Mecula, Mozambique 118/F2
Medain Salih, Saudi Arabia 59/C4
Medan, Indonesia 54/L9
Medan, Indonesia 85/B5
Médanos, Buenos Aires, Argentina 143/D4
Médanos, Entre Ríos, Argentina 143/G6
Médanos (isth.), Venezuela 124/D2
Medanosa (pt.), Argentina 143/D6
Medaryville, Ind. (47957) 227/D2
Meddybemps○, Maine (04657) 243/J5
Meddybemps (lake), Maine 243/J5
Médéa, Algeria 106/E1
Medel (mt.), Switzerland 39/D2
Medellín, Colombia 120/B2
Medellín, Colombia 126/C4
Medellín de Bravo, Mexico 150/Q2
Medemblik, Netherlands 27/G3
Médenine, Tunisia 106/F2
Mederdra, Mauritania 106/A5
Mederville, Iowa (†52043) 229/K3
Medetsiz Tepe (mt.), Turkey 63/F4
Medfield, Mass. (02052) 249/B8
Medfield○, Mass. (02052) 249/B8
Medford, Maine (†04453) 243/F5
Medford○, Maine (†04453) 243/F5
Medford, Mass. (02155) 249/C6
Medford, Minn. (55049) 255/E6
Medford, N.J. (08055) 273/D4
Medford, Okla. (73759) 288/L1
Medford, Oreg. 188/B2
Medford, Oreg. 146/F5
Medford, Oreg. (97501) 291/E5
Medford, Wis. (54451) 317/F5
Medford Center, Maine (†04453) 243/F5
Medford Lakes, N.J. (08055) 273/D4
Medgidia, Romania 45/J3
Medgun (creek), N.S. Wales 97/E1
Media, Ill. (61460) 222/C3
Media, Pa. (*19063) 294/L7
Media Agua, Argentina 143/C3
Media Luna, Cuba 158/G4
Mediapolis, Iowa (52637) 229/L6
Mediaş, Romania 45/G2
Medical Lake, Wash. (99022) 310/H3
Medical Springs, Oreg. (97860) 291/K2
Medicine (lake), Mont. 262/M2
Medicine (creek), Nebr. 264/D4
Medicine (creek), S. Dak. 298/J6
Medicine Bow (range), Colo. 208/G1
Medicine Bow, Wyo. (82329) 319/F4
Medicine Bow (range), Wyo. 319/F4
Medicine Bow (riv.), Wyo. 319/F3
Medicine Creek (dam), Nebr. 264/D4
Medicine Hat, Alberta 182/E4
Medicine Hat, Alta. 146/H4
Medicine Hat, Alta. 162/E5
Medicine Knoll (creek), S. Dak. 298/J5
Medicine Lake, Minn. (55441) 255/G5
Medicine Lake, Mont. (59247) 262/M2
Medicine Lodge (creek), Idaho 220/F5
Medicine Lodge, Kansas (67104) 232/D4
Medicine Lodge (riv.), Kansas 232/D4
Medicine Mound, Texas (†79252) 303/E3
Medicine Park, Okla. (73557) 288/J5
Medill, Mo. (†63445) 261/J2
Medina, Colombia 126/D5
Medina (Hamel), Minn. (†55340) 255/F5
Medina, N.Y. (14103) 276/D4
Medina, N. Dak. (58467) 282/M6
Medina (co.), Ohio 284/G3
Medina, Ohio (44256) 284/G3
Medina, Saudi Arabia 54/F7
Medina, Saudi Arabia 59/D5
Medina, Tenn. (38355) 237/D9
Medina (co.), Texas 303/E8
Medina, Texas (78055) 303/E8
Medina (lake), Texas 303/E8
Medina (riv.), Texas 303/J11
Medina, Wash. (98039) 310/B2
Medinaceli, Spain 33/E2
Medina del Campo, Spain 33/D2
Medina de Rioseco, Spain 33/D2
Medina-Sidonia, Spain 33/D4
Mediodía, Colombia 126/D8
Mediterranean (sea) 2/K4
Mediterranean (sea) 7/E5
Mediterranean (sea), Algeria 106/E1
Mediterranean (sea), Egypt 111/E1
Mediterranean (sea), France 28/E7
Mediterranean (sea), Italy 34/B6
Mediterranean (sea), Libya 111/C1
Mediterranean (sea), Morocco 106/D1
Mediterranean (sea), Tunisia 106/F1
Medix Run, Pa. (†15868) 294/F3
Medjerda (riv.), Algeria 106/F1
Medjerda (riv.), Tunisia 106/F1
Medley, Fla. (†33101) 212/B4
Medley, W. Va. (26734) 312/H4
Mednogorsk, U.S.S.R. 52/J4
Mednogorsk, U.S.S.R. 48/F4
Médoc (reg.), France 28/C5
Médog, China 77/E6
Medon, Tenn. (38356) 237/D10
Medora, Ill. (62063) 222/C4
Medora, Ind. (47260) 227/E7
Medora, Kansas (67558) 232/E3
Medora, Manitoba 179/B5
Medora, N. Dak. (58645) 282/C6
Médouneu, Gabon 115/B3
Medstead, Sask. 181/C2
Meductic, New Bruns. 170/C3
Medveditsa (riv.), U.S.S.R. 52/F4
Medvezh'yegorsk, U.S.S.R. 48/D3
Medvezh'yegorsk, U.S.S.R. 52/D2
Medway (riv.), England 13/H6
Medway○, Maine (04460) 243/G4
Medway○, Mass. (02053) 249/J4
Medway (harb.), Nova Scotia 168/D4
Medway (riv.), Nova Scotia 168/C4
Medzilaborce, Czech. 41/F2
Meeandah, Queensland 88/K2
Meehan, Miss. (†39301) 256/G6
Meekatharra, Australia 87/B8
Meekatharra, W. Australia 88/B5
Meekatharra, W. Australia 92/B4
Meeker, Colo. (81641) 208/D2
Meeker, La. (71346) 238/F4
Meeker (co.), Minn. 255/D5
Meeker, Ohio (†43302) 284/D4
Meeker, Okla. (74855) 288/N4
Meeks, Georgia (†31049) 217/G5
Meeks Bay, Calif. (†95730) 204/E5
Meelpaeg (lake), Newf. 166/C4
Meerane, E. Germany 22/E3
Meerhout, Belgium 27/G6
Meers, Okla. (73558) 288/J5
Meersburg, W. Germany 22/C5
Meerssen, Netherlands 27/H7
Meerut, India 54/J7
Meerut, India 68/D3
Meeteetse, Wyo. (82433) 319/D1
Meeting (lake), Sask. 181/D2
Meeting Creek, Alberta 182/D3
Mega, Ethiopia 111/G7
Mega (isl.), Indonesia 85/C6
Megalópolis, Greece 45/E7
Mégantic (co.), Québec 172/F3
Mégantic (lake), Québec 172/G4
Mégara, Greece 45/F6
Megargel, Ala. (36457) 195/D8
Megargel, Texas (76370) 303/F4
Meggett, S.C. (29460) 296/G6
Meghalaya (state), India 68/G3
Megiddo, Israel 65/C2
Mehama, Oreg. (97384) 291/E3
Mehan, Okla. (†74074) 288/M2
Meherrin (riv.), N.C. 281/P1
Meherrin, Va. (23954) 307/M6
Meherrin (riv.), Va. 307/M7
Mehetia (isl.), Fr. Poly. 87/M7
Mehlville, Mo. (†63129) 261/P4
Mehoopany, Pa. (18629) 294/K2
Mehran, Iran 66/E4
Mehran (riv.), Iran 59/F4
Mehran (riv.), Iran 66/J7
Mehsana, India 68/C4
Mehun-sur-Yèvre, France 28/E4
Meifa, P.D.R. Yemen 59/E7
Meiganga, Cameroon 115/B2
Meighen (isl.), N.W.T. 162/M3
Meighen (isl.), N.W. Terrs. 187/H1
Meigle, Scotland 15/E4
Meigs, Georgia (31765) 217/D8
Meigs (co.), Ohio 284/F7
Meigs (co.), Tenn. 237/M9
Meikle (riv.), Alberta 182/A1
Meiktila, Burma 72/B2
Meilen, Switzerland 39/G2
Meiners Oaks-Mira Monte, Calif. (93023) 204/F9
Meiningen, E. Germany 22/D3
Meire Grove, Minn. (†56352) 255/C5
Meiringen, Switzerland 39/F3
Meiron (mt.), Israel 65/C1
Meise, Belgium 27/E7
Meissen, E. Germany 22/E3
Mei Xian, China 77/J7
Mejillones, Chile 120/B5
Mejillones, Chile 138/A4
Mejillones del Sur (bay), Chile 138/A4
Mekambo, Gabon 115/B3
Mekerrhane, Sebkha (salt lake), Algeria 106/E3
Mekili, Libya 111/D1
Mékinac (lake), Québec 172/E2
Mekinock, N. Dak. (58258) 282/R4
Meknès, Morocco 102/B1
Meknès, Morocco 106/C2
Mekong (riv.) 54/M8
Mekong (riv.) 2/Q4
Mekong (riv.), Burma 72/D2
Mekong (riv.), Cambodia 72/E4
Mekong (Lancang Jiang) (riv.), China 77/F7
Mekong (riv.), Laos 72/D3
Mekong (riv.), Thailand 72/E3
Mekong, Mouths of the (delta), Vietnam 72/E5
Mekoryuk, Alaska (99630) 196/E2
Melaka (state), Malaysia 72/D7
Melaka, Malaysia 54/M9
Melaka, Malaysia 72/D7
Melanesia (reg.), Pacific 87/E5
Melaval, Sask. 181/E6
Melba, Idaho (83641) 220/B6
Melber, Ky. (42069) 237/D7
Melbern, Ohio (†43506) 284/A3
Melbeta, Nebr. (69355) 264/A3
Melbourne, Ark. (72556) 202/G1
Melbourne, Australia 2/R7
Melbourne, Australia 87/E9
Melbourne, Fla. 188/K5
Melbourne, Fla. (*32901) 212/F3
Melbourne, Iowa (50162) 229/G5
Melbourne, Ky. (41059) 237/T2
Melbourne, Mo. (†64642) 261/E2
Melbourne (isl.), N.W. Terrs. 187/H3
Melbourne, Ontario 177/C5
Melbourne, Québec 172/E4
Melbourne (cap.), Victoria 88/H7
Melbourne (cap.), Victoria 97/H5
Melbourne, Wash. (†98563) 310/B4
Melbourne Airport, Victoria 88/K7
Melbourne Beach, Fla. (32951) 212/F3
Melby, Minn. (56351) 255/C4
Melcher, Honduras 154/D3
Melcher, Iowa (50163) 229/G6
Melchor (isl.), Chile 138/D6
Melchor Múzquiz, Mexico 150/H3
Melchor Ocampo, Mexico 150/H4
Melchor Ocampo del Balsas, Mexico 150/H8
Melder, La. (71451) 238/E4
Meldorf, W. Germany 22/C1
Meldrim, Georgia (31318) 217/K6
Meldrum Bay, Ontario 177/A2
Meldrum Creek, Br. Col. 184/F4
Meleb, Manitoba 179/E4
Melenki, U.S.S.R. 52/F3
Meleuz, U.S.S.R. 52/J4
Mélèzes (riv.), Québec 174/C1
Melfa, Va. (23410) 307/S5
Melfi, Chad 111/C5
Melfi, Italy 34/E4
Melfort, Sask. 162/F5
Melfort, Sask. 181/G3
Melfort, Loch (inlet), Scotland 15/C4
Melgaço, Portugal 33/B1
Melgar de Fernamental, Spain 33/D1
Melide, Switzerland 39/G5
Meligalá, Greece 45/F7
Melilla, Spain 106/D1
Melilla, Spain 102/B1
Melilla, Spain 7/D5
Melimoyu (mt.), Chile 138/D5
Melinca, Chile 138/D5
Melincué, Argentina /F6
Melipilla, Chile 138/F4
Melita, Manitoba 179/A5
Melitopol', U.S.S.R. 7/H4
Melitopol', U.S.S.R. 52/D5
Melitota, Md. (†21620) 245/O4
Melk, Austria 41/C2
Melkbosstrand, S. Africa 118/E6
Melksham, England 13/E6
Melksham, England 10/E5
Mellansel, Sweden 18/L5
Melle, W. Germany 22/C2
Mellen, Wis. (54546) 317/E3
Mellerud, Sweden 18/H7
Mellette (co.), S. Dak. 298/H6
Mellette, S. Dak. (57461) 298/N3
Mellingen, Switzerland 39/F2
Mellott, Ind. (47958) 227/C4
Mellwood, Ark. (72367) 202/H5
Melmore, Ohio (44845) 284/D3
Mělník, Czech. 41/C1
Melo, Uruguay 120/D6
Melo, Uruguay 145/E3
Melocheville, Québec 172/C4
Melozitna (riv.), Alaska 196/H1
Melrhir, Chott (salt lake), Algeria 106/F2
Melrose, Conn. (06049) 210/E1
Melrose, Fla. (32666) 212/D2
Melrose, Iowa (52569) 229/G7
Melrose, La. (71452) 238/E3
Melrose, Md. (†21102) 245/L2
Melrose, Mass. (02176) 249/D6
Melrose, Minn. (56352) 255/D5
Melrose, Mont. (59743) 262/D5
Melrose, New Bruns. 170/F2
Melrose, Newf. 166/D2
Melrose, N. Mex. (88124) 274/F4
Melrose, N.S. Wales 97/D3
Melrose, Ohio (45861) 284/B3
Melrose, Oreg. (†97470) 291/D4
Melrose, Scotland 15/F5
Melrose, Scotland 10/E3
Melrose, Wis. (54642) 317/E7
Melrose Park, Fla. (†33301) 212/B4
Melrose Park, Ill. (*60160) 222/B5
Melrose Park, N.Y. (†13021) 276/G5
Melrude, Minn. (55766) 255/F3
Mels, Switzerland 39/H2
Melsetter, Zimbabwe 118/E3
Melstone, Mont. (59054) 262/H4
Melsungen, W. Germany 22/C3
Melton, Victoria 97/C5
Melton Hill (lake), Tenn. 237/N9
Melton Mowbray, England 10/F4
Melton Mowbray, England 13/G5
Meltonville, Iowa (†50472) 229/G2
Melun, France 28/E3
Melut, Sudan 111/F5
Melvaig, Scotland 15/C3
Melvern, Kansas (66510) 232/G3
Melvern (lake), Kansas 232/G3
Melvern Square, Nova Scotia 168/C3
Melvich, Scotland 15/E2
Melville (isl.), Australia 87/D7
Melville (isl.), Canada 4/B15
Melville (pen.), Canada 4/C14
Melville (bay), Greenl. 4/B13
Melville, La. (71353) 238/G5
Melville, Mont. (59055) 262/F4
Melville (pen.), N.W.T. 146/K3
Melville (pen.), N.W.T. 162/H2
Melville (isl.), N.W.T. 146/G2
Melville (isl.), N.W.T. 162/E1
Melville (lake), N.W.T. 162/L5
Melville (lake), Newf. 166/C3
Melville, N.Y. (11746) 276/O9
Melville, N. Dak. (†58421) 282/M5
Melville (isl.), N.W. Terrs. 187/G2
Melville (pen.), N.W. Terrs. 187/K3
Melville (isl.), North. Terr. 88/E2
Melville (bay), North. Terr. 88/F2
Melville (bay), North. Terr. 93/E2
Melville (isl.), North. Terr. 93/B1
Melville (cape), Queensland 88/G2
Melville (cape), Queensland 95/C2
Melville, Sask. 162/F5
Melville, Sask. 181/J5
Melville, W. Australia 92/A1
Melvin, Ala. (36913) 195/B7
Melvin, Ill. (60952) 222/E3
Melvin, Iowa (51350) 229/B2
Melvin, Lough (lake), Ireland 10/B3
Melvin (lake), Ireland 17/E3
Melvin, Mich. (48454) 250/G5
Melvin, Minn. (†56540) 255/B3
Melvin, Lough (lake), N. Ireland 10/B3
Melvin, Texas (76858) 303/E6
Melvina, Wis. (54619) 317/E8
Melvindale, Mich. (48122) 250/B7
Melvin Mills, N.H. (†03278) 268/D5
Melvin Village, N.H. (03850) 268/E4
Mélykút, Hungary 41/E3
Memaliaj, Albania 45/D5
Memba, Mozambique 118/G2
Membij, Syria 63/G4
Memel (Klaipeda), U.S.S.R. 52/B3
Memel (Klaipeda), U.S.S.R. 53/A3
Memmingen, W. Germany 22/D5
Mempawah, Indonesia 85/D5
Memphis, Ala. (†35442) 195/B4
Memphis (ruins), Egypt 111/J3
Memphis, Fla. (†33561) 212/D4
Memphis, Ind. (47143) 227/F8
Memphis, Mich. (48041) 250/G6
Memphis, Miss. (†38680) 256/D1
Memphis, Mo. (63555) 261/H2
Memphis, Nebr. (68042) 264/H3
Memphis, Tenn. 146/K6
Memphis, Tenn. 188/J3
Memphis, Tenn. (*38101) 237/B10
Memphis, Texas (79245) 303/D3
Memphis Naval Air Sta., Tenn. 237/B10
Memphremagog (lake), Québec 172/E4
Memphremagog (lake), Vt. 268/C1
Memramcook, New Bruns. 170/F2
Mena, Ark. (71953) 202/B4
Menafra, Uruguay 145/B3
Menahga, Minn. (56464) 255/C4
Menai (str.), Wales 13/C4
Menai Bridge, Wales 13/C4
Menaik, Alberta 182/D3
Ménaka, Mali 106/E5
Menan, Idaho (83434) 220/F6
Menands, N.Y. (†12201) 276/N5
Menarandra (riv.), Madagascar 118/H4
Menard (co.), Ill. 222/D3
Menard (co.), Texas 303/E7
Menard, Texas (76859) 303/E7
Menasalbas, Spain 33/D3
Menasha, Wis. (54952) 317/J7
Mencué, Argentina 143/C5
Mendak, Saudi Arabia 59/D5
Mende, France 28/E5
Mendenhall (cape), Alaska 196/E3
Mendenhall, Miss. (39114) 256/E7
Menderes, Büyük (riv.), Turkey 59/A2
Menderes, Büyük (riv.), Turkey 63/C4
Mendes, Georgia (†30427) 217/H7
Méndez, Ecuador 128/C4
Mendham, N.J. (07945) 273/D2
Mendham, Sask. 181/B5
Mendi, Ethiopia 111/G6
Mendi, Papua N.G. 85/B7
Mendip (hills), England 13/E6
Mendocino (cape), Calif. 146/F5
Mendocino (cape), Calif. 188/A2
Mendocino (co.), Calif. 204/B4
Mendocino, Calif. (95460) 204/B4
Mendocino (cape), Calif. 204/A3
Mendon, Ill. (62351) 222/B3
Mendon○, Mass. (01756) 249/H4
Mendon, Mich. (49072) 250/D7
Mendon, Mo. (64660) 261/F3
Mendon, N.Y. (14506) 276/E4
Mendon, Ohio (45862) 284/A4
Mendon, Utah (84325) 304/B2
Mendon○, Vt. (†05701) 268/B4
Mendooran, N.S. Wales 97/E2
Mendota, Calif. (93640) 204/E7
Mendota, Ill. (61342) 222/D2
Mendota, Minn. (55050) 255/G5
Mendota, Va. (24270) 307/D7
Mendota (lake), Wis. 317/H9
Mendota Heights, Minn. (†55050) 255/G6
Mendoza (prov.), Argentina 143/C4
Mendoza, Argentina 120/C6
Mendoza, Argentina 143/C3
Mendoza (riv.), Argentina 143/C3
Mendoza, Cuba 158/A2
Mendoza, Peru 128/D6
Mendoza, Uruguay 145/C5
Mendrisio, Switzerland 39/G5
Mene de Mauroa, Venezuela 124/C2
Mene Grande, Venezuela 124/C3
Menemen, Turkey 63/B3
Menemsha, Mass. (02552) 249/L7
Menen, Belgium 27/C7
Meneses, Cuba 158/F2
Menfi, Italy 34/D6
Menfro, Mo. (63765) 261/N7
Mengcheng, China 77/J5
Mengen, Turkey 63/D2
Menggala, Indonesia 85/D6
Menghai, China 77/E7
Mengla, China 77/F7
Mengshan, China 77/H7
Mengzi, China 77/F7
Menifee, Ark. (72107) 202/E3
Menifee (co.), Ky. 237/O5
Menihek, Newf. 166/A3
Menihek (lakes), Newf. 166/A3
Menin (Menen), Belgium 27/C7
Menindee, N.S. Wales 97/B3
Menindee (lake), N.S. Wales 97/B3
Meningie, S. Australia 94/F6
Menisino, Manitoba 179/F5
Menistouc (lake), Newf. 166/A3
Menlo, Georgia (30731) 217/B2
Menlo, Iowa (50164) 229/E6
Menlo, Kansas (67746) 232/B2
Menlo, Wash. (98561) 310/B4
Menlo Park, Calif. (94025) 204/J3
Menlo Park, N.J. (08837) 273/E2
Menneval, New Bruns. 170/C1
Menno, S. Dak. (57045) 298/P7
Meno, Okla. (73760) 288/K2
Menoken, N. Dak. (58558) 282/J6
Menominee, Ill. (†61025) 222/C1
Menominee (co.), Mich. 250/B3
Menominee, Mich. (49858) 250/B3
Menominee (riv.), Mich. 250/B3
Menominee (co.), Wis. 317/J5
Menominee (riv.), Wis. 317/L5
Menominee Ind. Res., Wis. 317/J5
Menomonee Falls, Wis. (53051) 317/K1
Menomonie, Wis. (54751) 317/C6
Menongue, Angola 115/C6
Menorca (Minorca) (isl.), Spain 33/J2
Mentasta (pass), Alaska 196/K2
Mentasta Lake, Alaska (†99586) 196/K2
Mentawai (isls.), Indonesia 54/L10
Mentawai (isls.), Indonesia 85/B6
Mentmore, N. Mex. (87319) 274/A3
Menton, France 28/G6
Mentone, Ala. (35984) 195/G1
Mentone, Calif. (92359) 204/H9
Mentone, Ind. (46539) 227/E2
Mentone, Texas (79754) 303/D10
Mentor, Kansas (67465) 232/E3
Mentor, Ky. (†41060) 237/N3
Mentor, Minn. (56736) 255/B3
Mentor, Ohio (44060) 284/H2
Mentor-on-the-Lake, Ohio (44060) 284/G2
Menunketesuck (riv.), Conn. 210/E3
Menye, Turkey 63/C3
Menyuan, China 77/F4
Menzel Bourguiba, Tunisia 106/F1
Menzel Temime, Tunisia 106/G1
Menzie, Manitoba 179/B4
Menzies, W. Australia 88/C5
Menzies, W. Australia 92/C5
Menzingen, Switzerland 39/G2
Menznau, Switzerland 39/E2
Meoqui, Mexico 150/G2
Meota, Sask. 181/C2
Meppel, Netherlands 27/J3
Meppen, W. Germany 22/B2
Mequinenza (res.), Spain 33/F2
Mequon, Wis. (53092) 317/L1
Mera, Ecuador 128/C3
Mera (riv.), Switzerland 39/E2
Merabéllou (gulf), Greece 45/H8
Meraia (reg.), Mauritania 106/C5
Meråker, Norway 18/G5
Meramangye (lake), S. Australia 94/C3
Meramec (riv.), Mo. 261/N3
Merano, Italy 34/C1
Merasheen (isl.), Newf. 166/C2

Miguelete 409

Merauke, Indonesia 85/K7
Merbein, Victoria 97/A4
Mercaderes, Colombia 126/B7
Mercara, India 68/D6
Merced (co.), Calif. 204/E6
Merced, Calif. (95340) 204/E6
Merced (riv.), Calif. 204/E6
Mercedario, Cerro (mt.), Argentina 143/B3
Mercedes, Buenos Aires, Argentina 143/G7
Mercedes, San Luis, Argentina 143/C3
Mercedes, Argentina 120/C6
Mercedes, Corrientes, Argentina 143/G4
Mercedes, Texas (78570) 303/F12
Mercedes, Uruguay 120/D6
Mercedes, Uruguay 145/B4
Merceditas, Chile 138/B7
Mercer (co.), Ill. 222/C2
Mercer (co.), Ky. 237/M5
Mercer○, Maine (04957) 243/D6
Mercer (co.), Mo. 261/E2
Mercer, Mo. (64661) 261/F2
Mercer (co.), N.J. 273/D3
Mercer, N. Zealand 100/E2
Mercer (co.), N. Dak. 282/G5
Mercer, N. Dak. (58559) 282/J5
Mercer (co.), Ohio 284/A4
Mercer, Ohio (†45862) 284/A4
Mercer (co.), Pa. 294/B3
Mercer, Pa. (16137) 294/B3
Mercer, Tenn. (38392) 237/D10
Mercer (co.), W. Va. 312/D8
Mercer, Wis. (54547) 317/F3
Mercer Island (city), Wash. (98040) 310/B2
Mercersburg, Pa. (17236) 294/G6
Mercerville-Hamilton Square, N.J. (08619) 273/D3
Merchantville, N.J. (08109) 273/B3
Merchtem, Belgium 27/E7
Mercier, Bolivia 136/B2
Mercier, Kansas (†66439) 232/G2
Mercier, Québec 172/H4
Mercier (dam), Québec 172/A3
Mercoal, Alberta 182/B3
Mercury, Nev. (89023) 266/E6
Mercury (bay), N. Zealand 100/F2
Mercury (isls.), N. Zealand 100/F2
Mercury, Texas (†76872) 303/E6
Mercy (bay), N.W. Terrs. 187/G2
Mercy (cape), N.W. Terrs. 187/M3
Mere, England 13/E6
Meredith, Colo. (81642) 208/F4
Meredith (lake), Colo. 208/M6
Meredith, N.H. (03253) 268/D4
Meredith○, N.H. (03253) 268/D4
Meredith Center, N.H. (†03253) 268/D4
Meredosia, Ill. (62665) 222/C4
Merefa, U.S.S.R. 52/E5
Meregh, Somalia 115/J3
Merelbeke, Belgium 27/D7
Merevari (riv.), Venezuela 124/F5
Mergui, Burma 54/L8
Mergui, Burma 72/C4
Mergui (arch.), Burma 72/C5
Meriç, Turkey 63/B2
Meriç (riv.), Turkey 63/B2
Merid, Sask. 181/B4
Mérida, Mexico 146/J7
Mérida, Mexico 150/P6
Mérida, Spain 7/D5
Mérida, Spain 33/C3
Mérida (state), Venezuela 124/C3
Mérida, Venezuela 120/B2
Mérida, Venezuela 124/C3
Mérida, Cordillera de (range), Venezuela 124/C3
Meriden, Conn. (06450) 210/D2
Meriden, Iowa (51037) 229/B3
Meriden, Kansas (66512) 232/G2
Meriden, Minn. (56067) 255/E6
Meriden, N.H. (03770) 268/C4
Meriden, Wyo. (82081) 319/H4
Meridian, Georgia (31319) 217/K8
Meridian, Idaho (83642) 220/B6
Meridian, Miss. 146/K6
Meridian, Miss. 188/J4
Meridian, Miss. (39301) 256/G6
Meridian, N.Y. (13113) 276/G4
Meridian, Okla. (73058) 288/M3
Meridian, Texas (76665) 303/G6
Meridian Naval Air Sta., Miss. 256/G5
Meridianville, Ala. (35759) 195/F1
Merigold, Miss. (38759) 256/C3
Merigomish, Nova Scotia 168/F3
Merigomish (harb.), Nova Scotia 168/F3
Merimbula, N.S. Wales 97/F5
Merín (lag.), Uruguay 145/F4
Merino, Colo. (80741) 208/N2
Merino, Victoria 97/A5
Merino Jarpa (isl.), Chile 138/D7
Merinos, Uruguay 145/C3
Merino Village, Mass. (†01570) 249/G4
Merion Station, Pa. (19066) 294/M6
Merir (isl.), Belau 87/D5
Meriwether (co.), Georgia 217/C4
Meriwether Lewis Park, Natchez Trace Pkwy., Tenn. 237/G10
Merj 'Uyun, Lebanon 63/F6
Mérk, Hungary 41/G3
Merkel, Texas (79536) 303/E5
Merksem, Belgium 27/E6
Merksplas, Belgium 27/F6
Merlin, Ontario 177/B5
Merlin, Oreg. (97532) 291/D5
Merlo, Argentina 143/G7
Mermentau, La. (70556) 238/E6
Mermentau (riv.), La. 238/E7
Merna, Nebr. (68856) 264/E3
Merna, Wyo. (†83115) 319/B3
Meroe (ruins), Sudan 111/F4
Merom, Ind. (47861) 227/B6
Merowe, Sudan 111/F4
Merowe, Sudan 59/B6
Merredin, W. Australia 88/B6
Merredin, W. Australia 92/B5
Merri (riv.), Victoria 88/L7
Merriam, Ind. (†46701) 227/G2
Merriam, Kansas (66203) 232/H3
Merrick (co.), Nebr. 264/F3
Merrick, N.Y. (11566) 276/R7
Merrick (mt.), Scotland 15/D5
Merrickville, Ontario 177/J3
Merricourt, N. Dak. (58469) 282/N7
Merrifield, Minn. (56465) 255/D4
Merrifield (bay), Newf. 166/B2
Merrifield, N. Dak. (†58201) 282/R4
Merrifield, Va. (22116) 307/S3
Merrill (pass), Alaska 196/H2
Merrill, Iowa (51038) 229/A3
Merrill, Mich. (48637) 250/E5
Merrill, Miss. (†39452) 256/G9
Merrill, N.Y. (12955) 276/N1
Merrill, Oreg. (97633) 291/F5
Merrill, Wis. (54452) 317/G5
Merrillan, Wis. (54754) 317/E7
Merrillville, Georgia (†31792) 217/E9
Merrillville, Ind. (46410) 227/C2
Merrimac, Ky. (†40009) 237/L6
Merrimac○, Mass. (01860) 249/L1
Merrimac, W. Va. (†25661) 312/B7
Merrimac, Wis. (53561) 317/G9
Merrimack (riv.), Mass. 249/K1
Merrimack (co.), N.H. 268/D5
Merrimack○, N.H. (03054) 268/D6
Merrimack (riv.), N.H. 268/D5
Merrimacport, Mass. (†01860) 249/L1
Merriman, Nebr. (69218) 264/C2
Merrimon, N.C. (†28516) 281/R5
Merrionette Park, Ill. (†60601) 222/B6
Merritt, Br. Col. 162/D5
Merritt, Br. Col. 184/G5
Merritt (isl.), Fla. 212/F3
Merritt, Ill. (†62650) 222/C4
Merritt, Mich. (49667) 250/D4
Merritt (res.), Nebr. 264/D2
Merritt, Wash. (†98826) 310/E3
Merritt Island, Fla. (32952) 212/F3
Merriwa, N.S. Wales 97/F3
Merriwagga, N.S. Wales 97/C3
Merriweather, Mich. (49947) 250/F1
Mer Rouge, La. (71261) 238/G1
Merrow, Conn. (06251) 210/F1
Merry Hill, N.C. (27957) 281/R2
Merrymeeting (lake), N.H. 268/E5
Merry Oaks, N.C. (†27559) 281/L3
Merryville, La. (70653) 238/D5
Mersa Fatma, Ethiopia 111/H5
Mersá Matrûh, Egypt 111/E1
Mersa Matrûh, Egypt 102/E1
Mersch, Luxembourg 27/J9
Mersea (dist.), England 13/J6
Merseburg, E. Germany 22/D3
Mersey (riv.), England 10/F2
Mersey (riv.), England 13/G2
Mersey (riv.), Nova Scotia 168/C4
Mersey (riv.), Tasmania 99/C3
Merseyside (co.), England 13/G2
Mershon, Georgia (31551) 217/H8
Mersin, Turkey 63/F4
Mersin, Turkey 59/B2
Mersin, Turkey 54/E6
Mersing, Malaysia 72/E7
Mërsrags, U.S.S.R. 53/B2
Mertert, Luxembourg 27/J9
Merthyr Tydfil, Wales 13/A6
Merthyr Tydfil, Wales 10/E5
Mértola, Portugal 33/C4
Merton, England 10/B5
Merton, England 13/H8
Merton, Wis. (53056) 317/K1
Mertz Glacier Tongue 5/C8
Mertzon, Texas (76941) 303/C6
Mertztown, Pa. (19539) 294/L4
Meru, Kenya 115/G3
Meru (mt.), Tanzania 115/G4
Merv (Mary), U.S.S.R. 48/F8
Merville, Br. Col. 184/E5
Mervin, Sask. 181/C2
Merwin, Mo. (†64723) 261/C6
Merwin (lake), Wash. 310/C5
Merzifon, Turkey 63/F2
Merzig, W. Germany 22/B4
Mesa, Ariz. 146/G6
Mesa, Ariz. 188/D4
Mesa, Ariz. (*85201) 198/D5
Mesa (co.), Colo. 208/B5
Mesa, Colo. (81005) 208/C4
Mesa, Idaho (83643) 220/B5
Mesa, Miss. (†39667) 256/D8
Mesa, Wash. (99343) 310/G4
Mesabi (range), Minn. 255/E3
Mesa Bolívar, Venezuela 124/C3
Mesachie Lake, Br. Col. 184/J3
Mesa del Seri, Mexico 150/D2
Mesagne, Italy 34/G4
Mesai (riv.), Colombia 126/D7
Mesará (gulf), Greece 45/G8
Mesa Verde National Park, Colo. (81330) 208/C8
Mesa Verde Nat'l Park, Colo. 208/C8
Mescalero, N. Mex. (88340) 274/D5
Mescalero (ridge), N. Mex. 274/F6
Mescalero (valley), N. Mex. 274/F5
Mescalero Apache Ind. Res., N. Mex. 274/D5
Meschede, W. Germany 22/C3
Mesena, Georgia (30819) 217/G4
Meservey, Iowa (50457) 229/G3
Meshed, Iran 54/G6
Meshed, Iran 66/L2
Meshed, Iran 59/H2
Meshed-i-Sar (Babol Sar), Iran 66/H2
Meshik, Alaska (†99579) 196/G3
Meshoppen, Pa. (18630) 294/L2
Meshra er Req, Sudan 111/E6
Mesic, N.C. (†28515) 281/R4
Mesick, Mich. (49668) 250/D4
Mesilla, N. Mex. (88046) 274/C6
Mesilla Park, N. Mex. (88047) 274/C6
Mesita, Colo. (81142) 208/H8
Meskanaw, Sask. 181/F3
Meskene, Syria 63/H5
Meskene, Syria 59/C2
Mesocco, Switzerland 39/H4
Mesolóngion, Greece 45/E6
Mesopotamia (reg.), Iraq 66/B3
Mesopotamia (reg.), Iraq 59/D3
Mesopotamia, Ohio (44439) 284/J3
Mesquite, Nev. (89024) 266/G6
Mesquite, N. Mex. (88048) 274/C6
Mesquite, Texas (*75149) 303/H2
Messancy, Belgium 27/H9
Messina (prov.), Italy 34/E5
Messina, Italy 34/E5
Messina, Italy 7/F5
Messina (str.), Italy 34/E6
Messina, S. Africa 118/D4
Messines, Québec 172/B3
Messíni, Greece 45/E7
Messíni (gulf), Greece 45/E7
Mesta (riv.), Bulgaria 45/F5
Mestre, Italy 34/D2
Mesudiye, Turkey 63/F4
Meta (riv.) 120/B2
Meta (dept.), Colombia 126/D6
Meta (riv.), Colombia 126/E5
Meta, Ky. (41501) 237/S5
Meta, Mo. (65058) 261/H6
Meta (riv.), Venezuela 124/E4
Métabetchouan, Québec 172/F1
Métabetchouane (riv.), Québec 172/F1
Metairie, La. (*70001) 238/O4
Metaline, Wash. (99152) 310/H2
Metaline Falls, Wash. (99153) 310/H2
Metamma, Ethiopia 111/G5
Metamora, Ill. (61548) 222/D3
Metamora, Ind. (47030) 227/G6
Metamora, Mich. (48455) 250/F6
Metamora, Ohio (43540) 284/C2
Metán, Argentina 143/D2
Metangula, Mozambique 118/F2
Metapán, El Salvador 154/C3
Métascouac (lake), Québec 172/F2
Metasville, Georgia (†30673) 217/G3
Metauro (riv.), Italy 34/D3
Metcalf, Georgia (†31792) 217/E9
Metcalf, Ill. (61940) 222/F4
Metcalfe (co.), Ky. 237/K7
Metcalfe, Miss. (38760) 256/B4
Metcalfe, Ontario 177/J2
Metchin (riv.), Newf. 166/B3
Metchosin, Br. Col. 184/K4
Metea, Ind. (†46950) 227/E3
Metedeconk (riv.), N.J. 273/E3
Meteghan, Nova Scotia 168/B4
Meteghan Centre, Nova Scotia 168/B4
Meteghan River, Nova Scotia 168/B4
Meteor (crater), Ariz. 198/E3
Metepec, Mexico 150/M2
Methlick, Scotland 15/F3
Methow, Wash. (98834) 310/E2
Methow (riv.), Wash. 310/E2
Methuen○, Mass. (01844) 249/K2
Methven, N. Zealand 100/C5
Methven, Scotland 15/E4
Metica (riv.), Colombia 126/D6
Metigoshe (lake), N. Dak. 282/K2
Metinic (isl.), Maine 243/E8
Metinota, Sask. 181/C2
Metiskow, Alberta 182/E3
Métis-sur-Mer, Québec 172/A1
Metlakatla, Alaska (99926) 196/N2
Metlakatla, Br. Col. 184/B3
Metlatonoc, Mexico 150/K8
Metlili Chaamba, Algeria 106/E2
Meto (bayou), Ark. 202/H5
Metolius, Oreg. (†97741) 291/F3
Metolius (riv.), Oreg. 291/F3
Metompkin (inlet), Va. 307/T5
Metompkin (isl.), Va. 307/T5
Metonga (lake), Wis. 317/J4
Metropolis, Ill. (62960) 222/E6
Metropolitan, Mich. (†49381) 250/A3
Métsovon, Greece 45/E6
Mettawa, Ill. (†60048) 222/B4
Mettawee (riv.), Vt. 268/A5
Metter, Georgia (30439) 217/H6
Mettet, Belgium 27/F8
Mettler, Calif. (93307) 204/G8
Metuchen, N.J. (08840) 273/E2
Metula, Israel 65/D1
Metz, France 7/E4
Metz, France 28/G3
Metz, Ind. (†46703) 227/H1
Metz, Mich. (†49776) 250/F3
Metz, Mo. (64765) 261/C6
Metz, W. Va. (26585) 312/F3
Metzger, Oreg. (†97223) 291/A2
Metzingen, W. Germany 22/C4
Meudon, France 28/A2
Meulaboh, Indonesia 85/B5
Meulebeke, Belgium 27/C7
Meung-sur-Loire, France 28/D4
Meurthe-et-Moselle (dept.), France 28/G3
Meuse (riv.), Belgium 27/F8
Meuse (dept.), France 28/F3
Meuse (riv.), France 28/F3
Meuselwitz, E. Germany 22/E3
Mexia, Ala. (36458) 195/D8
Mexia, Texas (76667) 303/H6
Mexiana (isl.), Brazil 132/D2
Mexicali, Mexico 150/B1
Mexicali, Mexico 146/G6
Mexican Hat, Utah (84531) 304/E6
Mexican Springs, N. Mex. (87320) 274/A3
Mexico 2/D4
MEXICO 150
Mexico 146/H7
Mexico (gulf) 188/J5
Mexico (gulf) 2/E4
Mexico (gulf) 146/K7
Mexico (gulf), Ala. 195/E10
Mexico (gulf), Cuba 158/A1
Mexico (gulf), Fla. 212/C4
Mexico, Ind. (46958) 227/E3
Mexico, Ky. (†42411) 237/E6
Mexico (gulf), La. 238/F8
Mexico, Maine (04257) 243/B6
Mexico○, Maine (04257) 243/B6
México (state), Mexico 150/K7
Mexico (gulf), Mexico 150/N4
Mexico, Mo. (65265) 261/J4
Mexico, N.Y. (13114) 276/H4
Mexico, Pa. (17056) 294/H4
Mexico (gulf), Texas 303/K9
Mexico Beach, Fla. (32410) 212/D6
Mexico City (cap.), Mexico 150/L1
Mexico City (cap.), Mexico 146/J7
Mexico City (cap.), Mexico 2/E5
Meyadin, Syria 59/C3
Meyadin, Syria 63/J5
Meybod, Iran 66/J4
Meydani, Ras-e (cape), Iran 59/G4
Meydani, Ras-e (cape), Iran 66/L8
Meyer, Iowa (†50456) 229/H2
Meyers Chuck, Alaska (99903) 196/N2
Meyersdale, Pa. (15552) 294/E6
Meyers Lake, Ohio (†44701) 284/H4
Meyerton, S. Africa 118/H7
Meymaneh, Afghanistan 68/A1
Meymaneh, Afghanistan 54/H6
Meymaneh, Afghanistan 59/H2
Meyrin, Switzerland 39/B4
Meyronne, Sask. 181/E6
Mezcala (riv.), Mexico 150/J8
Mezen', U.S.S.R. 4/C7
Mezen', U.S.S.R. 7/J2
Mezen' (riv.), U.S.S.R. 7/J2
Mezen', U.S.S.R. 48/E3
Mezen', U.S.S.R. 52/F1
Mezen' (bay), U.S.S.R. 52/F1
Mezen' (riv.), U.S.S.R. 52/G1
Mezen' (riv.), U.S.S.R. 48/E3
Mézenc (mt.), France 28/E5
Mezhdurechenskiy, U.S.S.R. 48/G4
Mezhdusharskiy (isl.), U.S.S.R. 52/G1
Meziadin (lake), Br. Col. 184/C2
Mézin, France 28/D5
Mezőberény, Hungary 41/F3
Mezőcsát, Hungary 41/F3
Mezőfalva, Hungary 41/E3
Mezőhegyes, Hungary 41/F3
Mezőkovácsháza, Hungary 41/F3
Mezőkövesd, Hungary 41/F3
Mezőszilas, Hungary 41/E3
Mezőtúr, Hungary 41/F3
Mezquital, Mexico 150/G5
Mezquital (riv.), Mexico 150/G5
Mhor, Loch (lake), Scotland 15/D3
Mhow, India 68/D4
Miacatlán, Mexico 150/K2
Miahuatlán de Porfirio Díaz, Mexico 150/L8
Miajadas, Spain 33/D3
Miami, Ariz. (85539) 198/E5
Miami, Fla. 188/K5
Miami, Fla. 146/K7
Miami, Fla. (*33101) 212/B5
Miami (canal), Fla. 212/F5
Miami (riv.), Fla. 212/B5
Miami (co.), Ind. 227/E3
Miami, Ind. (46959) 227/E3
Miami (co.), Kansas 232/H3
Miami, Manitoba 179/D5
Miami, Mo. (65344) 261/F4
Miami, N. Mex. (87729) 274/E2
Miami (co.), Ohio 284/B5
Miami, Okla. (74354) 288/S1
Miami, Texas (79059) 303/D2
Miami, U.S. 2/F4
Miami Beach, Fla. 188/L5
Miami Beach, Fla. (33139) 212/C5
Miami Lakes, Fla. (†33101) 212/B4
Miamisburg, Ohio (45342) 284/B6
Miami Shores, Fla. (33153) 212/B4
Miami Springs, Fla. (33166) 212/B5
Miamitown, Ohio (45041) 284/A9
Miamiville, Ohio (45147) 284/D9
Miandowab, Iran 66/E2
Miandrivazo, Madagascar 118/G3
Mianeh, Iran 59/E2
Mianeh, Iran 66/E2
Mianus, Conn. (†06830) 210/A4
Mianus (riv.), Conn. 210/A4
Mianwali, Pakistan 68/C2
Mianwali, Pakistan 59/K3
Mianyang, Hubei, China 77/H5
Mianyang, Sichuan, China 77/G5
Mianzhu, China 77/F5
Miass, U.S.S.R. 48/G4
Miastko, Poland 47/C2
Miazal, Ecuador 128/D4
Mica, Wash. (99023) 310/H3
Mica Creek, Br. Col. 184/H4
Micanopy, Fla. (32667) 212/D2
Micawber, Okla. (†74882) 288/N3
Micay, Colombia 126/B6
Micco, Fla. (†32960) 212/F4
Miccosukee, Fla. (32309) 212/B1
Miccosukee (lake), Fla. 212/B1
Michael, I. of Man 13/C3
Michael (lake), Newf. 166/C3
Michalovce, Czech. 41/G2
Michaud (pt.), Nova Scotia 168/H3
Michelago, N.S. Wales 97/E4
Michelson (mt.), Alaska 196/K1
Michelstadt, W. Germany 22/C4
Miches, Dom. Rep. 158/F6
Michiana, Mich. (†49117) 250/C7
Michiana Shores, Ind. (†49117) 227/D1
Michichi, Alberta 182/D4
Michie, Tenn. (38357) 237/E10
Michigamme, Mich. (49861) 250/B2
Michigamme (lake), Mich. 250/A2
Michigamme (res.), Mich. 250/B2
Michigamme (riv.), Mich. 250/A2
Michigan 188/J1
Michigan (lake) 188/J2
Michigan (lake), Ill. 222/F1
Michigan (lake), Ind. 227/C1
MICHIGAN 250/80
Michigan (lake), Mich. 250/B5
Michigan, N. Dak. (58259) 282/O3
Michigan (state), U.S. 146/K5
Michigan (lake), U.S. 146/K5
Michigan (isl.), Wis. 317/F2
Michigan (lake), Wis. 317/M9
Michigan Bar, Calif. (†95683) 204/C8
Michigan Center, Mich. (49254) 250/E6
Michigan City, Ind. (46360) 227/C1
Michigan City, Miss. (38647) 256/F1
Michigantown, Ind. (46057) 227/E4
Michigan Valley, Kansas (†66528) 232/G3
Michipicoten (isl.), Ontario 177/H5
Michipicoten (isl.), Ontario 175/C3
Michipicoten River, Ontario 177/H5
Michipicoten River, Ontario 175/C3
Michoacán (state), Mexico 150/H7
Michurin, Bulgaria 45/H4
Michurinsk, U.S.S.R. 52/F4
Michurinsk, U.S.S.R. 48/E4
Mickleton, N.J. (08056) 273/C4
Micotrin (mt.), Dominica 161/F6
Micoua, Québec 174/D3
Micoud, St. Lucia 161/G6
Micro, N.C. (27555) 281/N3
Micronesia, Federated States of 87/F5
Micronesia (reg.), Pacific 87/E4
Midale, Sask. 181/H6
Midas, Nev. (†89414) 266/E1
Middelburg, Netherlands 27/C6
Middelburg, C. of Good Hope, S. Africa 118/D6
Middelburg, Transvaal, S. Africa 118/D5
Middelfart, Denmark 21/C7
Middelfart, Denmark 18/G9
Middelharnis, Netherlands 27/E5
Middelkerke, Belgium 27/B6
Middelvlei, S. Africa 118/G7
Middenmeer, Netherlands 27/F3
Middle (riv.), Ontario 201/F1
Middle (pt.), Fla. 212/E6
Middle, Iowa (52307) 229/K5
Middle (riv.), Minn. 255/B2
Middle Alkali (lake), Calif. 204/E2
Middle Andaman (isl.), India 68/G6
Middle Arm, Newf. 166/C4
Middle Atlas (ranges), Morocco 106/C2
Middle Bass, Ohio (43446) 284/E2
Middle Bass (isl.), Ohio 284/E2
Middle Beaver (creek), Colo. 208/P4
Middleboro, Mass. (02346) 249/L5
Middleboro○, Mass. (02346) 249/L5
Middleboro (McKean), Pa. (16426) 294/B2
Middlebourne, W. Va. (26149) 312/E3
Middlebranch, Ohio (44652) 284/H4
Middlebro, Manitoba 179/G5
Middlebrook, Va. (24459) 307/K4
Middleburg, Fla. (32068) 212/E1
Middleburg, Ky. (42541) 237/M6
Middleburg, Md. (21768) 245/K2
Middleburg, N.C. (27556) 281/N2
Middleburg, Ohio (43336) 284/C5
Middleburg, Pa. (17842) 294/H4
Middleburg, Va. (22117) 307/N3
Middleburgh, N.Y. (12122) 276/M5
Middleburg Heights, Ohio (†44017) 284/G10
Middlebury○, Conn. (06762) 210/C2
Middlebury, Ind. (46540) 227/F1
Middlebury, Vt. (05753) 268/A3
Middlebury○, Vt. (05753) 268/A3
Middlebury Center, Pa. (16935) 294/H2
Middlebury Gap (pass), Vt. 268/B4
Middlebush, N.J. (08874) 273/D3
Middlechurch, Manitoba 179/E4
Middle Concho (riv.), Texas 303/C6
Middledam, Maine (†04216) 243/B6
Middle Falls, N.Y. (12848) 276/O4
Middlefield○, Conn. (06455) 210/E2
Middlefield○, Mass. (01243) 249/B3
Middlefield, Ohio (44062) 284/H3
Middle Fork (peak), Idaho 220/D5
Middlefork, Ind. (†46039) 227/E4
Middle Fork, Powder (riv.), Wyo. 319/F2
Middlegate, Norfolk Is. 88/L6
Middle Granville, N.Y. (12849) 276/O4
Middlegrove, Ill. (61549) 222/C3
Middle Grove, Mo. (†65263) 261/H4
Middle Haddam, Conn. (06456) 210/E2
Middle Harbour (creek), N. S. Wales 88/K3
Middle Harbour (creek), N.S. Wales 97/J3
Middle Hope, N.Y. (12550) 276/M7
Middle Inlet, Wis. (54148) 317/K5
Middle Lake, Sask. 181/F3
Middle Loch (inlet), Hawaii 218/A3
Middle Loup (riv.), Nebr. 264/D3
Middlemarch, N. Zealand 100/B6
Middle Musquodoboit, Nova Scotia 168/E3
Middle Patuxent (riv.), Md. 245/L3
Middle Piney (creek), Wyo. 319/B3
Middle Point, Ohio (45863) 284/B4
Middleport, N.Y. (14105) 276/C4
Middleport, Ohio (45760) 284/F7
Middleport, Pa. (17953) 294/K4
Middle River, Md. (21220) 245/N3
Middle River, Minn. (56737) 255/B2
Middle River, Nova Scotia 168/G2
Middle Saranac (lake), N.Y. 276/M2
Middlesboro, Ky. (40965) 237/O7
Middlesboro, Ky. 188/K3
Middlesbrough, England 7/D3
Middlesbrough, England 13/F3
Middlesbrough, England 10/F3
Middlesex (co.), Conn. 210/E3
Middlesex (co.), Mass. 249/J3
Middlesex (co.), N.J. 273/E3
Middlesex, N.J. (08846) 273/E2
Middlesex, N.Y. (14507) 276/F5
Middlesex, N.C. (27557) 281/N3
Middlesex (county), Ontario 177/C4
Middlesex○, Vt. (†05602) 268/B3
Middlesex (co.), Va. 307/R5
Middle Stewiacke, Nova Scotia 168/E3
Middleton (isl.), Alaska 196/J3
Middleton, England 13/H2
Middleton, England 10/G2
Middleton, Georgia (†30635) 217/G2
Middleton, Idaho (83644) 220/B6
Middleton○, Mass. (01949) 249/K2
Middleton, Mich. (48856) 250/E5
Middleton○, N.H. (†03887) 268/E5
Middleton, Nova Scotia 168/C4
Middleton, Tenn. (38052) 237/D10
Middleton, Wis. (53562) 317/G9
Middletown, Calif. (95461) 204/C5
Middletown, Conn. (06457) 210/E2
Middletown, Del. (19709) 245/R3
Middletown, Ill. (62666) 222/D3
Middletown, Ind. (47356) 227/F4
Middletown, Iowa (52638) 229/L7
Middletown, Ky. (40243) 237/L2
Middletown, Md. (21769) 245/J3
Middletown, Mo. (63359) 261/J4
Middletown○, N.J. (07748) 273/E3
Middletown, N.Y. (10940) 276/L8
Middletown, N.C. (†27824) 281/T4
Middletown, N. Ireland 17/H3
Middletown, Ohio (45042) 284/A6
Middletown, Pa. (17057) 294/J5
Middletown○, R.I. (02840) 249/J6
Middletown, Va. (22645) 307/M2
Middletown Springs○, Vt. (05757) 268/A5
Middle Valley, N.J. (†07853) 273/D2
Middleville, Mich. (49333) 250/D6
Middleville, N.J. (07855) 273/D1
Middleville, N.Y. (13406) 276/K4
Middleville, Ontario 177/H2
Middle Water, Texas (†79022) 303/B2
Middleway, W. Va. (†25430) 312/K4
Middlewich, England 13/H2
Middlewich, England 10/G2
Middlewood, Nova Scotia 168/D4
Midfield, Ala. (35228) 195/E4
Midgic Station, New Bruns. 170/F3
Mid Glamorgan, Wales 13/D6
Midhurst, Ontario 177/E3
Midian (dist.), Saudi Arabia 59/C4
Midkiff, W. Va. (25540) 312/B6
Midland, Ark. (72945) 202/B3
Midland, Ind. (47445) 227/C6
Midland, La. (70557) 238/F6
Midland, Md. (21542) 245/C2
Midland (co.), Mich. 250/E5
Midland, Mich. (48640) 250/E5
Midland, N.C. (28107) 281/J4
Midland, Ohio (45148) 284/C7
Midland, Ontario 177/D3
Midland, Oreg. (97634) 291/F5
Midland, Pa. (15059) 294/A4
Midland, S. Dak. (57552) 298/G5
Midland, Tex. 188/F4
Midland (co.), Texas 303/B6
Midland, Texas (*79701) 303/C6
Midland, Va. (22728) 307/N3
Midland City, Ala. (36350) 195/H8
Midland Park, N.J. (07432) 273/B1
Midlandvale, Alberta 182/D4
Midleton, Ireland 17/E8
Midleton, Ireland 10/B5
Midlothian, Ill. (60445) 222/B6
Midlothian (trad. co.), Scotland 15/B5
Midlothian, Texas (76065) 303/G5
Midlothian, Va. (23113) 307/N6
Midnapore, India 68/F4
Midnight, Miss. (39115) 256/C4
Midnight (lake), Sask. 181/C2
Midongy Atsimo, Madagascar 118/H4
Midvale, Idaho (83645) 220/B5
Midvale, Ohio (44653) 284/H5
Midvale, Utah (84047) 304/B3
Midville, Georgia (30441) 217/H5
Midway (isls.) 188/E6
Midway, Ala. (36053) 195/H6
Midway, Br. Col. 184/H6
Midway, Del. (†19971) 245/T6
Midway, Fla. (32343) 212/B1
Midway, Georgia (31320) 217/K7
Midway, Ind. (†47635) 227/C8
Midway, Ky. (40347) 237/M4
Midway (Sedalia), Ohio (†43151) 284/D6
Midway, Pa. (15060) 294/B5
Midway, Tenn. (37809) 237/P8
Midway (isls.), U.S. 87/J3
Midway, Utah (84049) 304/C3
Midway City, Calif. (92655) 204/D11
Midway Park, N.C. (28544) 281/O5
Midwest, Wyo. (82643) 319/F2
Midwest City, Okla. (73110) 288/M4
Midyat, Turkey 63/J4
Midye, Turkey 63/C2
Mid Yell, Scotland 15/G2
Midzhur (mt.), Bulgaria 45/F4
Midzhur (mt.), Yugoslavia 45/F4
Mie (pref.), Japan 81/H6
Miechów, Poland 47/E4
Międzychód, Poland 47/B2
Międzylesie, Poland 47/C3
Międzyrzec Podlaski, Poland 47/F3
Międzyrzecz, Poland 47/B2
Mielec, Poland 47/E3
Mier, Ind. (†46919) 227/F3
Mier, Mexico 150/K3
Miercurea Ciuc, Romania 45/G2
Mieres, Spain 33/D1
Miesso, Ethiopia 111/H6
Miesso, Ethiopia 102/G4
Miesville, Minn. (†55033) 255/F6
Miette, Alberta 182/B3
Mifflin, Ohio (†44805) 284/F4
Mifflin (co.), Pa. 294/G4
Mifflin, Pa. (17058) 294/H4
Mifflin, Wis. (†53580) 317/F10
Mifflinburg, Pa. (17844) 294/H4
Mifflintown, Pa. (17059) 294/H4
Miflin, Ala. (†36530) 195/C10
Migdal, Israel 65/C2
Migdal Ha 'Emeq, Israel 65/C2
Mignon, Ala. (†35150) 195/F4
Migori, Kenya 115/F4
Miguel Alves, Brazil 132/F4
Miguel Auza, Mexico 150/H4
Miguel de la Borda, Panama 154/G6
Miguelete, Uruguay 145/B5

Monomoy 411

Mirjaveh, Pakistan 59/H4
Mirnyy 5/C5
Mirnyy, U.S.S.R. 54/N3
Mirnyy, U.S.S.R. 48/M3
Mirpur, Pakistan 68/C2
Mirpur Khas, Pakistan 68/B3
Mirror, Alberta 182/D3
Mirror Lake, N.H. (03853) 268/E4
Mirtoön (sea), Greece 45/F7
Miryang, S. Korea 81/D6
Mirzapur-cum-Vindhyachal, India 68/E4
Misamis Occidental (prov.), Philippines 82/D6
Misamis Oriental (prov.), Philippines 82/E6
Misantla, Mexico 150/P1
Misawa, Japan 81/K3
Miscou (isl.), New Bruns. 170/F1
Miscou (pt.), New Bruns. 170/F1
Miscou Centre, New Bruns. 170/F1
Miscouche, Pr. Edward I. 168/D2
Miscou Harbour, New Bruns. 170/F1
Misenheimer, N.C. (28109) 281/J4
Misery (bay), Mich. 250/G1
Misery (riv.), Mich. 250/G1
Misery (mt.), St. Chris.-Nevis 161/C10
Misgar, Pakistan 68/C1
Misha'ab, Ras (cape), Saudi Arabia 59/E4
Mishagua, Peru 128/F8
Mishan, China 77/M2
Mishaum (pt.), Mass. 249/L6
Mishawaka, Ind. (46544) 227/E1
Misheguk (mt.), Alaska 196/F1
Mishicot, Wis. (54228) 317/L7
Mishmar Hanegev, Israel 65/B5
Mishmar Hayarden, Israel 65/D1
Mishmi (hills), India 68/H3
Misima (isl.), Papua N.G. 85/C8
Misiones (prov.), Argentina 143/F2
Misiones (dept.), Paraguay 144/D5
Miskitos (cays), Nicaragua 154/F3
Miskolc, Hungary 41/F2
Miskolc, Hungary 7/G4
Misool (isl.), Indonesia 85/J6
Mispec, New Bruns. 170/E3
Mispillion (riv.), Del. 245/S5
Misquah (hills), Minn. 255/F2
Missanabie, Ontario 177/J5
Missanabie, Ontario 175/D3
Missaukee (co.), Mich. 250/D4
Missi Falls, Manitoba 179/J2
Missinaibi (riv.), Ont. 162/H6
Missinaibi (lake), Ontario 175/D3
Missinaibi (riv.), Ontario 177/J5
Missinaibi (riv.), Ontario 175/D2
Mission, Br. Col. 184/L3
Mission, Kansas (66205) 232/H2
Mission (range), Mont. 262/C3
Mission, S. Dak. (57555) 298/H7
Mission, Texas (78572) 303/F11
Mission Beach, Alberta 182/C3
Mission City, Br. Col. 184/L3
Mission Hill, S. Dak. (57046) 298/P8
Mission Ridge, S. Dak. (57557) 298/H4
Mission Viejo, Calif. (92691) 204/D11
Missisa (lake), Ontario 175/D2
Missisquoi (co.), Québec 172/D4
Missisquoi (riv.), Vt. 268/B2
Mississagi (riv.), Ontario 177/A1
Mississagi (str.), Ontario 177/A2
Mississauga, Ontario 177/J4
Mississinewa (lake), Ind. 227/F3
Mississinewa (riv.), Ind. 227/F3
Mississippi 188/J4
MISSISSIPPI 256
Mississippi (riv.) 188/H4
Mississippi (sound), Ala. 195/B10
Mississippi (co.), Ark. 202/K2
Mississippi (riv.), Ark. 202/H7
Mississippi (riv.), Ill. 222/C5
Mississippi (riv.), Iowa 229/L7
Mississippi (riv.), Ky. 237/A10
Mississippi (delta), La. 146/K7
Mississippi (delta), La. 188/J5
Mississippi (delta), La. 238/M8
Mississippi (riv.), La. 238/H3
Mississippi (sound), La. 238/M6
Mississippi (riv.), Minn. 255/D4
Mississippi (riv.), Miss. 256/A8
Mississippi (sound), Miss. 256/G10
Mississippi (co.), Mo. 261/O9
Mississippi (riv.), Mo. 261/L4
Mississippi (lake), Ontario 177/H2
Mississippi (riv.), Tenn. 237/A10
Mississippi (state), U.S. 146/K6
Mississippi (riv.), U.S. 2/E4
Mississippi (riv.), U.S. 146/J6
Mississippi (riv.), Wis. 317/D10
Mississippi River Gulf Outlet (canal), La. 238/L7
Mississippi State, Miss. (39762) 256/G4
Missoula, Mont. 146/G5
Missoula, Mont. 188/D1
Missoula (co.), Mont. 262/C3
Missoula, Mont. (*59801) 262/C4
Missouri 188/H3
MISSOURI 261
Missouri (riv.) 188/H3
Missouri (riv.), Iowa 229/A4
Missouri (riv.), Kansas 232/G1
Missouri (riv.), Mo. 261/H5
Missouri (riv.), Mont. 262/L3
Missouri (riv.), Nebr. 264/H3
Missouri (riv.), N. Dak. 282/H5
Missouri (riv.), S. Dak. 298/P8
Missouri (state), U.S. 146/J6
Missouri (riv.), U.S. 2/D3
Missouri (riv.), U.S. 146/J5
Missouri Branch, W. Va. (†25511) 312/A7
Missouri City, Mo. (64072) 261/R5
Missouri City, Texas (77459) 303/J2
Missouri Coteau (hills), Sask. 181/F5
Missouri Valley, Iowa (51555) 229/B5
Mist, Ark. (†71646) 202/G7
Mist, Oreg. (97016) 291/D1
Mistake (bay), N.W. Terrs. 187/J3
Mistake Creek, North. Terr. 93/A4
Mistaken (pt.), Newf. 166/D2
Mistassibi (riv.), Que. 162/J5
Mistassibi (riv.), Québec 174/C3
Mistassini (lake), Que. 162/J5
Mistassini (lake), Que. 146/L4
Mistassini (terr.), Québec 174/B2
Mistassini, Québec 172/E1
Mistassini, Québec 174/C3
Mistassini (Baie-du-Poste), Québec 174/C2
Mistassini (lake), Québec 174/C2
Mistastin (lake), Newf. 166/B2
Mistastin (riv.), Newf. 166/B2
Mistatim, Sask. 181/H3
Mistehae (lake), Alberta 182/C2
Mistelbach an der Zaya, Austria 41/D2
Misteriosa (bank), Cayman Is. 156/A3
Misti, El (mt.), Peru 120/B4
Misti, El (mt.), Peru 128/G11
Mistinippi (lake), Newf. 166/B3
Miston, Tenn. (38056) 237/B8
Mistretta, Italy 34/E6
Misty Fjords Nat'l Mon., Alaska 196/N2
Misurata, Libya 102/D1
Misurata, Libya 111/C1
Mita (pt.), Mexico 150/G6
Mitaka, Japan 81/O2
Mitcham, S. Australia 88/D8
Mitcham, S. Australia 94/B8
Mitchell (lake), Ala. 188/J4
Mitchell (dam), Ala. 195/E5
Mitchell (lake), Ala. 195/F5
Mitchell, Ark. (†72583) 202/G1
Mitchell (co.), Georgia 217/D8
Mitchell, Georgia (30820) 217/G4
Mitchell, Ind. (47446) 227/E7
Mitchell (co.), Iowa 229/H2
Mitchell, Iowa (†50461) 229/H2
Mitchell (co.), Kansas 232/D2
Mitchell, La. (71453) 238/C3
Mitchell, Nebr. (69357) 264/A3
Mitchell (co.), N.C. 281/E2
Mitchell (mt.), N.C. 188/K3
Mitchell (mt.), N.C. 281/E3
Mitchell, Ontario 177/C4
Mitchell, Oreg. (97750) 291/G3
Mitchell, Queensland 88/H5
Mitchell, Queensland 95/C5
Mitchell (riv.), Queensland 88/G3
Mitchell (riv.), Queensland 95/B2
Mitchell, S. Dak. 188/G2
Mitchell, S. Dak. (57301) 298/N6
Mitchell (creek), S. Dak. 298/G5
Mitchell (co.), Texas 303/D5
Mitchell (riv.), Victoria 97/D5
Mitchell Bay, Ontario 177/B5
Mitchell Heights, W. Va. (†25601) 312/B7
Mitchells, Va. (22729) 307/N4
Mitchellsburg, Ky. (40452) 237/M5
Mitchellsville, Ill. (†62946) 222/E6
Mitchellton, Sask. 181/F6
Mitchellville, Ark. (†71639) 202/H6
Mitchellville, Iowa (50169) 229/G5
Mitchellville, Tenn. (37119) 237/J7
Mitchelstown, Ireland 10/B4
Mitchelstown, Ireland 17/E7
Mitchelton, Queensland 88/J2
Mitchelton, Queensland 95/D2
Mitchinamécus (res.), Québec 172/C2
Mithi, Pakistan 68/C4
Mithimna, Greece 45/G6
Mitiaro, Cook Is. 87/L7
Mitilini, Greece 45/H6
Mitkof (isl.), Alaska 196/N2
Mitla (ruin), Mexico 150/M8
Mito, Japan 81/K5
Mitrofania (isl.), Alaska 196/G3
Mitsamiouli, Comoros 118/G2
Mitsinjo, Madagascar 118/H3
Mitsue, Alberta 182/C2
Mitsukaido, Japan 81/P2
Mittagong, N.S. Wales 97/F4
Mitta Mitta (riv.), Victoria 97/D5
Mittenwald, W. Germany 22/D5
Mittersill, Austria 41/B3
Mittie, La. (70654) 238/E5
Mittweida, E. Germany 22/E3
Mitú, Colombia 126/E7
Mitú, Colombia 120/B2
Mituas, Colombia 126/F6
Mitwaba, Zaire 115/E5
Mitzic, Gabon 115/B3
Miura, Japan 81/O3
Miura (pen.), Japan 81/O3
Mivtahim, Israel 65/A5
Mix, La. (†70760) 238/G5
Miyagi (pref.), Japan 81/K4
Miyako, Japan 81/L4
Miyako (isl.), Japan 81/L7
Miyako (isls.), Japan 81/L7
Miyakonojo, Japan 81/E8
Miyazaki (pref.), Japan 81/E8
Miyazaki, Japan 81/E8
Miyazu, Japan 81/G6
Miyoshi, Japan 81/F6
Mizan Teferi, Ethiopia 111/G6
Mizda, Libya 111/B1
Mize, Georgia (†30577) 217/F2
Mize, Miss. (39116) 256/E7
Mizen (head), Ireland 10/A5
Mizen (head), Ireland 17/B9
Mizen (head), Ireland 17/K6
Mizhi, China 77/H4
Mizil, Romania 45/H3
Mizo (hill), India 68/G4
Mizoram (terr.), India 68/G4
Mizpah, Minn. (56660) 255/D3
Mizpah, N.J. (08342) 273/D5
Mizpe Ramon, Israel 65/D5
Mizque, Bolivia 136/C5
Mizque (riv.), Bolivia 136/C6
Mizusawa, Japan 81/K4
Mjölby, Sweden 18/J7
Mkokotoni, Tanzania 115/G5
Mkushi, Zambia 115/E6
Mladá Boleslav, Czech. 41/C1
Mladá Vožice, Czech. 41/C2
Mława, Poland 47/E2
Mljet (isl.), Yugoslavia 45/C4
Mmabatho (cap.), Bophuthatswana, S. Africa 102/E7
Mmabatho, S. Africa 118/D5
Mnichovo Hradiště, Czech. 41/C1
Mo, Norway 7/F2
Mo, Norway 18/J3
Moa, Cuba 158/K3
Moa (riv.), Guinea 106/B7
Moa (isl.), Indonesia 85/H7
Moa (riv.), S. Leone 106/B7
Moab, Utah (84532) 304/E5
Moak Lake, Manitoba 179/J2
Moala (isl.), Fiji 86/Q11
Moama, N.S. Wales 97/C5
Moamba, Mozambique 118/E5
Moanalua (stream), Hawaii 218/B3
Moanda, Gabon 115/B4
Moanda, Zaire 115/B5
Moapa, Nev. (89025) 266/G6
Moapa River Ind. Res., Nev. 266/G6
Moar (lake), Manitoba 179/G2
Moark, Ark. (†72422) 202/J1
Moate, Ireland 17/F5
Moatsville, W. Va. (26405) 312/G4
Mobara, Japan 81/K6
Mobaye, Cent. Afr. Rep. 115/D3
Mobayi-Mbongo, Zaire 115/D3
Mobayi-Mbongo, Zaire 102/E4
Mobeetie, Texas (79061) 303/D2
Moberly, Br. Col. 184/J4
Moberly (lake), Br. Col. 184/F2
Moberly, Mo. (65270) 261/G4
Moberly, Mo. 188/H3
Moberly Lake, Br. Col. 184/G2
Mobile, Ala. 146/K6
Mobile, Ala. 188/J4
Mobile (bay), Ala. 188/J5
Mobile (co.), Ala. 195/B9
Mobile, Ala. (*36601) 195/B9
Mobile (bay), Ala. 195/B10
Mobile (pt.), Ala. 195/B10
Mobile (riv.), Ala. 195/C9
Mobile, Ariz. (†85239) 198/C5
Mobile, Newf. 166/D2
Mobile Big (pond), Newf. 166/D2
Mobjack, Va. (23118) 307/R6
Mobjack (bay), Va. 307/R6
Mobridge, S. Dak. (57601) 298/J2
Mobuto Sese Seko (lake) 102/F4
Mobuto Sese Seko (lake), Uganda 115/F3
Mobuto Sese Seko (lake), Zaire 115/F3
Moca, Dom. Rep. 156/D3
Moca, Dom. Rep. 158/D5
Moca, P. Rico 161/A1
Mocajuba, Brazil 132/D3
Moçambique, Mozambique 118/G3
Moçambique, Mozambique 102/F6
Moçâmedes (dist.), Angola 115/B7
Moçâmedes, Angola 102/D6
Moçâmedes, Angola 115/B7
Mocanaqua, Pa. (18655) 294/K3
Moccasin, Ariz. (†86022) 198/C2
Moccasin, Mont. (59462) 262/F3
Mocha (isl.), Chile 138/B2
Mocha, Yemen Arab Rep. 59/D7
Moc Hoa, Vietnam 72/E5
Mochudi, Botswana 118/D4
Mochudi, Botswana 102/E7
Mocímboa da Praia, Mozambique 118/G2
Mociu, Romania 45/G2
Mocksville, N.C. (27028) 281/H3
Moclips, Wash. (98562) 310/A3
Moco (mt.), Angola 115/C6
Mocoa, Colombia 126/B7
Mococa, Brazil 135/C2
Mocodome (cape), Nova Scotia 168/G3
Mocomoco, Bolivia 136/A4
Mocoretá, Argentina 143/G5
Mocorito, Mexico 150/F4
Moctezuma, San Luis Potosí, Mexico 150/J5
Moctezuma, Sonora, Mexico 150/E2
Moctezuma (riv.), Mexico 150/K6
Mocuba, Mozambique 118/F3
Modale, Iowa (51556) 229/B5
Modane, France 28/G5
Modasa, India 68/C4
Modderfontein, S. Africa 118/H6
Mode, Ill. (62444) 222/E4
Model, Colo. (81059) 208/L8
Modena (prov.), Italy 34/C2
Modena, Italy 7/F4
Modena, Italy 34/C2
Modena, Utah (84753) 304/A6
Modena, Wis. (†54755) 317/C7
Modeste, La. (70376) 238/K3
Modesto, Calif. 188/B3
Modesto, Calif. (*95350) 204/D6
Modesto, Ill. (62667) 222/D4
Modest Town, Va. (23412) 307/T5
Modica, Italy 34/E6
Mödling, Austria 41/D2
Modoc (co.), Calif. 204/E2
Modoc, Georgia (†30401) 217/H5
Modoc, Ill. (62261) 222/C5
Modoc, Ind. (47358) 227/G4
Modoc, Kansas (67866) 232/A3
Modoc, S.C. (29838) 296/C4
Modoc Point, Oreg. (†97624) 291/F5
Modra, Czech. 41/D2
Modriča, Yugoslavia 45/D3
Modrý Kameň, Czech. 41/E2
Mo Duc, Vietnam 72/F4
Moe, Victoria 88/H7
Moe, Victoria 97/D6
Moen (isl.), Micronesia 87/F5
Moencopi (plat.), Ariz. 198/D3
Moengo, Suriname 131/D3
Moenkopi, Ariz. (†86045) 198/D2
Moenkopi Wash (dry riv.), Ariz. 198/D2
Moerai, Fr. Poly. 87/L8
Moerdijk, Netherlands 27/F5
Moerewa, N. Zealand 100/E1
Moësa (riv.), Switzerland 39/H4
Moeskroen (Mouscron), Belgium 27/C7
Moffat (co.), Colo. 208/C1
Moffat, Colo. (81143) 208/H6
Moffat, Scotland 15/E5
Moffat, Scotland 10/E3
Moffet (peak), N. Zealand 100/B6
Moffett, Okla. (74946) 288/S4
Moffett Nav. Air Sta., Calif. 204/K3
Moffit, N. Dak. (58560) 282/K6
Mogadiscio (prov.), Somalia 115/J3
Mogadishu (cap.), Somalia 2/M5
Mogadishu (cap.), Somalia 102/G4
Mogadishu (cap.), Somalia 115/J3
Mogador (Essaouira), Morocco 106/B2
Mogadore, Ohio (44260) 284/H3
Mogadouro, Portugal 33/C2
Mogami (riv.), Japan 81/K4
Mogaung, Burma 72/C1
Møgeltønder, Denmark 21/B8
Mogi das Cruzes, Brazil 132/E9
Mogi das Cruzes, Brazil 135/C3
Mogi Guaçu (riv.), Brazil 135/C2
Mogi-Guaçu, Brazil 135/C3
Mogilev, U.S.S.R. 7/G3
Mogilev, U.S.S.R. 52/C4
Mogilev, U.S.S.R. 48/D4
Mogilev-Podol'skiy, U.S.S.R. 52/C5
Mogil Mogil, N.S. Wales 97/E1
Mogilno, Poland 47/C2
Mogi-Mirim, Brazil 135/C3
Mogincual, Mozambique 118/G3
Mogocha, U.S.S.R. 48/N4
Mogok, Burma 72/C2
Mogollon (plat.), Ariz. 198/D4
Mogollon, N. Mex. (†88039) 274/A5
Mogollon (mts.), N. Mex. 274/A5
Mogollon Baldy (peak), N. Mex. 274/A5
Mogollon Rim (cliffs), Ariz. 198/D4
Mogororo, Chad 111/D5
Mogotes (pt.), Argentina 143/E4
Moguer, Spain 33/C4
Mohács, Hungary 41/E4
Mohaka (riv.), N. Zealand 100/F3
Mohaleshoek, Lesotho 118/D6
Mohall, N. Dak. (58761) 282/G2
Mohammadia, Algeria 106/D1
Mohammedia, Morocco 106/C2
Mohave (co.), Ariz. 198/A3
Mohave (lake), Ariz. 198/A3
Mohave (mts.), Ariz. 198/A4
Mohave (lake), Nev. 266/G7
Mohawk (mts.), Ariz. 198/B6
Mohawk (mt.), Conn. 210/B1
Mohawk, Ind. (†46140) 227/F5
Mohawk, Mich. (49950) 250/A1
Mohawk (riv.), N.H. 268/E2
Mohawk (lake), N.J. 273/D1
Mohawk, N.Y. (13407) 276/L4
Mohawk (riv.), N.Y. 276/L5
Mohawk, Oreg. (†97477) 291/E3
Mohawk, Tenn. (37810) 237/P8
Mohawk, W. Va. (24862) 312/C7
Mohe, China 77/K1
Mohegan, Conn. (†06382) 210/G3
Mohéli (isl.), Comoros 102/G6
Mohéli (isl.), Comoros 118/G2
Mohelnice, Czech. 41/D2
Mohenjo Daro (ruins), Pakistan 68/B3
Moher (cliffs), Ireland 17/B6
Mohican (cape), Alaska 196/E2
Mohican (riv.), Ohio 284/F4
Mohill, Ireland 17/F4
Mohler, Wash. (99154) 310/G3
Möhlin, Switzerland 39/E1
Mohn, Kapp (cape), Norway 18/E1
Mohnton, Pa. (19540) 294/L5
Mohnyin, Burma 72/C1
Moho, Peru 128/H10
Mohoro, Tanzania 115/G5
Mohrsville, Pa. (19541) 294/K5
Moi, Norway 18/E7
Moidart (dist.), Scotland 15/C4
Moiese, Mont. (59824) 262/B3
Moiliili, Hawaii (96828) 218/C4
Moinești, Romania 45/H2
Moingona, Iowa (†50036) 229/F4
Moira, N.Y. (12957) 276/M1
Moîrai, Greece 45/G8
Moirones, Uruguay 145/E2
Mõisaküla, U.S.S.R. 53/C1
Moise (riv.), Que. 146/M4
Moisés Ville, Argentina 143/E5
Moisie (riv.), Que. 162/K5
Moisie, Québec 174/D2
Moisie (riv.), Québec 174/D2
Moissac, France 28/D5
Moïssala, Chad 111/C6
Moitaco, Venezuela 124/F4
Mojácar, Spain 33/F4
Mojave, Calif. (93501) 204/G8
Mojave (des.), Calif. 204/H9
Mojave (riv.), Calif. 204/J9
Mojo, Bolivia 136/C7
Mojocoya, Bolivia 136/C6
Mojokerto, Indonesia 85/K2
Mokane, Mo. (65059) 261/J5
Mokapu, Hawaii (†96734) 218/F2
Mokapu (pen.), Hawaii 218/F2
Mokau (riv.), N. Zealand 100/E3
Mokelumne (riv.), Calif. 204/C9
Mokelumne Hill, Calif. (95245) 204/E5
Mokena, Ill. (60448) 222/B6
Mokil (atoll), Micronesia 87/G5
Moknine, Tunisia 106/G1
Mokohinau (isl.), N. Zealand 100/E1
Mokokchung, India 68/G3
Mokolo, Cameroon 115/B1
Mokp'o, S. Korea 81/C6
Moksha (riv.), U.S.S.R. 52/F4
Mokuauia (isl.), Hawaii 218/E1
Mokuaweoweo (crater), Hawaii 218/H6
Mokuhooniki (isl.), Hawaii 218/J1
Mokuleia, Hawaii (†96791) 218/D1
Mol, Belgium 27/G6
Mola di Bari, Italy 34/F4
Molalla, Oreg. (97038) 291/B3
Molalla (riv.), Oreg. 291/B3
Moland, Minn. (†55946) 255/E6
Molanosa, Sask. 181/M4
Molái, Greece 45/F7
Molare (peak), Switzerland 39/G3
Mold, Wales 13/G2
Moldau (Vltava) (riv.), Czech. 41/C2
Moldava nad Bodvou, Czech. 41/F2
Moldavian S.S.R., U.S.S.R. 7/G4
Moldavian S.S.R., U.S.S.R. 52/C5
Moldavian S.S.R., U.S.S.R. 48/C5
Molde, Norway 18/E5
Moldova Nouă, Romania 45/E3
Moldoveanul (mt.), Romania 45/G3
Mole (riv.), England 13/H8
Môle (cape), Haiti 158/B5
Mole Creek, Tasmania 99/C3
Molega (lake), Nova Scotia 168/D4
Molena, Georgia (30258) 217/D4
Molenbeek-Saint-Jean, Belgium 27/B9
Molepolole, Botswana 118/C4
Molepolole, Botswana 102/E7
Môle Saint Nicolas, Haiti 158/B5
Molfetta, Italy 34/F4
Molina, Chile 138/A10
Molina, Colo. (81646) 208/D4
Molina, Spain 33/F2
Molinas, Argentina 143/C2
Moline, Ill. 188/J2
Moline, Ill. (61265) 222/C2
Moline, Kansas (67353) 232/F4
Moline, Manitoba 179/B4
Moline, Mich. (49335) 250/D6
Moline Acres, Mo. (†63101) 261/R2
Molinicos, Spain 33/E3
Molinière (pt.), Grenada 161/C8
Molino, Fla. (32577) 212/B6
Molinos (pt.), P. Rico 161/G1
Moliro, Zaire 115/E5
Molise (reg.), Italy 34/E4
Mollebjerg (mt.), Denmark 21/C6
Mollendo, Peru 120/B4
Mollendo, Peru 128/F11
Mollerusa, Spain 33/G2
Molles (pt.), Chile 138/A9
Mollis, Switzerland 39/H2
Mölln, W. Germany 22/D2
Mollusk, Va. (22517) 307/P5
Mollys Falls (pond), Vt. 268/C3
Mölndal, Sweden 18/H8
Moloaa, Hawaii (†96703) 218/D1
Molodechno, U.S.S.R. 48/C4
Molodechno, U.S.S.R. 52/C4
Molokai (isl.), Hawaii 87/L3
Molokai (isl.), Hawaii 188/F5
Molokai (isl.), Hawaii 218/G1
Molokini (isl.), Hawaii 218/J2
Molong, N.S. Wales 97/E3
Molopo (riv.), Botswana 118/C5
Molopo (riv.), S. Africa 118/C5
Molotov (Perm'), U.S.S.R. 52/J3
Moloundou, Cameroon 115/C3
Molson (lake), Manitoba 179/J3
Molson, Wash. (†98844) 310/F2
Molt, Mont. (59057) 262/H5
Molteno, S. Africa 118/D6
Molucca (isls.), Indonesia 54/O10
Molucca (sea), Indonesia 54/O10
Molucca (sea), Indonesia 85/H6
Moluccas (isls.), Indonesia 85/H6
Molunkus (lake), Maine 243/G4
Moma, Mozambique 118/F3
Mombasa, Kenya 115/G4
Mombasa, Kenya 102/G5
Mombetsu, Japan 81/L1
Mombo, Tanzania 115/G4
Momchilgrad, Bulgaria 45/G5
Momence, Ill. (60954) 222/F2
Momeyer, N.C. (†27856) 281/N3
Momignies, Belgium 27/E8
Momostenango, Guatemala 154/B3
Mompog (passage), Philippines 82/D4
Mompós, Colombia 126/C3
Mon (state), Burma 72/C3
Mon (riv.), Burma 72/B2
Møn (isl.), Denmark 21/F8
Møn (isl.), Denmark 18/H9
Mona (passg.) 146/M8
Mona, Cyprus 63/E5
Mona (passage), Dom. Rep. 156/E3
Mona (passage), Dom. Rep. 158/F6
Mona (isl.), P. Rico 156/E3
Mona (passage), P. Rico 156/E3
Mona (passage), P. Rico 161/A2
Mona, Utah (84645) 304/C4
Mona (res.), Utah 304/C4
Monaca, Pa. (15061) 294/B4
Monach (isls.), Scotland 15/A3
Monach (sound), Scotland 15/A3
Monaco 7/E4
MONACO 28/G6
Monadhliath (mts.), Scotland 15/D3
Monadnock (mt.), N.H. 268/C6
Monagas (state), Venezuela 124/G3
Monaghan (co.), Ireland 17/H3
Monaghan, Ireland 10/C3
Monaghan, Ireland 17/G3
Monahans, Texas (79756) 303/B6
Monango, N. Dak. (58471) 282/N7
Monapo, Mozambique 118/G2
Monar, Loch (lake), Scotland 15/C3
Monarch, Alberta 182/D5
Monarch, Mont. (59463) 262/F3
Monarch Mills, S.C. (†29379) 296/D2
Monarda, Maine (†04776) 243/G4
Monaro (range), N.S. Wales 97/E5
Monashee (mts.), Br. Col. 184/H4
Monasterevan, Ireland 17/H5
Monastery, Nova Scotia 168/G3
Monastir, Tunisia 106/G1
Monatélé, Cameroon 115/B3
Mona Vale, N. S. Wales 88/L3
Mona Vale, N. S. Wales 97/K2
Monaville, W. Va. (25636) 312/B7
Monavullagh (mts.), Ireland 17/F7
Monbetsu, Japan 81/L2
Moncalieri, Italy 34/A2
Monçao, Portugal 33/B1
Moncayo (mt.), Spain 33/F2
Moncayo, Sierra de (range), Spain 33/F2
Monchegorsk, U.S.S.R. 7/H2
Monchegorsk, U.S.S.R. 48/C3
Monchegorsk, U.S.S.R. 52/D1
Mönchengladbach, W. Germany 22/B3
Monches, Wis. (†53029) 317/J1
Monchique, Portugal 33/B4
Monchique, Serra de (mts.), Portugal 33/B4
Monción, Dom. Rep. 158/D5
Moncks Corner, S.C. (29461) 296/G5
Monclo, W. Va. (†25183) 312/C7
Monclova, Mexico 146/H7
Monclova, Mexico 150/J3
Monclova, Ohio (43542) 284/C2
Moncouche (lake), Québec 172/G1
Moncton, N. Br. 146/M5
Moncton, N. Br. 162/K6
Moncton, New Bruns. 170/F2
Moncure, N.C. (27559) 281/L3
Mondamin, Iowa (51557) 229/B5
Monday (riv.), Paraguay 144/E4
Mondego (cape), Portugal 33/B2
Mondego (riv.), Portugal 33/B2
Mondéjar, Spain 33/E2
Mondonac (lake), Québec 172/D2
Mondoñedo, Spain 33/C1
Mondovi, Wis. (54755) 317/C6
Mondovì Breo, Italy 34/A2
Mondragon, Philippines 85/H3
Mondragon, Philippines 82/E4
Mondsee, Austria 41/B3
Moneague, Jamaica 158/J6
Monee, Ill. (60449) 222/F2
Monero, N. Mex. (†87547) 274/C2
Monessen, Pa. (15062) 294/C5
Monesterio, Spain 33/C3
Moneta, Iowa (51352) 229/C2
Moneta, Va. (24121) 307/J6
Moneta, Wyo. (†82601) 319/E2
Monett, Mo. (65708) 261/E9
Monetta, S.C. (29105) 296/D4
Monette, Ark. (72447) 202/K2
Money (isl.), China 85/E2
Money, Miss. (38945) 256/D3
Moneygall, Ireland 17/F6
Moneymore, N. Ireland 17/H2
Monfalcone, Italy 34/D2
Monforte, Portugal 33/C3
Monforte, Spain 33/C1
Monga, Zaire 115/D3
Mongalla, Sudan 111/F6
Mong Cai, Vietnam 72/E2
Möng Hsat, Burma 72/C2
Monghyr, India 68/F3
Möng Maü, Burma 72/C3
Möng Mit, Burma 72/C2
Mongo, Chad 111/C5
Mongo, Chad 102/D3
Mongo, Ind. (46771) 227/G1
Mongolia 2/P3
Mongolia 54/M5
Mongoumba, Cent. Afr. Rep. 115/C3
Möng Pan, Burma 72/C2
Möng Si, Burma 72/C2
Möng Tõn, Burma 72/C2
Möng Tung, Burma 72/C2
Mongu, Zambia 102/E6
Mongu, Zambia 115/D7
Monhegan○, Maine (04852) 243/E8
Monhegan (isl.), Maine 243/E8
Mönhhaan, Mongolia 77/H2
Moniac, Georgia (†31646) 217/H9
Moniaive, Scotland 10/D3
Moniaive, Scotland 15/E5
Monica, Ill. (†61559) 222/D3
Monico, Wis. (54549) 317/H4
Monida, Mont. (†59739) 262/D6
Monie, Md. (†21853) 245/P8
Monifieth, Scotland 15/F4
Moniquirá, Colombia 126/D5
Moniteau (co.), Mo. 261/G5
Monitor, Alberta 182/E4
Monitor, Ind. (†47901) 227/D4
Monitor (range), Nev. 266/E4
Monitor, Oreg. (†97072) 291/B3
Monitor, Wash. (98836) 310/E3
Monivea, Ireland 17/D5
Monkayo, Philippines 82/E7
Monkey (pt.), Nicaragua 154/F5
Monkey (hill), St. Chris.-Nevis 161/C10
Monkey River Town, Belize 154/C2
Mońki, Poland 47/F2
Monkoto, Zaire 115/D4
Monkton, Md. (21111) 245/M2
Monkton, Ontario 177/C4
Monkton○, Vt. (05469) 268/A3
Monkton Ridge, Vt. (†05473) 268/A3
Monmouth, Ill. (61462) 222/C3
Monmouth, Ind. (†46733) 227/H3
Monmouth, Iowa (52309) 229/M4
Monmouth, Maine (04259) 243/D7
Monmouth○, Maine (04259) 243/D7
Monmouth (co.), N.J. 273/E3
Monmouth, Oreg. (97361) 291/D3
Monmouth, Wales 13/E6
Monmouth, Wales 10/E5
Monmouth Beach, N.J. (07750) 273/F3
Monmouth Junction, N.J. (08852) 273/D3
Monnickendam, Netherlands 27/C4
Mono (riv.), Benin 106/E7
Mono (lake), Calif. 188/C3
Mono (co.), Calif. 204/F5
Mono (lake), Calif. 204/G5
Mono (riv.), Togo 106/E7
Monocacy (riv.), Md. 245/J3
Monocacy Nat'l Battlefield, Md. 245/J3
Mono Lake, Calif. (†93541) 204/F5
Monolith, Calif. (†93561) 204/G8
Monólithos, Greece 45/H7
Monomonac (lake), Mass. 249/G2
Monomoy (isl.), Mass. 249/O6

412 Monomoy

Monomoy (pt.), Mass. 249/O6
Monon, Ind. (47959) 227/D3
Monona (co.), Iowa 229/B4
Monona, Iowa (52159) 229/L2
Monona, Wis. (53716) 317/H9
Monongah, W. Va. (26554) 312/F4
Monongahela, Pa. (15063) 294/B5
Monongahela (riv.), Pa. 294/C6
Monongahela (riv.), W. Va. 312/G3
Monongalia (co.), W. Va. 312/F3
Monopoli, Italy 34/F4
Monor, Hungary 41/E3
Monos (isl.), Trin. & Tob. 161/A10
Monóvar, Spain 33/F3
Monoville, Tenn. (37121) 237/K8
Monowi, Nebr. (†68746) 264/F2
Monreal del Campo, Spain 33/F2
Monreale, Italy 34/D5
Monroe (co.), Ala. 195/D7
Monroe (co.), Ark. 202/H4
Monroe, Ark. (72108) 202/H4
Monroe○, Conn. (06468) 210/C3
Monroe (co.), Fla. 212/E7
Monroe (lake), Fla. 212/E3
Monroe (co.), Georgia 217/E4
Monroe, Georgia (30655) 217/E3
Monroe (co.), Ill. 222/C5
Monroe (co.), Ind. 227/D6
Monroe, Ind. (46772) 227/H3
Monroe (lake), Ind. 227/E6
Monroe (co.), Iowa 229/H7
Monroe, Iowa (50170) 229/G5
Monroe (co.), Ky. 237/K7
Monroe, La. 188/H4
Monroe, La. 146/J6
Monroe, La. (*71201) 238/F1
Monroe○, Maine (04951) 243/E6
Monroe (co.), Mich. 250/F7
Monroe, Mich. (48161) 250/F7
Monroe (co.), Miss. 256/H3
Monroe (co.), Mo. 261/H3
Monroe, Nebr. (68647) 264/G3
Monroe○, N.H. (03771) 268/C3
Monroe (mt.), N.H. 268/E3
Monroe○, N.J. (07434) 273/E3
Monroe (co.), N.Y. 276/E4
Monroe, N.Y. (10950) 276/M8
Monroe, N.C. (28110) 281/J5
Monroe (co.), Ohio 284/H6
Monroe, Ohio (45050) 284/B7
Monroe, Okla. (74947) 288/S4
Monroe, Oreg. (97456) 291/D3
Monroe (co.), Pa. 294/M3
Monroe (Monroeton), Pa. (18832) 294/J2
Monroe, S. Dak. (57047) 298/P7
Monroe (co.), Tenn. 237/N10
Monroe, Tenn. (38573) 237/L8
Monroe, Utah (84754) 304/B5
Monroe (peak), Utah 304/B5
Monroe, Va. (24574) 307/K6
Monroe, Wash. (98272) 310/D3
Monroe (co.), W. Va. 312/E7
Monroe (co.), Wis. 317/E8
Monroe, Wis. (53566) 317/G10
Monroe Bridge, Mass. (01350) 249/C2
Monroe Center, Ill. (61052) 222/E1
Monroe City, Ind. (47557) 227/C7
Monroe City, Mo. (63456) 261/J3
Monroe P.O. (Stepney), Conn. (06468) 210/B3
Monroeton, Pa. (18832) 294/J2
Monroeville, Ala. (36460) 195/D7
Monroeville, Ind. (46773) 227/H3
Monroeville, N.J. (08343) 273/C4
Monroeville, Ohio (44847) 284/E3
Monroeville, Pa. (15146) 294/C7
Monrovia, Ala. (†35804) 195/E1
Monrovia, Calif. (91016) 204/D10
Monrovia, Ind. (46157) 227/E5
Monrovia (cap.), Liberia 106/B7
Monrovia (cap.), Liberia 2/J5
Monrovia (cap.), Liberia 102/A4
Monrovia, Md. (21770) 245/J3
Mons, Belgium 27/E8
Monsanto, Portugal 33/C2
Monschau, W. Germany 22/B3
Monse, Wash. (†98812) 310/F2
Monsefú, Peru 128/C6
Monselice, Italy 34/C2
Monserrate (isl.), Mexico 150/D4
Monsey, N.Y. (10952) 276/J8
Møns Klint (cliff), Denmark 21/F8
Monson○, Maine (04464) 243/E5
Monson, Mass. (01057) 249/E4
Monson○, Mass. (01057) 249/E4
Mönsterås, Sweden 18/K8
Montagu, S. Africa 118/C6
Montague (isl.), Alaska 196/D1
Montague (str.), Alaska 196/D1
Montague, Calif. (96064) 204/C2
Montague○, Mass. (01351) 249/E2
Montague (isl.), Mexico 150/B1
Montague, Mich. (49437) 250/C5
Montague, Mont. (†59442) 262/F3
Montague, N.J. (†07851) 273/D1
Montague, N.C. (†28435) 281/N6
Montague, Pr. Edward I. 168/F2
Montague (co.), Texas 303/G4
Montague, Texas (76251) 303/G4
Montague (sound), W. Australia 88/C2
Montague (sound), W. Australia 92/D1
Montague City, Mass. (†01351) 249/D2
Montalba, Texas (75853) 303/J6
Montalbán, Spain 33/F2
Montalcino, Italy 34/C3
Mont Alto, Pa. (17237) 294/G6
Montalto Uffugo, Italy 34/E5
Montalvão, Portugal 33/C3
Montalvo, Calif. (93003) 204/F9
Montana 188/E1
MONTANA 262
Montana, Alaska (†99676) 196/B1
Montaña, La (reg.), Peru 128/F8
Montana, Switzerland 39/D4
Montana (state), U.S. 146/H5
Montana Mines, W. Va. (26586) 312/F3
Montánchez, Spain 33/D3
Montanja di Reij, Neth. Ant. 161/G9
Montara, Calif. (94037) 204/H3
Montargil, Portugal 33/B3
Montargis, France 28/E3
Montauban, France 28/D5
Montauban, Québec 172/E3
Montauk, N.Y. (11954) 276/S8
Montauk (pt.), N.Y. 276/S8
Montbard, France 28/F4
Montbéliard, France 28/G4
Mont Belvieu, Texas (77580) 303/L1
Montblanch, Spain 33/G2
Montbrison, France 28/E5
Montbrook, Fla. (†32696) 212/D2
Montcalm (co.), Mich. 250/D5
Montcalm (co.), Québec 172/C3
Montcalm (county), Québec 174/B3
Mont-Carmel, Québec 172/H2
Montceau-les-Mines, France 28/F4
Mont Cenis (tunnel), France 28/G5
Mont Cenis (tunnel), Italy 34/A2
Montcerf, Québec 172/A3
Montclair, Calif. (91763) 204/D10
Montclair, N.J. (*07042) 273/B2
Montclare, S.C. (†29532) 296/H3
Montcoal, W. Va. (25135) 312/D7
Mont-de-Marsan, France 28/C6
Montdidier, France 28/E3
Mont-Dore, France 28/E5
Monteagle, Tenn. (37356) 237/K10
Monteagudo, Bolivia 136/D6
Monte Alegre, Brazil 132/C3
Montealegre del Castillo, Spain 33/F3
Monte Alegre de Minas, Brazil 132/D7
Monte Aprazível, Brazil 135/A2
Monte Azul, Brazil 132/F6
Monte Bello (isls.), Australia 87/B8
Montebello, Calif. (90640) 204/C10
Montebello, Québec 172/B4
Monte Bello (isls.), W. Australia 88/A4
Monte Bello (isls.), W. Australia 92/A3
Montebelluna, Italy 34/D2
Monte Carlo, Monaco 28/G6
Monte Caseros, Argentina 143/G5
Montecito, Calif. (93103) 204/F9
Monte Comán, Argentina 143/C3
Monte Creek, Br. Col. 184/G5
Montecristi (prov.), Dom. Rep. 158/D5
Monte Cristi, Dom. Rep. 156/D2
Montecristi, Dom. Rep. 158/C5
Montecristi, Ecuador 128/B3
Monte Cristo, Bolivia 136/E4
Montecristo (isl.), Italy 34/C3
Monte Cristo (range), Nev. 266/D4
Monte Dourado, Brazil 132/C2
Montefiascone, Italy 34/D3
Montefrío, Spain 33/D4
Montego (bay), Jamaica 158/G5
Montego Bay, Jamaica 158/H5
Montego Bay, Jamaica 156/B3
Montego Bay (pt.), Jamaica 158/G5
Montegut, La. (70377) 238/J8
Montehermoso, Spain 33/C2
Monteiro, Brazil 132/G4
Monteith, Iowa (†50115) 229/D5
Montejinnie, North. Terr. 93/C4
Monte Lake, Br. Col. 184/G5
Montélimar, France 28/F5
Montelindo (riv.), Paraguay 144/C3
Montellano, Spain 33/D4
Montello, Nev. (89830) 266/G1
Montello, Wis. (53949) 317/H8
Montemayor (plat.), Argentina 143/C5
Montemorelos, Mexico 150/K4
Montemor-o-Novo, Portugal 33/B3
Montemor-o-Velho, Portugal 33/B2
Monte Ne, Ark. (†72756) 202/B1
Montenegro, Brazil 132/D10
Montenegro, Chile 138/G2
Montenegro (rep.), Yugoslavia 45/D4
Monte Patria, Chile 138/A8
Monte Plata, Dom. Rep. 158/E6
Montepuez, Mozambique 118/F2
Montepulciano, Italy 34/C3
Monte Quemado, Argentina 143/D2
Monte Real, Brazil 132/A5
Monterey, Ala. (†36030) 195/E7
Monterey, Calif. 188/B3
Monterey (bay), Calif. 188/B3
Monterey (co.), Calif. 204/D7
Monterey, Calif. (93940) 204/D7
Monterey (bay), Calif. 204/K4
Monterey, Ind. (46960) 227/D2
Monterey, Ky. (†40359) 237/M4
Monterey, La. (71354) 238/G4
Monterey○, Mass. (01245) 249/B4
Monterey, Tenn. (38574) 237/L8
Monterey, Va. (24465) 307/K4
Monterey, Wis. (†53066) 317/J1
Monterey Park, Calif. (91754) 204/C10
Montería, Colombia 120/B2
Montería, Colombia 126/B3
Monte Río, Calif. (95462) 204/B5
Montero, Bolivia 136/D5
Monteros, Argentina 143/C2
Monterotondo, Italy 34/F6
Monterrey, Mexico 2/D4
Monterrey, Mexico 146/J7
Monterrey, Mexico 150/J4
Monterville, W. Va. (26282) 312/F5
Montes, Uruguay 145/D5
Montesano, Wash. (98563) 310/B4
Monte Sant'Angelo, Italy 34/F4
Monte Santo, Brazil 132/G5
Montes Claros, Brazil 120/E4
Montes Claros, Brazil 132/E7
Monte Sereno, Calif. (95030) 204/K4
Montevallo, Ala. (35115) 195/E4
Montevallo, Mo. (†64767) 261/D7
Montevarchi, Italy 34/C3
Montevideo, Minn. (56265) 255/C6
Montevideo (dept.), Uruguay 145/B7
Montevideo (cap.), Uruguay 145/B7
Montevideo (cap.), Uruguay 120/D6
Montevideo (cap.), Uruguay 2/G7
Monteview, Idaho (83435) 220/F6
Monte Vista, Colo. (81144) 208/G7
Montezuma (co.), Colo. 208/B8
Montezuma, Colo. (†80435) 208/H3
Montezuma (peak), Colo. 208/F8
Montezuma, Georgia (31063) 217/E6
Montezuma, Ind. (47862) 227/C5
Montezuma, Iowa (50171) 229/H5
Montezuma, Kansas (67867) 232/B4
Montezuma, N. Mex. (87731) 274/D3
Montezuma, Ohio (45866) 284/A4
Montezuma, Tenn. (†38340) 237/D10
Montezuma (creek), Utah 304/E6
Montezuma Castle Nat'l Mon., Ariz. 198/D4
Montezuma Creek, Utah (84534) 304/E6
Montfoort, Netherlands 27/G4
Montfort, France 28/C3
Montfort, Wis. (53569) 317/E10
Montgomery (cap.), Ala. 188/J4
Montgomery (cap.), Ala. 146/K6
Montgomery (co.), Ala. 195/F6
Montgomery (cap.), Ala. (*36101) 195/F6
Montgomery (co.), Ark. 202/C4
Montgomery (co.), Georgia 217/G6
Montgomery (co.), Ill. 222/D4
Montgomery, Ill. (60538) 222/E2
Montgomery (co.), Ind. 227/D4
Montgomery, Ind. (47558) 227/C7
Montgomery (co.), Iowa 229/C6
Montgomery, Iowa (51353) 229/C2
Montgomery (co.), Kansas 232/G4
Montgomery (co.), Ky. 237/O4
Montgomery, La. (71454) 238/E3
Montgomery (co.), Md. 245/J4
Montgomery, Mich. (49255) 250/E7
Montgomery, Minn. (56069) 255/E6
Montgomery (co.), Miss. 256/E4
Montgomery (co.), Mo. 261/K5
Montgomery (co.), N.Y. 276/M5
Montgomery, N.Y. (12549) 276/M7
Montgomery (co.), N.C. 281/K4
Montgomery (co.), Ohio 284/B6
Montgomery, Ohio (45242) 284/C9
Montgomery (co.), Pa. 294/M5
Montgomery, Pa. (17752) 294/H3
Montgomery (co.), Tenn. 237/G8
Montgomery (co.), Texas 303/J7
Montgomery, Texas (77356) 303/J7
Montgomery○, Vt. (05470) 268/B2
Montgomery (co.), Va. 307/H6
Montgomery, Wales 13/D5
Montgomery, Wales 10/E4
Montgomery, W. Va. (25136) 312/D6
Montgomery Center, Vt. (05471) 268/B2
Montgomery City, Mo. (63361) 261/K5
Monthey, Switzerland 39/C4
Monticello, Ark. (71655) 202/G6
Monticello, Fla. (32344) 212/C1
Monticello, Georgia (31064) 217/E4
Monticello, Ill. (61856) 222/E3
Monticello, Ind. (47960) 227/D3
Monticello, Iowa (52310) 229/L4
Monticello, Ky. (42633) 237/M7
Monticello○, Maine (04760) 243/H3
Monticello, Minn. (55362) 255/E5
Monticello, Miss. (39654) 256/D7
Monticello, Mo. (63457) 261/J2
Monticello, N. Mex. (87939) 274/B5
Monticello, N.Y. (12701) 276/L7
Monticello, Ohio (†45887) 284/B4
Monticello, S.C. (29106) 296/E3
Monticello, Utah (84535) 304/E6
Monticello, Wis. (53570) 317/G10
Mont Ida, Kansas (†66091) 232/G3
Montier, Mo. (65546) 261/J8
Montigny-les-Metz, France 28/G3
Montigny-le-Tilleul, Belgium 27/E8
Montijo, Panama 154/G6
Montijo (gulf), Panama 154/G7
Montijo, Portugal 33/B3
Montijo, Spain 33/C3
Montilla, Spain 33/D4
Montjoie (lake), Québec 172/B3
Mont-Joli, Que. 162/K6
Mont-Joli, Québec 174/D3
Mont-Joli, Québec 172/J1
Mont-Laurier, Que. 162/J6
Mont-Laurier, Québec 172/B3
Mont-Laurier, Québec 174/B3
Mont-Louis, Québec 172/C1
Montluçon, France 28/E4
Montmagny (co.), Québec 172/G3
Montmagny, Québec 174/C3
Montmagny, Québec 172/G3
Montmartre, Sask. 181/H5
Montmédy, France 28/F3
Montmorenci, Ind. (47962) 227/D4
Montmorenci, S.C. (29839) 296/D4
Montmorency (co.), Mich. 250/E3
Montmorency, Québec 172/J3
Montmorency (riv.), Québec 172/F2
Montmorency, Victoria 97/J4
Montmorency No. 1 (co.), Québec 172/F2
Montmorency No. 2 (co.), Québec 172/G3
Montmorency No. I (county), Québec 174/C3
Montmorillon, France 28/D4
Mont Nebo, Sask. 181/E2
Montney, Br. Col. 184/G2
Monto, Queensland 95/D5
Monto, Queensland 88/J4
Montoire-sur-le-Loir, France 28/D4
Montoro, Spain 33/D3
Montosa (mesa), N. Mex. 274/E3
Montour, Idaho (83617) 220/B6
Montour, Iowa (50173) 229/H5
Montour (co.), Pa. 294/J3
Montour Falls, N.Y. (14865) 276/G6
Montoursville, Pa. (17754) 294/J3
Montowese, Conn. (†06473) 210/D3
Montoya, N. Mex. (†88401) 274/F3
Montoz (mt.), Switzerland 39/D2
Montpelier, Idaho 188/D2
Montpelier, Idaho (83254) 220/G7
Montpelier, Ind. (47359) 227/G3
Montpelier, Iowa (52759) 229/M6
Montpelier, Jamaica 158/H6
Montpelier, La. (†70422) 238/M1
Montpelier, Miss. (39754) 256/G3
Montpelier, N. Dak. (58472) 282/N6
Montpelier, Ohio (43543) 284/A2
Montpelier (cap.), Vt. (05602) 268/B3
Montpelier (cap.), Vt. 146/L5
Montpelier (cap.), Vt. 188/M2
Montpellier, France 7/E4
Montpellier, France 28/E6
Montpellier, Québec 172/B4
Montréal, Canada 2/F3
Montreal (riv.), Mich. 250/F1
Montreal, Mo. (65591) 261/G7
Montréal, Que. 146/L5
Montréal, Que. 162/J7
Montréal, Québec 172/H4
Montreal (lake), Sask. 181/F1
Montreal, Wis. (54550) 317/F3
Montreal (riv.), Wis. 317/F2
Montréal-Est, Québec 172/J4
Montreal Lake, Sask. 181/F1
Montréal-Nord, Québec 172/H4
Montreal River Harbor, Ontario 177/J5
Montreat, N.C. (28757) 281/E3
Montreuil, Pas-de-Calais, France 28/D2
Montreuil, Seine-Saint-Denis, France 28/B2
Montreux, Switzerland 39/C4
Montricher, Switzerland 39/B3
Mont-Rolland, Québec 172/C4
Montrose, Ala. (36559) 195/C9
Montrose, Ark. (71658) 202/H7
Montrose, Br. Col. 184/J5
Montrose (co.), Colo. 208/C6
Montrose, Colo. (81401) 208/D6
Montrose, Georgia (31065) 217/F5
Montrose, Ill. (62445) 222/E4
Montrose, Iowa (52639) 229/L7
Montrose, Kansas (†66956) 232/D2
Montrose, La. (†71457) 238/D3
Montrose, Md. (†20850) 245/K4
Montrose, Mich. (48457) 250/F5
Montrose, Minn. (55363) 255/E5
Montrose, Miss. (†39338) 256/F6
Montrose, Mo. (64770) 261/E6
Montrose, Pa. (18801) 294/L2
Montrose, Scotland 10/E2
Montrose, Scotland 15/F4
Montrose, S. Dak. (57048) 298/P6
Montrose, Victoria 97/K5
Montrose, W. Va. (26283) 312/G4
Montrose-La Crescenta, Calif. (91214) 204/C10
Montross, Va. (22520) 307/P4
Montrouge, France 28/B2
Mont-Royal, Québec 172/H4
Monts (pt.), Québec 172/B1
Mont-Saint-Hilaire, Québec 172/D4
Mont-Saint-Michel, France 28/C3
Mont-Saint-Michel, Québec 172/B3
Mont-Saint-Pierre, Québec 172/C1
MONTSERRAT 156/G3
Montserrat (mt.), Spain 33/G2
Montsinéry, Fr. Guiana 131/E3
Mont-Tremblant, Québec 172/C3
Mont-Tremblant Prov. Park, Québec 172/C3
Mont-Tremblant Prov. Park, Québec 174/C3
Montvale, N.J. (07645) 273/B1
Montvale, Va. (24122) 307/J6
Montverde, Fla. (32756) 212/E3
Mont Vernon○, N.H. (03057) 268/D6
Montville, Conn. (06353) 210/G3
Montville○, Conn. (06353) 210/G3
Montville, Maine (†04941) 243/E7
Montville○, Maine (†04941) 243/E7
Montville, Mass. (†01255) 249/B4
Montville○, N.J. (07045) 273/E2
Montville, Ohio (44064) 284/H2
Montz, La. (†70068) 238/M3
Monument, Colo. (80132) 208/K4
Monument (peak), Idaho 220/B4
Monument, Kansas (67747) 232/A2
Monument, N. Mex. (88265) 274/F6
Monument, Oreg. (97864) 291/H3
Monument (valley), Utah 304/D6
Monument Beach, Mass. (02553) 249/M6
Monument Valley, Utah (84536) 304/D6
Monywa, Burma 72/B2
Monza, Italy 34/B2
Monze, Zambia 115/E7
Monzón, Spain 33/G2
Mooar, Iowa (†52632) 229/L8
Moodie (isl.), N.W. Terrs. 187/M3
Moodus, Conn. (06469) 210/F2
Moodus (res.), Conn. 210/F2
Moody, Ala. (†35125) 195/F3
Moody, Maine (04054) 243/B9
Moody, Mo. (65770) 261/J9
Moody (co.), S. Dak. 298/R5
Moody, Texas (76557) 303/G6
Moody A.F.B., Georgia 217/F9
Moodys, Okla. (74444) 288/S2
Moodyville, Tenn. (†38549) 237/L7
Mooers, N.Y. (12958) 276/N1
Mooka, Japan 81/K5
Mooleyville, Ky. (40154) 237/H4
Mooloo Downs, W. Australia 92/B4
Moomin (creek), N.S. Wales 97/E1
Moon (lake), Calif. 204/E2
Moon (lake), Nebr. 264/E2
Moon, Okla. (†71821) 288/S7
Moonachie, N.J. (†07070) 273/B2
Moonah (creek), Queensland 95/A4
Moonbeam, Ontario 177/J5
Mooncoin, Ireland 17/G7
Moonie (riv.), N.S. Wales 97/E1
Moonie, Queensland 95/D5
Moon Run, Pa. (†15244) 294/B5
Moonta, S. Australia 94/E5
Moora, W. Australia 88/B6
Moora, W. Australia 92/B5
Moorabbin, Victoria 88/L7
Moorabbin, Victoria 97/J5
Moorcroft, Wyo. (82721) 319/H1
Moore, Idaho (83255) 220/E6
Moore, Mont. (59464) 262/G4
Moore (dam), N.H. 268/D3
Moore (res.), N.H. 268/D3
Moore (co.), N.C. 281/L4
Moore, Okla. (73160) 288/M4
Moore, S.C. (29369) 296/D2
Moore (co.), Tenn. 237/J10
Moore (co.), Texas 303/C2
Moore, Texas (78057) 303/E9
Moore, Utah (†84523) 304/C5
Moore (dam), Vt. 268/D3
Moore (res.), Vt. 268/D3
Moore (lake), W. Australia 88/B5
Moore (lake), W. Australia 92/B5
MOOREA, Fr. Poly. 86/S13
Moorea (isl.), Fr. Poly. 87/L7
Moorea (isl.), Fr. Poly. 86/S13
Moorefield, Ark. (†72501) 202/G2
Moorefield, Ind. (†47043) 227/G7
Moorefield, Ky. (40350) 237/O4
Moorefield, Nebr. (69039) 264/D4
Moorefield, Ontario 177/D4
Moorefield, W. Va. (26836) 312/J4
Moore Haven, Fla. (33471) 212/E5
Mooreland, Ind. (47360) 227/G5
Mooreland, Okla. (73852) 288/H2
Moore Park, Manitoba 179/C4
Mooresboro, N.C. (28114) 281/F4
Moores Bridge, Ala. (†35458) 195/C4
Mooresburg, Tenn. (37811) 237/P8
Moores Creek, Ky. (40453) 237/O6
Moores Creek Nat'l Battlefield, N.C. 281/N6
Moores Hill, Ind. (47032) 227/G6
Moores Mills, New Bruns. 170/C3
Moorestown, Mich. (49651) 250/D4
Moorestown, N.J. (08057) 273/B3
Mooresville, Ala. (35649) 195/E1
Mooresville, Ind. (46158) 227/E5
Mooresville, Mo. (64664) 261/E3
Mooresville, N.C. (28115) 281/H3
Mooreton, N. Dak. (58061) 282/S7
Moore Town, Jamaica 158/K6
Mooretown, Ontario 177/B5
Mooreville, Miss. (38857) 256/G2
Moorfoot (hills), Scotland 15/E5
Moorhead, Iowa (51558) 229/B5
Moorhead, Minn. 188/G1
Moorhead, Minn. (56560) 255/B4
Moorhead, Miss. (38761) 256/C4
Mooringsport, La. (71060) 238/B1
Moorland, Iowa (50566) 229/E4
Moorland, Ky. (†40223) 237/L2
Moorman, Ky. (42357) 237/G6
Moorooka, Queensland 88/K3
Moorooka, Queensland 95/D3
Mooroopna, Victoria 97/C5
Moorpark, Calif. (93021) 204/G9
Moorreesburg, S. Africa 118/B6
Moorslede, Belgium 27/B7
Moosburg an der Isar, W. Germany 22/D4
Moose (creek), Idaho 220/D3
Moose (pond), Maine 243/B7
Moose (riv.), Maine 243/D4
Moose (isl.), Manitoba 179/E3
Moose (riv.), Minn. 255/C2
Moose (riv.), N.Y. 276/K3
Moose (mt.), Sask. 181/J6
Moose (riv.), Vt. 268/D2
Moose (lake), Wis. 317/E3
Moose (lake), Wis. 317/F3
Moose, Wyo. (83012) 319/B2
Moose Creek, Ontario 177/K2
Moose Factory, Ontario 175/D2
Moosehead, Maine (†04478) 243/D4
Moosehead (lake), Maine 243/D4
Mooseheart, Ill. (60539) 222/E2
Moose Heights, Br. Col. 184/F3
Moosehorn, Manitoba 179/D3
Moose Jaw, Sask. 146/H4
Moose Jaw, Sask. 162/F6
Moose Jaw, Sask. 181/F5
Moose Jaw (riv.), Sask. 181/G5
Moose Lake, Manitoba 179/H3
Moose Lake, Minn. (55767) 255/F4
Mooseland, Nova Scotia 168/F4
Mooseleuk (stream), Maine 243/F2
Mooselookmeguntic (lake), Maine 243/B6
Moose Mountain (creek), Sask. 181/J6
Moose Mountain Prov. Park, Sask. 181/J6
Moose Pass, Alaska (99631) 196/C1
Moose Range, Sask. 181/H2
Moose River○, Maine (†04945) 243/C4
Moose River, Ontario 175/D2
Moosic, Pa. (18507) 294/F7
Moosilauke (mt.), N.H. 268/D3
Moosomin, Sask. 162/F5
Moosomin, Sask. 181/K5
Moosonee, Ont. 162/H5
Moosonee, Ont. 146/K4
Moosonee, Ontario 175/D2
Moosup, Conn. (06354) 210/H2
Moosup (riv.), Conn. 210/H2
Mopang (lake), Maine 243/H6
Mopeia, Mozambique 118/F3
Mopti, Mali 102/B3
Mopti, Mali 106/D6
Moqatta, Sudan 59/C7
Moqor, Afghanistan 68/B2
Moqor, Afghanistan 59/J3
Moquah, Wis. (†54806) 317/D2
Moquegua (dept.), Peru 128/G11
Moquegua, Peru 120/B4
Moquegua, Peru 128/G11
Mór, Hungary 41/E3
Mora, Cameroon 115/B1
Mora, India 68/B7
Mora, La. (71455) 238/E4
Mora, Minn. (55051) 255/E5
Mora, Mo. (65345) 261/F5
Mora (co.), N. Mex. 274/E3
Mora, N. Mex. (87732) 274/D3
Mora (riv.), N. Mex. 274/E3
Mora, Portugal 33/B3
Mora, Spain 33/E3
Mora, Sweden 18/J6
Moradabad, India 54/J7
Moradabad, India 68/D3
Mora de Rubielos, Spain 33/F2
Morado, Quebrado (riv.), Chile 138/A6
Morafenobe, Madagascar 118/G3
Morąg, Poland 47/E2
Moraga, Calif. (94556) 204/K2
Moraine, Ohio (†45439) 284/B6
Moraleda (chan.), Chile 138/D5
Morales, Guatemala 154/C3
Morales, Peru 128/D6
Moramanga, Madagascar 118/H3
Moramanga, Madagascar 102/G6
Moran, Ind. (†46041) 227/D4
Moran, Kansas (66755) 232/G4
Moran, Mich. (49760) 250/E2
Moran, Texas (76464) 303/E5
Moran, Wyo. (83013) 319/B2
Moranbah, Queensland 95/C9
Morane (isl.), Fr. Poly. 87/N8
Morant (pt.), Jamaica 156/C3
Morant Bay, Jamaica 158/K7
Morar, Scotland 15/C4
Morar, Loch (lake), Scotland 15/C4
Morat (lake), Switzerland 39/D3
Morata de Tajuña, Spain 33/G4
Moratalla, Spain 33/E3
Morattico, Va. (22523) 307/P5
Moratuwa, Sri Lanka 68/D7
Morava (riv.), Czech. 41/D2
Morava (riv.), Yugoslavia 45/E3
Moravia, Iowa (52571) 229/H7
Moravia, N.Y. (13118) 276/H5
Moravian Falls, N.C. (28654) 281/G2
Moravská Třebová, Czech. 41/D2
Moravské Budějovice, Czech. 41/D2
Morawa, W. Australia 88/B5
Morawa, W. Australia 92/B5
Morawhanna, Guyana 120/D2
Morawhanna, Guyana 131/B1
Moray (firth), Scotland 7/D3
Moray (firth), Scotland 15/E3
Moray (firth), Scotland 10/E2
Moray (trad. co.), Scotland 15/A5
Morazán, Honduras 154/D3
Morbihan (dept.), France 28/B4
Mörbylånga, Sweden 18/K8
Morden, Man. 162/G6
Morden, Manitoba 179/D5
Mordialloc, Victoria 97/J6
Mordialloc, Victoria 88/L7
Mordvinian A.S.S.R., U.S.S.R. 52/G4
Mordvinian A.S.S.R., U.S.S.R. 48/E4
More, Loch (lake), Scotland 15/E2
More, Loch (lake), Scotland 15/D2
Morea, Victoria 97/A5
Moreau (riv.), S. Dak. 298/G3
Moreauville, La. (71355) 238/G4
Morebattle, Scotland 15/F5
Morecambe, Alberta 182/E3
Morecambe (bay), England 10/oe3
Morecambe (bay), England 13/D3
Moree, N. S. Wales 88/H5
Moree, N.S. Wales 97/E1
Morehead, Kansas (†66776) 232/G4
Morehead, Ky. (40351) 237/P4
Morehead City, N.C. (28557) 281/R5
Morehouse (par.), La. 238/G1
Morehouse, Mo. (63868) 261/N9
Moreland, Ark. (72849) 202/E3
Moreland, Georgia (30259) 217/C4
Moreland, Idaho (83256) 220/F6
Moreland Hills, Ohio (†44022) 284/J9
Morelia, Mexico 150/J7
Morelia, Mexico 146/H8
Morella, Queensland 95/B4
Morell, Pr. Edward I. 168/F2
Morella, Queensland 88/G4
Morella, Spain 33/F2
Morelos (state), Mexico 150/K7
Morelos, Mexico 150/J2
Morelos Cañada, Mexico 150/O2
Morena, India 68/D3
Morena, Sierra (mts.), Spain 7/D5
Morena, Sierra (range), Spain 33/E3
Morenci, Ariz. (85540) 198/F5
Morenci, Mich. (49256) 250/E7
Moreni, Romania 45/G3
Moreno, Bolivia 136/B2
Moreno, Calif. (92360) 204/H10
Moreno (bay), Chile 138/A4
Møre og Romsdal (co.), Norway 18/E5
Mores (creek), Idaho 220/C6
Moresby, Br. Col. 184/B3
Moresby (isl.), Br. Col. 184/B4
Moreton (isl.), Queensland 88/J5
Moreton (bay), Queensland 88/K2
Moreton (bay), Queensland 95/E5
Moreton (isl.), Queensland 95/E5
Moretonhampstead, England 13/C7
Moreton-in-Marsh, England 13/F6
Moretown○, Vt. (05660) 268/B3
Morewood, Ontario 177/J2
Morgan (co.), Ala. 195/E2
Morgan (co.), Colo. 208/M2
Morgan (pt.), Conn. 210/D4
Morgan (co.), Georgia 217/F3
Morgan, Georgia (31766) 217/C7
Morgan (co.), Ill. 222/C4
Morgan (co.), Ind. 227/E6
Morgan (co.), Ky. 237/P5
Morgan, Ky. (†41040) 237/N3
Morgan, Minn. (56266) 255/D6
Morgan (co.), Mo. 261/G6
Morgan, Mo. (†65706) 261/G7
Morgan (co.), Ohio 284/G6
Morgan (co.), Tenn. 237/M8
Morgan, Texas (76671) 303/G5
Morgan (co.), Utah 304/C2
Morgan, Utah (84050) 304/C2
Morgan○, Vt. (05853) 268/D2
Morgan (co.), W. Va. 312/K3
Morgan Center, Vt. (05854) 268/D2
Morgan City, La. (70380) 238/H7
Morgan City, Miss. (38946) 256/D4

414 Mount Washington

Mount Washington○, Mass. (†12517) 249/A4
Mount Wellington, N. Zealand 100/C1
Mount Willing, Ala. (†36012) 195/E6
Mount Wolf, Pa. (17347) 294/J5
Mount Zion, Georgia (30150) 217/B3
Mount Zion, Ill. (62549) 222/E4
Mount Zion, Ind. (†46792) 227/G3
Mount Zion, Iowa (†52565) 229/K7
Mount Zion, W. Va. (26151) 312/D5
Moura, Portugal 33/C3
Moura, Queensland 95/D5
Moura, Queensland 88/J4
Mourão, Portugal 33/C3
Mourdi (depr.), Chad 111/D4
Mourne (Newry and Mourne) (dist.), N. Ireland17/J3
Mourne (mts.), N. Ireland 17/J3
Mourne (riv.), N. Ireland 17/G2
Mouscron, Belgium 27/C7
Moussoro, Chad 111/C5
Mouthcard, Ky. (41548) 237/S6
Mouth of Wilson, Va. (24363) 307/F7
Moutier, Switzerland 39/D2
Moûtiers, France 28/G5
Mouton (isl.), Nova Scotia 168/D5
Mouydir (mts.), Algeria 106/E3
Moville, Iowa (51039) 229/A4
Moville, Ireland 17/G1
Mowbray, Manitoba 179/D5
Mowdok Mual (mt.), Bangladesh 68/G4
Moweaqua, Ill. (62550) 222/E4
Mower (co.), Minn. 255/F7
Mowming (Maoming), China 77/H7
Mowrystown, Ohio (45155) 284/C7
Moxahala, Ohio (43761) 284/F6
Moxee City, Wash. (98936) 310/E4
Moxico (dist.), Angola 115/D6
Moxie (lake), Maine 243/D5
Moxley, Georgia (†30477) 217/H5
Moy (riv.), Ireland 17/C3
Moy, N. Ireland 17/H3
Moyale, Ethiopia 111/G7
Moyale, Kenya 115/G3
Moyamba, S. Leone 106/B7
Moycullen, Ireland 17/C5
Moyers, Okla. (74557) 288/P6
Moyers, W. Va. (26813) 312/H6
Moyeuvre-Grande, France 28/G3
Moygashel, N. Ireland 17/H3
Moyie, Br. Col. 184/K5
Moyie (riv.), Idaho 220/B1
Moyie Springs, Idaho (83845) 220/B1
Moyle (dist.), N. Ireland 17/J1
Moynalty, Ireland 17/H4
Moyo, Uganda 115/F3
Moyobamba, Peru 120/B3
Moyobamba, Peru 128/D6
Moyock, N.C. (27958) 281/S1
Moyogalpa, Nicaragua 154/E5
Moyu (Karakax), China 77/A4
Moza Illit, Israel 65/C4
Mozambique 2/L6
Mozambique 102/F6
Mozambique (chan.) 2/L7
Mozambique (chan.) 102/G6
Mozambique (pt.), La. 238/M7
Mozambique (chan.), Madagascar 118/G3
MOZAMBIQUE 118/E4
Mozambique (chan.), Mozambique 118/G3
Mozart, Sask. 181/G4
Mozer, W. Va. (†26866) 312/H5
Mozhaysk, U.S.S.R. 52/E3
Mozhga, U.S.S.R. 52/H3
Mozier, Ill. (62070) 222/C4
Mozyr', U.S.S.R. 48/C4
Mozyr', U.S.S.R. 52/C4
Mpanda, Tanzania 115/F5
Mpika, Zambia 115/F6
Mporokoso, Zambia 115/F5
M'Pouya, Congo 115/C4
Mpraeso, Ghana 106/D7
Mpulungu, Zambia 115/F5
Mpwapwa, Tanzania 115/G5
Mrągowo, Poland 47/E2
Msaken, Tunisia 106/G1
M'Sila, Algeria 106/E1
Msta (riv.), U.S.S.R. 52/D3
Mtakuja, Tanzania 115/F5
Mtsensk, U.S.S.R. 52/E4
Mtwara (reg.), Tanzania 115/G5
Mtwara-Mikindani, Tanzania 102/G6
Mtwara-Mikindani, Tanzania 115/H6
Mu (riv.), Burma 72/B2
Mualama, Mozambique 118/F3
Muang Hinboun, Laos 72/E3
Muang Kènthao, Laos 72/D3
Muang Khammouan, Laos 72/E3
Muang Không, Laos 72/E4
Muang Khôngxédôn, Laos 72/E4
Muang Khoua, Laos 72/D2
Muang May, Laos 72/E4
Muang Ou Tai, Laos 72/D2
Muang Pak-Lay, Laos 72/D3
Muang Paktha, Laos 72/D2
Muang Pakxan, Laos 72/D2
Muang Phin, Laos 72/E3
Muang Sing, Laos 72/D2
Muang Tahoi, Laos 72/E3
Muang Vangviang, Laos 72/D3
Muang Vapi, Laos 72/E4
Muang Xaignabouri (Sayaboury), Laos 72/D3
Muang Xay, Laos 72/D3
Muang Xépôn, Laos 72/E3
Muang Xon, Laos 72/D2
Muar, Malaysia 72/D7
Muarabungo, Indonesia 85/C6
Muarasiberut, Indonesia 85/B6
Muaratewe, Indonesia 85/F6
Muari, Ras (cape), Pakistan 68/B4
Muari, Ras (cape), Pakistan 59/J5
Mubarraz, Saudi Arabia 59/E4
Mubende, Uganda 115/F3
Mubi, Nigeria 106/G6
Muchanes, Bolivia 136/B4
Mücheln, E. Germany 22/D3
Muck (isl.), Scotland 10/C2
Muck (isl.), Scotland 15/B4
Muckamore, N. Ireland 17/J2
Muckle Flugga (isl.), Scotland 15/G2
Muckleshoot Ind. Res., Wash. 310/C3
Muckno (lake), Ireland 17/H3
Muco (riv.), Colombia 126/E5
Mucojo, Mozambique 118/G2
Mucope, Angola 115/B7
Mucuchachí, Venezuela 124/C3
Mucuchíes, Venezuela 124/C3
Mucugê, Brazil 132/F6
Mucur, Turkey 63/F3
Mucurapo, Trin. & Tob. 161/A10
Mucuri, Brazil 132/G7
Mucuripe (pt.), Brazil 132/G3
Mucusso, Angola 115/D7
Mud (lake), Idaho 220/F6
Mud (riv.), Ky. 237/H7
Mud (lake), La. 238/D7
Mud (lake), Minn. 255/B3
Mud (lake), Minn. 255/B5
Mud (riv.), Minn. 255/C2
Mud (isl.), Nova Scotia 168/B5
Mud (creek), Okla. 288/L6
Mud (creek), Oreg. 291/K2
Mud (creek), S. Dak. 298/N3
Mud (lake), S. Dak. 298/R2
Mud, W. Va. (†25565) 312/C6
Mud (riv.), W. Va. 312/B6
Mudanjiang (Mutankiang), China 77/M3
Mudanjiang, China54/O5
Mudan Jiang (riv.), China 77/L3
Mudanya, Turkey 63/C2
Mudauwara, Jordan 59/C4
Mud Bay, Br. Col. 184/H2
Mud Butte, S. Dak. (57758) 298/D4
Muddy (creek), Colo. 208/E4
Muddy (brook), Conn. 210/H1
Muddy (pond), Conn. 210/G1
Muddy (riv.), Conn. 210/D3
Muddy, Ill. (62965) 222/E6
Muddy (mts.), Nev. 266/G6
Muddy (creek), N. Dak. 282/G6
Muddy (pt.), St. Chris.-Nevis 161/C10
Muddy (lake), Sask. 181/B3
Muddy (creek), Utah 304/A2
Muddy (creek), Utah 304/C4
Muddy (creek), Wyo. 319/F3
Muddy (creek), Wyo. 319/D2
Muddy (mt.), Wyo. 319/F3
Muddy Boggy (creek), Okla. 288/O5
Mudge (pond), Conn. 210/B1
Mudgee, N. S. Wales 88/J6
Mudgee, N.S. Wales 97/E3
Mudhnib, Saudi Arabia 59/D4
Mudjatik (riv.), Sask. 181/L3
Mud Lake, Idaho (†83450) 220/F6
Mud Lake, Newf. 166/B3
Mud Lake (res.), S. Dak. 298/N2
Mud Mountain (lake), Wash. 310/D3
Mudon, Burma 72/C3
Mudug (prov.), Somalia 115/J2
Mudurnu, Turkey 63/D2
Muecate, Mozambique 118/F2
Mueda, Mozambique 118/F2
Muenster, Sask. 181/F3
Muenster, Texas (76252) 303/G4
Muerto, Mar (lag.), Mexico 150/N9
Muezerskiy, U.S.S.R. 52/D2
Muff, Ireland 17/G1
Mufulira, Zambia 115/E6
Mufulira, Zambia 102/E6
Muge, Portugal 33/B3
Mugford (cape), Newf. 166/B2
Mughar, Israel 65/C2
Muğla (prov.), Turkey 63/C4
Muğla, Turkey 59/A2
Muğla, Turkey 63/C4
Muglad, Sudan 111/E5
Muhammad, Ras (cape), Egypt 59/B4
Muhammad, Ras (cape), Egypt 111/F2
Muhammad Qol, Sudan 59/C5
Muhammad Qol, Sudan 111/G3
Muharraq, Bahrain 59/F4
Mühldorf am Inn, W. Germany 22/E4
Muhlenberg (co.), Ky. 237/G6
Mühlhausen (Thomas-Müntzer-Stadt), E. Germany 22/D3
Mühlviertel (reg.), Austria 41/C2
Muhu (isl.), U.S.S.R. 53/B1
Mui Bai Bung (pt.), Vietnam 54/M9
Muiden, Netherlands 27/G4
Muinebeag, Ireland 17/H6
Muir (glac.), Alaska 196/M1
Muir, Mich. (48860) 250/D5
Muir, Pa. (17957) 294/J4
Muirkirk, Md. (†20705) 245/L4
Muirkirk, Scotland 15/E5
Muir of Ord, Scotland 15/D3
Muiron (isls.), W. Australia 88/A4
Muiron (isls.), W. Australia 92/A3
Muir Woods Nat'l Mon., Calif. 204/H2
Muizenberg, S. Africa 118/E7
Muju, S. Korea 81/C6
Mukachevo, U.S.S.R. 52/B5
Mukah, Malaysia 85/E5
Mukalla, P.D.R. Yemen 54/F8
Mukalla, P.D.R. Yemen 59/E7
Mukdahan, Thailand 72/E3
Mukden, Bolivia 136/A2
Mukden (Shenyang), China 77/K3
Mukilteo, Wash. (98275) 310/C3
Mukinbudin, W. Australia 92/B5
Muko, Japan 81/J7
Muko (isl.), Japan 81/M3
Muko (riv.), Japan 81/H7
Mukutawa (lake), Manitoba 179/G2
Mukutawa (riv.), Manitoba 179/E1
Mukwonago, Wis. (53149) 317/J2
Mula, Spain 33/F3
Mulaló, Ecuador 128/C3
Mulanje (mt.), Malawi 102/F6
Mulanje (mts.), Malawi 115/G7
Mulatos, Colombia 126/B3
Mulberry (creek), Ala. 195/E5
Mulberry, Ark. (72947) 202/B2
Mulberry (riv.), Ark. 202/C2
Mulberry, Calif. (†95926) 204/D4
Mulberry, Fla. (33860) 212/E4
Mulberry, Ind. (46058) 227/D4
Mulberry, Kansas (66756) 232/H4
Mulberry, Ohio (†45150) 284/B7
Mulberry, Tenn. (37359) 237/H10
Mulberry Fork (riv.), Ala. 195/E3
Mulberry Grove, Ill. (62262) 222/D5
Mulchatna (riv.), Alaska 196/G2
Mulchén, Chile 138/E1
Mulde (riv.), E. Germany 22/E3
Muldon, Miss. (†39730) 256/G3
Muldoon, Texas (78949) 303/G8
Muldraugh, Ky. (40155) 237/J5
Muldrow, Okla. (74948) 288/S4
Mule (mts.), Ariz. 198/E7
Mule (creek), Kansas 232/C4
Mule Creek, N. Mex. (88051) 274/A5
Mule Creek, Wyo. (†57735) 319/H2
Muleculus, Nicaragua 154/E4
Mulegé, Mexico 150/C3
Mulegns, Switzerland 39/J3
Muleshoe, Texas (79347) 303/B3
Mulgrave, Nova Scotia 168/G3
Mulgrave (lake), Nova Scotia 168/F3
Mulhacén (mt.), Spain 33/E4
Mulhall, Okla. (73063) 288/M2
Mülheim an der Ruhr, W. Germany 22/B3
Mulhouse, France 7/E4
Mulhouse, France 28/G4
Mulhurst, Alberta 182/D3
Muli, China 77/F6
Muli (str.), Indonesia 85/K7
Mulino, Oreg. (97042) 291/B2
Mulinu'u (cape), W. Samoa 86/L8
Mulkear (riv.), Ireland 17/E6
Mull (head), Scotland 15/F2
Mull (head), Scotland 15/F1
Mull (isl.), Scotland 10/D2
Mull (isl.), Scotland 15/C4
Mull (sound), Scotland 15/C4
Mullagh, Ireland 17/H4
Mullaghareirk (mts.), Ireland 17/C7
Mullaghcarn (mt.), N. Ireland 17/G2
Mullaghmore, Ireland 17/D3
Mullaittivu, Sri Lanka 68/E7
Mullaley, N.S. Wales 97/E2
Mullan, Idaho (83846) 220/C2
Mullardoch, Loch (lake), Scotland 15/C3
Mullen, Nebr. (69152) 264/C2
Mullens, W. Va. (25882) 312/D7
Müller (mts.), Indonesia 85/E5
Mullet (key), Fla. 212/D4
Mullett (lake), Mich. 250/E3
Mullett Lake, Mich. (49761) 250/E3
Mullewa, W. Australia 88/B5
Mullewa, W. Australia 92/A5
Müllheim, Switzerland 39/G1
Müllheim, W. Germany 22/B5
Mullica (riv.), N.J. 273/D4
Mullica Hill, N.J. (08062) 273/C4
Mulliken, Mich. (48861) 250/E6
Mullin, Texas (76864) 303/F6
Mullinahone, Ireland 17/F7
Mullinavat, Ireland 17/G7
Mullingar, Ireland 10/C4
Mullingar, Ireland 17/G4
Mullingar, Sask. 181/D2
Mullins, S.C. (29574) 296/J3
Mullinville, Kansas (67109) 232/C4
Mullion, England 13/B7
Mull of Galloway (prom.), Scotland 15/D6
Mull of Kintyre (prom.), Scotland 15/C5
Mull of Oa (prom.), Scotland 15/B5
Mullumbimby, N.S. Wales 97/G1
Mulobezi, Zambia 115/E7
Mulongo, Zaire 115/E5
Mulroy (bay), Ireland 17/F1
Multan, Pakistan 54/J6
Multan, Pakistan 68/C2
Multan, Pakistan 59/K3
Multnomah (co.), Oreg. 291/E2
Mulund, India 68/B6
Mulungushi (dam), Zambia 115/E6
Mulvane, Kansas (67110) 232/E4
Mulvihill, Manitoba 179/D4
Mulwala, N.S. Wales 97/D4
Mumbwa, Zambia 115/E6
Mumford, N.Y. (14511) 276/E4
Mümliswil-Ramiswil, Switzerland 39/E2
Mumra, U.S.S.R. 52/G5
Mun, Mae Nam (riv.), Thailand 72/D4
Muna (isl.), Indonesia 85/G7
Muna, Mexico 150/P6
Munbura, Queensland 95/C2
Munbura, Queensland 88/G2
Müncheberg, E. Germany 22/F2
München (Munich), W. Germany 22/D4
Münchenbuchsee, Switzerland 39/E2
Muncho Lake, Br. Col. 184/L2
Muncho Lake Prov. Park, Br. Col. 184/L2
Muncie, Ill. (61857) 222/F3
Muncie, Ind. 188/J2
Muncie, Ind. (*47302) 227/G4
Muncy, Pa. (17756) 294/J3
Muncy Valley, Pa. (17758) 294/J3
Munda, Solomon Is. 86/D3
Mundabullangana, W. Australia 92/B3
Mundare, Alberta 182/D3
Mundaring (res.), W. Australia 88/B2
Munday, Texas (76371) 303/E4
Mundelein, Ill. (60060) 222/A4
Munden, Kansas (66959) 232/E2
Münden, W. Germany 22/C3
Mundesley, England 13/J5
Mundijong, W. Australia 88/B3
Mundijong, W. Australia 92/A2
Mundiwindi, W. Australia 92/B3
Mundo Novo, Brazil 132/F5
Mundrabilla, W. Australia 92/E5
Mundubbera, Queensland 88/J5
Munera, Spain 33/E3
Munford, Ala. (36268) 195/F3
Munford, Tenn. (38058) 237/B10
Munfordville, Ky. (42765) 237/J6
Mungbere, Zaire 115/E3
Munger, Mich. (48747) 250/F5
Mungindi, N.S. Wales 97/E1
Mungindi, Queensland 95/D6
Munguba, Brazil 132/C2
Munhall, Pa. (15120) 294/C7
Munhango, Angola 115/C6
Munich, N. Dak. (58352) 282/N2
Munich, W. Germany 7/F4
Munich, W. Germany 22/D4
Munising, Mich. (49862) 250/C2
Munith, Mich. (49259) 250/E6
Munjor, Kansas (†67601) 232/C3
Munku-Sardyk (mt.), Mongolia 77/F1
Munnerlyn, Georgia (†30830) 217/H5
Munning (pt.), N. Zealand 100/E7
Munnsville, N.Y. (13409) 276/J4
Muñoz Gamero (pen.), Chile 138/D10
Munro (mt.), Tasmania 99/E2
Munroe Falls, Ohio (44262) 284/H3
Münsingen, Switzerland 39/E3
Munson, Alberta 182/D4
Munson, Fla. (†32570) 212/B5
Munson, Pa. (16860) 294/F4
Munsonville, N.H. (03457) 268/C5
Munster, Ind. (46321) 227/B1
Munster (prov.), Ireland 17/D7
Munster (trad. prov.), Ireland 17
Munster, Ontario 177/J2
Münster, Switzerland 39/F4
Münster, W. Germany 22/B3
Munsungan (lake), Maine 243/E3
Muntendam, Netherlands 27/K2
Muntok, Indonesia 85/D6
Munuscong (lake), Mich. 250/E2
Muojärvi (lake), Finland 18/R4
Muong Khuong, Vietnam 72/E2
Muonio (riv.) 7/G2
Muonio, Finland 18/O3
Muonio (riv.), Finland 18/M2
Muonioälv (riv.), Sweden 18/M2
Muota (riv.), Switzerland 39/G3
Muotathal, Switzerland 39/G3
Muqaddam, Wadi (dry riv.), Sudan 111/F4
Muqdadiyah, Iraq 66/D4
Muqdisho (Mogadishu) (cap.), Somalia 115/J3
Muqdisho (Mogadishu) (cap.), Somalia 102/G4
Muqeible, Israel 65/C2
Muqui, Brazil 132/F8
Mur (riv.), Austria 41/C3
Mur (riv.), Yugoslavia 45/B2
Mura (riv.), Hungary 41/D3
Muradiye, Turkey 63/K3
Murakami, Japan 81/J4
Murallón, Cerro (mt.), Argentina 143/B6
Murallón, Cerro (mt.), Chile 138/D8
Murarrie, Queensland 88/K2
Murashi, U.S.S.R. 52/G3
Murat, France 28/E5
Murat (riv.), Turkey 59/C2
Murat (riv.), Turkey 63/H3
Murat Dağı (mt.), Turkey 63/C3
Murau, Austria 41/C3
Murbat, Oman 59/G6
Murchison, N. Zealand 100/D4
Murchison (range), North. Terr. 93/D6
Murchison (falls), Uganda 115/F3
Murchison (riv.), W. Australia 88/B5
Murchison (mt.), W. Australia 92/B4
Murchison (riv.), W. Australia 92/B4
Murchison Downs, W. Australia 88/B5
Murcia (prov.), Spain 33/F4
Murcia, Spain 7/D5
Murcia, Spain 33/F4
Murcia (reg.), Spain 33/F3
Murderers (creek), Oreg. 291/H3
Murderkill (riv.), Del. 245/R5
Murdo, S. Dak. (57559) 298/H6
Murdochville, Québec 172/C1
Murdock, Fla. (33938) 212/D4
Murdock, Ill. (61941) 222/E4
Murdock, Kansas (67111) 232/E4
Murdock, Minn. (56271) 255/C5
Murdock, Nebr. (68407) 264/H4
Muren (Mörön), Mongolia 77/F2
Mureş (riv.), Romania 45/E2
Muret, France 28/D6
Muretto (pass), Switzerland 39/J4
Murfreesboro, Ark. (71958) 202/C5
Murfreesboro, N.C. (27855) 281/R2
Murfreesboro, Tenn. (37130) 237/J9
Murg (riv.), Switzerland 39/G1
Murgab, U.S.S.R. 48/H6
Murgab (riv.), U.S.S.R. 48/G6
Murghab (riv.), Afghanistan 59/H2
Murgon, Queensland 88/J5
Murgon, Queensland 95/D5
Murgoo, W. Australia 92/B4
Muri, Switzerland 39/F2
Muriaé, Brazil 135/E2
Muriaé, Brazil 132/F8
Murias de Paredes, Spain 33/C1
Muri bei Bern, Switzerland 39/E3
Muriel (lake), Alberta 182/E2
Murindó, Colombia 126/B4
Müritzsee (lake), E. Germany 22/E2
Murjek, Sweden 18/M3
Murl, Ky. (†42633) 237/M7
Murle, Ethiopia 111/G6
Murmansk, U.S.S.R. 7/H2
Murmansk, U.S.S.R. 2/L2
Murmansk, U.S.S.R. 4/C8
Murmansk, U.S.S.R. 48/D3
Murmansk, U.S.S.R. 52/D1
Murnau, W. Germany 22/D5
Murnpeowie, S. Australia 94/F3
Murom, U.S.S.R. 52/F3
Murongo, Tanzania 115/F4
Muroran, Japan 81/K2
Muros, Spain 33/B1
Muroto, Japan 81/G7
Muroto (pt.), Japan 81/G7
Murphy, Idaho (83650) 220/B6
Murphy, Miss. (†38748) 256/C4
Murphy, Mo. (†63088) 261/O4
Murphy, N.C. (28906) 281/B4
Murphy, Oreg. (97533) 291/D5
Murphy (isl.), S.C. 296/J5
Murphy, Texas (†75074) 303/H1
Murphys, Calif. (95247) 204/E5
Murphysboro, Ill. (62966) 222/D6
Murphytown, W. Va. (†26142) 312/D4
Murra Murra, Queensland 95/C6
Murray (riv.) 88/G6
Murray (river), Australia 87/E9
Murray (riv.), Br. Col. 184/G3
Murray (co.), Georgia 217/C1
Murray, Idaho (83874) 220/C2
Murray, Ind. (†46714) 227/G3
Murray, Iowa (50174) 229/F6
Murray, Ky. (42071) 237/E7
Murray (co.), Minn. 255/C6
Murray, Nebr. (68409) 264/J4
Murray (riv.), N.S. Wales 97/A4
Murray (co.), Okla. 288/M6
Murray (lake), Okla. 288/M6
Murray (lake), Papua N.G. 85/B7
Murray (riv.), S. Australia 94/F6
Murray (lake), S.C. 188/K4
Murray (lake), S.C. 296/D4
Murray, Utah (84107) 304/C3
Murray, Utah 188/D2
Murray (riv.), Victoria 97/A4
Murray (bay), Victoria 88/H7
Murray (riv.), W. Australia 92/A2
Murray Bridge, S. Australia 88/F7
Murray Bridge, S. Australia 94/F6
Murray City, Ohio (43144) 284/F6
Murray Corner, New Bruns. 170/G2
Murray Downs, North. Terr. 93/D6
Murray Harbour, Pr. Edward I. 168/F2
Murray Lake Hills, Tenn. (37416) 237/L10
Murray River, Pr. Edward I. 168/F2
Murraysville, W. Va. (26153) 312/C4
Murrayville, Georgia (30564) 217/E2
Murrayville, Ill. (62668) 222/C4
Murrayville, Victoria 97/A4
Murree, Pakistan 68/C2
Murrells Inlet, S.C. (29576) 296/K4
Mürren, Switzerland 39/E3
Murrieta, Calif. (92362) 204/H10
Murringo, N.S. Wales 97/E4
Murrumbidgee (riv.), N. S. Wales 88/H6
Murrumbidgee (riv.), N.S. Wales 97/C4
Murrumburrah, N.S. Wales 97/E4
Murrupula, Mozambique 118/F3
Murrurundi, N.S. Wales 97/F2
Murrysville, Pa. (15668) 294/C5
Murska Sobota, Yugoslavia 45/C2
Murtarol (peak), Switzerland 39/K3
Murtaugh, Idaho (83344) 220/D7
Murten, Switzerland 39/D3
Murtle (lake), Br. Col. 184/H4
Murtoa, Victoria 97/B5
Murud, India 68/C5
Murupara, N. Zealand 100/F3
Mururoa (isl.), Fr. Poly. 87/M8
Murwara, India 68/E4
Murwillumbah, N. S. Wales 88/J5
Murwillumbah, N.S. Wales 97/G1
Muryo (mt.), Indonesia 85/J2
Mürz (riv.), Austria 41/C3
Murzuk, Libya 102/D2
Murzuk, Libya 111/B2
Mürzzuschlag, Austria 41/C3
Muş (prov.), Turkey 63/J3
Muş, Turkey 63/J3
Muş, Turkey 59/D2
Musa Khel Bazar, Pakistan 59/K3
Musa Khel Bazar, Pakistan 68/B2
Musala (mt.), Bulgaria 45/F4
Musan, N. Korea 81/D2
Musandam, Ras (cape), Oman 59/G4
Musashino, Japan 81/O2
Muscadine, Ala. (36269) 195/H3
Muscat (cap.), Oman 54/G7
Muscat (cap.), Oman 2/M4
Muscat (cap.), Oman 59/G5
Muscatatuck (riv.), Ind. 227/E7
Muscatine (co.), Iowa 229/L5
Muscatine, Iowa 188/H2
Muscatine, Iowa (52761) 229/L6
Muscle Shoals, Ala. (35660) 195/C1
Muscoda, Wis. (53573) 317/F9
Muscogee (co.), Georgia 217/C6
Musconetcong (beach), N.J. 273/C2
Muscongus (bay), Maine 243/E8
Muscotah, Kansas (66058) 232/G2
Muscoy, Calif. (92405) 204/E10
Muse, Okla. (74949) 288/S5
Musella, Georgia (31066) 217/E5
Musgrave (ranges), Australia 87/D8
Musgrave, Queensland 95/B2
Musgrave (range), S. Australia 88/E5
Musgrave (ranges), S. Australia 94/B2
Musgrave Harbour, Newf. 166/D4
Musgravetown, Newf. 166/C2
Mushaboom, Nova Scotia 168/F4
Mushandike Nat'l Park, Zimbabwe 118/D4
Mushie, Zaire 102/D5
Mushie, Zaire 115/C4
Musi (riv.), Indonesia 85/C6
Musidora, Alberta 182/E3
Muskeg (bay), Manitoba 179/G6
Muskeg (bay), Minn. 255/C2
Muskeget (chan.), Mass. 249/N7
Muskeget (isl.), Mass. 249/N7
Muskego, Wis. (53150) 317/K2
Muskegon (co.), Mich. 250/C5
Muskegon, Mich. 188/J2
Muskegon, Mich. (*49440) 250/C5
Muskegon (riv.), Mich. 250/C5
Muskegon Heights, Mich. (49444) 250/C5
Muskeg River, Alberta 182/A3
Muskingum (co.), Ohio 284/G5
Muskingum (riv.), Ohio 284/G6
Muskogee, Okla. 188/H3
Muskogee (co.), Okla. 288/R3
Muskogee, Okla. (74401) 288/R3
Muskoka (dist. munic.), Ontario 177/E3
Muskoka (lake), Ontario 177/E2
Muskrat (creek), Wyo. 319/E2
Muskwa (lake), Alberta 182/C1
Muskwa (riv.), Alberta 182/C1
Muskwa (riv.), Br. Col. 184/M2
Muslimiya, Syria 63/G4
Musmar, Sudan 111/G4
Musoma, Tanzania 115/F4
Musoma, Tanzania 102/F5
Musquacook (lakes), Maine 243/E2
Musquash (harb.), New Bruns. 170/D3
Musquodoboit (riv.), Nova Scotia 168/E4
Musquodoboit Harbour, Nova Scotia 168/E4
Mussau (isl.), Papua N.G. 86/B1
Musselburgh, Scotland 15/D2
Musselburgh, Scotland 10/C1
Musselshell (riv.) 188/E1
Musselshell (co.), Mont. 262/H4
Musselshell, Mont. (59059) 262/H4
Musselshell (riv.), Mont. 262/J3
Mustafakemalpaşa, Turkey 63/C3
Mustahil, Ethiopia 111/H6
Müstair, Switzerland 39/K3
Mustang, Nepal 68/E3
Mustang, Okla. (73064) 288/L4
Mustang (creek), Texas 303/A1
Mustang (isl.), Texas 303/G10
Mustang Draw (dry riv.), Texas 303/B5
Musters (lake), Argentina 143/C6
Mustinka (riv.), Minn. 255/B5
Mustoe, Va. (24468) 307/J4
Mustvee, U.S.S.R. 53/D1
Muswellbrook, N. S. Wales 88/J6
Muswellbrook, N.S. Wales 97/F3
Mût, Egypt 111/E2
Mût, Egypt 59/A4
Mût, Egypt 102/E2
Mut, Turkey 63/E4
Mutankiang (Mudanjiang), China 77/M3
Mutarara (Dona Ana), Mozambique 118/F3
Mutare (Umtali), Zimbabwe 118/E3
Muthanna (gov.), Iraq 66/D5
Muthill, Scotland 15/E4
Muting, Indonesia 85/K7
Mutki, Turkey 63/J3
Mutrie, Sask. 181/H5
Mutsamudu, Comoros 118/G2
Mutshatsha, Zaire 115/D6
Mutsu, Japan 81/K3
Mutsu (bay), Japan 81/K3
Muttaburra, Queensland 95/C4
Muttalip, Turkey 63/D3
Muttenz, Switzerland 39/E1
Muttler (mt.), Switzerland 39/K3
Mutton (isl.), Ireland 17/B6
Mutton Bird (isl.), N.S. Wales 97/J2
Muttonville, Mich. (†48062) 250/G6
Mutual, Ohio (†43078) 284/C5
Mutual, Okla. (73853) 288/H2
Mutum, Brazil 135/F1
Mu Us Shamo (des.), China 77/G4
Muwailih, Saudi Arabia 59/C4
Muwale, Tanzania 115/F5
Muxima, Angola 115/B5
Muy Muy, Nicaragua 154/E4
Muy Muy Viejo, Nicaragua 154/E4
Muynak, U.S.S.R. 48/F5
Muyumba, Zaire 115/E5
Muzaffarabad, Pakistan 68/C2
Muzaffarnagar, India 68/D3
Muzaffarpur, India 68/E3
Muzambinho, Brazil 135/C2
Muzo, Colombia 126/D5
Muzon (cape), Alaska 196/M2
Muztag (mt.), China 77/B4
Muztagata (mt.), China 77/A4
Mvadhi-Ousyé, Gabon 115/B3
M'Vouti, Congo 115/B4
Mwadingusha, Zaire 115/E6
Mwadui, Tanzania 115/F4
Mwanza, Malawi 115/F7
Mwanza (reg.), Tanzania 115/F4
Mwanza, Tanzania 115/F4
Mwanza, Tanzania 102/F5
Mwanza, Zaire 115/E5
Mwaya, Tanzania 115/F5
Mweelrea (mt.), Ireland 17/B4
Mweenish (isl.), Ireland 17/B5
Mweka, Zaire 115/D4
Mwene-Ditu, Zaire 115/D5
Mwenga, Zaire 115/E4
Mweru (lake) 102/E5
Mweru (lake), Zaire 115/E5
Mweru (lake), Zambia 115/E5
Mwesi, Tanzania 115/F5
Mwinilunga, Zambia 115/D6
Mya, Wadi (dry riv.), Algeria 106/E2
Myakka (riv.), Fla. 212/D4
Myakka City, Fla. (33551) 212/D4
Myall (lake), N.S. Wales 97/G3
Myanaung, Burma 72/B3
Myaungmya, Burma 72/B3
Myebon, Burma 72/B2
Myers, Ky. (†40311) 237/O4
Myers, Mont. (†59038) 262/J4
Myerstown, Pa. (17067) 294/K5
Myersville, Md. (21773) 245/H3
Myingyan, Burma 72/B2
Myitkyina, Burma 54/L7
Myitkyina, Burma 72/C1
Myitnge, Burma 72/C2
Myitnge (riv.), Burma 72/C2
Myjava, Czech. 41/D2
Mylo, N. Dak. (†58317) 282/L2
Mymensingh (Nasirabad), Bangladesh 68/G4
Mynyddislwyn, Wales 13/B6
Myohaung, Burma 72/B2
Myohyang (mt.), N. Korea 81/C3
Myŏngch'ŏn, N. Korea 81/D3

Naturaliste 415

Myra, Texas (76253) 303/G4
Myra, W. Va. (25544) 312/B6
Myricks, Mass. (†02780) 249/K5
Myrnam, Alberta 182/E3
Myrtle, Idaho (†83540) 220/B3
Myrtle, Manitoba 179/E5
Myrtle, Minn. (56070) 255/E7
Myrtle, Miss. (38650) 256/F1
Myrtle, Mo. (65778) 261/K9
Myrtle (lake), N. Dak. 282/L5
Myrtle Beach, S.C. (29577) 296/K4
Myrtle Beach A.F.B., S.C. 296/K4
Myrtle Creek, Oreg. (97457) 291/D4
Myrtleford, Victoria 97/D5
Myrtle Grove, Fla. (32506) 212/B6
Myrtle Grove, La. (†70083) 238/K7
Myrtle Point, Oreg. (97458) 291/C4
Myrtlewood, Ala. (36763) 195/C6
Mysen, Norway 18/G7
Myślenice, Poland 47/E4
Myślibórz, Poland 47/B2
Mysłowice, Poland 47/C4
Mysore, India 68/D6
Mysore, India 54/J8
Mys Shmidta, U.S.S.R. 4/C1
Mys Shmidta, U.S.S.R. 48/T3
Mystery Lake, Manitoba 179/J2
Mystic, Conn. (06355) 210/H3
Mystic (riv.), Conn. 210/H3
Mystic, Georgia (31769) 217/F7
Mystic, Iowa (52574) 229/H7
Mystic (lake), Mass. 249/C6
Mystic (riv.), Mass. 249/C6
Mystic, S. Dak. (†57778) 298/B5
Mystic Islands, N.J. (08087) 273/E4
Myszków, Poland 47/D3
My Tho, Vietnam 72/E5
Mytishchi, U.S.S.R. 52/E3
Myton, Utah (84052) 304/D3
M'zab (oasis), Algeria 106/E2
Mže (riv.), Czech. 41/B2
Mzimba, Malawi 115/F6
Mzimba, Malawi 102/F6

N

Naab (riv.), W. Germany 22/E4
Naafkopf (mt.), Switzerland 39/J2
Naaldwijk, Netherlands 27/E4
Naalehu, Hawaii (96772) 218/H7
Naalehu, Hawaii 188/G6
Naantali, Finland 18/M6
Naarden, Netherlands 27/G4
Naas, Ireland 10/C4
Naas, Ireland 17/H5
Naba, Burma 72/B1
Nababeep, S. Africa 118/B5
Nabari, Kiribati 87/J6
Nabb, Ind. (47147) 227/F7
Nabburg, W. Germany 22/E4
Naberezhnye Chelny, U.S.S.R. 52/H3
Nabesna, Alaska (†99764) 196/K2
Nabeul, Tunisia 106/G1
Nabiac, N.S. Wales 97/G3
Nabire, Indonesia 85/K6
Nablus (Nabulus), West Bank 65/C3
Nabnasset, Mass. (01861) 249/J2
Nabua, Philippines 82/D4
Nacala, Mozambique 118/G2
Nacala, Mozambique 102/G6
Nacaome, Honduras 154/D4
Naches, Wash. (98937) 310/E4
Naches (pass), Wash. 310/D3
Naches (riv.), Wash. 310/E4
Nachikatsuura, Japan 81/H7
Nachingwea, Tanzania 115/G6
Náchod, Czech. 41/D1
Nachusa, Ill. (61057) 222/D2
Nachvak (fjord), Newf. 166/B2
Nacimiento (riv.), Calif. 204/D8
Nacimiento, Chile 138/D1
Nacimiento (mts.), N. Mex. 274/C3
Nacimiento (peak), N. Mex. 274/C2
Nacka, Sweden 18/H1
Nackawic, New Bruns. 170/C2
Nacmine, Alberta 182/D4
Naco, Ariz. (85620) 198/E7
Naco, Mexico 150/D1
Nacogdoches (co.), Texas 303/K6
Nacogdoches, Texas (75961) 303/J6
Nacozari, Mexico 150/E1
Ñacunday, Paraguay 144/E5
Nadadores, Mexico 150/H3
Nadawah, Ala. (†36726) 195/D7
Nadeau, Mich. (49863) 250/B3
Nadi, Fiji 86/P10
Nadi, Fiji 87/H7
Nadiad, India 68/C4
Nădlac, Romania 45/E2
Nador, Morocco 106/D1
Nádudvar, Hungary 41/F3
Nadvoitsy, U.S.S.R. 52/D2
Nadym, U.S.S.R. 48/H3
Nadym (riv.), U.S.S.R. 48/H3
Naestved, Denmark 21/E7
Naestved, Denmark 18/G9
Naf, Idaho (83342) 220/E7
Näfels, Switzerland 39/H2
Nafenen, Switzerland 39/H3
Naft-e Shah, Iran 66/D4
Naft Kaneh, Iraq 66/D3
Naga, Philippines 85/G3
Naga, Philippines 54/O8
Naga, Philippines 82/D4
Nagahama, Ehime, Japan 81/F7
Nagahama, Shiga, Japan 81/H6
Nagai (isl.), Alaska 196/F4
Nagaland (state), India 68/G3
Nagambie, Victoria 97/C5
Nagano (pref.), Japan 81/J5
Nagano, Japan 81/J5
Nagaoka, Kyoto, Japan 81/J7
Nagaoka, Niigata, Japan 81/J5
Nagaokakyo, Japan 81/J7
Nagapattinam, India 68/E6
Nagar, Pakistan 68/D1
Nagarote, Nicaragua 154/D4
Nagar Parkar, Pakistan 68/C4
Nagarzê, China 77/C6
Nagasaki (pref.), Japan 81/D7
Nagasaki, Japan 54/O6
Nagasaki, Japan 81/D7
Nagato, Japan 81/E6
Nagaur, India 68/C3
Nagawicka (lake), Wis. 317/J1
Nagele, Netherlands 27/H3
Nagercoil, India 68/D7
Nagina, India 68/D3
Nagishot, Sudan 111/F7
Nagles (mts.), Ireland 17/E7
Nago, Japan 81/N6
Nagold, W. Germany 22/C4
Nagorno-Karabakh Aut. Obl., U.S.S.R. 48/E5
Nagorno-Karabakh Aut. Obl., U.S.S.R. 52/G7
Nagornyy, U.S.S.R. 48/N4
Nagoya, Japan 81/H6
Nagoya, Japan 2/R4
Nagoya, Japan 54/P6
Nagpur, India 54/J7
Nagpur, India 68/D4
Nagqu, China 77/D5
Nags Head, N.C. (27959) 281/T3
Nagua, Dom. Rep. 158/E5
Naguabo, P. Rico 161/F2
Naguabo, P. Rico 156/G1
Nagyatád, Hungary 41/D3
Nagybajom, Hungary 41/D3
Nagyecsed, Hungary 41/G3
Nagyhalász, Hungary 41/F2
Nagykálló, Hungary 41/F3
Nagykanizsa, Hungary 41/D3
Nagykáta, Hungary 41/E3
Nagykőrös, Hungary 41/E3
Nagyszénás, Hungary 41/F3
Naha, Japan 54/O7
Naha, Japan 81/N6
Nahan, India 68/D2
Nahang (riv.), Iran 66/N7
Nahanni Butte, N.W. Terrs. 187/F3
Nahanni Nat'l Park, N.W.T. 162/D3
Nahanni Nat'l Park, N.W. Terrs. 187/F3
Nahant◯, Mass. (01908) 249/E6
Nahant (bay), Mass. 249/E6
Nahariyya, Israel 65/C1
Nahavand, Iran 59/E3
Nahavand, Iran 66/F3
Nahcotta, Wash. (98537) 310/A4
Nahhalin, West Bank 65/C4
Nahiku, Hawaii (†96713) 218/K2
Nahma, Mich. (49864) 250/C3
Nahmakanta (lake), Maine 243/E4
Nahuel Huapí (lake), Argentina 120/B7
Nahuel Huapí (lake), Argentina 143/B5
Nahuel Huapí Nat'l Park, Argentina 143/B5
Nahunta, Georgia (31553) 217/H8
Naica, Mexico 150/G2
Naicam, Sask. 181/G3
Naihati, India 68/F1
Nailsworth, England 13/E6
Naiman, China 77/K3
Na'in, Iran 66/H4
Na'in, Iran 59/F3
Nain, Jamaica 158/H6
Nain, Newf. 166/B2
Nain, Newf. 162/K4
Naini Tal, India 68/D3
Nainpur, India 68/E4
Naipo (isl.), Colombia 126/F6
Nairn, La. (†70082) 238/L8
Nairn, Ontario 177/C1
Nairn, Scotland 15/E3
Nairn, Scotland 10/E2
Nairn (trad. co.), Scotland 15/B5
Nairn (riv.), Scotland 15/D3
Nairne, S. Australia 94/C8
Nairobi, Kenya 115/G4
Nairobi (cap.), Kenya 2/L6
Nairobi (cap.), Kenya 115/G4
Nairobi (cap.), Kenya 102/F5
Naivasha, Kenya 115/G4
Najafabad, Iran 59/F3
Najafabad, Iran 66/G4
Najayo Abajo, Dom. Rep. 158/E6
Najin, N. Korea 81/E2
Najran (Aba as Sa'ud), Saudi Arabia 59/D6
Naka (riv.), Japan 81/K5
Nakalele (pt.), Hawaii 218/J1
Nakaminato, Japan 81/K5
Nakamti, Ethiopia 102/F4
Nakamti, Ethiopia 111/G6
Nakamura, Japan 81/F7
Nakasato, Japan 81/K3
Nakatane, Japan 81/E8
Nakatsu, Japan 81/E7
Na Keal, Loch (inlet), Scotland 15/B4
Naked (isl.), Alaska 196/D1
Nakfa, Ethiopia 111/G4
Nakhichevan', U.S.S.R. 7/J5
Nakhichevan', U.S.S.R. 48/E6
Nakhichevan', U.S.S.R. 52/F7
Nakhichevan' A.S.S.R., U.S.S.R. 52/F7
Nakhichevan' A.S.S.R., U.S.S.R. 48/E6
Nakhodka, U.S.S.R. 54/P5
Nakhodka, U.S.S.R. 48/O5
Nakhon Nayok, Thailand 72/D4
Nakhon Pathom, Thailand 72/C4
Nakhon Phanom, Thailand 72/D3
Nakhon Ratchasima, Thailand 72/D4
Nakhon Ratchasima, Thailand 54/M8
Nakhon Sawan, Thailand 72/D4
Nakhon Si Thammarat, Thailand 54/M9
Nakhon Si Thammarat, Thailand 72/D5
Nakina, N.C. (28455) 281/M6
Nakina, Ont. 162/H5
Nakina, Ontario 177/H4
Nakina, Ontario 175/C2
Nakło nad Notecia, Poland 47/C2
Naknek, Alaska (99633) 196/G3
Naknek (lake), Alaska 196/G3
Nakonde, Zambia 115/F5
Nakop, Namibia 118/B5
Nakskov, Denmark 21/E8
Nakskov, Denmark 18/G9
Naktong (riv.), S. Korea 81/D6
Nakuru, Kenya 102/F5
Nakuru, Kenya 115/G4
Nakusp, Br. Col. 184/J5
Nal, Pakistan 59/J4
Nal, Pakistan 68/B3
Nal (riv.), Pakistan 59/J4
Nal (riv.), Pakistan 68/B3
Nalate, Turkey 63/G4
Nalayh (Nalaikha), Mongolia 77/G2
Nalcayec (isl.), Chile 138/D6
Nal'chik, U.S.S.R. 7/J4
Nal'chik, U.S.S.R. 48/E5
Nal'chik, U.S.S.R. 52/F6
Nalgonda, India 68/D5
Nallen, W. Va. (26680) 312/E6
Nallıhan, Turkey 63/D2
Nalut, Libya 111/B1
Namacurra, Mozambique 118/F3
Namak, Daryacheh-ye (salt lake), Iran 59/F3
Namak, Daryacheh-ye (salt lake), Iran 66/G3
Namaka, Alberta 182/D4
Namaksar (salt lake), Afghanistan 59/H3
Namaksar (salt lake), Afghanistan 68/A2
Namaksar (lake), Iran 66/M4
Namaksar (salt lake), Iran 59/H3
Namakzar-e Shahdad (salt lake), Iran 59/G3
Namakzar-e Shahdad (salt lake), Iran 66/L5
Namanga, Kenya 115/G4
Namangan, U.S.S.R. 48/H5
N'amaniya, Iraq 66/D4
Namapa, Mozambique 118/F2
Namaqualand (reg.), S. Africa 118/B5
Namarrói, Mozambique 118/F3
Namasagali, Uganda 115/F3
Namasigüe, Honduras 154/D4
Namatanai, Papua N.G. 87/F6
Namatanai, Papua N.G. 86/C1
Nambe, N. Mex. (†87501) 274/D3
Nambour, Queensland 88/J5
Nambour, Queensland 95/E5
Nambucca Heads, N.S. Wales 97/G2
Nam Co (lake), China 77/D5
Nam Dinh, Vietnam 72/E2
Namekagon (lake), Wis. 317/D3
Namekagon (riv.), Wis. 317/C3
Namen (Namur), Belgium 27/F8
Náměstovo, Czech. 41/E2
Nametil, Mozambique 118/F3
Namhkam, Burma 72/C2
Namib (des.), Namibia 118/A3
Namibia 2/K7
Namibia 102/D7
Namibia (des.) 102/D6
NAMIBIA (SOUTH-WEST AFRICA) 118/B3
Naminga, U.S.S.R. 48/M4
Namiquipa, Mexico 150/F2
Namlan, Burma 72/C2
Namlea, Indonesia 85/H6
Namoi (riv.), N. S. Wales 88/H6
Namoi (riv.), N.S. Wales 97/E2
Namonuito (atoll), Micronesia 87/E5
Namorik (atoll), Marshall Is. 87/G5
Nampa, Alberta 182/B1
Nampa, Idaho 146/G5
Nampa, Idaho (83651) 220/B6
Nampa, Idaho 188/C2
Nampala, Mali 106/C5
Namp'o, N. Korea 81/B4
Nampo-Shoto (isls.), Japan 81/M3
Nampula (prov.), Mozambique 118/F2
Nampula, Mozambique 118/F3
Nampula, Mozambique 102/F6
Namsen (riv.), Norway 18/H4
Namsos, Norway 7/F2
Namsos, Norway 18/G4
Nam Tram, Mui (cape), Vietnam 72/F4
Namtu, Burma 72/C2
Namu, Br. Col. 184/D4
Namuac, Philippines 82/C1
Namuli, Serra (mt.), Mozambique 118/F3
Namuno, Mozambique 118/F2
Namur (lake), Alberta 182/D1
Namur (prov.), Belgium 27/F8
Namur, Belgium 27/F8
Namur, Québec 172/C4
Namutoni, Namibia 118/B3
Namwala, Zambia 115/E7
Namwŏn, S. Korea 81/C6
Namysłów, Poland 47/C3
Namzha Parwa (mt.), China 77/E6
Nan, Thailand 72/D3
Nan, Mae Nam (riv.), Thailand 72/D3
Nanacamilpa, Mexico 150/M1
Nana Candundo, Angola 115/D6
Nanafalia, Ala. (36764) 195/B6
Nanaimo, Br. Col. 146/F5
Nanaimo, Br. Col. 162/D6
Nanaimo, Br. Col. 184/J3
Nanakuli, Hawaii (96792) 218/D2
Nanao, Japan 81/H5
Nanay (riv.), Peru 128/E4
Nancagua, Chile 138/F6
Nance (co.), Nebr. 264/F3
Nanchang, China 77/J6
Nanchang, China 54/N7
Nancheng, China 77/J6
Nanchong (Nanchung), China 77/G5
Nanchong, China 54/M6
nan Clar, Loch (lake), Scotland 15/D2
Nancowry (isl.), India 68/G7
Nancy, France 28/G3
Nancy, France 7/E4
Nancy, Ky. (42544) 237/M6
Nanda Devi (mt.), India 68/D2
Nandaime, Nicaragua 154/E5
Nander, India 68/D5
Nandi (Nadi), Fiji 87/H7
Nando, Uruguay 145/F3
Nandurbar, India 68/C4
Nandyal, India 68/D5
Nanga-Eboko, Cameroon 115/B3
Nanga Parbat (mt.), Pakistan 68/D1
Nangapinoh, Indonesia 85/E6
Nangatayap, Indonesia 85/E6
Nangnim-sanmaek (range), N. Korea 81/C3
Nangong, China 77/H4
Nangqên, China 77/E5
Nang Rong, Thailand 72/D4
Nangwarry, S. Australia 94/G7
Nang Xian, China 77/D6
Nanika (dam), Br. Col. 184/D3
Nanika (lake), Br. Col. 184/D3
Nanisivik, N.W. Terrs. /K2
Nanjemoy, Md. (20662) 245/K7
Nanjing (Nanking), China 77/J5
Nanjing, China 2/Q4
Nanjing, China 54/N6
Nanking (Nanjing), China 77/J5
Nankoku, Japan 81/F7
Nan Ling (mts.), China 77/H6
Nannine, W. Australia 92/B4
Nanning, China 77/G7
Nanning, China 54/M7
Nannup, W. Australia 92/B6
Nanoose Bay, Br. Col. 184/J3
Nanortalik, Greenl. 4/D12
Nanpan Jiang (riv.), China 77/F7
Nanping, China 77/J6
Nansei Shoto (Ryukyu) (isls.), Japan 81/M6
Nansen (sound), N.W. Terrs. 187/J1
Nanson, N. Dak. (58354) 282/L2
Nantahala, N.C. (†28702) 281/B4
Nantahala (lake), N.C. 281/B4
Nantai (mt.), Japan 81/J5
Nantasket Beach, Mass. (†02045) 249/E7
Nanterre, France 28/A1
Nantes, France 28/C4
Nantes, France 7/D4
Nantes, Québec 172/F4
Nanticoke (riv.), Del. 245/R6
Nanticoke, Md. (21840) 245/P7
Nanticoke (riv.), Md. 245/P7
Nanticoke, Ontario 177/E5
Nanticoke, Pa. (18634) 294/E7
Nanton, Alberta 182/D4
Nantong, China 77/K5
Nantua, France 28/F4
Nantucket (co.), Mass. 249/O7
Nantucket, Mass. (02554) 249/O7
Nantucket◯, Mass. (02554) 249/O7
Nantucket (isl.), Mass. 188/N2
Nantucket (isl.), Mass. 249/O8
Nantucket (sound), Mass. 249/N6
Nanty Glo, Pa. (15943) 294/E5
Nantyglo and Blaina, Wales 13/B6
Nanuet, N.Y. (10954) 276/K8
Nanuktok (isls.), Newf. 166/C2
Nanuku (passage), Fiji 86/R10
Nanumea (atoll), Tuvalu 87/H6
Nanuque, Brazil 132/F7
Nanuque, Brazil 120/E4
Nanxiong, China 77/H6
Nanyang, China 77/H5
Nanyuki, Kenya 115/G3
Nanzhang, China 77/H5
Nanzhao, China 77/H5
Nao (cape), Spain 33/G3
Naococane (lake), Québec 174/C2
Naolinco de Victoria, Mexico 150/P1
Naomi, Ky. (†42544) 237/M6
Náousa, Greece 45/F5
Napa, Calif. 188/B3
Napa (co.), Calif. 204/C5
Napa, Calif. (94558) 204/C5
Napadogan, New Bruns. 170/D2
Napa Junction, Calif. (†94590) 204/J1
Napakiak, Alaska (99634) 196/F2
Napaktok (bay), Newf. 166/B2
Napanee, Ontario 177/G3
Napanoch, N.Y. (12458) 276/M7
Napaskiak, Alaska (99559) 196/F2
Napata (ruins), Sudan 111/F4
Napavine, Wash. (98565) 310/C4
Napè, Laos 72/E3
Naper, Nebr. (68755) 264/E2
Naperville, Ill. (60540) 222/A6
Napf (mt.), Switzerland 39/E3
Napier, Ky. (†40851) 237/P7
Napier, N. Zealand 100/F3
Napier, N. Zealand 87/H9
Napier (mt.), North Terr. 93/A4
Napier, W. Va. (26631) 312/E5
Napier Field, Ala. (36303) 195/H8
Napierville (co.), Québec 172/D4
Napierville, Québec 172/D4
Napili-Honokowai, Hawaii (†96761) 218/H1
Napinka, Manitoba 179/B5
Naplate, Ill. (†61350) 222/E2
Naples, Fla. (*33940) 212/E5
Naples, Idaho (83847) 220/B1
Naples, Ill. (62669) 222/C4
Naples (prov.), Italy 34/E4
Naples, Italy 7/F4
Naples, Italy 34/E4
Naples◯, Maine (04055) 243/B8
Naples, N.Y. (14512) 276/F5
Naples, S. Dak. (†57271) 298/O4
Naples, Texas (75568) 303/K4
Naples Park, Fla. (†33940) 212/E5
Napo (riv.) 120/B3
Napo, China 77/G7
Napo (prov.), Ecuador 128/D3
Napo (riv.), Ecuador 128/D3
Napo (riv.), Peru 128/F4
Napoleon, Ind. (47034) 227/G6
Napoleon, Mich. (49261) 250/E6
Napoleon, Mo. (64074) 261/E4
Napoleon, N. Dak. (58561) 282/L6
Napoleon, Ohio (43545) 284/B3
Naponee, Nebr. (68960) 264/E4
Nappa Merri, Queensland 95/B5
Nappan, Nova Scotia 168/D3
Nappanee, Ind. (46550) 227/F2
Napperby, North. Terr. 93/C7
Napton, Mo. (65346) 261/F4
Naqa (ruins), Sudan 111/F4
Nara (pref.), Japan 81/J8
Nara, Japan 81/J8
Nara, Mali 106/C5
Naracoopa, Tasmania 99/B1
Naracoorte, S. Australia 88/F7
Naracoorte, S. Australia 94/G7
Naradhan, N.S. Wales 97/D3
Naramata, Br. Col. 184/H5
Naranja, Fla. (33032) 212/F6
Naranjal (riv.), Ecuador 128/C4
Naranjito, Honduras 154/C3
Naranjito, P. Rico 161/D1
Naranjos, Mexico 150/L6
Naraq, Iran 66/G3
Narashino, Japan 81/P2
Narathiwat, Thailand 72/D6
Nara Visa, N. Mex. (88430) 274/F3
Narayanganj, Bangladesh 68/G4
Narayanpet, India 68/D5
Narberth, Pa. (19072) 294/M6
Narberth, Wales 13/C6
Narbonne, France 28/E6
Narcissa, Okla. (†74354) 288/S1
Narcisse, Manitoba 179/E4
Narcondam (isl.), India 68/G6
Narcoossee, Fla. (†32769) 212/E3
Nardin, Okla. (74646) 288/M1
Nardò, Italy 34/F4
Naré, Argentina 143/F5
Nare, Colombia 126/C4
Narellan, N.S. Wales 97/F3
Nares (str.) 146/L2
Nares (str.), N.W.T. 162/N3
Nares (str.), N.W. Terrs. 187/L2
Narew (riv.), Poland 47/E2
Naricual, Venezuela 124/F2
Narinda, Madagascar 118/H3
Nariño (dept.), Colombia 126/B7
Nariva (swamp), Trin. & Tob. 161/B10
Narka, Kansas (66960) 232/E2
Narmada (riv.), India 54/J7
Narmada (riv.), India 68/D4
Narman, Turkey 63/J2
Narnaul, India 68/D3
Narni, Italy 34/D3
Naro, Italy 34/D6
Narodnaya (mt.), U.S.S.R. 7/K2
Narodnaya (mt.), U.S.S.R. 48/G3
Narodnaya (mt.), U.S.S.R. 52/J1
Narok, Kenya 115/G4
Narooma, N.S. Wales 97/F5
Narrabeen, N.S. Wales 88/L3
Narrabeen, N.S. Wales 97/K3
Narrabri, N. S. Wales 88/J6
Narrabri, N.S. Wales 97/E2
Narragansett, R.I. (02882) 249/J7
Narragansett◯, R.I. (02882) 249/J7
Narragansett (bay), R.I. 249/J6
Narran (lake), N.S. Wales 97/D1
Narran (riv.), N.S. Wales 97/D1
Narrandera, N. S. Wales 88/H6
Narrandera, N.S. Wales 97/D4
Narre Warren North, Victoria 97/K5
Narrogin, W. Australia 88/B6
Narrogin, W. Australia 92/B2
Narromine, N. S. Wales 88/H6
Narromine, N.S. Wales 97/E3
Narrows, Ky. (42358) 237/H5
Narrows, Oreg. (†97721) 291/H4
Narrows, The (str.), St. Chris.-Nevis 161/D11
Narrows, The (str.), Virgin Is. (Br.) 161/C4
Narrows, The (str.), Virgin Is. (U.S.) 161/C4
Narrows, Va. (24124) 307/G6
Narrowsburg, N.Y. (12764) 276/L7
Narrows Park-La Vale, Md. (†21502) 245/C2
Narsimhapur, India 68/D4
Narsinghgarh, India 68/D4
Narssaq, Greenl. 4/C12
Naruna, Va. (24576) 307/L6
Narva, U.S.S.R. 52/C3
Narva, U.S.S.R. 53/E1
Narva (res.), U.S.S.R. 53/D1
Narvik, Norway 4/C9
Narvik, Norway 7/F2
Narvik, Norway 18/K2
Nary, Minn. (†56601) 255/D3
Nar'yan-Mar, U.S.S.R. 4/C7
Nar'yan-Mar, U.S.S.R. 7/K2
Nar'yan-Mar, U.S.S.R. 48/F3
Nar'yan-Mar, U.S.S.R. 52/H1
Naryn, U.S.S.R. 48/H5
Nasarawa, Nigeria 106/F7
Năsăud, Romania 45/G2
Naseby, N. Zealand 100/C6
Naseby, Sask. 181/C3
Naselle, Wash. (98638) 310/B4
Naselle (riv.), Wash. 310/B4
Nash (stream), N.H. 268/E2
Nash (co.), N.C. 281/O2
Nash, N. Dak. (58264) 282/P3
Nash, Okla. (73761) 288/K1
Nash, Texas (75569) 303/K4
Nashawena (isl.), Mass. 249/L7
Nash Creek, New Bruns. 170/D1
Nashoba, Okla. (74558) 288/R6
Nashotah, Wis. (53058) 317/J1
Nashport, Ohio (43830) 284/F5
Nashua, Iowa (50658) 229/J3
Nashua (riv.), Mass. 249/H3
Nashua, Minn. (56565) 255/B4
Nashua, Mont. (59248) 262/K2
Nashua, N.H. 188/M2
Nashua, N.H. (03060) 268/D6
Nashville, Ark. (71852) 202/C6
Nashville, Georgia (31639) 217/F8
Nashville, Ill. (62263) 222/D5
Nashville, Ind. (47448) 227/E6
Nashville, Kansas (67112) 232/D4
Nashville, Mich. (49073) 250/D6
Nashville, Mo. (†64855) 261/D8
Nashville, N.C. (27856) 281/O3
Nashville, Ohio (44661) 284/F4
Nashville, Oreg. (†97370) 291/D3
Nashville (cap.), Tenn. 146/K6
Nashville (cap.), Tenn. 188/J3
Nashville (cap.), Tenn. (*37201) 237/H8
Nashwaak (riv.), New Bruns. 170/D2
Nashwaak Bridge, New Bruns. 170/D2
Nashwaak Village, New Bruns. 170/D2
Nashwauk, Minn. (55769) 255/E3
Našice, Yugoslavia 45/C3
Nasielsk, Poland 47/E2
Näsijärvi (lake), Finland 18/O6
Nasik, India 68/C5
Nasik, India 54/J8
Nasir, Sudan 111/F6
Nasirabad, Bangladesh 68/G4
Nasirabad, India 68/C3
Naskaupi (riv.), Newf. 166/B3
Naso (pt.), Philippines 82/C5
Nason, Ill. (†62816) 222/D5
Nasonville, R.I. (†02830) 249/H5
Nasratabad (Zabol), Iran 59/H3
Nasratabad (Zabol), Iran 66/M5
Nass (riv.), Br. Col. 184/C2
Nassau (cap.), Bahamas 146/L7
Nassau (cap.), Bahamas 156/C1
Nassau (bay), Chile 120/C8
Nassau (bay), Chile 138/F11
Nassau (isl.), Cook Is. 87/K7
Nassau, Del. (19969) 245/T6
Nassau (co.), Fla. 212/E1
Nassau (riv.), Fla. 212/E1
Nassau (sound), Fla. 212/E1
Nassau, Minn. (56272) 255/B5
Nassau (co.), N.Y. 276/N9
Nassau, N.Y. (12123) 276/N5
Nassau Bay, Texas (†77598) 303/K2
Nassawadox, Va. (23413) 307/S6
Nassawango (creek), Md. 245/S8
Nasser (lake), Egypt 102/F2
Nasser (lake), Egypt 111/F3
Nasser (lake), Egypt 59/F3
Nassereith, Austria 41/A3
Nässjö, Sweden 18/J8
Nassogne, Belgium 27/G8
Nasty (creek), S. Dak. 298/C2
Nasu (mt.), Japan 81/J5
Nata, Botswana 118/D4
Natá, Panama 154/G6
Natagaima, Colombia 126/C6
Natal, Brazil 2/H6
Natal, Brazil 132/H4
Natal, Brazil 120/F3
Natal, Br. Col. 184/K5
Natal (prov.), S. Africa 102/F7
Natal (prov.), S. Africa 118/E5
Natalbany, La. (70451) 238/N1
Natalia, Texas (78059) 303/J11
Natalicio Talavera, Paraguay 144/D4
Natanz, Iran 59/F3
Natanz, Iran 66/H4
Natashquan (riv.) 162/K5
Natashquan (riv.), Newf. 166/B3
Natashquan, Québec 174/E3
Natashquan (riv.), Québec 174/E2
Natashquan-Est (riv.), Newf. 166/B3
Natchaug (riv.), Conn. 210/G1
Natchez, Ala. (†36425) 195/D7
Natchez, La. (71456) 238/D3
Natchez, Miss. 188/H4
Natchez, Miss. (39120) 256/B7
Natchitoches (par.), La. 238/D3
Natchitoches, La. (71457) 238/D3
Naters, Switzerland 39/E4
Natewa (bay), Fiji 86/Q10
Nathalia, Victoria 97/C5
Nathalie, Va. (24577) 307/L7
Nathan, Mich. (†49821) 250/B3
Nathrop, Colo. (81236) 208/H5
Natick◯, Mass. (01760) 249/A7
Natick, R.I. (†02887) 249/H6
Natimuk, Victoria 97/A5
Nation (riv.), Br. Col. 184/F2
National Agricultural Research Center, Md. 245/G3
National Capital Region (Manila) (prov.), Philippines 82/C3
National City, Calif. (92050) 204/J11
National City, Mich. (48748) 250/F4
National Gardens, Fla. (†32074) 212/E2
National Mills, Manitoba 179/A2
National Mine, Mich. (49865) 250/B2
National Park, N.J. (08063) 273/B3
National Park, Switzerland 39/K3
National Reactor Testing Sta. (U.S.A.E.C), Idaho 220/F6
National Stock Yards, Ill. (62071) 222/A2
Natitingou, Benin 106/E6
Natividade, Brazil 132/E5
Natmauk, Burma 72/B2
Natoma, Kansas (67651) 232/D2
Natron (lake), Kenya 115/G4
Natron (lake), Tanzania 115/G4
Natrona (co.), Wyo. 319/F3
Natrona, Wyo. (82646) 319/F2
Natrona Heights, Pa. (15065) 294/C4
Nattavaara, Sweden 18/M3
Natuna (isls.), Indonesia 54/M9
Natuna (isls.), Indonesia 85/D5
Natural Bridge, Ala. (35577) 195/C2
Natural Bridge, N.Y. (13665) 276/K2
Natural Bridge, Va. (24578) 307/J5
Natural Bridge Nat'l Mon., Utah 304/E6
Natural Bridge Station, Va. (24579) 307/K5
Natural Dam, N.Y. (†13642) 276/J2
Naturaliste (cape), Tasmania 99/E2
Naturaliste (cape), W. Australia 88/A6
Naturaliste (chan.), W. Australia 88/A5
Naturaliste (cape), W. Australia 92/A6

N'Gounié 417

New Britain, Pa. (18901) 294/M5
New Brockton, Ala. (36351) 195/G8
Newbrook, Alberta 182/D2
New Brunswick (prov.) 162/K6
New Brunswick (prov.), Canada 146/M5
NEW BRUNSWICK 170
New Brunswick, N.J. (*08901) 273/E3
New Buena Vista, Pa. (†15550) 294/E5
New Buffalo, Mich. (49117) 250/C7
New Buffalo, Pa. (17069) 294/H5
Newburg, Ark. (72556) 202/G1
Newburg, Iowa (†50135) 229/H5
Newburg, Md. (20664) 245/L7
Newburg, Mo. (65550) 261/J7
Newburg, N. Dak. (58762) 282/J2
Newburg, Pa. (17240) 294/G5
Newburg (La Jose), Pa. (†15753) 294/E4
Newburg, W. Va. (26410) 312/G4
Newburg, Wis. (53060) 317/K9
Newburgh, Ind. (47630) 227/C9
Newburgh○, Maine (†04445) 243/F6
Newburgh, N.Y. 188/M2
Newburgh, N.Y. (12550) 276/M7
Newburgh, Ontario 177/H3
Newburgh, Scotland 10/E2
Newburgh, Grampian, Scotland 15/G3
Newburgh, Fife, Scotland 15/E4
Newburgh Heights, Ohio (†44101) 284/H9
New Burlington, Ind. (†47302) 227/G4
New Burlington, Ohio (†45201) 284/B9
New Burnside, Ill. (62967) 222/E6
Newbury, England 13/F6
Newbury, England 10/F5
Newbury○, Mass. (01950) 249/L1
Newbury○, N.H. (03255) 268/C5
Newbury, Ohio (44065) 284/H3
Newbury, Ontario 177/C5
Newbury, Vt. (05051) 268/C3
Newbury○, Vt. (05051) 268/C3
Newburyport, Mass. (01950) 249/L1
New Bussa, Nigeria 106/E6
New Caledonia (isl.) 2/T7
NEW CALEDONIA 86
New Caledonia 87/G8
New Caledonia (isl.), New Caled. 87/G8
New Caledonia (isl.), New Caled. 86/G4
New Cambria, Kansas (67470) 232/E3
New Cambria, Mo. (63558) 261/G3
New Canaan○, Conn. (06840) 210/B4
New Canton, Ill. (62356) 222/B4
New Canton, Va. (23123) 307/M5
New Carlisle, Ind. (46552) 227/E1
New Carlisle, Ohio (45344) 284/C6
New Carlisle, Québec 172/D2
New Carlisle, Québec 174/E3
New Carrollton, Md. (20784) 245/G4
New Castile (reg.), Spain 33/E3
Newcastle, Australia 2/S7
Newcastle, Calif. (95658) 204/C8
New Castle, Colo. (81647) 208/E3
New Castle (co.), Del. 245/R2
New Castle, Del. (19720) 245/R2
New Castle, Ind. (47362) 227/G5
Newcastle, Ireland 10/B4
Newcastle, Ireland 17/D7
New Castle, Ky. (40050) 237/L4
Newcastle○, Maine (04553) 243/D7
Newcastle, N. Br. 162/K6
Newcastle, N. S. Wales 88/J6
Newcastle, Nebr. (68757) 264/H2
Newcastle, New Bruns. 170/E2
New Castle○, N.H. (03854) 268/F5
Newcastle, N.S. Wales 97/F3
Newcastle, N. Ireland 10/D3
Newcastle, N. Ireland 17/J3
Newcastle (creek), North. Terr. 93/C4
New Castle, Ohio (†43843) 284/F5
Newcastle, Okla. (73065) 288/L4
Newcastle, Ontario 177/F4
New Castle, Pa. 188/K2
New Castle, Pa. (*16101) 294/B3
Newcastle, St. Chris.-Nevis 161/D11
Newcastle, S. Africa 118/E5
Newcastle, Texas (76372) 303/F4
Newcastle, Utah (84756) 304/A6
New Castle, Va. (24127) 307/H5
Newcastle, Wyo. (82701) 319/H2
Newcastle Creek, New Bruns. 170/D2
Newcastle-Damariscotta, Maine (04553) 243/E7
Newcastle Emlyn, Wales 13/C5
Newcastleton, Scotland 15/F5
Newcastle-under-Lyme, England 13/E4
Newcastle-under-Lyme, England 10/E4
Newcastle upon Tyne, England 7/D3
Newcastle upon Tyne, England 10/E3
Newcastle upon Tyne, England 13/H3
Newcastle Waters, North. Terr. 93/C4
New Centerville, Pa. (†15557) 294/D6
New Chelsea, Newf. 166/D2
New Chicago, Ind. (†46342) 227/C1
New Church, Va. (23415) 307/S5
New Cinema, Br. Col. 184/F3
New City, N.Y. (10956) 276/K8
New Columbia, Pa. (17856) 294/H3
New Columbus, Pa. (†17878) 294/K3
Newcomb, N. Mex. (†87325) 274/A2
Newcomb, N.Y. (12852) 276/M3
Newcomb, Tenn. (37819) 237/N7
Newcomerstown, Ohio (43832) 284/G5
New Concord, Ky. (42076) 237/E7
New Concord, Ohio (43762) 284/G6
New Cordell (Cordell), Okla. (†73632) 288/H4
New Corydon, Ind. (†47326) 227/H3
New Court, Mo. (†63452) 261/J2
New Creek, W. Va. (26743) 312/J4
New Cumberland, Pa. (17070) 294/J5
New Cumberland, W. Va. (26047) 312/E2
New Cumnock, Scotland 15/D5
Newdale, Idaho (83436) 220/G6
Newdale, Manitoba 179/B4
New Dayton, Alberta 182/D5
New Deal, Texas (79350) 303/C4
New Deer, Scotland 15/F3
Newdegate, W. Australia 92/B6
New Delhi (cap.), India 2/N4
New Delhi, India 54/J7
New Delhi (cap.), India 68/D3
New Denmark, New Bruns. 170/C1
New Denver, Br. Col. 184/J5
New Diggings, Wis. (†61075) 317/F10
New Douglas, Ill. (62074) 222/D5
New Dover, Ohio (†43040) 284/D5
New Durham○, N.H. (03855) 268/E5
New Eagle, Pa. (15067) 294/B5
New Edinburg, Ark. (71660) 202/F6
New Effington, S. Dak. (57255) 298/R2
New Egypt, N.J. (08533) 273/E3
Newell, Ala. (36270) 195/H4
Newell (lake), Alberta 182/E4
Newell, Iowa (50568) 229/D3
Newell, S. Dak. (57760) 298/C4
Newell, W. Va. (26050) 312/E1
New Ellenton, S.C. (29809) 296/D5
Newellton, La. (71357) 238/H2
Newellton, Nova Scotia 168/C5
New England (range), N.S. Wales 97/F1
New England, N. Dak. (58647) 282/E6
New England, W. Va. (26154) 312/C4
Newenham (cape), Alaska 196/F3
New Enterprise, Pa. (16664) 294/F5
New Era, La. (†71354) 238/G4
New Era, Mich. (49446) 250/C5
New Era, Oreg. (†97013) 291/B2
New Yam, Israel 65/B2
New Zohar, Israel 65/C5
New Fairfield○, Conn. (06810) 210/B3
Newfane, N.Y. (14108) 276/C4
Newfane, Vt. (05345) 268/B6
Newfane○, Vt. (05345) 268/B6
Newfield, Maine (04056) 243/B8
Newfield○, Maine (04056) 243/B8
Newfield, N.J. (08344) 273/D4
Newfield, N.Y. (14867) 276/G6
Newfields○, N.H. (03856) 268/F5
New Fish Creek, Alberta 182/B2
New Florence, Mo. (63363) 261/K5
New Florence, Pa. (15944) 294/D5
Newfolden, Minn. (56738) 255/B2
New Fork (lakes), Wyo. 319/C2
Newfound (lake), N.H. 268/D4
Newfoundland (prov.) 162/L5
Newfoundland (isl.) 162/L6
Newfoundland (prov.), Canada 146/M4
Newfoundland (isl.), Canada 2/G3
Newfoundland, Ky. (41162) 237/P4
NEWFOUNDLAND 166
Newfoundland (isl.), Newf. 166/C4
Newfoundland (isl.), Newf. 146/N5
Newfoundland, N.J. (07435) 273/D1
Newfoundland, Pa. (18445) 294/M3
Newfoundland (mts.), Utah 304/A2
New Franken, Wis. (54229) 317/L6
New Frankfort, Mo. (†65349) 261/F4
New Franklin, Mo. (65274) 261/G4
New Freedom, Pa. (17349) 294/J6
New Freeport, Pa. (15352) 294/B6
New Galilee, Pa. (16141) 294/A4
New Galloway, Scotland 10/D3
New Galloway, Scotland 15/D5
Newgate, Br. Col. 184/K5
New Georgia (isl.), Solomon Is. 87/F6
New Georgia (isl.), Solomon Is. 86/D3
New Germantown, Pa. (17071) 294/G5
New Germany, Minn. (55367) 255/E6
New Germany, Nova Scotia 168/D4
New Glarus, Wis. (53574) 317/G10
New Glasgow, Nova Scotia 168/F3
New Glasgow, Québec 172/D4
New Gloucester, Maine (04260) 243/C8
New Gloucester○, Maine (04260) 243/C8
New Goshen, Ind. (47863) 227/B5
New Gretna, N.J. (08224) 273/E4
New Guinea (isl.) 2/S6
New Guinea (isl.) 54/P10
New Guinea (isl.) 87/E6
New Guinea (isl.), Papua N.G. 86/B2
Newgulf, Texas (77462) 303/J8
Newhalem, Wash. (†98283) 310/D2
Newhalen, Alaska (†99606) 196/H3
Newhall, Calif. (91321) 204/G9
Newhall, Iowa (52315) 229/K5
Newhall, W. Va. (24866) 312/C8
Newham, England 13/H8
Newham, England 10/B5
New Hamburg, Mo. (†63736) 261/O8
New Hamburg, Ontario 177/D4
New Hampshire 188/M2
NEW HAMPSHIRE 268
New Hampshire, Ohio (45870) 284/C4
New Hampshire (state), U.S. 146/L5
New Hampton, Iowa (50659) 229/J2
New Hampton, Mo. (64471) 261/D2
New Hampton○, N.H. (03256) 268/D4
New Hampton, N.J. (†08827) 273/D2
New Hanover (co.), N.C. 281/O6
New Hanover (Lavongai) (isl.), Papua N.G. 87/F6
New Hanover (isl.), Papua N.G. 86/B1
New Harbor, Maine (04554) 243/E8
New Harbour, Newf. 166/C4
New Harbour, Newf. 166/D2
New Harbour, Nova Scotia 168/G3
New Harmony, Ind. (47631) 227/B8
New Harmony, Utah (84757) 304/A6
New Hartford, Conn. (06057) 210/C1
New Hartford○, Conn. (06057) 210/C1
New Hartford, Iowa (50660) 229/H3
New Hartford, Mo. (63364) 261/K4
New Hartford, N.Y. (13413) 276/K4
New Haven, Conn. 188/M2
New Haven (co.), Conn. 210/D3
New Haven, Conn. (*06501) 210/D3
New Haven (harb.), Conn. 210/D3
Newhaven, England 10/F5
Newhaven, England 13/H7
New Haven, Ill. (62867) 222/E6
New Haven, Ind. (46774) 227/H2
New Haven, Ky. (40051) 237/K5
New Haven, Mich. (48048) 250/G6
New Haven, Mo. (63068) 261/K5
New Haven, N.Y. (13121) 276/H4
New Haven, Nova Scotia 168/H2
New Haven, Ohio (44850) 284/E3
New Haven○, Vt. (05472) 268/A3
New Haven, W. Va. (25265) 312/C5
New Haven, Wyo. (†82720) 319/H1
New Hazelton, Br. Col. 184/D2
New Hebrides (Vanuatu) 87/G7
Newhebron, Miss. (39140) 256/D7
New Hill, N.C. (27562) 281/M3
New Holland, Georgia (†30501) 217/E2
New Holland, Ill. (62671) 222/D3
New Holland, N.C. (27885) 281/S4
New Holland, Ohio (43145) 284/D6
New Holland, Pa. (17557) 294/K5
New Holland, S. Dak. (57364) 298/M7
New Holstein, Wis. (53061) 317/K8
New Home, Texas (79383) 303/C4
New Hope, Ala. (35760) 195/F1
Newhope, Ark. (71959) 202/C5
New Hope, Ky. (40052) 237/L5
New Hope, Minn. (†55428) 255/G5
New Hope, Ohio (†45320) 284/A6
New Hope, Pa. (18938) 294/N5
New Hope, Tenn. (†37380) 237/K11
New Hope, Va. (24469) 307/L4
New Horse Springs, N. Mex. (†87821) 274/A5
New Houlka (Houlka), Miss. (38850) 256/G2
New Hradec, N. Dak. (58648) 282/E5
New Hyde Park, N.Y. (11040) 276/P7
New Iberia, La. (70560) 238/G6
Newington○, Conn. (06111) 210/E2
Newington, Georgia (30446) 217/J5
Newington○, N.H. (†03801) 268/F5
Newington, Ontario 177/K2
Newington, Va. (22122) 307/S3
New Ipswich○, N.H. (03071) 268/D6
New Ireland (isl.), Papua N.G. 87/F6
New Ireland (isl.), Papua N.G. 86/B1
New Jersey 188/M3
NEW JERSEY 273
New Jersey, New Bruns. 170/E1
New Jersey (state), U.S. 146/L5
New Johnsonville, Tenn. (37134) 237/E8
New Kensington, Pa. (15068) 294/C4
New Kent (co.), Va. 307/P5
New Kent, Va. (23124) 307/P5
Newkirk, N. Mex. (88431) 274/E3
Newkirk, Okla. (74647) 288/N1
New Knoxville, Ohio (45871) 284/B5
New Laguna, N. Mex. (87038) 274/B4
New Lancaster, Kansas (†66040) 232/H3
Newland, Ind. (†47978) 227/C2
Newland, N.C. (28657) 281/F2
New Lebanon, Ind. (47864) 227/C6
New Lebanon, N.Y. (12125) 276/O6
New Lebanon, Ohio (45345) 284/B6
New Lebanon, Pa. (†16145) 294/B3
New Leipzig, N. Dak. (58562) 282/G7
New Lenox, Ill. (60451) 222/B6
New Lexington, Ohio (43764) 284/F6
New Liberty, Iowa (52765) 229/M5
New Liberty, Ky. (40355) 237/M3
New Lima, Okla. (74884) 288/O4
New Limerick○, Maine (04761) 243/G3
Newlin, Texas (†79245) 303/D3
New Lisbon, Ind. (47366) 227/G5
New Lisbon, N.J. (08064) 273/D4
New Lisbon, Wis. (53950) 317/F8
New Liskeard, Ont. 162/H6
New Liskeard, Ontario 177/K5
New Liskeard, Ontario 175/E3
Newllano, La. (71461) 238/D4
New London, Ark. (†71765) 202/F7
New London, Conn. 188/M2
New London (co.), Conn. 210/G2
New London, Conn. (06320) 210/G3
New London, Ind. (†46979) 227/E4
New London, Iowa (52645) 229/L7
New London, Minn. (56273) 255/C5
New London, Mo. (63459) 261/K3
New London, N.H. (03257) 268/D5
New London○, N.H. (03257) 268/D5
New London, N.C. (28127) 281/J4
New London, Ohio (44851) 284/F3
New London (bay), Pr. Edward I. 168/E2
New London, Texas (75682) 303/K5
New London, Wis. (54961) 317/J7
New Lothrop, Mich. (48460) 250/F5
New Lowell, Ontario 177/E3
New Lyme, Ohio (44066) 284/J2
New Lynn, N. Zealand 100/B1
New Madison, Ohio (45346) 284/A6
New Madrid (co.), Mo. 261/N9
New Madrid, Mo. (63869) 261/O9
Newmains, Scotland 15/C2
Newman, Calif. (95360) 204/D6
Newman, Ill. (61942) 222/E4
Newman, Ky. (†42301) 237/G5
Newman (sound), Newf. 166/D2
Newman, W. Australia 88/C4
Newman (lake), Wash. 310/H3
Newman, W. Australia 92/B3
New Manchester, W. Va. (26056) 312/E1
Newman Grove, Nebr. (68758) 264/G3
Newman Lake, Wash. (99025) 310/J3
Newmans Cove, Newf. 166/D2
New Marion, Ind. (†47023) 227/G6
New Market, Ala. (35761) 195/F1
Newmarket, England 13/H5
Newmarket, England 10/G4
New Market, Ind. (47965) 227/D5
New Market, Iowa (51646) 229/D7
Newmarket, Ireland 10/B4
Newmarket, Ireland 17/C7
Newmarket, Jamaica 158/H6
New Market, Md. (21774) 245/J3
New Market, Minn. (55054) 255/E6
New Market, Mo. (†64439) 261/C4
New Market, New Bruns. 170/D3
Newmarket, N.H. (03857) 268/F5
Newmarket○, N.H. (03857) 268/F5
New Market, Ohio (†45133) 284/C7
Newmarket, Ontario 177/E3
Newmarket, Queensland 88/K2
Newmarket, Queensland 95/D2
Newmarket, Scotland 15/B2
New Market, Tenn. (37820) 237/O8
New Market, Va. (22844) 307/L3
Newmarket-on-Fergus, Ireland 17/D6
New Marlborough○, Mass. (†01230) 249/B4
New Martinsburg, Ohio (†43160) 284/D7
New Martinsville, W. Va. (26155) 312/E3
New Maryland, New Bruns. 170/D3
New Matamoras, Ohio (45767) 284/J6
New Meadows, Idaho (83654) 220/B4
New Melle, Mo. (63365) 261/L5
New Memphis, Ill. (62266) 222/D5
Newmerella, Victoria 97/E5
New Mexico 188/E4
NEW MEXICO 274
New Mexico (state), U.S. 146/H6
New Miami, Ohio (45011) 284/A7
New Middleton, Tenn. (†38563) 237/J8
New Middletown, Ind. (47160) 227/E8
New Middletown, Ohio (44442) 284/J4
New Milford, Conn. (06776) 210/B2
New Milford○, Conn. (06776) 210/B2
New Milford, N.J. (07646) 273/B1
New Milford, Ohio (†44272) 284/H3
New Milford, Pa. (18834) 294/L2
Newmill, Scotland 15/E3
New Mills, England 13/J2
New Mills, England 10/G2
Newmilns and Greenholm, Scotland 15/D5
New Milton, W. Va. (26411) 312/E4
New Minas, Nova Scotia 168/D3
New Minden, Ill. (†62263) 222/D5
New Mount Pleasant, Ind. (†47371) 227/G4
New Munich, Minn. (56356) 255/D5
Newnan, Georgia (30263) 217/C4
Newnans (lake), Fla. 212/D2
New Norcia, W. Australia 92/A5
New Norfolk, Tasmania 88/H8
New Norfolk, Tasmania 99/C4
New Norway, Alberta 182/D3
New Offenburg, Mo. (63661) 261/M7
New Orleans, La. 188/H5
New Orleans, La. 146/K7
New Orleans, La. (*70101) 238/O4
New Orleans, U.S. 2/E4
New Osgoode, Sask. 181/H3
New Oxford, Pa. (17350) 294/H6
New Palestine, Ind. (46163) 227/F5
New Pallas, Ireland 17/E6
New Paltz, N.Y. (12561) 276/M7
New Paris, Ind. (46553) 227/F2
New Paris, Ohio (45347) 284/A6
New Paris, Pa. (15554) 294/E5
New Pass (range), Nev. 266/D3
New Pekin, Ind. (†47165) 227/F7
New Perlican, Newf. 166/D2
New Petersburg, Ohio (†45123) 284/D7
New Philadelphia, Ill. (†61459) 222/C3
New Philadelphia, Ind. (†47167) 227/F7
New Philadelphia, Ohio (44663) 284/G5
New Philadelphia, Pa. (17959) 294/K4
New Pine Creek, Oreg. (97635) 291/G5
New Pitsligo, Scotland 15/F3
New Pittsburg, Ohio (†44691) 284/F4
New Plymouth, Idaho (83655) 220/B6
New Plymouth, N. Zealand 100/D3
New Plymouth, Ohio (45654) 284/F7
New Point, Ind. (47263) 227/G6
New Point, Mo. (64473) 261/B2
Newport, Ark. (72112) 202/H2
Newport, Del. (19804) 245/R2
Newport, England 13/F7
Newport, England 13/E5
Newport, England 10/F5
Newport, Ind. (47966) 227/C5
Newport, Mayo, Ireland 17/C4
Newport, Tipperary, Ireland 17/E6
Newport, Ky. (*41071) 237/S2
Newport, Ky. 188/K3
Newport, Maine (04953) 243/E6
Newport○, Maine (04953) 243/E6
Newport, Md. (†20622) 245/L7
Newport, Minn. (55055) 255/F6
Newport, Miss. (†38641) 256/D1
Newport, Nebr. (68759) 264/E2
New Port, Neth. Ant. 161/G9
Newport, N.H. (03773) 268/C5
Newport○, N.H. (03773) 268/C5
Newport, N.J. (08345) 273/C5
Newport, N.Y. (13416) 276/K4
Newport, N.C. (28570) 281/R5
Newport, Nova Scotia 168/E3
Newport, Ohio (†43140) 284/C6
Newport, Ohio (45768) 284/H7
Newport, Oreg. (97365) 291/C3
Newport, Pa. (17074) 294/H5
Newport, Québec 172/D2
Newport, R.I. 188/M2
Newport (co.), R.I. 249/K6
Newport, R.I. (02840) 249/J7
Newport, Tenn. (37821) 237/P9
Newport, Texas (76254) 303/F4
Newport, Vt. (05855) 268/C2
Newport○, Vt. (05855) 268/C2
Newport, Va. (24128) 307/H6
Newport, Wales 10/E5
Newport, Dyfed, Wales 13/C5
Newport, Gwent, Wales 13/B6
Newport, Wash. (99156) 310/H2
Newport Beach, Calif. (*92660) 204/D11
Newport Center, Vt. (05857) 268/C2
New Portland, Maine (04954) 243/C6
New Portland○, Maine (04954) 243/C6
Newport News, Va. 188/L3
Newport News (I.C.), Va. (*23601) 307/P6
Newport-on-Tay, Scotland 15/F4
Newport Pagnell, England 13/G5
New Port Richey, Fla. (*33552) 212/D3
New Prague, Minn. (56071) 255/E6
New Preston, Conn. (06777) 210/B2
New Providence (isl.), Bahamas 156/C1
New Providence (Borden), Ind. (†47106) 227/F8
New Providence, Iowa (50206) 229/G4
New Providence, N.J. (07974) 273/E2
New Providence, Pa. (17560) 294/K6
New Prue (Prue), Okla. (†74060) 288/O2
Newquay, England 10/D5
Newquay, England 13/B7
New Quay, Wales 10/D4
New Quay, Wales 13/C5
New Raymer, Colo. (80742) 208/M1
New Richland, Minn. (56072) 255/E7
New Richmond, Ind. (47967) 227/D4
New Richmond, Ohio (45157) 284/B8
New Richmond, Québec 172/C2
New Richmond, Wis. (54017) 317/A5
New Riegel, Ohio (44853) 284/D3
New River, N.C. (28540) 281/O5
New River (inlet), N.C. 281/P6
New River, Tenn. (†37755) 237/M8
New River, Va. (24129) 307/G6
New River Beach, New Bruns. 170/D3
New Road, Nova Scotia 168/E4
New Roads, La. (70760) 238/G5
New Rochelle, N.Y. (*10801) 276/P7
New Rockford, N. Dak. (58356) 282/N4
New Romney, England 13/J7
New Ross, Ind. (47968) 227/D5
New Ross, Ireland 10/C4
New Ross, Ireland 17/H7
New Ross, Nova Scotia 168/D4
Newry, Maine (04261) 243/B6
Newry○, Maine (04261) 243/B6
Newry, N. Ireland 17/J3
Newry, N. Ireland 10/C3
Newry, North. Terr. 93/A3
Newry, Pa. (16665) 294/F5
Newry, S.C. (29665) 296/B2
New Salem, Ill. (62357) 222/C4
New Salem, Ind. (†46173) 227/G5
New Salem, Kansas (†67156) 232/F4
New Salem○, Mass. (01355) 249/E2
New Salem, N. Dak. (58563) 282/G6
New Salem, Nova Scotia 168/D3
New Salem, Ohio (†43148) 284/E6
New Salem, Pa. (15468) 294/C6
New Salem (Delmont), Pa. (†15626) 294/D5
New Salisbury, Ind. (47161) 227/E8
New Sarepta, Alberta 182/D3
New Sarpy, La. (70078) 238/N4
New Schwabenland (reg.) 5/B1
New Scone, Scotland 15/E4
New Sharon, Iowa (50207) 229/H6
New Sharon○, Maine (04955) 243/C6
New Sharon, N.J. (†08691) 273/D3
New Shoreham (Block Island)○, R.I. (†02807) 249/H8
New Siberian (isls.), U.S.S.R. 54/R2
New Siberian (isls.), U.S.S.R. 4/B2
New Siberian (isls.), U.S.S.R. 2/S2
New Siberian (isls.), U.S.S.R. 48/P2
New Site, Ala. (†35010) 195/G4
New Site, Miss. (38859) 256/H1
New Smyrna Beach, Fla. (32069) 212/F2
Newsoms, Va. (23874) 307/O7
New South Wales, /H6
New South Wales (state), Australia 87/E9
NEW SOUTH WALES 97
New Spadra, Ark. (†72830) 202/C3
New Square, N.Y. (†10901) 276/K8
New Stanton, Pa. (15672) 294/C5
New Straitsville, Ohio (43766) 284/F6
New Strawn (Strawn), Kansas (66839) 232/G3
New Stuyahok, Alaska (99636) 196/G3
New Sweden, Maine (04762) 243/G2
New Sweden○, Maine (04762) 243/G2
New Tazewell, Tenn. (37825) 237/O8
Newtok, Alaska (99681) 196/F2
Newton, Ala. (36352) 195/G8
Newton (co.), Ark. 202/D2
Newton (co.), Georgia 217/E3
Newton, Georgia (31770) 217/D8
Newton, Ill. (62448) 222/E5
Newton (co.), Ind. 227/C3
Newton, Iowa 188/H2
Newton, Iowa (50208) 229/H5
Newton, Kansas (67114) 232/E3
Newton, Mass. (†02158) 249/C7
Newton (co.), Miss. 256/F6
Newton, Miss. (39345) 256/F6
Newton (co.), Mo. 261/D9
Newton○, N.H. (03858) 268/E6
Newton, N.J. (07860) 273/D1
Newton, N.C. (28658) 281/G3
Newton, Québec 172/C4
Newton, Scotland 15/E5
Newton (co.), Texas 303/L7
Newton, Texas (75966) 303/L7
Newton, Utah (84327) 304/C2
Newton, W. Va. (25266) 312/D5
Newton Abbot, England 13/D7
Newton Abbot, England 10/E5
Newton Center, Mass. (02159) 249/C7
Newton Falls, N.Y. (13666) 276/K2
Newton Falls, Ohio (44444) 284/J3
Newtongrange, Scotland 15/D2
Newton Grove, N.C. (28366) 281/N4
Newton Hamilton, Pa. (17075) 294/G5
Newton Highlands, Mass. (02161) 249/C7
Newtonia, Mo. (64853) 261/D9
Newton Junction, N.H. (03859) 268/E6
Newton-le-Willows, England 13/H2
Newton Lower Falls, Mass. (†02162) 249/B7
Newton Mearns, Scotland 15/B2
Newton Mills, Nova Scotia 168/F3
Newtonmore, Scotland 15/D3
Newton Siding, Manitoba 179/D5
Newton Stewart, Scotland 10/D3
Newton Stewart, Scotland 15/D6
Newtonsville, Ohio (45158) 284/B7
Newton Upper Falls, Mass. (†02164) 249/C7
Newtonville, Ind. (47632) 227/D8
Newtonville, Mass. (02160) 249/C7
Newtonville, N.J. (08346) 273/D4
Newtown, Conn. (06470) 210/B3
Newtown○, Conn. (06470) 210/B3
Newtown, Ind. (47969) 227/C4
Newtown, Ky. (†40324) 237/N4
Newtown, Mo. (64667) 261/F2
Newtown, New Bruns. 170/E3
Newtown, Newf. 166/D4
Newtown, N.S. Wales 97/C6
New Town, N. Dak. (58763) 282/F4
Newtown, Ohio (45244) 284/C10
Newtown, Pa. (18940) 294/N5
New Town, S.C. (†29536) 296/J3
Newtown, Victoria 97/C6
Newtown, Wales 13/D5
Newtown, Wales 10/E4
Newtownabbey (dist.), N. Ireland 17/J2
Newtownabbey, N. Ireland 17/K2
Newtownards, N. Ireland 17/K2
Newtownbutler, N. Ireland 17/G3
Newtown Forbes, Ireland 17/F4
Newtownhamilton, N. Ireland 17/H3
Newtownmountkennedy, Ireland 17/J5
Newtown Saint Boswells, Scotland 15/F5
Newtownsandes, Ireland 17/C6
Newtown Square○, Pa. (19073) 294/L6
Newtownstewart, N. Ireland 17/G2
New Trenton, Ind. (47035) 227/H6
New Trier, Minn. (†55031) 255/F6
New Tripoli, Pa. (18066) 294/L4
New Troy, Mich. (49119) 250/C7
New Tulsa, Okla. (†74080) 288/P2
Newtyle, Scotland 15/E4
New Ulm, Minn. (56073) 255/D6
New Ulm, Texas (78950) 303/H8
New Underwood, S. Dak. (57761) 298/D5
New Vernon, N.J. (07976) 273/D2
New Victoria, Nova Scotia 168/H2
New Vienna, Iowa (52065) 229/L3
New Vienna, Ohio (45159) 284/C7
Newville, Ala. (36353) 195/H8
Newville, Ind. (†46721) 227/H2
Newville, Pa. (17241) 294/H5
Newville, W. Va. (26632) 312/E5
New Vineyard○, Maine (04956) 243/C6
New Virginia, Iowa (50210) 229/F6
New Washington, Ind. (47162) 227/F7
New Washington, Ohio (44854) 284/E4
New Washington, Philippines 82/D5
New Waterford, Nova Scotia 168/J2
New Waterford, Ohio (44445) 284/J4
New Waverly, Ind. (46961) 227/E3
New Waverly, Texas (77358) 303/J7
New Westminster, Br. Col. 162/D6
New Westminster, Br. Col. 184/K3
New Weston, Ohio (45348) 284/A5
New Whiteland, Ind. (46184) 227/E5
New Wilmington, Pa. (16142) 294/B3
New Winchester, Ind. (†46122) 227/D5
New Winchester, Ohio (†44820) 284/D4
New Windsor, England 13/G8
New Windsor, England 10/F5
New Windsor, Ill. (61465) 222/C2
New Windsor, Md. (21776) 245/K2
New Windsor, N.Y. (12550) 276/N8
New Witten, S. Dak. (†57584) 298/K7
New Woodstock, N.Y. (13122) 276/J5
New World (isl.), Newf. 166/C4
New York 188/L2
NEW YORK 276
New York, N.Y. 146/L5
New York, N.Y. 188/M2
New York (co.), N.Y. 276/M9
New York, N.Y. (*10001) 276/M9
New York (state), U.S. 146/L5
New York, U.S. 2/F3
New York Mills, Minn. (56567) 255/C4
New York Mills, N.Y. (13417) 276/K4
New York State Barge (canal), N.Y. 276/C4
New Zealand 2/T8
New Zealand 87/G9
NEW ZEALAND 100
New Zion, New Bruns. 170/D2
New Zion, S.C. (29111) 296/H4
Ney, Ohio (43549) 284/B3
Neyagawa, Japan 81/J7
Neyland, Wales 13/B6
Neyriz, Iran 66/J6
Neyshabur, Iran 59/G2
Neyshabur, Iran 66/L2
Nezhin, U.S.S.R. 52/D4
Nez Perce (co.), Idaho 220/B3
Nezperce, Idaho (83543) 220/B3
Nez Perce Nat'l Hist. Park, Idaho 220/B-C3
Nezwar (mt.), Iran 66/H3
Ngabang, Indonesia 85/D5
N'gage, Angola 115/C5
Ngage, Angola 102/D5
Ngahere, N. Zealand 100/C5
Ngami (lake), Botswana 118/C4
Ngamiland (reg.), Botswana 118/C3
Ngamring, China 77/C6
Ngangla Ringco (lake), China 77/B5
Ngangzê Co (lake), China 77/C5
Ngao, Thailand 72/D3
Ngaoundéré, Cameroon 115/B2
Ngaoundéré, Cameroon 102/D4
Ngapara, N. Zealand 100/C6
Ngara, Tanzania 115/F4
Ngaruawahia, N. Zealand 100/E2
Ngatapa, N. Zealand 100/F3
Ngatik (atoll), Micronesia 87/F5
Ngau (isl.), Fiji 86/Q10
Ngauruhoe (mt.), N. Zealand 100/E3
Ngawi, Indonesia 85/K2
Nghia Lo, Vietnam 72/D2
Ngiva, Angola 102/D6
Ngiva, Angola 115/C7
Ngoc Linh (mt.), Vietnam 72/E4
Ngom Qu (riv.), China 77/E5
Ngong, Kenya 115/G4
Ngoring Hu (lake), China 77/E4
Ngorongoro (crater), Tanzania 115/F4
N'Gounié (riv.), Congo 115/B4

Northwood 419

North (riv.), Mass. 249/D2
North (riv.), Mass. 249/L4
North (chan.), Mich. 250/F2
North (pt.), Mich. 250/F3
North (lake), Minn. 255/F1
North (sea), Netherlands 27/E3
North (lake), New Bruns. 170/C3
North (riv.), Newf. 166/C3
North (riv.), Newf. 166/B2
North (isl.), N. Zealand 87/H9
North (cape), N. Zealand 87/H9
North (cape), N. Zealand 100/D1
North (isl.), N. Zealand 100/F1
North (lake), N. Dak. 282/J3
North (chan.), N. Ireland 10/D3
North (chan.), N. Ireland 17/K1
North (Nordkapp) (cape), Norway 7/G1
North (cape), Norway 4/B8
North (cape), N.S. 162/K6
North (cape), Nova Scotia 168/H1
North (mt.), Nova Scotia 168/D3
North (chan.), Ontario 177/A1
North (chan.), Ontario 175/D3
North (mt.), Pa. 294/K3
North (pt.), Pr. Edward I. 168/E1
North (chan.), Scotland 10/D3
North (chan.), Scotland 15/C5
North (sound), Scotland 15/G4
North (sound), Scotland 15/F1
North (isl.), Seychelles 118/H5
North, S.C. (29112) 296/E4
North (inlet), S.C. 296/J5
North (isl.), S.C. 296/J5
North (pt.), Tasmania 99/E1
North (creek), Utah 304/C6
North (lake), Utah 304/B2
North (riv.), Wash. 310/B4
North (sea), W. Germany 22/B2
North (riv.), W. Va. 312/J4
North (lake), Wis. 317/J1
North Abington, Mass. (02351) 249/L4
North Acton, Mass. (†01720) 249/J2
North Adams, Mass. (01247) 249/B2
North Adams, Mich. (49262) 250/E7
Northallerton, England 10/F3
Northallerton, England 13/F3
Northam, England 13/C6
Northam, W. Australia 88/B6
Northam, W. Australia 92/B1
NORTH AMERICA 146
North America 2/C4
North Amherst, Mass. (01059) 249/E3
North Amity, Maine (04465) 243/H4
Northampton, England 13/F5
Northampton, England 10/F4
Northampton, Mass. (01060) 249/D3
Northampton (co.), N.C. 281/P2
Northampton (co.), Pa. 294/M4
Northampton, Pa. (18067) 294/M4
Northampton (co.), Va. 307/S6
Northampton, W. Australia 88/A5
Northampton, W. Australia 92/A5
Northamptonshire (co.), England 13/G5
North Andaman (isl.), India 68/G6
North Andover○, Mass. (01845) 249/K2
North Anna (riv.), Va. 307/M4
North Anson, Maine (04958) 243/D6
North Apollo, Pa. (15673) 294/D4
North Arlington, N.J. (07032) 273/B2
North Arm (inlet), N.W. Terrs. 187/G3
North Asheboro, N.C. (†27203) 281/K3
North Ashford, Conn. (†06282) 210/G1
North Aspy (riv.), Nova Scotia 168/H2
North Atlantic Ocean 2/H3
North Attleboro○, Mass. (*02760) 249/J5
North Augusta, Ontario 177/J3
North Augusta, S.C. (29841) 296/C5
North Aulatsivik (isl.), Newf. 166/B2
North Aurora, Ill. (60542) 222/E2
North Avondale, Colo. (†81022) 208/L6
North Ballachulish, Scotland 15/C4
North Baltimore, Ohio (45872) 284/C3
North Bangor, N.Y. (12966) 276/M1
North Barrington, Ill. (†60010) 222/A5
North Bass (isl.), Ohio 284/E2
North Battleford, Sask. 146/H4
North Battleford, Sask. 162/F5
North Battleford, Sask. 181/C3
North Bay, N.Y. (13123) 276/J4
North Bay, Ont. 146/L5
North Bay, Ont. 162/J6
North Bay, Ontario 177/E1
North Bay, Ontario 175/E3
North Bay, Wis. (†53401) 317/M3
North Bay Ingonish (bay), Nova Scotia 168/H2
North Bay Village, Fla. (33141) 212/B4
North Beach, Md. (20831) 245/N6
North Belgrade, Maine (†04963) 243/D7
North Bellingham, Mass. (†02019) 249/J4
North Bend, Br. Col. 184/G5
North Bend, Nebr. (68649) 264/H3
North Bend, Ohio (45052) 284/B9
North Bend, Oreg. (97459) 291/C4
North Bend, Pa. (17760) 294/G3
North Bend, Wash. (98045) 310/D3
North Bend, Wis. (†54642) 317/D7
North Bennington, Vt. (05257) 268/A6
North Bergen○, N.J. (07047) 273/B2
North Berwick, Maine (03906) 243/B9
North Berwick○, Maine (03906) 243/B9
North Berwick, Scotland 15/F4
North Berwick, Scotland 10/E2
North Beveland (isl.), Netherlands 27/D5
North Billerica, Mass. (01862) 249/J2
North Bloomfield, Conn. (†06002) 210/E1
North Bloomfield, Ohio (44450) 284/J3
North Bonneville, Wash. (98639) 310/C5
North Borneo (Sabah) (state), Malaysia 85/F3
Northboro, Iowa (51647) 229/C7
Northborough, Mass. (01532) 249/H3
Northborough○, Mass. (01532) 249/H3
North Boston, N.Y. (14110) 276/C5
North Bourke, N.S. Wales 97/C2
North Brabant (prov.), Netherlands 27/F5
North Braddock, Pa. (15104) 294/C7
North Bradford, Maine (†04410) 243/F5
North Bradley, Mich. (†48618) 250/E5
Northbranch, Kansas (†66936) 232/D2
North Branch, Md. (†21502) 245/D2
North Branch, Mich. (48461) 250/F5
North Branch, Minn. (55056) 255/F5
North Branch, N.H. (†03440) 268/D5
North Branch, N.J. (08876) 273/D2
North Branch Oromocto (riv.), New Bruns. 170/D3
North Branford○, Conn. (06471) 210/E3
North Brentwood, Md. (†20722) 245/F4
Northbridge○, Mass. (01534) 249/H4
North Bridgton, Maine (04057) 243/B7
Northbrook, Ill. (60062) 222/B5
North Brook, Ontario 177/G3
North Brookfield, Mass. (01535) 249/F3
North Brookfield○, Mass. (01535) 249/F3
North Brooksville, Maine (†04617) 243/F7
North Brunswick○, N.J. (08902) 273/D3
North Bruny (isl.), Tasmania 99/D5
North Buena Vista, Iowa (52066) 229/L3
North Calais, Vt. (†05648) 268/C3
North Caldwell, N.J. (†07006) 273/B2
North Calling Lake, Alberta 182/D2
North Canadian (riv.) 188/G3
North Canadian (riv.), Okla. 288/K3
North Canton, Conn. (06059) 210/D1
North Canton, Georgia (†30114) 217/C2
North Canton, Ohio (44720) 284/H4
North Cape (Nordkapp) (pt.), Norway 18/P1
North Cape May, N.J. (08204) 273/C6
North Caribou (lake), Ontario 175/B2
North Carolina 188/L3
NORTH CAROLINA 281
North Carolina (state), U.S. 146/K6
North Carrizo (creek), Colo. 208/N8
North Carrizo (riv.), Okla. 288/A1
North Carrollton, Miss. (38947) 256/E3
North Carter (mt.), N.H. 268/E3
North Carver, Mass. (02355) 249/L5
North Cascades Nat'l Park, Wash. 310/D2
North Catasauqua, Pa. (†18032) 294/L4
North Charleston, S.C. (29406) 296/G6
North Charlestown, N.H. (†03603) 268/C5
North Chatham, Mass. (02650) 249/O6
North Chatham, N.H. (†04058) 268/E3
North Chelmsford, Mass. (01863) 249/J2
North Chesterville, Maine (†04938) 243/C6
North Chicago, Ill. (60064) 222/B4
North Chichester, N.H. (†03263) 268/E5
North Chili, N.Y. (14514) 276/E4
North City (Coello), Ill. (†62825) 222/E5
North Clarendon, Vt. (05759) 268/B4
Northcliffe, W. Australia 92/B6
North Cohasset, Mass. (†02025) 249/F7
North Colebrook, Conn. (†06021) 210/C1
North College Hill, Ohio (45239) 284/B9
North Collins, N.Y. (14111) 276/C5
North Concho (riv.), Texas 303/C6
North Concord, Vt. (05858) 268/D3
North Conway, N.H. (03860) 268/E3
North Cooking Lake, Alberta 182/D3
North Cotabato (prov.), Philippines 82/E7
Northcote, Minn. (†56728) 255/A2
Northcote, N. Zealand 100/B1
Northcote, Victoria 88/L7
Northcote, Victoria 97/J5
North Cove, N.C. (†28752) 281/F3
North Cove, Wash. (†98590) 310/A4
North Cowichan, Br. Col. 184/J3
North Creek, N.Y. (12853) 276/M3
North Crossett, Ark. (71635) 202/G7
North Cutler, Maine (†04626) 243/J6
North Dakota 188/F1
NORTH DAKOTA 282
North Dakota (state), U.S. 146/H5
North Dandalup, W. Australia 88/B3
North Danger (reef), Philippines 85/E3
North Danville, Vt. (†05819) 268/C3
North Dartmouth, Mass. (02747) 249/K6
North Dexter, Maine (†04930) 243/E5
North Dighton, Mass. (02764) 249/K5
North Dixmont, Maine (†04932) 243/E6
North Down (dist.), N. Ireland 17/K2
North Downs (hills), England 13/G6
North Eagle Butte, S. Dak. (†57625) 298/G3
Northeast (cape), Alaska 196/E2
North East (pt.), Jamaica 158/K6
Northeast (pass), La. 238/M8
North East, Md. (21901) 245/P2
North East, Pa. (16428) 294/C1
North East Breakers, Bermuda 156/H2
North East Cape Fear (riv.), N.C. 281/O4
North East Carry, Maine (†04441) 243/D4
North-Eastern (prov.), Kenya 115/G3
Northeast Foreland (pen.), Greenl. 4/A10
North Eastham, Mass. (02651) 249/O5
Northeast Harbor, Maine (04662) 243/G7
Northeast Land (isl.), Norway 4/B8
North East Margaree (riv.), Nova Scotia 168/H2
North Easton, Mass. (02356) 249/K4
North East Polder, Netherlands 27/H3
North East Providence (chan.), Bahamas 156/C1
North Edisto (riv.), S.C. 296/G6
North Edwards, Calif. (93523) 204/H8
North Egremont, Mass. (01252) 249/A4
Northeim, W. Germany 22/C3
North English, Iowa (52316) 229/J5
North Enid, Okla. (†73701) 288/L2
Northern (dist.), Israel 65/C2
Northern (head), New Bruns. 170/D4
Northern (prov.), Sudan 111/E3
Northern Cheyenne Ind. Res., Mont. 262/K5
Northern Dvina (riv.), U.S.S.R. 52/F2
Northern Dvina (riv.), U.S.S.R. 48/E3
Northern Indian (lake), Manitoba 179/J2
NORTHERN IRELAND 17
NORTHERN IRELAND 10/C3
Nottoway (riv.), Va. 307/O7
Notukeu (creek), Sask. 181/D6
Notus, Idaho (83656) 220/B6
Nouadhibou, Mauritania 106/A4
Nouadhibou, Mauritania 102/A2
Nouakchott (cap.), Mauritania 106/A5
Nouakchott (cap.), Mauritania 102/A3
Nouakchott (cap.), Mauritania 2/J5
Nouméa (cap.), New Caled. 87/G8
Nouméa (cap.), New Caledonia 2/T7
Nouméa (cap.), New Caled. 86/H5
Nounan, Idaho (†83254) 220/G7
Noup (head), Scotland 15/E1
Noupoort, S. Africa 118/C6
Nouveau-Comptoir, Québec 174/B2
Northern Ireland, U.K. 7/D3
Northern Marianas 87/E4
Northern Marianas, U.S. 2/S5
Northern Peninsula Aboriginal Reserve, Queensland 88/G2
Northern Peninsula Aboriginal Res., Queensland 95/B1
Northern Samar (prov.), Philippines 82/E4
Northern Sporades (isls.), Greece 45/F6
Northern Territory, 88/E3
NORTHERN TERRITORY 93
Northern Territory (terr.), Australia 87/D7
North Esk (riv.), Scotland 15/F4
North Esk (riv.), Tasmania 99/D3
North Fairfield, Ohio (44855) 284/E3
North Falmouth, Mass. (02556) 249/M6
North Ferrisburg, Vt. (05473) 268/A3
Northfield, Conn. (06778) 210/C2
Northfield, Ill. (60093) 222/B5
Northfield, Ky. (†40201) 237/K1
Northfield○, Maine (†04654) 243/H6
Northfield, Mass. (01360) 249/E2
Northfield○, Mass. (01360) 249/E2
Northfield, Minn. (55057) 255/E6
Northfield○, N.H. (†03276) 268/D5
Northfield, N.J. (08225) 273/D5
Northfield, Ohio (44067) 284/J10
Northfield, Texas (79246) 303/D3
Northfield, Vt. (05663) 268/B3
Northfield○, Vt. (05663) 268/B3
Northfield, Wis. (†54635) 317/D7
Northfield Falls, Vt. (05664) 268/B3
Northfield Farms, Mass. (†01360) 249/E2
Northfield-Tilton, N.H. (†03276) 268/D5
Northfleet, England 10/C5
Northfleet, England 13/J8
North Fond du Lac, Wis. (†54935) 317/J8
Northford, Conn. (06472) 210/D3
North Foreland (prom.), England 10/G5
North Foreland (prom.), England 13/J6
North Fork, Calif. (93643) 204/F6
North Fork, Frenchman (creek), Colo. 208/O1
North Fork, Gunnison (riv.), Colo. 208/D5
North Fork, Smoky Hill (riv.), Colo. 208/P4
North Fork, Idaho (83466) 220/D4
North Fork (riv.), Idaho 220/B7
North Fork, Flathead (riv.), Mont. 262/B2
North Fork, Little Humboldt (riv.), Nev. 266/D1
North Fork, Grand (riv.), N. Dak. 282/E8
Northfork, W. Va. (24868) 312/D8
North Fork, Powder (riv.), Wyo. 319/F2
North Fork, Shoshone (riv.), Wyo. 319/C1
North Fork, Wind (riv.), Wyo. 319/C2
North Fort Myers, Fla. (33903) 212/E5
North Foster, R.I. (†02857) 249/H5
North Fourchu, Nova Scotia 168/H3
North Fox (isl.), Mich. 250/D3
North Franklin, Conn. (06254) 210/G2
North Freedom, Wis. (53951) 317/G9
North Friars (bay), St. Chris.-Nevis 161/D10
North Friesland (reg.), W. Germany 22/C1
North Frisian (isls.), Denmark 21/B7
North Frisian (isls.), W. Germany 22/B1
North Fryeburg, Maine (04058) 243/B7
North Galiano, Br. Col. 184/K3
North Garden, Va. (22959) 307/L5
Northgate, N. Dak. (58767) 282/F2
Northgate, Sask. 181/J6
Northglenn, Colo. (80233) 208/K3
North Gorham, Maine (†04075) 243/B8
North Gosforth, England 13/J3
North Gower, Ontario 177/J2
North Grafton, Mass. (01536) 249/H4
North Granby, Conn. (06060) 210/D1
North Grant, Nova Scotia 168/G3
North Grosvenor Dale, Conn. (06255) 210/H1
North Groton, N.H. (†03266) 268/D4
North Grove, Ind. (†46911) 227/F3
North Guilford, Conn. (†06437) 210/E3
North Hadley, Mass. (†01035) 249/D3
North Haledon, N.J. (07508) 273/B1
North Hampton○, N.H. (03862) 268/F6
North Hampton, Ohio (45349) 284/C5
North Hanover, Mass. (†02339) 249/L4
North Hansel (mts.), Utah 304/B2
North Harbour, Newf. 166/D2
North Harlowe, N.C. (†28532) 281/R5
North Hartland, Vt. (05052) 268/C4
North Hartsville, S.C. (†29550) 296/G3
North Harwich, Mass. (02645) 249/O6
North Hatfield, Mass. (01066) 249/D3
North Hatley, Québec 172/F4
North Haven○, Conn. (06473) 210/D3
North Haven, Maine (04853) 243/F7
North Haven○, Maine (04853) 243/F7
North Haverhill, N.H. (03774) 268/D3
North Havre, Mont. (†59501) 262/G2
North Hayden, Ind. (†46356) 227/B2
North Head, New Bruns. 170/D4
North Henderson, Ill. (61466) 222/C2
North Hero, Vt. (05474) 268/A2
North Highlands, Calif. (95660) 204/B8
North High Shoals, Georgia (†30645) 217/F3
North Hills, W. Va. (†26101) 312/D4
North Hodge, La. (†71247) 238/E2
North Holland (prov.), Netherlands 27/F3
North Holland (canal), Netherlands 27/C4
North Hollywood, Calif. (*91601) 204/B10
North Hornell, N.Y. (†14843) 276/E6
North Horr, Kenya 115/G3
North Hudson, N.Y. (12855) 276/N3
North Hudson, Wis. (†54016) 317/A5
North Hyde Park, Vt. (05665) 268/B2
North Hykeham, England 13/G4
North Industry, Ohio (44707) 284/H4
North Inishkea (isl.), Ireland 17/A3
North Java, N.Y. (14113) 276/D5
North Jay, Maine (04262) 243/C6
North Johns, Ala. (35086) 195/D4
North Judson, Ind. (46366) 227/D2
North Kansas City, Mo. (64116) 261/P5
North Kedgwick (riv.), New Bruns. 170/C1
North Kent, Conn. (†06757) 210/B1
North Kent (isl.), N.W. Terrs. 187/J2
North Kingstown○, R.I. (02852) 249/J6
North Kingsville, Ohio (44068) 284/J2
North Knife (lake), Manitoba 179/J2
North Knife Lake, Manitoba 179/J2
North Korea 54/O5
North La Junta, Colo. (†81050) 208/N7
Northlake, Ill. (60164) 222/B5
Northlake, Texas (75238) 303/F1
North Lake, Wis. (53064) 317/J1
North Lakhimpur, India 68/G3
Northland, Mich. (49869) 250/B2
Northland, Wis. (†54945) 317/H6
North Landgrove, Vt. (†05148) 268/B5
North Laramie (riv.), Wyo. 319/G3
North Las Vegas, Nev. (89030) 266/F6
North Lauderdale, Fla. (†33063) 212/B3
North Lawrence, N.Y. (12967) 276/L1
North Lawrence, Ohio (44666) 284/G4
North Leeds, Maine (04263) 243/C7
North Lewisburg, Ohio (43060) 284/C5
North Liberty, Ind. (46554) 227/E1
North Liberty, Iowa (52317) 229/K5
North Lima, Ohio (44452) 284/J4
North Limington, Maine (†04049) 243/B8
North Little Rock, Ark. (*72114) 202/F4
North Livermore, Maine (†04254) 243/C7
North Loup, Nebr. (68859) 264/F3
North Loup (riv.), Nebr. 264/E3
North Lovell, Maine (†04231) 243/B7
North Lubec, Maine (†04652) 243/J6
North Luconia (shoals), Philippines 85/E4
North Madison, Conn. (†06443) 210/E3
North Madison, Ohio (†44057) 284/H2
North Magnetic Pole (dist.) 162/F1
North Magnetic Pole, Canada 4/B15
North Magnetic Pole, N.W. Terrs. 187/H2
North Manchester, Ind. (46962) 227/F3
North Manitou, Mich. (†49654) 250/C3
North Manitou (isl.), Mich. 250/C3
North Mankato, Minn. (56001) 255/D6
North Marshfield, Mass. (02059) 249/M4
North Merritt (isl.), Fla. 212/F3
North Miami, Fla. (33161) 212/B4
North Miami, Okla. (74358) 288/R1
North Miami Beach, Fla. (33161) 212/C4
North Middleboro, Mass. (02346) 249/L5
North Middletown, Ky. (40357) 237/N4
North Minch (sound), Scotland 10/D1
North Minch (sound), Scotland 15/B3
North Montpelier, Vt. (05666) 268/C3
Northmoor, Mo. (†64152) 261/P5
North Motton, Tasmania 99/C3
North Mountain, W. Va. (†25427) 312/K3
North Muskegon, Mich. (49445) 250/C5
North Myrtle Beach, S.C. (29582) 296/K4
North Naples, Fla. (33940) 212/E5
North Natuna (isl.), Indonesia 85/D4
North Negril (pt.), Jamaica 158/G6
North Newport, N.H. (†03773) 268/C5
North New Portland, Maine (04961) 243/C6
North New River (canal), Fla. 212/F5
North Newry, Maine (†04261) 243/B6
North Newton, Kansas (67117) 232/E3
North Oaks, Minn. (†55101) 255/G5
North Ogden, Utah (†84404) 304/C2
North Olmsted, Ohio (44070) 284/G9
Northome, Minn. (56661) 255/D3
North Ossetian A.S.S.R., U.S.S.R. 48/E5
North Ossetian A.S.S.R., U.S.S.R. 52/F6
North Oxford, Mass. (01537) 249/G4
North Pacific (ocean) 87/F4
North Pacific Ocean 2/B5
North Pacific Ocean 2/T4
North Pagai (isl.), Indonesia 85/C6
North Palm Beach, Fla. (33403) 212/F5
North Park, Ill. (†61111) 222/D1
North Parsonfield, Maine (†04047) 243/A8
North Pease (riv.), Texas 303/D3
North Pekin, Ill. (†61554) 222/D3
North Pembroke, Mass. (02358) 249/M4
North Pender Island, Br. Col. 184/K3
North Penobscot, Maine (†04476) 243/F7
North Perry, Maine (†04667) 243/J5
North Perry, Ohio (†44081) 284/H2
North Petherton, England 13/D6
North Pine, Br. Col. 184/G2
North Plain, Conn. (†06371) 210/F3
North Plainfield, N.J. (07060) 273/E2
North Plains, Oreg. (97133) 291/A2
North Platte (riv.) 188/F2
North Platte (riv.), Colo. 208/G1
North Platte, Nebr. 188/F2
North Platte, Nebr. (69101) 264/D3
North Platte (riv.), Nebr. 264/B3
North Platte (riv.), U.S. 146/H5
North Platte (riv.), Wyo. 319/H3
North Plymouth, Mass. (02360) 249/L5
North Pole 4/A1
North Pole 2/F1
North Pole, Alaska (99705) 196/J2
North Pole (brook), New Bruns. 170/D1
North Pomfret, Vt. (05053) 268/B4
Northport, Ala. (35476) 195/C4
North Port, Fla. (33595) 212/D4
Northport○, Maine (†04849) 243/E7
Northport, Mich. (49670) 250/D3
Northport, Nebr. (†69336) 264/B3
Northport, N.Y. (11768) 276/O9
Northport, Nova Scotia 168/E3
Northport, Wash. (99157) 310/H2
North Portal, Sask. 181/J6
North Potomac, Md. (†20857) 245/K4
North Powder, Oreg. (97867) 291/K2
North Pownal, Vt. (05260) 268/A6
North Prairie, Wis. (53153) 317/J2
North Providence○, R.I. (02908) 249/J5
North Pulaski, Va. (†24301) 307/G6
North Randall, Ohio (†44101) 284/H9
North Randolph, Vt. (†05061) 268/B4
North Raymond, Maine (†04274) 243/C8
North Reading○, Mass. (01864) 249/C5
North Redington Beach, Fla. (†33708) 212/B3
North Redwood, Minn. (56275) 255/D6
North Renous (riv.), New Bruns. 170/D2
North Rhine-Westphalia (state), W. Germany 22/B3
North Richland Hills, Texas (76118) 303/F2
Northridge, Ohio (45414) 284/B6
North Ridgeville, Ohio (44039) 284/F3
North Rim, Ariz. (86052) 198/C2
North River, Newf. 166/D2
North River, N.Y. (12856) 276/M3
North River, N. Dak. (†58102) 282/S6
North River, Nova Scotia 168/D4
North Riverside, Ill. (60546) 222/B5
North Robinson, Ohio (44856) 284/E4
North Ronaldsay (firth), Scotland 15/F1
North Ronaldsay (isl.), Scotland 15/F1
North Ronaldsay (isl.), Scotland 10/E1
Northrop, Minn. (56075) 255/D7
North Rose, N.Y. (14516) 276/G4
North Roxboro, N.C. (†27573) 281/L2
North Royalton, Ohio (44133) 284/H10
North Rustico, Pr. Edward I. 168/E2
North Saanich, Br. Col. 184/K3
North Saint Paul, Minn. (55109) 255/G5
North Salem, Ind. (46165) 227/D5
North Salem, N.H. (03073) 268/E6
North Salt Lake, Utah (†84010) 304/C3
North Sandwich, N.H. (03259) 268/E4
North San Juan, Calif. (95960) 204/E4
North Santiam (riv.), Oreg. 291/E3
North Saskatchewan (riv.) (dist.) 162/E5
North Saskatchewan (riv.), Alberta 182/E3
North Saskatchewan (riv.), Canada 146/G4
North Saskatchewan (riv.), Sask. 181/D3
North Scituate, Mass. (02060) 249/F8
North Scituate, R.I. (02857) 249/H5
North Sea (canal), Netherlands 27/F4
North Seal (riv.), Manitoba 179/H2
North Searsmont, Maine (†04973) 243/E7
North Sentinel (isl.), India 68/G6
North Sevogle (riv.), New Bruns. 170/D1
North Shapleigh, Maine (04060) 243/B8
North Shoal (lake), Manitoba 179/E4
North Shore, Wis. 317/M1
Northside, N.C. (27564) 281/M2
Northside, Sask. 181/F2
North Sioux City, S. Dak. (57049) 298/R8
North Skunk (riv.), Iowa 229/H5
North Somercotes, England 10/G4
North Somercotes, England 13/H4
North Somers, Conn. (†06071) 210/F1
North Spectacle (lake), Conn. 210/B2
North Spirit Lake, Ontario 175/B2
North Springfield, Pa. (16430) 294/A1
North Springfield, Vt. (05150) 268/B5
North Springfield, Va. (22151) 307/S3
North Star, Alberta 182/B1
North Star, Mich. (48862) 250/E5
North Star, Ohio (45350) 284/A5
North Stonington○, Conn. (06359) 210/H3
North Stratford, N.H. (03590) 268/D2
North Sunderland, England 13/F2
North Sutton, N.H. (03260) 268/D5
North Swansea, Mass. (†02777) 249/K5
North Sydney, N. S. Wales 88/L4
North Sydney, N.S. Wales 97/J3
North Sydney, Nova Scotia 168/H2
North Syracuse, N.Y. (13212) 276/H4
North Taranaki (bight), N. Zealand 100/D3
North Tarrytown, N.Y. (10591) 276/O6
North Terre Haute, Ind. (47805) 227/C5
North Thetford, Vt. (05054) 268/C4
North Thompson (riv.), Br. Col. 184/G4
North Tidworth, England 13/F6
North Tiverton, R.I. (†02722) 249/K6
North Tolsta, Scotland 15/B2
Northton, Scotland 15/B3
North Tonawanda, N.Y. (14120) 276/C4
North Trap (isl.), N. Zealand 100/B7
North Troy, Vt. (05859) 268/C2
North Truchas (peak), N. Mex. 274/D3
North Truro, Mass. (02652) 249/O4
North Tunbridge, Vt. (†05077) 268/C4
North Turner, Maine (04266) 243/C7
North Twin (mt.), N.H. 268/D3
North Tyne (riv.), England 13/E2
North Uist (isl.), Scotland 15/A3
North Uist (isl.), Scotland 10/C2
Northumberland (co.), England 13/E2
Northumberland (co.), New Bruns. 170/D2
Northumberland (str.), New Bruns. 170/F2
Northumberland○, N.H. (†03582) 268/D2
Northumberland (str.), Nova Scotia 168/E2
Northumberland (county), Ontario 177/G3
Northumberland (co.), Pa. 294/J4
Northumberland, Pa. (17857) 294/J4
Northumberland (str.), Pr. Edward I. 168/D2
Northumberland (isls.), Queensland 95/D4
Northumberland (cape), S. Australia 94/F8
Northumberland (co.), Va. 307/R5
Northumberland National Park, England 13/E2
North Umpqua (riv.), Oreg. 291/E4
North Ural (mts.), U.S.S.R. 52/K1
North Utica (Utica), Ill. (†61373) 222/E2
North Uxbridge, Mass. (01538) 249/H4
Northvale, N.J. (07647) 273/F1
North Vancouver, Br. Col. 162/D6
North Vancouver, Br. Col. 184/K3
North Vassalboro, Maine (04962) 243/D7
North Vernon, Ind. (47265) 227/F6
Northview, Mo. (†65706) 261/G8
Northville, Conn. (†06776) 210/B2
Northville, Mich. (48167) 250/F6
Northville, N.Y. (12134) 276/M4
Northville, S. Dak. (57465) 298/M3
North Wabasca (lake), Alberta 182/D1
North Wakefield, N.H. (†03872) 268/E4
North Waldoboro, Maine (†04572) 243/E7
North Wales, Pa. (19454) 294/M5
North Walpole, N.H. (†03608) 268/C5
North Walsham, England 13/J5
North Walsham, England 10/G4
North Waltham, Mass. (02154) 249/B6
North Warren, Pa. (†16365) 294/D2
North Washington, Iowa (50661) 229/J2
North Waterboro, Maine (04061) 243/B8
North Waterford, Maine (04267) 243/B7
Northway, Alaska (99764) 196/K2
North Wayne, Maine (†04284) 243/C7
North Weare, N.H. (†03281) 268/D5
North Webster, Ind. (46555) 227/F2
Northwest (pt.), Fla. 212/E6
North West (dist.), Guyana 131/A2
North West (pt.), Jamaica 158/G5
North West (cape), Australia 87/B8
North West (cape), W. Australia 88/A4
North West (cape), W. Australia 92/A3
North-West Aboriginal Reserve, S. Australia 88/E5
North-West Aboriginal Res., W. Australia 92/E4
North West Arm (inlet), Newf. 166/D2
North West Brook, Newf. 166/C2
North West Brook (riv.), Newf. 166/D2
North Westchester, Conn. (06474) 210/F2
Northwestern (sen. dist.), Alaska 196/E2
North-West Frontier (prov.), Pakistan 68/C2
North West Gander (riv.), Newf. 166/C4
North Westminster, Vt. (†05101) 268/B5
Northwest Miramichi (riv.), New Bruns. 170/D1
Northwest Oromocto (riv.), New Bruns. 170/D3
North Westport, Mass. (02790) 249/K6
North West Providence (chan.), Bahamas 156/B1
North West River, Newf. 166/B3
Northwest Territories 162/E2
Northwest Territories (prov.), Canada 146/G3
NORTHWEST TERRITORIES 187
Northwest Upsalquitch (riv.), New Bruns. 170/D1
North Weymouth, Mass. (02191) 249/D8
North Whitefield, Maine (04353) 243/D7
Northwich, England 13/H2
Northwich, England 10/G2
North Wilbraham, Mass. (†01095) 249/E4
North Wildwood, N.J. (08260) 273/D6
North Wilkesboro, N.C. (28659) 281/G2
North Williston, Vt. (†05495) 268/A3
North Wilton, Conn. (†06897) 210/B4
North Windham, Conn. (06256) 210/G1
North Windham, Maine (04062) 243/C8
North Wolcott, Vt. (†05680) 268/C2
Northwood, Iowa (50459) 229/G2
Northwood○, N.H. (03261) 268/E5
Northwood, N. Dak. (58267) 282/P4

O

Pátzcuaro 425

Panjab, Afghanistan 68/B2
Panjab, Afghanistan 59/J3
Panjang, Hon (Hon Tho Chau) (isl.), Vietnam 72/D5
Panjgur, Pakistan 68/A3
Panjgur, Pakistan 59/H4
Panjim, India 54/J8
Panjim (Panaji), India 68/C5
Pankow, E. Germany 22/F3
Pankshin, Nigeria 106/F7
P'anmunjŏm, N. Korea 81/C5
P'anmunjŏm, S. Korea 81/C5
Panmure (isl.), Pr. Edward I. 168/F2
Panna, India 68/E4
Pannawonica, W. Australia 92/B3
Pannonhalma, Hungary 41/D3
Panny (riv.), Alberta 182/C1
Panola, Ala. (35477) 195/B5
Panola, Ill. (†61738) 222/E3
Panola (co.), Miss. 256/E2
Panola, Okla. (74559) 288/R5
Panola (co.), Texas 303/K5
Panora, Iowa (50216) 229/E5
Panorama Park, Iowa (†52722) 229/N5
Panquehue, Chile 138/G2
Panruti, India 68/D6
Pansey, Ala. (36370) 195/H8
Pantanal (reg.), Brazil 120/D4
Pantar (isl.), Indonesia 85/G7
Pantego, N.C. (27860) 281/R3
Pantego, Texas (76013) 303/F2
Pantelleria, Italy 34/C6
Pantelleria (isl.), Italy 7/F5
Pantelleria (isl.), Italy 34/D6
Pantha, Burma 72/B2
Panther (creek), Idaho 220/D4
Panther (creek), Ky. 237/G5
Panther, W. Va. (24872) 312/C8
Panther Burn, Miss. (38765) 256/C4
Panthersville, Georgia (†30032) 217/L1
Pantin, France 28/B1
Pantoja, Peru 128/E3
Panton○, Vt. (†05491) 268/A3
Pánuco, Mexico 150/K6
Pánuco (riv.), Mexico 150/K5
Panuke (lake), Nova Scotia 168/D4
Pan Xian, China 77/G6
Panyam, Nigeria 106/F7
Panzós, Guatemala 154/C3
Pao (riv.), Venezuela 124/D3
Pao (riv.), Venezuela 124/F3
Paoki (Baoji), China 77/G5
Paola, Italy 34/E5
Paola, Kansas (66071) 232/H3
Paoli, Colo. (80746) 208/P1
Paoli, Ind. (47454) 227/E7
Paoli, Okla. (73074) 288/M5
Paoli, Pa. (19301) 294/M5
Paoli, Wis. (†53508) 317/G10
Paonia, Colo. (81428) 208/D5
Paopao (bay), Fr. Poly. 86/S12
Paoting (Baoding), China 77/J4
Paotow (Baotou), China 77/G3
Paoua, Cent. Afr. Rep. 115/C2
Paoy Pet, Cambodia 72/D4
Papa, Hawaii (†96704) 218/G6
Pápa, Hungary 41/D3
Papaaloa, Hawaii (96780) 218/J4
Papagaio (riv.), Brazil 132/B6
Papagayo (gulf), C. Rica 154/E5
Papago Ind. Res., Ariz. 198/C6
Papaikou, Hawaii 188/G6
Papaikou, Hawaii (96781) 218/J5
Papakura, N. Zealand 100/E2
Papallacta, Ecuador 128/D3
Papanoa, Mexico 150/J8
Papantla de Olarte, Mexico 150/L6
Papar, Malaysia 85/F4
Papara, Fr. Poly. 86/S13
Papa Stour (isl.), Scotland 10/G1
Papa Stour (isl.), Scotland 15/F2
Papatoetoe, N. Zealand 100/C1
Papa Westray (isl.), Scotland 15/F1
Papa Westray (isl.), Scotland 10/E1
Papeete (cap.), Fr. Polynesia 2/B6
Papeete (cap.), Fr. Poly. 86/S13
Papeete (cap.), Fr. Poly. 87/M7
Papelón, Venezuela 124/D3
Papenburg, W. Germany 22/B2
Papenoo, Fr. Poly. 86/T12
Papetoai, Fr. Poly. 86/S12
Paphos, Cyprus 63/E5
Papillion, Nebr. (68046) 264/J3
Papineau, Ill. (60956) 222/F3
Papineau (lake), Ontario 177/G2
Papineau (co.), Québec 172/B4
Papineau (lake), Québec 172/C4
Papineauville, Québec 172/C4
Paposo, Chile 138/A5
Papradno, Czech. 41/E2
Paps, The (mt.), Ireland 17/C7
Paps of Jura (mt.), Scotland 15/C5
Papua (gulf), Papua N.G. 87/E6
Papua New Guinea 2/S6
PAPUA NEW GUINEA 86/B1
PAPUA NEW GUINEA 85/B7
Papua New Guinea 87/E6
Papudo, Chile 138/A9
Papun, Burma 72/C3
Papunáua (riv.), Colombia 126/E6
Papunya, North. Terr. 93/B7
Papurí (riv.), Colombia 126/F7
Paquera, C. Rica 154/E6
Paquette, Québec 172/F4
Paquetville, New Bruns. 170/E1
Pará (state), Brazil 132/C4
Pará (Belém), Brazil 132/E3
Pará (est.), Brazil 120/E3
Pará (riv.), Brazil 132/D3
Para (dist.), Suriname 131/D3
Paraburdoo, W. Australia 88/B4
Paraburdoo, W. Australia 92/B3
Paracale, Philippines 82/D3
Paracas (pen.), Peru 128/D9
Paracatu, Brazil 132/E7
Paracatu (riv.), Brazil 132/E7
Paracel (isls.), China 85/E2
Parachilna, S. Australia 88/F6
Parachilna, S. Australia 94/F4
Parachute, Colo. 208/C4
Paraćin, Yugoslavia 45/E4
Parada Esperanza, Uruguay 145/B3
Parada Liebigs, Uruguay 145/A4
Parada Rivas, Uruguay 145/B2
Parade, S. Dak. (57647) 298/G3
Pará de Minas, Brazil 132/E7
Pará de Minas, Brazil 135/D1
Paradip, India 68/F4
Paradis, La. (70080) 238/M4
Paradise, Ariz. (†85632) 198/F7
Paradise, Calif. (95969) 204/D4
Paradise, Guyana 131/C3
Paradise, Kansas (67658) 232/D2
Paradise, Mich. (49768) 250/D2
Paradise (lake), Mich. 250/E3
Paradise, Mo. (†64089) 261/D4
Paradise, Mont. (59856) 262/B3
Paradise, Newf. 166/D2
Paradise (riv.), Newf. 166/C3
Paradise, Nova Scotia 168/C4
Paradise (lake), Nova Scotia 168/C4
Paradise, Pa. (17562) 294/K5
Paradise, Texas (76073) 303/G5
Paradise, Utah (84328) 304/C2
Paradise, W. Va. (†25124) 312/C5
Paradise Hill, Okla. (†74435) 288/R3
Paradise Hill, Sask. 181/B2
Paradise Inn, Wash. (98398) 310/D4
Paradise River, Newf. 166/C3
Paradise Valley, Alberta 182/E3
Paradise Valley, Ariz. (85253) 198/D5
Paradise Valley, Nev. (89119) 266/F6
Paradise Valley, Nev. (89426) 266/D1
Paradise Valley, Wyo. (†82601) 319/F3
Paradisino (peak), Switzerland 39/K4
Paradiso, Switzerland 39/G5
Paradox, Colo. (81429) 208/B6
Paragon, Ind. (46166) 227/D6
Paragonah, Utah (84760) 304/B6
Paragould, Ark. (72450) 202/J1
Paraguá (riv.), Bolivia 136/E4
Paragua (riv.), Venezuela 124/G4
Paraguaçu (riv.), Brazil 120/F4
Paraguaçu (riv.), Brazil 132/F6
Paraguaçu Paulista, Brazil 132/D8
Paraguai (riv.) 120/D4
Paraguai (riv.), Brazil 132/B8
Paraguaipoa, Venezuela 124/C2
Paraguaná (pen.), Venezuela 124/C1
Paraguarí (dept.), Paraguay 144/D4-5
Paraguay 2/F7
Paraguay 120/D5
PARAGUAY 144
Paraguay (riv.), Argentina 143/E1
Paraguay (riv.), Bolivia 136/F7
Paraguay (riv.), Paraguay 144/D4
Paraíba (state), Brazil 132/G4
Paraíba (riv.), Brazil 120/E5
Paraíba (riv.), Brazil 135/E2
Paraíba do Sul, Brazil 135/E3
Parainen, Finland 18/M6
Paraíso, C. Rica 154/F6
Paraíso, Dom. Rep. 158/D7
Paraíso, Mexico 150/N7
Paraíso de Chabasquén, Venezuela 124/D3
Parakou, Benin 106/E7
Parallel, Kansas (†66933) 232/F2
Paraloma, Ark. (†71846) 202/B6
Paramaribo (dist.), Suriname 131/D2
Paramaribo (cap.), Suriname 131/D2
Paramaribo (cap.), Suriname 2/G5
Paramaribo (cap.), Suriname 120/D2
Paramithia, Greece 45/E6
Paramonga, Peru 128/C8
Paramount, Calif. (90723) 204/C11
Paramus, N.J. (07652) 273/B1
Paramushir (isl.) 54/S5
Paramushir (isl.), U.S.S.R. 48/Q4
Paran (dry riv.), Israel 65/D5
Paraná (riv.) 2/G7
Paraná (riv.) 120/D5
Paraná, Argentina 143/F5
Paraná, Argentina 120/D6
Paraná (riv.), Argentina 143/E2
Paraná (state), Brazil 132/D9
Paraná (state), Brazil 135/B4
Paranã, Brazil 132/E6
Paranã (riv.), Brazil 132/C8
Paranã (riv.), Brazil 132/E6
Paranaguá, Brazil 120/E5
Paranaguá, Brazil 132/E9
Paranaguá, Brazil 135/B4
Paranaíba, Brazil 132/D7
Paranam, Suriname 131/D3
Paranapanema (riv.), Brazil 132/C8
Paranapanema (riv.), Brazil 135/B3
Paranapiacaba (range), Brazil 135/B4
Paranatinga (riv.), Brazil 120/D4
Paranatinga (riv.), Brazil 132/C6
Parang, Maguindanao, Philippines 82/E7
Parang, Sulu, Philippines 82/C8
Parao (riv.), Uruguay 145/E3
Paraparaumu, N. Zealand 100/E4
Parapetí (riv.), Bolivia 136/D6
Para Station, N. S. Wales 97/B3
Parati, Brazil 135/D3
Paratinga, Brazil 132/F6
Paray-le-Monial, France 28/F4
Parbhani, India 68/D5
Parchim, E. Germany 22/D2
Parchman, Miss. (38738) 256/D3
Parchment, Mich. (49004) 250/D6
Parczew, Poland 47/F3
Pardee (res.), Calif. 204/C9
Pardee, Va. (†24285) 307/C6
Pardeeville, Wis. (53954) 317/H8
Pardes Hanna-Karkur, Israel 65/B2
Parding, China 77/C5
Pardo (riv.), Brazil 132/D8
Pardo (riv.), Brazil 132/F6
Pardo (riv.), Brazil 135/B2
Pardo (riv.), Brazil 132/C8
Pardoe, Pa. (†16137) 294/B3
Pardoo, W. Australia 92/B3
Pardubice, Czech. 41/C1
Pare, Indonesia 85/K2
Parece Vela (isl.), Japan 54/P7
Parece Vela (isl.), Japan 87/D3
Parecis (mts.), Brazil 120/C4
Parecis, Serra dos (range), Brazil 132/B6
Paredes de Nava, Spain 33/D1
Paredones, Chile 138/A10
Parent, Québec 174/C3
Pareora, N. Zealand 100/C6
Parepare, Indonesia 85/F6
Parguera, P. Rico 161/A3
Parham, Ant. & Bar. 161/E11
Parham, Ontario 177/H3
Parhams, La. (†71343) 238/G4
Paria (gulf) 120/C1
Paria (plat.), Ariz. 198/D2
Paria (riv.), Ariz. 198/D1
Paria, Bolivia 136/B5
Paria (gulf), Trin. & Tob. 156/G5
Paria (gulf), Trin. & Tob. 161/A11
Paria (riv.), Utah 304/B6
Paria (gulf), Venezuela 124/H2
Paria (pen.), Venezuela 124/G2
Pariaguán, Venezuela 124/F3
Pariaman, Indonesia 85/B6
Paricutín (vol.), Mexico 150/H7
Parida (isl.), Panama 154/F6
Parika, Guyana 131/B2
Parikkala, Finland 18/Q6
Parima, Sierra (mts.), Venezuela 124/F6
Parinacochas (lake), Peru 128/F10
Parinacota, Cerro (mt.), Chile 138/B1
Parinari, Peru 128/E5
Pariñas (pt.), Peru 128/B5
Parintins, Brazil 120/D3
Parintins, Brazil 132/B3
Paris, Ark. (72855) 202/C3
Paris (city) (dept.), France 28/B2
Paris (cap.), France 2/J3
Paris (cap.), France 7/E4
Paris (cap.), France 28/B2
Paris, Idaho (83261) 220/G7
Paris, Ill. (61944) 222/F4
Paris, Iowa (†52214) 229/K4
Paris, Ky. (40361) 237/N4
Paris○, Maine (04271) 243/B7
Paris, Mich. (49338) 250/D5
Paris, Miss. (38949) 256/F2
Paris, Mo. (65275) 261/J4
Paris, Ohio (44669) 284/H4
Paris, Ontario 177/D4
Paris, Tenn. (38242) 237/E8
Paris, Texas (75460) 303/J4
Paris, Texas 188/G4
Paris, Va. (22130) 307/N3
Paris Crossing, Ind. (47270) 227/F7
Parish, N.Y. (13131) 276/H4
Parish, Uruguay 145/C3
Parishville, N.Y. (13672) 276/L1
Parisville, Mich. (†48470) 250/G5
Parisville, Québec 172/F3
Parita, Panama 154/G6
Parita (bay), Panama 154/G6
Park (co.), Colo. 208/H4
Park (range), Colo. 208/F1
Park (riv.), Conn. 210/E2
Park, Kansas (67751) 232/B2
Park (co.), Mont. 262/F5
Park (riv.), N. Dak. 282/R3
Park (dist.), Scotland 15/B2
Park (co.), Wyo. 319/C1
Parkano, Finland 18/N6
Parkbeg, Sask. 181/E5
Park City, Ill. (†60085) 222/B4
Park City, Kansas (†67201) 232/E4
Park City, Ky. (42160) 237/J6
Park City, Mont. (59063) 262/H5
Park City, Utah (84060) 304/C3
Parkdale, Ark. (71661) 202/H7
Parkdale, Colo. (†81212) 208/H6
Parkdale, Oreg. (97041) 291/F2
Parkdale, Pr. Edward I. 168/E2
Parke (co.), Ind. 227/C5
Parker, Ariz. (85344) 198/A4
Parker (dam), Ariz. 198/A4
Parker, Colo. (80134) 208/K4
Parker, Fla. (32401) 212/C6
Parker, Idaho (83438) 220/G6
Parker, Kansas (66072) 232/H3
Parker, Pa. (16049) 294/C3
Parker, S. Dak. (57053) 298/P7
Parker (lake), S. Dak. 298/P3
Parker (co.), Texas 303/G5
Parker, Texas (†75069) 303/H1
Parker, Wash. (98939) 310/E4
Parker City, Ind. (47368) 227/G4
Parker Dam, Calif. (92267) 204/L9
Parkersburg, Ill. (62452) 222/F5
Parkersburg, Ind. (†47954) 227/D5
Parkersburg, Iowa (50665) 229/H3
Parkersburg, W. Va. 188/K3
Parkersburg, W. Va. (26101) 312/D4
Parkers Cove, Newf. 166/D4
Parkers Cove, Nova Scotia 168/C4
Parkers Lake, Ky. (42634) 237/M7
Parkers Prairie, Minn. (56361) 255/C4
Parkertown, N.J. (†08087) 273/E4
Parkerview, Sask. 181/H4
Parkerville, Kansas (†66846) 232/F3
Parkes, N. S. Wales 88/H6
Parkes, N.S. Wales 97/E3
Parkesburg, Pa. (19365) 294/L6
Park Falls, Wis. (54552) 317/F4
Park Forest, Ill. (60466) 222/B6
Park Forest South, Ill. (60466) 222/F2
Park Hall, Md. (20667) 245/N8
Park Hill, Okla. (74451) 288/R3
Parkhill, Ontario 177/C4
Park Hills, Ky. (†41011) 237/S2
Parkin, Ark. (72373) 202/J3
Parkland, Alberta 182/D4
Parkland, Fla. (†33441) 212/F5
Parkland, Okla. (†74824) 288/N3
Parkland, Wash. (98444) 310/C3
Parkman○, Maine (†04443) 243/D5
Parkman, Ohio (44080) 284/H3
Parkman, Sask. 181/K6
Parkman, Wyo. (82838) 319/E1
Park Place, Oreg. (†97045) 291/B2
Park Rapids, Minn. (56470) 255/D4
Park Rapids, Wash. (†99114) 310/H2
Park Ridge, Ill. (60068) 222/B5
Park Ridge, N.J. (07656) 273/B1
Park Ridge, Wis. (†54481) 317/H6
Park River, N. Dak. (58270) 282/P3
Parks, Ariz. (86018) 198/C3
Parks, Ark. (72950) 202/B4
Parks, La. (70582) 238/G6
Parks, Nebr. (69041) 264/C4
Parkside, Pa. (†19013) 294/M7
Parkside, Sask. 181/E2
Parksley, Va. (23421) 307/S5
Parkston, S. Dak. (57366) 298/O7
Parksville, Br. Col. 184/J3
Parksville, Ky. (40464) 237/M5
Parksville, N.Y. (12768) 276/L7
Parksville, S.C. (29844) 296/C4
Parkton, Md. (21120) 245/M2
Parkton, N.C. (28371) 281/M5
Park Valley, Utah (84329) 304/A2
Parkview (mt.), Colo. 208/G2
Parkville, Md. (21234) 245/M3
Parkville, Mo. (64152) 261/O5
Parkville, Pa. (†17331) 294/J6
Parkville, Victoria 97/H5
Parkway, Mo. (64130) 261/L6
Parkway Village, Ky. (†40201) 237/J2
Parkwood, N.C. (27707) 281/M3
Parlakhemundi, India 68/E5
Parlier, Calif. (93648) 204/F7
Parlin, Colo. (81239) 208/F6
Parlin (pond), Maine 243/C4
Parma, Idaho (83660) 220/B6
Parma (prov.), Italy 34/C2
Parma, Italy 7/E4
Parma, Italy 34/C2
Parma (riv.), Italy 34/C2
Parma, Mich. (49269) 250/E6
Parma, Mo. (63870) 261/N9
Parma, Ohio (44129) 284/H9
Parmachenee (lake), Maine 243/B5
Parma Heights, Ohio (†44130) 284/G9
Parmana, Venezuela 124/F4
Parmele, N.C. (27861) 281/P3
Parmelee, S. Dak. (57566) 298/G7
Parmer (co.), Texas 303/B3
Parnaguá, Brazil 132/E5
Parnaíba, Brazil 132/F3
Parnaíba, Brazil 120/E3
Parnaíba (riv.), Brazil 120/E3
Parnaíba (riv.), Brazil 132/F3
Parnamirim, Brazil 132/F4
Parnassus (mt.), Greece 45/F6
Parnassus, N. Zealand 100/D5
Parndana, S. Australia 94/E6
Parnell, Iowa (52325) 229/J5
Parnell, Mo. (64475) 261/C2
Pärnu, U.S.S.R. 7/G3
Pärnu, U.S.S.R. 53/C1
Pärnu, U.S.S.R. 52/C3
Pärnu, U.S.S.R. 48/C4
Paro, Bhutan 68/F3
Paron, Ark. (72132) 202/E4
Paroo (riv.), N. S. Wales 88/G5
Paroo (chan.), N.S. Wales 97/B2
Paroo (riv.), N.S. Wales 97/C1
Paroo (riv.), Queensland 95/C6
Paropamisus (mts.), Afghanistan 59/H3
Paropamisus (range), Afghanistan 68/A2
Páros (isl.), Greece 45/G7
Parow, S. Africa 118/F6
Parowan, Utah (84761) 304/B6
Parpan, Switzerland 39/J3
Parr, Ind. (†47978) 227/C2
Parr, S.C. (29066) 296/E3
Parral, Chile 138/A11
Parral, Mexico 150/G3
Parral, Ohio (†44622) 284/G4
Parramatta, N. S. Wales 88/K4
Parramatta (riv.), N. S. Wales 88/K4
Parramatta, N.S. Wales 97/H3
Parramatta (riv.), N.S. Wales 97/J3
Parramore (isl.), Va. 307/S5
Parran, Md. (†20639) 245/M6
Parras de la Fuente, Mexico 150/H4
Parratah, Tasmania 99/D4
Parrett (riv.), England 13/E6
Parrish, Ala. (35580) 195/D3
Parrish, Fla. (33564) 212/D4
Parrish, Wis. (†54435) 317/H5
Parris Island Marine Base, S.C. 296/F7
Parrott, Georgia (31777) 217/D7
Parrott, Va. (24132) 307/G6
Parrottsville, Tenn. (37843) 237/P8
Parrsboro, Nova Scotia 168/D3
Parry (isls.), N.W.T. 146/G2
Parry (chan.), N.W.T. 146/G2
Parry (chan.), N.W.T. 162/E-H1
Parry (bay), N.W. Terrs. 187/K3
Parry (cape), N.W. Terrs. 187/F2
Parry (chan.), N.W. Terrs. 187/G2
Parry (isls.), N.W. Terrs. 187/G2
Parry (pen.), N.W. Terrs. 187/F2
Parry (isl.), Ontario 177/D2
Parry (sound), Ontario 177/D2
Parry, Sask. 181/G6
Parry Sound, Ont. 162/J6
Parry Sound (terr. dist.), Ontario 175/E3
Parry Sound, Ontario 175/D3
Parry Sound, Ontario 177/E2
Parseierspitze (mt.), Austria 41/A3
Parshall, Colo. (80468) 208/G2
Parshall, N. Dak. (58770) 282/F4
Parsippany-Troy Hills○, N.J. (07054) 273/E2
Parsnip (riv.), Br. Col. 184/F3
Parson, Br. Col. 184/J4
Parsons, Kans. 188/G3
Parsons, Kansas (67357) 232/G4
Parsons, Tenn. (38363) 237/E9
Parsons, W. Va. (26287) 312/G4
Parsonsburg, Md. (21849) 245/R7
Parson's Pond, Newf. 166/C3
Partanna, Italy 34/D6
Partapgarh, India 68/C4
Parthenay, France 28/C4
Partinico, Italy 34/D6
Partizansk, U.S.S.R. 48/O5
Partizánske, Czech. 41/E2
Partlow, Va. (22534) 307/N4
Partridge, Kansas (67566) 232/D4
Partridge (riv.), Minn. 255/G3
Partridge (bay), Newf. 166/C3
Partridge (pt.), Newf. 166/C3
Partry (mts.), Ireland 17/C4
Paru (riv.), Brazil 132/C3
Paru de Oeste (riv.), Brazil 120/D3
Paru de Oeste (riv.), Brazil 132/B3
Paruro, Peru 128/F9
Parvatipuram, India 68/E5
Parys, S. Africa 118/D5
Pas, De (riv.), Québec 174/D1
Pasadena, Calif. 188/C4
Pasadena, Calif. (*91101) 204/C10
Pasadena, Md. (21122) 245/M4
Pasadena, Newf. 166/C4
Pasadena, Texas (*77501) 303/J2
Pasado (cape), Ecuador 128/B3
Pasaje, Ecuador 128/C4
Pa Sak, Mae Nam (riv.), Thailand 72/D4
Pasangkayu, Indonesia 85/F6
Pasargadae (ruins), Iran 66/H5
Pasatiempo, Calif. (†95060) 204/K4
Pasawng, Burma 72/C3
Pasayten (riv.), Wash. 310/E2
Pascagoula, Miss. (39567) 256/G10
Pascagoula (riv.), Miss. 256/G9
Pascalis, Québec 174/B3
Paşcani, Romania 45/H2
Paschall, N.C. (†27589) 281/N1
Pasco (co.), Fla. 212/D3
Pasco (dept.), Peru 128/E8
Pasco, Wash. (99301) 310/F4
Pascoag, R.I. (02859) 249/H5
Pascola, Mo. (63871) 261/N10
Pascua (riv.), Chile 138/D7
Pas-de-Calais (dept.), France 28/E2
Pasewalk, E. Germany 22/F2
Pasighat, India 68/G3
Pasinler, Turkey 63/J3
Pasión (riv.), Guatemala 154/B2
Paskenta, Calif. (96074) 204/C4
Pasłek, Poland 47/D1
Pasley (bay), N.W. Terrs. 187/J2
Pasni, Pakistan 68/A3
Pasni, Pakistan 54/H7
Pasni, Pakistan 59/H4
Paso Ataques, Uruguay 145/D2
Paso Barreto, Paraguay 144/D3
Paso de Andrés Pérez, Uruguay 145/B3
Paso de Indios, Argentina 143/C5
Paso de la Laguna, Salto, Uruguay 145/B2
Paso de la Laguna, Tacuarembó, Uruguay 145/D3
Paso de las Piedras, Uruguay 145/C2
Paso del Borracho, Uruguay 145/D2
Paso del Cerro, Uruguay 145/C2
Paso de León, Uruguay 145/B1
Paso del Horno, Uruguay 145/C2
Paso de Los Libres, Argentina 143/E2
Paso de los Toros, Uruguay 145/C3
Paso del Parque, Uruguay 145/B2
Paso de Ovejas, Mexico 150/Q2
Paso de Patria, Paraguay 144/C5
Paso de Ramos, Uruguay 145/C1
Paso de Uleste, Uruguay 145/B3
Paso Flores, Argentina 143/C5
Paso Hondo, Uruguay 145/B4
Paso Potrero, Uruguay 145/C2
Pasorapa, Bolivia 136/C6
Paso Real, Honduras 154/E3
Paso Robles, Calif. (93446) 204/E8
Paspébiac, Québec 172/D2
Pasqua, Sask. 181/F5
Pasque (isl.), Mass. 249/L7
Pasquia (hills), Sask. 181/J2
Pasquia (riv.), Sask. 181/K2
Pasquotank (co.), N.C. 281/S2
Pass (creek), Wyo. 319/F4
Passaconaway (mt.), N.H. 268/E4
Passadumkeag○, Maine (04475) 243/F5
Passage (isl.), Mich. 250/E1
Passage East, Ireland 17/G7
Passagem Franca, Brazil 132/E4
Passage West, Ireland 17/E8
Passage West, Ireland 10/B5
Passaic, Mo. (64777) 261/D6
Passaic (co.), N.J. 273/E1
Passaic, N.J. (07055) 273/E2
Passaic (riv.), N.J. 273/E2
Passamaquoddy (bay), Maine 243/J5
Passamaquoddy (bay), New Bruns. 170/C3
Passamaquoddy Ind. Res., Maine 243/J6
Passau, W. Germany 22/E4
Pass Christian, Miss. (39571) 256/F10
Passero (cape), Italy 7/F5
Passero (cape), Italy 34/E6
Passes (lake), Québec 172/F2
Passi, Philippines 82/D5
Passo Fundo, Brazil 120/D5
Passo Fundo, Brazil 132/D10
Passos, Brazil 132/E8
Passos, Brazil 135/C2
Passumpsic, Vt. (05861) 268/D3
Passumpsic (riv.), Vt. 268/D2
Pastaza (riv.) 120/B3
Pastaza (prov.), Ecuador 128/D3
Pastaza (riv.), Ecuador 128/D4
Pastaza (riv.), Peru 128/D5
Pasto, Colombia 120/B2
Pasto, Colombia 126/B7
Pastol (bay), Alaska 196/F2
Pastora (peak), Ariz. 198/F2
Pastos Bons, Brazil 132/E4
Pastrana, Spain 33/E2
Pastura, N. Mex. (88435) 274/E4
Pasuquin, Philippines 82/C1
Pasuruan, Indonesia 85/K2
Pasvalys, U.S.S.R. 53/C2
Pasvikelv (riv.), Norway 18/Q2
Paswegin, Sask. 181/H4
Pásztó, Hungary 41/E3
Pata, Bolivia 136/A4
Patacamaya, Bolivia 136/B5
Patagonia (reg.), Argentina 120/C7
Patagonia (reg.), Argentina 143/C5
Patagonia, Ariz. (85624) 198/E7
Pataguanset (lake), Conn. 210/G3
Pataha, Wash. (†99347) 310/H4
Pataha (creek), Wash. 310/H4
Patan, India 68/C4
Patapédia (riv.), New Bruns. 170/C1
Patapédia (riv.), Québec 172/B2
Patapsco, Md. (†21048) 245/L2
Patapsco (riv.), Md. 245/M4
Pataskala, Ohio (43062) 284/E5
Pataz, Peru 128/D6
Patchewollock, Victoria 97/A4
Patch Grove, Wis. (53817) 317/D10
Patchogue, N.Y. (11772) 276/P9
Patea, N. Zealand 100/E3
Paternion, Austria 41/B3
Paterno, Italy 34/E6
Pateros, Wash. (98846) 310/E2
Pateros (lake), Wash. 310/F2
Paterson, N.J. 188/M2
Paterson, N.J. (*07501) 273/B2
Paterson, Wash. (99345) 310/F5
Patesville, Ky. (†42364) 237/H5
Pathankot, India 68/D2
Pathfinder (res.), Wyo. 188/E2
Pathfinder (res.), Wyo. 319/F3
Pathiu, Thailand 72/C5
Pathlow, Sask. 181/G3
Pati (pt.), Guam 86/K6
Pati, Indonesia 85/J2
Patía, Colombia 126/B6
Patía (riv.), Colombia 126/B6
Patiala, India 68/D2
Patillas, P. Rico 161/E2
Patillas (lake), P. Rico 161/E2
Pativilca (riv.), Peru 128/D8
Patmos, Ark. (†71801) 202/C7
Pátmos (isl.), Greece 45/H7
Patna, India 54/K7
Patna, India 68/F3
Patna, Scotland 15/D5
Patnanongan (isl.), Philippines 82/D3
Patnos, Turkey 63/K3
Patoka, Ill. (62875) 222/D5
Patoka, Ind. (47666) 227/B8
Patoka (riv.), Ind. 227/C8
Paton, Iowa (50217) 229/E4
Patos, Brazil 120/F3
Patos, Brazil 132/G4
Patos (lake), Brazil 120/D6
Patos (lag.), Brazil 132/D10
Patos de Minas, Brazil 120/E4
Patos de Minas, Brazil 132/E7
Patoutville, La. (†70544) 238/G7
Patquía, Argentina 143/C3
Pátrai, Greece 7/G5
Pátrai, Greece 45/E6
Patricia, Alberta 182/E4
Patricia, S. Dak. (†57551) 298/G7
Patricia, Texas (79352) 303/B5
Patricio Lynch (isl.), Chile 138/D7
Patrick, Neth. Ant. 161/F8
Patrick, S.C. (29584) 296/G2
Patrick (co.), Va. 307/H7
Patrick A.F.B., Fla. 212/F3
Patricksburg, Ind. (47455) 227/D6
Patrick's Cove, Newf. 166/C2
Patrick Springs, Va. (24133) 307/H7
Patrickswell, Ireland 17/D6
Patriot, Ind. (47038) 227/H7
Patriot, Ohio (45658) 284/F8
Patrocínio, Brazil 132/E7
Patronville, Ind. (†47635) 227/C9
Patroon, Texas (75967) 303/L6
Patsaliga (creek), Ala. 195/F7
Patsburg, Ala. (†36049) 195/F7
Patta (isl.), Kenya 115/H4
Pattani, Thailand 72/D6
Patten, Maine (04765) 243/F4
Patten○, Maine (04765) 243/F4
Pattenburg, N.J. (†08802) 273/C2
Patterson, Ark. (72123) 202/H3
Patterson, Calif. (95363) 204/D6
Patterson, Georgia (31557) 217/H8
Patterson, Idaho (†83253) 220/E5
Patterson, Ill. (62078) 222/C4
Patterson, Iowa (50218) 229/F6
Patterson, La. (70392) 238/H7
Patterson (pt.), Mich. 250/D3
Patterson, Mo. (63956) 261/L8
Patterson, N.Y. (12563) 276/N7
Patterson, N.C. (28661) 281/F3
Patterson, Edward A. (lake), N. Dak. 282/E6
Patterson, Ohio (45843) 284/C4
Patterson, Va. (24633) 307/D6
Patterson (creek), W. Va. 312/J4
Patterson Creek, W. Va. (26746) 312/J3
Pattersonville, N.Y. (12137) 276/M5
Patti, Italy 34/E5
Pattison, Miss. (39144) 256/C7
Patton, Mo. (63662) 261/M8
Patton, Pa. (16668) 294/E4
Pattonsburg, Mo. (64670) 261/D2
Patuanak, Sask. 181/L3
Patuca, Honduras 154/E3
Patuca (pt.), Honduras 154/E3
Patuca (riv.), Honduras 154/E3
Patuha (mt.), Indonesia 85/H2
Pătulele, Romania 45/F3
Patutahi, N. Zealand 100/F3
Patuxent (riv.), Md. 245/M7
Patuxent River Nav. Air Test Ctr., Md. 245/N7
Patzau, Wis. (†54836) 317/B3
Pátzcuaro, Mexico 150/J7

Piedmont 427

Pequea, Pa. (17565) 294/K6
Pequest (riv.), N.J. 273/D2
Pequonnock (riv.), Conn. 210/C3
Pequop (mts.), Nev. 266/G2
Pequot Lakes, Minn. (56472) 255/D4
Pera (head), Queensland 88/G2
Pera (head), Queensland 95/B2
Pera (Beyoğlu), Turkey 63/D6
Perabumulih, Indonesia 85/C6
Peraitepuí, Venezuela 124/H5
Perak (state), Malaysia 72/D6
Perak, Gunong (mt.), Malaysia 72/D6
Perales (riv.), Spain 33/F4
Peralta, Dom. Rep. 158/D6
Peralta, N. Mex. (87042) 274/C4
Peralta, Spain 33/F1
Peralta, Uruguay 145/C3
Peravia (prov.), Dom. Rep. 158/E6
Percé (cape), Nova Scotia 168/J2
Percé, Québec 172/D1
Percé, Québec 174/E3
Perch (lake), Mich. 250/G2
Perch (riv.), Mich. 250/G2
Perche (reg.), France 28/D3
Percival, Iowa (51648) 229/B7
Percival, Sask. 181/J5
Percival (lakes), W. Australia 88/C4
Percival (lakes), W. Australia 92/D3
Percy, Ill. (62272) 222/D5
Percy, Miss. (†38748) 256/C4
Percy, N.H. (†03582) 268/E2
Perdido, Ala. (36562) 195/C8
Perdido (bay), Ala. 195/D10
Perdido (riv.), Ala. 195/C9
Perdido (riv.), Fla. 212/B6
Perdido (mt.), Spain 33/G1
Perdido Beach, Ala. (36530) 195/C10
Pérdika, Greece 45/E6
Perdue, Sask. 181/D3
Perdue Hill, Ala. (36470) 195/C8
Pereira, Colombia 126/C5
Pereira, Colombia 120/B2
Perelló, Spain 33/G2
Pere Marquette (riv.), Mich. 250/D5
Perené (riv.), Peru 128/E8
Perenjori, W. Australia 92/B5
Pérez, Argentina 143/F6
Pérez (isl.), Mexico 150/P5
Perg, Austria 41/C2
Pergamino, Argentina 143/F6
Pergamino, Argentina 120/C6
Pergine Valsugana, Italy 34/C1
Pergola, Italy 34/D3
Perham○, Maine (04766) 243/G2
Perham, Minn. (56573) 255/C4
Perhentian, Kepulauan (isls.), Malaysia 72/D6
Periam, Romania 45/E2
Péribonca (riv.), Que. 162/J5
Péribonca (riv.), Québec 174/C3
Péribonca (riv.), Québec 172/F1
Péribonka, Québec 172/E1
Perico, Cuba 158/D1
Perico, Texas (†79087) 303/B1
Pericos, Mexico 150/F4
Peridot, Ariz. (85542) 198/E5
Perigord, Sask. 181/H3
Périgueux, France 28/D5
Perijá, Serranía de (mts.), Colombia 126/D2
Perijá, Sierra de (mts.), Venezuela 124/B2
Perim (isl.), P.D.R. Yemen 59/D7
Perintown, Ohio (†45150) 284/B7
Perito F.P. Moreno Nat'l Park, Argentina 143/B6
Perito Moreno, Argentina 143/B6
Periyar (lake), India 68/D7
Perkam (cape), Indonesia 85/K6
Perkasie, Pa. (18944) 294/M5
Perkatkin, U.S.S.R. 48/T2
Perkins (mt.), Conn. 210/F1
Perkins, Georgia (30822) 217/J5
Perkins, Iowa (†51239) 229/A2
Perkins, Mich. (49872) 250/B3
Perkins, Mo. (63774) 261/N8
Perkins (co.), Nebr. 264/C4
Perkins, Okla. (74059) 288/M3
Perkins, Québec 172/B4
Perkins (co.), S. Dak. 298/D3
Perkins, S. Dak. (†57062) 298/08
Perkins, W. Va. (26634) 312/E5
Perkinsfield, Ontario 177/E3
Perkinston, Miss. (39573) 256/F9
Perkinstown, Wis. (†54451) 317/E5
Perkinsville, Ind. (†46011) 227/F4
Perkinsville, N.Y. (14529) 276/E5
Perkinsville, Vt. (05151) 268/B5
Perks, Ill. (62973) 222/D6
Perla, Ark. (†72104) 202/E5
Perlas (lag.), Nicaragua 154/F4
Perlas (pt.), Nicaragua 154/F4
Perlas (arch.), Panama 154/H6
Perleberg, E. Germany 22/D2
Perley, Minn. (56574) 255/B3
Perlis (state), Malaysia 72/D6
Perm', U.S.S.R. 2/M3
Perm', U.S.S.R. 7/K3
Perm', U.S.S.R. 52/J3
Perm', U.S.S.R. 48/F4
Perma, Mont. (59857) 262/B3
Përmet, Albania 45/E5
Pernambuco (state), Brazil 132/G5
Pernambuco (Recife), Brazil 132/H5
Pernell, Okla. (73076) 288/M5
Pernik, Bulgaria 45/F4
Peron (isls.), North. Terr. 88/D2
Peron (isls.), North. Terr. 93/A2
Peron (cape), Tasmania 99/E4
Peron (cape), W. Australia 88/A2
Peron (pen.), W. Australia 92/A4
Péronne, France 28/E3
Perote, Ala. (36061) 195/G7
Perote, Mexico 150/O1
Perow, Br. Col. 184/D3
Perpetua (cape), Oreg. 291/C3
Perpignan, France 7/E4
Perpignan, France 28/E6
Perquilauquén (riv.), Chile 138/A11
Perquimans (co.), N.C. 281/S2
Perrin, Mo. (†64477) 261/D3
Perrin, Texas (76075) 303/G5
Perrin, Va. (†23072) 307/R6
Perrine, Fla. (33157) 212/F6
Perrineville, N.J. (08535) 273/E3
Perrinton, Mich. (48871) 250/E5
Perris, Calif. (92370) 204/F11
Perro (mts.), N. Mex. 274/D4
Perronville, Mich. (49873) 250/B3
Perros (bay), Cuba 158/G2
Perry (co.), Ala. 195/D5
Perry (isl.), Alaska 196/C1
Perry (co.), Ark. 202/E4
Perry, Ark. (72125) 202/E3
Perry, Fla. (32347) 212/C1
Perry, Georgia (31069) 217/E6
Perry (co.) Ill. 222/D5
Perry, Ill. (62362) 222/C4
Perry (co.), Ind. 227/D8
Perry, Iowa (50220) 229/E5
Perry, Kansas (66073) 232/G2
Perry (lake), Kansas 232/G2
Perry (co.), Ky. 237/P6
Perry, La. (70575) 238/F7
Perry○, Maine (04667) 243/J6
Perry, Mich. (48872) 250/E6
Perry (co.), Miss. 256/G8
Perry (co.), Mo. 261/N7
Perry, Mo. (63462) 261/J4
Perry (stream), N.H. 268/E1
Perry, N.Y. (14530) 276/D5
Perry (co.), Ohio 284/F6
Perry, Ohio (44081) 284/H2
Perry, Okla. (73077) 288/M2
Perry, Oreg. (†97850) 291/J2
Perry (co.), Pa. 294/H5
Perry, S.C. (29124) 296/E4
Perry (co.), Tenn. 237/F9
Perry, Utah (†84302) 304/C2
Perry, W. Va. (†26851) 312/J5
Perrydale, Oreg. (†97101) 291/D2
Perrygo Place, Wis. (†53511) 317/J10
Perry Hall, Md. (21128) 245/N3
Perryman, Md. (21130) 245/O3
Perryopolis, Pa. (15473) 294/C5
Perrysburg, Ind. (†46951) 227/E3
Perrysburg, N.Y. (14129) 276/B6
Perrysburg, Ohio (43551) 284/C2
Perry's Cove, Newf. 166/D2
Perry's Victory and Int'l Peace Mem., Ohio 284/E2
Perrysville, Ind. (47974) 227/C4
Perrysville, Ohio (44864) 284/F4
Perrysville, Pa. (15237) 294/B6
Perryton, Ohio (†43822) 284/F5
Perryton, Texas (79070) 303/D1
Perrytown, Ark. (71801) 202/C6
Perryvale, Alberta 182/D2
Perryville, Alaska (99648) 196/G3
Perryville, Ark. (72126) 202/E3
Perryville, Ky. (40468) 237/M5
Perryville, La. (†71220) 238/G1
Perryville, Md. (21903) 245/O2
Perryville, Mo. (63775) 261/N7
Perryville, Tenn. (38364) 237/F9
Perşembe, Turkey 63/G2
Persepolis (ruins), Iran 66/H6
Perseverance (bay), Virgin Is. (U.S.) 161/A4
Perseverancia, Bolivia 136/D4
Pershing, Ind. (†46975) 227/E2
Pershing, Ind. (47370) 227/G5
Pershing, Iowa (50221) 229/G6
Pershing (co.), Nev. 266/C2
Pershing, Okla. (†74002) 288/O1
Pershore, England 13/E5
Persia, Iowa (51563) 229/B5
Persia, Tenn. (†37857) 237/P8
Persian (gulf) 54/G7
Persian (gulf), Bahrain 59/F4
Persian (gulf), Iran 66/F6
Persian (gulf), Iran 59/F4
Persian (gulf), Iraq 59/F4
Persian (gulf), Kuwait 59/F4
Persian (gulf), Qatar 59/F4
Persian (gulf), Saudi Arabia 59/F4
Persinger, W. Va. (†26651) 312/E6
Person (co.), N.C. 281/M2
Pertek, Turkey 63/H3
Perth, Australia 2/Q7
Perth, Kansas (†67152) 232/E4
Perth, N. Dak. (58363) 282/M2
Perth (county), Ontario 177/C4
Perth, Ontario 177/H3
Perth, Scotland 10/E2
Perth, Scotland 15/E4
Perth (trad. co.), Scotland 15/A5
Perth, Tasmania 99/D3
Perth (cap.), W. Australia 88/B2
Perth (cap.), W. Australia 92/A1
Perth Airport, W. Australia 88/B2
Perth Amboy, N.J. (*08861) 273/E2
Perth-Andover, New Bruns. 170/C2
Perthshire, Miss. (†38746) 256/C3
Perthville, N.S. Wales 97/E3
Pertominsk, U.S.S.R. 52/E2
Peru 2/F6
Peru 120/B4
PERU 128
Peru, Ill. (61354) 222/D2
Peru, Ind. (46970) 227/E3
Peru, Iowa (50222) 229/F6
Peru, Kansas (67360) 232/F4
Peru, Maine (04272) 243/C6
Peru○, Maine (04272) 243/C6
Peru, Nebr. (68421) 264/J4
Peru, N.Y. (12972) 276/N1
Peru○, Vt. (05152) 268/B5
Perugia (prov.), Italy 34/D3
Perugia, Italy 34/D3
Perugia, Italy 7/F4
Perugorría, Argentina 143/G4
Péruwelz, Belgium 27/D8
Pervari, Turkey 63/K4
Pervomaysk, U.S.S.R. 52/F3
Pervomaysk, U.S.S.R. 52/D5
Pervoural'sk, U.S.S.R. 48/F4
Perwez, Belgium 27/F7
Péry, Switzerland 39/D2
Pesaro, Italy 34/D3
Pesaro e Urbino (prov.), Italy 34/D3
Pescadero, Calif. (94060) 204/J4
Pescadero (creek), Calif. 204/J3
Pescadero (pt.), Calif. 204/J3
Pescadero, Mexico 150/D5
Pescadores (Penghu) (isls.), China 77/J7
Pescara (prov.), Italy 34/E3
Pescara, Italy 34/E3
Pescara, Italy 7/F4
Pescara (riv.), Italy 34/D3
Pescia, Italy 34/C3
Peseux, Switzerland 39/C3
Peshastin, Wash. (98847) 310/E3
Peshawar, Pakistan 54/H6
Peshawar, Pakistan 59/K3
Peshawar, Pakistan 68/C2
Peshkopi, Albania 45/E5
Peshtera, Bulgaria 45/G4
Peshtigo, Wis. (54157) 317/L5
Peshtigo (riv.), Wis. 317/K5
Peskovka, U.S.S.R. 52/H3
Peskowesk (lake), Nova Scotia 168/C4
Peso da Régua, Portugal 33/C2
Pesotum, Ill. (61863) 222/E4
Pespire, Honduras 154/D4
Pessac, France 28/C5
Pest (co.), Hungary 41/E3
Pestel, Haiti 158/A6
Pestovo, U.S.S.R. 52/D3
Péta, Greece 45/E6
Petaca, N. Mex. (87554) 274/C2
Petacalco (bay), Mexico 150/H8
Petah Tiqwa, Israel 65/B3
Petal, Miss. (39465) 256/F8
Petaluma, Calif. (94952) 204/H1
Pétange, Luxembourg 27/H9
Petas, Las (riv.), Bolivia 136/F5
Petatlán, Mexico 150/J8
Petauke, Zambia 115/F6
Petawaga (lake), Québec 172/A2
Petawawa, Ontario 177/G2
Petawawa (riv.), Ontario 177/G2
Petén-Itzá (lake), Guatemala 154/B2
Petenwell (lake), Wis. 317/G7
Peter (isl.), Virgin Is. (Br.) 156/H1
Peter (isl.), Virgin Is. (Br.) 161/D4
Peterborough, England 13/G5
Peterborough, England 10/F4
Peterborough, N.H. (03458) 268/D6
Peterborough○, N.H. (03458) 268/D6
Peterborough, Ont. 162/J7
Peterborough (county), Ontario 177/F3
Peterborough, Ontario 177/F3
Peterborough, S. Australia 88/F6
Peterborough, S. Australia 94/F5
Peterculter, Scotland 15/F3
Peterhead, Scotland 15/G3
Peterhead, Scotland 10/E2
Peter I (isl.) 5/B14
Peter I (isl.), Norway 2/E9
Peterlee, England 13/J3
Peterman, Ala. (36471) 195/D7
Petermann (ranges), North. Terr. 93/A8
Petermann (ranges), W. Australia 92/E4
Petermann Ranges Aboriginal Reserve, North. Terr. 88/D4
Petermann Ranges Aboriginal Res., North. Terr. 93/A8
Peteroa (vol.), Argentina 143/B4
Peteroa (vol.), Chile 138/B10
Peter Pond (lake), Sask. 181/L3
Peter's (riv.), Newf. 166/D2
Petersburg, Alaska 188/E6
Petersburg, Alaska (99833) 196/N2
Petersburg, Ill. (62675) 222/D4
Petersburg, Ind. (47567) 227/C7
Petersburg, Ky. (41080) 237/M2
Petersburg, Mich. (49270) 250/F7
Petersburg, Minn. (†56143) 255/C7
Petersburg, Nebr. (68652) 264/G3
Petersburg, N.J. (†08270) 273/D5
Petersburg, N.Y. (12138) 276/O5
Petersburg, N. Dak. (58272) 282/P3
Petersburg, Pa. (16669) 294/G4
Petersburg, Tenn. (37144) 237/H10
Petersburg, Texas (79250) 303/C4
Petersburg, Va. 188/L3
Petersburg (I.C.), Va. (23803) 307/N6
Petersburg, W. Va. (26847) 312/H5
Petersburg Nat'l Battlefield, Va. 307/O6
Petersfield, England 13/F6
Petersfield, Jamaica 158/G6
Petersfield, Manitoba 179/E4
Petersham○, Mass. (01366) 249/F3
Peterson, Ala. (35478) 195/D4
Peterson, Iowa (51047) 229/C3
Peterson, Minn. (55962) 255/G7
Peterson, Sask. 181/F3
Peterson Air Force Base, Colo. 208/K5
Peterstown, W. Va. (24963) 312/E8
Petersville, Ind. (†47201) 227/F6
Petersville, Ky. (†41179) 237/P4
Petersville, Md. (†21758) 245/H3
Pétervására, Hungary 41/F3
Peterview, Newf. 166/C4
Pétionville, Haiti 158/C6
Petit Bois (isl.), Miss. 256/H10
Petit-Bourg, Guadeloupe 161/A6
Petit-Canal, Guadeloupe 161/A6
Petit Cap, Québec 172/D1
Petitcodiac, New Bruns. 170/E3
Petitcodiac (riv.), New Bruns. 170/F3
Petit Cul-de-Sac Marin (bay), Guadeloupe 161/A6
Petit-de-Grat, Nova Scotia 168/H3
Petit-de-Grat (isl.), Nova Scotia 168/H3
Petite Cascapédia (riv.), Québec 172/C1
Petite-Matane, Québec 172/B1
Petite Nation (riv.), Québec 172/B4
Petite Riviere Bridge, Nova Scotia 168/D4
Petite Rivière de l'Artibonite, Haiti 158/B5
Petite-Rivière-de-l'Île, New Bruns. 170/F1
Petite-Rivière-Ouest, Québec 172/D2
Petites, Newf. 166/C4
Petit-Étang, Nova Scotia 168/G2
Petite-Terre (isls.), Guadeloupe 161/B6
Petite-Vallée, Québec 172/D1
Petit-Goâve, Haiti 156/D3
Petit Goâve, Haiti 158/B6
Petit Jean (mt.), Ark. 202/C3
Petit Jean (riv.), Ark. 202/D3
Petitjean (Sidi-Kacem), Morocco 106/C2
Petit Mécatina (isl.), Québec 174/F2
Petit Mécatina (riv.), Québec 174/E2
Petitot (riv.), Br. Col. 184/M2
Petitot (riv.), N.W. Terrs. 187/F4
Petit Piton (mt.), St. Lucia 161/G6
Petit Rocher, New Bruns. 170/E1
Petit Rocher Sud, New Bruns. 170/E1
Petit-Saguenay (Saint-François-d'Assise), Québec 172/G1
Petitsikapau (lake), Newf. 166/A3
Petit Soufrière, Dominica 161/F6
Petley, Newf. 166/D2
Peto, Mexico 150/P6
Petone, N. Zealand 100/B2
Petorca, Chile 138/A9
Petoskey, Mich. (49770) 250/E3
Petpeswick (head), Nova Scotia 168/E4
Petra (ruins), Jordan 65/D5
Petre (bay), N. Zealand 100/D7
Petre (pt.), Ontario 177/G4
Petrey, Ala. (36062) 195/F7
Petrich, Bulgaria 45/F5
Petrified Forest, Ariz. (86028) 198/F3
Petrified Forest Nat'l Park, Ariz. 198/F4
Petrila, Romania 45/F3
Petrinja, Yugoslavia 45/B3
Petrohué, Chile 138/E3
Petrokrepost', U.S.S.R. 52/D3
Petrólea, Colombia 126/D3
Petroleum, Ind. (46778) 227/G3
Petroleum, Ky. (†42120) 237/J7
Petroleum (co.), Mont. 262/H3
Petroleum, W. Va. (26161) 312/D4
Petrolia, Kansas (†66720) 232/G4
Petrolia, Ontario 177/B5
Petrolia, Pa. (16050) 294/C3
Petrolia, Texas (76377) 303/F4
Petrolina, Brazil 120/E3
Petrolina, Brazil 132/G5
Petrona (pt.), P. Rico 161/D3
Petropavlovsk, U.S.S.R. 54/J4
Petropavlovsk, U.S.S.R. 48/G4
Petropavlovsk-Kamchatskiy, U.S.S.R. 2/S3
Petropavlovsk-Kamchatskiy, U.S.S.R. 54/T4
Petropavlovsk-Kamchatskiy, U.S.S.R. 48/R4
Petrópolis, Brazil 132/F8
Petrópolis, Brazil 135/E3
Petros, Tenn. (37845) 237/M8
Petroşeni, Romania 45/F3
Petrovsk, U.S.S.R. 52/G4
Petrovsk-Zabaykal'skiy, U.S.S.R. 48/L4
Petrozavodsk, U.S.S.R. 7/H2
Petrozavodsk, U.S.S.R. 48/D3
Petrozavodsk, U.S.S.R. 52/D2
Petsamo (Pechenga), U.S.S.R. 52/D1
Pettibone, N. Dak. (58475) 282/L5
Pettigo, Ireland 17/F2
Pettigo, N. Ireland 17/F2
Pettigrew, Ark. (72752) 202/C2
Pettis (co.), Mo. 261/F5
Pettisville, Ohio (43553) 284/B2
Pettus, Texas (78146) 303/G9
Petty Harbour, Newf. 166/D2
Petworth, D.C. (20011) 245/F4
Peu, Solomon Is. 87/G7
Peuco, Chile 138/G4
Peuerbach, Austria 41/B2
Peumo, Chile 138/F5
Pevas, Peru 128/G4
Pevek, U.S.S.R. 54/U3
Pevek, U.S.S.R. 48/S3
Pevely, Mo. (63070) 261/M6
Pewamo, Mich. (48873) 250/E5
Pewaukee, Wis. (53072) 317/K1
Pewaukee (lake), Wis. 317/K1
Pewee Valley, Ky. (40056) 237/L4
Peyrano, Argentina 143/F6
Peyton, Colo. (80831) 208/K4
Peytona, W. Va. (25154) 312/C6
Pézenas, France 28/E6
Pezinok, Czech. 41/D2
Pfaffenhofen an der Ilm, W. Germany 22/D4
Pfäffnau, Switzerland 39/E2
Pfarrkirchen, W. Germany 22/E4
Pfeifer, Kansas (67660) 232/C3
Pflugerville, Texas (78660) 303/G7
Pforzheim, W. Germany 22/C4
Pfronten, W. Germany 22/D5
Pfullingen, W. Germany 22/C4
Pfunds, Austria 41/A3
Pha Hom Pok, Doi (mt.), Thailand 72/C2
Phalaborwa, S. Africa 118/E4
Phalodi, India 68/C3
Phanat Nikhom, Thailand 72/D4
Phangan, Ko (isl.), Thailand 72/D5
Phangnga, Thailand 72/C5
Phan Rang, Vietnam 72/F5
Phan Thiet, Vietnam 72/F5
Phan Thiet, Vietnam 54/M8
Phantom (lake), Wis. 317/J2
Pharoah, Okla. (74862) 288/O4
Pharr, Texas (78577) 303/F11
Phatthalung, Thailand 72/D6
Phayao, Thailand 72/C3
Pheasant (hills), Sask. 181/J5
Pheba, Miss. (39755) 256/G3
Phelps (mt.) 120/C2
Phelps, Ky. (41553) 237/S6
Phelps (co.), Mo. 261/J7
Phelps (co.), Nebr. 264/E4
Phelps, N.Y. (14532) 276/F5
Phelps (lake), N.C. 281/S3
Phelps (peak), Venezuela 124/E7
Phelps, Wis. (54554) 317/H3
Phelps City, Mo. (†64482) 261/A2
Phenix, Va. (23959) 307/L6
Phenix City, Ala. 188/J4
Phenix City, Ala. (36867) 195/H6
Phet Buri, Thailand 72/C4
Phetchabun, Thailand 72/D3
Phiafai, Laos 72/E4
Phichai, Thailand 72/D3
Phichit, Thailand 72/D3
Phil, Ky. (†42539) 237/M6
Philadelphia, Ill. (†62612) 222/C4
Philadelphia, Miss. (39350) 256/F5
Philadelphia, Mo. (63463) 261/J3
Philadelphia, N.Y. (13673) 276/J2
Philadelphia, Pa. 188/M2
Philadelphia, Pa. 146/L6
Philadelphia (city county), Pa. 294/M6
Philadelphia, Pa. (*19101) 294/N6
Philadelphia, Tenn. (37846) 237/M9
Philadelphia, U.S. 2/F4
Philbrook, Minn. (†56466) 255/D4
Phil Campbell, Ala. (35581) 195/C2
Philip (riv.), Nova Scotia 168/E3
Philip, S. Dak. (57567) 298/F5
Philipp, Miss. (38950) 256/D3
Philippeville (Skikda), Algeria 106/F1
Philippeville, Belgium 27/E8
Philippi, W. Va. (26416) 312/G4
Philippine (sea) 54/O8
Philippine (sea), Guam 86/K6
Philippine (sea), Philippines 85/G2
Philippine (sea), Philippines 82/D3
Philippines 2/R5
Philippines 54/O8
PHILIPPINES 85/H4
PHILIPPINES 82
Philipsburg, Mont. (59858) 262/C4
Philipsburg, Pa. (16866) 294/F4
Philipsburg, Québec 172/D4
Philip Smith (mts.), Alaska 196/J1
Phillip (pt.), N.S. Wales 97/J2
Phillip (isl.), Victoria 97/C6
Phillippy, Tenn. (†38079) 237/C8
Phillips (co.), Ark. 202/J5
Phillips (co.), Colo. 208/P1
Phillips (co.), Kansas 232/C2
Phillips○, Maine (04966) 243/C6
Phillips (co.), Mont. 262/J2
Phillips, Nebr. (68865) 264/F4
Phillips (bay), N.W. Terrs. 187/J1
Phillips, Okla. (†74538) 288/O6
Phillips, Texas (†79007) 303/C2
Phillips, Wis. (54555) 317/E4
Phillipsburg, Georgia (†31794) 217/E8
Phillipsburg, Kansas (67661) 232/C2
Phillipsburg, Mo. (65722) 261/G7
Phillipsburg, N.J. (08865) 273/C2
Phillipsburg, Ohio (45354) 284/B6
Phillipston○, Mass. (†01331) 249/F2
Phillipstown, Ill. (†62827) 222/F5
Phillipsville, N.C. (†28716) 281/D3
Philmont, N.Y. (12565) 276/N6
Philo, Calif. (95466) 204/B4
Philo, Ill. (61864) 222/E3
Philo, Ohio (43771) 284/G6
Philomath, Georgia (30659) 217/G3
Philomath, Oreg. (97370) 291/D3
Philomont, Va. (22131) 307/N2
Philpot, Ky. (42366) 237/H5
Philpots (isl.), N.W. Terrs. 187/L2
Philpott (lake), Va. 307/H7
Phippen, Sask. 181/C3
Phippsburg, Colo. (80469) 208/F2
Phippsburg, Maine (04562) 243/D8
Phippsburg○, Maine (04562) 243/D8
Phitsanulok, Thailand 72/D3
Phlox, Wis. (54464) 317/J5
Phnom Penh (cap.), Cambodia 54/M8
Phnom Penh (cap.), Cambodia 72/E5
Phnum Tbeng Meanchey, Cambodia 72/E4
Phoenix (cap.), Ariz. 146/G6
Phoenix (cap.), Ariz. 188/D4
Phoenix (cap.), Ariz. (*85001) 198/C5
Phoenix, Ill. (†60426) 222/C6
Phoenix (isls.), Kiribati 87/J6
Phoenix, La. (†70042) 238/L7
Phoenix, Md. (21131) 245/M2
Phoenix, N.Y. (13135) 276/H4
Phoenix, Oreg. (97535) 291/E5
Phoenixville, Conn. (†06235) 210/G1
Phoenixville, Pa. (19460) 294/L5
Phôngsali, Laos 72/D2
Phon Phisai, Thailand 72/D3
Phoques (bay), Tasmania 99/A1
Phou Bia (mt.), Laos 72/D3
Phou Cô Pi (mt.), Laos 72/E3
Phou Loi (mt.), Laos 72/D2
Phou San (mt.), Laos 72/D3
Phrae, Thailand 72/D3
Phra Nakhon Si Ayutthaya, Thailand 72/D4
Phsar Ream, Cambodia 72/D5
Phuc Loi, Vietnam 72/E3
Phu Cuong, Vietnam 72/E5
Phu Dien, Vietnam 72/E3
Phuket, Thailand 54/L9
Phuke, Thailand 72/C6
Phuket, Ko (isl.), Thailand 72/C5
Phu Lang Thuong (Bac Giang), Vietnam 72/E2
Phulbani, India 68/E4
Phu Ly, Vietnam 72/E2
Phumi Banam, Cambodia 72/E5
Phumi Phsar, Cambodia 72/E4
Phumi Prek Kak, Cambodia 72/E4
Phumi Samraong, Cambodia 72/D4
Phu My, Vietnam 72/F4
Phu Qui, Vietnam 72/E3
Phu Quoc, Dao (isl.), Vietnam 72/D5
Phu Rieng, Vietnam 72/E5
Phu Tho, Vietnam 72/E2
Phutthaisong, Thailand 72/D4
Phu Vinh, Vietnam 72/E5
Piaçabuçu, Brazil 132/H5
Piacenza (prov.), Italy 34/B2
Piacenza, Italy 34/B2
Piacoa, Venezuela 124/H3
Pia Fai, Doi (mt.), Thailand 72/D4
Piai, Tanjong (pt.), Malaysia 72/E6
Pian (creek), N.S. Wales 97/E1
Piankatank (riv.), Va. 307/R5
Pianosa (isl.), Italy 34/C3
Pianosa (isl.), Italy 34/E3
Piapoco, Colombia 126/F6
Piapot, Sask. 181/B6
Piarco, Trin. & Tob. 161/B10
Piat, Philippines 82/C2
Piatra Neamţ, Romania 45/G2
Piatt (co.), Ill. 222/E4
Piauí (state), Brazil 132/F4
Piauí, Serra do (range), Brazil 132/F5
Piauí (riv.), Brazil 132/F5
Piave (riv.), Italy 34/D2
Piave, Miss. (†39476) 256/G8
Piazza Armerina, Italy 34/E6
Piazzi (isl.), Chile 138/D9
Pibor (riv.), Sudan 111/F6
Pibor Post, Sudan 111/F6
Pibrac, Québec 172/F1
Pibroch, Alberta 182/D2
Pica, Chile 138/B2
Picabo, Idaho (83348) 220/D6
Picacho, Ariz. (85241) 198/D6
Picacho, N. Mex. (88343) 274/D5
Picadilly, Newf. 166/C4
Picara (pt.), Virgin Is. (U.S.) 161/B4
Picard (lake), Québec 172/D2
Picardville, Alberta 182/D2
Picardy (trad. prov.), France 29
Picatinny Arsenal, N.J. 273/D2
Picayune, Miss. (39466) 256/E9
Piceance (creek), Colo. 208/C3
Picher, Okla. (74360) 288/S1
Pichidegua, Chile 138/F5
Pichilemu, Chile 138/A10
Pichincha (prov.), Ecuador 128/C3
Pichis (riv.), Peru 128/E8
Pichones (cays), Honduras 154/F3
Pichucalco, Mexico 150/N8
Pickard, Ind. (†46069) 227/E4
Pickaway (co.), Ohio 284/D6
Pickaway, W. Va. (24964) 312/E7
Pick City, N. Dak. (†58545) 282/G5
Pickens (co.), Ala. 195/B4
Pickens, Ark. (71662) 202/H6
Pickens (co.), Georgia 217/D2
Pickens, Miss. (39146) 256/E5
Pickens, Okla. (74752) 288/S6
Pickens (co.), S.C. 296/B2
Pickens, S.C. (29671) 296/B2
Pickens, W. Va. (26230) 312/F5
Pickensville, Ala. (†35447) 195/B4
Pickerel (lake), Conn. 210/F2
Pickerel (lake), Manitoba 179/C2
Pickerel, Wis. (54465) 317/J5
Pickering, England 13/G3
Pickering, Mo. (64476) 261/C2
Pickering, Ontario 177/K4
Pickerington, Ohio (43147) 284/E6
Pickersgill, Guyana 131/B2
Pickert, N. Dak. (†58230) 282/P5
Pickett (co.), Tenn. 237/M7
Pickett, Wis. (54964) 317/J8
Pickford, Mich. (49774) 250/E2
Pickle Lake, Ontario 175/C2
Pickrell, Nebr. (68422) 264/H4
Pickstown, S. Dak. (57367) 298/M7
Pickton, Texas (75471) 303/J5
Pickwick (lake), Ala. 195/B1
Pickwick, Minn. (†55948) 255/G7
Pickwick (lake), Miss. 256/H1
Pickwick (lake), Tenn. 237/E11
Pickwick Dam, Tenn. (38365) 237/E10
Pico (isl.), Portugal 33/C1
Pico (peak), Vt. 268/B4
Pico Rivera, Calif. (90660) 204/C10
Picos, Brazil 132/F4
Picos, Brazil 120/E3
Picota, Peru 128/D6
Pico Truncado, Argentina 143/C6
Pictograph (rocks), Ariz. 198/B5
Picton (isl.), Argentina 143/C8
Picton (isl.), Chile 138/F11
Picton, N.S. Wales 97/F4
Picton, N. Zealand 100/D4
Picton, Ontario 177/G3
Picton (mt.), Tasmania 99/C5
Pictou (co.), Nova Scotia 168/F3
Pictou, Nova Scotia 168/F3
Pictou (harb.), Nova Scotia 168/F3
Pictou (isl.), Nova Scotia 168/F3
Pictou Landing, Nova Scotia 168/F3
Picture Butte, Alberta 182/D5
Pictured Rocks (cliff), Mich. 250/C2
Pictured Rocks Nat'l Lakeshore, Mich. 250/C2
Picture Rocks, Pa. (17762) 294/J3
Pidurutalagala (mt.), Sri Lanka 68/E7
Pie, W. Va. (25689) 312/B7
Piedade, Brazil 135/C3
Piedade do Rio Grande, Brazil 135/D2
Piedecuesta, Colombia 126/D4
Piedmont, Ala. (36272) 195/G3
Piedmont, Calif. (94611) 204/J2
Piedmont, Georgia (†30204) 217/D4
Piedmont (reg.), Italy 34/A2
Piedmont, Kansas (67122) 232/F4
Piedmont, Mo. (63957) 261/L8
Piedmont, Ohio (43983) 284/H5

Plainview, Ark. (72857) 202/D4
Plain View, Iowa (†52773) 229/M5
Plainview, Minn. (55964) 255/F6
Plainview, Nebr. (68769) 264/G2
Plainview, N.Y. (11803) 276/R
Plainview, S. Dak. (57771) 298/E4
Plainview, Texas (79072) 303/C3
Plainville○, Conn. (06062) 210/D2
Plainville, Georgia (30733) 217/C2
Plainville, Ill. (62365) 222/B4
Plainville, Ind. (47568) 227/C7
Plainville, Kansas (67663) 232/C2
Plainville○, Mass. (02762) 249/J4
Plainwell, Mich. (49080) 250/D6
Plaisance, Haiti 158/C5
Plaisance, Québec 172/B4
Plaisted, Maine (04767) 243/F1
Plaistow○, N.H. (03865) 268/E6
Plaju, Indonesia 85/D6
Plamondon, Alberta 182/D2
Plana (cays), Bahamas 156/D2
Planá, Czech. 41/B2
Planada, Calif. (95365) 204/E6
Planeta Rica, Colombia 126/C3
Plánice, Czech. 41/B2
Plankinton, S. Dak. (57368) 298/N6
Plano, Ill. (60545) 222/E2
Plano, Iowa (52581) 229/G7
Plano, Texas (75074) 303/G1
Plant, Tenn. (†37054) 237/F9
Plantagenet, Ontario 177/K2
Plantation, Fla. (33317) 212/B4
Plantation (key), Fla. 212/F7
Plantation, Ky. (†40201) 237/K1
Plant City, Fla. (33566) 212/D3
Plantersville, Ala. (36758) 195/E5
Plantersville, Miss. (38862) 256/G2
Plantersville, S.C. (29441) 296/J4
Plantsite, Ariz. (†85540) 198/F5
Plantsville, Conn. (06479) 210/D2
Plaquemine, La. (70764) 238/J2
Plaquemines (par.), La. 238/L8
Plasencia, Spain 33/C2
Plaster City, Calif. (92269) 204/K11
Plaster Rock, New Bruns. 170/C2
Plastun, U.S.S.R. 48/O5
Plasy, Czech. 41/B2
Plat, Wis. (†53017) 317/K1
Plata (riv.) 2/G7
Plata, Río de la (est.), Argentina 143/E4
Plata (riv.), P. Rico 161/D2
Plata, La (riv.), Uruguay 145/B5
Platanal, Venezuela 124/F6
Platanilla, C. Rica 154/F6
Platea, Pa. (†16417) 294/B2
Plateau (creek), Colo. 208/C4
Plateau (state), Nigeria 106/F7
Plateau, Nova Scotia 168/H2
Plateau City, Colo. (†81624) 208/D4
Plate Cove, Newf. 166/D2
Platen, Kapp (pt.), Norway 18/D1
Platina, Calif. (96076) 204/B3
Platinum, Alaska (99651) 196/F3
Platner, Colo. (†80743) 208/N2
Plato, Colombia 126/C3
Plato, Minn. (55370) 255/D6
Plato, Mo. (65552) 261/H8
Plato, Sask. 181/C4
Platoro (res.), Colo. 208/F8
Platte (riv.), Iowa 229/D8
Platte (lake), Mich. 250/C4
Platte (co.), Mo. 261/C4
Platte (riv.), Mo. 261/C3
Platte (riv.), Nebr. 146/J5
Platte (riv.), Nebr. 188/G2
Platte (co.), Nebr. 264/G3
Platte (riv.), Nebr. 264/E4
Platte, S. Dak. (57369) 298/M7
Platte (lake), S. Dak. 298/M6
Platte (co.), Wyo. 319/H4
Platte Center, Nebr. (68653) 264/G3
Platte City, Mo. (64079) 261/C4
Plattenville, La. (70393) 238/K4
Platter, Okla. (74753) 288/O7
Platteville, Colo. (80651) 208/K2
Platteville, Wis. (53818) 317/F10
Platte Woods, Mo. (†64152) 261/O5
Platt Nat'l Park, Okla. 288/N6
Plattsburg, Mo. (64477) 261/D3
Plattsburgh, N.Y. (12901) 276/O1
Plattsburgh A.F.B., N.Y. 276/N1
Plattsmouth, Nebr. (68048) 264/J3
Plattsville, Ontario 177/D4
Plau, E. Germany 22/E2
Plaucheville, La. (71362) 238/G5
Plauen, E. Germany 22/E3
Plauersee (lake), E. Germany 22/E2
Plav, Yugoslavia 45/D4
Plaviņas, U.S.S.R. 53/C2
Playa (pt.), Guyana 131/B1
Playa Azul, Mexico 150/H7
Playa Bonita, C. Rica 154/E6
Playa de Fajardo, P. Rico 161/F1
Playa de Humacao, P. Rico 161/F2
Playa Grande, Nicaragua 154/D4
Playas, Ecuador 128/B4
Playas (lake), N. Mex. 274/A7
Playón Chico, Panama 154/H6
Playón Grande, Panama 154/H6
Plaza, N. Dak. (58771) 282/G3
Plaza, Wash. (99028) 310/H3
Plaza Huincul, Argentina 143/B4
Pleasant (isl.), Alaska 196/M1
Pleasant (lake), Ariz. 198/C5
Pleasant, Ind. (†47043) 227/G7
Pleasant (lake), Maine 243/H5
Pleasant (lake), Maine 243/E3
Pleasant (lake), Maine 243/G3
Pleasant (riv.), Maine 243/H6
Pleasant (mt.), New Bruns. 170/D3
Pleasant (lake), N.Y. 276/M4
Pleasant (bay), Nova Scotia 168/H2
Pleasant Bay, Nova Scotia 168/H2
Pleasant City, Ohio (43772) 284/G6
Pleasant Dale, Nebr. (68423) 264/G4
Pleasantdale, Sask. 181/G3
Pleasant Gap, Ala. (†36272) 195/H3
Pleasant Gap, Pa. (16823) 294/G4
Pleasant Green, Mo. (†65276) 261/F5
Pleasant Grove, Ala. (35127) 195/D4
Pleasant Grove, Calif. (95668) 204/B8
Pleasant Grove, Miss. (38657) 256/D2
Pleasant Grove, N.J. (†07865) 273/D2
Pleasant Grove, Utah (84062) 304/C3
Pleasant Hill, Ala. (†36701) 195/E6
Pleasant Hill, Calif. (94523) 204/K2
Pleasant Hill, Ill. (62366) 222/C4
Pleasant Hill, La. (71065) 238/C3
Pleasant Hill, Miss. (†38651) 256/E1
Pleasant Hill, Mo. (64080) 261/D5
Pleasant Hill, N.C. (27866) 281/O1
Pleasant Hill, Ohio (45359) 284/B5
Pleasant Hill, S.C. (†29058) 296/F2
Pleasant Hill, Tenn. (38578) 237/L9
Pleasant Hills, Md. (†21087) 245/N3
Pleasant Hills, Pa. (15236) 294/B7
Pleasant Hope, Mo. (65725) 261/F8
Pleasant Island, Maine (†04964) 243/B5
Pleasant Lake, Ind. (46779) 227/H1
Pleasant Lake, Mass. (†02645) 249/O6
Pleasant Lake, Minn. (†56301) 255/D5
Pleasant Lake, N. Dak. (58364) 282/L3
Pleasant Lane, S.C. (†29824) 296/D4
Pleasant Mills, Ind. (46780) 227/H3
Pleasant Mound, Ill. (†62284) 222/D5
Pleasant Mount, Pa. (18453) 294/M2
Pleasanton, Calif. (94566) 204/L2
Pleasanton, Iowa (50224) 229/F7
Pleasanton, Kansas (66075) 232/H3
Pleasanton, Nebr. (68866) 264/E4
Pleasanton, N. Mex. (†88039) 274/A5
Pleasanton, Texas (78064) 303/F9
Pleasant Plain, Iowa (†52540) 229/K6
Pleasant Plain, Ohio (45162) 284/B7
Pleasant Plains, Ark. (72568) 202/G2
Pleasant Plains, Ill. (62677) 222/D4
Pleasant Point, N. Zealand 100/C6
Pleasant Pond, Maine (†04925) 243/D5
Pleasant Prairie, Wis. (53158) 317/L10
Pleasant Ridge, Mich. (48069) 250/B6
Pleasants (co.), W. Va. 312/D4
Pleasant Shade, Tenn. (37145) 237/K8
Pleasant Valley, Conn. (06063) 210/C1
Pleasant Valley, Md. (†21157) 245/L2
Pleasant Valley, Mo. (†64836) 261/R5
Pleasant Valley, Oreg. (†97814) 291/K3
Pleasant Valley (creek), S. Dak. 298/B6
Pleasant Valley, Va. (22848) 307/L4
Pleasant View, Colo. (81331) 208/B7
Pleasant View, Ill. (†62681) 222/C3
Pleasant View, Ky. (40769) 237/N7
Pleasant View, Tenn. (37146) 237/G8
Pleasant View, Utah (†84401) 304/B2
Pleasantville, Ind. (†47838) 227/C7
Pleasantville, Iowa (50225) 229/G6
Pleasantville, N.J. (08232) 273/D5
Pleasantville, N.Y. (10570) 276/N8
Pleasantville, Ohio (43148) 284/F6
Pleasantville (Alum Bank), Pa. (†15521) 294/E5
Pleasantville, Pa. (16341) 294/C2
Pleasantville, Tenn. (37147) 237/F9
Pleasure Beach, Conn. (†06385) 210/G3
Pleasure Ridge Park, Ky. (40258) 237/J4
Pleasureville, Ky. (40057) 237/L4
Pleiku, Vietnam 72/E4
Plenița, Romania 45/F3
Plenty (bay), N. Zealand 100/F2
Plenty, Sask. 181/C4
Plenty (riv.), Victoria 97/J4
Plenty (riv.), Victoria 88/L6
Plenty River Mine, North. Terr. 93/D7
Plentywood, Mont. (59254) 262/M2
Plesetsk, U.S.S.R. 52/F2
Plessis, N.Y. (13675) 276/J2
Plessisville, Québec 172/F3
Plessur (riv.), Switzerland 39/J3
Pleszew, Poland 47/C3
Pletcher, Ala. (†36750) 195/E5
Plétipi (lake), Que. 162/J5
Plétipi (lake), Québec 174/C2
Plettenberg (bay), S. Africa 118/C6
Plettenberg, W. Germany 22/C3
Pleven, Bulgaria 7/G4
Pleven, Bulgaria 45/G4
Plevna, Ala. (†35761) 195/F1
Plevna, Ind. (†46901) 227/E3
Plevna, Kansas (67568) 232/D4
Plevna, Mo. (63464) 261/H3
Plevna, Mont. (59344) 262/M4
Plevna, Ontario 177/H3
Pliny, W. Va. (25158) 312/B5
Pljevlja, Yugoslavia 45/D4
Ploče, Yugoslavia 45/C4
Płock (prov.), Poland 47/D2
Płock, Poland 47/D2
Plockton, Scotland 15/C3
Ploërmel, France 28/B4
Ploiești, Romania 45/H3
Ploiești, Romania 7/G4
Plomárion, Greece 45/H6
Plomb du Cantal (mt.), France 28/E5
Plombières, Belgium 27/F7
Plomer (pt.), N.S. Wales 97/G2
Plomosa (mts.), Ariz. 198/A5
Plön, W. Germany 22/D1
Płonia (riv.), Poland 47/B2
Płońsk, Poland 47/E2
Plovdiv, Bulgaria 7/G4
Plovdiv, Bulgaria 45/G4
Plover, Iowa (50573) 229/D3
Plover, Wis. (54467) 317/G7
Pluckemin, N.J. (07978) 273/D2
Plum (riv.), Ill. 222/C1
Plum (creek), Manitoba 179/B5
Plum (lake), Manitoba 179/B5
Plum (isl.), Mass. 249/L2
Plum (isl.), N.Y. 276/R8
Plum, Pa. (15239) 294/C5
Plumas (co.), Calif. 204/E4
Plumas, Manitoba 179/D4
Plumber (creek), Utah 304/C2
Plum Branch, S.C. (29845) 296/C4
Plum City, Wis. (54761) 317/B6
Plum Coulee, Manitoba 179/E5
Plumerville, Ark. (72127) 202/E3
Plummer, Idaho (83851) 220/B2
Plummer, Ind. (†47424) 227/C7
Plummer, Minn. (56748) 255/B3
Plummers Landing, Ky. (41081) 237/P4
Plum Point, Md. (†20639) 245/N6
Plum Springs, Ky. (†42101) 237/J7
Plumsteadville, Pa. (18949) 294/M5
Plum Tree, Ind. (†46792) 227/G3
Plumtree, Zimbabwe 118/D4
Plumville, Pa. (16246) 294/D4
Plumwood, Ohio (†43140) 284/D6
Plunge, U.S.S.R. 53/B3
Plunkett, Sask. 181/F4
Plunkettville, Okla. (†74963) 288/S6
Plush, Oreg. (97637) 291/H5
Plymouth (cap.), 156/F3
Plymouth, Calif. (95669) 204/C8
Plymouth○, Conn. (06782) 210/C2
Plymouth, England 7/D3
Plymouth, England 10/E5
Plymouth, England 13/C7
Plymouth (sound), England 13/C7
Plymouth, Fla. (32768) 212/E3
Plymouth, Ill. (62367) 222/C3
Plymouth, Ind. (46563) 227/E2
Plymouth (co.), Iowa 229/A3
Plymouth, Iowa (50464) 229/G2
Plymouth○, Maine (04969) 243/E6
Plymouth (co.), Mass. 249/L5
Plymouth, Mass. (02360) 249/M5
Plymouth○, Mass. (02360) 249/M5
Plymouth (bay), Mass. 249/M5
Plymouth, Mich. (*48170) 250/F6
Plymouth, Minn. (†55441) 255/G5
Plymouth, Nebr. (68424) 264/G4
Plymouth, N.H. (03264) 268/D4
Plymouth○, N.H. (03264) 268/D4
Plymouth, N.C. (27962) 281/R3
Plymouth, Ohio (44865) 284/E4
Plymouth, Pa. (18651) 294/E7
Plymouth, Utah (84330) 304/B2
Plymouth○, Vt. (05056) 268/B4
Plymouth, Wash. (99346) 310/F5
Plymouth, W. Va. (†25011) 312/C5
Plymouth, Wis. (53073) 317/L8
Plymouth Union, Vt. (†05056) 268/B4
Plympton○, Mass. (02367) 249/L5
Plympton, Nova Scotia 168/C4
Plynlimon (mt.), Wales 13/D5
Plzeň, Czech. 7/F4
Plzeň, Czech. 41/B2
Pniel, S. Africa 118/F6
Pniewy, Poland 47/C2
Po (riv.), Italy 7/E4
Po (riv.), Italy 34/C2
Po, Upper Volta 106/D6
Po (riv.), Va. 307/N4
Poá, Brazil 135/C3
Poatina, Tasmania 99/C3
Pobeda (peak), China 77/A3
Pobeda (peak), U.S.S.R. 48/J5
Población, Chile 138/F5
Pobla de Segur, Spain 33/G1
Poca, W. Va. (25159) 312/C6
Pocahontas, Alberta 182/B3
Pocahontas, Ark. (72455) 202/H1
Pocahontas, Ill. (62275) 222/D5
Pocahontas (co.), Iowa 229/D3
Pocahontas, Iowa (50574) 229/D3
Pocahontas, Miss. (39072) 256/D6
Pocahontas, Mo. (63779) 261/N8
Pocahontas, Tenn. (38061) 237/D10
Pocahontas, Va. (24635) 307/F6
Pocahontas (co.), W. Va. 312/F6
Pocasset, Mass. (02559) 249/M6
Pocasset, Okla. (73079) 288/L4
Pocatalico (riv.), W. Va. 312/C5
Pocatello, Idaho 146/G5
Pocatello, Idaho (*83201) 220/F7
Pocatello, Idaho 188/D2
Počátky, Czech. 41/C2
Pochep, U.S.S.R. 52/D4
Pöchlarn, Austria 41/C2
Pocklington, England 13/G4
Pocoata, Bolivia 136/B6
Poções, Brazil 132/F6
Pocola, Okla. (74902) 288/T4
Pocologan, New Bruns. 170/D3
Pocomoke (riv.), Md. 245/S8
Pocomoke (sound), Md. 245/P9
Pocomoke (sound), Va. 307/S5
Pocomoke City, Md. (21851) 245/R8
Pocomoonshine (lake), Maine 243/H5
Pocona, Bolivia 136/C5
Poconé, Brazil 132/B7
Pocono (mts.), Pa. 294/M3
Pocono Lake, Pa. (18347) 294/L3
Pocono Pines, Pa. (18350) 294/M3
Poços de Caldas, Brazil 120/E5
Poços de Caldas, Brazil 135/C2
Poços de Caldas, Brazil 132/E8
Pocotalago, Georgia (†30633) 217/F2
Pocotalico, W. Va. (†25301) 312/C6
Pocotaligo (riv.), S.C. 296/G4
Pocotopaug (lake), Conn. 210/E2
Pocpo, Bolivia 136/C6
Podbořany, Czech. 41/B1
Poděbrady, Czech. 41/C1
Podol'sk, U.S.S.R. 7/H3
Podol'sk, U.S.S.R. 52/E3
Podol'sk, U.S.S.R. 48/D4
Podor, Senegal 106/B5
Podporozh'ye, U.S.S.R. 52/D2
Podunk (riv.), Conn. 210/E1
Poe, Alberta 182/D3
Poe, Ind. (†46802) 227/G3
Poel (isl.), E. Germany 22/D1
Poenari Burchi, Romania 45/G3
Poge (cape), Mass. 249/N7
Poggibonsi, Italy 34/C3
Pogradec, Albania 45/E5
Pohakuloa (pt.), Hawaii 218/H2
P'ohang, S. Korea 81/D5
Pohatcong (creek), N.J. 273/C2
Pohénégamook, Québec 172/H2
Pohjois-Karjala (prov.), Finland 18/Q5
Pohořelice, Czech. 41/D2
Pohsien (Bo Xian), China 77/J5
Poiana Mare, Romania 45/F4
Poigan (lake), Québec 172/A2
Poinsett (co.), Ark. 202/J2
Poinsett (lake), Fla. 212/F3
Poinsett (lake), S. Dak. 298/P4
Point, La. (†71234) 238/F1
Point (lake), N.W. Terrs. 187/G3
Point, Texas (75472) 303/J5
Point Alexander, Ontario 177/G1
Point Arena, Calif. (95468) 204/B5
Point au Fer (isl.), La. 238/H8
Point au Fer (pt.), La. 238/H8
Point Baker, Alaska (99927) 196/M2
Point Cedar, Ark. (†71921) 202/D5
Point Clear, Ala. (36564) 195/C10
Point Comfort, Texas (77978) 303/H9
Point Cross, Nova Scotia 168/G2
Point de Bute, New Bruns. 170/F3
Point du Bois, Manitoba 179/G4
Pointe-à-la-Croix, Québec 172/C2
Pointe-à-la-Frégate, Québec 172/D1
Pointe-à-la-Garde, Québec 172/B2
Pointe a la Hache, La. (70082) 238/L7
Pointe-à-Pitre, Guadeloupe 161/B6
Pointe-à-Pitre, Guadeloupe 156/G3
Pointe à Raquette, Haiti 158/B6
Pointe au Baril Station, Ontario 177/D2
Pointe-au-Chêne, Québec 172/C4
Pointe-au-Père, Québec 172/J1
Pointe-au-Pic, Québec 172/G2
Pointe Aux Barques, Mich. (48467) 250/G4
Pointe-aux-Outardes, Québec 172/A1
Pointe Aux Pins, Mich. (49775) 250/E3
Pointe-aux-Trembles, Québec 172/J4
Pointe-Bleue, Québec 172/E1
Pointe-Calumet, Québec 172/G4
Pointe-Claire, Québec 172/H4
Pointe Coupee (par.), La. 238/G5
Pointe du Bout, Martinique 161/C6
Pointe-du-Chêne, New Bruns. 170/F2
Pointe-du-Lac, Québec 172/E3
Pointe-du-Moulin, Québec 172/H4
Point Edward, Ontario 177/B4
Pointe-Gatineau, Québec 172/B4
Pointe-Lebel, Québec 172/A1
Pointe-Noire, Congo 102/D5
Pointe-Noire, Congo 115/B4
Pointe-Noire, Guadeloupe 161/A6
Pointe-Sapin, New Bruns. 170/F2
Pointe-Verte, New Bruns. 170/E1
Point Fortin, Trin. & Tob. 161/A11
Point Harbor, N.C. (27964) 281/T2
Point Hope, Alaska 188/C5
Point Hope, Alaska (99766) 196/E1
Point Isabel, Ind. (†46928) 227/F4
Point La Haye, Newf. 166/D2
Point Lance, Newf. 166/C2
Point Lay, Alaska (†99723) 196/F1
Point Leamington, Newf. 166/C4
Point Marion, Pa. (15474) 294/C6
Point Mugu Pacific Missile Test Center, Calif. 204/F9
Point of Rocks, Md. (21777) 245/J3
Point of Rocks, Wyo. (82942) 319/D4
Point Pelee, Ontario 177/B6
Point Pelee Nat'l Park, Ontario 177/B5
Point Pleasant, Mo. (63873) 261/O10
Point Pleasant, N.J. (08742) 273/E3
Point Pleasant, Ohio (45163) 284/B8
Point Pleasant, Pa. (18950) 294/N5
Point Pleasant, W. Va. (25550) 312/B5
Point Pleasant Beach, N.J. (08742) 273/E3
Point Reyes Nat'l Seashore, Calif. 204/H1
Point Reyes Station, Calif. (94956) 204/H1
Point Roberts, Wash. (98281) 310/B2
Points, W. Va. (25437) 312/J4
Point Salvation Aboriginal Reserve, W. Australia 88/C5
Point Salvation Aboriginal Res., W. Australia 92/D5
Point Tupper, Nova Scotia 168/G3
Point Verde, Newf. 166/C2
Point Washington, Fla. (32454) 212/C6
Poipu, Hawaii (†96756) 218/C2
Poison (creek), Wyo. 319/E2
Poison Spider (creek), Wyo. 319/F3
Poisson Blanc (lake), Québec 172/B4
Poissons (riv.), Newf. 166/A3
Poitiers, France 7/E4
Poitiers, France 28/D4
Poitou (trad. prov.) France 29
Pojo, Bolivia 136/C5
Pojoaque, N. Mex. (†87501) 274/C3
Pokaran, India 68/C3
Pokataroo, N.S. Wales 97/E1
Pokegama (lake), Minn. 255/E3
Pokemouche (riv.), New Bruns. 170/E1
Pokesudie (isl.), New Bruns. 170/F1
Pokhara, Nepal 68/E3
Pokhvistnevo, U.S.S.R. 52/H4
Poko, Zaire 115/E3
Pokrovsk, U.S.S.R. 48/N3
Pola, Philippines 82/C4
Pola (Pula), Yugoslavia 45/A3
Polacca, Ariz. (86042) 198/E3
Polacca Wash (dry riv.), Ariz. 198/E3
Pola de Lena, Spain 33/C1
Pola de Siero, Spain 33/D1
Polanco del Yi, Uruguay 145/D4
Poland 2/K3
Poland 7/F3
POLAND 47
Poland (riv.), Conn. 210/C2
Poland, Ind. (47868) 227/C6
Poland, Maine (04273) 243/C7
Poland○, Maine (04273) 243/C7
Poland, N.Y. (13431) 276/L4
Poland, Ohio (44514) 284/J3
Poland Spring, Maine (04274) 243/C7
Polar, Wis. (54418) 317/H5
Polar Bear Prov. Park, Ontario 175/D2
Polaris, Mont. (59746) 262/C5
Polatlı, Turkey 63/E3
Polatlı, Turkey 59/B2
Połczyn-Zdrój, Poland 47/C2
Polebridge, Mont. (59928) 262/B2
Pol-e Khomri, Afghanistan 68/B1
Pol-e Khomri, Afghanistan 59/J2
Polgár, Hungary 41/F3
Polgárdi, Hungary 41/E3
Poli, Cameroon 115/B2
Policastro (gulf), Italy 34/E5
Police, Poland 47/B2
Polička, Czech. 41/D2
Poligny, France 28/F4
Poligus, U.S.S.R. 48/K3
Polikastron, Greece 45/F5
Polikhnitos, Greece 45/G6
Polillo, Philippines 82/D3
Polillo (isl.), Philippines 85/G3
Polillo (isl.), Philippines 82/C3
Polillo (str.), Philippines 82/C3
Polis, Cyprus 63/E5
Políyiros, Greece 45/F5
Polk (co.), Ark. 202/B5
Polk (co.), Fla. 212/E4
Polk (co.), Georgia 217/B3
Polk (co.), Iowa 229/F5
Polk (co.), Minn. 255/B3
Polk (co.), Mo. 261/F7
Polk, Mo. (65727) 261/F7
Polk (co.), Nebr. 264/G3
Polk, Nebr. (68654) 264/G3
Polk (co.), N.C. 281/E4
Polk, Ohio (44866) 284/F4
Polk (co.), Oreg. 291/D3
Polk, Pa. (16342) 294/C3
Polk (co.), Tenn. 237/N10
Polk (co.), Texas 303/K7
Polk (co.), Wis. 317/B5
Polk City, Fla. (33868) 212/E3
Polk City, Iowa (50226) 229/F5
Polkowice, Poland 47/C3
Polkton, N.C. (28135) 281/J4
Polkville, Miss. (39118) 256/E6
Polkville, N.C. (28136) 281/F4
Pollaphuca (res.), Ireland 17/J5
Pollard, Ala. (†36441) 195/D8
Pollard, Ark. (72456) 202/K1
Pollards Point, Newf. 166/C4
Pöllau, Austria 41/C3
Pollensa, Spain 33/H3
Pollett (riv.), New Bruns. 170/E3
Pollett River, New Bruns. 170/E3
Pollock, Idaho (83547) 220/B4
Pollock, La. (71467) 238/F3
Pollock, Mo. (63560) 261/F2
Pollock, S. Dak. (57648) 298/J2
Pollock Pines, Calif. (95726) 204/E5
Pollocksville, N.C. (28573) 281/P5
Pollockville, Alberta 182/E4
Polmak, Norway 18/Q2
Polná, Czech. 41/C2
Polo, Dom. Rep. 158/D6
Polo, Ill. (61074) 222/D1
Polo, Mo. (64671) 261/D3
Polomka, Czech. 41/E2
Polonia, Chile 138/G6
Polonia, Wis. (†54423) 317/H6
Polonio, Uruguay 145/F5
Polonio (cape), Uruguay 145/F5
Polonnaruwa, Sri Lanka 68/E7
Polonnoye, U.S.S.R. 52/C4
Polotsk, U.S.S.R. 52/C3
Polperro, England 13/C7
Polson, Mont. (59860) 262/B3
Poltava, U.S.S.R. 7/H4
Poltava, U.S.S.R. 52/D5
Poltava, U.S.S.R. 48/D5
Poltimore, Québec 172/B4
Põltsamaa, U.S.S.R. 53/D1
Polvadera, N. Mex. (87828) 274/B4
Polyarnyy, U.S.S.R. 52/D1
Polyarnyy, U.S.S.R. 48/D3
Polynesia (reg.), Pacific 87/K7
Pomabamba, Peru 128/D7
Pomaire, Chile 138/F4
Pomán, Argentina 143/C2
Pomaria, S.C. (29126) 296/E3
Pombal, Brazil 132/G4
Pombal, Portugal 33/B3
Pomerania (reg.), E. Germany 22/E2
Pomeranian (bay), E. Germany 22/F1
Pomeranian (bay), Poland 47/B1
Pomerene, Ariz. (85627) 198/E6
Pomeroon (riv.), Guyana 131/B2
Pomeroy, Iowa (50575) 229/D3
Pomeroy, N. Ireland 17/H2
Pomeroy, Ohio (45769) 284/G7
Pomeroy, Wash. (99347) 310/H4
Pomezia, Italy 34/F7
Pomfret○, Conn. (06258) 210/H1
Pomfret, Md. (20675) 245/L6
Pomfret○, Vt. (†05067) 268/B4
Pomfret Center, Conn. (06259) 210/H1
Pomme de Terre (riv.), Minn. 255/C5
Pomme de Terre (lake), Mo. 261/E7
Pomona, Calif. 188/C4
Pomona, Calif. (*91766) 204/D10
Pomona, Kansas (66076) 232/G3
Pomona (lake), Kansas 232/G3
Pomona, Md. (†21620) 245/O4
Pomona, Mo. (65789) 261/J9
Pomona, N.J. (08240) 273/D5
Pomona Park, Fla. (32081) 212/E2
Pomonkey, Md. (†20640) 245/K6
Pomorie, Bulgaria 45/H4
Pomos (pt.), Cyprus 63/E5
Pompano Beach, Fla. (*33060) 212/F5
Pompanoosuc, Vt. (†05078) 268/C4
Pompéia, Brazil 135/A3
Pompeii (ruins), Italy 34/E4
Pompeii, Mich. (48874) 250/E5
Pomperaug, Conn. (†06798) 210/C2
Pomperaug (riv.), Conn. 210/C3
Pompey, N.Y. (13138) 276/J5
Pompeys Pillar, Mont. (59064) 262/J5
Pompton (lake), N.J. 273/B1
Pompton Lakes, N.J. (07442) 273/A1
Pompton Plains, N.J. (07444) 273/B1
Pomquet, Nova Scotia 168/G3
Pomy, Switzerland 39/C3
Ponape (isl.), Micronesia 87/F5
Ponass (lakes), Sask. 181/H3
Ponca, Ark. (72670) 202/D1
Ponca, Nebr. (68770) 264/H2
Ponca (creek), S. Dak. 298/L7
Ponca City, Okla. 188/G3
Ponca City, Okla. (74601) 288/M1
Ponce (dist.), P. Rico 161/C2
Ponce, P. Rico 161/C3
Ponce, P. Rico 156/F1
Ponce de Leon, Fla. (32455) 212/C6
Ponce de Leon (bay), Fla. 212/E6
Ponce Inlet, Fla. (†32019) 212/F2
Poncha Springs, Colo. (81242) 208/G6
Ponchatoula, La. (70454) 238/N2
Pond (pt.), Conn. 210/C4
Pond (riv.), Ky. 237/G6
Pond, Miss. (†39669) 256/B8
Pond, Mo. (†63038) 261/M3
Pond (inlet), N.W. Terrs. 187/L2
Pond Creek, Okla. (73766) 288/L1
Pond Eddy, Pa. (†12770) 294/N3
Pondera (co.), Mont. 262/D2
Ponderay, Idaho (83852) 220/B1
Ponderosa, N. Mex. (87044) 274/C3
Pond Fork (riv.), W. Va. 312/C6
Pondicherry (terr.), India 68/E6
Pondicherry, India 68/E6
Pond Inlet, Canada 4/B13
Pond Inlet, N.W.T. 162/J1
Pond Inlet, N.W. Terrs. 187/L2
Pondoland (reg.), S. Africa 118/D6
Pondosa, Calif. (96007) 204/D2
Ponds (isl.), Newf. 166/C3
Poneloya, Nicaragua 154/D4
Ponemah, Minn. (56666) 255/D2
Ponemah, N.H. (†03055) 268/D6
Poneto, Ind. (46781) 227/G3
Ponferrada, Spain 33/C1
Pongara (pt.), Gabon 115/A3
Ponhook (lake), Nova Scotia 168/D4
Poniatowa, Poland 47/E3
Ponnani, India 68/D6
Ponoka, Alberta 182/D3
Ponomarevka, U.S.S.R. 52/H4
Ponorogo, Indonesia 85/J2
Ponoy, U.S.S.R. 48/E3
Ponoy, U.S.S.R. 52/F1
Ponoy (riv.), U.S.S.R. 52/E1
Pons, France 28/C5
Ponset, Conn. (†06441) 210/E3
Ponsford, Minn. (56575) 255/C4
Pont-à-Celles, Belgium 27/E8
Ponta Delgada (dist.), Portugal 33/D2
Ponta Delgada, Portugal 33/C2
Ponta de Pedras, Brazil 132/D3
Ponta do Sol, Portugal 33/A2
Ponta Grossa, Brazil 120/D5
Ponta Grossa, Brazil 132/D9
Ponta Grossa, Brazil 135/B4
Pont-à-Mousson, France 28/G3
Ponta Porã, Brazil 132/C8
Ponta Porã, Paraguay 144/E3
Pontarlier, France 28/G4
Pontbriand, Québec 172/F3
Pont Canavese, Italy 34/A2
Pontchartrain (lake), U.S. 188/J5
Pontchartrain (lake), La. 238/O3
Pontchartrain Causeway, La. 238/O3
Pontecorvo, Italy 34/D4
Ponte de Sor, Portugal 33/C3
Ponte do Lima, Portugal 33/B2
Ponteix, Sask. 181/D6
Ponteland, England 13/H3
Ponte Nova, Brazil 132/F8
Ponte Nova, Brazil 135/E2
Pontevedra, Philippines 82/D5
Pontevedra (prov.), Spain 33/B1
Pontevedra, Spain 33/B1
Ponte Vedra Beach, Fla. (32082) 212/E1
Pontgrave, New Bruns. 170/F1
Pontiac, Ill. (61764) 222/E3
Pontiac, Mich. 188/K2
Pontiac, Mich. (*48053) 250/F6
Pontiac, Mo. (65729) 261/G9
Pontiac (co.), Québec 172/A3
Pontiac (county), Québec 174/B3
Pontiac, R.I. (†02887) 249/J6
Pontiac, S.C. (†29045) 296/F3
Pontianak, Indonesia 85/D6
Pontianak, Indonesia 54/N10
Pontian Kechil, Malaysia 72/E5
Pontic (mts.), Turkey 59/C1
Pontic (mts.), Turkey 63/H2
Pontine (isls.), Italy 34/D4
Pontinia, Italy 34/D4
Pontivy, France 28/B3
Pont-l'Abbe, France 28/A4
Pont-Lafrance, New Bruns. 170/E1
Pont-Landry, New Bruns. 170/F1
Pont-l'Évêque, France 28/D3
Ponto da Divisão, Brazil 132/B5
Pontoise, France 28/E3
Pontoon Beach, Ill. (†62040) 222/A2
Pontoosuc, Ill. (†62330) 222/B3
Pontoosuc (lake), Mass. 249/A3
Pontorson, France 28/C3
Pontotoc (co.), Miss. 256/F2
Pontotoc, Miss. (38863) 256/G2
Pontotoc (co.), Okla. 288/N5
Pontotoc, Okla. (74863) 288/N6
Pontotoc, Texas (76869) 303/E7
Pontremoli, Italy 34/B2
Pontresina, Switzerland 39/J3
Pontrilas, Sask. 181/H2
Pont-Rouge, Québec 172/F3
Pontypool, Ontario 177/F3
Pontypool, Wales 13/B6
Pontypridd, Wales 13/A6
Pontypridd, Wales 10/E5
Pony, Mont. (59747) 262/E5
Pony (creek), Okla. 288/C1

Rangeley 433

Quay (co.), N. Mex. 274/F3
Quay, N. Mex. (88433) 274/F4
Quay, Okla. (†74085) 288/N2
Quchan, Iran 66/L2
Quchan, Iran 59/G2
Quealy, Wyo. (†82901) 319/C4
Queanbeyan, N. S. Wales 88/H7
Queanbeyan, N. S. Wales 97/E4
Québec (prov.) 162/J5
QUÉBEC 172
Québec, Canada 2/F3
Québec (prov.), Que. 146/L4
Québec (cap.), Que. 146/L5
Québec (cap.) Que. 162/J6
Québec (co.), Québec 172/F3
Québec (county), Québec 174/C3
Québec (cap.), Québec 172/H3
Québec (cap.), Québec 174/C3
Quebeck, Tenn. (38579) 237/K9
Quebracho, Uruguay 145/B2
Quebracho Coto, Argentina 143/D2
Quebrada de Alvarado, Chile 138/F2
Quebradillas, P. Rico 161/B1
Quechee, Vt. (05059) 268/C4
Quechisla, Bolivia 136/C7
Quecholac, Mexico 150/O2
Quecreek, Pa. (15555) 294/D5
Quedlinburg, E. Germany 22/D3
Queen (cape), N.W. Terrs. 187/L3
Queen, Pa. (16670) 294/E5
Queen Anne, Md. (21657) 245/O5
Queen Annes (co.), Md. 245/P4
Queenborough, England 13/H6
Queenborough, England 10/G5
Queen Charlotte (isls.), Br. Col. 146/E4
Queen Charlotte (isls.), Br. Col. 162/C5
Queen Charlotte, Br. Col. 184/A3
Queen Charlotte (isls.), Br. Col. 184/B3
Queen Charlotte (sound), Br. Col. 184/C4
Queen Charlotte (str.), Br. Col. 184/D5
Queen Charlotte (sound), N.W.T. 162/D5
Queen City, Mo. (63561) 261/H2
Queen City, Texas (75572) 303/L4
Queen Creek, Ariz. (85242) 198/D5
Queen Elizabeth (isls.), Canada 2/C2
Queen Elizabeth (isls.), Canada 4/B15
Queen Elizabeth (isls.), N.W.T. 146/G2
Queen Elizabeth (isls.), N.W.T. 162/M3
Queen Elizabeth (isls.), N.W. Terrs. 187/H1
Queen Mary Coast (reg.) 5/C5
Queen Maud (mts.) 5/A12
Queen Maud (gulf), N.W.T. 162/F2
Queen Maud (gulf), N.W. Terrs. 187/H3
Queen Maud Land (reg.), Ant. 2/K10
Queen Maud Land (reg.) 5/B1
Queens (sound), Br. Col. 184/C4
Queen's (co.), New Bruns. 170/D3
Queens (co.), N.Y. 276/N9
Queens (borough), N.Y. (*11101) 276/N9
Queens (chan.), N.W. Terrs. 187/J2
Queens (co.), Nova Scotia 168/C4
Queens (co.), Pr. Edward I. 168/E2
Queens, W. Va. (†26237) 312/F5
Queensberry (mt.), Scotland 15/E5
Queenscliff, Victoria 97/C6
Queensferry, Scotland 10/C1
Queensferry, Scotland 15/D1
Queen Shoals, W. Va. (†25045) 312/D6
Queensland, 88/G4
QUEENSLAND 95
Queensland (state), Australia 87/E8
Queensport, Nova Scotia 168/G3
Queenstown, Alberta 182/D4
Queenstown, Guyana 131/B2
Queenstown (Cóbh), Ireland 10/B5
Queenstown (Cóbh), Ireland 17/E8
Queenstown, Md. (21658) 245/O5
Queenstown, New Bruns. 170/D3
Queenstown, N. Zealand 100/B6
Queenstown, S. Africa 102/E8
Queenstown, S. Africa 118/D6
Queenstown, Tasmania 99/B4
Queenstown, Tasmania 88/H8
Queensville, Ind. (†47265) 227/F6
Queets, Wash. (†98331) 310/A3
Queets (riv.), Wash. 310/A3
Queilén, Chile 138/D4
Queimadas, Brazil 132/F5
Quela, Angola 115/C5
Quelimane, Mozambique 118/F3
Quelimane, Mozambique 102/F6
Quelpart (Cheju) (isl.), S. Korea 81/C7
Queluz, Portugal 33/A1
Quemado (pt.), Cuba 158/K4
Quemado, N. Mex. (87829) 274/A4
Quemado, Texas (78877) 303/D9
Quemado de Güines, Cuba 158/E1
Quemchi, Chile 138/D4
Quemoy (Jinmen) (isl.), China 77/J7
Quemú-Quemú, Argentina 143/D4
Quenemo, Kansas (66528) 232/G3
Quentin, Miss. (39647) 256/C8
Quepos, C. Rica 154/E6
Quequay Chico (riv.), Uruguay 145/B3
Quequay Grande (riv.), Uruguay 145/B3
Que Que, Zimbabwe 118/D3
Que Que, Zimbabwe 102/E6
Quequén, Argentina 143/E4
Querecotillo, Peru 128/B5
Querétaro (state), Mexico 150/J6
Querétaro, Mexico 146/J7
Querétaro, Mexico 150/J6
Quesada, Spain 33/E4
Queshan, China 77/H5
Quesnel, Br. Col. 162/D5
Quesnel (lake), Br. Col. 162/D5
Quesnel, Br. Col. 184/F4
Quesnel (lake), Br. Col. 184/G4
Quesnel (riv.), Br. Col. 184/F4
Quesnel (lake), Manitoba 179/G4
Questa, N. Mex. (87556) 274/D2
Queteña, Bolivia 136/B8
Quetico Prov. Park, Ontario 175/B3
Quetico Prov. Park, Ontario 177/G5
Quetta, Pakistan 54/H6
Quetta, Pakistan 59/J3
Quetta, Pakistan 68/B2
Queule, Chile 138/D2
Quevedo, Ecuador 128/C3
Quévy, Belgium 27/D8
Quezaltenango, Guatemala 154/B3
Quezaltepeque, Guatemala 154/C3
Quezon (prov.), Philippines 82/C3
Quibala, Angola 115/C6
Quibaxe, Angola 115/B5
Quibdó, Colombia 126/B5
Quiberon, France 28/B4
Quibor, Venezuela 124/D3
Quicacha, Peru 128/F10
Quick, Br. Col. 184/D3
Quick, W. Va. (25045) 312/D6
Quicksand, Ky. (41363) 237/P5
Quicksburg, Va. (22847) 307/L3
Quiebra Hacha, Cuba 158/B1
Quiévrain, Belgium 27/D8
Quigley, Alberta 182/E1
Quiindy, Paraguay 144/B5
Quijotoa, Ariz. (†85634) 198/C6
Quilalí, Nicaragua 154/E4
Quilán (cape), Chile 138/D4
Quilán (isl.), Chile 138/D5
Quilca, Peru 128/F11
Quilcene, Wash. (98376) 310/B3
Quilchena, Br. Col. 184/G5
Quilengues, Angola 115/B6
Quilicura, Chile 138/G3
Quill (lakes), Sask. 181/G4
Quillabamba, Peru 128/F9
Quillacas, Bolivia 136/B6
Quillacollo, Bolivia 136/B5
Quillacollo, Bolivia 120/C4
Quillagua, Chile 138/B3
Quillaicillo, Chile 138/A8
Quillan, France 28/E6
Quillayute Ind. Res., Wash. 310/A3
Quilleco, Chile 138/E1
Quill Lake, Sask. 181/G3
Quillota, Chile 138/F2
Quilon, India 68/D7
Quilpie, Queensland 88/G5
Quilpie, Queensland 95/C5
Quilpué, Chile 138/F2
Quimby, Iowa (51049) 229/B3
Quimby, Maine (04770) 243/F2
Quime, Bolivia 136/B5
Quimili, Argentina 143/D2
Quimper, France 28/A4
Quimperlé, France 28/B4
Quinault, Wash. (98575) 310/B3
Quinault (lake), Wash. 310/B3
Quinault (riv.), Wash. 310/A3
Quinault Ind. Res., Wash. 310/A3
Quinby, S.C. (†29501) 296/H3
Quinby, Va. (23423) 307/S5
Quinby (inlet), Va. 307/S6
Quince Mil, Peru 128/G9
Quincy, Calif. (95971) 204/E4
Quincy, Fla. (32351) 212/B1
Quincy, Ill. 188/H3
Quincy, Ill. (62301) 222/B4
Quincy, Ind. (47456) 227/D6
Quincy, Kansas (†66870) 232/F4
Quincy, Ky. (41166) 237/P3
Quincy, Mass. (02169) 249/D7
Quincy (bay), Mass. 249/D7
Quincy, Mich. (49082) 250/E7
Quincy, Miss. (†38848) 256/H3
Quincy, Mo. (65735) 261/F6
Quincy, N.H. (†03266) 268/D4
Quincy, Ohio (43343) 284/C5
Quincy, Wash. (98848) 310/F3
Quincy, W. Va. (†25015) 312/C6
Quindío (dept.), Colombia 126/C5
Quinebaug, Conn. (06262) 210/H1
Quinebaug (riv.), Conn. 210/H2
Quinebaug (riv.), Mass. 249/F4
Quines, Argentina 143/C3
Quinhagak, Alaska (99655) 196/F3
Qui Nhon, Vietnam 72/F4
Qui Nhon, Vietnam 54/M8
Quiniluban (isls.), Philippines 82/C5
Quinlan, Okla. (†73852) 288/J2
Quinlan, Texas (75474) 303/H5
Quinn (riv.), Nev. 266/D1
Quinn, S. Dak. (57775) 298/E5
Quinn Canyon (range), Nev. 266/F4
Quinnesec, Mich. (49876) 250/A3
Quinnimont, W. Va. (25910) 312/D7
Quinnipiac, Conn. (†06492) 210/D3
Quinnipiac (riv.), Conn. 210/D3
Quinta de Tilcoco, Chile 138/G5
Quintana de la Serena, Spain 33/D3
Quintanar de la Orden, Spain 33/E3
Quintana Roo (state), Mexico 150/P7
Quintay, Chile 138/F3
Quinter, Kansas (67752) 232/B2
Quintero, Chile 138/F2
Quinto (riv.), Argentina 143/D3
Quinto, Spain 33/F2
Quinto, Switzerland 39/G3
Quinton, Ky. (†42518) 237/M7
Quinton, N.J. (08072) 273/C4
Quinton, Okla. (74561) 288/R4
Quinton, Sask. 181/G4
Quinton, Va. (23141) 307/O5
Quinwood, W. Va. (25981) 312/E6
Quinzau, Angola 115/B5
Quionga, Mozambique 118/G2
Quipapá, Brazil 132/G5
Quirey, Colombia 126/F5
Quirihue, Chile 138/E1
Quirindi, N.S. Wales 97/F2
Quirino (prov.), Philippines 82/C2
Quirino, Philippines 82/C2
Quiriquire, Venezuela 124/G3
Quirke (lake), Ontario 177/B1
Quiroga, Argentina 143/F7
Quiroga, Bolivia 136/C6
Quiroga, Spain 33/C1
Quirusillas, Bolivia 136/D6
Quisiro, Venezuela 124/C2
Quispamsis, New Bruns. 170/E3
Quissanga, Mozambique 118/G2
Quissett, Mass. (†02540) 249/M6
Quissico, Mozambique 118/F4
Quitaque, Texas (79255) 303/C3
Quitasueño (bank), Colombia 126/A8
Quitilipi, Argentina 143/D2
Quitman, Ark. (72131) 202/F3
Quitman (co.), Georgia 217/B7
Quitman, Georgia (31643) 217/E9
Quitman, La. (71268) 238/E2
Quitman (co.), Miss. 256/D2
Quitman, Miss. (39355) 256/G6
Quitman, Mo. (†64428) 261/C2
Quitman, Texas (75783) 303/J5
Quitman (mts.), Texas 303/B11
Quito (cap.), Ecuador 2/F6
Quito (cap.), Ecuador 128/C3
Quito (cap.), Ecuador 120/B2
Quixadá, Brazil 120/F3
Quixadá, Brazil 132/G4
Quixeramobim, Brazil 132/F4
Qujing, China 77/F6
Qulin, Mo. (63961) 261/M9
Qum, Iran 54/G6
Qum (Qom), Iran 59/F3
Qum (Qom), Iran 66/G3
Qumar He (riv.), China 77/D4
Qumarlêb, China 77/D5
Qumeim, Jordan 65/D2
Qunfidha, Saudi Arabia 59/D6
Quogue, N.Y. (11959) 276/P9
Quoich (riv.), N.W. Terrs. 187/J3
Quoich, Loch (lake), Scotland 15/C3
Quonnipaug (lake), Conn. 210/E3
Quorn, S. Australia 88/F6
Quorn, S. Australia 94/F5
Quryat, Oman 59/G5
Qusaiba, Saudi Arabia 59/D4
Quteife, Syria 63/G6
Qu Xian, Sichuan, China 77/G5
Qu Xian, Zhejiang, China 77/J6
Qüxü, China 77/D6
Quyon, Québec 172/A4
Quyquyó, Paraguay 144/D5

R

Raab (riv.), Austria 41/C3
Raabs an der Thaya, Austria 41/C2
Raahe, Finland 18/O4
Raalte, Netherlands 27/J4
Ra'anana, Israel 65/B3
Raanes (pen.), N.W. Terrs. 187/K2
Raasay (isl.), Scotland 15/C3
Raasay (sound), Scotland 15/B3
Rab, Yugoslavia 45/B3
Rab (isl.), Yugoslavia 45/B3
Rába (riv.), Hungary 41/D3
Raba, Indonesia 85/F7
Rabat (cap.), Morocco 2/J4
Rabat (cap.), Morocco 106/C2
Rabat (cap.), Morocco 102/B1
Rabaul, Papua N.G. 87/F6
Rabaul, Papua N.G. 86/B2
Rabbit (riv.), Mich. 250/D6
Rabbit (isl.), N.S. Wales 97/J2
Rabbit (creek), S. Dak. 298/E3
Rabbit Ears (peak), Colo. 208/G2
Rabbit Ears (range), Colo. 208/F2
Rabbithash, Ky. (†41091) 237/M3
Rabbit Lake, Sask. 181/D2
Rabbit Lake, Sask. 181/M2
Rabigh, Saudi Arabia 59/C5
Rabinal, Guatemala 154/B3
Rabka, Poland 47/D4
Rabocheostrovsk, U.S.S.R. 52/D1
Rabun, Ala. (†36507) 195/C8
Rabun (co.), Georgia 217/F1
Rabun (lake), Georgia 217/E1
Rabun Gap, Georgia (30568) 217/F1
Raccoon (pt.), Fla. 212/D3
Raccoon, Ind. (†46172) 227/D5
Raccoon (riv.), Iowa 229/D4
Raccoon (pt.), La. 238/H8
Raccoon (creek), N.J. 273/C4
Raccoon (creek), Ohio 284/F8
Race (pt.), Mass. 249/N4
Race (cape), Newf. 166/D2
Race (cape.), Newf. 146/N5
Race (cape), Newf. 162/L6
Raceland, Ky. (41169) 237/R3
Raceland, La. (70394) 238/J7
Racepond, Georgia (†31537) 217/H8
Rachel, W. Va. (26587) 312/F3
Rach Gia, Vietnam 72/E5
Racibórz, Poland 47/C3
Racine, Minn. (55967) 255/F7
Racine, Mo. (64858) 261/C9
Racine, Ohio (45771) 284/G8
Racine, Québec 172/E4
Racine, W. Va. (25165) 312/C6
Racine, Wis. 188/J2
Racine (co.), Wis. 317/K10
Racine, Wis. (*53401) 317/M3
Ráckeve, Hungary 41/E3
Rackham, Manitoba 179/B4
Raco, Mich. (49778) 250/E2
Racola, Mo. (†63630) 261/L6
Radama (isls.), Madagascar 118/H2
Rădăuţi, Romania 45/G2
Radbuza (riv.), Czech. 41/B2
Radcliff, Ky. (40160) 237/K5
Radcliff, Ohio (45670) 284/F7
Radcliffe, England 13/H2
Radcliffe, Iowa (50230) 229/G4
Radeberg, E. Germany 22/E3
Radebeul, E. Germany 22/E3
Radenthein, Austria 41/B3
Rader, Tenn. (†37743) 237/R8
Radersburg, Mont. (59641) 262/E4
Radford (I.C.), Va. (24141) 307/G6
Radhanpur, India 68/C4
Radiant, Va. (22732) 307/M4
Radisson, Québec 174/B2
Radisson, Sask. 181/D3
Radisson, Wis. (54867) 317/D4
Radium, Colo. (80472) 208/G3
Radium, Kansas (67571) 232/D3
Radium, Minn. (56749) 255/B2
Radium Hill, S. Australia 88/G6
Radium Hill, S. Australia 94/G5
Radium Hot Springs, Br. Col. 184/J5
Radium Springs, N. Mex. (88054) 274/B6
Radkersburg, Austria 41/C3
Radley, Ind. (†46938) 227/F4
Radnice, Czech. 41/B2
Radnor, Ind. (†46923) 227/D3
Radnor, Ohio (43066) 284/D5
Radnor (for.), Wales 13/D5
Radnor, W. Va. (25556) 312/A6
Radolfzell, W. Germany 22/C5
Radom, Ill. (62876) 222/D5
Radom (prov.), Poland 47/E3
Radom, Poland 7/G3
Radom, Poland 47/E3
Radomir, Bulgaria 45/F4
Radomsko, Poland 47/D3
Radoviš, Yugoslavia 45/F5
Radstadt, Austria 41/B3
Radviliškis, U.S.S.R. 53/B3
Radville, Sask. 162/F6
Radville, Sask. 181/G6
Radway, Alberta 182/D2
Radziejów, Poland 47/D2
Radzyń Podlaski, Poland 47/F3
Rae (isth.), N.W.T. 162/H2
Rae (isth.), N.W. Terrs. 187/K3
Rae (riv.), N.W. Terrs. 187/G3
Rae (str.), N.W. Terrs. 187/J3
Rae-Edzo, N.W.T. 162/E3
Rae-Edzo, N.W. Terrs. 187/G3
Raeford, N.C. (28376) 281/L5
Rae Lake, N.W. Terrs. 187/G3
Raeren, Belgium 27/J7
Raeside (lake), W. Australia 88/C5
Raeside (lake), W. Australia 92/C5
Raetihi, N. Zealand 100/E3
Raeville, Nebr. (68656) 264/F3
Rafaela, Argentina 143/F5
Rafaela, Argentina 120/C6
Rafah, Gaza Strip 65/A5
Rafai, Cent. Afr. Rep. 115/D2
Rafidiya, West Bank 65/C3
Rafsanjan, Iran 59/G3
Rafsanjan, Iran 66/K5
Raft (riv.), Idaho 220/E7
Raft (riv.), Utah 304/A1
Raft River (mts.), Utah 304/A2
Rafz, Switzerland 39/G1
Raga, Sudan 111/E6
Ragan, Nebr. (68969) 264/E4
Ragang (vol.), Philippines 82/E7
Ragay (gulf), Philippines 82/D4
Ragged (isl.), Bahamas 156/C2
Ragged (pt.), Barbados 161/C8
Ragged (isl.), Maine 243/F8
Ragged (lake), Maine 243/E4
Ragged (isls.), Newf. 166/C2
Raglan, N. Zealand 100/E2
Raglan (harb.), N. Zealand 100/E2
Ragland, Ala. (35131) 195/F3
Ragley, La. (70657) 238/D5
Rago, Kansas (67128) 232/D4
Ragsdale, Ind. (47573) 227/C7
Ragusa (prov.), Italy 34/E6
Ragusa, Italy 34/E6
Ragusa (Dubrovnik), Yugoslavia 45/C4
Raha, Indonesia 85/G6
Raheng (Tak), Thailand 72/C3
Rahan, Ireland 17/F5
Rahimyar Khan, Pakistan 68/C3
Rahotu, N. Zealand 100/D3
Rahue (riv.), Chile 138/D3
Rahway, N.J. (*07065) 273/E2
Raiatea (isl.), Fr. Poly. 87/L7
Raices, Argentina 143/G6
Raichur, India 68/D5
Raiford, Fla. (32083) 212/D1
Raigarh, India 68/E4
Railley (mt.), Mont. 262/C3
Railroad (valley), Nev. 266/F4
Railroad, Pa. (17355) 294/J6
Railroad Canyon (res.), Calif. 204/E11
Railton, Tasmania 99/C3
Rainbow (lake), Alberta 182/A5
Rainbow (plat.), Ariz. 198/D2
Rainbow, Conn. (†06095) 210/E1
Rainbow (mt.), Idaho 220/C4
Rainbow (lake), Maine 243/E4
Rainbow, Victoria 97/A4
Rainbow Bridge Nat'l Mon., Utah 304/C6
Rainbow City, Ala. (35901) 195/F3
Rainbow Lake, Alberta 182/A5
Rainelle, W. Va. (25962) 312/E7
Rainier, Alberta 182/D4
Rainier, Oreg. (97048) 291/E1
Rainier (mt.), Wash. 188/B1
Rainier, Wash. (98576) 310/C4
Rainier (mt.), Wash. 310/D4
Rains, S.C. (29589) 296/J3
Rains (co.), Texas 303/J5
Rainsboro, Ohio (45165) 284/C7
Rainsburg, Pa. (†15522) 294/F6
Rainsville, Ala. (35986) 195/G2
Rainsville, Ind. (†47918) 227/C4
Rainsville, N. Mex. (87736) 274/D2
Rainy (riv.), Minn. 188/H1
Rainy (lake), Minn. 188/H1
Rainy (lake), Minn. 255/E2
Rainy (riv.), Minn. 255/D2
Rainy (lake), Ont. 162/G6
Rainy (lake), Ontario 177/G5
Rainy (lake), Ontario 175/B3
Rainy River, Ont. 162/G6
Rainy River (terr. dist.), Ontario 177/G5
Rainy River (terr. dist.), Ontario 175/B3
Rainy River, Ontario 175/A3
Rainy River, Ontario 177/F5
Raipur, India 54/K7
Raipur, India 68/E4
Raisin, Calif. (93652) 204/E7
Raisin (riv.), Mich. 250/F7
Raisio, Finland 18/M6
Raith, Ontario 175/C3
Raith, Ontario 177/G5
Raivavae (isl.), Fr. Poly. 87/M8
Raja Ampat Group (isls.), Indonesia 85/H6
Rajahmundry, India 68/E5
Rajang (riv.), Malaysia 85/E5
Rajapalaiyam, India 68/D7
Rajapur, India 68/C5
Rajasthan (state), India 68/C3
Rajec, Czech. 41/E2
Rajgarh, India 68/D4
Rajka, Hungary 41/D3
Rajkot, India 54/H7
Rajkot, India 68/C4
Rajnandgaon, India 68/E4
Rajpipla, India 68/C4
Rajpur, India 68/F2
Rajpura, India 68/D2
Rajshahi, Bangladesh 68/F4
Rakahanga (atoll), Cook Is. 87/K7
Rakaia, N. Zealand 100/C5
Rakaia (riv.), N. Zealand 100/C5
Rakamaz, Hungary 41/F2
Rakan, Ras (cape), Qatar 59/F4
Rakaposhi (mt.), Pakistan 68/C1
Rakaposhi (mt.), Pakistan 59/K2
Rakata (isl.), Indonesia 85/C7
Rake, Iowa (50465) 229/F2
Rakhov, U.S.S.R. 52/B5
Rakino (isl.), N. Zealand 100/C1
Rakitu (isl.), N. Zealand 100/E2
Rakkestad, Norway 18/G7
Rakof (isls.), Alaska 196/M1
Rákospalota, Hungary 41/E3
Rakovník, Czech. 41/B1
Rakvere, U.S.S.R. 53/D1
Rakvere, U.S.S.R. 52/C3
Raleigh, Fla. (†32696) 212/D2
Raleigh, Georgia (†30293) 217/C5
Raleigh, Ill. (62977) 222/E6
Raleigh, Ind. (†46173) 227/G5
Raleigh, Miss. (39153) 256/F6
Raleigh, Newf. 166/C3
Raleigh (cap.), N.C. 146/L6
Raleigh (cap.), N.C. 188/L3
Raleigh (cap.), N.C. (*27601) 281/M3
Raleigh (bay), N.C. 281/S5
Raleigh, N. Dak. (58564) 282/H7
Raleigh, Tenn. (38128) 237/B10
Raleigh (co.), W. Va. 312/D7
Raleigh, W. Va. (25911) 312/D7
Ralik Chain (isls.), Marshall Is. 87/G5
Ralls (co.), Mo. 261/J3
Ralls, Texas (79357) 303/C4
Ralph, Ala. (35480) 195/C4
Ralph, Mich. (49877) 250/B2
Ralph, Sask. 181/H6
Ralph, S. Dak. (57650) 298/C2
Ralphton, Pa. (†15563) 294/D5
Ralston, Alberta 182/E4
Ralston, Iowa (51459) 229/D4
Ralston, Nebr. (68127) 264/J3
Ralston, N.J. (†07945) 273/D2
Ralston, Okla. (74650) 288/N2
Ralston, Pa. (17763) 294/H2
Ralston, Tenn. (†38237) 237/D8
Ralston, Wash. (†99169) 310/G4
Ralston, Wyo. (82440) 319/D1
Ram (head), Virgin Is. (U.S.) 161/C5
Rama, Nicaragua 154/E4
Rama, Sask. 181/H4
Ramadi, Iraq 59/D3
Ramadi, Iraq 66/C4
Ramage, W. Va. (25166) 312/C7
Ramah, Colo. (80832) 208/L4
Ramah (bay), Newf. 166/B2
Ramah, N. Mex. (87321) 274/A3
Ramallah, West Bank 65/C4
Ramallo, Argentina 143/F6
Ramapo (riv.), N.J. 273/E1
Ramat Gan, Israel 65/B3
Ramat Hasharon, Israel 65/B3
Rambi (isl.), Fiji 86/R10
Ramblewood, N.J. (†08054) 273/D4
Rambouillet, France 28/D3
Rame, Israel 65/C2
Ramea, Newf. 166/C4
Ramea (isls.), Newf. 166/C4
Ramechhap, Nepal 68/F3
Ramelton, Ireland 17/F1
Ramer, Ala. (36069) 195/F6
Ramer, Tenn. (38367) 237/D10
Rameswaram, India 68/D7
Ramey, Minn. (†56329) 255/E5
Ramey, Pa. (16671) 294/F4
Ramey A.F.B., P. Rico 161/A1
Ramhormoz, Iran 66/F5
Ramhurst, Georgia (†30705) 217/C1
Ramiers (isl.), Martinique 161/C6
Ramla, Israel 65/B4
Ramm, Jebel (mt.), Jordan 65/D5
Ramme, Denmark 21/B4
Rammun, West Bank 65/C4
Ramnäs, Sweden 18/J7
Ramon (mt.), Israel 65/D5
Ramon, N. Mex. (†88136) 274/D4
Ramona, Calif. (92065) 204/J10
Ramona, Kansas (67475) 232/E3
Ramona, Okla. (74061) 288/P1
Ramona, S. Dak. (57054) 298/P5
Ramón Castilla, Peru 128/G5
Ramón de las Yaguas, Cuba 158/J4
Ramón Santana, Dom. Rep. 158/F6
Ramón Trigo, Uruguay 145/E3
Ramor (lake), Ireland 17/G4
Ramore, Ontario 177/K5
Ramos (riv.), Mexico 150/G4
Ramos Arizpe, Mexico 150/J4
Ramosch, Switzerland 39/K3
Ramotswa, Botswana 118/C4
Rampart, Alaska (99767) 196/H1
Ramparts (riv.), N.W. Terrs. 187/E3
Rampur, Him. Pradesh, India 68/D2
Rampur, Uttar Pradesh, India 68/D3
Ramree (isl.), Burma 72/B3
Ramsar, Iran 66/G2
Ramsay, Mich. (49959) 250/F2
Ramsay, Mont. (59748) 262/D4
Ramsay, Ontario 177/J5
Ramsbottom, England 13/H2
Ramsele, Sweden 18/K5
Ramsen, Switzerland 39/G1
Ramseur, N.C. (27316) 281/K3
Ramsey, England 10/F4
Ramsey, England 13/G5
Ramsey, Ill. (62080) 222/D4
Ramsey, Ind. (47166) 227/E8
Ramsey, I. of Man 13/C3
Ramsey, I. of Man 10/D3
Ramsey (bay), I. of Man 13/C3
Ramsey (co.), Minn. 255/E5
Ramsey, Minn. (†55303) 255/E5
Ramsey, N.J. (07446) 273/B1
Ramsey (co.), N. Dak. 282/N3
Ramsey (mt.), Tasmania 99/B3
Ramsey (isl.), Wales 13/B6
Ramsgate, England 10/G5
Ramsgate, England 13/J6
Ramsjö, Sweden 18/J5
Ramu (riv.), Papua N.G. 85/B7
Ramunia, Tanjong (pt.), Malaysia 72/F6
Ramville (isl.), Martinique 161/D6
Rana (fjord), Norway 18/H3
Rana (riv.), Norway 18/J3
Ranau, Malaysia 85/F4
Ranburne, Ala. (36273) 195/H3
Rancagua, Chile 138/G5
Rancagua, Chile 120/B6
Ranches of Taos, N. Mex. (87557) 274/D2
Ranchester, Wyo. (82839) 319/E1
Ranchi, India 68/F4
Rancho Cordova, Calif. (95670) 204/C8
Rancho Cucamonga, Calif. (91730) 204/E10
Rancho Mirage, Calif. (92270) 204/J10
Rancho Palos Verdes, Calif. (90274) 204/B11
Rancho Santa Clarita, Calif. (†91321) 204/G9
Rancho Santa Fe, Calif. (92067) 204/H10
Rancho Veloz, Cuba 158/D1
Ranchuelo, Cuba 158/E2
Ranchwood Manor, Okla. (†73160) 288/L4
Ranco (lake), Chile 138/E3
Rancocas, N.J. (08073) 273/D3
Rancocas (creek), N.J. 273/D3
Rand, Colo. (80473) 208/G2
Randalia, Iowa (52164) 229/K3
Randall, Iowa (50231) 229/F4
Randall, Kansas (66963) 232/D2
Randall, Minn. (56475) 255/D4
Randall (co.), Texas 303/C2
Randall (mt.), W. Australia 88/B3
Randallstown, Md. (21133) 245/L3
Randalstown, N. Ireland 17/J2
Randburg, S. Africa 118/H6
Randers, Denmark 18/G8
Randers, Denmark 21/C5
Randfontein, S. Africa 118/G6
Randle, Wash. (98377) 310/D4
Randleman, N.C. (27317) 281/K3
Randles, Mo. (†63740) 261/N8
Randlett, Okla. (73562) 288/K6
Randlett, Utah (84063) 304/E3
Randolph (co.), Ala. 195/H4
Randolph, Ala. (36792) 195/E5
Randolph, Ariz. (85243) 198/D6
Randolph (co.), Ark. 202/H1
Randolph (co.), Georgia 217/C7
Randolph (co.), Ill. 222/D5
Randolph (co.), Ind. 227/G4
Randolph, Iowa (51649) 229/B7
Randolph, Kansas (66554) 232/F2
Randolph○, Maine (†04345) 243/D7
Randolph, Md. (†20853) 245/K4
Randolph○, Mass. (02368) 249/D8
Randolph, Minn. (55065) 255/E6
Randolph, Miss. (38864) 256/F2
Randolph (co.), Mo. 261/G3
Randolph, Mo. (†64101) 261/P5
Randolph, Nebr. (68771) 264/G2
Randolph○, N.H. (03593) 268/E3
Randolph○, N.J. (†07801) 273/D2
Randolph, N.Y. (14772) 276/C6
Randolph (co.), N.C. 281/K3
Randolph, Ohio (44265) 284/H3
Randolph, Utah (84064) 304/C2
Randolph, Vt. (05060) 268/B4
Randolph○, Vt. (05060) 268/B4
Randolph, Va. (23962) 307/L7
Randolph (co.), W. Va. 312/G5
Randolph, Wis. (53956) 317/H8
Randolph A.F.B., Texas 303/K10
Randolph Center, Vt. (05061) 268/B4
Random (isl.), Newf. 166/D2
Random (sound), Newf. 166/D2
Random Lake, (53075) 317/K8
Randsburg, Calif. (93554) 204/H8
Randwick, N. S. Wales 88/L4
Randwick, N.S. Wales 97/J3
Ranelagh, Tasmania 99/C4
Ranfurly, Alberta 182/E3
Ranfurly, N. Zealand 100/B6
Rangamati, Bangladesh 68/G4
Rangasa (cape), Indonesia 85/F6
Rangatira (isl.), N. Zealand 100/E7
Range, Ala. (36473) 195/D8
Range (creek), Utah 304/D4
Rangeley, Maine (04970) 243/B6

434 Rangeley

Rangeley○, Maine (04970) 243/B6
Rangeley (lake), Maine 243/B6
Rangely, Colo. (81648) 208/B2
Ranger, Georgia (30734) 217/C2
Ranger (peak), Idaho 220/D3
Ranger, N.C. (†28906) 281/A4
Ranger, Sask. 181/D2
Ranger, Texas (76470) 303/F5
Ranger, W. Va. (25557) 312/B6
Rangiauria (Pitt) (isl.), N. Zealand 100/E7
Rangiora, N. Zealand 100/D5
Rangiroa (atoll), Fr. Poly. 87/M7
Rangitaiki (riv.), N. Zealand 100/F3
Rangitata (riv.), N. Zealand 100/C5
Rangitikei (riv.), N. Zealand 100/E3
Rangitoto (isl.), N. Zealand 100/C1
Rangkasbitung, Indonesia 85/G2
Rangoon (div.), Burma 72/C3
Rangoon (cap.), Burma 2/P5
Rangoon (cap.), Burma 54/L8
Rangoon (cap.), Burma 72/C3
Rangoon, W. Va. (†26238) 312/F4
Rangpur, Bangladesh 68/F3
Rania, Iraq 66/D2
Ranier, Minn. (56668) 255/E2
Ranken (riv.), North. Terr. 93/E6
Rankin, Ill. (60960) 222/F3
Rankin (co.), Miss. 256/E6
Rankin, Pa. (†15104) 294/C7
Rankin, Texas (79778) 303/B6
Rankine Store, North. Terr. 93/E5
Rankin Inlet, N.W. Terrs. 187/J3
Rankins Springs, N.S. Wales 97/D3
Rankweil, Austria 41/A3
Ranlo, N.C. (28052) 281/G4
Rannoch (dist.), Scotland 15/D4
Rannoch, Loch (lake), Scotland 10/D2
Rannoch, Loch (lake), Scotland 15/D4
Ranong, Thailand 72/C5
Ransiki, Indonesia 85/J6
Ransom, Ill. (60470) 222/E2
Ransom, Kansas (67572) 232/C3
Ransom (co.), N. Dak. 282/P7
Ransom, Pa. (18653) 294/F7
Ransomville, N.Y. (14131) 276/C4
Ranson, W. Va. (25438) 312/L4
Rantauprapat, Indonesia 85/C5
Rantekombola (mt.), Indonesia 85/F6
Rantis, West Bank 65/C3
Rantoul, Ill. (61866) 222/E3
Rantoul, Kansas (66079) 232/G3
Ranua, Finland 18/P4
Ranui, N. Zealand 100/B1
Ranum, Denmark 21/C4
Ranya, Wadi (dry riv.), Saudi Arabia 59/D5
Rao Co (mt.), Laos 72/E3
Rao Co (mt.), Vietnam 72/E3
Raohe, China 77/M2
Raoui, Erg er (des.), Algeria 106/D3
Raoul (isl.), N. Zealand 87/J8
Raoul (cape), Tasmania 99/D5
Rapa (isl.), Fr. Poly. 87/M8
Rapallo, Italy 34/B2
Rapa Nui (Easter) (isl.), Chile 87/Q8
Rapch (riv.), Iran 66/L8
Rapel, Chile 138/F4
Rapel (riv.), Chile 138/F4
Rapelje, Mont. (59067) 262/G5
Raper (cape), N.W.T. 162/K2
Raper (cape), N.W. Terrs. 187/M3
Raphine, Va. (24472) 307/K5
Raphoe, Ireland 17/F2
Rapid (riv.), Mich. 250/B2
Rapid (riv.), Minn. 255/D2
Rapidan, Va. (22733) 307/M4
Rapidan (riv.), Va. 307/M4
Rapid City, Manitoba 179/B4
Rapid City, Mich. (49676) 250/D4
Rapid City, S. Dak. 146/H5
Rapid City, S. Dak. 188/F2
Rapid City, S. Dak. (57701) 298/C5
Rapide-Blanc, Québec 174/C3
Rapides (par.), La. 238/E4
Rapide Taureau (dam), Québec 172/D3
Rapid River, Mich. (49878) 250/C3
Rapids City, Ill. (61278) 222/C2
Rapid View, Sask. 181/C1
Rāpina, U.S.S.R. 53/D1
Raposos, Brazil 135/E2
Rappahannock (co.), Va. 307/M3
Rappahannock (riv.), Va. 307/P4
Rapperswil, Switzerland 39/G2
Rápulo (riv.), Bolivia 136/C4
Rapu-Rapu (isl.), Philippines 82/E4
Raqqa (El Rashid), Syria 63/H5
Raquette (lake), N.Y. 276/L3
Raquette (riv.), N.Y. 276/L1
Raquette Lake, N.Y. (13436) 276/L3
Raraka (atoll), Fr. Poly. 87/M7
Rarden, Ohio (45671) 284/D8
Rardin, Ill. (61948) 222/E4
Raritan, Ill. (61471) 222/C3
Raritan, N.J. (08869) 273/D2
Raritan (bay), N.J. 273/E3
Raritan (riv.), N.J. 273/D2
Raroia (atoll), Fr. Poly. 87/M7
Raron, Switzerland 39/E4
Rarotonga (isl.), Cook Is. 87/K8
Rasa (isl.), Philippines 82/B6
Ra's al Khafji, Saudi Arabia 59/E4
Ras al Khaimah, U.A.E. 59/G4
Rasar, Tenn. (†37878) 237/O9
Ras Asèr (cape), Somalia 102/H3
Ras Dashan (mt.), Ethiopia 102/F3
Ras Dashan (mt.), Ethiopia 111/G5
Raseiniai, U.S.S.R. 53/B3
Ra's en Naqb, Jordan 65/E5
Ras Ghārib, Egypt 111/F2
Rashad, Sudan 111/F5
Ras Hafun (cape), Somalia 102/H3
Rasharkin, N. Ireland 17/J2
Rasheiya, Lebanon 63/F6
Rashid (Rosetta), Egypt 111/J2
Rashid (Rosetta), Egypt 59/B3
Rashid (prov.), Syria 63/H5
Rasht, Iran 59/E2
Rasht, Iran 54/G6
Rasht, Iran 66/F2
Rask, Iran 66/M7
Raška, Yugoslavia 45/E4
Ras Lanuf, Libya 111/C1
Rason (lake), W. Australia 88/C5
Rason (lake), W. Australia 92/D5
Rasskazovo, U.S.S.R. 52/F4
Ras Tanura, Saudi Arabia 59/F4
Rastatt, W. Germany 22/C4
Rastede, W. Germany 22/C2
Rat (isls.), Alaska 196/K4
Rat (riv.), Manitoba 179/F5
Ratak Chain (isls.), Marshall Is. 87/G5
Ratangarh, India 68/C3
Rat Buri, Thailand 72/C4
Ratcliff, Ark. (72951) 202/C3
Ratcliff, Texas (75858) 303/J6
Ratcliffe, Sask. 181/G6
Rathangan, Ireland 17/G5
Rathbun, Iowa (52545) 229/H7
Rathbun (lake), Iowa 229/G7
Rathcoole, Ireland 17/J5
Rathcormac, Ireland 17/E7
Rathdowney, Ireland 17/F6
Rathdrum, Idaho (83858) 220/A2
Rathdrum, Ireland 17/J6
Rathedaung, Burma 72/B2
Rathenow, E. Germany 22/E2
Rathfriland, N. Ireland 17/J3
Rathgormuck, Ireland 17/F7
Rathkeale, Ireland 17/D7
Rathkeale, Ireland 10/B4
Rathlin (isl.), N. Ireland 10/C3
Rathlin (isl.), N. Ireland 17/J1
Rathlin (sound), N. Ireland 17/J1
Rathlin O'Birne (isl.), Ireland 17/C2
Rathluirc, Ireland 10/B4
Rathluirc, Ireland 17/D7
Rathmore, Ireland 17/J5
Rathmullen, Ireland 17/F1
Rathnew-Merrymeeting, Ireland 17/J6
Rathowen, Ireland 17/F4
Rathvilly, Ireland 17/H6
Rathwell, Manitoba 179/D5
Ratibor (Racibórz), Poland 47/C3
Ratingen, W. Germany 22/B3
Ratio, Ark. (†72333) 202/J5
Ratlam, India 68/C4
Ratliff City, Okla. (73081) 288/M6
Ratnagiri, India 68/C5
Ratnapura, Sri Lanka 68/D7
Ratoath, Ireland 17/J5
Raton, N. Mex. 188/F3
Raton, N. Mex. (87740) 274/E2
Rats (riv.), Québec 172/D2
Rattan, Okla. (74562) 288/R6
Ratten, Austria 41/C3
Rattlesnake (creek), Kansas 232/D4
Rattlesnake (creek), Ohio 284/C7
Rattlesnake (creek), Oreg. 291/K5
Rattlesnake (hills), Wyo. 319/E3
Rattlesnake (range), Wyo. 319/E3
Rattray (head), Scotland 15/G3
Rättvik, Sweden 18/J6
Ratzeburg, W. Germany 22/D2
Raub, Ind. (47976) 227/C3
Raub, Malaysia 72/D7
Raub, N. Dak. (58774) 282/F4
Rauch, Argentina 143/E4
Rauch, Minn. (†55740) 255/E3
Raukumara (range), N. Zealand 100/F3
Raul Leoni (dam), Venezuela 124/G4
Raul Soares, Brazil 135/E2
Rauma, Finland 18/M6
Rauma (riv.), Norway 18/F5
Raunds, England 13/G5
Raung (mt.), Indonesia 85/L2
Raurkela, India 68/F4
Rausu, Japan 81/M1
Rauville, S. Dak. (†57201) 298/P3
Ravalli (co.), Mont. 262/B4
Ravalli, Mont. (59863) 262/B3
Ravanna, Ark. (†75556) 202/C7
Ravanna, Mo. (†64673) 261/E2
Ravar, Iran 59/G3
Ravar, Iran 66/K5
Ravelo, Bolivia 136/C6
Ravels, Belgium 27/G6
Raven, Va. (24639) 307/E6
Ravena, N.Y. (12143) 276/N6
Ravencliff, W. Va. (25913) 312/C7
Ravendale, Calif. (96123) 204/E3
Ravenden, Ark. (72459) 202/H1
Ravenden Springs, Ark. (72460) 202/H1
Ravenel, S.C. (29470) 296/G6
Ravenna (prov.), Italy 34/D2
Ravenna, Italy 34/D2
Ravenna, Ky. (40472) 237/O5
Ravenna, Mich. (49451) 250/D5
Ravenna, Nebr. (68869) 264/F4
Ravenna, Ohio (44266) 284/H3
Ravenna, Texas (75476) 303/H4
Raven Rock, W. Va. (†26170) 312/D4
Ravensburg, W. Germany 22/C5
Ravenscrag, Sask. 181/C6
Ravensdale, Wash. (98051) 310/D3
Ravenshoe, Queensland 88/H3
Ravenshoe, Queensland 95/C3
Ravensthorpe, W. Australia 88/C6
Ravensthorpe, W. Australia 92/B6
Ravenswood, W. Va. (26164) 312/C5
Ravenwood, Mo. (64479) 261/C2
Ravi (riv.), Pakistan 68/C2
Ravia, Okla. (73455) 288/N6
Ravine, Pa. (17966) 294/K4
Ravinia, S. Dak. (57357) 298/N7
Ravne na Koroškem, Yugoslavia 45/B2
Rawalpindi, Pakistan 54/J6
Rawalpindi, Pakistan 68/C2
Rawalpindi, Pakistan 59/K3
Rawa Mazowiecka, Poland 47/E3
Rawdon, Québec 172/D3
Rawene, N. Zealand 100/D2
Rawhide (creek), Wyo. 319/G1
Rawhide (creek), Wyo. 319/H3
Rawi, Ko (isl.), Thailand 72/C6
Rawicz, Poland 47/C3
Rawlings, Md. (21557) 245/C2
Rawlings, Va. (23876) 307/N7
Rawlinna, W. Australia 88/C6
Rawlinna, W. Australia 92/D5
Rawlins (co.), Kansas 232/A2
Rawlins, Wyo. 188/E2
Rawlins, Wyo. (82301) 319/E4
Rawson, Argentina 120/C7
Rawson, Buenos Aires, Argentina 143/F7
Rawson, Chubut, Argentina 143/D5
Rawson, N. Dak. (†58831) 282/C4
Rawson, Ohio (45881) 284/C4
Rawtenstall, England 13/H1
Rawtenstall, England 10/G2
Raxaul, India 68/E3
Ray (mts.), Alaska 196/H1
Ray, Ill. (†62681) 222/C3
Ray, Ind. (46737) 227/H1
Ray, Minn. (56669) 255/E2
Ray (co.), Mo. 261/E4
Ray (cape), Newf. 166/C4
Ray (cape), Newf. 162/K6
Ray, N. Dak. (58849) 282/D3
Ray, Ohio (45672) 284/E7
Raya (mt.), Indonesia 85/E6
Rayagada, India 68/E5
Rayak, Lebanon 63/G6
Raybon, Georgia (†31553) 217/H8
Rayborn, Mo. (†65703) 261/H8
Raychikhinsk, U.S.S.R. 48/N5
Ray City, Georgia (31645) 217/F8
Ray Hubbard (lake), Texas 303/H2
Rayland, Ohio (43943) 284/J5
Rayle, Georgia (30660) 217/G3
Rayleigh, Br. Col. 184/G5
Rayleigh, England 13/J8
Raymer (New Raymer), Colo. (80742) 208/M1
Raymond, Alberta 182/D5
Raymond, Alta. 162/E6
Raymond, Calif. (93653) 204/F6
Raymond, Idaho (†83114) 220/G7
Raymond, Ill. (62560) 222/D4
Raymond, Ind. (†45056) 227/H6
Raymond, Iowa (50667) 229/J4
Raymond, Kansas (67573) 232/D3
Raymond, Maine (04071) 243/B8
Raymond○, Maine (04071) 243/B8
Raymond, Minn. (56282) 255/C5
Raymond, Miss. (39154) 256/D6
Raymond, Mont. (59256) 262/M2
Raymond, Nebr. (68428) 264/H4
Raymond, N.H. (03077) 268/E5
Raymond○, N.H. (03077) 268/E5
Raymond, Ohio (43067) 284/C5
Raymond, S. Dak. (57258) 298/O4
Raymond, Wash. (98577) 310/B4
Raymond, Wis. (†53126) 317/L2
Raymond City, W. Va. (†25159) 312/C6
Raymond Terrace, N.S. Wales 97/F3
Raymondville, Mo. (65555) 261/J8
Raymondville, N.Y. (13678) 276/L1
Raymondville, Texas (78580) 303/G11
Raymore, Mo. (64083) 261/D5
Raymore, Sask. 181/G4
Rayne, La. (70578) 238/F6
Raynesford, Mont. (59469) 262/F3
Raynham○, Mass. (02767) 249/K5
Raynham, N.C. (†28340) 281/L5
Raynham Center, Mass. (02768) 249/K5
Rayón, San Luis Potosí, Mexico 150/K6
Rayón, Sonora, Mexico 150/D2
Rayong, Thailand 72/D4
Rays (lake), Idaho 220/F6
Rays Crossing, Ind. (†46176) 227/F5
Rayside-Balfour, Ontario 177/K5
Raystown (lake), Pa. 294/F5
Raystown Branch, Juniata (riv.), Pa. 294/F5
Raysut (Risut), Oman 59/F6
Raytown, Mo. (64133) 261/P6
Rayville, La. (71269) 238/G2
Rayville, Mo. (64084) 261/E4
Raywick, Ky. (40060) 237/L5
Razan, Iran 66/F3
Razaza (res.), Iraq 66/C4
Razdan, U.S.S.R. 52/G6
Razgrad, Bulgaria 45/H4
Razlog, Bulgaria 45/F5
Ré (isl.), France 28/C4
Rea, Mo. (64480) 261/C2
Reader, Ark. (71726) 202/D6
Reader, W. Va. (26167) 312/E3
Readfield, Maine (04355) 243/D7
Readfield○, Maine (04355) 243/D7
Readfield, Wis. (54969) 317/J7
Reading, England 13/G8
Reading, England 10/F5
Reading, Kansas (66868) 232/F3
Reading○, Mass. (01867) 249/C5
Reading, Mich. (49274) 250/E7
Reading, Minn. (56165) 255/C7
Reading, Ohio (45215) 284/C9
Reading, Pa. 188/L2
Reading, Pa. (*19601) 294/L5
Reading○, Vt. (05062) 268/B5
Readington, N.J. (08870) 273/D2
Readland, Ark. (71664) 202/H7
Readlyn, Iowa (50668) 229/J3
Readlyn, Sask. 181/F6
Readsboro, Vt. (05350) 268/B6
Readsboro○, Vt. (05350) 268/B6
Reads Landing, Minn. (55968) 255/F6
Reads Mill, Ala. (†36279) 195/G3
Readstown, Wis. (54652) 317/E9
Readsville, Mo. (†65067) 261/J5
Readville, Mass. (02137) 249/C8
Ready, Ky. (†42721) 237/J6
Readyville, Tenn. (37149) 237/J9
Reagan, Okla. (†73460) 288/N6
Reagan, Tenn. (38368) 237/E9
Reagan (co.), Texas 303/C6
Reagan, Texas (76680) 303/H6
Real, Cordillera (range), Bolivia 136/A5
Real (co.), Texas 303/E8
Real de San Carlos, Uruguay 145/A5
Realitos, Texas (78376) 303/F10
Realp, Switzerland 39/F3
Reamstown, Pa. (17567) 294/K5
Reao (atoll), Fr. Poly. 87/N7
Reardan, Wash. (99029) 310/H3
Reasnor, Iowa (50232) 229/G5
Reaville, N.J. (†08822) 273/D3
Reay, Scotland 15/E2
Rebecca, Georgia (31783) 217/E7
Rebecca (lake), W. Australia 88/C6
Rebecca (lake), W. Australia 92/C5
Rebecq, Belgium 27/E7
Rebersburg, Pa. (16872) 294/H4
Rebiana (oasis), Libya 111/D3
Rebiana Sand Sea (des.), Libya 111/D3
Reboledo, Uruguay 145/D4
Rebun (isl.), Japan 81/K1
Recanati, Italy 34/D3
Recherche (arch.), Australia 87/C9
Recherche (arch.), W. Australia 88/C6
Recherche (arch.), W. Australia 92/C6
Rechitsa, U.S.S.R. 52/C4
Rechnitz, Austria 41/D3
Rechthalten, Switzerland 39/D3
Recife, Brazil 132/H5
Recife, Brazil 120/F3
Recife, Brazil 2/H6
Reckingen, Switzerland 39/F4
Recklinghausen, W. Germany 22/B3
Recluse, Wyo. (82725) 319/G1
Reconquista, Argentina 143/F4
Recreo, Argentina 143/C2
Rector, Ark. (72461) 202/K1
Rectortown, Va. (22140) 307/N3
Recuay, Peru 128/D7
Red (riv.) 146/J5
Red (riv.) 188/H4
Red (sea) 2/L4
Red (sea) 54/E7
Red (riv.) 54/M7
Red (sea) 102/F2
Red (riv.), Ark. 202/C6
Red (mt.), Conn. 210/B1
Red (sea), Egypt 111/G3
Red (sea), Ethiopia 111/H4
Red (riv.), Idaho 220/C4
Red (riv.), Ky. 237/G7
Red (riv.), Ky. 237/O5
Red (riv.), La. 238/G4
Red (riv.), Manitoba 179/F4
Red (lake), Minn. 188/H1
Red (isl.), Newf. 166/C2
Red (bay), N. Ireland 17/K1
Red, North Fork (riv.), Okla. 288/H4
Red (riv.), Okla. 288/R7
Red (lake), Ontario 175/B2
Red (sea), Saudi Arabia 59/C5
Red (lake), S. Dak. 298/L6
Red (sea), Sudan 111/G3
Red (riv.), Tenn. 237/G7
Red (riv.), Texas 303/F3
Red (riv.), U.S. 146/J6
Red (riv.), Utah 304/D3
Red (riv.), Vietnam 72/E2
Red (pt.), Virgin Is. (U.S.) 161/D4
Red (sea), Yemen Arab Rep. 59/C5
Reda, Poland 47/D1
Redang, Pulau (isl.), Malaysia 72/D6
Redange, Luxembourg 27/H9
Red Ash, Va. (24640) 307/E6
Red Bank, New Bruns. 170/E2
Red Bank, N.J. (07701) 273/E3
Redbank (creek), Pa. 294/E3
Red Bank, Tenn. (37415) 237/L10
Red Banks, Miss. (38661) 256/F1
Red Bay, Ala. (35582) 195/B2
Red Bay, Fla. (†32455) 212/C6
Red Bay, Newf. 166/C3
Red Bay, Ontario 177/C3
Red Beach, Maine (04670) 243/J5
Red Bird, Mo. (†65014) 261/J6
Redbird, Okla. (74458) 288/P3
Red Bluff, Calif. (96080) 204/C3
Red Bluff (lake), N. Mex. 274/E7
Red Bluff (lake), Texas 188/F4
Red Bluff (lake), Texas 303/A6
Red Boiling Springs, Tenn. (37150) 237/K7
Redbridge, England 13/H8
Redbridge, England 10/C5
Red Bud, Ill. (62278) 222/D5
Redbush, Ky. (41251) 237/P5
Redby, Minn. (56670) 255/D3
Redcar, England 10/F3
Redcar, England 13/F3
Red Cedar (riv.), Wis. 317/C5
Red Chute (bayou), La. 238/C1
Redcliff, Alberta 182/E4
Red Cliff, Colo. (81649) 208/G4
Red Cliff, Wis. (†54814) 317/E2
Redcliffe, Queensland 95/E5
Red Cliffe, Queensland 88/J5
Red Cliff Ind. Res., Wis. 317/E2
Red Cliffs, Victoria 97/B4
Redcloud (peak), Colo. 208/E6
Red Cloud, Nebr. (68970) 264/F4
Red Creek, N.Y. (13143) 276/G4
Red Creek, W. Va. (26289) 312/H4
Redcrest, Calif. (95569) 204/A3
Red Deer, Alberta 182/D3
Red Deer (lake), Alberta 182/D3
Red Deer (riv.), Alberta 182/D4
Red Deer, Alta. 146/G4
Red Deer, Alta. 162/E5
Red Deer (lake), Manitoba 179/A2
Red Deer (riv.), Manitoba 179/A2
Red Deer (riv.), Sask. 181/K3
Red Deer (riv.), Sask. 181/A5
Red Deer Hill, Sask. 181/F2
Reddell, La. (70580) 238/F5
Redden, Del. (†19947) 245/S5
Red Devil, Alaska (99656) 196/G2
Reddick, Fla. (32686) 212/D2
Reddick, Ill. (60961) 222/E2
Redding, Calif. 146/F5
Redding, Calif. 188/B2
Redding, Calif. (96001) 204/C3
Redding○, Conn. (06875) 210/B3
Redding, Iowa (50860) 229/E7
Redding Ridge, Conn. (06876) 210/B3
Reddington, Ind. (†47274) 227/F6
Redditch, England 13/E5
Redditch, England 10/G3
Red Earth Creek, Alberta 182/C1
Red Elm, S. Dak. (†57623) 298/F3
Redeye (riv.), Minn. 255/D4
Red Feather Lakes, Colo. (80545) 208/H1
Redfield, Ark. (72132) 202/F5
Redfield, Iowa (50233) 229/E5
Redfield, Kansas (66769) 232/H4
Redfield, N.Y. (13437) 276/J3
Redfield, Sask. 181/D2
Redfield, S. Dak. (57469) 298/N4
Redfish (lake), Idaho 220/D5
Redford, Mo. (63665) 261/L8
Redford, Texas (79846) 303/C12
Red Fork, Powder (riv.), Wyo. 319/F2
Redgranite, Wis. (54970) 317/J7
Redhead, Trin. & Tob. 161/B10
Red Head Cove, Newf. 166/D2
Red Hill (mt.), Hawaii 218/K2
Red Hill, Pa. (18076) 294/L5
Red Hook, N.Y. (12571) 276/N7
Redhouse, Ky. (†40475) 237/N5
Red House, Nev. (†89414) 266/D2
Red House, Va. (23963) 307/L6
Red House, W. Va. (25168) 312/C5
Redig, S. Dak. (57776) 298/C3
Red Indian (lake), Newf. 166/C4
Redington, Nebr. (†69336) 264/A3
Redington Beach, Fla. (33708) 212/B3
Redington Shores, Fla. (†33708) 212/B3
Red Jacket, W. Va. (25692) 312/B7
Redkey, Ind. (47373) 227/G4
Red Lake (co.), Minn. 255/B3
Redlake, Minn. (56671) 255/C3
Red Lake (riv.), Minn. 255/B2
Red Lake, Ont. 162/G6
Red Lake, Ontario 175/B2
Red Lake Falls, Minn. (56750) 255/B3
Red Lake Ind. Res., Minn. 255/C2
Red Lake Road, Ontario 177/G5
Red Lake Road, Ontario 175/B2
Redland, Alberta 182/D4
Redland, Oreg. (†97045) 291/B2
Redlands, Calif. (92373) 204/H9
Red Level, Ala. (36474) 195/E8
Red Lick, Miss. (†39096) 256/B7
Red Lion, Del. (†19701) 245/R2
Red Lion, N.J. (08088) 273/D4
Red Lion, Ohio (†45005) 284/B7
Red Lion, Pa. (17356) 294/J6
Red Lodge, Mont. (59068) 262/G5
Redman, Mich. (†48468) 250/G5
Red Mesa, Colo. (81326) 208/C8
Redmon, Ill. (61949) 222/F4
Redmond, Oreg. (97756) 291/F3
Redmond, Utah (84652) 304/C4
Redmond, Wash. (98052) 310/B1
Red Mountain, Calif. (93558) 204/H8
Red Oak, Georgia (30272) 217/J2
Red Oak, Iowa (51566) 229/C6
Red Oak, Mich. (†49756) 250/E4
Red Oak, N.C. (27868) 281/N2
Red Oak, Okla. (74563) 288/R5
Red Oak, Texas (75154) 303/H5
Red Oak, Va. (23964) 307/L7
Red Oaks Mill, N.Y. (†12601) 276/N7
Redon, France 28/C4
Redonda (isl.), Ant. & Bar. 156/F3
Redondela, Spain 33/B1
Redondo, Portugal 33/C3
Redondo, Wash. (98054) 310/C3
Redondo Beach, Calif. (*90277) 204/B11
Redoubt (vol.), Alaska 196/H2
Redowl, S. Dak. (57777) 298/D4
Red Owl (creek), S. Dak. 298/E4
Redpa, Tasmania 99/A2
Red Pass, Br. Col. 184/H4
Redridge, Mich. (†49931) 250/G1
Red River (par.), La. 238/D2
Red River, N. Mex. (87558) 274/D2
Red River, Nova Scotia 168/H2
Red River, S.C. (†29730) 296/F2
Red River (co.), Texas 303/J4
Red River Hot Springs, Idaho (†83525) 220/C4
Red River of the North (riv.) 188/G1
Red River of the North (riv.), Minn. 255/A2
Red River of the North (riv.), N. Dak. 282/S4
Red Rock, Ariz. (85245) 198/D6
Red Rock, Br. Col. 184/F3
Red Rock (lake), Iowa 229/G6
Red Rock (lakes), Mont. 262/E6
Red Rock (riv.), Mont. 262/D6
Redrock, N. Mex. (88055) 274/A6
Red Rock, Okla. (74651) 288/M2
Red Rock, Ontario 177/H5
Red Rock, Ontario 175/C3
Red Rock, Texas (78662) 303/G8
Red Scaffold (creek), S. Dak. 298/F4
Red Sea (prov.), Sudan 111/G4
Red Sea Hills (mts.), Sudan 59/C5
Red Springs, N.C. (28377) 281/L5
Red Springs, Texas (76378) 303/E4
Redstar, W. Va. (25914) 312/D7
Redstone, Br. Col. 184/F4
Redstone, Colo. (†81623) 208/E4
Redstone, Mont. (59257) 262/M2
Redstone, N.H. (†03813) 268/E3
Redstone (riv.), N.W. Terrs. 187/F3
Redstone (lake), Ontario 177/F2
Redstone (creek), S. Dak. 298/O5
Redstone Arsenal, Ala. 195/E1
Red Sucker Lake, Manitoba 179/K3
Red Sulphur Springs, W. Va. (†24963) 312/E7
Redtop, Minn. (†56342) 255/E4
Redvale, Colo. (81431) 208/B6
Redvers, Sask. 181/K6
Red Volta (riv.), Ghana 106/D6
Red Volta (riv.), Upper Volta 106/D6
Redwater, Alberta 182/D3
Redwater (riv.), Mont. 262/L3
Redwater (creek), S. Dak. 298/A4
Redway, Calif. (95560) 204/B3
Red Willow, Alberta 182/D3
Red Willow (co.), Nebr. 264/D4
Redwine, Ky. (†41477) 237/P4
Red Wine (riv.), Newf. 166/B3
Red Wing, Colo. (81066) 208/J7
Redwing, Kansas (†67544) 232/D3
Red Wing, Minn. (55066) 255/F6
Redwood (co.), Minn. 255/C6
Redwood (riv.), Minn. 255/C6
Redwood, Miss. (39156) 256/C6
Redwood, N.Y. (13679) 276/J2
Redwood City, Calif. (*94061) 204/J3
Redwood Estates-Chemeketa Park, Calif. (95044) 204/K4
Redwood Falls, Minn. (56283) 255/C6
Redwood Nat'l Park, Calif. 204/A2
Redwood Valley, Calif. (95470) 204/B4
Ree, Lough (lake), Ireland 10/B4
Ree (lake), Ireland 17/F5
Reece, Kansas (†67045) 232/F4
Reece City, Ala. (†35954) 195/G2
Reed, Ark. (71670) 202/H6
Reed, Ky. (42451) 237/G5
Reed, Okla. (73563) 288/G5
Reed (mt.), Québec 174/D2
Reed City, Mich. (49677) 250/D5
Reeder, Manitoba 179/A4
Reeder, N. Dak. (58649) 282/E7
Reedley, Calif. (93654) 204/F7
Reedpoint, Mont. (59069) 262/G5
Reeds, Mo. (64859) 261/D8
Reedsburg (res.), Mich. 250/E4
Reedsburg, Ohio (†44691) 284/F4
Reedsburg, Wis. (53959) 317/G8
Reeds Ferry, N.H. (†03054) 268/D6
Reedsport, Oreg. (97467) 291/C4
Reeds Spring, Mo. (65737) 261/F9
Reedsville, Ohio (45772) 284/G7
Reedsville, Pa. (17084) 294/G4
Reedsville, W. Va. (26547) 312/G3
Reedsville, Wis. (54230) 317/L7
Reedville, Oreg. (†97005) 291/A2
Reedville, Va. (22539) 307/R5
Reedy (lake), Fla. 212/E4
Reedy (riv.), S.C. 296/C2
Reedy, W. Va. (25270) 312/D5
Reedy (creek), W. Va. 312/D5
Reedyville, Ky. (†42275) 237/H6
Reef (bay), Virgin Is. (U.S.) 161/C4
Reefton, N. Zealand 100/C5
Ree Heights, S. Dak. (57371) 298/L4
Reelfoot (lake), Tenn. 237/C8
Reelsville, Ind. (46171) 227/D5
Reeman, Mich. (†49412) 250/D5
Reese, Mich. (48757) 250/F5
Reese (riv.), Nev. 266/D3
Reese A.F.B., Texas 303/B4
Reeseville, Wis. (53579) 317/J9
Reesville, Ohio (45166) 284/C7
Reeves, La. (70658) 238/D5
Reeves (co.), Texas 303/D11
Reeves Knob (mt.), Ark. 202/E2
Reevesville, Ill. (†62943) 222/E6
Reevesville, S.C. (29471) 296/F5
Refahiye, Turkey 63/H3
Refa'i, Iraq 66/E5
Reform, Ala. (35481) 195/C4
Reform, Miss. (39757) 256/F4
Refton, Pa. (17568) 294/K6
Refuge Cove, Br. Col. 184/E5
Refugio (isl.), Chile 138/D5
Refugio (co.), Texas 303/G9
Refugio, Texas (78377) 303/G9
Rega (riv.), Poland 47/B2
Regal, Minn. (†56312) 255/D5
Regan, N. Dak. (58477) 282/K5
Regen, W. Germany 22/E4
Regen (riv.), W. Germany 22/E4
Regeneração, Brazil 132/F4
Regensburg, W. Germany 7/F4
Regensburg, W. Germany 22/E4
Regensdorf, Switzerland 39/F2
Regent, Manitoba 179/B5
Regent, N. Dak. (58650) 282/E7
Reger, Mo. (†63556) 261/F2
Reggane, Algeria 106/D3
Regge (riv.), Netherlands 27/K4
Reggio, La. (†70085) 238/L7
Reggio di Calabria (prov.), Italy 34/E5
Reggio di Calabria, Italy 7/F5
Reggio di Calabria, Italy 34/E5
Reggio nell'Emilia (prov.), Italy 34/C2
Reggio nell'Emilia, Italy 34/C2
Reghin, Romania 45/G2
Régina, Fr. Guiana 131/E3
Regina, Mont. (59539) 262/J3
Regina, N. Mex. (87046) 274/B2
Regina (cap.), Sask. 162/F5
Regina (cap.), Sask. 146/H4
Regina (cap.), Sask. 181/G5
Regina Beach, Sask. 181/F5
Register, Georgia (30452) 217/J6
Registro, Brazil 135/C4
Regla, Cuba 158/C1
Regnitz (riv.), W. Germany 22/D4
Reguengos de Monsaraz, Portugal 33/C3
Regway, Sask. 181/G6
Rehau, W. Germany 22/D3
Rehoboth, Ala. (†36720) 195/D6
Rehoboth○, Mass. (02769) 249/K5
Rehoboth, Namibia 118/B4
Rehoboth, Namibia 102/D7
Rehoboth, N. Mex. (87322) 274/A3
Rehoboth, Va. (†23974) 307/M7
Rehoboth Beach, Del. (19971) 245/T6
Rehovot, Israel 65/B4
Rehrersburg, Pa. (19550) 294/K5
Reichenau an der Rax, Austria 41/C3
Reichenbach, E. Germany 22/E3
Reichenbach im Kandertal, Switzerland 39/E3

Reid, Md. (†21740) 245/H2
Reid (lake), S. Dak. 298/O3
Reid (rocks), Tasmania 99/B1
Reid, W. Australia 92/E5
Reiden, Switzerland 39/F2
Reids Grove, Md. (†21869) 245/P6
Reidsville, Georgia (30453) 217/H6
Reidsville, N.C. (27320) 281/K2
Reidville, S.C. (29375) 296/C2
Reigate, England 13/H8
Reigate, England 10/F5
Reile's Acres, N. Dak. (†58078) 282/S6
Reily, Ohio (45060) 284/A7
Re'im, Israel 65/A5
Reims, France 7/E4
Reims, France 28/E3
Reina Adelaida (arch.), Chile 120/B8
Reina Adelaida (arch.), Chile 138/D9
Reinach in Aargau, Switzerland 39/F2
Reinach in Baselland, Switzerland 39/E2
Reinbeck, Iowa (50669) 229/H4
Reindeer (lake) 162/F4
Reindeer (lake), Canada 146/H4
Reindeer (isl.), Manitoba 179/E2
Reindeer (lake), Manitoba 179/H2
Reindeer (lake), Sask. 181/N3
Reindeer (riv.), Sask. 181/M3
Reinersville, Ohio (43756) 284/G6
Reinfeld, W. Germany 22/D2
Reinga (cape), N. Zealand 100/D1
Reinland, Manitoba 179/E5
Reinosa, Spain 33/D1
Reisaelv (riv.), Norway 18/M2
Reisduoddarhal'di (Haltiatunturi), Norway 18/M2
Reiss, Scotland 15/E2
Reisterstown, Md. (21136) 245/L3
Reitz, S. Africa 118/D5
Rejaf, Sudan 111/F7
Reliance, Md. (†19973) 245/P6
Reliance, N.W. Terrs. 187/H3
Reliance, S. Dak. (57569) 298/K6
Reliance, Tenn. (37369) 237/N10
Reliance, Va. (22649) 307/M3
Reliance, Wyo. (82943) 319/C4
Relief, Ky. (41463) 237/P5
Relizane, Algeria 106/E1
Reloncaví (bay), Chile 138/D4
Remada, Tunisia 106/F2
Remagen, W. Germany 22/B3
Remanso, Brazil 132/F5
Remates, Cuba 158/A2
Rembang, Indonesia 85/K2
Rembert, S.C. (29128) 296/G3
Rembrandt, Iowa (50576) 229/C3
Rembrandt, Manitoba 179/E4
Remedios, Colombia 126/C4
Remedios, Cuba 156/B2
Remedios, Cuba 158/E2
Remedios (pt.), El Salvador 154/B4
Remer, Minn. (56672) 255/E3
Remerton, Georgia (31601) 217/F9
Remich, Luxembourg 27/J9
Reminderville, Ohio (†44202) 284/J10
Remington, Ind. (47977) 227/C3
Remington, Ohio (†45202) 284/C9
Remington, Va. (22734) 307/N3
Rémire, Fr. Guiana 131/E3
Rémire (isls.), Fr. Guiana 131/F3
Remiremont, France 28/G3
Remlap, Ala. (35133) 195/E3
Remmel (mt.), Wash. 310/E2
Remo, Br. Col. 184/C3
Remolino, Colombia 126/C2
Remote, Oreg. (97468) 291/D5
Remscheid, W. Germany 22/B3
Remsen, Iowa (51050) 229/B3
Remsen, N.Y. (13438) 276/K4
Remus, Mich. (49340) 250/D5
Remus, Okla. (†74801) 288/N4
Remy, La. (†70763) 238/L3
Rena, Ark. (†72956) 202/B3
Rena, Norway 18/G6
Reñaca, Chile 138/F2
Renaix (Ronse), Belgium 27/D7
Rena Lara, Miss. (38767) 256/C2
Renan, Switzerland 39/C2
Renault, Ill. (62279) 222/C5
Renca, Chile 138/G3
Rencona, N. Mex. (†87562) 274/D3
Rencontre East, Newf. 166/C4
Rend (lake), Ill. 222/E5
Rendeux, Belgium 27/H8
Rendova (isl.), Solomon Is. 86/D3
Rendsburg, W. Germany 22/C1
Rendville, Ohio (†43730) 284/F6
Renens, Switzerland 39/C3
Renews, Newf. 166/D2
Renforth, New Bruns. 170/E3
Renfrew, Ont. 162/J6
Renfrew (county), Ontario 177/G2
Renfrew (county), Ontario 175/E3
Renfrew, Ontario 177/H2
Renfrew, Ontario 175/E3
Renfrew, Pa. (16053) 294/C4
Renfrew, Scotland 10/A1
Renfrew, Scotland 15/B2
Renfrew (trad. co.), Scotland 15/A5
Renfroe, Ala. (†35160) 195/F4
Renfroe, Georgia (†31805) 217/C6
Renfroe, Miss. (†39051) 256/F5
Renfrow, Okla. (†73759) 288/L1
Rengam, Malaysia 72/E5
Rengat, Indonesia 85/C6
Rengo, Chile 138/G5
Reni, U.S.S.R. 52/C5
Renick, Mo. (65278) 261/H4
Renick, W. Va. (24966) 312/F6
Renigunta, India 68/E6
Renish (pt.), Scotland 15/B3
Renk, Sudan 111/F5
Renkum, Netherlands 27/H5
Renmark, S. Australia 88/G6
Renmark, S. Australia 94/G5
Rennell (isl.), Solomon Is. 87/F7
Rennell (isl.), Solomon Is. 86/E5
Renner, S. Dak. (57055) 298/R6
Rennert, N.C. (†28386) 281/L5
Rennes, France 7/D4
Rennes, France 28/C3
Rennie, Manitoba 179/G5
Rennie (lake), N.W. Terrs. 187/H3
Renno, S.C. (†29325) 296/D2
Reno, Alberta 182/B2
Reno, Georgia (†31728) 217/D9
Reno, Ill. (†62086) 222/D5
Reno (co.), Kansas 232/D4
Reno (lake), Minn. 255/C5
Reno, Nev. 146/G6
Reno, Nev. 188/C3
Reno, Nev. (*89501) 266/B3
Reno, Ohio (45773) 284/H7
Reno, Texas (†76020) 303/E2
Reno Beach, Ohio (†43412) 284/D2
Renous, New Bruns. 170/E2
Renous (riv.), New Bruns. 170/D2
Renova, Miss. (†38732) 256/C3
Renovo, Pa. (17764) 294/G3
Renown, Sask. 181/F4
Rensburg, S. Africa 118/J7
Rensselaer, Ind. (47978) 227/C3
Rensselaer, Mo. (†63401) 261/J3
Rensselaer (co.), N.Y. 276/O5
Rensselaer, N.Y. (12144) 276/N5
Rensselaer Falls, N.Y. (13680) 276/K1
Rentchler, Ill. (†62220) 222/B3
Rentiesville, Okla. (74459) 288/R4
Renton, Scotland 15/A1
Renton, Wash. (98055) 310/B2
Rentz, Georgia (31075) 217/G6
Renville (co.), Minn. 255/C6
Renville, Minn. (56284) 255/C6
Renville (co.), N. Dak. 282/G2
Renwer, Manitoba 179/B2
Renwick, Iowa (50577) 229/E3
Répcelak, 41/D3
Repentigny, Québec 172/J4
Replete, W. Va. (†26222) 312/F5
Repos (lake), Québec 172/C2
Repton, Ala. (36475) 195/D8
Republic, Ala. (†35203) 195/E3
Republic (co.), Kansas 232/E2
Republic, Kansas (66964) 232/E2
Republic, Mich. (49879) 250/B2
Republic, Mo. (65738) 261/E8
Republic, Ohio (44867) 284/D3
Republic, Wash. (99166) 310/G2
República Dominicana, Cuba 158/F2
Republican (riv.) 188/F2
Republican (riv.), Colo. 208/P3
Republican (riv.), Kansas 232/E2
Republican (riv.), Nebr. 264/G5
Republican City, Nebr. (68971) 264/E4
Republican Grove, Va. (24585) 307/K7
Repulse (bay), Queensland 88/H4
Repulse Bay, Canada 4/C14
Repulse Bay, N.W.T. 162/H2
Repulse Bay, N.W. Terrs. 187/K3
Requa, Calif. (†95548) 204/A2
Requegua, Chile 138/G5
Requena, Peru 128/F5
Requena, Spain 33/F3
Requinoa, Chile 138/G5
Rera, Brazil 132/A1
Resaca, Georgia (30735) 217/C1
Reşadiye, Turkey 63/G2
Research, Victoria 97/J4
Reseda, Calif. (91335) 204/B10
Resende, Brazil 135/D3
Resende, Portugal 33/B2
Reserve, Kansas (66529) 232/G2
Reserve, La. (70084) 238/M3
Reserve, Mont. (59258) 262/M2
Reserve, N. Mex. (87830) 274/A5
Reserve, Sask. 181/J3
Reserve, Wis. (†54876) 317/D4
Reserve Mines, Nova Scotia 168/H2
Resht (Rasht), Iran 66/F2
Reshui, China 77/E4
Resistencia, Argentina 143/E2
Resistencia, Argentina 120/D5
Reşiţa, Romania 45/E3
Resolute, Canada 4/B14
Resolute Bay, N.W.T. 162/G1
Resolute Bay, N.W. Terrs. 187/J2
Resolution (isl.), N.W.T. 146/M3
Resolution (isl.), N.W.T. 162/K3
Resolution (isl.), N. Zealand 100/A6
Resolution (isl.), N.W. Terrs. 187/M3
Resolution Island, N.W. Terrs. 187/M3
Resort, Loch (inlet), Scotland 15/A2
Resource, Sask. 181/G3
Respenda de la Peña, Spain 33/D1
Restauración, Dom. Rep. 158/D5
Rest Haven, Georgia (†30518) 217/E2
Restigouche (co.), New Bruns. 170/C1
Restigouche (riv.), New Bruns. 170/C1
Restigouche, Québec 172/C2
Reston, Manitoba 179/A5
Reston, Va. (22090) 307/R2
Restoule, Ontario 177/E1
Restoule (lake), Ontario 177/E1
Restrepo, Colombia 126/D5
Reszel, Poland 47/E1
Retalhuleu, Guatemala 154/B3
Retamosa, Uruguay 145/E4
Rethel, France 28/F3
Réthimnon, Greece 45/G8
Retie, Belgium 27/G6
Retiro, Chile 138/A11
Retlaw, Alberta 182/D4
Rétság, Hungary 41/E3
Retsil, Wash. (98378) 310/A2
Retsof, N.Y. (14539) 276/E5
Retz, Austria 41/D2
Reubens, Idaho (83548) 220/B3
Réunion (isl.), (Fr.) 2/M7
RÉUNION 118/F5
Reus, Spain 33/G2
Reusel, Netherlands 27/G6
Reuss (riv.), Switzerland 39/F2
Reutlingen, W. Germany 22/C4
Reutte, Austria 41/A3
Reva, S. Dak. (57651) 298/C2
Revadim, Israel 65/B4
Reveille (peak), Nev. 266/E5
Reveille (range), Nev. 266/E4
Revel, France 28/E6
Revel (Tallinn), U.S.S.R. 52/B3
Revelo, Ky. (42638) 237/N7
Revelstoke, Br. Col. 162/E5
Revelstoke, Br. Col. 184/J5
Reventazón, Peru 128/B6
Revenue, Sask. 181/B3
Revere, Mass. (02151) 249/D6
Revere, Minn. (56166) 255/C6
Revere, Mo. (63465) 261/J2
Revere, N. Dak. (†58484) 282/O5
Revere, W. Va. (†26158) 312/E5
Reverie, Tenn. (38062) 237/A9
Revillagigedo (chan.), Alaska 196/N2
Revillagigedo (isl.), Alaska 196/N2
Revillagigedo (isls.), Mexico 146/G8
Revillagigedo (isls.), Mexico 2/D5
Revillagigedo (isls.), Mexico 150/C7
Revillo, S. Dak. (57259) 298/R3
Révin, France 28/F3
Revivim, Israel 65/D5
Revúca, Czech. 41/F2
Revuelto (creek), N. Mex. 274/F3
Rew, Pa. (16744) 294/F2
Rewa, India 68/E4
Reward, Sask. 181/B3
Rewataya (reef), Indonesia 85/F7
Rewey, Wis. (53580) 317/F10
Rex, N.C. (28378) 281/M5
Rex, Oreg. (†97132) 291/A2
Rexburg, Idaho (83440) 220/G6
Rexford, Kansas (67753) 232/B2
Rexford, Mont. (59930) 262/A2
Rexton, Mich. (†49734) 250/D2
Rexton, New Bruns. 170/F2
Rexville, Ind. (†47250) 227/G7
Rexville, N.Y. (14877) 276/E6
Rey, Iran 59/F2
Rey, Iran 66/G3
Rey (isl.), Panama 154/H6
Rey Bouba, Cameroon 115/B2
Reydell, Ark. (72133) 202/G5
Reydon, Okla. (73660) 288/G3
Reyes, Bolivia 136/B4
Reyes (pt.), Calif. 204/B6
Reyhanlı, Turkey 63/G4
Reykjanestá (cape), Iceland 7/B2
Reykjanestá (cape), Iceland 21/A2
Reykjavík (cap.), Iceland 4/C11
Reykjavík (cap.), Iceland 2/J2
Reykjavík (cap.), Iceland 21/B1
Reykjavík (cap.), Iceland 7/B2
Reynaud, Sask. 181/F3
Reyno, Ark. (72462) 202/J1
Reynolds, Georgia (31076) 217/D5
Reynolds (creek), Idaho 220/B6
Reynolds, Ill. (61279) 222/C2
Reynolds, Ind. (47980) 227/D3
Reynolds (co.), Mo. 261/L8
Reynolds, Mo. (63666) 261/K8
Reynolds, Nebr. (68429) 264/G4
Reynolds, N. Dak. (58275) 282/R4
Reynolds Bridge, Conn. (†06787) 210/C2
Reynoldsburg, Ohio (43068) 284/E6
Reynolds Station, Ky. (42368) 237/H5
Reynoldsville, Pa. (15851) 294/D3
Reynosa, Mexico 150/K3
Rezaiyeh (Urmia), Iran 66/D2
Reza'iyeh (Urmia), Iran 59/D2
Rezé, France 28/C4
Rēzekne, U.S.S.R. 52/C3
Rēzekne, U.S.S.R. 53/D2
Rhaetian Alps (range), Switzerland 39/J3
Rhame, N. Dak. (58651) 282/C7
Rhätikon (mts.), Liecht. 39/J2
Rhätikon (mts.), Switzerland 39/J2
Rhayader, Wales 13/D5
Rhea (creek), Oreg. 291/H2
Rhea (co.), Tenn. 237/M9
Rheatown, Tenn. (†37641) 237/R8
Rheda-Wiedenbrück, W. Germany 22/C3
Rheden, Netherlands 27/H4
Rheims (Reims), France 28/E4
Rhein, Sask. 181/J4
Rheinau, Switzerland 39/G1
Rheine, W. Germany 22/B2
Rheineck, Switzerland 39/J2
Rheinfeld, Sask. 181/D5
Rheinfelden, Switzerland 39/E1
Rheinfelden, W. Germany 22/B5
Rheinsberg, E. Germany 22/E2
Rheinwaldhorn (mt.), Switzerland 39/G4
Rhems, S.C. (†29440) 296/H4
Rhenen, Netherlands 27/H5
Rhéris, Wadi (dry riv.), Morocco 106/D2
Rheydt, W. Germany 22/B3
Rhine (riv.) 7/E4
Rhine (riv.), Austria 41/A3
Rhine (riv.), France 28/G3
Rhine, Georgia (31077) 217/F7
Rhine (riv.), Liecht. 39/J2
Rhine (riv.), Netherlands 27/J5
Rhine (riv.), Switzerland 39/J2
Rhine (riv.), W. Germany 22/B3
Rhinebeck, N.Y. (12572) 276/N7
Rhinecliff, N.Y. (12574) 276/N7
Rhineland, Mo. (65069) 261/J5
Rhineland, Sask. 181/D5
Rhinelander, Wis. (54501) 317/H4
Rhineland-Palatinate (state), W. Germany 22/B4
Rhinns, The (pen.), Scotland 15/C6
Rhinns (pt.), Scotland 15/B5
Rhino Camp, Uganda 115/F3
Rhir, Wadi (dry riv.), Algeria 106/F2
Rhir (cape), Morocco 106/B2
Rho, Italy 34/B2
Rhode Island 188/M2
RHODE ISLAND 249
Rhode Island (isl.), R.I. 249/J6
Rhode Island (sound), R.I. 249/J7
Rhode Island (state), U.S. 146/M5
Rhodell, W. Va. (25915) 312/D7
Rhodes (Ródhos), Greece 45/J7
Rhodes (isl.), Greece 7/G5
Rhodes (isl.), Greece 45/H7
Rhodes (peak), Idaho 220/D3
Rhodes, Iowa (50234) 229/G5
Rhodes, Mich. (48652) 250/E5
Rhodes Inyanga Nat'l Park, Zimbabwe 118/E3
Rhodes Point, Md. (21858) 245/O9
Rhodhiss, N.C. (28667) 281/F3
Rhododendron, Oreg. (97073) 291/F2
Rhodope (mts.), Bulgaria 45/G5
Rhodope (mts.), Greece 45/G5
Rhome, Texas (76078) 303/E1
Rhön (mts.), E. Germany 22/D3
Rhön (mts.), W. Germany 22/D3
Rhondda, Wales 13/A6
Rhondda, Wales 10/E5
Rhône (dept.), France 28/F5
Rhône (riv.), France 7/E4
Rhône (riv.), France 28/F5
Rhône (riv.), Switzerland 39/D4
Rhosllanerchrugog, Wales 13/D4
Rhu, Scotland 15/A1
Rhu Coigeach (cape), Scotland 15/C2
Rhyl, Wales 13/D4
Rhymney, Wales 13/A6
Rhymney (riv.), Wales 13/B6
Rhynie, Scotland 15/F3
Rhyolite (Ghost Town), Nev. (†89003) 266/E6
Riachão, Brazil 132/E4
Riachuelo, Uruguay 145/B5
Rialto, Calif. (92376) 204/E10
Riana, Tasmania 99/B3
Riaño, Spain 33/D1
Riau (arch.), Indonesia 85/C5
Riaza, Spain 33/E2
Rib (mt.), Wis. 317/G6
Ribadavia, Spain 33/B1
Ribadeo, Spain 33/C1
Ribamar, Brazil 132/F3
Ribas do Rio Pardo, Brazil 132/C8
Ribat Qila, Pakistan 68/A3
Ribat Qila, Pakistan 59/H4
Ribáuè, Mozambique 118/F3
Ribble (riv.), England 10/E4
Ribble (riv.), England 13/E4
Ribe (co.), Denmark 21/B7
Ribe, Denmark 21/B7
Ribe, Denmark 18/F9
Ribeira, Brazil 135/B4
Ribeira (riv.), Brazil 135/B4
Ribeira Brava, Portugal 33/A2
Ribeira de Iguape, Brazil 135/C4
Ribeira de Pena, Portugal 33/C2
Ribeira Grande, C. Verde 106/B7
Ribeirão Preto, Brazil 120/E5
Ribeirão Preto, Brazil 135/C2
Ribeirão Preto, Brazil 132/E8
Ribera, N. Mex. (87560) 274/D3
Ribérac, France 28/D5
Riberach an der Riss, W. Germany 22/C4
Riberalta, Bolivia 136/C2
Riberalta, Bolivia 120/C4
Rib Falls, Wis. (†54426) 317/G6
Ribla, Kuh-e (riv.), Iran 66/J6
Rib Lake, Wis. (54470) 317/F5
Ribnitz-Damgarten, E. Germany 22/E1
Ribstone, Alberta 182/E3
Říčany u Prahy, Czech. 41/C2
Ricaurte, Colombia 126/A7
Riccarton, N. Zealand 100/D5
Rice, Calif. (†92280) 204/L9
Rice (co.), Kansas 232/D3
Rice, Kansas (66965) 232/E2
Rice (co.), Minn. 255/E6
Rice, Minn. (56367) 255/D5
Rice (lake), Minn. 255/E4
Rice (mt.), N.H. 268/E2
Rice (lake), Ontario 177/F3
Rice, Texas (75155) 303/H5
Rice, Va. (23966) 307/M6
Rice, Wash. (99167) 310/G2
Riceboro, Georgia (31323) 217/K7
Rice Lake, Wis. (54868) 317/C5
Rices Landing, Pa. (15357) 294/C6
Riceton, Sask. 181/G5
Ricetown, Ky. (41364) 237/O6
Riceville, Iowa (50466) 229/H2
Riceville, Pa. (16432) 294/C2
Riceville, Tenn. (37370) 237/M10
Rich, Miss. (38662) 256/D2
Rich (cape), Ontario 177/D3
Rich (co.), Utah 304/C2
Richard, Sask. 181/D3
Richard City, Tenn. (†37380) 237/K11
Richard Collinson (inlet), N.W. Terrs. 187/G2
Richards, Iowa (†50579) 229/D4
Richards, Mo. (64778) 261/D7
Richards (isl.), N.W. Terrs. 187/E3
Richards Bay, S. Africa 118/E5
Richards Gebaur A.F.B., Mo. 261/P6
Richards Landing, Ontario 177/J5
Richardson (riv.), Alberta 182/C5
Richardson, Ky. (41253) 237/R5
Richardson (lakes), Maine 243/B6
Richardson (co.), Nebr. 264/J4
Richardson (isls.), N.W. Terrs. 187/G3
Richardson (mts.), N.W. Terrs. 187/E3
Richardson, Sask. 181/G5
Richardson, Texas (75080) 303/G2
Richardson, W. Va. (†26151) 312/D5
Richardson (mts.), Yukon 187/E3
Richardsons Landing, Tenn. (†38023) 237/B10
Richardsville, Ky. (42270) 237/J6
Richardsville, New Bruns. 170/D1
Richard Toll, Senegal 106/A5
Richardton, N. Dak. (58652) 282/F6
Richburg, N.Y. (14774) 276/D6
Richburg, S.C. (29729) 296/E2
Rich Creek, Va. (24147) 307/G6
Richdale, Alberta 182/E4
Riche (pt.), Newf. 166/C3
Richelieu, Ky. (42271) 237/H7
Richelieu (co.), Québec 172/D4
Richelieu, Québec 172/D4
Richer, Manitoba 179/F5
Richey, Mont. (59259) 262/L3
Richfield, Idaho (83349) 220/D6
Richfield, Kansas (67953) 232/A4
Richfield, Minn. (55423) 255/G6
Richfield, N.C. (28137) 281/J4
Richfield, Nova Scotia 168/C4
Richfield, Ohio (44286) 284/G3
Richfield, Pa. (17086) 294/H4
Richfield, Utah (84701) 304/B5
Richfield, Wis. (53076) 317/K1
Richfield Springs, N.Y. (13439) 276/K5
Richford, N.Y. (13835) 276/H6
Richford, Vt. (05476) 268/B2
Richford○, Vt. (05476) 268/B2
Richford, Wis. (†54930) 317/H7
Rich Fountain, Mo. (65070) 261/J6
Richgrove, Calif. (93261) 204/F8
Rich Hill, Mo. (64779) 261/D6
Richhill, N. Ireland 17/H3
Richibucto, New Bruns. 170/E2
Richibucto (harb.), New Bruns. 170/F2
Richibucto (riv.), New Bruns. 170/E2
Richibucto Village, New Bruns. 170/F2
Rich Lake, Alberta 182/E2
Richland, Fla. (†33599) 212/D3
Richland, Georgia (31825) 217/C6
Richland (co.), Ill. 222/E5
Richland, Ind. (47634) 227/C9
Richland (creek), Ind. 227/D6
Richland, Iowa (52585) 229/K6
Richland, Kansas (†66409) 232/G3
Richland (par.), La. 238/G2
Richland, Mich. (49083) 250/D6
Richland, Miss. (†39218) 256/D6
Richland, Mo. (65556) 261/H7
Richland (co.), Mont. 262/M3
Richland, Mont. (59260) 262/K2
Richland, Nebr. (68657) 264/G3
Richland, N.J. (08350) 273/D5
Richland, N.Y. (13144) 276/H3
Richland (co.), N. Dak. 282/R7
Richland (co.), Ohio 284/E4
Richland, Oreg. (97870) 291/K3
Richland, Pa. (17087) 294/K5
Richland (co.), S.C. 296/F4
Richland, S.C. (29675) 296/A2
Richland, S. Dak. (†57025) 298/R8
Richland (creek), Tenn. 237/G10
Richland, Texas (76681) 303/H6
Richland, Wash. 188/B1
Richland, Wash. (99352) 310/F4
Richland (co.), Wis. 317/F9
Richland Balsam (mt.), N.C. 281/D4
Richland Center, Wis. (53581) 317/F9
Richland Hills, Texas (76118) 303/F2
Richland-Kennewick, Wash. 310/80
Richlands, N.C. (28574) 281/O5
Richlands, Va. (24641) 307/E6
Richland Springs, Texas (76871) 303/F6
Richlandtown, Pa. (18955) 294/M5
Richlea, Sask. 181/C4
Richmond, Ala. (†36761) 195/D6
Richmond, Ark. (†71822) 202/B6
Richmond, Br. Col. 184/K3
Richmond, Calif. (*94801) 204/J1
Richmond, England 13/F3
Richmond, England 10/E3
Richmond (co.), Georgia 217/H4
Richmond, Ill. (60071) 222/E1
Richmond, Ind. (47374) 227/H5
Richmond, Iowa (52247) 229/K6
Richmond, Jamaica 158/J6
Richmond, Kansas (66080) 232/G3
Richmond, Ky. (40475) 237/N5
Richmond, La. (†71282) 238/H2
Richmond, Maine (04357) 243/D7
Richmond○, Maine (04357) 243/D7
Richmond○, Mass. (01254) 249/A3
Richmond, Mich. (48062) 250/G6
Richmond, Minn. (56368) 255/D5
Richmond, Mo. (64085) 261/D4
Richmond○, N.H. (†03470) 268/C6
Richmond (range), N.S. Wales 97/G1
Richmond (riv.), N.S. Wales 97/G1
Richmond (co.), N.Y. 276/M9
Richmond (Staten Island) (borough), N.Y. 276/M9
Richmond, N. Zealand 100/D4
Richmond (range), N. Zealand 100/D4
Richmond (co.), N.C. 281/K4
Richmond (co.), Nova Scotia 168/H3
Richmond (Grand River), Ohio (†44045) 284/H2
Richmond, Ohio (43944) 284/J5
Richmond, Ontario 177/J2
Richmond (co.), Québec 172/E4
Richmond, Québec 172/E4
Richmond, Queensland 88/G4
Richmond, Queensland 95/B4
Richmond (peak), St. Vin. & Grens. 161/A8
Richmond, S. Africa 118/C6
Richmond, Tasmania 99/D4
Richmond, Texas (77469) 303/J8
Richmond, Utah (84333) 304/C2
Richmond, Vt. (05477) 268/A3
Richmond○, Vt. (05477) 268/A3
Richmond, Victoria 88/L7
Richmond, Victoria 97/J5
Richmond (cap.), Va. 188/L3
Richmond (cap.), Va. 146/L6
Richmond (co.), Va. 307/P5
Richmond (cap.) (I.C.), Va. (*23201) 307/O5
Richmond Beach-Innis Arden, Wash. (98160) 310/A1
Richmond Corner, Maine (†04357) 243/D7
Richmond Corner, New Bruns. 170/C2
Richmond Dale, Ohio (45673) 284/E7
Richmond Furnace, Mass. (†01254) 249/A3
Richmond Heights, Fla. (†33158) 212/F6
Richmond Heights, Mo. (63117) 261/P3
Richmond Heights, Ohio (44143) 284/H9
Richmond Highlands, Wash. (†98133) 310/A1
Richmond Hill, Georgia (31324) 217/K7
Richmond Hill, Ontario 177/J4
Richmond Nat'l Battlefield Park, Va. 307/O6
Richmond upon Thames, England 10/B5
Richmond upon Thames, England 13/H8
Richmondville, N.Y. (12149) 276/M5
Richmond-Windsor, N.S. Wales 97/F3
Richmound, Sask. 181/B5
Rich Mountain, Ark. (†71953) 202/B4
Rich Square, N.C. (27869) 281/P2
Richterswil, Switzerland 39/G2
Richthofen (mt.), Colo. 208/G2
Richton, Miss. (39476) 256/G8
Richton Park, Ill. (60471) 222/B6
Richvale, Calif. (95974) 204/D4
Richvalley, Ind. (†46992) 227/F3
Richview, Ill. (62877) 222/D5
Richville, Mich. (48758) 250/F5
Richville, Minn. (56576) 255/C4
Richville, N.Y. (13681) 276/K2
Richwood, La. (†71201) 238/F2
Richwood, Minn. (56577) 255/C4
Richwood, N.J. (08074) 273/C4
Richwood, Ohio (43344) 284/D5
Richwood, W. Va. (26261) 312/F6
Richwood, Wis. (†53094) 317/J9
Richwoods, Mo. (63071) 261/L6
Rickardsville, Iowa (†52039) 229/M3
Rickenbacker Air Force Base, Ohio 284/E6
Ricketts, Iowa (51460) 229/B4
Ricketts (pt.), Victoria 97/J6
Ricketts (pt.), Victoria 88/L8
Rickman, Tenn. (38580) 237/L8
Rickmansworth, England 13/G8
Rickmansworth, England 10/A5
Rickreall, Oreg. (97371) 291/D3
Ricla, Spain 33/F2
Rico, Colo. (81332) 208/C7
Ricobayo (res.), Spain 33/D2
Ricse, Hungary 41/G2
Ridderkerk, Netherlands 27/F5
Riddle, Idaho (†89832) 220/B7
Riddle, Oreg. (97469) 291/D5
Riddlesburg, Pa. (16672) 294/F5
Riddleton, Tenn. (37151) 237/J8
Riddleville, Georgia (†31018) 217/G5
Riddon, Loch (inlet), Scotland 15/C5
Rideau (lake), Ontario 177/H3
Riderwood, Ala. (†36904) 195/B6
Ridge, Md. (20680) 245/N8
Ridge, Mont. (†59314) 262/M5
Ridgecrest, Calif. (93555) 204/H8
Ridgecrest, La. (†71334) 238/G3
Ridgedale, Mo. (65739) 261/F9
Ridgedale, Sask. 181/H2
Ridge Farm, Ill. (61870) 222/F4
Ridgefield, Conn. (06877) 210/B3
Ridgefield○, Conn. (06877) 210/B3
Ridgefield, N.J. (07657) 273/B2
Ridgefield, Wash. (98642) 310/C5
Ridgefield Park, N.J. (07660) 273/B2
Ridgeland, Miss. (39157) 256/D6
Ridgeland, S.C. (29936) 296/E7
Ridgeland, Wis. (54763) 317/B5
Ridgeley, W. Va. (26753) 312/J3
Ridgely, Md. (21660) 245/P5
Ridgely, Mo. (†64444) 261/C4
Ridgely, Tenn. (38080) 237/B8
Ridgeside, Tenn. (†37401) 237/L10
Ridge Spring, S.C. (29129) 296/D4
Ridgetop, Tenn. (37152) 237/H8
Ridgetown, Ontario 177/C5
Ridgeview, S. Dak. (57652) 298/H3
Ridgeville, Georgia (†31331) 217/K8
Ridgeville, Ind. (47380) 227/G4
Ridgeville, Manitoba 179/E5
Ridgeville, S.C. (29472) 296/G5
Ridgeville Corners, Ohio (43555) 284/B3
Ridgeway, Iowa (52165) 229/K2
Ridgeway, Minn. (†55943) 255/G7
Ridgeway, Mo. (64481) 261/D2
Ridgeway, N.C. (27570) 281/N2
Ridgeway, Ohio (43345) 284/C4
Ridgeway, S.C. (29130) 296/F3
Ridgeway, Va. (24148) 307/J7
Ridgeway, W. Va. (25440) 312/K4
Ridgeway, Wis. (53582) 317/F10
Ridgeway Branch, Toms (riv.), N.J. 273/E3
Ridgewood, N.J. (*07450) 273/B1
Ridgley, Tasmania 99/B3
Ridgway, Colo. (81432) 208/D6
Ridgway, Ill. (62979) 222/E6
Ridgway, Pa. (15853) 294/E3
Ridi, Nepal 68/E3
Riding (mt.), Manitoba 179/B4
Riding Mountain, Manitoba 179/C4
Riding Mountain Nat'l Park, Man. 162/F5
Riding Mountain Nat'l Park, Manitoba 179/B4
Ridley, Tenn. (†38474) 237/G9
Ridley Park, Pa. (19078) 294/M7
Ridott, Ill. (61067) 222/D1
Ridotto, Iowa (†50546) 229/D3
Ried im Innkreis, Austria 41/B2
Riegelsville, N.J. (†08865) 273/C2
Riegelsville, Pa. (18077) 294/M4
Riegelwood, N.C. (28456) 281/N6
Riehen, Switzerland 39/E1
Rienzi, Miss. (38865) 256/G1
Riesa, E. Germany 22/E3
Riesco (isl.), Chile 138/E10
Riesel, Texas (76682) 303/H6
Riesi, Italy 34/E6
Rietavas, U.S.S.R. 53/A3
Rietberg, W. Germany 22/C3
Rietfontein, Namibia 118/C4
Rieth, Oreg. (†97801) 291/J2
Rieti (prov.), Italy 34/D3
Rieti, Italy 34/D3
Rif, Er (range), Morocco 106/D2

436 Riffelalp

Riffelalp, Switzerland 39/E5
Rifle, Colo. (81650) 208/D3
Rifle (creek), Colo. 208/D3
Rifle (riv.), Mich. 250/E4
Rifle (lake), Wash. 310/C4
Rifstangi (cape), Iceland 21/C1
Rift Valley (prov.), Kenya 115/G3
Riga (lake), Conn. 210/B1
Riga, U.S.S.R. 2/L3
Riga, U.S.S.R. 7/G3
Riga (gulf), U.S.S.R. 7/G3
Riga (cap.), U.S.S.R. 53/C2
Riga, U.S.S.R. 48/C4
Riga, U.S.S.R. 52/B3
Riga (gulf), U.S.S.R. 52/B3
Riga (gulf), U.S.S.R. 53/B2
Riga (gulf), U.S.S.R. 48/C4
Rigan, Iran 66/L6
Rigaud, Québec 172/C4
Rigby, Idaho (83442) 220/F6
Rigdon, Ind. (†46928) 227/F4
Rigestan (reg.), Afghanistan 59/H3
Riggins, Idaho (83549) 220/B4
Riggisberg, Switzerland 39/E3
Rigi (mt.), Switzerland 39/F2
Rigo, Papua N.G. 85/C7
Rigolet, Newf. 166/C3
Rigolet, Newf. 162/L5
Rig Rig, Chad 111/B5
Rigside, Scotland 15/E5
Riihimäki, Finland 18/O6
Riiser-Larsen (pen.), Ant. 2/L9
Riiser-Larsen (pen.) 5/C2
Rijeka, Yugoslavia 45/B3
Rijeka, Yugoslavia 7/F4
Rijen, Netherlands 27/F5
Rijnsburg, Netherlands 27/F4
Rijssen, Netherlands 27/J4
Rijswijk, Netherlands 27/E4
Rikitea, Fr. Poly. 87/N8
Rikuchu-Kaigan National Park, Japan 81/L4
Rikuzentakata, Japan 81/K4
Riley, Ind. (47871) 227/C6
Riley (co.), Kansas 232/F2
Riley, Kansas (66531) 232/F2
Riley, Ky. (†40328) 237/L5
Riley, Maine (†04262) 243/C6
Riley, Oreg. (97758) 291/H4
Riley Brook, New Bruns. 170/C1
Rileysburg, Ind. (†47932) 227/B4
Rillito, Ariz. (85246) 198/D6
Rillton, Pa. (15678) 294/C5
Rima (riv.), Niger 106/F6
Rima (riv.), Nigeria 106/F6
Rima, Wadi (dry riv.), Saudi Arabia 59/D4
Rimac (riv.), Peru 128/D9
Rimal, Ar (des.), Saudi Arabia 59/F5
Rimatara (isl.), Fr. Poly. 87/L8
Rimavská Sobota, Czech. 41/E2
Rimbey, Alberta 182/C3
Rimbo, Sweden 18/L7
Rimersburg, Pa. (16248) 294/D3
Rimini, Italy 34/D2
Rimini, S.C. (29131) 296/G4
Rîmnicu Sărat, Romania 45/H3
Rîmnicu Vîlcea, Romania 45/G3
Rimouski, Que. 162/K6
Rimouski (co.), Québec 172/J1
Rimouski (county), Québec 174/D3
Rimouski, Québec 172/J1
Rimouski, Québec 174/D3
Rimouski (riv.), Québec 172/J1
Rimouski-Est, Québec 172/J1
Rimpfischhorn (mt.), Switzerland 39/E4
Rimrock, Ariz. (86335) 198/D4
Rimrock (lake), Wash. 310/D4
Rimutaka (range), N. Zealand 100/B3
Rinard, Ill. (62878) 222/E5
Rinard, Iowa (50587) 229/D4
Rincón, Cerro (mt.), Argentina 143/C1
Rincon (peak), Ariz. 198/E6
Rincón, Cerro (mt.), Chile 138/C4
Rincón, Dom. Rep. 158/E5
Rincón (bay), Dom. Rep. 158/F5
Rincon, Georgia (31326) 217/K6
Rincon, Neth. Ant. 161/E8
Rincon, N. Mex. (87940) 274/C6
Rincón (pt.), Panama 154/G6
Rincón, P. Rico 161/A1
Rincón (bay), P. Rico 161/D3
Rinconada, Argentina 143/C1
Rinconada San Martín, Chile 138/G2
Rincón de Romos, Mexico 150/H5
Rindge○, N.H. (03461) 268/C6
Riner, Va. (24149) 307/H6
Rineyville, Ky. (40162) 237/K5
Ringarooma, Tasmania 99/D3
Ringarooma (bay), Tasmania 99/D2
Ringe, Denmark 21/D7
Ringebu, Norway 18/G6
Ringelspitz (mt.), Switzerland 39/H3
Ringerike, Norway 18/C3
Ringgold, Georgia (30736) 217/B1
Ringgold (co.), Iowa 229/E7
Ringgold, La. (71068) 238/D2
Ringgold, Md. (†21783) 245/H2
Ringgold, Nebr. (†69167) 264/D3
Ringgold, Texas (76261) 303/G4
Ringgold, Va. (24586) 307/K7
Ringim, Nigeria 106/F6
Ringkøbing (co.), Denmark 21/B5
Ringkøbing, Denmark 18/E8
Ringkøbing, Denmark 21/A5
Ringkøbing (fjord), Denmark 21/B6
Ringling, Mont. (59642) 262/F4
Ringling, Okla. (73456) 288/L6
Ringmer, England 13/H7
Ringoes, N.J. (08551) 273/D3
Ringold, Okla. (74754) 288/R6
Ringsted, Denmark 21/E7
Ringsted, Iowa (50578) 229/D2
Ringtown, Pa. (17967) 294/K4
Ringvassøy (isl.), Norway 18/L2
Ringwood, England 13/F7
Ringwood, Ill. (60072) 222/E1
Ringwood, N.J. (07456) 273/E1
Ringwood, N.C. (†27823) 281/O2
Ringwood, North. Terr. 93/D7
Ringwood, Okla. (73768) 288/K2
Ringwood, Victoria 88/M7
Ringwood, Victoria 97/K5
Rinn (lake), Ireland 17/F4
Rinteln, W. Germany 22/C2
Rio, Ill. (61472) 222/C2
Rio, La. (†70427) 238/L5
Rio, W. Va. (26755) 312/J4
Rio, Wis. (53960) 317/H9
Rio Arriba (co.), N. Mex. 274/B2
Riobamba, Ecuador 128/C3
Riobamba, Ecuador 120/B3
Río Blanco, Chile 138/B9
Rio Blanco (co.), Colo. 208/C3
Rio Blanco, Colo. (†81650) 208/C3
Río Blanco, P. Rico 161/F2
Rio Bonito, Brazil 135/E3
Rio Branco, Brazil 120/C3
Rio Branco, Brazil 132/G10
Río Branco, Uruguay 145/F3
Rio Brazos (riv.), N. Mex. 274/C2
Rio Brilhante, Brazil 132/C8
Río Bueno, Chile 138/D3
Rio Bueno, Jamaica 158/H5
Río Caribe, Venezuela 124/G2
Río Cauto, Cuba 158/H4
Rio Chama (riv.), N. Mex. 274/C2
Río Chico, Venezuela 124/F2
Río Cisnes, Chile 138/E5
Rio Claro, Brazil 132/E8
Rio Claro, Brazil 135/C3
Rio Claro, Trin. & Tob. 161/B11
Río Claro, Venezuela 124/D3
Río Colorado, Argentina 120/C6
Río Colorado, La Pampa, Argentina 143/D4
Río Colorado, Río Negro, Argentina 143/D4
Rio Creek, Wis. (54231) 317/L6
Río Cuarto, Argentina 143/D3
Río Cuarto, Argentina 120/C6
Rio de Janeiro (state), Brazil 135/E3
Rio de Janeiro (state), Brazil 132/F8
Rio de Janeiro, Brazil 2/G7
Rio de Janeiro, Brazil 120/E5
Rio de Janeiro, Brazil 135/E3
Rio de Janeiro, Brazil 132/F8
Rio Dell, Calif. (95562) 204/A3
Río de Oro, Colombia 126/D3
Rio do Sul, Brazil 132/D9
Rio Felix (riv.), N. Mex. 274/E5
Río Gallegos, Argentina 120/C8
Río Gallegos, Argentina 143/C7
Ritidian (pt.), Guam 86/K6
Rio Grande (riv.) 2/D4
Rio Grande (riv.) 146/H7
Rio Grande (riv.) 188/F5
Río Grande, Argentina 143/C7
Río Grande, Bolivia 136/B7
Rio Grande, Brazil 120/D6
Rio Grande, Brazil 132/D11
Rio Grande (co.), Colo. 208/G7
Rio Grande (res.), Colo. 208/E7
Rio Grande (riv.), Colo. 208/H8
Rio Grande, N.J. (08242) 273/D5
Rio Grande (riv.), N. Mex. 274/C5
Rio Grande, Ohio (45674) 284/F8
Río Grande, P. Rico 161/E1
Rio Grande (riv.), Texas 303/D9
Rio Grande City, Texas (78582) 303/F11
Rio Grande do Norte (state), Brazil 132/G4
Rio Grande do Sul (state), Brazil 132/C10
Rio Grande Pyramid (mt.), Colo. 208/E7
Rio Grande Wild and Scenic River, Texas 303/B8
Riohacha, Colombia 120/B1
Riohacha, Colombia 126/D2
Río Hondo, Guatemala 154/C3
Rio Hondo (riv.), N. Mex. 274/E5
Rio Hondo, Texas (78583) 303/G11
Rioja, Peru 128/D6
Río Lagartos, Mexico 150/P6
Rio Linda, Calif. (95673) 204/B8
Rio Maior, Portugal 33/B3
Río Mulato, Bolivia 136/B6
Río Muni (terr.), Equat. Guinea 115/B3
Rion, S.C. (29132) 296/E3
Riondel, Br. Col. 184/J5
Río Negro (prov.), Argentina 143/C5
Rio Negro, Brazil 132/D9
Río Negro, Chile 138/D3
Rionegro, Antioquia, Colombia 126/C4
Rionegro, Santander, Colombia 126/D4
Río Negro (dept.), Uruguay 145/B3
Río Negro (res.), Uruguay 145/D3
Rionero in Vulture, Italy 34/E4
Rio Pardo, Brazil 132/C10
Rio Pardo de Minas, Brazil 132/F6
Rio Penasco (riv.), N. Mex. 274/E6
Río Piedras, P. Rico 161/E1
Rio Pomba, Brazil 135/E2
Rio Puerco (riv.), N. Mex. 274/C4
Rio Rancho, N. Mex. (87124) 274/C3
Rio Real, Brazil 132/G5
Rio Rico, Ariz. (85621) 198/E7
Rio Salado (riv.), N. Mex. 274/B4
Río San Juan, Dom. Rep. 158/E5
Río Seco, Cuba 158/A2
Río Segundo, Argentina 143/D3
Riosucio, Caldas, Colombia 126/C5
Riosucio, Chocó, Colombia 126/B4
Río Tercero, Argentina 143/D3
Río Tigre, Ecuador 128/D4
Rio Tinto, Brazil 132/H4
Río Tocuyo, Venezuela 124/C2
Riou (lake), Sask. 181/M2
Rio Verde, Brazil 132/D7
Rio Verde, Brazil 120/D4
Río Verde, Chile 138/E10
Ríoverde, Mexico 150/J6
Rio Verde de Mato Grosso, Brazil 132/C7
Rio Vista, Calif. (94571) 204/L1
Riparia, Wash. (†99359) 310/G4
Riparius, N.Y. (12862) 276/M3
Ripley, Calif. (92272) 204/L10
Ripley, England 13/F4
Ripley, Ill. (†62353) 222/C3
Ripley (co.), Ind. 227/G6
Ripley○, Maine (†04930) 243/E5
Ripley, Miss. (38663) 256/G1
Ripley (co.), Mo. 261/L9
Ripley, N.Y. (14775) 276/A6
Ripley, Ohio (45167) 284/C8
Ripley, Okla. (74062) 288/N2
Ripley, Ontario 177/C3
Ripley, Tenn. (38063) 237/B9
Ripley, W. Va. (25271) 312/C5
Riplinger, Wis. (†54479) 317/E6
Ripoll, Spain 33/H1
Ripon, Calif. (95366) 204/D6
Ripon, England 10/F3
Ripon, England 13/F3
Ripon, Québec 172/B4
Ripon, Wis. (54971) 317/J8
Rippey, Iowa (50235) 229/E5
Ripplemead, Va. (24150) 307/G6
Ripples, New Bruns. 170/D3
Rippon, W. Va. (25441) 312/L4
Rippowam (riv.), Conn. 210/A4
Ripton○, Vt. (05766) 268/A4
Ririe, Idaho (83443) 220/G6
Risafe, Syria 63/H5
Risalpur Cantonment, Pakistan 68/C2
Risaralda (dept.), Colombia 126/B5
Risca, Wales 13/B6
Risco, Mo. (63874) 261/N9
Rishiri (isl.), Japan 81/K1
Rishon Le Ziyyon, Israel 65/B4
Rishra, India 68/F1
Rising City, Nebr. (68658) 264/G3
Rising Fawn, Georgia (30738) 217/A1
Rising Star, Texas (76471) 303/F5
Rising Sun, Ind. (47040) 227/H7
Rising Sun, Md. (21911) 245/O2
Risingsun, Ohio (43457) 284/C3
Rising Sun, Wis. (†54628) 317/D9
Risle (riv.), France 28/D3
Rison, Ark. (71665) 202/F6
Risør, Norway 18/F7
Risoux (mt.), Switzerland 39/B3
Ristigouche (riv.), Québec 172/B2
Ristijärvi, Finland 18/Q4
Rita Blanca (creek), Texas 303/B2
Ritchey, Mo. (†64844) 261/D9
Ritchie, Md. (†20027) 245/G5
Ritchie (co.), W. Va. 312/D4
Ritchies (arch.), India 68/G6
Ritidian (pt.), Guam 86/K6
Ritner, Ky. (42639) 237/M7
Ritter, Oreg. (97872) 291/H3
Ritter, S.C. (29488) 296/F6
Rittman, Ohio (44270) 284/G4
Ritzville, Wash. (99169) 310/G3
Rivadavia, Mendoza, Argentina 143/C3
Rivadavia, Salta, Argentina 143/D1
Rivadavia, San Juan, Argentina 143/C3
Rivadavia, Chile 138/A7
Riva del Garda, Italy 34/C2
Rivanna (riv.), Va. 307/M5
Rivas, Nicaragua 154/E5
Riva San Vitale, Switzerland 39/G5
Rive-de-Gier, France 28/F5
Rivera, Switzerland 39/G4
Rivera (dept.), Uruguay 145/D2
Rivera, Uruguay 145/D1
Rivera, Uruguay 120/D6
Riverbank, Calif. (95367) 204/E6
River Bourgeois, Nova Scotia 168/H3
River Cess, Liberia 106/C7
Rivercourse, Alberta 182/E3
Riverdale, Calif. (93656) 204/E7
Riverdale, Georgia (*30274) 217/K2
Riverdale, Ill. (60627) 222/C6
Riverdale, Iowa (†52722) 229/N5
Riverdale, Kansas (†67152) 232/E4
Riverdale, Md. (20840) 245/F4
Riverdale, Mich. (48877) 250/E5
Riverdale, Nebr. (68870) 264/E4
Riverdale, N.H. (†03045) 268/D5
Riverdale, N.J. (07457) 273/A1
Riverdale, N. Dak. (58565) 282/H4
Riverdale Heights, Md. (†20840) 245/G4
River de Chute, New Bruns. 170/C2
River Denys, Nova Scotia 168/G3
River Edge, N.J. (07661) 273/B1
River Falls, Ala. (36476) 195/E8
River Falls, Wis. (54022) 317/A6
River Forest, Ill. (60305) 222/B5
River Forest, Ind. (†46011) 227/F4
River Glade, New Bruns. 170/E3
River Grove, Ill. (60171) 222/B5
River Grove, Oreg. (†97223) 291/B2
Riverhead, Newf. 166/D2
Riverhead, N.Y. (11901) 276/P9
Riverhead, N. Zealand 100/B1
River Hébert, Nova Scotia 168/D3
River Heights, Utah (†84321) 304/C2
River Hills, Manitoba 179/G4
River Hills, Wis. (†53201) 317/M1
Riverhurst, Sask. 181/E5
Riverina (reg.), N. S. Wales 88/H7
Riverina (reg.), N.S. Wales 97/C4
River John, Nova Scotia 168/E3
River Jordan, Br. Col. 184/J3
Riverland, Fla. (†33301) 212/B4
Riverlea, Ohio (†43085) 284/D5
Rivermines, Mo. (†63601) 261/L7
Rivero (isl.), Chile 138/D6
River Oaks, Texas (77019) 303/E2
River of Ponds, Newf. 166/C3
River of Ponds (lake), Newf. 166/C3
Riverport, Nova Scotia 168/D4
River Rouge, Mich. (48218) 250/B7
Rivers (inlet), Br. Col. 184/D4
Rivers, Manitoba 179/B4
Rivers (state), Nigeria 106/F8
Rivers (lake), Sask. 181/F6
Riversdale, Jamaica 158/J6
Riversdale, S. Africa 118/H7
Riversdale, S. Africa 118/C6
Riverside, Ala. (35135) 195/F3
Riverside, Calif. 188/C4
Riverside (co.), Calif. 204/J10
Riverside, Calif. (*92501) 204/E11
Riverside (res.), Colo. 208/L2
Riverside, Conn. (06878) 210/A4
Riverside, Georgia (†30759) 217/B2
Riverside, Georgia (†31768) 217/E8
Riverside, Ill. (60546) 222/B6
Riverside, Ind. (†47918) 227/C4
Riverside, Iowa (52327) 229/K6
Riverside, Ky. (42272) 237/J6
Riverside, Md. (†20662) 245/K7
Riverside, Mass. (†01376) 249/D2
Riverside, Mich. (49084) 250/C6
Riverside, Mo. (64168) 261/O5
Riverside○, N.J. (08075) 273/B3
Riverside, N.Y. (†14830) 276/F6
Riverside, N. Dak. (†58078) 282/S6
Riverside, Oreg. (97917) 291/J4
Riverside, Pa. (17868) 294/J4
Riverside, R.I. (02915) 249/J5
Riverside, Sask. 181/G6
Riverside, Texas (77367) 303/J7
Riverside, Utah (84334) 304/B2
Riverside, Wash. (98849) 310/F2
Riverside, Wyo. (†82325) 319/F4
Riverside-Albert, New Bruns. 170/F3
Riverside Stage Stop, Ariz. (85237) 198/D5
Rivers Inlet, Br. Col. 184/D4
River Sioux, Iowa (†51545) 229/B5
Riverstown, Ireland 17/E3
Riverton, Conn. (06065) 210/D1
Riverton, Ill. (62561) 222/D4
Riverton, Ind. (†47861) 227/B6
Riverton, Iowa (51650) 229/B7
Riverton, Kansas (66770) 232/H4
Riverton, La. (†71418) 238/F2
Riverton, Man. 162/G5
Riverton, Manitoba 179/E3
Riverton, Minn. (†56455) 255/D4
Riverton, Nebr. (68972) 264/F4
Riverton, N.J. (08077) 273/B3
Riverton, N. Zealand 100/B7
Riverton, Nova Scotia 168/F3
Riverton, Oreg. (†97423) 291/C4
Riverton, Utah (84065) 304/B3
Riverton, Vt. (05668) 268/B3
Riverton, Va. (22651) 307/M3
Riverton, Wash. (†98188) 310/B2
Riverton, W. Va. (26814) 312/H5
Riverton, Wyo. (82501) 319/D2
Riverton Heights, Wash. (98188) 310/B2
Rivervale, Ark. (72377) 202/K2
River Vale○, N.J. (07675) 273/B1
River Valley, Ontario 177/D1
Riverview, Ala. (†36426) 195/D8
River View, Ala. (36872) 195/H5
Riverview, Fla. (33569) 212/D4
Riverview, Mich. (48192) 250/B7
Riverview, Mo. (†63101) 261/R2
Riverview, New Bruns. 170/F2
Riverville, Va. (†24553) 307/L5
Riverwood, Ky. (†40222) 237/K1
Riverwoods, Ill. (†60015) 222/B5
Rives, Mo. (63875) 261/M10
Rives, Tenn. (38253) 237/C8
Rives Junction, Mich. (49277) 250/E6
Rivesville, W. Va. (26588) 312/F3
Riviera (reg.), France 28/G6
Riviera, Texas (78379) 303/G10
Riviera Beach, Fla. (33404) 212/G5
Riviera Beach, Md. (†21061) 245/N4
Riviera-Bullhead, Ariz. (86440) 198/A3
Rivière-à-Claude, Québec 172/C1
Rivière-à-Pierre, Québec 172/E3
Rivière-au-Renard, Québec 172/D1
Rivière-au-Tonnerre, Québec 174/D2
Rivière-Bleue, Québec 172/J2
Rivière-Bois-Clair, Québec 172/F3
Rivière-du-Loup, Que. 162/K6
Rivière-du-Loup (co.), Québec 172/H2
Rivière-du-Loup, Québec 174/D3
Rivière-du-Loup, Québec 172/H2
Rivière-du-Moulin, Québec 172/G1
Rivière-du-Portage, New Bruns. 170/F1
Rivière-Éternité, Québec 172/G1
Rivière-la-Madeleine, Québec 172/C1
Rivière-Matawin, Québec 172/E3
Rivière-Ouelle, Québec 172/G2
Rivière-Pentecôte, Québec 174/D3
Rivière-Pilote, Martinique 161/D7
Rivière-Port-Daniel, Québec 172/D2
Rivière-Portneuf, Québec 172/H1
Rivière-Saint-Paul, Québec 174/F2
Rivière-Salée, Martinique 161/D7
Rivière-Trois-Pistoles, Québec 172/J1
Rivière Verte, New Bruns. 170/B1
Rivière-Verte, Québec 172/H2
Riwaka, N. Zealand 100/D4
Riwoqê, China 77/E5
Rixeyville, Va. (22737) 307/M3
Rixford, Pa. (16745) 294/F2
Riyadh (cap.), Saudi Arabia 2/M4
Riyadh (cap.), Saudi Arabia 54/F7
Riyadh (cap.), Saudi Arabia 59/E5
Riyan, P.D.R. Yemen 59/E7
Rizal (prov.), Philippines 82/C3
Rize (prov.), Turkey 63/J2
Rize, Turkey 59/D1
Rize, Turkey 63/J2
Rizokarpasso, Cyprus 63/F5
Rjukan, Norway 18/F7
Roa, Norway 18/G6
Roa, Spain 33/E2
Roachdale, Ind. (46172) 227/D5
Road (bay), Virgin Is. (Br.) 161/D3
Roadside, Scotland 15/F4
Roadstown, N.J. (†08302) 273/C5
Road Town (cap.), Virgin Is. (Br.) 161/D3
Road Town (cap.), Virgin Is. (Br.) 156/H1
Roag, Loch (inlet), Scotland 15/B2
Roan (creek), Colo. 208/C4
Roan (plat.), Colo. 208/B3
Roan, Norway 18/G4
Roan (isl.), Scotland 15/D2
Roan (cliffs), Utah 304/E4
Roane (co.), Tenn. 237/M9
Roane (co.), W. Va. 312/D5
Roan Mountain, Tenn. (37687) 237/S8
Roann, Ind. (46974) 227/F3
Roanne, France 28/F4
Roanoke (riv.) 188/L3
Roanoke, Ala. (36274) 195/H4
Roanoke, Ill. (61561) 222/D3
Roanoke, Ind. (46783) 227/G3
Roanoke, La. (70581) 238/E6
Roanoke, Mo. (†65230) 261/G4
Roanoke (isl.), N.C. 281/T3
Roanoke (riv.), N.C. 281/P2
Roanoke, Texas (76262) 303/F1
Roanoke, Va. 146/L6
Roanoke, Va. 188/K3
Roanoke (co.), Va. 307/H6
Roanoke (I.C.), Va. (*24001) 307/H6
Roanoke (riv.), Va. 307/N8
Roanoke, W. Va. (26423) 312/F5
Roanoke Rapids, N.C. (27870) 281/O2
Roaring (brook), Conn. 210/F1
Roaring (brook), Conn. 210/E2
Roaring Branch, Pa. (17765) 294/J2
Roaring Fork, Colorado (riv.), Colo. 208/E4
Roaring Gap, N.C. (28668) 281/H2
Roaring River, N.C. (28669) 281/G2
Roaring Spring, Pa. (16673) 294/F5
Roaring Springs, Texas (79256) 303/D4
Roaringwater (bay), Ireland 17/B9
Roark, Ky. (40979) 237/P6
Roatán, Honduras 154/D2
Roatán (isl.), Honduras 154/D2
Roba, Ala. (†36089) 195/G6
Robards, Ky. (42452) 237/F5
Robat Karim, Iran 66/G3
Robb, Alberta 182/B3
Robben (isl.), S. Africa 118/E6
Robbins, Calif. (95676) 204/B8
Robbins, Ill. (60472) 222/B6
Robbins, N.C. (27325) 281/K4
Robbins (isl.), Tasmania 99/B2
Robbins, Tenn. (37852) 237/M8
Robbinsdale, Minn. (55422) 255/G5
Robbinston, Maine (04671) 243/J5
Robbinston○, Maine (04671) 243/J5
Robbinsville, N.J. (08691) 273/D3
Robbinsville, N.C. (28771) 281/B4
Robe (mt.), N.S. Wales 97/A2
Robe, S. Australia 94/F7
Robe, Wash. (†98252) 310/D2
Robeline, La. (71469) 238/D3
Roberdel, N.C. (†28379) 281/K5
Robersonville, N.C. (27871) 281/P3
Robert (isl.), China 85/E2
Robert, La. (70455) 238/N1
Robert (harb.), Martinique 161/D6
Roberta, Georgia (31078) 217/D5
Roberta, Okla. (†74701) /K7
Robert Lee, Texas (76945) 303/D6
Roberto Payán, Colombia 126/A7
Roberts, Idaho (83444) 220/F6
Roberts, Ill. (60962) 222/E3
Roberts, Mont. (59070) 262/G5
Roberts (co.), S. Dak. 298/P2
Roberts (co.), Texas 303/D2
Roberts, Wis. (54023) 317/A6
Robert's Arm, Newf. 166/C4
Robertsburg, W. Va. (25172) 312/C5
Roberts Creek, Br. Col. 184/J3
Robertsdale, Ala. (36567) 195/C9
Robertsdale, Pa. (16674) 294/F5
Roberts Field Int'l Airport, Liberia 106/C7
Robertsfors, Sweden 18/M4
Robertsganj, India 68/E4
Robertson (co.), Ky. 237/N3
Robertson, S. Africa 118/C6
Robertson (co.), Tenn. 237/H7
Robertson (co.), Texas 303/H6
Robertson, Wyo. (82944) 319/B4
Robertsonville, Québec 172/F3
Robertsport, Liberia 102/A4
Robertsport, Liberia 106/B7
Robertstown, Georgia (†30545) 217/E1
Robertsville, Conn. (†06098) 210/C1
Robertsville, Ohio (44670) 284/H4
Robertville, New Bruns. 170/E1
Roberval, Que. 162/J6
Roberval, Québec 174/C3
Roberval, Québec 172/E1
Robeson (co.), N.C. 281/L5
Robeson (chan.), N.W. Terrs. 187/M1
Robesonia, Pa. (19551) 294/K5
Robichaud, New Bruns. 170/F2
Robinhood, Sask. 181/C2
Robins, Iowa (52328) 229/K4
Robins, Ohio (†43723) 284/H6
Robins A.F.B., Georgia 217/F5
Robinson, Ill. (62454) 222/F5
Robinson, Iowa (†52330) 229/K4
Robinson, Kansas (66532) 232/G2
Robinson, Ky. (41082) 237/N4
Robinson, N. Dak. (58478) 282/L5
Robinson (riv.), North. Terr. 93/E4
Robinson, Pa. (15949) 294/D5
Robinson (lake), S.C. 296/G3
Robinson (ranges), W. Australia 92/B4
Robinson Creek, Ky. (41560) 237/S6
Robinson Crusoe (isl.), Chile 120/B6
Robinson River, North. Terr. 93/E4
Robinsons, Maine (†04734) 243/H3
Robinsonville, Miss. (38664) 256/D1
Robinsonville, New Bruns. 170/C1
Robinvale, Victoria 97/B4
Robles, Colombia 126/D2
Roblin, Manitoba 179/A3
Roblin, Ontario 177/G3
Roboré, Bolivia 136/F6
Roboré, Bolivia 120/D4
Rob Roy, Ind. (†47918) 227/C4
Robsart, Sask. 181/B6
Robson (mt.), Br. Col. 162/D5
Robson, Br. Col. 184/J5
Robson (mt.), Br. Col. 184/H3
Robstown, Texas (78380) 303/G10
Roby, Mo. (65557) 261/H7
Roby, Texas (79543) 303/D5
Roca, Nebr. (68430) 264/H4
Roca (cape), Portugal 33/B3
Rocafuerte, Ecuador 128/B3
Rocanville, Sask. 181/K5
Roca Partida (isl.), Mexico 150/C7
Roca que Vela (cay), Colombia 126/B8
Rocas (isl.), Brazil 120/F3
Rocas de Santo Domingo, Chile 138/F4
Roccastrada, Italy 34/C3
Rocha (dept.), Uruguay 145/E4
Rocha, Uruguay 145/E5
Rocha (lag.), Uruguay 145/E5
Rochdale, England 13/H2
Rochdale, England 10/G2
Rochdale, Mass. (01542) 249/G4
Roche, Switzerland 39/C4
Rochechouart, France 28/D5
Rochefort, Belgium 27/G8
Rochefort, France 28/C4
Roche Harbor, Wash. (98250) 310/B2
Rochelle, Georgia (31079) 217/F7
Rochelle, Ill. (61068) 222/D2
Rochelle, Texas (76872) 303/E6
Rochelle, Wyo. (†82701) 319/H2
Rochelle Park○, N.J. (07662) 273/B2
Roche Percé, Sask. 181/J6
Rocheport, Mo. (65279) 261/H5
Rocher River, N.W.T. 162/E3
Rocher River, N.W. Terrs. 187/G3
Rochert, Minn. (56578) 255/C4
Rochester, Alberta 182/D2
Rochester, England 13/J8
Rochester, England 10/G5
Rochester, Ill. (62563) 222/D4
Rochester, Ind. (46975) 227/E2
Rochester, Iowa (†52772) 229/L5
Rochester, Ky. (42273) 237/H6
Rochester○, Mass. (02770) 249/L6
Rochester, Mich. (48063) 250/F6
Rochester, Minn. 188/H2
Rochester, Minn. (55901) 255/F6
Rochester, N.H. (03867) 268/E5
Rochester, N.Y. 188/L2
Rochester, N.Y. 146/L5
Rochester, N.Y. (*14601) 276/E4
Rochester, Ohio (†44090) 284/F3
Rochester, Pa. (15074) 294/B4
Rochester, Texas (79544) 303/E4
Rochester○, Vt. (05767) 268/B4
Rochester, Victoria 97/C5
Rochester, Wash. (98579) 310/C4
Rochester, Wis. (53167) 317/K3
Rochester Mills, Pa. (15771) 294/D4
Rochford, S. Dak. (57778) 298/B5
Rochfort Bridge, Alberta 182/C3
Rochon Sands, Alberta 182/D3
Rociada, N. Mex. (87742) 274/D3
Rock (creek), Idaho 220/F7
Rock (creek), Ill. 222/D2
Rock (riv.), Ill. 222/C2
Rock (riv.), Iowa 229/A2
Rock, Kansas (67131) 232/F4
Rock (lake), Manitoba 179/C5
Rock (creek), Md. 245/K4
Rock, Mass. (†02346) 249/L5
Rock, Mich. (49880) 250/B2
Rock (co.), Minn. 255/B7
Rock (riv.), Minn. 255/B7
Rock (creek), Mont. 262/C4
Rock (co.), Nebr. 264/E2
Rock (creek), Nev. 266/E2
Rock (creek), Oreg. 291/E4
Rock (creek), Oreg. 291/G2
Rock (creek), Oreg. 291/H3
Rock (creek), S. Dak. 298/O6
Rock (creek), Wash. 310/H3
Rock (lake), Wash. 310/H3
Rock (co.), Wis. 317/H10
Rock (riv.), Wis. 317/J9
Rockall (isl.), Scotland 7/C3
Rockaway, N.J. (07866) 273/D2
Rockaway, Oreg. (97136) 291/C2
Rockaway Beach, Mo. (65740) 261/F9
Rock Bluff, Fla. (†32321) 212/B1
Rockbridge, Ill. (62081) 222/C4
Rockbridge, Mo. (65741) 261/H9
Rockbridge, Ohio (43149) 284/E6
Rockbridge (co.), Va. 307/K5
Rockbridge, Wis. (†53581) 317/F9
Rockcastle (co.), Ky. 237/N6
Rockcastle (riv.), Ky. 237/N6
Rock Castle, W. Va. (25272) 312/C5
Rock Cave, W. Va. (26234) 312/F5
Rock City, Ill. (61070) 222/D1
Rockcliffe Park, Ontario 177/J2
Rockcorry, Ireland 17/H3
Rock Creek, Br. Col. 184/H6
Rock Creek, Kansas (†66512) 232/G2
Rock Creek, Minn. (55067) 255/F5
Rock Creek, Ohio (44084) 284/J2
Rock Creek, Yukon 187/E3
Rockdale (co.), Georgia 217/D3
Rockdale, Ill. (60436) 222/E2
Rockdale, N. S. Wales 88/K4
Rockdale, N.S. Wales 97/J4
Rockdale, Texas (76567) 303/G7
Rockdale, Wis. (†53523) 317/J10
Rock Dell, Minn. (†55920) 255/F7
Rockerville, S. Dak. (†57701) 298/C6
Rockfall, Conn. (06481) 210/E2
Rock Falls, Ill. (61071) 222/D2
Rock Falls, Iowa (50467) 229/G2
Rock Falls, Wis. (54764) 317/C6
Rockfield, Ind. (46977) 227/D3
Rockfield, Ky. (42274) 237/J7
Rockfield, Wis. (53077) 317/L1
Rockfish, N.C. (†28302) 281/L5
Rockford, Ala. (35136) 195/F5
Rockford, Idaho (†83221) 220/F6
Rockford, Ill. 146/K5
Rockford, Ill. 188/J2
Rockford, Ill. (*61101) 222/D1
Rockford, Iowa (50468) 229/H2
Rockford, Mich. (49341) 250/D5

Rosston 437

Rockford, Minn. (55373) 255/F5
Rockford, N.C. (27044) 281/H2
Rockford, Ohio (45882) 284/A4
Rockford, Sask. 181/J3
Rockford, Tenn. (37853) 237/O9
Rockford, Wash. (99030) 310/H3
Rock Forest, Québec 172/F4
Rock Glen, Pa. (18246) 294/K4
Rockglen, Sask. 181/F6
Rock Grove, Ill. (†61070) 222/D1
Rock Hall, Md. (21661) 245/O4
Rockham, S. Dak. (57470) 298/M4
Rockhampton, Australia 2/S7
Rockhampton, Australia 87/F8
Rockhampton, Queensland 88/H4
Rockhampton, Queensland 95/D4
Rockhampton Downs, North. Terr. 93/D5
Rockhaven, Sask. 181/B3
Rock Hill, Mo. (†63119) 261/P3
Rock Hill, S.C. 188/K4
Rock Hill, S.C. (29730) 296/E2
Rockholds, Ky. (40759) 237/N7
Rockingham, Georgia (†31510) 217/H7
Rockingham (co.), N.H. 268/E5
Rockingham (co.), N.C. 281/K2
Rockingham, N.C. (28379) 281/K5
Rockingham○, Vt. (†05101) 268/B5
Rockingham (co.), Va. 307/L4
Rockingham, W. Australia 88/B2
Rockingham, W. Australia 92/A2
Rock Island, Ill. 188/J2
Rock Island (co.), Ill. 222/C2
Rock Island, Ill. (61201) 222/C2
Rock Island, Okla. (†74932) 288/T4
Rock Island, Québec 172/E4
Rock Island, Tenn. (38581) 237/K9
Rock Island, Texas (77470) 303/H8
Rock Island, Wash. (†98801) 310/E3
Rock Island (dam), Wash. 310/E3
Rock Island Arsenal, Ill. 222/C2
Rocklake, N. Dak. (58365) 282/M2
Rockland, Conn. (†06443) 210/E3
Rockland, Del. (19732) 245/R1
Rockland, Idaho (83271) 220/F7
Rockland, Maine (04841) 243/E7
Rockland○, Mass. (02370) 249/L4
Rockland, Mich. (49960) 250/G1
Rockland (co.), N.Y. 276/M8
Rockland, Ontario 177/J2
Rockland, Texas (75970) 303/K6
Rockland, Wis. (54653) 317/D8
Rocklands (res.), Victoria 97/B5
Rockledge, Fla. (32955) 212/F3
Rockledge, Georgia (30454) 217/G6
Rockledge, Pa. (†19101) 294/M5
Rockleigh, N.J. (07647) 273/C1
Rocklin, Calif. (95677) 204/B8
Rockmart, Georgia (30153) 217/B2
Rock Mills, Ala. (36274) 195/H4
Rock Oak, W. Va. (†26756) 312/J4
Rock Point, Md. (20682) 245/L7
Rockport, Ark. (†72104) 202/E5
Rockport, Calif. (†95488) 204/B4
Rockport, Ill. (62370) 222/B4
Rockport, Ind. 227/C9
Rockport, Ky. (42369) 237/H6
Rockport, Maine (04856) 243/F7
Rockport○, Maine (04856) 243/F7
Rockport○, Mass. (01966) 249/M2
Rockport, Miss. (†39083) 256/D7
Rock Port, Mo. (64482) 261/B2
Rockport, Texas (78382) 303/H9
Rockport (lake), Utah 304/C3
Rockport, Wash. (98283) 310/D2
Rockport, W. Va. (26169) 312/C4
Rock Rapids, Iowa (51246) 229/A2
Rock River, Wyo. (82083) 319/G4
Rock Run, Ala. (†36272) 195/G2
Rocks, Md. (†21084) 245/N2
Rocks (pt.), N. Zealand 100/C4
Rock Springs, Mont. (59312) 262/K4
Rocksprings, Texas (78880) 303/D8
Rock Springs, Wis. (53961) 317/F8
Rock Springs, Wyo. 146/H5
Rock Springs, Wyo. 188/E2
Rock Springs, Wyo. (82901) 319/C4
Rockstone, Guyana 131/B2
Rockton, Ill. (61072) 222/E1
Rockvale, Colo. (81244) 208/J6
Rockvale, Mont. (†59080) 262/H5
Rockvale, Tenn. (37153) 237/J9
Rock Valley, Iowa (51247) 229/A2
Rockville, Conn. (†06066) 210/F1
Rockville, Ind. (47872) 227/C5
Rockville, Maine (†04841) 243/E7
Rockville, Md. (*20850) 245/K4
Rockville, Mass. (†02054) 249/A8
Rockville, Minn. (56369) 255/D5
Rockville, Mo. (64780) 261/D6
Rockville, Nebr. (68871) 264/F3
Rockville, Nova Scotia 168/B5
Rockville, R.I. (02873) 249/G6
Rockville, S.C. (†29487) 296/G6
Rockville, Utah (84763) 304/A6
Rockville, Va. (23146) 307/N5
Rockville, Wis. (†53820) 317/E10
Rockville Centre, N.Y. (*11570) 276/R7
Rockwall (co.), Texas 303/H5
Rockwall, Texas (75087) 303/H5
Rockwell, Iowa (50469) 229/G3
Rockwell, N.C. (28138) 281/J3
Rockwell City, Iowa (50579) 229/D4
Rockwood, Ala. (†35653) 195/C2
Rockwood, Ill. (62280) 222/D6
Rockwood, Maine (04478) 243/D4
Rockwood, Mich. (48173) 250/F6
Rockwood, Ontario 177/D4
Rockwood, Pa. (15557) 294/D6
Rockwood, Tenn. (37854) 237/M9
Rockwood, Texas (76873) 303/E6
Rocky (mts.) 162/D4
Rocky (mts.) 146/F4
Rocky (mts.) 188/E3
Rocky (mts.), Alberta 182/BC4
Rocky (mts.), Br. Col. 184/F2
Rocky (mts.), Canada 4/D16
Rocky (mts.), Colo. 208/F1
Rocky (mts.), Idaho 220/D1
Rocky (lake), Maine 243/J6
Rocky (mts.), Mont. 262/D4
Rocky (bay), Newf. 166/C3
Rocky (riv.), Newf. 166/D2
Rocky (mts.), N. Mex. 274/C1
Rocky (pt.), Norfolk I. 88/K6
Rocky (riv.), N.C. 281/H4
Rocky (riv.), Ohio 284/G9
Rocky, Okla. (73661) 288/J4
Rocky (riv.), S.C. 296/B3
Rocky (cape), Tasmania 99/B2
Rocky (mts.), Wash. 310/H2
Rocky (mts.), Wyo. 319/C1
Rocky (mts.), Yukon 187/F4
Rocky Bottom, S.C. (†29685) 296/B1
Rocky Boy, Mont. (†59521) 262/G2
Rocky Boy's Ind. Res., Mont. 262/G2
Rocky Comfort, Mo. (64861) 261/D9
Rocky Face, Georgia (30740) 217/C1
Rockyford, Alberta 182/D4
Rocky Ford, Colo. (81067) 208/M6
Rocky Ford, Georgia (30455) 217/J5
Rocky Fork (lake), Ohio 284/D7
Rocky Gap, Va. (24366) 307/F6
Rocky Gorge (res.), Md. 245/L4
Rocky Harbour, Newf. 166/C4
Rocky Hill○, Conn. (06067) 210/E2
Rocky Hill, Ky. (42163) 237/J6
Rocky Hill, N.J. (08553) 273/D3
Rocky Lane, Alberta 182/B5
Rocky Mount, Georgia (†30251) 217/C4
Rocky Mount, La. (†71064) 238/C1
Rocky Mount, Mo. (65072) 261/G6
Rocky Mount, N.C. 188/L3
Rocky Mount, N.C. (27801) 281/O3
Rocky Mount, Va. (24151) 307/J7
Rocky Mountain Arsenal, Colo. 208/K3
Rocky Mountain House, Alberta 182/C3
Rocky Mountain House, Alta. 162/E5
Rocky Mountain Nat'l Park, Colo. 208/H2
Rocky Point, N.C. (28457) 281/O6
Rocky Point, Wash. (†98626) 310/A2
Rockypoint, Wyo. (†82721) 319/G1
Rocky Rapids, Alberta 182/C3
Rocky Reach (dam), Wash. 310/E3
Rocky Ridge (mt.), Idaho 220/C3
Rocky Ridge, Ohio (43458) 284/D2
Rocky River, Ohio (44116) 284/G9
Rodanthe, N.C. (27968) 281/U3
Rodarte, N. Mex. (87561) 274/D2
Rodas, Cuba 158/E2
Rødby, Denmark 21/E8
Rødby, Denmark 18/G9
Roddickton, Newf. 166/C3
Rødding, Denmark 21/B7
Roddy, Tenn. (†37381) 237/M9
Rødekro, Denmark 21/C7
Roden, Netherlands 27/J2
Rodeo, Calif. (94572) 204/J1
Rodeo, Mexico 150/G4
Rodeo, N. Mex. (88056) 274/A7
Roderfield, W. Va. (24881) 312/C8
Roderick (isl.), Br. Col. 184/C4
Rodessa, La. (71069) 238/B1
Rodez, France 28/E5
Ródhos, Greece 45/J7
Roding (riv.), England 13/J7
Rodinga, North. Terr. 93/D8
Rødkaersbro, Denmark 21/C5
Rodman, Iowa (50580) 229/D2
Rodman, N.Y. (13682) 276/J3
Rodman, S.C. (†29706) 296/E2
Rodney, Mich. (49342) 250/D5
Rodney, Miss. (†39096) 256/B7
Rodney, Ontario 177/C5
Rodney Village, Del. (19901) 245/R4
Rodrigues, Brazil 132/F10
Rodríguez, Uruguay 145/C5
Rødvig, Denmark 21/F7
Roe, Ark. (72134) 202/H4
Roe (riv.), N. Ireland 17/H1
Roebling-Florence, N.J. (08554) 273/D3
Roebourne, W. Australia 88/B4
Roebourne, W. Australia 92/B3
Roebuck (bay), W. Australia 88/C3
Roebuck (bay), W. Australia 92/C2
Roebuck Plains, W. Australia 92/C2
Roeland Park, Kansas (†66205) 232/H2
Roer (riv.), Netherlands 27/J6
Roermond, Netherlands 27/J6
Roeselare, Belgium 27/C7
Roes Welcome (sound), N.W.T. 162/H2
Roes Welcome (sound), N.W. Terrs. 187/K3
Roff, Okla. (74865) 288/N5
Rogachev, U.S.S.R. 52/D4
Rogagua (lake), Bolivia 136/B3
Rogaguado (lake), Bolivia 136/C3
Rogaland (co.), Norway 18/E7
Rogatica, Yugoslavia 45/D4
Roger Mills (co.), Okla. 288/G3
Rogers, Ark. (72756) 202/B1
Rogers, Br. Col. 184/J4
Rogers (lake), Calif. 204/H9
Rogers, Conn. (06263) 210/H1
Rogers (lake), Conn. 210/F3
Rogers, La. (†71342) 238/F3
Rogers, Minn. (55374) 255/E5
Rogers, Nebr. (68659) 264/H3
Rogers, N. Mex. (88132) 274/F5
Rogers, N. Dak. (58479) 282/O5
Rogers, Ohio (44455) 284/J4
Rogers (co.), Okla. 288/P2
Rogers, Texas (76569) 303/G7
Rogers (mt.), Va. 307/E7
Rogers City, Mich. (49779) 250/F3
Rogerson, Idaho (83302) 220/D7
Rogers Springs, Tenn. (†38052) 237/D10
Rogersville, Ala. (35652) 195/D1
Rogersville, Mo. (65742) 261/G8
Rogersville, New Bruns. 170/E2
Rogersville, Pa. (15359) 294/B6
Rogersville, Tenn. (37857) 237/P8
Roger Williams Nat'l Mem., R.I. 249/J5
Roggen, Colo. (80652) 208/L2
Roggwil, Switzerland 39/E2
Rogliano, France 28/B6
Rogozno, Poland 47/C2
Rogue (riv.), Oreg. 291/C5
Rogue River, Oreg. (97537) 291/D5
Roha, India 68/C5
Rohnert Park, Calif. (94928) 204/C5
Rohnerville, Calif. (†95540) 204/B3
Rohrbach in Oberösterreich, Austria 41/B2
Rohrersville, Md. (21779) 245/H3
Rohri, Pakistan 68/B3
Rohtak, India 68/C5
Rohwer, Ark. (71666) 202/H6
Roi Et, Thailand 72/D4
Roja, U.S.S.R. 53/B2
Rojas, Argentina 143/F7
Rojo (cape), Mexico 150/L6
Rojo (cape), P. Rico 161/A3
Rojo (cape), P. Rico 156/F1
Rokan (riv.), Indonesia 85/C5
Rokeby, Sask. 181/J4
Rokiškis, U.S.S.R. 53/C2
Rokycany, Czech. 41/B2
Rokytnice nad Jizerou, Czech. 41/C1
Rola Co (lake), China 77/C4
Roland, Ark. (72135) 202/E4
Roland, Iowa (50236) 229/F4
Roland, Manitoba 179/D5
Roland, Okla. (74954) 288/S4
Røldal, Norway 18/E7
Roldán, Argentina 143/F6
Rolecha, Chile 138/D4
Rolesville, N.C. (27571) 281/N3
Rolette (co.), N. Dak. 282/L2
Rolette, N. Dak. (58366) 282/L2
Roleystone, W. Australia 88/B2
Rolfe, Iowa (50581) 229/D3
Roll, Ariz. (85347) 198/A6
Rolla, Ark. (†72104) 202/E5
Rolla, Br. Col. 184/G2
Rolla, Kansas (67954) 232/A4
Rolla, Mo. (65401) 261/J7
Rolla, N. Dak. (58367) 282/L2
Rollag, Minn. (†56549) 255/B4
Rolle, Switzerland 39/B4
Rollingbay, Wash. (98061) 310/A2
Rollingdam, New Bruns. 170/C3
Rolling Fields, Ky. (†40201) 237/K2
Rolling Fork (riv.), Ky. 237/L5
Rolling Fork, Miss. (39159) 256/C5
Rolling Hills, Alberta 182/E4
Rolling Hills, Calif. (90274) 204/B11
Rolling Hills, Ky. (†40201) 237/L1
Rolling Hills Estates, Calif. (90274) 204/B11
Rolling Meadows, Ill. (60008) 222/A5
Rolling Prairie, Ind. (46371) 227/D1
Rollingstone, Minn. (55969) 255/G6
Rollins, Mont. (59931) 262/B3
Rollo (bay), Pr. Edward I. 168/F2
Rolphton, Ontario 177/G1
Roma, Australia 87/E8
Roma (Rome) (cap.), Italy 34/F6
Roma, Queensland 88/H5
Roma, Queensland 95/D5
Roma, Sweden 18/L8
Romain (cape), S.C. 296/J6
Romaine (riv.), Newf. 166/B3
Romaine (riv.), Que. 162/K5
Romaine, Québec 174/E2
Romaine (riv.), Québec 174/E2
Roma-Los Saenz, Texas (78584) 303/E11
Roman, Romania 45/H2
Romance, Ark. (72136) 202/F3
Romance, Sask. 181/G3
Romance, W. Va. (25175) 312/C5
Romang, Argentina 143/F4
Romang (isl.), Indonesia 85/H7
Romania 2/L3
Romania 7/G4
ROMANIA 45/F3
Romano (cay), Cuba 158/G2
Romano (cay), Cuba 156/C2
Romano (cape), Fla. 212/E6
Romanshorn, Switzerland 39/H1
Romans-sur-Isère, France 28/F5
Romanzof (cape), Alaska 196/E2
Rombauer, Mo. (63962) 261/M9
Romblon (prov.), Philippines 82/D4
Romblon, Philippines 82/D4
Romblon (isl.), Philippines 82/D4
Rome, Ga. 188/K4
Rome, Georgia (30161) 217/B2
Rome, Ill. (61562) 222/D3
Rome, Ind. (47574) 227/D9
Rome, Iowa (52642) 229/K7
Rome (prov.), Italy 34/F6
Rome (cap.), Italy 7/F4
Rome (cap.), Italy 34/F6
Rome (cap.), Italy 2/K3
Rome○, Maine (†04957) 243/D6
Rome, Miss. (38768) 256/C3
Rome, N.Y. 188/M2
Rome, N.Y. (13440) 276/J4
Rome (Stout), Ohio (†45684) 284/D8
Rome, Ohio (44085) 284/J2
Rome, Oreg. (†97910) 291/K5
Rome, Pa. (18837) 294/K2
Rome, Wis. (†53178) 317/H1
Rome City, Ind. (46784) 227/G1
Romeo, Colo. (81148) 208/G8
Romeo, Mich. (48065) 250/F6
Romeoville, Ill. (60441) 222/B6
Romeroville, N. Mex. (†87701) 274/D3
Romeville, La. (†70723) 238/L3
Romilly-sur-Seine, France 28/F3
Romney, Ind. (47981) 227/D4
Romney, W. Va. (26757) 312/J4
Romny, U.S.S.R. 52/D4
Rømø, Denmark 21/B7
Rømø (isl.), Denmark 21/B7
Rømø (isl.), Denmark 18/F9
Romont, Switzerland 39/C3
Romorantin-Lanthenay, France 28/D4
Romsdalsfjorden (fjord), Norway 18/E5
Romsey, England 10/F5
Romsey, England 13/F6
Romulus, Mich. (48174) 250/F6
Romulus, N.Y. (14541) 276/G5
Ron, Vietnam 72/E3
Ron, Mui (cape), Vietnam 72/E3
Rona (isl.), Scotland 15/B3
Ronald, Wash. (98940) 310/E3
Ronan, Mont. (59864) 262/C3
Ronay (isl.), Scotland 15/A3
Roncador, Serra do (range), Brazil 132/D5
Roncador (cays), Colombia 126/B9
Ronceverte, W. Va. (24970) 312/F7
Ronciglione, Italy 34/C3
Ronda, N.C. (28670) 281/H2
Ronda, Spain 33/D4
Rønde, Denmark 21/D5
Ronde (isl.), Grenada 161/D7
Rondeau Prov. Park, Ontario 177/C5
Rondo, Ark. (†72355) 202/J4
Rondônia (terr.), Brazil 132/H10
Rondônia, Brazil 132/H10
Rondonópolis, Brazil 120/D4
Rondout (res.), N.Y. 276/M7
Rondu, Pakistan 68/D1
Rong, Koh (isl.), Cambodia 72/D5
Rong'an, China 77/G6
Ronge, Lac La (lake), Sask. 162/F4
Ronge, La (lake), Sask. 181/M3
Rongelap (atoll), Marshall Is. 87/G4
Rongjiang, China 77/G6
Rong Kwang, Thailand 72/D3
Rong Xian, China 77/H7
Ronju (mt.), Fr. Poly. 86/T13
Ronkonkoma, N.Y. (11779) 276/O9
Rønne, Denmark 21/F9
Rønne, Denmark 18/J9
Ronneby, Minn. (†56324) 255/E5
Ronneby, Sweden 18/J8
Ronne Entrance (inlet) 5/B15
Ronne Ice Shelf, Ant. 2/F10
Ronne Ice Shelf 5/B15
Ronse, Belgium 27/D7
Ronuro (riv.), Brazil 132/C6
Roodepoort, S. Africa 118/H6
Roodhouse, Ill. (62082) 222/C4
Roof Butte (mt.), Ariz. 198/F2
Rooi, Neth. Ant. 161/E8
Rooks (co.), Kansas 232/C2
Roopville, Georgia (30170) 217/B4
Roosendaal, Netherlands 27/F5
Roosevelt (isl.), Ant. 2/A10
Roosevelt (isl.) 5/A10
Roosevelt (res.), Ariz. 188/D4
Roosevelt, Ariz. (85545) 198/D5
Roosevelt (riv.), Brazil 120/C3
Roosevelt (riv.), Brazil 132/A5
Roosevelt, La. (†71276) 238/H1
Roosevelt, Minn. (55673) 255/C2
Roosevelt (co.), Mont. 262/L2
Roosevelt, N.J. (08555) 273/E3
Roosevelt (co.), N. Mex. 274/F4
Roosevelt, N.Y. (11575) 276/R7
Roosevelt, Okla. (73564) 288/J5
Roosevelt, Texas (76874) 303/D7
Roosevelt, Utah (84066) 304/D3
Roosevelt, Wash. (99356) 310/E5
Roosevelt Campobello Int'l Park, New Bruns. 170/D4
Roosevelt City, Ala. (35020) 195/E4
Roosevelt Park, Mich. (49444) 250/C5
Roosevelt Road Naval Res., P. Rico 161/F2
Roosville, Br. Col. 184/K5
Root (riv.), Minn. 255/G7
Rootstown, Ohio (44272) 284/H3
Roper, N.C. (27970) 281/R3
Roper (riv.), North. Terr. 88/E3
Roper (riv.), North. Terr. 93/C3
Roper River, North. Terr. 93/D3
Roper River Mission, North. Terr. 88/E2
Roper Valley, North. Terr. 93/D3
Ropesville, Texas (79358) 303/B4
Roque Bluffs○, Maine (†04654) 243/H6
Roque González de Santa Cruz, Paraguay 144/B5
Roque Pérez, Argentina 143/G7
Roquetas, Spain 33/G2
Rora (head), Scotland 15/E2
Roraima (mt.) 120/C2
Roraima (terr.), Brazil 132/H8
Roraima (mt.), Guyana 131/A3
Roraima (mt.), Venezuela 124/H5
Rørby, Denmark 21/E6
Rorketon, Manitoba 179/C3
Røros, Norway 18/G5
Rorschach, Switzerland 39/H2
Rosa, Ala. (†35049) 195/E3
Rosa (cape), Ecuador 128/B10
Rosa (mt.), Italy 34/A1
Rosa, La. (71364) 238/G5
Rosa, Manitoba 179/F5
Rosa (mt.), Switzerland 39/E5
Rosaire, Québec 172/G3
Rosaireville, New Bruns. 170/E2
Rosalia, Kansas (67132) 232/F4
Rosalia, Wash. (99170) 310/H3
Rosalie, Dominica 161/F6
Rosalie, Nebr. (68055) 264/H2
Rosalina, Paraguay 144/D3
Rosalind, Alberta 182/D3
Rosamond, Calif. (93560) 204/G9
Rosamond (lake), Calif. 204/G9
Rosamond, Ill. (62083) 222/D4
Rosamorada, Mexico 150/G5
Rosapenna, Ireland 17/F1
Rosario, Argentina 143/F6
Rosario, Argentina 120/C6
Rosário, Brazil 132/F3
Rosario, Chile 138/F5
Rosario (cay), Cuba 158/C2
Rosario, Sinaloa, Mexico 150/G5
Rosario, Sonora, Mexico 150/E3
Rosario, Paraguay 144/D4
Rosario, P. Rico 161/A2
Rosario, Uruguay 145/B5
Rosario, Venezuela 124/B2
Rosario (str.), Wash. 310/C2
Rosario de la Frontera, Argentina 143/D2
Rosario de Lerma, Argentina 143/C1
Rosario del Tala, Argentina 143/G6
Rosáriodo Sul, Brazil 132/C10
Rosário Oeste, Brazil 132/C6
Rosas, Spain 33/H1
Rosas (gulf), Spain 33/H1
Rosati, Mo. (†65559) 261/J6
Rosa Zárate, Ecuador 128/C2
Rosburg, Wash. (98643) 310/B4
Rosbys Rock, W. Va. (†26041) 312/E3
Roscoe, Ill. (61073) 222/D1
Roscoe, Minn. (56371) 255/D5
Roscoe, Mo. (64781) 261/E7
Roscoe, Mont. (59071) 262/G5
Roscoe, Nebr. (†69153) 264/C3
Roscoe, N.Y. (12776) 276/L7
Roscoe, Pa. (15477) 294/C5
Roscoe, S. Dak. (57471) 298/L3
Roscoe, Texas (79545) 303/D5
Roscoff, France 28/A3
Roscommon (co.), Ireland 17/E4
Roscommon, Ireland 10/B4
Roscommon, Ireland 17/E4
Roscommon (co.), Mich. 250/E4
Roscommon, Mich. (48653) 250/E4
Roscrea, Ireland 10/B4
Roscrea, Ireland 17/F6
Rose (peak), Ariz. 198/F5
Rose (pt.), Br. Col. 184/B3
Rose (pt.), Martinique 161/D6
Rose, Nebr. (68772) 264/E2
Rose, N.Y. (14542) 276/G4
Rose (riv.), North. Terr. 93/D2
Rose, Okla. (74364) 288/R2
Roseau (cap.), Dominica 156/G4
Roseau (cap.), Dominica 161/E7
Roseau (riv.), Dominica 161/E7
Roseau (co.), Minn. 255/C2
Roseau, Minn. (56751) 255/C2
Roseau (riv.), Minn. 255/B2
Roseau (riv.), St. Lucia 161/G6
Roseau River, Manitoba 179/F5
Roseaux, Haiti 158/A6
Rosebank, Manitoba 179/D5
Roseberry, Br. Col. 184/J5
Rosebery, Tasmania 99/B3
Rose Blanche, Newf. 166/C4
Roseboom, N.Y. (13450) 276/L5
Roseboro, N.C. (28382) 281/N5
Rosebud, Alberta 182/D4
Rosebud (riv.), Alberta 182/D4
Rose Bud, Ark. (72137) 202/F3
Rosebud, Mo. (63091) 261/K6
Rosebud (co.), Mont. 262/K4
Rosebud, Mont. (59347) 262/K4
Rosebud (creek), Mont. 262/K4
Rosebud, S. Dak. (57570) 298/H7
Rosebud, Texas (76570) 303/G7
Rosebud (creek), Utah 304/A2
Rosebud Ind. Res., S. Dak. 298/H7
Roseburg, Oreg. (97470) 291/D4
Rosebush Mich. (48878) 250/E5
Rose City, Mich. (48654) 250/E4
Rose Creek, Minn. (55970) 255/F7
Rosedale, Ind. (47874) 227/C5
Rosedale, La. (70772) 238/G6
Rosedale, Md. (21237) 245/M3
Rosedale, Miss. (38769) 256/B3
Rosedale, Okla. (†74831) 288/M5
Rosedale, Tenn. (†37728) 237/N8
Rosedale, Va. (24280) 307/E7
Rosedale, W. Va. (26636) 312/E5
Rosefield, La. (†71435) 238/G3
Roseglen, N. Dak. (58775) 282/G4
Rosehearty, Scotland 15/F3
Rosehill, Ala. (†36028) 195/F8
Rose Hill, Barbados 161/B8
Rose Hill, Ill. (†62448) 222/E4
Rose Hill, Iowa (52586) 229/J6
Rose Hill, Kansas (67133) 232/E4
Rose Hill, Ky. (†40330) 237/M5
Rose Hill, Miss. (39356) 256/F6
Rose Hill, N.C. (28458) 281/N5
Rose Hill, Va. (24281) 307/B7
Roseisle, Manitoba 179/D5
Rose Lake, Br. Col. 184/E3
Roseland, Ark. (72463) 202/K2
Roseland, Fla. (32957) 212/F4
Roseland, Ind. (†46601) 227/E1
Roseland, Kansas (†66773) 232/H4
Roseland, La. (70456) 238/J5
Roseland, Minn. (†56216) 255/C6
Roseland, Nebr. (68973) 264/F4
Roseland, N.J. (07068) 273/A2
Roseland, Va. (22967) 307/K5
Roselawn, Ind. (†46310) 227/C2
Roselle, Ill. (60172) 222/A5
Roselle, N.J. (07203) 273/B2
Roselle Park, N.J. (07204) 273/A2
Rose Lodge, Oreg. (97372) 291/D3
Rose Lynn, Alberta 182/E4
Rosemark, Tenn. (38053) 237/B10
Rosemary, Alberta 182/E4
Rosemead, Calif. (91770) 204/C10
Rosemère, Québec 172/H4
Rosemont, Ill. (60018) 222/B5
Rosemont, Md. (†21758) 245/H3
Rosemont, N.J. (08556) 273/D3
Rosemont, Pa. (19010) 294/M5
Rosemount, Minn. (55068) 255/E6
Rosemount, Ohio (†45662) 284/D8
Rosen, Minn. (†56212) 255/B5
Rosenberg, Texas (77471) 303/J8
Rosendale, Minn. (†56243) 255/D5
Rosendale, Mo. (64483) 261/C2
Rosendale, N.Y. (12472) 276/M7
Rosendale, Wis. (54974) 317/J8
Rosenfeld, Manitoba 179/E5
Rosengart, Manitoba 179/E5
Rosenhayn, N.J. (08352) 273/C5
Rosenheim, W. Germany 22/D5
Rosenhof, Sask. 181/D5
Rosenlaui, Switzerland 39/F3
Rosenort, Manitoba 179/E5
Rosepine, La. (70659) 238/D5
Rose Prairie, Br. Col. 184/G2
Roseray, Sask. 181/C5
Roseto, Pa. (18013) 294/M4
Rosetown, Sask. 162/F5
Rosetown, Sask. 181/D4
Rosetta, Egypt 111/J2
Rosetta, Egypt 59/B3
Rosetta, Miss. (†39633) 256/B8
Rosette, Utah (†84329) 304/A2
Rose Valley, Pa. (†19065) 294/L7
Rose Valley, Sask. 181/H3
Roseville, Calif. (95678) 204/B8
Roseville, Ill. (61473) 222/C3
Roseville, Mich. (48066) 250/B6
Roseville, Minn. (55113) 255/G5
Roseville, Ohio (43777) 284/F6
Roseville, Pa. (†16933) 294/H2
Roseway (riv.), Nova Scotia 168/C4
Rosewood, North. Terr. 93/A4
Rosewood, Ohio (43070) 284/C5
Rosewood Heights, Ill. (†62024) 222/B2
Roseworthy, S. Australia 94/B6
Roshage (cape), Denmark 18/F8
Rosharon, Texas (77583) 303/J3
Rosh Ha 'Ayin, Israel 65/B3
Rosholt, S. Dak. (57260) 298/R2
Rosholt, Wis. (54473) 317/H6
Rosh Pinna, Israel 65/D2
Rosice, Czech. 41/D2
Rosiclare, Ill. (62982) 222/E6
Rosie, Ark. (72571) 202/G2
Rosier, Georgia (†30434) 217/H5
Rosignano Marittimo, Italy 34/C3
Rosignol, Guyana 131/C2
Rosine, Ky. (42370) 237/H6
Roşiori de Vede, Romania 45/G3
Rositsa, Bulgaria 45/H4
Roskilde (co.), Denmark 21/E6
Roskilde, Denmark 21/E6
Roskilde, Denmark 18/G9
Roslavl', U.S.S.R. 52/D4
Roslev, Denmark 21/B4
Roslin, Ontario 177/G3
Roslin, Tenn. (†38556) 237/M8
Roslyn, N.Y. (11576) 276/R6
Roslyn, S. Dak. (57261) 298/P2
Roslyn, Wash. (98941) 310/E3
Rosman, N.C. (28772) 281/D4
Rosmaninhal, Portugal 33/C3
Røsnaes (pen.), Denmark 21/D6
Rosneath, Scotland 15/A1
Rosneath, Scotland 10/A1
Ross (isl.), Ant. 2/T10
Ross (sea), Ant. 2/A10
Ross (isl.) 5/B9
Ross (sea) 5/B10
Ross, Calif. (94957) 204/H1
Ross, Iowa (†50025) 229/D5
Ross, Manitoba 179/F5
Ross (isl.), Manitoba 179/J3
Ross, Minn. (56753) 255/C2
Ross (isl.), New Bruns. 170/D4
Ross, N. Zealand 100/C5
Ross (pt.), Norfolk I. 88/L6
Ross, N. Dak. (58776) 282/E3
Ross (co.), Ohio 284/D7
Ross, Ohio (45061) 284/B9
Ross, Tasmania 99/D4
Ross (dam), Wash. 310/D2
Ross (lake), Wash. 310/D2
Rossa, Switzerland 39/H4
Rossall (pt.), England 13/D4
Rossan (pt.), Ireland 10/B3
Ross and Cromarty (trad. co.), Scotland 15/A5
Rossano, Italy 34/F5
Rossarden, Tasmania 99/D3
Ross Barnett (res.), Miss. 256/D6
Ross Bay Junction, Newf. 166/A3
Rossbear (lake), Alberta 182/C1
Rossburg, Ohio (45362) 284/A5
Rossburn, Manitoba 179/B4
Rosscarbery, Ireland 17/C8
Rosscarbery (bay), Ireland 10/B5
Rosscarbery (bay), Ireland 17/D9
Rosseau, Ontario 177/E2
Rosseau (lake), Ontario 177/E2
Rossel (isl.), Papua N.G. 85/D8
Rossendale, Manitoba 179/D5
Rosser, Manitoba 179/E4
Rosses (bay), Ireland 17/D1
Rosses Point, Ireland 17/D3
Rossford, Ohio (43460) 284/C2
Ross Fork, Mont. (†59457) 262/G3
Ross Ice Shelf, Ant. 2/A11
Ross Ice Shelf 5/A10
Rossie, Iowa (51356) 229/C2
Rossie, N.Y. (†13646) 276/J2
Rossignol (lake), Nova Scotia 168/C4
Rossing, Namibia 118/B4
Rossiter, Pa. (15772) 294/E4
Rosskeeragh (pt.), Ireland 17/D3
Ross Lake Nat'l Rec. Area, Wash. 310/E2
Rossland, Br. Col. 162/E6
Rossland, Br. Col. 184/H6
Rosslare, Ireland 10/C4
Rosslare, Ireland 17/J7
Rosslare (bay), Ireland 17/J7
Rosslare Harbour (Ballygeary), Ireland 17/J7
Rosslau, E. Germany 22/E3
Rosslyn Farms, Pa. (†15106) 294/B7
Rosslyn Village, Ontario 177/G5
Rosslyn Village, Ontario 175/C3
Rossmore, W. Va. (25643) 312/C7
Rossmoyne, Ohio (45236) 284/C9
Rosso, Mauritania 106/A5
Rosso, Mauritania 102/A3
Ross of Mull (pen.), Scotland 15/B4
Ross-on-Wye, England 10/E5
Ross-on-Wye, England 13/E6
Rossosh', U.S.S.R. 52/E4
Rossport, Ontario 177/H5
Ross River, Yukon 187/E3
Rosstock (mt.), Switzerland 39/G3
Rosston, Ark. (71858) 202/D6
Rosston, Ind. (†46077) 227/E4
Rosston, Okla. (73855) 288/G1

Sainte-Marguerite 439

Saas, Switzerland 39/J3
Saas Fee, Switzerland 39/E4
Saba (isl.), Neth. Ant. 156/F3
Saba (isl.), Virgin Is. (U.S.) 161/A4
Šabac, Yugoslavia 45/D3
Sabadell, Spain 7/E4
Sabadell, Spain 33/H2
Sabae, Japan 81/H5
Sabah (state), Malaysia 2/Q5
Sabah (state), Malaysia 85/F4
Sabah (reg.), Malaysia 54/N9
Sábalo, Cuba 158/A2
Sabana, Cuba 158/K4
Sabana (arch.), Cuba 158/E1
Sabana de la Mar, Dom. Rep. 156/E3
Sabana de la Mar, Dom. Rep. 158/F5
Sabana Grande, Dom. Rep. 158/E6
Sabanagrande, Honduras 154/D4
Sabana Grande, P. Rico 161/B2
Sabanalarga, Colombia 126/C2
Sabana Seca, P. Rico 161/D1
Sabancuy, Mexico 150/O7
Sabaneta, Dom. Rep. 158/D5
Sabaneta, Barinas, Venezuela 124/D3
Sabaneta, Falcón, Venezuela 124/D2
Sabang, Celebes, Indonesia 85/F5
Sabang, Weh, Indonesia 85/B4
Şabanözü, Turkey 63/E2
Sabará, Brazil 135/E1
Sabattus, Maine (04280) 243/C7
Sabattus○, Maine (04280) 243/C7
Sabaudia, Italy 34/D4
Sabaya, Bolivia 136/A6
Saberi, Hamun-e (lake), Iran 66/M5
Sabetha, Kansas (66534) 232/G2
Sabi (riv.), Zimbabwe 118/E3
Sabile, U.S.S.R. 53/B2
Sabillasville, Md. (21780) 245/J2
Sabin, Minn. (56580) 255/B4
Sabina, Ohio (45169) 284/C7
Sabinal (cay), Cuba 158/H2
Sabinal, Texas (78881) 303/E8
Sabinas, Mexico 150/J3
Sabinas (riv.), Mexico 150/J3
Sabinas Hidalgo, Mexico 150/J3
Sabine (riv.) 188/H4
Sabine (mt.) 5/B9
Sabine (par.), La. 238/C3
Sabine (lake), La. 238/C7
Sabine (passage), La. 238/C7
Sabine (riv.), La. 238/C5
Sabine (pen.), N.W. Terrs. 187/H2
Sabine (co.), Texas 303/L6
Sabine, Texas (†77640) 303/L8
Sabine (lake), Texas 303/L8
Sabine (riv.), Texas 303/L7
Sabine Pass, Texas (77655) 303/L8
Sabinópolis, Brazil 132/F7
Sabinoso, N. Mex. (†87746) 274/E3
Sabinov, Czech. 41/F2
Sabinsville, Pa. (16943) 294/G2
Sabir, Jebel (mt.), Yemen Arab Rep. 59/D7
Sabirabad, U.S.S.R. 52/G6
Sabkha, Syria 63/H5
Sablayan, Philippines 82/C4
Sable (cape), Fla. 188/K5
Sable (cape), Fla. 212/E6
Sable (cape), N.S. 146/M5
Sable (isl.), N.S. 146/N5
Sable (cape), N.S. 162/K7
Sable (isl.), N.S. 162/L7
Sable (cape), Nova Scotia 168/C5
Sable (isl.), Nova Scotia 168/J5
Sable (riv.), Ontario 177/B1
Sable (riv.), Québec 174/D1
Sable River, Nova Scotia 168/C5
Sables (lake), Québec 172/B3
Sables (lake), Québec 172/H1
Sablé-sur-Sarthe, France 28/C4
Sabougla, Miss. (†38955) 256/F3
Sabra (cape), Indonesia 85/J6
Sabrathaa, Libya 111/B1
Sabrina Coast (reg.) 5/C6
Sabtang, Philippines 82/B2
Sabtang (isl.), Philippines 82/B2
Sabugal, Portugal 33/C2
Sabula, Iowa (52070) 229/N4
Sabula, Mo. (†63620) 261/L8
Sabula, Pa. (†15801) 294/E3
Sabya, Saudi Arabia 59/D6
Sabzevar, Iran 54/G6
Sabzevar, Iran 59/G2
Sabzevar, Iran 66/K2
Sabzvaran, Iran 66/K6
Sabzvaran, Iran 59/G4
Sac (co.), Iowa 229/C4
Sac (riv.), Mo. 261/E7
Sacaba, Bolivia 136/C5
Sacaca, Bolivia 136/B6
Sacajawea (peak), Oreg. 291/K2
Sacajawea (lake), Wash. 310/G4
Sácama, Colombia 126/D4
Sacandaga (lake), N.Y. 276/L3
Sac and Fox Ind. Res., Iowa 229/H5
Sacapulas, Guatemala 154/B3
Sacaton, Ariz. (85247) 198/D5
Sacavém, Portugal 33/A1
Sac City, Iowa (50583) 229/C4
Sacedón, Spain 33/E2
Săcele, Romania 45/G3
Sac-Fox-Iowa Ind. Res., Kansas 232/G2
Sacheen (lake), Wash. 310/H2
Sachem (head), Conn. 210/E4
Sachem Head, Conn. (†06437) 210/E3
Sachigo (riv.), Ont. 162/G5
Sachigo (riv.), Ontario 175/B2
Sachojere, Bolivia 136/C4
Sachse, Texas (†75040) 303/H2
Sachseln, Switzerland 39/F3
Sachs Harbour, Canada 4/B16
Sachs Harbour, N.W.T. 162/D1
Sachs Harbour, N.W. Terrs. 187/F2
Sackets (harb.), N.Y. 276/H3
Sackets Harbor, N.Y. (13685) 276/H3
Säckingen, W. Germany 22/C5
Sackville, New Bruns. 170/F3
Sackville, Nova Scotia 168/E4
Saco, Ala. (†36081) 195/G7
Saco, Maine (04072) 243/C8
Saco (riv.), Maine 243/B8
Saco, Mo. (†63645) 261/M8
Saco, Mont. (59261) 262/J2
Saco (riv.), N.H. 268/E3
Sacol (isl.), Philippines 82/D7
Sacramento, Brazil 132/D7
Sacramento, Brazil 135/C1
Sacramento (cap.), Calif. 146/F6
Sacramento (cap.), Calif. 188/B3
Sacramento (riv.), Calif. 188/B3
Sacramento (co.), Calif. 204/D5
Sacramento (cap.), Calif. (*95801) 204/B8
Sacramento (riv.), Calif. 204/D5
Sacramento, Ky. (42372) 237/G6
Sacramento, N. Mex. (88347) 274/D6
Sacramento (mts.), N. Mex. 274/D6
Sacramento Army Depot, Calif. 204/B8
Sacramento Wash (dry riv.), Ariz. 198/A4
Sacratif (cape), Spain 33/E4
Sacré-Coeur-de-Saguenay, Québec 172/H1
Sacred Heart, Minn. (56285) 255/C6
Sacul, Texas (75788) 303/K6
Sádaba, Spain 33/F1
Sadani, Tanzania 115/G5
Saddle (hills), Alberta 182/A2
Saddle, Ark. (†72554) 202/G1
Saddle (mt.), Idaho 220/F6
Saddle (mt.), Idaho 220/D3
Saddle (riv.), N.J. 273/B1
Saddle (mts.), Wash. 310/E4
Saddle Brook○, N.J. (07662) 273/B1
Saddle Mountain, Okla. (†73023) 288/J5
Saddle River, N.J. (07458) 273/B1
Saddlestring, Wyo. (82840) 319/F1
Saddleworth, England 13/J2
Saddleworth, England 10/G2
Sa Dec, Vietnam 72/E5
Sadhoowa, Trin. & Tob. 161/B11
Sadieville, Ky. (40370) 237/M4
Sadij (riv.), Iran 66/L8
Sadiya, India 68/H3
Sa'diya, Iraq 66/D3
Sa'diya, Hor (lake), Iraq 66/E4
Sadlers Village, St. Chris.-Nevis 161/C10
Sadlersville, Tenn. (37154) 237/G7
Sado (isl.), Japan 81/J4
Sado (riv.), Portugal 33/B3
Sadon, Burma 72/C1
Sadorus, Ill. (61872) 222/E4
Saeby, Denmark 18/G8
Saeby, Denmark 21/D3
Saegertown, Pa. (16433) 294/B2
Saetermoen, Norway 18/L2
Saetermoen, Norway 18/L2
Safad (Zefat), Israel 65/C2
Safaniya, Ras (cape), Saudi Arabia 59/E4
Šafárikovo, Czech. 41/F2
Safata (bay), W. Samoa 86/M9
Safe, Mo. (†65559) 261/J6
Safety Harbor, Fla. (33572) 212/B2
Säffle, Sweden 18/H7
Safford, Ala. (36773) 195/D6
Safford, Ariz. (85546) 198/F6
Saffordville, Kansas (†66869) 232/F3
Saffron Walden, England 10/G4
Saffron Walden, England 13/H5
Safi, Jordan 65/E5
Safi, Morocco 102/B1
Safi, Morocco 106/C2
Safidar, Kuh-e (mt.), Iran 59/F4
Safidar, Kuh-e (mt.), Iran 66/H6
Safid Rud (riv.), Iran 66/F2
Safien, Switzerland 39/H3
Safita, Syria 63/G5
Safonovo, U.S.S.R. 52/D3
Safranbolu, Turkey 63/E2
Safut, Jordan 65/D3
Saga, China 77/B6
Saga (pref.), Japan 81/E7
Saga, Japan 81/E7
Sagadahoc (co.), Maine 243/D7
Sagaing (div.), Burma 72/B1
Sagaing, Burma 72/B2
Sagami (bay), Japan 81/O3
Sagami (riv.), Japan 81/O2
Sagami (sea), Japan 81/J6
Sagamihara, Japan 81/O2
Sagamore, Mass. (02561) 249/M5
Sagamore, Pa. (16250) 294/D4
Sagamore Hill Nat'l Hist. Site, N.Y. 276/R6
Sagamore Hills, Ohio (†44067) 284/J10
Saganaga (lake), Minn. 255/H2
Saganaga (lake), Ontario 175/B3
Sagar, India 68/D4
Sagavanirktok (riv.), Alaska 196/J1
Sagay, Camiguin, Philippines 82/E6
Sagay, Negros Occ., Philippines 82/D5
Sage, Ark. (72573) 202/G1
Sage (creek), Mont. 262/F2
Sage (mt.), Virgin Is. (Br.) 161/D4
Sage, Wyo. (†83101) 319/B4
Sagemace (bay), Manitoba 179/B3
Sagerton, Texas (79548) 303/E4
Sageville, Iowa (†52001) 229/M3
Sag Harbor, N.Y. (11963) 276/R8
Saginaw, Ala. (35137) 195/E4
Saginaw, Mich. 188/K2
Saginaw (bay), Mich. 188/K2
Saginaw (co.), Mich. 250/E5
Saginaw, Mich. (*48601) 250/F5
Saginaw (bay), Mich. 250/F5
Saginaw (riv.), Mich. 250/F5
Saginaw, Minn. (55779) 255/F4
Saginaw, Mo. (64864) 261/C8
Saginaw, Oreg. (97472) 291/E4
Saginaw, Texas (76179) 303/E2
Sagle, Idaho (83860) 220/B1
Saglek (bay), Newf. 166/B2
Saglek (fjord), Newf. 166/B2
Saglouc, Que. 162/J3
Saglouc, Québec 174/E1
Sagnay, Philippines 82/D4
Sagola, Mich. (49881) 250/B2
Saguache (co.), Colo. 208/G6
Saguache, Colo. (81149) 208/G6
Saguache (creek), Colo. 208/F6
Sagua de Tánamo, Cuba 158/K3
Sagua la Grande, Cuba 156/B2
Sagua la Grande, Cuba 158/E1
Sagua la Grande (riv.), Cuba 158/E1
Saguaro (lake), Ariz. 198/D5
Saguaro Nat'l Mon., Ariz. 198/E6
Saguenay (county), Québec 174/D2
Saguenay (co.), Québec 172/H1
Saguenay (riv.), Québec 174/C3
Saguenay (riv.), Québec 172/G1
Saguia el Hamra (dry riv.), Western Sahara 106/B3
Sagunto, Spain 33/F3
Sa'gya, China 77/C6
Sahagún, Colombia 126/C3
Sahagún, Spain 33/D1
Sahand, Kuh-e (mt.), Iran 66/E2
Sahara (desert) 2/J4
Sahara (des.) 102/C2
Sahara (des.), Algeria 106/E4
Sahara (des.), Chad 111/C3
Sahara (des.), Egypt 111/E3
Sahara (des.), Libya 111/C3
Sahara (des.), Mali 106/D4
Sahara (des.), Mauritania 106/C4
Sahara (des.), Niger 106/F4
Sahara (des.), Sudan 111/E3
Saharan Atlas (ranges), Algeria 106/E2
Saharanpur, India 68/D3
Saharsa, India 68/F3
Şahinli, Turkey 63/C6
Sahiwal, Pakistan 68/C2
Sahiwal, Pakistan 59/K3
Sahuaripa, Mexico 150/E2
Sahuarita, Ariz. (85629) 198/E7
Sahuayo de Díaz, Mexico 150/H7
Šahy, Czech. 41/E2
Saïda, Algeria 106/E2
Saida, Lebanon 63/F6
Sa'idabad, Iran 66/J6
Sa'idabad, Iran 59/G4
Saïdia, Morocco 106/D2
Saidor, Papua N.G. 85/B7
Saidu, Pakistan 68/C2
Saignelégier, Switzerland 39/D2
Saigo, Japan 81/F5
Saigon (Ho Chi Minh City), Vietnam 54/M8
Saihut, P.D.R. Yemen 54/G8
Saihut, P.D.R. Yemen 59/F6
Saikai National Park, Japan 81/D7
Saiki, Japan 81/E7
Sailes, La. (†71028) 238/D2
Sailor (creek), Idaho 220/C7
Sailor Springs, Ill. (62879) 222/E5
Saimaa (lake), Finland 18/Q6
Saimbeyli, Turkey 63/G4
Sain Alto, Mexico 150/H5
Sain-ni, N. Korea 81/B4
Saint Abbs, Scotland 15/F5
Saint Abbs (head), Scotland 15/F5
Saint-Adalbert, Québec 172/H3
Saint-Adelme, Québec 172/B1
Saint-Adelphe, Québec 172/E3
Saint Adolphe, Manitoba 179/E5
Saint-Adolphe, Québec 172/F2
Saint-Adolphe-d'Howard, Québec 172/C4
Saint-Adrien, Québec 172/F4
Saint-Affrique, France 28/E6
Saint-Agapitville, Québec 172/F3
Saint Agatha○, Maine (04772) 243/G1
Saint Agnes, England 13/B7
Saint-Aimé-des-Lacs, Québec 172/G2
Saint-Alban, Québec 172/E3
Saint Albans, England 13/H7
Saint Albans, England 10/F5
Saint Alban's (head), England 13/F7
Saint Albans○, Maine (04971) 243/E6
Saint Albans, Mo. (63073) 261/L5
Saint Alban's, Newf. 166/C4
Saint Albans, Vt. (05478) 268/A2
Saint Albans○, Vt. (05478) 268/A2
Saint Albans, W. Va. (25177) 312/C6
Saint Albans Bay, Vt. (05481) 268/A2
Saint Albert, Alberta 182/D3
Saint Albert, Ontario 177/J2
Saint-Albert, Québec 172/E3
Saint-Alexandre, Québec 172/D4
Saint-Alexandre-de-Kamouraska, Québec 172/H2
Saint-Alexis, Québec 172/D4
Saint-Alexis-de-Matapédia, Québec 172/B2
Saint-Alexis-des-Monts, Québec 172/D3
Saint Almo, New Bruns. 170/C2
Saint Alphonse, Manitoba 179/C5
Saint-Alphonse, Québec 172/D3
Saint Alphonse de Clare, Nova Scotia 168/B4
Saint-Alphonse-de-Caplan, Québec 172/C2
Saint-Amable, Québec 172/J4
Saint-Amand-Mont-Rond, France 28/E4
Saint Amant, La. (70774) 238/L2
Saint Ambroise, Manitoba 179/E4
Saint-Ambroise, Québec 172/F1
Saint-Anaclet, Québec 172/J1
Saint-André (cape), Madagascar 118/G3
Saint-André, New Bruns. 170/C1
Saint-André, Québec 172/B2
Saint-André, Réunion 118/G5
Saint-André-Avellin, Québec 172/B4
Saint-André-de-Kamouraska, Québec 172/H2
Saint-André-du-Lac-Saint-Jean, Québec 172/E1
Saint-André-Est, Québec 172/C4
Saint Andrew (pt.), Fla. 212/D6
Saint Andrew (sound), Georgia 217/K9
Saint Andrew (lake), Manitoba 179/E3
Saint Andrew (mt.), St. Vin. & Grens. 161/A9
Saint Andrews, New Bruns. 170/C3
Saint Andrew's, Newf. 166/C4
Saint Andrews, Nova Scotia 168/F3
Saint Andrews (chan.), Nova Scotia 168/H2
Saint Andrews, Scotland 15/F4
Saint Andrews, Scotland 10/E2
Saint Andrews (bay), Scotland 15/F4
Saint Andrews, S.C. (29407) 296/G6
Saint Andrews, Tenn. (37372) 237/K10
Saint-Anicet, Québec 172/C4
Saint Ann, Mo. (63074) 261/O2
Saint Anne, Chan. Is. 13/E8
Saint Anne, Ill. (60964) 222/F2
Saint Anns (bay), Nova Scotia 168/H2
Saint Anns, Ontario 177/E4
Saint Ann's Bay, Jamaica 156/C3
Saint Ann's Bay, Jamaica 158/J5
Saint-Anselme, Québec 172/F3
Saint Ansgar, Iowa (50472) 229/H2
Saint Anthony, Idaho (83445) 220/G6
Saint Anthony, Ind. (47575) 227/D8
Saint Anthony, Iowa (50239) 229/G4
Saint Anthony, Minn. (†56307) 255/D5
Saint Anthony, Minn. (55414) 255/G5
Saint Anthony, Newf. 166/C3
Saint Anthony, N. Dak. (58566) 282/H6
Saint-Antoine, New Bruns. 170/F2
Saint-Antoine, Québec 172/H4
Saint-Antoine-Abbé, Québec 172/D4
Saint-Antoine-sur-Richelieu, Québec 172/D4
Saint-Antonin, Québec 172/H2
Saint-Antonin-Noble-Val, France 28/D5
Saint Arnaud, Victoria 97/B5
Saint-Arsène, Québec 172/H2
Saint Arthur, New Bruns. 170/D1
Saint-Astier, France 28/D5
Saint-Athanase, Québec 172/H2
Saint-Aubert, Québec 172/G2
Saint Aubin, Chan. Is. 13/E8
Saint-Aubin-Sauges, Switzerland 39/C3
Saint Augustin (riv.), Newf. 166/C3
Saint-Augustin, Québec 172/G4
Saint-Augustin, Québec 174/F2
Saint-Augustin (riv.), Québec 174/F2
Saint-Augustin-de-Québec, Québec 172/E3
Saint Augustine, Fla. 188/K5
Saint Augustine, Fla. 146/K7
Saint Augustine, Fla. (32084) 212/E2
Saint Augustine, Ill. (61474) 222/C3
Saint Augustine, Md. (†21915) 245/P3
Saint Augustine Beach, Fla. (32084) 212/E2
Saint Austell (bay), England 13/C7
Saint Austell-with-Fowey, England 13/C7
Saint Austell with Fowey, England 10/D5
Saint-Barnabé, Québec 172/D4
Saint-Barthélemy (isl.), Guadeloupe 156/F3
Saint-Barthélemy, Québec 172/D3
Saint Basile, New Bruns. 170/B1
Saint-Basile-le-Grand, Québec 172/J4
Saint-Basile-Sud, Québec 172/F3
Saint Bees (head), England 13/D3
Saint Benedict, Kansas (†66538) 232/F2
Saint Benedict, La. (70457) 238/K5
Saint Benedict, Oreg. (97373) 291/B3
Saint Benedict, Pa. (15773) 294/E4
Saint Benedict, Sask. 181/F3
Saint-Benjamin, Québec 172/G3
Saint-Benoît, Réunion 118/G5
Saint-Benoît-Labre, Québec 172/G3
Saint Bernard, Ala. (35138) 195/E2
Saint Bernard (par.), La. 238/L7
Saint Bernard, La. (70085) 238/L7
Saint Bernard, Nova Scotia 168/B4
Saint Bernard, Ohio (45217) 284/B9
Saint-Bernard, Québec 172/F3
Saint Bernard, Great (pass), Switzerland 39/D5
Saint-Bernard-sur-Mer, Québec 172/G2
Saint Bernice, Ind. (47875) 227/C5
Saint Bethlehem, Tenn. (37155) 237/G7
Saint Blaise, Québec 172/E4
Saint-Blaise, Switzerland 39/D2
Saint-Bonaventure-de-Yamaska, Québec 172/E4
Saint-Boniface-de-Shawinigan, Québec 172/D3
Saint Bonifacius, Minn. (55375) 255/F5
Saint Brendan's, Newf. 166/D4
Saint Brides, Alberta 182/E2
Saint Bride's, Newf. 166/C2
Saint Brides (bay), Wales 10/D5
Saint Brides (bay), Wales 13/B6
Saint-Brieuc, France 28/B3
Saint Brieux, Sask. 181/G3
Saint-Bruno, Québec 172/F1
Saint-Bruno-de-Montarville, Québec 172/J4
Saint-Calais, France 28/D4
Saint-Calixte-de-Kilkenny, Québec 172/D4
Saint-Camille, Québec 172/F4
Saint-Camille-de-Bellechasse, Québec 172/G3
Saint-Casimir, Québec 172/E3
Saint Catharine, Mo. (64677) 261/G3
Saint Catharines, Ontario 177/E4
Saint Catherine, Fla. (†33513) 212/D3
Saint Catherine (mt.), Grenada 161/D8
Saint Catherine (lake), Vt. 268/A5
Saint Catherines (isl.), Georgia 217/K7
Saint Catherines (sound), Georgia 217/K7
Saint-Céré, France 28/D5
Saint-Cergue, Switzerland 39/B4
Saint-Césaire, Québec 172/D4
Saint-Chamond, France 28/F5
Saint Charles, Ark. (72140) 202/H5
Saint Charles, Idaho (83272) 220/G7
Saint Charles, Ill. (60174) 222/E2
Saint Charles, Iowa (50240) 229/F6
Saint Charles, Ky. (42453) 237/F6
Saint Charles (par.), La. 238/K7
Saint Charles, Mich. (48655) 250/E5
Saint Charles, Minn. (55972) 255/F7
Saint Charles (co.), Mo. 261/M2
Saint Charles, Mo. (63301) 261/N1
Saint-Charles, New Bruns. 170/F2
Saint Charles, Ontario 177/D1
Saint-Charles, Bellechasse, Québec 172/G3
Saint Charles, S.C. (29134) 296/G3
Saint Charles, S. Dak. (57571) 298/L7
Saint Charles, Va. (24282) 307/B7
Saint-Charles-de-Mandeville, Québec 172/D3
Saint-Charles-Garnier, Québec 172/J1
Saint-Charles-sur-Richelieu, Québec 172/D4
SAINT CHRISTOPHER-NEVIS 156/F3
SAINT CHRISTOPHER (SAINT KITTS)-NEVIS 161/D11
Saint Christopher (isl.), St. Chris.-Nevis 156/F3
Saint Christopher (isl.), St. Chris.-Nevis 161/D10
Saint Chrysostom, Pr. Edward I. 168/E2
Saint-Chrysostome, Québec 172/D4
Saint Clair (co.), Ala. 195/F3
Saint Clair, Ala. (36774) 195/E6
Saint Clair, Georgia (†30816) 217/H4
Saint Clair (co.), Ill. 222/D5
Saint Clair (lake), Mich. 188/K2
Saint Clair (co.), Mich. 250/G6
Saint Clair, Mich. (48079) 250/G6
Saint Clair (lake), Mich. 250/G6
Saint Clair (riv.), Mich. 250/G6
Saint Clair, Minn. (56080) 255/E6
Saint Clair (co.), Mo. 261/E6
Saint Clair, Mo. (63077) 261/K6
Saint Clair (lake), Ontario 177/B5
Saint Clair (riv.), Ontario 177/B5
Saint Clair, Pa. (17970) 294/K4
Saint Clair (lake), Tasmania 99/C4
Saint Clair Beach, Ontario 177/B5
Saint Clair Shores, Mich. (*48080) 250/B6
Saint Clair Springs, Ala. (†35146) 195/F3
Saint Clairsville, Ohio (43950) 284/J5
Saint Clairsville, Pa. (16676) 294/F5
Saint-Claude, France 28/F4
Saint-Claude, Guadeloupe 161/A7
Saint Claude, Manitoba 179/D5
Saint-Claude, Québec 172/F4
Saint Clears, Wales 13/C6
Saint-Clément, Québec 172/H2
Saint Clements, Ontario 177/D4
Saint-Cléophas, Québec 172/D3
Saint-Clet, Québec 172/C4
Saint Cloud, Fla. (32769) 212/E3
Saint-Cloud, France 28/A2
Saint Cloud, Minn. 188/H1
Saint Cloud, Minn. (56301) 255/D5
Saint Cloud, Wis. (53079) 317/K8
Saint Columb Major, England 13/B7
Saint Combs, Scotland 15/G3
Saint-Côme, Québec 172/D3
Saint-Constant, Québec 172/H4
Saint Croix (riv.) 188/H1
Saint Croix, Ind. (47576) 227/D8
Saint Croix (riv.), Maine 243/J5
Saint Croix (riv.), Minn. 255/F5
Saint Croix, New Bruns. 170/C3
Saint Croix (riv.), New Bruns. 170/C3
Saint Croix, Nova Scotia 168/E4
Saint Croix (isl.), Virgin Is. (U.S.) 156/H2
Saint Croix (isl.), Virgin Is. (U.S.) 161/G4
Saint Croix (co.), Wis. 317/B5
Saint Croix (lake), Wis. 317/A6
Saint Croix (riv.), Wis. 317/A4
Saint Croix Falls, Wis. (54024) 317/A5
Saint Croix Flowage (res.), Wis. 317/C3
Saint Croix Isl. Nat'l Mon., Maine 243/J5
Saint-Cuthbert, Québec 172/D3
Saint-Cyprien, Québec 172/J2
Saint-Cyrille, Québec 172/E4
Saint-Cyrille-de-L'Islet, Québec 172/G3
Saint Cyrus, Scotland 15/F4
Saint-Damase, Québec 172/B1
Saint-Damase-des-Aulnaies, Québec 172/C2
Saint-Damien-de-Brandon, Québec 172/D3
Saint-Damien-de-Buckland, Québec 172/G3
Saint David, Ariz. (85630) 198/E7
Saint David, Ill. (61563) 222/C3
Saint David, Maine (04773) 243/G1
Saint-David, Québec 172/J3
Saint-David-de-Falardeau, Québec 172/F1
Saint-David-d'Yamaska, Québec 172/E4
Saint Davids (isl.), Bermuda 156/H2
Saint David's, Wales 13/B6
Saint David's (head), Wales 10/D5
Saint David's (head), Wales 13/B6
Saint-Denis, France 28/B1
Saint-Denis, Québec 172/D4
Saint-Denis (cap.), Réunion 118/F5
Saint Denis, Sask. 181/F3
Saint-Denis-de-la-Bouteillerie, Québec 172/G2
Saint-Didace, Québec 172/D3
Saint-Dié, France 28/G3
Saint-Dizier, France 28/F3
Saint-Dominique, Québec 172/E4
Saint-Donat-de-Montcalm, Québec 172/C3
Saint-Donat-de-Rimouski, Québec 172/J1
Saint Donatus, Iowa (52071) 229/M4
Sainte-Adèle, Québec 172/C4
Sainte Agathe, Manitoba 179/E5
Sainte-Agathe, Québec 172/F3
Sainte-Agathe-des-Monts, Québec 172/C3
Sainte-Agnes-de-Charlevoix, Québec 172/G2
Sainte Amélie, Manitoba 179/C4
Sainte-Anastasie, Québec 172/F3
Sainte-Angèle-de-Mérici, Québec 172/J1
Sainte Anne (lake), Alberta 182/C3
Sainte-Anne, Guadeloupe 161/B6
Sainte Anne, Manitoba 179/F5
Sainte-Anne, Martinique 161/D7
Sainte-Anne, New Bruns. 170/E1
Sainte-Anne (lake), Québec 172/H2
Sainte-Anne (riv.), Québec 172/C1
Sainte-Anne (riv.), Québec 172/G2
Sainte-Anne (riv.), Québec 172/F3
Sainte Anne (isl.), Seychelles 118/H5
Sainte-Anne-de-Beaupré, Québec 172/F2
Sainte-Anne-de-Bellevue, Québec 172/H4
Sainte-Anne-de-Kent, New Bruns. 170/F2
Sainte-Anne-de-Madawaska, New Bruns. 170/B1
Sainte-Anne-des-Monts, Québec 172/C1
Sainte-Anne-des-Plaines, Québec 172/H4
Sainte-Anne-du-Lac, Québec 172/B3
Sainte-Apolline, Québec 172/G3
Sainte-Aurélie, Québec 172/G3
Sainte-Béatrix, Québec 172/D3
Sainte-Bernadette, Québec 172/G1
Sainte-Blandine, Québec 172/J1
Sainte-Brigide, Québec 172/D4
Sainte-Catherine, Québec 172/F3
Sainte-Cécile-de-Frontenac, Québec 172/G4
Sainte-Cécile-de-Masham, Québec 172/A4
Sainte-Claire, Québec 172/G3
Sainte-Clothilde-de-Horton, Québec 172/E4
Sainte-Croix, Québec 172/F3
Sainte-Croix, Switzerland 39/B3
Saint-Édouard-de-Kent, New Bruns. 170/F2
Saint-Édouard-de-Maskinongé, Québec 172/D3
Saint-Édouard-de-Napierville, Québec 172/D4
Saint Edward, Nebr. (68660) 264/G3
Saint Edward, Pr. Edward I. 168/D2
Sainte-Edwidge, Québec 172/F4
Sainte-Élisabeth, Québec 172/D3
Sainte-Émélie-de-l'Énergie, Québec 172/D3
Sainte-Eulalie, Québec 172/E3
Sainte-Euphémie, Québec 172/G3
Sainte-Famille-d'Aumond, Québec 172/B3
Sainte-Famille-d'Orléans, Québec 172/G3
Sainte-Félicité, Québec 172/B1
Sainte-Flavie, Québec 172/J1
Sainte-Florence, Québec 172/B2
Sainte-Foy, Québec 172/H3
Sainte-Françoise, Québec 172/H1
Sainte-Geneviève, Manitoba 179/F5
Sainte Genevieve (co.), Mo. 261/M7
Sainte Genevieve, Mo. (63670) 261/M6
Sainte-Geneviève, Québec 172/H4
Sainte-Geneviève-de-Batiscan, Québec 172/E3
Sainte-Hedwidge-de-Roberval, Québec 172/E1
Sainte-Hélène-de-Bagot, Québec 172/E4
Sainte-Hélène-de-Kamouraska, Québec 172/H2
Sainte-Hénédine, Québec 172/F3
Sainte-Julie-de-Verchères, Québec 172/J4
Sainte-Julienne, Québec 172/D4
Sainte-Julie-Station, Québec 172/F3
Sainte-Justine, Québec 172/G3
Sainte-Justine-de-Newton, Québec 172/C4
Saint Eleanors, Pr. Edward I. 168/E2
Saint-Éleuthère, Québec 172/H2
Saint Elias (mt.), Alaska 188/D5
Saint Elias (cape), Alaska 196/K3
Saint Elias (mt.), Alaska 196/K3
Saint Elias (mts.), Alaska 196/L2
Saint Elias (mt.), Yukon 162/B3
Saint Elias (mt.), Yukon 187/D3
Saint Elias (mts.), Yukon 187/E3
Saint-Élie, Fr. Guiana 131/E3
Saint-Élie, Québec 172/E3
Saint Elizabeth, Mo. (65075) 261/H6
Saint Elmo, Ala. (36568) 195/B10
Saint Elmo, Colo. (†81236) 208/G5
Saint Elmo, Ill. (62458) 222/E4
Saint-Éloi, Québec 172/H1
Sainte-Louise, Québec 172/G2
Sainte-Luce, Martinique 161/D7
Sainte-Luce, Québec 172/J1
Sainte-Lucie-de-Beauregard, Québec 172/H3
Sainte-Lucie-de-Doncaster, Québec 172/C3
Saint-Elzéar, Québec 172/F3
Saint-Elzéar-de-Bonaventure, Québec 172/C2
Sainte-Marguerite, Guadeloupe 161/B6
Sainte-Marguerite-de-Dorchester, Québec 172/G3
Sainte-Marguerite-Marie, Québec 172/B2
Sainte-Marguerite (riv.), Québec 172/G1
Sainte-Marguerite Nord-Est (riv.), Québec 172/H1
Sainte-Marguerite (riv.), Québec 174/D2

444 Santiago

Santiago de Cuba, Cuba 156/C3
Santiago de Cuba, Cuba 158/J4
Santiago de Huata, Bolivia 136/A5
Santiago de las Vegas, Cuba 158/C1
Santiago del Estero (prov.), Argentina 143/D2
Santiago del Estero, Argentina 120/C5
Santiago del Estero, Argentina 143/D2
Santiago de Machaca, Bolivia 136/A5
Santiago de Pacaguaras, Bolivia 136/A3
Santiago do Cacem, Portugal 33/B3
Santiago Ixcuintla, Mexico 150/G6
Santiago Jamiltepec, Mexico 150/K8
Santiago Juxtlahuaca, Mexico 150/K8
Santiago Miahuatlán, Mexico 150/O2
Santiago Papasquiaro, Mexico 150/F4
Santiago Pinotepa Nacional, Mexico 150/K8
Santiago Rodríguez (prov.), Dom. Rep. 158/D5
Santiago Tuxtla, Mexico 150/M7
Santiago Vázquez, Uruguay 145/A7
Santiaguillo (lake), Mexico 150/G4
San Timoteo, Venezuela 124/C3
Santipur, India 68/F4
Säntis (mt.), Switzerland 39/H2
Santo, Texas (76472) 303/F5
Santo Amaro, Brazil 132/G6
Santo André, Brazil 135/C3
Santo Ângelo, Brazil 132/C10
Santo Antão (isl.), C. Verde 106/A7
Santo António, São Tomé e Príncipe 106/F8
Santo Antônio da Platina, Brazil 132/D8
Santo Antônio da Platina, Brazil 135/A3
Santo Antônio do Leverger, Brazil 132/C6
Santo Corazón, Bolivia 136/F5
Santo Domingo, C. Rica 154/F6
Santo Domingo, Cuba 158/E1
Santo Domingo (cap.), Dom. Rep. 146/L8
Santo Domingo (cap.), Dom. Rep. 156/E3
Santo Domingo (cap.), Dom. Rep. 158/E6
Santo Domingo, Nicaragua 154/E4
Santo Domingo de la Calzada, Spain 33/E1
Santo Domingo de los Colorados, Ecuador 128/C3
Santo Domingo Pueblo, N. Mex. (87052) 274/C3
San Tomé, Venezuela 124/F3
Santoña, Spain 33/E1
Santos, Brazil 2/G7
Santos, Brazil 132/E9
Santos, Brazil 120/E5
Santos, Brazil 135/C3
Santos, Fla. (†32670) 212/D2
Santos Dumont, Brazil 132/F8
Santos Dumont, Brazil 135/E2
Santos Mercado, Bolivia 136/B1
Santo Tomás, Mexico 150/A1
Santo Tomás, Nicaragua 154/E5
Santo Tomás, Amazonas, Peru 128/C6
Santo Tomás, Cusco, Peru 128/G10
Santo Tomas, Davao, Philippines 82/E7
Santo Tomas, La Union, Philippines 82/C2
Santo Tomas (mt.), Philippines 82/C2
Santo Tomás de Andoas, Peru 128/D4
Santo Tomás de Castilla, Guatemala 154/C3
Santo Tomé, Corrientes, Argentina 143/E2
Santo Tomé, Santa Fe, Argentina 143/F5
Santuck, S.C. (†29031) 296/D2
Santuit, Mass. (†02635) 249/N6
Santurce, P. Rico 161/E1
San Urbano, Argentina 143/F6
San Valentín, Cerro (mt.), Chile 138/D6
San Vicente, Chile 138/F4
San Vicente (San Vicente de Tagua Tagua), Chile 138/F5
San Vicente, El Salvador 154/C4
San Vicente, Mexico 150/B1
San Vicente, Amazonas, Venezuela 124/E5
San Vicente, Apure, Venezuela 124/D4
San Vicente de Alcántara, Spain 33/C3
San Vicente de Cañete, Peru 128/D9
San Vicente del Caguán, Colombia 126/C6
San Vito, Italy 34/B5
San Vito (cape), Italy 34/D5
San Vito al Tagliamento, Italy 34/D2
San Vito dei Normanni, Italy 34/F4
San Vito Romano, Italy 34/F6
San Xavier Ind. Res., Ariz. 198/D6
Sanyati (riv.), Zimbabwe 118/D3
San Ygnacio, Texas (78067) 303/E10
San Ysidro, N. Mex. (87053) 274/C3
Sanyuan, China 77/G5
Sanza Pombo, Angola 115/C5
São Bento, Brazil 132/E3
São Bernardo do Campo, Brazil 135/C3
São Borja, Brazil 132/C10
São Brás de Alportel (Alportel), Portugal 33/C4
São Carlos, Brazil 135/C3
São Cristóvão, Brazil 132/G5
São Domingos, Brazil 132/E6
São Félix, Brazil 132/G6
São Fidélis, Brazil 132/F8
São Fidélis, Brazil 135/F2
São Francisco, Brazil 132/E6
São Francisco (riv.), Brazil 120/E4
São Francisco (riv.), Brazil 2/G6
São Francisco (riv.), Brazil 132/F5
São Francisco (riv.), Brazil 135/D2
São Francisco do Sul, Brazil 132/E9
São Gabriel, Brazil 132/C10
São Gonçalo, Brazil 132/F8
São Gonçalo, Brazil 135/E3
São Gonçalo do Sapucaí, Brazil 135/D2
São João da Boa Vista, Brazil 132/E8
São João da Boa Vista, Brazil 135/C2
São João da Madeira, Portugal 33/B2
São João da Pesqueira, Portugal 33/C2
São João del Rei, Brazil 132/E8
São João del Rei, Brazil 135/D2
São João de Meriti, Brazil 135/E3
São João do Piauí, Brazil 132/F5
São João dos Patos, Brazil 132/F4
São João Nepomuceno, Brazil 135/E2
São Joaquim da Barra, Brazil 135/C2
São Jorge (isl.), Portugal 33/B1
São José, Brazil 132/D9
São José da Laje, Brazil 132/H5
São José do Gurupi, Brazil 132/E3
São José do Rio Pardo, Brazil 135/C2
São José do Rio Preto, Brazil 120/E5
São José do Rio Preto, Brazil 132/D8
São José do Rio Preto, Brazil 135/B2
São José dos Campos, Brazil 135/D3
São José dos Pinhais, Brazil 132/D9
São Leopoldo, Brazil 132/D10
São Lourenço, Brazil 135/D3
São Lourenço (riv.), Brazil 132/C7
São Lourenço do Sul, Brazil 132/C10
São Luís, Brazil 132/F3
São Luís, Brazil 120/E3
São Luís Gonzaga, Brazil 132/C10
São Manuel, Brazil 135/B3
São Marcos (bay), Brazil 120/E3
São Marcos (bay), Brazil 132/F3
São Martinho do Porto, Portugal 33/B3
São Mateus, Brazil 132/G7
São Miguel (isl.), Portugal 33/D2
São Miguel Arcanjo, Brazil 135/C3
São Miguel do Guamá, Brazil 132/E3
São Miguel dos Campos, Brazil 132/G5
Saona (isl.), Dom. Rep. 156/E3
Saona (isl.), Dom. Rep. 158/F6
Saône (riv.), France 28/F4
Saône-et-Loire (dept.), France 28/F4
Saonek, Indonesia 85/J6
São Nicolau, Angola 115/B6
São Nicolau (isl.), C. Verde 106/B8
São Paulo (state), Brazil 135/B3
São Paulo (state), Brazil 132/D8
São Paulo, Brazil 120/E5
São Paulo, Brazil 2/G6
São Paulo, Brazil 132/E8
São Paulo, Brazil 135/C3
São Paulo de Olivença, Brazil 132/G9
São Pedro do Piauí, Brazil 132/F4
São Pedro do Sul, Portugal 33/B2
São Raimundo das Mangabeiras, Brazil 132/E4
São Raimundo Nonato, Brazil 132/F5
São Romão, Brazil 132/E7
São Roque, Brazil 135/C3
São Roque (cape), Brazil 2/H6
São Roque (cape), Brazil 120/F3
São Roque (cape), Brazil 132/H4
São Sebastião, Brazil 135/D3
São Sebastião (isl.), Brazil 120/E5
São Sebastião (isl.), Brazil 135/D3
São Sebastião (isl.), Brazil 132/E8
São Sebastião (pt.), Mozambique 118/F4
São Sebastião do Paraíso, Brazil 135/C2
São Sebastião do Paraíso, Brazil 132/E8
São Simão, Brazil 135/C2
São Teotónio, Portugal 33/B4
São Tiago (isl.), C. Verde 106/B8
São Tomé (cape), Brazil 120/F5
São Tomé (cape), Brazil 132/F8
São Tomé (cap.), São Tomé e Príncipe 106/F8
São Tomé (isl.), São T. & Pr. 106/F8
São Tomé e Príncipe 102/C4
SÃO TOMÉ E PRÍNCIPE 106/F8
Saoura, Wadi (dry riv.), Algeria 106/D3
São Vicente, Brazil 135/C4
São Vicente (isl.), C. Verde 106/B7
São Vicente, Portugal 33/A2
São Vicente (cape), Portugal 7/C5
São Vicente Ferrer, Brazil 132/E3
São Vincent (cape), Portugal 33/B4
Sapahaqui, Bolivia 136/B5
Sápai, Greece 45/G5
Sapanca, Turkey 63/D2
Saparua, Indonesia 85/H6
Sapawe, Ontario 177/G5
Sapawe, Ontario 175/B3
Sapele, Nigeria 106/F7
Sapello, N. Mex. (87745) 274/D3
Sapelo (isl.), Georgia 217/K8
Sapelo (sound), Georgia 217/K7
Sapelo Island, Georgia (31327) 217/K8
Şaphane, Turkey 63/C3
Saponac, Maine (†04417) 243/G5
Saposoa, Peru 128/D6
Sappa (creek), Kansas 232/B2
Sappemeer-Hoogezand, Netherlands 27/K2
Sapphire, N.C. (28774) 281/D4
Sappho, Wash. (†98305) 310/A2
Sappington, Mo. (63126) 261/O4
Sapporo, Japan 2/S3
Sapporo, Japan 54/P5
Sapporo, Japan 81/K2
Sapse, Bolivia 136/C6
Sapucaí (riv.), Brazil 135/D2
Sapucaí, Paraguay 144/B5
Sapulpa, Okla. (74066) 288/O3
Saqqez, Iran 59/E2
Saqqez, Iran 66/E2
Saquena, Peru 128/F5
Sara (riv.), Cent. Afr. Rep. 115/C2
Sara (riv.), Chad 111/C6
Sara, Philippines 82/D5
Sarab, Iran 66/E2
Sara Buri, Thailand 72/D4
Saragosa, Texas (79780) 303/D11
Saragossa, Ala. (†35578) 195/D3
Saragossa, Spain 7/D4
Saragossa, Spain 33/F2
Saraguro, Ecuador 128/C4
Sarah (lake), Minn. 255/F5
Sarah, Miss. (38665) 256/D1
Sarahsville, Ohio (43779) 284/H6
Sarajevo, Yugoslavia 7/F4
Sarajevo, Yugoslavia 45/D4
Sarakhs, Iran 66/M2
Saraland, Ala. (36571) 195/B9
Saramacca (dist.), Suriname 131/C3
Saramacca (riv.), Suriname 131/D3
Sarampiuni, Bolivia 136/A4
Saran', U.S.S.R. 48/H5
Saranac, Mich. (48881) 250/D6
Saranac, N.Y. (12981) 276/N1
Saranac (lakes), N.Y. 276/M2
Saranac (riv.), N.Y. 276/N1
Saranac Lake, N.Y. (12983) 276/M2
Sarandë, Albania 45/E6
Sarandí del Yí, Uruguay 145/D4
Sarandí de Navarro, Uruguay 145/C3
Sarandí Grande, Uruguay 145/C4
Sarangani (bay), Philippines 82/E8
Sarangani (isls.), Philippines 82/E8
Sarangani (isls.), Philippines 85/G4
Sarangani (str.), Philippines 82/E8
Saransk, U.S.S.R. 7/J3
Saransk, U.S.S.R. 48/E4
Saransk, U.S.S.R. 52/G4
Sarapul, U.S.S.R. 7/K3
Sarapul, U.S.S.R. 48/F4
Sarapul, U.S.S.R. 52/H3
Sarare, Venezuela 124/D3
Sarare (riv.), Venezuela 124/C4
Sarasota, Fla. 188/K5
Sarasota (co.), Fla. 212/D4
Sarasota, Fla. (*33577) 212/D4
Sarasota (pt.), Fla. 212/D4
Sarasota Springs, Fla. (†33577) 212/D4
Saraswati (riv.), India 68/F1
Saratoga, Ark. (71859) 202/C6
Saratoga, Calif. (95070) 204/K4
Saratoga, Ind. (47382) 227/H4
Saratoga, Iowa (52167) 229/J2
Saratoga, Miss. (†39111) 256/E7
Saratoga (co.), N.Y. 276/N4
Saratoga (lake), N.Y. 276/N4
Saratoga, Texas (77585) 303/K7
Saratoga, Wyo. (82331) 319/F4
Saratoga Nat'l Hist. Park, N.Y. 276/N4
Saratoga Springs, N.Y. (12866) 276/N4
Saratov, U.S.S.R. 7/J3
Saratov, U.S.S.R. 48/E4
Saratov, U.S.S.R. 52/G4
Saravan, Iran 59/H4
Saravan, Iran 66/N7
Saravan, Laos 72/E4
Sarawak (state), Malaysia 2/Q5
Sarawak (state), Malaysia 85/E5
Sarawak (reg.), Malaysia 54/N9
Sarayacu, Ecuador 128/D3
Sarayköy, Turkey 63/C4
Sarayönü, Turkey 63/E3
Sarbaz, Iran 66/M7
Sarbaz, Iran 59/H4
Sarben, Nebr. (†69155) 264/C3
Sárbogárd, Hungary 41/E3
Sarco (bay), Chile 138/A7
Sarcoxie, Mo. (64862) 261/D8
Sardarshahr, India 68/C3
Sar Dasht, Iran 66/D2
Sardina (pt.), P. Rico 161/A1
Sardinata, Colombia 126/D3
Sardinia, Ind. (†47283) 227/F6
Sardinia (reg.), Italy 34/B4
Sardinia (isl.), Italy 7/E4
Sardinia (isl.), Italy 34/B4
Sardinia, N.Y. (14134) 276/C5
Sardinia, Ohio (45171) 284/C7
Sardinia, S.C. (29143) 296/G4
Sardis, Ala. (36775) 195/E6
Sardis, Ala. (†35957) 195/F2
Sardis, Br. Col. 184/M3
Sardis, Georgia (30456) 217/J5
Sardis, Ky. (41056) 237/O3
Sardis (lake), Miss. 188/J4
Sardis, Miss. (38666) 256/E2
Sardis (dam), Miss. 256/E2
Sardis (lake), Miss. 256/E2
Sardis, Ohio (43946) 284/J6
Sardis, Okla. (74564) 288/R5
Sardis, Tenn. (38371) 237/E10
Sardis, W. Va. (†26461) 312/F4
Sar-e Pol, Afghanistan 68/B1
Sar-e Pol, Afghanistan 59/J2
Sarepta, La. (71071) 238/D1
Sarepta, Miss. (38867) 256/F2
Sar Eskand Khan, Iran 66/E2
Sargans, Switzerland 39/H2
Sargeant, Minn. (55973) 255/F7
Sargent, Georgia (30275) 217/C4
Sargent, Nebr. (68874) 264/E3
Sargent (co.), N. Dak. 282/P7
Sargents, Colo. (81248) 208/F6
Sargodha, Pakistan 59/K3
Sargodha, Pakistan 68/C2
Sarh, Chad 111/C6
Sarh, Chad 102/D4
Sarhro, Jebel (mts.), Morocco 106/C2
Sari, Iran 59/F2
Sari, Iran 66/H2
Saria (isl.), Greece 45/H8
Sarigan (isl.), No. Marianas 87/E4
Sarıgöl, Turkey 63/C3
Sarih, Jordan 65/D2
Sarıkamış, Turkey 63/K2
Sarıkamış, Turkey 59/D1
Sarıkaya, Turkey 63/F3
Sarıköy, Turkey 63/B2
Sarina, Queensland 88/H4
Sarina, Queensland 95/D4
Sarine (Saane) (riv.), Switzerland 39/D3
Sariñena, Spain 33/F2
Sarıoğlan, Turkey 63/G3
Sarita, Texas (78385) 303/G10
Sariwŏn, N. Korea 81/B4
Sarıyer, Turkey 63/D5
Sarız, Turkey 63/G3
Sark (isl.), Chan. Is. 13/E8
Sark (isl.), Chan. Is. 10/E6
Sarkad, Hungary 41/F3
Sarkand, U.S.S.R. 48/J5
Şarkikaraağaç, Turkey 63/D3
Şarkışla, Turkey 63/G3
Şarköy, Turkey 63/B2
Sarlat-La-Canéda, France 28/D5
Sarles, N. Dak. (58372) 282/N2
Sarmi, Indonesia 85/K6
Sarmiento, Argentina 143/B6
Sarmiento, Argentina 120/C7
Sarmiento, Cerro (mt.), Chile 138/E11
Särna, Sweden 18/H6
Sarnath, India 68/E3
Sarnen, Switzerland 39/F3
Sarnen (lake), Switzerland 39/F3
Sarnia, Ont. 162/H7
Sarnia, Ontario 177/B5
Sarny, U.S.S.R. 52/C4
Sarona, Wis. (54870) 317/C4
Saronic (gulf), Greece 45/F7
Saronno, Italy 34/B2
Saronville, Nebr. (68975) 264/G4
Saros (gulf), Turkey 63/B2
Sárospatak, Hungary 41/F2
Sarpsborg, Norway 18/D4
Sarpy (co.), Nebr. 264/H3
Sarra (well), Libya 111/D3
Sarralbe, France 28/G3
Sarrebourg, France 28/G3
Sarreguemines, France 28/G3
Sarria, Spain 33/C1
Sarroch, Italy 34/B5
Sarsati (riv.), India 68/F1
Sarstún (riv.), Belize 154/C3
Sarstún (riv.), Guatemala 154/C3
Sartell, Minn. (56377) 255/D5
Sartène, France 28/B7
Sarthe (dept.), France 28/D3
Sarthe (riv.), France 28/D4
Sartrouville, France 28/A1
Sarufutsu, Japan 81/L1
Sarur, Oman 59/G5
Sárvár, Hungary 41/D3
Sarver, Pa. (16055) 294/C4
Sárviz csatorna (canal), Hungary 41/E3
Sarysh̄agan, U.S.S.R. 48/H5
Sary Su (riv.), U.S.S.R. 48/H5
Sasabe, Ariz. (85633) 198/D7
Sasabe, Mexico 150/C1
Sasaginnigak (lake), Manitoba 179/G3
Sasakwa, Okla. (74867) 288/N5
Sasaram, India 68/E4
Sasebo, Japan 81/D7
Saseenos, Br. Col. 184/J3
Saskatchewan (prov.) 162/F5
Saskatchewan (riv.) 162/F5
Saskatchewan (prov.), Canada 146/H4
Saskatchewan (riv.), Canada 2/D3
SASKATCHEWAN 181
Saskatchewan (riv.), Sask. 181/H2
Saskatchewan Beach, Sask. 181/G5
Saskatchewan Landing Prov. Park, Sask. 181/C5
Saskatoon, Sask. 162/F5
Saskatoon, Sask. 146/H4
Saskatoon, Sask. 181/E3
Saskeram (riv.), Sask. 181/K2
Sason, Turkey 63/J3
Sasovo, U.S.S.R. 52/F4
Saspamco, Texas (78153) 303/K11
Sassafras, Md. (†21637) 245/P3
Sassafras (riv.), Md. 245/P3
Sassafras (mt.), S.C. 296/B1
Sassafras, Tasmania 99/C3
Sassandra, Ivory Coast 106/C8
Sassandra (riv.), Ivory Coast 106/C7
Sassari (prov.), Italy 34/B4
Sassari, Italy 34/B4
Sassari, Italy 7/E4
Sasseneire (mt.), Switzerland 39/E4
Sasser, Georgia (31785) 217/D7
Sassnitz, E. Germany 22/E1
Sasstown, Liberia 106/C8
Sassuolo, Italy 34/C2
Sástago, Spain 33/F2
Sasu (mt.), N. Korea 81/C4
Sata (cape), Japan 81/E8
Satadougou, Mali 106/B6
Satanta, Kansas (67870) 232/B4
Satara, India 68/C5
Satartia, Miss. (39162) 256/C5
Satawal (isl.), Micronesia 87/E5
Satellite Beach, Fla. (32935) 212/F3
Säter, Sweden 18/J6
Saticoy, Calif. (93004) 204/F9
Satigny, Switzerland 39/A4
Satilla (riv.), Georgia 217/G8
Satipo, Peru 128/E8
Satluj (Sutlej) (riv.), India 68/C3
Satna, India 68/E4
Sátoraljaújhely, Hungary 41/F2
Satpura (range), India 68/D4
Satsop, Wash. (98583) 310/B3
Satsuma, Ala. (36572) 195/B9
Satsuma, Fla. (32089) 212/E2
Satsuma, La. (†70754) 238/L1
Satte, Japan 81/O1
Satu Mare, Romania 45/F2
Satu Mare, Romania 7/G4
Satun, Thailand 72/C6
Satupaitea, W. Samoa 86/L8
Saturna Island, Br. Col. 184/K3
Saturnia, Italy 34/C3
Satus (creek), Wash. 310/E4
Sauble Beach, Ontario 177/C3
Sauce, Argentina 143/G5
Sauce, Peru 128/D6
Sauce, Canelones, Uruguay 145/B6
Sauce, Rocha, Uruguay 145/E5
Sauce (lag.), Uruguay 145/D5
Sauceda (mts.), Ariz. 198/C6
Sauce de Luna, Argentina 143/G5
Sauce del Yí, Uruguay 145/D4
Saucedo, Uruguay 145/B2
Sauchie, Scotland 15/C1
Saucier, Miss. (39574) 256/F9
Saucillo, Mexico 150/G2
Sauda, Qurnet es (mt.), Lebanon 63/G5
Saudhárkrókur, Iceland 21/B1
Saudi Arabia 2/M4
Saudi Arabia 54/F7
SAUDI ARABIA 59/D4
Sauer (riv.), Luxembourg 27/J9
Sauer (riv.), W. Germany 22/B4
Sauerland (reg.), W. Germany 22/B3
Saugatuck, Conn. (†06880) 210/B4
Saugatuck (res.), Conn. 210/B3
Saugatuck (riv.), Conn. 210/B3
Saugatuck, Mich. (49453) 250/C6
Saugeen (riv.), Ontario 177/C3
Saugerties, N.Y. (12477) 276/M6
Sauget, Ill. (62201) 222/A2
Saugus○, Mass. (01906) 249/D6
Saugus Iron Works Nat'l Hist. Site, Mass. 249/D6
Sauiá, Brazil 132/B3
Sauk (riv.), Wash. 310/D2
Sauk (co.), Wis. 317/G9
Sauk Centre, Minn. (56378) 255/C5
Sauk City, Wis. (53583) 317/G9
Sauk Rapids, Minn. (56379) 255/D5
Sauk Village, Ill. (60411) 222/C6
Saukville, Wis. (53080) 317/L9
Saül, Fr. Guiana 131/E4
Saulgau, W. Germany 22/C5
Saulkrasti, U.S.S.R. 53/C2
Saulnierville, Nova Scotia 168/B4
Saulsbury, Tenn. (38067) 237/C10
Saulsville, W. Va. (25876) 312/C7
Sault-au-Mouton, Québec 172/H1
Sault au Mouton (riv.), Québec 172/H1
Saulteaux (riv.), Alberta 182/C2
Sault Sainte Marie, Mich. 188/J1
Sault Sainte Marie, Mich. (49783) 250/E2
Sault Sainte Marie, Ont. 162/H6
Sault Sainte Marie, Ontario 177/J5
Sault Sainte Marie, Ontario 175/D3
Sault Ste. Marie, Ont. 146/K5
Saum, Minn. (56674) 255/D3
Saumarez (reef), 95/E4
Saumarez (reef), Coral Sea Is. Terr. 88/J4
Saumarez, New Bruns. 170/E1
Saumâtre (lake), Haiti 158/C6
Saumlaki, Indonesia 85/J7
Saumur, France 28/D4
Saunders (isl.), 143/E7
Saunders (co.), Nebr. 264/H3
Saundersville, Mass. (†01560) 249/G4
Saunemin, Ill. (61769) 222/E3
Sauqira (bay), Oman 59/G6
Sauqira, Ras (cape), Oman 59/G6
Sauquoit, N.Y. (13456) 276/K5
Saurimo, Angola 115/D5
Saurimo, Angola 102/E6
Sausalito, Calif. (94965) 204/H2
Sautatá, Colombia 126/B4
Sautee-Nacoochee, Georgia (30571) 217/E1
Sauteurs, Grenada 161/D8
Saut-Tigre, Fr. Guiana 131/E3
Sauzal, Chile 138/G5
Sava (riv.) 7/F4
Sava (riv.), Yugoslavia 45/D3
Savage, (riv.), Md. 245/B2
Savage, Minn. (55337) 255/G6
Savage, Miss. (38667) 256/D1
Savage, Mont. (59262) 262/M3
Savage (harb.), Pr. Edward I. 168/F2
Savage (riv.), Tasmania 99/B3
Savage-Guilford, Md. (20863) 245/L4
Savage River (lake), Md. 245/B2
Savage River, Tasmania 99/B3
Savageton, Wyo. (†82716) 319/G2
Savah, Ind. (†47620) 227/B8
Savai'i (isl.), W. Samoa 87/J7
Savai'i (isl.), W. Samoa 86/L8
Savalou, Benin 106/E7
Savana (isl.), Virgin Is. (U.S.) 161/A4
Savanat (Estahbanat), Iran 66/J6
Savaneta, Neth. Ant. 161/E10
Savanette, Haiti 158/C6
Savanna, Ill. (61074) 222/C1
Savanna, Okla. (74565) 288/P5
Savanna Army Depot, Ill. 222/C1
Savannah (riv.) 188/K4
Savannah, Ga. 146/K6
Savannah, Ga. 188/K4
Savannah, Georgia (*31401) 217/L6
Savannah (riv.), Georgia 217/K5
Savannah, Mo. (64485) 261/C3
Savannah○, N.Y. (13146) 276/G4
Savannah, Ohio (44874) 284/F4
Savannah (riv.), S.C. 296/E6
Savannah, Tenn. (38372) 237/E10
Savannah, U.S. 2/F4
Savannah (riv.), U.S. 146/K6
Savannah River Plant Atomic Energy Commission, S.C. 296/D5
Savannakhét, Laos 72/E3
Savanna-la-Mar, Jamaica 158/G6
Savanna-la-Mar, Jamaica 156/B3
Savannes (bay), St. Lucia 161/G7
Savant (lake), Ontario 177/G4
Savant (lake), Ontario 175/B2
Savant Lake, Ontario 177/G4
Savant Lake, Ontario 175/B2
Savantvadi, India 68/C5
Savanur, India 68/D6
Savaştepe, Turkey 63/B3
Save (riv.) 102/F7
Savé, Benin 106/E7
Save (riv.), Mozambique 118/E4
Saveh, Iran 59/F2
Saveh, Iran 66/G3
Săveni, Romania 45/H1
Saverne, France 28/G3
Saverton, Mo. (63467) 261/K3
Savery, Wyo. (82332) 319/E4
Savery (creek), Wyo. 319/E4
Savièse, Switzerland 39/D4
Savigliano, Italy 34/A2
Savo (isl.), Solomon Is. 86/D3
Savognin, Switzerland 39/J3
Savoie (Savoy) (dept.), France 28/G5
Savona, Br. Col. 184/G5
Savona (prov.), Italy 34/B2
Savona, Italy 34/B2
Savona, N.Y. (14879) 276/F6
Savonburg, Kansas (66772) 232/G4
Savonet, Neth. Ant. 161/F8
Savonlinna, Finland 18/Q6
Savoonga, Alaska (99769) 196/E2
Savoy, Ill. (61874) 222/E3
Savoy, Ky. (†40769) 237/N7
Savoy○, Mass. (01256) 249/B2
Savoy, Mont. (†59526) 262/H2
Savoy, S. Dak. (†57754) 298/B5
Şavşat, Turkey 63/K2
Sävsjö, Sweden 18/J8
Savu (sea), Indonesia 54/O10
Savukoski, Finland 18/Q3
Savur, Turkey 63/J4
Savusavu (bay), Fiji 86/Q10
Sawahlunto, Indonesia 85/C6
Sawankhalok, Thailand 72/C3
Sawara, Japan 81/K6
Sawatch (range), Colo. 208/G4
Sawbill, Newf. 166/A3
Sawbill Landing, Minn. (†55603) 255/G3
Sawbridgeworth, England 13/H7
Saweba (cape), Indonesia 85/J6
Sawi, India 68/G7
Sawmill Bay, N.W. Terrs. 187/G3
Sawpit, Colo. (†81430) 208/D7
Sawston, England 13/H5
Sawtell, N.S. Wales 97/G2
Sawtooth (range), Idaho 220/C6
Sawtooth (ridge), Wash. 310/E2
Sawtooth Nat'l Rec. Area, Idaho 220/D5
Sawu (isl.), Indonesia 85/G8
Sawu (isls.), Indonesia 85/G8
Sawu (sea), Indonesia 85/G7
Sawyer, Kansas (67134) 232/D4
Sawyer, Ky. (42643) 237/N7
Sawyer, Mich. (49125) 250/C7
Sawyer, Minn. (55780) 255/F4
Sawyer, N. Dak. (58781) 282/H3
Sawyer, Okla. (74756) 288/R7
Sawyer (co.), Wis. 317/D4
Sawyers Bar, Calif. (96027) 204/B2
Sawyerville, Ala. (36776) 195/C5
Sawyerville, Ill. (62085) 222/D4
Sawyerville, Québec 172/F4
Saxapahaw, N.C. (27340) 281/L3
Saxe, Va. (23967) 307/L7
Saxeville, Wis. (54976) 317/H7
Saxis, Va. (23427) 307/S5
Saxman, Alaska (†99901) 196/N2
Saxmundham, England 13/J5
Saxon, S.C. (†29301) 296/D2
Saxon, Switzerland 39/D4
Saxon, Wis. (54559) 317/F3
Saxonburg, Pa. (16056) 294/C4
Saxonville, Mass. (01701) 249/A7
Saxony (reg.), E. Germany 22/E3
Saxton, Ky. (†40769) 237/N7
Saxton, Pa. (16678) 294/F5
Saxtons River, Vt. (05154) 268/B5
Say, Niger 106/E6
Saya, Bolivia 136/B5
Sayabec, Québec 172/B2
Sayaboury (Muang Xaignabouri), Laos 72/D3
Sayama, Japan 81/O2
Sayán, Peru 128/D8
Sayan (mts.), U.S.S.R. 48/K4
Saybrook, Ill. (61770) 222/E3
Saybrook, Pa. (†16347) 294/D2
Saybrook Point, Conn. (†06475) 210/F3
Sayhan-Ovoo, Mongolia 77/F2
Saylesville, R.I. (†02865) 249/J5
Saylorsburg, Pa. (18353) 294/M4
Saylorville (lake), Iowa 229/F5
Sayner, Wis. (54560) 317/H4
Saynshand, Mongolia 77/H3
Saynshand, Mongolia 54/M5
Sayre, Ala. (35139) 195/E3
Sayre, Okla. (73662) 288/G4
Sayre, Pa. (18840) 294/K2
Sayreville, N. J. (08872) 273/E3
Sayula, Mexico 150/H7
Sayula de Alemán, Mexico 150/M8
Sayville, N.Y. (11782) 276/O9
Sayward, Br. Col. 184/D5
Sazan (isl.), Albania 45/D5
Sázava (riv.), Czech. 41/C2
Sbaa, Algeria 106/D3
Sbeïtla, Tunisia 106/F1
Scafell Pike (mt.), England 13/D3
Scafell Pike (mt.), England 10/E3
Scalasaig, Scotland 15/B4
Scalby, England 13/G3
Scales Mound, Ill. (61075) 222/C1
Scaletta (pass), Switzerland 39/J3
Scalf, Ky. (40982) 237/O7
Scalloway, Scotland 10/G1
Scalloway, Scotland 15/G2
Scalpay (isl.), Scotland 15/B3
Scalpay (isl.), Scotland 15/C3
Scalp Level, Pa. (†15963) 294/E5
Scaly Mountain, N.C. (28775) 281/C4
Scammon, Kansas (66773) 232/H4
Scammon Bay, Alaska (99662) 196/E2
Scandia, Alberta 182/E4
Scandia, Kansas (66966) 232/E2
Scandia, Minn. (55073) 255/F5
Scandia, Wash. (†98370) 310/A1
Scandinavia 18
Scandinavia, Wis. (54977) 317/H7
Scanlon, Minn. (†55720) 255/F4
Scanterbury, Manitoba 179/F4
Scantic, Conn. (†06097) 210/E1
Scantic (riv.), Conn. 210/E1

Seminoe 445

Scapa, Alberta 182/D4
Scapa Flow (chan.), Scotland 15/E2
Scapa Flow (chan.), Scotland 10/E1
Scappoose, Oreg. (97056) 291/E2
Scarba (isl.), Scotland 15/C4
Scarboro, Barbados 161/B9
Scarboro, Georgia (†30442) 217/J5
Scarborough, England 10/F3
Scarborough, England 13/G3
Scarborough, Maine (04074) 243/C8
Scarborough○, Maine (04074) 243/C8
Scarborough, Ontario 177/K4
Scarborough, Trin. & Tob. 156/G5
Scarbro, W. Va. (25917) 312/D7
Scarinish, Scotland 15/B4
Scarp (isl.), Scotland 15/A2
Scarriff, Ireland 17/E6
Scarriff (isl.), Ireland 17/A8
Scarsdale, N.Y. (10583) 276/P6
Scarth, Manitoba 179/B5
Scarville, Iowa (50473) 229/F2
Scatarie (isl.), Nova Scotia 168/J2
Scavaig, Loch (inlet), Scotland 15/B3
Sceaux, France 28/A2
Scenic, S. Dak. (57780) 298/D6
Scenic, Wash. (†98288) 310/D3
Sceptre, Sask. 181/B5
Schaal, Ark. (†71851) 202/C6
Schaalsee (lake), E. Germany 22/D2
Schaalsee (lake), W. Germany 22/D2
Schaan, Liecht. 39/H2
Schaefferstown, Pa. (17088) 294/K5
Schaerbeek, Belgium 27/C9
Schaffer, Mich. (49882) 250/B3
Schaffhausen (canton), Switzerland 39/G1
Schaffhausen, Switzerland 39/G1
Schagen, Netherlands 27/F3
Schaghticoke, N.Y. (12154) 276/N5
Schaller, Iowa (51053) 229/C4
S-chanf, Switzerland 39/J3
Schangnau, Switzerland 39/E3
Schänis, Switzerland 39/H2
Scharans, Switzerland 39/J3
Schärding, Austria 41/B2
Scharhörn (isl.), W. Germany 22/C2
Schattdorf, Switzerland 39/G3
Schaumburg, Ill. (60194) 222/A5
Schawana, Wash. (†99321) 310/F4
Schefferville, Que. 146/L4
Schefferville, Que. 162/K5
Schefferville, Québec 174/D2
Scheibbs, Austria 41/C2
Scheinfeld, W. Germany 22/D4
Schelde (Scheldt) (riv.), Belgium 27/C7
Scheldt (riv.), Belgium 27/C7
Schell City, Mo. (64783) 261/D6
Schell Creek (range), Nev. 266/G3
Schellsburg, Pa. (15559) 294/E5
Schellville, Calif. (†95476) 204/J1
Schenectady, N.Y. 188/M2
Schenectady (co.), N.Y. 276/M5
Schenectady, N.Y. (*12301) 276/M5
Schenevus, N.Y. (12155) 276/L5
Schererville, Ind. (46375) 227/C2
Scherhorn (mt.), Switzerland 39/G3
Schertz, Texas (78154) 303/K10
Scherzingen, Switzerland 39/H1
Schesaplana (mt.), Switzerland 39/J2
Scheveningen, Netherlands 27/E4
Schichallion (mt.), Scotland 15/D4
Schiedam, Netherlands 27/E5
Schiermonnikoog, Netherlands 27/J1
Schiermonnikoog (isl.), Netherlands 27/J1
Schiers, Switzerland 39/J3
Schijndel, Netherlands 27/G5
Schiller Park, Ill. (60176) 222/B5
Schinznach-Dorf, Switzerland 39/F2
Schio, Italy 34/C2
Schiphol, Netherlands 27/B5
Schkeuditz, E. Germany 22/E3
Schladming, Austria 41/B3
Schlater, Miss. (38952) 256/D3
Schlei (inlet), W. Germany 22/C1
Schleicher (co.), Texas 303/D7
Schleitheim, Switzerland 39/G1
Schleswig, Iowa (51461) 229/B4
Schleswig, W. Germany 22/C1
Schleswig-Holstein (state), W. Germany 22/C1
Schleusingen, E. Germany 22/D3
Schley (co.), Georgia 217/D6
Schley, Minn. (†56633) 255/D3
Schlieren, Switzerland 39/F2
Schliersee, W. Germany 22/D5
Schlitz, W. Germany 22/C3
Schlüchtern, W. Germany 22/C3
Schmalkalden, E. Germany 22/D3
Schmölln, E. Germany 22/E3
Schnecksville, Pa. (18078) 294/L4
Schneeberg, E. Germany 22/E3
Schneeberg (mt.), W. Germany 22/D3
Schnee Eifel (plat.), Belgium 27/J8
Schneidemühl (Piła), Poland 47/C2
Schneider, Ind. (46376) 227/C2
Schnellville, Ind. (47580) 227/D8
Schoelcher, Martinique 161/C6
Schoenchen, Kansas (67667) 232/C3
Schoenfeld, Sask. 181/D5
Schoen Lake Prov. Park, Br. Col. 184/E5
Schofield, Wis. (54476) 317/H6
Schofield Barracks, Hawaii (96786) 218/E2
Schoharie (co.), N.Y. 276/M5
Schoharie, N.Y. (12157) 276/M5
Schoharie (creek), N.Y. 276/M6
Schoharie (res.), N.Y. 276/M6
Scholle, N. Mex. (†87036) 274/C4
Scholls, Oreg. (†97123) 291/A2
Schomberg, Ontario 177/J3
Schönberg, E. Germany 22/D2
Schönberg, W. Germany 22/D1
Schönebeck, E. Germany 22/D2
Schöneberg, W. Germany 22/E4
Schöneiche, E. Germany 22/E2
Schönenwerd, Switzerland 39/E2
Schongau, W. Germany 22/D5
Schöningen, W. Germany 22/D2
Schoodic (lake), Maine 243/F5
Schoolcraft (co.), Mich. 250/C2
Schoolcraft, Mich. (49087) 250/D6
Schoolcraft (riv.), Minn. 255/C3
Schooleys Mountain, N.J. (07870) 273/D2
School Hill, Wis. (†53042) 317/L8
Schoonhoven, Netherlands 27/F5
Schoten, Belgium 27/F6
Schottegat (bay), Neth. Ant. 161/G9
Schouten (isls.), Indonesia 85/K6
Schouten (isls.), Papua N.G. 85/B6
Schouten (isl.), Tasmania 99/E4
Schouwen (isl.), Netherlands 27/D5
Schramberg, W. Germany 22/C4
Schram City, Ill. (†62049) 222/D4
Schreckhorn (mt.), Switzerland 39/F3
Schreiber, Ontario 177/H5
Schreiber, Ontario 175/C3
Schrems, Austria 41/C2
Schriever, La. (70395) 238/J7
Schroeder, Minn. (55613) 255/G3
Schroon (lake), N.Y. 276/N3
Schroon (riv.), N.Y. 276/N3
Schroon Lake, N.Y. (12870) 276/N3
Schruns, Austria 41/A3
Schübelbach, Switzerland 39/G2
Schulenburg, Texas (78956) 303/H8
Schuler, Alberta 182/E4
Schull, Ireland 10/B5
Schull, Ireland 17/B8
Schulter, Okla. (74460) 288/P3
Schultz (lake), N.W. Terrs. 187/J3
Schumacher, Ontario 175/D3
Schüpfheim, Switzerland 39/F3
Schurz, Nev. (89427) 266/C4
Schussenried, W. Germany 22/C4
Schuyler (co.), Ill. 222/C3
Schuyler (co.), Mo. 261/G2
Schuyler, Nebr. (68661) 264/G3
Schuyler (co.), N.Y. 276/G6
Schuyler, Va. (22969) 307/L5
Schuyler Lake, N.Y. (13457) 276/L5
Schuylerville, N.Y. (12871) 276/N4
Schuylkill (co.), Pa. 294/K4
Schuylkill (riv.), Pa. 294/M5
Schuylkill Haven, Pa. (17972) 294/K4
Schwaan, E. Germany 22/E2
Schwabach, W. Germany 22/D4
Schwäbisch Gmünd, W. Germany 22/C4
Schwäbisch Hall, W. Germany 22/C4
Schwalmstadt, W. Germany 22/C3
Schwanden, Switzerland 39/H2
Schwandorf im Bayern, W. Germany 22/E4
Schwaner (mts.), Indonesia 85/E6
Schwarzach im Pongau, Austria 41/B3
Schwarzenburg, Switzerland 39/D3
Schwarzhorn (mt.), Switzerland 39/E4
Schwarzhorn (mt.), Switzerland 39/F3
Schwarzwald (Black) (for.), W. Germany 22/C4
Schwatka (mts.), Alaska 196/G1
Schwaz, Austria 41/A3
Schwechat, Austria 41/D2
Schwedt, E. Germany 22/F2
Schweidnitz (Świdnica), Poland 47/C3
Schweinfurt, W. Germany 22/D3
Schwelm, W. Germany 22/B3
Schwenksville, Pa. (19473) 294/L5
Schwerin (dist.), E. Germany 22/D2
Schwerin, E. Germany 22/D2
Schweriner see (lake), E. Germany 22/D2
Schwertberg, Austria 41/C2
Schwetzingen, W. Germany 22/C4
Schwyz (canton), Switzerland 39/G2
Schwyz, Switzerland 39/G2
Sciacca, Italy 34/D6
Scicli, Italy 34/E6
Science Hill, Ky. (42553) 237/M6
Scilly (isls.), England 13/A7
Scilly (isls.), England 10/C6
Scio, N.Y. (14880) 276/E6
Scio, Ohio (43988) 284/H5
Scio, Oreg. (97374) 291/E3
Sciota, Ill. (61475) 222/C3
Sciota, Pa. (18354) 294/M4
Scioto (co.), Ohio 284/D8
Scioto (riv.), Ohio 284/D8
Sciotodale, Ohio (†45662) 284/E8
Scioto Furnace, Ohio (45677) 284/E8
Scipio, Ind. (47273) 227/F6
Scipio, Ind. (†45053) 227/H6
Scipio, Okla. (†74501) 288/P4
Scipio, Utah (84656) 304/B4
Scircleville, Ind. (46066) 227/E4
Scitico, Conn. (†06036) 210/E1
Scituate, Mass. (02066) 249/F8
Scituate○, Mass. (02066) 249/F8
Scituate (res.), R.I. 249/H5
Sclater, Manitoba 179/B3
Scobey, Miss. (38953) 256/E3
Scobey, Mont. (59263) 262/L2
Scofield, Utah (†84526) 304/C4
Scofield (res.), Utah 304/C4
Scollard, Alberta 182/D4
Scone, N.S. Wales 97/F3
Scooba, Miss. (39358) 256/G5
Scopi (mt.), Switzerland 39/G3
Scopus, Mo. (63762) 261/N8
Scoresby (sound), Greenl. 4/B10
Scoresbysund, Greenl. 4/B10
Scotch Grove, Iowa (52331) 229/L4
Scotch Plains○, N.J. (07076) 273/E2
Scotchtown, Nova Scotia 168/H2
Scotch Village, Nova Scotia 168/E3
Scotfield, Alberta 182/E4
Scotia (sea) 2/G8
Scotia (sea) 5/D16
Scotia, Calif. (95565) 204/A3
Scotia, Nebr. (68875) 264/F3
Scotia, N.Y. (12302) 276/N5
Scotia, S.C. (29939) 296/E6
SCOTLAND 15
SCOTLAND 10/D2
Scotland, Ark. (72141) 202/E2
Scotland○, Conn. (06264) 210/G2
Scotland, Georgia (31083) 217/G6
Scotland, Ind. (47457) 227/D7
Scotland, Md. (20687) 245/N8
Scotland (co.), Mo. 261/H2
Scotland (co.), N.C. 281/L5
Scotland, Ontario 177/D4
Scotland, Pa. (17254) 294/G6
Scotland, S. Dak. (57059) 298/O7
Scotland, Texas (76379) 303/F4
Scotland, U.K. 7/D3
Scotland Neck, N.C. (27874) 281/P2
Scotlandville, La. (70807) 238/J1
Scots (bay), Nova Scotia 168/D3
Scots Bay, Nova Scotia 168/D3
Scotsburn, Nova Scotia 168/F3
Scotsguard, Sask. 181/C6
Scotstown, Ireland 17/H3
Scotstown, Québec 172/F4
Scotsville, Nova Scotia 168/G2
Scott (isl.), Ant. 2/A9
Scott (isl.), Ant. 5/C10
Scott (co.), Ark. 202/B4
Scott, Ark. (72142) 202/F4
Scott (cape), Br. Col. 162/D5
Scott (cape), Br. Col. 184/C5
Scott (isls.), Br. Col. 184/C5
Scott (riv.), Calif. 204/B2
Scott, Georgia (31095) 217/G5
Scott (co.), Ill. 222/C4
Scott (co.), Ind. 227/F7
Scott, Ind. (†46746) 227/F1
Scott (co.), Iowa 229/M5
Scott (co.), Kansas 232/B3
Scott (co.), Ky. 237/M4
Scott, La. (70583) 238/F6
Scott (co.), Minn. 255/E6
Scott (co.), Miss. 256/E6
Scott, Miss. (38772) 256/B3
Scott (co.), Mo. 261/N8
Scott, Ohio (45886) 284/A4
Scott (mt.), Okla. 288/K5
Scott, Sask. 181/C3
Scott (lake), Sask. 181/M2
Scott (co.), Tenn. 237/M8
Scott (co.), Va. 307/C7
Scott A.F.B., Ill. 222/B3
Scott City, Kansas (67871) 232/B3
Scott City, Mo. (63780) 261/O8
Scottdale, Georgia (30079) 217/L1
Scottdale, Pa. (15683) 294/C5
Scott-Jonction, Québec 172/F3
Scottland, Ill. (†61924) 222/F4
Scotts (head), Dominica 161/E7
Scotts, N.C. (28699) 281/H3
Scottsbluff, Nebr. 188/F2
Scottsbluff, Nebr. 146/H5
Scotts Bluff (co.), Nebr. 264/A3
Scottsbluff, Nebr. (69361) 264/A3
Scotts Bluff Nat'l Mon., Nebr. 264/A3
Scottsboro, Ala. (35768) 195/F1
Scottsburg, Ind. (47170) 227/F7
Scottsburg, Ky. (†42445) 237/F6
Scottsburg, Oreg. (97473) 291/D4
Scottsburg, Va. (24589) 307/L7
Scottsdale, Ariz. (*85251) 198/D5
Scottsdale, Tasmania 99/D3
Scotts Hill, N.C. (†28401) 281/O6
Scotts Hill, Tenn. (38374) 237/E10
Scotts Mills, Oreg. (97375) 291/B3
Scottsmoor, Fla. (32775) 212/F3
Scotts Ridge (hills), Conn. 210/A3
Scott Station, Ant. 5/B9
Scotts Valley, Calif. (95060) 204/K4
Scottsville, Ark. (†72843) 202/D3
Scottsville, Kansas (67477) 232/D2
Scottsville, Ky. (42164) 237/J7
Scottsville, N.Y. (14546) 276/E4
Scottsville, Va. (24590) 307/L5
Scottville, Ill. (62683) 222/C4
Scottville, Mich. (49454) 250/C5
Scoudouc, New Bruns. 170/F2
Scourie, Scotland 15/C2
Scout Lake, Sask. 181/F6
Scrabster, Scotland 15/E2
Scraggly (lake), Maine 243/H5
Scraggly (lake), Maine 243/F3
Scranage, Ala. (†36552) 195/C8
Scranton, Ark. (72863) 202/C3
Scranton, Iowa (51462) 229/D4
Scranton, Kansas (66537) 232/G3
Scranton, Ky. (40373) 237/O5
Scranton, N.Y. (†14075) 276/C5
Scranton, N.C. (27875) 281/S4
Scranton, N. Dak. (58653) 282/D7
Scranton, Pa. 188/L2
Scranton, Pa. 146/L5
Scranton, Pa. (*18501) 294/F7
Scranton, S.C. (29591) 296/H4
Scraper, Okla. (†74359) 288/S2
Screven (co.), Georgia 217/J5
Screven, Georgia (31560) 217/H7
Scriba, N.Y. (†13827) 276/H4
Scribner, Nebr. (68057) 264/H3
Scridain, Loch (inlet), Scotland 15/B4
Scugog (lake), Ontario 177/F3
Scullin, Okla. (†73086) 288/N5
Scunthorpe, England 10/F4
Scunthorpe, England 13/G4
Scuol, Switzerland 39/K3
Scurdie Ness (prom.), Scotland 15/F4
Scurrival (pt.), Scotland 15/A3
Scurry (co.), Texas 303/D5
Scurry, Texas (75158) 303/H5
Scusciuban, Somalia 115/J1
Scutari (lake), Albania 45/D4
Scutari (lake), Yugoslavia 45/D4
Scyrene, Ala. (†36436) 195/C7
Sea (isls.), Georgia 217/K9
Sea (isls.), S.C. 296/G7
Seabeck, Wash. (98380) 310/C3
Seaboard, N.C. (27876) 281/O1
Seabold, Wash. (†98110) 310/A1
Sea Breeze, N.Y. (†14617) 276/F4
Sea Bright, N.J. (07760) 273/F3
Seabrook○, N.H. (03874) 268/F6
Seabrook, N.J. (08302) 273/C5
Seabrook, S.C. (29940) 296/F6
Seabrook (isl.), S.C. 296/G6
Seabrook, Texas (77586) 303/K2
Seabrook-Lanham, Md. (20801) 245/G4
Sea Cliff, N.Y. (11579) 276/R6
Seadrift, Texas (77983) 303/H9
Seaford, Del. (19973) 245/R6
Seaford, England 10/G5
Seaford, England 13/H7
Seaford, N.Y. (11783) 276/R7
Seaford, Va. (23696) 307/R6
Seaforth, Minn. (56287) 255/C6
Seaforth, Ontario 177/C4
Seaforth, Loch (inlet), Scotland 15/B3
Sea Girt, N.J. (08750) 273/E3
Seagoville, Texas (75159) 303/H3
Seagraves, Texas (79359) 303/B5
Seagrove, N.C. (27341) 281/K3
Seaham, England 10/F3
Seaham, England 13/J3
Seahorse (lake), Newf. 166/A3
Seahorse (pt.), N.W. Terrs. 187/L3
Seahurst, Wash. (98062) 310/A2
Sea Island, Georgia (31561) 217/K8
Sea Isle City, N.J. (08243) 273/D5
Seal (isl.), Maine 243/F8
Seal (riv.), Man. 162/G4
Seal (riv.), Manitoba 179/J2
Seal (lake), Newf. 166/B3
Seal (isl.), Nova Scotia 168/B5
Seal (isl.), S. Africa 118/F7
Sea Lake, Victoria 97/B4
Seal Beach, Calif. (90740) 204/C11
Seal Cove, Maine (04674) 243/G7
Seal Cove, New Bruns. 170/D4
Seal Cove, Newf. 166/C4
Seal Cove, Newf. 166/C3
Seale, Ala. (36875) 195/H6
Sealevel, N.C. (28577) 281/S5
Seal Harbor, Maine (04675) 243/G7
Seal Rock, Oreg. (97376) 291/C3
Sealston, Va. (22547) 307/O4
Sealy, Texas (77474) 303/H8
Seaman, Ohio (45679) 284/C8
Seamer, England 13/G3
Sea Pines, S.C. (†29928) 296/F7
Sea Ranch Lakes, Fla. (†33301) 212/C3
Searchlight, Nev. (89046) 266/F7
Searchmont, Ontario 177/J5
Searcy (co.), Ark. 202/E2
Searcy, Ark. (72143) 202/G3
Searight, Ala. (†36028) 195/F8
Searles, Ala. (†35468) 195/D4
Searles (lake), Calif. 204/H8
Searles, Minn. (56084) 255/D6
Sears, Mich. (49679) 250/D5
Searsboro, Iowa (50242) 229/H5
Searsburg○, Vt. (†05363) 268/A6
Searsmont, Maine (04973) 243/E7
Searsmont○, Maine (04973) 243/E7
Searsport, Maine (04974) 243/F7
Searsport○, Maine (04974) 243/F7
Seascale, England 10/E2
Seascale, England 13/D3
Seaside, Calif. (93955) 204/D7
Seaside, Oreg. (97138) 291/D2
Seaside Heights, N.J. (08751) 273/E4
Seaside Park, N.J. (08752) 273/E4
Seaton, England 13/D7
Seaton, Ill. (61476) 222/C2
Seaton Valley, England 13/J3
Seatonville, Ill. (61359) 222/D2
Seat Pleasant, Md. (20027) 245/G5
Seattle, U.S. 2/C3
Seattle, Wash. 146/F5
Seattle, Wash. 188/B1
Seattle, Wash. (*98101) 310/A2
Seaview, Wash. (98644) 310/A4
Seaward Kaikouras (range), N. Zealand 100/D5
Seawell, Barbados 161/B9
Seba, Indonesia 85/G8
Seba Beach, Alberta 182/C3
Sebago (lake), Maine 243/B8
Sebago Lake, Maine (04075) 243/B8
Sebastian (co.), Ark. 202/B3
Sebastian, Fla. (32958) 212/F4
Sebastian (cape), Oreg. 291/C5
Sebastián Vizcaíno (bay), Mexico 150/B2
Sebasticook (lake), Maine 243/E6
Sebastopol, Calif. (95472) 204/C5
Sebastopol, Miss. (39359) 256/F5
Sebastopol, Victoria 97/B5
Sebatik (isl.), Indonesia 85/F5
Sebatik (isl.), Malaysia 85/F5
Sebec, Maine (04481) 243/E5
Sebec○, Maine (04481) 243/E5
Sebec Lake, Maine (04482) 243/E5
Sebec Station, Maine (†04426) 243/E5
Sebeka, Minn. (56477) 255/C4
Seben, Turkey 63/D2
Sebeş, Romania 45/F3
Sebes Körös (riv.), Hungary 41/F3
Sebewaing, Mich. (48759) 250/F5
Sebha, Libya 102/D2
Sebha, Libya 111/B2
Şebinkarahisar, Turkey 63/H2
Sebiş, Romania (2) 45/F2
Sebnitz, E. Germany 22/F3
Seboeis○, Maine (04484) 243/F5
Seboeis (lake), Maine 243/F5
Seboeis (riv.), Maine 243/F4
Seboomook, Maine (†04478) 243/D4
Seboomook (lake), Maine 243/D4
Seboruco, Venezuela 124/B3
Sebou (riv.), Morocco 106/C2
Seboyeta, N. Mex. (87055) 274/B3
Sebree, Ky. (42455) 237/F5
Sebrell, Va. (†23837) 307/O7
Sebring, Fla. (33870) 212/E4
Sebring, Ohio (44672) 284/H4
Sebringville, Ontario 177/C4
Sebuku (bay), Indonesia 85/F5
Secane, Pa. (†19018) 294/M7
Secas (isls.), Panama 154/G7
Secaucus, N.J. (07094) 273/B2
Secesh (riv.), Idaho 220/C4
Sechelt, Br. Col. 184/J2
Sechura, Peru 128/B5
Sechura (bay), Peru 128/B5
Seco, Ky. (41849) 237/R6
Second (lake), N.H. 268/E1
Second Cataract, Sudan 59/B5
Second Cataract, Sudan 111/F3
Secondcreek, W. Va. (24974) 312/F7
Second Mesa, Ariz. (86043) 198/E3
Secor, Ill. (61771) 222/D3
Sečovce, Czech. 41/F2
Secretan, Sask. 181/E5
Secretary, Md. (21664) 245/P6
Secretary (isl.), N. Zealand 100/A6
Section, Ala. (35771) 195/G1
Secunderabad, India 68/D5
Sécure (riv.), Bolivia 136/C4
Security-Widefield, Colo. (80911) 208/K5
Sedalia, Alberta 182/E4
Sedalia, Colo. (80135) 208/K4
Sedalia, Ind. (46067) 227/E4
Sedalia, Ky. (42079) 237/D7
Sedalia, Mo. (65301) 261/F5
Sedalia, Mo. 188/H3
Sedalia, Ohio (43151) 284/D6
Sedalia, S.C. (†29379) 296/D2
Sedan, France 28/F3
Sedan, Ind. (†46793) 227/G2
Sedan, Kansas (67361) 232/F4
Sedan, Minn. (56380) 255/C5
Sedan, N. Mex. (88436) 274/F2
Sedano, Spain 33/E1
Sedbergh (co.), England 10/E3
Sedbergh, England 13/E3
Seddon, N. Zealand 100/E4
Seddonville, N. Zealand 100/C4
Seddülbahir, Turkey 63/B6
Sede Boqer, Israel 65/D5
Sederot, Israel 65/B4
Sedgewick, Alberta 182/E3
Sedgewickville, Mo. (63781) 261/N7
Sedgwick, Ark. (72465) 202/J2
Sedgwick (co.), Colo. 208/P1
Sedgwick, Colo. (80749) 208/O1
Sedgwick (co.), Kansas 232/E4
Sedgwick, Kansas (67135) 232/E4
Sedgwick○, Maine (04676) 243/F7
Sedhiou, Senegal 106/A6
Sedili Kechil, Tanjong (pt.), Malaysia 72/F5
Sedlčany, Czech. 41/C2
Sedley, Sask. 181/H5
Sedley, Va. (23878) 307/P7
Sedom, Israel 65/D5
Sedona, Ariz. (86336) 198/D4
Sedot Yam, Israel 65/B3
Sedro-Woolley, Wash. (98284) 310/C2
Šeduva, U.S.S.R. 53/B3
Seebe, Alberta 182/C4
Seebert, W. Va. (24975) 312/F6
Seechelt (inlet), Br. Col. 184/J2
Seechelt (pen.), Br. Col. 184/J2
Seeheim, Namibia 118/B5
Seeis, Namibia 118/B4
Seekonk○, Mass. (02771) 249/J5
Seeley, Calif. (92273) 204/K11
Seeley, Wis. (†54843) 317/D3
Seeley Lake, Mont. (59868) 262/C3
Seeleys Bay, Ontario 177/H3
Seelyville, Ind. (47878) 227/C6
Seelyville, Pa. (18431) 294/M2
Seesen, W. Germany 22/D3
Seewis im Prättigau, Switzerland 39/J2
Seez (riv.), Switzerland 39/H2
Şefaatlı, Turkey 63/F3
Seferihisar, Turkey 63/B3
Seffner, Fla. (33584) 212/D4
Sefrou, Morocco 106/D2
Sefton, N. Zealand 100/D5
Seg (lake), U.S.S.R. 52/D2
Segamat, Malaysia 72/D7
Segarcea, Romania 45/F3
Segezha, U.S.S.R. 52/D2
Segezha, U.S.S.R. 48/D3
Segnes (pass), Switzerland 39/H3
Segni, Italy 34/F7
Segorbe, Spain 33/F3
Ségou, Mali 106/C6
Ségou, Mali 102/B3
Segovia, Colombia 126/C4
Segovia (Coco) (riv.), Honduras 154/E3
Segovia (Coco) (riv.), Nicaragua 154/E3
Segovia (prov.), Spain 33/D2
Segovia, Spain 33/D2
Segré, France 28/C4
Segre (riv.), Spain 33/G2
Segreganset, Mass. (02773) 249/K5
Seguam (isl.), Alaska 196/D4
Seguam (passage), Alaska 196/D4
Séguéla, Ivory Coast 106/C7
Segui, Argentina 143/F6
Seguin, Kansas (†67740) 232/B2
Séguin (lake), Québec 172/B2
Seguin, Texas (78155) 303/G8
Segula (isl.), Alaska 196/K4
Segundo, Colo. (81070) 208/K8
Segura (riv.), Spain 33/F3
Sehore, India 68/D4
Sehwan, Pakistan 59/J4
Sehwan, Pakistan 68/B3
Seiad Valley, Calif. (96086) 204/B2
Seibert (lake), Alberta 182/E2
Seibert, Colo. (80834) 208/O4
Seibo, Dom. Rep. 156/E3
Seil (isl.), Scotland 15/C4
Seiland (isl.), Norway 18/N1
Seiling, Okla. (73663) 288/J2
Sein (isl.), France 28/A3
Seinäjoki, Finland 18/N5
Seine (riv.), France 7/E4
Seine (bay), France 28/C3
Seine (riv.), France 28/D3
Seine (riv.), Ontario 175/B3
Seine-et-Marne (dept.), France 28/E3
Seine-Saint-Denis (dept.), France 28/C1
Seistan (reg.), Iran 66/M5
Seixal, Portugal 33/A1
Seiyun, P.D.R. Yemen 59/E6
Sejerø (isl.), Denmark 21/E6
Sejny, Poland 47/F1
Seke-Banza, Zaire 115/B5
Sekenke, Tanzania 115/F4
Se Khong (riv.), Cambodia 72/E4
Se Khong (riv.), Laos 72/E4
Sekiu, Wash. (98381) 310/A2
Sekkane, Erg (des.), Mali 106/D4
Sekondi, Ghana 106/D8
Selah, Wash. (98942) 310/E4
Selama, Malaysia 72/D6
Selangor (state), Malaysia 72/D7
Selaphum, Thailand 72/E3
Selaru (isl.), Indonesia 85/J7
Selatan (cape), Indonesia 85/E6
Selawik, Alaska (99770) 196/G1
Selawik (lake), Alaska 196/F1
Selayar (isl.), Indonesia 85/G7
Selb, W. Germany 22/E3
Selby, England 13/F4
Selby, S. Dak. (57472) 298/J3
Selby, Victoria 97/K5
Selby-on-the-Bay, Md. (†21037) 245/N5
Selbyville, Del. (19975) 245/S7
Selbyville, W. Va. (26236) 312/F5
Selçuk, Turkey 63/B3
Selden, Kansas (67757) 232/B2
Seldom, Newf. 166/D4
Seldovia, Alaska (99663) 196/B2
Sele (riv.), Italy 34/E4
Selebi-Pikwe, Botswana 118/D4
Selemdzha (riv.), U.S.S.R. 48/O4
Selemiya, Syria 63/G5
Selendi, Turkey 63/C3
Selenga (riv.) 54/M5
Selenge, Mongolia 77/G2
Selenge, Mongolia 77/F2
Selenge (Selenga) Mörön (riv.), Mongolia 77/G2
Sélestat, France 28/G3
Selfridge, N. Dak. (58568) 282/J7
Sélibaby, Mauritania 106/B5
Seligman, Ariz. (86337) 198/B3
Seligman, Mo. (65745) 261/D9
Selim, Turkey 63/K2
Selima (oasis), Sudan 111/E3
Selima (oasis), Sudan 59/A5
Selimiye, Turkey 63/B4
Selinsgrove, Pa. (17870) 294/J4
Selje, Norway 18/D5
Selkirk (mts.), Br. Col. 184/J4
Selkirk (mts.), Idaho 220/B1
Selkirk, Kansas (67873) 232/A3
Selkirk, Man. 162/G5
Selkirk, Manitoba 179/F4
Selkirk (isl.), Manitoba 179/C1
Selkirk, Mich. (†48661) 250/E4
Selkirk, Scotland 10/E3
Selkirk, Scotland 15/F5
Selkirk (trad. co.) Scotland 15/B5
Sella, Bolivia 136/C7
Selle (peak), Haiti 158/C6
Selleck, Wash. (†98051) 310/D3
Sellers, Ala. (†36046) 195/F6
Sellers, S.C. (29592) 296/H3
Sellersburg, Ind. (47172) 227/F8
Sellersville, Pa. (18960) 294/M5
Sells, Ariz. (85634) 198/D7
Sells, Georgia (†30548) 217/E2
Sellye, Hungary 41/D4
Selma, Ala. 188/J4
Selma, Ala. (36701) 195/E6
Selma, Ark. (†71670) 202/G6
Selma, Calif. (93662) 204/F7
Selma, Ind. (47383) 227/G4
Selma, Iowa (52588) 229/J7
Selma, Miss. (†39120) 256/B7
Selma, N.C. (27576) 281/N3
Selma, Ohio (45364) 284/C6
Selma, Oreg. (97538) 291/D5
Selma, Texas (†78201) 303/K10
Selma, Va. (24474) 307/J5
Selmah, Nova Scotia 168/E3
Selman, Okla. (73856) 288/H1
Selmer, Tenn. (38375) 237/D10
Selmont, Ala. (†36701) 195/E6
Selous (mt.), Yukon 187/E3
Selsey, England 13/G7
Selsey Bill (prom.), England 13/G7
Selukwe, Zimbabwe 118/E3
Selva, Argentina 143/D2
Selvas (for.), Brazil 120/C3
Selvin, Ind. (†47523) 227/C8
Selway (riv.), Idaho 220/C3
Selwyn (lake), N.W. Terrs. 187/H4
Selwyn, Queensland 95/B4
Selwyn (range), Queensland 95/B4
Selwyn (lake), Sask. 181/M2
Selwyn, W. Va. (†25674) 312/B7
Selwyn (mts.), Yukon 187/E3
Selz, N. Dak. (58373) 282/L4
Seman, Ala. (†36092) 195/F5
Semans, Sask. 181/G4
Semara, W. Sahara 102/A2
Semara, Western Sahara 106/B3
Semarang, Indonesia 54/N10
Semarang, Indonesia 85/J2
Sematan, Malaysia 85/D5
Sembé, Congo 115/B3
Sembrancher, Switzerland 39/D4
Şemdinli, Turkey 63/L4
Semenov, U.S.S.R. 52/F3
Semeru (mt.), Indonesia 85/K2
Semichi (isls.), Alaska 196/J3
Semidi (isls.), Alaska 196/G3
Semiluki, U.S.S.R. 52/E4
Semily, Czech. 41/C1
Seminary, Miss. (39479) 256/E7
Seminoe (res.), Wyo. 188/E2

Starogard Gdański 451

South Willington, Conn. (06265) 210/F1
South Wilmington, Ill. (60474) 222/E2
South Wilton, Conn. (†06897) 210/B4
South Windham, Conn. (06266) 210/G2
South Windham (Little Falls-South Windham), Maine (04082) 243/C8
South Windham, Vt. (†05359) 268/B5
South Windsor○, Conn. (06074) 210/E1
Southwold, England 13/J5
Southwold, England 10/G4
South Wolf (isl.), Newf. 166/C3
South Wolfeboro, N.H. (†03894) 268/E4
South Woodbury, Vt. (†05681) 268/C3
South Woodstock, Conn. (06267) 210/G1
South Woodstock, Vt. (05071) 268/B4
Southworth, Wash. (98386) 310/A2
South Worthington, Mass. (†01098) 249/C3
South Yadkin (riv.), N.C. 281/H3
South Yarmouth, Mass. (02664) 249/O6
South Yorkshire (co.), England 13/F4
South Zanesville, Ohio (43701) 284/F6
Sovata, Romania 45/G2
Sovereign, Sask. 181/D4
Sovetsk, U.S.S.R. 7/J3
Sovetsk, U.S.S.R. 52/G3
Sovetsk (Tilsit), U.S.S.R. 52/B4
Sovetskaya Gavan', U.S.S.R. 54/R5
Sovetskaya Gavan', U.S.S.R. 48/P5
SOVIET UNION (U.S.S.R.) 48
Sowerby Bridge, England 13/H1
Sowerby Bridge, England 10/G2
Soweto, S. Africa 118/H6
Soya (pt.), Japan 81/L1
Soyhières, Switzerland 39/D2
Soyo, Angola 115/B5
Soyo, Angola 102/D5
Sozopol, Bulgaria 45/H4
Spa, Belgium 27/H8
Spades, Ind. (†47041) 227/G6
Spain 2/J3
Spain 7/D4
SPAIN 33
Spalding, England 13/G5
Spalding, England 10/F4
Spalding (co.), Georgia 217/D4
Spalding, Mich. (49886) 250/B3
Spalding, Mo. (†63401) 261/J3
Spalding, Nebr. (68665) 264/F3
Spalding, Sask. 181/G3
Spaldings, Jamaica 158/H6
Spallumcheen, Br. Col. 184/H5
Spanaway, Wash. (98387) 310/C3
Spandau, W. Germany 22/E3
Spangle, Wash. (99031) 310/H3
Spangler, Pa. (15775) 294/E4
Spaniard's Bay, Newf. 166/D2
Spanish (head), I. of Man 13/C3
Spanish, Ontario 177/J5
Spanish (riv.), Ontario 177/C1
Spanishburg, W. Va. (25922) 312/D8
Spanish Fork, Utah (84660) 304/C3
Spanish Fork (riv.), Utah 304/C3
Spanish Fort, Ala. (36527) 195/C9
Spanish Fort, Texas (†76255) 303/G4
Spanish Lake, Mo. (†63138) 261/R1
Spanish Ship Bay, Nova Scotia 168/G4
Spanish Town, Jamaica 158/J6
Spanish Town, Jamaica 156/C3
Sparkill, N.Y. (10976) 276/K8
Sparkman, Ark. (71763) 202/E6
Sparks, Georgia (31647) 217/F8
Sparks, Kansas (†66035) 232/G2
Sparks, Nebr. (69220) 264/D2
Sparks, Nev. 188/C3
Sparks, Nev. (89431) 266/B3
Sparks, Okla. (74869) 288/N3
Sparks (lake), Oreg. 291/F3
Sparksville, Ky. (42778) 237/L6
Sparland, Ill. (61565) 222/D2
Sparlingville, Mich. (†48060) 250/G6
Sparr, Fla. (32690) 212/D2
Sparrow Bush, N.Y. (12780) 276/L8
Sparrows Point, Md. (21219) 245/N4
Sparta, Georgia (31087) 217/F4
Sparta, Greece 45/F7
Sparta, Ill. (62286) 222/D5
Sparta, Ky. (41086) 237/M3
Sparta, Mich. (49345) 250/D5
Sparta, Mo. (65753) 261/F9
Sparta○, N.J. (07871) 273/D1
Sparta, N.C. (28675) 281/G1
Sparta, Ohio (43350) 284/E5
Sparta, Ontario 177/C5
Sparta, Oreg. (†97870) 291/K3
Sparta, Tenn. (38583) 237/K9
Sparta, Va. (22552) 307/O4
Sparta, Wis. (54656) 317/E8
Spartanburg, Ind. (†47355) 227/H4
Spartanburg, S.C. 188/K4
Spartanburg (co.), S.C. 296/D2
Spartanburg, S.C. (*29301) 296/C1
Spartansburg, Pa. (16434) 294/C2
Spartivento (cape), Italy 34/B5
Spartivento (cape), Italy 34/F6
Sparwood, Br. Col. 184/K5
Spassk-Dal'niy, U.S.S.R. 48/O5
Spátha (cape), Greece 45/F8
Spaulding, Ill. (†62561) 222/D4
Spavinaw, Okla. (74366) 288/R2
Spavinaw (lake), Okla. 288/S2
Spean (riv.), Scotland 15/D4
Spean Bridge, Scotland 15/D4
Spear (cape), New Bruns. 170/G2
Spear (cape), Newf. 166/D2
Spearfish, S. Dak. (57783) 298/B5
Spearman, Texas (79081) 303/C1
Spearsville, Ind. (†46181) 227/E6
Spearsville, La. (71277) 238/E1
Spearville, Kansas (67876) 232/C4
Spectacle (lakes), Conn. 210/B2
Specter (range), Nev. 266/E6
Speculator, N.Y. (12164) 276/M3
Spedden, Alberta 182/E2
Spednik (lake), New Bruns. 170/C3
Speed, Ind. (47172) 227/F8
Speed, Kansas (†67639) 232/C2
Speed, N.C. (27881) 281/P3
Speedway, Ind. (46224) 227/E5
Speedwell, Tenn. (37870) 237/O8
Speedwell, Va. (24374) 307/F8
Speer (mt.), Switzerland 39/H2
Speers, Sask. 181/D3
Speightstown, Barbados 161/B8
Speightstown, Barbados 156/G4
Speigner, Ala. (†36025) 195/F5
Spelterville, Ind. (†47808) 227/C5
Spelve, Loch (inlet), Scotland 15/C4
Spenard, Alaska (99503) 196/C1
Spenborough, England 13/J1
Spence Bay, N.W. Terrs. 187/J3
Spencer (cape), Alaska 196/L1
Spencer (pt.), Alaska 196/E1
Spencer (lake), Alberta 182/E2
Spencer (gulf), Australia 87/D9
Spencer, Idaho (†83423) 220/F5
Spencer (co.), Ind. 227/C9
Spencer, Ind. (47460) 227/D6
Spencer, Iowa (51301) 229/C2
Spencer (co.), Ky. 237/L4
Spencer, La. (71278) 238/F1
Spencer (pond), Maine 243/D4
Spencer (stream), Maine 243/C5
Spencer, Mass. (01562) 249/F3
Spencer○, Mass. (01562) 249/F3
Spencer, Nebr. (68777) 264/F2
Spencer (cape), New Bruns. 170/E3
Spencer, N.Y. (14883) 276/H6
Spencer, N.C. (28159) 281/H3
Spencer, Ohio (44275) 284/F3
Spencer, Okla. (73084) 288/M3
Spencer (creek), Oreg. 291/E5
Spencer (gulf), S. Australia 88/F6
Spencer (cape), S. Australia 88/F7
Spencer (cape), S. Australia 94/E6
Spencer (gulf), S. Australia 94/E6
Spencer, S. Dak. (57374) 298/O6
Spencer, Tenn. (38585) 237/L9
Spencer, Va. (24165) 307/J7
Spencer, W. Va. (25276) 312/D5
Spencer, Wis. (54479) 317/F6
Spencerburg, Mo. (†63441) 261/K4
Spencerport, N.Y. (14559) 276/E4
Spencers Island, Nova Scotia 168/D3
Spencerville, Ind. (46788) 227/G2
Spencerville, Ohio (45887) 284/B4
Spencerville, Okla. (74760) 288/R6
Spencerville, Ontario 177/J3
Spences Bridge, Br. Col. 184/G5
Spennymoor, England 13/F3
Spennymoor, England 10/F3
Spenser (mts.), N. Zealand 100/D5
Sperling, Manitoba 179/E5
Sperrin (mts.), N. Ireland 17/G2
Sperry, Iowa (52650) 229/L7
Sperry, Okla. (74073) 288/P2
Sperryville, Va. (22740) 307/M3
Spessart (range), W. Germany 22/C4
Spétsai, Greece 45/F7
Spey (riv.), Scotland 10/E2
Spey (riv.), Scotland 15/E3
Speyer, W. Germany 22/C4
Sphinx (mt.), Mont. 262/E5
Spiceland, Ind. (47385) 227/F5
Spicer, Minn. (56288) 255/C5
Spicer (isls.), N.W. Terrs. 187/L3
Spicewood, Texas (78669) 303/F7
Spickard, Mo. (64679) 261/F2
Spiddal, Ireland 17/C5
Spider (lake), Maine 243/E3
Spider (lake), Wis. 317/D3
Spiekeroog (isl.), W. Germany 22/B2
Spies, N.C. (†27325) 281/K4
Spiez, Switzerland 39/E3
Spíli, Greece 45/G8
Spillimacheen, Br. Col. 184/J5
Spillville, Iowa (52168) 229/J2
Spilsby, England 13/H4
Spin Buldak, Afghanistan 68/B2
Spin Buldak, Afghanistan 59/J3
Spindale, N.C. (28160) 281/F4
Spink (co.), S. Dak. 298/N4
Spink, S. Dak. (†57010) 298/R8
Spinnerstown, Pa. (18968) 294/M5
Spirit (lake), Idaho 220/B2
Spirit (lake), Iowa 229/C2
Spirit (lake), S. Dak. 298/O4
Spirit (lake), Wash. 310/C4
Spirit, Wis. (†54513) 317/F5
Spirit Lake, Idaho (83869) 220/A2
Spirit Lake, Iowa (51360) 229/C2
Spirit River, Alberta 182/A2
Spirit River, Alta. 162/E4
Spiritwood, N. Dak. (58481) 282/N6
Spiritwood, Sask. 181/D2
Spiro, Okla. (74959) 288/S4
Spišská Belá, Czech. 41/F2
Spišská Nová Ves, Czech. 41/F2
Spital am Pyhrn, Austria 41/C3
Spithead (chan.), England 13/F7
Spitsbergen (isl.), Norway 4/B9
Spitsbergen (isl.), Norway 18/C2
Spittal an der Drau, Austria 41/B3
Spitz, Austria 41/C2
Spivey, Kansas (67142) 232/D4
Splendora, Texas (77372) 303/J7
Split (lake), Manitoba 179/J2
Split (cape), Nova Scotia 168/D3
Split, Yugoslavia 7/F4
Split, Yugoslavia 45/C4
Split Lake, Manitoba 179/J2
Split Rock, Wis. (†54486) 317/H6
Splügen (pass), Italy 34/B1
Splügen, Switzerland 39/H3
Splügen (pass), Switzerland 39/H3
Spofford, N.H. (03462) 268/C6
Spofford, Texas (78877) 303/D8
Spokane, Mo. (65754) 261/F9
Spokane, Wash. 146/G5
Spokane, Wash. 188/C1
Spokane (co.), Wash. 310/H3
Spokane, Wash. (*99201) 310/H3
Spokane (mt.), Wash. 310/H3
Spokane (riv.), Wash. 310/H3
Spokane Ind. Res., Wash. 310/G3
Spöl (riv.), Switzerland 39/F2
Spoleto, Italy 34/D3
Spoon (riv.), Ill. 222/C3
Spooner, Wis. (54801) 317/B4
Spot (pond), Mass. 249/C6
Spotswood, N.J. (08884) 273/E3
Spotsylvania (co.), Va. 307/N4
Spotsylvania, Va. (22553) 307/N4
Spotted (range), Nev. 266/F6
Spotted Horse, Wyo. (†82831) 319/G1
Spottsville, Ky. (42458) 237/G5
Spottswood, Va. (24475) 307/K5
Spotville, Ark. (†71753) 202/D7
Spragge, Ontario 177/J5
Sprague, Ala. (36076) 195/F6
Sprague, Manitoba 179/G5
Sprague, Nebr. (68438) 264/H4
Sprague (riv.), Oreg. 291/F5
Sprague, Wash. (99032) 310/G3
Sprague (lake), Wash. 310/G3
Sprague River, Oreg. (97639) 291/F5
Spragueville, Iowa (52074) 229/N4
Spratly (isl.), Philippines 85/E4
Spratt, Mich. (†49753) 250/F3
Spray (mts.), Alberta 182/C4
Spray, Oreg. (97874) 291/H3
Spray Lakes, Alberta 182/C4
Spraytown, Ind. (†47228) 227/E6
Spread Eagle, Wis. (†54121) 317/K4
Spreckelsville, Hawaii (96779) 218/J1
Spree (riv.), E. Germany 22/F3
Spreewald (for.), E. Germany 22/F3
Spremberg, E. Germany 22/F3
Sprent, Tasmania 99/C3
Sprigg, W. Va. (25693) 312/B7
Sprimont, Belgium 27/H8
Spring (riv.), Ark. 202/H1
Spring (creek), Nev. 266/D2
Spring (mts.), Nev. 266/F6
Spring (valley), Nev. 266/G3
Spring (creek), N. Dak. 282/E5
Spring (creek), S. Dak. 298/J2
Spring (creek), S. Dak. 298/C6
Spring, Texas (*77373) 303/J7
Spring Arbor, Mich. (49283) 250/E6
Spring Bay, Ill. (†61601) 222/D3
Spring Bay, Ontario 177/B2
Springbok, S. Africa 118/B5
Springboro, Ohio (45066) 284/B6
Springboro, Pa. (16435) 294/B2
Springbrook, Iowa (52075) 229/N4
Spring Brook, N. Dak. (58850) 282/D3
Springbrook, Ontario 177/G3
Springbrook, Oreg. (†97132) 291/A2
Springbrook, Wis. (54875) 317/C4
Spring City, Mo. (†64801) 261/C9
Spring City, Pa. (19475) 294/L5
Spring City, Tenn. (37381) 237/M9
Spring City, Utah (84662) 304/C4
Spring Coulée, Alberta 182/D5
Spring Creek, Pa. (16436) 294/D2
Spring Creek, Tenn. (38378) 237/D9
Spring Creek, W. Va. (†24966) 312/F7
Springdale, Ark. (72764) 202/B1
Springdale, Iowa (†52776) 229/L5
Springdale, Mont. (59082) 262/F5
Springdale, Newf. 166/C4
Springdale, Ohio (45246) 284/B9
Springdale, Pa. (15144) 294/C6
Springdale, S.C. (†29720) 296/F2
Springdale, S.C. (29169) 296/E4
Springdale, Utah (84767) 304/B6
Springdale, Wash. (99173) 310/H2
Springe, W. Germany 22/C2
Springer (mt.), Georgia 217/D1
Springer (lake), Ill. 222/E4
Springer, N. Mex. (87747) 274/E2
Springer, Okla. (73458) 288/M6
Springerton, Ill. (62887) 222/E5
Springerville, Ariz. (85938) 198/F4
Springfield, Ark. (72157) 202/E3
Springfield, Colo. (81073) 208/O8
Springfield, Fla. (32401) 212/D6
Springfield, Georgia (31329) 217/K6
Springfield, Idaho (83277) 220/F6
Springfield (cap.), Ill. 146/J6
Springfield (cap.), Ill. 188/H3
Springfield (cap.), Ill. (*62701) 222/D4
Springfield (lake), Ill. 222/D4
Springfield, Ind. (†47638) 227/B8
Springfield, Ky. (40069) 237/L5
Springfield, La. (70462) 238/M2
Springfield○, Maine (04487) 243/G5
Springfield, Mass. 188/M2
Springfield, Mass. (*01101) 249/D4
Springfield, Mich. (49015) 250/D6
Springfield, Minn. (56087) 255/C6
Springfield, Mo. (*65801) 261/F8
Springfield, Mo. 188/H3
Springfield, Mo. 146/J6
Springfield, Nebr. (68059) 264/H3
Springfield, King's, New Bruns. 170/E3
Springfield, York, New Bruns. 170/C2
Springfield○, N.H. (†03284) 268/C4
Springfield○, N.J. (07081) 273/E2
Springfield, Nova Scotia 168/D4
Springfield, Ohio 188/K2
Springfield, Ohio (*45501) 284/C6
Springfield, Ontario 177/C5
Springfield, Oreg. (97477) 291/E3
Springfield○, Pa. (19064) 294/M7
Springfield, Queensland 88/G5
Springfield, Queensland 95/B5
Springfield, S.C. (29146) 296/E4
Springfield, S. Dak. (57062) 298/N8
Springfield, Tenn. (37172) 237/H8
Springfield, Vt. (05156) 268/B5
Springfield○, Vt. (05156) 268/B5
Springfield, Va. (*22150) 307/S3
Springfield, W. Va. (26763) 312/J4
Springfield Armory Nat'l Hist. Site, Mass. 249/D4
Springford, Ontario 177/D5
Spring Garden, Ala. (36275) 195/G3
Spring Garden, Calif. (95971) 204/D4
Spring Garden, Ill. (†62846) 222/E5
Spring Green, Wis. (53588) 317/G9
Spring Grove, Ill. (60081) 222/E1
Spring Grove, Ind. (†47374) 227/H5
Spring Grove, Minn. (55974) 255/G7
Spring Grove, Pa. (17362) 294/J6
Spring Grove, Va. (23881) 307/P6
Spring Hall, Barbados 161/B8
Springhaven, Nova Scotia 168/C5
Spring Hill, Ark. (†71801) 202/C6
Spring Hill, Iowa (†50125) 229/F6
Spring Hill, Kansas (66083) 232/H3
Springhill, La. (71075) 238/D1
Spring Hill, Minn. (†56352) 255/D5
Springhill, Nova Scotia 168/E3
Spring Hill, Tenn. (37174) 237/H9
Springhill Junction, Nova Scotia 168/D3
Springhills, Ohio (†43357) 284/C5
Springholm, Scotland 15/E5
Spring Hope, N.C. (27882) 281/N3
Springhouse, Br. Col. 184/G4
Spring Lake, Ind. (†46140) 227/F5
Spring Lake, Mich. (49456) 250/C5
Spring Lake, Minn. (†55056) 255/E5
Spring Lake, Minn. (56680) 255/E3
Spring Lake, N.J. (07762) 273/F3
Spring Lake, N.C. (28390) 281/M4
Springlake, Texas (79082) 303/B3
Spring Lake, Wis. (†54960) 317/H8
Spring Lake Heights, N.J. (†07762) 273/E3
Spring Lake Park, Minn. (†55432) 255/E5
Springlee, Ky. (†40201) 237/K2
Spring Lick, Ky. (42779) 237/H6
Spring Mills, Pa. (16875) 294/G4
Spring Mills, S.C. (†29067) 296/F2
Spring Park, Minn. (55384) 255/F5
Spring Place, Georgia (†30705) 217/C1
Springport, Ind. (47386) 227/G4
Springport, Mich. (49284) 250/E6
Spring Ridge, La. (†71047) 238/B2
Springs, S. Africa 118/J6
Springside, Sask. 181/J4
Springstein, Manitoba 179/E5
Springsure, Queensland 95/D5
Springton (res.), Pa. 294/L6
Springtown, Ark. (72767) 202/B1
Springtown, Texas (76082) 303/G5
Springvale, Georgia (31788) 217/C7
Springvale, Maine (04083) 243/B9
Springvale, Victoria 88/L7
Springvale, Victoria 97/J5
Spring Valley, Ala. (†35674) 195/C1
Spring Valley, Ill. (61362) 222/D2
Spring Valley, Minn. (55975) 255/F7
Spring Valley, N.Y. (10977) 276/K8
Spring Valley, Ohio (45370) 284/C6
Spring Valley, Sask. 181/F6
Spring Valley, Texas (†77001) 303/J1
Spring Valley, Wis. (54767) 317/B6
Springview, Nebr. (68778) 264/E2
Springville, Ala. (35146) 195/E3
Springville, Calif. (93265) 204/G7
Springville, Ind. (47462) 227/D7
Springville, Iowa (52336) 229/L4
Springville, La. (†70754) 238/L2
Springville, Miss. (†38863) 256/F2
Springville, N.Y. (14141) 276/C5
Springville, Pa. (18844) 294/L2
Springville, Tenn. (38256) 237/E8
Springville, Utah (84663) 304/C3
Springwater, N.Y. (14560) 276/E5
Springwater, Sask. 181/C4
Springwood, Va. (†24066) 307/J5
Sproat Lake, Br. Col. 184/H3
Sprott, Ala. (36779) 195/D5
Sprowston, England 13/J5
Spruce (isl.), Manitoba 179/B1
Spruce, Mich. (48762) 250/F4
Spruce (mt.), Vt. 268/C3
Spruce Creek, Pa. (16683) 294/F4
Sprucedale, Ontario 177/E2
Spruce Grove, Alberta 182/D3
Spruce Home, Sask. 181/F2
Spruce Knob (mt.), W. Va. 312/G5
Spruce Knob-Seneca Rocks Nat'l Rec. Area, W. Va. 312/H5
Spruce Lake, Sask. 181/B2
Spruce Pine, Ala. (35585) 195/C2
Spruce Pine, N.C. (28777) 281/E3
Spruce Run (res.), N.J. 273/D2
Spruce View, Alberta 182/C3
Spruce Woods, Manitoba 179/C5
Spruce Woods Prov. Park, Manitoba 179/C5
Sprule, Ky. (40986) 237/O7
Spry (harb.), Nova Scotia 168/F4
Spry Harbour, Nova Scotia 168/F4
Spur, Texas (79370) 303/D4
Spurgeon, Ind. (47584) 227/C8
Spurlockville, W. Va. (25565) 312/B6
Spurn (head), England 13/H4
Spurn (head), England 10/G4
Spurr (mt.), Alaska 196/B1
Spur Tree, Jamaica 158/H6
Spuzzum, Br. Col. 184/G5
Spy (pond), Mass. 249/C6
Spy Hill, Sask. 181/K5
Squam (lake), N.H. 268/E4
Squamish, Br. Col. 184/F5
Squa Pan, Maine (†04732) 243/G2
Squa Pan (lake), Maine 243/G2
Square (lake), Maine 243/G1
Square Butte, Mont. (†59442) 262/F3
Square Islands, Newf. 166/C3
Squatec, Québec 172/J2
Squatec (lake), Québec 172/J2
Squaw (creek), Idaho 220/B5
Squaw (peak), Idaho 220/D4
Squaw (creek), Oreg. 291/F3
Squaw (creek), S. Dak. 298/B3
Squaw Harbor, Alaska (†99661) 196/F3
Squaw Lake, Minn. (56681) 255/D3
Squaw Rapids, Sask. 181/H2
Squibnocket (pt.), Mass. 249/M7
Squillace (gulf), Italy 34/F5
Squinzano, Italy 34/G4
Squire, W. Va. (24884) 312/C8
Squires, Mo. (65755) 261/G9
Squires Mem. Park, Newf. 166/C4
Squirrel, Idaho (83447) 220/G5
Sragen, Indonesia 85/J2
Sre Ambel, Cambodia 72/D5
Srebrenica, Yugoslavia 45/D3
Srednekolymsk, U.S.S.R. 4/C2
Srednekolymsk, U.S.S.R. 48/Q3
Sre Khtum, Cambodia 72/E4
Śrem, Poland 47/C2
Sremska Mitrovica, Yugoslavia 45/D3
Srepok (riv.), Cambodia 72/E4
Sretensk, U.S.S.R. 54/N4
Sretensk, U.S.S.R. 48/M4
Srikakulam, India 68/E5
Sri Lanka 54/K9
SRI LANKA (CEYLON) 68/E7
Srinagar, India 68/D2
Srinagar, India 54/J6
Srivardhan, India 68/C5
Środa Śląska, Poland 47/C3
Środa Wielkopolska, Poland 47/C2
Staaten (riv.), Queensland 88/G3
Staaten (riv.), Queensland 95/B3
Staatsburg, N.Y. (12580) 276/N7
Stab, Ky. (42557) 237/N6
Stacks (mts.), Ireland 17/B7
Stacy, Minn. (55079) 255/E5
Stacy, N.C. (28581) 281/S5
Stacy, Va. (24616) 307/E6
Stacyville, Iowa (50476) 229/H2
Stacyville, Maine (04782) 243/F4
Stacyville○, Maine (04782) 243/F4
Stade, W. Germany 22/C2
Staden, Belgium 27/B7
Stadskanaal, Netherlands 27/L3
Stadthagen, W. Germany 22/C2
Stäfa, Switzerland 39/G2
Staffa (isl.), Scotland 15/B4
Staffelstein, W. Germany 22/D3
Staffhorst, W. Germany 22/C2
Stafford○, Conn. (06075) 210/F1
Stafford, England 10/G2
Stafford, England 13/E5
Stafford (lake), Fla. 212/D2
Stafford (co.), Kansas 232/D3
Stafford, Kansas (67578) 232/D4
Stafford, N.Y. (14143) 276/D5
Stafford, Ohio (43786) 284/H6
Stafford, Okla. (†73601) 288/H3
Stafford, Queensland 88/K2
Stafford, Queensland 95/D2
Stafford, Texas (77477) 303/J2
Stafford (co.), Va. 307/O4
Stafford, Va. (22554) 307/O4
Staffordshire (co.), England 13/E5
Stafford Springs, Conn. (06076) 210/F1
Staffordsville, Ky. (41256) 237/R5
Staffordville, Conn. (06077) 210/G1
Staffordville, N.J. (†08092) 273/E4
Staines (pen.), Chile 138/D9
Staines, England 10/B5
Staines, England 13/G8
Stainville, Tenn. (†37710) 237/N8
Staked (Llano Estacado) (plain), N. Mex. 274/F5
Staked (Llano Estacado) (plain), Texas 303/B4
Stakhanov, U.S.S.R. 52/E5
Stalden, Switzerland 39/E4
Staley, N.C. (27355) 281/K3
Stalham, England 13/J5
Stalheim, Norway 18/E6
Stalin, Albania 45/D5
Stalingrad (Volgograd), U.S.S.R. 7/J4
Stalingrad (Volgograd), U.S.S.R. 48/E5
Stalingrad (Volgograd), U.S.S.R. 52/F5
Stallings, N.C. (†28079) 281/H4
Stallo, Miss. (†39350) 256/F5
Stallworthy (cape), N.W. Terrs. 187/J1
Stalowa Wola, Poland 47/F3
Stalwart, Mich. (49789) 250/E2
Stalwart, Sask. 181/F4
Stambaugh, Mich. (49964) 250/G2
Stamford, Conn. (*06901) 210/A4
Stamford, England 13/G5
Stamford, England 10/F4
Stamford, Nebr. (68977) 264/E4
Stamford, N.Y. (12167) 276/L6
Stamford, Queensland 88/G4
Stamford, Texas (79553) 303/E5
Stamford (lake), Texas 303/E4
Stamford○, Vt. (05352) 268/A6
Stampa, Switzerland 39/J4
Stamping Ground, Ky. (40379) 237/M4
Stampriet, Namibia 118/B4
Stamps, Ark. (71860) 202/D7
Stanardsville, Va. (22973) 307/L4
Stanberry, Mo. (64489) 261/C2
Stanbridge-Est, Québec 172/D4
Stanchfield, Minn. (55080) 255/E5
Standard, Alberta 182/D4
Standard, Calif. (95373) 204/E6
Standard, Ill. (61363) 222/D2
Standard, La. (†71465) 238/F3
Standard City, Ill. (62686) 222/D4
Standerton, S. Africa 118/D5
Standfast (pt.), Ant. & Bar. 161/E11
Standing Rock, Ala. (36878) 195/H4
Standing Rock Ind. Res., N. Dak. 282/J7
Standish, Calif. (96128) 204/E3
Standish, Maine (04084) 243/B8
Standish○, Maine (04084) 243/B8
Standish, Mich. (48658) 250/F5
Standish-with-Langtree, England 13/G2
Stand Off, Alberta 182/D5
Stanfield, Ariz. (85272) 198/C6
Stanfield, N.C. (28163) 281/J4
Stanfield, Oreg. (97875) 291/H2
Stanford, Calif. (94305) 204/J3
Stanford, Ill. (61774) 222/D3
Stanford, Ind. (47463) 227/D6
Stanford, Ky. (40484) 237/M5
Stanford, Mont. (59479) 262/F3
Stanfordville, N.Y. (12581) 276/N7
Stangelville, Wis. (†54208) 317/L7
Stanger, S. Africa 118/E5
Stanhope, England 13/E3
Stanhope, Iowa (50246) 229/F4
Stanhope, N.J. (07874) 273/D2
Stanhope, Pr. Edward I. 168/E2
Stanhope, Québec 172/F4
Stanislaus (co.), Calif. 204/D6
Stanke Dimitrov, Bulgaria 45/F4
Stanley, England 13/H3
Stanley (cap.), Falk. Is. 120/D8
Stanley (cap.), Falk. Is. 143/E7
Stanley, Idaho (83278) 220/D5
Stanley, Iowa (50671) 229/K3
Stanley, Kansas (†66223) 232/H3
Stanley, Ky. (42375) 237/G5
Stanley, La. (†71049) 238/C3
Stanley, New Bruns. 170/D2
Stanley, N. Mex. (87056) 274/D3
Stanley, N.Y. (14561) 276/F5
Stanley, N.C. (28164) 281/G4
Stanley, N. Dak. (58784) 282/F3
Stanley (mt.), North. Terr. 93/B7
Stanley, Nova Scotia 168/E3
Stanley, Okla. (†74536) 288/R5
Stanley, Scotland 15/E4
Stanley (co.), S. Dak. 298/H5
Stanley, Tasmania 99/B2
Stanley (mt.), Tasmania 99/A1
Stanley, Va. (22851) 307/L3
Stanley, Wis. (54768) 317/E6
Stanley (falls), Zaire 102/E5
Stanley (falls), Zaire 115/D3
Stanley Pool (lake), Zaire 115/C4
Stanleytown, Va. (24168) 307/H7
Stanleyville, N.C. (†27045) 281/J2
Stanly (co.), N.C. 281/J4
Stanmore, Alberta 182/E4
Stannards, N.Y. (†14895) 276/E6
Stann Creek Town, Belize 154/C2
Stanovoy (range), U.S.S.R. 54/N4
Stanovoy (range), U.S.S.R. 48/N4
Stans, Switzerland 39/F3
Stanstead (co.), Québec 172/F4
Stanstead Plain, Québec 172/F4
Stanthorpe, Queensland 88/J5
Stanthorpe, Queensland 95/D6
Stanton, Ala. (36790) 195/E5
Stanton, Calif. (90680) 204/D11
Stanton, England 13/H5
Stanton, Iowa (51573) 229/C7
Stanton (co.), Kansas 232/A4
Stanton, Ky. (40380) 237/O5
Stanton, Mich. (48888) 250/D5
Stanton, Miss. (†39120) 256/B7
Stanton, Mo. (63079) 261/K6
Stanton (co.), Nebr. 264/G3
Stanton, Nebr. (68779) 264/G3
Stanton, N.J. (08885) 273/D2
Stanton, N. Dak. (58571) 282/H5
Stanton, Tenn. (38069) 237/C10
Stanton, Texas (79782) 303/C5
Stantonsburg, N.C. (27883) 281/O3
Stantonville, Tenn. (38379) 237/E10
Stanwood, Iowa (52337) 229/L5
Stanwood, Mich. (49346) 250/D5
Stanwood, Wash. (98292) 310/C2
Stanzel, Iowa (†50849) 229/E6
Staphorst, Netherlands 27/J3
Staplehurst, Nebr. (68439) 264/G4
Staples, Minn. (56479) 255/D4
Staples, Ontario 177/B5
Stapleton, Ala. (36578) 195/C9
Stapleton, Georgia (30823) 217/H4
Stapleton, Nebr. (69163) 264/D3
Stapylton (bay), N.W. Terrs. 187/G3
Star, Alberta 182/D3
Star, Idaho (83669) 220/B6
Star (lake), Minn. 255/C4
Star, Miss. (39167) 256/D6
Star, N.C. (27356) 281/K4
Star, Texas (76880) 303/F6
Starachowice, Poland 47/E3
Stará L'ubovňa, Czech. 41/F2
Staraya Russa, U.S.S.R. 52/D3
Stara Zagora, Bulgaria 7/G4
Stara Zagora, Bulgaria 45/G4
Starbuck (isl.), Kiribati 87/L6
Starbuck, Manitoba 179/E5
Starbuck, Minn. (56381) 255/C5
Starbuck, Wash. (99359) 310/G4
Star City, Ark. (71667) 202/G6
Star City, Ind. (46985) 227/D3
Star City, Sask. 181/G3
Star City, W. Va. (26505) 312/F3
Staré Město, Czech. 41/D2
Stargard Szczeciński, Poland 47/B2
Stargo, Ariz. (†85540) 198/F5
Starhill, La. (†70748) 238/H5
Stark (co.), Ill. 222/D2
Stark, Kansas (66775) 232/G4
Stark, Minn. (†55032) 255/E5
Stark, Mont. (†59846) 262/B3
Stark○, N.H. (†03582) 268/E2
Stark (co.), N. Dak. 282/E6
Stark (co.), Ohio 284/H4
Stark City, Mo. (64866) 261/D9
Starke, Fla. (32091) 212/D2
Starke (co.), Ind. 227/D2
Starkey, Oreg. (†97850) 291/J2
Star Keys (isls.), N. Zealand 100/E7
Starks, La. (70661) 238/C6
Starks○, Maine (†04980) 243/D6
Starks, Wis. (†54501) 317/H4
Starksboro○, Vt. (05487) 268/A3
Starkville, Colo. (81074) 208/L8
Starkville, Miss. (39759) 256/G4
Starkweather, N. Dak. (58377) 282/N3
Star Lake, N.Y. (13690) 276/K2
Star Lake, Wis. (54561) 317/G3
Starlight, Ind. (†47119) 227/F8
Starnberg, W. Germany 22/H4
Starnbergersee (lake), W. Germany 22/D5
Starodub, U.S.S.R. 52/D4
Starogard Gdański, Poland 47/D2

T

Taurianova 455

Taichung, China 77/K7
Taichung, Taiwan 54/O7
Taieri (riv.), N. Zealand 100/C7
Taif, Saudi Arabia 54/F7
Taif, Saudi Arabia 59/D5
Taigu, China 77/H4
Taihape, N. Zealand 100/E3
Taihe, China 77/J6
Tai Hu (lake), China 77/J5
Tailem Bend, S. Australia 88/F7
Tailem Bend, S. Australia 94/F6
Tailfingen, W. Germany 22/C4
Taima, Saudi Arabia 59/C4
Tain, Scotland 15/D3
Tain, Scotland 10/D2
Tainan, China 77/J7
Tainaron (cape), Greece 7/G5
Tainaron (cape), Greece 45/F7
Taintor, Iowa (50253) 229/H6
Taipei, China 77/K7
Taipei (cap.), Rep. of China 54/O7
Taipei (cap.), Rep. of China 2/R4
Taiping, Malaysia 72/D6
Taitao (pen.), Chile 120/B7
Taitao (cape), Chile 138/D6
Taitao (pen.), Chile 138/D6
Taits Gap, Ala. (†35121) 195/F3
Taitung, China 77/K7
Taivalkoski, Finland 18/P4
Taiwan 54/N7
Taiwan 2/R4
Taiwan (str.) 54/N7
Taiwan (isl.) 54/N7
Taiwan, China 77/K7
Taiwan (Formosa) (isl.), China 77/K7
Taiwan (Formosa) (str.), China 77/J7
Taiyuan, China 77/H4
Taiyuan, China 54/N6
Taizhou (Tachen) (isls.), China 77/K6
Taizhou (Taichow), China 77/K5
Ta'izz, Yemen Arab Rep. 54/F8
Ta'izz, Yemen Arab Rep. 59/D7
Tajimi, Japan 81/H6
Tajique, N. Mex. (87057) 274/C4
Tajo (Tagus) (riv.), Spain 33/D3
Tajrish, Iran 66/G3
Tajumulco (vol.), Guatemala 154/B3
Tak, Thailand 72/C3
Takaishi, Japan 81/H8
Takaka, N. Zealand 100/D4
Takalar, Indonesia 85/F7
Takama, Guyana 131/C3
Takamatsu, Japan 81/F6
Takaoka, Japan 81/H5
Takapau, N. Zealand 100/F4
Takapuna, N. Zealand 100/B1
Takarazuka, Japan 81/H7
Takaroa (atoll), Fr. Poly. 87/M7
Takasaki, Japan 81/J5
Takatsuki, Japan 81/J7
Takayama, Japan 81/H5
Takefu, Japan 81/G6
Takeshima (isls.), Japan 81/F5
Takestan, Iran 66/F2
Takev, Cambodia 72/E5
Takhiatash, U.S.S.R. 48/F5
Takhta-Bazar, U.S.S.R. 48/G6
Takikawa, Japan 81/K2
Takingeun, Indonesia 85/B5
Takitimu (mts.), N. Zealand 100/A6
Takkaze (riv.), Ethiopia 111/G5
Takla (lake), Br. Col. 184/D2
Takla Makan (des.), China 54/K6
Takla Makan (Taklimakan Shamo) (des.), China 77/B4
Taklimakan Shamo (des.), China 77/B4
Tako, Sask. 181/B3
Takoma Park, Md. (20912) 245/F4
Takoradi, Ghana 106/D8
Takoradi-Sekondi, Ghana 102/B4
Taksimo, U.S.S.R. 48/M4
Taku (glac.), Alaska 196/N1
Taku (riv.), Alaska 196/N1
Taku (riv.), Br. Col. 184/J2
Takua Pa, Thailand 72/C5
Takutu (riv.), Guyana 131/B4
Tala, Mexico 150/H6
Tala, Uruguay 145/D5
Talab (riv.), Iran 59/H4
Talab (riv.), Iran 66/N6
Talab (riv.), Pakistan 68/A3
Talagante, Chile 138/G4
Talai (Da'an, Dalai), China 77/K2
Talak (reg.), Niger 106/E5
Talala, Okla. (74080) 288/P1
Talamanca (range), C. Rica 154/F6
Talangbetutu, Indonesia 85/C6
Talara, Peru 128/B5
Talara, Peru 120/A3
Talaud (isls.), Indonesia 54/O9
Talaud (isls.), Indonesia 85/H5
Talavera de la Reina, Spain 33/D2
Talawe (mt.), Papua N.G. 86/B2
Talbert, Ky. (41377) 237/P6
Talbingo, N.S. Wales 97/E4
Talbot, Alberta 182/E3
Talbot (isl.), Fla. 212/E1
Talbot (co.), Georgia 217/C5
Talbot, Ind. (47984) 227/C3
Talbot (co.), Md. 245/O5
Talbot (inlet), N.W. Terrs. 187/L2
Talbot (cape), W. Australia 88/D2
Talbot (cape), W. Australia 92/D1
Talbott, Tenn. (37877) 237/P8
Talbotton, Georgia (31827) 217/C5
Talca, Chile 138/A11
Talca, Chile 120/B6
Talca (pt.), Chile 138/E3
Talcahuano, Chile 138/D1
Talcahuano, Chile 120/B6
Talcán (isl.), Chile 138/D4
Talco, Texas (75487) 303/K4
Talcott (range), Conn. 210/D1
Talcott, W. Va. (24981) 312/E7
Talcottville, Conn. (†06066) 210/F1
Taldy-Kurgan, U.S.S.R. 54/J5
Taldy-Kurgan, U.S.S.R. 48/H5
Taleh, Somalia 115/J2
Talent, Oreg. (97540) 291/E5
Talgar, U.S.S.R. 48/H5
Talgarth, Wales 13/D5
Tali (Dali), China 77/E6
Taliabu (isl.), Indonesia 85/G6
Taliaferro (co.), Georgia 217/G3
Talibon, Philippines 82/E5
Talihina, Okla. (74571) 288/S5
Talina, Bolivia 136/B7
Tali Post, Sudan 111/F6
Talisayan, Philippines 82/E6
Talisheek, La. (70464) 238/L5
Talita, Uruguay 145/D4
Tal Kaif, Iraq 66/C2
Talkeetna, Alaska (99676) 196/B1
Talkeetna (mts.), Alaska 196/J2
Talkheh (riv.), Iran 66/E1
Talking Rock, Georgia (30175) 217/D1
Tallaboa, P. Rico 161/B3
Talladega (co.), Ala. 195/F4
Talladega, Ala. (35160) 195/F4
Talladega Springs, Ala. (†35150) 195/F4
Tallaght, Ireland 17/J5
Tallahaga (creek), Miss. 256/F4
Tallahala (creek), Miss. 256/F7
Tallahassee (cap.), Fla. 146/K6
Tallahassee (cap.), Fla. 188/K4
Tallahassee (cap.), Fla. (*32301) 212/B1
Tallahatchie (co.), Miss. 256/D3
Tallahatchie (riv.), Miss. 256/D3
Tallahatta Springs, Ala. (†36784) 195/C7
Tallangatta, Victoria 97/D5
Tallant, Okla. (†74002) 288/O1
Tallapoosa (co.), Ala. 195/G5
Tallapoosa (riv.), Ala. 195/G4
Tallapoosa, Georgia (30176) 217/B3
Tallapoosa, Mo. (63878) 261/N9
Tallassee, Ala. (36078) 195/G5
Tallinn, U.S.S.R. 7/G3
Tallinn (cap.), U.S.S.R. 53/C1
Tallinn, U.S.S.R. 48/C4
Tallinn, U.S.S.R. 52/B3
Tallmadge, Ohio (44278) 284/H3
Tallman, N.Y. (10982) 276/J8
Tallman, Sask. 181/E3
Tallmansville, W. Va. (26237) 312/F5
Tallow, Ireland 17/F7
Tallula, Ill. (62688) 222/D4
Tallulah, La. (71282) 238/H2
Tallulah Falls, Georgia (30573) 217/F1
Talma, Ind. (†46975) 227/E2
Talmage, Kansas (67482) 232/E2
Talmage, Nebr. (68448) 264/H4
Talmage, Sask. 181/H6
Talmage, Utah (84073) 304/D3
Talmo, Georgia (30575) 217/E2
Talmo, Kansas (†66935) 232/E2
Talmoon, Minn. (56637) 255/E3
Talodi, Sudan 111/F5
Talofofo (bay), Guam 86/K7
Taloga, Okla. (73667) 288/J2
Talon (lake), Ontario 177/E1
Taloqan, Afghanistan 68/B1
Taloqan, Afghanistan 59/J2
Talpa, Texas (76882) 303/E6
Talpa de Allende, Mexico 150/G6
Talparo, Trin. & Tob. 161/B10
Talquin (lake), Fla. 212/B1
Talsi, U.S.S.R. 53/B2
Taltal, Chile 138/A5
Taltal, Chile 120/B5
Taltal, Quebrada de (riv.), Chile 138/B5
Taltson (riv.), N.W. Terrs. 187/G3
Talvik, Norway 18/N2
Talyawalka (creek), N.S. Wales 97/B2
Talyawalka Ana Branch, Darling (riv.), N.S. Wales 97/B3
Tama (co.), Iowa 229/H4
Tama, Iowa (52339) 229/H5
Tama (riv.), Japan 81/O2
Tamaha, Okla. (†74462) 288/S4
Tamaki (str.), N. Zealand 100/C1
Tamale, Ghana 102/B4
Tamale, Ghana 106/D7
Tamalpais (mt.), Calif. 204/H1
Tamana (mt.), Trin. & Tob. 161/B10
Tamanrasset, Algeria 106/F4
Tamanrasset, Algeria 102/C2
Tamanrasset, Wadi (dry riv.), Algeria 106/E4
Tamaqua, Pa. (18252) 294/L4
Tamar (riv.), England 13/C7
Tamar (riv.), England 10/D5
Tamar (riv.), Tasmania 99/D3
Támara, Colombia 126/D5
Tamarac, Fla. (†33321) 212/B3
Tamarac (riv.), Minn. 255/A2
Tamarack, Idaho (†83654) 220/B5
Tamarack (isl.), Manitoba 179/F3
Tamarack, Minn. (55787) 255/E4
Tamarack (riv.), Minn. 255/D2
Tamarack, Pa. (†17729) 294/G3
Tamarite de Litera, Spain 33/G2
Tamaro (mt.), Switzerland 39/G4
Tamaroa, Ill. (62888) 222/D5
Tamarugal, Pampa del (plain), Chile 138/B3
Tamási, Hungary 41/E3
Tamassee, S.C. (29686) 296/A2
Tamatama, Venezuela 124/F6
Tamatave (Toamasina), Madagascar 118/H3
Tamaulipas (state), Mexico 150/K4
Tamaya, Chile 138/A8
Tamayo, Dom. Rep. 158/D6
Tamazula, Mexico 150/F4
Tamazulapan del Progreso, Mexico 150/L8
Tamazunchale, Mexico 150/K6
Tambacounda, Senegal 106/B6
Tambar Springs, N.S. Wales 97/E2
Tambelan (isls.), Indonesia 85/D5
Tamberías, Argentina 143/C3
Tambey, U.S.S.R. 48/G2
Tambo (riv.), Peru 128/G11
Tambo, Queensland 88/H4
Tambo, Queensland 95/C5
Tambo de Mora, Peru 128/D9
Tambo Grande, Peru 128/B5
Tambohorano, Madagascar 118/G3
Tambopata (riv.), Peru 128/H9
Tambores, Uruguay 145/C2
Tamboril, Dom. Rep. 158/D5
Tamboritha (mt.), Victoria 97/D5
Tambov, U.S.S.R. 7/J3
Tambov, U.S.S.R. 52/F4
Tambov, U.S.S.R. 48/E4
Tambura, Sudan 111/E6
Tamchakett, Mauritania 106/B5
Tame, Colombia 126/E4
Tame (riv.), England 10/G3
Tâmega (riv.), Portugal 33/C2
Tamentit, Algeria 106/D3
Tamiahua, Mexico 150/L6
Tamiami (canal), Fla. 212/E6
Tamil Nadu (state), India 68/D6
Tamin (gov.), Iraq 66/D3
Tamina (riv.), Switzerland 39/H3
Tamins, Switzerland 39/H3
Tamise (Temse), Belgium 27/E6
Tam Ky, Vietnam 72/F4
Tammisaari (Ekenäs), Finland 18/N6
Tamms, Ill. (62988) 222/D6
Tammun, West Bank 65/C3
Tamo, Ark. (71644) 202/G5
Tamora, Nebr. (†68434) 264/G4
Tampa, Fla. 188/K5
Tampa, Fla. 146/K7
Tampa (bay), Fla. 188/K5
Tampa, Fla. (*33601) 212/C2
Tampa (bay), Fla. 212/D4
Tampa, Kansas (67483) 232/E3
Tampere, Finland 7/G2
Tampere, Finland 18/N6
Tampico, Ill. (61283) 222/D2
Tampico, Ind. (†47220) 227/F7
Tampico, Mexico 146/J7
Tampico, Mexico 150/L5
Tampico, Mont. (†59230) 262/K2
Tampico, Wash. (†98901) 310/E4
Tampoc (riv.), Fr. Guiana 131/E4
Tam Quan, Vietnam 72/F4
Tamra, Saudi Arabia 59/E5
Tams, W. Va. (25933) 312/D7
Tamsagbulag, Mongolia 77/J2
Tamsagout, Mauritania 106/C4
Tamshiyacu, Peru 128/F5
Tamsweg, Austria 41/B3
Tamuin, Mexico 150/K6
Tamuning, Guam 86/K7
Tamworth, Australia 87/E9
Tamworth, England 13/F5
Tamworth, England 10/G3
Tamworth◯, N.H. (03886) 268/E4
Tamworth, N.S. Wales 88/J6
Tamworth, N.S. Wales 97/F2
Tamworth, Ontario 177/H3
Tamyang, S. Korea 81/C6
Tana (lake), Ethiopia 102/F3
Tana (lake), Ethiopia 111/G5
Tana (riv.), Finland 18/P2
Tana (riv.), Kenya 102/G5
Tana (riv.), Kenya 115/G4
Tana, Norway 18/Q1
Tana (riv.), Norway 18/P1
Tanabe, Kyoto, Japan 81/J7
Tanabe, Wakayama, Japan 81/G7
Tanacross, Alaska (99776) 196/K2
Tanafjord (fjord), Norway 18/Q1
Tanaga (isl.), Alaska 196/K4
Tanaga (vol.), Alaska 196/K4
Tanahgrogot, Indonesia 85/F6
Tanahmerah, Indonesia 85/K7
Tanah Merah, Malaysia 72/D6
Tanamá (riv.), P. Rico 161/B1
Tanami (des.), North. Terr. 88/E3
Tanami, North. Terr. 93/A5
Tanami (des.), North. Terr. 93/C5
Tánamo, Cuba 158/J3
Tan An, Vietnam 72/E5
Tanana, Alaska 188/D5
Tanana, Alaska (99777) 196/H1
Tanana (riv.), Alaska 146/D3
Tanana (riv.), Alaska 188/D5
Tanana (riv.), Alaska 196/J2
Tananarive (Antananarivo) (cap.), Madagascar 118/H3
Tanaro (riv.), Italy 34/B2
Tanch'ŏn, N. Korea 81/D3
Tancook Island, Nova Scotia 168/D4
Tanda, India 68/E3
Tandag, Philippines 82/F6
Tandil, Argentina 143/E4
Tandil, Argentina 120/D6
Tando Adam, Pakistan 68/B3
Tando Allahyar, Pakistan 68/B3
Tandou (lake), N.S. Wales 97/A3
Tandragee, N. Ireland 17/J3
Tanega (isl.), Japan 81/E8
Taney (co.), Mo. 261/F9
Taneycomo (lake), Mo. 261/F9
Taneytown, Md. (21787) 245/K2
Taneyville, Mo. (65759) 261/F9
Tanezrouft (des.), Algeria 102/C2
Tanezrouft (des.), Algeria 106/E4
Tang, Kas (isl.), Cambodia 72/D5
Tanga (isls.), Papua N.G. 86/C1
Tanga (reg.), Tanzania 115/G5
Tanga, Tanzania 115/G4
Tanga, Tanzania 102/F5
Tangainony, Madagascar 118/H4
Tangalla, Sri Lanka 68/E7
Tanganyika (lake) 102/F5
Tanganyika (lake), Burundi 115/E5
Tanganyika (lake), Tanzania 115/E5
Tanganyika (lake), Zaire 115/E5
Tanganyika (lake), Zambia 115/E5
Tangent (pt.), Alaska 196/H1
Tangent, Alberta 182/B2
Tangent, Oreg. (97389) 291/D3
Tangerang, Indonesia 85/G1
Tangermünde, E. Germany 22/D2
Tanggula Shan (range), China 77/D5
Tangier, Ind. (47985) 227/C5
Tangier (sound), Md. 245/P8
Tangier (Tanger), Morocco 106/C1
Tangier, Morocco 102/B1
Tangier, Nova Scotia 168/F4
Tangier (riv.), Nova Scotia 168/F4
Tangier, Okla. (†73801) 288/G2
Tangier, Va. (23440) 307/R5
Tangier (isl.), Va. 307/R5
Tangier (sound), Va. 307/S5
Tangipahoa (par.), La. 238/K5
Tangipahoa, La. (70465) 238/J5
Tangipahoa (riv.), La. 238/N1
Tangra Yumco (lake), China 77/C5
Tangshan, China 77/J4
Tangshan, China 54/N5
Tangub, Philippines 82/D6
Tangyanika (lake) 2/L6
Tangyuan, China 77/L2
Tanimbar (isls.), Indonesia 54/P10
Tanimbar (isls.), Indonesia 85/J7
Tanjay, Philippines 82/D6
Tanjore (Thanjavur), India 68/D6
Tanjungbalai, Indonesia 85/C5
Tanjungkarang, Indonesia 54/M10
Tanjungkarang, Indonesia 85/C7
Tanjungpandan, Indonesia 85/D6
Tanjungpinang, Indonesia 85/C5
Tanjungpriok, Indonesia 85/H1
Tanjungpura, Indonesia 85/B5
Tanjungredeb, Indonesia 85/F5
Tanjungselor, Indonesia 85/F5
Tanna (isl.), Vanuatu 87/H7
Tanner, Ala. (35671) 195/E1
Tanner, W. Va. (26179) 312/E5
Tannersville, N.Y. (12485) 276/M6
Tannersville, Pa. (18372) 294/M3
Tannis (bay), Denmark 21/D2
Tannu-Ola (range), Mongolia 77/D1
Tannu-Ola (range), U.S.S.R. 48/K5
Tanon (str.), Philippines 82/D6
Tanout, Niger 106/F6
Tanque Verde, Ariz. (†85701) 198/E6
Tanta, Egypt 111/J3
Tanta, Egypt 59/B3
Tantallon, Sask. 181/K5
Tantalus (mt.), Hawaii 218/D4
Tan-Tan, Morocco 106/B3
Tantoyuca, Mexico 150/L6
Tantung (Dandong), China 77/K3
Tanumshede, Sweden 18/G7
Tanunda, S. Australia 94/C6
Tanzania 2/L6
Tanzania 102/F5
TANZANIA 115/F5
Tao, Ko (isl.), Thailand 72/C5
Tao'an, China 77/K2
Taole, China 77/G4
Taongi (atoll), Marshall Is. 87/G4
Taopi, Minn. (55977) 255/F7
Taormina, Italy 34/E6
Taos, Mo. (†65101) 261/H5
Taos (co.), N. Mex. 274/D2
Taos, N. Mex. (87571) 274/D2
Taos Pueblo, N. Mex. (†87571) 274/D2
Taoudenni, Mali 106/D4
Taoudenni, Mali 102/B2
Taourirt, Algeria 106/E3
Taourirt, Morocco 106/D2
Taouz, Morocco 106/D2
Taoyuan, China 77/K6
Tapa, U.S.S.R. 53/C1
Tapacarí, Bolivia 136/B5
Tapachula, Mexico 150/N9
Tapajós (riv.), Brazil 2/G6
Tapajós (riv.), Brazil 120/D3
Tapajós (riv.), Brazil 132/B4
Tapaktuan, Indonesia 85/B5
Tapalquén, Argentina 143/E4
Tapanahoni (riv.), Suriname 131/D4
Tapani (lake), Québec 172/B3
Tapanui, N. Zealand 100/B6
Tapaz, Philippines 82/D5
Tapera do Jeronimo, Brazil 132/C2
Tapeta, Liberia 106/C7
Tapi, Mae Nam (riv.), Thailand 72/C5
Tapiantana Group (isls.), Philippines 82/D7
Tapiche (riv.), Peru 128/E6
Taping (riv.), Burma 72/C1
Tápiószele, Hungary 41/E3
Tapirapecó, Sierra (mts.), Venezuela 124/F7
Tapiutan (isl.), Philippines 82/B5
Tapoco, N.C. (28780) 281/A4
Tapolca, Hungary 41/D3
Tappahannock, Va. (22560) 307/O5
Tappan (lake), N.J. 273/C1
Tappan, N.Y. (10983) 276/K8
Tappan (lake), Ohio 284/H5
Tappen, N. Dak. (58487) 282/L6
Tappi (cape), Japan 81/K3
Tapti (riv.), India 68/D4
Tapul (isl.), Philippines 82/C8
Tapul Group (isls.), Philippines 85/G4
Tapul Group (isls.), Philippines 82/C8
Taputapu (cape), Amer. Samoa 86/N9
Taquari (riv.), Brazil 132/C7
Taquaritinga, Brazil 132/D8
Taquaritinga, Brazil 135/B2
Tar (riv.), N.C. 281/O3
Tara (hill), Ireland 17/H4
Tara, Ontario 177/C3
Tara (isl.), Philippines 82/C4
Tara, Queensland 95/D5
Tara, Queensland 88/J5
Tara, U.S.S.R. 48/H4
Tara (riv.), Yugoslavia 45/D4
Tarabuco, Bolivia 136/C6
Tarabulus, Lebanon 63/F5
Tarabulus, Lebanon 59/C3
Taradale, N. Zealand 100/F3
Taraira (riv.), Colombia 126/F8
Tarairí, Bolivia 136/D7
Tarakan, Indonesia 54/N9
Tarakan, Indonesia 85/F5
Taralga, N.S. Wales 97/E4
Tarama (isl.), Japan 81/L7
Tarancón, Spain 33/E3
Tarangire Nat'l Park, Tanzania 115/G4
Taranna, Tasmania 99/D5
Taransay (isl.), Scotland 15/A3
Taranto (prov.), Italy 34/F4
Taranto, Italy 34/F4
Taranto, Italy 7/F4
Taranto (gulf), Italy 7/F5
Taranto (gulf), Italy 34/F5
Tarapacá (reg.), Chile 138/B2
Tarapacá, Chile 138/B2
Tarapacá, Colombia 126/F9
Tarapaya, Bolivia 136/B6
Tarapoto, Peru 120/B3
Tarapoto, Peru 128/D6
Tarare, France 28/F5
Tararua (range), N. Zealand 100/E4
Tarascon, France 28/F6
Tarasp, Switzerland 39/K3
Tarata, Bolivia 136/C5
Tarata, Peru 128/H11
Tarauacá, Brazil 132/G10
Tarauaca, Brazil 120/C3
Taravao (bay), Fr. Poly. 86/T13
Taravao (isth.), Fr. Poly. 86/T13
Tarawa (atoll), Kiribati 87/H5
Tarazona, Spain 33/E2
Tarazona de la Mancha, Spain 33/F3
Tarbat Ness (prom.), Scotland 15/E3
Tarbert, Ireland 17/C6
Tarbert, Strathclyde, Scotland 15/C5
Tarbert, W. Isles, Scotland 15/B3
Tarbert, East Loch (inlet), Scotland 15/B3
Tarbert, Loch (inlet), Scotland 15/B5
Tarbert, West Loch (inlet), Scotland 15/C5
Tarbert, West Loch (inlet), Scotland 15/A3
Tarbes, France 7/E4
Tarbes, France 28/D6
Tarbolton, Scotland 15/D5
Tarboro, Georgia (†31568) 217/J8
Tarboro, N.C. (27886) 281/O3
Tarbot, Nova Scotia 168/H2
Tarcoola, S. Australia 88/E6
Tarcoola, S. Australia 94/D4
Tarcutta, N.S. Wales 97/D4
Tardienta, Spain 33/F2
Tardošked, Czech. 41/E2
Taree, N. S. Wales 88/J6
Taree, N.S. Wales 97/G2
Tärendö, Sweden 18/N3
Tarentum, Pa. (15084) 294/C4
Tarfaya, Morocco 106/B3
Tarfaya, Morocco 102/A2
Tar Heel, N.C. (28392) 281/M5
Tarhuna, Libya 102/D1
Tarhuna, Libya 111/B1
Tariana, Colombia 126/F7
Táriba, Venezuela 124/B4
Tarifa, Spain 33/D4
Tariff, W. Va. (25281) 312/D5
Tariffville, Conn. (06081) 210/D1
Tarija (riv.), Argentina 143/D1
Tarija (dept.), Bolivia 136/D7
Tarija, Bolivia 120/C5
Tarija, Bolivia 136/C7
Tarija, Rio Grande de (riv.), Bolivia 136/C8
Tariku (riv.), Indonesia 85/K6
Tarim (riv.), China 54/K5
Tarim, P.D.R. Yemen 59/E6
Tarim He (riv.), China 77/B3
Tarim Pendi (basin), China 77/B4
Tar Island, Alberta 182/E1
Taritatu (riv.), Indonesia 85/K6
Tarkio, Mo. (64491) 261/B2
Tarkio, Mont. (†59872) 262/B4
Tarko-Sale, U.S.S.R. 48/H3
Tarkwa, Ghana 106/D7
Tarlac (prov.), Philippines 82/C3
Tarlac, Philippines 82/C3
Tarlac, Philippines 85/G2
Tarland, Scotland 15/F3
Tarleton (lake), N.H. 268/D4
Tarlton, Ohio (43156) 284/E6
Tarlton, Tenn. (†37301) 237/K9
Tarlton Downs, North. Terr. 93/E7
Tarm, Denmark 21/B6
Tarma, Peru 128/E8
Tarn (dept.), France 28/E6
Tarn (riv.), France 28/E6
Tarna (riv.), Hungary 41/F3
Tärnaby, Sweden 18/J4
Tarnak (riv.), Afghanistan 68/B2
Tårnby, Denmark 21/F6
Tarn-et-Garonne (dept.), France 28/D5
Tarnobrzeg (prov.), Poland 47/E3
Tarnobrzeg, Poland 47/E3
Tarnopol, Sask. 181/F3
Tarnov, Nebr. (68642) 264/G3
Tarnów (prov.), Poland 47/E4
Tarnów, Poland 7/G3
Tarnów, Poland 47/E4
Tarnowskie Góry, Poland 47/A3
Tarom, Iran 66/J6
Tarom, Iran 59/G4
Taroom, Queensland 95/D5
Tarouca, Portugal 33/C2
Taroudannt, Morocco 106/C2
Taroudant, Morocco 102/A2
Tarpa, Hungary 41/G2
Tarpon Springs, Fla. (*33589) 212/D3
Tarqui, Peru 128/E3
Tarquinia, Italy 34/C3
Tarqumiya, West Bank 65/C4
Tarragona (prov.), Spain 33/G2
Tarragona, Spain 33/G2
Tarragona, Spain 7/E4
Tarraleah, Tasmania 99/C4
Tarrant (co.), Texas 303/G5
Tarrant City, Ala. (35217) 195/E3
Tarrants, Mo. (†63334) 261/K4
Tarrasa, Spain 33/G2
Tárrega, Spain 33/G2
Tarryall (creek), Colo. 208/H4
Tarrytown, Georgia (30470) 217/H6
Tarrytown, N.Y. (10591) 276/O6
Tarsney Lakes, Mo. (†64063) 261/R6
Tarsus, Turkey 59/C2
Tarsus, Turkey 63/F4
Tart, China 77/D4
Tartagal, Argentina 143/D1
Tartagal, Argentina 120/C5
Tartas, France 28/C6
Tartu, U.S.S.R. 7/G3
Tartu, U.S.S.R. 53/D1
Tartu, U.S.S.R. 48/C4
Tartu, U.S.S.R. 52/C3
Tartus (prov.), Syria 63/G5
Tartus, Syria 63/F5
Tarutung, Indonesia 85/B5
Tarver, Georgia (†31648) 217/G9
Tarzan, Texas (79783) 303/B5
Tarzana, Calif. (91356) 204/B10
Täsch, Switzerland 39/E4
Tasco, Kansas (†67740) 232/B2
Tashauz, U.S.S.R. 48/F5
Tashk (lake), Iran 59/F4
Tashk (lake), Iran 66/J6
Tashkent, U.S.S.R. 54/H5
Tashkent, U.S.S.R. 2/N3
Tashkent, U.S.S.R. 48/G5
Tasikmalaya, Indonesia 85/H2
Tasisuak (lake), Newf. 166/B2
Taşkent, Turkey 63/E4
Taşköprü, Turkey 63/F2
Taşlıçay, Turkey 63/K3
Tasman (sea) 2/S7
Tasman (sea) 87/G9
Tasman (sea) 88/J7
Tasman (sea), N.S. Wales 97/F5
Tasman (bay), N. Zealand 100/D4
Tasman (mt.), N. Zealand 100/C5
Tasman (mts.), N. Zealand 100/D4
Tasman (sea), N. Zealand 100/B4
Tasman (pen.), Tasmania 88/H8
Tasman (head), Tasmania 99/D5
Tasman (pen.), Tasmania 99/E5
Tasman (sea), Tasmania 99/E4
Tasman (sea), Victoria 97/F5
Tasmania, 87/H8
Tasmania (state), Australia 87/E10
TASMANIA 99
Tasmania (isl.), Australia 2/S8
Tâşnad, Romania 45/F2
Taşova, Turkey 63/F4
Tassili N'Ahagger (plat.), Algeria 106/E4
Tassili N'Ajjer (plat.), Algeria 106/F3
Tåstrup, Denmark 21/F6
Tasu, Br. Col. 184/A4
Taşucu (gulf), Turkey 63/E4
Taswell, Ind. (47175) 227/D8
Tata, Hungary 41/E3
Tataa (pt.), Fr. Poly. 86/S13
Tatabánya, Hungary 41/E3
Tatahouine, Tunisia 106/G2
Tatalrose, Br. Col. 184/D3
Tatamagouche, Nova Scotia 168/E3
Tatamba, Solomon Is. 86/D3
Tatamy, Pa. (18085) 294/M4
Tatar (str.), U.S.S.R. 54/R5
Tatar (str.), U.S.S.R. 48/P4
Tatar A.S.S.R., U.S.S.R. 52/G3
Tatar A.S.S.R., U.S.S.R. 48/F4
Tatarsk, U.S.S.R. 48/H4
Tate, Georgia (30177) 217/D2
Tate (co.), Miss. 256/E1
Tate, Sask. 181/G4
Tateville, Ky. (42558) 237/M7
Tateyama, Japan 81/K6
Tathlina (lake), N.W. Terrs. 187/G3
Tathlith, Saudi Arabia 59/D6
Tathra, N.S. Wales 97/F5
Tati (riv.), Botswana 118/D4
Tatitlek, Alaska (99677) 196/D1
Tatla Lake, Br. Col. 184/E4
Tatlatui (lake), Br. Col. 184/D2
Tatlayoko (lake), Br. Col. 184/E4
Tatnam (cape), Manitoba 179/K2
Tatnum (cape), Man. 162/G4
Tatoosh (isl.), Wash. 310/A2
Tatra, High (mts.), Czech. 41/E2
Tatra, High (range), Poland 47/D4
Tatta, Pakistan 59/J5
Tatta, Pakistan 68/B4
Tattnall (co.), Georgia 217/J6
Tatuí, Brazil 135/C3
Tatum, N. Mex. (88267) 274/F5
Tatum, S.C. (29594) 296/H2
Tatum, Texas (75691) 303/K5
Tatums, Okla. (73087) 288/M6
Tatung (Datong), China 77/H3
Tatura, Victoria 97/C5
Tatvan, Turkey 63/K3
Taubaté, Brazil 132/E8
Taubaté, Brazil 135/D3
Tauber (riv.), W. Germany 22/C4
Täuffelen, Switzerland 39/D2
Taumarunui, N. Zealand 100/E3
Taum Sauk (mt.), Mo. 261/L7
Taung, S. Africa 118/C5
Taungdwingyi, Burma 72/C2
Taunggyi, Burma 72/C2
Taungthonton (mt.), Burma 72/B1
Taungup, Burma 72/B3
Taunton, England 13/D6
Taunton, England 10/E5
Taunton, Mass. (02780) 249/K5
Taunton (riv.), Mass. 249/K5
Taunton, Minn. (56291) 255/B6
Taunus (range), W. Germany 22/C3
Taupo, N. Zealand 100/F3
Taupo (lake), N. Zealand 100/F3
Tauq, Iraq 66/D3
Taurage, U.S.S.R. 53/B3
Taurage, U.S.S.R. 52/B3
Tauranga, N. Zealand 100/F2
Taureau (res.), Québec 172/D3
Taurianova, Italy 34/E5

Timor 457

Thailand (gulf), Cambodia 72/D5
THAILAND (SIAM) 72
Thailand (gulf), Thailand 72/D5
Thai Nguyen, Vietnam 72/E2
Thakhek (Muang Khammouan), Laos 72/E3
Thal, Pakistan 59/K3
Thal, Switzerland 39/J2
Thalberg, Manitoba 179/F4
Thale, E. Germany 22/D3
Thale Luang (lag.), Thailand 72/D6
Thalia, Texas (79227) 303/E4
Thalmann, Georgia (†31520) 217/J8
Thalu, Ko (isls.), Thailand 72/C5
Thalwil, Switzerland 39/G2
Thame, England 13/G6
Thame (riv.), England 13/G7
Thames (riv.), Conn. 210/G3
Thames (riv.), England 10/F5
Thames (riv.), England 13/H6
Thames, N. Zealand 100/E2
Thames (firth), N. Zealand 100/E2
Thames (riv.), Ontario 177/B5
Thamesford, Ontario 177/C4
Thamesville, Conn. (†06360) 210/G2
Thamesville, Ontario 177/C5
Thana, India 68/B6
Thana (creek), India 68/B7
Thane, Alaska (†99801) 196/N1
Thangool, Queensland 95/D5
Thanh Hoa, Vietnam 72/E3
Thanh Tri, Vietnam 72/E5
Thanjavur, India 68/D6
Thann, France 28/G4
Thar (des.), Pakistan 68/C3
Thargomindah, Queensland 88/G5
Thargomindah, Queensland 95/C5
Tharrawaddy, Burma 72/C3
Tharthar, Wadi (dry riv.), Iraq 66/C3
Tharthar (res.), Iraq 66/C3
Thásos, Greece 45/G5
Thásos (isl.), Greece 45/G5
Thatch (cay), Virgin Is. (U.S.) 161/B4
Thatcham, England 13/F6
Thatcher, Ariz. (85552) 198/F6
Thatcher, Colo. (†81082) 208/L7
Thatcher, Idaho (83283) 220/G7
That Khe, Vietnam 72/E2
Thaton, Burma 72/C3
Thau (mts.), France 28/F6
Thaungdut, Burma 72/B1
Thawville, Ill. (60968) 222/E3
Thaxton, Miss. (38871) 256/F2
Thaxton, Va. (24174) 307/K6
Thaya (riv.), Austria 41/C2
Thayawthadangyi Kyun (isl.), Burma 72/C4
Thayer, Ill. (62689) 222/D4
Thayer, Ind. (46381) 227/C2
Thayer, Iowa (50254) 229/E6
Thayer, Kansas (66776) 232/G4
Thayer, Mo. (65791) 261/J9
Thayer (co.), Nebr. 264/G4
Thayer, Nebr. (†68467) 264/G4
Thayer, W. Va. (†25936) 312/E7
Thayer Junction, Wyo. (†82901) 319/D4
Thayetmyo, Burma 72/B3
Thayne, Wyo. (83127) 319/A3
Thayngen, Switzerland 39/G1
Thazi, Burma 72/C2
The Alberga (riv.), S. Australia 94/D2
Thealka, Ky. (41259) 237/R5
Theano (pt.), Ontario 177/J5
Thebarton, S. Australia 88/D8
Thebarton, S. Australia 94/A7
The Battlefords Prov. Park, Sask. 181/C2
Thebes, Ill. (62990) 222/D6
The Colony, Texas 303/G1
The Coorong (lag.), S. Australia 94/F6
The Dalles, Oreg. 188/B1
The Dalles, Oreg. (97058) 291/F2
The Dalles (dam), Oreg. 291/F2
The Dalles (dam), Wash. 310/D5
Thedford, Nebr. (69166) 264/D3
Thedford, Ontario 177/C4
The Entrance, N. S. Wales 88/J6
The Entrance, N.S. Wales 97/F3
The Gap, N.S. Wales 97/A2
The Gap, Queensland 88/J2
The Glen, N.Y. (†12885) 276/N3
The Granites, North. Terr. 93/B6
The Hamilton (riv.), S. Australia 94/D2
The Hawk, Nova Scotia 168/C5
The Heads (prom.), Oreg. 291/C5
The Hermitage, N. Zealand 100/C5
Theilman, Minn. (55978) 255/F6
Thelon (riv.), N.W.T. 146/H3
Thelon (riv.), N.W.T. 162/F3
Thelon (riv.), N.W. Terrs. 187/H3
Them, Denmark 21/C5
The Macumba (riv.), S. Australia 94/E2
The Narrows (str.), N.J. 273/E2
Thendara, N.Y. (13472) 276/K3
The Neales (riv.), S. Australia 94/E3
Theodore, Ala. (36582) 195/B9
Theodore, Queensland 95/D5
Theodore, Sask. 181/J4
Theodore Roosevelt (dam), Ariz. 198/D5
Theodore Roosevelt (lake), Ariz. 198/D5
Theodore Roosevelt Nat'l Park, N. Dak. 282/D4
Theodore Roosevelt Nat'l Park, N. Dak. 282/C5
Theodore Roosevelt Nat'l Park, N. Dak. 282/D6
Theodosia, Mo. (65761) 261/G9
The Pas, Man. 162/F5
The Pas, Manitoba 179/H3
The Plains, Ohio (45780) 284/F7
The Plains, Va. (22171) 307/N3
The Range, New Bruns. 170/E2
Theresa, N.Y. (13691) 276/J2
Theresa, Wis. (53091) 317/K8
Therien, Alberta 182/E2
Theriot, La. (70397) 238/J8
Thermaic (gulf), Greece 45/F6
Thermal, Calif. (92274) 204/J10
Thermalito, Calif. (†95965) 204/D4
Thermopolis, Wyo. (82443) 319/D2
The Rock, Georgia (30285) 217/D5
The Rock, N.S. Wales 97/D4
The Round (mt.), N.S. Wales 97/G2
Therwil, Switzerland 39/E1
The Salt (lake), N.S. Wales 97/B2
Thesiger (bay), N.W. Terrs. 187/F2
The Skaw (Skagens Odde) (cape), Denmark 21/D2
Thessalon, Ont. 162/H6
Thessalon, Ontario 177/J5
Thessalon, Ontario 175/D3
Thessaloníki, Greece 7/G4
Thessaloníki, Greece 45/F5
Thessaly (reg.), Greece 45/F6
The Stevenson (riv.), S. Australia 94/D2
Thetford, England 13/H5
Thetford, England 10/G4
Thetford○, Vt. (05074) 268/C4
Thetford Center, Vt. (05075) 268/C4
Thetford Mines, Québec 172/F3
Thetis Island, Br. Col. 184/J3
The Twins (mt.), Alberta 182/B3
Theux, Belgium 27/H8
The Village, Okla. (73120) 288/L3
The Warburton (riv.), S. Australia 94/F2
Thibault, New Bruns. 170/C1
Thibodaux, La. (70301) 238/J7
Thicket Portage, Manitoba 179/J3
Thickwood (hills), Alberta 182/D1
Thickwood (hills), Sask. 181/D2
Thida, Ark. (72165) 202/H2
Thief (lake), Minn. 255/C2
Thief (riv.), Minn. 255/B2
Thief River Falls, Minn. (56701) 255/B2
Thielsen (mt.), Oreg. 291/F4
Thiensville, Wis. (53092) 317/L1
Thiers, France 28/E5
Thiès, Senegal 106/A5
Thiès, Senegal 102/A3
Thika, Kenya 102/F5
Thika, Kenya 115/G4
Thimphu (cap.), Bhutan 54/L7
Thimphu (cap.), Bhutan 68/G3
Thio, Ethiopia 111/H5
Thio, New Caled. 86/H4
Thionville, France 28/G3
Thíra, Greece 45/G7
Thíra (isl.), Greece 45/G7
Third (lake), Maine 243/H5
Third (lake), N.H. 268/E1
Third Cataract, Sudan 111/E4
Third Cataract (dam), Sudan 102/E3
Third Cataract, Sudan 59/B6
Third Lake, Ill. (†60046) 222/B4
Thirsk, England 13/F3
Thirty Mile (creek), N. Dak. 282/F6
Thirtymile (creek), Oreg. 291/G2
Thisted, Denmark 21/B4
Thisted, Denmark 18/F8
Thistle (isl.), S. Australia 94/E6
Thistle, Utah (†84629) 304/C4
Thithia (isl.), Fiji 86/R10
Thívai, Greece 45/F6
Thiviers, France 28/D5
Thjórsá (riv.), Iceland 21/C1
Thlewiaza (riv.), N.W. Terrs. 187/J3
Thoa (riv.), N.W. Terrs. 187/H3
Tho Chau, Hon (isl.), Vietnam 72/D5
Thoen, Thailand 72/C3
Thohoyandou, S. Africa 118/E4
Thohoyandou (cap.), Venda, S. Africa 102/F7
Tholen, Netherlands 27/E5
Thomas (co.), Georgia 217/E9
Thomas (co.), Kansas 232/A2
Thomas, Md. (†21613) 245/N6
Thomas (co.), Nebr. 264/D3
Thomas, Okla. (73669) 288/J3
Thomas (creek), Oreg. 291/G5
Thomas, S. Dak. (†57242) 298/P4
Thomas (lake), Texas 303/C5
Thomas (range), Utah 304/A4
Thomas, W. Va. (26292) 312/H4
Thomasboro, Ill. (61878) 222/E3
Thomas-Müntzer-Stadt, E. Germany 22/D3
Thomas Stone Nat'l Hist. Site, Md. 245/K6
Thomaston, Ala. (36783) 195/C6
Thomaston○, Conn. (06787) 210/C2
Thomaston (res.), Conn. 210/C2
Thomaston, Georgia (30286) 217/D5
Thomaston, Maine (04861) 243/E7
Thomaston○, Maine (04861) 243/E7
Thomaston, N.Y. (†11020) 276/P7
Thomastown, Ireland 10/C4
Thomastown, Ireland 17/G7
Thomastown, La. (†71262) 238/H2
Thomastown, Miss. (39171) 256/E5
Thomastown, Victoria 97/J4
Thomasville, Ala. (36784) 195/C7
Thomasville, Ga. 188/K4
Thomasville, Georgia (31792) 217/E9
Thomasville, Miss. (†39073) 256/E6
Thomasville, Mo. (†65438) 261/J9
Thomasville, N.C. (27360) 281/J3
Thomasville, Pa. (17364) 294/J6
Thomonde, Haiti 158/C6
Thompson, Ala. (†36089) 195/G6
Thompson (riv.), Br. Col. 184/G5
Thompson○, Conn. (06277) 210/H1
Thompson (peak), Idaho 220/C5
Thompson, Iowa (50478) 229/F2
Thompson (riv.), Iowa 229/E7
Thompson, Man. 162/G4
Thompson, Man. 146/J4
Thompson, Manitoba 179/J2
Thompson (isl.), Mass. 249/D7
Thompson, Mich. (49889) 250/C3
Thompson (creek), Miss. 256/G8
Thompson, Mo. (65285) 261/J4
Thompson (peak), N. Mex. 274/D3
Thompson, N. Dak. (58278) 282/R4
Thompson, Ohio (44086) 284/H2
Thompson, Pa. (18465) 294/L2
Thompson (riv.), Queensland 95/B5
Thompson (lake), S. Dak. 298/O5
Thompson, Utah (84540) 304/E5
Thompson (mt.), Wyo. 319/B3
Thompson Falls, Mont. (59873) 262/A3
Thompsons (creek), S.C. 296/G2
Thompsons Station, Tenn. (37179) 237/H9
Thompsontown, Pa. (17094) 294/H4
Thompson Valley (res.), Oreg. 291/F5
Thompsonville, Conn. (†06082) 210/E1
Thompsonville, Ill. (62890) 222/E6
Thompsonville, Mich. (49683) 250/C4
Thomsen (riv.), N.W. Terrs. 187/G2
Thomson, Georgia (30824) 217/H4
Thomson, Ill. (61285) 222/C2
Thomson, Minn. (†56319) 255/F4
Thomson (riv.), Queensland 88/G4
Thomson's Falls, Kenya 115/G3
Thon Buri, Thailand 72/D4
Thongwa, Burma 72/C3
Thonon-les-Bains, France 28/G4
Thonotosassa, Fla. (33592) 212/D3
Thor, Iowa (50591) 229/E3
Thorburn, Nova Scotia 168/F3
Thoreau, N. Mex. (87323) 274/A3
Thoresby (mt.), Newf. 166/B2
Thorhild, Alberta 182/D2
Thorn, Miss. (†38851) 256/F3
Thornaby-on-Tees, England 10/F3
Thornaby-on-Tees, England 13/F3
Thornburg, Iowa (50255) 229/J6
Thornburg, Va. (22565) 307/N4
Thornbury, England 13/E6
Thornbury, Ontario 177/D3
Thorndale, Ontario 177/C4
Thorndale, Texas (76577) 303/G7
Thorndike○, Maine (04986) 243/E6
Thorndike, Mass. (01079) 249/E4
Thorne, England 13/F4
Thorne, N. Dak. (†58366) 282/L2
Thorne, Ontario 175/E3
Thorne Bay, Alaska (†99901) 196/M2
Thornfield, Mo. (65762) 261/G9
Thornhill, Br. Col. 184/C3
Thornhill, Ky. (†40222) 237/K1
Thornhill, Manitoba 179/D5
Thornhill, Central, Scotland 15/D4
Thornhill, Dumf. & Gall., Scotland 15/E5
Thorn Hill, Tenn. (37881) 237/P8
Thornhurst, Pa. (†18424) 294/L3
Thornley, England 13/J4
Thornloe, Ontario 175/E3
Thornloe, Ontario 177/K5
Thornton, Ark. (71766) 202/F6
Thornton, Calif. (95686) 204/B9
Thornton, Colo. (80229) 208/K3
Thornton, Idaho (†83453) 220/G6
Thornton, Ill. (60476) 222/C6
Thornton, Iowa (50479) 229/G3
Thornton, Miss. (39172) 256/D4
Thornton○, N.H. (†03285) 268/D4
Thornton, Ontario 177/E3
Thornton, Texas (76687) 303/H6
Thornton, Wash. (99176) 310/H3
Thornton, W. Va. (26440) 312/G4
Thornton Cleveleys, England 13/G1
Thornton Cleveleys, England 10/F1
Thorntown, Ind. (46071) 227/D4
Thornville, Ohio (43076) 284/F6
Thornwell, La. (†70549) 238/E6
Thornwood, W. Va. (†24920) 312/G5
Thorofare, N.J. (08086) 273/B4
Thorold, Ontario 177/E4
Thorp, Wash. (98946) 310/E3
Thorp, Wis. (54771) 317/E6
Thorpe (lake), N.C. 281/C4
Thorpe, W. Va. (24888) 312/D8
Thorp Spring, Texas (†76048) 303/F5
Thorsby, Ala. (35171) 195/E5
Thorsby, Alberta 182/C3
Thouars, France 28/C4
Thouin (pt.), W. Australia 88/B4
Thouin (pt.), W. Australia 92/B3
Thousand (isls.), N.Y. 276/H2
Thousand (isls.), Ontario 177/H3
Thousand Island Park, N.Y. (13692) 276/J2
Thousand Lake (mt.), Utah 304/C5
Thousand Oaks, Calif. (*91360) 204/G9
Thousand Palms, Calif. (92276) 204/J10
Thousand Spring (creek), Nev. 266/G1
Thousand Springs, Nev. (†89835) 266/G1
Thrace (reg.), Greece 45/G5
Thrall, Kansas (†66853) 232/F3
Thrasher, Miss. (†38829) 256/G1
Three (isls.), New Bruns. 170/D4
Three Bridges, N.J. (08887) 273/D2
Three Churches, W. Va. (26765) 312/J4
Three Creek, Idaho (†83302) 220/C7
Three Creeks, Alberta 182/B1
Three Creeks, Ark. (†71749) 202/E7
Three Forks, Mont. (59752) 262/E5
Three Guardsmen (mt.), Br. Col. 184/H1
Three Hills, Alberta 182/D4
Three Hummock (isl.), Tasmania 99/B2
Three Kings (isls.), N. Zealand 100/D1
Three Lakes, Wis. (54562) 317/H4
Three Mile Bay, N.Y. (13693) 276/H2
Three Mile Plains, Nova Scotia 168/D4
Three Notch, Ala. (†36053) 195/G6
Three Oaks, Mich. (49128) 250/C7
Three Pagodas (pass), Burma 72/C4
Three Pagodas (pass), Thailand 72/C4
Three Points (cape), Ghana 106/D8
Three Rivers, Mass. (01080) 249/E4
Three Rivers, Mich. (49093) 250/D7
Three Rivers, N. Mex. (†88352) 274/C5
Three Rivers (Trois-Rivières), Que. 172/E3
Three Rivers, Texas (78071) 303/F9
Three Rivers, W. Australia 92/B4
Three Sisters (mt.), Oreg. 291/F3
Three Springs, Pa. (17264) 294/G5
Three Springs, W. Australia 88/B5
Three Springs, W. Australia 92/A5
Throckmorton (co.), Texas 303/E4
Throckmorton, Texas (76083) 303/F4
Throne, Alberta 182/E3
Throop, Pa. (18512) 294/F7
Thrums, Br. Col. 184/J5
Thrumster, Scotland 15/E2
Thuin, Belgium 27/E8
Thule, Greenl. 4/B13
Thule, Greenland 2/F2
Thule, Greenland 146/M2
Thule A.F.B. (Dundas), Greenl. 4/B13
Thule A.F.B. (Dundas), Greenland 146/M2
Thumail, Iraq 66/C4
Thun, Switzerland 39/E3
Thunder (bay), Mich. 250/F4
Thunder (hills), Sask. 181/L4
Thunder (creek), S. Dak. 298/N4
Thunder (lake), Wis. 317/H4
Thunder Bay (riv.), Mich. 250/F3
Thunder Bay, Ont. 162/H6
Thunder Bay, Ont. 146/K5
Thunder Bay (terr. dist.), Ontario 175/C3
Thunder Bay (terr. dist.), Ontario 177/H5
Thunder Bay, Ontario 175/C3
Thunder Bay, Ontario 177/H5
Thunderbird (lake), Okla. 288/M4
Thunderbolt, Georgia (†31404) 217/K6
Thunder Butte (creek), S. Dak. 298/E3
Thunder Hawk, S. Dak. (†57638) 298/F2
Thunder Lake, Alberta 182/C2
Thunersee (lake), Switzerland 39/E3
Thunstetten, Switzerland 39/E2
Thur (riv.), Switzerland 39/G1
Thurgau (canton), Switzerland 39/H1
Thüringer Wald (for.), E. Germany 22/D3
Thuringia (reg.), E. Germany 22/D3
Thurles, Ireland 10/B4
Thurles, Ireland 17/F6
Thurloo Downs, N.S. Wales 97/B1
Thurlow (dam), Ala. 195/G6
Thurlow, Mont. (†59347) 262/K4
Thurman, Iowa (51654) 229/B7
Thurman, N.Y. (†12885) 276/M3
Thurman, Ohio (45685) 284/F8
Thurmond, W. Va. (25936) 312/D7
Thurmont, Md. (21788) 245/J2
Thurrock, England 13/J8
Thurrock, England 10/C5
Thursday Island, Queensland 88/G2
Thursday Island, Queensland 95/B1
Thurso, Québec 172/B4
Thurso, Scotland 10/E1
Thurso, Scotland 15/E2
Thurso (riv.), Scotland 15/E2
Thurston (isl.) 5/C14
Thurston (co.), Nebr. 264/H2
Thurston, Nebr. (68062) 264/H2
Thurston, Ohio (43157) 284/E6
Thurston (co.), Wash. 310/C4
Thusis, Switzerland 39/H3
Thutade (lake), Br. Col. 184/D2
Thyatira, Miss. (†38668) 256/E1
Thyborøn, Denmark 21/A4
Thyolo, Malawi 115/F7
Thyregod, Denmark 21/C6
Tia, N.S. Wales 97/F2
Tiahuanacu, Bolivia 136/A5
Tía Juana, Venezuela 124/C2
Tiandong, China 77/G7
Tianjin, China 2/Q4
Tianjin, China 54/N6
Tianjin (Tientsin), China 77/J4
Tianjun, China 77/E4
Tianlin, China 77/G7
Tian Shan (range), China 77/C3
Tianshui, China 77/F5
Tianzhu, China 77/F4
Tiaret, Algeria 106/E1
Tiatucurá, Uruguay 145/C3
Tiavea, W. Samoa 86/M8
Tiawah, Okla. (†74017) 288/P2
Tib, Ras el (Bon) (cape), Tunisia 106/G1
Tibagi, Brazil 135/A4
Tibagi (riv.), Brazil 135/A4
Tibaná, Colombia 126/D5
Tibati, Cameroon 115/B2
Tibbie, Ala. (36583) 195/B8
Tibbita, N.S. Wales 97/C4
Tiber (riv.), Italy 7/F4
Tiber (riv.), Italy 34/D3
Tiberias, Israel 65/C2
Tiberias (lake), Israel 65/D2
Tibesti (mts.) 102/D2
Tibesti, Serir (des.), Chad 111/C3
Tibesti (mts.), Chad 111/C3
Tibesti, Serir (des.), Libya 111/C3
Tibet (reg.), China 2/P4
Tibet (reg.), China 54/K6
Tibet (reg.), China 77/B5
Tibet Aut. Reg. (Xizang), China 77/B5
Tibooburra, N. S. Wales 88/G5
Tibooburra, N.S. Wales 97/B1
Tibro, Sweden 18/J7
Tibugá (gulf), Colombia 126/B5
Tiburon, Calif. (94920) 204/J2
Tiburon, Haiti 158/A6
Tiburon (cape), Haiti 156/C3
Tiburon (cape), Haiti 158/A6
Tiburón (isl.), Mexico 150/C2
Tiburón (pt.), Panama 154/J6
Ticaco, Peru 128/H11
Ticao (isl.), Philippines 82/D4
Tice, Fla. (33905) 212/E5
Ticehurst, England 13/H6
Tichfield, Sask. 181/D4
Tichigan, Wis. (†53185) 317/K2
Tichigan (lake), Wis. 317/K2
Tichitt, Mauritania 106/C5
Tichlá (well), Western Sahara 106/B4
Tichnor, Ark. (72166) 202/H5
Ticino (canton), Switzerland 39/G4
Ticino (riv.), Switzerland 39/G4
Tickfaw, La. (70466) 238/M1
Tickfaw (riv.), La. 238/M1
Tickle (bay), Newf. 166/D2
Ticonderoga, N.Y. (12883) 276/N3
Ticonic, Iowa (†51010) 229/B4
Ticul, Mexico 150/P6
Tidaholm, Sweden 18/J7
Tide Head, New Bruns. 170/D1
Tidewater, Oreg. (97390) 291/D3
Tidikelt (oasis), Algeria 106/E3
Tidioute, Pa. (16351) 294/D2
Tidjikja, Mauritania 102/A3
Tidjikja, Mauritania 106/B5
Tidnish, Nova Scotia 168/E3
Tidore (isl.), Indonesia 85/H5
Tidra (isl.), Mauritania 106/A5
Tiedemann (mt.), Br. Col. 184/E4
Tiefencastel, Switzerland 39/J3
Tiel, Netherlands 27/G5
Tieling, China 77/K3
Tielt, Belgium 27/C7
Tielt-Winge, Belgium 27/F7
Tienen, Belgium 27/F7
Tien Shan (range) 54/K5
Tienshui (Tianshui), China 77/F5
Tientsin (Tianjin), China 77/J4
Tie Yen, Vietnam 72/E2
Tie Plant, Miss. (38960) 256/E3
Tiernan, Oreg. (†97453) 291/C3
Tierp, Sweden 18/K6
Tierra Amarilla, Chile 138/A6
Tierra Amarilla, N. Mex. (87575) 274/C2
Tierra Blanca, Mexico 150/L7
Tierra Blanca (creek), N. Mex. 274/B6
Tierra Blanca (creek), Texas 303/B3
Tierra del Fuego (isl.) 2/F8
Tierra del Fuego (isl.) 120/C8
Tierra del Fuego, Antártida, e Islas del Atlántico del sur (prov.) Argentina 143/C7
Tierra del Fuego, Grande de (isl.), Argentina 143/C7
Tierra del Fuego, Grande de (isl.), Chile 138/E11
Tierralta, Colombia 126/C3
Tie Siding, Wyo. (82084) 319/G4
Tietê, Brazil 135/C3
Tietê (riv.), Brazil 120/E5
Tietê (riv.), Brazil 132/D8
Tietê (riv.), Brazil 135/B2
Tieton, Wash. (98947) 310/E4
Tieton (riv.), Wash. 310/D4
Tieyon, S. Australia 94/C2
Tiff, Mo. (63674) 261/L6
Tiffany, Colo. (†81137) 208/D8
Tiffany (mt.), Wash. 310/F2
Tiff City, Mo. (64868) 261/C9
Tiffin, Iowa (52340) 229/K5
Tiffin, Mo. (†64744) 261/E7
Tiffin, Ohio (44883) 284/D3
Tiffin (riv.), Ohio 284/B3
Tiflis (Tbilisi), U.S.S.R. 52/F6
Tift (co.), Georgia 217/E7
Tifton, Georgia (31794) 217/F8
Tiftona, Tenn. (†37401) 237/L11
Tigalda (isl.), Alaska 196/F4
Tigard, Oreg. (97223) 291/A2
Tiger, Georgia (30576) 217/F1
Tiger (falls), Guyana 131/C4
Tiger (Macan) (isls.), Indonesia 85/G7
Tiger (falls), Suriname 131/C4
Tiger, Wash. (†99180) 310/H2
Tiger Lily, Alberta 182/C2
Tigerton, Wis. (54486) 317/H6
Tigerville, S.C. (29688) 296/C1
Tighina (Bendery), U.S.S.R. 52/C5
Tigieglo, Somalia 115/H3
Tignall, Georgia (30668) 217/G3
Tignamar, Chile 138/B1
Tignéré, Cameroon 115/B2
Tignish, Pr. Edward I. 168/D2
Tigre, Argentina 143/G7
Tigre (prov.), Ethiopia 111/H5
Tigre (riv.), Peru 128/E4
Tigre (isl.), Uruguay 145/A7
Tigre (riv.), Venezuela 124/G3
Tigrett, Tenn. (38070) 237/C9
Tigris (riv.) 54/F6
Tigris (riv.), Iran 59/E3
Tigris (riv.), Iraq 59/E3
Tigris (riv.), Iraq 66/E4
Tigris (riv.), Syria 59/E3
Tigris (riv.), Syria 63/K4
Tigris (Dicle) (riv.), Turkey 63/J4
Tigris (riv.), Turkey 59/E3
Tiguentourine, Algeria 106/F3
Tihama (reg.), Saudi Arabia 59/C5
Tihama (reg.), Yemen Arab Rep. 59/C5
Tihany, Hungary 41/D3
Tihwa (Ürümqi), China 77/C3
Tijamuchi (riv.), Bolivia 136/C4
Tijeras, N. Mex. (87059) 274/C3
Tijuana, Mexico 150/A1
Tijuana, Mexico 146/G6
Tijucas, Brazil 132/D9
Tikal, Guatemala 154/C2
Tikamgarh, India 68/D4
Tikchik (lkes), Alaska 196/G2
Tikhoretsk, U.S.S.R. 52/F5
Tikhvin, U.S.S.R. 52/D3
Tiko, Cameroon 102/C4
Tiko, Cameroon 115/A3
Tikopia (isl.), Solomon Is. 87/G7
Tikrit, Iraq 59/D3
Tikrit, Iraq 66/C3
Tiksi, U.S.S.R. 4/B3
Tiksi, U.S.S.R. 54/P2
Tiksi, U.S.S.R. 48/N2
Tila, Mexico 150/N8
Tilburg, Netherlands 27/G5
Tilbury, Ontario 177/B5
Tilcara, Argentina 143/C1
Tilcha, S. Australia 94/G3
Tilden, Ill. (62292) 222/D5
Tilden, Ky. (†42409) 237/F5
Tilden, Miss. (†38843) 256/H2
Tilden, Nebr. (68781) 264/G2
Tilden, Texas (78072) 303/F9
Tilehurst, England 13/F6
Tilemsi (valley), Mali 106/E5
Tilford, S. Dak. (†57769) 298/C5
Tilghman, Md. (21671) 245/N6
Tilin, Burma 72/B2
Tiline, Ky. (42083) 237/E6
Till (riv.), Englnd 13/E2
Tillabéry, Niger 106/E6
Tillamook (co.), Oreg. 291/D2
Tillamook, Oreg. (97141) 291/D2
Tillamook (head), Oreg. 291/C2
Tillanchong (isl.), India 68/G7
Tillar, Ark. (71670) 202/H6
Tillatoba, Miss. (38961) 256/E3
Tilleda, Wis. (54978) 317/J6
Tiller, Oreg. (97484) 291/E5
Tillery, N.C. (27887) 281/O2
Tillery (lake), N.C. 281/J4
Tilley, Alberta 182/E4
Tilley, New Bruns. 170/C2
Tillicoultry, Scotland 10/B1
Tillicoultry, Scotland 15/C1
Tillicum, Wash. (98492) 310/C3
Tillman, Miss. (†39150) 256/C7
Tillman (co.), Okla. 288/J6
Tillman, S.C. (29943) 296/E7
Tillson, N.Y. (12486) 276/M7
Tillsonburg, Ontario 177/D5
Tilney, Sask. 181/F5
Tilomonte, Chile 138/B4
Tílos (isl.), Greece 45/H7
Tilpa, N.S. Wales 97/C2
Tilsit (Sovetsk), U.S.S.R. 52/B4
Tilston, Manitoba 179/A5
Tilt (riv.), Scotland 15/E4
Tiltagara, N.S. Wales 97/C2
Tiltil, Chile 138/G2
Tilting, Newf. 166/D4
Tilton, Ark. (†72347) 202/J3
Tilton, Georgia (†30720) 217/B1
Tilton, Ill. (†61832) 222/F3
Tilton○, N.H. (03276) 268/D5
Tilton-Northfield, N.H. (03276) 268/D5
Tiltonsville, Ohio (43963) 284/J5
Tim, Denmark 21/B5
Timagami, Ontario 177/K5
Timagami, Ontario 175/E3
Timagami (lake), Ontario 177/K5
Timagami (lake), Ontario 175/D3
Timan (ridge), U.S.S.R. 52/G1
Timaná, Colombia 126/C7
Timane (riv.), Paraguay 144/B2
Timaru, N. Zealand 100/C6
Timashevsk, U.S.S.R. 52/E5
Timbákion, Greece 45/G8
Timbalier (bay), La. 238/K8
Timbalier (isl.), La. 238/K8
Timbarra (riv.), N.S. Wales 97/G1
Timbédra, Mauritania 106/C5
Timber (mt.), Nev. 266/E5
Timber (mt.), Nev. 266/F4
Timber, Oreg. (97144) 291/D2
Timber Bay, Sask. 181/F1
Timber Creek, North. Terr. 88/E3
Timberlake, N.C. (27583) 281/M2
Timberlake, Ohio (†44094) 284/J8
Timber Lake, S. Dak. (57656) 298/H3
Timberlea, Nova Scotia 168/E4
Timberville, Va. (22853) 307/L3
Timbío, Colombia 126/B6
Timbiquí, Colombia 126/B6
Timblin, Pa. (15778) 294/D4
Timbo, Ark. (72680) 202/F2
Timboulaga (well), Niger 106/F5
Timbuktu (Tombouctou), Mali 106/D5
Timbuktu, Mali 102/B3
Time, Ill. (†62363) 222/C4
Times Beach, Mo. (†63025) 261/N4
Timewell, Ill. (62375) 222/C3
Timgad, Algeria 106/F1
Timia, Niger 106/F4
Timia, Niger 102/C2
Timimoun, Algeria 102/C2
Timimoun, Algeria 106/E3
Timiris (cape), Mauritania 106/A5
Timiș (riv.), Romania 45/E3
Timiskaming (lake) 162/J6
Timiskaming (terr. dist.), Ontario 177/K5
Timiskaming (terr. dist.), Ontario 175/D3
Timiskaming (lake), Ontario 175/E3
Timișoara, Romania 7/G4
Timișoara, Romania 45/E3
Timken, Kansas (67582) 232/C3
Timmendorfer Strand, W. Germany 22/D1
Timmins, Ont. 146/K5
Timmins, Ont. 162/H6
Timmins, Ontario 177/J5
Timmins, Ontario 175/D3
Timmissao (well), Algeria 106/E4
Timmonsville, S.C. (29161) 296/H3
Timms Hill (mt.), Wis. 317/F5
Timnath, Colo. (80547) 208/J2
Timok (riv.), Bulgaria 45/F3
Timok (riv.), Yugoslavia 45/F3
Timoleague, Ireland 17/D8
Timon, Brazil 132/F4
Timonium-Lutherville, Md. (21093) 245/M3
Timor (sea) 54/O11
Timor (sea) 88/D2
Timor (isl.), Indonesia 54/O10
Timor (isl.), Indonesia 2/R6

Trousdale 459

Toronto, Canada 2/F3
Toronto, Iowa (52343) 229/M5
Toronto, Kansas (66777) 232/G4
Toronto (lake), Kansas 232/F4
Toronto (res.), N.Y. 276/L7
Toronto, Ohio (43964) 284/J5
Toronto (cap.), Ont. 146/K5
Toronto (cap.), Ont. 162/H7
Toronto (metro. munic.), Ontario 177/K4
Toronto (cap.), Ontario 177/K4
Toronto, S. Dak. (57268) 298/R4
Toropalca, Bolivia 136/B7
Toropets, U.S.S.R. 52/D3
Tororo, Uganda 115/F3
Torote (riv.), Spain 33/G4
Torotoro, Bolivia 136/C6
Torpedo, Pa. (†16340) 294/D2
Torphins, Scotland 15/F3
Torpoint, England 13/C7
Torquay (Torbay), England 13/D7
Torquay, Sask. 181/H6
Torquemada, Spain 33/D1
Torr (head), N. Ireland 17/K1
Torrance, Calif. 188/C4
Torrance, Calif. (*90501) 204/C11
Torrance (co.), N. Mex. 274/D4
Torrance, Ontario 177/E3
Torrance, Pa. (15779) 294/D5
Torre, Cerro de la (mt.), Chile 138/E4
Torre Annunziata, Italy 34/E4
Torreblanca, Spain 33/G2
Torrecilla (lag.), P. Rico 161/E1
Torre del Greco, Italy 34/E4
Torre de Moncorvo, Portugal 33/C2
Torredonjimeno, Spain 33/D4
Torre Gaia, Italy 34/F6
Torrejón (res.), Spain 33/D3
Torrejoncillo, Spain 33/C3
Torrejón de Ardoz, Spain 33/G4
Torrelaguna, Spain 33/E2
Torrelavega, Spain 33/D1
Torremaggiore, Italy 34/E4
Torremolinos, Spain 33/D4
Torrens (riv.) 88/E7
Torrens (lake), Australia 87/D9
Torrens (isl.), S. Australia 88/D7
Torrens (lake), S. Australia 88/F6
Torrens (lake), S. Australia 94/E4
Torrens (riv.), S. Australia 94/C7
Torrente, Spain 33/F3
Torreón, Mexico 146/H7
Torreón, Mexico 150/H4
Torreon, N. Mex. (87061) 274/C4
Torre-Pacheco, Spain 33/F4
Torres (strait) 87/E7
Torres (str.), Papua N.G. 85/A7
Torres (str.), Queensland 88/G2
Torres (str.), Queensland 95/B1
Torres (isls.), Vanuatu 87/G7
Torres Martinez Ind. Res., Calif. 204/J10
Torres Novas, Portugal 33/B3
Torres Vedras, Portugal 33/B3
Torrevieja, Spain 33/F4
Torrey, Utah (84775) 304/C5
Torridge (riv.), England 13/C7
Torridon, Loch (inlet), Scotland 15/C3
Torriente, Cuba 158/D1
Torrijos, Philippines 82/D4
Torrijos, Spain 33/D2
Tørring, Denmark 21/C6
Torringford, Conn. (†06790) 210/C1
Torrington, Alberta 182/D4
Torrington, Conn. (06790) 210/C1
Torrington, Wyo. (82240) 319/H3
Torroella de Montgrí, Spain 33/H1
Torrowangee, N.S. Wales 97/A2
Torrox, Spain 33/E4
Torsby, Sweden 18/H6
Tors Cove, Newf. 166/D2
Torshälla, Sweden 18/K7
Tórshavn, Denmark 7/D2
Tórshavn (cap.), Faerøe Is., Denmark 21/A3
Tortilla Flat, Ariz. (85290) 198/D5
Tortola (isl.), Virgin Is. (Br.) 161/D3
Tortola (isl.), Virgin Is. (Br.) 156/H1
Tórtolas, Cerro de las (mt.), Chile 138/B8
Tortona, Italy 34/B2
Tortorici, Italy 34/E6
Tortosa, Spain 33/G2
Tortosa (cape), Spain 33/G2
Tortue (chan.), Haiti 158/C5
Tortue (Tortuga) (isl.), Haiti 156/D2
Tortue (Tortuga) (isl.), Haiti 158/C4
Tortuga (isl.), Haiti 158/C4
Tortuga (isl.), Haiti 156/D2
Tortugas (gulf), Colombia 126/B6
Tortuguero (lag.), P. Rico 161/D1
Tortuguilla (pt.), Cuba 158/K4
Tortum, Turkey 63/J2
Torud, Iran 59/F2
Torud, Iran 66/J3
Torul, Turkey 63/H2
Toruń (prov.), Poland 47/D2
Toruń, Poland 7/F3
Toruń, Poland 47/D2
Torunos, Venezuela 124/C3
Tõrva, U.S.S.R. 53/C1
Tory (isl.), Ireland 17/E1
Tory (isl.), Ireland 10/B3
Tory (sound), Ireland 17/E1
Torysa (riv.), Czech. 41/F2
Torzhok, U.S.S.R. 52/D3
Tosa, Japan 81/F7
Tosa (bay), Japan 81/F7
Tosashimizu, Japan 81/F7
Toson Hu (lake), China 77/E4
Töss (riv.), Switzerland 39/G1
Tostado, Argentina 143/D2
Toston, Mont. (59643) 262/E4
Tosu, Japan 81/E7
Tosya, Turkey 63/F2
Tota, Laguna de (lake), Colombia 126/D5
Totana, Spain 33/F4
Tótkomlós, Hungary 41/F3
Tot'ma, U.S.S.R. 48/E4
Tot'ma, U.S.S.R. 52/F3
Totnes, England 13/D7
Totnes, England 10/E5
Totnes, Sask. 181/C4
Totness, Suriname 131/C3
Toto, Ind. (†46534) 227/D2
Totoket, Conn. (†06405) 210/D3
Totonicapán, Guatemala 154/B3
Totora, Cochabamba, Bolivia 136/C5
Totora, Oruro, Bolivia 136/A5
Totoral, Chile 138/A6
Totoral, Quebrada (riv.), Chile 138/A6
Totoral, Uruguay 145/C3
Totowa, N.J. (07512) 273/B1
Totoya (isl.), Fiji 86/R11
Tottenham, N.S. Wales 97/D3
Tottenham, Ontario 177/E3
Tottori (pref.), Japan 81/G6
Tottori, Japan 81/G6
Touat (oasis), Algeria 106/E3
Touba, Ivory Coast 106/C7
Touba, Senegal 106/A6
Toubkal, Jebel (mt.), Morocco 102/B1
Toubkal, Jebel (mt.), Morocco 106/C2
Touchet, Wash. (99360) 310/G4
Touchet (riv.), Wash. 310/G4
Touchwood (lake), Alberta 182/E2
Touchwood (hills), Sask. 181/G4
Toufourine (well), Mali 106/C4
Tougaloo, Miss. (39174) 256/D6
Tougan, Upper Volta 106/D6
Touggourt, Algeria 106/F2
Touggourt, Algeria 102/C1
Toughkenamon, Pa. (19374) 294/L6
Tougué, Guinea 106/B6
Touila (well), Algeria 106/C3
Touila (well), Mauritania 106/C3
Toukoto, Mali 106/C6
Toul, France 28/F3
Touladi, Grand Lac (lake), Québec 172/J1
Toulnustouc (riv.), Québec 174/D2
Toulon, France 7/E4
Toulon, France 28/F6
Toulon, Ill. (61483) 222/D2
Toulouse, France 7/E4
Toulouse, France 28/D6
Toumodi, Ivory Coast 106/D7
Toungo, Nigeria 106/G7
Toungoo, Burma 72/C3
Touraine (trad. prov.), France 29
Tourakom, Laos 72/D3
Tourbis (lake), Québec 172/C2
Tourcoing, France 28/E2
Tour d'Aï (mt.), Switzerland 39/C4
Tourelle, Québec 172/C1
Tournai, Belgium 27/C7
Tournavista, Peru 128/E7
Tournon, France 28/F5
Tournus, France 28/F4
Touros, Brazil 132/H4
Touro Synagogue Nat'l Hist. Site, R.I. 249/J7
Tours, France 28/D4
Tours, France 7/E4
Tourville, Québec 172/H2
Toutes Aides, Manitoba 179/C3
Toutle, Wash. (98649) 310/C4
Toutle, North Fork (riv.), Wash. 310/C4
Toutle, South Fork (riv.), Wash. 310/C4
Toužim, Czech. 41/B1
Töv, Mongolia 77/G2
Tovar, Venezuela 124/C3
Tovey, Ill. (62570) 222/D4
Towaco, N.J. (07082) 273/E2
Towada, Japan 81/K3
Towada (lake), Japan 81/K3
Towada-Hachimantai National Park, Japan 81/K3
Towakaima, Guyana 131/B2
Towanda, Ill. (61776) 222/E3
Towanda, Kansas (67144) 232/E4
Towanda, Pa. (18848) 294/J2
Towanda (creek), Pa. 294/J2
Towaoc, Colo. (81334) 208/B8
Towcester, England 13/F5
Tower, Mich. (49792) 250/E3
Tower, Minn. (55790) 255/F3
Tower, Wyo. (†82190) 319/B1
Tower City, N. Dak. (58071) 282/P6
Tower City, Pa. (17980) 294/J4
Tower Hamlets, England 13/H8
Tower Hill, Ill. (62571) 222/E4
Tower Lakes, Ill. (†60010) 222/A4
Towers of Silence, India 68/B7
Tow Law, England 13/H4
Town (creek), Ala. 195/C1
Town (creek), Md. 245/E2
Town and Country, Mo. (†63101) 261/O3
Town and Country, Wash. (†99218) 310/H3
Town Creek, Ala. (35672) 195/D1
Towner, Colo. (81080) 208/P6
Towner (co.), N. Dak. 282/M2
Towner, N. Dak. (58788) 282/K3
Townley, Ala. (35587) 195/D3
Town of Pines, Ind. (†46360) 227/D1
Town Point, Md. (†21915) 245/P3
Towns (co.), Georgia 217/E1
Towns, Georgia (†31055) 217/G7
Townsend, Del. (19734) 245/R3
Townsend, Georgia (31331) 217/J7
Townsend, Mass. (01469) 249/H2
Townsend○, Mass. (01469) 249/H2
Townsend, Mont. (59644) 262/E4
Townsend (inlet), N.J. 273/D5
Townsend, Tenn. (37882) 237/O9
Townsend, Va. (23443) 307/R6
Townsend, Wis. (54175) 317/K5
Townsend Harbor, Mass. (†01469) 249/G2
Townsends Inlet, N.J. (†08243) 273/D5
Townshend○, Vt. (05353) 268/B5
Townsville, Australia 2/S6
Townsville, Australia 87/E7
Townsville, N.C. (27584) 281/N1
Townsville, Queensland 88/H3
Townsville, Queensland 95/C3
Townville, Pa. (16360) 294/C2
Townville, S.C. (29689) 296/B2
Towot, Sudan 111/F6
Towraghondi, Afghanistan 68/A1
Towson, Md. (21204) 245/M3
Towuti (lake), Indonesia 85/G6
Towy (riv.), Wales 13/D6
Towy (riv.), Wales 10/E5
Toxey, Ala. (36921) 195/B7
Toya (lake), Japan 81/K2
Toyah, Texas (79785) 303/D11
Toyah (creek), Texas 303/D11
Toyah (lake), Texas 303/A6
Toyahvale, Texas (79786) 303/D11
Toyama (pref.), Japan 81/H5
Toyama, Japan 81/H5
Toyama (bay), Japan 81/H5
Toyohashi, Japan 81/H6
Toyonaka, Japan 81/J7
Toyooka, Japan 81/G6
Toyota, Japan 81/H6
Tozeur, Tunisia 106/F2
Trabzon (prov.), Turkey 63/H2
Trabzon, Turkey 54/E5
Trabzon, Turkey 63/H2
Trabzon, Turkey 59/C1
Tracadie, New Bruns. 170/F1
Tracadie, Nova Scotia 168/G3
Tracadie (bay), Pr. Edward I. 168/F2
Trachselwald, Switzerland 39/E2
Tracy, Calif. (95376) 204/D6
Tracy, Conn. (†06492) 210/D2
Tracy, Iowa (50256) 229/H6
Tracy, Ky. (†42123) 237/K7
Tracy, Minn. (56175) 255/C6
Tracy, Mo. (64079) 261/C4
Tracy, New Bruns. 170/D3
Tracy, Québec 172/D3
Tracy Arm (inlet), Alaska 196/N1
Tracy City, Tenn. (37387) 237/K10
Tracyton, Wash. (98393) 310/A2
Trade, Tenn. (37691) 237/T8
Trade Lake, Wis. (†54837) 317/A4
Tradespark, Scotland 15/E3
Tradesville, S.C. (†29720) 296/F2
Tradewater (riv.), Ky. 237/F6
Trading (bay), Alaska 196/B1
Trading Post, Kansas (†66075) 232/H3
Traer, Iowa (50675) 229/J4
Traer, Kansas (†67749) 232/B2
Trafalgar, Ind. (46181) 227/E6
Trafalgar, Nova Scotia 168/F3
Trafalgar (cape), Spain 33/C4
Trafaria, Portugal 33/A1
Trafford, Ala. (35172) 195/E3
Trafford, Pa. (15085) 294/C5
Traghen, Libya 111/B2
Traiguén, Chile 138/D2
Traiguén (isl.), Chile 138/D6
Trail, Br. Col. 162/E6
Trail, Br. Col. 146/G4
Trail, Br. Col. 184/J6
Trail, Minn. (56684) 255/C3
Trail, Oreg. (97541) 291/E5
Trail City, S. Dak. (57657) 298/H3
Trail Creek, Ind. (†46360) 227/D1
Traill (isl.), Greenl. 4/B10
Traill (co.), N. Dak. 282/R5
Traîne (lake), Québec 172/D2
Trainer, Pa. (†19013) 294/L7
Traiskirchen, Austria 41/D2
Trakai, U.S.S.R. 53/C3
Tralake, Miss. (38757) 256/C4
Tralee, Ireland 10/B4
Tralee, Ireland 17/B7
Tralee (bay), Ireland 17/B7
Tramán-tepuí (mt.), Venezuela 124/G5
Tramelan, Switzerland 39/D2
Trammel, Va. (24289) 307/D6
Tramore, Ireland 10/C4
Tramore, Ireland 17/G7
Tramore (bay), Ireland 17/G7
Trampas, N. Mex. (87576) 274/D2
Tramperos (creek), N. Mex. 274/F2
Tramping (lake), Sask. 181/C3
Tramping Lake, Sask. 181/B3
Tranås, Sweden 18/J7
Trancoso, Portugal 33/C2
Tranebjerg, Denmark 21/D6
Tranebjerg (mt.), Denmark 21/C6
Tranent, Scotland 15/F5
Trang, Thailand 72/C6
Trangan (isl.), Indonesia 85/J7
Trangie, N.S. Wales 97/D3
Trani, Italy 34/F4
Tranquebar, India 68/E6
Tranqueras, Uruguay 145/D2
Tranqui (isl.), Chile 138/D4
Tranquility, N.J. (07879) 273/D2
Tranquillity, Calif. (93668) 204/E7
Transantarctic (mts.) 5/B17
Trans-Carpathian Oblast, U.S.S.R. 52/B5
Transfer, Pa. (16154) 294/A3
Transkei (aut. rep.), S. Africa 102/E8
Transkei (aut. rep.), S. Africa 118/D6
Transquaking (riv.), Md. 245/P7
Transvaal (prov.), S. Africa 102/E7
Transvaal (prov.), S. Africa 118/D4
Transylvania, La. (71286) 238/H1
Transylvania (co.), N.C. 281/D4
Transylvanian Alps (mts.), Romania 45/G3
Trapani (prov.), Italy 34/D5
Trapani, Italy 7/F5
Trapani, Italy 34/D5
Trap Falls (res.), Conn. 210/C3
Traphill, N.C. (28685) 281/H2
Trappe, Md. (21673) 245/O6
Trappers (lake), Colo. 208/E3
Traralgon, Victoria 97/D6
Traralgon, Victoria 88/H7
Trarza (reg.), Mauritania 106/A5
Trasimeno (lake), Italy 34/D3
Traskwood, Ark. (72167) 202/E5
Trat, Thailand 72/D4
Traun, Austria 41/C2
Traun (riv.), Austria 41/C2
Traun See (lake), Austria 41/B3
Traunstein, W. Germany 22/E5
Travancore (reg.), India 68/D7
Travelers Rest, S.C. (29690) 296/C2
Travellers (lake), N.S. Wales 97/B3
Travellers Rest, Ky. (†41314) 237/O6
Travemünde, W. Germany 22/D2
Travers, Alberta 182/D4
Travers (res.), Alberta 182/D4
Traverse (bay), Manitoba 179/F4
Traverse (isl.), Mich. 250/A1
Traverse (pt.), Mich. 250/A1
Traverse (co.), Minn. 255/B5
Traverse, Minn. (†56082) 255/D6
Traverse (lake), Minn. 255/B5
Traverse (lake), S. Dak. 298/R2
Traverse City, Mich. 188/K2
Traverse City, Mich. (49684) 250/D4
Tra Vinh (Phu Vinh), Vietnam 72/E5
Travis (co.), Texas 303/G7
Travis (lake), Texas 303/G7
Travis A.F.B., Calif. 204/L1
Travnik, Yugoslavia 45/C3
Trawbreaga (bay), Ireland 17/F1
Traynor, Sask. 181/C3
Traytown, Newf. 166/D1
Trbovlje, Yugoslavia 45/B2
Treadway, Tenn. (37883) 237/P8
Treasure (isl.), Fla. 212/B3
Treasure (co.), Mont. 262/J4
Treasure Island, Fla. (33740) 212/B3
Treasury (isls.), Solomon Is. 86/C2
Treaty, Ind. (†46992) 227/F3
Trebbia (riv.), Italy 34/B2
Třebíč, Czech. 41/C2
Trebinje, Yugoslavia 45/D4
Trebišov, Czech. 41/F2
Trebizond (Trabzon), Turkey 63/H2
Trebloc, Miss. (38875) 256/G3
Třeboň, Czech. 41/C2
Trece Martires, Philippines 82/C3
Tredegar, Wales 13/B6
Treece, Kansas (66778) 232/H4
Treelon, Sask. 181/C6
Trees, La. (71081) 238/B1
Treesbank, Manitoba 179/C5
Tregaron, Wales 13/D5
Tregaron, Wales 10/E4
Tregarva, Sask. 181/G5
Trego (co.), Kansas 232/C3
Trego, Mont. (59934) 262/B2
Trego, Wis. (54888) 317/C4
Treherne, Manitoba 179/D5
Treig, Loch (lake), Scotland 15/D4
Treinta y Tres (dept.), Uruguay 145/E4
Treinta y Tres, Uruguay 145/E4
Trelew, Argentina 143/C5
Trelleborg, Sweden 18/H9
Tremadoc (bay), Wales 10/D4
Tremadoc (prom.), Wales 13/C5
Tremblant (lake), Québec 172/C3
Trembleur (lake), Br. Col. 184/E3
Trementina, N. Mex. (88439) 274/E3
Tremiti (isls.), Italy 34/E3
Tremont, Ill. (61568) 222/D3
Tremont, Maine (†04653) 243/G7
Tremont○, Maine (†04653) 243/G7
Tremont, Miss. (38876) 256/H2
Tremont, Pa. (17981) 294/K4
Tremont City, Ohio (45372) 284/C5
Tremonton, Utah (84337) 304/B2
Tremp, Spain 33/G1
Trempealeau (co.), Wis. 317/D7
Trempealeau, Wis. (54661) 317/C8
Trempealeau (riv.), Wis. 317/C7
Trenary, Mich. (49891) 250/C2
Trenčín, Czech. 41/E2
Trenel, Argentina 143/D4
Trenggalek, Indonesia 85/K2
Trenque Lauquen, Argentina 143/D4
Trent (riv.), England 13/G4
Trent (riv.), England 10/F4
Trent (riv.), N.C. 281/P4
Trent, Oreg. (†97431) 291/E4
Trent, S. Dak. (57065) 298/R6
Trent, Texas (79561) 303/D5
Trente et un Milles (lake), Québec 172/B3
Trentham, Manitoba 179/F5
Trentham Cliffs, N.S. Wales 97/B4
Trentino-Alto Adige (reg.), Italy 34/C1
Trento (prov.), Italy 34/C1
Trento, Italy 34/C1
Trenton, Ala. (35774) 195/F1
Trenton, Ark. (†72374) 202/J5
Trenton, Fla. (32693) 212/D2
Trenton, Georgia (30752) 217/A1
Trenton, Ill. (62293) 222/D5
Trenton, Iowa (†52641) 229/K6
Trenton, Ky. (42286) 237/G7
Trenton, Maine (†04605) 243/G7
Trenton○, Maine (†04605) 243/G7
Trenton, Md. (†21155) 245/L2
Trenton, Mich. (48183) 250/B7
Trenton, Miss. (†39153) 256/E6
Trenton, Mo. (64683) 261/E2
Trenton, Nebr. (69044) 264/D4
Trenton (cap.), N.J. 146/L5
Trenton (cap.), N.J. 188/M2
Trenton (cap.), N.J. (*08601) 273/D3
Trenton, N.C. (28585) 281/P4
Trenton, N. Dak. (58853) 282/C3
Trenton, Nova Scotia 168/F3
Trenton, Ohio (45067) 284/B7
Trenton, Ontario 177/G3
Trenton, S.C. (29847) 296/D4
Trenton, Tenn. (38382) 237/D9
Trenton, Texas (75490) 303/H4
Trenton, Utah (84338) 304/B2
Trent Woods, N.C. (†28560) 281/P4
Trepassey, Newf. 166/D2
Treptow, E. Germany 22/F4
Tres Árboles, Uruguay 145/C3
Tres Arroyos, Argentina 143/D4
Tres Arroyos, Argentina 120/C6
Tres Bocas, Uruguay 145/B2
Tresckow, Pa. (18254) 294/K4
Tresco (isl.), England 13/A8
Três Corações, Brazil 132/E8
Três Corações, Brazil 135/D2
Tres Cruces, Nevado (mt.), Chile 138/B6
Tres Esquinas, Colombia 126/C7
Treshnish (isls.), Scotland 15/B4
Tres Islas, Uruguay 145/E3
Três Lagoas, Brazil 120/D5
Três Lagoas, Brazil 132/C8
Três Marias (res.), Brazil 120/E4
Tres Montes (cape), Chile 120/B7
Tres Montes (cape), Chile 138/C7
Tres Montes (gulf), Chile 138/D6
Tres Montes (pen.), Chile 138/C6
Tres Palmas, Colombia 126/B3
Trespassey (bay), Newf. 166/D2
Tres Picos, Cerro (mt.), Argentina 143/B5
Tres Piedras, N. Mex. (87577) 274/D2
Tres Pinos, Calif. (95075) 204/D7
Três Pontas, Brazil 135/D2
Tres Puntas (cape), Argentina 120/C7
Tres Puntas (cape), Argentina 143/D6
Tres Puntas (cape), Guatemala 154/C3
Três Rios, Brazil 135/E3
Três Rios, Brazil 132/F8
Tres Ritos, N. Mex. (†87579) 274/D2
Třešť, Czech. 41/C2
Treuchtlingen, W. Germany 22/D4
Treungen, Norway 18/F7
Treutlen (co.), Georgia 217/G6
Trevelin, Argentina 143/B5
Trevett, Maine (04571) 243/D8
Treviglio, Italy 34/B2
Treviño, Spain 33/E1
Treviso (prov.), Italy 34/D2
Treviso, Italy 34/D2
Trevlac, Ind. (†47448) 227/E6
Trevorton, Pa. (17881) 294/J4
Trevose (head), England 13/B7
Trévoux, France 28/F5
Treynor, Iowa (51575) 229/B6
Treyvaux, Switzerland 39/D3
Trezevant, Tenn. (38258) 237/D8
Trhové Sviny, Czech. 41/C2
Triabunna, Tasmania 99/D4
Triadelphia (lake), Md. 245/L4
Triadelphia, W. Va. (26059) 312/E2
Triana, Ala. (†35758) 195/E1
Triangle, Alberta 182/B2
Triangle, Va. (22172) 307/O3
Triángulo Este (isl.), Mexico 150/N6
Triángulo Oeste (isl.), Mexico 150/N6
Tribbett, Miss. (38779) 256/C4
Tribbey, Okla. (†74852) 288/M4
Triberg im Schwarzwald, W. Germany 22/C4
Tribune, Kansas (67879) 232/A3
Tribune, Sask. 181/H6
Tricase, Italy 34/G5
Trichur, India 68/D6
Trida, N.S. Wales 97/C3
Tridell, Utah (84076) 304/E3
Trident, Mont. (59752) 262/E5
Trident (peak), Nev. 266/C1
Trieben, Austria 41/C3
Trier, W. Germany 22/B4
Triesen, Liecht. 39/H2
Trieste (prov.), Italy 34/E2
Trieste, Italy 34/E2
Trieste, Italy 7/F4
Trieste (gulf), Italy 34/D2
Trigal, Bolivia 136/C6
Trigg (co.), Ky. 237/F7
Triglav (mt.), Yugoslavia 45/A2
Trigueros, Spain 33/C4
Tríkkala, Greece 45/E6
Tri Lakes, Ind. (†46725) 227/G2
Trilby, Fla. (33593) 212/D3
Trilla, Ill. (62469) 222/E4
Trillick, N. Ireland 17/G3
Trim, Ireland 17/H4
Trim, Ireland 10/C4
Trimble, Ill. (†62454) 222/F4
Trimble (co.), Ky. 237/L3
Trimble, Ky. (42559) 237/M6
Trimble, Mo. (64492) 261/D4
Trimble, Ohio (45782) 284/F7
Trimble, Tenn. (38259) 237/C8
Trim Cane (creek), Miss. 256/G4
Trimmis, Switzerland 39/J3
Trimont, Minn. (56176) 255/D7
Trin, Switzerland 39/H3
Trinchera, Colo. (81081) 208/M8
Trinchera (peak), Colo. 208/J8
Trinchera (riv.), Colo. 208/H8
Trincheras, Mexico 150/D1
Trincomalee, Sri Lanka 54/K9
Trincomalee, Sri Lanka 68/E7
Trindade, Brazil 132/D7
Třinec, Czech. 41/E2
Tring, England 13/G7
Tring, England 10/F5
Tring-Jonction, Québec 172/F3
Trinidad (isl.), Argentina 143/D4
Trinidad, Bolivia 120/C4
Trinidad, Bolivia 136/C4
Trinidad, Calif. (95570) 204/A2
Trinidad (head), Calif. 204/A2
Trinidad (gulf), Chile 138/D8
Trinidad, Colombia 126/E5
Trinidad, Colo. 146/H6
Trinidad, Colo. 188/F3
Trinidad, Colo. (81082) 208/L8
Trinidad, Cuba 158/E2
Trinidad, Cuba 156/B2
Trinidad, Honduras 154/C3
Trinidad, Paraguay 144/E5
Trinidad, Texas (75163) 303/J5
Trinidad (isl.), Trin. & Tob. 156/G5
Trinidad (isl.), Trin. & Tob. 161/A9
Trinidad, Uruguay 145/B4
Trinidad, Wash. (†98848) 310/F3
Trinidad and Tobago 2/G5
Trinidad and Tobago 146/N8
TRINIDAD and TOBAGO 161
TRINIDAD and TOBAGO 156/G5
Trinity, Ala. (35673) 195/D1
Trinity (isls.), Alaska 196/H3
Trinity (co.), Calif. 204/B3
Trinity (riv.), Calif. 204/B3
Trinity (mt.), Idaho 220/C6
Trinity, Ky. (†41179) 237/O3
Trinity (range), Nev. 266/C2
Trinity, Newf. 166/D4
Trinity, Newf. 166/D2
Trinity (bay), Newf. 166/D2
Trinity (bay), Queensland 88/H3
Trinity (bay), Queensland 95/C3
Trinity (co.), Texas 303/J6
Trinity, Texas (75862) 303/J7
Trinity (bay), Texas 303/L2
Trinity (riv.), Texas 188/G4
Trinity (riv.), Texas 303/H5
Trinity, West Fork (riv.), Texas 303/G2
Trinity Center, Calif. (96091) 204/C2
Trinity Springs, Ind. (†47581) 227/D7
Trinity Ville, Jamaica 158/K6
Trinkitat, Sudan 111/G4
Trinkitat, Sudan 59/C6
Trino, Italy 34/B2
Trinway, Ohio (43842) 284/F5
Trio, S.C. (29595) 296/H5
Trion, Georgia (30753) 217/B1
Triplet, Va. (23886) 307/N7
Triplett, Mo. (65286) 261/F4
Tripoli, Iowa (50676) 229/J3
Tripoli (Tarabulus), Lebanon 59/C3
Tripoli (Tarabulus), Lebanon 63/F5
Tripoli (cap.), Libya 2/K4
Tripoli (cap.), Libya 102/D1
Tripoli (cap.), Libya 111/B1
Tripoli, Wis. (54564) 317/G4
Tripolis, Greece 45/F7
Tripolitania (reg.), Libya 102/D1
Tripolitania (reg.), Libya 111/B1
Tripp (co.), S. Dak. 298/K7
Tripp, S. Dak. (57376) 298/N7
Tripura (state), India 68/G4
Trischen (isl.), W. Germany 22/C1
Tristan da Cunha (isl.), St. Helena 2/J7
Triste (gulf), Venezuela 124/D2
Triton (isl.), China 85/E2
Triumph, Ill. (61371) 222/E2
Triumph-Buras, La. (†70041) 238/L8
Triune, Tenn. (†37014) 237/H9
Trivandrum, India 54/J9
Trivandrum, India 68/D7
Trivoli, Ill. (61569) 222/D3
Trnava, Czech. 41/D2
Trobriand (isls.), Papua N.G. 87/F6
Trobriand (isls.), Papua N.G. 85/C7
Trochu, Alberta 182/D4
Troense, Denmark 21/D7
Trofaiach, Austria 41/C3
Trogir, Yugoslavia 45/C4
Troisdorf, W. Germany 22/B3
Trois-Pistoles, Québec 172/H1
Trois Pitons, Morne (mt.), Dominica 161/E6
Trois-Ponts, Belgium 27/H8
Trois-Rivières, Guadeloupe 161/A7
Trois-Rivières (riv.), Haiti 158/B5
Trois-Rivières, Que. 162/J6
Trois-Rivières, Que. 146/L5
Trois-Rivières, Que. 172/E3
Trois-Rivières-Ouest, Québec 172/E3
Trois-Saumons, Québec 172/G2
Troistorrents, Switzerland /C4
Troisvierges, Luxembourg 27/J9
Troitsa (lake), Br. Col. 184/D3
Troitsk, U.S.S.R. 48/G4
Troitsko-Pechorsk, U.S.S.R. 52/J2
Trojan, S. Dak. (†57754) 298/B5
Trollhättan, Sweden 18/H7
Trombay, India 68/B7
Trombetas (riv.), Brazil 132/B3
Tromie (riv.), Scotland 15/D4
Trommald, Minn. (†56455) 255/D4
Troms (co.), Norway 18/L2
Tromsø, Norway 4/B9
Tromsø, Norway 7/F2
Tromsø, Norway 18/L2
Trona, Calif. (93562) 204/H8
Tronador (mt.), Argentina 143/B5
Tronador, Cerro (mt.), Chile 138/E3
Trondheim, Norway 7/F2
Trondheim, Norway 18/F5
Trondheimsfjorden (fjord), Norway 7/F2
Trondheimsfjorden (fjord), Norway 18/G5
Troodos (mt.), Cyprus 63/E5
Troon, Scotland 10/D3
Troon, Scotland 15/D5
Tropic, Utah (84776) 304/B6
Trosa, Sweden 18/K7
Trosky, Minn. (56177) 255/B7
Trossachs, Sask. 181/G6
Trossachs, The, (valley), Scotland 15/D4
Trostan (mt.), N. Ireland 17/J1
Trotternish (dist.), Scotland 15/B3
Trotters, N. Dak. (58657) 282/C5
Trotwood, Ohio (45426) 284/B6
Trou Bonbon, Haiti 158/A6
Trou du Nord, Haiti 158/C5
Troup (co.), Georgia 217/B4
Troup (head), Scotland 15/F3
Troup, Texas (75789) 303/J5
Troupsburg, N.Y. (14885) 276/F6
Trousdale, Kansas (†67059) 232/C4
Trousdale, Okla. (†74878) 288/M4

Victoria Harbour 463

Vandenberg A.F.B., Calif. 204/E9
Vanderbijl Park, S. Africa 118/D5
Vanderbilt, Mich. (49795) 250/E3
Vanderbilt, Pa. (15486) 294/C5
Vanderbilt, Texas (77991) 303/H9
Vanderburgh (co.), Ind. 227/B8
Vandergrift, Pa. (15690) 294/D4
Vanderhoof, Br. Col. 162/D5
Vanderhoof, Br. Col. 184/E3
Vanderlin (isl.), North. Terr. 88/F3
Vanderlin (isl.), North. Terr. 93/E3
Vanderpool, Texas (78885) 303/E8
Vanderpool, Va. (†24465) 307/J4
Vandervoort, Ark. (71972) 202/B5
Van Diemen (cape), North. Terr. 88/D2
Van Diemen (cape), North. Terr. 93/A1
Van Diemen (gulf), North. Terr. 88/E2
Van Diemen (gulf), North. Terr. 93/B1
Vandiver, Ala. (35176) 195/F4
Vandiver, Mo. (†65265) 261/J4
Vandling, Pa. (18421) 294/M2
Vändra, U.S.S.R. 53/C1
Vandura, Sask. 181/K5
Vanduser, Mo. (63784) 261/N9
Vanegas, Mexico 150/J5
Vänern (lake), Sweden 7/F3
Vänern (lake), Sweden 18/H7
Vänersborg, Sweden 18/G7
Van Etten, N.Y. (14889) 276/G6
Vanga, Kenya 115/G4
Vangaindrano, Madagascar 118/H4
Vanguard, Sask. 181/D6
Vangunu (isl.), Solomon Is. 86/D3
Van Hoa, Vietnam 72/E2
Van Horn, Texas (79855) 303/C11
Van Horne, Iowa (52346) 229/J4
Van Hornesville, N.Y. (13475) 276/L5
Vanier, Ontario 177/J2
Vanier, Québec 172/J3
Vanikoro (isl.), Solomon Is. 87/G7
Vanil Noir (mt.), Switzerland 39/D3
Vanimo, Papua N.G. 87/E6
Vanimo, Papua N.G. 85/B6
Vanino, U.S.S.R. 48/P5
Vaniyambadi, India 68/D6
Vankleek Hill, Ontario 177/K2
Van Lear, Ky. (41265) 237/R5
Vanleer, Tenn. (37181) 237/G8
Vanlue, Ohio (45890) 284/C4
Van Meter, Iowa (50261) 229/E5
Vanna, Georgia (30672) 217/F2
Vännäs, Sweden 18/L5
Vanndale, Ark. (72387) 202/J3
Vannes, France 28/B4
Van Ninh, Vietnam 72/F4
Vannøy (isl.), Norway 18/L1
Van Nuys, Calif. (*91401) 204/B10
Van Orin, Ill. (61374) 222/D2
Vanoss, Okla. (†74820) 288/N5
Vanrhynsdorp, S. Africa 118/B6
Van Rook, Queensland 95/B3
Vansant, Va. (24656) 307/D6
Vansbro, Sweden 18/H6
Vanscoy, Sask. 181/D4
Vansittart (isl.), N.W. Terrs. 187/K3
Vansittart (isl.), Tasmania 99/E2
Vantage, Sask. 181/F6
Vantage, Wash. (98950) 310/E4
Van Tassell, Wyo. (82242) 319/H3
Vanua Levu (isl.), Fiji 87/H7
Vanua Levu (isl.), Fiji 86/Q10
Vanuatu 2/T6
Vanuatu 87/G7
Van Vleet, Miss. (†38851) 256/G3
Vanvoorhis, W. Va. (†26505) 312/G3
Van Wert, Georgia (†30153) 217/B3
Van Wert, Iowa (50262) 229/F7
Van Wert (co.), Ohio 284/A4
Van Wert, Ohio (45891) 284/A4
Van Wyck, S.C. (29744) 296/F2
Van Yen, Vietnam 72/E2
Vanylven, Norway 18/E5
Van Zandt (co.), Texas 303/J5
Van Zandt, Wash. (†98244) 310/C2
Vanzant, Mo. (65768) 261/H9
Var (dept.), France 28/G6
Vara, Sweden 18/H7
Vara de María, Venezuela 124/C4
Varadero, Cuba 158/D1
Varakļāni, U.S.S.R. 53/D2
Varallo Pombia, Italy 34/B2
Varamin, Iran 66/G3
Varanasi, India 54/K7
Varanasi, India 68/E3
Varangerfjorden (fjord), Norway 18/Q2
Varangerfjorden (fjord), Norway 7/H1
Varangerhalvøya (pen.), Norway 18/Q1
Varano (lake), Italy 34/F3
Varaždin, Yugoslavia 45/B2
Varazze, Italy 34/B2
Varberg, Sweden 18/G8
Vardaman, Miss. (38878) 256/F3
Vardar (riv.), Greece 45/F5
Vardar (riv.), Yugoslavia 45/E5
Varde, Denmark 18/F9
Varde, Denmark 21/B6
Varde (riv.), Denmark 21/B6
Vardø, Norway 18/R1
Varel, W. Germany 22/C2
Varella, Mui (cape), Vietnam 72/F4
Varena, U.S.S.R. 53/C3
Varennes, Québec 172/J4
Vareš, Yugoslavia 45/D3
Varese (prov.), Italy 34/B2
Varese, Italy 34/B2
Vargem Bonita, Brazil 135/E3
Varginha, Brazil 135/D2
Varginha, Brazil 132/E8
Varina, Iowa (50593) 229/D3
Varkaus, Finland 18/Q5
Värmland (co.), Sweden 18/H7
Varna, Bulgaria 7/G4
Varna, Bulgaria 45/J4
Varna, Ill. (61375) 222/D2
Varnado, La. (70467) 238/L5
Värnamo, Sweden 18/J8
Varnek, U.S.S.R. 52/J1
Varnell, Georgia (30756) 217/C1
Varner, Kansas (†67068) 232/D4
Varney, Ontario 177/D3
Varney, W. Va. (25696) 312/B7
Varnsdorf, Czech. 41/C1
Varnville, S.C. (29944) 296/E6
Várpalota, Hungary 41/E3
Vars, Ontario 177/J2
Vartholomión, Greece 45/E7
Varto, Turkey 63/J3
Varysburg, N.Y. (14167) 276/D5
Varzarin, Kuh-e (mt.), Iran 59/E3
Varzarin, Kuh-e (mt.), Iran 66/E4
Vas (co.), Hungary 41/D3
Vasa (Vaasa), Finland 18/M5
Vasa, Minn. (†55089) 255/F6
Vasa Barris (riv.), Brazil 132/G5
Vásárosnamény, Hungary 41/G2
Vascongadas (reg.), Spain 33/E1
Vashi, India 68/B7
Vashka (riv.), U.S.S.R. 52/G2
Vashon, Wash. (98070) 310/A2
Vasile Roaită, Romania 45/J3
Vasil'kov, U.S.S.R. 52/D4
Vaslui, Romania 45/H2
Vass, N.C. (28394) 281/L4
Vassalboro, Maine (04989) 243/D7
Vassalboro○, Maine (04989) 243/D7
Vassar, Kansas (66543) 232/G3
Vassar, Manitoba 179/G5
Vassar, Mich. (48768) 250/F5
Vassouras, Brazil 135/E3
Västenjaure (lake), Sweden 18/K3
Västerås, Sweden 7/F3
Västerås, Sweden 18/K7
Västerbotten (co.), Sweden 18/K4
Västerdalälven (riv.), Sweden 18/H6
Västerhaninge, Sweden 18/H1
Västernorrland (co.), Sweden 18/K5
Västervik, Sweden 18/K8
Västmanland (co.), Sweden 18/K7
Vasto, Italy 34/E3
Vasvár, Hungary 41/D3
Vaternish (dist.), Scotland 15/B3
Vaternish (pt.), Scotland 15/B3
Vatersay (isl.), Scotland 15/A4
Vathí, Greece 45/H7
Vatican City 7/F4
VATICAN CITY 34
Vatican City, Vatican City 34/B6
Vaticano (cape), Italy 34/E5
Vatnajökull (glac.), Iceland 21/C1
Vatomandry, Madagascar 118/H3
Vatra Dornei, Romania 45/G2
Vättern (lake), Sweden 7/F3
Vättern (lake), Sweden 18/J7
Vatukoula, Fiji 86/P10
Vatulele (isl.), Fiji 86/P11
Vauclin (mt.), Martinique 161/D6
Vaucluse (dept.), France 28/F6
Vaucluse, S.C. (29850) 296/D7
Vaud (canton), Switzerland 39/B3
Vaudreuil (co.), Québec 172/C4
Vaudreuil, Québec 172/C4
Vaughan, Miss. (39179) 256/D5
Vaughan, N.C. (27586) 281/N2
Vaughan, Ontario 177/J4
Vaughan, W. Va. (†26656) 312/D6
Vaughn, Mont. (59487) 262/E3
Vaughn, N. Mex. (88353) 274/D4
Vaughn, Wash. (98394) 310/C3
Vaughnsville, Ohio (45893) 284/B4
Vaupés (comm.), Colombia 126/E7
Vaupés (riv.), Colombia 120/B2
Vaupés (riv.), Colombia 126/E7
Vauxhall, Alberta 182/D4
Vauxhall, N.J. (07088) 273/A2
Vaux-sur-Sûre, Belgium 27/H9
Vava'u Group (isls.), Tonga 87/J7
Vavenby, Br. Col. 184/H4
Vavuniya, Sri Lanka 68/E7
Vawn, Sask. 181/C2
Vaxholm, Sweden 18/J1
Växjö, Sweden 7/F3
Växjö, Sweden 18/J8
Vaygach (isl.), U.S.S.R. 4/C6
Vaygach (isl.), U.S.S.R. 52/K1
Vayland, S. Dak. (†57381) 298/M5
Važec, Czech. 41/E2
Vazhgort, U.S.S.R. 52/G2
Vaz-Obervaz, Switzerland 39/J3
Vázquez, Cuba 158/H3
Veagh (lake), Ireland 17/F1
Vealmoor, Texas (79720) 303/C5
Veazie○, Maine (04401) 243/F6
Veblen, S. Dak. (57270) 298/P2
Vechigen, Switzerland 39/E3
Vecht (riv.), Netherlands 27/F4
Vechta, W. Germany 22/C2
Vechte (riv.), Netherlands 27/J3
Vechte (riv.), W. Germany 22/B2
Vecsés, Hungary 41/E3
Vedaranniyam, India 68/E6
Vedia, Argentina 143/F7
Veedersburg, Ind. (47987) 227/C4
Veendam, Netherlands 27/K2
Veenendaal, Netherlands 27/G4
Veenhuizen, Netherlands 27/J2
Veere, Netherlands 27/D5
Veersche Meer (lake), Netherlands 27/D5
Vega (pt.), Alaska 196/J4
Vega, Alberta 182/C2
Vega (isl.), Norway 18/G4
Vega, Texas (79092) 303/B2
Vega Alta, P. Rico 161/D1
Vega Baja, P. Rico 161/D1
Vegafjorden (fjord), Norway 18/G4
Vegas Creek, Nev. (89121) 266/G6
Veghel, Netherlands 27/H5
Vegreville, Alberta 182/E3
Vègreville, Alta. 162/E5
Veguita, N. Mex. (87062) 274/C4
Vehar (lake), India 68/B7
Veinticinco (25) de Agosto, Uruguay 145/A6
Veinticinco (25) de Diciembre, Paraguay 144/D4
Veinticinco de Mayo, Argentina 143/F7
Veinticinco de Mayo, Ecuador 128/C4
Veinticinco (25) de Mayo, Uruguay 145/C5
Veintiocho de Noviembre, Argentina 143/B7
Vejen, Denmark 21/C7
Vejer de la Frontera, Spain 33/C4
Vejle (co.), Denmark 21/C6
Vejle, Denmark 21/C6
Vejle, Denmark 18/F9
Vejle (fjord), Denmark 21/C6
Vejprty, Czech. 41/B1
Vela, La (cape), Colombia 126/D1
Vela, Roca que (cay), Colombia 126/B8
Vélan (mt.), Switzerland 39/D5
Velarde, N. Mex. (87582) 274/C2
Velas (cape), C. Rica 154/D5
Velasco, Ciego de Ávila, Cuba 158/G2
Velasco, Holguín, Cuba 158/H3
Velázquez, Uruguay 145/E5
Velda, Mo. (†63101) 261/P2
Velden am Wörthersee, Austria 41/C3
Veldhoven, Netherlands 27/G6
Veldrif, S. Africa 118/B6
Velence, Hungary 41/E3
Velenje, Yugoslavia 45/B2
Vélez, Colombia 126/D4
Vélez-Blanco, Spain 33/E4
Vélez-Málaga, Spain 33/E4
Vélez-Rubio, Spain 33/E4
Velhas (riv.), Brazil 132/E7
Velika Plana, Yugoslavia 45/E3
Velikaya (riv.), U.S.S.R. 48/S3
Velikaya (riv.), U.S.S.R. 52/C3
Veliki Bečkerek (Zrenjanin), Yugoslavia 45/E3
Velikiye Luki, U.S.S.R. 7/H3
Velikiye Luki, U.S.S.R. 52/D3
Velikiye Luki, U.S.S.R. 48/D4
Velikiy Ustyug, U.S.S.R. 7/J2
Velikiy Ustyug, U.S.S.R. 48/E3
Velikiy Ustyug, U.S.S.R. 52/F2
Veliko Tŭrnovo, Bulgaria 45/G4
Velikovisochnoye, U.S.S.R. 52/H1
Velizh, U.S.S.R. 52/D3
Velká Bíteš, Czech. 41/D2
Velká Bystřice, Czech. 41/D2
Vel'ké Kapušany, Czech. 41/G2
Velké Meziříčí, Czech. 41/D2
Vel'ké Rovné, Czech. 41/E2
Vella Lavella (isl.), Solomon Is. 86/D2
Velletri, Italy 34/F7
Vellore, India 68/D6
Velluda, Sierra (mt.), Chile 138/E1
Velma, Okla. (73091) 288/L6
Velp, Netherlands 27/J5
Velpen, Ind. (47590) 227/C8
Velsen, Netherlands 27/F4
Vel'sk, U.S.S.R. 52/F2
Vel'sk, U.S.S.R. 48/E3
Velten, E. Germany 22/E2
Veluwe (reg.), Netherlands 27/H4
Velva, N. Dak. (58790) 282/J3
Velvendós, Greece 45/F5
Vemb, Denmark 21/B5
Vémend, Hungary 41/E3
Venadillo, Colombia 126/C5
Venado, Mexico 150/J5
Venado Tuerto, Argentina 143/D3
Venafro, Italy 34/E4
Venaissin (trad. prov.), France 29
Venamo (mt.), Guyana 131/A3
Venamo, Cerro (mt.), Venezuela 124/H4
Venamo (riv.), Venezuela 124/H4
Venango, Nebr. (69168) 264/C4
Venango (co.), Pa. 294/C3
Venango, Pa. (16440) 294/B2
Vena Park, Queensland 95/B3
Vence, France 28/G6
Venda (aut. rep.), S. Africa 102/F7
Venda (aut. rep.), S. Africa 118/E4
Vendas Novas, Portugal 33/B3
Vendée (dept.), France 28/C4
Vendôme, France 28/D4
Vendrell, Spain 33/G2
Venedocia, Ohio (45894) 284/B4
Venedy, Ill. (62296) 222/D5
Veneta, Oreg. (97487) 291/D3
Venetie, Alaska (99781) 196/J1
Veneto (reg.), Italy 34/D3
Venezia (Venice), Italy 34/D2
Venezuela 2/F5
Venezuela 120/C2
Venezuela, Cuba 158/F2
VENEZUELA 124
Venezuela (gulf), Venezuela 120/B1
Venezuela (gulf), Venezuela 124/C2
Vengurla, India 68/C5
Veniaminof (crater), Alaska 196/F3
Venice, Alberta 182/E2
Venice, Calif. (90291) 204/B11
Venice, Fla. (*33595) 212/D4
Venice, Ill. (62090) 222/A2
Venice (prov.), Italy 34/D2
Venice, Italy 7/F4
Venice, Italy 34/D2
Venice (gulf), Italy 34/D2
Venice, La. (70091) 238/M8
Venice, Utah (†84701) 304/C5
Vénissieux, France 28/F5
Venkatagiri, India 68/D6
Venlo, Netherlands 27/J6
Venn, Sask. 181/F4
Venosa, Italy 34/E4
Venraij, Netherlands 27/H6
Venta (riv.), U.S.S.R. 53/B2
Venterspos, S. Africa 118/G6
Ventimiglia, Italy 34/A3
Ventnor, England 10/F5
Ventnor, England 13/F7
Ventnor City, N.J. (08406) 273/E5
Ventotene (isl.), Italy 34/D4
Ventspils, U.S.S.R. 48/B4
Ventspils, U.S.S.R. 53/A2
Ventspils, U.S.S.R. 52/B3
Ventuari (riv.), Venezuela 124/E5
Ventura (co.), Calif. 204/F9
Ventura, Calif. (*93001) 204/F9
Ventura, Iowa (50482) 229/F2
Venturia, N. Dak. (58489) 282/L7
Venus, Fla. (33960) 212/E4
Venus (pt.), Fr. Poly. 86/T12
Venus, Pa. (16364) 294/C3
Venus (bay), Victoria 97/C6
Venustiano Carranza, Mexico 150/N8
Venustiano Carranza (res.), Mexico 150/J3
Ver (riv.), England 13/H7
Vera, Argentina 143/F5
Vera, Ill. (†62080) 222/D4
Vera, Okla. (74082) 288/P2
Vera (lag.), Paraguay 144/D5
Vera, Spain 33/F4
Vera, Texas (76383) 303/E4
Vera, Va. (†24522) 307/L6
Vera Cruz, Brazil 135/B3
Vera Cruz, Ind. (†46714) 227/G3
Veracruz (state), Mexico 150/L7
Veracruz, Mexico 150/Q1
Veracruz, Mexico 2/E5
Veracruz, Mexico 146/J8
Veradale, Wash. (99037) 310/H3
Veragua Abajo, Dom. Rep. 158/E5
Veras, Uruguay 145/C2
Veraval, India 68/C4
Verbania, Italy 34/B2
Verbena, Ala. (36091) 195/E5
Verboort, Oreg. (†97116) 291/A2
Vercelli (prov.), Italy 34/B2
Vercelli, Italy 34/B2
Verchères (co.), Québec 172/J4
Verchères, Québec 172/J4
Verçinin Tepesi (mt.), Turkey 63/J2
Verda, Ky. (†40828) 237/P7
Verda, La. (71481) 238/E3
Verde (riv.), Ariz. 188/D4
Verde (riv.), Ariz. 198/D5
Verde (cay), Bahamas 156/C2
Verde (riv.), Brazil 132/C7
Verde (riv.), Mexico 150/F3
Verde (riv.), Mexico 150/L8
Verde (riv.), Paraguay 144/C3
Verde (cape), Senegal 102/A3
Verde (cape), Senegal 106/A6
Verde Island (passage), Philippines 82/C4
Verdel, Nebr. (68782) 264/F2
Verden, Okla. (73092) 288/K4
Verden, W. Germany 22/C2
Verdery, S.C. (†29819) 296/C3
Verdi, Minn. (56179) 255/B6
Verdi, Nev. (89439) 266/B3
Verdigre, Nebr. (68783) 264/F2
Verdigris (riv.), Kansas 232/G5
Verdigris, Okla. (†74017) 288/P2
Verdigris (riv.), Okla. 288/P2
Verdinho (riv.), Brazil 132/D7
Verdon, Nebr. (68457) 264/J4
Verdon, S. Dak. (57478) 298/N3
Verdun, Québec 172/H4
Verdún, Uruguay 145/D5
Verdun-sur-Meuse, France 28/F3
Verdunville, W. Va. (25649) 312/B7
Vereeniging, S. Africa 102/E7
Vereeniging, S. Africa 118/D5
Veregin, Sask. 181/K4
Verendrye, N. Dak. (†58717) 282/J3
Vereshchagino, U.S.S.R. 52/H3
Verga (cape), Guinea 106/B6
Vergara, Argentina 143/H7
Vergara, Spain 33/E1
Vergara, Uruguay 145/E3
Vergas, Minn. (56587) 255/C4
Vergeletto, Switzerland 39/G4
Vergennes, Ill. (62994) 222/D6
Vergennes, Vt. (05491) 268/A3
Veribest, Texas (76886) 303/D6
Verín, Spain 33/C2
Veríssimo, Brazil 135/B1
Verkhnevilyuysk, U.S.S.R. 48/N3
Verkhnyaya Toyma, U.S.S.R. 52/G2
Verkhoyansk, U.S.S.R. 2/R2
Verkhoyansk, U.S.S.R. 4/C3
Verkhoyansk, U.S.S.R. 54/P3
Verkhoyansk, U.S.S.R. 48/N3
Verkhoyansk (range), U.S.S.R. 48/N3
Verkhoyansk (range), U.S.S.R. 4/C3
Verkhoyansk (range), U.S.S.R. 54/O3
Verkniy At-Uryakh, U.S.S.R. 48/Q3
Verlo, Sask. 181/C5
Vermejo (riv.), N. Mex. 274/E2
Vermejo Park, N. Mex. (†81091) 274/D2
Vermilion, Alberta 182/E3
Vermilion (riv.), Alberta 182/E3
Vermilion (cliffs), Ariz. 198/D2
Vermilion (co.), Ill. 222/F3
Vermilion, Ill. (61955) 222/F4
Vermilion (riv.), Ind. 227/B4
Vermilion (par.), La. 238/F7
Vermilion (bay), La. 238/F7
Vermilion (lake), Minn. 188/H1
Vermilion (lake), Minn. 255/F3
Vermilion (range), Minn. 255/F3
Vermilion (riv.), Minn. 255/F2
Vermilion, Ohio (44089) 284/F3
Vermilion (riv.), Ohio 284/F3
Vermilion (hills), Sask. 181/E5
Vermilion (cliffs), Utah 304/B6
Vermilion Bay, Ontario 177/G4
Vermilion Bay, Ontario 175/B3
Vermilion Grove, Ill. (†61870) 222/F4
Vermillion (co.), Ind. 227/C5
Vermillion, Kansas (66544) 232/F2
Vermillion, Minn. (55085) 255/F6
Vermillion, S. Dak. (57069) 298/R8
Vermillion (riv.), S. Dak. 298/P6
Vermillion (riv.), Québec 172/D2
Vermont 188/M2
Vermont, Ill. (61484) 222/C3
Vermont (state), U.S. 146/L5
VERMONT 268
Vermontville, Mich. (49096) 250/E6
Vernal, Utah (84078) 304/E3
Vernayaz, Switzerland 39/D4
Verndale, Minn. (56481) 255/C4
Verndon, Minn. (†55752) 255/E4
Verner, Ontario 177/D1
Verneuil-sur-Avre, France 28/D3
Vernon, Ala. (35592) 195/B3
Vernon, Ariz. (85940) 198/F4
Vernon, Br. Col. 162/E5
Vernon, Br. Col. 184/H5
Vernon, Colo. (80755) 208/P3
Vernon○, Conn. (06066) 210/F1
Vernon, Fla. (32462) 212/C6
Vernon, France 28/D3
Vernon, Ill. (62892) 222/D5
Vernon, Ind. (47282) 227/F7
Vernon, Ky. (†42151) 237/L7
Vernon (par.), La. 238/D4
Vernon, La. (†71228) 238/E2
Vernon (lake), La. 238/D4
Vernon, Mich. (48476) 250/F6
Vernon (co.), Mo. 261/D7
Vernon, N.J. (07462) 273/E1
Vernon, Okla. (74877) 288/P4
Vernon, Ontario 177/J2
Vernon (lake), Ontario 177/E2
Vernon, Pr. Edward I. 168/E2
Vernon, Texas (76384) 303/E3
Vernon, Utah (84080) 304/B3
Vernon○, Vt. (05354) 268/B6
Vernon (co.), Wis. 317/E8
Vernonburg, Georgia (†31401) 217/K7
Vernon Center, Conn. (†06066) 210/F1
Vernon Center, Minn. (56090) 255/D7
Vernon Fork (creek), Ind. 227/F7
Vernon Hill, Va. (24597) 307/K7
Vernon Hills, Ill. (60061) 222/B4
Vernonia, Oreg. (97064) 291/D2
Vero Beach, Fla. (32960) 212/F4
Veroli, Italy 34/D4
Verona, Ill. (60479) 222/E2
Verona (prov.), Italy 34/C2
Verona, Italy 34/C2
Verona, Italy 7/F4
Verona, Ky. (41092) 237/M3
Verona, Miss. (38879) 256/G2
Verona, Mo. (65769) 261/E9
Verona, N.J. (07044) 273/B2
Verona, N. Dak. (58490) 282/O7
Verona, Ohio (45378) 284/A6
Verona, Ontario 177/H3
Verona, Pa. (15147) 294/C6
Verona, Va. (24482) 307/K4
Verona, Wis. (53593) 317/G9
Verónica, Argentina 143/H7
Verpelét, Hungary 41/F2
Verret (lake), La. 238/H7
Verret, New Bruns. 170/B1
Verrettes, Haiti 158/C5
Vérroia, Greece 45/F5
Versailles, Conn. (06383) 210/G2
Versailles, France 28/A2
Versailles, France 7/E4
Versailles, Ill. (62378) 222/C4
Versailles, Ind. (47042) 227/G6
Versailles, Ky. (40383) 237/M4
Versailles, Mo. (65084) 261/G6
Versailles, N.Y. (14168) 276/B6
Versailles, Ohio (45380) 284/A5
Versailles, Pa. (15132) 294/C7
Versalles, Bolivia 136/D3
Vershire○, Vt. (05079) 268/C4
Versoix, Switzerland 39/B4
Verte (bay), New Bruns. 170/G2
Verte (bay), Nova Scotia 168/D2
Verte (isl.), Québec 172/H1
Vertientes, Cuba 158/G3
Vert-Pré, Martinique 161/D6
Vertus, France 28/E3
Verviers, Belgium 27/H7
Verwoerd, Hendrik (dam), S. Africa 118/D6
Verwood, Sask. 181/F6
Vesava, India 68/B7
Vesdre (riv.), Belgium 27/H7
Veseleyville, N. Dak. (†58237) 282/R3
Veseli, Minn. (55086) 255/E6
Veselí nad Lužnicí, Czech. 41/C2
Veselí nad Moravou, Czech. 41/D2
Vesoul, France 28/F4
Vesper, Kansas (†67455) 232/D2
Vesper, Sask. 181/D5
Vesper, Wis. (54489) 317/F7
Vesta, C. Rica 154/F6
Vesta, Minn. (56292) 255/C6
Vesta, Va. (24177) 307/H7
Vestaburg, Mich. (48891) 250/E5
Vest-Agder (co.), Norway 18/E7
Vestal○, N.Y. (13850) 276/H6
Vestavia Hills, Ala. (35216) 195/E4
Vesterålen (isls.), Norway 7/F2
Vesterålen (isls.), Norway 18/J2
Vester Skerninge, Denmark 21/D7
Vestervig, Denmark 21/B4
Vestfjord (fjord), Norway 18/H3
Vestfjorden (fjord), Norway 7/F2
Vestfold (co.), Norway 18/G7
Vestmannaeyjar, Iceland 7/C2
Vestmannaeyjar, Iceland 21/B2
Vestsjaelland (co.), Denmark 21/E6
Vestvågøya (isl.), Norway 18/H3
Vesuvius (vol.), Italy 34/E4
Vesuvius, Va. (24483) 307/K5
Veszprém (co.), Hungary 41/D3
Veszprém, Hungary 41/D3
Vésztő, Hungary 41/F3
Vetal, S. Dak. (57575) 298/G7
Veteran, Alberta 182/E3
Veteran, Wyo. (82243) 319/H4
Vetlanda, Sweden 18/J8
Vetluga (riv.), U.S.S.R. 52/G3
Veurne, Belgium 27/B6
Vevay, Ind. (47043) 227/G7
Vevey, Switzerland 39/C4
Vex, Switzerland 39/D4
Veyo, Utah (†84722) 304/A6
Veys, Iran 66/F5
Veytaux, Switzerland 39/C4
Vezirköprü, Turkey 63/F2
Viacha, Bolivia 120/C4
Viacha, Bolivia 136/A5
Viadana, Italy 34/C2
Viale, Argentina 143/F5
Vian, Okla. (74962) 288/S4
Viana, Brazil 132/E3
Viana del Bollo, Spain 33/C1
Viana do Alentejo, Spain 33/C3
Viana do Castelo, Portugal 33/B2
Vianden, Luxembourg 27/J9
Vianen, Netherlands 27/G5
Viangchan (Vientiane), Laos 72/D3
Viangphoukha, Laos 72/D2
Viano do Castelo (dist.), Portugal 33/B2
Viareggio, Italy 34/C3
Vibank, Sask. 181/H5
Vibbard, Mo. (†64062) 261/D4
Viborg (co.), Denmark 21/C4
Viborg, Denmark 18/F8
Viborg, Denmark 21/C5
Viborg, S. Dak. (57070) 298/P7
Vibo Valentia, Italy 34/F5
Viburnum, Mo. (65566) 261/K7
Viby, Denmark 21/F6
Vicálvaro, Spain 33/G4
Vicam, Mexico 150/D3
Vicco, Ky. (41773) 237/P6
Vicente Guerrero, Baja California, Mexico 150/A1
Vicente Guerrero, Durango, Mexico 150/G5
Vicente López, Argentina 143/G7
Vicenza (prov.), Italy 34/C2
Vicenza, Italy 34/C2
Viceroy, Sask. 181/F6
Vich, Spain 33/H2
Vichacla, Bolivia 136/C7
Vichada (comm.), Colombia 126/F5
Vichada (riv.), Colombia 126/F5
Vichadero, Uruguay 145/E2
Vichaya, Bolivia 136/A5
Viche, Ecuador 128/C2
Vichuga, U.S.S.R. 52/F3
Vichy, France 28/E4
Vichy, Mo. (65580) 261/J6
Vici, Okla. (73859) 288/H2
Vick, Ark. (†71648) 202/F7
Vick, La. (71372) 238/F4
Vickers (lake), Manitoba 179/F3
Vickery, Ohio (43464) 284/D3
Vicksburg, Ariz. (†85348) 198/B5
Vicksburg, Ind. (†47441) 227/C6
Vicksburg, Mich. (49097) 250/D6
Vicksburg, Miss. 188/H4
Vicksburg, Miss. (39180) 256/C6
Vicksburg Nat'l Mil. Park, Miss. 256/C6
Viçosa, Brazil 135/E2
Viçosa, Brazil 132/G5
Vicosoprano, Switzerland 39/J4
Vicovaro, Italy 34/F6
Victoire, Sask. 181/D2
Victor, Calif. (95253) 204/C9
Victor, Colo. (80860) 208/J5
Victor, Idaho (83455) 220/G6
Victor, Iowa (52347) 229/J5
Victor, Mont. (59875) 262/B4
Victor, N.Y. (14564) 276/F5
Victor, S. Dak. (†57260) 298/R2
Victor, W. Va. (25938) 312/D6
Victor Harbor, S. Australia 88/F7
Victor Harbor, S. Australia 94/F6
Victoria 88/G7
Victoria (lake) 2/L6
Victoria (lake) 102/F5
Victoria (Mosi-Oa-Tunya) (falls) 102/E6
Victoria, Argentina 143/F6
Victoria, Ark. (72388) 202/K2
Victoria (state), Australia 87/E9
Victoria (cap.), Br. Col. 146/F5
Victoria (cap.), Br. Col. 162/D6
Victoria (cap.), Br. Col. 184/K4
Victoria (mt.), Burma 72/B2
Victoria (Limbe), Cameroon 115/A3
Victoria (isl.), Canada 2/D2
Victoria (isl.), Canada 4/B15
Victoria, Malleco, Chile 138/D2
Victoria, Tarapacá, Chile 138/A3
Victoria, Grenada 161/D8
Victoria, Guinea 106/B6
Victoria, Ill. (61485) 222/C2
Victoria, Kansas (67671) 232/C3
Victoria (lake), Kenya 115/F4
Victoria, Malta 34/E6
Victoria, Minn. (55386) 255/F6
Victoria, Miss. (38679) 256/E1
Victoria, Mo. (†63020) 261/M6
Victoria (co.), New Bruns. 170/C1
Victoria, Newf. 166/D2
Victoria (lake), Newf. 166/C4
Victoria (lake), N.S. Wales 97/A3
Victoria (riv.), North. Terr. 88/E3
Victoria (riv.), North. Terr. 93/B3
Victoria (isl.), N.W.T. 146/G2
Victoria (isl.), N.W.T. 162/E1
Victoria (isl.), N.W. Terrs. 187/G2
Victoria (str.), N.W.T. 162/F2
Victoria (str.), N.W. Terrs. 187/H3
Victoria (co.), Nova Scotia 168/H2
Victoria (county), Ontario 177/F3
Victoria (lake), Ontario 177/F2
Victoria (peaks), Philippines 82/B6
Victoria, Pr. Edward I. 168/E2
Victoria (cap.), Seychelles 118/H5
Victoria (lake), Tanzania 115/F4
Victoria, Tenn. (†37397) 237/K10
Victoria (co.), Texas 303/H9
Victoria, Texas 188/G5
Victoria, Texas (77901) 303/H9
Victoria (lake), Uganda 115/F4
VICTORIA 97
Victoria, Va. (23974) 307/M6
Victoria (falls), Zambia 115/E7
Victoria (falls), Zimbabwe 118/C3
Victoria Beach, Manitoba 179/F4
Victoria Beach, Nova Scotia 168/C4
Victoria de las Tunas, Cuba 158/H3
Victoria Harbour, Ontario 177/E3

Wamic 465

Vordingborg, Denmark 21/E7
Vordingborg, Denmark 18/G9
Vorgod (riv.), Denmark 21/B6
Vorkuta, U.S.S.R. 4/C6
Vorkuta, U.S.S.R. 7/L2
Vorkuta, U.S.S.R. 52/K1
Vorkuta, U.S.S.R. 48/G3
Vormsi (isl.), U.S.S.R. 53/B1
Vorona (riv.), U.S.S.R. 52/F4
Voronezh, U.S.S.R. 7/H3
Voronezh, U.S.S.R. 52/E4
Voronezh, U.S.S.R. 48/E4
Voroshilovgrad, U.S.S.R. 7/H4
Voroshilovgrad, U.S.S.R. 52/E5
Voroshilovgrad, U.S.S.R. 48/E5
Vorskla (riv.), U.S.S.R. 52/E4
Vorst (Forest), Belgium 27/B9
Võrtsjärv (lake), U.S.S.R. 53/D1
Võru, U.S.S.R. 52/C2
Võru, U.S.S.R. 53/D2
Vosges (dept.), France 28/G3
Vosges (mts.), France 28/G3
Voskresensk, U.S.S.R. 52/E3
Voss, N. Dak. (58280) 282/R3
Voss, Norway 18/E6
Vossburg, Miss. (39366) 256/F7
Vostochnyy, U.S.S.R. 48/O5
Vostok (isl.), Kiribati 2/B6
Vostok (isl.), Kiribati 87/L7
Votamo (riv.), Venezuela 124/F6
Votice, Czech. 41/C2
Votkinsk, U.S.S.R. 48/F4
Votkinsk, U.S.S.R. 52/H3
Votuporanga, Brazil 135/B2
Vouvry, Switzerland 39/C4
Voúxa (cape), Greece 45/F8
Vouziers, France 28/F3
Voyageurs Nat'l Park, Minn. 255/F2
Voy-Vozh, U.S.S.R. 48/F3
Voy-Vozh, U.S.S.R. 52/H2
Vozhe (lake), U.S.S.R. 52/F2
Vozhega, U.S.S.R. 52/F2
Vozhma, U.S.S.R. 52/G3
Voznesensk, U.S.S.R. 52/D5
Vrå, Denmark 21/C3
Vráble, Czech. 41/E2
Vracov, Czech. 41/D2
Vrangelya (isl.), U.S.S.R. 54/U2
Vranje, Yugoslavia 45/F4
Vranov nad Teplou, Czech. 41/F2
Vratsa, Bulgaria 45/F4
Vrbas, Yugoslavia 45/D3
Vrbas (riv.), Yugoslavia 45/C3
Vrbno pod Pradědem, Czech. 41/D1
Vrbovce, Czech. 41/D1
Vrbové, Czech. 41/D2
Vrchlabí, Czech. 41/C1
Vrede, S. Africa 118/D5
Vredenburg, S. Africa 118/B6
Vredenburgh, Ala. (36481) 195/D7
Vredendal, S. Africa 118/B6
Vreed-en-Hoop, Guyana 131/B2
Vresse-sur-Semois, Belgium 27/F9
Vriezenveen, Netherlands 27/K4
Vrondádhes, Greece 45/G6
Vršac, Yugoslavia 45/E3
Vrútky, Czech. 41/E2
Vryburg, S. Africa 118/C5
Vryheid, S. Africa 118/E5
Vsetín, Czech. 41/D2
Vsevidof (mt.), Alaska 196/E4
Vuadens, Switzerland 39/C3
Vučitrn, Yugoslavia 45/E4
Vught, Netherlands 27/G5
Vukovar, Yugoslavia 45/D3
Vulcan, Alberta 182/D4
Vulcan, Mich. (49892) 250/B3
Vulcan, Mo. (63675) 261/L8
Vulcan, W. Va. (25697) 312/B7
Vulcano (isl.), Italy 34/E5
Vu Liet, Vietnam 72/E3
Vung Tau, Vietnam 72/E5
Vuollerim, Sweden 18/M3
Vuolvojaure (lake), Sweden 18/L3
Vuotso, Finland 18/P2
Vya, Nev. (†96104) 266/B1
Vyatka (riv.), U.S.S.R. 52/H3
Vyatskiye Polyany, U.S.S.R. 52/H3
Vyazemskiy, U.S.S.R. 48/O5
Vyaz'ma, U.S.S.R. 52/D3
Vyborg, U.S.S.R. 7/G2
Vyborg, U.S.S.R. 52/C2
Vyborg, U.S.S.R. 48/C3
Vychegda (riv.), U.S.S.R. 52/G2
Východočeský (reg.), Czech. 41/C1
Východoslovenský (reg.), Czech. 41/F2
Vyg (lake), U.S.S.R. 52/E2
Vyksa, U.S.S.R. 52/F3
Vym' (riv.), U.S.S.R. 52/H2
Vyshniy Volochek, U.S.S.R. 7/H2
Vyshniy Volochek, U.S.S.R. 52/D3
Vyshniy Volochek, U.S.S.R. 48/D4
Vyškov, Czech. 41/D2
Vysoké Mýto, Czech. 41/D2
Vysoké Tatry, Czech. 41/F2
Vyšší Brod, Czech. 41/C2
Vytegra, U.S.S.R. 52/E2

W

Wa, Ghana 106/D6
Waal (riv.), Netherlands 27/G5
Waalre, Netherlands 27/G6
Waalwijk, Netherlands 27/G5
Waarschoot, Belgium 27/D6
Waas (mt.), Utah 304/E5
Waasis, New Bruns. 170/D3
Wabamun, Alberta 182/C3
Waban, Mass. (†02168) 249/B7
Wabana, Newf. 166/D2
Wabaningo, Mich. (49463) 250/C5
Wabasca, Alberta 182/D2
Wabasca (riv.), Alberta 182/C1
Wabasca (riv.), Alta. 162/E4
Wabash (riv.) 188/J3
Wabash, Ark. (72389) 202/J5
Wabash (co.), Ill. 222/F5
Wabash (riv.), Ill. 222/F5
Wabash (co.), Ind. 227/F3
Wabash, Ind. (46992) 227/F3
Wabash (riv.), Ind. 227/B7
Wabash, Ohio (†45822) 284/A4
Wabash (riv.), Ohio 284/A5
Wabasha (co.), Minn. 255/F6
Wabasha, Minn. (55981) 255/G6
Wabasso, Fla. (32970) 212/F4
Wabasso, Minn. (56293) 255/C6
Wabatawangang (lake), Minn. 255/D3
Wabaunsee (co.), Kansas 232/F3
Wabaunsee, Kansas (†66547) 232/F2
Wabbaseka, Ark. (72175) 202/G5
Wabeno, Wis. (54566) 317/J5
Wabi (riv.), Ethiopia 111/H6
Wabigoon, Ontario 175/B3
Wabigoon, Ontario 177/G5
Wabi Shebelle (riv.) 102/G4
Wabi Shebelle (riv.), Ethiopia 111/H6
Wabowden, Manitoba 179/J3
Wąbrzeźno, Poland 47/D2
Wabuk (pt.), Ontario 175/D1
Wabush, Newf. 166/A3
Wabush, Newf. 162/K5
Wabuska, Nev. (†89447) 266/B3
Waccamaw (lake), N.C. 281/N6
Waccamaw (riv.), N.C. 281/M7
Waccamaw (riv.), S.C. 296/J5
Waccasassa (bay), Fla. 212/D2
Waccasassa (riv.), Fla. 212/D2
Wachapreague, Va. (23480) 307/S5
Wachapreague (inlet), Va. 307/T6
Wachtebeke, Belgium 27/D6
Wachusett (mt.), Mass. 249/G3
Wachusett (res.), Mass. 249/G3
Wacissa, Fla. (32361) 212/B1
Waco, Georgia (30182) 217/B3
Waco, Ky. (40385) 237/N5
Waco, Mo. (63869) 261/C8
Waco, Nebr. (68460) 264/G4
Waco, N.C. (28169) 281/G4
Waco, Texas 188/G4
Waco, Texas 146/J6
Waco, Texas (*76701) 303/G6
Waconda (lake), Kansas 232/D2
Waconia, Minn. (55387) 255/E6
Wadai (reg.), Chad 111/D5
Waddamana, Tasmania 99/C4
Waddan, Libya 102/D2
Waddan, Libya 111/C2
Waddell, Ariz. (85355) 198/C5
Waddenzee (sound), Netherlands 27/G2
Waddington (mt.), Br. Col. 162/D5
Waddington (mt.), Br. Col. 184/E4
Waddington, N.Y. (13694) 276/K1
Waddy, Ky. (40076) 237/L4
Wade, Miss. (†39567) 256/G9
Wade (lake), Newf. 166/A3
Wade, N.C. (28395) 281/M4
Wade, Okla. (†74723) 288/O7
Wadebridge, England 13/C7
Wade-Hampton, S.C. (†29607) 296/C2
Wadena, Ind. (†47944) 227/C3
Wadena, Iowa (52169) 229/K3
Wadena (co.), Minn. 255/D4
Wadena, Minn. (56482) 255/C4
Wadena, Sask. 181/H4
Wädenswil, Switzerland 39/G2
Wadesboro, La. (†70454) 238/M2
Wadesboro, N.C. (28170) 281/J5
Wadestown, W. Va. (26589) 312/F3
Wadesville, Ind. (47638) 227/B8
Wadeville, N.C. (†27306) 281/J4
Wadhams, N.Y. (12990) 276/N2
Wadi Dra, Morocco 102/B2
Wadi es Sir, Jordan 65/D4
Wadi Halfa, Sudan 111/F3
Wadi Musa, Jordan 65/E5
Wading (riv.), N.J. 273/D4
Wading River, N.Y. (11792) 276/P9
Wadley, Ala. (36276) 195/G4
Wadley, Georgia (30477) 217/H5
Wadmalaw (isl.), S.C. 296/G6
Wad Medani, Sudan 111/F5
Wad Medani, Sudan 59/B7
Wad Medani, Sudan 102/F3
Wadowice, Poland 47/D4
Wadsworth, Ala. (†36022) 195/E5
Wadsworth, Ill. (60083) 222/B4
Wadsworth, Nev. (89442) 266/B3
Wadsworth, Ohio (44281) 284/G3
Wadsworth, Texas (77483) 303/J9
Waelder, Texas (78959) 303/G8
Wagait Aboriginal Res., North. Terr. 93/B2
Wagarville, Ala. (36585) 195/B8
Wagener, S.C. (29164) 296/E4
Wageningen, Netherlands 27/H5
Wageningen, Suriname 131/C3
Wager (bay), N.W.T. 146/J3
Wager (bay), N.W.T. 162/G2
Wager (bay), N.W. Terrs. 187/K3
Wagga Wagga, Australia 87/E9
Wagga Wagga, N. S. Wales 88/H7
Wagga Wagga, N.S. Wales 97/D4
Waggoner, Ill. (62572) 222/D4
Waggrakine, W. Australia 92/A5
Wagin, W. Australia 88/B6
Wagin, W. Australia 92/B2
Wagner, Alberta 182/C2
Wagner, Mont. (59543) 262/H2
Wagner, S. Dak. (57380) 298/N7
Wagoner (co.), Okla. 288/P3
Wagoner, Okla. (74467) 288/R3
Wagon Mound, N. Mex. (87752) 274/E2
Wagontire, Oreg. (†97720) 291/H4
Wagon Wheel Gap, Colo. (†81130) 208/F7
Wagram, N.C. (28396) 281/L5
Wągrowiec, Poland 47/C2
Wah, Pakistan 68/C2
Wahai, Indonesia 85/H6
Wahalak, Miss. (†39358) 256/G5
Wahiawa, Hawaii (96786) 218/E2
Wahiawa, Hawaii 188/F5
Wahkiacus, Wash. (98670) 310/D5
Wahkiakum (co.), Wash. 310/B4
Wahkon, Minn. (56386) 255/E4
Wahlern, Switzerland 39/D3
Wahoo, Nebr. (68066) 264/H3
Wahpeton, Iowa (†51360) 229/C2
Wahpeton, N. Dak. 188/G1
Wahpeton, N. Dak. (58075) 282/S7
Wahsatch, Utah (†82930) 304/C2
Wah Wah (mts.), Utah 304/A5
Wahwashkesh (lake), Ontario 177/D2
Wahweap (creek), Utah 304/C6
Wai, Poulo (isls.), Vietnam 72/E4
Waiakoa, Hawaii (†96788) 218/J2
Waialae, Hawaii (96816) 218/D4
Waialeale (mt.), Hawaii 218/C1
Waialee, Hawaii (†96731) 218/E1
Waialua, Hawaii 188/F5
Waialua, Molokai, Hawaii (†96748) 218/H1
Waialua, Oahu, Hawaii (96791) 218/E1
Waianae, Hawaii (96792) 218/D2
Waiau, N. Zealand 100/D5
Waiau (riv.), N. Zealand 100/A6
Waidhofen an der Thaya, Austria 41/C2
Waidhofen an der Ybbs, Austria 41/C3
Waidsboro, Va. (†24088) 307/J7
Waigama, Indonesia 85/H6
Waigeo (isl.), Indonesia 85/J5
Waihee, Hawaii (†96793) 218/J2
Waiheke (isl.), N. Zealand 100/E2
Waihi, N. Zealand 100/E2
Waikabubak, Indonesia 85/F7
Waikanae, N. Zealand 100/E4
Waikane, Hawaii (†96744) 218/F2
Waikapu, Hawaii (†96793) 218/J2
Waikaremoana (lake), N. Zealand 100/F3
Waikari, N. Zealand 100/D5
Waikato (riv.), N. Zealand 100/E2
Waikawa, N. Zealand 100/B7
Waikerie, S. Australia 94/F6
Waikiki, Hawaii (†96743) 218/H4
Waikiki (canton), Hawaii (96815) 218/C4
Waikiki (beach), Hawaii 218/C4
Waikouaiti, N. Zealand 100/C6
Wailau, Hawaii (†96748) 218/H1
Wailea, Hawaii (†96710) 218/J4
Wailea, Maui, Hawaii (†96790) 218/J2
Wailua, Hawaii (†96746) 218/D2
Wailuku, Hawaii (96793) 218/J2
Wailuku, Hawaii 188/F5
Wailuku (riv.), Hawaii 218/J5
Waimakariri (riv.), N. Zealand 100/D5
Waimalu, Hawaii (†96701) 218/B3
Waimanalo, Hawaii (96795) 218/F2
Waimanalo Bch., Hawaii (†96795) 218/F2
Waimangaroa, N. Zealand 100/C4
Waimate, N. Zealand 100/C6
Waimea (Kamuela), Hawaii, (†96743) 218/G3
Waimea, Kauai, Hawaii (96796) 218/B2
Waimea, Oahu, Hawaii (†96712) 218/E1
Waimea (bay), Hawaii 218/B2
Waimea (riv.), Hawaii 218/C2
Waimes, Belgium 27/J8
Wainaku, Hawaii (†96720) 218/J5
Wainfleet, Ontario 177/E4
Wainfleet All Saints, England 13/H4
Waingapu, Indonesia 85/G7
Waini (riv.), Guyana 131/B2
Wainiha, Hawaii (†96714) 218/C1
Wainiha (riv.), Hawaii 218/C1
Wainuiomata, N. Zealand 100/B3
Wainui-o-mata (riv.), N. Zealand 100/B3
Wainwright, Alaska (99782) 196/F1
Wainwright, Alberta 182/E3
Wainwright, Ohio (44686) 284/G5
Wainwright, Okla. (74468) 288/R3
Wainwright, U.S. 4/B18
Waiohinu, Hawaii (†96772) 218/G7
Waipa (riv.), N. Zealand 100/E2
Waipahu, Hawaii 188/F5
Waipahu, Hawaii (96797) 218/A3
Waipara, N. Zealand 100/D5
Waipawa, N. Zealand 100/F3
Waipio, Hawaii (†96758) 218/H3
Waipio (bay), Hawaii 218/H3
Waipio (pen.), Hawaii 218/A3
Waipio (pt.), Hawaii 218/A4
Waipio Acres, Hawaii (†96786) 218/E2
Waipiro Bay, N. Zealand 100/G3
Waipukurau, N. Zealand 100/F4
Wairau (riv.), N. Zealand 100/D4
Wairoa, N. Zealand 100/F3
Wairoa (riv.), N. Zealand 100/E1
Waitakere, N. Zealand 100/B1
Waitakere (range), N. Zealand 100/A1
Waitaki (riv.), N. Zealand 100/C6
Waitangi, N. Zealand 100/D7
Waitara, N. Zealand 100/E3
Waite○, Maine (04492) 243/H5
Waite Hill, Ohio (†44094) 284/H2
Waitemata (harb.), N. Zealand 100/B1
Waite Park, Minn. (56387) 255/D5
Waiteville, W. Va. (24984) 312/F8
Waitotara, N. Zealand 100/E3
Waits (riv.), Vt. 268/C3
Waitsburg, Wash. (99361) 310/G4
Waitsfield○, Vt. (05673) 268/B3
Waits River, Vt. (†05076) 268/C3
Waitville, Sask. 181/F3
Waiuku, N. Zealand 100/E2
Waiyevu, Fiji 86/R10
Wajabula, Indonesia 85/H5
Wajima, Japan 81/H5
Wajir, Kenya 115/H3
Wajir, Kenya 102/F4
Waka, Ethiopia 111/G6
Waka, Texas (79093) 303/D1
Waka, Zaire 115/D3
Wakarusa, Ind. (46573) 227/F1
Wakarusa, Kansas (66546) 232/G3
Wakasa, Japan 81/G6
Wakasa (bay), Japan 81/G6
Wakatipu (lake), N. Zealand 100/B6
Wakaw, Sask. 181/F3
Wakaw Lake, Sask. 181/F3
Wakayama (pref.), Japan 81/G6
Wakayama, Japan 54/P6
Wakayama, Japan 81/G6
Wakde (isl.), Indonesia 85/K6
Wake (co.), N.C. 281/M3
Wake (isl.), Pacific 87/G4
WaKeeney, Kansas (67672) 232/C2
Wakefield, England 10/F4
Wakefield, England 13/J2
Wakefield, Kansas (67487) 232/E2
Wakefield, La. (70784) 238/H5
Wakefield○, Mass. (01880) 249/C5
Wakefield, Mich. (49968) 250/F2
Wakefield, Nebr. (68784) 264/H2
Wakefield○, N.H. (†03872) 268/F4
Wakefield, Ohio (45687) 284/E8
Wakefield, Va. (23888) 307/O7
Wakefield-Peace Dale, R.I. (*02879) 249/J7
Wake Forest, N.C. (27587) 281/M3
Wakema, Burma 72/B3
Wakeman, Ohio (44889) 284/F3
Wakenda, Mo. (64687) 261/F4
Wake Village, Texas (75501) 303/K4
Wakita, Okla. (73771) 288/L1
Wakkanai, Japan 81/K1
Wakonda, S. Dak. (57073) 298/P7
Wakool, N.S. Wales 97/C4
Wakopa, Manitoba 179/C5
Wakpala, S. Dak. (57658) 298/H2
Wakulla (co.), Fla. 212/B1
Wakulla, Fla. (†32327) 212/B1
Wakwekobi (lake), Ontario 177/A1
Wala, Kuh-i- (mt.), Afghanistan 59/H3
Walbridge, Ohio (43465) 284/C2
Wałbrzych (prov.), Poland 47/C3
Wałbrzych, Poland 47/C3
Walcha, N.S. Wales 97/F2
Walchensee (lake), W. Germany 22/D5
Walcheren (isl.), Netherlands 27/C5
Walcott, Ark. (72474) 202/J1
Walcott, Br. Col. 184/D3
Walcott (lake), Idaho 220/E7
Walcott, Iowa (52773) 229/M5
Walcott, N. Dak. (58077) 282/R6
Walcott, Wyo. (82335) 319/F4
Walcourt, Belgium 27/F8
Wałcz, Poland 47/C2
Wald, Switzerland 39/G2
Waldeck, Sask. 181/D5
Walden, Colo. (80480) 208/G1
Walden, Georgia (†31201) 217/E5
Walden, Ky. (40768) 237/N7
Walden (pond), Mass. 249/A6
Walden, N.Y. (12586) 276/M7
Walden, Ontario 175/D3
Walden, Ontario 177/J5
Walden, Tenn. (†37377) 237/L10
Walden○, Vt. (†05873) 268/C3
Waldenburg, Ark. (72475) 202/J2
Waldenburg (Wałbrzych), Poland 47/C3
Waldenburg, Switzerland 39/E2
Walden Heights, Vt. (†05873) 268/C3
Waldersee, Manitoba 179/D4
Waldheim, E. Germany 22/E3
Waldheim, La. (†70433) 238/L5
Waldheim, Sask. 181/E3
Waldia, Ethiopia 111/G5
Waldkirch, Switzerland 39/H2
Waldkirch, W. Germany 22/B4
Waldkraiburg, W. Germany 22/E4
Waldo, Ala. (†35150) 195/F4
Waldo, Ark. (71770) 202/D7
Waldo, Br. Col. 184/K5
Waldo, Fla. (32694) 212/D2
Waldo, Kansas (67673) 232/D2
Waldo (co.), Maine 243/E6
Waldo○, Maine (†04915) 243/E7
Waldo, Ohio (43356) 284/D5
Waldo (lake), Oreg. 291/E4
Waldo, Wis. (53093) 317/L8
Waldoboro, Maine (04572) 243/E7
Waldoboro○, Maine (04572) 243/E7
Waldorf, Md. (20601) 245/L6
Waldorf, Minn. (56091) 255/E7
Waldport, Oreg. (97394) 291/C3
Waldron, Ark. (72958) 202/B4
Waldron, Ind. (46182) 227/F6
Waldron, Kansas (67150) 232/D4
Waldron, Mich. (49288) 250/E7
Waldron, Mo. (64092) 261/O5
Waldron, Sask. 181/J5
Waldron, Wash. (98297) 310/B2
Waldrup, Miss. (†39422) 256/F7
Waldsassen, W. Germany 22/E3
Waldshut-Tiengen, W. Germany 22/C5
Waldwick, N.J. (07463) 273/B1
Waldwick, Wis. (†53565) 317/G10
Walensee (lake), Switzerland 39/H2
Walenstadt, Switzerland 39/H2
Wales, Alaska (99783) 196/E1
Wales, Alaska 188/C5
Wales○, Mass. (01081) 249/F4
Wales, Minn. (†55616) 255/G3
Wales, N. Dak. (58281) 282/N2
Wales (isl.), N.W. Terrs. 187/K3
Wales, Tenn. (†38478) 237/G10
Wales, U.K. 7/D3
Wales, Utah (84667) 304/C4
WALES 13
WALES, Wales 10/E4
Wales, Wis. (53183) 317/J1
Walesboro, Ind. (†47201) 227/F6
Waleska, Georgia (30183) 217/D2
Walford, Iowa (52351) 229/K5
Walford, Ontario 177/B1
Walgett, N. S. Wales 88/H6
Walgett, N.S. Wales 97/E2
Walgreen Coast (reg.) 5/B13
Walhachin, Br. Col. 184/G5
Walhalla, Mich. (49458) 250/C5
Walhalla, N. Dak. (58282) 282/P2
Walhalla, S.C. (29691) 296/A2
Walhonding, Ohio (43843) 284/F5
Walikale, Zaire 115/E4
Walker (co.), Ala. 195/D3
Walker (creek), Ariz. 198/F2
Walker (mt.), Ark. 202/E2
Walker (co.), Georgia 217/B1
Walker, Iowa (52352) 229/K4
Walker, Kansas (67674) 232/C3
Walker, Ky. (40997) 237/O7
Walker, La. (70785) 238/L1
Walker, Mich. (49504) 250/D6
Walker, Minn. (56484) 255/D3
Walker, Mo. (64790) 261/D7
Walker (lake), Nev. 188/C3
Walker (lake), Nev. 266/C4
Walker (riv.), Nev. 266/C3
Walker, N.Y. (†14468) 276/E4
Walker (bay), N.W. Terrs. 187/G2
Walker, Oreg. (†97426) 291/D4
Walker, S. Dak. (57659) 298/G2
Walker (isl.), Tasmania 99/B2
Walker (co.), Texas 303/J7
Walker (creek), Va. 307/F6
Walker, W. Va. (26180) 312/D4
Walkerburn, Scotland 15/F5
Walker Mill, Md. (†20023) 245/F5
Walker River Ind. Res., Nev. 266/C3
Walker Springs, Ala. (36586) 195/C7
Walkerston, Queensland 88/H4
Walkerston, Queensland 95/D4
Walkersville, Md. (21793) 245/J3
Walkersville, W. Va. (26447) 312/F5
Walkerton, Ind. (46574) 227/E2
Walkerton, Ontario 177/C3
Walkerton, Va. (23177) 307/O5
Walkertown, N.C. (27051) 281/J2
Walkerville, Mich. (49459) 250/C5
Walkerville, Mont. (59701) 262/D4
Walkerville, S. Australia 88/E8
Wall○, N.J. (07719) 273/E3
Wall, Pa. (†15148) 294/C5
Wall, S. Dak. (57790) 298/E6
Wall, Texas (76957) 303/D6
Wallace, Ala. (†36426) 195/D8
Wallace (mt.), Alberta 182/C2
Wallace, Calif. (95254) 204/C9
Wallace, Idaho (83873) 220/C2
Wallace, Ind. (47988) 227/C5
Wallace (co.), Kansas 232/A3
Wallace, Kansas (67761) 232/A3
Wallace, La. (†70049) 238/M3
Wallace (lake), La. 238/C2
Wallace, Mich. (49893) 250/B3
Wallace, Nebr. (69169) 264/C4
Wallace, N.Y. (14890) 276/E6
Wallace, N.C. (28466) 281/N5
Wallace, Nova Scotia 168/E3
Wallace (harb.), Nova Scotia 168/E3
Wallace, S.C. (29596) 296/H2
Wallace, S. Dak. (57272) 298/P3
Wallace, W. Va. (26448) 312/E4
Wallaceburg, Ontario 177/B5
Wallace Lake, Manitoba 179/G3
Wallaceton, Pa. (16876) 294/F4
Wallacetown, Ontario 177/C5
Wallaga (prov.), Ethiopia 111/G6
Wallal Station, W. Australia 92/C2
Walland, Tenn. (37886) 237/O9
Wallaroo, S. Australia 94/E5
Wallasey, England 13/G2
Wallasey, England 10/F2
Walla Walla, N.S. Wales 97/D4
Walla Walla (riv.), Oreg. 291/J1
Walla Walla, Wash. 188/C1
Walla Walla (co.), Wash. 310/G4
Walla Walla, Wash. (99362) 310/G4
Walla Walla (riv.), Wash. 310/G4
Wallback, W. Va. (25285) 312/D5
Wallburg, N.C. (27373) 281/J3
Walldürn, W. Germany 22/C4
Walled Lake, Mich. (48088) 250/F6
Wallen, Ind. (†46802) 227/G2
Wallendbeen, N.S. Wales 97/E4
Wallenpaupack (lake), Pa. 294/M3
Waller (co.), Texas 303/J8
Wallerawang, N.S. Wales 97/F3
Wallerville, Miss. (†38652) 256/G2
Wallibu, St. Vin. & Grens. 161/A8
Walling, Tenn. (38587) 237/K9
Wallingford, Conn. (06492) 210/D3
Wallingford○, Conn. (06492) 210/D3
Wallingford, England 13/F6
Wallingford, Iowa (51365) 229/D2
Wallingford, Ky. (41093) 237/O4
Wallingford, Pa. (19086) 294/L7
Wallingford, Vt. (05773) 268/B5
Wallingford○, Vt. (05773) 268/B5
Wallington, N.J. (07057) 273/B2
Wallins Creek, Ky. (40873) 237/O7
Wallis (lake), N.S. Wales 97/G3
Wallis, Texas (77485) 303/H8
Wallis (isls.), Wallis and Futuna 87/J7
Wallis and Futuna 87/J7
Wallisellen, Switzerland 39/G2
Wallisville, Texas (77597) 303/L1
Wallkill (riv.), N.J. 273/D1
Wallkill, N.Y. (12589) 276/M7
Wallkill (riv.), N.Y. 276/L8
Wall Lake, Iowa (51466) 229/C4
Wallo (prov.), Ethiopia 111/H5
Wallonia, Ky. (†42405) 237/F7
Walloon (lake), Mich. 250/E3
Walloon Lake, Mich. (49796) 250/E3
Wallops (isl.), Va. 307/T5
Wallowa (co.), Oreg. 291/K2
Wallowa, Oreg. (97885) 291/K2
Wallowa (mts.), Oreg. 291/K2
Wallowa (riv.), Oreg. 291/K2
Wallpack Center, N.J. (07881) 273/D1
Walls, Miss. (38680) 256/D1
Walls, Scotland 15/G2
Wallsburg, Utah (84082) 304/C3
Wallsend, England 13/J3
Wallula (lake), Oreg. 291/H1
Wallula, Wash. (99363) 310/G4
Wallula (lake), Wash. 310/F4
Walney, Isle of (isl.), England 13/D3
Walney, Isle of (isl.), England 10/E3
Walnut, Calif. (91789) 204/D10
Walnut (creek), Calif. 204/K1
Walnut, Ill. (61376) 222/D2
Walnut, Iowa (51577) 229/C6
Walnut, Kansas (66780) 232/G4
Walnut (creek), Kansas 232/B3
Walnut (riv.), Kansas 232/E4
Walnut, Miss. (38683) 256/G1
Walnut, N.C. (28753) 281/D3
Walnut, Pa. (†17082) 294/G4
Walnut (creek), Texas 303/F3
Walnut Bottom, Pa. (17266) 294/H5
Walnut Canyon Nat'l Mon., Ariz. 198/D3
Walnut Cove, N.C. (27052) 281/J2
Walnut Creek, Calif. (*94595) 204/K2
Walnut Creek, N.C. (†27530) 281/O4
Walnut Creek, Ohio (44687) 284/G4
Walnut Grove, Ala. (35990) 195/F2
Walnut Grove, Calif. (95690) 204/B9
Walnut Grove, Georgia (†30209) 217/E3
Walnut Grove, Ill. (†61470) 222/C3
Walnut Grove, Ky. (42563) 237/M6
Walnut Grove, Minn. (56180) 255/C6
Walnut Grove, Miss. (39189) 256/F5
Walnut Grove, Mo. (65770) 261/F8
Walnut Hill, Ark. (†71826) 202/C7
Walnut Hill, Fla. (32568) 212/B5
Walnut Hill, Ill. (62893) 222/E5
Walnut Hill, Maine (†04021) 243/C8
Walnutport, Pa. (18088) 294/L4
Walnut Ridge, Ark. (72476) 202/J1
Walnut Springs, Texas (76690) 303/G5
Walpole, Mass. (02081) 249/B8
Walpole○, Mass. (02081) 249/B8
Walpole○, N.H. (03608) 268/C5
Walpole (isl.), Ontario 177/B5
Walpole, Sask. 181/K6
Walpole, W. Australia 92/B6
Walrus (isl.), Alaska 196/E3
Walrus (isls.), Alaska 196/F3
Walsall, England 10/G3
Walsall, England 13/E5
Walsenburg, Colo. (81089) 208/K7
Walsh, Alberta 182/E5
Walsh, Colo. (81090) 208/P8
Walsh (co.), N. Dak. 282/P3
Walsh, Queensland 95/B3
Walshville, Ill. (62091) 222/D4
Walsingham, England 13/H5
Walsingham (cape), N.W.T. 162/K2
Walsingham (cape), N.W. Terrs. 187/M3
Walsrode, W. Germany 22/C2
Walston, Pa. (15781) 294/D4
Walstonburg, N.C. (27888) 281/O3
Walterboro, S.C. (29488) 296/F6
Walter F. George (dam), Ala. 195/H7
Walter F. George (res.), Ala. 195/H7
Walter F. George (dam), Georgia 217/B7
Walter F. George (res.), Georgia 217/B7
Walterhill, Tenn. (†37130) 237/J9
Walter Reed Army Med. Ctr., D.C. 245/E4
Walter Reed Army Med. Ctr. Annex, Md. 245/E4
Walters, La. (71374) 238/G3
Walters, Minn. (56092) 255/E7
Walters, Okla. (73572) 288/K6
Walters Falls, Ontario 177/D3
Waltershausen, E. Germany 22/D3
Waltersville, Ky. (†40312) 237/N5
Waltersville, Miss. (†39180) 256/C6
Walterville, Oreg. (97489) 291/E3
Walthall (co.), Miss. 256/D8
Walthall, Miss. (39771) 256/F3
Waltham○, Maine (†04605) 243/G6
Waltham, Mass. (02154) 249/B6
Waltham, Minn. (55982) 255/F7
Waltham○, Vt. (†05491) 268/A3
Waltham Forest, England 13/H8
Waltham Forest, England 10/B5
Waltham Holy Cross, England 13/H7
Waltham Holy Cross, England 10/B5
Walthill, Nebr. (68067) 264/H2
Walthourville, Georgia (31333) 217/J7
Waltman, Wyo. (†82648) 319/E2
Walton (co.), Fla. 212/C6
Walton, Fla. (†33457) 212/F4
Walton (co.), Georgia 217/E3
Walton, Ind. (46994) 227/E3
Walton, Kansas (67151) 232/E3
Walton, Ky. (41094) 237/M3
Walton, Nebr. (68461) 264/H4
Walton, N.Y. (13856) 276/K6
Walton, Nova Scotia 168/E3
Walton, Ontario 177/C4
Walton, Oreg. (97490) 291/D3
Walton, W. Va. (25286) 312/D5
Walton and Weybridge, England 13/G8
Walton and Weybridge, England 10/B6
Walton Hills, Ohio (†44146) 284/J10
Walton-le-Dale, England 13/G1
Walton-le-Dale, England 10/F1
Waltonville, Ill. (62894) 222/D5
Waltreak, Ark. (†72833) 202/C4
Waltz, Mich. (†48164) 250/F6
Walum, N. Dak. (†58448) 282/O5
Walupt (lake), Wash. 310/D4
Walvis (bay), S. Africa 118/A4
Walvis Bay, S. Africa 2/K7
Walvis Bay, S. Africa 102/D7
Walvis Bay, S. Africa 118/A4
Walworth, N.Y. (14568) 276/F4
Walworth, S. Dak. 298/J3
Walworth (co.), Wis. 317/J10
Walworth, Wis. (53184) 317/J10
Walzenhausen, Switzerland 39/J2
Wamac, Ill. (†62801) 222/D5
Wamba, Kenya 115/G3
Wamba, Nigeria 106/F7
Wamba, Zaire 115/E3
Wamego, Kansas (66547) 232/F2
Wamel, Netherlands 27/H5
Wamena, Indonesia 85/K6
Wamgumbaug (lake), Conn. 210/F1
Wami (riv.), Tanzania 115/G5
Wamic, Oreg. (97063) 291/F2

Westernport 467

Waver (Wavre), Belgium 27/F7
Waverley, Mass. (02179) 249/B6
Waverley, N. S. Wales 88/L4
Waverley, N.S. Wales 97/K3
Waverley, N. Zealand 100/E3
Waverley, Nova Scotia 168/E4
Waverley, Ontario 177/E3
Waverley, Victoria 97/J5
Waverley, Victoria 88/L7
Waverley Downs, N.S. Wales 97/B1
Waverly, Ala. (36879) 195/G5
Waverly, Fla. (33877) 212/E4
Waverly, Georgia (31565) 217/J8
Waverly, Ill. (62692) 222/D4
Waverly, Iowa (50677) 229/J3
Waverly, Kansas (66871) 232/G3
Waverly, Ky. (42462) 237/F5
Waverly, La. (71232) 238/H2
Waverly, Minn. (55390) 255/E5
Waverly, Mo. (64096) 261/E4
Waverly, Nebr. (68462) 264/H4
Waverly, N.Y. (14892) 276/G7
Waverly, Ohio (45690) 284/D7
Waverly, S. Dak. (57202) 298/R3
Waverly, Tenn. (37185) 237/F8
Waverly, Va. (23890) 307/O6
Waverly, Wash. (99039) 310/H3
Waverly, W. Va. (26184) 312/D4
Waverly Hall, Georgia (31831) 217/C5
Waves, N.C. (27982) 281/U3
Wavre, Belgium 27/F7
Wawa (riv.), Nicaragua 154/E3
Wawa, Ontario 175/C3
Wawa, Ontario 177/J5
Wawaka, Ind. (46794) 227/F2
Wawanesa, Manitoba 179/C5
Wawasee, Ind. (†46567) 227/F2
Wawasee (lake), Ind. 227/F2
Wawayanda (lake), N.J. 273/E1
Waweig, New Bruns. 170/C3
Wawina, Minn. (55794) 255/E3
Wawota, Sask. 181/J6
Wawpecong, Ind. (†46901) 227/F3
Wax, Ky. (42787) 237/J6
Waxahachie, Texas (75165) 303/H5
Waxhaw, N.C. (28173) 281/H5
Way, Miss. (†39046) 256/E5
Way (lake), W. Australia 88/C5
Way (lake), W. Australia 92/C4
Wayagamac (lake), Québec 172/E2
Wayan, Idaho (83285) 220/G7
Wayatinah, Tasmania 99/C4
Waycross, Ga. 188/K4
Waycross, Georgia (31501) 217/H8
Wayerton, New Bruns. 170/E1
Wayland, Iowa (52654) 229/K6
Wayland, Ky. (41666) 237/R6
Wayland○, Mass. (01778) 249/A7
Wayland, Mich. (49348) 250/D6
Wayland, Mo. (63472) 261/J2
Wayland, N.Y. (14572) 276/E5
Wayland, Ohio (44285) 284/H3
Waymansville, Ind. (†47201) 227/E6
Waymart, Pa. (18472) 294/M2
Wayne, Ala. (†36763) 195/C6
Wayne, Alberta 182/D4
Wayne (co.), Georgia 217/J7
Wayne (co.), Ill. 222/E5
Wayne, Ill. (60184) 222/E2
Wayne (co.), Ind. 227/G5
Wayne (co.), Iowa 229/G7
Wayne, Kansas (†66930) 232/E2
Wayne (co.), Ky. 237/M7
Wayne, Maine (04284) 243/D7
Wayne○, Maine (04284) 243/D7
Wayne (co.), Mich. 250/F6
Wayne, Mich. (48184) 250/F6
Wayne (co.), Miss. 256/G7
Wayne (co.), Mo. 261/L8
Wayne (co.), Nebr. 264/G2
Wayne, Nebr. (68787) 264/G2
Wayne○, N.J. (07470) 273/A1
Wayne (co.), N.Y. 276/F4
Wayne, N.Y. (14893) 276/F6
Wayne (co.), N.C. 281/N4
Wayne (co.), Ohio 284/G4
Wayne, Ohio (43466) 284/C3
Wayne, Okla. (73095) 288/M5
Wayne (co.), Pa. 294/M2
Wayne, Pa. (19087) 294/M6
Wayne (co.), Tenn. 237/F10
Wayne (co.), Utah 304/C5
Wayne (co.), W. Va. 312/B6
Wayne, W. Va. (25570) 312/B6
Wayne City, Ill. (62895) 222/E5
Waynesboro, Georgia (30830) 217/J4
Waynesboro, Miss. (39367) 256/G7
Waynesboro, Pa. (17268) 294/G6
Waynesboro, Tenn. (38485) 237/F10
Waynesboro (I.C.), Va. (22980) 307/K4
Waynesburg, Ky. (40489) 237/M6
Waynesburg, Ohio (44688) 284/H4
Waynesburg, Pa. (15370) 294/B6
Waynesfield, Ohio (45896) 284/C4
Waynesville, Georgia (31566) 217/J8
Waynesville, Ill. (61778) 222/D3
Waynesville, Ind. (†47201) 227/F6
Waynesville, Mo. (65583) 261/H7
Waynesville, N.C. (28786) 281/D4
Waynesville, Ohio (45068) 284/B6
Waynetown, Ind. (47990) 227/C4
Waynoka, Okla. (73860) 288/J1
Wayside, Georgia (†31032) 217/E4
Wayside, Kansas (†67301) 232/G4
Wayside, Miss. (38780) 256/C4
Wayside, Texas (79094) 303/C3
Wayside, Wis. (†54126) 317/L7
Wayzata, Minn. (55391) 255/G5
Wazirabad, Pakistan 59/K3
We (isl.), Indonesia 85/B4
Wé, New Caled. 86/H4
Weagamow Lake, Ontario 175/B2
Weakley (co.), Tenn. 237/D8
Weald, The (reg.), England 13/H6
Wear (riv.), England 13/F3
Wear (riv.), England 10/F3
Weare○, N.H. (03281) 268/D5
Weare P.O. (North Weare), N.H. (03281) 268/D5
Weatherby, Mo. (64497) 261/D3
Weatherby Lake, Mo. (†64152) 261/O5
Weatherford, Okla. (73096) 288/J4
Weatherford, Texas (76086) 303/G5
Weatherly, Pa. (18255) 294/L4
Weathers, Okla. (†74560) 288/P5
Weathersby, Miss. (†39114) 256/E7
Weatogue, Conn. (06089) 210/D1
Weaubleau, Mo. (65774) 261/F7
Weaver, Ala. (36277) 195/G3
Weaver (riv.), England 13/G2
Weaver (lake), Manitoba 179/F2
Weaver, Minn. (†55958) 255/G6
Weaver, New Bruns. 170/E2
Weaver, N. Dak. (†58352) 282/N2
Weaverville, Calif. (96093) 204/B3
Weaverville, N.C. (28787) 281/D3
Webb, Ala. (36376) 195/H8
Webb, Iowa (51366) 229/C3
Webb (lake), Maine 243/C6
Webb, Miss. (38966) 256/D3
Webb (bay), Newf. 166/B2
Webb, Sask. 181/C5
Webb (co.), Texas 303/E10
Webb, Texas (†76010) 303/F3
Webb City, Ark. (†72949) 202/C3
Webb City, Mo. (64870) 261/C8
Webb City, Okla. (74654) 288/N1
Webber, Kansas (66970) 232/D2
Webbers Falls, Okla. (74470) 288/R3
Webbers Falls (res.), Okla. 288/R3
Webberville, Mich. (48892) 250/E6
Webb Lake, Wis. (54892) 317/B3
Webbs Cross Roads, Ky. (42652) 237/L6
Webbville, Ky. (41180) 237/R4
Webbwood, Ontario 177/C1
Webequie, Ontario 175/C2
Weber (co.), Utah 304/B2
Weber (riv.), Utah 304/C3
Weber City, Va. (24251) 307/C7
Webi Shabelle (riv.), Somalia 115/H3
Webster, Fla. (33597) 212/D3
Webster (co.), Georgia 217/C6
Webster, Ind. (47392) 227/H5
Webster (co.), Iowa 229/E4
Webster, Iowa (52355) 229/J6
Webster (res.), Kansas 232/C2
Webster (co.), Ky. 237/F5
Webster, Ky. (40176) 237/J5
Webster (par.), La. 238/D1
Webster (brook), Maine 243/E3
Webster, Mass. (01570) 249/G4
Webster○, Mass. (01570) 249/G4
Webster (lake), Mass. 249/G4
Webster, Minn. (55088) 255/E6
Webster (co.), Miss. 256/F3
Webster (co.), Mo. 261/G8
Webster (co.), Nebr. 264/F4
Webster○, N.H. (†03301) 268/D5
Webster, N.Y. (14580) 276/F4
Webster, N.C. (28788) 281/C4
Webster, N. Dak. (58382) 282/N3
Webster, Pa. (15087) 294/C5
Webster, S. Dak. (57274) 298/P3
Webster, Texas (77598) 303/K2
Webster (co.), W. Va. 312/F6
Webster, Wis. (54893) 317/B4
Webster City, Iowa (50595) 229/F4
Webster Groves, Mo. (63119) 261/P3
Webster Mills, Pa. (†17233) 294/F6
Webster Springs, W. Va. (26288) 312/F6
Websterville, Vt. (05678) 268/B3
Wecota, S. Dak. (57480) 298/L3
Weda, Indonesia 85/H5
Wedau, Papua N.G. 85/C7
Weddel (isl.), 143/D7
Weddell (sea), Ant. 2/H10
Weddell (sea) 5/C16
Wedderburn, Oreg. (97491) 291/C5
Wedderburn, Victoria 97/B5
Weddington, Ark. (†72701) 202/B1
Wedel, W. Germany 22/C2
Wedgefield, S.C. (29168) 296/F4
Wedgeport, Nova Scotia 168/C5
Wedgeworth, Ala. (†36776) 195/C5
Wedowee, Ala. (36278) 195/H4
Weed, Calif. (96094) 204/C2
Weed, N. Mex. (88354) 274/D6
Weed (hills), Sask. 181/J5
Weed Heights, Nev. (89443) 266/B4
Weedon-Centre, Québec 172/F4
Weedsport, N.Y. (13166) 276/G4
Weedville, Pa. (15868) 294/F3
Weehawken○, N.J. (07087) 273/C2
Week (isls.), Chile 138/D10
Weekapaug, R.I. (02891) 249/G7
Weekes, Sask. 181/J3
Weeki Wachee, Fla. (†33512) 212/D3
Weeks, La. (†70569) 238/G7
Weeks, Nev. (†89447) 266/B3
Weeks (isl.), N. Zealand 100/B1
Weeksbury, Ky. (41667) 237/R6
Weeks Mills, Maine (04361) 243/E7
Weeksville, N.C. (27909) 281/S2
Weems, Va. (22576) 307/P5
Weeping Water, Nebr. (68463) 264/J4
Weert, Netherlands 27/H6
Weesatche, Texas (77993) 303/G9
Weesen, Switzerland 39/H2
Weesp, Netherlands 27/C5
Weethalle, N.S. Wales 97/D3
Wee Waa, N.S. Wales 97/E2
Wegdahl, Minn. (†56265) 255/C6
Weggis, Switzerland 39/F2
Węgorzewo, Poland 47/E1
Wegra-Flat Creek, Ala. (†35129) 195/D3
Węgrów, Poland 47/E2
Weichang, China 77/J3
Weida, E. Germany 22/D3
Weiden in der Oberpfalz, W. Germany 22/D4
Weidman, Mich. (48893) 250/D5
Weifang, China 77/J4
Weihai (Weihaiwei), China 77/K4
Wei He (riv.), China 77/G5
Weilburg, W. Germany 22/C3
Weilheim im Oberbayern, W. Germany 22/D5
Weimar, E. Germany 22/D3
Weimar, Texas (78962) 303/H8
Weinan, China 77/H5
Weiner, Ark. (72479) 202/J2
Weinert, Texas (76388) 303/E4
Weinfelden, Switzerland 39/H1
Weingarten, W. Germany 22/C5
Weinheim, W. Germany 22/C4
Weining, China 77/F6
Weinsberg, W. Germany 22/C4
Weipa, Queensland 88/G1
Weipa, Queensland 95/B2
Weippe, Idaho (83553) 220/C3
Weir (lake), Fla. 212/E2
Weir, Kansas (66781) 232/H4
Weir, Miss. (39772) 256/F4
Weirdale, Sask. 181/F2
Weirgor, Wis. (†54835) 317/D4
Weir River, Manitoba 179/J2
Weirsdale, Fla. (32695) 212/D3
Weirton, W. Va. (26062) 312/E2
Weirwood, Va. (23484) 307/S6
Weisburg, Ind. (†47041) 227/H6
Weiser, Idaho (83672) 220/B5
Weiser (riv.), Idaho 220/B5
Weishan, China 77/F6
Weismes (Waimes), Belgium 27/J8
Weiss (lake), Ala. 195/G2
Weiss (lake), Georgia 217/A2
Weissenburg im Bayern, W. Germany 22/D4
Weissenfels, E. Germany 22/D3
Weissensee, E. Germany 22/F3
Weissenstein (mts.), Switzerland 39/D2
Weisserstein (mt.), Belgium 27/J8
Weissert, Nebr. (68880) 264/E3
Weisshorn (mt.), Switzerland 39/J3
Weisshorn (mt.), Switzerland 39/E4
Weissmies (mt.), Switzerland 39/F4
Weisswasser, E. Germany 22/F3
Weitchpec, Calif. (†95546) 204/B2
Weitensfeld-Flattnitz, Austria 41/B3
Weitra, Austria 41/C2
Weixi, China 77/E6
Weixin, China 77/F6
Weiz, Austria 41/C3
Wejh, Saudi Arabia 59/C4
Wejh, Saudi Arabia 54/E7
Wejherowo, Poland 47/D1
Welaka, Fla. (32093) 212/E2
Welbekend, S. Africa 118/J6
Welch, Okla. (74369) 288/R1
Welch, Texas (79377) 303/B5
Welch, W. Va. (24801) 312/C8
Welches, Oreg. (†97067) 291/E2
Welchman Hall, Barbados 161/B8
Welchville, Maine (†04270) 243/C7
Welcome, La. (†70086) 238/L3
Welcome, Md. (20693) 245/K7
Welcome, Minn. (56181) 255/D7
Welcome, N.C. (27374) 281/J3
Welcome, Ontario 177/F4
Welcome All, Georgia (†30304) 217/J2
Weld (co.), Colo. 208/L1
Weld○, Maine (04285) 243/C6
Weld (range), W. Australia 92/B4
Welda, Kansas (66091) 232/G3
Weldon, Ark. (72177) 202/H3
Weldon, Calif. (93283) 204/G8
Weldon, Ill. (61882) 222/E3
Weldon, Iowa (50264) 229/F7
Weldon, New Bruns. 170/F3
Weldon, N.C. (27890) 281/O2
Weldon, Sask. 181/F2
Weldon, Texas (75863) 303/J6
Weldona, Colo. (80653) 208/M2
Weldon Spring Heights, Mo. (†63301) 261/M2
Weleetka, Okla. (74880) 288/O4
Welford, Queensland 95/C5
Welkom, S. Africa 102/E7
Welkom, S. Africa 118/D5
Welland (riv.), England 13/G5
Welland (riv.), England 10/F4
Welland, Ontario 177/E5
Welland (canal), Ontario 177/E5
Wellandport, Ontario 177/E4
Wellborn, Fla. (32094) 212/D1
Wellersburg, Pa. (15564) 294/E6
Wellesley (isls.), Australia 87/D7
Wellesley○, Mass. (02181) 249/B7
Wellesley, Ontario 177/D4
Wellesley (isls.), Queensland 88/F3
Wellesley (isls.), Queensland 95/A3
Wellesley Hills, Mass. (02181) 249/B7
Wellfleet○, Mass. (02667) 249/O5
Wellfleet (harb.), Mass. 249/O5
Wellfleet, Nebr. (69170) 264/D4
Wellford, S.C. (29385) 296/C2
Wellin, Belgium 27/G8
Welling, Alberta 182/D5
Welling, Okla. (74471) 288/S3
Wellingborough, England 13/G5
Wellingborough, England 10/F4
Wellington, Ala. (36279) 195/G3
Wellington (isl.), Chile 120/B7
Wellington (isl.), Chile 138/D8
Wellington, Colo. (80549) 208/K1
Wellington, England 13/D7
Wellington, England 10/E5
Wellington, Ill. (60973) 222/F3
Wellington, Kansas (67152) 232/E4
Wellington, Ky. (†40201) 237/K2
Wellington, Ky. (40387) 237/O5
Wellington○, Maine (04990) 243/D5
Wellington, Mo. (64097) 261/E4
Wellington, Nev. (89444) 266/B4
Wellington, N.S. Wales 97/E3
Wellington (cap.), N. Zealand 2/T8
Wellington (cap.), N. Zealand 87/H10
Wellington (cap.), N. Zealand 100/A3
Wellington (bay), N.W. Terrs. 187/H3
Wellington (chan.), N.W.T. 162/G1
Wellington (chan.), N.W. Terrs. 187/J2
Wellington, Nova Scotia 168/E4
Wellington, Ohio (44090) 284/F3
Wellington (county), Ontario 177/D4
Wellington, Ontario 177/G4
Wellington, Pr. Edward I. 168/D2
Wellington, S. Africa 118/B6
Wellington, Texas (79095) 303/D3
Wellington, Utah (84542) 304/D4
Wellington (lake), Victoria 97/D6
Wellington, Va. (†22308) 307/T3
Wellman, Iowa (52356) 229/K6
Wellman (lake), Manitoba 179/B3
Wellman, Texas (79378) 303/B5
Wellpinit, Wash. (99040) 310/G3
Wells, Br. Col. 184/G3
Wells, England 13/E6
Wells, England 10/E5
Wells (co.), Ind. 227/G3
Wells, Kansas (67488) 232/E2
Wells, Maine (04090) 243/B9
Wells○, Maine (04090) 243/B9
Wells, Mich. (49894) 250/B3
Wells, Minn. (56097) 255/E7
Wells, Nev. (89835) 266/G1
Wells, N.Y. (12190) 276/M4
Wells (co.), N. Dak. 282/L4
Wells, Texas (75976) 303/J6
Wells○, Vt. (05774) 268/A5
Wells (riv.), Vt. 268/C3
Wells (dam), Wash. 310/F3
Wells (lake), W. Australia 88/C5
Wells (lake), W. Australia 92/C4
Wells Beach, Maine (04090) 243/B9
Wellsboro, Ind. (†46382) 227/D1
Wellsboro, Pa. (16901) 294/H2
Wells Bridge, N.Y. (13859) 276/K6
Wellsburg, Iowa (50680) 229/H4
Wellsburg, N.Y. (14894) 276/G6
Wellsburg, N. Dak. (†58341) 282/L4
Wellsburg, W. Va. (26070) 312/E2
Wellsford, N. Zealand 100/E2
Wells Gray Prov. Park, Br. Col. 184/H4
Wells-next-the-Sea, England 13/H5
Wells-next-the-Sea, England 10/G4
Wells River, Vt. (05081) 268/C3
Wellston, Mich. (49689) 250/D4
Wellston, Mo. (63112) 261/R2
Wellston, Ohio (45692) 284/F7
Wellston, Okla. (74881) 288/M3
Wellsville, Kansas (66092) 232/G3
Wellsville, Mo. (63384) 261/K4
Wellsville, N.Y. (14895) 276/E6
Wellsville, Ohio (43968) 284/J4
Wellsville, Pa. (17365) 294/J5
Wellsville, Utah (84339) 304/C2
Wellton, Ariz. (85356) 198/A6
Wellwood, Manitoba 179/C4
Wels, Austria 41/C2
Welsford, New Bruns. 170/D3
Welsford, Nova Scotia 168/E3
Welsh, La. (70591) 238/E6
Welshfield, Ohio (†44021) 284/H3
Welshpool, New Bruns. 170/D4
Welshpool, Wales 10/E4
Welshpool, Wales 13/D5
Welton, Iowa (52774) 229/M5
Welty, Okla. (74882) 288/O3
Welwyn, England 13/H7
Welwyn, England 10/F5
Welwyn, Sask. 181/K5
Wem, England 13/E5
Wembere (riv.), Tanzania 115/F4
Wembley, Alberta 182/A2
Wemmel, Belgium 27/B9
Wemyss Bay, Scotland 15/A2
Wenamu (riv.), Guyana 131/A2
Wenas (creek), Wash. 310/E4
Wenasoga, Miss. (†38834) 256/G1
Wenatchee, Wash. 188/B1
Wenatchee, Wash. (98801) 310/E3
Wenatchee (lake), Wash. 310/E3
Wenatchee (mts.), Wash. 310/E3
Wenatchee (riv.), Wash. 310/E3
Wenchi, Ghana 106/D7
Wenchow (Wenzhou), China 77/J6
Wendel, Calif. (96136) 204/E3
Wendel, W. Va. (26450) 312/F4
Wendell, Idaho (83355) 220/D7
Wendell○, Mass. (01379) 249/E2
Wendell, Minn. (56590) 255/B4
Wendell, N.H. (03783) 268/C5
Wendell, N.C. (27591) 281/N3
Wendell Depot, Mass. (01380) 249/E2
Wenden, Ariz. (85357) 198/B5
Wendeng, China 77/K4
Wendover, England 13/G7
Wendover, Ontario 177/J2
Wendover, Utah (84083) 304/A3
Wendover, Wyo. (†82214) 319/H3
Wendron, England 13/B7
Wendte, S. Dak. (†57532) 298/H5
Wenham○, Mass. (01984) 249/L2
Wenling, China 77/K6
Wenlock (riv.), Queensland 88/G2
Wenman (isl.), Ecuador 128/B8
Wenona, Georgia (†31015) 217/E7
Wenona, Ill. (61377) 222/E2
Wenona, Md. (21870) 245/P8
Wenona, N.C. (†27860) 281/R3
Wenonah, Ill. (†62075) 222/D4
Wenonah, N.J. (08090) 273/C4
Wenquan, Qinghai, China 77/D5
Wenquan, Xinjiang Uygur, China 77/B3
Wenshan, China 77/F7
Wensum (riv.), England 13/J5
Wentworth, Mo. (64873) 261/D8
Wentworth○, N.H. (03282) 268/D4
Wentworth (lake), N.H. 268/E4
Wentworth, N.S. Wales 97/B4
Wentworth, N.C. (27375) 281/K2
Wentworth, Nova Scotia 168/E3
Wentworth, S. Dak. (57075) 298/R6
Wentworth, Wis. (54894) 317/C2
Wentworths Location○, N.H. (†03579) 268/E2
Wentzville, Mo. (63385) 261/L5
Wen Xian, China 77/G5
Wenzhou (Wenchow), China 77/J6
Wenzhou, China 54/N7
Weogufka, Ala. (35183) 195/F4
Weohyakapka (lake), Fla. 212/E4
Weott, Calif. (95571) 204/A3
Wepawaug (riv.), Conn. 210/C3
Wequetequock, Conn. (†02891) 210/H3
Werdau, E. Germany 22/E3
Werder, E. Germany 22/E2
Werner Lake, Ontario 175/A2
Wernersville, Pa. (19565) 294/K5
Wernigerode, E. Germany 22/D3
Werra (riv.), E. Germany 22/D3
Werra (riv.), W. Germany 22/D3
Werribee, Victoria 88/G7
Werrimull, Victoria 97/A4
Werris Creek, N.S. Wales 97/F2
Wertheim, W. Germany 22/C4
Wervik, Belgium 27/B7
Wesco, Mo. (65586) 261/K7
Wesel, W. Germany 22/B3
Weser (riv.), Germany 7/E3
Weser (riv.), W. Germany 22/C2
Weskan, Kansas (67762) 232/A3
Weslaco, Texas (78596) 303/F11
Weslemkoon (lake), Ontario 177/G2
Wesley, Ark. (72773) 202/C1
Wesley, Dominica 161/F5
Wesley, Georgia (†30401) 217/H6
Wesley, Iowa (50483) 229/E2
Wesley, Maine (04686) 243/H6
Wesley○, Maine (04686) 243/H6
Wesley Vale, Tasmania 99/C3
Wesleyville, Newf. 166/D4
Wesleyville, Pa. (16510) 294/C1
Wes-Rand, S. Africa 118/G6
Wessel (isls.), Australia 87/D7
Wessel (cape), North. Terr. 88/F2
Wessel (cape), North. Terr. 93/E1
Wessel (isls.), North. Terr. 88/F2
Wessel (isls.), North. Terr. 93/E1
Wessington, S. Dak. (57381) 298/M5
Wessington Springs, S. Dak. (57382) 298/M5
Wesson, Ark. (†71749) 202/E7
Wesson, Miss. (39191) 256/D7
West (riv.), Conn. 210/D3
West (riv.), Conn. 210/E3
West, Iowa (52357) 229/J5
West (bay), La. 238/M8
West (isl.), Mass. 249/L6
West (riv.), Mass. 249/H4
West, Miss. (39192) 256/E4
West (isls.), New Bruns. 170/D4
West (cape), N. Zealand 100/A6
West (bay), Nova Scotia 168/G3
West (pt.), Nova Scotia 168/H5
West (riv.), Nova Scotia 168/F3
West (pt.), Pr. Edward I. 168/D2
West (pt.), Tasmania 99/A2
West, Texas (76691) 303/G6
West (bay), Texas 303/K3
West (riv.), Vt. 268/B5
West Acton, Mass. (01720) 249/H3
West Alexander, Pa. (15376) 294/B5
West Alexandria, Ohio (45381) 284/A6
West Allis, Wis. (53214) 317/L1
West Alton, Mo. (63386) 261/M5
West Alton, N.H. (†03246) 268/E4
West Amboy, N.Y. (†13493) 276/J4
West Arichat, Nova Scotia 168/G3
West Ashford, Conn. (†06251) 210/G1
West Aspetuck (riv.), Conn. 210/B2
West Athens, Maine (†04912) 243/D6
West Augusta, Va. (24485) 307/K4
West Avon, Conn. (†06001) 210/D1
West Baden Springs, Ind. (47469) 227/D7
West Baines (riv.), North. Terr. 93/A4
West Baldwin, Maine (04091) 243/B8
Westbank, Br. Col. 184/H5
WEST BANK 59/C3
WEST BANK 65/C3
West Bank (reg.), 65/C3
West Baraboo, Wis. (†53913) 317/G9
West Barnet, Vt. (05870) 268/C3
West Barns, Scotland 15/F5
West Barnstable, Mass. (02668) 249/N6
West Barrington, R.I. (†02806) 249/J5
West Bath○, Maine (†04530) 243/D8
West Baton Rouge (par.), La. 238/H6
West Bay, Fla. (32407) 212/C6
West Bay, Nova Scotia 168/G3
West Bay Road, Nova Scotia 168/G3
West Bend, Iowa (50597) 229/D3
Westbend, Ky. (40388) 237/N5
West Bend, Sask. 181/H4
West Bend, Wis. (53095) 317/K9
West Bengal (state), India 68/F4
West Berkshire, Vt. (†05450) 268/B2
West Berlin, Mass. (†01503) 249/H3
West Berlin, N.J. (08091) 273/D4
West Bethel, Maine (04286) 243/B7
West Blocton, Ala. (35184) 195/D4
West Bloomfield, Wis. (†54983) 317/J7
Westboro, Mo. (64498) 261/B1
Westboro, Ohio (†45148) 284/C7
Westboro, Wis. (54490) 317/F5
Westborough, Mass. (01581) 249/H3
Westborough○, Mass. (01581) 249/H3
West Bountiful, Utah (†84087) 304/B3
Westbourne, Manitoba 179/D4
Westbourne, Tenn. (†37766) 237/O7
West Boxford, Mass. (01885) 249/K2
West Boylston○, Mass. (01583) 249/G3
West Braintree, Vt. (†05669) 268/B4
West Branch (res.), Conn. 210/C1
West Branch, Iowa (52358) 229/L5
West Branch, Farmington (riv.), Mass. 249/B4
West Branch, Mich. (48661) 250/E4
West Branch, Rocky (riv.), Ohio 284/G10
West Brattleboro, Vt. (05301) 268/B6
West Brentwood, N.H. (†03848) 268/E6
West Brewster, Mass. (†02631) 249/O5
Westbridge, Br. Col. 184/H5
West Bridgewater○, Mass. (02379) 249/K4
West Bridgewater, Vt. (†05034) 268/B4
West Bridgford, England 13/F5
West Bromwich, England 13/F5
West Bromwich, England 10/G3
Westbrook, Conn. (06498) 210/F3
Westbrook○, Conn. (06498) 210/F3
Westbrook, Maine (04092) 243/C8
Westbrook, Minn. (56183) 255/C6
West Brook, Nova Scotia 168/D3
Westbrook, Texas (79565) 303/C5
West Brookfield, Mass. (01585) 249/F4
West Brookfield○, Mass. (01585) 249/F4
West Brooklyn, Ill. (61378) 222/D2
West Brooksville, Maine (†04617) 243/F7
West Brownsville, Pa. (15417) 294/C5
West Buechel, Ky. (†40218) 237/K2
West Burke, Vt. (05871) 268/C2
West Burlington, Iowa (52655) 229/L7
West Burra (isl.), Scotland 15/G2
Westbury, England 10/E5
Westbury, England 13/E6
Westbury, N.Y. (11590) 276/R7
Westbury, Tasmania 99/C3
West Buxton, Maine (04093) 243/B8
Westby, Mont. (59275) 262/M2
Westby, Wis. (54667) 317/E8
West Calder, Scotland 15/C2
West Caldwell, N.J. (07006) 273/A2
West Campton, N.H. (03228) 268/D4
West Canaan, N.H. (03741) 268/C4
West Cape May, N.J. (†08204) 273/D6
West Carroll (par.), La. 238/H1
West Carrollton, Ohio (45449) 284/B6
West Carthage, N.Y. (†13619) 276/J3
West Charleston, Vt. (05872) 268/C2
West Chatham, Mass. (02669) 249/O6
West Chazy, N.Y. (12992) 276/N1
West Chelmsford, Mass. (†01824) 249/J2
Westchester, Conn. (†06474) 210/F2
Westchester, Ill. (60153) 222/B5
West Chester, Iowa (52359) 229/K6
Westchester (co.), N.Y. 276/N8
West Chester, Ohio (45069) 284/C9
West Chester, Pa. (19380) 294/L6
West Chesterfield, Mass. (01084) 249/C3
Westchester Station, Nova Scotia 168/E3
West Chicago, Ill. (60185) 222/A5
West Chop (pt.), Mass. 249/M7
West City, Ill. (†62812) 222/E5
Westcliffe, Colo. (81252) 208/H6
West College Corner, Ind. (†47353) 227/H5
West Columbia, S.C. (29169) 296/E4
West Columbia, Texas (77486) 303/J8
West Columbia, W. Va. (25287) 312/B5
West Concord, Mass. (†01742) 249/A6
West Concord, Minn. (55985) 255/F6
West Corinth, Vt. (†05039) 268/C3
West Cornwall, Conn. (06796) 210/B1
West Cornwall, Vt. (†05753) 268/A4
West Cote Blanche (bay), La. 238/G7
Westcott, Alberta 182/C4
Westcott Cove (bay), Conn. 210/A4
West Covina, Calif. (*91790) 204/D10
Westcreek, Colo. (†80135) 208/J4
West Creek, N.J. (08092) 273/E4
West Crossett, Ark. (†71635) 202/F7
West Cummington, Mass. (†01026) 249/B3
West Danville, Vt. (05873) 268/C3
West Dean, England 13/F6
West Demerara-Essequibo Coast (dist.), Guyana 131/B2
West Dennis, Mass. (02670) 249/O6
West Deptford○, N.J. (†08086) 273/B3
West Des Moines, Iowa (50318) 229/F5
West Dover, Nova Scotia 168/E4
West Dover, Vt. (05356) 268/B6
West Dublin, Nova Scotia 168/D4
West Dudley, Mass. (†01550) 249/F4
West Dummerston, Vt. (05357) 268/B6
West Dundee (Dundee), Ill. (†60118) 222/E1
West Eau Gallie, Fla. (32935) 212/F3
West Elizabeth, Pa. (15088) 294/C5
West Elkton, Ohio (45070) 284/A6
West Elmira, N.Y. (†14901) 276/G6
West Eminence, Mo. (†65466) 261/J8
Westend, Calif. (†93562) 204/H8
West End, N.C. (27376) 281/K4
West End, Sask. 181/J5
West End, Virgin Is. (Br.) 161/C4
West End-Cobb Town, Ala. (†36201) 195/G3
Westend Saltpond (lag.), Virgin Is. (U.S.) 161/E4
West Enfield, Maine (04493) 243/F5
West Epping, N.H. (†03042) 268/E5
Wester Eems (chan.), Netherlands 27/K1
Westerland, W. Germany 22/C1
Westerlo, Belgium 27/F6
Westerlo, N.Y. (12193) 276/M6
Westerly, R.I. (02891) 249/G7
Westerly○, R.I. (02891) 249/G7
Western (prov.), Kenya 115/G3
Western, Nebr. (68464) 264/G4
Western (head), Nova Scotia 168/D5
Western Australia 88/B5
WESTERN AUSTRALIA 92
Western Australia (state), Australia 87/C8
Western Bay, Newf. 166/D2
Western Channel (str.), Japan 81/D6
Western Dvina (riv.), U.S.S.R. 53/C2
Western Dvina (riv.), U.S.S.R. 52/C3
Western Dvina (riv.), U.S.S.R. 48/C4
Western Ghats (mts.), India 68/C5
Western Grove, Ark. (72685) 202/D1
Western Institute, Tenn. (38074) 237/C10
Western Isles (islands area), Scotland 15/A3
Westernport, Md. (21562) 245/B3

Willow Springs 469

White City, Sask. 181/G5
Whiteclay, Nebr. (69365) 264/B2
White Cliffs, N.S. Wales 97/B2
White Cloud, Ind. (†47112) 227/E8
White Cloud, Kansas (66094) 232/G2
White Cloud, Mich. (49349) 250/D5
White Coomb (mt.), Scotland 15/E5
White Cottage, Ohio (43791) 284/F6
Whitecourt, Alberta 182/C2
White Deer, Pa. (17887) 294/J3
White Deer, Texas (79097) 303/C2
White Earth, Minn. (56591) 255/C3
White Earth, N. Dak. (58794) 282/E3
White Earth (riv.), N. Dak. 282/E3
White Earth Ind. Res., Minn. 255/C3
White Elster (riv.), E. Germany 22/E3
Whiteface (riv.), Minn. 255/F3
Whiteface, N.H. (†03259) 268/E4
Whiteface (mt.), N.H. 268/E4
Whiteface (mt.), N.Y. 276/N2
Whiteface, Texas (79379) 303/B4
White Face (mt.), Vt. 268/B2
Whitefield, Maine (04362) 243/D7
Whitefield○, Maine (04362) 243/D7
Whitefield, N.H. (03598) 268/D3
Whitefield○, N.H. (03598) 268/D3
Whitefield, Okla. (74472) 288/R4
Whitefish (bay), Mich. 250/E2
Whitefish (pt.), Mich. 250/E2
Whitefish (riv.), Mich. 250/C2
Whitefish (lake), Minn. 255/D4
Whitefish, Mont. (59937) 262/B2
Whitefish (lake), Mont. 262/B2
Whitefish Falls, Ontario 177/C1
Whitefish Point, Mich. (†49768) 250/E2
Whiteflat, Texas (†79234) 303/D3
Whiteford, Md. (21160) 245/N2
White Fox, Sask. 181/H2
White Fox (riv.), Sask. 181/G2
Whitegate, Ireland 17/E8
White Gull (creek), Sask. 181/G2
White Hall, Ala. (†36040) 195/E6
Whitehall, Ark. (†72432) 202/J3
White Hall, Ark. (71602) 202/F5
White Hall, Georgia (†30601) 217/F3
White Hall, Ill. (62092) 222/C4
Whitehall, Ind. (†47401) 227/D6
Whitehall, La. (†70462) 238/M2
White Hall, Md. (21161) 245/M2
Whitehall, Mich. (49461) 250/C5
Whitehall, Mont. (59759) 262/D5
Whitehall, N.Y. (12887) 276/O3
Whitehall, Ohio (43213) 284/E6
Whitehall, Pa. (†15234) 294/B7
Whitehall, Scotland 15/F1
White Hall, S.C. (†29945) 296/F6
White Hall, Va. (22987) 307/L4
Whitehall, Wis. (54773) 317/D7
White Handkerchief (cape), Newf. 166/B2
Whitehaven, England 13/D3
Whitehaven, England 10/E3
Whitehaven, Md. (21873) 245/P7
Whitehaven (harb.), Nova Scotia 168/G3
White Haven, Pa. (18661) 294/L3
White Head, New Bruns. 170/D4
White Head (isl.), New Bruns. 170/D4
Whitehead, N. Ireland 17/K2
Whitehead, Nova Scotia 168/G3
White Heath, Ill. (61884) 222/E3
Whitehills, Scotland 15/F3
White Horn, Tenn. (†37711) 237/R8
Whitehorse, Canada 4/C16
Whitehorse, Canada 2/C3
Whitehorse, S. Dak. (57661) 298/H3
Whitehorse (cap.), Yukon 187/E3
Whitehorse (cap.), Yukon 162/C3
Whitehorse (cap.), Yukon 146/E3
White Horse Lake, N. Mex. (87073) 274/B3
Whitehouse, Ky. (41269) 237/R5
Whitehouse, N.J. (08888) 273/D2
Whitehouse, Ohio (43571) 284/C2
White House, Tenn. (37188) 237/H8
White House Station, N.J. (08889) 273/D2
White Iron (lake), Minn. 255/G3
White Knob (mts.), Idaho 220/E6
White Lake, N.C. (28337) 281/M5
White Lake, Ontario 177/H2
White Lake, S. Dak. (57383) 298/M6
White Lake, Wis. (54491) 317/J5
Whiteland, Ind. (46184) 227/E5
Whitelaw, Alberta 182/A1
Whitelaw, Wis. (54247) 317/L7
Whiteman A.F.B., Mo. 261/E5
Whitemark, Tasmania 99/D2
White Marsh, Md. (21162) 245/N3
White Meadow Lake, N.J. (†07866) 273/D2
White Mills, Ky. (42788) 237/J5
White Mills, Pa. (18473) 294/M2
White Mountain, Alaska (99784) 196/F2
White Mountains Nat'l Rec. Area, Alaska 196/J1
Whitemouth, Manitoba 179/G5
Whitemouth (lake), Manitoba 179/G5
Whitemouth (riv.), Manitoba 179/G5
Whitemud (riv.), Alberta 182/A1
Whiten (head), Scotland 15/D2
White Nile (riv.) 2/L5
White Nile (riv.) 102/F4
White Nile (prov.), Sudan 111/F5
White Nile (riv.), Sudan 111/F5
White Nile (riv.), Sudan 59/B7
White Oak (lake), Ark. 202/D6
White Oak, Georgia (31568) 217/J8
White Oak, Md. (†20901) 245/F3
Whiteoak, Mo. (63880) 261/M10
White Oak, N.C. (28399) 281/M5
Whiteoak (swamp), N.C. 281/P5
Whiteoak (creek), Ohio 284/C7
White Oak, Okla. (†74301) 288/R1
White Oak, Pa. (15131) 294/C7
White Oak, S.C. (29176) 296/E3
Whiteoak (creek), Tenn. 237/F8
White Oak, Texas (75693) 303/K5
White Oaks, Conn. (†06488) 210/C2
White Oaks, N. Mex. (†88301) 274/D5
White Owl, S. Dak. (57792) 298/E4
White Partridge (lake), Ontario 177/G2
White Pass, Wash. (†98937) 310/D4
White Pigeon, Mich. (49099) 250/D7
White Pine, Mich. (49971) 250/F1
Whitepine, Mont. (†59874) 262/A3
White Pine (co.), Nev. 266/F3
White Pine (range), Nev. 266/F3
White Pine, Tenn. (37890) 237/P8
White Pines, Calif. (†95223) 204/E5
White Plains, Ala. (†36862) 195/G3
White Plains, Georgia (30678) 217/F4
White Plains, Ky. (42464) 237/G6
White Plains, Md. (20695) 245/L6
White Plains, N.Y. (*10601) 276/P6
White Plains, N.C. (27031) 281/H2
White Plains, Va. (23893) 307/N7
White Pond, S.C. (29854) 296/D5
White Post, Va. (22663) 307/M2
White Quartz Hill, North. Terr. 93/D7
White Rapids, New Bruns. 170/E2
Whiteriver, Ariz. (85941) 198/E5
White River, Ont. 162/H6
White River, Ontario 175/C3
White River, Ontario 177/J5
White River, S. Dak. (57579) 298/H6
White River (lake), Texas 303/C4
White River Junction, Vt. (05001) 268/C4
White Rock, Br. Col. 184/K3
White Rock (creek), Kansas 232/D2
White Rock, N. Mex. (87544) 274/C3
Whiterock, N.C. (†28753) 281/D3
White Rock, S.C. (29177) 296/E3
White Rock, S. Dak. (†57260) 298/R2
White Rock (creek), Texas 303/G2
Whiterocks, Utah (84085) 304/E3
White Russian S.S.R., U.S.S.R. 7/G3
White Russian S.S.R., U.S.S.R. 52/C4
White Russian S.S.R., U.S.S.R. 48/C4
Whites, Wash. (†98541) 310/B3
Whitesail (lake), Br. Col. 184/D3
White Salmon, Wash. (98672) 310/D5
White Salmon (riv.), Wash. 310/D4
White Sands (des.), N. Mex. 274/C5
White Sands Missile Range, N. Mex. (88002) 274/C6
White Sands Missile Range, N. Mex. 274/C5
White Sands Nat'l Mon., N. Mex. 274/C6
Whitesbog, N.J. (†08015) 273/E4
Whitesboro, N.J. (08252) 273/D5
Whitesboro, N.Y. (13492) 276/K4
Whitesboro, Okla. (74577) 288/S5
Whitesboro, Texas (76273) 303/H4
Whitesburg, Georgia (30185) 217/B4
Whitesburg, Ky. (41858) 237/R6
Whitesburg, Tenn. (37891) 237/P8
Whites Chapel, Ala. (†35094) 195/F3
Whites City, N. Mex. (88268) 274/E6
Whites Creek, W. Va. (†25530) 312/A6
White Settlement, Texas (76108) 303/E2
Whiteshell Prov. Park, Manitoba 179/G4
White Shield, N. Dak. (†58534) 282/G4
Whiteshore (lake), Sask. 181/C3
Whiteside (chan.), Chile 138/E10
Whiteside (co.), Ill. 222/D2
Whiteside, Mo. (63387) 261/K4
Whiteside, Tenn. (37396) 237/K10
Whites Lake, Nova Scotia 168/E4
Whiteson, Oreg. (†97128) 291/D2
White Springs, Fla. (32096) 212/D1
Whitestone, Georgia (30186) 217/C1
White Stone, Va. (22578) 307/R5
Whitestown, Ind. (46075) 227/E5
White Sulphur Springs, Georgia (†31822) 217/C5
White Sulphur Springs, La. (†71371) 238/F3
White Sulphur Springs, Mont. (59645) 262/E4
White Sulphur Springs, W. Va. (24986) 312/F7
Whitesville, Georgia (†31833) 217/C5
Whitesville, Ky. (42378) 237/H5
Whitesville, Mo. (†64480) 261/C2
Whitesville, N.J. (†08701) 273/E3
Whitesville, N.Y. (14897) 276/E6
Whitesville, W. Va. (25209) 312/C6
Whiteswan (lakes), Sask. 181/F1
White Swan, Wash. (98952) 310/E4
Whitetail, Mont. (59276) 262/L2
Whitetop, Va. (24292) 307/E7
Whiteville, La. (71376) 238/F5
Whiteville, N.C. (28472) 281/M6
Whiteville, Tenn. (38075) 237/C10
White Volta (riv.) 102/B4
White Volta (riv.), Ghana 106/D6
White Volta (riv.), Upper Volta 106/D6
Whitewater, Colo. (81527) 208/C5
Whitewater (bay), Fla. 212/F6
Whitewater, Ind. (†47374) 227/H5
Whitewater (riv.), Ind. 227/H6
Whitewater, Kansas (67154) 232/E4
Whitewater, Manitoba 179/B5
Whitewater (lake), Manitoba 179/B5
Whitewater, Mo. (63785) 261/N8
Whitewater, Mont. (59544) 262/J2
Whitewater, Wis. (53190) 317/J10
Whitewater Baldy (mt.), N. Mex. 274/A5
Whitewood, Sask. 181/J5
Whitewood, S. Dak. (57793) 298/B5
Whitewood (creek), S. Dak. 298/B4
Whitewood, Va. (24657) 307/E6
Whitewright, Texas (75491) 303/H4
Whitfield, Ala. (†36925) 195/B6
Whitfield (co.), Georgia 217/B1
Whitfield, Miss. (39193) 256/E6
Whitford, Alberta 182/D3
Whitharral, Texas (79380) 303/B4
Whithorn, Scotland 10/D3
Whithorn, Scotland 15/D6
Whitianga, N. Zealand 100/E2
Whiting, Ind. (46394) 227/C1
Whiting, Iowa (51063) 229/A4
Whiting, Kansas (66552) 232/G2
Whiting○, Maine (04691) 243/J6
Whiting, Mo. (†63845) 261/O9
Whiting, N.J. (08759) 273/E4
Whiting○, Vt. (05778) 268/A4
Whiting, Wis. (†54481) 317/H7
Whiting Bay, Scotland 15/C5
Whiting Field Naval Air Sta., Fla. 212/B6
Whitingham○, Vt. (05361) 268/B6
Whitinsville, Mass. (01588) 249/H4
Whitkow, Sask. 181/D3
Whitla, Alberta 182/E5
Whitlash, Mont. (59545) 262/E2
Whitley (co.), Ind. 227/F2
Whitley (co.), Ky. 237/N7
Whitley Bay, England 13/J3
Whitley City, Ky. (42653) 237/N7
Whitleyville, Tenn. (38588) 237/K8
Whitlock, Tenn. (†38242) 237/E8
Whitman○, Mass. (02382) 249/L4
Whitman (riv.), Mass. 249/G2
Whitman, Nebr. (69366) 264/C2
Whitman, N. Dak. (58283) 282/O3
Whitman (co.), Wash. 310/H4
Whitman Mission Nat'l Hist. Site, Wash. 310/G4
Whitmer, W. Va. (26296) 312/G5
Whitmire, S.C. (29178) 296/D3
Whitmore, Calif. (96096) 204/D3
Whitmore Lake, Mich. (48189) 250/F6
Whitmore Village, Hawaii (†96786) 218/E1
Whitnel, N.C. (28645) 281/F3
Whitney (mt.), Calif. 188/C3
Whitney (mt.), Calif. 204/G7
Whitney (lake), Conn. 210/D3
Whitney, Nebr. (69367) 264/A2
Whitney, New Bruns. 170/E2
Whitney, Ontario 177/F2
Whitney, Pa. (15693) 294/D5
Whitney, S.C. (29303) 296/D1
Whitney, Texas (76692) 303/G6
Whitney Point, N.Y. (13862) 276/J6
Whitney Point (lake), N.Y. 276/J6
Whitneyville, Conn. (06517) 210/D3
Whitneyville○, Maine (04692) 243/H6
Whitsett, Texas (78075) 303/F9
Whitsunday (isl.), Queensland 88/H4
Whitsunday (isl.), Queensland 95/D4
Whitt, Texas (76090) 303/G5
Whittaker, Mich. (48190) 250/F6
Whittemore, Iowa (50598) 229/E2
Whittemore, Mich. (48770) 250/F4
Whitten, Iowa (50269) 229/H4
Whittier, Alaska (99693) 196/C1
Whittier, Calif. (*90601) 204/D11
Whittier, Iowa (52360) 229/K4
Whittier, N.C. (28789) 281/C4
Whittle (cape), Québec 174/F2
Whittlesea, Victoria 97/C5
Whittlesey, England 13/G5
Whittlesey, Wis. (†54451) 317/F5
Whitton, N.S. Wales 97/D4
Whitwell, Tenn. (37397) 237/K10
Wholdaia (lake), N.W. Terrs. 187/H3
Why, Ariz. (85321) 198/C6
Whyalla, Australia 87/D9
Whyalla, S. Australia 94/E5
Whycocomagh, Nova Scotia 168/G3
Whyjonta, N.S. Wales 97/B1
Wiarton, Ontario 177/C3
Wiau (lake), Alberta 182/E2
Wiawso, Ghana 106/D7
Wiay (isl.), Scotland 15/A3
Wibaux (co.), Mont. 262/M4
Wibaux, Mont. (59353) 262/M3
Wichabai, Guyana 131/B4
Wichita, Kans. 188/G3
Wichita (co.), Kansas 232/A3
Wichita, Kansas 146/J6
Wichita, Kansas (*67201) 232/E4
Wichita (mts.), Okla. 288/J5
Wichita (co.), Texas 303/F3
Wichita (riv.), Texas 303/F4
Wichita Falls, Texas 146/H6
Wichita Falls, Texas (*76301) 303/F4
Wichita Falls, Texas 188/G4
Wick, Iowa (†50240) 229/F6
Wick, Scotland 10/E1
Wick, Scotland 15/E2
Wick (riv.), Scotland 15/E2
Wick, W. Va. (26185) 312/E4
Wickahoney (creek), Idaho 220/C7
Wickatunk, N.J. (07765) 273/E3
Wicked (pt.), Manitoba 179/D2
Wickenburg, Ariz. (85358) 198/C5
Wickepin, W. Australia 92/B2
Wickersham, Wash. (†98284) 310/C2
Wickes, Ark. (71973) 202/B5
Wickes, Mont. (†59638) 262/D4
Wickett, Texas (79788) 303/A6
Wickham, New Bruns. 170/D3
Wickham, Québec 172/E4
Wickham (cape), Tasmania 99/A1
Wickham, W. Australia 92/B3
Wickiup (res.), Oreg. 291/F4
Wickliffe, Ky. (42087) 237/C7
Wickliffe, Ohio (44092) 284/J9
Wicklow (co.), Ireland 17/J5
Wicklow, Ireland 10/C4
Wicklow, Ireland 17/K6
Wicklow (head), Ireland 17/K6
Wicklow (head), Ireland 10/D4
Wicklow (mts.), Ireland 17/J6
Wicklow, New Bruns. 170/C2
Wicksburg, Ala. (†36352) 195/G8
Wicomico (co.), Md. 245/P7
Wicomico, Md. (†20611) 245/L7
Wicomico (riv.), Md. 245/R7
Wicomico (riv.), Md. 245/L7
Wicomico Church, Va. (22579) 307/R5
Wiconisco, Pa. (17097) 294/J4
Wide (chan.), Chile 138/D8
Wide (bay), Papua N.G. 86/C2
Wide (bay), Queensland 95/E5
Wideman, Ark. (72585) 202/G1
Widemouth, W. Va. (†24736) 312/D8
Widen, W. Va. (25211) 312/E6
Widener, Ark. (72394) 202/J3
Widewater, Alberta 182/C2
Widgiemooltha, W. Australia 88/C6
Widgiemooltha, W. Australia 92/C5
Widnes, England 10/F2
Widnes, England 13/G2
Widnoon, Pa. (16261) 294/D4
Więcbork, Poland 47/C2
Wiederkehr Village, Ark. 202/C3
Wiehl, W. Germany 22/B3
Wiek, E. Germany 22/E1
Wieliczka, Poland 47/E3
Wieluń, Poland 47/D3
Wien (Vienna) (cap.), Austria 41/D2
Wiener Neustadt, Austria 41/D3
Wieprz (riv.), Poland 47/F3
Wierden, Netherlands 27/K4
Wieringermeer Polder, Netherlands 27/G3
Wierum, Netherlands 27/H2
Wieruszów, Poland 47/D3
Wiesbaden, W. Germany 7/E3
Wiesbaden, W. Germany 22/B3
Wiese (isl.), U.S.S.R. 4/B6
Wiese (isl.), U.S.S.R. 48/H2
Wiesmoor, W. Germany 22/B2
Wigan, England 13/G2
Wigan, England 10/G2
Wiggins, Colo. (80654) 208/L2
Wiggins, Miss. (39577) 256/F9
Wiggins, S.C. (†29446) 296/F6
Wight (isl.), England 13/F7
Wight (isl.), England 10/F5
Wigston, England 13/F5
Wigton, England 13/D3
Wigtown, Scotland 10/D3
Wigtown, Scotland 15/D6
Wigtown (trad. co.), Scot. 15/A5
Wigtown (bay), Scotland 10/D3
Wigtown (bay), Scotland 15/D6
Wijhe, Netherlands 27/J4
Wijk bij Duurstede, Netherlands 27/G5
Wijk en Aalburg, Netherlands 27/F5
Wikel, W. Va. (†24945) 312/E7
Wikieup, Ariz. (85360) 198/B4
Wikwemikong, Ontario 177/C2
Wil, Switzerland 39/H2
Wilawana, Pa. (†18840) 294/J2
Wilbarger (co.), Texas 303/E3
Wilber, Nebr. (68465) 264/G4
Wilberforce, Ontario 177/F3
Wilbert, Minn. (†56031) 255/D7
Wilbraham, Mass. (01095) 249/E4
Wilbraham○, Mass. (01095) 249/E4
Wilbur, Ind. (†46151) 227/D5
Wilbur, Ky. (†41124) 237/R5
Wilbur, Oreg. (97494) 291/D4
Wilbur, Wash. (99185) 310/G3
Wilbur, W. Va. (26459) 312/E4
Wilbur Park, Mo. (†63101) 261/P3
Wilburton, Kansas (†67950) 232/A4
Wilburton, Okla. (74578) 288/R5
Wilcannia, N.S. Wales 88/G6
Wilcannia, N.S. Wales 97/B2
Wilchingen, Switzerland 39/F1
Wilcox (co.), Ala. 195/D7
Wilcox, Fla. (†32693) 212/D2
Wilcox (co.), Georgia 217/F7
Wilcox, Mo. (†64468) 261/C2
Wilcox, Nebr. (68982) 264/E4
Wilcox, Pa. (15870) 294/E2
Wilcox, Sask. 181/G5
Wilczek Land (isl.), U.S.S.R. 4/B6
Wilczek Land (isl.), U.S.S.R. 48/G1
Wild Ammonoosuc (riv.), N.H. 268/D3
Wildbad im Schwarzwald, W. Germany 22/C4
Wildcat (creek), Ind. 227/E4
Wild Cat, Ky. (40998) 237/O6
Wild Cherry, Ark. (†72576) 202/F1
Wild Cove, Newf. 166/C3
Wilder, Idaho (83676) 220/A6
Wilder, Minn. (56184) 255/C7
Wilder (dam), N.H. 268/C4
Wilder, Tenn. (38589) 237/L8
Wilder, Vt. (05088) 268/C4
Wilder (dam), Vt. 268/C4
Wilderness, Va. (†22553) 307/N4
Wilders, Ky. (†41071) 237/S2
Wildersville, Tenn. (38388) 237/E9
Wilderswil, Switzerland 39/E3
Wildervank, Netherlands 27/K2
Wilderville, Oreg. (97543) 291/D5
Wildeshausen, W. Germany 22/C2
Wild Goose, Ontario 177/H5
Wild Goose, Ontario 175/C3
Wildhaus, Switzerland 39/H2
Wildhay (riv.), Alberta 182/B3
Wildhorn (mt.), Switzerland 39/D4
Wild Horse, Colo. (80862) 208/N5
Wild Horse (res.), Nev. 266/E1
Wildhorse (creek), Okla. 288/L5
Wildie, Ky. (40492) 237/N6
Wildomar, Calif. (92395) 204/H10
Wildon, Austria 41/C3
Wildorado, Texas (79098) 303/B2
Wild Rice (lake), Minn. 255/F4
Wild Rice (riv.), Minn. 255/B3
Wild Rice, N. Dak. (†58047) 282/S6
Wild Rice (riv.), N. Dak. 282/R7
Wildrose, N. Dak. (58795) 282/D2
Wild Rose, Wis. (54984) 317/H7
Wildspitze (mt.), Austria 41/A3
Wildstrubel (mt.), Switzerland 39/E4
Wildsville, La. (71377) 238/G3
Wildwood, Alberta 182/C3
Wildwood, Fla. (32785) 212/D3
Wildwood, Minn. (†56643) 255/E3
Wildwood, N.J. (08260) 273/D6
Wildwood Crest, N.J. (08260) 273/D6
Wileville, Nova Scotia 168/D4
Wiley, Colo. (81092) 208/O6
Wiley, Georgia (30581) 217/F1
Wiley (creek), Oreg. 291/E3
Wiley City, Wash. (98906) 310/E4
Wiley Ford, W. Va. (26767) 312/J3
Wileyville, W. Va. (26186) 312/E3
Wilfred, Ind. (†47879) 227/C6
Wilhelm (mt.), Papua N.G. 85/B7
Wilhelm II Coast (reg.) 5/C5
Wilhelmina (canal), Netherlands 27/G6
Wilhelmina (mts.), Suriname 131/C4
Wilhelm-Pieck-Stadt, E. Germany 22/F3
Wilhelmsburg, Austria 41/C2
Wilhelmshaven, W. Germany 22/B2
Wilkes (co.), Georgia 217/G3
Wilkes (co.), N.C. 281/G2
Wilkes (lake), Ontario 177/F1
Wilkes-Barre, Pa. 188/L2
Wilkes-Barre, Pa. (*18701) 294/F7
Wilkesboro, N.C. (28697) 281/G2
Wilkes Land (reg.), Ant. 2/R10
Wilkes Land (reg.) 5/B7
Wilkeson, Wash. (98396) 310/D3
Wilkesville, Ohio (45695) 284/F7
Wilke, Sask. 181/C3
Wilkin (co.), Minn. 255/B4
Wilkins, Nev. (†89835) 266/G1
Wilkinsburg, Pa. (15221) 294/C7
Wilkinson (co.), Georgia 217/F5
Wilkinson, Ind. (46186) 227/F5
Wilkinson, Minn. (†56633) 255/D3
Wilkinson (co.), Miss. 256/B8
Wilkinson, Miss. (†39669) 256/B8
Wilkinson (lakes), S. Australia 94/C3
Wilkinson, W. Va. (25653) 312/B7
Wilkinsonville, Mass. (01590) 249/G4
Will (co.), Ill. 222/F2
Willacoochee, Georgia (31650) 217/G8
Willacy (co.), Texas 303/G11
Willamette (riv.), Oreg. 291/A3
Willamette, Middle Fork (riv.), Oreg. 291/E4
Willamina, Oreg. (97396) 291/D2
Willandra Billabong (creek), N.S. Wales 97/C3
Willapa, Wash. (†98577) 310/B4
Willapa (bay), Wash. 310/A4
Willard, Kansas (†66601) 232/G2
Willard, Mich. (†48611) 250/E5
Willard, Mo. (65781) 261/F8
Willard, Mont. (59354) 262/M4
Willard, N. Mex. (87063) 274/D4
Willard, N.Y. (14588) 276/G5
Willard, N.C. (28478) 281/O5
Willard, Ohio (44890) 284/E3
Willard, Utah (84340) 304/C2
Willard, Wis. (54493) 317/E6
Willards, Md. (21874) 245/S7
Willaumez (pen.), Papua N.G. 86/B2
Willaura, Victoria 97/B5
Willcox, Ariz. (85643) 198/F6
Willebroek, Belgium 27/E6
Willems (canal), Netherlands 27/G5
Willemstad, Netherlands 27/F5
Willemstad (cap.), Neth. Ant. 161/F9
Willemstad (cap.), Neth. Ant. 156/E4
Willen, Manitoba 179/A4
Willernie, Minn. (55090) 255/G5
Willeroo, North. Terr. 93/B3
Willette, Tenn. (†37150) 237/K8
Willey, Iowa (†51401) 229/D5
Willey House, N.H. (†03812) 268/E3
William (riv.), Sask. 181/L2
William Creek, S. Australia 94/E3
William H. Taft Nat'l Hist. Site, Ohio 284/C10
William L. Springer (lake), Ill. 222/E4
Williams, Ariz. (86046) 198/C3
Williams, Calif. (95987) 204/C4
Williams, Ind. (47470) 227/D7
Williams, Iowa (50271) 229/F3
Williams, Minn. (56686) 255/D2
Williams (co.), N. Dak. 282/C3
Williams (co.), Ohio 284/A2
Williams, Okla. (†74932) 288/T4
Williams, Oreg. (97544) 291/D5
Williams, S.C. (29493) 296/F5
Williams, W. Australia 92/B2
Williams (riv.), W. Va. 312/F6
Williams A.F.B., Ariz. 198/D5
Williams Bay, Wis. (53191) 317/J10
Williamsboro, N.C. (†27536) 281/M2
Williamsburg, Colo. (†81226) 208/J6
Williamsburg, Iowa (52361) 229/J5
Williamsburg, Kansas (66095) 232/G3
Williamsburg, Ky. (40769) 237/N7
Williamsburg, Md. (21674) 245/P6
Williamsburg○, Mass. (01096) 249/C3
Williamsburg, Mich. (49690) 250/D4
Williamsburg, Mo. (63388) 261/J5
Williamsburg, New Bruns. 170/D2
Williamsburg, N. Mex. (87942) 274/B5
Williamsburg, Ohio (45176) 284/B7
Williamsburg, Ontario 177/J3
Williamsburg, Pa. (16693) 294/F5
Williamsburg (co.), S.C. 296/H4
Williamsburg (I.C.), Va. (23185) 307/P6
Williamsburg, W. Va. (24991) 312/F7
Williamsfield, Ill. (61489) 222/C3
Williamsfield, Jamaica 158/H6
Williamsfield, Ohio (44093) 284/J2
Williamsford, Ontario 177/D3
Williamsford, Tasmania 99/B3
Williams Fork, Colorado (riv.), Colo. 208/G3
Williams Fork, Yampa (riv.), Colo. 208/E2
Williams Harbour, Newf. 166/C3
Williams Lake, Br. Col. 162/D5
Williams Lake, Br. Col. 184/F4
Williamson, Georgia (30292) 217/D4
Williamson (co.), Ill. 222/E6
Williamson, Ill. (†62088) 222/D5
Williamson, Iowa (50272) 229/G6
Williamson, N.Y. (14589) 276/F4
Williamson (riv.), Oreg. 291/F5
Williamson (co.), Tenn. 237/H9
Williamson (co.), Texas 303/G7
Williamson, W. Va. (25661) 312/B7
Williamsport, Ind. (47993) 227/C4
Williamsport, Ky. (41271) 237/R5
Williamsport, Md. (21795) 245/G2
Williamsport, Newf. 166/C3
Williamsport, Ohio (43164) 284/D6
Williamsport, Pa. 188/L2
Williamsport, Pa. (17701) 294/H3
Williamsport, Tenn. (38487) 237/G9
Williamston, Mich. (48895) 250/E6
Williamston, N.C. (27892) 281/R3
Williamston, S.C. (29697) 296/B2
Williamstown, Kansas (†66073) 232/G2
Williamstown, Ky. (41097) 237/M3
Williamstown, Mass. (01267) 249/B2
Williamstown○, Mass. (01267) 249/B2
Williamstown, Mo. (63473) 261/J2
Williamstown, New Bruns. 170/C2
Williamstown, N.J. (08094) 273/D4
Williamstown, N.Y. (13493) 276/J4
Williamstown, Ontario 177/K2
Williamstown, Pa. (17098) 294/J4
Williamstown, S. Australia 94/C7
Williamstown○, Vt. (05679) 268/B3
Williamstown, Victoria 97/H5
Williamstown, Victoria 88/K7
Williamstown, W. Va. (26187) 312/C4
Williamsville, Ill. (62693) 222/D4
Williamsville, Miss. (†39090) 256/F4
Williamsville, Mo. (63977) 261/L9
Williamsville, N.Y. (14221) 276/C5
Williamsville, Vt. (05362) 268/B6
Williamsville, Va. (24487) 307/J4
Willies (range), Queensland 95/C6
Williford, Ark. (72482) 202/H1
Willimantic, Conn. (06226) 210/G2
Willimantic (riv.), Conn. 210/F1
Willimantic, Maine (†04443) 243/E5
Willimantic○, Maine (†04443) 243/E5
Willingboro○, N.J. (08046) 273/D3
Willingdon, Alberta 182/E3
Willington○, Conn. (†06279) 210/F1
Willington, S.C. (29852) 296/C4
Willis (islets), Australia 87/F7
Willis (isls.), Coral Sea Is. Terr. 88/J3
Willis, Kansas (66435) 232/G2
Willis, Mich. (48191) 250/F6
Willis, Okla. (†73439) 288/M7
Willis, Texas (77378) 303/J7
Willis, Va. (24380) 307/H7
Willis (riv.), Va. 307/M5
Willisau, Switzerland 39/F2
Willisburg, Ky. (40078) 237/L5
Williston (lake), Br. Col. 162/D4
Williston (lake), Br. Col. 184/F2
Williston, Fla. (32696) 212/D2
Williston, N. Dak. 188/F1
Williston, N. Dak. (58801) 282/C3
Williston, S.C. (29853) 296/E5
Williston, Tenn. (38076) 237/C10
Williston○, Vt. (05495) 268/A3
Williston Park, N.Y. (11596) 276/R7
Willisville, Ark. (71864) 202/D6
Willisville, Ill. (62997) 222/D6
Willisville, Ontario 177/C1
Willis Wharf, Va. (23486) 307/S5
Williton, England 13/D6
Willits, Calif. (95490) 204/B4
Willmar, Minn. (56201) 255/C5
Willmar, Sask. 181/J6
Willmathsville, Mo. (†63546) 261/G2
Willmore Wilderness Prov. Park, Alberta 182/A3
Willoughby (bay), Ant. & Bar. 161/E11
Willoughby, N. S. Wales 88/K3
Willoughby, N.S. Wales 97/J3
Willoughby, Ohio (44094) 284/J8
Willoughby, Vt. (†05822) 268/C2
Willoughby (lake), Vt. 268/D2
Willoughby Hills, Ohio (†44094) 284/J9
Willow, Alaska (99688) 196/B1
Willow, Ark. (†72084) 202/E5
Willow (creek), Calif. 204/E3
Willow (creek), Idaho 220/G6
Willow (riv.), Minn. 255/E4
Willow (creek), Mont. 262/E2
Willow, Okla. (73673) 288/G4
Willow (creek), Oreg. 291/H2
Willow (creek), Oreg. 291/K3
Willow (creek), S. Dak. 298/C4
Willow (creek), Utah 304/E4
Willow (res.), Wis. 317/F4
Willow (creek), Wyo. 319/F2
Willow (lake), Wyo. 319/C2
Willow Bend, W. Va. (24992) 312/F7
Willow Branch, Ind. (46187) 227/F5
Willowbrook, Ill. (†60521) 222/B6
Willowbrook, Kansas (†67501) 232/D3
Willowbrook, Sask. 181/J4
Willow Bunch, Sask. 181/F6
Willow Bunch (lake), Sask. 181/F6
Willow City, N. Dak. (58384) 282/K2
Willow City, Texas (78675) 303/F7
Willow Creek, Calif. (95573) 204/B3
Willow Creek, Mont. (59760) 262/E5
Willow Creek (res.), Mont. 262/D3
Willowcreek, Oreg. (†97918) 291/K3
Willow Creek, Sask. 181/B6
Willowdale, Oreg. (†97741) 291/G3
Willow Grove, Del. (†19934) 245/R4
Willow Grove, New Bruns. 170/E3
Willow Grove, Pa. (19090) 294/M5
Willow Hill, Ill. (62480) 222/E5
Willow Hill, Pa. (17271) 294/G5
Willowick, Ohio (44094) 284/J8
Willow Island, Nebr. (69171) 264/D4
Willowlake (riv.), N.W. Terrs. 187/F3
Willow Lake, S. Dak. (57278) 298/O4
Willowmore, S. Africa 118/C6
Willowra, North. Terr. 93/C6
Willow Ranch, Calif. (96108) 204/E2
Willow River, Br. Col. 184/F3
Willow River, Minn. (55795) 255/F4
Willows, Calif. (95988) 204/C4
Willows, Md. (†20732) 245/M6
Willows, Sask. 181/F6
Willow Springs, Ill. (60480) 222/B6

Woodburn, Iowa (50275) 229/F7
Woodburn, Ky. (42170) 237/J7
Woodburn, N.S. Wales 97/F2
Woodburn, Oreg. (97071) 291/A3
Woodbury, Conn. (06798) 210/C2
Woodbury○, Conn. (06798) 210/C2
Woodbury, Georgia (30293) 217/C5
Woodbury (co.), Iowa 229/B4
Woodbury, Ky. (42288) 237/H6
Woodbury, Minn. (†55798) 255/F6
Woodbury, N.J. (08096) 273/B4
Woodbury, Pa. (16695) 294/F5
Woodbury, Tenn. (37190) 237/J9
Woodbury○, Vt. (05681) 268/C3
Woodbury Heights, N.J. (08097) 273/B4
Woodbury P.O. (North Woodbury), Conn. (06798) 210/C2
Woodchopper, Alaska (†99733) 196/K1
Woodcliff, Georgia (†30467) 217/J5
Woodcliff Lake, N.J. (07675) 273/B1
Woodcock, Pa. (†16335) 294/B2
Woodcrest, Calif. (†92504) 204/E11
Wood Dale, Ill. (60191) 222/B5
Wooden Ball (isl.), Maine 243/F8
Woodenbong, N.S. Wales 97/G1
Woodenbridge, Ireland 17/J6
Woodend, Victoria 97/C5
Woodfibre, Br. Col. 184/K2
Woodfin, N.C. (†28804) 281/D3
Woodford, Grenada 161/C8
Woodford (co.), Ill. 222/D3
Woodford, Ireland 17/E5
Woodford (co.), Ky. 237/M4
Woodford, Okla. (†73451) 288/M6
Woodford, S.C. (†29112) 296/E4
Woodford○, Vt. (†05201) 268/A6
Woodford, Wis. (†53504) 317/G10
Woodgate, N.Y. (13494) 276/K3
Woodhall Spa, England 13/G4
Woodhaven, La. (†70466) 238/M1
Woodhaven, Mich. (†48183) 250/F6
Woodhouse, Alberta 182/D5
Woodhull, Ill. (61490) 222/C2
Woodhull, N.Y. (14898) 276/F6
Woodhull (lake), N.Y. 276/L3
Woodington, Ohio (†45331) 284/A5
Woodinville, Wash. (98072) 310/B1
Wood Islands, Pr. Edward I. 168/F2
Woodlake, Calif. (93286) 204/G7
Wood Lake, Minn. (56297) 255/C6
Wood Lake, Nebr. (69221) 264/D2
Woodland, Ala. (36280) 195/H4
Woodland, Calif. (95695) 204/B8
Woodland, Georgia (31836) 217/D5
Woodland, Ill. (60974) 222/F3
Woodland, Ind. (†46624) 227/E1
Woodland, La. (†70722) 238/J5
Woodland○, Maine (04694) 243/H5
Woodland, Mich. (48897) 250/D6
Woodland, Miss. (39776) 256/F3
Woodland, N.C. (27897) 281/P2
Woodland, Pa. (16881) 294/F4
Woodland, Utah (†84036) 304/C3
Woodland, Wash. (98674) 310/C5
Woodland Hills, Calif. (*91364) 204/B10
Woodland Hills, Ky. (†40201) 237/L2
Woodland Mills, Tenn. (38271) 237/C8
Woodland Park, Colo. (80863) 208/J4
Woodlands, Manitoba 179/E4
Woodlands, Singapore 72/F6
Woodlands, W. Va. (†26055) 312/E3
Woodlark (isl.), Papua N.G. 85/C7
Woodlawn, Hawaii (†96801) 218/D4
Woodlawn, Ill. (62898) 222/D5
Woodlawn, Ky. (†41071) 237/T2
Woodlawn, La. (†70647) 238/E6
Woodlawn, Md. (†21201) 245/M3
Woodlawn, Ohio (†45201) 284/C9
Woodlawn, Tenn. (37191) 237/G7
Woodlawn, Va. (24381) 307/G7
Woodlawn Heights, Ind. (†46011) 227/F4
Woodlawn-Oakdale, Ky. (†42001) 237/D6
Woodlawn Park, Ky. (†40201) 237/K2
Woodleaf, N.C. (27054) 281/H3
Woodley, Sask. 181/J6
Woodley and Sandford, England 13/G8
Woodlyn, Pa. (19094) 294/M7
Wood-Lynne, N.J. (†08107) 273/B3
Woodman, Wis. (53827) 317/E9
Woodmere, N.Y. (11598) 276/P7
Woodmere, Ohio (†44101) 284/J9
Woodmont, Conn. (†06460) 210/D4
Woodmoor, Md. (†21207) 245/L3
Wood Mountain, Sask. 181/E6
Wood Mountain Hist. Park, Sask. 181/E6
Woodnorth, Manitoba 179/A5
Woodport, N.J. (†07885) 273/D2
Woodridge, Ill. (†60517) 222/B6
Woodridge, Manitoba 179/G5
Wood-Ridge, N.J. (07075) 273/B2
Woodridge, N.Y. (12789) 276/L7
Wood River, Ill. (62095) 222/B2
Wood River, Nebr. (68883) 264/F4
Wood River Junction, R.I. (02894) 249/H7
Woodroffe (mt.), S. Australia 88/E5
Woodroffe (mt.), S. Australia 94/B2
Woodrow, Colo. (80757) 208/M3
Woodrow, Sask. 181/E6
Woodruff, Ariz. (85942) 198/E4
Woodruff (co.), Ark. 202/H3
Woodruff, Kansas (†67661) 232/C2
Woodruff, S.C. (29388) 296/D2
Woodruff, Utah (84086) 304/C2
Woodruff, Wis. (54568) 317/G4
Woods (lake) 146/J5
Woods (lake) 162/G6
Woods (lake), Ind. 227/E2
Woods (lake), Manitoba 179/H5
Woods (lake), Minn. 188/G1
Woods (lake), Minn. 255/D1
Woods (lake), Newf. 166/B3
Woods (lake), North. Terr. 88/E3
Woods (lake), North. Terr. 93/C4
Woods (co.), Okla. 288/J1
Woods (lake), Ontario 177/F5
Woods (lake), Ontario 175/B3
Woods (res.), Tenn. 237/J10
Woodsbend, Ky. (†41472) 237/P5
Woodsboro, Md. (21798) 245/J2
Woodsboro, Texas (78393) 303/G9
Woods Cross, Utah (84087) 304/B3
Woodsdale, N.C. (27595) 281/M2
Woodsfield, Ohio (43793) 284/H6
Woods Heights, Mo. (†64024) 261/S4
Woods Hole, Mass. (02543) 249/M6
Woodside, Calif. (94062) 204/J3
Woodside, Del. (19980) 245/R4
Woodside, Manitoba 179/D4
Woodside, Mont. (†59875) 262/B4
Woodside, S. Australia 94/C8
Woodside, Utah (†84501) 304/D4
Woodson, Ark. (72180) 202/F4
Woodson, Ill. (62695) 222/C4
Woodson (co.), Kansas 232/G4
Woodson, Texas (76091) 303/E5
Woodson Terrace, Mo. (†63101) 261/P2
Wood's Point, Victoria 97/D5
Woodstock, Ala. (35188) 195/D4
Woodstock○, Conn. (06281) 210/H1
Woodstock, England 13/F6
Woodstock, England 10/F5
Woodstock, Georgia (30188) 217/D2
Woodstock, Ill. (60098) 222/E1
Woodstock, Md. (21163) 245/L3
Woodstock, Minn. (56186) 255/B7
Woodstock, N. Br. 162/K6
Woodstock, New Bruns. 170/C2
Woodstock○, N.H. (03293) 268/D4
Woodstock, N.S. Wales 97/E3
Woodstock, N.Y. (12498) 276/M6
Woodstock, Ohio (43084) 284/C5
Woodstock, Ontario 177/D4
Woodstock, Vt. (05091) 268/B4
Woodstock○, Vt. (05091) 268/B4
Woodstock, Va. (22664) 307/L3
Woodstock Valley, Conn. (06282) 210/G1
Woodston, Kansas (67675) 232/C2
Woodstown, N.J. (08098) 273/C4
Woodsville, N.H. (03785) 268/C3
Wood Village, Oreg. (†97060) 291/B2
Woodville, Ala. (35776) 195/F1
Woodville, Conn. (†06777) 210/B2
Woodville, Fla. (32362) 212/B1
Woodville, Georgia (30670) 217/F3
Woodville, Mass. (01784) 249/H4
Woodville, Miss. (39669) 256/B8
Woodville, N.Y. (13698) 276/H3
Woodville, N. Zealand 100/F4
Woodville, N.C. (†27849) 281/P2
Woodville, Ohio (43469) 284/D3
Woodville, Okla. (73466) 288/N7
Woodville, Ontario 177/F3
Woodville, Pa. (†15106) 294/B7
Woodville, S. Australia 88/D7
Woodville, S. Australia 94/A7
Woodville, S.C. (†29669) 296/C2
Woodville, Texas (75979) 303/K7
Woodville, Va. (22749) 307/M3
Woodville, W. Va. (25572) 312/C6
Woodville, Wis. (54028) 317/B6
Woodward, Iowa (50276) 229/E5
Woodward (co.), Okla. 288/H2
Woodward, Okla. (73801) 288/H2
Woodward, S.C. (†29014) 296/E2
Woodwards Cove, New Bruns. 170/D4
Woodway, Texas (†76712) 303/G6
Woodway, Va. (†24277) 307/C7
Woodway, Wash. (†98020) 310/C3
Woodworth, Ill. (†60953) 222/F3
Woodworth, La. (71485) 238/E4
Woodworth, N. Dak. (58496) 282/M5
Woody (mt.), Ariz. 198/D3
Woody, Calif. (93287) 204/G8
Woody (isl.), China 85/E2
Woody Creek, Colo. (81656) 208/F4
Woody Island, Alaska (†99615) 196/H3
Woody Island, Newf. 166/C2
Woody Point, Newf. 166/C4
Wool, England 13/E7
Woolbridge, Mo. (65287) 261/G5
Wooler, England 13/F2
Woolford, Alberta 182/D5
Woolford, Md. (21677) 245/O7
Woolgar, Queensland 95/B3
Woolgoolga, N.S. Wales 97/G2
Wooli, N.S. Wales 97/G1
Woollahra, N. S. Wales 88/L4
Woollahra, N.S. Wales 97/K3
Woollum, Ky. (40999) 237/O6
Woolrich, Pa. (17779) 294/H3
Woolsey, Georgia (30294) 217/D4
Woolsington, England 13/H3
Woolstock, Iowa (50599) 229/F3
Wooltana, S. Australia 88/F6
Wooltana, S. Australia 94/F4
Woolwich○, Maine (04579) 243/D8
Woolwine, Va. (24185) 307/H7
Woomera, Australia 87/D9
Woomera, S. Australia 88/F6
Woomera, S. Australia 94/E4
Woonsocket, R.I. (02895) 249/J4
Woonsocket, S. Dak. (57385) 298/N5
Wooramel, W. Australia 92/A4
Wooramel (riv.), W. Australia 88/A5
Wooramel (riv.), W. Australia 92/A4
Wooroloo, W. Australia 88/B2
Wooster, Ark. (72181) 202/F3
Wooster, Ohio (44691) 284/G4
Woosung, Ill. (61091) 222/D2
Wooton, Ky. (41776) 237/P6
Wootton Basset, England 13/E6
Woqooyi Galbeed (prov.), Somalia 115/H1
Worb, Switzerland 39/E3
Worcester, England 13/E5
Worcester, England 10/E4
Worcester (co.), Md. 245/S8
Worcester, Mass. 188/M2
Worcester (co.), Mass. 249/G3
Worcester, Mass. (*01601) 249/H3
Worcester, N.Y. (12197) 276/L5
Worcester, S. Africa 102/D8
Worcester, S. Africa 118/B6
Worcester○, Vt. (05682) 268/B3
Worden, Ark. (†72010) 202/H3
Worden, Ill. (62097) 222/B2
Worden, Kansas (†66006) 232/G3
Worden, Mont. (59088) 262/H5
Worden, Oreg. (†97601) 291/E5
Wordsworth, Sask. 181/J6
Wörgl, Austria 41/A3
Work (chan.), Br. Col. 184/C3
Workai (isl.), Indonesia 85/K7
Workington, England 13/D3
Workington, England 10/E3
Worksop, England 10/F4
Worksop, England 13/F4
Workum, Netherlands 27/G3
Worland, Mo. (†64752) 261/C6
Worland, Wyo. (82401) 319/E1
WORLD 2
Worley, Idaho (83876) 220/B2
Wormerveer, Netherlands 27/F4
Worms, W. Germany 22/C4
Woronoco, Mass. (01097) 249/C4
Woronora (riv.), N. S. Wales 88/K5
Woronora (riv.), N.S. Wales 97/J4
Worpswede, W. Germany 22/C2
Worsbrough, England 13/J2
Worsley, Alberta 182/A1
Worsley, England 13/H2
Worth (co.), Georgia 217/E8
Worth, Georgia (†31714) 217/E7
Worth, Ill. (60482) 222/B6
Worth (co.), Iowa 229/G2
Worth (co.), Mo. 261/D2
Worth, Mo. (†64456) 261/C2
Worth (lake), Texas 303/E2
Wortham, Texas (76693) 303/H6
Worthing, England 13/G7
Worthing, England 10/F5
Worthing, S. Dak. (57077) 298/R7
Worthington, Ind. (47471) 227/C6
Worthington, Iowa (52078) 229/L4
Worthington, Ky. (41183) 237/R3
Worthington○, Mass. (01098) 249/C3
Worthington, Minn. (56187) 255/C7
Worthington, Mo. (63567) 261/G2
Worthington, Ohio (43085) 284/E5
Worthington, Pa. (16262) 294/C4
Worthington, W. Va. (26591) 312/F4
Worthington Springs, Fla. (32697) 212/D2
Worthville, Ky. (41098) 237/L3
Worthville, N.C. (27378) 281/K3
Worthville, Pa. (15784) 294/D3
Worton, Md. (21678) 245/O3
Woss Lake, Br. Col. 184/D5
Wostok, Alberta 182/D3
Wotje (atoll), Marshall Is. 87/H5
Wottonville, Québec 172/F4
Wounded Knee, S. Dak. (57794) 298/D7
Wounded Knee (creek), S. Dak. 298/E7
Wour, Chad 111/C3
Wowoni (isl.), Indonesia 85/G6
Wragby, England 13/G4
Wrangel (isl.), U.S.S.R. 4/B18
Wrangel (isl.), U.S.S.R. 48/T2
Wrangell, Alaska (99929) 196/N2
Wrangell (cape), Alaska 196/H3
Wrangell (isl.), Alaska 196/N2
Wrangell (mts.), Alaska 196/K2
Wrangell-St. Elias Nat'l Preserve, Alaska 196/K2
Wrangell-St. Elias Nat'l Park, Alaska 196/K2
Wrangle, England 13/H4
Wrath (cape), Scotland 15/C2
Wrath (cape), Scotland 10/D1
Wray, Colo. (80758) 208/P2
Wray, Georgia (31798) 217/F7
Wreck Cove, Nova Scotia 168/H2
Wren, Ala. (†35650) 195/D2
Wren, Miss. (†39730) 256/G3
Wren, Ohio (45899) 284/A4
Wrens, Georgia (30833) 217/H4
Wrenshall, Minn. (55797) 255/F4
Wrentham, Alberta 182/D5
Wrentham○, Mass. (02093) 249/J4
Wrexham, Wales 13/E4
Wrexham, Wales 10/E4
Wright, Ala. (†35677) 195/C1
Wright, Ark. (72182) 202/F5
Wright (co.), Iowa 229/F3
Wright, Kansas (67882) 232/C4
Wright, La. (†70548) 238/F6
Wright (co.), Minn. 255/D5
Wright, Minn. (55798) 255/E4
Wright (co.), Mo. 261/H8
Wright (mt.), Québec 174/D2
Wright (lake), S. Australia 94/A2
Wright, Wyo. (82732) 319/G2
Wright Brothers Nat'l Mem., N.C. 281/T2
Wright City, Mo. (63390) 261/K5
Wright City, Okla. (74766) 288/R6
Wright Patman (lake), Texas 303/K4
Wright-Patterson Air Force Base, Ohio 284/B6
Wrights, Ill. (62098) 222/C4
Wrights, Pa. (†16743) 294/F2
Wrightstown, Minn. (†56453) 255/C4
Wrightstown, N.J. (08562) 273/D3
Wrightstown, Wis. (54180) 317/K7
Wrightsville, Ark. (72183) 202/F4
Wrightsville, Georgia (31096) 217/G5
Wrightsville, Pa. (17368) 294/J5
Wrightsville Beach, N.C. (28480) 281/O6
Wrightwood, Calif. (92397) 204/D10
Wrigley, Ky. (41477) 237/P4
Wrigley, N.W.T. 162/D3
Wrigley, N.W. Terrs. 187/F3
Wrigley, Tenn. (37098) 237/G9
Wrocław (prov.), Poland 47/C3
Wrocław, Poland 47/C3
Wrocław, Poland 7/F3
Wrong (lake), Manitoba 179/F2
Wroughton, England 13/F6
Wroxeter, Ontario 177/C4
Wroxton, Sask. 181/K4
Września, Poland 47/C2
Wschowa, Poland 47/C3
W. Scott Kerr (res.), N.C. 281/G2
Wuchang, China 77/L3
Wuchow (Wuzhou), China 77/H7
Wuchuan, Guizhou, China 77/G6
Wuchuan, Nei Monggol, China 77/H3
Wuchung (Wuzhong), China 77/G4
Wuda, China 77/G4
Wudaoliang, China 77/D5
Wuding, China 77/F6
Wudinna, S. Australia 88/E6
Wudinna, S. Australia 94/D5
Wudu, China 77/F5
Wugang, China 77/H6
Wuhai, China 77/G4
Wuhan, China 77/H5
Wuhan, China 54/N6
Wuhan, China 2/Q4
Wuhing (Wuxing), China 77/K5
Wuhu, China 77/J5
Wuhu, China 54/N6
Wu Jiang (riv.), China 77/G6
Wukari, Nigeria 106/F7
Wum, Cameroon 115/A2
Wun, India 68/D5
Wundowie, W. Australia 88/C2
Wundowie, W. Australia 92/B1
Wünnewil, Switzerland 39/D3
Wunnummin Lake, Ontario 175/C2
Wunsiedel, W. Germany 22/E3
Wunstorf, W. Germany 22/C2
Wupatki Nat'l Mon., Ariz. 198/D3
Wuppertal, W. Germany 22/B3
Wuqi, China 77/G4
Wuqia, China 77/A4
Würmsee (Starnbergersee) (lake), W. Germany 22/D5
Wurong, Queensland 95/B3
Wurtland, Ky. (41144) 237/R3
Wurtsboro, N.Y. (12790) 276/L7
Wurtsmith A.F.B., Mich. 250/F4
Würzburg, W. Germany 22/C4
Wurzen, E. Germany 22/E3
Wushi, China 77/A3
Wusih (Wuxi), China 77/J5
Wusuli Jiang (Ussuri) (riv.), China 77/M2
Wutai, China 77/H4
Wuwei, China 77/F4
Wuxi (Wusih), China 77/K5
Wuxi, China 54/O6
Wuxing (Wuhing), China 77/K5
Wuyang, China 77/H4
Wuyiling, China 77/L2
Wuyi Shan (range), China 77/J6
Wuyuan, China 77/G3
Wuzhong (Wuchung), China 77/G4
Wuzhou (Wuchow), China 77/H7
Wyaconda, Mo. (63474) 261/J2
Wyalkatchem, W. Australia 88/B6
Wyalkatchem, W. Australia 92/B5
Wyalla, S. Australia 88/F6
Wyalusing, Pa. (18853) 294/K2
Wyalusing, Wis. (†53801) 317/D10
Wyandanch, N.Y. (11798) 276/N9
Wyandot (co.), Ohio 284/D4
Wyandotte, Ind. (†47137) 227/E8
Wyandotte (co.), Kansas 232/H2
Wyandotte, Mich. (48192) 250/B7
Wyandotte, Okla. (74370) 288/S1
Wyandra, Queensland 95/C5
Wyanet, Ill. (61379) 222/D2
Wyangala (res.), N.S. Wales 97/E3
Wyarno, Wyo. (82845) 319/G2
Wyassup (lake), Conn. 210/H3
Wyatt, Ind. (46595) 227/E1
Wyatt, La. (†71251) 238/E2
Wyatt, Mo. (63882) 261/O9
Wycheproof, Victoria 97/B5
Wyckoff○, N.J. (07481) 273/B1
Wye (riv.), England 13/J2
Wye (riv.), England 13/D5
Wye (riv.), Wales 13/D5
Wye (riv.), Wales 10/E4
Wye Mills, Md. (21679) 245/O5
Wyeville, Wis. (54671) 317/F7
Wyk auf Föhr, W. Germany 22/C1
Wykoff, Minn. (55990) 255/F7
Wylie, Minn. (†56750) 255/B3
Wylie (lake), S.C. 296/E1
Wylie, Texas (75098) 303/H1
Wylliesburg, Va. (23976) 307/L7
Wyman, Iowa (†52621) 229/L6
Wyman (lake), Maine 243/C5
Wyman Dam, Maine (†04920) 243/D5
Wymark, Sask. 181/D5
Wymer, W. Va. (26297) 312/G5
Wymondham, England 13/J5
Wymore, Nebr. (68466) 264/H4
Wynberg, S. Africa 118/E6
Wynbring, S. Australia 94/C4
Wyndham, Australia 87/C7
Wyndham, N. Zealand 100/B7
Wyndham, W. Australia 88/D3
Wyndham, W. Australia 92/E1
Wyndmere, N. Dak. (58081) 282/R7
Wynigen, Switzerland 39/E2
Wynnburg, Tenn. (38077) 237/C8
Wynndel, Br. Col. 184/J5
Wynne, Ark. (72396) 202/J3
Wynne, Md. (†20680) 245/N8
Wynnewood, Okla. (73098) 288/M5
Wynnewood, Pa. (19096) 294/M6
Wynniatt (bay), N.W. Terrs. 187/G2
Wynnum, Queensland 95/E5
Wynnum, Queensland 88/L2
Wynona, Okla. (74084) 288/O1
Wynoochee (lake), Wash. 310/B3
Wynoochee (riv.), Wash. 310/B3
Wynot, Nebr. (68792) 264/G2
Wynyard, Sask. 162/F5
Wynyard, Sask. 181/G4
Wynyard, Tasmania 88/H8
Wynyard, Tasmania 99/B3
Wyocena, Wis. (53969) 317/H9
Wyola, Mont. (59089) 262/J5
Wyoming 188/E2
WYOMING 319
Wyoming, Del. (19934) 245/R4
Wyoming, Ill. (61491) 222/D2
Wyoming, Iowa (52362) 229/L4
Wyoming, Mich. (49509) 250/D6
Wyoming, Minn. (55092) 255/F5
Wyoming (co.), N.Y. 276/D5
Wyoming, N.Y. (14591) 276/D5
Wyoming, Ohio (45215) 284/C9
Wyoming, Ontario 177/B5
Wyoming (co.), Pa. 294/K2
Wyoming, Pa. (18644) 294/E7
Wyoming, R.I. (02898) 249/H6
Wyoming (state), U.S. 146/H5
Wyoming (co.), W. Va. 312/C7
Wyoming (peak), Wyo. 319/B3
Wyoming (range), Wyo. 319/B2
Wyomissing, Pa. (19610) 294/K5
Wyong, N.S. Wales 97/F3
Wyre (riv.), England 13/G1
Wyre (isl.), Scotland 15/F1
Wyrzysk, Poland 47/C2
Wysokie Mazowieckie, Poland 47/F2
Wysox, Pa. (18854) 294/K2
Wyszków, Poland 47/E2
Wythe (co.), Va. 307/F7
Wytheville, Va. (24382) 307/G7
Wytopitlock, Maine (04497) 243/G4
Wytopitlock (lake), Maine 243/G4

X

Xainza, China 77/C5
Xaitongmoin, China 77/C6
Xai-Xai, Mozambique 118/E5
Xai-Xai, Mozambique 102/F7
Xaltocan, Mexico 150/N1
Xangongo, Angola 115/C7
Xanten, W. Germany 22/B3
Xánthi, Greece 45/G5
Xapuri, Brazil 132/G10
Xar Moron He (riv.), China 77/J3
Xarrama (riv.), Portugal 33/B3
Xau (lake), Botswana 118/C4
Xavantina, Brazil 132/C6
Xcalak, Mexico 150/Q7
Xenia, Ill. (62899) 222/E5
Xenia, Ohio (45385) 284/C6
Xiadong, China 77/E3
Xiaguan (Siakwan), China 77/E6
Xiamen (Amoy), China 77/J7
Xiamen, China 54/N7
Xi'an (Sian), China 77/G5
Xi'an, China 54/M6
Xi'an, China 2/Q4
Xianfeng, China 77/G6
Xiangfan (Siangfan), China 77/H5
Xianghoang (plat.), Laos 72/D3
Xiang Jiang (riv.), China 77/H6
Xiangkhoang, Laos 72/D3
Xiangshan, China 77/K6
Xiangtan (Siangtan), China 77/H6
Xiangtan, China 54/N7
Xianyang (Sienyang), China 77/G5
Xiaogan, China 77/H5
Xiapu (Siapu), China 77/K6
Xichang (Sichang), China 77/F6
Xicoténcatl, Mexico 150/K5
Xicotepec de Juárez, Mexico 150/L6
Xicute, Colombia 126/E7
Xigazê (Shigatse), China 77/C6
Xigazê, China 54/K7
Xiji, China 77/G4
Xi Jiang (riv.), China 77/H7
Xilin, China 77/F7
Ximiao, China 77/F3
Xin Barag Zuoqi, China 77/J2
Xinghai, China 77/E4
Xingtai (Singtai), China 77/H4
Xingu (riv.), Brazil 120/D3
Xingu (riv.), Brazil 132/C3
Xingyi, China 77/G6
Xinhe (Toksu), China 77/B3
Xining (Sining), China 77/F4
Xining, China 54/M6
Xinjiang Uygur (Sinkiang-Uigur Aut. Reg.), China 77/B3
Xinjin, China 77/K4
Xintai, China 77/J4
Xin Xian, China 77/H4
Xinxiang (Sinsiang), China 77/H4
Xinyang (Sinyang), China 77/H5
Xinyi, China 77/J5
Xinyi He (riv.), China 77/J5
Xinyuan (Künes), China 77/B3
Xique-Xique, Brazil 132/F5
Xisha (isls.), China 85/E2
Xishui, China 77/G6
Xi Ujimqin, China 77/J3
Xiushui, China 77/H6
Xiuyan, China 77/K3
Xixia, China 77/H5
Xizang (Tibet Aut. Reg.), China 77/B5
Xochihuehuetlán, Mexico 150/K8
Xochimilco, Mexico 150/L1
Xochitlán, Mexico 150/N2
Xpujil, Mexico 150/P7
Xuanhan, China 77/G5
Xuan Loc, Vietnam 72/E5
Xuanwei, China 77/F6
Xuchang (Hsüchang), China 77/H5
Xuguit, China 77/K2
Xunke, China 77/L2
Xuwen, China 77/H7
Xuzhou (Süchow), China 77/J5
Xuzhou, China 54/N6

Y

Yaak, Mont. (†59935) 262/A2
Ya'an, China 77/F6
Yaapeet, Victoria 97/B4
Ya'bad, West Bank 65/C3
Yaballo, Ethiopia 111/G6
Yabassi, Cameroon 115/B3
Yabebyry, Paraguay 144/D5
Yabis, Wadi el (dry riv.), Jordan 65/D3
Yablis, Nicaragua 154/F4
Yablonovyy (range), U.S.S.R. 54/N4
Yablonovyy (range), U.S.S.R. 48/M4
Yabrud, West Bank 65/C4
Yabucoa, P. Rico 161/E2
Yachats, Oreg. (97498) 291/C3
Yacimientos de Río Turbio, Argentina 120/B8
Yaco, Bolivia 136/B5
Yacolt, Wash. (98675) 310/C5
Yacuiba, Bolivia 120/C5
Yacuiba, Bolivia 136/D7
Yacuma (riv.), Bolivia 136/B3
Yadgir, India 68/D5
Yadkin (co.), N.C. 281/H2
Yadkin (riv.), N.C. 281/J3
Yadkinville, N.C. (27055) 281/H2
Yad Mordekhai, Israel 65/A4
Yadong, China 77/C6
Yaeyama (isls.), Japan 81/K7
Yagoua, Cameroon 115/B1
Yagra, China 77/B5
Yagradagzê Shan (mt.), China 77/D4
Yaguachi Nuevo, Ecuador 128/B4
Yaguajay, Cuba 158/F2
Yaguaraparo, Venezuela 124/G2
Yaguarí, Uruguay 145/E2
Yaguarón, Paraguay 144/B5
Yaguarón (riv.), Uruguay 145/F3
Yaguarú, Bolivia 136/D4
Yaguas (riv.), Peru 128/G4
Yaguate, Dom. Rep. 158/E6
Yagüez (riv.), P. Rico 161/A2
Yagur, Israel 65/C2
Yahav, Israel 65/D5
Yahk, Br. Col. 184/J5
Yahuma, Zaire 115/D3
Yahyalı, Turkey 63/F3
Yaizu, Japan 81/J6
Yajalón, Mexico 150/N8
Yakima, Wash. 146/F5
Yakima, Wash. 188/B1
Yakima (co.), Wash. 310/E4
Yakima, Wash. (*98901) 310/E4
Yakima (ridge), Wash. 310/E4
Yakima (riv.), Wash. 310/E4
Yakima Ind. Res., Wash. 310/E4
Yako, Upper Volta 106/D6
Yakobi (isl.), Alaska 196/M1
Yakoma, Zaire 115/D3
Yaku (isl.), Japan 81/E8
Yakumo, Japan 81/J2
Yakut A.S.S.R., U.S.S.R. 48/N3
Yakutat, Alaska 188/D6
Yakutat, Alaska (99689) 196/L3
Yakutat (bay), Alaska 196/K3
Yakutsk, U.S.S.R. 54/O3
Yakutsk, U.S.S.R. 2/R2
Yakutsk, U.S.S.R. 48/N3
Yala, Thailand 72/D6
Yalaha, Fla. (32797) 212/E3
Yalata Aboriginal Reserve, S. Australia 88/E6
Yalata Aboriginal Res., S. Australia 94/B4
Yale, Br. Col. 184/M2
Yale (mt.), Colo. 208/G5
Yale (lake), Fla. 212/E3
Yale, Ill. (62481) 222/E4
Yale, Iowa (50277) 229/E5
Yale, Mich. (48097) 250/G5
Yale, Okla. (74085) 288/N2
Yale, S. Dak. (57386) 298/O5
Yale, Va. (23897) 307/O7
Yale (lake), Wash. 310/C4
Yalesville, Conn. (†06492) 210/D3
Yalgoo, W. Australia 92/B5
Yali, Estero (riv.), Chile 138/F4
Yalinga, Cent. Afr. Rep. 115/D2
Yallahs, Jamaica 158/K6
Yallock, N.S. Wales 97/C3
Yallourn, Victoria 97/D6
Yalmer, Mich. (†49885) 250/B2
Yalobusha (co.), Miss. 256/E2
Yalobusha (riv.), Miss. 256/E3
Yalong (riv.), China 54/M7
Yalong Jiang (riv.), China 77/F6
Yalova, Çanakkale, Turkey 63/B6
Yalova, İstanbul, Turkey 63/C2
Yalpunga, N.S. Wales 97/A1
Yalta, U.S.S.R. 7/H4
Yalta, U.S.S.R. 52/D6
Yalu (riv.) 54/O5
Yalu (riv.), China 77/L3
Yalu (riv.), N. Korea 81/C3
Yalutorsk, U.S.S.R. 48/G4
Yalvaç, Turkey 63/D3
Yalvaç, Turkey 59/B2
Yamachiche, Québec 172/E3
Yamagata (pref.), Japan 81/K4
Yamagata, Japan 81/K4
Yamaguchi (pref.), Japan 81/E6
Yamaguchi, Japan 81/E6
Yamal (pen.), U.S.S.R. 54/H2
Yamal (pen.), U.S.S.R. 4/B6
Yamal (pen.), U.S.S.R. 48/G2
Yamal-Nenets Aut. Okr., U.S.S.R. 48/H3
Yamama, Saudi Arabia 59/E5
Yamanashi (pref.), Japan 81/J6
Yamantau (mt.), U.S.S.R. 52/J4
Yamarna Aboriginal Reserve, W. Australia 88/C5
Yamarna Aboriginal Res., W. Australia 92/D4
Yamasá, Dom. Rep. 158/E6
Yamaska (co.), Québec 172/E3
Yamaska, Québec 172/E4
Yamaska (riv.), Québec 172/E4
Yamaska-Est, Québec 172/E4
Yamato, Japan 81/O2
Yamatokoriyama, Japan 81/J8

472 Yamatotakada

Yamatotakada, Japan 81/J8
Yamba, N.S. Wales 97/G1
Yambah, North. Terr. 93/C7
Yambio, Sudan 111/E7
Yambio, Sudan 102/E4
Yambol, Bulgaria 45/H4
Yambou (head), St. Vin. & Grens. 161/A9
Yambrasbamba, Peru 128/D5
Yamdena (isl.), Indonesia 85/J7
Yamethin, Burma 72/C2
Yamhill (co.), Oreg. 291/D2
Yamhill, Oreg. (97148) 291/D2
Y'Ami (isl.), Philippines 82/B2
Yamma Yamma (lake), Queensland 88/G5
Yamma Yamma (lake), Queensland 95/B5
Yampa, Colo. (80483) 208/F2
Yampa (riv.), Colo. 208/B2
Yamparaéz, Bolivia 136/C6
Yampi Sound, W. Australia 88/C3
Yampi Sound, W. Australia 92/C2
Yamsk, U.S.S.R. 48/Q4
Yamun, West Bank 65/C3
Yamuna (Jumna) (riv.), Pakistan 68/E3
Yamzho Yumco (lake), China 77/C6
Yan, Nigeria 106/G7
Yana, U.S.S.R. 54/P3
Yana (riv.), U.S.S.R. 4/C3
Yana (riv.), U.S.S.R. 48/O3
Yanac, Victoria 97/A5
Yanacachi, Bolivia 136/B5
Yanahuanca, Peru 128/D8
Yanam, India 68/E5
Yan'an (Yenan), China 77/G4
Yanaoca, Peru 128/G10
Yanaul, U.S.S.R. 52/J3
Yancannia, N.S. Wales 97/B2
Yancey, Ky. (†40831) 237/P7
Yancey (co.), N.C. 281/E3
Yanceyville, N.C. (27379) 281/L2
Yancheng, China 77/K5
Yanchi, China 77/G4
Yanco, N.S. Wales 97/D4
Yandé (isl.), New Caled. 86/F4
Yandeyarra Aboriginal Reserve, W. Australia 88/B4
Yandina, Solomon Is. 86/D3
Yandoon, Burma 72/B3
Yanfolila, Mali 106/C6
Yanga, Mexico 150/P2
Yangambi, Zaire 115/D3
Yangambi, Zaire 102/E4
Yangcheng, China 77/H4
Yangchow (Yangzhou), China 77/J5
Yangchüan (Yangquan), China 77/H4
Yangchun, China 77/H7
Yangdŏk, N. Korea 81/C4
Yanggao, China 77/H3
Yanggu, S. Korea 81/C4
Yangjiang, China 77/H7
Yangquan (Yangchüan), China 77/H4
Yangshan, China 77/H7
Yang Sin, Chu (mt.), Vietnam 72/F4
Yangtze (riv.), China 54/N6
Yangtze (riv.), China 2/Q4
Yangtze (Chang Jiang) (riv.), China 77/K5
Yangyang, S. Korea 81/D4
Yangzhou (Yangchow), China 77/J5
Yanhuqu, China 77/B5
Yanji (Yenki), China 77/L3
Yankee Fork, Salmon (riv.), Idaho 220/D5
Yankee Lake, Ohio (†44403) 284/J3
Yankeetown, Fla. (32698) 212/D2
Yankeetown, Ind. (†47630) 227/C9
Yanko (creek), N.S. Wales 97/C4
Yankton, S. Dak. 188/G2
Yankton (co.), S. Dak. 298/P7
Yankton, S. Dak. (57078) 298/P8
Yanqi, China 77/C3
Yanrey, W. Australia 92/A3
Yantabulla, N.S. Wales 97/C1
Yantai (Chefoo), China 77/K4
Yantai, China 54/O6
Yantara, N.S. Wales 97/B1
Yantara (lake), N.S. Wales 97/B1
Yantic, Conn. (06389) 210/G2
Yantic (riv.), Conn. 210/G2
Yantis, Texas (75497) 303/J5
Yantley, Ala. (36924) 195/B6
Yanush, Okla. (†74574) 288/R5
Yao, Japan 81/J8
Yaoundé (cap.), Cameroon 2/K5
Yaoundé (cap.), Cameroon 102/D4
Yaoundé (cap.), Cameroon 115/B3
Yap (isl.), Micronesia 87/D5
Yapacani (riv.), Bolivia 136/C5
Yapei, Ghana 106/D7
Yapen (isl.), Indonesia 85/K6
Yapen (str.), Indonesia 85/K6
Yapraklı, Turkey 63/E2
Yaque del Norte (riv.), Dom. Rep. 158/D5
Yaque del Sur (riv.), Dom. Rep. 158/D6
Yaqui, Mexico 150/D3
Yaqui (riv.), Mexico 146/H7
Yaqui (riv.), Mexico 150)E2
Yaquina, Oreg. (†97365) 291/C3
Yara, Cuba 158/H4
Yaracuy (state), Venezuela 124/D2
Yaraka, Queensland 95/C5
Yaraligöz Daği (mt.), Turkey 59/B1
Yaralıgöz Dağı (mt.), Turkey 63/F2
Yaransk, U.S.S.R. 52/G3
Yarbo, Ala. (†36558) 195/B7
Yarbo, Sask. 181/K5
Yarboutenda, Senegal 106/B6
Yarda, Chad 111/C4
Yardley, Pa. (19067) 294/N5
Yardville, N.J. (08620) 273/D3
Yare (riv.), England 13/J5
Yare (riv.), England 10/G4
Yarega, U.S.S.R. 52/H2
Yaretas de Vizcachas, Cerro (mt.), Chile 138/G3
Yarí, Colombia 126/D7
Yarí (riv.), Colombia 126/D8
Yarim, Yemen Arab Rep. 59/D7
Yaritagua, Venezuela 124/D2
Yarkand (Shache), China 77/A4
Yarkand (riv.), China 54/K6
Yarkant He (riv.), China 77/A4
Yarker, Ontario 177/H3
Yarle (lakes), S. Australia 94/B4
Yarmouth, Iowa (52660) 229/L6
Yarmouth, Maine (04096) 243/C8
Yarmouth○, Maine (04096) 243/C8
Yarmouth○, Mass. (02675) 249/O6
Yarmouth, N.S. 162/K7
Yarmouth (co.), Nova Scotia 168/C5
Yarmouth, Nova Scotia 168/B5
Yarmouth (sound), Nova Scotia 168/B5
Yarmouth Port, Mass. (02675) 249/N6
Yarmuk (riv.), Israel 65/D2
Yarnell, Ariz. (85362) 198/C4
Yaroslavl', U.S.S.R. 7/H3
Yaroslavl', U.S.S.R. 48/D4
Yaroslavl', U.S.S.R. 52/E3
Yarqon (riv.), Israel 65/B3
Yarra (riv.), Victoria 97/C5
Yarra (riv.), Victoria 88/L6
Yarram, Victoria 97/D6
Yarrawonga, Victoria 97/C5
Yarrow, Br. Col. 184/M3
Yarrow, Mo. (†63501) 261/G2
Yarrow (riv.), Scotland 15/E5
Yarrowitch, N.S. Wales 97/F2
Yarrow Point, Wash. (†98004) 310/B2
Yartsevo, U.S.S.R. 48/J4
Yartsevo, U.S.S.R. 52/D3
Yarumal, Colombia 126/C4
Yaruu, Mongolia 77/E2
Yas (isl.), U.A.E. 59/F5
Yasawa Group (isls.), Fiji 86/P10
Yásica Abajo, Dom. Rep. 158/E5
Yasin, Pakistan 59/K2
Yasin, Pakistan 68/C1
Yasnyy, U.S.S.R. 52/J4
Yasothon, Thailand 72/D4
Yass, N.S. Wales 97/E4
Yasuj, Iran 66/G5
Yasun (cape), Turkey 63/G2
Yata (riv.), Bolivia 136/C3
Yatabe, Japan 81/P2
Yatağan, Turkey 63/C4
Yataity, Paraguay 144/C5
Yateley, England 13/G8
Yates (dam), Ala. 195/G5
Yates (co.), N.Y. 276/F5
Yates Center, Kansas (66783) 232/G4
Yates City, Ill. (61572) 222/C3
Yatesville, Georgia (31097) 217/D5
Yathkyed (lake), N.W.T. 162/F3
Yathkyed (lake), N.W. Terrs. 187/J3
Yatina, Bolivia 136/C7
Yatsushiro, Japan 81/E7
Yatta, West Bank 65/C5
Yatton, England 13/E6
Yatua (riv.), Venezuela 124/E7
Yauca, Peru 128/E10
Yauco, P. Rico 161/B2
Yauco, P. Rico 156/F1
Yauco (lake), P. Rico 161/B2
Yauli, Peru 128/D8
Yaúna Moloca, Colombia 126/E8
Yaupi, Ecuador 128/D4
Yaupon Beach, N.C. (†28461) 281/N7
Yauri, Peru 128/G10
Yautepec, Mexico 150/L2
Yauyos, Peru 128/E9
Yava, Ariz. (†86301) 198/C4
Yavapai (co.), Ariz. 198/C4
Yavapai Ind. Res., Ariz. 198/C4
Yavaraté, Colombia 126/F7
Yavarí (riv.) 120/B3
Yavarí (riv.), Peru 128/G5
Yavaros, Mexico 150/E3
Yavero (riv.), Peru 128/F9
Yavita, Venezuela 124/E6
Yavne, Israel 65/B4
Yavne'el, Israel 65/D2
Yawata, Japan 81/J7
Yawatahama, Japan 81/F7
Yawkey, W. Va. (25573) 312/C6
Yawri (bay), S. Leone 106/B7
Ya Xian, China 77/G8
Yaxley, England 13/G5
Yaylıdağı, Turkey 63/F5
Yazd (governorate), Iran 66/J5
Yazd (Yezd), Iran 66/J5
Yazd, Iran 59/F3
Yazd, Iran 54/G6
Yazdan, Iran 66/M4
Yazdan, Iran 59/H3
Yazd-e Khvasat, Iran 66/H5
Yazoo (co.), Miss. 265/D5
Yazoo (riv.), Miss. 188/H4
Yazoo (riv.), Miss. 256/C5
Yazoo City, Miss. (39194) 256/D5
Ybbs an der Donau, Austria 41/C2
Ybycuí, Paraguay 144/B5
Ybytymí, Paraguay 144/B5
Yding Skovhøj (mt.), Denmark 21/C6
Ye, Burma 72/C4
Yea, Victoria 97/C5
Yeaddiss, Ky. (41777) 237/P6
Yeadon, Pa. (19050) 294/N7
Yeager, Okla. (†74848) 288/O4
Yeagertown, Pa. (17099) 294/G4
Yebbi-Bou, Chad 111/C3
Yecheng, China 77/A4
Yecla, Spain 33/F3
Yécora, Mexico 150/E2
Yecuatla, Mexico 150/P1
Yeddo, Ind. (†47952) 227/C4
Yeeda River, W. Australia 92/C2
Yeelirrie, W. Australia 92/C4
Yefremov, U.S.S.R. 52/E4
Yegros, Paraguay 144/D5
Yeguas (pt.), P. Rico 161/F3
Yehualtepec, Mexico 150/O2
Yehud, Israel 65/B3
Yei, Sudan 111/F7
Yelabuga, U.S.S.R. 52/H3
Yelan', U.S.S.R. 52/F4
Yelcho (lake), Chile 138/E4
Yelets, U.S.S.R. 7/H3
Yelets, U.S.S.R. 48/D4
Yelets, U.S.S.R. 52/E4
Yélimané, Mali 106/B5
Yelizavety (cape), U.S.S.R. 54/R4
Yelizavety (cape), U.S.S.R. 48/P4
Yelizovo, U.S.S.R. 48/Q4
Yell (co.), Ark. 202/D3
Yell (isl.), Scotland 15/G2
Yell (isl.), Scotland 10/G1
Yell (sound), Scotland 15/G2
Yellamanchili, India 68/E5
Yelleq, Jebel (mt.), Egypt 59/B3
Yellow (sea) 54/O6
Yellow (Huang He) (riv.), China 77/J4
Yellow (sea), China 77/K4
Yellow (creek), Colo. 208/C3
Yellow (riv.), Fla. 212/B6
Yellow (riv.), Ind. 227/D2
Yellow (brook), N.J. 273/E3
Yellow (sea), N. Korea 81/B6
Yellow (creek), Ohio 284/J4
Yellow (sea), S. Korea 81/B6
Yellow (creek), Tenn. 237/F8
Yellow (creek), W. Va. 312/E1
Yellow (lake), Wis. 317/B4
Yellow (riv.), Wis. 317/F7
Yellow Bluff, Ala. (†36769) 195/C7
Yellowbud, Ohio (†45601) 284/D7
Yellowcreek, N.C. (†28771) 281/A4
Yellow Creek, Sask. 181/F3
Yellow Dog (riv.), Mich. 250/B2
Yellow Grass, Sask. 181/H6
Yellowhead (pass), Alberta 182/A3
Yellowhead (pass), Br. Col. 184/H4
Yellow Jacket, Colo. (81335) 208/B7
Yellowknife, Canada 4/C15
Yellowknife, Canada 2/D2
Yellowknife, N.W.T. 146/G3
Yellowknife (cap.), N.W.T. 162/E3
Yellowknife (cap.), N.W. Terrs. 187/G3
Yellowknife (riv.), N.W. Terrs. 187/G3
Yellow Medicine (co.), Minn. 255/B6
Yellow Pine, Ala. (36588) 195/B8
Yellow Pine, Idaho (83677) 220/C4
Yellow Pine, La. (†71039) 238/D2
Yellow Spring, W. Va. (26865) 312/J4
Yellow Springs, Md. (†21701) 245/H3
Yellow Springs, Ohio (45387) 284/C6
Yellowstone (riv.) 188/E1
Yellowstone (co.), Mont. 262/H4
Yellowstone (riv.), Mont. 262/M3
Yellowstone (riv.), N. Dak. 282/B4
Yellowstone (riv.), U.S. 146/H5
Yellowstone (lake), Wyo. 188/E2
Yellowstone (lake), Wyo. 319/B1
Yellowstone (riv.), Wyo. 319/B1
Yellowstone Nat'l Park, Idaho 262/F6
Yellowstone Nat'l Park, Mont. 262/F6
Yellowstone Nat'l Park, Wyo. (82190) 31/B1
Yellowstone Nat'l Park, Wyo. 188/E2
Yellowstone Nat'l Park, Wyo. 319/B1
Yellville, Ark. (72687) 202/E1
Yelm, Wash. (98597) 310/C4
Yelverton (bay), N.W. Terrs. 187/K1
Yelwa, Nigeria 106/F6
Yemassee, S.C. (29945) 296/F6
Yemen, People's Dem. Rep. of 2/M5
Yemen, People's Democratic Republic of 54/F8
YEMEN, PEOPLE'S DEM. REPUBLIC OF, 59/E7
YEMEN ARAB REP. 59/D7
Yemen Arab Republic 2/M5
Yemen Arab Republic 54/F8
Yemetsk, U.S.S.R. 52/F2
Yenakiyevo, U.S.S.R. 52/E5
Yenan (Yan'an), China 77/G4
Yenangyaung, Burma 72/B2
Yen Bai, Vietnam 72/E2
Yenbo, Saudi Arabia 54/E7
Yenbo, Saudi Arabia 59/C5
Yenda, N.S. Wales 97/D4
Yendi, Ghana 106/D7
Yengisar, China 77/A4
Yenice, Çanakkale, Turkey 63/B3
Yenice, İçel, Turkey 63/F4
Yenice, Zonguldak, Turkey 63/E2
Yeniceoba, Turkey 63/E3
Yeniköy, Çanakkale, Turkey 63/B6
Yeniköy, Çanakkale, Turkey 63/C5
Yeniköy, İstanbul, Turkey 63/D6
Yenimahalle, Turkey 63/E3
Yenişehir, Turkey 63/C2
Yenisey (riv.), U.S.S.R. 4/C5
Yenisey (riv.), U.S.S.R. 2/P2
Yenisey (riv.), U.S.S.R. 54/K3
Yenisey (riv.), U.S.S.R. 48/J3
Yeniseysk, U.S.S.R. 54/L4
Yeniseysk, U.S.S.R. 48/K4
Yenki (Yanji), China 77/L3
Yen Minh, Vietnam 72/E2
Yentai (Yantai), China 77/K4
Yentna (riv.), Alaska 196/A1
Yeo (lake), W. Australia 88/D5
Yeo (lake), W. Australia 92/D5
Yeola, India 68/C4
Yeoman, Ind. (47997) 227/D3
Yeotmal, India 68/D4
Yeoval, N.S. Wales 97/E3
Yeovil, England 10/E5
Yeovil, England 13/E7
Yeppoon, Queensland 95/D4
Yeppoon, Queensland 88/J4
Yerevan (Erivan), U.S.S.R. 52/F6
Yerichaña, Venezuela 124/F5
Yerington, Nev. (89447) 266/B4
Yerington Ind. Res., Nev. 266/B3
Yerkesik, Turkey 63/C4
Yerköy, Turkey 63/F3
Yerlisu, Turkey 63/C5
Yermak, U.S.S.R. 48/H4
Yermentau, 48/H4
Yermo, Calif. (92398) 204/J9
Yeroham, Israel 65/B6
Yerolimin, Greece 45/F7
Yeronga, Queensland 95/D3
Yeronga, Queensland 88/K3
Yerseke, Netherlands 27/E6
Yershov, U.S.S.R. 52/G4
Yesagyo, Burma 72/B2
Yeshbum, P.D.R. Yemen 59/E7
Yesil', 48/G4
Yeşilhisar, Turkey 63/F3
Yeşilırmak (riv.), Turkey 63/G2
Yeşilköy, Turkey 63/D6
Yeşilova, Burdur, Turkey 63/C4
Yeşilova, Niğde, Turkey 63/E3
Yeşilyurt, Turkey 63/H3
Yeso, N. Mex. (88136) 274/E4
Yeso (creek), N. Mex. 274/E4
Yesodot, Israel 65/B4
Yessentuki, U.S.S.R. 52/F6
Yessey, U.S.S.R. 48/L3
Yeste, Spain 33/E3
Yesud Hama'ala, Israel 65/D1
Yetholm, Scotland 15/F5
Yetman, N.S. Wales 97/F1
Yettem, Calif. (93670) 204/F7
Yetter, Iowa (51433) 229/D4
Ye-u, Burma 72/B2
Yeu (isl.), France 28/B4
Yevlakh, U.S.S.R. 52/G6
Yevpatoriya, U.S.S.R. 52/D5
Ye Xian, China 77/K4
Yeysk, U.S.S.R. 52/E5
Ygatimí, Paraguay 144/E4
Yhú, Paraguay 144/E4
Yi (riv.), Uruguay 145/B4
Yialousa, Cyprus 63/E5
Yiannitsá, Greece 45/F5
Yibin (Ipin), China 77/F6
Yibin, China 54/M7
Yibug Caka (lake), China 77/C5
Yichang (Ichang), China 77/H5
Yichun, Heilongjiang, China 77/L2
Yichun, Jiangxi, China 77/H6
Yidu, Hubei, China 77/H5
Yidu, Shandong, China 77/J4
Yiftah, Israel 65/D1
Yığılca, Turkey 63/D2
Yıldızeli, Turkey 63/G3
Yiliang, China 77/F7
Yinchuan (Ningsia, Yinchwan), China 77/G4
Yinchuan, China 54/M6
Yingjiang, China 77/E7
Yingkou (Yinkow), China 77/K3
Yingshan, Hubei, China 77/H5
Yingshan, Sichuan, China 77/G5
Yining, China 77/B3
Yining, China 54/K5
Yinjiang, China 77/G6
Yin Shan (mts.), China 77/G3
Yirga-Alam, Ethiopia 102/F4
Yirga Alam, Ethiopia 111/G6
Yirka, Israel 65/C2
Yirol, Sudan 111/F6
Yirrkala, North. Terr. 93/E2
Yishan, China 77/G7
Yíthion, Greece 45/F7
Yiwu (Aratürük), China 77/D3
Yiyang, China 77/H6
Ylikitka (lake), Finland 18/Q3
Ylitornio, Finland 18/O3
Ylivieska, Finland 18/O4
Ymir, Br. Col. 184/J5
Ynys Môn (Anglesey) (ridge), Wales 13/C4
Ynys Môn (Anglesey) (isl.), Wales 10/D4
Yoakum (co.), Texas 303/B4
Yoakum, Texas (77995) 303/G8
Yocalla, Bolivia 136/B6
Yocemento, Kansas (†67601) 232/C3
Yockanookany (riv.), Miss. 256/E5
Yoco, Venezuela 124/G2
Yocón, Honduras 154/D3
Yocum, Ky. (41478) 237/P5
Yoder, Colo. (80864) 208/L5
Yoder, Ind. (46798) 227/G3
Yoder, Kansas (67585) 232/E4
Yoder, Wyo. (82244) 319/H4
Yodo (riv.), Japan 81/J7
Yog (pt.), Philippines 82/E3
Yogyakarta, Indonesia 54/M10
Yogyakarta, Indonesia 85/J2
Yoho Nat'l Park, Br. Col. 162/E5
Yoho Nat'l Park, Br. Col. 184/J4
Yoichi, Japan 81/K2
Yojoa (lake), Honduras 154/D3
Yokadouma, Cameroon 115/B3
Yokawa, Japan 81/H7
Yokena, Miss. (†39180) 256/C6
Yokkaichi, Japan 81/H6
Yoko, Cameroon 115/B2
Yokohama, Japan 2/R4
Yokohama, Japan 81/O3
Yokohama, Japan 54/R6
Yokosuka, Japan 81/O3
Yokote, Japan 81/K4
Yola, Nigeria 106/G7
Yola, Nigeria 102/D4
Yolla, Tasmania 99/B3
Yolo (co.), Calif. 204/D5
Yolo, Calif. (95697) 204/B8
Yolyn, W. Va. (25654) 312/C7
Yona, Guam 86/K7
Yonago, Japan 81/F6
Yonaguni (isl.), Japan 81/K7
Yoncalla, Oreg. (97499) 291/D4
Yonezawa, Japan 81/K5
Yongamp'o, N. Korea 81/B4
Yongchang, China 77/F4
Yŏngch'ŏn, S. Korea 81/D6
Yongchuan, China 77/G6
Yongdeng, China 77/F4
Yŏngdŏk, S. Korea 81/D5
Yonges Island, S.C. (29494) 296/G6
Yonghe, China 77/H4
Yŏnghŭng, N. Korea 81/C4
Yŏngju, S. Korea 81/D5
Yongning, China 77/G4
Yongren, China 77/F6
Yongxin, China 77/H6
Yongxing, China 77/H6
Yonkers, Georgia (†31014) 217/F6
Yonkers, N.Y. (*10701) 276/O6
Yonne (dept.), France 28/E4
Yonne (riv.), France 28/E3
Yono, Japan 81/O2
Yopal, Colombia 126/D5
Yorba Linda, Calif. (92686) 204/D11
Yorito, Honduras 154/D3
York, Ala. (36925) 195/B6
York (cape), Australia 2/S6
York (cape), Australia 87/E7
York, England 13/F4
York, England 10/F4
York (cape), Greenl. 4/B13
York, Ky. (41184) 237/P3
York (co.), Maine 243/B9
York, Maine (03909) 243/B9
York○, Maine (03909) 243/B9
York (co.), Nebr. 264/G4
York, Nebr. (68467) 264/G4
York (co.), New Bruns. 170/C3
York, N.Y. (14592) 276/E5
York, N. Dak. (58386) 282/L3
York (reg. munic.), Ontario 177/E4
York, Ontario 177/J4
York, Pa. 188/L3
York (co.), Pa. 294/J6
York, Pa. (*17401) 294/J6
York (riv.), Québec 172/D1
York (cape), Queensland 88/G2
York (cape), Queensland 95/B1
York (co.), S.C. 296/E2
York, S.C. (29745) 296/E1
York (co.), Va. 307/P6
York (riv.), Va. 307/P6
York, W. Australia 88/B6
York, W. Australia 92/B1
York (sound), W. Australia 88/C2
York (sound), W. Australia 92/D1
York, Wis. (†54758) 317/D7
York Beach, Maine (03910) 243/B9
Yorke (pen.), S. Australia 88/F7
Yorke (pen.), S. Australia 94/E6
Yorketown, S. Australia 88/F6
Yorketown, S. Australia 94/E6
York Factory, Man. 162/G4
York Factory, Manitoba 179/K2
York Harbor, Maine (03911) 243/B9
York Haven, Pa. (17370) 294/J5
York Landing, Man. 146/J4
York Landing, Manitoba 179/J2
Yorklyn, Del. (19736) 245/R1
Yorkshire, North (co.), England 13/F3
Yorkshire, South (co.), England 13/F4
Yorkshire, West (co.), England 13/J1
Yorkshire, N.Y. (14173) 276/D5
Yorkshire, Ohio (45388) 284/B5
Yorkshire Dales National Park, England 13/E3
York Springs, Pa. (17372) 294/H6
Yorkton, Sask. 146/H4
Yorkton, Sask. 162/F5
Yorkton, Sask. 181/J4
Yorktown, Ark. (71678) 202/G5
Yorktown, Ind. (47396) 227/G4
Yorktown, Iowa (51656) 229/C7
Yorktown, N.J. (†08098) 273/C4
Yorktown, Texas (78164) 303/G9
Yorktown, Va. (23690) 307/R6
Yorktown Heights, N.Y. (10598) 276/N8
Yorkville, Ill. (60560) 222/E2
Yorkville, Ind. (†47022) 227/H6
Yorkville, N.Y. (13495) 276/K4
Yorkville, Ohio (43971) 284/J5
Yorkville, Tenn. (38389) 237/C8
Yoro, Honduras 154/D3
Yoron (isl.), Japan 81/N6
Yorosso, Mali 106/C6
Yosemite, Ky. (42566) 237/M6
Yosemite National Park, Calif. (95389) 204/F6
Yosemite Nat'l Park, Calif. 188/C3
Yosemite Nat'l Park, Calif. 204/F6
Yoshino (riv.), Japan 81/G6
Yoshino-Kumano National Park, Japan 81/H7
Yoshkar-Ola, U.S.S.R. 7/J3
Yoshkar-Ola, U.S.S.R. 52/G3
Yoshkar-Ola, U.S.S.R. 48/E4
Yost, Utah (†84329) 304/A2
Yŏsu, S. Korea 81/C6
Yotala, Bolivia 136/C6
Yotaú, Bolivia 136/D5
Yotvata, Israel 65/D5
Youanmi, W. Australia 92/B5
Youbou, Br. Col. 184/J3
Youghal, Ireland 10/B5
Youghal, Ireland 17/F8
Youghal (bay), Ireland 10/C5
Youghal (bay), Ireland 17/F8
Youghiogheny (riv.), Md. 245/A3
Youghiogheny (dam), Pa. 294/D6
Youghiogheny River (lake), Md. 245/A2
Youghiogheny River (lake), Pa. 294/D6
Young, Ariz. (85554) 198/D4
Young, N. S. Wales 88/H6
Young, N.S. Wales 97/E4
Young (cape), N. Zealand 100/D7
Young (mt.), North. Terr. 93/D3
Young, Sask. 181/F4
Young (co.), Texas 303/F4
Young, Uruguay 145/B3
Young America, Ind. (46998) 227/E3
Young America, Minn. (55397) 255/E6
Youngcane, Georgia (†30512) 217/D1
Young Cove, Nova Scotia 168/C4
Young Harris, Georgia (30582) 217/E1
Youngs Cove, New Bruns. 170/E3
Youngs Creek, Ind. (†47454) 227/D8
Youngs Creek, Ky. (†40759) 237/N7
Youngstown, Alberta 182/E4
Youngstown, Fla. (32466) 212/D6
Youngstown, Ind. (†47808) 227/C6
Youngstown, N.Y. (14174) 276/C4
Youngstown, Ohio (*44501) 284/J3
Youngstown, Ohio 188/K2
Youngsville, La. (70592) 238/G6
Youngsville, N. Mex. (87064) 274/C2
Youngsville, N.Y. (12791) 276/L7
Youngsville, N.C. (27596) 281/N2
Youngsville, Pa. (16371) 294/D2
Youngtown, Ariz. (85363) 198/C5
Youngwood, Pa. (15697) 294/D5
Yountville, Calif. (94599) 204/C5
Youshashan, China 77/D4
Youssoufia, Morocco 106/C2
Youyang, China 77/G6
Yozgat (prov.), Turkey 63/F3
Yozgat, Turkey 59/B2
Yozgat, Turkey 63/F3
Ypacaraí, Paraguay 144/B5
Ypané, Paraguay 144/B5
Ypané (riv.), Paraguay 144/D3
Ypé Jhú, Paraguay 144/E3
Ypoá (lake), Paraguay 144/B5
Ypres (Ieper), Belgium 27/B7
Ypsilanti, Georgia (†31827) 217/D5
Ypsilanti, Mich. (48197) 250/F6
Ypsilanti, N. Dak. (58497) 282/N6
Yreka, Calif. 188/B2
Yreka, Calif. (96097) 204/C2
Yser (riv.), Belgium 27/B7
Yssingeaux, France 28/F5
Ystad, Sweden 18/H9
Ystradgynlais, Wales 13/D6
Ythan (riv.), Scotland 15/F3
Yuan (riv.), China 54/M7
Yuan Jiang (riv.), China 77/H6
Yuanling, China 77/G6
Yuanmou, China 77/F6
Yuanping, China 77/H4
Yuba (co.), Calif. 204/D4
Yuba (riv.), Calif. 204/D4
Yuba, Okla. (†74721) 288/O7
Yuba, Wis. (54672) 317/F8
Yuba City, Calif. (95991) 204/D4
Yubari, Japan 81/L2
Yubetsu, Japan 81/L1
Yucaipa, Calif. (92399) 204/J9
Yucatán (chan.) 146/K7
Yucatán (state), Mexico 150/P6
Yucatán (pen.), Mexico 146/K7
Yucatán (pen.), Mexico 150/P7
Yucca, Ariz. (86438) 198/A4
Yucca Flat (basin), Nev. 266/E6
Yucca House Nat'l Mon., Colo. 208/B8
Yucca Valley, Calif. (92284) 204/J9
Yuci (Yütze), China 77/H4
Yudu, China 77/J6
Yuendumu, North. Terr. 93/B7
Yuexi, China 77/F6
Yueyang, China 77/H6
Yug (riv.), U.S.S.R. 52/G2
Yugorskiy (pen.), U.S.S.R. 52/K1
Yugoslavia 2/K3
Yugoslavia 7/F4
YUGOSLAVIA 45/C3
Yuhuan (isl.), China 77/K6
Yukon (riv.) 2/B2
Yukon (riv.) 146/C3
Yukon (riv.) 4/C17
Yukon (riv.), Alaska 188/C5
Yukon (riv.), Alaska 196/F2
Yukon, Mo. (65589) 261/J8
Yukon, Okla. (73099) 288/L3
Yukon, Pa. (15698) 294/C5
Yukon (riv.), Yukon 162/C3
Yukon (riv.), Yukon 187/E3
Yukon-Charley Rivers Nat'l Preserve, Alaska 196/K2
Yukon Territory 162/C3
Yukon Territory (terr.), Canada 146/E3
YUKON TERRITORY 187
Yüksekova, Turkey 63/L4
Yukuhashi, Japan 81/E7
Yule (riv.), W. Australia 92/B3
Yulee, Fla. (32097) 212/E1
Yuli (Lopnur), China 77/C3
Yulin, Guangxi Zhuangzu, China 77/G7
Yulin, Shanxi, China 77/G4
Yuma, Ariz. 188/D4
Yuma, Ariz. 146/G6
Yuma (co.), Ariz. 198/A5
Yuma, Ariz. (85364) 198/A6
Yuma (des.), Ariz. 198/A6
Yuma (co.), Colo. 208/P2
Yuma, Colo. (80759) 208/O2
Yuma (bay), Dom. Rep. 158/F6
Yuma, Tenn. (38390) 237/E9
Yuma Ind. Res., Calif. 204/L11
Yuma Marine Corps Air Sta., Ariz. 198/A6
Yuma Proving Ground, Ariz. 198/A6
Yumbel, Chile 138/E1
Yumbo, Colombia 126/B6
Yumen, China 77/E4
Yumen, China 54/L6
Yumenzhen, China 77/E3
Yumin, China 77/B2
Yumurtalık, Turkey 63/F4
Yuna (riv.), Dom. Rep. 158/E5
Yuna, W. Australia 92/A5
Yunak, Turkey 63/D3
Yunan, China 77/H7
Yunaska (isl.), Alaska 196/D4
Yuncheng, China 77/H4
Yungas, Las (reg.), Bolivia 136/B5
Yungay, Chile 138/E1
Yungkia (Wenzhou), China 77/J6
Yunguyo, Peru 128/H11
Yunnan (prov.), China 77/F7
Yunta, S. Australia 94/F5
Yunxi, China 77/G5
Yunxiao, China 77/J7
Yunyang, China 77/G5
Yupukari, Guyana 131/B4

Zzyzx 473

Yura, Bolivia 136/B7
Yuraguanal, Cuba 158/G2
Yurga, U.S.S.R. 48/J4
Yurimaguas, Peru 128/E5
Yuruá (riv.), Peru 128/F7
Yuruari (riv.), Venezuela 124/H4
Yurungkax He (riv.), China 77/A4
Yur'yevets, U.S.S.R. 52/F3
Yuscarán, Honduras 154/D4
Yushan (isls.), China 77/K6
Yü Shan (mt.), China 77/K7
Yushu, Jilin, China 77/L3
Yushu, Qinghai, China 77/E5
Yusufeli, Turkey 63/J2
Yutan, Nebr. (68073) 264/H3
Yutian, Hebei, China 77/J4
Yutian, Xinjiang Uygur, China 77/B4
Yuty, Paraguay 144/D5
Yütze (Yuci), China 77/H4
Yuxi, China 77/F7
Yu Xian, China 77/H4
Yuzawa, Japan 81/K4
Yuzhno-Kuril'sk, U.S.S.R. 48/P5
Yuzhno-Sakhalinsk, U.S.S.R. 54/R5
Yuzhno-Sakhalinsk, U.S.S.R. 48/P5
Yvelines (dept.), France 28/D3
Yverdon, Switzerland 39/C3
Yvetot, France 28/D3
Yvoir, Belgium 27/F8
Yvonand, Switzerland 39/C3
Ywathit, Burma 72/C3

Z

Zaachila, Mexico 150/L8
Zaandam (Zaanstad), Netherlands 27/B4
Zaandijk, Netherlands 27/B4
Zabaykal'sk, U.S.S.R. 48/M5
Zabid, Yemen Arab Rep. 59/D7
Ząbki, Poland 47/E2
Ząbkowice, Poland 47/B3
Ząbkowice Śląskie, Poland 47/C3
Žabljak, Yugoslavia 45/D4
Zabol, Iran 59/H3
Zabol, Iran 66/M5
Zabré, Upper Volta 106/D6
Zábřeh, Czech. 41/D2
Zabrze, Poland 7/F3
Zabrze, Poland 47/A4
Zacapa, Guatemala 154/C3
Zacapoaxtla, Mexico 150/O1
Zacapu, Mexico 150/J7
Zacatecas (state), Mexico 150/H5
Zacatecas, Mexico 150/H5
Zacatecoluca, El Salvador 154/C4
Zacatelco, Mexico 150/N1
Zacatepec, Mexico 150/L2
Zacatlán, Mexico 150/N1
Zach, Tenn. (†38580) 237/E8
Zachariah, Ky. (41396) 237/O5
Zachary, La. (70791) 238/K1
Zachow, Wis. (54182) 317/K6
Zacoalco de Torres, Mexico 150/H6
Zadar, Yugoslavia 45/B3
Zadetkyi Kyun (isl.), Burma 72/C5
Zadi, Burma 72/C4
Zadoi, China 77/E5
Zafra, Spain 33/C3
Żagań, Poland 47/B3
Žagare, U.S.S.R. 53/B2
Zagarolo, Italy 34/F7
Zagazig, Egypt 59/B3
Zagazig, Egypt 111/K3
Zagheh, Iran 66/F4
Zagora, Morocco 106/C2
Zagorsk, U.S.S.R. 7/H3
Zagorsk, U.S.S.R. 52/E3
Zagreb, Yugoslavia 7/F4
Zagreb, Yugoslavia 45/C3
Zagros (mts.), Iran 59/E3
Zagros (mts.), Iran 66/E4
Zagyva (riv.), Hungary 41/F3
Zahedan, Iran 59/H4
Zahedan, Iran 66/M6
Zahedan, Iran 54/G7
Zahl, N. Dak. (58856) 282/C2
Zahle, Lebanon 63/F6
Záhony, Hungary 41/G2
Zahran, Saudi Arabia 59/D6
Zaidín, Spain 33/G2
Zaire 2/K6
Zaire 102/E5
ZAIRE 115/D4
Zaire (Congo) (riv.) 102/E4
Zaire (dist.), Angola 115/B5
Zaire (Congo) (riv.), Zaire 115/C4
Zaječar, Yugoslavia 45/E4
Zakamensk, U.S.S.R. 48/L4
Zakho, Iraq 66/C2
Zákinthos, Greece 45/E7
Zákinthos (Zante) (isl.), Greece 45/E7
Zako, Cent. Afr. Rep. 115/D2
Zakopane, Poland 47/D4
Zala (co.), Hungary 41/D3
Zala (riv.), Hungary 41/D3
Zalaegerszeg, Hungary 41/D3
Zalamea de la Serena, Spain 33/D3
Zalamea la Real, Spain 33/C4
Zalaszentgrót, Hungary 41/D3
Zalău, Romania 45/F2
Zaleski, Ohio (45698) 284/F7
Zalim, Saudi Arabia 59/D5
Zalingei, Sudan 111/D5
Zalma, Mo. (63787) 261/N8
Zaltbommel, Netherlands 27/G5
Zalun, Burma 72/B3
Zama (lake), Alberta 182/A5
Zama, Miss. (†39090) 256/F5
Zambales (prov.), Philippines 82/C3
Žamberk, Czech. 41/D1
Zambezi (riv.) 2/L6
Zambezi (riv.) 102/E6
Zambezi (riv.), Angola 115/D6
Zambezi (riv.), Mozambique 118/E3
Zambezi (riv.), Namibia 118/C3
Zambezi, Zambia 115/D6
Zambezi (riv.), Zambia 115/D7
Zambezi (riv.), Zimbabwe 118/E3
Zambézia (prov.), Mozambique 118/F3
Zambia 2/L6
Zambia 102/E6
ZAMBIA 115/E7
Zamboanga, Philippines 85/G4
Zamboanga, Philippines 82/C7
Zamboanga, Philippines 54/N9
Zamboanga del Norte (prov.), Philippines 82/D6
Zamboanga del Sur (prov.), Philippines 82/D7
Zambrów, Poland 47/E2
Zamora, Calif. (95698) 204/C5
Zamora, Ecuador 128/C5
Zamora (riv.), Ecuador 128/B4
Zamora (prov.), Spain 33/D2
Zamora, Spain 33/D2
Zamora-Chinchipe (prov.), Ecuador 128/C5
Zamora de Hidalgo, Mexico 150/H7
Zamość (prov.), Poland 47/F3
Zamość, Poland 47/F3
Zams, Austria 41/A3
Zamtang, China 77/F5
Zanaga, Congo 115/B4
Zanda, China 77/A5
Zanderij, Suriname 131/D3
Zanderij, Suriname 120/D2
Zandvoort, Netherlands 27/E4
Zanesfield, Ohio (43360) 284/C5
Zanesville, Ind. (46799) 227/G3
Zanesville, Ohio 188/K3
Zanesville, Ohio (43701) 284/G6
Zanja de Lira, Venezuela 124/E3
Zanjan (governorate), Iran 66/F2
Zanjan, Iran 59/E2
Zanjan, Iran 66/K5
Zanjan (riv.), Iran 66/F2
Zanoni, Mo. (65784) 261/H9
Zante (Zákinthos), Greece 45/E7
Zanthus, W. Australia 92/C5
Zanzibar, Tanzania 102/F5
Zanzibar, Tanzania 115/G5
Zanzibar (isl.), Tanzania 2/M6
Zanzibar (isl.), Tanzania 102/F5
Zanzibar (isl.), Tanzania 115/G5
Zanzibar Mjini (reg.), Tanzania 115/G5
Zanzibar Shambani North (reg.), Tanzania 115/G5
Zanzibar Shambani South (reg.), Tanzania 115/G5
Zao (mt.), Japan 81/K5
Zaouiet Kounta, Algeria 106/D3
Zaoyang, China 77/H5
Zaozernyy, U.S.S.R. 48/K4
Zaozhuang, China 77/J5
Zap, N. Dak. (58580) 282/G5
Západočeský (reg.), Austria 41/B2
Západoslovenský (reg.), Austria 41/D2
Zapala, Argentina 143/B4
Zapala, Argentina 120/B6
Zapaleri, Cerro (mt.), Argentina 143/C1
Zapaleri, Cerro (mt.), Bolivia 136/B8
Zapaleri, Cerro (mt.), Chile 138/C4
Zapallar, Chile 138/A9
Zapata (pen.), Cuba 158/C2
Zapata (co.), Texas 303/E11
Zapata, Texas (78076) 303/E11
Zapata Occidental (swamp), Cuba 158/D2
Zapata Oriental (swamp), Cuba 158/D2
Zapatera (isl.), Nicaragua 154/E5
Zapatoca, Colombia 126/D4
Zapatosa, Ciénaga de (swamp), Colombia 126/D3
Zapicán, Uruguay 145/E4
Zapiga, Chile 138/B2
Zapolyarnyy, U.S.S.R. 52/D1
Zaporozh'ye, U.S.S.R. 7/H4
Zaporozh'ye, U.S.S.R. 48/D5
Zaporozh'ye, U.S.S.R. 52/E5
Zapotillo, Ecuador 128/B5
Zapucay, Uruguay 145/D2
Zapug, China 77/B5
Za Qu (riv.), China 77/E5
Zara, Turkey 59/C1
Zara, Turkey 63/G3
Zara (Zadar), Yugoslavia 45/B3
Zarafshan, 48/G5
Zaragoza, Colombia 126/C4
Zaragoza, Chihuahua, Mexico 150/F1
Zaragoza, Coahuila, Mexico 150/J2
Zaragoza, Puebla, Mexico 150/O1
Zaragoza (prov.), Spain 33/F2
Zaragoza (Saragossa), Spain 33/F2
Zarand, Iran 59/G3
Zarand, Iran 66/H6
Zaranj, Afghanistan 68/A2
Zaranj, Afghanistan 59/H3
Zarasai, U.S.S.R. 53/C3
Zárate, Argentina 143/G6
Zaraza, Venezuela 124/F3
Zard Kuh (mt.), Iran 66/F4
Zarembo (isl.), Alaska 196/N2
Zarephath, N.J. (08890) 273/D2
Zaria, Nigeria 106/F6
Zaria, Nigeria 102/C3
Zarineh (riv.), Iran 66/E2
Zărnești, Romania 45/G3
Zarqa' (riv.), Jordan 65/D3
Zarqam, Iran 66/H6
Zaruma, Ecuador 128/C4
Zarumilla, Peru 128/B4
Żary, Poland 47/B3
Zarzal, Colombia 126/B5
Zarza la Mayor, Spain 33/C3
Zarzis, Tunisia 106/G2
Zarzis, Tunisia 102/D1
Zaskar (mts.), India 68/D2
Zastron, S. Africa 118/D6
Žatec, Czech. 41/B1
Zavala (co.), Texas 303/E9
Zavalla, Argentina 143/F6
Zavalla, Texas (75980) 303/K6
Zavdi'el, Israel 65/B4
Zaventem, Belgium 27/C9
Zavitinsk, U.S.S.R. 48/O4
Zawi, Zimbabwe 118/D3
Zawia, Libya 102/D1
Zawia, Libya 111/B1
Zawiercie, Poland 47/D3
Zayandeh (riv.), Iran 66/H4
Zayar, China 77/B3
Zaysan, U.S.S.R. 48/J5
Zaysan (lake), U.S.S.R. 54/K5
Zaysan (lake), U.S.S.R. 48/J5
Zayü, China 77/E6
Zaza del Medio, Cuba 158/F2
Zázrivá, Czech. 41/E2
Zbąszyń, Poland 47/B2
Zbiroh, Czech. 41/B2
Zborov, Czech. 41/F2
Žďár nad Sázavou, Czech. 41/C2
Zduńska Wola, Poland 47/D3
Zealand (Sjaelland) (isl.), Den. 21/E6
Zealand, New Bruns. 170/D2
Zealandia, Sask. 181/D4
Zearing, Iowa (50278) 229/G4
Zeballos, Br. Col. 184/D5
Zebdani, Syria 63/G6
Zebirget (isl.), Egypt 59/C5
Zebulon, Georgia (30295) 217/D4
Zebulon, Ky. (†41501) 237/S5
Zebulon, N.C. (27597) 281/N3
Zedelgem, Belgium 27/C6
Zeebrugge, Belgium 27/C6
Zeehan, Tasmania 99/B3
Zeeland, Mich. (49464) 250/D6
Zeeland (prov.), Netherlands 27/D6
Zeeland, N. Dak. (58581) 282/L8
Ze'elim, Israel 65/A5
Zeerust, S. Africa 118/D5
Zeewolde, Netherlands 27/G4
Zefat, Israel 65/C2
Zegharta, Lebanon 63/G5
Zegrzyńskie (lake), Poland 47/E2
Zehdenick, E. Germany 22/E2
Zehner, Sask. 181/G5
Zeigler, Ill. (62999) 222/D6
Zeila, Somalia 115/H1
Zeil am Main, W. Germany 22/D4
Zeist, Netherlands 27/G4
Zeitz, E. Germany 22/E3
Zekiah Swamp (riv.), Md. 245/L7
Zêkog, China 77/F5
Zele, Belgium 27/E6
Zelenoborskiy, U.S.S.R. 52/D1
Zelenodol'sk, U.S.S.R. 52/G3
Zelenokumsk, U.S.S.R. 52/F6
Zelienople, Pa. (16063) 294/B4
Želiezovce, Czech. 41/E2
Zell, S. Dak. (57483) 298/M4
Zell, Luzern, Switzerland 39/E2
Zell, Zürich, Switzerland 39/G2
Zell, W. Germany 22/B4
Zella, Libya 102/D2
Zella, Libya 111/C2
Zella-Mehlis, E. Germany 22/D3
Zell am See, Austria 41/B3
Zell am Ziller, Austria 41/A3
Zellersee (lake), Switzerland 39/G1
Zellwood, Fla. (32798) 212/E3
Zelma, Sask. 181/F4
Zelow, Poland 47/D3
Zelten, Jebel (mts.), Libya 111/D2
Zeltweg, Austria 41/C3
Zelzate, Belgium 27/D6
Zemio, Cent. Afr. Rep. 115/D2
Zemongo, Cent. Afr. Rep. 115/E2
Zemple, Minn. (†56636) 255/E3
Zempoala, Mexico 150/Q1
Zemst, Belgium 27/E7
Zenas, Ind. (†47223) 227/G6
Zenda, Kansas (67159) 232/D4
Zeneta, Sask. 181/J5
Zenia, Calif. (95495) 204/B3
Zenica, Yugoslavia 45/C3
Zenith, Ill. (†62899) 222/E5
Zenith, Kansas (†67578) 232/D4
Zenith, W. Va. (†24951) 312/F7
Zenith-Saltwater, Wash. (†98101) 310/C3
Zenjan (Zanjan), Iran 66/F2
Zenobia (peak), Colo. 208/B1
Zenon Park, Sask. 181/H2
Zenoria, La. (†71371) 238/F3
Zent, Ark. (†72021) 202/H4
Zenta (Senta), Yugo. 45/D3
Zeona, S. Dak. (57795) 298/D3
Žepče, Yugoslavia 45/D3
Zepernick, E. Germany 22/F3
Zephyr, Ontario 177/E3
Zephyr, Texas (76890) 303/F6
Zephyr Cove, Nev. (89448) 266/A3
Zephyrhills, Fla. (33599) 212/D3
Zepp, Va. (†22654) 307/L3
Zerbst, E. Germany 22/E3
Zereh, Gowd-e (depr.), Afghanistan 68/A3
Zermatt, Switzerland 39/E4
Zernez, Switzerland 39/K3
Zernograd, U.S.S.R. 52/F5
Zessfontein, Namibia 118/A3
Zêtang, China 77/G6
Zetland (trad. co.), Scot. 15/B4
Zeulenroda, E. Germany 22/D3
Zeven, W. Germany 22/C2
Zevenaar, Netherlands 27/J5
Zevenbergen, Netherlands 27/E5
Zeya, U.S.S.R. 48/N4
Zeya (riv.), U.S.S.R. 48/N4
Zeytinburnu, Turkey 63/D6
Zeytindağ, Turkey 63/B3
Zgierz, Poland 47/D3
Zgorzelec, Poland 47/B3
Zhanang, China 77/D6
Zhanghei, China 77/J3
Zhangjiakou (Kalgan), China 77/J3
Zhangjiakou, China 54/N5
Zhangping, China 77/J6
Zhangye (Changyeh), China 77/F4
Zhangye, China 54/M6
Zhangzhou (Changchow), China 77/J7
Zhanjiang (Chankiang), China 77/H7
Zhanjiang, China 54/N7
Zhanyi, China 77/F6
Zhaodong, China 77/K2
Zhaojue, China 77/F6
Zhaoqing, China 77/H7
Zhaosu, China 77/B3
Zhaotong (Chaotung), China 77/F6
Zhari Namco (lake), China 77/C5
Zhashui, China 77/G5
Zhatay, U.S.S.R. 48/O3
Zhaxi Co (lake), China 77/C5
Zhdanov, U.S.S.R. 7/H4
Zhdanov, U.S.S.R. 48/D5
Zhdanov, U.S.S.R. 52/E5
Zhejiang (Chekiang) (prov.), China 77/K6
Zhelaniye (cape), U.S.S.R. 48/H2
Zheleznodorozhnyy, U.S.S.R. 52/H2
Zheleznogorsk, U.S.S.R. 52/E4
Zheleznogorsk-Ilimskiy, U.S.S.R. 48/L4
Zhenba, China 77/G5
Zheng'an, China 77/G6
Zhenglan, China 77/J3
Zhengzhou (Chengchow), China 77/H5
Zhengzhou, China 54/N6
Zhenjiang (Chinkiang), China 77/J5
Zhenxiong, China 77/F6
Zhenyuan, China 77/G6
Zhido, China 77/E5
Zhigalovo, U.S.S.R. 48/L4
Zhigansk, U.S.S.R. 4/C3
Zhigansk, U.S.S.R. 54/N3
Zhigansk, U.S.S.R. 48/N3
Zhigulevsk, U.S.S.R. 52/G4
Zhi Qu (Tongtian He) (riv.), China 77/E5
Zhirnovsk, U.S.S.R. 52/G4
Zhitomir, U.S.S.R. 7/G3
Zhitomir, U.S.S.R. 48/C4
Zhitomir, U.S.S.R. 52/C4
Zhlobin, U.S.S.R. 52/D4
Zhmerinka, U.S.S.R. 52/C5
Zhob (riv.), Pakistan 59/J3
Zhob (riv.), Pakistan 68/B2
Zhodino, U.S.S.R. 52/C4
Zhongba, China 77/B6
Zhongdian, China 77/F6
Zhongning, China 77/G4
Zhongshan (Chungshan), China 77/H7
Zhongwei, China 77/F4
Zhoushan (arch.), China 77/K5
Zhovtnevoye, U.S.S.R. 52/D5
Zhuanghe, China 77/K4
Zhucheng, China 77/J4
Zhukovka, U.S.S.R. 52/D4
Zhumadian (Chumatien), China 77/H5
Zhushan, China 77/G5
Zhuzhou (Chuchow), China 77/H6
Zhuzhou, China 54/N7
Zia Pueblo, N. Mex. (†87053) 274/C3
Žiar nad Hronom, Czech. 41/E2
Zibak, Afghanistan 59/K2
Zibak, Afghanistan 68/C1
Zibo (Tzepo), China 77/J4
Zibo, China 54/N6
Zichang, China 77/G4
Židlochovice, Czech. 41/D2
Ziebach (co.), S. Dak. 298/F4
Ziębice, Poland 47/C3
Ziel (mt.), North. Terr. 88/E4
Ziel (mt.), North. Terr. 93/C7
Zielona Góra (prov.), Poland 47/B3
Zielona Góra, Poland 47/B3
Zierikzee, Netherlands 27/D5
Zifta, Egypt 111/J3
Zigong (Tzekung), China 77/F6
Ziguei, Chad 111/C5
Zigui, China 77/H5
Ziguinchor, Senegal 106/A6
Ziguinchor, Senegal 102/A3
Zihuantanejo, Mexico 150/J8
Zikhron Ya'aqov, Israel 65/B2
Zilbir (riv.), Iran 66/D1
Zile, Turkey 59/C1
Zile, Turkey 63/G2
Zilfi, Saudi Arabia 59/E4
Žilina, Czech. 41/E2
Zillah, Wash. (98953) 310/E4
Zillis-Reischen, Switzerland 39/H3
Zilupe, U.S.S.R. 53/D2
Zilwaukee, Mich. (†48601) 250/F5
Zim, Minn. (55799) 255/F3
Zima, U.S.S.R. 48/L4
Zimatlán de Álvarez, Mexico 150/L8
Zimbabwe 2/L6
Zimbabwe 102/E6
ZIMBABWE 118/D4
Zimbabwe Nat'l Park, Zimbabwe 118/E4
Zimmerdale, Kansas (†67117) 232/E3
Zimmerman, La. (†71409) 238/E4
Zimmerman, Minn. (55398) 255/E5
Zimnicea, Romania 45/G4
Zimnitsa, Bulgaria 45/H4
Zinal, Switzerland 39/E4
Zinc, Ark. (†72601) 202/E1
Zinder, Niger 106/F6
Zinder, Niger 102/C3
Zingren, China 77/G6
Zingst, E. Germany 22/E1
Zinhui, China 77/H7
Zinjibar, P.D.R. Yemen 59/E7
Zinnik (Soignies), Belgium 27/D7
Zion, Ark. (72589) 202/G1
Zion, Ill. (60099) 222/F1
Zion, Md. (†21901) 245/P2
Zion, Mo. (†63645) 261/M8
Zion, N.J. (†08853) 273/D3
Zion, S.C. (†29574) 296/J3
Zion Hill, St. Chris.-Nevis 161/D11
Zion National Park, Utah (84767) 304/B6
Zion Nat'l Park, Utah 304/A6
Zionsville, Ind. (46077) 227/E5
Zionville, N.C. (28698) 281/F2
Zipaquirá, Colombia 126/D5
Zippori, Israel 65/C2
Zirc, Hungary 41/D3
Žirje (isl.), Yugoslavia 45/B4
Zirkel (mt.), Colo. 208/F1
Zirko (isl.), U.A.E. 59/F5
Zirl, Austria 41/A3
Zirndorf, W. Germany 22/D4
Zistersdorf, Austria 41/D2
Zitácuaro, Mexico 150/J7
Zittau, E. Germany 22/F3
Zitterwald (plat.), Belgium 27/J8
Zivarık, Turkey 63/E3
Ziwa Magharibi (West Lake) (reg.), Tanzania 115/F4
Ziyang, China 77/F5
Ziz, Wadi (dry riv.), Morocco 106/D2
Zizers, Switzerland 39/J3
Zlaté Moravce, Czech. 41/E2
Zlatograd, Bulgaria 45/G5
Zlatoust, U.S.S.R. 54/G4
Zlatoust, U.S.S.R. 48/F4
Zlín (Gottwaldov), Czech. 41/D2
Zliten, Libya 111/C1
Złocieniec, Poland 47/C2
Złotoryja, Poland 47/C3
Złotów, Poland 47/C2
Žlutice, Czech. 41/B1
Znamenka, U.S.S.R. 52/D5
Żnin, Poland 47/C2
Znojmo, Czech. 41/D2
Zoar (lake), Conn. 210/C3
Zoar, Ohio (44697) 284/H4
Zoarville, Ohio (44698) 284/H4
Zofingen, Switzerland 39/F2
Zogang, China 77/E5
Zohreh (riv.), Iran 66/F5
Zoigê, China 77/F5
Zolfo Springs, Fla. (33890) 212/E4
Zollikofen, Switzerland 39/E3
Zollikon, Switzerland 39/G2
Zolotonosha, U.S.S.R. 52/D5
Zomba, Malawi 115/G7
Zomba, Malawi 102/F6
Zonderend (riv.), S. Africa 118/G6
Zongo, Bolivia 136/B5
Zongo, Zaire 115/C3
Zongolica, Mexico 150/P2
Zonguldak (prov.), Turkey 63/D2
Zonguldak, Turkey 63/D2
Zonguldak, Turkey 59/B1
Zonhoven, Belgium 27/G6
Zoo Baba (well), Niger 106/G5
Zook, Kansas (†67550) 232/C3
Zorbatiya, Iraq 66/D4
Zorita, Spain 33/D3
Zorritos, Peru 128/B4
Zortman, Mont. (59546) 262/H3
Zottegem, Belgium 27/D7
Zouar, Chad 111/C3
Zouîrât, Mauritania 106/B4
Zoutkamp, Netherlands 27/J2
Zrenjanin, Yugoslavia 45/E3
Zuata, Venezuela 124/F3
Zuata (riv.), Venezuela 124/F3
Zububa, West Bank 65/C2
Zucchero (mt.), Switzerland 39/G4
Zudáñez, Bolivia 136/C6
Zug (canton), Switzerland 39/G2
Zug, Switzerland 39/G2
Zugdidi, U.S.S.R. 52/F6
Zugersee (lake), Switzerland 39/F2
Zugspitze (mt.), Austria 41/A3
Zugspitze (mt.), W. Germany 22/D5
Zuidelijke IJsselmeerpolders (prov.), Netherlands 27/H4
Zuienkerke, Belgium 27/C6
Zuila, Libya 111/C2
Zújar, Spain 33/E4
Zújar (res.), Spain 33/D3
Zula, Ethiopia 111/G4
Zula, Ethiopia 59/C6
Zula, Ky. (†42603) 237/M7
Zulia (state), Venezuela 124/B2
Zulia (riv.), Venezuela 124/B3
Zülpich, W. Germany 22/B3
Zulu, Ind. (†46773) 227/H2
Zulueta, Cuba 158/E2
Zululand (reg.), S. Africa 118/E5
Zumba, Ecuador 128/C5
Zumbo, Mozambique 118/E3
Zumbro (riv.), Minn. 255/F6
Zumbro Falls, Minn. (55991) 255/F6
Zumbrota, Minn. (55992) 255/F6
Zumpango del Río, Mexico 150/J8
Zumpango de Ocampo, Mexico 150/L1
Zundert, Netherlands 27/F6
Zungeru, Nigeria 106/F7
Zunhua, China 77/J3
Zuni (riv.), Ariz. 198/F4
Zuni, N. Mex. (87327) 274/A3
Zuni (mts.), N. Mex. 274/A3
Zuni (riv.), N. Mex. 274/A3
Zuni, Va. (23898) 307/P7
Zuni Ind. Res., N. Mex. 274/A3
Zunyi (Tsunyi), China 77/G6
Zunyi, China 54/M7
Zuoz, Switzerland 39/J3
Zuqar (isl.), Yemen Arab Rep. 59/D7
Zurabad, Iran 66/M3
Zurich, Kansas (67676) 232/C2
Zurich, Mont. (59547) 262/G2
Zurich, Ontario 177/C4
Zürich (canton), Switzerland 39/G2
Zürich, Switzerland 39/F2
Zürich, Switzerland 7/E4
Zürichsee (lake), Switzerland 39/G2
Żuromin, Poland 47/E2
Zurzach, Switzerland 39/F1
Zushi, Japan 81/O3
Zutphen, Netherlands 27/J4
Zuweiza, Jordan 65/D4
Zuyevka, U.S.S.R. 52/H3
Zvolen, Czech. 41/E2
Zvornik, Yugoslavia 45/D3
Zwai (lake), Ethiopia 111/G6
Zwanenburg, Netherlands 27/A4
Zwara, Libya 111/B1
Zwart (riv.), S. Africa 118/G7
Zwartsluis, Netherlands 27/H3
Zweibrücken, W. Germany 22/B4
Zweisimmen, Switzerland 39/D3
Zwelitsha, S. Africa 118/D6
Zwenkau, E. Germany 22/E3
Zwettl-Niederösterreich, Austria 41/C2
Zwickau, E. Germany 22/E3
Zwijndrecht, Netherlands 27/E5
Zwingle, Iowa (52079) 229/M4
Zwischenahn, W. Germany 22/B2
Zwoleń, Poland 47/E3
Zwolle, La. (71486) 238/C3
Zwolle, Netherlands 27/J3
Zychlin, Poland 47/D2
Żyrardów, Poland 47/E2
Zyryanka, U.S.S.R. 4/C2
Zyryanka, U.S.S.R. 54/S3
Zyryanka, U.S.S.R. 48/Q3
Zyryanovsk, U.S.S.R. 48/J5
Żywiec, Poland 47/D4
Zzyzx, Calif. (†92309) 204/J8

GEOGRAPHICAL TERMS

A. = Arabic Burm. = Burmese Camb. = Cambodian Ch. = Chinese Czech. = Czechoslovakian Dan. = Danish Du. = Dutch Finn. = Finnish Fr. = French Ger. = German Ice. = Icelandic
It. = Italian Jap. = Japanese Mong. = Mongol Nor. = Norwegian Per. = Persian Port. = Portuguese Russ. = Russian Sp. = Spanish Sw. = Swedish Turk. = Turkish

Term	Language	Meaning
Å	Nor., Sw.	Stream
Aas	Dan., Nor.	Hills
Abajo	Sp.	Lower
Ada, Adasi	Turk.	Island
Altipiano	It.	Plateau
Altiplano	Sp.	Plateau
Alv, Alf, Elf	Sw.	River
Arrecife	Sp.	Reef
Asa	Nor., Sw.	Hill
Asaga	Turk.	Lower
Austral	Sp.	Southern
Baai	Du.	Bay
Bab	Arabic	Gate or Strait
Bahia	Sp.	Bay
Bahr	Arabic	Marsh, Lake, Sea, River
Baia	Port.	Bay
Baie	Fr.	Bay, Gulf
Baizo	Port.	Low
Bakke	Dan.	Hill
Bana	Jap.	Cape
Bañados	Sp.	Marshes
Band	Per.	Mt. Range
Bandao	Ch.	Peninsula
Bandar	Per.	Harbor
Barra	Sp.	Reef
Bel	Turk.	Pass
Belt	Ger.	Strait
Ben	Gaelic	Mountain
Bera	Du.	Mountain
Berg	Ger., Du.	Mountain
Bir	Arabic	Well
Boca	Sp.	Gulf, Inlet
Boğhaz	Turk.	Strait
Bolshoi, Bolshaya	Russ.	Big
Bolson	Sp.	Depression
Bong	Korean	Mountain
Boreal	Sp.	Northern
Breen	Nor.	Glacier
Bro	Dan., Nor., Sw.	Bridge
Bucht	Ger.	Bay
Bugt	Dan.	Bay
Bukhta	Russ.	Bay
Bukit	Malay	Hill, Mountain
Bukt	Nor., Sw.	Bay, Gulf
Burnu, Burun	Turk.	Cape, Point
By	Dan., Nor., Sw.	Town
Cabo	Port., Sp.	Cape
Campos	Port.	Plains
Canal	Port., Sp.	Channel
Cap, Capo	Fr., It.	Cape
Cataratas	Sp.	Falls
Catena	It.	Mt. Range
Catingas	Port.	Open Woodlands
Cayos	Sp.	Islands
Central, Centrale	Fr., It.	Middle
Cerrito, Cerro	Sp.	Hill
Cerros	Sp.	Hills, Mountains
Chai	Turk.	River
Chott	Arabic	Salt Lake
Ciénaga	Sp.	Swamp
Ciudad	Sp.	City
Col	Fr.	Pass
Cordillera	Sp.	Mt. Range, Mts.
Côte	Fr.	Coast
Csatoria	Magyar	Canal
Cuchilla	Sp.	Mt. Range
Curiche	Sp.	Swamp
Dağ, Daği	Turk.	Mountain, Peak
Dağlari	Turk.	Mt. Range
Dal	Nor., Sw.	Valley
Dar	Arabic	Land
Dar'ya	Russ.	River
Daryacheh	Per.	Marshy Lake
Dasht	Per.	Desert, Plain
Deniz, Denizi	Turk.	Sea, Lake
Desierto	Sp.	Desert
Détroit	Fr.	Strait
Djeziret	Arabic, Turk.	Island
Do	Korean	Island
Doi	Thai	Mountain
Eiland	Du.	Island
Elv	Dan., Nor.	River
Embalse	Sp.	Reservoir
Emi	Berber	Mountain
Erg	Arabic	Dune, Desert
Eski	Turk.	Old
Est, Este	Fr., Port., Sp.	East
Estero	Sp.	Estuary, Creek
Estrecho, Estreito	Sp., Port.	Strait
Etang	Fr.	Pond, Lagoon, Lake
Feng	Ch.	Mountain
Fiume	It.	River
Fjäll	Sw.	Mountain
Fjeld, Fjell	Nor.	Hills, Mountain
Fjord	Dan., Nor., Sw.	Fiord
Fleuve	Fr.	River
Fljót	Ice.	Stream
Fluss	Ger.	River
Fors	Sw.	Waterfall
Fos, Foss	Dan., Nor.	Waterfall
Gamla	Nor.	Old
Gamle	Dan.	Old
Gata	Jap.	Lake
Gawa	Jap.	River
Gebel	Arabic	Mountain
Gebergte	Du.	Mt. Range
Gebirge	Ger.	Mt. Range
Gobi	Mongol	Desert
Goe	Jap.	Pass
Gol	Mongol, Turk.	Lake, Stream
Golf	Ger., Du.	Gulf
Golfe	Fr.	Gulf
Golfo	Sp., It., Port.	Gulf
Gölü	Turk.	Lake
Gora	Russ.	Mountain
Grand, Grande	Fr., Sp.	Big
Groot	Du.	Big
Gross	Ger.	Big
Grosso	It., Port.	Big
Guba	Russ.	Bay, Gulf
Gunto	Jap.	Archipelago
Gunung	Malay	Mountain
Hai	Ch.	Sea
Haixia	Ch.	Strait
Halbinsel	Ger.	Peninsula
Hamáda, Hammada	Arabic	Rocky Plateau
Hamn	Sw.	Harbor
Hamún	Per.	Marsh
Hanto	Jap.	Peninsula
Has, Hassi	Arabic	Well
Hav	Dan., Nor., Sw.	Sea, Ocean
Havet	Nor.	Bay
Havn	Dan., Nor.	Harbor
Havre	Fr.	Harbor
He	Ch.	River, Stream
Higashi, Higasi	Jap.	East
Hochebene	Ger.	Plateau
Hoek	Du.	Cape
Hoku	Jap.	North
Holm	Dan., Nor., Sw.	Island
Hory	Czech.	Mountains
Hoved	Dan., Nor.	Cape, Promontory
Hu	Ch.	Lake
Huang	Ch.	Yellow
Huk	Dan., Nor., Sw.	Point
Hus, Huus	Dan., Nor., Sw.	House
Idehan	Arabic	Desert
Ile	Fr.	Island
Ilet	Fr.	Islet
Ilot	Fr.	Islet
Indre	Dan., Nor.	Inner
Inferieur, Inferiore	Fr., It.	Lower
Inner, Inre	Sw.	Inner
Insel	Ger.	Island
Irmak	Turk.	River
Isla	Sp.	Island
Isola	It.	Island
Jabal, Jebel	Arabic	Mountains
Järvi	Finn.	Lake
Jaure	Sw.	Lake
Jiang	Ch.	River, Stream
Jima	Jap.	Island
Joki	Finn.	River
Kaap	Du.	Cape
Kabir, Kebir	Arabic	Big
Kai	Jap.	Sea
Kaikyo	Jap.	Strait
Kami	Turk.	Upper
Kanaal	Du.	Canal
Kanal	Russ., Ger.	Canal, Channel
Kao	Thai	Mountain
Kap, Kapp	Nor., Sw., Ice.	Cape
Kaupunki	Finn.	Town
Kawa	Jap.	River
Khao	Thai	Mountain
Khrebet	Russ.	Mt. Range
Kita	Jap.	North
Klein	Du., Ger.	Small
Klint	Dan.	Promontory
Kô	Jap.	Lake
Ko	Thai	Island
Koh	Camb., Khmer.	Island
Kop	Du.	Peak, Head
Köping	Sw.	Market, Borough
Körfez, Körfezi	Turk.	Gulf
Kosa	Russ.	Spit
Kosui	Jap.	Lake
Kraal	Du.	Native Village
Kuchuk	Turk.	Small
Kuh, Kuhha	Per.	Mt. Range, Mts.
Kul	Sinkiang Turki	Lake
Kum	Turk.	Desert
Kuro	Jap.	Black
Laag	Du.	Low
Lac	Fr.	Lake
Lago	Port., Sp., It.	Lake
Lagoa	Port.	Lagoon
Laguna	Sp.	Lagoon
Lagune	Fr.	Lagoon
Lahti	Finn.	Bay, Bight
Län	Sw.	County
Liedao	Ch.	Islands, Archipelago
Lilla	Sw.	Small
Lille	Dan., Nor.	Small
Ling	Ch.	Mountain
Llanos	Sp.	Plains
Mae Nam	Thai	River
Mali, Malaya	Russ.	Small
Man	Korean	Bay
Mar	Sp., Port.	Sea
Mare	It.	Sea
Medio	Sp.	Middle
Meer	Du.	Lake
Meer	Ger.	Sea
Mer	Fr.	Sea
Meridionale	It.	Southern
Meseta	Sp.	Plateau
Middelst, Midden	Du.	Middle
Minami	Jap.	Southern
Mis	Russ.	Cape
Misaki	Jap.	Cape
Mittel	Ger.	Middle
Mont	Fr.	Mountain
Montagne	Fr.	Mountain
Montaña	Sp.	Mountains
Monte	Sp., It., Port.	Mountain
More	Russ.	Sea
Mörön	Mong.	Stream
Morro	Port., Sp.	Mountain, Promontory
Morue	Fr.	Hill
Moyen	Fr.	Middle
Muang	Siamese	Town
Mui	Vietnamese	Cape, Point
Mys	Russ.	Cape
Nada	Jap.	Sea
Naka	Jap.	Middle
Nam	Burm., Lao.	River
Namakzar	Per.	Salt Waste
Nan	Jap.	South
Nes	Nor.	Cape, Point
Nevado	Sp.	Snow-covered Peak
Nieder	Ger.	Lower
Nishi, Nisi	Jap.	West
Nizhni, Nizhnyaya	Russ.	Lower
Njarga	Finn.	Peninsula, Promontory
Nong	Thai	Lake
Noord	Du.	North
Nord	Fr., Ger.	North
Norte	Sp., It., Port.	North
Nos	Russ.	Cape
Novi, Novaya	Russ.	New
Nur, Nuur	Ch., Mong.	Lake
Nuruu	Mong.	Mountains
Nusa	Malay	Island
Ny, Nya	Nor., Sw.	New
O	Jap.	Big
Ö	Nor., Sw.	Island
Ober	Ger.	Upper
Occidental, Occidentale	Sp., It.	Western
Odde	Dan.	Point
Oeste	Port.	West
Ooster	Du.	Eastern
Opper, Over	Du.	Upper
Oriental	Sp., Fr.	Eastern
Orientale	It.	Eastern
Orta	Turk.	Middle
Ost	Ger.	East
Ostrov	Russ.	Island
Ouest	Fr.	West
Öy	Nor.	Island
Ozero	Russ.	Lake
Pampa	Sp.	Plain
Pas	Fr.	Channel, Strait
Paso	Sp.	Pass
Passo	It., Port.	Pass
Peña	Sp.	Rock, Mountain
Pendi	Ch.	Basin
Penisola	It.	Peninsula
Pequeño	Sp.	Small
Pereval	Russ.	Pass
Peski	Russ.	Desert
Petit, Petite	Fr.	Small
Phu	Lao, Annamese.	Mtn.
Pic	Fr.	Mountain
Piccolo	It.	Small
Pico	Port., Sp.	Mountain, Peak
Pik	Russ.	Mountain, Peak
Piton	Fr.	Mountain, Peak
Planalto	Port.	Plateau
Plato	Russ.	Plateau
Pointe	Fr.	Point
Poluostrov	Russ.	Peninsula
Ponta	Port.	Point
Presa	Sp.	Reservoir
Presqu'île	Fr.	Peninsula
Proliv	Russ.	Strait
Pulou, Pulo	Malay	Island
Punt	Du.	Point
Punta	Sp., It., Port.	Point
Qiryat	Hebrew	City, Settlement
Qum	Turk.	Desert
Qundao	Ch.	Islands
Rada	Sp.	Inlet
Rade	Fr.	Bay, Inlet
Ras	Arabic	Cape
Reka	Russ.	River
Retto	Jap.	Archipelago
Ria	Sp.	Estuary
Río	Sp.	River
Rivier, Rivière	Du., Fr.	River
Rud	Per.	River
Sai	Jap.	West
Saki	Jap.	Cape
Salar, Salina	Sp.	Salt Deposit
Salto	Sp., Port.	Falls
San	Jap., Korean	Hill
Sanmaek	Korean	Mt. Range
Schiereiland	Du.	Peninsula
Se	Camb., Khmer.	River
See	Ger.	Sea, Lake
Selvas	Sp., Port.	Woods, Forest
Seno	Sp.	Bay, Gulf
Serra	Port.	Mts.
Serranía	Sp.	Mts.
Seto	Jap.	Strait
Settentrionale	It.	Northern
Severni, Severnaya	Russ.	North
Shamo	Ch.	Desert
Shan	Ch., Jap.	Hill, Mts.
Shankou	Ch.	Pass
Shatt	Arabic	River
Shima	Jap.	Island
Shimo	Jap.	Lower
Shin	Jap.	Land
Shiro	Jap.	White
Shoto	Jap.	Islands
Si	Ch.	West
Sierra	Sp.	Mt. Range, Mts.
Sjö	Nor., Sw.	Lake, Sea
Sok, Suk, Souk	Arabic	Market
Song	Annamese	River
Sopka	Russ.	Volcano
Spitze	Ger.	Mt. Peak
Sredni, Srednyaya	Russ.	Middle
Stad	Dan., Nor., Sw.	City
Stari, Staraya	Russ.	Old
Step	Russ.	Treeless Plain
Straat	Du.	Strait
Strasse	Ger.	Strait
Stretto	It.	Strait
Ström	Dan., Nor., Sw.	Sound
Stung	Camb., Khmer.	River
Su	Turk.	River
Sud, Süd	Sp., Fr., Ger.	South
Suido	Jap.	Strait, Channel
Sul	Port.	South
Sund	Dan., Nor., Sw.	Sound
Sungei	Malay	River
Supérieur	Fr.	Upper
Superior, Superiore	Sp., It.	Upper
Sur	Sp.	South
Suyu	Turk.	River
Ta	Ch.	Big
Tafelland	Du.	Plateau
Tagh	Turk.	Mt. Range
Take	Jap.	Peak, Ridge
Takht	Arabic	Lower
Tal	Ger.	Valley
Tanjung	Malay	Cape, Point
Tell	Arabic	Hill
Thale	Thai	Sea, Lake
Tind	Nor.	Peak
Tö	Jap.	East
To	Jap.	Island
Toge	Jap.	Pass
Trask	Finn.	Lake
Tugh	Somali	Dry River
Ujung	Malay	Point
Umi	Jap.	Bay
Unter	Ger.	Lower
Ura	Jap.	Inlet
Uul	Mong.	Mountain
Val	Fr.	Valley
Vatn	Nor.	Lake
Vecchio	It.	Old
Veld	Du.	Plain, Field
Velho	Port.	Old
Verkhni	Russ.	Upper
Vesi	Finn.	Lake
Viejo	Sp.	Old
Vik	Nor., Sw.	Bay
Vishni, Vishnyaya	Russ.	High
Vodokhranilishche	Russ.	Reservoir
Volcán	Sp.	Volcano
Vostochni, Vostochnaya	Russ.	East, Eastern
Wadi	Arabic	Dry River
Wald	Ger.	Forest
Wan	Jap.	Bay
Westersch	Du.	Western
Wüste	Ger.	Desert
Yama	Jap.	Mountain
Yug, Yuzhni, Yuzhnaya	Russ.	South, Southern
Zaki	Jap.	Cape
Zaliv	Russ.	Bay, Gulf
Zangbo	Tibetan	River, Stream
Zapadni, Zapadnaya	Russ.	Western
Zee	Du.	Sea
Zemlya	Russ.	Land
Zizhiqu	Ch.	Autonomous Region
Zuid	Du.	South

MAP PROJECTIONS

by Erwin Raisz

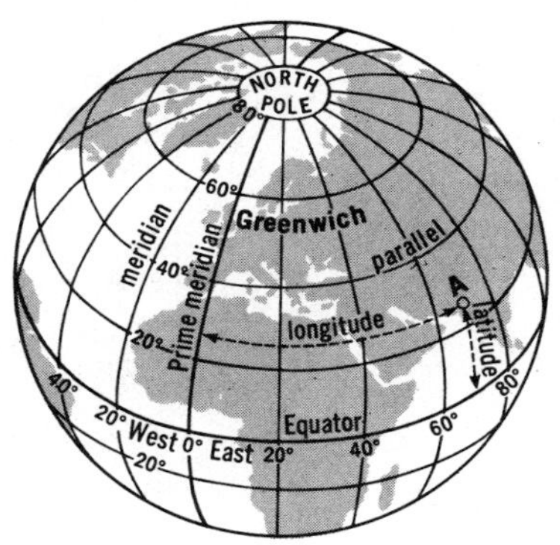

Our earth is rotating around its *axis* once a day. The two end points of its axis are the *poles;* the line circling the earth midway between the poles is the *equator.* The arc from either of the poles to the equator is divided into 90 *degrees.* The distance, expressed in degrees, from the equator to any point is its *latitude* and circles of equal latitude are the *parallels.* On maps it is customary to show parallels of evenly-spaced degrees such as every fifth or every tenth.

The equator is divided into 360 degrees. Lines circling from pole to pole through the degree points on the equator are called *meridians.* They are all equal in length but by international agreement the meridian passing through the Greenwich Observatory in London has been chosen as *prime meridian.* The distance, expressed in degrees, from the prime meridian to any point is its *longitude.* While meridians are all equal in length, parallels become shorter and shorter as they approach the poles. Whereas one degree of latitude represents everywhere approximately 69 miles, one degree of longitude varies from 69 miles at the equator to nothing at the poles.

Each degree is divided into 60 minutes and each minute into 60 seconds. One minute of latitude equals a nautical mile.

The map is flat but the earth is nearly spherical. Neither a rubber ball nor any part of a rubber ball may be flattened without stretching or tearing unless the part is very small. To present the curved surface of the earth on a flat map is not difficult as long as the areas under consideration are small, but the mapping of countries, continents, or the whole earth requires some kind of *projection.* Any regular set of parallels and meridians upon which a map can be drawn makes a map projection. Many systems are used.

In any projection only the parallels or the meridians or some other set of lines can be *true* (the same length as on the globe of corresponding scale); all other lines are too long or too short. Only on a globe is it possible to have both the parallels and the meridians true. The scale given on a flat map cannot be true everywhere. The construction of the various projections begins usually with laying out the parallels or meridians which have true lengths.

Rectangular Projection

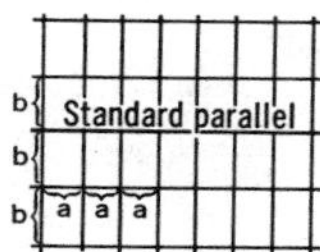

RECTANGULAR PROJECTION — This is a set of evenly-placed meridians and horizontal parallels. The central or *standard parallel* and all meridians are true. All other parallels are either too long or too short. The projection is used for simple maps of small areas, as city plans, etc.

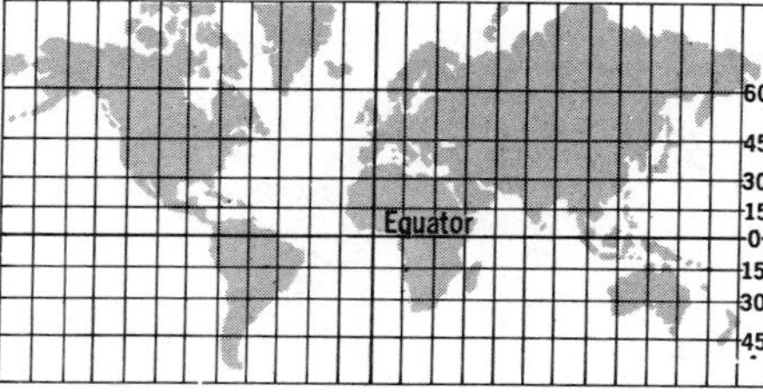

Mercator Projection

MERCATOR PROJECTION — In this projection the meridians are evenly-spaced vertical lines. The parallels are horizontal, spaced so that their length has the same relation to the meridians as on a globe. As the meridians converge at higher latitudes on the globe, while on the map they do not, the parallels have to be drawn also farther and farther apart to maintain the correct relationship. When every very small area has the same shape as on a globe we call the projection *conformal.* The most interesting quality of this projection is that all *compass directions* appear as straight lines. For this reason it is generally used for marine charts. It is also frequently used for world maps in spite of the fact that the high latitudes are very much exaggerated in size. Only the equator is true to scale; all other parallels and meridians are too long. The Mercator projection did *not* derive from projecting a globe upon a cylinder.

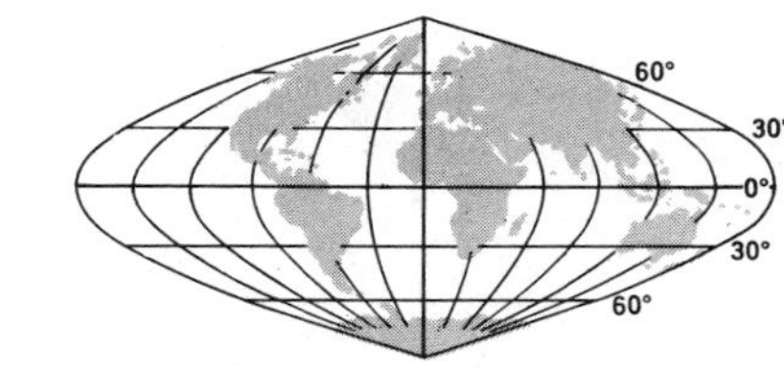

Sinusoidal Projection

SINUSOIDAL PROJECTION — The parallels are truly-spaced horizontal lines. They are divided truly and the connecting curves make the meridians. It does not make a good world map because the outer regions are distorted, but the central portion is good and this part is often used for maps of Africa and South America. Every part of the map has the same area as the corresponding area on the globe. It is an *equal-area* projection.

MOLLWEIDE PROJECTION — The meridians are equally-spaced ellipses; the parallels are horizontal lines spaced so that every belt of latitude should have the same area as on a globe. This projection is popular for world maps, especially in European atlases.

GOODE'S INTERRUPTED PROJECTIONS—Only the good central part of the Mollweide or sinusoidal (or both) projection is used and the oceans are cut. This makes an equal-area map with little distortion of shape. It is commonly used for world maps.

ECKERT PROJECTIONS — These are similar to the sinusoidal or the Mollweide projections, but the poles are shown as lines half the length of the equator. There are several variants; the meridians are either sine curves or ellipses; the parallels are horizontal and spaced either evenly or so as to make the projection equal area. Their use for world maps is increasing. The figure shows the elliptical equal-area variant.

CONIC PROJECTION — The original idea of the conic projection is that of capping the globe by a cone upon which both the parallels and meridians are projected from the center of the globe. The cone is then cut open and laid flat. A cone can be made tangent to any chosen *standard parallel*.

The actually-used conic projection is a modification of this idea. The radius of the standard parallel is obtained as above. The meridians are straight radiating lines spaced truly on the standard parallel. The parallels are concentric circles spaced at true distances. All parallels except the standard are too long. The projection is used for maps of countries in middle latitudes, as it presents good shapes with small scale error.

There are several variants: The use of *two standard parallels*, one near the top, the other near the bottom of the map, reduces the scale error. In the *Albers projection* the parallels are spaced unevenly, to make the projection equal-area. This is a good projection for the United States. In the *Lambert conformal conic projection* the parallels are spaced so that any small quadrangle of the grid should have the same shape as on the globe. This is the best projection for air-navigation charts as it has relatively straight azimuths.

An *azimuth* is a great-circle direction reckoned clockwise from north. A *great-circle direction* points to a place along the shortest line on the earth's surface. This is not the same as compass direction. The center of a great circle is the center of the globe.

BONNE PROJECTION — The parallels are laid out exactly as in the conic projection. All parallels are divided truly and the connecting curves make the meridians. It is an equal-area projection. It is used for maps of the northern continents, as Asia, Europe, and North America.

POLYCONIC PROJECTION — The central meridian is divided truly. The parallels are non-concentric circles, the radii of which are obtained by drawing tangents to the globe as though the globe were covered by several cones rather than by only one. Each parallel is divided truly and the connecting curves make the meridians. All meridians except the central one are too long. This projection is used for large-scale topographic sheets — less often for countries or continents.

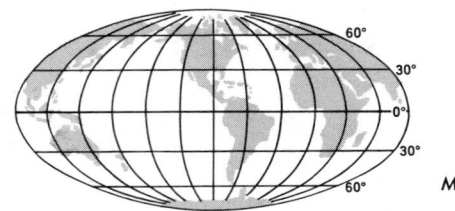

Mollweide Projection

Goode's Interrupted Projection

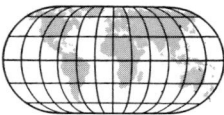

Eckert Projection

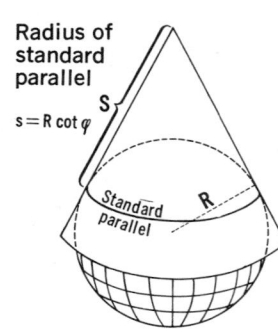

Radius of standard parallel

$s = R \cot \varphi$

Conic Projection

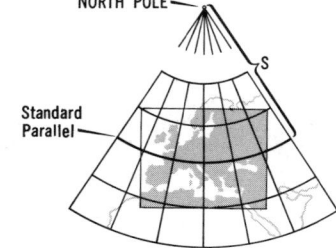

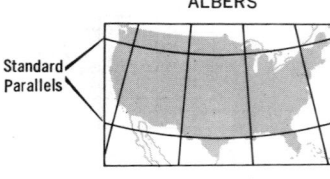

ALBERS

Albers Projection

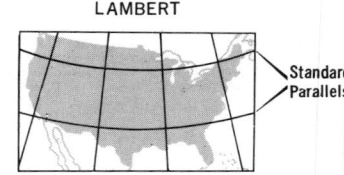

LAMBERT

Lambert Conformal Conic Projection

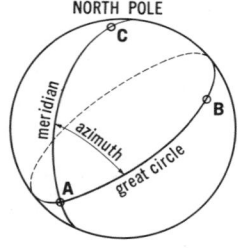

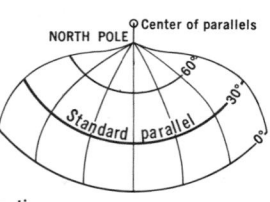

Bonne Projection

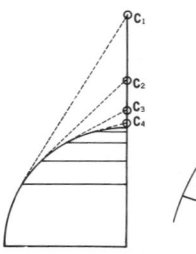
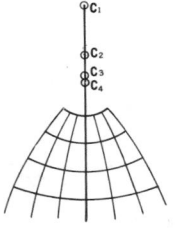

Polyconic Projection

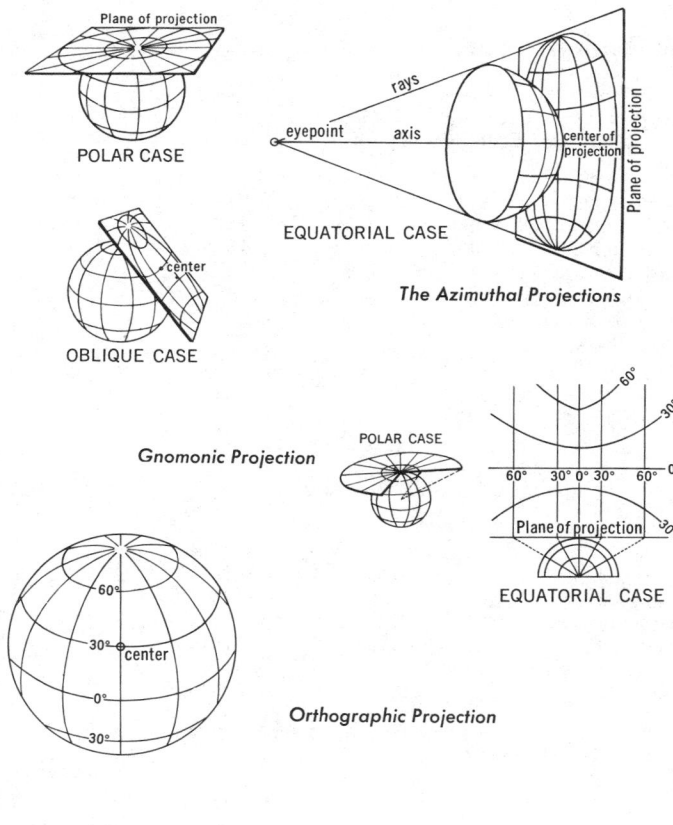

POLAR CASE

EQUATORIAL CASE

The Azimuthal Projections

OBLIQUE CASE

Gnomonic Projection

POLAR CASE

EQUATORIAL CASE

Orthographic Projection

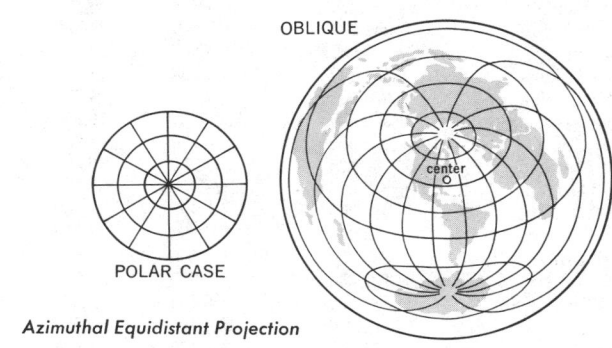

OBLIQUE

POLAR CASE

Azimuthal Equidistant Projection

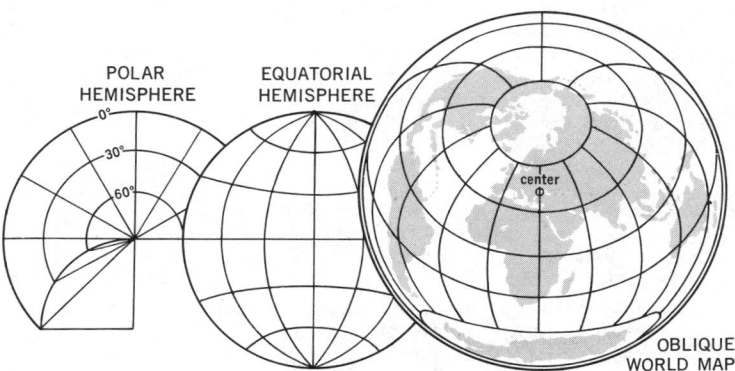

POLAR HEMISPHERE

EQUATORIAL HEMISPHERE

OBLIQUE WORLD MAP

Lambert Azimuthal Equal-Area Projection

THE AZIMUTHAL PROJECTIONS — In this group a part of the globe is projected from an eyepoint onto a plane. The eyepoint can be at different distances, making different projections. The plane of projection can be tangent at the equator, at a pole, or at any other point on which we want to focus attention. The most important quality of all azimuthal projections is that they show every point at its true direction (azimuth) from the center point, and all points equally distant from the center point will be equally distant on the map also.

GNOMONIC PROJECTION — This projection has the eyepoint at the center of the globe Only the central part is good; the outer regions are badly distorted. Yet the projection has one important quality, all great circles being shown as straight lines. For this reason it is used for laying out the routes for long range flying or trans-oceanic navigation.

ORTHOGRAPHIC PROJECTION — This projection has the eyepoint at infinite distance and the projecting rays are parallel. The polar or equatorial varieties are rare but the oblique case became very popular on account of its visual quality. It looks like a picture of a globe. Although the distortion on the peripheries is extreme, we see it correctly because the eye perceives it not as a map but as a picture of a three-dimensional globe. Obviously only a hemisphere (half globe) can be shown.

Some azimuthal projections do not derive from the actual process of projecting from an eyepoint, but are arrived at by other means:

AZIMUTHAL EQUIDISTANT PROJECTION — This is the only projection in which every point is shown both at true great-circle direction and at true distance from the center point, but all other directions and distances are distorted. The principle of the projection can best be understood from the polar case. Most polar maps are in this projection. The oblique case is used for radio direction finding, for earthquake research, and in long-distance flying. A separate map has to be constructed for each central point selected.

LAMBERT AZIMUTHAL EQUAL-AREA PROJECTION—The construction of this projection can best be understood from the polar case. All three cases are widely used. It makes a good polar map and it is often extended to include the southern continents. It is the most common projection used for maps of the Eastern and Western Hemispheres, and it is a good projection for continents as it shows correct areas with relatively little distortion of shape. Most of the continent maps in this atlas are in this projection.

IN THIS ATLAS, on almost all maps, parallels and meridians have been marked because they are useful for the following:

(a) They show the north-south and east-west directions which appear on many maps at oblique angles especially near the margins.

(b) With the help of parallels and meridians every place can be exactly located; for instance, New York City is at 41° N and 74° W on any map.

(c) They help to measure distances even in the distorted parts of the map. The scale given on each map is true only along certain lines which are specified in the foregoing discussion for each projection. One degree of latitude equals nearly 69 statute miles or 60 nautical miles. The length of one degree of longitude varies (1° long. = 1° lat. × cos lat.).

WORLD STATISTICAL TABLES

Elements of the Solar System

	Mean Distance from Sun: in Miles	in Kilometers	Period of Revolution around Sun	Period of Rotation on Axis	Equatorial Diameter: in Miles	in Kilometers	Surface Gravity (Earth = 1)	Mass (Earth = 1)	Mean Density (Water = 1)	Number of Satellites
MERCURY	35,990,000	57,900,000	87.97 days	59 days	3,032	4,880	0.38	0.055	5.5	0
VENUS	67,240,000	108,200,000	224.70 days	243 days†	7,523	12,106	0.90	0.815	5.25	0
EARTH	93,000,000	149,700,000	365.26 days	23h 56m	7,926	12,755	1.00	1.00	5.5	1
MARS	141,730,000	228,100,000	687.00 days	24h 37m	4,220	6,790	0.38	0.107	4.0	2
JUPITER	483,880,000	778,700,000	·11.86 years	9h 50m	88,750	142,800	2.87	317.9	1.3	16
SATURN	887,130,000	1,427,700,000	29.46 years	10h 14m	74,580	120,020	1.32	95.2	0.7	17
URANUS	1,783,700,000	2,870,500,000	84.01 years	10h 49m†	31,600	50,900	0.93	14.6	1.3	5
NEPTUNE	2,795,500,000	4,498,800,000	164.79 years	15h 48m	30,200	48,600	1.23	17.2	1.8	3
PLUTO	3,667,900,000	5,902,800,000	247.70 years	6.39 days (?)	1,500	2,400	0.03 (?)	0.01(?)	0.7(?)	1

†Retrograde motion

Facts About the Sun

Equatorial diameter	865,000 miles	1,392,000 kilometers
Period of rotation on axis	25-35 days*	
Orbit of galaxy	every 225 million years	
Surface gravity (Earth = 1)	27.8	
Mass (Earth = 1)	333,000	
Density (Water = 1)	1.4	
Mean distance from Earth	93,000,000 miles	149,700,000 kilometers

*Rotation of 25 days at Equator, decreasing to about 35 days at the poles.

Facts About the Moon

Equatorial diameter	2,160 miles	3,476 kilometers
Period of rotation on axis	27 days, 7 hours, 43 minutes	
Period of revolution around Earth (sidereal month)	27 days, 7 hours, 43 minutes	
Phase period between new moons (synodic month)	29 days, 12 hours, 44 minutes	
Surface gravity (Earth = 1)	0.16	
Mass (Earth = 1)	0.0123	
Density (Water = 1)	3.34	
Maximum distance from Earth	252,710 miles	406,690 kilometers
Minimum distance from Earth	221,460 miles	356,400 kilometers
Mean distance from Earth	238,860 miles	384,400 kilometers

Dimensions of the Earth

	Area in Sq. Miles	Sq. Kilometers
Superficial area	197,751,000	512,175,090
Land surface	57,970,000	150,142,300
Water surface	139,781,000	362,032,790

	Miles	Kilometers
Equatorial circumference	24,902	40,075
Polar circumference	24,860	40,007
Equatorial diameter	7,926.68	12,756.4
Polar diameter	7,899.99	12,713.4
Equatorial radius	3,963.34	6,378.2
Polar radius	3,949.99	6,356.7
Volume of the Earth	2.6×10^{11} cubic miles	10.84×10^{11} cubic kilometers
Mass or weight	6.6×10^{21} short tons	6.0×10^{21} metric tons
Maximum distance from Sun	94,600,000 miles	152,000,000 kilometers
Minimum distance from Sun	91,300,000 miles	147,000,000 kilometers

The Continents

	Area in: Sq. Miles	Sq. Km.	Percent of World's Land
Asia	17,128,500	44,362,815	29.5
Africa	11,707,000	30,321,130	20.2
North America	9,363,000	24,250,170	16.2
South America	6,875,000	17,806,250	11.8
Antarctica	5,500,000	14,245,000	9.5
Europe	4,057,000	10,507,630	7.0
Australia	2,966,136	7,682,300	5.1

Oceans and Major Seas

	Area in: Sq. Miles	Sq. Km.	Greatest Depth in: Feet	Meters
Pacific Ocean	64,186,000	166,241,700	36,198	11,033
Atlantic Ocean	31,862,000	82,522,600	28,374	8,648
Indian Ocean	28,350,000	73,426,500	25,344	7,725
Arctic Ocean	5,427,000	14,056,000	17,880	5,450
Caribbean Sea	970,000	2,512,300	24,720	7,535
Mediterranean Sea	969,000	2,509,700	16,896	5,150
Bering Sea	875,000	2,266,250	15,800	4,800
Gulf of Mexico	600,000	1,554,000	12,300	3,750
Sea of Okhotsk	590,000	1,528,100	11,070	3,370
East China Sea	482,000	1,248,400	9,500	2,900
Sea of Japan	389,000	1,007,500	12,280	3,740
Hudson Bay	317,500	822,300	846	258
North Sea	222,000	575,000	2,200	670
Black Sea	185,000	479,150	7,365	2,245
Red Sea	169,000	437,700	7,200	2,195
Baltic Sea	163,000	422,170	1,506	459

Major Ship Canals

	Length in: Miles	Kms.	Minimum Feet	Depth in: Meters
Volga-Baltic, U.S.S.R.	225	362	—	—
Baltic-White Sea, U.S.S.R.	140	225	16	5
Suez, Egypt	100.76	162	42	13
Albert, Belgium	80	129	16.5	5
Moscow-Volga, U.S.S.R.	80	129	18	6
Volga-Don, U.S.S.R.	62	100	—	—
Göta, Sweden	54	87	10	3
Kiel (Nord-Ostsee), W. Ger.	53.2	86	38	12
Panama Canal, Panama	50.72	82	41.6	13
Houston Ship, U.S.A.	50	81	36	11

Largest Islands

	Area in: Sq. Mi.	Sq. Km.		Area in: Sq. Mi.	Sq. Km.		Area in: Sq. Mi.	Sq. Km.
Greenland	840,000	2,175,600	South I., New Zealand	58,393	151,238	Hokkaido, Japan	28,983	75,066
New Guinea	305,000	789,950	Java, Indonesia	48,842	126,501	Banks, Canada	27,038	70,028
Borneo	290,000	751,100	North I., New Zealand	44,187	114,444	Ceylon, Sri Lanka	25,332	65,610
Madagascar	226,400	586,376	Newfoundland, Canada	42,031	108,860	Tasmania, Australia	24,600	63,710
Baffin, Canada	195,928	507,454	Cuba	40,533	104,981	Svalbard, Norway	23,957	62,049
Sumatra, Indonesia	164,000	424,760	Luzon, Philippines	40,420	104,688	Devon, Canada	21,331	55,247
Honshu, Japan	88,000	227,920	Iceland	39,768	103,000	Novaya Zemlya (north isl.), U.S.S.R.	18,600	48,200
Great Britain	84,400	218,896	Mindanao, Philippines	36,537	94,631	Marajó, Brazil	17,991	46,597
Victoria, Canada	83,896	217,290	Ireland	31,743	82,214	Tierra del Fuego, Chile & Argentina	17,900	46,360
Ellesmere, Canada	75,767	196,236	Sakhalin, U.S.S.R.	29,500	76,405	Alexander, Antarctica	16,700	43,250
Celebes, Indonesia	72,986	189,034	Hispaniola, Haiti & Dom. Rep.	29,399	76,143			

Principal Mountains of the World

	Feet	Meters		Feet	Meters		Feet	Meters
Everest, Nepal-China	29,028	8,848	Pissis, Argentina	22,241	6,779	Kazbek, U.S.S.R.	16,512	5,033
Godwin Austen (K2), Pakistan-China	28,250	8,611	Mercedario, Argentina	22,211	6,770	Puncak Jaya, Indonesia	16,503	5,030
Kanchenjunga, Nepal-India	28,208	8,598	Huascarán, Peru	22,205	6,768	Tyree, Antarctica	16,289	4,965
Lhotse, Nepal-China	27,923	8,511	Llullaillaco, Chile-Argentina	22,057	6,723	Blanc, France	15,771	4,807
Makalu, Nepal-China	27,824	8,481	Nevada Ancohuma, Bolivia	21,489	6,550	Klyuchevskaya Sopka, U.S.S.R.	15,584	4,750
Dhaulagiri, Nepal	26,810	8,172	Illampu, Bolivia	21,276	6,485	Fairweather (Br. Col., Canada)	15,300	4,663
Nanga Parbat, Pakistan	26,660	8,126	Chimborazo, Ecuador	20,561	6,267	Dufourspitze (Mte. Rosa), Italy-Switzerland	15,203	4,634
Annapurna, Nepal	26,504	8,078	McKinley, Alaska	20,320	6,194	Ras Dashan, Ethiopia	15,157	4,620
Gasherbrum, Pakistan-China	26,740	8,068	Logan, Canada (Yukon)	19,524	5,951	Matterhorn, Switzerland	14,691	4,478
Nanda Devi, India	25,645	7,817	Cotopaxi, Ecuador	19,347	5,897	Whitney, California, U.S.A.	14,494	4,418
Rakaposhi, Pakistan	25,550	7,788	Kilimanjaro, Tanzania	19,340	5,895	Elbert, Colorado, U.S.A.	14,433	4,399
Kamet, India	25,447	7,756	El Misti, Peru	19,101	5,822	Rainier, Washington, U.S.A.	14,410	4,392
Gurla Mandhada, China	25,355	7,728	Pico Cristóbal Colón, Colombia	19,029	5,800	Shasta, California, U.S.A.	14,162	4,350
Kongur Shan, China	25,325	7,719	Huila, Colombia	18,865	5,750	Pikes Peak, Colorado, U.S.A.	14,110	4,301
Tirich Mir, Pakistan	25,230	7,690	Citlaltépetl (Orizaba), Mexico	18,855	5,747	Finsteraarhorn, Switzerland	14,022	4,274
Gongga Shan, China	24,790	7,556	El'brus, U.S.S.R.	18,510	5,642	Mauna Kea, Hawaii, U.S.A.	13,796	4,205
Muztagata, China	24,757	7,546	Damavand, Iran	18,376	5,601	Mauna Loa, Hawaii, U.S.A.	13,677	4,169
Communism Peak, U.S.S.R.	24,599	7,498	St. Elias, Alaska-Canada (Yukon)	18,008	5,489	Jungfrau, Switzerland	13,642	4,158
Pobeda Peak, U.S.S.R.	24,406	7,439	Vilcanota, Peru	17,999	5,486	Cameroon, Cameroon	13,350	4,069
Chomo Lhari, Bhutan-China	23,997	7,314	Popocatépetl, Mexico	17,887	5,452	Grossglockner, Austria	12,457	3,797
Muztag, China	23,891	7,282	Dykhtau, U.S.S.R.	17,070	5,203	Fuji, Japan	12,389	3,776
Cerro Aconcagua, Argentina	22,831	6,959	Kenya, Kenya	17,058	5,199	Cook, New Zealand	12,349	3,764
Ojos del Salado, Chile-Argentina	22,572	6,880	Ararat, Turkey	16,946	5,165	Etna, Italy	11,053	3,369
Bonete, Chile-Argentina	22,541	6,870	Vinson Massif, Antarctica	16,864	5,140	Kosciusko, Australia	7,310	2,228
Tupungato, Chile-Argentina	22,310	6,800	Margherita (Ruwenzori), Africa	16,795	5,119	Mitchell, North Carolina, U.S.A.	6,684	2,037

Longest Rivers of the World

	Length in: Miles	Kms.		Length in: Miles	Kms.		Length in: Miles	Kms.
Nile, Africa	4,145	6,671	São Francisco, Brazil	1,811	2,914	Ohio-Allegheny, U.S.A.	1,306	2,102
Amazon, S. Amer.	3,915	6,300	Indus, Asia	1,800	2,897	Kama, U.S.S.R.	1,262	2,031
Chang Jiang (Yangtze), China	3,900	6,276	Danube, Europe	1,775	2,857	Red, U.S.A.	1,222	1,966
Mississippi-Missouri-Red Rock, U.S.A.	3,741	6,019	Salween, Asia	1,770	2,849	Don, U.S.S.R.	1,222	1,967
Ob'Irtysh-Black Irtysh, U.S.S.R.	3,362	5,411	Brahmaputra, Asia	1,700	2,736	Columbia, U.S.A.-Canada	1,214	1,953
Yenisey-Angara, U.S.S.R.	3,100	4,989	Euphrates, Asia	1,700	2,736	Saskatchewan, Canada	1,205	1,939
Huang He (Yellow), China	2,877	4,630	Tocantins, Brazil	1,677	2,699	Peace-Finlay, Canada	1,195	1,923
Amur-Shilka-Onon, Asia	2,744	4,416	Xi (Si), China	1,650	2,655	Tigris, Asia	1,181	1,901
Lena, U.S.S.R.	2,734	4,400	Amudar'ya, Asia	1,616	2,601	Darling, Australia	1,160	1,867
Congo (Zaire), Africa	2,718	4,374	Nelson-Saskatchewan, Canada	1,600	2,575	Angara, U.S.S.R.	1,135	1,827
Mackenzie-Peace-Finlay, Canada	2,635	4,241	Orinoco, S. Amer.	1,600	2,575	Sungari, Asia	1,130	1,819
Mekong, Asia	2,610	4,200	Zambezi, Africa	1,600	2,575	Pechora, U.S.S.R.	1,124	1,809
Missouri-Red Rock, U.S.A.	2,564	4,125	Paraguay, S. Amer.	1,584	2,549	Snake, U.S.A.	1,000	1,609
Niger, Africa	2,548	4,101	Kolyma, U.S.S.R.	1,562	2,514	Churchill, Canada	1,000	1,609
Paraná-La Plata, S. Amer.	2,450	3,943	Ganges, Asia	1,550	2,494	Pilcomayo, S. Amer.	1,000	1,609
Mississippi, U.S.A.	2,348	3,778	Ural, U.S.S.R.	1,509	2,428	Magdalena, Colombia	1,000	1,609
Murray-Darling, Australia	2,310	3,718	Japurá, S. Amer.	1,500	2,414	Uruguay, S. Amer.	994	1,600
Volga, U.S.S.R.	2,194	3,531	Arkansas, U.S.A.	1,450	2,334	Platte-N. Platte, U.S.A.	990	1,593
Madeira, S. Amer.	2,013	3,240	Colorado, U.S.A.-Mexico	1,450	2,334	Ohio, U.S.A.	981	1,578
Purus, S. Amer.	1,995	3,211	Negro, S. Amer.	1,400	2,253	Pecos, U.S.A.	926	1,490
Yukon, Alaska-Canada	1,979	3,185	Dnieper, U.S.S.R.	1,368	2,202	Oka, U.S.S.R.	918	1,477
St. Lawrence, Canada-U.S.A.	1,900	3,058	Orange, Africa	1,350	2,173	Canadian, U.S.A.	906	1,458
Rio Grande, Mexico-U.S.A.	1,885	3,034	Irrawaddy, Burma	1,325	2,132	Colorado, Texas, U.S.A.	894	1,439
Syrdar'ya-Naryn, U.S.S.R.	1,859	2,992	Brazos, U.S.A.	1,309	2,107	Dniester, U.S.S.R.	876	1,410

Principal Natural Lakes

	Area in: Sq. Miles	Sq. Km.	Max. Depth in: Feet	Meters		Area in: Sq. Miles	Sq. Km.	Max. Depth in: Feet	Meters
Caspian Sea, U.S.S.R.-Iran	143,243	370,999	3,264	995	Lake Eyre, Australia	3,500-0	9,000-0	—	—
Lake Superior, U.S.A.-Canada	31,820	82,414	1,329	405	Lake Titicaca, Peru-Bolivia	3,200	8,288	1,000	305
Lake Victoria, Africa	26,724	69,215	270	82	Lake Nicaragua, Nicaragua	3,100	8,029	230	70
Aral Sea, U.S.S.R.	25,676	66,501	256	78	Lake Athabasca, Canada	3,064	7,936	400	122
Lake Huron, U.S.A.-Canada	23,010	59,596	748	228	Reindeer Lake, Canada	2,568	6,651	—	—
Lake Michigan, U.S.A.	22,400	58,016	923	281	Lake Turkana (Rudolf), Africa	2,463	6,379	240	73
Lake Tanganyika, Africa	12,650	32,764	4,700	1,433	Issyk-Kul', U.S.S.R.	2,425	6,281	2,303	702
Lake Baykal, U.S.S.R.	12,162	31,500	5,316	1,620	Lake Torrens, Australia	2,230	5,776	—	—
Great Bear Lake, Canada	12,096	31,328	1,356	413	Vänern, Sweden	2,156	5,584	328	100
Lake Nyasa (Malawi), Africa	11,555	29,928	2,320	707	Nettiling Lake, Canada	2,140	5,543	—	—
Great Slave Lake, Canada	11,031	28,570	2,015	614	Lake Winnipegosis, Canada	2,075	5,374	38	12
Lake Erie, U.S.A.-Canada	9,940	25,745	210	64	Lake Mobutu Sese Seko (Albert), Africa	2,075	5,374	160	49
Lake Winnipeg, Canada	9,417	24,390	60	18	Kariba Lake, Zambia-Zimbabwe	2,050	5,310	295	90
Lake Ontario, U.S.A.-Canada	7,540	19,529	775	244	Lake Nipigon, Canada	1,872	4,848	540	165
Lake Ladoga, U.S.S.R.	7,104	18,399	738	225	Lake Mweru, Zaire-Zambia	1,800	4,662	60	18
Lake Balkhash, U.S.S.R.	7,027	18,200	87	27	Lake Manitoba, Canada	1,799	4,659	12	4
Lake Maracaibo, Venezuela	5,120	13,261	100	31	Lake Taymyr, U.S.S.R.	1,737	4,499	85	26
Lake Chad, Africa	4,000-10,000	10,360-25,900	25	8	Lake Khanka, China-U.S.S.R.	1,700	4,403	33	10
Lake Onega, U.S.S.R.	3,710	9,609	377	115	Lake Kioga, Uganda	1,700	4,403	25	8

Foreign City Weather

Two figures are given for each of the months, thus 88/73. The first figure is the average daily high temperature (°F) and the second is the average daily low temperature (°F) for the month. The boldface figures indicate the average number of days with rain for each month.

City	January	February	March	April	May	June	July	August	September	October	November	December
ABIDJAN, Ivory Coast	88/73 **3**	90/75 **4**	90/75 **6**	90/75 **9**	88/75 **16**	85/73 **18**	83/73 **8**	82/71 **7**	83/73 **8**	85/74 **13**	87/74 **13**	88/74 **6**
ACAPULCO, Mexico	85/70	87/70 **0**	87/70 **0**	87/71 **1**	89/74 **4**	89/76 **15**	89/75 **11**	89/75 **14**	88/75 **18**	88/74 **12**	88/72 **4**	87/70 **1**
ACCRA, Ghana	87/73 **1**	88/75 **2**	88/76 **4**	88/76 **6**	87/75 **9**	84/74 **10**	81/73 **4**	80/71 **3**	81/73 **4**	85/74 **6**	87/75 **3**	88/75 **2**
ADDIS ABABA, Ethiopia	75/43	76/47	77/49 **8**	77/50 **10**	77/50 **10**	74/49 **20**	69/50 **28**	69/50 **27**	72/49 **21**	75/45 **3**	73/43 **2**	73/41 **2**
ALGIERS, Algeria	59/49 **11**	61/49 **9**	63/52 **9**	68/55 **5**	73/59 **5**	78/65 **2**	83/70 **1**	85/71 **1**	81/69 **4**	74/63 **7**	66/56 **11**	60/51 **12**
AMSTERDAM, Netherlands	40/34 **19**	41/34 **15**	46/37 **13**	52/43 **14**	60/50 **12**	65/55 **12**	69/59 **14**	68/59 **14**	64/56 **15**	56/48 **18**	47/41 **19**	41/35 **19**
ANKARA, Turkey	39/24 **8**	42/26 **8**	51/31 **7**	63/40 **7**	73/49 **7**	78/53 **5**	86/59 **2**	87/59 **1**	78/52 **3**	69/44 **5**	57/37 **6**	43/29 **9**
APIA, Western Samoa	86/75 **22**	85/76 **19**	86/74 **19**	86/75 **14**	85/74 **12**	85/74 **7**	85/74 **5**	84/75 **3**	84/74 **11**	85/75 **14**	86/74 **16**	85/74 **19**
ATHENS, Greece	54/42 **7**	55/43 **6**	60/46 **5**	67/52 **3**	77/60 **3**	85/67 **2**	90/72 **1**	90/72 **1**	83/66 **2**	74/60 **4**	64/52 **6**	57/46 **7**
BAGHDAD, Iraq	60/39 **4**	64/42 **3**	71/48 **4**	85/57 **3**	97/67 **1**	105/73 **0**	110/76 **0**	110/76 **0**	104/70 **0**	92/61 **1**	77/51 **3**	64/42 **5**
BALI, Indonesia	88/74 **19**	88/74 **14**	88/74 **13**	88/74 **7**	88/73 **5**	87/71 **3**	87/70 **1**	87/70 **1**	89/71 **1**	90/73 **2**	90/75 **6**	88/74 **14**
BANGKOK, Thailand	89/68 **1**	91/72 **1**	93/75 **3**	95/77 **3**	93/77 **9**	91/76 **10**	90/76 **13**	90/76 **13**	89/76 **15**	88/75 **14**	87/72 **5**	87/68 **1**
BARCELONA, Spain	56/42 **5**	57/44 **7**	61/47 **5**	64/51 **5**	71/57 **9**	77/63 **5**	81/69 **4**	82/69 **5**	78/65 **7**	71/58 **8**	62/50 **7**	57/44 **6**
BEIRUT, Lebanon	62/51 **15**	63/51 **12**	66/54 **9**	72/58 **5**	78/64 **2**	83/73 **1**	84/73 **0**	85/74 **0**	84/74 **1**	81/69 **4**	74/63 **7**	65/53 **15**
BELFAST, Northern Ireland	45/34 **22**	47/34 **18**	49/35 **20**	53/39 **18**	59/43 **17**	64/49 **15**	65/52 **14**	65/52 **14**	61/49 **15**	55/43 **19**	49/38 **20**	46/35 **25**
BELGRADE, Yugoslavia	37/27 **8**	41/27 **6**	53/35 **7**	64/45 **9**	74/53 **9**	79/58 **11**	84/61 **6**	83/60 **8**	77/58 **9**	66/50 **8**	53/44 **12**	40/30 **9**
BERLIN, Germany	35/26 **10**	38/27 **8**	46/32 **9**	55/38 **9**	65/46 **9**	72/56 **10**	74/55 **10**	72/54 **10**	66/48 **8**	55/41 **8**	43/33 **8**	37/29 **11**
BIARRITZ, France	54/40 **10**	52/38 **11**	57/41 **11**	63/44 **11**	69/53 **11**	72/56 **9**	76/60 **7**	77/61 **9**	74/55 **11**	66/50 **11**	58/44 **12**	53/41 **14**
BOGOTA, Colombia	67/48 **6**	68/49 **7**	67/50 **13**	67/51 **20**	66/51 **17**	65/51 **16**	64/50 **18**	65/50 **16**	66/50 **13**	66/50 **16**	66/50 **16**	66/49 **15**
BOMBAY, India	83/67 **1**	83/67 **1**	86/72 **1**	89/76 **1**	91/80 **1**	89/79 **14**	85/77 **21**	85/76 **19**	85/76 **13**	89/76 **6**	89/73 **1**	87/69 **1**
BONN, West Germany	39/30 **7**	37/26 **6**	50/35 **7**	58/39 **14**	67/46 **13**	72/52 **14**	73/55 **15**	72/54 **14**	66/48 **12**	56/44 **12**	47/37 **11**	44/36 **15**
BRASILIA, Brazil	80/65 **17**	81/64 **20**	82/64 **7**	82/62 **10**	79/56 **4**	80/64 **2**	78/51 **3**	84/56 **1**	84/60 **5**	82/64 **11**	82/66 **17**	78/64 **16**
BRINDISI, Italy	55/43 **10**	57/43 **6**	60/45 **5**	65/50 **5**	73/57 **5**	80/64 **2**	84/68 **1**	84/69 **3**	80/65 **4**	70/58 **8**	64/52 **10**	58/46 **8**
BUCHAREST, Romania	33/20 **6**	38/24 **5**	51/33 **6**	63/41 **6**	74/51 **8**	81/58 **7**	86/61 **7**	86/60 **5**	76/53 **7**	65/44 **5**	49/35 **9**	37/26 **6**
BUDAPEST, Hungary	35/26 **7**	40/28 **6**	51/36 **7**	62/44 **8**	72/52 **9**	78/57 **9**	82/61 **7**	81/59 **6**	74/53 **7**	61/45 **6**	47/37 **11**	38/31 **9**
BUENOS AIRES, Argentina	85/63 **7**	83/63 **6**	79/60 **7**	72/53 **8**	64/47 **7**	60/45 **7**	57/42 **8**	60/43 **9**	64/46 **8**	69/50 **9**	76/56 **9**	82/61 **8**
CAIRO, Egypt	65/47 **1**	69/48 **1**	75/52 **1**	83/57 **1**	91/63 **1**	95/68 **0**	96/70 **0**	95/71 **0**	90/68 **0**	86/65 **1**	78/58 **1**	68/50 **1**
CALCUTTA, India	80/55 **1**	84/59 **2**	93/69 **2**	97/75 **3**	96/77 **7**	92/79 **13**	89/79 **18**	89/78 **18**	90/78 **13**	89/74 **6**	84/64 **1**	79/55 **1**
CAPE TOWN, South Africa	78/60 **3**	79/60 **2**	77/58 **3**	72/53 **6**	67/49 **9**	65/46 **9**	63/45 **10**	64/46 **9**	65/49 **7**	70/52 **5**	73/55 **3**	76/58 **3**
CARACAS, Venezuela	75/56 **6**	77/56 **6**	79/58 **3**	81/60 **4**	80/62 **9**	78/62 **14**	78/61 **16**	79/61 **13**	80/61 **13**	79/61 **12**	77/60 **13**	78/58 **10**
CHARLOTTE AMALIE, Virgin Islands	82/73 **18**	81/72 **13**	82/73 **12**	83/74 **13**	85/76 **15**	86/77 **15**	87/78 **16**	88/78 **19**	87/78 **17**	87/77 **18**	85/76 **19**	83/74 **18**
COLOMBO, Sri Lanka	86/72 **7**	87/72 **2**	88/74 **8**	88/76 **14**	87/78 **19**	85/77 **18**	85/77 **12**	85/77 **11**	85/77 **13**	85/75 **19**	85/73 **16**	85/72 **10**
COPENHAGEN, Denmark	36/29 **9**	36/28 **7**	41/31 **8**	50/37 **9**	61/44 **8**	64/48 **8**	72/55 **9**	69/54 **12**	63/49 **8**	53/42 **9**	43/35 **10**	38/32 **11**
DARWIN, Australia	90/77 **20**	90/77 **18**	91/77 **17**	92/76 **6**	91/73 **1**	88/69 **0**	87/67 **0**	89/70 **1**	91/74 **2**	93/77 **5**	94/78 **10**	92/78 **15**
DJAKARTA, Indonesia	84/74 **18**	84/74 **17**	86/74 **15**	87/75 **11**	87/75 **11**	87/74 **10**	87/73 **5**	88/73 **5**	88/75 **5**	87/74 **5**	86/74 **12**	85/74 **14**
DUBLIN, Ireland	47/35 **13**	47/35 **11**	51/36 **11**	54/38 **11**	59/42 **11**	65/48 **11**	67/51 **13**	67/51 **13**	63/47 **12**	57/43 **12**	51/38 **12**	47/36 **13**
EDINBURGH, Scotland	43/35 **18**	43/35 **15**	47/36 **15**	50/39 **16**	55/43 **15**	62/48 **15**	65/52 **17**	64/52 **16**	60/48 **16**	53/44 **18**	47/39 **18**	44/36 **17**
FLORENCE, Italy	49/35 **9**	53/36 **9**	60/40 **7**	68/46 **7**	75/53 **9**	84/58 **5**	89/63 **4**	88/62 **4**	81/58 **6**	69/51 **9**	58/42 **10**	50/37 **9**
GENEVA, Switzerland	39/29 **10**	43/30 **9**	51/35 **10**	58/41 **11**	66/48 **12**	73/55 **11**	77/58 **10**	76/57 **10**	69/52 **10**	58/44 **11**	47/37 **11**	40/31 **10**
GUAYAQUIL, Ecuador	88/70 **20**	87/71 **25**	88/72 **24**	89/71 **14**	88/68 **9**	87/68 **2**	84/67 **2**	86/65 **2**	87/66 **2**	86/68 **3**	88/68 **4**	88/70 **10**
HAMBURG, West Germany	35/28 **12**	37/30 **10**	42/33 **10**	51/39 **11**	60/47 **9**	67/53 **10**	69/56 **12**	69/56 **12**	63/51 **11**	53/44 **11**	44/36 **11**	38/31 **12**
HAMILTON, Bermuda	68/58 **14**	68/57 **13**	68/57 **12**	71/59 **9**	76/64 **7**	81/69 **7**	85/73 **10**	86/74 **12**	84/72 **10**	79/69 **12**	74/63 **13**	70/60 **15**
HAVANA, Cuba	79/65 **6**	79/65 **4**	81/67 **4**	84/69 **4**	86/72 **7**	88/74 **10**	89/75 **9**	89/75 **10**	88/75 **11**	85/73 **11**	81/69 **7**	79/67 **6**
HELSINKI, Finland	27/17 **11**	26/15 **8**	32/22 **8**	43/31 **8**	55/41 **8**	63/49 **8**	71/57 **8**	66/55 **12**	57/46 **11**	45/37 **12**	37/30 **11**	31/22 **11**
HONG KONG	64/56 **4**	63/55 **5**	67/60 **7**	75/67 **7**	82/74 **13**	85/78 **19**	87/78 **17**	87/78 **15**	85/77 **12**	81/73 **6**	74/65 **3**	68/59 **3**
JERUSALEM, Israel	55/41 **9**	56/42 **11**	65/46 **9**	73/50 **3**	81/57 **1**	85/60 **0**	87/63 **0**	87/64 **0**	85/62 **1**	81/59 **4**	70/53 **4**	59/45 **7**
JOHANNESBURG, South Africa	78/58 **12**	77/58 **9**	75/55 **9**	72/50 **4**	66/43 **3**	62/39 **1**	63/39 **1**	68/43 **1**	73/48 **2**	77/53 **7**	77/55 **10**	78/57 **11**
KARACHI, Pakistan	77/55 **1**	79/58 **1**	85/67 **1**	90/73 **1**	93/79 **1**	93/82 **2**	91/81 **2**	88/79 **2**	88/77 **1**	91/72 **1**	87/64 **1**	80/57 **1**
KINGSTON, Jamaica	86/67 **3**	86/67 **3**	86/68 **2**	87/70 **3**	87/72 **4**	89/74 **3**	90/73 **4**	90/73 **6**	89/73 **6**	88/73 **9**	87/71 **5**	87/69 **4**
LAGOS, Nigeria	88/74 **2**	89/77 **3**	89/78 **7**	89/77 **10**	87/76 **16**	85/74 **20**	83/74 **16**	82/73 **14**	83/74 **14**	85/74 **16**	88/75 **7**	88/75 **2**
LA PAZ, Bolivia	63/43 **21**	63/43 **18**	64/42 **16**	65/40 **9**	64/37 **5**	62/34 **2**	62/33 **2**	63/35 **3**	64/38 **9**	66/40 **9**	67/42 **11**	65/42 **18**

Foreign City Weather

	January	February	March	April	May	June	July	August	September	October	November	December
LAS PALMAS, Canary Is.	70/58 8	71/58 5	71/59 5	71/61 3	73/62 1	75/65 1	77/67 1	79/70 1	79/69 1	79/67 5	76/64 7	72/60 8
LENINGRAD, USSR	23/12 17	24/12 15	33/18 13	45/31 11	58/42 12	66/51 12	71/57 13	66/53 15	57/45 14	45/37 15	34/27 17	26/18 18
LIMA, Peru	82/66 1	83/67 1	83/66 1	80/63 1	74/60 1	68/58 1	67/57 1	66/56 2	68/57 1	71/58 1	74/60 1	78/62 1
LISBON, Portugal	56/46 9	58/47 8	61/49 10	64/52 7	69/56 6	75/60 2	79/63 1	80/64 1	76/62 4	69/57 7	62/52 10	57/47 10
LIVERPOOL, England	44/36 18	44/36 13	48/38 13	52/41 14	58/46 14	63/51 13	66/55 15	65/55 16	61/51 15	55/46 17	48/41 17	45/37 18
LONDON, England	44/35 17	45/35 13	51/47 11	56/40 14	63/45 13	69/51 11	73/55 13	72/54 13	67/51 13	58/44 14	49/39 16	45/36 16
MADRID, Spain	47/33 9	51/35 9	57/40 11	64/44 9	71/50 9	80/57 6	87/62 3	86/62 2	77/56 6	66/48 8	54/40 10	48/35 9
MANILA, Philippines	86/69 6	88/69 3	91/71 4	93/73 4	93/75 12	91/75 17	88/75 24	87/75 23	88/75 22	88/74 19	87/72 14	86/70 11
MARACAIBO, Venezuela	90/73 1	90/73 1	91/74 1	92/76 1	92/77 6	93/77 6	94/76 5	94/77 7	94/77 6	92/76 9	91/76 8	91/75 2
MARSEILLE, France	53/38 10	52/37 9	55/38 8	59/41 10	65/46 10	72/52 6	78/58 6	83/61 6	76/57 7	67/57 9	67/50 10	59/43 11
MELBOURNE, Australia	78/57 9	78/57 7	75/55 9	68/51 13	62/47 14	57/44 16	56/42 17	59/43 17	63/46 15	67/48 14	71/51 13	75/54 11
MEXICO CITY, Mexico	66/42 4	69/43 5	75/47 9	77/51 14	78/54 17	76/55 21	73/53 27	73/54 27	74/53 23	70/50 13	68/46 6	66/43 4
MILAN, Italy	40/29 7	47/33 6	56/38 6	66/46 6	72/54 9	80/61 6	84/64 6	82/63 6	76/58 6	64/49 7	51/39 7	42/33 7
MONTEVIDEO, Uruguay	83/62 6	82/61 5	78/59 5	71/53 6	64/48 6	59/43 6	58/43 6	59/43 7	63/46 6	68/49 6	74/54 6	79/59 7
MOSCOW, USSR	21/9 11	23/10 9	32/17 8	47/31 9	65/44 9	73/51 10	76/55 12	72/52 12	61/43 9	46/34 11	31/23 9	23/13 9
MUNICH, West Germany	33/23 10	37/25 9	45/31 10	54/37 13	63/45 13	69/51 14	72/54 14	71/53 13	64/48 11	53/40 10	42/31 9	36/26 11
NAIROBI, Kenya	77/54 5	79/55 6	77/57 11	75/58 16	72/56 17	70/53 9	69/51 6	70/52 7	75/52 6	76/55 8	74/56 15	74/55 11
NAPLES, Italy	54/42 11	55/43 11	60/46 6	67/50 6	73/56 6	81/62 3	86/67 1	86/67 3	81/63 6	72/56 9	63/49 11	57/45 11
NASSAU, Bahamas	77/65 6	77/64 5	79/66 5	81/69 6	84/71 9	87/74 12	88/75 14	88/75 14	88/75 15	85/73 13	81/70 9	79/67 7
NEW DELHI, India	70/44 2	75/49 2	87/58 1	97/68 1	105/79 3	102/83 4	96/81 8	93/79 8	93/75 4	93/65 1	84/52 1	73/46 1
NICE, France	56/40 8	56/41 8	59/45 8	64/49 7	69/56 8	76/62 5	81/66 2	81/66 5	77/62 6	70/55 9	62/48 7	58/43 8
NOUMEA, New Caledonia	86/72 10	85/73 12	85/72 16	83/70 13	79/66 15	77/64 13	76/62 13	76/61 12	78/63 8	80/65 7	83/68 7	86/70 6
ODESSA, USSR	28/22 7	31/26 4	39/32 5	52/41 6	67/55 6	74/62 7	79/65 6	78/65 5	68/56 4	57/47 5	43/35 5	33/27 6
OSLO, Norway	30/20 8	32/20 7	40/25 7	50/34 7	62/43 7	69/51 8	73/56 10	69/53 11	60/45 8	49/37 10	37/29 9	31/24 10
PALERMO, Sicily, Italy	58/42 14	60/47 10	62/49 7	67/53 5	73/59 5	82/66 1	86/71 1	87/72 1	83/69 4	75/62 10	67/55 9	61/50 11
PALMA, Majorca, Spain	57/42 8	59/43 8	62/45 8	66/49 5	73/55 5	80/61 3	84/66 1	86/67 2	81/64 6	74/57 8	65/50 9	59/44 10
PAPEETE, Tahiti	89/72 16	89/72 16	89/72 17	89/72 10	87/70 10	86/69 8	86/68 9	86/68 6	86/69 6	87/70 8	88/71 13	88/72 14
PARIS, France	42/32 15	45/33 13	52/36 15	60/41 14	67/47 13	73/52 11	76/55 12	75/55 12	69/50 11	59/44 14	49/38 15	43/33 17
PEKING, China	35/15 3	41/20 3	53/30 3	68/44 4	80/56 6	88/65 8	89/71 13	87/69 11	80/58 7	69/44 5	50/30 2	37/19 2
PHNOM PENH, Cambodia	87/68 3	90/72 1	93/74 3	94/76 6	92/76 14	91/76 15	89/75 13	89/76 17	88/76 19	87/76 17	86/74 9	86/71 3
PORT-AU-PRINCE, Haiti	87/68 3	88/68 5	89/69 7	89/71 11	90/72 13	92/73 8	94/74 7	93/73 11	91/73 12	90/72 12	88/71 7	87/69 3
PORT OF SPAIN, Trinidad	85/67 14	86/67 8	87/67 8	88/69 7	89/70 10	87/71 17	87/70 20	87/71 21	88/71 18	88/71 16	87/70 17	86/69 16
PRAGUE, Czechoslovakia	34/25 12	38/28 11	45/33 13	55/40 12	63/45 13	72/55 14	74/58 14	73/57 12	65/52 11	54/44 11	41/35 12	34/29 13
RANGOON, Burma	89/65 1	92/67 1	96/71 1	97/76 2	92/77 14	86/76 23	85/76 25	85/76 25	86/76 20	88/76 10	88/73 5	88/67 1
RIO DE JANEIRO, Brazil	84/73 13	85/73 11	83/72 12	80/69 10	77/66 10	76/64 7	75/63 7	76/64 7	75/65 11	77/66 13	79/68 13	82/71 14
ROME, Italy	54/39 8	56/39 11	62/42 5	68/46 6	74/55 6	82/60 3	88/64 2	88/64 3	83/61 6	73/53 9	63/46 8	56/41 9
SAIGON (HO CHI MINH CITY), Vietnam	89/70 2	91/71 1	93/74 2	95/76 4	92/76 16	89/75 21	88/75 23	88/75 21	88/74 21	88/74 20	87/73 11	87/71 7
SAN JUAN, Puerto Rico	80/70 20	80/70 15	81/70 15	82/72 14	84/74 16	85/75 17	85/75 19	85/76 20	85/75 18	85/75 18	84/73 19	81/72 21
SANTIAGO, Chile	85/53 0	84/52 0	80/49 1	74/45 5	65/41 5	58/37 8	59/37 8	62/39 5	66/42 3	72/45 3	78/48 1	83/51 0
SAO PAULO, Brazil	81/63 19	82/64 17	81/62 15	78/58 10	73/54 10	71/51 8	71/49 6	73/51 8	74/54 11	76/57 13	79/59 14	80/61 13
SEOUL, South Korea	32/15 8	37/20 6	47/29 7	62/41 8	72/51 10	80/61 10	84/70 16	87/71 13	78/59 9	67/45 7	51/32 9	37/20 8
SEVILLE, Spain	59/41 8	62/44 9	67/48 9	73/51 8	80/57 5	89/63 2	96/67 1	97/68 1	89/64 3	78/57 5	67/49 9	60/44 8
SHANGHAI, China	46/33 6	47/34 9	55/40 9	66/50 9	77/59 9	82/67 11	90/74 7	90/74 7	82/66 11	74/57 4	63/45 6	53/36 6
SINGAPORE, Singapore	86/73 17	88/73 11	88/75 14	88/75 15	89/75 15	88/75 13	88/75 13	87/75 14	87/75 14	87/74 16	87/74 18	87/74 19
SOFIA, Bulgaria	34/22 6	39/25 6	51/32 8	62/41 8	70/49 11	76/54 9	82/57 7	82/56 6	74/50 6	63/42 7	50/35 7	37/26 7
STOCKHOLM, Sweden	31/23 8	31/22 7	37/26 7	45/32 6	57/41 8	65/49 7	70/55 9	66/53 10	58/46 8	48/39 9	38/31 9	33/26 7
SYDNEY, Australia	78/65 14	78/65 13	76/63 14	71/58 14	66/52 13	61/48 12	60/46 12	63/48 11	67/51 12	71/56 12	74/60 12	77/63 13
TAIPEI, Taiwan, China	66/54 9	65/53 13	70/57 12	77/63 14	83/69 12	89/73 13	92/76 10	91/76 13	88/73 10	81/67 9	75/62 7	69/57 8
TEHRAN, Iran	45/27 4	50/32 4	59/39 5	71/49 3	82/58 2	93/66 1	99/72 1	97/71 1	90/64 1	76/53 3	63/43 3	51/33 4
TEL AVIV, Israel	63/48 10	65/48 8	67/50 6	74/54 2	81/60 1	84/65 0	87/69 0	87/70 0	86/68 1	84/64 2	77/59 7	66/52 11
TOKYO, Japan	47/29 5	48/31 6	54/36 10	63/46 10	71/54 10	76/63 12	83/70 10	86/72 9	79/66 12	69/55 11	60/43 7	52/33 5
VALPARAISO, Chile	72/56 1	72/56 1	70/54 1	67/52 5	63/50 5	60/48 7	60/47 7	61/47 5	62/48 2	65/50 2	69/52 1	71/54 1
VENICE, Italy	43/33 6	46/35 5	54/41 5	63/49 5	71/57 7	78/64 8	82/67 5	82/67 5	78/62 5	65/52 7	54/43 7	46/37 9
VIENNA, Austria	34/26 8	38/28 7	47/34 7	57/41 9	66/50 9	71/56 9	75/59 9	73/58 10	66/52 7	55/44 8	44/36 8	37/30 9
WELLINGTON, New Zealand	69/56 10	69/56 9	67/54 11	63/51 13	58/47 16	55/44 17	53/42 18	54/43 17	57/46 15	60/48 14	63/50 13	67/54 12
ZURICH, Switzerland	48/14 11	52/15 11	62/22 14	70/32 14	77/39 14	83/47 15	86/51 15	84/49 14	78/42 11	68/32 14	57/25 12	49/16 13

U.S. City Weather

City	Record Temperature High (F°)	Record Temperature Low (F°)	Annual Average: Precip. (Water equiv.) (in.)	Annual Average: Snow and Sleet (in.)	Annual Average: Wind Speed (mph)	First Freeze Date 32 F° or less Average	First Freeze Date 32 F° or less Earliest on record	Last Freeze Date 32 F° or less Average	Last Freeze Date 32 F° or less Latest on record	Elevation of Station (feet)
Albany	104	—28	36.46	65.7	8.8	Oct. 13	Sept. 23	Apr. 27	May 20	292
Albuquerque	105	—17	8.33	10.7	9.0	Oct. 29	Oct. 11	Apr. 16	May 18	5,314
Atlanta	103	— 9	48.66	1.5	9.1	Nov. 12	Oct. 24	Mar. 24	Apr. 15	1,034
Baltimore	107	— 7	41.62	21.9	9.5	Oct. 26	Oct. 8	Apr. 15	May 11	155
Birmingham	107	—10	53.46	1.2	7.4	Nov. 10	Oct. 17	Mar. 17	Apr. 21	630
Bismarck	114	—45	16.15	38.4	10.6	Sept. 22	Sept. 6	May 11	May 30	1,660
Boise	111	—23	11.97	21.7	9.0	Oct. 12	Sept. 9	May 6	May 31	2,868
Boston	104	—18	41.55	41.9	12.6	Nov. 7	Oct. 5	Apr. 8	May 3	29
Buffalo	99	—21	35.19	88.6	12.3	Oct. 25	Sept. 23	Apr. 30	May 24	706
Burlington, Vt.	101	—30	32.54	78.4	8.8	Oct. 3	Sept. 13	May 10	May 24	340
Charleston, W. Va.	108	—24	43.66	28.8	6.5	Oct. 28	Sept. 29	Apr. 18	May 11	951
Charlotte	104	— 5	45.00	5.6	7.6	Nov. 4	Oct. 15	Apr. 2	Apr. 16	769
Cheyenne	100	—38	14.48	52.0	13.3	Sept. 27	Aug. 25	May 18	June 18	6,141
Chicago	105	—23	33.47	40.7	10.3	Oct. 26	Sept. 25	Apr. 20	May 14	623
Cincinnati	102	—19	40.40	23.2	9.1	Oct. 25	Sept. 28	Apr. 15	May 25	877
Cleveland	103	—19	34.15	51.5	10.8	Nov. 2	Sept. 29	Apr. 21	May 14	805
Columbia, S.C.	107	— 2	45.23	1.8	6.9	Nov. 3	Oct. 4	Mar. 30	Apr. 21	225
Columbus, Ohio	106	—20	36.98	27.7	8.7	Oct. 31	Oct. 7	Apr. 16	May 9	833
Concord, N.H.	102	—37	38.13	64.1	6.7	Sept. 24	Sept. 13	May 17	June 6	346
Dallas-Ft. Worth, Tex.	112	— 8	32.11	2.7	11.1	Nov. 21	Oct. 27	Mar. 16	Apr. 13	596
Denver	105	—30	14.60	60.1	9.0	Oct. 14	Sept. 16	May 2	May 28	5,332
Des Moines	110	—30	31.49	33.2	11.1	Oct. 10	Sept. 28	Apr. 20	May 11	963
Detroit	105	—24	31.49	31.7	10.2	Oct. 21	Sept. 23	Apr. 23	May 12	626
El Paso	109	— 8	8.47	4.4	9.6	Nov. 11	Oct. 31	Mar. 13	Apr. 11	3,916
Great Falls	107	—49	14.83	57.7	13.1	Sept. 26	Sept. 7	May 14	June 8	3,657
Hartford	102	—26	43.00	53.1	9.0	Oct. 15	Sept. 27	Apr. 22	May 10	179
Houston	108	5	47.07	0.4	7.6	Dec. 11	Oct. 25	Feb. 5	Mar. 27	108
Indianapolis	107	—25	39.98	21.3	9.7	Oct. 22	Sept. 27	Apr. 23	May 27	808
Jackson	107	— 5	50.96	0.8	7.7	Nov. 8	Oct. 9	Mar. 18	Apr. 25	331
Jacksonville	105	10	51.75	Trace	8.6	Dec. 16	Nov. 3	Feb. 6	Mar. 31	31
Juneau	90	—22	53.95	109.1	8.5	Oct. 21	Sept. 9	Apr. 22	June 8	24
Kansas City, Mo.	113	—22	36.66	19.7	10.2	Oct. 26	Sept. 30	Apr. 7	May 6	1,025
Little Rock	110	—13	48.17	5.3	8.2	Nov. 15	Oct. 23	Mar. 16	Apr. 13	265
Los Angeles	110	23	11.94	Trace	7.4	—	Dec. 9	—	Jan. 21	104
Louisville	107	—20	42.94	17.3	8.4	Oct. 25	Oct. 15	Apr. 10	Apr. 19	488
Memphis	106	—13	48.74	5.7	9.2	Nov. 5	Oct. 17	Mar. 20	Apr. 15	284
Miami	100	26	59.21	—	9.1	—	—	—	Feb. 6	12
Milwaukee	105	—25	30.18	45.2	11.8	Oct. 23	Sept. 20	Apr. 25	May 27	693
Minneapolis-St. Paul	108	—34	26.62	45.8	10.6	Oct. 13	Sept. 3	Apr. 29	May 24	838
Mobile	104	— 1	63.26	0.4	9.3	Dec. 12	Nov. 15	Feb. 17	Mar. 20	221
Nashville	107	—15	46.61	10.9	7.9	Oct. 31	Oct. 7	Apr. 3	Apr. 24	605
New Orleans	102	7	58.93	0.2	8.4	Dec. 3	Nov. 11	Feb. 15	Apr. 8	30
New York City	106	—15	43.56	29.1	9.4	Nov. 12	Oct. 19	Apr. 7	Apr. 24	87
Norfolk	105	2	45.22	7.2	10.6	Nov. 21	Nov. 7	Mar. 22	Apr. 14	30
Oklahoma City	113	—17	31.71	9.2	12.9	Nov. 7	Oct. 7	Apr. 1	May 3	1,304
Omaha	114	—32	28.48	32.5	10.9	Oct. 20	Sept. 24	Apr. 14	May 11	982
Philadelphia	106	—11	41.18	20.3	9.6	Nov. 17	Oct. 19	Mar. 30	Apr. 20	28
Phoenix	118	16	7.41	Trace	6.1	Dec. 11	Nov. 4	Jan. 27	Mar. 3	1,107
Pittsburgh	103	—20	36.21	45.5	9.4	Oct. 20	Oct. 10	Apr. 21	May 4	1,225
Portland, Me.	103	—39	42.15	74.3	8.8	Sept. 27	Sept. 17	May 12	May 31	63
Portland, Ore.	107	— 3	37.98	7.5	7.8	Dec. 1	Oct. 26	Feb. 25	May 4	39
Providence	104	—17	40.90	37.8	10.8	Oct. 26	Oct. 3	Apr. 14	Apr. 24	62
Reno	106	—19	7.65	26.8	6.4	Oct. 2	Aug. 30	May 14	June 25	4,400
Richmond	107	—12	43.77	14.3	7.6	Nov. 8	Oct. 5	Apr. 2	May 11	177
Sacramento	115	17	17.33	Trace	8.3	Dec. 11	Nov. 4	Jan. 24	Mar. 14	25
St. Louis	115	—23	36.70	17.8	9.5	Oct. 20	Sept. 28	Apr. 15	May 10	564
Salt Lake City	107	—30	15.63	58.1	8.7	Nov. 1	Sept. 25	Apr. 12	Apr. 30	4,227
San Francisco	106	20	18.88	Trace	10.5	—	Dec. 11	—	Jan. 21	18
Seattle	100	0	40.30	15.2	9.3	Dec. 1	Oct. 19	Feb. 23	Apr. 3	450
Spokane	108	—30	16.19	54.0	8.7	Oct. 12	Sept. 13	Apr. 20	May 16	2,365
Washington, D.C.	106	—15	40.00	16.8	9.2	Nov. 10	Oct. 2	Mar. 29	May 12	65
Wichita	114	—22	30.06	16.3	12.6	Nov. 1	Sept. 27	Apr. 5	Apr. 21	1,340
Wilmington, Del.	107	—15	43.63	20.1	9.1	Oct. 26	Sept. 27	Apr. 18	May 9	80

SOURCE: National Climatic Center

U.S. City Weather

City	Jan.	Feb.	Mar.	April	May	June	July	Aug.	Sept.	Oct.	Nov.	Dec.	ANNUAL
Albany	23.0°	23.7°	33.5°	46.5°	58.4°	67.7°	72.5°	70.2°	62.7°	51.4°	39.7°	27.7°	48.1°
Albuquerque	34.5	39.5	46.3	54.8	63.8	73.3	77.1	75.1	68.4	56.8	43.9	35.1	55.7
Atlanta	43.5	45.6	52.6	61.3	69.6	76.4	78.5	77.8	73.1	62.9	52.0	44.7	61.5
Baltimore	33.2	35.0	42.6	53.6	63.1	72.1	76.8	75.3	68.5	57.3	46.0	36.4	55.0
Birmingham	45.6	47.1	55.0	62.9	70.7	77.8	79.9	79.6	75.2	64.6	53.4	46.3	63.2
Bismarck	8.1	12.2	25.3	42.9	54.6	64.1	70.6	68.5	57.9	45.7	28.6	15.4	41.1
Boise	29.9	35.5	42.3	49.6	57.8	65.4	74.5	72.5	62.7	52.3	40.6	32.1	51.3
Boston	28.9	29.1	36.9	46.9	57.7	67.0	72.6	70.7	64.0	54.2	43.5	32.6	50.3
Buffalo	25.1	24.5	32.3	43.3	54.6	64.7	70.3	68.9	62.6	51.8	40.0	29.5	47.3
Burlington, Vt.	18.0	18.4	29.3	42.6	55.2	64.8	69.7	67.3	59.6	48.8	36.6	23.3	44.5
Charleston, W. Va.	36.6	38.0	46.0	56.0	64.8	72.3	76.0	74.8	69.3	58.0	46.7	38.2	56.4
Charlotte	42.0	43.9	51.0	60.0	68.9	76.0	78.7	77.4	72.2	61.6	50.9	43.1	60.5
Cheyenne	26.1	27.7	32.4	41.4	51.0	61.0	67.7	66.4	57.3	46.4	35.2	28.6	45.1
Chicago	24.7	27.1	36.4	47.8	58.2	68.4	73.8	72.5	65.6	54.5	40.4	29.4	49.9
Cincinnati	30.8	33.6	41.7	53.5	63.3	71.9	75.5	74.2	67.3	56.3	43.6	34.4	53.9
Cleveland	27.5	27.8	35.9	47.0	58.3	67.9	72.2	70.6	64.6	53.8	41.6	31.3	49.9
Columbia, S.C.	46.6	48.1	55.1	63.5	71.9	78.5	80.8	79.9	75.1	64.5	54.4	47.2	63.8
Columbus, Ohio	29.4	30.8	40.0	51.1	61.9	70.9	74.8	72.9	66.6	55.0	42.3	32.4	52.3
Concord, N.H.	21.3	22.8	31.9	44.4	56.2	64.9	70.0	67.3	59.7	49.2	37.5	25.6	45.9
Dallas-Ft. Worth, Tex.	45.6	48.8	56.9	65.2	72.7	80.9	84.5	84.6	77.8	67.8	56.1	47.7	65.7
Denver	30.1	32.8	38.7	47.4	56.7	66.6	72.6	71.3	62.6	51.6	39.6	32.3	50.2
Des Moines	20.8	24.7	36.3	50.4	61.5	71.1	76.1	73.7	65.3	54.2	38.5	26.1	49.9
Detroit	25.3	25.8	34.5	46.7	58.1	68.2	73.0	71.1	64.2	53.1	40.1	29.5	49.2
El Paso	44.7	49.3	55.6	63.8	72.2	80.8	81.9	80.2	74.8	64.7	52.5	45.2	63.8
Great Falls	21.2	26.1	31.4	43.3	53.3	60.9	69.7	67.9	57.6	48.3	34.8	27.1	45.1
Hartford	27.1	27.7	36.9	47.9	59.0	67.9	73.1	70.9	63.7	53.3	42.1	30.4	50.0
Houston	53.2	54.6	62.0	67.9	74.3	79.8	82.4	81.3	77.5	70.2	59.6	55.5	68.2
Indianapolis	28.5	30.8	40.1	52.0	62.5	71.8	75.7	73.7	66.9	55.5	42.0	31.9	52.6
Jackson	48.4	50.9	57.3	65.3	72.6	79.6	81.8	81.5	76.9	66.5	55.7	49.5	65.5
Jacksonville	55.0	56.6	61.8	67.5	73.7	78.5	80.4	80.1	77.1	68.9	60.6	54.9	67.9
Juneau	22.2	27.3	31.2	38.4	46.4	52.8	55.5	54.1	49.0	41.5	32.0	26.9	39.8
Kansas City, Mo.	29.7	33.1	43.2	55.5	65.3	74.7	79.5	78.0	70.0	59.1	44.7	33.6	55.6
Little Rock	41.7	44.8	52.9	62.5	70.1	78.2	81.3	80.5	74.1	63.8	51.9	43.8	62.1
Los Angeles	54.6	55.9	56.9	59.3	62.1	64.9	68.3	69.5	68.5	65.2	60.4	56.4	61.8
Louisville	34.7	36.8	45.6	56.3	66.0	74.6	78.3	76.8	70.4	58.9	46.4	37.2	56.9
Memphis	41.3	44.1	52.2	62.1	70.5	78.2	81.2	80.0	74.1	63.5	51.6	43.6	61.9
Miami	67.5	68.0	71.3	74.9	78.0	80.9	82.2	82.7	81.6	77.8	72.3	68.5	75.5
Milwaukee	20.9	23.2	32.6	44.3	54.3	64.5	70.7	69.7	62.5	51.5	37.7	26.1	46.5
Minneapolis-St. Paul	13.2	16.7	29.6	45.7	57.9	67.8	73.1	70.7	61.5	50.0	33.0	19.5	44.9
Mobile	51.9	54.4	60.1	67.1	74.3	80.3	81.8	81.5	78.1	68.9	58.9	53.1	67.6
Nashville	39.1	41.0	49.5	59.5	68.2	76.3	79.4	78.3	72.2	61.1	48.9	41.1	59.6
New Orleans	54.3	56.5	61.7	68.9	75.4	80.8	82.2	82.0	78.8	70.7	60.7	55.6	69.0
New York City	32.3	32.7	40.6	51.1	61.9	70.9	76.1	74.6	68.0	58.0	46.7	35.7	54.1
Norfolk	41.6	42.3	48.8	57.4	66.7	74.7	78.6	77.5	72.4	62.2	52.1	43.6	59.8
Oklahoma City	37.2	40.8	49.8	60.2	68.2	77.0	81.4	81.1	73.7	62.7	49.4	39.9	60.1
Omaha	22.0	26.5	37.5	51.7	62.7	72.3	77.4	75.1	66.3	55.0	39.3	27.5	51.1
Philadelphia	33.1	33.8	41.6	52.2	63.0	71.8	76.6	74.7	68.4	57.5	46.2	36.2	54.6
Phoenix	51.6	55.4	60.5	67.7	76.0	85.2	90.8	89.0	83.6	71.7	59.8	52.4	70.3
Pittsburgh	30.7	31.3	39.9	51.1	62.0	70.6	74.6	72.8	66.6	55.2	43.2	33.6	52.7
Portland, Me.	22.4	23.4	32.3	42.8	53.2	62.4	68.2	66.6	59.6	49.6	38.6	26.9	45.5
Portland, Ore.	38.5	43.0	45.9	50.6	57.0	60.2	65.8	65.3	62.7	54.0	45.7	41.1	52.5
Providence	29.4	29.3	37.6	47.5	57.8	66.9	72.7	71.0	63.9	54.0	43.4	32.6	50.5
Reno	31.8	36.6	41.2	47.4	54.9	62.5	70.2	68.5	60.7	50.9	41.0	33.4	49.9
Richmond	38.0	39.4	46.9	56.9	66.1	74.0	77.6	76.1	69.9	58.9	48.7	39.7	57.7
Sacramento	44.9	49.8	53.1	58.1	64.5	70.8	75.4	74.3	71.6	63.4	52.9	45.7	60.4
St. Louis	31.7	34.8	44.3	56.1	65.9	75.1	79.3	77.5	70.1	59.0	45.3	35.3	56.2
Salt Lake City	28.0	33.2	40.7	49.0	58.3	68.1	77.2	75.4	65.1	53.1	40.5	31.4	51.7
San Francisco	48.0	50.9	52.9	54.6	57.3	60.3	61.5	62.0	62.9	60.0	54.3	49.3	56.2
Seattle	38.2	42.2	43.9	48.1	55.0	59.9	64.4	63.8	59.6	51.8	44.6	40.5	51.0
Spokane	26.8	31.7	39.4	47.6	55.8	62.5	70.2	68.7	59.5	48.7	37.0	30.4	48.2
Washington, D.C.	36.1	37.7	45.7	56.1	65.8	74.3	78.4	76.9	70.3	59.6	48.4	38.4	57.3
Wichita	31.6	35.2	44.7	56.3	65.4	75.3	80.3	79.3	70.9	59.6	45.2	35.0	56.5
Wilmington, Del.	32.6	33.1	41.9	52.2	62.7	71.4	76.0	74.1	67.9	56.8	45.7	35.2	54.2

AVERAGE MONTHLY TEMPERATURES (in °F)

SOURCE: National Climatic Center (data based on normals for 1936-1975)

TABLES OF AIRLINE DISTANCES

All Distances in Statute Miles

Between Principal Cities of the World

FROM/TO	Azores	Bagdad	Berlin	Bombay	Buenos Aires	Callao	Cairo	Cape Town	Chicago	Istanbul	Guam	Honolulu	Juneau	London	Los Angeles	Melbourne	Mexico City	Montreal	New Orleans	New York	Panama	Paris	Rio de Janeiro	San Francisco	Santiago	Seattle	Shanghai	Singapore	Tokyo	Wellington
Azores	....	3906	2148	5930	5385	4825	3325	5670	3305	2880	8985	7421	4715	1562	5034	12190	4584	2548	3718	2604	3918	1617	4312	5114	5718	4720	7324	8338	7370	11475
Bagdad	3906	....	2040	2022	8215	8618	785	4923	6490	1085	6380	8445	6180	2568	7695	8150	8155	5814	7212	6066	7807	2385	7012	7521	8876	6848	4468	4443	5242	9782
Berlin	2148	2040	....	3947	7411	6937	1823	5949	4458	1068	7158	7384	4638	575	5849	9992	6119	3776	5182	4026	5902	540	6246	5744	7842	5121	5323	6226	5623	11384
Bombay	5930	2022	3947	....	9380	10530	2698	5133	8144	3043	4831	8172	6992	4526	8810	6140	9818	7582	8952	7875	9832	4391	8438	8523	10127	7830	3219	2425	4247	7752
Buenos Aires	5385	8215	7411	9380	....	1982	7428	4332	5598	7638	10516	7653	7964	6919	6148	7336	4609	5619	4902	5295	3319	6891	1230	6487	731	6956	12295	9940	11601	6341
Callao	4825	8618	6937	10530	1982	....	7870	6195	3765	7666	9760	5993	5806	6376	4155	8196	2619	3954	2990	3633	1450	6455	2400	4500	1548	4964	10760	11700	9740	6696
Cairo	3325	785	1823	2698	7428	7870	....	4476	6231	780	7175	8925	6352	2218	7675	8720	7807	5502	6862	5701	7230	2020	6242	7554	8100	6915	5290	5152	6005	10360
Cape Town	5670	4923	5949	5133	4332	6195	4476	....	8551	5210	8918	11655	10382	5975	10165	6510	8620	7975	8390	7845	7090	5732	3850	10340	5080	10305	8179	6025	9234	7149
Chicago	3305	6490	4458	8144	5598	3765	6231	8551	....	5530	7510	4315	2310	4015	1741	9837	1690	750	827	727	2320	4219	5320	1875	5325	1753	7155	9475	6410	8465
Istanbul	2880	1085	1068	3043	7638	7666	780	5210	5530	....	7015	8200	5665	1540	6895	9189	7160	4825	6220	5060	6797	1390	6420	6770	8230	6124	5084	5440	5649	10790
Guam	8985	6380	7158	4831	10516	9760	7175	8918	7510	7015	....	3896	5225	7605	6255	3497	7690	7840	7895	8115	9220	7675	11710	5952	9946	5785	1945	2990	1596	4206
Honolulu	7421	8445	7384	8172	7653	5993	8925	11655	4315	8200	3896	....	2825	7320	2620	5581	3846	4992	4305	5051	5347	7525	8400	2407	6935	2707	5009	6874	3940	4676
Juneau	4715	6180	4638	6992	7964	5806	6352	10382	2310	5665	5225	2825	....	4496	1835	8162	3210	2647	2860	2874	4456	4700	7611	1530	7320	870	4968	7375	4117	7501
London	1562	2568	575	4526	6919	6376	2218	5975	4015	1540	7605	7320	4496	....	5496	10590	5605	3370	4656	3500	5310	210	5747	5440	7275	4850	5841	6818	6050	11790
Los Angeles	5034	7695	5849	8810	6148	4155	7675	10165	1741	6895	6255	2620	1835	5496	....	8098	1445	2468	1695	2466	3025	5711	6330	345	5595	961	6598	8955	5600	6806
Melbourne	12190	8150	9992	6140	7336	8196	8720	6510	9837	9189	3497	5581	8162	10590	8098	....	8599	10553	9455	10541	9211	10500	8340	7970	7130	8330	4967	3768	5172	1655
Mexico City	4584	8155	6119	9818	4609	2619	7807	8620	1690	7160	7690	3846	3210	5605	1445	8599	....	2247	940	2110	1532	5800	4810	1870	4122	2339	8120	10495	7190	7003
Montreal	2548	5814	3776	7582	5619	3954	5502	7975	750	4825	7840	4992	2647	3370	2468	10553	2247	....	1390	340	2545	3490	5110	2557	5461	2309	7141	9280	6546	9206
New Orleans	3718	7212	5182	8952	4902	2990	6862	8390	827	6220	7895	4305	2860	4656	1695	9455	940	1390	....	1161	1600	4846	4798	1960	4553	2137	7830	10255	6993	7950
New York	2604	6066	4026	7875	5295	3633	5701	7845	727	5060	8115	5051	2874	3500	2466	10541	2110	340	1161	....	2211	3600	4810	2606	5134	2440	7460	9617	6846	9067
Panama	3918	7807	5902	9832	3319	1450	7230	7090	2320	6797	9220	5347	4456	5310	3025	9211	1532	2545	1600	2211	....	5440	3311	3349	3000	3680	9430	11800	8560	7580
Paris	1617	2385	540	4391	6891	6455	2020	5762	4219	1390	7675	7525	4700	210	5711	10500	5800	3490	4846	3600	5440	....	5710	5680	7300	5080	5855	6730	6132	11865
Rio de Janeiro	4312	7012	6246	8438	1230	2400	6242	3850	5320	6420	11710	8400	7611	5747	6330	8340	4810	5110	4798	4810	3311	5710	....	6655	1852	6945	11510	9875	11600	7510
San Francisco	5114	7521	5744	8523	6487	4500	7554	10340	1875	6770	5952	2407	1530	5440	345	7970	1870	2557	1960	2606	3349	5680	6655	....	5960	692	6245	8440	5250	6800
Santiago	5718	8876	7842	10127	731	1548	8100	5080	5325	8230	9946	6935	7320	7275	5595	7130	4122	5461	4553	5134	3000	7300	1852	5960	....	6466	11850	10270	10850	5925
Seattle	4720	6848	5121	7830	6956	4964	6915	10305	1753	6124	5785	2707	870	4850	961	8330	2339	2309	2137	2440	3680	5080	6945	692	6466	....	5780	8200	4863	7310
Shanghai	7324	4468	5323	3219	12295	10760	5290	8179	7155	5084	1945	5009	4968	5841	6598	4967	8120	7141	7830	7460	9430	5855	11510	6245	11850	5780	....	2395	1095	6080
Singapore	8338	4443	6226	2425	9940	11700	5152	6025	9475	5440	2990	6874	7375	6818	8955	3768	10495	9280	10255	9617	11800	6730	9875	8440	10270	8200	2395	....	3350	5360
Tokyo	7370	5242	5623	4247	11601	9740	6005	9234	6410	5649	1596	3940	4117	6050	5600	5172	7190	6546	6993	6846	8560	6132	11600	5250	10850	4863	1095	3350	....	5730
Wellington	11475	9782	11384	7752	6341	6696	10360	7149	8465	10790	4206	4676	7501	11790	6806	1655	7003	9206	7950	9067	7580	11865	7510	6800	5925	7310	6080	5360	5730	......

Between Principal Cities of Europe

	Amsterdam	Athens	Baku	Barcelona	Belgrade	Berlin	Brussels	Bucharest	Budapest	Cologne	Copenhagen	Istanbul	Dresden	Dublin	Frankfort	Hamburg	Leningrad	Lisbon	London	Lyon	Madrid	Marseilles	Milan	Moscow	Munich	Oslo	Paris	Riga	Rome	Sofia	Stockholm	Toulouse	Warsaw	Vienna	Zurich
Amsterdam	....	1340	2218	770	875	365	105	1100	710	128	381	1360	385	468	228	232	1090	1140	220	458	912	627	517	1325	415	568	257	820	808	1073	695	625	673	580	375
Athens	1340	....	1395	1160	500	1112	1292	460	698	1200	1320	350	1022	1765	1113	1250	1535	1770	1476	1100	1463	1025	900	1388	925	1610	1300	1310	650	335	1495	1215	990	795	1000
Baku	2218	1395	....	2427	1487	1867	2240	1220	1562	2127	1980	1070	1837	2490	2055	2020	1570	3050	2435	2238	2742	2238	2028	1175	1912	2118	2335	1590	1900	1360	1862	2425	1555	1700	2050
Barcelona	770	1160	2427	....	998	925	658	1210	924	692	1085	1380	860	919	665	910	1740	610	707	327	316	211	450	1852	648	1330	518	1440	530	1072	1410	156	1150	830	513
Belgrade	875	500	1487	998	....	618	850	295	205	750	840	502	530	1327	652	760	1165	1555	1040	752	1235	750	540	1160	475	1112	890	855	440	231	1005	930	510	300	590
Berlin	365	1112	1867	925	618	....	401	798	425	300	225	1068	95	815	268	165	815	1410	575	601	1149	730	570	995	310	520	540	520	730	810	503	815	320	322	410
Brussels	105	1292	2240	658	850	401	....	1110	700	110	475	1345	407	480	198	301	1175	998	202	352	807	521	435	1392	372	672	170	900	730	945	793	515	720	568	312
Bucharest	1100	460	1220	1210	295	798	1110	....	295	982	970	272	725	1560	890	950	1080	1842	1285	1025	1518	1020	819	920	725	1245	1152	870	700	194	1080	1210	580	520	855
Budapest	710	698	1562	924	205	425	700	295	....	590	629	650	345	1176	504	572	965	1515	900	680	1214	718	476	965	350	920	770	685	500	395	820	883	342	128	498
Cologne	128	1200	2127	692	750	300	110	982	590	....	400	1240	292	585	93	228	1090	1126	308	370	875	528	390	1285	282	635	250	805	675	945	722	875	602	460	259
Copenhagen	381	1320	1960	1085	840	225	475	970	629	400	....	1240	315	768	412	180	708	1520	590	760	1272	906	720	970	520	303	634	453	948	1010	330	962	415	538	595
Istanbul	1360	350	1070	1380	502	1068	1345	272	650	1240	1240	....	995	1830	1150	1222	1292	2005	1540	1238	1690	1205	1030	1180	975	1505	1390	1115	840	315	1340	1400	852	790	1090
Dresden	385	1022	1837	860	530	95	407	725	345	292	315	995	....	852	236	238	885	1380	592	540	1100	655	435	1200	227	620	523	585	630	730	598	762	325	235	342
Dublin	468	1765	2490	919	1327	815	480	1560	1176	585	768	1830	852	....	671	668	1440	1015	300	720	902	875	880	1728	855	786	480	1210	1175	1525	1010	761	1130	1040	768
Frankfort	228	1113	2055	665	652	268	198	890	504	93	412	1150	236	671	....	250	1075	1160	392	350	888	492	323	1240	193	675	295	780	698	860	730	560	550	370	193
Hamburg	232	1250	2020	910	760	165	301	950	572	228	180	1222	238	668	250	....	880	1301	448	580	1098	730	570	1100	378	445	459	600	810	954	502	780	462	460	432
Leningrad	1090	1535	1570	1740	1165	815	1175	1080	965	1090	708	1292	885	1440	1075	880	....	2235	1300	1420	1980	1540	1315	391	1100	670	1335	300	1440	1218	435	1635	640	975	1225
Lisbon	1140	1770	3050	610	1555	1410	998	1842	1515	1126	1520	2005	1380	1015	1160	1301	2235	....	975	850	313	810	1350	430	1208	1690	890	1940	1150	1685	1848	640	1700	1415	1058
London	220	1476	2435	707	1040	575	202	1285	900	308	590	1540	592	300	392	448	1300	975	....	455	777	620	595	1540	526	720	210	1035	890	1235	885	550	890	762	480
Lyon	458	1100	2238	327	752	601	352	1025	680	370	760	1238	540	720	350	580	1420	850	455	....	577	170	210	1560	352	1005	248	1122	462	928	1080	228	850	562	206
Madrid	912	1463	2742	316	1235	1149	807	1518	1214	875	1272	1690	1100	902	888	1098	1980	313	777	557	....	394	728	2120	910	1474	645	1670	840	1385	1598	344	1410	1110	765
Marseilles	627	1025	2238	211	750	730	521	1020	718	528	906	1205	655	875	492	730	1540	810	620	170	394	....	238	1642	445	1165	410	1238	372	895	1225	196	950	620	318
Milan	517	900	2028	450	540	570	435	819	476	390	720	1030	435	880	323	570	1315	1350	595	210	728	238	....	1408	215	1000	400	1010	295	715	1020	400	705	385	137
Moscow	1325	1388	1175	1852	1160	995	1392	920	965	1285	970	1180	1200	1728	1240	1100	391	430	1540	1560	2120	1642	1408	....	1220	1030	1538	520	1462	1100	770	1770	710	1028	1350
Munich	415	925	1912	648	475	310	372	725	350	282	520	975	227	855	193	378	1100	1208	526	352	910	445	215	1220	....	810	425	800	430	672	811	570	500	222	158
Oslo	568	1610	2118	1330	1112	520	672	1245	920	635	303	1505	620	786	675	445	670	1690	720	1005	1474	1165	1000	1030	810	....	830	531	1242	1295	267	1140	653	835	869
Paris	257	1300	2335	518	890	540	170	1152	770	250	634	1390	523	480	295	459	1335	890	210	248	645	410	400	1538	425	830	....	1050	690	1080	950	431	845	770	295
Riga	820	1310	1590	1440	855	520	900	870	685	805	453	1115	585	1210	780	600	300	1940	1035	1122	1670	1238	1010	520	800	531	1050	....	1155	985	276	1335	350	685	930
Rome	808	650	1900	530	440	730	730	700	500	675	948	840	630	1175	698	810	1440	1150	890	462	840	372	295	1462	430	1242	690	1155	....	545	1220	569	810	470	421
Sofia	1073	335	1360	1072	231	810	945	194	395	945	1010	315	730	1525	860	954	1218	1685	1235	928	1385	895	715	1100	672	1295	1080	985	545	....	1170	1080	662	500	780
Stockholm	695	1495	1862	1410	1005	503	793	1080	820	722	330	1340	598	1010	730	502	435	1848	885	1080	1598	1225	1020	770	811	267	950	276	1220	1170	....	1281	500	770	908
Toulouse	625	1215	2425	156	930	815	515	1210	883	875	962	1400	762	761	560	780	1635	640	550	228	344	196	400	1770	570	1140	431	1335	569	1080	1281	....	1062	725	425
Warsaw	673	990	1555	1150	510	320	720	580	342	602	415	852	325	1130	550	462	640	1700	890	850	1410	950	705	710	500	653	845	350	810	662	500	1062	....	345	640
Vienna	580	795	1700	830	300	322	568	520	128	460	538	790	235	1040	370	460	975	1415	762	562	1110	620	385	1028	222	835	770	685	470	500	770	725	345	....	365
Zurich	375	1000	2050	513	590	410	312	855	498	259	595	1090	342	768	193	432	1225	1058	480	206	765	318	137	1350	158	869	295	930	421	780	908	425	640	365	....